CAMRY
1983-92 REPAIR MANUAL

CHILTON'S™

President Dean F. Morgantini, S.A.E.
Vice President–Finance Barry L. Beck
Vice President–Sales Glenn D. Potere

Executive Editor Kevin M. G. Maher
Production Manager Ben Greisler, S.A.E.
Project Managers Michael Abraham, George B. Heinrich III, Will Kessler, A.S.E., Richard Schwartz

Editors Dean Morgantini, Jeff H. Fisher, Jeffry M. Hoffman

CHILTON™ Automotive Books
PUBLISHED BY **W. G. NICHOLS, INC.**

Manufactured in USA

1020 Andrew Drive
West Chester, PA 19380
ISBN 0-8019-8265-0
Library of Congress Catalog Card No. 91-058870
6789012345 7654321098

Contents

1 General Information and Maintenance

- 1-2 How to Use this Book
- 1-3 Tools and Equipment
- 1-10 Routine Maintenance and Lubrication
- 1-26 Jump Starting
- 1-74 Capacities Chart

2 Engine Performance and Tune-Up

- 2-2 Tune-Up Specifications
- 2-2 Tune-Up Procedures
- 2-7 Firing Orders
- 2-8 Electronic Ignition

3 Engine and Engine Overhaul

- 3-2 Engine Electrical Systems
- 3-23 Engine Mechanical Service
- 3-26 Engine Specifications
- 3-103 Exhaust Systems

4 Engine Controls

- 4-5 Engine Emission Control System And Service
- 4-13 Electronic Engine Control System
- 4-26 Vacuum Diagrams

5 Fuel System

- 5-2 Fuel Injection System
- 5-18 Diesel Fuel System
- 5-18 Fuel Tank

6 Chassis Electrical

- 6-6 Heating and Air Cond.
- 6-28 Cruise Control
- 6-33 Radio
- 6-35 Windshield Wipers
- 6-37 Instruments and Switches
- 6-40 Lighting
- 6-47 Circuit Protection
- 6-58 Wiring Diagram

Contents

7-2 Manual Transmission	**7-63** Clutch	Drive Train	7
7-46, 71 Halfshafts	**7-63** Automatic Transmission		
7-82 Driveshaft and U-Joints	**7-77** Transfer Case		
8-2 Front Suspension	**8-17** Rear Suspension	Suspension and Steering	8
8-15 Wheel Alignment Specs.	**8-24** Steering		
9-9 Front Disc Brakes	**9-25** Parking Brake	Brakes	9
9-14 Drum Brakes	**9-27** Anti-Lock Brakes		
9-23 Rear Disc Brakes	**9-39** Brake Specifications		
10-2 Exterior	**10-28** Stain Removal	Body	10
10-12 Interior			
10-29 Glossary		Glossary	
10-33 Master Index		Master Index	

SAFETY NOTICE

Proper service and repair procedures are vital to the safe, reliable operation of all motor vehicles, as well as the personal safety of those performing repairs. This manual outlines procedures for servicing and repairing vehicles using safe, effective methods. The procedures contain many NOTES, CAUTIONS and WARNINGS which should be followed along with standard procedures to eliminate the possibility of personal injury or improper service which could damage the vehicle or compromise its safety.

It is important to note that the repair procedures and techniques, tools and parts for servicing motor vehicles, as well as the skill and experience of the individual performing the work vary widely. It is not possible to anticipate all of the conceivable ways or conditions under which vehicles may be serviced, or to provide cautions as to all of the possible hazards that may result. Standard and accepted safety precautions and equipment should be used when handling toxic or flammable fluids, and safety goggles or other protection should be used during cutting, grinding, chiseling, prying, or any other process that can cause material removal or projectiles.

Some procedures require the use of tools specially designed for a specific purpose. Before substituting another tool or procedure, you must be completely satisfied that neither your personal safety, nor the performance of the vehicle will be endangered.

Although information in this manual is based on industry sources and is complete as possible at the time of publication, the possibility exists that some vehicle manufacturers made later changes which could not be included here. While striving for total accuracy, W. G. Nichols, Inc. cannot assume responsibility for any errors, changes or omissions that may occur in the compilation of this data.

PART NUMBERS

Part numbers listed in this reference are not recommendations by Chilton for any product by brand name. They are references that can be used with interchange manuals and aftermarket supplier catalogs to locate each brand supplier's discrete part number.

SPECIAL TOOLS

Special tools are recommended by the vehicle manufacturer to perform their specific job. Use has been kept to a minimum, but where absolutely necessary, they are referred to in the text by the part number of the tool manufacturer. These tools can be purchased, under the appropriate part number, from your local dealer or regional distributor, or an equivalent tool can be purchased locally from a tool supplier or parts outlet. Before substituting any tool for the one recommended, read the SAFETY NOTICE at the top of this page.

ACKNOWLEDGMENTS

W. G. Nichols, Inc. expresses appreciation to Toyota Motor Sales, USA, Inc., Torrance, CA for their generous assistance.

1

GENERAL INFORMATION AND MAINTENANCE

AIR CLEANER 1-14
AIR CONDITIONING
Charging 1-37
Discharging 1-37
Evacuating 1-37
Gauge sets 1-36
General service 1-33
Inspection 1-35
Safety precautions 1-34
Troubleshooting 1-87
ANTIFREEZE 1-59
AUTOMATIC TRANSMISSION
Application chart 1-9
Fluid change 1-52
BATTERY
Cables 1-24
General maintenance 1-23
Fluid level and maintenance 1-23
Jump starting 1-26, 74
Replacement 1-25
Testing 1-24
BELTS 1-27
CAPACITIES CHART 1-74
CHASSIS LUBRICATION 1-65
COOLING SYSTEM 1-59
CRANKCASE VENTILATION VALVE 1-19
DRIVE AXLE
Lubricant level 1-57
EVAPORATIVE CANISTER 1-17
FILTERS
Air 1-14
Crankcase 1-19
Fuel 1-17
Oil 1-48
FLUIDS AND LUBRICANTS
Automatic transmission 1-52
Battery 1-23
Chassis greasing 1-65
Coolant 1-60
Engine oil 1-45
Fuel recommendations 1-46
Manual transmission 1-51
Master cylinder 1-62
Power steering pump 1-63
Transfer case 1-55
FRONT DRIVE AXLE
Lubricant level 1-57
FUEL FILTER 1-17
HISTORY 1-6
HOSES 1-32
HOW TO USE THIS BOOK 1-2
IDENTIFICATION
Drive axle 1-8
Engine 1-8
Model 1-6
Serial number 1-6
Transmission
Automatic 1-9
Manual 1-9
Vehicle 1-6
JACKING POINTS 1-5, 69
JUMP STARTING 1-26
MAINTENANCE INTERVALS CHART 1-75
MASTER CYLINDER 1-62
MODEL IDENTIFICATION 1-6
OIL AND FUEL RECOMMENDATIONS 1-45
OIL AND FILTER CHANGE (ENGINE) 1-48
OIL LEVEL CHECK
Differential 1-57
Engine 1-47
Transfer case 1-55
Tranqmission 1-51
PCV VALVE 1-19
POWER STEERING PUMP 1-63
PREVENTIVE MAINTENANCE CHARTS 1-75
PUSHING 1-67
RADIATOR 1-62
ROUTINE MAINTENANCE 1-10
SAFETY MEASURES 1-5
SERIAL NUMBER LOCATION 1-6
SPECIAL TOOLS 1-3
SPECIFICATIONS CHARTS
Capacities 1-74
Preventive Maintenance 1-75
TIRES
Inflation 1-44
Rotation 1-43
Storage 1-44
Tread depth 1-43
Troubleshooting 1-89
Usage 1-43
Wear problems 1-43
TOOLS AND EQUIPMENT 1-3
TOWING 1-67
TRAILER TOWING 1-65
TRANSFER CASE
Fluid level 1-55
TRANSMISSION
Application charts 1-9
Routine maintenance 1-51
TROUBLESHOOTING CHARTS
Air conditioning 1-87
Tires 1-89
Wheels 1-89
VEHICLE IDENTIFICATION 1-6
WHEEL BEARINGS 1-65
WHEELS 1-43
WINDSHIELD WIPERS 1-39

Air Cleaner 1-14
Air Conditioning 1-33
Automatic Transmission Application Chart 1-9
Capacities Chart 1-74
Cooling System 1-59
Fuel Filter 1-17
Jump Starting 1-26, 74
Manual Transmission Application Chart 1-9
Oil and Filter Change 1-48
Windshield Wipers 1-39

HOW TO USE THIS BOOK

Chilton's Total Car Manual for the Toyota Camry is intended to teach you about the inner workings of your car and save you money on its upkeep.

The first two sections will be the most used, since they contain maintenance and tune-up information and procedures. Studies have shown that a properly tuned and maintained car can get at least 10% better gas mileage (which translates into lower operating costs) and periodic maintenance will catch minor problems before they turn into major repair bills. The other sections deal with the more complex systems of your car. Operating systems from engine through brakes are covered. It will give you the detailed instructions to help you change your own brake pads and shoes, tune-up the engine, replace spark plugs and filters, and do many more jobs that will save you money, give you personal satisfaction and help you avoid expensive problems.

A secondary purpose of this book is a reference guide for owners who want to understand their car and/or their mechanics better. In this case, no tools at all are required. Knowing just what a particular repair job requires in parts and labor time will allow you to evaluate whether or not you're getting a fair price quote and help decipher itemized bills from a repair shop.

Before attempting any repairs or service on your car, read through the entire procedure outlined in the appropriate section. This will give you the overall view of what tools and supplies will be required. There is nothing more frustrating than having to walk to the bus stop on Monday morning because you were short one gasket on Sunday afternoon. So read ahead and plan ahead. Each operation should be approached logically and all procedures thoroughly understood before attempting any work. Some special tools that may be required can often be rented from local automotive jobbers or places specializing in renting tools and equipment. Check the yellow pages of your phone book.

All sections contain adjustments, maintenance, removal and installation procedures, and overhaul procedures. When overhaul is not considered practical, we tell you how to remove the failed part and then how to install the new or rebuilt replacement. In this way, you at least save the labor costs. Backyard overhaul of some components (such as the alternator or water pump) is just not practical, but the removal and installation procedure is often simple and well within the capabilities of the average car owner.

Two basic mechanic's rules should be mentioned here. First, whenever the LEFT side of the car or engine is referred to, it is meant to specify the DRIVER'S side of the car. Conversely, the RIGHT side of the car means the PASSENGER'S side. Second, all screws and bolts are removed by turning counterclockwise, and tightened by turning clockwise.

Safety is always the most important rule. Constantly be aware of the dangers involved in working on or around an automobile and take proper precautions to avoid the risk of personal injury or damage to the vehicle. See the section, Servicing Your Vehicle Safely, and the SAFETY NOTICE on the acknowledgment page before attempting any service procedures and pay attention to the instructions provided. There are 3 common mistakes in mechanical work:

1. Incorrect order of assembly, disassembly or adjustment. When taking something apart or putting it together, doing things in the wrong order usually just costs you extra time; however it CAN break something. Read the entire procedure before beginning disassembly. Do everything in the order in which the instructions say you should do it, even if you can't immediately see a reason for it. When you're taking apart something that is very intricate (for example a carburetor), you might want to draw a picture of how it looks when assembled at one point in order to make sure you get everything back in its proper position. We will supply exploded views whenever possible, but sometimes the job requires more attention to detail than an illustration provides. When making adjustments (especially tune-up adjustments), do them in order. One adjustment often affects another and you cannot expect satisfactory results unless each adjustment is made only when it cannot be changed by any other.

2. Overtorquing (or undertorquing) nuts and bolts. While it is more common for overtorquing to cause damage, undertorquing can cause a fastener to vibrate loose and cause serious damage, especially when dealing with aluminum parts. Pay attention to torque specifications and utilize a torque wrench in assembly. If a torque figure is not available remember that, if you are using the right tool to do the job, you will probably not have to strain yourself to get a fastener tight enough. The pitch of most threads is so slight that the tension you put on the wrench will be multiplied many times in actual force on what you are tightening. A good example of how critical torque is can be seen in the case of spark plug installation, especially where you are putting the plug into an aluminum cylinder head. Too little torque can fail to crush the gasket, causing leakage of combustion gases and consequent overheating of the plug and engine parts. Too much torque can damage the threads or distort the plug, which changes the spark gap at the electrode. Since more and more manufacturers are using aluminum in their engine and chassis parts to save weight, a torque wrench should be in any serious do-it-yourselfer's tool box.

There are many commercial chemical products available for ensuring that fasteners won't come loose, even if they are not torqued just right (a very common brand is Loctite®). If you're worried about getting something together tight enough to hold, but loose enough to avoid mechanical damage during assembly, one of these products might offer substantial insurance. Read the label on the package and make sure the product is compatible with the materials, fluids, etc. involved before choosing one.

3. Crossthreading. This occurs when a part such as a bolt is screwed into a nut or casting at the wrong angle and forced, causing the threads to become damaged. Crossthreading is more likely to occur if access is difficult. It helps to clean and lubricate fasteners, and to start threading with the part to be installed going straight in, using your fingers. If you encounter resistance, unscrew the part and start over again at a different angle until it can be inserted and turned several times without much effort. Keep in mind that many parts, especially spark plugs, use tapered threads so that gentle turning will automatically bring the part you're threading to the proper angle if you don't force it or resist a change in angle. Don't put a wrench on the part until it's been turned in a couple of times by hand. If you suddenly encounter resistance and the part has not seated fully, don't force it. Pull it back out and make sure it's clean and threading properly.

Always take your time and be patient; once you have some experience, working on your car will become an enjoyable hobby.

TOOLS AND EQUIPMENT

The service procedures in this book presuppose a familiarity with hand tools and their proper use. However, it is possible that you may have a limited amount of experience with the sort of equipment needed to work on an automobile. This section is designed to help you assemble a basic set of tools that will handle most of the jobs you may undertake.

In addition to the normal assortment of screwdrivers and pliers, automotive service work requires an investment in wrenches, sockets and the handles needed to drive them, and various measuring tools such as torque wrenches and feeler gauges.

You will find that virtually every nut and bolt on your Toyota is metric. Therefore, despite a few close size similarities, standard inch-size tools will not fit and must not be used. You will need a set of metric wrenches as your most basic tool kit, ranging from about 6mm to 17mm in size. High quality forged wrenches are available in three styles: open end, box end, and combination open/box end. The combination tools are generally the cost desirable as a starter set; the wrenches shown in the illustration are of the combination type.

The other set of tools inevitably required is a ratchet handle and socket set. This set should have the same size range as your wrench set. The ratchet, extension, and flex drives for the sockets are available in many sizes; it is advisable to choose a 3/8 in. drive set initially. One break in the inch/metric sizing war is that metric-sized sockets sold in the U.S. have inch-sized drive (1/4, 3/8, 1/2, etc.). Thus, if you already have an inch-size socket set, you need only buy new metric sockets in the sizes needed. Sockets are available in 6- and 12-point versions; 6-point types are stronger and are a good choice for a first set. The choice of a drive handle for the sockets should be made with some care. If this is your first set, take the plunge and invest in a flex-head ratchet; it will get into many places otherwise accessible only through a long chain of universal joints, extensions, and adapters. An alternative is a flex handle, which lacks the ratcheting feature but has a head which pivots 180°; such a tool is shown below the ratchet handle in the illustration. In addition to the range of sockets mentioned, a rubber-lined spark plug socket should be purchased. The correct size for the plugs in your Toyota's engine is 13/16 in. If your car is equipped with a diesel engine, spark plugs are not used. These type of engines use a system of glow plugs and fuel injection nozzles. A 12mm deep well socket will be required to remove the glow plugs and a Toyota injection nozzle wrench set #SST 09628-64010 may also be wise investments.

The most important thing to consider when purchasing hand tools is quality. Don't be misled by the low cost of bargain tools. Forged wrenches, tempered screwdriver blades and fine tooth ratchets are much better investments than their less expensive counterparts. The skinned knuckles and frustration inflicted by poor quality tools make any job an unhappy chore. Another consideration is that quality tools come with an unbeatable replacement guarantee, if the tool breaks, you get a new one, no questions asked.

Most jobs can be accomplished using the tools on the accompanying lists. There will be an occasional need for a special tool, such as snap ring pliers; that need will be mentioned in the text. It would not be wise to buy a large assortment of tools on the premise that someday they will be needed. Instead, the tools should be acquired one at a time, each for a specific job, both to avoid unnecessary expense and to be certain that you have the right tool.

The tools needed for basic maintenance jobs, in addition to the wrenches and sockets mentioned, include:

1. Jackstands, for support
2. Oil filter wrench
3. Oil filter spout or funnel
4. Grease gun
5. Battery post and clamp cleaner
6. Container for draining oil
7. Many rags for the inevitable spills

In addition to these items there are several others which are not absolutely necessary, but handy to have around. These include a transmission funnel and filler tube, a drop (trouble) light on a long cord, an adjustable (crescent) wrench, and slip joint pliers.

A more advanced list of tools, suitable for tune-up work, can be drawn up easily. While the tools are slightly more sophisticated, they need not be outrageously expensive. The key to these purchases is to make them with an eye towards adaptability and wide range. A basic list of tune-up tools could include:

1. Tachometer/dwell meter.
2. Spark plug gauge and gapping tool.
3. Feeler gauges for valve adjustment.
4. Timing light.

You will need both wire-type and flat-type feeler gauges, the former for the spark plugs and the latter for the valves. The choice of a timing light should be made carefully. A light which works on the DC current supplied by the car battery is the best choice; it should have a xenon tube for brightness. Since most late model cars have electronic ignition, and since nearly all cars will have it in the future, the light should have an inductive pickup which clamps around the number one spark plug cable (the timing light illustrated has one of these pickups). In addition to these basic tools, there are several other tools and gauges which you may find useful. These include:

1. A compression gauge. The screw-in type is slower to use, but eliminates the possibility of a faulty reading due to escaping pressure
2. A manifold vacuum gauge
3. A test light
4. A combination volt/ohmmeter
5. An induction meter, used to determine whether or not there is current flowing in a wire, an extremely helpful tool for electrical troubleshooting

Finally, you will find a torque wrench necessary for all but the most basic of work. The beam-type models are perfectly adequate. The newer click-type (breakaway) torque wrenches are more accurate, but are much more expensive, and must be periodically recalibrated.

Torque specification for each fastener will be given in the procedure in any case that a specific torque value is required. If no torque specifications are given, use the following values as a guide, based upon fastener size:

Bolts marked 6T

6mm bolt/nut — 5–7 ft. lbs.
8mm bolt/nut — 12–17 ft. lbs.
10mm bolt/nut — 23–34 ft. lbs.
12mm bolt/nut — 41–59 ft. lbs.
14mm bolt/nut — 56–76 ft. lbs.

Bolts marked 8T

6mm bolt/nut — 6–9 ft. lbs.
8mm bolt/nut — 13–20 ft. lbs.
10mm bolt/nut — 27–40 ft. lbs.
12mm bolt/nut — 46–69 ft. lbs.
14mm bolt/nut — 75–101 ft. lbs.

Special Tools

➡ **Special tools are occasionally necessary to perform a specific job**

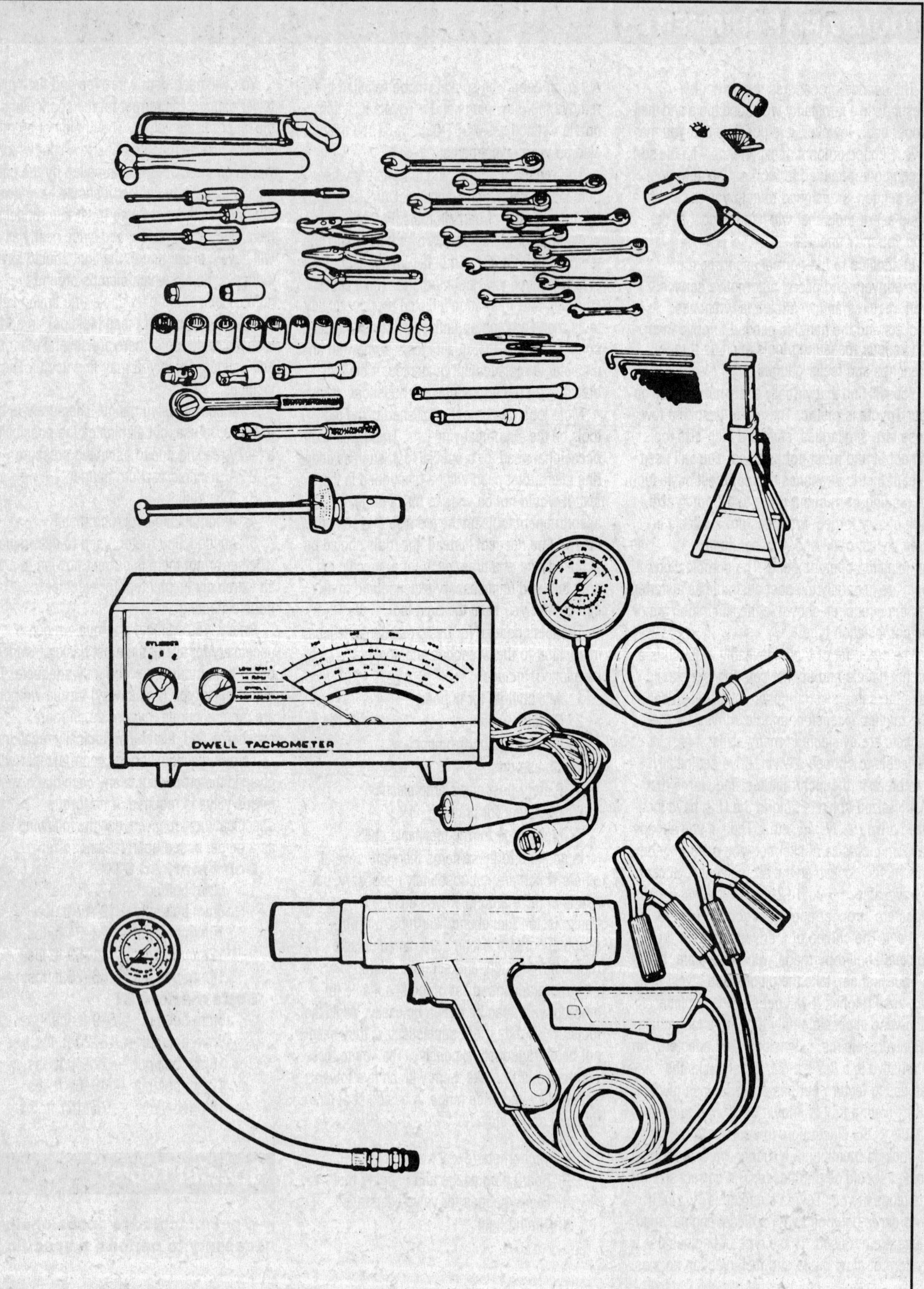

FIG. 1 This basic collection of hand tools will handle most service needs

or are recommended to make the job easier. Their use has been kept tot minimum. When a special tool is indicated, it will be referred to by manufacturer's part number, and, where possible, an illustration of the tool will be provided so that an equivalent tool may be used. A list of tool manufactures and their addresses follows:

Owattona Tool Company
Major Motor Division
2013 Fourth St. NW
PO Box 314
Owatonna, MN 55060

SERVICING YOUR CAR SAFELY

It is virtually impossible to anticipate all of the hazards involved with automotive maintenance and service, but care and common sense will prevent most accidents. The rules of safety for mechanics range from "don't smoke around gasoline," to "use the proper tool for the job." The trick to avoiding injuries is to develop safe work habits and take every possible precaution.

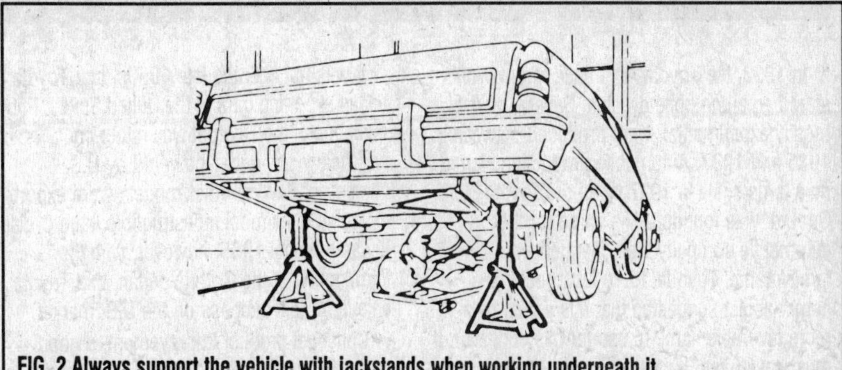

FIG. 2 Always support the vehicle with jackstands when working underneath it

Dos

- Do keep a fire extinguisher and first aid kit within easy reach.
- Do wear safety glasses or goggles when cutting, drilling or prying. If you wear glasses for the sake of vision, they should be made of hardened glass that can also serve as safety glasses, or wear safety goggles over your regular glasses.
- Do shield your eyes whenever you work around the battery. Batteries contain sulphuric acid. In case of contact with the eyes or skin, flush the area with water or a mixture of water and baking soda and get medical attention immediately.
- Do use safety stands for any undercar service. Jacks are for raising vehicles. Safety stands are for making sure the vehicle stays raised until you want it to come down. Whenever the vehicle is raised, block the wheels remaining on the ground and set the parking brake.
- Do use adequate ventilation when working with any chemicals or hazardous materials. Like carbon monoxide, the asbestos dust resulting from brake lining wear can be poisonous in sufficient quantities.
- Do disconnect the negative battery cable when working on the electrical system. The secondary ignition system can contain more than 40,000 volts.
- Do follow manufacturer's directions whenever working with potentially hazardous materials. Both brake fluid and antifreeze are poisonous if taken internally.
- Do properly maintain your tools. Loose hammerheads, mushroomed punches and chisels, frayed or poorly grounded electrical cords, excessively worn screwdrivers, spread wrenches (open end), cracked sockets, slipping ratchets, or faulty droplight sockets can cause accidents.
- Do use the proper size and type of tool for the job being done.
- Do when possible, pull on a wrench handle rather than push on it, and adjust your stance to prevent a fall.
- Do be sure that adjustable wrenches are tightly adjusted on the nut or bolt and pulled so that the face is on the side of the fixed jaw.
- Do select a wrench or socket that fits the nut or bolt. The wrench or socket should sit straight, not cocked.
- Do strike squarely with a hammer; avoid glancing blows.
- Do set the parking brake and block the drive wheels if the work requires that the engine be running.

Don'ts

- Don't run an engine in a garage or anywhere else without proper ventilation — EVER! Carbon monoxide is poisonous; it takes a long time to leave the human body and you can build up a deadly supply of it in your system by simply breathing in a little every day. You may not realize you are slowly poisoning yourself. Always use power vents, windows, fans or open the garage doors.
- Don't work around moving parts while wearing a necktie or other loose clothing. Short sleeves are much safer than long, loose sleeves and hard-toed shoes with neoprene soles protect your toes and give a better grip on slippery surfaces. Jewelry such as watches, fancy belt buckles, beads or body adornment of any kind is not safe working around a car. Long hair should be hidden under a hat or cap.
- Don't use pockets for toolboxes. A fall or bump can drive a screwdriver deep into you body. Even a wiping cloth hanging from the back pocket can wrap around a spinning shaft or fan.
- Don't smoke when working around gasoline, cleaning solvent or other flammable material.
- Don't smoke when working around the battery. When the battery is being charged, it gives off explosive hydrogen gas.
- Don't use gasoline to wash your hands; there are excellent soaps available. Gasoline may contain lead, and lead can enter the body through a cut, accumulating in the body until you are very ill. Gasoline also removes all the natural oils from the skin so that bone-dry hands will suck up oil and grease.

• Don't service the air conditioning system unless you are equipped with the necessary tools and training. The refrigerant, R-12, is extremely cold and when exposed to the air, will instantly freeze any surface it comes in contact with, including your eyes. Although the refrigerant is normally non-toxic, R-12 becomes a deadly poisonous gas in the presence of an open flame. One good whiff of the vapors from burning refrigerant can be fatal.

• Don't loose track of your tools or parts. Wrenches left on fan shrouds and in the area of drive belts become potential missile hazards. Items like these usually find their way to an eye, face or limb or the engine. Scan the engine compartment for any loose tools or any parts that may have been replaced. It's great to be able to fix your car and save money and get satisfaction, but it's not worth the price of personal injury.

HISTORY

In 1933, the Toyota Automatic Loom Works stared an automobile division. Several models, mostly experimental, were produced between 1935 and 1937. Automobile production started on a large scale in 1937 when the Toyota Motor Co. Ltd. was founded. The name for the automobile company was changed from the family name. Toyoda, to Toyota, because a numerologist suggested that this would be a more favorable name to use for this endeavor. It must have been; by 1947, Toyota had produced 100,000 vehicles. Today Toyota is Japan's largest producer of motor vehicles and ranks among the largest in world production.

It was not until the late 1950s, that Toyota began exporting cars to the United States. Public reception of the Toyopet was rather cool. The car was heavy and under-powered by U.S. standards. Several other models were exported, including the almost indestructible Land Cruiser. It was not until 1965, however, with the introduction of the Corona sedan, that Toyota enjoyed a real success on the U.S. market.

Continual product improvement, a good dealer network, and an ability to blanket the economy end of the market are responsible for this success. Today, Toyota produces a full range of models, from the economical to the luxurious. Camry is just an extension of Toyota's commitment to quality and customer satisfaction in the mid-sized sedan and station wagon market.

The most recent introduction to the Camry family, came in the form of the All-Trac 4-Wheel Drive models that appeared on the market in 1988. Basically, the All-Trac 4-Wheel Drive is the same as the conventional sedan in interior and exterior appearance; however, the chassis and drive train components have been modified to accept the new 4-Wheel Drive system. All-Trac 4-Wheel Drive vehicles are one in the same. The All-Trac designation has been chosen for the United States and the 4-Wheel Drive designation has been selected for Canadian vehicles.

SERIAL NUMBER IDENTIFICATION

Vehicle

➧ SEE FIGS. 3–7

All models have the vehicle identification number (VIN) stamped on a plate which is attached to the left side of the instrument panel. This plate is visible through the windshield. The VIN is the legal identifier of your vehicle. The VIN consists of seventeen symbols (letters and numbers). The first two digits "JT" of the VIN are are standard on all Toyota manufactured vehicles, and they represent "Japan Toyota". The remaining fifteen digits are a combination of alpha/numerical codes that provide information ranging from the vehicle designation to the frame number.

The VIN is also stamped on the manufacturer's plate in the engine compartment which is usually located on the firewall cowl panel and on the certification regulation plate affixed to the driver's door post.

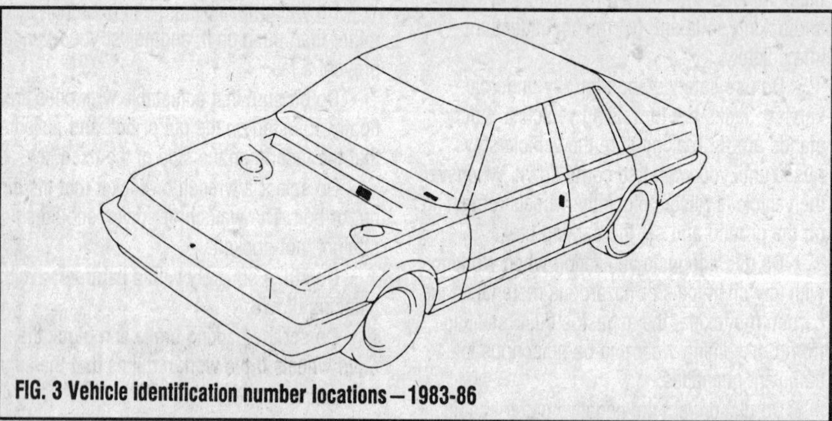

FIG. 3 Vehicle identification number locations—1983-86

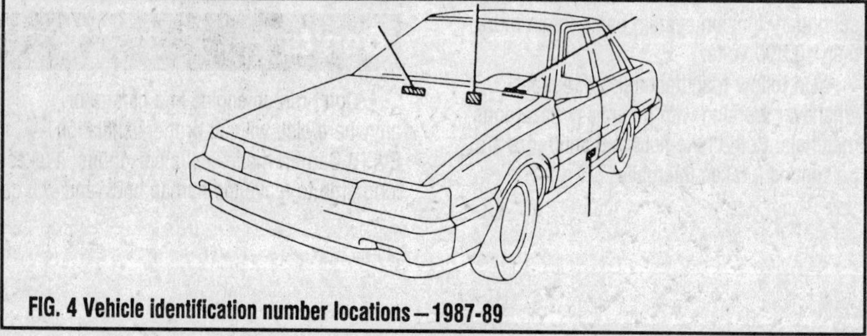

FIG. 4 Vehicle identification number locations—1987-89

FIG. 6 VIN tag and Body Certification tag on a 1991 Camry

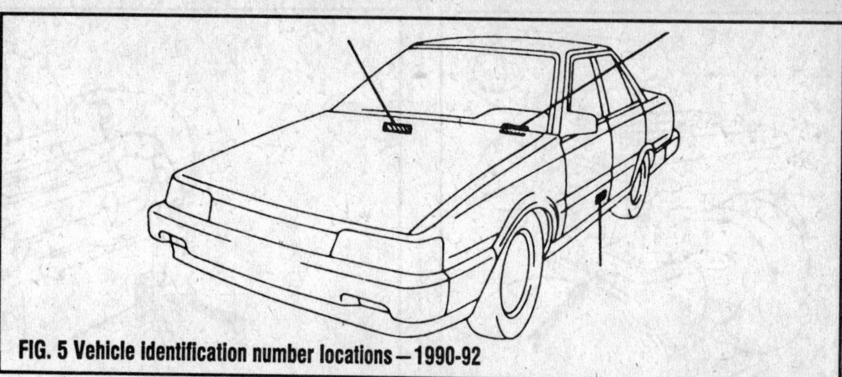

FIG. 5 Vehicle identification number locations — 1990-92

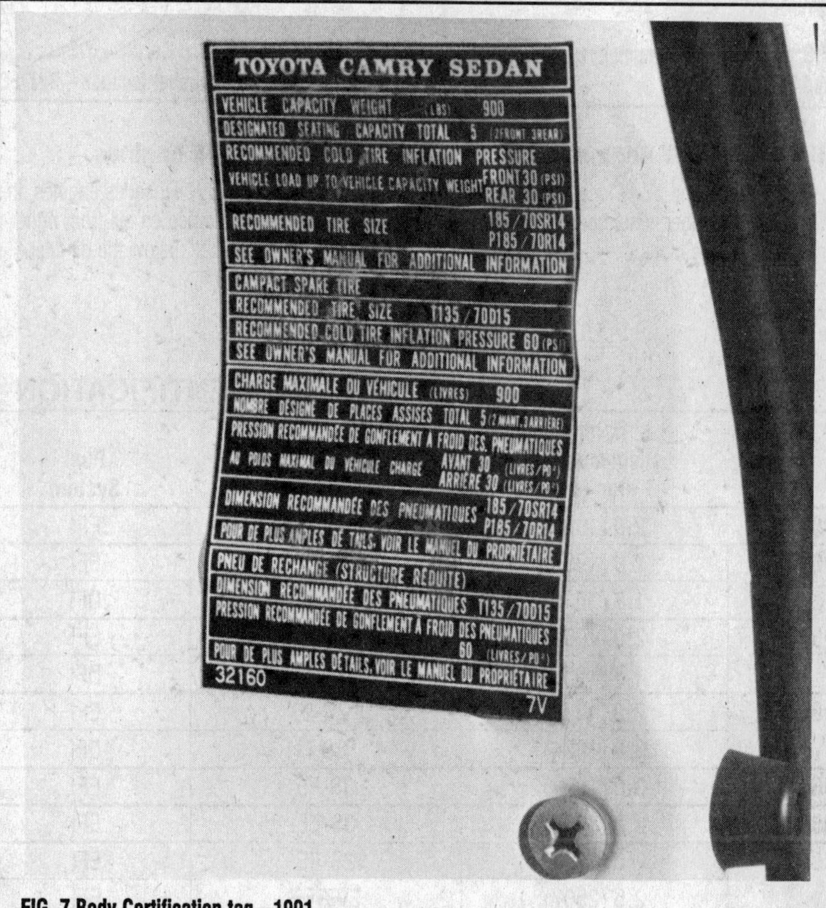

FIG. 7 Body Certification tag — 1991

Engine

➧ SEE FIGS. 8–11

The engine serial number consists of an engine series identification number, followed by a 6-digit production number.

1C-T and 2C-T Engines

On the 1C-T and 2C-T series engines, the serial numbers are stamped on the right side of the cylinder block, below the oil filter.

2S-E Engines

On the 2S-E series engines, the serial numbers are stamped on the right side of the cylinder block, below the oil filter.

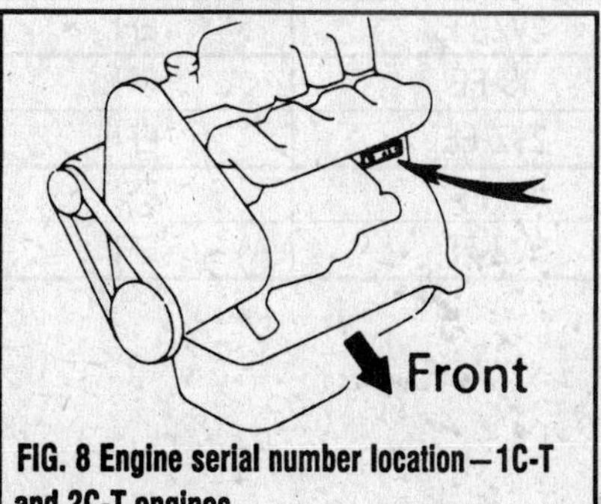

FIG. 8 Engine serial number location — 1C-T and 2C-T engines

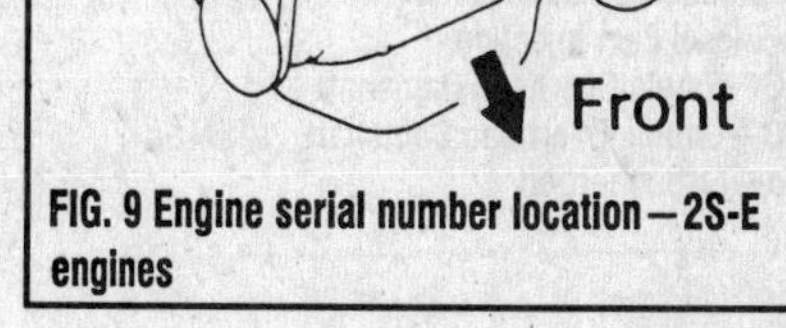

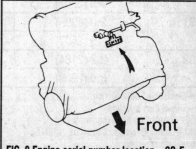

FIG. 9 Engine serial number location — 2S-E engines

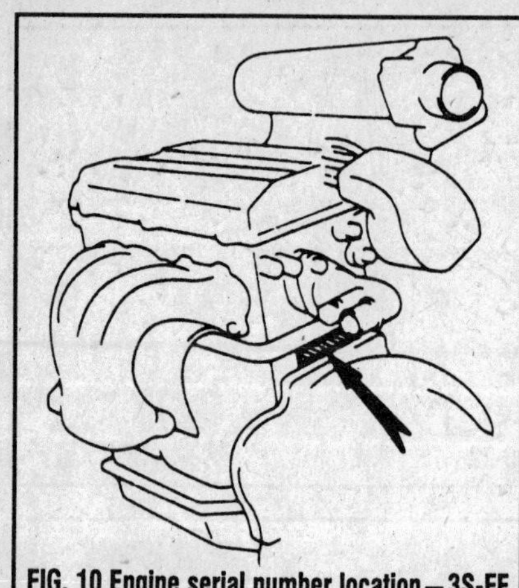
FIG. 10 Engine serial number location—3S-FE and 5S-FE engines

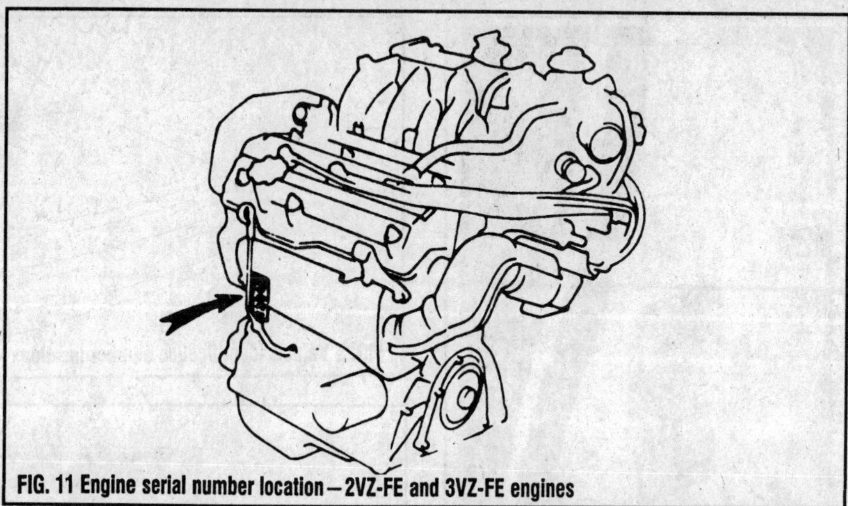
FIG. 11 Engine serial number location—2VZ-FE and 3VZ-FE engines

3S-FE and 5S-FE Engines

On the 3S-FE and 5S-FE engine series, the engine serial number is stamped on the left rear side of the engine block.

2VZ-FE and 3VZ-FE Engines

On the 2VZ-FE and 3VZ-FE series engines, the serial numbers are stamped on the front right side of the cylinder block, below the oil filter.

Transaxle

Transaxle identification codes are located on the vehicle identification number under the hood.

ENGINE IDENTIFICATION

Year	Engine Displacement liter (cc)	Engine Series (ID/VIN)	Fuel System	No. of Cylinders	Engine Type
1983	2.0 (1995)	2S-E	EFI	4	SOHC
1984	2.0 (1995)	2S-E	EFI	4	SOHC
	1.8 (1839)	1C-T	DFI	4	SOHC, Turbo
1985	2.0 (1995)	2S-E	EFI	4	SOHC
	1.8 (1839)	1C-T	DFI	4	SOHC, Turbo
1986	2.0 (1995)	2S-E	EFI	4	SOHC
	2.0 (1974)	2C-T	DFI	4	SOHC, Turbo
1987	2.0 (1998)	3S-FE	EFI	4	DOHC
1988	2.0 (1998)	3S-FE	EFI	4	DOHC
1989	2.0 (1998)	3S-FE	EFI	4	DOHC
	2.5 (2507)	2VZ-FE	EFI	6	DOHC
1990	2.0 (1998)	3S-FE	EFI	4	DOHC
	2.5 (2507)	2VZ-FE	EFI	6	DOHC
1991	2.0 (1998)	3S-FE	EFI	4	DOHC
	2.5 (2507)	2VZ-FE	EFI	6	DOHC
1992	2.2 (2164)	5S-FE	EFI	4	DOHC
	3.0 (2959)	3VZ-FE	EFI	6	DOHC

EFI—Electronic Fuel Injection
DFI—Diesel Fuel Injection
SOHC—Single Overhead Camshaft
DOHC—Double Overhead Camshaft
Turbo—Turbocharged

MANUAL TRANSAXLE APPLICATION CHART

Year	Model	Transmission Identification	Transmission Type
1983	Camry	S51	5 Spd.
1984	Camry	S51	5 Spd.
1985	Camry	S51	5 Spd.
1986	Camry	S51	5 Spd.
1987	Camry	S51	5 Spd.
1988	Camry (2WD)	S51	5 Spd.
	(4WD)	E56F2 ①, E56F5 ②	5 Spd.
1989	Camry (2WD, 4 cyl.)	S51	5 Spd.
	(2WD, 6 cyl.)	E52	5 Spd.
	(4WD)	E56F5	5 Spd.
1990	Camry (2WD, 4 cyl.)	S51	5 Spd.
	(2WD, 6 cyl.)	E52	5 Spd.
	(4WD)	E56F5	5 Spd.
1991	Camry (4 cyl.)	S51	5 Spd.
	(6 cyl.)	E52	5 Spd.
1992	Camry (4 cyl.)	S51	5 Spd.
	(6 cyl.)	E53	5 Spd.

① 4WD center differential with viscous coupling control
② 4WD center differential with differential lock-up

AUTOMATIC TRANSAXLE APPLICATION CHART

Year	Model	Transmission Identification	Transmission Type
1983	Camry	A140E	ECT
1984	Camry	A140E	ECT
1985	Camry	A140E	ECT
		A140L	OVER
1986	Camry	A140E	ECT
		A140L	OVER
1987	Camry	A140E	ECT
		A140L	OVER
1988	Camry	A140E	ECT
		A140L	OVER
1989	Camry (Sedan)	A140L	OVER
	(LX, DLX)	A140E, A540E ①	ECT
	(All-Trac)	A540H	ECT
1990	Camry (Sedan)	A140E	OVER
	(LX, DLX)	A140E, A540E ①	ECT
	(All-Trac)	A540H	ECT
1991	Camry (Sedan)	A140L	OVER
	(LX, DLX)	A140E, A540E ①	ECT
	(All-Trac)	A540H	ECT
1992	Camry (4 cyl.)	A140E	ECT
	(6 cyl.)	A540E	ECT

OVER—Overdrive
ECT—Electronically Controlled Transmission
① A540E used w/V6

ROUTINE MAINTENANCE

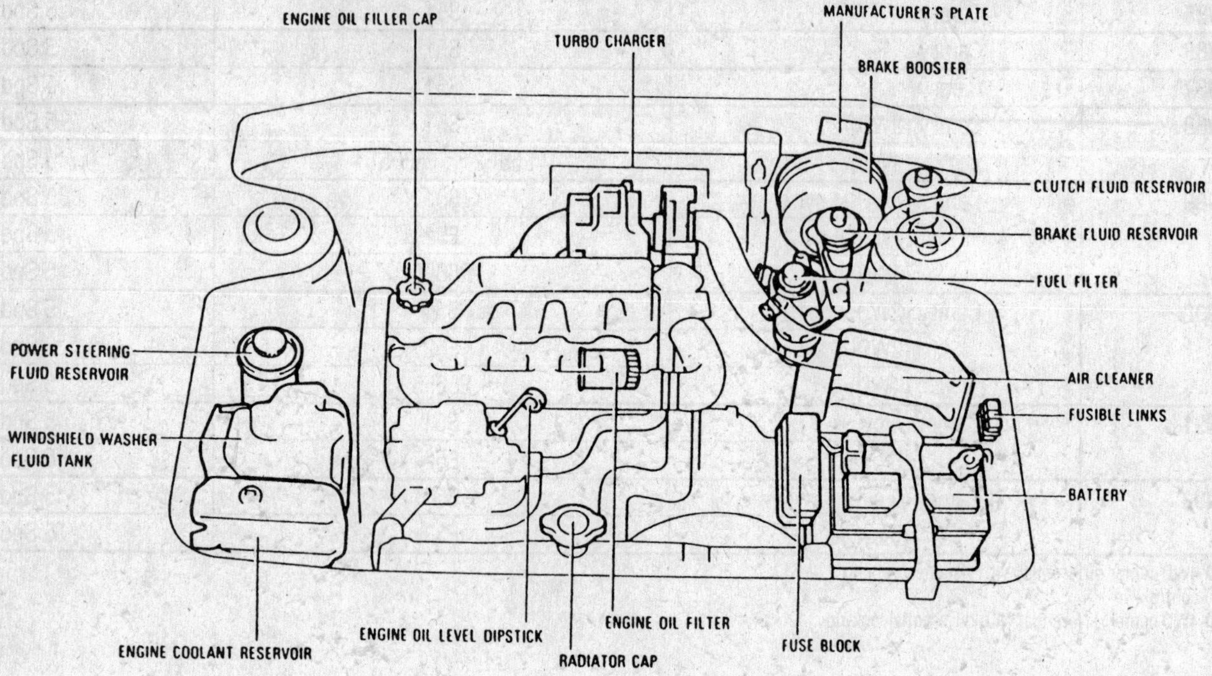

ENGINE OIL FILLER CAP
TURBO CHARGER
MANUFACTURER'S PLATE
BRAKE BOOSTER
CLUTCH FLUID RESERVOIR
BRAKE FLUID RESERVOIR
FUEL FILTER
POWER STEERING FLUID RESERVOIR
WINDSHIELD WASHER FLUID TANK
AIR CLEANER
FUSIBLE LINKS
BATTERY
ENGINE COOLANT RESERVOIR
ENGINE OIL LEVEL DIPSTICK
RADIATOR CAP
ENGINE OIL FILTER
FUSE BLOCK

FIG. 12 View of the engine compartment—1C-T engines

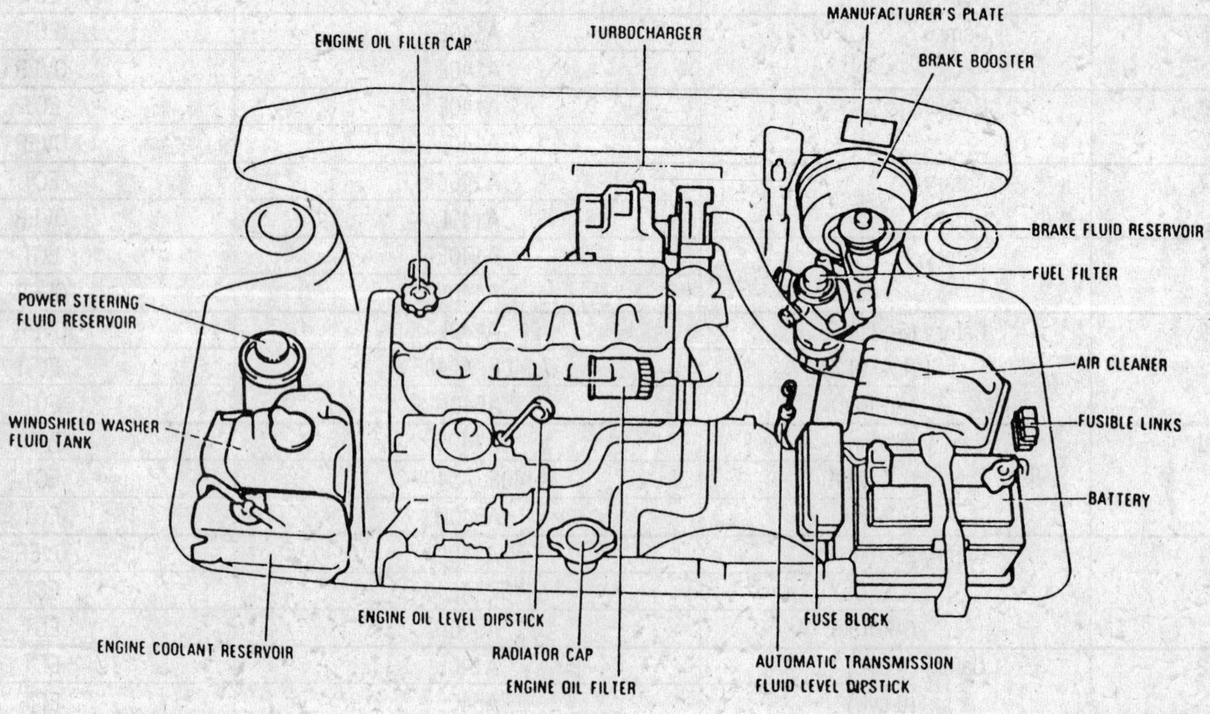

ENGINE OIL FILLER CAP
TURBOCHARGER
MANUFACTURER'S PLATE
BRAKE BOOSTER
BRAKE FLUID RESERVOIR
FUEL FILTER
POWER STEERING FLUID RESERVOIR
WINDSHIELD WASHER FLUID TANK
AIR CLEANER
FUSIBLE LINKS
BATTERY
ENGINE COOLANT RESERVOIR
ENGINE OIL LEVEL DIPSTICK
RADIATOR CAP
ENGINE OIL FILTER
FUSE BLOCK
AUTOMATIC TRANSMISSION FLUID LEVEL DIPSTICK

FIG. 13 View of the engine compartment—2C-T engines

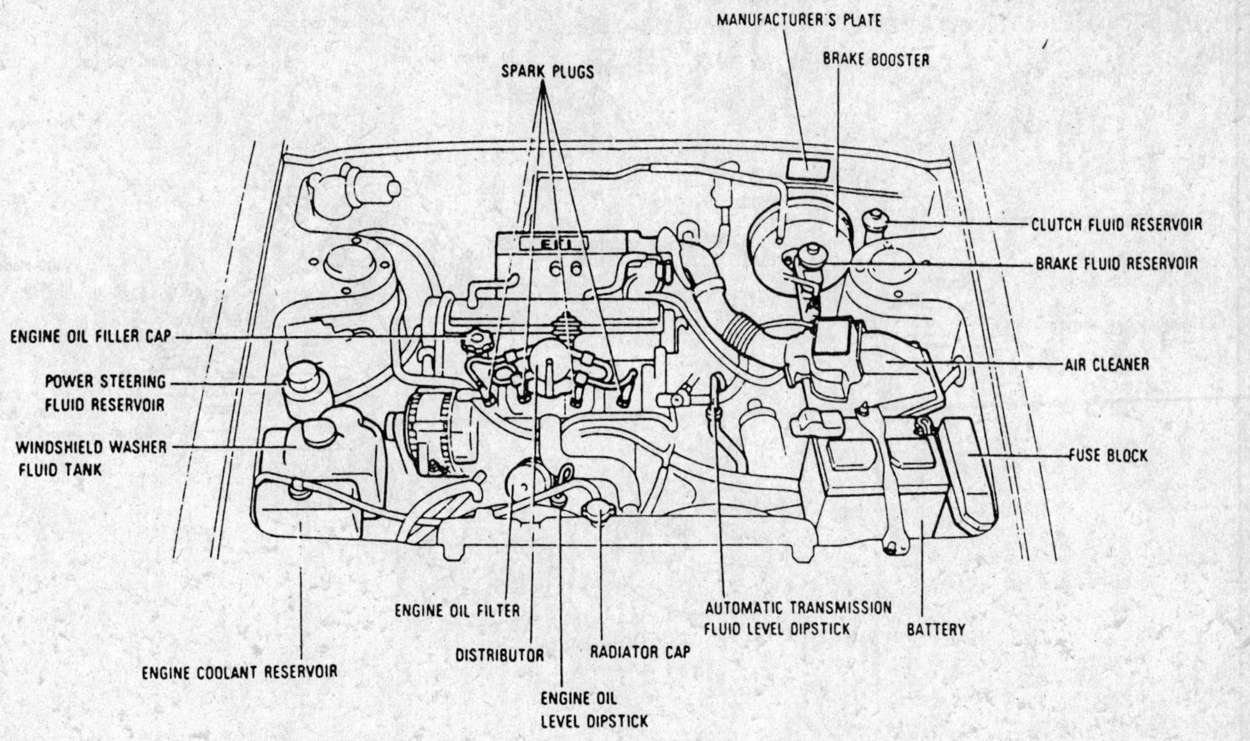

MANUFACTURER'S PLATE
BRAKE BOOSTER
SPARK PLUGS
CLUTCH FLUID RESERVOIR
BRAKE FLUID RESERVOIR
ENGINE OIL FILLER CAP
AIR CLEANER
POWER STEERING FLUID RESERVOIR
WINDSHIELD WASHER FLUID TANK
FUSE BLOCK
ENGINE OIL FILTER
AUTOMATIC TRANSMISSION FLUID LEVEL DIPSTICK
BATTERY
DISTRIBUTOR
RADIATOR CAP
ENGINE COOLANT RESERVOIR
ENGINE OIL LEVEL DIPSTICK

FIG. 14 View of the engine compartment — 2S-E engines

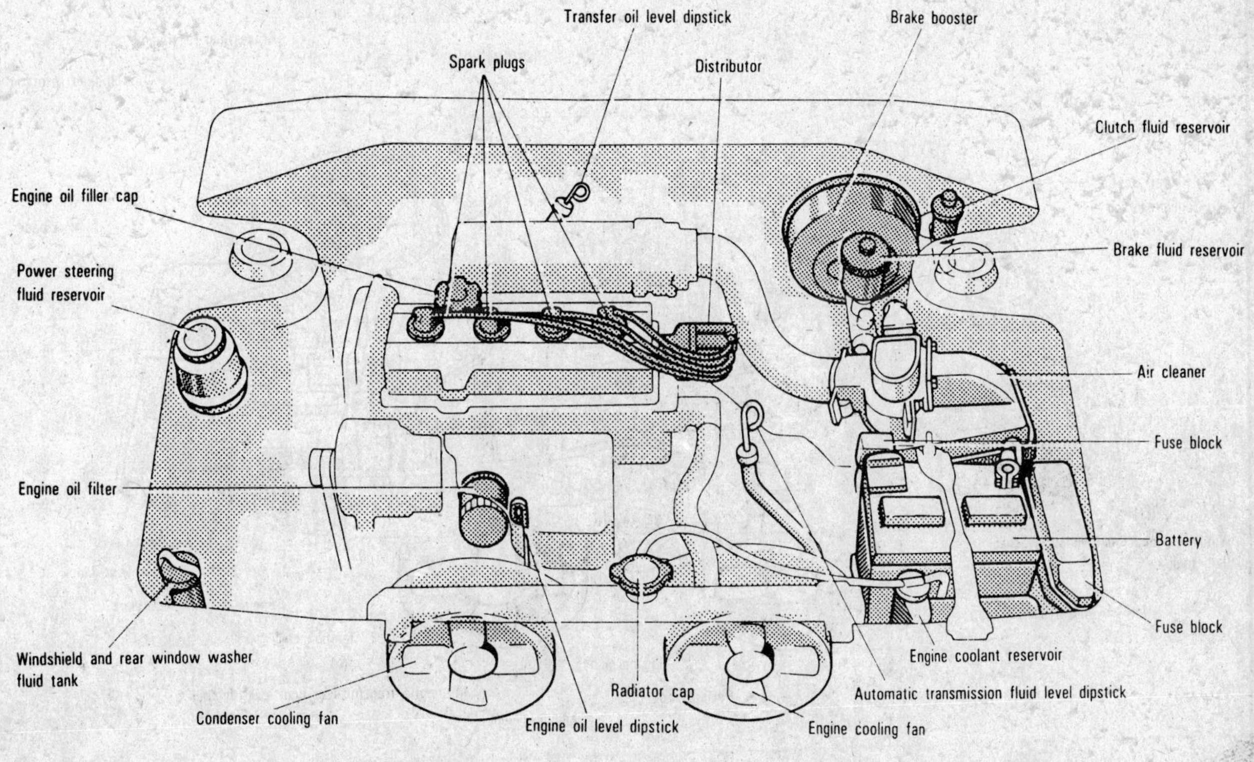

Transfer oil level dipstick
Brake booster
Spark plugs
Distributor
Clutch fluid reservoir
Engine oil filler cap
Brake fluid reservoir
Power steering fluid reservoir
Air cleaner
Fuse block
Engine oil filter
Battery
Fuse block
Windshield and rear window washer fluid tank
Engine coolant reservoir
Radiator cap
Automatic transmission fluid level dipstick
Condenser cooling fan
Engine oil level dipstick
Engine cooling fan

FIG. 15 View of the engine compartment — 3S-FE engines

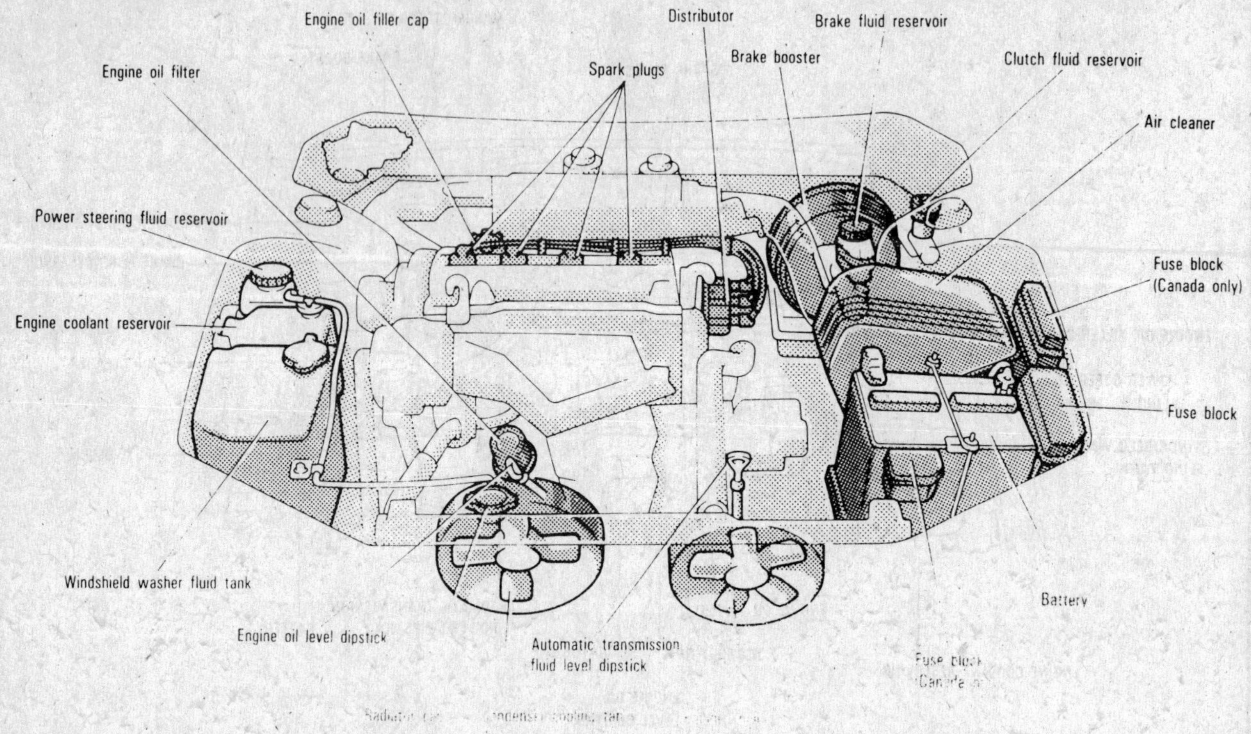

FIG. 16 View of the engine compartment—5S-FE engines

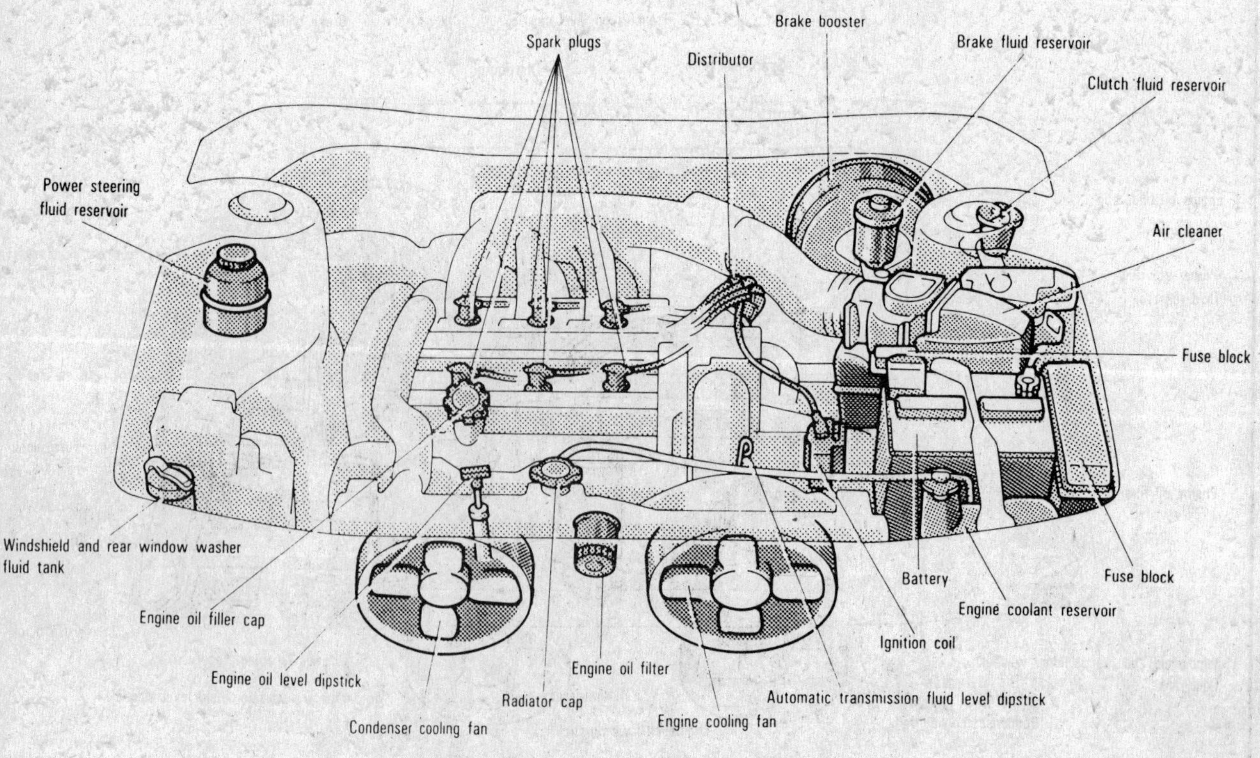

FIG. 17 View of the engine compartment—2VZ-FE engines

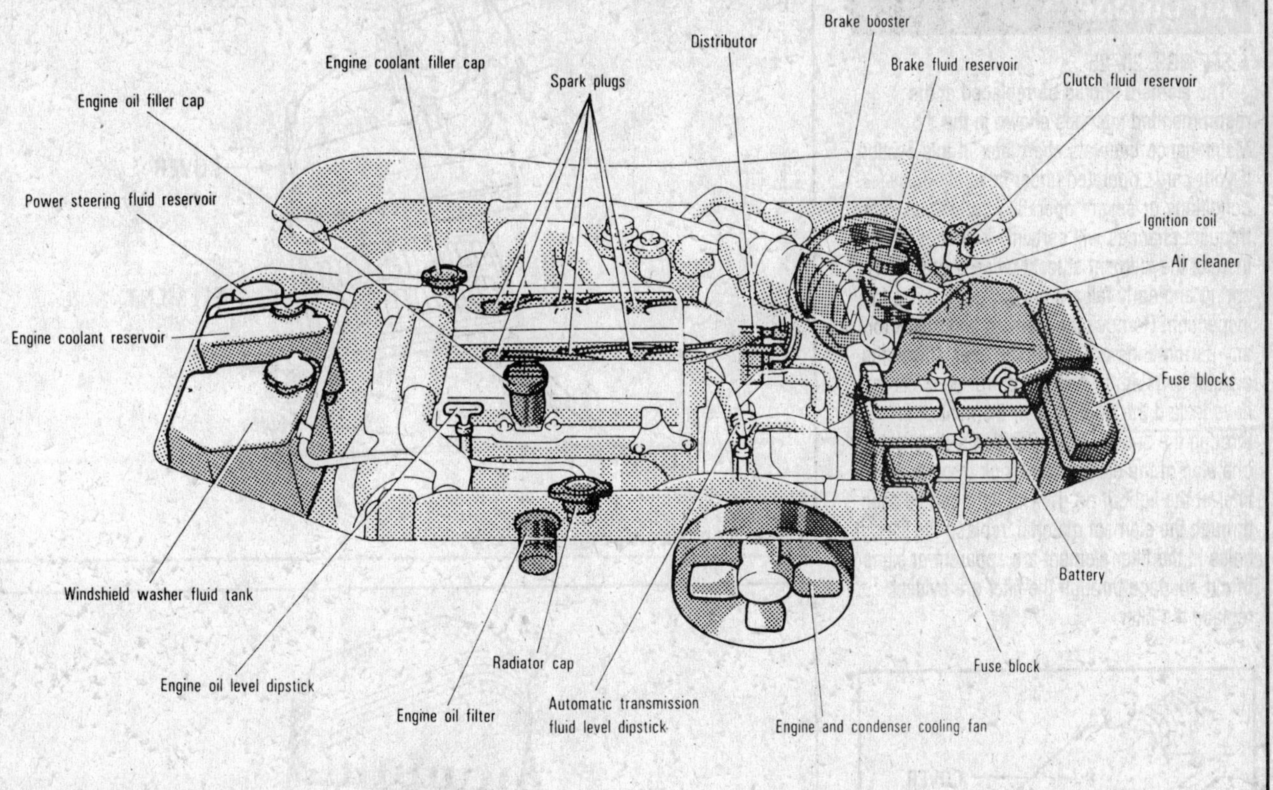

FIG. 18 View of the engine compartment – 3VZ-FE engines

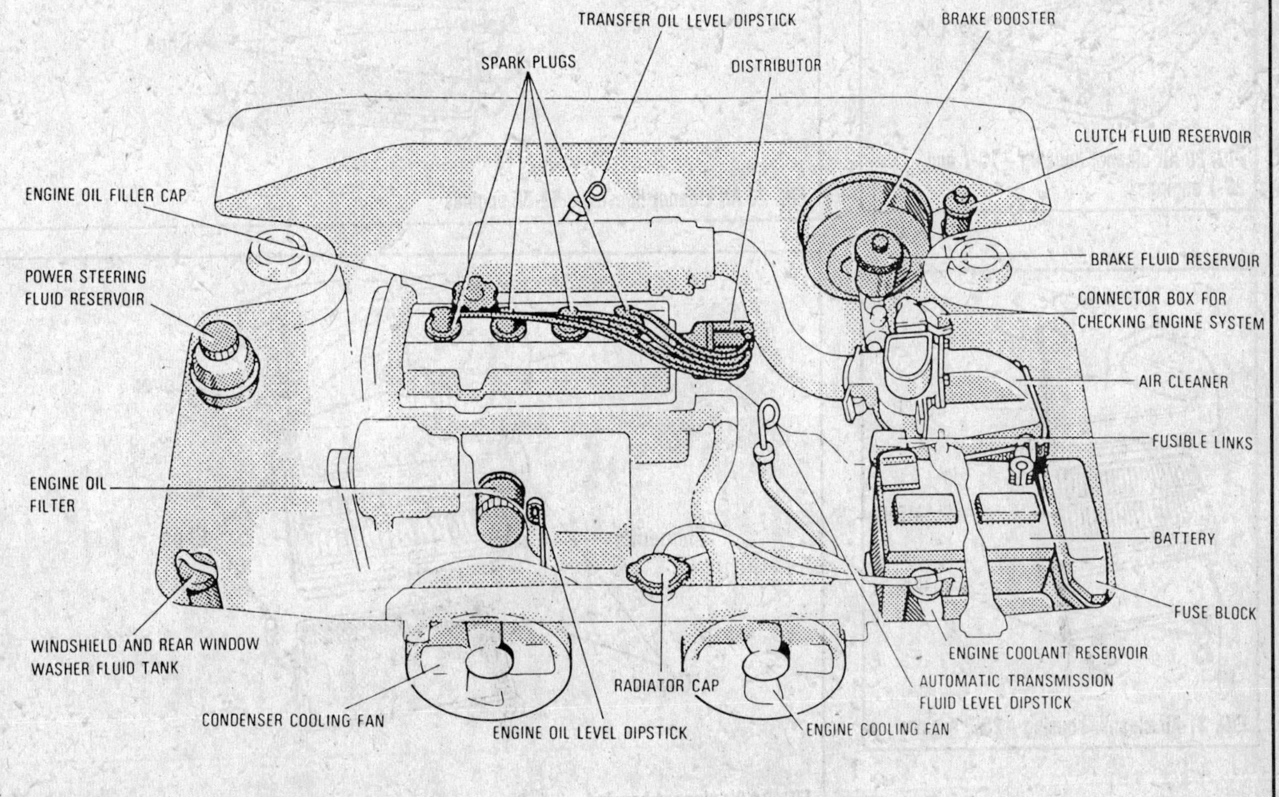

FIG. 19 Underhood component locations – 3S-FE engines

Air Cleaner

➧ SEE FIGS. 20–25

The element should be replaced at the recommended intervals shown in the Maintenance Intervals chart later in this section. If your car is operated under severely dusty conditions or severe operating conditions, more frequent changes will certainly be necessary. Inspect the element at least twice a year. Early spring and early fall are always good times for inspection. Remove the element and check for any perforations or tears in the filter. Check the cleaner housing for signs of dirt or dust that may have leaked through the filter element or in through the snorkel tube. Position a droplight on one side of the element and look through the filter at the light. If no glow of light can be seen through the element material, replace the filter. If holes in the filter element are apparent or signs of dirt seapage through the filter are evident, replace the filter.

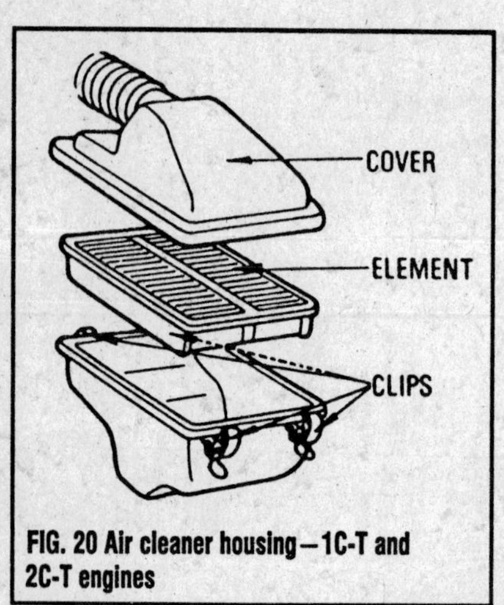

FIG. 20 Air cleaner housing—1C-T and 2C-T engines

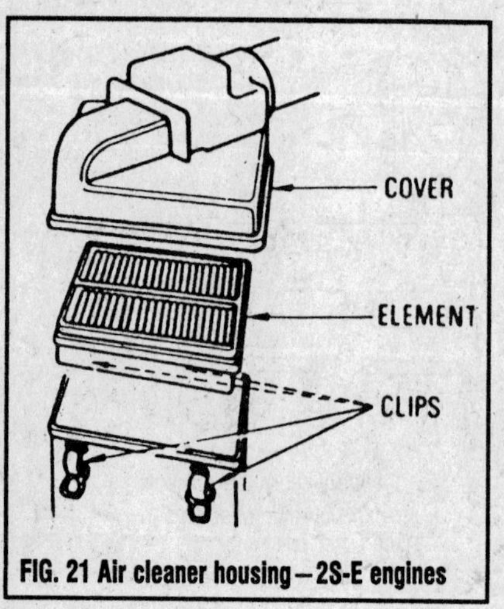

FIG. 21 Air cleaner housing—2S-E engines

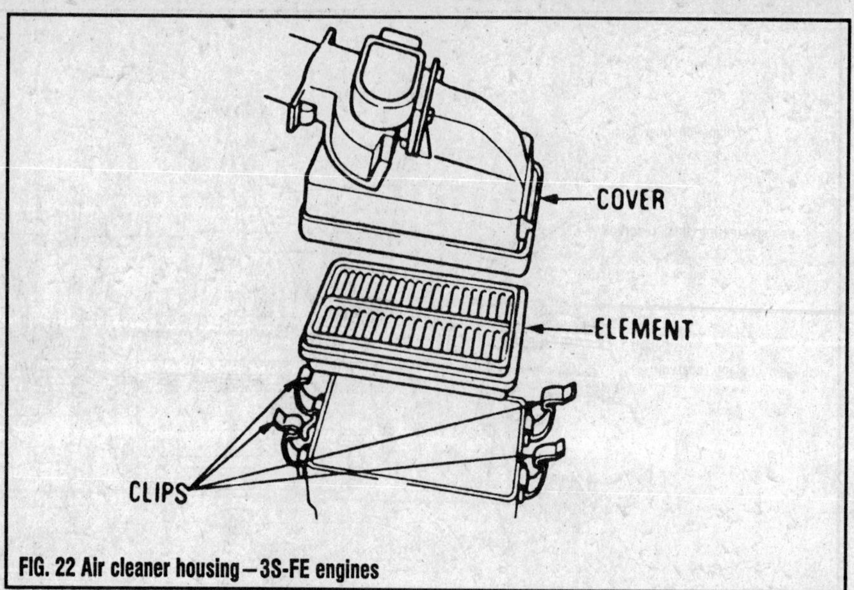

FIG. 22 Air cleaner housing—3S-FE engines

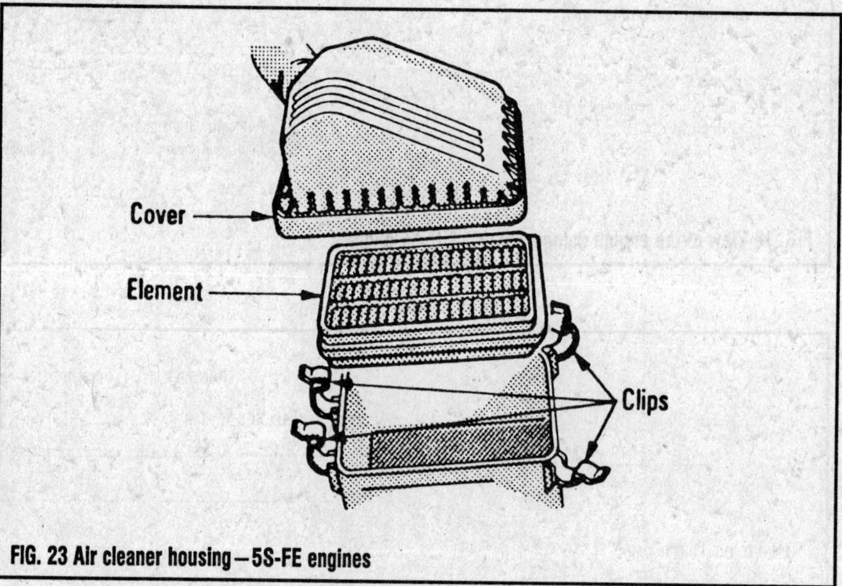

FIG. 23 Air cleaner housing—5S-FE engines

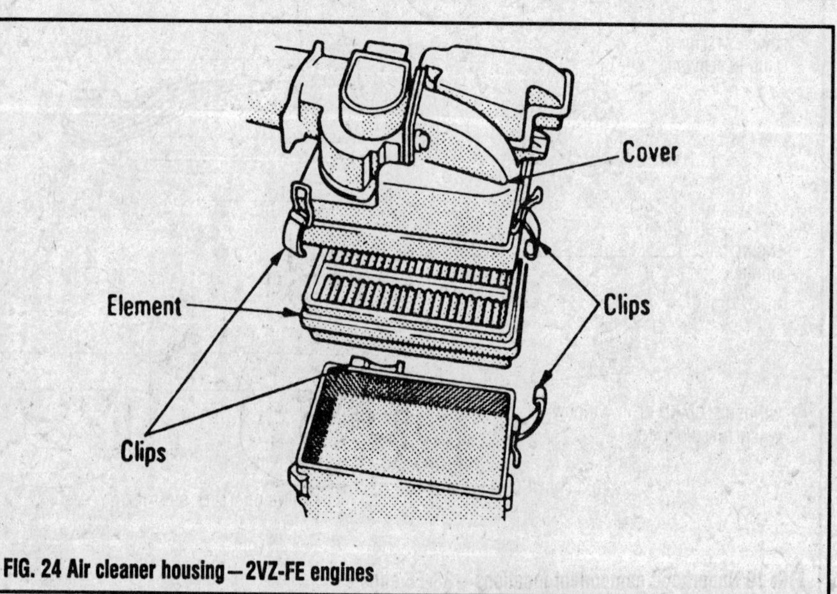

FIG. 24 Air cleaner housing—2VZ-FE engines

Cover
Element
Clips

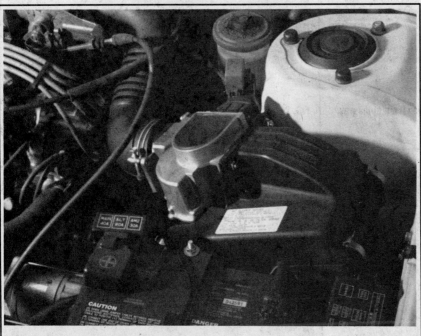

FIG. 25 Air cleaner housing—3VZ-FE engines

FIG. 26 View of the air cleaner housing—3S-FE engines

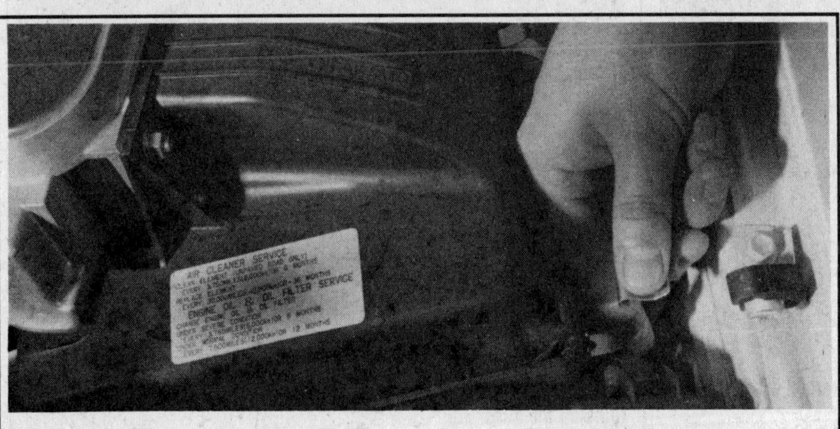

FIG. 27 Press and release all retaining clips

REMOVAL & INSTALLATION

➧ SEE FIGS. 26–32

1. Lift the wire tabs to release the four retaining clips on the bottom of the housing and lift off the top cover.
2. Position the cover with the air flow meter and the air cleaner flexible hose off to the side.
3. Withdraw the element from the housing and discard it.
4. With a clean rag, remove any dirt or dust from the front cover and also from the element seating surface.
5. Position and install the new filter element so that it seats properly in the housing.
6. Position the cover with the attached air flow meter and hose over the element. Secure it with the retaining clips.

CAUTION

Do not drive the vehicle with air cleaner removed. Doing so will allow dirt and a variety of other foreign particles to enter the engine and cause damage and wear. Also, backfiring could cause a fire in the engine compartment.

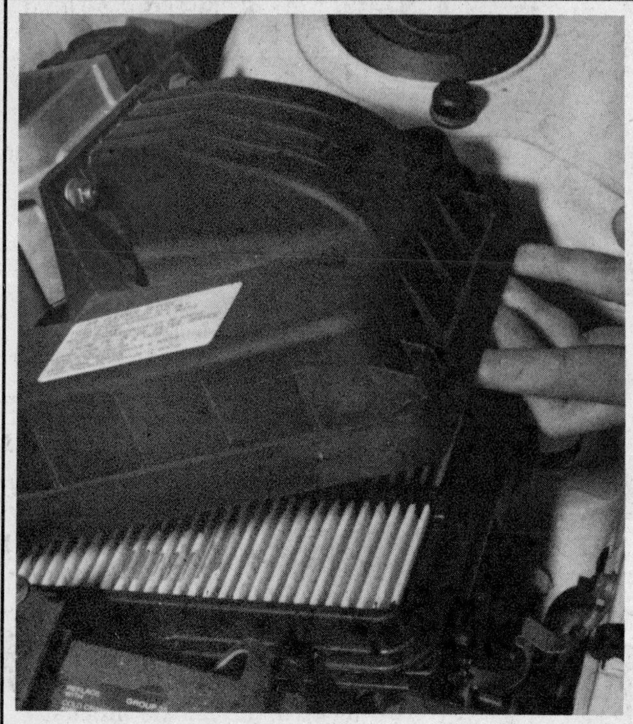

FIG. 28 Carefully lift up the upper housing and position it out of the way

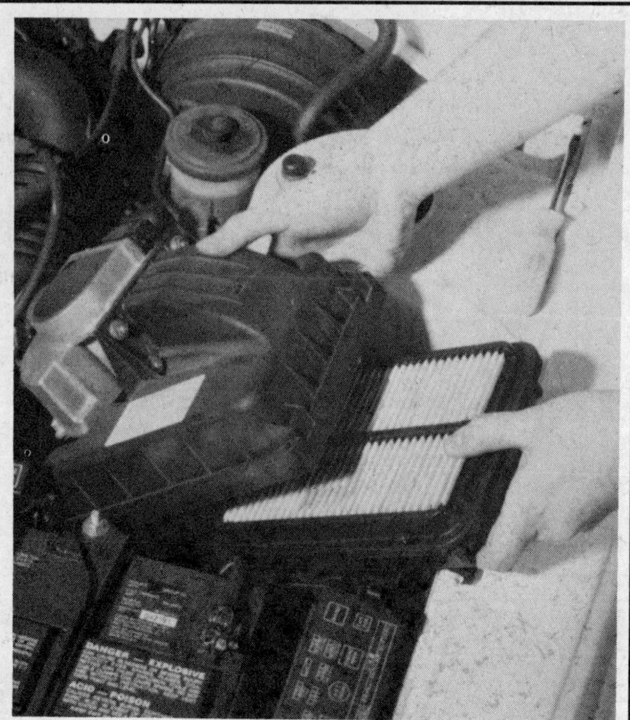

FIG. 29 Slide out the filter element

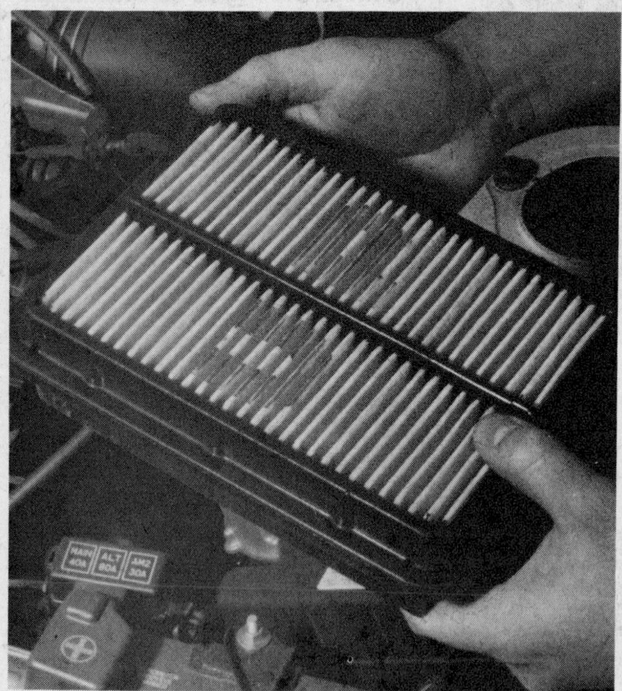

FIG. 30 Checking the filter element. Most filters are marked with UP for the top side

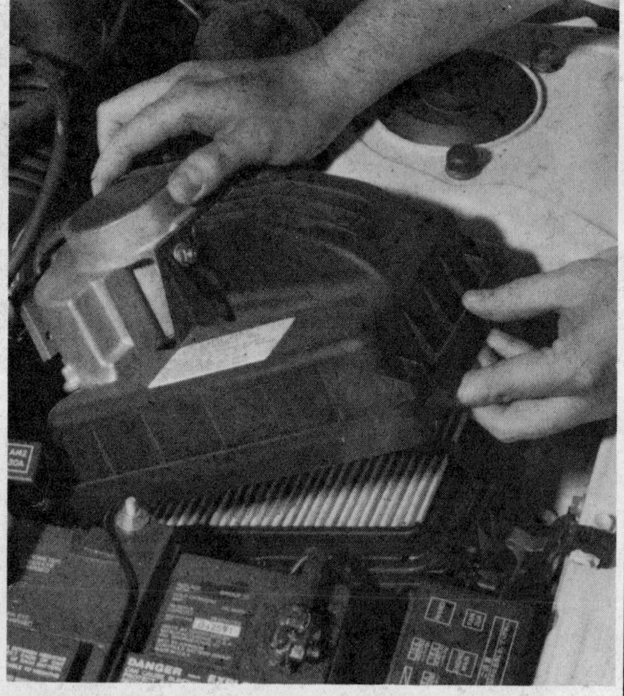

FIG. 31 After inserting the element, lower the upper housing and reinstall the clips

Inside

Outside

FIG. 32 To remove moderate accumulations of dust, low pressure air may be used

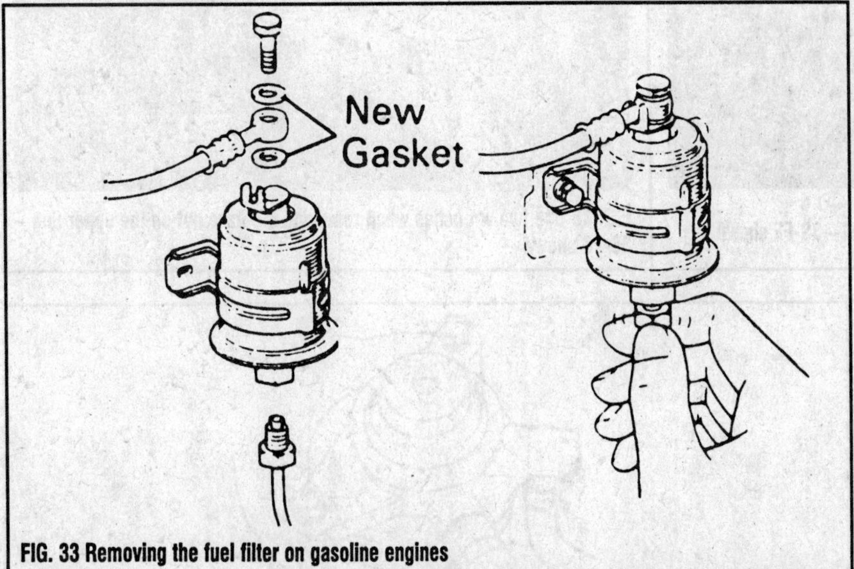

FIG. 33 Removing the fuel filter on gasoline engines

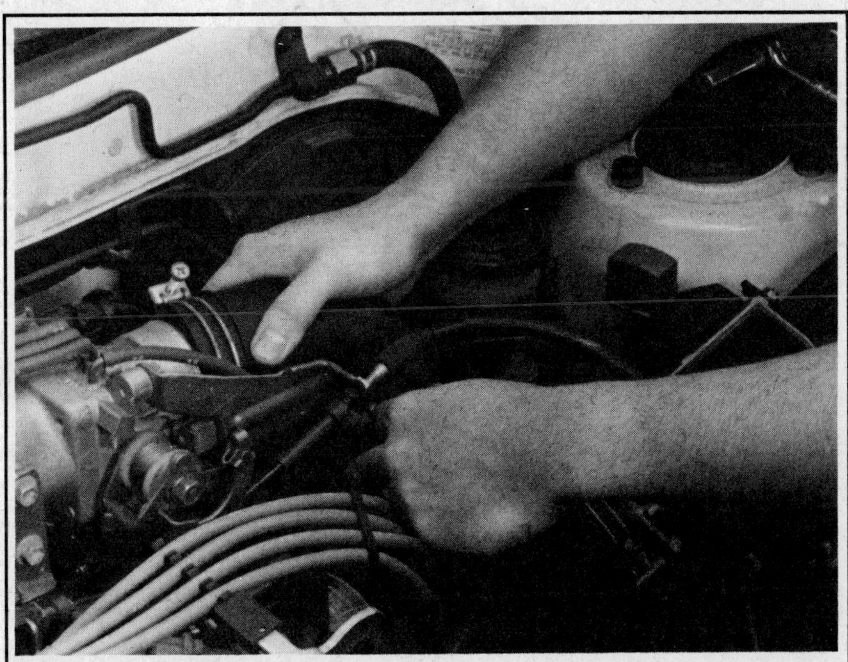

FIG. 34 Removing the air intake tube will afford easy access to the fuel filter — 3S-FE shown

Fuel Filter

REMOVAL & INSTALLATION

Gasoline Engines

➧ SEE FIGS. 33–36

✲✲ CAUTION

The fuel filter inlet and outlet lines may contain from 33–44 psi depending on how long the vehicle was allowed to sit between uses. When the fuel filter lines are disconnected, a large amount of fuel may be released from the connections. To be prepared for this occurance, have a couple of clean rags on hand and also obtain a small plastic container to place under the fuel filter to collect any excess fuel.

1. Disconnect the negative battery cable from its terminal.
2. Place a drain pan or plastic container under the fuel filter.
3. Slowly loosen the lower flare nut fitting until all the pressure is relieved and all the fuel is collected.
4. Loosen the union bolt on the upper portion of the filter and remove the banjo fitting and two metal gaskets. Discard the gaskets.
5. Pull the filter from the mounting bracket and install a new filter in its place.
6. Install the banjo fitting with a new metal gasket on each side and install the union bolt. Torque the union bolt to 22 ft. lbs. (30 Nm).
7. Connect the flare nut to the lower connection and make hand tight. Torque the flare nut to 22 ft. lbs. (30 Nm).
8. Remove the drain pan and/or rags and connect the negative battery cable.
9. Start the engine and visually inspect the upper and lower connections for leaks. Run the tip of your finger around both connections to ensure that the connections are leak-free. If any leaks are found they must be repaired immediately.

FIG. 35 The filter is attached to the inner fender well—3S-FE shown

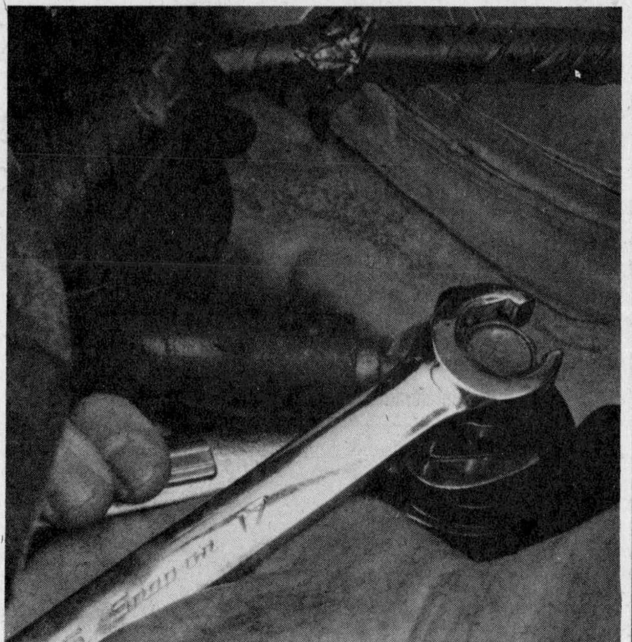

FIG. 36 Use two wrenches when removing the flare nut on the upper line—3S-FE shown

Diesel Engines

SEE FIGS. 37–38

1. Unplug the fuel filter warning switch connector located at the bottom of the filter housing.
2. Loosen the filter clamp bolt and remove the clamp.
3. Place a small plastic container under the drain plug at the bottom of the filter. Loosen the drain plug and drain the fuel from the filter.
4. With a strap or filter wrench, remove the fuel filter and the warning switch from the filter housing.
5. With pliers, remove the warning switch from the filter. Remove the O-ring and replace with new. Discard the filter.

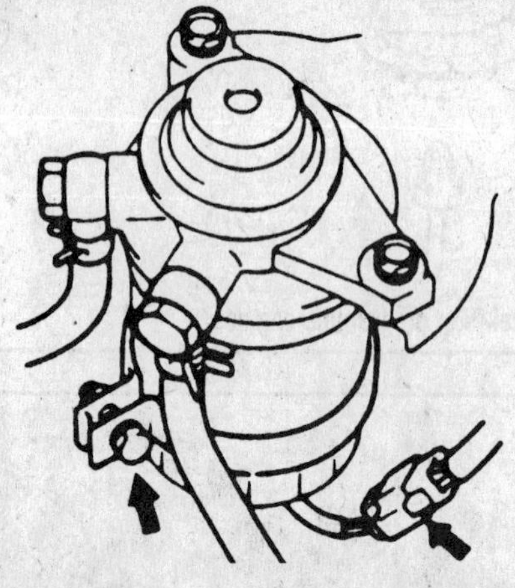

CAUTION

The switch is sensitive. Remove the switch carefully to avoid causing damage.

6. Coat the new O-ring with clean diesel fuel and install the O-ring onto the switch. Thread the switch into the new filter by hand to ensure proper seating of the O-ring. Properly tighten the switch. Check the drain plug to make sure it is tight.
7. Coat the fuel filter O-ring with clean diesel fuel and install the O-ring into the new filter. On 1C-T engines, screw the filter handtight only. On 2C-T engines, thread the filter into the housing

FIG. 37 Remove the clamp bolt and disconnect the warning switch on diesel engine fuel filters

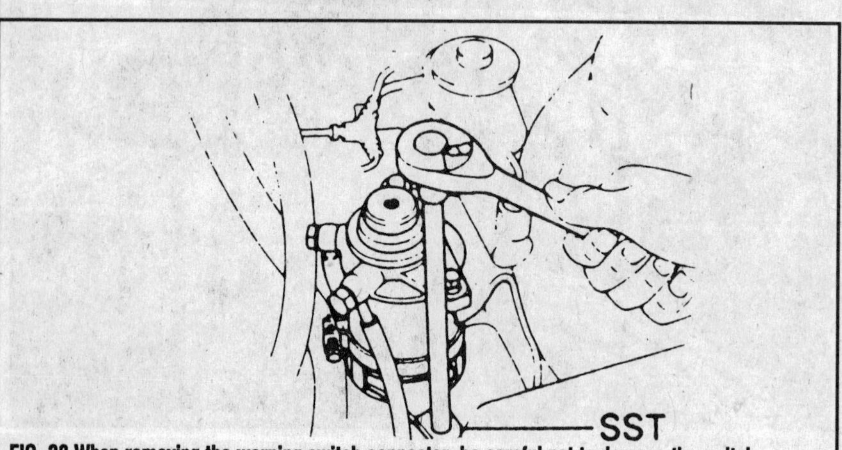

FIG. 38 When removing the warning switch connector, be careful not to damage the switch—diesel engines

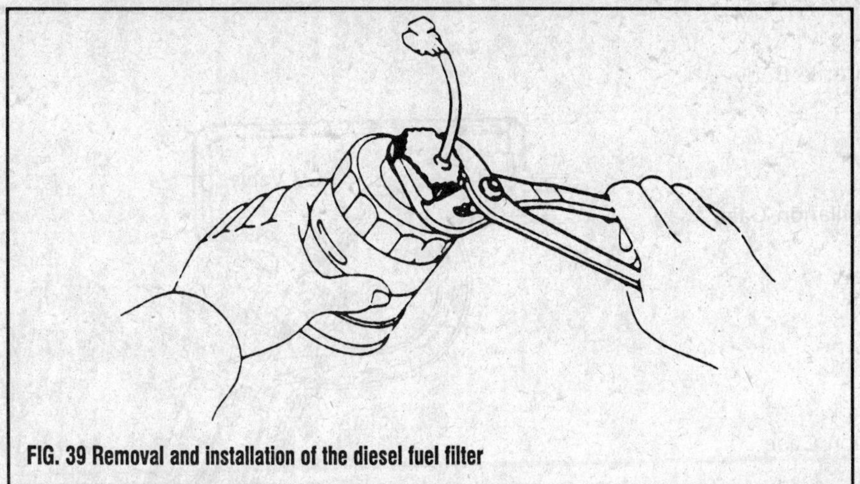

FIG. 39 Removal and installation of the diesel fuel filter

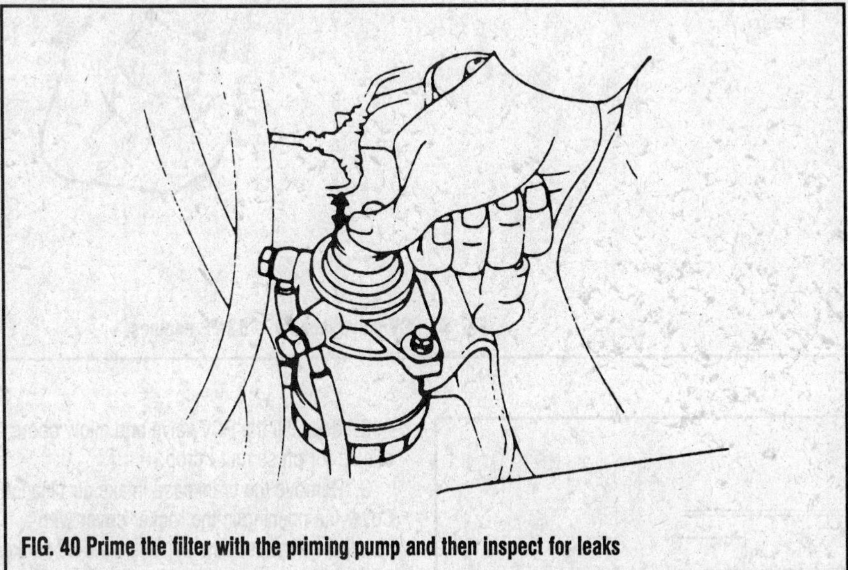

FIG. 40 Prime the filter with the priming pump and then inspect for leaks

by hand until a slight resistance is felt. With the strap wrench, tighten the filter and additional 3/4 turn.

8. Install the filter clamp and tighten the bolt.
9. Connect the warning switch electrical lead.
10. Push the priming pump on top of the filter housing several times to fill the filter. Start the engine and inspect for leaks. Correct all leaks immediately.

DRAINING THE FUEL FILTER

Diesel Engines Only

➧ SEE FIGS. 39–40

➡ In addition to filtration, the fuel filter also separates water from the fuel. A switch in the bottom of the filter senses the amount of water accumulated in the filter. When the warning light or buzzer on the dash comes on, the water in the fuel filter must be drained immediately.

1. Raise the hood and place a small drain pan or plastic container under the drain plug to catch the water.
2. Loosen the drain plug about 2–2 1/2 turns.

➡ Loosening the drain plug more than the indicated amount, will cause water to ooze from around the threads of the drain plug.

3. Press the priming pump on top of the filter until clean fuel only is discharged from the drain plug.
4. Tighten the drain plug by hand, do not use a tool.

PCV Valve

➧ SEE FIGS. 41–49

➡ Diesel engines do not utilize a PCV system. Additionally, the 3S-FE engine series, while equipped with a PCV system, do not utilize a PCV valve.

The PCV valve, which is the heart of the positive crankcase ventilation system, should be changed as noted in the Maintenance Intervals chart at the end of this section. The main thing to keep in mind is that the valve should be free of dirt and residue and should be in working order. As long as the valve is kept clean and is not showing signs of becoming damaged or gummed up, it should perform its function properly. When the valve cannot be cleaned sufficiently or becomes sticky and will not operate freely, it should be replaced.

The PCV valve is used to control the rate at which crankcase vapors are returned to the intake manifold. The action of the valve plunger is controlled by intake manifold vacuum and the spring. During deceleration and idle, when manifold vacuum is high, it overcomes the tension of the valve spring and the plunger bottoms in the manifold end of the valve housing. Because of the valve construction, it reduces, but dies not stop, the passage of vapors to the intake manifold. When the engine is lightly accelerated or operated at constant speed, spring tension matches intake manifold vacuum pull and the plunger takes a mid-position in the valve body, allowing more vapors to flow into the manifold.

The valve is either mounted on the valve cover or in the line which runs from the intake manifold to the crankcase. Do not attempt to adjust or repair the valve. If the valve is faulty, replace it.

TESTING

An inoperative PCV system will cause rough idling, sludge and oil dilution. In the event erratic idle, never attempt to compensate by disconnecting the PCV system. Disconnecting the PCV system will adversely affect engine ventilation. It could also shorten engine life through the buildup of sludge.

To inspect the PCV valve, proceed as follows:

1. With the engine idling, remove the PCV valve from the rocker cover or line. If the valve is not plugged, a hissing sound will be heard. A strong vacuum should be felt when you place your finger over the valve.

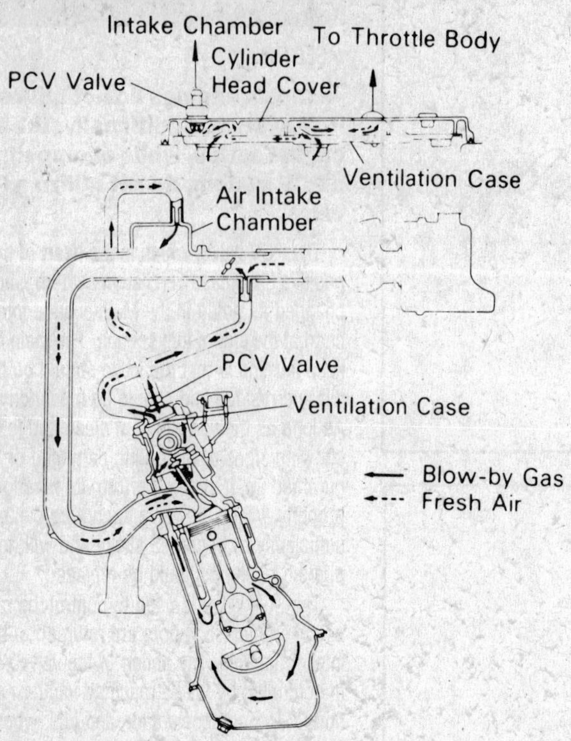

Intake Chamber
To Throttle Body
Cylinder Head Cover
PCV Valve
Ventilation Case
Air Intake Chamber
PCV Valve
Ventilation Case
Blow-by Gas
Fresh Air

FIG. 41 PCV valve location – 2S-E engines

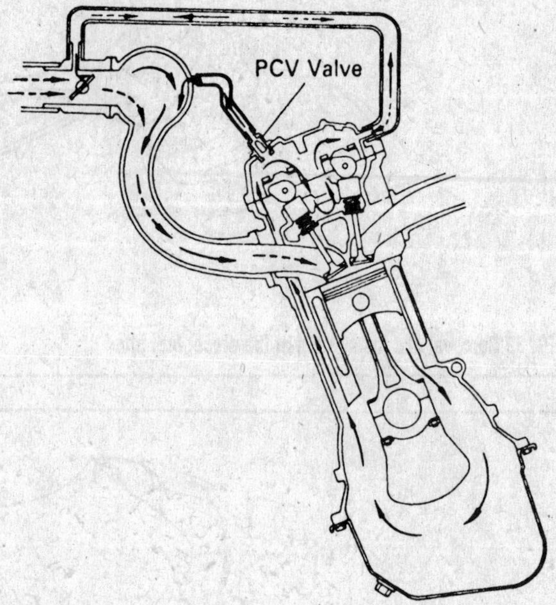

PCV Valve

FIG. 42 PCV valve location – 5S-FE engines

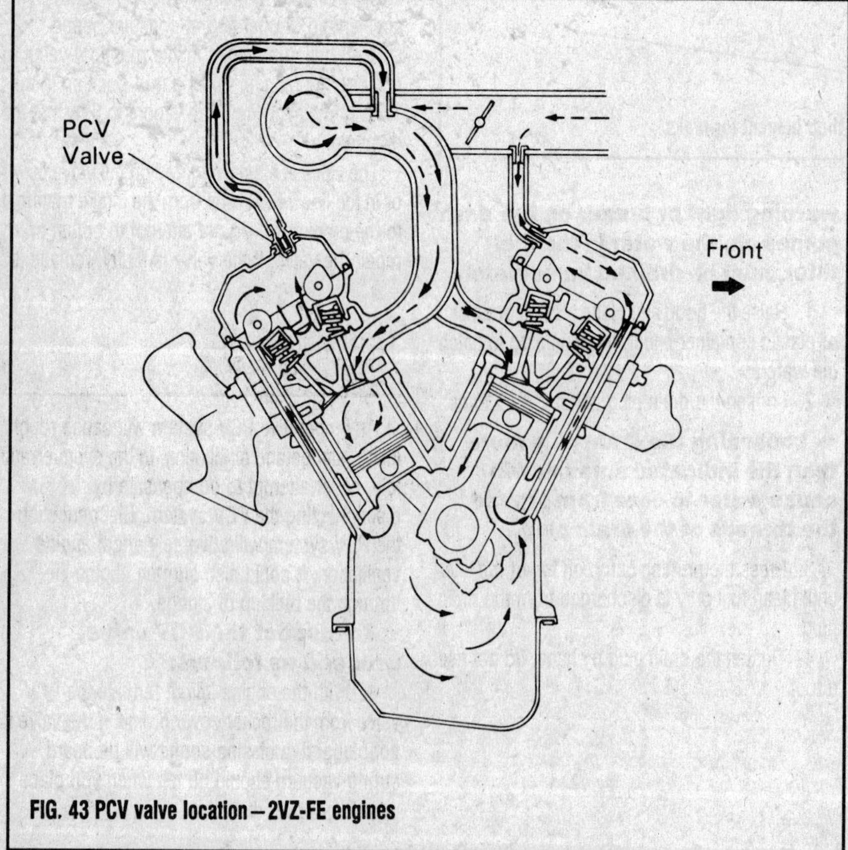

FIG. 43 PCV valve location – 2VZ-FE engines

2. Reinstall the PCV valve and allow about a minute for pressure to drop.

3. Remove the crankcase intake air cleaner. Cover the opening in the rocker cover with a piece of stiff paper. The paper should be sucked against the opening with noticeable force.

4. With the engine stopped, remove the PCV valve and shake it. A rattle or clicking should be heard to indicate that the valve is free.

5. If the system meets the tests in Steps 1, 2, 3, and 4 (above), no further service is required, unless replacement is specified in the Maintenance Intervals Chart. If the system does not meet the tests, the valve should be replaced with a new one.

➡ Do not attempt to clean a PCV valve.

6. With a new PCV valve installed, if the paper is not sucked against the crankcase air intake opening (see Step 2), it will be necessary to clean the PCV valve hose and the passage in the manifold.

7. Clean the line with Combustion Chamber Conditioner or similar solvent. Do not leave the hoses in solvent for more than 1/2 hour. Allow the line to air dry.

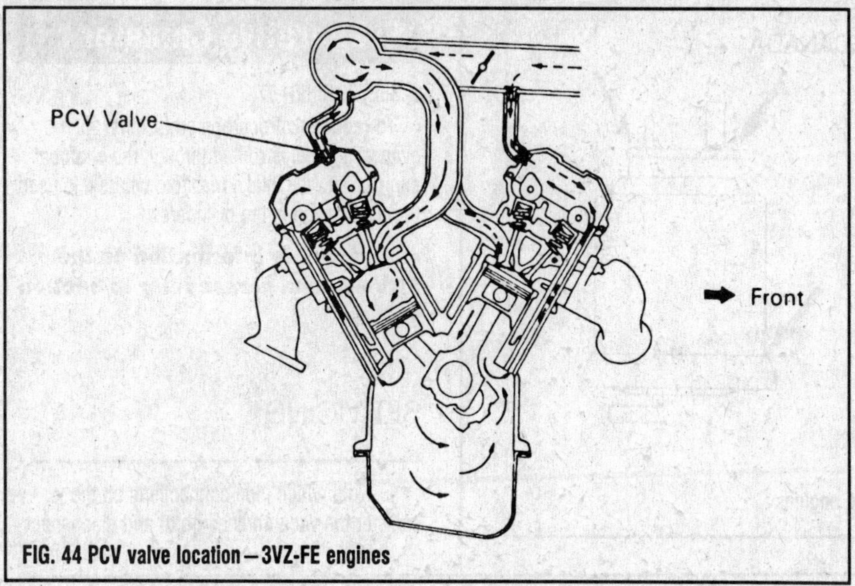

FIG. 44 PCV valve location—3VZ-FE engines

FIG. 45 Inspection of the PCV hoses and connections—2S-E engines

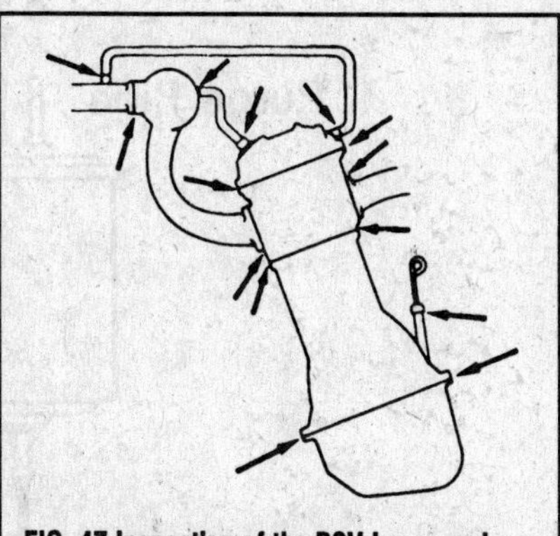

FIG. 47 Inspection of the PCV hoses and connections—5S-FE engines

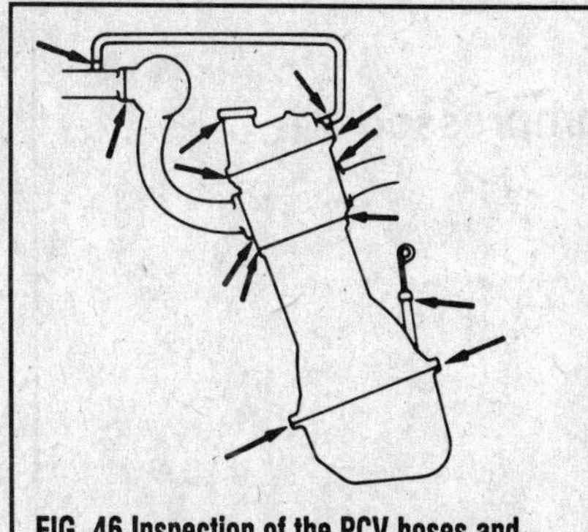

FIG. 46 Inspection of the PCV hoses and connections—3S-FE engines

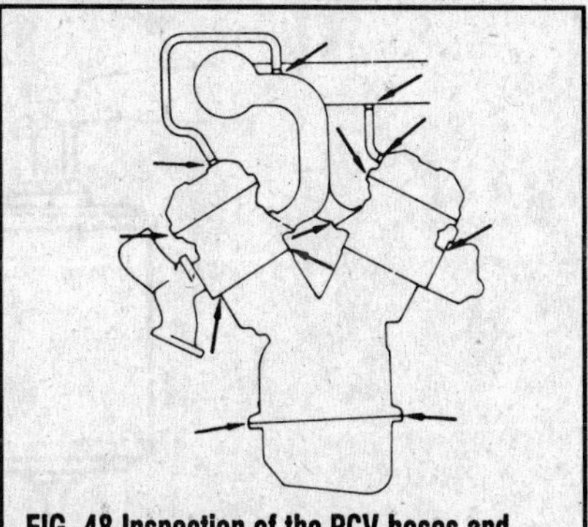

FIG. 48 Inspection of the PCV hoses and connections—2VZ-FE engines

➡ It is not necessary to disassembly the carburetor for this operation. If necessary, use a smaller drill, so that no metal is removed.

8. After checking and/or servicing the Crankcase Ventilation System, any components that do not allow passage or air to the intake manifold should be replaced.

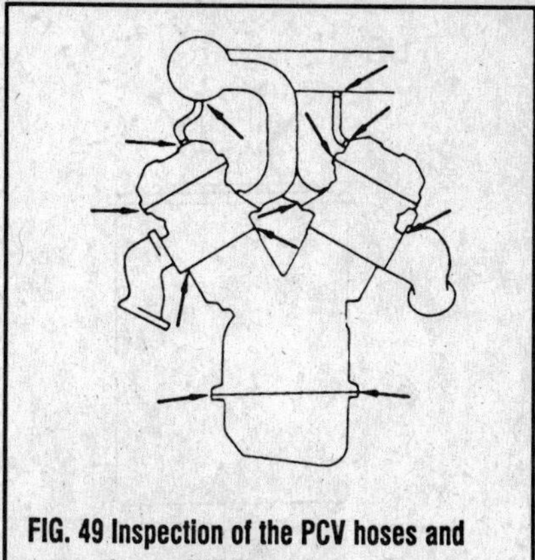

FIG. 49 Inspection of the PCV hoses and connections—3VZ-FE engines

REMOVAL & INSTALLATION

1. Remove the PCV valve from the cylinder head cover or from the manifold-to-crankcase hose. Clean any gum deposits from the orifices by spraying the valve with carburetor or contact cleaner.
2. Attach a length of clean rubber hose to the crankcase end of the valve. Blow into the hose and place your finger over the other end. Air should pass freely through the valve.

CAUTION

Do not suck air through the valve because the petroleum substances inside the valve are harmful to your health. Besides, they taste bad.

3. Remove the hose and connect it to the other end (intake manifold) end of the valve. Blow into the valve through the hose and place your finger over the other end. Very little air should pass through.
4. If the valve fails either of the tests, replace it.
5. Visually inspect all hose connections and hoses for cracks, clogs or deterioration and replace as necessary.
6. Install the PCV valve. Make sure all hose connections are tight.

➡ For further information on the PCV system, please refer to Section 4.

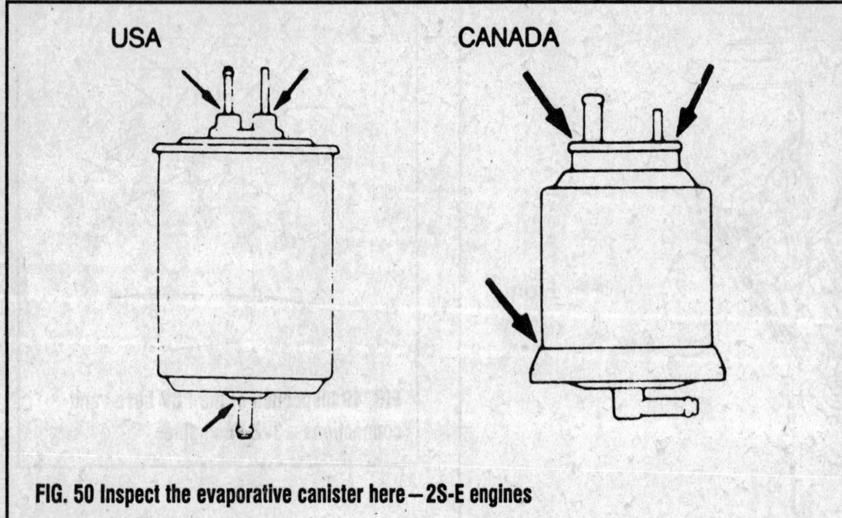

FIG. 50 Inspect the evaporative canister here—2S-E engines

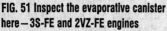

Evaporative Canister

➧ SEE FIGS. 50–57

To reduce hydrocarbon emissions, evaporated fuel is routed through the charcoal canister into the intake manifold where it is used for combustion in the cylinders.

➡ For further information on the PCV system. please refer to Section 4.

SERVICING

1. Note which pipe connections on the canister the vacuum lines go to and disconnect

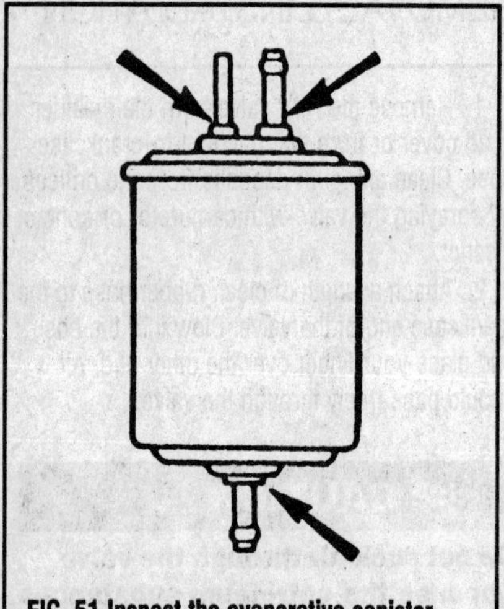
FIG. 51 Inspect the evaporative canister here—3S-FE and 2VZ-FE engines

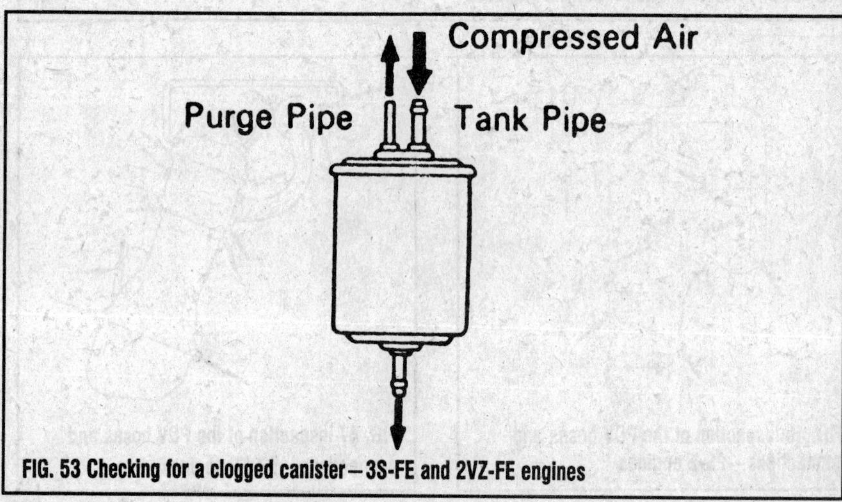

FIG. 53 Checking for a clogged canister—3S-FE and 2VZ-FE engines

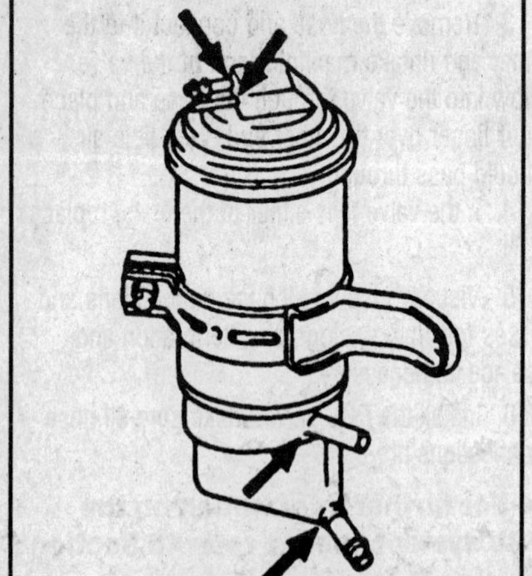
FIG. 52 Inspect the evaporative canister here—5S-FE and 3VZ-FE engines

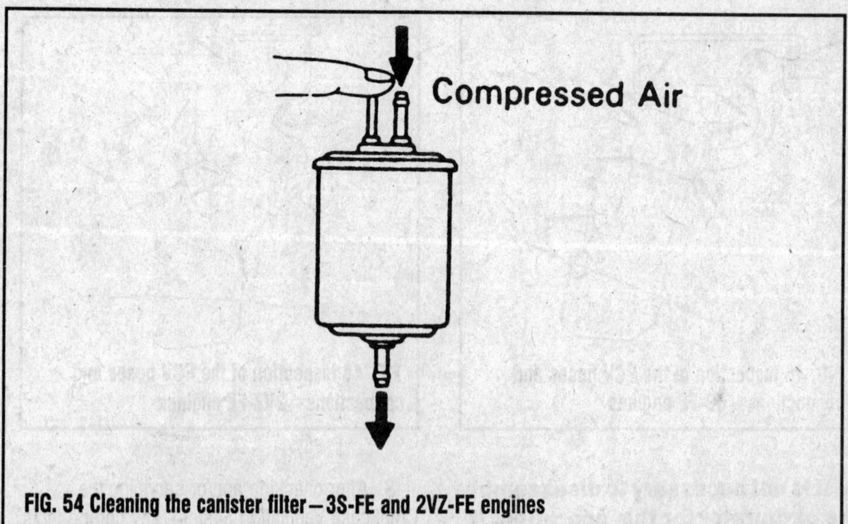

FIG. 54 Cleaning the canister filter—3S-FE and 2VZ-FE engines

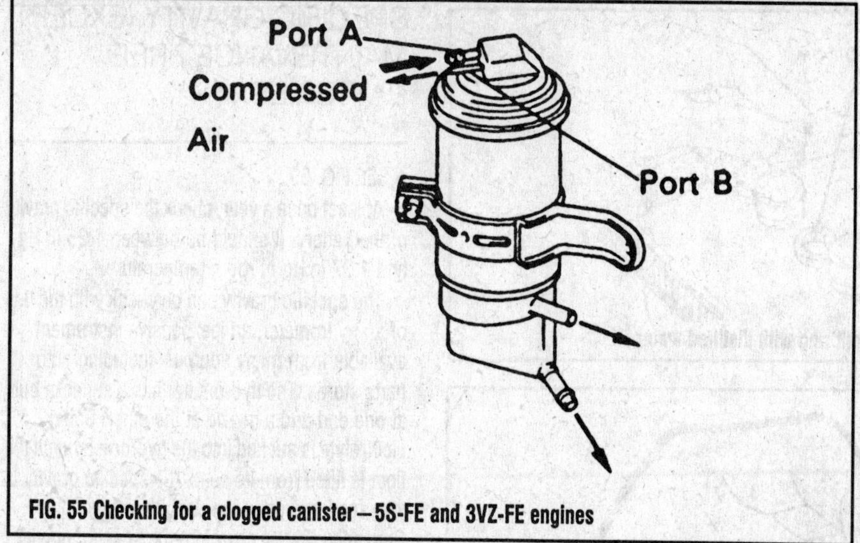

FIG. 55 Checking for a clogged canister—5S-FE and 3VZ-FE engines

Port A
Compressed
Air
Port B

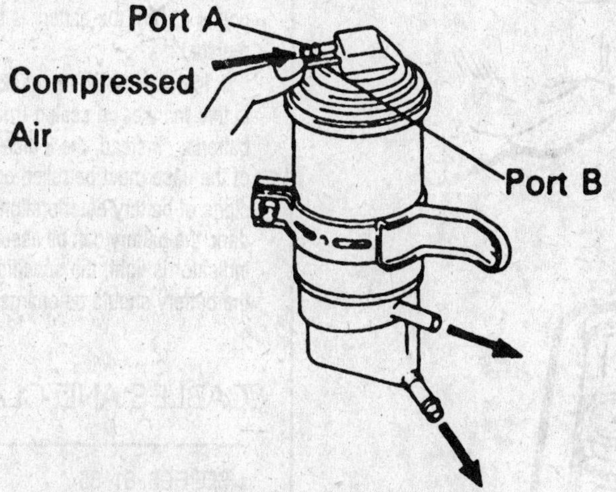

FIG. 56 Cleaning the canister filter—5S-FE and 3VZ-FE engines

FIG. 57 The evaporative canister is under the master cylinder, near the fuel filter—3S-FE engine shown

them. This can be done easily with lettered or numbered strips of masking tape.

2. Remove the charcoal canister.

3. The canister should be checked for clogging and a stuck check valve. Using low pressure compressed air, blow into the tank pipe, and place your hand over the other pipes to ensure that the air flows freely. Blow compressed air into the purge pipe and make sure that air does not flow from the other pipes. If the air does not flow as outlined, replace the canister.

4. If the canister is clogged, it may be cleaned using low pressure compressed air. To clean the canister, blow low pressure compressed air into the tank pipe while holding the upper canister pipe closed. If any of the activated carbon comes out, replace the canister.

➡ Do not attempt to wash the canister to clean it.

5. The charcoal canister vacuum lines and pipe connections should be checked for clogging, pinching, looseness and cracks. Replace all damaged vacuum lines.

6. Install the charcoal canister and connect the canister hoses to their proper connections.

Battery

FLUID LEVEL (EXCEPT MAINTENANCE FREE BATTERIES)

➧ SEE FIG. 58

Check the battery electrolyte level at least once a month, or more often in hot weather or during periods of extended operation. The level can be checked through the case on translucent polypropylene batteries; the cell caps must be removed on other models. The electrolyte level in each cell should be kept filled to the split ring inside, or the line marked on the outside of the case.

If the level is low, add only distilled water, or colorless, odorless drinking water, through the opening until the level is correct. Each cell is completely separate from the others, so each must be checked and filled individually.

If water is added in freezing weather, the car should be driven several miles to allow the water to mix with the electrolyte. Otherwise, the battery could freeze.

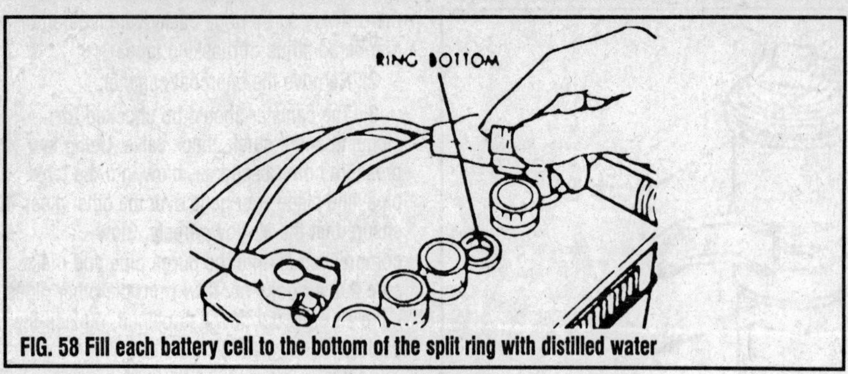

FIG. 58 Fill each battery cell to the bottom of the split ring with distilled water

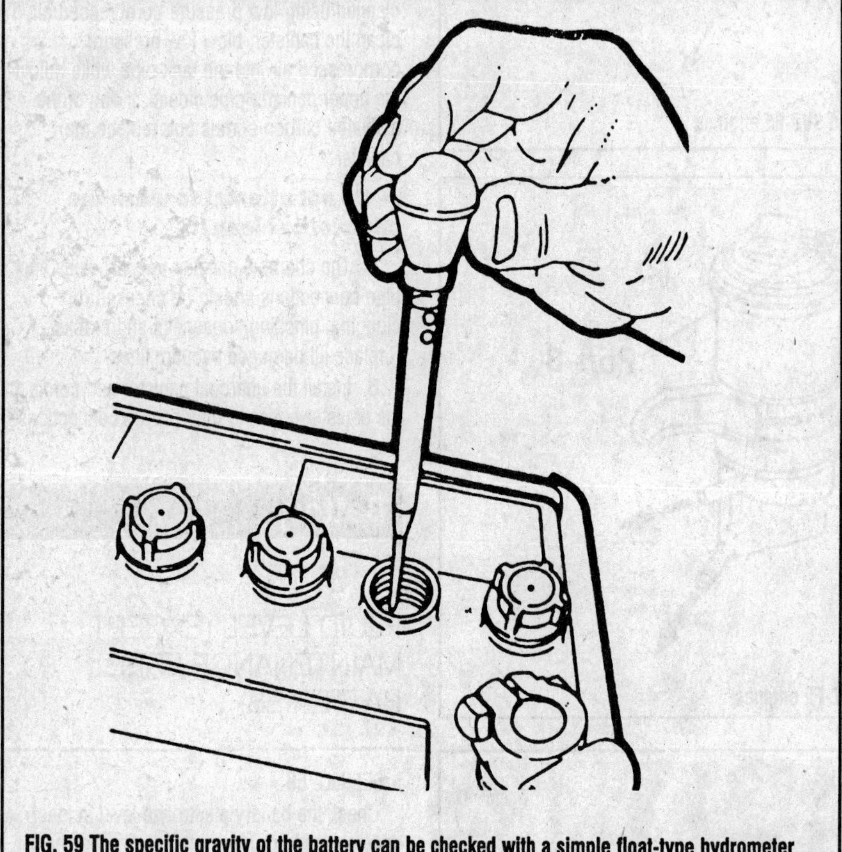
FIG. 59 The specific gravity of the battery can be checked with a simple float-type hydrometer

SPECIFIC GRAVITY (EXCEPT MAINTENANCE FREE BATTERIES)

➧ SEE FIG. 59

At least once a year, check the specific gravity of the battery. It should be between 1.25 in.Hg and 1.27 in.Hg at room temperature.

The specific gravity can be check with the use of an hydrometer, an inexpensive instrument available from many sources, including auto parts stores. The hydrometer has a squeeze bulb at one end and a nozzle at the other. Battery electrolyte is sucked into the hydrometer until the float is lifted from its seat. The specific gravity is then read by noting the position of the float. Generally, if after charging, the specific gravity between any two cells varies more than 50 points (0.50), the battery is bad and should be replaced.

It is not possible to check the specific gravity in this manner on sealed (maintenance-free) batteries. Instead, the indicator built into the top of the case must be relied on to display any signs of battery deterioration. If the indicator is dark, the battery can be assumed to be OK. If the indicator is light, the specific gravity is low, and the battery should be charged or replaced.

CABLES AND CLAMPS

➧ SEE FIGS. 61–65

Once a year, the battery terminals and the cable clamps should be cleaned. Loosen the clamps and remove the cables, negative cable first. On batteries with posts on top, the use of a puller specially made for the purpose is recommended. These are inexpensive, and available in auto parts stores. Side terminal battery cables are secured with a bolt.

BATTERY STATE OF CHARGE AT ROOM TEMPERATURE

Specific Gravity Reading	Charged Condition
1.260–1.280	Fully Charged
1.230–1.250	3/4 Charged
1.200–1.220	1/2 Charged
1.170–1.190	1/4 Charged
1.140–1.160	Almost no Charge
1.110–1.130	No Charge

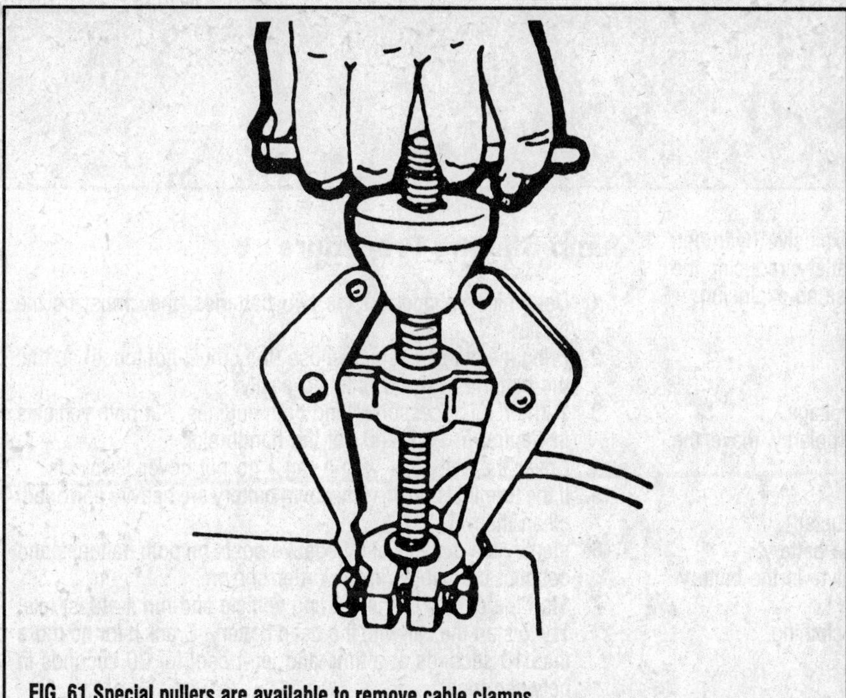

FIG. 61 Special pullers are available to remove cable clamps

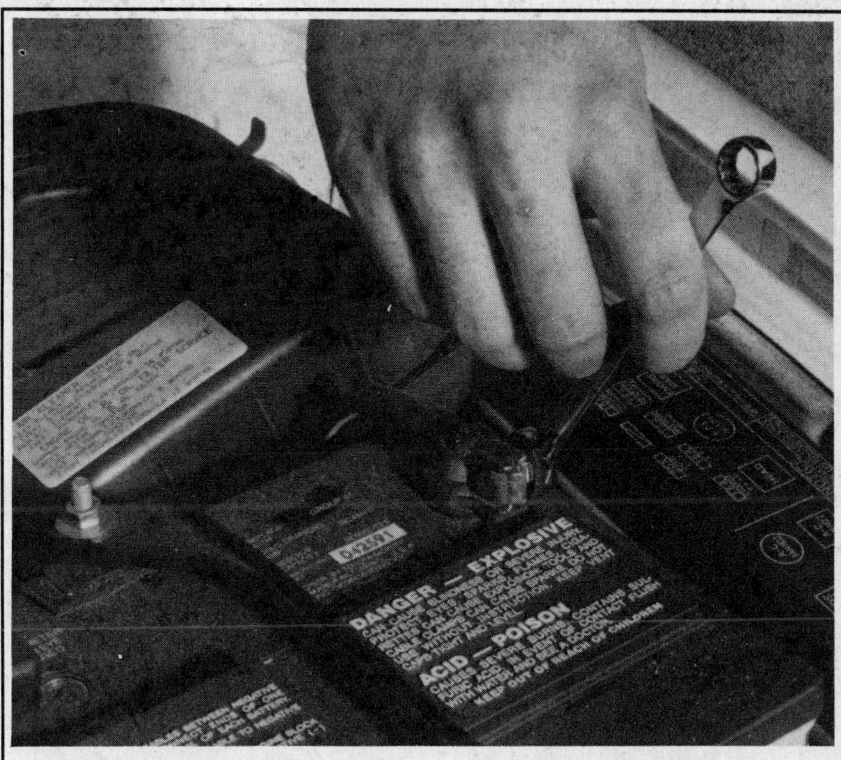

FIG. 62 Disconnecting the battery cable

Clean the cable lamps and the battery terminal with a wire brush, until all corrosion, grease, etc., is removed and the metal is shiny. It is especially important to clean the inside of the clamp thoroughly, since a small deposit of foreign material or oxidation there will prevent a sound electrical connection and inhibit either starting or charging. Special tools are available for cleaning these parts, one type for conventional batteries and another type for side terminal batteries.

Before installing the cables, loosen the battery holddown clamp or strap, remove the battery and check the battery tray. Clear it of any debris, and check it for soundness. Rust should be wire brushed away, and the metal given a coat of anti-rust paint. Replace the battery and tighten the holddown clamp or strap securely, but be careful not to overtighten, which will crack the battery case.

After the clamps and terminals are clean, reinstall the cables, negative cable last; do not hammer on the clamps to install. Tighten the clamps securely, but do not distort them. Give the clamps and terminals a thin external coat of grease after installation, to retard corrosion.

Check the cables at the same time that the terminals are cleaned. If the cable insulation is cracked or broken, or if the ends are frayed, the cable should be replaced with a new cable of the same length and gauge.

**** CAUTION**

Keep flame or sparks away from the battery; it gives off explosive hydrogen gas! Battery electrolyte contains sulphuric acid! If you should splash any on your skin or in your eyes, flush the affected area with plenty of clear water. If it lands in your eyes, get medical help immediately!

REPLACEMENT

When it becomes necessary to replace the battery, be sure to select a new battery with a cold cranking power rating equal to or greater than the battery originally installed. Deterioration, embrittlement and just plain aging of the battery cables, starter motor and associated wires makes the battery's job all the more difficult in successive years. The slow increase in electrical resistance over time makes it prudent to install a new battery with a greater capacity than the old. Details on battery removal and installation are covered in Section 3.

JUMP STARTING A DEAD BATTERY

The chemical reaction in a battery produces explosive hydrogen gas. This is the safe way to jump start a dead battery, reducing the chances of an accidental spark that could cause an explosion.

Jump Starting Precautions

1. Be sure both batteries are of the same voltage.
2. Be sure both batteries are of the same polarity (have the same grounded terminal).
3. Be sure the vehicles are not touching.
4. Be sure the vent cap holes are not obstructed.
5. Do not smoke or allow sparks around the battery.
6. In cold weather, check for frozen electrolyte in the battery. Do not jump start a frozen battery.
7. Do not allow electrolyte on your skin or clothing.
8. Be sure the electrolyte is not frozen.

CAUTION: Make certin that the ignition key, in the vehicle with the dead battery, is in the OFF position. Connecting cables to vehicles with on-board computers will result in computer destruction if the key is not in the OFF position.

Jump Starting Procedure

1. Determine voltages of the two batteries; they must be the same.
2. Bring the starting vehicle close (they must not touch) so that the batteries can be reached easily.
3. Turn off all accessories and both engines. Put both vehicles in Neutral or Park and set the handbrake.
4. Cover the cell caps with a rag—do not cover terminals.
5. If the terminals on the run-down battery are heavily corroded, clean them.
6. Identify the positive and negative posts on both batteries and connect the cables in the order shown.
7. Start the engine of the starting vehicle and run it at fast idle. Try to start the car with the dead battery. Crank it for no more than 10 seconds at a time and let it cool for 20 seconds in between tries.
8. If it doesn't start in 3 tries, there is something else wrong.
9. Disconnect the cables in the reverse order.
10. Replace the cell covers and dispose of the rags.

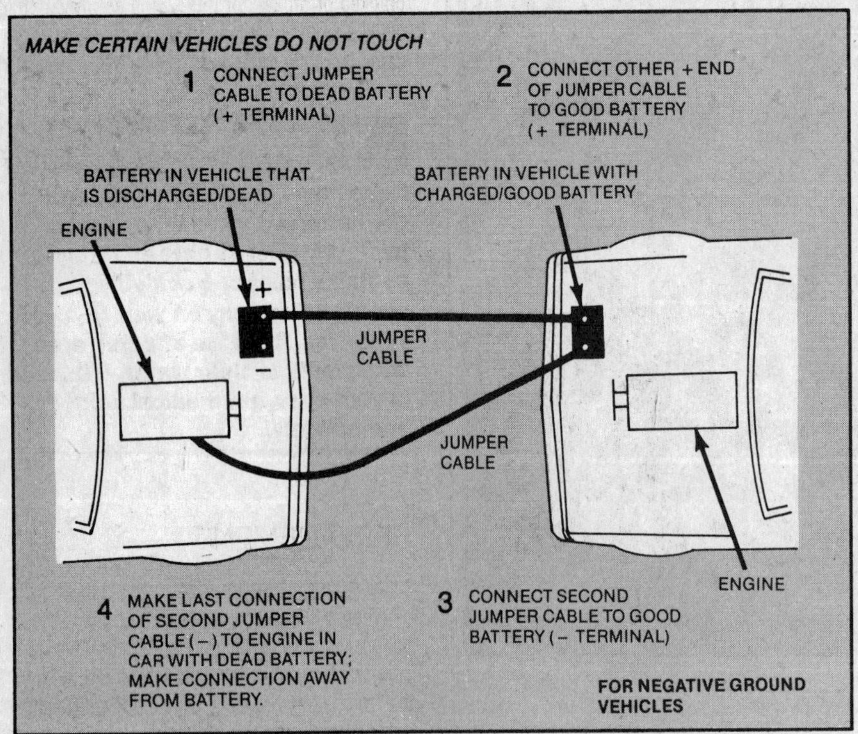
MAKE CERTAIN VEHICLES DO NOT TOUCH
1 CONNECT JUMPER CABLE TO DEAD BATTERY (+ TERMINAL)
2 CONNECT OTHER + END OF JUMPER CABLE TO GOOD BATTERY (+ TERMINAL)
BATTERY IN VEHICLE THAT IS DISCHARGED/DEAD
BATTERY IN VEHICLE WITH CHARGED/GOOD BATTERY
ENGINE
+
−
JUMPER CABLE
JUMPER CABLE
ENGINE
4 MAKE LAST CONNECTION OF SECOND JUMPER CABLE (−) TO ENGINE IN CAR WITH DEAD BATTERY; MAKE CONNECTION AWAY FROM BATTERY.
3 CONNECT SECOND JUMPER CABLE TO GOOD BATTERY (− TERMINAL)
FOR NEGATIVE GROUND VEHICLES

Side terminal batteries occasionally pose a problem when connecting jumper cables. There frequently isn't enough room to clamp the cables without touching sheet metal. Side terminal adaptors are available to alleviate this problem and should be removed after use

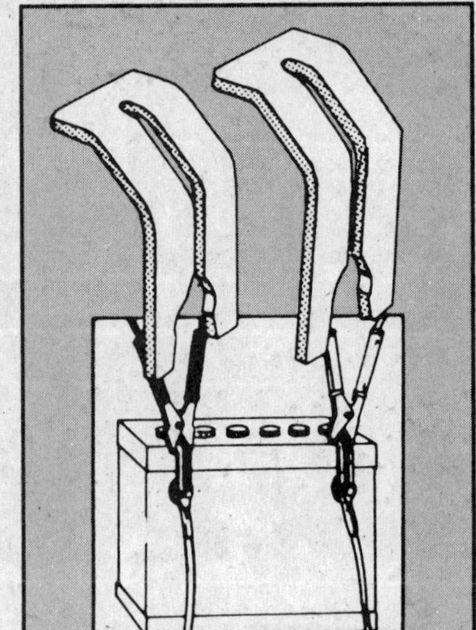

FIG. 63 Clean the battery posts with a wire brush; or the special tool shown

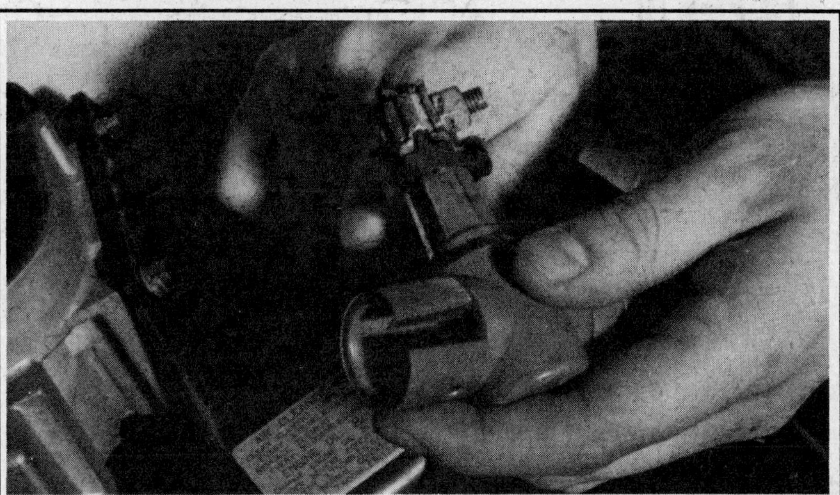

FIG. 64 Clean the inside of the clamps with a wire brush; or the special tool shown

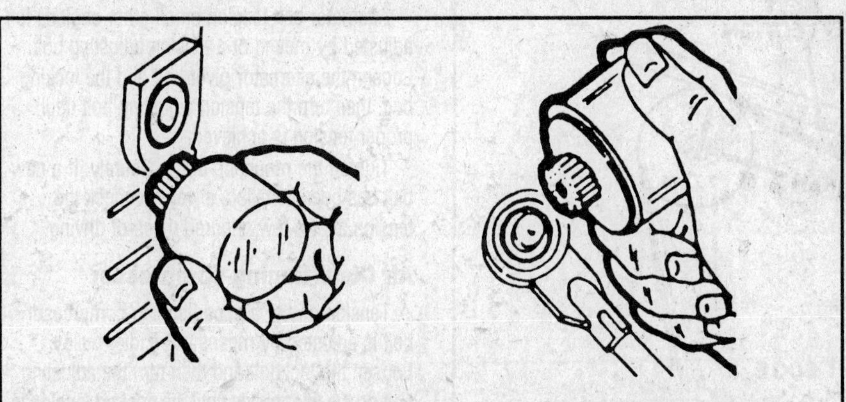

FIG. 65 Special tools are also available for cleaning the posts and clamps of side terminal batteries

Belts

INSPECTION

➧ SEE FIGS. 65A–65D

The belts which drive the engine accessories such as the alternator or generator, the air pump, power steering pump, air conditioning compressor and water pump are of either the V-belt design or flat, serpentine design. Gasoline engines use only the serpentine belts while diesel engines use a combination of both. V-belts show wear and damage readily, since their basic design was a belt with a rubber casing. As the casing wore, cracks and fibers were readily apparent. Newer design, caseless belts do not show wear as readily, and an untrained eye cannot distinguish between a good, serviceable belt and one that is worn to the point of failure. It is sound maintenance practice to visually inspect the belts regularly and replace them, as required.

Visually inspect the serpentine belt for the following: separation of the adhesive rubber above and below the core, core separation from the belt side, a severed core, separation of the rib from the adhesive rubber, cracking or separation of the ribs, torn or worn or cracks in the inner ridges of the ribs.

On diesel engines, inspect the alternator V-belt for cracks, accumulations of oil and wear. Check that the belt does not touch the bottom of the pulley groove. The belt should ride slightly above the edge of the pulley.

Its not a bad idea to replace all drive belts at 60,000 miles (96,000 km) regardless of their condition.

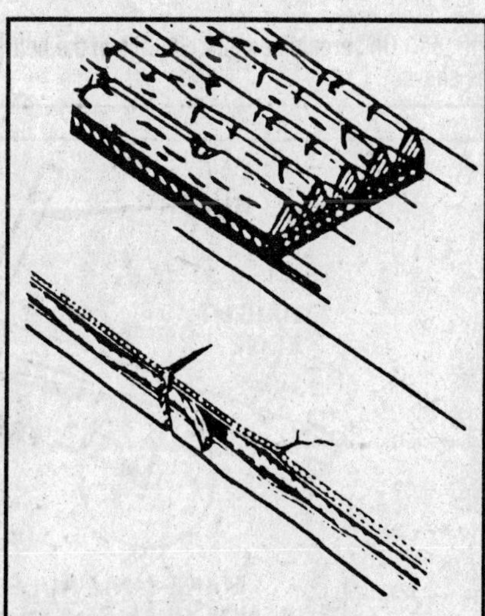

FIG. 65A Visually inspect the serpentine belt for damage and wear

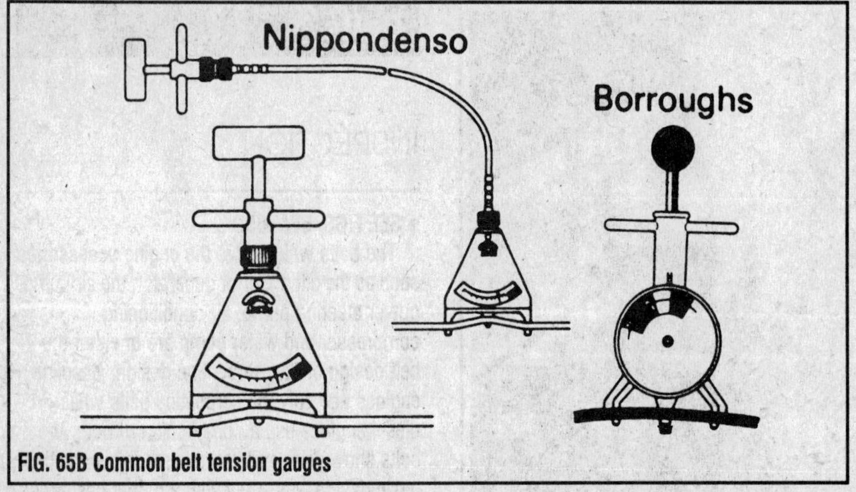

FIG. 65B Common belt tension gauges

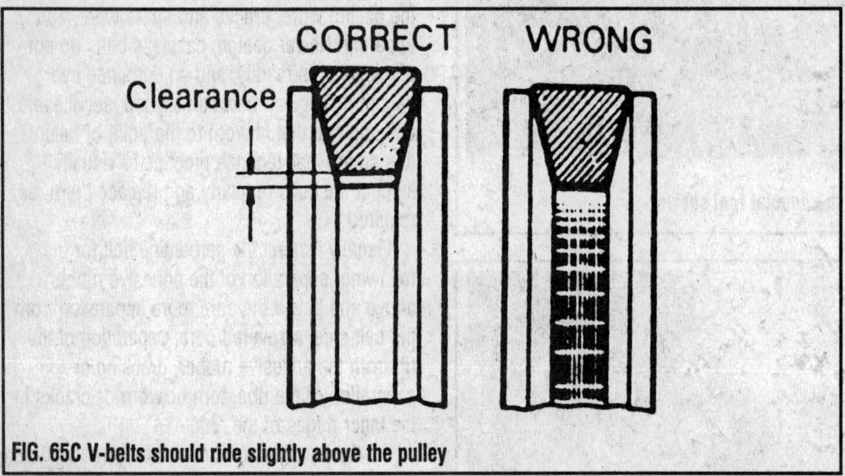

FIG. 65C V-belts should ride slightly above the pulley

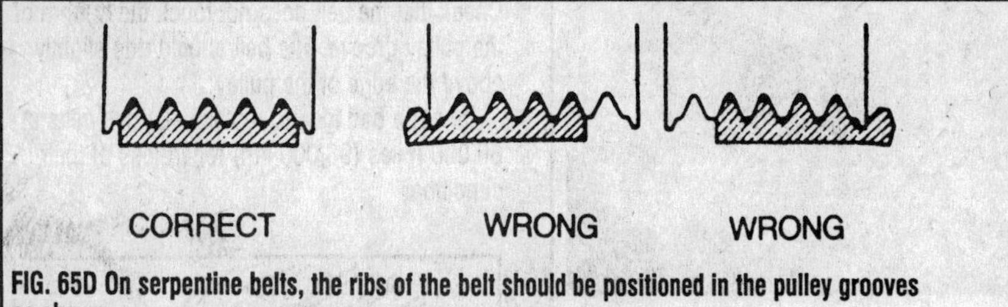

FIG. 65D On serpentine belts, the ribs of the belt should be positioned in the pulley grooves as shown

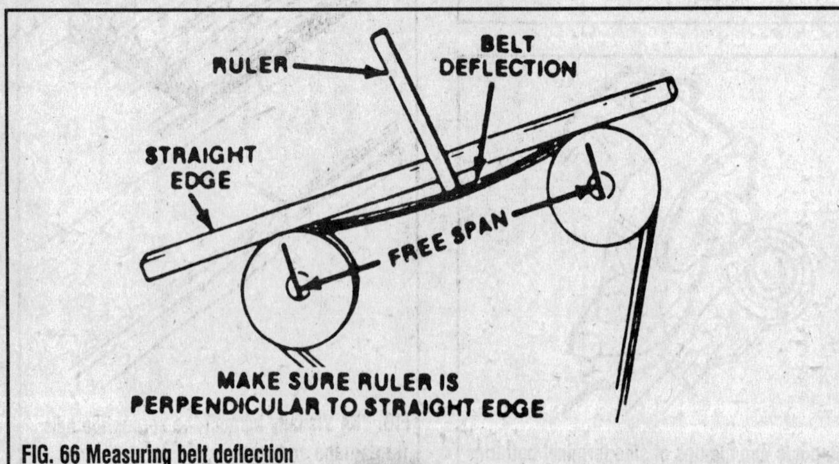

FIG. 66 Measuring belt deflection

ADJUSTING

➧ SEE FIGS. 66–67

Belts are normally adjusted by loosening the bolts of the accessory being driven and moving that accessory on its pivot points until the proper tension is applied to the belt. The accessory is held in this position while the bolts are tightened. To determine proper belt tension, you can purchase a belt tension gauge or simply use the deflection method. To determine deflection, press inward on the belt at the mid-point of its longest straight run. The belt should deflect (move inward) $^3/_8$–$^1/_2$ in. (10–13mm). Some long V-belts and most serpentine belts have idler pulleys which are used for adjusting purposes. Just loosen the idler pulley and move it to take up or release tension on the belt.

➡ Proper belt tension is important because it will allow the belt to run quietly and will maximize the belt's service life.

Alternator

➧ SEE FIGS. 68–69

On early engines, adjust the tension of the alternator drive belt, loosen the pivot and mounting bolts on the alternator. Using a wooden hammer handle or a broomstick, or even your hand if you're strong enough, move the alternator one way or the other until the tension is within acceptable limits.

CAUTION

Never use a screwdriver or any other metal device such as a prybar, as a lever when adjusting the alternator belt tension!

Tighten the mounting bolts securely. If a new belt has been installed, always recheck the tension after a few hundred miles of driving.

Alternator belt tension on all other engines is adjusted by means of a tension adjusting bolt. Loosen the alternator pivot bolt and the locking bolt, then turn the tension adjusting bolt until proper tension is achieved.

Tighten the mounting bolts securely. If a new belt has been installed, always recheck the tension after a few hundred miles of driving.

Air Conditioning Compressor

Tension on the air conditioning compressor belt is adjusted by means of an idler pulley. Loosen the lockbolt and then turn the adjusting bolt on the idler pulley until the desired tension is achieved. Retighten the idler pulley lockbolt.

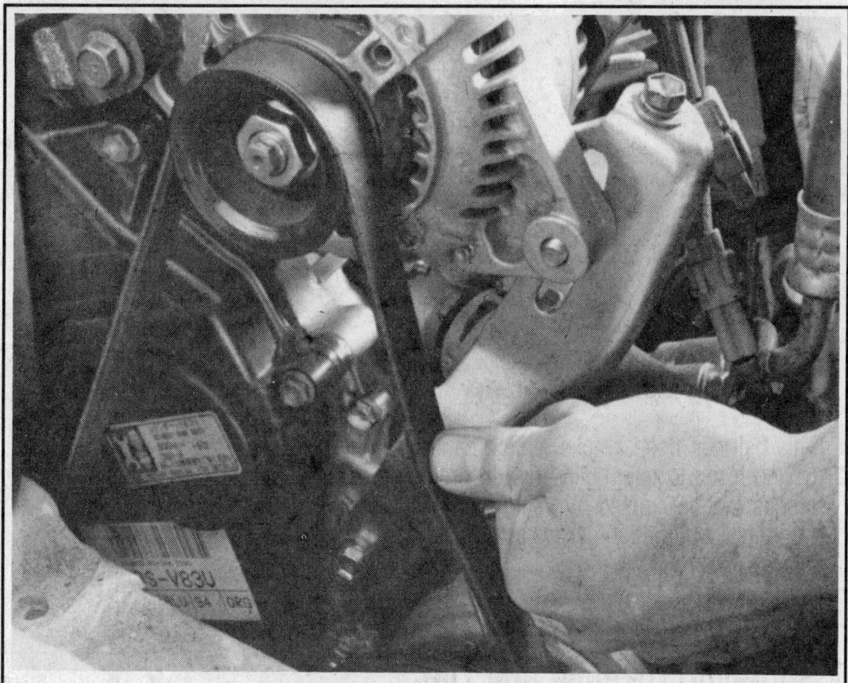

FIG. 67 Measuring belt deflection

FIG. 69 Rotate the adjusting bolt to change the drive belt tension

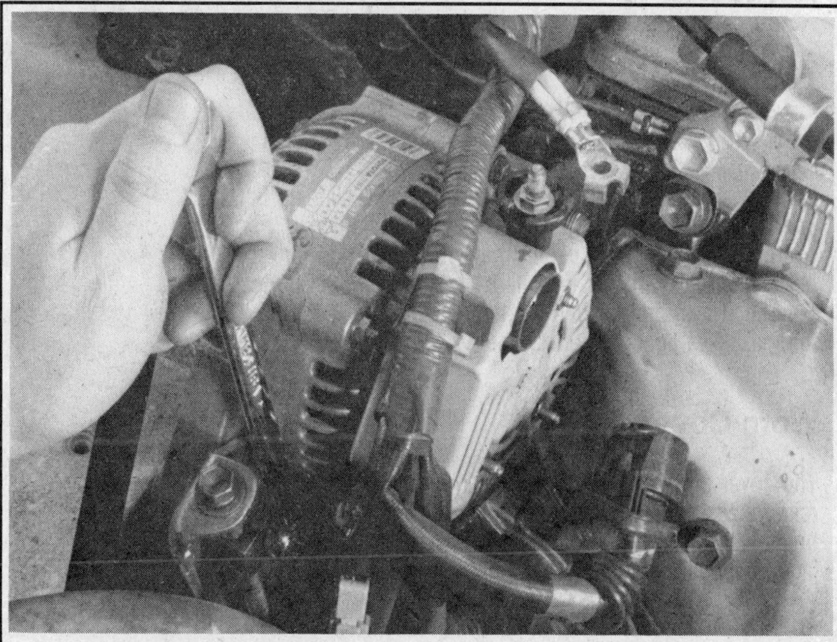

FIG. 68 Loosen the tension adjustment lock bolt

Tighten the lockbolt securely. If a new belt has been installed, always recheck the tension after a few hundred miles of driving.

Power Steering Pump

On some models, tension on the power steering pump belt is adjusted by means of an idler pulley. Loosen the lockbolt and then turn the adjusting bolt on the idler pulley until the desired tension is achieved. Retighten the idler pulley lockbolt.

Tighten the lockbolt securely. If a new belt has been installed, always recheck the tension after a few hundred miles of driving.

Power steering pump belt tension on other models is adjusted by means of a tension adjusting bolt. Loosen the power steering pump pivot bolt and then turn the tension adjusting bolt until proper tension is achieved.

Tighten the mounting bolts securely. If a new belt has been installed, always recheck the tension after a few hundred miles of driving.

HOW TO SPOT WORN V-BELTS

V–Belts are vital to efficient engine operation – they drive the fan, water pump and other accessories. They require little maintenance (occasional tightening) but they will not last forever. Slipping or failure of the V–belt will lead to overheating. If your V–belt looks like any of these, it should be replaced.

Cracking or Weathering

This belt has deep cracks, which cause it to flex. Too much flexing leads to heat build–up and premature failure. These cracks can be caused by using the belt on a pulley that is too small. Notched belts are available for small diameter pulleys.

Softening (Grease and Oil)

Oil and grease on a belt can cause the belt's rubber compounds to soften and separate from the reinforcing cords that hold the belt together. The belt will first slip, then finally fail altogether.

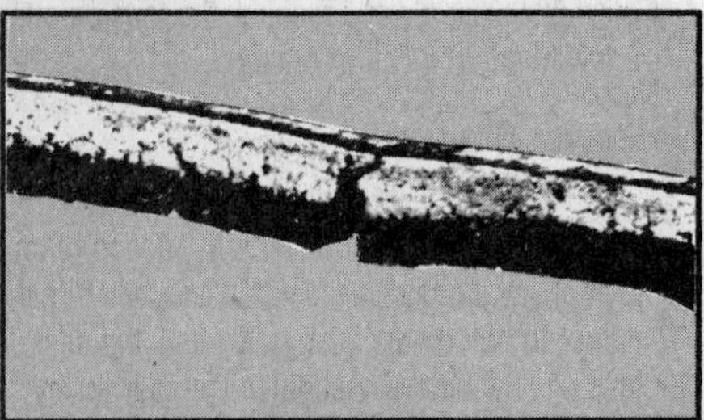

Glazing

Glazing is caused by a belt that is slipping. A slipping belt can cause a run-down battery, erratic power steering, overheating or poor accessory performance. The more the belt slips, the more glazing will be built up on the surface of the belt. The more the belt is glazed, the more it will slip. If the glazing is light, tighten the belt.

Worn Cover

The cover of this belt is worn off and is peeling away. The reinforcing cords will begin to wear and the belt will shortly break. When the belt cover wears in spots or has a rough jagged appearance, check the pulley grooves for roughness.

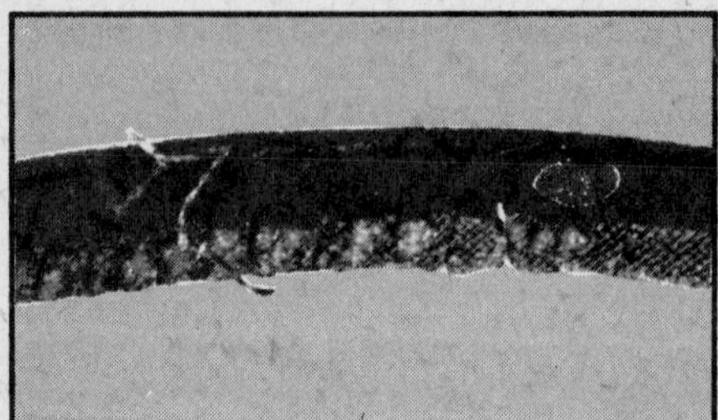

Separation

This belt is on the verge of breaking and leaving you stranded. The layers of the belt are separating and the reinforcing cords are exposed. It's just a matter of time before it breaks completely.

HOW TO SPOT BAD HOSES

Both the upper and lower radiator hoses are called upon to perform difficult jobs in an inhospitable environment. They are subject to nearly 18 psi at under hood temperatures often over 280°F, and must circulate nearly 7500 gallons of coolant an hour—3 good reasons to have good hoses.

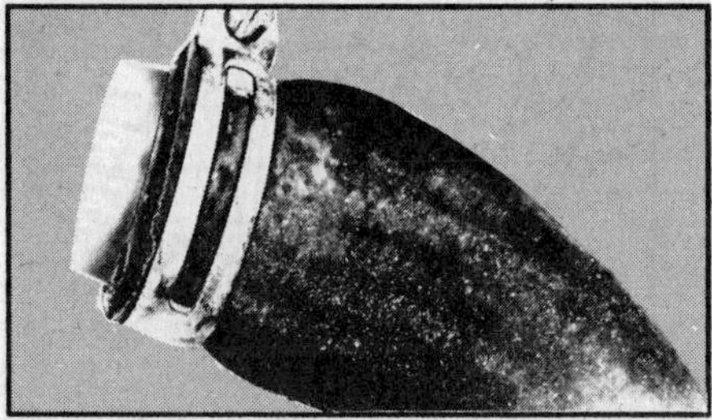

Swollen Hose

A good test for any hose is to feel it for soft or spongy spots. Frequently these will appear as swollen areas of the hose. The most likely cause is oil soaking. This hose could burst at any time, when hot or under pressure.

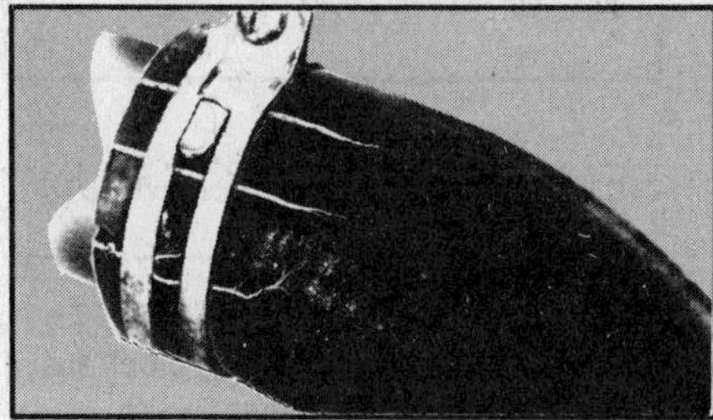

Cracked Hose

Cracked hoses can usually be seen but feel the hoses to be sure they have not hardened; a prime cause of cracking. This hose has cracked down to the reinforcing cords and could split at any of the cracks.

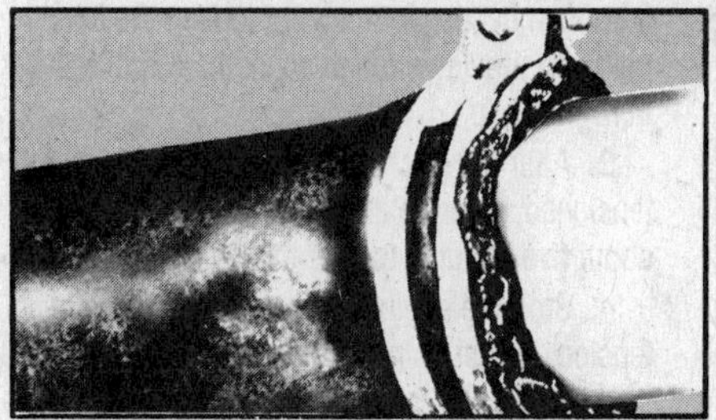

Frayed Hose End (Due to Weak Clamp)

Weakened clamps frequently are the cause of hose and cooling system failure. The connection between the pipe and hose has deteriorated enough to allow coolant to escape when the engine is hot.

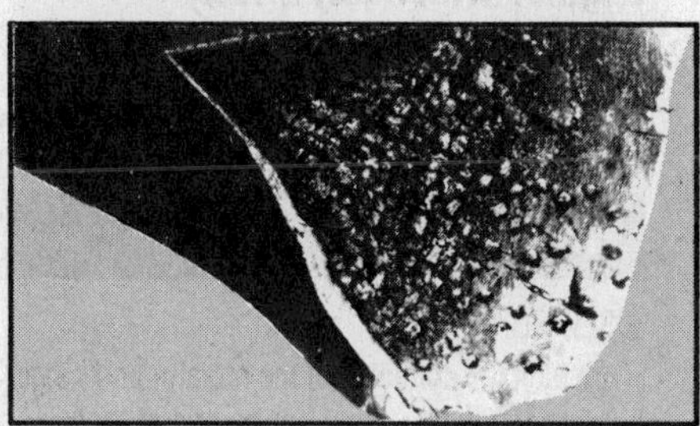

Debris in Cooling System

Debris, rust and scale in the cooling system can cause the inside of a hose to weaken. This can usually be felt on the outside of the hose as soft or thinner areas.

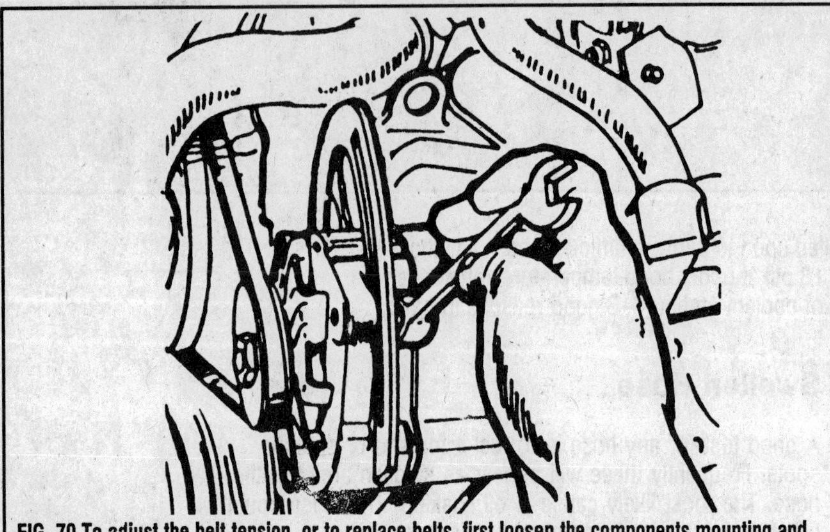
FIG. 70 To adjust the belt tension, or to replace belts, first loosen the components mounting and adjusting bolts slightly

FIG. 71 Push the component toward the engine and slip off the belt

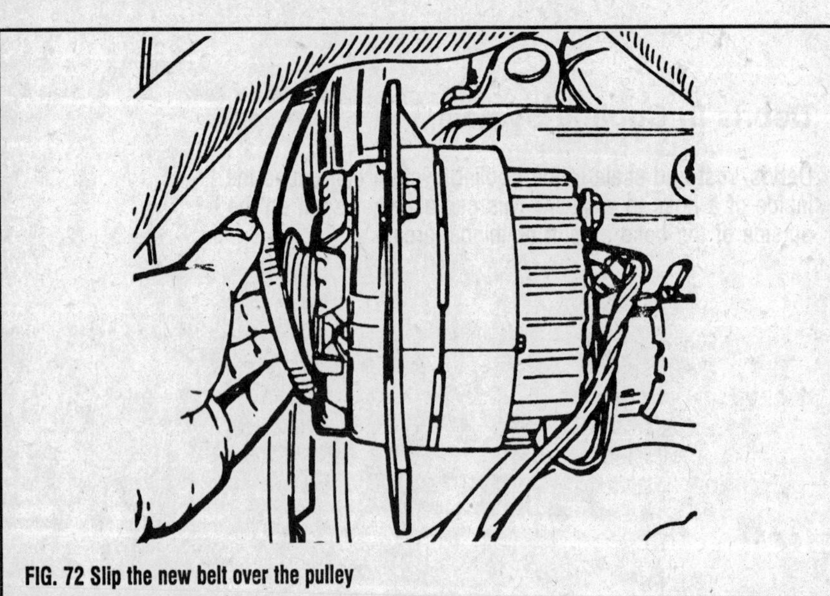
FIG. 72 Slip the new belt over the pulley

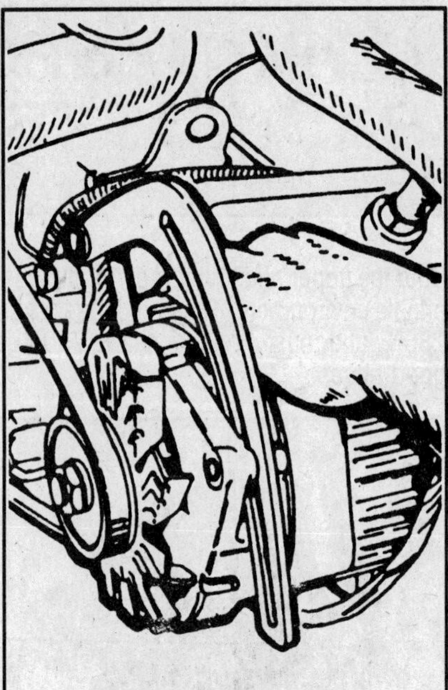
FIG. 73 Pull outward on the component and tighten the mounting bolts

REMOVAL & INSTALLATION

➧ SEE FIGS. 70–73

1. Loosen the accessory being driven and move it on its pivot point to free the belt.
2. Remove the belt. If an idler pulley is used, it is often necessary, only, to loosen the idler pulley to provide enough slack the remove the belt.
3. After the new belt is in place and properly tensioned, start the engine and allow it to run for about five minutes to seat the new belt(s)
4. Stop the engine and recheck the belt tension. Adjust as necessary.

➡ It is important to note that on engines with many driven accessories, several or all of the belts may have to be removed to get at the one to be replaced.

Hoses

➧ SEE FIG. 74

Inspect the condition of the radiator and heater hoses periodically. Early spring and at the beginning of the fall or winter, when you are performing other maintenance, are good times. Make sure the engine and cooling system are cold. Visually inspect for cracking, rotting or collapsed hoses, replace as necessary. Run your hand along the length of the hose. If a weak or swollen spot is noted when squeezing the hose wall, replace the hose.

REMOVAL & INSTALLATION

⁂ CAUTION

When draining the coolant, keep in mind that dogs and cats are attracted by the ethylene glycol antifreeze, and are quite likely to drink any that is left in an uncovered container or in puddles left on the ground. This will prove fatal in sufficient quantity. Always drain the coolant into a sealable container. Coolant should be reused unless it is contaminated or several years old.

1. Place a large drain pan under the radiator drain cock. The drain cock is located on the lower right side of the radiator.

➡ To prevent unnecessary spillage, before draining the radiator, obtain a length of rubber hose or tubing and connect it to the end of the drain cock. The length should be sufficient enough to direct the coolant from the drain cock to the drain pan. Save this item, because it will be useful whenever the engine coolant is drained.

2. Open the drain cock and drain the radiator. Only a few turns is required to establish a good flow.
3. Once all the coolant is removed from the radiator, close the drain cock and move the drain pan out of the way.
4. Release the tension of the two upper radiator hose clamps and slide the clamps away from the hose connections. With a moderate twisting and pulling motion, remove the upper radiator hose from its attaching points. Remove the clamps and transfer them to the new hose.
5. Loosen the two lower radiator hose clamps and push the clamps away from the hose connections. Remove the lower hose in the same manner as the upper hose. Remove the clamps and transfer them to the new hose.

➡ It is not necessary to discard the old hoses as long as they are not severely cracked or swollen. Shake them out to remove the coolant, seal them in a plastic bag and store the hoses in the trunk or luggage compartment. Old hoses provide a good short term repair if, by chance, a new hose fails. Also, if new clamps are being installed, throw the old clamps in with the hoses.

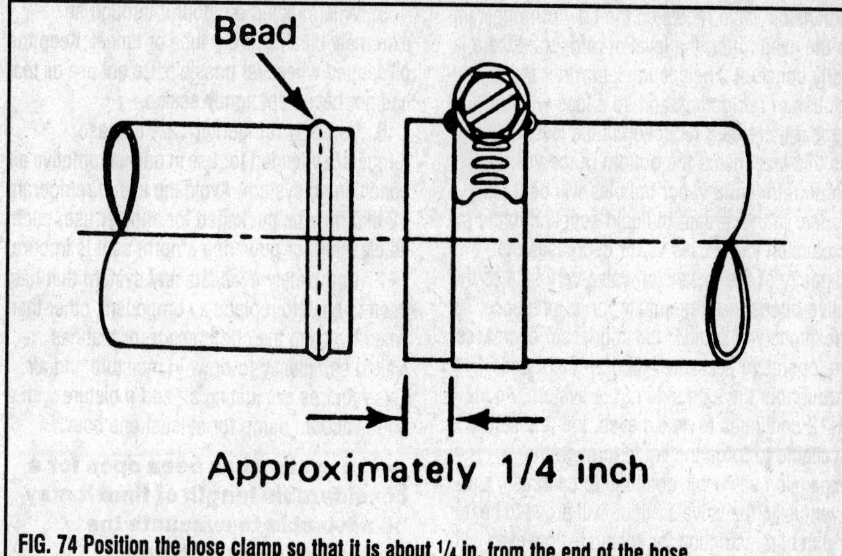

FIG. 74 Position the hose clamp so that it is about 1/4 in. from the end of the hose

6. Before installing the new hoses, ensure that the radiator and engine hose connections are clean. This is important for proper sealing.
7. Install the lower radiator hose with the two clamps. Make sure the clamps are even and tight.
8. Install the upper radiator hose with the two clamps. Make sure the clamps are even and tight.
9. Fill the reserve tank to a level between the **LOW** and **FULL** lines on the tank with a suitable ethylene glycol based coolant mixed with the proper amount of water (follow instructions on coolant container). Make sure the radiator cap is tight.
10. Start the engine and allow to idle for several minutes. Check the hose connections for leaks.

Air Conditioning System

The purpose of the air conditioning system is to maintain a comfortable environment inside the passenger compartment by controlling air temperature, circulation, humidity and purifying the air. The air conditioning system is designed to cycle a compressor on and off to maintain the desired cooling within the passenger compartment. Passenger compartment comfort is maintained by the temperature lever located on the control head. The system is also designed to prevent the evaporator from freezing.

When an air conditioning mode is selected, electrical current is sent to the compressor clutch coil. The clutch plate and the hub assembly is then drawn rearward which engages the pulley. The clutch plate and the pulley are then locked together and act as one unit. This in turn drives the compressor shaft which compresses low pressure refrigerant vapor from the evaporator into high pressure. The compressor also circulates refrigerant oil and refrigerant through the air conditioner system. On certain models, the compressor, is equipped with a cut-off solenoid which will shut the compressor off momentarily under certain conditions. These include wide-open throttle and low idle speeds.

The switches on the control head are used to control the operation of the air conditioning system.

GENERAL SERVICING PROCEDURES

The most important aspect of air conditioning service is the maintenance of pure and adequate charge of refrigerant in the system. A refrigeration system cannot function properly if a significant percentage of the charge is lost. Leaks are common because the severe vibration encountered in an automobile can easily cause cracking or loosening of the air conditioning fittings. As a result, the operating pressures of the system force refrigerant out.

The problem can be understood by considering what happens to the system as it is operated with a continuous leak. Because the expansion valve regulates the flow of refrigerant to the evaporator, the level of refrigerant there is fairly constant. The accumulator/drier stores any excess of refrigerant, and so a loss will first appear there as a reduction in the level of liquid. As this level nears the bottom of the vessel, some refrigerant vapor bubbles will begin to appear in the stream of liquid supplied to the expansion valve. This vapor decreases the capacity of the expansion valve very little as the valve opens to compensate for its presence. As the quantity of liquid in the condenser decreases, the operating pressure will drop there and throughout the high side of the system. As the R-12 continues to be expelled, the pressure available to force the liquid through the expansion valve will continue to decrease, and, eventually, the valve's orifice will prove to be too much of a restriction for adequate flow even with the needle fully withdrawn.

At this point, low side pressure will start to drop, and severe reduction in cooling capacity, marked by freeze-up of the evaporator coil, will result. Eventually, the operating pressure of the evaporator will be lower than the pressure of the atmosphere surrounding it, and air will be drawn into the system wherever there are leaks in the low side.

Because all atmospheric air contains at least some moisture, water will enter the system and mix with the R-12 and the oil. Trace amounts of moisture will cause sludging of the oil, and corrosion of the system. Saturation and clogging of the filter-drier, and freezing of the expansion valve orifice will eventually result. As air fills the system to a greater and greater extent, it will interfere more and more with the normal flows of refrigerant and heat.

GENERAL PRECAUTIONS

A list of general precautions that should be observed while doing this follows:

1. Keep all tools as clean and dry as possible.
2. Thoroughly purge the service gauges and hoses of air and moisture before connecting them to the system. Keep them capped when not in use.
3. Thoroughly clean any refrigerant fitting before disconnecting it, in order to minimize the entrance of dirt into the system. Before connecting any O-ring type fitting, apply a few drops of clean compressor oil onto the O-ring.
4. Plan any operation that requires opening the system beforehand in order to minimize the length of time it will be exposed to open air. Cap or seal the open ends to minimize the entrance of foreign material.
5. When adding oil, pour it through an extremely clean and dry tube or funnel. Keep the oil capped whenever possible. Do not use oil that has not been kept tightly sealed.
6. Use only refrigerant 12. Purchase refrigerant intended for use in only automotive air conditioning system. Avoid the use of refrigerant 12 that may be packaged for another use, such as cleaning, or powering a horn, as it is impure.
7. Completely evacuate any system that has been opened to replace a component, other than when isolating the compressor, or that has leaked sufficiently to draw in moisture and air. This requires evacuating air and moisture with a good vacuum pump for at least one hour.

➡ **If a system has been open for a considerable length of time it may be advisable to evacuate the system for up to 12 hours (overnight).**

8. Use a wrench on both halves of a fitting that is to be disconnected, so as to avoid twisting the refrigerant lines.

ADDITIONAL PREVENTIVE MAINTENANCE CHECKS

Antifreeze

In order to prevent heater core freeze-up during A/C operation, it is necessary to maintain permanent type antifreeze protection of +15°F (-9°C) or lower. A reading of -15°F (-26°C) is ideal since this protection also supplies sufficient corrosion inhibitors for the protection of the engine cooling system.

➡ **The same antifreeze should not be used longer than the manufacturer specified.**

Radiator Cap

For efficient operation of an air conditioned car's cooling system, the radiator cap should have a holding pressure which meets manufacturer's specifications. A cap which fails to hold these pressure should be replaced.

Condenser

Any obstruction of or damage to the condenser configuration will restrict the air flow which is essential to its efficient operation. It is therefore, a good rule to keep this unit clean and in proper physical shape.

➡ **Bug screens are regarded as obstructions.**

Condensation Drain Tube

This single molded drain tube expels the condensation, which accumulates on the bottom of the evaporator housing, into the engine compartment.

If this tube is obstructed, the air conditioning performance can be restricted and condensation buildup can spill over onto the vehicle's floor.

SAFETY PRECAUTIONS

Because of the importance of the necessary safety precautions that must be exercised when working with air conditioning systems and R-12 refrigerant, a recap of the safety precautions are outlined.

1. Avoid contact with a charged refrigeration system, even when working on another part of the air conditioning system or vehicle. If a heavy tool comes into contact with a section of copper tubing or a heat exchanger, it can easily cause the relatively soft material to rupture.
2. When it is necessary to apply force to a fitting which contains refrigerant, as when checking that all system couplings are securely tightened, use a wrench on both parts of the fitting involved, if possible. This will avoid putting excessive torsional stress on refrigerant tubing. (It is advisable, when possible, to use tube or line wrenches when tightening these flare nut fittings).
3. Do not attempt to discharge the system by merely loosening a fitting, or removing the service valve caps and cracking these valves. Precise control is possibly only when using the service gauges. Place a rag under the open end of the center charging hose while discharging the system to catch any drops of liquid that might escape. Wear protective gloves when connecting or disconnecting service gauge hoses. Escaping refrigerant will immediately freeze any part of the body that it comes in contact with (frostbite). If frostbite does occur, consult a physician immediately.
4. Discharge the system only in a well ventilated area, as high concentrations of the gas can exclude oxygen and act as an anesthesia. When leak testing or soldering, this is particularly important, as toxic phosgene gas is formed when R-12 contacts any flame. Phosgene gas is fatal to both humans and animals. Never smoke near R-12 or allow it to discharge into an open flame.
5. Never start a system without first verifying that both service valves are backseated, if equipped, and that all fittings are throughout the system are snugly connected.

6. Avoid applying heat to any refrigerant line or storage vessel. Charging may be aided by using water heated to less than +125°F (+51°C) to warm the refrigerant container. Never allow a refrigerant storage container to sit out in the sun, or near any other source of heat, such as a radiator.

7. Always wear goggles when working on a system to protect the eyes. If refrigerant contacts the eye, it is advisable in all cases to see a physician as soon as possible. Goggles are a cheap insurance policy that could save your sight.

8. Always keep refrigerant can fittings capped when not in use. Avoid sudden shock to the can which might occur from dropping it, or from banging a heavy tool against it. NEVER carry a can in the passenger compartment of a car.

9. Always completely discharge the system before painting the vehicle (if the paint is to be baked on), or before welding anywhere near the refrigerant lines.

SYSTEM INSPECTION

System Off Checks

1. Check the fins of the condenser for blockage or damage. Carefully remove any debris (bugs, dirt, etc.) from the fins. Be careful not to damage the fins. Any obstruction of or damage to the condenser configuration will restrict the air flow which is essential to its efficient heat transfer operation. It is therefore, a good rule to keep this unit clean and in proper physical shape.

2. Check that the drive belt is properly tensioned and is positioned properly in the grooves of the compressor pulley. Adjust the tension of the belt as required.

3. Check for kinks in the refrigerant lines or loose electrical wiring.

4. Check the antifreeze. In order to prevent heater core freeze-up during air conditioning operation, it is necessary to maintain permanent type antifreeze protection of +15°F (9°C) or lower. A reading of –15°F (–26°C) is ideal since this protection also supplies sufficient corrosion inhibitors for the protection of the engine cooling system.

5. Check the radiator cap. For efficient operation of an air conditioned car's cooling system, the radiator cap should have a holding pressure of 14.9 psi. A cap which fails to hold these pressure should be replaced.

6. Check the condensation drain tube. This single molded drain tube expels the condensation, which accumulates on the bottom of the evaporator housing, into the engine compartment. If this tube is obstructed, the air conditioning performance can be restricted and condensation buildup can spill over onto the vehicle's floor.

System Operational Checks

1. Start the engine and turn the air conditioning switch to the **On** position. Have a companion cycle the blower switch and make sure the air conditioning unit operates at all positions of the switch. Don't let the companion leave leave just yet, he or she will be needed to assist you in the next step.

2. Check the operation of the magnetic clutch. If the clutch does not engage, check the air conditioning fuse. When the clutch is engaged the engine idle rpm should increase to 900-1000 rpm. Depress the accelerator pedal. The air conditioning clutch should remain engaged when the engine rpm is raised. Also, check the clutch bearing for noise and grease leakage.

3. Lighty touch the compressor lines. The suction line (low pressure) should be cold and the discharge line (high pressure) should be hot.

4. Listen for any unusual noises or vibration. Look for loose tubing and hose clamps.

5. Check the refrigerant level in the sight glass (refer to "Operational Checks").

6. Check the operation of the condenser fan cooling motor. The fan operates at two speeds depending on the water temperature and the position of the air conditioning switch. The fan must rotate smoothly.

7. If you have a leak detector, check all hoses and fittings for leaks.

REFRIGERANT LEVEL CHECKS

➧ SEE FIGS. 75–77

✲✲ CAUTION

The compressed refrigerant used in the air conditioning system expands into the atmosphere at a temperature of -21.7°F (-29.4°C) or lower. This will freeze any surface that it contacts, including your eyes. In addition, the refrigerant decomposes into a poisonous gas in the presence of a flame. Do not open or disconnect any part of the air conditioning system.

You can safely make a few simple checks to determine if your air conditioning system needs service. The tests work best if the temperature is warm, about 70°F (21.1°C).

➡ If your vehicle is equipped with an aftermarket air conditioner, the following system check may not apply. You should contact the manufacturer of the unit for instructions on systems checks.

1. Place the automatic transaxle in Park or the manual transaxle in Neutral. Set the parking brake.

2. Have a companion run the engine at a fast idle (about 1,500 rpm).

3. Set the controls for maximum cold with the blower on High.

4. Locate the sight glass on the top of the receiver. They sight glass may be dirty, so wipe it first to ensure a good view.

5. If you see foam or bubbles, the system is low and must be recharged.

6. If there are no bubbles, there is either no refrigerant at all or the system is fully charged. Feel the two hoses going to the belt driven compressor. If they are both at the same temperature, the system is empty and must be recharged.

7. If one hose (high pressure) is warm and the other (low pressure) is cold, the system may be all right.

8. Have a companion turn the fan control on and off to operate the compressor clutch. Watch the sight glass.

9. If bubbles appear when the clutch is disengaged and disappear when it is engaged, the system is properly charged.

10. If the refrigerant takes more than 45 seconds to bubble when the clutch is disengaged, the system is overcharged. This usually causes poor cooling at low speeds.

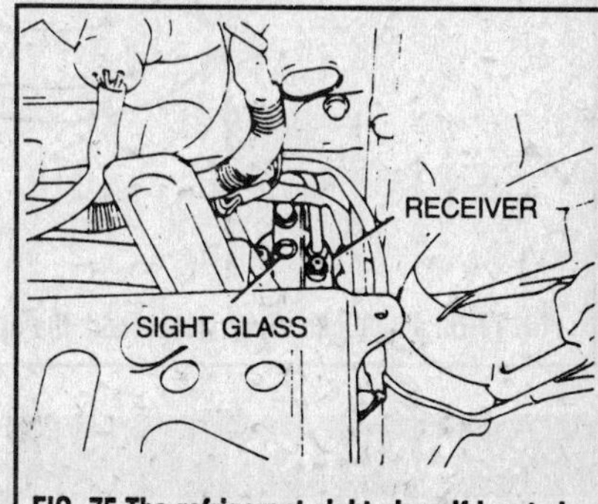

FIG. 75 The refrigerant sight glass if located on top of the receiver

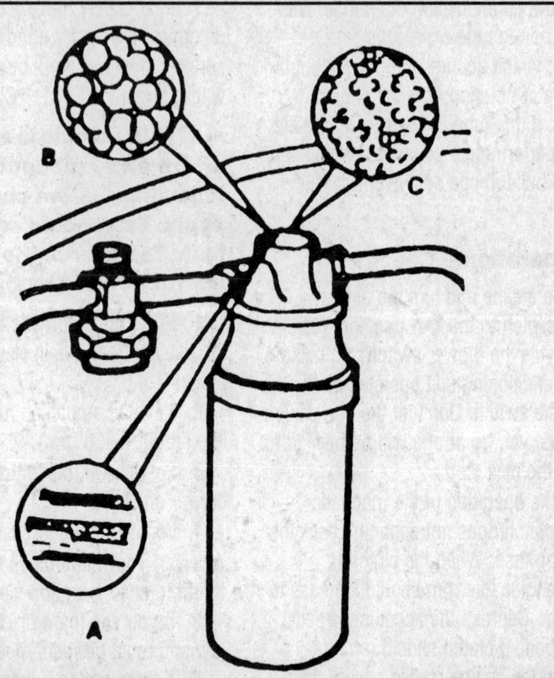

FIG. 76 Oil streaks (A), constant bubbles (B) or foam (C) indicate that there is not enough refrigerant in the system. Occasional bubbling during initial operation is normal. A clear sight glass indicates a proper charge of refrigerant, or no refrigerant at all, which can be determined by the presence of cold air at the outlets of the car. If the glass is clouded with a white milky substance, have the receiver/drier checked

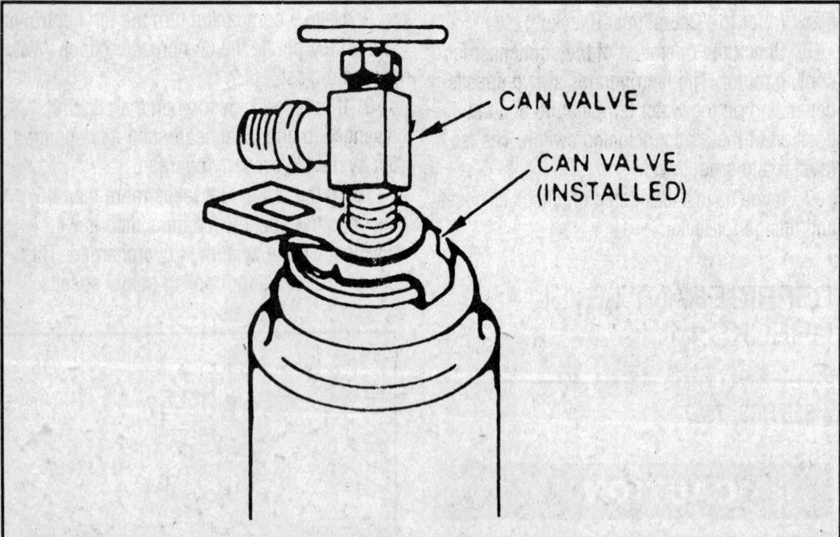

FIG. 77 On pound can of refrigerant with the opener valve connected

⁂ CAUTION

If it determined that the system has a leak, it should be corrected as soon as possible. Leaks may allow moisture to enter the system and cause a very expensive rust problem.

➡ Exercise the air conditioner for a few minutes, every two weeks or so, during the cold months. This avoids the possibility of the compressor seals drying out from lack of lubrication.

GAUGE SETS

Most of the service work performed in air conditioning requires the use of a set of two gauges, one for the high (head) pressure side of the system, the other for the low (suction) side. Vacuum and pressure gauges enable you to tell what is happening inside the system and are necessary components for effective troubleshooting and system maintenance.

The low side gauge records both pressure and vacuum. Vacuum readings are calibrated from 0 to 30 inches and the pressure graduations vary according to the type of gauge set that you are using.

The high side gauge measures pressure from 0 to at least 60 psi.

Both gauges are threaded into a manifold that contains two hand shut-off valves. Proper manipulation of these valves and the use of the attached test hoses allow the user to perform the following services:

1. Test high and low side pressures.
2. Remove air, moisture, and contaminated refrigerant.
3. Purge the system (of refrigerant).
4. Charge the system (with refrigerant).

The manifold valves are designed so that they have no direct effect on gauge readings, but serve only to provide for, or cut off, flow of refrigerant through the manifold. During all testing and hook-up operations, the valves are kept in a closed position to avoid disturbing the refrigeration system. The valves are opened only to purge the system or refrigerant or to charge it. The gauges sense pressure (or vacuum) from the source through the connection on the bottom of the gauge. This pressure or vacuum causes a flattened metal tube (Bourden tube) to straighten. The straightening of the tube is transmitted through a linkage to the pointer needle.

Accuracy is important when measuring refrigerant pressure readings. Frequent use of the gauge sets may cause the gauges to lose their calibration and give false or inaccurate readings. The gauges should be periodically calibrated in accordance with the intervals recommended by the manufacturer.

DISCHARGING THE SYSTEM

➧ SEE FIGS. 78–85

CAUTION

R-12 refrigerant is a chlorofluorocarbon which, when released into the atmosphere, can contribute to the depletion of the ozone layer in the upper atmosphere. Ozone filters out harmful radiation from the sun. If possible, an approved R-12 Recovery/Recycling machine that meets SAE standards should be employed when discharging the system. Follow the operating instructions provided with the approved equipment exactly to properly discharge the system.

➡ The fittings for attaching the manifold gauge set are located on the compressor suction and discharge service valves.

1. Close both service valves on the manifold gauge. Support the gauge set from the hood so that the face of the gauges can be read easily.
2. Connect the low pressure hose to the suction service valve and the high presssure hose to the discharge service valve. Tighten the hose nuts by hand.

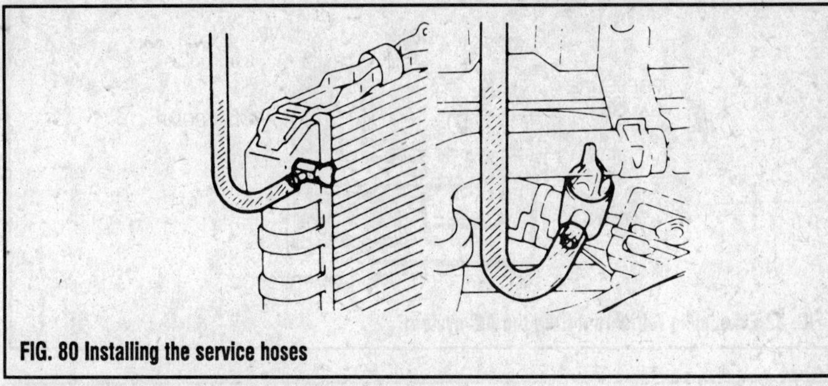

FIG. 80 Installing the service hoses

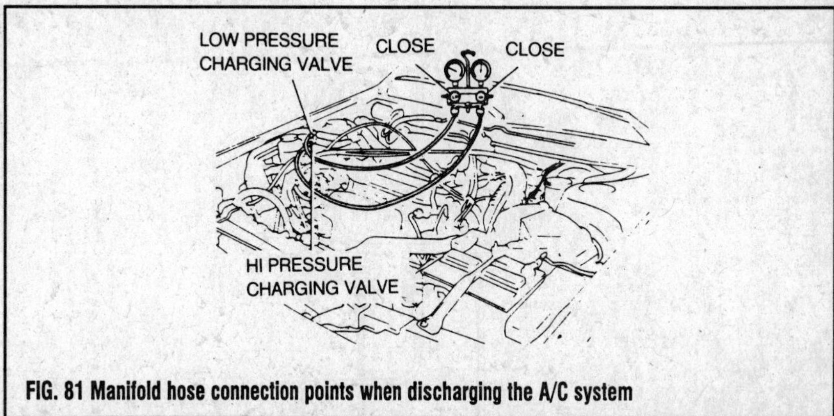

FIG. 81 Manifold hose connection points when discharging the A/C system

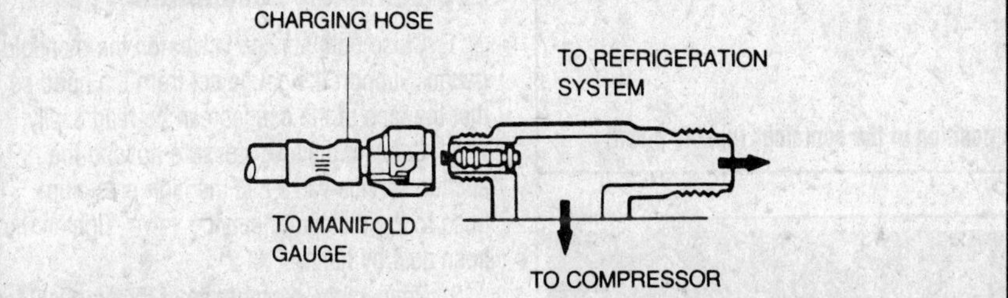

➡ Do not apply oil to the seat of the connection.

3. Place the free end of the center hose in a clean rag or towel.

FIG. 78 Charging hose connections

CHARGING HOSE
TO REFRIGERATION SYSTEM
TO MANIFOLD GAUGE
TO COMPRESSOR

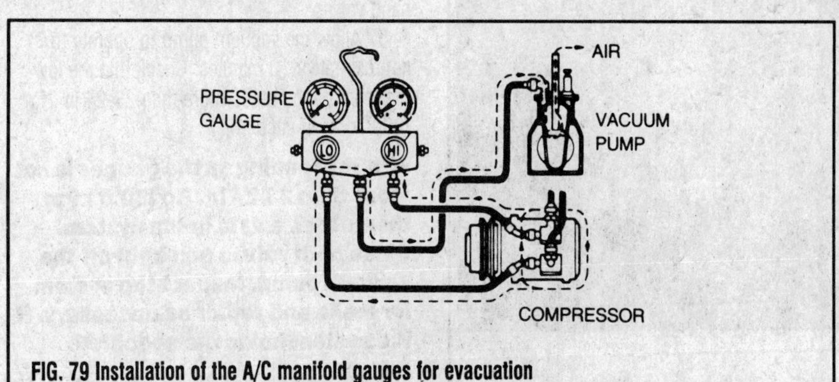

FIG. 79 Installation of the A/C manifold gauges for evacuation

4. Slowly open the high pressure valve on the manifold to adjust the flow of refrigerant. Do not open the valve very much.

➡ If the refrigerant is allowed to escape too fast, the oil from the compressor will be drawn out with the refrigerant.

5. Check the shop towel to ensure that no oil is being discharged. If there is evidence of oil in the towel, close down on the manifold valve to reduce the refrigerant flow.
6. Once a good flow of refrigerant is established, observe the high presure gauge. After the reading drops below 50 psi (3.5 kg/cm^2, 343 kPa), slowly open the low pressure gauge.
7. As the system pressure drops, completely open both manifold valves until a reading of **0** is indicated on both gauges.

CHARGING

Evacuating The System

➡ Whenever the air conditioning system has been discharged and opened for service and repair, air and moisture must be evacuated from the system. After the

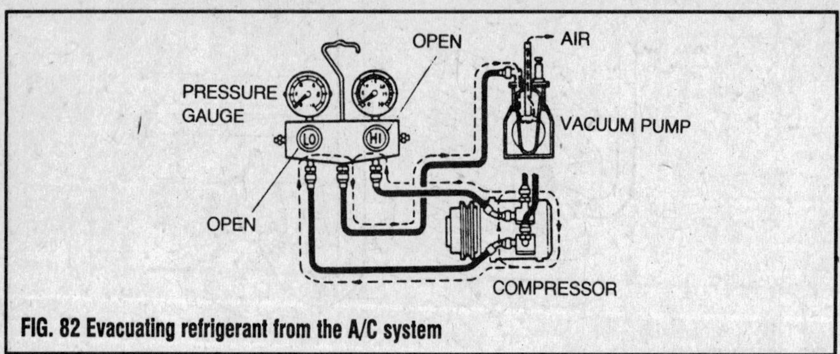

FIG. 82 Evacuating refrigerant from the A/C system

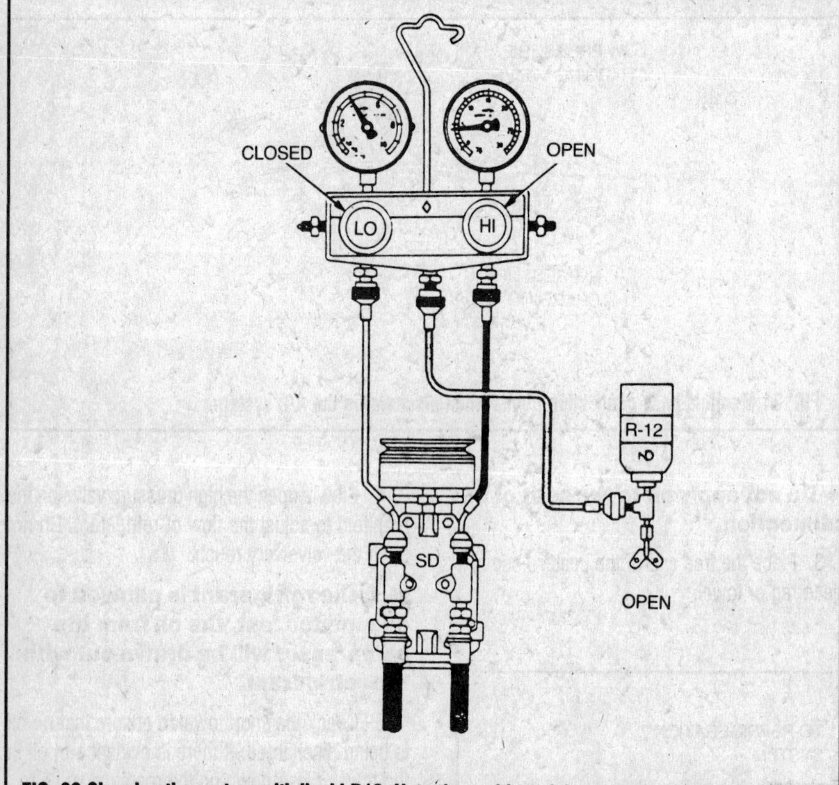

FIG. 83 Charging the system with liquid R12. Note the position of the container (upside down)

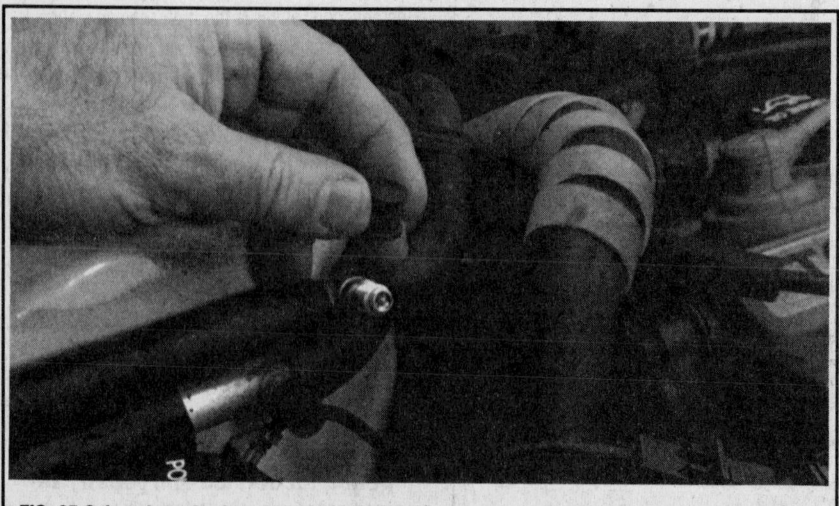
FIG. 85 Schraeder valve location—1991 Camry

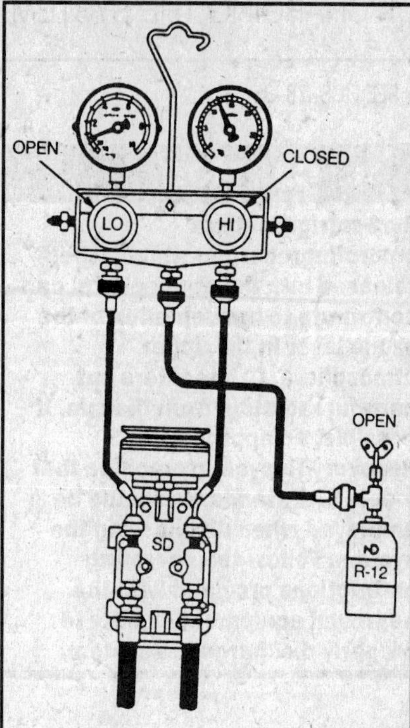

FIG. 84 Charging the system with vapor R12. With this method, the can is positioned right-side up

Installation of a new component, the system should be evacuated for approximately 15 minutes. If an old component has been serviced, evacuate the system for approximately 30 minutes.

1. Close both service valves on the manifold gauge. Support the gauge set from the hood so that the face of the gauges can be read easily.
2. Connect the low pressure hose to the suction service valve and the high presssure hose to the discharge service valve. Tighten the hose nuts by hand.
3. Connect the center hose of the manifold to the inlet connection of a suitable vacuum pump.
4. Turn the vacuum pump on and open both hand valves.
5. Allow the vacuum pump to operate for approximately 10 minutes. Check that the low pressure gauge reads more than 23-24 in. Hg (80.0 kPa) of vacuum.

➡ If the reading on the gauges is not more than 23-24 in. Hg (80.0 kPa, then a leak exists in the system. Close both valves and shut off the vacuum pump. Inspect the system for leaks and repair as necessary. If the system holds the specified

vacuum, turn the vacuum pump on, open the manifold valvesand continue evacuating the system.

6. Continue evacuating the system down to 29.5 in. Hg. It may take a while to reach this point, but be patient because the last few inches of vacuum are important for obtaining a good evacuation.
7. Close the hand valves on the manifold.
8. Turn the vacuum pump off.
9. Disconnect the manifold center hose from the vacuum pump.
10. The system is now ready for charging.

Charging The System

Using one lb. cans of R-12 purchased a local retail store, the air conditioning system may be charged as a **liquid**, with the can turned upside down, or as a **vapor** with the can turned right-side up. Liquid charging is faster, but sometimes vapor must be drawn into the system to complete the charge. Always read the service precautions and instructions on the can before attempting to charge the system. The system holds approximately two lbs. (two cans) of refrigerant.

LIQUID CHARGE

CAUTION

Make sure that the engine is off when charging the system with liquid R-12.

1. Evacuate the system and make sure that both of the service valves on the gauge manifold are closed. Locate the sight glass on top of the receiver and wipe it off if it is dirty.
2. Connect the center hose of the gauge manifold to the can of refrigerant. Open the valve at the top of the can.
3. Bleed the air from the center hose by loosening the hose collar at the gauge manifold. When vapor is observed, tighten the collar.
4. Open the high pressure valve on the manifold and turn the R-12 can upside down. Due the properties of R-12, when the can is upside down, refrigerant will enter the system as a liquid.

WARNING

Keep the low presure gauge manifold valve closed and DO NOT run the engine. If the engine is operated, the compressor will force refrigerant back into the drum and may cause it to explode.

5. The system holds approximately two lbs. of refrigerant. To change cans, close the high pressure gauge manifold valve. Disconnect the discharged can from the center hose and connect a new can to the hose with the can valve closed. Bleed the air from the center hose by loosening the hose fitting at the can connection. Open the can valve. Open the high pressure valve and continue charging.
6. The system is fully charged when the sight glass is free of bubbles. If a full charge cannot be obtained, use the vapor charge method to complete the charge.
7. If a satisfactory charge was obtained, close the high pressure valve. Close the can valve and disconnect the can from the center hose. Disconnect the mainfold hoses from the suction and discharge service fittings.

VAPOR CHARGE

➡ Before attempting to charge the system by the vapor method, make sure the system has been charged with at least one lb. of liquid. The vapor method charges the system through the low pressure side by place the refrigerant can right side up. With the can right-side up, the refrigerant can enter the system as a vapor. A pan of warm water (104°F [40°C]) will be needed in this procedure. The R-12 can is placed in the warm water to keep the pressure in the container slightly higher than the vapor pressure in the system.

1. Close the high pressure valve on the manifold.
2. Place the refrigerant container in a pan of warm water right-side up.
3. Open the low pressure valve on the manifold.
4. Start the engine, turn the air conditioner to maximum cool and the blower switch on high.
5. Step on the accelerator pedal and raise the engine idle to 1500 rpm to allow the compressor to draw the vapor into the system.

CAUTION

Do not turn the R-12 can upside down. Doing so will allow the vapor refrigerant to become a liquid and severely damage the compressor. Liquids cannot be compressed.

6. Observe the sight glass. The system is fully charged when all the bubbles have disappeared from the sight glass.

Windshield Wipers

➧ SEE FIGS. 86–94

For maximum effectiveness and longest element life, the windshield and wiper blades should be kept clean. Dirt, tree sap, road tar and so on will cause streaking, smearing and blade deterioration if left on the windshield. It is advisable to wash the windshield carefully with a commercial glass cleaner at least once a month. Wipe off the rubber blades with a wet rag afterwards. Do not attempt to move the wipers back and forth by hand; damage to the motor and drive mechanism will result.

If the blades are found to be cracked, broken or torn, they should be replaced immediately. Replacement intervals will vary with usage, although ozone deterioration usually limits blade lift to about one year. If the wiper pattern is smeared or streaked, or if the blade chatters across the glass, the blades should be replaced. It is easiest and most sensible to replace them in pairs.

There are basically three different types of wiper blade refills, which differ in their method of replacement. One type has two release buttons, approximately 1/3 of the way up from the ends of the blade frame. Pushing the buttons down releases a lock and allows the rubber blade to be removed from the frame. The new blade slides back into the frame and locks in place.

The second type of refill has two metal tabs which are unlocked by squeezing them together. The rubber blade can then be withdrawn from the frame jaws. A new one is installed by inserting it into the front frame jaws and sliding it rearward to engage the remaining frame jaws. There are usually four jaws, be certain when installing that the refill is engaged in all of them. At the end of its travel, the tabs will lock into place on the front jaws of the wiper blade frame.

The third type is a refill made from polycarbonate. The refill has a simple locking device at one end which flexes downward out of the groove into which the jaws of the holder fit, allowing easy release. By sliding the new refill through all the jaws and pushing through the

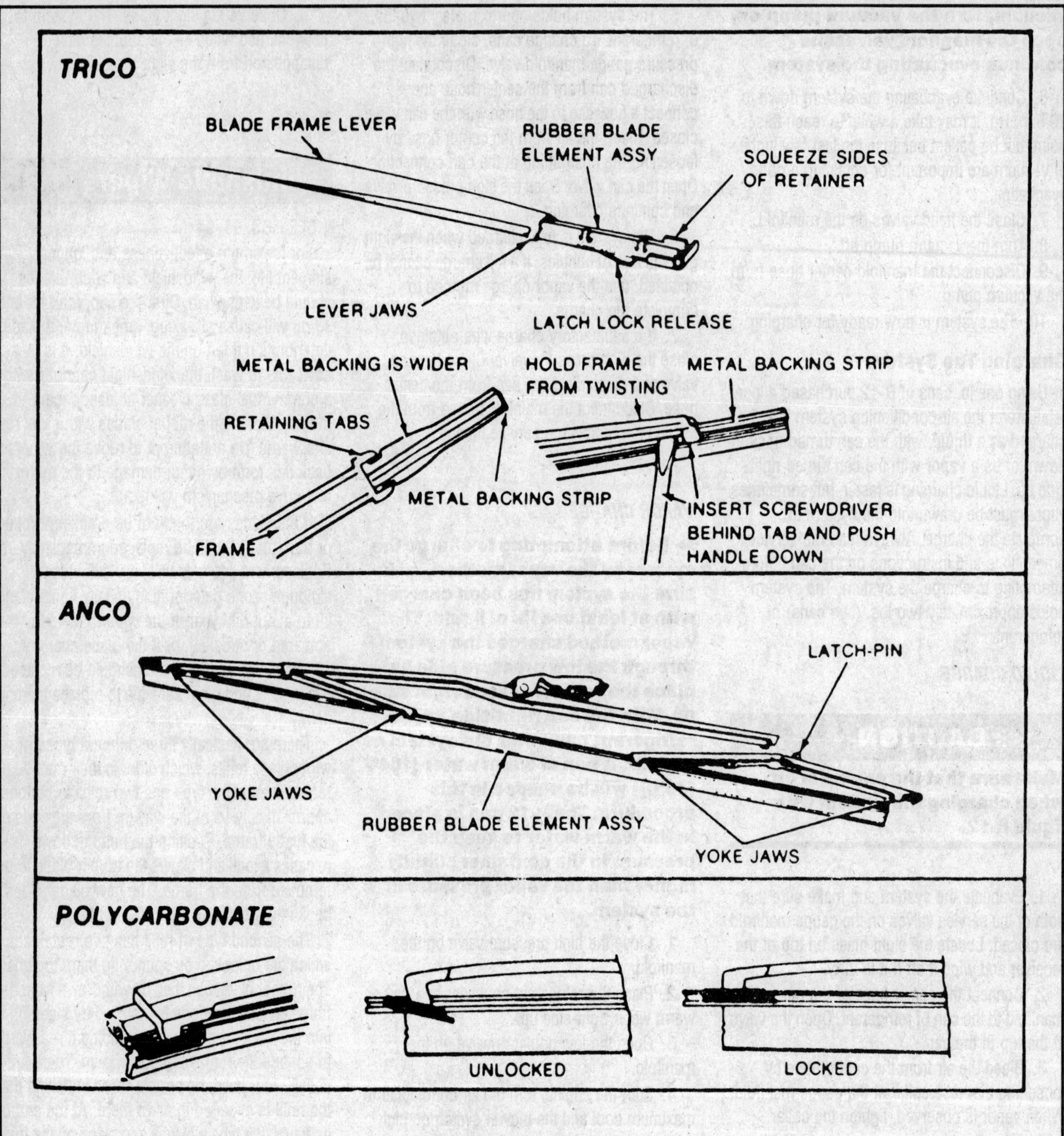

FIG. 86 The three types of wiper element retention

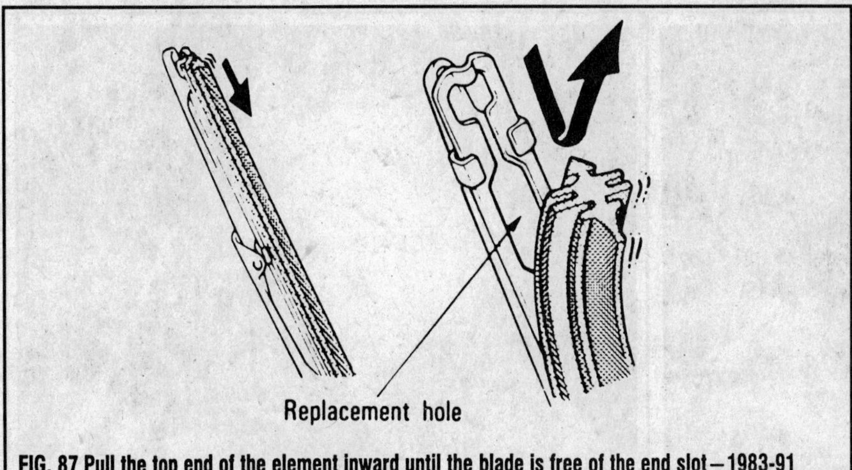

FIG. 87 Pull the top end of the element inward until the blade is free of the end slot—1983-91

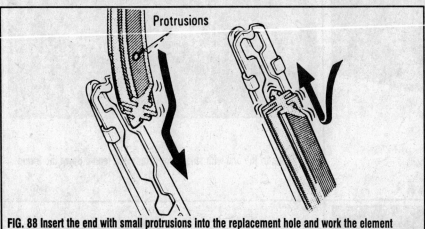

FIG. 88 Insert the end with small protrusions into the replacement hole and work the element along the slot in the blade—1983-91

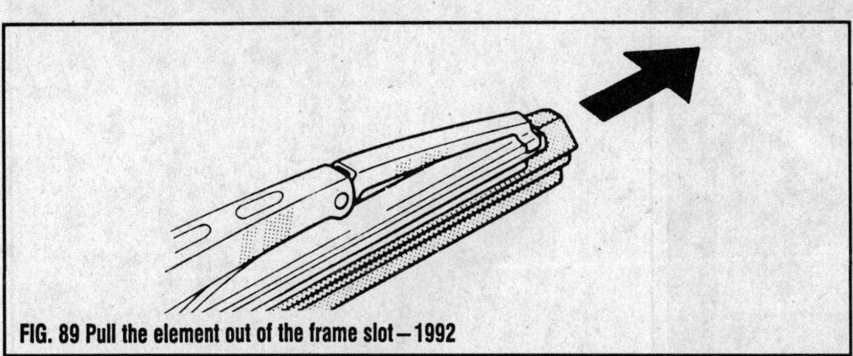

FIG. 89 Pull the element out of the frame slot—1992

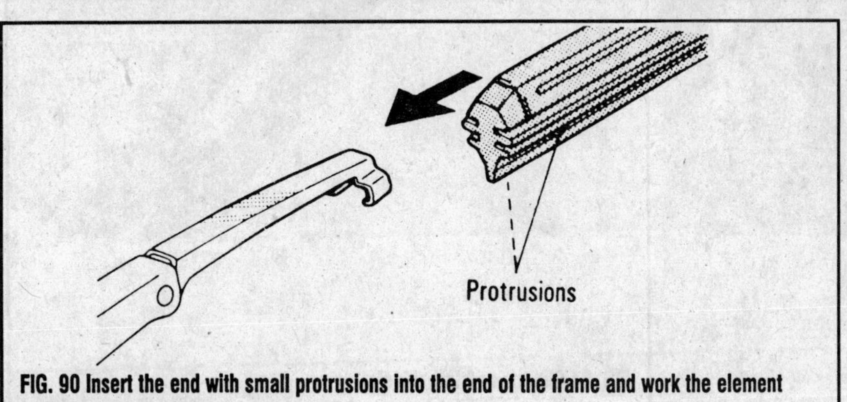

FIG. 90 Insert the end with small protrusions into the end of the frame and work the element along the slot in the blade—1992

slight resistance when it reaches the end of its travel, the refill will lock into position. Regardless of the type of refill used, make sure that all of the frame jaws are engaged as the refill is pushed into place and locked. The metal blade holder and frame will scratch the glass if allowed to touch it.

To replace the original factory-equipped wiper blades on 1983–91 models, pull the top end of the rubber inward until the rubber blade is free of the end slot and the replacement hole is visible. Pull the rubber blade out of the replacement hole. Insert the end new rubber wiper blade with the protrusions into the replacement hole and work the rubber along the slot in the blade frame. Once all the rubber is in the frame slot, allow it to expand and fill in the end. Check the wipers for proper operation.

On 1992 models, simply pull the element out of the frame slots from the right (as you face the car!) side of the blade. Install a new element into the same side from which it was removed by inserting the end with the small protrusions and working it along the slot. Check the wipers for proper operation.

ARM AND BLADE REPLACEMENT

A detailed description and procedures for replacing the wiper arm and blade is found in Section 6.

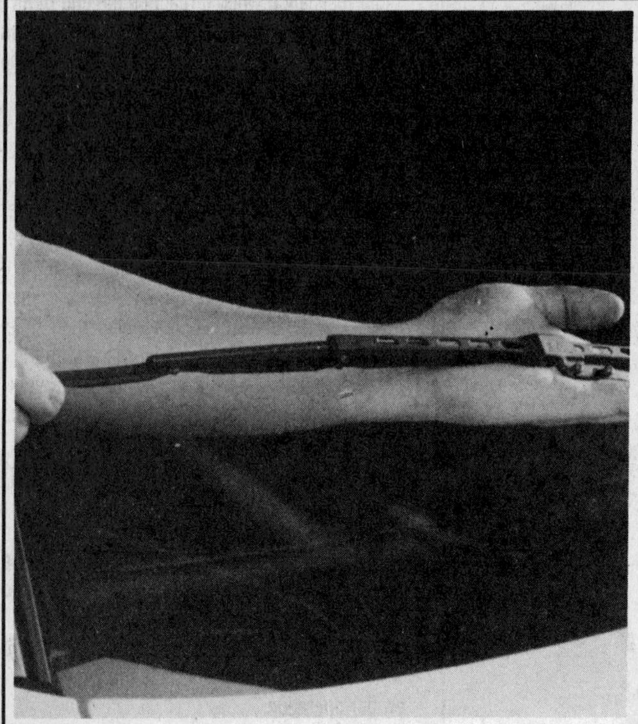

FIG. 91 Slide the old element out of the frame

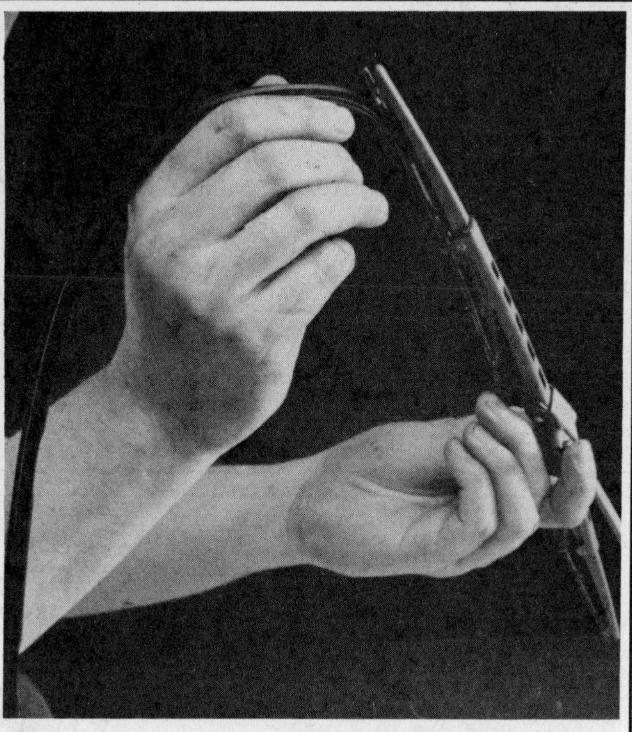

FIG. 92 Insert the end with small protrusions and feed it down the frame

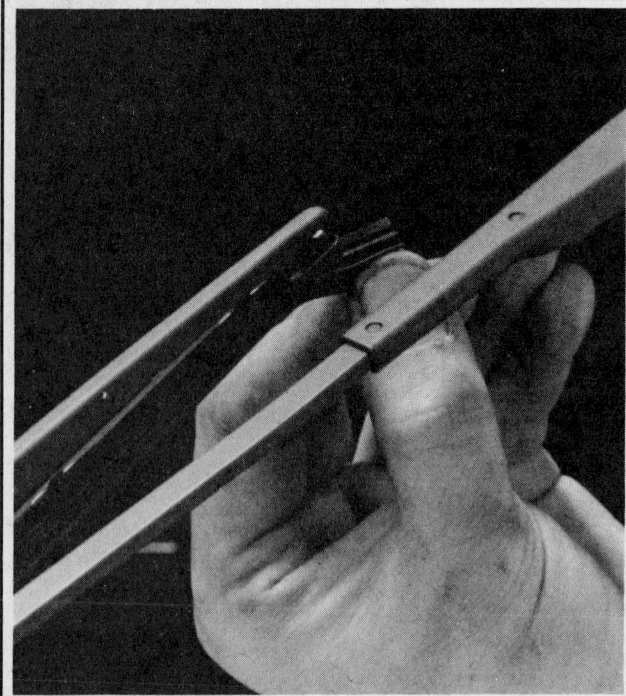

FIG. 93 Pull the end through and then reinsert it

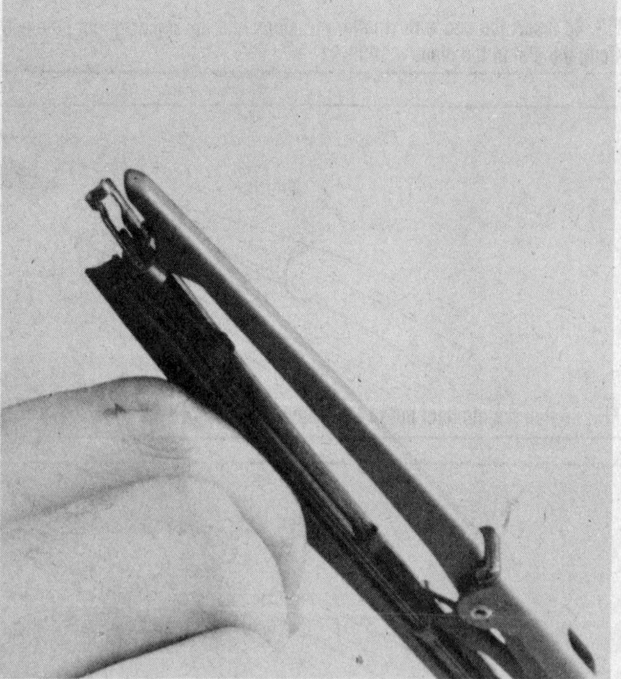

FIG. 94 Clip the end into the slot

Tires and Wheels

➧ SEE FIGS. 95–98

Inspect the tires regularly for wear and damage. Remove stones or other foreign particles which may be lodged in the tread. If tread wear is excessive or irregular it could be a sign of front end problems, or simply improper inflation.

The inflation should be checked at least once per month and adjusted if necessary. The tires must be cold (driven less than one mile) or an inaccurate reading will result. Do not forget to check the spare.

The correct inflation pressure for your vehicle can be found on a decal mounted to the car. Depending upon model and year, the decal can be located at the driver's door, the passenger's door or the glove box. If you cannot find the decal a local automobile tire dealer can furnish you with information.

Inspect tires for uneven wear that might indicate the need for front end alignment or tire rotation. Tires should be replaced when a tread wear indicator appears as a solid band across the tread.

When you buy new tires, give some thought to these points, especially if you are switching to larger tires or to another profile series (50, 60, 70, 78):

1. The wheels must be the correct width for the tire. Tire dealers have charts of tire and rim compatibility. A mismatch can cause sloppy handling and rapid tread wear. The old rule of thumb is that the tread width should match the rim width (inside bead to inside bead) within 1 in. (25mm). For radial tires, the rim width should be 80% or less of the tire (not tread) width.

2. The height (mounted diameter) of the new tires can greatly change speedometer accuracy, engine speed at a given road speed, fuel mileage, acceleration, and ground clearance. Tire makers furnish full measurement specifications. Speedometer drive gears are available from Toyota dealers for correction.

➡ **Dimensions of tires marked the same size may vary significantly, even among tires from the same maker.**

3. The spare tire should be usable, at least for low speed operation, with the new tires.

4. There shouldn't be any body interference when loaded, on bumps, or in turning.

The only sure way to avoid problems with these points is to stick to tire and wheel sizes available as factory options.

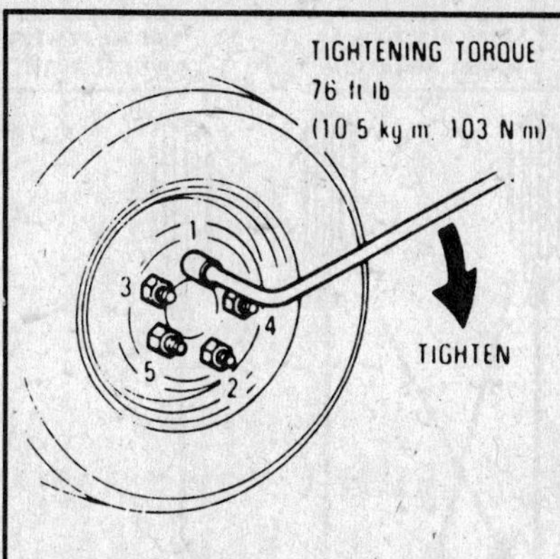

FIG. 95 Tighten the wheel lug nuts in a criss-cross pattern

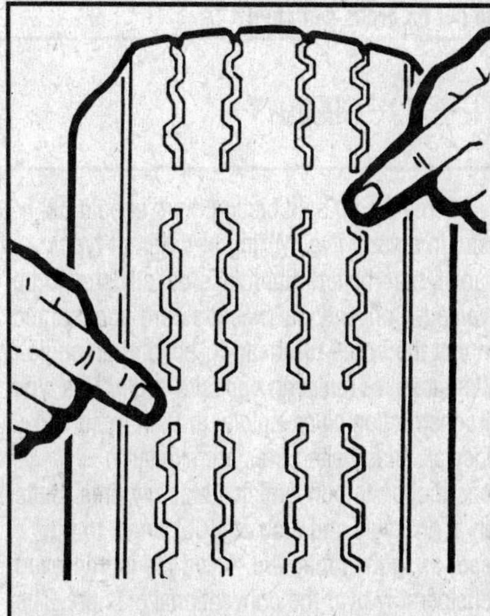

FIG. 96 Tread wear indicators will appear when the tire is worn out

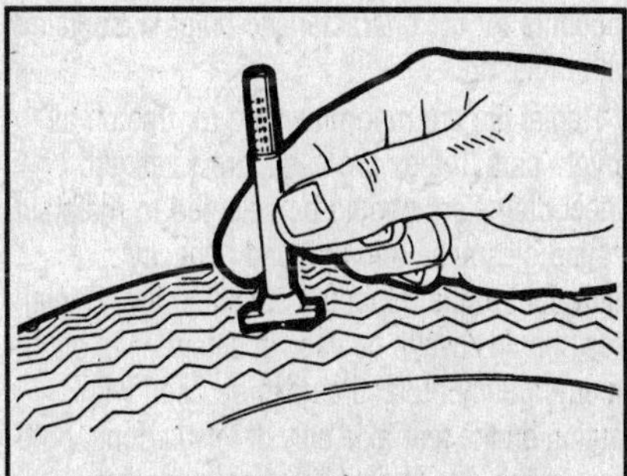

FIG. 97 Tread depth can also be checked with an inexpensive gauge

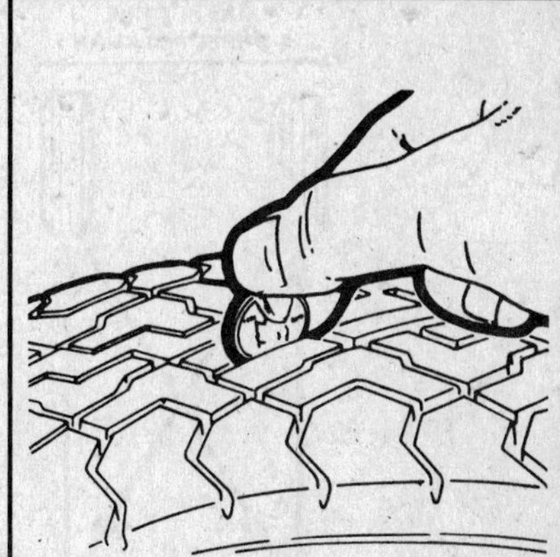

FIG. 98 A penny works as well as anything for checking tread depth; when the top of Lincoln's head is visible, its time for the new tires

TIRE ROTATION

➧ SEE FIG. 99

The rotation is recommended every 7500 miles (12,000 Km) or so, to obtain maximum tire wear. The pattern you use depends on whether or not your car has a usable spare. Radial tires should not be cross-switched (from one side of the car to the other); they last longer if their direction of rotation is not changed. Snow tires sometimes have directional arrows molded into the side of the carcass; the arrow shows the direction of rotation. They will wear very rapidly if the rotation is reversed. Studded tires will lose their studs if their rotational direction is reversed.

➡ **On the All-Trac/4wd, it is a good idea to rotate the tires at 3000 mile (5000 Km) intervals.**

➡ **Mark the wheel position or direction of rotation on radial tires or studded snow tires before removing them.**

If your car is equipped with tires having different load ratings on the front and the rear, the tires should not be rotated front to rear. Rotating these tires could affect tire life (the tires with the lower rating will wear faster, and could become overloaded), and upset the handling of the car.

TIRE USAGE

The tires on your car were selected to provide the best all around performance for normal operation when inflated as specified. Oversize

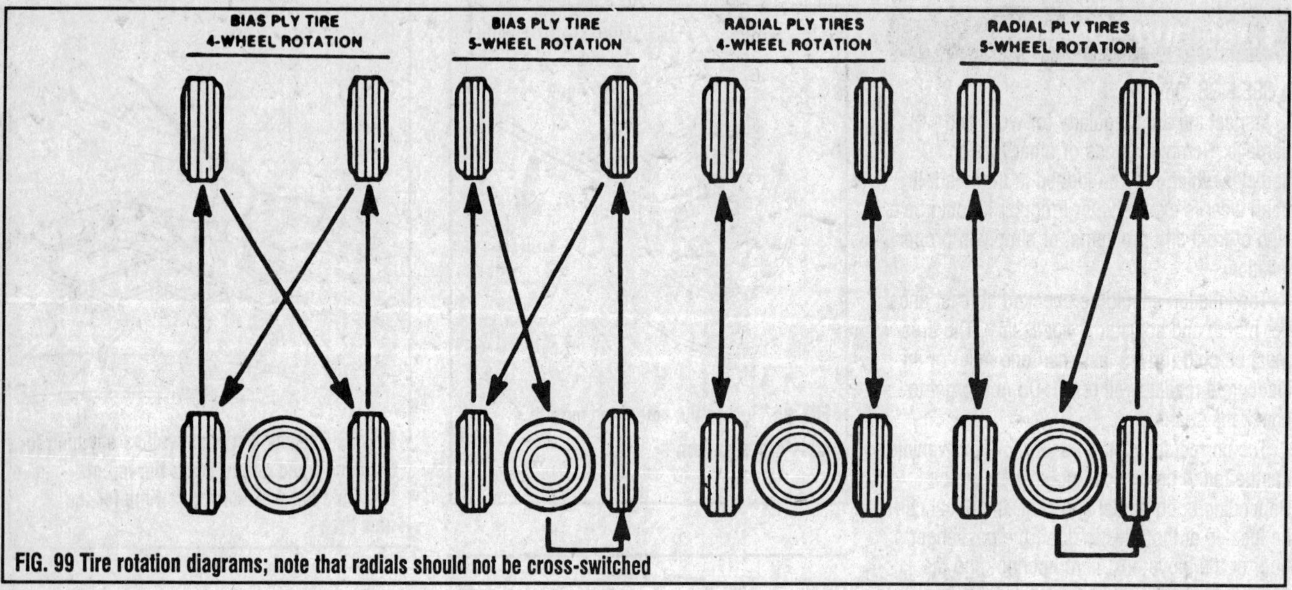

FIG. 99 Tire rotation diagrams; note that radials should not be cross-switched

tires (Load Range D) will not increase the maximum carrying capacity of the vehicle, although they will provide an extra margin of tread life. Be sure to check overall height before using larger size tires which may cause interference with suspension components or wheel wells. When replacing conventional tire sizes with other tire size designations, be sure to check the manufacturer's recommendations. Interchangeability is not always possible because of differences in load ratings, tire dimensions, wheel well clearances, and rim size. Also due to differences in handling characteristics, 70 Series and 60 Series tires should be used only in pairs on the same axle; radial tires should be used only in sets of four.

The wheels must be the correct width for the tire. Tire dealers have charts of tire and rim compatibility. A mismatch can cause sloppy handling and rapid tread wear. The old rule of thumb is that the tread width should match the rim width (inside bead to inside bead) within an inch. For radial tires, the rim width should be 80% or less of the tire (not tread) width.

The height (mounted diameter) of the new tires can greatly change speedometer accuracy, engine speed at a given road speed, fuel mileage, acceleration, and ground clearance. Tire manufacturers furnish full measurement specifications. Speedometer drive gears are available for correction.

➡ **Dimensions of tires marked the same size may vary significantly, even among tires from the same manufacturer.**

The spare tire should be usable, at least for low speed operation, with the new tires.

TIRE DESIGN

For maximum satisfaction, tires should be used in sets of five. Mixing or different types (radial, bias-belted, fiberglass belted) should be avoided. Conventional bias tires are constructed so that the cords run bead-to-bead at an angle. Alternate plies run at an opposite angle. This type of construction gives rigidity to both tread and sidewall. Bias-belted tires are similar in construction to conventional bias ply tires. Belts run at an angle and also at a 90° angle to the bead, as in the radial tire. Tread life is improved considerably over the conventional bias tire. The radial tire differs in construction, but instead of the carcass plies running at an angle of 90° to each other, they run at an angle of 90° to the bead. This gives the tread a great deal of rigidity and the sidewall a great deal of flexibility and accounts for the characteristic bulge associated with radial tires.

Radial tire are recommended for use on all Toyota cars. If they are used, tire sizes and wheel diameters should be selected to maintain ground clearance and tire load capacity equivalent to the minimum specified tire. Radial tires should always be used in sets of five, but in an emergency radial tires can be used with caution on the rear axle only. If this is done, both tires on the rear should be of radial design.

➡ **Radial tires should never be used on only the front axle.**

STORAGE

Store the tires at the proper inflation pressure if they are mounted on wheels. Keep them in a cool dry place, laid on their sides. If the tires are stored in the garage or basement, do not let them stand on a concrete floor; set them on strips of wood.

INFLATION PRESSURE

Tire inflation is the most ignored item of auto maintenance. Gasoline mileage can drop as much as 0.8% for every 1 pound per square inch (psi of under inflation).

Two items should be a permanent fixture in every glove compartment; a tire pressure gauge and a tread depth gauge. Check the tire air pressure (including the spare) regularly with a pocket type gauge. Kicking the tires won't tell you a thing, and the gauge on the service station air hose is notoriously inaccurate.

The tire pressures recommended for your care are usually found on the glove box door, on the door jam, or in the owners manual. Ideally, inflation pressure should be checked when the tires are cool. When the air becomes heated it expands and the pressure increases. Every 10 degree rise (or drop) in temperature means a difference of 1 psi, which also explains why the tire appears to lose air on a very cold night. When it is impossible to check the tires cold, allow for pressure build-up due to heat. If the hot pressure exceeds the cold pressure by more than 15 psi, reduce your speed, load or both. Otherwise internal heat is created in the tire.

When the heat approaches the temperature at which the tire was cured, during manufacture, the tread can separate from the body.

CAUTION

Never counteract excessive pressure build-up by bleeding off air pressure (letting some air out). This will only further raise the tire operating temperature.

Before starting a long trip with lots of luggage, you can add about 2–4 psi to the tires to make them run cooler, but never exceed the maximum inflation pressure on the side of the tire.

CARE OF SPECIAL WHEELS

An aluminum wheel may be porous and leak air. Locate the leak by inflating the tire to 40 psi and submerging the tire/wheel assembly in water. Mark the leak areas. Remove the tire from the wheel and scuff the inside rim surface with 80 grit sandpaper. Apply a thick layer of adhesive sealant or equivalent to the leak area and allow to dry for approximately 6 hours.

Clean wheels with a special mag wheel cleaner or mild soap and water. Do not use harsh detergents or solvents or else the protective coating may be damaged.

FLUIDS AND LUBRICANTS

Oil and Fuel Recommendations

OIL

SEE FIGS. 100–103

The SAE (Society of Automotive Engineers) grade number indicates the viscosity of the engine oil; its resistance to flow at a given temperature. The lower the SAE grade number, the lighter the oil. For example, the mono-grade oils begin with SAE 5 weight, which is a thin light oil, and continue in viscosity up to SAE 80 or 90 weight, which are heavy gear lubricants. These oils are also known as "straight weight", meaning they are of a single viscosity, and do not vary with engine temperature.

Multi-viscosity oils offer the important advantage of being adaptable to temperature extremes. These oils have designations such as 10W-40, 20W-50, etc. The "10W-40" means that in winter (the "W" in the designation) the oil acts like a thin 10 weight oil, allowing the engine to spin easily when cold and offering rapid lubrication. Once the engine has warmed up, however, the oil acts like a straight 40 weight, maintaining good lubrication and protection for the engine's internal components. A 20W-50 oil would therefore be slightly heavier than and not as ideal in cold weather as the 10W-40, but would offer better protection at higher rpm and temperatures because when warm it acts like a

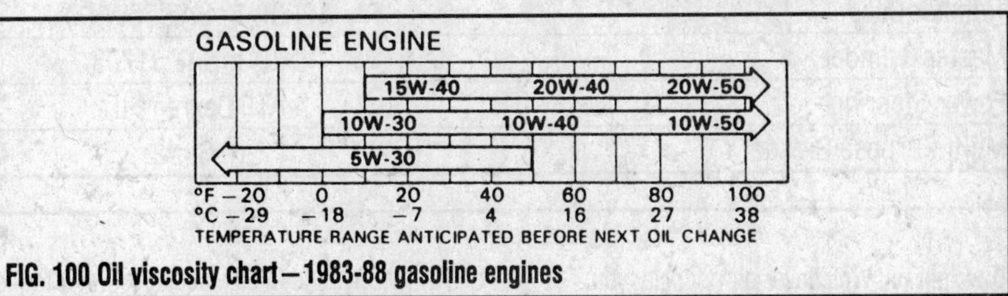

FIG. 100 Oil viscosity chart—1983-88 gasoline engines

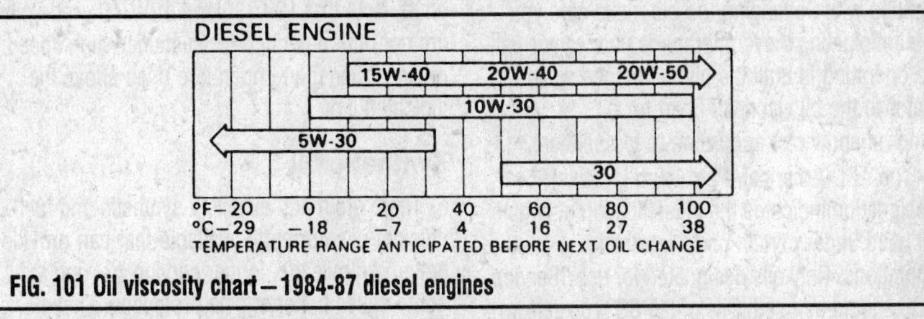

FIG. 101 Oil viscosity chart—1984-87 diesel engines

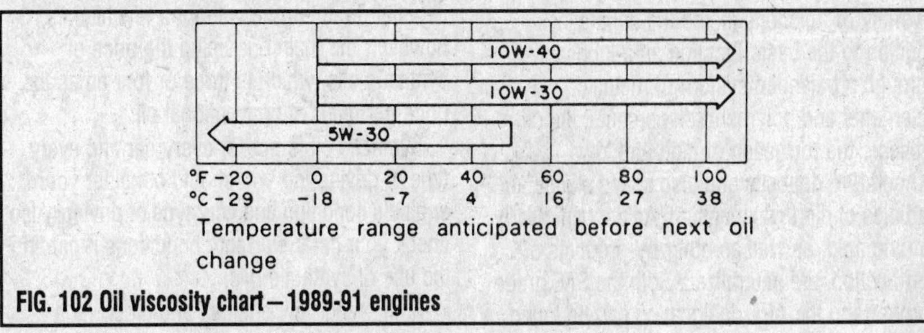

FIG. 102 Oil viscosity chart—1989-91 engines

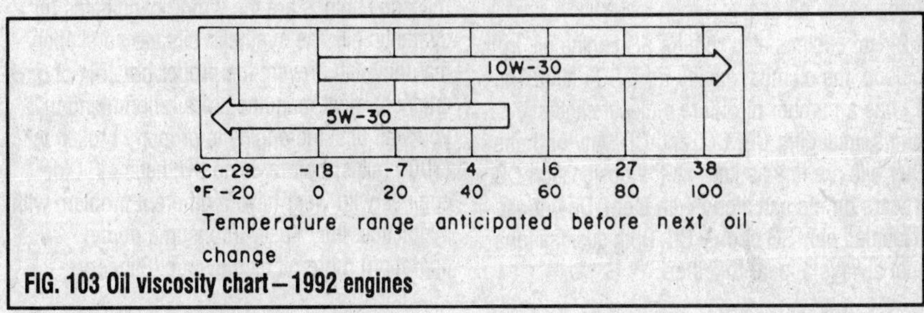

FIG. 103 Oil viscosity chart—1992 engines

RECOMMENDED LUBRICANTS

Component		Lubricant
Engine Oil		API SG/CC
Coolant		Ethylene Glycol Anti-freeze
Manual Transaxle		
	S51	ATF Dexron® II
	E52	API GL-4 or GL-5, SAE 75W-90
	E53	API GL-4 or GL-5, SAE 75W-90
	E56F2, E56F5	API GL-5, SAE 75W-90 or 80W-90
Automatic Transaxle		
	A140L, A140E, A540E	ATF Dexron® II
	A540H	ATF Type T
Differential (Front)		
	2WD w/S51 MT	ATF Dexron® II
	2WD w/E52 MT	API GL-4, SAE 75W-90
	4WD w/MT	API GL-5, SAE 75W-90
	AT	ATF Dexron® II
Differential (Rear)		API GL-5, SAE 90W
Transfer Case		API GL-5, SAE 75W-90
Master Cylinder		DOT 3, SAE J1703
Power Steering		ATF Dexron® II
Multi-Purpose Grease		NLGI #2

50 weight oil. Whichever oil viscosity you choose when changing the oil, make sure you are anticipating the temperatures your engine will be operating in until the oil is changed again. Refer to the oil viscosity chart for oil recommendations according to temperature.

The API (American Petroleum Institute) designation indicates the classification of engine oil used under certain given operating conditions. Only oils designated for use "Service SG" should be used. Oils of the SG type perform a variety of functions inside the engine in addition to the basic function as a lubricant. Through a balanced system of metallic detergents and polymeric dispersants, the oil prevents the formation of high and low temperature deposits and also keeps sludge and particles of dirt in suspension. Acids, particularly sulfuric acid, as well as other by-products of combustion, are neutralized. Both the SAE grade number and the APE designation can be found on top of the oil can.

Diesel engines also require SG engine oil. In addition, the oil must qualify for a CC rating. The API has a number of different diesel engine ratings, including CB, CC, and CD. Any of these other oils are fine as long as the designation CC appears on the can along with them. Do not use oil labeled only SG or only CC. Both designations must always appear together.

For recommended oil viscosities, refer to the chart. Note that 10W-30 and 10W-40 grade oils are not recommended for sustained high speed driving when the temperature rises above the indicated limit.

Synthetic Oil

There are many excellent synthetic and fuel-efficient oils currently available that can provide better gas mileage, longer service life, and in some cases better engine protection. These benefits do not come without a few hitches, however; the main one being the price of synthetic oils, which is three or four times the price per quart of conventional oil.

Synthetic oil is not for every car and every type of driving, so you should consider your engine's condition and your type of driving. Also, check your car's warranty conditions regarding the use of synthetic oils.

Both brand new engines and older, high mileage engines are the wrong candidates for synthetic oil. The synthetic oils are so slippery that they can prevent the proper break-in of new engines; most manufacturers recommend that you wait until the engine is properly broken in (3000 miles) before using synthetic oil. Older engines with wear have a different problem with synthetics: they "use" (consume during operation) more oil as they age. Slippery synthetic oils get past these worn parts easily. If your engine is "using" conventional oil, it will use synthetics much faster. Also, if your car is leaking oil past old seals you'll have a much greater leak problem with synthetics.

Consider your type of driving. If most of your accumulated mileage is high speed, highway type driving, the more expensive synthetic oils may be a benefit. Extended highway driving gives the engine a chance to warm up, accumulating less acids in the oil and putting less stress on the engine over the long run. Under these conditions, the oil change interval can be extended (as long as your oil filter can last the extended life of the oil) up to the advertised mileage claims of the synthetics. Cars with synthetic oils may show increased fuel economy in highway driving, due to less internal friction. However, many automotive experts agree that 50,000 miles (80,000 km) is too long to keep any oil in your engine.

Cars used under harder circumstances, such as stop-and-go, city type driving, short trips, or extended idling, should be serviced more frequently. For the engines in these cars, the much greater cost of synthetic or fuel-efficient oils may not be worth the investment. Internal wear increase much quicker on these cars, causing greater oil consumption and leakage.

➡ The mixing of conventional and synthetic oils is not recommended. If you are using synthetic oil, it might be wise to carry two or three quarts with you no matter where you drive, as not all service stations carry this type of lubricant. Non-detergent or straight mineral oils must never be used.

FUEL

Gasoline Engines

It is important to use fuel of the proper octane rating in your car. Octane rating is based on the quantity of anti-knock compounds added to the fuel and it determines the speed at which the gas will burn. The lower the octane rating, the faster it burns. The higher the octane, the slower the fuel will burn and a greater percentage of compounds in the fuel prevent spark ping (knock), detonation and preignition (dieseling).

As the temperature of the engine increases, the air/fuel mixture exhibits a tendency to ignite before the spark plug is fired. If fuel of an octane rating too low for the engine is used, this will allow combustion to occur before the piston has completed its compression stroke, thereby creating a very high pressure very rapidly.

Fuel of the proper octane rating, for the compression ratio and ignition timing of your car, will slow the combustion process sufficiently to allow the spark plug enough time to ignite the mixture completely and smoothly. Many non-catalyst models are designed to run on regular fuel. The use of some super-premium fuel is no substitution for a properly tuned and maintained engine. Chances are that if your engine exhibits any signs of spark ping, detonation or pre-ignition when using regular fuel, the ignition timing should be checked against specifications or the cylinder head should be removed for decarbonizing.

Vehicles equipped with catalytic converters must use UNLEADED GASOLINE ONLY. Use of unleaded fuel shortened the life of spark plugs, exhaust systems and EGR valves and can damage the catalytic converter. Most converter equipped models are designed to operate using unleaded gasoline with a minimum rating of 87 octane. Use of unleaded gas with octane ratings lower than 87 can cause persistent spark knock which could lead to engine damage.

Light spark knock may be noticed when accelerating or driving up hills. The slight knocking may be considered normal (with 87 octane) because the maximum fuel economy is obtained under condition of occasional light spark knock. Gasoline with an octane rating higher than 87 may be used, but it is not necessary (in most cases) for proper operation.

If spark knock is constant, when using 87 octane, at cruising speeds on level ground, ignition timing adjustment may be required.

➡ Your engine's fuel requirement can change with time, mainly due to carbon buildup, which changes the compression ratio. If your engine pings, knocks or runs on, switch to a higher grade of fuel. Sometimes just changing brands will cure the problem. If it becomes necessary to retard the timing from specifications, don't change it more than a few degrees. Retarded timing will reduce power output and fuel mileage and will increase the engine temperature.

Diesel Engines

Diesel engines require the use of diesel fuel. At no time should gasoline be substituted. Two grades of diesel fuel are manufactured, #1 and #2, although #2 grade is generally more available. Better fuel economy results from the use of #2 grade fuel. In some northern parts of the U.S. and in most parts of Canada, #1 grade fuel is available in the winter or a winterized blend of #2 grade is supplied in winter months. When the temperature falls below 20°F (–7°C), #1 grade or winterized #2 grade fuel are the only fuels that can be used. Cold temperatures cause unwinterized #2 to thicken (it actually gels), blocking the fuel lines and preventing the engine from running.

DIESEL CAUTIONS:

- Do not use home heating oil in your car.
- Do not use ether or starting assist fluids in your car.
- Do not use any fuel additives recommended for use in gasoline engines.

It is normal that the engine noise level is louder during the warm-up period in winter. It is also normal that whitish/blue smoke may be emitted from the exhaust after starting and during warm-up. The amount of smoke depends upon the outside temperature.

OPERATION IN FOREIGN COUNTRIES

If you plan to drive your car outside the United States or Canada, there is a possibility that fuels will be too low in anti-knock quality and could produce engine damage. It is wise to consult with local authorities upon arrival in a foreign country to determine the best fuels available.

Engine

CAUTION

Prolonged and repeated skin contact with used engine oil, with no effort to remove the oil, may be harmful. Always follow these simple precautions when handling used motor oil:

- Avoid prolonged skin contact with used motor oil.
- Remove oil from skin by washing thoroughly with soap and water or waterless hand cleaner. Do not use gasoline, thinners or other solvents.
- Avoid prolonged skin contact with oil-soaked clothing.

OIL LEVEL CHECK

➡ SEE FIGS. 104–105

Every time you stop for fuel, check the engine oil as follows:

1. Park the car on level ground.
2. When checking the oil level it is best for the engine to be at operating temperature, although checking the oil immediately after a stopping will lead to a false reading. Wait a few minutes after turning off the engine to allow the oil to drain back into the crankcase.
3. Open the hood and locate the dipstick which is on the left side of the engine. Pull the dipstick from its tube, wipe it clean and reinsert it.
4. Pull the dipstick out again and, holding it horizontally, read the oil level. The oil should be between the **F** and **L** marks on the dipstick. If the oil is below the **L** mark, add oil of the proper viscosity through the capped opening on the top of the cylinder head cover. See the "Oil and Fuel Recommendations" chart in this section for the proper viscosity ad rating of oil to use.
5. Replace the dipstick and check the oil level again after adding any oil. Be careful not to overfill the crankcase. Approximately one quart of oil will raise the level from the **L** to the **F**. Excess oil will generally be consumed at an accelerated rate.

FIG. 104 Dipstick location on the 3S-FE engine

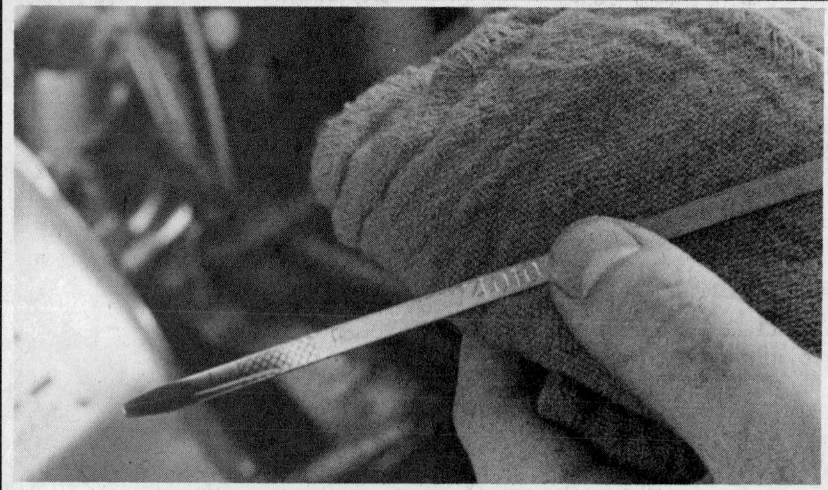

FIG. 105 The oil level should be between the L and the F marks on the dipstick

OIL AND FILTER CHANGE

➧ SEE FIGS. 106–109

The oil should be changed every 7500 miles (12,000 km). Nissan recommends changing the oil filter with every other oil change; we suggest that the filter be changed with every oil change. There is approximately 1 quart of dirty oil left remaining in the old oil filter if it is not changed! A few dollars more every year seems a small price to pay for extended engine life — so change the filter every time you change the oil!

✲✲ CAUTION

Prolonged and repeated skin contact with used engine oil, with no effort to remove the oil, may be harmful. Always follow these simple precautions when handling used motor oil.

- Avoid prolonged skin contract with used motor oil.
- Remove oil from skin by washing thoroughly with soap and water or waterless hand cleaner. Do not use gasoline, thinners or other solvents.
- Avoid prolonged skin contact with oil-soaked clothing.

The oil drain plug is located on the bottom, rear of the oil pan (bottom of the engine, underneath the car). The oil filter is located on the front side of the engine on all models.

The mileage figures given are the Toyota recommended intervals assuming normal driving and conditions. If your car is being used under dusty, polluted or off-road conditions, change the oil and filter more frequently than specified. The same goes for cars driven in stop-and-go traffic or only for short distances. Always

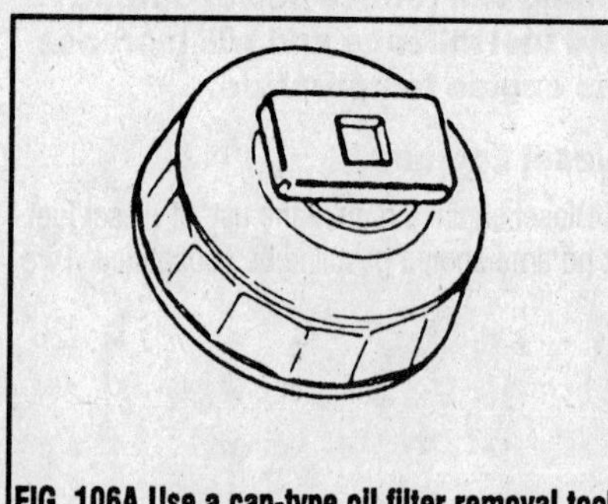

FIG. 106A Use a cap-type oil filter removal tool

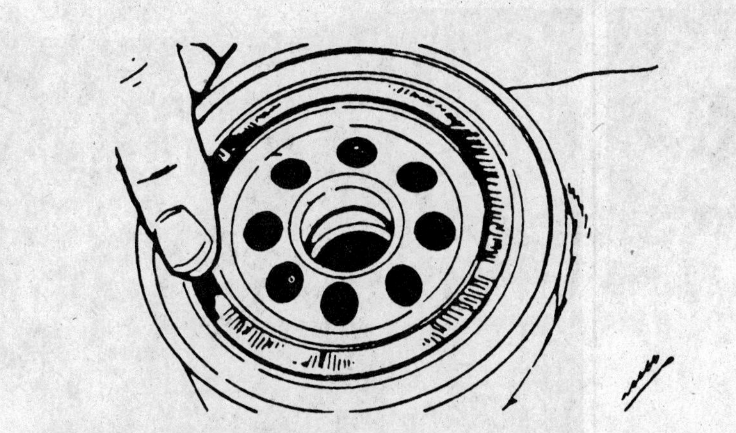

FIG. 107A Lubricate the gasket on the new filter with clean engine oil. A dry gasket may not make as good a seal and could allow the filter to leak

drain the oil after the engine has been running long enough to bring it to normal operating temperature. Hot oil will flow easier and more contaminants will be removed along with the oil than if it were drained cold. To change the oil and filter:

CAUTION

The EPA warns that prolonged contact with used engine oil may cause a number of skin disorders, including cancer! You should make every effort to minimize your exposure to used engine oil. Protective gloves should be worn when changing the oil. Wash your hands and any other exposed skin areas as soon as possible after exposure to used engine oil. Soap and water, or waterless hand cleaner should be used.

1. Warm the oil by running the engine for a short period of time or at least until the needle on the temperature gauge rises above the **C** mark. This will make the oil flow more freely from the oil pan.
2. Park on a level surface, apply the parking brake and block the wheels. Stop the engine. Raise the hood and remove the oil filler cap from the top of the valve cover. This allows the air to enter the engine as the oil drains. Remove the dipstick, wipe it off and set it aside.
3. Position a suitable oil drain pan under the drain plug.

➡ **All diesel and gasoline engines hold approximately 4 quarts of oil (give or take 0.2 or 0.3), so choose a drain pan that exceeds this amount to allow for movement of the oil when the pan is pulled from under the vehicle. This will prevent time lost to the cleaning up of messy oil spills.**

4. With the proper size metric socket or closed end wrench (DO NOT use pliers or vise grips), loosen the drain plug. Back out the drain plug while maintaining a slight upward force on it to keep the oil from running out around it (and your hand). Allow the oil to drain into the drain pan.

CAUTION

The engine oil will be hot. Keep your arms, face and hands away from the oil as it is draining

5. Remove the drain pan and wipe any excess oil from the area around the hole using a clean rag. Clean the threads of the drain plug and the drain plug gasket to remove any sludge deposits that may have accumulated.
6. With a filter wrench, loosen the oil filter counterclockwise and back the filter off the filter post the rest of the way by hand. Keep the filter end up so that the oil does not spill out. Tilt the filter into the drain pan to drain the oil.
7. Remove the drain pan from under the vehicle and position it off to the side.
8. With a clean rag, wipe off the filter seating surface to ensure a proper seal. Make sure that the old gasket is not stuck to the seating surface. If it is, remove it and thoroughly clean the seating surface of the old gasket material.
9. Open a container of new oil and smear some of this oil onto the rubber gasket of the new oil filter. Get a feel for where the filter post is and start the filter by hand until the gasket contacts the seat. Using the filter wrench, turn the filter an additional 3/4 turn.
10. Install the drain plug and metal gasket. Be sure that the plug is tight enough that the oil does not leak out, but not tight enough to strip the threads. Over time you will develop a sense of what the proper tightness of the drain plug is. If a torque wrench is available, tighten the plug to the following specifications:
   - 1C-T, 2C-T, 2S-E engines—18 ft. lbs. (25 Nm)
   - 3S-FE, 5S-FE engines—29 ft. lbs. (39 Nm)
   - 2VZ-FE engines—18 ft. lbs. (25 Nm)
   - 3VZ-FE engines—27 ft. lbs. (37 Nm)

➡ **Replace the drain plug gasket at every third or fourth oil change.**

11. Through a suitable plastic or metal funnel, add clean new oil of the proper grade and viscosity through the oil filler on the top of the valve cover. Be sure that the oil level registers near the **F** (full) mark on the dipstick.
12. Install and tighten the oil filler cap.
13. Start the engine and allow it to run for several minutes. Check for leaks at the filter and drain plug. Sometimes leaks will not be revealed until the engine reaches normal operating temperature.
14. Stop the engine and recheck the oil level. Add oil as necessary.

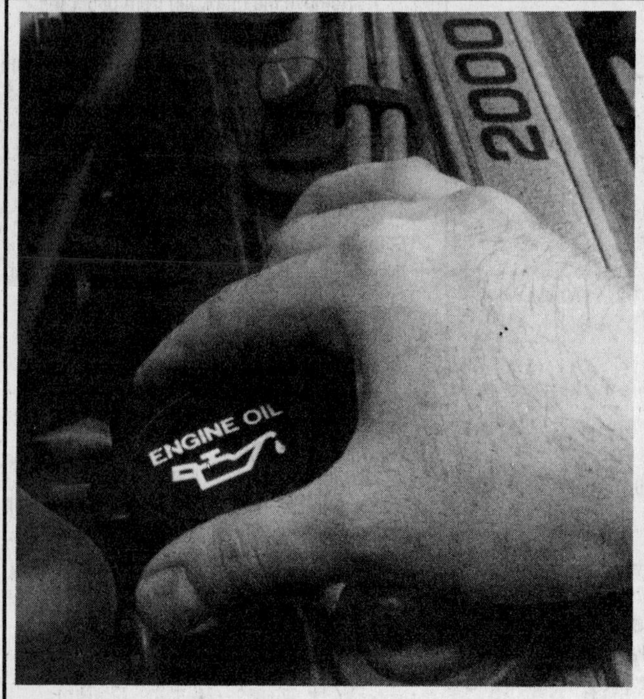

FIG. 106 Remove the oil filler cap

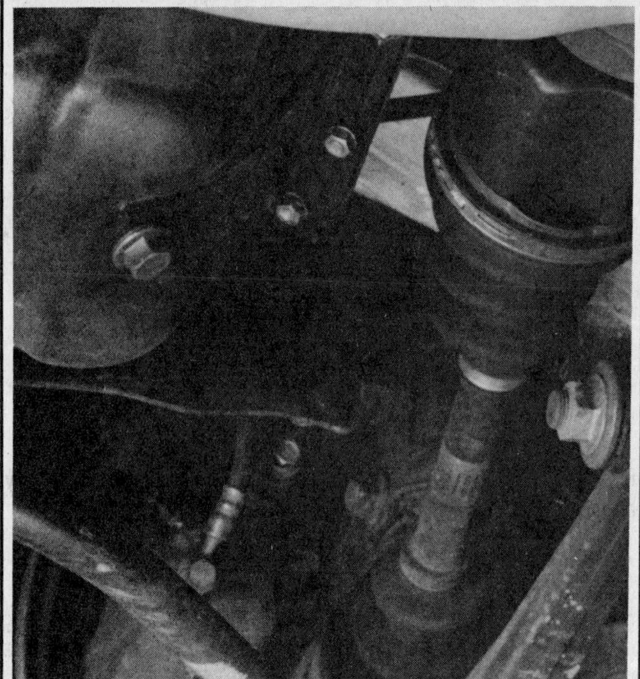
FIG. 107 The oil drain plug is at the bottom of the oil pan

FIG. 108 Remove the oil filter carefully

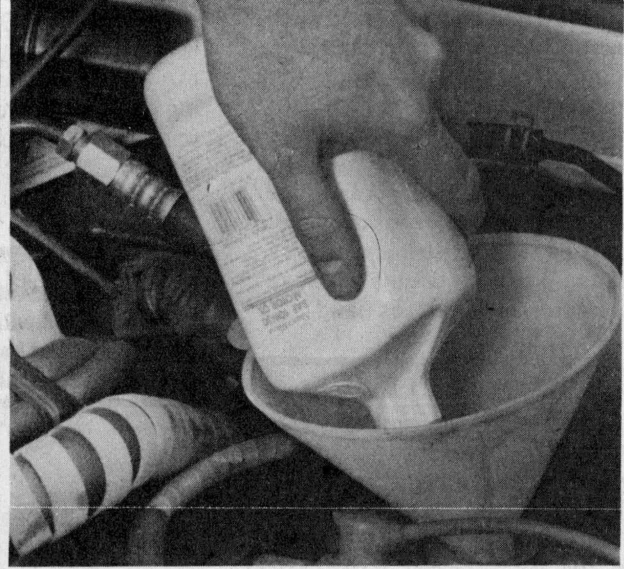
FIG. 109 Its always a good idea to use a funnel when adding oil

Manual Transaxle

FLUID RECOMMENDATIONS

- All 2wd, 4 cyl. models: DEXRON® II ATF
- All 2wd, 6 cyl. models: multipurpose gear oil API GL-4 or GL-5; SAE 80W-90
- All 4wd models: multipurpose gear oil API GL-4; SAE 75W-90 or 80W-90

FLUID LEVEL CHECK

➧ SEE FIG. 110

The oil in the manual transaxle should be checked at least every 15,000 miles (24,000 km) and replaced every 25,000–30,000 miles (40,000–48,000 km), even more frequently if driven in deep water.

1. With the car parked on a level surface, remove the filler plug (24mm hex head on gasoline models, 17mm hex head on diesel models) from the front side of the transaxle housing.
2. If the lubricant begins to trickle out of the hole, there is enough. Otherwise, carefully insert your finger (watch out for sharp threads!) and check to see if the oil is up to the edge of the hole.
3. If not, add oil through the hole until the level is at the edge of the hole. Most gear lubricants come in a plastic squeeze bottle with a nozzle; making additions simple. You can also use a common everyday kitchen baster.
4. Replace the filler plug and tighten it to 36 ft. lbs. (49 Nm). Run the engine and check for leaks.

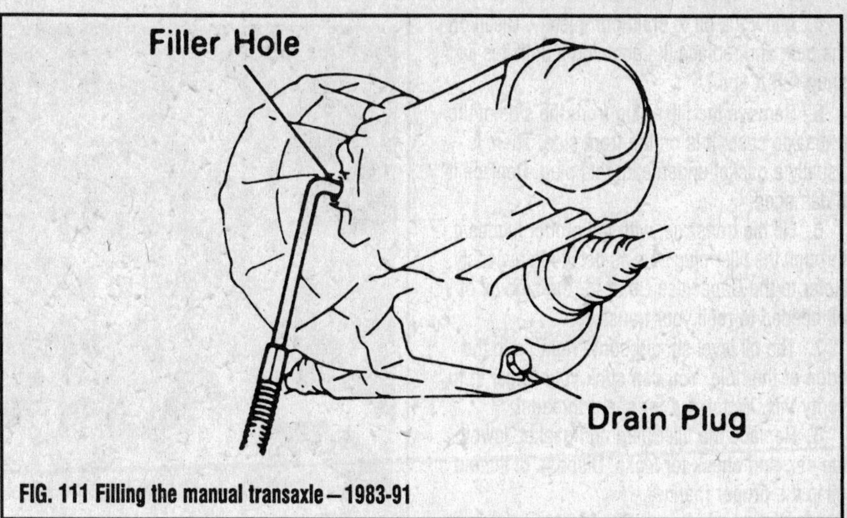

FIG. 111 Filling the manual transaxle—1983-91

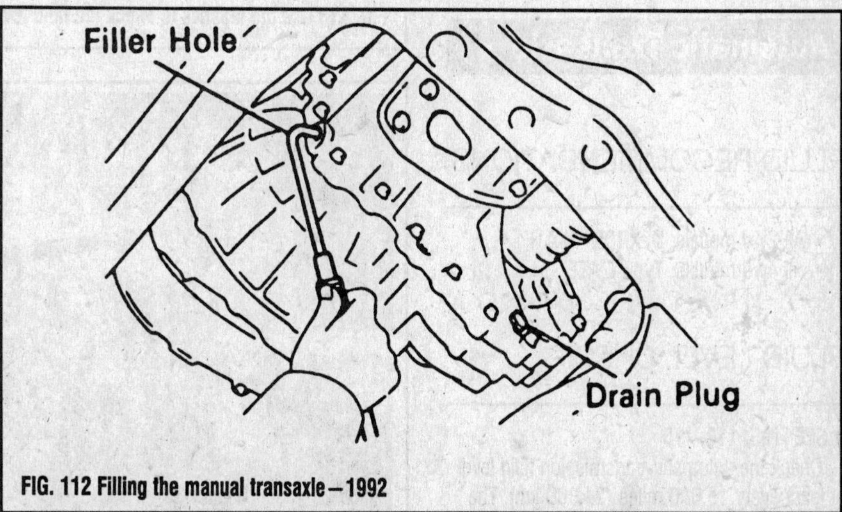

FIG. 112 Filling the manual transaxle—1992

DRAIN AND REFILL

➧ SEE FIGS. 11–112

Once every 30,000 miles (48,000 km), the oil in the manual transaxle should be changed.

1. The transaxle oil should be hot before it is drained. If the engine is at normal operating temperature, the transaxle oil should be hot enough.
2. Raise the car and support it properly on jackstands so that you can safely work underneath. You will probably not have enough room to work if the car is not raised.
3. The drain plug is located on the bottom of the transaxle, it should be a 24mm hex head. Place a pan under the drain plug and remove it. Keep a slight upward pressure on the plug while unscrewing it, this will keep the oil from pouring out until the plug is removed.

✲✲ CAUTION

The oil will be HOT! Be careful when you remove the plug so that you don't take a bath in hot gear oil.

FIG. 110 Use your finger to check the oil level on the manual transaxle

4. Allow the oil to drain completely. Clean off the plug and replace it, tightening it until it is just snug (36 ft. lbs.).

5. Remove the filler plug from the side of the transaxle case. It is on the front side. There is usually a gasket underneath this plug. Replace it if damaged.

6. Fill the transaxle, with the proper lubricant, through the filler plug hole as detailed previously. Refer to the Capacities Chart for the amount of oil needed to refill your transaxle.

7. The oil level should come right up to the edge of the hole. You can stick your finger in to verify this. Watch out for sharp threads!

8. Replace the filler plug and gasket, lower the car, and check for leaks. Dispose of the old oil in the proper manner.

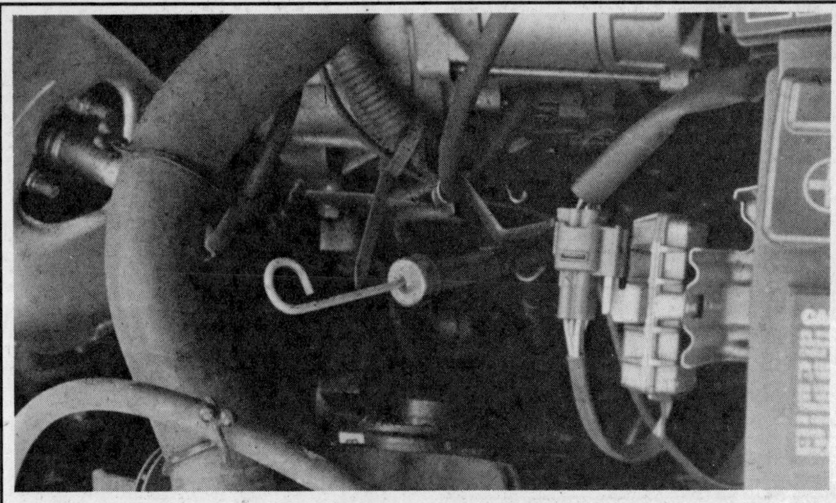

FIG. 113 Use the dipstick to check the fluid level in an automatic transaxle

Automatic Transaxle

FLUID RECOMMENDATIONS

- All 2wd models: DEXRON® II ATF
- All 4wd models: Type T ATF

FLUID LEVEL CHECK

➧ SEE FIGS. 113–115

Check the automatic transmission fluid level at least every 15,000 miles (24,000 km). The dipstick is in the left front of the engine compartment, near the battery. The fluid level should be checked only when the transmission is hot (normal operating temperature). The transmission is considered hot after about 20 miles of highway driving.

1. Park the car on a level surface with the engine idling. Shift the transmission into **P** and set the parking brake.

2. Remove the dipstick, wipe it clean and reinsert if firmly. Be sure that it has been pushed all the way in. Remove the dipstick and check the fluid level while holding it horizontally. All models have a HOT and a COLD side to the dipstick.

- **COLD**: the fluid level should fall in this range when the engine has been running for only a short time.
- **HOT**: the fluid level should fall in this range when the engine has reached normal running temperatures.

3. If the fluid level is not within the proper area on either side of the dipstick, pour ATF into the dipstick tube. This is easily done with the aid

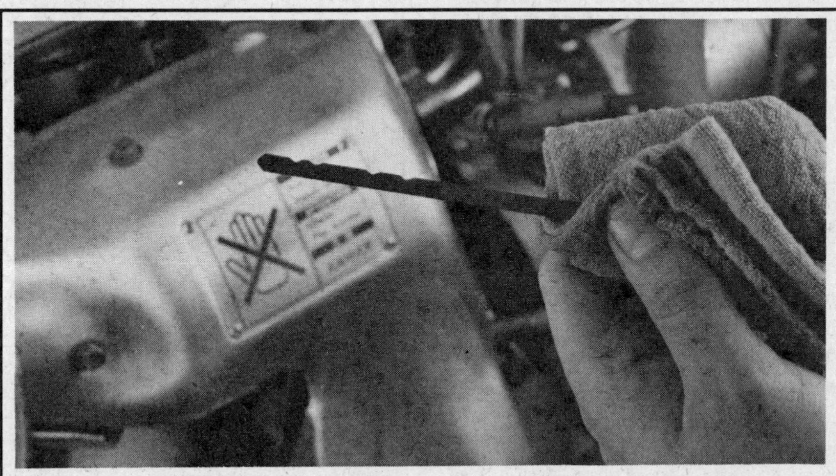

FIG. 114 The level should be between the notches

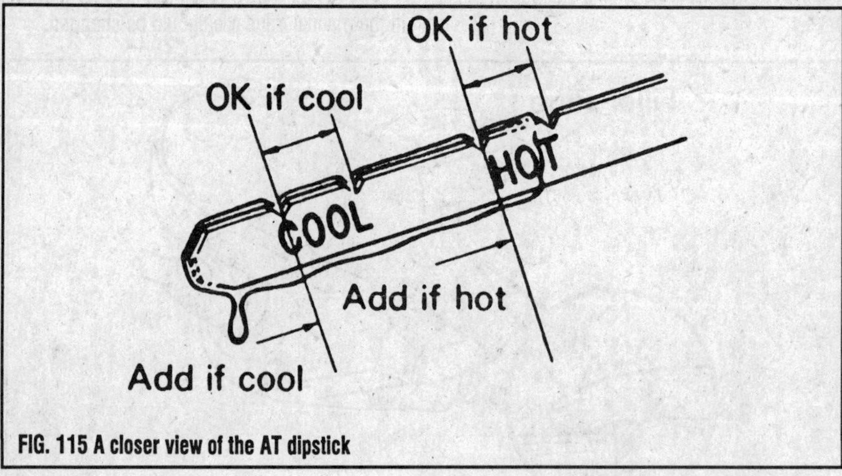

FIG. 115 A closer view of the AT dipstick

of a funnel. Check the level often as you are filling the transaxle. Be extremely careful not to overfill it. Overfilling will cause slippage, seal damage and overheating. Approximately one pint of ATF will raise the level from one notch to the other.

➡ **Always use the proper transmission fluid when filling your car's transaxle. All 2wd models use DEXRON® II; all 4wd models use Type T. Always check with the owner's manual to be sure. NEVER use Type F or Type T in a transaxle requiring DEXRON® II or vice versa, as severe damage will result.**

⁂ CAUTION

The fluid on the dipstick should always be a bright red color. It if is discolored (brown or black), or smells burnt, serious transmission troubles, probably due to overheating, should be suspected. The transmission should be inspected by a qualified service technician to locate the cause of the burnt fluid.

DRAIN AND REFILL

➧ SEE FIGS. 116–120

The automatic transaxle fluid should be changed at least every 25,000–30,000 miles (40,000–48,000 km). If the car is normally used in severe service, such as stop-and-go driving, trailer towing or the like, the interval should be halved. The fluid should be hot before it is drained; a 20 minute drive will accomplish this.

➡ **The removal of the transaxle oil pan drain plug requires the use of Toyota special tool #SST 09043-38100 or its equivalent (a 10mm hex head wrench).**

1. Remove the dipstick from the filler tube and install a funnel in the opening.
2. Position a suitable drain pan under the drain plug. Loosen the drain plug with a 10mm hex head wrench and allow the fluid to drain.
3. Install and tighten the drain plug to 36 ft. lbs. (49 Nm)..
4. Through the filler tube opening, add the proper amount of transmission fluid as specified in the Capacities Chart.
5. Check the fluid level and add as required.

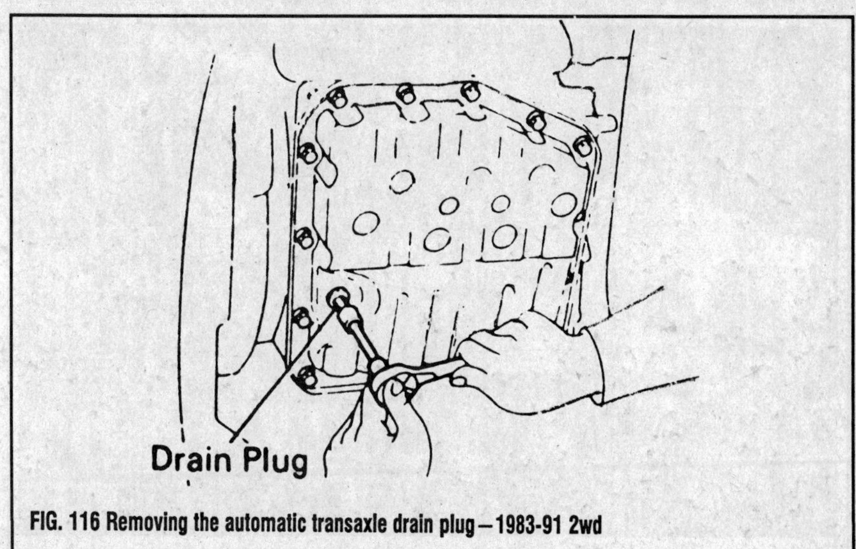

FIG. 116 Removing the automatic transaxle drain plug – 1983-91 2wd

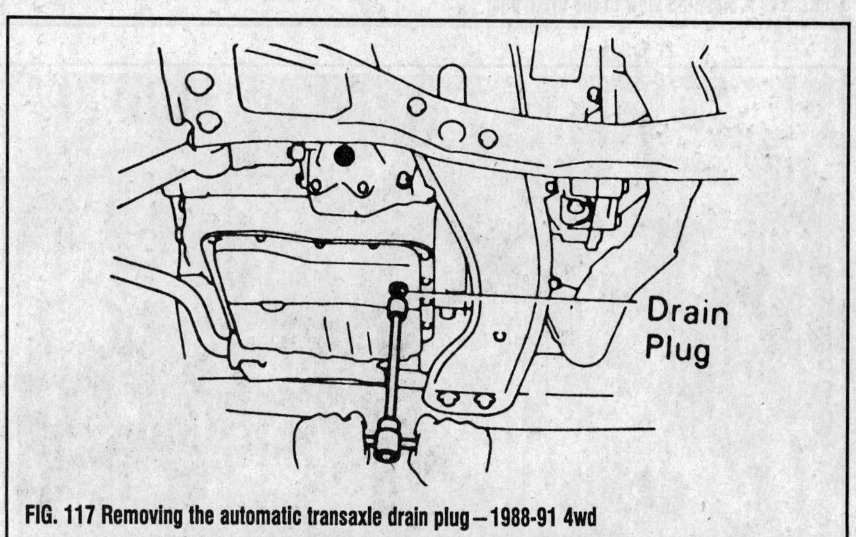

FIG. 117 Removing the automatic transaxle drain plug – 1988-91 4wd

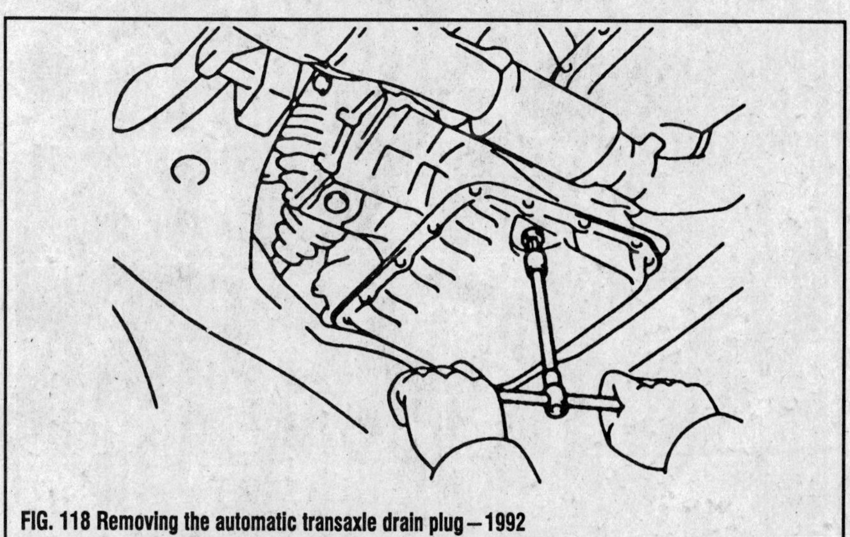

FIG. 118 Removing the automatic transaxle drain plug – 1992

FIG. 119 A close-up view of the drain plug

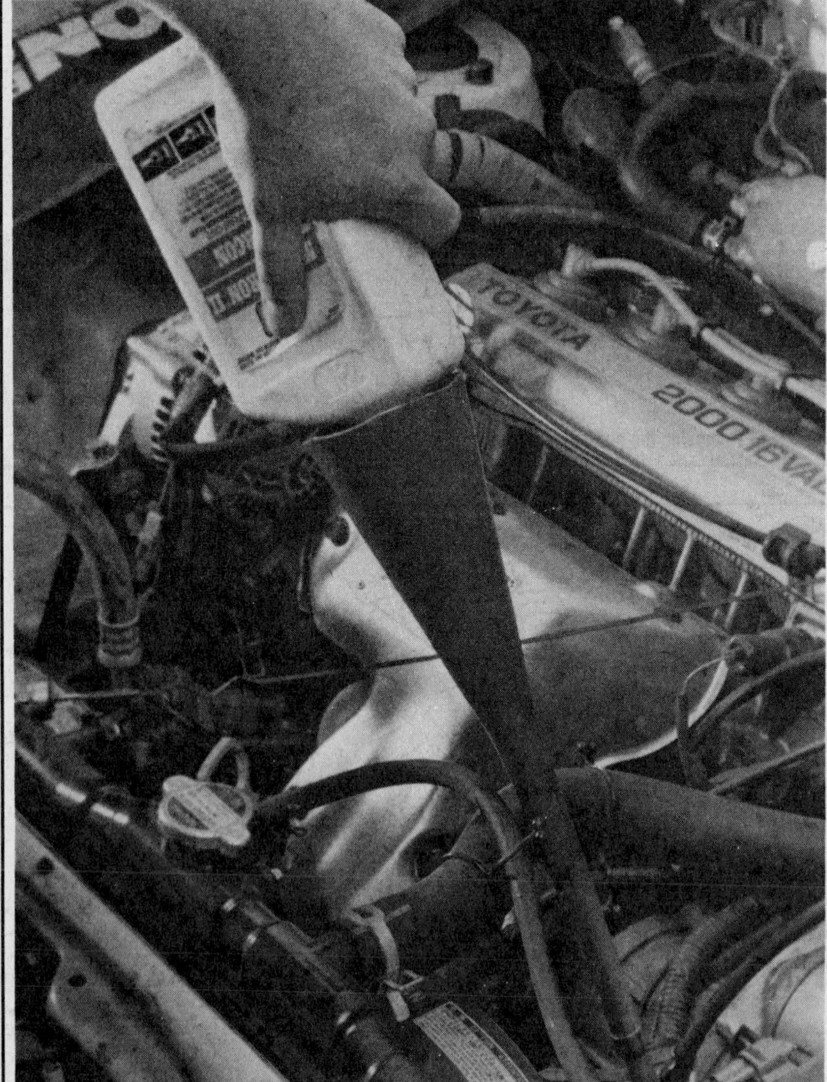

FIG. 120 Always use a funnel when adding fluid to the automatic transaxle

✲✲ WARNING

Do not overfill the transaxle.

PAN AND FILTER SERVICE

➧ SEE FIGS. 121–123

➡ The removal of the transaxle oil pan drain plug requires the use of Toyota special tool #SST 09043-38100 or its equivalent (a 10mm hex head wrench).

1. To avoid contamination of the transaxle, thoroughly clean the exterior of the oil pan and surrounding area to remove any deposits of dirt and grease.
2. Position a suitable drain pan under the oil pan and remove the drain plug. Allow the oil to drain from the pan. Set the drain plug aside.
3. Loosen and remove all but two of the fifteen oil pan retaining bolts.
4. Support the pan by hand and slowly remove the remaining two bolts.
5. Carefully lower the pan to the ground. There will be some fluid still inside the pan, so be careful.
6. Remove the three oil strainer attaching bolts and carefully remove the strainer. The strainer will also contain some fluid.

➡ One of the three oil strainer bolts is slightly longer than the other two. Make a mental note of where the longer bolt goes so that it may be reinstalled in the original position.

7. Discard the strainer. Remove the gasket from the pan and discard it.
8. Drain the remainder of the fluid from the oil pan and wipe the pan clean with a rag. With a gasket scraper, remove any old gasket material from the flanges of the pan and the transaxle. Remove the gasket from the drain plug and replace it with a new one.

➡ Depending on the year and maintenance schedule of the vehicle, there may be from one to three small magnets on the bottom of the pan. These magnets were installed by the manufacturer at the time the transaxle was assembled. The magnets function to collect metal chips and filings from clutch plates, bushings and bearings that accumulate during the normal break-in process that a

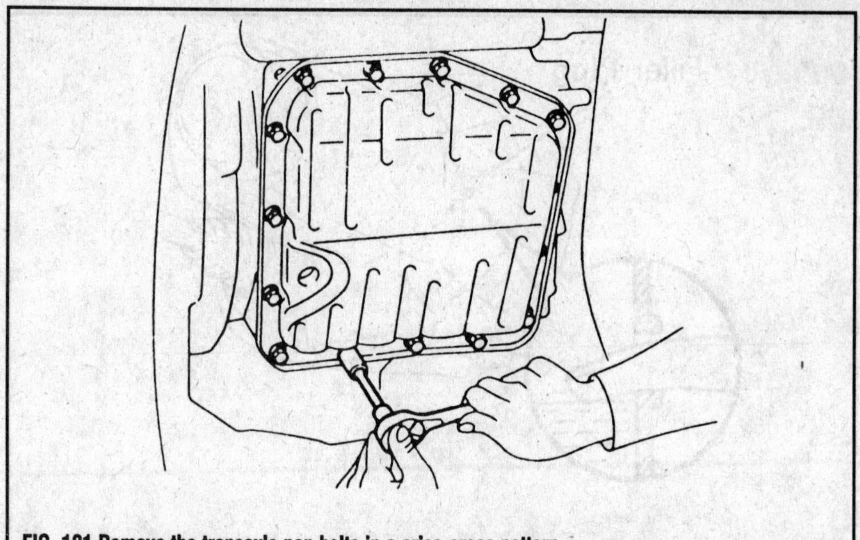
FIG. 121 Remove the transaxle pan bolts in a criss-cross pattern

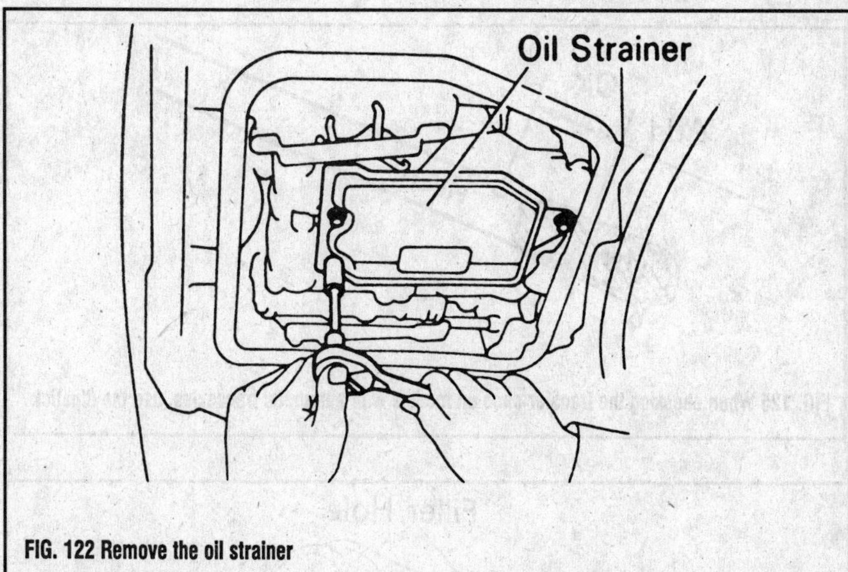

FIG. 122 Remove the oil strainer

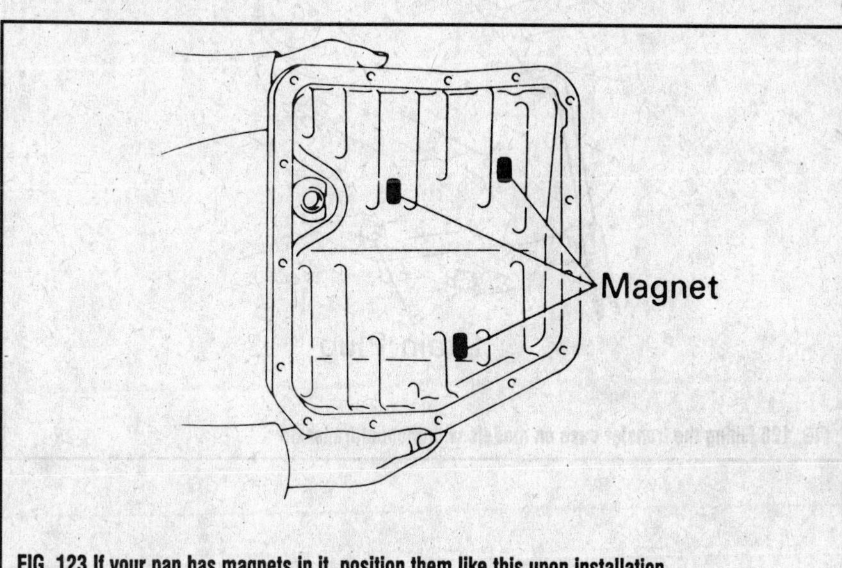

FIG. 123 If your pan has magnets in it, position them like this upon installation

new transaxle experiences. So, don't be alarmed if such accumulations are present. Clean the magnets and reinstall them. They are useful tools for determining transaxle component wear.

To install the filter and pan:

9. Install the new oil strainer. Install and tighten the retaining bolts in their proper locations.

10. Install the new gasket onto the oil pan making sure that the holes in the gasket are aligned evenly with those of the pan. Position the magnets so that they will not interfere with the oil tubes.

11. Raise the pan and gasket into position on the transaxle and install the retaining bolts. Torque the retaining bolts in a criss-cross pattern to 43 in. lbs. (4.9 Nm).

12. Install and tighten the drain plug to 36 ft. lbs. (49 Nm).

13. Fluid is added only through the dipstick tube. Use only the proper automatic transmission fluid; do not overfill.

14. Replace the dipstick after filling. Start the engine and allow it to idle. DO NOT race the engine!

15. After the engine has idled for a few minutes, shift the transmission slowly through the gears and then return it to **P**. With the engine still idling, check the fluid level on the dipstick. If necessary, add more fluid to raise the level to where it is supposed to be.

CAUTION

Check the fluid in the drain pan, it should always be a bright red color. It if is discolored (brown or black), or smells burnt, serious transmission troubles, probably due to overheating, should be suspected. The transmission should be inspected by a qualified service technician to locate the cause of the burnt fluid.

Transfer Case

FLUID RECOMMENDATIONS

- All models: multipurpose gear oil API GL-5; SAE 75W-90 or 80W-90

FLUID LEVEL CHECK

➧ SEE FIGS. 124–125

The oil in the transfer case should be checked at least every 15,000 miles (24,000 km) and replaced every 25,000–30,000 miles (40,000–48,000 km), even more frequently if driven in deep water or mud.

Manual Transaxle

1. With the car parked on a level surface, remove the filler plug from the front of the transaxle housing. The plug should use a 24mm hex head wrench.
2. If the lubricant begins to trickle out of the hole, there is enough. Otherwise, carefully insert your finger (watch out for sharp threads!) and check to see if the oil is up to the edge of the hole.
3. If not, add oil through the hole until the level is at the edge of the hole. Most gear lubricants come in a plastic squeeze bottle with a nozzle; making additions simple. You can also use a common everyday kitchen baster.
4. Replace the filler plug and tighten it to 36 ft. lbs. (49 Nm). Run the engine and check for leaks.

Automatic Transaxle

1. Park the car on a level surface with the engine idling. Shift the transmission into **P** and set the parking brake.
2. Remove the dipstick, wipe it clean and reinsert if firmly. Be sure that it has been pushed all the way in. Remove the dipstick and check the fluid level while holding it horizontally. All models have a LOW and a HIGH notch on the dipstick.
3. If the fluid level is not within the proper area on either side of the dipstick, pour the proper lubricant into the dipstick tube. This is easily done with the aid of a funnel. Check the level often as you are filling the transfer case. Be extremely careful not to overfill it.

DRAIN AND REFILL

➧ SEE FIGS. 126–128

Once every every 30,000 miles (48,000 km), the oil in the transfer case should be changed.

1. The transfer case oil should be hot before it is drained. If the engine is at normal operating temperature, the oil should be hot enough.

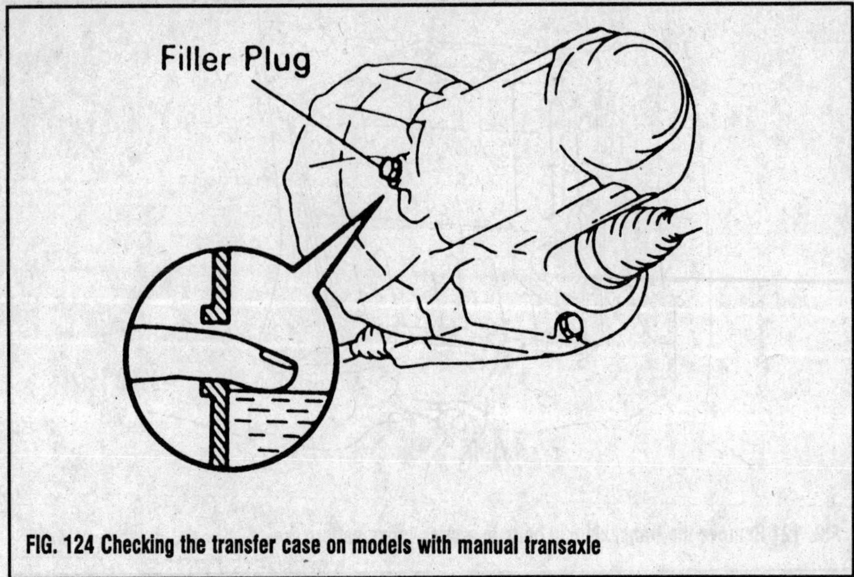

FIG. 124 Checking the transfer case on models with manual transaxle

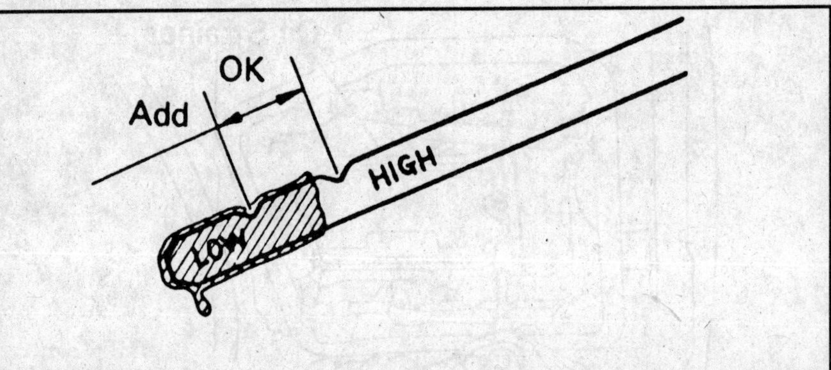

FIG. 125 When checking the transfer case on models with automatic transaxles, use the dipstick

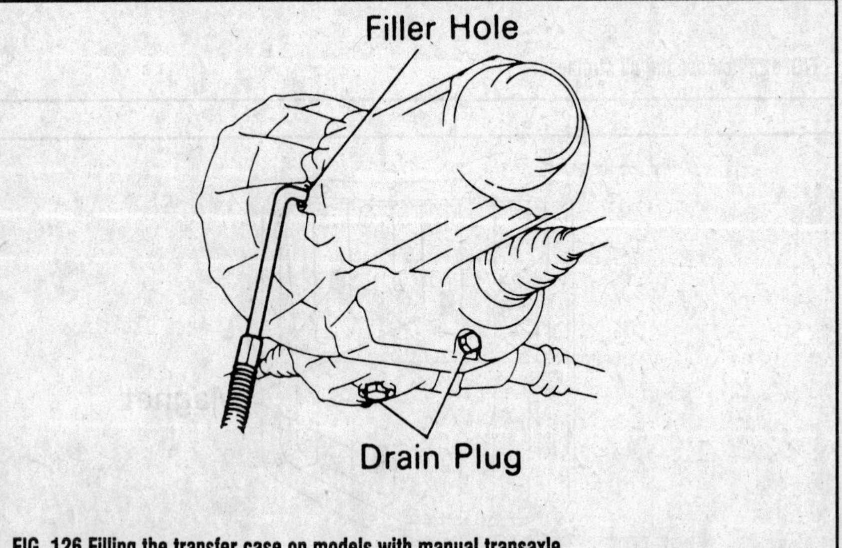

FIG. 126 Filling the transfer case on models with manual transaxle

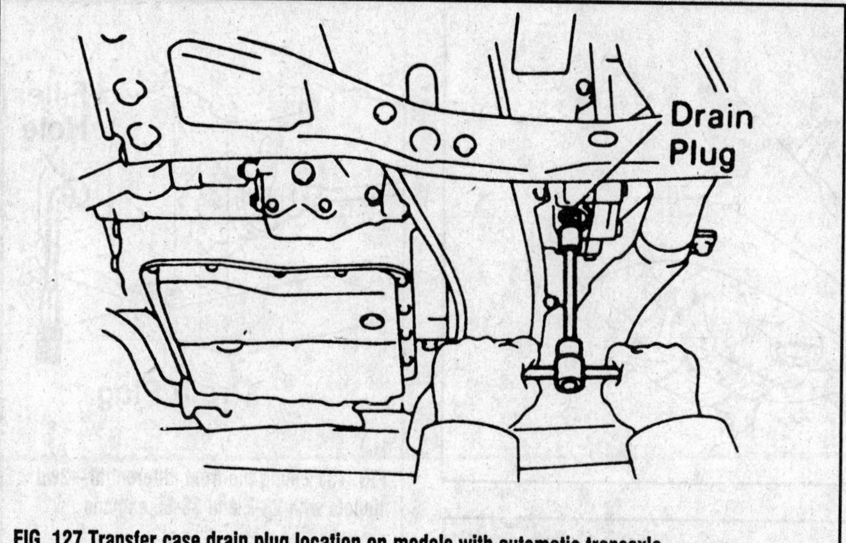

FIG. 127 Transfer case drain plug location on models with automatic transaxle

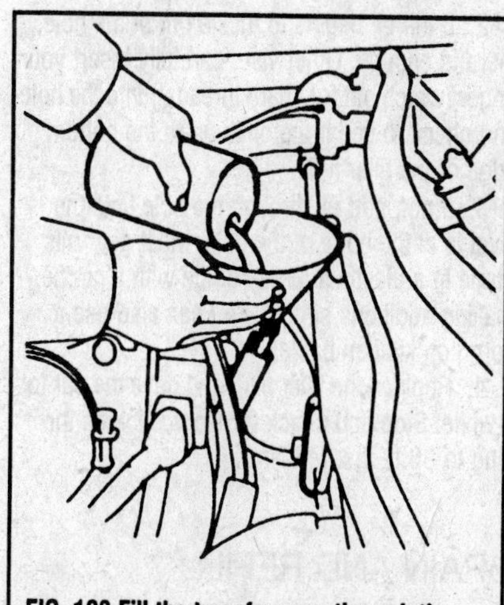
FIG. 128 Fill the transfer case through the dipstick tube on models with automatic transaxles

2. Raise the car and support it properly on jackstands so that you can safely work underneath. You will probably not have enough room to work if the car is not raised.

3. The drain plug is located on the bottom of the transfer case. It should require a hex head wrench (24mm on models with MT and 10mm on those with AT). Place a pan under the drain plug and remove it. Keep a slight inward pressure on the plug while unscrewing it, this will keep the oil from pouring out until the plug is removed.

⁂ CAUTION

The oil will be HOT. Be careful when you remove the plug so that you don't take a bath in hot gear oil.

4. Allow the oil to drain completely. Clean off the plug and replace it, tightening it until it is just snug – 36 ft. lbs. (49 Nm).

5. Remove the filler plug from the side of the case on models with MT. There will be a gasket underneath this plug. Replace it if damaged.

6. Fill the transfer case with gear oil through the filler plug hole as detailed previously (remember, on models with AT, simply use the dipstick tube!). Refer to the Capacities Chart for the amount of oil needed to refill your transfer case.

7. The oil level should come right up to the edge of the hole. You can stick your finger in to verify this. Watch out for sharp threads. On models with AT, use the dipstick as detailed previously.

8. Replace the filler plug and gasket, lower the car, and check for leaks. Dispose of the old oil in the proper manner.

Drive Axles (Differentials)

FLUID RECOMMENDATIONS

Front

- All 2wd models (4 cyl., MT): DEXRON® II ATF
- All 2wd models (6 cyl., MT): Hypoid gear oil API GL-4, SAE 75W-90
- All 4wd models (MT): Hypoid gear oil API GL-5, SAE 75W-90
- All models (AT): DEXRON® II ATF

Rear

- All 4wd models: Hypoid gear oil API GL-5, SAE 90W

FLUID LEVEL CHECK

➧ SEE FIGS. 129–130

The oil in the front and/or rear differential should be checked at least every 15,000 miles (24,000 km) and replaced every 25,000–30,000 miles (40,000–48,000 km). If driven in deep water it should be replaced immediately.

1. With the car parked on a level surface, remove the filler plug (usually a 10mm hex head) from the back of the differential.

➡ The plug on the bottom is the drain plug on rear differentials and most front. The lower of the two plugs on the back of the housing is the drain plug on the front differential of models with V6 engines.

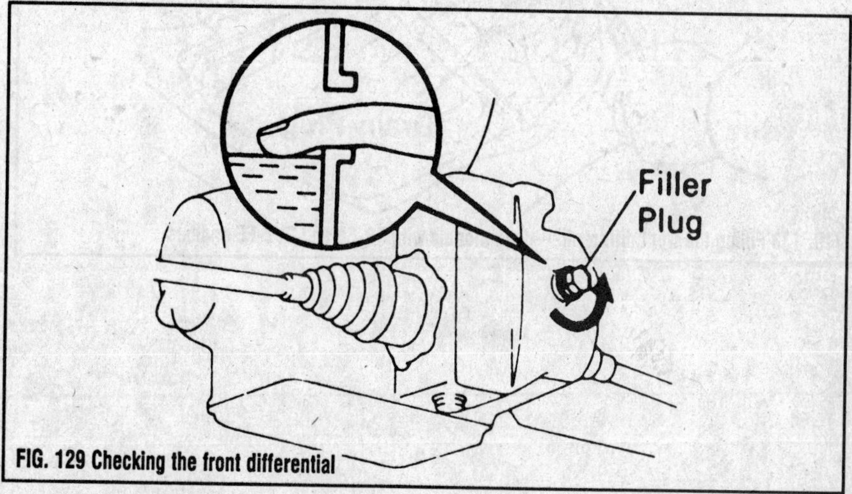

FIG. 129 Checking the front differential

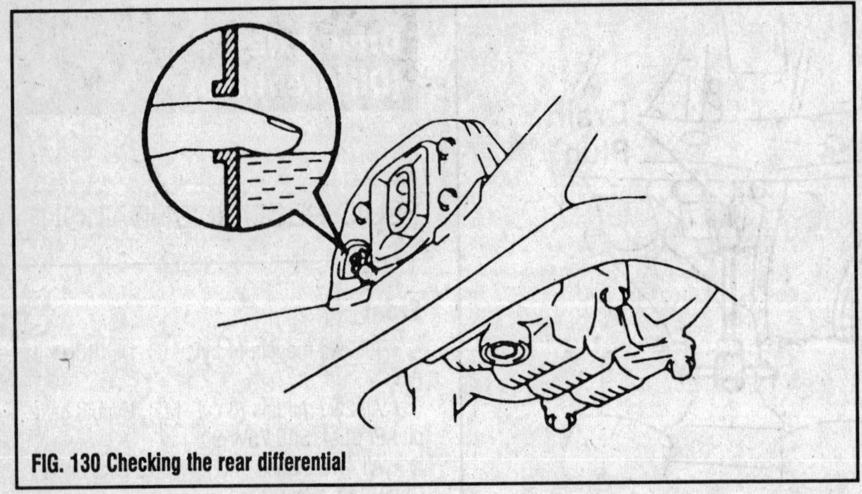
FIG. 130 Checking the rear differential

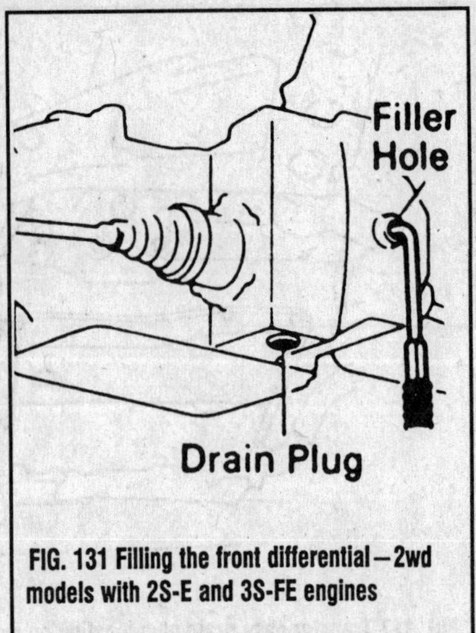

FIG. 131 Filling the front differential—2wd models with 2S-E and 3S-FE engines

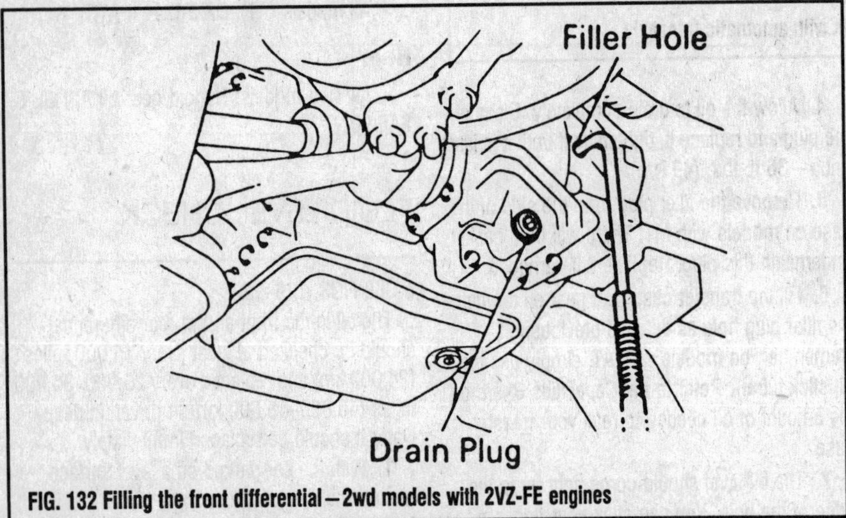

FIG. 132 Filling the front differential—2wd models with 2VZ-FE engines

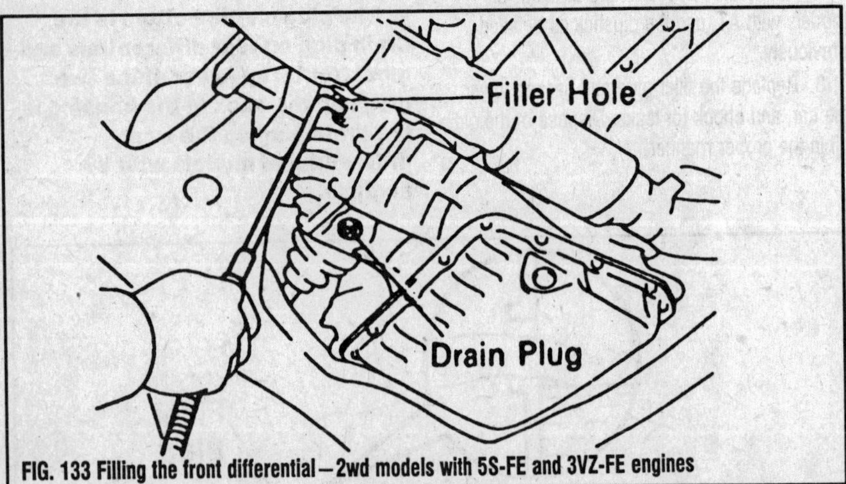

FIG. 133 Filling the front differential—2wd models with 5S-FE and 3VZ-FE engines

2. If the oil begins to trickle out of the hole, there is enough. Otherwise, carefully insert your finger (watch out for sharp threads!) into the hole and check to see if the oil is up to the bottom edge of the filler hole.

3. If not, add oil through the hole until the level is at the edge of the hole. Most gear oils come in a plastic squeeze bottle with a nozzle, making additions simple. You can also use a common kitchen baster.

4. Replace the filler plug and drive the car for a while. Stop and check for leaks. Tighten the plug to 36 ft. lbs. (49 Nm).

DRAIN AND REFILL

➧ SEE FIGS. 131–134

The gear oil in the front or rear differential should be changed at least every 25,000–30,000 miles (40,000–48,000 km); immediately if driven in deep water.

To drain and fill the differential, proceed as follows:

1. Park the vehicle on a level surface. Set the parking brake.

2. Remove the filler (upper) plug. Place a container which is large enough to catch all of the differential oil, under the drain plug.

3. Remove the drain (lower) plug (usually a 10mm hex head) and gasket, if so equipped. Allow all of the oil to drain into the container.

4. Install the drain plug. Tighten it so that it will not leak, but do not overtighten. Tighten to 36 ft. lbs. (49 Nm).

➡ Its usually a good idea to replace the drain plug gasket at this time.

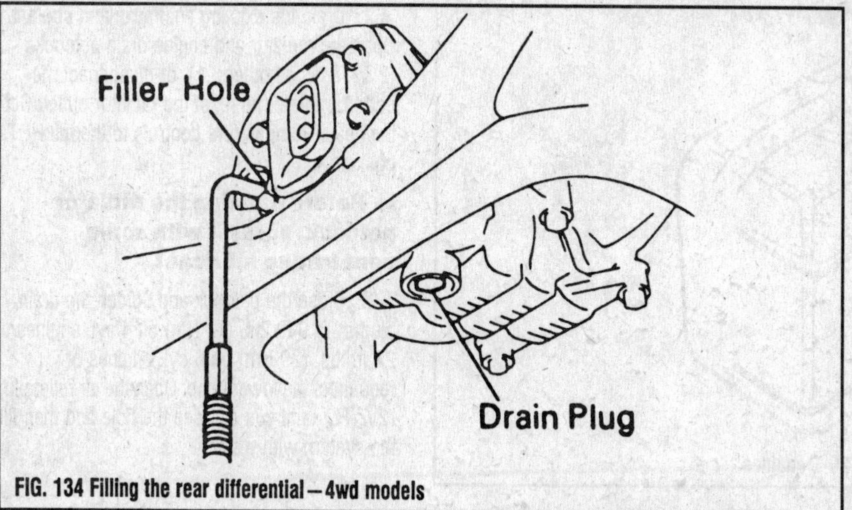

FIG. 134 Filling the rear differential — 4wd models

5. Refill with the proper grade and viscosity of axle lubricant (see "Recommended Lubricants" chart). Be sure that the level reaches the bottom of the filler plug. DO NOT overfill!
6. Install the filler plug and check for leakage.

Cooling System

FLUID RECOMMENDATIONS

When additional coolant is required to maintain the proper level, always add a 50/50 mixture of ethylene glycol antifreeze/coolant and water.

FLUID LEVEL CHECK

➧ SEE FIGS. 135–136

Dealing with the cooling system can be a tricky matter unless the proper precautions are observed. It is best to check the coolant level in the radiator when the engine is cold. This is done by checking the expansion tank. If coolant is visible above the **LOW** mark on the tank, the level is satisfactory. Always be certain that the filler caps on both the radiator and the reservoir are tightly closed.

In the event that the coolant level must be checked when the engine is warm or on engines without the expansion tank, place a thick rag over the radiator cap and slowly turn the cap counterclockwise until it reaches the first detent. Allow all the hot steam to escape. This will allow the pressure in the system to drop gradually, preventing an explosion of hot coolant. When the hissing noise stops, remove the cap the rest of the way.

It's a good idea to check the coolant every time that you stop for fuel. If the coolant level is low, add equal amount of ethylene glycol-based antifreeze and clean water. On models without an expansion tank, add coolant through the radiator filler neck. Fill the expansion tank to the **FULL** level.

✲✲ CAUTION

Never add cold coolant to a hot engine unless the engine is running, to avoid cracking the engine block.

Avoid using water that is known to have a high alkaline content or is very hard, except in emergency situations. Drain and flush the cooling system as soon as possible after using such water.

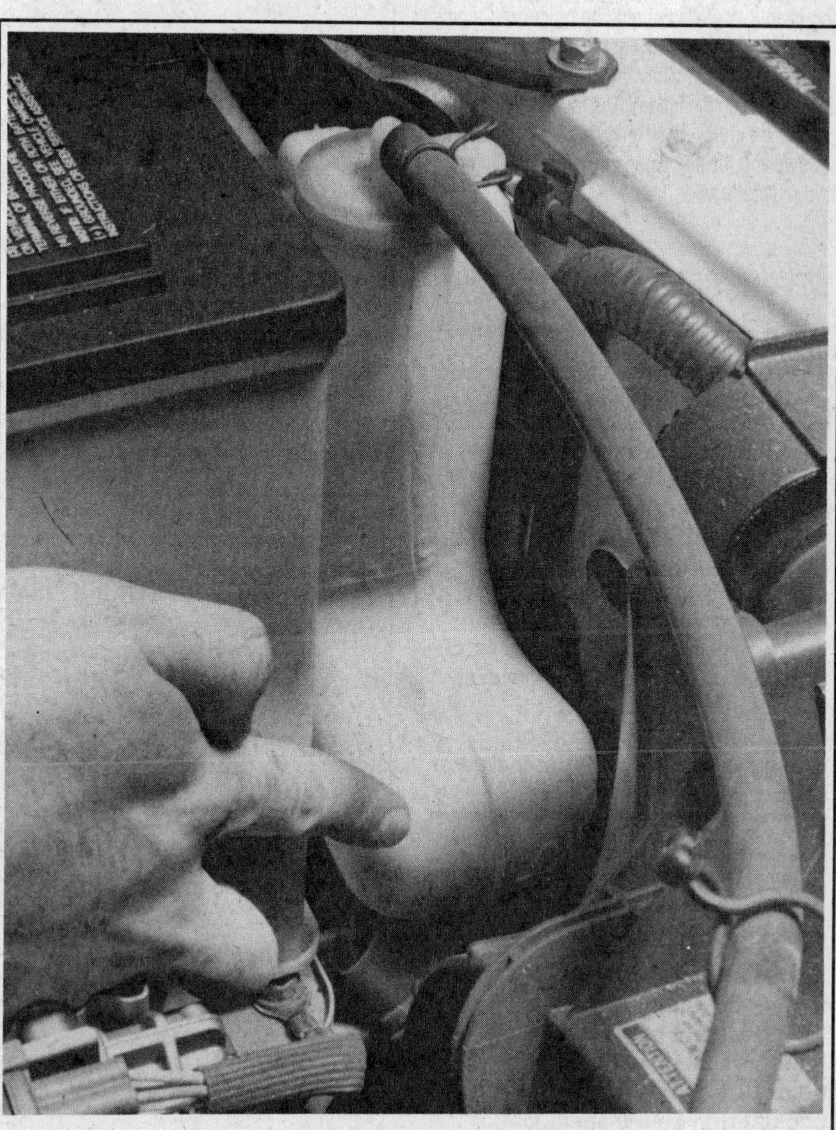

FIG. 135 Coolant reservoir tank — 3S-FE, 5S-FE, 2VZ-FE and 3VZ-FE engines

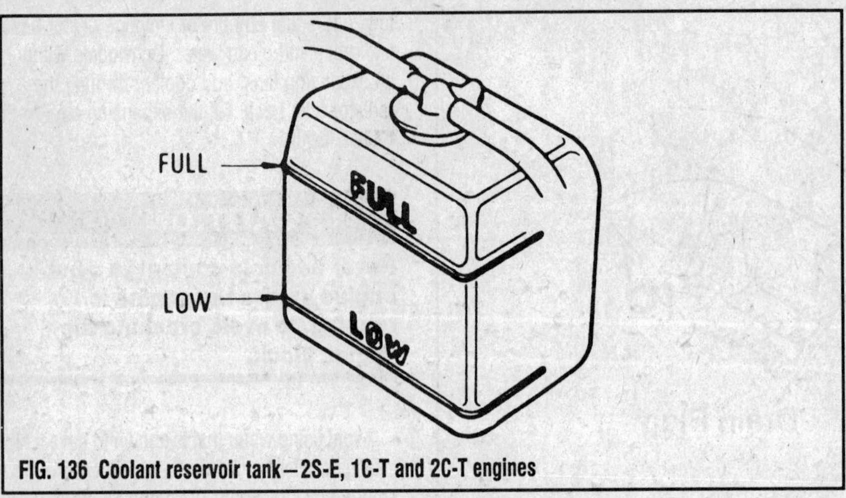

FIG. 136 Coolant reservoir tank—2S-E, 1C-T and 2C-T engines

1. Drain the existing antifreeze and coolant. Open the radiator and engine drain petcocks (2VZ-FE: 2; all others: 1), or disconnect the bottom radiator hose, at the radiator outlet. Set the heater temperature controls to the full HOT position.

➡ **Before opening the radiator petcock, spray it with some penetrating lubricant.**

2. Close the petcock and tighten the drain plug(s) to 9 ft. lbs. (13 Nm) on 4 cyl. engines or 22 ft. lbs. (29 Nm) on 6 cyl. engines or reconnect the lower hose. Open the air relief plug (2VZ-FE) until you can see the hole and then fill the system with water.

The radiator hoses and clamps and the radiator cap should be checked at the same time as the coolant level. Hoses which are brittle, cracked, or swollen should be replaced. Clamps should be checked for tightness (screwdriver tight only! Do not allow the clamp to cut into the hose or crush the fitting). The radiator cap gasket should be checked for any obvious tears, cracks or swelling, or any signs of incorrect seating in the radiator neck.

DRAIN, REFILL AND FLUSH

➧ SEE FIGS. 137–142

CAUTION

When draining the coolant, keep in mind that cats and dogs are attracted by the ethylene glycol antifreeze, and are quite likely to drink any that is left in an uncovered container or in puddles on the ground. This will prove fatal in sufficient quantity. Always drain the coolant into a sealable container. Coolant should be reused unless it is contaminated or several years old.

Completely draining and refilling the cooling system every two years at least will remove accumulated rust, scale and other deposits.

➡ **Use a good quality antifreeze with water pump lubricants, rust inhibitors and other corrosion inhibitors along with acid neutralizers. Use a permanent type coolant that meets specification ESE-M97B44A or the equivalent.**

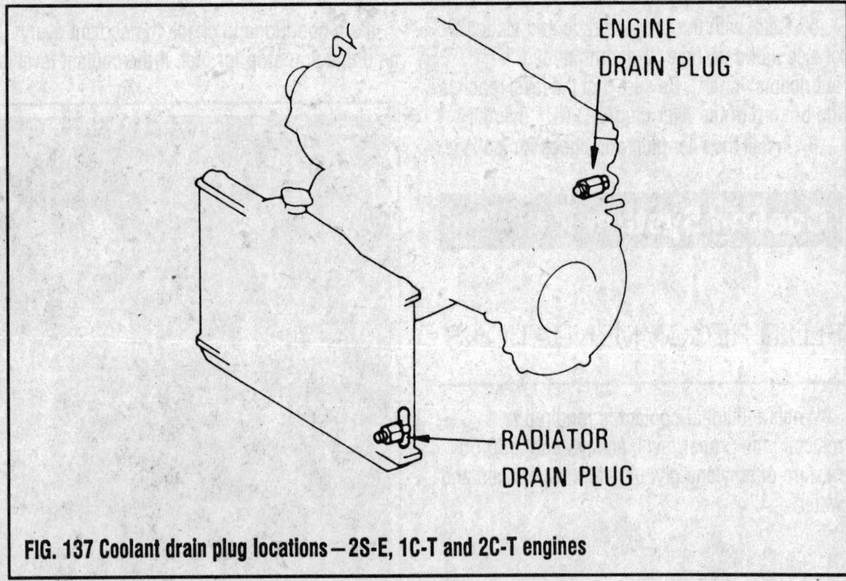

FIG. 137 Coolant drain plug locations—2S-E, 1C-T and 2C-T engines

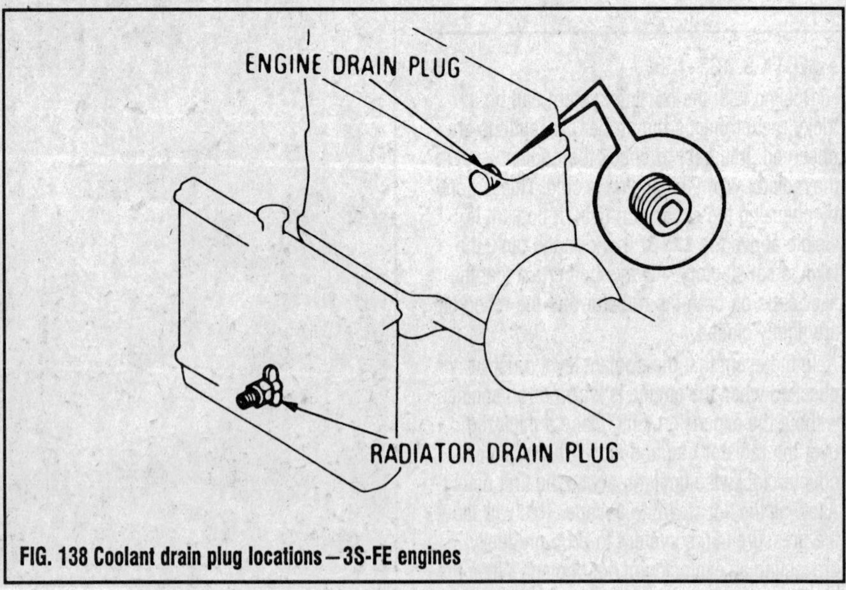

FIG. 138 Coolant drain plug locations—3S-FE engines

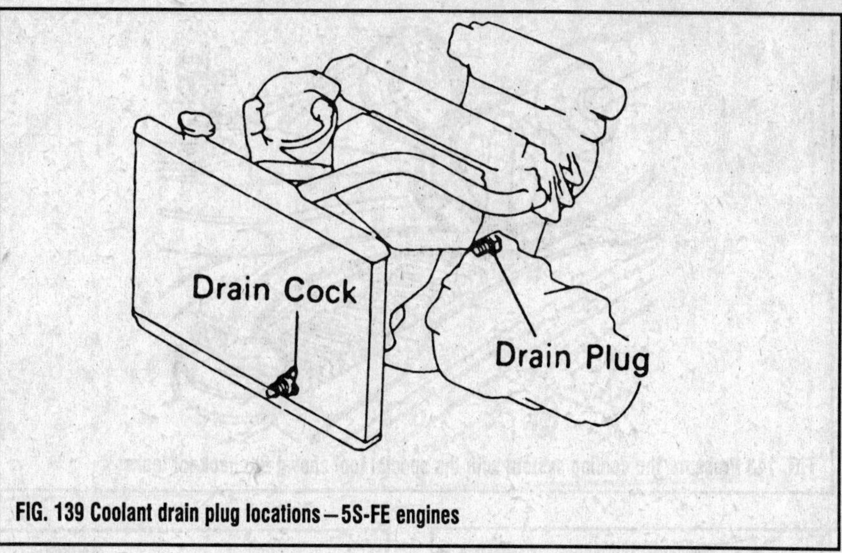

FIG. 139 Coolant drain plug locations – 5S-FE engines

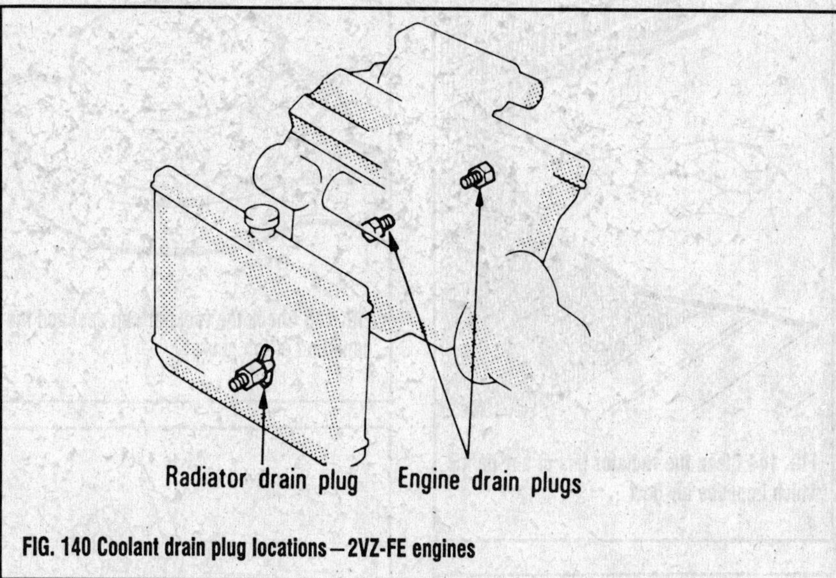

FIG. 140 Coolant drain plug locations – 2VZ-FE engines

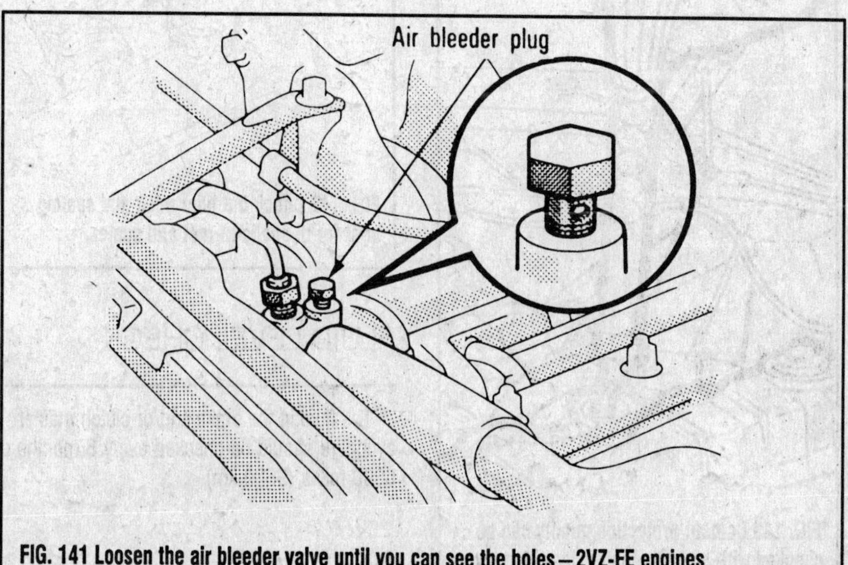

FIG. 141 Loosen the air bleeder valve until you can see the holes – 2VZ-FE engines

FIG. 142 Coolant drain plug locations – 3VZ-FE engines

3. Add a can of quality radiator flush. Be sure the flush is safe to use in engines having aluminum components.

4. Idle the engine until the upper radiator hose gets hot. Race it 2 or 3 times and then shut it off. Let the engine cool down.

5. Drain the system again.

6. Repeat this process until the drained water is clear and free of scale.

7. Close all petcocks and connect all the hoses.

8. If equipped with a coolant recovery system, flush the reservoir with water and leave empty.

9. Determine the capacity of your cooling system (see Capacities specifications). Add a 50/50 mix of quality antifreeze (ethylene glycol) and water to provide the desired protection. Add through the radiator filler neck until full and then fill the expansion tank to the **FULL** line.

SYSTEM INSPECTION

➧ SEE FIGS. 143–147

Most permanent antifreeze/coolant have a colored dye added which makes the solution an excellent leak detector. When servicing the cooling system, check for leakage at:

- All hoses and hose connections.
- Radiator seams, radiator core, and radiator draincock.
- All engine block and cylinder head freeze (core) plugs, and drain plugs.
- Edges of all cooling system gaskets (head gaskets, thermostat gasket).

- Transmission fluid cooler.
- Heating system components, water pump.
- Check the engine oil dipstick for signs of coolant in the engine oil.
- Check the coolant in the radiator for signs of oil in the coolant.

Investigate and correct any indication of coolant leakage.

Check the Radiator Cap

While you are checking the coolant level, check the radiator cap for a worn or cracked gasket. If the cap doesn't seal properly, fluid will be lost and the engine will overheat.

A worn cap should be replaced with a new one.

Clean Radiator of Debris

Periodically clean any debris such as leaves, paper, insects, etc., from the radiator fins. Pick the large pieces off by hand. The smaller pieces can be washed away with water pressure from a hose.

Carefully straighten any bent radiator fins with a pair of needle nose pliers. Be careful, the fins are very soft. Don't wiggle the fins back and forth too much. Straighten them once and try not to move them again.

CHECKING SYSTEM PROTECTION

A 50/50 mix of coolant concentrate and water will usually provide protection to −35°F (−37°C). Freeze protection may be checked by using a cooling system hydrometer. Inexpensive hydrometers (floating ball types) may be obtained from a local department store (automotive section) or an auto supply store. Follow the directions packaged with the coolant hydrometer when checking protection.

Master Cylinders

➧ SEE FIGS. 148–150

All models utilize both a brake and a clutch master cylinder. Both are located above the brake booster unit at the driver's side firewall.

FLUID RECOMMENDATIONS

Use only Heavy Duty Brake fluid meeting DOT 3 or SAE J1703 specifications.

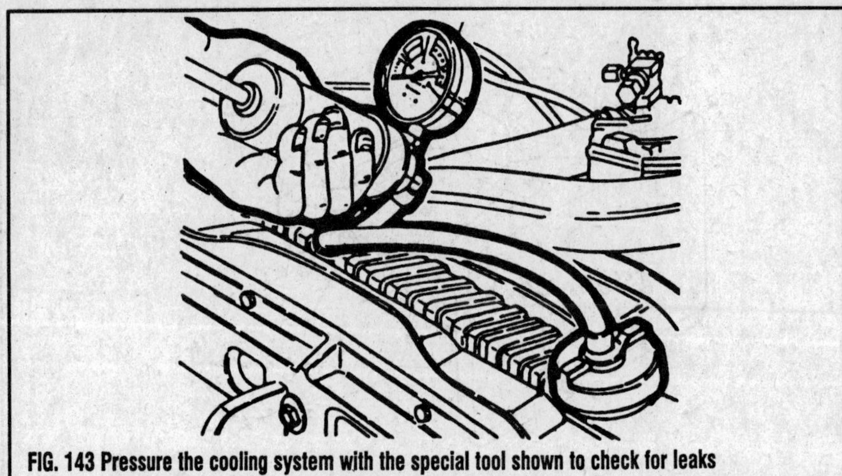

FIG. 143 Pressure the cooling system with the special tool shown to check for leaks

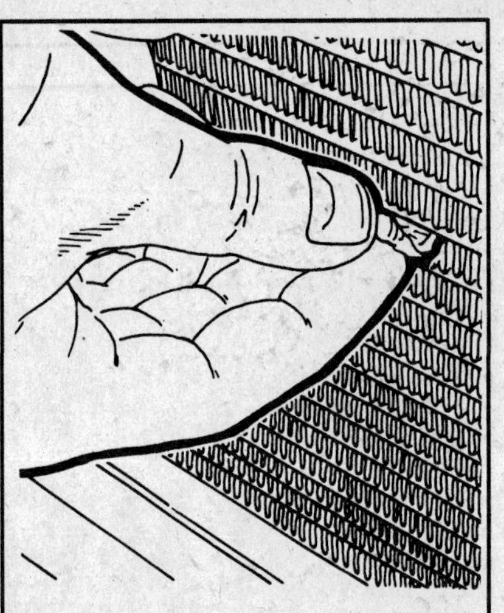

FIG. 144 Clean the radiator fins of any debris which impedes air flow

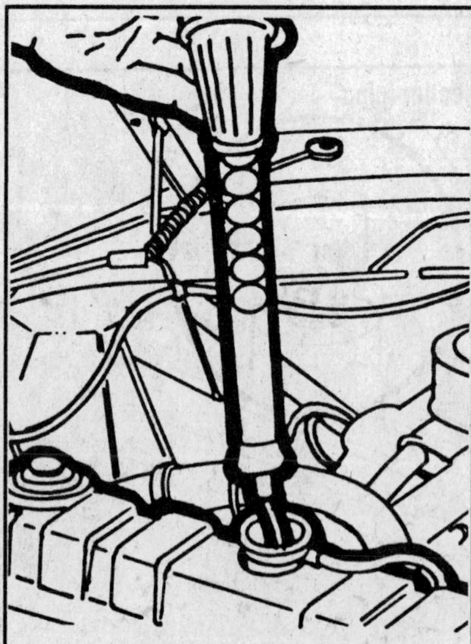

FIG. 145 Coolant protection quality can be checked with an inexpensive float-type tester

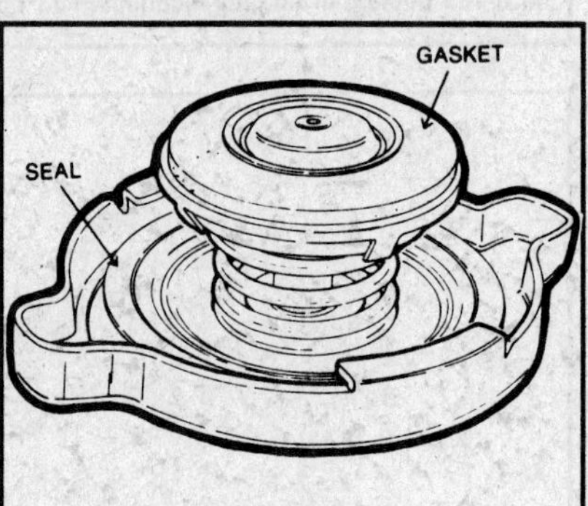

FIG. 146 Check the radiator cap seal and the condition of the gasket

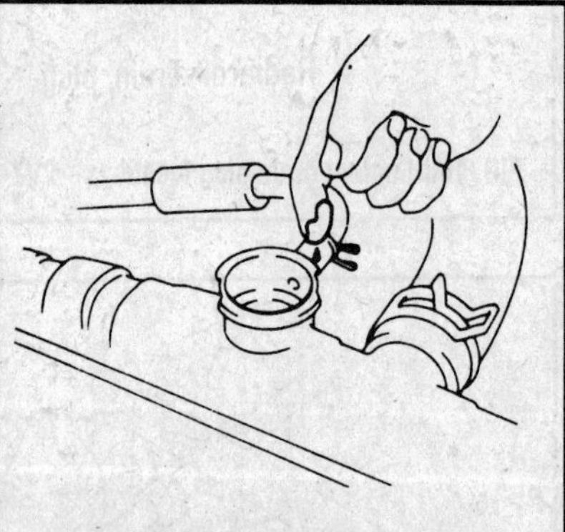

FIG. 147 Check the filler neck and sealing seat for deposits of rust and scale

FLUID LEVEL CHECK

The fluid in the brake and/or clutch master cylinders should be checked every 6 months or 6000 miles (9600 km).

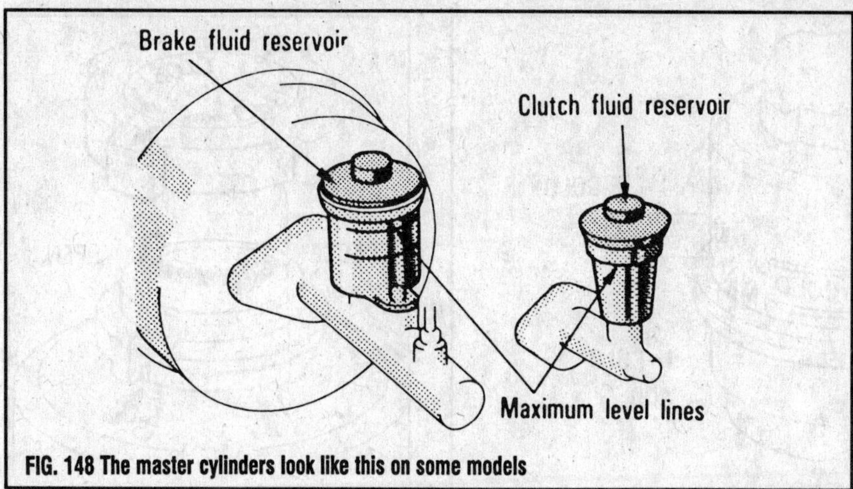

FIG. 148 The master cylinders look like this on some models

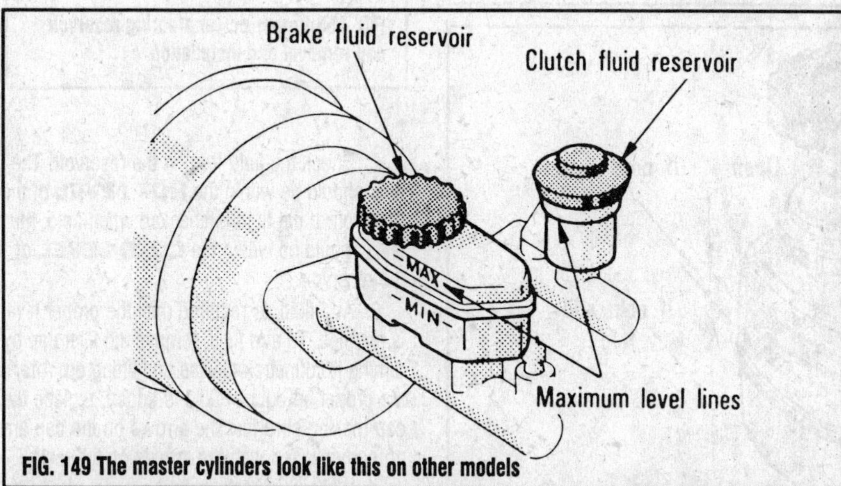

FIG. 149 The master cylinders look like this on other models

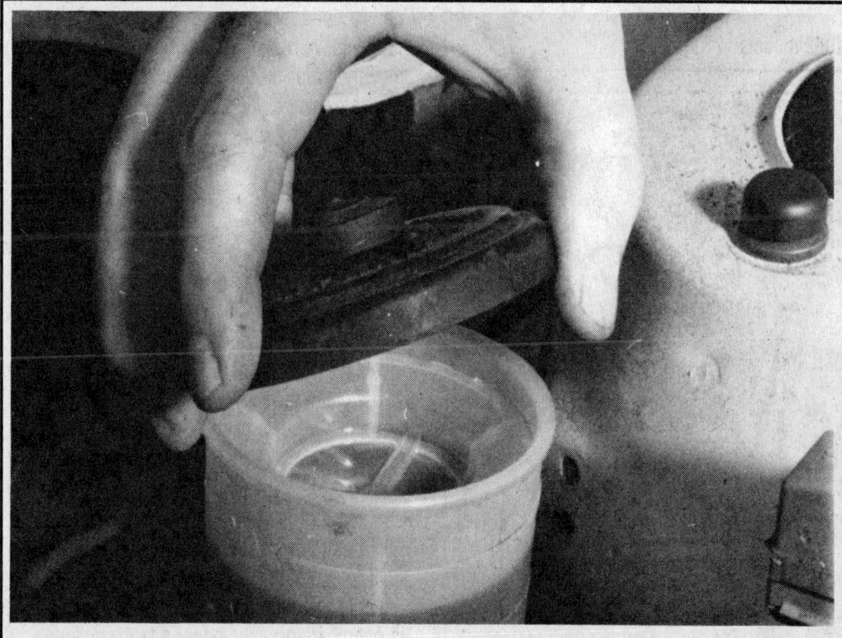
FIG. 150 Lift the cap up and slowly pour brake fluid in

Check the fluid level on the side of the reservoir. If fluid is required, remove the filler cap and gasket from the master cylinder. Fill the reservoir to the **MAX** line on the reservoir. Install the filler cap, making sure the gasket is properly seated in the cap.

➡ **It is normal for the fluid level to fall as the disc brake pads wear. However, if the master cylinder requires filling frequently, you should check the system for leaks in the hoses, master cylinder, or wheel cylinders. Brake fluid dissolves paint. It also absorbs moisture from the air; never leave a container or the master cylinder or the clutch cylinder uncovered any longer than necessary. The clutch master cylinder uses the same fluid as the brakes, and should be checked at the same time as the brake master cylinder.**

Power Steering Pump

➧ SEE FIGS. 151–154

FLUID RECOMMENDATIONS

• Use only DEXRON® II ATF in the power steering system.

FLUID LEVEL CHECK

Check the power steering fluid level every 6 months or 6000 miles (9600 km).

1. Make sure that the vehicle is level. If the reservoir is dirty, wipe it off.
2. Start the engine and allow it to idle.
3. With the engine at idle, move the steering wheel from LOCK to LOCK several times to raise the temperature of the fluid.
4. The power steering pump reservoir is translucent, so the fluid level may be checked without removing the cap. Look through the reservoir and check for foaming or emulsification.

➡ **Foaming or emulsification indicates the either there is air in the system or the fluid level is low.**

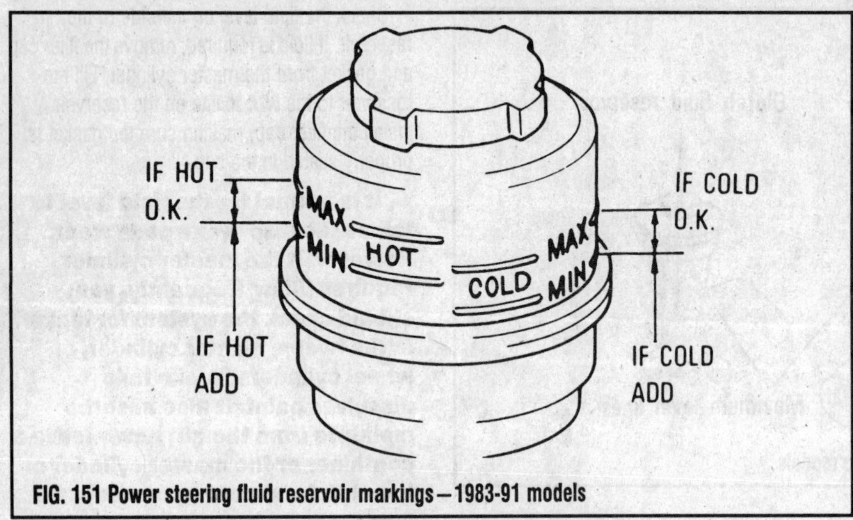

FIG. 151 Power steering fluid reservoir markings – 1983-91 models

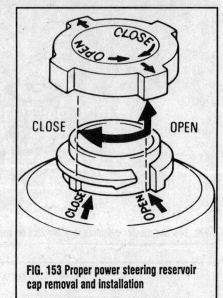

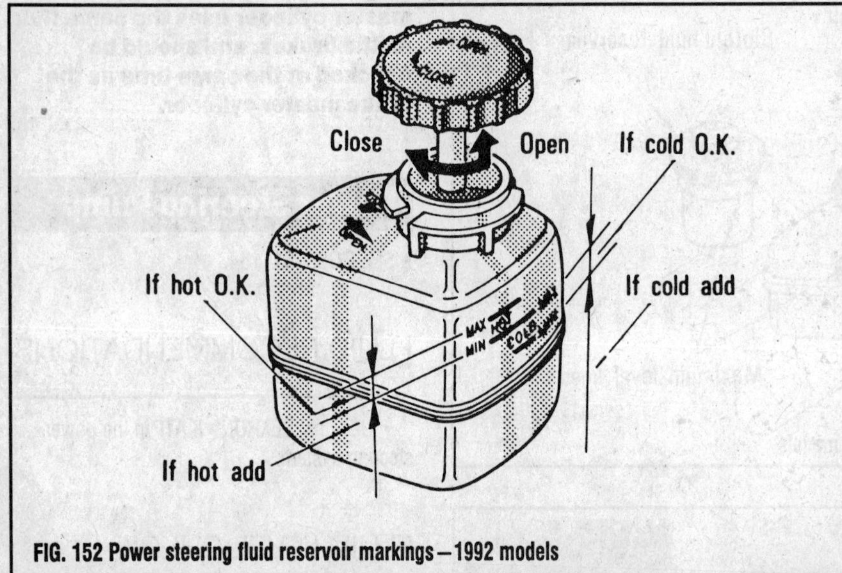

FIG. 152 Power steering fluid reservoir markings – 1992 models

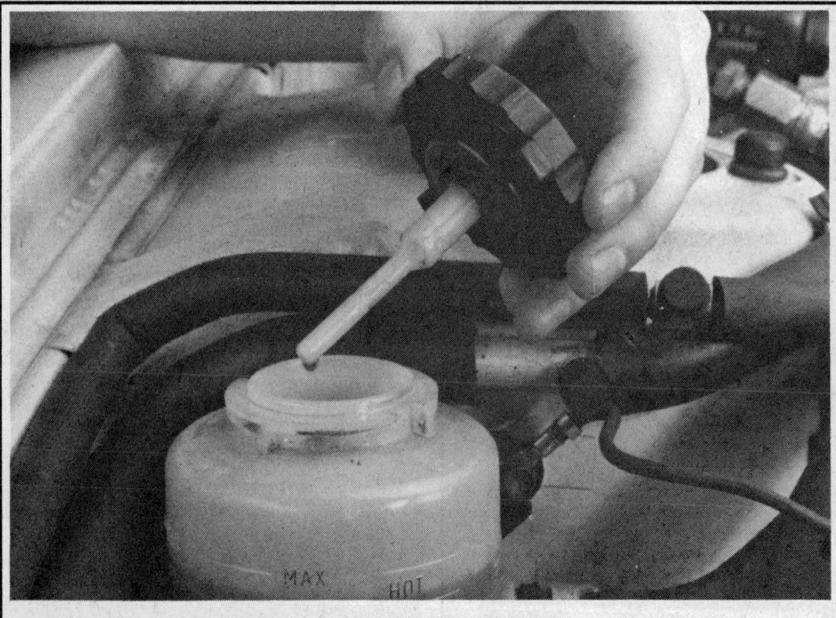

FIG. 154 Remove the cap and slowly pour fluid in

FIG. 153 Proper power steering reservoir cap removal and installation

5. Check the fluid level in the reservoir. The fluid should be within the **HOT LEVEL** of the reservoir. If the fluid is checked when cold, the level should be within the **COLD LEVEL** of the reservoir.

6. Add fluid as required until the proper level is reached. To add fluid, remove the filler cap by turning it counetrclockwise and lifting up. After the proper amount of fluid is added, replace the cap making sure that the arrows on the cap are properly aligned with the arrows on the tank.

7. While your in the neighborhood, check the steering box case, vane pump and hose connections for leaks and damage. Simple preventative maintenance checks like these can identify minor problems before turn into major problems and also increase your familiarity with the locations of steering system components.

Battery

At every fuel stop the level of the battery electrolyte should be checked. The level should be maintained between the upper and lower levels marked on the battery case or the bottom of the vent well in each cell.

If the electrolyte level is low, distilled water should be added until the proper level is reached. Each cell is completely separate from the others, so each must be filled individually. It is a good idea to add the distilled water with a squeeze bulb to avoid having electrolyte splash out. If water is frequently needed, the most likely cause is overcharging, caused by a faulty voltage regulator. If any acid solution should escape, it can be neutralized with a baking soda and water solution, but don't let the stuff get in the battery.

In winter, add water only before driving to prevent the battery from freezing and cracking. When replacing a battery, it is important that the replacement have an out put rating equal to or greater than original equipment. See Section 3 for details on battery replacement.

✻✻ CAUTION

If you get acid on you skin or in your eyes, rinse it off immediately with lots of water. Go to a doctor if it gets in you eyes. The gases formed inside the battery cells are highly explosive. Never check the level of the electrolyte in the presence of flame or while smoking.

Chassis Greasing

The chassis components are self-contained and therefore require no periodic internal lubrication (no grease fittings). Coat the outside of the ball joints and the steering gear housing with NLGI No. 2 lithium based grease or its equivalent.

MANUAL TRANSAXLE AND CLUTCH LINKAGE

On models so equipped, apply a small amount of chassis grease to the pivot points of the transaxle and clutch linkage.

AUTOMATIC TRANSAXLE LINKAGE

On models so equipped, apply a small amount of 10W engine oil to the kickdown and shift linkage at the pivot points.

PARKING BRAKE LINKAGE

At yearly intervals or whenever binding is noticeable in the parking brake linkage, lubricate the cable guides, levers and linkage with a suitable chassis grease.

Body Lubrication And Maintenance

There is no set period recommended by Toyota for body lubrication. However, it is a good idea to lubricate the following body points at least once a year, especially in the fall before cold weather.

LOCK CYLINDERS

Apply graphite lubricant sparingly thought the key slot. Insert the key and operate the lock several times to be sure that the lubricant is worked into the lock cylinder.

DOOR HINGES AND HINGE CHECKS

Spray a silicone lubricant or apply white lithium grease on the hinge pivot points to eliminate any binding conditions. Open and close the door several times to be sure that the lubricant is evenly and thoroughly distributed. When applying grease, the use of a small acid brush is very helpful in getting the grease to those hard to reach areas.

TAILGATE

Spray a silicone lubricant on all of the pivot and friction surfaces to eliminate any squeaks or binds. Work the tailgate to distribute the lubricant

BODY DRAIN HOLES

Be sure that the drain holes in the doors and rocker panels are cleared of obstruction. A small screwdriver can be used to clear them of any debris.

Wheel Bearings

REMOVAL, PACKING, INSTALLATION, ADJUSTMENT

In order to replace the rear wheel bearings the axle hub and carrier and rear axle shaft must be removed and the bearings pressed out. Removal of the axle hub and carrier is detailed in Section 7.

TRAILER TOWING

General Recommendations

Your Camry can be used for trailer towing; however, the vehicle is designed primarily as a passenger carrying vehicle. The towing of a trailer will have an effect on, handling, performance, braking, durability and fuel consumption. Keep the following in mind when towing a trailer.

- Before beginning a trip, check that all the lights and turn signals are operational and physically check that the trailer-vehicle electrical connectors are tight. At random intervals during the trip, repeat this check.
- Avoid jerky starts and sudden acceleration. If equipped with a manual transaxle, prevent

excessive clutch slippage by keeping the engine rpm low and always start out in first gear.

• When backing in a trailer, always have someone to guide you to reduce the possibilty of an accident.

• When towing a trailer vehicle-to-vehicle stopping distances are increased. For each 10 mph of speed, allow at least one vehicle and one trailer length between you and the vehicle ahead. Avoid sudden braking on wet and slippery surfaces.

• In order to maintain braking and charging system efficiency, do not use the fifth (manual transaxles) or overdrive (automatic transaxles).

• Slow down and shift into a lower gear before descending steep or long downhill grades. Do not make sudden downshifts.

• Avoid holding the brake pedal down to long or too frequently. This could cause he brakes to overheat and reduce their efficiency.

• Because of the additional load placed on the engine by the trailer, the engine is more susceptible to overheating during hot weather, especially when pulling the trailer up a long or steep hill. Be more conscious of the temperature gauge when operating with a trailer during hot weather.

• When parking, always place wheel chocks under both the wheels of the vehicle and the wheels of the trailer. Apply the parking brake firmly and place the transaxle in **P** (automatic) or in reverse (manual). Avoid parking on a slope whenever possible. But, if you have to park on a slope, perform the following:

1. Apply the parking brake and hold it.
2. Have someone place a set chocks under the wheels of the vehicle and a set under the wheels of the trailer.
3. When the chocks are properly in place, slowly release the parking brake until the chocks absorb the load.
4. Apply the parking brake firmly.
5. Shift into reverse (manual) or **P** (automatic) and stop the engine.

When pulling away from the parking spot on a slope, perform the following:

1. With the transaxle in **P** (automatic) or the clutch pedal depressed (manual), start the engine. With automatic transaxles, be sure to keep the brake pedal depressed.
2. Shift into gear.
3. Release the parking brake (with the foot on the brake pedal for automatic transaxles) and slowly back or pull away from the wheel chocks. Stop the vehicle and apply the brakes.
4. Have somebody remove the wheel chocks.

Trailer Weight

Trailer weight is the first, and most important, factor in determining whether or not your vehicle is suitable for towing the trailer you have in mind. The horsepower-to-weight ratio should be calculated. The basic standard is a ratio of 35:1. That is, 35 pounds of GVW for every horsepower.

To calculate this ratio, multiply you engine's rated horsepower by 35, then subtract the weight of the vehicle, including passengers and luggage. The resulting figure is the ideal maximum trailer weight that you can tow. One point to consider: a numerically higher axle ratio can offset what appears to be a low trailer weight. If the weight of the trailer that you have in mind is somewhat higher than the weight you just calculated, you might consider changing your rear axle ratio to compensate.

Hitch Weight

There are three kinds of hitches: bumper mounted, frame mounted, and load equalizing.

Bumper mounted hitches are those which attach solely to the vehicle's bumper. Many states prohibit towing with this type of hitch, when it attaches to the vehicle's stock bumper, since it subjects the bumper to stresses for which it was not designed. Aftermarket rear step bumpers, designed for trailer towing, are acceptable for use with bumper mounted hitches.

Frame mounted hitches can be of the type which bolts to two or more points on the frame, plus the bumper, or just to several points on the frame. Frame mounted hitches can also be of the tongue type, for Class I towing, or, of the receiver type, for classes II and III.

Load equalizing hitches are usually used for large trailers. Most equalizing hitches are welded in place and use equalizing bars and chains to level the vehicle after the trailer is hooked up.

The bolt-on hitches are the most common, since they are relatively easy to install.

Check the gross weight rating of your trailer. Tongue weight is usually figured as 10% of gross trailer weight. Therefore, a trailer with a maximum gross weight of 2000 lb. will have a maximum tongue weight of 200 lb. Class I tarilers fall into this category. Class II trailers are those with a gross weight rating of 2000–3500 lb., while Class III trailers fall into the 3500–6000 lb. category. Class IV trailers are those over 6000 lb. and are for use with fifth wheel trucks, only.

When you've determined the hitch that you'll need, follow the manufacturer's installation instructions, exactly, especially when it comes to fastener torques. The hitch will subjected to a lot of stress and good hitches come with hardened bolts. Never substitute an inferior bolt for a hardened bolt. And as far as the hitch ball goes, it should be coated with a light film of grease.

➡ On All-Trac 4-Wheel Drive vehicles, in order to provide maximum protection and guard against personal injury, it is necessary to use a trailer hitch that which includes a protector designed to help to prevent fuel tank leakage and possible fire in the event of a rear end collision.

Chains

If the coupling unit or hitch ball is damaged, there is the danger of the trailer wandering into another lane. A safety chain must always be used between the vehicle and the trailer. For proper safety chain installation procedures and precautions, follow the manufacturer's recommendations.

Tires

Make certain that the tires are properly inflated. Adjust the tire pressure to the recommended cold tire pressure on the plate on the drivers side door post.

Trailer Wiring

Wiring your Toyota for towing is fairly easy. There are a number of good wiring kits available and these should be used, rather than trying to design your own. All trailers will need brake lights and turn signals as well as tail lights and side marker lights. Most states require extra marker lights for overly wide trailers. Also, most states have recently required back-up lights for trailers, and most trailer manufacturers have been building trailers with back-up lights for several years.

Additionally, some Class I, most Class II and just about all Class III trailers will have electric brakes.

Add to this number an accessories wire, to operate trailer internal equipment or to charge the trailer's battery, and you can have as many as seven wires in the harness.

Determine the equipment on your trailer and

buy the wiring kit necessary. The kit will contain all the wires needed, plus a plug adapter set which included the female plug, mounted on the bumper or hitch, and the male plug, wired into, or plugged into the trailer harness.

When installing the kit, follow the manufacturer's instructions. The color coding of the wires is standard throughout the industry.

One point to note, most imported vehicles, have separate turn signals. On most domestic vehicles, the brake lights and rear turn signals operate with the same bulb. For those vehicles with separate turn signals, you can purchase an isolation unit so that the brake lights won't blink whenever the turn signals are operated, or, you can go to your local electronics supply house and buy four diodes to wire in series with the brake and turn signal bulbs. Diodes will isolate the brake and turn signals. The choice is yours. The isolation units are simple and quick to install, but far more expensive than the diodes. The diodes, however, require more work to install properly, since they require the cutting of each bulb's wire and soldering in place of the diode.

One final point, the best kits are those with a spring loaded cover on the vehicle mounted socket. This cover prevents dirt and moisture from corroding the terminals. Never let the vehicle socket hang loosely. Always mount it securely to the bumper or hitch.

Cooling Systems

ENGINE

One of the most common, if not THE most common, problem associated with trailer towing is engine overheating.

With factory installed trailer towing packages, a heavy duty cooling system is usually included. Heavy duty cooling systems are available as optional equipment on most cars, with or without a trailer package. If you have one of these extra-capacity systems, you shouldn't have any overheating problems.

If you have a standard cooling system, without an expansion tank, you'll definitely need to get an aftermarket expansion tank kit, preferably one with at least a 2 quart capacity. These kits are easily installed on the radiator's overflow hose, and come with a pressure cap designed for expansion tanks.

Another helpful accessory is a Flex Fan. These fan are large diameter units are designed to provide more airflow at low speeds, with blades that have deeply cupped surfaces. The blades then flex, or flatten out, at high speed, when less cooling air is needed. These fans are far lighter in weight than stock fans, requiring less horsepower to drive them. Also, they are far quieter than stock fans.

If you do decide to replace your stock fan with a flex fan, note that if your car has a fan clutch, a spacer between the flex fan and water pump hub will be needed.

Aftermarket engine oil coolers are helpful for prolonging engine oil life and reducing overall engine temperatures. Both of these factors increase engine life.

While not absolutely necessary in towing Class I and some Class II trailers, they are recommended for heavier Class II and all Class III towing.

Engine oil cooler systems consist of an adapter, screwed on in place of the oil filter, a remote filter mounting and a multi-tube, finned heat exchanger, which is mounted in front of the radiator or air conditioning condenser.

TRANSAXLE

An automatic transaxle is usually recommended for trailer towing. Automatic transaxles have proven reliable and, of course, easy to operate, in trailer towing.

The increased load of a trailer, however, causes an increase in the temperature of the automatic transmission fluid. Heat is the worst enemy of an automatic transaxle. As the temperature of the fluid increases, the life of the fluid decreases.

It is essential, therefore, that you install an automatic transmission cooler.

The cooler, which consists of a multi-tube, finned heat exchanger, is usually installed in front of the radiator or air conditioning compressor, and hooked inline with the transmission cooler tank inlet line. Follow the cooler manufacturer's installation instructions.

Select a cooler of at least adequate capacity, based upon the combined gross weights of the car and trailer.

Cooler manufacturers recommend that you use an aftermarket cooler in addition to, and not instead of, the present cooling tank in your car radiator. If you do want to use it in place of the radiator cooling tank, get a cooler at least two sizes larger than normally necessary.

➡ **A transmission cooler can, sometimes, cause slow or harsh shifting in the transmission during cold weather, until the fluid has a chance to come up to normal operating temperature. Some coolers can be purchased with or retrofitted with a temperature bypass valve which will allow fluid flow through the cooler only when the fluid has reached operating temperature, or above.**

PUSHING AND TOWING

SEE FIGS. 155–159

WARNING

Push-starting is not recommended for cars equipped with a catalytic converter. Raw gas collecting in the converter may cause damage. Jump starting is recommended.

If your vehicle ever needs to be towed, use a safety chain system for all towing. The wheels and axle on the ground must be in operational condition. If they are damaged, a towing dolly must be used.

If the vehicle is towed with the front or all four wheels on the ground, the ignition key must be in the **ACC** position.

If the vehicle is equipped with All-Trac 4-Wheel Drive, special methods and precautions must be followed.

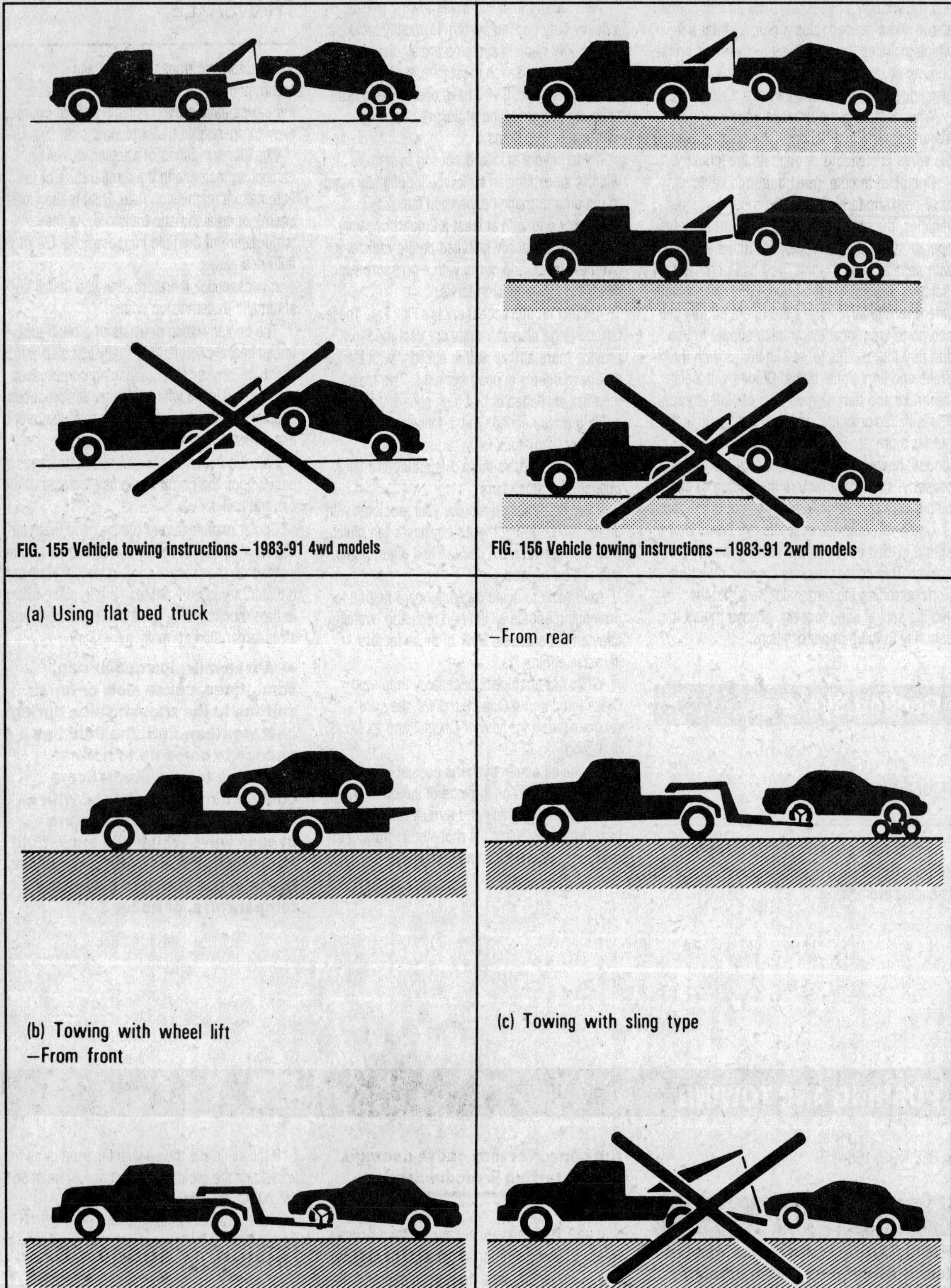

FIG. 155 Vehicle towing instructions—1983-91 4wd models

FIG. 156 Vehicle towing instructions—1983-91 2wd models

FIG. 157 Vehicle towing instructions—1992 models

FIG. 158 Vehicle towing instructions—1992 models

Manual Transaxles

ALL-TRAC 4-WHEEL DRIVE WITH CENTER DIFFERENTIAL LOCK BUTTON

On these type vehicles, towing can be accomplished in the following two ways only:

- **Towing with rear wheels on a dolly**: Be sure to raise the front wheel using a towing sling.
- **Towing with four wheels on the ground**: Make sure the center differential is unlocked (the indicator light must be off with the ignition on). Release the parking brake and put the transmission in neutral. The ignition key must be in the **ACC** position.

ALL-TRAC 4-WHEEL DRIVE WITHOUT CENTER DIFFERENTIAL LOCK BUTTON

On these type vehicles, towing can be accomplished in the following two ways only:

- **Towing with rear wheels on a dolly**: Be sure to raise the front wheel using a towing sling.
- **Towing with four wheels on the ground**: Release the parking brake and put the transmission in neutral. The ignition key must be in the **ACC** position.

EXCEPT ALL-TRAC 4-WHEEL DRIVE

- **Towing with the front wheels on the ground**: Place the transaxle in neutral and turn the ignition key to the **ACC** position. The use of a towing dolly is recommended.
- **Towing with the rear wheels on the ground**: Release the parking brake.

Automatic Transaxles

- **Towing with the rear wheels on the ground**: Release the parking brake.
- **Towing with four wheels on the ground**: The vehicle can be towed from the front only. Release the parking brake and place the transaxle in the **N** position. The ignition key must be in the **ACC** position. Before towing check the transaxle fluid level. If the level is lower than the HOT line, add fluid or use a towing dolly.

✻✻ WARNING

Never tow a vehicle with an automatic transaxle from the rear with the front wheel on the ground, as this may cause damage to the transaxle! If the vehicle must be towed from the rear, use a towing dolly under the front wheels.

Emergency Towing

In case of an an emergency, secure a cable to one of the tie-down tabs located under the front of the vehicle.

Use this method only on hard surfaced roads. A driver must remain in the vehicle to steer and apply the brakes. Remember that the power assist for the steering and brakes will not work with the engine off, so steering and braking will be more difficult. This method cannot be used if the wheels, steering, brakes, drive axle or transaxle are damaged.

Before towing, release the parking brake and place the transaxle in neutral. The key must be in the **ACC** position.

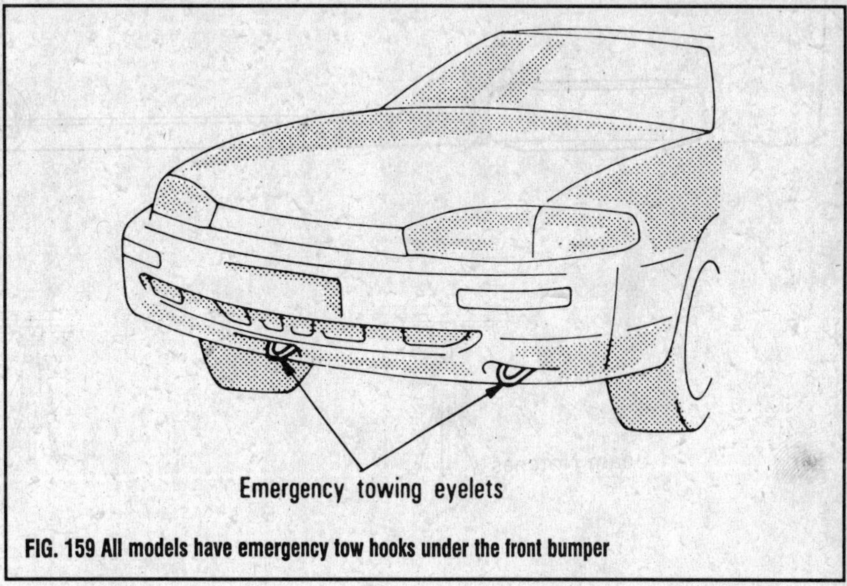

FIG. 159 All models have emergency tow hooks under the front bumper

JACKING

➧ SEE FIGS. 159A–162

There are certain safety precautions which should be observed when jacking the vehicle. They are as follows:

- Always jack the car on a level surface.
- Set the parking brake if the front wheels are to be raised. This will keep the car from rolling forward.
- If the rear wheels are to be raised, block the front wheel to keep the car from rolling forward.
- Block the wheel diagonally opposite the one which is being raised.

• If the vehicle is being raised in order to work underneath it, support it with jackstands. Do not place the jackstands against the sheet metal panels beneath the car or they will become distorted.

• Do not use a bumper jack to raise the vehicle; bumpers are not designed for this purpose.

➡ **The tool which is supplied with Toyota passenger cars includes a wheel block.**

✻✻ CAUTION

Do not work beneath a vehicle supported only by a tire-changing jack!

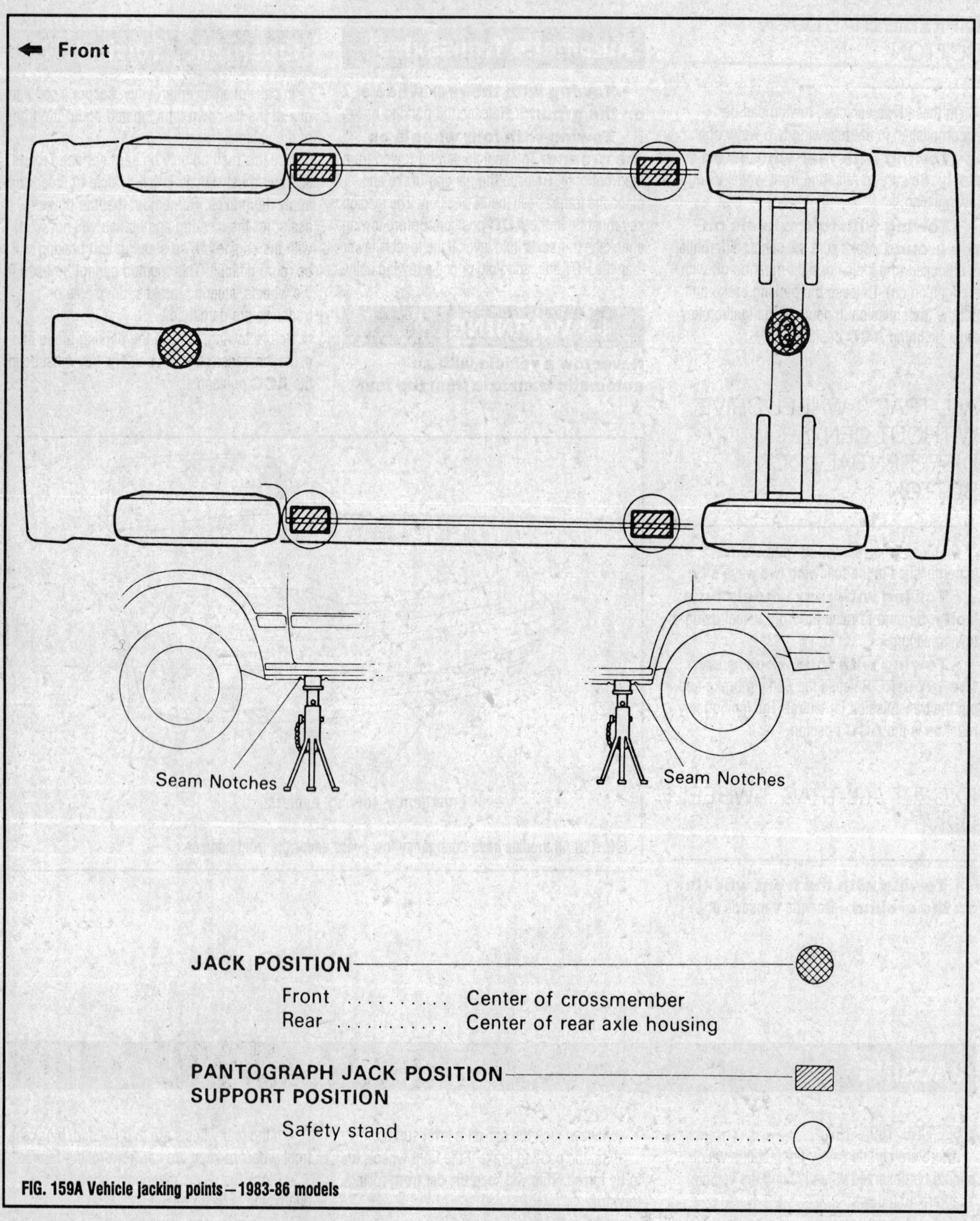

FIG. 159A Vehicle jacking points—1983-86 models

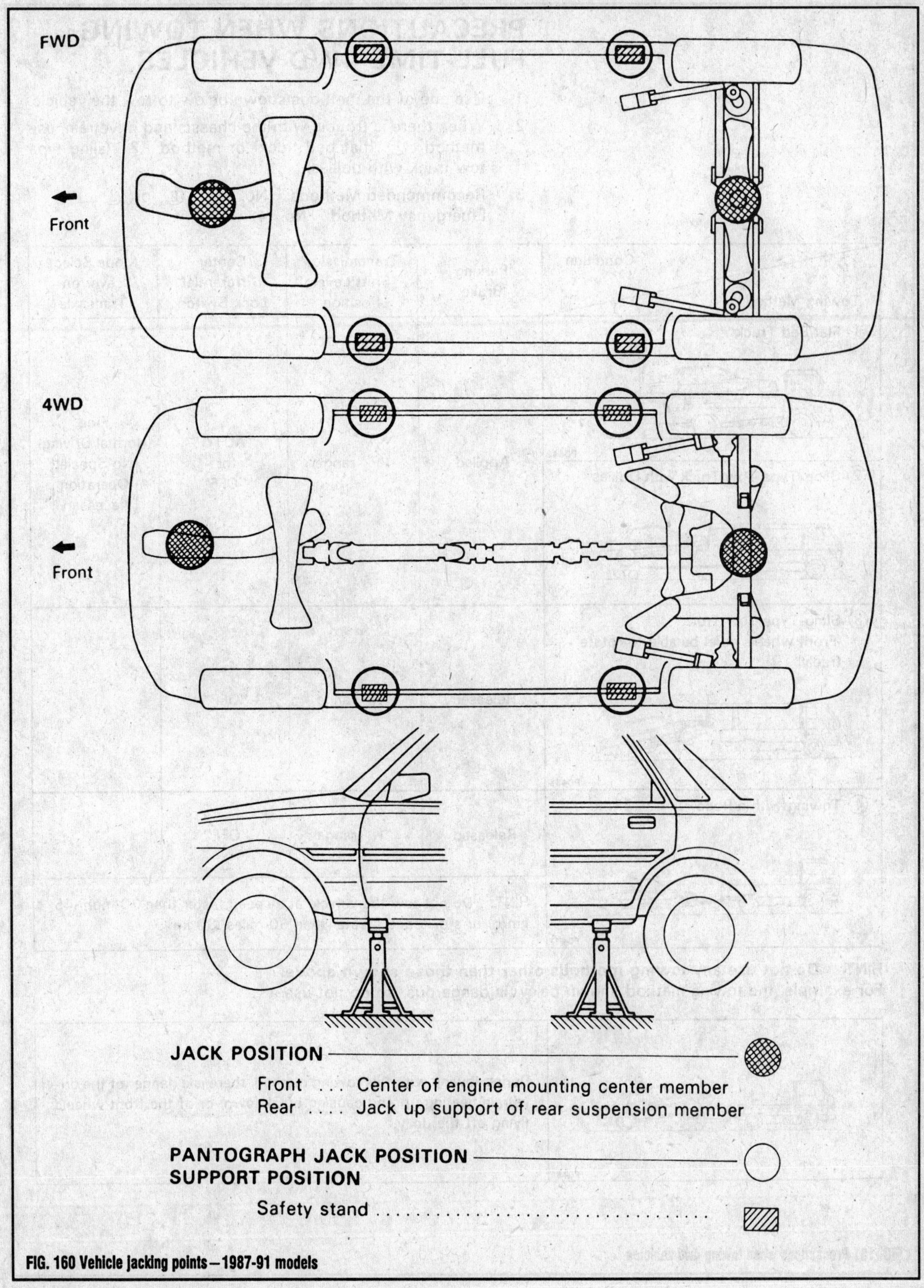

FIG. 160 Vehicle jacking points—1987-91 models

PRECAUTIONS WHEN TOWING FULL-TIME 4WD VEHICLES

1. Use one of the methods shown below to tow the vehicle.
2. When there is trouble with the chassis and drivetrain, use method ① (flat bed truck) or method ② (sling type tow truck with dollies)
3. Recommended Methods: No. ①, ② or ③
   Emergency Method: No. ④

<table>
<tr><th>Condition / Towing Method</th><th>Parking Brake</th><th>Transmission Shift Lever Position</th><th>Center Differential Lock Switch</th><th>Mode Select Lever on Transaxle</th></tr>
<tr><td>① Flat Bed Truck
P0442</td><td rowspan="2">Applied</td><td rowspan="2">"P" range</td><td rowspan="2">"AUTO" or "OFF"</td><td rowspan="2">Free (Normal Driving) (No Special Operation Necessary)</td></tr>
<tr><td>② Sling-Type Tow Truck with Dollies</td></tr>
<tr><td>③ Sling-Type Tow Truck (Front wheels must be able to rotate freely)
P0438</td><td>Released</td><td>"N" range</td><td>"OFF"</td><td>↑</td></tr>
<tr><td rowspan="2">④ Towing with a Rope
P0437</td><td>Released</td><td>"N" range</td><td>"OFF"</td><td>↑</td></tr>
<tr><td colspan="4">HINT: Do not tow the vehicle at a speed faster than 30 mph (45 km/h) or a distance greater than 50 miles (80 km).</td></tr>
</table>

HINT: **Do not use any towing methods other than those shown above.**
For example, the towing method shown below is dangerous, so do not use it.

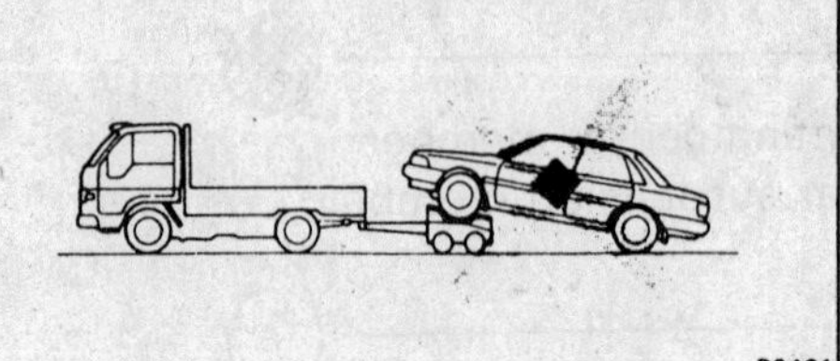

P0481

During towing with this towing method, there is a danger of the drivetrain heating up and causing breakdown, or of the front wheels flying off the dolly.

FIG. 161 Precautions when towing 4wd vehicles

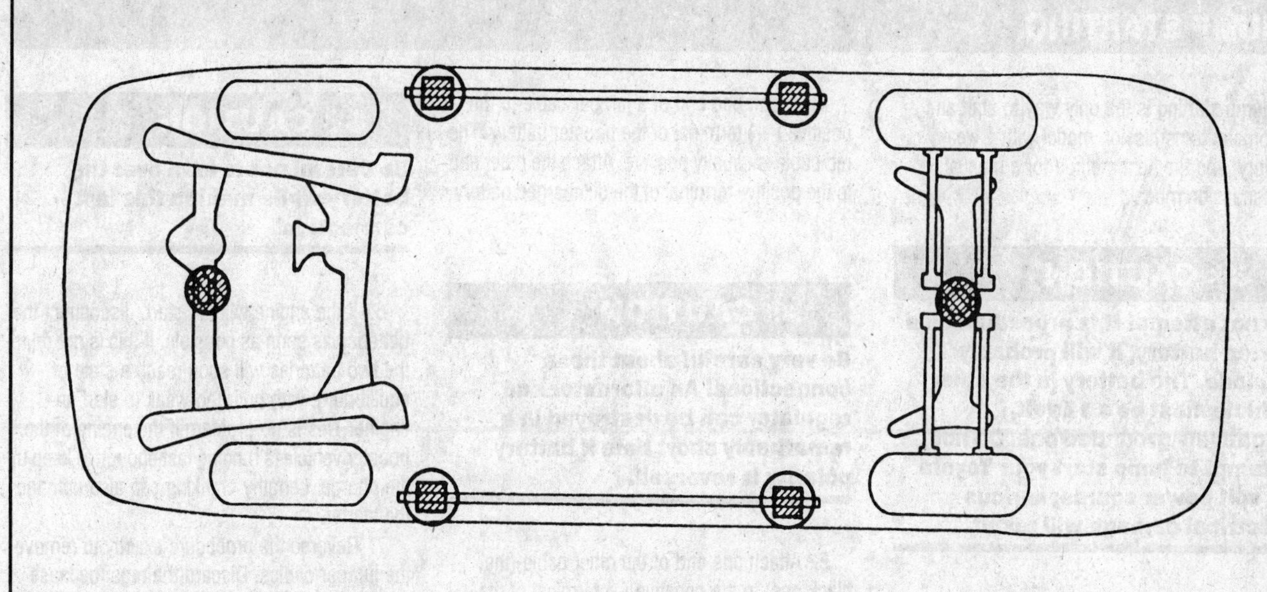

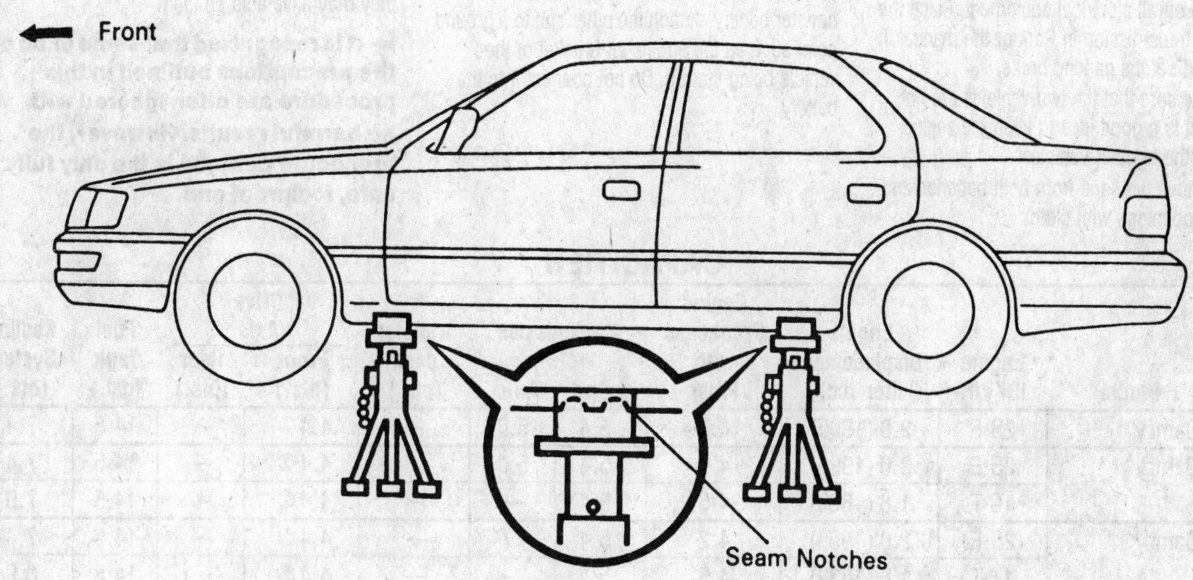

JACK POSITION

Front .... Front crossmember
Rear .... Rear axle beam

CAUTION: When jack-up the rear and front, make sure the car is not carrying any extra weight.

PANTOGRAPH JACK POSITION

SUPPORT POSITION

Safety stand and swing arm type lift ....

FIG. 162 Vehicle jacking points—1992 models

JUMP STARTING

Jump starting is the only way to start an automatic transmission model with a weak battery, and the best method for a manual transmission model.

✲✲ CAUTION

Do not attempt this procedure on a frozen battery, it will probably explode. The battery in the other vehicle must be a 12 volt, negatively grounded one. Do not attempt to jump start your Toyota 24 volt power source; serious electrical damage will result.

1. Turn off all electrical equipment. Place the automatic transmission in Park or the manual in Neutral and set the parking brake.
2. Make sure that the two vehicles are not touching. It is a good idea to keep the engine running in the booster vehicle.
3. Remove the caps from both batteries and cover the openings with cloths.
4. Attach one end of a jumper cable to the positive (+) terminal of the booster battery. The red cable is usually positive. Attach the other end to the positive terminal of the discharged battery.

✲✲ CAUTION

Be very careful about these connections! An alternator and regulator can be destroyed in a remarkably short time if battery polarity is reversed.

5. Attach one end of the other cable (the black one) to the negative (–) terminal of the booster battery. Attach the other end to a ground point such as the engine lift bracket of the vehicle being started. Do not connect it to the battery.

✲✲ CAUTION

Be careful not to lean over the battery while making this last connection!

6. If the engine will not start, disconnect the batteries as soon as possible. If this is not done, the two batteries will soon reach a state of equilibrium, with both too weak to start an engine. This is no problem if the engine of the booster vehicle is running fast enough to keep up the charge. Lengthy cranking can also damage the starter.
7. Reverse the procedure exactly to remove the jumper cables. Discard the rags, because they may have acid on them.

➡ It is recognized that some or all of the precautions outlined in this procedure are often ignored with no harmful results. However, the procedure outlined is the only fully safe, foolproof one.

CAPACITIES

Year	Model	Engine ID/VIN	Engine Displacement liter (cc)	Engine Crankcase with Filter	Transmission (pts.)		Transfer case (pts.)	Drive Axle		Fuel Tank (gal.)	Cooling System (qts.)
					5-Spd	Auto.		Front (pts.)	Rear (pts.)		
1983	Camry	2S-E	2.0 (1995)	4.2	5.4	5.0	—	4.4②	—	14.5	7.4
1984	Camry	2S-E	2.0 (1995)	4.2	5.4	5.0	—	4.4②	—	14.5	7.4
		1C-T	1.8 (1839)	4.5	5.4	—	—	4.4②	—	14.5	7.9
1985	Camry	2S-E	2.0 (1995)	4.2	5.4	①	—	4.4②	—	14.5	7.4
		1C-T	1.8 (1839)	4.5	5.4	—	—	4.4②	—	14.5	8.9
1986	Camry	2S-E	2.0 (1995)	4.2	5.4	①	—	3.4②	—	14.5	7.4
		2C-T	2.0 (1974)	4.5	5.4	—	—	3.4②	—	14.5	8.9
1987	Camry	3S-FE	2.0 (1998)	4.3	5.4	5.2	—	3.4②	—	15.9	6.8
1988	Camry (2WD)	3S-FE	2.0 (1998)	4.1	5.4	5.2	—	3.4②	—	15.9	6.8
	Camry (4WD)	3S-FE	2.0 (1998)	4.1	10.6③	—	④	④	2.4	15.9	6.8
1989	Camry (2WD)	3S-FE	2.0 (1998)	4.1	5.4	5.2	—	3.4②	—	15.9	6.8
	Camry (2WD)	2VZ-FE	2.5 (2507)	4.1	8.8	5.2	—	2.2②	—	15.9	9.0
	Camry (4WD)	3S-FE	2.0 (1998)	4.1	10.6	5.2	④	2.2②	2.4	15.9	6.8
1990	Camry (2WD)	3S-FE	2.0 (1998)	4.1	5.4	5.2	—	3.4②	—	15.9	6.8
	Camry (2WD)	2VZ-FE	2.5 (2507)	4.1	8.8	5.2	—	2.2②	—	15.9	9.9
	Camry (4WD)	3S-FE	2.0 (1998)	4.1	10.6	5.2	④	3.4	2.4	15.9	6.8
1991	Camry (2WD)	3S-FE	2.0 (1998)	4.3	5.4	5.2	—	3.4②	—	15.9	6.8
	Camry (2WD)	2VZ-FE	2.5 (2507)	4.1	8.8	5.2	—	2.2②	—	15.9	9.9
	Camry (4WD)	3S-FE	2.0 (1998)	4.3	—	7.0	1.5	3.4	2.4	15.9	6.8
1992	Camry	5S-FE	2.2 (2164)	4.3	5.4	5.2	—	3.4	—	18.5	6.7
		3VZ-FE	3.0 (2959)	4.5	8.8	5.2	—	1.6	—	18.5	9.0

① A140E: 5.0 A140L: 4.2 ② AT only, MT included w/transmission capacity ③ Includes differential and transfer case
④ Included w/transmission capacity

MAINTENANCE SCHEDULE

Maintenance operations: A = Check and/or adjust if necessary;
R = Replace, change or lubricate;
I = Inspect and correct or replace if necessary

System	Maintenance items	Service interval	15	30	45	60	SV series	CV series
		Odometer reading or months, whichever comes first						
		Miles x 1,000	15	30	45	60		
		Kilometers x 1,000	24	48	72	96		
		Months	12	24	36	48		
ENGINE	Valve clearance (2) (Diesel)		A	A	A	A	–	●
	Timing belt (Diesel)					R	–	●
	Drive belts(4) (including PS and A/C drive belt)	Gasoline				I	●	–
		Diesel	I	R	I	R	–	●
	Engine oil and oil filter (1)	Gasoline	Change every 10,000 miles (16,000 km) or 8 months				●	–
		Diesel	Change every 5,000 miles (8,000 km) or 4 months				–	●
	Engine coolant(5)					R	●	●
	Vacuum pump oil hoses (Diesel)		I	I	I	R	–	●
	Exhaust pipes and mountings(1)		I		I		●	●
FUEL	Idle speed(2)	Gasoline	A*	A*	A*	A	●	–
		Diesel	A	A			–	●
	Fuel filter (Diesel)			R		R	–	●
	Air filter(1)			R		R	●	●
	Fuel lines and connections			I			●	●
	Fuel filler cap gasket					R	●	●
IGNITION	Spark plugs (Gasoline)			R		R	●	–
	Ignition wiring and distributor cap(1) (Gasoline)		(3)				●	–
EMISSION CONTROL	Charcoal canister (Gasoline)					I	●	–
	Fuel evaporative emission control system, hoses and connections (Gasoline)					I	●	–
TRANSAXLE	Transmission and differential oil(1)		I	I	I	I	●	●
BRAKES	Brake lining and drums(1)			I		I	●	●
	Brake pads and discs(1)		I	I	I	I	●	●
	Brake line pipes and hoses(6)			I	I	I	●	●
CHASSIS	Steering linkage(1),(6)			I	I	I	●	●
	Drive shaft boots(1),(6)			I	I	I	●	●
	Ball joints and dust covers(1),(6)			I	I	I	●	●
	Bolts and nuts on chassis and body(1)		I		I		●	●

* The items marked with an asterisk are recommended maintenance items for California vehicles only, but are required for Federal and Canada.

FIG. 163 Maintenance intervals chart—1983-84 models

NOTE:

(1) For vehicles normally used under any of the following severe conditions, the applicable items of maintenance should be performed as indicated in the table below.

Maintenance items		Service interval		Severe condition
Engine oil and oil filter	Gasoline	R	Every 3,750 miles (6,000 km) or 3 months	A . . D . F
	Diesel	R	Every 1,875 miles (3,000 km) or 1.5 months	A . . D . F
Exhaust pipes and mountings		I	Every 7,500 miles (12,000 km) or 6 months	A B C . E .
Air filter		I	Every 3,750 miles (6,000 km) or 3 months	. . . D . .
		R	Every 30,000 miles (48,000 km) or 24 months	
Ignition wiring (3) (Gasoline)		I	Every 12 months	. . . . E .
Distributor cap (3) (Gasoline)		I	Every 12 months	. . . . E .
Brake linings and drums		I	Every 7,500 miles (12,000 km) or 6 months	A B C D . .
Brake pads and discs		I	Every 7,500 miles (12,000 km) or 6 months	A B C D . .
Steering linkage, gear housing and steering wheel freeplay		I	Every 7,500 miles (12,000 km) or 6 months	. . C . . .
Ball joints and dust covers		I	Every 7,500 miles (12,000 km) or 6 months	. . C D E .
Drive shaft boots		I	Every 7,500 miles (12,000 km) or 6 months	. . C . E .
Transmission and differential oil		R	Every 15,000 miles (24,000 km) or 12 months	A . C . . .
Automatic transmission fluid		R	Every 15,000 miles (24,000 km) or 12 months	A . C . . .
Bolts and nuts on chassis and body		I	Every 7,500 miles (12,000 km) or 6 months	. . C . . .

"Severe conditions"

A – Pulling trailers
B – Repeated short trips
C – Driving on rough and/or muddy roads
D – Driving on dusty roads
E – Operating in extremely cold weather and/or driving in areas using road salt
F – Repeated short trips in extremely cold weather

(2) Specifications appear on the information label.

(3) In areas where road salt is used, inspection and cleaning of the distributor cap and ignition wiring should be performed each year just after the snow season.

(4) Inspect every 15,000 miles (24,000 km) or 12 months after 60,000 miles (96,000 km) or 48 months.

(5) Replace every 30,000 miles (48,000 km) or 24 months after 60,000 miles (96,000 km) or 48 months, due to possible use of poor quality coolant locally available.

(6) First inspection at 30,000 miles (48,000 km) or 24 months and every 15,000 miles (24,000 km) or 12 months thereafter.

FIG. 164 Maintenance intervals chart—1983-84 models

MAINTENANCE SCHEDULE

(GASOLINE ENGINE)

Maintenance operations: A = Check and/or adjust if necessary;
R = Replace, change or lubricate;
I = Inspect and correct or replace if necessary

NORMAL CONDITION SCHEDULE

System	Service interval (Odometer reading or months, whichever comes first) / Maintenance items	Maintenance services beyond 60,000 miles (96,000 km) should be performed at the same intervals shown in each maintenance schedule.						
		Miles x 1,000	10	20	30	40	50	60
		Km x 1,000	16	32	48	64	80	96
		Months	12	24	36	48	60	72
ENGINE	Drive belts (V-ribbed belt)(1)							I
	Engine oil and oil filter ★•		R	R	R	R	R	R
	Engine coolant(2)							R
	Exhaust pipes and mountings				I			I
FUEL	Idle speed •(3)		A		A			A
	Air filter ★•				R			R
	Fuel line and connections				I			I
	Fuel filler cap gasket							R
IGNITION	Spark plugs ★•				R			R
EVAP	Charcoal canister							I
BRAKES	Brake lining and drums			I		I		I
	Brake pads and discs			I		I		I
	Brake line pipes and hoses			I		I		I
CHASSIS	Steering linkage			I		I		I
	Drive shaft boots			I		I		I
	Ball joints and dust covers			I		I		I
	Automatic transaxle, manual transaxle, differential and steering gear housing oil			I		I		I
	Bolts and nuts on chassis and body			I		I		I

Maintenance services indicated by a star (★) or asterisk (•) are required under the terms of the Emission Control Systems Warranty (ECSW). See Owner's Guide for complete warranty information.

★ For vehicles sold in California

• For vehicles sold outside California

NOTE:

(1) After 60,000 miles (96,000 km) or 72 months, inspect every 10,000 miles (16,000 km) or 12 months.

(2) After 60,000 miles (96,000 km) or 72 months, replace every 30,000 miles (48,000 km) or 36 months.

(3) After 30,000 miles (48,000 km) or 36 months, adjust every 30,000 miles (48,000 km) or 36 months. Maintenance services performed only at 30,000 miles (48,000 km) or 36 months under the terms of the ECSW.

FIG. 165 Maintenance intervals chart—1985-86 models with gasoline engines (normal conditions)

Follow the severe condition schedule if vehicle is operated mainly under one or more of the following severe conditions:

- Pulling a trailer
- Repeated short trips
- Driving on rough and/or muddy roads
- Driving on dusty roads
- Driving in extremely cold weather and/or on salted roads

SEVERE CONDITION SCHEDULE

System	Service interval (Odometer reading or months, whichever comes first) / Maintenance items		Maintenance services beyond 60,000 miles (96,000 km) should be performed at the same intervals shown in each maintenance schedule.											
		Miles x 1,000	5	10	15	20	25	30	35	40	45	50	55	60
		Km x 1,000	8	16	24	32	40	48	56	64	72	80	88	96
		Months	6	12	18	24	30	36	42	48	54	60	66	72
ENGINE	Drive belts (V-ribbed belt)(1)													I
	Engine oil and oil filter ★•		R	R	R	R	R	R	R	R	R	R	R	R
	Engine coolant(2)													R
	Exhaust pipes and mountings				I			I			I			I
FUEL	Idle speed • (3)			A				A						A
	Air filter ★• (5)		I	I	I	I	I	R	I	I	I	I	I	R
	Fuel line and connections							I						I
	Fuel filler cap gasket													R
IGNITION	Spark plugs ★•							R						R
	Ignition wiring and distributor cap ★•		(4)											
EVAP	Charcoal canister													I
BRAKES	Brake lining and drums			I		I		I		I		I		I
	Brake pads and discs			I		I		I		I		I		I
	Brake line pipes and hoses					I				I				I
CHASSIS	Steering linkage(6)			I		I		I		I		I		I
	Drive shaft boots			I		I		I		I		I		I
	Ball joints and dust covers			I		I		I		I		I		I
	Automatic transaxle, manual transaxle, differential and steering gear housing(7) oil					R				R				R
	Bolts and nuts on chassis and body(6)			I		I		I		I		I		I

Maintenance servies indicated by a star (★) or asterisk (•) are required under the terms of the Emission Control Systems Warranty (ECSW).
See Owner's Guide for complete warranty information.

★ For vehicles sold in California

• For vehicles sold outside California

NOTE:

(1) After 60,000 miles (96,000 km) or 72 months, inspect every 10,000 miles (16,000 km) or 12 months.

(2) After 60,000 miles (96,000 km) or 72 months, replace every 30,000 miles (48,000 km) or 36 months.

(3) After 30,000 miles (48,000 km) or 36 months, adjust every 30,000 miles (48,000 km) or 36 months. Maintenance services performed only at 30,000 miles (48,000 km) or 36 months under the terms of the ECSW.

(4) In areas where road salt is used, inspect and clean each year just after the snow season.

(5) Applicable when operating mainly on dusty roads. If not, follow the normal condition schedule.

(6) Applicable when operating mainly on rough and/or muddy roads. If not, follow the normal condition schedule.

(7) Inspect the steering gear housing for oil leakage only.

FIG. 166 Maintenance intervals chart—1985-86 models with gasoline engines (severe conditions)

MAINTENANCE SCHEDULE

(DIESEL ENGINE)

Maintenance operations: A = Check and/or adjust if necessary;
R = Replace, change or lubricate;
I = Inspect and correct or replace if necessary

NORMAL CONDITION SCHEDULE

System	Service interval (Odometer reading or months, whichever comes first) / Maintenance items	Maintenance services beyond 60,000 miles (96,000 km) should be performed at the same intervals shown in each maintenance schedule.						
		Miles x 1,000	10	20	30	40	50	60
		Km x 1,000	16	32	48	64	80	96
		Months	12	24	36	48	60	72
ENGINE	Timing belt							R
	Valve clearance ★•				A			A
	Drive belts				R			R
	Engine oil ★•		Change every 5,000 miles (8,000 km) or 6 months					
	Engine oil filter ★•		R	R	R	R	R	R
	Engine coolant(1)							R
	Vacuum pump oil hoses				I			R
	Exhaust pipes and mountings				I			I
FUEL	Idle speed ★• (2)				A			
	Air filter ★•				R			R
	Fuel filter				R			R
	Fuel line and connections				I			I
	Fuel filler cap gasket							R
BRAKES	Brake lining and drums			I		I		I
	Brake pads and discs			I		I		I
	Brake line pipes and hoses			I		I		I
CHASSIS	Steering linkage			I		I		I
	Drive shaft boots			I		I		I
	Ball joints and dust covers			I		I		I
	Automatic transaxle, differential and steering gear housing oil			I		I		I
	Bolts and nuts on chassis and body			I		I		I

Maintenance services indicated by a star (★) or asterisk (•) are required under the terms of the Emission Control Systems Warranty.
See Owner's Guide for complete warranty information.

★ For vehicles sold in California
• For vehicles sold outside California

NOTE:
(1) After 60,000 miles (96,000 km) or 72 months, replace every 30,000 miles (48,000 km) or 36 months.
(2) Adjustment at 30,000 miles (48,000 km) or 36 months only.

FIG. 167 Maintenance intervals chart—1985-86 models with diesel engines (normal conditions)

Follow the severe condition schedule if vehicle is operated mainly under one or more of the following severe conditions:

- Pulling a trailer
- Repeated short trips
- Driving on rough and/or muddy roads
- Driving on dusty roads
- Driving in extremely cold weather and/or on salted roads

SEVERE CONDITION SCHEDULE

System	Service interval (Odometer reading or months, whichever comes first) / Maintenance items	Maintenance services beyond 60,000 miles (96,000 km) should be performed at the same intervals shown in each maintenance schedule.												
		Miles x 1,000	5	10	15	20	25	30	35	40	45	50	55	60
		Km x 1,000	8	16	24	32	40	48	56	64	72	80	88	96
		Months	6	12	18	24	30	36	42	48	54	60	66	72
ENGINE	Timing belt													R
	Valve clearance ★•							A						A
	Drive belts							R						R
	Engine oil ★•		Change every 2,500 miles (4,000 km) or 3 months											
	Engine oil filter ★•		R	R	R	R	R	R	R	R	R	R	R	R
	Engine coolant (1)													R
	Vacuum pump oil hoses							I						R
	Exhaust pipes and mountings				I			I			I			I
FUEL	Idle speed ★•(2)							A						
	Air filter ★• (3)		I	I	I	I	I	R	I	I	I	I	I	R
	Fuel filter							R						R
	Fuel line and connections							I						I
	Fuel filler cap gasket													R
BRAKES	Brake lining and drums			I		I		I		I		I		I
	Brake pads and discs			I		I		I		I		I		I
	Brake line pipes and hoses					I				I				I
CHASSIS	Steering linkage (4)			I		I		I		I		I		I
	Drive shaft boots			I		I		I		I		I		I
	Ball joints and dust covers			I		I		I		I		I		I
	Automatic transaxle, differential and steering gear housing (5) oil					R				R				R
	Bolts and nuts on chassis and body (4)			I		I		I		I		I		I

Maintenance services indicated by a star (★) or asterisk (*) are required under the terms of the Emission Control Systems Warranty.
See Owner's Guide for complete warranty information.

★ For vehicles sold in California
• For vehicles sold outside California

NOTE:
(1) After 60,000 miles (96,000 km) or 72 months, replace every 30,000 miles (48,000 km) or 36 months.
(2) Adjustment at 30,000 miles (48,000 km) or 36 months only.
(3) Applicable when operating mainly on dusty roads. If not, follow the normal condition schedule.
(4) Applicable when operating mainly on rough and/or muddy roads. If not, follow the normal condition schedule.
(5) Inspect the steering gear housing for oil leakage only.

FIG. 168 Maintenance intervals chart—1985-86 models with diesel engines (severe conditions)

MAINTENANCE SCHEDULE

Maintenance operations: A = Check and adjust if necessary;
R = Replace, change or lubricate;
I = Inspect and correct or replace if necessary

NORMAL CONDITION SCHEDULE

System	Service interval (Odometer reading or months, whichever, comes first) / Maintenance items	Maintenance services beyond 60,000 miles (96,000 km) should be performed at the same intervals shown in each maintenance schedule.						
		Miles × 1,000	10	20	30	40	50	60
		Km × 1,000	16	32	48	64	80	96
		Months	12	24	36	48	60	72
ENGINE	Valve clearance							A
	Drive belts[(1)]							I
	Engine oil and oil filter★		R	R	R	R	R	R
	Engine coolant[(2)]							R
	Exhaust pipes and mountings				I			I
FUEL	Air filter★				R			R
	Fuel lines and connections				I			I
	Fuel tank cap gasket							R
IGNITION	Spark plugs★•				R			R
EVAP	Charcoal canister							I
BRAKES	Brake linings and drums			I		I		I
	Brake pads and discs			I		I		I
	Brake line pipes and hoses			I		I		I
CHASSIS	Steering linkage			I		I		I
	Drive shaft boots			I		I		I
	Ball joints and dust covers			I		I		I
	Automatic transaxle, manual transaxle, differential and steering gear housing oil[(3)]			I		I		I
	Bolts and nuts on chassis and body			I		I		I

Maintenance services indicated by a star (★) or asterisk (•) are required under the terms of the Emission Control Systems Warranty (ECSW). See Owner's Guide or Warranty Booklet for complete warranty information.

★ For vehicles sold in California
• For vehicles sold outside California

NOTE:

(1) After 60,000 miles (96,000 km), inspect every 10,000 miles (16,000 km) or 12 months.
(2) After 60,000 miles (96,000 km), replace every 30,000 miles (48,000 km) or 36 months.
(3) Inspect the steering gear housing oil for leakage only.

FIG. 169 Maintenance intervals chart—1987-88 models (normal conditions)

Follow the severe condition schedule if vehicle is operated mainly under one or more of the following severe conditions:

- Towing a trailer, using a camper or car top carrier.
- Repeat short trips less than 5 miles (8 km) and outside temperatures remain below freezing.
- Extensive idling and/or low speed driving for a long distance such as police, taxi or door-to-door delivery use.
- Operating on dusty, rough, muddy or salt spread roads.

SEVERE CONDITION SCHEDULE

System	Service interval (Odometer reading or months, whichever comes first) / Maintenance items	Maintenance services beyond 60,000 miles (96,000 km) should be performed at the same intervals shown in each maintenance schedule.												
		Miles x 1,000	5	10	15	20	25	30	35	40	45	50	55	60
		Km x 1,000	8	16	24	32	40	48	56	64	72	80	88	96
		Months	6	12	18	24	30	36	42	48	54	60	66	72
ENGINE	Timing belt		R(1)											
	Valve clearance													A
	Drive belts(2)													I
	Engine oil and oil filter ★		R	R	R	R	R	R	R	R	R	R	R	R
	Engine coolant(3)													R
	Exhaust pipes and mountings				I			I			I			I
FUEL	Air filter ★ (4)		I	I	I	I	I	R	I	I	I	I	I	R
	Fuel line and connections							I						I
	Fuel tank cap gasket													R
IGNITION	Spark plugs ★ *							R						R
EVAP	Charcoal canister													I
BRAKES	Brake linings and drums			I		I		I		I		I		I
	Brake pads and discs			I		I		I		I		I		I
	Brake line pipes and hoses					I				I				I
CHASSIS	Steering linkage(5)			I		I		I		I		I		I
	Drive shaft boots			I		I		I		I		I		I
	Ball joints and dust covers			I		I		I		I		I		I
	Transaxle, rear differential, and steering gear housing(6) oil					R				R				R
	Bolts and nuts on chassis and body(5)			I		I		I		I		I		I

Maintenance services indicated by a star (★) or asterisk (*) are required under the terms of the Emission Control Systems Warranty (ECSW). See Owner's Guide for complete warranty information.

★ For vehicles sold in California

* For vehicles sold outside California

NOTE:

(1) For the vehicles frequently idled for extensive periods and/or driven for long distance at low speeds such as taxi, police and door-to-door delivery, it is recommended to change at 60,000 miles (96,000 km).

(2) After 60,000 miles (96,000 km), inspect every 10,000 miles (16,000 km) or 12 months.

(3) After 60,000 miles (96,000 km), replace every 30,000 miles (48,000 km) or 36 months.

(4) Applicable when operating mainly on dusty roads. If not, follow the normal condition schedule.

(5) Applicable when operating mainly on rough and/or muddy roads. If not, follow the normal condition schedule.

(6) Inspect the steering gear housing for oil leakage only.

FIG. 170 Maintenance intervals chart—1987-88 models (severe conditions)

MAINTENANCE SCHEDULE

Maintenance operations: A = Check and adjust if necessary;
R = Replace, change or lubricate;
I = Inspect and correct or replace if necessary

SCHEDULE A

CONDITIONS:

- Towing a trailer, using a camper or car top carrier.
- Repeated short trips less than 5 miles (8 km) and outside temperatures remain below freezing.
- Extensive idling and/or low speed driving for a long distance such as police, taxi or door-to-door delivery use.
- Operating on dusty, rough, muddy or salt spread roads.

System	Service interval (Odometer reading or months, whichever comes first) / Maintenance items		Maintenance services beyond 60,000 miles (96,000 km) should be performed at the same intervals shown in each maintenance schedule.											
			Miles × 1,000	5	10	15	20	25	30	35	40	45	50	55	60
			Km × 1,000	8	16	24	32	40	48	56	64	72	80	88	96
			Months	6	12	18	24	30	36	42	48	54	60	66	72
ENGINE	Timing belt														R[1]
	Valve clearance														A
	Drive belts[2]														I
	Engine oil and oil filter★			R	R	R	R	R	R	R	R	R	R	R	R
	Engine coolant[3]														R
	Exhaust pipes and mountings					I			I			I			I
FUEL	Air filter★*[4]			I	I	I	I	I	R	I	I	I	I	I	R
	Fuel lines and connections								I						I
	Fuel tank cap gasket														R
IGNITION	Spark plugs	3S-FE**							R						R
		2VZ-FE													R
EVAP	Charcoal canister														I
BRAKES	Brake linings and drums				I		I		I		I		I		I
	Brake pads and discs				I		I		I		I		I		I
	Brake line pipes and hoses						I				I				I
CHASSIS	Steering linkage[5]				I		I		I		I		I		I
	Drive shaft boots				I		I		I		I		I		I
	Ball joints and dust covers				I		I		I		I		I		I
	Automatic transaxle, manual transaxle, transfer differential and steering gear housing[6] oil						R				R				R
	Bolts and nuts on chassis and body[5]				I		I		I		I		I		I

Maintenance services indicated by a star (★) or asterisk (*) are required under the terms of the Emission Control Systems Warranty (ECSW). See Owner's Guide or Warranty Booklet for complete warranty information.

★ For vehicles sold in California
* For vehicles sold outside California

NOTE:

(1) For vehicles frequently idled for extensive periods and/or driven for long distance at low speeds such as taxi, police and door-to-door delivery, it is recommended to change at 60,000 miles (96,000 km).
(2) After 60,000 miles (96,000 km) or 72 months, inspect every 10,000 miles (16,000 km) or 12 months.
(3) After 60,000 miles (96,000 km) or 72 months, replace every 30,000 miles (48,000 km) or 36 months.
(4) Applicable when operating mainly on dusty roads. If not, follow the schedule B.
(5) Applicable when operating mainly on rough and/or muddy roads. If not, follow the schedule B.
(6) Inspect the steering gear housing for oil leakage only

FIG. 171 Maintenance intervals chart—1989 models (severe conditions)

SCHEDULE B

CONDITIONS: Conditions other than those listed for SCHEDULE A.

System	Service interval (Odometer reading or months, whichever comes first) / Maintenance items		Maintenance services beyond 60,000 miles (96,000 km) should be performed at the same intervals shown in each maintenance schedule.						
			Miles × 1,000	10	20	30	40	50	60
			Km × 1,000	16	32	48	64	80	96
			Months	12	24	36	48	60	72
ENGINE	Valve clearance								A
	Drive belts(1)								I
	Engine oil and filter★			R	R	R	R	R	R
	Engine coolant(2)								R
	Exhaust pipes and mountings					I			I
FUEL	Air filter★					R			R
	Fuel lines and connections					I			I
	Fuel tank cap gasket								R
IGNITION *	Spark plugs	3S-FE engine★*				R			R
		2VZ-FE engine							R
EVAP	Charcoal canister								I
BRAKES	Brake linings and drums				I		I		I
	Brake pads and discs				I		I		I
	Brake line pipes and hoses				I		I		I
CHASSIS	Steering linkage				I		I		I
	Drive shaft boots				I		I		I
	Ball joints and dust covers				I		I		I
	Automatic transaxle, manual transaxle, transfer differential and steering gear housing oil				I		I		I
	Bolts and nuts on chassis and body				I		I		I

Maintenance services indicated by a star (★) or asterisk (*) are required under the terms of the Emission Control Systems Warranty (ECSW). See Owner's Guide or Warranty Booklet for complete warranty information.

★ For vehicles sold in California

* For vehicles sold outside California

NOTE:

(1) After 60,000 miles (96,000 km) or 72 months, inspect every 10,000 miles (16,000 km) or 12 months.

(2) After 60,000 miles (96,000 km) or 72 months, replace every 30,000 miles (48,000 km) or 36 months.

FIG. 172 Maintenance intervals chart—1989 models (normal conditions)

MAINTENANCE SCHEDULE

SCHEDULE A

CONDITIONS:

- Towing a trailer, using a camper or car top carrier.
- Repeated short trips less than 5 miles (8 km) and outside temperature remains below freezing.
- Extensive idling and/or low speed driving for long distances such as police, taxi or door-to-door delivery use.
- Operating on dusty, rough muddy or salt spread roads.

Maintenance operations: A = Check and adjust if necessary; R = Replace, change or lubricate; I = Inspect and correct or replace if necessary

System	Service interval (Odometer reading or months, whichever comes first)	Maintenance services beyond 60,000 miles (96,000 km) should continue to be performed at the same intervals shown for each maintenance schedule.																
		Miles x 1,000	3.75	7.5	11.25	15	18.75	22.5	26.25	30	33.75	37.5	41.25	45	48.75	52.5	56.25	60	Months
	Maintenance items	km x 1,000	6	12	18	24	30	36	42	48	54	60	66	72	78	84	90	96	
ENGINE	Timing belt[1]																	R	–
	Valve clearance																	A	A: Every 72 months
	Drive belts		I: First period, 60,000 miles (96,000 km) or 72 months. I: After that every 7,500 miles (12,000 km) or 12 months																
	Engine oil and oil filter*		R	R	R	R	R	R	R	R	R	R	R	R	R	R	R	R	R: Every 6 months
	Engine coolant		R: First period, 45,000 miles (72,000 km) or 36 months. R: After that every 30,000 miles (48,000 km) or 24 months																
	Exhaust pipes and mountings					I				I				I				I	I: Every 24 months
FUEL	Air filter[2]*		I	I	I	I	I	I	I	R	I	I	I	I	I	I	I	R	I: Every 36 months R: Every 36 months
	Fuel lines and connections[3]									I								I	I: Every 36 months
	Fuel tank cap gasket																	R	R: Every 72 months
IGNITION	Spark plugs (Platinum tipped type)																	R	R: Every 72 months
EVAP	Charcoal canister																	I	I: Every 72 months
BRAKES	Brake linings and drums[4]			I		I		I		I		I		I		I		I	I: Every 12 months
	Brake pads and discs (Front and rear)			I		I		I		I		I		I		I		I	I: Every 12 months
	Brake line pipes and hoses					I				I				I				I	I: Every 24 months
CHASSIS	Steering linkage			I		I		I		I		I		I		I		I	I: Every 12 months
	SRS airbag		I: First period, 10 years. I: After that every 2 years.																
	Drive shaft boots			I		I		I		I		I		I		I		I	I: Every 12 months
	Ball joints and dust covers			I		I		I		I		I		I		I		I	I: Every 12 months
	Manual transaxle, automatic transaxle and differential					R				R				R				R	R: Every 24 months
	Steering gear housing oil[6]					I				I				I				I	I: Every 24 months
	Bolts and nuts on chassis and body[7]			I		I		I		I		I		I				I	I: Every 12 months

* Mark indicates maintenance which is part of the warranty conditions for the Emission Control System. The warranty period is in accordance with the owner's guide or the warranty booklet. (*: California specification vehicles)

(1) Applicable to vehicles operated under conditions of extensive idling and/or low speed driving for a long distance such as police, taxi or door-to-door delivery use.

(2) Applicable when operating mainly on dusty road. If not, apply SCHEDULE B.

(3) Includes inspection of fuel tank band and vapor vent system.

(4) Also applicable to lining drum for parking brake.

(5) Check for leakage.

(6) Check for oil leaks from steering gear housing.

(7) Applicable only when operating mainly on rough, muddy roads. The applicable parts are listed below. For other usage conditions, refer to SCHEDULE B.

- Front and rear suspension member to cross body
- Strut bar bracket to body bolts
- Bolts for sheet installation

FIG. 173 Maintenance intervals chart—1990-92 models (severe conditions)

SCHEDULE B

CONDITIONS: Conditions other than those listed for SCHEDULE A.

System	Service interval (Odometer reading or months, whichever comes first)	Maintenance service beyond 60,000 miles (96,000 km) should continue to be performed at the same intervals shown for each maintenance schedule.								
	Miles x 1,000	7.5	15	22.5	30	37.5	45	52.5	60	Months
	Maintenance items / km x 1,000	12	24	36	48	60	72	84	96	
ENGINE	Valve clearance								A	A: Every 72 months
	Drive belts	I: First period, 60,000 miles (96,000 km) or 72 months. I: After that every 7,500 miles (12,000 km) or 12 months								
	Engine oil and oil filter*	R	R	R	R	R	R	R	R	R: Every 12 months
	Engine coolant	R: First period, 45,000 miles (72,000 km) or 36 months. R: After that every 30,000 miles (48,000 km) or 24 months								
	Exhaust pipes and mountings				I				I	I: Every 36 months
FUEL	Air filter*				R				R	R: Every 36 months
	Fuel lines and connections(1)				I				I	I: Every 36 months
	Fuel tank cap gasket								R	R: Every 72 months
IGNITION	Spark plugs (Platinum tipped type)								R	R: Every 72 months
EVAP	Charcoal canister								I	I: Every 72 months
BRAKES	Brake linings and drums(2)		I		I		I		I	I: Every 24 months
	Brake pads and discs (Front and rear)		I		I		I		I	I: Every 24 months
	Brake line pipes and hoses		I		I		I		I	I: Every 24 months
CHASSIS	Steering linkage		I		I		I		I	I: Every 24 months
	SRS airbag	I: First period, 10 years. I: After that every 2 years.								
	Drive shaft boots		I		I		I		I	I: Every 24 months
	Ball joints and dust covers		I		I		I		I	I: Every 24 months
	Manual transaxle, automatic transaxle and differential(3)		I		I		I		I	I: Every 24 months
	Steering gear housing oil(4)		I		I		I		I	I: Every 24 months
	Bolts and nuts on chassis and body(5)		I		I		I		I	I: Every 24 months

* Mark indicates maintenance which is part of the warranty conditions for the Emission Control System. The warranty period is in accordance with the owner's guide or the warranty booklet. (*: California specification vehicles)

(1) Includes inspection of fuel tank band and vapor vent system.
(2) Also applicable to lining drum for parking brake.
(3) Check for leakage.
(4) Check for oil leaks from steering gear housing.
(5) The applicable parts are listed below.
- Front and rear suspension member to cross body
- Strut bar bracket to body bolt
- Bolts for sheet installation

FIG. 174 Maintenance intervals chart—1990-92 models (normal conditions)

Troubleshooting Basic Air Conditioning Problems

Problem	Cause	Solution
There's little or no air coming from the vents (and you're sure it's on)	• The A/C fuse is blown • Broken or loose wires or connections • The on/off switch is defective	• Check and/or replace fuse • Check and/or repair connections • Replace switch
The air coming from the vents is not cool enough	• Windows and air vent wings open • The compressor belt is slipping • Heater is on • Condenser is clogged with debris • Refrigerant has escaped through a leak in the system • Receiver/drier is plugged	• Close windows and vent wings • Tighten or replace compressor belt • Shut heater off • Clean the condenser • Check system • Service system
The air has an odor	• Vacuum system is disrupted • Odor producing substances on the evaporator case • Condensation has collected in the bottom of the evaporator housing	• Have the system checked/repaired • Clean the evaporator case • Clean the evaporator housing drains
System is noisy or vibrating	• Compressor belt or mountings loose • Air in the system	• Tighten or replace belt; tighten mounting bolts • Have the system serviced
Sight glass condition Constant bubbles, foam or oil streaks Clear sight glass, but no cold air Clear sight glass, but air is cold Clouded with milky fluid	 • Undercharged system • No refrigerant at all • System is OK • Receiver drier is leaking dessicant	 • Charge the system • Check and charge the system • Have system checked
Large difference in temperature of lines	• System undercharged	• Charge and leak test the system
Compressor noise	• Broken valves • Overcharged • Incorrect oil level • Piston slap • Broken rings • Drive belt pulley bolts are loose	• Replace the valve plate • Discharge, evacuate and install the correct charge • Isolate the compressor and check the oil level. Correct as necessary. • Replace the compressor • Replace the compressor • Tighten with the correct torque specification
Excessive vibration	• Incorrect belt tension • Clutch loose • Overcharged • Pulley is misaligned	• Adjust the belt tension • Tighten the clutch • Discharge, evacuate and install the correct charge • Align the pulley
Condensation dripping in the passenger compartment	• Drain hose plugged or improperly positioned • Insulation removed or improperly installed	• Clean the drain hose and check for proper installation • Replace the insulation on the expansion valve and hoses

Troubleshooting Basic Air Conditioning Problems (cont.)

Problem	Cause	Solution
Frozen evaporator coil	• Faulty thermostat • Thermostat capillary tube improperly installed • Thermostat not adjusted properly	• Replace the thermostat • Install the capillary tube correctly • Adjust the thermostat
Low side low—high side low	• System refrigerant is low • Expansion valve is restricted	• Evacuate, leak test and charge the system • Replace the expansion valve
Low side high—high side low	• Internal leak in the compressor—worn	• Remove the compressor cylinder head and inspect the compressor. Replace the valve plate assembly if necessary. If the compressor pistons, rings or
Low side high—high side low (cont.)	 • Cylinder head gasket is leaking • Expansion valve is defective • Drive belt slipping	cylinders are excessively worn or scored replace the compressor • Install a replacement cylinder head gasket • Replace the expansion valve • Adjust the belt tension
Low side high—high side high	• Condenser fins obstructed • Air in the system • Expansion valve is defective • Loose or worn fan belts	• Clean the condenser fins • Evacuate, leak test and charge the system • Replace the expansion valve • Adjust or replace the belts as necessary
Low side low—high side high	• Expansion valve is defective • Restriction in the refrigerant hose	• Replace the expansion valve • Check the hose for kinks—replace if necessary
Low side low—high side high	• Restriction in the receiver/drier • Restriction in the condenser	• Replace the receiver/drier • Replace the condenser
Low side and high normal (inadequate cooling)	**• Air in the system** **• Moisture in the system**	**• Evacuate, leak test and charge the system** **• Evacuate, leak test and charge the system**

Troubleshooting Basic Wheel Problems

Problem	Cause	Solution
The car's front end vibrates at high speed	· The wheels are out of balance · Wheels are out of alignment	· Have wheels balanced · Have wheel alignment checked/adjusted
Car pulls to either side	· Wheels are out of alignment · Unequal tire pressure · Different size tires or wheels	· Have wheel alignment checked/adjusted · Check/adjust tire pressure · Change tires or wheels to same size
The car's wheel(s) wobbles	· Loose wheel lug nuts · Wheels out of balance · Damaged wheel · Wheels are out of alignment · Worn or damaged ball joint · Excessive play in the steering linkage (usually due to worn parts) · Defective shock absorber	· Tighten wheel lug nuts · Have tires balanced · Raise car and spin the wheel. If the wheel is bent, it should be replaced · Have wheel alignment checked/adjusted · Check ball joints · Check steering linkage · Check shock absorbers
Tires wear unevenly or prematurely	· Incorrect wheel size · Wheels are out of balance · Wheels are out of alignment	· Check if wheel and tire size are compatible · Have wheels balanced · Have wheel alignment checked/adjusted

Troubleshooting Basic Tire Problems

Problem	Cause	Solution
The car's front end vibrates at high speeds and the steering wheel shakes	· Wheels out of balance · Front end needs aligning	· Have wheels balanced · Have front end alignment checked
The car pulls to one side while cruising	· Unequal tire pressure (car will usually pull to the low side) · Mismatched tires · Front end needs aligning	· Check/adjust tire pressure · Be sure tires are of the same type and size · Have front end alignment checked
Abnormal, excessive or uneven tire wear See "How to Read Tire Wear"	· Infrequent tire rotation · Improper tire pressure · Sudden stops/starts or high speed on curves	· Rotate tires more frequently to equalize wear · Check/adjust pressure · Correct driving habits
Tire squeals	· Improper tire pressure · Front end needs aligning	· Check/adjust tire pressure · Have front end alignment checked

Tire Size Comparison Chart

"Letter" sizes			Inch Sizes	Metric-inch Sizes		
"60 Series"	"70 Series"	"78 Series"	1965–77	"60 Series"	"70 Series"	"80 Series"
			5.50-12, 5.60-12	165/60-12	165/70-12	155-12
		Y78-12	6.00-12			
		W78-13	5.20-13	165/60-13	145/70-13	135-13
		Y78-13	5.60-13	175/60-13	155/70-13	145-13
			6.15-13	185/60-13	165/70-13	155-13, P155/80-13
A60-13	A70-13	A78-13	6.40-13	195/60-13	175/70-13	165-13
B60-13	B70-13	B78-13	6.70-13	205/60-13	185/70-13	175-13
			6.90-13			
C60-13	C70-13	C78-13	7.00-13	215/60-13	195/70-13	185-13
D60-13	D70-13	D78-13	7.25-13			
E60-13	E70-13	E78-13	7.75-13			195-13
			5.20-14	165/60-14	145/70-14	135-14
			5.60-14	175/60-14	155/70-14	145-14
			5.90-14			
A60-14	A70-14	A78-14	6.15-14	185/60-14	165/70-14	155-14
	B70-14	B78-14	6.45-14	195/60-14	175/70-14	165-14
	C70-14	C78-14	6.95-14	205/60-14	185/70-14	175-14
D60-14	D70-14	D78-14				
E60-14	E70-14	E78-14	7.35-14	215/60-14	195/70-14	185-14
F60-14	F70-14	F78-14, F83-14	7.75-14	225/60-14	200/70-14	195-14
G60-14	G70-14	G77-14, G78-14	8.25-14	235/60-14	205/70-14	205-14
H60-14	H70-14	H78-14	8.55-14	245/60-14	215/70-14	215-14
J60-14	J70-14	J78-14	8.85-14	255/60-14	225/70-14	225-14
L60-14	L70-14		9.15-14	265/60-14	235/70-14	
	A70-15	A78-15	5.60-15	185/60-15	165/70-15	155-15
B60-15	B70-15	B78-15	6.35-15	195/60-15	175/70-15	165-15
C60-15	C70-15	C78-15	6.85-15	205/60-15	185/70-15	175-15
	D70-15	D78-15				
E60-15	E70-15	E78-15	7.35-15	215/60-15	195/70-15	185-15
F60-15	F70-15	F78-15	7.75-15	225/60-15	205/70-15	195-15
G60-15	G70-15	G78-15	8.15-15/8.25-15	235/60-15	215/70-15	205-15
H60-15	H70-15	H78-15	8.45-15/8.55-15	245/60-15	225/70-15	215-15
J60-15	J70-15	J78-15	8.85-15/8.90-15	255/60-15	235/70-15	225-15
	K70-15		9.00-15	265/60-15	245/70-15	230-15
L60-15	L70-15	L78-15, L84-15	9.15-15			235-15
	M70-15	M78-15				255-15
		N78-15				

NOTE: Every size tire is not listed and many size comaprisons are approximate, based on load ratings. Wider tires than those supplied new with the vehicle should always be checked for clearance

ELECTRONIC IGNITION 2-8
FIRING ORDERS 2-7
IDLE SPEED AND MIXTURE ADJUSTMENT 2-23
IGNITION TIMING 2-10
SPARK PLUGS 2-3
SPARK PLUG WIRES 2-5
SPECIFICATIONS CHARTS 2-2
TIMING 2-10
TUNE-UP
- Idle speed and mixture 2-23
- Ignition timing 2-10
- Procedures 2-2
- Spark plugs 2-3
- Spark plug wires 2-5
- Specifications 2-2
- Troubleshooting 2-29
- Valve lash adjustment 2-13

WIRING
- Spark plug 2-5

2

ENGINE PERFORMANCE AND TUNE-UP

Electronic Ignition 2-8
Firing Orders 2-7
Idle Speed and Mixture Adjustment 2-23
Ignition Timing 2-10
Tune-up Charts 2-2
Valve Lash Adjustment 2-13

TUNE-UP PROCEDURES

In order to extract the best performance and economy from your engine it is essential that it be properly tuned at regular intervals. A regular tune-up will keep your Toyota's engine running smoothly and will prevent the annoying minor breakdowns and poor performance associated with an untuned engine.

A complete tune-up should be performed every 15,000 miles (24,000 km) or twelve months, whichever comes first. This interval should be halved if the car is operated under severe conditions, such as trailer towing, prolonged idling, continual stop and start driving, or if starting or running problems are noticed. It is assumed that the routine maintenance described in Section 1 has been kept up, as this will have a decided effect on the results of a tune-up. All of the applicable steps of a tune-up should be followed in order, as the result is a cumulative one.

➡ If the specifications on the tune-up sticker in the engine compartment of your Toyota disagree with the "Tune-Up Specifications" chart in this section, the figures on the sticker must be used. The sticker often reflects changes made during the production run.

GASOLINE ENGINE TUNE-UP SPECIFICATIONS

Year	Engine ID/VIN	Engine Displacement liter (cc)	Spark Plugs Gap (in.)	Ignition Timing (deg.)		Fuel Pump (psi)	Idle Speed (rpm)		Valve Clearance	
				MT	AT		MT	AT	In.	Ex.
1983	2S-E	2.0 (1995)	0.043	5B	5B	28–36	700	700	Hyd.	Hyd.
1984	2S-E	2.0 (1995)	0.043	5B	5B	28–36	700	700	Hyd.	Hyd.
1985	2S-E	2.0 (1995)	0.043	5B	5B	33–38	700 ①	750 ①	Hyd.	Hyd.
1986	2S-E	2.0 (1995)	0.043	10B ②	10B ②	33–38	700 ①	750 ①	Hyd.	Hyd.
1987	3S-FE	2.0 (1998)	0.043	10B ③	10B ③	38–44	650 ④	650 ④	0.007–0.011	0.011–0.015
1988	3S-FE	2.0 (1998)	0.043	10B ③	10B ③	38–44	650 ④	650 ④	0.007–0.011	0.011–0.015
1989	3S-FE	2.0 (1998)	0.043	10B ⑤	10B ⑤	38–44	700 ④	700 ④	0.007–0.011	0.011–0.015
	2VZ-FE	2.5 (2507)	0.043	10B ⑤	10B ⑤	38–44	700 ④	700 ④	0.005–0.009	0.011–0.015
1990	3S-FE	2.0 (1998)	0.043	10B ⑤	10B ⑤	38–44	700 ④	700 ④	0.007–0.011	0.011–0.015
	2VZ-FE	2.5 (2507)	0.043	10B ⑤	10B ⑤	38–44	700 ④	700 ④	0.005–0.009	0.011–0.015
1991	3S-FE	2.0 (1998)	0.043	10B ⑤	10B ⑤	38–44	650 ④	650 ④	0.007–0.011	0.011–0.015
	2VZ-FE	2.5 (2507)	0.043	10B ⑤	10B ⑤	38–44	700 ④	700 ④	0.005–0.009	0.011–0.015
1992	5S-FE	2.2 (2164)	0.043	10B ⑤	10B ⑤	38–44	750 ④	750 ④	0.007–0.011	0.011–0.015
	3VZ-FE	3.0 (2959)	0.043	10B ⑤	10B ⑤	38–44	700 ④	700 ④	0.005–0.009	0.011–0.015

① Cooling fan off, trans. in neutral, vacuum advance off
② @ idle, check connector terminals T and E_1 connected
③ Check connector terminals T and E_1 connected
④ ± 50 rpm
⑤ Check connector terminals TE and E_1 connected

DIESEL ENGINE TUNE-UP SPECIFICATIONS

Year	Engine ID/VIN	Engine Displacement liter (cc)	Valve Clearance Intake (in.)	Valve Clearance Exhaust (in.)	Intake Valve Opens (deg.)	Injection Pump Setting (deg.)	Injection Nozzle Pressure (psi) New	Injection Nozzle Pressure (psi) Used	Idle Speed (rpm)	Cranking Compression Pressure (psi)
1984	1C-T	1.8 (1839)	0.008–0.012	0.010–0.014	11B	25–30B	2062–2205	1920–2205	750	427①
1985	1C-T	1.8 (1839)	0.008–0.012	0.010–0.014	11B	25–30B	2062–2205	1920–2205	750	427①
1986	2C-T	2.0 (1974)	0.008–0.012	0.010–0.014	11B	25–30B	2062–2205	1920–2205	750	427①

① Minimum: 356. Difference between each cylinder should be no less than 71 psi

Spark Plugs

Spark plugs ignite the air and fuel mixture in the cylinder as the piston reaches the top of the compression stroke. The controlled explosion that results forces the piston down, turning the crankshaft and the rest of the drive train.

The average life of a spark plug is 15,000 miles (24,000 km), although manufacturers are now claiming spark plug lives of up to 60,000 miles (96,000 km) or more with the new platinum tipped plugs; in fact, your car may be equipped with just such plugs. This is, however, dependent on a number of factors: the mechanical condition of the engine; the type of fuel; the driving conditions; and the driver.

When you remove the spark plugs, check their condition. They are a good indicator of the condition of the engine. It is a good idea to remove the spark plugs every 7500 miles (12,000 km) or so to keep an eye on the mechanical state of the engine.

A small deposit of light tan or gray material (or rust red with unleaded fuel) on a spark plug that has been used for any period of time is to be considered normal. Any other color, or abnormal amounts of deposit, indicates that there is something amiss in the engine.

The gap between the center electrode and the side or ground electrode can be expected to increase not more than 0.025mm every 1,000 miles (1600 km) under normal conditions.

When a spark plug is functioning normally or, more accurately, when the plug is installed in an engine that is functioning properly, the plugs can be taken out, cleaned, regapped, and reinstalled in the engine without doing the engine any harm.

When, and if, a plug fouls and begins to misfire, you will have to investigate, correct the cause of the fouling, and either clean or replace the plug.

There are several reasons why a spark plug will foul and you can learn which is at fault by just looking at the plug.

There are many spark plugs suitable for use in your Toyota's engine and are offered in a number of different heat ranges. The amount of heat which the plug absorbs is determined by the length of the lower insulator. The longer the insulator the hotter the plug will operate; the shorter the insulator, the cooler it will operate. A spark plug that absorbs (or retains) little heat and remains too cool will accumulate deposits of lead, oil, and carbon, because it is not hot enough to burn them off. This leads to fouling and consequent misfiring. A spark plug that absorbs too much heat will have no deposits, but the electrodes will burn away quickly and, in some cases, pre-ignition may result. Pre-ignition occurs when the spark plug tips get so hot that they ignite the air/fuel mixture before the actual spark fires. This premature ignition will usually cause a pinging sound under conditions of low speed and heavy load. In severe cases, the heat may become high enough to start the air/fuel mixture burning throughout the combustion chamber rather than just to the front of the plug. In this case, the resultant explosion will be strong enough to damage pistons, rings, and valves.

In most cases the factory recommended heat range is correct; it is chosen to perform well under a wide range of operating conditions. However, if most of your driving is long distance, high speed travel, you may want to install a spark plug one step colder than standard. If most of your driving is of the short trip variety, when the engine may not always reach operating temperature, a hotter plug may help burn off the deposits normally accumulated under those conditions.

REMOVAL

SEE FIGS. 1-4

1. Number the wires so that you won't cross them when you replace them.
2. Remove the wire from the end of the spark lug by grasping the wire by the rubber boot. If the boot sticks to the plug, remove it by twisting and pulling at the same time. Do not pull wire itself or you will damage the core.

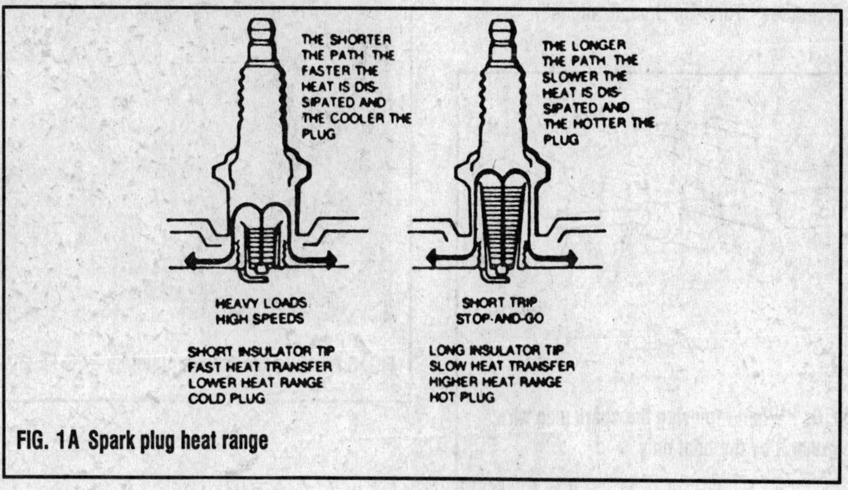

FIG. 1A Spark plug heat range

3. Use a 16mm spark plug socket to loosen all of the plugs about two turns.

➡ **The cylinder head is cast from aluminum. Remove the spark plugs when the engine is cold, if possible, to prevent damage to the threads. If removal of the plugs is difficult, apply a few drops of penetrating oil or silicone spray to the area around the base of the plug, and allow it a few minutes to work.**

4. If compressed air is available, apply it to the area around the spark plug holes. Otherwise, use a rag or a brush to clean the area. Be careful not to allow nay foreign material to drop into the spark plug holes.

5. Remove the plugs by unscrewing them the rest of the way from the engine.

INSPECTION

♦ SEE FIGS. 5-7

Check the plugs for deposits and wear (see the "Spark Plug Diagnosis" chart). If they are not going to be replaced, clean the plugs thoroughly. Remember that nay kind of deposit will decrease the efficiency of the plug. Plugs can be cleaned on a spark plug cleaning machine, which can sometimes be found in service stations, or you can do an acceptable job of cleaning with a stiff brush. If the plugs are cleaned, the electrodes must be filed flat. Use an ignition points file, not an emery board or the like, which will leave deposits. The electrodes must be filed perfectly flat with sharp edges; rounded edges reduce the spark plug voltage by as much as 50%.

Check spark plug gap before installation. The ground electrode (the L-shaped one connected to the body of the plug) must be parallel to the center electrode and the specified size wire gauge (see "Tune-Up Specifications").

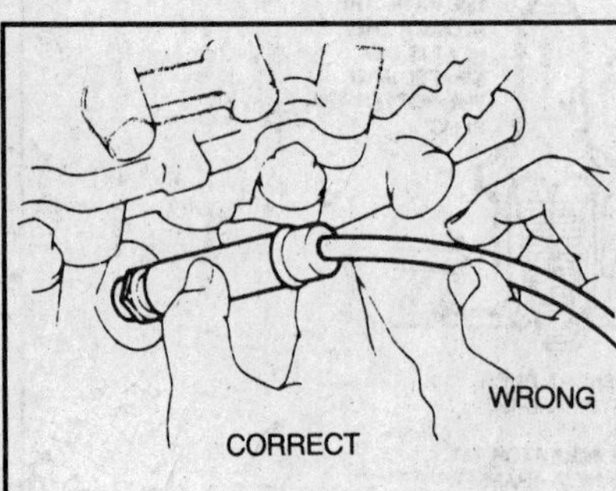

FIG. 1 When removing the spark plug wire, grasp it by the boot only

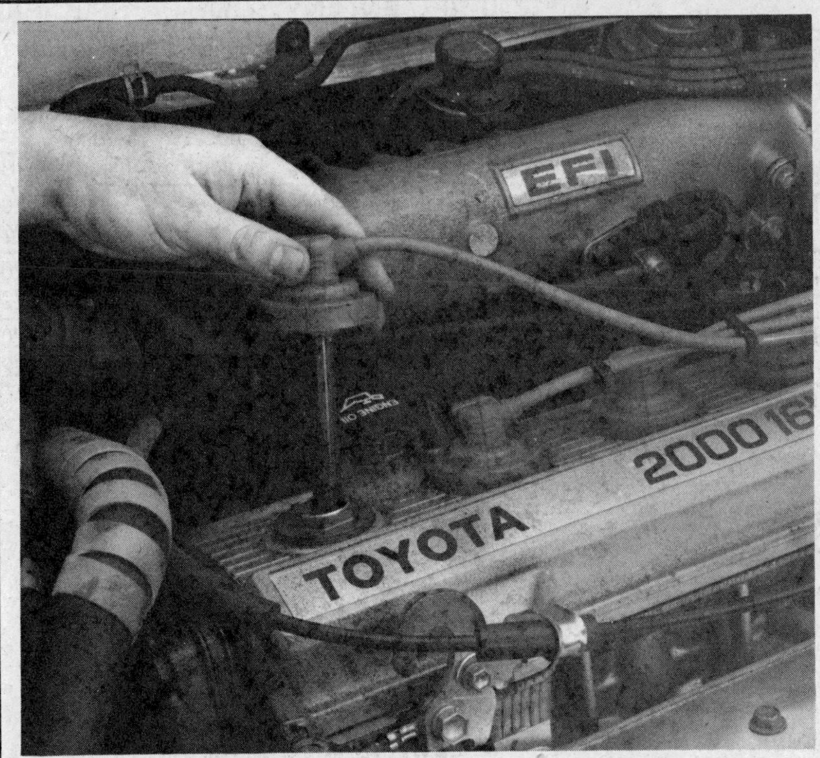

FIG. 2 Removing the spark plug tube on a 3S-FE engine

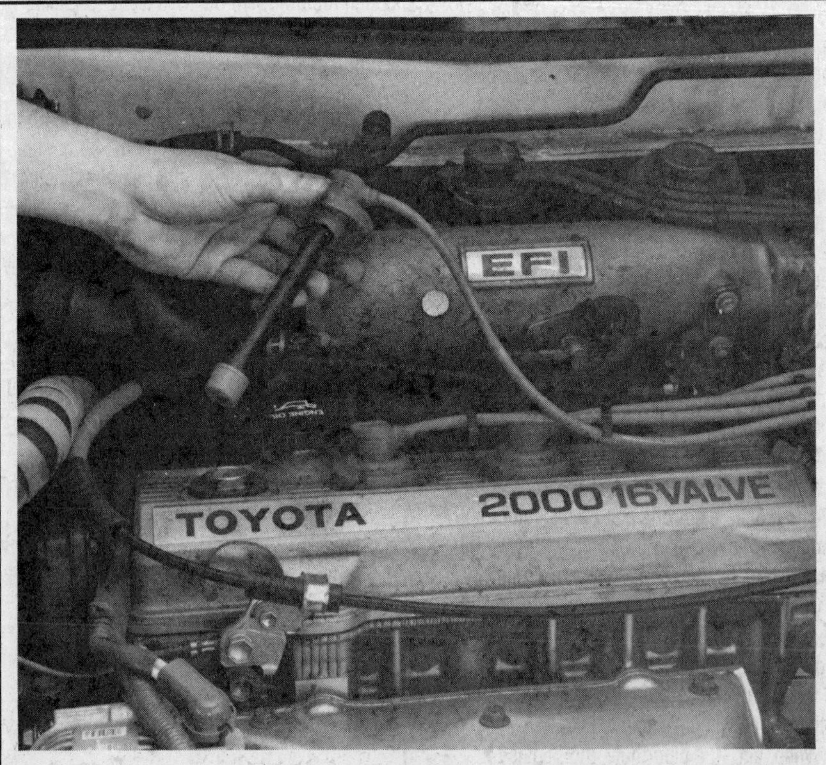

FIG. 3 Remove the tube completely—3S-FE engines

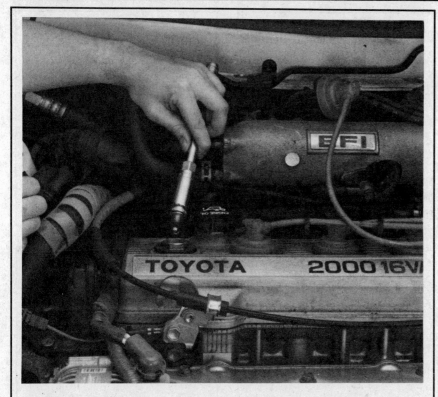

FIG. 4 Use the proper ratchet and extension to get to the spark plug – 3S-FE engines

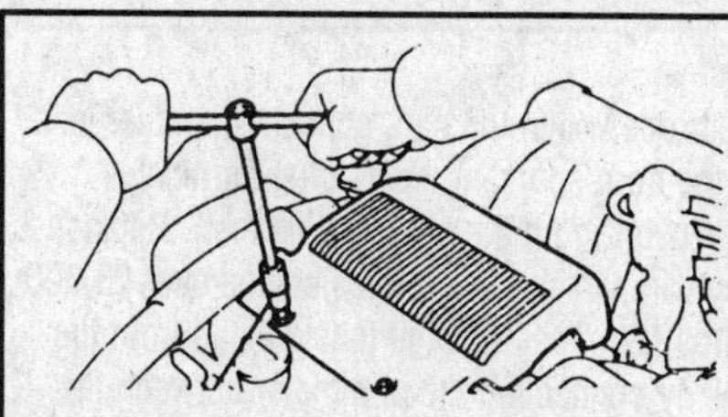

FIG. 4A Remove the V-bank cover to get at the plug wires – 3VZ-FE engines

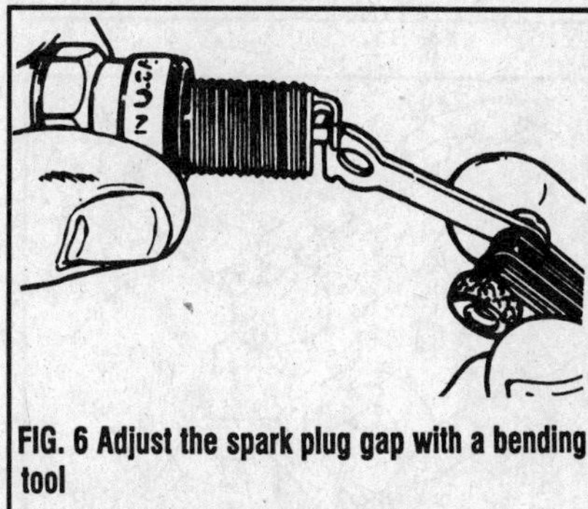

FIG. 6 Adjust the spark plug gap with a bending tool

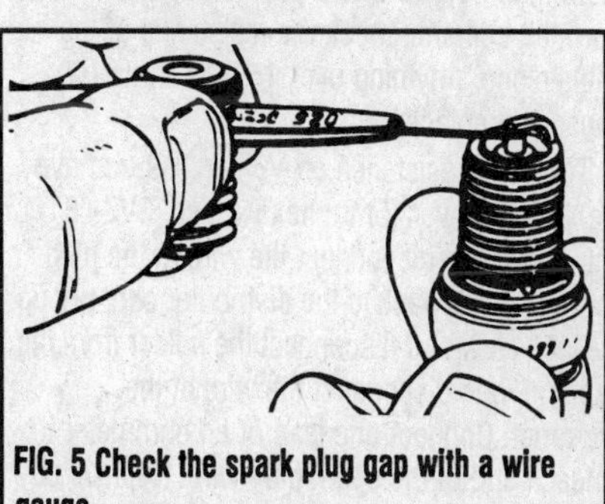

FIG. 5 Check the spark plug gap with a wire gauge

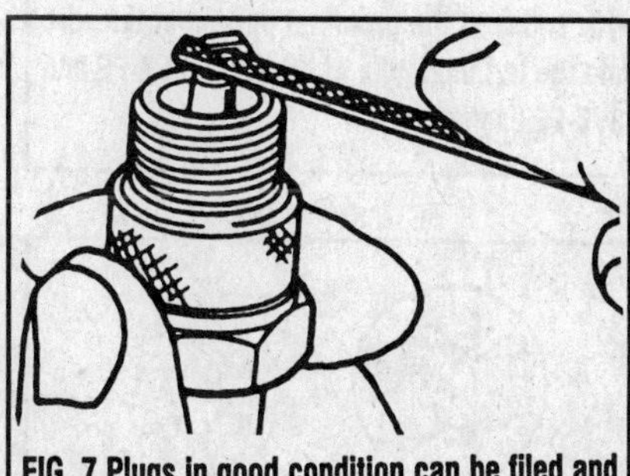

FIG. 7 Plugs in good condition can be filed and reused

WARNING

NEVER adjust the gap on a used platinum tipped spark plug!

Always check the gap on new plugs, too; they are not always set correctly at the factory. Do not use a flat feeler gauge when measuring the gap, because the reading will be inaccurate. Wire gapping tools usually have a bending tool attached. Use that to adjust the side electrode until the proper distance is obtained. Absolutely never bend the center electrode. Also, be careful not to bend the side electrode too far or too often; it may weaken and break off within the engine, requiring removal of the cylinder head to retrieve it.

INSTALLATION

1. Lubricate the threads of the spark plugs with a drop of oil. Install the plugs and tighten them hand tight. Take care not to cross-thread them.
2. Tighten the spark plugs with the socket. Do not apply the same amount of force you would use for a bolt; just snug them in. If a torque wrench is available, tighten to 11–15 ft. lbs. (16–20 Nm)
3. Install the wires on their respective plugs. Make sure the wires are firmly connected. You will be able to feel them click into place.

Spark Plug Wires

CHECKING AND REPLACEMENT

➧ SEE FIG. 4, 9-17

At every tune-up, visually inspect the spark plug cables for burns cuts, or breaks in the insulation. Check the boots and the nipples on the distributor cap and coil. Replace any damaged wiring.

Every 36,000 miles (58,000 km) or so, the resistance of the wires should be checked with an ohmmeter. Wires with excessive resistance will cause misfiring, and may make the engine difficult to start in damp weather. Generally, the useful life of the cables is 36,000–50,000 miles (58,000–80,000 km).

To check resistance on 4 cyl. engines, remove the distributor cap, leaving the wires attached. Connect one lead of an ohmmeter to an

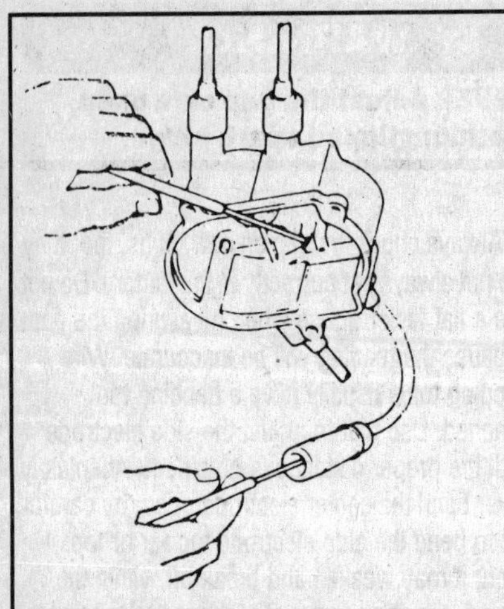
FIG. 9 Checking the resistance of the spark plug wires with the distributor cap removed—2S-E engines

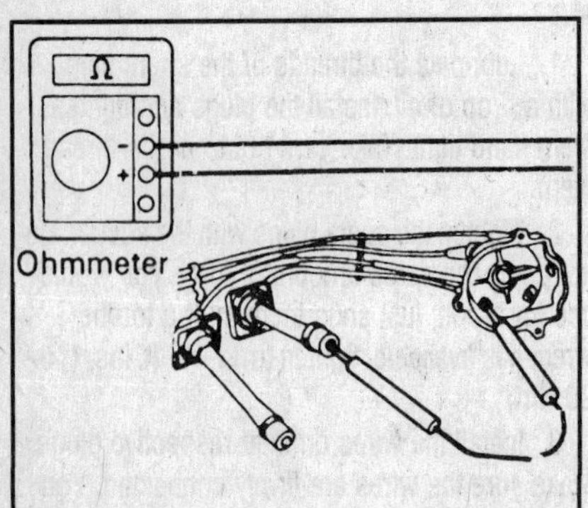

FIG. 10 Checking the resistance of the spark plug wires—3S-FE and 5S-FE engines

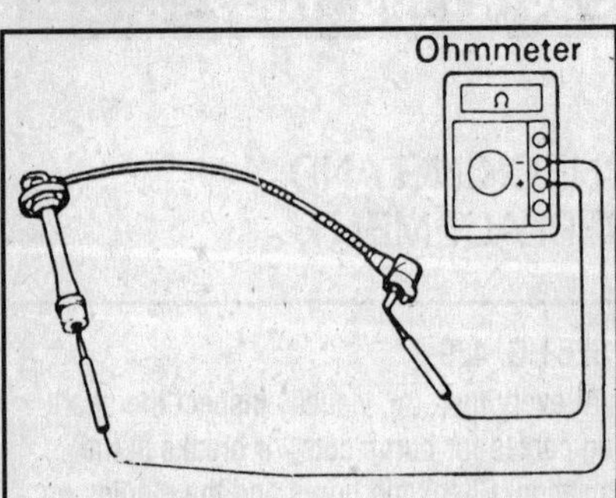

FIG. 11 Checking the resistance of the spark plug wires—2VZ-FE and 3VZ-FE engines

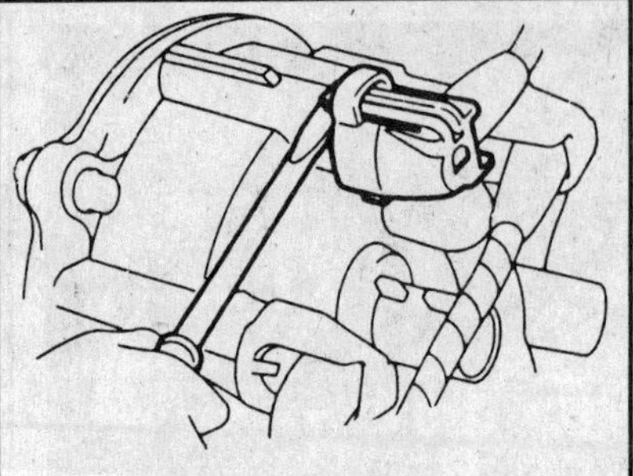
FIG. 12 Lift up the lock claw and disconnect the holder from the cap—2VZ-FE and 3VZ-FE engines

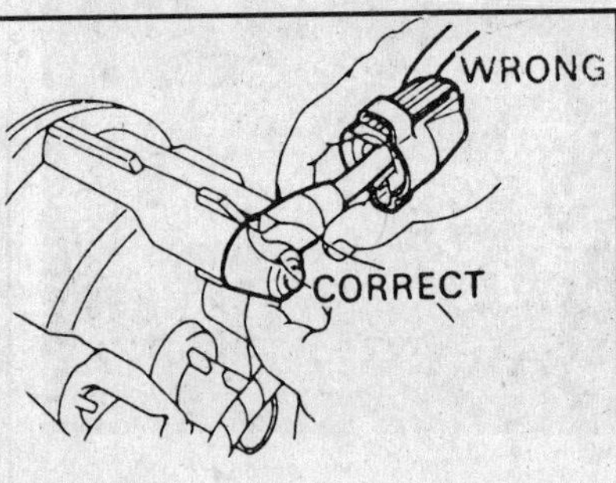

FIG. 13 Disconnect the spark plug wire from the cap at the grommet—2VZ-FE and 3VZ-FE engines

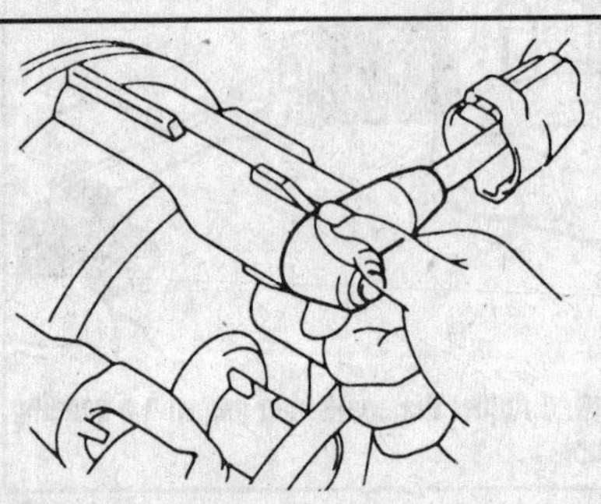
FIG. 14 Insert the grommet portion of the wire into the terminal hole of the cap—2VZ-FE and 3VZ-FE engines

FIG. 15 Align the two splines and slide the holder onto the cap—2VZ-FE and 3VZ-FE engines

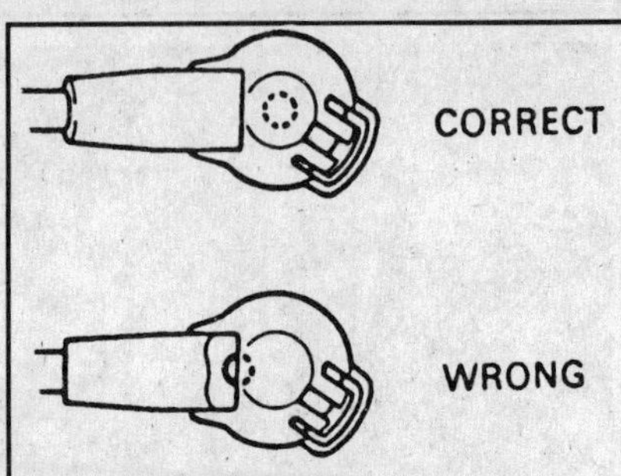

FIG. 16 Always check that the holder is correctly installed to the grommet and cap—2VZ-FE and 3VZ-FE engines

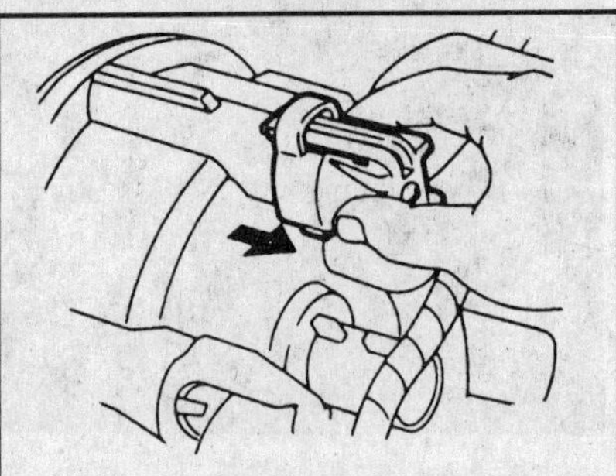
FIG. 17 Pull lightly on the holder to check that the lock claw is engaged—2VZ-FE and 3VZ-FE engines

electrode within the cap; connect the other lead to the corresponding spark plug terminal (remove it from the plug for this test). Replace any wire which shows a resistance over 25,000 ohms (Ω). Test the high tension lead from the coil by connecting the ohmmeter between the center contact in the distributor cap and either of the primary terminals of the coil (remember, on the 3S-FE, the coil is in the cap!). If resistance is more than 25,000 ohms (Ω), remove the cable from the coil and check the resistance of the cable alone. Anything over 15,000 ohms (Ω) is cause for replacement.

To check resistance on V6 engines, remove the V-bank cover (5mm hex wrench, 3VZ-FE only) and then disconnect the wire at the plug. Trace the wire back to the distributor cap, pry up the lock claw and disconnect the holder from the cap and then disconnect the wire at the grommet. Connect one lead of an ohmmeter to an each end of the spark plug wire. Replace any wire which shows a resistance over 25,000 ohms (Ω). Test the high tension lead from the coil by connecting the ohmmeter between the center contact in the distributor cap and either of the primary terminals of the coil. If resistance is more than 25,000 ohms (Ω), remove the cable from the coil and check the resistance of the cable alone. Anything over 15,000 ohms (Ω) is cause for replacement.

It should be remembered that resistance is also a function of length; the longer the cable, the greater the resistance. Thus, if the cables on your car are longer than the factory originals, resistance will be higher, quite possibly outside these limits.

When installing new cables, always replace them one at a time to avoid mixups. Start by replacing the longest one first. Install the boot firmly over the spark plug. Route the wire over the same path as the original. Insert the nipple firmly into the tower on the cap or the coil. On the V6, insert the grommet portion into the terminal hole of the cap, align the spline on the cap with that on the holder and slide the holder onto the terminal. Make sure that the lock claw is properly engaged by giving it a slight tug.

FIRING ORDERS

To avoid confusion, always replace the spark plug wires one at a time.

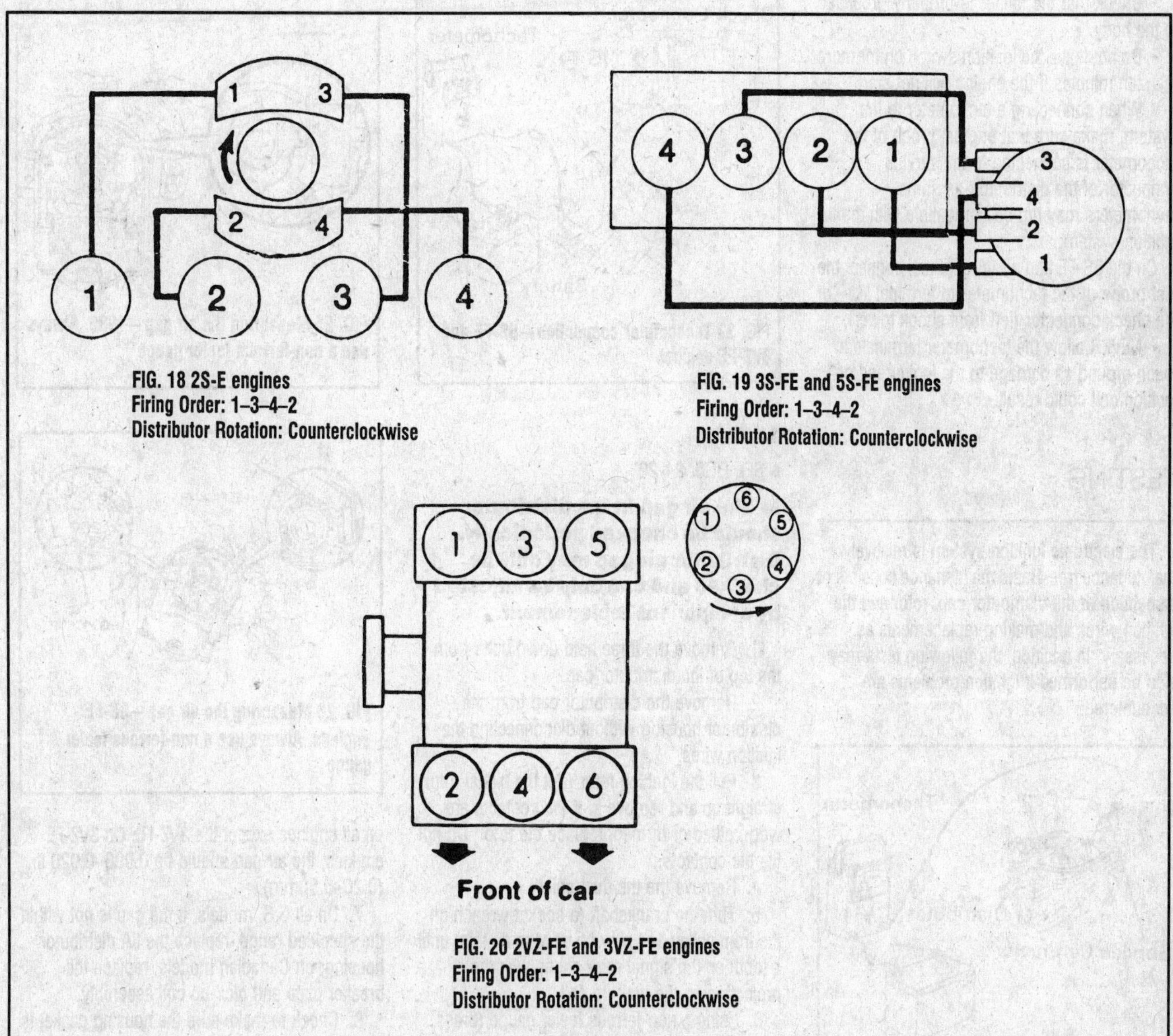

FIG. 18 2S-E engines
Firing Order: 1–3–4–2
Distributor Rotation: Counterclockwise

FIG. 19 3S-FE and 5S-FE engines
Firing Order: 1–3–4–2
Distributor Rotation: Counterclockwise

FIG. 20 2VZ-FE and 3VZ-FE engines
Firing Order: 1–3–4–2
Distributor Rotation: Counterclockwise

Electronic Ignition

The Integrated Ignition Assembly (IIA) system or the Electronic Spark Advance (ESA) system is used on all Camrys with gasoline engines. Diesel engines do not require the use of ignition systems.

PRECAUTIONS

➧ SEE FIGS. 21-23

- Do not disconnect the battery while the engine is running.
- Check that the igniter is properly grounded to the body.
- Do not leave the ignition switch on for more than ten minutes if the engine will not start.
- When connecting a tachometer to the system, make sure that the test probe of the tachometer is connected to the service connector of the distributor, as some tachometers may not be compatible with the IIA ignition system.

On the 5S-FE and all V6 engines, connect the test probe of the tachometer to terminal **IG–** of the check connector (left front shock tower).

- NEVER allow the tachometer terminals to touch ground as damage to the igniter and/or ignition coil could result.

TESTING

The electronic ignition system is relatively maintenance free. Basic maintenance consists of inspection of the distributor cap, rotor and the ignition wires and making replacements as necessary. In addition, the following tests may also be performed if ignition problems are encountered.

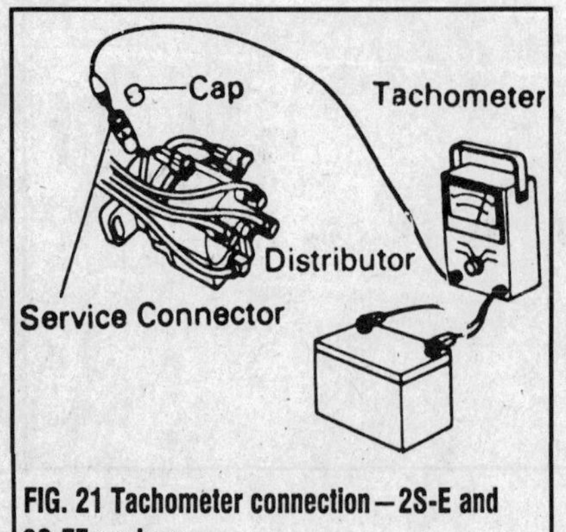

FIG. 21 Tachometer connection—2S-E and 3S-FE engines

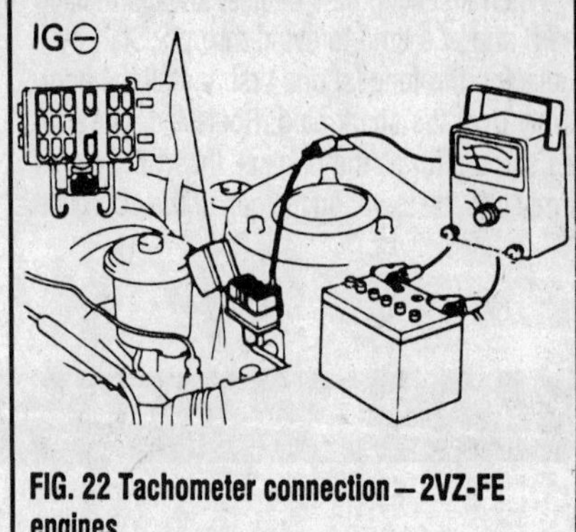

FIG. 22 Tachometer connection—2VZ-FE engines

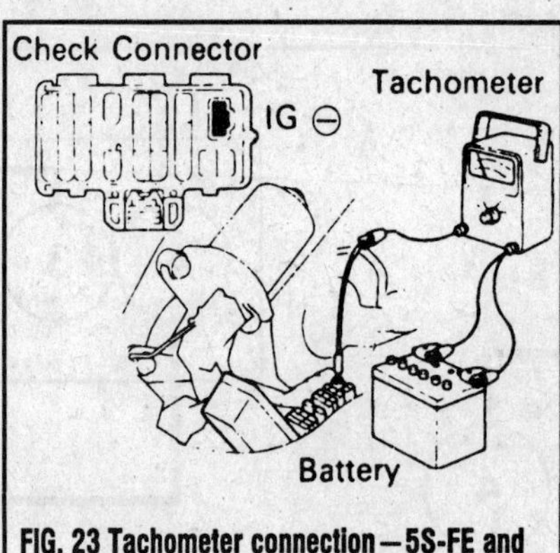
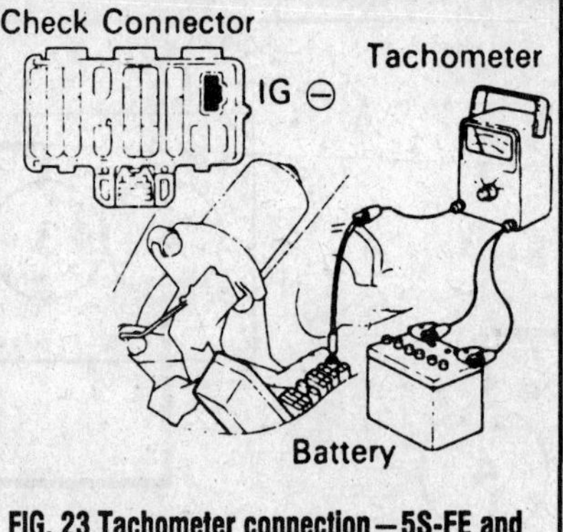

FIG. 23 Tachometer connection—5S-FE and 3VZ-FE engines

Air Gap

➧ SEE FIGS. 24-29

➡ **The air gap in the distributor should be checked periodically. Distributor air gap may only be checked and can only be adjusted by component replacement.**

1. Remove the three hold down bolts from the top of the distributor cap.
2. Remove the distributor cap from the distributor housing without disconnecting the ignition wires.
3. Pull the ignition rotor (not the signal rotor) straight up and remove it. If the contacts are worn, pitted or burned, replace the rotor. Do not file the contacts.
4. Remove the the dust shield.
5. Turn the crankshaft (a socket wrench on the front pulley bolt may be used to do this) until a tooth on the signal rotor aligns with the projection on the pick-up coil.
6. Using a non-ferrous feeler gauge (brass, copper, or plastic) measure the gap between the signal rotor and the pick-up coil projection. DO NOT USE AN ORDINARY METAL FEELER GAUGE! The gauge should just touch either side of the gap (snug fit). The acceptable range for the air gap is 0.008–0.016 in. (0.20-0.40mm) on all engines except the 3VZ-FE. On 3VZ-FE engines, the air gap should be 0.008–0.020 in. (0.20–0.50mm).
7. On all U.S. models, if the gap is not within the specified range, replace the IIA distributor housing; on Canadian models, replace the breaker plate and pick-up coil assembly.
8. Check to make sure the housing gasket is properly positioned on the housing.
9. Install the rotor and dust shield.
10. Install the distributor cap with attached wiring. Attach the cap to the housing with the holddown bolts.

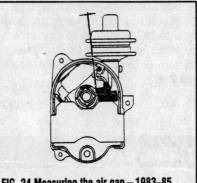

FIG. 24 Measuring the air gap—1983–85. Always use a non-ferrous feeler gauge

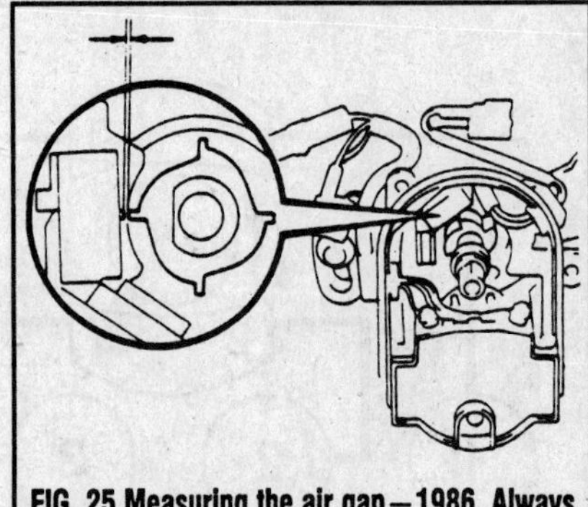

FIG. 25 Measuring the air gap—1986. Always use a non-ferrous feeler gauge

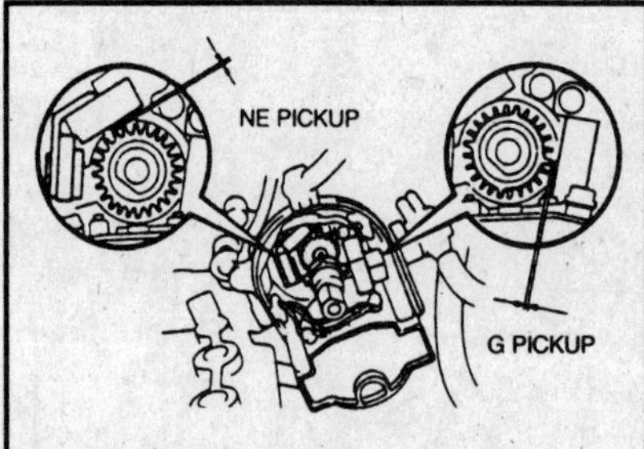

FIG. 26 Measuring the air gap—3S-FE engines. Always use a non-ferrous feeler gauge

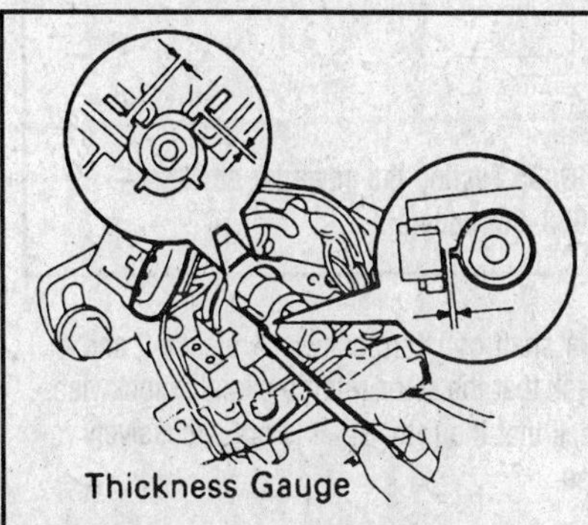

FIG. 27 Measuring the air gap—2VZ-FE engines. Always use a non-ferrous feeler gauge

Thickness Gauge

FIG. 28 Measuring the air gap—5S-FE engines. Always use a non-ferrous feeler gauge

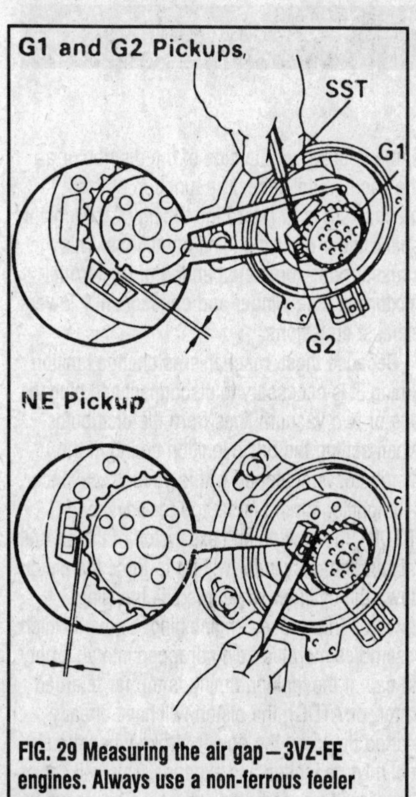

FIG. 29 Measuring the air gap—3VZ-FE engines. Always use a non-ferrous feeler gauge

Signal Generator (Pick-Up Coil) Resistance

3S-FE ENGINES

➧ SEE FIG. 30

Using a suitable ohmmeter, measure the resistance between the following terminals:

- For **G** pick-up coil resistance: terminals **G** and **G–**. Resistance should be: 1987–90: 140–180Ω, 1991: 205–255Ω.
- For **NE** pick-up coil resistance: terminals **NE** and **G–**. Resistance should be: 1987–90: 140–180Ω, 1991: 205–255Ω.

If the resistance is not as specified, replace the distributor housing assembly.

5S-FE ENGINES

➧ SEE FIG. 31

Using a suitable ohmmeter, measure the resistance between the following terminals:

- For **G** pick-up coil resistance: terminals **G**+ and **G–**. Resistance should be 185–265Ω (cold).
- For **NE** pick-up coil resistance: terminals **NE**+ and **NE–**. Resistance should be 370–530Ω (cold).

If the resistance is not as specified, replace the distributor housing assembly.

2VZ-FE ENGINES

➧ SEE FIG. 32

Using a suitable ohmmeter, measure the resistance between the following terminals:

- For **G1** pick-up coil resistance: terminals **G1** and **G–**. Resistance should be 140–180Ω.
- For **G2** pick-up coil resistance: terminals **G2** and **G–**. Resistance should be 140–180Ω.
- For **NE** pick-up coil resistance: terminals **NE** and **G–**. Resistance should be 140–180Ω.

If the resistance is not as specified, replace the distributor housing assembly.

3VZ-FE ENGINES

➧ SEE FIG. 33

Using a suitable ohmmeter, measure the resistance between the following terminals:

- For **G1** pick-up coil resistance: terminals **G1** and **G–**. Resistance should be 125–190Ω (cold).
- For **G2** pick-up coil resistance: terminals **G2** and **G–**. Resistance should be 125–190Ω (cold).

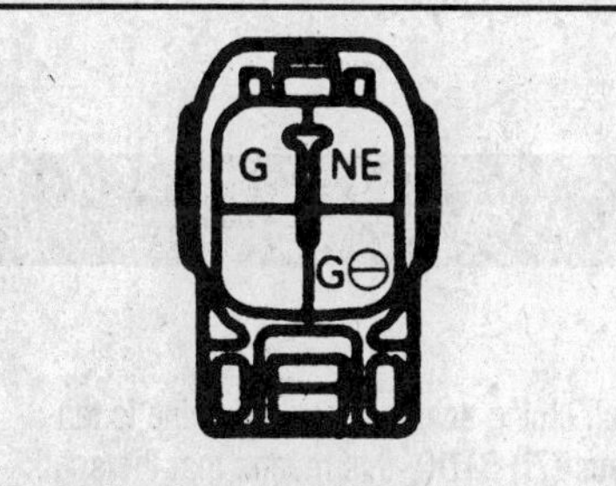

FIG. 30 Signal generator (pick-up coil) resistance test—3S-FE engines

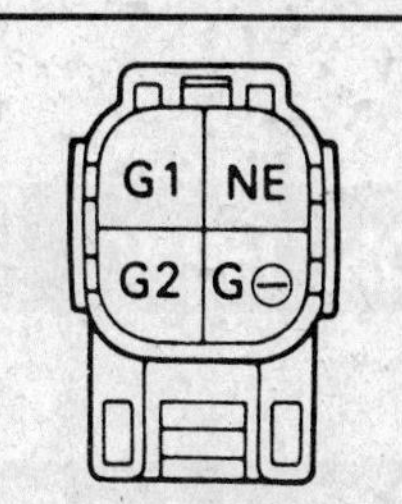

FIG. 32 Signal generator (pick-up coil) resistance test—2VZ-FE engines

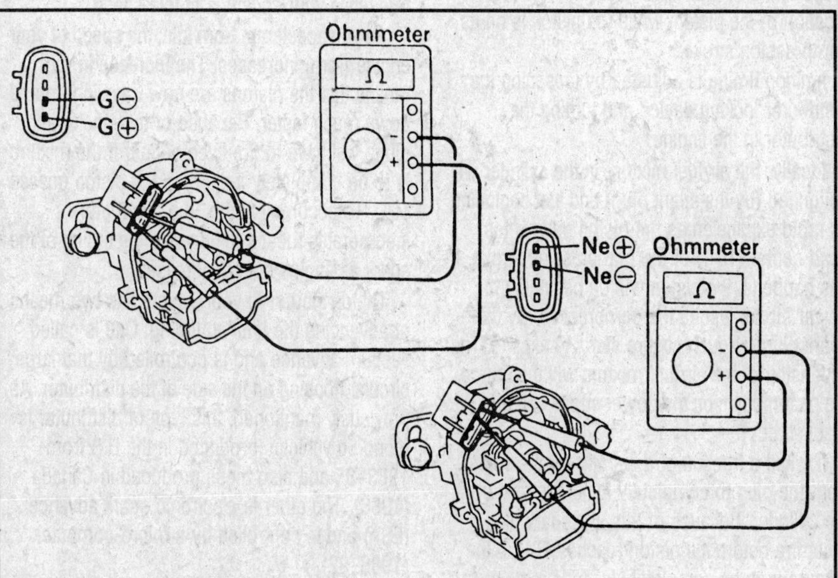

FIG. 31 Signal generator (pick-up coil) resistance test—5S-FE engines

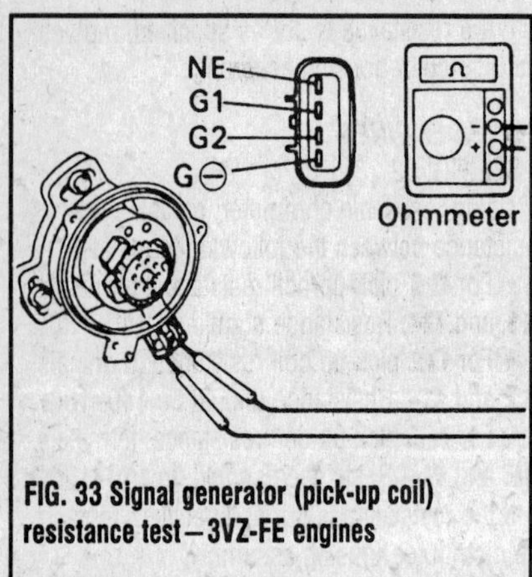

FIG. 33 Signal generator (pick-up coil) resistance test – 3VZ-FE engines

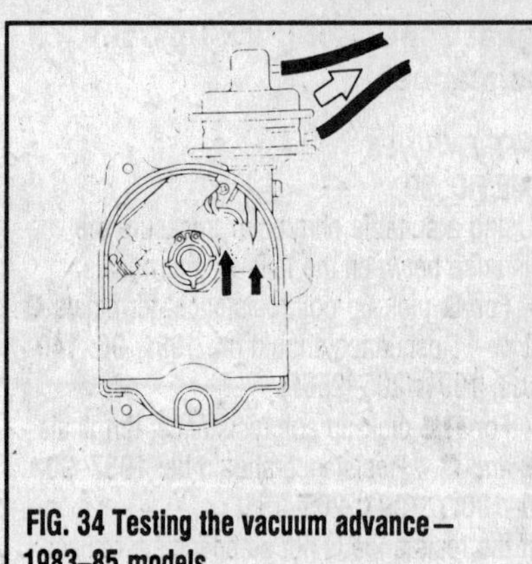
FIG. 34 Testing the vacuum advance – 1983–85 models

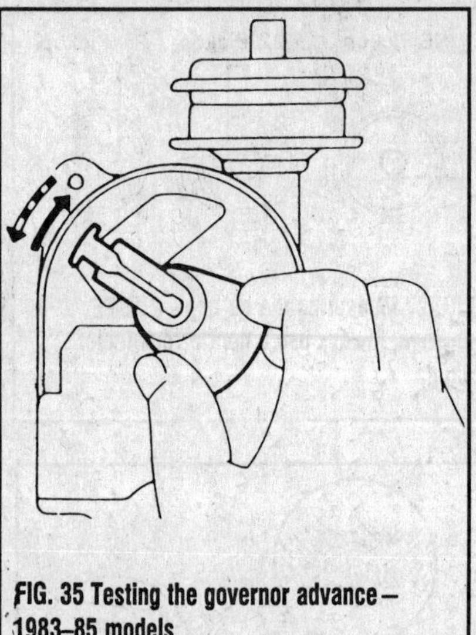
FIG. 35 Testing the governor advance – 1983–85 models

• For **NE** pick-up coil resistance: terminals **NE** and **G–**. Resistance should be 155–240Ω (cold).

If the resistance is not as specified, replace the distributor housing assembly.

Vacuum Advance

1983-85 AND CANADA MODELS ONLY

➧ SEE FIG. 34

Inspect the vacuum advance by disconnecting the vacuum hose and connecting a vacuum pump to the diaphragms. Apply a vacuum and check that the vacuum advance moves freely. If the advance unit does not respond to the vacuum, replace it.

Governor Advance

1983-85 AND CANADA MODELS ONLY

➧ SEE FIG. 35

Inspect the governor advance by turning the rotor shaft counterclockwise, release it and check that the rotor returns slightly clockwise. Check that the rotor shaft is not excessively loose.

IGNITION TIMING

Gasoline Engines Only

Ignition timing is the measurement in degrees of crankshaft rotation of the instant the spark plugs in the cylinders fire, in relation to the location of the piston, while the piston is on its compression stroke.

Ignition timing is adjusted by loosening the distributor locking device and turning the distributor in the engine.

Ideally, the air/fuel mixture in the cylinder will be ignited (by the spark plug) and just beginning its rapid expansion as the piston passes top dead center (TDC) of the compression stroke. If this happens, the piston will be beginning the power stroke just as the compressed (by the spark plug) air/fuel mixture starts to expand. The expansion of the air/fuel mixture will then force the piston down on the power stroke and turn the crankshaft.

It takes a fraction of a second for the spark from the plug to completely ignite the mixture in the cylinder. Because of this, the spark plug must fire before the piston reaches TDC, if the mixture is to be completely ignited as the piston passes TDC. This measurement is given in degrees (of top dead center (BTDC). If the ignition timing setting for your engine is ten degrees (7°) BTDC, this means that the spark plug must fire at a time when the piston for that cylinder is 10° before top dead center of the compression stroke. However, this only holds true while your engine is at idle speed.

As you accelerate from idle, the speed of your engine (rpm) increases. The increase in rpm means that the pistons are now traveling up and down much faster. Because of this, the spark plugs will have to fire even sooner if the mixture is to be completely ignited as the piston passes TDC. To accomplish this, the distributor incorporates means to advance the timing of the spark as engine speed increases.

The distributor in your Toyota has two means of advancing the ignition timing. One is called vacuum advance and is controlled by that large circular housing on the side of the distributor. As previously mentioned, this type of distributor is found on vehicles produced in the U.S from 1983–85 and also those produced in Canada (1986). The other is electronic spark advance (ESA) and is controlled by a micro-computer (1986–92).

In addition, some distributors have a vacuum-retard mechanism which is contained in the same housing on the side of the distributor as the vacuum advance. The function of this mechanism is to retard the timing of the ignition spark under certain engine conditions. This causes more complete burning of the air/fuel mixture in the cylinder and consequently lowers exhaust emissions.

Because these mechanisms change ignition timing, it is necessary to disconnect and plug the one or two vacuum lines from the distributor when setting the basic ignition timing, if the distributor is equipped with a vacuum advancer.

If ignition timing is set too far advanced (BTDC), the ignition and expansion of the air/fuel mixture in the cylinder will try to force the piston down the cylinder while it is still traveling upward. This causes engine ping, a sound which resembles marbles being dropped into an empty tin can. If the ignition timing is too far retarded (after, or ATDC), the piston will have already started down on the power stroke when the air/fuel mixture ignites and expands. This will cause the piston to be forced down only a portion of its travel and will result in poor engine performance and lack of power.

Ignition timing adjustment is checked with a tachometer and a timing light.

➡ **All engines require the use of a special tachometer that can be connected to the IIA service connector coming out of the distributor or the check connector (see Electronic Ignition System Precautions). Many tachometers are not compatible with this configuration, so consult with the manufacturer before purchasing a tachometer.**

The tachometer test probe is connected to the distributor service connector or the check connector.

The timing light is connected to the number one (No. 1) spark plug of the engine. The timing light flashes every time an electrical current is sent from the distributor, through the No.1 spark plug wire, to the spark plug. The crankshaft pulley and the front cover of the engine are marked with a timing pointer and a timing scale. When the timing pointer is aligned with the **O** mark on the timing scale, the piston in No. 1 cylinder is at TDC of its compression stroke. With the engine running, and the timing light aimed at the timing pointer and timing scale, the stroboscopic flashes from the timing light will allow you to check the ignition timing setting of the engine. The timing light flashes every time the spark plug in the No. 1 cylinder of the engine fires. Since the flash from the timing light makes the crankshaft pulley seem stationary for a moment, you will be able to read the exact position of the piston in the No. 1 cylinder on the timing scale on the front of the front of the engine.

There are three basic types of timing lights available. The first is a simple neon bulb with two wire connections (one for the spark plug and one for the plug wire, connecting the light in series). This type of light is quite dim, and must be held closely to the marks to be seen, but it is inexpensive. The second type of light operates from the battery. Two alligator clips connect to the battery terminals, while a third wire connects to the spark plug with an adapter. This type of light is more expensive, but the xenon bulb provides a nice bright flash which can even be seen in sunlight. The third type replaces the battery source with 110 volt house current. Some timing lights have other functions built into them, such as dwell meters, tachometers, or remote starting switches. These are convenient, in that they reduce the tangle of wires under the hood, but may duplicate the functions of tools you already have.

Use a timing light with an inductive pickup. This pickup simply clamps onto the No. 1 plug wire, eliminating the adapter. It is not susceptible to crossfiring or false triggering, which may occur with a conventional light, due to the greater voltages produced by electronic ignition.

CHECKING AND ADJUSTMENT

1983-85 and Canada

➧ SEE FIGS. 21, 36-37

1. Warm up the engine, apply the parking brake and block the wheels. Stop the engine when warm.
2. Locate the IIA service connector coming from the distributor and remove the rubber protective cap.

➡ **All engines require the use of a special tachometer that is connected to the service connector. Many tachometers are not compatible with this hook-up, so we recommend that you consult with the manufacturer before purchasing a certain type.**

3. Connect the test probe of the tachometer to the service connector. Check the idle speed with the tachometer and make sure that it is correct. Adjust as necessary.
4. Connect a timing light to the engine according to the manufacturer's instructions. If the timing marks are difficult to see, use chalk or a dab of paint to make them more visible.
5. Disconnect the two vacuum lines from the distributor vacuum advance and plug the lines.
6. Start and run the engine at idle with the transaxle in Neutral on manual transaxles, or Park on automatic transaxles. Make sure the parking brake is securely set and the wheels are blocked.
7. Point the timing light at the timing marks. With the engine at idle, the timing mark on the crankshaft pulley should be aligned with the degree mark specified in the tune-up chart at the beginning of this section, or according to the values listed on the underhood emission control sticker.
8. If the timing is not as specified, loosen the pinch bolt at the base of the distributor and move the distributor to advance or retard the timing as required.
9. Stop the engine and tighten the pinch bolt. Start the engine and recheck the timing and the idle speed.
10. Stop the engine and disconnect the timing light and the tachometer. Install the rubber cap on the service connector.
11. Reconnect the vacuum lines to the distributor advance unit.

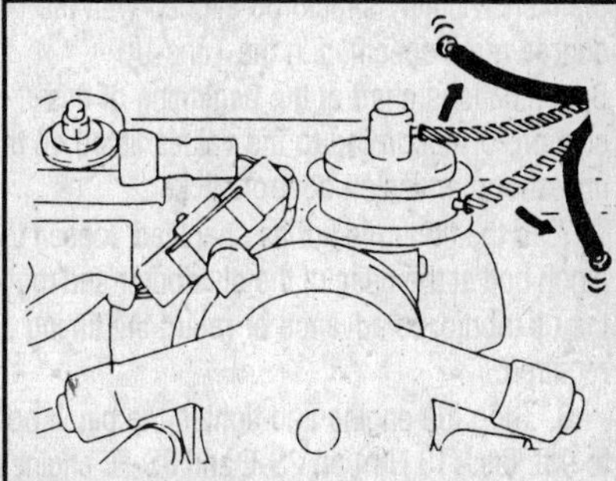

FIG. 36 On distributors equipped with a vacuum advance, disconnect and plug the vacuum lines before adjusting the timing

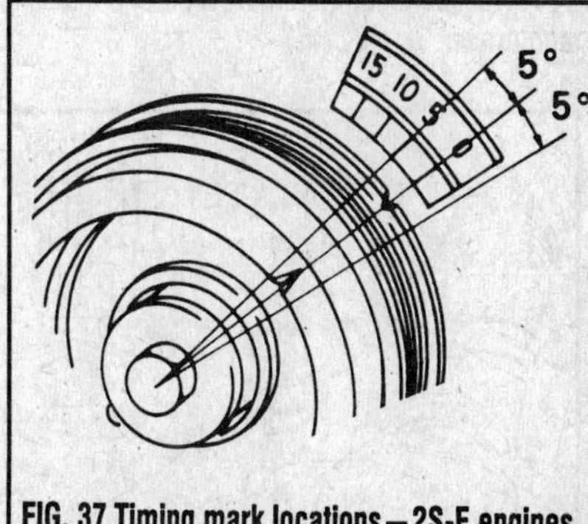

FIG. 37 Timing mark locations — 2S-E engines

1986-92

➧ SEE FIGS. 22, 23, 38-45

1. Connect a timing light to the engine following the manufacturer's instructions.

➡ **The 2S-E and 3S-FE engines require a special type of tachometer which hooks up to the service connector wire coming out of the distributor. The 5S-FE, 2VZ-FE and 3VZ-FE engines require that the tach connects to the check connector. As many tachometers are not compatible with this hookup, we recommend that you consult with the manufacturer before purchasing a certain type.**

3. Start and run the engine at idle with the transaxle in Neutral on manual transaxles, or Park on automatic transaxles. Make sure the parking brake is securely set and the wheels are blocked.
4. Check the idle speed and adjust as required.
5. Open the lid on the check connector (a grey or black box attached to the front, left shock tower) and short the connector at terminals **T** and $\mathbf{E_1}$ (1986–88) or $\mathbf{TE_1}$ and $\mathbf{E_1}$ (1989–92).
6. Point the timing light at the timing marks. With the engine at idle, the timing mark on the

crankshaft pulley should be aligned with the degree mark specified in the Tune-Up Specifications chart at the beginning of this section, or according to the values listed on the underhood emission control sticker.

7. If the timing is not as specified, loosen the pinch bolt at the base of the distributor and move the distributor to advance or retard the timing as required.

8. Stop the engine and tighten the pinch bolt to 9 ft. lbs. (13 Nm) on 2S-E and 3S-FE engines, 14 ft. lbs. (19 Nm) on 5S-FE engines, or 13 ft. lbs. (18 Nm) on 2VZ-FE and 3VZ-FE engines. Start the engine and recheck the timing and the idle speed.

9. Unshort the connector and close the lid.

10. Disconnect the timing light and the tachometer.

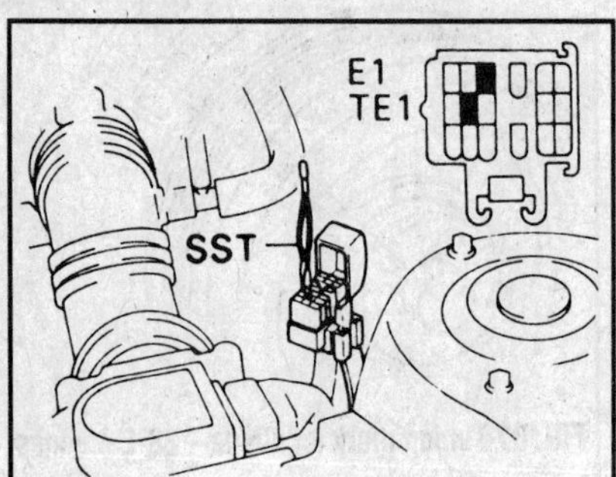

FIG. 38 Short the check connector before checking the ignition timing—3S-FE and 2VZ-FE engines

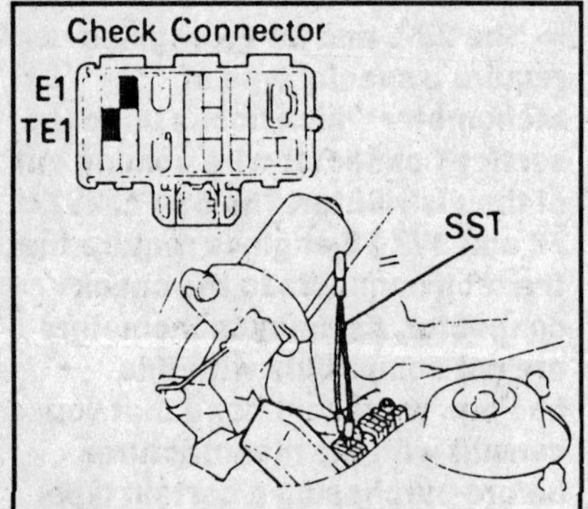

FIG. 39 Short the check connector before checking the ignition timing—5S-FE and 3VZ-FE engines

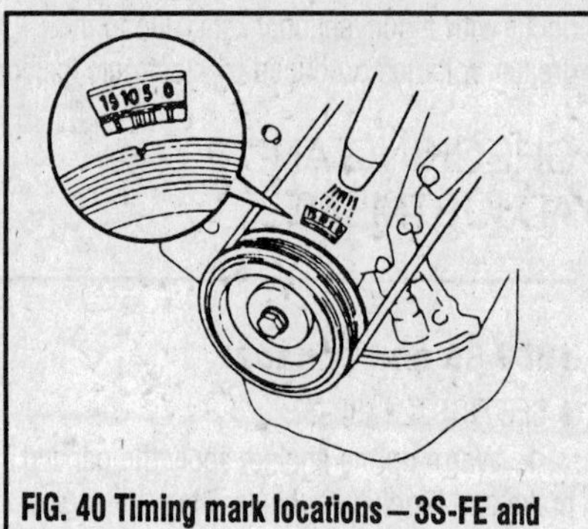
FIG. 40 Timing mark locations—3S-FE and 5S-FE engines

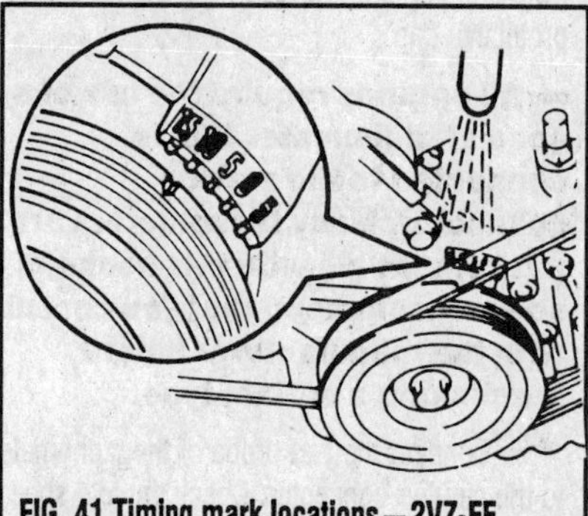
FIG. 41 Timing mark locations—2VZ-FE engines

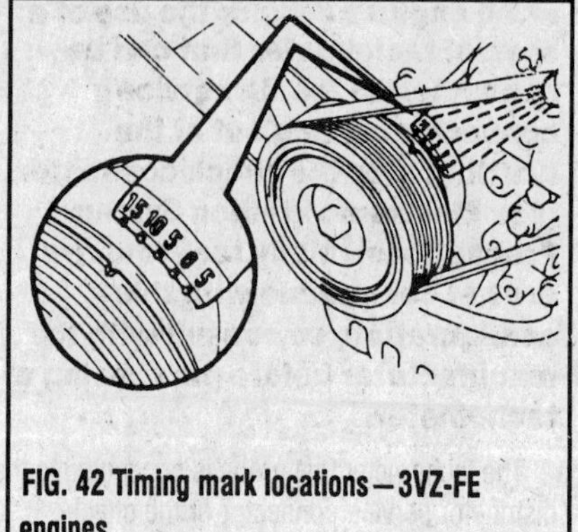
FIG. 42 Timing mark locations—3VZ-FE engines

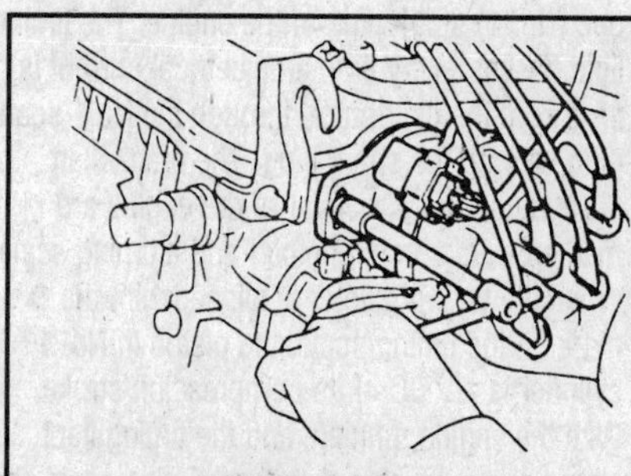
FIG. 43 To adjust the timing, loosen the pinch bolt(s) and rotate the distributor

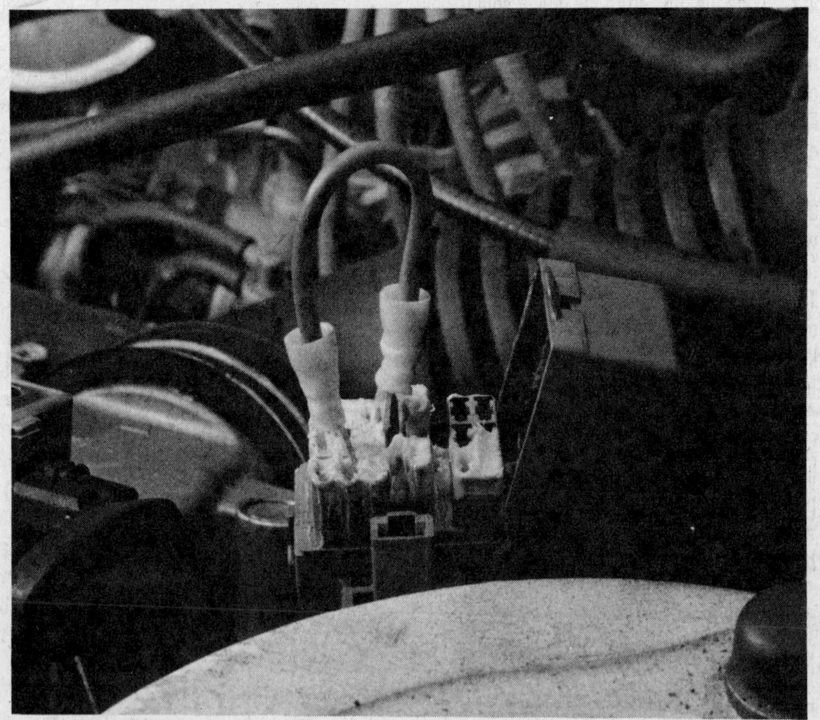
FIG. 45 The check connector is attached to the left, front shock tower

VALVE LASH

As part of every major tune-up or once every 15,000 miles (24,000 km) the valve clearance should be checked and adjusted if necessary.

Valve lash is one factor which determines how far the intake and exhaust valves will open into the cylinder.

If the valve clearance is too large, part of the lift of the camshaft will be used up in removing the excessive clearance, thus the valves will not be opened far enough. This condition has two effects, the valve train components will emit a tapping noise as they take up the excessive clearance, and the engine will perform poorly, since the less the intake valves open, the smaller the amount of air/fuel mixture admitted to the cylinders will be. The less the exhaust valves open, the greater the back-pressure in the cylinder which prevents the proper air/fuel mixture from entering the cylinder.

If the valve clearance is too small, the intake and exhaust valves will not fully seat on the cylinder head when they close. When a valve seats on the cylinder head it does two things; it seals the combustion chamber so none of the gases in the cylinder can escape and it cools itself by transferring some of the heat it absorbed from the combustion process through the cylinder head and into the engine cooling system. Therefore, if the valve clearance is too small, the engine will run poorly (due to gases escaping from the combustion chamber), and the valves will overheat and warp (since they cannot transfer heat unless they are touching the seat in the cylinder head).

➡ Although Toyota recommends that the valve lash on certain models be set while the engine is running, we feel that for the average owner/mechanic it is more convenient to adjust the valves statically (engine off). Thus, running valve lash and adjustment procedures have been omitted from the manual. While all valve adjustments must be as accurate as possible, it is better to have the valve adjustment slightly loose than slightly tight, as burnt valves may result from overly tight adjustments.

ADJUSTMENTS

2S-E Engines

These engines are equipped with hydraulic valve adjusters in the valve train. The adjusters automatically maintain a zero valve clearance between the rocker arm and valve stem and no periodic adjustment is possible or necessary. The best way to maintain hydraulic lash adjusters is through regular and frequent oil and filter changes.

1C-T and 2C-T Engines

➧ SEE FIGS. 46-50

➡ Adjust the valve clearance when the engine is cold.

1. Remove the cylinder head cover and gasket by removing the six seal nuts and washers.
2. With a socket wrench, turn the crankshaft pulley until the notch in the pulley aligns with the timing pointer on the front cover. The engine will now be at TDC No. 1 cylinder. The lifters on No. 1 cylinder should both be loose, and both those on No. 4 should be tight. If not, turn the crankshaft one complete revolution (360°) and then realign the marks.
3. Using a flat feeler gauge measure the gap between the lifter and the camshaft lobe on each valve of the No. 1 cylinder. Then, check each valve shown in the illustration. If the clearance is not within specifications, note what it is and write it down on a piece of paper. The readings will be used later to determine the proper adjustment shims.
4. Turn the crankshaft 360°, in the direction of normal rotation, and align the pointer and notch. Measure the clearance on the valves marked in the illustration.
5. If all the valve measurements were within specifications, you need go no further. If not, record the measurements on a piece of paper and proceed to Step 7 to begin the valve adjustment procedure.
6. Turn the crankshaft so that the intake lobe of the camshaft on any cylinder in need of adjustment, is pointing straight up. Both valves on that cylinder may now be adjusted.
7. Using a small screwdriver, turn the lifter so that the notch is easily accessible.
8. Install SST No. 09248-64010 (a depressor) between the two lobes and turn the handle so that the tool presses down both lifters evenly.
9. Using a small screwdriver and a finger magnet, remove the shims.

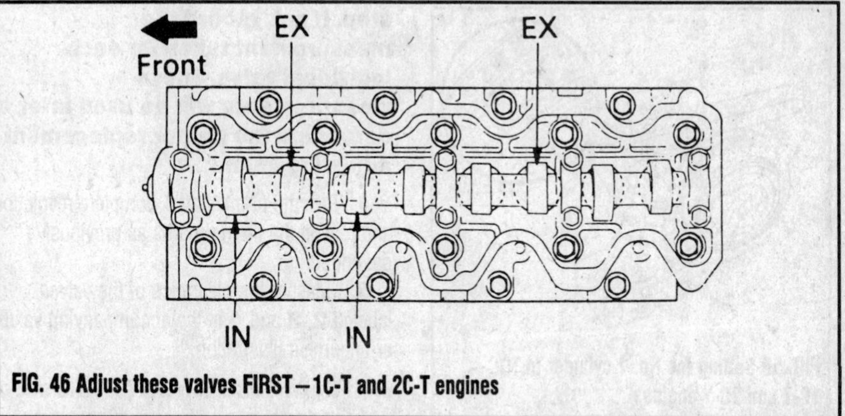

FIG. 46 Adjust these valves FIRST—1C-T and 2C-T engines

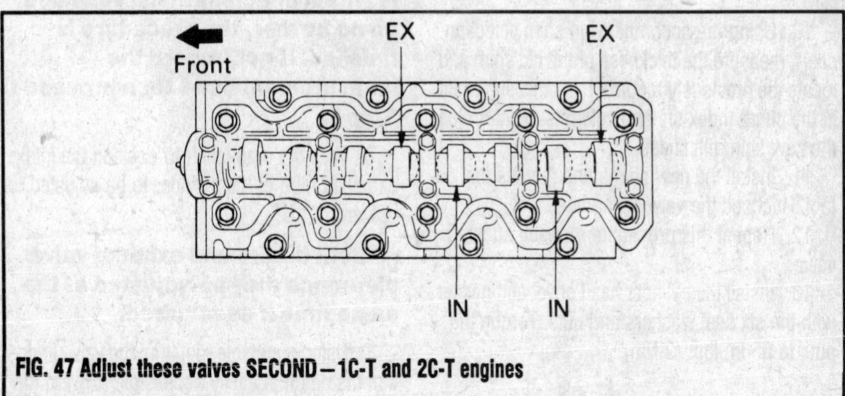

FIG. 47 Adjust these valves SECOND—1C-T and 2C-T engines

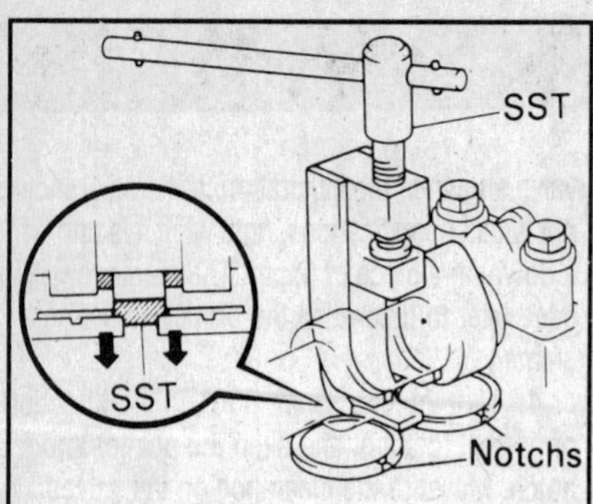

FIG. 48 Service tool installation—1C-T and 2C-T engines

Intake side:
New shim thickness
= T + [A − 0.25 mm (0.010 in.)]

Exhaust side:
New shim thickness
= T + [A − 0.30 mm (0.012 in.)]

FIG. 49 Shim selection formula—1C-T and 2C-T engines

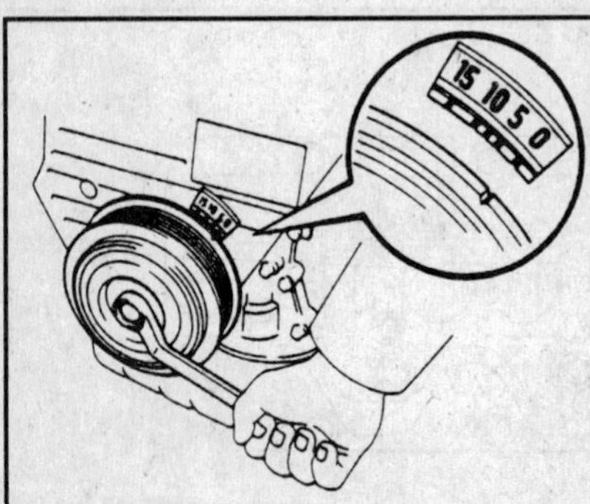

FIG. 50 Setting the No. 1 cylinder to TDC—1C-T and 2C-T engines

10. Using the accompanying shim selection chart, measure the thickness of the old shim and locate the previously recorded gap measurement in the chart. Index the two columns to determine the new shim thickness.
11. Install the new shims and remove the tool. Recheck the valve clearance.
12. Repeat this procedure for each affected valve.
13. Install the cylinder head cover and gasket with the six seal washers and nuts. Torque the nuts to 65 in. lbs. (9 Nm).

3S-E and 5S-FE Engines

SEE FIGS. 51-64

➡ Adjust valve clearance when the engine is cold.

1. Remove the cylinder head cover by removing the four nuts, grommets and gasket. Note the position of the grommets before removing them. Keep the grommets in order so that they may be reinstalled in their original positions. This will minimize the possibility of oil leakage when the cover is reinstalled.
2. Use a wrench and turn the crankshaft until the notch in the pulley aligns with the timing mark **0** of the No. 1 timing belt cover. This will insure that engine is at TDC.

➡ Check that the valve lifters on the No. 1 cylinder are loose and those on No. 4 cylinder are tight. If not, turn the crankshaft 1 complete revolution (360°) and then realign the marks.

3. Using a feeler gauge measure the clearance between the camshaft lobe and the valve lifter. This measurement should correspond to specification. Check only the valves labeled **1**, **2** and **3** in the accompanying valve arrangement illustration.

➡ If the measurement is within specifications, go on to the next step. If not, record the measurement taken for each individual valve. These measurements will be used later to determine the proper replacement adjusting shim.

4. Turn the crankshaft 1 complete revolution and realign the timing marks as previously described.
5. Measure the clearance of the valves labeled **2**, **3** and **4** in the accompanying valve arrangement illustration.

➡ If the measurement for this set of valves (and also the previous one) is within specifications, you need go no further, the procedure is finished. If not, record the measurements and then proceed to Step 6.

6. Turn the crankshaft to position the intake camshaft lobe of the cylinder to be adjusted, upward.

➡ Both intake and exhaust valve clearance may be adjusted at the same time if so required.

7. Using a suitable tool, turn the valve lifter so that the notch is easily accessible (toward the spark plug).

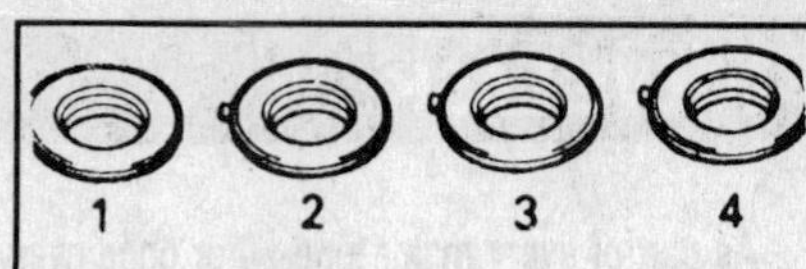

FIG. 51 Arrange the grommets in correct order to ease installation—3S-FE and 5S-FE engines

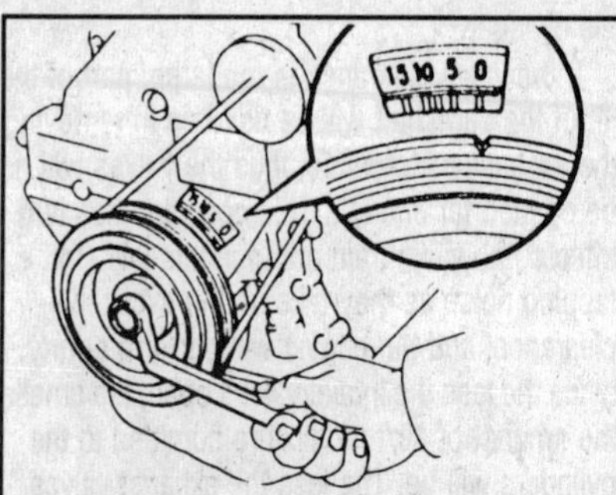

FIG. 52 Setting the No. 1 cylinder to TDC—3S-FE and 5S-FE engines

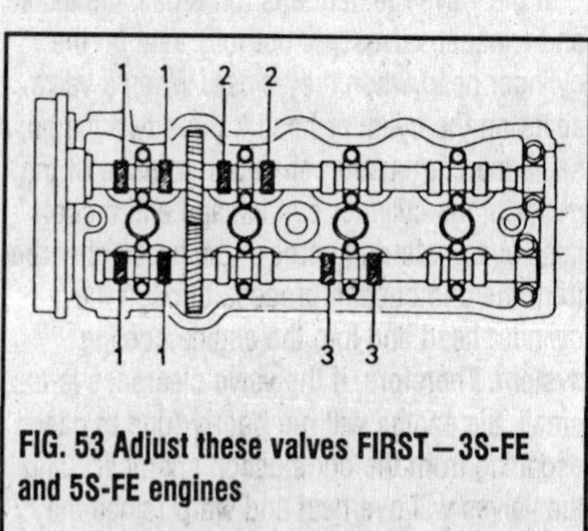

FIG. 53 Adjust these valves FIRST—3S-FE and 5S-FE engines

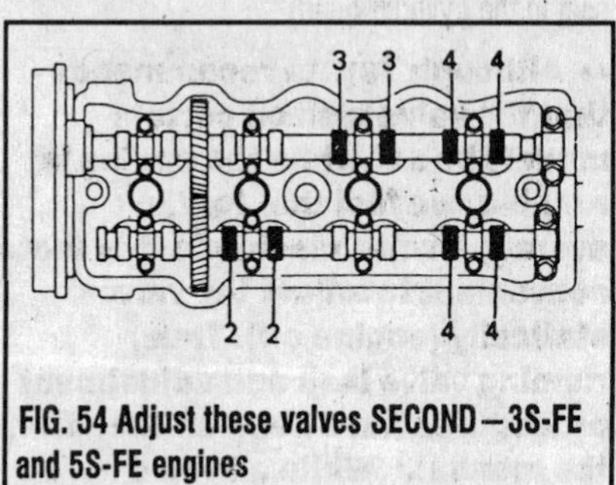

FIG. 54 Adjust these valves SECOND—3S-FE and 5S-FE engines

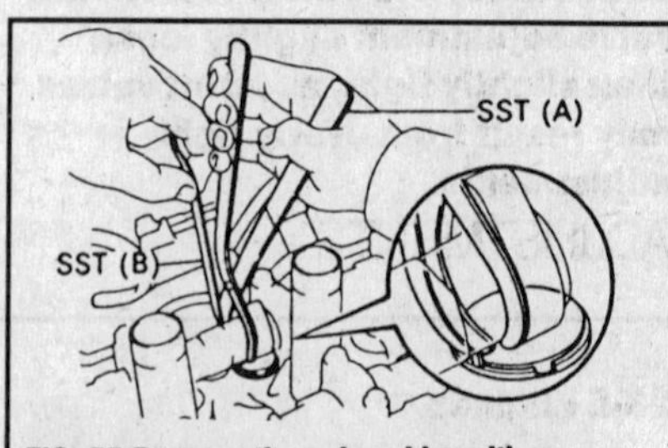

FIG. 55 Remove the valve shim with a depressing tool—3S-FE and 5S-FE engines

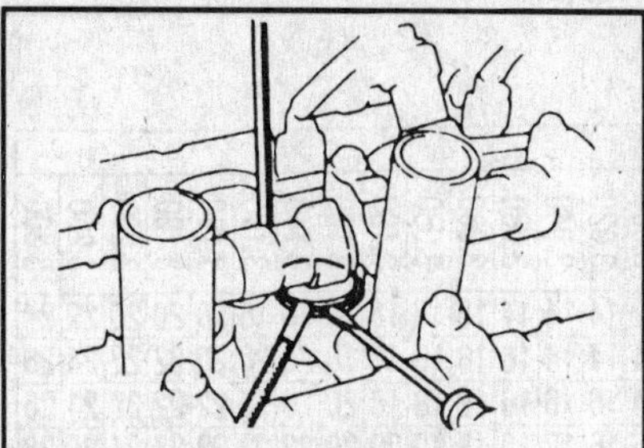
FIG. 56 Remove the shim with a magnet—3S-FE and 5S-FE engines

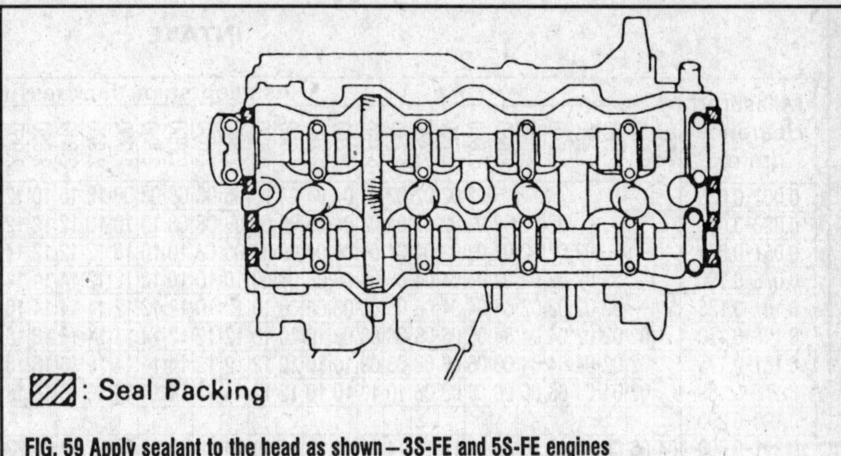

FIG. 59 Apply sealant to the head as shown—3S-FE and 5S-FE engines

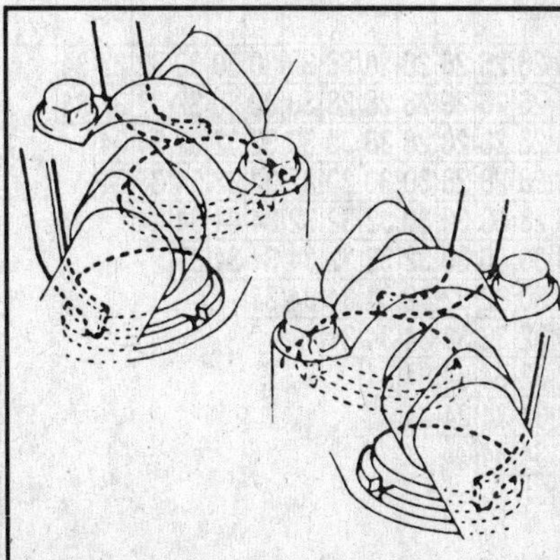
FIG. 57 Position the tool on the lifter so that there is enough space to remove the shim—3S-FE and 5S-FE engines

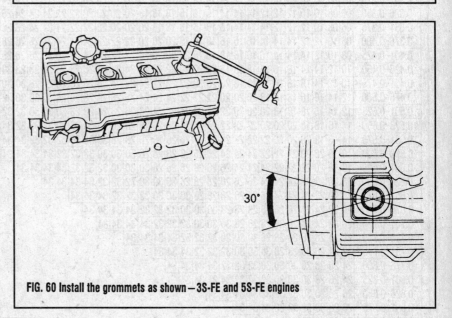

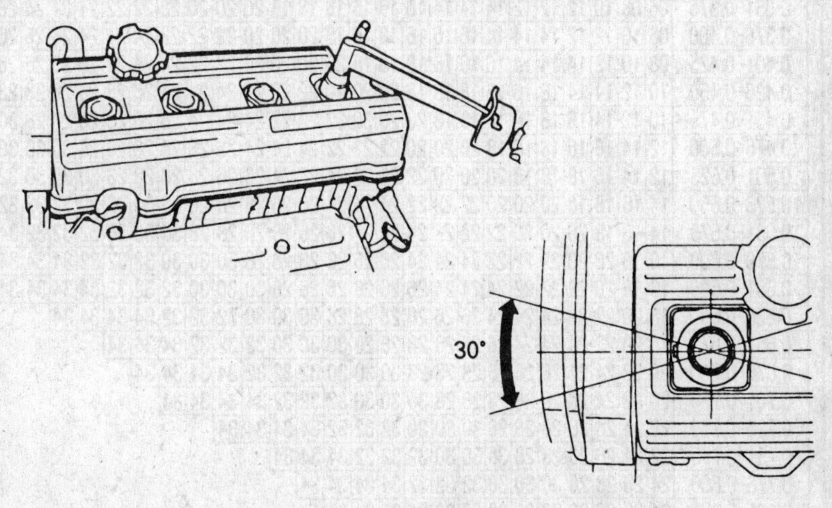

FIG. 60 Install the grommets as shown—3S-FE and 5S-FE engines

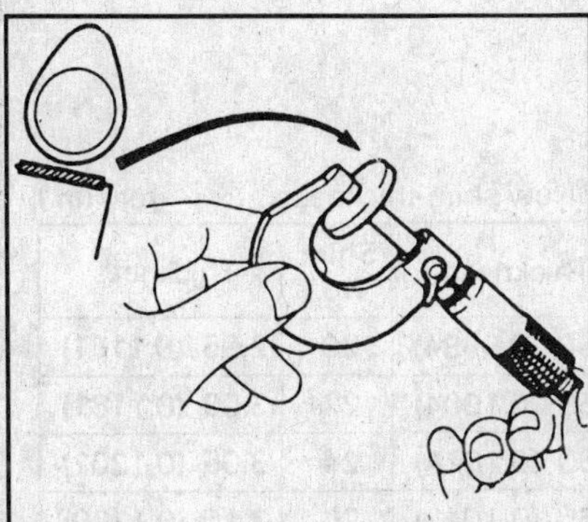
FIG. 58 Check the thickness of the shim with a micrometer—3S-FE and 5S-FE engines

8. Install a valve lifter depressing tool between the 2 camshaft lobes and then turn the handle so that the tool presses down both (intake and exhaust) valve lifters evenly.

9. Using a suitable tool and a magnet, remove the valve shims.

10. Measure the thickness of the old shim with a micrometer. Locate that particular measurement in the "Installed Shim Thickness" column of the accompanying charts, then locate the previously recorded measurement (from Step 3 or 5) for that valve in the "Measured Clearance " column of the charts. Index the 2 columns to arrive at the proper replacement shim thickness.

11. The new replacement shim thickness may also be determined by the following formula:

T ..... THICKNESS OF USED SHIM
A ..... MEASURED VALVE CLEARANCE
N ..... THICKNESS OF NEW SHIM

INTAKE N = T + (A − 0.24 MM (0.009 IN.))
EXHAUST N = T + (A − 0.33 MM (0.013 IN.))

FIG.60A Shim selection formula—3S-FE and 5S-FE engines

Select a new shim with a thickness as close as possible to the value arrived at in the formula. To convert millimeters to inches, multiply by 0.039. To convert inches to millimeters, multiply by 25.4.

➡ Replacement shims are available in 27 sizes, in increments of 0.05mm, from 2.00mm to 3.300mm.

12. Place the new shim on the valve lifter. Remove the special tool and then recheck the valve clearance.

13. Install the gasket onto the cylinder head cover. install the head cover with the four grommets and nuts. Torque the nuts to 13 ft. lbs. (18 Nm).

2VZ-FE and 3VZ-FE Engines

➧ SEE FIGS. 66-74

➡ Adjust and inspect the valve clearance when the engine is cold.

1. Disconnect the negative battery cable.

INTAKE

Measured clearance (mm)	Installed shim thickness (mm)																																								
	2.500	2.550	2.600	2.620	2.640	2.650	2.660	2.680	2.700	2.720	2.740	2.750	2.760	2.780	2.800	2.820	2.840	2.850	2.860	2.880	2.900	2.920	2.940	2.950	2.960	2.980	3.000	3.020	3.040	3.050	3.060	3.080	3.100	3.120	3.140	3.150	3.160	3.180	3.200	3.250	3.300
0.000-0.025								02	02	02	02	02	04	04	04	06	06	06	08	08	08	10	10	10	12	12	12	14	14	14	16	16	16	18	18	18	20	20	20	22	24
0.026-0.050					02	02	02	02	02	02	04	04	04	06	06	06	08	08	08	10	10	10	12	12	12	14	14	14	16	16	16	18	18	18	20	20	20	22	22	24	26
0.051-0.075				02	02	02	02	02	02	04	04	04	06	06	06	08	08	08	10	10	10	12	12	12	14	14	14	16	16	16	18	18	18	20	20	20	22	22	22	24	26
0.076-0.100			02	02	02	02	02	04	04	04	06	06	06	08	08	08	10	10	10	12	12	12	14	14	14	16	16	16	18	18	18	20	20	20	22	22	22	24	24	26	28
0.101-0.125			02	02	02	02	04	04	04	06	06	06	08	08	08	10	10	10	12	12	12	14	14	14	16	16	16	18	18	18	20	20	20	22	22	22	24	24	24	26	28
0.126-0.150		02	02	02	04	04	04	06	06	06	08	08	08	10	10	10	12	12	12	14	14	14	16	16	16	18	18	18	20	20	20	22	22	22	24	24	24	26	26	28	30
0.151-0.175		02	02	04	04	04	06	06	06	08	08	08	10	10	10	12	12	12	14	14	14	16	16	16	18	18	18	20	20	20	22	22	22	24	24	24	26	26	26	28	30
0.176-0.189		02	04	04	06	06	06	06	08	08	10	10	10	10	12	12	14	14	14	14	16	16	18	18	18	18	20	20	22	22	22	22	24	24	26	26	26	26	28	30	32
0.190-0.290																																									
0.291-0.300	04	06	08	10	10	10	10	12	12	14	14	14	14	16	16	18	18	18	18	20	20	22	22	22	22	24	24	26	26	26	26	28	28	30	30	30	30	32	32	34	
0.301-0.325	04	06	08	10	10	10	12	12	12	14	14	14	16	16	16	18	18	18	20	20	20	22	22	22	24	24	24	26	26	26	28	28	28	30	30	30	32	32	32	34	
0.326-0.350	06	08	10	10	12	12	12	14	14	14	16	16	16	18	18	18	20	20	20	22	22	22	24	24	24	26	26	26	28	28	28	30	30	30	32	32	32	34	34		
0.351-0.375	06	08	10	12	12	12	14	14	14	16	16	16	18	18	18	20	20	20	22	22	22	24	24	24	26	26	26	28	28	28	30	30	30	32	32	32	34	34	34		
0.376-0.400	08	10	12	12	14	14	14	16	16	16	18	18	18	20	20	20	22	22	22	24	24	24	26	26	26	28	28	28	30	30	30	32	32	32	34	34	34	34			
0.401-0.425	08	10	12	14	14	14	16	16	16	18	18	18	20	20	20	22	22	22	24	24	24	26	26	26	28	28	28	30	30	30	32	32	32	34	34	34	34				
0.426-0.450	10	12	14	14	16	16	16	18	18	18	20	20	20	22	22	22	24	24	24	26	26	26	28	28	28	30	30	30	32	32	32	34	34	34	34						
0.451-0.475	10	12	14	16	16	16	18	18	18	20	20	20	22	22	22	24	24	24	26	26	26	28	28	28	30	30	30	32	32	32	34	34	34								
0.476-0.500	12	14	16	16	18	18	18	20	20	20	22	22	22	24	24	24	26	26	26	28	28	28	30	30	30	32	32	32	34	34	34	34									
0.501-0.525	12	14	16	18	18	18	20	20	20	22	22	22	24	24	24	26	26	26	28	28	28	30	30	30	32	32	32	34	34	34	34										
0.526-0.550	14	16	18	18	20	20	20	22	22	22	24	24	24	26	26	26	28	28	28	30	30	30	32	32	32	34	34	34	34												
0.551-0.575	14	16	18	20	20	20	22	22	22	24	24	24	26	26	26	28	28	28	30	30	30	32	32	32	34	34	34														
0.576-0.600	16	18	20	20	22	22	22	24	24	24	26	26	26	28	28	28	30	30	30	32	32	32	34	34	34	34															
0.601-0.625	16	18	20	22	22	22	24	24	24	26	26	26	28	28	28	30	30	30	32	32	32	34	34	34	34																
0.626-0.650	18	20	22	22	24	24	24	26	26	26	28	28	28	30	30	30	32	32	32	34	34	34	34																		
0.651-0.675	18	20	22	24	24	24	26	26	26	28	28	28	30	30	30	32	32	32	34	34	34																				
0.676-0.700	20	22	24	24	26	26	26	28	28	28	30	30	30	32	32	32	34	34	34	34																					
0.701-0.725	20	22	24	26	26	26	28	28	28	30	30	30	32	32	32	34	34	34	34																						
0.726-0.750	22	24	26	26	28	28	28	30	30	30	32	32	32	34	34	34	34																								
0.751-0.775	22	24	26	28	28	28	30	30	30	32	32	32	34	34	34																										
0.776-0.800	24	26	28	28	30	30	30	32	32	32	34	34	34	34																											
0.801-0.825	24	26	28	30	30	30	32	32	32	34	34	34	34																												
0.826-0.850	26	28	30	30	32	32	32	34	34	34	34																														
0.851-0.875	26	28	30	32	32	32	34	34	34																																
0.876-0.900	28	30	32	32	34	34	34	34																																	
0.901-0.925	28	30	32	34	34	34	34																																		
0.926-0.950	30	32	34	34	34																																				
0.951-0.975	30	32	34																																						
0.976-1.000	32	34																																							
1.001-1.025	34	34																																							
1.026-1.090	34																																								

New shim thickness mm (in.)

Shim No.	Thickness	Shim No.	Thickness
02	2.50 (0.0984)	20	2.95 (0.1161)
04	2.55 (0.1004)	22	3.00 (0.1181)
06	2.60 (0.1024)	24	3.05 (0.1201)
08	2.65 (0.1043)	26	3.10 (0.1220)
10	2.70 (0.1063)	28	3.15 (0.1240)
12	2.75 (0.1083)	30	3.20 (0.1260)
14	2.80 (0.1102)	32	3.25 (0.1280)
16	2.85 (0.1122)	34	3.30 (0.1299)
18	2.90 (0.1142)		

Intake valve clearance (Cold):
0.19 — 0.29 mm (0.007 — 0.011 in.)

EXAMPLE: The 2.800 mm (0.1102 in.) shim is installed and the measured clearance is 0.450 mm (0.0177 in.). Replace the 2.800 mm (0.1102 in.) shim with a No. 22 shim.

FIG. 61 Valve shim selection chart (intake)—3S-FE engines

EXHAUST

Measured clearance (mm)	Installed shim thickness (mm)																																							
	2.500	2.550	2.600	2.620	2.640	2.650	2.660	2.680	2.700	2.720	2.740	2.750	2.760	2.780	2.800	2.820	2.840	2.850	2.860	2.880	2.900	2.920	2.940	2.950	2.960	2.980	3.000	3.020	3.040	3.050	3.060	3.080	3.100	3.120	3.140	3.150	3.160	3.180	3.200	3.250	3.300
0.000-0.025													02	02	02	02	02	04	04	04	06	06	06	08	08	08	10	10	10	12	12	12	14	14	14	16	16	16	18	20	22
0.026-0.050											02	02	02	02	02	04	04	04	04	06	06	08	08	08	08	10	10	12	12	12	12	14	14	16	16	16	16	18	18	20	22
0.051-0.075										02	02	02	02	02	04	04	04	06	06	06	08	08	08	10	10	10	12	12	12	14	14	14	16	16	16	18	18	18	20	22	24
0.076-0.100								02	02	02	02	02	02	04	04	06	06	06	06	08	08	10	10	10	10	12	12	14	14	14	14	16	16	18	18	18	18	20	20	22	24
0.101-0.125							02	02	02	02	02	04	04	04	06	06	06	08	08	08	10	10	10	12	12	12	14	14	14	16	16	16	18	18	18	20	20	20	22	24	26
0.126-0.150					02	02	02	02	02	04	04	04	04	06	06	08	08	08	08	10	10	12	12	12	12	14	14	16	16	16	16	18	18	20	20	20	20	22	22	24	26
0.150-0.175				02	02	02	02	02	04	04	04	06	06	06	08	08	08	10	10	10	12	12	12	14	14	14	16	16	16	18	18	18	20	20	20	22	22	22	24	26	28
0.176-0.200			02	02	02	02	02	04	04	06	06	06	06	08	08	10	10	10	10	12	12	14	14	14	14	16	16	18	18	18	18	20	20	22	22	22	22	24	24	26	28
0.201-0.225			02	02	02	04	04	04	06	06	06	08	08	08	10	10	10	12	12	12	14	14	14	16	16	16	18	18	18	20	20	20	22	22	22	24	24	24	26	28	30
0.226-0.250		02	02	04	04	04	04	06	06	08	08	08	08	10	10	12	12	12	12	14	14	16	16	16	16	18	18	20	20	20	20	22	22	24	24	24	24	26	26	28	30
0.251-0.275		02	04	04	04	06	06	08	08	08	08	10	10	10	12	12	12	14	14	14	16	16	16	18	18	18	20	20	20	22	22	22	24	24	24	26	26	26	28	30	32
0.275-0.279		02	04	04	06	06	06	08	08	08	10	10	10	12	12	12	14	14	14	16	16	16	18	18	18	20	20	20	22	22	22	24	24	24	26	26	26	28	28	30	32
0.280-0.380																																									
0.381-0.400	04	06	08	10	10	10	10	12	12	14	14	14	14	16	16	18	18	18	18	20	20	22	22	22	22	24	24	26	26	26	26	28	28	30	30	30	30	32	32	34	
0.401-0.425	06	08	10	10	10	12	12	12	14	14	14	16	16	16	18	18	18	20	20	20	22	22	22	24	24	24	26	26	26	28	28	28	30	30	30	32	32	32	34	34	
0.426-0.450	06	08	10	12	12	12	12	14	14	16	16	16	16	18	18	20	20	20	20	22	22	24	24	24	24	26	26	28	28	28	28	30	30	32	32	32	32	34	34		
0.451-0.475	08	10	12	12	12	14	14	14	16	16	16	18	18	18	20	20	20	22	22	22	24	24	24	26	26	26	28	28	28	30	30	30	32	32	32	34	34	34	34		
0.476-0.500	08	10	12	14	14	14	14	16	16	18	18	18	18	20	20	22	22	22	22	24	24	26	26	26	26	28	28	30	30	30	30	32	32	34	34	34	34				
0.501-0.525	10	12	14	14	14	16	16	16	18	18	18	20	20	20	22	22	22	24	24	24	26	26	26	28	28	28	30	30	30	32	32	32	34	34	34	34					
0.526-0.550	10	12	14	16	16	16	16	18	18	20	20	20	20	22	22	24	24	24	24	26	26	28	28	28	28	30	30	32	32	32	32	34	34	34							
0.551-0.575	12	14	16	16	16	18	18	18	20	20	20	22	22	22	24	24	24	26	26	26	28	28	28	30	30	30	32	32	32	34	34	34	34								
0.576-0.600	12	14	16	18	18	18	18	20	20	22	22	22	22	24	24	26	26	26	26	28	28	30	30	30	30	32	32	34	34	34	34	34									
0.601-0.625	14	16	18	18	18	20	20	20	22	22	22	24	24	24	26	26	26	28	28	28	30	30	30	32	32	32	34	34	34	34											
0.626-0.650	14	16	18	20	20	20	20	22	22	24	24	24	24	26	26	28	28	28	28	30	30	32	32	32	32	34	34	34													
0.651-0.675	16	18	20	20	20	22	22	22	24	24	24	26	26	26	28	28	28	30	30	30	32	32	32	34	34	34	34														
0.676-0.700	16	18	20	22	22	22	22	24	24	26	26	26	26	28	28	30	30	30	30	32	32	34	34	34	34	34															
0.701-0.725	18	20	22	22	22	24	24	24	26	26	26	28	28	28	30	30	30	32	32	32	34	34	34	34																	
0.726-0.750	18	20	22	24	24	24	24	26	26	28	28	28	28	30	30	32	32	32	32	34	34	34																			
0.751-0.775	20	22	24	24	24	26	26	26	28	28	28	30	30	30	32	32	32	34	34	34	34																				
0.776-0.800	20	22	24	26	26	26	26	28	28	30	30	30	30	32	32	34	34	34	34	34																					
0.801-0.825	22	24	26	26	26	28	28	28	30	30	30	32	32	32	34	34	34																								
0.826-0.850	22	24	26	28	28	28	28	30	30	32	32	32	32	34	34	34																									
0.851-0.875	24	26	28	28	28	30	30	30	32	32	32	34	34	34	34																										
0.876-0.900	24	26	28	30	30	30	30	32	32	34	34	34	34	34																											
0.901-0.925	26	28	30	30	30	32	32	32	34	34	34	34																													
0.926-0.950	26	28	30	32	32	32	32	34	34	34																															
0.951-0.975	28	30	32	32	32	34	34	34	34																																
0.976-1.000	28	30	32	34	34	34	34	34																																	
1.001-1.025	30	32	34	34	34	34																																			
1.026-1.050	30	32	34	34																																					
1.051-1.075	32	34	34																																						
1.076-1.100	32	34																																							
1.101-1.125	34	34																																							
1.126-1.180	34																																								

New shim thickness mm (in.)

Shim No.	Thickness	Shim No.	Thickness
02	2.50 (0.0984)	20	2.95 (0.1161)
04	2.55 (0.1004)	22	3.00 (0.1181)
06	2.60 (0.1024)	24	3.05 (0.1201)
08	2.65 (0.1043)	26	3.10 (0.1220)
10	2.70 (0.1063)	28	3.15 (0.1240)
12	2.75 (0.1083)	30	3.20 (0.1260)
14	2.80 (0.1102)	32	3.25 (0.1280)
16	2.85 (0.1122)	34	3.30 (0.1299)
18	2.90 (0.1142)		

Exhaust valve clearance:

0.28 — 0.38 mm (0.011 — 0.015 in.)

EXAMPLE: The 2.800 mm (0.1102 in.) shim is installed and the measured clearance is 0.450 mm (0.0177 in.). Replace the 2.800 mm (0.1102 in.) shim with a No. 18 shim.

FIG. 62 Valve shim selection chart (exhaust)—3S-FE engines

Measured clearance mm (in.) \ Installed shim thickness mm (in.)	2.50 (0.0984)	2.52 (0.0992)	2.54 (0.1000)	2.56 (0.1008)	2.58 (0.1016)	2.60 (0.1024)	2.62 (0.1031)	2.64 (0.1039)	2.65 (0.1043)	2.66 (0.1047)	2.67 (0.1051)	2.68 (0.1055)	2.69 (0.1059)	2.70 (0.1063)	2.71 (0.1067)	2.72 (0.1071)	2.73 (0.1075)	2.74 (0.1079)	2.75 (0.1083)	2.76 (0.1087)	2.77 (0.1091)	2.78 (0.1094)	2.79 (0.1098)	2.80 (0.1102)	2.81 (0.1106)	2.82 (0.1110)	2.83 (0.1114)	2.84 (0.1118)	2.85 (0.1122)	2.86 (0.1126)	2.87 (0.1130)	2.88 (0.1134)	2.89 (0.1138)	2.90 (0.1142)	2.91 (0.1146)	2.92 (0.1150)	2.93 (0.1154)	2.94 (0.1157)	2.95 (0.1161)	2.96 (0.1165)	2.97 (0.1169)	2.98 (0.1173)	2.99 (0.1177)	3.00 (0.1181)	3.01 (0.1185)	3.02 (0.1189)	3.03 (0.1193)	3.04 (0.1197)	3.05 (0.1201)	3.06 (0.1205)	3.08 (0.1213)	3.10 (0.1220)	3.12 (0.1228)	3.14 (0.1236)	3.15 (0.1240)	3.16 (0.1244)	3.18 (0.1252)	3.20 (0.1260)	3.22 (0.1268)	3.24 (0.1276)	3.25 (0.1280)	3.26 (0.1283)	3.28 (0.1291)	3.30 (0.1299)
0.000 - 0.020 (0.0000 - 0.0008)													1	1	1	1	1	1	1	2	2	2	2	2	3	3	3	3	3	4	4	4	4	4	5	5	5	5	5	6	6	6	6	6	7	7	7	7	7	8	8	8	9	9	9	10	10	10	11	11	11	12	12	12
0.021 - 0.040 (0.0008 - 0.0016)											1	1	1	1	1	1	1	2	2	2	2	2	3	3	3	3	3	4	4	4	4	4	5	5	5	5	5	6	6	6	6	6	7	7	7	7	7	8	8	8	8	9	9	10	10	10	10	11	11	12	12	12	12	13
0.041 - 0.060 (0.0016 - 0.0024)									1	1	1	1	1	1	1	2	2	2	2	2	3	3	3	3	3	4	4	4	4	4	5	5	5	5	5	6	6	6	6	6	7	7	7	7	7	8	8	8	8	8	9	9	10	10	10	10	11	11	12	12	12	12	13	13
0.061 - 0.080 (0.0024 - 0.0031)								1	1	1	1	1	1	2	2	2	2	2	3	3	3	3	3	4	4	4	4	4	5	5	5	5	5	6	6	6	6	6	7	7	7	7	7	8	8	8	8	8	9	9	9	10	10	10	11	11	11	12	12	12	13	13	13	14
0.081 - 0.100 (0.0032 - 0.0039)							1	1	1	1	1	2	2	2	2	2	3	3	3	3	3	4	4	4	4	4	5	5	5	5	5	6	6	6	6	6	7	7	7	7	7	8	8	8	8	8	9	9	9	9	10	10	10	11	11	11	12	12	12	13	13	13	14	14
0.101 - 0.120 (0.0040 - 0.0047)						1	1	1	1	2	2	2	2	2	3	3	3	3	3	4	4	4	4	4	5	5	5	5	5	6	6	6	6	6	7	7	7	7	7	8	8	8	8	8	9	9	9	9	9	10	10	10	11	11	11	12	12	12	13	13	13	14	14	14
0.121 - 0.140 (0.0048 - 0.0055)					1	1	1	2	2	2	2	2	3	3	3	3	3	4	4	4	4	4	5	5	5	5	5	6	6	6	6	6	7	7	7	7	7	8	8	8	8	8	9	9	9	9	9	10	10	10	10	11	11	12	12	12	12	13	13	14	14	14	14	15
0.141 - 0.160 (0.0056 - 0.0063)				1	1	1	2	2	2	2	3	3	3	3	3	4	4	4	4	4	5	5	5	5	5	6	6	6	6	6	7	7	7	7	7	8	8	8	8	8	9	9	9	9	9	10	10	10	10	10	11	11	12	12	12	12	13	13	14	14	14	14	15	15
0.161 - 0.180 (0.0063 - 0.0071)			1	1	1	2	2	2	3	3	3	3	3	4	4	4	4	4	5	5	5	5	5	6	6	6	6	6	7	7	7	7	7	8	8	8	8	8	9	9	9	9	9	10	10	10	10	10	11	11	11	12	12	12	13	13	13	14	14	14	15	15	15	16
0.181 - 0.189 (0.0071 - 0.0074)		1	1	1	1	2	2	3	3	3	3	3	4	4	4	4	4	5	5	5	5	5	6	6	6	6	6	7	7	7	7	7	8	8	8	8	8	9	9	9	9	9	10	10	10	10	10	11	11	11	11	12	12	13	13	13	13	14	14	15	15	15	15	16
0.190 - 0.290 (0.0075 - 0.0114)																																																																
0.291 - 0.300 (0.0115 - 0.0118)	2	3	3	3	4	4	5	5	5	5	6	6	6	6	6	7	7	7	7	7	8	8	8	8	8	9	9	9	9	9	10	10	10	10	10	11	11	11	11	11	12	12	12	12	12	13	13	13	13	13	14	14	15	15	15	15	16	16	17	17	17	17	17	
0.301 - 0.320 (0.0119 - 0.0126)	2	3	3	4	4	4	5	5	5	6	6	6	6	6	7	7	7	7	7	8	8	8	8	8	9	9	9	9	9	10	10	10	10	10	11	11	11	11	11	12	12	12	12	12	13	13	13	13	13	14	14	14	15	15	15	16	16	16	17	17	17	17		
0.321 - 0.340 (0.0126 - 0.0134)	3	3	4	4	4	5	5	6	6	6	6	6	7	7	7	7	7	8	8	8	8	8	9	9	9	9	9	10	10	10	10	10	11	11	11	11	11	12	12	12	12	12	13	13	13	13	13	14	14	14	14	15	15	16	16	16	16	17	17	17	17			
0.341 - 0.360 (0.0134 - 0.0142)	3	4	4	4	5	5	6	6	6	6	7	7	7	7	7	8	8	8	8	8	9	9	9	9	9	10	10	10	10	10	11	11	11	11	11	12	12	12	12	12	13	13	13	13	13	14	14	14	14	14	15	15	16	16	16	16	17	17	17					
0.361 - 0.380 (0.0142 - 0.0150)	4	4	4	5	5	6	6	6	7	7	7	7	7	8	8	8	8	8	9	9	9	9	9	10	10	10	10	10	11	11	11	11	11	12	12	12	12	12	13	13	13	13	13	14	14	14	14	14	15	15	15	16	16	16	17	17	17	17						
0.381 - 0.400 (0.0150 - 0.0157)	4	4	5	5	6	6	6	7	7	7	7	8	8	8	8	8	9	9	9	9	9	10	10	10	10	10	11	11	11	11	11	12	12	12	12	12	13	13	13	13	13	14	14	14	14	14	15	15	15	15	16	16	16	17	17	17	17							
0.401 - 0.420 (0.0158 - 0.0165)	4	5	5	6	6	6	7	7	7	8	8	8	8	8	9	9	9	9	9	10	10	10	10	10	11	11	11	11	11	12	12	12	12	12	13	13	13	13	13	14	14	14	14	14	15	15	15	15	15	16	16	16	17	17	17	17								
0.421 - 0.440 (0.0166 - 0.0173)	5	5	6	6	6	7	7	8	8	8	8	8	9	9	9	9	9	10	10	10	10	10	11	11	11	11	11	12	12	12	12	12	13	13	13	13	13	14	14	14	14	14	15	15	15	15	15	16	16	16	16	17	17	17	17									
0.441 - 0.460 (0.0174 - 0.0181)	5	6	6	6	7	7	8	8	8	8	9	9	9	9	9	10	10	10	10	10	11	11	11	11	11	12	12	12	12	12	13	13	13	13	13	14	14	14	14	14	15	15	15	15	15	16	16	16	16	16	17	17	17											
0.461 - 0.480 (0.0181 - 0.0189)	6	6	6	7	7	8	8	8	9	9	9	9	9	10	10	10	10	10	11	11	11	11	11	12	12	12	12	12	13	13	13	13	13	14	14	14	14	14	15	15	15	15	15	16	16	16	16	16	17	17	17	17												
0.481 - 0.500 (0.0189 - 0.0197)	6	6	7	7	8	8	8	9	9	9	9	10	10	10	10	10	11	11	11	11	11	12	12	12	12	12	13	13	13	13	13	14	14	14	14	14	15	15	15	15	15	16	16	16	16	16	17	17	17	17	17													
0.501 - 0.520 (0.0197 - 0.0205)	6	7	7	8	8	8	9	9	9	10	10	10	10	10	11	11	11	11	11	12	12	12	12	12	13	13	13	13	13	14	14	14	14	14	15	15	15	15	15	16	16	16	16	16	17	17	17	17	17	17														
0.521 - 0.540 (0.0205 - 0.0213)	7	7	8	8	8	9	9	10	10	10	10	10	11	11	11	11	11	12	12	12	12	12	13	13	13	13	13	14	14	14	14	14	15	15	15	15	15	16	16	16	16	16	17	17	17	17	17	17	17															
0.541 - 0.560 (0.0213 - 0.0220)	7	8	8	8	9	9	10	10	10	10	11	11	11	11	11	12	12	12	12	12	13	13	13	13	13	14	14	14	14	14	15	15	15	15	15	16	16	16	16	16	17	17	17	17	17	17	17																	
0.561 - 0.580 (0.0221 - 0.0228)	8	8	8	9	9	10	10	10	11	11	11	11	11	12	12	12	12	12	13	13	13	13	13	14	14	14	14	14	15	15	15	15	15	16	16	16	16	16	17	17	17	17	17	17	17																			
0.581 - 0.600 (0.0229 - 0.0236)	8	8	9	9	10	10	10	11	11	11	11	12	12	12	12	12	13	13	13	13	13	14	14	14	14	14	15	15	15	15	15	16	16	16	16	16	17	17	17	17	17	17	17																					
0.601 - 0.620 (0.0237 - 0.0244)	8	9	9	10	10	10	11	11	11	12	12	12	12	12	13	13	13	13	13	14	14	14	14	14	15	15	15	15	15	16	16	16	16	16	17	17	17	17	17	17	17																							
0.621 - 0.640 (0.0244 - 0.0252)	9	9	10	10	10	11	11	12	12	12	12	12	13	13	13	13	13	14	14	14	14	14	15	15	15	15	15	16	16	16	16	16	17	17	17	17	17	17	17																									
0.641 - 0.660 (0.0252 - 0.0260)	9	10	10	10	11	11	12	12	12	12	13	13	13	13	13	14	14	14	14	14	15	15	15	15	15	16	16	16	16	16	17	17	17	17	17	17	17																											
0.661 - 0.680 (0.0260 - 0.0268)	10	10	10	11	11	12	12	12	13	13	13	13	13	14	14	14	14	14	15	15	15	15	15	16	16	16	16	16	17	17	17	17	17	17	17																													
0.681 - 0.700 (0.0268 - 0.0276)	10	10	11	11	12	12	12	13	13	13	13	14	14	14	14	14	15	15	15	15	15	16	16	16	16	16	17	17	17	17	17	17	17																															
0.701 - 0.720 (0.0276 - 0.0283)	10	11	11	12	12	12	13	13	13	14	14	14	14	14	15	15	15	15	15	16	16	16	16	16	17	17	17	17	17	17	17																																	
0.721 - 0.740 (0.0284 - 0.0291)	11	11	12	12	12	13	13	14	14	14	14	14	15	15	15	15	15	16	16	16	16	16	17	17	17	17	17	17	17																																			
0.741 - 0.760 (0.0292 - 0.0299)	11	12	12	12	13	13	14	14	14	14	15	15	15	15	15	16	16	16	16	16	17	17	17	17	17	17	17																																					
0.761 - 0.780 (0.0300 - 0.0307)	12	12	12	13	13	14	14	14	15	15	15	15	15	16	16	16	16	16	17	17	17	17	17	17	17																																							
0.781 - 0.800 (0.0307 - 0.0315)	12	12	13	13	14	14	14	15	15	15	15	16	16	16	16	16	17	17	17	17	17	17	17																																									
0.801 - 0.820 (0.0315 - 0.0323)	12	13	13	14	14	14	15	15	15	16	16	16	16	16	17	17	17	17	17	17	17																																											
0.821 - 0.840 (0.0323 - 0.0331)	13	13	14	14	14	15	15	16	16	16	16	16	17	17	17	17	17	17	17																																													
0.841 - 0.860 (0.0331 - 0.0339)	13	14	14	14	15	15	16	16	16	16	17	17	17	17	17	17	17																																															
0.861 - 0.880 (0.0339 - 0.0346)	14	14	14	15	15	16	16	16	17	17	17	17	17	17	17																																																	
0.881 - 0.900 (0.0347 - 0.0354)	14	14	15	15	16	16	16	17	17	17	17	17	17																																																			
0.901 - 0.920 (0.0355 - 0.0362)	14	15	15	16	16	16	17	17	17	17	17																																																					
0.921 - 0.940 (0.0363 - 0.0370)	15	15	16	16	16	17	17	17	17																																																								
0.941 - 0.960 (0.0370 - 0.0378)	15	16	16	16	17	17	17																																																									
0.961 - 0.980 (0.0378 - 0.0386)	16	16	16	17	17	17																																																										
0.981 - 1,000 (0.0386 - 0.0394)	16	16	17	17	17																																																											
1.001 - 1.020 (0.0394 - 0.0402)	16	17	17	17																																																												
1.021 - 1.040 (0.0402 - 0.0409)	17	17	17																																																													
1.041 - 1.060 (0.0410 - 0.0417)	17	17																																																														
1.061 - 1.080 (0.0418 - 0.0425)	17																																																															
1.081 - 1.090 (0.0426 - 0.0429)	17																																																															

Intake valve clearance (Cold):
0.19 – 0.29 mm (0.007 – 0.011 in.)

EXAMPLE: The 2.800 mm (0.1102 in.) shim is installed, and the measured clearance is 0.450 mm (0.0177 in.). Replace the 2.800 mm (0.1102 in.) shim with a No. 11 shim.

New shim thickness mm (in.)

Shim No.	Thickness	Shim No.	Thickness
1	2.50 (0.0984)	10	2.95 (0.1161)
2	2.55 (0.1004)	11	3.00 (0.1181)
3	2.60 (0.1024)	12	3.05 (0.1201)
4	2.65 (0.1043)	13	3.10 (0.1220)
5	2.70 (0.1063)	14	3.15 (0.1240)
6	2.75 (0.1083)	15	3.20 (0.1260)
7	2.80 (0.1102)	16	3.25 (0.1280)
8	2.85 (0.1122)	17	3.30 (0.1299)
9	2.90 (0.1142)		

FIG. 63 Valve shim selection chart (intake) – 5S-FE engines

Measured clearance mm (in.) \ Installed shim thickness mm (in.)	2.50 (0.0984)	2.52 (0.0992)	2.54 (0.1000)	2.56 (0.1008)	2.58 (0.1016)	2.60 (0.1024)	2.62 (0.1031)	2.64 (0.1039)	2.65 (0.1043)	2.66 (0.1047)	2.67 (0.1051)	2.68 (0.1055)	2.69 (0.1059)	2.70 (0.1063)	2.71 (0.1067)	2.72 (0.1071)	2.73 (0.1075)	2.74 (0.1079)	2.75 (0.1083)	2.76 (0.1087)	2.77 (0.1091)	2.78 (0.1094)	2.79 (0.1098)	2.80 (0.1102)	2.81 (0.1106)	2.82 (0.1110)	2.83 (0.1114)	2.84 (0.1118)	2.85 (0.1122)	2.86 (0.1126)	2.87 (0.1130)	2.88 (0.1134)	2.89 (0.1138)	2.90 (0.1142)	2.91 (0.1146)	2.92 (0.1150)	2.93 (0.1154)	2.94 (0.1157)	2.95 (0.1161)	2.96 (0.1165)	2.97 (0.1169)	2.98 (0.1173)	2.99 (0.1177)	3.00 (0.1181)	3.01 (0.1185)	3.02 (0.1189)	3.03 (0.1193)	3.04 (0.1197)	3.05 (0.1201)	3.06 (0.1205)	3.08 (0.1213)	3.10 (0.1220)	3.12 (0.1228)	3.14 (0.1236)	3.15 (0.1240)	3.16 (0.1244)	3.18 (0.1252)	3.20 (0.1260)	3.22 (0.1268)	3.24 (0.1276)	3.25 (0.1280)	3.26 (0.1283)	3.28 (0.1291)	3.30 (0.1299)
0.000 - 0.020 (0.0000 - 0.0008)																								1	1	1	1	1	2	2	2	2	2	3	3	3	3	3	4	4	4	4	4	5	5	5	5	5	6	6	6	7	7	7	8	8	8	9	9	9	10	10	10	11
0.021 - 0.040 (0.0008 - 0.0016)																				1	1	1	1	1	1	1	2	2	2	2	2	3	3	3	3	3	4	4	4	4	4	5	5	5	5	5	6	6	6	6	7	7	7	8	8	8	9	9	9	10	10	10	11	11
0.041 - 0.060 (0.0016 - 0.0024)																		1	1	1	1	1	1	1	2	2	2	2	2	3	3	3	3	3	4	4	4	4	4	5	5	5	5	5	6	6	6	6	6	7	7	7	8	8	8	9	9	9	10	10	10	11	11	11
0.061 - 0.080 (0.0024 - 0.0031)																1	1	1	1	1	1	1	2	2	2	2	2	3	3	3	3	3	4	4	4	4	4	5	5	5	5	5	6	6	6	6	6	7	7	7	7	8	8	9	9	9	9	10	10	11	11	11	11	12
0.081 - 0.100 (0.0032 - 0.0039)														1	1	1	1	1	1	1	2	2	2	2	2	3	3	3	3	3	4	4	4	4	4	5	5	5	5	5	6	6	6	6	6	7	7	7	7	7	8	8	9	9	9	9	10	10	11	11	11	11	12	12
0.101 - 0.120 (0.0040 - 0.0047)												1	1	1	1	1	1	1	2	2	2	2	2	3	3	3	3	3	4	4	4	4	4	5	5	5	5	5	6	6	6	6	6	7	7	7	7	7	8	8	8	9	9	9	10	10	10	11	11	11	12	12	12	13
0.121 - 0.140 (0.0048 - 0.0055)										1	1	1	1	1	1	1	2	2	2	2	2	3	3	3	3	3	4	4	4	4	4	5	5	5	5	5	6	6	6	6	6	7	7	7	7	7	8	8	8	8	9	9	9	10	10	10	11	11	11	12	12	12	13	13
0.141 - 0.160 (0.0056 - 0.0063)								1	1	1	1	1	1	1	2	2	2	2	2	3	3	3	3	3	4	4	4	4	4	5	5	5	5	5	6	6	6	6	6	7	7	7	7	7	8	8	8	8	8	9	9	9	10	10	10	11	11	11	12	12	12	13	13	13
0.161 - 0.180 (0.0063 - 0.0071)							1	1	1	1	1	1	2	2	2	2	2	3	3	3	3	3	4	4	4	4	4	5	5	5	5	5	6	6	6	6	6	7	7	7	7	7	8	8	8	8	8	9	9	9	9	10	10	11	11	11	11	12	12	13	13	13	13	14
0.181 - 0.200 (0.0071 - 0.0079)						1	1	1	1	1	2	2	2	2	2	3	3	3	3	3	4	4	4	4	4	5	5	5	5	5	6	6	6	6	6	7	7	7	7	7	8	8	8	8	8	9	9	9	9	9	10	10	11	11	11	11	12	12	13	13	13	13	14	14
0.201 - 0.220 (0.0079 - 0.0087)					1	1	1	1	2	2	2	2	2	3	3	3	3	3	4	4	4	4	4	5	5	5	5	5	6	6	6	6	6	7	7	7	7	7	8	8	8	8	8	9	9	9	9	9	10	10	10	11	11	11	12	12	12	13	13	13	14	14	14	15
0.221 - 0.240 (0.0087 - 0.0094)				1	1	1	1	2	2	2	2	3	3	3	3	3	4	4	4	4	4	5	5	5	5	5	6	6	6	6	6	7	7	7	7	7	8	8	8	8	8	9	9	9	9	9	10	10	10	10	11	11	11	12	12	12	13	13	13	14	14	14	15	15
0.241 - 0.260 (0.0095 - 0.0102)			1	1	1	1	2	2	2	3	3	3	3	3	4	4	4	4	4	5	5	5	5	5	6	6	6	6	6	7	7	7	7	7	8	8	8	8	8	9	9	9	9	9	10	10	10	10	10	11	11	11	12	12	12	13	13	13	14	14	14	15	15	15
0.261 - 0.279 (0.0103 - 0.0110)		1	1	1	1	2	2	3	3	3	3	3	4	4	4	4	4	5	5	5	5	5	6	6	6	6	6	7	7	7	7	7	8	8	8	8	8	9	9	9	9	9	10	10	10	10	10	11	11	11	11	12	12	13	13	13	13	14	14	15	15	15	15	16
0.280 - 0.380 (0.0110 - 0.0150)																																																																
0.381 - 0.400 (0.0150 - 0.0157)	2	3	3	3	4	4	5	5	5	5	6	6	6	6	6	7	7	7	7	7	8	8	8	8	8	9	9	9	9	9	10	10	10	10	10	11	11	11	11	11	12	12	12	12	12	13	13	13	13	13	14	14	15	15	15	15	16	16	17	17	17	17	17	
0.401 - 0.420 (0.0158 - 0.0165)	3	3	3	4	4	5	5	5	6	6	6	6	6	7	7	7	7	7	8	8	8	8	8	9	9	9	9	9	10	10	10	10	10	11	11	11	11	11	12	12	12	12	12	13	13	13	13	13	14	14	14	15	15	15	16	16	16	17	17	17	17	17		
0.421 - 0.440 (0.0166 - 0.0173)	3	3	4	4	5	5	5	6	6	6	6	7	7	7	7	7	8	8	8	8	8	9	9	9	9	9	10	10	10	10	10	11	11	11	11	11	12	12	12	12	12	13	13	13	13	13	14	14	14	14	15	15	15	16	16	16	17	17	17	17				
0.441 - 0.460 (0.0174 - 0.0181)	3	4	4	5	5	5	6	6	6	7	7	7	7	7	8	8	8	8	8	9	9	9	9	9	10	10	10	10	10	11	11	11	11	11	12	12	12	12	12	13	13	13	13	13	14	14	14	14	14	15	15	15	16	16	16	17	17	17	17					
0.461 - 0.480 (0.0181 - 0.0189)	4	4	5	5	5	6	6	7	7	7	7	7	8	8	8	8	8	9	9	9	9	9	10	10	10	10	10	11	11	11	11	11	12	12	12	12	12	13	13	13	13	13	14	14	14	14	14	15	15	15	15	16	16	17	17	17	17	17						
0.481 - 0.500 (0.0189 - 0.0197)	4	5	5	5	6	6	7	7	7	7	8	8	8	8	8	9	9	9	9	9	10	10	10	10	10	11	11	11	11	11	12	12	12	12	12	13	13	13	13	13	14	14	14	14	14	15	15	15	15	15	16	16	17	17	17	17	17							
0.501 - 0.520 (0.0197 - 0.0205)	5	5	5	6	6	7	7	7	8	8	8	8	8	9	9	9	9	9	10	10	10	10	10	11	11	11	11	11	12	12	12	12	12	13	13	13	13	13	14	14	14	14	14	15	15	15	15	15	16	16	16	17	17	17	17	17								
0.521 - 0.540 (0.0205 - 0.0213)	5	5	6	6	7	7	7	8	8	8	8	9	9	9	9	9	10	10	10	10	10	11	11	11	11	11	12	12	12	12	12	13	13	13	13	13	14	14	14	14	14	15	15	15	15	15	16	16	16	16	17	17	17	17										
0.541 - 0.560 (0.0213 - 0.0220)	5	6	6	7	7	7	8	8	8	9	9	9	9	9	10	10	10	10	10	11	11	11	11	11	12	12	12	12	12	13	13	13	13	13	14	14	14	14	14	15	15	15	15	15	16	16	16	16	16	17	17	17	17											
0.561 - 0.580 (0.0221 - 0.0228)	6	6	7	7	7	8	8	9	9	9	9	9	10	10	10	10	10	11	11	11	11	11	12	12	12	12	12	13	13	13	13	13	14	14	14	14	14	15	15	15	15	15	16	16	16	16	16	17	17	17	17	17												
0.581 - 0.600 (0.0229 - 0.0236)	6	7	7	7	8	8	9	9	9	9	10	10	10	10	10	11	11	11	11	11	12	12	12	12	12	13	13	13	13	13	14	14	14	14	14	15	15	15	15	15	16	16	16	16	16	17	17	17	17	17	17													
0.601 - 0.620 (0.0237 - 0.0244)	7	7	7	8	8	9	9	9	10	10	10	10	10	11	11	11	11	11	12	12	12	12	12	13	13	13	13	13	14	14	14	14	14	15	15	15	15	15	16	16	16	16	16	17	17	17	17	17	17															
0.621 - 0.640 (0.0244 - 0.0252)	7	7	8	8	9	9	9	10	10	10	10	11	11	11	11	11	12	12	12	12	12	13	13	13	13	13	14	14	14	14	14	15	15	15	15	15	16	16	16	16	16	17	17	17	17	17	17	17																
0.641 - 0.660 (0.0252 - 0.0260)	7	8	8	9	9	9	10	10	10	11	11	11	11	11	12	12	12	12	12	13	13	13	13	13	14	14	14	14	14	15	15	15	15	15	16	16	16	16	16	17	17	17	17	17	17	17																		
0.661 - 0.680 (0.0260 - 0.0268)	8	8	9	9	9	10	10	11	11	11	11	11	12	12	12	12	12	13	13	13	13	13	14	14	14	14	14	15	15	15	15	15	16	16	16	16	16	17	17	17	17	17	17	17																				
0.681 - 0.700 (0.0268 - 0.0276)	8	9	9	9	10	10	11	11	11	11	12	12	12	12	12	13	13	13	13	13	14	14	14	14	14	15	15	15	15	15	16	16	16	16	16	17	17	17	17	17	17	17																						
0.701 - 0.720 (0.0276 - 0.0283)	9	9	9	10	10	11	11	11	12	12	12	12	12	13	13	13	13	13	14	14	14	14	14	15	15	15	15	15	16	16	16	16	16	17	17	17	17	17	17	17																								
0.721 - 0.740 (0.0284 - 0.0291)	9	9	10	10	11	11	11	12	12	12	12	13	13	13	13	13	14	14	14	14	14	15	15	15	15	15	16	16	16	16	16	17	17	17	17	17	17	17																										
0.741 - 0.760 (0.0292 - 0.0299)	9	10	10	11	11	11	12	12	12	13	13	13	13	13	14	14	14	14	14	15	15	15	15	15	16	16	16	16	16	17	17	17	17	17	17	17																												
0.761 - 0.780 (0.0300 - 0.0307)	10	10	11	11	11	12	12	13	13	13	13	13	14	14	14	14	14	15	15	15	15	15	16	16	16	16	16	17	17	17	17	17	17	17																														
0.781 - 0.800 (0.0307 - 0.0315)	10	11	11	11	12	12	13	13	13	13	14	14	14	14	14	15	15	15	15	15	16	16	16	16	16	17	17	17	17	17	17	17																																
0.801 - 0.820 (0.0315 - 0.0323)	11	11	11	12	12	13	13	13	14	14	14	14	14	15	15	15	15	15	16	16	16	16	16	17	17	17	17	17	17	17																																		
0.821 - 0.840 (0.0323 - 0.0331)	11	11	12	12	13	13	13	14	14	14	14	15	15	15	15	15	16	16	16	16	16	17	17	17	17	17	17	17																																				
0.841 - 0.860 (0.0331 - 0.0339)	11	12	12	13	13	13	14	14	14	15	15	15	15	15	16	16	16	16	16	17	17	17	17	17	17	17																																						
0.861 - 0.880 (0.0339 - 0.0346)	12	12	13	13	13	14	14	15	15	15	15	15	16	16	16	16	16	17	17	17	17	17	17	17																																								
0.881 - 0.900 (0.0347 - 0.0354)	12	13	13	13	14	14	15	15	15	15	16	16	16	16	16	17	17	17	17	17	17	17																																										
0.901 - 0.920 (0.0355 - 0.0362)	13	13	13	14	14	15	15	15	16	16	16	16	16	17	17	17	17	17	17	17																																												
0.921 - 0.940 (0.0363 - 0.0370)	13	13	14	14	15	15	15	16	16	16	16	17	17	17	17	17	17	17																																														
0.941 - 0.960 (0.0370 - 0.0378)	13	14	14	15	15	15	16	16	16	17	17	17	17	17	17	17																																																
0.961 - 0.980 (0.0378 - 0.0386)	14	14	15	15	15	16	16	17	17	17	17	17	17	17																																																		
0.981 - 1.000 (0.0386 - 0.0394)	14	15	15	15	16	16	17	17	17	17	17	17																																																				
1.001 - 1.020 (0.0394 - 0.0402)	15	15	15	16	16	17	17	17	17	17																																																								
1.021 - 1.040 (0.0402 - 0.0409)	15	15	16	16	17	17	17	17																																																										
1.041 - 1.060 (0.0410 - 0.0417)	15	16	16	17	17	17	17																																																												
1.061 - 1.080 (0.0418 - 0.0425)	16	16	17	17	17	17																																																														
1.081 - 1.100 (0.0426 - 0.0433)	16	17	17	17	17																																																																
1.101 - 1.120 (0.0433 - 0.0441)	17	17	17	17																																																																	
1.121 - 1.140 (0.0441 - 0.0449)	17	17	17																																																																		
1.141 - 1.160 (0.0449 - 0.0457)	17	17																																																																			
1.161 - 1.180 (0.0457 - 0.0465)	17																																																																				

Exhaust valve clearance (Cold):
0.28 – 0.38 mm (0.011 – 0.015 in.)

EXAMPLE: The 2.800 mm (0.1102 in.) shim is installed, and the measured clearance is 0.450 mm (0.0177 in.). Replace the 2.800 mm (0.1102 in.) shim with a No. 9 shim.

New shim thickness mm (in.)

Shim No.	Thickness	Shim No.	Thickness
1	2.50 (0.0984)	10	2.95 (0.1161)
2	2.55 (0.1004)	11	3.00 (0.1181)
3	2.60 (0.1024)	12	3.05 (0.1201)
4	2.65 (0.1043)	13	3.10 (0.1220)
5	2.70 (0.1063)	14	3.15 (0.1240)
6	2.75 (0.1083)	15	3.20 (0.1260)
7	2.80 (0.1102)	16	3.25 (0.1280)
8	2.85 (0.1122)	17	3.30 (0.1299)
9	2.90 (0.1142)		

FIG. 64 Valve shim selection chart (exhaust)—5S-FE engines

CAUTION

On models with an airbag, wait at least 30 seconds from the time that the ignition switch is turned to the LOCK position and the battery is disconnected before performing any further work.

2. Drain the engine coolant.
3. Disconnect and remove the air intake tube as detailed in Section 4.
4. Remove the cylinder head covers by removing the six nuts, seal washers and gaskets. Note that this is a fairly lengthy procedure! We suggest that you refer to Section 4 for the proper steps.
5. Use a wrench and turn the crankshaft until the notch in the pulley aligns with the timing mark **O** of the No. 1 timing belt cover. This will insure that engine is at TDC.

➡ Check that the valve lifters on the No. 1 (IN) cylinder are loose and that those on the No. 1 (EX) cylinder are tight. If not, turn the crankshaft one complete revolution (360°) and then realign the mark.

6. Using a feeler gauge measure the clearance between the camshaft lobe and the valve lifter. This measurement should correspond to specification. Check only the valves detailed in the accompanying valve arrangement illustration (FIRST).

➡ If the measurement is within specifications, go on to the next step. If not, record the measurement taken for each individual valve. These measurements will be used later to determine the proper replacement adjusting shim.

7. Turn the crankshaft ⅔ of a revolution (240°).
8. Now measure the clearance of the valves detailed in the accompanying valve arrangement illustration (SECOND).

➡ If the measurement for this set of valves (and also the previous one) is within specifications, you need go no further, the procedure is finished. If not, record the measurements and then proceed to Step 9.

9. Turn the crankshaft a further ⅔ of a revolution (240°).
10. Now measure the clearance of the valves detailed in the accompanying valve arrangement illustration (THIRD).

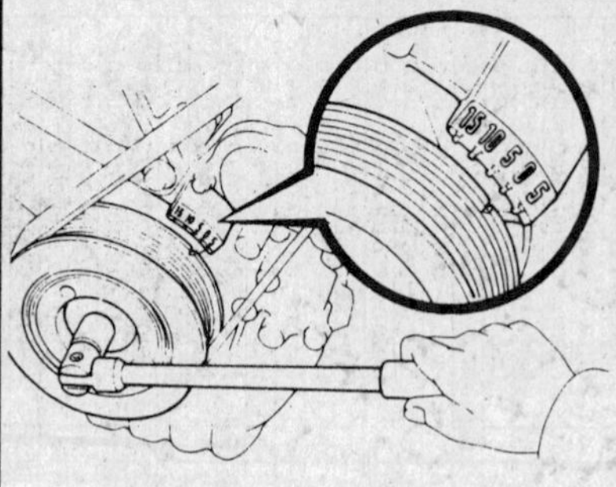

FIG. 66 Set the No. 1 cylinder to TDC—2VZ-FE and 3VZ-FE engines

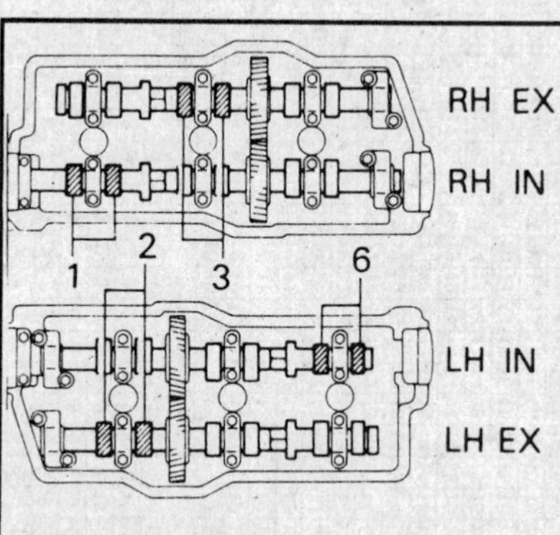

FIG. 67 Adjust these valves FIRST—2VZ-FE and 3VZ-FE engines

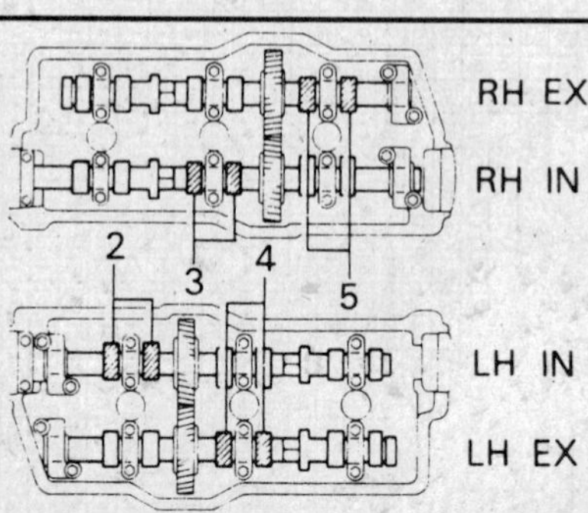

FIG. 68 Adjust these valves SECOND—2VZ-FE and 3VZ-FE engines

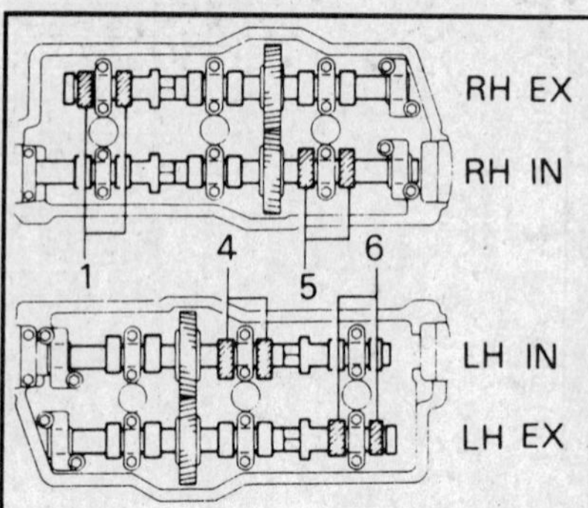

FIG. 69 Adjust these valves THIRD—2VZ-FE and 3VZ-FE engines

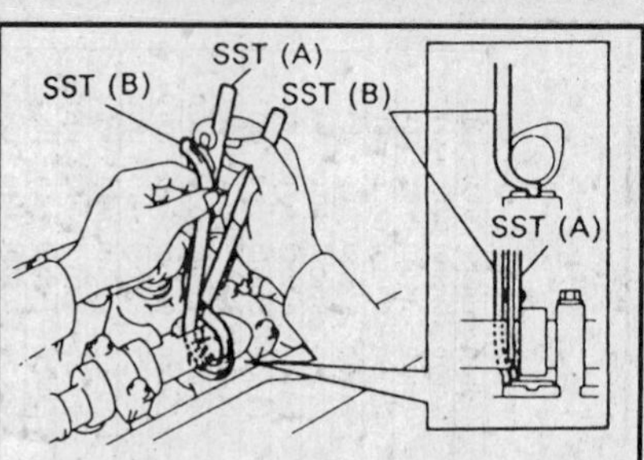

FIG. 70 Press down on the valve lifter with the tool—2VZ-FE and 3VZ-FE engines

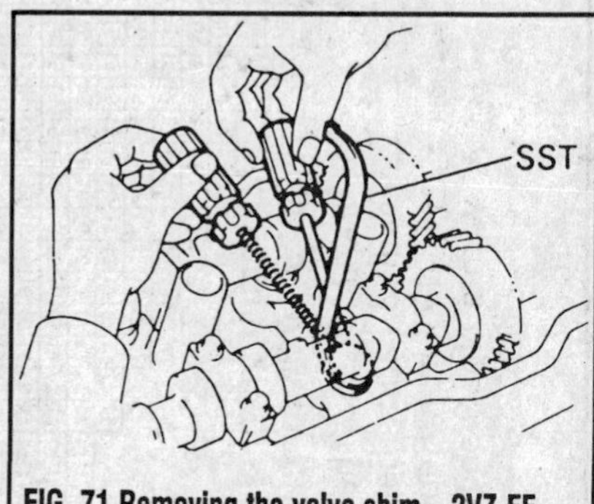

FIG. 71 Removing the valve shim—2VZ-FE and 3VZ-FE engines

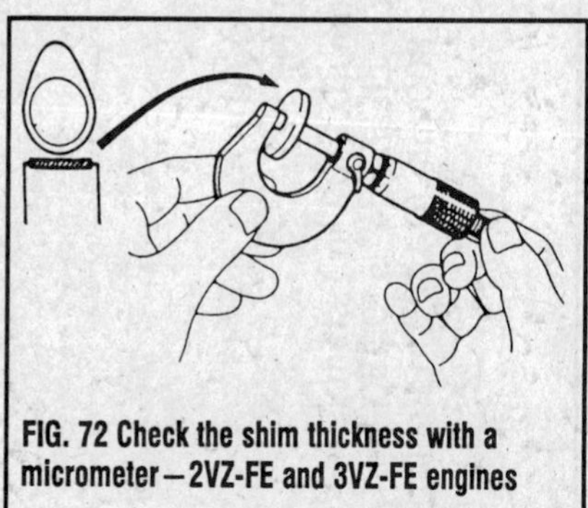

FIG. 72 Check the shim thickness with a micrometer—2VZ-FE and 3VZ-FE engines

➡ If the measurement for this set of valves (and also the previous two) is within specifications, you need go no further, the procedure is finished. If not, record the measurements and then proceed to Step 11.

11. Turn the crankshaft to position the camshaft lobe of the valve to be adjusted faces upward.
12. Using a suitable tool, turn the valve lifter so that the notch is easily accessible (toward the spark plug).
13. Install a valve lifter depressing tool between the camshaft lobe and the valve and then turn the handle so that the tool presses down the valve lifter evenly.
14. Using a suitable tool and a magnet, remove the valve adjusting shim.
15. Measure the thickness of the old shim

INTAKE

Measured clearance (mm)	Installed shim thickness (mm)																																												
	2.500	2.525	2.550	2.575	2.600	2.620	2.640	2.650	2.660	2.680	2.700	2.720	2.740	2.750	2.760	2.780	2.800	2.820	2.840	2.850	2.860	2.880	2.900	2.920	2.940	2.950	2.960	2.980	3.000	3.020	3.040	3.050	3.060	3.080	3.100	3.120	3.140	3.150	3.160	3.180	3.200	3.225	3.250	3.275	3.300
0.000 – 0.025						02	02	02	02	02	04	04	04	06	06	06	08	08	08	10	10	10	12	12	12	14	14	14	16	16	16	18	18	18	20	20	20	22	22	22	24	24	26	26	28
0.026 – 0.050					02	02	02	02	02	04	04	06	06	06	06	08	08	10	10	10	10	12	12	14	14	14	14	16	16	18	18	18	18	20	20	22	22	22	22	24	24	26	26	28	28
0.051 – 0.075				02	02	02	02	04	04	04	06	06	06	08	08	08	10	10	10	12	12	12	14	14	14	16	16	16	18	18	18	20	20	20	22	22	22	24	24	24	26	26	28	28	30
0.076 – 0.100			02	02	02	04	04	04	04	06	06	08	08	08	08	10	10	12	12	12	12	14	14	16	16	16	16	18	18	20	20	20	20	22	22	24	24	24	24	26	26	28	28	30	30
0.101 – 0.125		02	02	02	04	04	04	06	06	06	08	08	08	10	10	10	12	12	12	14	14	14	16	16	16	18	18	18	20	20	20	22	22	22	24	24	24	26	26	26	28	28	30	30	32
0.126 – 0.129		02	02	04	04	04	06	06	06	08	08	08	10	10	10	12	12	12	14	14	14	16	16	16	18	18	18	20	20	20	22	22	22	24	24	24	26	26	26	28	28	28	30	30	32
0.130 – 0.230																																													
0.231 – 0.250	04	06	06	08	08	10	10	10	10	12	12	14	14	14	14	16	16	18	18	18	18	20	20	22	22	22	22	24	24	26	26	26	26	28	28	30	30	30	30	32	32	34	34	34	
0.251 – 0.275	06	06	08	08	10	10	10	12	12	12	14	14	14	16	16	16	18	18	18	20	20	20	22	22	22	24	24	24	26	26	26	28	28	28	30	30	30	32	32	32	34	34	34	34	
0.276 – 0.300	06	08	08	10	10	12	12	12	12	14	14	16	16	16	16	18	18	20	20	20	20	22	22	24	24	24	24	26	26	28	28	28	28	30	30	32	32	32	32	34	34	34	34		
0.301 – 0.325	08	08	10	10	12	12	12	14	14	14	16	16	16	18	18	18	20	20	20	22	22	22	24	24	24	26	26	26	28	28	28	30	30	30	32	32	32	34	34	34	34	34			
0.326 – 0.350	08	10	10	12	12	14	14	14	14	16	16	18	18	18	18	20	20	22	22	22	22	24	24	26	26	26	26	28	28	30	30	30	30	32	32	34	34	34	34	34	34				
0.351 – 0.375	10	10	12	12	14	14	14	16	16	16	18	18	18	20	20	20	22	22	22	24	24	24	26	26	26	28	28	28	30	30	30	32	32	32	34	34	34	34	34						
0.376 – 0.400	10	12	12	14	14	16	16	16	16	18	18	20	20	20	20	22	22	24	24	24	24	26	26	28	28	28	28	30	30	32	32	32	32	34	34	34	34	34							
0.401 – 0.425	12	12	14	14	16	16	16	18	18	18	20	20	20	22	22	22	24	24	24	26	26	26	28	28	28	30	30	30	32	32	32	34	34	34	34	34									
0.426 – 0.450	12	14	14	16	16	18	18	18	18	20	20	22	22	22	22	24	24	26	26	26	26	28	28	30	30	30	30	32	32	34	34	34	34	34	34										
0.451 – 0.475	14	14	16	16	18	18	18	20	20	20	22	22	22	24	24	24	26	26	26	28	28	28	30	30	30	32	32	32	34	34	34	34	34												
0.476 – 0.500	14	16	16	18	18	20	20	20	20	22	22	24	24	24	24	26	26	28	28	28	28	30	30	32	32	32	32	34	34	34	34	34													
0.501 – 0.525	16	16	18	18	20	20	20	22	22	22	24	24	24	26	26	26	28	28	28	30	30	30	32	32	32	34	34	34	34	34															
0.526 – 0.550	16	18	18	20	20	22	22	22	22	24	24	26	26	26	26	28	28	30	30	30	30	32	32	34	34	34	34	34	34																
0.551 – 0.575	18	18	20	20	22	22	22	24	24	24	26	26	26	28	28	28	30	30	30	32	32	32	34	34	34	34	34																		
0.576 – 0.600	18	20	20	22	22	24	24	24	24	26	26	28	28	28	28	30	30	32	32	32	32	34	34	34	34	34																			
0.601 – 0.625	20	20	22	22	24	24	24	26	26	26	28	28	28	30	30	30	32	32	32	34	34	34	34	34																					
0.626 – 0.650	20	22	22	24	24	26	26	26	26	28	28	30	30	30	30	32	32	34	34	34	34	34	34																						
0.651 – 0.675	22	22	24	24	26	26	26	28	28	28	30	30	30	32	32	32	34	34	34	34	34																								
0.676 – 0.700	22	24	24	26	26	28	28	28	28	30	30	32	32	32	32	34	34	34	34	34																									
0.701 – 0.725	24	24	26	26	28	28	28	30	30	30	32	32	32	34	34	34	34	34																											
0.726 – 0.750	24	26	26	28	28	30	30	30	30	32	32	34	34	34	34	34																													
0.751 – 0.775	26	26	28	28	30	30	30	32	32	32	34	34	34	34	34																														
0.776 – 0.800	26	28	28	30	30	32	32	32	32	34	34	34	34	34																															
0.801 – 0.825	28	28	30	30	32	32	32	34	34	34	34	34																																	
0.826 – 0.850	28	30	30	32	32	32	34	34	34	34	34																																		
0.851 – 0.875	30	30	32	32	34	34	34	34	34																																				
0.876 – 0.900	30	32	32	34	34	34	34	34																																					
0.901 – 0.925	32	32	34	34	34	34																																							
0.926 – 0.950	32	34	34	34	34																																								
0.951 – 0.975	34	34	34	34																																									
0.976 – 1.000	34	34	34																																										
1.001 – 1.025	34	34																																											
1.026 – 1.030	34																																												

New shim thicknesses mm (in.)

Shim No.	Thickness	Shim No.	Thickness
02	2.500 (0.0984)	20	2.950 (0.1161)
04	2.550 (0.1004)	22	3.000 (0.1181)
06	2.600 (0.1024)	24	3.050 (0.1201)
08	2.650 (0.1043)	26	3.100 (0.1220)
10	2.700 (0.1063)	28	3.150 (0.1240)
12	2.750 (0.1083)	30	3.200 (0.1260)
14	2.800 (0.1102)	32	3.250 (0.1280)
16	2.850 (0.1122)	34	3.300 (0.1299)
18	2.900 (0.1142)		

Intake valve clearance (Cold):
0.13 – 0.23 mm (0.005 – 0.009 in.)

EXAMPLE: The 2.800 mm (0.1102 in.) shim is installed and the measured clearance is 0.450 mm (0.0177 in.). Replace the 2.800 mm (0.1102 in.) shim with a No. 24 shim.

FIG. 73 Valve shim selection chart (intake)—2VZ-FE and 3VZ-FE engines

EXHAUST

Measured clearance (mm)	Installed Shim thickness (mm)																																												
	2.500	2.525	2.550	2.575	2.600	2.620	2.640	2.650	2.660	2.680	2.700	2.720	2.740	2.750	2.760	2.780	2.800	2.820	2.840	2.850	2.860	2.880	2.900	2.920	2.940	2.950	2.960	2.980	3.000	3.020	3.040	3.050	3.060	3.080	3.100	3.120	3.140	3.150	3.160	3.180	3.200	3.225	3.250	3.275	3.300
0.000 – 0.025														02	02	02	02	02	04	04	04	04	06	06	08	08	08	08	10	10	12	12	12	12	14	14	16	16	16	16	18	18	20	20	22
0.026 – 0.050												02	02	02	02	02	02	04	04	04	06	06	06	08	08	08	10	10	10	12	12	12	14	14	14	16	16	16	18	18	18	20	20	22	22
0.051 – 0.075											02	02	02	02	02	02	04	04	06	06	06	06	08	08	10	10	10	10	12	12	14	14	14	14	16	16	18	18	18	18	20	20	22	22	24
0.076 – 0.100										02	02	02	02	02	04	04	04	06	06	06	08	08	08	10	10	10	12	12	12	14	14	14	16	16	16	18	18	18	20	20	20	22	22	24	24
0.101 – 0.125								02	02	02	02	02	04	04	04	04	06	06	08	08	08	08	10	10	12	12	12	12	14	14	16	16	16	16	18	18	20	20	20	20	22	22	24	24	26
0.126 – 0.150						02	02	02	02	02	02	04	04	04	06	06	06	08	08	08	10	10	10	12	12	12	14	14	14	16	16	16	18	18	18	20	20	20	22	22	22	24	24	26	26
0.151 – 0.175					02	02	02	02	02	02	04	04	06	06	06	06	08	08	10	10	10	10	12	12	14	14	14	14	16	16	18	18	18	18	20	20	22	22	22	22	24	24	26	26	28
0.176 – 0.200				02	02	02	02	02	04	04	04	06	06	06	08	08	08	10	10	10	12	12	12	14	14	14	16	16	16	18	18	18	20	20	20	22	22	22	24	24	24	26	26	28	28
0.201 – 0.225			02	02	02	02	04	04	04	04	06	06	08	08	08	08	10	10	12	12	12	12	14	14	16	16	16	16	18	18	20	20	20	20	22	22	24	24	24	24	26	26	28	28	30
0.226 – 0.250		02	02	02	02	04	04	04	06	06	06	08	08	08	10	10	10	12	12	12	14	14	14	16	16	16	18	18	18	20	20	20	22	22	22	24	24	24	26	26	26	28	28	30	30
0.251 – 0.269		02	02	02	04	04	06	06	06	06	08	08	10	10	10	10	12	12	14	14	14	14	16	16	18	18	18	18	20	20	22	22	22	22	24	24	26	26	26	26	28	28	30	30	32
0.270 – 0.370																																													
0.371 – 0.375	04	06	06	08	08	08	10	10	10	12	12	12	14	14	14	16	16	16	18	18	18	20	20	20	22	22	22	24	24	24	26	26	26	28	28	28	30	30	30	32	32	34	34	34	
0.376 – 0.400	04	06	06	08	08	10	10	10	12	12	12	14	14	14	16	16	16	18	18	18	20	20	20	22	22	22	24	24	24	26	26	26	28	28	28	30	30	30	32	32	32	34	34	34	
0.401 – 0.425	06	06	08	08	10	10	12	12	12	12	14	14	16	16	16	16	18	18	20	20	20	20	22	22	24	24	24	24	26	26	28	28	28	28	30	30	32	32	32	32	34	34	34		
0.426 – 0.450	06	08	08	10	10	12	12	12	14	14	14	16	16	16	18	18	18	20	20	20	22	22	22	24	24	24	26	26	26	28	28	28	30	30	30	32	32	32	34	34	34	34			
0.451 – 0.475	08	08	10	10	12	12	14	14	14	14	16	16	18	18	18	18	20	20	22	22	22	22	24	24	26	26	26	26	28	28	30	30	30	30	32	32	34	34	34	34	34				
0.476 – 0.500	08	10	10	12	12	14	14	14	16	16	16	18	18	18	20	20	20	22	22	22	24	24	24	26	26	26	28	28	28	30	30	30	32	32	32	34	34	34	34	34					
0.501 – 0.525	10	10	12	12	14	14	16	16	16	16	18	18	20	20	20	20	22	22	24	24	24	24	26	26	28	28	28	28	30	30	32	32	32	32	34	34	34	34	34						
0.526 – 0.550	10	12	12	14	14	16	16	16	18	18	18	20	20	20	22	22	22	24	24	24	26	26	26	28	28	28	30	30	30	32	32	32	34	34	34	34	34								
0.551 – 0.575	12	12	14	14	16	16	18	18	18	18	20	20	22	22	22	22	24	24	26	26	26	26	28	28	30	30	30	30	32	32	34	34	34	34	34										
0.576 – 0.600	12	14	14	16	16	18	18	18	20	20	20	22	22	22	24	24	24	26	26	26	28	28	28	30	30	30	32	32	32	34	34	34	34	34											
0.601 – 0.625	14	14	16	16	18	18	20	20	20	20	22	22	24	24	24	24	26	26	28	28	28	28	30	30	32	32	32	32	34	34	34	34	34												
0.626 – 0.650	14	16	16	18	18	20	20	20	22	22	22	24	24	24	26	26	26	28	28	28	30	30	30	32	32	32	34	34	34	34	34														
0.651 – 0.675	16	16	18	18	20	20	22	22	22	22	24	24	26	26	26	26	28	28	30	30	30	30	32	32	34	34	34	34	34																
0.676 – 0.700	16	18	18	20	20	22	22	22	24	24	24	26	26	26	28	28	28	30	30	30	32	32	32	34	34	34	34	34																	
0.701 – 0.725	18	18	20	20	22	22	24	24	24	24	26	26	28	28	28	28	30	30	32	32	32	32	34	34	34	34	34																		
0.726 – 0.750	18	20	20	22	22	24	24	24	26	26	26	28	28	28	30	30	30	32	32	32	34	34	34	34	34																				
0.751 – 0.775	20	20	22	22	24	24	26	26	26	28	28	30	30	30	30	32	32	34	34	34	34	34	34																						
0.776 – 0.800	20	22	22	24	24	26	26	26	28	28	28	30	30	30	32	32	32	34	34	34	34	34																							
0.801 – 0.825	22	22	24	24	26	26	28	28	28	28	30	30	32	32	32	32	34	34	34	34	34																								
0.826 – 0.850	22	24	24	26	26	28	28	28	30	30	30	32	32	32	34	34	34	34	34																										
0.851 – 0.875	24	24	26	26	28	28	30	30	30	30	32	32	34	34	34	34	34																												
0.876 – 0.900	24	26	26	28	28	30	30	30	32	32	32	34	34	34	34	34																													
0.901 – 0.925	26	26	28	28	30	30	32	32	32	32	34	34	34	34	34																														
0.926 – 0.950	26	28	28	30	30	32	32	32	34	34	34	34	34																																
0.951 – 0.975	28	28	30	30	32	32	34	34	34	34	34																																		
0.976 – 1.000	28	30	30	32	32	34	34	34	34	34																																			
1.001 – 1.025	30	30	32	32	34	34	34	34	34																																				
1.026 – 1.050	30	32	32	34	34	34	34																																						
1.051 – 1.075	32	32	34	34	34																																								
1.076 – 1.100	32	34	34	34																																									
1.101 – 1.125	34	34	34																																										
1.126 – 1.150	34	34																																											
1.151 – 1.170	34																																												

New shim thicknesses mm (in.)

Shim No.	Thickness	Shim No.	Thickness
02	2.500 (0.0984)	20	2.950 (0.1161)
04	2.550 (0.1004)	22	3.000 (0.1181)
06	2.600 (0.1024)	24	3.050 (0.1201)
08	2.650 (0.1043)	26	3.100 (0.1220)
10	2.700 (0.1063)	28	3.150 (0.1240)
12	2.750 (0.1083)	30	3.200 (0.1260)
14	2.800 (0.1102)	32	3.250 (0.1280)
16	2.850 (0.1122)	34	3.300 (0.1299)
18	2.900 (0.1142)		

Exhaust valve clearance:
0.27 – 0.37 mm (0.011 – 0.015 in.)

EXAMPLE: The 2.800 mm (0.1102 in.) shim is installed and the measured clearance is 0.450 mm (0.0177 in.). Replace the 2.800 mm (0.1102 in.) shim with a No. 18 shim.

FIG. 74 Valve shim selection chart (exhaust)—2VZ-FE and 3VZ-FE engines

with a micrometer. Locate that particular measurement in the "Installed Shim Thickness" column of the accompanying charts, then locate the previously recorded measurement (from Step 6, 8 or 10) for that valve in the "Measured Clearance " column of the charts. Index the 2 columns to arrive at the proper replacement shim thickness.

16. The new replacement shim thickness may also be determined by a formula.

- T...Thickness of used shim
- A...Measured valve clearance
- N...Thickness of new shim
- Intake:
  N = T + (A–0.18mm)
- Exhaust:
  N = T + (A–0.32mm)

Select a new shim with a thickness as close as possible to the value arrived at in the formula. To convert millimeters to inches, multiply by 0.039. To convert inches to millimeters, multiply by 25.4.

➡ **Replacement shims are available in 17 sizes, in increments of 0.05mm (0.0020 in.), from 2.50mm (0.0984 in.) to 3.30mm (0.1299 in.).**

17. Place the new shim on the valve lifter. Remove the special tool and then recheck the valve clearance.

18. Install the gasket onto the cylinder head cover. install the head cover with the seal washers and nuts. Torque the nuts to 52 inch lbs. (6 Nm).

19. Install the intake tube.

20. Refill the engine with coolant and connect the battery cable.

IDLE SPEED AND MIXTURE

Gasoline Engines

IDLE SPEED ADJUSTMENT

2S-E Engines

➧ SEE FIGS. 21, 75, 76

1. Leave the air cleaner installed and all the air pipes and hoses of the air intake system connected. Leave all vacuum lines connected to the ESA and EGR systems, etc.

2. Make sure that the Electronic Fuel Injection wiring connectors are fully plugged in. Apply the emergency brake and block the wheels. Start the engine and let it warm up.

3. Turn all the accessories OFF and place the transaxle in the neutral range.

4. Remove the rubber cap from the IIA service connector coming from the distributor. Remove the plug covering the idle speed adjusting screw. Place the cap and the plug in your pocket.

➡ **These engines require the use of a special tachometer that can be connected to this service connector. Many tachometers are not compatible with this hook-up, so we recommend that you consult with the manufacturer before purchasing a certain type.**

5. Connect the test probe of the tachometer to the service connector. Please refer to the proper connection illustrations detailed in the Ignition Timing section.

❊❊ WARNING

Never allow the tachometer terminal to touch the ground as it could result in damage to the ignition igniter and/or the ignition coil.

6. Race the engine at 2,500 rpm for approximately two minutes. Return the engine to idle and disconnect the vacuum switching valve (VSV) for the idle speed control (ISC).

7. Set the idle speed by turning the idle speed adjusting screw. The idle speed should be as detailed in the Tune-Up Specifications chart.

8. After setting the idle speed, shut off the engine. Connect the VSV connector and remove

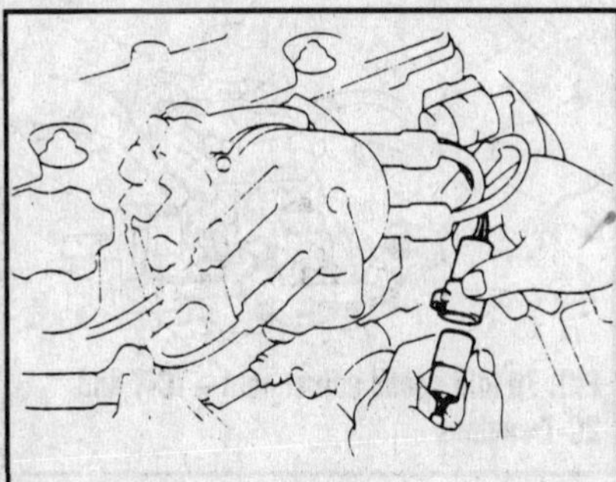

FIG. 75 Disconnect the ISV connector—2S-E engines

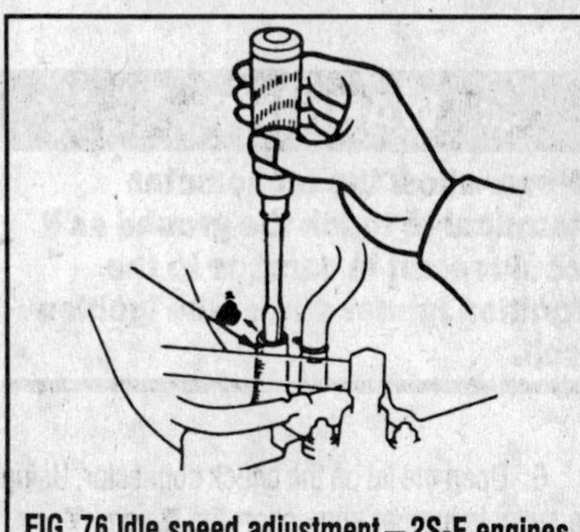

FIG. 76 Idle speed adjustment—2S-E engines

the tachometer. Install the plug and the rubber cap.

3S-FE Engines

➧ SEE FIG. 21, 38, 77

1. Leave the air cleaner installed and all the air pipes and hoses of the air intake system connected. Leave all vacuum lines connected to the ESA and EGR systems, etc.

2. Make sure that the Electronic Fuel Injection wiring connectors are fully plugged in. Apply the emergency brake and block the wheels. Start the engine and allow it to warm up.

3. Turn all the accessories OFF and place the transaxle in the neutral range.

4. Remove the rubber cap from the IIA service connector coming from the distributor. Remove the rubber boot covering the idle speed adjusting screw.

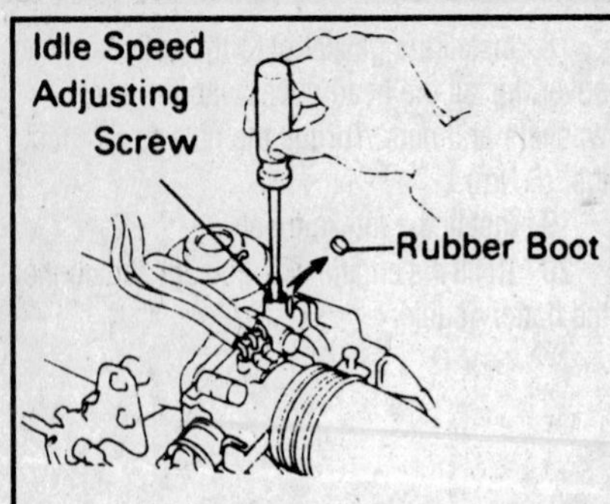

FIG. 77 Idle speed adjustment—3S-FE engines

➡ **These engines require the use of a special tachometer that can be connected to the service connector. Many tachometers are not compatible with this hook-up, so we recommend that you consult with the manufacturer before purchasing a certain type.**

5. Connect the test probe of the tachometer to the IIA service connector coming from the distributor.

WARNING

Never allow the tachometer terminal to touch the ground as it could result in damage to the ignition igniter and/or the ignition coil.

6. Open the lid on the check connector. Using a suitable jumper wire, short the **E_1** and **T** terminals on 1987–88 models; or the **E_1** and **TE_1** terminals on 1989–91 models.
7. Check the idle speed with the tachometer. If the idle speed is not as specified, set the idle speed by turning the idle speed adjusting screw. The idle speed should be as detailed in the Tune-Up Specifications chart.
8. Remove the jumper wire and close the lid of the service connector. Disconnect the tachometer and install the plug and rubber boot.

5S-FE, 2VZ-FE and 3VZ-FE Engines

Idle speed on these engines is controlled completely by the Electronic Control Unit (ECU). Idle speed is not adjustable on these engines.

IDLE MIXTURE ADJUSTMENT

Idle mixture is controlled completely by the Electronic Control Unit (ECU). Idle mixture is not adjustable on these engines.

Diesel Engines

IDLE SPEED ADJUSTMENT

1C-T and 2C-T Engines

➧ SEE FIGS. 78, 79

1. This adjustment should be made with the engine at normal operating temperature under the following conditions:
   a. Air cleaner installed.
   b. All accessories switched OFF.
   c. Transaxle in Neutral.
   d. Wheels blocked and parking brake firmly applied.
2. Connect a suitable diesel tachometer to the engine according to the manufacturer's instructions.
3. Disconnect the accelerator cable from the injection pump.
4. Start the engine and allow it to warm up.
5. Check the idle speed with the tachometer. It should be 750 rpm. If not, adjust the idle speed by loosening the locknut and turning the idle speed adjusting screw located on the injection pump.

FIG. 78 Disconnecting the injection pump accelerator cable—1C-T and 2C-T engines

FIG. 79 Idle speed adjustment—1C-T and 2C-T engines

MAXIMUM IDLE SPEED ADJUSTMENT

1C-T and 2C-T Engines

1. This adjustment should be made with a warm engine under the following conditions:
   a. Air cleaner installed.
   b. All accessories switched OFF.
   c. Transaxle in Neutral.
   d. Wheels blocked and parking brake firmly applied.
2. Connect a suitable diesel tachometer to the engine according to the manufacturer's instructions.
3. Disconnect the accelerator cable from the injection pump.
4. Check the normal idle speed and adjust as necessary.
5. Fully depress the injection pump adjusting lever and check the maximum idle speed with the tachometer. The maximum idle speed should be 5,200 rpm.

WARNING

This check should be done quickly. Hold the lever in the maximum idle position just long enough to read the tachometer and perform any necessary adjustments.

6. If the maximum idle speed is not as specified, perform the following adjustment:
   a. Remove the lockwire from the maximum speed adjusting screw.
   b. Loosen the locknut on the maximum adjusting screw.
   c. Adjust the maximum idle speed by turning the screw.
   d. When the maximum idle speed adjusted, tighten the locknut.
   e. Lock the maximum adjusting screw with a new piece of wire.
7. Check the normal idle speed and adjust as necessary. Recheck the maximum idle speed.
8. Disconnect the tachometer.
9. Connect the accelerator cable to the adjusting lever so that there is no slack in the cable.
10. Depress the accelerator pedal all the way and have an assistant observe the adjusting lever on the injection pump. The adjusting lever should be stopped by the maximum idle speed adjusting bolt when the pedal is fully depressed.

ON-VEHICLE INSPECTION

SPARK TEST

CHECK THAT SPARK OCCURS

(a) Disconnect high-tension cords from spark plugs.

(b) Remove the spark plugs.

(c) Install the spark plugs to each high-tension cord.

(d) Ground the spark plug.

(e) Check if spark occurs while engine is being cranked.

NOTE: To prevent gasoline from being injected from injectors during this test, crank the engine for no more than 1 — 2 seconds at a time.

If the spark does not occurs, perform the test as follows:

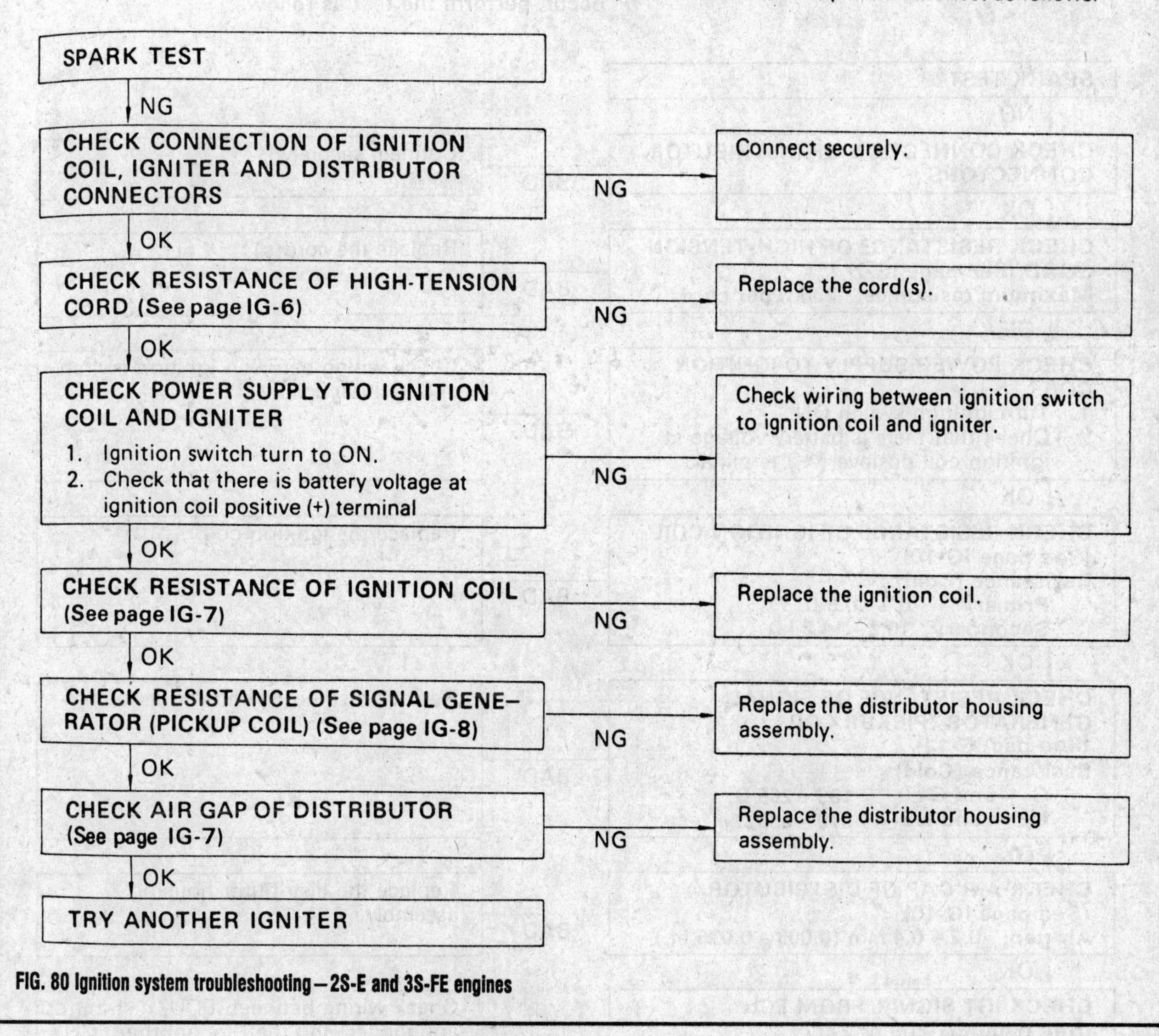

FIG. 80 Ignition system troubleshooting—2S-E and 3S-FE engines

ON–VEHICLE INSPECTION
SPARK TEST

CHECK THAT SPARK OCCURS

(a) Disconnect the high–tension cords from the spark plugs. (See page IG–7)
(b) Remove the spark plugs. (See page IG–8)
(c) Install the spark plugs to the each high–tension cord.
(d) Ground the spark plug.
(e) Check if spark occurs while engine is being cranked. HINT: To prevent gasoline from being injected from injectors during this test, crank the engine for no more than 1 – 2 seconds at a time.If the spark does not occur, perform the test as follows:

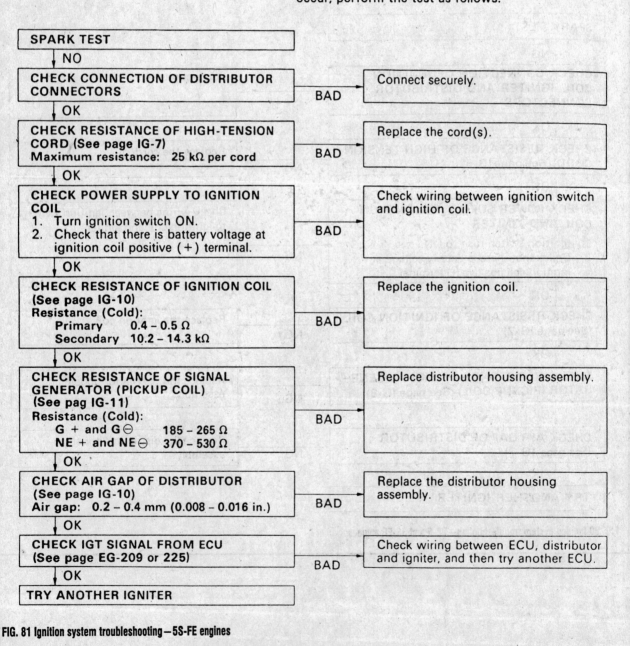

Check	Result	Action
SPARK TEST		
↓ NO		
CHECK CONNECTION OF DISTRIBUTOR CONNECTORS	BAD →	Connect securely.
↓ OK		
CHECK RESISTANCE OF HIGH-TENSION CORD (See page IG-7) **Maximum resistance: 25 kΩ per cord**	BAD →	Replace the cord(s).
↓ OK		
CHECK POWER SUPPLY TO IGNITION COIL 1. Turn ignition switch ON. 2. Check that there is battery voltage at ignition coil positive (+) terminal.	BAD →	Check wiring between ignition switch and ignition coil.
↓ OK		
CHECK RESISTANCE OF IGNITION COIL (See page IG-10) **Resistance (Cold):** **Primary 0.4 – 0.5 Ω** **Secondary 10.2 – 14.3 kΩ**	BAD →	Replace the ignition coil.
↓ OK		
CHECK RESISTANCE OF SIGNAL GENERATOR (PICKUP COIL) (See pag IG-11) **Resistance (Cold):** **G + and G⊖ 185 – 265 Ω** **NE + and NE⊖ 370 – 530 Ω**	BAD →	Replace distributor housing assembly.
↓ OK		
CHECK AIR GAP OF DISTRIBUTOR (See page IG-10) **Air gap: 0.2 – 0.4 mm (0.008 – 0.016 in.)**	BAD →	Replace the distributor housing assembly.
↓ OK		
CHECK IGT SIGNAL FROM ECU (See page EG-209 or 225)	BAD →	Check wiring between ECU, distributor and igniter, and then try another ECU.
↓ OK		
TRY ANOTHER IGNITER		

FIG. 81 Ignition system troubleshooting—5S-FE engines

ON-VEHICLE INSPECTION

SPARK TEST

CHECK THAT SPARK OCCURS

(a) Disconnect the high-tension cord from the distributor.

(b) Hold the end approx. 12.5 mm (0.50 in.) from body of vehicle.

(c) See if spark occurs while engine is being cranked.

HINT: To prevent gasoline from being injected from injectors during this test, crank the engine for no more than 1 – 2 seconds at a time.

If the spark does not occur, perform the test as follows:

SPARK TEST

↓ NO

CHECK CONNECTION OF IGNITION COIL, IGNITER AND DISTRIBUTOR CONNECTORS — BAD → Connect securely.

↓ OK

CHECK RESISTANCE OF HIGH-TENSION CORDS (See page IG-10)
Maximum resistance: 25 kΩ per cord — BAD → Replace the cord (s).

↓ OK

CHECK POWER SUPPLY TO IGNITION COIL
1. Turn ignition switch ON.
2. Check that there is battery voltage at ignition coil positive (+) terminal.

— BAD → Check wiring between ignition switch to ignition coil and igniter.

↓ OK

CHECK RESISTANCE OF IGNITION COIL (See page IG-12)
Resistance (Cold):
Primary 0.41 – 0.50 Ω
Secondary 10.2 – 13.8 kΩ

— BAD → Replace the ignition coil.

↓ OK

CHECK RESISTANCE OF SIGNAL GENERATOR (PICKUP COIL) (See page IG-8)
Resistance: 140 — 180 Ω — BAD → Replace the distributor.

↓ OK

CHECK AIR GAP OF DISTRIBUTOR (See page IG-12)
Air gap: 0.2 – 0.4 mm (0.008 – 0.016 in.) — BAD → Replace the distributor.

↓ OK

CHECK IGT SIGNAL FROM ECU (See page FI-62) — BAD → Check wiring between ECU and distributor, and then try another ECU.

↓ OK

TRY ANOTHER IGNITER

FIG. 82 Ignition system troubleshooting—2VZ-FE engines

ON—VEHICLE INSPECTION

SPARK TEST

CHECK THAT SPARK OCCURS

(a) Disconnect the high—tension cord from the distributor. (See page IG—27)

(b) Hold the end approx. 12.5 mm (0.50 in.) from the body of vehicle.

(c) See if spark occurs while engine is being cranked.
HINT: To prevent gasoline from being injected from injectors during this test, crank the engine for no more than 1 — 2 seconds at time.

If the spark does not occur, perform the test as follows:

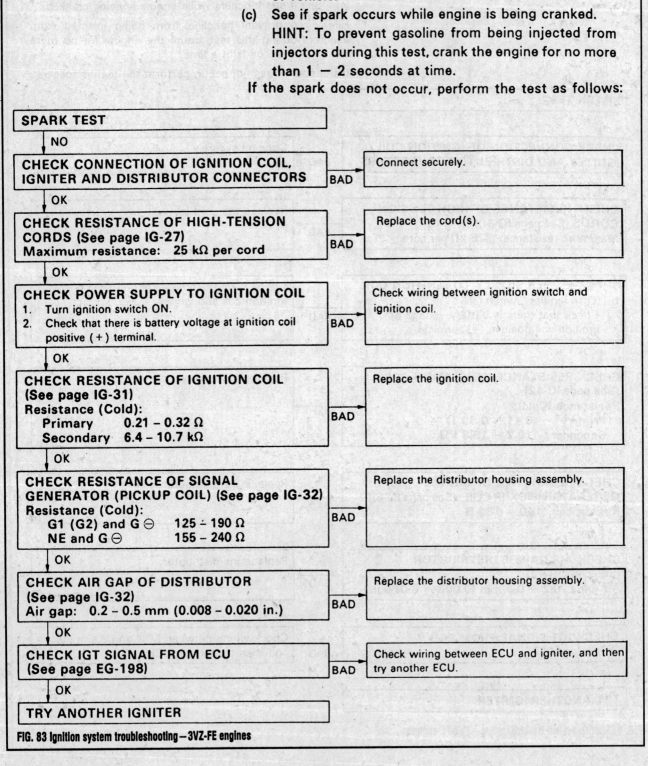

Step	Result	Action if BAD
SPARK TEST	NO → next step	
CHECK CONNECTION OF IGNITION COIL, IGNITER AND DISTRIBUTOR CONNECTORS	OK → next step; BAD →	Connect securely.
CHECK RESISTANCE OF HIGH-TENSION CORDS (See page IG-27) Maximum resistance: 25 kΩ per cord	OK → next step; BAD →	Replace the cord(s).
CHECK POWER SUPPLY TO IGNITION COIL 1. Turn ignition switch ON. 2. Check that there is battery voltage at ignition coil positive (+) terminal.	OK → next step; BAD →	Check wiring between ignition switch and ignition coil.
CHECK RESISTANCE OF IGNITION COIL (See page IG-31) Resistance (Cold): Primary 0.21 – 0.32 Ω Secondary 6.4 – 10.7 kΩ	OK → next step; BAD →	Replace the ignition coil.
CHECK RESISTANCE OF SIGNAL GENERATOR (PICKUP COIL) (See page IG-32) Resistance (Cold): G1 (G2) and G ⊖ 125 – 190 Ω NE and G ⊖ 155 – 240 Ω	OK → next step; BAD →	Replace the distributor housing assembly.
CHECK AIR GAP OF DISTRIBUTOR (See page IG-32) Air gap: 0.2 – 0.5 mm (0.008 – 0.020 in.)	OK → next step; BAD →	Replace the distributor housing assembly.
CHECK IGT SIGNAL FROM ECU (See page EG-198)	OK → next step; BAD →	Check wiring between ECU and igniter, and then try another ECU.
TRY ANOTHER IGNITER		

FIG. 83 Ignition system troubleshooting—3VZ-FE engines

Diagnosis of Spark Plugs

Problem	Possible Cause	Correction
Brown to grayish-tan deposits and slight electrode wear.	• Normal wear.	• Clean, regap, reinstall.
Dry, fluffy black carbon deposits.	• Poor ignition output.	• Check distributor to coil connections.
Wet, oily deposits with very little electrode wear.	• "Break-in" of new or recently overhauled engine. • Excessive valve stem guide clearances. • Worn intake valve seals.	• Degrease, clean and reinstall the plugs. • Refer to Section 3. • Replace the seals.
Red, brown, yellow and white colored coatings on the insulator. Engine misses intermittently under severe operating conditions.	• By-products of combustion.	• Clean, regap, and reinstall. If heavily coated, replace.
Colored coatings heavily deposited on the portion of the plug projecting into the chamber and on the side facing the intake valve.	• Leaking seals if condition is found in only one or two cylinders.	• Check the seals. Replace if necessary. Clean, regap, and reinstall the plugs.
Shiny yellow glaze coating on the insulator.	• Melted by-products of combustion.	• Avoid sudden acceleration with wide-open throttle after long periods of low speed driving. Replace the plugs.
Burned or blistered insulator tips and badly eroded electrodes.	• Overheating.	• Check the cooling system. • Check for sticking heat riser valves. Refer to Section 1. • Lean air-fuel mixture. • Check the heat range of the plugs. May be too hot. • Check ignition timing. May be over-advanced. • Check the torque value of the plugs to ensure good plug-engine seat contact.
Broken or cracked insulator tips.	• Heat shock from sudden rise in tip temperature under severe operating conditions. Improper gapping of plugs.	• Replace the plugs. Gap correctly.

TORQUE SPECIFICATIONS

Component	English	Metric
Spark Plug:	11–15 ft. lbs.	16–20 Nm
Distributor Pinch Bolt(s):		
2S-E, 3S-FE:	9 ft. lbs.	13 Nm
5S-FE:	14 ft. lbs.	19 Nm
2VZ-FE:	13 ft. lbs.	18 Nm
3VZ-FE:	13 ft. lbs.	18 Nm
Cylinder Head Cover Nuts:		
3S-FE:	13 ft. lbs.	18 Nm
5S-FE:	17 ft. lbs.	23 Nm
2VZ-FE, 3VZ-FE:	52 inch. lbs.	6 Nm

3

ENGINE AND ENGINE OVERHAUL

ALTERNATOR
- Alternator precautions 3-12
- Brush replacement 3-15
- Removal and installation 3-13
- Specifications 3-17

BATTERY 3-16
CAMSHAFT 3-82
CATALYTIC CONVERTER 3-103
CHARGING SYSTEM 3-12
COIL (IGNITION) 3-5
COMPRESSION TESTING 3-25
CONNECTING RODS AND BEARINGS
- Service 3-88, 96
- Specifications 3-28

CRANKSHAFT
- Service 3-98
- Specifications 3-28

CYLINDER HEAD
- Removal and installation 3-53
- Resurfacing 3-62

DISTRIBUTOR 3-8
ENGINE
- Camshaft 3-82
- Compression testing 3-25
- Connecting rods and bearings 3-88
- Crankshaft 3-98
- Cylinder head 3-53
- Cylinders 3-96
- Exhaust manifold 3-41
- Fan 3-45
- Flywheel 3-102
- Freeze plugs 3-97
- Front (timing) cover 3-72
- Front seal 3-72
- Intake manifold 3-39
- Main bearings 3-101
- Oil pan 3-67
- Oil pump 3-69
- Overhaul techniques 3-23
- Piston pin 3-95
- Pistons 3-88
- Rear main seal 3-98
- Removal and installation 3-30
- Ring gear 3-102
- Rings 3-95
- Rocker arms 3-38
- Specifications 3-26, 109
- Thermostat 3-38
- Timing belt 3-78
- Timing covers 3-72
- Timing gears 3-81
- Turbocharger 3-44
- Valve (rocker) cover 3-36
- Valve guides 3-66
- Valves 3-62
- Valve seats 3-65
- Valve springs 3-65
- Water pump 3-49

EXHAUST MANIFOLD 3-41
EXHAUST PIPE 3-103
EXHAUST SYSTEM 3-103
FAN 3-45
FLYWHEEL AND RING GEAR 3-102
FREEZE PLUGS 3-97
IC REGULATOR 3-15
IGNITER 3-7
IGNITION COIL 3-5
INTAKE MANIFOLD 3-39
MAIN BEARINGS 3-101
MANIFOLDS
- Intake 3-39
- Exhauqt 3-41

MUFFLER 3-104
OIL COOLER 3-70
OIL PAN 3-67
OIL PUMP 3-69
PICKUP COIL 3-5
PISTON PIN 3-95
PISTONS 3-88
RADIATOR 3-47
REAR MAIN OIL SEAL 3-98
RING GEAR 3-102
RINGS 3-95
ROCKER ARMS 3-38
SENDING UNITS & SENSORS 3-22
SPECIFICATIONS CHARTS
- Alternator and regulator 3-17
- Camshaft 3-27
- Crankshaft and connecting rod 3-28
- General engine 3-26, 109
- Piston and ring 3-29
- Starter 3-17
- Torque 3-30, 114
- Valves 3-26

STARTER
- Overhaul 3-21
- Removal and installation 3-19
- Solenoid or relay replacement 3-21
- Specifications 3-17

STRIPPED THREADS 3-24
TAILPIPE 3-104
THERMOSTAT 3-38
TIMING BELT 3-78
TIMING GEARS 3-81
TORQUE SPECIFICATIONS 3-30, 114
VALVE GUIDES 3-66
VALVE SEATS 3-65
VALVE SERVICE 3-62
VALVE SPECIFICATIONS 3-26
VALVE SPRINGS 3-65
WATER PUMP 3-49

Alternator and Regulator Specifications Chart 3-17
Camshaft Specifications Chart 3-27
Crankshaft and Connecting Rod Specifications Chart 3-28
Engine Electrical Systems 3-2
Engine Mechanical Systems 3-23
Engine Torque Specifications Chart 3-30, 114
Exhaust System 3-103
General Engine Specifications Chart 3-26, 109
Piston Specifications Chart 3-29
Piston Ring Specifications Chart 3-29
Starter Specifications Chart 3-17
Valve Specifications Chart 3-26

ENGINE ELECTRICAL

Understanding Basic Electricity

Understanding the basic theory of electricity makes electrical troubleshooting much easier. Several gauges are used in electrical troubleshooting to see inside the circuit being tested. Without a basic understanding, it will be difficult to understand testing procedures.

Electricity is the flow of electrons, hypothetical particles thought to constitute the basic "stuff" of electricity. In a comparison with water flowing in a pipe, the electrons would be the water. As the flow of water can be measured, the flow of electricity can be measured. The unit of measurement is amperes, frequently abbreviated "amps". An ammeter will measure the actual amount of current flowing in the circuit.

Just as the water pressure is measured in units such as pounds per square inch, electrical pressure is measured in volts. When a voltmeter's two probes are placed on two "live" portions of an electrical circuit with different electrical pressures, current will flow through the voltmeter and produce a reading which indicates the difference in electrical pressure between the two parts of the circuit.

While increasing the voltage in a circuit will increase the flow of current, the actual flow depends not only on voltage, but on the resistance of the circuit. The standard unit for measuring circuit resistance is an ohm, measured by an ohmmeter. The ohmmeter is somewhat similar to an ammeter, but incorporates its own source of power so that a standard voltage is always present.

An actual electric circuit consists of four basic parts. These are: the power source such as a generator or battery; a hot wire, which conducts the electricity under a relatively high voltage to the component supplied by the circuit; the load, such as a lamp, motor, resistor, or relay coil; and the ground wire, which carries the current back to the source under very low voltage. In such a circuit the bulk of the resistance exists between the point where the hot wire is connected to the load, and the point where the load is grounded. In an automobile, the vehicle's frame, which is made of steel, is used as a part of the ground circuit for many of the electrical devices.

Remember that, in electrical testing, the voltmeter is connected in parallel with the circuit being tested (without disconnecting any wires) and measures the difference in voltage between the locations of the two probes; that the ammeter is connected in series with the load (the circuit is separated at one point and the ammeter inserted so it becomes a part of the circuit); and the ohmmeter is self-powered, so that all the power in the circuit should be off and the portion of the circuit to be measured contacted at either end by one of the probes of the meter.

For any electrical system to operate, it must make a complete circuit. This simply means that the power flow from the battery must make a complete circle. When an electrical component is operating, power flows from the battery to the component, passes through the component causing it to perform its function (lighting a light bulb) and then returns to the battery through the ground of the circuit. This ground is usually (but not always) the metal part of the car on which the electrical component is mounted.

Perhaps the easiest way to visualize this is to think of connecting a light bulb with two wires attached to it to your battery. The battery in your car has two posts (negative and positive). If one of the two wires attached to the light bulb was attached to the negative post of the battery and the other wire was attached to the positive post of the battery, you would have a complete circuit. Current from the battery would flow out one post, through the wire attached to it and then to the light bulb, where it would pass through causing it to light. It would then leave the light bulb, travel through the other wire, and return to the other post of the battery.

The normal automotive circuit differs from this simple example in two ways. First, instead of having a return wire from the bulb to the battery, the light bulb returns the current to the battery through the chassis of the vehicle. Since the negative battery cable is attached to the chassis and the chassis is made of electrically conductive metal, the chassis of the vehicle can serve as a ground wire to complete the circuit. Secondly, most automotive circuits contain switches to turn components on and off.

Some electrical components which require a large amount of current to operate also have a relay in their circuit. Since these circuits carry a large amount of current, the thickness of the wire in the circuit (gauge size) is also greater. If this large wire were connected from the component to the control switch on the instrument panel, and then back to the component, a voltage drop would occur in the circuit. To prevent this potential drop in voltage, an electromagnetic switch (relay) is used. The large wires in the circuit are connected from the battery to one side of the relay, and from the opposite side of the relay to the component. The relay is normally open, preventing current from passing through the circuit. An additional, smaller, wire is connected from the relay to the control switch for the circuit. When the control switch is turned on, it grounds the smaller wire from the relay and completes the circuit. When the control switch is turned on, it grounds the smaller wire from the relay. If you were to disconnect the light bulb (from the previous example of a light bulb being connected to the battery by two wires) from the wires and touch the two wires together (please take our word for this; don't try it), the result will be a shower of sparks. A similar thing happens (on a smaller scale) when the power supply wire to a component or the electrical component itself becomes grounded before the normal ground connection for the circuit. To prevent damage to the system, the fuse for the circuit blows to interrupt the circuit, protecting the components from damage. Because grounding a wire from a power source makes a complete circuit, less the required component to see the power, the phenomenon is called a short circuit. The most common causes of short circuits are: the rubber insulation on the wire breaking or rubbing through to expose the current carrying core of the wire to a metal part of the car, or a shorted switch.

Some electrical systems on the car are protected by a circuit breaker which is, basically, a self-repairing fuse. When either of the above described events takes place in a system which is protected by a circuit breaker, the circuit breaker opens the circuit the same way a fuse does. However, when either the short is removed from the circuit or the surge subsides, the circuit breaker resets itself and does not have to be replaced as a fuse does.

The final protective device in the chassis electrical system is a fuse link. A fuse link is a wire that acts as a fuse. It is connected between the starter relay and the main wiring harness for the car. This connection is under the hood, very near a similar fuse link which protects the engine electrical system. Since the fuse link protects all the chassis electrical components, it is the probably cause of trouble when none of the electrical components function, unless the battery is disconnected or dead.

Electrical problems generally fall into one of three areas:

1. The component that is not functioning is not receiving current.
2. The component itself is not functioning.
3. The component is not properly grounded.

Problems that fall into the first category are by far the most complicated. It is the current supply system to the component which contains all the switches, relays, fuses., etc.

The electrical system can be checked with a test light and a jumper wire. A test light is a device that looks like a pointed screwdriver with a wire attached to it. It has a light bulb in its handle. A jumper wire is a piece of insulated wire with an alligator clip attached to each end.

If a light bulb is not working, you must follow a systematic plan to determine which of the three causes is the villain.

1. Turn on the switch that controls the inoperable bulb.
2. Disconnect the power supply wire from the bulb.
3. Attach the ground wire on the test light to a good metal ground.
4. Touch the probe end of the test light to the end of the power supply wire that was disconnected form the bulb. If the bulb is receiving current, the test light will go on.

➡ If the bulb is one which works only when the ignition key is turned on (turn signal), make sure the key is turned on.

If the test light does not go on, then the problem is in the circuit between the battery and the bulb. As mentioned before, this includes all the switches, fuses, and relays in the system. Turn to the wiring diagram and find the bulb on the diagram. Follow the wire that runs back to the battery. The problem is an open circuit between the battery and the bulb. If the fuse is blown and, when replaced, immediately blows again, there is a short circuit in the system which must be located and repaired. If there is a switch in the system, bypass it with a jumper wire. This is done by connecting one end of the jumper wire to the power supply wire into the switch and the other end of the jumper wire to the wire coming out of the switch. Again, consult the wiring diagram. If the test light lights with the jumper wire installed, the switch or whatever was bypassed is defective.

➡ Never substitute the jumper wire for the bulb, as the bulb is the component required to use the power from the power source.

5. If the bulb in the test light goes on, then the current is getting to the bulb that is not working in the car. This eliminates the first of the three possible causes. Connect the power supply wire and connect a jumper wire from the bulb to a good metal ground. Do this with the switch which controls the bulb turned on, and also the ignition switch turned on if it is required for the light to work. If the bulb works with jumper wire installed, then it has a bad ground. This is usually caused by the metal area on which the bulb mounts to the car being coated with some type of foreign matter.
6. If neither test located the source of the trouble, then the light bulb itself is defective.

The above test procedure can be applied to any of the components of the chassis electrical system by substituting the component that is not working for the light bulb. Remember that for any electrical system to work, all connections must be clean and tight.

UNDERSTANDING THE ENGINE ELECTRICAL SYSTEM

The engine electrical system can be broken down into three separate and distinct systems:

1. The starting system.
2. The charging system.
3. The ignition system.

Battery and Starting System

The battery is the first link in the chain of mechanisms which work together to provide cranking of the automobile engine. The battery is a lead/acid electrochemical device consisting of six 2V subsections connected in series so the unit is capable of producing approximately 12V of electrical pressure. Each subsection, or cell, consists of a series of positive and negative plates held a short distance apart in a solution of sulfuric acid and water. The two types of plates are of dissimilar metals. This causes a chemical reaction to be set up, and it is this reaction which produces current flow from the battery when its positive and negative terminals are connected to an electrical appliance such as a lamp or motor. The continued transfer of electrons would eventually convert the sulfuric acid in the electrolyte to water, and make the two plates identical in chemical composition. As electrical energy is removed from the battery, its voltage output tends to drop. Thus, measuring battery voltage and battery electrolyte composition are two ways of checking the ability of the unit to supply power. During the starting of the engine, electrical energy is removed from the battery. However, if the charging circuit is in good condition and the operating conditions are normal, the power removed from the battery will be replaced by the alternator which will force electrons back through the battery, reversing the normal flow, and restoring the battery to its original chemical state.

The battery and starting motor are linked by very heavy electrical cables designed to minimize resistance to the flow of current. Generally, the major power supply cable that leaves the battery goes directly to the starter, while other electrical system needs are supplied by a smaller cable. During starter operation, power flows from the battery to the starter and is grounded through the car's frame and the battery's negative ground strap.

The starting motor is a specially designed, direct current electric motor capable of producing a very great amount of power for its size. One thing that allows the motor to produce a great deal of power is its tremendous rotating speed. It drives the engine through a tiny pinion gear (attached to the starter's armature), which drives the very large flywheel ring gear at a greatly reduced speed. Another factor allowing it to produce so much power is that only intermittent operation is required of it. This, little allowance for air circulation is required, and the windings can be built into a very small space.

A magnetic switch mounted on the starter housing, is supplied by current from the starting switch circuit of the ignition switch. This magnetic action of the switch mechanically engages the starter clutch assembly and electrically closes the heavy switch which connects it to the battery. The starting switch circuit consists of the starting switch contained within the ignition switch, a transmission neutral safety switch or clutch pedal switch, and the wiring necessary to connect these in series with the starter solenoid or relay.

A pinion, which is a small gear, is mounted to a one-way drive clutch. This clutch is splined to the starter armature shaft. When the ignition switch is moved to the **START** position, the solenoid plunger slides the pinion toward the flywheel ring gear via a collar and spring. If the teeth on the pinion and flywheel match properly, the pinion will engage the flywheel immediately. If the gear teeth butt one another, the spring will be compressed and will force the gears to mesh as soon as the starter turns far enough to allow them to do so. As the solenoid plunger reaches the end of its travel, it closes the contacts that connect the battery and starter and then the engine is cranked.

As soon as the engine starts, the flywheel gear begins turning fast enough to drive the pinion at an extremely high rate of speed. At this point, the one-way clutch begins allowing the pinion to spin faster than the starter shaft so that the starter will not operate at excessive speed. When the ignition switch is released from the starter position, the solenoid is de-energized, and a spring contained within the solenoid assembly pulls the gear out of mesh and interrupts the current flow to the starter.

The starter uses a separate relay, mounted on the left hand cowl, to switch the motor and magnetic switch current on and off. The relay is used to reduce the amount of current the starting switch must carry.

Charging System

An alternator differs from a conventional DC shunt generator in that the armature is stationary, and is called the stator, while the field rotates and is called the rotor. The higher current values in the alternator's stator are conducted to the external circuit through fixed leads and connections, rather than through a rotating commutator and brushes as in a DC generator. This eliminates a major point of maintenance.

The alternator uses a 3-phase stator winding. The rotor consists of a field coil encased between 6-poled, interleaved sections, producing a 12-pole magnetic field with alternating north and south poles. By rotating the rotor inside the stator, and alternating current is induced in the stator windings. This alternating current is changed to direct current by diodes and is routed out of the alternator through the output terminal. Diode rectifiers act as one way electrical valves. Half of the diodes have a negative polarity and are grounded. The other half of the diodes have a positive polarity and are connected to the output terminal.

Since the diodes have a high resistance to the flow of current in one direction, and a low resistance in the opposite direction, they are connected in a manner which allows current to flow from the alternator to the battery in the low resistance direction.

The high resistance in the other direction prevents the flow of current from the battery to the alternator. Because of this feature, there is no need for a circuit breaker between the alternator and the battery.

Residual magnetism in the rotor field poles is minimal. The starting field current must, therefore, be supplied by the battery. It is connected to the field winding through the ignition switch and the charge indicator lamp or ammeter.

As in the DC shunt generator, the alternator voltage is regulated by varying the field current. This is accomplished electronically in the transistorized voltage regulator. No current regulator is required because all alternators have self limiting current characteristics.

An alternator is better than a conventional DC shunt generator because it is lighter and more compact, because it is designed to supply the battery and accessory circuits through a wide range of engine speeds, and because it eliminates the necessary maintenance of replacing brushes and servicing commutators.

The transistorized voltage regulator is an electronic switching device that is located on the alternator housing. It senses the voltage at the auxiliary terminal of the alternator and supplies the necessary field current for maintaining the system voltage at the output terminal. The output current is determined by the battery electrical load, such as operating headlights or heater blower. The regulator is a sealed unit on which no adjustments are possible.

Ignition System

The electronic ignition system offers many advantages over the conventional breaker points ignition system. By eliminating the points, maintenance requirements are greatly reduced. An electronic ignition system is capable of producing a much higher voltage which in turn aids in starting, reduces spark plug fouling and provides improved emission control.

The Integrated Ignition Assembly (IIA) ignition system is used on all Camrys and also on a variety of other Toyota vehicles (except diesel engines, as they do not have ignition systems). The distributor used on vehicles sold in the United States from 1983–85 was discontinued in 1986 and appeared in Canadian vehicles sold in that year. That distributor used a vacuum advancer to control the spark advance. The later 1986–92 ignition systems control the spark advance electronically through a micro-computer.

The Integrated Ignition Assembly (IIA) ignition system consists of a distributor with a signal generator, ignition coil(s), electronic igniter and a micro-computer (ECU). The ECU is programmed with data for optimum ignition timing for a wide range of driving and operating conditions. Using the data provided by the various engine mounted sensors (intake air volume, engine temperature, rpm, etc.), the ECU converts the data into a reference voltage signal and sends this signal to the igniter mounted inside the distributor. The signal generator receives a reference voltage from the ECU and activates the components of the igniter. The signal generator consists of three main components: the signal rotor, the pick-up coil and the permanent magnet. The signal rotor (not to be confused with the normal distributor rotor) revolves with the distributor shaft, while the pick-up coil and permanent magnet are stationary. As the signal rotor spins, the teeth on it pass a projection leading from the pick-up coil. When this occurs, voltage is allowed to flow through the system and fire the spark plugs. This process happens without physical contact or electrical arcing; therefore, there is no need to replace burnt or worn parts.

Ignition Coil

➡ The ignition coil is found in the distributor on all models except the 2VZ-FE and 3VZ-FE. On these models the coil is a separate unit, attached to the front left fender well, near the fuse box.

TESTING

Primary Coil Resistance

➧ SEE FIGS. 1-2

Using a suitable ohmmeter, measure the resistance between the positive and negative terminals. The primary coil resistance (cold) should be as follows:

- **1983–86**: 0.3–0.5Ω (USA); 1.2–1.5Ω (Canada)
- **1987–91 3S-FE**: 0.38–0.46Ω
- **1992 5S-FE**: 0.4–0.5Ω
- **1989–91 2VZ-FE**: 0.41–0.50Ω
- **1992 3VZ-FE**: 0.21–0.32Ω

If the primary coil resistance is not as specified, replace the ignition coil.

Secondary Coil Resistance

➧ SEE FIGS. 3-4

Using a suitable ohmmeter, measure the resistance between the positive terminal and the high tension terminal. The secondary coil resistance (cold) should be as follows:

- **1983–88 2S-E, 3S-FE**: 7.5–10.5Ω
- **1989–91 3S-FE**: 7.7–10.4Ω
- **1992 5S-FE**: 10.2–14.3kΩ
- **1989–91 2VZ-FE**: 10.2–13.8Ω
- **1992 3VZ-FE**: 6.4–10.7kΩ

If the resistance is not as specified, replace the ignition coil.

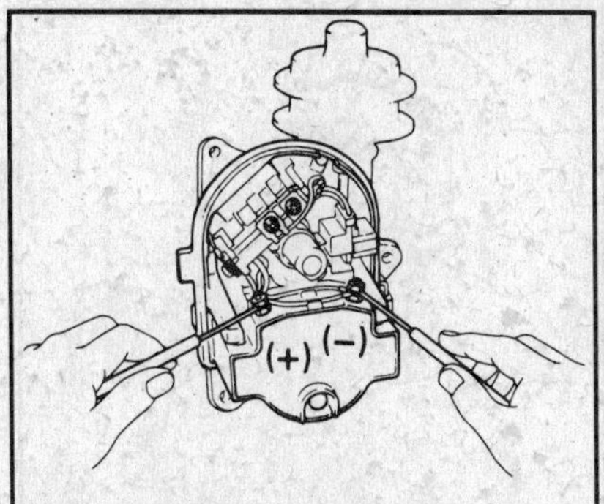

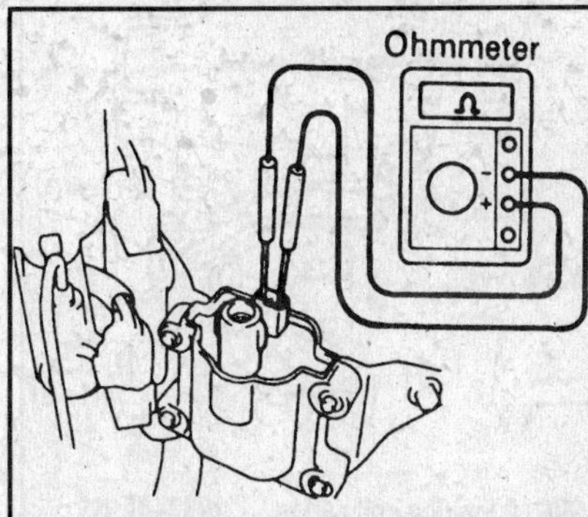

FIG. 1 Primary coil resistance test — all except 2VZ-FE and 3VZ-FE engines

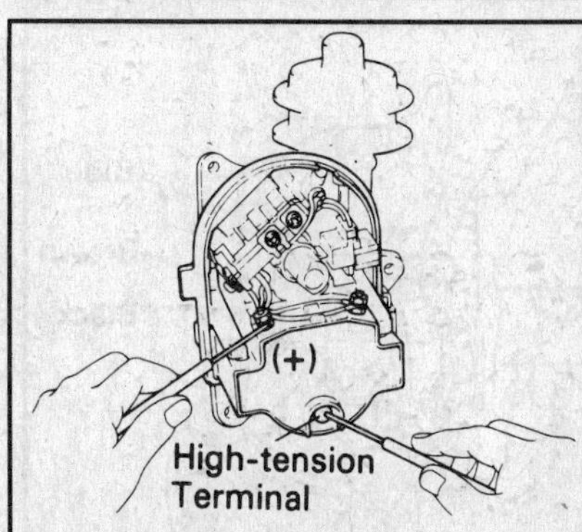

FIG. 2 Primary coil resistance test — 2VZ-FE and 3VZ-FE engines

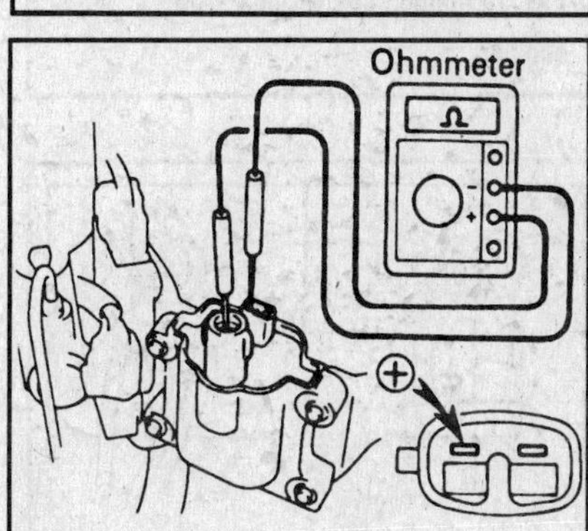

FIG. 3 Secondary coil resistance test — all except 2VZ-FE and 3VZ-FE engines

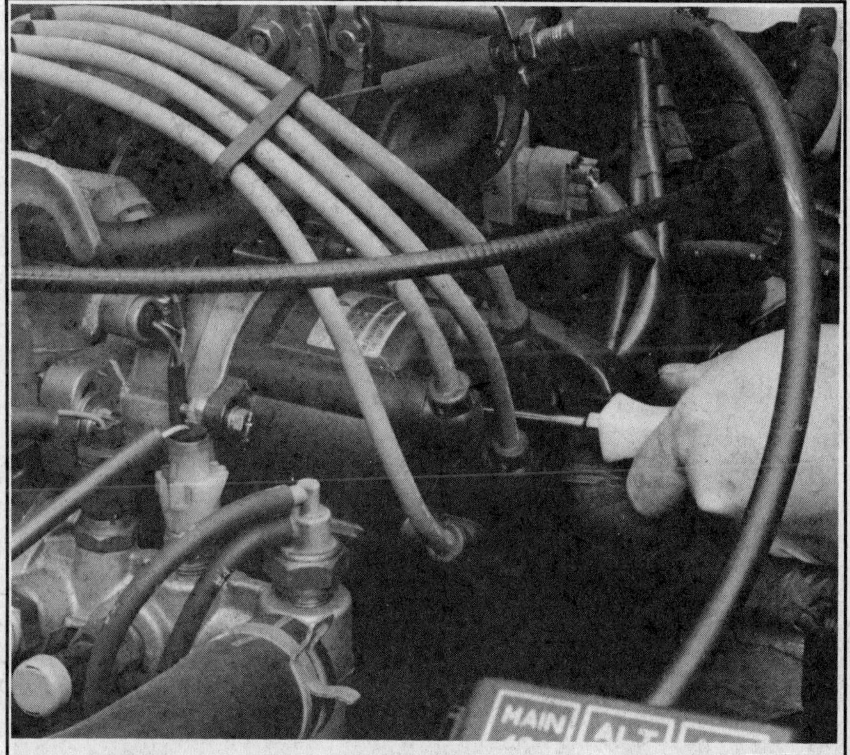

FIG. 4 Secondary coil resistance test — 2VZ-FE and 3VZ-FE engines

Air Gap

The air gap in the distributor should be checked periodically. Distributor air gap may only be checked and can only be adjusted by component replacement. The air gap checking and adjustment procedure is described in Section 2.

REMOVAL & INSTALLATION

1983–92 2S-E, 3S-FE and 5S-FE Engines

➧ SEE FIGS. 5-11

1. Disconnect the cable from the negative battery terminal.

✲✲ CAUTION

On models with an airbag, wait at least 30 seconds from the time that the ignition switch is turned to the LOCK position and the battery is disconnected before performing any further work.

2. Mark the position of the distributor flange in relation to the camshaft housing. Remove the distributor assembly.

3. Remove the distributor cap with the wires attached, and remove the packing. Mark the position of the rotor relative to the housing and pull the rotor straight up and off the shaft. The distributor cap is held to the housing with three retaining screws.

4. Remove the ignition coil dust cover.

5. Remove the two nuts and spring washers and disconnect the three or four wires from the terminals on the side of the ignition coil.

➡ 1983–85 models and 1983–86 Canadian models, use four ignition coil wires color coded yellow, blue, brown and red. 1986–91 models use three wires color coded blue, brown and black.

6. Remove the four retaining screws and remove the ignition coil and packing.

7. Install the new ignition coil with packing and four retaining screws.

8. Connect the three or four wires to the proper terminals on the side of the coil and install the two nuts and spring washers.

FIG. 5 Removing the distributor cap

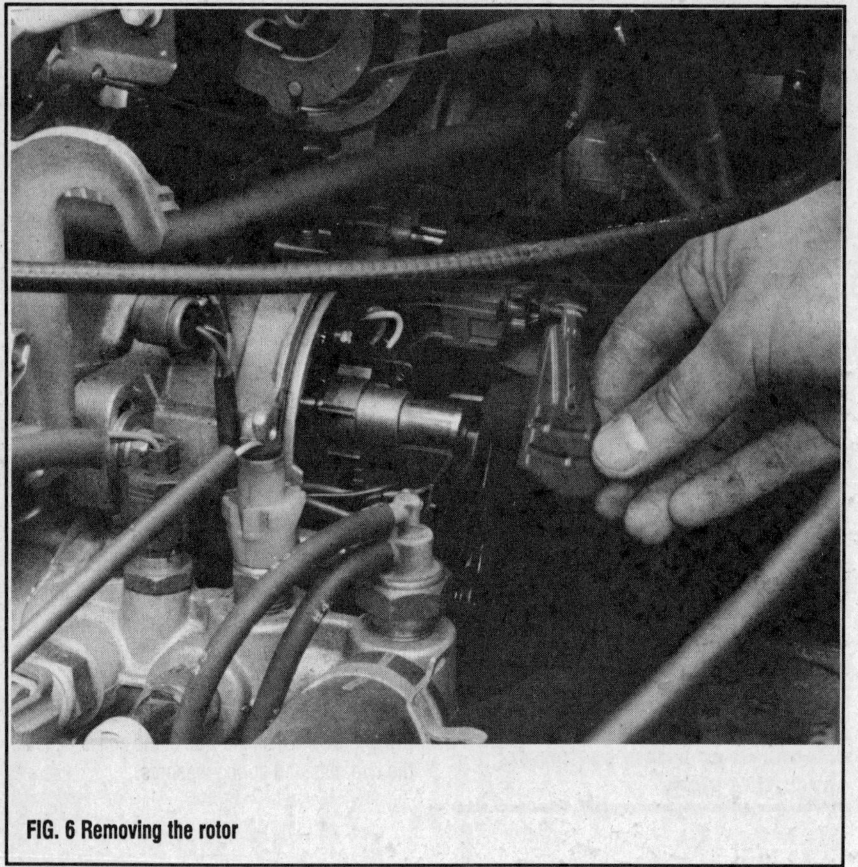

FIG. 6 Removing the rotor

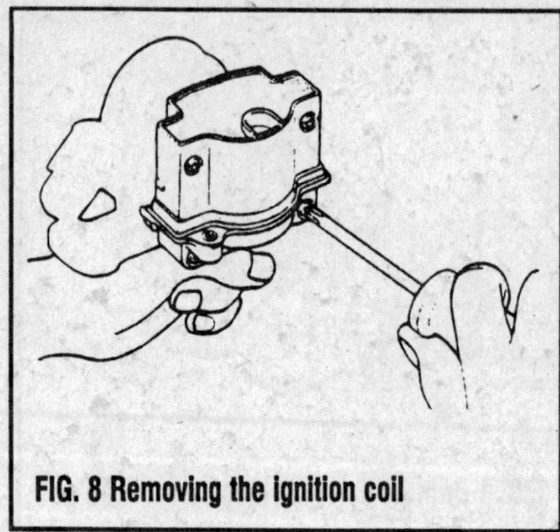

FIG. 8 Removing the ignition coil

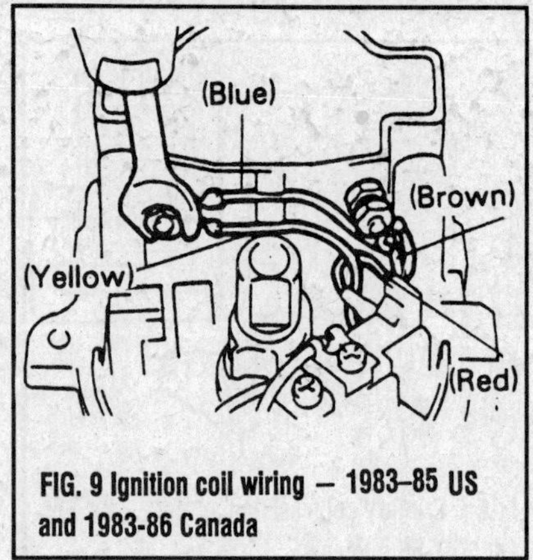

FIG. 9 Ignition coil wiring – 1983–85 US and 1983-86 Canada

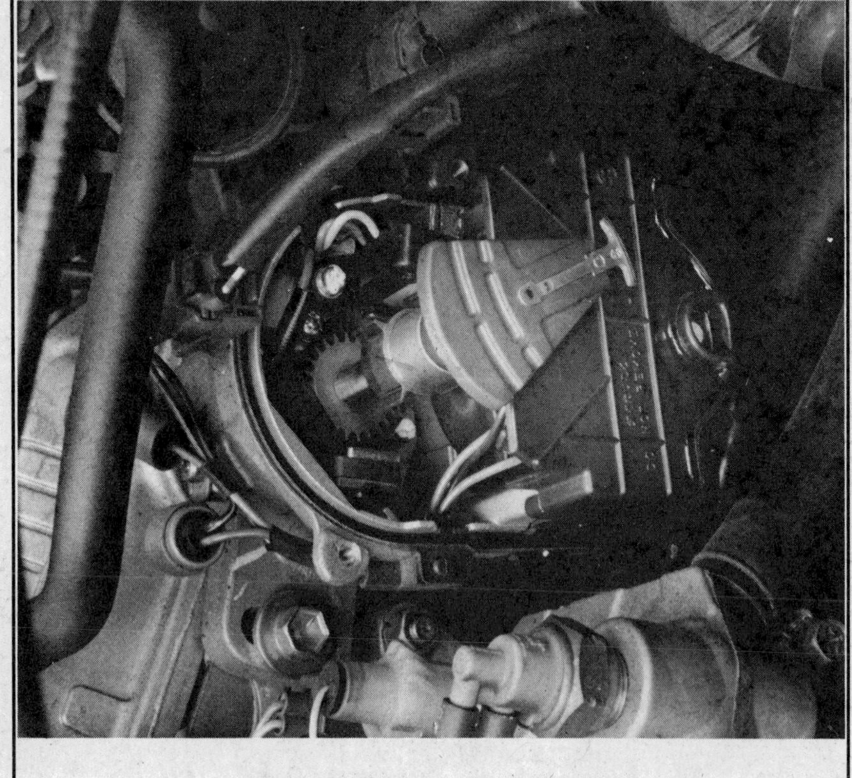

FIG. 7 The ignition coil is in the distributor

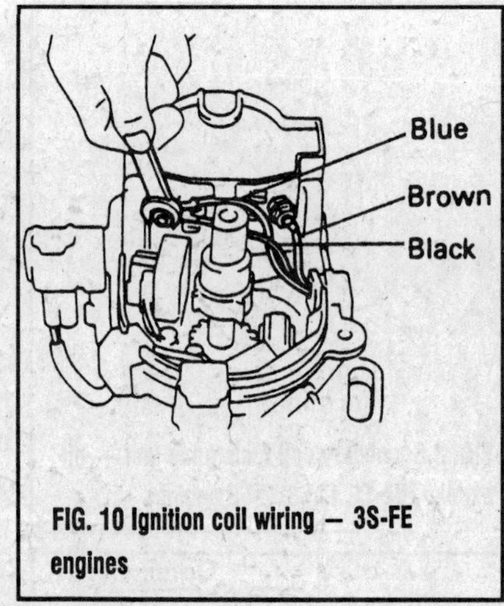

FIG. 10 Ignition coil wiring – 3S-FE engines

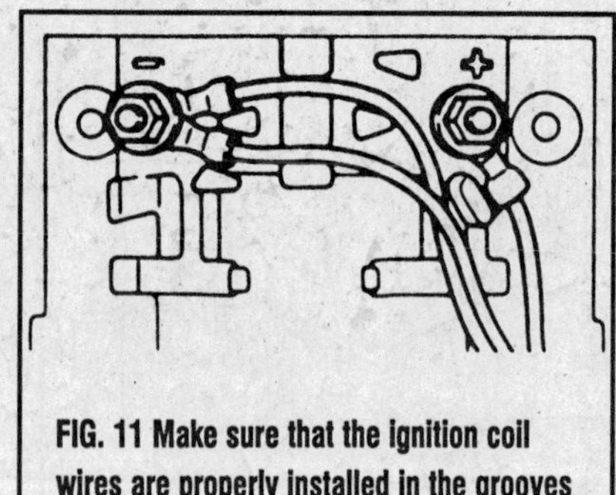

FIG. 11 Make sure that the ignition coil wires are properly installed in the grooves

CAUTION

When connecting the wires to the ignition coil terminals, make sure they are inserted properly into the grooves on the side of the coil. The wires must not make contact with the signal rotor or distributor housing.

9. Install the coil dust cover and push the rotor onto the shaft.
10. Place the distributor cap with packing and wires into position. Install the three retaining screws.
11. Install the distributor assembly and connect the negative battery cable.
12. Connect a tachometer and timing light to the engine and adjust the ignition timing.

1989–92 2VZ-FE and 3VZ-FE Engines

1. Disconnect the negative battery cable.

CAUTION

On models with an airbag, wait at least 30 seconds from the time that the ignition switch is turned to the LOCK position and the battery is disconnected before performing any further work.

2. Unplug and disconnect the coil electrical lead.
3. Disconnect the spark plug wire from the distributor.
4. Remove the four mounting screws and remove the ignition coil from its mounting bracket.

To install:

5. Install the ignition coil in the bracket and tighten the mounting screws.
6. Reconnect the spark plug lead and the electrical lead.
7. Connect the negative battery cable.

Igniter

TESTING

Spark Test

ALL MODELS

The igniter is responsible for firing the spark plugs. This test determines if spark is occurring.

1. Disconnect the spark plug wires from the spark plugs. Do them ONE AT A TIME and mark them as to cylinder number to ensure proper installation.
2. Remove the spark plugs. Mark them also.
3. Install the spark plugs into their respective coil wires.
4. Pick one plug/wire assembly using a suitable pair of spark plug wire boot pullers and ground it.
5. Have an assistant crank the engine and see if spark is present at the plug.

CAUTION

To prevent fuel from being injected from the injectors during this test, crank the engine for not more than one to two seconds at a time.

6. Repeat Steps 4–5 for the remaining plugs.
7. If spark does not occur, use the charts at the end of Section 2 to troubleshoot the igniter.

Igniter Line Source and Power Transistor Voltage

1883–85 AND 1983–867 CANADA MODELS ONLY

➧ SEE FIGS. 12-14

1. To test line source voltage, turn the ignition switch to the ON position. Using a suitable voltmeter, connect the positive probe to the ignition coil positive terminal and the negative probe to a suitable body ground. The voltage should be approximately 12 volts.
2. To test igniter power transistor voltage, proceed as follows:
   a. With the ignition switch in the ON position, connect the voltmeter positive probe to the ignition coil negative terminal and the negative probe to the body ground. The voltmeter should read approximately 12 volts.
   b. Using a dry cell (1.5V) battery, connect the positive terminal of the battery to the pink wire terminal and the negative terminal to the white terminal.

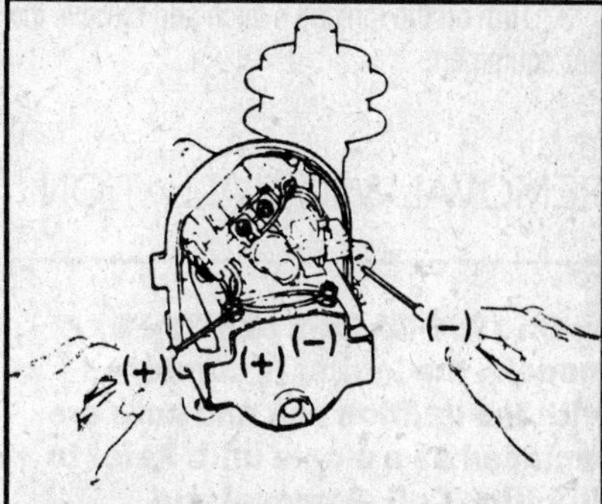

FIG. 12 Checking igniter power source line voltage

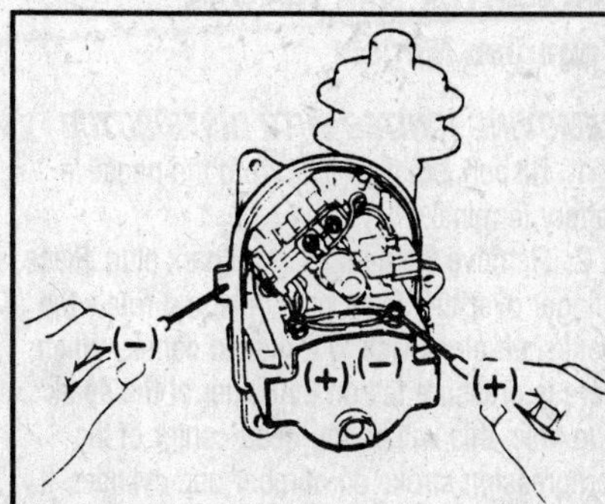

FIG. 13 Checking igniter power transistor voltage

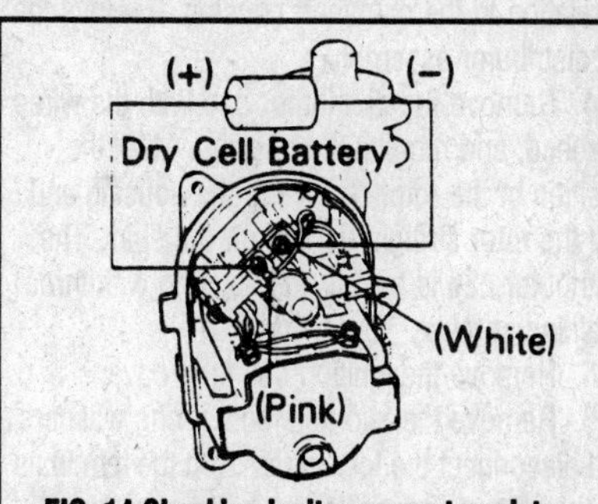

FIG. 14 Checking igniter power transistor voltage

CAUTION

Do not apply battery voltage for more than five seconds to avoid destroying the power transistor in the igniter.

   c. Using a voltmeter, connect the positive probe to the ignition coil negative terminal and the negative probe to a suitable body ground. Check the voltage reading, it should read 5 volts, less the battery voltage (USA), and 0–3 volts (Canada). If there is a problem with the igniter, replace it with a new one.

3. Turn off the ignition switch and remove the test equipment.

REMOVAL & INSTALLATION

➡ On 1986–91 2S-E and 3S-FE models, the igniter is combined with the ignition coil and both are replaced as a single unit. Refer to "Ignition Coil, Removal and Installation" described in this section.

1983–85 U.S. and 1983–86 Canadian Models

REMOVING IGNITER WITH DISTRIBUTOR

1. Disconnect the cable from the negative battery terminal.
2. Remove the number one spark plug. Place a finger over the spark plug hole and rotate the crankshaft clockwise to top dead center. When there is pressure felt on the finger at the spark plug hole, this will be top dead center of the compression stroke on number one cylinder. If not, repeat the procedure. Install the number one spark plug.
3. Mark the position of the distributor flange in relation to the camshaft housing. Remove the IIA distributor assembly.
4. Remove the distributor cap with the wires attached, and remove the packing. Mark the position of the rotor relative to the housing and pull the rotor straight up and off the shaft. The distributor cap is held to the housing with three retaining screws.
5. Remove the ignition coil dust cover.
6. Remove the two nuts and spring washers and disconnect the four wires from the terminals on the side of the ignition coil. The wires are color coded yellow, blue, brown and red.
7. Remove the four retaining screws and remove the ignition coil and packing.
8. Remove the nuts and disconnect the pink, white and black wires from the igniter terminals. Remove the two igniter retaining screws and remove the igniter.

To install:

1. Attach the new igniter with the two retaining screws. Connect the pink, black and white wires to their respective terminals and install the nuts. Make sure that the pick-up coil wires are secured in their clips and that there is slack in the wires.
2. Install the ignition coil and attach it with the four retaining screws.
3. Connect the four ignition coil wires to their respective terminals and install the two nuts and spring washers.

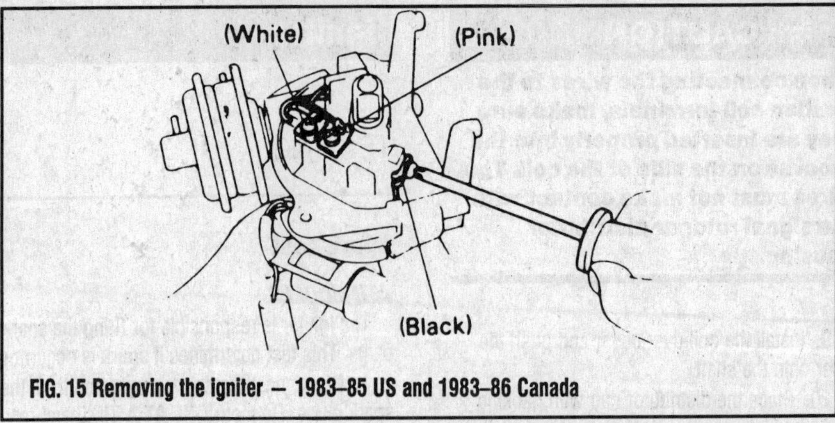

FIG. 15 Removing the igniter — 1983–85 US and 1983–86 Canada

4. Install the coil dust cover and push the rotor onto the shaft.
5. Place the distributor cap and wires into position. Install and tighten the retaining screws.
6. Install the distributor assembly and connect the negative battery cable.
7. Connect a tachometer and timing light to the engine and adjust the ignition timing.

REMOVING IGNITER WITHOUT REMOVING DISTRIBUTOR

1. Remove the distributor cap, rotor and dielectric insulator covers. Disconnect the red and yellow wires from the coil and the pink, white and black wires from the igniter.
2. Remove the igniter. It may be necessary to mark and rotate the distributor to gain access to the igniter retaining screws. The timing should be checked after the distributor is returned to the mark.
3. Install the new igniter using the two new retaining screws.
4. Twist the pick-up coil wires together, install the white wire first then pink and black wires to their original locations. Make sure the wires do not touch the housing generator or advance plate.
5. Route the red and yellow wires from the igniter so they do not contact moving parts. Connect the red wire to the right coil terminal (with the brown wire) and the yellow wire to the left terminal (with the blue wire). Replace the covers, rotor and cap.
6. Connect a tachometer and timing light to the engine and adjust the ignition timing.

1989–92 2VZ-FE and 3VZ-FE Engines

1. Disconnect the negative battery cable.

⁂ CAUTION

On models with an airbag, wait at least 30 seconds from the time that the ignition switch is turned to the LOCK position and the battery is disconnected before performing any further work.

2. Unplug and disconnect the igniter electrical lead.
3. Remove the four mounting screws and remove the igniter from its mounting bracket.

To install:

4. Install the igniter in the bracket and tighten the mounting screws.
5. Reconnect the electrical lead.
6. Connect the negative battery cable.

Distributor

REMOVAL & INSTALLATION

1983–85 U.S. and 1983–86 Canada

➧ SEE FIGS. 16-18

1. Disconnect the negative battery cable.
2. Disconnect the IIA connector.
3. Label and disconnect the hoses from he vacuum advancer.
4. Label and disconnect the wires from the spark plugs. Leave the wires connected to the distributor cap.
5. Mark the distributor flange in relation to the camshaft housing. Remove the holddown bolts and pull the distributor assembly from the camshaft housing.

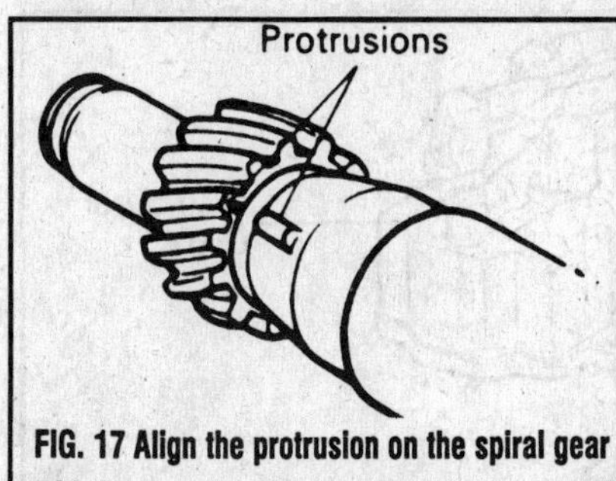

FIG. 17 Align the protrusion on the spiral gear with the protrusions on the housing

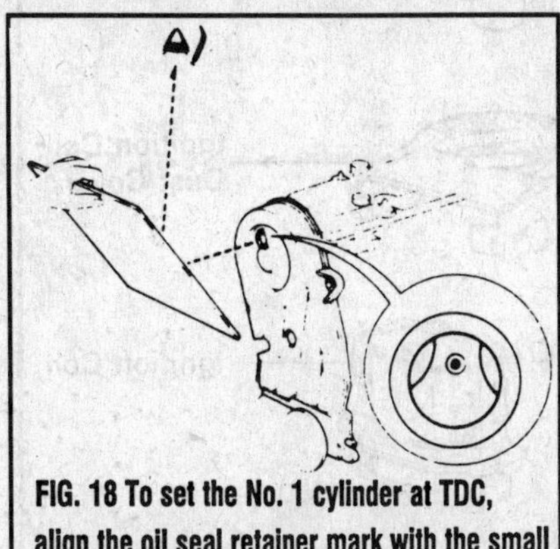
FIG. 18 To set the No. 1 cylinder at TDC, align the oil seal retainer mark with the small hole on the crankshaft — 2S-E engines

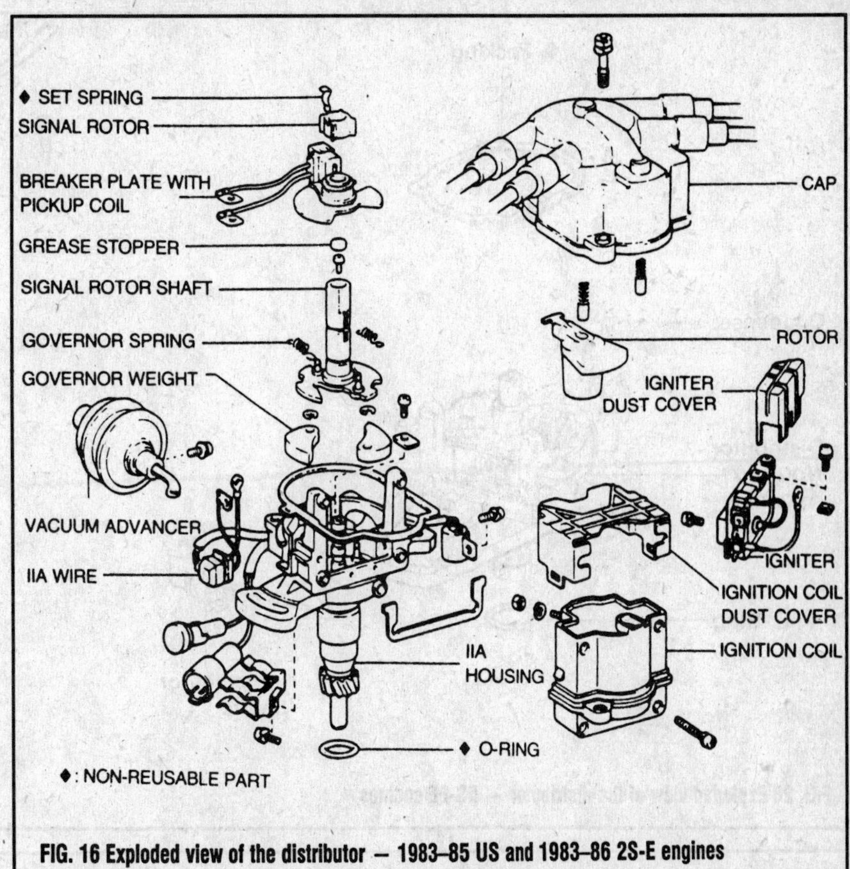

FIG. 16 Exploded view of the distributor — 1983–85 US and 1983–86 2S-E engines

6. Before the distributor can be installed (especially in cases where the engine has been disturbed, cranked or dismantled) set the No. 1 piston at TDC by performing the following:

a. Remove the right front wheel and fender apron seal.

b. Remove the inspection plug from the hole of the No. 2 timing belt cover.

c. With the use of a mirror, align the oil seal retainer mark with the center of the small hole on the camshaft timing pulley. Perform the alignment by turning the crankshaft pulley clockwise using a socket wrench.

d. Install the inspection plug and the right fender seal.

e. Also the timing mark on the crankshaft pulley should be aligned with the **O** mark on the timing indicator.

7. Coat the spiral gear and governor shaft tip with clean engine oil.

8. Align the protrusions on the housing with the spiral gear.

9. Insert the distributor by aligning the center of the flange with the hole in the camshaft housing. Lightly tighten the holddown bolts.

10. Connect the spark plug wires to their respective plugs.

11. Connect the vacuum advancer hoses, IIA connector and negative battery cable.

12. Connect a tachometer and timing light to the engine and adjust the ignition timing.

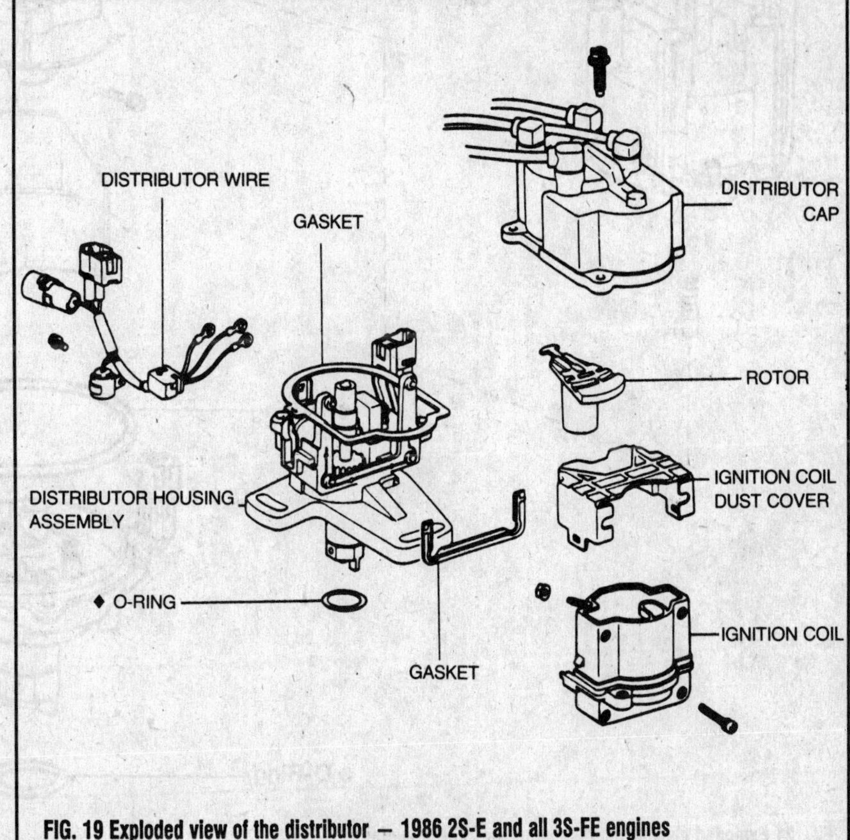

FIG. 19 Exploded view of the distributor — 1986 2S-E and all 3S-FE engines

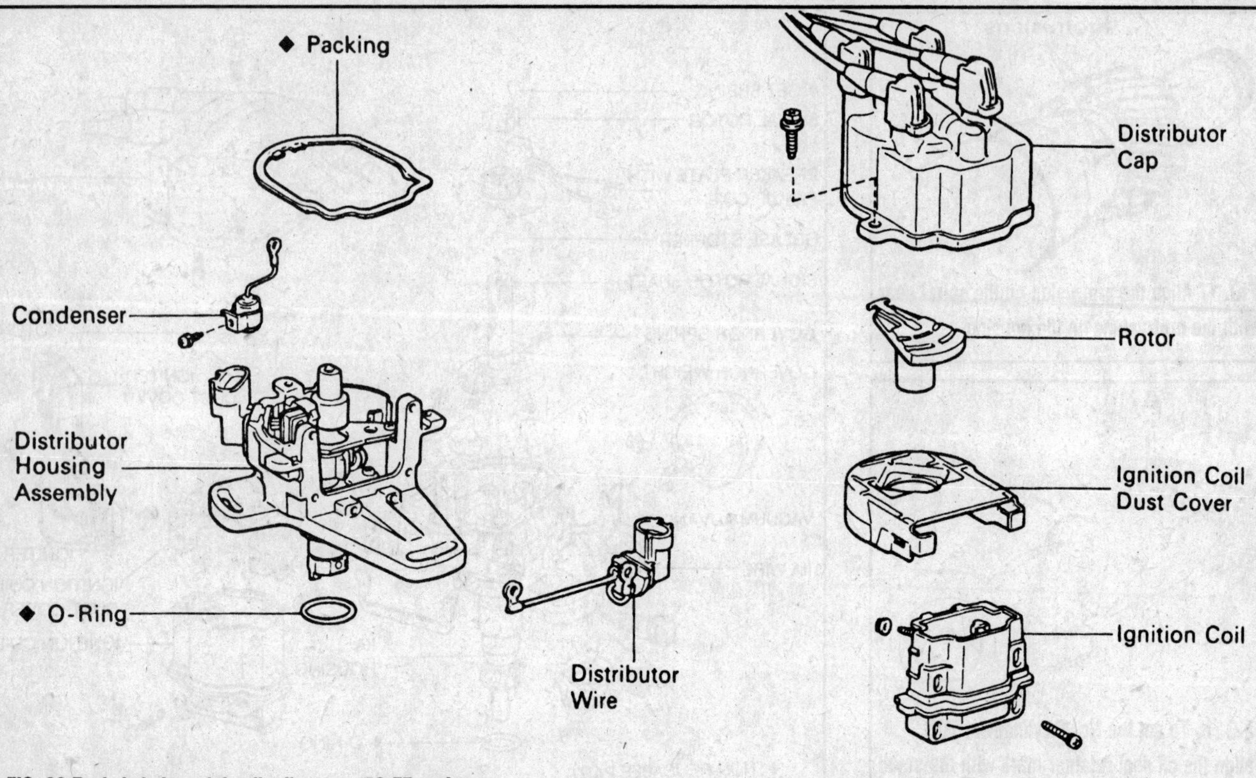

◆ Packing
Condenser
Distributor Housing Assembly
◆ O-Ring
Distributor Wire
Distributor Cap
Rotor
Ignition Coil Dust Cover
Ignition Coil

FIG. 20 Exploded view of the distributor — 5S-FE engines

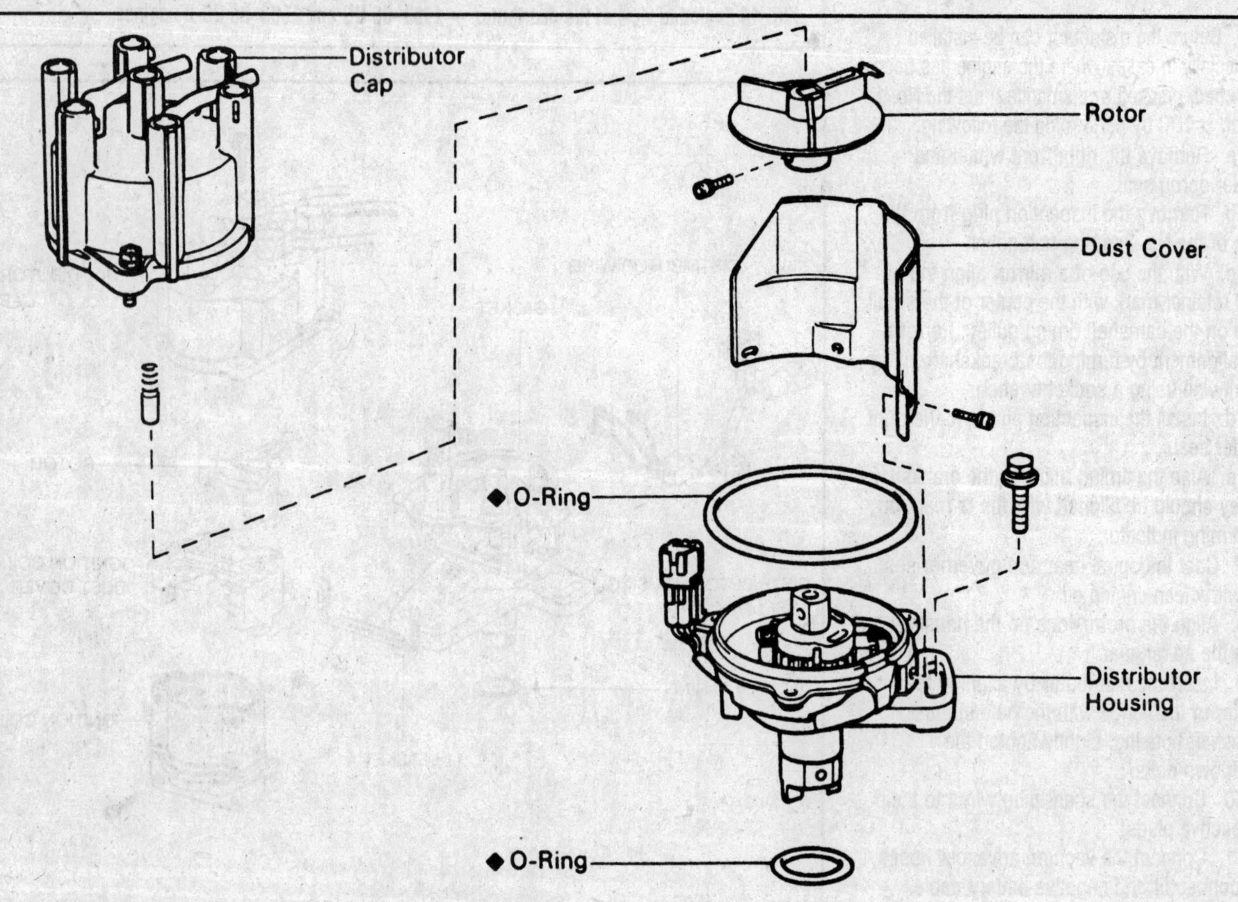

Distributor Cap
Rotor
Dust Cover
◆ O-Ring
Distributor Housing
◆ O-Ring

FIG. 21 Exploded view of the distributor — 2VZ-FE engines

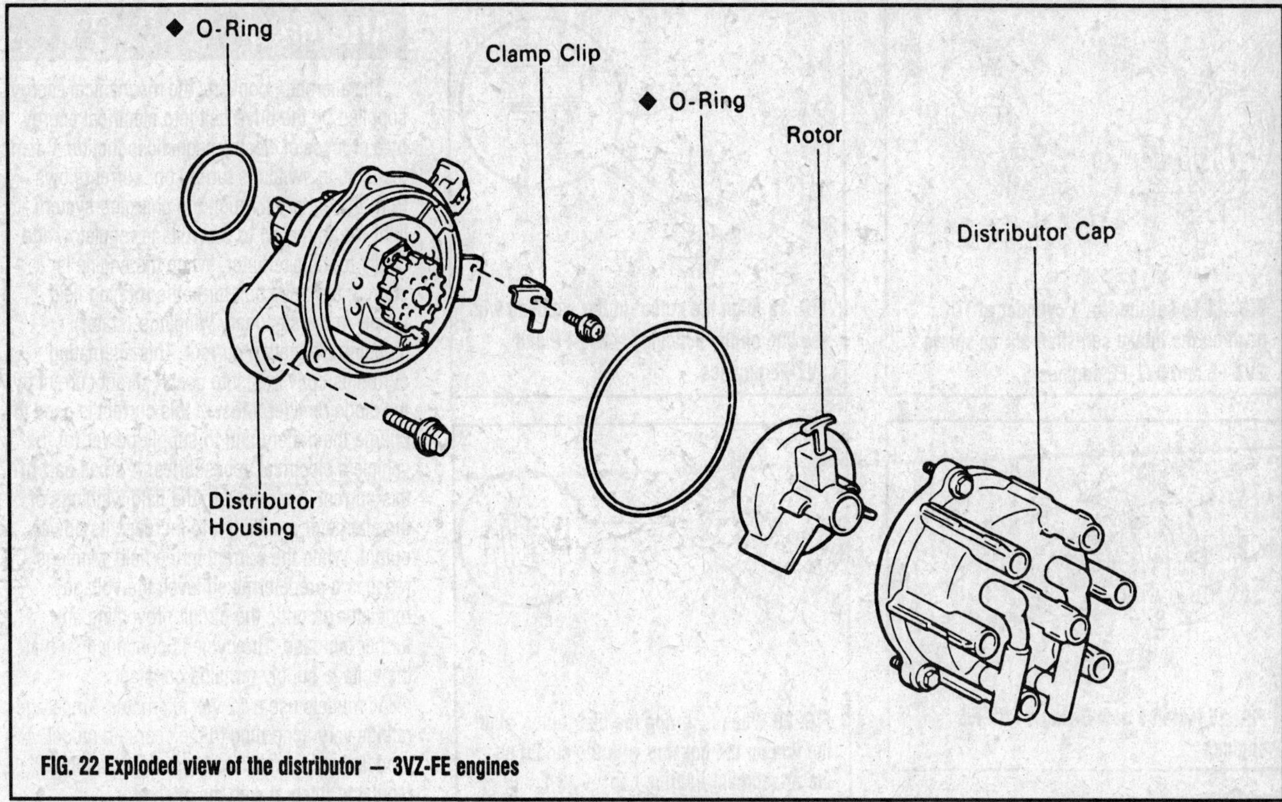

FIG. 22 Exploded view of the distributor — 3VZ-FE engines

1986–92

➧ SEE FIGS. 19-31

1. Disconnect the cable from the negative battery terminal.

> **✲✲ CAUTION**
>
> **On models with an airbag, wait at least 30 seconds from the time that the ignition switch is turned to the LOCK position and the battery is disconnected before performing any further work.**

2. Remove the air cleaner hose. On the 5S-FE, disconnect the accelerator cable from the throttle linkage and the remove the air cleaner cap, resonator and the air cleaner hose
3. Disconnect the connectors from the distributor.
4. Label and disconnect the spark plug wires from the spark plugs. Leave the wires connected to the distributor cap.
5. Mark the distributor flange in relation to the cylinder head. Loosen and remove the distributor hold down bolts and remove the distributor assembly.
6. Remove the O-ring from the distributor housing and replace with new.
7. Before the distributor can be installed (especially in cases where the engine has been disturbed, cranked or dismantled), set the No. 1 piston at TDC by performing the following: with a socket wrench or equivalent, turn the crankshaft clockwise and position the slit in the intake camshaft as shown in the accompanying illustrations. Also the timing mark on the crankshaft pulley should be aligned with the **0** mark on the No. 1 timing belt cover indicator.
8. Coat the new distributor housing O-ring with clean engine oil and install the O-ring.
9. Align the cut-out of the coupling with the line of the housing.
10. Insert the distributor into the cylinder head by aligning the center of the flange with the bolt hole in the cylinder head. Now align the flange with the match mark made previously on the cylinder head. Lightly tighten the holddown bolts.
11. Connect the spark plug wires to their respective spark plugs.
12. Connect the distributor connectors and the air cleaner hose.
13. Connect the negative battery cable.
14. Connect a tachometer and timing light to the engine and adjust the ignition timing.
15. Tighten the holddown bolts to 9 ft. lbs. (13 Nm) on 2S-E and 3S-FE engines; 14 ft. lbs. (19 Nm) on 5S-FE engines; or , 13 ft. lbs. (18 Nm) on 2VZ-FE and 3VZ-FE engines.

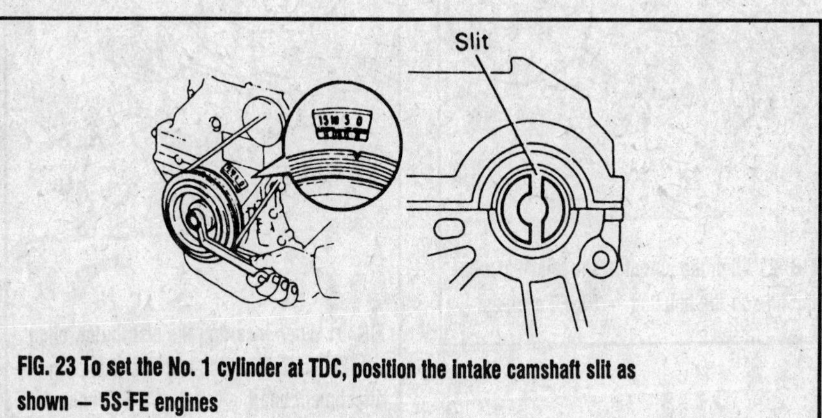

FIG. 23 To set the No. 1 cylinder at TDC, position the intake camshaft slit as shown — 5S-FE engines

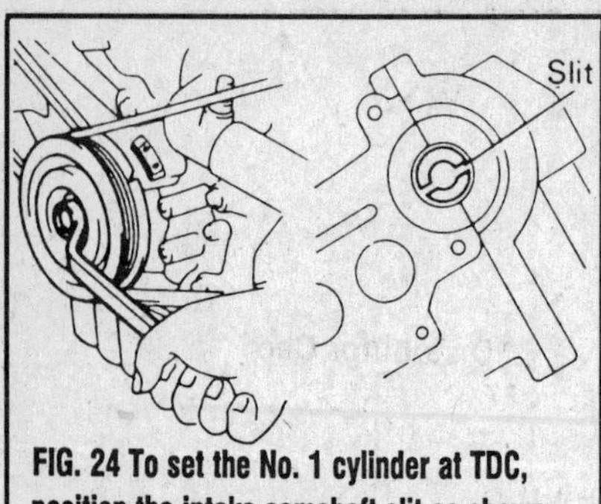

FIG. 24 To set the No. 1 cylinder at TDC, position the intake camshaft slit as shown 2VZ-FE and 3VZ-FE engines

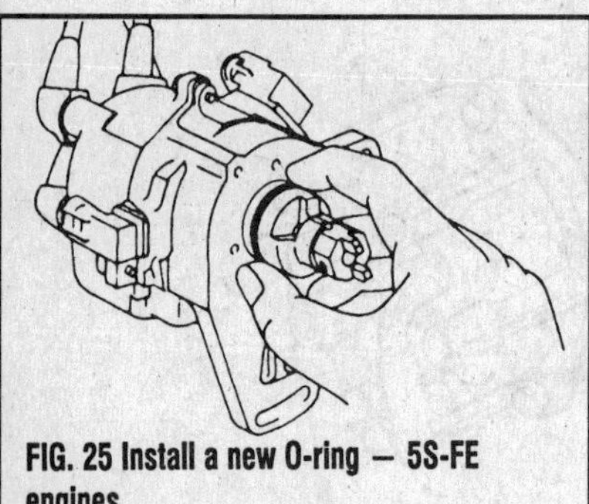
FIG. 25 Install a new O-ring — 5S-FE engines

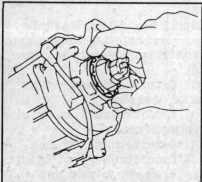

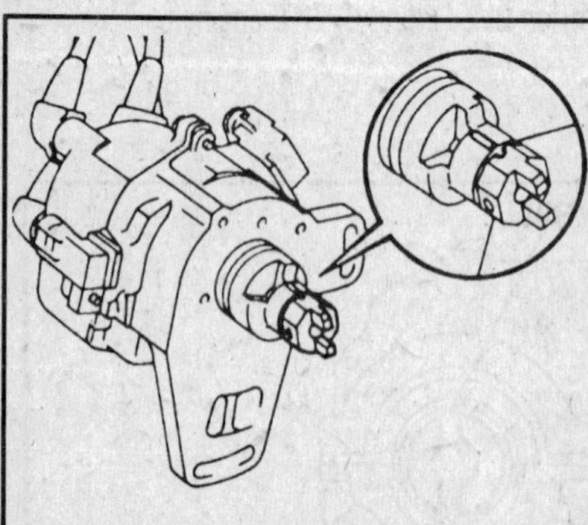
FIG. 26 Install a new O-ring — 2VZ-FE and 3VZ-FE engines

FIG. 27 Align the cutout of the coupling with the line on the housing — 5S-FE engines

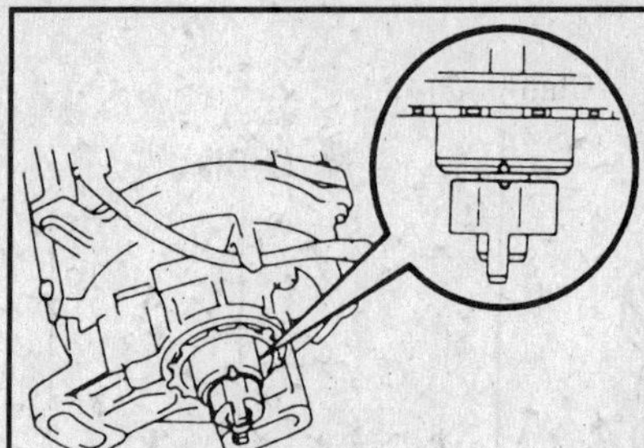
FIG. 28 Align the cutout of the coupling with the line on the housing — 2VZ-FE and 3VZ-FE engines

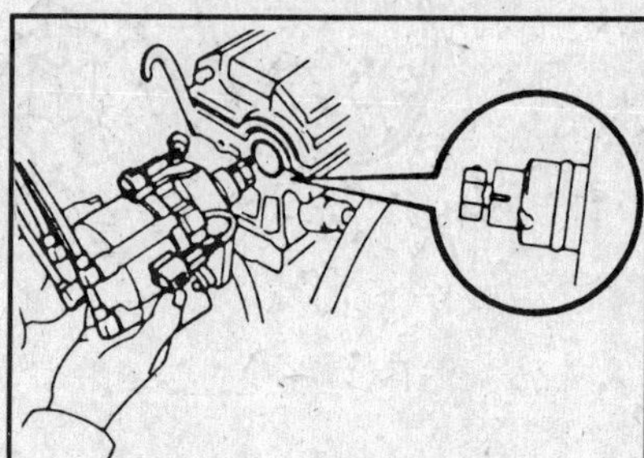
FIG. 29 When inserting the distributor, align the line on the housing with the cutout on the attachment bearing cap — 2S-E and 3S-FE engines

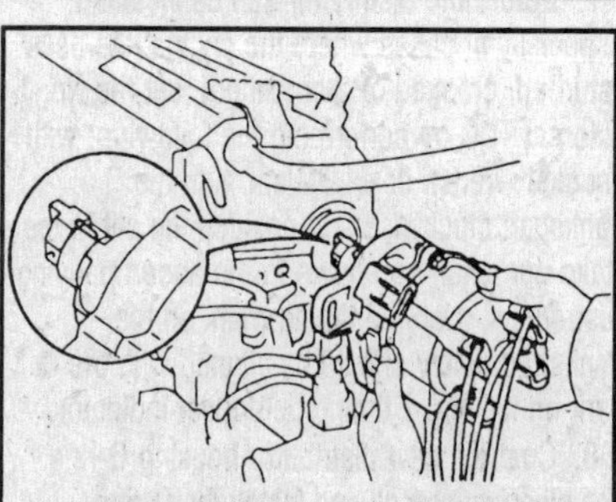
FIG. 30 Align the center of the flange with the center of the bolt hole on the head — 5S-FE engines

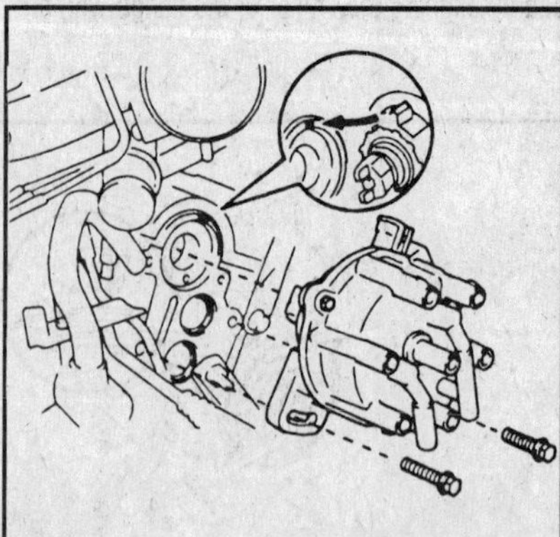
FIG. 31 When inserting the distributor, align the line on the housing with the cutout on the attachment bearing cap — 5S-FE engines

Alternator

The alternator converts the mechanical energy supplied by the drive belt into electrical energy by a process of electromagnetic induction. When the ignition switch is turned on, current flows from the battery through the charging system light (or ammeter) to the voltage regulator, and finally to the alternator. When the engine is started, the drive belt turns the rotating field (rotor) in the stationary windings (stator), inducing alternating current. This alternating current is converted into usable direct current by the diode rectifier. Most of this current is used to charge the battery and to supply power for the vehicle's electrical accessories. A small part of this current is returned to the field windings of the alternator enabling it to increase its power output. When the current in the field windings reaches a predetermined level, the voltage regulator grounds the circuit preventing any further increase. The cycle is continued so that the voltage supply remains constant.

All models use a 12 volt alternator. Amperage ratings vary according to the year and model. All models have a transistorized, nonadjustable regulator, integral with the alternator.

ALTERNATOR PRECAUTIONS

To prevent damage to the alternator and regulator, the following precautionary measures must be taken when working with the electrical system.

1. Never reverse the battery connections. Always check the battery polarity visually. This is to be done before any connections are made to ensure that all of the connections correspond to the battery ground polarity of the car.
2. Booster batteries must be connected properly. Make sure the positive cable of the booster battery is connected to the positive terminal of the battery which is getting the boost.
3. Disconnect the battery cables before using a fast charger; the charger has a tendency to force current through the diodes in the opposite direction for which they were designed.
4. Never use a fast charger as a booster for starting the car.
5. Never disconnect the voltage regulator while the engine is running, unless as noted for testing purposes.
6. Do not ground the alternator output terminal.
7. Do not operate the alternator on an open circuit with the field energized.

8. Do not attempt to polarize the alternator.
9. Disconnect the battery cables and remove the alternator before using an electric arc welder on the car.
10. Protect the alternator from excessive moisture. If the engine is to be steam cleaned, cover or remove the alternator.

REMOVAL & INSTALLATION

➧ SEE FIGS. 32-35

1. Disconnect the negative battery cable.

⁂ CAUTION

On models with an airbag, wait at least 30 seconds from the time that the ignition switch is turned to the LOCK position and the battery is disconnected before performing any further work.

2. Remove the two bolts and the No. 3 right hand engine mounting stay on the 3VZ-FE. Remove the bolt and nut and then remove the No. 2 right hand engine mounting stay on 2VZ-FE and 3VZ-FE engines.
3. Disconnect the electrical connector and wire (and nut) from the alternator.
4. Remove the air cleaner (2S-E), if necessary, to gain access to the alternator.
5. Unfasten the bolts which attach the adjusting link to the alternator.
6. Remove the alternator drive belt from the pulley.
7. Unfasten the alternator attaching bolt and then withdraw the alternator from its bracket.

To install:

1. To install; mount the alternator on the alternator brackets with the pivot and adjusting bolts. Do not tighten the bolts at this time.
2. Install the drive belt onto the pulley making sure that the grooves on the belt and the grooves on the pulley are properly aligned.
3. Adjust the drive belt tension and properly tighten the pivot and adjusting bolts.
4. Connect the wire (and nut) and connector to the alternator.
5. Connect the negative and starter battery cables.
6. Start the engine and allow it warm to warm up. Visually inspect the drive belt and listen for any abnormal vibration. Stop the engine and recheck the belt tension.

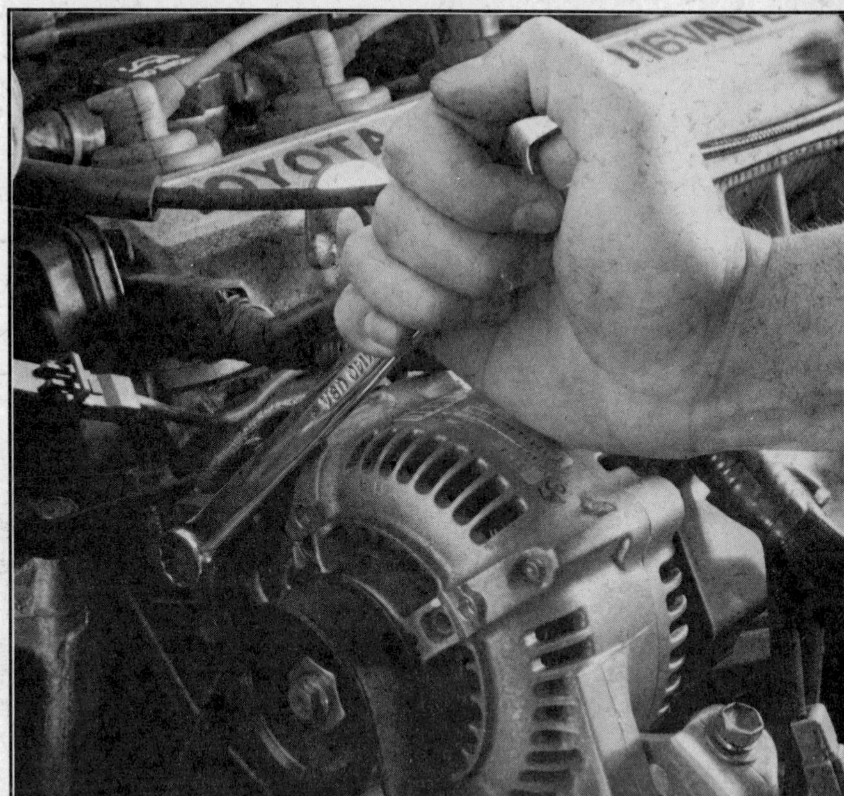

FIG. 34 Loosen the alternator pivot bolt

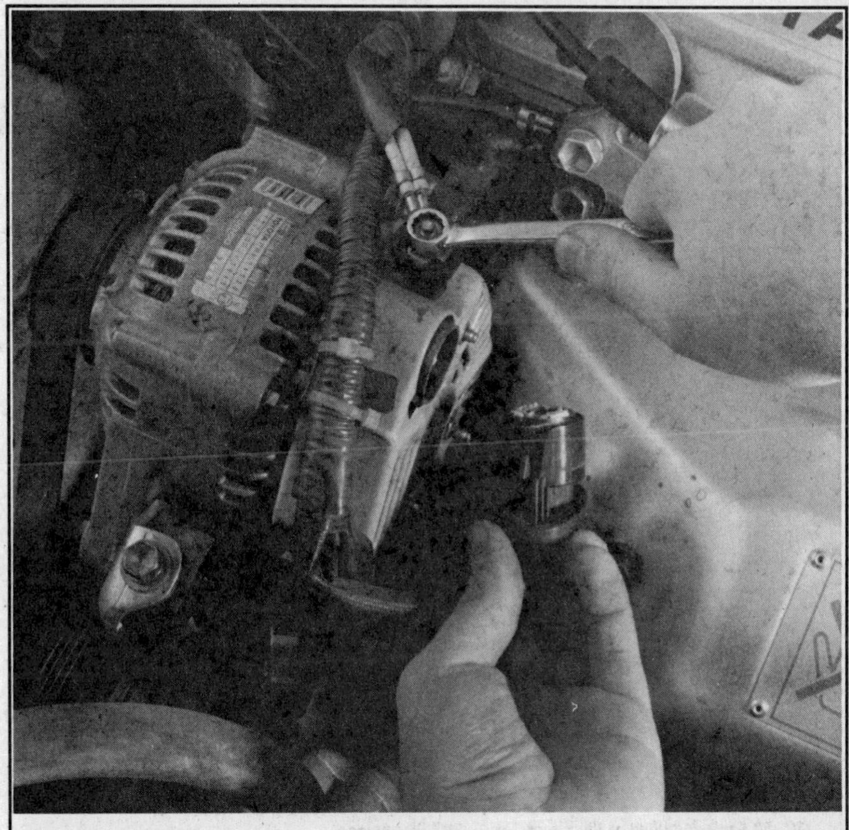

FIG. 35 Disconnect the electrical leads at the alternator

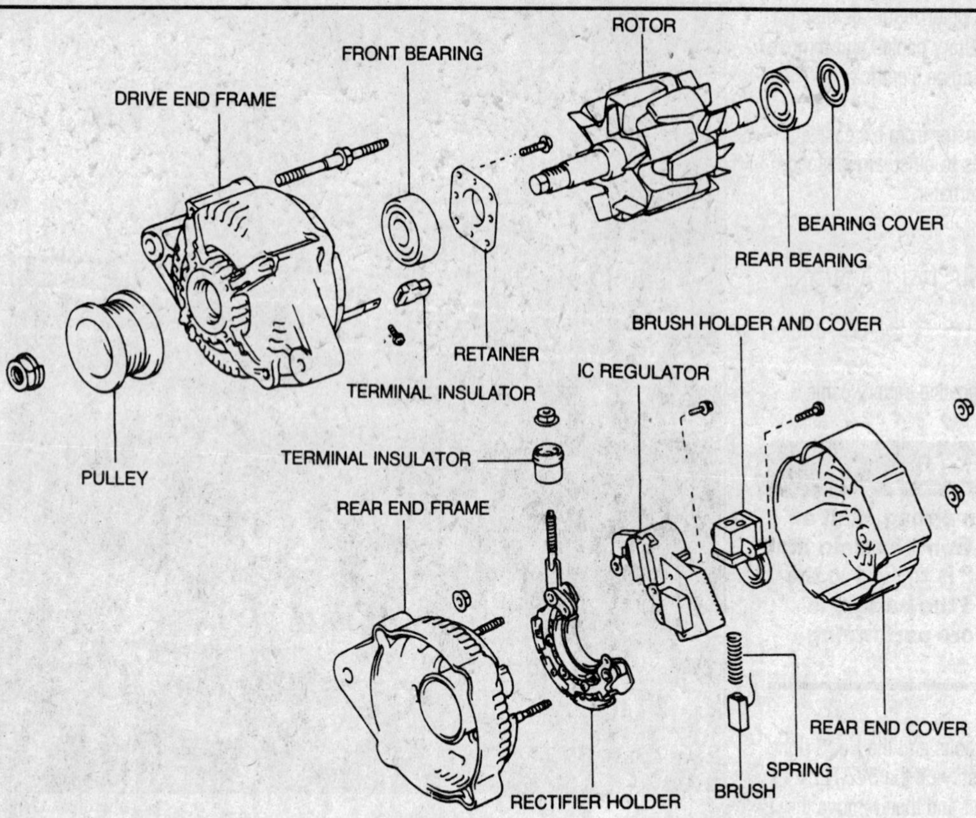

FIG. 32 Exploded view of the alternator — 2S-E, 3S-FE, 5S-FE and 2VZ-FE engines

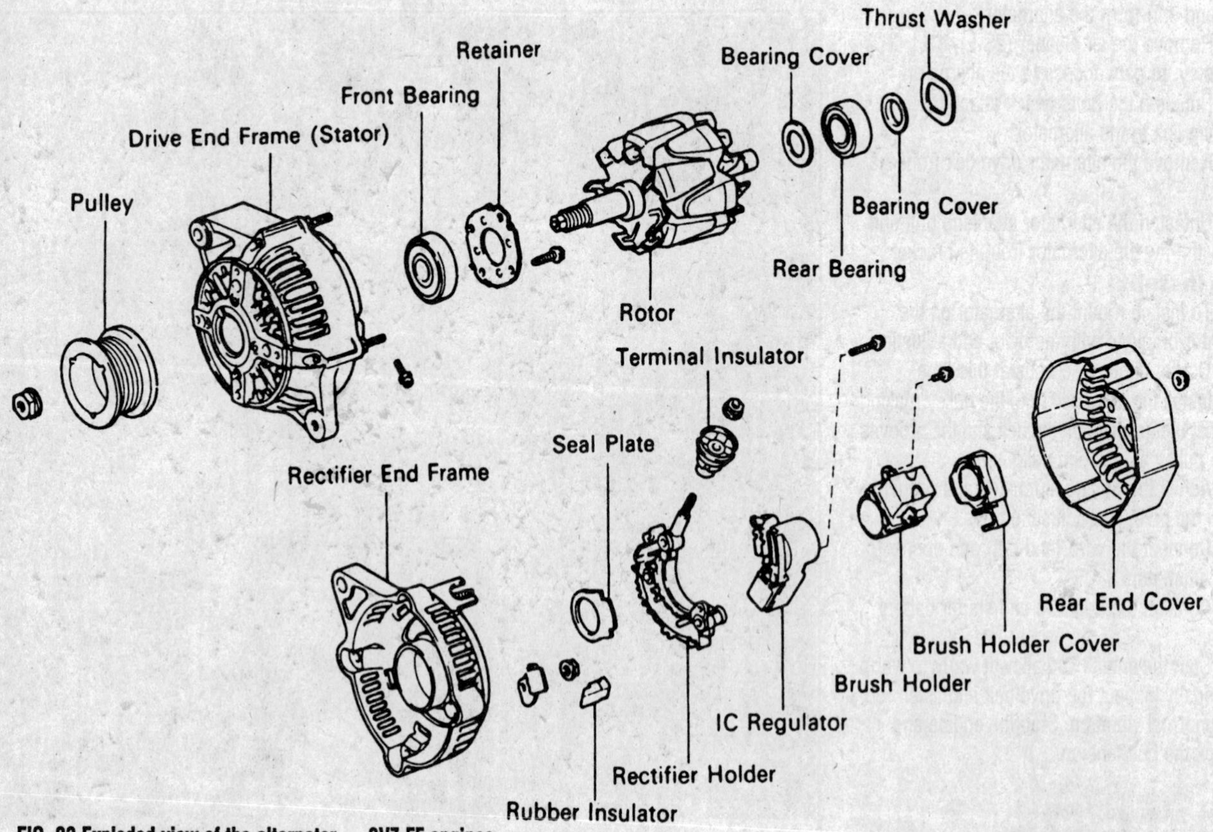

FIG. 33 Exploded view of the alternator — 3VZ-FE engines

BRUSH REPLACEMENT

➧ SEE FIGS. 36-42

1. Disconnect the negative battery cable and remove the alternator.

✲✲ CAUTION

On models with an airbag, wait at least 30 seconds from the time that the ignition switch is turned to the LOCK position and the battery is disconnected before performing any further work.

2. On the back of the alternator, remove the nut and the terminal insulator, remove the three mounting nuts and pull off the rear end cover.
3. Remove the five mounting screws and then lift out the brush holder and the regulator. On the 3VZ-FE, remove the brush holder cover first.

To Inspect:

1. Use a ruler (the 3VZ-FE will require a vernier caliper) and measure the exposed brush length. Standard length should be 0.413 in. (10.5mm); minimum should be 0.059 in. (1.5mm). If less than minimum, replace the brushes (the brushes and the holder assembly on the 3VZ-FE are replaced as a unit).
2. Unsolder and remove the brush and its spring.
3. Thread the wire of a new brush through the hole in the holder and then insert the spring and brush into the holder.
4. Solder the brush wire to the holder so its exposed length is 0.413 in. (10.5mm). Check that the brush moves smoothly in the holder and then cut off any excess wire.

To Install:

1. Position the brush/holder assembly and the regulator on the end frame. Be careful of the holder direction!
2. Install the five screws and tighten them until there is clearance of approximately 0.04 in. (1mm) between the holder and the connector.
3. Install the brush holder cover and then install the rear end cover.
4. Install the alternator and connect the battery cable.

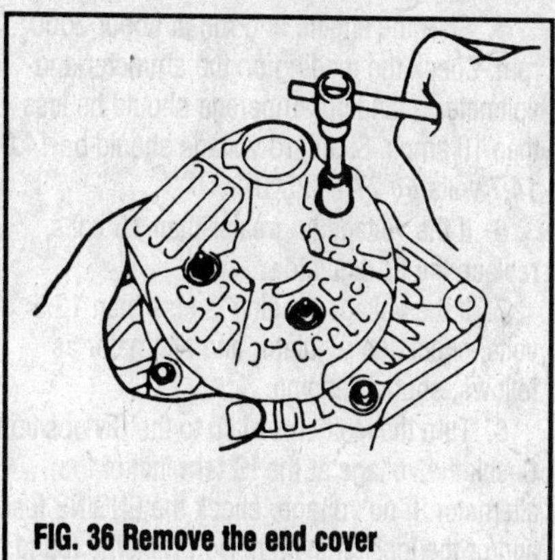

FIG. 36 Remove the end cover

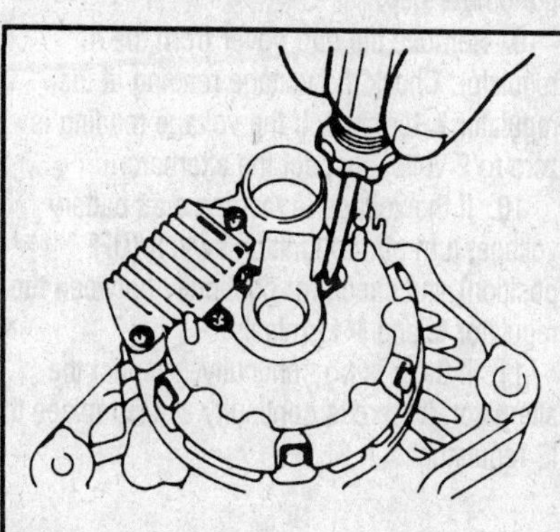

FIG. 37 Loosen the screws and lift out the brush holder and regulator assembly

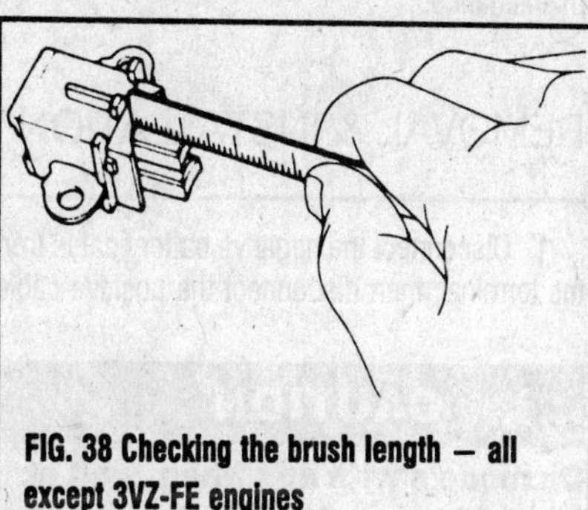

FIG. 38 Checking the brush length — all except 3VZ-FE engines

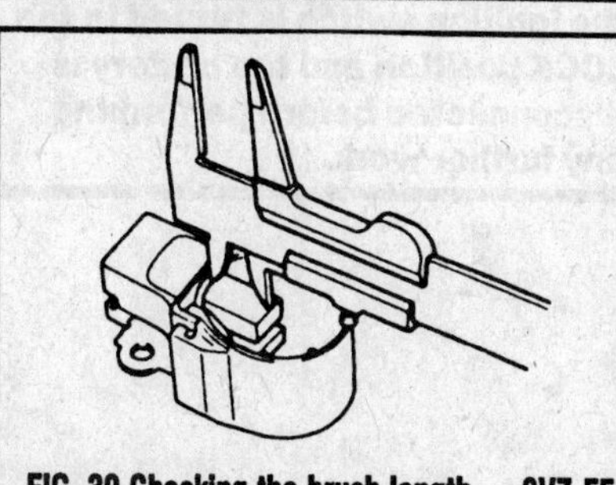

FIG. 39 Checking the brush length — 3VZ-FE engines

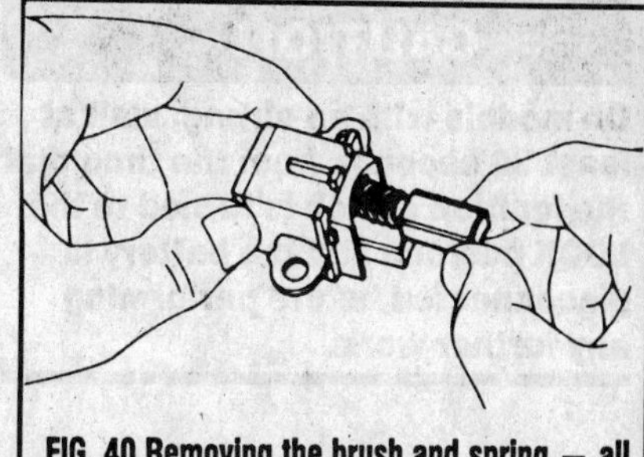

FIG. 40 Removing the brush and spring — all except 3VZ-FE engines

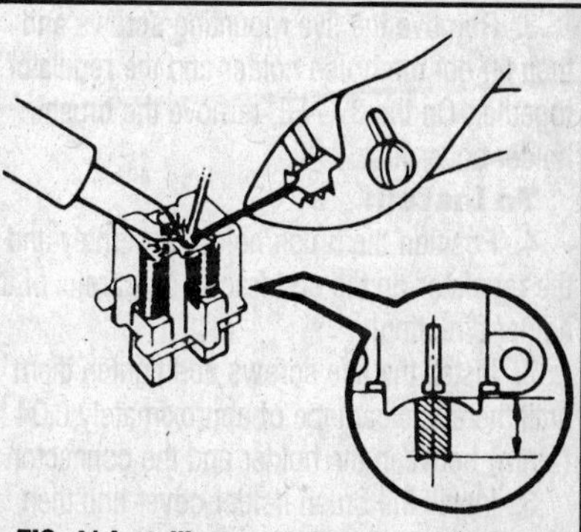

FIG. 41 Installing a new brush — all except 3VZ-FE engines

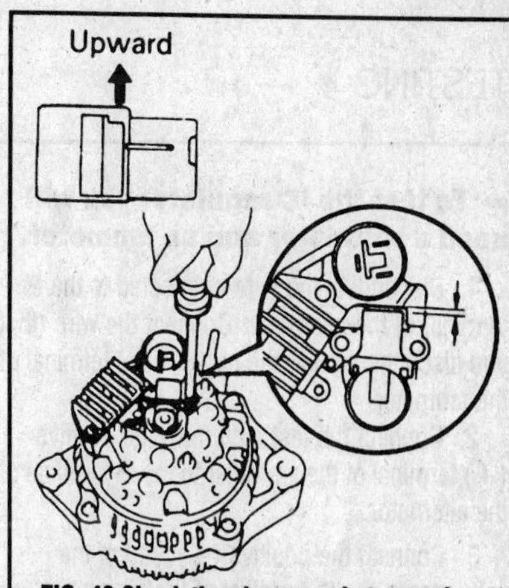

FIG. 42 Check the clearance between the brush holder and connector — 3VZ-FE engines

IC Regulator

The IC regulator is mounted inside the alternator housing and is non-adjustable.

REMOVAL & INSTALLATION

➧ SEE FIGS. 36, 37, 42

1. Disconnect the negative battery cable and remove the alternator.

CAUTION

On models with an airbag, wait at least 30 seconds from the time that the ignition switch is turned to the LOCK position and the battery is disconnected before performing any further work.

2. On the back of the alternator, remove the nut and the terminal insulator, remove the three mounting nuts and pull off the rear end cover.
3. Remove the five mounting screws and then lift out the brush holder and the regulator together. On the 3VZ-FE, remove the brush holder cover first.

To Install:

4. Position the brush/holder assembly and the regulator on the end frame. Be careful of the holder direction!
5. Install the five screws and tighten them until there is clearance of approximately 0.04 in. (1mm) between the holder and the connector.
6. Install the brush holder cover and then install the rear end cover.
7. Install the alternator and connect the battery cable.

TESTING

➡ To test the IC regulator you will need a voltmeter and an ammeter.

1. Disconnect the wire connected to the **B** terminal of the alternator. Connect the wire (that you disconnected) to the negative (–) terminal of the ammeter.
2. Connect the test lead from the positive (+) terminal of the ammeter to the **B** terminal of the alternator.
3. Connect the positive (+) lead of the voltmeter to the **B** terminal of the alternator.
4. Connect the negative (–) lead of the voltmeter to ground.
5. Start the engine and run at about 2000 rpm. Check the reading on the ammeter and voltmeter. Standard amperage should be less than 10 amps. Standard voltage should be 14.0-14.7 volts @ 77°F (25°C).
6. If the voltage is greater than 15 volts, replace the IC regulator.
7. If the voltage reading is less than 13.5 volts, check the regulator and alternator as follows; shut off engine.
8. Turn the ignition switch to the ON position. Check the voltage at the IG terminal of the alternator. If no voltage, check the ENGINE fuse and/or the ignition switch. No problems found, go to next step.
9. Remove the end cover from the IC regulator. Check the voltage reading at the regulator **L** terminal. If the voltage reading is zero to 2 volts, suspect the alternator.
10. If the voltage is the same as battery voltage, turn off the ignition switch (OFF position) and check for continuity between the regulator **L** and **F** terminals.
11. If there is no continuity, suspect the alternator. If there is continuity at 4Ω replace the IC regulator.

Battery

Refer to Section 1 for details on battery maintenance.

REMOVAL & INSTALLATION

1. Disconnect the negative battery cable from the terminal, then disconnect the positive cable.

CAUTION

On models with an airbag, wait at least 30 seconds from the time that the ignition switch is turned to the LOCK position and the battery is disconnected before performing any further work.

➡ To avoid sparks, always disconnect the negative cable first and reconnect it last.

2. Unscrew and remove the battery holddown clamp.
3. Remove the battery, being careful not to spill any of the acid.

➡ Spilled acid can be neutralized with a baking soda and water solution. If you somehow get acid into your eyes, flush it out with lots of clean water and get to a doctor as quickly as possible.

To Install:

4. Clean the battery posts thoroughly before reinstalling or when installing a new one.
5. Clean the cable clamps using the special tools or a wire brush, both inside and out.
6. Install the battery, and the holddown clamp. Connect the positive and then the negative cable. Do not hammer them into place. The terminals should be coated with grease to prevent corrosion.

CAUTION

Make absolutely sure that the battery is connected properly before you turn on the ignition switch. Reversed polarity can burn out our alternator and regulator in a matter of seconds.

ALTERNATOR AND REGULATOR SPECIFICATIONS

			Alternator		Regulator		
Year	Engine ID/Vin	Engine Displacement liter (cc)	Output (amps)	Regulated Volts @ 75°F	Air Gap (in.)	Point Gap (in.)	Back Gap (in.)
1983	2S-E	2.0 (1995)	70	13.5–15.1		—Not Adjustable—	
1984	2S-E	2.0 (1995)	70	13.5–15.1		—Not Adjustable—	
	1C-T	1.8 (1839)	55, 60	13.8–14.4		—Not Adjustable—	
1985	2S-E	2.0 (1995)	70	13.5–15.1		—Not Adjustable—	
	1C-T	1.8 (1839)	55, 60	13.8–14.4		—Not Adjustable—	
1986	2S-E	2.0 (1995)	70	13.5–15.1		—Not Adjustable—	
	2C-T	2.0 (1974)	55, 60	13.8–14.4		—Not Adjustable—	
1987	3S-FE	2.0 (1998)	70	13.5–15.1		—Not Adjustable—	
1988	3S-FE	2.0 (1998)	70	13.5–15.1		—Not Adjustable—	
1989	3S-FE	2.0 (1998)	70	13.9–15.1		—Not Adjustable—	
	2VZ-FE	2.5 (2507)	70	13.9–15.1		—Not Adjustable—	
1990	3S-FE	2.0 (1998)	70	13.9–15.1		—Not Adjustable—	
	2VZ-FE	2.5 (2507)	70	13.9–15.1		—Not Adjustable—	
1991	3S-FE	2.0 (1998)	70	13.9–15.1		—Not Adjustable—	
	2VZ-FE	2.5 (2507)	70	13.9–15.1		—Not Adjustable—	
1992	5S-FE	2.2 (2164)	70	14.0–15.0		—Not Adjustable—	
	3VZ-FE	3.0 (2959)	80	14.0–14.3		—Not Adjustable—	

STARTER SPECIFICATIONS

			Lock Test			No-Load Test			
Year	Engine ID/VIN	Engine Displacement liter (cc)	Amps	Volts	Torque (ft. lbs.)	Amps	Volts	RPM	Brush Spring Tension (oz.)
1983	2S-E	2.0 (1995)	—Not Recommended—			90 ①	11.5	3000 ②	62.4–84.8
1984	2S-E	2.0 (1995)	—Not Recommended—			90 ①	11.5	3000 ②	62.4–84.8
	1C-T	1.8 (1839)	—Not Recommended—			180 ①	11.0	3500 ②	113.6–140.8
1985	2S-E	2.0 (1995)	—Not Recommended—			90 ①	11.5	3000 ②	62.4–84.8
	1C-T	1.8 (1839)	—Not Recommended—			180 ①	11.0	3500 ②	113.6–140.8
1986	2S-E	2.0 (1995)	—Not Recommended—			90 ①	11.5	3000 ②	62.4–84.8
	2C-T	2.0 (1974)	—Not Recommended—			180 ①	11.0	3500 ②	113.6–140.8
1987	3S-FE	2.0 (1998)	—Not Recommended—			90 ①	11.5	3000 ②	62.4
1988	3S-FE	2.0 (1998)	—Not Recommended—			90 ①	11.5	3000 ②	62.4
1989	3S-FE	2.0 (1998)	—Not Recommended—			90 ①	11.5	3000 ②	57–83
	2VZ-FE	2.5 (2507)	—Not Recommended—			90 ①	11.5	3000 ②	57–83
1990	3S-FE	2.0 (1998)	—Not Recommended—			90 ①	11.5	3000 ②	57–83
	2VZ-FE	2.5 (2507)	—Not Recommended—			90 ①	11.5	3000 ②	57–83
1991	3S-FE	2.0 (1998)	—Not Recommended—			90 ①	11.5	3000 ②	57–83
	2VZ-FE	2.5 (2507)	—Not Recommended—			90 ①	11.5	3000 ②	57–83
1992	5S-FE	2.2 (2164)	—Not Recommended—			90 ①	11.5	3000 ②	57–83
	3VZ-FE	3.0 (2959)	—Not Recommended—			90 ①	11.5	3000 ②	57–83

① Or less
② Or more

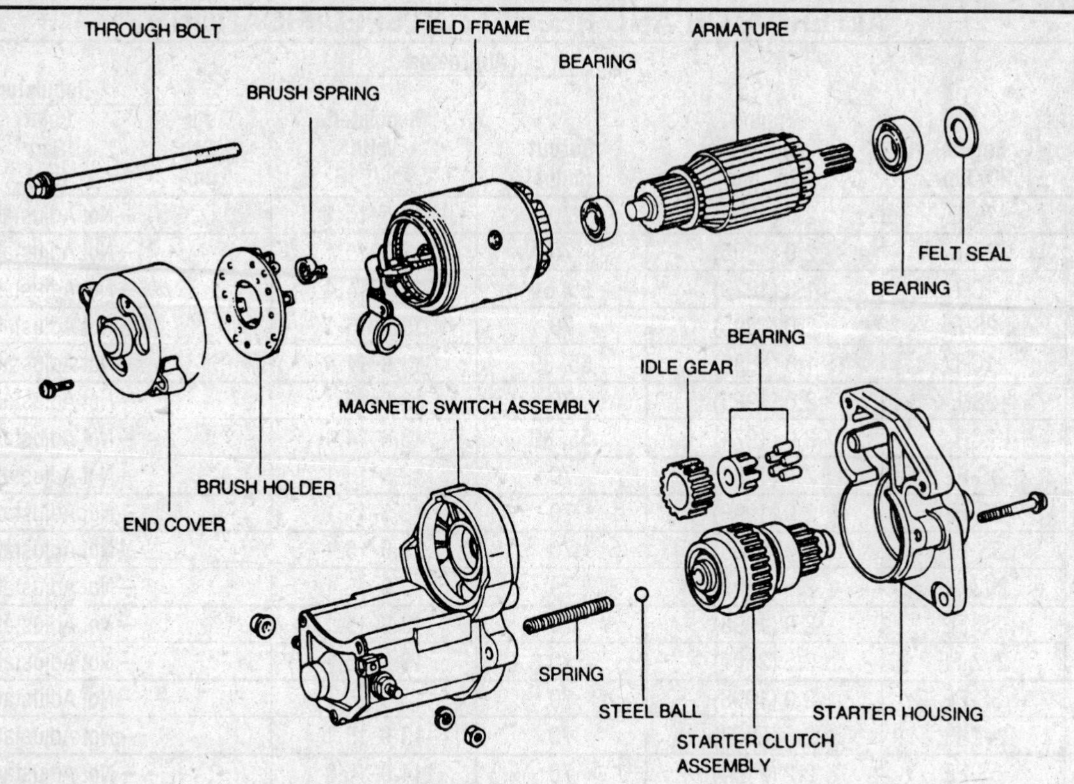

THROUGH BOLT
FIELD FRAME
ARMATURE
BEARING
BRUSH SPRING
FELT SEAL
BEARING
BEARING
IDLE GEAR
MAGNETIC SWITCH ASSEMBLY
BRUSH HOLDER
END COVER
SPRING
STEEL BALL
STARTER HOUSING
STARTER CLUTCH
ASSEMBLY

FIG. 43 Exploded view of the 1.0 Kw starter — 1983–91 gasoline engines

O-RING
END COVER
O-RING
FIELD FRAME
BRUSH SPRING
FRONT BEARING
ARMATURE
O-RING
REAR BEARING
PINION GEAR
IDLE GEAR
BRUSH HOLDER
THROUGH BOLT
STEEL BALL
BEARING
SPRING
STARTER HOUSING
STARTER CLUTCH ASSEMBLY
MAGNETIC SWITCH ASSEMBLY

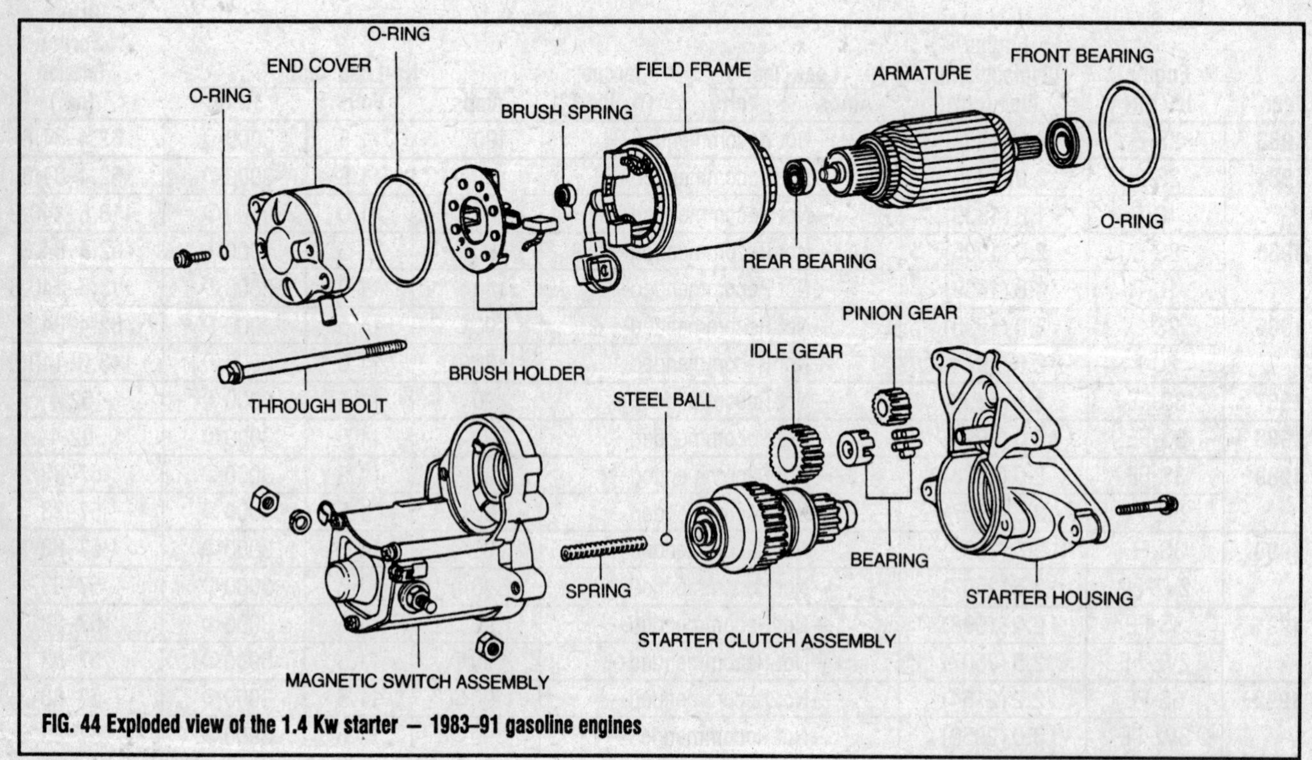

FIG. 44 Exploded view of the 1.4 Kw starter — 1983–91 gasoline engines

Starter

REMOVAL & INSTALLATION

Gasoline Engines

SEE FIGS. 43-47

1. Disconnect the cable from the negative terminal of the battery.

CAUTION

On models with an airbag, wait at least 30 seconds from the time that the ignition switch is turned to the LOCK position and the battery is disconnected before performing any further work.

2. On 1992 models with cruise control, remove the battery.
3. Also on 1992 models with cruise control, remove the actuator cover and disconnect the connector. Remove the three bolts and then lift out the cruise control actuator.
4. Peel the rubber boot away and remove the nut and disconnect the negative battery cable from the magnetic switch terminal on the starter. Disconnect the electrical connector also located on the magnetic switch.
5. Support the starter by hand and remove the two mounting bolts.
6. Remove the starter from the transaxle.
7. Place the starter motor in the transaxle and support by hand.
8. Install the two mounting bolts and torque them to 29 ft. lbs. (39 Nm)
9. Connect the connector to the magnetic switch. Place the battery cable on the switch terminal and install the nut. Tighten the nut and position the rubber boot over the cable.
10. Using the ignition switch, "bump" the starter over a few times and check for proper operation.

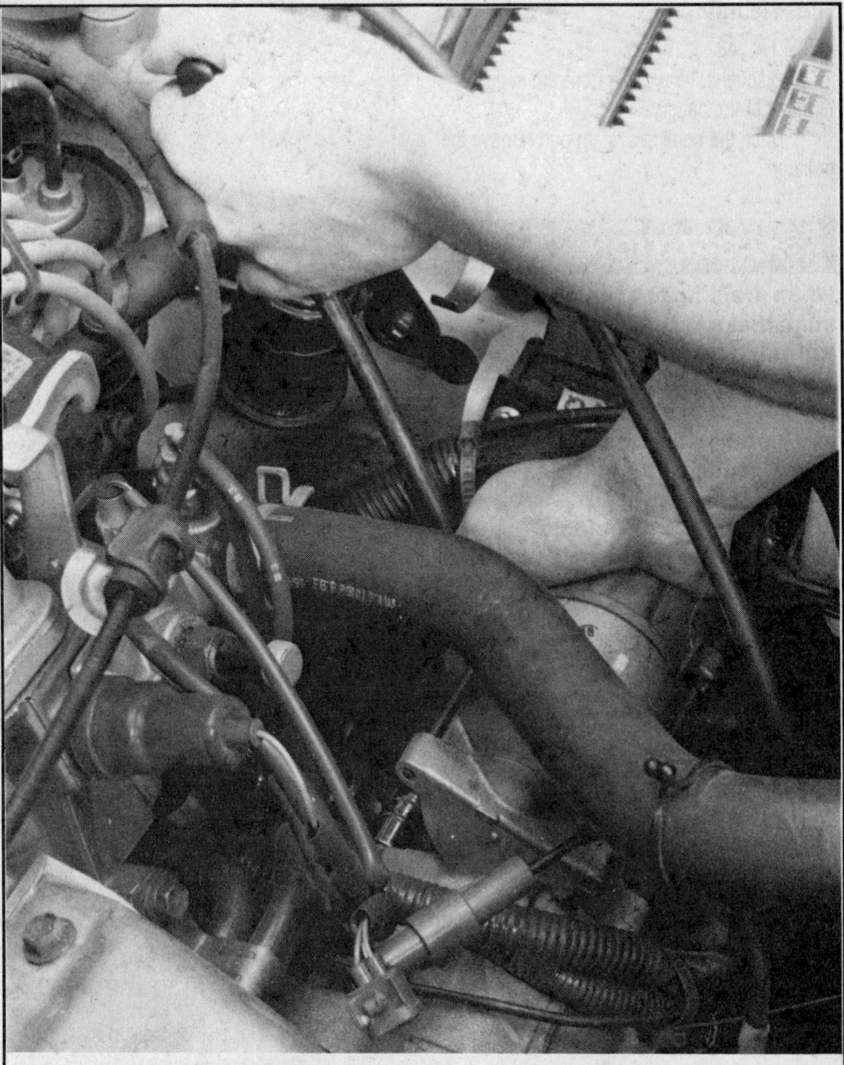

FIG. 45 Removing the starter bolts

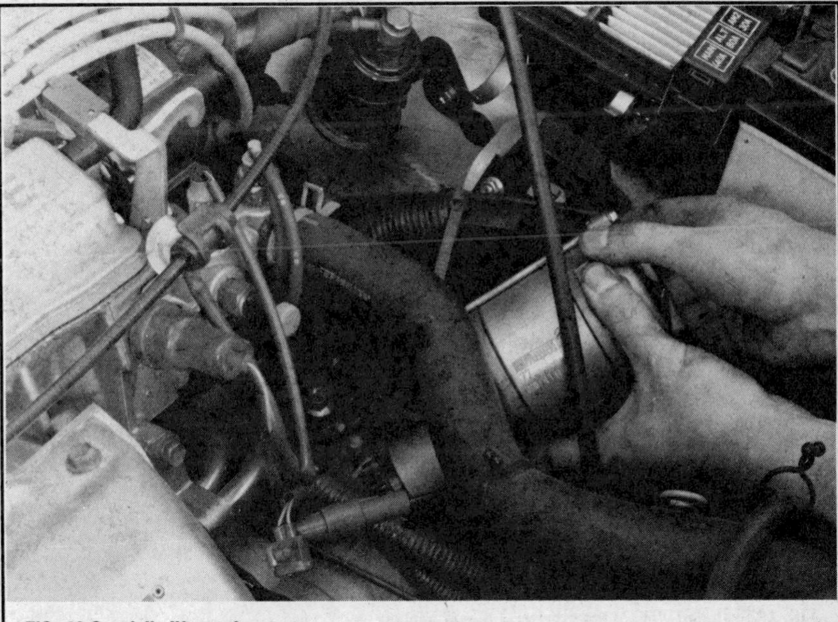

FIG. 46 Carefully lift out the starter

Diesel Engines

➧ SEE FIG. 48

1. Disconnect the cable from the negative terminal of the battery.
2. Drain the cooling system and remove the radiator.

✲✲ CAUTION

When draining the coolant, keep in mind that cats and dogs are attracted by the ethylene glycol antifreeze, and are quite likely to drink any that is left in an uncovered container or in puddles on the ground. This will prove fatal in sufficient quantity. Always drain the coolant into a sealable container. Coolant should be reused unless it is contaminated or several years old.

3. Remove the nut and bolt from the starter motor stay bracket and remove the bracket.
4. Peel the rubber boot away and remove the nut and disconnect the negative battery cable from the magnetic switch terminal on the starter. Disconnect the electrical connector also located on the magnetic switch.

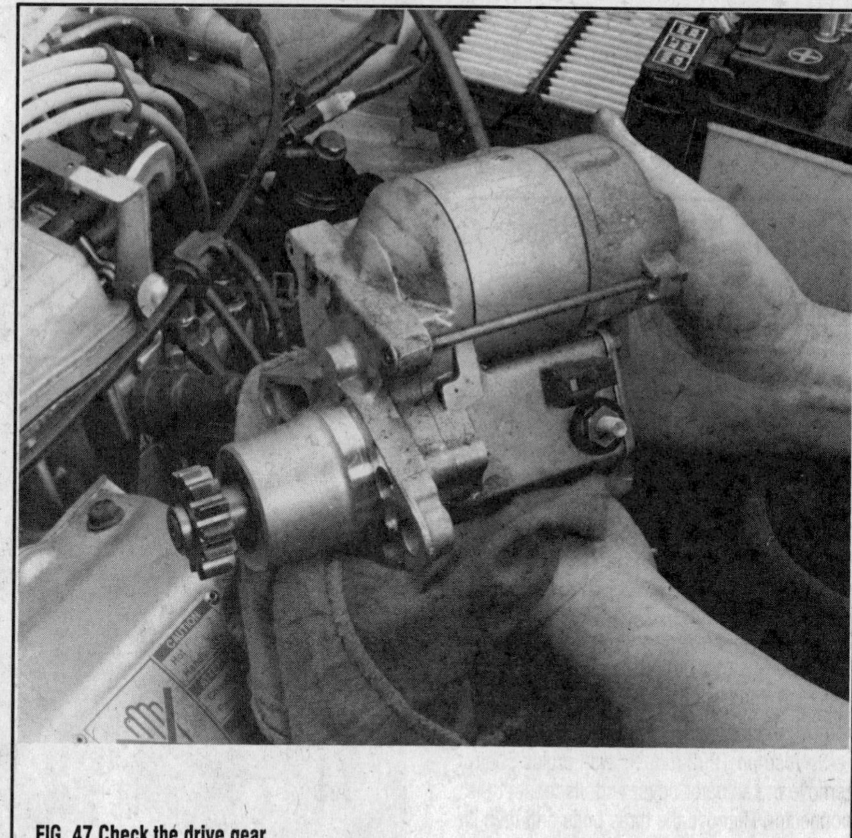

FIG. 47 Check the drive gear

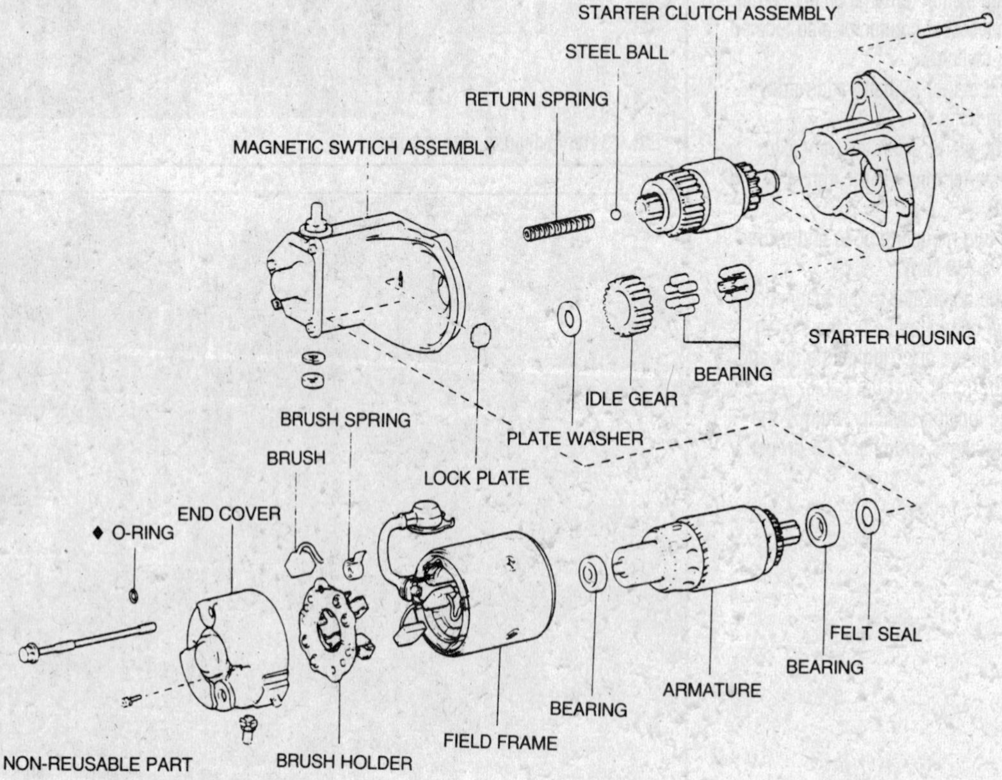

STARTER CLUTCH ASSEMBLY
STEEL BALL
RETURN SPRING
MAGNETIC SWTICH ASSEMBLY
STARTER HOUSING
BEARING
IDLE GEAR
BRUSH SPRING
PLATE WASHER
BRUSH
LOCK PLATE
END COVER
◆ O-RING
FELT SEAL
BEARING
ARMATURE
BEARING
FIELD FRAME
◆ NON-REUSABLE PART
BRUSH HOLDER

FIG. 48 Exploded view of the starter — diesel engines

5. Support the starter by hand and remove the two mounting bolts. Remove the lead wire from terminal 50 of the starter

6. Remove the starter from the transaxle.

To Install:

1. Connect the lead wire to terminal 50 of the starter.

2. Place the starter motor in the transaxle and support by hand.

3. Install the two mounting bolts and torque them to 29 ft. lbs. (39 Nm).

4. Connect the connector to the magnetic switch. Place the battery cable on the switch terminal and install the nut. Tighten the nut and position the rubber boot over the cable.

5. Install the starter motor stay bracket with the nut and bolt.

6. Install the radiator and fill the cooling system.

7. Connect the cable to the negative terminal of the battery.

8. Start the engine and check for leaks.

RELAY REPLACEMENT

A starter relay is used on vehicles equipped with manual transmissions. The relay is located on the left hand cowl (on later models, behind the glove box). If the relay is found to be faulty, remove it and replace with a new relay.

OVERHAUL

There are two types of starters available on the Camry: 1.0 kw and 1.4 kw. Both the part number and the type are listed on the starter itself. Consult the information on the starter before attempting any overhaul procedure.

Disassembly

➧ SEE FIGS. 49, 50

1. Disconnect the negative cable from the battery terminal.

CAUTION

On models with an airbag, wait at least 30 seconds from the time that the ignition switch is turned to the LOCK position and the battery is disconnected before performing any further work.

2. Disconnect and label all the starter electrical wiring/connectors. Remove the starter from the vehicle and place on a suitable workstand.

3. Remove the nut and disconnect the lead wire from the terminal of the magnetic switch.

4. Remove the two thru-bolts and pull out the field frame together with the armature. On the 1.4 kw type, remove the O-ring and discard it.

5. Remove the starter housing, clutch assembly and gears by removing the two screws.

6. Remove the following components from the magnetic switch assembly:

a. Starter housing and clutch assembly
b. Return spring
c. Pinion gear (1983-91)
d. Roller (1992)
e. Retainer (1992)
f. Idler gear.
g. Bearing

7. With the use of a magnetic finger, remove the steel ball from the clutch shaft hole.

8. Remove the two screws from the field cover on the end frame. On the 1.4 kw type, remove the O-ring and discard it. With the use of a screw driver, hold the spring back and disconnect the brush from the brush holder. Disconnect the four brushes and remove the brush holder.

9. Remove the armature from the field frame.

Inspection and Repair

ARMATURE COIL

1. Using an ohmmeter, check that there is continuity between the segments of the commutator. If no continuity exists, replace the armature.

2. Using an ohmmeter, check that there is no continuity between the commutator and the armature coil core. If continuity exists, replace the armature.

COMMUTATOR

1. Inspect the surface of the commutator for burning and dirt. If the surface is burnt and dirty, polish the surface with No. 400 grit sandpaper or have it turned down on a lathe.

2. Place the commutator on a pair of V-blocks. Using a dial indicator, measure the runout of the commutator. Maximum permissible runout is 0.05mm. If the runout exceeds the limit, have it turned down on a lathe.

3. With calipers, measure the diameter of the commutator. The standard diameter is 29.000mm and the maximum allowable limit is 30.000mm.

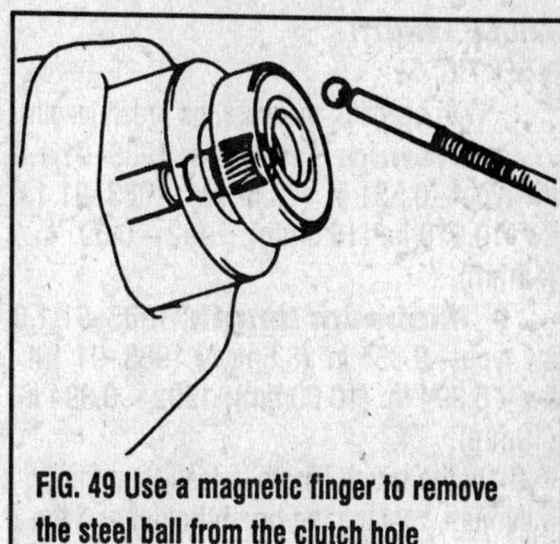

FIG. 49 Use a magnetic finger to remove the steel ball from the clutch hole

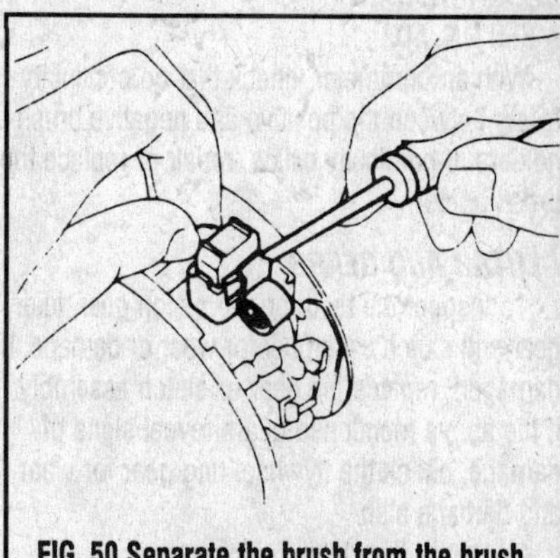

FIG. 50 Separate the brush from the brush holder by holding back the spring

4. Check that the undercover depth is clean and free of dirt. Smooth the edges as required. The standard undercut depth is 0.60mm and the minimum allowable limit is 0.20mm. If the undercut length is less than the minimum, correct it with a hacksaw blade.

FIELD COIL (FIELD FRAME)

1. With an ohmmeter, check for continuity between the lead wire and the field coil brush lead. If continuity does not exist, replace the filed frame.

2. With an ohmmeter, check that there is no continuity between the lead wire and the field coil brush lead. If continuity exists, replace the field frame.

BRUSH LENGTH

➧ SEE FIG. 51

1. With calipers, measure the brush length:

a. **Standard length**: 1983–91 1.0 kw type—0.531 in. (13.5mm); 1983–91 1.4 kw—0.610 in. (15.5mm); 1992—0.591 in. (15mm).

b. **Minimum length**: 1983–91 1.0 kw type—0.335 in. (8.5mm); 1983–91 1.4 kw—0.394 in. (10.00mm); 1992—0.394 in. (10mm).

2. In the brush length is less than the minimum, replace the brush holder and the field frame.

BRUSH HOLDER

➧ SEE FIG. 50

With an ohmmeter, check that no continuity exists between the positive and negative brush holders. If continuity exists, repair or replace the brush holder.

CLUTCH AND GEARS

1. Inspect the teeth on the pinion gear, idler gear and clutch assembly for wear or damage. If damaged, replace the gear or clutch assembly. If the above mentioned gears reveal signs of damage, check the flywheel ring gear for wear and damage also.

2. Rotate the clutch pinion gear counterclockwise and make sure that the gear rotates freely. Attempt to rotate the pinion gear clockwise and make sure that it locks. If necessary, replace the clutch assembly.

BEARINGS

➧ SEE FIG. 52

1. Rotate each bearing by hand and push inward. If resistance is felt or the bearing sticks, replace the bearing.

2. To replace the bearing remove the old bearing (front and rear) with a suitable bearing puller.

3. Using SST No.s 09285-76010 (1.0 kw type), SST No. 09201-41020 (1.4 kw type) and a press, press in the front bearing.

4. For the rear bearing only a press is required for installation.

MAGNETIC SWITCH

➧ SEE 53, 54

1. **Pull-in coil open circuit test**: with an ohmmeter, check that there is continuity between terminals 50 and C. If there is no continuity, replace the magnetic switch.

2. **Hold-in coil open circuit test**: with an ohmmeter, check that there is continuity between terminal 50 and the body. If there is no continuity, replace the magnetic switch.

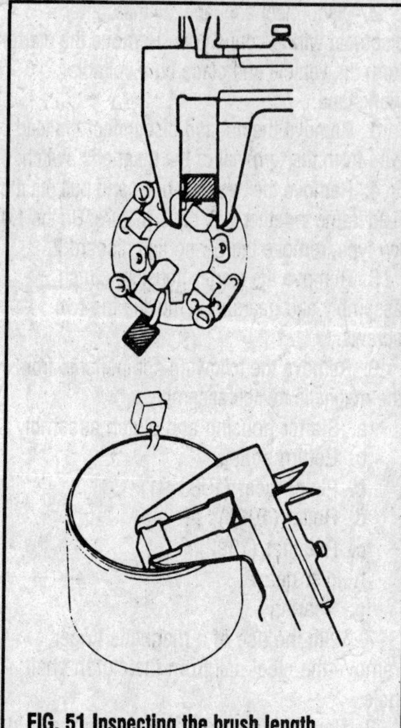

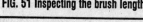

FIG. 51 Inspecting the brush length

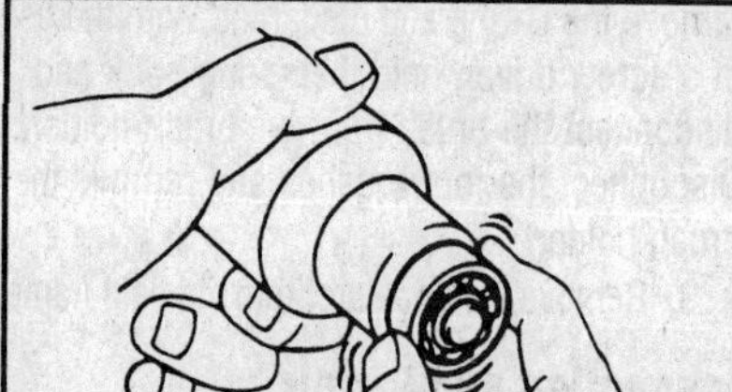

FIG. 52 Inspecting the starter bearing

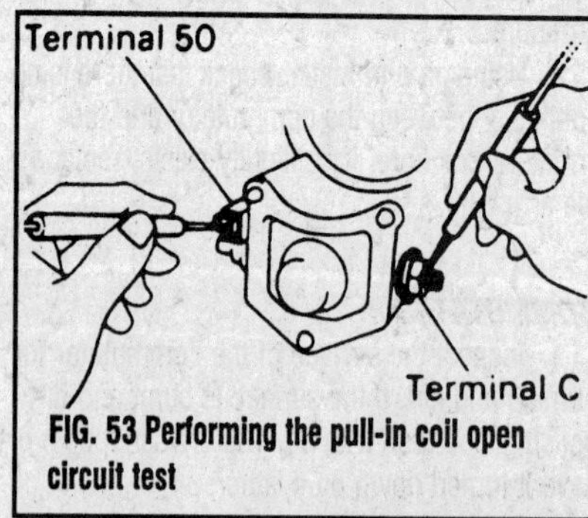

FIG. 53 Performing the pull-in coil open circuit test

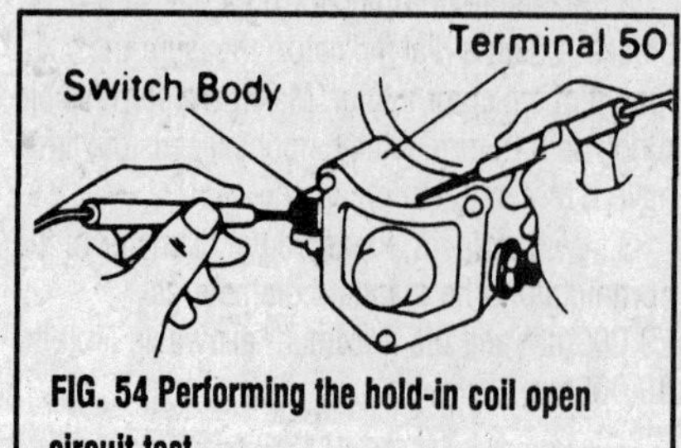

FIG. 54 Performing the hold-in coil open circuit test

Assembly

➡ When assembling the starter, use a suitable high temperature grease to lubricate the bearings, springs and gears.

1. Lubricate the armature bearing and insert the armature into the field frame.

2. Place the brush holder in position on the armature. Using a screwdriver, hold the brush spring back and connect the brush in the brush holder. Make sure that the positive lead wires are not grounded. On the 1.4 kw type, place a new O-ring on the filed frame. Install the end cover with the two screws.

3. Apply a bead of grease to the the steel ball and place the ball on the end of the magnetic finger. Install the ball into the clutch shaft hole.

4. Lubricate the return spring with grease and insert the spring into the magnetic switch hole.

5. Place the following parts on the starter housing:

a. Starter housing and clutch assembly
b. Return spring
c. Pinion gear (1983-91)
d. Roller (1992)
e. Retainer (1992)
f. Idler gear.
g. Bearing

6. Attach the starter housing and the magnetic switch with the two screws.

7. On the 1.4 kw type, install a new O-ring on the field frame. Align the protrusion of the field frame with the cut-out of the magnetic switch.

8. Install the field frame and armature assembly with the two through bolts.

9. Connect the lead wire to terminal **C** and install the nut.

Sending Units and Sensors

REMOVAL & INSTALLATION

⁂ CAUTION

When draining the coolant, keep in mind that cats and dogs are attracted by the ethylene glycol antifreeze, and are quite likely to drink any that is left in an

uncovered container or in puddles on the ground. This will prove fatal in sufficient quantity. Always drain the coolant into a sealable container. Coolant should be reused unless it is contaminated or several years old.

Engine Coolant Temperature Sensor

1. Disconnect the negative battery cable.

CAUTION

On models with an airbag, wait at least 30 seconds from the time that the ignition switch is turned to the LOCK position and the battery is disconnected before performing any further work.

2. Drain the cooling system.
3. Disconnect the sensor electrical connector.
4. Remove the sensor from coolant flange or the thermostat housing.
5. Install the sensor and connect the electrical lead. Tighten the sensor to 12–18 ft. lbs. (16–24 Nm). Fill the cooling system.

Cooling Fan Switches

1. Disconnect the negative battery cable.

CAUTION

On models with an airbag, wait at least 30 seconds from the time that the ignition switch is turned to the LOCK position and the battery is disconnected before performing any further work.

2. Drain the cooling system.
3. Disconnect the switch electrical connector.
4. Remove the switch from the thermostat housing.
5. Installation is the reverse of the removal procedure. Fill the cooling system.

Oil Pressure Sender

1. Disconnect the negative battery cable.

CAUTION

On models with an airbag, wait at least 30 seconds from the time that the ignition switch is turned to the LOCK position and the battery is disconnected before performing any further work.

2. Raise and safely support the vehicle.
3. Disconnect the electrical connector from the oil pressure sender, which is located on the left rear side of the engine block, near the starter.
4. Remove the oil pressure sender.
5. Installation is the reverse of the removal procedure.

Fuel Sender

1. Disconnect the negative battery cable.

CAUTION

On models with an airbag, wait at least 30 seconds from the time that the ignition switch is turned to the LOCK position and the battery is disconnected before performing any further work.

2. Remove the matt in the trunk.
3. Lift up the access plate if equipped. Disconnect the sender electrical connector.
4. Remove the sender from the fuel tank.
5. Installation is the reverse of the removal procedure. Tighten the screws to 17 inch lbs. (2 Nm).

ENGINE MECHANICAL

Engine Overhaul Tips

Most engine overhaul procedures are fairly standard. In addition to specific parts replacement procedures and complete specifications for your individual engine, this section also is a guide to accepted rebuilding procedures.

Competent and accurate machine shop services will ensure maximum performance, reliability and engine life.

In most instances it is more profitable for the do-it-yourself mechanic to remove, clean and inspect the component, buy the necessary parts and deliver these to a shop for actual machine work.

On the other hand, much of the rebuilding work (crankshaft, block, bearings, piston rods, and other components) is well within the scope of the do-it-yourself mechanic.

TOOLS

The tools required for an engine overhaul or parts replacement will depend on the depth of your involvement. With a few exceptions, they will be the tools found in a mechanic's tool kit (see Section 1). More in-depth work will require any or all of the following:

- a dial indicator (reading in thousandths) mounted on a universal base
- micrometers and telescope gauges
- jaw and screw-type pullers
- scraper
- valve spring compressor
- ring groove cleaner
- piston ring expander and compressor
- ridge reamer
- cylinder hone or glaze breaker
- Plastigage®
- engine stand

The use of most of these tools is illustrated in this section. Many can be rented for a one-time use from a local parts jobber or tool supply house specializing in automotive work.

Occasionally, the use of special tools is called for. See the information on Special Tools and Safety Notice in the front of this book before substituting another tool.

INSPECTION TECHNIQUES

Procedures and specifications are given in this section for inspecting, cleaning and assessing the wear limits of most major components. Other procedures such as Magnaflux® and Zyglo® can be used to locate material flaws and stress cracks. Magnaflux® is a magnetic process applicable only to ferrous materials. The Zyglo® process coats the material with a fluorescent dye penetrant and can be used on any material Check for suspected surface cracks can be more readily made using spot check dye. The dye is sprayed onto the suspected area, wiped off and the area sprayed with a developer. Cracks will show up brightly.

OVERHAUL TIPS

Aluminum has become extremely popular for use in engines, due to its low weight. Observe the following precautions when handling aluminum parts:

- Never hot tank aluminum parts (the caustic hot tank solution will eat the aluminum.
- Remove all aluminum parts (identification tag, etc.) from engine parts prior to the tanking.
- Always coat threads lightly with engine oil or anti-seize compounds before installation, to prevent seizure.
- Never overtorque bolts or spark plugs especially in aluminum threads.

Stripped threads in any component can be repaired using any of several commercial repair kits (Heli-Coil®, Microdot®, Keenserts®, etc.).

When assembling the engine, any parts that will be frictional contact must be prelubed to provide lubrication at initial start-up. Any product specifically formulated for this purpose can be used, but engine oil is not recommended as a prelube.

When semi-permanent (locked, but removable) installation of bolts or nuts is desired, threads should be cleaned and coated with Loctite® or other similar, commercial non-hardening sealant.

REPAIRING DAMAGED THREADS

Several methods of repairing damaged threads are available. Heli-Coil®, Keenserts® and Microdot® are among the most widely used. All involve basically the same principle, drilling out stripped threads, tapping the hole and installing a prewound insert — making welding, plugging and oversize fasteners unnecessary.

Two types of thread repair inserts are usually supplied: a standard type for most Inch Coarse, Inch Fine, Metric Course and Metric Fine thread sizes and a spark lug type to fit most spark plug port sizes. Consult the individual manufacturer's catalog to determine exact applications. Typical thread repair kits will contain a selection of prewound threaded inserts, a tap (corresponding to the outside diameter threads of the insert) and an installation tool. Spark plug inserts usually differ because they require a tap equipped with pilot threads and a combined reamer/tap section. Most manufacturers also supply blister-packed thread repair inserts separately in addition to a master kit containing a variety of taps and inserts plus installation tools.

Before effecting a repair to a threaded hole, remove any snapped, broken or damaged bolts or studs. Penetrating oil can be used to free frozen threads. The offending item can be removed with locking pliers or with a screw or stud extractor. After the hole is clear, the thread can be repaired, as shown in the series of accompanying illustrations.

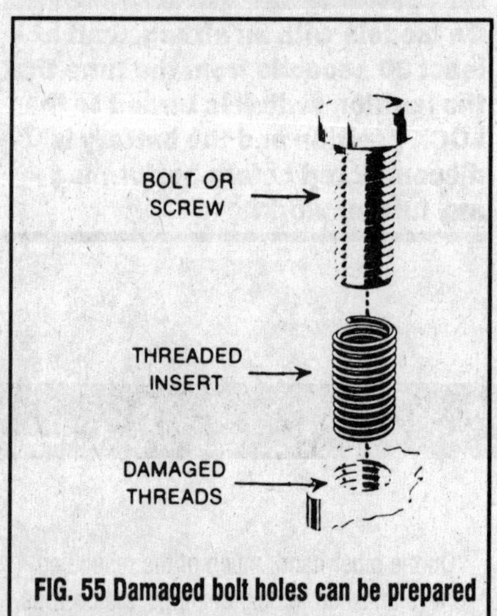

FIG. 55 Damaged bolt holes can be prepared with thread repair inserts

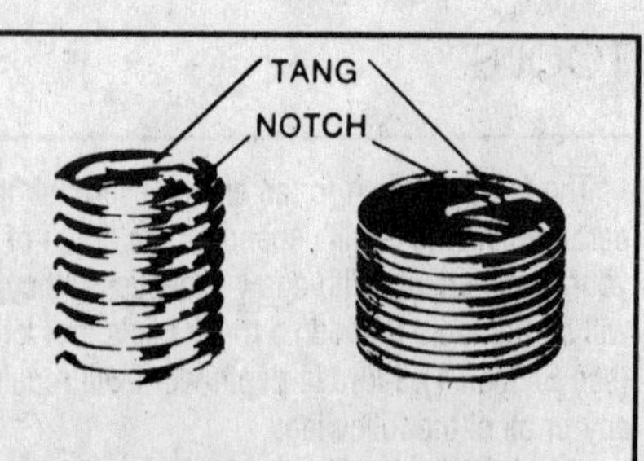

FIG. 56 Standard thread repair insert (left) and spark plug thread insert (right)

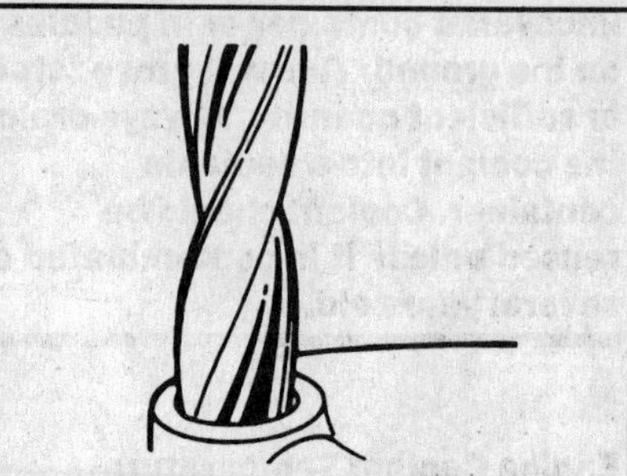

FIG. 57 Drill out the damaged threads with the specified drill. Drill completely through the hole or to the bottom of a blind hole

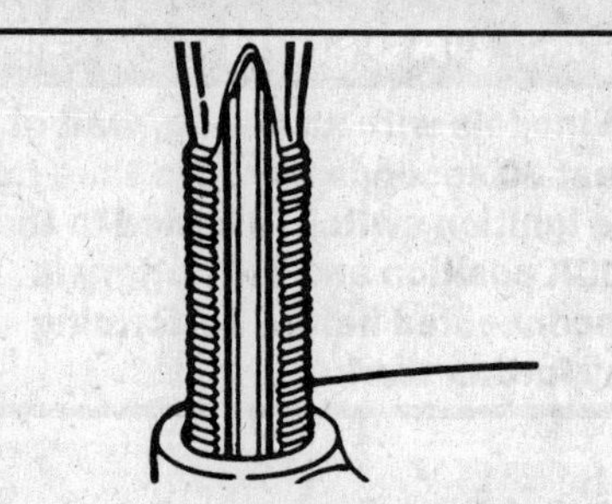

FIG. 58 With the tap supplied, tap the hole to receive the thread insert. Keep the tap well oiled and back it out frequently to avoid clogging the threads

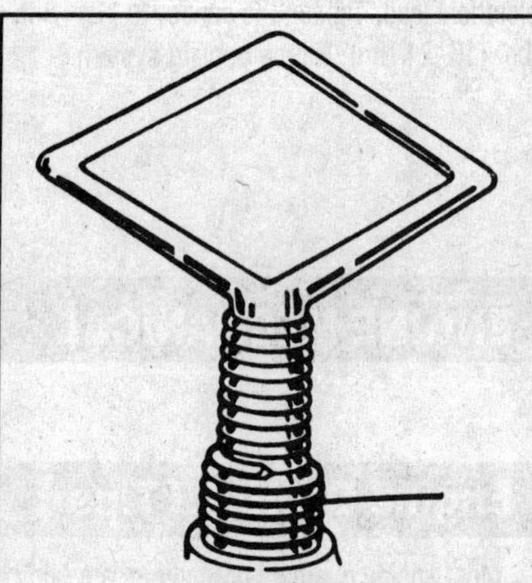

FIG. 59 Screw the threaded insert onto the installation tool until the tang engages the slot. Screw the insert into the tapped hole until it is 1/4–1/2 turn below the top surface. After installation, break off the tang with a hammer and punch

Checking Engine Compression

A noticeable lack of engine power, excessive oil consumption and/or poor fuel mileage measured over an extended period are all indicators of internal engine wear. Worn piston rings, scored or worn cylinder bores, blown head gaskets, sticking or burnt valves and worn valve seats are all possible culprits here. A check of each cylinder's compression will help you locate the problems.

As mentioned in the Tools and Equipment section of Section 1, a screw-in type compression gauge is more accurate that the type you simply hold against the spark plug hole, although it takes slightly longer to use. It's worth it to obtain a more accurate reading. Follow the procedures below.

Gasoline Engines

➧ SEE FIG. 60

1. Warm up and stop the engine.
2. Disconnect the cold start injector and distributor connectors.
3. Remove all the spark plugs.
4. Insert a compression gauge into the hole of the No. 1 spark plug until the fitting is snug.

WARNING

Be careful not to crossthread the plug hole. On aluminum cylinder heads use extra care, as the threads in these heads are easily ruined.

5. Ask an assistant to depress the accelerator pedal fully. Then, while you read the compression gauge, ask the assistant to crank the engine two or three times in short bursts using the ignition switch.

➡ The battery must be fully charged to produce a revolution of at least 250 rpm.

6. Read the compression gauge at the end of each series of cranks, and record the highest of these readings. Repeat this procedure for each of the engine's cylinders. Compare the highest reading of each cylinder to the compression pressure specification in the Tune-Up Specifications chart in Section 2. The specifications given in this chart are maximum values.

A cylinder's compression pressure is usually acceptable if it is not less than 80% of maximum. The difference between any two cylinders should be no more than 12–14 pounds.

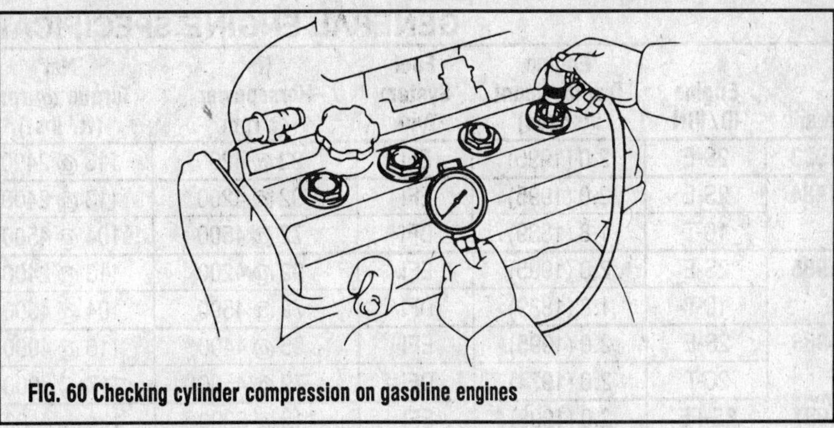

FIG. 60 Checking cylinder compression on gasoline engines

7. If a cylinder is unusually low, pour a tablespoon of clean engine oil into the cylinder through the spark plug hole and repeat the compression test. If the compression comes up after adding the oil, it appears that the cylinder's piston rings or bore are damaged or worn. If the pressure remains low, the valves may not be seating properly (a valve job is needed), or the head gasket may be blown near that cylinder. If compression in any two adjacent cylinders is low, and if the addition of oil doesn't help the compression, there is leakage past the head gasket. Oil and coolant water in the combustion chamber can result from this problem. There may be evidence of water droplets on the engine dipstick when a head gasket has blown.
8. Remove the compression gauge and install the spark plugs.
9. Reconnect the distributor and cold start injector connectors.

Diesel Engines

1. Warm up and stop the engine.
2. Disconnect the fuel cut-off solenoid wire connector.
3. Remove the glow plugs.

CAUTION

Make sure the load wire is not grounded.

➡ A special compression gauge and adaptor suitable for diesel engines (because these engines have much greater compression pressures) must be used. Use SST No.s 09992-00023 (gauge) and 09992-00160 (adapter) or their equivalents to measure the compression pressure.

4. Install and tighten the adapter into glow plug opening and connect a compression gauge to the adapter.
5. While you read the compression gauge, have an assistant crank the engine two or three times in short bursts using the ignition switch.

➡ The battery must be fully charged to produce a revolution of at least 250 rpm.

6. Read the compression gauge at the end of each series of cranks, and record the highest of these readings. Repeat this procedure for each of the engine's cylinders. Compare the highest reading of each cylinder to the compression pressure specification in the Tune-Up Specifications chart in Section 2. The specifications given in this chart are maximum values.

A cylinder's compression pressure is usually acceptable if it is not less than 80% of maximum. The difference between any two cylinders should be no more than 12-14 psi

7. If a cylinder is unusually low, pour a tablespoon of clean engine oil into the cylinder through the spark plug hole and repeat the compression test. If the compression comes up after adding the oil, it appears that the cylinder's piston rings or bore are damaged or worn. If the pressure remains low, the valves may not be seating properly (a valve job is needed), or the head gasket may be blown near that cylinder. If compression in any two adjacent cylinders is low, and if the addition of oil doesn't help the compression, there is leakage past the head gasket. Oil and coolant water in the combustion chamber can result from this problem. There may be evidence of water droplets on the engine dipstick when a head gasket has blown.
8. Remove the compression gauge and adapter.
9. Reinstall the glow plugs and reconnect the fuel cut-off solenoid wire connector.

GENERAL ENGINE SPECIFICATIONS

Year	Engine ID/VIN	Engine Displacement liter (cc)	Fuel System Type	Net Horsepower @ rpm	Net Torque @ rpm (ft. lbs.)	Bore × Stroke (in.)	Com-pression Ratio	Oil Pressure @ rpm
1983	2S-E	2.0 (1995)	EFI	92 @ 4200	113 @ 2400	3.31 × 3.54	8.7:1	①
1984	2S-E	2.0 (1995)	EFI	92 @ 4200	113 @ 2400	3.31 × 3.54	8.7:1	①
	1C-T	1.8 (1839)	DFI	72 @ 4500	104 @ 4500	3.27 × 3.35	22.5:1	②
1985	2S-E	2.0 (1995)	EFI	92 @ 4200	113 @ 2400	3.31 × 3.54	8.7:1	①
	1C-T	1.8 (1839)	DFI	72 @ 4500	104 @ 4500	3.27 × 3.35	22.5:1	②
1986	2S-E	2.0 (1995)	EFI	95 @ 4400	116 @ 4000	3.31 × 3.54	8.7:1	①
	2C-T	2.0 (1974)	DFI	79 @ 4500	117 @ 3000	3.39 × 3.39	23.0:1	②
1987	3S-FE	2.0 (1998)	EFI	115 @ 5200	124 @ 4400	3.39 × 3.39	9.3:1	①
1988	3S-FE	2.0 (1998)	EFI	115 @ 5200	124 @ 4400	3.39 × 3.39	9.3:1	①
1989	3S-FE	2.0 (1998)	EFI	115 @ 5200	124 @ 4400	3.39 × 3.39	9.3:1	④
	2VZ-FE	2.5 (2507)	EFI	156 @ 5600	160 @ 4400	3.44 × 2.74	9.0:1	④
1990	3S-FE	2.0 (1998)	EFI	115 @ 5200	124 @ 4400	3.39 × 3.39	9.3:1	④
	2VZ-FE	2.5 (2507)	EFI	156 @ 5600	160 @ 4400	3.44 × 2.74	9.0:1	④
1991	3S-FE	2.0 (1998)	EFI	115 @ 5200	124 @ 4400	3.39 × 3.39	9.3:1	④
	2VZ-FE	2.5 (2507)	EFI	156 @ 5600	160 @ 4400	3.44 × 2.74	9.0:1	④
1992	5S-FE	2.2 (2164)	EFI	130 @ 5400 ③	145 @ 4400	3.43 × 3.58	9.5:1	④
	3VZ-FE	3.0 (2959)	EFI	185 @ 5200	195 @ 4400	3.44 × 3.23	9.6:1	④

NOTE: Horsepower and torque are SAE net figures. They are measured at the rear of the transmission with all accessories installed and operating. Since the figures vary when a given engine is installed in different models, some are representative rather than exact.

① 4.3 @ idle; 36–71 @ 3000
② 4.3 @ idle; 36–85 @ 3000
③ 125 @ 5400—Calif.
④ 4.3 @ idle; 43–78 @ 3000

VALVE SPECIFICATIONS

Year	Engine ID/VIN	Engine Displacement liter (cc)	Seat Angle (deg.)	Face Angle (deg.)	Spring Test Pressure (lbs. @ in.)	Spring Installed Height (in.)	Stem-to-Guide Clearance (in.)		Spring Diameter (in.)	
							Intake	Exhaust	Intake	Exhaust
1983	2S-E	2.0 (1995)	45.5	45.5	68 @ 1.555	1.555	0.0010–0.0024	0.0012–0.0026	0.3138–0.3144	0.3136–0.3142
1984	2S-E	2.0 (1995)	45.5	45.5	68 @ 1.555	1.555	0.0010–0.0024	0.0012–0.0026	0.3138–0.3144	0.3136–0.3142
	1C-T	1.8 (1839)	45	45.5	53 @ 1.557	1.557	0.0008–0.0022	0.0014–0.0028	0.3140–0.3146	0.3134–0.3140
1985	2S-E	2.0 (1995)	45.5	45.5	68 @ 1.555	1.555	0.0010–0.0024	0.0012–0.0026	0.3138–0.3144	0.3136–0.3142
	1C-T	1.8 (1839)	45	45.5	53 @ 1.557	1.557	0.0008–0.0022	0.0014–0.0028	0.3140–0.3146	0.3134–0.3140
1986	2S-E	2.0 (1995)	45.5	45.5	68 @ 1.555	1.555	0.0010–0.0024	0.0012–0.0026	0.3138–0.3144	0.3136–0.3142
	2C-T	2.0 (1974)	45	45.5	53 @ 1.557	1.557	0.0008–0.0022	0.0014–0.0028	0.3140–0.3146	0.3134–0.3140
1987	3S-FE	2.0 (1998)	45	44.5	39.6 @ 1.366	1.366	0.0010–0.0024	0.0012–0.0026	0.2350–0.2356	0.2348–0.2354
1988	3S-FE	2.0 (1998)	45	44.5	39.6 @ 1.366	1.366	0.0010–0.0024	0.0012–0.0026	0.2350–0.2356	0.2348–0.2354

VALVE SPECIFICATIONS

Year	Engine ID/VIN	Engine Displacement liter (cc)	Seat Angle (deg.)	Face Angle (deg.)	Spring Test Pressure (lbs. @ in.)	Spring Installed Height (in.)	Stem-to-Guide Clearance (in.)		Spring Diameter (in.)	
							Intake	Exhaust	Intake	Exhaust
1989	3S-FE	2.0 (1998)	45	44.5	39.6 @ 1.366	1.366	0.0010–0.0024	0.0012–0.0026	0.2350–0.2356	0.2348–0.2354
	2VZ-FE	2.5 (2507)	45	44.5	44.1 @ 1.331	1.331	0.0010–0.0024	0.0012–0.0026	0.2350–0.2356	0.2348–0.2354
1990	3S-FE	2.0 (1998)	45	44.5	39.6 @ 1.366	1.366	0.0010–0.0024	0.0012–0.0026	0.2350–0.2356	0.2348–0.2354
	2VZ-FE	2.5 (2507)	45	44.5	44.1 @ 1.331	1.331	0.0010–0.0024	0.0012–0.0026	0.2350–0.2356	0.2348–0.2354
1991	3S-FE	2.0 (1998)	45	44.5	39.6 @ 1.366	1.366	0.0010–0.0024	0.0012–0.0026	0.2350–0.2356	0.2348–0.2354
	2VZ-FE	2.5 (2507)	45	44.5	44.1 @ 1.331	1.331	0.0010–0.0024	0.0012–0.0026	0.2350–0.2356	0.2348–0.2354
1992	5S-FE	2.2 (2164)	45	44.5	39.6 @ 1.366	1.366	0.0010–0.0024	0.0012–0.0026	0.2350–0.2356	0.2348–0.2354
	3VZ-FE	3.0 (2959)	45	44.5	39.6 @ 1.311	1.311	0.0010–0.0024	0.0012–0.0026	0.2350–0.2356	0.2348–0.2354

CAMSHAFT SPECIFICATIONS

All measurements given in inches.

Year	Engine ID/VIN	Engine Displacement liter (cc)	Journal Diameter					Elevation		Bearing Clearance	Camshaft End Play
			1	2	3	4	5	In.	Ex.		
1983	2S-E	2.0 (1995)	1.8291–1.8297	1.8192–1.8199	1.8094–1.8100	1.7996–1.8002	1.7897–1.7904 ①	1.5325–1.5365	1.5325–1.5365	0.0010–0.0026	0.0031–0.0091
1984	2S-E	2.0 (1995)	1.8291–1.8297	1.8192–1.8199	1.8094–1.8100	1.7996–1.8002	1.7897–1.7904 ①	1.5325–1.5365	1.5325–1.5365	0.0010–0.0026	0.0031–0.0091
	1C-T	1.8 (1839)	1.1015–1.1022	1.1015–1.1022	1.1015–1.1022	1.1015–1.1022	1.1015–1.1022	1.8081	1.8478	0.0015–0.0029	0.0031–0.0071
1985	2S-E	2.0 (1995)	1.8291–1.8297	1.8192–1.8199	1.8094–1.8100	1.7996–1.8002	1.7897–1.7904 ①	1.5325–1.5365	1.5325–1.5365	0.0010–0.0026	0.0031–0.0091
	1C-T	1.8 (1839)	1.1015–1.1022	1.1015–1.1022	1.1015–1.1022	1.1015–1.1022	1.1015–1.1022	1.8081	1.8478	0.0015–0.0029	0.0031–0.0071
1986	2S-E	2.0 (1995)	1.8291–1.8297	1.8192–1.8199	1.8094–1.8100	1.7996–1.8002	1.7897–1.7904 ①	1.5325–1.5365	1.5325–1.5365	0.0010–0.0026	0.0031–0.0091
	2C-T	2.0 (1974)	1.1015–1.1022	1.1015–1.1022	1.1015–1.1022	1.1015–1.1022	1.1015–1.1022	1.8081	1.8478	0.0015–0.0029	0.0031–0.0071
1987	3S-FE	2.0 (1998)	1.0614–1.0620	1.0614–1.0620	1.0614–1.0620	1.0614–1.0620	—	1.3744–1.3783	1.4000–1.4039	0.0010–0.0024	0.0018–0.0039
1988	3S-FE	2.0 (1998)	1.0614–1.0620	1.0614–1.0620	1.0614–1.0620	1.0614–1.0620	—	1.3744–1.3783	1.4000–1.4039	0.0010–0.0024	0.0018–0.0039
1989	3S-FE	2.0 (1998)	1.0614–1.0620	1.0614–1.0620	1.0614–1.0620	1.0614–1.0620	—	1.3744–1.3783	1.4000–1.4039	0.0010–0.0024	0.0018–0.0039
	2VZ-FE	2.5 (2507)	1.0610–1.0616	1.0610–1.0616	1.0610–1.0616	1.0610–1.0616	1.0610–1.0616	1.5555–1.5594	1.5339–1.5378	0.0014–0.0028	0.0012–0.0031
1990	3S-FE	2.0 (1998)	1.0614–1.0620	1.0614–1.0620	1.0614–1.0620	1.0614–1.0620	—	1.3744–1.3783	1.4000–1.4039	0.0010–0.0024	0.0018–0.0039
	2VZ-FE	2.5 (2507)	1.0610–1.0616	1.0610–1.0616	1.0610–1.0616	1.0610–1.0616	1.0610–1.0616	1.5555–1.5594	1.5339–1.5378	0.0014–0.0028	0.0012–0.0031

CAMSHAFT SPECIFICATIONS

All measurements given in inches.

Year	Engine ID/VIN	Engine Displacement liter (cc)	Journal Diameter 1	2	3	4	5	Elevation In.	Ex.	Bearing Clearance	Camshaft End Play
1991	3S-FE	2.0 (1998)	1.0614–1.0620	1.0614–1.0620	1.0614–1.0620	1.0614–1.0620	—	1.3744–1.3783	1.4000–1.4039	0.0010–0.0024	0.0018–0.0039
	2VZ-FE	2.5 (2507)	1.0610–1.0616	1.0610–1.0616	1.0610–1.0616	1.0610–1.0616	1.0610–1.0616	1.5555–1.5594	1.5339–1.5378	0.0014–0.0028	0.0012–0.0031
1992	5S-FE	2.2 (2164)	1.0614–1.0620	1.0614–1.0620	1.0614–1.0620	1.0614–1.0620	—	1.6539–1.6579	1.5722–1.5811	0.0010–0.0024	①
	3VZ-FE	3.0 (2959)	1.0610–1.0616	1.0610–1.0616	1.0610–1.0616	1.0610–1.0616	1.0610–1.0616	1.6598–1.6638	1.6520–1.6559	0.0014–0.0028	0.0013–0.0031

① Intake: 0.0018–0.0039
Exhaust: 0.0012–0.0033

CRANKSHAFT AND CONNECTING ROD SPECIFICATIONS

All measurements are given in inches.

Year	Engine ID/VIN	Engine Displacement liter (cc)	Crankshaft Main Brg. Journal Dia.	Crankshaft Main Brg. Oil Clearance	Crankshaft Shaft End-play	Crankshaft Thrust on No.	Connecting Rod Journal Diameter	Connecting Rod Oil Clearance	Connecting Rod Side Clearance
1983	2S-E	2.0 (1995)	2.1648–2.1654	0.0008–0.0019 ①	0.0008–0.0087	3	1.8892–1.8898	0.0009–0.0022	0.0063–0.0083
1984	2S-E	2.0 (1995)	2.1648–2.1654	0.0008–0.0019 ①	0.0008–0.0087	3	1.8892–1.8898	0.0009–0.0022	0.0063–0.0083
	1C-T	1.8 (1839)	2.2435–2.2441	0.0013–0.0026	0.0016–0.0094	3	1.9877–1.9882	0.0014–0.0025	0.0031–0.0118
1985	2S-E	2.0 (1995)	2.1648–2.1654	0.0008–0.0019 ①	0.0008–0.0087	3	1.8892–1.8898	0.0009–0.0022	0.0063–0.0083
	1C-T	1.8 (1839)	2.2435–2.2441	0.0013–0.0026	0.0016–0.0094	3	1.9877–1.9882	0.0014–0.0025	0.0031–0.0118
1986	2S-E	2.0 (1995)	2.1648–2.1654	0.0008–0.0019 ①	0.0008–0.0087	3	1.8892–1.8898	0.0009–0.0022	0.0063–0.0083
	2C-T	2.0 (1974)	2.2435–2.2441	0.0013–0.0026	0.0016–0.0094	3	1.9877–1.9882	0.0014–0.0025	0.0031–0.0118
1987	3S-FE	2.0 (1998)	2.1649–2.1655	0.0006–0.0013 ①	0.0008–0.0087	3	1.8892–1.8898	0.0009–0.0022	0.0063–0.0123
1988	3S-FE	2.0 (1998)	2.1649–2.1655	0.0006–0.0013 ①	0.0008–0.0087	3	1.8892–1.8898	0.0009–0.0022	0.0063–0.0123
1989	3S-FE	2.0 (1998)	2.1649–2.1655	0.0006–0.0013 ①	0.0008–0.0087	3	1.8892–1.8898	0.0009–0.0022	0.0063–0.0123
	2VZ-FE	2.5 (2507)	2.5191–2.5197	0.0011–0.0022	0.0008–0.0087	3	1.8892–1.8898	0.0011–0.0026	0.0059–0.0130
1990	3S-FE	2.0 (1998)	2.1649–2.1655	0.0006–0.0013 ①	0.0008–0.0087	3	1.8892–1.8898	0.0009–0.0022	0.0063–0.0123
	2VZ-FE	2.5 (2507)	2.5191–2.5197	0.0011–0.0022	0.0008–0.0087	3	1.8892–1.8898	0.0011–0.0026	0.0059–0.0130
1991	3S-FE	2.0 (1998)	2.1649–2.1655	0.0006–0.0013 ①	0.0008–0.0087	3	1.8892–1.8898	0.0009–0.0022	0.0063–0.0123
	2VZ-FE	2.5 (2507)	2.5191–2.5197	0.0011–0.0022	0.0008–0.0087	3	1.8892–1.8898	0.0011–0.0026	0.0059–0.0130

CRANKSHAFT AND CONNECTING ROD SPECIFICATIONS

All measurements are given in inches.

Year	Engine ID/VIN	Engine Displacement liter (cc)	Crankshaft Main Brg. Journal Dia.	Crankshaft Main Brg. Oil Clearance	Crankshaft Shaft End-play	Crankshaft Thrust on No.	Connecting Rod Journal Diameter	Connecting Rod Oil Clearance	Connecting Rod Side Clearance
1992	5S-FE	2.2 (2164)	2.1653–2.1655	0.0006–0.0013 ①	0.0008–0.0087	3	1.8892–1.8898	0.0009–0.0022	0.0063–0.0123
	3VZ-FE	3.0 (2959)	2.5191–2.5197	0.0011–0.0022	0.0008–0.0087	3	2.1648–2.1654	0.0011–0.0026	0.0059–0.0130

① No. 3: 0.0012–0.0022 (1987)
No. 3: 0.0011–0.0019 (1988)
No. 3: 0.0010–0.0017 (1989–92)

PISTON AND RING SPECIFICATIONS

All measurements are given in inches.

Year	Engine ID/VIN	Engine Displacement liter (cc)	Piston Clearance	Ring Gap Top Compression	Ring Gap Bottom Compression	Ring Gap Oil Control	Ring Side Clearance Top Compression	Ring Side Clearance Bottom Compression	Ring Side Clearance Oil Control
1983	2S-E	2.0 (1995)	0.0006–0.0014	0.0110–0.0197	0.0079–0.0177	0.0079–0.0311	0.0012–0.0028	0.0012–0.0028	Snug
1984	2S-E	2.0 (1995)	0.0006–0.0014	0.0110–0.0197	0.0079–0.0177	0.0079–0.0311	0.0012–0.0028	0.0012–0.0028	Snug
	1C-T	1.8 (1839)	0.0016–0.0024	0.0098–0.0193	0.0079–0.0113	0.0079–0.0193	0.0079–0.0081	0.0079–0.0081	Snug
1985	2S-E	2.0 (1995)	0.0006–0.0014	0.0110–0.0197	0.0079–0.0177	0.0079–0.0311	0.0012–0.0028	0.0012–0.0028	Snug
	1C-T	1.8 (1839)	0.0016–0.0024	0.0106–0.0213	0.0098–0.0205	0.0079–0.0205	0.0080	0.0080	Snug
1986	2S-E	2.0 (1995)	0.0006–0.0014	0.0110–0.0197	0.0079–0.0177	0.0079–0.0311	0.0012–0.0028	0.0012–0.0028	Snug
	2C-T	2.0 (1974)	0.0018–0.0026	0.0106–0.0213	0.0098–0.0205	0.0079–0.0323	0.0080	0.0080	Snug
1987	3S-FE	2.0 (1998)	0.0018–0.0026	0.0106–0.0197	0.0106–0.0201	0.0079–0.0323	0.0012–0.0028	0.0012–0.0028	Snug
1988	3S-FE	2.0 (1998)	0.0018–0.0026	0.0106–0.0205	0.0106–0.0209	0.0079–0.0323	0.0018–0.0028	0.0018–0.0028	Snug
1989	3S-FE	2.0 (1998)	0.0018–0.0026	0.0106–0.0197	0.0106–0.0201	0.0079–0.0207	0.0012–0.0028	0.0012–0.0028	Snug
	2VZ-FE	2.5 (2507)	0.0018–0.0026	0.0118–0.0205	0.0138–0.0236	0.0079–0.0207	0.0004–0.0031	0.0012–0.0028	Snug
1990	3S-FE	2.0 (1998)	0.0018–0.0026	0.0106–0.0197	0.0106–0.0201	0.0079–0.0207	0.0012–0.0028	0.0012–0.0028	Snug
	2VZ-FE	2.5 (2507)	0.0018–0.0026	0.0118–0.0205	0.0138–0.0236	0.0079–0.0207	0.0004–0.0031	0.0012–0.0028	Snug
1991	3S-FE	2.0 (1998)	0.0018–0.0026	0.0106–0.0197	0.0106–0.0201	0.0079–0.0207	0.0012–0.0028	0.0012–0.0028	Snug
	2VZ-FE	2.5 (2507)	0.0018–0.0026	0.0118–0.0205	0.0138–0.0236	0.0079–0.0207	0.0004–0.0031	0.0012–0.0028	Snug
1992	5S-FE	2.2 (2164)	0.0055–0.0063	0.0106–0.0197	0.0138–0.0234	0.0017–0.0207	0.0016–0.0031	0.0012–0.0028	Snug
	3VZ-FE	3.0 (2959)	0.0051–0.0059	0.0110–0.0197	0.0150–0.0236	0.0059–0.0224	0.0004–0.0031	0.0012–0.0028	Snug

TORQUE SPECIFICATIONS

All readings in ft. lbs.

Year	Engine ID/VIN	Engine Displacement liter (cc)	Cylinder Head Bolts	Main Bearing Bolts	Rod Bearing Bolts	Crankshaft Damper Bolts	Flywheel Bolts	Manifold Intake	Manifold Exhaust	Spark Plugs	Lug Nut
1983	2S-E	2.0 (1995)	45–50	40–45	33–38	78–82	70–75	30–33	30–33	11–15	76
1984	2S-E	2.0 (1995)	45–50	40–45	33–38	78–82	70–75	30–33	30–33	11–15	76
	1C-T	1.8 (1839)	60–65	75–78	45–50	70–75	63–68	10–15	32–36	—	76
1985	2S-E	2.0 (1995)	45–50	40–45	33–38	78–82	70–75	30–33	30–33	11–15	76
	1C-T	1.8 (1839)	60–65	75–78	45–50	70–75	63–68	10–15	32–36	—	76
1986	2S-E	2.0 (1995)	45–50	40–45	33–38	78–82	70–75	30–33	30–33	11–15	76
	2C-T	2.0 (1974)	①	75–78	45–50	70–75	63–68	10–15	32–36	—	76
1987	3S-FE	2.0 (1998)	45–50	40–45	33–38	78–82	70–75	11–17	27–33	11–15	76
1988	3S-FE	2.0 (1998)	45–50	40–45	33–38	78–82	70–75	11–17	27–33	11–15	76
1989	3S-FE	2.0 (1998)	45–50	40–45	33–38	78–82	70–75	11–17	27–33	11–15	76
	2VZ-FE	2.5 (2507)	①	43–47	16–20	176–186	58–64	11–15	26–32	11–15	76
1990	3S-FE	2.0 (1998)	45–50	40–45	33–38	78–82	70–75	11–17	27–33	11–15	76
	2VZ-FE	2.5 (2507)	①	45 ①	18 ①	176–186	58–64	11–15	26–32	11–15	76
1991	3S-FE	2.0 (1998)	36 ①	40–45	33–38	78–82	58–64 ②	11–15	32–40	11–15	76
	2VZ-FE	2.5 (2507)	①	45 ①	18 ①	176–186	58–64	11–15	26–32	11–15	76
1992	5S-FE	2.2 (2164)	36 ①	40–45	18 ①	78–82	58–64 ②	11–15	32–40	11–15	76
	3VZ-FE	3.0 (2959)	①	45 ①	18 ①	176–186	58–64	11–15	26–32	11–15	76

① See text
② AT only. MT—63–67

Engine

REMOVAL & INSTALLATION

CAUTION

When draining the coolant, keep in mind that cats and dogs are attracted by the ethylene glycol antifreeze, and are quite likely to drink any that is left in an uncovered container or in puddles on the ground. This will prove fatal in sufficient quantity. Always drain the coolant into a sealable container. Coolant should be reused unless it is contaminated or several years old. The EPA warns that prolonged contact with used engine oil may cause a number of skin disorders, including cancer! You should make every effort to minimize your exposure to used engine oil. Protective gloves should be worn when changing the oil. Wash your hands and any other exposed skin areas as soon as possible after exposure to used engine oil. Soap and water, or waterless hand cleaner should be used.

1C-T and 2C-T Engines

1. Disconnect and remove the battery. Drain the coolant from the radiator and engine drain cocks. Matchmark and remove the hood.
2. Remove the relay block bracket and position the assembly out of the way without disconnecting any electrical connectors. Remove the cruise control actuator.
3. If the vehicle is not equipped with cruise control, disconnect the accelerator cable at the injection pump. Disconnect the throttle cable at the injection pump. Remove the air cleaner assembly with the air cleaner hose.
4. Disconnect and remove the heater hoses. Remove the radiator.
5. Disconnect, plug and label the fuel inlet and outlet hoses, the vacuum pump vacuum hoses, the pressure hose for the turbocharger warning switch, the idle up vacuum hoses and the HAC vacuum hose.
6. Disconnect and label all electrical wires, vacuum hoses and cables from their various engine parts.
7. Disconnect the speedometer cable. Remove the transaxle case protection shield. Disconnect the transaxle control cable at the swivel and bracket and lift it out.
8. Remove the windshield washer and radiator reservoir tanks.
9. Unbolt the power steering pump, remove the drive belt and then position the pump out of the way with the hoses still connected. Support the pump with a piece of string or wire. Unbolt and position the air condition compressor on the radiator support. Support the compressor with a piece of string or wire.
10. Raise and support the vehicle safely. Drain the engine oil. Drain the transaxle fluid.
11. Unbolt both halfshafts. Unbolt the left side steering knuckle for halfshaft removal.
12. Disconnect the exhaust pipe at the turbocharger elbow manifold.
13. Remove the rear engine insulator. Lower the vehicle and remove the front engine mount bolts.
14. Attach an engine lifting hoist to the lifting brackets. Take up the weight of the engine with the hoist and then remove the right and left engine mounts.
15. Slowly and carefully, remove the engine/transaxle assembly from the vehicle. Be careful to avoid striking the crankshaft pulley or the transaxle against any part of the body.

To Install:

1. Slowly and carefully, lower the engine/ transaxle assembly into the engine compartment and align each mounting with its bracket. Temporarily install the transaxle case and mounting through bolts. Remove the lifting hoist from the engine.
2. Raise and safely support the vehicle. Install the engine rear mounting insulator.
3. Connect the exhaust pipe to the exhaust elbow using a new gasket. Connect the left steering knuckle to the ball joint. Torque the bolts to 65 ft. lbs. (88 Nm).
4. Connect both front drive shafts. Torque the nuts to 27 ft. lbs. (36 Nm). Depress the brake pedal as each nut is torqued. Lower the vehicle.
5. Lower the vehicle. Tighten the left and right mounting through bolts and nuts. Install the air conditioning compressor.
6. Install the power steering pump and adjust the belt tension. Install the washer and radiator reservoir tanks.
7. Install the engine front mounting bolts. Connect the transaxle control cable to the bracket and swivel and secure with the retaining clips.
8. Install the transaxle case connector and connect the speedometer cable.
9. Route, connect and clamp all the electrical wires to their various engine parts. Connect all the vacuum hoses.
10. Install the radiator. Connect the throttle cable to the injection pump. Install the air cleaner assembly and the air cleaner hose.
11. On vehicles equipped with cruise control, connect the accelerator cable to the injection pump. Install the cruise control actuator. Install the relay block and bracket. Install the battery.
12. Fill the radiator with coolant to the proper level. Fill the trasaxle with ATF. Install a new oil filter and replace the engine oil.
13. Start the engine and check for leaks of any kind. Correct all leaks as necessary.
14. Adjust the engine idle and maximum idle speeds.
15. Install and adjust the hood.
16. Perform a road test. Recheck the coolant and engine oil levels.

2S-E Engines

1. Drain the engine coolant from the radiator and engine drain cocks.
2. Remove the hood. Disconnect and remove the battery. On vehicles equipped with an automatic transaxle, disconnect the throttle cable and bracket from the throttle body.
3. Disconnect and label all cables, electrical wires and vacuum lines attached to various engine parts.
4. Remove the cruise control actuator and bracket. Disconnect the radiator and heater hoses. Disconnect the automatic transaxle cooler lines. Remove the radiator.
5. Remove the air cleaner assembly and air flow meter. Disconnect all wiring and linkage at the transaxle.
6. Pull out the fuel injection system wiring harness. Secure the assembly to the right side of fender apron.
7. Disconnect and plug the fuel lines at the fuel filter and return pipes. Unbolt the air conditioning compressor and position it out of the way. DO NOT disconnect any refrigerant lines.
8. Disconnect the speedometer cable at the transaxle. Remove the clutch release cylinder without disconnecting the fluid line.
9. Raise and support the vehicle safely. Drain the engine oil. Drain the transaxle fluid. Wrap both drive shaft boots with shop towels an unbolt both halfshafts.
10. Unbolt the power steering pump (leaving the hoses connected) and position it out of the way. Disconnect the exhaust pipe from the manifold. Disconnect the front and rear engine mounts at the frame member.
11. Attach an engine hoist chain to the lifting eyes and connect a suitable engine lifting device to the hoist. Take up the engine weight with the crane and remove the right and left side engine mounts.
12. Carefully, raise and remove the engine and transaxle assembly from the vehicle. Clear the right side of the mounting while lowering the transaxle and clear the power steering gear while lowering the neutral start switch. Make sure that the engine clears all wiring hoses and cables.
13. Position the engine in a suitable engine holding stand and disconnect the lifting device and the chains.

To Install:

1. Connect the engine hoist chains to the lifting eyes and connect the lifting device to the hoist. Remove the engine from the holding stand.
2. Carefully lower the engine and transaxle assembly into the engine compartment. Keep the engine level and align each mounting with its bracket. Temporarily install both the left and right mountings through their nuts and bolts. Remove the lifting device and chain hoist from the engine.
3. Raise the vehicle and support safely. Install the front and rear mounting insulators onto the frame member. Torque the bolts to 29 ft. lbs. (38 Nm). Connect the exhaust pipe to the exhaust manifold using new gaskets. Install the power steering pump onto the bracket. Install the drive belt and adjust the belt tension.
4. On vehicles equipped with manual transaxle, insert the drive shaft to the transaxle and connect the steering knuckle to the ball joint. Torque the bolts to 65 ft. lbs. (88 Nm). Connect both front drive shafts, torque the nuts to 27 ft. lbs. (36 Nm) and remove the shop towels from the drive boots.
5. Lower the vehicle and tighten the left and right mounting through bolts. Install the front mounting insulator through bolt. Install the air conditioning compressor and adjust the drive belt tension.
6. On vehicles equipped with automatic transaxle, connect the transaxle control cable to both the bracket and swivel and install the retaining clips. On vehicles equipped with manual transaxle, connect each cable to the bracket, select and shaft levers and install the the retaining clips and plate washers. Install the transaxle case protector.
7. On vehicles equipped with manual transaxle, install the clutch release cylinder and hose bracket. Connect the speedometer cable. Connect the fuel inlet and return hoses. Torque the fuel filter inlet bolt to 22 ft. lbs. (29 Nm).
8. Connect the heater hoses to the cylinder block. Pull the EFI wiring harness from the right fender apron through between the engine and the air intake manifold. Connect all EFI and electrical wiring and all vacuum hoses to their various engine components.
9. Install the air cleaner assembly with the air flow meter and the air cleaner hose. Install the radiator. Install the cruise control actuator and bracket. Connect the accelerator cable to the throttle body and adjust it. On vehicles equipped with automatic transaxle, connect the throttle cable with bracket and adjust it.
10. Install the battery making sure that the original polarity is observed. Close the radiator and engine drain cocks and fill the radiator with coolant to the proper level. Fill the transaxle and differential. Replace the engine oil with a new filter.
11. Adjust the ignition timing and the engine idle speed. Check for leaks and correct as required. Install and adjust the hood. Perform a road test. Recheck the coolant and engine oil levels.

3S-FE Engines

2-WHEEL DRIVE

1. Disconnect the negative battery cable. Remove the hood. Drain the engine coolant. Tag and disconnect all vacuum hoses, electrical wires and cables that are necessary to remove the engine.
2. Remove the radiator. On vehicles equipped with automatic transaxle, disconnect the throttle cable and bracket from the throttle body.
3. Disconnect the accelerator cable from the throttle body. Remove the cruise control actuator and bracket, if equipped.

4. Disconnect the ground wire from the alternator upper bracket. Remove the air cleaner assembly, air flow meter and air cleaner hose.

5. Remove the igniter. Remove the heater hoses. Disconnect and plug the fuel lines. Disconnect the speedometer cable.

**** CAUTION**

Catch the excess fuel in a small plastic container.

6. On vehicles equipped with manual transaxle, remove the clutch release cylinder and tube bracket. DO NOT disconnect the tube from the bracket. Disconnect the transaxle control cable (manual transmission and automatic transmission).

7. Remove the air conditioning compressor and position it to the side. DO NOT disconnect the refrigerant lines. Disconnect and label all electrical wires, connectors and vacuum hoses from their various engine parts.

8. Raise and support the vehicle safely. Drain the engine oil. Remove the engine under covers.

9. Remove the suspension lower crossmember. Remove the driveshafts and wrap the boots with shop towels. Remove the power steering pump and position it to the side. DO NOT disconnect the lines. Position the pump against the cowl and support it with a piece of string or wire.

10. Disconnect the exhaust pipe from the catalytic converter. Disconnect the engine mounting center member.

11. Lower the vehicle. Disconnect the TCCS (Toyota Computer Control System) and the ECU (Electronic Control Unit) electrical connectors.

12. Properly attach a chain hoist the lifting device to the engine. Raise the engine slightly and remove the engine retaining brackets and bolts.

13. Carefully remove the engine/transaxle assembly from the vehicle. Be careful not to hit the power steering gear housing or the neutral safety switch.

14. Position the engine on a suitable workstand and remove the lifting device and chain hoist.

To install:

1. Attach the chain hoist and lifting device to the engine and remove the engine from the engine stand.

2. Carefully lower the engine into the engine compartment being careful not to hit the power steering housing or the neutral start switch. Once the engine is in place and all the mountings are properly aligned with the body brackets, install the mounting insulators and temporarily install the thru-bolts. Torque the bolts on the left mount to 38 ft. lbs. (52 Nm), the thru-bolt to 64 ft. lbs. (87 Nm). On the right mount, tighten the bracket nut to 38 ft. lbs. (52 Nm), the body nut to 65 ft. lbs. (88 Nm), and the bolt to 47 ft. lbs. (64 Nm).

3. Connect the TCCS and ECU connectors. Raise and safely support the vehicle.

4. Install the engine mounting center member and torque the bolts to 29 ft. lbs. (39 Nm). Install the front and rear engine mounting insulators and nuts and bolts. Torque the bolts to 32 ft. lbs. (43 Nm). Connect the exhaust pipe to the catalytic converter using new gaskets. Torque the bolts to 46 ft. lbs. (62 Nm).

5. Install the power steering pump and drive shafts. Install the suspension lower crossmember.

6. Install the engine under covers. Torque the bolts of the left and right mounting insulators to 58 ft. lbs. (78 Nm). Reconnect all the vacuum hoses, wires and connectors.

7. Install the air conditioning compressor. Connect the transaxle control cable. On vehicles equipped with manual transaxle, install the clutch release cylinder and tube clamp.

8. Connect the speedometer cable. Unplug and connect the fuel hoses. Connect the heater hoses. Install the igniter.

9. Install the air cleaner assembly, air flow meter and air cleaner hose. Connect the ground strap to the alternator upper bracket. Install the cruise control actuator and bracket. On vehicles equipped with manual transaxle, install the throttle cable and adjust it. Install the accelerator cable and adjust it.

10. Install the radiator and the battery. Fill the engine with coolant to the proper level. Install a new filter and replace the engine oil. Start the engine and check for leaks. Correct all leaks as required.

11. Adjust the power steering pump and the alternator drive belt tension. Adjust the ignition timing and the valve clearance.

12. Install the hood and check the toe-in.

13. Perform a road test. Recheck the coolant and engine oil levels.

ALL-TRAC 4-WHEEL DRIVE

1. Disconnect the negative battery cable and drain the engine coolant. Remove the hood.

2. Disconnect the accelerator cable from the throttle body. Remove the radiator.

3. Disconnect the heater hoses.

4. Disconnect the inlet hose at the fuel filter. Disconnect the return hose at the fuel return pipe.

5. Disconnect and remove the cruise control actuator.

6. Remove the air cleaner assembly.

7. Remove the clutch slave cylinder and hose bracket without disconnecting the hose. Position the assembly out of the way. Disconnect the speedometer cable and the transaxle control cables.

8. Disconnect and remove the air conditioning compressor with the refrigerant lines still attached; position it out of the way. DO NOT disconnect the refrigerant lines.

9. Disconnect and label all wires, connecters and vacuum lines from their various engine parts.

10. Raise the front of the vehicle so that there is sufficient clearance to lower the engine. Drain the engine oil and remove the engine undercovers.

11. Remove the lower suspension crossmember and the halfshafts. Disconnect and remove the propeller shaft. Cover the drive boots with shop towels.

12. Remove the power steering pump with the hydraulic lines still attached and place it against the cowl. Secure the pump with a piece of string or wire. Remove the front exhaust pipe.

13. Remove the engine mounting center member and the stabilizer bar. Lower the vehicle.

14. Disconnect the TCCS (Toyota Computer Control System) and ECU (Electronic Control Unit) connectors and pull them out through the firewall. Remove the power steering pump reservoir tank mounting bolts.

15. Attach an engine lifting device to the engine lift brackets. Remove the right side engine mount stay and then remove the insulator and bracket. Remove the left side engine mount insulator and bracket.

16. Lower the engine and transaxle as an assembly from the engine compartment. Be careful not to hit the power steering gear housing or the neutral safety switch.

17. Place the engine in a suitable engine holding stand.

To install:

1. Remove the engine from the holding stand. Carefully raise the engine into the engine compartment being careful not to strike the power steering gear housing or the neutral start switch.

2. Keep the engine level and align each mounting with the bracket. Install the left and right mounting insulators and temporarily install the through bolts. Torque the left mount bolts to 38 ft. lbs. (52 Nm), the thru-bolt to 64 ft. lbs. (87 Nm) and right mounting bracket bolts to 64 ft. lbs. (87 Nm), the nuts to 38 ft. lbs. (52 Nm) and the right mounting stay bolt and nut to 54 ft. lbs. (73 Nm). Remove the lifting device from the engine.

3. Install the power steering pump reservoir mounting bolts. Connect the TCCS and ECU connectors. Raise the vehicle and support safely.

4. Install the stabilizer bar. Install the engine mounting center member and torque the member body bolts to 29 ft. lbs. (39 Nm) and all other member bolts to 38 ft. lbs. (52 Nm).

5. Install the front exhaust pipe and torque the bolts to 46 ft. lbs. (62 Nm). Attach the power steering pump to the bracket. Install the propeller shaft and connect the front drive shafts. Install the suspension lower crossmember. Torque the member body bolts to 153 ft. lbs. (207 Nm) and all other member bolts to 29 ft. lbs. (39 Nm).

6. Install the engine covers and lower the vehicle. Connect all electrical wires, connectors and vacuum hoses. Install the air conditioning compressor and the drive belt.

7. Connect the transaxle control and speedometer cables. Install the clutch release cylinder and release bracket.

8. Install the air cleaner, air cleaner hose and flow meter assembly. Install the cruise control actuator.

9. Unplug and connect the fuel hoses. Connect the heater water hoses.

10. Install the radiator. Install the accelerator cable and adjust it. Install the battery.

11. Fill the engine with coolant to the proper level. Install a new oil filter and replace the engine oil. Start the engine and check for leaks of any kind. Correct all leaks as necessary.

12. Adjust the power steering pump and the alternator drive belt tension. Adjust the ignition timing and the valve clearance.

13. Install the hood and check the toe-in.

14. Perform a road test. Recheck the coolant and engine oil levels.

5S-FE Engines

➧ SEE FIGS. 61-63

1. Disconnect the negative battery cable.

CAUTION

On models with an airbag, wait at least 30 seconds from the time that the ignition switch is turned to the LOCK position and the battery is disconnected before performing any further work.

2. Remove the battery and its tray.

3. Remove the hood.

4. Remove the engine under cover and then drain the engine coolant and oil.

5. Disconnect the accelerator cable from the throttle body. On models with AT, its the throttle cable, not the accelerator.

6. Remove the air cleaner assembly, resonator and the air intake hose.

7. On models with cruise control, remove the actuator cover, unplug the connector, remove the three bolts and then disconnect the actuator with the bracket.

8. Disconnect the ground strap at the battery carrier.

9. Remove the radiator and then disconnect the coolant reservoir hose.

10. Remove the three washer tank mounting bolts, disconnect the connector and hose and then lift out the tank.

11. Tag and disconnect the:

a. Three connectors to the engine relay box

b. Two connectors from the left side fender apron

c. Igniter connector

d. Noise filter connector

e. Connector at the fender apron

f. Check connector

g. A/C magnet switch connector (if equipped)

h. Ground strap at the right fender apron

i. Vacuum sensor connector

j. Back-up light switch and speed sensor (models with MT)

12. Disconnect the heater hoses and the fuel return hose and the fuel inlet hose. All of these may leak coolant of fuel, so have a container handy!

13. On models with MT, remove the starter and then remove the clutch release cylinder. Don't disconnect the hydraulic line, simply hang the cylinder out of the way.

14. Disconnect the transaxle control cables at the transaxle.

15. Tag and disconnect all remaining vacuum hoses.

16. Remove the under cover beneath the glove box. Remove the lower instrument panel, the glove box door and the box itself. Tag and disconnect the two ECU connectors and the four cowl wire connector. Remove the two nuts and then pull the engine harness into the engine compartment.

17. Without disconnecting the refrigerant lines, remove the A/C compressor and hang it carefully out of the way.

18. Loosen the two bolts and disconnect the front exhaust pipe bracket. Use a deep 14mm socket and remove the three nuts attaching the front pipe to the manifold. Disconnect the pipe.

19. Remove the halfshafts.

20. Without disconnecting the hydraulic lines, remove the power steering pump and hang it aside; carefully!

21. Remove the three bolts (MT) or four bolts (AT) and then disconnect the left engine mounting insulator. Pop out the plugs, remove the three nuts and then remove the right engine mounting insulator. Remove the three bolts and disconnect the front engine mounting insulator.

22. Attach an engine lifting device to the lift hooks. Remove the three bolts and disconnect the control rod. Slowly and carefully, lift the engine/transaxle assembly out of the engine compartment.

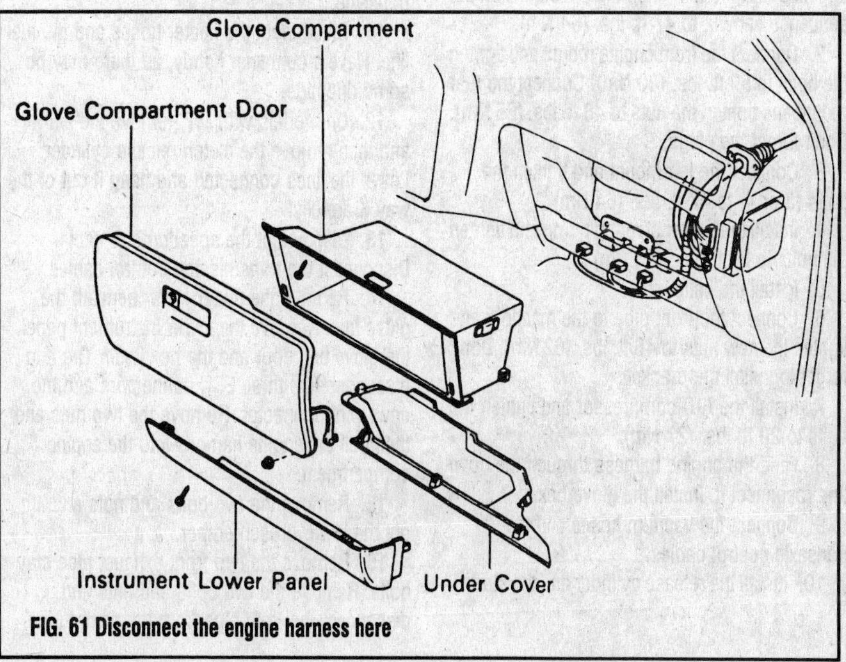

FIG. 61 Disconnect the engine harness here

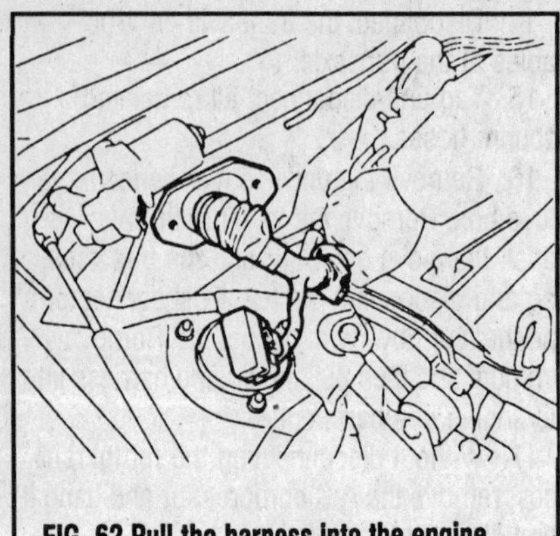

FIG. 62 Pull the harness into the engine compartment — 5S-FE engines

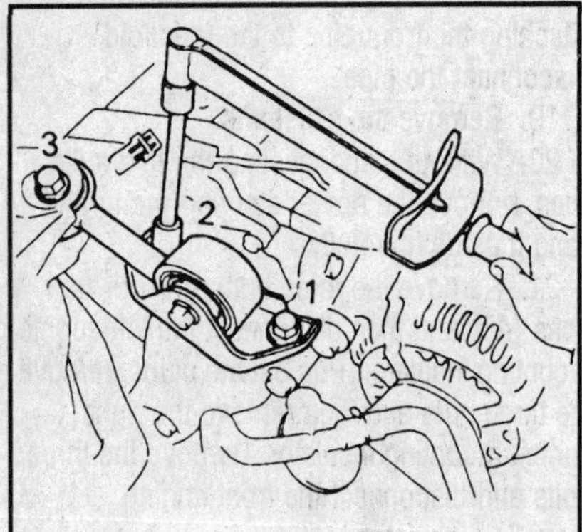

FIG. 63 Tighten the engine control rod in this sequence — 5S-FE engines

To install:

1. Carefully lower the engine into the engine compartment. With the engine level and all the mounts aligned with their brackets, install the engine control rod. Tighten the three bolts, in the sequence shown, to 47 ft. lbs. (64 Nm).
2. Connect the front engine mount and tighten the bolts to 59 ft. lbs. (80 Nm). Connect the rear mount and tighten the nuts to 48 ft. lbs. (66 Nm). Don't forget the plugs.
3. Connect the left mount and tighten the bolts (3 or 4) to 47 ft. lbs. (64 Nm).
4. Install the power steering pump and tighten the bolts to 31 ft. lbs. (43 Nm).
5. Install the halfshafts.
6. Connect the front pipe to the manifold and tighten the new nuts to 46 ft. lbs. (62 Nm). Don't forget to install the bracket.
7. Install the A/C compressor and tighten the bolts to 20 ft. lbs. (27 Nm).
8. Feed the engine harness through the cowl and reconnect it. Install the glove box.
9. Connect the vacuum hoses and the transaxle control cables.
10. Install the release cylinder and the starter.
11. Connect the fuel inlet hose and tighten it to 22 ft. lbs. (29 Nm). Connect the return hose and the two heater hoses.
12. Reconnect all wires disconnected previously.
13. Install the washer tank and connect the electrical lead and hose.
14. Install the coolant reservoir hose and the radiator.
15. Connect the ground strap to the battery carrier and then install the cruise control actuator. Install the air cleaner assembly.
16. Connect the throttle/accelerator cable and adjust it.
17. Fill the engine with oil and coolant. Connect the battery cable, start the engine and check for any leaks.

2VZ-FE Engines

➧ SEE FIGS. 64-67

1. Remove the battery. Drain the engine coolant and remove the hood.
2. Remove the engine under covers and drain the oil.
3. Remove the ignition coil, igniter and bracket.
4. Remove the radiator. Remove the overflow tank.
5. Remove the alternator and the belt adjusting bar.
6. Disconnect the accelerator/throttle cable from the throttle body.
7. On models with cruise control, remove the actuator and vacuum pump.
8. Remove the air cleaner assembly.
9. Tag and disconnect all wires and vacuum hoses.
10. Disconnect the ground strap at the transaxle.
11. Disconnect the heater hoses and the fuel line. Have a container handy, as there may be some drippage.
12. On models with MT, remove the starter and then remove the clutch release cylinder. Leave the lines connected and hang it out of the way. Carefully!
13. Disconnect the speedometer cable. Disconnect the transmission control cables.
14. Remove the under cover beneath the glove box. Remove the lower instrument panel, the glove box door and the box itself. Tag and disconnect the three ECU connectors and the cowl wire connector. Remove the two nuts and then pull the engine harness into the engine compartment.
15. Remove the two bolts and nuts and lift out the lower crossmember.
16. Remove the two front exhaust pipe stay bolts. Remove the two bolts and nuts and disconnect the front pipe from the center pipe. Remove the three nuts and disconnect the pipe from the manifold.
17. Without disconnecting the refrigerant lines, remove the A/C compressor and hang it carefully out of the way.
18. Remove the halfshafts.
19. Without disconnecting the hydraulic lines, remove the power steering pump and hang it aside; carefully!
20. Remove the eight bolts and two nuts and remove the engine mount center member.
21. Remove the nut and the thru-bolt and remove the front engine mount. Remove the three bolts and remove the bracket also.
22. Remove the three bolts and lift out the center engine mount.
23. Remove the nut and the thru-bolt and remove the rear engine mount. Remove the three bolts and remove the bracket also.
24. Remove the engine mounting stays.
25. Attach an engine lifting device to the lift hooks. remove the three bolts and disconnect the control rod. Slowly and carefully, lift the engine/transaxle assembly out of the engine compartment.

To install:

1. Carefully lower the engine into the engine compartment. With the engine level and all the mounts aligned with their brackets, install the right engine mount and temporarily install the bolt and nuts. Temporarily install the No. 2 mounting stay bolt (A). Install the left mount bracket to the transaxle case and tighten the three bolts to 38 ft. lbs. (52 Nm). Position the left mount on the bracket and tighten the three bolts to 38 ft. lbs. (52 Nm); tighten the thru-bolt to 64 ft. lbs. (87 Nm).
2. Position the right mount and tighten the bolt to 47 ft. lbs. (64 Nm), the bracket nut to 38 ft. lbs. (52 Nm), and the body nut to 65 ft. lbs. (88 Nm).
3. Install the No. 1 right mounting stay and tighten the bolts to 38 ft. lbs. (52 Nm). Install the No. 2 stay and tighten the bolt (A) to 48 ft. lbs. (66 Nm) and the nut to 38 ft. lbs. (52 Nm).
4. Install the left mounting stay. On models with MT, tighten the nut to 38 ft. lbs. (52 Nm) and the bolt to 14 ft. lbs. (19 Nm). On models with AT, tighten the 12mm nut to 15 ft. lbs. (21 Nm) and the 14mm nut to 38 ft. lbs. (52 Nm).
5. Install the power steering pump reservoir.
6. Install the front engine mount and bracket. Tighten the bracket bolts to 57 ft. lbs. (77 Nm). Use a new nut on the mount and tighten it and the bolt finger tight.
7. Install the center mount and tighten the bolts to 38 ft. lbs. (52 Nm).
8. Install the rear engine mount and bracket. Tighten the bracket bolts to 57 ft. lbs. (77 Nm). Use a new nut on the mount and tighten it and the bolt finger tight.

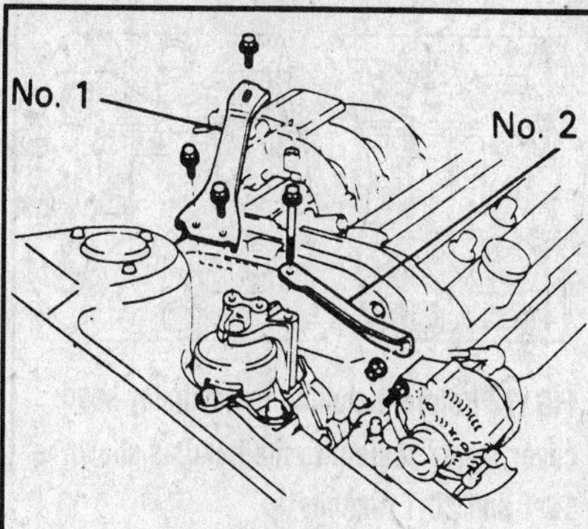

FIG. 64 Installing the right side engine stays — 5S-FE engines

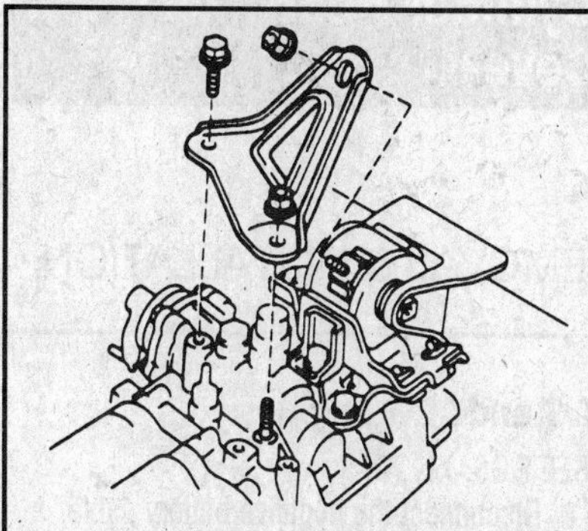
FIG. 65 Installing the left side engine stays manual transaxle — 5S-FE engines

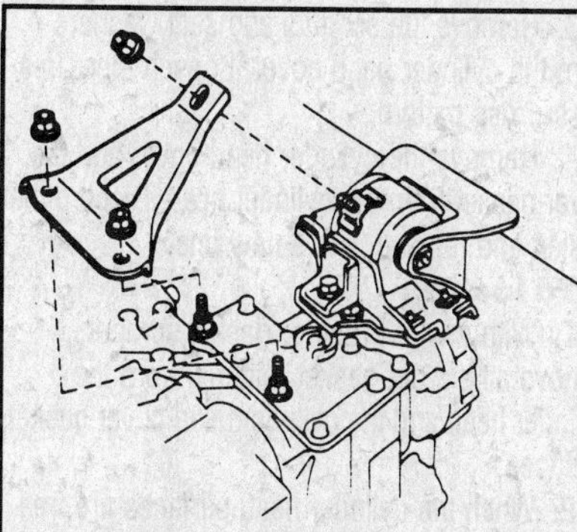
FIG. 66 Installing the left side engine stays automatic transaxle — 5S-FE engines

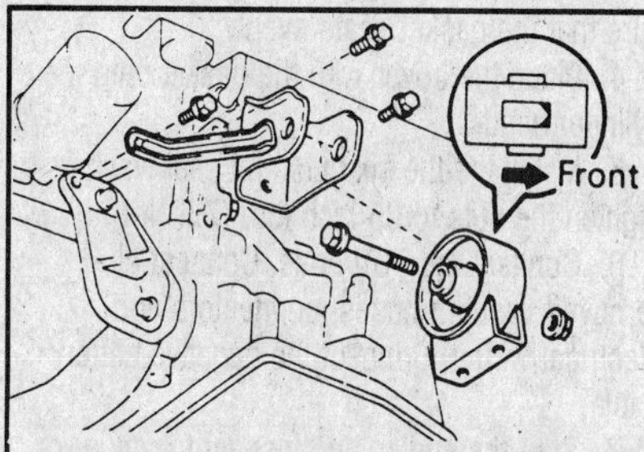

FIG. 67 Installing the front engine mount and bracket — 5S-FE engines

9. Install the center mounting member and tighten the four bolts to 29 ft. lbs. (39 Nm). Install the four bolts and two nuts holding the front, center and rear mounts to the center member and tighten them to 54 ft. lbs. (73 Nm). Tighten the front and rear mount thru-bolts to 64 ft. lbs. (87 Nm).

10. Install the power steering pump and tighten the bolts to 31 ft. lbs. (43 Nm).

11. Install the halfshafts.

12. Install the A/C compressor.

13. Install the front exhaust pipe and tighten the manifold nuts to 46 ft. lbs. (62 Nm) and the converter nuts to 32 ft. lbs. (43 Nm).

14. Install the lower cross member and tighten the bolts to 153 ft. lbs. (207 Nm).

15. Feed the engine harness into the car and install the glove box.

16. Connect the transaxle control cables and the speedometer cable.

17. Install the release cylinder and the starter.

18. Connect the fuel and heater hoses. Connect the ground strap to the transaxle. Connect all vacuum hoses and electrical leads.

19. Install the air cleaner assembly and the cruise control actuator.

20. Install and adjust the throttle/accelerator cable. Install the coolant overflow tank.

21. Install the alternator belt adjusting bar and then install the alternator. Install the radiator.

22. Install the ignition coil assembly and then install the battery.

23. Fill the engine with oil and coolant. Connect the battery cable, start the engine and check for any leaks.

3VZ-FE Engines

➧ SEE FIGS. 68-70

1. Disconnect the negative battery cable.

CAUTION

On models with an airbag, wait at least 30 seconds from the time that the ignition switch is turned to the LOCK position and the battery is disconnected before performing any further work.

2. Remove the battery and its tray.

3. Remove the hood.

4. Remove the engine under cover and then drain the engine coolant and oil.

5. Disconnect the accelerator cable from the throttle body. On models with AT, its the throttle cable, not the accelerator.

6. Remove the air cleaner assembly, resonator and the air intake hose.

7. On models with cruise control, remove the actuator cover, unplug the connector, remove the three bolts and then disconnect the actuator with the bracket.

8. Disconnect the ground strap at the battery carrier.

9. Remove the radiator and then disconnect the coolant reservoir hose.

10. Remove the three washer tank mounting bolts, disconnect the connector and hose and then lift out the tank.

11. Tag and disconnect the:

a. Three connectors to the engine relay box

b. Two connectors from the left side fender apron

c. Igniter connector

d. Noise filter connector

e. Connector at the fender apron

f. Check connector

g. Ground strap at the right fender apron

h. Back-up light switch and speed sensor (models with MT)

12. Disconnect the heater hoses and the fuel return hose and the fuel inlet hose. All of these may leak coolant of fuel, so have a container handy!

13. On models with MT, remove the starter and then remove the clutch release cylinder. Don't disconnect the hydraulic line, simply hang the cylinder out of the way.

14. Disconnect the transaxle control cables at the transaxle.

15. Tag and disconnect all remaining vacuum hoses.

16. Remove the under cover beneath the glove box. Remove the lower instrument panel, the glove box door and the box itself. Tag and disconnect the three ECU connectors, the five cowl wire connectors and the cooling fan ECU connector. Remove the two nuts and then pull the engine harness into the engine compartment.

17. Without disconnecting the refrigerant lines, remove the A/C compressor and hang it carefully out of the way.

18. Loosen the two bolts and disconnect the front exhaust pipe bracket. Use a deep 14mm socket and remove the three nuts attaching the front pipe to the manifold. Disconnect the pipe.

19. Remove the halfshafts.

20. Without disconnecting the hydraulic lines, remove the power steering pump and hang it aside; carefully! Disconnect the hydraulic cooling fan pressure hose.

21. Remove the three bolts (MT) or four bolts (AT) and then disconnect the left engine mounting insulator. Pop out the plugs, remove the four nuts and then remove the rear engine mounting insulator. Remove the four bolts and

remove the mount absorber. Remove the three bolts and disconnect the front engine mounting insulator.

22. Attach an engine lifting device to the lift hooks. Remove the three bolts and disconnect the control rod. Slowly and carefully, lift the engine/transaxle assembly out of the engine compartment.

To install:

1. Carefully lower the engine into the engine compartment. With the engine level and all the mounts aligned with their brackets, install the engine control rod. Tighten the three bolts, in the sequence shown, to 47 ft. lbs. (64 Nm). Install the right side mounting stays and tighten the bolt (A) to 23 ft. lbs. (31 Nm) and the bolts (B) to 46 ft. lbs. (62 Nm).
2. Connect the front engine mount and tighten the bolts to 59 ft. lbs. (80 Nm). Connect the engine mount absorber and tighten the bolts to 35 ft. lbs. (48 Nm). Connect the rear mount and tighten the nuts to 48 ft. lbs. (66 Nm). Don't forget the plugs.
3. Connect the left mount and tighten the bolts (3 or 4) to 47 ft. lbs. (64 Nm).
4. Install the power steering pump and tighten the bolts to 31 ft. lbs. (43 Nm).
5. Install the halfshafts. Connect the cooling fan pressure hose.
6. Connect the front pipe to the manifold and tighten the new nuts to 46 ft. lbs. (62 Nm), tighten the converter nuts to 32 ft. lbs. (43 Nm). Don't forget to install the bracket.
7. Install the A/C compressor and tighten the cylinder block bolts to 20 ft. lbs. (27 Nm); tighten the bracket bolts to 14 ft. lbs. (20 Nm).
8. Feed the engine harness through the cowl and reconnect it. Install the glove box.
9. Connect the vacuum hoses and the transaxle control cables.
10. Install the release cylinder and the starter.
11. Connect the fuel inlet hose and tighten it to 22 ft. lbs. (29 Nm). Connect the return hose and the two heater hoses.
12. Reconnect all wires disconnected previously.
13. Install the washer tank and connect the electrical lead and hose.
14. Install the coolant reservoir hose and the radiator.
15. Connect the ground strap to the battery carrier and then install the cruise control actuator. Install the air cleaner assembly.
16. Connect the throttle/accelerator cable and adjust it.
17. Fill the engine with oil and coolant. Connect the battery cable, start the engine and check for any leaks.

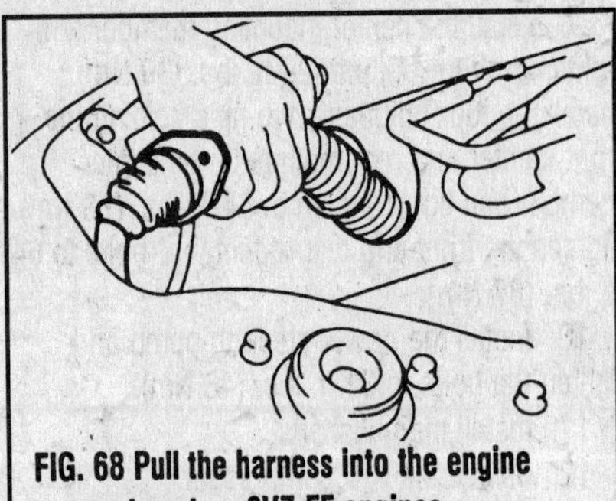

FIG. 68 Pull the harness into the engine compartment — 3VZ-FE engines

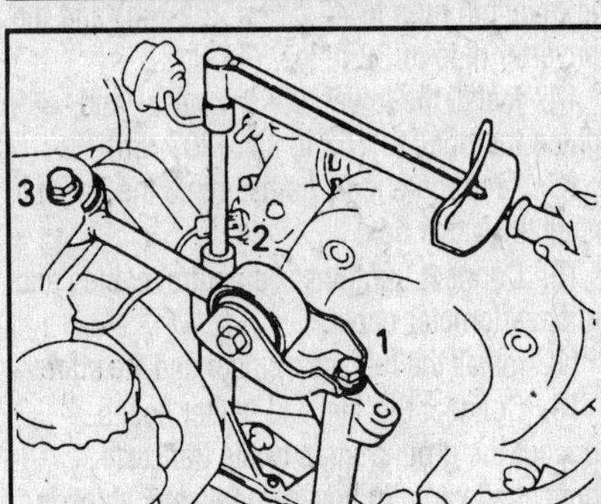

FIG. 69 Tighten the engine control rod in this sequence — 3VZ-FE engines

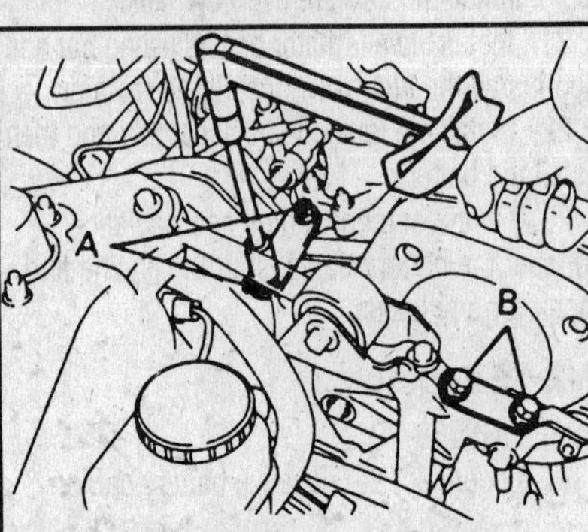

FIG. 70 Installing the right side engine stays — 5S-FE engines

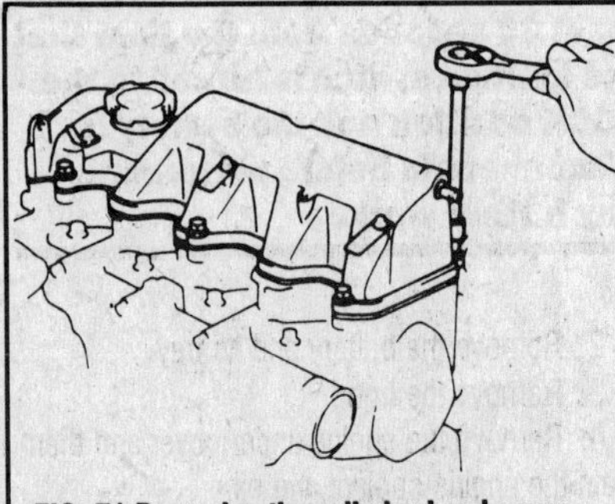

FIG. 71 Removing the cylinder head cover 1C-T and 2C-T engines

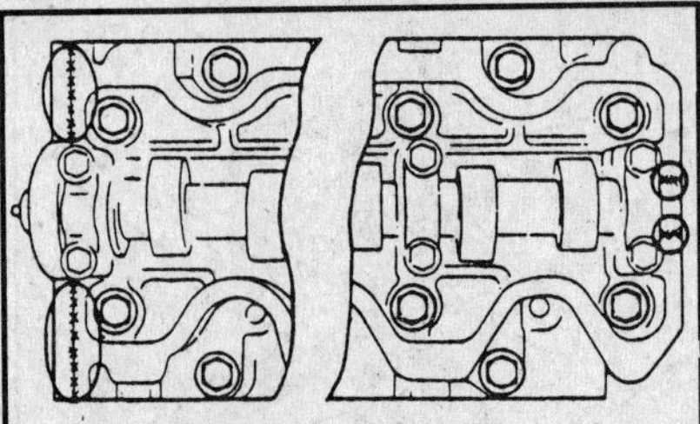

FIG. 72 Before installing the cylinder head cover, apply sealant to the head as shown — 1C-T and 2C-T engines

Cylinder Head Cover

REMOVAL & INSTALLATION

1C-T and 2C-T Engines

➧ SEE FIGS. 71, 72

1. Disconnect the negative battery cable. Remove and label all electrical wiring, connectors and vacuum hoses necessary to gain removal clearance.
2. Disconnect the PCV hose.
3. Remove the six nuts and seal washers from the cylinder head cover. Loosen them in a criss-cross pattern.
4. Remove the cylinder head cover and the cover gasket from the cylinder head. Discard the gasket and replace with a new one.

To install:

1. With a wire brush or gasket scraper, remove all the old gasket material from the cylinder head and the cylinder head cover gasket surfaces.
2. When the cylinder head surfaces are free and clean, apply beads of sealant to the cylinder head in the locations shown in the accompanying illustrations.
3. Install the new gasket in the cover. Make sure that the gasket seats evenly.
4. Place the cover with the gasket onto the cylinder head.
5. Install the the six nuts and seal washers. Tighten the nuts to 65 inch lbs. (7.5 Nm).
6. Connect the PCV hose. Connect all removed vacuum hoses, connectors and electrical wiring. Connect the negative battery cable.
7. Start the engine and inspect for oil leaks. Repair any leaks as necessary.

2S-E, 3S-FE and 5S-FE Engines

➧ SEE FIGS. 73-76

1. Disconnect the negative battery cable. Remove and label all electrical wiring, connectors and vacuum hoses necessary to gain removal clearance.
2. Remove the spark plug wires. Disconnect the PCV hose.
3. Remove the four nuts and grommets located on top of the cylinder head cover.

➡ On 3S-FE engines, label or arrange the grommets so that they may be reinstalled in the same order. This will minimize the possibility of oil leakage when the cylinder head cover is reinstalled.

4. Remove the cylinder head cover and the cover gasket from the cylinder head. Discard the gasket and replace with a new one.

To install:

1. With a wire brush or gasket scraper, remove all the old gasket material from the cylinder head and the cylinder head cover gasket surfaces.
2. When the cylinder head surfaces are free and clean, apply beads of sealant to the cylinder head in the locations shown in the accompanying illustrations.
3. Install the new cylinder head gasket in the cover. Make sure that the gasket seats evenly.
4. Place the cylinder head cover with the gasket onto the cylinder head.
5. Install the four grommets and nuts. Tighten the nuts to 13 ft. lbs. (18 Nm) on the 2S-E; 17 ft. lbs. (23 Nm) on the 3S-FE and 5S-FE.

➡ On 3S-FE engines, align the grommets as shown in the accompanying illustration to ensure proper sealing of the cylinder head cover.

6. Connect the PCV hose. Connect all removed vacuum hoses, connectors and electrical wiring. Connect the negative battery cable.
7. Start the engine and inspect for oil leaks. Repair any leaks as necessary.

2VZ-FE and 3VZ-FE Engines

➧ SEE FIG. 77

1. Disconnect the negative battery cable. Remove and label all electrical wiring, connectors and vacuum hoses necessary to gain removal clearance.
2. On the 3VZ-FE, remove the V-bank cover.
3. Remove the spark plug wires. Disconnect the PCV hose.
4. Remove the six (2VZ-FE) or eight (3VZ-FE) nuts and seal washers located on top of the cylinder head cover.
5. Remove the cylinder head cover and the cover gasket from the cylinder head. Discard the gasket and replace with a new one.

To install:

1. With a wire brush or gasket scraper, remove all the old gasket material from the cylinder head and the cylinder head cover gasket surfaces.
2. When the cylinder head surfaces are free and clean, apply beads of sealant to the cylinder head in the locations shown in the accompanying illustrations.
3. Install the new cylinder head gasket in the cover. Make sure that the gasket seats evenly.
4. Place the cylinder head cover with the gasket onto the cylinder head.
5. Install the six/eight nuts and seal washers. Tighten the nuts to 52 inch lbs. (5.9 Nm).
6. Install the spark plug wires. On the 3VZ-FE, install the V-bank cover.
7. Connect the PCV hose. Connect all removed vacuum hoses, connectors and electrical wiring. Connect the negative battery cable.
8. Start the engine and inspect for oil leaks. Repair any leaks as necessary.

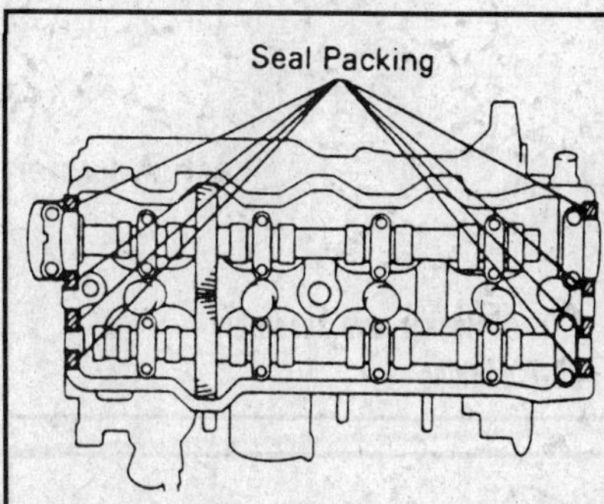

FIG. 73 Before installing the cylinder head cover, apply sealant to the head as shown — 3S-FE engines

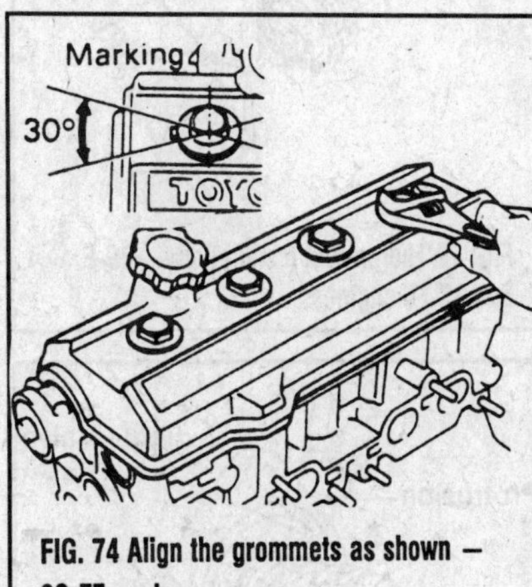

FIG. 74 Align the grommets as shown — 3S-FE engines

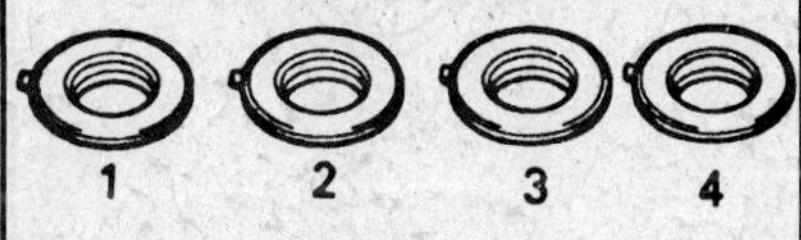

FIG. 75 Keep the grommets in correct order — 3S-FE and 5S-FE engines

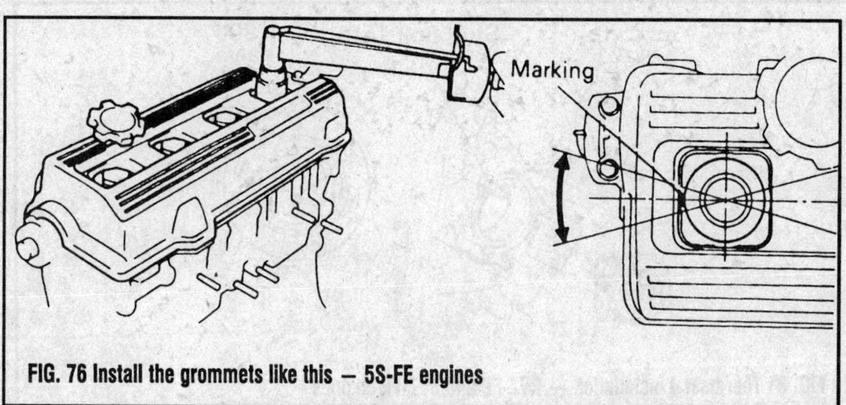

FIG. 76 Install the grommets like this — 5S-FE engines

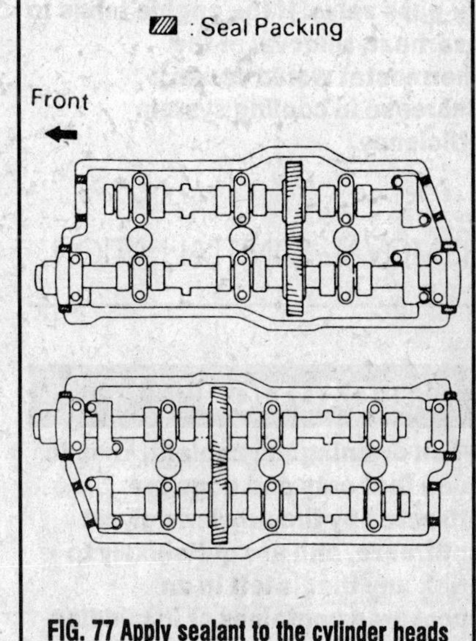

FIG. 77 Apply sealant to the cylinder heads here — 2VZ-FE and 3VZ-FE engines

Rocker Arms and Lash Adjusters

REMOVAL & INSTALLATION

2S-E Engines Only

➧ SEE FIG. 78

The 2S-E engine is the only engine in the Camry family that uses rocker arms and lash adjusters to activate the valves. Valve operation in on all other engines is accomplished directly by the camshaft and accessory valve components.

1. Disconnect the negative battery cable.
2. Remove the cylinder head cover and gasket.
3. Remove the rocker arms and lash adjusters. Label each rocker arm/lash adjuster pair as it is removed to that they are installed in their original positions.
4. Install the rocker arms and lash adjuster in the same order as they were removed.
5. Install the cylinder head cover and gasket.
6. Connect the negative battery cable.
7. Start the engine and inspect for leaks.

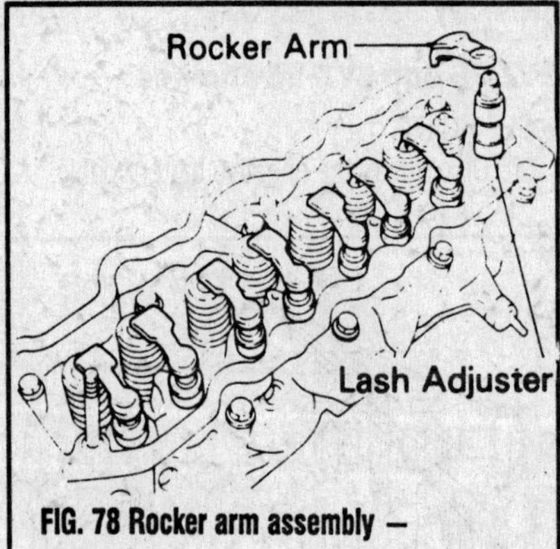

FIG. 78 Rocker arm assembly — 2S-E engines

Thermostat

On both diesel and gasoline engines, the thermostat is located in the water inlet housing that is connected to the lower radiator hose.

➡ **The thermostat is equipped with a by-pass valve. If the engine tends to overheat, removal of the thermostat would cause a decrease in cooling system efficiency.**

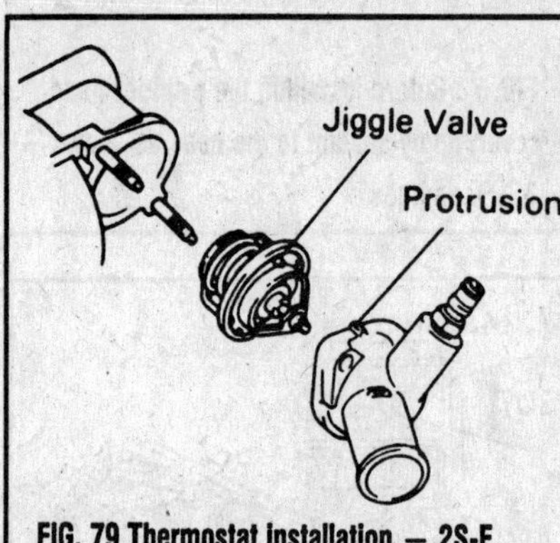

FIG. 79 Thermostat installation — 2S-E and 3S-FE engines

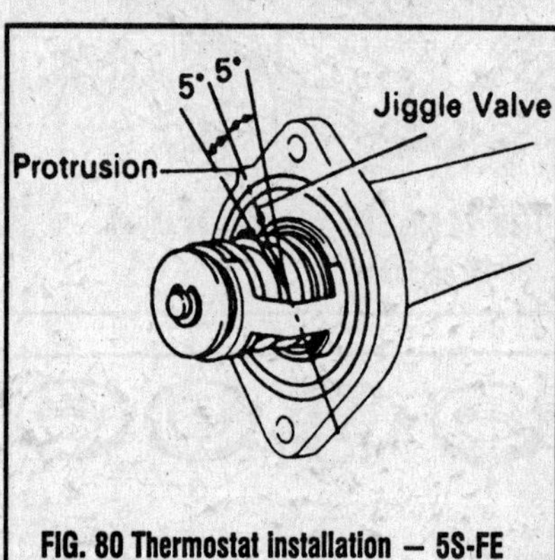

FIG. 80 Thermostat installation — 5S-FE engines

REMOVAL & INSTALLATION

✲✲ CAUTION

When draining the coolant, keep in mind that cats and dogs are attracted by the ethylene glycol antifreeze, and are quite likely to drink any that is left in an uncovered container or in puddles on the ground. This will prove fatal in sufficient quantity. Always drain the coolant into a sealable container. Coolant should be reused unless it is contaminated or several years old.

Gasoline Engines

➧ SEE FIGS. 79-81

1. Position a suitable drain pan under the radiator drain cock and drain the cooling system.
2. Disconnect the water temperature switch connector from the water inlet housing (except 5S-FE engines).
3. Remove the oil filter on 5S-FE engines.
4. Loosen the hose clamp and disconnect the lower radiator hose from the water inlet housing.
5. Remove the two nuts from the water inlet housing and remove the housing from the water pump studs.
6. Remove the thermostat and rubber O-ring gasket from the water inlet housing.

To install:

1. Make sure all the gasket surfaces are clean. Clean the inside of the inlet housing and the radiator hose connection with a rag.
2. Install the new rubber O-ring gasket onto the thermostat. On 2SE and 3S-FE engines, align the jiggle valve of the thermostat with the protrusion on the water inlet housing. On 5S-FE engines, align the jiggle valve with the upper side of the stud bolt. On 2VZ-FE and 3VZ-FE engines, align the jiggle valve with the stud bolt (A). Insert the thermostat into the housing.
3. Position the water inlet housing with the thermostat over the studs on the water pump and install the two nuts. Torque the two nuts to 78 inch lbs. (8.8 Nm) on 4 cyl. engines or 14 ft. lbs. (20 Nm) on V6 engines.
4. Connect the lower radiator hose to the inlet housing and install the hose clamp. on the 3VZ-FE, tighten the bolt holding the water inlet hose to the alternator belt adjusting bar to 14 ft. lbs. (20 Nm).
5. Connect the water temperature switch connector.

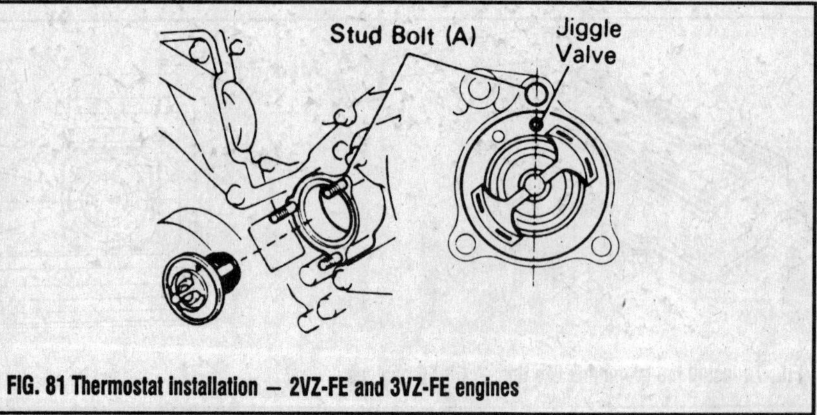

FIG. 81 Thermostat installation — 2VZ-FE and 3VZ-FE engines

6. Install the oil filter and check the oil level.
7. Fill the cooling system with a good brand of eythylene glycol based coolant.
8. Start the engine and inspect for leaks.

Diesel Engines

➧ SEE FIG. 82

1. Position a suitable drain pan under the radiator drain cock and drain the cooling system.
2. Disconnect the radiator cooling fan connector.
3. Remove the right engine under cover. Unbolt and remove the radiator cooling fan shroud fan with the fan and motor.
4. Loosen the lower radiator hose from the water inlet housing.
5. Loosen the air conditioning compressor pulley lock bolt and drive belt adjusting bolt. Remove the drive belt from the pulley. Remove the three compressor mounting bolts and position the air conditioning compressor off to the side.

CAUTION

DO NOT disconnect the refrigeration lines from the compressor.

6. Remove the two bolts from the water inlet housing and remove the housing, rubber O-ring gasket and thermostat from the cylinder block.

To Install:

1. Make sure all the inlet and cylinder block gasket surfaces are clean. Clean the inside of the inlet housing and the radiator hose connection with a rag.
2. Install the new rubber O-ring gasket onto the thermostat and place the thermostat into the cylinder block with the jiggle valve facing outward.
3. Place the water inlet with the thermostat and gasket onto the cylinder block and install the two bolts. Tighten the bolts to 65 inch lbs. (7 Nm).
4. Place the air conditioning compressor back into position and install the three mounting bolts. Install the drive belt onto the compressor pulley and adjust the drive belt tension.
5. Connect the lower radiator hose to the water inlet and install the hose clamp.
6. Install the radiator cooling fan shroud/fan/motor assembly. Install the right engine under cover.
7. Connect the radiator cooling fan motor connector.
8. Fill the cooling system with a good brand of eythylene glycol based coolant to the proper level.

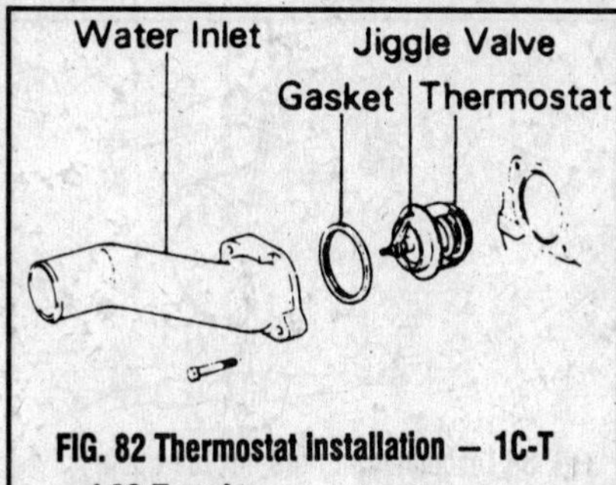

FIG. 82 Thermostat installation — 1C-T and 2C-T engines

9. Start the engine and inspect for leaks. Recheck the air conditioning compressor drive belt tension.

Intake Manifold

REMOVAL & INSTALLATION

CAUTION

When draining the coolant, keep in mind that cats and dogs are attracted by the ethylene glycol antifreeze, and are quite likely to drink any that is left in an uncovered container or in puddles on the ground. This will prove fatal in sufficient quantity. Always drain the coolant into a sealable container. Coolant should be reused unless it is contaminated or several years old.

1C-T and 2C-T Engines

➧ SEE FIG. 83

1. Disconnect the negative battery cable.
2. Position a suitable drain pan under the radiator and drain the cooling system.
3. Remove the turbocharger (as described in this section).
4. Remove the intake manifold with the fuel pipe by removing the six bolts and two nuts. Remove the intake manifold gasket.

To Install:

1. Thoroughly clean the intake manifold and cylinder head surfaces with a soft brush and solvent.
2. Place the new gasket onto the intake manifold and attach the manifold to the cylinder head with six bolts and two nuts. Torque the bolts and nuts to 13 ft. lbs. (18 Nm).
3. Install the turbocharger.
4. Fill the cooling system to the proper level.
5. Connect the negative battery cable.
6. Start the engine and inspect for leaks.
7. Check and/or adjust the engine idle and maximum idle speeds.

2S-E, 3S-FE and 5S-FE Engines

➧ SEE FIGS. 84-86

1. Disconnect the negative battery cable. Position a suitable drain pan under the radiator drain cock and drain the cooling system.

CAUTION

On models with an airbag, wait at least 30 seconds from the time that the ignition switch is turned to the LOCK position and the battery is disconnected before performing any further work.

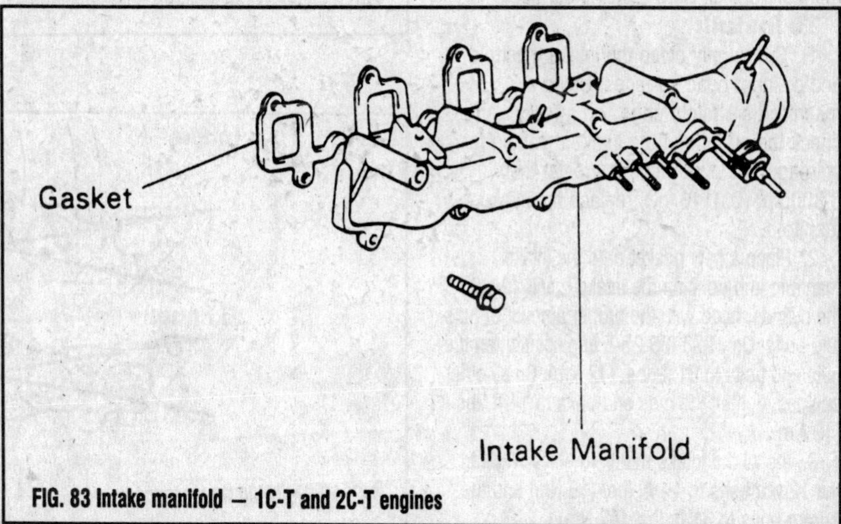

FIG. 83 Intake manifold — 1C-T and 2C-T engines

2. On vehicles equipped with automatic transaxle, disconnect the throttle cable from the throttle linkage.
3. Remove the accelerator cable return spring and remove the cable with bracket from the throttle body.
4. Loosen the clamp and disconnect the air cleaner hose.
5. Disconnect the throttle position sensor connector. On 3S-FE engines, disconnect the ISC (Idle Speed Control) valve connector also.
6. Disconnect, label and plug the following hoses:
a. Two water by-pass hoses.
b. PCV hoses from the throttle body.
c. Inlet hose to the air valve.
d. All emission vacuum hoses connected to the throttle body.
e. Vacuum hose between the EGR valve and modulator.
f. Power steering pump air hose (if equipped).
7. Loosen the union nut of the EGR pipe. Remove the two bolts, EGR valve modulator and gasket. Remove the bolt and the EGR valve.
8. Remove the four bolts attaching the throttle body to the intake manifold. Remove the throttle body and throttle body gasket.
9. Remove the intake manifold stays by removing the 12mm and 14mm bolts.
10. Disconnect the vacuum sensing hose.
11. Remove the two nuts and seven bolts (1983–85 2S-E engines) or two nuts and six bolts (1986 2S-E and 1987–92 3S-FE and 5S-FE engines) that attach the intake manifold to the cylinder head.
12. On 5S-FE engines, remove the bolt, vacuum hose bracket and the main engine wire harness. On Calif. 5S-FE, remove the wire bracket.
13. Remove the intake manifold and intake manifold gasket from the cylinder head.

To Install:

1. Thoroughly clean the intake manifold and cylinder head surfaces. Using a machinist's straight edge and a feeler gauge, check the surface of the intake manifold for warpage. If the warpage is greater than 0.300mm (0.0118 in.), replace the intake manifold.
2. Place a new gasket onto the intake manifold and position the intake manifold onto the cylinder head with the proper amount of nuts and bolts. On 1983–85 2S-E engines tighten the nuts and bolts to 31 ft. lbs. (42 Nm). On all other engines, tighten the nuts and bolts to 14 ft. lbs. (19 Nm).
3. Install the intake manifold stays. Tighten the 12mm bolts to 14 ft. lbs. (19 Nm) and the 14mm bolts to 31 ft. lbs. (42 Nm).

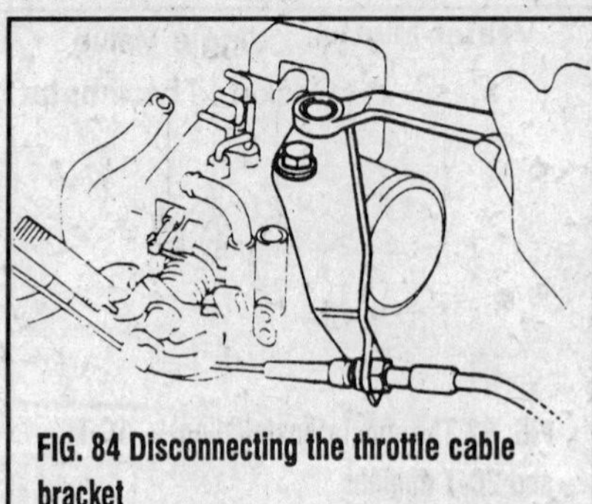

FIG. 84 Disconnecting the throttle cable bracket

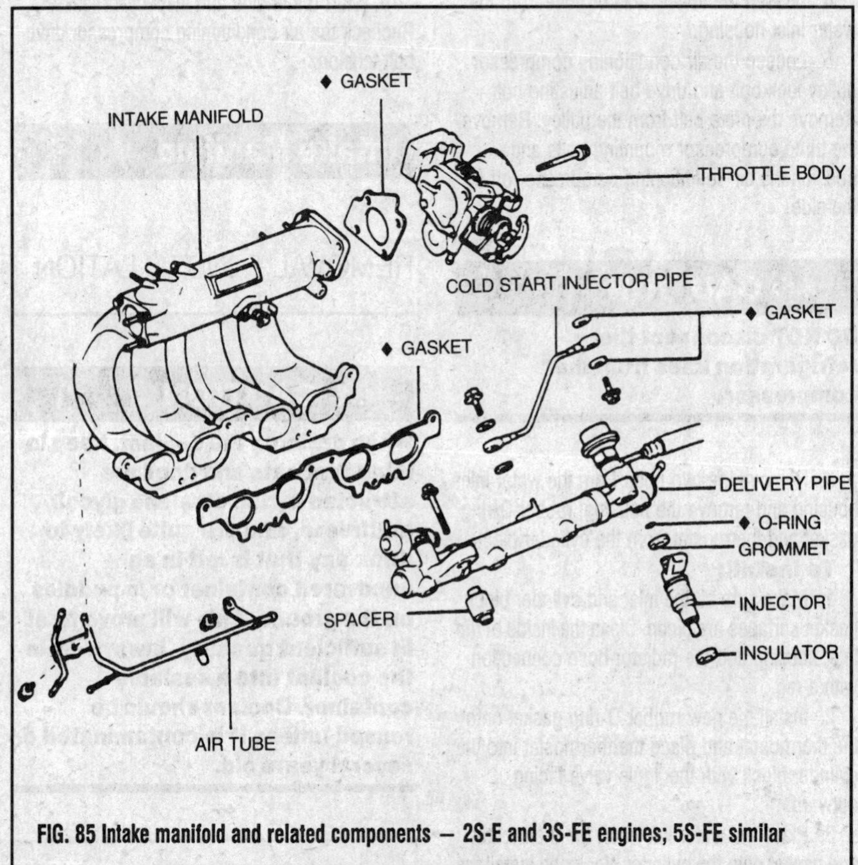

FIG. 85 Intake manifold and related components — 2S-E and 3S-FE engines; 5S-FE similar

4. Place a new gasket onto the throttle body and attach the throttle body to the intake manifold with the four bolts. Tighten the bolts to 14 ft. lbs. (19 Nm).
5. Install the EGR valve with new gasket and the modulator. Torque the pipe union nut to 43 ft. lbs. (59 Nm) and the bolts to 9 ft. lbs. (13 Nm).
6. Unplug and connect all hoses.
7. Connect the throttle position sensor and ISC valve connectors.
8. Connect the air cleaner hose and tighten the hose clamp.

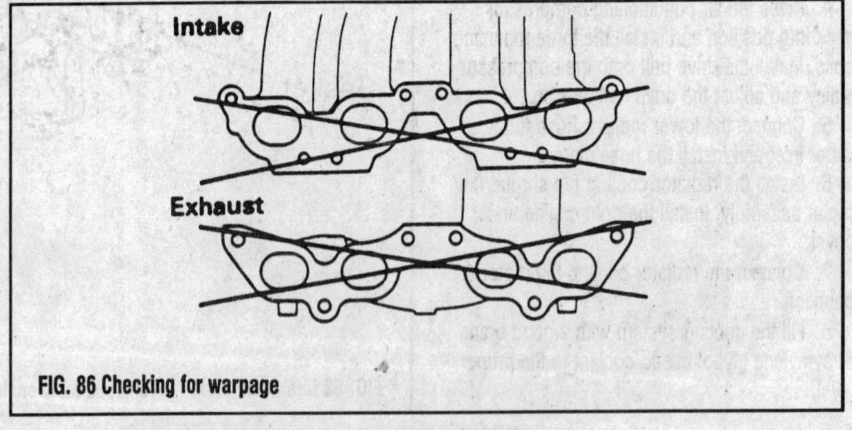

FIG. 86 Checking for warpage

9. Connect the throttle cable with bracket onto the throttle body. Install the return spring.

10. On vehicles equipped with automatic transaxle, connect the accelerator cable and adjust it.

11. Fill the cooling system to the proper level and connect the negative battery cable.

12. Start the engine and inspect for leaks.

2VZ-FE and 3VZ-FE Engines

➧ SEE FIG. 87

1. Disconnect the negative battery cable. Drain the engine coolant.

✱✱ CAUTION

On models with an airbag, wait at least 30 seconds from the time that the ignition switch is turned to the LOCK position and the battery is disconnected before performing any further work.

2. Disconnect the throttle/accelerator cable from the throttle body.

3. Disconnect the air cleaner hose at the air intake chamber and remove it.

4. Remove the V-bank cover on the 3VZ-FE.

5. Tag and disconnect all lines and hoses and then remove both the ISC valve and the throttle body.

6. Remove the EGR valve and vacuum modulator. Remove the distributor.

7. On the 3VZ-FE, remove the emission control valve set and then disconnect the left side engine harness.

8. Remove the cylinder head rear plate.

9. Remove the intake chamber stays, any wires and then remove the air intake chamber.

10. Remove the fuel injection delivery pipe and the injectors.

11. Remove the water outlet and the by-pass outlet.

12. Remove the two bolts and the No. 2 idler pulley bracket stay. Remove the eight bolts and four nuts and then lift out the intake manifold.

To install:

1. Thoroughly clean the intake manifold and cylinder head surfaces. Using a machinist's straight edge and a feeler gauge, check the surface of the intake manifold for warpage. If the warpage is greater than 0.10mm (0.0039 in.), replace the intake manifold.

2. Place new gaskets onto the intake manifold and position the intake manifold between the cylinder heads. Tighten the nuts and bolts to 13 ft. lbs. (18 Nm). Tighten the No. 2 pulley bracket bolts to 13 ft. lbs. (18 Nm).

3. Install the water by-pass outlet and tighten the bolts to 14 ft. lbs. (20 Nm) on the 2VZ-FE, or 74 inch lbs. (8.3 Nm) on the 3VZ-FE. Tighten the water outlet to 74 inch lbs. (8.3 Nm).

4. Install the injectors and delivery pipe.

5. Install the air intake chamber and tighten the two bolts and two nuts to 32 ft. lbs. (43 Nm); use an 8mm hex wrench. Install the chamber stays and tighten the mounting bolts to 27 ft. lbs. (37 Nm) on the 2VZ-FE, or 29 ft. lbs. (39 Nm) on the 3VZ-FE.

6. Install the distributor. Install the emission control valve set on the 3VZ-FE and tighten the two bolts to 73 inch lbs. (8.3 Nm).

7. Install the EGR valve and modulator (with new gaskets). Tighten the bolts and nuts to 13 ft. lbs. (18 Nm).

8. Place a new gasket onto the throttle body and attach the throttle body to the intake manifold with the four bolts. Tighten the bolts to 14 ft. lbs. (19 Nm).

9. Install the ISC valve and tighten it to 9 ft. lbs. (13 Nm).

10. Unplug and connect all hoses.

11. Connect the throttle position sensor and ISC valve connectors.

12. Connect the air cleaner hose and tighten the hose clamp.

13. Connect the throttle cable with bracket onto the throttle body. Install the return spring.

14. On vehicles equipped with automatic transaxle, connect the accelerator cable and adjust it.

15. Fill the cooling system to the proper level and connect the negative battery cable.

16. Start the engine and inspect for leaks.

Exhaust Manifold

REMOVAL & INSTALLATION

1C-T and 2-CT Engines

➧ SEE FIG. 88

1. Disconnect the negative battery cable.

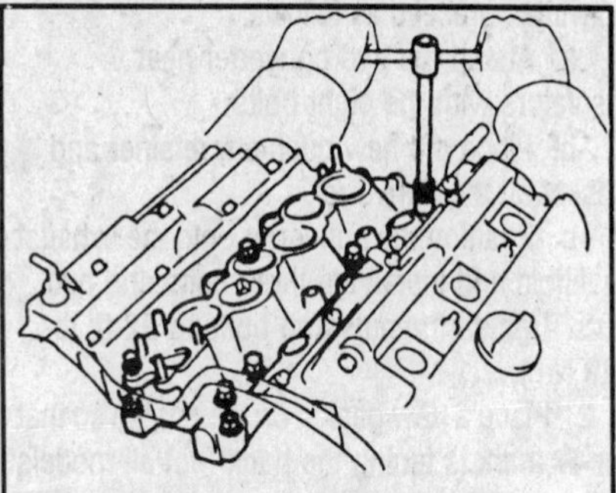

FIG. 87 Removing the intake manifold — 2VZ-FE and 3VZ-FE engines

2. Remove the turbocharger from the exhaust manifold as described in this section.

3. Remove the heat insulator from the exhaust manifold by removing the two bolts.

4. Remove the exhaust manifold from the engine by removing the six bolts and two nuts.

To install:

1. Remove the exhaust manifold gasket and replace it with a new one.

2. Thoroughly clean the exhaust manifold and cylinder block to remove any carbon or gasket material deposits. If the carbon deposits are not removed, there is the possibility of them entering the turbine and causing damage.

3. Place the new gasket onto the manifold and install the exhaust manifold onto the engine with the six bolts. Tighten the bolts in an alternate pattern to 31 ft. lbs. (42 Nm).

4. Install the heat insulator onto the manifold and secure with the two bolts.

5. Install the turbocharger.

6. Connect the negative battery cable. Start the engine and inspect for leaks.

2S-E Engines

✱✱ CAUTION

Be careful when working on or near the catalytic converter. External temperatures can reach 1,500°F (816°C) and more causing severe burns. Removal and installation of the exhaust manifold should be accomplished only on a cold engine.

1. Disconnect the negative battery cable.

2. Raise the front of the vehicle and support safely.

3. Disconnect the oxygen sensor connector (USA only). The oxygen sensor is located in the exhaust manifold.

4. Loosen the front and rear flange bolts of the catalytic converter so that they can be turned by hand (there are two nuts and bolts per flange).

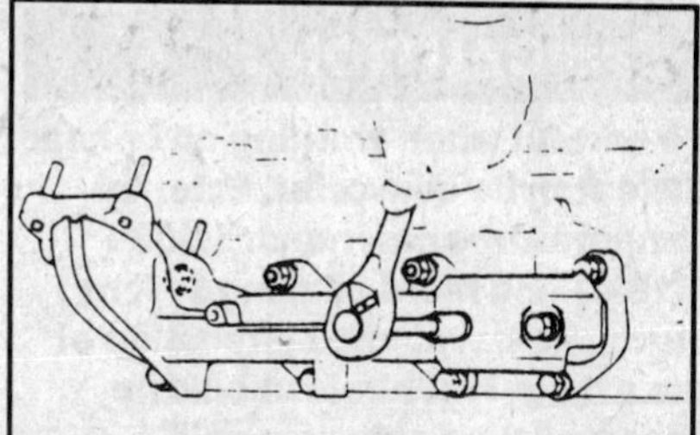

FIG. 88 Removing the exhaust manifold and heat insulator — 1C-T and 2C-T engines

5. Support the catalytic converter and disconnect the exhaust pipe by removing the loosened flange bolts and nuts. Remove the flange gaskets and set them aside.

6. Remove the exhaust pipe stay bolts from the cylinder block.

7. Remove the three nuts from the exhaust manifold flange.

8. Disconnect the exhaust pipe from the manifold and remove the two exhaust manifold gaskets. You may have to "coax" the manifold from the block with a few sharp blows from a heavy rubber mallet. Remove the two exhaust manifold gaskets.

CAUTION

When removing the exhaust manifold, be careful not to damage the oxygen sensor.

9. With a wire brush and solvent, thoroughly clean the surfaces of the exhaust manifold and cylinder block to remove any carbon or gasket material residue. While your in the area, run the wire brush across the converter flange also. If the converter flange gaskets are damaged, replace them with new ones.

To install:

1. Lay the two new gaskets onto the exhaust manifold and attach the manifold to the cylinder block with the three nuts. Tighten the manifold nuts to 31 ft. lbs. (42 Nm).

2. Attach the exhaust manifold stay to the cylinder block with the two bolts.

3. Support the converter and install the flange gaskets and nuts and bolts. Tighten the front and rear flange bolts to 32 ft. lbs. (43 Nm).

4. Connect the oxygen sensor connector (USA only).

5. Lower the vehicle and connect the negative battery cable.

6. Start the engine and inspect for exhaust leaks.

3S-FE Engines

SEE FIGS. 89-92

CAUTION

Be careful when working on or near the catalytic converter. External temperatures can reach 1,500°F (816°C) and more causing severe burns. Removal and installation of the exhaust manifold should be accomplished only on a cold engine.

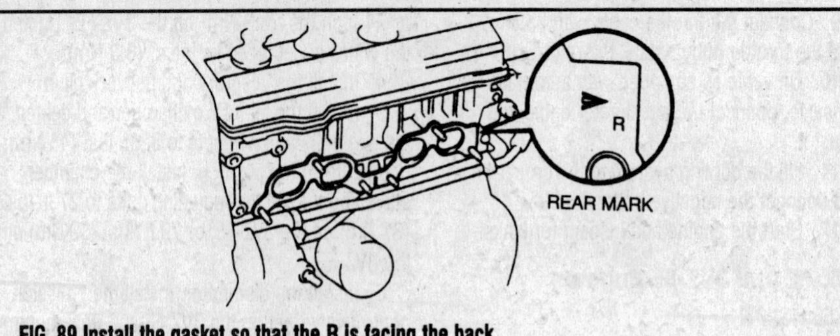

FIG. 89 Install the gasket so that the R is facing the back

1. Disconnect the negative battery cable.

2. Raise the front of the vehicle and support safely.

3. Disconnect the oxygen sensor connector.

4. Loosen the bolt and disconnect the clamp from the catalytic converter bracket. Remove the nuts and disconnect the exhaust pipe from the catalytic converter. Remove the gasket and discard it.

5. Remove the upper manifold heat insulator by removing the six retaining bolts.

6. Remove the six nuts and lower the exhaust manifold and catalytic converter assembly. Discard the nuts and replace with new.

7. Disconnect the catalytic converter stay by removing the two bolts and two nuts.

8. To separate the exhaust manifold from the converter, proceed as follows:

a. Unbolt the lower manifold heat insulator (five bolts).

b. Unbolt the two catalytic converter heat insulators (eight bolts).

c. Unbolt and separate the exhaust manifold from the catalytic converter (three bolts and two nuts).

d. Remove the gasket, retainer and cushion.

9. Thoroughly clean the exhaust manifold and cylinder block to remove any carbon or gasket material deposits. Replace the two exhaust manifold gaskets, catalytic converter gasket, retainer and cushion.

To install:

1. To connect the exhaust manifold to the converter, proceed as follows:

a. Attach the two converter heat insulators with the eight bolts.

b. Place the new cushion, retainer and gasket on the converter.

c. Position the converter onto the exhaust manifold and install the three bolts and two nuts. Tighten the nuts and bolts to 22 ft. lbs. (29 Nm).

2. Place a new gasket on the engine so that the **R** mark is facing the back (not all models will have this mark). If the gasket is not installed properly, it will not seal.

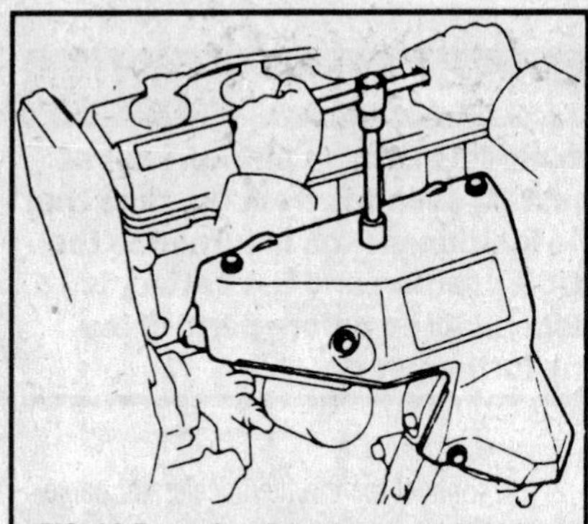

FIG. 90 Removing the exhaust manifold heat shield — 3S-FE engines

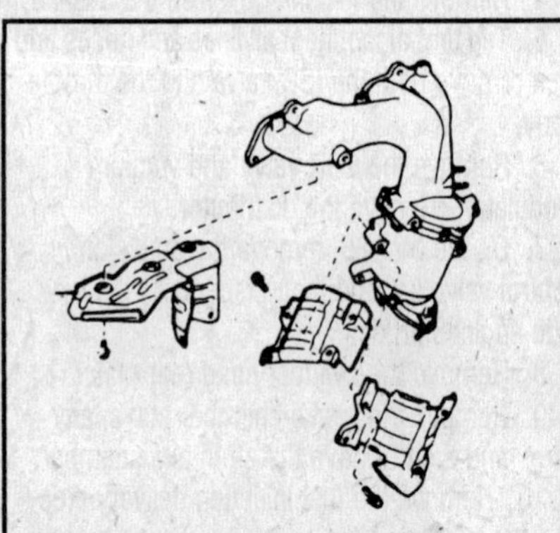

FIG. 91 Removing the converter heat insulators — 3S-FE engines

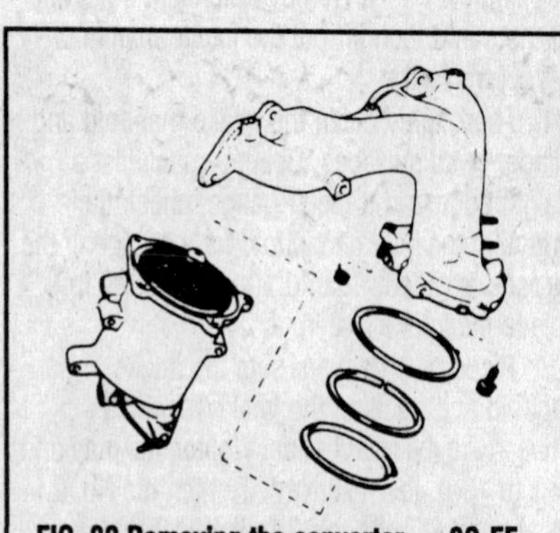

FIG. 92 Removing the converter — 3S-FE engines

3. Support the exhaust manifold and catalytic converter assembly by hand and guide the assembly over the mounting studs. Install the six new nuts and tighten them to 31 ft. lbs. (41 Nm) on 1987–88 models , or 37 ft. lbs. (48 Nm) on 1989–91 models.

4. Install the converter stay with the two bolts and two nuts. Tighten the bolts and nuts to 31 ft. lbs. (41 Nm).

5. Install the manifold upper heat insulator with the six bolts.

6. Place a new gasket onto the exhaust pipe and connect the exhaust pipe to the catalytic converter with the three nuts. Tighten the nuts to 46 ft. lbs. (62 Nm). Install the clamp and the clamp bolt.

7. Connect the oxygen sensor connector.

8. Lower the vehicle and connect the negative battery cable.

9. Start the engine and inspect for leaks.

5S-FE Engines

➧ SEE FIGS. 93-96

1. Disconnect the negative battery cable.

CAUTION

On models with an airbag, wait at least 30 seconds from the time that the ignition switch is turned to the LOCK position and the battery is disconnected before performing any further work.

2. Raise the front of the vehicle and support safely.

3. Disconnect the oxygen sensor connector.

4. Loosen the two bolts and disconnect the front exhaust pipe bracket. Use a 14mm deep socket and remove the nuts and disconnect the exhaust pipe from the catalytic converter. Remove the gasket and discard it.

Except Calif.:

5. Remove the upper manifold heat insulator by removing the six retaining bolts.

6. Remove the two manifold stays.

7. Remove the six nuts and lower the exhaust manifold. Discard the nuts and replace with new ones.

8. Remove the four bolts and lift off the lower heat insulator.

Calif.:

9. Remove the upper manifold heat insulator by removing the four retaining bolts.

10. Remove the two manifold stays.

11. Remove the six nuts and lower the exhaust manifold and catalytic converter assembly. Discard the nuts and replace with new ones.

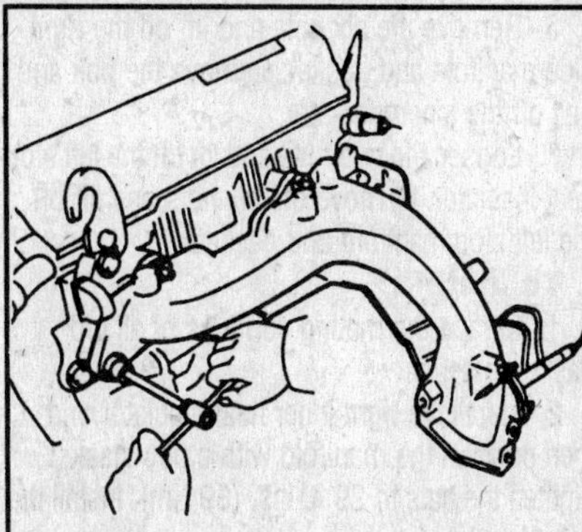

FIG. 93 Removing the exhaust manifold — 5S-FE engines

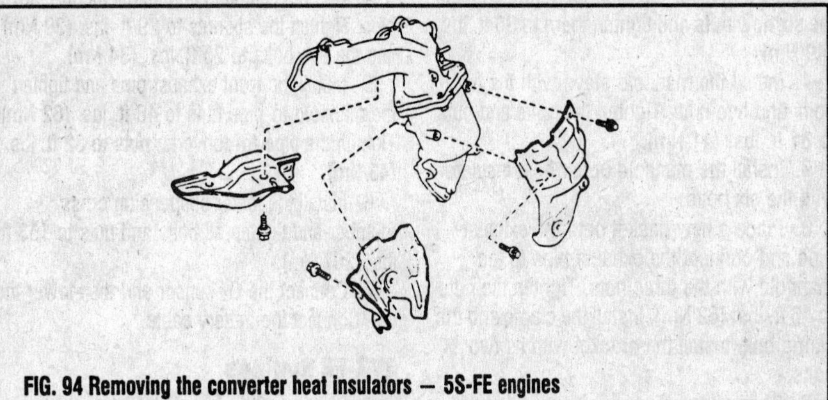

FIG. 94 Removing the converter heat insulators — 5S-FE engines

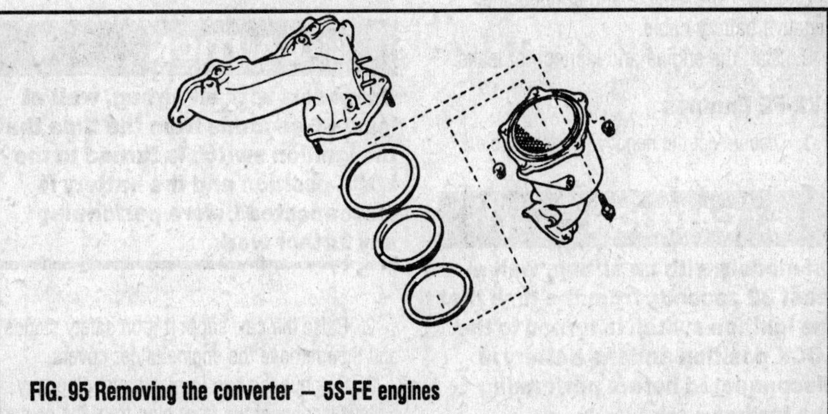

FIG. 95 Removing the converter — 5S-FE engines

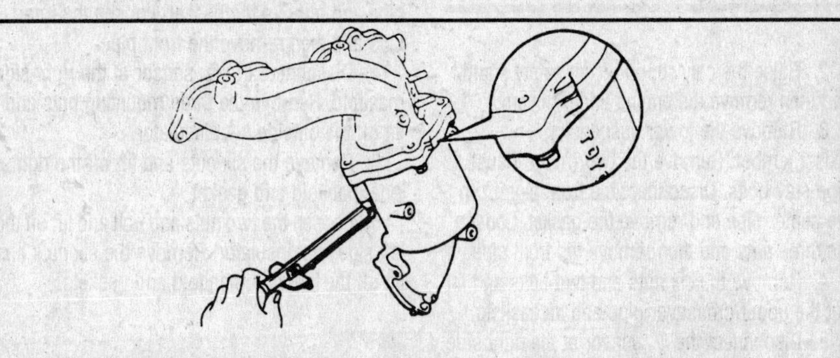

FIG. 96 When connecting the converter to the manifold, make sure that the two marks align — 5S-FE engines

12. To separate the exhaust manifold from the converter, proceed as follows:

a. Unbolt the lower manifold heat insulator (three bolts).

b. Unbolt the two catalytic converter heat insulators (eight bolts).

c. Unbolt and separate the exhaust manifold from the catalytic converter (three bolts and two nuts).

d. Remove the gasket, retainer and cushion.

13. Thoroughly clean the exhaust manifold and cylinder block to remove any carbon or gasket material deposits. Replace the two exhaust manifold gaskets, catalytic converter gasket, retainer and cushion.

To Install:

1. To connect the exhaust manifold to the converter on Calif. models, proceed as follows:
   a. Attach the two converter heat insulators with the eight bolts.
   b. Place the new cushion, retainer and gasket on the converter.
   c. Position the converter onto the exhaust manifold and install the three bolts and two nuts. Tighten the nuts and bolts to 22 ft. lbs. (29 Nm).
2. Place a new gasket on the engine. If the gasket is not installed properly, it will not seal.
3. Support the exhaust manifold (exc. Calif.) or the exhaust manifold/catalytic converter assembly (Calif.) by hand and guide the assembly over the mounting studs. Install the six new nuts and tighten them to 36 ft. lbs. (49 Nm).
4. Install the manifold stays with the two bolts and two nuts. Tighten the bolts and nuts to 31 ft. lbs. (41 Nm).
5. Install the manifold upper heat insulator with the six bolts.
6. Place a new gasket onto the exhaust pipe and connect the exhaust pipe to the manifold with the three nuts. Tighten the nuts to 46 ft. lbs. (62 Nm). Install the clamp and the clamp bolt. Install the bracket with its two bolts.
7. Connect the oxygen sensor connector.
8. Lower the vehicle and connect the negative battery cable.
9. Start the engine and inspect for leaks.

2VZ-FE Engines

1. Disconnect the negative battery cable.

CAUTION

On models with an airbag, wait at least 30 seconds from the time that the ignition switch is turned to the LOCK position and the battery is disconnected before performing any further work.

2. Raise the car, support it on safety stands and then remove the engine under covers.
3. Remove the lower suspension crossmember. Remove the two front exhaust pipe stay bolts. Disconnect the front pipe from the center pipe and remove the gasket. Loosen the three nuts and then remove the front pipe.
4. Remove the six nuts and two bolts and lift out the upper crossover pipe and its gaskets.
5. Disconnect the O_2 sensor at the right side manifold. Remove the three mounting nuts and lift off the outside heat insulator.
6. Remove the six nuts and lift off the right side manifold and gasket. Remove the bolt and pull off the inner insulator.
7. Loosen the two nuts and lift off the left side heat insulator. Remove the six nuts and lift off the left side manifold and gaskets.

To Install:

1. Scrape the mating surfaces of all old gasket material.
2. Install the right inner heat insulator and then position the manifold with a new gasket. Tighten the nuts to 29 ft. lbs. (39 Nm). Install the outer insulator.
3. Use a new gasket and install the left manifold. Tighten the nuts to 29 ft. lbs. (39 Nm). Install the outer insulator.
4. Use new gaskets and install the crossover pipe. Tighten the six nuts to 29 ft. lbs. (39 Nm) and the two bolts to 25 ft. lbs. (34 Nm).
5. Install the front exhaust pipe and tighten the manifold-to-pipe nuts to 46 ft. lbs. (62 Nm). Tighten the pipe-to-converter nuts to 32 ft. lbs. (43 Nm).
6. Install the lower suspension cross member and tighten all bolts and nuts to 153 ft. lbs. (207 Nm).
7. Connect the O_2 sensor and then lower the car. Connect the battery cable.

3VZ-FE Engines

1. Disconnect the negative battery cable.

CAUTION

On models with an airbag, wait at least 30 seconds from the time that the ignition switch is turned to the LOCK position and the battery is disconnected before performing any further work.

2. Raise the car, support it on safety stands and then remove the engine under covers.
3. Remove the two front exhaust pipe stay bolts. Disconnect the front pipe from the center pipe and remove the gasket. Loosen the three nuts and then remove the front pipe.
4. Disconnect the O_2 sensor at the right side manifold. Remove the three mounting nuts and lift off the outside heat insulator.
5. Remove the six nuts and lift off the right side manifold and gasket.
6. Loosen the two nuts and bolt and lift off the left side heat insulator. Remove the six nuts and lift off the left side manifold and gaskets.

To Install:

1. Scrape the mating surfaces of all old gasket material.
2. Install the right manifold with a new gasket. Tighten the nuts to 29 ft. lbs. (39 Nm). Install the outer insulator.
3. Use a new gasket and install the left manifold. Tighten the nuts to 29 ft. lbs. (39 Nm). Install the outer insulator.
4. Install the front exhaust pipe and tighten the manifold-to-pipe nuts to 46 ft. lbs. (62 Nm). Tighten the pipe-to-converter nuts to 32 ft. lbs. (43 Nm).
5. Connect the O_2 sensor, install the under covers and then lower the car. Connect the battery cable.

Turbocharger

REMOVAL & INSTALLATION

1C-T and 2C-T Engines Only

➧ SEE FIGS. 97

1. Disconnect the negative battery cable.
2. Disconnect the PCV hose from the cylinder head cover.
3. Loosen the clamp and disconnect the air cleaner hose from the turbocharger.
4. Undo the clips and remove the air cleaner hose with the air cleaner cover.
5. Disconnect the turbocharger pressure hose to the compressor elbow.
6. Disconnect the air intake hose from the intake manifold.
7. Remove the bolt attaching the compressor elbow stay to the engine hanger.
8. Loosen the two bolts and remove the compressor elbow with the relief valve and the air intake hose attached.
9. Unbolt and remove the turbocharger heat insulators.
10. Disconnect the exhaust pipe from the turbine elbow by removing the three nuts from the flange. Remove the gasket and replace it with a new one.
11. Remove the nuts from the turbocharger oil pipe flange.
12. Remove the four nuts and remove the turbocharger, turbocharger and flange gaskets from the exhaust manifold.
13. Cover the exhaust pipe with masking tape to prevent the entry of foreign material into the engine.

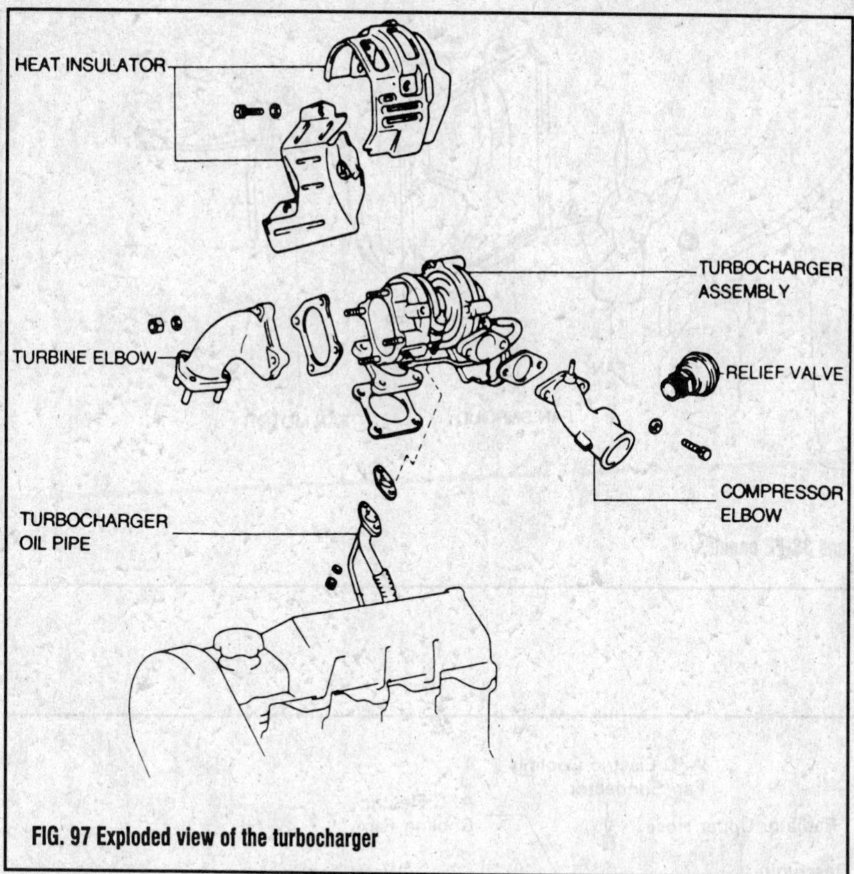

FIG. 97 Exploded view of the turbocharger

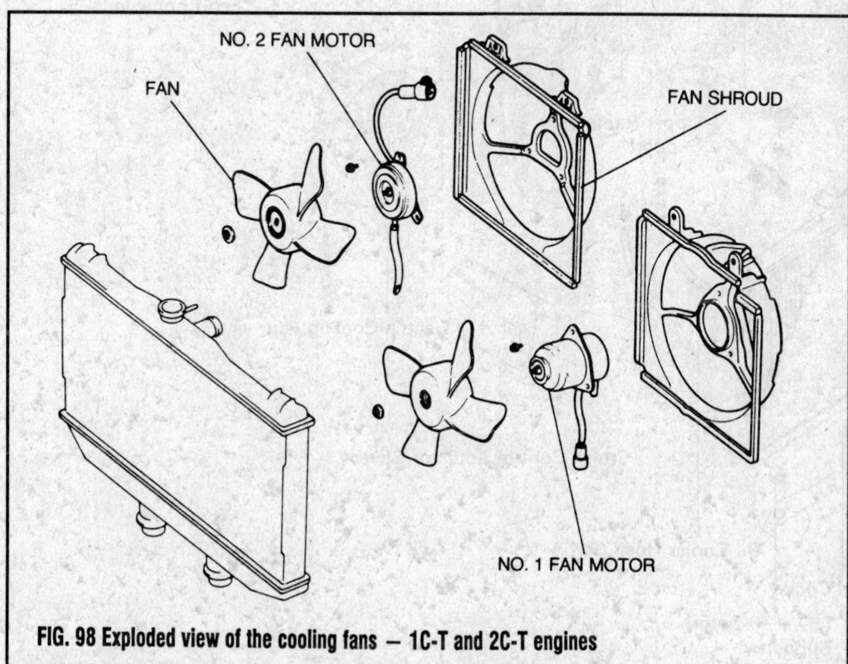

FIG. 98 Exploded view of the cooling fans — 1C-T and 2C-T engines

To Install:

1. Remove the masking tape and thoroughly clean all the exhaust manifold and turbocharger flanges to remove any deposits of carbon or gasket material.
2. Place the new gasket so that the protrusion is on the opposite side of the cylinder head.
3. Carefully place the turbocharger, with a new oil pipe gasket into position on the exhaust manifold and oil pipe. Install the four nuts and tighten them to 38 ft. lbs. (52 Nm).
4. Install the oil pipe flange nuts and tighten them to 13 ft. lbs. (18 Nm).
5. Place a new gasket on the exhaust pipe.
6. Connect the exhaust pipe to the turbine elbow and install the flange nuts. Tighten the nuts to 9 ft. lbs. (13 Nm).
7. Install the turbocharger heat insulators.
8. Using a new gasket, install the compressor elbow with the relief valve and air intake hose with the two bolts. Tighten the bolts to 9 ft. lbs. (13 Nm).
9. Connect the compressor elbow stay to the engine hanger.
10. Connect the air intake hose to the intake manifold and tighten the hose clamp.
11. Connect the turbocharger pressure hose to the compressor elbow.
12. Install the air cleaner case cover and the air cleaner hose by securing the four clips.
13. Connect the air cleaner hose to the turbocharger and tighten the clamp.
14. Connect the PCV hose to the cylinder head cover.
15. Connect the negative battery cable. Start the engine and inspect for leaks.

Electric Cooling Fans

REMOVAL & INSTALLATION

➧ SEE FIGS. 98-101

1. Disconnect the cable at the negative battery terminal.

⁂ CAUTION

On models with an airbag, wait at least 30 seconds from the time that the ignition switch is turned to the LOCK position and the battery is disconnected before performing any further work.

2. Tag and disconnect the cooling fan and temperature switch connectors.

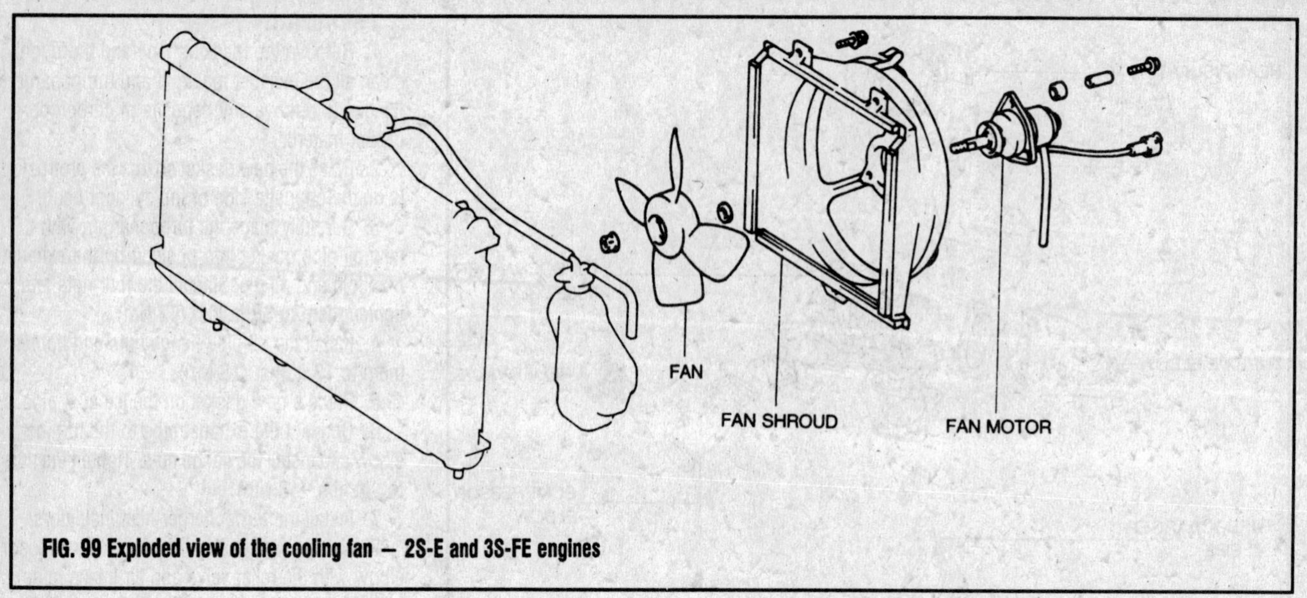

FIG. 99 Exploded view of the cooling fan — 2S-E and 3S-FE engines

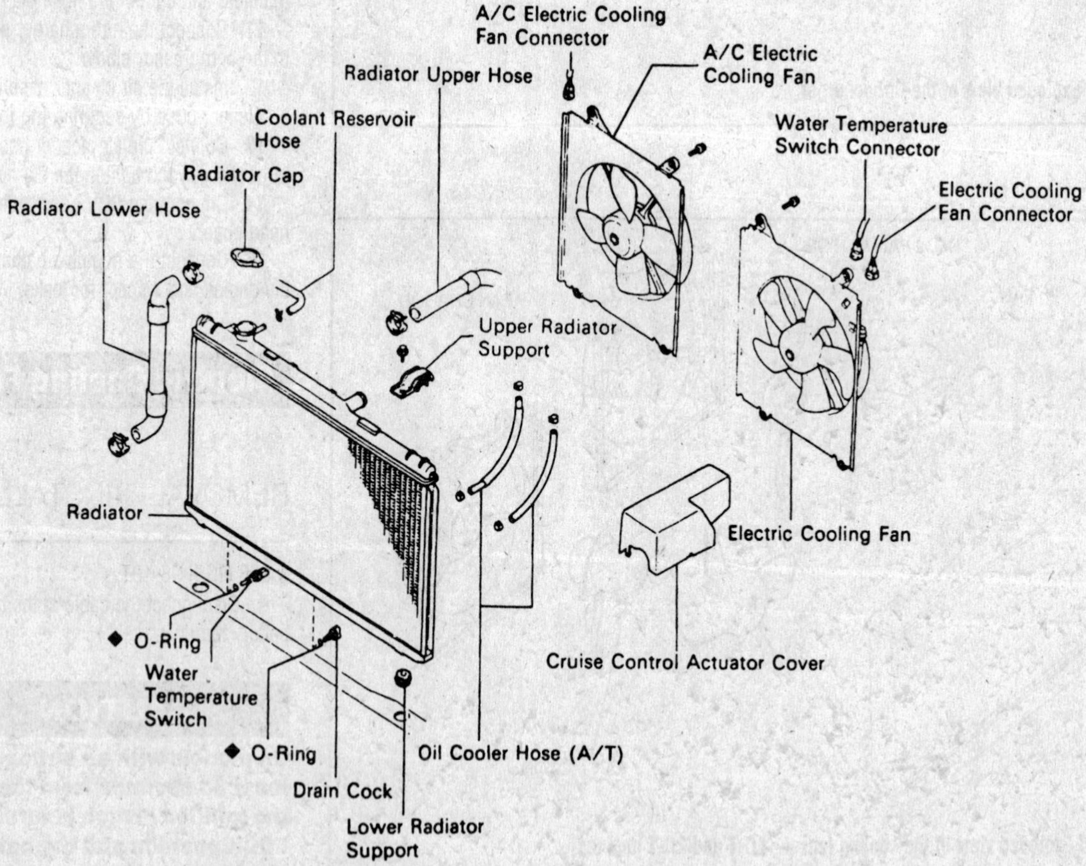

FIG. 100 Exploded view of the cooling fan — 5S-FE engines

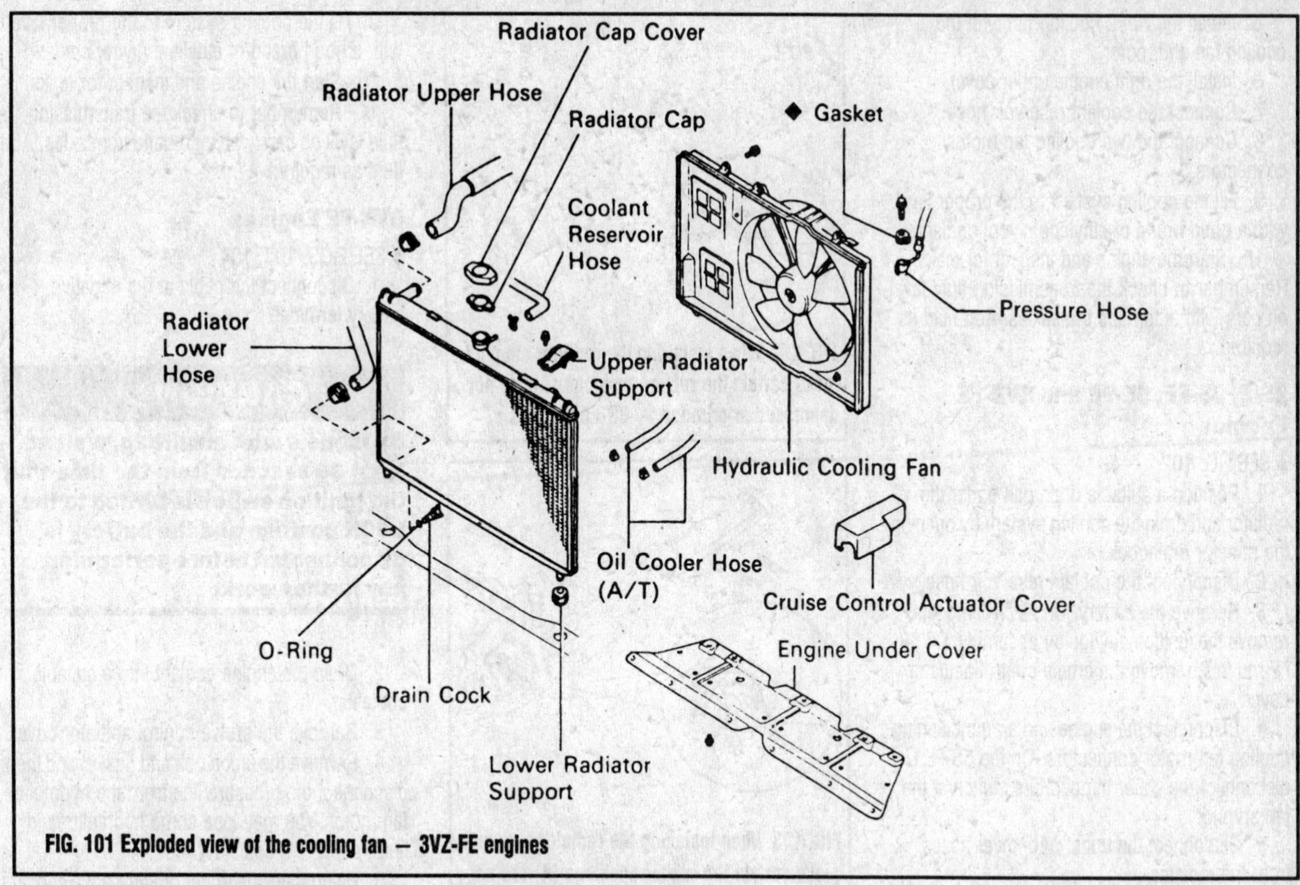

FIG. 101 Exploded view of the cooling fan — 3VZ-FE engines

3. Loosen the union bolt and remove the hydraulic line on models with the 3VZ-FE engine—that's right, these models use an electrically operated hydraulic cooling fan!

4. Remove the mounting bolts and lift out the fan shroud/motor/fan assembly.

5. Unbolt the fan from the shaft, remove the motor mounting bolts and remove the motor from the shroud bracket.

6. Position the motor in the bracket and tighten the mounting bolts. Press the fan onto the shaft and tighten the bolt.

7. Install the shroud/fan assembly to the radiator.

8. Connect the electrical leads. Connect the hydraulic line on the 3VZ-FE and tighten the union bolt to 47 ft. lbs. (64 Nm).

9. Connect the battery.

Radiator

REMOVAL & INSTALLATION

CAUTION

When draining the coolant, keep in mind that cats and dogs are attracted by the ethylene glycol antifreeze, and are quite likely to drink any that is left in an uncovered container or in puddles on the ground. This will prove fatal in sufficient quantity. Always drain the coolant into a sealable container. Coolant should be reused unless it is contaminated or several years old.

1C-T and 2C-T Engines

1. Position a suitable drain pan under the radiator and drain the cooling system by opening the radiator draincock.

2. Disconnect the two cooling fan connectors.

3. Disconnect the coolant reservoir hose.

4. Remove the right engine under cover.

5. Unbolt and remove the No. 2 fan shroud with cooling fan and motor.

6. Disconnect the upper and lower hoses from the radiator.

7. Disconnect the water temperature switch connector.

8. On vehicles equipped with automatic transaxle, disconnect the two cooler hoses from the cooler pipes.

➡ Take care when disconnecting the cooler lines because some of the transmission oil will leak from the line. Place a small plastic container under the lines to collect the oil and plug each connection to prevent further leakage.

9. Remove the two bolts and radiator supports.

10. Remove the radiator from the vehicle.

To install:

1. Place the radiator in position and support it by hand. Install the two radiator supports with bolts. Make sure that the rubber cushion of each support is not depressed or crimped

2. On vehicles equipped with automatic transaxle, connect and tighten the two oil cooler hoses.

3. Connect the water temperature switch connector.

4. Connect the upper and lower radiator hoses.

5. Install the No. 2 cooling fan with the cooling fan and motor.
6. Install the right engine under cover.
7. Connect the coolant reservoir hose.
8. Connect the two cooling fan motor connectors.
9. Fill the cooling system to the proper level with a good brand of ethylene glycol coolant.
10. Start the engine and inspect for leaks. Remember to check the transmission fluid level on cars with automatic transaxles. Add fluid as required.

2S-E, 3S-FE, 5S-FE and 2VZ-FE Engines

➧ SEE FIG. 102

1. Position a suitable drain pan under the radiator and drain the cooling system by opening the radiator draincock.
2. Disconnect the coolant reservoir hose.
3. Remove the battery. On 2VZ-FE models, remove the ignition coil/ignitor assembly. On 5S-FE models, remove the cruise control actuator cover.
4. Disconnect the engine and air conditioning cooling fan motor connectors. On the 5S-FE, disconnect the water temperature switch at the fan shroud.
5. Disconnect the upper and lower hoses from the radiator.
6. Unbolt and remove the engine electric cooling fan assembly (shroud and motor).
7. On vehicles equipped with air conditioning, remove the air conditioning electric cooling fan assembly (shroud and motor).
8. On vehicles equipped with automatic transaxle, disconnect the two cooler hoses from the cooler pipes at the bottom of the radiator.

➡ Take care when disconnecting the cooler lines because some of the transmission oil will leak from the line. Place a small plastic container under the lines to collect the oil and plug each connection to prevent further leakage.

9. Support the radiator by hand and remove the two bolts and radiator supports.
10. Remove the radiator from the vehicle.

To Install:

1. Place the radiator in position and support it by hand. Install the two radiator supports with bolts Tighten the bolts to 9 ft. lbs. (13 Nm). Make sure that the rubber cushion of each support is not depressed or crimped.
2. On vehicles equipped with automatic transaxle, connect and tighten the two oil cooler hoses.
3. On vehicles equipped with air conditioning, install the air conditioning electric cooling fan assembly.

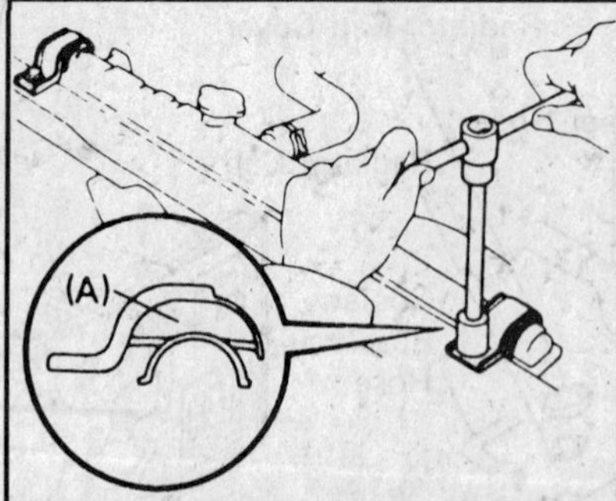

FIG. 102 When installing the radiator supports, make certain the rubber cushions (A) are not depressed or crimped — 3S-FE engines

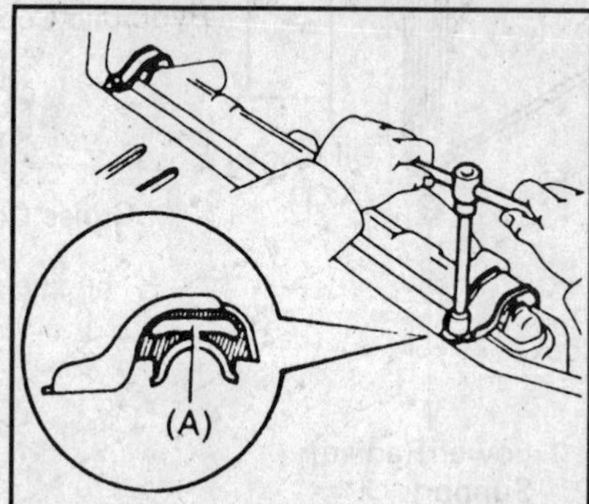

FIG. 103 When installing the radiator supports, make certain the rubber cushions (A) are not depressed or crimped — 3VZ-FE engines

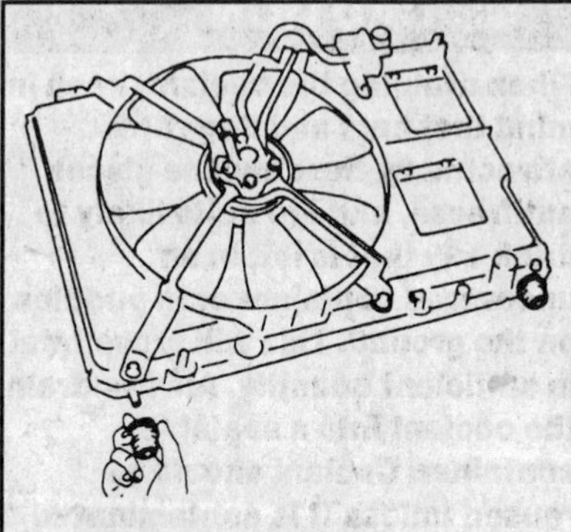
FIG. 104 Slide on the lower radiator supports — 3VZ-FE engines

4. Install the engine electric cooling fan assembly.
5. Connect the cooling fan motor connectors. Connect the water temperature switch.
6. Connect the upper and lower hoses to the radiator.
7. Connect the coolant reservoir hose.
8. Install the battery. Install the ignition coil/ignitor assembly and the cruise control actuator cover if removed.
9. Fill the cooling system to the proper level with a good brand of ethylene glycol coolant.
10. Start the engine and inspect for leaks.
11. Remember to check the transmission fluid level on cars with automatic transaxles. Add fluid as required.

3VZ-FE Engines

➧ SEE FIGS. 103, 104

1. Disconnect the cable at the negative battery terminal.

✻✻ CAUTION

On models with an airbag, wait at least 30 seconds from the time that the ignition switch is turned to the LOCK position and the battery is disconnected before performing any further work.

2. Drain the engine coolant into a suitable container.
3. Remove the cruise control actuator cover.
4. Remove the union bolt and gasket and then disconnect the pressure line from the hydraulic fan motor. You may lose some hydraulic fluid here, so have a container ready.
5. Disconnect the upper radiator hose and the coolant reservoir hose. Disconnect the hydraulic motor return hose.
6. Remove the engine under cover.
7. Disconnect the lower radiator hose and the oil cooler lines.
8. Remove the two bolts and the upper supports and lift out the radiator/fan assembly. Remove the six bolts and separate the fan from the radiator.

To Install:

1. Install the fan assembly to the radiator and then install the radiator. Tighten the two support bolts to 9 ft. lbs. (13 Nm). Be sure that the rubber support cushions are not pinched.
2. Connect the oil cooler hoses and the lower radiator hose.
3. Install the engine under cover.
4. Connect the hydraulic motor return line.
5. Connect the reservoir and upper radiator hoses.
6. Connect the pressure line to the hydraulic motor with a new gasket. Tighten the union bolt to 47 ft. lbs. (64 Nm).
7. Install the actuator cover.
8. Fill the engine with coolant, connect the battery, start the car and check for leaks.

Water Pump

REMOVAL & INSTALLATION

CAUTION

When draining the coolant, keep in mind that cats and dogs are attracted by the ethylene glycol antifreeze, and are quite likely to drink any that is left in an uncovered container or in puddles on the ground. This will prove fatal in sufficient quantity. Always drain the coolant into a sealable container. Coolant should be reused unless it is contaminated or several years old.

1C-T and 2C-T Engines

SEE FIG. 105

1. Drain the cooling system.
2. Remove the timing belt covers, timing belt and injection pump pulley as described in this section.
3. Remove the seven bolts and two injection pump holding nuts and remove the water pump and the water pump gasket.
4. Place the new water pump gasket onto the water pump and attach the water pump to the engine with the seven bolts and two holding nuts. Tighten the nuts and bolts to 13 ft. lbs. (18 Nm).
5. Install the injection pump pulley, timing belt and timing belt covers.
6. Fill the cooling system to the proper level with a good brand of ethylene glycol based coolant.
7. Start the engine and check for leaks.
8. Check and adjust the engine idle and maximum speeds.

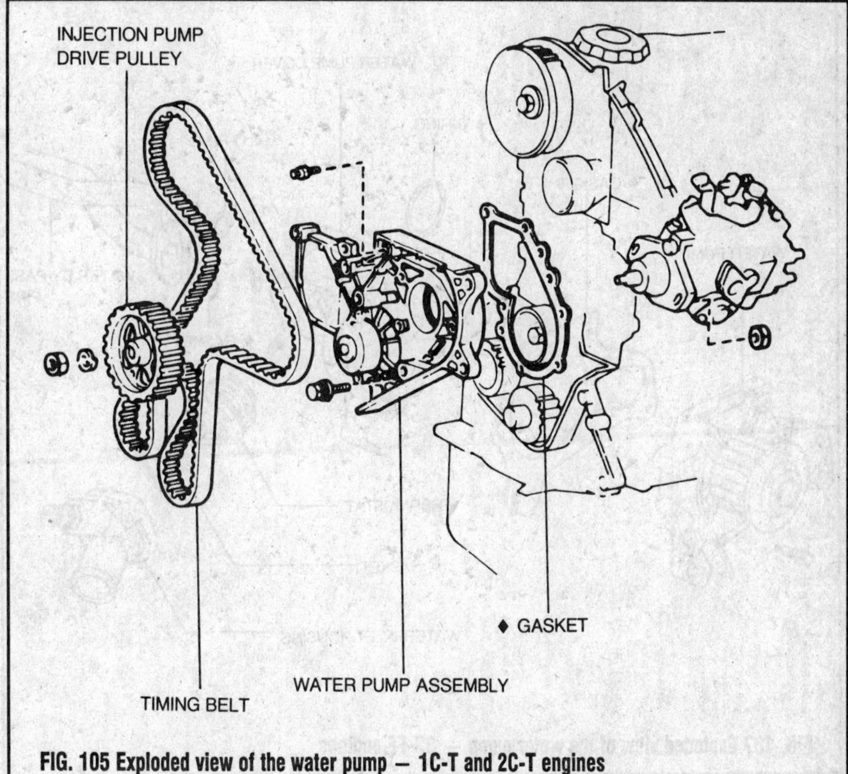

FIG. 105 Exploded view of the water pump — 1C-T and 2C-T engines

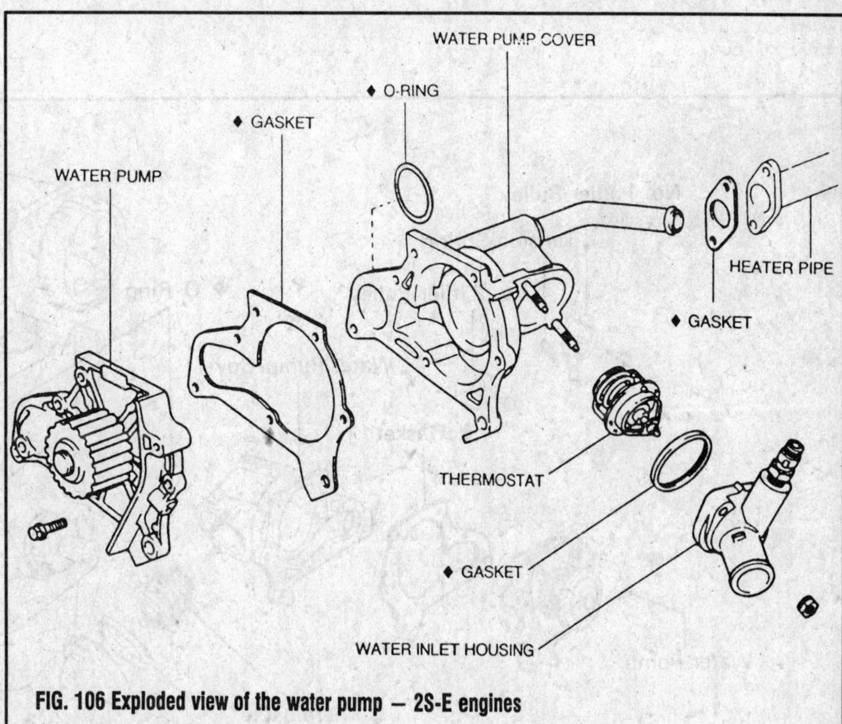

FIG. 106 Exploded view of the water pump — 2S-E engines

2S-E Engines

SEE FIG. 106, 108, 109

1. Drain the cooling system.
2. Remove the timing belt as described in this section.
3. Remove the alternator adjusting bar.
4. Disconnect the lower radiator hose from the water inlet housing.
5. Disconnect the water temperature switch from the water inlet housing.
6. Disconnect the water by-pass hose from the water pump.
7. Remove the two heater pipe clamp bolt. Remove the two nuts and heater pipe with gasket. Replace the gasket.
8. Loosen the three water pump mounting bolts in the indicated sequence.
9. Remove the water pump and O-ring. If the water pump is stubborn, tap it a few times with a rubber mallet.

To Install:

1. Make sure all the water pump and engine contact surfaces are clean and install the new O-ring into the pump cover groove.
2. Install the water pump with the three bolts. Torque the bolts in the indicated sequence to 82 inch lbs. (9.3 Nm).

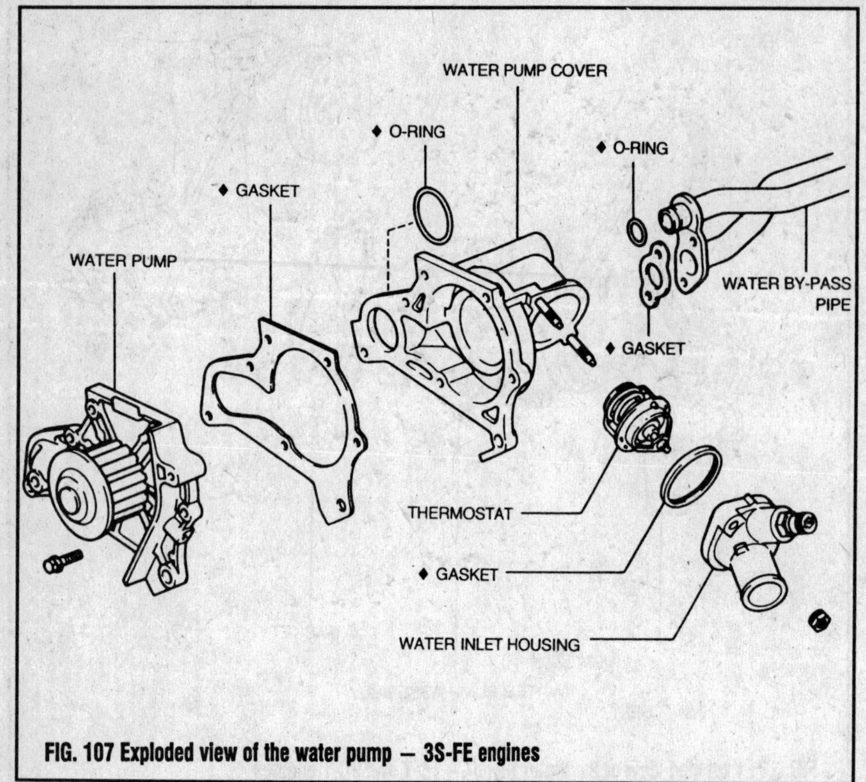

FIG. 107 Exploded view of the water pump — 3S-FE engines

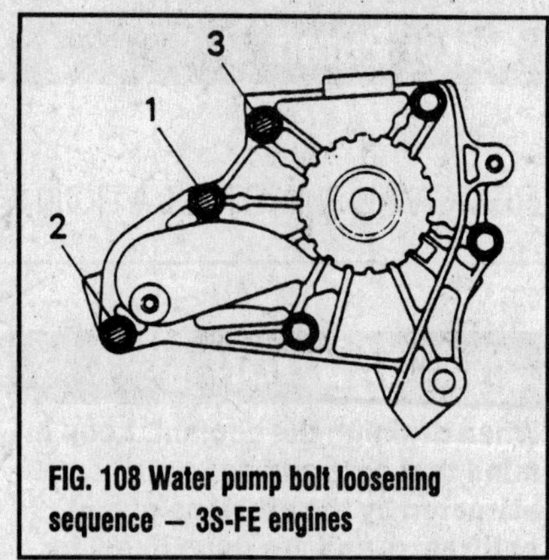

FIG. 108 Water pump bolt loosening sequence — 3S-FE engines

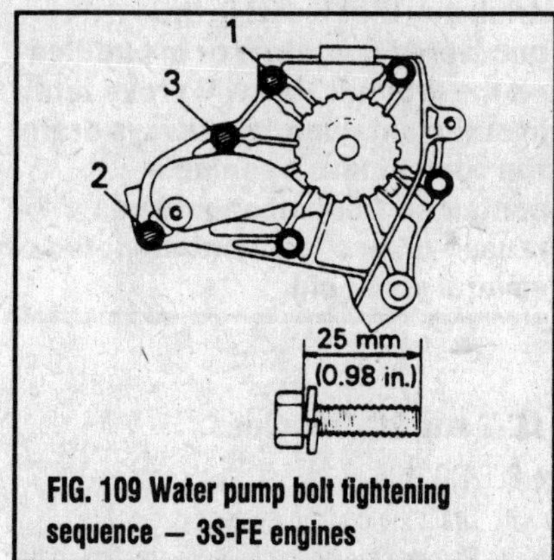

FIG. 109 Water pump bolt tightening sequence — 3S-FE engines

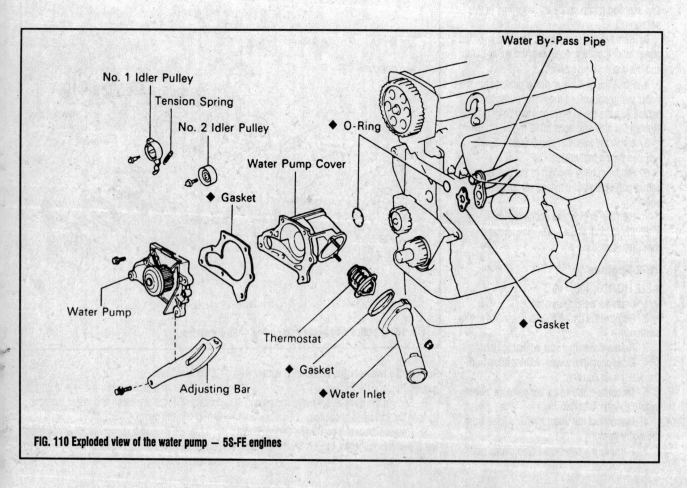

Water By-Pass Pipe
No. 1 Idler Pulley
Tension Spring
No. 2 Idler Pulley
◆ O-Ring
Water Pump Cover
◆ Gasket
Water Pump
Thermostat
◆ Gasket
Adjusting Bar
◆ Water Inlet
◆ Gasket

FIG. 110 Exploded view of the water pump — 5S-FE engines

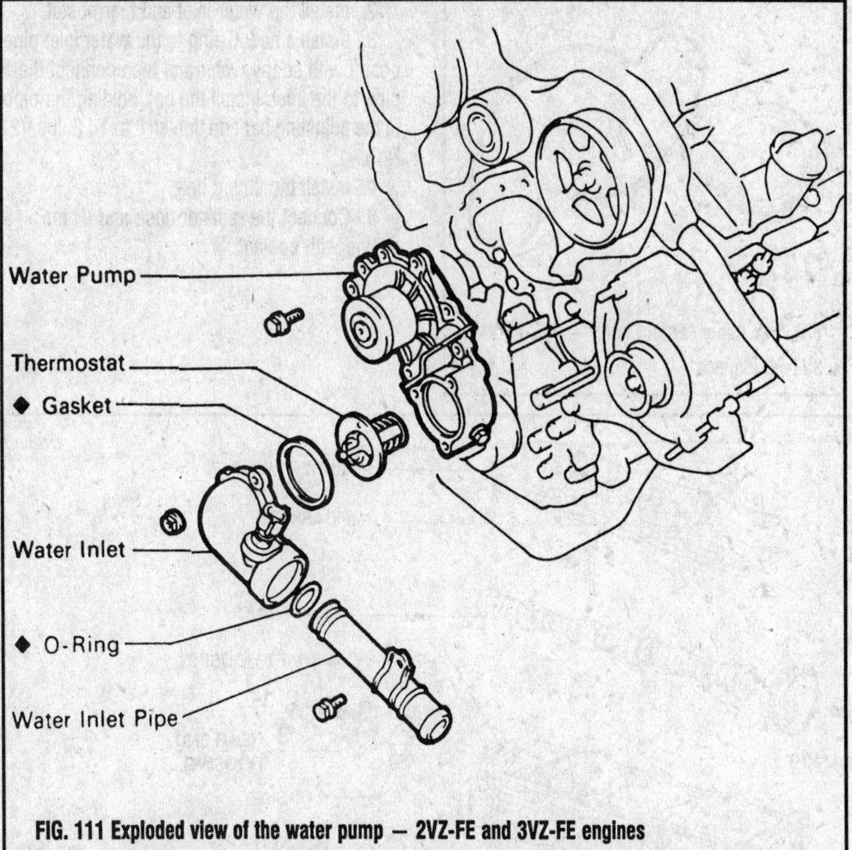

FIG. 111 Exploded view of the water pump — 2VZ-FE and 3VZ-FE engines

3. Place the new gasket between the heater pipe and the water pump. Connect the heater pipe to the water pump with the two nuts. Install the heater pipe clamp bolt.
4. Connect the water by-pass hose to the water pump.
5. Connect the lower radiator hose to the water inlet housing.
6. Connect the temperature switch connector.
7. Install the alternator adjusting bar.
8. Fill the cooling system to the proper level with a good brand of ethylene glycol based coolant.
9. Start the engine and inspect for leaks.

3S-FE Engines

➧ SEE FIGS. 107-109

1. Drain the cooling system.
2. Disconnect the water temperature switch connector from the water inlet housing.
3. Disconnect the lower radiator hose from the water inlet housing.
4. Remove the timing belt and timing belt pulleys as described in this section.
5. Remove the two nuts attaching the water by-pass pipe to the water pump cover.
6. Remove the three water pump-to-engine attaching bolts.
7. Pull the water pump and the water pump cover out from the engine.
8. Remove the two O-rings and gasket. Discard them and replace with new.

To install:

1. Make sure the water pump and engine contact surfaces are clean and free of gasket material. Install the two new O-rings and gasket onto the water pump cover and the water by-pass pipe. Coat the water by-pass pipe O-ring with a coating of clean engine oil.
2. Connect the water pump cover to the by-pass pipe but do not install the nuts just yet.
3. Place the water pump onto the engine and install the three bolts. Tighten the bolts in an alternate pattern to 82 inch lbs. (9.3 Nm). Install the by-pass pipe attaching nuts and torque them to 82 inch lbs. (9.3 Nm) also.
4. Install the timing belt and timing belt pulleys.
5. Connect the lower radiator hose to the water inlet housing.
6. Connect the water temperature switch connector.
7. Fill the cooling system to the proper level with a good brand of ethylene glycol based coolant.
8. Start the engine and check for leaks.

5S-FE Engines

➧ SEE FIG. 110

1. Disconnect the cable from the negative battery terminal.

CAUTION

On models with an airbag, wait at least 30 seconds from the time that the ignition switch is turned to the LOCK position and the battery is disconnected before performing any further work.

2. Drain the engine coolant.
3. Remove the timing belt.
4. Remove the No. 1 idler pulley and tension spring. Remove the No. 2 idler pulley.
5. Disconnect the lower radiator hose at the water inlet.
6. Remove the alternator belt adjusting bar.
7. Loosen the two nuts and disconnect the water by-pass pipe.
8. Remove the three pump mounting bolts in sequence (middle, top, bottom) and then pull out the water pump and cover. Remove the gasket and two O-rings.

To install:

1. Replace the two O-rings and gasket with new ones, coat the by-pass O-ring with soapy water and then connect the pump cover to the by-pass pipe—do not install the nuts yet!
2. With the pump loosely connected to the pipe, install the pump and tighten the three bolts to 82 inch lbs. (9.3 Nm), in sequence (top, bottom, middle). Install the two by-pass pipe nuts and tighten them to 78 inch lbs. (8.8 Nm).
3. Install the belt adjusting bar.
4. Connect the lower hose to the water inlet.
5. Install the No. 2 idler pulley with a 35mm (1.38 in.) bolt and tighten it to 31 ft. lbs. (42 Nm). Check that the pulley moves smoothly.
6. Install the No. 1 idler pulley and spring. Use a 42mm (1.65 in.) bolt, but don't tighten it. Install the spring, pry it as far left as it will go and then tighten the bolt.
7. Install the timing belt.
8. Connect the battery cable and fill the engine with coolant.

2VZ-FE and 3VZ-FE Engines

➧ SEE FIG. 111, 112

1. Drain the engine coolant.
2. Disconnect the lower radiator hose at the water inlet.
3. Disconnect the timing belt from the water pump pulley.

4. Remove the bolt holding the inlet pipe to the alternator belt adjusting bar and then remove the inlet pipe and O-ring.
5. Remove the water inlet and thermostat.
6. Remove the seven bolts and then pry off the water pump.

To Install:

1. Scrape any remaining gasket material off the pump mating surface. Apply a 2–3mm (0.08–0.12 in.) bead of sealant to the groove in the pump and then install the pump. Tighten the bolts to 14 ft. lbs. (20 Nm).

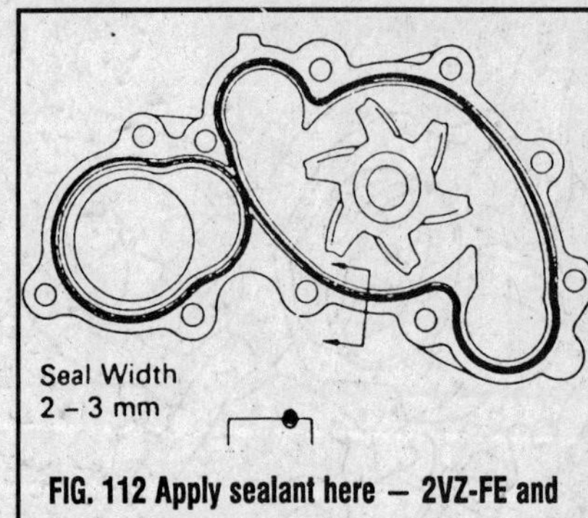

FIG. 112 Apply sealant here — 2VZ-FE and 3VZ-FE engines

2. Install the water inlet and thermostat.
3. Install a new O-ring to the water inlet pipe, coat it with soapy water and then connect the pipe to the inlet. Install the bolt holding the pipe to the adjusting bar and tighten it to 14 ft. lbs. (20 Nm).
4. Install the timing belt.
5. Connect the radiator hose and fill the engine with coolant.

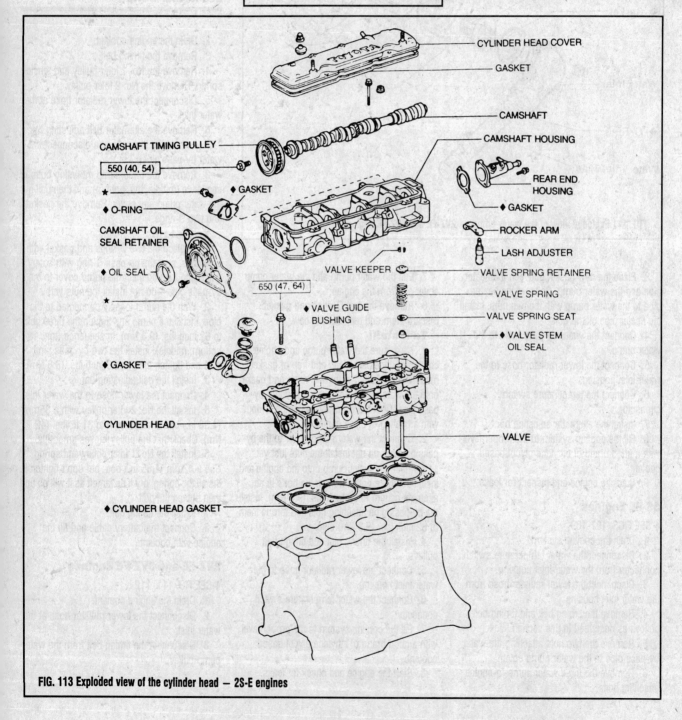

FIG. 113 Exploded view of the cylinder head — 2S-E engines

Cylinder Head

REMOVAL & INSTALLATION

CAUTION

When draining the coolant, keep in mind that cats and dogs are attracted by the ethylene glycol antifreeze, and are quite likely to drink any that is left in an uncovered container or in puddles on the ground. This will prove fatal in sufficient quantity. Always drain the coolant into a sealable container. Coolant should be reused unless it is contaminated or several years old.

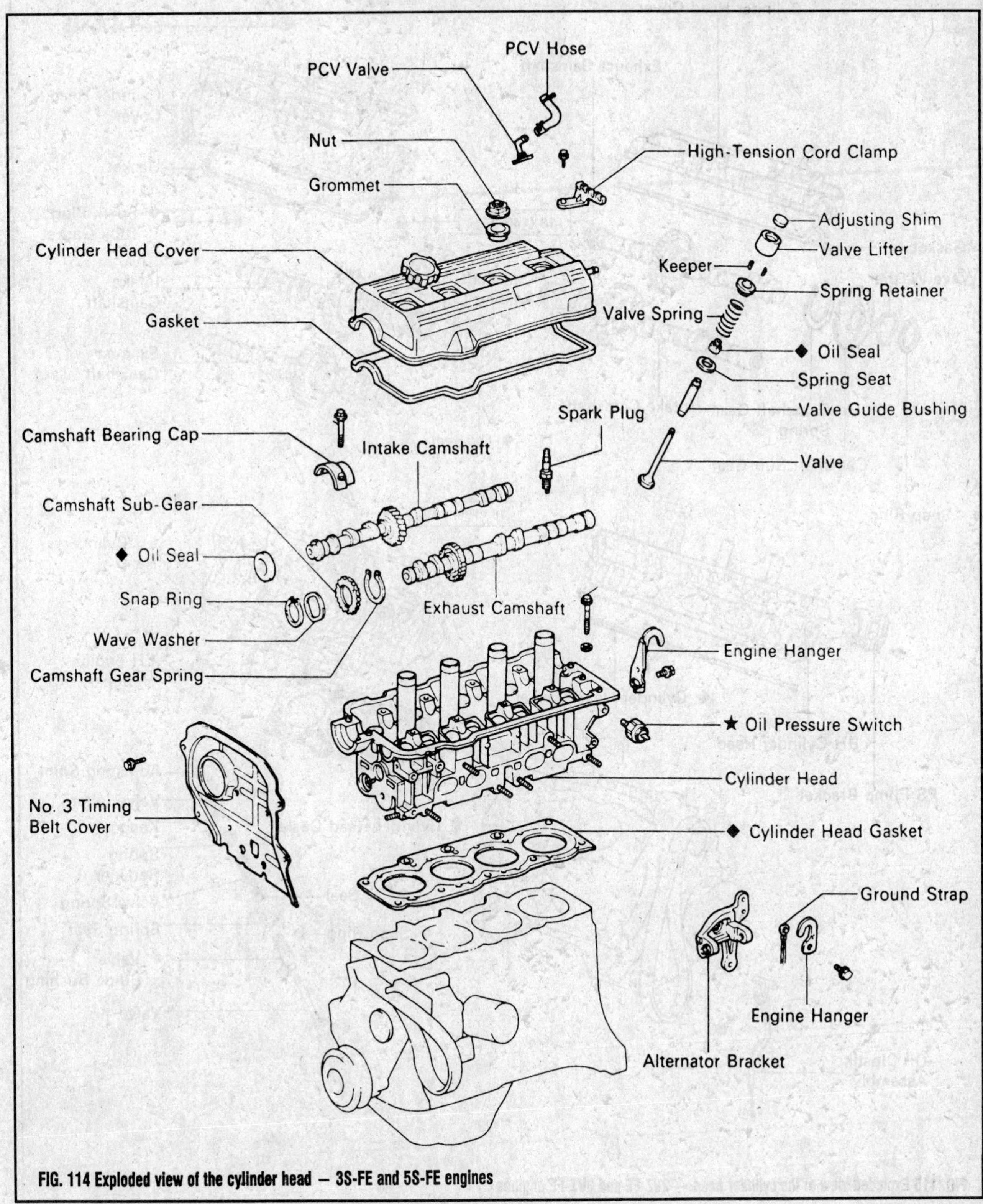

FIG. 114 Exploded view of the cylinder head — 3S-FE and 5S-FE engines

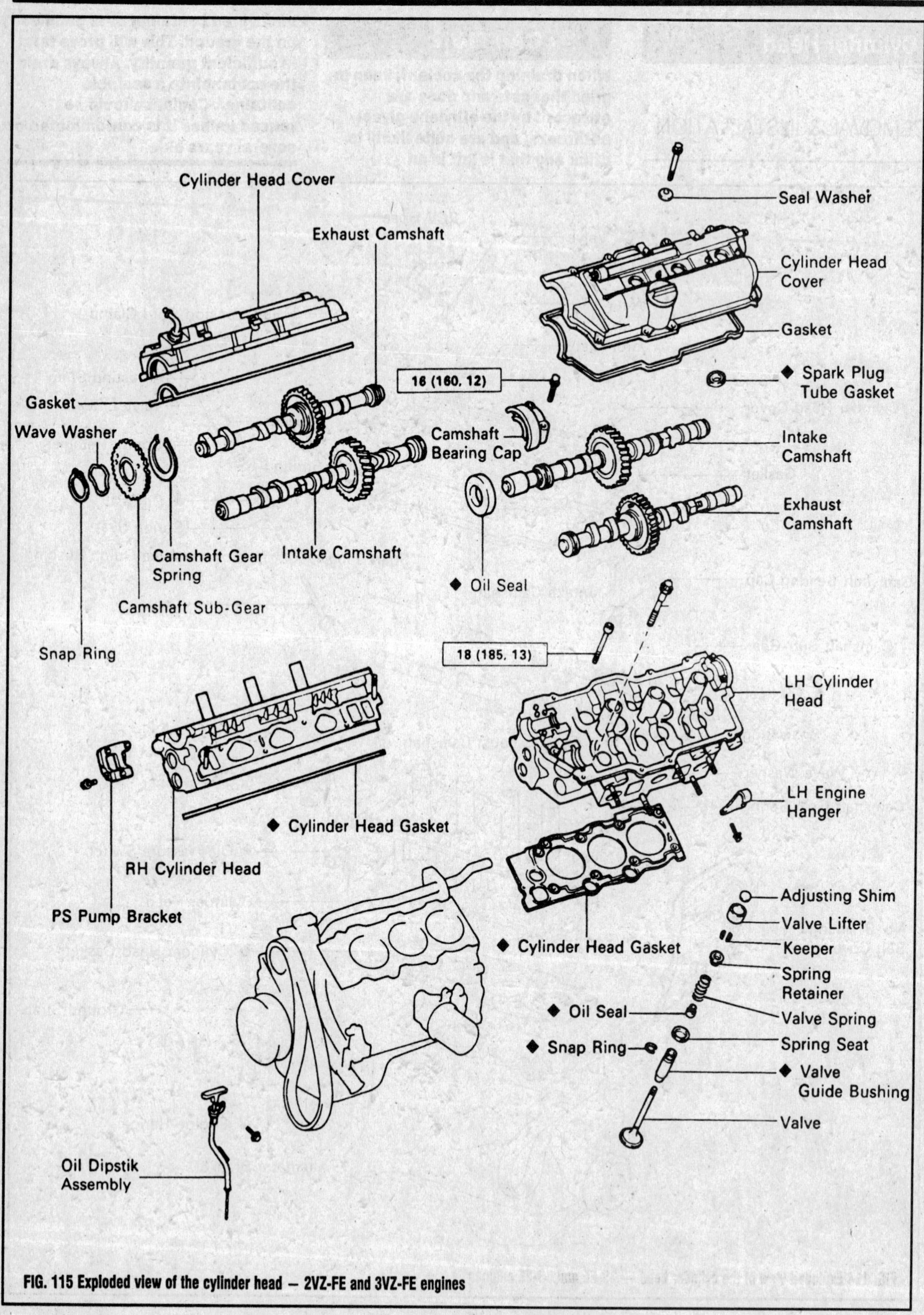

FIG. 115 Exploded view of the cylinder head — 2VZ-FE and 3VZ-FE engines

1C-T and 2C-T Engines

SEE FIGS. 116-119

1. Disconnect the negative battery cable.
2. Drain the cooling system.
3. Remove the cruise control actuator.
4. Disconnect and tag all wires connected to or running across the head.
5. Disconnect the accelerator control rod from the injection pump.
6. Disconnect the PCV hose from the cylinder head cover. Remove the air cleaner hose with case cover.
7. Disconnect the following hoses:
   a. Air intake hose.
   b. Fuel inlet and outlet hoses.
   c. Radiator inlet hose.
   d. Heater inlet and outlet hoses.
   e. Pressure hose from the turbocharger indicator and warning switch.
   f. Vacuum hose to the HAC.
   g. Air conditioning or heater idle-up vacuum hose.
8. Remove the electronic vacuum regulating valve assembly, pipe and hoses.
9. Remove the current sensor.
10. Disconnect the water temperature sender gauge connector, heater or idle-up water temperature sensor and air conditioning cut water temperature sensor.
11. Raise and support the vehicle safely.
12. Drain the engine oil.
13. Disconnect the exhaust pipe from the turbine elbow.
14. Remove the exhaust manifold stay mounting bolt.
15. Lower the vehicle.
16. Remove the turbocharger.
17. Remove the water outlet with pipe.
18. Remove the EGR valve and pipe.
19. Remove the heater pipe.
20. Disconnect the by-pass hose from the cylinder head union.
21. Disconnect the current sensor plate and glow plug connectors. Using a 12mm deep socket, loosen and remove the four glow plugs.
22. Remove the injection nozzle holders.
23. Remove the level gauge guide support mounting bolt.
24. Remove the No. 2 timing cover.
25. Turn the engine so that the No. 1 cylinder is at TDC of the firing stroke. Make sure that the line mark on the camshaft pulley is aligned with the top end of the head.
26. Place matchmarks on the camshaft timing pulley, injection pump pulley and belt. Remove the camshaft timing pulley.

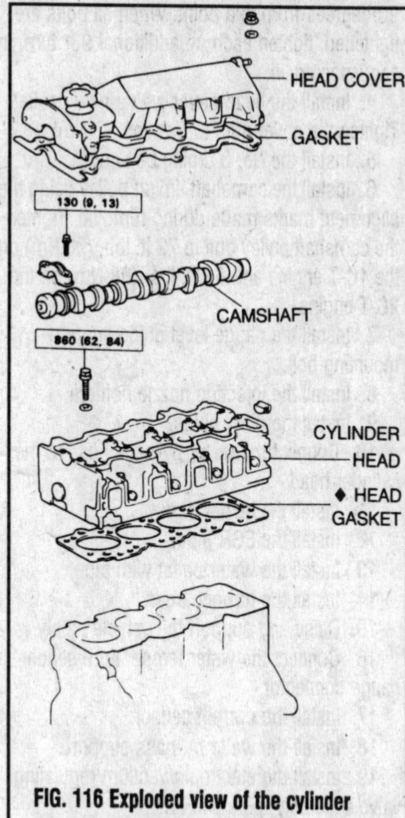

FIG. 116 Exploded view of the cylinder head — 1C-T and 2C-T engines

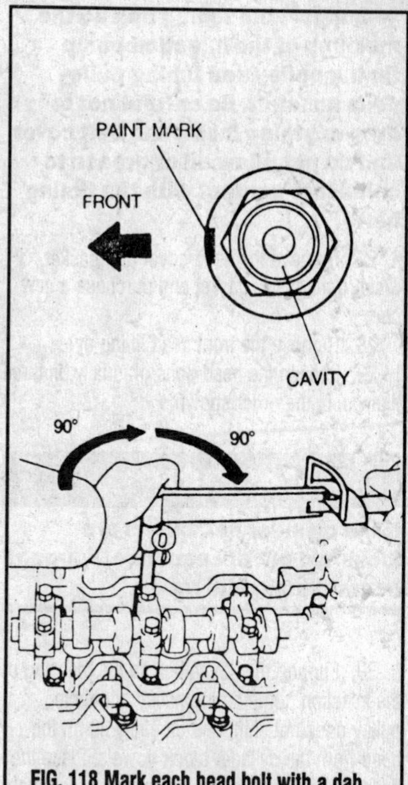

FIG. 118 Mark each head bolt with a dab of paint prior to angle-torquing — 1C-T and 2C-T engines

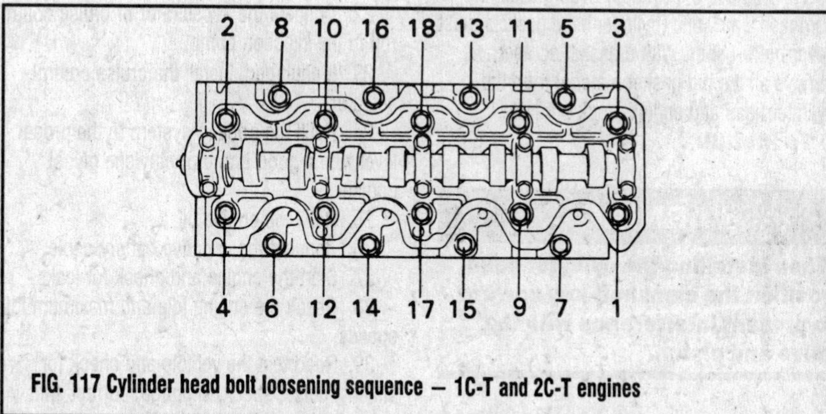

FIG. 117 Cylinder head bolt loosening sequence — 1C-T and 2C-T engines

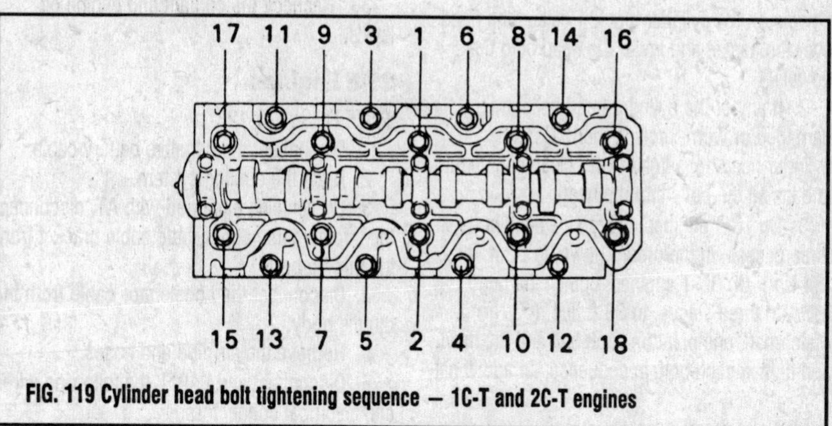

FIG. 119 Cylinder head bolt tightening sequence — 1C-T and 2C-T engines

➡ **Support the timing belt so the meshing of the injection pump timing pulley and timing pulley does not shift. Be careful not to drop anything inside the belt cover and do not allow oil or grease to come into contact with the timing belt.**

27. Remove the head cover and gasket. Discard the cover gasket and purchase a new one.
28. Remove the front head lifting eye.
29. Loosen the head bolts gradually, in three passes, in the order shown.

⁂ CAUTION

If the cylinder head bolts are loosened out of sequence, warpage or cracking could result.

30. Support the timing belt so the meshing of the injection pump timing pulley and timing pulley does not shift, and carefully lift off the head from the cylinder block dowels. Place the head on wooden blocks on a clean work bench. If the head is difficult to break loose, there is a recess at the front end in which you may pry with a suitable tool.
31. Remove the cylinder head gasket and purchase a new one (cylinder head gaskets must never be re-used). With a gasket scraper, remove all the old gasket material from the cylinder head and engine block surfaces.

To install:

⁂ WARNING

When installing the cylinder head, position the camshaft key upward to prevent interference with the valve and piston.

1. Position the new head gasket over the dowels on the cylinder block. Position the head over the gasket and lower the head onto the dowels.
2. If any of the cylinder head bolts are damaged or worn, replace them. Coat the cylinder head bolts lightly with clean engine oil and install the bolts into the head.
3. On 1C-T engines, tighten the head bolts, in three passes, in the order shown, to 62 ft. lbs. (84 Nm). On 2C-T engines, tighten the head bolts, in three stages, to 33 ft. lbs. (46 Nm). Matchmark one point on each bolt and the head, and tighten each bolt, in sequence, an additional 90 degrees from that point. When all bolts are tightened, tighten each an additional 90° turn, in sequence again.
4. Install the head cover with a new gasket. Tighten the cover nuts to 5 ft. lbs. (7 Nm).
5. Install the No. 3 timing belt cover.
6. Install the camshaft timing pulley using the alignment marks made during removal. Tighten the camshaft pulley bolt to 72 ft. lbs. (98 Nm) on the 1C-T engine and 65 ft. lbs. (88 Nm) on the 2C-T engine.
7. Install the gauge level guide support mounting bolt.
8. Install the injection nozzle holders.
9. Install the glow plugs.
10. Connect the water by-pass hose to the cylinder head.
11. Install the heater pipe.
12. Install the EGR pipe.
13. Install the water outlet with pipe.
14. Install the turbocharger.
15. Raise and support the vehicle safely.
16. Connect the water temperature sender gauge connector.
17. Install the current sensor.
18. Install the water by-pass support.
19. Install the electronic vacuum regulating valve assembly, pipe and hoses.
20. Connect all hoses removed in Step 7.
21. Install the air cleaner case with the cover. Connect the PCV hose to the head cover.
22. Connect the accelerator or cruise control rod to the injection pump.
23. If equipped, install the cruise control actuator.
24. Refill the cooling system to the proper level with a good brand of ethylene glycol coolant.
25. Refill the engine oil.
26. Connect the negative battery cable.
27. Start the engine and check for leaks.
28. Check the engine idle and maximum idle speeds.
29. Road test the vehicle and check for unusual noise, shock, slippage, correct shift points and smooth operation.
30. Recheck the coolant and engine oil levels.

2S-E Engines

➧ SEE FIGS. 120-123

1. Disconnect the negative battery cable.
2. Drain the cooling system.
3. On vehicles equipped with AT, disconnect the throttle cable and throttle cable bracket from the throttle body.
4. Disconnect the accelerator cable from the throttle body.
5. Remove the air pipe and hoses.
6. Disconnect and LABEL the following wires and electrical connectors.
   a. Ground strap connector.
   b. IIA connector.
   c. Igniter connector (USA only).
   d. Water temperature sensor gauge connector.
   e. Idle-up VSV connector (USA) only.
   f. Water temperature switch connector (automatic transmission only).
   g. Alternator terminal wiring and connector.
7. Disconnect and LABEL the following vacuum hoses:
   a. Air conditioning idle-up vacuum hoses.
   b. Cruise control actuator vacuum hose.
   c. Brake booster vacuum hose from the air intake manifold.
   d. Vacuum hose to the charcoal canister.
   e. Emission control hoses.
8. Remove the vacuum pipe from the head cover.
9. Disconnect and LABEL the following wires and electrical connectors:
   a. Oxygen sensor connector (USA only).
   b. Cold start injector time switch connector.
   c. Injector connectors.
   d. Throttle position sensor connector.
   e. Air flow meter connector.
   f. Check connector.
   g. Solenoid resistor connector.
   h. LH fender apron connectors.
   i. Air valve connector.
   j. Water temperature sensor connector.
   k. Start injector time switch connector (normal).
   l. Engine ground strap.
10. Pull the EFI harness to the right fender apron side.
11. Remove the alternator.
12. Remove the distributor assembly.
13. Remove the upper radiator hose and bypass hose.
14. Unbolt and remove the water outlet housing.
15. Disconnect the heater water outlet hose.
16. Disconnect the two air hoses from the fuel injection air valve.
17. Unbolt and remove the rear end housing with the air valve attached.
18. Remove the heater pipe by disconnecting the water by-pass and heater water inlet hoses and removing the two nuts with the gasket.
19. Disconnect the fuel line at the filter and the fuel return line at the return pipe. Collect all the excess fuel in a small plastic container.
20. Raise and support the vehicle on jackstands.
21. Drain the oil.

22. Disconnect the exhaust pipe at the manifold.
23. Disconnect the two power steering pump vacuum hoses.
24. Remove the intake manifold stay.
25. Lower the vehicle.
26. Remove the timing belt from the camshaft pulley.
27. Remove the No. 1 idler pulley and tension spring.
28. Remove the throttle body.
29. Disconnect the PCV hoses and remove the valve cover.
30. Unbolt and remove the camshaft housing using a small prybar positioned between the cylinder head and camshaft housing projections. Loosen the bolts gradually in the sequence shown.

CAUTION

If the bolts are loosened out of sequence, warpage of the camshaft housing could occur.

31. Remove the rocker arms and lash adjusters. Label each assembly as it is removed and keep all the assemblies together.
32. Loosen and remove the head bolts evenly, in three passes, in the order shown. Carefully lift the head from the engine and place it on wood blocks in a clean work area.

CAUTION

If the cylinder head bolts are loosened out of sequence, warpage or cracking could result.

33. Remove the cylinder head gasket and purchase a new one (cylinder head gaskets must never be re-used). With a gasket scraper, remove all the old gasket material from the cylinder head and engine block surfaces.

To install:

1. Place the new cylinder head gasket onto the cylinder block. Place the cylinder head onto the gasket.
2. Coat the threads of the eighteen cylinder head bolts with clean engine oil and install the bolts into the cylinder head. Uniformly torque the bolts in three passes to 47 ft. lbs. (64 Nm); 15 (20), 30 (47), 47 (64); using the sequence shown.
3. Install the rocker arms and lash adjusters in their original locations.

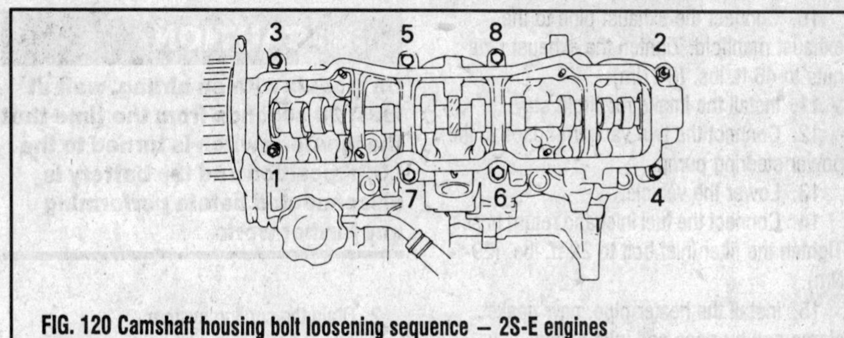

FIG. 120 Camshaft housing bolt loosening sequence — 2S-E engines

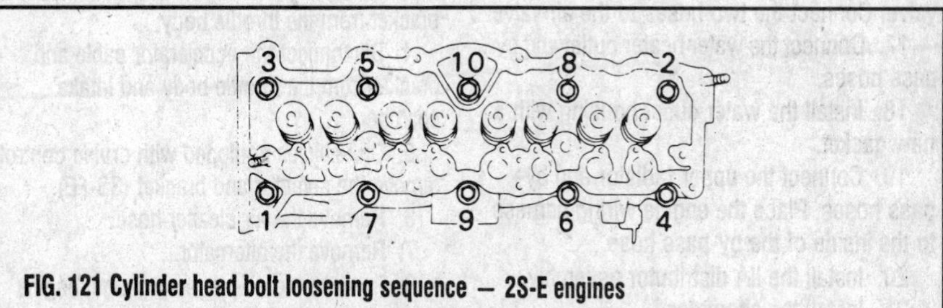

FIG. 121 Cylinder head bolt loosening sequence — 2S-E engines

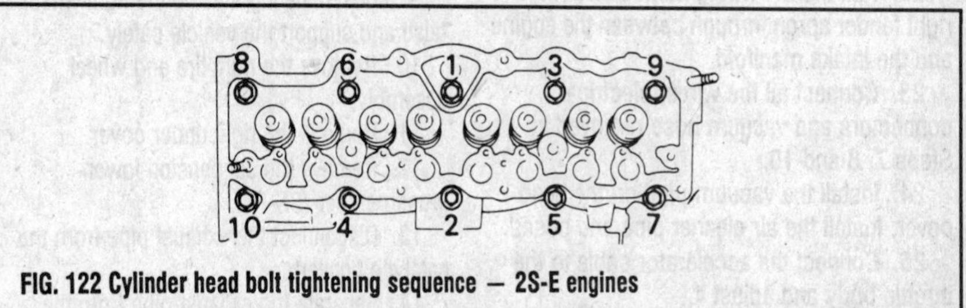

FIG. 122 Cylinder head bolt tightening sequence — 2S-E engines

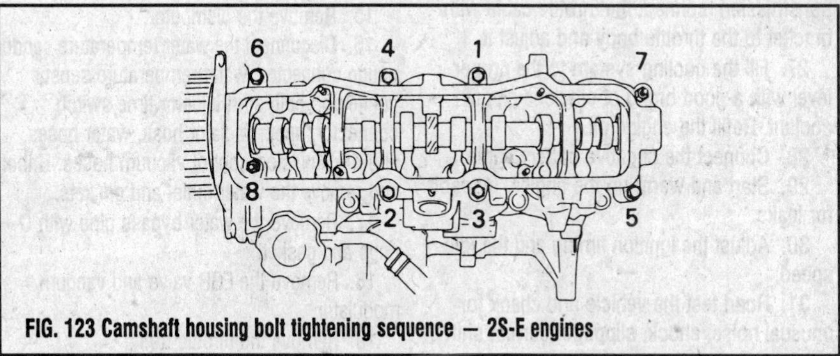

FIG. 123 Camshaft housing bolt tightening sequence — 2S-E engines

4. Install the camshaft housing by performing the following:
   a. Using a gasket scraper, thoroughly clean all the old packing material from the gasket surfaces and sealing grooves. Clean the surfaces again with a suitable cleaning solvent.
   b. Apply a bead of seal packing (No. 08826-00080 or equivalent) to the camshaft housing contact surface. Do not use to much sealant. The sealant hardens within 3 minutes after application. If the sealant hardens, it must be removed and reapplied.
   c. Place the camshaft housing onto the cylinder head.
   d. Install the camshaft housing bolts. Tighten the bolts in three passes to 11 ft. lbs. (16 Nm).
   e. Install the vacuum idle-up pipe.
5. Install the valve cover with a new gasket. Connect the PCV hoses to the cover.
6. Install the throttle body.
7. Temporarily install the the No. idler pulley and tension spring.
8. Install the timing belt to the pulley.
9. Raise the vehicle and support it safely.

10. Connect the exhaust pipe to the exhaust manifold. Tighten the exhaust pipe nuts to 46 ft. lbs. (64 Nm).

11. Install the intake manifold stay.

12. Connect the two vacuum hoses to the power steering pump.

13. Lower the vehicle.

14. Connect the fuel inlet and return hoses. Tighten the filter inlet bolt to 22 ft. lbs. (29 Nm).

15. Install the heater pipe, new gasket, clamp and by-pass and inlet hoses.

16. Install the rear end housing with air valve. Connect the two hoses to the air valve.

17. Connect the water heater outlet and by-pass hoses.

18. Install the water outlet housing with a new gasket.

19. Connect the upper radiator and by-pass hoses. Place the engine wiring harness to the inside of the by-pass hose.

20. Install the IIA distributor assembly.

21. Install the alternator.

22. Pull the EFI wiring harness from the right fender apron through between the engine and the intake manifold.

23. Connect all the wires, electrical connectors and vacuum hose removed in Steps 7, 8 and 10.

24. Install the vacuum pipe on the head cover. Install the air cleaner pipe and hoses.

25. Connect the accelerator cable to the throttle body and adjust it.

26. On vehicles equipped with automatic transmission, connect the throttle cable with bracket to the throttle body and adjust it.

27. Fill the cooling system to the proper level with a good brand of ethylene glycol coolant. Refill the engine oil.

28. Connect the negative battery cable.

29. Start and warm up the engine. Inspect for leaks.

30. Adjust the ignition timing and the idle speed.

31. Road test the vehicle and check for unusual noise, shock, slippage, correct shift points and smooth operation.

32. Recheck the coolant and engine oil levels.

3S-FE and 5S-FE Engines

➧ SEE FIGS. 124-127

1. Disconnect the negative battery cable.

CAUTION

On models with an airbag, wait at least 30 seconds from the time that the ignition switch is turned to the LOCK position and the battery is disconnected before performing any further work.

2. Drain the cooling system.

3. On vehicles equipped with automatic transmission, disconnect the throttle cable and bracket from the throttle body.

4. Disconnect the accelerator cable and bracket from the throttle body and intake chamber.

5. On vehicles equipped with cruise control, remove the actuator and bracket (3S-FE).

6. Remove the air cleaner hose.

7. Remove the alternator.

8. Remove the oil pressure gauge, engine hangers and alternator upper bracket.

9. Loosen the lug nuts on the right wheel and raise and support the vehicle safely.

10. Remove the right tire and wheel assembly.

11. Remove the right under cover.

12. Remove the suspension lower crossmember (3S-FE).

13. Disconnect the exhaust pipe from the catalytic converter.

14. Separate the exhaust pipe from the catalytic converter.

15. Remove the distributor.

16. Disconnect the water temperature sender gauge connector, water temperature sensor connector, cold start injector time switch connector, upper radiator hose, water hoses, and the emission control vacuum hoses. Unbolt and remove the water outlet and gaskets.

17. Remove the water bypass pipe with O-rings and gasket.

18. Remove the EGR valve and vacuum modulator.

19. Remove the throttle body.

20. Remove the cold start injector pipe (3S-FE).

21. Disconnect the air chamber hose, throttle body air hose and power steering hoses (if equipped). Remove the air tube.

22. Remove the intake manifold stay and disconnect the vacuum sensing hose. Remove the intake manifold and gasket. Purchase a new gasket.

23. Remove the fuel delivery pipe and the injectors.

24. Remove the spark plugs.

25. Remove the camshaft timing pulley. Remove the No. 1 idler pulley and tension spring. Remove the No. 3 timing belt cover. Properly support the timing belt so that meshing of the crankshaft timing pulley does not occur and the timing belt does not shift.

26. Remove the cylinder head cover. Label and arrange the grommets in order so that they can be reinstalled in the correct order. Remove the engine hangers, and the alternator bracket on the 5S-FE.

27. Remove the intake and exhaust camshafts as described in this section.

28. Loosen and remove the ten head bolts evenly, in three passes, in the order shown. Carefully lift the head from the engine and place it on wood blocks in a clean work area.

CAUTION

If the cylinder head bolts are loosened out of sequence, warpage or cracking could result.

29. Remove the cylinder head gasket and purchase a new one (cylinder head gaskets must never be re-used). With a gasket scraper, remove all the old gasket material from the cylinder head and engine block surfaces.

To Install:

1. Place the new cylinder head gasket onto the cylinder block. Place the cylinder head onto the gasket.

2. Coat the threads of the ten cylinder head bolts with clean engine oil and install the bolts into the cylinder head. Uniformly torque the bolts in three passes to an ultimate torque of 47 ft. lbs. (64 Nm) on 1986–88 models, or 36 ft. lbs. (49 Nm) on 1989–92 models, using the sequence shown. If any of the bolts does not meet the torque, replace it. On 1989–92 models, mark the forward edge of each bolt with paint and then retighten each bolt an additional 90°. Check that each painted mark is now at a 90° angle to the front.

3. Using a 30mm socket, install the spark plug tubes and tighten them to 29 ft. lbs. (39 Nm).

4. Install the intake and exhaust camshafts.

5. Install the cylinder head cover. Tighten the cover nuts to 13 ft. lbs. (18 Nm) on 1986–88 models, or 17 ft. lbs. (23 Nm) on 1989–92 models.

6. Install the No. 3 timing belt cover with the four cover bolts; tighten them to 69 inch lbs. (7.8 Nm). Install the hangers and alternator bracket on the 5S-FE. Tighten the hangers to 18 ft. lbs. (25 Nm) and the bracket to 31 ft. lbs. (42 Nm).

7. Install the No. 1 idler pulley and tension spring.

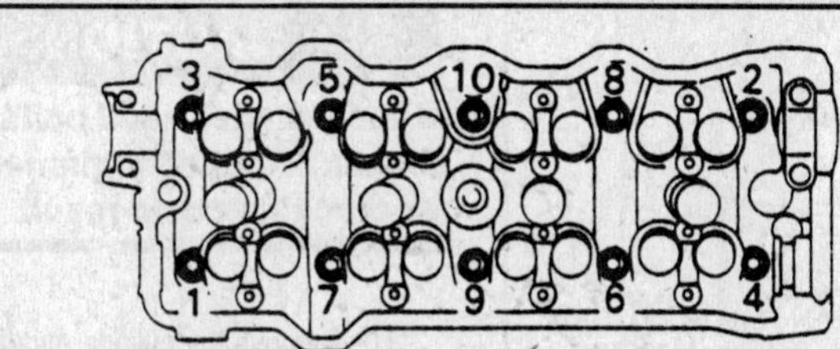

FIG. 124 Cylinder head bolt loosening sequence — 3S-FE and 5S-FE engines

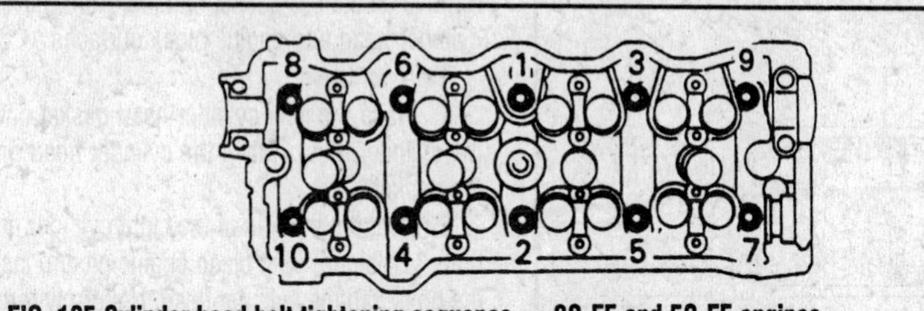

FIG. 125 Cylinder head bolt tightening sequence — 3S-FE and 5S-FE engines

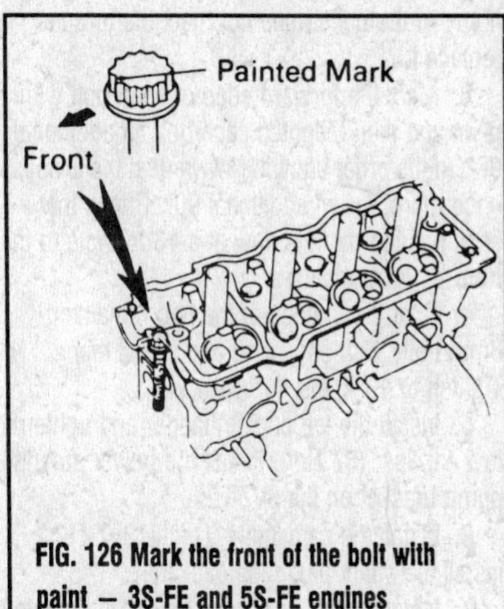

FIG. 126 Mark the front of the bolt with paint — 3S-FE and 5S-FE engines

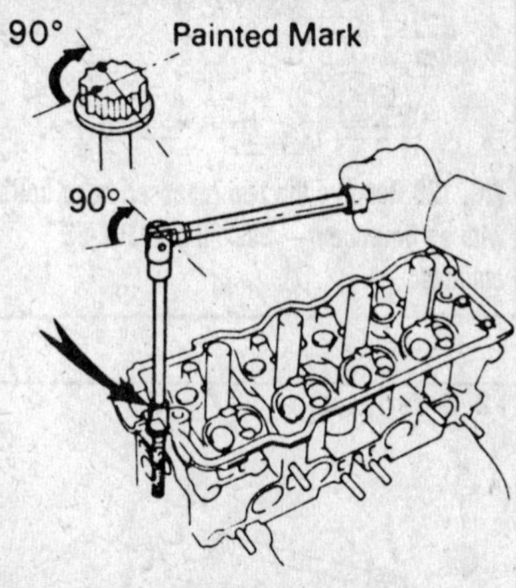

FIG. 127 Check that the painted mark is at 90° to the front — 3S-FE and 5S-FE engines

8. Install the camshaft timing pulley.
9. Install the spark plugs.
10. Install the injector and delivery pipe. Tighten the mounting bolts to 9 ft. lbs. (13 Nm).
11. Install the intake manifold with new gasket. Tighten the nuts and bolts to 14 ft. lbs. (19 Nm).
12. Install the air tube and connect the air intake chamber hose, throttle body air hose and power steering pump hoses (if equipped).
13. Install the cold start injector pipe.
14. Install the throttle body.
15. Install the EGR valve and modulator with new gaskets. Tighten the union nut to 43 ft. lbs. (59 Nm) and the bolt to 9 ft. lbs. (13 Nm).
16. Install the water by-pass pipe with new O-ring and gasket. Coat the O-ring with clean engine oil after installing it into the groove in the pipe. Tighten the bolts to 82 inch lbs. (9.3 Nm) on the 3S-FE, 78 inch lbs. (88 Nm) on the 5S-FE. Connect the water hoses.
17. Install the water outlet with a new gasket. Torque the bolts to 11 ft. lbs. (15 Nm). Connect the upper radiator hose, water hose, emission control vacuum hoses, water temperature sender gauge connector, water temperature sensor connector and cold start injector time switch connector.
18. Install the distributor assembly.
19. Assemble the exhaust manifold and the catalytic converter with new gaskets. Torque the bolts to 22 ft. lbs.
20. Install the exhaust manifold and catalytic converter with new gasket to the engine. The exhaust manifold gasket should be installed so that the **R** mark (most models) is toward the back.
21. Connect the exhaust pipe to the catalytic converter.
22. Install the suspension lower crossmember.
23. Install the engine right under cover.
24. Install the right front wheel and make the lug nuts snug.
25. Lower the vehicle.
26. Install the oil pressure gauge, engine hangers and alternator bracket on the 3S-FE. Tighten the bolts to 31 ft. lbs. (41 Nm).
27. Install the alternator and adjust the drive belt tension.
28. Install the air cleaner hose.
29. If equipped, install the cruise control actuator and bracket.
30. Install the radiator reservoir tank.
31. Install and adjust the accelerator cable.
32. If equipped with automatic transaxle, connect and adjust the throttle cable.
33. Fill the cooling system to the proper level with a good brand of ethylene glycol coolant.
34. Connect the negative battery cable.
35. Start the engine and check for leaks.
36. Adjust the valves and the ignition timing.
37. Check the toe-in.
38. Road test the vehicle and check for unusual noise, shock, slippage, correct shift points and smooth operation.
39. Recheck the coolant and engine oil levels.

2VZ-FE and 3VZ-FE Engines

➧ SEE FIG. 128-133

1. Disconnect the negative battery cable.

CAUTION

On models with an airbag, wait at least 30 seconds from the time that the ignition switch is turned to the LOCK position and the battery is disconnected before performing any further work.

2. Drain the cooling system.
3. On vehicles equipped with automatic transmission, disconnect the throttle cable and bracket from the throttle body.
4. Disconnect the accelerator cable and bracket from the throttle body and intake chamber.
5. On vehicles equipped with cruise control, remove the actuator, vacuum pump and bracket (2VZ-FE).
6. Remove the air cleaner hose.
7. Remove the alternator.
8. Remove the oil pressure gauge, engine hangers and alternator upper bracket.
9. Loosen the lug nuts on the right wheel and raise and support the vehicle safely.
10. Remove the right tire and wheel assembly.

11. Remove the right under cover.
12. Remove the suspension lower crossmember (2VZ-FE).
13. Disconnect the exhaust pipe from the catalytic converter.
14. Separate the exhaust pipe from the catalytic converter.
15. Remove the distributor. Remove the V-bank cover on the 3VZ-FE.
16. Disconnect the water temperature sender gauge connector, water temperature sensor connector, cold start injector time switch connector, upper radiator hose, water hoses, and the emission control vacuum hoses. Unbolt and remove the water outlet and gaskets.
17. Remove the water bypass pipe with O-rings and gasket.
18. Remove the EGR valve and vacuum modulator. Remove the exhaust crossover pipe
19. Remove the throttle body.
20. Remove the cold start injector pipe (2VZ-FE).
21. Disconnect the air chamber hose, throttle body air hose and power steering hoses (if equipped). Remove the air tube.
22. Remove the intake manifold stay and disconnect the vacuum sensing hose. Remove the intake manifold and gasket. Purchase a new gasket.
23. Remove the fuel delivery pipe and the injectors.
24. Remove the rear cylinder head plate. On the 3VZ-FE, remove the emission control valve set and the left side engine harness.
25. Remove the exhaust manifolds. Remove the spark plugs. On the 3VZ-FE, remove the oil dipstick.
26. Remove the timing belt, all camshaft timing pulleys and the No. 2 idler pulley.
27. Remove the No. 3 timing belt cover. Support the belt carefully so that the belt and pulley mesh does not shift.
28. Remove the cylinder head covers. Remove the spark plug tube gaskets on the 2VZ-FE.
28. Remove the intake and exhaust camshafts from each head as described in this section.
29. On the 3VZ-FE, remove the power steering pump bracket and the left side engine hanger.
30. Remove the two (one on each head) 8mm hex bolts. Loosen and remove the eight head bolts evenly, in three passes, in the order shown. Carefully lift the head from the engine and place it on wood blocks in a clean work area.

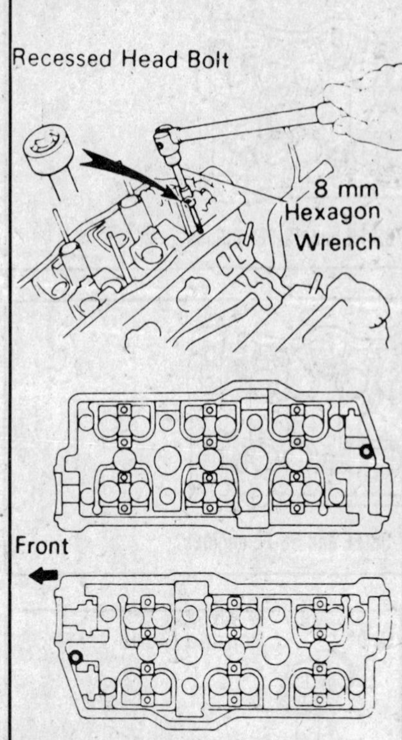

FIG. 128 Remove the two recessed head bolts with an 8mm hex — 2VZ-FE and 3VZ-FE engines

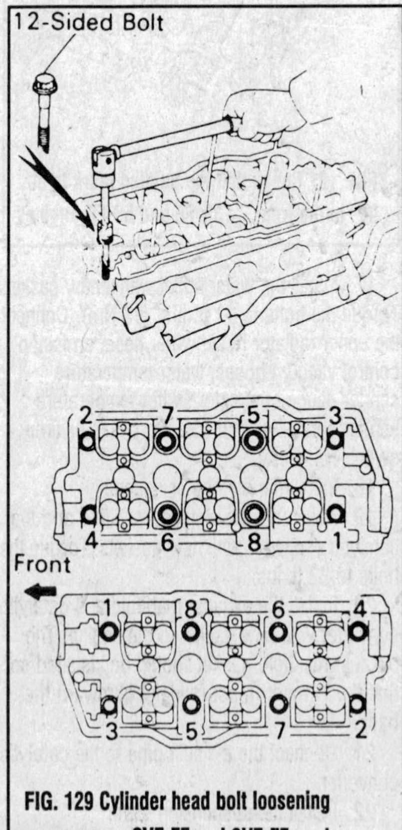

FIG. 129 Cylinder head bolt loosening sequence — 2VZ-FE and 3VZ-FE engines

✱✱ CAUTION

If the cylinder head bolts are loosened out of sequence, warpage or cracking could result.

31. Remove the cylinder head gasket and purchase a new one (cylinder head gaskets must never be re-used). With a gasket scraper, remove all the old gasket material from the cylinder head and engine block surfaces.

To install:

1. Place the new cylinder head gasket onto the cylinder block. Place the cylinder head onto the gasket.
2. Coat the threads of the eight cylinder head bolts (12-sided) with clean engine oil and install the bolts into the cylinder head. Uniformly torque the bolts in three passes to an ultimate torque of 25 ft. lbs. (34 Nm), using the sequence shown. If any of the bolts does not meet the torque, replace it.
3. Mark the forward edge of each bolt with paint and then retighten each bolt an additional 90°, in the order shown. Now repeat the process once more, for an additional 90°. Check that each painted mark is now at a 180° angle to the front — facing the rear.
4. Coat the threads of the two remaining 8mm bolts with engine oil and install them. Tighten to 13 ft. lbs. (18 Nm).
5. Install the left engine hanger and tighten it to 27 ft. lbs. (37 Nm). Install the power steering pump bracket on the 3VZ-FE.
6. Install the camshafts. On the 2VZ-FE, install the spark plug tube gaskets.
7. Install the cylinder head covers and tighten the bolts to 52 inch lbs. (5.9 Nm).
8. Install the No. 3 timing belt cover and tighten the six bolts to 65 inch lbs. (7.4 Nm). Install the No. 2 idler pulley, the camshaft timing pulleys and the timing belt.
9. Install the spark plugs.
10. Install the right and left side exhaust manifolds and tighten them to 29 ft. lbs. (39 Nm).
11. Install the intake manifold and the No. 2 idler pulley bracket. Tighten all bolts to 13 ft. lbs. (18 Nm).
12. Install the cylinder head rear plate and the oil dipstick tube.
13. Install the water by-pass outlet and tighten the bolts to 14 ft. lbs. (20 Nm) on the 2VZ-FE, or 74 inch lbs. (8.3 Nm) on the 3VZ-FE. On the 2VZ-FE, install the water outlet.
14. Install the injectors and delivery pipe. Tighten the bolts to 9 ft. lbs. (13 Nm).

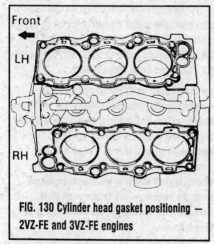

Front
LH
RH

FIG. 130 Cylinder head gasket positioning — 2VZ-FE and 3VZ-FE engines

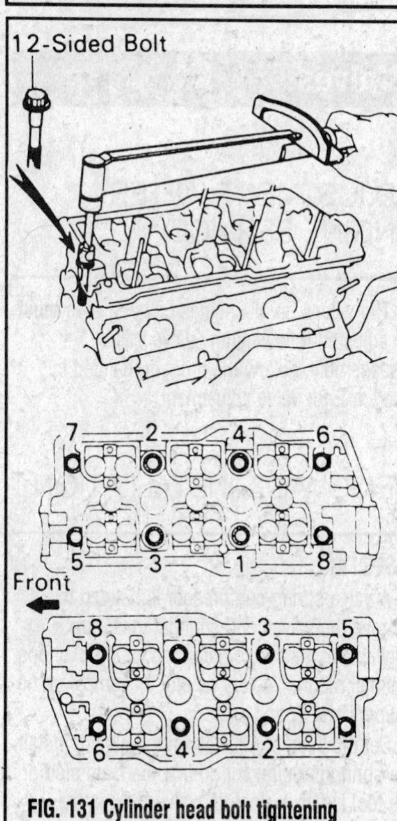

FIG. 131 Cylinder head bolt tightening sequence — 2VZ-FE and 3VZ-FE engines

FIG. 132 Mark the front of the bolt with paint — 2VZ-FE and 3VZ-FE engines

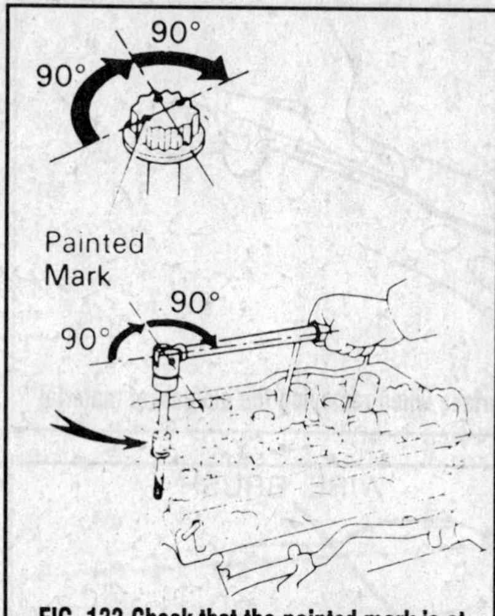

FIG. 133 Check that the painted mark is at 180° to the front — 2VZ-FE and 3VZ-FE engines

15. On the 3VZ-FE, install the air pipe, the engine harness and the No. 1 EGR cooler. Tighten the pipe to 73 inch lbs. (8.3 Nm) and the cooler to 13 ft. lbs. (18 Nm).
16. Install the air intake chamber. Tighten the mounting bolts to 32 ft. lbs. (43 Nm), the stays to 27 ft. lbs. (37 Nm) on the 2VZ-FE or 29 ft. lbs. (39 Nm) on the 3VZ-FE.
17. Install the cold start injector. Install the distributor and the EGR assembly. Tighten the EGR bolts to 13 ft. lbs. (18 Nm).
18. On the 2VZ-FE, install the crossover pipe and tighten the bolts to 25 ft. lbs. (34 Nm) and the nuts to 29 ft. lbs. (39 Nm). On the 3VZ-FE, install the emission control valve set and tighten it to 73 inch lbs. (8.3 Nm).
19. Install the EGR pipe and tighten the bolt to 13 ft. lbs. (18 Nm) and the union nut to 58 ft. lbs. (78 Nm).
20. Install the throttle body and the ISC valve. Tighten both sets of bolts to 9 ft. lbs. (13 Nm).
21. On the 3VZ-FE, install the V-bank cover.
22. Install the front exhaust pipe and tighten the manifold nuts to 46 ft. lbs. (62 Nm), tighten the converter nuts to 32 ft. lbs. (43 Nm). Install the engine under cover on the 2VZ-FE.
23. Install the alternator and adjust the drive belt tension.
24. Install the air cleaner hose.
25. If equipped, install the cruise control actuator and bracket.
26. Install and adjust the accelerator cable.
27. If equipped with automatic transaxle, connect and adjust the throttle cable.
28. Fill the cooling system to the proper level with a good brand of ethylene glycol coolant.
29. Connect the negative battery cable. Start the engine and check for leaks.
30. Adjust the valves and the ignition timing. Check the toe-in.
31. Road test the vehicle and check for unusual noise, shock, slippage, correct shift points and smooth operation.
32. Recheck the coolant and engine oil levels.

CLEANING & INSPECTION

➧ SEE FIGS. 134, 135

When the rocker assembly and valve train have been removed from the cylinder head (see Valves and Springs below), set the cylinder head on two wooden blocks on the bench, combustion chamber side up. Using a scraper or putty knife, carefully scrape away any gasket material that may have stuck to the head-to-block mating surface when the head was removed. Make sure you DO NOT gouge the mating surface with the tool.

Using a wire brush chucked into your electric drill, remove the carbon in each combustion chamber. Make sure the brush is actually removing the carbon and not merely burnishing it.

Clean all the valve guides using a valve guide brush (available at most auto parts or auto tool shops) and solvent. A fine-bristled rifle bore cleaning brush also works here.

Inspect the threads of each spark plug hole by screwing a plug into each, making sure it screws down completely. Heli-coil® any plug hole this is damaged.

✱✱ CAUTION

DO NOT hot tank the cylinder head! The head material on most engines is aluminum, which is ruined if subjected to the hot tank solution. Some of the early engines were equipped with cast iron heads, which can be hot-tanked (a service performed by most machine shops which immerses the head in a hot, caustic solution for cleaning). To be sure your engine's cylinder head is aluminum, check around its perimeter with a magnet. Your engine has an iron head if the magnet sticks.

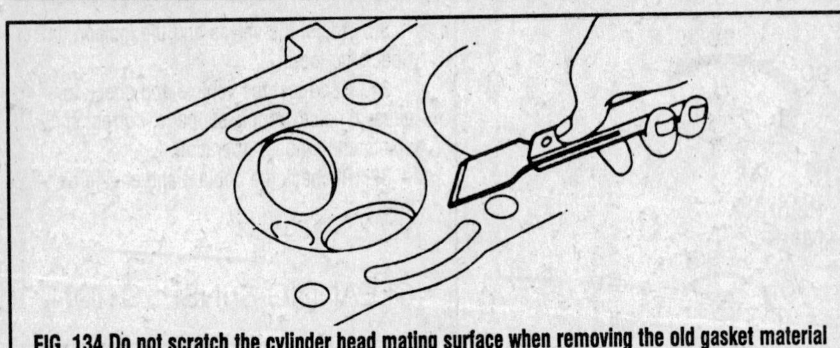

FIG. 134 Do not scratch the cylinder head mating surface when removing the old gasket material

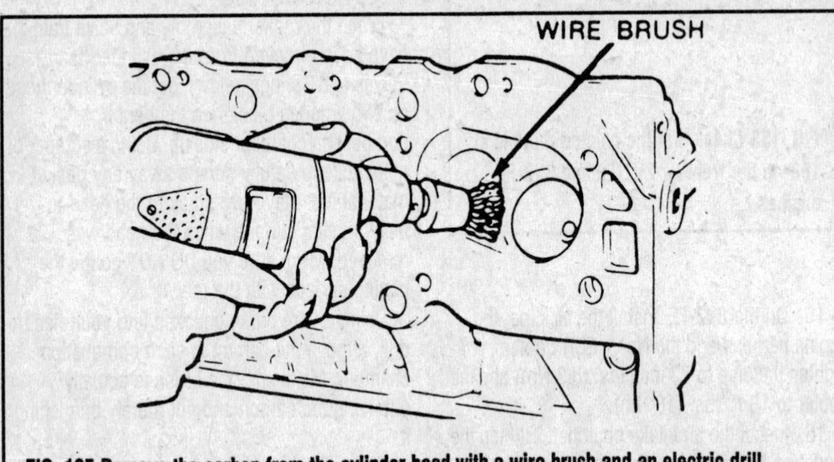

FIG. 135 Remove the carbon from the cylinder head with a wire brush and an electric drill

➡ Before hot-tanking any overhead cam head, check with the machine shop doing the work. Some cam bearings are easily damaged by the hot tank solution.

Finally, go over the entire head with a clean shop rag soaked in solvent to remove any grit, old gasket particles, etc. Blow out the bolt holes, coolant galleys, intake and exhaust ports, valve guides and plug holes with compressed air.

RESURFACING

➧ SEE FIGS. 136, 137

While the head is removed, check the head-to-block mating surface for straightness. If the engine has overheated and blown a head gasket, this must be done as a matter of course. A warped mating surface must be resurfaced (milled); this is done on a milling machine and is quite similar to planing a piece of wood.

Using a precision steel straightedge and a blade-type feeler gauge, check the surface of the head across its length, width and diagonal length as shown in the illustrations. Also check the intake and exhaust manifold mating surfaces and cam cover (all) mating surfaces. If warpage exceed 0.08mm in a 152mm span, or 0.15mm over the total length, the head must be milled. If warpage is highly excessive, the head must be replaced. Again, consult the machine shop operator on head milling limitations.

CYLINDER BLOCK CLEANING

➧ SEE FIG. 138

While the cylinder head is removed, the top of the cylinder block and pistons should also be cleaned. Before you begin, rotate the crankshaft until one or more pistons are flush with the top of the block (on the four cylinder engines, you will either have Nos. 1 and 4 up, or Nos. 2 and 3 up). Carefully stuff clean rags into the cylinders in which the pistons are down. This will help keep grit and carbon chips out during cleaning. Using care not to gouge or scratch the block-to-head mating surface and the piston top(s), clean away any old gasket material with a wire brush and/or scraper. On the piston tops, make sure you are actually removing the carbon and not merely burnishing it.

Remove the rags from the down cylinders after you have wiped the top of the block with a solvent soaked rag. Rotate the crankshaft until the other pistons come up flush with the top of the block, and clean those pistons.

➡ Because you have rotated the crankshaft, you will have to re-time the engine following the procedure listed under the Timing Belt removal procedure. Make sure you wipe out each cylinder thoroughly with a solvent-soaked rag, to remove all traces of grit, before the head is reassembled to the block.

Valves

ADJUSTMENT (AFTER ENGINE SERVICE)

The valves on all engines covered here must be adjusted following any valve train disassembly. Follow the procedure listed in Section 2 for valve adjustment.

REMOVAL & INSTALLATION

➧ SEE FIGS. 139-142

A valve spring compressor is needed to remove the valves and springs; these are available at most auto parts and auto tool shops. A small magnet is very helpful for removing the keepers and spring seats.

Set the head on its side on the bench. Install the spring compressor so that the fixed side of the tool is flat against the valve head in the combustion chamber, and the screw side is against the retainer. Slowly turn the screw in towards the head, compressing the spring. As the spring compresses, the keepers will be revealed; pick them off of the valve stem with the magnet as they are easily fumbled and lost. When the keepers are removed, back the screw out and remove the retainers and springs. Remove the compressor and pull the valves out of the head from the other side. Remove the valve seals by hand and remove the spring seats with the magnet.

Since it is very important that each valve and its spring, retainer, spring seat and keepers is reassembled in its original location, you must keep these parts in order. The best way to do this to to cut either eight or sixteen (four cylinder) or

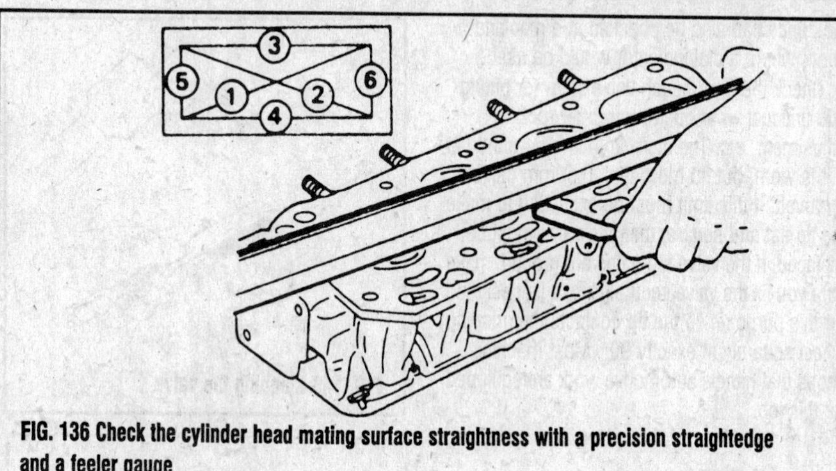

FIG. 136 Check the cylinder head mating surface straightness with a precision straightedge and a feeler gauge

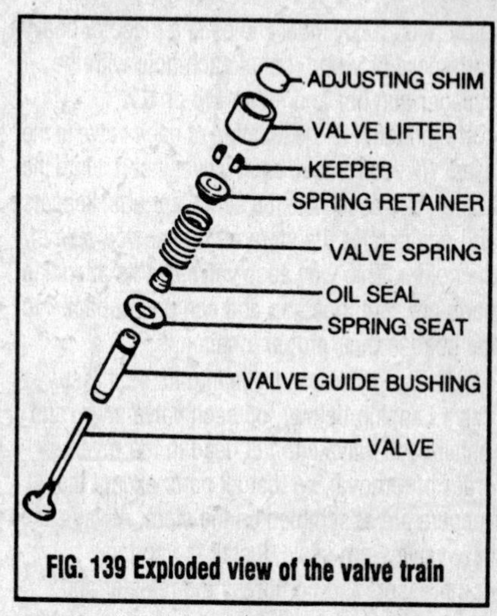

FIG. 139 Exploded view of the valve train

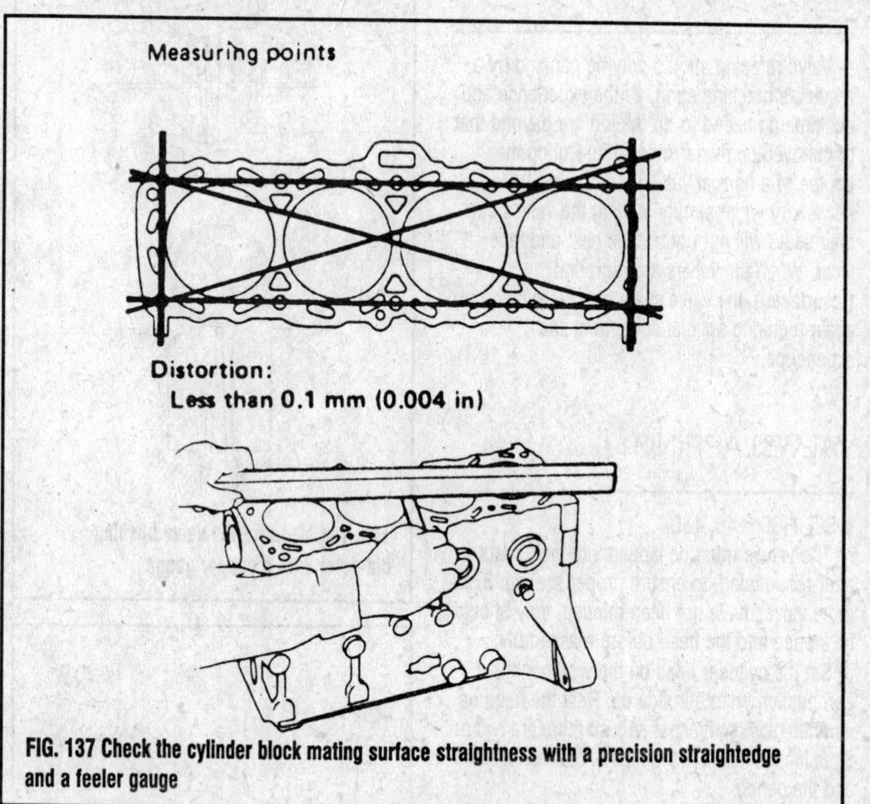

FIG. 137 Check the cylinder block mating surface straightness with a precision straightedge and a feeler gauge

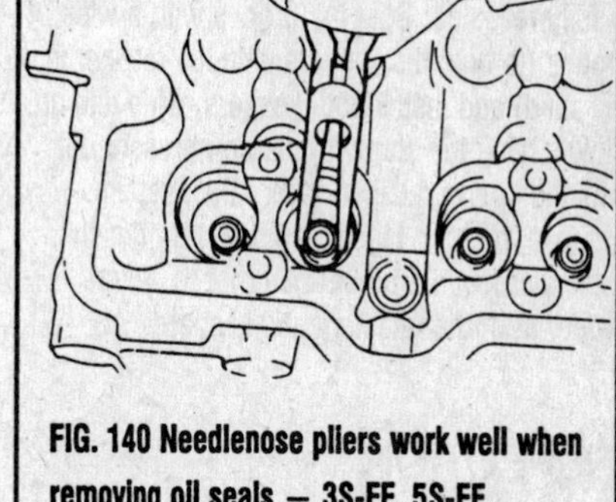
FIG. 140 Needlenose pliers work well when removing oil seals — 3S-FE, 5S-FE, 2VZ-FE and 3VZ-FE engines

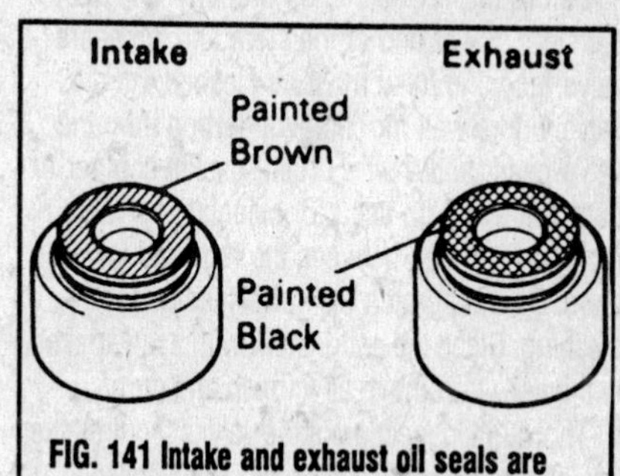

FIG. 141 Intake and exhaust oil seals are color coded — 3S-FE and 5S-FE engines

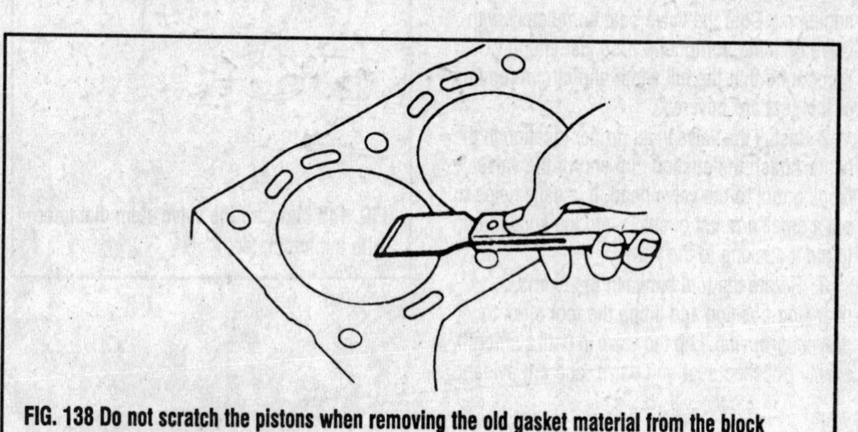
FIG. 138 Do not scratch the pistons when removing the old gasket material from the block

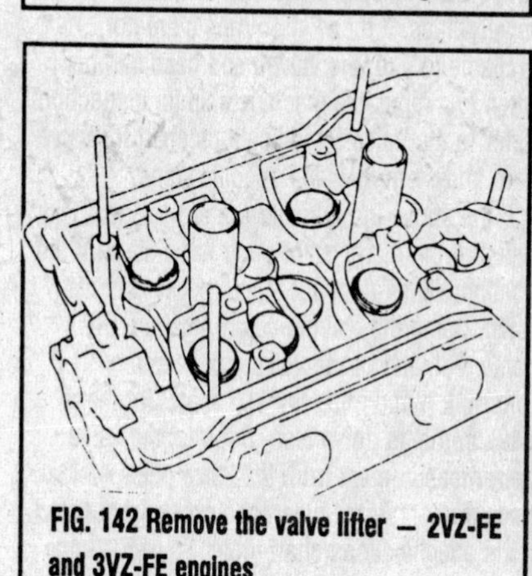
FIG. 142 Remove the valve lifter — 2VZ-FE and 3VZ-FE engines

thirty two (six cylinder) holes in a piece of heavy cardboard or wood. Label each hole with the cylinder number and either **IN** or **EX**, corresponding to the location of each valve in the head. As you remove each valve, insert it into the holder, and assemble the seats, springs, keepers and retainers to the stem on the labeled side of the holder. This way each valve and its attending parts are kept together, and can be put back into the head in their proper locations.

After lapping each valve into its seat (see Valve Lapping below), oil each valve stem, and install each valve into the head in the reverse order of removal, so that all parts except the keepers are assembled on the stem. Always use new valve stem seals. Install the spring compressor, and compress the retainer and spring until the keeper groove on the valve stem is fully revealed. Coat the groove with a wipe of grease (to hold the keepers until the retainer is released) and install both keepers, wide end up. Slowly back the screw of the compressor out until the spring retainer covers the keepers. Remove the tool. Lightly tap the end of each valve stem with a rubber hammer to ensure proper fit of the retainers and keepers.

INSPECTION

➧ SEE FIGS. 143-148

Before the valves can be properly inspected, the stem, lower end of the stem and the entire valve face and head must be cleaned. An old valve works well for chipping carbon from the valve head, and a wire brush, gasket scraper or putty knife can be used for cleaning the valve face and the area between the face and lower stem. Do not scratch the valve face during cleaning. Clean the entire stem with a rag soaked in thinners to remove all varnish and gum.

Thorough inspection of the valves requires the use of a micrometer, and a dial indicator is needed to measure the inside diameter of the valve guides. If these instruments are not available to you, the valves and head can be taken to a reputable machine ship for inspection. Refer to the Valve Specifications chart for valve stem and stem-to-guide specifications.

If the above instruments are at your disposal, measure the diameter of each valve stem at the locations illustrated. Jot these measurements down. Using the dial indicator, measure the inside diameter of the valve guides at their bottom, top and midpoint 90° apart. Jot these measurements down also. Subtract the valve stem measurement from the valve guide inside measurement; if the clearance exceed that listed in the specifications chart under Stem-to-Guide Clearance, replace the valve(s). Stem-to-guide clearance can also be checked at a machine shop, where a dial indicator would be used.

Check the top of each valve stem for pitting and unusual wear due to improper rocker adjustment, etc. The stem tip can be ground flat if it is worn, but no more than 0.50mm can be removed; if this limit must be exceeded to make the tip flat and square, then the valve must be replaced. If the valve stem tips are ground, make sure you fix the valve securely into a jig designed for this purpose, so the tip contacts the grinding wheel squarely at exactly 90°. Most machine shops that handle automotive work are equipped for this job.

REFACING

Valve refacing should only be handled by a reputable machine shop, as the experience and equipment needed to do the job are beyond that of the average owner/mechanic. During the course of a normal valve job, refacing is necessary when simply lapping the valves into their seats will not correct the seat and face wear. When the valves are reground (resurfaced), the valve seats must also be recut, again requiring special equipment and experience.

VALVE LAPPING

➧ SEE FIGS. 149, 150

The valves must be lapped into their seats after resurfacing, to ensure proper sealing. Even if the valves have not been refaced, they should be lapped into the head before reassembly.

Set the cylinder head on the workbench, combustion chamber side up. Rest the head on wooden blocks on either end, so there are two or three inches between the tops of the valve guides and the bench.

1. Lightly lube the valve stem with clean engine oil. Coat the valve seat completely with valve grinding compound. Use just enough compound that the full width and circumference of the seat are covered.
2. Install the valve in its proper location in the head. Attach the suction cup end of the valve lapping tool to the valve head. It usually helps to put a small amount of saliva into the suction cup to aid it sticking to the valve.
3. Rotate the tool between the palms, changing position and lifting the tool often to prevent grooving. Lap the valve in until a smooth, evenly polished seat and valve face are evident.

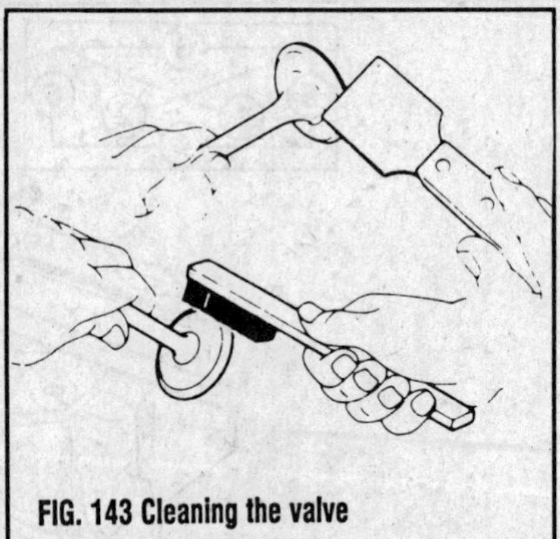

FIG. 143 Cleaning the valve

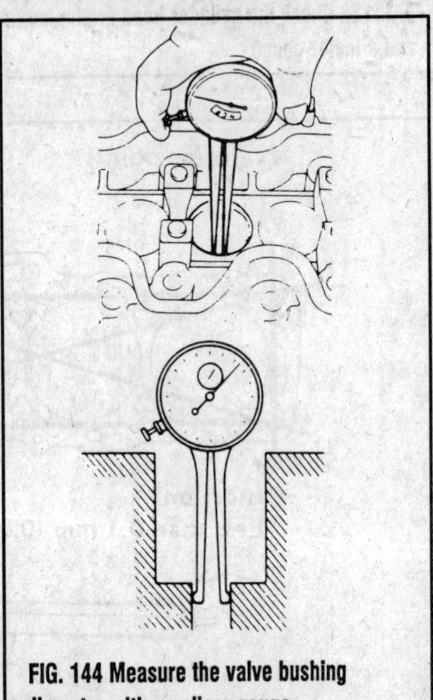

FIG. 144 Measure the valve bushing diameter with a caliper gauge

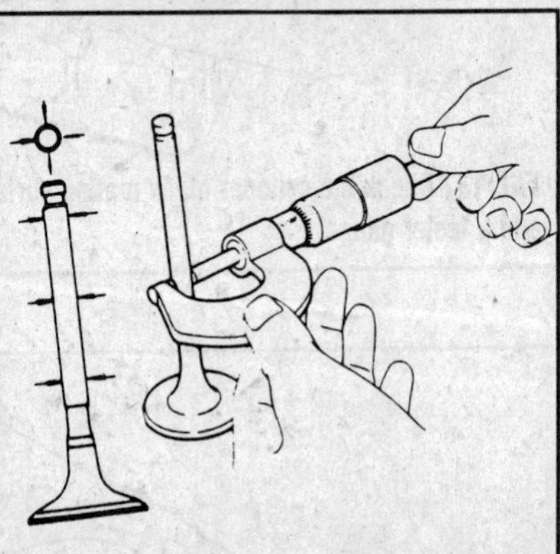

FIG. 145 Measure the valve stem diameter with a micrometer

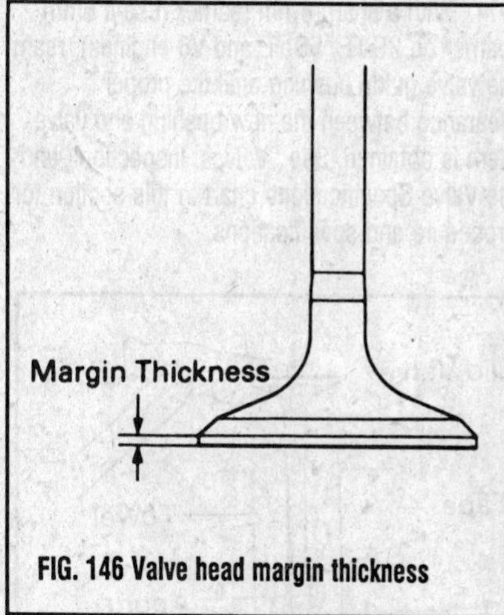

FIG. 146 Valve head margin thickness

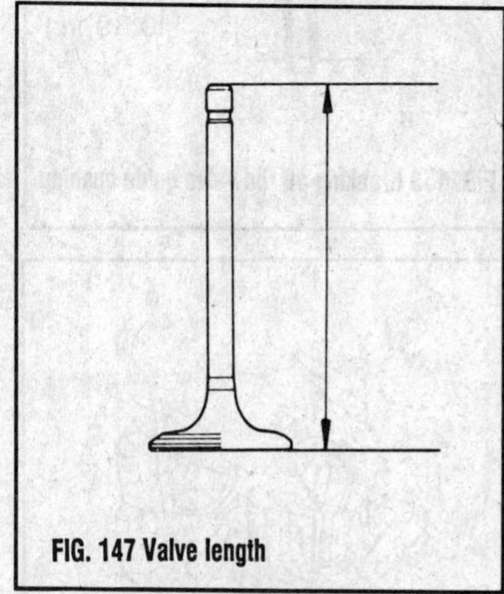

FIG. 147 Valve length

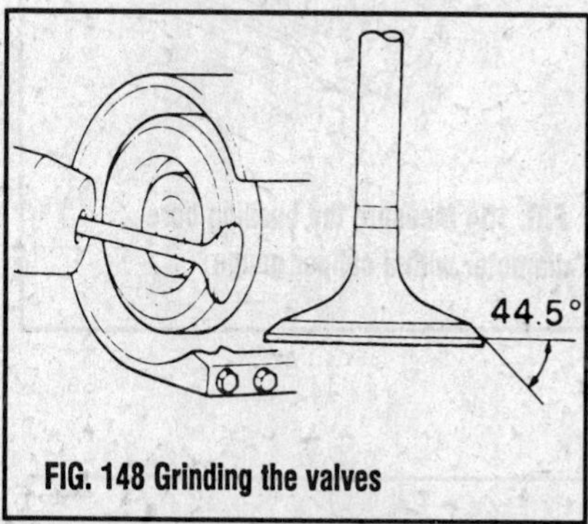

FIG. 148 Grinding the valves

4. Remove the valve from the head. Wipe away all traces of grinding compound from the valve face and seat. Wipe out the port with a solvent soaked rag, and swab out the valve guide with a piece of solvent soaked rag to make sure there are no traces of compound grit inside the guide. This cleaning is important.

5. Proceed through the remaining valves, one at a time. Make sure the valve faces, seats, cylinder ports and valve guides are clean before reassembling the valve train.

FIG. 149 Lapping the valves by hand

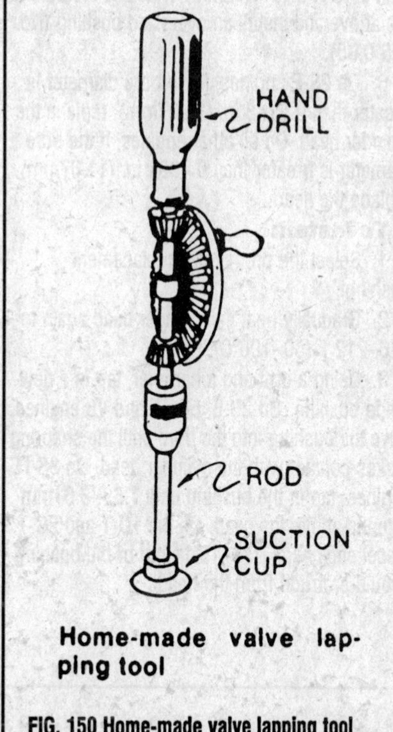

FIG. 150 Home-made valve lapping tool

Valve Springs

REMOVAL & INSTALLATION

Valve spring removal and installation is part of the "Valves, Removal and Installation" procedure covered in this section.

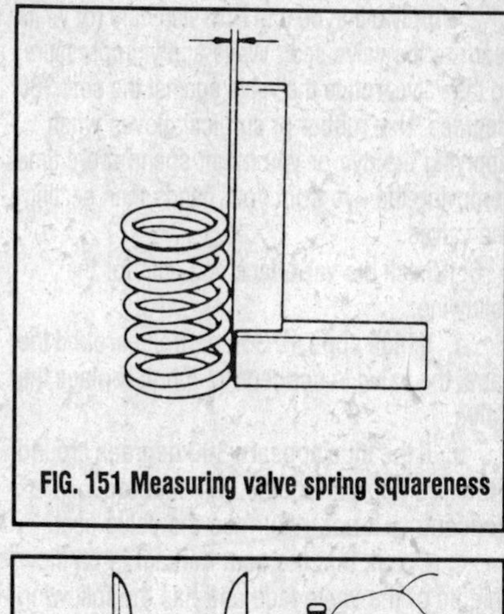

FIG. 151 Measuring valve spring squareness

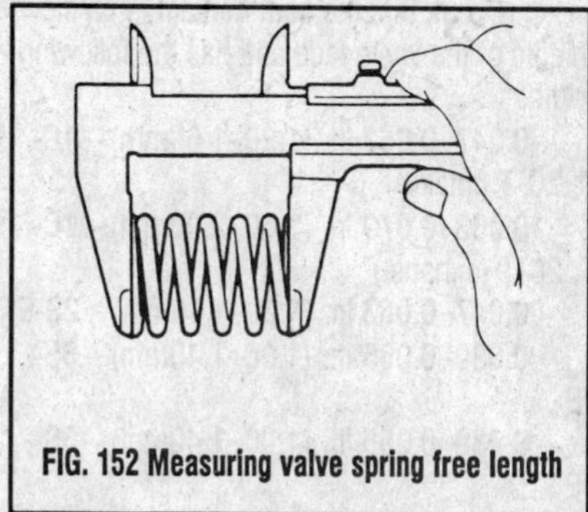

FIG. 152 Measuring valve spring free length

INSPECTION

➧ SEE FIGS. 151, 152

Valve spring squareness, length and tension should be checked while the valve train is disassembled. Place each valve spring on a flat surface next to a steel square. Measure the length of the spring, and rotate it against the edge of the square to measure distortion. If spring length varies (by comparison) by more than 1.6mm or if distortion exceeds 1.6mm, replace the spring.

Spring tension must be checked on a spring tester. Springs used on most engines should be within one pound of each other when tested at their specified installed heights.

Valve Seats

INSPECTION AND CLEANING

All Engines

1. Using a 45 degree carbide cutter, resurface the valve seats lightly removing only enough of the seat metal to clean it.

2. Apply a thin coat of Prussian blue (or white lead) to the valve seat. While applying pressure to the valve, rotate the valve against the seat 360 degrees. Use rubber or surgical gloves when applying the dye or you might spend more time removing the dye from your hands than seating the valves.

3. Check the valve face and seat for the following:

a. If blue appears 360 degrees around the face, the valve is concentric. If not, replace the valve.

b. If the blue appears 360 degrees around the valve seat, the guide and seat are concentric. If not, resurface the valve seat.

c. Check that the seat contact is on the middle of the valve face and has the following widths:

0.047–0.063 in. (1.20–1.60mm) — 1C-T, 2C-T (intake)

0.063–0.079 in. (1.60–2.00mm) — 1C-T, 2C-T (exhaust)

0.047–0.063 in. (1.20–1.60mm) — 2S-E

0.039–0.055 in. (1.00–1.40mm) — 3S-FE

0.039–0.055 in. (1.00–1.40mm) — 5S-FE

0.039–0.055 in. (1.00–1.40mm) — 2VZ-FE

0.039–0.055 in. (1.00–1.40mm) — 3VZ-FE

4. If the valve seat width is not as specified, it must be resurfaced as follows:

a. If the seating is too high on the valve face, use 30 and 45 degree cutters to correct the seat.

b. If the seating is too low on the valve face, use 60 and 45 degree cutters to correct the seat. On 3S-FE and 5S-FE engines, use 75 and 45 degree cutters to correct the seat.

c. Hand lap the valve and valve seat using an abrasive lapping compound.

d. Clean the valve and valve seat after lapping.

Valve Guides

REMOVAL & INSTALLATION

➧ SEE FIG. 153-155

1. Gradually heat the cylinder head in water to 176-212°F (80-100°C), before beginning the replacement procedure.

2. On 2S-E engines, use a brass rod and hammer to break the valve guide off above its snapring.

3. Allow the head to cool. Using SST. No. 09201-70010 (SST No. 09201-60011 for diesel engines) or equivalent (a drift), tap out the guide bushing from the bore.

4. Using a caliper gauge, measure the bushing bore diameter of the cylinder head. The guide bore diameter range should be as follows:

1C-T, 2C-T — 0.5138–0.5148 in. (13.050–13.077mm)

2S-E — 0.5138–0.5148 in. (13.050–13.077mm)

3S-FE, 5S-FE — 0.4350–0.4361 in. (11.05–11.07mm)

2VZ-FE, 3VZ-FE — 0.4350–0.4361 in. (11.05–11.07mm) If the diameter falls within the given ranges, use the standard size replacement bushing (No. STD).

5. On 2S-E, 2C-T and 1C-T engines, if the bushing bore diameter is more than 0.5129 in. (13.02mm) machine the bore to the above and install an oversized bushing (No. O/S 0.05). On all other engines, if the bushing bore is greater than 0.4341 in. (11.02mm), machine the bore to the above and install an oversized bushing (No. O/S 0.05).

6. On 2S-E engines, if the bore diameter is greater than 0.5148 in. (13.07mm), replace the cylinder head. On all other engines, if the bore diameter is greater than 0.4361 in. (11.07mm), replace the head.

To Install:

1. Select the proper size replacement bushing.

2. Gradually heat the cylinder head again to 176–212°F (80–100°C).

3. Using a drift and a hammer, tap in a new guide bushing. On 2S-E, 5S-FE and V6 engines, drive the bushing into the bore until the snapring makes contact with the cylinder head. On 3S-FE engines, tap in the bushing until 7.69–8.61mm extends above the head. On the 1C-T and 2C-T diesel engines, 17.30–18.11mm of the bushing should protrude from the head.

4. With a sharp 8mm reamer (use a 6mm reamer on 3S-FE, 5S-FE and V6 engines), ream the valve guide bushing until the proper clearance between the new bushing and valve stem is obtained. See "Valves, Inspection" and the Valve Specifications chart in this section for procedure and specifications.

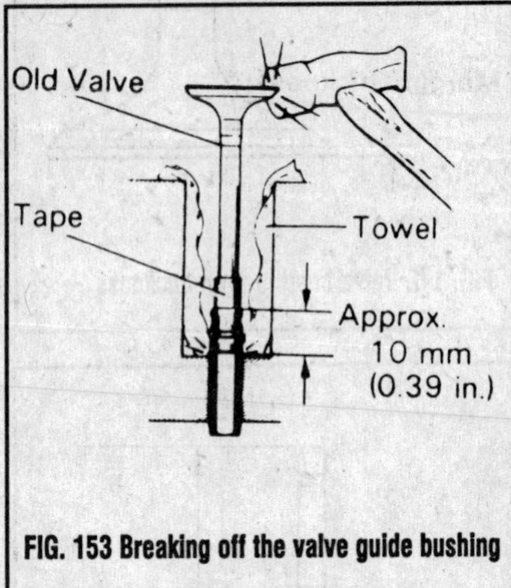

FIG. 153 Breaking off the valve guide bushing

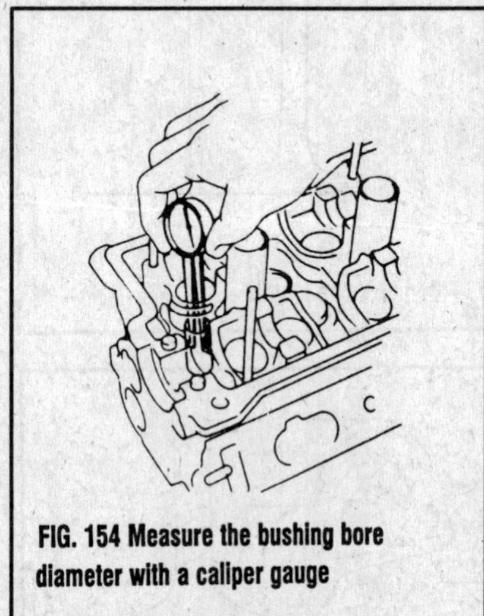

FIG. 154 Measure the bushing bore diameter with a caliper gauge

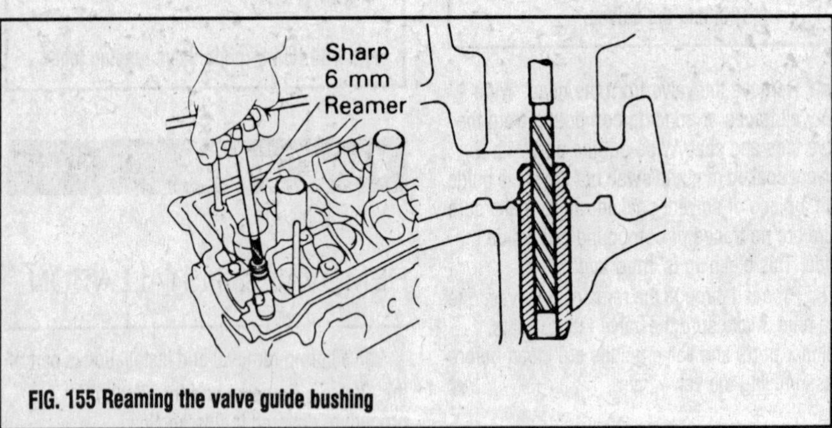

FIG. 155 Reaming the valve guide bushing

Oil Pan

REMOVAL & INSTALLATION

CAUTION

The EPA warns that prolonged contact with used engine oil may cause a number of skin disorders, including cancer! You should make every effort to minimize your exposure to used engine oil. Protective gloves should be worn when changing the oil. Wash your hands and any other exposed skin areas as soon as possible after exposure to used engine oil. Soap and water, or waterless hand cleaner should be used.

Diesel Engines

➧ SEE FIG. 157

1. Raise and support the front end of jackstands.
2. Drain the oil.
3. Remove the engine undercovers.
4. Remove the timing belt.
5. Remove the lower idler pulley and crankshaft pulley.
6. With the engine supported by a hoist or jack, remove the center crossmember.
7. Remove the nineteen bolts and three nuts from the oil pan.
8. Using a small prybar, separate the oil pan from the cylinder block.

To Install:

1. Using a gasket scraper and a wire brush, remove all the old packing material from the oil pan and cylinder block gasket surfaces. Wipe the oil pan interior with a rag. Clean the contact surfaces with a non-residue type solvent.
2. Apply a thin 1/8" bead of No. 102 seal packing or equivalent to the oil pan as shown in the illustration. To ensure the proper size bead, cut the nozzle on the tube.

➡ Avoid applying too much sealant to the oil pan. The oil pan must be assembled to the block within three minutes after the sealant is applied. If not, the sealant must be removed and re-applied.

3. Place the oil pan against the block and install the bolts and nuts. Torque the nuts and bolts to 5 ft. lbs. (7 Nm).
4. Install the center engine mounting member. Torque the center, front and rear mounting bolts to 29 ft. lbs. (39 Nm).
5. Install the lower idler and crankshaft pulleys.
6. Install the timing belt.
7. Lower the engine and disconnect the hoist.
8. Install the engine under covers.
9. Lower the vehicle. Refill the engine oil. Start the engine and inspect for leaks. Recheck the oil level.
10. Check and adjust the engine and maximum idle speeds.

Gasoline Engines

➧ SEE FIG. 156, 157

1. Raise the support the front end on jackstands.
2. Drain the oil and remove the dipstick.
3. Remove the right engine undercover or covers (exc. 2S-E).
4. On all engines except the 2S-E, disconnect the exhaust pipe, remove the lower suspension crossmember, engine mounting center member and the stiffener plate.
5. Remove the three nuts and eighteen bolts (there are seventeen bolts and two nuts on the 3S-FE and 5S-FE; fifteen bolts and four nuts on the V6) from the oil pan flange.
6. Using SST No. 09032-00100 or equivalent (prybar), separate the oil pan from the cylinder block.
7. Lower the oil pan to the ground being careful not to damage the oil pan flange.

To Install:

1. Using a gasket scraper and a wire brush, remove all the old packing material from the oil pan and cylinder block gasket surfaces. Wipe the oil pan interior with a rag. Clean the contact surfaces with a non-residue type solvent.
2. Apply a thin 1/8" bead of No. 102 seal packing or equivalent to the oil pan as shown in the illustration. To ensure the proper size bead, cut the nozzle on the tube.

➡ Avoid applying too much sealant to the oil pan. The oil pan must be assembled to the block within three minutes after the sealant is applied. If not, the sealant must be removed and re-applied.

3. Place the oil pan against the block and install the bolts and nuts. Torque the nuts and bolts to 4 ft. lbs. (5.4 Nm)

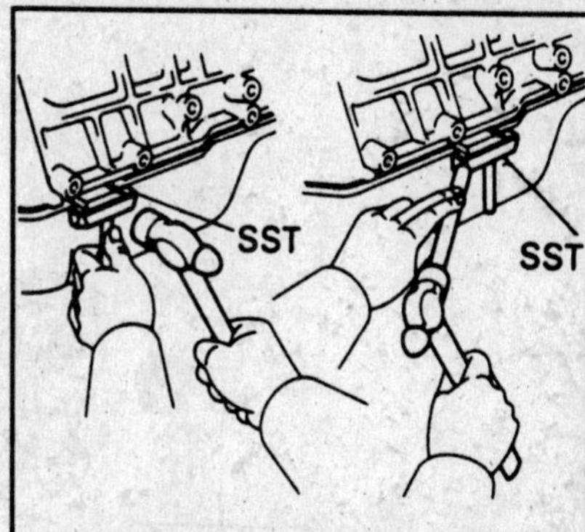

FIG. 156 Insert the blade of the special tool between the oil pan and cylinder block to cut the sealant

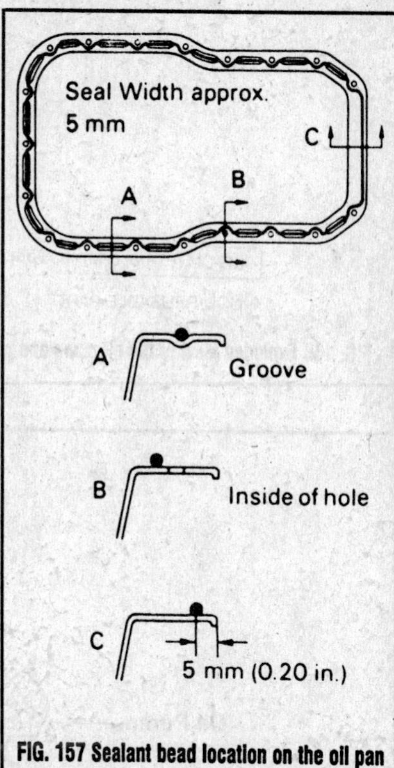

FIG. 157 Sealant bead location on the oil pan

4. Install the stiffener plate and torque the mounting bolts to 27 ft. lbs. (37 Nm). Install the engine mounting center member. Connect the exhaust pipe.
5. Install the right engine cover or covers.
6. Fill the engine with oil to the proper level.
7. Start the engine and check for leaks. Recheck the engine oil level.

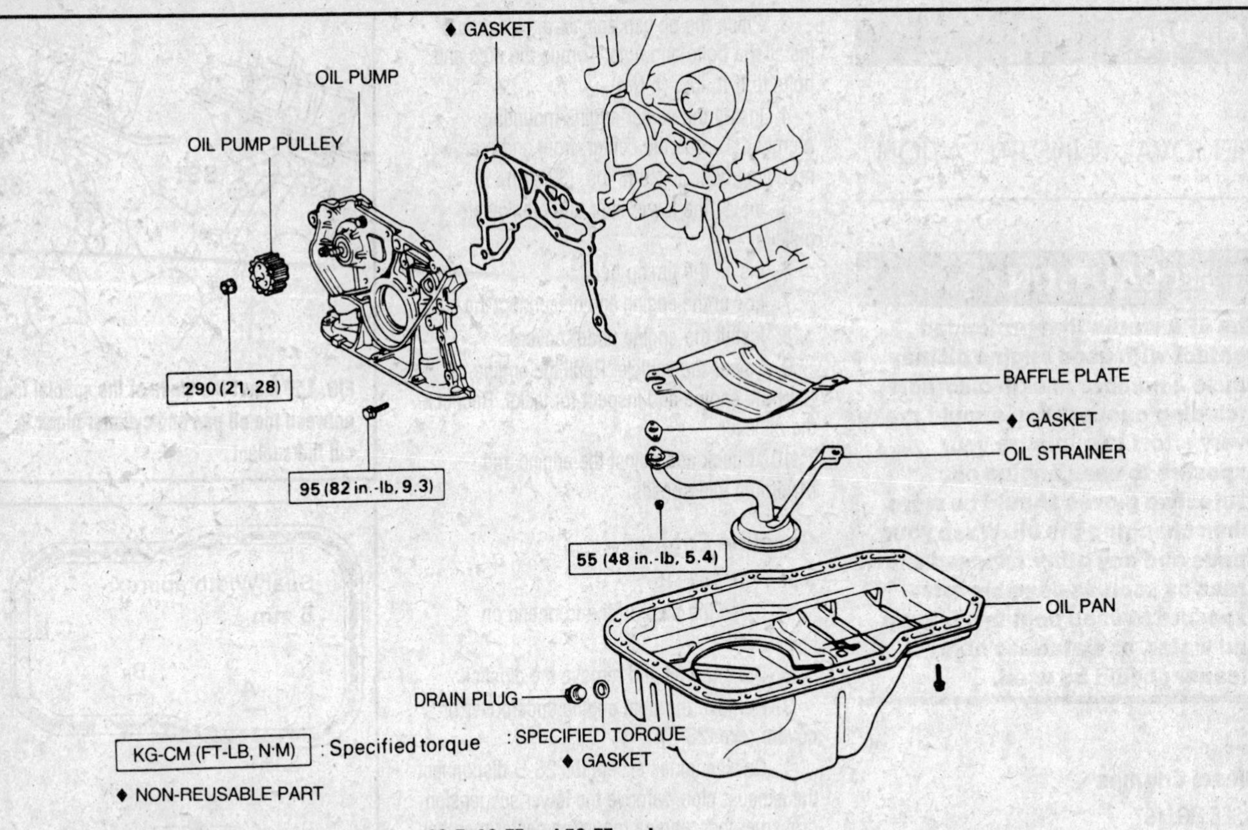

FIG. 158 Exploded view of the oil pump and pan — 2S-E, 3S-FE and 5S-FE engines

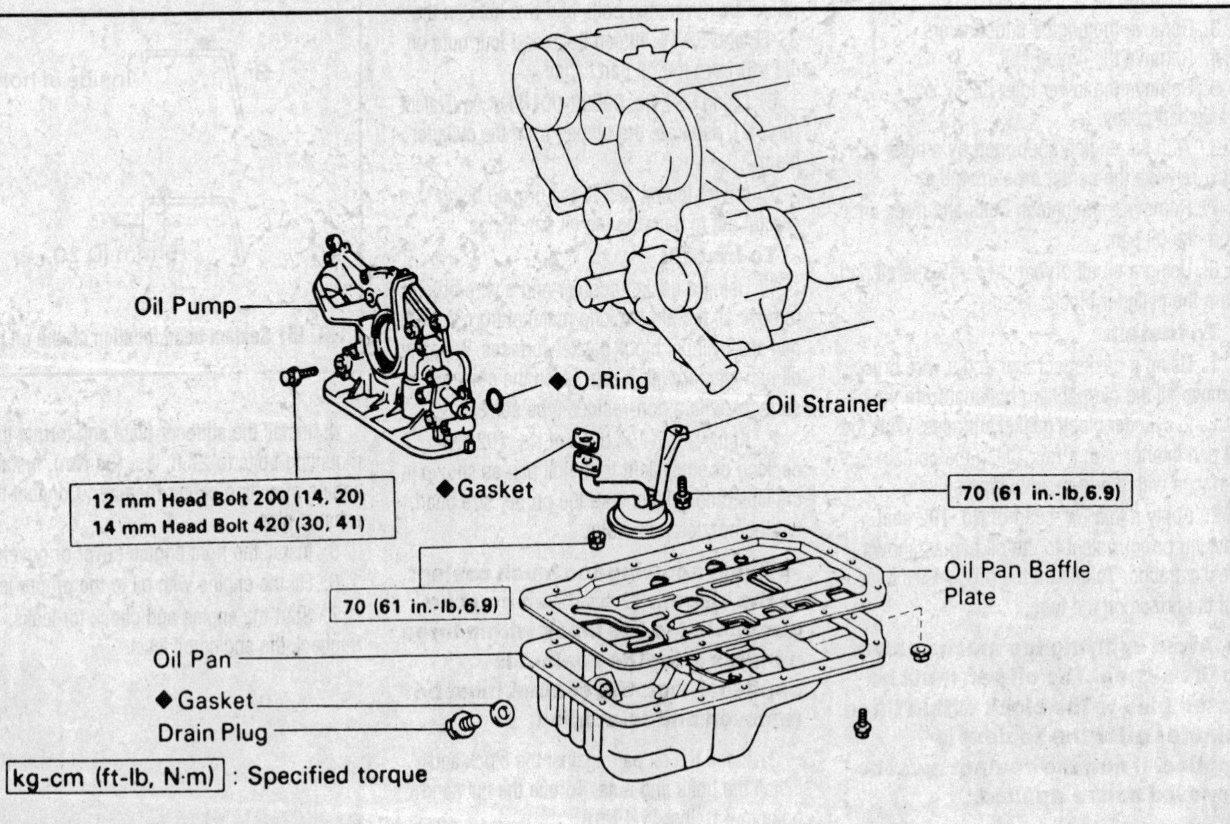

FIG. 159 Exploded view of the oil pump and pan — 2VZ-FE and 3VZ-FE engines

Oil Pump

REMOVAL & INSTALLATION

Diesel Engines

➧ SEE FIGS. 160, 161

1. Remove the oil pan.
2. Remove the two nuts, bolts, gasket and oil strainer.
3. Remove the eleven bolts and alternator stay. Tap the oil pump loose from the block with a soft-faced or rubber mallet.
4. Group the bolts according to length and set them aside (you'll see why later!).

✽✽ WARNING

During removal, be careful not to damage the crankshaft oil seal with the crankshaft Woodruff key. Do not drop the oil pump rotor.

5. Remove the O-ring seal from the oil pump groove and purchase a new one.

To install:

1. With a gasket scraper or wire brush, remove the old packing material from the oil pump and cylinder block contact surfaces.
2. Place a new O-ring seal into the oil pump groove.
3. Apply No. 102 packing sealant to the oil pump body indicated by the dotted line on the accompanying figure.

➡ There are three different size oil pump mounting bolts: 20mm, 30mm and 32mm. Make sure the bolts are installed in their proper locations (use the figure as a guide).

4. Attach the oil pump and alternator stay to the block with the bolts. Torque the bolts to 13 ft. lbs. (18 Nm).
5. Install the strainer with the two bolts, two nuts and new gasket. Torque the bolts to 9 ft. lbs. (13 Nm) and the nuts to 5 ft. lbs. (9 Nm).
6. Install the oil pan and refill the engine oil.
7. Start the engine and inspect for leaks.
8. Recheck the engine oil level.

Gasoline Engines

➧ SEE FIGS. 162-164

1. Remove the oil pan.
2. Remove the oil pan baffle plate.
3. Remove the oil strainer and O-ring.
4. Remove the timing belt. On V6 engines, remove the No. 1 idler and the crankshaft timing pulleys.
5. On the V6, remove the alternator and the A/C compressor. Also, remove the compressor bracket and the power steering pump adjusting bar.
6. Remove the twelve (nine – V6) oil pump retaining bolts.
7. With a soft-faced hammer or rubber mallet, tap the oil pump loose from the block.
8. Remove the oil pump gasket and replace a new one.

To install:

1. Clean the cylinder block and oil pump gasket contact surfaces.
2. Place a new gasket onto the cylinder block on 4 cyl. engines. On the V6, draw a 2–3mm bead of seal packing as shown in the illustration (you've got 5 min.).
3. Position the oil pump onto the block and install the bolts. On the V6 engines, insert a new O-ring and then engage the spline teeth on the drive gear with the large teeth on the end of the crankshaft.

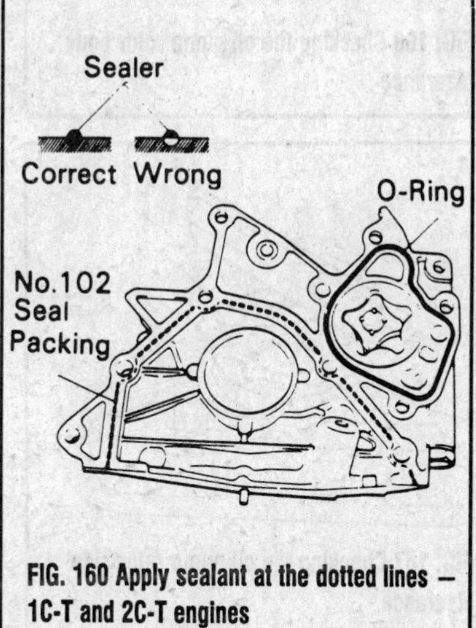

FIG. 160 Apply sealant at the dotted lines – 1C-T and 2C-T engines

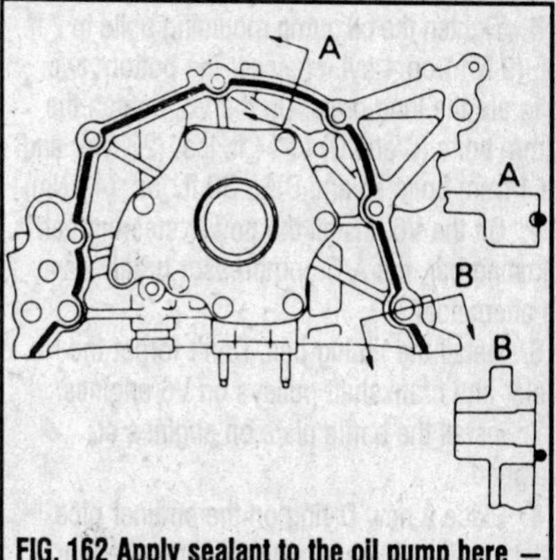

FIG. 162 Apply sealant to the oil pump here – 2VZ-FE and 3VZ-FE engines

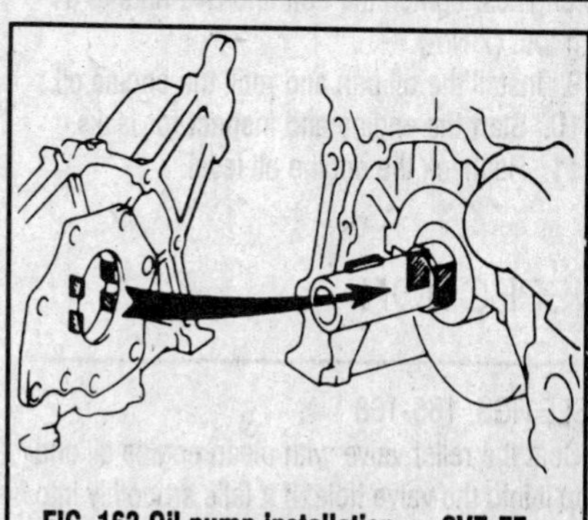

FIG. 163 Oil pump installation – 2VZ-FE and 3VZ-FE engines

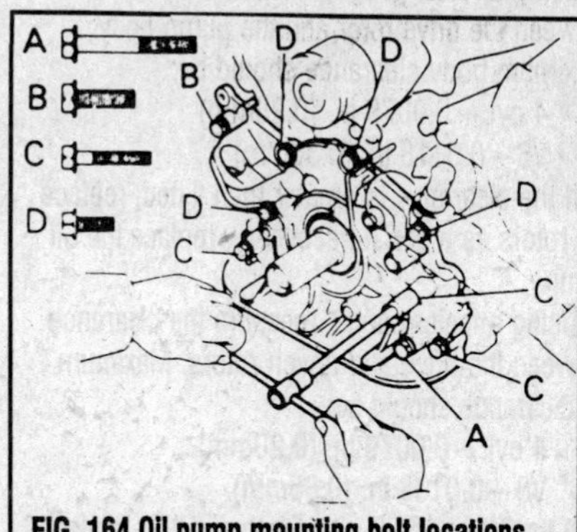

FIG. 164 Oil pump mounting bolt locations – 2VZ-FE and 3VZ-FE engines

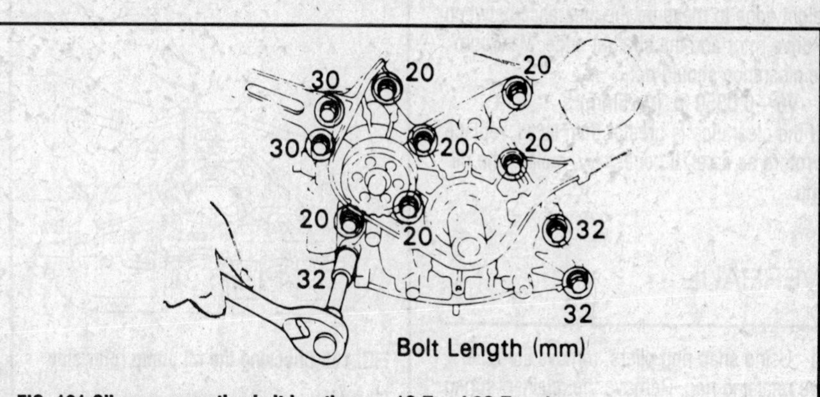

FIG. 161 Oil pump mounting bolt locations – 1C-T and 2C-T engines

4. Tighten the oil pump mounting bolts to 7 ft. lbs. (9 Nm) on 4 cyl. engines; the bottom two bolts are the long ones. On the V6, tighten the 12mm bolts (C and D) to 14 ft. lbs. (20 Nm) and the 14mm bolts (A and B) to 30 ft. lbs. (41 Nm)

5. On the V6, install the power steering belt adjusting bar, the A/C compressor bracket and the alternator.

6. Install the timing belt. Don't forget the No. 1 idler and crankshaft pulleys on V6 engines.

7. Install the baffle plate on engines so equipped.

8. Place a new O-ring on the strainer pipe outlet and install the strainer. Tighten the four bolts on 4 cyl. engines to 4 ft. lbs. (5.5 Nm). On V6 engines, tighten the bolt and two nuts to 61 inch lbs. (7 Nm).

9. Install the oil pan and refill the engine oil.

10. Start the engine and inspect for leaks.

11. Recheck the engine oil level.

INSPECTION

➧ SEE FIGS. 165-168

Coat the relief valve with clean engine oil and drop it into the valve hole. If it falls smoothly into the hole under its own weight, its OK. If not, replace the valve or pump.

Using a feeler gauge, measure the clearance between the drive rotor and the pump body. Maximum body clearance should be:

4 cyl.—0.0079 in. (0.20mm)
V6—0.0118 in. (0.30mm)

If the clearance is greater than listed, replace the rotors as a set. If necessary, replace the oil pump.

Using a feeler gauge, measure the clearance between the drive and driven rotors. Maximum tip clearance should be:

4 cyl.—0.0079 in. (0.20mm)
V6—0.0138 in. (0.35mm)

If the clearance is greater than listed, replace the rotors as a set.

On V6 engines only, use a feeler gauge and a straight edge to measure the clearance between the drive rotor and the straight edge. Maximum side clearance should be:

V6—0.0059 in. (0.15mm)

If the clearance is greater than listed, replace the rotors as a set. If necessary, replace the oil pump.

OVERHAUL

1. Using snap ring pliers, remove the relief valve retaining ring. Remove the retainer, spring and valve.

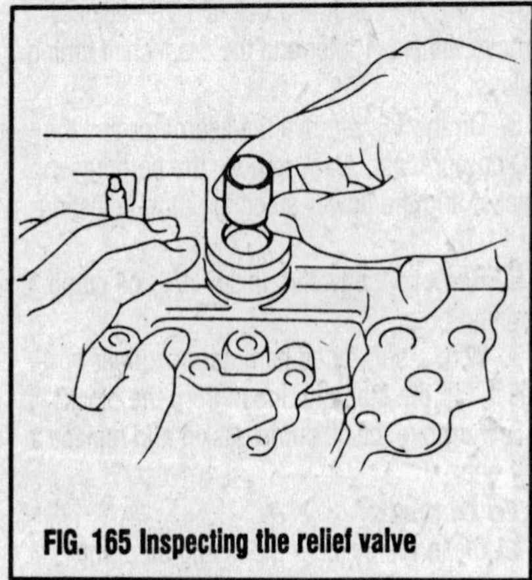

FIG. 165 Inspecting the relief valve

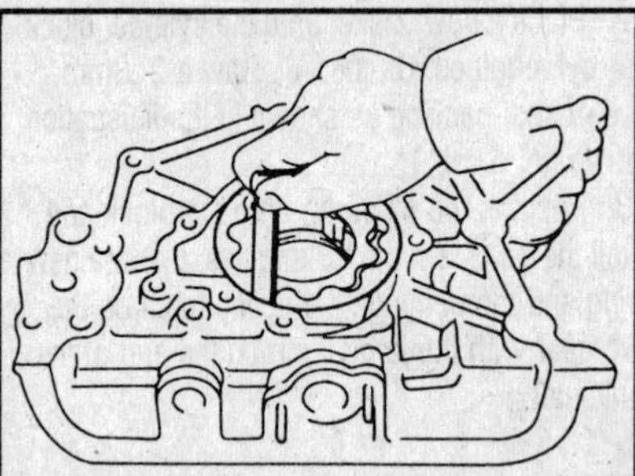

FIG. 166 Checking the oil pump rotor body clearance

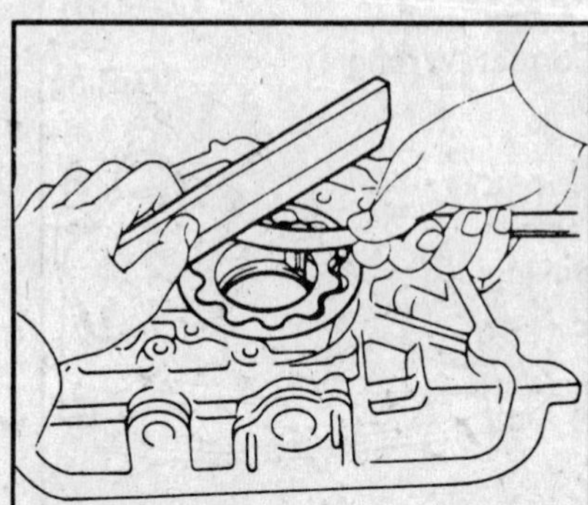

FIG. 167 Checking the oil pump rotor side clearance

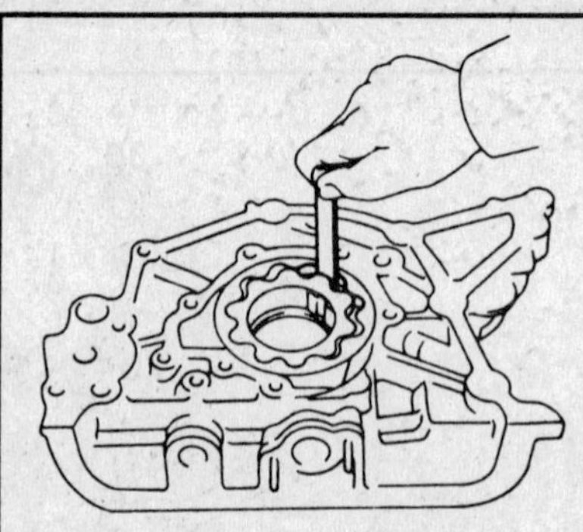

FIG. 168 Checking the oil pump rotor side clearance

2. Loosen the mounting screws and lift off the pump body cover. Lift out the drive and driven rotors as a set.

3. Position the rotor set in the body. On V6 engines, make sure that the marks face upward.

4. Check all clearances and then install the pump body cover over the rotor set. Tighten the screws to 78 inch lbs. (8.8 Nm).

5. Install the relief valve with its spring and retainer and then pop the snap ring into place. On the 3VZ-FE, tighten the plug to 27 ft. lbs. (37 Nm).

Oil Cooler and Relief Valve

REMOVAL & INSTALLATION

CAUTION

When draining the coolant, keep in mind that cats and dogs are attracted by the ethylene glycol antifreeze, and are quite likely to drink any that is left in an uncovered container or in puddles on the ground. This will prove fatal in sufficient quantity. Always drain the coolant into a sealable container. Coolant should be reused unless it is contaminated or several years old.

1C-T and 2C-T Engines

➧ SEE FIG. 169

1. Open the engine and radiator drain cocks and drain the cooling system.

2. Disconnect the oil pressure switch connector and remove the oil pressure switch.

3. Remove the two union bolts from the oil cooler.

4. Disconnect the two water hoses and remove the oil cooler and the two O-rings. Discard the O-rings and purchase new ones.

5. Remove the oil filter.

6. Disconnect the oil hose from the oil filter bracket.

7. Remove the five bolts, filter bracket and O-ring. Discard the O-ring and purchase a new one.

8. Unbolt and remove the exhaust manifold stay.

9. Loosen and unscrew the relief valve.

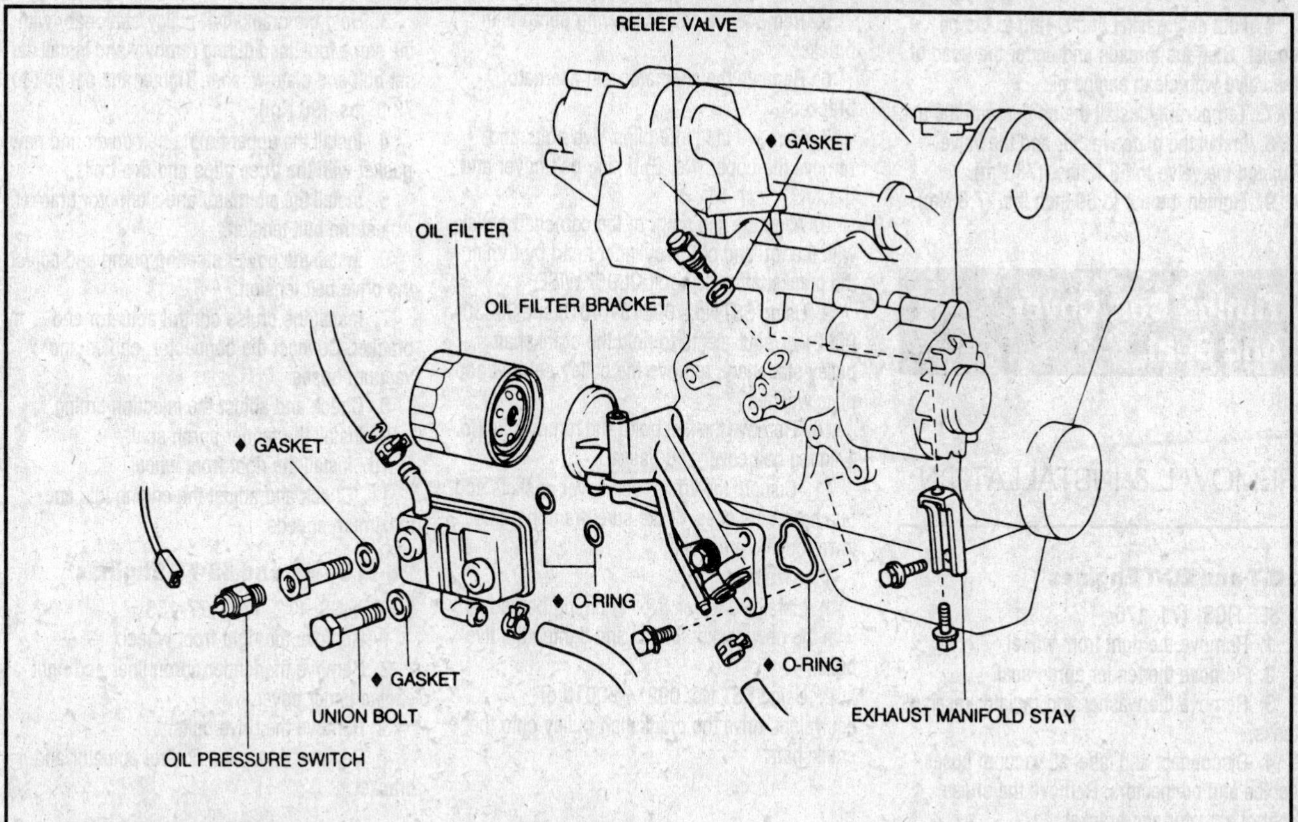

FIG. 169 Oil cooler and relief valve components — 1C-T and 2C-T engines

To Install:

1. Install and tighten the relief valve.
2. Install the exhaust manifold stay.
3. Place a new O-ring into the filter bracket and attach the bracket to the engine with the five bolts. Tighten the bolts to 27 ft. lbs. (37 Nm).
4. Connect the oil hose to the filter bracket.
5. Install a new oil filter.
6. Place two new O-rings in the oil cooler and connect the two water hoses.
7. Install the oil cooler with the two union bolts. Tighten the bolts to 38 ft. lbs. (49 Nm).
8. Install the oil pressure switch and connect the switch connector.
9. Fill the cooling system to the proper level with a good brand of ethylene glycol coolant.
10. Start the engine and check for leaks.
11. Check the engine oil and coolant levels and add as necessary.

5S-FE Engines

➧ SEE FIG. 170

1. Drain the engine oil and coolant.
2. Remove the oil filter.
3. Disconnect the two water by-pass hoses at the oil cooler.
4. Unscrew the relief valve and remove the plate washer.
5. Remove the nut and spin out the cooler. Remove the gasket and O-ring.

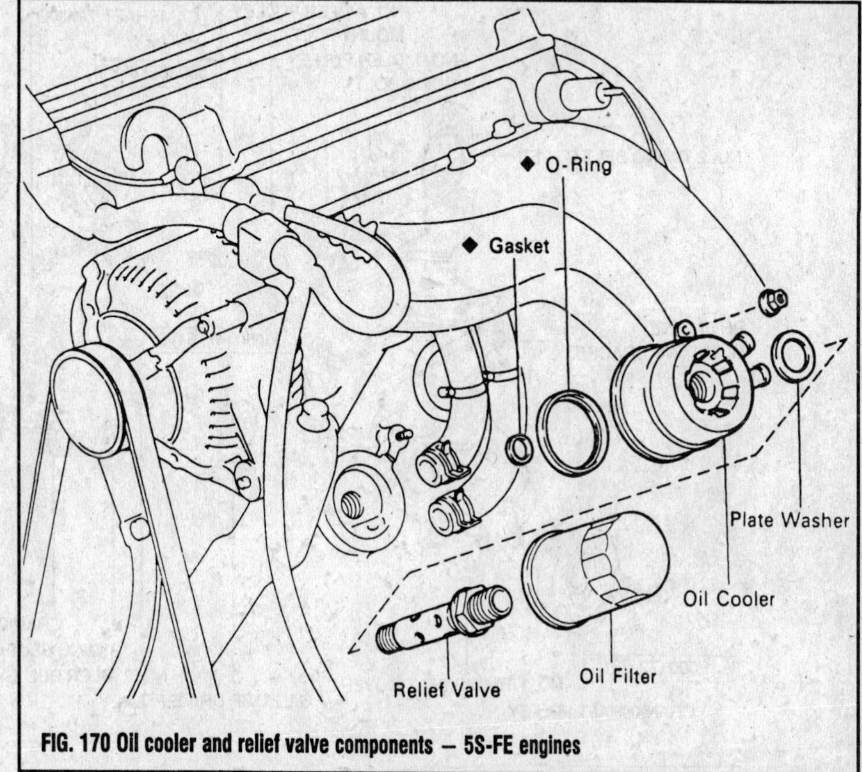

FIG. 170 Oil cooler and relief valve components — 5S-FE engines

6. Fit a new gasket and O-ring to the oil cooler. Coat the threads and under the head of the valve with clean engine oil.
7. Temporarily install the cooler with the nut.
8. Install the plate washer and the valve. Tighten the valve to 58 ft. lbs. (78 Nm).
9. Tighten the nut to 69 inch lbs. (7.8 Nm).

Timing Belt Cover And Seal

REMOVAL & INSTALLATION

1C-T and 2C-T Engines

➧ SEE FIGS. 171, 176

1. Remove the right front wheel.
2. Remove the fender apron seal.
3. Remove the washer and radiator reservoir tanks.
4. Disconnect and label all vacuum hoses, cables and connectors. Remove the cruise control actuator and bracket.
5. Remove the power steering pump with bracket.
6. Remove the alternator and alternator bracket.
7. Remove the three clips, five bolts and remove the upper (No. 2) timing belt cover and gasket.
8. Align the line mark of the camshaft pulley with the top end of the cylinder head by turning the crankshaft pulley bolt CLOCKWISE.
9. Using SST No.s 09213-14010 and 09330-00021 or equivalents to hold the crankshaft pulley stationary, remove the pulley set bolt and plate washer.
10. Remove the five bolts and remove the No. 1 timing belt cover and gasket.
11. Discard the timing belt cover gaskets and purchase new ones. Make sure the upper and lower covers are clean.

To Install:

1. Install the lower (No. 1) timing belt cover with the new gasket. Install and tighten the five bolts.
2. Using SST No. 09214-60010 or equivalent, drive the crankshaft pulley onto the crankshaft.
3. Hold the crankshaft pulley stationary with the same tool used during removal and install the set bolt and plate washer. Tighten the set bolt to 72 ft. lbs. (98 Nm).
4. Install the upper timing belt cover and new gasket with the three clips and five bolts.
5. Install the alternator and alternator bracket. Adjust the belt tension.
6. Install the power steering pump and adjust the drive belt tension.
7. Install the cruise control actuator and bracket. Connect the connector, cables and vacuum hoses.
8. Check and adjust the injection timing.
9. Install the fender apron seal.
10. Install the right front wheel.
11. Check and adjust the engine idle and maximum speeds.

2S-E, 3S-FE and 5S-FE Engines

➧ SEE FIGS. 172, 173, 177-186

1. Remove the right front wheel.
2. Remove the fender apron liner and right engine under cover.
3. Remove the drive belts.
4. Remove the cruise control actuator and bracket.

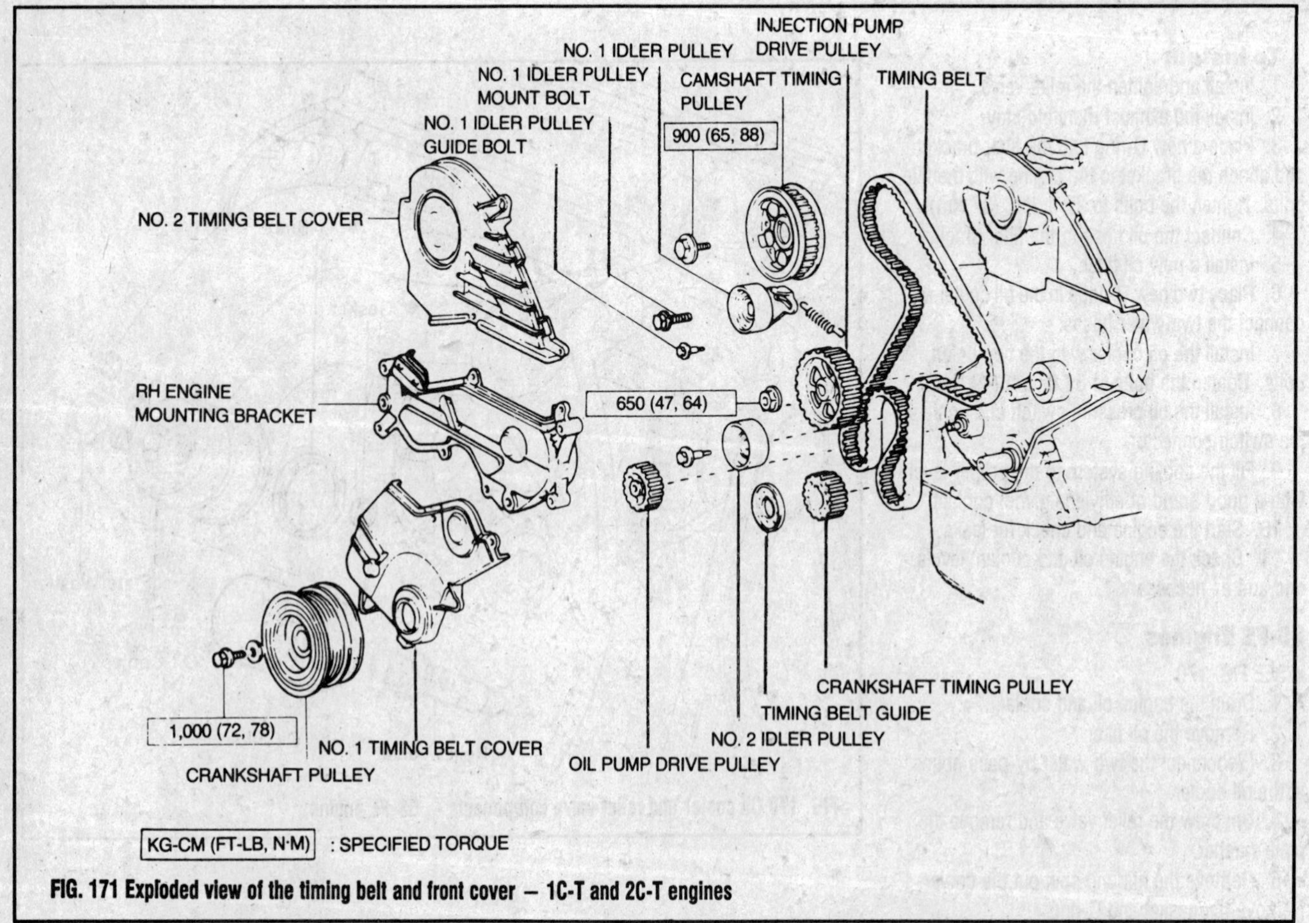

FIG. 171 Exploded view of the timing belt and front cover — 1C-T and 2C-T engines

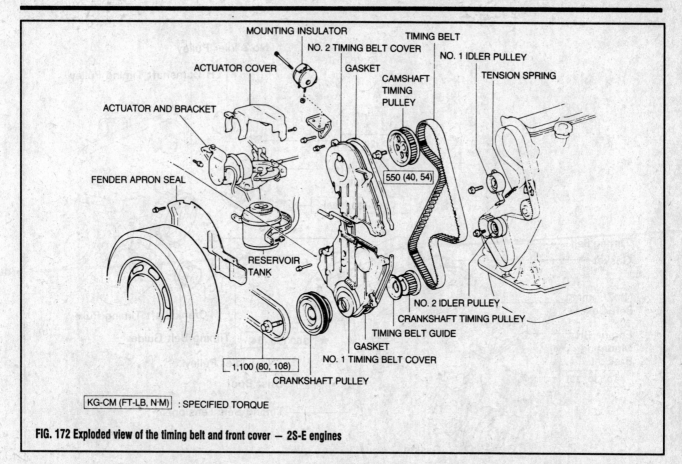

FIG. 172 Exploded view of the timing belt and front cover — 2S-E engines

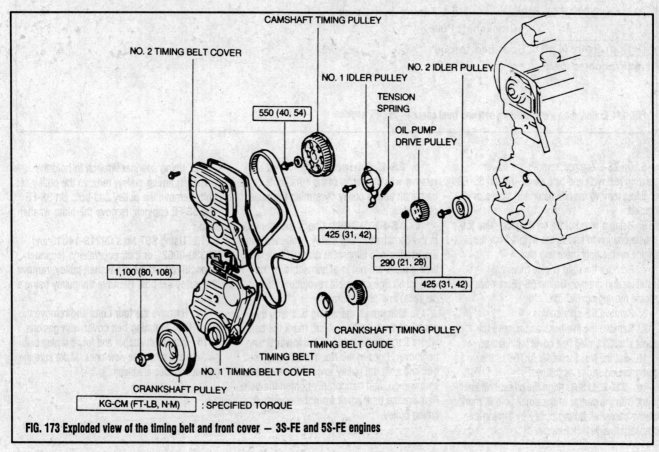

FIG. 173 Exploded view of the timing belt and front cover — 3S-FE and 5S-FE engines

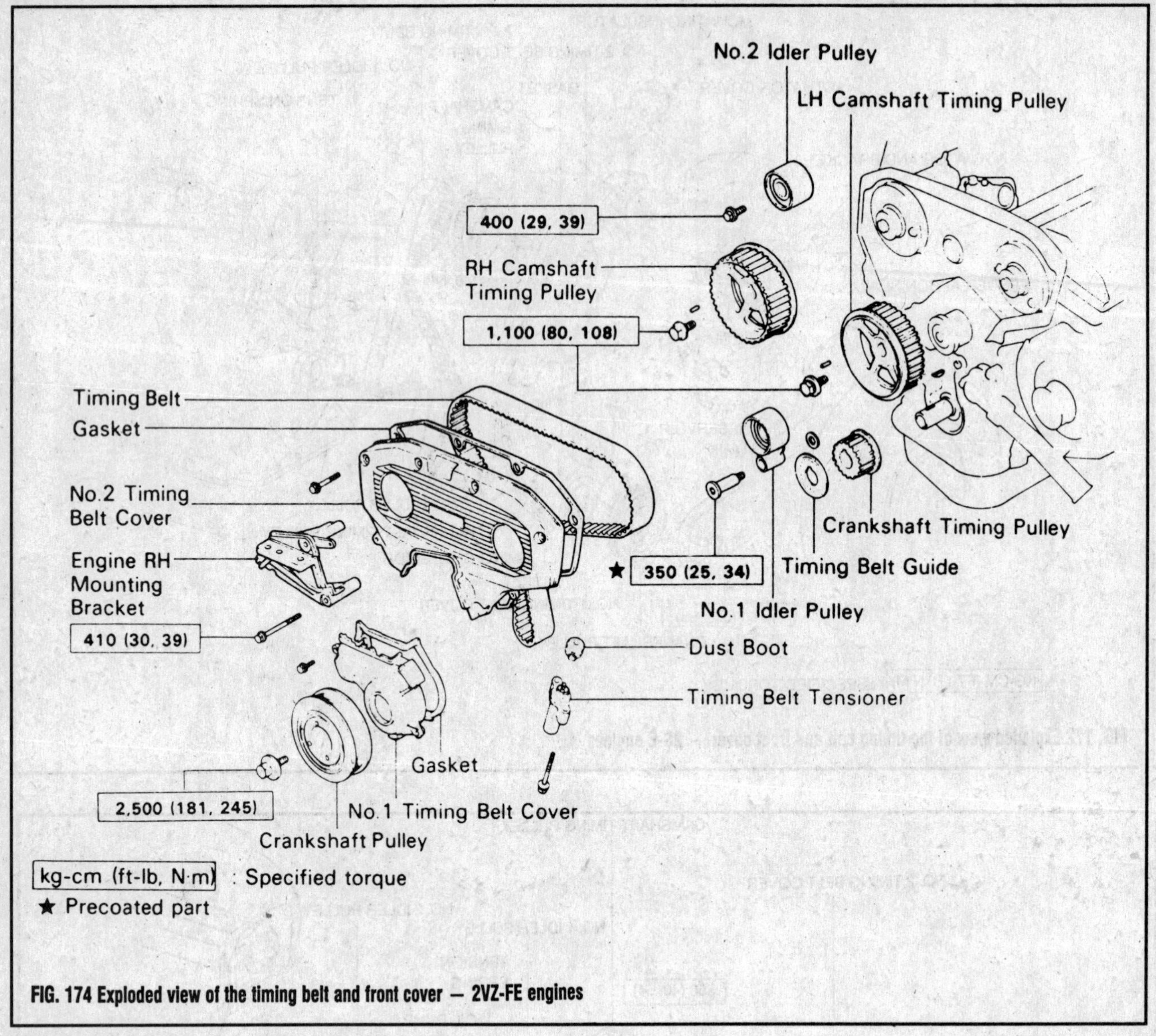

FIG. 174 Exploded view of the timing belt and front cover — 2VZ-FE engines

5. On 2S-E engines, remove the power steering reservoir and belt. On 3S-FE and 5S-FE engines, remove the alternator and alternator bracket.

6. Using a wood block on the jack, raise the engine enough to relieve the weight from the engine on the right mounting side.

7. Remove the right engine mounting insulator and bracket. On the 5S-FE, remove the engine moving control rod.

8. Remove the spark plugs.

9. Remove the five bolts and remove the upper (No. 2) timing belt cover with gasket.

10. Set the No. 1 cylinder to TDC of the compression stroke as follows:

a. **2S-E/USA**: Align the oil seal retainer mark with the center of the small hole **E** mark on the camshaft timing pulley by turning the crankshaft pulley clockwise.

b. **2S-E/Canada**: Align the oil seal retainer with the center of the small hole on the camshaft timing pulley by turning the pulley clockwise.

c. **3S-FE/5S-FE**: Check that the hole in the camshaft timing pulley is aligned with the bearing cap alignment mark. If hole and timing mark are not in alignment, turn the crankshaft one complete revolution (360 degrees) and align them.

11. Matchmark the timing belt with the camshaft timing pulley. Also, mark the belt where it meets the edge of the lower timing belt cover. Loosen the No. 1 idler pulley set bolt and shift the pulley toward the left as far as it will go, and temporarily tighten the bolt. Remove the timing belt from the camshaft timing pulley.

12. Using spanner wrench to hold the camshaft timing pulley, remove the pulley set bolt. Remove the pulley and bolt. On 3S-FE and 5S-FE engines, remove the plate washer also.

13. Using SST No.s 09213-14010 and 09330-00021 or their equivalents (spanner wrench) to hold the crankshaft pulley, remove the pulley set bolt. Remove the pulley using a puller.

14. Remove the four bolts and remove the lower (No. 1) timing belt cover with gaskets.

15. Discard the upper and lower timing belt gaskets and purchase new ones. Make sure the gasket surfaces are clean.

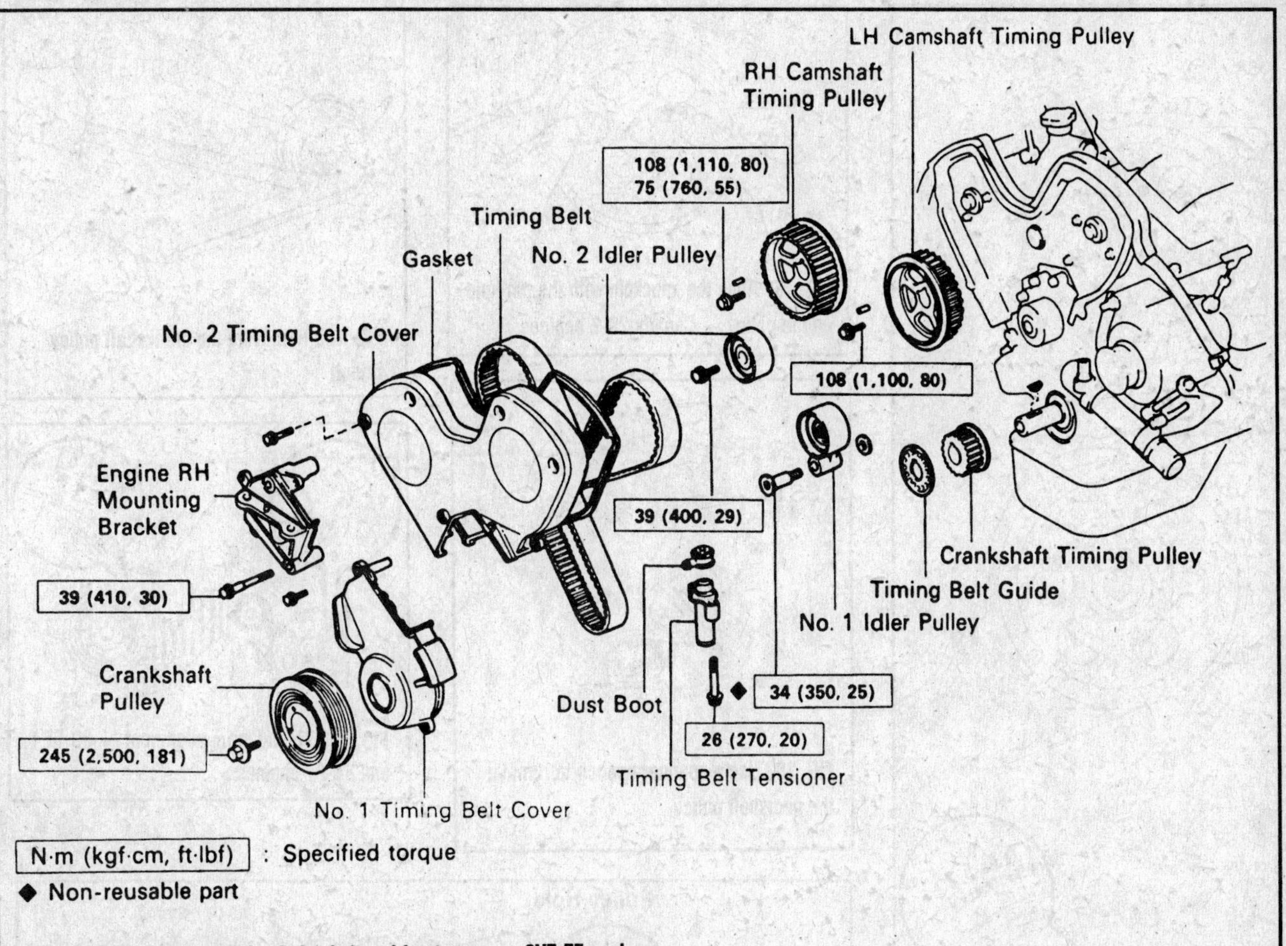

N·m (kgf·cm, ft·lbf) : Specified torque

◆ Non-reusable part

FIG. 175 Exploded view of the timing belt and front cover — 3VZ-FE engines

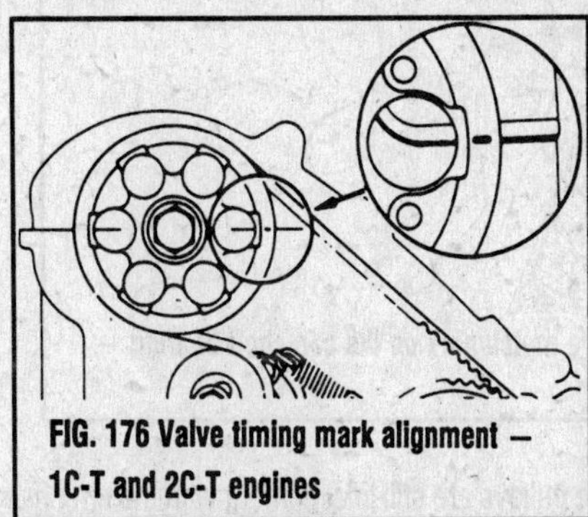

FIG. 176 Valve timing mark alignment — 1C-T and 2C-T engines

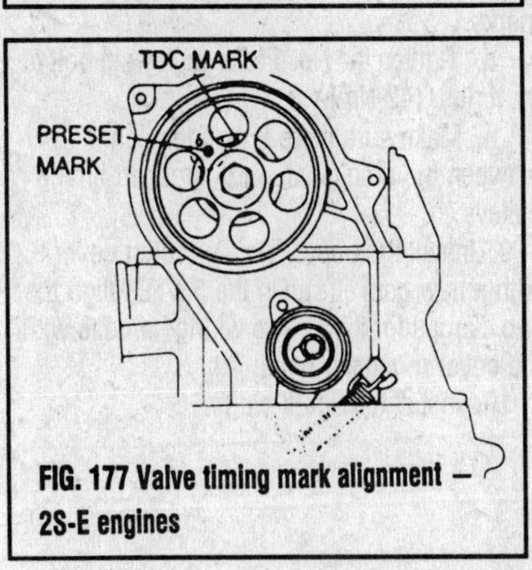

FIG. 177 Valve timing mark alignment — 2S-E engines

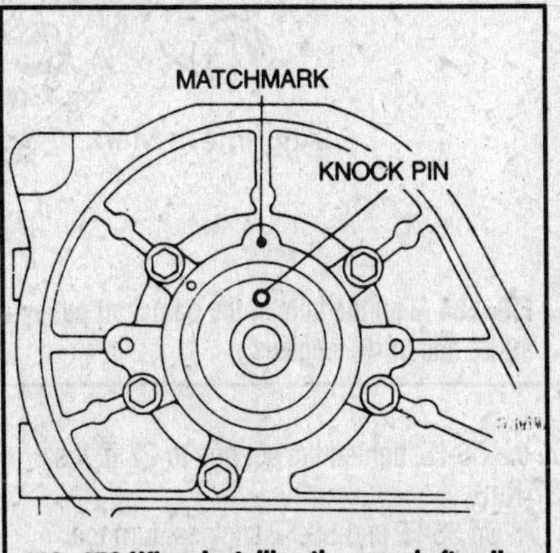

FIG. 178 When installing the camshaft pulley, align the knockpin with the matchmarks on the oil seal retainer

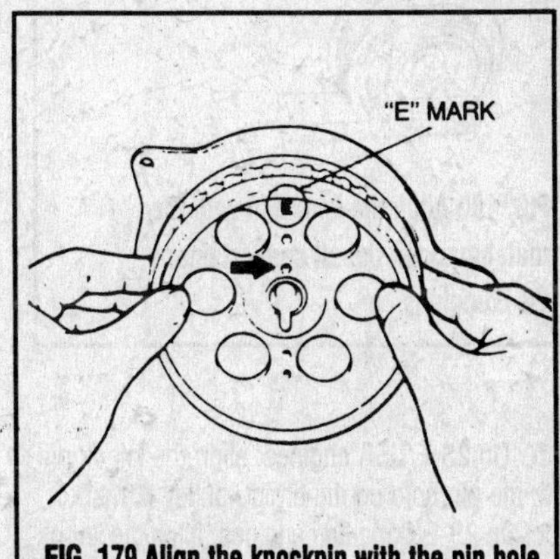

FIG. 179 Align the knockpin with the pin hole on the timing pulley "E" mark side — U.S. 2S-E engines

To Install:

1. Install the lower (No.1) timing belt cover and new gasket with the four bolts.

2. Align the crankshaft pulley set key with the pulley key groove. Install the pulley. Tighten the pulley bolt to 80 ft. lbs. (108 Nm).

3. On 2S-E engines, turn the crankshaft pulley and align the **O** mark on the lower (No. 1) timing belt cover.

4. Align the camshaft knock pin with the matchmarks on the oil seal retainer.

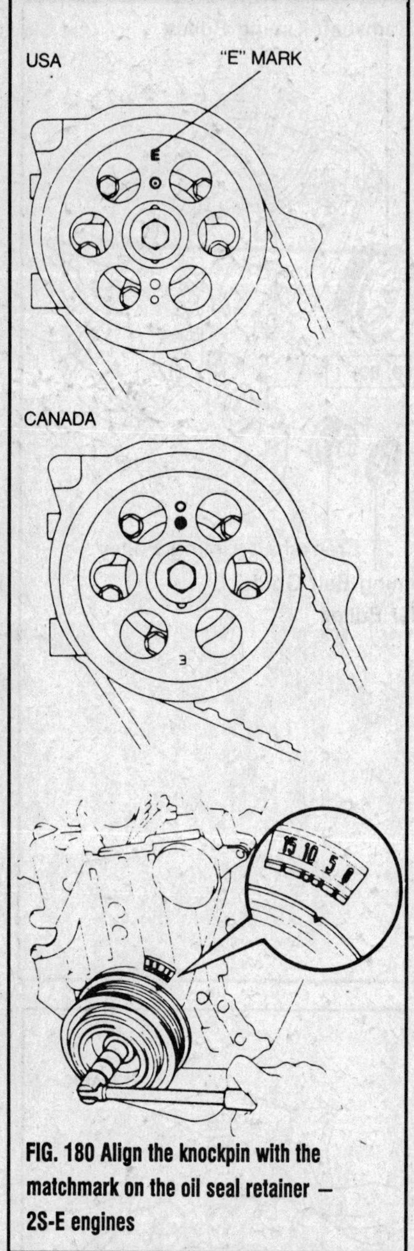

FIG. 180 Align the knockpin with the matchmark on the oil seal retainer — 2S-E engines

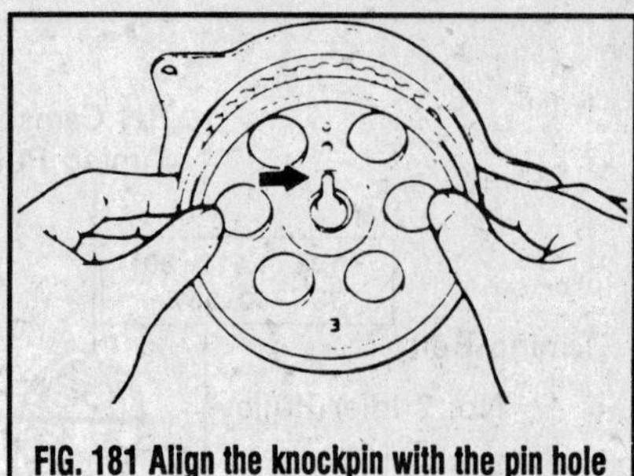
FIG. 181 Align the knockpin with the pin hole on the pulley — Canada 2S-E engines

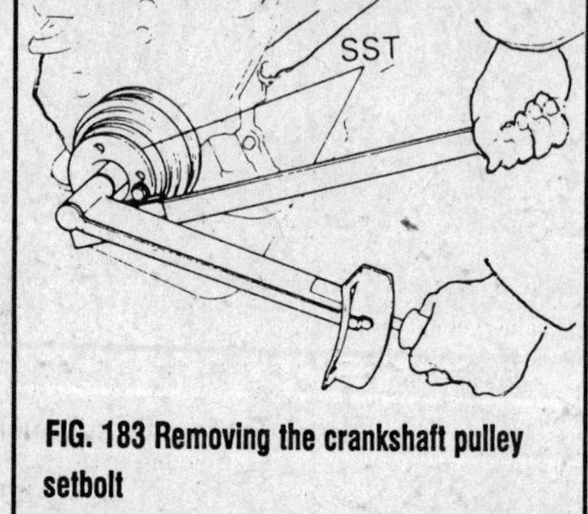

FIG. 183 Removing the crankshaft pulley setbolt

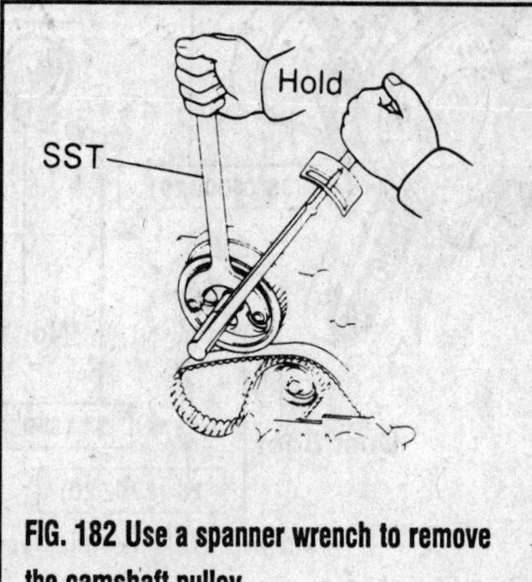

FIG. 182 Use a spanner wrench to remove the camshaft pulley

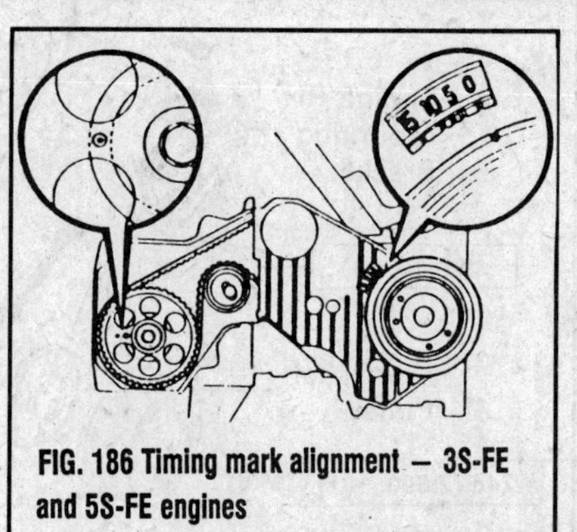
FIG. 186 Timing mark alignment — 3S-FE and 5S-FE engines

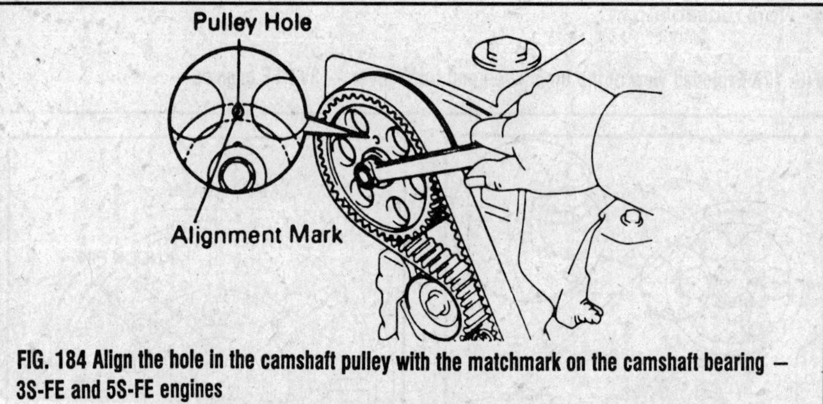

FIG. 184 Align the hole in the camshaft pulley with the matchmark on the camshaft bearing — 3S-FE and 5S-FE engines

5. On 2S-E/USA engines, align the knock pin with the pin hole on the timing pulley **E** mark side. On 2S-E/Canadian engines, align the knock pin with the pin hole on the timing pulley. On 3S-FE and 5S-FE engines, align the knock pin with the groove of the pulley, and slide the pulley onto the camshaft with the plate washer and set bolt.

➡ On 2S-E engines, make sure that the matchmark on the oil seal retainer and center hole of the small hole on the camshaft timing pulley are aligned.

6. Using the removal tool to hold the pulley stationary, install and tighten the pulley set bolt to 40 ft. lbs. (54 Nm) on the 2S-E and the 3S-FE. On the 5S-FE, tighten the set bolt to 27 ft. lbs. (37 Nm).

7. On 3S-FE and 5S-FE engines, turn the crankshaft pulley and align the **O** mark on the lower (No. 1) timing belt cover.

8. Install the timing belt and check the valve timing as follows:

a. Align the matchmarks that you made previously, and install the timing belt onto the camshaft pulley.

b. Loosen the No. 1 idler pulley set bolt $1/2$ turn.

c. Turn the crankshaft pulley two complete revolutions TDC to TDC. ALWAYS turn the crankshaft CLOCKWISE. Check that the pulleys are still in alignment with the timing marks.

d. Tighten the No. 1 idler pulley set bolt to 31 ft. lbs. (42 Nm).

e. Make sure there is belt tension between the crankshaft and camshaft timing pulleys.

9. Install the upper (No. 2) timing cover with a new gasket(s). On the 5S-FE, align the two clamps for the engine wiring harness with the cover mounting bolts.

10. Install the spark plugs.

11. Install the right mounting insulator with bracket. Tighten the bracket bolts to 38 ft. lbs. (52 Nm), insulator nuts to 38 ft. lbs. (52 Nm) and thru-bolt to 52 ft. lbs. (71 Nm). On the 5S-FE, install the No. 2 engine mount bracket and tighten to 38 ft. lbs. (52 Nm); install the control rod and tighten the bolts to 47 ft. lbs. (64 Nm).

12. Lower the engine.

13. On 3S-FE and 5S-FE engines, install the alternator and alternator bracket. On 2S-E engines, install the power steering reservoir tank.

14. Install the drive belt and adjust the tension.

15. Install the cruise control actuator with bracket.

16. Install the fender apron seal and right engine under cover.

17. Install the right front wheel.

2VZ-FE and 3VZ-FE Engines

➧ SEE FIGS. 174, 175, 187-197

1. Disconnect the cable from the negative battery terminal.

✲✲ CAUTION

On models with an airbag, wait at least 30 seconds from the time that the ignition switch is turned to the LOCK position and the battery is disconnected before performing any further work.

2. Remove the power steering pump reservoir and position it out of the way. Remove the right fender apron seal and then remove the alternator and power steering belts. On 2VZ-FE, remove the cruise control actuator and vacuum pump.

3. On the 3VZ-FE, remove the coolant reservoir hose, the washer tank and then the coolant overflow tank.

4. Remove the right side engine mount stays.

5. Position a piece of wood on a floor jack and then slide the jack under the oil pan. Raise the jack slightly until the pressure is off the engine mounts.

6. On the 2VZ-FE, remove the right side engine mount insulator. On the 3VZ-FE, remove the engine control rod.

7. Remove the spark plugs.

8. Remove the right side engine mounting bracket.

9. Remove the eight bolts and lift off the upper (No. 2) cover.

10. Paint matchmarks on the timing belt at all points where it meshes with the pulleys and the lower timing cover.

11. Set the No. 1 cylinder to TDC of the compression stroke and check that the timing marks on the camshaft timing pulleys are aligned with those on the No. 3 timing cover. If not, turn the engine one complete revolution (360°) and check again.

12. Remove the timing belt tensioner and the dust boot.

13. Turn the right camshaft pulley clockwise slightly to release tension and then remove the timing belt from the pulleys.

14. Use a spanner wrench to hold the pulley, loosen the set bolt and then remove the camshaft timing pulleys along with the knock pin. Be sure to keep track of which is which.

15. Remove the No. 2 idler pulley.

16. Remove the crankshaft pulley and then pull off the lower (No. 1) timing belt cover.

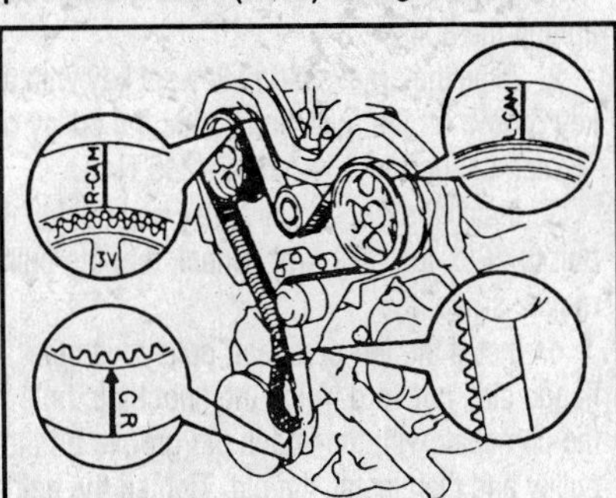

FIG. 187 Before removing the timing belt, make sure that all the matchmarks are there — 2VZ-FE and 3VZ-FE engines

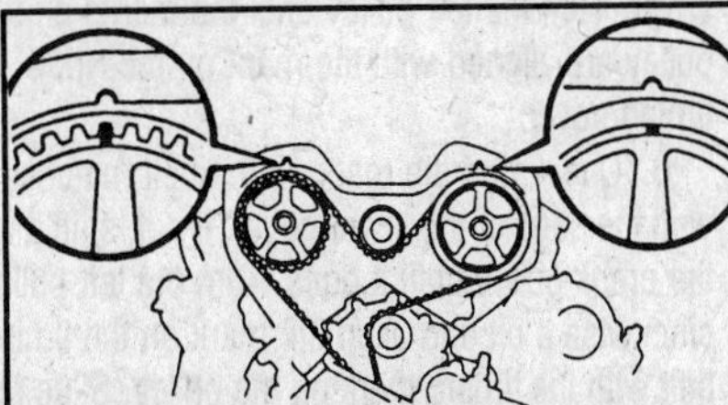
FIG. 188 Check that the marks on the camshaft pulleys and the No. 3 timing cover are in alignment — 2VZ-FE and 3VZ-FE engines

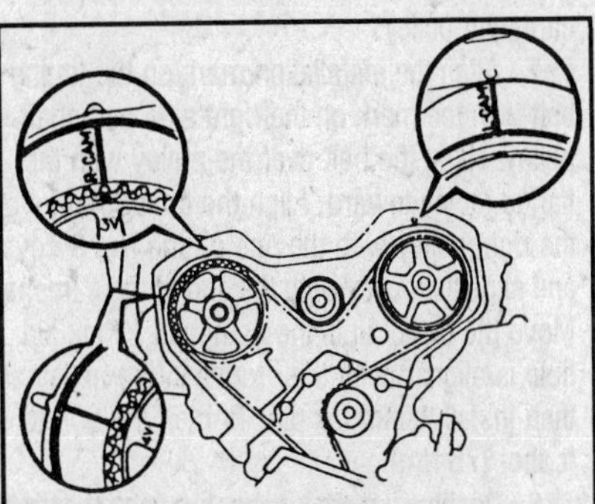

FIG. 189 Before removing the timing belt, make sure that all the matchmarks are there — 2VZ-FE and 3VZ-FE engines

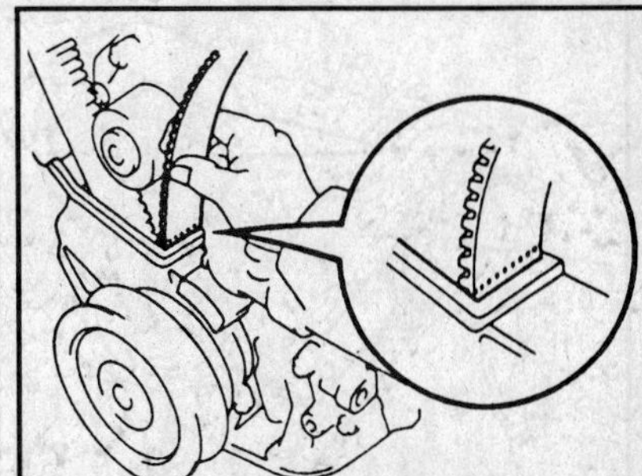
FIG. 190 Mark the timing belt where it passes the lower timing cover — 2VZ-FE and 3VZ-FE engines

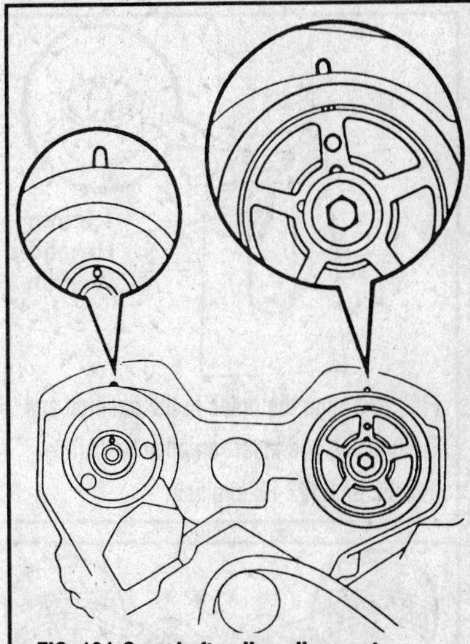
FIG. 191 Camshaft pulley alignment — 2VZ-FE and 3VZ-FE engines

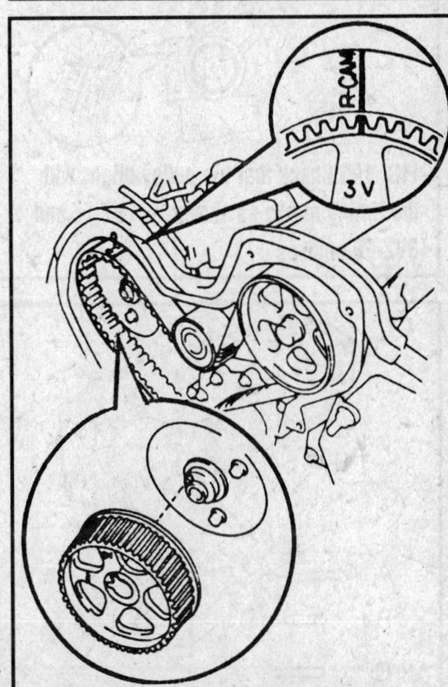

FIG. 192 Align the installation mark on the belt with the mark on the right side pulley — 2VZ-FE and 3VZ-FE engines

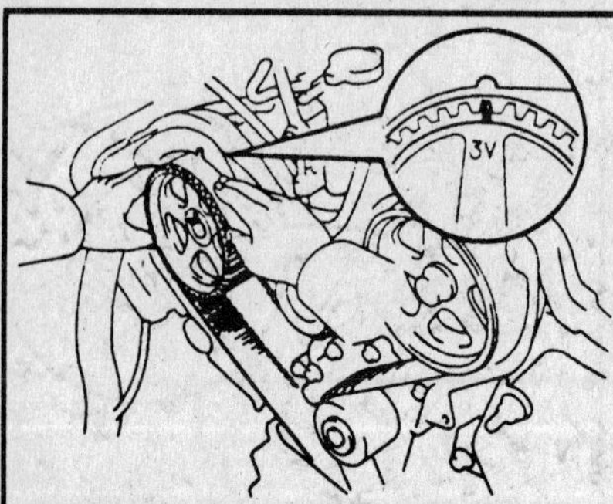

FIG. 193 Align the marks on the right pulley and the No. 3 timing pulley and then slide the belt on — 2VZ-FE and 3VZ-FE engines

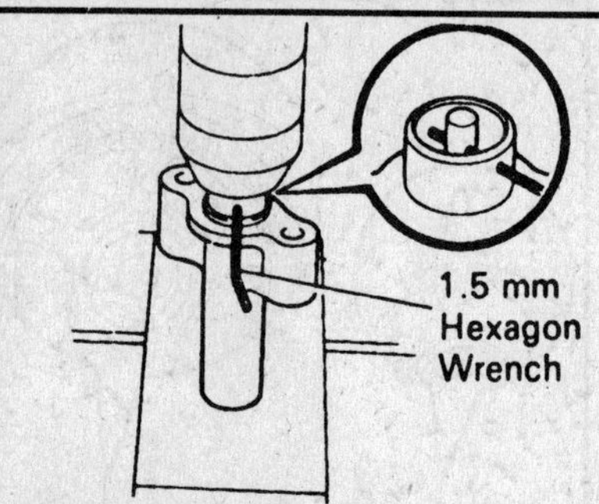

FIG. 194 Align the holes in the pushrod and the housing and insert an allen wrench — 2VZ-FE and 3VZ-FE engines

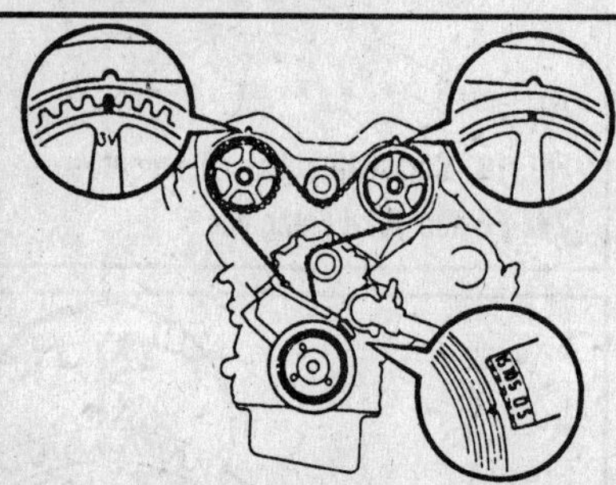

FIG. 195 Check that the pulley aligns with the timing marks as shown — 2VZ-FE and 3VZ-FE engines

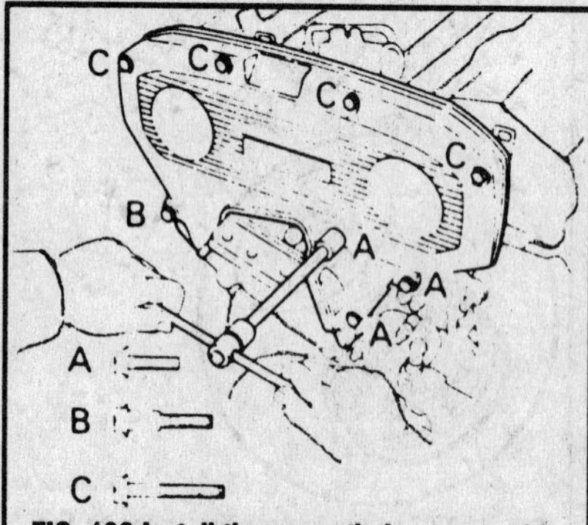

FIG. 196 Install the upper timing cover with the bolts as shown — 2VZ-FE engines

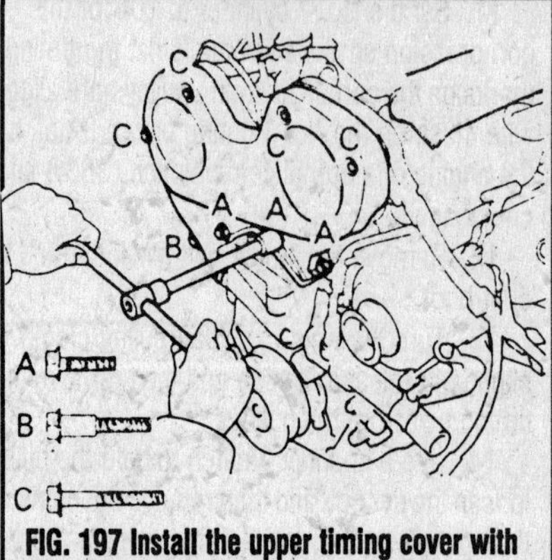

FIG. 197 Install the upper timing cover with the bolts as shown — 3VZ-FE engines

To Install:

1. Install the lower (No. 1) timing cover and tighten the bolts.
2. Align the crankshaft pulley set key with the key groove on the pulley and slide the pulley on. Tighten the bolt to 181 ft. lbs. (245 Nm).
3. Install the No. 2 idler pulley and tighten the bolt to 29 ft. lbs. (39 Nm). Check that the pulley moves smoothly.
4. Install the left camshaft pulley with the flange side outward. Align the knock pin hole in the camshaft with the knock pin groove on the pulley and then install the pin. Tighten the bolt to 80 ft. lbs. (108 Nm).
5. Set the No. 1 cylinder to TDC again. Turn the right camshaft until the knock pin hole is aligned with the timing mark on the No. 3 belt cover. Turn the left pulley until the marks on the pulley are aligned with the mark on the No. 3 timing cover.
6. Check that the mark on the belt matches with the edge of the lower cover. If not, shift it on the crank pulley until it does. Turn the left pulley clockwise a bit and align the mark on the timing belt with the timing mark on the pulley. Slide the belt over the left pulley. Now move the pulley until the marks on it align with the one on the No. 3 cover. There should be tension on the belt between the crankshaft pulley and the left camshaft pulley.
7. Align the installation mark on the timing belt with the mark on the right side camshaft pulley. Hang the belt over the pulley with the flange facing inward. Align the timing marks on the right pulley with the one on the No. 3 cover and slide the pulley onto the end of the camshaft. Move the pulley until the camshaft knock pin hole is aligned with the groove in the pulley and then install the knock pin. Tighten the bolt to 55 ft. lbs. (75 Nm).
8. Position a plate washer between the timing belt tensioner and the a block and then press in the pushrod until the holes are aligned between it and the housing. Slide a 1.27mm (3VZ-FE—1.5mm) allen wrench through the hole to keep the push rod set. Install the dust boot and then install the tensioner. Tighten the bolts to 20 ft. lbs. (26 Nm). Don't forget to pull out the allen wrench!
9. Turn the crankshaft **clockwise** two complete revolutions and check that all marks are still in alignment. If they aren't, remove the timing belt and start over again.
10. Install the right engine mount bracket and tighten it to 30 ft. lbs. (39 Nm).
11. Position a new gasket and then install the upper (No. 2) timing cover. refer to the illustration for bolt positioning.
12. Install the spark plugs.
13. On the 2VZ-FE, install the right engine mount insulator. Tighten the bolt to 47 ft. lbs. (64 Nm), the bracket nut to 38 ft. lbs. (52 Nm) and the body nut to 65 ft. lbs. (88 Nm). Install the No. 1 stay and tighten it to 38 ft. lbs. (52 Nm). Install the No. 2 stay and tighten the bolt to 48 ft. lbs. (66 Nm) and the nut to 38 ft. lbs (52 Nm).
14. On the 3VZ-FE, install the control rod and tighten the bolts to 47 ft. lbs. (64 Nm). Install the right stay and tighten it to 23 ft. lbs. (31 Nm).
15. Install and adjust the drive belts.
16. Install the fender apron seal and the wheel.
17. On the 3VZ-FE, install the No. 2 stay and tighten the bolt to 55 ft. lbs. (75 Nm), the nut to 46 ft. lbs. (62 Nm). Install the No. 3 stay and tighten it to 54 ft. lbs. (73 Nm).
18. Install the coolant overflow tank and the washer tank.
19. Install the power steering reservoir tank and the cruise control actuator.
20. Connect the battery cable, start the car and check for any leaks.

Timing Belt

REMOVAL & INSTALLATION

1C-T and 2C-T Engines

➧ SEE FIGS. 198, 199

1. Remove the right hand front wheel.
2. Remove the fender apron seal.
3. Remove the windshield washer and radiator reservoir tanks.
4. Disconnect and label all vacuum hoses, cables, electrical connector and remove the cruise control actuator and bracket.
5. Remove the power steering pump with bracket.
6. Remove the alternator and alternator bracket.

7. Undo the three clips, remove the five bolts and remove the upper (No. 2) timing belt cover and gasket.

8. Align the line mark of the camshaft pulley with the top end of the cylinder head by turning the crankshaft pulley bolt CLOCKWISE.

9. Using a spanner wrench to hold the crankshaft pulley stationary, remove the pulley set bolt and plate washer.

10. Remove the five bolts and remove the No. 1 timing belt cover and gasket.

11. Using a small prybar or similar tool, remove the tension spring. The use of any tool that will pinch the spring is not recommended.

12. Loosen the No. 1 idler pulley mounting bolt.

➡ **If the timing belt is to be reused draw a directional arrow on the belt in the direction of normal engine rotation and place match marks on the belt and the camshaft, crankshaft and injection pump pulleys.**

13. Remove the timing belt.

To install:

1. Align the mark of the camshaft pulley with the top end of the cylinder head. DO NOT align the cylinder head cover with the boss.

2. Align the grooves of the crankshaft timing pulley and the oil pump.

3. Align the cavity of the injection pump drive pulley with the line mark on the water pump.

➡ **Hold the injection pump drive pulley in place until the timing belt is completely installed.**

4. Install the timing belt onto the camshaft pulley.

➡ **If the OLD timing belt is being installed make sure the direction arrow is facing in the direction of engine rotation an that the match marks made on the belt and timing pulleys are properly aligned. If a NEW belt is being installed, install the belt so that the numbers and letters can be read from the rear end of the engine.**

5. Hold the injection pump pulley still with a wrench and install the timing belt onto the pulley. The timing belt should be evenly meshed with the pulley and should not be loose.

6. Install the timing belt onto the water pump and crankshaft pulleys. The timing belt should be evenly meshed with the pulley and should not be loose.

7. Install the timing belt onto the No. 2 idler and oil pump pulleys. The timing belt should be evenly meshed with the pulley and should not be loose.

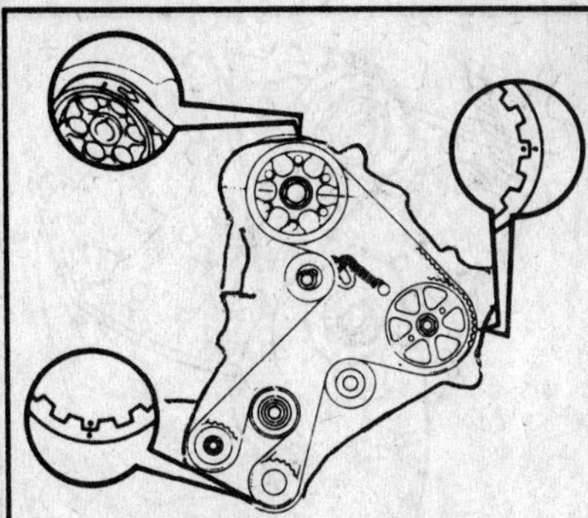

FIG. 198 When planning to reuse the timing belt, matchmark the belt to the pulleys — 1C-T and 2C-T engines

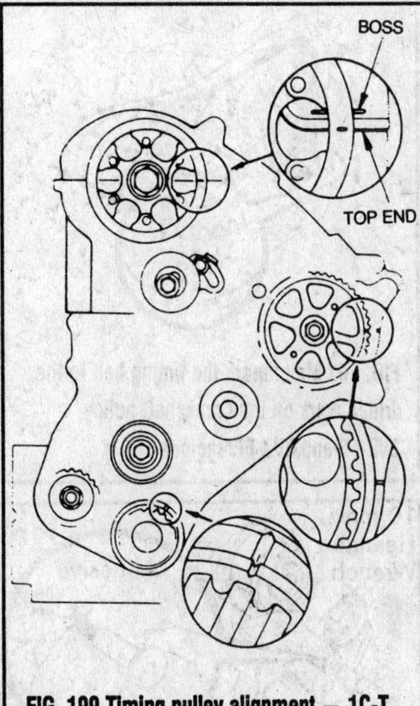

FIG. 199 Timing pulley alignment — 1C-T and 2C-T engines

8. Install the tension spring.

9. Using the crankshaft pulley mounting bolt and the proper size socket. Turn the crankshaft CLOCKWISE two complete revolutions from TDC to TDC.

10. Visually check that each pulley is aligned with its timing mark. If the marks do not align, remove the belt end reinstall it.

11. Tighten the No. 1 idler pulley set bolt to 27 ft. lbs. (37 Nm). DO NOT move the idler pulley bracket while tightening the set bolt.

12. Install the right hand engine mounting bracket with the retaining bolts. Tighten the 10mm bolts to 27 ft. lbs. (37 Nm) and the 12mm bolts to 47 ft. lbs. (64 Nm). If the vehicle is equipped with power steering and/or air conditioning, do not install the 12mm bolts.

13. Install the right hand mounting insulator.

14. Lower the engine.

15. Install the timing belt guide. Make sure that the cup is facing outward.

16. Install the upper (No. 1) timing belt cover with the new gasket. Install and tighten the five bolts.

17. Drive the crankshaft pulley onto the crankshaft.

18. Hold the crankshaft pulley stationary with the same tool used during removal and install the set bolt and plate washer. Tighten the set bolt to 72 ft. lbs. (98 Nm).

19. Install the lower timing belt cover and new gasket with the three clips and five bolts.

20. Install the alternator and alternator bracket. Adjust the belt tension.

21. Install the power steering pump and adjust the drive belt tension.

22. Install the cruise control actuator and bracket. Connect the connector, cables and vacuum hoses.

23. Check and adjust the injection timing.

24. Install the fender apron seal.

25. Install the right front wheel.

26. Check and adjust the engine idle and maximum speeds.

2S-E, 3S-FE and 5S-FE Engines

➧ SEE FIGS. 172, 173, 177-186, 200-201

1. Remove the timing belt covers as previously detailed.

2. Raise the engine just enough to remove the weight from the engine mount on the right side.

3. Remove the thru-bolt, two nuts, and right hand mounting insulator.

4. Remove the retaining bolts and remove the right hand mounting bracket (from the side the alternator was removed from).

5. Remove the timing belt and timing belt guide.

➡ **If the timing belt is to be reused, draw a directional arrow on the timing belt in the direction of engine rotation (clockwise) and place matchmarks on the timing belt and crankshaft gear.**

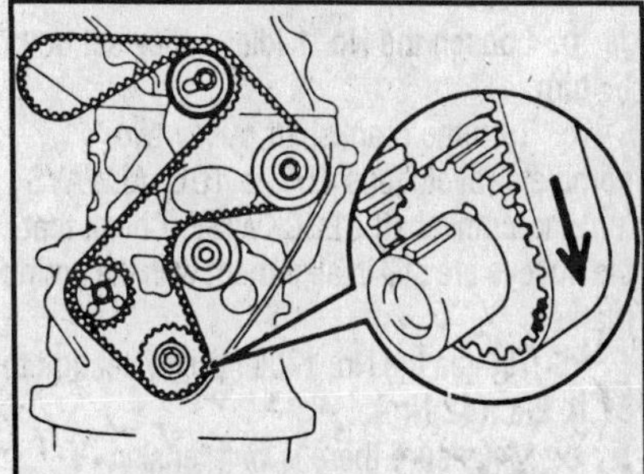

FIG. 200 When reusing a timing belt, draw a directional arrow on the belt and matchmark the belt to the crankshaft gear

To Install:

1. Turn the crankshaft until the key groove in the crankshaft timing pulley is facing upward. Install the timing belt on the crankshaft timing, oil pump, No. 2 idler and water pump pulleys.

➡ If the old timing belt is being reinstalled, make sure the directional arrow is facing in the original direction and that the belt and crankshaft gear matchmarks are properly aligned.

2. Install the lower (No. 1) timing belt cover and new gasket with the four bolts.
3. Align the crankshaft pulley set key with the pulley key groove. Install the pulley. Tighten the pulley bolt to 80 ft. lbs. (108 Nm).
4. On 2S-E engines, turn the crankshaft pulley and align the **O** mark on the lower (No. 1) timing belt cover.
5. Align the camshaft knock pin with the matchmarks on the oil seal retainer.
6. On 2S-E/USA engines, align the knock pin with the pin hole on the timing pulley **E** mark side. On 2S-E/Canadian engines, align the knock pin with the pin hole on the timing pulley. On 3S-FE and 5S-FE engines, align the knock pin with the groove of the pulley, and slide the pulley onto the camshaft with the plate washer and set bolt.

➡ On 2S-E engines, make sure that the matchmark on the oil seal retainer and center hole of the small hole on the camshaft timing pulley are aligned.

7. Using the removal tool to hold the pulley stationary, install and tighten the pulley set bolt to 40 ft. lbs. (54 Nm) on the 2S-E and the 3S-FE. On the 5S-FE, tighten the set bolt to 27 ft. lbs. (37 Nm).
8. On 3S-FE and 5S-FE engines, turn the crankshaft pulley and align the **O** mark on the lower (No. 1) timing belt cover.
9. Install the timing belt and check the valve timing as follows:
   a. Align the matchmarks that you made previously, and install the timing belt onto the camshaft pulley.
   b. Loosen the No. 1 idler pulley set bolt 1/2 turn.
   c. Turn the crankshaft pulley two complete revolutions TDC to TDC. ALWAYS turn the crankshaft CLOCKWISE. Check that the pulleys are still in alignment with the timing marks.
   d. Tighten the No. 1 idler pulley set bolt to 31 ft. lbs. (42 Nm).
   e. Make sure there is belt tension between the crankshaft and camshaft timing pulleys.

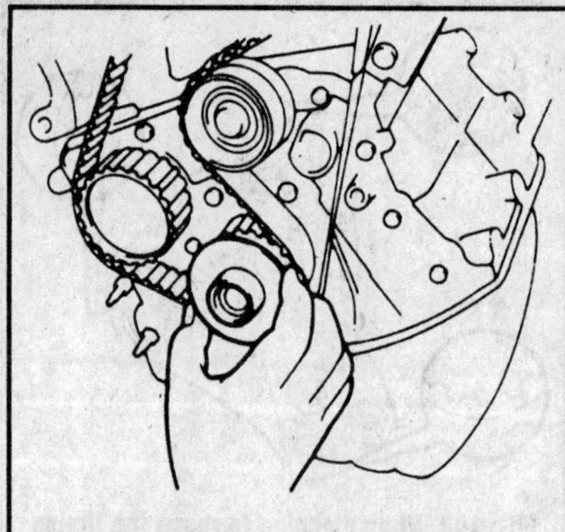

FIG. 201 Removing the timing belt guide

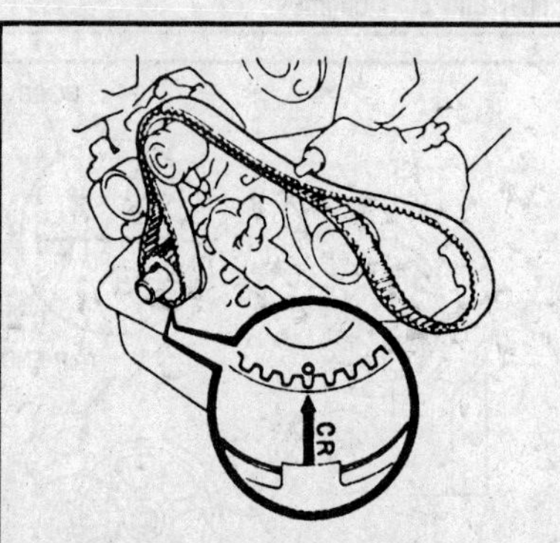

FIG. 202 Matchmark the timing belt to the drilled mark on the crankshaft pulley — 2VZ-FE and 3VZ-FE engines

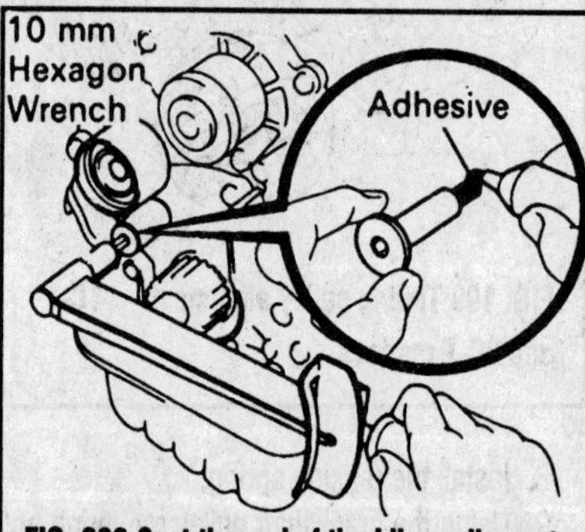

FIG. 203 Coat the end of the idler pulley set bolt with adhesive — 2VZ-FE and 3VZ-FE engines

10. Install the upper (No. 2) timing cover with a new gasket(s). On the 5S-FE, align the two clamps for the engine wiring harness with the cover mounting bolts.
11. Install the spark plugs.
12. Install the right mounting insulator with bracket. Tighten the bracket bolts to 38 ft. lbs. (52 Nm), insulator nuts to 38 ft. lbs. (52 Nm) and thru-bolt to 52 ft. lbs. (71 Nm). On the 5S-FE, install the No. 2 engine mount bracket and tighten to 38 ft. lbs. (52 Nm); install the control rod and tighten the bolts to 47 ft. lbs. (64 Nm).
13. Lower the engine.
14. On 3S-FE and 5S-FE engines, install the alternator and alternator bracket. On 2S-E engines, install the power steering reservoir tank.
15. Install the drive belt and adjust the tension.
16. Install the cruise control actuator with bracket.
17. Install the fender apron seal and right engine under cover.
18. Install the right front wheel.

2VZ-FE and 3VZ-FE Engines

➧ SEE FIGS. 174-175, 187-197, 202-203

1. Remove the upper and lower timing belt covers as previously detailed.
2. Remove the timing belt guide.
3. Remove the timing belt.

➡ If the timing belt is to be reused, draw a directional arrow on the timing belt in the direction of engine rotation (clockwise) and place matchmarks on the timing belt and crankshaft gear to match the drilled mark on the pulley.

4. With a 10mm hex wrench, remove the set bolt, plate washer and the No. 1 idler pulley.

To Install:

1. Turn the crankshaft until the key groove in the crankshaft timing pulley is facing upward. Slide the timing pulley on so that the flange side faces inward.
2. Apply bolt adhesive to the first few threads of the No. 1 idler pulley set bolt, install the plate washer and pulley and then tighten the bolt to 25 ft. lbs. (34 Nm).
3. Install the timing belt on the crankshaft timing, No. 1 idler and water pump pulleys.

➡ If the old timing belt is being reinstalled, make sure the directional arrow is facing in the original direction and that the belt and crankshaft gear matchmarks are properly aligned.

4. Install the lower (No. 1) timing cover and tighten the bolts.
5. Align the crankshaft pulley set key with the key groove on the pulley and slide the pulley on. Tighten the bolt to 181 ft. lbs. (245 Nm).
6. Install the No. 2 idler pulley and tighten the bolt to 29 ft. lbs. (39 Nm). Check that the pulley moves smoothly.
7. Install the left camshaft pulley with the flange side outward. Align the knock pin hole in the camshaft with the knock pin groove on the pulley and then install the pin. Tighten the bolt to 80 ft. lbs. (108 Nm).

8. Set the No. 1 cylinder to TDC again. Turn the right camshaft until the knock pin hole is aligned with the timing mark on the No. 3 belt cover. Turn the left pulley until the marks on the pulley are aligned with the mark on the No. 3 timing cover.

9. Check that the mark on the belt matches with the edge of the lower cover. If not, shift it on the crank pulley until it does. Turn the left pulley clockwise a bit and align the mark on the timing belt with the timing mark on the pulley. Slide the belt over the left pulley. Now move the pulley until the marks on it align with the one on the No. 3 cover. There should be tension on the belt between the crankshaft pulley and the left camshaft pulley.

10. Align the installation mark on the timing belt with the mark on the right side camshaft pulley. Hang the belt over the pulley with the flange facing inward. Align the timing marks on the right pulley with the one on the No. 3 cover and slide the pulley onto the end of the camshaft. Move the pulley until the camshaft knock pin hole is aligned with the groove in the pulley and then install the knock pin. Tighten the bolt to 55 ft. lbs. (75 Nm).

11. Position a plate washer between the timing belt tensioner and the a block and then press in the pushrod until the holes are aligned between it and the housing. Slide a 1.27mm (3VZ-FE—1.5mm) allen wrench through the hole to keep the push rod set. Install the dust boot and then install the tensioner. Tighten the bolts to 20 ft. lbs. (26 Nm). Don't forget to pull out the allen wrench!

12. Turn the crankshaft **clockwise** two complete revolutions and check that all marks are still in alignment. If they aren't, remove the timing belt and start over again.

13. Install the right engine mount bracket and tighten it to 30 ft. lbs. (39 Nm).

14. Position a new gasket and then install the upper (No. 2) timing cover. refer to the illustration for bolt positioning.

15. Install the spark plugs.

16. On the 2VZ-FE, install the right engine mount insulator. Tighten the bolt to 47 ft. lbs. (64 Nm), the bracket nut to 38 ft. lbs. (52 Nm) and the body nut to 65 ft. lbs. (88 Nm). Install the No. 1 stay and tighten it to 38 ft. lbs. (52 Nm). Install the No. 2 stay and tighten the bolt to 48 ft. lbs. (66 Nm) and the nut to 38 ft. lbs (52 Nm).

17. On the 3VZ-FE, install the control rod and tighten the bolts to 47 ft. lbs. (64 Nm). Install the right stay and tighten it to 23 ft. lbs. (31 Nm).

18. Install and adjust the drive belts.

19. Install the fender apron seal and the wheel.

20. On the 3VZ-FE, install the No. 2 stay and tighten the bolt to 55 ft. lbs. (75 Nm), the nut to 46 ft. lbs. (62 Nm). Install the No. 3 stay and tighten it to 54 ft. lbs. (73 Nm).

21. Install the coolant overflow tank and the washer tank.

22. Install the power steering reservoir tank and the cruise control actuator.

23. Connect the battery cable, start the car and check for any leaks.

Camshaft Timing Gear

REMOVAL & INSTALLATION

Diesel Engines

➧ SEE FIGS. 204, 205

1. Remove the timing belt as previously detailed.

2. Using a spanner wrench to hold the camshaft pulley, remove the set bolt.

3. Install a two-armed puller and remove the camshaft pulley. Be careful, the pulley may spring off so don't drop it!

3. Using a spanner wrench to hold the injection pump drive pulley, remove the set bolt.

4. Install a two-armed puller and remove the drive pulley. Be careful, the pulley may spring off so don't drop it!

To install:

1. Slide the injection pump drive pulley over the pump key and tighten the bolt to 47 ft. lbs. (64 Nm).

2. Align the camshaft knockpin with the camshaft timing pulley and slide the pulley onto the shaft. Install the set bolt and plate washer and tighten it to 65 ft. lbs. (88 Nm).

3. Install the timing belt and covers.

Gasoline Engines

➧ SEE FIGS. 206-208

1. Remove the timing belt as previously detailed.

2. Using a spanner wrench to hold the camshaft pulley, remove the set bolt.

3. Install a two-armed puller and remove the camshaft pulley. Be careful, the pulley may spring off so don't drop it!

To install:

1. Align the camshaft knockpin with the groove in the camshaft timing pulley and slide the pulley onto the shaft (flange side outward on V6 engines). Install the set bolt and plate washer and tighten it to 40 ft. lbs. (54 Nm) on the 2S-FE

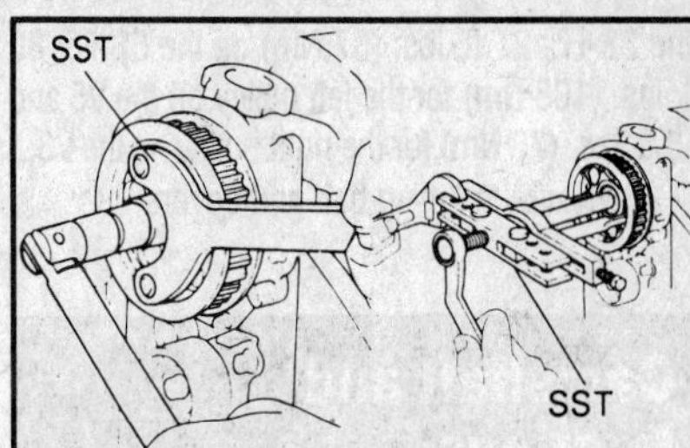

FIG. 204 Removing the camshaft timing pulley — 1C-T and 2C-T engines

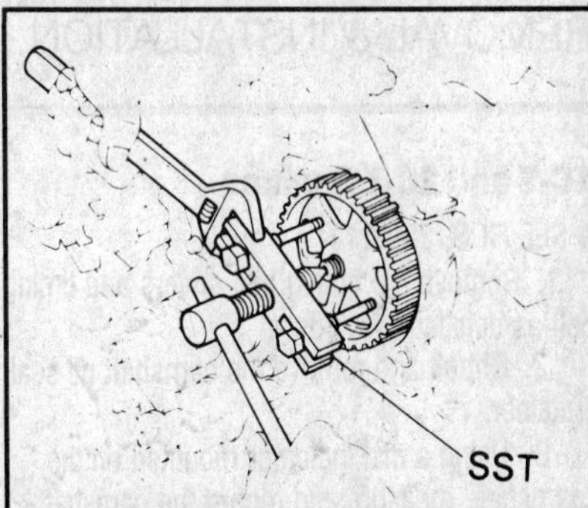

FIG. 205 Removing the injection pump drive pulley — 1C-T and 2C-T engines

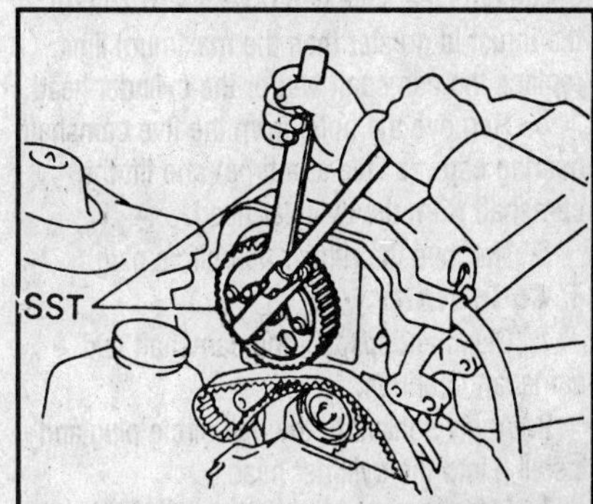

FIG. 206 Removing the camshaft timing pulley — 2S-E, 3S-FE and 5S-FE engines

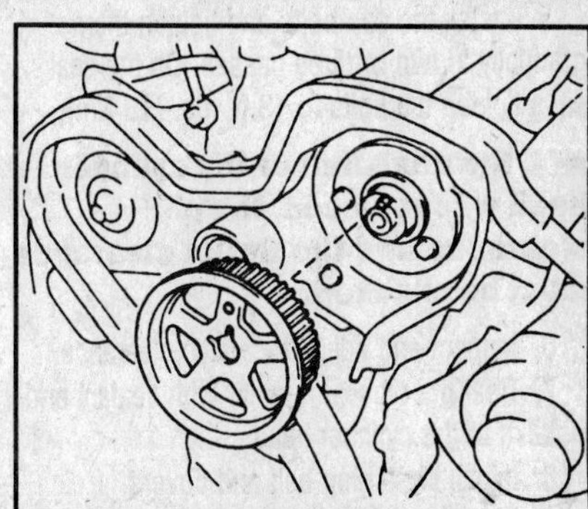

FIG. 207 When installing the left side camshaft pulley, align the camshaft knockpin hole with the groove on the pulley — 2VZ-FE and 3VZ-FE engines

and 3S-FE; 27 ft. lbs. (37 Nm) on the 5S-FE; 80 ft. lbs. (108 Nm) for the left pulley on the V6 and 55 ft. lbs. (75 Nm) for the right pulley on the V6.

2. Install the timing belt and covers.

Camshaft and Bearings

REMOVAL & INSTALLATION

1C-T and 2C-T Engines

➧ SEE FIGS. 209-211

1. Remove the timing belt covers and timing belt as detailed previously.
2. Unbolt and remove the camshaft oil seal retainer.
3. Using a dial indicator mounted on the camshaft, measure and record the camshaft thrust clearance by moving the camshaft back and forth. The standard clearance is 0.0031–0.0071 in. (0.0787–0.180mm) and the maximum clearance is 0.0098 in. (0.25mm). If the thrust is greater than the maximum limit, replace the camshaft and/or the cylinder head.
4. Remove the bolts from the five camshaft bearing caps (a little at a time) and lift the camshaft from the cylinder head.
5. Remove the rubber half circle plug.

To install:

1. Clean and inspect the camshaft and camshaft bearings.
2. Apply sealant to the half circle plug and install it into the cylinder head.
3. Place the camshaft in the cylinder head.
4. Position the bearing caps so that number on the top of the cap is pointing toward the front.
5. Install the cap bolts and tighten them gradually in two or three passes. On the final pass tighten the bolts to 13 ft. lbs. (18 Nm).

➡ **If the camshaft or the cylinder head was replaced, the oil clearance and the thrust clearance must be checked.**

6. Inspect and adjust the valve clearance.
7. Coat the oil seal retainer with sealant and install it to the cylinder head.
8. Install the timing belt and covers.
9. Start the engine and inspect for leaks.
10. Check the engine idle and maximum idle speeds and adjust as necessary.

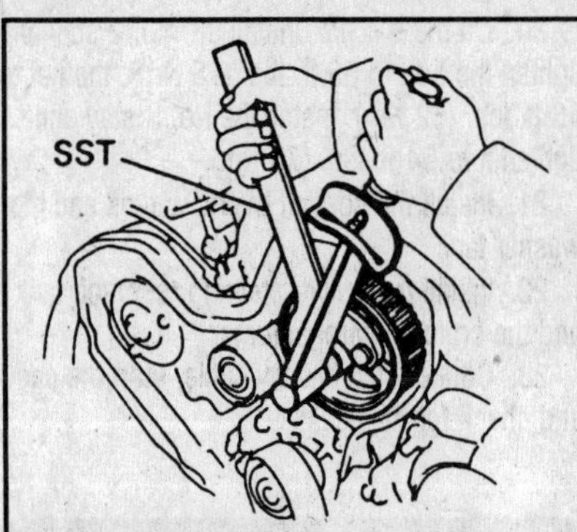

FIG. 208 Removing the camshaft timing pulley — 2VZ-FE and 3VZ-FE engines

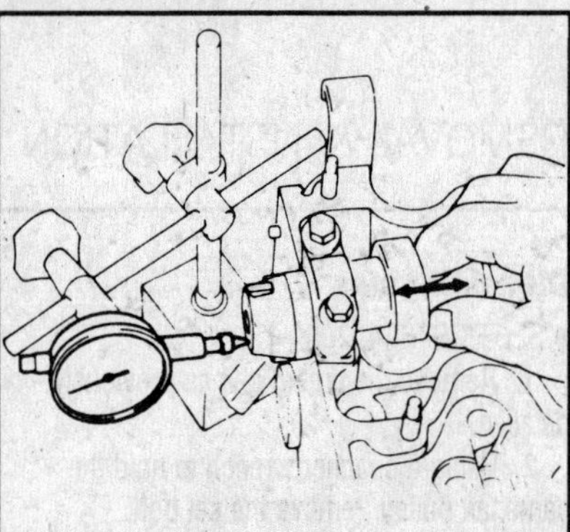

FIG. 209 Checking the camshaft end play

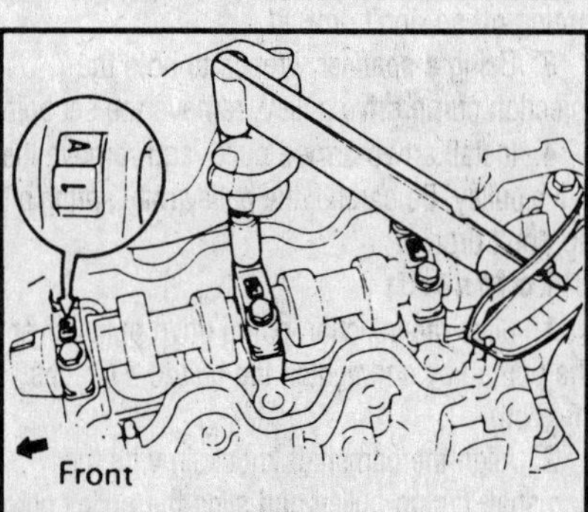

FIG. 210 Install the bearing caps so that the number points toward the front

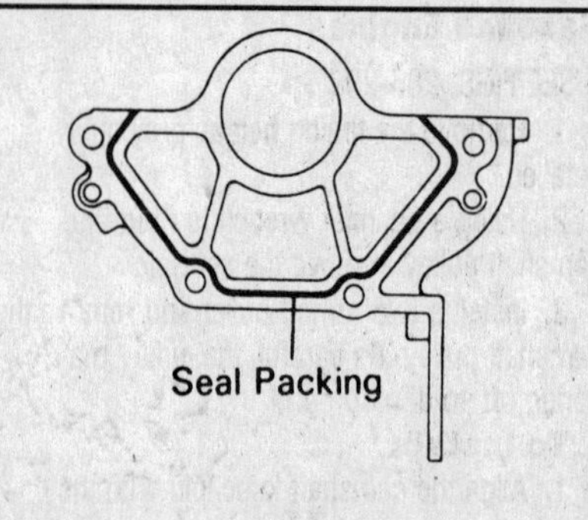

FIG. 211 Apply sealant to the oil seal retainer

2S-E Engines

➧ SEE FIGS. 212-214

The camshaft is located in the camshaft housing.

1. Disconnect the negative battery cable.
2. Remove the valve cover.
3. Loosen the camshaft housing bolts gradually in the sequence shown in Cylinder Head Removal and Installation procedure.

CAUTION

If the bolts are loosened out of sequence, warpage of the camshaft housing could occur.

4. Position a small prybar between the cylinder head and camshaft housing projections, separate the camshaft housing from the cylinder head.
5. Once separated, lift the housing from the engine and place it on a clean work bench.
6. Using a spanner wrench, hold the camshaft pulley stationary and remove the pulley set bolt. Remove the pulley.
7. Inspect the camshaft thrust clearance as follows:
   a. Mount a dial indicator (of recent calibration) to the pulley end of the camshaft.
   b. Preload the dial indicator and zero it.
   c. Move the camshaft back and forth by hand and record the thrust clearance. The standard thrust clearance is 0.0031–0.0090 in. (0.0787–0.228mm). Maximum thrust clearance is 0.0138 in. (0.35mm).
   d. If the thrust is greater than the maximum limit, replace the camshaft and/or the camshaft housing.
8. Remove the five bolts that attach the oil seal retainer to the housing. Remove the oil seal retainer and O-ring. Discard the O-ring.
9. With a slight twisting motion, slowly withdraw the camshaft from the camshaft housing. This must be done slowly to avoid damaging the housing.
10. With a gasket scraper and cleaning solvent, remove the old sealing material from the housing and head contact surfaces.
11. Inspect the camshaft and camshaft housing.

To install:

1. Good maintenance practice suggests that whenever a seal is removed or disturbed, it should be replaced. Replace the camshaft oil seal as follows:
   a. Tap the old seal from the retainer with a screwdriver and hammer.
   b. Install the new seal by pressing it in with the proper size deep well socket.

c. Lubricate the new seal with multi-purpose grease.

2. Slowly insert the camshaft into the housing.

3. Clean the retainer bolts thoroughly with a wire brush to remove all the old sealant, grease or dirt.

4. Apply sealant to the last two or three threads of the bolt end.

5. Place the new O-ring into the retainer and attach the retainer with the five bolts. Tighten the bolts to 82 inch lbs. (9.3 Nm).

6. Remove any oil or grease from the camshaft pulley and then install it as previously detailed.

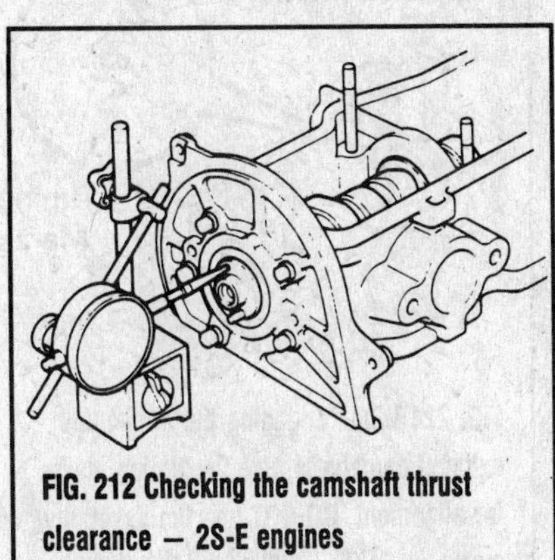

FIG. 212 Checking the camshaft thrust clearance — 2S-E engines

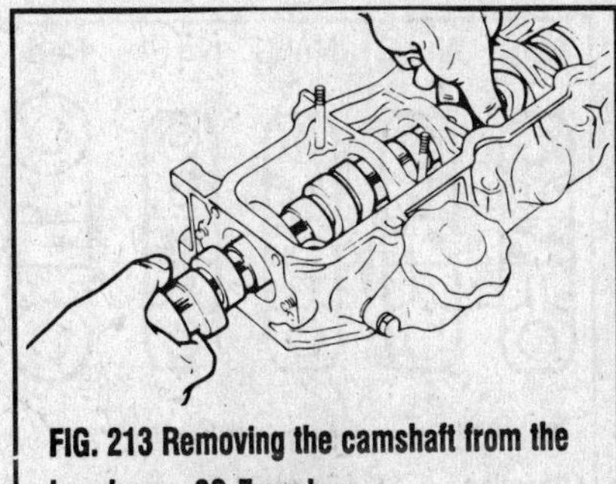

FIG. 213 Removing the camshaft from the housing — 2S-E engines

7. Apply a bead of sealant to the camshaft housing contact surface. Do not use too much sealant. The sealant hardens within 3 minutes after application. If the sealant hardens, it must be removed and re-applied.

8. Place the camshaft housing onto the cylinder head. Install the camshaft housing bolts. Tighten the bolts in three passes to 11 ft. lbs. (15 Nm) in the sequence shown in the Cylinder Head Removal and Installation section.

9. Install the head cover. Connect the negative battery cable. Start and warm up the engine. Inspect for leaks. Adjust the ignition timing and the idle speed.

3S-FE and 5S-FE Engines

➧ SEE FIGS. 215-223

1. Remove the cylinder head cover.

➡ Being that the thrust clearance on both the intake and exhaust camshafts is small, the camshafts must be kept level during removal. If the camshafts are removed without being kept level, the camshaft may be caught in the cylinder head causing the head to break or the camshaft to seize.

2. To remove the exhaust camshaft proceed as follows:

a. Set the knock pin of the intake camshaft at 10–45° BTDC of camshaft angle. This angle will help to lift the exhaust camshaft level and evenly by pushing No. 2 and No. 4 cylinder camshaft lobes of the exhaust camshaft toward their valve lifters.

b. Secure the exhaust camshaft sub-gear to the main gear using a service bolt. The manufacturer recommends a bolt 0.63–0.79 in. (16–20mm) long with a thread diameter of 6mm and a 1mm thread pitch. When removing the exhaust camshaft be sure that the torsional spring force of the sub-gear has been eliminated (you guessed it; that's what the bolt is for!).

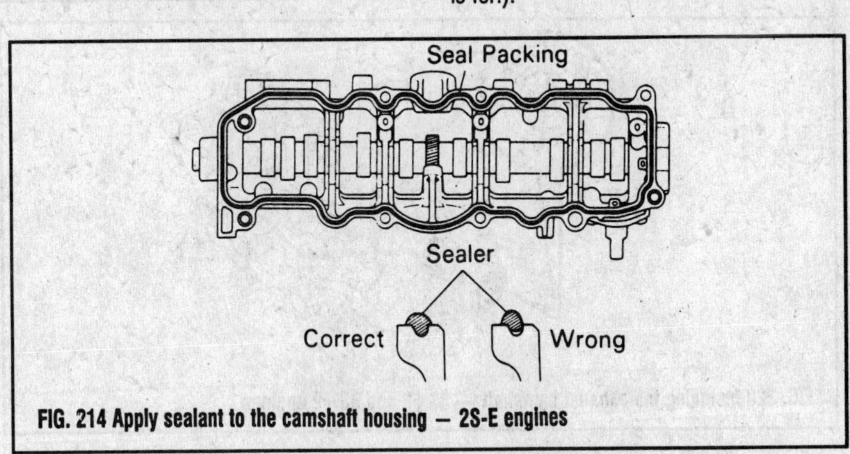

FIG. 214 Apply sealant to the camshaft housing — 2S-E engines

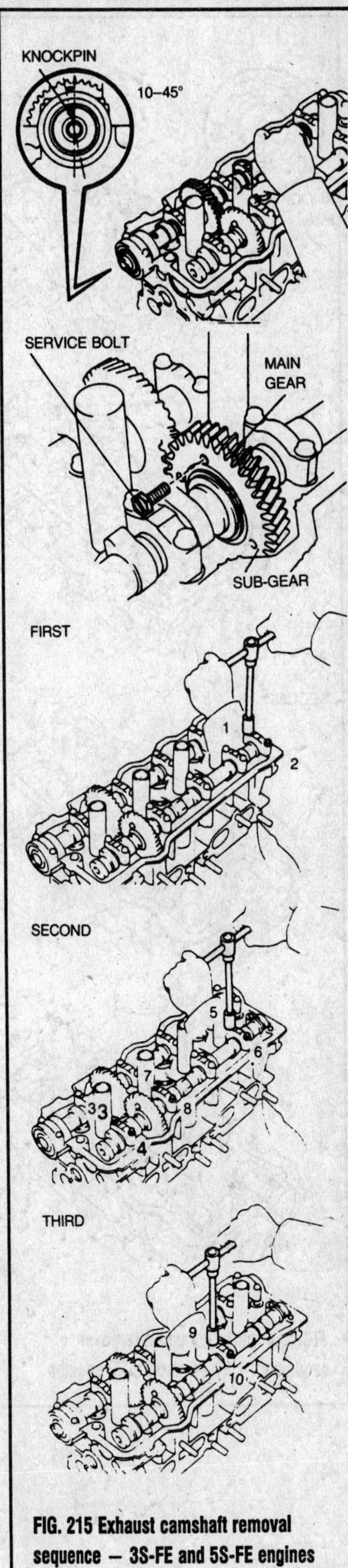

FIG. 215 Exhaust camshaft removal sequence — 3S-FE and 5S-FE engines

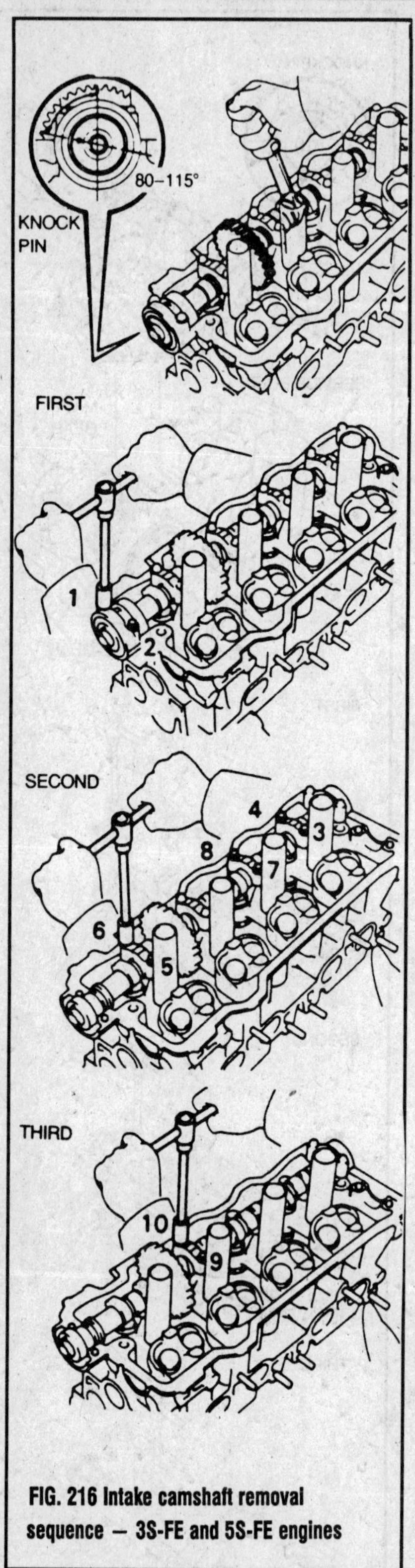

FIG. 216 Intake camshaft removal sequence — 3S-FE and 5S-FE engines

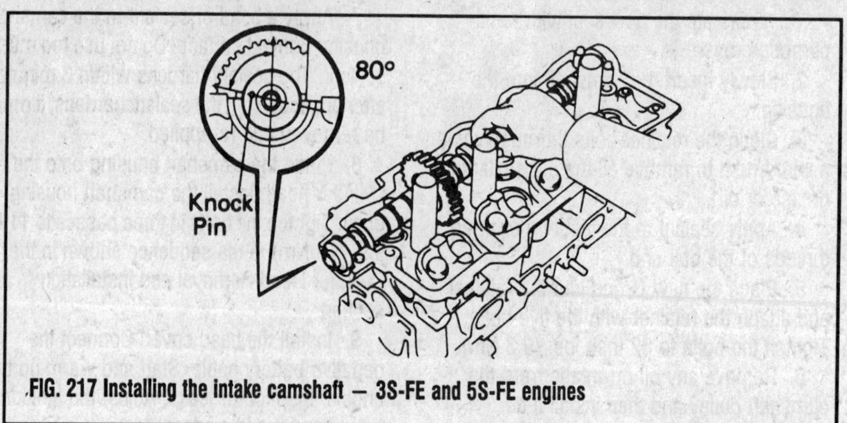

FIG. 217 Installing the intake camshaft — 3S-FE and 5S-FE engines

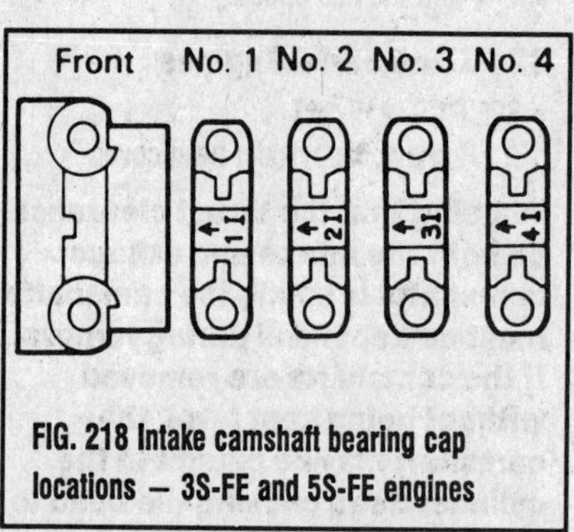

FIG. 218 Intake camshaft bearing cap locations — 3S-FE and 5S-FE engines

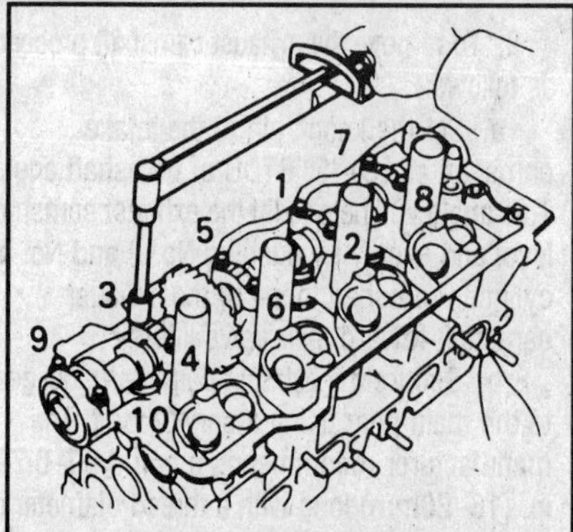

FIG. 219 Intake camshaft bearing cap bolt tightening sequence — 3S-FE and 5S-FE engines

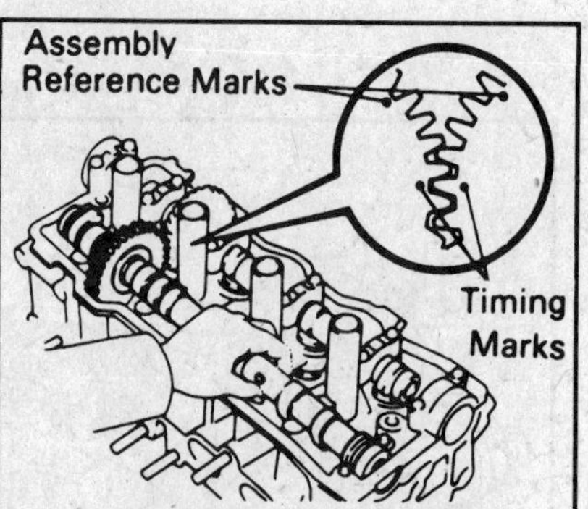

FIG. 221 When engaging the intake and exhaust camshafts, use the timing marks for alignment, DO NOT use the assembly marks — 3S-FE and 5S-FE engines

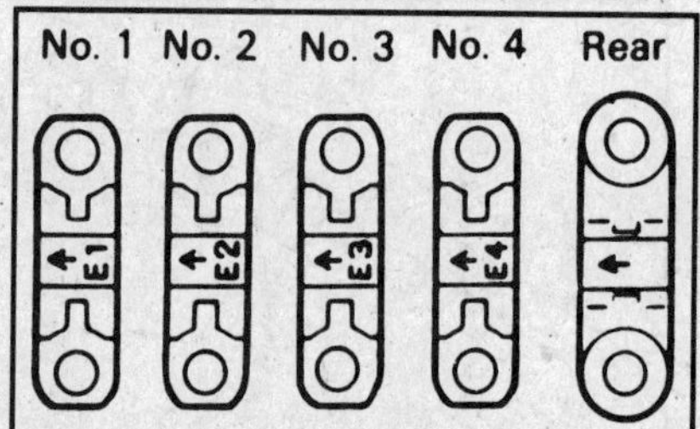

FIG. 222 Exhaust camshaft bearing cap locations — 3S-FE and 5S-FE engines

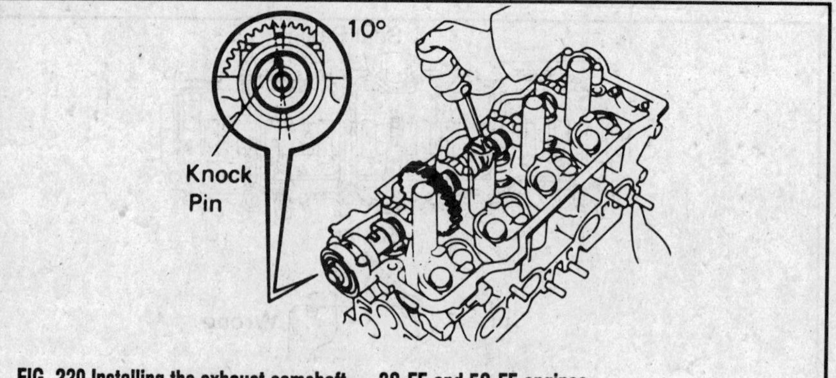

FIG. 220 Installing the exhaust camshaft — 3S-FE and 5S-FE engines

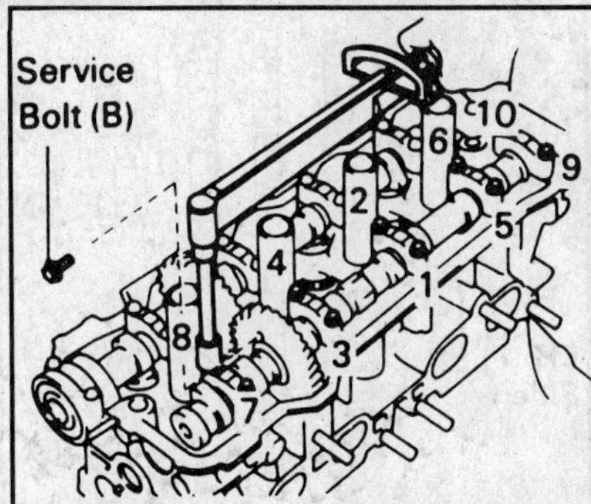

FIG. 223 Exhaust camshaft bearing cap bolt tightening sequence — 3S-FE and 5S-FE engines

c. Remove the No. 1 and No. 2 rear bearing cap bolts and remove the cap. Uniformly loosen and remove bearing cap bolts No. 3 to No. 8 in several passes and in the proper sequence. Do not remove bearing cap bolts No. 9 and 10 at this time. Remove the No. 1, 2, and 4 bearing caps.

d. Alternately loosen and remove bearing cap bolts No. 9 and 10. As these bolts are loosened check to see that the camshaft is being lifted out straight and level.

➡ If the camshaft is not lifting out straight and level retighten No. 9 and 10 bearing cap bolts. Reverse the order of Steps c through a and reset the intake camshaft knock pin to 10-45 degrees BTDC and repeat Steps a through c again. Do not attempt to pry the camshaft from its mounting.

e. Remove the No. 3 bearing cap and exhaust camshaft from the engine.

3. To remove the intake camshaft, proceed as follows:

a. Set the knock pin of the intake camshaft at 80–115° BTDC of camshaft angle. This angle will help to lift the intake camshaft level and evenly by pushing No. 1 and No. 3 cylinder camshaft lobes of the intake camshaft toward their valve lifters.

b. Remove the No. 1 and No. 2 front bearing cap bolts and remove the front bearing cap and oil seal. If the cap will not come apart easily, leave it in place without the bolts.

c. Uniformly loosen and remove bearing cap bolts No. 3 to No. 8 in several phases and in the proper sequence. Do not remove bearing cap bolts No. 9 and 10 at this time. Remove No. 1, 3, and 4 bearing caps.

d. Alternately loosen and remove bearing cap bolts No. 9 and 10. As these bolts are loosened and after breaking the adhesion on the front bearing cap, check to see that the camshaft is being lifted out straight and level.

➡ If the camshaft is not lifting out straight and level retighten No. 9 and 10 bearing cap bolts. Reverse Steps b through d, than start over from Step b. Do not attempt to pry the camshaft from its mounting.

e. Remove the No. 2 bearing cap with the intake camshaft from the engine.

To install:

1. Before installing the intake camshaft, apply multi-purpose grease to the thrust portion of the camshaft.

2. To install the intake camshaft, proceed as follows:

a. Position the camshaft at 80–115° BTDC of camshaft angle on the cylinder head.

b. Apply sealant to the front bearing cap.

c. Coat the bearing cap bolts with clean engine oil.

d. Tighten the camshaft bearing caps evenly and in several passes to 14 ft. lbs. (19 Nm) in the proper sequence.

3. To install the exhaust camshaft, proceed as follows:

a. Set the knock pin of the camshaft at 10–45° BTDC of camshaft angle.

b. Apply multipurpose grease to the thrust portion of the camshaft.

c. Position the exhaust camshaft gear with the intake camshaft gear so that the timing marks are in alignment with one another. Be sure to use the proper alignment marks on the gears. Do not use the assembly reference marks.

d. Turn the intake camshaft clockwise or counterclockwise little by little until the exhaust camshaft sits in the bearing journals evenly without rocking the camshaft on the bearing journals.

e. Coat the bearing cap bolts with clean engine oil.

f. Tighten the camshaft bearing caps evenly and in several passes to 14 ft. lbs. (19 Nm). Remove the service bolt from the assembly.

4. Install the head cover.

5. Start the engine and check for leaks.

6. Adjust the valves and the ignition timing.

2VZ-FE and 3VZ-FE engines

➧ SEE FIGS. 224-239

1. Remove the cylinder head covers.

➡ Being that the thrust clearance on both the intake and exhaust camshafts is small, the camshafts must be kept level during removal. If the camshafts are removed without being kept level, the camshaft may be caught in the cylinder head causing the head to break or the camshaft to seize.

2. To remove the exhaust camshaft from the right side cylinder head,proceed as follows:

a. Turn the camshaft with a wrench until the two pointed marks on the drive and driven gears are aligned.

b. Secure the exhaust camshaft sub-gear to the main gear using a service bolt. The manufacturer recommends a bolt 0.63–0.79 in. (16–20mm) long with a thread diameter of 6mm and a 1mm thread pitch. When removing the exhaust camshaft be sure that the torsional spring force of the sub-gear has been eliminated (you guessed it; that's what the bolt is for!).

c. Remove eight bearing cap bolts and remove the caps. Uniformly loosen and remove bearing cap bolts in several passes and in the proper sequence.

d. Remove the exhaust camshaft from the engine.

3. Uniformly loosen and remove the ten bearing cap bolts in several passes, in the sequence shown. Remove the bearing caps and oil seal and then lift out the intake camshaft.

4. To remove the exhaust camshaft from the left side cylinder head, proceed as follows:

a. Turn the camshaft with a wrench until the pointed marks on the drive and driven gears are aligned.

b. Secure the exhaust camshaft sub-gear to the main gear using a service bolt. The manufacturer recommends a bolt 0.63–0.79 in. (16–20mm) long with a thread diameter of 6mm and a 1mm thread pitch. When removing the exhaust camshaft be sure that the torsional spring force of the sub-gear has been eliminated (you guessed it; that's what the bolt is for!).

c. Remove eight bearing cap bolts and remove the caps. Uniformly loosen and remove bearing cap bolts in several passes and in the proper sequence.

d. Remove the exhaust camshaft from the engine.

5. Uniformly loosen and remove the ten bearing cap bolts in several passes, in the sequence shown. Remove the bearing caps and oil seal and then lift out the intake camshaft.

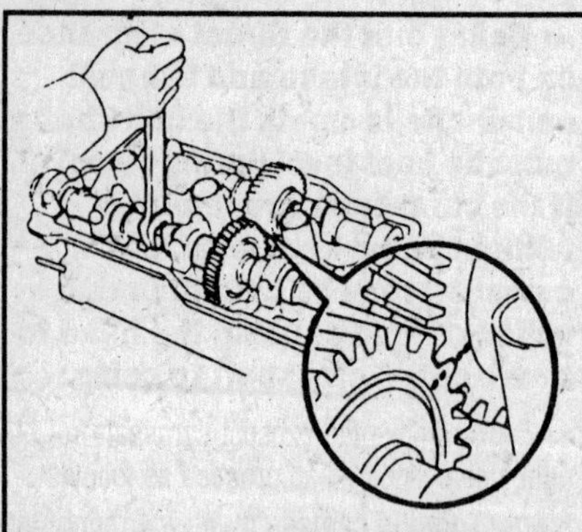
FIG. 224 Align the two pointed marks on the gears — 2VZ-FE and 3VZ-FE engines

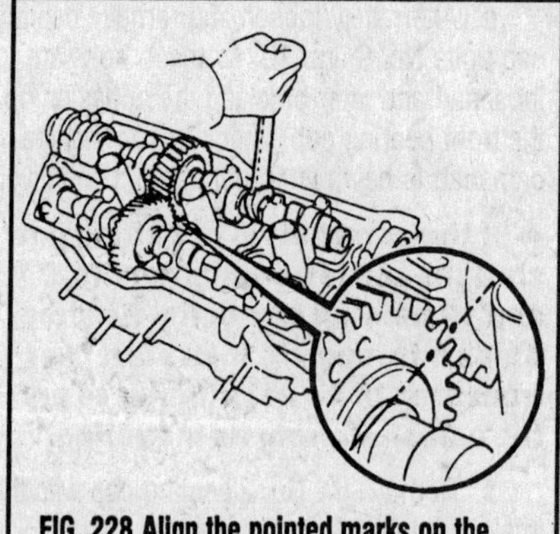
FIG. 228 Align the pointed marks on the gears — 2VZ-FE and 3VZ-FE engines

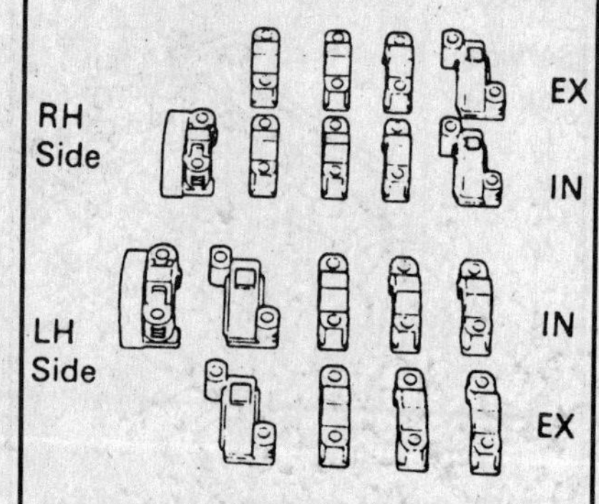

FIG. 232 Arrange the bearing caps in order — 2VZ-FE and 3VZ-FE engines

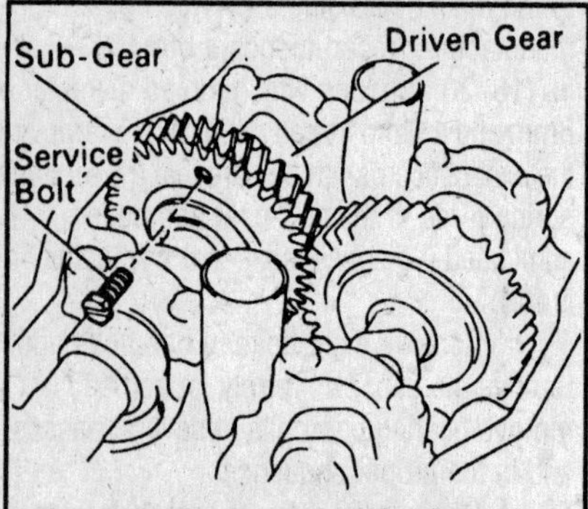

FIG. 225 Secure the right side exhaust camshaft sub-gear with a service bolt — 2VZ-FE and 3VZ-FE engines

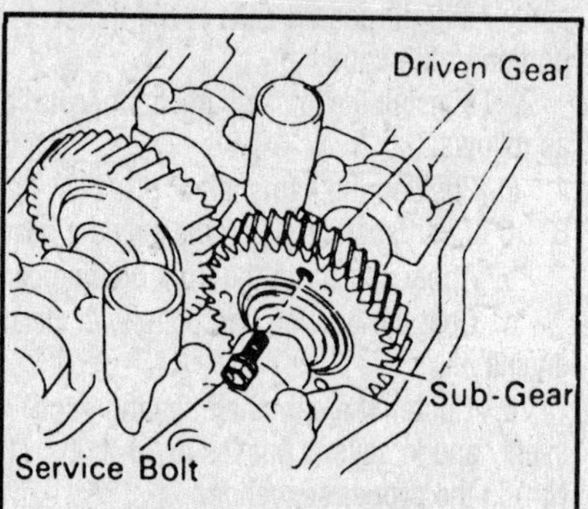

FIG. 229 Secure the left side exhaust camshaft sub-gear with a service bolt — 2VZ-FE and 3VZ-FE engines

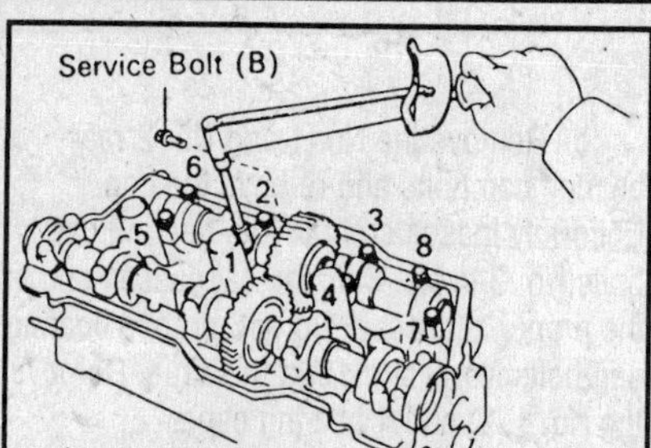

FIG. 233 Right side exhaust camshaft bearing cap bolt tightening sequence — 2VZ-FE and 3VZ-FE engines

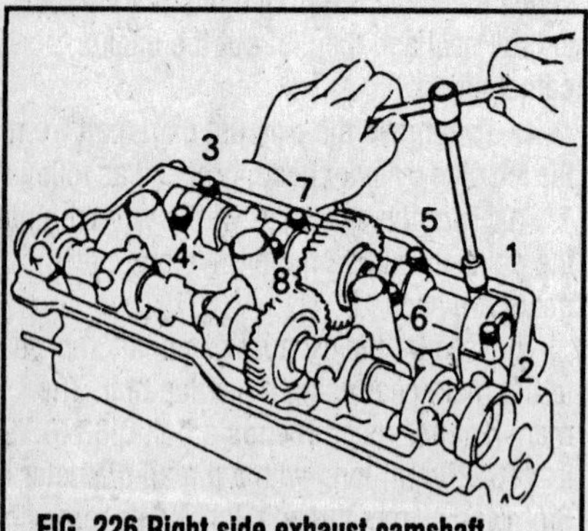
FIG. 226 Right side exhaust camshaft bearing cap bolt loosening sequence — 2VZ-FE and 3VZ-FE engines

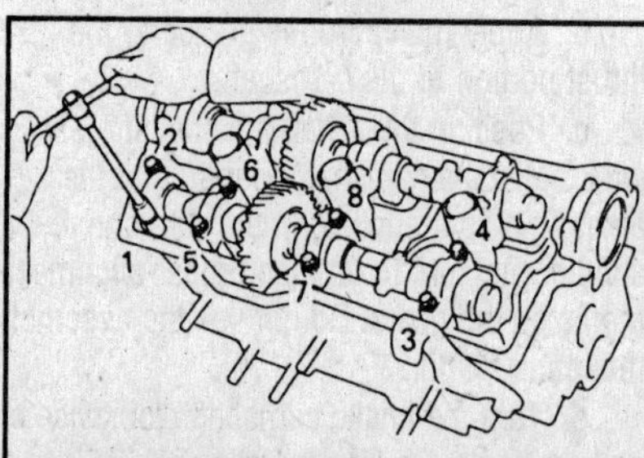
FIG. 230 Left side exhaust camshaft bearing cap bolt loosening sequence — 2VZ-FE and 3VZ-FE engines

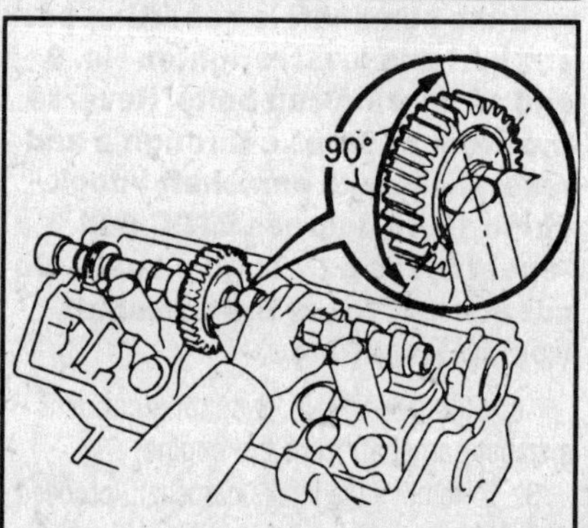

FIG. 234 Install the left side intake camshaft like this — 2VZ-FE and 3VZ-FE engines

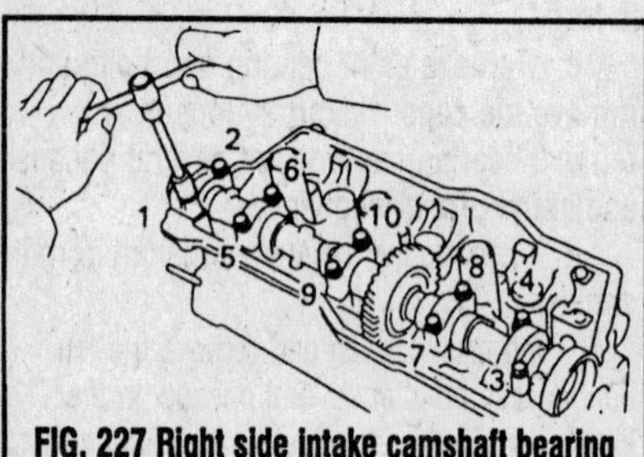
FIG. 227 Right side intake camshaft bearing cap bolt loosening sequence — 2VZ-FE and 3VZ-FE engines

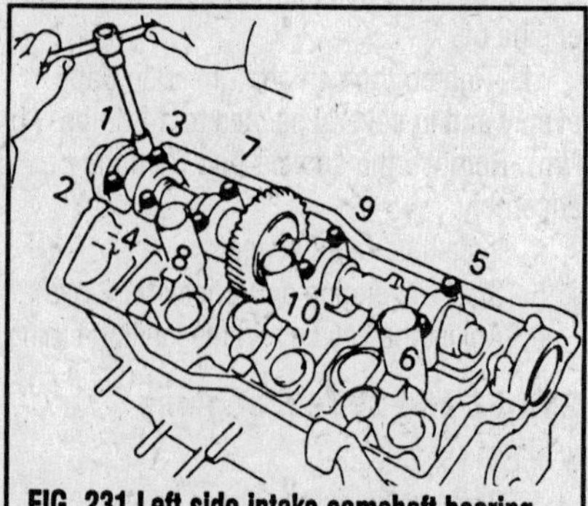
FIG. 231 Left side intake camshaft bearing cap bolt loosening sequence — 2VZ-FE and 3VZ-FE engines

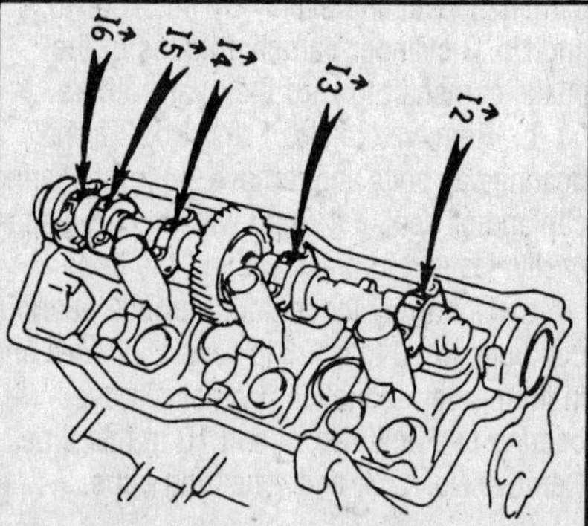

FIG. 235 Install the left side intake camshaft bearing caps — 2VZ-FE and 3VZ-FE engines

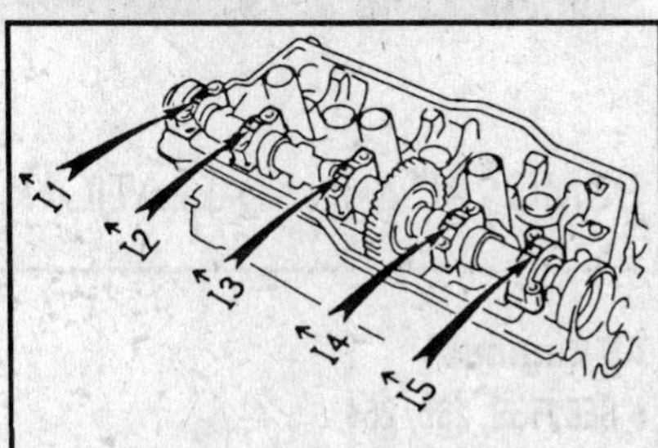

FIG. 236 Left side intake camshaft bearing cap bolt tightening sequence — 2VZ-FE and 3VZ-FE engines

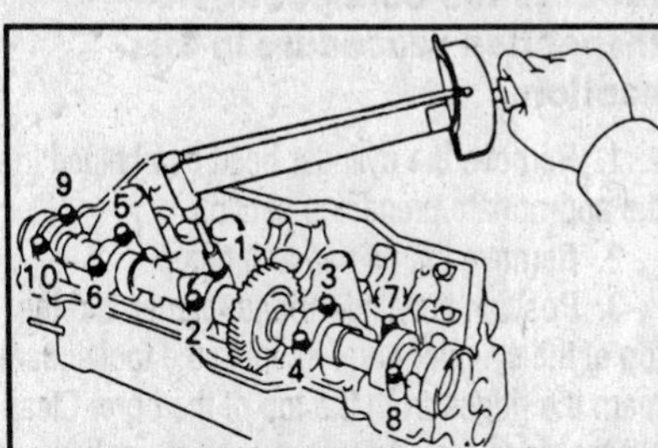

FIG. 237 Install the right side intake camshaft bearing caps — 2VZ-FE and 3VZ-FE engines

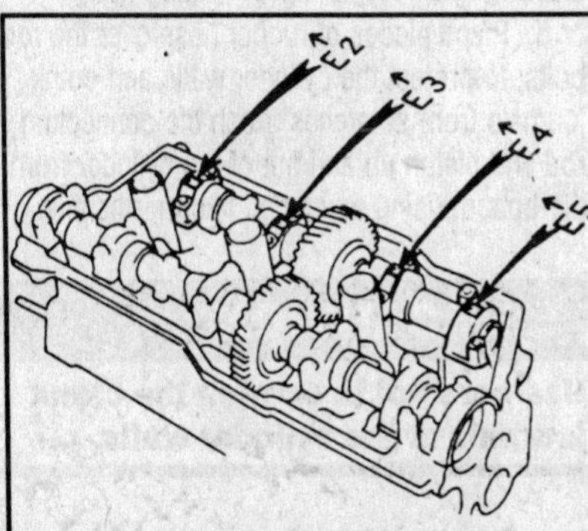

FIG. 238 Right side intake camshaft bearing cap bolt tightening sequence — 2VZ-FE and 3VZ-FE engines

FIG. 239 Install the right side exhaust camshaft bearing caps — 2VZ-FE and 3VZ-FE engines

To Install:

1. Before installing the intake camshaft in the right side cylinder head, apply multi-purpose grease to the thrust portion of the camshaft.
2. To install the intake camshaft, proceed as follows:
   a. Position the camshaft at a 90° angle to the two pointed marks on the cylinder head.
   b. Apply sealant to the No. 1 bearing cap.
   c. Coat the bearing cap bolts with clean engine oil.
   d. Tighten the camshaft bearing caps evenly and in several passes to 12 ft. lbs. (16 Nm) in the proper sequence.
3. Apply multi-purpose grease to the thrust portion of the exhaust camshaft (right side head).
4. Position the camshaft into the head so that the two pointed marks are aligned on the drive and driven gears. Install the bearing caps and tighten the bolts to 12 ft. lbs. (16 Nm), in several passes, in the sequence shown.
5. Remove the service bolt.
6. Before installing the intake camshaft in the left side cylinder head, apply multi-purpose grease to the thrust portion of the camshaft.
7. To install the intake camshaft, proceed as follows:
   a. Position the camshaft at a 90° angle to the pointed mark on the cylinder head.
   b. Apply sealant to the No. 1 bearing cap.
   c. Coat the bearing cap bolts with clean engine oil.
   d. Tighten the camshaft bearing caps evenly and in several passes to 12 ft. lbs. (16 Nm) in the proper sequence.
8. Apply multi-purpose grease to the thrust portion of the exhaust camshaft (left side head).
9. Position the camshaft into the head so that the pointed marks are aligned on the drive and driven gears. Install the bearing caps and tighten the bolts to 12 ft. lbs. (16 Nm), in several passes, in the sequence shown.
10. Remove the service bolt.
11. Install the head cover.
12. Start the engine and check for leaks.
13. Adjust the valves and the ignition timing.

CHECKING CAMSHAFT RUNOUT

➧ SEE FIG. 240

Camshaft runout should be checked when the camshaft has been removed from the engine. An accurate dial indicator is needed for this procedure; engine specialists and most machine shops have this equipment. If you have access to a dial indicator, or can take your camshaft to someone who does, measure the camshaft bearing journal runout. The maximum (limit) runout on the 2S-E, 3S-FE and 5S-FE camshafts is 0.0016 in. (0.04mm). The runout limit on the 2VZ-FE and 3VZ-FE camshafts is 0.0024 in. (0.06mm). The maximum (limit) runout on the 1C-T and 2C-T camshafts is 0.0024 in. (0.06mm) If the runout exceeds the limit replace the camshaft.

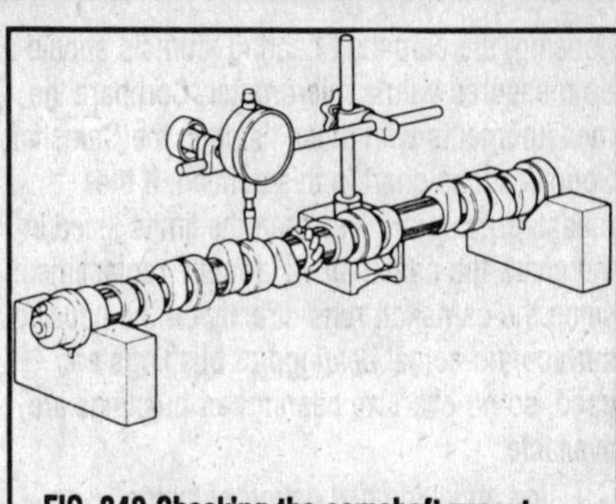

FIG. 240 Checking the camshaft runout

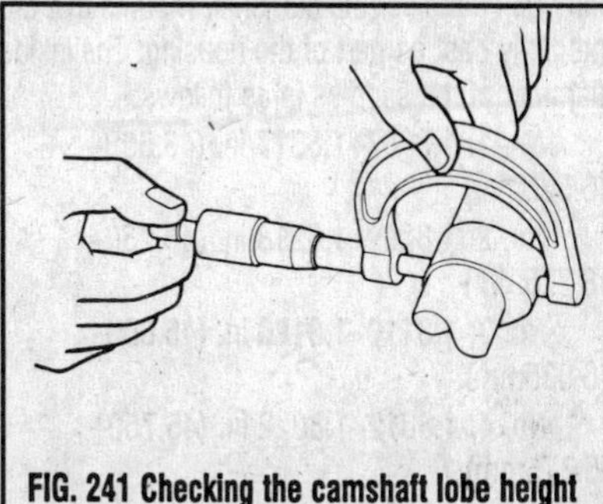

FIG. 241 Checking the camshaft lobe height

CHECKING CAMSHAFT LOBE HEIGHT

➧ SEE FIG. 241

Use a micrometer to check camshaft (lobe) height, making sure the anvil and the spindle of the micrometer are positioned directly on the heel and tip of the camshaft lobe as shown in the accompanying illustration.

CHECKING CAMSHAFT JOURNALS AND CAMSHAFT BEARING SADDLES

2S-E Engines Only

➧ SEE FIGS. 242, 243

While the camshaft is still removed from the

housing, the camshaft bearing journals should be measured with a micrometer. Compare the measurements with those listed in the Camshaft Specifications chart in this section. If the measurements are less than the limits listed in the chart, the camshaft will require replacement, since the camshaft runs directly on the housing surface; no actual bearings or bushings are used, so no oversize bearings or bushings are available.

Using an inside dial gauge or inside micrometer, measure the inside diameter of the camshaft saddles (the camshaft mounts that are integrally cast as part of the housing. The inside diameter of the saddles is as follows:

No. 1: 1.8307–1.8317 in. (46.500–46.525mm)

No. 2: 1.8209–1.8218 in. (46.250–46.275mm)

No. 3: 1.8110–1.8120 in. (46.000–46.025mm)

No. 4: 1.8012–1.8022 in. (45.750–45.775mm)

No. 5: 1.7913–1.7923 in. (45.500–45.525mm)

No. 6: 1.7815–1.7825 in. (45.250–45.275mm)

The camshaft journal oil clearances are listed in the Camshaft Specifications chart in this section. Simply subtract the journal diameter from the inside diameter. If clearances are off, the housing must be replaced (again, because oversize bearings or bushings are not available).

CHECKING BEARING OIL CLEARANCE

All Engines Except 2S-E

➧ SEE FIG. 244

Measure the bearing oil clearance by placing a piece of Plastigage® on each bearing journal. Replace the bearing caps and tighten the bolts to the proper torque.

➡ NOTE: Do not turn the camshaft.

Remove the caps and measure each piece of Plastigage®. If the clearance is greater than the values on the Camshaft Specifications chart, replace the camshaft. If necessary, replace the bearing caps and cylinder head as a set.

Check the camshaft bearings for flaking and scoring. If the bearings show any signs of damage, replace the bearing caps and the cylinder head as a set.

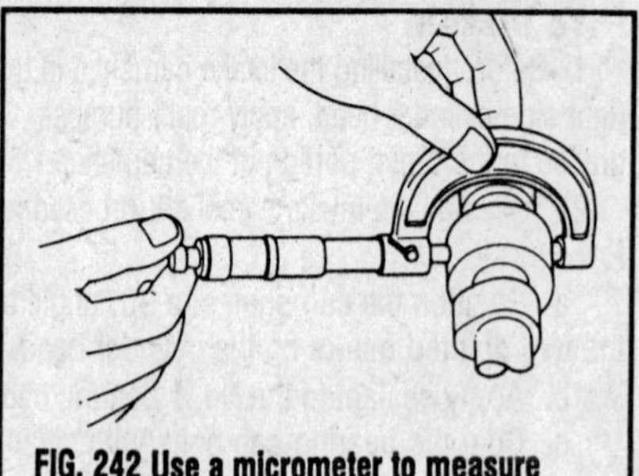

FIG. 242 Use a micrometer to measure camshaft journal diameter

FIG. 243 Use an inside micrometer to measure the camshaft housing bore diameter — 2S-E engines

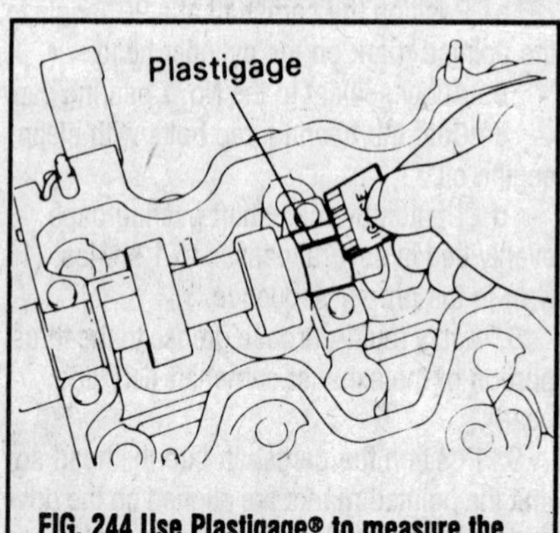

FIG. 244 Use Plastigage® to measure the camshaft oil clearance

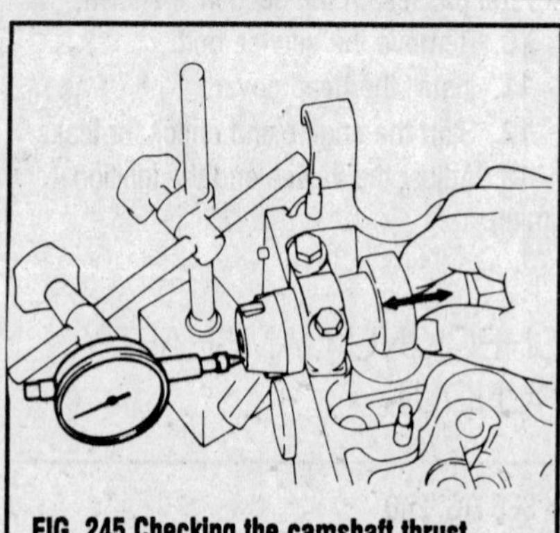

FIG. 245 Checking the camshaft thrust clearance

CHECKING CAMSHAFT ENDPLAY

➧ SEE FIG. 245

After the camshaft has been installed, endplay should be checked. The camshaft sprocket should **not** be installed on the cam. Use a dial gauge to check the endplay, by moving the camshaft forward and backward in the cylinder head. Endplay specifications should be as noted in the Camshaft Specifications chart.

Pistons and Connecting Rods

REMOVAL & INSTALLATION

All Engines

➧ SEE FIGS. 250, 251

➡ Before removing the piston assemblies, connecting rod bearing clearance and side clearance should be checked. Refer to the Connecting Rod Inspection procedure in this section.

1. Remove the cylinder head as outlined in the appropriate preceding section.
2. Remove the oil pan and pump.
3. Position a cylinder ridge reamer into the top of the cylinder bore. Keeping the tool square, ream the ridges from the top of the bore. Clean out the ridge material with a solvent-soaked rag, or blow it out with compressed air.
4. Remove the oil strainer if it is in the way. Unbolt the connecting rod caps, after match marking each cap to its connecting rod.
5. Place pieces of rubber hose over the rod bolts, to protect the cylinder walls and crank journals from scratches. Push the connecting rod and piston up and out of the cylinder from the bottom using a wooden hammer handle.

CAUTION

Use care not to scratch the crank journals or the cylinder walls.

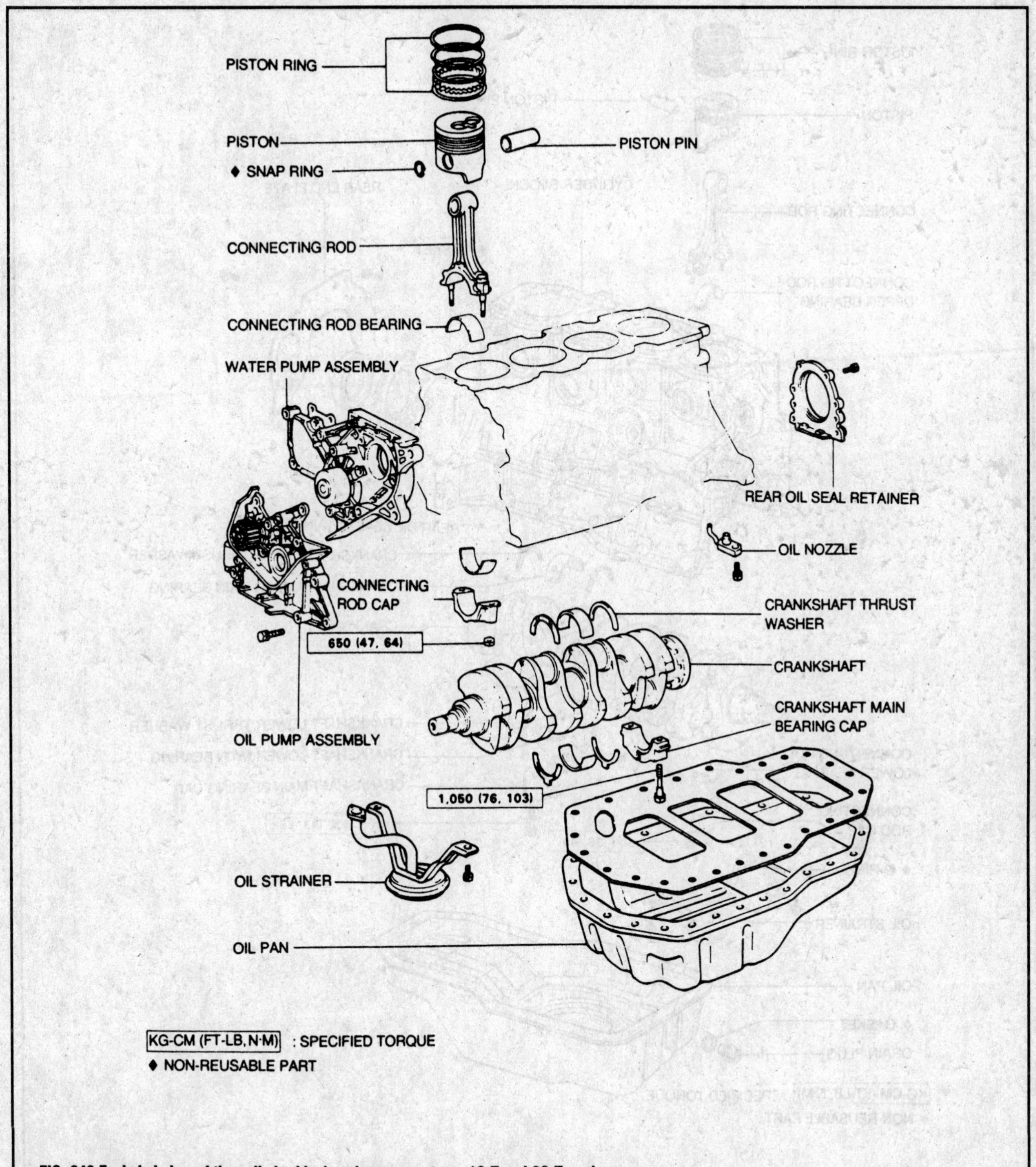

FIG. 246 Exploded view of the cylinder block and components — 1C-T and 2C-T engines

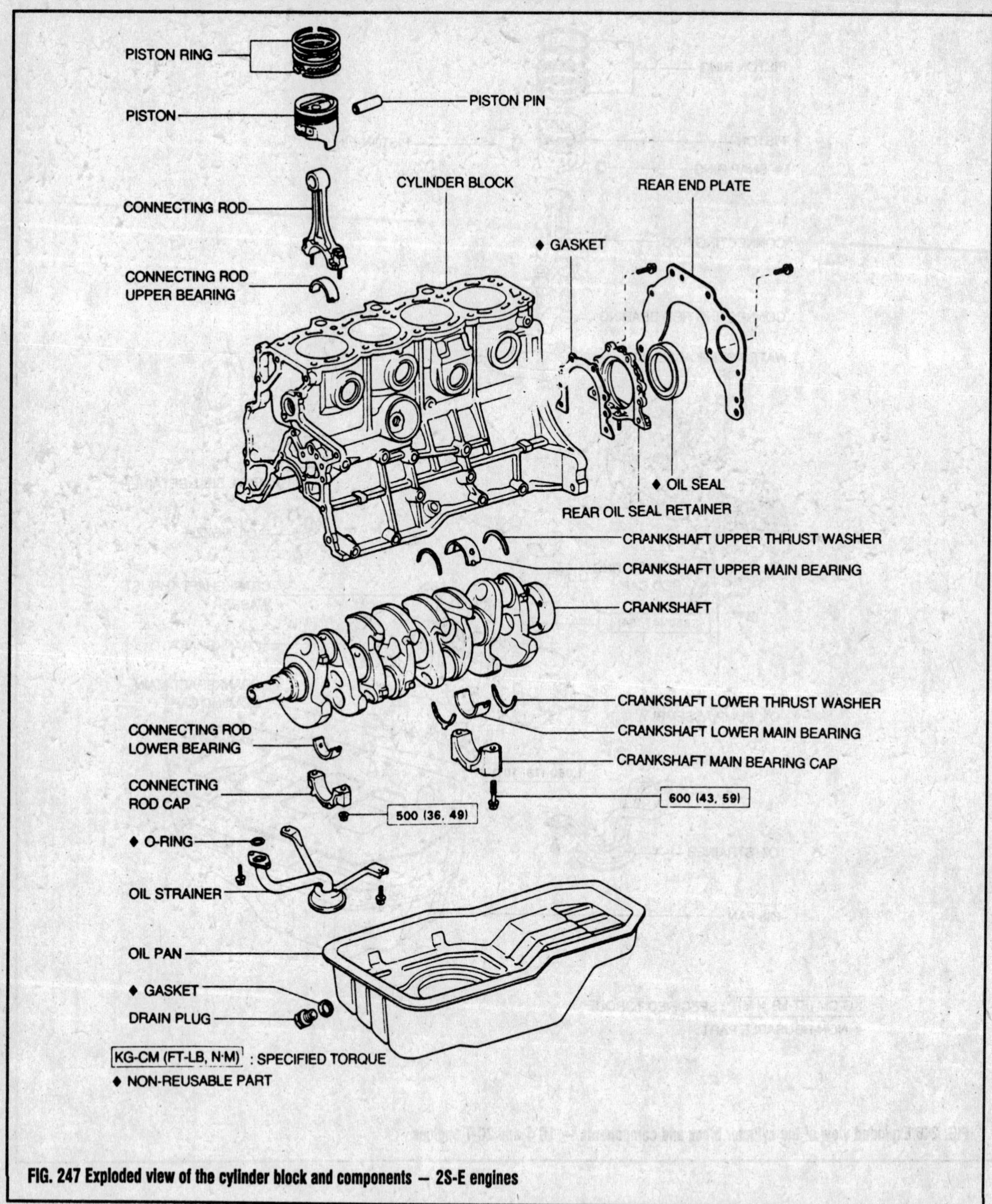

FIG. 247 Exploded view of the cylinder block and components — 2S-E engines

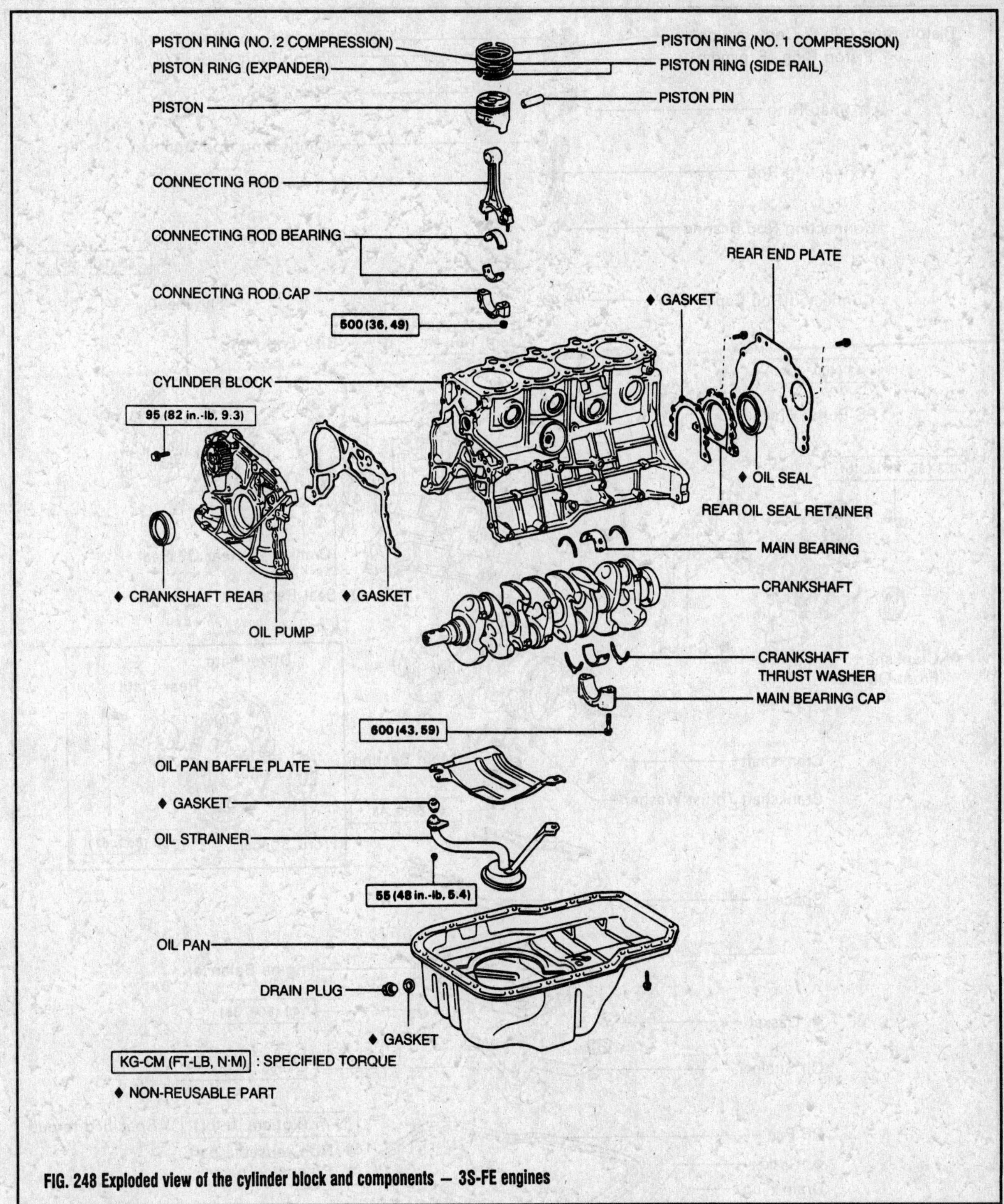

FIG. 248 Exploded view of the cylinder block and components — 3S-FE engines

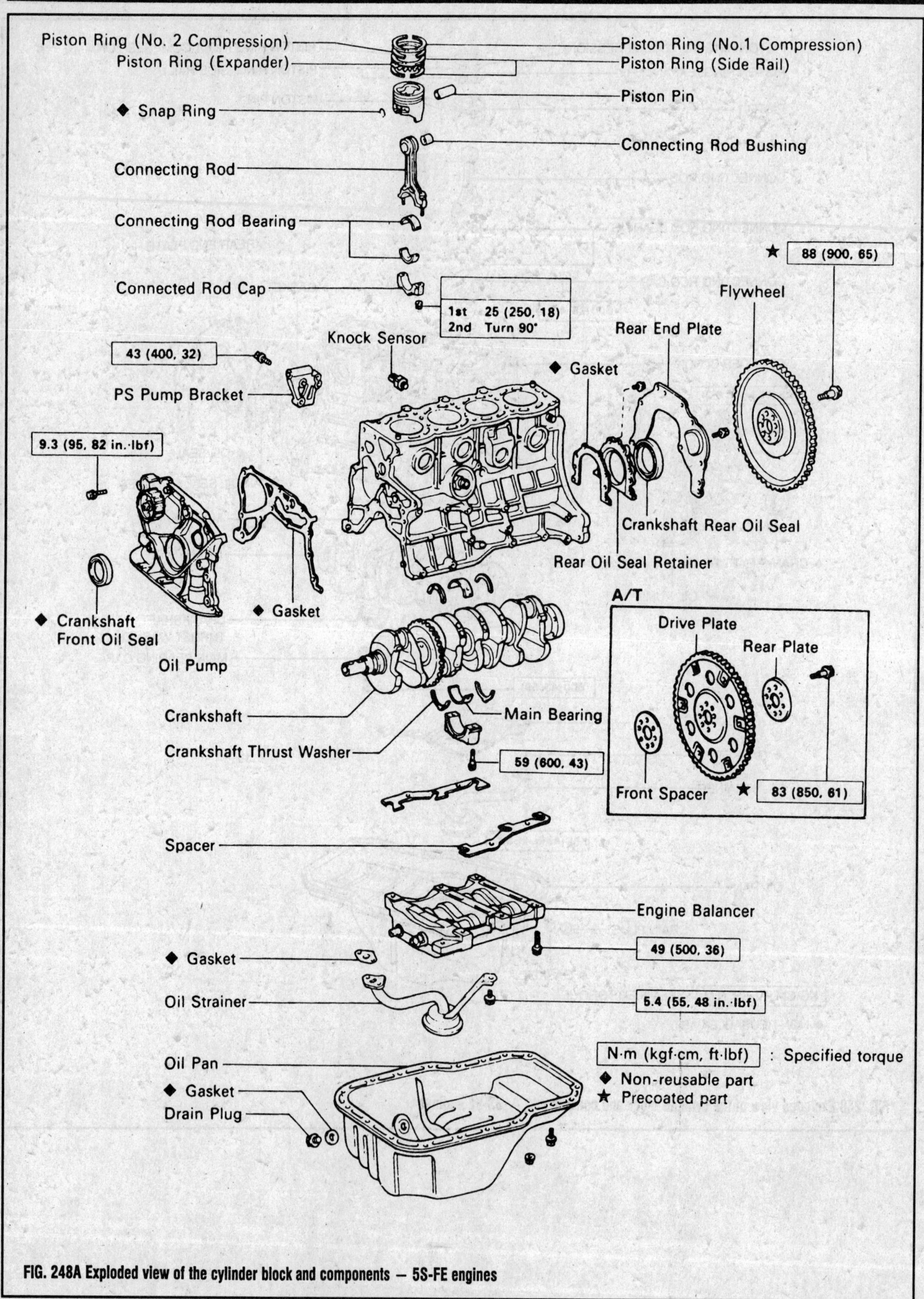
Piston Ring (No. 2 Compression)
Piston Ring (Expander)
Piston Ring (No.1 Compression)
Piston Ring (Side Rail)
Piston Pin
◆ Snap Ring
Connecting Rod Bushing
Connecting Rod
Connecting Rod Bearing
★ 88 (900, 65)
Connected Rod Cap
1st 25 (250, 18)
2nd Turn 90°
Flywheel
Rear End Plate
Knock Sensor
43 (400, 32)
◆ Gasket
PS Pump Bracket
9.3 (95, 82 in.·lbf)
Crankshaft Rear Oil Seal
Rear Oil Seal Retainer
A/T
◆ Gasket
◆ Crankshaft
Front Oil Seal
Drive Plate
Rear Plate
Oil Pump
Crankshaft
Main Bearing
Crankshaft Thrust Washer
59 (600, 43)
Front Spacer
★ 83 (850, 61)
Spacer
Engine Balancer
49 (500, 36)
◆ Gasket
Oil Strainer
5.4 (55, 48 in.·lbf)
N·m (kgf·cm, ft·lbf) : Specified torque
◆ Non-reusable part
★ Precoated part
Oil Pan
◆ Gasket
Drain Plug

FIG. 248A Exploded view of the cylinder block and components — 5S-FE engines

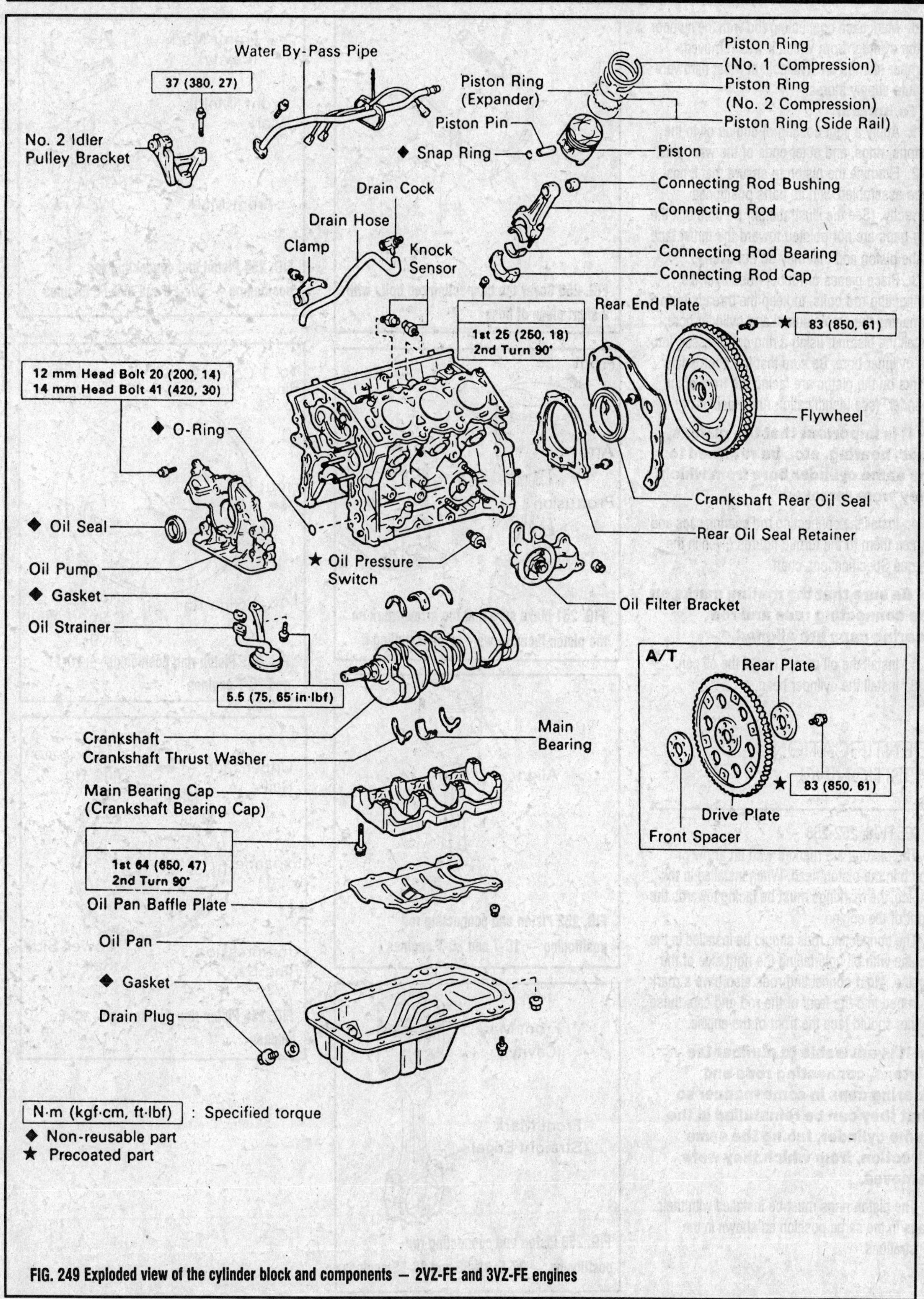
Water By-Pass Pipe
37 (380, 27)
No. 2 Idler
Pulley Bracket
Piston Ring
(No. 1 Compression)
Piston Ring
(Expander)
Piston Ring
(No. 2 Compression)
Piston Ring (Side Rail)
Piston Pin
◆ Snap Ring
Piston
Connecting Rod Bushing
Drain Cock
Connecting Rod
Drain Hose
Clamp
Knock
Sensor
Connecting Rod Bearing
Connecting Rod Cap
Rear End Plate
1st 25 (250, 18)
2nd Turn 90°
★ 83 (850, 61)
12 mm Head Bolt 20 (200, 14)
14 mm Head Bolt 41 (420, 30)
◆ O-Ring
Flywheel
Crankshaft Rear Oil Seal
◆ Oil Seal
Rear Oil Seal Retainer
Oil Pump
★ Oil Pressure
Switch
◆ Gasket
Oil Filter Bracket
Oil Strainer
A/T
Rear Plate
5.5 (75, 65 in·lbf)
Crankshaft
Main
Bearing
Crankshaft Thrust Washer
★ 83 (850, 61)
Main Bearing Cap
(Crankshaft Bearing Cap)
Drive Plate
Front Spacer
1st 64 (650, 47)
2nd Turn 90°
Oil Pan Baffle Plate
Oil Pan
◆ Gasket
Drain Plug
N·m (kgf·cm, ft·lbf) : Specified torque
◆ Non-reusable part
★ Precoated part

FIG. 249 Exploded view of the cylinder block and components — 2VZ-FE and 3VZ-FE engines

6. Mark each connecting rod with the number of the cylinder from which it was removed. Number stamps are available at most hardware or auto supply stores.

To Install:

1. Apply a light coating of engine oil to the pistons, rings, and outer ends of the wrist pins.
2. Examine the piston to ensure that it has been assembled with its parts positioned correctly. (See the illustrations.) Be sure that the ring gaps are not pointed toward the thrust face of the piston and that they do not overlap.
3. Place pieces of rubber hose over the connecting rod bolts, to keep the threads from damaging the crank journal and cylinder bore. Install the pistons, using a ring compressor, into the cylinder bore. Be sure that the appropriate marks on the piston are facing the front of the cylinder. (see Identification And Positioning)

➡ **It is important that the pistons, rods, bearing, etc., be returned to the same cylinder bore from which they were removed.**

4. Install the connecting rod bearing caps and tighten them to the torque figures given in the Torque Specifications chart.

➡ **Be sure that the mating marks on the connecting rods and rod bearing caps are aligned.**

5. Install the oil pump. Install the oil pan.
6. Install the cylinder head.

IDENTIFICATION AND POSITIONING

➧ SEE FIGS. 252-258

The pistons are marked with an arrow or notch in the piston head. When installed in the engine, the markings **must** be facing towards the front of the engine.

The connecting rods should be installed in the engine with oil hole facing the right side of the engine. **Most** connecting rods also have a mark stamped into the front of the rod and cap, these marks should face the front of the engine.

➡ **It is advisable to number the pistons, connecting rods and bearing caps in some manner so that they can be reinstalled in the same cylinder, facing the same direction, from which they were removed.**

The piston rings must be installed with their gaps in the same position as shown in the illustrations.

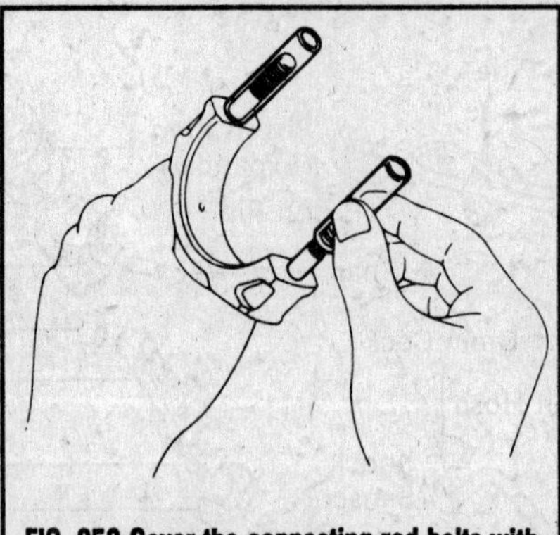
FIG. 250 Cover the connecting rod bolts with a short piece of hose

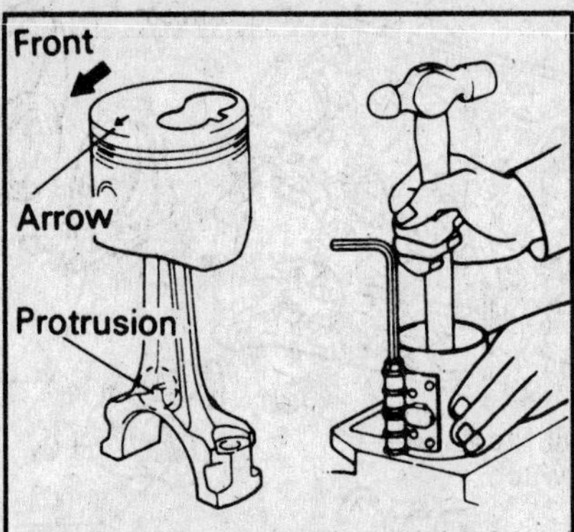

FIG. 251 Make sure that the arrow/mark on the piston faces forward when installing it

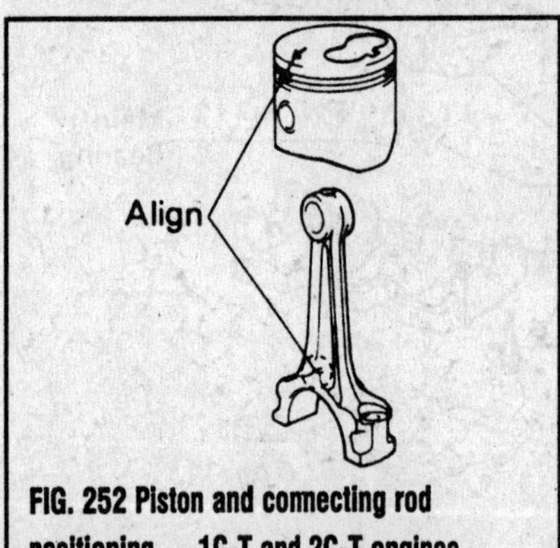

FIG. 252 Piston and connecting rod positioning — 1C-T and 2C-T engines

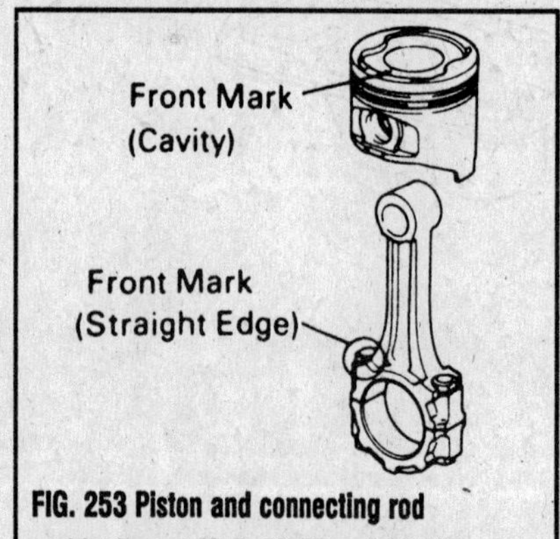

FIG. 253 Piston and connecting rod positioning — 2S-E, 3S-FE and 5S-FE engines

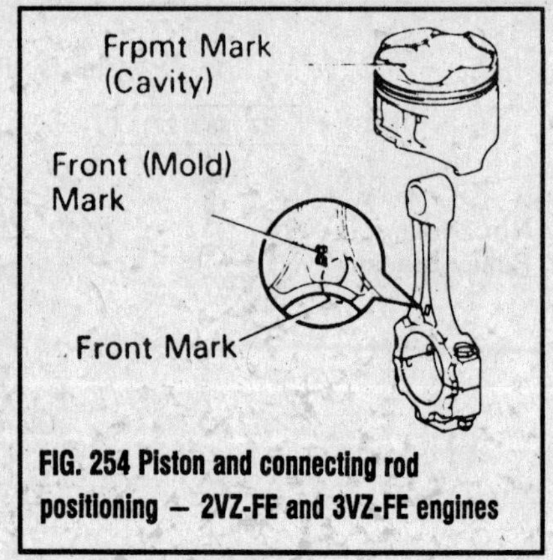

FIG. 254 Piston and connecting rod positioning — 2VZ-FE and 3VZ-FE engines

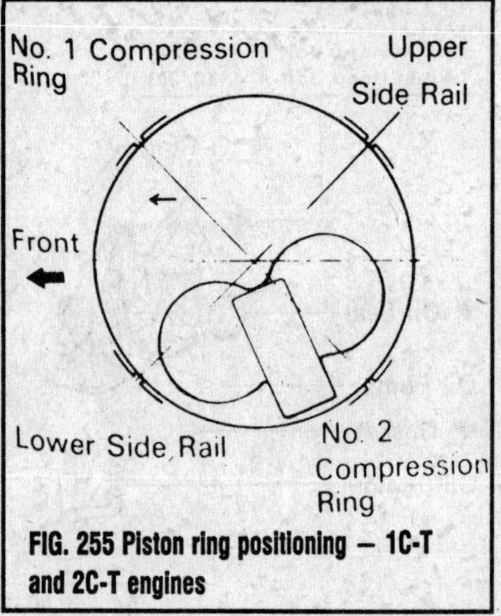

FIG. 255 Piston ring positioning — 1C-T and 2C-T engines

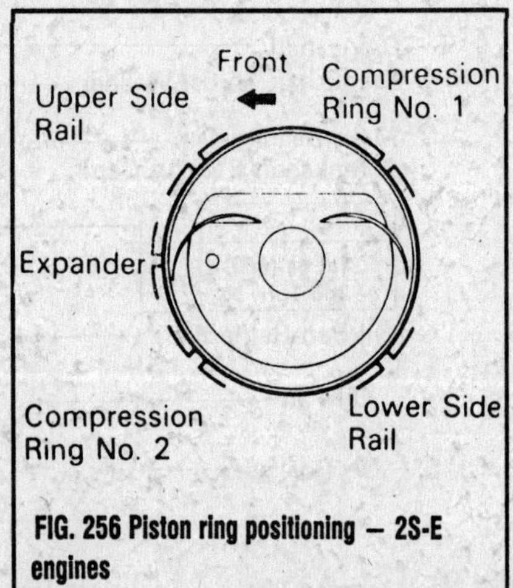

FIG. 256 Piston ring positioning — 2S-E engines

Upper Side Rail
No. 1 Compression Ring
Expander
Front Mark (Cavity)
No. 2 Compression Ring
Lower Side Rail

FIG. 257 Piston ring positioning — 3S-FE and 5S-FE engines

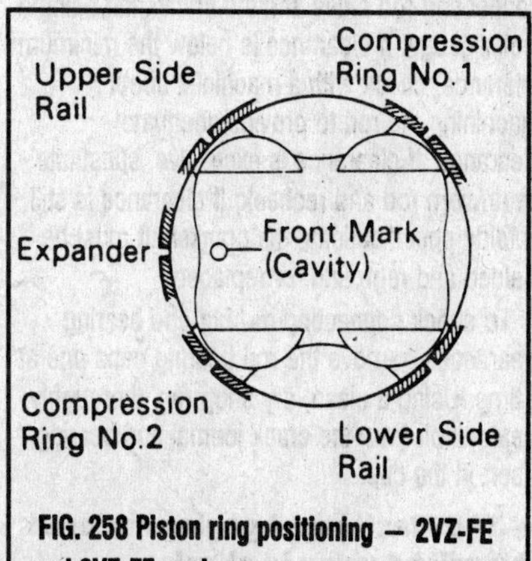

FIG. 258 Piston ring positioning — 2VZ-FE and 3VZ-FE engines

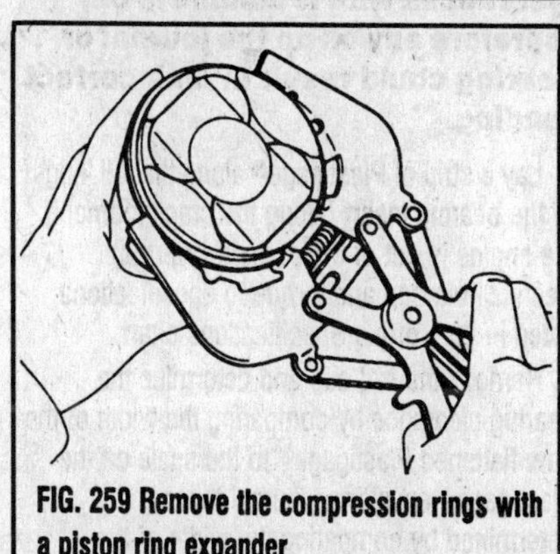

FIG. 259 Remove the compression rings with a piston ring expander

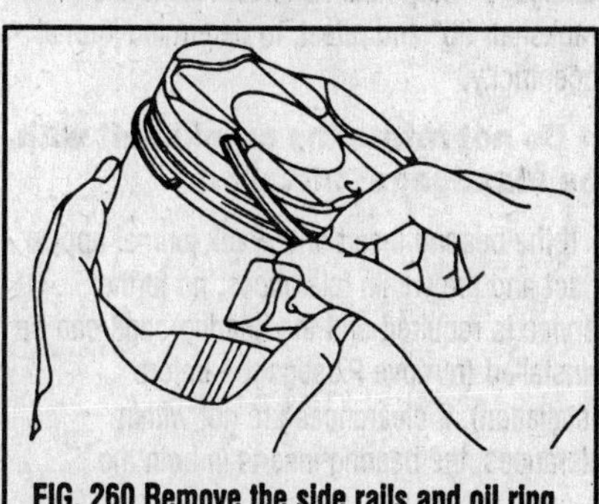

FIG. 260 Remove the side rails and oil ring expander by hand

PISTON RING REPLACEMENT

➧ SEE FIGS. 259, 260

➡ **The cylinder walls must be de-glazed (honed) when the piston rings are replaced. De-glazing ensures proper ring seating and oil retention.**

Using a piston ring expander, remove the two compression rings one by one. Remove the two side rails and oil ring expander by hand. Always remove and replace the rings of each piston before going on to the next. This helps avoid mixing up the rings. When the rings have been removed from each piston, perform the end gap and piston inspection and cleaning procedure detailed below (Cleaning and Inspection). The rings are marked with a code on one side, the mark denoting the up side for installation.

Install the rings using the ring expander, starting with the top compression ring and working down. Make sure the code marks are facing up on each ring. Position the rings so that the ring and gaps are set as in the illustrations. Never align the end gaps!

WRIST PIN REMOVAL AND INSTALLATION

➧ SEE FIGS. 261-263

Wrist pin and/or connecting rod small-end bushing wear can be checked by rocking the piston at a right angle to the wrist pin by hand. If more than very **slight** movement is felt, the pin and/or rod busing must be replaced.

The pistons on the engines covered here must be heated in hot water to expand them before the wrist pins can be removed and installed. The four cylinder pistons must be heated to 176°F (80°C), and all six cylinder pistons must be heated to 140°F (60°C). This job can be performed at a machine shop if the idea of boiling pistons in the kitchen doesn't appeal to you. If you decide to do it, however, remember that each piston, pin and connecting rod assembly is a matched set and must be kept together until reassembly.

1. Using needlenose or snapring pliers, remove the snaprings from the piston (if so equipped).

2. Heat the piston(s) in hot water (as noted above depending on engine).

3. Using a plastic-faced hammer and driver, lightly tap the wrist pin out of the piston. Remove the piston from the connecting rod.

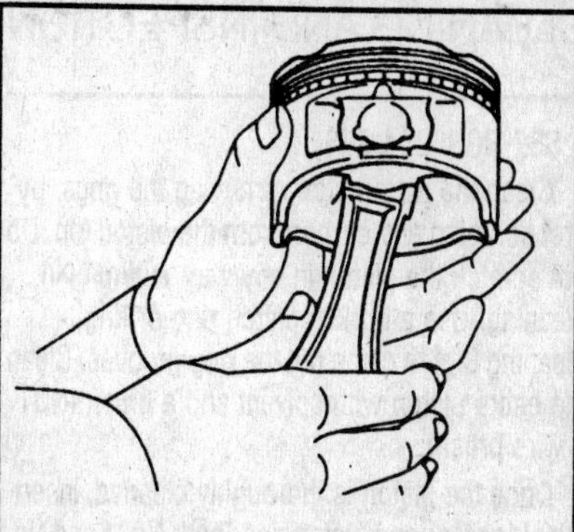

FIG. 261 Checking the connecting rod and wrist pin

FIG. 262 Removing the snap ring

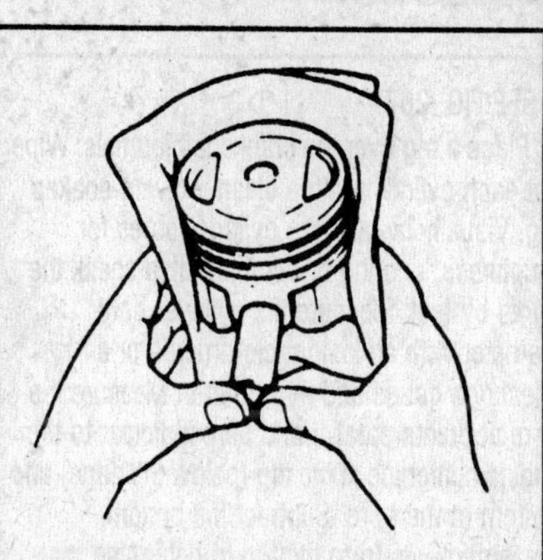

FIG. 263 When fully heated, the wrist pin can then be pressed out

4. Assembly is in the opposite order of disassembly. The piston must again be heated to install the wrist pin and rod; it should be able to be pushed into place with your thumb when heated. When assembling, make sure the marks on the piston and connecting rod are aligned on the same side as shown.

CLEANING AND INSPECTION

➧ SEE FIGS. 264-266

Clean the piston after removing the rings, by first scraping any carbon from the piston top. Do not scratch the piston in any way during cleaning. Use a broken piston ring or ring cleaning tool to clean out the ring grooves. Clean the entire piston with solvent and a brush (NOT a wire brush).

Once the piston is thoroughly cleaned, insert the side of a good piston ring (both No. 1 and No. 2 compression on each piston) into its respective groove. Using a feeler gauge, measure the clearance between the ring and its groove. If clearance is greater than the maximum listed under Ring Side Clearance in the Piston and Ring chart, replace the ring(s) and if necessary, the piston.

To check ring end-gap, insert a compression ring into the cylinder. Lightly oil the cylinder bore and push the ring down into the cylinder with a piston, to the bottom of its travel. Measure the ring end-gap with a feeler gauge. If the gap is not within specification, replace the ring; DO NOT file the ring ends.

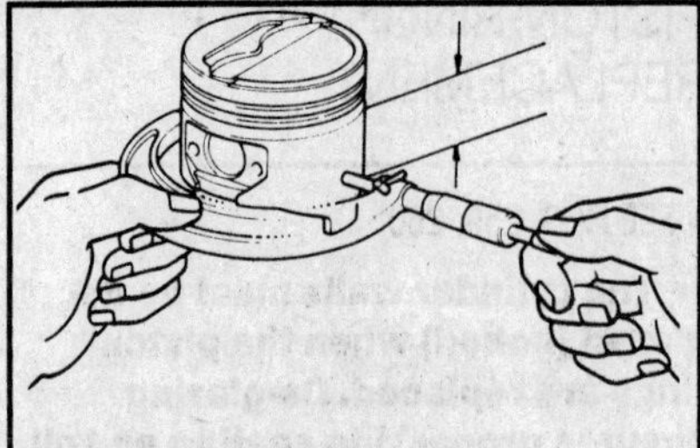

FIG. 264 Measure the piston diameter and oil clearance with a micrometer

FIG. 265 Checking the piston ring side clearance

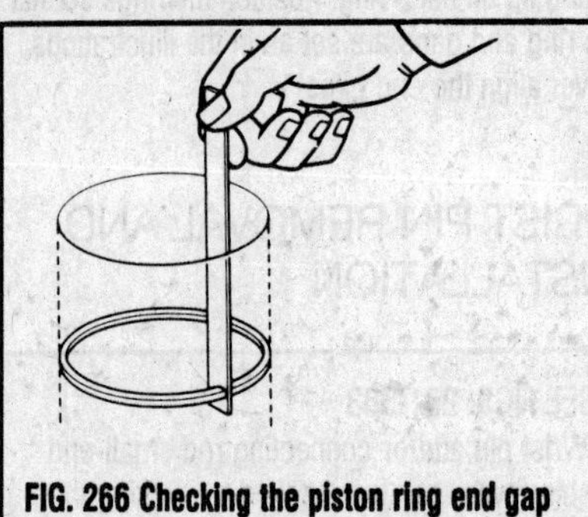

FIG. 266 Checking the piston ring end gap

CYLINDER BORE INSPECTION

➧ SEE FIG. 267

Place a rag over the crankshaft journals. Wipe out each cylinder with a clean, solvent-soaked rag. Visually inspect the cylinder bores for roughness, scoring or scuffing; also check the bores by feel. Measure the cylinder bore diameter with an inside micrometer, or a telescope gauge and micrometer. Measure the bore at points parallel and perpendicular to the engine centerline at the top (below the ridge) and bottom of the bore. Subtract the bottom measurements from the top to determine cylinder taper.

Measure the piston diameter with a micrometer; since this micrometer may not be part of your tool kit as it is necessarily large, you have to have the pistons miked at a machine shop. Take the measurements at right angles to the wrist pin center line, about an inch down the piston skirt from the top. Compare this measurement to the bore diameter of each cylinder. The difference is the piston clearance. If the clearance is greater than that specified in the Piston and Ring Specifications chart, have the cylinders honed or rebored and replace the pistons with an oversize set. Piston clearance can also be checked by inverting a piston into an oiled cylinder, and sliding in a feeler gauge between the two.

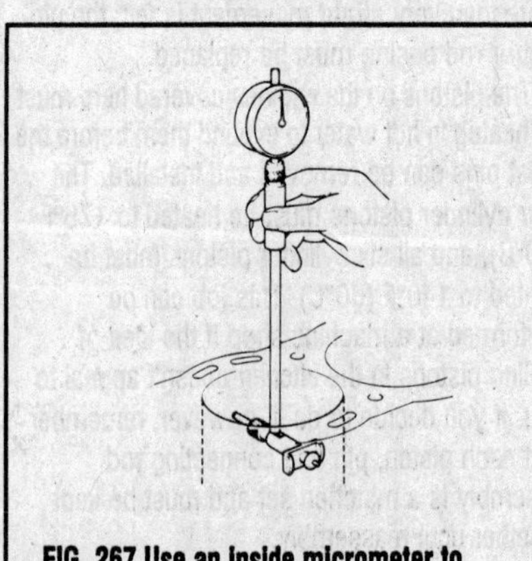

FIG. 267 Use an inside micrometer to measure the bore

CONNECTING ROD INSPECTION AND BEARING REPLACEMENT

➧ SEE FIGS. 268-271

Connecting rod side clearance and big-end bearing inspection and replacement should be performed while the rods are still installed in the engine. Determine the clearance between the connecting rod sides and the crankshaft using a feeler gauge. If clearance is below the minimum tolerance, check with a machinist about machining the rod to provide adequate clearance. If clearance is excessive, substitute an unworn rod and recheck; if clearance is still outside specifications, the crankshaft must be welded and reground, or replaced.

To check connecting rod big-end bearing clearances, remove the rod bearing caps one at a time. Using a clean, dry shop rag, thoroughly clean all oil from the crank journal and bearing insert in the cap.

➡ The Plastigage® gaging material you will be using to check clearances with is soluble in oil; therefore any oil on the journal or bearing could result in an incorrect reading.

Lay a strip of Plastigage® along the full length of the bearing insert (along the crank journal if the engine is out of the car and inverted). Reinstall the cap and torque to specifications listed in the Torque Specifications chart.

Remove the rod cap and determine the bearing clearance by comparing the width of the now flattened Plastigage® to the scale on the Plastigage® envelope. Journal taper is determined by comparing the width of the Plastigage® strip near its ends. Rotate the crankshaft 90° and retest, to determine journal eccentricity.

➡ Do not rotate the crankshaft with the Plastigage® installed.

If the bearing insert and crank journal appear intact and are within tolerances, no further service is required and the bearing caps can be reinstalled (remove Plastigage® before installation). If clearances are not within tolerances, the bearing inserts in both the

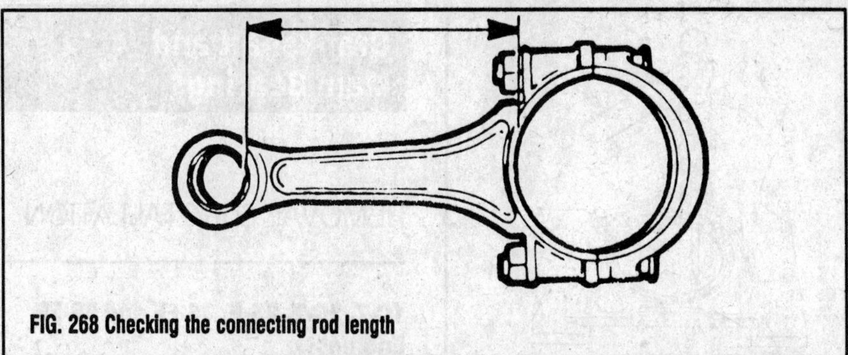
FIG. 268 Checking the connecting rod length

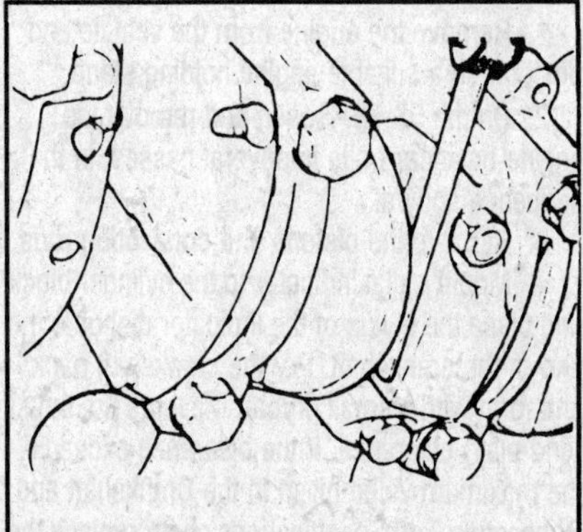
FIG. 269 Check the connecting rod side clearance

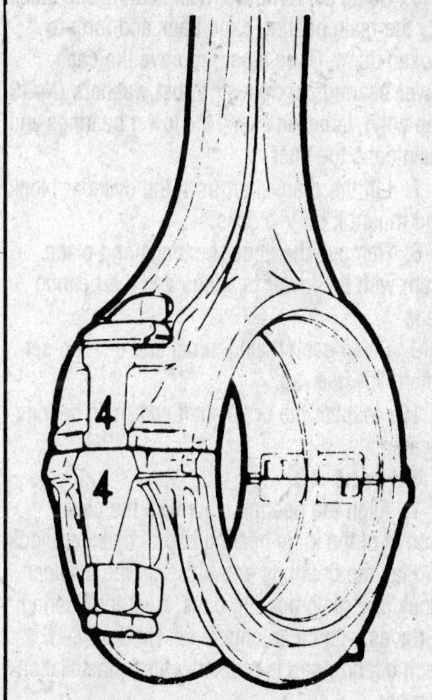

FIG. 270 Match the connecting rod to the cylinder with a stamp

connecting rod and rod cap must be replaced with undersize inserts, and/or the crankshaft must be reground. To install the bearing insert halves, press them into the bearing caps and connecting rods. Make sure the tab in each insert fits into the notch in each rod and cap. Lube the face of each insert with engine oil prior to installing each rod into the engine.

The connecting rods can be further inspected when they are removed from the engine and separated from their pistons. Rod alignment (straightness and squareness) must be checked by a machinist, as the rod must be set in a special fixture. Many machine shops also perform a Magnafluxing service, which is a process that shows up any tiny cracks that you may be unable to see.

Core (Freeze) Plugs

REPLACEMENT

Core plugs need replacement only if they are found to be leaking, are excessively rusty, have popped due to freezing or, if the engine is being overhauled.

If the plugs are accessible with the engine in the car, they can be removed as-is. If not, the engine will have to be removed.

1. If necessary, remove the engine and mount it on a work stand. If the engine is being left in the car, drain the engine coolant and engine oil.

CAUTION

When draining the coolant, keep in mind that cats and dogs are attracted by the ethylene glycol antifreeze, and are quite likely to drink any that is left in an uncovered container or in puddles on the ground. This will prove fatal in sufficient quantity. Always drain the coolant into a sealable container. Coolant should be reused unless it is contaminated or several years old.

2. Remove anything blocking access to the plug or plugs to be replaced.
3. Drill or center-punch a hole in the plug. For large plugs, drill a $^1/_2$ in. hole; for small plugs, drill a $^1/_4$ in. hole.
4. For large plugs, using a slide-hammer, thread a machine screw adapter or insert 2-jawed puller adapter into the hole in the plug. Pull the plug from the block; for small plugs, pry the plug out with a pin punch.
5. Thoroughly clean the opening in the block, using steel wool or emery paper to polish the hole rim.
6. Coat the outer diameter of the new plug with sealer and place it in the hole. For cup-type core plugs: These plugs are installed with the flanged end outward. The maximum diameter of this type of plug is located at the outer edge of the flange. Carefully and evenly, drive the new plug into place. For expansion-type plugs: These plugs are installed with the flanged end inward. The maximum diameter of this type of plug is located at the base of the flange. It is imperative that the correct type of installation tool is used with this type of plug. Under no

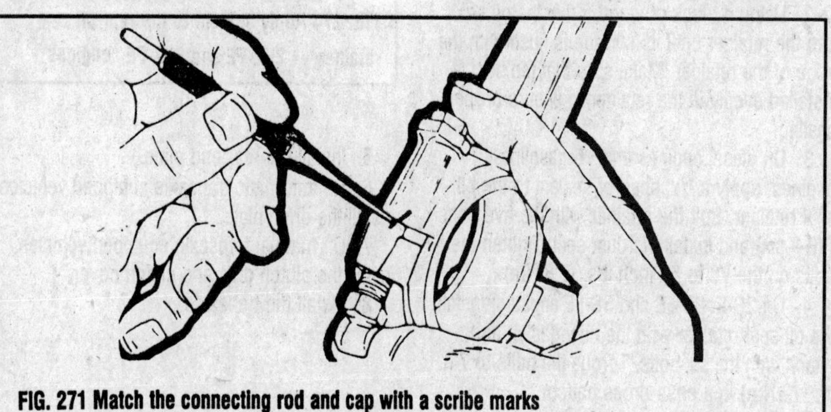
FIG. 271 Match the connecting rod and cap with a scribe marks

circumstances is this type of plug to be driven in using a tool that contacts the crowned portion of the plug. Driving in this plug incorrectly will cause the plug to expand prior to installation. When installed, the trailing (maximum) diameter of the plug MUST be below the chamfered edge of the bore to create an effective seal. If the core plug replacing tool has a depth seating surface, do not seat the tool against a non-machined (casting) surface.

7. Install any removed parts and, if necessary, install the engine in the car.
8. Refill the cooling system and crankcase.
9. Start the engine and check for leaks.

Rear Main Seal

REMOVAL & INSTALLATION

All Engines

➧ SEE FIGS. 272-274

1. Remove the transmission.
2. On manual transaxle equipped vehicles, remove the clutch cover assembly and flywheel.
3. On automatic transaxle equipped vehicles, remove the drive plate.
4. Remove the rear end plate.
5. On gasoline engines, remove the six bolts and remove the oil seal retainer and gasket. Discard the gasket and purchase a new one. V6 engines use sealant instead of a gasket.
6. On diesel engines, remove the dust seal. Remove the five bolts and remove the oil seal retainer.
7. Use a small prybar to pry the oil seal from the retaining plate. Be careful not to damage the plate.

To Install:

1. Clean the retainer contact surfaces thoroughly and lubricate the new oil seal with multi-purpose grease.
2. Using a block of wood, drive the oil seal into the retainer until its surface is flush with the edge of the retainer. Make sure that the seal is installed evenly in the retainer to ensure proper sealing.
3. On diesel engines and V6 gasoline engines, apply a 1/8" bead of sealant to the oil seal retainer. Bolt the retainer with the five bolts (V6 – six) and install the dust seal. Tighten the bolts on the V6 to 69 inch lbs. (7.8 Nm).
4. On 2S-E, 3S-FE and 5S-FE engines, install the oil seal retainer with the new gasket and attach with the six bolts. Torque the bolts to 7 ft. lbs. (9 Nm) in a criss-cross pattern.

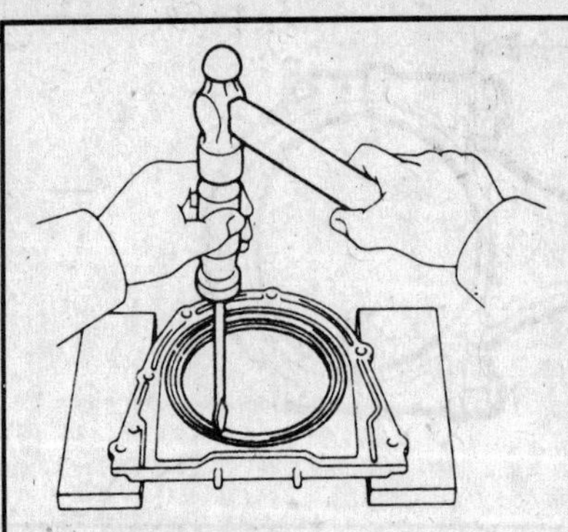

FIG. 272 Removing the rear main seal from the retainer

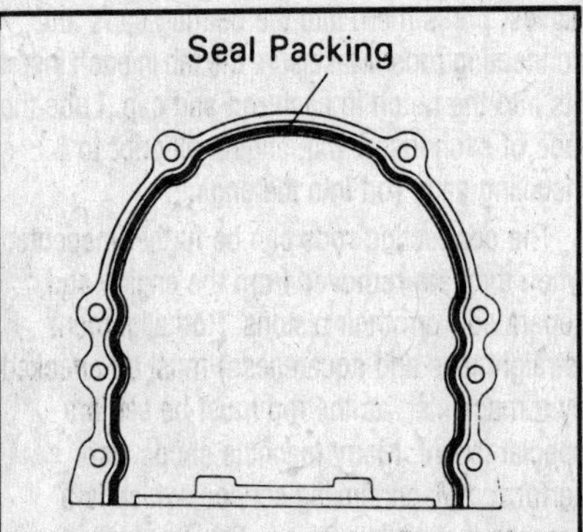

FIG. 273 Apply sealant to the rear oil seal retainer – 1C-T and 2C-T engines

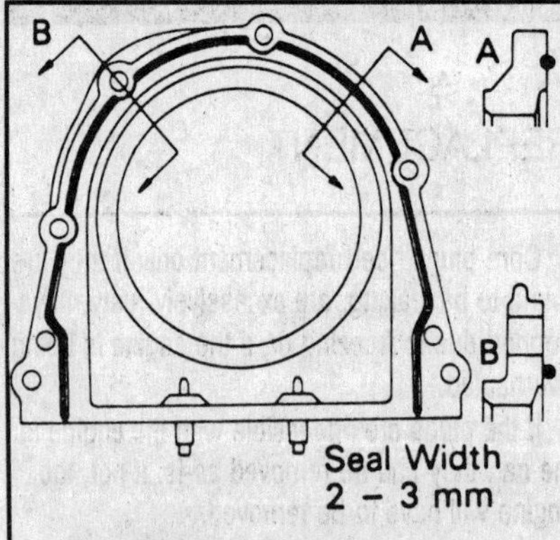

FIG. 274 Apply sealant to the rear oil seal retainer – 2VZ-FE and 3VZ-FE engines

5. Install the rear end plate.
6. On automatic transaxle equipped vehicles, install the drive plate.
7. On manual transaxle equipped vehicles, install the clutch disc and clutch cover.
8. Install the transaxle.

Crankshaft and Main Bearings

REMOVAL & INSTALLATION

1C-T, 2C-T, 2S-E, 3S-FE and 5S-FE Engines

➧ SEE FIGS. 275-285

1. Remove the engine from the vehicle and position on a suitable engine holding stand.
2. On the 5S-FE, loosen and remove the engine balancer bolts in several passes, in the sequence shown.
3. Remove the pistons and connecting rods.
4. Mount a dial indicator to the cylinder block and place the stylus of the indicator dial onto the end of the crankshaft. Pry the crankshaft back and forth with a small prybar. Measure the thrust (end play) clearance. If the clearance exceeds the maximum value given in the Crankshaft and Connecting Rod Specifications chart, replace the entire set of thrust washers.
5. Loosen the ten main bearing cap bolts in the sequence shown. For the diesel engines reverse the tightening sequence.
6. Using the removed main bearing cap bolts, pry the main bearing caps back and forth to loosen them. Once loose, remove the caps, lower bearings and lower thrust washers (No. 3 cap only). Label and keep the lower bearings and main caps together.
7. Lift the crankshaft from the cylinder block and mount it on V-blocks.
8. Remove the upper bearings and place them with the lower bearings and the bearing caps.
9. Clean each main journal and bearing set with a lint-free rag.
10. Inspect the crankshaft and main bearing clearances.

To Install:

1. Align the bearing claw with the claw groove of the main bearing cap or cylinder block and lay the bearings into place on the cylinder block and main bearing caps. Coat the bearing surfaces with clean engine oil. On the 5S-FE, each bearing cap is marked with an installation number.

CAUTION

The bearing with the oil hole must be installed in the cylinder block bearing saddle.

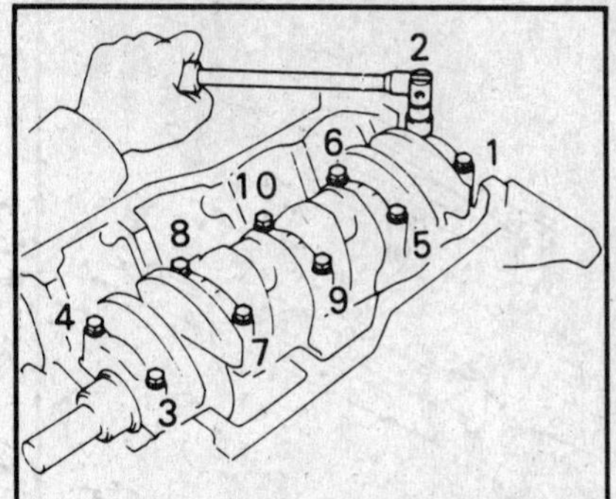

FIG. 275 Main bearing cap bolt loosening sequence — 2S-E, 3S-FE and 5S-FE engines

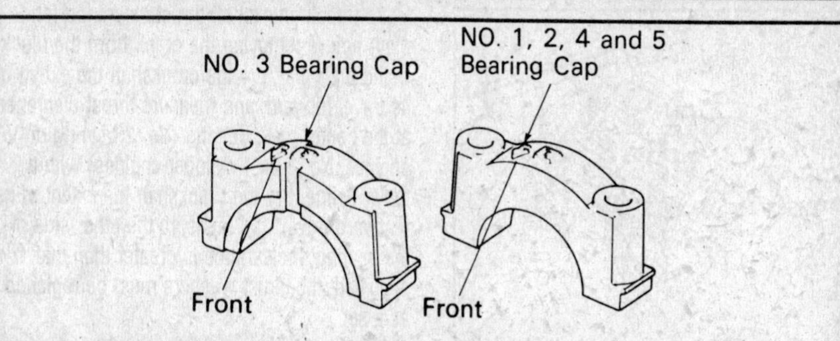

FIG. 279 Install the main bearing caps in the proper order with the arrow facing forward — 1C-T and 2C-T engines

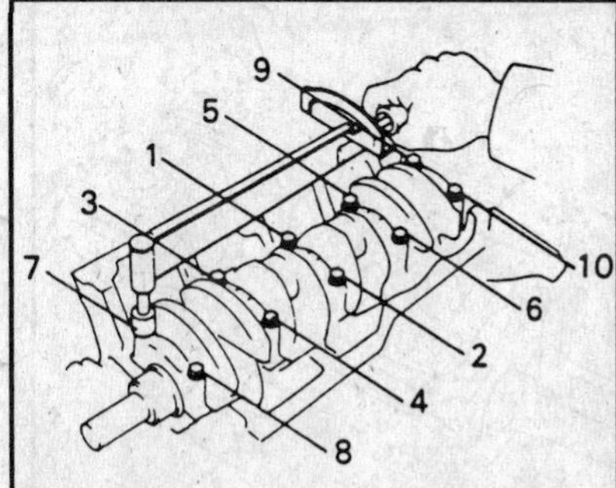

FIG. 276 Main bearing cap bolt tightening sequence — 2S-E, 3S-FE and 5S-FE engines

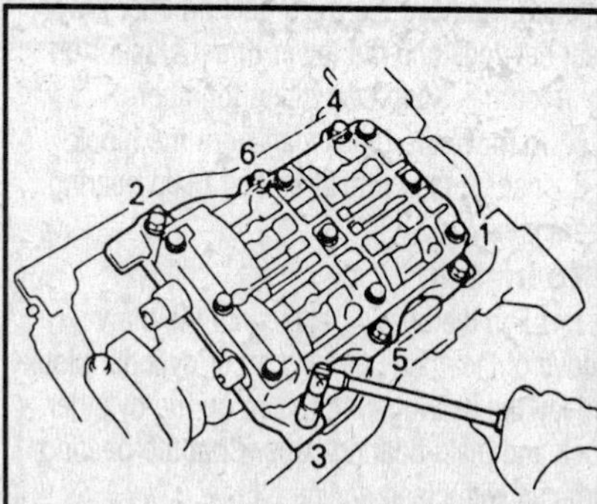

FIG. 280 Engine balancer bolt loosening sequence — 5S-FE engines

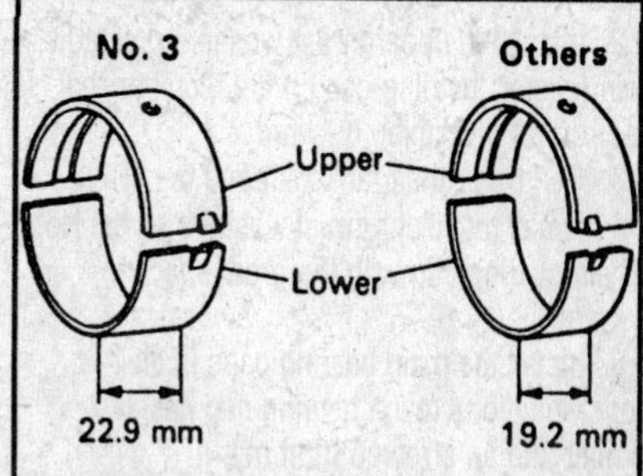

FIG. 282 Main bearing installation — 5S-FE engines

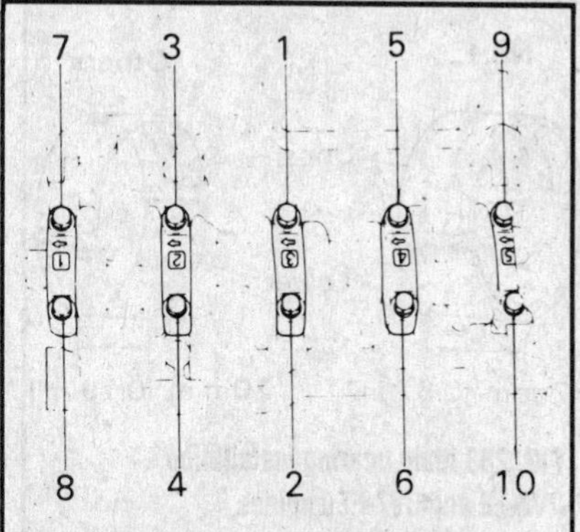

FIG. 277 Main bearing cap bolt tightening sequence — 1C-T and 2C-T engines

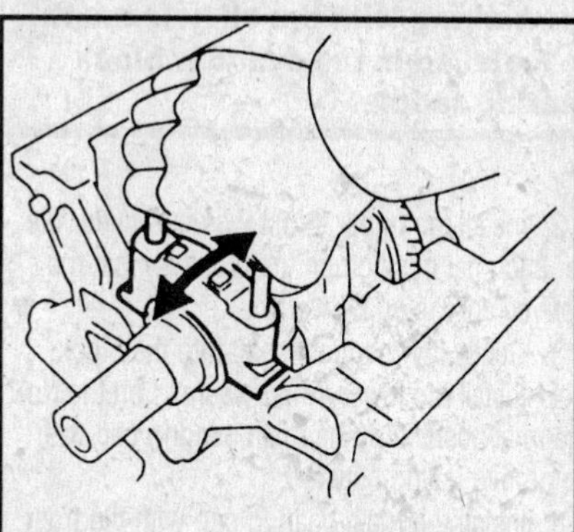
FIG. 281 Wiggle the main bearing cap back and forth until it comes loose

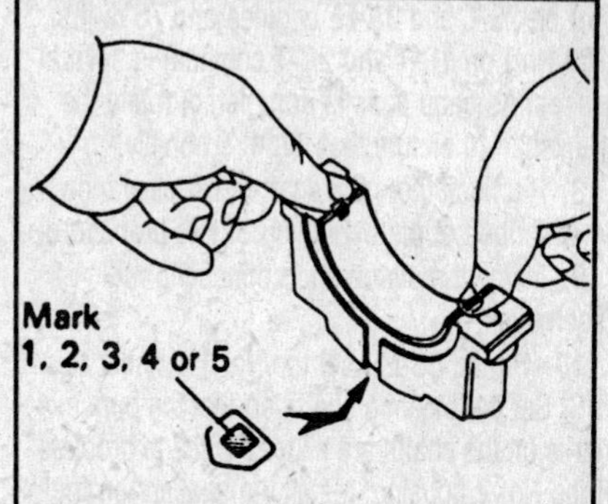

FIG. 283 Each main bearing is marked for installation — 5S-FE engines

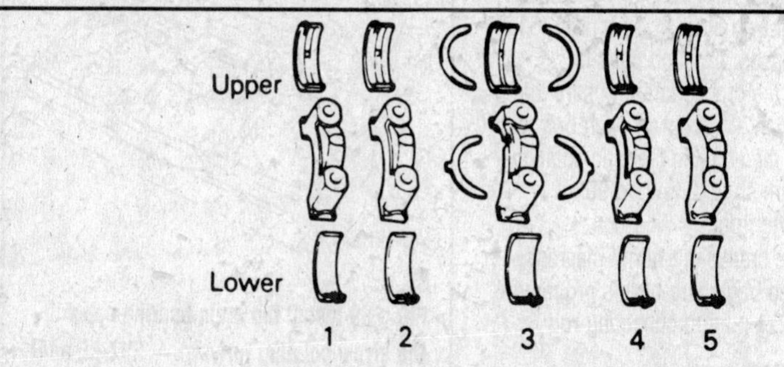

FIG. 278 Arrange the main bearings and caps — 2S-E, 3S-FE and 5S-FE engines

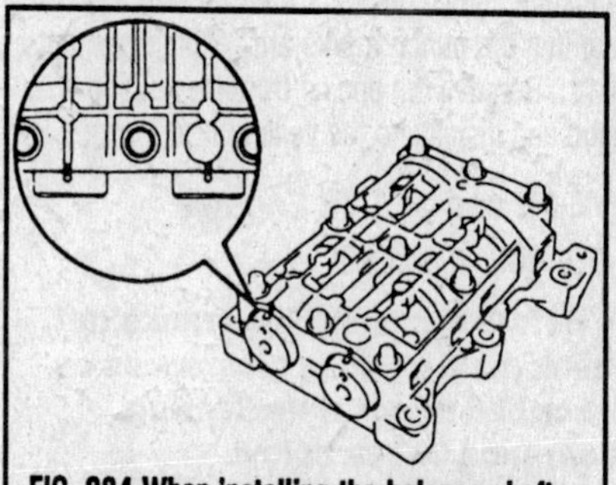
FIG. 284 When installing the balance shafts the punch marks should be aligned with the grooves in the No. 2 housing — 5S-FE engines

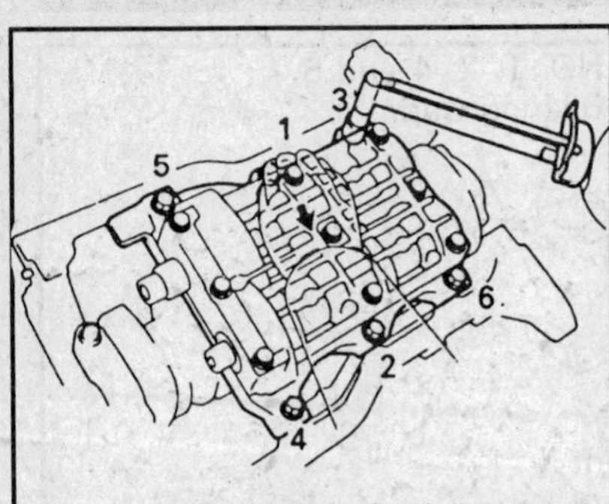

FIG. 285 Pull the balancer in the direction of the arrow and then tighten the bolts in this order — 5S-FE engines

2. Install the upper thrust washers under the main (center) bearing cap on the block so that the grooves are facing outward.

3. Gently lay the crankshaft into the block.

4. Install the lower thrust washers on the No. 3 main bearing cap with the groove facing outward.

5. Install the main bearing caps in their proper locations (each bearing cap has a number and an arrowed front mark).

6. Coat the threads and under the heads of the caps with clean engine oil.

7. Install the ten main bearing bolts and tighten the bolts in sequence to 43 ft. lbs. (59 Nm) on 2S-E and 3S-FE engines and 76 ft. lbs. (103 Nm) on 1C-T and 2C-T engines) in several passes. As each pass is completed, rotate the crankshaft to ensure that it turn smoothly.

8. Recheck the crankshaft thrust clearance as described at the beginning of this procedure.

9. Install the piston and connecting rod assemblies.

10. On the 5S-FE, set the No. 1 cylinder to TDC. Set the balance shafts so that the punch marks on the shafts are aligned with the grooves of the No. 2 housing. Install the spacers on the cylinder block and then position the balancer. Pull the balancer in the direction of the arrow and tighten the bolts in several passes, in the sequence shown, to 36 ft. lbs. (49 Nm). Make sure that the punch marks are still in alignment.

11. Remove the engine from the holding stand and install into the vehicle.

2VZ-FE and 3VZ-FE Engines

➧ SEE FIGS. 286-291

➡ Before removing the crankshaft, check main bearing clearances as described under Main Bearing Clearance Check below.

1. Remove the piston and connecting rod assemblies following the procedure in this section.

2. Check crankshaft thrust clearance (end play) before removing the crank from the block. Using a pry bar, pry the crankshaft the extent of its travel forward, and measure thrust clearance at the center main bearing (No. 2 bearing on V6 engines, No. 3 on 4 cylinder engines) with a feeler gauge. Pry the crankshaft the extent of its rearward travel, and measure the other side of the bearing. If clearance is greater than that specified, the thrust washers must be replaced as a set.

3. Loosen and remove the main bearing cap bolts, in several passes, in the sequence shown.

4. Use a small prybar and lift up the main bearing cap (its one big assembly on these engines). Remove the main bearing cap, lower main bearings and the lower thrust washer on No. 2 journal. Keep everything together.

5. Remove the crankshaft from the block.

6. Inspect the crankshaft and main bearing clearances.

To install:

1. Align the bearing claw with the claw groove of the main bearing cap or cylinder block and lay the bearings into place on the cylinder block and main bearing caps. Coat the bearing surfaces with clean engine oil.

⁂ CAUTION

The bearing with the oil hole must be installed in the cylinder block bearing saddle.

2. Install the upper thrust washers under the No. 2 journal position on the block so that the grooves are facing outward.

3. Gently lay the crankshaft into the block.

4. Install the lower thrust washers on the No. 2 journal position of the main bearing cap with the groove facing outward.

5. Install the main bearing cap with the front mark facing forward.

6. Coat the threads and under the heads of the caps with clean engine oil.

7. Install the eight main bearing bolts and tighten the bolts in sequence to 45 ft. lbs. (61 Nm) in several passes. As each pass is completed, rotate the crankshaft to ensure that it turns smoothly. Mark the front of each bolt with a dab of paint and then tighten them an additional 90°. The paint mark should now be 90° perpendicular to the front.

8. Recheck the crankshaft thrust clearance as described at the beginning of this procedure.

9. Install the piston and connecting rod assemblies.

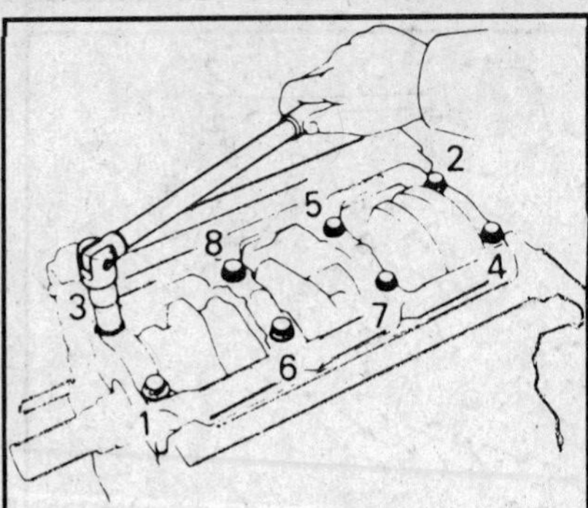

FIG. 286 Loosen the main bearing cap bolts in this order — 2VZ-FE and 3VZ-FE engines

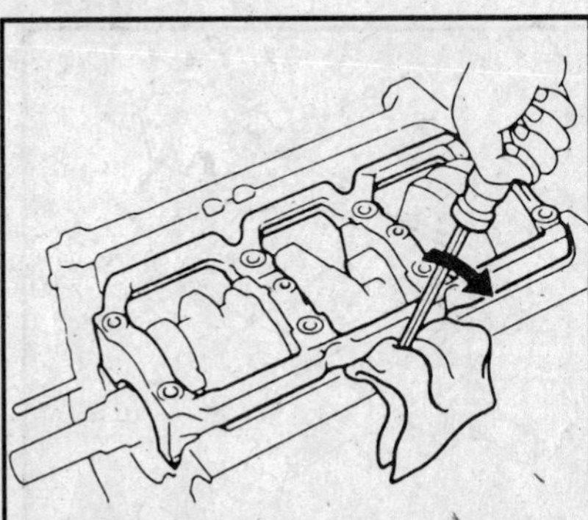
FIG. 287 Pry the main bearing cap from the cylinder block — 2VZ-FE and 3VZ-FE engines

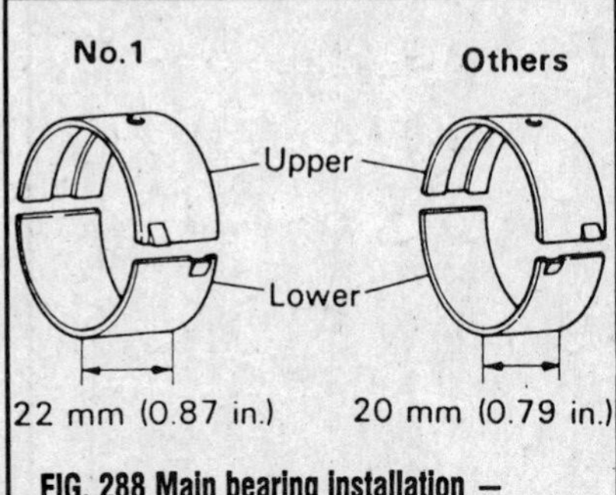

FIG. 288 Main bearing installation — 2VZ-FE and 3VZ-FE engines

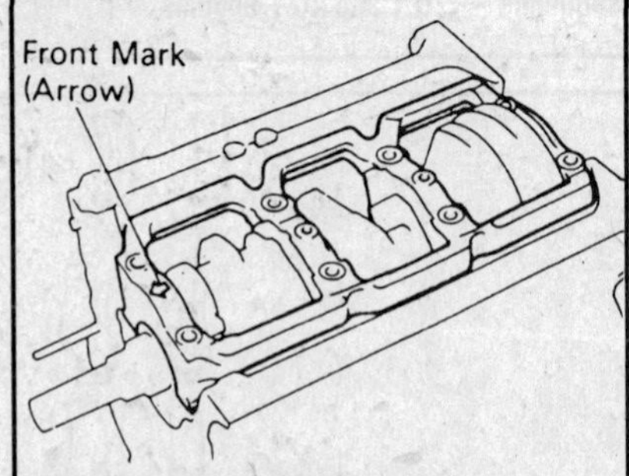

FIG. 289 Install the main bearing cap with the arrow pointing forward — 2VZ-FE and 3VZ-FE engines

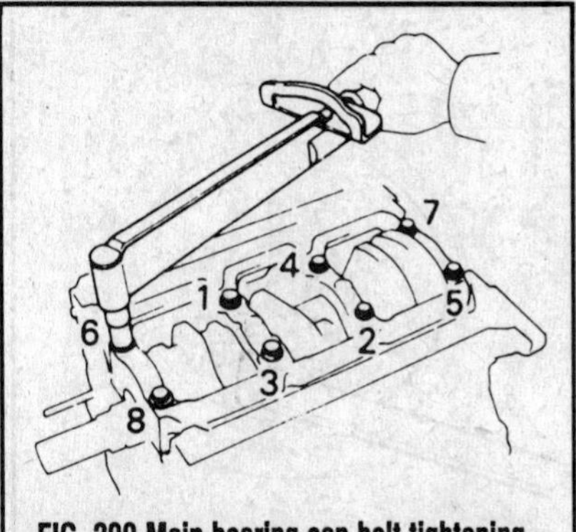

FIG. 290 Main bearing cap bolt tightening sequence — 2VZ-FE and 3VZ-FE engines

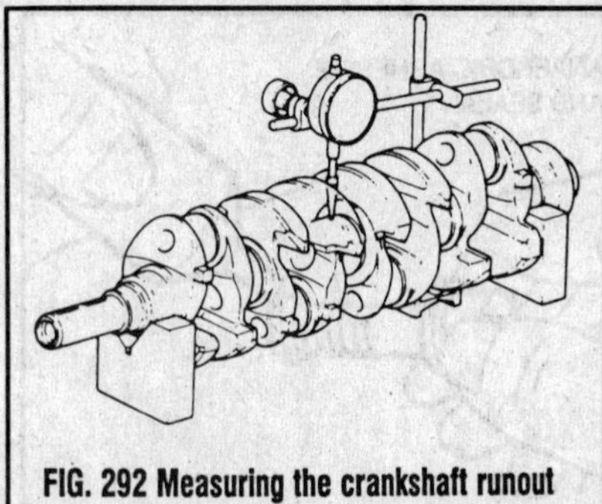
FIG. 292 Measuring the crankshaft runout

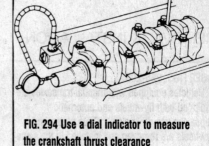

FIG. 294 Use a dial indicator to measure the crankshaft thrust clearance

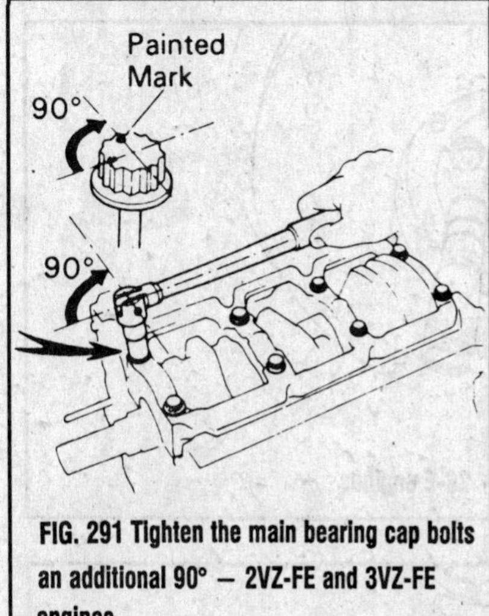

FIG. 291 Tighten the main bearing cap bolts an additional 90° — 2VZ-FE and 3VZ-FE engines

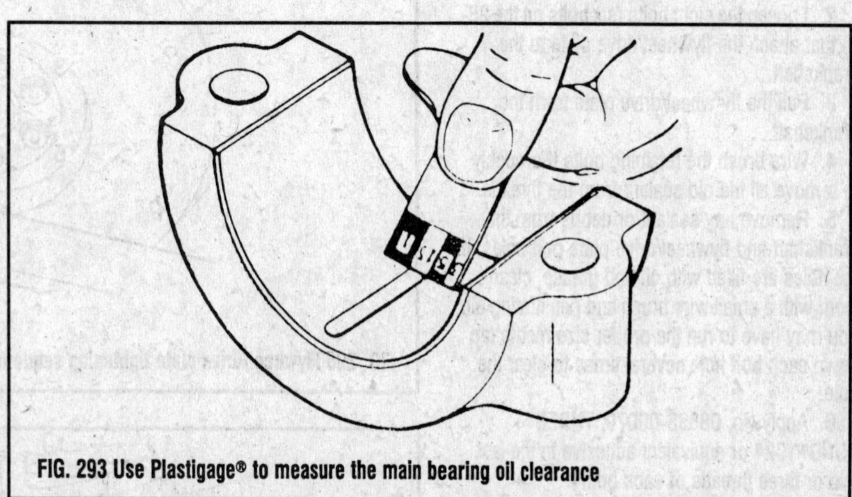
FIG. 293 Use Plastigage® to measure the main bearing oil clearance

10. Remove the engine from the holding stand and install into the vehicle.

INSPECTION

Crankshaft inspection and servicing should be handled exclusively by a reputable machinist, as most of the necessary procedures require a dial indicator and fixing jig, a large micrometer, and machine tools such as a crankshaft grinder. While at the machine shop, the crankshaft should be thoroughly cleaned (especially the oil passages). Magnafluxed (to check for minute cracks) and the following checks made: main journal diameter, crank pin (connecting rod journal) diameter, taper and out-of-round, and run-out. Wear, beyond specification limits, in any of these areas means the crankshaft must be reground or replaced.

MAIN BEARING CLEARANCE CHECK

➧ SEE FIGS. 292-294

Checking main bearing clearances is done in the same manner as checking connecting rod big-end clearances.

1. With the crankshaft installed, remove the main bearing cap. Clean all oil form the bearing insert in the cap and from the crankshaft journal, as the Plastigage® material is oil-soluble.
2. Lay a strip of Plastigage® along the full width of the bearing cap (or along the width of the crank journal if the engine is out of the car and inverted).
3. Install the bearing cap and torque to specification.

➡ Do not rotate the crankshaft with the Plastigage® installed.

4. Remove the bearing cap and determine bearing clearance by comparing the width of the now-flattened Plastigage® with the scale on the Plastigage® envelope. Journal taper is determined by comparing the width of the Plastigage® strip near its ends. Rotate the crankshaft 90° and retest, to determine journal eccentricity.
5. Repeat the above for the remaining bearings. If the bearing journal and insert appear in good shape (with not unusual wear visible) and are within tolerances, no further main bearing service is required. If unusual wear is evident and/or the clearances are outside specifications, the bearings must be replaced and the cause of their wear found.

Flywheel and Drive Plate

REMOVAL & INSTALLATION

➧ SEE FIGS. 295-298

Vehicles equipped with manual transaxles are equipped with flywheels and automatic transaxles use drive plates. Drive plates and flywheels are removed and installed in the same manner.

1. Remove the engine from the vehicle and disconnect the transaxle from the engine.
2. Loosen the eight bolts (six bolts on the 2S-E) that attach the flywheel/drive plate to the crankshaft.
3. Pull the fly wheel/drive plate from the crankshaft.
4. Wire brush the retaining bolts thoroughly to remove all the old sealant from the threads.
5. Remove any sealant or debris from the crankshaft and flywheel/drive plate bolt holes. If the holes are filled with oil and grease, clean them with a small wire brush and penetrating oil. You may have to run the proper size metric tap down each bolt hole several times to clear the hole.
6. Apply No. 08833-00070, THREE BOND®1324 or equivalent adhesive to the last two or three threads of each bolt.
7. Support and position the flywheel/drive plate onto the crankshaft.
8. Install the retaining bolts. On flywheel equipped engines, tighten the bolts in sequence to:

   2S-E: 72 ft. lbs. (98 Nm)
   1C-T, 2C-T: 65 ft. lbs. (88 Nm)
   3S-FE, 5S-FE: 65 ft. lbs. (88 Nm)
   2VZ-FE, 3VZ-FE: 61 ft. lbs. (83 Nm)

   On drive plate equipped engines, tighten the bolts in sequence to:

   2S-E: 61 ft. lbs. (83 Nm)
   1C-T, 2C-T: 65 ft. lbs. (88 Nm)
   3S-FE, 5S-FE: 61 ft. lbs. (83 Nm)
   2VZ-FE, 3VZ-FE: 61 ft. lbs. (83 Nm)
9. Connect the transaxle to the engine and install the engine into the vehicle.

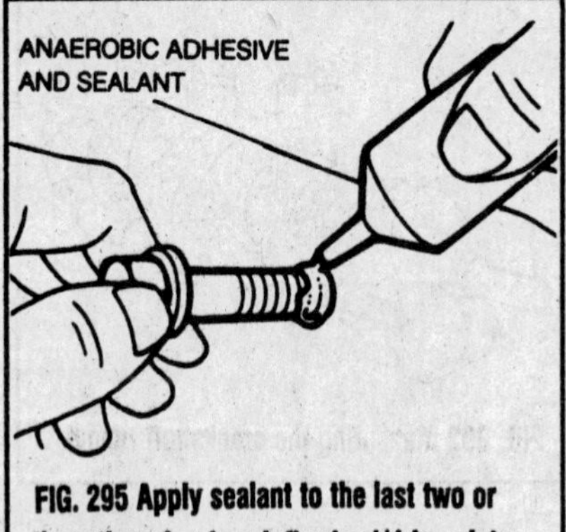

FIG. 295 Apply sealant to the last two or three threads of each flywheel/drive plate bolt prior to installation

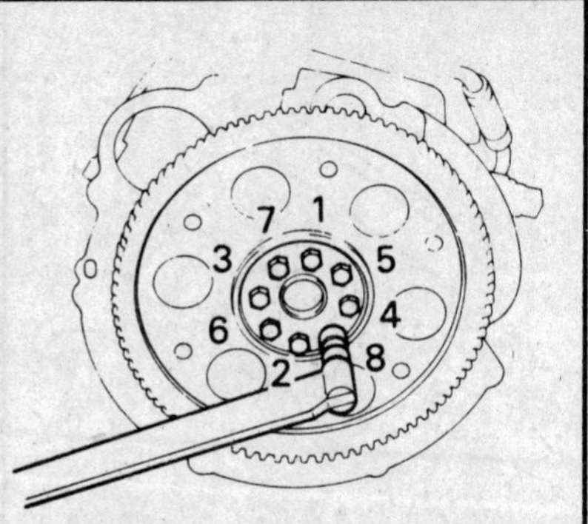

FIG. 298 Flywheel/drive plate tightening sequence — 1C-T and 2C-T engines

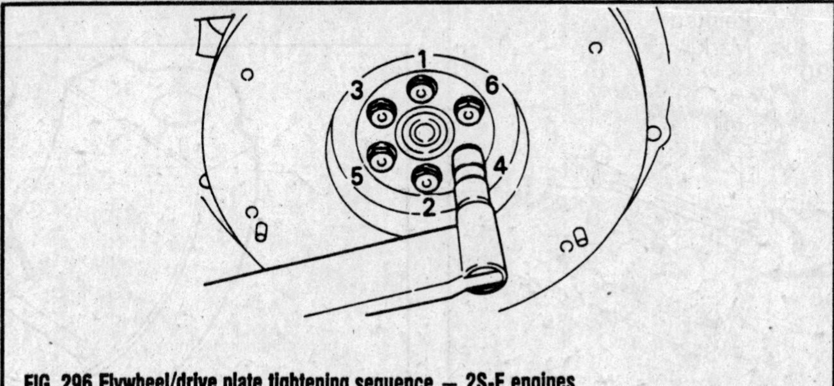

FIG. 296 Flywheel/drive plate tightening sequence — 2S-E engines

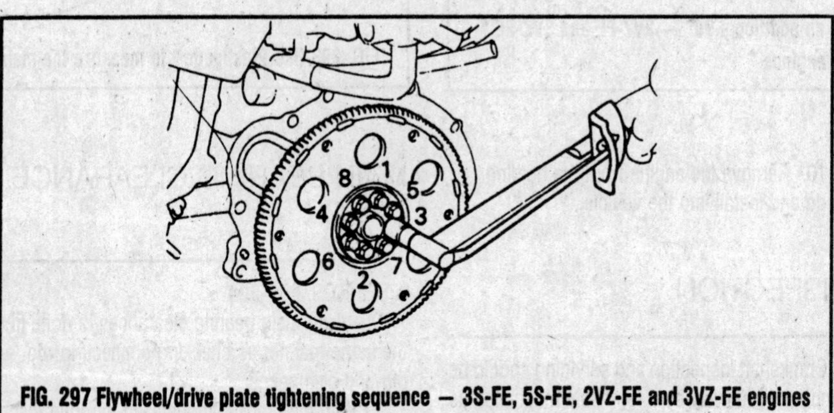

FIG. 297 Flywheel/drive plate tightening sequence — 3S-FE, 5S-FE, 2VZ-FE and 3VZ-FE engines

EXHAUST SYSTEM

Safety Precautions

For a number of reasons, exhaust system work can be the most dangerous type of work you can do on your car. Always observe the following precautions:

- Support the car extra securely. Not only will you often be working directly under it, but you'll frequently be using a lot of force, say, heavy hammer blows, to dislodge rusted parts. This can cause a car that's improperly supported to shift and possibly fall.
- Wear goggles. Exhaust system parts are always rusty. Metal chips can be dislodged, even when you're only turning rusted bolts. Attempting to pry pipes apart with a chisel makes the chips fly even more frequently.
- If you're using a cutting torch, keep it a great distance from either the fuel tank or lines. Stop what you're doing and feel the temperature of the fuel bearing pipes on the tank frequently. Even slight heat can expand and/or vaporize fuel, resulting in accumulated vapor, or even a liquid leak, near your torch.
- Watch where your hammer blows fall and make sure you hit squarely. You could easily tap a brake or fuel line when you hit an exhaust system part with a glancing blow. Inspect all lines and hoses in the area where you've been working.

CAUTION

Be very careful when working on or near the catalytic converter. External temperatures can reach 1,500°F (816°C) and more, causing severe burns. Removal or installation should be performed only on a cold exhaust system.

Special Tools

A number of special exhaust system tools can be rented from auto supply houses or local stores that rent special equipment. A common one is a tail pipe expander, designed to enable you to join pipes of identical diameter.

It may also be quite helpful to use solvents designed to loosen rusted bolts or flanges. Soaking rusted parts the night before you do the job can speed the work of freeing rusted parts considerably. Remember that these solvents are often flammable. Apply only to parts after they are cool!

Catalytic Converter

CAUTION

Be very careful when working on or near the catalytic converter. External temperatures can reach 1,500°F (816°C) and more causing severe burns. Removal and installation should only be performed on a cold exhaust system.

INSPECTION

Diesel engines do not have catalytic converters.

1. Physically check all the exhaust pipe connections for looseness or damage.
2. Check the clamps for weakness, cracks or any other form of damage.
3. On 2S-E engines, check the catalytic converter protector for dents or damage. If any part of the protector is damaged or dented, to the point where the damaged area makes contact with the catalyst, repair or replace it.
4. On 2S-E engines, check the heat insulator for damage and make sure that there is sufficient clearance between the converter and the heat insulator.

FIG. 299 Make sure that the protector is not contacting the converter — 2S-E engines

Front Pipe

REMOVAL & INSTALLATION

1. Support the vehicle securely by using jackstands or equivalent under the frame of the vehicle.
2. Remove the exhaust pipe clamps and any front exhaust pipe shield.
3. Soak the exhaust manifold front pipe mounting studs with penetrating oil. Remove attaching nuts and gasket from the manifold.

➡ **If these studs snap off, while removing the front pipe the manifold will have to be removed and the stud will have to be drilled out and the hole tapped.**

4. Remove any exhaust pipe mounting hanger or bracket.
5. Remove front pipe from the muffler/catalytic converter.
6. Install the front pipe on the manifold with seal if so equipped.
7. Connect the pipe to the muffler/catalytic converter. Assemble all parts loosely and position the pipe to insure proper clearance from body of vehicle.
8. Tighten mounting studs, bracket bolts and exhaust clamps.
9. Install exhaust pipe shield.
10. Start engine and check for exhaust leaks.

Catalytic Converter

REMOVAL & INSTALLATION

1. Remove the converter lower shield.
2. Disconnect converter from front pipe or manifold.
3. Disconnect converter from center pipe or tail pipe assembly.
4. Remove catalytic converter.

➡ **Assemble all parts loosely and position the converter before tightening the exhaust clamps.**

5. To install, reverse the removal procedures. Always use new clamps and exhaust seals, start the engine and check for leaks.

Center Pipe

REMOVAL & INSTALLATION

1. Raise the vehicle and support it with safety stands.
2. Soak all nuts and bolts at the converter and muffler connections with penetrating oil.
3. Disconnect the pipe at the converter.
4. While supporting the pipe, disconnect it at the muffler and remove it.
5. Position the pipe and connect it to the muffler.
6. Connect the pipe to the converter and then install any other mounting brackets or hardware.

Tailpipe And Muffler

REMOVAL & INSTALLATION

1. Disconnect the tailpipe at the center pipe, catalytic converter or front pipe.
2. Remove all brackets and exhaust clamps.
3. Remove the tailpipe from muffler. On some models the tailpipe and muffler are one piece.
4. To install reverse the removal procedures. Always use new clamps and exhaust seals, start engine and check for leaks.

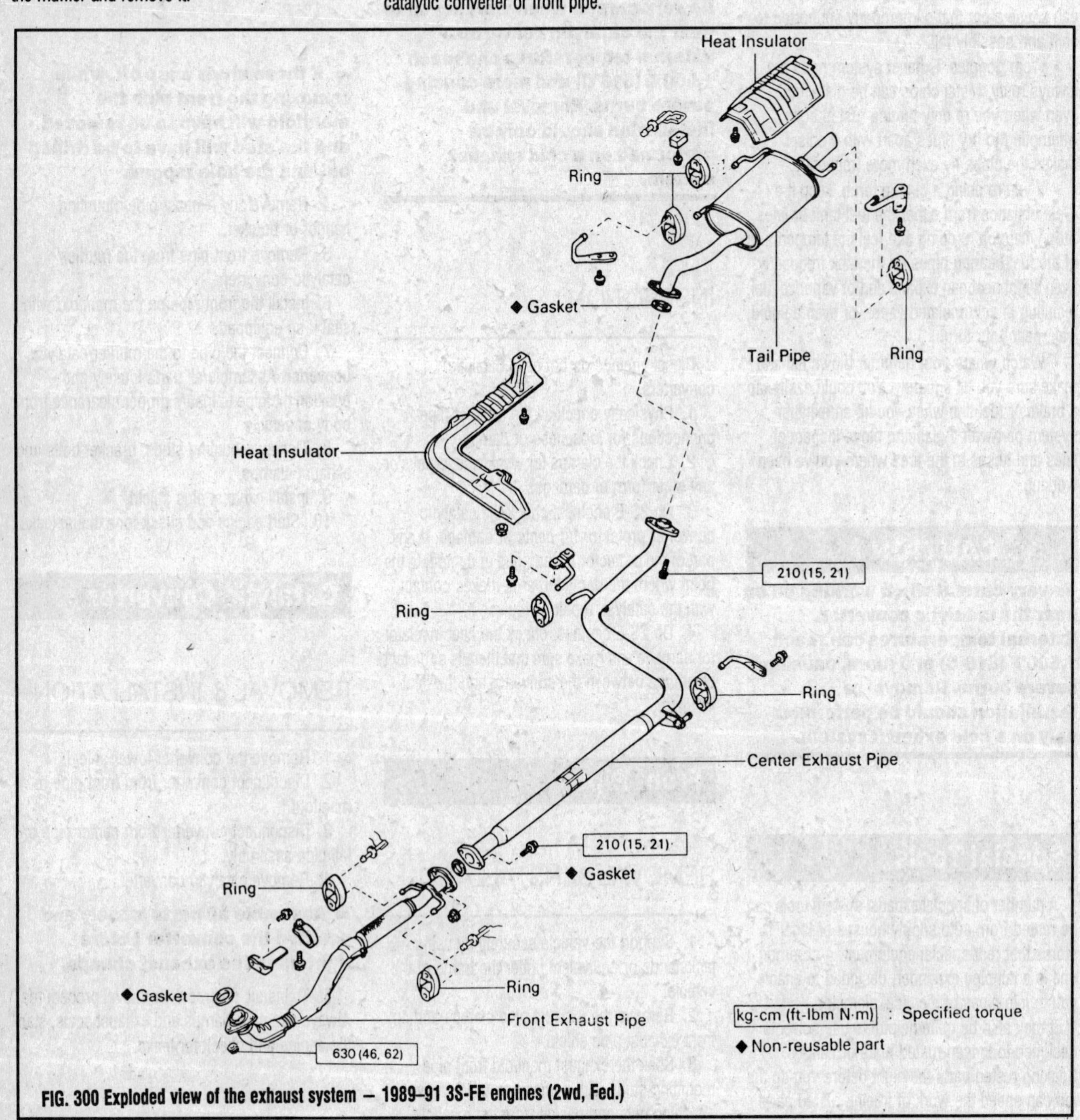

FIG. 300 Exploded view of the exhaust system — 1989–91 3S-FE engines (2wd, Fed.)

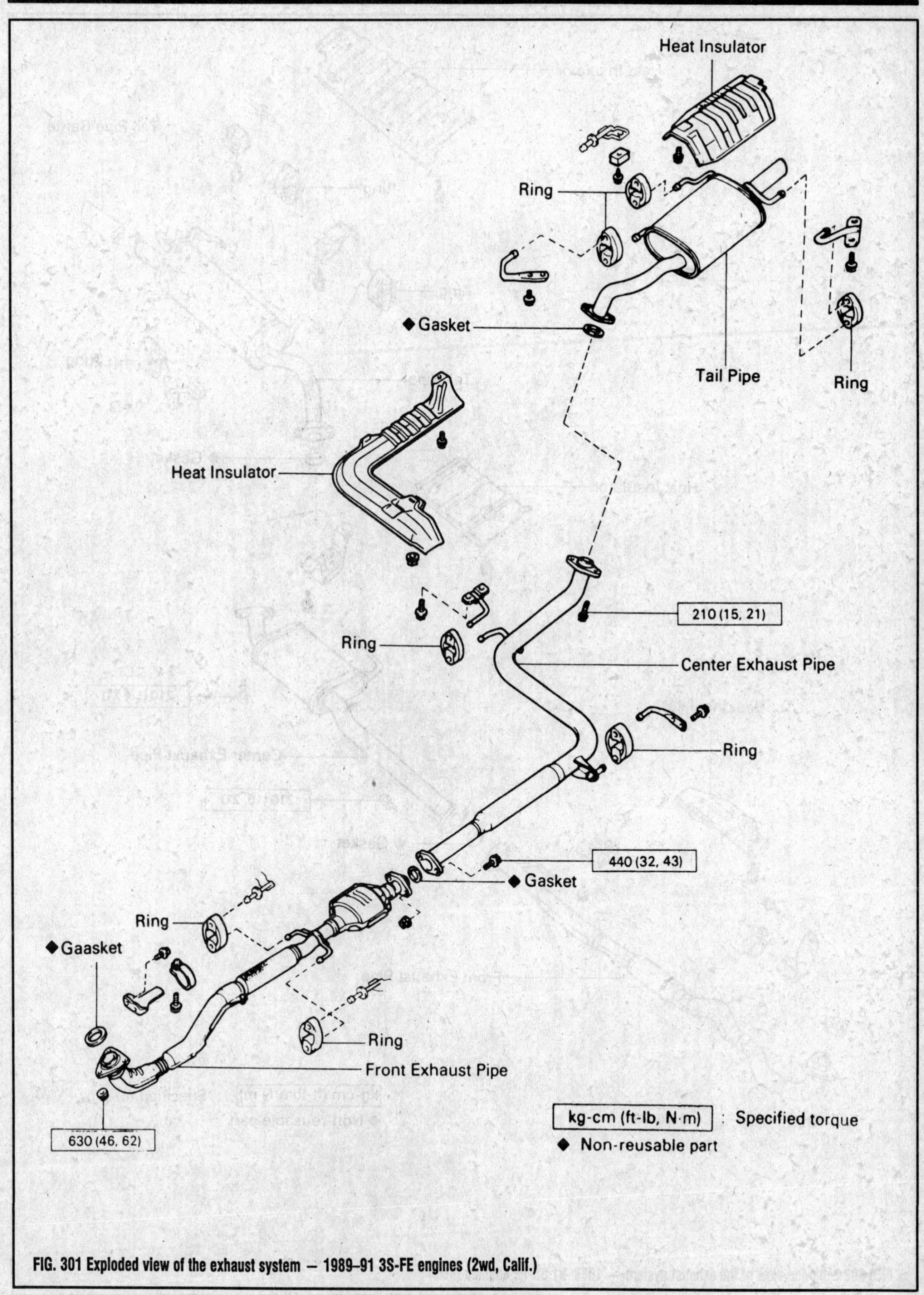

FIG. 301 Exploded view of the exhaust system — 1989–91 3S-FE engines (2wd, Calif.)

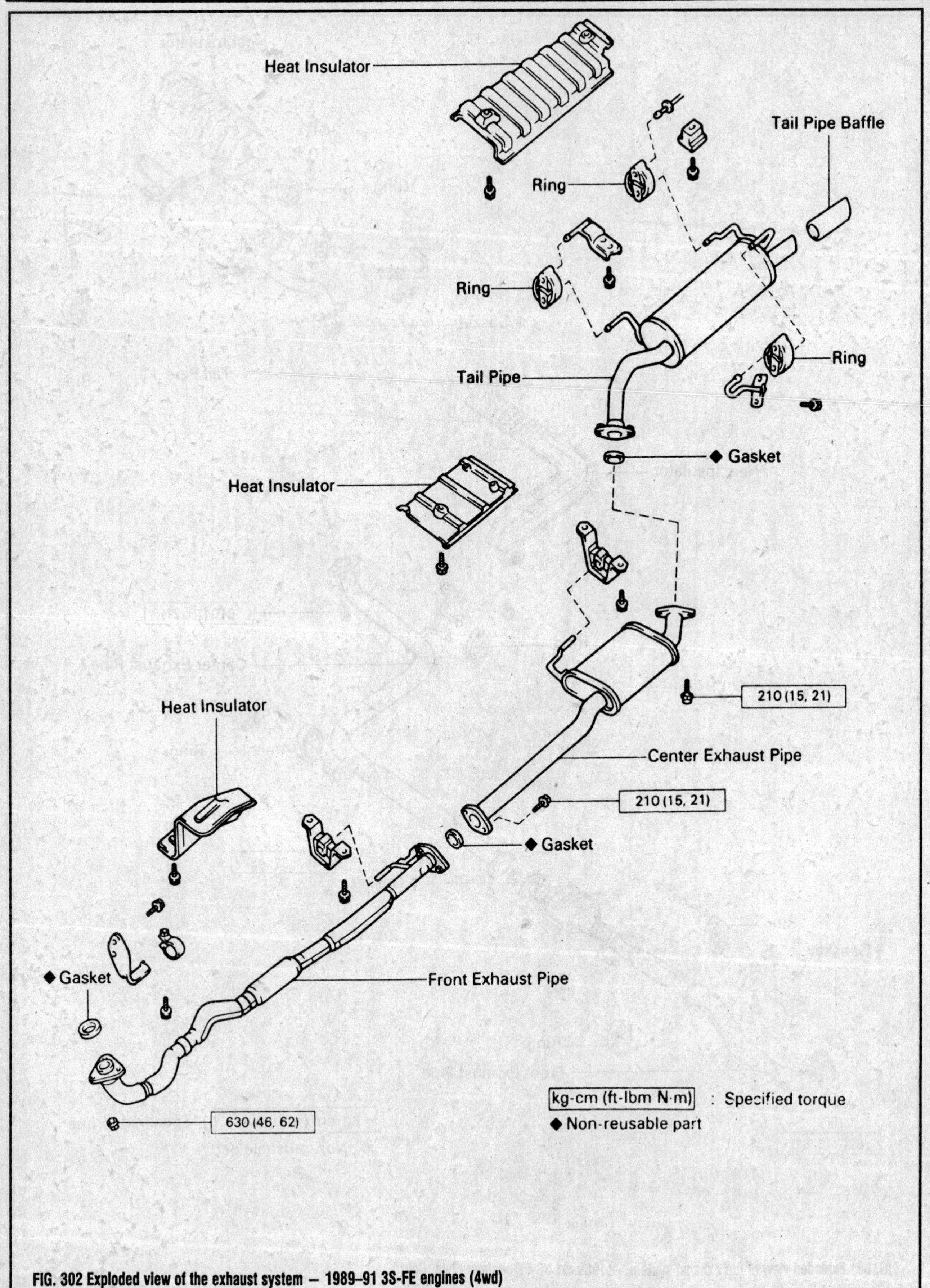

FIG. 302 Exploded view of the exhaust system – 1989–91 3S-FE engines (4wd)

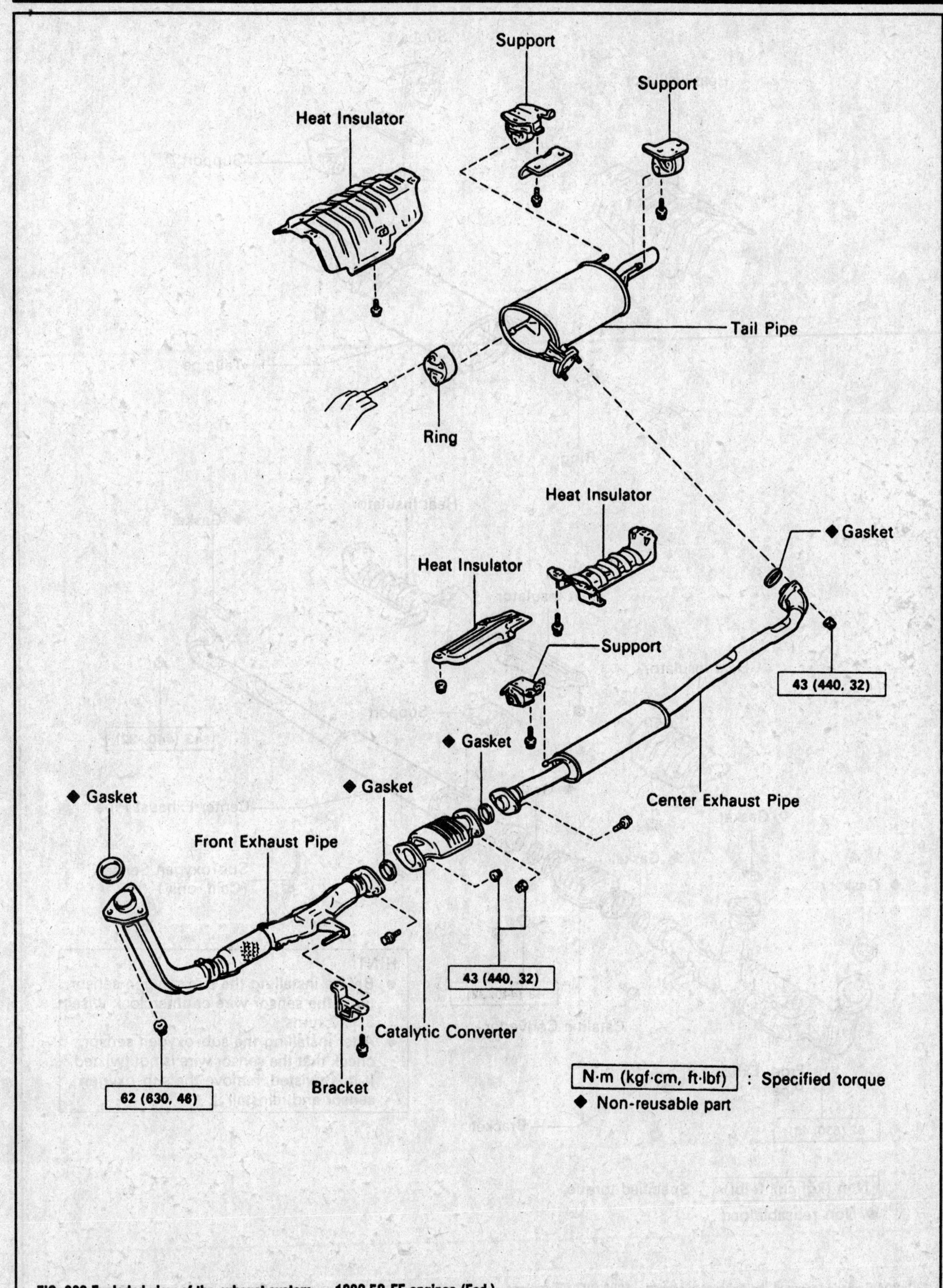

FIG. 303 Exploded view of the exhaust system — 1992 5S-FE engines (Fed.)

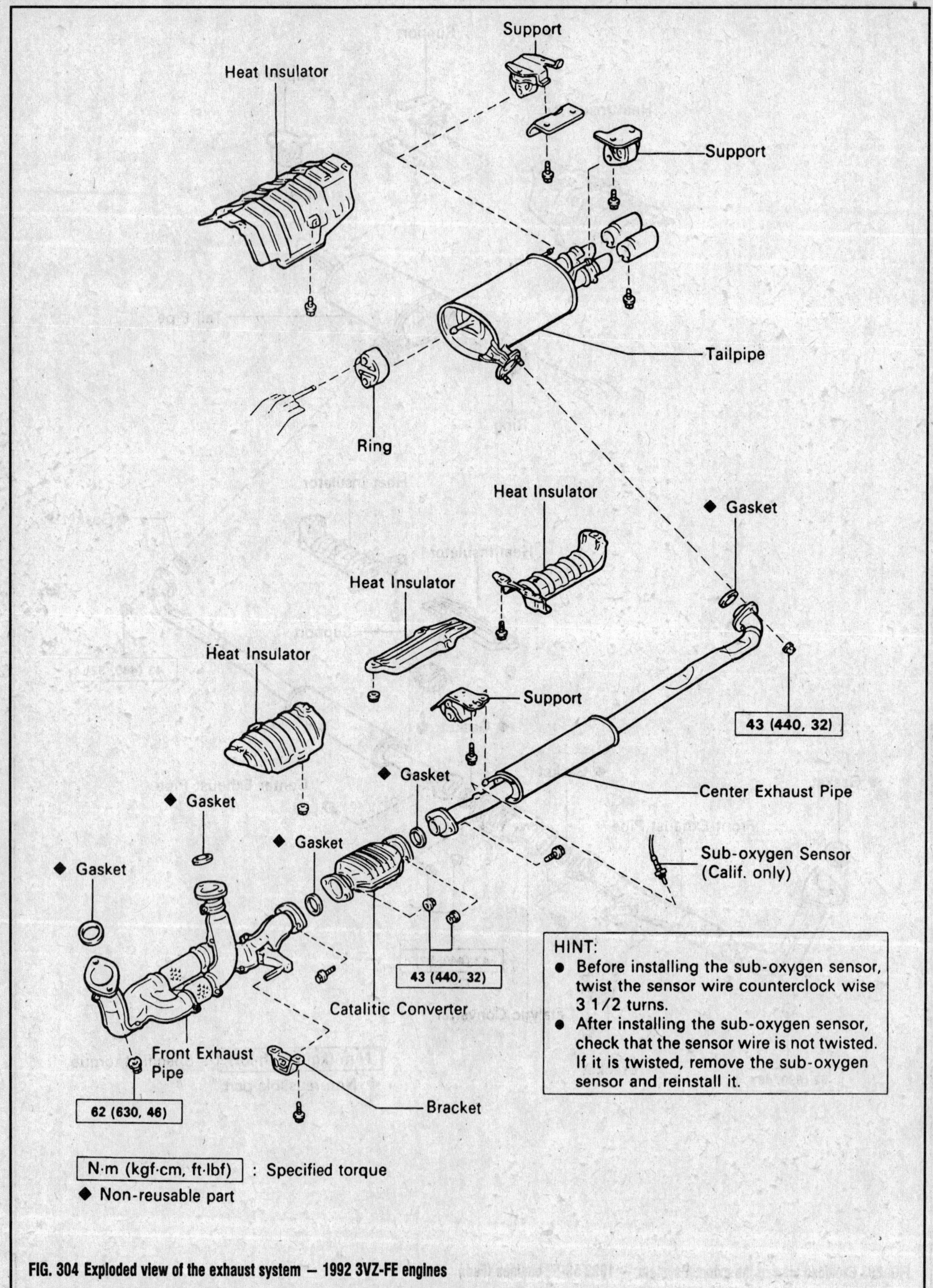

FIG. 304 Exploded view of the exhaust system — 1992 3VZ-FE engines

ENGINE REBUILDING SPECIFICATIONS

Component	English	Metric
Camshaft		
Lobe Height		
1C-T		
Intake	1.8081 in.	45.925mm
Exhaust	1.8478 in.	46.935mm
2C-T		
Intake	1.8081 in.	45.925mm
Exhaust	1.8440 in.	46.835mm
2S-E	1.5325–1.5365 in.	38.926–39.026mm
2VZ-FE		
Intake	1.5555–1.5594 in.	39.510–39.610mm
Exhaust	1.5339–1.5378 in.	38.960–39.060mm
3VZ-FE		
Intake	1.6598–1.6638 in.	42.160–42.260mm
Exhaust	1.6520–1.6559 in.	41.960–42.060mm
3S-FE	1.3744–1.3783 in.	34.910–35.010mm
5S-FE		
Intake	1.6539–1.6579 in.	42.010–42.110mm
Exhaust	1.5772–1.5811 in.	40.060–40.160mm
Journal Diameter		
1C-T, 2C-T		
All	1.1014–1.1022 in.	27.975–27.995mm
2S-E		
No. 1	1.8291–1.8297 in.	46.459–46.475mm
No. 2	1.8192–1.8199 in.	46.209–46.225mm
No. 3	1.8094–1.8100 in.	45.959–45.975mm
No. 4	1.7996–1.8002 in.	45.709–45.725mm
No. 5	1.7897–1.7904 in.	45.459–45.475mm
No. 6	1.7799–1.7805 in.	45.209–45.225mm
2VZ-FE, 3VZ-FE		
All	1.0610–1.0616 in.	26.949–26.965mm
3S-FE, 5S-FE		
All	1.0614–1.0620 in.	26.959–26.975mm
Journal Oil Clearance		
1C-T, 2C-T		
All	0.0015–0.0029 in.	0.037–0.073mm
2S-E		
All	0.0010–0.0026 in.	0.025–0.067mm
2VZ-FE, 3VZ-FE		
All	0.0014–0.0028 in.	0.035–0.072mm
3S-FE, 5S-FE		
All	0.0010–0.0024 in.	0.025–0.062mm
Thrust Clearance		
1C-T, 2C-T	0.0031–0.0071 in.	0.08–0.18mm
2S-E	0.0031–0.0091 in.	0.08–0.23mm
2VZ-FE, 3VZ-FE	0.0012–0.0031 in.	0.030–0.080mm
3S-FE, 5S-FE		
Intake	0.0018–0.0039 in.	0.045–0.100mm
Exhaust	0.0012–0.0033 in.	0.030–0.085mm
Camshaft Runout		
1C-T, 2C-T	0.0024 in.	0.06mm
2S-E	0.0016 in.	0.04mm
2VZ-FE, 3VZ-FE	0.0024 in.	0.06mm
3S-FE, 5S-FE	0.0016 in.	0.04mm
Cylinder Block		
Cylinder Bore		
Diameter		
1C-T	3.2677–3.2689 in.	83.0–83.03mm
2C-T	3.3858–3.3870 in.	86.00–86.03mm
2S-E	3.3071–3.3083 in.	84.0–84.03mm
2VZ-FE, 3VZ-FE		
Mark 1	3.4449–3.4453 in.	87.500–87.510mm
Mark 2	3.4453–3.4457 in.	87.510–87.520mm
Mark 3	3.4457–3.4461 in.	87.520–87.530mm

ENGINE REBUILDING SPECIFICATIONS

Component	English	Metric
3S-FE		
Mark 1	3.3858–3.3862 in.	86.000–86.010mm
Mark 2	3.3862–3.3866 in.	86.010–86.020mm
Mark 3	3.3866–3.3870 in.	86.020–86.030mm
5S-FE		
Mark 1	3.4252–3.4256 in.	87.000–87.010mm
Mark 2	3.4256–3.4260 in.	87.010–87.020mm
Mark 3	3.4260–3.4264 in.	87.020–87.030mm
Wear		
1C-T	3.2768 in.	83.23mm
2C-T	3.3949 in.	86.23mm
2S-E	3.3181 in.	84.28mm
Warpage		
1C-T, 2C-T	0.008 in.	0.2mm
2S-E	0.0020 in.	0.05mm
2VZ-FE, 3VZ-FE	0.0020 in.	0.05mm
3S-FE, 5S-FE	0.0020 in.	0.05mm
Cylinder Head		
Valve Stem Diameter		
1C-T, 2C-T		
Intake	0.3140–0.3146 in.	7.975–7.990mm
Exhaust	0.3134–0.2746 in.	7.960–6.975mm
2S-E		
Intake	0.3138–0.3134 in.	7.970–7.985mm
Exhaust	0.3136–0.3142 in.	7.965–7.980mm
2VZ-FE, 3VZ-FE		
Intake	0.2350–0.2356 in.	5.970–5.985mm
Exhaust	0.2348–0.2354 in.	5.965–5.980mm
3S-FE, 5S-FE		
Intake	0.2350–0.2356 in.	5.970–5.985mm
Exhaust	0.2348–0.2354 in.	5.965–5.980mm
Valve Stem-to-Guide Clearance		
1C-T, 2C-T		
Intake	0.0008–0.0022 in.	0.020–0.055mm
Exhaust	0.0014–0.0028 in.	0.035–0.070mm
2S-E		
Intake	0.0010–0.0024 in.	0.025–0.060mm
Exhaust	0.0012–0.0026 in.	0.030–0.065mm
2VZ-FE, 3VZ-FE		
Intake	0.0010–0.0024 in.	0.025–0.060mm
Exhaust	0.0012–0.0026 in.	0.030–0.065mm
3S-FE, 5S-FE		
Intake	0.0010–0.0024 in.	0.025–0.060mm
Exhaust	0.0012–0.0026 in.	0.030–0.065mm
Valve Face Angle		
1C-T, 2C-T	44.5°	44.5°
2S-E	45.5°	45.5°
2VZ-FE, 3VZ-FE	44.5°	44.5°
3S-FE, 5S-FE	44.5°	44.5°
Valve Seat Angle		
1C-T, 2C-T	45°	45°
2S-E	45°	45°
2VZ-FE, 3VZ-FE	45°	45°
3S-FE, 5S-FE	45°	45°
Valve Spring Pressure		
1C-T, 2C-T		
Installed	50.5–55.8 lbs. @ 1.587 in.	225–248N @ 40.3mm
2S-E		
Installed	68 lbs. @ 1.555 in.	302N @ 39.5mm
2VZ-FE		
Installed	41.0–47.2 lbs. @ 1.331 in.	182–210N @ 33.8mm

ENGINE REBUILDING SPECIFICATIONS

Component	English	Metric
3VZ-FE		
Installed	38.4–42.4 lbs. @ 1.331 in.	186–206N @ 33.3mm
3S-FE, 5S-FE		
Installed	36.8–42.5 lbs. @ 1.366 in.	164–189N @ 34.7mm
Valve Spring Free Length		
1C-T, 2C-T	1.870 in.	47.5mm
2S-E	1.839 in.	46.7mm
2VZ-FE	1.677 in.	42.6mm
3VZ-FE	1.630 in.	41.4mm
3S-FE	1.772 in.	45.0mm
5S-FE	1.6520–1.6531 in.	41.96–41.99mm
Valve Overall Length		
1C-T		
Intake	4.1949 in.	106.55mm
Exhaust	4.1850 in.	106.30mm
2C-T		
Intake	4.1614 in.	105.70mm
Exhaust	4.1476 in.	105.35mm
2S-E		
Intake	4.319 in.	109.7mm
Exhaust	4.303 in.	109.3mm
2VZ-FE		
Intake	3.783 in.	96.1mm
Exhaust	3.787 in.	96.2mm
3VZ-FE		
Intake	3.7461 in.	95.15mm
Exhaust	3.7362 in.	94.90mm
3S-FE		
Intake	3.9606 in.	100.60mm
Exhaust	3.9547 in.	100.45mm
5S-FE		
Intake	3.8425 in.	97.60mm
Exhaust	3.8760 in.	98.45mm
Valve Lifter Oil Clearance		
1C-T, 2C-T	0.0011–0.0021 in.	0.028–0.053mm Max.
2VZ-FE	0.0005–0.0018 in.	0.015–0.046mm Max.
3VZ-FE	0.0009–0.0020 in.	0.024–0.052mm Max.
3S-FE	0.0005–0.0018 in.	0.015–0.046mm Max.
5S-FE	0.0009–0.0020 in.	0.024–0.052mm Max.
Piston and Connecting Rod		
Piston Diameter		
1C-T	3.2659–3.2671 in.	82.955–82.985mm
2C-T	3.3837–3.3848 in.	85.945–85.975mm
2S-E	3.3061–3.3073 in.	83.975–84.005mm
2VZ-FE		
Mark 1	3.4427–3.4431 in.	87.445–87.455mm
Mark 2	3.4431–3.4435 in.	87.455–87.465mm
Mark 3	3.4435–3.4439 in.	87.465–87.475mm
3VZ-FE		
Mark 1	3.4394–3.4398 in.	87.360–87.370mm
Mark 2	3.4398–3.4402 in.	87.370–87.380mm
Mark 3	3.4402–3.4405 in.	87.380–87.390mm
3S-FE		
Mark 1	3.3836–3.3840 in.	85.945–85.955mm
Mark 2	3.3840–3.3844 in.	85.955–85.965mm
Mark 3	3.3844–3.3848 in.	85.965–85.975mm
5S-FE		
Mark 1	3.4193–3.4197 in.	86.850–86.860mm
Mark 2	3.4197–3.4201 in.	86.860–86.870mm
Mark 3	3.4201–3.4205 in.	86.870–86.880mm

ENGINE REBUILDING SPECIFICATIONS

Component	English	Metric
Piston-to-Bore Clearance		
1C-T	0.0016–0.0024 in.	0.04–0.06mm
2C-T	0.0018–0.0026 in.	0.045–0.065mm
2S-E	0.0006–0.0014 in.	0.015–0.035mm
2VZ-FE	0.0018–0.0026 in.	0.045–0.065mm
3VZ-FE	0.0051–0.0059 in.	0.013–0.015mm
3S-FE	0.0018–0.0026 in.	0.045–0.065mm
5S-FE	0.0055–0.0063 in.	0.014–0.016mm
Piston Pin Diameter		
1C-T	1.0633–1.0638 in.	27.008–27.020mm
2C-T	1.0630–1.0635 in.	27.000–27.012mm
2S-E	1.8892–1.8898 in.	47.985–48.000mm
2VZ-FE	1.8892–1.8898 in.	47.985–48.000mm
3VZ-FE	0.8860–1.8864 in.	21.997–22.006mm
3S-FE	1.8892–1.8898 in.	47.985–48.000mm
5S-FE	0.8860–1.8865 in.	21.997–22.009mm
Piston Pin-to-Bushing Clearance		
1C-T, 2C-T	0.0003–0.0006 in.	0.007–0.015mm
2S-E	0.0009–0.0022 in.	0.024–0.055mm
Ring Groove Clearance		
1C-T, 2C-T	0.008 in.	0.2mm
2S-E	0.0012–0.0028 in.	0.03–0.07mm
2VZ-FE, 3VZ-FE		
No. 1	0.0004–0.0031 in.	0.10–0.080mm
No. 2	0.0012–0.0028 in.	0.30–0.070mm
3S-FE	0.0012–0.0028 in.	0.03–0.07mm
5S-FE		
No. 1	0.0016–0.0031 in.	0.40–0.080mm
No. 2	0.0012–0.0028 in.	0.30–0.070mm
Ring End Gap		
1C-T		
No. 1	0.0098–0.0193 in.	0.25–0.49mm
No. 2	0.0079–0.0173 in.	0.20–0.44mm
Oil	0.0079–0.0193 in.	0.20–0.49mm
2C-T		
No. 1	0.0106–0.0213 in.	0.27–0.54mm
No. 2	0.0098–0.0205 in.	0.25–0.52mm
Oil	0.0079–0.0323 in.	0.20–0.82mm
2S-E		
No. 1	0.0110–0.0197 in.	0.28–0.50mm
No. 2	0.0079–0.0177 in.	0.20–0.45mm
Oil	0.0079–0.0311 in.	0.20–0.79mm
2VZ-FE		
No. 1	0.0118–0.0205 in.	0.300–0.520mm
No. 2	0.0138–0.0236 in.	0.350–0.600mm
Oil	0.0079–0.0217 in.	0.200–0.550mm
3VZ-FE		
No. 1	0.0110–0.0197 in.	0.280–0.500mm
No. 2	0.0150–0.0236 in.	0.380–0.600mm
Oil	0.0059–0.0224 in.	0.150–0.570mm
3S-FE		
No. 1	0.0106–0.0197 in.	0.270–0.500mm
No. 2	0.0106–0.0201 in.	0.270–0.510mm
Oil	0.0079–0.0217 in.	0.200–0.550mm
5S-FE		
No. 1	0.0106–0.0197 in.	0.270–0.500mm
No. 2	0.0138–0.0234 in.	0.350–0.600mm
Oil	0.0079–0.0217 in.	0.200–0.550mm
Connecting Rod Alignment		
1C-T, 2C-T		
Twist	0.0059 in. per 3.94 in.	0.15mm per 100mm
Bend	0.0020 in. per 3.94 in.	0.05mm per 100mm

ENGINE REBUILDING SPECIFICATIONS

Component	English	Metric
2S-E		
Twist	0.0059 in. per 3.94 in.	0.015mm per 100mm
Bend	0.0020 in. per 3.94 in.	0.05mm per 100mm
2VZ-FE, 3VZ-FE		
Twist	0.0059 in. per 3.94 in.	0.015mm per 100mm
Bend	0.0020 in. per 3.94 in.	0.05mm per 100mm
3S-FE, 5S-FE		
Twist	0.0059 in. per 3.94 in.	0.015mm per 100mm
Bend	0.0020 in. per 3.94 in.	0.05mm per 100mm
Connecting Rod Thrust Clearance		
1C-T, 2C-T	0.0031–0.0118 in.	0.08–0.30mm
2S-E	0.0063–0.0083 in.	0.16–0.21mm
2VZ-FE, 3VZ-FE	0.0059–0.0130 in.	0.15–0.33mm
3S-FE, 5S-FE	0.0063–0.0123 in.	0.160–0.312mm
Connecting Rod Bearing Oil Clearance		
1C-T	0.0014–0.0025 in.	0.036–0.064mm
2C-T	0.0017–0.0028 in.	0.036–0.064mm
2S-E	0.0009–0.0022 in.	0.024–0.055mm
2VZ-FE, 3VZ-FE	0.0011–0.0026 in.	0.028–0.065mm
3S-FE	0.0009–0.0022 in.	0.024–0.055mm
5S-FE	0.0063–0.0123 in.	0.160–0.312mm
Crankshaft		
Main Journal Diameter		
1C-T, 2C-T	2.2435–2.2441 in.	56.985–57.000mm
2S-E	2.1648–2.1654 in.	54.985–55.000mm
2VZ-FE, 3VZ-FE	2.5191–2.5197 in.	63.985–64.000mm
3S-FE	2.1649–2.1655 in.	54.988–55.003mm
5S-FE	2.1653–2.1655 in.	54.988–55.003mm
Main Journal Out-of-Round Limit		
1C-T, 2C-T	0.0008 in.	0.02mm
2S-E	0.0008 in.	0.02mm
2VZ-FE, 3VZ-FE	0.0008 in.	0.02mm
3S-FE, 5S-FE	0.0008 in.	0.02mm
Main Journal Oil Clearance		
1C-T, 2C-T	0.0013–0.0026 in.	0.034–0.065mm
2S-E		
No. 3	0.0012–0.0022 in.	0.030–0.057mm
All Others	0.0008–0.0019 in.	0.020–0.047mm
2VZ-FE, 3VZ-FE	0.0011–0.0022 in.	0.029–0.056mm
3S-FE, 5S-FE		
No. 3	0.0010–0.0017 in.	0.025–0.044mm
All Others	0.0006–0.0013 in.	0.015–0.034mm
Connecting Rod Journal Diameter		
1C-T, 2C-T	1.9877–1.9882 in.	50.488–50.500mm
2S-E	1.8892–1.8898 in.	47.985–48.000mm
2VZ-FE	1.8892–1.8898 in.	47.985–48.000mm
3S-FE	1.8892–1.8898 in.	47.985–48.000mm
Connecting Rod Journal Out-of-Round Limit		
1C-T, 2C-T	0.0008 in.	0.02mm
2S-E	0.0008 in.	0.02mm
2VZ-FE, 3VZ-FE	0.0008 in.	0.02mm
3S-FE, 5S-FE	0.0008 in.	0.02mm
Connecting Rod Bearing-to-Crankshaft Oil Clearance		
1C-T	0.0014–0.0025 in.	0.036–0.064mm
2C-T	0.0017–0.0028 in.	0.044–0.072mm
2S-E	0.0009–0.0022 in.	0.024–0.055mm
2VZ-FE, 3VZ-FE	0.0011–0.0026 in.	0.028–0.065mm
3S-FE, 5S-FE	0.0009–0.0022 in.	0.024–0.055mm

ENGINE REBUILDING SPECIFICATIONS

Component	English	Metric
Crankshaft Runout		
1C-T, 2C-T	0.004 in.	0.1mm
2S-E	0.0024 in.	0.06mm
2VZ-FE, 3VZ-FE	0.0024 in.	0.06mm
3S-FE, 5S-FE	0.0024 in.	0.06mm
Crankshaft Thrust Clearance		
1C-T, 2C-T	0.0016–0.0094 in.	0.04–0.24mm
2S-E	0.0008–0.0087 in.	0.02–022mm
2VZ-FE, 3VZ-FE	0.0008–0.0087 in.	0.02–022mm
3S-FE, 5S-FE	0.0008–0.0087 in.	0.02–022mm
Oil Pump		
1C-T, 2C-T		
Body Clearance	0.0039–0.0067 in.	0.10–0.17mm
Tip Clearance	0.0020–0.0059 in.	0.05–0.15mm
2S-E		
Body Clearance	0.0039–0.0067 in.	0.10–0.17mm
Tip Clearance	0.0016–0.0063 in.	0.04–0.16mm
2VZ-FE, 3VZ-FE		
Body Clearance	0.0039–0.0069 in.	0.100–0.175mm
Tip Clearance	0.0043–0.0094 in.	0.11–0.24mm
Side Clearance	0.0012–0.0035 in.	0.03–0.09mm
3S-FE, 5S-FE		
Body Clearance	0.0039–0.0063 in.	0.10–0.16mm
Tip Clearance	0.0016–0.0063 in.	0.04–0.16mm

TORQUE SPECIFICATIONS

Component	English	Metric
A/C Compressor:	20 ft. lbs.	27 Nm
Air Intake Chamber:		
2VZ-FE, 3VZ-FE:	32 ft. lbs.	43 Nm
Air Intake Chamber Stays:		
2VZ-FE:	27 ft. lbs.	37 Nm
3VZ-FE:	29 ft. lbs.	39 Nm
Camshaft Bearing Cap:		
1C-T, 2C-T:	13 ft. lbs.	18 Nm
2S-E, 3S-FE, 5S-FE:	14 ft. lbs.	19 Nm
2VZ-FE, 3VZ-FE:	12 ft. lbs.	16 Nm
Camshaft Housing:		
2S-E	11 ft. lbs.	15 Nm
Camshaft Timing Pulley:		
1C-T, 2C-T:	65 ft. lbs.	88 Nm
2S-E, 3S-FE:	40 ft. lbs.	54 Nm
5S-FE:	27 ft. lbs.	37 Nm
2VZ-FE, 3VZ-FE:		
Left:	80 ft. lbs.	108 Nm
Right:	55 ft. lbs.	75 Nm
Coolant Temperature Sensor:	15 ft. lbs.	20 Nm
Cooling Fan Hydraulic Line:		
3VZ-FE:	47 ft. lbs.	64 Nm
Crankshaft Balancer:		
5S-FE:	36 ft. lbs.	49 Nm
Crankshaft Pulley:		
1C-T, 2C-T:	72 ft. lbs.	98 Nm
2S-E, 3S-FE, 5S-FE:	80 ft. lbs.	108 Nm
2VZ-FE, 3VZ-FE:	181 ft. lbs.	245 Nm

TORQUE SPECIFICATIONS

Component	English	Metric
Cylinder head:		
1C-T:	62 ft. lbs.	84 Nm
2C-T:		
1st:	33 ft. lbs.	44 Nm
2nd:	90°	
3rd:	90°	
2S-E:		
1st:	15 ft. lbs.	20 Nm
2nd:	30 ft. lbs.	47 Nm
3rd:	47 ft. lbs.	64 Nm
3S-FE, 5S-FE:		
1986–88:	47 ft. lbs.	64 Nm
1989–92		
1st:	36 ft. lbs.	49 Nm.
2nd:	90°	
2VZ-FE, 3VZ-FE:		
12mm:		
1st	25 ft. lbs.	34 Nm
2nd:	90°	
3rd:	90°	
8mm:	13 inch lbs.	18 Nm
Cylinder head cover:		
1C-T, 2C-T:	65 inch lbs.	7.5 Nm
2S-E:	13 ft. lbs.	18 Nm
3S-FE, 5S-FE:	17 ft. lbs.	23 Nm
2VZ-FE, 3VZ-FE:	52 inch lbs.	5.9 Nm
Distributor Pinch Bolt:		
2S-E, 3S-FE:	9 ft. lbs.	13 Nm
5S-FE:	14 ft. lbs.	19 Nm
2VZ-FE, 3VZ-FE:	13 ft. lbs.	18 Nm
Drive Plate:		
1C-T, 2C-T:	65 ft. lbs.	88 Nm
2S-E:	61 ft. lbs.	83 Nm
3S-FE, 5S-FE:	61 ft. lbs.	83 Nm
2VZ-FE, 3VZ-FE:	61 ft. lbs.	83 Nm
EGR Valve:		
4 cyl.:		
Pipe:	43 ft. lbs.	59 Nm
Bolt:	9 ft. lbs.	13 Nm
6 cyl.:	13 ft. lbs.	18 Nm
Engine Mounts:		
2S-E:		
Front & Rear:	29 ft. lbs.	39 Nm
3S-FE (2wd):		
Left Bolts:	38 ft. lbs.	52 Nm
Left Thru-bolts:	64 ft. lbs.	87 Nm
Right:		
Bracket Bolts:	38 ft. lbs.	52 Nm
Body Bolts:	65 ft. lbs.	88 Nm
Bolts:	47 ft. lbs.	64 Nm
Center Member:	29 ft. lbs.	39 Nm
Front & Rear:	32 ft. lbs.	43 Nm
3S-FE (4wd):		
Left Bolts:	38 ft. lbs.	52 Nm
Left Thru-bolts:	64 ft. lbs.	87 Nm
Right:		
Bracket Bolts:	64 ft. lbs.	87 Nm
Nuts:	38 ft. lbs.	52 Nm
Stays:	54 ft. lbs.	73 Nm
Center Member:		
Body Bolts:	29 ft. lbs.	39 Nm
Other Bolts:	38 ft. lbs.	52 Nm

TORQUE SPECIFICATIONS

Component	English	Metric
5S-FE:		
Front:	59 ft. lbs.	80 Nm
Rear:	48 ft. lbs.	66 Nm
Left:	47 ft. lbs.	64 Nm
2VZ-FE:		
Left Mount Bracket:	38 ft. lbs.	52 Nm
Left Mount:		
Bolts:	38 ft. lbs.	52 Nm
Thru-bolts:	64 ft. lbs.	87 Nm
Right:		
Bolt:	47 ft. lbs.	64 Nm
Bracket Nut:	38 ft. lbs.	52 Nm
Body Nut:	65 ft. lbs.	88 Nm
No. 1 Stay (right):	38 ft. lbs.	53 Nm
No. 2 Stay (right):		
Bolt:	48 ft. lbs.	66 Nm
Nut:	38 ft. lbs.	52 Nm
Lower Mount Stay:		
MT (nut):	38 ft. lbs.	52 Nm
MT (bolt):	14 ft. lbs.	20 Nm
AT (12mm):	15 ft. lbs.	21 Nm
AT (14mm):	38 ft. lbs.	52 Nm
Front & Rear Mount Bracket:	57 ft. lbs.	77 Nm
Center Mount:	38 ft. lbs.	52 Nm
Center mount Member	29 ft. lbs.	39 Nm
Front, Rear & Center Mount:		
Bolts:	54 ft. lbs.	73 Nm
Thru-bolts:	64 ft. lbs.	87 Nm
3VZ-FE:		
Engine Control Rod:	47 ft. lbs.	64 Nm
Rear Mounting Stays:		
A:	23 ft. lbs.	31 Nm
B:	46 ft. lbs.	62 Nm
Front Mounting Stays:	59 ft. lbs.	80 Nm
Front Absorber:	35 ft. lbs.	48 Nm
Right:	48 ft. lbs.	66 Nm
Left:	47 ft. lbs.	64 Nm
Exhaust Manifold		
1C-T, 2C-T:	31 ft. lbs.	42 Nm
2S-E:	31 ft. lbs.	42 Nm
3S-FE, 5S-FE:	22 ft. lbs.	29 Nm
2VZ-FE, 3VZ-FE:		
Manifold:	29 ft. lbs.	39 Nm
Crossover Nut:	29 ft. lbs.	39 Nm
Crossover Bolts:	25 ft. lbs.	34 Nm
Exhaust Pipe:	46 ft. lbs.	62 Nm
Flywheel:		
1C-T, 2C-T:	65 ft. lbs.	88 Nm
2S-E:	72 ft. lbs.	98 Nm
3S-FE, 5S-FE:	65 ft. lbs.	88 Nm
2VZ-FE, 3VZ-FE:	61 ft. lbs.	83 Nm
Fuel Filter Inlet Nut:	22 ft. lbs.	29 Nm
Fuel Sender:	17 inch lbs.	2 Nm
Idler Pulley:		
1C-T, 2C-T:	27 ft. lbs.	37 Nm
2S-E, 3S-FE, 5S-FE:	31 ft. lbs.	42 Nm
2VZ-FE, 3VZ-FE:	29 ft. lbs.	29 Nm
Injection Pump Pulley:		
Diesel:	47 ft. lbs.	64 Nm

TORQUE SPECIFICATIONS

Component	English	Metric
Intake Manifold:		
1C-T, 2C-T:	13 ft. lbs.	18 Nm
2S-E (1983–85):	31 ft. lbs.	42 Nm
2S-E, 3S-FE, 5S-FE:	14 ft. lbs.	19 Nm
2VZ-FE, 3VZ-FE:	13 ft. lbs.	18 Nm
ISC Valve:		
2VZ-FE, 3VZ-FE:	9 ft. lbs.	13 Nm
Lower Crossmember:		
3S-FE (4wd):		
Body:	153 ft. lbs.	207 Nm
Other:	29 ft. lbs.	39 Nm
5S-FE:	153 ft. lbs.	207 Nm
Main Bearing Cap:		
1C-T, 2C-T:	76 ft. lbs.	103 Nm
2S-E, 3S-FE, 5S-FE:	43 ft. lbs.	59 Nm
2VZ-FE, 3VZ-FE:		
1st:	45 ft. lbs.	61 Nm
2nd:	90°	
Oil Cooler:		
1C-T, 2C-T:	38 ft. lbs.	49 Nm
Oil Pan:		
Diesel:	5 ft. lbs.	7 Nm
Gasoline:	4 ft. lbs.	5.4 Nm
Oil Pan Stiffener Plate:	27 ft. lbs.	37 Nm
Oil Pump:		
Diesel:	13 ft. lbs.	18 Nm
4 cyl.:	7 ft. lbs.	9 Nm
6 cyl.:		
12mm:	14 ft. lbs.	20 Nm
14mm:	30 ft. lbs.	41 Nm
Oil Pump Relief Valve Plug:	27 ft. lbs.	37 Nm
Power Steering Pump:	31 ft. lbs.	43 Nm
Rear Main Seal Retainer:		
2S-E, 3S-FE, 5S-FE:	7 ft. lbs.	9 Nm
2VZ-FE, 3VZ-FE:	69 inch lbs.	7.9 Nm
Radiator:	9 ft. lbs.	13 Nm
Relief Valve:		
5S-FE:	58 ft. lbs.	78 Nm
Spark Plug Tubes:		
3S-FE, 5S-FE:	29 ft. lbs.	39 Nm
Starter:	29 ft. lbs.	39 Nm
Thermostat Housing:		
Diesel:	65 inch lbs.	7 Nm
4 cyl.:	78 inch lbs.	8.8 Nm
6 cyl.:	14 ft. lbs.	20 Nm
Throttle Body:		
4 cyl.:	14 ft. lbs.	20 Nm
Timing Belt Tensioner:		
2VZ-FE, 3VZ-FE:	20 ft. lbs.	26 Nm
Turbocharger:	38 ft. lbs.	52 Nm

TORQUE SPECIFICATIONS

Component	English	Metric
Water Bypass Outlet:		
2VZ-FE:	14 ft. lbs.	20 Nm
3VZ-FE:	74 inch lbs.	8.3 Nm
Water Pump:		
1C-T, 2C-T:	13 ft. lbs.	18 Nm
2S-E, 3S-FE, 5S-FE:	82 inch lbs.	9.3 Nm
2VZ-FE, 3VZ-FE:	14 ft. lbs.	20 Nm

AIR FLOW METER 4-19
APPLICATION CHART 4-
CHECK ENGINE LIGHT 4-13
COOLANT TEMPERATURE
SENSOR 4-22
CRANKCASE VENTILATION VALVE 4-6
EGR VALVE 4-8
ELECTRONIC ENGINE CONTROLS 4-13
ENGINE EMISSION CONTROLS
Evaporative canister 4-6
Exhaust gas recirculation (EGR) system 4-8
Oxygen (O_2) sensor 4-15
PCV valve 4-6
EVAPORATIVE CANISTER 4-6
EXHAUST EMISSION CONTROLS 4-3
EXHAUST GAS RECIRCULATION (EGR) SYSTEM 4-8
IDLE SPEED CONTROL VALVE 4-22
INTAKE AIR TEMPERATURE SENSOR 4-21
MAIN RELAYS 4-24
MANIFOLD PRESSURE SENSOR 4-20
OXYGEN (O_2) SENSOR 4-15
PCV VALVE 4-6
THROTTLE POSITION SENSOR 4-17
VACUUM DIAGRAMS 4-26
VACUUM SOLENOID VALVES 4-22
ELECTRONIC ENGINE CONTROLS 4-13

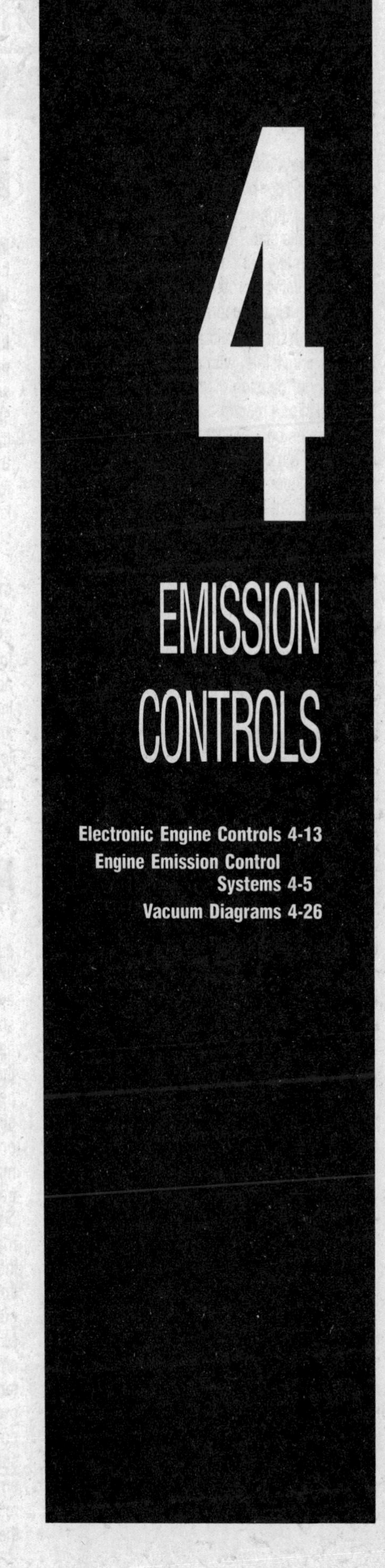

4

EMISSION CONTROLS

Electronic Engine Controls 4-13
Engine Emission Control Systems 4-5
Vacuum Diagrams 4-26

AIR POLLUTION

The earth's atmosphere, at or near sea level, consists of 78% nitrogen, 21% oxygen and 1% other gases, approximately. If it were possible to remain in this state, 100% clean air would result. However, many varied causes allow other gases and particulates to mix with the clean air, causing the air to become unclean or polluted.

Certain of these pollutants are visible while others are invisible, with each having the capability of causing distress to the eyes, ears, throat, skin and respiratory system. Should these pollutants be concentrated in a specific area and under the right conditions, death could result due to the displacement or chemical change of the oxygen content in the air. These pollutants can cause much damage to the environment and to the many man made objects that are exposed to the elements.

To better understand the causes of air pollution, the pollutants can be categorized into 3 separate types, natural, industrial and automotive.

Natural Pollutants

Natural pollution has been present on earth before man appeared and is still a factor to be considered when discussing air pollution, although it causes only a small percentage of the present overall pollution problem existing in our country. It is the direct result of decaying organic matter, wind born smoke and particulates from such natural events as plains and forest fires (ignited by heat or lightning), volcanic ash, sand and dust which can spread over a large area of the countryside.

Such a phenomenon of natural pollution has been recent volcanic eruptions, with the resulting plume of smoke, steam and volcanic ash blotting out the sun's rays as it spreads and rises higher into the atmosphere, where the upper air currents catch and carry the smoke and ash, while condensing the steam back into water vapor. As the water vapor, smoke and ash traveled on their journey, the smoke dissipates into the atmosphere while the ash and moisture settle back to earth in a trail hundred of miles long. In many cases, lives are lost and millions of dollars of property damage result, and ironically, man can only stand by and watch it happen.

Industrial Pollution

Industrial pollution is caused primarily by industrial processes, the burning of coal, oil and natural gas, which in turn produces smoke and fumes. Because the burning fuels contain much sulfur, the principal ingredients of smoke and fumes are sulfur dioxide (SO_2) and particulate matter. This type of pollutant occurs most severely during still, damp and cool weather, such as at night. Even in its less severe form, this pollutant is not confined to just cities. Because of air movements, the pollutants move for miles over the surrounding countryside, leaving in its path a barren and unhealthy environment for all living things.

Working with Federal, State and Local mandated rules, regulations and by carefully monitoring the emissions, industries have greatly reduced the amount of pollutant emitted from their industrial sources, striving to obtain an acceptable level. Because of the mandated industrial emission clean up, many land areas and streams in and around the cities that were formerly barren of vegetation and life, have now begun to move back in the direction of nature's intended balance.

Automotive Pollutants

The third major source of air pollution is the automotive emissions. The emissions from the internal combustion engine were not an appreciable problem years ago because of the small number of registered vehicles and the nation's small highway system. However, during the early 1950's, the trend of the American people was to move from the cities to the surrounding suburbs. This caused an immediate problem in the transportation areas because the majority of the suburbs were not afforded mass transit conveniences. This lack of transportation created an attractive market for the automobile manufacturers, which resulted in a dramatic increase in the number of vehicles produced and sold, along with a marked increase in highway construction between cities and the suburbs. Multi-vehicle families emerged with much emphasis placed on the individual vehicle per family member. As the increase in vehicle ownership and usage occurred, so did the pollutant levels in and around the cities, as the suburbanites drove daily to their businesses and employment in the city and its fringe area, returning at the end of the day to their homes in the suburbs.

It was noted that a fog and smoke type haze was being formed and at times, remained in suspension over the cities and did not quickly dissipate. At first this "smog", derived from the words "smoke" and "fog", was thought to result from industrial pollution but it was determined that the automobile emissions were largely to blame. It was discovered that as normal automobile emissions were exposed to sunlight for a period of time, complex chemical reactions would take place.

It was found the smog was a photo chemical layer and was developed when certain oxides of nitrogen (NOx) and unburned hydrocarbons (HC) from the automobile emissions were exposed to sunlight and was more severe when the smog would remain stagnant over an area in which a warm layer of air would settle over the top of a cooler air mass at ground level, trapping and holding the automobile emissions, instead of the emissions being dispersed and diluted through normal air flows. This type of air stagnation was given the name "Temperature Inversion".

Temperature Inversion

In normal weather situations, the surface air is warmed by the heat radiating from the earth's surface and the sun's rays and will rise upward, into the atmosphere, to be cooled through a convection type heat expands with the cooler upper air. As the warm air rises, the surface pollutants are carried upward and dissipated into the atmosphere.

When a temperature inversion occurs, we find the higher air is no longer cooler but warmer than the surface air, causing the cooler surface air to become trapped and unable to move. This warm air blanket can extend from above ground level to a few hundred or even a few thousand feet into the air. As the surface air is trapped, so are the pollutants, causing a severe smog condition. Should this stagnant air mass extend to a few thousand feet high, enough air movement with the inversion takes place to allow the smog layer to rise above ground level but the pollutants still cannot dissipate. This inversion can remain for days over an area, with only the smog level rising or lowering from ground level to a few hundred feet high. Meanwhile, the pollutant levels increases, causing eye irritation, respirator problems, reduced visibility, plant damage and in some cases, cancer type diseases.

This inversion phenomenon was first noted in the Los Angeles, California area. The city lies in a basin type of terrain and during certain weather conditions, a cold air mass is held in the basin while a warmer air mass covers it like a lid.

Because this type of condition was first documented as prevalent in the Los Angeles area, this type of smog was named Los Angeles Smog, although it occurs in other areas where a large concentration of automobiles are used and the air remains stagnant for any length of time.

Internal Combustion Engine Pollutants

Consider the internal combustion engine as a machine in which raw materials must be placed so a finished product comes out. As in any machine operation, a certain amount of wasted material is formed. When we relate this to the internal combustion engine, we find that by putting in air and fuel, we obtain power from this mixture during the combustion process to drive the vehicle. The by-product or waste of this power is, in part, heat and exhaust gases with which we must concern ourselves.

HEAT TRANSFER

The heat from the combustion process can rise to over 4000°F (2204°C). The dissipation of this heat is controlled by a ram air effect, the use of cooling fans to cause air flow and having a liquid coolant solution surrounding the combustion area and transferring the heat of combustion through the cylinder walls and into the coolant. The coolant is then directed to a thin-finned, multi-tubed radiator, from which the excess heat is transferred to the outside air by 1 or all of the 3 heat transfer methods, conduction, convection or radiation.

The cooling of the combustion area is an important part in the control of exhaust emissions. To understand the behavior of the combustion and transfer of its heat, consider the air/fuel charge. It is ignited and the flame front burns progressively across the combustion chamber until the burning charge reaches the cylinder walls. Some of the fuel in contact with the walls is not hot enough to burn, thereby snuffing out or Quenching the combustion process. This leaves unburned fuel in the combustion chamber. This unburned fuel is then forced out of the cylinder along with the exhaust gases and into the exhaust system.

Many attempts have been made to minimize the amount of unburned fuel in the combustion chambers due to the snuffing out or "Quenching", by increasing the coolant temperature and lessening the contact area of the coolant around the combustion area. Design limitations within the combustion chambers prevent the complete burning of the air/fuel charge, so a certain amount of the unburned fuel is still expelled into the exhaust system, regardless of modifications to the engine.

EXHAUST EMISSIONS

Composition Of The Exhaust Gases

The exhaust gases emitted into the atmosphere are a combination of burned and unburned fuel. To understand the exhaust emission and its composition review some basic chemistry.

When the air/fuel mixture is introduced into the engine, we are mixing air, composed of nitrogen (78%), oxygen (21%) and other gases (1%) with the fuel, which is 100% hydrocarbons (HC), in a semi-controlled ratio. As the combustion process is accomplished, power is produced to move the vehicle while the heat of combustion is transferred to the cooling system. The exhaust gases are then composed of nitrogen, a diatomic gas (N_2), the same as was introduced in the engine, carbon dioxide (CO2), the same gas that is used in beverage carbonation and water vapor (H_2O). The nitrogen (N_2), for the most part passes through the engine unchanged, while the oxygen (O_2) reacts (burns) with the hydrocarbons (HC) and produces the carbon dioxide (CO_2) and the water vapors (H_2O). If this chemical process would be the only process to take place, the exhaust emissions would be harmless. However, during the combustion process, other pollutants are formed and are considered dangerous. These pollutants are carbon monoxide (CO), hydrocarbons (HC), oxides of nitrogen (NOx) oxides of sulfur (SOx) and engine particulates.

Lead (Pb), is considered 1 of the particulates and is present in the exhaust gases whenever leaded fuels are used. Lead (Pb) does not dissipate easily. Levels can be high along roadways when it is emitted from vehicles and can pose a health threat. Since the increased usage of unleaded gasoline and the phasing out of leaded gasoline for fuel, this pollutant is gradually diminishing. While not considered a major threat lead is still considered a dangerous pollutant.

HYDROCARBONS

Hydrocarbons (HC) are essentially unburned fuel that have not been successfully burned during the combustion process or have escaped into the atmosphere through fuel evaporation. The main sources of incomplete combustion are rich air/fuel mixtures, low engine temperatures and improper spark timing. The main sources of hydrocarbon emission through fuel evaporation come from the vehicle's fuel tank and carburetor bowl.

To reduce combustion hydrocarbon emission, engine modifications were made to minimize dead space and surface area in the combustion chamber. In addition the air/fuel mixture was made more lean through improved carburetion, fuel injection and by the addition of external controls to aid in further combustion of the hydrocarbons outside the engine. Two such methods were the addition of an air injection system, to inject fresh air into the exhaust manifolds and the installation of a catalytic converter, a unit that is able to burn traces of hydrocarbons without affecting the internal combustion process or fuel economy.

To control hydrocarbon emissions through fuel evaporation, modifications were made to the fuel tank and carburetor bowl to allow storage of the fuel vapors during periods of engine shut-down, and at specific times during engine operation, to purge and burn these same vapors by blending them with the air/fuel mixture.

CARBON MONOXIDE

Carbon monoxide is formed when not enough oxygen is present during the combustion process to convert carbon (C) to carbon dioxide (CO_2). An increase in the carbon monoxide (CO) emission is normally accompanied by an increase in the hydrocarbon (HC) emission because of the lack of oxygen to completely burn all of the fuel mixture.

Carbon monoxide (CO) also increases the rate at which the photo chemical smog is formed by speeding up the conversion of nitric oxide (NO) to nitrogen dioxide (NO_2). To accomplish this, carbon monoxide (CO) combines with oxygen (O_2) and nitrogen dioxide (NO_2) to produce carbon dioxide (CO_2) and nitrogen dioxide (NO_2). ($CO + O_2 + NO = CO_2 + NO_2$).

The dangers of carbon monoxide, which is an odorless, colorless toxic gas are many. When carbon monoxide is inhaled into the lungs and passed into the blood stream, oxygen is replaced by the carbon monoxide in the red blood cells, causing a reduction in the amount of oxygen being supplied to the many parts of the body. This lack of oxygen causes headaches, lack of coordination, reduced mental alertness and should the carbon monoxide concentration be high enough, death could result.

NITROGEN

Normally, nitrogen is an inert gas. When heated to approximately 2500°F (1371°C) through the combustion process, this gas becomes active and causes an increase in the nitric oxide (NOx) emission.

Oxides of nitrogen (NOx) are composed of approximately 97–98% nitric oxide (NO2). Nitric oxide is a colorless gas but when it is passed into the atmosphere, it combines with oxygen and forms nitrogen dioxide (NO2). The nitrogen dioxide then combines with chemically active hydrocarbons (HC) and when in the presence of sunlight, causes the formation of photo chemical smog.

OZONE

To further complicate matters, some of the nitrogen dioxide (NO_2) is broken apart by the sunlight to form nitric oxide and oxygen. (NO_2 + sunlight = NO + O). This single atom of oxygen then combines with diatomic (meaning 2 atoms) oxygen (O_2) to form ozone (O_3). Ozone is 1 of the smells associated with smog. It has a pungent and offensive odor, irritates the eyes and lung tissues, affects the growth of plant life and causes rapid deterioration of rubber products. Ozone can be formed by sunlight as well as electrical discharge into the air.

The most common discharge area on the automobile engine is the secondary ignition electrical system, especially when inferior quality spark plug cables are used. As the surge of high voltage is routed through the secondary cable, the circuit builds up an electrical field around the wire, acting upon the oxygen in the surrounding air to form the ozone. The faint glow along the cable with the engine running that may be visible on a dark night, is called the "corona discharge." It is the result of the electrical field passing from a high along the cable, to a low in the surrounding air, which forms the ozone gas. The combination of corona and ozone has been a major cause of cable deterioration. Recently, different types and better quality insulating materials have lengthened the life of the electrical cables.

Although ozone at ground level can be harmful, ozone is beneficial to the earth's inhabitants. By having a concentrated ozone layer called the 'ozonosphere', between 10 and 20 miles (16–32km) up in the atmosphere much of the ultra violet radiation from the sun's rays are absorbed and screened. If this ozone layer were not present, much of the earth's surface would be burned, dried and unfit for human life.

There is much discussion concerning the ozone layer and its density. A feeling exists that this protective layer of ozone is slowly diminishing and corrective action must be directed to this problem. Much experimenting is presently being conducted to determine if a problem exists and if so, the short and long term effects of the problem and how it can be remedied.

OXIDES OF SULFUR

Oxides of sulfur (SOx) were initially ignored in the exhaust system emissions, since the sulfur content of gasoline as a fuel is less than $\frac{1}{10}$ of 1%. Because of this small amount, it was felt that it contributed very little to the overall pollution problem. However, because of the difficulty in solving the sulfur emissions in industrial pollutions and the introduction of catalytic converter to the automobile exhaust systems, a change was mandated. The automobile exhaust system, when equipped with a catalytic converter, changes the sulfur dioxide (SO_2) into the sulfur trioxide (SO_3).

When this combines with water vapors (H_2O), a sulfuric acid mist (H_2SO_4) is formed and is a very difficult pollutant to handle and is extremely corrosive. This sulfuric acid mist that is formed, is the same mist that rises from the vents of an automobile storage battery when an active chemical reaction takes place within the battery cells.

When a large concentration of vehicles equipped with catalytic converters are operating in an area, this acid mist will rise and be distributed over a large ground area causing land, plant, crop, paints and building damage.

PARTICULATE MATTER

A certain amount of particulate matter is present in the burning of any fuel, with carbon constituting the largest percentage of the particulates. In gasoline, the remaining percentage of particulates is the burned remains of the various other compounds used in its manufacture. When a gasoline engine is in good internal condition, the particulate emissions are low but as the engine wears internally, the particulate emissions increase. By visually inspecting the tail pipe emissions, a determination can be made as to where an engine defect may exist. An engine with light gray smoke emitting from the tail pipe normally indicates an increase in the oil consumption through burning due to internal engine wear. Black smoke would indicate a defective fuel delivery system, causing the engine to operate in a rich mode. Regardless of the color of the smoke, the internal part of the engine or the fuel delivery system should be repaired to a "like new" condition to prevent excess particulate emissions.

Diesel and turbine engines emit a darkened plume of smoke from the exhaust system because of the type of fuel used. Emission control regulations are mandated for this type of emission and more stringent measures are being used to prevent excess emission of the particulate matter. Electronic components are being introduced to control the injection of the fuel at precisely the proper time of piston travel, to achieve the optimum in fuel ignition and fuel usage. Other particulate after-burning components are being tested to achieve a cleaner particular emission.

Good grades of engine lubricating oils should be used, meeting the manufacturers specification. "Cut-rate" oils can contribute to the particulate emission problem because of their low "flash" or ignition temperature point. Such oils burn prematurely during the combustion process causing emissions of particulate matter.

The cooling system is an important factor in the reduction of particulate matter. With the cooling system operating at a temperature specified by the manufacturer, the optimum of combustion will occur. The cooling system must be maintained in the same manner as the engine oiling system, as each system is required to perform properly in order for the engine to operate efficiently for a long time.

Other Automobile Emission Sources

Before emission controls were mandated on the internal combustion engines, other sources of engine pollutants were discovered, along with the exhaust emission. It was determined the engine combustion exhaust produced 60% of the total emission pollutants, fuel evaporation from the fuel tank and carburetor vents produced 20%, with the another 20% being produced through the crankcase as a by-product of the combustion process.

CRANKCASE EMISSIONS

Crankcase emissions are made up of water, acids, unburned fuel, oil fumes and particulates. The emissions are classified as hydrocarbons (HC) and are formed by the small amount of unburned, compressed air/fuel mixture entering the crankcase from the combustion area during the compression and power strokes, between the cylinder walls and piston rings. The head of the compression and combustion help to form the remaining crankcase emissions.

Since the first engines, crankcase emissions were allowed to go into the air through a road draft tube, mounted on the lower side of the engine block. Fresh air came in through an open oil filler cap or breather. The air passed through the crankcase mixing with blow-by gases. The motion of the vehicle and the air blowing past the open end of the road draft tube caused a low pressure area at the end of the tube. Crankcase emissions were simply drawn out of the road draft tube into the air.

To control the crankcase emission, the road draft tube was deleted. A hose and/or tubing was routed from the crankcase to the intake manifold so the blow-by emission could be burned with the air/fuel mixture. However, it was found that intake manifold vacuum, used to draw the crankcase emissions into the manifold, would vary in strength at the wrong time and not allow the proper emission flow. A regulating type valve was needed to control the flow of air through the crankcase.

Testing, showed the removal of the blow-by gases from the crankcase as quickly as possible, was most important to the longevity of the engine. Should large accumulations of blow-by gases remain and condense, dilution of the engine oil would occur to form water, soots, resins, acids and lead salts, resulting in the formation of sludge and varnishes. This condensation of the blow-by gases occur more frequently on vehicles used in numerous starting and stopping conditions, excessive idling and when the engine is not allowed to attain normal operating temperature through short runs. The crankcase purge control or PCV system will be described in detail later in this section.

FUEL EVAPORATIVE EMISSIONS

Gasoline fuel is a major source of pollution, before and after it is burned in the automobile engine. From the time the fuel is refined, stored, pumped and transported, again stored until it is pumped into the fuel tank of the vehicle, the gasoline gives off unburned hydrocarbons (HC) into the atmosphere. Through redesigning of the storage areas and venting systems, the pollution factor has been diminished but not eliminated, from the refinery standpoint. However, the automobile still remained the primary source of vaporized, unburned hydrocarbon (HC) emissions.

Fuel pumped form an underground storage tank is cool but when exposed to a warner ambient temperature, will expand. Before controls were mandated, an owner would fill the fuel tank with fuel from an underground storage tank and park the vehicle for some time in warm area, such as a parking lot. As the fuel would warm, it would expand and should no provisions or area be provided for the expansion, the fuel would spill out the filler neck and onto the ground, causing hydrocarbon (HC) pollution and creating a severe fire hazard. To correct this condition, the vehicle manufacturers added overflow plumbing and/or gasoline tanks with built in expansion areas or domes.

However, this did not control the fuel vapor emission from the fuel tank and the carburetor bowl. It was determined that most of the fuel evaporation occurred when the vehicle was stationary and the engine not operating. Most vehicles carry 5–25 gallons (19–95 liters) of gasoline. Should a large concentration of vehicles be parked in one area, such as a large parking lot, excessive fuel vapor emissions would take place, increasing as the temperature increases.

To prevent the vapor emission from escaping into the atmosphere, the fuel system is designed to trap the fuel vapors while the vehicle is stationary, by sealing the fuel system from the atmosphere. A storage system is used to collect and hold the fuel vapors from the carburetor and the fuel tank when the engine is not operating. When the engine is started, the storage system is then purged of the fuel vapors, which are drawn into the engine and burned with the air/fuel mixture.

The components of the fuel evaporative system will be described in detail later in this section.

EMISSION CONTROLS

Emission Systems Used

GASOLINE ENGINES

- Positive Crankcase ventilation (PCV): reduces blow-by gas.
- Fuel Evaporative Emission Control (EVAP): reduces evaporative hydrocarbons.
- Exhaust Gas Recirculation (EGR): reduces nitrogen oxide emissions.
- Three-Way Catalyst (TWC): reduces hydrocarbons, carbon monoxide and nitrogen oxides.
- Oxidation Catalyst (OC) — Canada: reduces hydrocarbons and carbon monoxides.
- Electronic Control Unit (ECU): regulates all conditions for exhaust emission reduction.

DIESEL ENGINES

- Exhaust Gas Recirculation (EGR): reduces nitrogen oxide emissions.

Crankcase Ventilation System

OPERATION

➧ SEE FIG. 1–2

A positive crankcase ventilation (PCV) system is used on all Toyota gasoline engines vehicles sold in the United States. Exhaust blow-by gases are routed from the crankcase to the intake manifold, where they are combined with the fuel/ air mixture and burned during combustion. This reduces the amount of hydrocarbons emitted by the exhaust.

A valve (PCV) is used in the line to prevent the gases in the crankcase from being ignited in case of a backfire. The amount of blow-by gases entering the mixture is also regulated by the PCV valve, which is spring loaded and has a variable orifice.

The important components of the PCV system are:

- PCV valve
- Valve cover
- Air intake chamber
- Ventilation case
- Hoses, connections and gaskets

SERVICING

PCV system service is relative easy, as it consists of making sure that the PCV valve is working and that all the hoses and connection are tight and in good shape. A clogged PCV valve and/or restricted hoses can cause the engine to run poorly.

Check the attaching hoses for cracks or clogs by visually and physically inspecting them. Check the PCV system hoses and connections to ensure that there are no leaks, then replace or tighten, as necessary.

To check the valve, remove it and blow through both of its ends. When blowing from the side which goes toward the intake manifold, very little air should pass through. When blowing from the crankcase (valve cover) side, air should pass through freely.

Replace the valve with a new one, if the valve fails to function as outlined.

➡ **NOTE: Do not attempt to clean or adjust the valve. Replace it with a new one.**

REMOVAL & INSTALLATION

Remove the PCV valve from the cylinder head cover or from the manifold-to-crankcase hose.

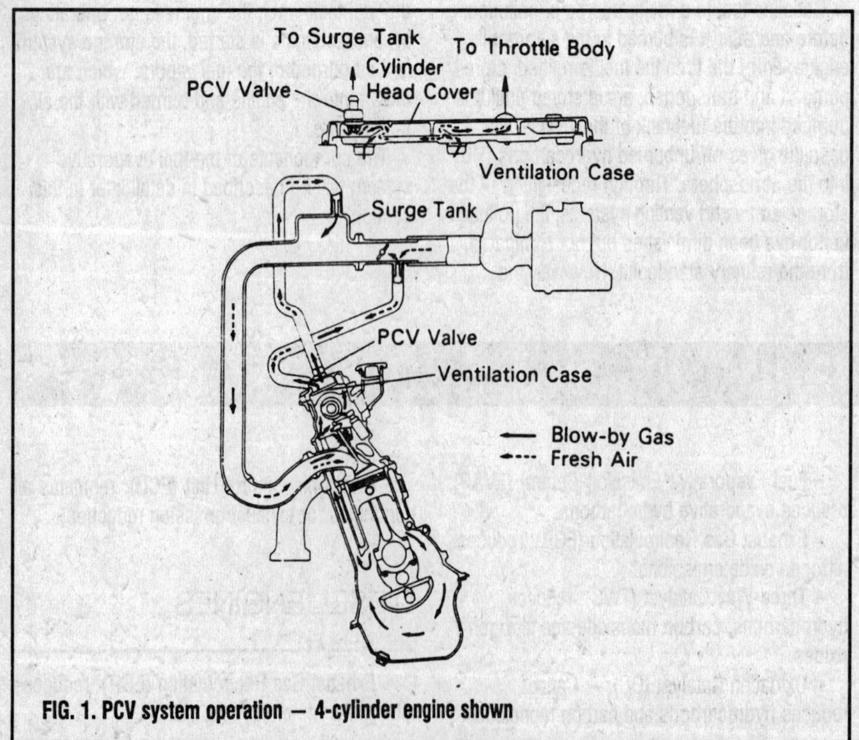

FIG. 1. PCV system operation — 4-cylinder engine shown

Evaporative Emission Controls

OPERATION

➧ SEE FIG. 3 & 6

To reduce the hydrocarbon emissions, evaporated fuel from the fuel tank is routed through the charcoal canister to the intake manifold for combustion in the cylinders.

SERVICING

Fuel Lines, Gas Cap and Charcoal Canister

Visually inspect all the fuel and vapor lines and connections for cracks, wear and sharp bends. Replace all damaged lines and tighten all loose connection.

Visually inspect the fuel tank for deformation, cracks and fuel leakage.

Remove the gas cap and check the cap and

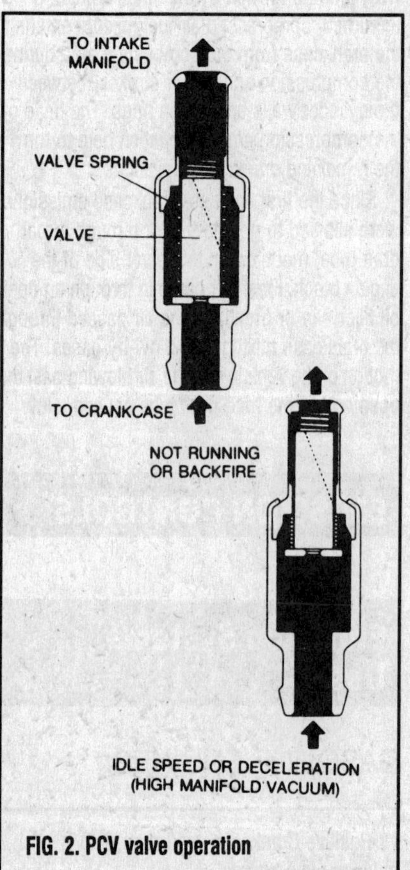

FIG. 2. PCV valve operation

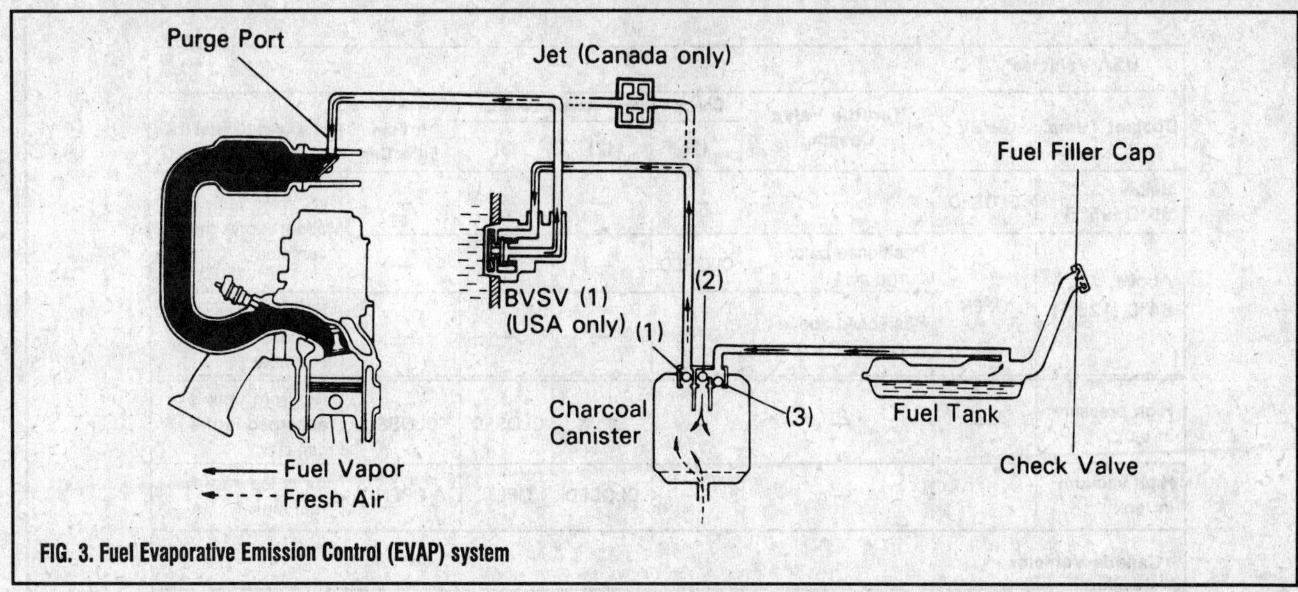

FIG. 3. Fuel Evaporative Emission Control (EVAP) system

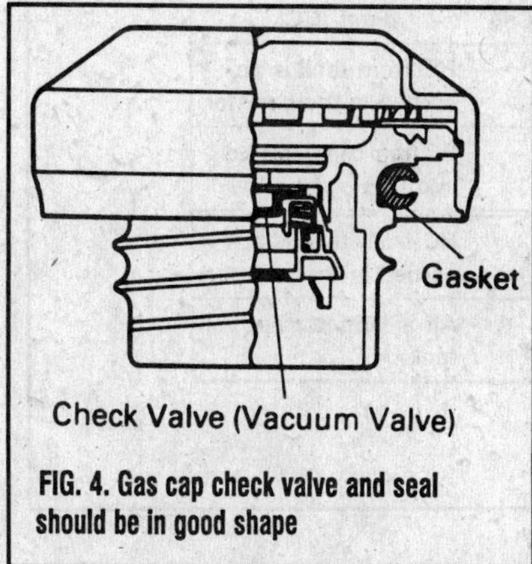

FIG. 4. Gas cap check valve and seal should be in good shape

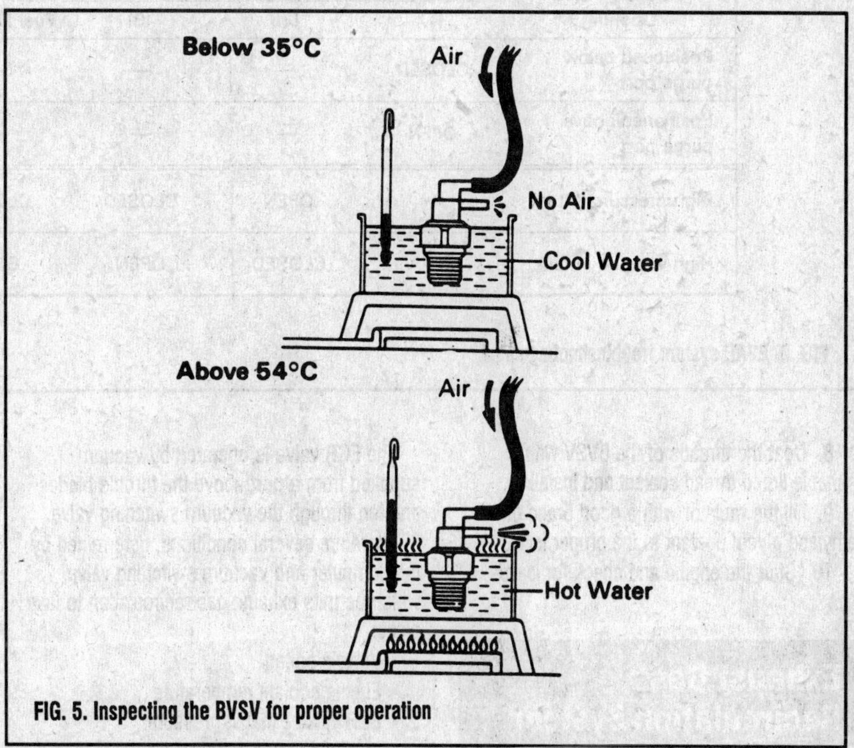

FIG. 5. Inspecting the BVSV for proper operation

gasket for cracks and damage. If the gasket is worn, replace it with new one. If the cap is damaged, it should be discarded and replaced.

Remove the charcoal canister from the vehicle and visually inspect and test the unit as described in Section 1. Remember that the charcoal canister should not be washed or cleaned and none of the activated carbon inside the unit should come out. If the canister is found to be inoperable, replace it with a new one.

Bimetal Vacuum Switching Valve (BVSV)

➧ SEE FIG. 5–6

The BVSV can be checked by blowing air into it at different temperatures.

1. Drain the coolant from the radiator into a suitable drain container.

❊❊ CAUTION

When draining the coolant, keep in mind that cats and dogs are attracted by the ethylene glycol antifreeze, and are quite likely to drink any that is left in an uncovered container or in puddles on the ground. This will prove fatal in sufficient quantity. Always drain the coolant into a sealable container. Coolant should be reused unless it is contaminated or several years old.

2. Unscrew and remove the BVSV.
3. Place the BVSV into a container filled with cool water (below 95°F [35°C]).
4. Blow air into the unit and make sure the valve is closed.
5. Remove the unit from the container and place into a container filled with hot water (129°F [54°C]).
6. Blow air into the unit and make sure that the valve is open.
7. If the valve does not operate as described, replace it.

USA Vehicles							
Coolant Temp.	BVSV	Throttle Valve Opening	Check Valve in Carcoal Canister (1)	(2)	(3)	Check Valve in Fuel Filler Cap	Evaporated Fuel (HC)
Below 35°C (95°F)	CLOSED	—	—	—	—	—	HC from tank is absorbed in the canister
Above 54°C (129°F)	OPEN	Positioned below purge port	CLOSED	—	—	—	
		Positioned above purge port	OPEN	—	—	—	HC from canister is led into air intake chamber
High pressure in tank	—	—	—	OPEN	CLOSED	CLOSED	HC from tank is absorbed in the canister
High vacuum in tank	—	—	—	CLOSED	OPEN	OPEN	Air is led into the fuel tank.

Canada Vehicles					
Throttle Valve Opening	Check Valve in Carcoal Canister (1)	(2)	(3)	Check Valve in Fuel Filler Cap	Evaporated Fuel (HC)
Positioned below purge port	CLOSED	—	—	—	HC from tank is absorbed in the canister.
Positioned above purge port	OPEN	—	—	—	HC from canister is led into air intake chamber.
High pressure in tank	—	OPEN	CLOSED	CLOSED	HC from tank is absorbed in the canister.
High vacuum in tank	—	CLOSED	OPEN	OPEN	Air is led into the fuel tank.

FIG. 6. EVAP system troubleshooting chart

8. Coat the threads of the BVSV with a suitable liquid thread sealant and install.
9. Fill the radiator with a good brand of ethylene glycol coolant to the proper level.
10. Start the engine and check for leaks.

Exhaust Gas Recirculation System

OPERATION

To reduce emissions, a portion of the exhaust gasses are recirculated through the EGR valve to the intake manifold to lower the maximum combustion temperature. The EGR system is used on both diesel and gasoline engines.

In all cases, the EGR valve is controlled by the same computer and vacuum switching valve which is used to operate other emission control system components.

The EGR valve is operated by vacuum supplied from a port above the throttle blades and fed through the vacuum switching valve.

There are several conditions, determined by the computer and vacuum switching valve, which permits exhaust gas recirculation to take place:

- Vehicle speed.
- Engine coolant temperature.
- EGR valve exhaust pressure.
- Manifold flange temperature.

SERVICE

Gasoline Engines

➧ SEE FIG. 7–9

EGR VACUUM MODULATOR FILTER CHECK

Check the EGR vacuum modulator filters for contamination and clogging. If only moderate accumulations exist, clean the filters with compressed air, otherwise replace them.

BVSV CHECK WITH COLD ENGINE

Using a three-way Tee connector, connect a vacuum gauge to the hose between the EGR valve and the vacuum pipe. Start the engine and check that the engine starts and runs at idle speed. With the engine cool (113°F [45°C]), verify the vacuum gauge reads 0 in. Hg.

BVSV AND EGR VACUUM MODULATOR CHECK WITH HOT ENGINE

Using a three-way Tee connector, connect a vacuum gauge to the hose between the EGR valve and the vacuum pipe. Start the engine and allow it to warm up to normal operating temperature. The gauge should read low vacuum at 2,500 rpm. Disconnect the vacuum hose from port **R** of the EGR vacuum modulator and connect port **R** directly to the intake manifold with another hose. Check that the vacuum gauge reads a high vacuum at 2,500 rpm. As large amounts of EGR gases enter the engine will misfire slightly, this indicates the EGR valve is functioning properly. Remove the vacuum gauge and reconnect the hoses to their original locations.

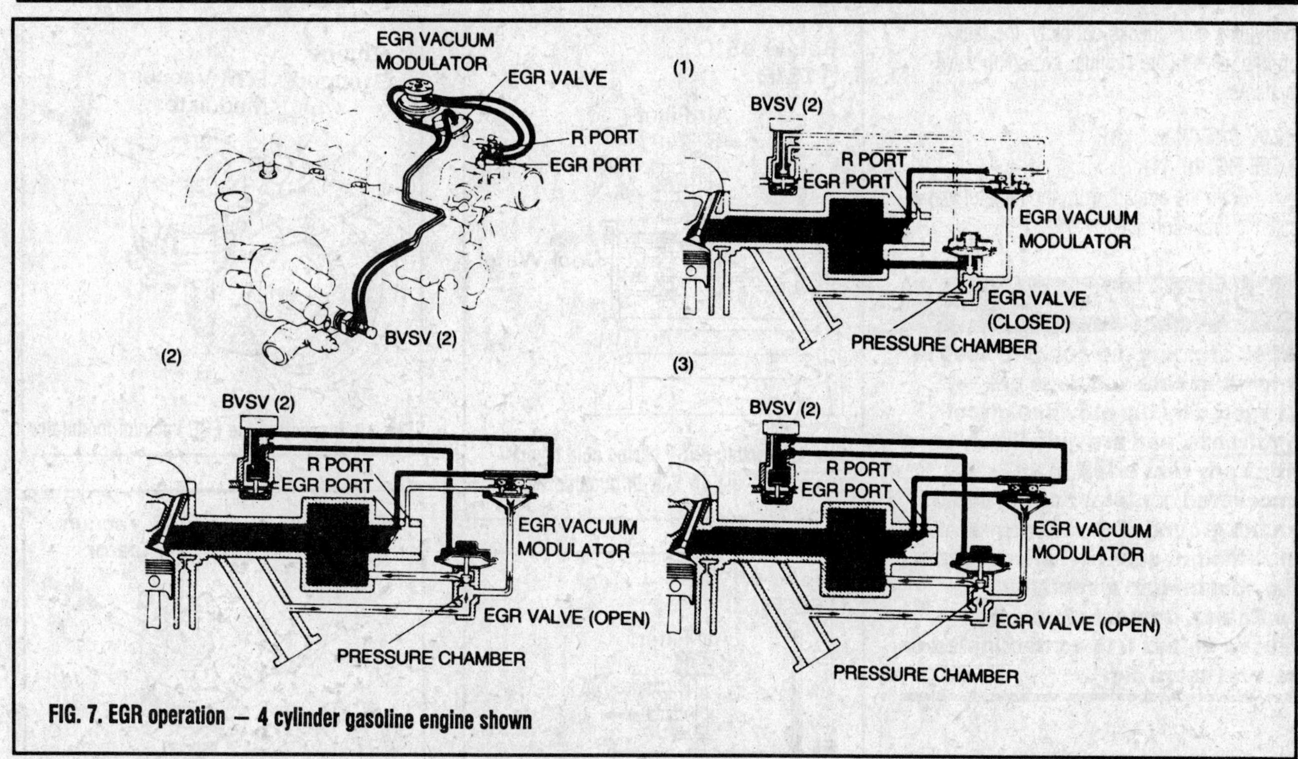

FIG. 7. EGR operation — 4 cylinder gasoline engine shown

To reduce NOx emission, part of the exhaust gases are recirculated through the EGR valve to the intake manifold to lower the maximum combustion temperature

Coolant Temp.	BVSV	Throttle Valve Opening Angle	Pressure in the EGR Valve Pressure Chamber		EGR Vacuum Modulator	EGR Valve	Exhaust Gas
Below 45°C (113°F)	CLOSED	—	—		—	CLOSED	Not recirculated
Above 66°C (151°F)	OPEN	Positioned below EGR port	—		—	CLOSED	Not recirculated
		Positioned between EGR port and R port	(1) LOW	*Pressure constantly alternating between low and high	OPENS passage to atmosphere	CLOSED	Not recirculated
			(2) HIGH		CLOSES passage to atmosphere	OPEN	Recirculated
		Positioned above R port	(3) HIGH	**	CLOSES passage to atmosphere	OPEN	Recirculated (increase)

Remarks: *Pressure increase → Modulator closes → EGR valve opens → Pressure drops
↑——— EGR valve closes ← Modulator opens ←——┘

**When the throttle valve is positioned above the R port, the EGR vacuum modulator will close the atmosphere passage and open the EGR valve to increase the EGR gas, even if the exhaust pressure is insufficiently low.

FIG. 8. EGR system operation — gasoline engine

EGR VALVE CHECK AND INSPECTION

With the engine idling, apply a vacuum directly to the EGR valve. The engine should run rough or die. Reconnect the vacuum hose to their original locations.

Remove the EGR valve and check for sticking and sludge and heavy carbon deposits. Reinstall the EGR valve with a new gasket.

If, after having completed the above tests, the EGR system still doesn't work correctly and

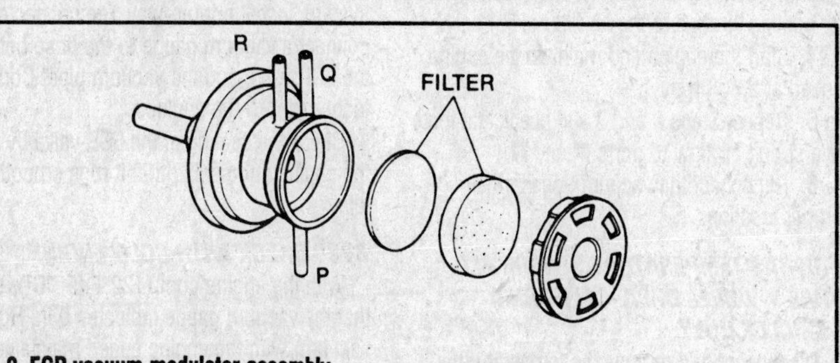

FIG. 9. EGR vacuum modulator assembly

everything else checks out okay, the fault probably lies in the vacuum switching valve systems.

BVSV CHECK

➧ SEE FIG. 10–11

1. Drain the coolant from the radiator into a suitable drain container.

❊ CAUTION

When draining the coolant, keep in mind that cats and dogs are attracted by the ethylene glycol antifreeze, and are quite likely to drink any that is left in an uncovered container or in puddles on the ground. This will prove fatal in sufficient quantity. Always drain the coolant into a sealable container. Coolant should be reused unless it is contaminated or several years old.

2. Unscrew and remove the BVSV from the water outlet.
3. Place the BVSV into a container filled with warm water (below 113°F [45°C]).
4. Blow air into the unit and check that air flows from the **J** pipe to the air filter.
5. Heat the BVSV to 151°F (66°C) in water.
6. Blow air into the unit and check that air flows from pipe **J** to pipe **K**.
7. If the valve does not operate as described, replace it.
8. Coat the threads of the BVSV with a suitable liquid thread sealant and install the valve into the water outlet.
9. Fill the radiator with a good brand of ethylene glycol coolant to the proper level.
10. Start the engine and check for leaks.

EGR VACUUM MODULATOR CHECK

➧ SEE FIG. 12–13

1. Disconnect the vacuum hoses from ports **P**, **Q** and **R** of the vacuum modulator.
2. Block ports **P** and **R** with your finger.
3. Blow air through port **Q** and check that the air passes through to the air filter side freely.
4. Start the engine and maintain the engine speed at 2,500 rpm.
5. Repeat Steps 2 and 3 and check that there is a strong air flow to ports **P** and **R**.
6. Reconnect the vacuum hose to their proper locations.

EGR GAS TEMPERATURE SENSOR ALL-TRAC 4-WHEEL DRIVE CALIFORNIA VEHICLES ONLY

Disconnect and remove the temperature sensor from the EGR valve. Place the sensor into a container of water with a thermometer. Connect the probes of an ohmmeter across the terminals of the sensor and slowly heat the water. At 122°F (50°C) the resistance should be 69.40-88.50kΩ. At 212°F (100°C) the resistance should drop to 11.89-14.37kΩ. If the resistance is not as specified, replace the sensor.

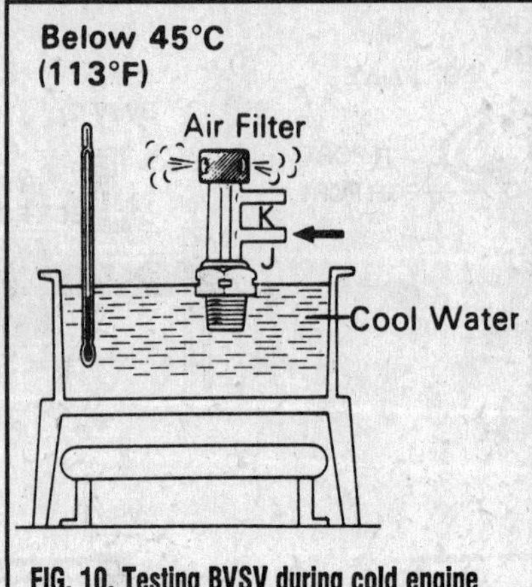

FIG. 10. Testing BVSV during cold engine operation — no air flow through port K

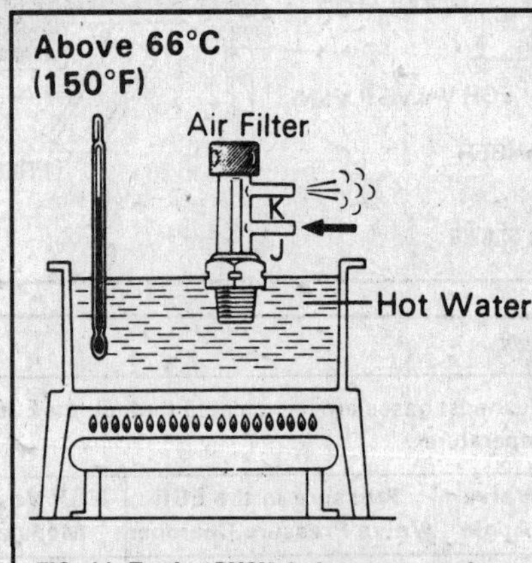

FIG. 11. Testing BVSV during warm engine operation — air should flow through port K

Diesel Engines

➧ SEE FIG. 14–16

Before beginning inspection of the EGR system, install a three-way Tee connector and connect a vacuum gauge to the hose between the EGR valve and the vacuum pipe. Connect a tachometer to the engine.

Check the seating of the EGR valve by starting the engine and seeing that it runs smoothly at idle.

BVSV CHECK WITH COLD ENGINE

With the engine cool (122°F [50°C]), check that the vacuum gauge indicates 0 in. Hg (no vacuum) with the engine speed maintained at 2,300 rpm.

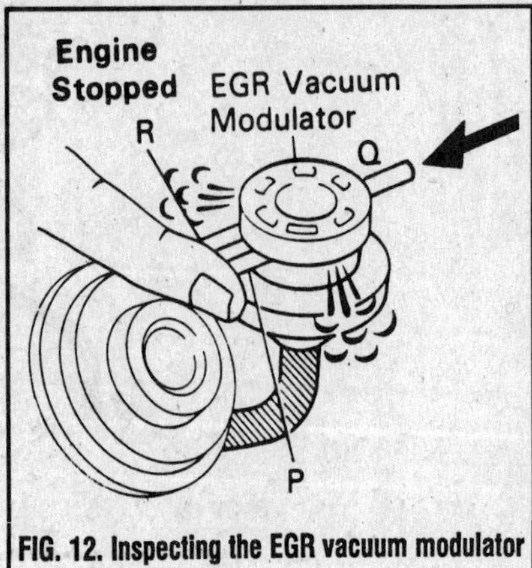

FIG. 12. Inspecting the EGR vacuum modulator

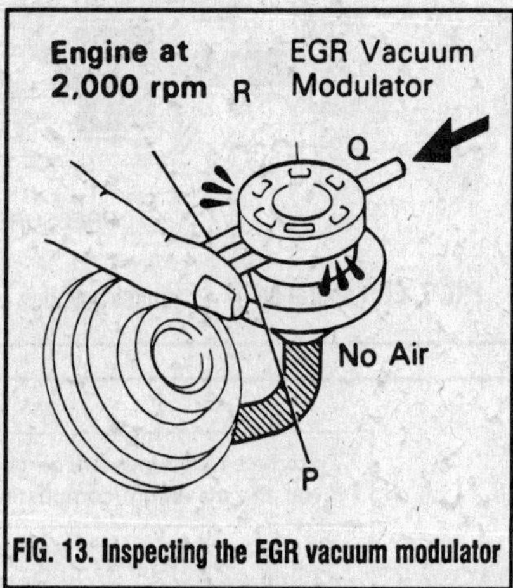

FIG. 13. Inspecting the EGR vacuum modulator

BVSV CHECK WITH HOT ENGINE

1. Warm the engine to normal operating temperature.
2. Check that the vacuum gauge reads 1.97 in. Hg, at idle speed.
3. Raise the engine idle to 2,300 rpm and check that the vacuum gauge reads above 11.02 in. Hg.
4. Increase the engine idle speed to 3,500 rpm and check that the vacuum gauge reads 1.97 in. Hg.
5. Disconnect the vacuum gauge and reconnect the vacuum hoses to their original locations.

➡ If the hot engine test does not indicate any system problems, perform the remaining system checks.

BVSV CHECK

1. Drain the coolant from the radiator into a suitable drain container.

❊ CAUTION

When draining the coolant, keep in mind that cats and dogs are attracted by the ethylene glycol

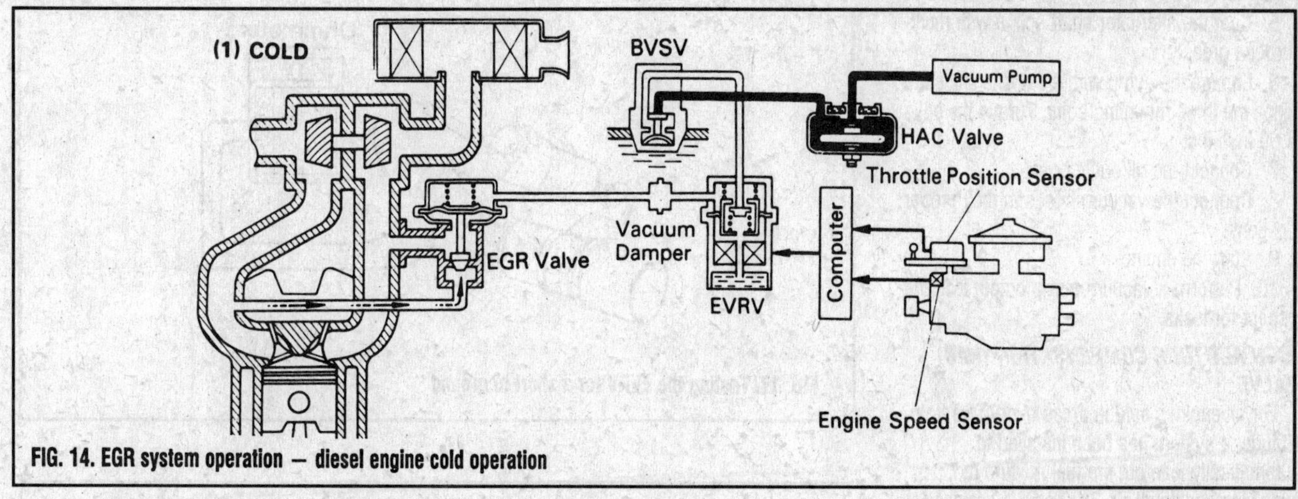

FIG. 14. EGR system operation — diesel engine cold operation

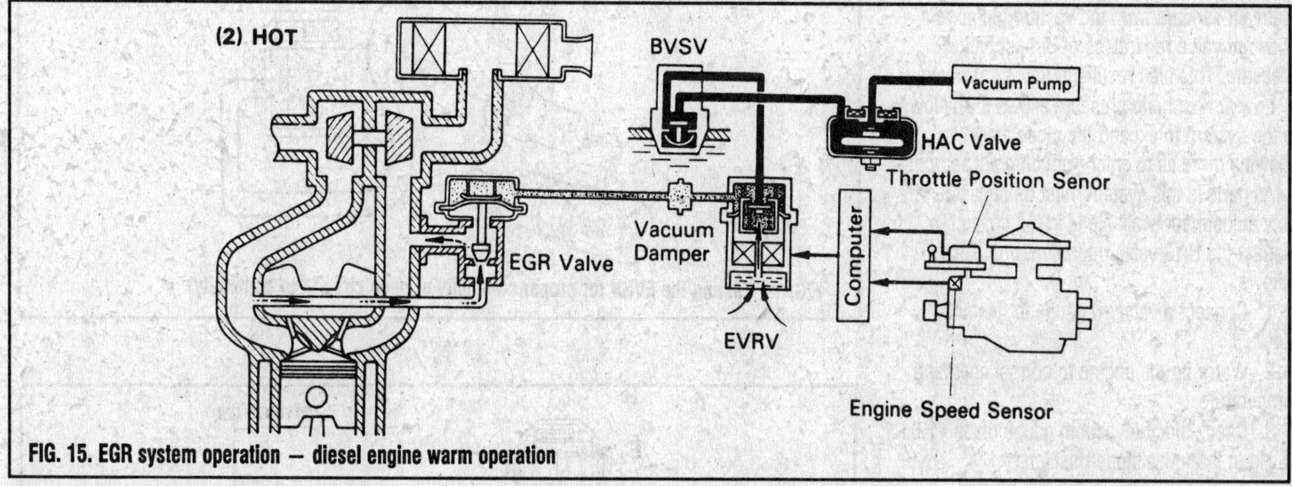

FIG. 15. EGR system operation — diesel engine warm operation

antifreeze, and are quite likely to drink any that is left in an uncovered container or in puddles on the ground. This will prove fatal in sufficient quantity. Always drain the coolant into a sealable container. Coolant should be reused unless it is contaminated or several years old.

2. Unscrew and remove the BVSV.
3. Place the BVSV into a container filled with cool water below 122°F (50°C).
4. Blow air into the unit and verify the BVSV is closed.
5. Heat the BVSV to above 157°F (69°C) in the water.
6. Blow air into the unit and check that the valve is open.
7. If the valve does not operate as described, replace it.
8. Coat the threads of the BVSV with a suitable liquid thread sealant and install the valve into the water outlet.
9. Fill the radiator with a good brand of ethylene glycol coolant to the proper level.
10. Start the engine and check for leaks.

EGR VALVE INSPECTION

Remove the EGR valve from the vehicle and inspect the valve for sludge and heavy carbon deposits. Replace the valve as required. Install the EGR valve with a new gasket.

VACUUM PUMP OUTPUT TEST

Connect a vacuum gauge to the outlet pipe and warm up the engine to normal operating temperature. Check that the vacuum gauge indicates 25.59 in. Hg. If the vacuum pump is not operating as specified, replace it.

FIG. 16. Connect a vacuum gauge between the EGR valve and vacuum damper

Removal and Installation

➧ SEE FIG. 21

Vacuum pumps are only used on diesel engines. The vacuum pump is located on the alternator rear end plate and is driven by the alternator rotor spline shaft.

1. Disconnect the vacuum hoses.
2. Disconnect the oil outlet hose.
3. Remove the three mounting bolts and pull the vacuum pump from the spline shaft at alternator end frame.
3. Remove the O-ring from the alternator end frame groove. Discard the O-ring and purchase a new one.
4. Install the new O-ring into the alternator end frame groove.

5. Coat the alternator shaft spline with multi-purpose grease.

6. Engage the pump with the spline shaft and install the three mounting bolts. Torque the bolts to 69 inch lbs.

7. Connect the oil outlet hose.

8. Connect the vacuum hoses to their proper locations.

9. Start the engine.

10. Perform a vacuum pump output test and inspect for leaks.

HIGH ALTITUDE COMPENSATION (HAC) VALVE

For all engines sold in areas over 4000 ft. in altitude, a system has been installed to automatically lean out the fuel mixture by supplying additional air. The valve is designed to maintain vacuum from the vacuum pump at a constant value regardless of atmospheric pressure. This also results in lower emissions.

Low atmospheric pressure allows the bellows in the system to expand the close a port, allowing more air to enter from different sources.

All parts in this system must be replaced. The only adjustment available is in the timing. To inspect the HAC valve operation, proceed as follows:

1. Connect a vacuum gauge to the outlet pipe.

2. Warm up the engine to normal operating temperature.

3. Check that the vacuum gauge reads 11.81 in. Hg in the low altitude position.

4. If the HAC valve is not operating as specified, replace it.

ELECTRONIC VACUUM REGULATING VALVE (EVRV) INSPECTION

➧ SEE FIG. 17–18

The EVRV is controlled by the computer. When the EVRV is off, air is led into the EGR valve diaphragm through its air filter and the EGR valve close the port so that the exhaust gas is not recirculated. When the EVRV is on, the computer controls the EVRV to maintain vacuum to the EGR valve diaphragm at optimum value by mixing air at constant volume from the HAC valve.

Inspection of the EVRV consists of checking the valve for open and short circuits with the valve installed and the electrical connector disconnected.

With an ohmmeter, check that there is no continuity between the terminals and the EVRV body. If there is continuity, there is a short circuit and the valve must be replaced.

To check for an open circuit, with an ohmmeter check for resistance between the valve terminals. The resistance should be from 11–13Ω at 68°F (20°C). If the resistance is not within the range, replace the EVRV.

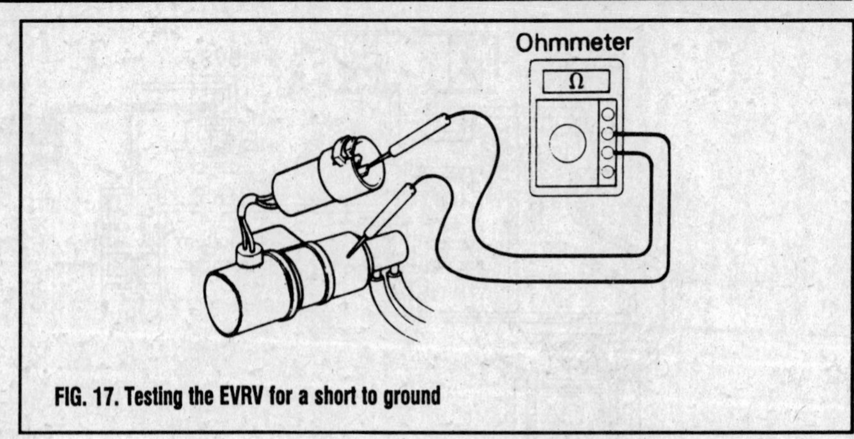

FIG. 17. Testing the EVRV for a short to ground

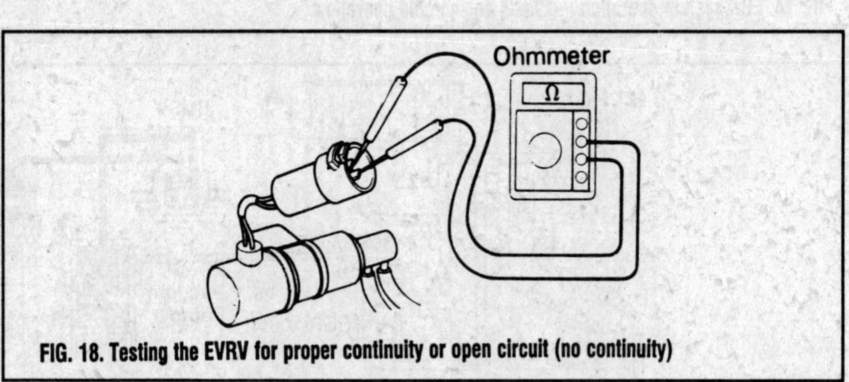

FIG. 18. Testing the EVRV for proper continuity or open circuit (no continuity)

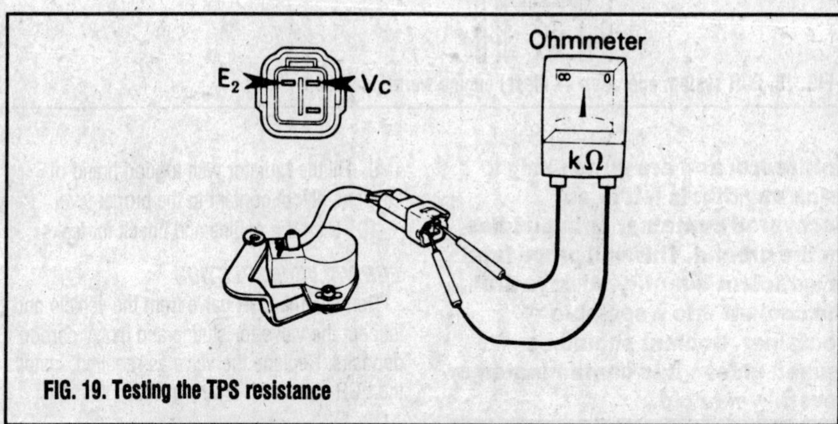

FIG. 19. Testing the TPS resistance

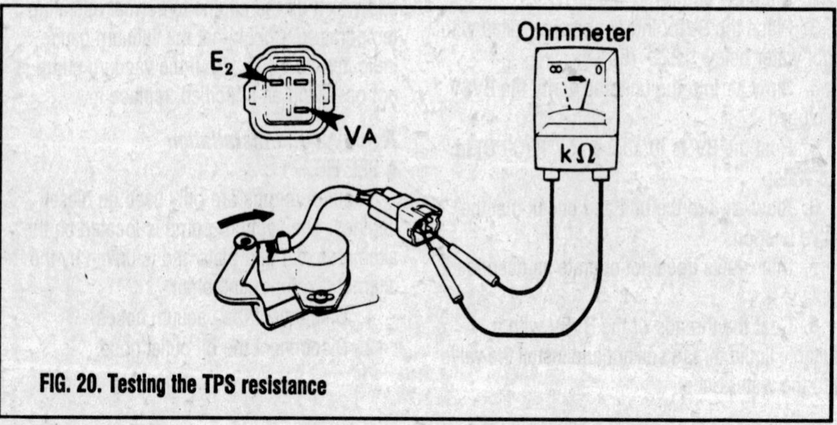

FIG. 20. Testing the TPS resistance

THROTTLE POSITION SENSOR (TPS) INSPECTION

➧ SEE FIG. 19–20

The TPS feeds the computer information on the opening angle of the accelerator lever to detect driving condition.

With an ohmmeter, measure the resistance between the **Vc** and **E2** terminals. The resistance should be from 3-7kΩ at 68°F (20°C).

Connect the ohmmeter probes to the **Va** and **E2** terminals and move the throttle lever from the open and closed position. When the throttle lever is moved in this manner, you should notice a decrease in the resistance.

If the TPS does not behave as described, replace it with a new one.

➡ **After replacement of the TPS, be sure to bring the vehicle to a garage or specialty shop to perform the fine adjustments that are necessary for proper functioning of the computer system.**

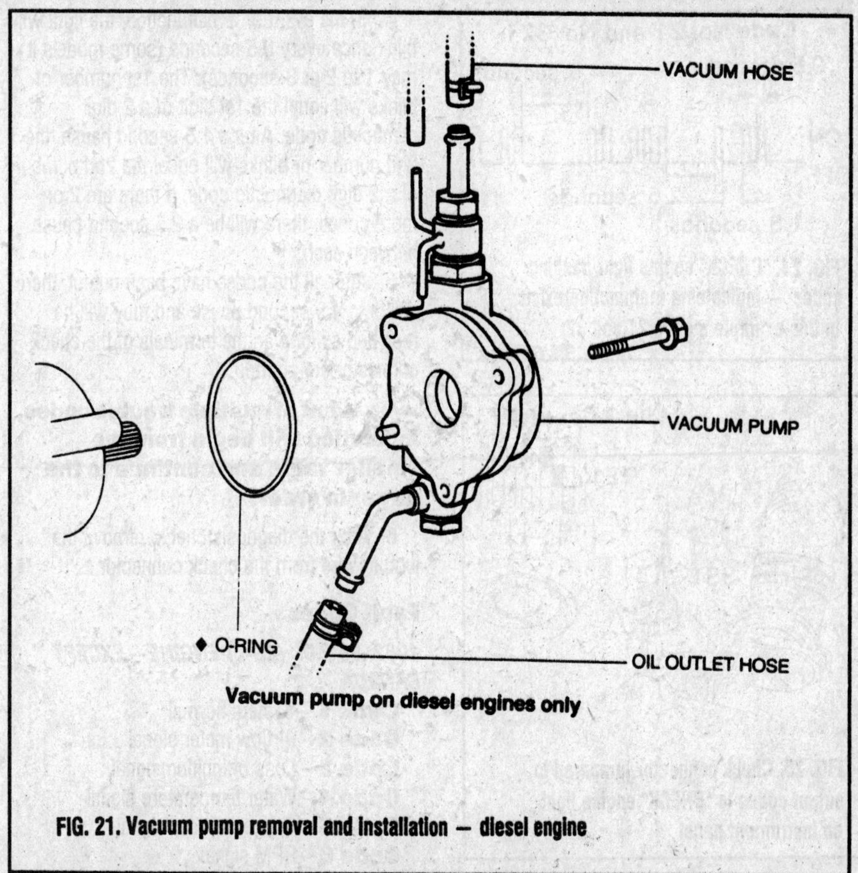

FIG. 21. Vacuum pump removal and installation — diesel engine

ELECTRONIC ENGINE CONTROLS

Check Engine Lights

RESETTING

The Electronic Control Unit (ECU) contains a self-diagnosis system. Troubles within the engine emission and fuel control system signal network are detected causing a "CHECK ENGINE" warning light on the dash to illuminate.

The light will illuminate briefly with the ignition key in the ON position and the engine not running and will normally go out when the engine is started. However, if the light comes on when the engine is running, the computer has detected a fault or malfunction within the system.

In the event you do get a fault indication light, the only way to reset the light is to diagnose the system and determine the component or components that are causing the malfunction. The light will automatically de-energize when the malfunction is identified and corrected. Identifying a malfunction involves a litany of complicated diagnosis procedures and fault codes that we are not able to address in this book and that are normally beyond the capabilities of the DIYer. "CHECK ENGINE" light problems are best left with those that have the proper experience and diagnosis equipment. However, if you wish to learn more about emissions related troubleshooting and diagnosis, you may want to explore "CHILTON'S GUIDE TO" books, which are available at your local retailer.

SELF-DIAGNOSIS

➧ SEE FIG. 22–25

The ECU contains a built-in self diagnosis system by which troubles with the engine signal the engine signal network are detected and a "Check Engine" warning light on the instrument panel flashes Code No. 1–71 (these code numbers vary from year to year). The "Check Engine" light on the instrument panel informs the

FIG. 22. "CHECK" engine light

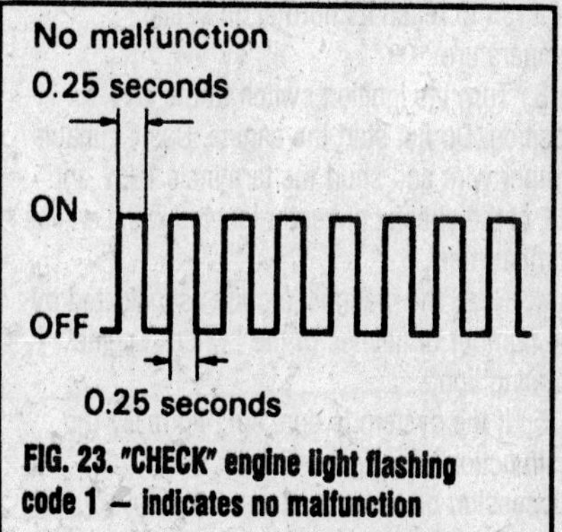

FIG. 23. "CHECK" engine light flashing code 1 — indicates no malfunction

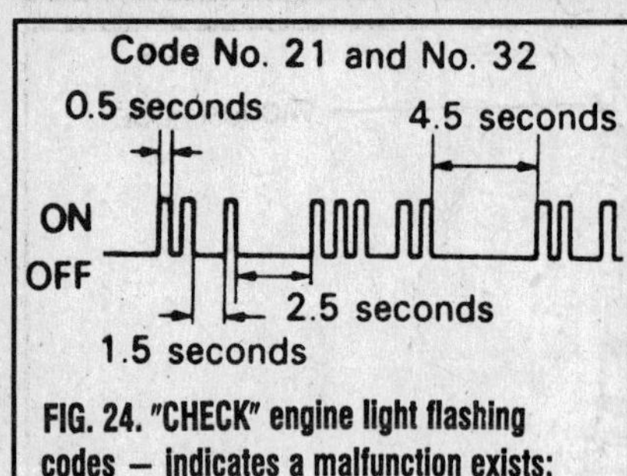

FIG. 24. "CHECK" engine light flashing codes — indicates a malfunction exists; in this example a code 21 and 32

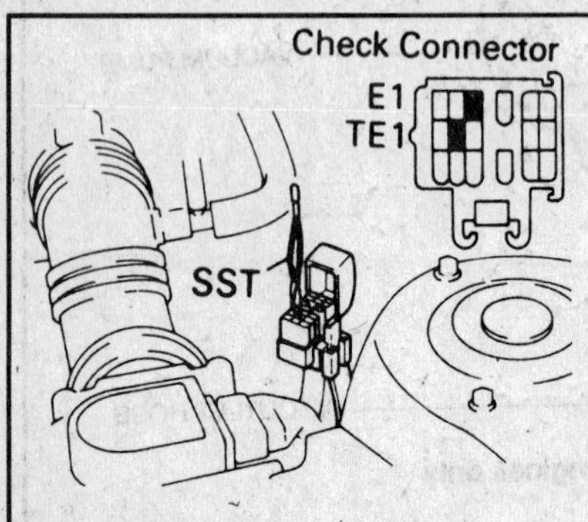

FIG. 25. Check connector jumpered to output codes to "CHECK" engine light on instrument panel

driver that a malfunction has been detected. The light goes out automatically when the malfunction has been cleared.

The diagnostic code can be read by the number of blinks of the "Check Engine" warning light when the proper terminals of the check connector are short-circuited. If the vehicle is equipped with a super monitor display, the diagnostic code is indicated on the display screen.

Output of Diagnostic Codes

1. The battery voltage should be above 11 volts. Throttle valve fully closed (throttle position sensor IDL points closed.
2. Place the transmission in **P** or **N** range. Turn the A/C switch **OFF**. Start the engine and let it run to reach its normal operating temperature.
3. Turn the ignition switch to the **ON** position. Do not start the engine. Use a suitable jumper wire and short the terminals **TE1** and **E1** of the check connector located in the engine compartment.
4. Read the diagnostic code as indicated by the number of flashes of the "Check Engine" warning light.
5. If the system is operating normally (no malfunction), the light will blink rapidly in succession on late models and once every 4.5 seconds on early models.
4. In the event of a malfunction, the light will blink once every 0.5 seconds (some models it may 1 to 2 or 3 seconds). The 1st number of blinks will equal the 1st digit of a 2 digit diagnostic code. After a 1.5 second pause, the 2nd number of blinks will equal the 2nd number of a 2 digit diagnostic code. If there are 2 or more codes, there will be a 2.5 second pause between each.
5. After all the codes have been output, there will be a 4.5 second pause and they will be repeated as long as the terminals of the check connector are shorted.

➡ **In event of multiple trouble codes, indication will begin from the smaller value and continue to the larger in order.**

6. After the diagnosis check, remove the jumper wire from the check connector.

Fault Codes

1982–86 2.0L (2S-E) ENGINE—EXCEPT CANADA

Code 1—System normal
Code 2—Airflow meter signal
Code 3—Loss of ignition signal
Code 4—Water temperature signal
Code 5—Oxygen sensor signal
Code 6—RPM signal
Code 7—Throttle position sensor signal
Code 8—Intake Air temperature sensor signal
Code 9—Vehicle speed sensor signal
Code 10—Starter signal
Code 11—A/C switch signal

1982–86 2.0L (2S-E) ENGINE—CANADA

Code 1—System normal
Code 2—Airflow meter signal (Vc)
Code 3—Airflow meter signal (Vs)
Code 4—Water temperature sensor signal (THW)
Code 6—Ignition signal
Code 7—Throttle position sensor signal

1987–91 2.0L (3S-FE) OR 1989–91 2.5L (2VZ-FE) ENGINES

Code 12—Loss of RPM signal after start signal
Code 13—Loss of RPM signal above 1,000 rpm
Code 14—Loss of ignition signal
Code 16—Loss of ECT Normal signal to ECU
Code 21—Main oxygen sensor signal out of range
Code 22—Faulty coolant temperature signal
Code 24—Faulty intake air temperature signal
Code 25—Air/Fuel ratio—lean malfunction
Code 26—Air/Fuel ratio—rich malfunction
Code 27—Calif. only; Sub-oxygen sensor signal out of range compared to main sensor
Code 31—Faulty air flow meter signal at idle
Code 32—Faulty air flow meter signal off idle
Code 41—Faulty throttle position sensor signal
Code 42—Faulty vehicle speed sensor signal
Code 43—No starter signal seen at ECU, engine cranking, up to 800 rpm
Code 51—Switch condition signal
Code 52—2VZ-FE only; loss of knock sensor signal
Code 53—2VZ-FE only; ECU knock control circuit failure
Code 71—Calif. only; EGR system malfunction based on signal from EGR temperature sensor

1992 2.2L (5S-FE) OR 3.0 (3VZ-FE) ENGINES

Code 12—Loss of RPM signal after start signal
Code 13—Loss of RPM signal above 1,000 rpm
Code 14—Loss of ignition signal
Code 16—Loss of ECT Normal signal to ECU
Code 21—Main oxygen sensor signal out of range; 3VZ-FE, left sensor
Code 22—Faulty coolant temperature signal
Code 24—Faulty intake air temperature signal
Code 25—Air/Fuel ratio—lean malfunction
Code 26—Air/fuel ratio—rich malfunction
Code 27—California only; Sub-oxygen sensor signal out of range compared to main sensor
Code 28—3VZ-FE, right oxygen sensor signal out of range
Code 31—5S-FE, faulty vacuum sensor signal; 3VZ-FE, air flow meter signal out of range at idle
Code 32—3VZ-FE, air flow meter signal out of range off idle
Code 41—Faulty throttle position sensor signal
Code 42—Faulty vehicle speed sensor signal
Code 43—No starter signal seen at ECU
Code 51—Switch condition signal
Code 52—Loss of knock sensor signal; 3VZ-FE, knock sensor on left bank
Code 53—ECU knock control circuit failure
Code 55—3VZ-FE, loss of knock sensor signal from right side sensor
Code 71—Calif. only; EGR system malfunction based on signal from EGR temperature sensor

Canceling Out The Diagnostic Code

1. After repairing the trouble area, the diagnostic code that is retained in the ECU memory must be canceled out by removing the EFI or ECU-B (15A) fuse for 30 seconds or more, depending on the ambient temperature (the lower temperature, the longer the fuse must be left out with the ignition switch **OFF**).

➡ Cancellation can also be done by removing the battery negative terminal, but keep in mind, when removing the negative battery cable, the other memory systems (radio, ETR, clock, etc.) will also be canceled out.

If the diagnostic code is not canceled out, it will be retained by the ECU and appear along with a new code in event of future trouble. If it is necessary to work on engine components requiring removal of the battery terminal, a check must first be made to see if a diagnostic code is detected.

2. After cancellation, perform a road test, if necessary, confirm that a normal code is now read on the "Check Engine" warning light or super monitor display.

3. If the same diagnostic code is still indicated, it indicates that the trouble area has not been repaired.

Diagnosis Indication

1. Including "Normal", the ECU is programmed several diagnostic codes.

2. When more than a single code is indicated, the lowest number code will appear first. However, no other code will appear along with Code 1 or 11.

3. All detected diagnostic codes, except Code 51 and 53, will be retained in memory by the ECU from the time of detection until canceled out.

4. Once the malfunction is cleared, the "Check Engine" warning light on the instrument panel will go out but the diagnostic code(s) remain stored in the ECU memory (except for Code 51).

Oxygen Sensor

The oxygen sensor is located in the exhaust system. It contains a zirconia element exposed on 1 side to outside air and exhaust gas on the other side. The difference in oxygen concentrations cause the element to generate a small electrical signal. By monitoring this signal, the ECU is advised of the oxygen content in the exhaust stream. The oxygen sensor is a main component in the emissions and fuel

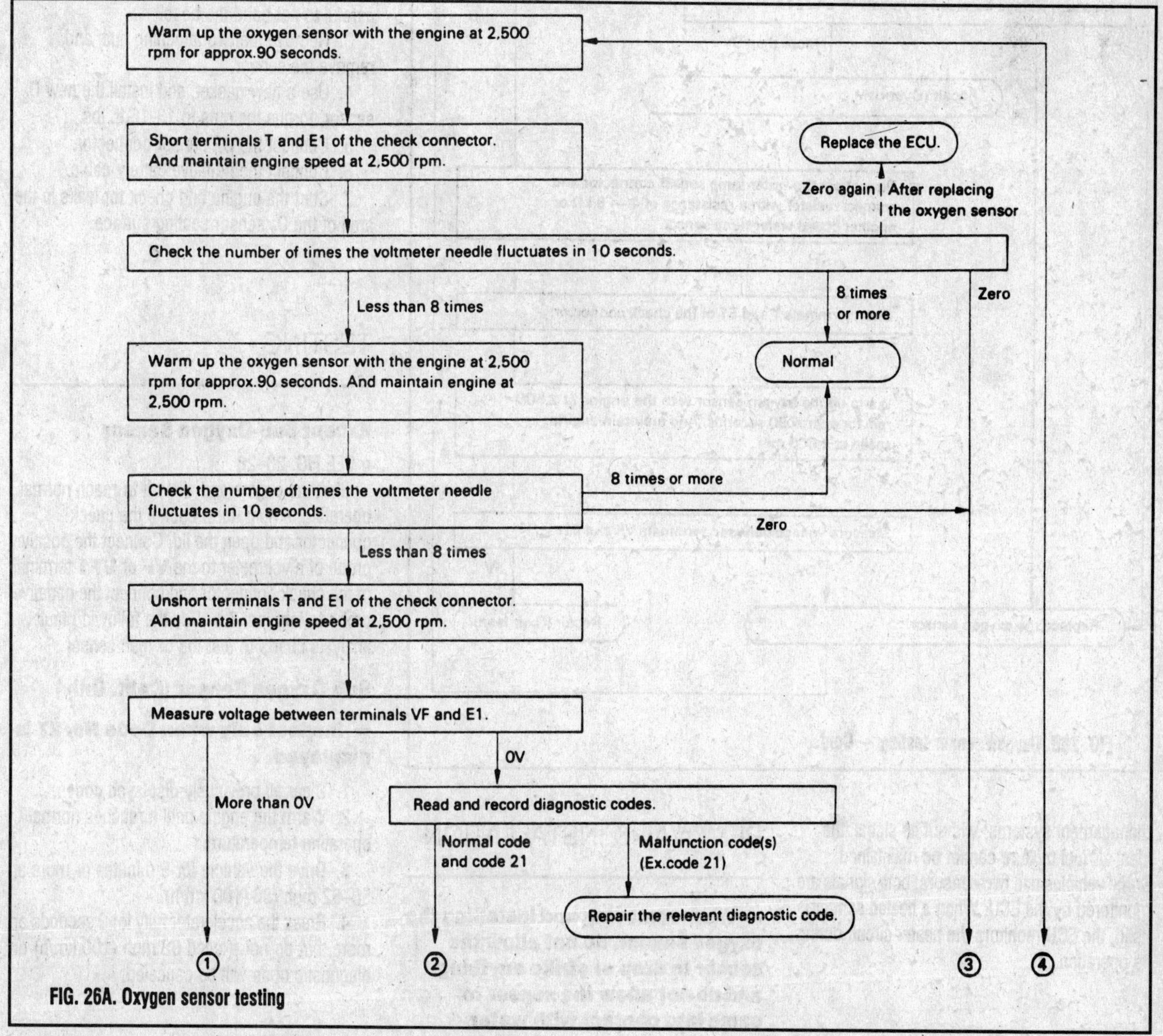

FIG. 26A. Oxygen sensor testing

①　②　③　④

Repair the relevant diagnostic code.

↑ Malfunction code(s) (Ex.code 21)

Read and record diagnostic codes.

↓ Normal code and code 21

Unshort terminals T and E1 of the check connector. And maintain engine at 2,500 rpm.

Measure voltage between terminals VF and E1.

0V ↓　　5V ↓

Disconnect the PCV hose.

Measure voltage between terminals VF and E1.

0V　　More than 0V ↓

Repair (Over rich)

Disconnect the water temp.sensor connector and connect resistor with a resistance of 4 — 8 kΩ or another coded water temp.sensor.

Short terminals T and E1 of the check connector.

Warm up the oxygen sensor with the engine at 2,500 rpm for approx.90 seconds. And maintain engine speed at 2,500 rpm.

Measure voltage between terminals VF and E1.

0V ↓　　5V ↓

Replace the oxygen sensor.　　Repair (Over lean)

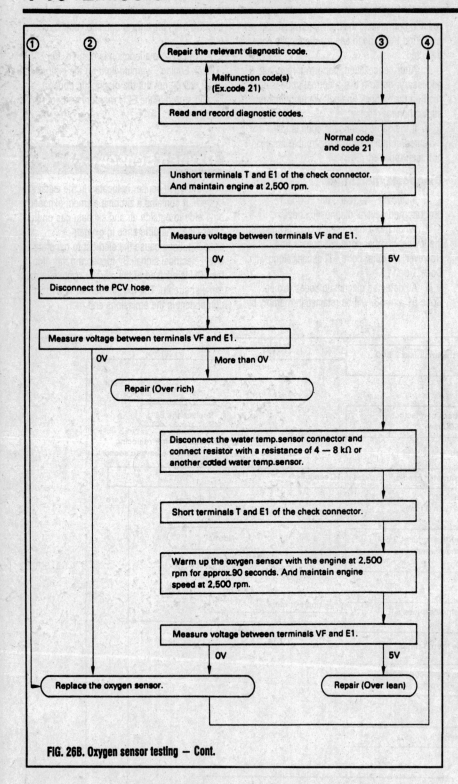

FIG. 26B. Oxygen sensor testing — Cont.

management systems; without its signal, the ideal air/fuel mixture cannot be maintained. Some vehicles use two sensors; both signals are monitored by the ECU. When a heated sensor is used, the ECU monitors the heater circuit during its operation.

REMOVAL & INSTALLATION

➡ When removing and installing the oxygen sensor, do not allow the sensor to drop or strike anything and do not allow the sensor to came into contact with water.

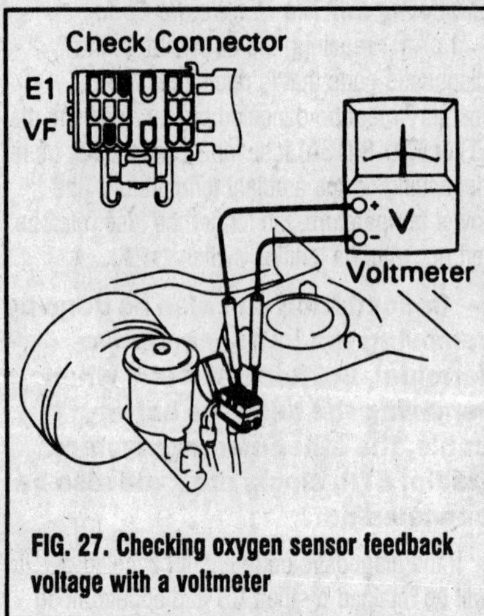

FIG. 27. Checking oxygen sensor feedback voltage with a voltmeter

1. Disconnect the battery ground cable.
2. Unplug the connector at the sensor. Be careful to not bend the hose.
3. Remove the two attaching nuts and remove the sensor.
4. Use a new gasket, and install the new O_2 sensor. torque the nuts to 13-16 ft. lbs.
5. Connect the O2 sensor connector.
6. Connect the negative battery cable.
7. Start the engine and check for leaks in the area of the O_2 sensor seating surface.

TESTING

Except Sub-Oxygen Sensor

➧ SEE FIG. 26–28

Start the engine and allow it to reach normal operating temperature. Locate the check connector and open the lid. Connect the positive probe of a voltmeter to the **VF** or **VF1** terminal of the check connector and connect the negative probe to terminal **E1**. Use the following fault analysis charts to test the oxygen sensor.

Sub-Oxygen Sensor (Calif. Only)

➡ Inspect only when Code No. 27 is displayed.

1. Clear all previously displayed codes.
2. Warm the engine until it reaches normal operating temperature.
3. Drive the vehicle for 5 minutes or more at 50–62 mph (80–100 km/h).
4. Press the accelerator fully for 2 seconds or more, but do not exceed 62 mph (100 km/h) or diagnostic code will be canceled.

Clearance between lever and stop screw		Continuity between terminals		
		IDL – E_1 (TL)	Psw – E_1 (TL)	IDL – Psw
0.50 mm	(0.0197 in.)	Continuity	No continuity	No continuity
0.90 mm	(0.0354 in.)	No continuity	No continuity	No continuity
Throttle valve fully opened		No continuity	Continuity	No continuity

FIG. 28. Testing the TPS with an ohmmeter – 2.0L (2S-E) engine

5. Stop the vehicle and turn the engine **OFF**.
6. Inspect the system for diagnostic code No. 27. If the code reappears, check the wiring and circuit. If the circuit is normal, replace the sub-oxygen sensor.

Throttle Position Sensor

Located on the throttle body, the sensor is connected to the throttle plate shaft; it translates the position of the throttle plate into an electrical signal. The sensor also contains contact points for idle and wide open throttle positions.

TESTING

➧ SEE FIG. 28–35, 44 & 45

1. Disconnect the sensor connector. Apply vacuum to the throttle opener, if equipped.
2. Insert a feeler gauge between the throttle stop screw and the stop lever.
3. Using a ohmmeter measure the resistance between the terminals using the corresponding illustrations.

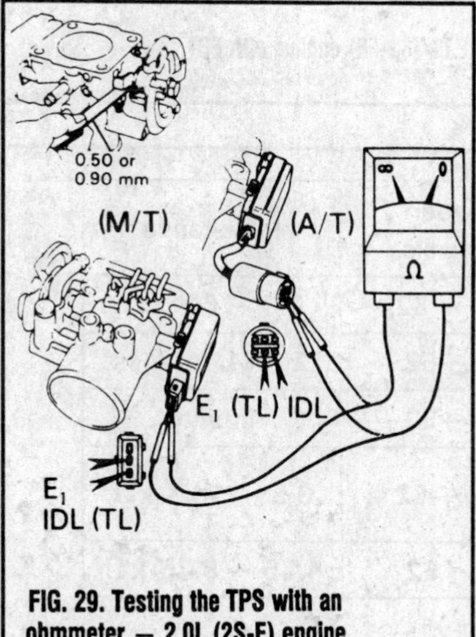

FIG. 29. Testing the TPS with an ohmmeter – 2.0L (2S-E) engine

Adjustment

2.0L ENGINE WITHOUT ECT

➧ SEE FIG. 36–37

1. Loosen the sensor screw.
2. Insert a 0.0276 in. (0.070mm) feeler gauge between the throttle stop screw and lever.
3. Connect and ohmmeter to terminals **IDL** and **E1**.

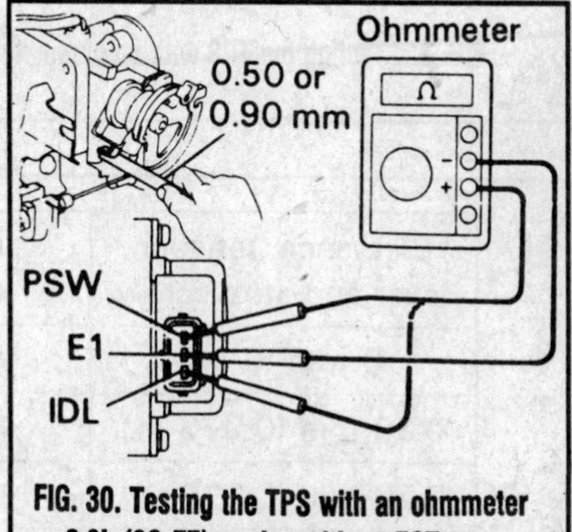

FIG. 30. Testing the TPS with an ohmmeter – 2.0L (3S-FE) engine without ECT

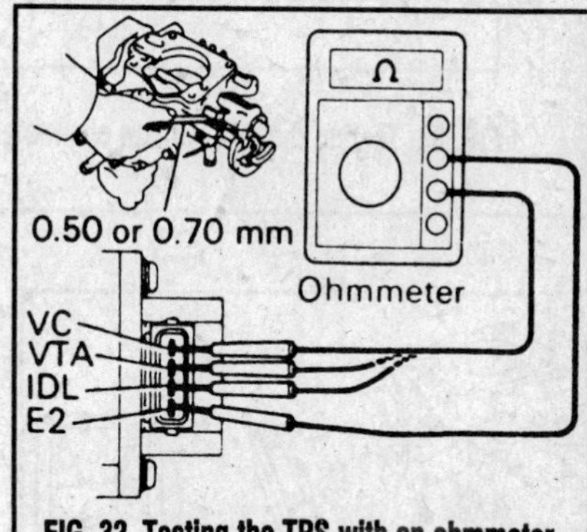

FIG. 32. Testing the TPS with an ohmmeter – 2.0L (3S-FE) engine with ECT

Clearance between lever and stop screw	Continuity between terminals	
	IDL – E1	PSW – E1
0.50 mm (0.020 in.)	Continuity	No continuity
0.90 mm (0.035 in.)	No continuity	No continuity
Throttle valve fully open	No continuity	Continuity

FIG. 31. Testing the TPS with an ohmmeter – 2.0L (3S-FE) engine without ECT

Clearance between lever and stop screw	Between terminals	Resistance
0 mm (0 in.)	VTA — E2	0.2 — 0.8 kΩ
0.50 mm (0.020 in.)	IDL — E2	2.3 kΩ or less
0.70 mm (0.028 in.)	IDL — E2	Infinity
Throttle valve fully open	VTA — E2	3.3 — 10 kΩ
—	VC — E2	3 — 7 kΩ

FIG. 33. Testing the TPS with an ohmmeter — 2.0L (3S-FE) engine with ECT

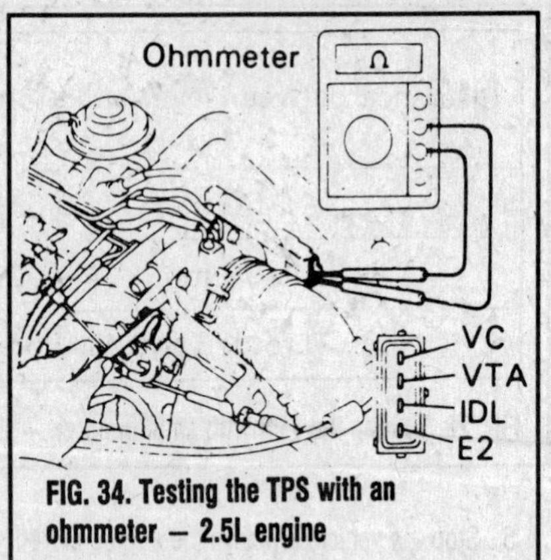

FIG. 34. Testing the TPS with an ohmmeter — 2.5L engine

Clearance between lever and stop screw	Between terminals	Resistance
0 mm (0 in.)	VTA - E2	0.3 - 6.3 kΩ
0.30 mm (0.012 in.)	IDL - E2	2.3 kΩ or less
0.70 mm (0.028 in.)	IDL - E2	Infinity
Throttle valve fully open	VTA - E2	3.5 - 10.3 kΩ
-	VC - E2	4.25 - 8.25 kΩ

FIG. 35. Testing the TPS with an ohmmeter — 2.5L engine

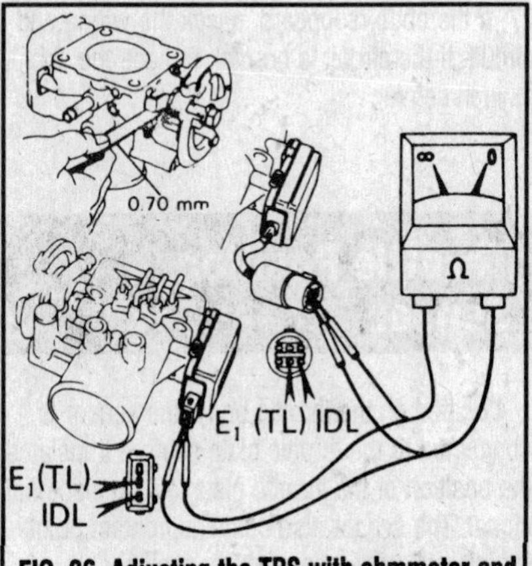

FIG. 36. Adjusting the TPS with ohmmeter and feeler gauge — 2.0L engine without ECT

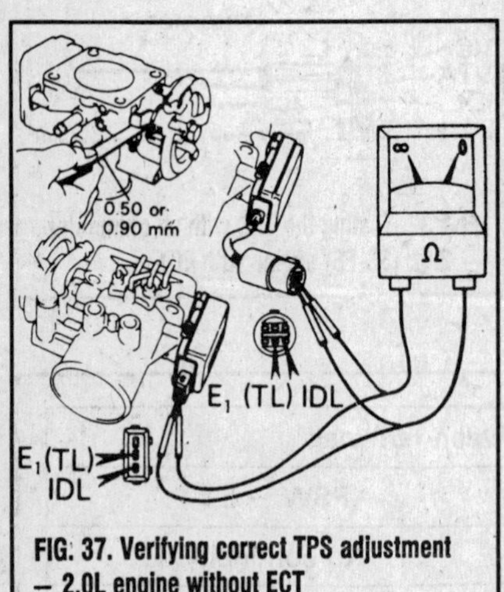

FIG. 37. Verifying correct TPS adjustment — 2.0L engine without ECT

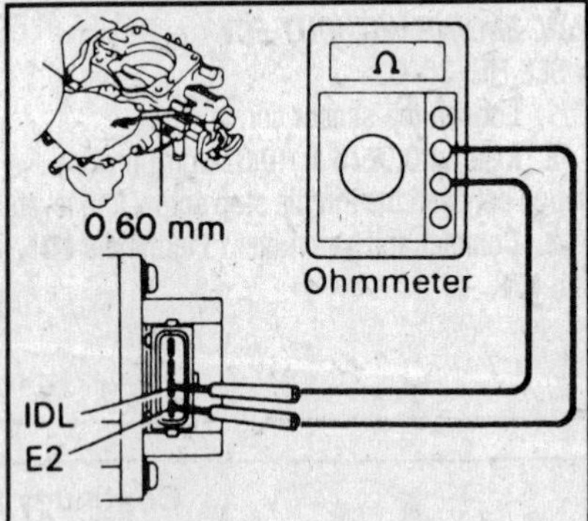

FIG. 38. Adjusting the TPS with ohmmeter and feeler gauge — 2.0L with ECT & 2.2L engines

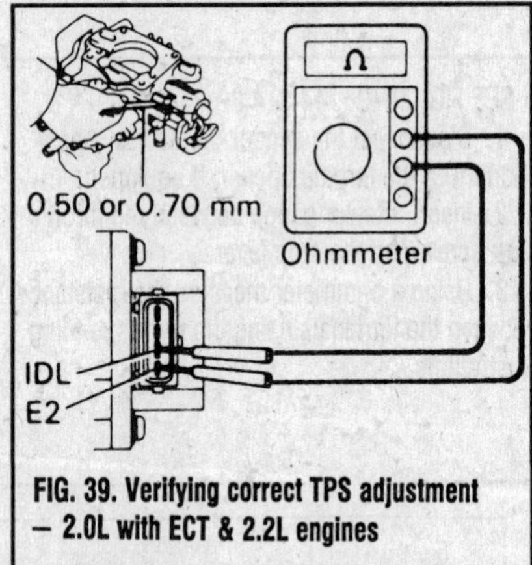

FIG. 39. Verifying correct TPS adjustment — 2.0L with ECT & 2.2L engines

4. Gradually turn the sensor counterclockwise until the ohmmeter deflects and then tighten the screws.

5. Using a 0.0197 in. (0.050mm) feeler gauge between the throttle stop screw and lever, verify with an ohmmeter that there is continuity.

6. Using a 0.0354 in. (0.090mm) feeler gauge between the throttle stop screw and lever, verify with an ohmmeter that there is no continuity.

7. If not as specified, replace the sensor.

2.0L WITH ECT & 2.2L ENGINES

➧ SEE FIG. 38–39

1. Loosen the sensor screws. Apply vacuum to the throttle opener, if equipped.

2. Insert a 0.024 in. (0.060mm) feeler gauge between the throttle stop screw and lever.

3. Connect and ohmmeter to terminals **IDL** and **E2** of the sensor.

4. Gradually turn the sensor clockwise until the ohmmeter deflects and then tighten the screws.

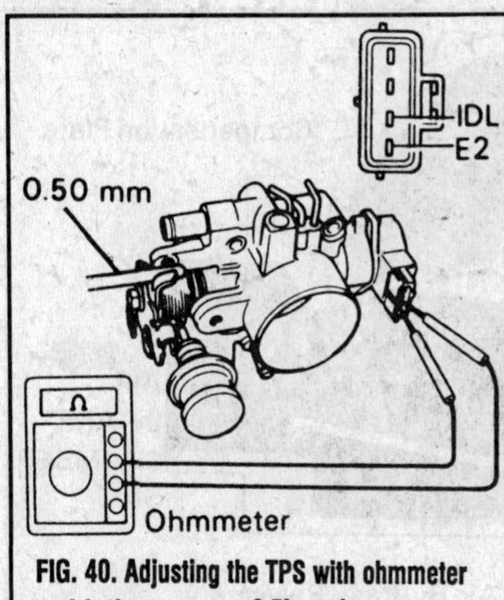

FIG. 40. Adjusting the TPS with ohmmeter and feeler gauge — 2.5L engine

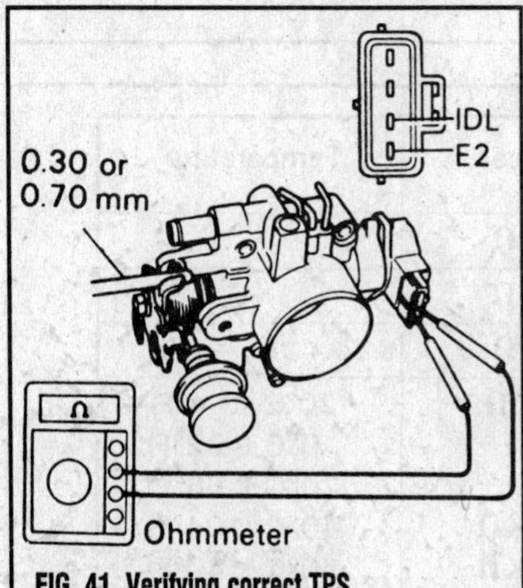

FIG. 41. Verifying correct TPS adjustment — 2.5L engine

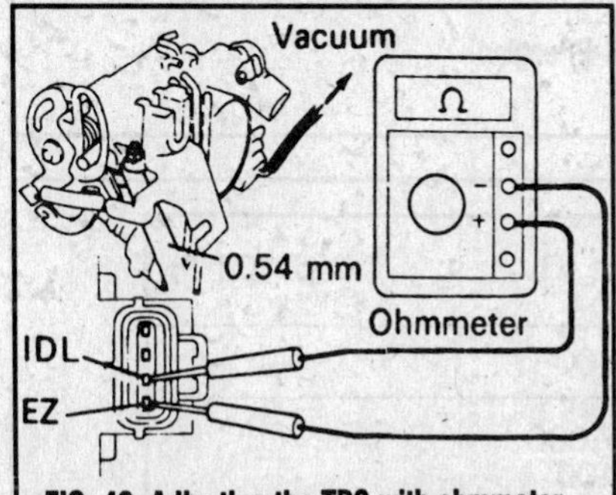

FIG. 42. Adjusting the TPS with ohmmeter and feeler gauge — 3.0L engine

5. Using a 0.020 in. (0.050mm) feeler gauge between the throttle stop screw and lever, verify with an ohmmeter that there is continuity.

6. Using a 0.028 in. (0.070mm) feeler gauge between the throttle stop screw and lever, verify with an ohmmeter that there is no continuity.

7. If not as specified, replace the sensor.

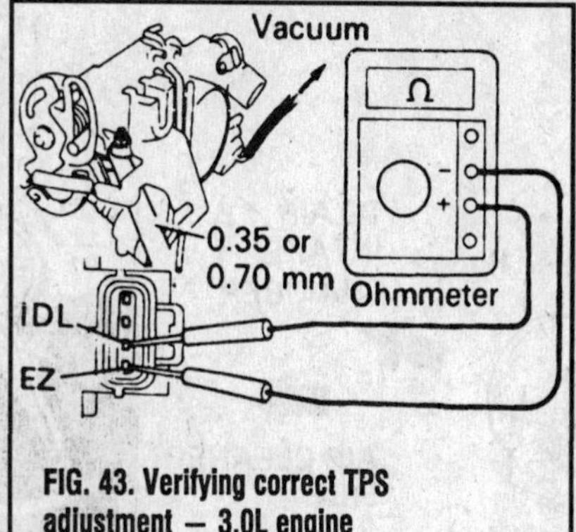

FIG. 43. Verifying correct TPS adjustment — 3.0L engine

2.5L ENGINE

➧ SEE FIG. 40–41

1. Loosen the sensor screws.
2. Insert a 0.020 in. (0.050mm) feeler gauge between the throttle stop screw and lever.
3. Connect and ohmmeter to terminals **IDL** and **E2** of the sensor.
4. Gradually turn the sensor clockwise until the ohmmeter deflects and then tighten the screws.
5. Using a 0.012 in. (0.030mm) feeler gauge between the throttle stop screw and lever, verify with an ohmmeter that there is continuity.
6. Using a 0.028 in. (0.070mm) feeler gauge between the throttle stop screw and lever, verify with an ohmmeter that there is no continuity.
7. If not as specified, replace the sensor.

Clearance between lever and stop screw	Between terminals	Resistance
0 mm (0 in.)	VTA – E2	0.2 – 5.7 kΩ
0.50 mm (0.020 in.)	IDL – E2	2.3 kΩ or less
0.70 mm (0.028 in.)	IDL – E2	Infinity
Throttle valve fully open	VTA – E2	2.0 – 10.2 kΩ
–	VC – E2	2.5 – 5.9 kΩ

FIG. 44. Testing the TPS with an ohmmeter — 2.2L engine

Clearance between lever and stop screw	Between terminals	Resistance
0 mm (0 in.)	VTA – E2	0.28 – 6.4 kΩ
0.35 mm (0.014 in.)	IDL – E2	0.5 kΩ or less
0.70 mm (0.028 in.)	IDL – E2	Infinity
Throttle valve fully open	VTA – E2	2.0 – 11.6 kΩ
–	VC – E2	2.7 – 7.7 kΩ

FIG. 45. Testing the TPS with an ohmmeter — 3.0L engine

3.0L ENGINE

➧ SEE FIG. 42–43

1. Loosen the sensor screws. Apply vacuum to the throttle opener.
2. Insert a 0.021 in. (0.054mm) feeler gauge between the throttle stop screw and lever.
3. Connect and ohmmeter to terminals **IDL** and **E2** of the sensor.
4. Gradually turn the sensor clockwise until the ohmmeter deflects and then tighten the screws.
5. Using a 0.014 in. (0.035mm) feeler gauge between the throttle stop screw and lever, verify with an ohmmeter that there is continuity.
6. Using a 0.028 in. (0.070mm) feeler gauge between the throttle stop screw and lever, verify with an ohmmeter that there is no continuity.
7. If not as specified, replace the sensor.

Air Flow Meter

➧ SEE FIG. 46

The air flow meter contains a spring-loaded measuring plate. The plate is connected to a potentiometer which controls the signal to the ECU. In this way, the control unit is advised of intake air volume and can control injector duration and ignition advance accordingly. All engines except the 2.2L use an Air Flow Meter. The 2.2L engine uses a Vacuum (MAP) sensor.

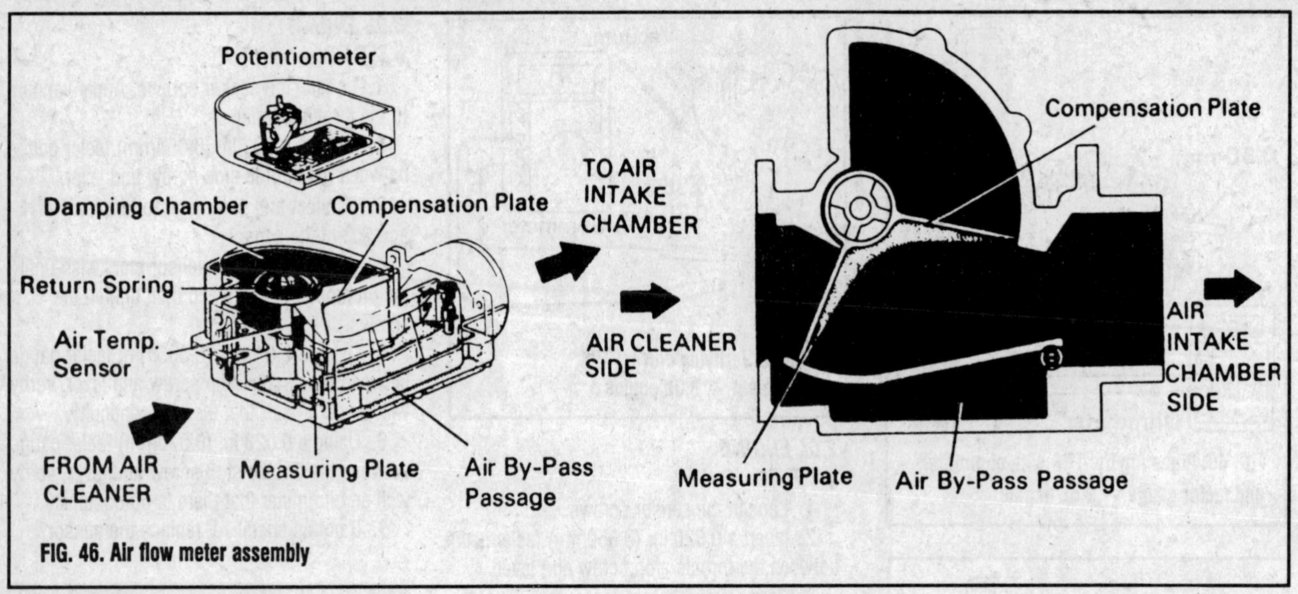

FIG. 46. Air flow meter assembly

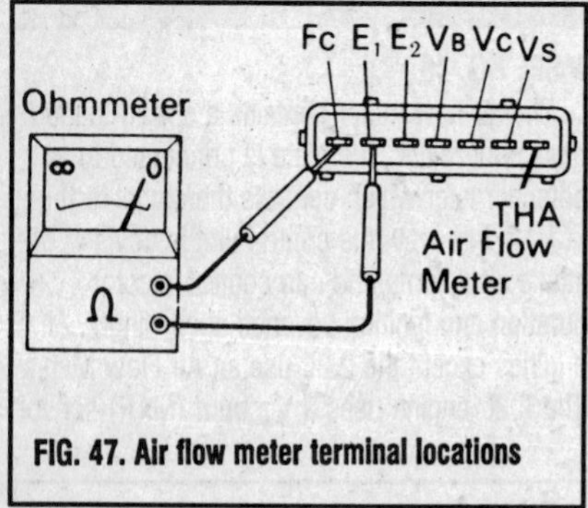

FIG. 47. Air flow meter terminal locations

Between terminals	Resistance	Temperature
E_2 – Vs	20 – 400 Ω	–
E_2 – Vc	100 – 300 Ω	–
E_2 – VB	200 – 400 Ω	–
E_2 – THA	10 – 20 KΩ 4 – 7 KΩ 2 – 3 KΩ 0.9 – 1.3 KΩ 0.4 – 0.7 KΩ	-20°C (-4°F) 0°C (32°F) 20°C (68°F) 40°C (104°F) 60°C (140°F)
E_1 – Fc	Infinity	–

FIG. 48. Air flow meter test chart — 2.0L (2S-E) engine

The air flow meter and temperature sensor are tested and serviced as a single unit. If only testing the air temperature sensor, perform the resistance tests on terminals THA and E2.

TESTING

➧ SEE FIG. 47–50

1. Disconnect the air flow meter connector.
2. Using a ohmmeter measure the resistance between the terminals as shown in chart.
3. If the resistance is not as specified, replace the air flow meter. The air temperature sensor and air flow meter are replaced as a single unit.

Between terminals		Resistance (Ω)	Temp. °C (°F)
VS — E2		200 — 600	—
VC — E2	3S-FE 2VZ-FE	3,000 — 7,000 200 — 400	—
THA — E2		10,000 — 20,000 4,000 — 7,000 2,000 — 3,000 900 — 1,300 400 — 700	-20 (-4) 0 (32) 20 (68) 40 (104) 60 (140)
FC — E1		Infinity	—

FIG. 49. Air flow meter test chart — 2.0L (3S-FE) & 2.5L engines

Vacuum Sensor

(Manifold Absolute Pressure [MAP])

The sensor converts a vacuum signal from the intake manifold to an electrical signal returned to the ECU. This signal is used to determine basic injection duration and basic ignition advance angle. The sensor does not use atmospheric pressure; rather, it senses the absolute pressure

Between terminals	Resistance (Ω)	Temp. °C (°F)
VS – E2	200 – 600	–
VC – E2	200 – 400	–
THA – E2	10,000 – 20,000	–20 (–4)
	4,000 – 7,000	0 (32)
FC – E1	Infinity	–

FIG. 50. Air flow meter test chart – 3.0L engine

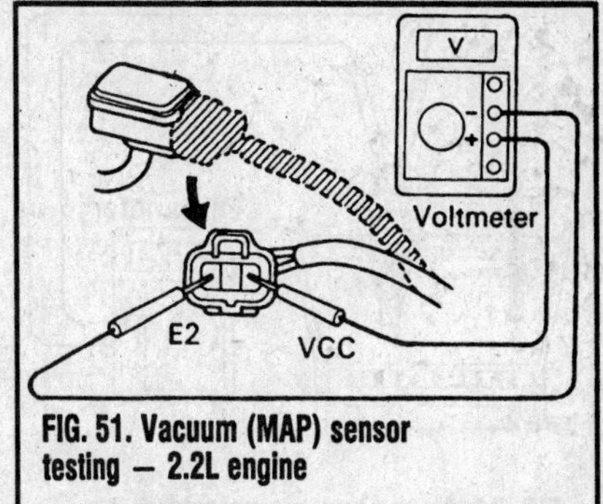

FIG. 51. Vacuum (MAP) sensor testing – 2.2L engine

within the intake manifold. Since it is not affected by atmospheric pressure changes, the ECU can maintain accurate fuel metering under all weather and altitude conditions. This sensor is only equipped on the 2.2L engine; all other engine use an Air Flow sensor.

A malfunctioning MAP sensor will usually set a Code 31.

TESTING

➧ SEE FIG. 51–52

1. Disconnect the vacuum sensor connector.
2. Turn the ignition switch **ON**.
3. Measure the voltage between terminal VC and ground of the vacuum sensor connector.
4. The voltage should read 4.75–5.25 volts. If not as specified, replace the ECU.
5. Turn ignition switch **OFF** and reconnect the sensor.
6. Disconnect the vacuum hose of the intake chamber side.
7. Turn the ignition switch **ON**.
8. Connect a voltmeter to terminals PIM and E2 of the ECU. Apply vacuum to the sensor and record the voltage drop.
9. The voltmeter should read:

- 0.3–0.5 volts – 3.94 in. Hg
- 0.7–0.9 volts – 7.87 in. Hg
- 1.1–1.3 volts – 11.8 in. Hg
- 1.5–1.7 volts – 15.8 in. Hg
- 1.9–2.1 volts – 19.7 in. Hg

10. If not as specified, repair the wiring to the sensor or replace the sensor.

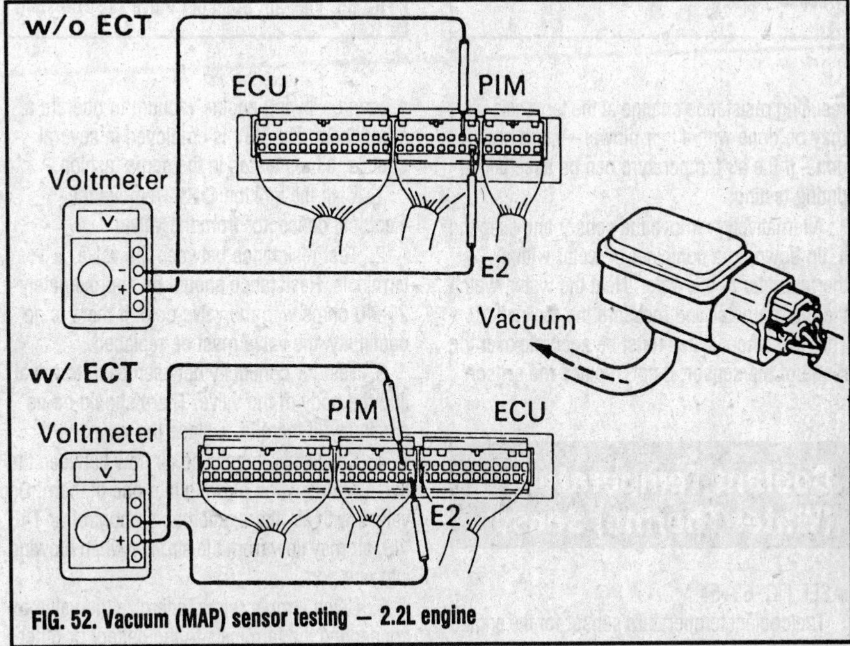

FIG. 52. Vacuum (MAP) sensor testing – 2.2L engine

Intake Air Temperature Sensor

➧ SEE FIG. 53–54

Vehicles using the vacuum sensor (2.2L engine) are equipped with a separate intake air temperature sensor mounted in the intake air stream. The sensor is tested by disconnecting the wire harness, then subjecting the sensor to changes in temperature and measuring the

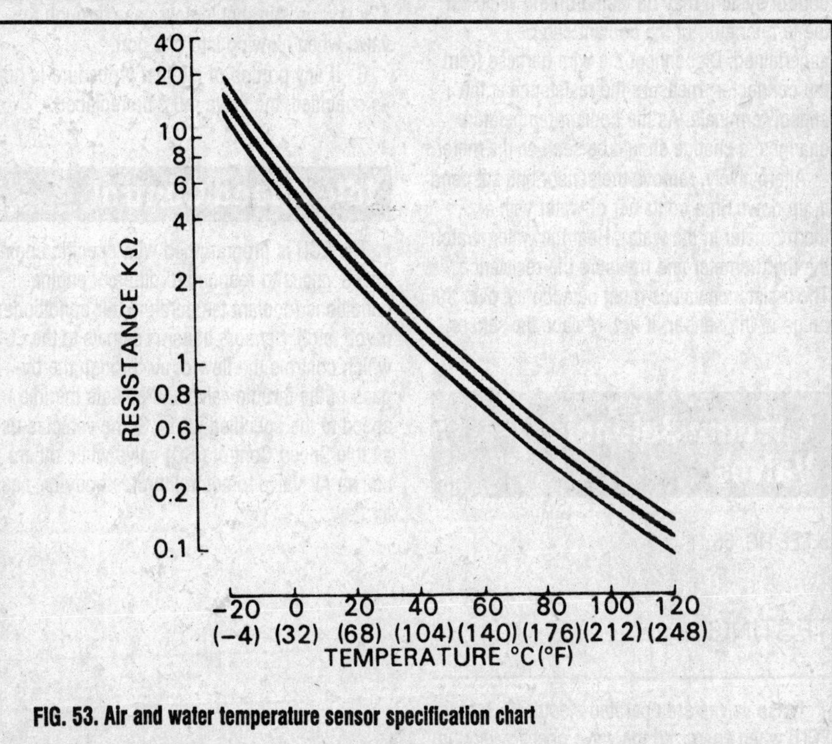

FIG. 53. Air and water temperature sensor specification chart

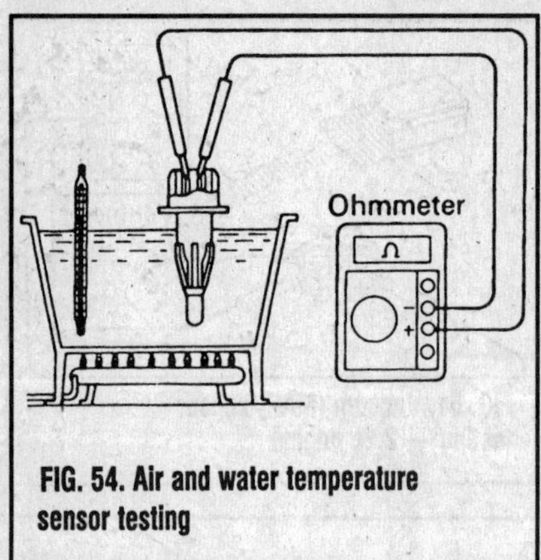

FIG. 54. Air and water temperature sensor testing

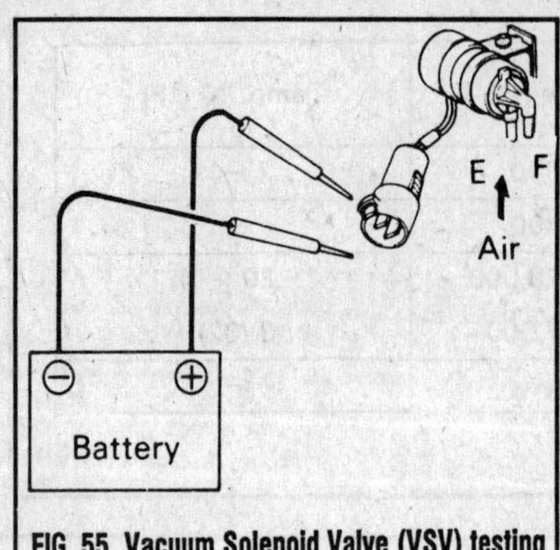

FIG. 55. Vacuum Solenoid Valve (VSV) testing

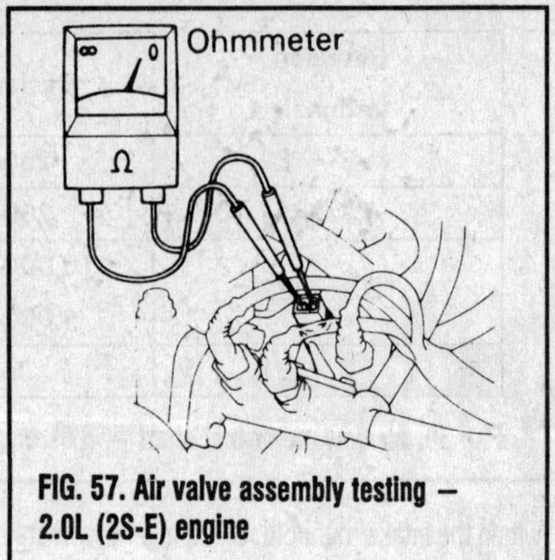

FIG. 57. Air valve assembly testing — 2.0L (2S-E) engine

resulting resistance change at the terminals. This may be done with a hair blower—not a heat gun—if the air temperature can be ascertained during testing.

Alternatively, remove the sensor and suspend it, tip down, in a container of water with a thermometer in the water. Heat the water, watch the thermometer and measure the resistance. The resistance values must be accurate over the range of the sensor; if not, replace the sensor.

Coolant Temperature (Water Thermo) Sensor

➧ SEE FIG. 53–54

The coolant temperature sensor for the engine control system may be tested on the vehicle if the temperature of the coolant can be ascertained. Disconnect the wire harness from the connector; measure the resistance at the sensor terminals. As the coolant temperature changes, a change should be seen on the meter.

Alternatively, remove the sensor and suspend it, tip down, in a container of water with a thermometer in the water. Heat the water, watch the thermometer and measure the resistance. The resistance values must be accurate over the range of the sensor; if not, replace the sensor.

Vacuum Solenoid Valves

➧ SEE FIG. 55

TESTING

These valves are operated electrically by the ECU; when energized the valve opens a vacuum passage allowing engine vacuum to operate a component. The VSV is employed in several circuits; all are tested in the same fashion.

1. With the ignition **OFF**, remove the electrical connector from the valve.
2. Test resistance between the valve terminals. Resistance should be approximately 26–40 ohms with the valve cold. If there is no continuity, the valve must be replaced.
3. Test for continuity between each terminal and the body of the valve. There should be no continuity; if there is, replace the valve.
4. Check that there is no air flow between the two air ports when blowing into one of them. On valves with air filters, such as air control or T-VIS, air may flow from the air filter when blowing into one port.
5. Using jumper wires, energize the valve by connecting the terminals to the battery or other 12v source. Air should now pass through the valve when blowing into one port.
6. If any portion of the test procedure is not as specified, the valve must be replaced.

Idle Speed Control

The ECU is programmed with specific engine speed values to respond to different engine conditions (coolant temperature, air conditioner on/off, etc.). Sensors transmit signals to the ECU which controls the flow of air through the by-pass of the throttle valve and adjusts the idle speed to the specified value. Some vehicles use an Idle Speed Control (ISC) valve while others use an Air Valve to control throttle body by-pass air flow.

TESTING

Air Valve

➧ SEE FIG. 56–57

2.0L (2S-E) ENGINE

1. With the engine running and the coolant temperature below 140°F (60°C), pinch off the Air Valve hose and verify that the idle is reduced by no more than a 100 rpm.
2. Disconnect the valve wire connector and measure the coil resistance. It should be 40–60 ohms with the coolant temperature at 176°F (80°C) and the air valve closed.
3. If not as specified, replace the valve.

Idle Speed Control (ISC) Valve

➧ SEE FIG. 58–61

2.0L (3S-FE) AND 2.2L ENGINES

➡ The idle speed must be set correctly before testing the ISC valve.

1. Bring the engine to normal operating temperature with transmission in **N**.
2. Using a jumper wire, connect the terminals TE1 and E1 of the check connector.
3. The engine rpm should rise to 1000–1300 rpm for 5 seconds. If rpm is as specified, the valve is functioning properly.
4. If rpm did not function as specified, stop the engine and disconnect the jumper wire.
5. Disconnect the ISC valve connector.
6. Using an ohmmeter, measure the resistance between the +B terminal (middle terminal) and the ISC1 (ISCC) and ISC2 (ISCO) outer terminals.
7. The resistance should be 16–17 ohms on the 2.0L engine or 19.3–22.3 ohms on the 2.2L engine.
8. If not as specified, replace the ISC valve.

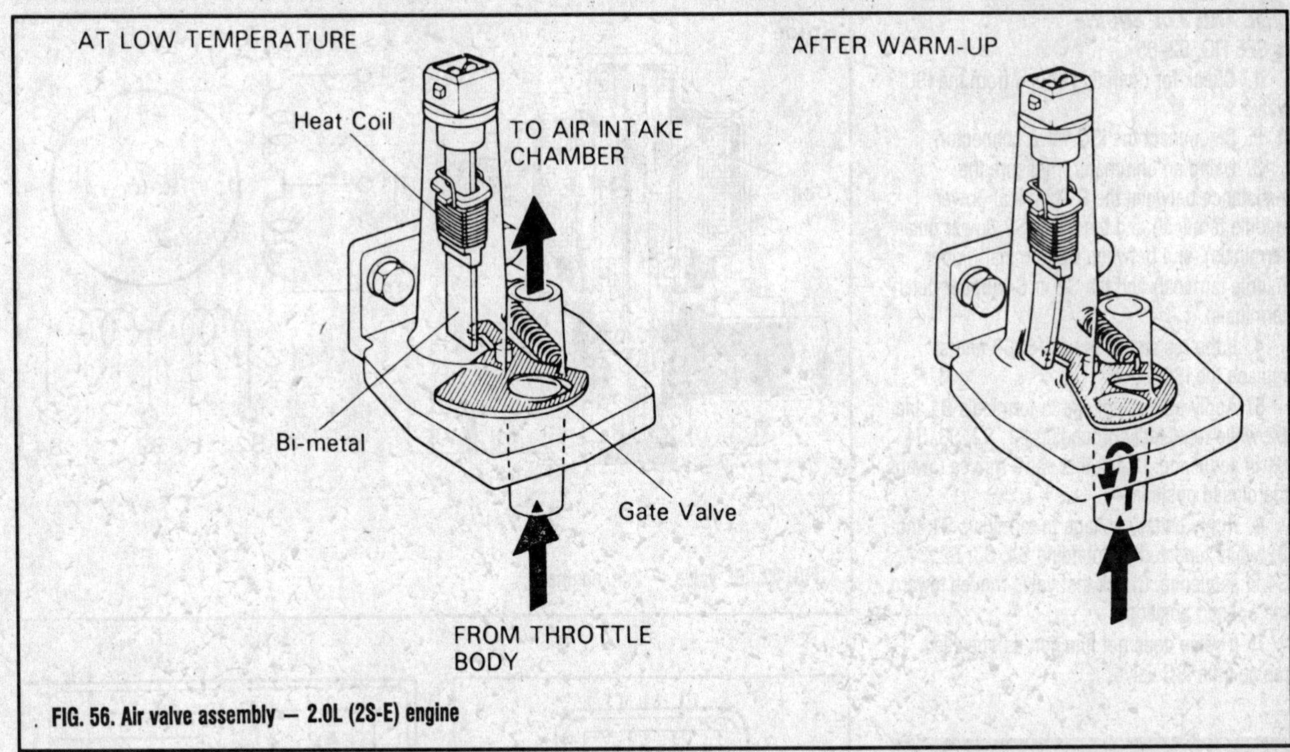

FIG. 56. Air valve assembly — 2.0L (2S-E) engine

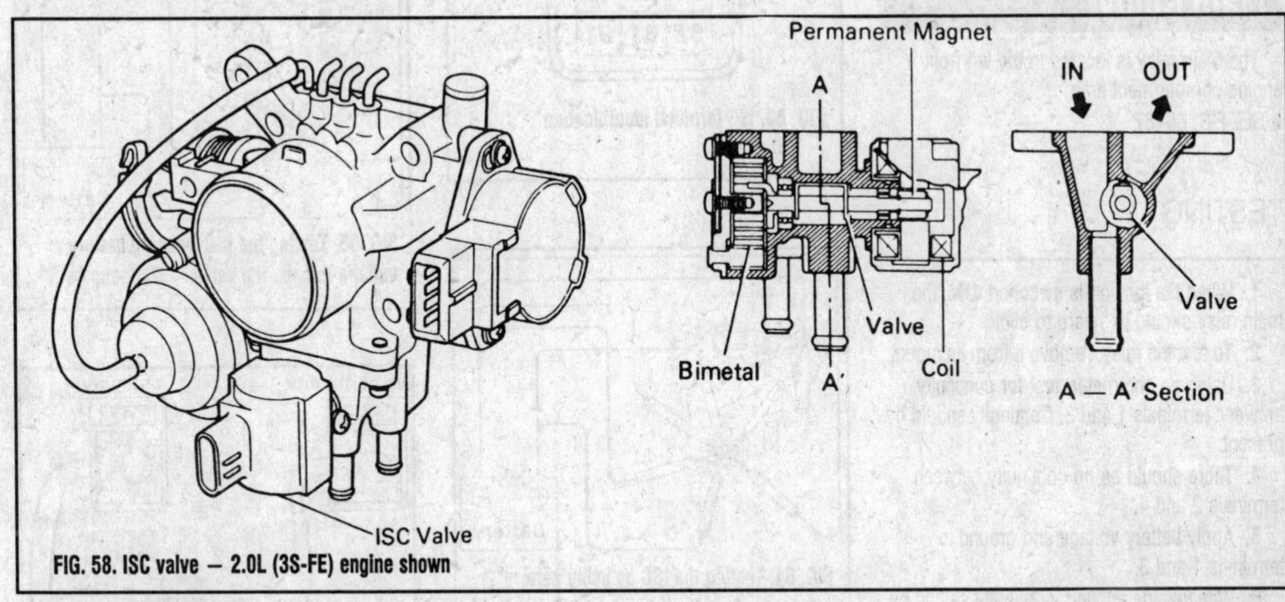

FIG. 58. ISC valve — 2.0L (3S-FE) engine shown

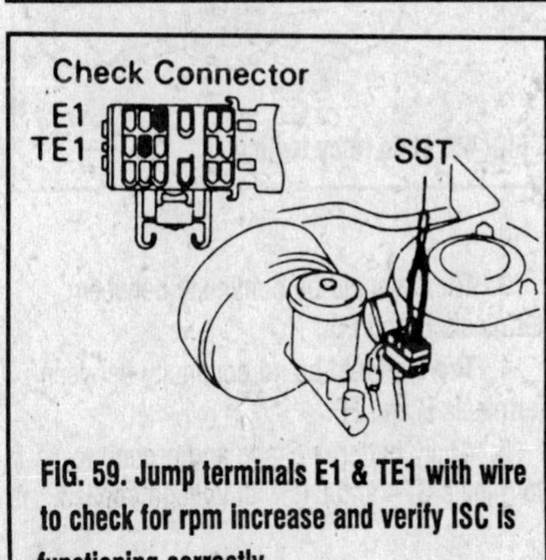

FIG. 59. Jump terminals E1 & TE1 with wire to check for rpm increase and verify ISC is functioning correctly

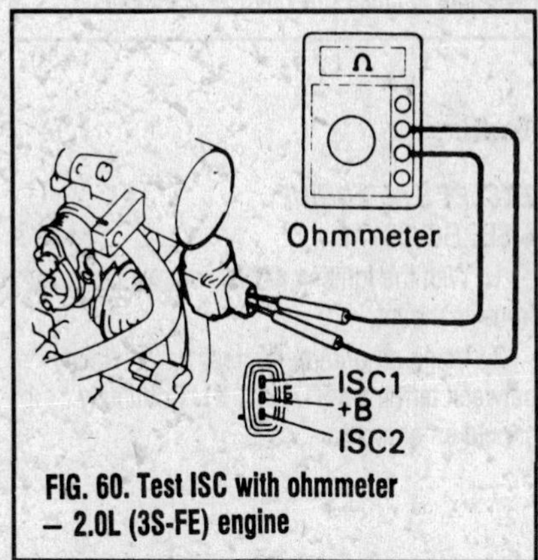

FIG. 60. Test ISC with ohmmeter — 2.0L (3S-FE) engine

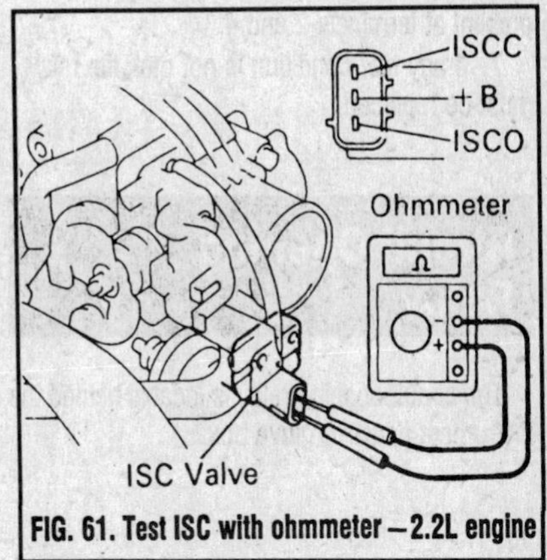

FIG. 61. Test ISC with ohmmeter —2.2L engine

2.5L AND 3.0L ENGINE

➧ SEE FIG. 62–65

1. Check for operating sound from the ISC valve.
2. Disconnect the ISC valve connector.
3. Using an ohmmeter, measure the resistance between the B1 terminal (lower middle terminal) and the S1 or S3 (lower outer terminals), and between B2 terminal (upper middle terminal) and the S2 or S4 (upper outer terminals).
4. If the resistance is not 10–30 ohms, replace the ISC valve.
5. Apply battery voltage to terminals B1 and B2 while repeatedly grounding S1, S2, S3, S4, S1 in sequence. Check that valve moves toward the closed position.
6. Apply battery voltage to terminals B1 and B2 while repeatedly grounding S4, S3, S2, S1, S4 in sequence. Check that valve moves toward the opened position.
7. If valve does not function as specified, replace the ISC valve.

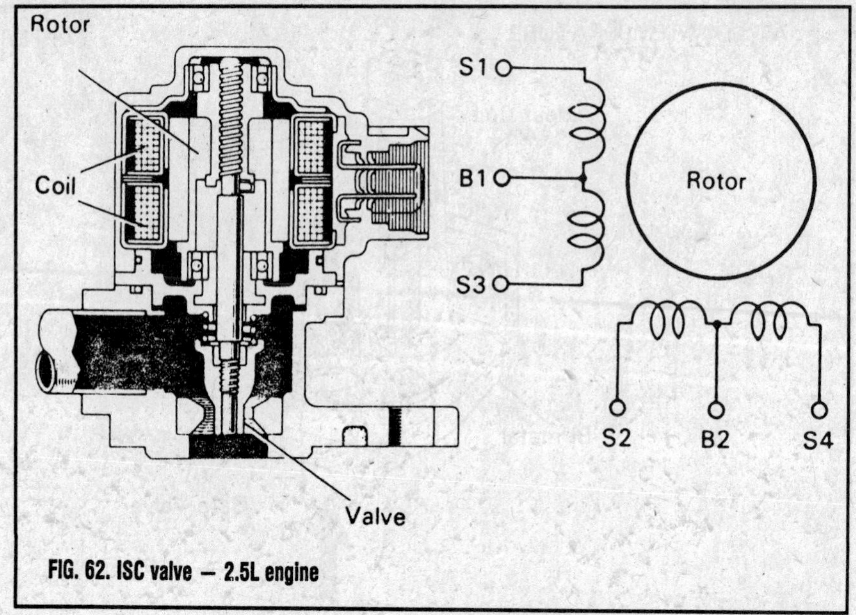

FIG. 62. ISC valve – 2.5L engine

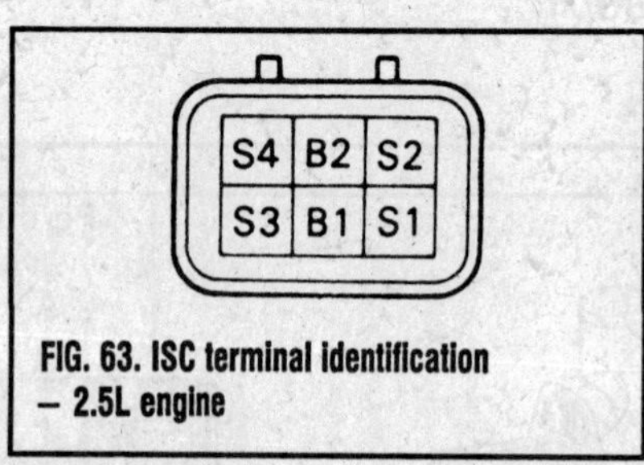

FIG. 63. ISC terminal identification – 2.5L engine

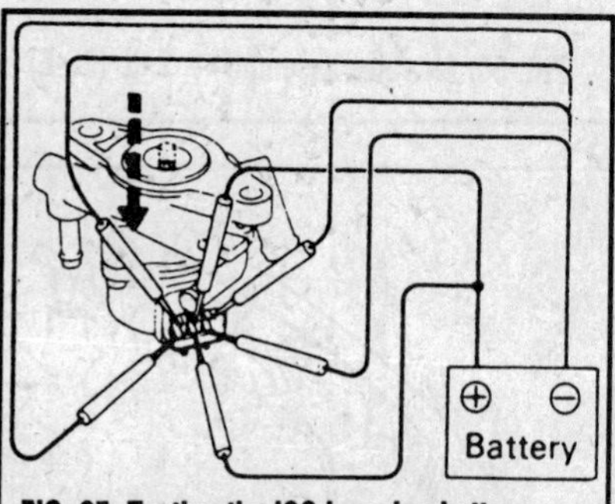

FIG. 65. Testing the ISC by using battery voltage to open the valve – 2.5L engine

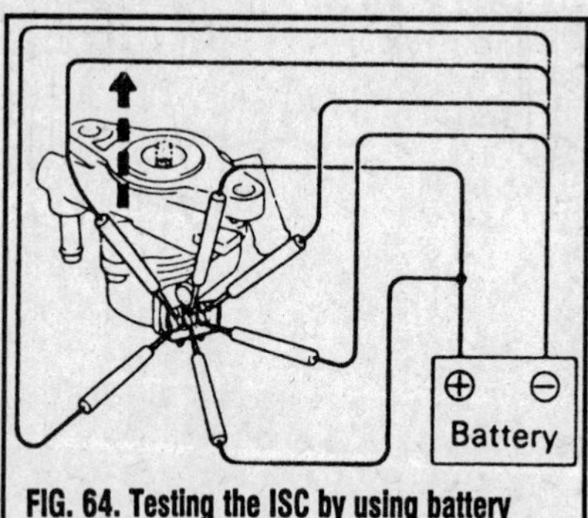

FIG. 64. Testing the ISC by using battery voltage to close the valve – 2.5L engine

Main Relay

The Main relay is located in the left front engine compartment area.

➧ SEE FIG. 66–67

TESTING

1. When the ignition is switched **ON**, the main relay should be heard to click.
2. To test the relay, remove it from its mount.
3. Using an ohmmeter, test for continuity between terminals 1 and 3. Continuity should be present.
4. There should be no continuity between terminals 2 and 4.
5. Apply battery voltage and ground to terminals 1 and 3.
6. With voltage applied, continuity should be present at terminals 2 and 4.
7. If any test condition is not met, the relay must be replaced.

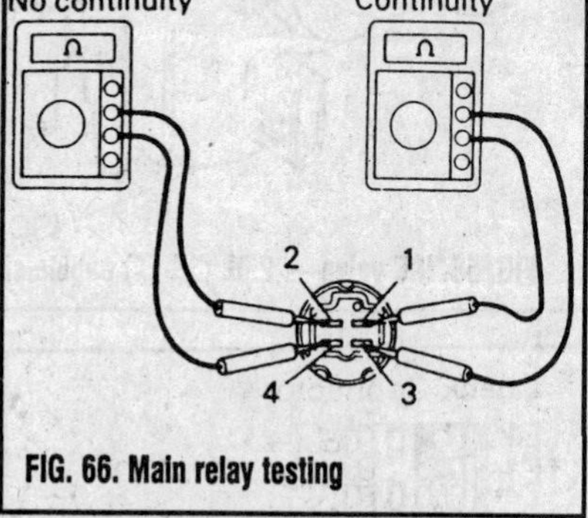

FIG. 66. Main relay testing

Circuit Opening Relay

The circuit opening relay is located behind the instrument panel or glove box.

Testing

EXCEPT 3.0L ENGINE

➧ SEE FIG. 68–71

1. With the ignition **OFF**, remove the relay from its mount.
2. Using an ohmmeter, test for continuity between terminals STA and E1. Continuity should be present.
3. There should be continuity between terminals B and FC.
4. There should be no continuity between terminals B and FP.
5. Apply battery voltage and ground to terminals STA and E1; with voltage applied,

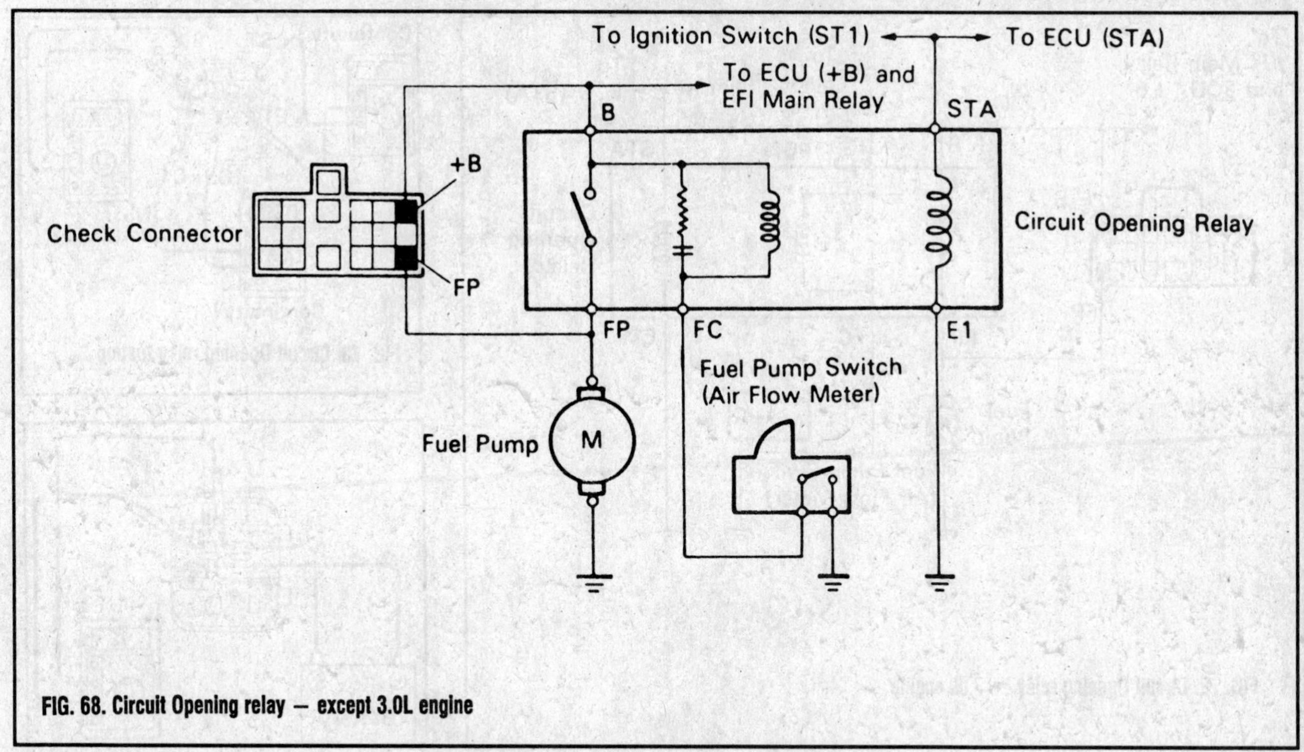

FIG. 68. Circuit Opening relay — except 3.0L engine

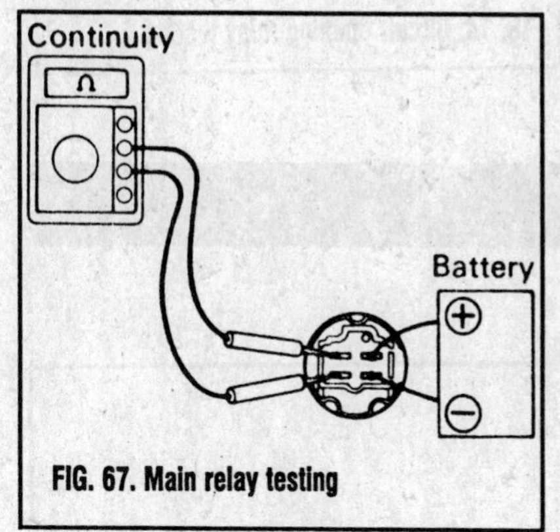

FIG. 67. Main relay testing

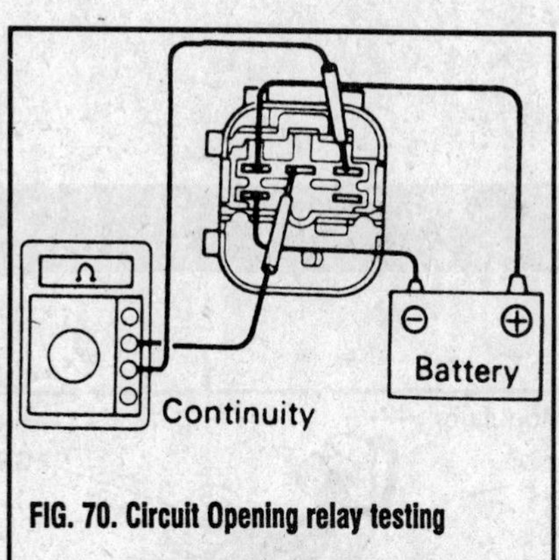

FIG. 70. Circuit Opening relay testing

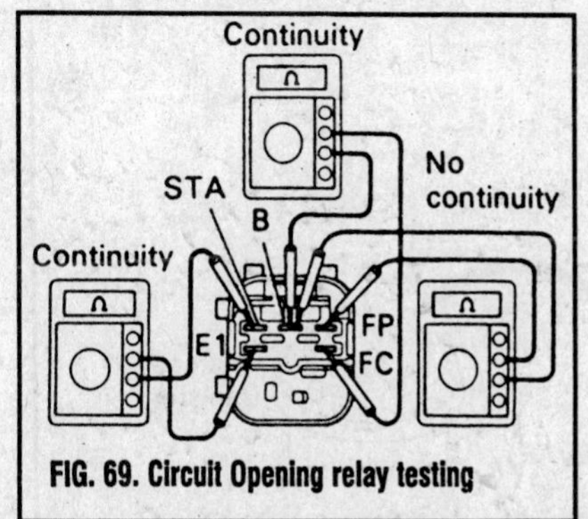

FIG. 69. Circuit Opening relay testing

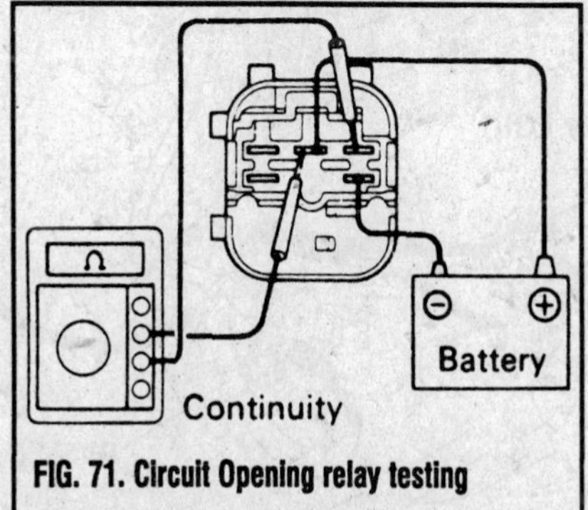

FIG. 71. Circuit Opening relay testing

continuity should be present at terminals B and FP.

6. Apply battery voltage and ground to terminals B and FC; with voltage applied, continuity should be present at terminals B and FP.

7. If any test condition is not met, the relay must be replaced.

3.0L ENGINE

➧ SEE FIG. 72–74

1. With the ignition **OFF**, remove the relay from its mount.

2. Using an ohmmeter, test for continuity between terminals ST and E1 Continuity should be present.

3. There should be continuity between terminals IG and FC.

4. There should be no continuity between terminals B and FP.

5. Apply battery voltage and ground to terminals ST and E1; with voltage applied, continuity should be present at terminals B and FP.

6. If any test condition is not met, the relay must be replaced.

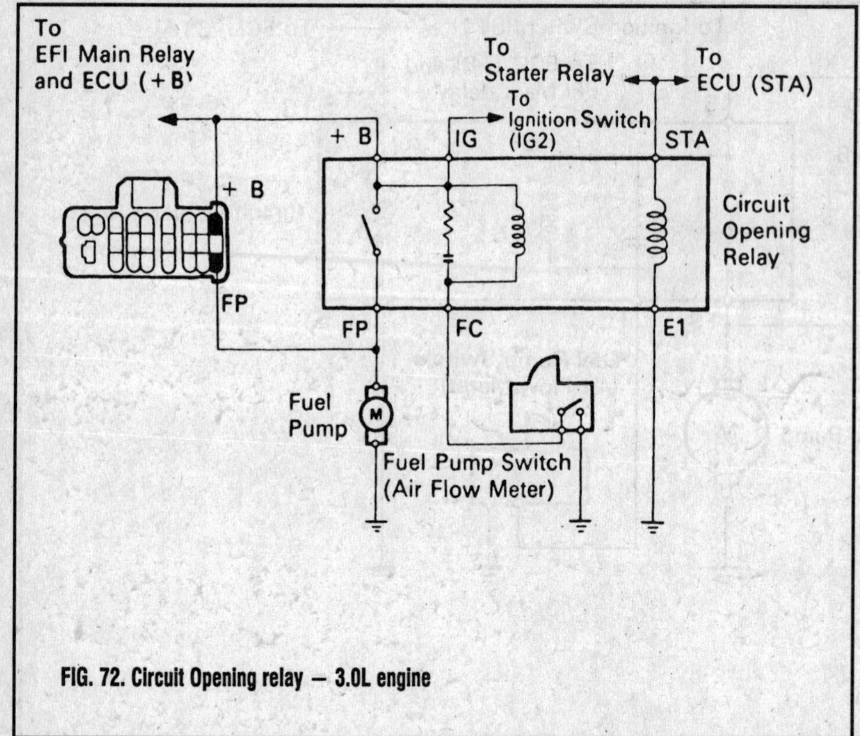

FIG. 72. Circuit Opening relay — 3.0L engine

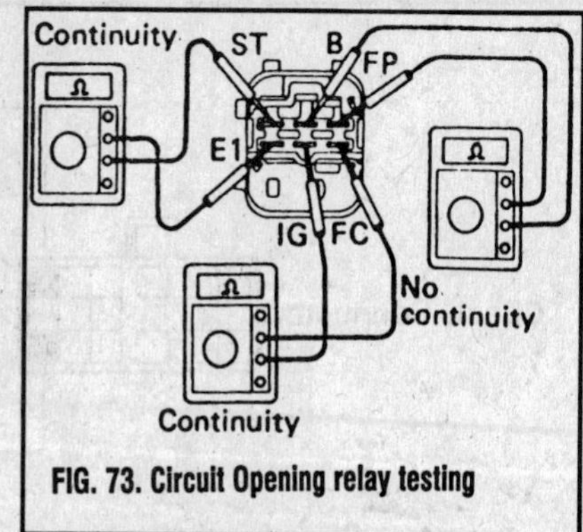

FIG. 73. Circuit Opening relay testing

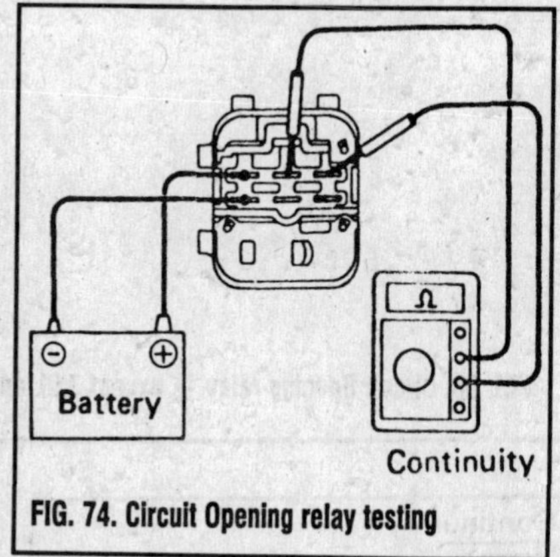

FIG. 74. Circuit Opening relay testing

VACUUM DIAGRAMS

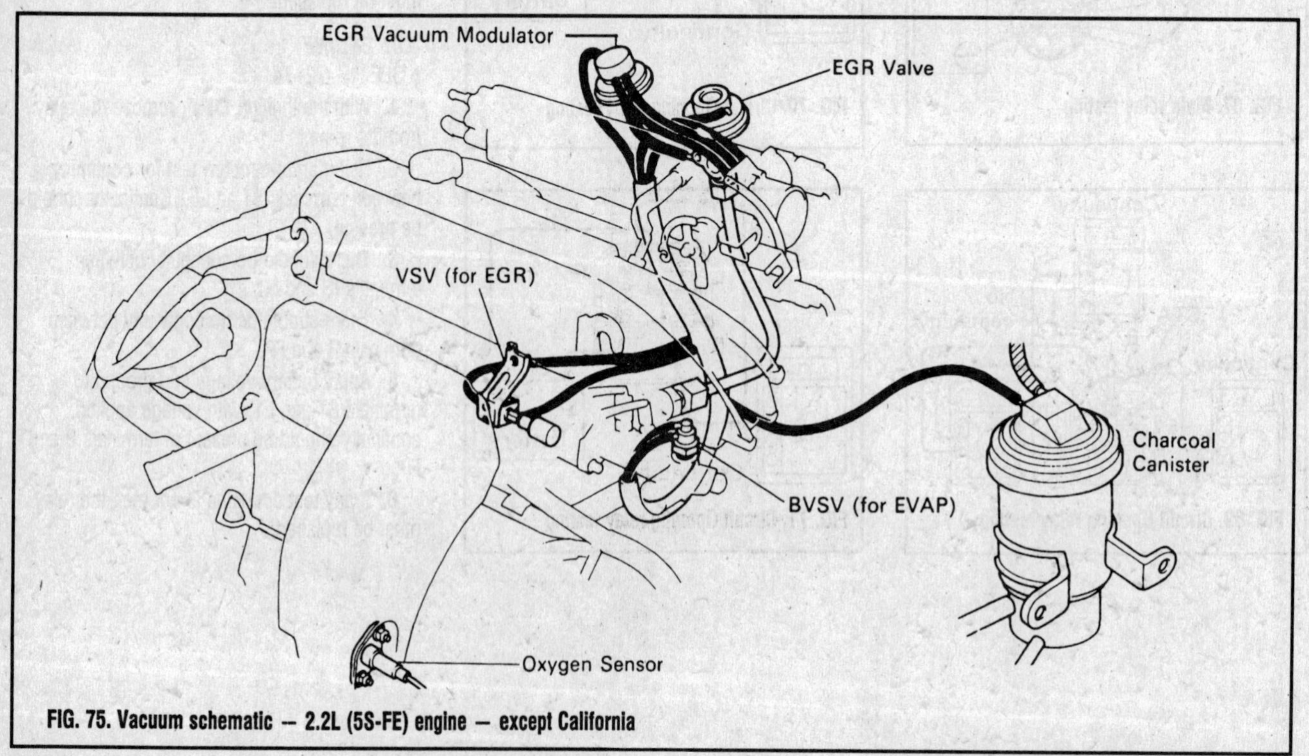

FIG. 75. Vacuum schematic — 2.2L (5S-FE) engine — except California

EGR Vacuum Modulator
EGR
Valve
VSV
(for EVAP)
Oxygen
Sensor
VSV (for EGR)
Charcoal
Canister
Check
Valve
TWC

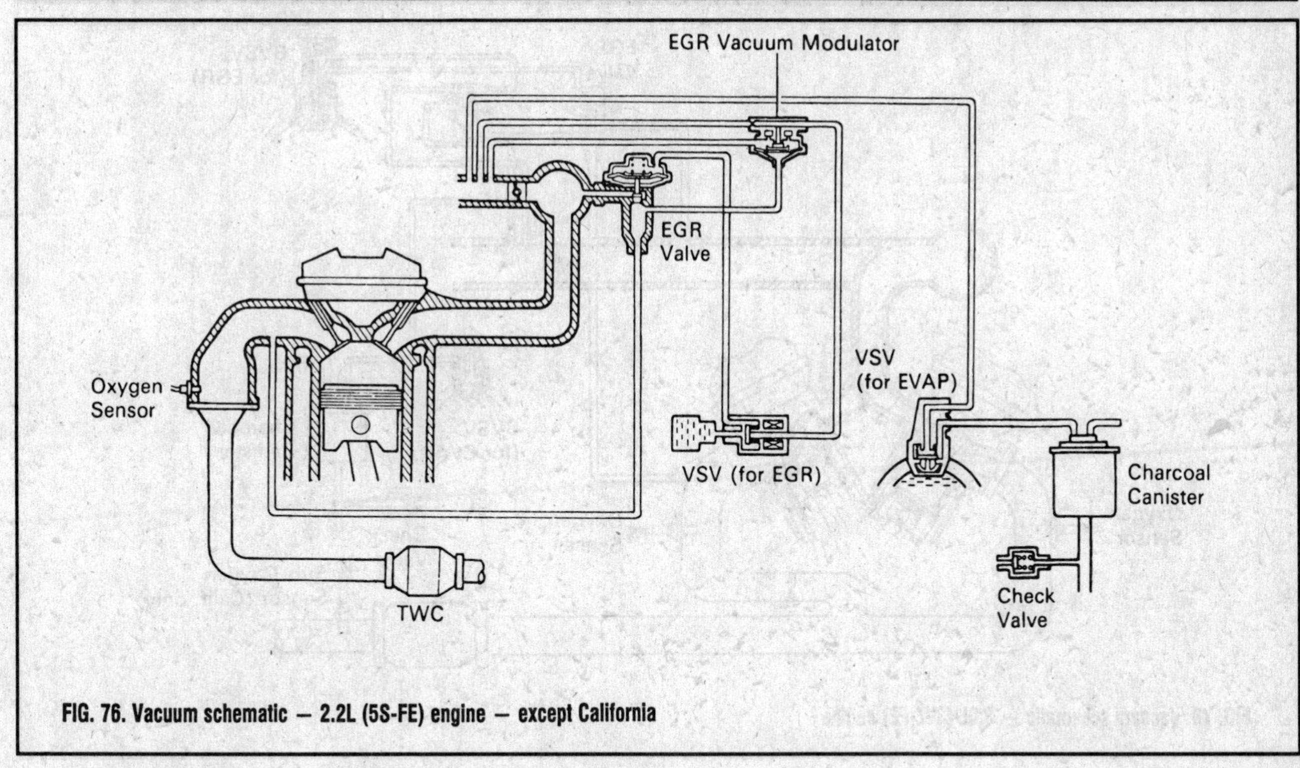

FIG. 76. Vacuum schematic — 2.2L (5S-FE) engine — except California

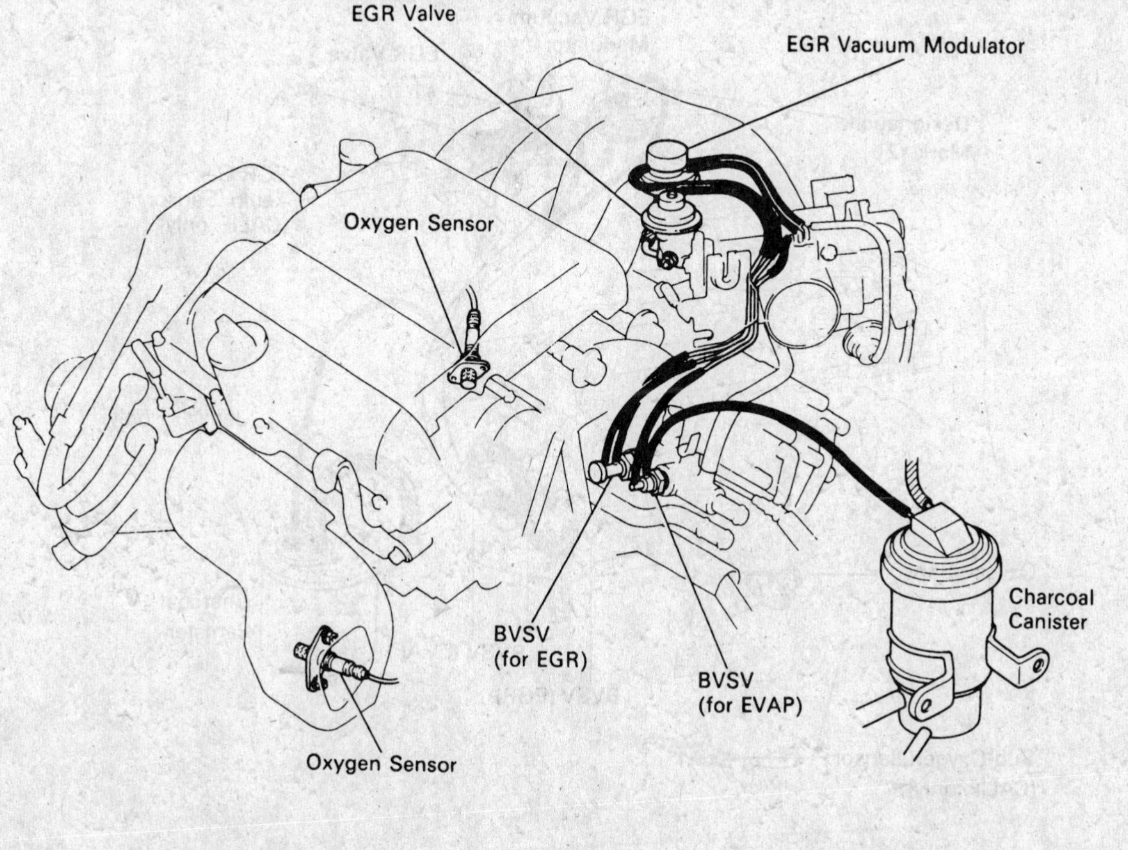

EGR Valve
EGR Vacuum Modulator
Oxygen Sensor
Charcoal
Canister
BVSV
(for EGR)
BVSV
(for EVAP)
Oxygen Sensor

FIG. 77. Vacuum schematic — 3.0L (3VZ-FE) engine

EGR
Valve
BVSV
(for EGR)
BVSV
(for EVAP)
Charcoal
Canister
Oxygen
Sensor
Oxygen
Sensor
Check
Valve
Sub-Oxygen
Sensor (Calif. only)

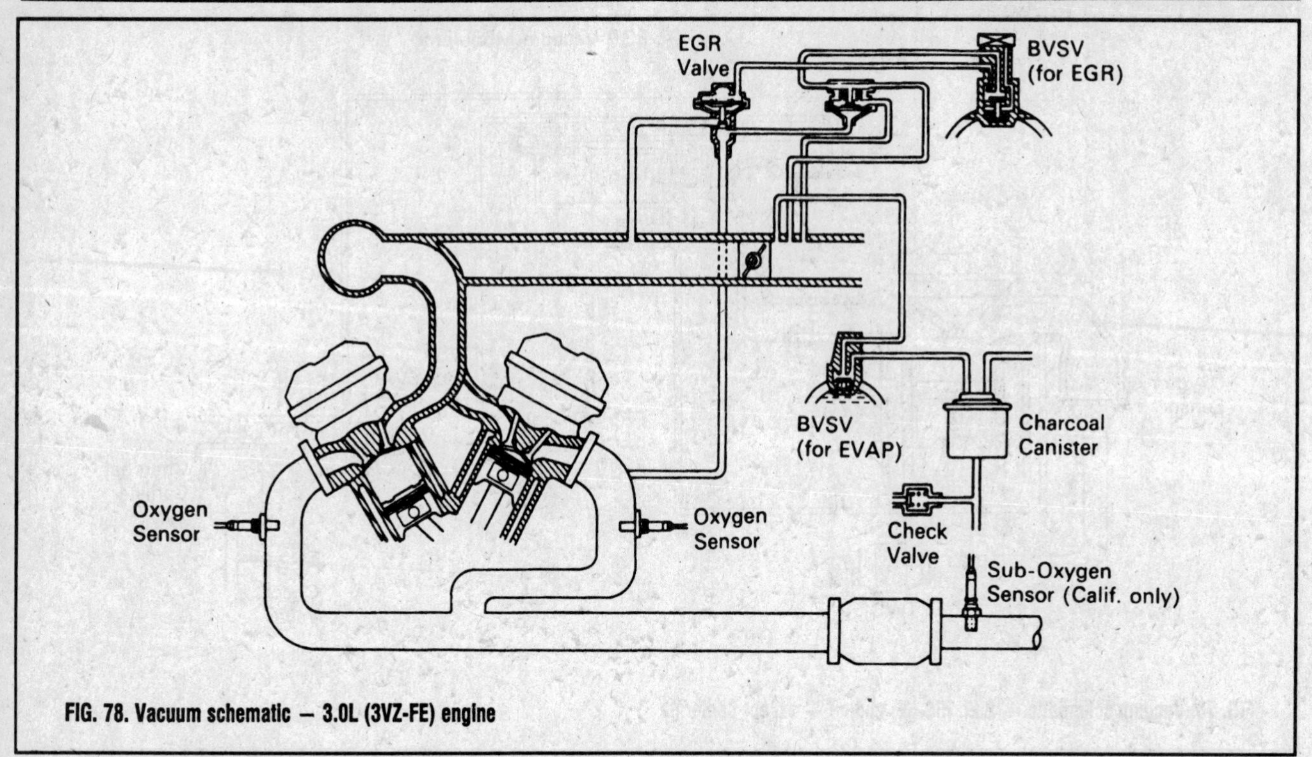

FIG. 78. Vacuum schematic — 3.0L (3VZ-FE) engine

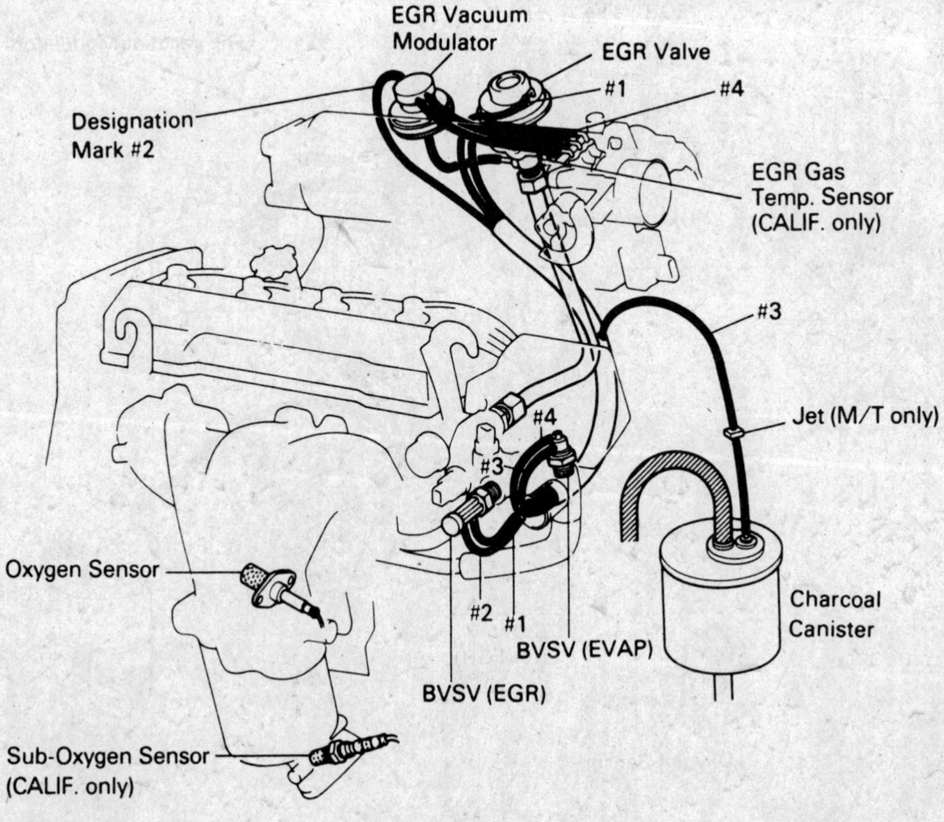

EGR Vacuum
Modulator
EGR Valve
#1
#4
Designation
Mark #2
EGR Gas
Temp. Sensor
(CALIF. only)
#3
Jet (M/T only)
#4
#3
Oxygen Sensor
#2
#1
BVSV (EVAP)
BVSV (EGR)
Charcoal
Canister
Sub-Oxygen Sensor
(CALIF. only)

FIG. 79. Vacuum schematic — 2.0L (3S-FE) engine

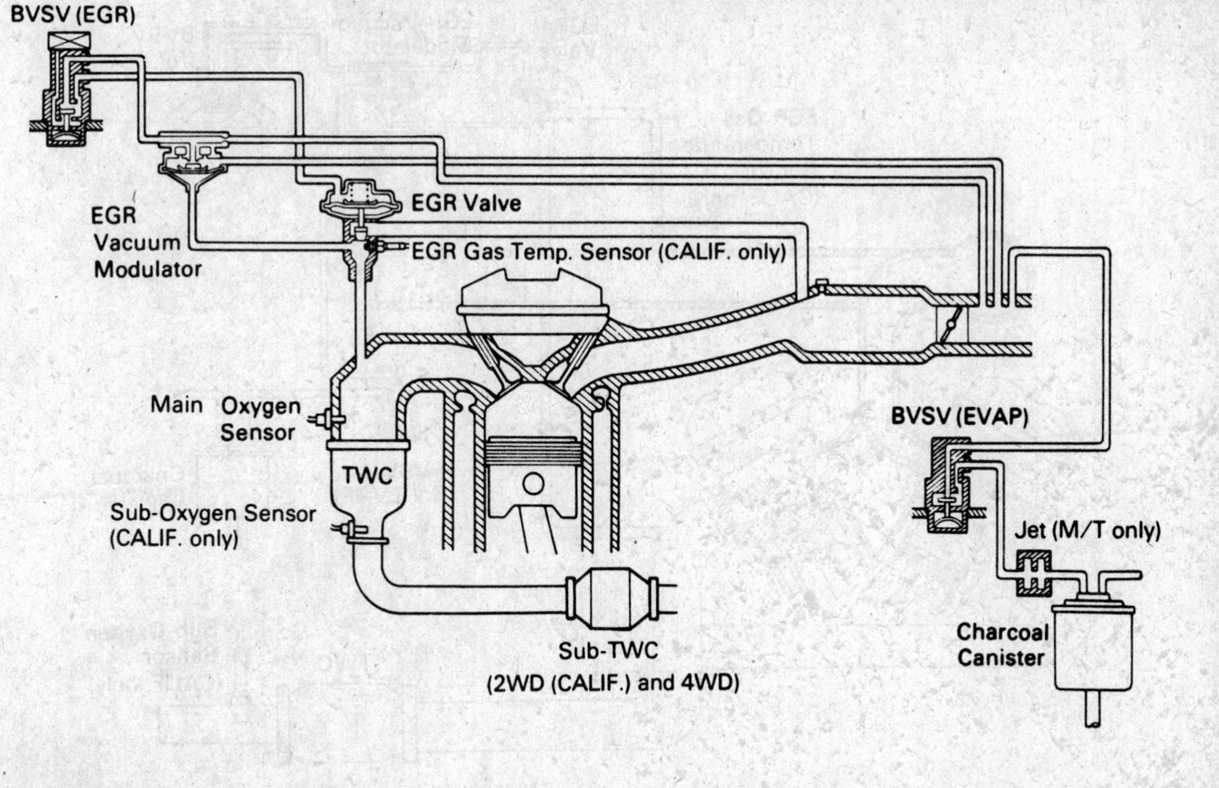

BVSV (EGR)
EGR Vacuum Modulator
EGR Valve
EGR Gas Temp. Sensor (CALIF. only)
Main Oxygen Sensor
TWC
Sub-Oxygen Sensor (CALIF. only)
Sub-TWC (2WD (CALIF.) and 4WD)
BVSV (EVAP)
Jet (M/T only)
Charcoal Canister

FIG. 80. Vacuum schematic – 2.0L (3S-FE) engine

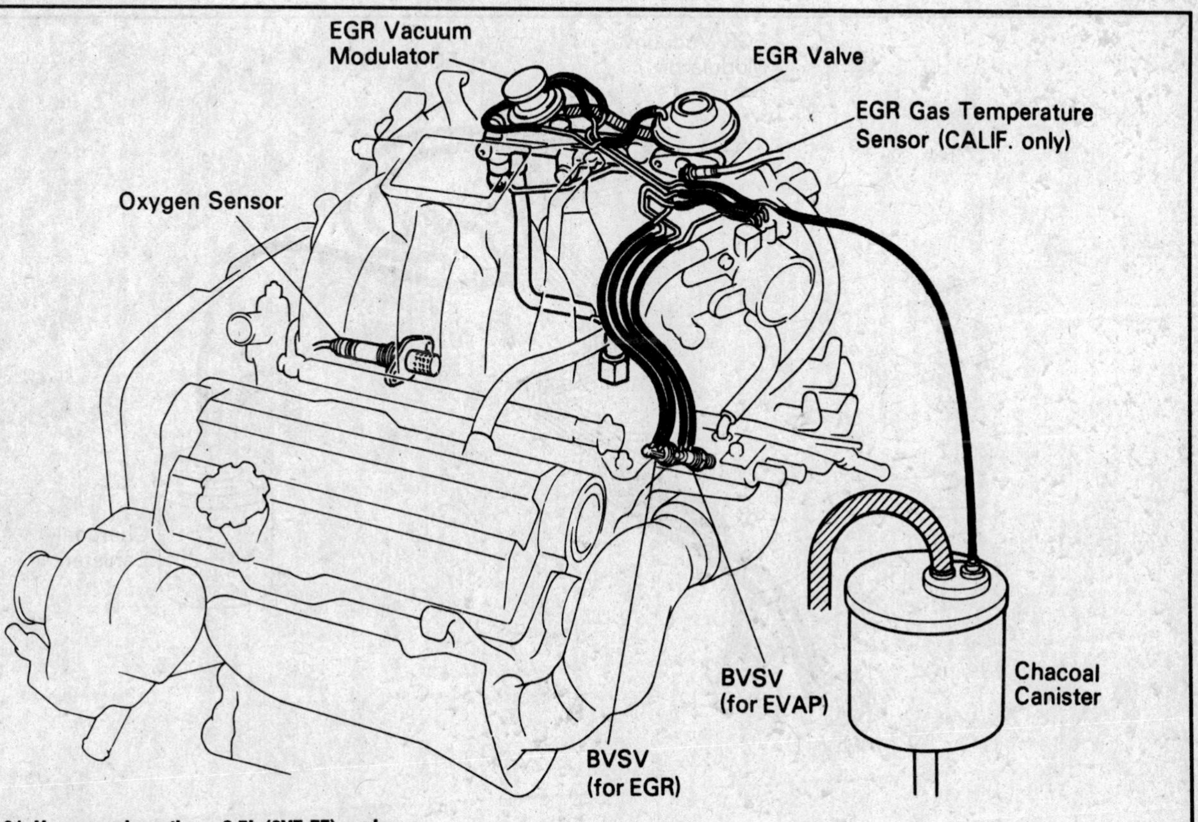

EGR Vacuum Modulator
EGR Valve
EGR Gas Temperature Sensor (CALIF. only)
Oxygen Sensor
BVSV (for EVAP)
Chacoal Canister
BVSV (for EGR)

FIG. 81. Vacuum schematic – 2.5L (2VZ-FE) engine

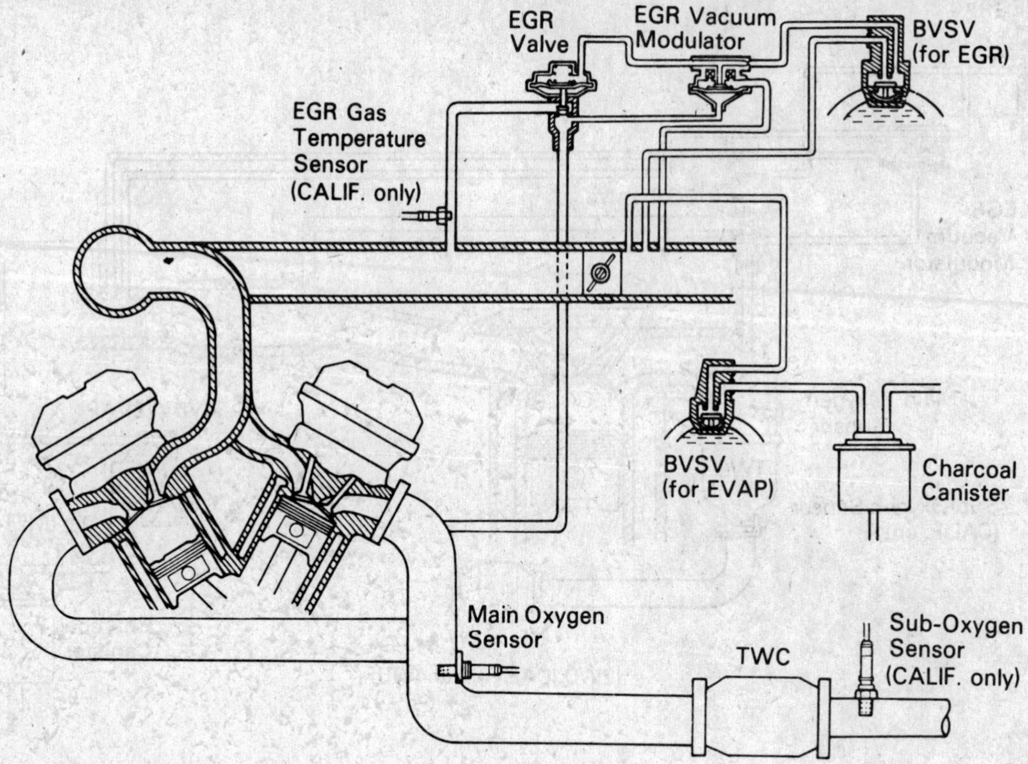

EGR Valve
EGR Vacuum Modulator
BVSV (for EGR)
EGR Gas Temperature Sensor (CALIF. only)
BVSV (for EVAP)
Charcoal Canister
Main Oxygen Sensor
TWC
Sub-Oxygen Sensor (CALIF. only)

FIG. 82. Vacuum schematic — 2.5L (2VZ-FE) engine

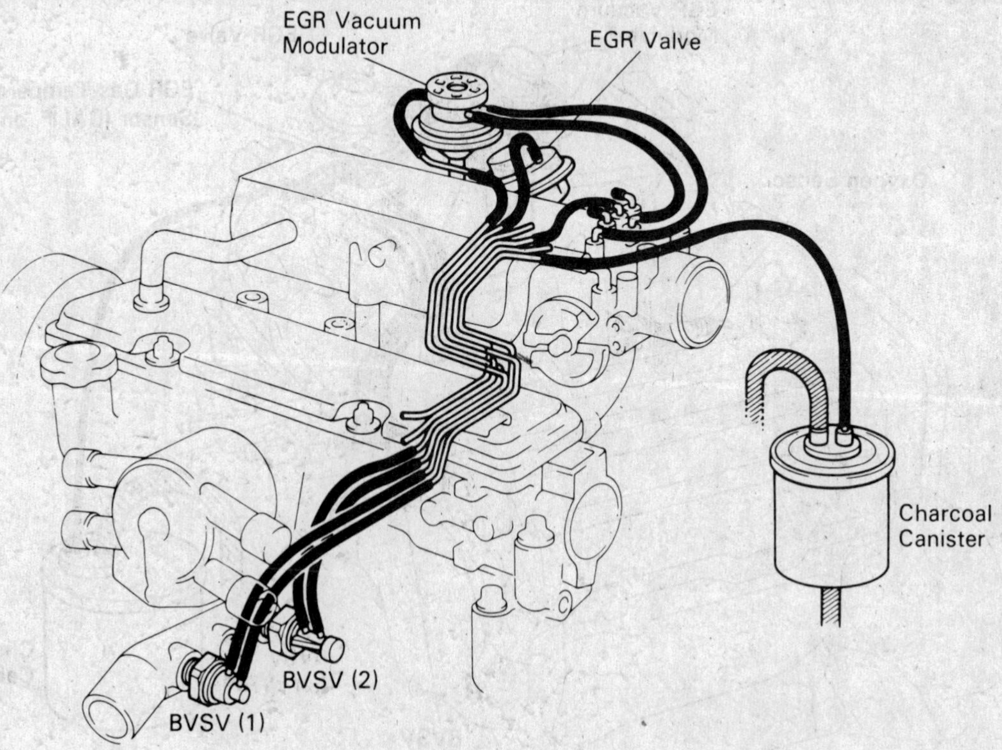

EGR Vacuum Modulator
EGR Valve
Charcoal Canister
BVSV (2)
BVSV (1)

FIG. 83. Vacuum schematic — 2.0L (2S-E) engine — except Canada

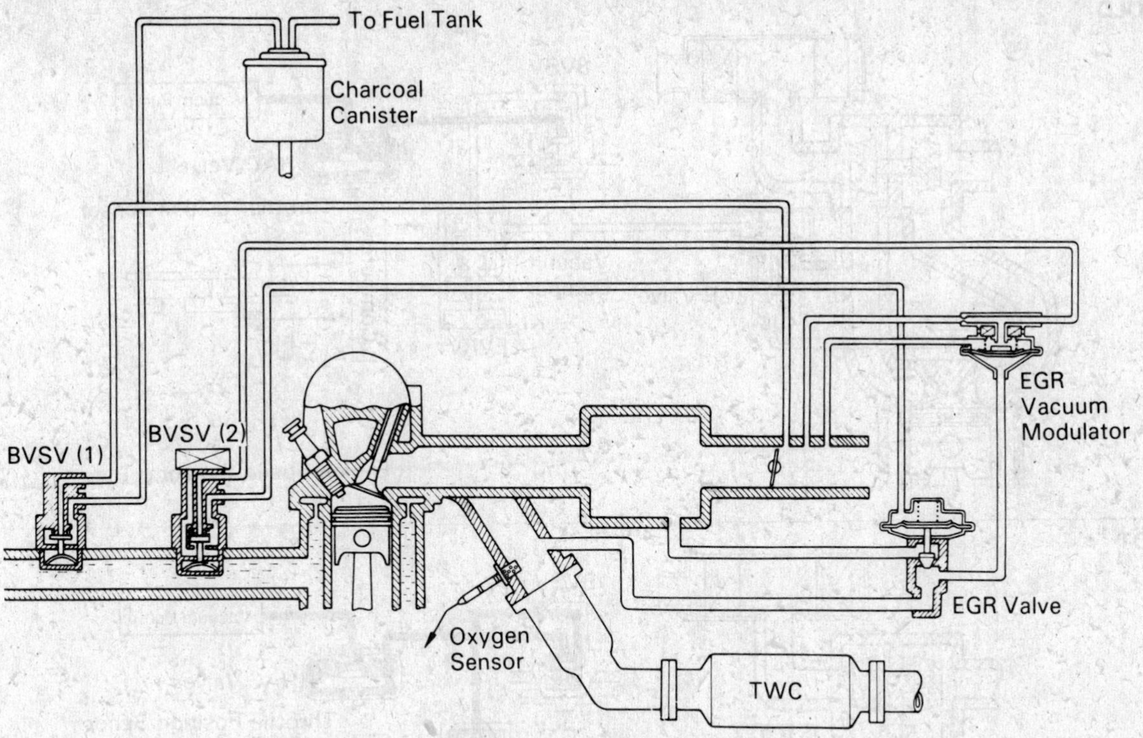

To Fuel Tank
Charcoal
Canister
BVSV (1)
BVSV (2)
EGR
Vacuum
Modulator
EGR Valve
Oxygen
Sensor
TWC

FIG. 84. Vacuum schematic – 2.0L (2S-E) engine – except Canada

Vacuum Damper
HAC Valve
EVRV
Vacuum Pump
EGR Valve
BVSV
Throttle
Position
Sensor

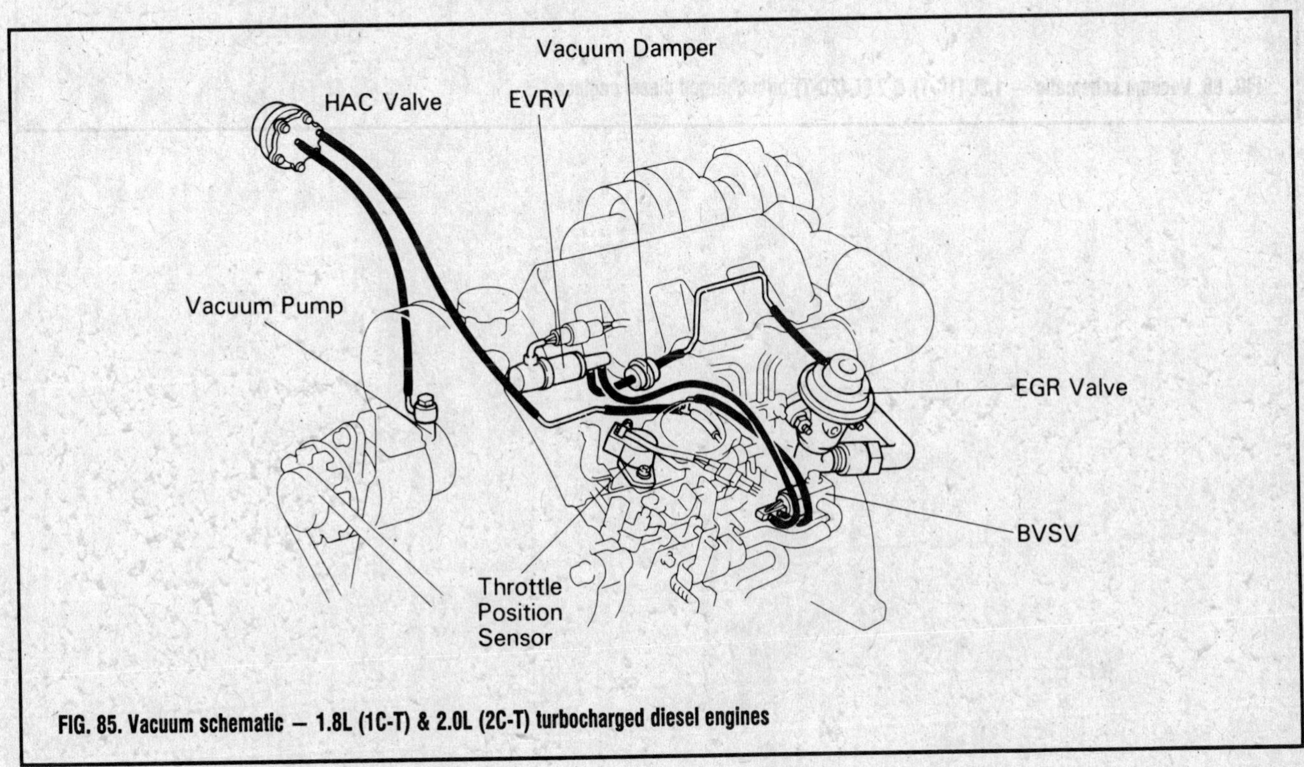

FIG. 85. Vacuum schematic – 1.8L (1C-T) & 2.0L (2C-T) turbocharged diesel engines

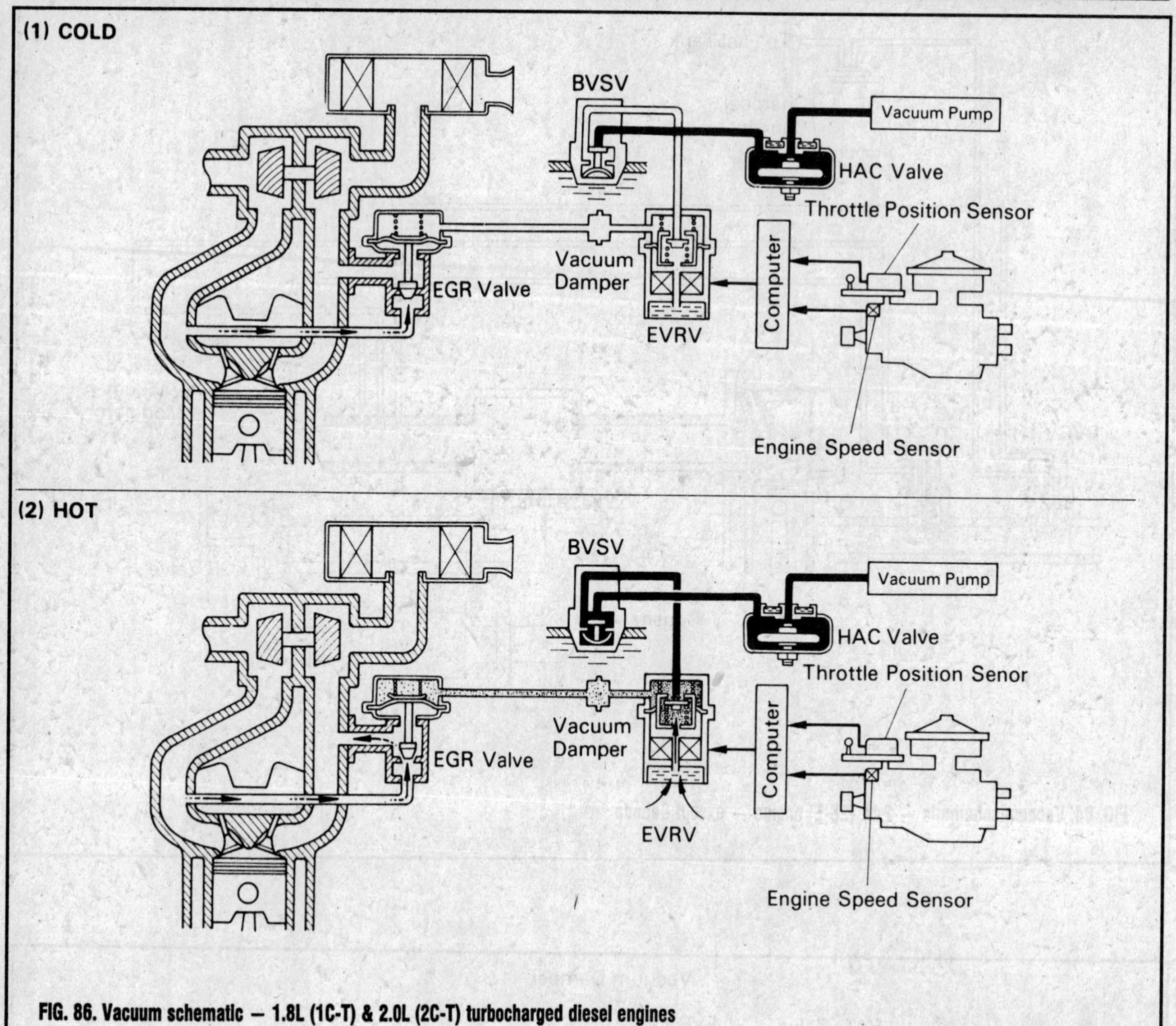

FIG. 86. Vacuum schematic – 1.8L (1C-T) & 2.0L (2C-T) turbocharged diesel engines

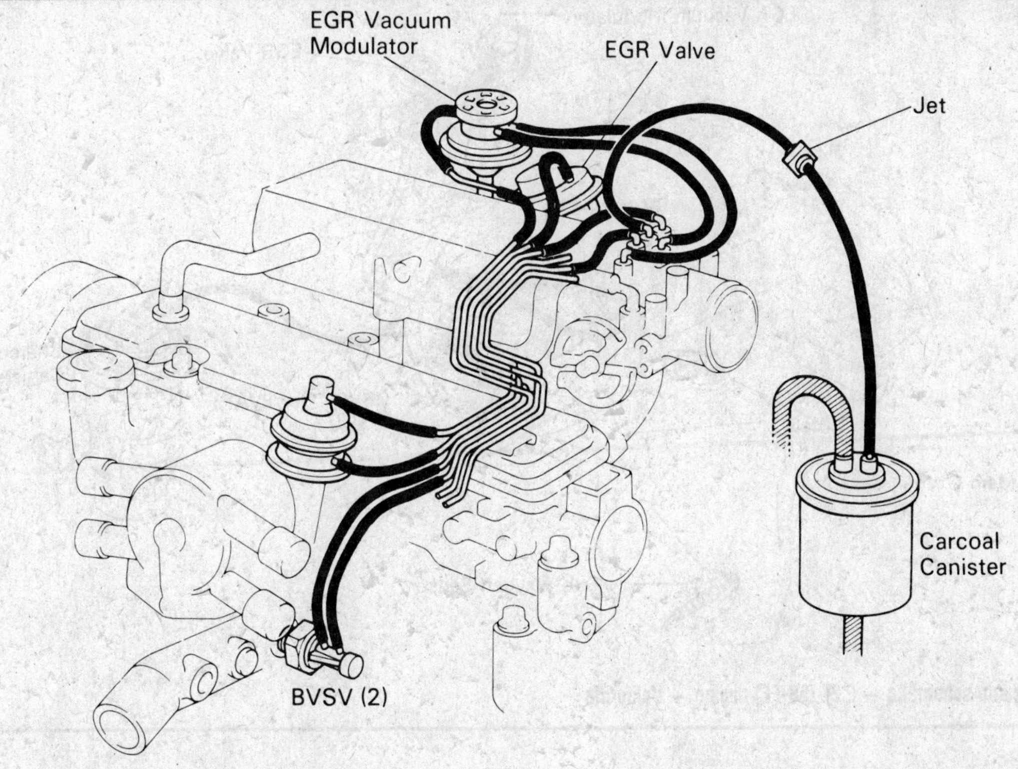

FIG. 87. Vacuum schematic — 2.0L (2S-E) engine — Canada

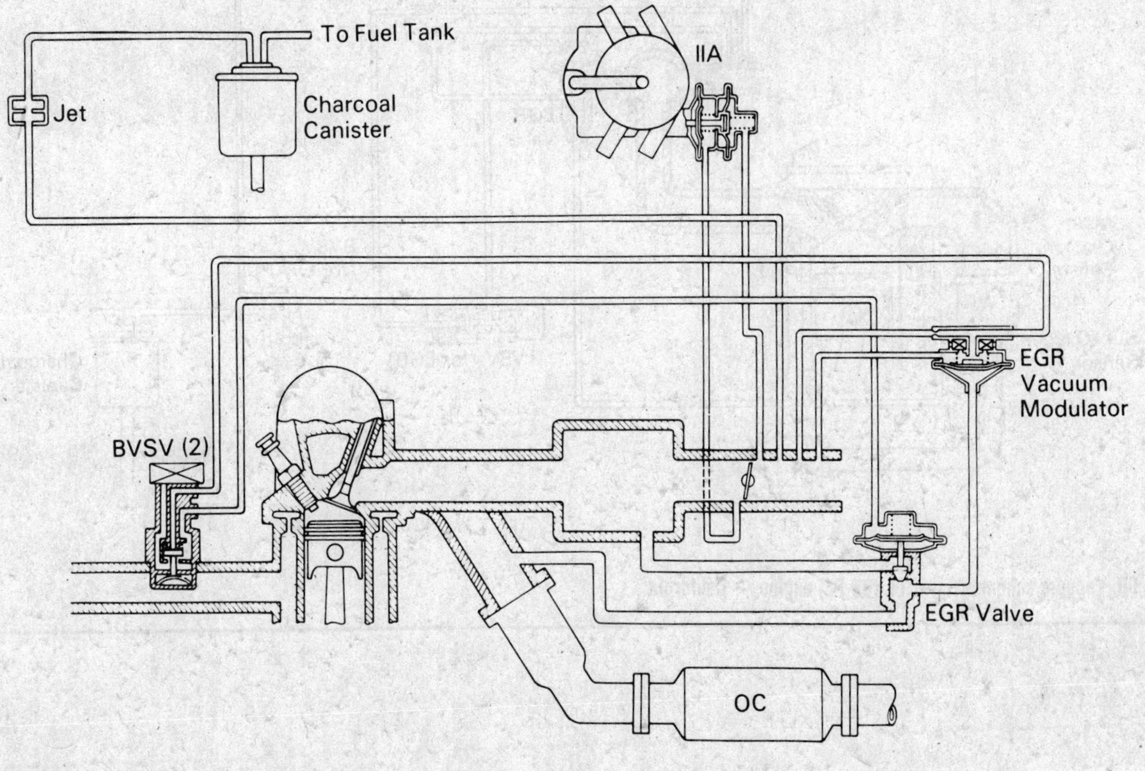

FIG. 88. Vacuum schematic — 2.0L (2S-E) engine — Canada

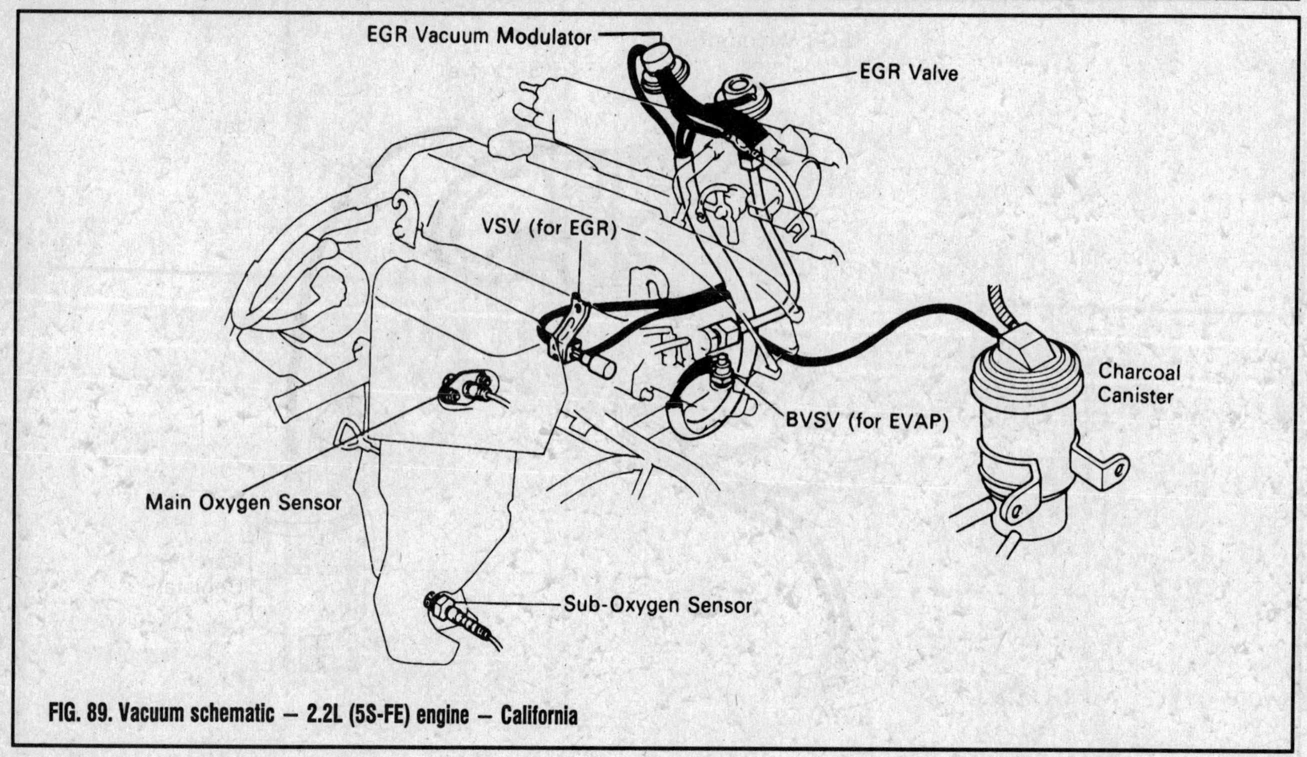

FIG. 89. Vacuum schematic – 2.2L (5S-FE) engine – California

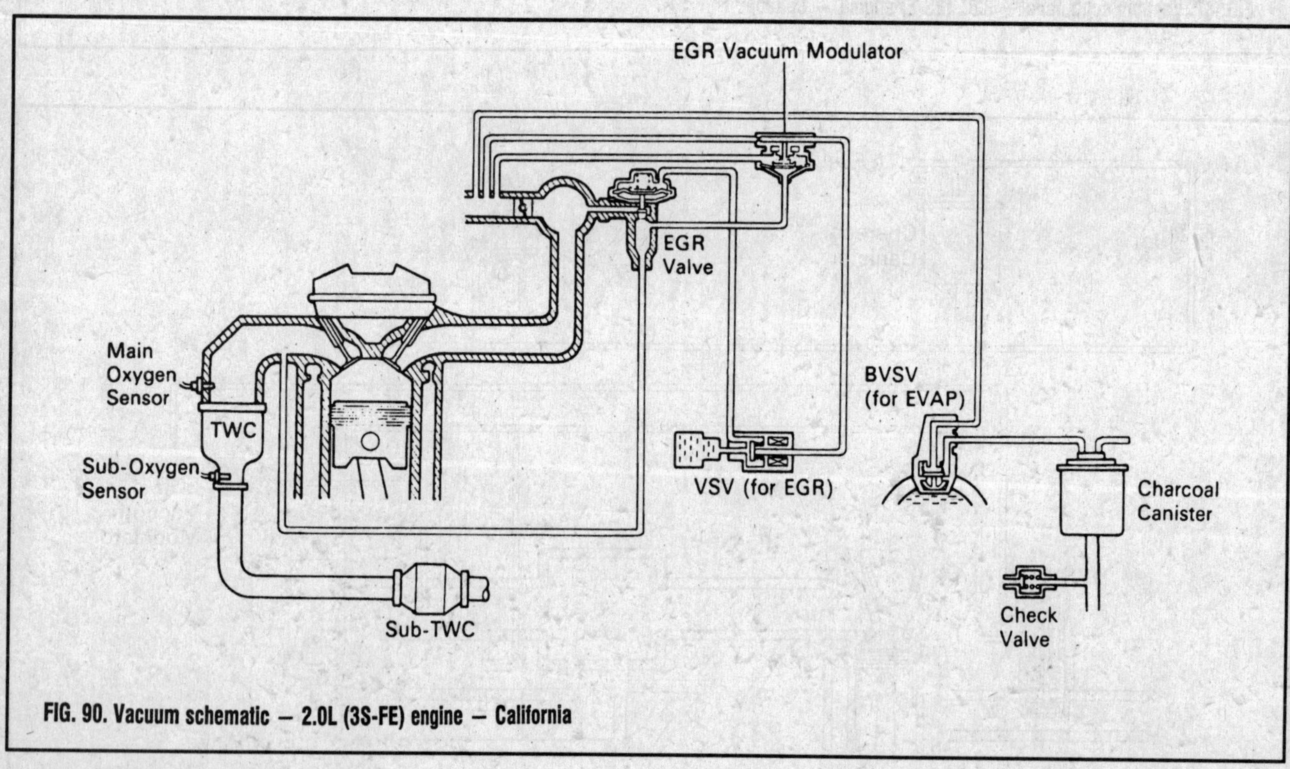

FIG. 90. Vacuum schematic – 2.0L (3S-FE) engine – California

5

FUEL SYSTEM

Fuel Injection Systems 5-2
Diesel Fuel System 5-18

DIESEL FUEL SYSTEM
- Glow plugs 5-21
- Injection lines 5-18
- Injection pump 5-20
- Injection timing 5-21
- Injectors 5-19

ELECTRONIC FUEL INJECTION
- Fuel pressure relief 5-3
- Fuel pump 5-3
- Idle speed control valve 5-9
- Injectors 5-9
- Throttle body 5-5
- Throttle position sensor 5-17

FUEL PUMP
- Electric 5-3

FUEL SYSTEM
- Diesel 5-18
- Fuel injection 5-2

FUEL TANK 5-18

GASOLINE FUEL INJECTION SYSTEM

Description of System

The EFI system precisely controls fuel injection to match engine requirements, reducing emissions and increasing driveability.

The electric fuel pump pumps fuel to the pressure regulator. The four fuel injectors are electric solenoid valves which open and close by signals from the control unit.

The EFI computer receives input from various sensors to determine engine operating condition.

1. Air flow meter: measures the amount of intake air.
2. Ignition coil: engine RPM.
3. Throttle position sensor: amount of throttle opening.
4. Water temperature sensor or cylinder head temperature sensors: temperature of coolant or engine.
5. Air temperature sensor: temperature of intake air (ambient temperature).
6. Starting switch: signals that the starter is operating.
7. Altitude switch: used to signal changes in atmospheric pressure.
8. Exhaust gas sensor: used to measure the oxygen content of the exhaust gas.
9. Vacuum sensor: measures the amount of intake manifold pressure in volts.

The sensors provide the input to the control unit, which determines the amount of fuel to be injected by its preset program.

Safety Precautions

Safety is the most important factor to adhere to when preforming maintenance on the EFI system. Failure to conduct fuel system maintenance and repairs in a safe manner may result in serious personal injury. Maintenance and testing of the vehicle's fuel system components can be accomplished safely and effectively by adhering to the following rules and guidelines.

GENERAL PRECAUTIONS

- To avoid the possibility of fire and personal injury, always disconnect the negative battery cable unless the repair or test procedure specifically requires that battery voltage be applied.
- Always relieve the fuel system pressure prior to disconnecting any fuel system component (injector, fuel rail, pressure regulator, etc...), fitting or fuel line connection. To relieve pressure wrap a shop rag around the fitting or connection being opened, a slowly open the system. Wait for pressure to relieve itself, then remove the rag and wipe up any spilled fuel. Exercise extreme caution whenever relieving fuel system pressure to avoid exposing skin, face and eyes to fuel spray. Be advised that fuel under pressure may penetrate the skin or any part of the body that it comes in contact with.
- Always place a shop towel or cloth around the fitting or connection prior to loosening to absorb any excess fuel due to spillage. Ensure that all fuel spillage (should it occur) is quickly removed from engine surfaces. Ensure that all fuel soaked cloths or towels are deposited into a suitable waste container.
- Always have a properly charged fire extinguisher in the vicinity of the work area and always ensure work areas are adequately ventilated.
- Do not allow fuel spray or fuel vapors to come in contact with spark or open flame. Remember that smoking and fuel maintenance do not mix!
- Always use a backup wrench when loosening and tightening fuel line connection fittings. This will prevent unnecessary stress and torsion to fuel line piping. Always follow the proper torque specifications.
- Always replace worn fuel fitting O-rings with new ones. Do not substitute fuel hose or equivalent where rigid fuel pipe is called for.
- Always use common sense.

MAINTENANCE PRECAUTIONS

- When connecting test equipment (tachometer, timing light, etc.) use the battery as the power source.
- Always ensure that the battery and ignition coil terminals are properly and securely connected.
- Handle the spark plug wires carefully. Always pull by the boots and never on the wires.
- During engine compartment cleaning, always protect electrical system components from water.
- Do not strike the oxygen sensor or place stress on the sensor wire. Do not allow the oxygen sensor to come in contact with water.

MOBILE RADIO PRECAUTIONS (HAM, CB, ETC.)

The ECU was designed so that it would not be affected by outside interference. However, if your Camry is equipped with a CB radio transceiver or similar device (even it has only a 10 Watt output), it may at times affect the operation of the ECU. There is an even more likelihood of the ECU being affected if the antenna and feeder are installed close by. If you do have this type of equipment installed, observe the following precautions:

- Install the antenna as far away as possible from the ECU. The ECU is located under the radio so the antenna should be installed in the rear side of the vehicle.
- Keep the antenna feeder as far away from the ECU wiring — about 8 in. (203mm) will suffice. DO NOT wind the feeder and ECU wires together.
- Make sure that the feeder and antenna are properly adjusted.
- Do not equip your Camry with a powerful mobile radio system.

AIR INDUCTION SYSTEM PRECAUTIONS

- Improper installation of the engine oil dipstick, oil filler cap, PCV valve hoses, etc. may cause the engine to run lean and idle poorly.
- Any loose, disconnected or cracked part of the air induction system between the throttle body and the air intake manifold may cause the engine to run lean and idle poorly.

ELECTRONIC CONTROL SYSTEM PRECAUTIONS

- Before disconnecting ECU connectors, terminals, etc., first disconnect the power by turning the ignition switch to the Off position or disconnecting the battery terminals.
- When installing the battery, make sure that

the proper polarity is observed when connecting the cables.

- Handle the EFI system components carefully during removal and installation, especially the ECU. These components are very susceptible to damage if dropped or handled roughly.
- Be careful When troubleshooting the EFI system. There are many transistor circuits involved and even the slightest contact between terminals can cause problems.
- Never open the ECU cover.
- If you must open the hood during rainy weather, don't allow the engine to be exposed too long.
- Always replace parts as an assembly.

The Electronic Fuel Injection (EFI) system is broken down into three major systems: The Fuel System, Air Induction System and Electronic Control System.

FUEL SYSTEM

An electric fuel pump supplies sufficient fuel, under a constant pressure, to the EFI injectors. These injectors inject a metered quantity of fuel into the intake manifold in accordance with signals from the ECU (Electronic Control Unit) computer. Each injector injects at the same time, one half of the fuel required for ideal combustion with each engine revolution.

AIR INDUCTION SYSTEM

The air induction system provides sufficient air for the engine operation. Major air intake system components include the air flow meter, air valve and throttle body.

ELECTRONIC CONTROL SYSTEMS

The engine is equipped with a Toyota Computer Control System (TCCS) which centrally controls the electronic fuel injection, electronic spark advance and the exhaust gas recirculation valve. The systems can be diagnosed by means of an Electronic Control Unit (ECU) which employs a microcomputer. The ECU and the TCCS control the following functions: electronic fuel injection (EFI), Electronic Spark Advance (ESA), idle speed control, exhaust gas recirculation, system diagnosis and fail-safe functions.

ELECTRONIC FUEL INJECTION (EFI)

The ECU receives signals from the various sensors indicating changing engine operations conditions such as:

- Intake air volume.
- Intake air temperature.
- Coolant temperature sensor.
- Engine rpm.
- Acceleration/deceleration.
- Exhaust oxygen content.

These signals are utilized by the ECU to determine the injection duration necessary for an optimum air-fuel ratio.

ELECTRONIC SPARK ADVANCE (ESA)

The ESA is programmed with data for optimum timing during any and all operating conditions. Using the data provided by sensors which monitor various engine functions (rpm, intake air volume, coolant temperature, etc.), the microcomputer (ECU) triggers the spark at precisely the right moment.

IDLE SPEED CONTROL

The ECU is programmed with specific engine speed values to respond to different engine conditions (coolant temperature, air conditioner on/off. etc.). Sensors transmit signals to the ECU which controls the flow of air through the by-pass of the throttle valve and adjusts the idle speed to the specified value.

EXHAUST GAS RECIRCULATION (EGR)

The ECU detects the coolant temperature and controls the EGR operations to lower combustion chamber temperatures accordingly.

DIAGNOSIS

Diagnosis functions are performed by the ECU and found in Section 4.

Relieving Fuel System Pressure

CAUTION

Failure to relieve fuel pressure before repairs or disassembly can cause serious personal injury and/or property damage.

Fuel pressure is maintained within the fuel lines, even if the engine is **OFF** or has not been run in a period of time. This pressure must be safely relieved before any fuel-bearing line or component is loosened or removed.

1. Place a catch-pan under the joint to be disconnected. A large quantity of fuel will be released when the joint is opened.
2. Wear eye or full face protection.
3. Slowly release the joint using a wrench of the correct size. Counterhold the joint with a second wrench if possible.
4. Allow the pressurized fuel to bleed off slowly before disconnecting the joint.
5. Plug the opened lines immediately to prevent fuel spillage or the entry of dirt.
6. Dispose of the released fuel properly.

Fuel Lines and Connections

INSPECTION

1. Visually inspect the fuel lines for cracks or leakage.
2. Visually inspect all connections for deformation.
3. Check the fuel tank vapor vent system hoses and connections for looseness, sharp bends or damage.
4. Check the fuel tank for deformation, cracks, fuel leakage or tank band looseness.
5. Check the filler neck for damage or signs of leakage.

Electrical Fuel Pump and Sending Unit

The fuel pump circuit is controlled by the ECU either directly or through the main/circuit opening relays. Under normal conditions, the controller will not energize the fuel pump unless other signals such as cranking, air flow and ignition are received. The fuel pump can be energized through the diagnostic connector for testing.

REMOVAL & INSTALLATION

➧ SEE FIG. 1

:::: CAUTION

The fuel pump is located inside the fuel tank and is attached to the sending unit. Do not smoke or have any open flame in the work area when removing the fuel pump!

1. Disconnect the negative battery cable.
2. Position a suitable waste container under the fuel tank and drain the fuel from the tank.
3. Remove the fuel tank.
4. On non-All-Trac 4-Wheel Drive vehicles, remove the six screws from the fuel pump bracket. On All-Trac 4-Wheel Drive vehicles, there are seven screws to remove.
5. Withdraw the fuel pump bracket from the fuel tank. Remove the gasket from the fuel tank and discard it.
6. Remove the two nuts that hold the pump to the bracket and disconnect the wires from the fuel pump.
7. Pull the bracket from the bottom of the fuel pump.
8. Disconnect the fuel hose (discharge) from the fuel pump.
9. Remove the fuel filter rubber cushion and clip. Remove the filter from the pump.

To install the fuel pump:

10. Install the fuel filter and secure with the clip. Install the rubber cushion.
11. Connect the fuel hose to the fuel pump.
12. Install the rubber cushion to the bottom of the fuel pump.
13. Push the bottom of the fuel pump and the rubber cushion into the fuel pump bracket.
14. Using a new gasket, place the bracket onto the fuel tank.
15. Install the bracket retaining screws and torque to 26–30 inch lbs.
16. Install the fuel tank.
17. Fill the fuel tank and check for leaks.
18. Connect the negative battery cable.

TESTING

Check Fuel Pump Operation

1. Turn the ignition switch to the ON position, but don't start the engine.
2. Remove the rubber cap from the fuel EFI check connector and short both the **+B** and **FP** terminals with a jumper wire.
3. Check that there is pressure in the hose to the cold start injector.
4. Remove the jumper wire and turn the ignition switch **OFF** position.
5. If no pressure can be felt in the line, check the following components:
   a. Fuseable links.
   b. Fuses (EFI 15A, IGN 7.5A).
   c. EFI main relay.
   d. Fuel pump.
   e. Wiring connections.
6. If there is no fuel pump pressure and an inspection of the related electrical components does not reveal a malfunction, replace the fuel pump.

Check Fuel Pump Pressure

➧ SEE FIG. 2–5

1. Before beginning the pressure test, make sure that the battery voltage is above 12 volts.
2. Disconnect the negative battery cable.

:::: CAUTION

Work must be started approximately 30 seconds or

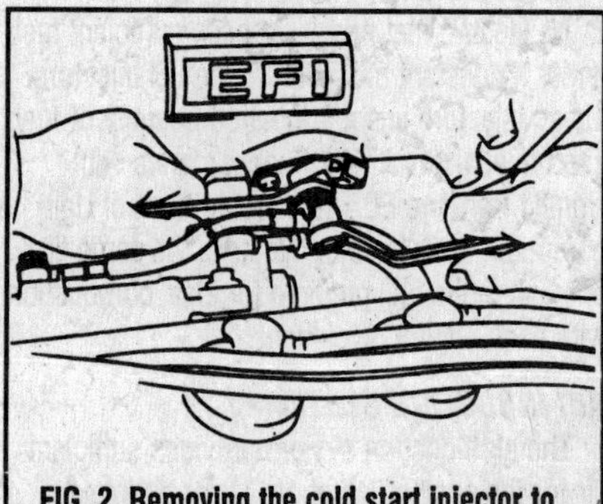

FIG. 2. Removing the cold start injector to test fuel pressure

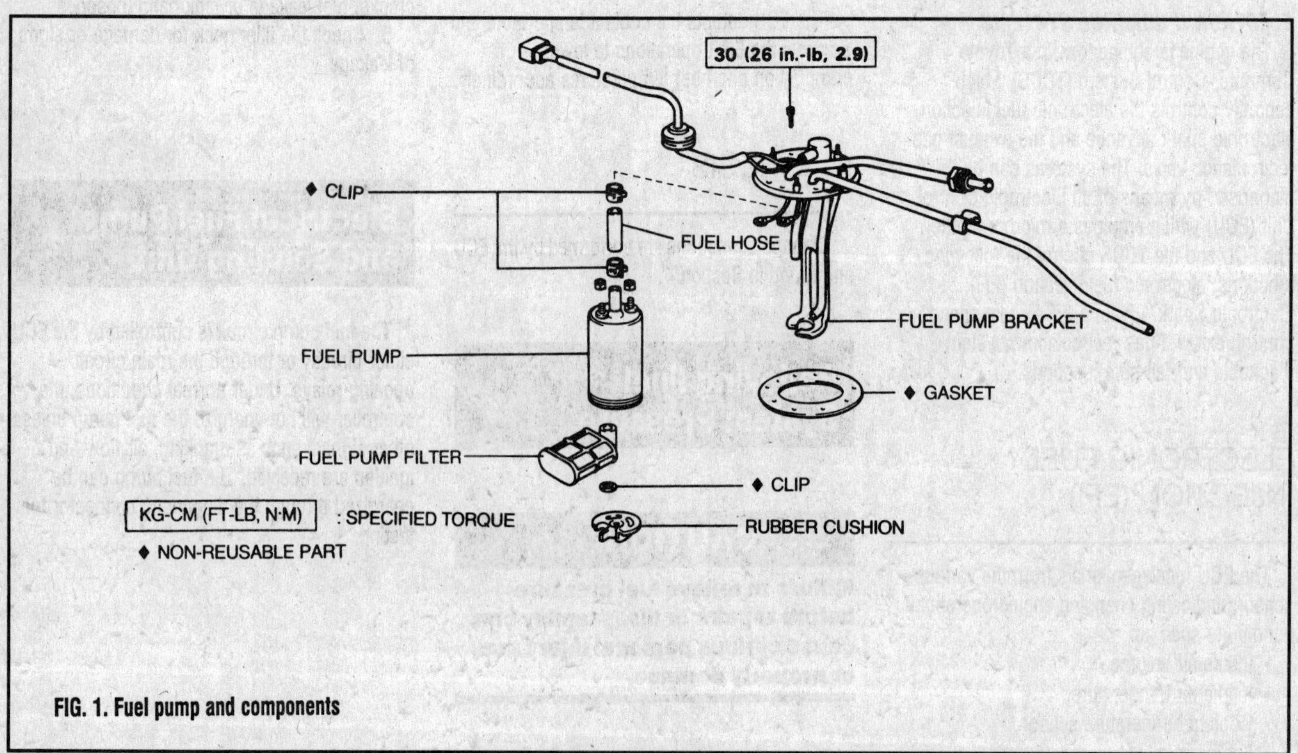

FIG. 1. Fuel pump and components

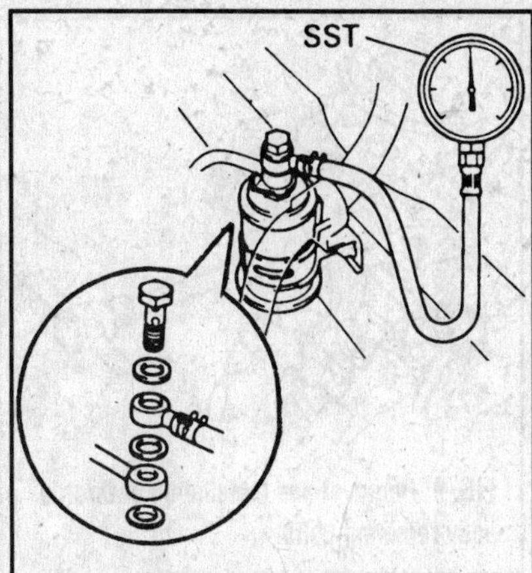

FIG. 3. Removing the fuel filter inlet hose to test fuel pressure

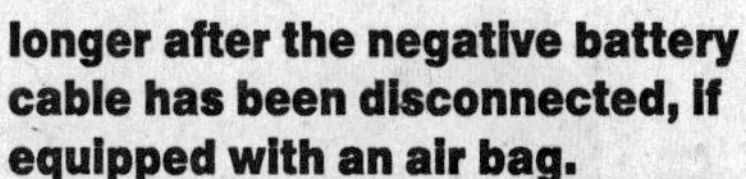

longer after the negative battery cable has been disconnected, if equipped with an air bag.

3. Disconnect the cold start injector connector or fuel filter inlet line.

4. Position a small plastic container or shop towel under the cold start injector pipe.

5. Remove the two union bolts, four gaskets and cold start injector pipe.

➡ **Loosen the union bolts slowly.**

6. Connect a suitable pressure gauge (SST No. 09628-45012 or equivalent) to the delivery pipe with two new gaskets and the union bolt. Torque the union bolt to 13 ft. lbs.

7. Thoroughly wipe up any fuel that may have spilled.

8. Connect the negative battery cable.

9. Remove the rubber cap from the fuel EFI check connector and short both the +**B** and **FP** terminals using a jumper wire.

10. Turn the ignition switch to the **ON** position.

11. Measure the fuel pressure on the gauge. On 1983–86 vehicles normal fuel pump pressure is 33–38 psi and on 1987–92 vehicles, 38–44 psi. If the fuel pressure exceeds the maximum limit, replace the fuel pressure regulator. If the pressure is below the minimum limit, check the following components:

a. fuel hose and connections.

b. Fuel pump.

c. Fuel filter.

d. Fuel pressure regulator.

12. Remove the jumper wire.

13. Start the engine.

14. Disconnect the vacuum hose from the fuel pressure regulator and plug the end of the hose.

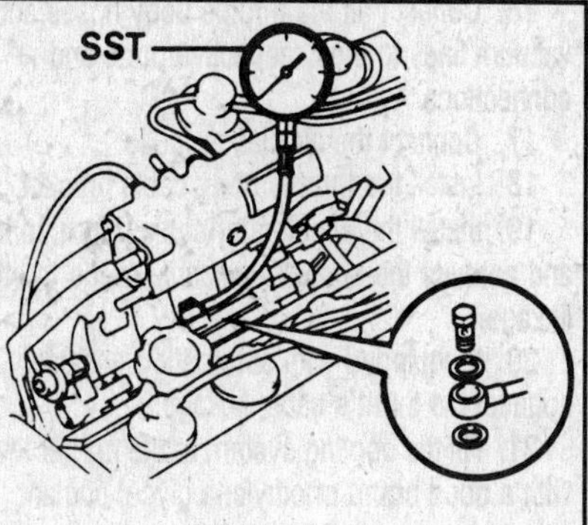

FIG. 4. Connecting the fuel pressure gauge to the fuel delivery pipe

15. Measure the fuel pressure at idle. On 1983–86 vehicles normal fuel pump pressure is 33–38 psi and on 1987–92 vehicles, 38–44 psi.

16. Unplug and reconnect the vacuum hose to the pressure regulator.

17. Measure the fuel pressure at idle again. On 1983–86 vehicles the pressure should be 27–31 psi and for 1987–92 vehicles, 31–37 psi.

18. If the pressure is not as specified, check the vacuum hose and pressure regulator.

19. Stop the engine and check that the fuel pressure remains at 21 psi or more for five minutes after the engine is turned off. If the fuel pressure is not as specified, check the fuel pump, pressure regulator and/or injectors.

20. Disconnect the negative battery cable and disconnect the test gauge carefully to prevent fuel spillage.

21. Install the cold start injector or filter pipe with new gaskets and the two new union bolts. Torque the bolts to 13 ft. lbs.

22. Connect the cold start injector connector.

23. Connect the negative battery cable.

24. Start the engine and check for leaks.

Throttle Body

➧ SEE FIG. 6–8

REMOVAL & INSTALLATION

2.0L (2S-E) Engine

1. On 1986 vehicles, drain the cooling system.

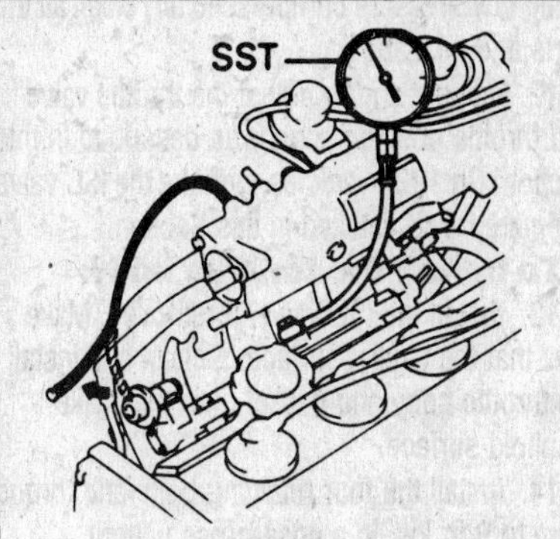

FIG. 5 Disconnect and plug the vacuum hose at the pressure regulator

CAUTION

When draining the coolant, keep in mind that cats and dogs are attracted by the ethylene glycol antifreeze, and are quite likely to drink any that is left in an uncovered container or in puddles on the ground. This will prove fatal in sufficient quantity. Always drain the coolant into a sealable container. Coolant should be reused unless it is contaminated or several years old.

2. On vehicles equipped with automatic transaxle, disconnect the throttle cable from the throttle linkage.

3. Disconnect the accelerator cable from the throttle linkage and remove the accelerator cable return spring.

4. Remove the cable bracket from the throttle body.

5. Disconnect the air cleaner hose.

6. Disconnect and label the two water by-pass hoses, PCV throttle body hose, air inlet valve hose and all emission control vacuum hoses.

7. Disconnect the throttle position sensor connector.

8. Remove the four bolts that secure the throttle body to the intake manifold.

9. Lift the throttle body and throttle body gasket from the intake manifold and remove from the vehicle.

10. Cover the intake manifold opening with masking tape to prevent the entry of foreign matter. Purchase a new gasket.

11. Using a soft bristle brush and carburetor cleaner, clean all the throttle body cast parts.

Using low pressure compressed air, clean all the ports and passages.

12. Inspect and/or adjust the throttle valve and throttle position sensor as described in this Section. On 1987 vehicles, remove the ISC valve if required also detailed in this Section.

To install the throttle body:

13. Install the ISC valve, if removed. Make sure that the gasket surface is clean and install the throttle body and gasket onto the intake manifold surface.

14. Install the four retaining bolts and torque them to 9 ft. lbs. in a criss-cross pattern.

15. Connect the throttle position sensor connector.

16. Connect all the throttle body hoses and vacuum lines to their respective ports and connections.

17. Connect the air cleaner hose.

18. Install the throttle body cable bracket.

19. Install the accelerator cable return spring and connect the accelerator cable to the throttle linkage.

20. If equipped with automatic transaxle, connect the throttle cable linkage.

21. Fill the cooling system to the proper level with a good brand of ethylene glycol coolant.

2.0L (3S-FE) Engine

1. Drain the cooling system.

FIG. 8. Removal and installation of throttle body retaining bolts

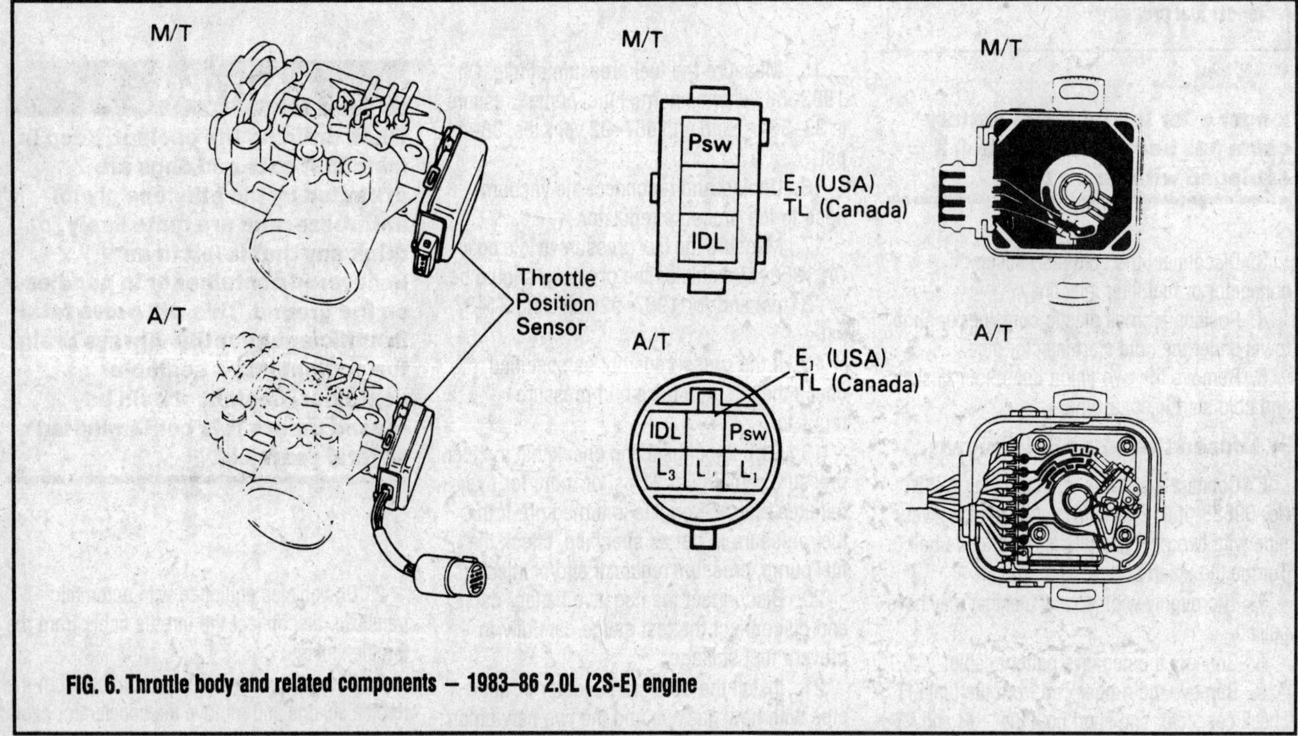

FIG. 6. Throttle body and related components – 1983–86 2.0L (2S-E) engine

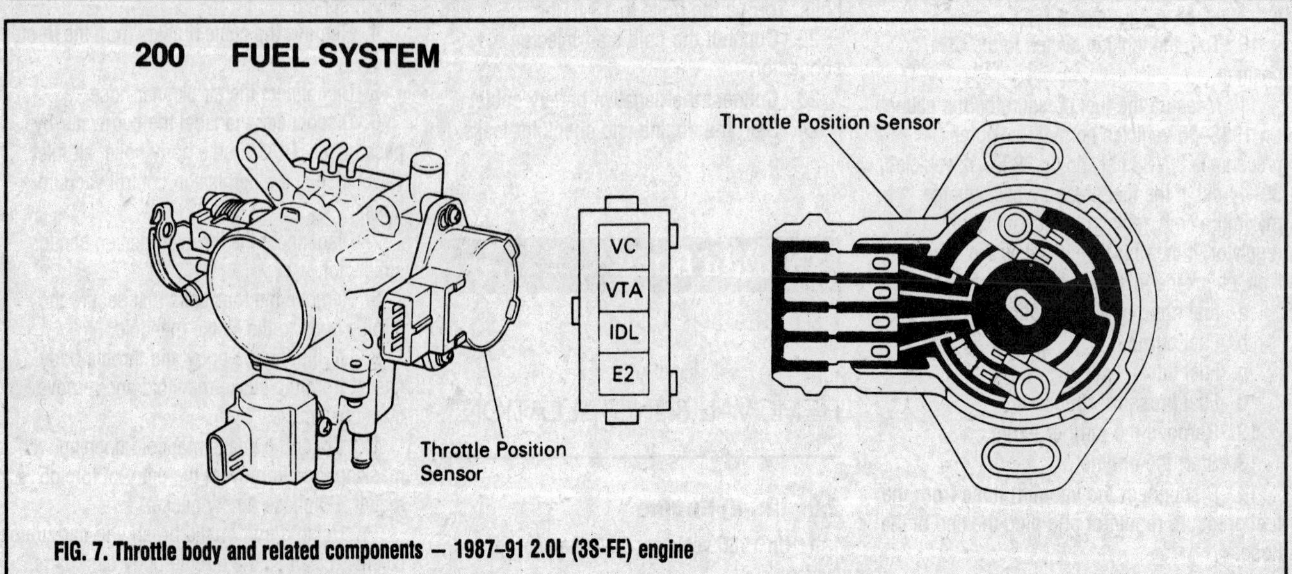

FIG. 7. Throttle body and related components – 1987–91 2.0L (3S-FE) engine

CAUTION

When draining the coolant, keep in mind that cats and dogs are attracted by the ethylene glycol antifreeze, and are quite likely to drink any that is left in an uncovered container or in puddles on the ground. This will prove fatal in sufficient quantity. Always drain the coolant into a sealable container. Coolant should be reused unless it is contaminated or several years old.

2. On vehicles equipped with automatic transaxle, disconnect the throttle cable from the throttle linkage.
3. Disconnect the accelerator cable from the throttle linkage.
4. Disconnect the air cleaner hose.
5. Disconnect the throttle position sensor connector.
6. Disconnect the idle speed control (ISC) control valve connector.
7. Disconnect and label the two water by-pass hoses, PCV throttle body hose, air inlet valve hose and all emission control vacuum hoses.
8. Remove the four bolts that secure the throttle body to the intake manifold.
9. Lift the throttle body and throttle body gasket from the intake manifold and remove it from the vehicle.
10. Cover the intake manifold opening with masking tape to prevent the entry of foreign matter. Purchase a new gasket.
11. Using a soft bristle brush and carburetor cleaner, clean all the throttle body cast parts. Using low pressure compressed air, clean all the ports and passages.
12. Inspect and/or adjust the throttle valve and throttle position sensor as described in Section 4. Remove the ISC valve, if required.

To install the throttle body:

13. Install the ISC valve, if removed.
14. Make sure that the gasket surface is clean and install the throttle body and gasket onto the intake manifold.
15. Install the four retaining bolts and torque them to 14 ft. lbs.
16. Connect all the throttle body hoses and vacuum lines to their respective ports and connections.
17. Connect the ISC valve and throttle position sensor connectors.
18. Connect the air cleaner hose.
19. If equipped with automatic transaxle, connect the throttle cable and adjust it.
20. Connect the accelerator cable and adjust it.
21. Fill the cooling system to the proper level with a good brand of ethylene glycol coolant.

2.2L (5S-FE) Engine

1. Disconnect the negative battery cable. Wait 30 seconds before performing any work, if equipped with an air bag.
2. Drain the engine coolant.
3. Disconnect the accelerator cable from the throttle linkage. If equipped with automatic transmission, disconnect the throttle cable from the linkage.
4. Remove the air cleaner cap and hose.
5. Disconnect the throttle position sensor and ISC valve wiring connectors.
6. Label and disconnect the PCV and vacuum hoses from the throttle body.
7. Remove the retaining bolts holding the throttle body; remove the throttle body and its gasket.
8. Remove the coolant by-pass hoses and air hose after the throttle body is partially removed.
9. Clean the cast parts of the throttle body using a bristle brush and carburetor cleaner. Do not expose the throttle position sensor or other external components to the solvent. Use compressed air to clean and dry all passages in the throttle body.
10. If the throttle position sensor is to be replaced:
    a. Remove the mounting screws and remove the sensor.
    b. Make certain the throttle plate is fully closed. Place the sensor onto the throttle body so that the electrical connector is positioned properly.
    c. Temporarily install the retaining screws for the sensor.
    d. Adjust the throttle position sensor.

To install:

11. Connect the coolant by-pass hoses and the air hose to the throttle body before installation.
12. Place a new gasket on the intake manifold. The gasket is correctly installed in only one position: the protrusion or bulge in the gasket must face downward. Install the throttle body, tightening the retaining nuts and bolts to 14 ft. lbs. (19 Nm).

➡ The bolts must be installed correctly; the upper bolts are shorter than the lowers.

13. Connect the PCV and vacuum hoses to the throttle body.
14. Attach the wiring connectors to the throttle position sensor and ISC valve.
15. Install the air cleaner cap and hose assembly.
16. Install and adjust the throttle cable and/or accelerator cable.
17. Refill the engine coolant.

2.5L (2VZ-FE) Engine

1. Drain the coolant from the throttle body.
2. If equipped with automatic transmission, disconnect the throttle cable.
3. Disconnect the accelerator cable.
4. Remove the air flow meter, air cleaner cap and air intake hose as an assembly. Label and disconnect the air and vacuum hoses before removal.
5. Disconnect the throttle position sensor wiring connector.
6. Disconnect the PCV, coolant by-pass and emission hoses from the throttle body. If equipped with automatic transmission, remove the throttle cable bracket.
7. Remove the nuts and bolts holding the throttle body; remove the throttle body and the gasket.
8. Clean the cast parts of the throttle body using a bristle brush and carburetor cleaner. Do not expose the throttle position sensor to the solvent. Use compressed air to clean and dry all passages in the throttle body.
9. If the throttle position sensor is to be replaced:
    a. Remove the mounting screws and remove the sensor.
    b. Make certain the throttle plate is fully closed. Place the sensor onto the throttle body.
    c. Temporarily install the retaining screws for the sensor.
    d. Adjust the throttle position sensor.

To install:

10. Place a new gasket on the intake manifold. Install the throttle body, tightening the retaining nuts and bolts to 9 ft. lbs. (13 Nm).
11. Install the throttle cable bracket if it was removed; tighten the bolts to 9 ft. lbs. (13 Nm).
12. Connect the PCV, coolant by-pass and emission hoses to the throttle body.
13. Attach the wiring connector to the throttle position sensor.
14. Install the air cleaner cap, air flow meter and intake hose. Make sure the components are correctly seated and that all clips and retainers are secured.
15. Connect and adjust the accelerator cable. Connect the throttle cable if it was removed and adjust it.
16. Refill the engine coolant.
17. Connect the negative battery cable.

3.0L (3S-FE) Engine

1. Drain the coolant from the engine.
2. Disconnect the accelerator cable and, if equipped with automatic transmission, the throttle cable.
3. Disconnect the air cleaner hose.

4. Detach the wiring connector from the throttle position sensor and the ISC valve.

5. Disconnect the PCV hose, the coolant by-pass hoses, the air tube hose and the emission system vacuum hoses.

6. Remove the retaining bolts; remove the throttle body and gasket.

7. Clean the cast parts of the throttle body using a bristle brush and carburetor cleaner. Do not expose the throttle position sensor or other external components to the solvent. Use compressed air to clean and dry all passages in the throttle body.

8. If the throttle position sensor is to be replaced:

a. Remove the mounting screws and remove the sensor.

b. Make certain the throttle plate is fully closed. With the throttle body held in its normal orientation, place the sensor onto the throttle body so that the electrical connector is in the correct position.

c. Temporarily install the retaining screws for the sensor.

d. Adjust the throttle position sensor.

To Install:

9. Using a new gasket, install the throttle

Throttle Body
ISC Valve
◆ Gasket
◆ Non-reusable part

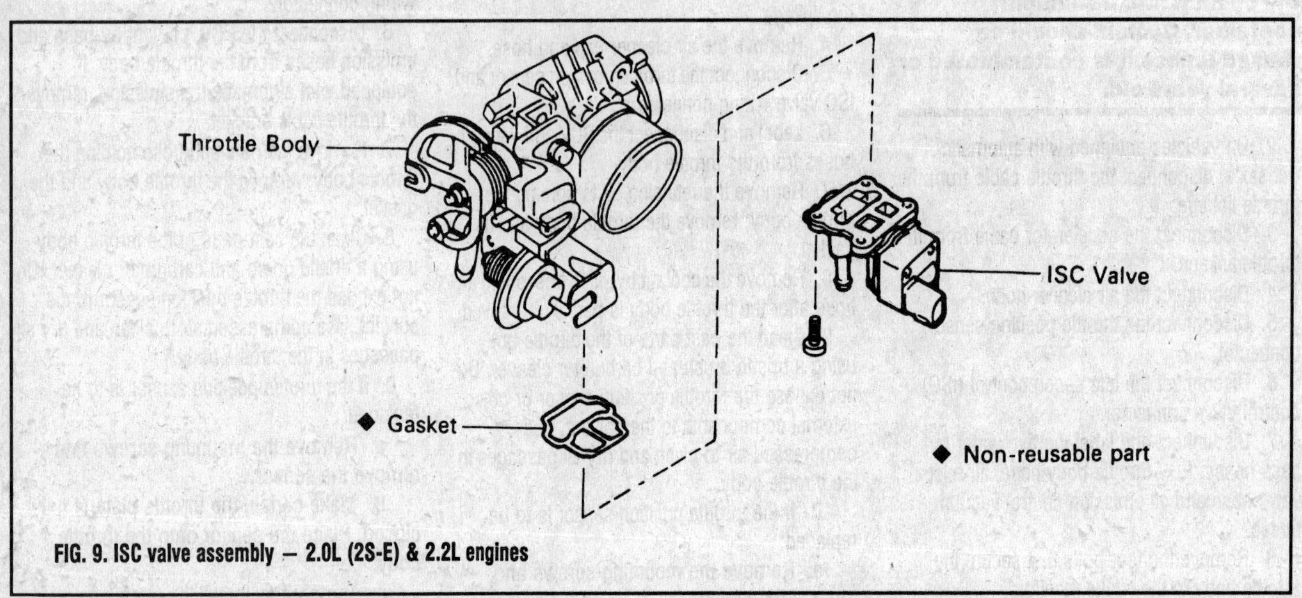

FIG. 9. ISC valve assembly – 2.0L (2S-E) & 2.2L engines

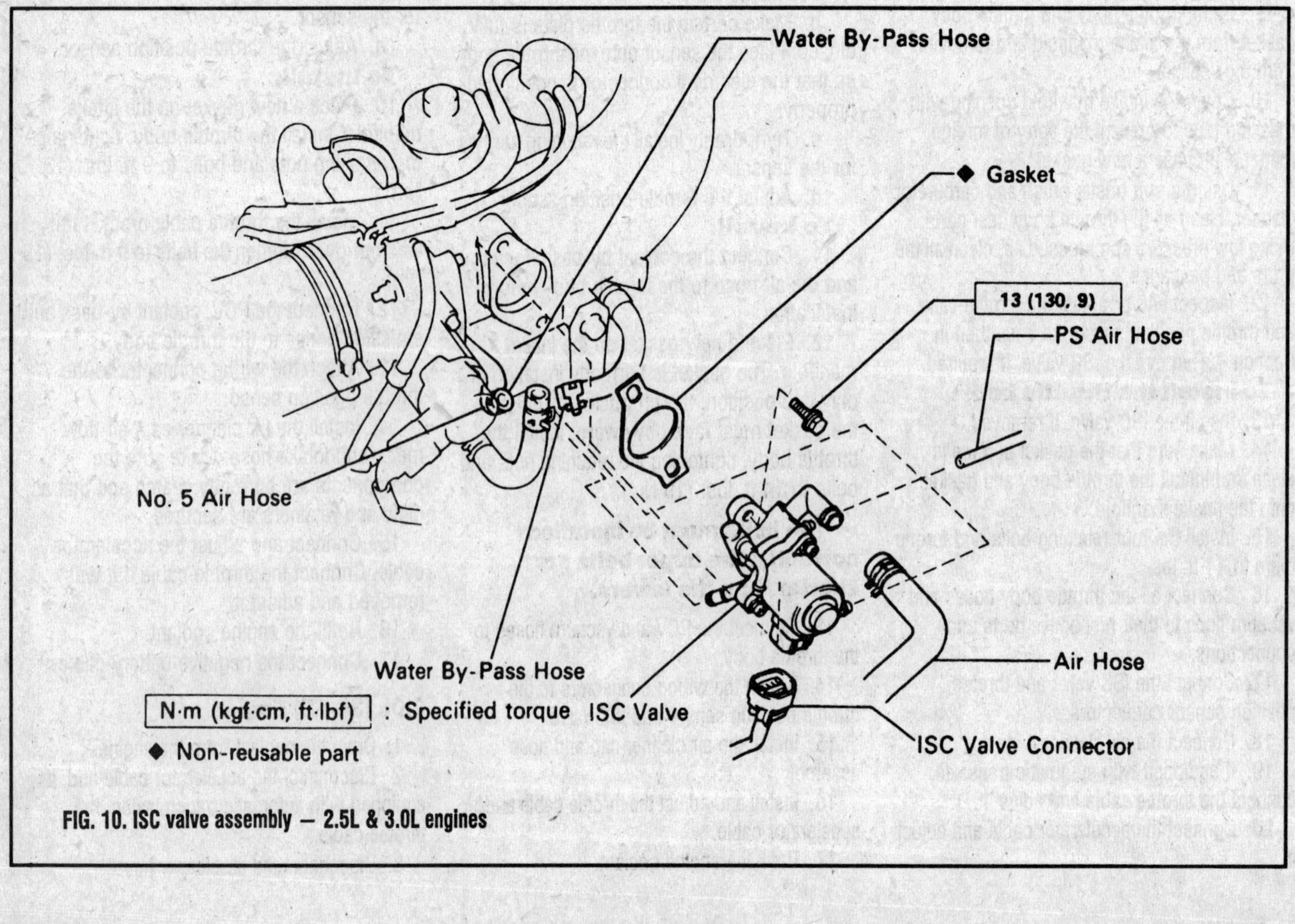

Water By-Pass Hose
◆ Gasket
13 (130, 9)
PS Air Hose
No. 5 Air Hose
Air Hose
Water By-Pass Hose
N·m (kgf·cm, ft·lbf) : Specified torque
ISC Valve
ISC Valve Connector
◆ Non-reusable part

FIG. 10. ISC valve assembly – 2.5L & 3.0L engines

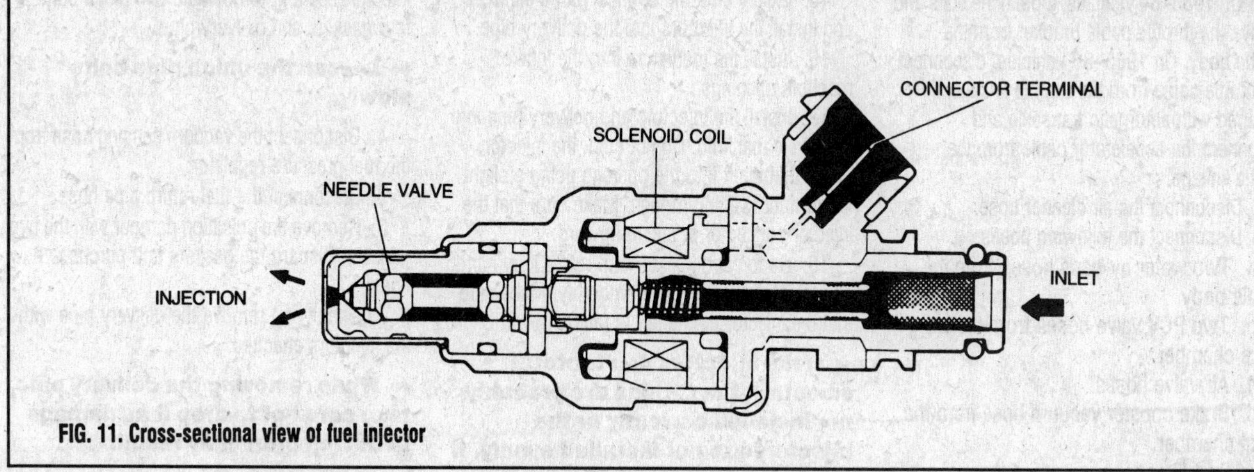

FIG. 11. Cross-sectional view of fuel injector

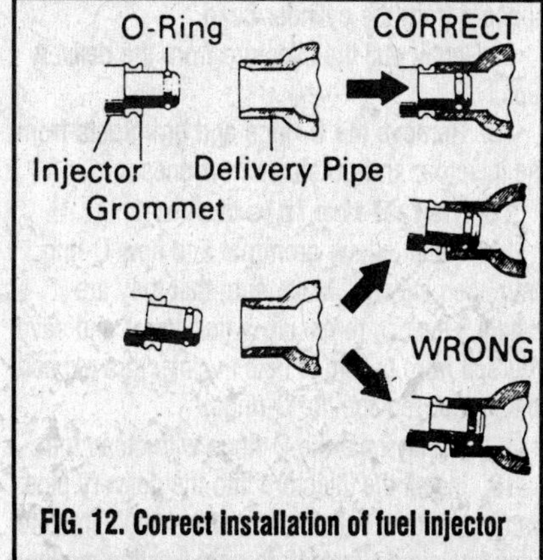

FIG. 12. Correct installation of fuel injector

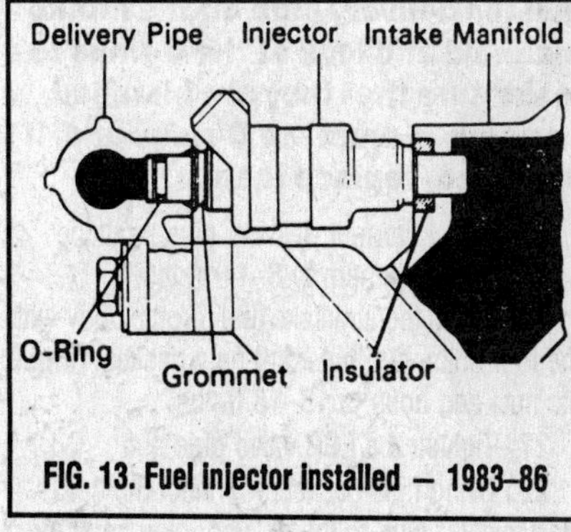

FIG. 13. Fuel injector installed — 1983–86

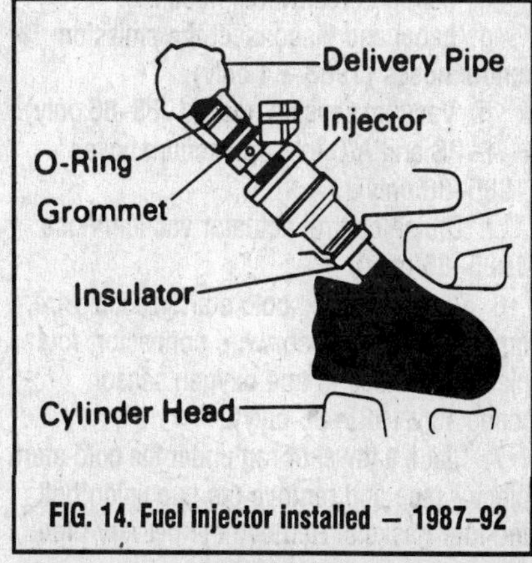

FIG. 14. Fuel injector installed — 1987–92

body and tighten the mounting bolts to 14 ft. lbs. (19 Nm).

10. Connect the vacuum hoses, the air tube hose, the coolant by-pass hoses, and the PCV hose.

11. Attach the wiring connectors to the throttle position sensor and ISC valve.

12. Install the air cleaner intake hose.

13. Install and adjust the throttle cable if it was disconnected. Install and adjust the accelerator cable.

14. Refill the coolant.

ISC VALVE REPLACEMENT

2.0L (3S-FE) and 2.2L Engine

➧ SEE FIG. 9

1. Remove the throttle body from the vehicle.

2. Remove the four screws that attach the idle speed control (ISC) valve to the throttle body.

3. Lift the ISC valve from the throttle body and remove the gasket.

4. Discard the gasket and purchase a new one.

5. Place the new gasket onto the throttle body.

6. Install the ISC valve onto the throttle body and install the four screws.

7. Install the throttle body into the vehicle.

8. Inspect the throttle linkage for freedom of movement.

2.5L and 3.0L ENGINE

➧ SEE FIG. 10

1. Drain the engine coolant.

2. Disconnect the ISC connector.

3. Disconnect the air, vacuum and coolant by-pass hoses.

4. Free the wire harness from the clamp; remove the retaining bolts and remove the valve with the gasket.

5. Install a new gasket. Install the valve and tighten the retaining bolts to 9 ft. lbs. (13 Nm).

6. Install the coolant by-pass hoses, the air or vacuum hoses and connect the wiring harness to the valve.

7. Refill the engine coolant.

Fuel Injectors

➧ SEE FIG. 11–14

REMOVAL & INSTALLATION

2.0L (2S-E) Engine

1. Disconnect the negative battery cable.

2. On 1985–86 vehicles, drain the cooling system.

⁂ CAUTION

When draining the coolant, keep in mind that cats and dogs are attracted by the ethylene glycol antifreeze, and are quite likely to drink any that is left in an uncovered container or in puddles on the ground. This will prove fatal in sufficient quantity. Always drain the coolant into a sealable container. Coolant should be reused unless it is contaminated or several years old.

3. On 1983–84 vehicles, loosen the bolts and remove the throttle cable bracket from the throttle body. On 1985–86 vehicles, disconnect the throttle cable from the throttle linkage, if equipped with automatic transaxle and disconnect the accelerator cable from the throttle linkage.

4. Disconnect the air cleaner hose.

5. Disconnect the following hoses:

a. Two water by-pass hoses from the throttle body.

b. Two PCV valve hoses from the air intake chamber.

c. Air valve hoses.

d. Brake booster vacuum hose from the intake chamber.

e. Fuel filter hose.

f. Main and return fuel hoses.

g. Label and disconnect the emission control hoses (1983–84 only).

h. Vacuum sensing hose (1985–86 only).

i. PS and A/C idle-up vacuum hoses (1985–86 only).

j. Cruise control actuator vacuum hose (1985–86 only).

6. Disconnect the cold start injector wire, throttle position sensor wire connector, four injector connectors and oxygen sensor connector (1985–86 only).

7. Place a towel or rag under the cold start injector pipe and remove the two union bolts and four gaskets. Remove the delivery pipe.

➡ Loosen the union pipe bolts slowly.

8. Loosen the EGR valve pipe nut.

9. Remove the two nuts and four bolts and remove the air intake chamber and throttle body. Remove the gasket and purchase a new one.

10. Unbolt and remove the delivery pipe with the injectors attached.

➡ When removing the delivery pipe, take care not to drop it as damage to the injectors may result. Also, do not remove the injector cover.

11. Remove the four insulators from the openings in the intake manifold.

12. Gently pull the injectors from the delivery pipe.

13. Remove the O-rings and grommets from the injectors and purchase new ones.

To install the injectors:

14. Install a new grommet and new O-ring onto each injector.

➡ Make sure that they are installed evenly to ensure a good seat and save yourself from having to take the injectors out and readjust or replace the O-rings.

15. Lightly coat the O-rings with clean fuel and install the injectors into the delivery pipe.

16. Install the insulators into the intake manifold openings.

17. Install the injectors and delivery pipe into the intake manifold. Do not cock the injector, install it straight into the opening using a slight left to right twisting motion. Make sure that the injector connector is facing upward.

18. Go to each injector and rotate it by hand. The injector should rotate smoothly. Make sure that the injector connector is facing upward.

➡ If the injectors don't rotate smoothly, the O-rings are probably not installed correctly or the injectors are not installed evenly. If this is the case, you will have the pull the delivery pipe off the intake manifold and look at the O-rings to make sure that they are installed correctly. Adjust the O-rings and, if damaged, replace them.

19. Install the four delivery pipe retaining bolts and torque them to 8–11 ft. lbs.

20. Install the air intake and throttle body with the four bolts, two nuts and new gasket. Torque the nuts and bolts to 15–18 ft. lbs.

21. Tighten the EGR valve pipe nut.

22. Using new gaskets, connect the cold start injector pipe to the delivery pipe and cold start injector. Torque the union bolts to 11–15 ft. lbs.

23. Connect the wires, wiring connectors and hoses.

24. Connect the air cleaner hose.

25. Install the throttle cable bracket to the throttle body. On 1985–86 vehicles, connect the accelerator (automatic transaxle) and throttle cables.

26. On 1985–86 vehicles, refill the cooling system with a good brand of ethylene glycol coolant to the proper level.

27. Connect the negative battery cable.

28. Turn the ignition switch to the On position. DO NOT start the engine.

29. On 1983–84 vehicles, short both terminals of the fuel pump check connector with a jumper wire. On 1985–86 vehicles, short the **+B** and **Fp** terminals of the engine check connector.

30. Check all fuel connections for leaks using the tip of your finger. Correct all fuel leaks immediately.

31. Remove the jumper wire.

2.0L (3S-FE) Engine

1. Disconnect the negative battery cable.

2. Disconnect the connector from the cold start injector.

3. Place a towel or rag under the cold start injector pipe and remove the two union bolts, four gaskets and delivery pipe.

➡ Loosen the union pipe bolts slowly.

4. Disconnect the vacuum sensing hose from the fuel pressure regulator.

5. Disconnect the fuel return pipe hose.

6. Remove the pulsation damper with the two gaskets. Discard the gaskets and purchase new ones.

7. Unbolt and remove the delivery pipe with the injectors attached.

➡ When removing the delivery pipe, take care not to drop it as damage to the injectors may result.

8. Remove the four insulators and two spacers from the cylinder head.

9. Gently pull the injectors from the delivery pipe.

10. Remove the O-rings and grommets from the injectors and purchase new ones.

To install the injectors:

11. Install a new grommet and new O-ring onto each injector. Make sure that they are installed evenly, to ensure a good seat and save yourself from having to take the injectors out and readjust or replace the O-rings.

12. Lightly coat the O-rings with clean fuel.

13. Install the injectors into the delivery pipe. Do not cock the injector, install it straight into the opening using a light left to right twisting motion.

14. Place the four insulators and two spacers on the cylinder head.

15. Install the injectors together with the delivery pipe onto the cylinder head.

16. Go to each injector and rotate it by hand. The injector should rotate smoothly.

➡ If the injectors don't rotate smoothly, the O-rings are probably not installed correctly or the injectors are not installed evenly. If this is the case, you will have the pull the delivery pipe off the intake manifold and look at the O-rings to make sure that they are installed correctly. Adjust the O-rings and, if damaged, replace them.

17. After the delivery pipe and injectors are properly in place, go to each injector and position the connector so that it is facing upward.

18. Install the two delivery pipe retaining bolts and torque them to 9 ft. lbs.

19. Install the pulsation damper with two new gaskets on both sides of the fuel hose "banjo" fitting. Tighten the damper.

20. Connect the fuel return hose.

21. Connect the injector connectors.

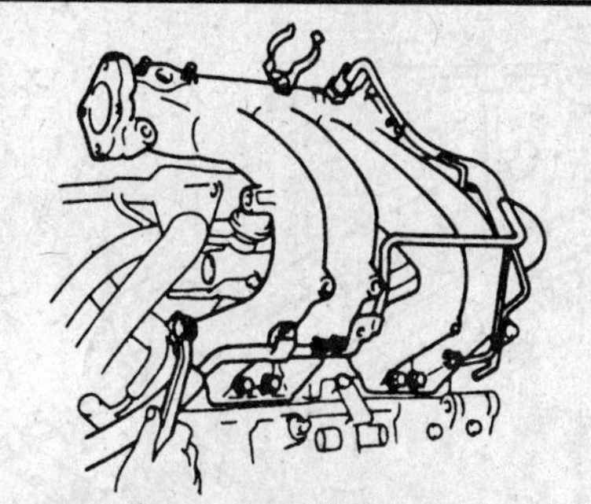
FIG. 15. Remove the intake manifold — 2.2L engine

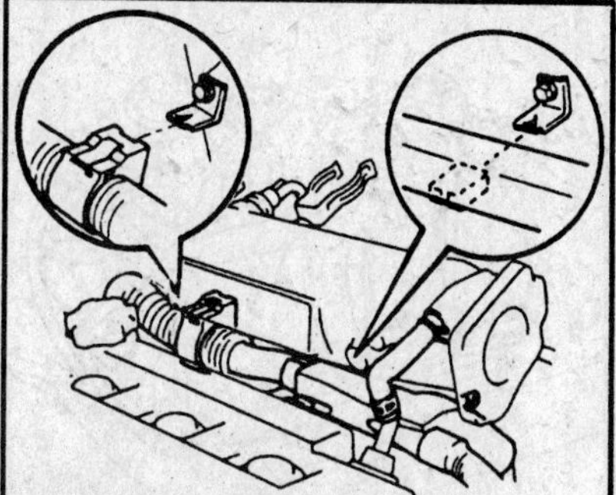
FIG. 16. Disconnect the wire harness clamps — 2.2L engine

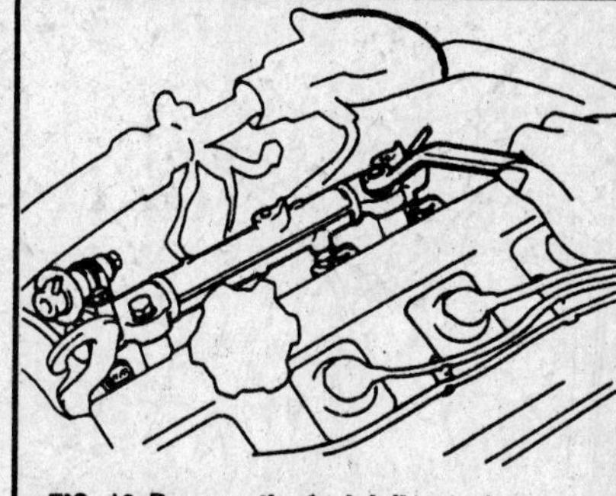
FIG. 18. Remove the fuel delivery pipe and injectors — 2.2L engine

22. Connect the vacuum sensing hose.

23. Using new gaskets, connect the cold start injector pipe to the delivery pipe and cold start injector. Torque the two union bolts to 13 ft. lbs.

23. Connect the cold start injector wiring connector.

24. Connect the negative battery cable.

25. Short the +**B** and **Fp** terminals of the engine check connector with a jumper wire.

26. While the connector is shorted, pinch the fuel return hose. When the pinched, this causes the pressure in the high pressure fuel line to rise to 57 psi. At this time any leaks in any part of the system should be apparent. Carefully look at each component for leakage and run the tip of your finger around each connection.

FIG. 17. Loosen the pulsation damper and disconnect the fuel inlet — 2.2L engine

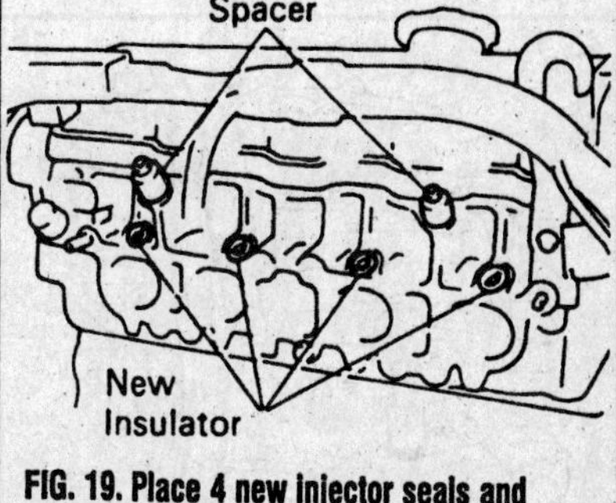

FIG. 19. Place 4 new injector seals and 2 spacers in position on cylinder head — 2.2L engine

2.2L (5S-FE) Engine

SEE FIG. 15–21

1. With the ignition in the **LOCK** position, disconnect the negative battery cable. On vehicles equipped with airbag systems, allow 30 seconds to pass before performing any other work.

2. Drain the engine coolant.

3. Disconnect the accelerator cable from the throttle body. If equipped with automatic transmission, disconnect the throttle cable.

4. Disconnect the air intake temperature sensor connector.

5. Disconnect the cruise control actuator cable from the clamp on the resonator.

6. Loosen the air cleaner hose clamp bolt. Disconnect the air cleaner hose from the throttle body. Release the air cleaner clips and remove the air cleaner cap with the resonator and air cleaner hose.

7. Disconnect the wiring to the throttle position sensor and the ISC valve.

8. Label and disconnect the hoses for the PCV, EGR vacuum modulator and EVAP VSV.

9. Remove the 4 bolts holding the throttle body. Label and disconnect the hoses from the throttle body.

10. Remove the throttle body with its gasket.

11. Disconnect the PS vacuum hoses.

12. Label and disconnect the hoses from the EVAP BVSV.

13. Remove the EGR valve and the vacuum modulator.

14. Disconnect the vacuum sensor hose at the air intake chamber, the brake booster vacuum hose and the vacuum sensing hose.

15. If equipped with air conditioning, disconnect the magnet switch VSV connector.

16. Disconnect the ground straps from the intake manifold.

17. Disconnect the knock sensor and EGR VSV connectors.

18. Free the engine wire harness by removing the bolt and wire clamp.

19. Remove the stays or supports holding the air intake chamber and the intake manifold.

20. Remove the intake manifold and remove the gasket.

21. Disconnect the wiring to each injector.

22. Loosen the pulsation damper and disconnect the fuel inlet pipe. Disconnect the fuel return hose.

23. Remove the retaining bolts; remove the delivery pipe or fuel rail along with the injectors. Do not drop any injectors during removal.

24. Remove the insulators and rail spacers from the head. Remove the injectors from the fuel rail.

25. Remove the O-ring and grommet from each injector.

To Install:

26. Install a new grommet on each injector. Apply a light coat of gasoline to new O-rings and install them on each injector.

27. Install the injectors into the fuel rail while turning each left and right. After installation, check that the injectors turn freely in place; if not, remove the injector and inspect the O-ring for damage or deformation.

28. Place new insulators and spacers on the head.

29. Install the fuel rail and injectors; check that the injectors still turn freely in position. Position the injector connectors upward.

30. Install the retaining bolts, tightening them to 9 ft. lbs. (13 Nm).

31. Connect the fuel return hose. Install the fuel inlet pipe and pulsation damper to the delivery pipe. Use new gaskets; tighten the union bolt to 25 ft. lbs. (34 Nm).

32. Connect the wiring to each injector.

33. Using a new gasket, install the intake manifold. Make certain all related wiring is in place before installation. Tighten the retaining

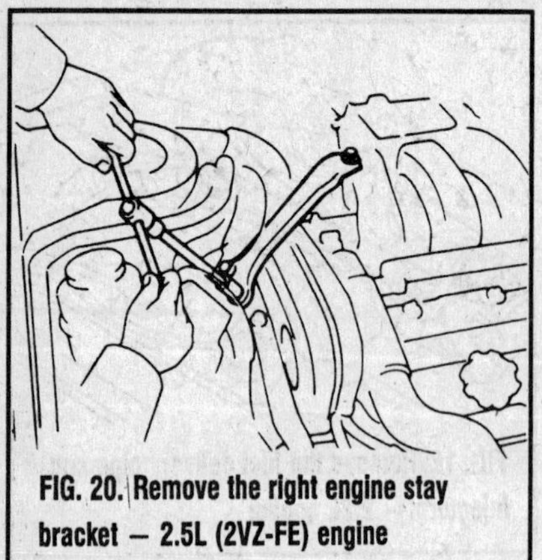

FIG. 20. Remove the right engine stay bracket — 2.5L (2VZ-FE) engine

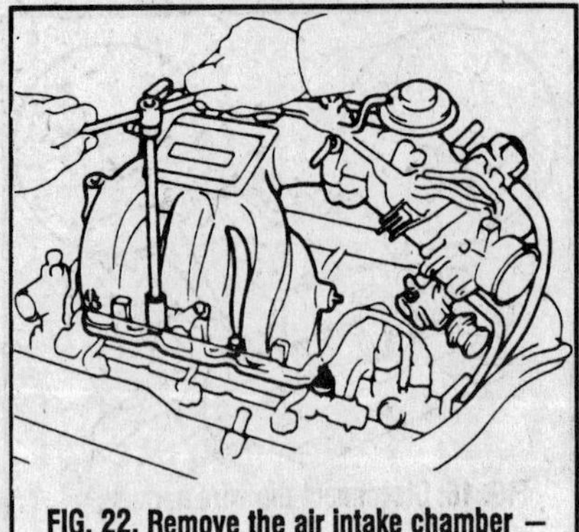

FIG. 22. Remove the air intake chamber — 2.5L (2VZ-FE) engine

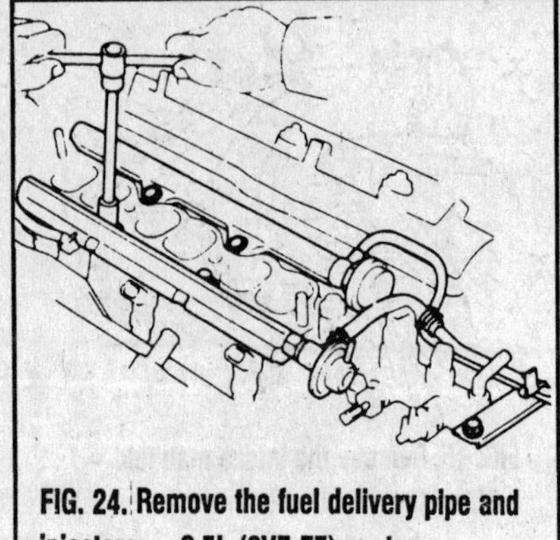

FIG. 24. Remove the fuel delivery pipe and injectors — 2.5L (2VZ-FE) engine

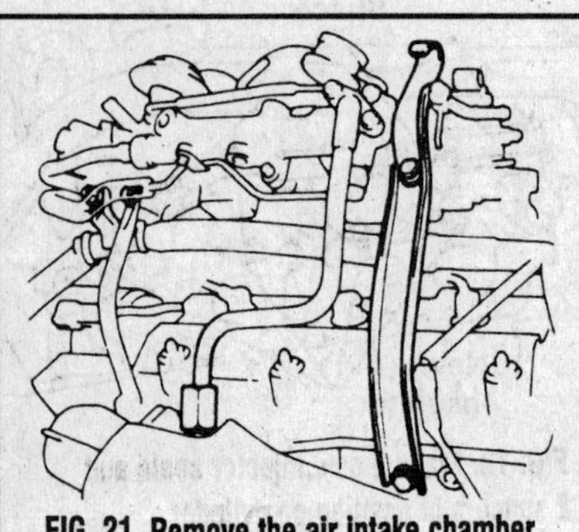

FIG. 21. Remove the air intake chamber stay bracket — 2.5L (2VZ-FE) engine

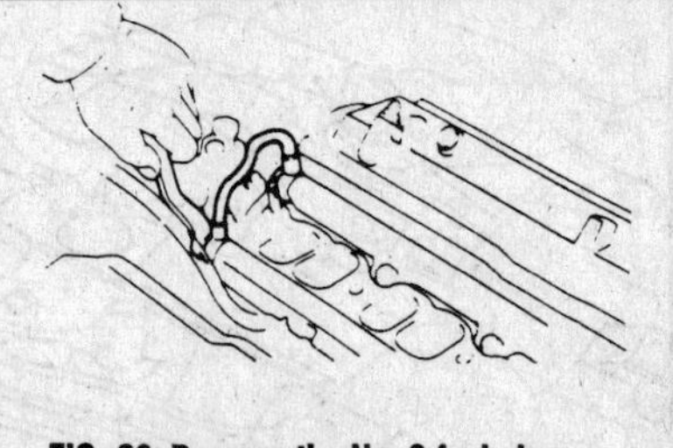

FIG. 23. Remove the No. 2 fuel pipe — 2.5L (2VZ-FE) engine

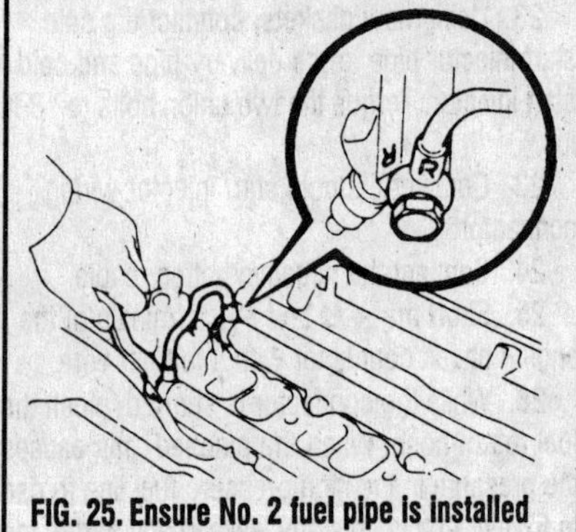

FIG. 25. Ensure No. 2 fuel pipe is installed properly — 2.5L (2VZ-FE) engine

nuts and bolts evenly in several passes to 14 ft. lbs (19 Nm).

34. Install the air chamber and manifold stays. Tighten the 14mm bolt to 31 ft. lbs. (42 Nm) and the 12mm bolt to 16 ft. lbs (22 Nm).

35. Position and secure the engine wire harness; tighten the clamp and bolt.

36. Connect the wiring to the knock sensor and the EGR VSV.

37. Connect both engine ground straps to the intake manifold.

38. Connect the A/C magnet switch wiring if it was removed.

39. Install the hoses for the vacuum sensor, brake booster and vacuum sensing hose.

40. Install the EGR valve and vacuum modulator. Use new gaskets. Tighten the union nut to 43 ft. lbs (59 Nm) and the bolt to 9 ft. lbs. (13 Nm).

41. Connect the hoses to the charcoal canister and EGR VSV; connect the wiring to the EGR temperature sensor if it was removed.

42. Connect the vacuum hoses to the EVAP BVSV. Install the 2 PS vacuum hoses.

43. Connect the air and coolant hoses to the throttle body. Install a new gasket, taking note of the correct gasket placement. Install the throttle body, tightening the bolts evenly and alternately to 14 ft. lbs. (19 Nm).

➡ The upper mounting bolts are shorter than the lower mounting bolts. Make certain the bolts are correctly placed before tightening.

44. Connect the PCV, EGR vacuum modulator and EGR VSV hoses to the throttle body. Connect the wiring for the throttle position sensor.

45. Install the air cleaner cap, resonator and intake hose.

46. Connect the wiring to the air intake temperature sensor; reinstall the cruise control actuator cable.

47. Reinstall and adjust the throttle control cable if it was removed. Connect the accelerator cable.

48. Refill the engine coolant.

49. Connect the negative battery terminal.

2.5L (2VZ-FE) Engine

➧ SEE FIG. 22–26

1. Disconnect the negative battery cable. On vehicles equipped with airbag systems, allow 30 seconds to pass before performing any other work.

2. Drain the engine coolant.

3. If equipped with automatic transmission, disconnect the throttle control cable from the throttle body and bracket. On all vehicles, disconnect the accelerator cable and bracket from the throttle body and air plenum or intake chamber.

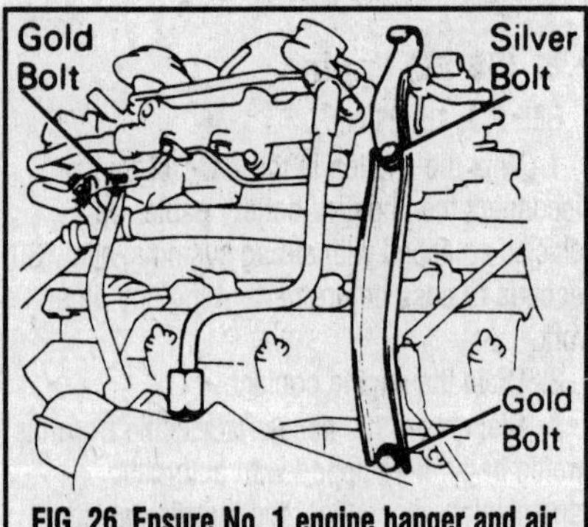

FIG. 26. Ensure No. 1 engine hanger and air intake chamber bracket are installed properly — 2.5L (2VZ-FE) engine

4. Disconnect the air flow meter connector and disconnect the air hoses. Loosen the clamp bolt and disconnect the cap clips; remove the air cleaner cover and the air flow meter with the air cleaner hose.

5. Label and disconnect the following hoses and electrical connectors: PCV hoses, vacuum sensing (MAP) hose, fuel pressure vacuum solenoid valve hose, emission system vacuum hoses, ISC connector, throttle position sensor and EGR temperature sensor if so equipped.

6. Remove the right upper engine stay.

7. Disconnect the cold start injector connector and fuel hose.

8. Label and disconnect the brake booster vacuum hose, PS vacuum hose and air hose, cruise control vacuum hose, wire harness clamp and fuel pressure vacuum solenoid valve hose.

9. Remove the wire harness clamp and free the wire harness. Disconnect the EGR tube.

10. Remove the 2 bolts holding the engine hanger. Disconnect and remove the air plenum stay from the air plenum.

11. Remove the air plenum or intake chamber with its gasket.

12. Disconnect the cold start injector connector, the coolant temperature sensor connector and the six injector connectors.

13. Disconnect the wire harness retaining clamps from the left side fuel rail.

14. Disconnect the fuel return hoses from the fuel pressure regulator and the No. 1 fuel rail. Disconnect the fuel inlet hose from the fuel filter.

15. Remove the No. 2 fuel line.

16. Remove the 2 bolts. Remove the left fuel rail together with the 3 injectors. Take great care not to drop an injector during removal.

17. Remove the 3 bolts, then remove the right fuel rail along with the injectors. Take great care not to drop an injector during removal.

18. Remove the injectors from the fuel rail. Remove the 6 insulators from the intake manifold and remove the spacers from the fuel rail mounting points.

To install:

19. Install a new grommet to each injector.

20. Lightly coat new O-rings with clean gasoline; install the O-rings on each injector.

21. Install the injectors into the fuel rails while turning the injector left and right. Once installed, the injector should turn freely. If any binding is felt, remove the injector and inspect the O-ring for crimping or damage.

22. Place the insulators and spacers in place on the manifold.

23. Install the right and left rail assemblies in position on the intake manifold. Again check that the injectors rotate freely. Turn the injector so the electrical connector faces upward.

24. Install the retaining bolts, tightening them to 9 ft. lbs. (13 Nm).

25. Install the No. 2 fuel pipe. The gaskets at the union bolts must be replaced. Tighten the fittings to 24 ft. lbs. (32 Nm).

26. Install the inlet hose to the fuel filter and connect the return hoses to the pressure regulator and No. 1 fuel line. The washers at the union bolts must be replaced with new ones.

27. Connect the wire harness clips to the left fuel rail.

28. Attach the wiring connectors to the injectors, the cold start injector and the coolant temperature sensor.

29. Install the air intake chamber, tightening the nuts and bolts to 32 ft. lbs. (43 Nm).

30. Connect the EGR tube. Tighten it to 58 ft. lbs. (78 Nm).

31. Connect the wire harness clamp.

32. Install the intake chamber support; install the No. 1 engine hanger. Tighten the mounting bolts for both to 27 ft. lbs. (37 Nm).

33. Install the wire harness clamp, brake booster vacuum hose, PS vacuum and air hoses, cruise control vacuum hose, ground strap connector and fuel pressure vacuum solenoid valve hose.

34. Connect the cold start injector hose.

35. Install the cold start injector wiring.

36. install the upper right engine stay, tightening the bolts to 38 ft. lbs. (52 Nm).

37. Install or connect the wiring or hoses to the ISC, throttle position sensor, EGR temperature sensor, PCV, vacuum components, fuel pressure VSV and coolant by-pass hoses.

38. With the air hose connected, install the air flow meter and air cleaner cover. Secure the 4 clips. Connect the air hoses and connect the wire harness to the air flow meter.

39. Reinstall the accelerator cable and bracket at the throttle body and the air plenum.

40. Install and adjust the throttle control cable if it was removed.

41. Refill the cooling system.

42. Connect the negative battery cable.

3.0L (3VZ-FE) Engine

➧ SEE FIG. 27

1. With the ignition switch in the LOCK position, disconnect the negative battery terminal. If vehicle is equipped with an airbag system, wait at least 30 seconds before performing any other work.

2. Drain the engine coolant.

3. Disconnect the accelerator cable from the throttle linkage.

4. If equipped with automatic transmission, disconnect the throttle cable from the throttle linkage.

5. Remove the air cleaner cap, air flow meter and the air cleaner hose as a unit.

6. Remove the two 5mm bolts holding the V-cover; remove the cover.

7. Disconnect the EGR temperature connector clamp from the set of emission control valves.

8. Label and remove the hoses from the fuel pressure control VSV. Disconnect the hoses from the IACV, disconnect the VSV wiring connectors and remove the emission control valve set.

9. Label and disconnect the brake booster vacuum hose, PS air hose, PCV hose and IACV vacuum hose.

10. Disconnect the two ground straps.

11. Remove the wiring connector from the cold start injector. Disconnect the fuel line from the cold start injector.

12. Remove the No. 1 engine hanger and the air intake chamber support.

13. Remove the EGR pipe.

14. Remove the bolt and disconnect the hydraulic pressure pipe from the air intake chamber.

15. Disconnect the 3 hoses at the air intake plenum, disconnect the two coolant by-pass hoses and disconnect the EGR temperature sensor connector if so equipped.

16. Disconnect the throttle position sensor connector. Detach the connector for the ISC valve and remove the air hoses from the ISC valve. Remove the PS air hose.

17. Remove the bolts and nuts holding the air plenum; remove the air plenum and gasket.

18. Disconnect the fuel return hoses from the No. 1 fuel pipe; then disconnect the fuel inlet hose from the filter.

19. Disconnect the wiring connectors from each injector.

20. Remove the No. 2 fuel pipe.

21. Remove the left delivery pipe or fuel rail; be careful not to drop the injectors during removal.

22. Remove the 3 injectors from the delivery pipe. Remove the rail spacers from the intake manifold.

23. Disconnect the two air hoses; remove the air pipe with the hoses attached.

24. Remove the right fuel rail and injectors. Take care not to drop an injector. Remove the injectors from the rail.

To install:

25. Install new grommets on each injector.

26. Apply a light coat of clean gasoline to new O-rings and install 2 on each injector.

27. Install each injector into the fuel rail while turning the injector left and right. Once installed, the injector should turn freely in the rail. If not, remove the injector and inspect the O-ring for damage or dislocation.

28. Place the rail spacers on the manifold. Clean the injector ports and install the right rail and injector assembly. Again check that the injectors turn freely in place.

29. Position the injector wiring connector upward. Install the bolts holding the delivery pipe and tighten them to 9 ft. lbs. (13 Nm).

30. Install the air pipe and hoses; tighten the retaining bolts only to 74 inch lbs. (8.3 Nm).

31. Repeat Steps 28 and 29 to install the left side delivery pipe and injectors.

32. Install the No. 2 fuel pipe connecting the two fuel rails. Use new gaskets at each union bolt. Tighten the union bolts to 25 ft. lbs. (34 Nm).

33. Connect the IACV vacuum hose.

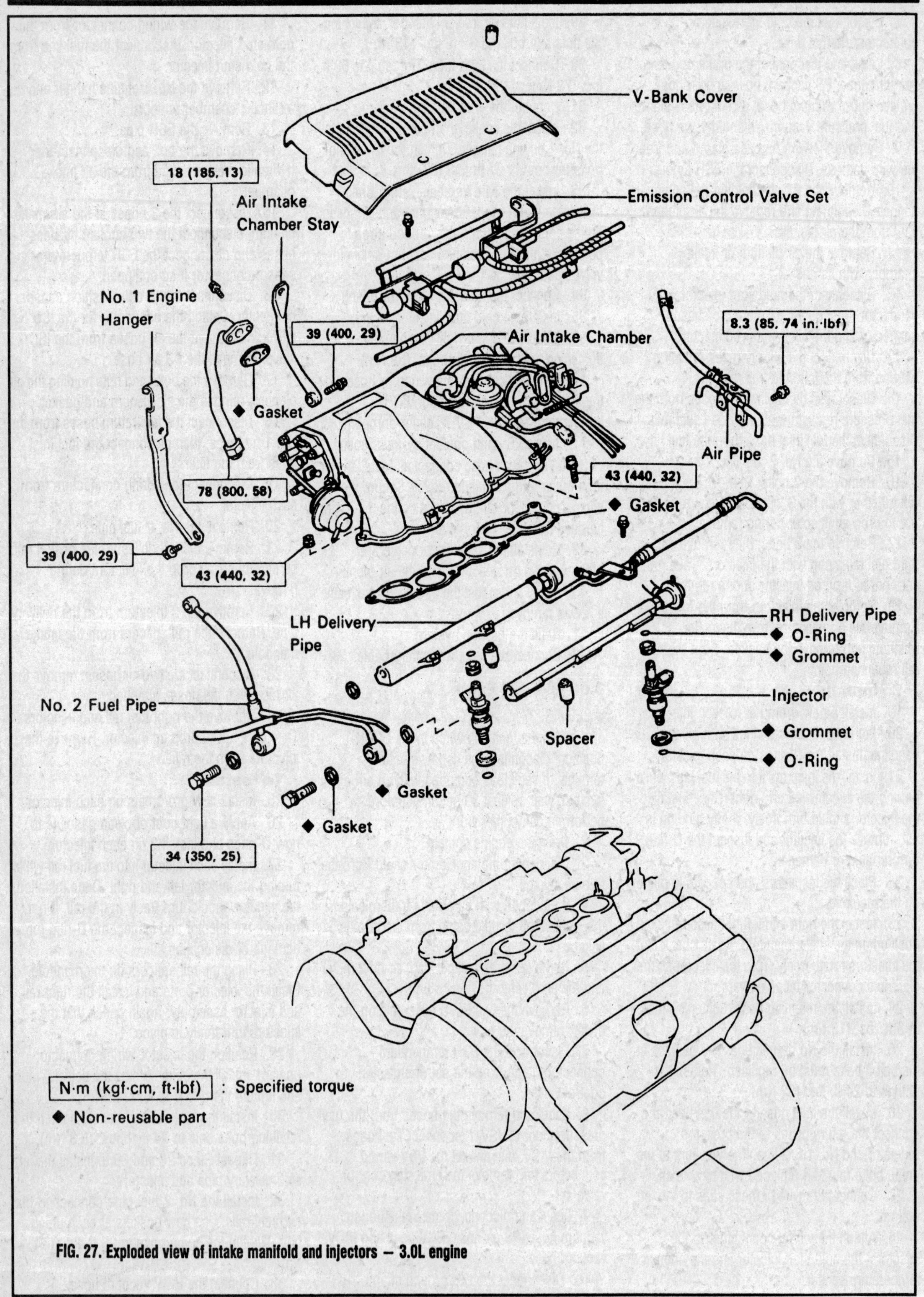

FIG. 27. Exploded view of intake manifold and injectors — 3.0L engine

34. Attach the wiring connectors to their proper injectors.

35. Install the inlet hose to the fuel filter using new gaskets; tighten the bolt to 22 ft. lbs. (29 Nm). Connect the return hose to the No. 1 fuel pipe.

36. Using a new gasket, install the air intake chamber. Tighten the mounting nuts to 32 ft. lbs (43 Nm).

37. Connect the throttle position sensor harness, ISC valve wiring, ISC air hose and PS air hose.

38. Connect the EGR temperature sensor wiring.

39. Install the coolant by-pass hose to the throttle body. Install the coolant by-pass hose to the EGR cooler.

40. Connect the vacuum hoses to the BVSV.

41. Attach the hydraulic pressure pipe to the air intake chamber.

42. Install the EGR pipe with a new gasket and new sleeve ball. Tighten the bolts to 13 ft. lbs (18 Nm) and the union nut to 58 ft. lbs (78 Nm).

43. Install the No. 1 engine hanger and the air intake chamber stay. Tighten the bolts to 29 ft. lbs. (39 Nm).

44. Connect the injector pipe with new gaskets to the cold start injector. Tighten the bolts to 11 ft. lbs (15 Nm). Attach the cold start injector wiring connector.

45. Connect the 2 ground straps.

46. Connect the brake booster vacuum hose, PS air hose, PCV hose and the IACV vacuum hose.

47. Install the emission valve set and tighten the bolts. Connect the VSV connectors and attach the 2 vacuum hoses to the IACV VSV. Install the two hoses to the fuel pressure VSV. Connect the EGR temperature sensor connector clamp to the valve set.

48. Install the V-bank cover on the engine.

49. Install the air cleaner cover, air flow meter and air hose as a unit. Make certain the clips are correctly engaged.

50. Connect and adjust the throttle control cable if it was removed.

51. Connect the accelerator cable and adjust it as needed.

52. Refill the engine coolant.

53. Connect the negative battery cable.

TESTING

On-Vehicle Inspection

CHECK INJECTOR OPERATION

➡ **This procedure requires the use of an engine stethoscope. If by chance a engine stethoscope is not available, you may use your finger.**

1. Start the engine.
2. Position the probe of the sound scope (or finger tip) under the base of the injector connector and have an assistant alternately increase the engine rpm and return it to idle.
3. Listen or feel for a change in the operating sound of the injector. The change should be proportional to the increase in engine rpm.
4. If no sound is heard or if the injector sound is unusual, check the connector and connector wiring, injector, resistor or the signal from the ECU.

CHECK INJECTOR RESISTANCE

Disconnect the connector from the injector. With an ohmmeter, measure the resistance between the injector terminals. The resistance should be approximately 1.5–3.0Ω for the 2.0L (2S-E) engine or 13.8Ω for all other engines. If the resistance is not as specified, replace the injector. Reconnect the injector connector.

Off-Vehicle Inspection

INJECTOR VOLUME TEST

CAUTION

To avoid personal injury, do not smoke or use any type of open flame when testing the injectors!

1. Remove the injector(s) from the vehicle and set aside.
2. Place a rag under the "banjo" fitting and, disconnect the fuel hose from the fuel filter outlet. Remove the gaskets and replace them with new ones.
3. Connect SST No. 09628-41045 to the fuel filter outlet connection with the new gaskets and tighten the union bolt.
4. Remove the fuel pressure regulator.
5. Connect the fuel return hose to the pressure regulator with the service union with a set of new gaskets and tighten the union bolt.
6. Install a new O-ring onto injector.
7. Connect the special service tool to the injector with the service union and clamp the union and the tool to the injector with the service clamp.
8. Connect a length of rubber or vinyl hose to the injector tip to prevent fuel splashing and overspray.
9. Place the injector into a graduated cylinder with metric increments and connect the negative battery cable.
10. Turn the ignition switch **ON**, but DO NOT start the engine.
11. With a jumper wire, short the +**B** and **FP** terminals of the check connector.
12. Connect SST No. 09842-30070 to the injector and the battery for 15 seconds.
13. Measure the volume injected into the cylinder during the 15 second period. The volume should be 3.3–3.9 cu. in. (54–64cc) for the 3.0L engine or 2.7–3.4 cu. in. (44–55cc) for all other engines. If all four injectors were tested, there should be no less than 0.3 cu. in. (5cc) difference between each injector.
14. If the actual volume does not agree with the specified volume, replace the injector.
15. Proceed to the "Check Leakage Rate" test.

CHECK LEAKAGE RATE

1. Leaving everything as it was from the injection test, disconnect the service tool test probes from the battery.
2. Check the injector tip for leakage for a period of one minute. An acceptable leakage rate is one drop.
3. If the leakage exceeds this amount, replace the injector.
4. Disconnect the negative battery cable and remove the all the test equipment.
5. Install the injector(s).

Fuel Pressure Regulator

REMOVAL & INSTALLATION

2.0L ENGINE

➧ SEE FIG. 28–29

1. Disconnect the negative battery cable. Disconnect the vacuum sensing hose at the regulator.
2. Disconnect the fuel return hose.
3. Remove the retaining bolts and remove the regulator.
4. Reinstall in reverse order. Tighten the 2 retaining bolts to 48 inch lbs. (5.4 Nm).
5. Connect the negative battery cable.

2.2L ENGINE

➧ SEE FIG. 30

1. Disconnect the negative battery cable. Disconnect the vacuum hose at the fuel pressure regulator.
2. Disconnect the fuel return pipe from the fuel pressure regulator.
3. Remove the retaining bolts and remove the fuel pressure regulator.

6. To install, replace the O-ring, coating the new one with clean gasoline.

7. Install the pressure regulator. Tighten the retaining bolts to 48 inch lbs. (5.4 Nm).

8. Connect the fuel return line to the regulator. Replace the gaskets; tighten the union bolt to 14 ft. lbs. (19 Nm).

9. Connect the vacuum hose and negative battery cable.

2.5L ENGINE

SEE FIG. 31

1. Disconnect the negative battery cable. Disconnect the vacuum sensing hose at the regulator.

2. Disconnect the fuel return hose.

3. Loosen the locknut and remove the fuel pressure regulator.

4. Before installation, fully loosen the locknut. Lightly coat a new O-ring with gasoline and install it on the regulator.

5. Press the regulator into the fuel delivery pipe by hand. Turn the pressure regulator so that the vacuum pipe is vertical.

6. Tighten the lock nut to 24 ft. lbs. (32 Nm).

7. Connect the fuel return hose and the vacuum hose. Connect the negative battery cable.

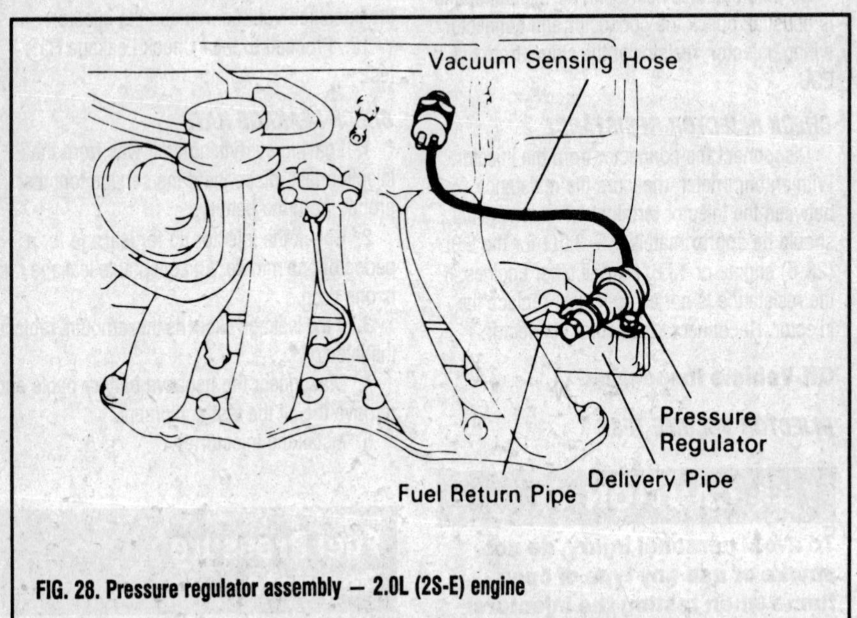

FIG. 28. Pressure regulator assembly — 2.0L (2S-E) engine

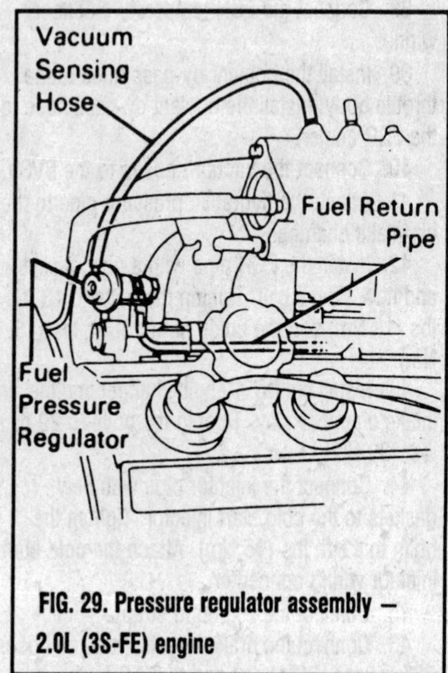

FIG. 29. Pressure regulator assembly — 2.0L (3S-FE) engine

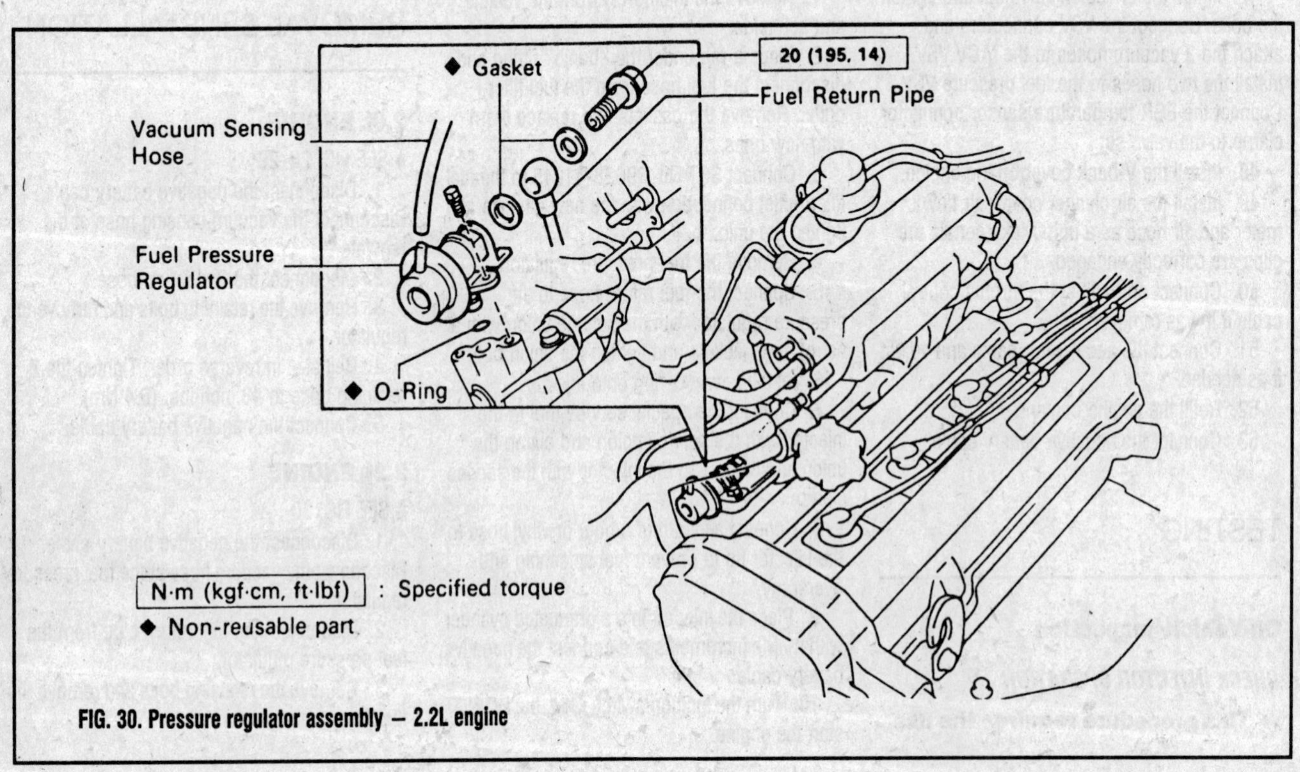

FIG. 30. Pressure regulator assembly — 2.2L engine

3.0L Engine

➧ SEE FIG. 32

1. Disconnect the negative battery cable. Remove the nuts holding the V-bank cover and remove the cover.
2. Disconnect the vacuum sensing hose and the fuel return hose from the pressure regulator.
3. Loosen the locknut and remove the pressure regulator.
4. Before installation, fully loosen the locknut. Lightly coat a new O-ring with gasoline and install it on the regulator.
5. Press the regulator into the fuel delivery pipe by hand. Turn the pressure regulator counterclockwise so that the fuel return pipe is pointing towards the air intake chamber and the vacuum port points straight up.
6. Tighten the locknut to 16 ft. lbs. (22 Nm).
7. Connect the fuel return hose. Install the vacuum hose.
8. Install the V-cover. Connect the negative battery cable.

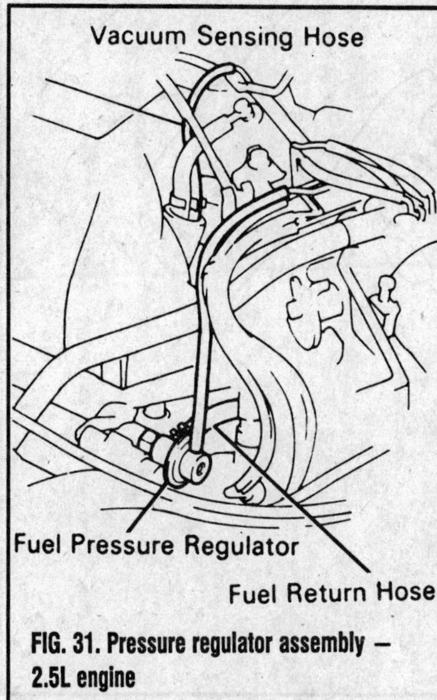

FIG. 31. Pressure regulator assembly — 2.5L engine

Throttle Position Sensor (TPS)

REMOVAL & INSTALLATION

1. Remove the mounting screws and remove the sensor.
2. Make certain the throttle plate is fully closed. With the throttle body held in its normal orientation, place the sensor onto the throttle body so that the electrical connector is in the correct position.
3. Temporarily install the retaining screws for the sensor.
4. Adjust the throttle position sensor.

Cold Start Injector

➧ SEE FIG. 33

The cold start injector is mounted in the intake air stream. Controlled by the ECU, it provides additional fuel during cold engine start-up. Its function is controlled by both a timer circuit and as a function of coolant temperature. The 2.2L engine is not equipped with a cold start injector.

REMOVAL & INSTALLATION

1. With the ignition **OFF**, disconnect the negative battery cable. For vehicles equipped with airbag systems, wait at least 30 seconds after disconnecting the battery before commencing any other work.

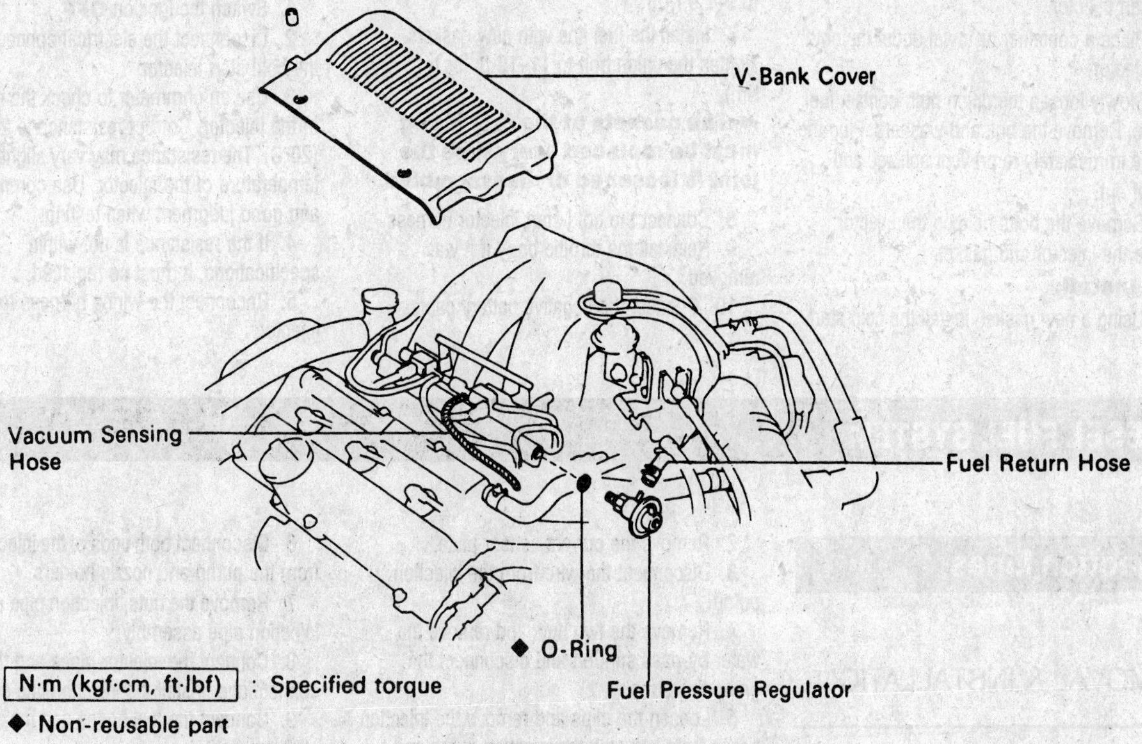

V-Bank Cover
Vacuum Sensing Hose
Fuel Return Hose
◆ O-Ring
Fuel Pressure Regulator
N·m (kgf·cm, ft·lbf) : Specified torque
◆ Non-reusable part

FIG. 32. Pressure regulator assembly — 3.0L engine

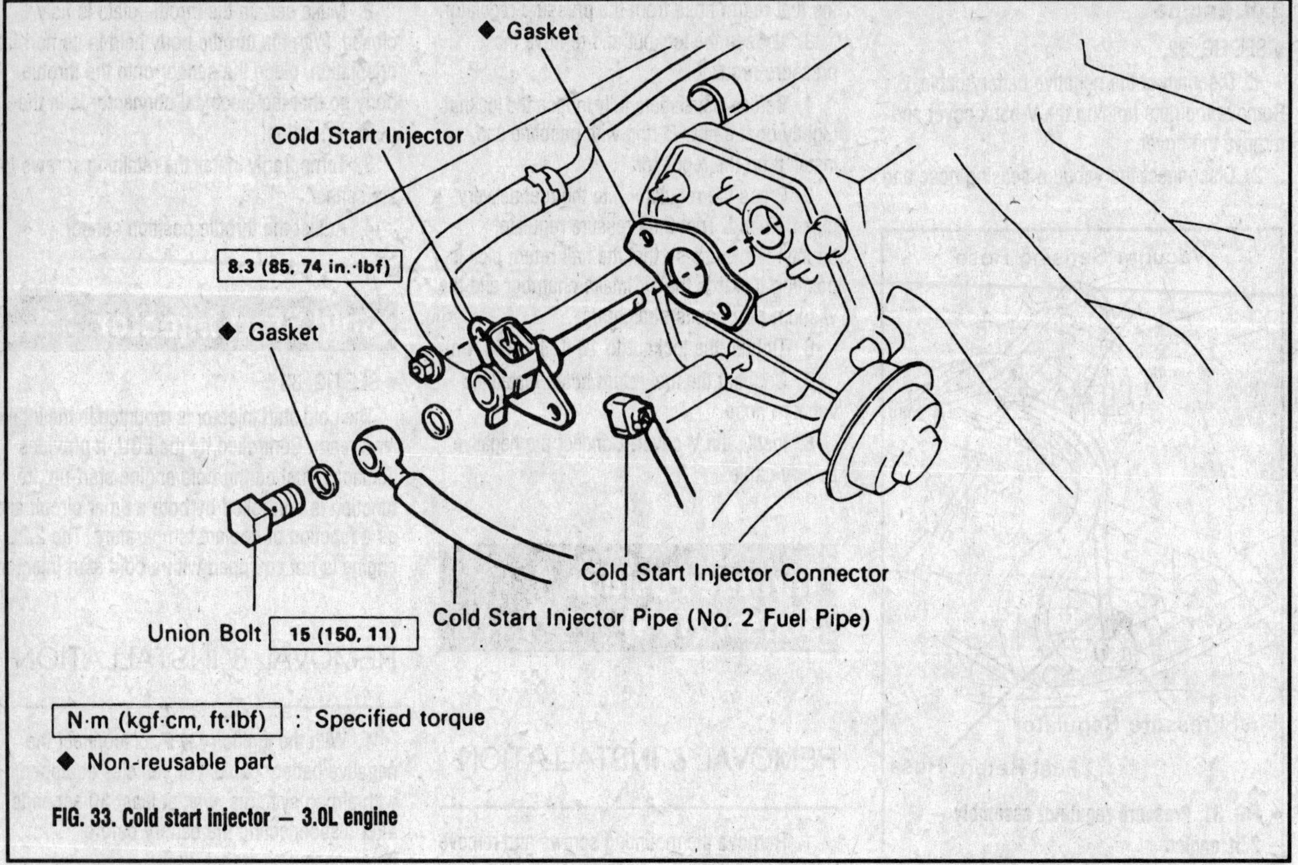

FIG. 33. Cold start injector — 3.0L engine

2. Disconnect the electrical harness from the cold start injector.

3. Place a container or towel under the cold start injector.

4. Slowly loosen the union bolt; contain fuel spillage. Remove the bolt and washers. Plug the fuel line immediately to prevent spillage and entry of dirt.

5. Remove the bolts holding the injector; remove the injector and gasket.

To install:

6. Using a new gasket, install the cold start injector. Tighten the bolts to 52–70 inch lbs. (5.9–7.9 Nm)

7. Install the fuel line with new gaskets. Tighten the union bolt to 11–15 ft. lbs. (15–20 Nm).

➡ The gaskets at the fuel fitting must be replaced every time the joint is loosened or disassembled.

8. Connect the cold start injector harness.

9. Reinstall the throttle body if it was removed.

10. Connect the negative battery cable.

Testing

1. Switch the ignition **OFF**.

2. Disconnect the electrical connector from the cold start injector

3. Use an ohmmeter to check the resistance of the injector. Correct resistance is 2–4Ω 68°F (20°C). The resistance may vary slightly with the temperature of the injector. Use common sense and good judgment when testing.

4. If the resistance is not within specifications, it must be replaced.

5. Reconnect the wiring harness to the injector.

DIESEL FUEL SYSTEM

Injection Lines

REMOVAL & INSTALLATION

1. Label and disconnect all the electronic vacuum regulating valve assembly pipe and hoses.

2. Remove the current sensor plate.

3. Disconnect the wire from the injection pump.

4. Remove the two nuts and remove the water by-pass support and disconnect the grounding strap.

5. Loosen the clips and remove the injection hoses from between the injection pump and pipe.

6. Disconnect both ends of the injection pipes from the pump and nozzle holders.

7. Remove the nuts, injection pipe clamp and injection pipe assembly.

8. Connect the injector pipes and tighten the connections. Install the injection line clamp.

9. Connect the fuel hoses and make sure the clips are tight.

10. Bleed the system by loosening the pipes

at the nozzles and cranking the engine until all air is expelled and fuel sprays.

11. Connect the ground strap and install the water by-pass support.
12. Connect the injection pump wire.
13. Install the current sensor plate.
14. Install the electronic vacuum regulating assembly, pipe and hoses.
15. Start the engine and inspect for leaks.

Injection Nozzle

SEE FIG. 34–35

REMOVAL & INSTALLATION

1. Label and disconnect all the electronic vacuum regulating valve assembly pipe and hoses.
2. Remove the current sensor plate.
3. Disconnect the wire from the injection pump.
4. Remove the two nuts and remove the water by-pass support and disconnect the grounding strap.
5. Loosen the clips and remove the injection hoses from between the injection pump and pipe.
6. Disconnect both ends of the injection pipes from the pump and nozzle holders.
7. Remove the nuts, injection pipe clamp and injection pipe assembly.
8. Disconnect the fuel hoses from the leakage pipes.
9. Remove the four nuts, leakage pipe and four washers.
10. Using SST No. 09268-64010 or equivalent, unscrew the injection nozzle holders and arrange them in order.
11. Remove the nozzle seats and gaskets. Discard these items and purchase new ones.

To install the injector nozzles:

12. Install new nozzle seats and gaskets onto the injectors.
13. Install the injector nozzle holders and torque them to 47 ft. lbs.

CAUTION

Follow the recommended torque value when tightening the injector nozzle holders. Over tightening the holders could cause nozzle deformation, needle binding, improper sealing and other problems.

14. Install the nozzle leakage pipe assembly onto the nozzle holder with the washers and four nuts. Torque the nuts to 22 ft. lbs.
15. Connect the fuel hose to the leakage pipe.
16. Connect the injector pipes and tighten the connections. Install the injection line clamp.
17. Connect the fuel hoses and make sure the clips are tight.
18. Bleed the system by loosening the pipes at the nozzles and cranking the engine until all air is expelled and fuel sprays.
19. Connect the ground strap and install the water by-pass support.
20. Connect the injection pump wire.
21. Install the current sensor plate.
22. Install the electronic vacuum regulating assembly, pipe and hoses.
23. Start the engine and inspect for leaks.

TESTING

Injection nozzle testing requires the use of an expensive diesel engine nozzle pressure tester, calibration fluid and also a reasonable familiarity with injection nozzle testing procedures. Normally, the purchase of such equipment is not made by the average DIYer. Injectors rely on close tolerances for proper fuel injection. Even the smallest speck of dirt caught between the injector nozzle and the nozzle body can lead to the failure of the injector. If you do have a set of injectors that need testing and/or opening pressure adjustment, the matter may be best handled by a qualified technician or an injector specialist.

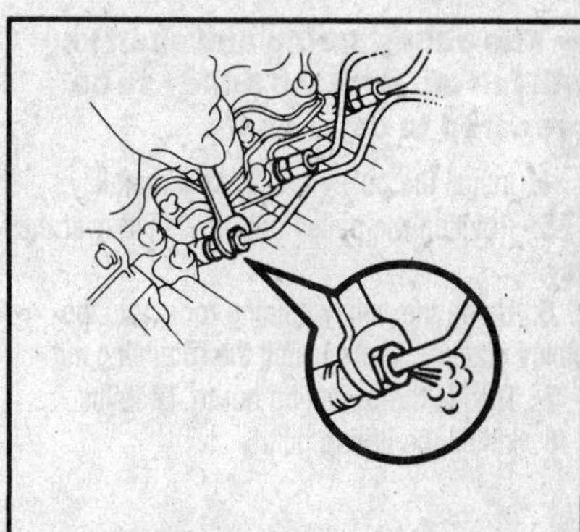

FIG. 34. Bleeding the air from diesel fuel lines

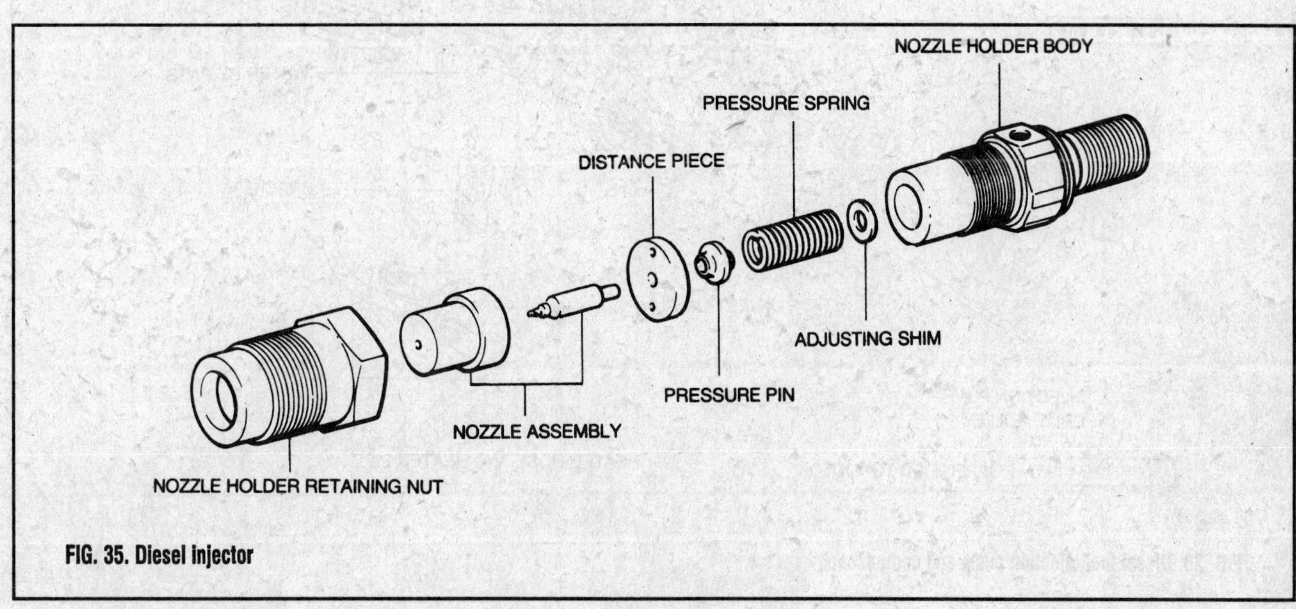

FIG. 35. Diesel injector

Injection Pump Drive Pulley

➧ SEE FIG. 36

REMOVAL & INSTALLATION

1. Remove the timing belt as described in Section 1.
2. Using SST No. 09278-54012 or suitable pulley holder to hold the injection pump pulley, remove the pulley mounting nut.
3. Using SST No. 09213-60017 or suitable gear puller, remove the drive pulley from the injection pump shaft.

➡ The pulley spring and shaft key will fall out with the pulley so be prepared to catch them.

4. Install the pulley spring and shaft key.
5. Position the pulley onto the shaft over the key.
6. Using the pulley holding tool, hold the pulley stationary and install the mounting nut.
7. Torque the mounting nut to 47 ft. lbs.
8. Install the timing belt.

Injection Pump

REMOVAL & INSTALLATION

➧ SEE FIG. 37–38

1. Disconnect the negative battery cable. Drain the cooling system.

CAUTION

When draining the coolant, keep in mind that cats and dogs are attracted by the ethylene glycol antifreeze, and are quite likely to drink any that is left in an uncovered container or in puddles on the ground. This will prove fatal in sufficient quantity. Always drain the coolant into a sealable container. Coolant should be reused unless it is contaminated or several years old.

2. Disconnect the accelerator and cruise control cables from the pump.
3. Disconnect the throttle sensor connector.
4. Disconnect the water by-pass hoses, the boost compensator hoses, the A/C or heater idle-up vacuum hoses and the heater hose.
5. Remove the injector pipes.
6. Remove the injection pump drive pulley as described in this Section.
7. Matchmark the raised timing mark on the pump flange (injection period line) with the block. Unbolt and remove the pump.

To install the injection pump:

8. Align the injection period line on the injection pump and water pump assembly.
9. Loosen the pump bracket bolts marked **A** in the illustration and ensure that there is no clearance between the bracket and the stay, and tighten the bolts.
10. Temporarily tighten the mounting bolt marked **B**. This bolt will be torqued to specification when the timing is adjusted.
11. Install the injection pump drive pulley.
12. Install the injection pipes.
13. Connect all the hoses and fill the cooling system to the proper level.
14. Prime the injection pump by operating the priming pump located on top of the fuel filter. Prime the pump until you can feel resistance.
15. Bleed the system by loosening the pipes at the nozzles and cranking the engine until all air is expelled and fuel sprays.

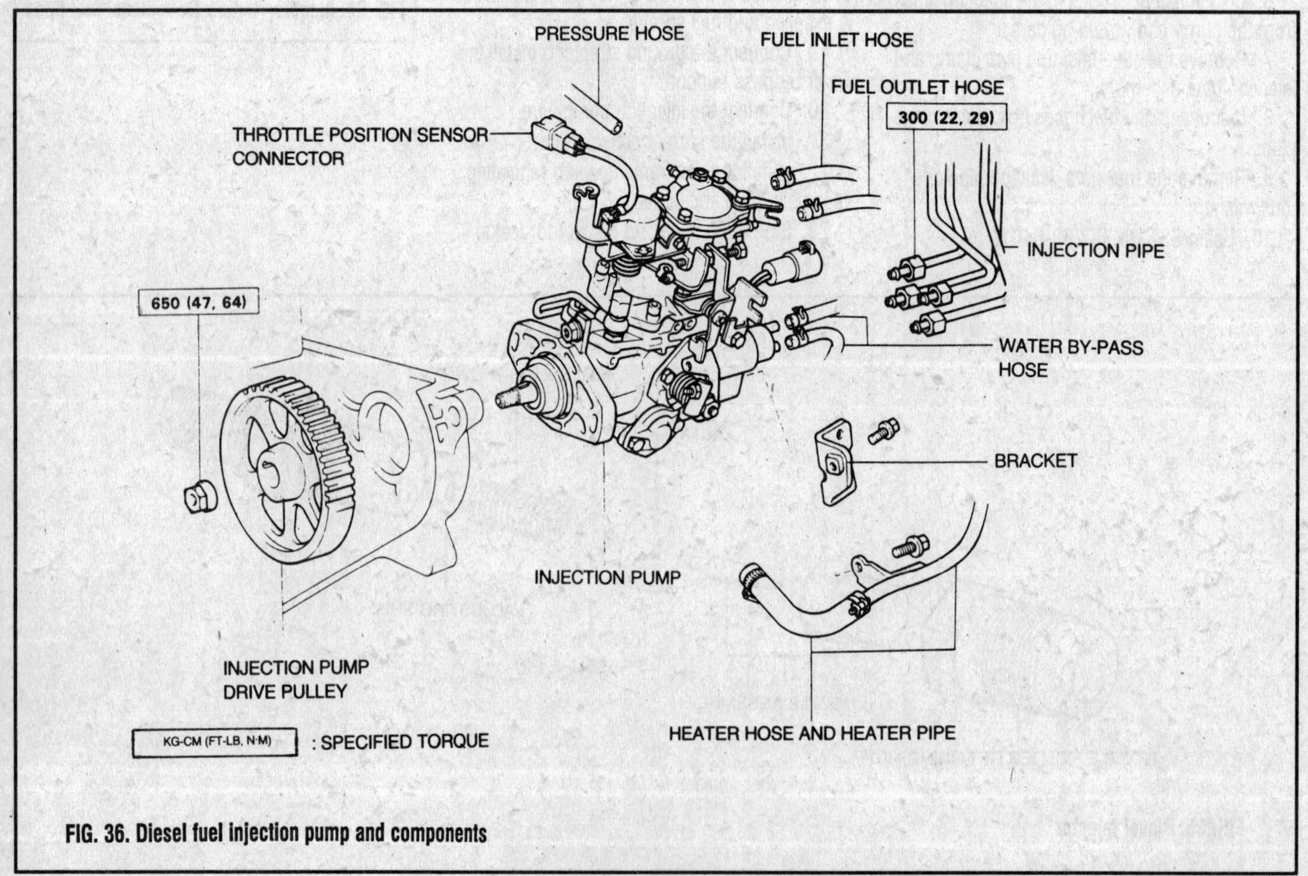

FIG. 36. Diesel fuel injection pump and components

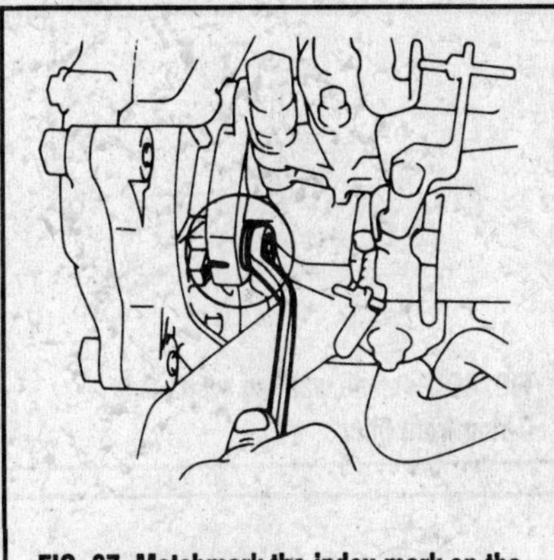
FIG. 37. Matchmark the index mark on the pump flange to the block

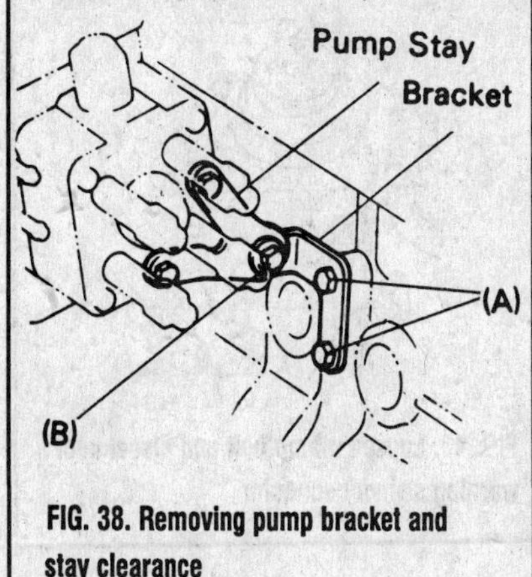

FIG. 38. Removing pump bracket and stay clearance

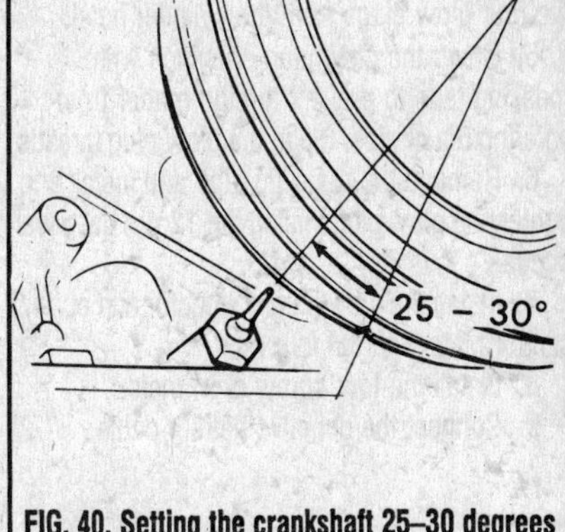

FIG. 40. Setting the crankshaft 25–30 degrees BTDC on the compression stroke

16. Connect the ground strap and install the water by-pass support.
17. Install the current sensor plate.
18. Install the electronic vacuum regulating assembly, pipe and hoses.
19. Connect the throttle position sensor connector.
20. Connect the throttle cable to the injection pump.
21. Connect the accelerator or cruise control cable and rod to the injection pump.
22. Check the engine idle and maximum idle speeds.
23. Check the coolant level and add as necessary.

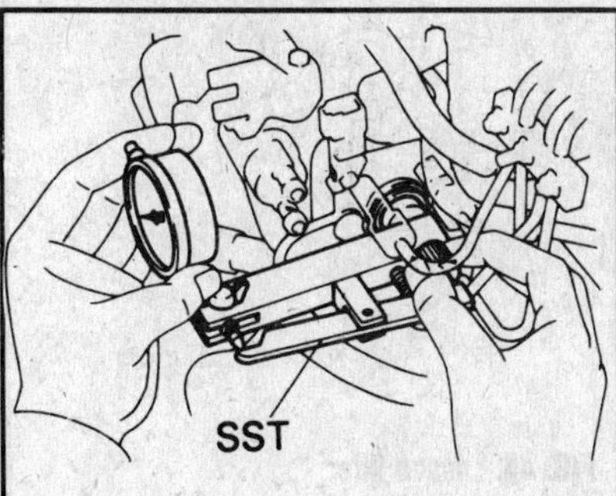

FIG. 39. Installing stroke measuring tool with dial indicator for setting injection pump timing

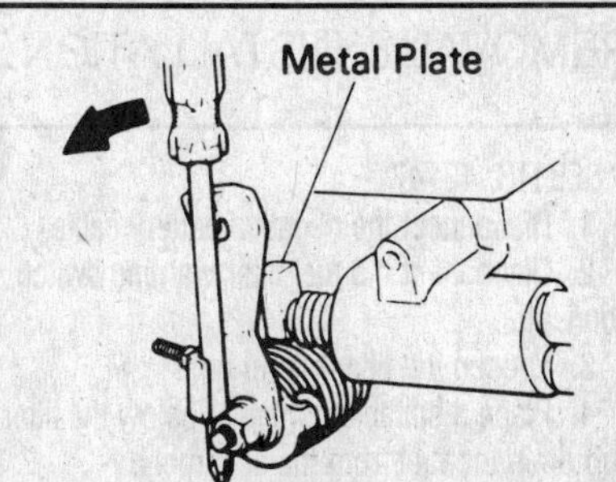

FIG. 41. Use a screwdriver to open cold starting lever and then insert 0.33–0.39 in. (8.5–10.0mm) block

INJECTION TIMING

➧ SEE FIG. 39–41

➡ **This procedure requires the use of a plunger stroke measuring tool and dial indicator.**

1. Remove the injection pump head bolt and install stroke measuring tool SST 09275-54010 or equivalent, along with the dial indicator.
2. Turn the crankshaft clockwise with a socket wrench to set No. 1 or No. 4 cylinder to approximately 25–30° BTDC on the compression stroke.
3. Use a screwdriver to turn the cold start lever 20° counterclockwise, then place a metal block 8.5–10.0mm thick between the cold start lever and thermo wax plunger.
4. Zero the dial indicator, then check to make sure the indicator remains at zero while rotating the crankshaft pulley slightly to the left and right.
5. Slowly rotate the crankshaft pulley until the No. 1 or No. 4 cylinder comes to TDC of the compression stroke, then measure the plunger stroke. It should read 0.70mm on the dial indicator.
6. To adjust the injection timing, loosen the four injection lines and the union bolt of the fuel inlet line. Loosen the injection pump mounting bolts and nuts.
7. Adjust the plunger stroke by slightly tilting the injection pump body. If the stroke is less than specifications given above, tilt the pump toward the engine. If greater than specifications, tilt the pump away from the engine.
8. Once the pump stroke is within specifications (as described in Step 5), tighten the injection pump mounting bolts and nuts. Torque the bolts to 34 ft. lbs. and the nuts to 13 ft. lbs. Torque all union nuts and bolts to 22 ft. lbs.
9. Remove the metal plate from the cold start lever and the pump stroke measuring tool from the injection pump. Install the distributor head bolt and torque to 12 ft. lbs. Replace the head bolt washer when installing. Bleed any air from the injection pump by cranking the starter motor, then start the engine and check for leaks.

Glow Plugs

REMOVAL & INSTALLATION

➧ SEE FIG. 42

1. Disconnect the negative battery cable.
2. Remove the four screw grommets.
3. Remove the four nuts, current sensor plate and glow plug connector.

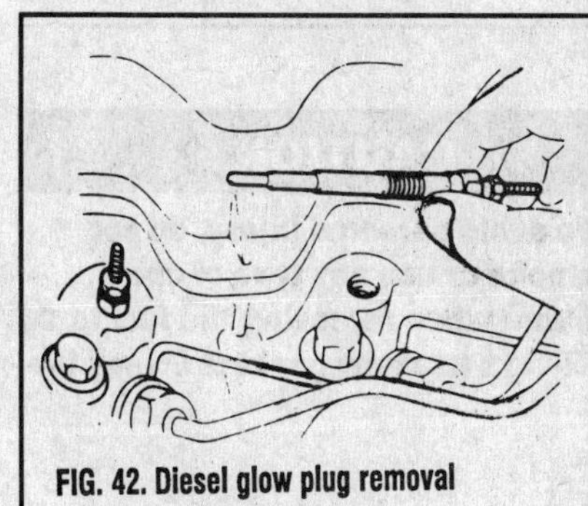
FIG. 42. Diesel glow plug removal

4. With a 12mm deep well socket, remove the four glow plugs from the cylinder head.
5. Cover the glow plug openings with masking tape to prevent foreign matter from entering the engine. Clean the glow plug threads.
6. Remove the masking tape and install and tighten the glow plugs using the 12mm deep well socket.
7. Install the glow plug connector and current sensor plate with the four nuts.
8. Install the four screw grommets.
9. Connect the negative battery cable.

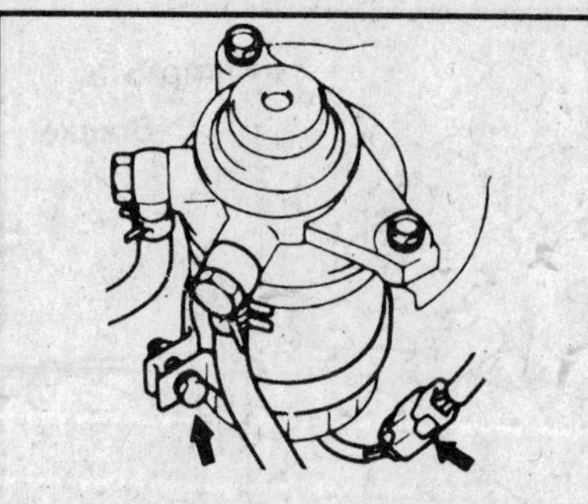

FIG. 43. Loosen clamp bolt and disconnect warning switch connector

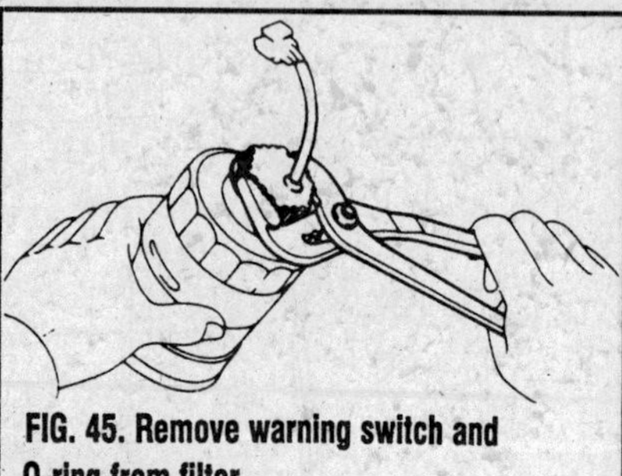

FIG. 45. Remove warning switch and O-ring from filter

Fuel Filter

REMOVAL & INSTALLATION

SEE FIG. 43–47

1. Disconnect the negative battery cable.
2. Disconnect the fuel filter warning switch connector.
3. Loosen the filter clamp bolt.
4. Place a suitable container below the filter and drain the fuel from the assembly.
5. Using SST tool 09228-64010, remove the filter with the warning switch and O-ring.
6. Remove the warning switch and O-ring. Use care not to damage the switch.

To install:

7. Install the warning switch with a new O-ring by hand and then using SST tool 09228-64010, turn the filter an additional $^3/_4$ turn. Put a light coat of fuel on the O-ring.

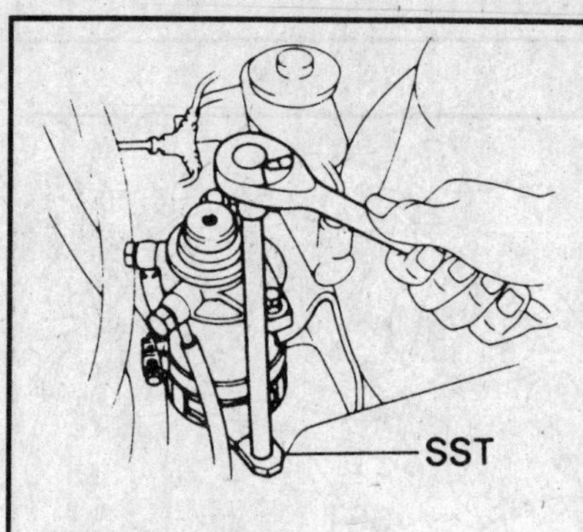

FIG. 44. Loosen filter

8. Tighten the filter clamp bolt and connect the warning switch.
9. Connect the negative battery cable. using the priming pump, fill the filter with fuel and check for leaks.

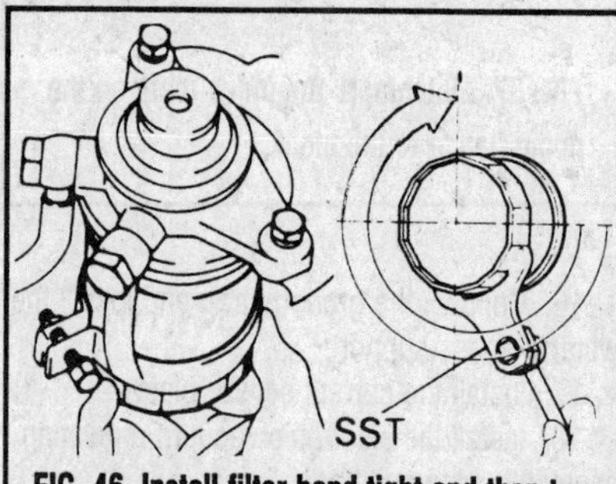

FIG. 46. Install filter hand tight and then turn an additional $^3/_4$ turn with filter wrench

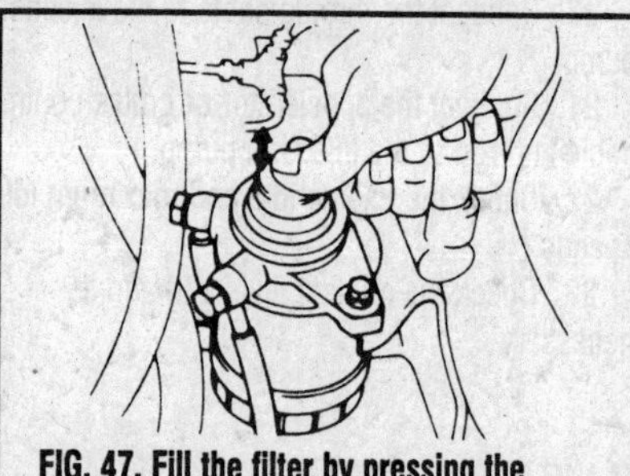

FIG. 47. Fill the filter by pressing the priming pump

FUEL TANK

SEE FIG. 48–52

REMOVAL & INSTALLATION

CAUTION

To avoid personal injury, do not smoke or use any type of open flame when removing the fuel tank! Always use new gaskets on any fuel tank or fuel line component. During installation, make sure that the rubber protectors are installed with the fuel tank and make sure that all line or plug torque specification are observed. To reduce the amount of fuel that you will have to dispose of, use as much of the fuel as possible before draining the tank.

1. Raise and safely support the vehicle. Disconnect the negative battery cable and properly relieve the fuel system pressure.
2. If equipped with a drain plug position a large capacity waste drain receptacle under the drain plug.
3. Remove the drain plug and gasket. Discard the gasket and purchase a new one.
4. If not equipped with a drain plug obtain an approved pumping device and drain a sufficient amount of fuel from the tank.
5. Remove the luggage compartment mat. Remove the cover over the tank sending unit and hose connections. Disconnect the gauge

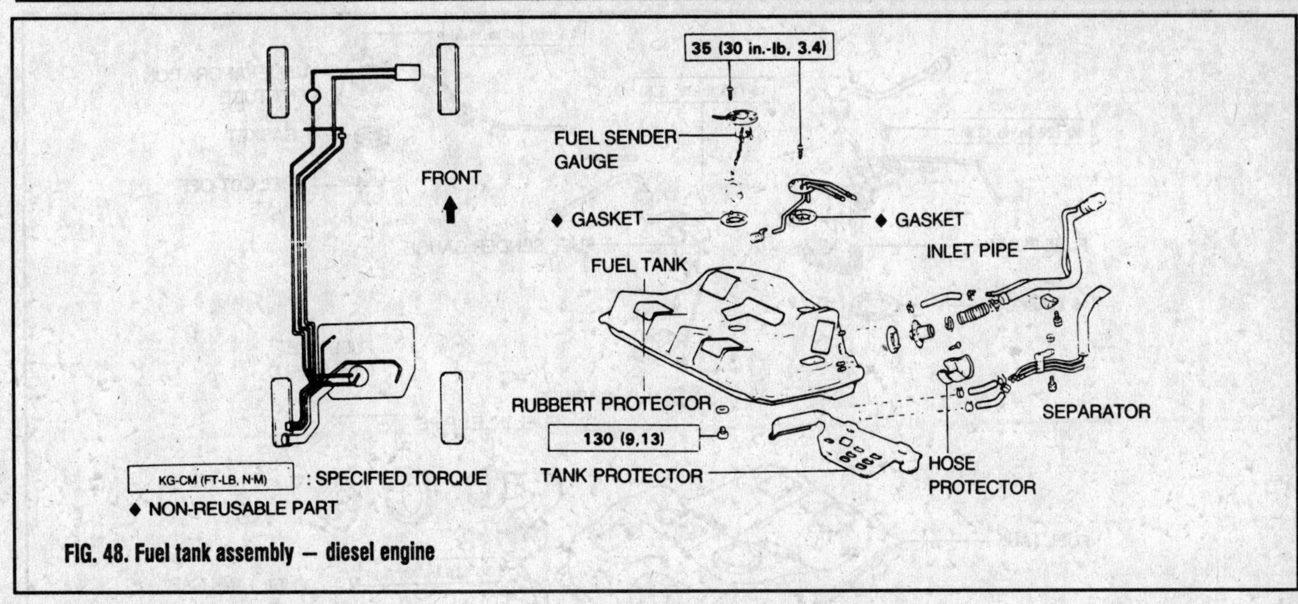

FIG. 48. Fuel tank assembly — diesel engine

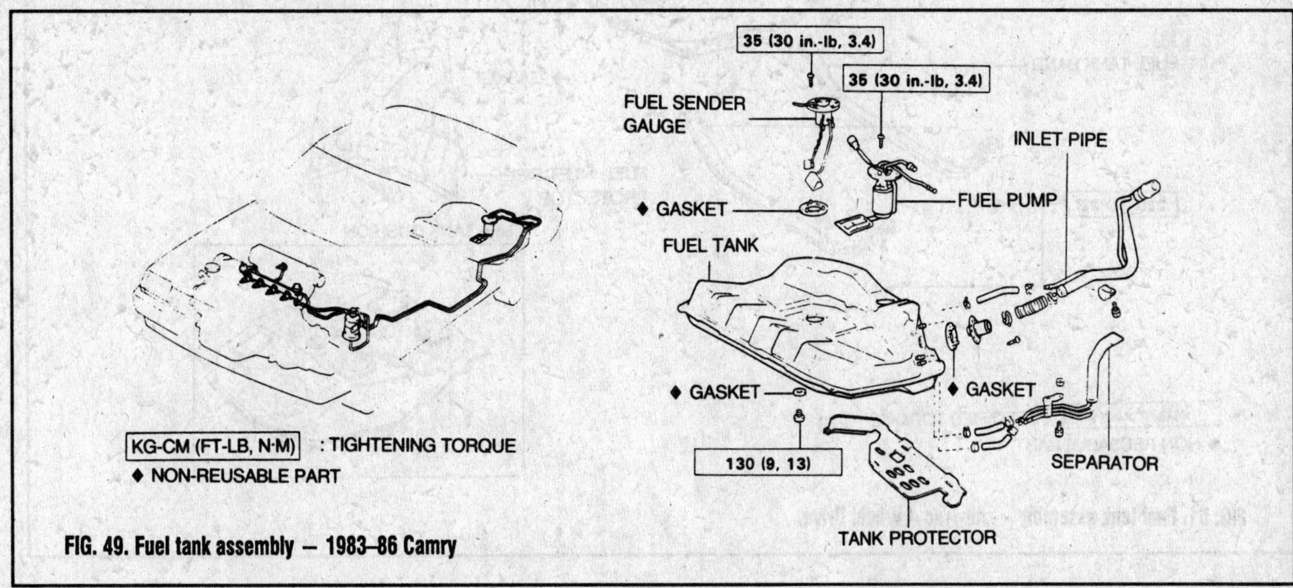

FIG. 49. Fuel tank assembly — 1983–86 Camry

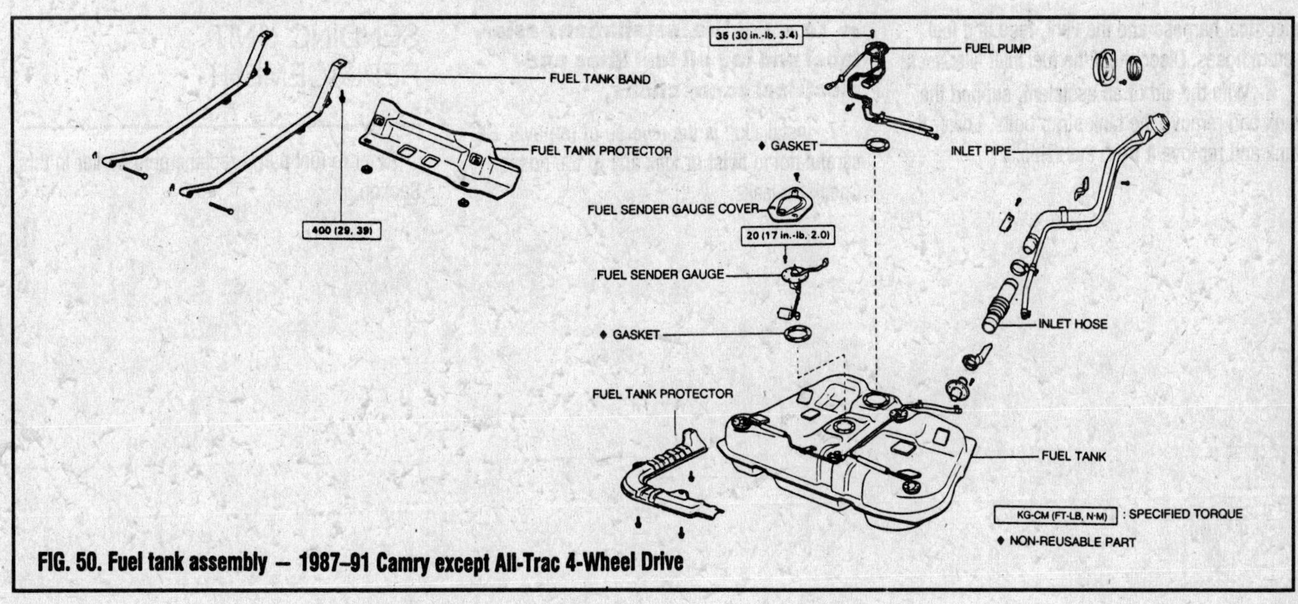

FIG. 50. Fuel tank assembly — 1987–91 Camry except All-Trac 4-Wheel Drive

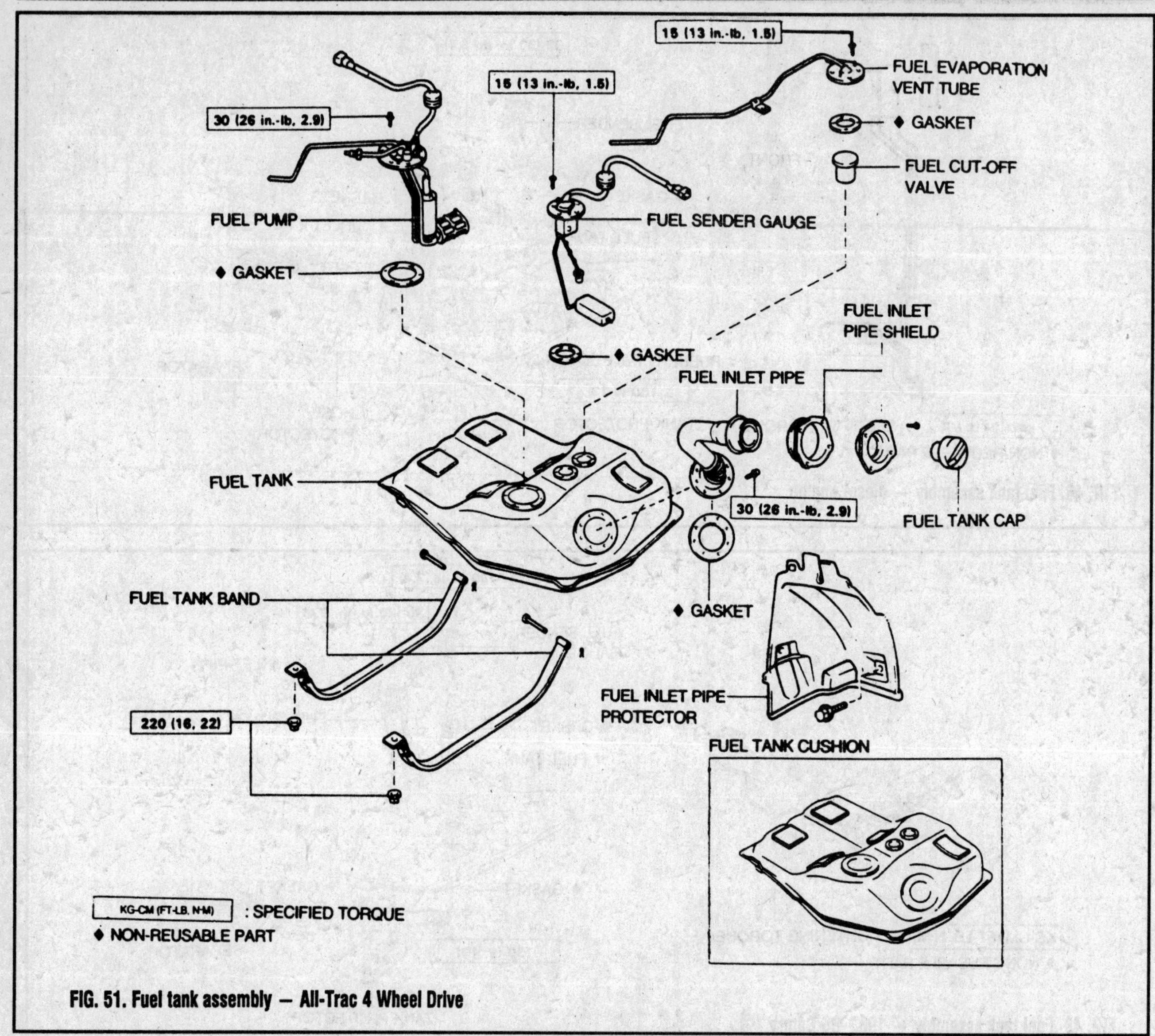

FIG. 51. Fuel tank assembly — All-Trac 4 Wheel Drive

electrical harness and the vent, feed and fuel return hoses. Disconnect the fuel inlet filler neck.

6. With the aid of an assistant, support the tank and remove the tank strap bolts. Lower the tank and remove it from the vehicle.

➡ **To make the installation easier, label and tag all fuel lines and electrical connections.**

7. Installation is the reverse of removal. Be careful not to twist or kink any of the hoses. Check for leaks.

SENDING UNIT REPLACEMENT

Refer to fuel pump replacement earlier in this Section.

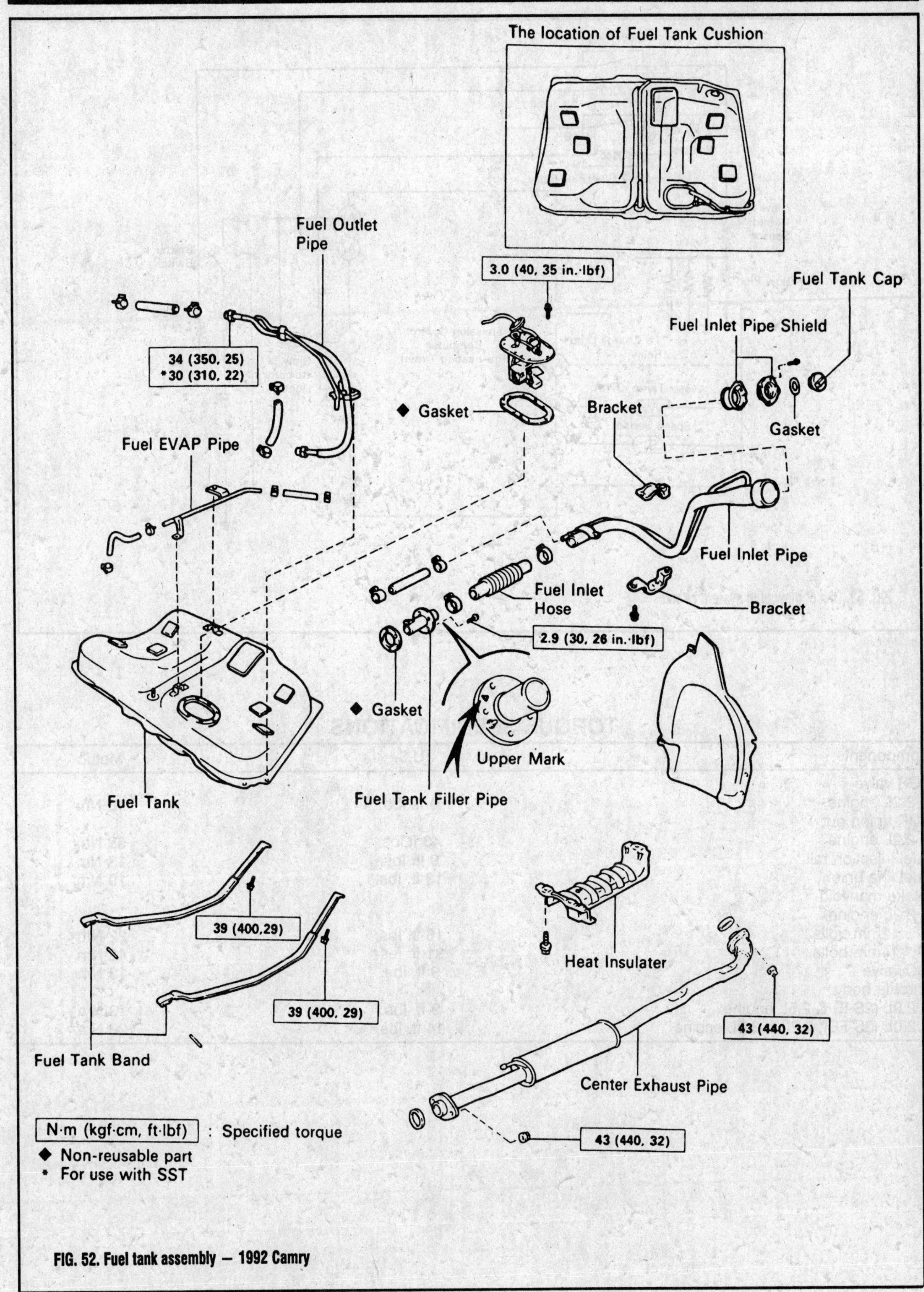

The location of Fuel Tank Cushion
Fuel Outlet Pipe
3.0 (40, 35 in.·lbf)
Fuel Tank Cap
Fuel Inlet Pipe Shield
34 (350, 25)
*30 (310, 22)
◆ Gasket
Bracket
Gasket
Fuel EVAP Pipe
Fuel Inlet Pipe
Fuel Inlet Hose
Bracket
2.9 (30, 26 in.·lbf)
◆ Gasket
Upper Mark
Fuel Tank
Fuel Tank Filler Pipe
39 (400,29)
Heat Insulater
39 (400, 29)
43 (440, 32)
Fuel Tank Band
Center Exhaust Pipe
N·m (kgf·cm, ft·lbf) : Specified torque
◆ Non-reusable part
* For use with SST
43 (440, 32)

FIG. 52. Fuel tank assembly — 1992 Camry

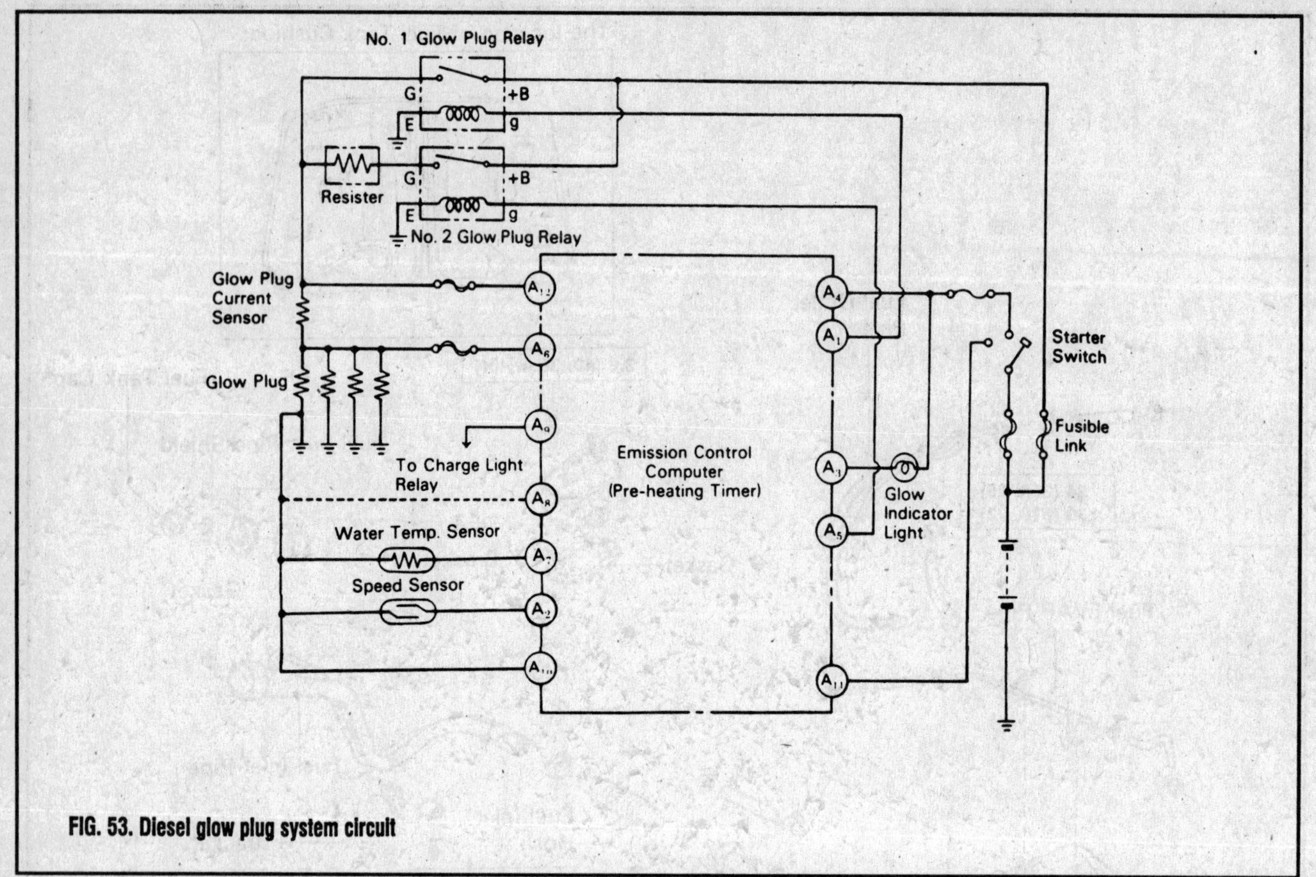

FIG. 53. Diesel glow plug system circuit

TORQUE SPECIFICATIONS

Component	U.S.	Metric
EGR valve		
2.2L engine	9 ft. lbs.	13 Nm
EGR union nut		
2.2L engine	43 ft.lbs.	59 Nm
Fuel injection rail	9 ft. lbs.	13 Nm
Fuel line union	13 ft. lbs.	19 Nm
Intake manifold		
2.2L engine		
12mm bolts	16 ft. lbs.	22 Nm
14mm bolts	31 ft. lbs.	42 Nm
ISC valve	9 ft. lbs.	13 Nm
Throttle body		
2.0L (2S-E) & 2.5L engine	9 ft. lbs.	13 Nm
2.0L (3S-FE), 2.2L & 3.0L engine	14 ft. lbs.	20 Nm

AIR CONDITIONING
Blower 6-9
Compressor 6-14
Condenser 6-16
Control panel 6-13
Evaporator 6-17
Pressure switch 6-25
A/C switch 6-23
Refrigerant lines 6-20
Receiver 6-19
Water control valve 6-11

BLOWER MOTOR 6-9

CHASSIS ELECTRICAL SYSTEM
Circuit breakers 6-47
Heater and air conditioning 6-9
Instrument cluster 6-37
Lighting 6-44
Windshield wipers 6-35
Control panel 6-34
Cruise control 6-28
Evaporator 6-17
Flashers 6-57
Fuses 6-47
Fusible linis 6-52
Headlights 6-40
Headlight switch 6-39

HEATER
Blower 6-9
Blower switch 6-13
Control cable 6-12
Control panel 6-13
Core 6-10

INSTRUMENT CLUSTER 6-37

INSTRUMENTS AND SWITCHES
Cluster 6-37
Gauges 6-38
Panel 6-34
Radio 6-33
Speakers 6-33
Speedometer 6-38

LIGHTING
Headlights 6-40
License plate light 6-45
Light bulb application chart 6-40
Signal and marker lights 6-43
Marker lights 6-43

RADIO 6-33

SPEEDOMETER CABLE 6-38

SWITCHES
Headlight 6-39
Windshield wiper 6-39

TRAILER WIRING 6-47

TROUBLESHOOTING
Cruise control 6-28
Gauges 6-260
Heater 6-261
Lights 6-258
Speed sensor & ratio controller 6-31
Thermistor 6-22
Pressure switch 6-27
Air conditioning switch 6-23
Turn signals and flashers 6-257
Windshield wipers 6-262

WINDSHIELD WIPERS
Arm and blade 6-35
Linkage and motor 6-35
Switch 6-39

WIRING DIAGRAMS 6-58

6 CHASSIS ELECTRICAL

Circuit Protection 6-47
Cruise Control 6-28
Heating and Air Conditioning 6-9
Instruments and Switches 6-37
Lighting 6-40
Radio 6-33
Troubleshooting Charts 6-257
Understanding Electrical Systems 6-2
Windshield Wipers 6-35
Wiring Diagrams 6-58

UNDERSTANDING AND TROUBLESHOOTING ELECTRICAL SYSTEMS

At the rate which both import and domestic manufacturers are incorporating electronic control systems into their production lines, it won't be long before every new vehicle is equipped with one or more on-board computer. These electronic components (with no moving parts) should theoretically last the life of the vehicle, provided nothing external happens to damage the circuits or memory chips.

While it is true that electronic components should never wear out, in the real world malfunctions do occur. It is also true that any computer-based system is extremely sensitive to electrical voltages and cannot tolerate careless or haphazard testing or service procedures. An inexperienced individual can literally do major damage looking for a minor problem by using the wrong kind of test equipment or connecting test leads or connectors with the ignition switch **ON**. When selecting test equipment, make sure the manufacturers instructions state that the tester is compatible with whatever type of electronic control system is being serviced. Read all instructions carefully and double check all test points before installing probes or making any test connections.

The following section outlines basic diagnosis techniques for dealing with computerized automotive control systems. Along with a general explanation of the various types of test equipment available to aid in servicing modern electronic automotive systems, basic repair techniques for wiring harnesses and connectors is given. Read the basic information before attempting any repairs or testing on any computerized system, to provide the background of information necessary to avoid the most common and obvious mistakes that can cost both time and money. Although the replacement and testing procedures are simple in themselves, the systems are not, and unless one has a thorough understanding of all components and their function within a particular computerized control system, the logical test sequence these systems demand cannot be followed. Minor malfunctions can make a big difference, so it is important to know how each component affects the operation of the overall electronic system to find the ultimate cause of a problem without replacing good components unnecessarily. It is not enough to use the correct test equipment; the test equipment must be used correctly.

Safety Precautions

CAUTION

Whenever working on or around any computer based microprocessor control system, always observe these general precautions to prevent the possibility of personal injury or damage to electronic components.

- Never install or remove battery cables with the key **ON** or the engine running. Jumper cables should be connected with the key **OFF** to avoid power surges that can damage electronic control units. Engines equipped with computer controlled systems should avoid both giving and getting jump starts due to the possibility of serious damage to components from arcing in the engine compartment when connections are made with the ignition **ON**.
- Always remove the battery cables before charging the battery. Never use a high output charger on an installed battery or attempt to use any type of "hot shot" (24 volt) starting aid.
- Exercise care when inserting test probes into connectors to insure good connections without damaging the connector or spreading the pins. Always probe connectors from the rear (wire) side, NOT the pin side, to avoid accidental shorting of terminals during test procedures.
- Never remove or attach wiring harness connectors with the ignition switch **ON**, especially to an electronic control unit.
- Do not drop any components during service procedures and never apply 12 volts directly to any component (like a solenoid or relay) unless instructed specifically to do so. Some component electrical windings are designed to safely handle only 4 or 5 volts and can be destroyed in seconds if 12 volts are applied directly to the connector.
- Remove the electronic control unit if the vehicle is to be placed in an environment where temperatures exceed approximately 176°F (80°C), such as a paint spray booth or when arc or gas welding near the control unit location in the car.

ORGANIZED TROUBLESHOOTING

When diagnosing a specific problem, organized troubleshooting is a must. The complexity of a modern automobile demands that you approach any problem in a logical, organized manner. There are certain troubleshooting techniques that are standard:

1. Establish when the problem occurs. Does the problem appear only under certain conditions? Were there any noises, odors, or other unusual symptoms?
2. Isolate the problem area. To do this, make some simple tests and observations; then eliminate the systems that are working properly. Check for obvious problems such as broken wires, dirty connections or split or disconnected vacuum hoses. Always check the obvious before assuming something complicated is the cause.
3. Test for problems systematically to determine the cause once the problem area is isolated. Are all the components functioning properly? Is there power going to electrical switches and motors? Is there vacuum at vacuum switches and/or actuators? Is there a mechanical problem such as bent linkage or loose mounting screws? Doing careful, systematic checks will often turn up most causes on the first inspection without wasting time checking components that have little or no relationship to the problem.
4. Test all repairs after the work is done to make sure that the problem is fixed. Some causes can be traced to more than one component, so a careful verification of repair work is important to pick up additional malfunctions that may cause a problem to reappear or a different problem to arise. A blown fuse, for example, is a simple problem that may require more than another fuse to repair. If you don't look for a problem that caused a fuse to blow, for example, a shorted wire may go undetected.

Experience has shown that most problems tend to be the result of a fairly simple and obvious cause, such as loose or corroded connectors or air leaks in the intake system; making careful inspection of components during testing essential to quick and accurate troubleshooting. Special, hand held computerized testers designed specifically for diagnosing the engine control system are available from a variety of after market sources, as well as from the vehicle manufacturer, but care should be taken that any test equipment being used is designed to diagnose that particular computer controlled system accurately without damaging the control unit (ECU) or components being tested.

➡ **Pinpointing the exact cause of trouble in an electrical system can sometimes only be accomplished by the use of special test equipment. The following describes commonly used test equipment and explains how to put it to best use in diagnosis. In addition to the information covered below, the manufacturer's instructions booklet provided with the tester should be read and clearly understood before attempting any test procedures.**

TEST EQUIPMENT

Jumper Wires

Jumper wires are simple, yet extremely valuable, pieces of test equipment. Jumper wires are merely wires that are used to bypass sections of a circuit. The simplest type of jumper wire is merely a length of multistrand wire with an alligator clip at each end. Jumper wires are usually fabricated from lengths of standard automotive wire and whatever type of connector (alligator clip, spade connector or pin connector) that is required for the particular vehicle being tested. The well equipped tool box will have several different styles of jumper wires in several different lengths. Some jumper wires are made with three or more terminals coming from a common splice for special purpose testing. In cramped, hard-to-reach areas it is advisable to have insulated boots over the jumper wire terminals in order to prevent accidental grounding, sparks, and possible fire, especially when testing fuel system components.

Jumper wires are used primarily to locate open electrical circuits, on either the ground (–) side of the circuit or on the hot (+) side. If an electrical component fails to operate, connect the jumper wire between the component and a good ground. If the component operates only with the jumper installed, the ground circuit is open. If the ground circuit is good, but the component does not operate, the circuit between the power feed and component is open. You can sometimes connect the jumper wire directly from the battery to the hot terminal of the component, but first make sure the component uses 12 volts in operation. Some electrical components, such as fuel injectors, are designed to operate on about 4 volts and running 12 volts directly to the injector terminals can burn out the wiring. By inserting an inline fuse holder between a set of test leads, a fused jumper wire can be used for bypassing open circuits. Use a 5 amp fuse to provide protection against voltage spikes. When in doubt, use a voltmeter to check the voltage input to the component and measure how much voltage is being applied normally. By moving the jumper wire successively back from the lamp toward the power source, you can isolate the area of the circuit where the open is located. When the component stops functioning, or the power is cut off, the open is in the segment of wire between the jumper and the point previously tested.

**** CAUTION**

Never use jumpers made from wire that is of lighter gauge than used in the circuit under test. If the jumper wire is of too small gauge, it may overheat and possibly melt. Never use jumpers to bypass high resistance loads (such as motors) in a circuit. Bypassing resistances, in effect, creates a short circuit which may, in turn, cause damage and fire. Never use a jumper for anything other than temporary bypassing of components in a circuit.

12 Volt Test Light

The 12 volt test light is used to check circuits and components while electrical current is flowing through them. It is used for voltage and ground tests. Twelve volt test lights come in different styles but all have three main parts; a ground clip, a probe, and a light. The most commonly used 12 volt test lights have pick-type probes. To use a 12 volt test light, connect the ground clip to a good ground and probe wherever necessary with the pick. The pick should be sharp so that it can penetrate wire insulation to make contact with the wire, without making a large hole in the insulation. The wrap-around light is handy in hard to reach areas or where it is difficult to support a wire to push a probe pick into it. To use the wrap around light, hook the wire to probed with the hook and pull the trigger. A small pick will be forced through the wire insulation into the wire core.

**** CAUTION**

Do not use a test light to probe electronic ignition spark plug or coil wires. Never use a pick-type test light to probe wiring on computer controlled systems unless specifically instructed to do so. Any wire insulation that is pierced by the test light probe should be taped and sealed with silicone after testing.

Like the jumper wire, the 12 volt test light is used to isolate opens in circuits. But, whereas the jumper wire is used to bypass the open to operate the load, the 12 volt test light is used to locate the presence of voltage in a circuit. If the test light glows, you know that there is power up to that point; if the 12 volt test light does not glow when its probe is inserted into the wire or connector, you know that there is an open circuit (no power). Move the test light in successive steps back toward the power source until the light in the handle does glow. When it does glow, the open is between the probe and point previously probed.

➡ **The test light does not detect that 12 volts (or any particular amount of voltage) is present; it only detects that some voltage is present. It is advisable before using the test light to touch its terminals across the battery posts to make sure the light is operating properly.**

Self-Powered Test Light

The self-powered test light usually contains a 1.5 volt pen light battery. One type of self-powered test light is similar in design to the 12 volt test light. This type has both the battery and the light in the handle and pick-type probe tip. The second type has the light toward the open tip, so that the light illuminates the contact point. The self-powered test light is dual purpose piece of test equipment. It can be used to test for either open or short circuits when power is isolated from the circuit (continuity test). A powered test light should not be used on any computer controlled system or component unless specifically instructed to do so. Many engine sensors can be destroyed by even this small amount of voltage applied directly to the terminals.

Open Circuit Testing

To use the self-powered test light to check for open circuits, first isolate the circuit from the vehicle's 12 volt power source by disconnecting the battery or wiring harness connector. Connect the test light ground clip to a good ground and probe sections of the circuit sequentially with the test light. (start from either end of the circuit). If the light is out, the open is between the probe and the circuit ground. If the light is on, the open is between the probe and end of the circuit toward the power source.

Short Circuit Testing

By isolating the circuit both from power and from ground, and using a self-powered test light, you can check for shorts to ground in the circuit. Isolate the circuit from power and ground. Connect the test light ground clip to a good ground and probe any easy-to-reach test point in the circuit. If the light comes on, there is a short somewhere in the circuit. To isolate the short, probe a test point at either end of the isolated circuit (the light should be on). Leave the test light probe connected and open connectors, switches, remove parts, etc., sequentially, until the light goes out. When the light goes out, the short is between the last circuit component opened and the previous circuit opened.

➡ The 1.5 volt battery in the test light does not provide much current. A weak battery may not provide enough power to illuminate the test light even when a complete circuit is made (especially if there are high resistances in the circuit). Always make sure that the test battery is strong. To check the battery, briefly touch the ground clip to the probe; if the light glows brightly the battery is strong enough for testing. Never use a self-powered test light to perform checks for opens or shorts when power is applied to the electrical system under test. The 12 volt vehicle power will quickly burn out the 1.5 volt light bulb in the test light.

Voltmeter

A voltmeter is used to measure voltage at any point in a circuit, or to measure the voltage drop across any part of a circuit. It can also be used to check continuity in a wire or circuit by indicating current flow from one end to the other. Voltmeters usually have various scales on the meter dial and a selector switch to allow the selection of different voltages. The voltmeter has a positive and a negative lead. To avoid damage to the meter, always connect the negative lead to the negative (–) side of circuit (to ground or nearest the ground side of the circuit) and connect the positive lead to the positive (+) side of the circuit (to the power source or the nearest power source). Note that the negative voltmeter lead will always be black and that the positive voltmeter will always be some color other than black (usually red). Depending on how the voltmeter is connected into the circuit, it has several uses.

A voltmeter can be connected either in parallel or in series with a circuit and it has a very high resistance to current flow. When connected in parallel, only a small amount of current will flow through the voltmeter current path; the rest will flow through the normal circuit current path and the circuit will work normally. When the voltmeter is connected in series with a circuit, only a small amount of current can flow through the circuit. The circuit will not work properly, but the voltmeter reading will show if the circuit is complete or not.

Available Voltage Measurement

Set the voltmeter selector switch to the 20V position and connect the meter negative lead to the negative post of the battery. Connect the positive meter lead to the positive post of the battery and turn the ignition switch ON to provide a load. Read the voltage on the meter or digital display. A well charged battery should register over 12 volts. If the meter reads below 11.5 volts, the battery power may be insufficient to operate the electrical system properly. This test determines voltage available from the battery and should be the first step in any electrical trouble diagnosis procedure. Many electrical problems, especially on computer controlled systems, can be caused by a low state of charge in the battery. Excessive corrosion at the battery cable terminals can cause a poor contact that will prevent proper charging and full battery current flow.

Normal battery voltage is 12 volts when fully charged. When the battery is supplying current to one or more circuits it is said to be "under load". When everything is off the electrical system is under a "no-load" condition. A fully charged battery may show about 12.5 volts at no load; will drop to 12 volts under medium load; and will drop even lower under heavy load. If the battery is partially discharged the voltage decrease under heavy load may be excessive, even though the battery shows 12 volts or more at no load. When allowed to discharge further, the battery's available voltage under load will decrease more severely. For this reason, it is important that the battery be fully charged during all testing procedures to avoid errors in diagnosis and incorrect test results.

Voltage Drop

When current flows through a resistance, the voltage beyond the resistance is reduced (the larger the current, the greater the reduction in voltage). When no current is flowing, there is no voltage drop because there is no current flow. All points in the circuit which are connected to the power source are at the same voltage as the power source. The total voltage drop always equals the total source voltage. In a long circuit with many connectors, a series of small, unwanted voltage drops due to corrosion at the connectors can add up to a total loss of voltage which impairs the operation of the normal loads in the circuit.

INDIRECT COMPUTATION OF VOLTAGE DROPS

1. Set the voltmeter selector switch to the 20 volt position.
2. Connect the meter negative lead to a good ground.
3. Probe all resistances in the circuit with the positive meter lead.
4. Operate the circuit in all modes and observe the voltage readings.

DIRECT MEASUREMENT OF VOLTAGE DROPS

1. Set the voltmeter switch to the 20 volt position.
2. Connect the voltmeter negative lead to the ground side of the resistance load to be measured.
3. Connect the positive lead to the positive side of the resistance or load to be measured.
4. Read the voltage drop directly on the 20 volt scale.

Too high a voltage indicates too high a resistance. If, for example, a blower motor runs too slowly, you can determine if there is too high a resistance in the resistor pack. By taking voltage drop readings in all parts of the circuit, you can isolate the problem. Too low a voltage drop indicates too low a resistance. If, for example, a blower motor runs too fast in the MED and/or LOW position, the problem can be isolated in the resistor pack by taking voltage drop readings in all parts of the circuit to locate a possibly shorted resistor. The maximum allowable voltage drop under load is critical, especially if there is more than one high resistance problem in a circuit because all voltage drops are cumulative. A small drop is normal due to the resistance of the conductors.

HIGH RESISTANCE TESTING

1. Set the voltmeter selector switch to the 4 volt position.
2. Connect the voltmeter positive lead to the positive post of the battery.
3. Turn on the headlights and heater blower to provide a load.
4. Probe various points in the circuit with the negative voltmeter lead.
5. Read the voltage drop on the 4 volt scale.

Some average maximum allowable voltage drops are:

FUSE PANEL — 7 volts
IGNITION SWITCH — 5 volts
HEADLIGHT SWITCH — 7 volts
IGNITION COIL (+) — 5 volts
ANY OTHER LOAD — 1.3 volts

➡ **Voltage drops are all measured while a load is operating; without current flow, there will be no voltage drop.**

Ohmmeter

The ohmmeter is designed to read resistance (ohms) in a circuit or component. Although there are several different styles of ohmmeters, all will usually have a selector switch which permits the measurement of different ranges of resistance (usually the selector switch allows the multiplication of the meter reading by 10, 100, 1,000, and 10,000). A calibration knob allows the meter to be set at zero for accurate measurement. Since all ohmmeters are powered by an internal battery (usually 9 volts), the ohmmeter can be used as a self-powered test light. When the ohmmeter is connected, current from the ohmmeter flows through the circuit or component being tested. Since the ohmmeter's internal resistance and voltage are known values, the amount of current flow through the meter depends on the resistance of the circuit or component being tested.

The ohmmeter can be used to perform continuity test for opens or shorts (either by observation of the meter needle or as a self-powered test light), and to read actual resistance in a circuit. It should be noted that the ohmmeter is used to check the resistance of a component or wire while there is no voltage applied to the circuit. Current flow from an outside voltage source (such as the vehicle battery) can damage the ohmmeter, so the circuit or component should be isolated from the vehicle electrical system before any testing is done. Since the ohmmeter uses its own voltage source, either lead can be connected to any test point.

➡ **When checking diodes or other solid state components, the ohmmeter leads can only be connected one way in order to measure current flow in a single direction. Make sure the positive (+) and negative (-) terminal connections are as described in the test procedures to verify the one-way diode operation.**

In using the meter for making continuity checks, do not be concerned with the actual resistance readings. Zero resistance, or any resistance readings, indicate continuity in the circuit. Infinite resistance indicates an open in the circuit. A high resistance reading where there should be none indicates a problem in the circuit. Checks for short circuits are made in the same manner as checks for open circuits except that the circuit must be isolated from both power and normal ground. Infinite resistance indicates no continuity to ground, while zero resistance indicates a dead short to ground.

RESISTANCE MEASUREMENT

The batteries in an ohmmeter will weaken with age and temperature, so the ohmmeter must be calibrated or "zeroed" before taking measurements. To zero the meter, place the selector switch in its lowest range and touch the two ohmmeter leads together. Turn the calibration knob until the meter needle is exactly on zero.

➡ **All analog (needle) type ohmmeters must be zeroed before use, but some digital ohmmeter models are automatically calibrated when the switch is turned on. Self-calibrating digital ohmmeters do not have an adjusting knob, but its a good idea to check for a zero readout before use by touching the leads together. All computer controlled systems require the use of a digital ohmmeter with at least 10 megohms impedance for testing. Before any test procedures are attempted, make sure the ohmmeter used is compatible with the electrical system or damage to the on-board computer could result.**

To measure resistance, first isolate the circuit from the vehicle power source by disconnecting the battery cables or the harness connector. Make sure the key is OFF when disconnecting any components or the battery. Where necessary, also isolate at least one side of the circuit to be checked to avoid reading parallel resistances. Parallel circuit resistances will always give a lower reading than the actual resistance of either of the branches. When measuring the resistance of parallel circuits, the total resistance will always be lower than the smallest resistance in the circuit. Connect the meter leads to both sides of the circuit (wire or component) and read the actual measured ohms on the meter scale. Make sure the selector switch is set to the proper ohm scale for the circuit being tested to avoid misreading the ohmmeter test value.

⁂ WARNING

Never use an ohmmeter with power applied to the circuit. Like the self-powered test light, the ohmmeter is designed to operate on its own power supply. The normal 12 volt automotive electrical system current could damage the meter!

Ammeters

An ammeter measures the amount of current flowing through a circuit in units called amperes or amps. Amperes are units of electron flow which indicate how fast the electrons are flowing through the circuit. Since Ohms Law dictates that current flow in a circuit is equal to the circuit voltage divided by the total circuit resistance, increasing voltage also increases the current level (amps). Likewise, any decrease in resistance will increase the amount of amps in a circuit. At normal operating voltage, most circuits have a characteristic amount of amperes, called "current draw" which can be measured using an ammeter. By referring to a specified current draw rating, measuring the amperes, and comparing the two values, one can determine what is happening within the circuit to aid in diagnosis. An open circuit, for example, will not allow any current to flow so the ammeter reading will be zero. More current flows through a heavily loaded circuit or when the charging system is operating.

An ammeter is always connected in series with the circuit being tested. All of the current that normally flows through the circuit must also flow through the ammeter; if there is any other path for the current to follow, the ammeter reading will not be accurate. The ammeter itself has very little resistance to current flow and therefore will not affect the circuit, but it will measure current draw only when the circuit is closed and electricity is flowing. Excessive current draw can blow fuses and drain the battery, while a reduced current draw can cause motors to run slowly, lights to dim and other components to not operate properly. The ammeter can help diagnose these conditions by locating the cause of the high or low reading.

Multimeters

Different combinations of test meters can be built into a single unit designed for specific tests. Some of the more common combination test devices are known as Volt/Amp testers, Tach/Dwell meters, or Digital Multimeters. The Volt/Amp tester is used for charging system, starting system or battery tests and consists of a voltmeter, an ammeter and a variable resistance carbon pile. The voltmeter will usually have at least two ranges for use with 6, 12 and 24 volt systems. The ammeter also has more than one range for testing various levels of battery loads and starter current draw and the carbon pile can be adjusted to offer different amounts of resistance. The Volt/Amp tester has heavy leads to carry large amounts of current and many later models have an inductive ammeter pickup that clamps around the wire to simplify test connections. On some models, the ammeter also has a zero-center scale to allow testing of charging and starting systems without switching leads or polarity. A digital multimeter is a voltmeter, ammeter and ohmmeter combined in an instrument which gives a digital readout. These are often used when testing solid state circuits because of their high input impedance (usually 10 megohms or more).

The tach/dwell meter combines a tachometer and a dwell (cam angle) meter and is a specialized kind of voltmeter. The tachometer scale is marked to show engine speed in rpm and the dwell scale is marked to show degrees of distributor shaft rotation. In most electronic ignition systems, dwell is determined by the control unit, but the dwell meter can also be used to check the duty cycle (operation) of some electronic engine control systems. Some tach/dwell meters are powered by an internal battery, while others take their power from the car battery in use. The battery powered testers usually require calibration much like an ohmmeter before testing.

Special Test Equipment

A variety of diagnostic tools are available to help troubleshoot and repair computerized engine control systems. The most sophisticated of these devices are the console type engine analyzers that usually occupy a garage service bay, but there are several types of after market electronic testers available that will allow quick circuit tests of the engine control system by plugging directly into a special connector located in the engine compartment or under the dashboard. Several tool and equipment manufacturers offer simple, hand held testers that measure various circuit voltage levels on command to check all system components for proper operation. Although these testers usually cost about $300-500, consider that the average computer control unit (or ECM) can cost just as much and the money saved by not replacing perfectly good sensors or components in an attempt to correct a problem could justify the purchase price of a special diagnostic tester the first time it's used.

These computerized testers can allow quick and easy test measurements while the engine is operating or while the car is being driven. In addition, the on-board computer memory can be read to access any stored trouble codes; in effect allowing the computer to tell you where it hurts and aid trouble diagnosis by pinpointing exactly which circuit or component is malfunctioning. In the same manner, repairs can be tested to make sure the problem has been corrected. The biggest advantage these special testers have is their relatively easy hookups that minimize or eliminate the chances of making the wrong connections and getting false voltage readings or damaging the computer accidentally.

➡ It should be remembered that these testers check voltage levels in circuits; they don't detect mechanical problems or failed components if the circuit voltage falls within the preprogrammed limits stored in the tester PROM unit. Also, most of the hand held testes are designed to work only on one or two systems made by a specific manufacturer.

A variety of after market testers are available to help diagnose different computerized control systems. Owatonna Tool Company (OTC), for example, markets a device called the OTC Monitor which plugs directly into the assembly line diagnostic link (ALDL) on some GM, Ford and Chrysler products. The OTC tester makes diagnosis a simple matter of pressing the correct buttons and, by changing the internal PROM or inserting a different diagnosis cartridge, it will work on any model from full size to subcompact, over a wide range of years. An adapter is supplied with the tester to allow connection to all types of ALDL links, regardless of the number of pin terminals used. By inserting an updated PROM into the OTC tester, it can be easily updated to diagnose any new modifications of computerized control systems.

Wiring Harnesses

The average automobile contains about 1/2 mile of wiring, with hundreds of individual connections. To protect the many wires from damage and to keep them from becoming a confusing tangle, they are organized into bundles, enclosed in plastic or taped together and called wire harnesses. Different wiring harnesses serve different parts of the vehicle. Individual wires are color coded to help trace them through a harness where sections are hidden from view.

A loose or corroded connection or a replacement wire that is too small for the circuit will add extra resistance and an additional voltage drop to the circuit. A ten percent voltage drop can result in slow or erratic motor operation, for example, even though the circuit is complete. Automotive wiring or circuit conductors can be in any one of three forms:

1. Single strand wire
2. Multistrand wire
3. Printed circuitry

Single strand wire has a solid metal core and is usually used inside such components as alternators, motors, relays and other devices. Multistrand wire has a core made of many small strands of wire twisted together into a single conductor. Most of the wiring in an automotive electrical system is made up of multistrand wire, either as a single conductor or grouped together in a harness. All wiring is color coded on the insulator, either as a solid color or as a colored wire with an identification stripe. A printed circuit is a thin film of copper or other conductor that is printed on an insulator backing. Occasionally, a printed circuit is sandwiched between two sheets of plastic for more protection and flexibility. A complete printed circuit, consisting of conductors, insulating material and connectors for lamps or other components is called a printed circuit board. Printed circuitry is used in place of individual wires or harnesses in places where space is limited, such as behind instrument panels.

Wire Gauge

Since computer controlled automotive electrical systems are very sensitive to changes in resistance, the selection of properly sized wires is critical when systems are repaired. The wire gauge number is an expression of the cross section area of the conductor. The most common system for expressing wire size is the American Wire Gauge (AWG) system.

Wire cross section area is measured in circular mils. A mil is 1/1000″ (0.001″); a circular mil is the area of a circle one mil in diameter. For example, a conductor 1/4″ in diameter is 0.250″ or 250 mils. The circular mil cross section area of the wire is 250 squared (250″)or 62,500 circular mils. Imported car models usually use metric wire gauge designations, which is simply the cross section area of the conductor in square millimeters (mm″).

Gauge numbers are assigned to conductors of various cross section areas. As gauge number increases, area decreases and the conductor becomes smaller. A 5 gauge conductor is smaller than a 1 gauge conductor and a 10 gauge is smaller than a 5 gauge. As the cross section area of a conductor decreases, resistance increases and so does the gauge number. A conductor with a higher gauge number will carry less current than a conductor with a lower gauge number.

➡ Gauge wire size refers to the size of the conductor, not the size of the complete wire. It is possible to have two wires of the same gauge with different diameters because one may have thicker insulation than the other.

A 2 volt automotive electrical systems generally use 10, 12, 14, 16 and 18 gauge wire. Main power distribution circuits and larger accessories usually use 10 and 12 gauge wire. Battery cables are usually 4 or 6 gauge, although 1 and 2 gauge wires are occasionally used. Wire length must also be considered when making repairs to a circuit. As conductor length increases, so does resistance. An 18 gauge wire, for example, can carry a 10 amp load for 10 feet without excessive voltage drop; however if a 15 foot wire is required for the same 10 amp load, it must be a 16 gauge wire.

An electrical schematic shows the electrical current paths when a circuit is operating properly. It is essential to understand how a circuit works before trying to figure out why it doesn't. Schematics break the entire electrical system down into individual circuits and show only one particular circuit. In a schematic, no attempt is made to represent wiring and components as they physically appear on the vehicle; switches and other components are shown as simply as possible. Face views of harness connectors show the cavity or terminal locations in all multi-pin connectors to help locate test points.

If you need to backprobe a connector while it is on the component, the order of the terminals must be mentally reversed. The wire color code can help in this situation, as well as a keyway, lock tab or other reference mark.

WIRING REPAIR

Soldering is a quick, efficient method of joining metals permanently. Everyone who has the occasion to make wiring repairs should know how to solder. Electrical connections that are soldered are far less likely to come apart and will conduct electricity much better than connections that are only "pig-tailed" together. The most popular (and preferred) method of soldering is with an electrical soldering gun. Soldering irons are available in many sizes and wattage ratings. Irons with higher wattage ratings deliver higher temperatures and recover lost heat faster. A small soldering iron rated for no more than 50 watts is recommended, especially on electrical systems where excess heat can damage the components being soldered.

There are three ingredients necessary for successful soldering; proper flux, good solder and sufficient heat. A soldering flux is necessary to clean the metal of tarnish, prepare it for soldering and to enable the solder to spread into tiny crevices. When soldering, always use a resin flux or resin core solder which is non-corrosive and will not attract moisture once the job is finished. Other types of flux (acid core) will leave a residue that will attract moisture and cause the wires to corrode. Tin is a unique metal with a low melting point. In a molten state, it dissolves and alloys easily with many metals. Solder is made by mixing tin with lead. The most common proportions are 40/60, 50/50 and 60/40, with the percentage of tin listed first. Low priced solders usually contain less tin, making them very difficult for a beginner to use because more heat is required to melt the solder. A common solder is 40/60 which is well suited for all-around general use, but 60/40 melts easier, has more tin for a better joint and is preferred for electrical work.

Soldering Techniques

Successful soldering requires that the metals to be joined be heated to a temperature that will melt the solder—usually 360-460°F (182-238°C). Contrary to popular belief, the purpose of the soldering iron is not to melt the solder itself, but to heat the parts being soldered to a temperature high enough to melt the solder when it is touched to the work. Melting flux-cored solder on the soldering iron will usually destroy the effectiveness of the flux.

➡ Soldering tips are made of copper for good heat conductivity, but must be "tinned" regularly for quick transference of heat to the project and to prevent the solder from sticking to the iron. To "tin" the iron, simply heat it and touch the flux-cored solder to the tip; the solder will flow over the hot tip. Wipe the excess off with a clean rag, but be careful as the iron will be hot.

After some use, the tip may become pitted. If so, simply dress the tip smooth with a smooth file and "tin" the tip again. An old saying holds that "metals well cleaned are half soldered." Flux-cored solder will remove oxides but rust, bits of insulation and oil or grease must be removed with a wire brush or emery cloth. For maximum strength in soldered parts, the joint must start off clean and tight. Weak joints will result in gaps too wide for the solder to bridge.

If a separate soldering flux is used, it should be brushed or swabbed on only those areas that are to be soldered. Most solders contain a core of flux and separate fluxing is unnecessary. Hold the work to be soldered firmly. It is best to solder on a wooden board, because a metal vise will only rob the piece to be soldered of heat and make it difficult to melt the solder. Hold the soldering tip with the broadest face against the work to be soldered. Apply solder under the tip close to the work, using enough solder to give a heavy film between the iron and the piece being soldered, while moving slowly and making sure the solder melts properly. Keep the work level or the solder will run to the lowest part and favor the thicker parts, because these require more heat to melt the solder. If the soldering tip overheats (the solder coating on the face of the tip burns up), it should be retinned. Once the soldering is completed, let the soldered joint stand until cool. Tape and seal all soldered wire splices after the repair has cooled.

Wire Harness and Connectors

The on-board computer (ECM) wire harness electrically connects the control unit to the various solenoids, switches and sensors used by the control system. Most connectors in the engine compartment or otherwise exposed to the elements are protected against moisture and dirt which could create oxidation and deposits on the terminals. This protection is important because of the very low voltage and current levels used by the computer and sensors. All connectors have a lock which secures the male and female terminals together, with a secondary lock holding the seal and terminal into the connector. Both terminal locks must be released when disconnecting ECM connectors.

These special connectors are weather-proof and all repairs require the use of a special terminal and the tool required to service it. This tool is used to remove the pin and sleeve terminals. If removal is attempted with an ordinary pick, there is a good chance that the terminal will be bent or deformed. Unlike standard blade type terminals, these terminals cannot be straightened once they are bent. Make certain that the connectors are properly seated and all of the sealing rings in place when connecting leads. On some models, a hinge-type flap provides a backup or secondary locking feature for the terminals. Most secondary locks are used to improve the connector reliability by retaining the terminals if the small terminal lock tangs are not positioned properly.

Molded-on connectors require complete replacement of the connection. This means splicing a new connector assembly into the harness. All splices in on-board computer systems should be soldered to insure proper contact. Use care when probing the connections or replacing terminals in them as it is possible to short between opposite terminals. If this happens to the wrong terminal pair, it is possible to damage certain components. Always use jumper wires between connectors for circuit checking and never probe through weatherproof seals.

Open circuits are often difficult to locate by sight because corrosion or terminal misalignment are hidden by the connectors. Merely wiggling a connector on a sensor or in the wiring harness may correct the open circuit condition. This should always be considered when an open circuit or a failed sensor is indicated. Intermittent problems may also be caused by oxidized or loose connections. When using a circuit tester for diagnosis, always probe connections from the wire side. Be careful not to damage sealed connectors with test probes.

All wiring harnesses should be replaced with identical parts, using the same gauge wire and connectors. When signal wires are spliced into a harness, use wire with high temperature insulation only. With the low voltage and current levels found in the system, it is important that the best possible connection at all wire splices be made by soldering the splices together. It is seldom necessary to replace a complete harness. If replacement is necessary, pay close attention to insure proper harness routing. Secure the harness with suitable plastic wire clamps to prevent vibrations from causing the harness to wear in spots or contact any hot components.

➡ **Weatherproof connectors cannot be replaced with standard connectors. Instructions are provided with replacement connector and terminal packages. Some wire harnesses have mounting indicators (usually pieces of colored tape) to mark where the harness is to be secured.**

In making wiring repairs, it's important that you always replace damaged wires with wires that are the same gauge as the wire being replaced. The heavier the wire, the smaller the gauge number. Wires are color-coded to aid in identification and whenever possible the same color coded wire should be used for replacement. A wire stripping and crimping tool is necessary to install solderless terminal connectors. Test all crimps by pulling on the wires; it should not be possible to pull the wires out of a good crimp.

Wires which are open, exposed or otherwise damaged are repaired by simple splicing. Where possible, if the wiring harness is accessible and the damaged place in the wire can be located, it is best to open the harness and check for all possible damage. In an inaccessible harness, the wire must be bypassed with a new insert, usually taped to the outside of the old harness.

When replacing fusible links, be sure to use fusible link wire, NOT ordinary automotive wire. Make sure the fusible segment is of the same gauge and construction as the one being replaced and double the stripped end when crimping the terminal connector for a good contact. The melted (open) fusible link segment of the wiring harness should be cut off as close to the harness as possible, then a new segment spliced in as described. In the case of a damaged fusible link that feeds two harness wires, the harness connections should be replaced with two fusible link wires so that each circuit will have its own separate protection.

➡ **Most of the problems caused in the wiring harness are due to bad ground connections. Always check all vehicle ground connections for corrosion or looseness before performing any power feed checks to eliminate the chance of a bad ground affecting the circuit.**

Repairing Hard Shell Connectors

Unlike molded connectors, the terminal contacts in hard shell connectors can be replaced. Weatherproof hard-shell connectors with the leads molded into the shell have non-replaceable terminal ends. Replacement usually involves the use of a special terminal removal tool that depress the locking tangs (barbs) on the connector terminal and allow the connector to be removed from the rear of the shell. The connector shell should be replaced if it shows any evidence of burning, melting, cracks, or breaks. Replace individual terminals that are burnt, corroded, distorted or loose.

➡ **The insulation crimp must be tight to prevent the insulation from sliding back on the wire when the wire is pulled. The insulation must be visibly compressed under the crimp tabs, and the ends of the crimp should be turned in for a firm grip on the insulation.**

The wire crimp must be made with all wire strands inside the crimp. The terminal must be fully compressed on the wire strands with the ends of the crimp tabs turned in to make a firm grip on the wire. Check all connections with an ohmmeter to insure a good contact. There should be no measurable resistance between the wire and the terminal when connected.

Mechanical Test Equipment

Vacuum Gauge

Most gauges are graduated in inches of mercury (in.Hg), although a device called a manometer reads vacuum in inches of water (in. H2O). The normal vacuum reading usually varies between 18 and 22 in.Hg at sea level. To test engine vacuum, the vacuum gauge must be connected to a source of manifold vacuum. Many engines have a plug in the intake manifold which can be removed and replaced with an adapter fitting. Connect the vacuum gauge to the fitting with a suitable rubber hose or, if no manifold plug is available, connect the vacuum gauge to any device using manifold vacuum, such as EGR valves, etc. The vacuum gauge can be used to determine if enough vacuum is reaching a component to allow its actuation.

Hand Vacuum Pump

Small, hand-held vacuum pumps come in a variety of designs. Most have a built-in vacuum gauge and allow the component to be tested without removing it from the vehicle. Operate the pump lever or plunger to apply the correct amount of vacuum required for the test specified in the diagnosis routines. The level of vacuum in inches of Mercury (in.Hg) is indicated on the pump gauge. For some testing, an additional vacuum gauge may be necessary.

Intake manifold vacuum is used to operate various systems and devices on late model vehicles. To correctly diagnose and solve problems in vacuum control systems, a vacuum source is necessary for testing. In some cases, vacuum can be taken from the intake manifold when the engine is running, but vacuum is normally provided by a hand vacuum pump. These hand vacuum pumps have a built-in vacuum gauge that allow testing while the device is still attached to the component. For some tests, an additional vacuum gauge may be necessary.

HEATER

➡ **For Discharging, evacuating, leak-testing and charging the air conditioning system, refer to Section 1.**

Blower Motor

REMOVAL & INSTALLATION

➡ **On most vehicles, the air conditioning assembly is integral with the heater assembly (including the blower motor) and therefore the blower motor removal may differ from the procedures detailed below. In some case it may be necessary to remove the air conditioning/heater housing and assembly to remove the blower motor. Due to the lack of information available at the time of this publication, a general heater core removal and installation procedure is outlined for the Camry from 1983-91. The removal steps can be altered as required.**

1983-87

➧ SEE FIG. 1

1. Disconnect the negative battery cable.
2. Remove the parcel tray located under the dash.
3. Remove the two discharge duct bracket mounting screens, and then remove the two brackets and the duct.
4. Remove the mounting screw, and remove the right side forward console cover.
5. Unscrew the mounting screw and remove the relay bracket located under the motor.
6. Disconnect the motor connector. If equipped, unscrew and remove the A/C amplifier and route the wiring harness out of the way.
7. Remove the three mounting screws, and remove the motor, gasket, and blower assembly. If necessary, remove the blower mounting nut and washers, and remove the blower from the shaft.

To install:

8. Install the blower wheel onto the shaft with washers and mounting nut.
9. Position the blower with gasket up into the blower case and install the retaining screws.
10. Install the A/C amplifier and route the wiring harness properly.
11. Connect the motor connector.
12. Install the relay bracket and fight side forward console cover.
13. Assemble the ducting with brackets and screens.
14. Install the parcel tray.
15. Reconnect the battery.
15. Cycle the blower through all the speeds to check for proper operation.

1988-91

➧ SEE FIG. 2

1. Disconnect the negative battery cable.
2. Remove the 3 screws attaching the retainer.
3. Remove the glove box. Remove the duct between the blower motor assembly and the heater assembly.
4. Disconnect the blower motor wire connector at the blower motor case.
5. Disconnect the air source selector control cable at the blower motor assembly.
6. Loosen the nuts and bolts attaching the blower motor to the blower case, remove the blower motor from the vehicle.

To install:

7. Installation is the reverse of the removal procedure.
8. Check the blower for proper operation at all speeds.

1992

➧ SEE FIGS. 3-5

1. Disconnect the negative battery cable.
2. Remove the glove compartment.
3. Remove the ECU and the ECU bracket.
4. Remove the connector bracket by disconnecting the connector and removing the 2 screws.
5. Disconnect the connector from the blower unit.
6. Disconnect the air inlet damper control cable.
7. Remove the 3 screws, the nut and the blower unit.

To install:

8. Installation is the reverse of removal.

FIG. 1 Heater blower motor—1983-87

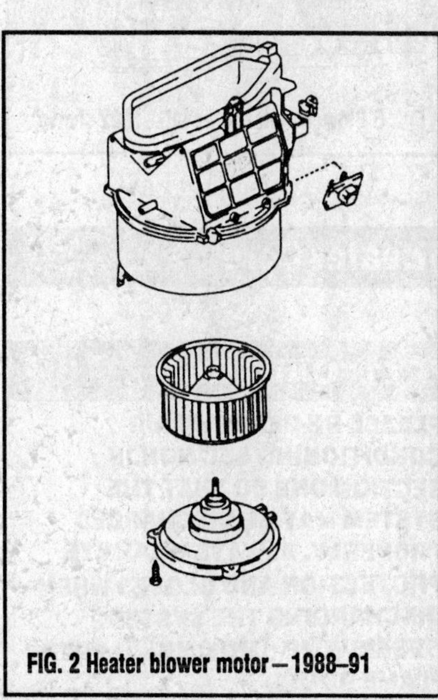

FIG. 2 Heater blower motor—1988-91

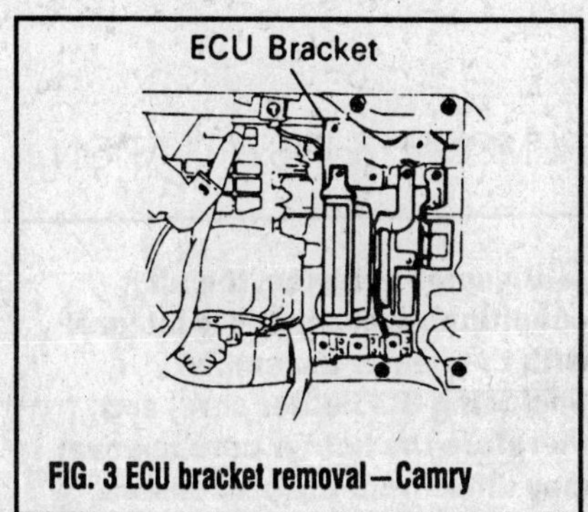

FIG. 3 ECU bracket removal—Camry

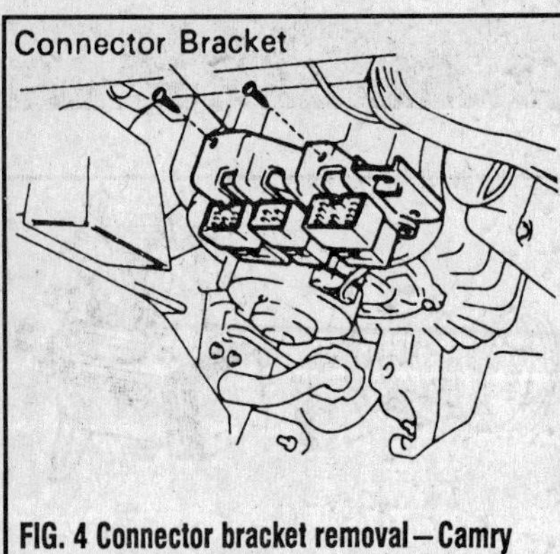

FIG. 4 Connector bracket removal—Camry

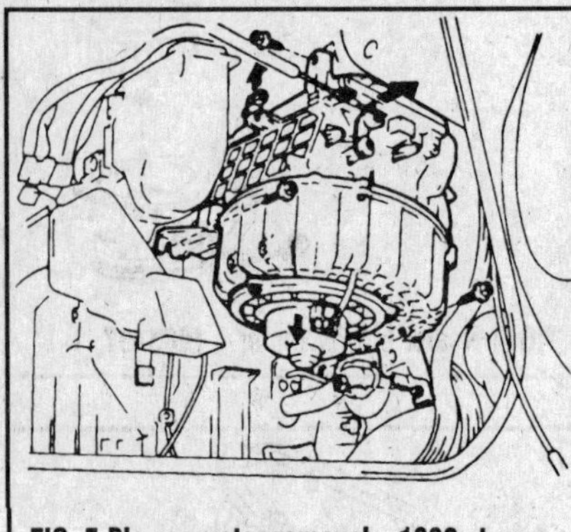
FIG. 5 Blower motor removal—1992 shown

Heater Core

CAUTION

PLEASE RE-READ THE AIR CONDITIONING SECTION IN SECTION ONE SO THAT THE SYSTEM MAY BE DISCHARGED PROPERLY. ALWAYS WEAR EYE PROTECTION AND GLOVES WHEN DISCHARGING THE SYSTEM. OBSERVE NO SMOKING/NO OPEN FLAME RULES.

REMOVAL & INSTALLATION

➡ **On some vehicles, the air conditioning assembly is integral with the heater assembly (including the heater core) and therefore the heater core removal may differ from the procedures detailed below. In some cases it may be necessary to remove the air conditioning/heater housing and assembly to remove the heater core. Due to the lack of information available at the time of this publication, a general heater core removal and installation procedure is outlined for each vehicle. The removal steps can be altered as required.**

CAUTION

When draining the coolant, keep in mind that cats and dogs are attracted by the ethylene glycol antifreeze, and are quite likely to drink any that is left in an uncovered container or in puddles on the ground. This will prove fatal in sufficient quantity. Always drain the coolant into a sealable container. Coolant should be reused unless it is contaminated or several years old.

1983–87

➧ SEE FIG. 6

1. Disconnect the negative battery cable.
2. Position a suitable drain pan under the radiator, and partially drain the cooling system.
3. Remove the console, if so equipped, by removing the shift knob (manual transaxles), wiring connector, and console attaching screws.
4. Remove the carpeting from the tunnel.
5. If equipped, remove the cigarette lighter and ash tray.
6. Remove the package tray, if it makes access to the heater core easier.
7. Unscrew and remove the center air outlet.
8. Remove the bottom cover/intake assembly screws and withdraw the assembly.
9. Remove the cover from the water valve.
10. Remove the water valve.
11. Loosen the hose clamps and disconnect the hoses from the core.
12. Remove the core from its housing.

To install:

13. Install the core into the housing and connect the inlet and outlet hoses. Tighten the hose clamps.
14. Install the water valve and valve cover.
15. Install the bottom cover intake assembly and tighten the screws.
16. Install the central air outlet and tighten the screws.
17. Install the package tray if it was removed.
18. Install the cigar lighter and ash tray if it was removed.
19. Install the tunnel carpeting.
20. Install the console components.
21. Fill the radiator to the proper level with a good brand of ethylene glycol brand coolant.
22. Fill the cooling system to the proper level.
23. Install the remaining components, reconnect the battery, then start and warm the engine, making sure that the cooling system stays full.
24. Stop the engine, pressurize the cooling system and check for leaks. Check the heater operation pressurized.

1988–91

➧ SEE FIG. 7

1. Disconnect the negative battery cable.
2. Position a suitable drain pan under the radiator, and partially drain the cooling system.
3. Remove the console, if equipped, by removing the shift knob (manual), wiring connector, and console attaching screws.
4. Remove the carpeting from the tunnel.
5. If necessary, remove the cigarette lighter and ash tray.
6. Remove the package tray, if it makes access to the heater core difficult.
7. Remove the bottom cover/intake assembly screws and withdraw the assembly.
8. Remove the cover from the water valve.
9. Remove the water valve.
10. Remove the hose clamps and remove the hoses from the core.
11. Remove the heater core.

To install:

12. Install the heater core into the heater housing, make sure to clean heater housing of all dirt, leaves, etc. before heater core installation.
13. Fill the cooling system to the proper level.
14. Install the remaining components and reconnect the battery, then start and warm the engine, making sure that the cooling system stays full.
15. Stop the engine, pressurize the cooling system and check for leaks. Check the heater operation pressurized.

1992

➧ SEE FIGS. 8 AND 9

1. Disconnect the negative battery cable.
2. Position a suitable drain pan under the radiator, and partially drain the cooling system.
3. Remove the heater protector by removing the screws and the 2 clips.
4. Remove the heater hoses from the heater pipes.
5. Remove the 3 screws and the 3 clamps that secure the heater core, then remove the core.

To install:

6. Install the heater core into the heater housing, make sure to clean heater housing of all

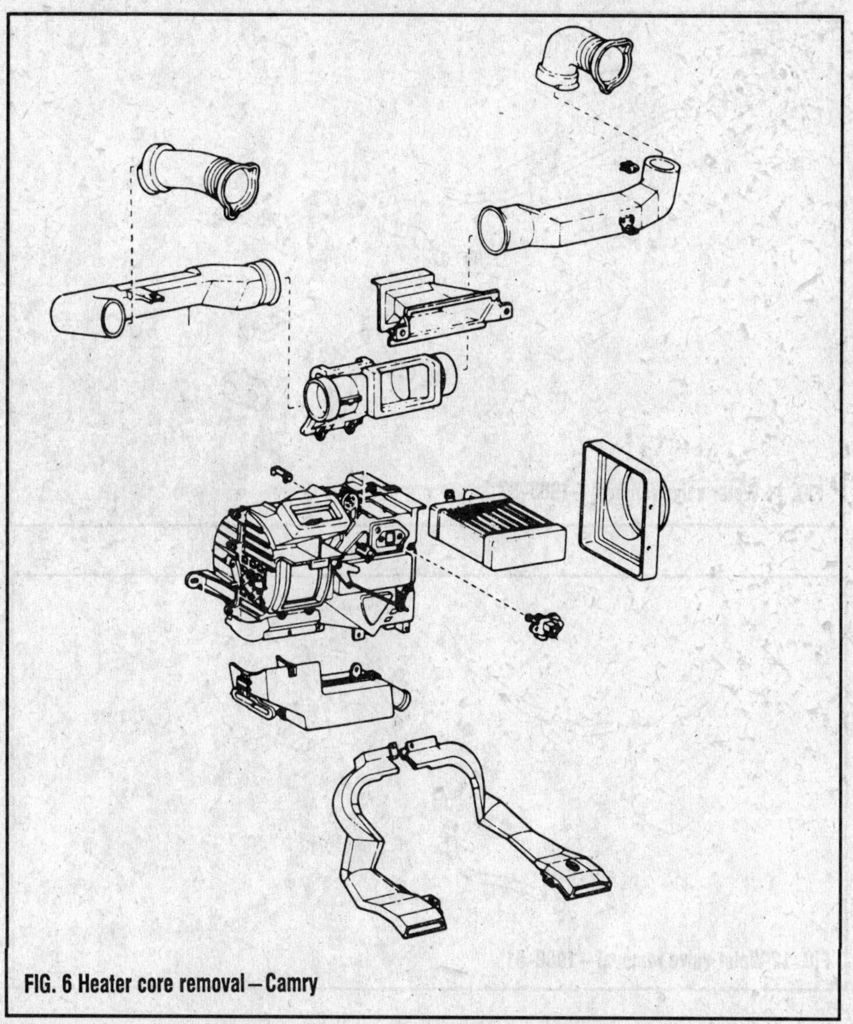

FIG. 6 Heater core removal—Camry

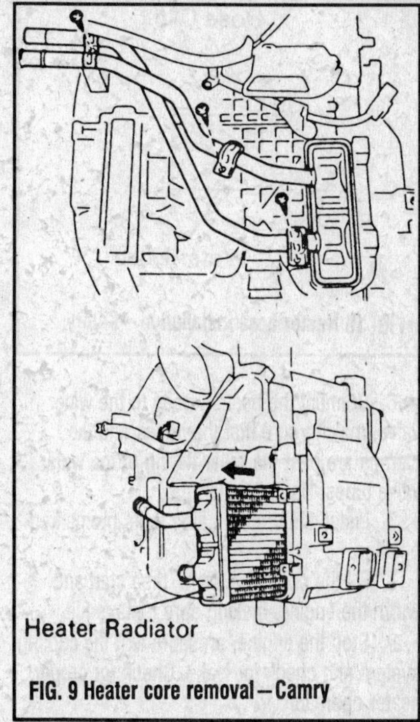

FIG. 9 Heater core removal—Camry

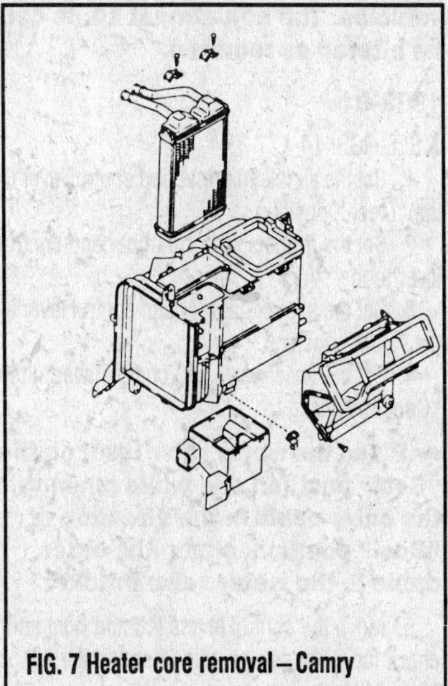

FIG. 7 Heater core removal—Camry

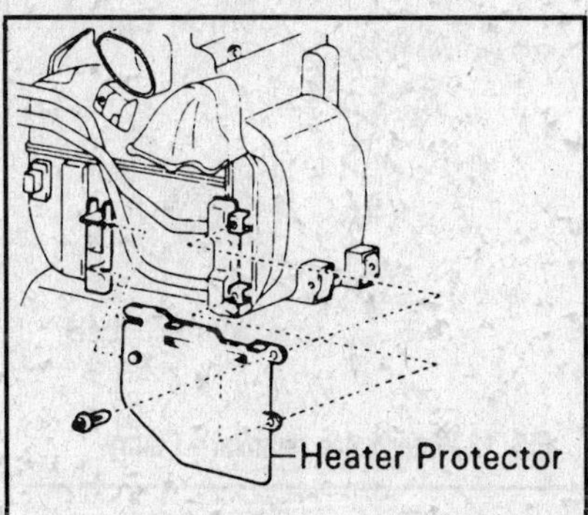

FIG. 8 Heater protector removal—Camry

dirt, leaves, etc. before heater core installation.

7. Fill the cooling system to the proper level.
8. Install the remaining components, reconnect the battery, then start and warm the engine, making sure that the cooling system stays full.
9. Stop the engine, pressurize the cooling system and check for leaks. Check the heater operation pressurized.

Heater Water Control Valve

REMOVAL & INSTALLATION

➡ **Due to the lack of information available at the time of this publication, a general heater water control valve removal and installation procedure is outlined for the Camry from 1983–91. The removal steps can be altered as required.**

1983-91

➧ SEE FIGS. 10-12

1. Partially drain the engine coolant from the radiator.
2. Mark and disconnect the water valve control cable from the water valve.
3. Disconnect the heater hoses from the water valve.

➡ **Be careful not to pull on the heater core tubes when removing the heater hoses, since the heater core can be easily damaged.**

4. Remove the bolt and the water valve.

To install:

5. Install the bolt and the water valve.

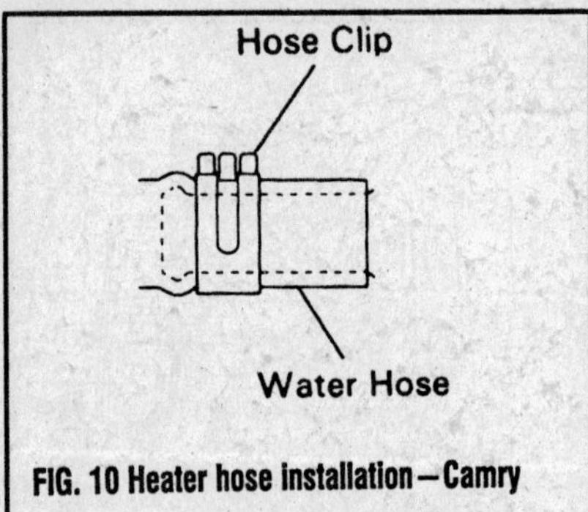

FIG. 10 Heater hose installation — Camry

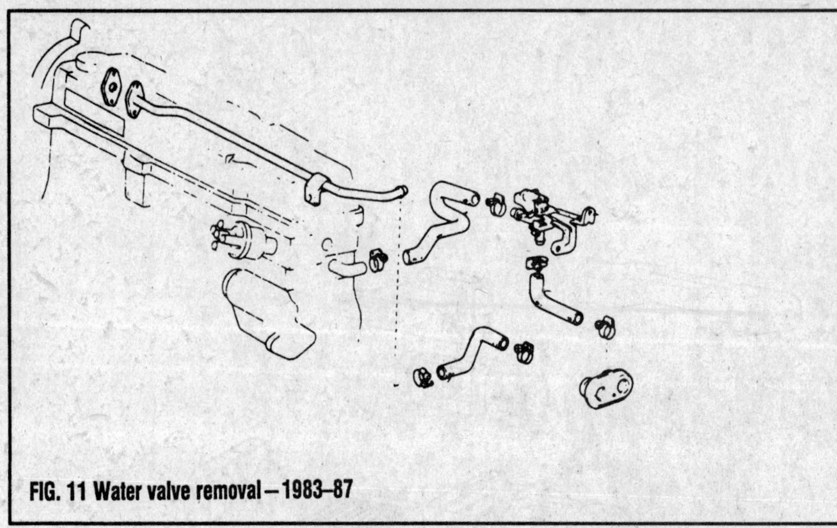
FIG. 11 Water valve removal — 1983–87

6. Connect the heater hoses to the water valve, making sure that the hoses and the clamps are past the outer flaring of the water valve tubes. Use new clamps.

7. Install the control cable to its premarked position.

8. Fill the cooling system, then start and warm the engine, making sure it stays full.

9. Stop the engine, pressure test the cooling system and check for leaks. Check for proper heater operation.

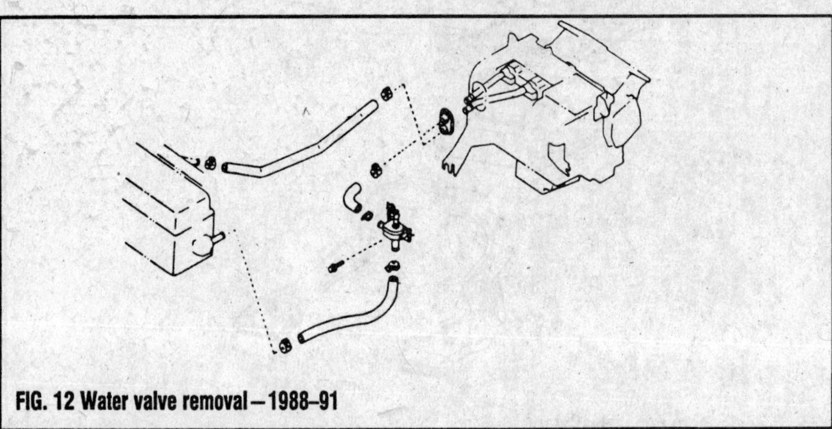
FIG. 12 Water valve removal — 1988–91

1992

➧ SEE FIGS. 10 AND 13

1. Partially drain the engine coolant from the radiator.

2. Mark and disconnect the water valve control cable from the water valve.

3. Disconnect the heater hoses from the water valve.

➡ Be careful not to pull on the heater core tubes when removing the heater hoses, since the heater core can be easily damaged.

4. Remove the bolt and the water valve.

To install:

5. Install the bolt and the water valve.

6. Connect the heater hoses to the water valve, making sure that the hoses and the clamps are past the outer flaring of the water valve tubes. Use new clamps.

7. Install the control cable to the premarked position.

8. Fill the cooling system, then start and warm the engine, making sure it stays full.

9. Stop the engine, pressure test the cooling system and check for leaks. Check for proper heater operation.

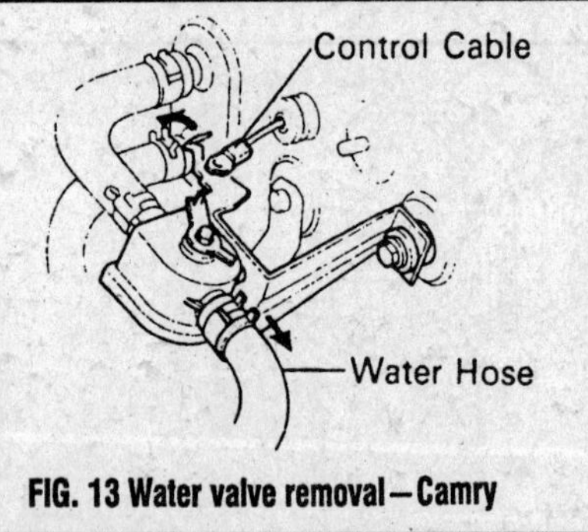

FIG. 13 Water valve removal — Camry

Control Cable

ADJUSTMENT

➡ Due to the lack of information available at the time of this publication, a general heater control cable adjustment procedure is outlined for 1983–91 vehicles. The adjustment steps can be altered as required.

1983–91

➧ SEE FIGS. 14-17

1. Set the air inlet damper and control lever to the "Fresh" position.

2. Set the mode selector damper and control lever to the "Vent" position.

3. Set the air mix damper and control lever to the "Cool" position.

4. Set the water valve and control lever to the "Cool" position.

➡ Place the water valve lever on the "Cool" position and while pushing the outer cable in the direction of "Cool" position, clamp the outer cable to the water valve bracket.

5. Move the control levers left and right and check for stiffness or binding through the full range of the levers.

FIG. 14 Setting the heater control cable to the "Fresh" position—Camry

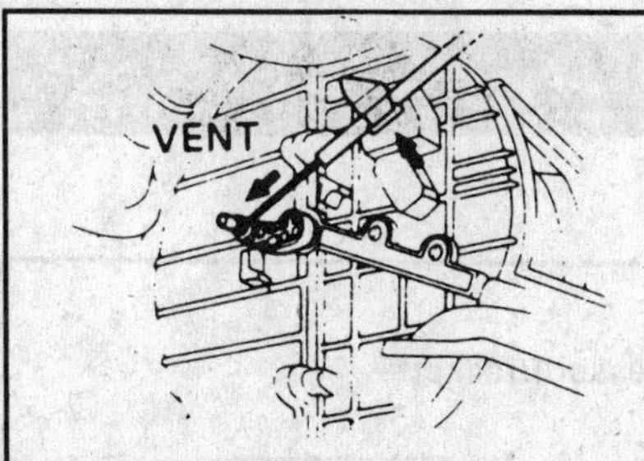

FIG. 15 Setting the heater control cable to the "Vent" position—Camry

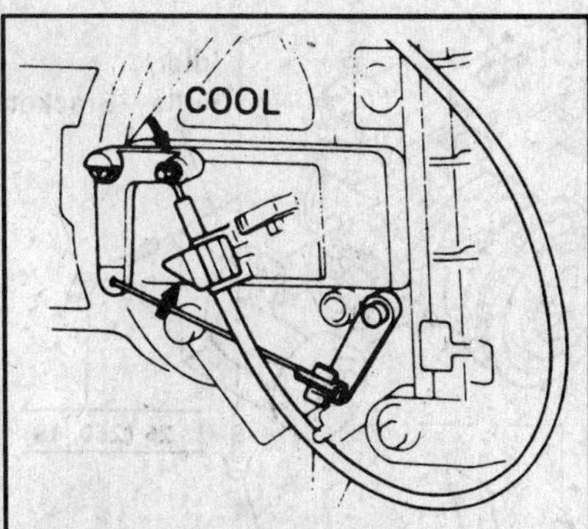

FIG. 16 Setting the heater control cable to the "Cool" position—Camry

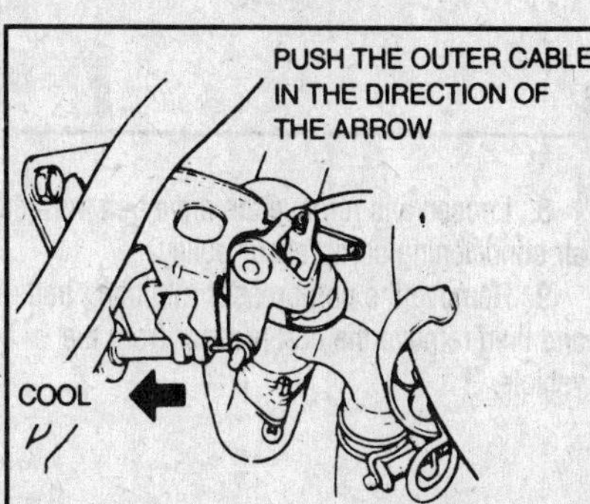

FIG. 17 Setting the water valve and control lever to the "Cool" position—Camry

1992

➧ SEE FIG. 18

1. Set the temperature control switch to "Cool" and set the water valve lever to "Cool".
2. Install the control cable and lock the clamp.

➡ Lock the clamp while lightly pushing the outer cable in the direction toward the "Cool" position of the valve.

Heater and Air Conditioning Control Panel

REMOVAL & INSTALLATION

➡ Due to the lack of information available at the time of this publication, a general control panel removal and installation procedure is outlined for the Camry. The removal steps can be altered as required.

➧ SEE FIGS. 19-20C

1. Disconnect the negative battery cable.
2. Remove the 2 screws or gently pry against the plastic clips, if so equipped.
3. Remove the ashtray by using a suitable tool and releasing the white plastic clip at the rear of the ash receptacle retainer.
4. Carefully pull out the center cluster finish panel.
5. Remove the heater control panel by removing the 4 screws.

To Install:

6. Installation is the reverse of removal. Use care when snapping back together plastic components, if so equipped.

Blower Switch

REMOVAL & INSTALLATION

1. Disconnect the negative battery cable.
2. Remove the blower switch control knob (if the switch is the lever type).
3. Remove the heater control panel.
4. Remove the screws or clips retaining the switch.

To Install:

5. Installation is the reverse of removal.

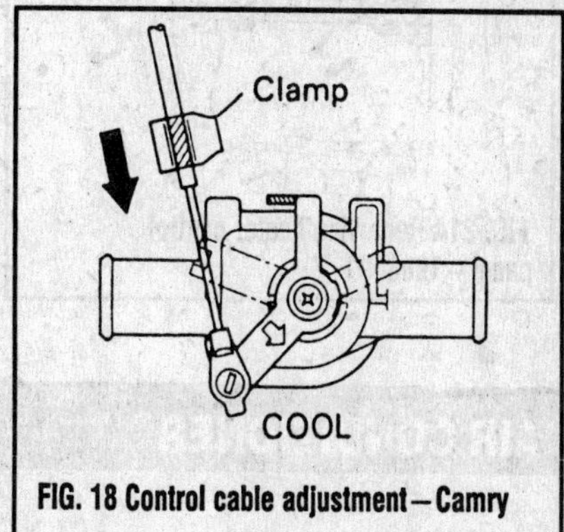

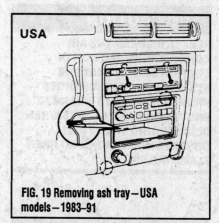

FIG. 18 Control cable adjustment—Camry

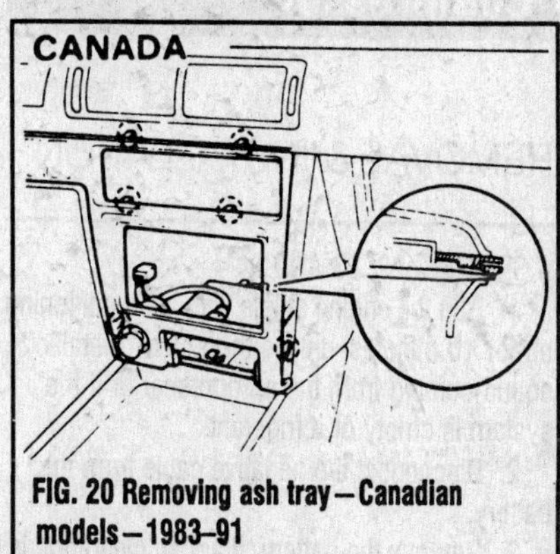

FIG. 19 Removing ash tray—USA models—1983–91

FIG. 20 Removing ash tray—Canadian models—1983–91

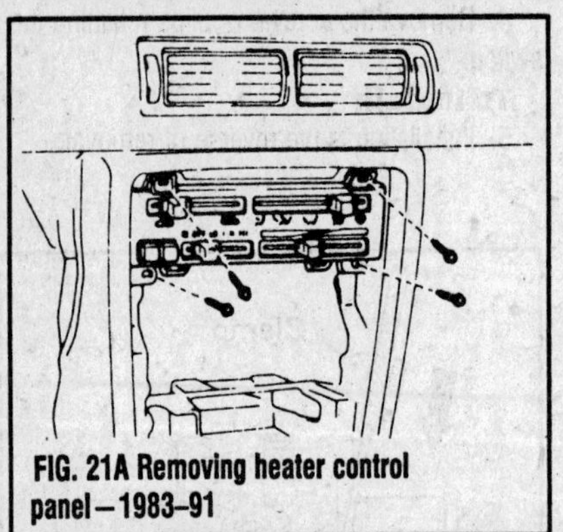
FIG. 21A Removing heater control panel – 1983–91

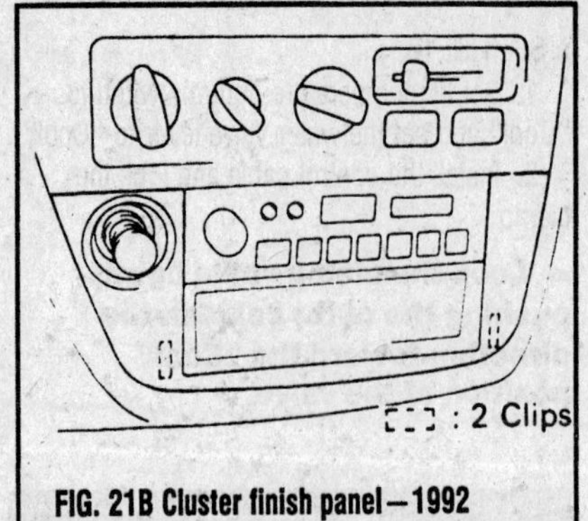

FIG. 21B Cluster finish panel – 1992

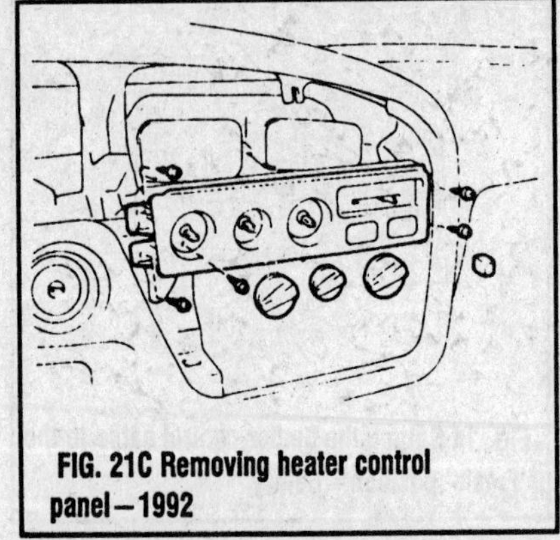
FIG. 21C Removing heater control panel – 1992

AIR CONDITIONER

CAUTION

PLEASE RE-READ THE AIR CONDITIONING SECTION IN SECTION ONE SO THAT THE SYSTEM MAY BE DISCHARGED PROPERLY. ALWAYS WEAR EYE PROTECTION AND GLOVES WHEN DISCHARGING THE SYSTEM. OBSERVE NO SMOKING/NO OPEN FLAME RULES.

Compressor

REMOVAL & INSTALLATION

SEE FIGS. 22, 23 AND 24

1. Run the engine at idle with air conditioning on for 10 minutes, unless there is a "metallic" sound coming from the compressor or if the system is empty of refrigerant.
2. Disconnect the negative cable from the battery.
3. Remove the battery, if added clearance is necessary. On the 1992 Camry with a V6 engine remove the battery bracket.
4. On 1989–91 models with V6 engines, remove the ignitor bracket, radiator fan and condensor fan. On the 1992 model, only remove the condensor fan and the cooling fan on cars with 4 cylinder and V6 engines, respectively.
5. Disconnect the clutch and sensor lead wires from the wiring harness.
6. Discharge and recover the refrigerant from the refrigeration system, using proper procedures.
7. Disconnect the two hoses from the compressor service valves.

Cap the open fittings immediately to keep moisture out of the system.

8. Loosen and remove the drive belt from the air conditioning compressor pulley.
9. Remove the compressor mounting bolts and then remove the compressor from the vehicle.

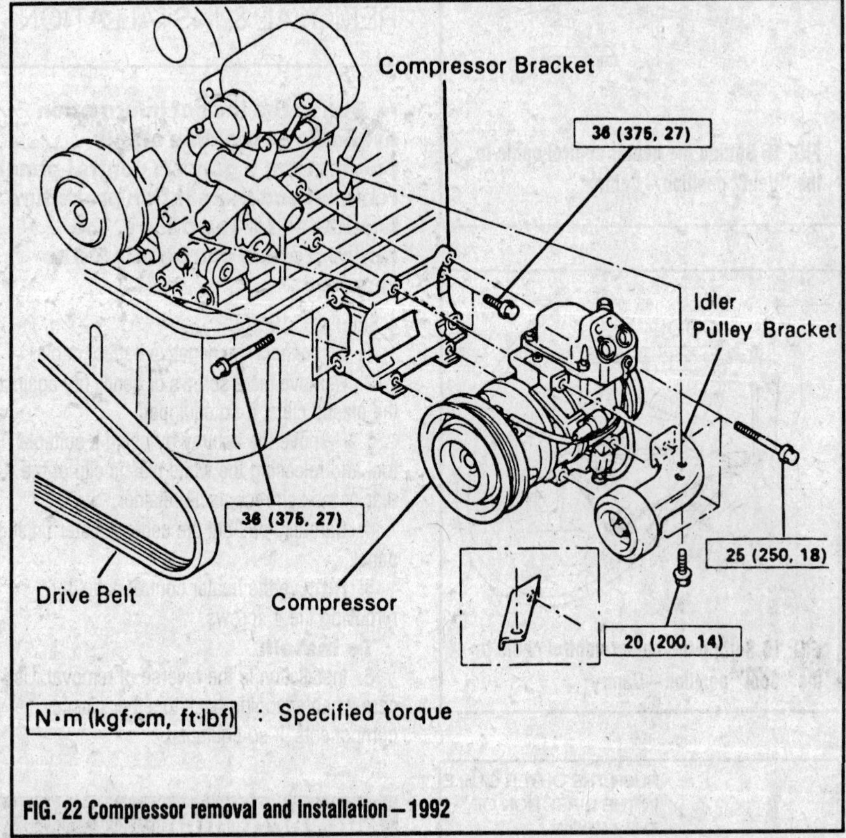

FIG. 22 Compressor removal and installation – 1992

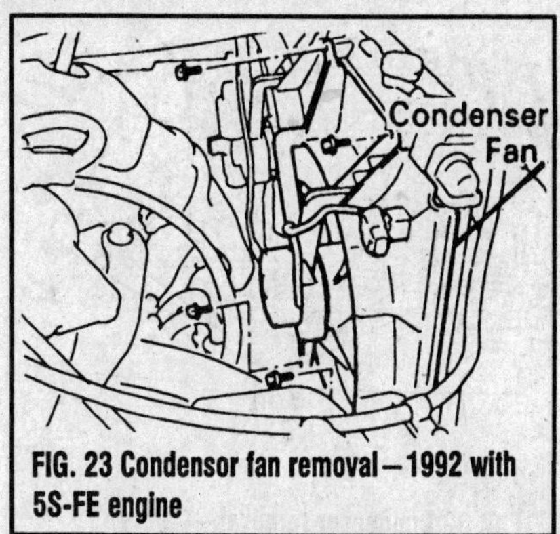

FIG. 23 Condensor fan removal—1992 with 5S-FE engine

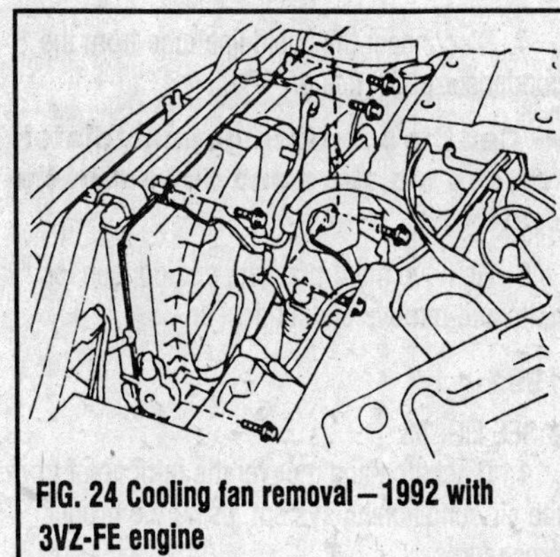
FIG. 24 Cooling fan removal—1992 with 3VZ-FE engine

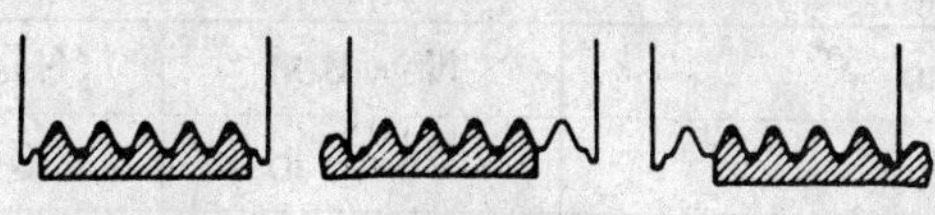

FIG. 25 Installing A/C belt—Camry

Engine	New belt	Used belt
2S-E	175 ± 5	130 ± 10
1C-T (w/o PS)	175 ± 5	115 ± 20
1C-T (w/ PS)	160 ± 20	100 ± 20

FIG. 26 A/C belt tension—1984

Engine	New belt	Used belt
2S-E	175 ± 5	130 ± 10
1C-T	160 ± 20	100 ± 20

FIG. 27 A/C belt tension—1985

Engine	New belt	Used belt
2S-E	175 ± 5	130 ± 10
2C-T	160 ± 20	100 ± 20

FIG. 28 A/C belt tension—1986

To Install:

1983–86

➧ SEE FIGS. 25–28

1. Install the compressor and torque the 3 mounting bolts evenly to 20 ft. lbs. (27 Nm).
2. Install the drive belt to the pulley, then tighten the belt to specifications with the adjusting bolts. (Check the belt tension with Burroughs tension guage BT-33-73F).

➡ Make sure that the drive belt is installed correctly.

a. On 1983 models, adjust the belt tension to 175±5 lbs. if a new belt is being used, or adjust the tension to 130±10 lbs. if the belt is a used belt.

b. On 1984–86 models, refer to the tension charts.

➡ "New belt" refers to a brand new belt that has never been used;"Used belt" refers to a belt that has been used on a running engine for 5 minutes or more.

3. Connect the two flexible hoses to the compressor service valves and torque the discharge line to 16 ft. lbs. (22 Nm), and the suction line to 24 ft. lbs. (32 Nm).
4. Connect the clutch lead and the sensor leads to the wiring harness.
5. Install the battery, if it was removed, and connect the positive cable, then the negative cable to the battery.
6. Evacuate, charge and test the refrigeration system.

1987–92

1. Install the compressor and torque the 4 mounting bolts evenly to 20 ft. lbs. (27 Nm) on 4-cylinder models through 1991, and 18 ft. lbs. (25 Nm) on 6-cylinder models through 1991. The bolts are torqued to 18 ft. lbs. (25 Nm) on the 1992 Camry.
2. Install the drive belt to the pulley, then tighten the belt to specifications with the adjusting bolts. (Check the belt tension with Burroughs tension guage BT-33-73F).

➡ Make sure that the drive belt is installed correctly.

a. On 1987–88 models, adjust the belt tension to 175±5 lbs. if a new belt is being used, or adjust the tension to 130±10 lbs. if the belt is a used belt.

b. On 1989–92 models, refer to the tension charts.

➡ "New belt" refers to a brand new belt that has never been used;"Used belt" refers to a belt that has been used on a running engine for 5 minutes or more.

3. Connect the two hoses to the compressor service valves and torque the discharge line and the suction line to 18 ft. lbs. (25 Nm).

Engine	New Belt	Used Belt
3S-FE	175 ± 5 lbs	130 ± 10 lbs
2VZ-FE	175 ± 5 lbs	115 ± 20 lbs

FIG. 29 A/C belt tension—1989–91

Engine	New Belt	Used Belt
3VZ–FE	165 ± 26 lb	88 ± 22 lb
5S–FE	165 ± 26 lb	110 ± 11 lb

FIG. 30 A/C belt tension—1992

4. Install the ignitor bracket, radiator fan and condensor fan, if they were removed.
5. Connect the clutch lead and the sensor leads to the wiring harness.
6. Install the battery (and the bracket, if removed) and connect the positive cable, then the negative cable to the battery.
7. Evacuate, charge and test the refrigeration system.

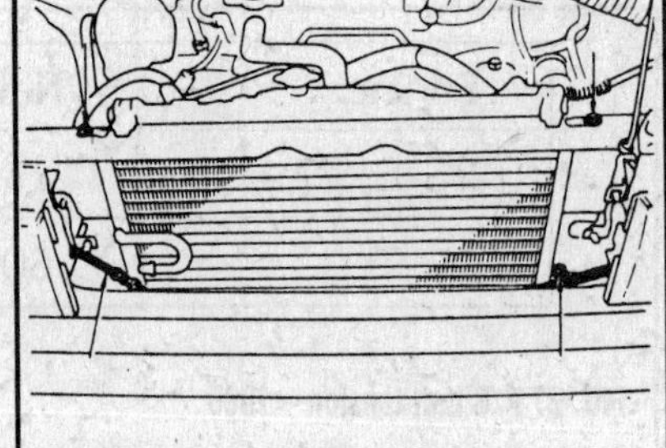

FIG. 31 Removing condensor bolts—Camry

Condenser

REMOVAL & INSTALLATION

1983–86

➧ SEE FIG. 31

1. Discharge and recover the refrigerant from the air conditioning system, using the proper procedures.
2. Remove the front grille, bumper and hood lock brace.
3. Disconnect the discharge flexible hose from the condensor inlet fitting.
4. Disconnect the liquid line tube from the condensor outlet fitting.

➡ Cap the open fittings immediately to keep moisture and dirt out of the system. Also, use the 2 proper type and size wrenches to avoid twisting the lines or rounding the fittings.

5. Remove the 4 condensor bolts and remove the condensor.

1987–88

➧ SEE FIG. 32

1. Discharge and recover the refrigerant from the air conditioning system, using the proper procedures.
2. Remove the front grille.
3. Disconnect the discharge hose from the condensor inlet fitting.
4. Disconnect the liquid line tube from the condensor outlet fitting.

➡ Cap the open fittings immediately to keep moisture and dirt out of the system.

5. Remove the 4 brackets and condensor bolts and remove the condensor.

1989–91

➧ SEE FIG. 32

1. Discharge and recover the refrigerant from the air conditioning system, using the proper procedures.
2. Remove the battery, ignitor bracket, radiator fan and condensor fan.
3. Disconnect the discharge hose from the condensor inlet fitting.

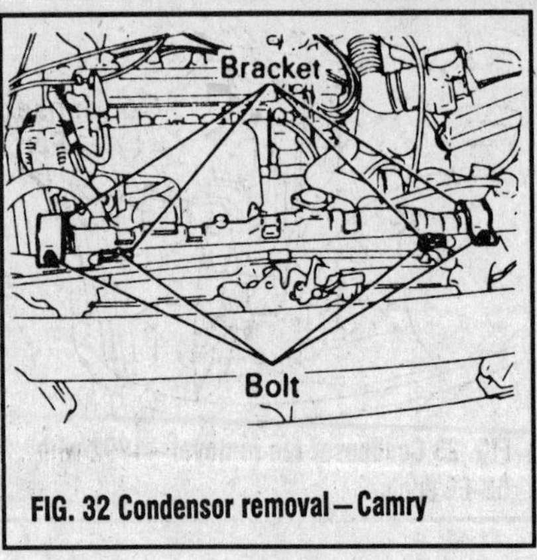

FIG. 32 Condensor removal—Camry

4. Disconnect the liquid line tube from the condensor outlet fitting.

➡ Cap the open fittings immediately to keep moisture and dirt out of the system.

5. Remove the 4 brackets and condensor bolts and remove the condensor.

1992

➧ SEE FIG. 33

1. Discharge and recover the refrigerant from the air conditioning system, using the proper procedures.
2. Remove the battery, upper cover and battery bracket.
3. Remove the 6 bolts retaining the cooling fan and remove the fan.
4. Remove the 2 bolts and the 2 upper supports.
5. Remove the 2 bolts and the 2 liquid tubes from the condensor.

➡ Cap the open fittings immediately to keep moisture and dirt out of the system.

6. Remove the headlights on both sides of the vehicle.
7. Remove the 2 condensor bolts and lean the radiator backward, then remove the condensor.

To install:

1983–86

1. Install the condensor with the 4 bolts, making sure that the rubber cushions fit on the mounting flanges correctly.
2. Connect the discharge hose to the condensor inlet fitting and torque to 15–18 ft. lbs. (20–24 Nm).
3. Connect the liquid line tube to the condensor outlet fitting and torque to 9–11 ft. lbs. (12–15 Nm).
4. Install the front grille, bumper and hood lock brace.
5. If the condensor was replaced, add 40–

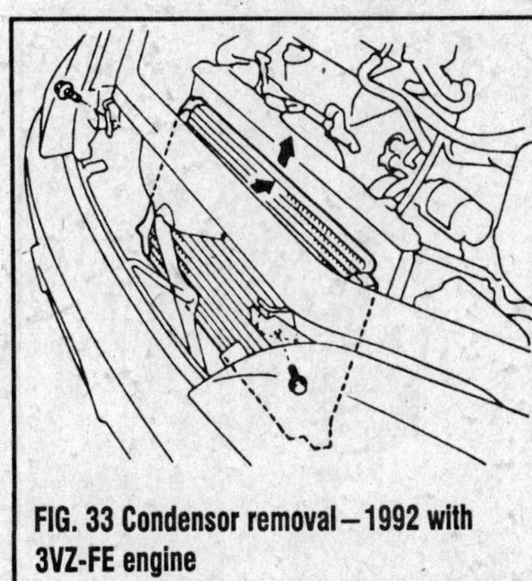
FIG. 33 Condensor removal—1992 with 3VZ-FE engine

50cc (1.4–1.7 oz.) compressor oil (Densoil 6, Suniso No. 5GS or equivalent) to the condensor.

6. Evacuate, charge and test the refrigeration system.

1987-88

1. Install the condensor with the brackets and bolts, making sure that the rubber cushions fit on the mounting flanges correctly.
2. Connect the discharge hose to the condensor inlet fitting and torque to 18 ft. lbs. (24 Nm).
3. Connect the liquid line tube to the condensor outlet fitting and torque to 10 ft. lbs. (14 Nm).
4. Install the front grille.
5. If the condensor was replaced, add 40–50cc (1.4–1.7 oz.) compressor oil (Densooil 6, Suniso No. 5GS or equivalent) to the condensor.
6. Evacuate, charge and test the refrigeration system.

1989-91

1. Install the condensor with the brackets and bolts, making sure that the rubber cushions fit on the mounting flanges correctly.
2. Connect the discharge hose to the condensor inlet fitting and torque to 9 ft. lbs. (13 Nm).
3. Connect the liquid line tube to the condensor outlet fitting and torque to 9 ft. lbs. (13 Nm).
4. Install the battery, ignitor bracket, radiator fan and condensor fan.
5. If the condensor was replaced, add 40–50cc (1.4–1.7 oz.) compressor oil (Densoil 6, Suniso No. 5GS or equivalent) to the condensor.
6. Evacuate, charge and test the refrigeration system.

1992

1. Install the condensor with the 2 bolts.
2. Install the liquid tubes and torque the 2 bolts to 7 ft. lbs. (9.8 Nm).
3. Install the cooling fan.
4. If the condensor was replaced, add 35cc (1.2 oz.) compressor oil (ND Oil 6, Suniso No. 5GS or equivalent) to the condensor.
5. Evacuate, charge and test the refrigeration system.
6. Install the removal parts in the reverse order of removal.

Cooling Unit and Evaporator Core

REMOVAL & INSTALLATION

➡ **Due to the lack of information available at the time of this publication, a general evaporator core removal and installation procedure is outlined for the Camry from 1983–91. The removal steps can be altered as required.**

1983-91

➧ SEE FIGS. 34–39

1. Disconnect the negative battery cable, then discharge and recover the refrigerant from the air conditioning system, using the proper procedures.
2. Disconnect the suction flexible hose from the cooling unit outlet fitting.
3. Disconnect the liquid line from the cooling unit inlet fitting. Cap the open fittings immediately to keep the moisture out of the system.

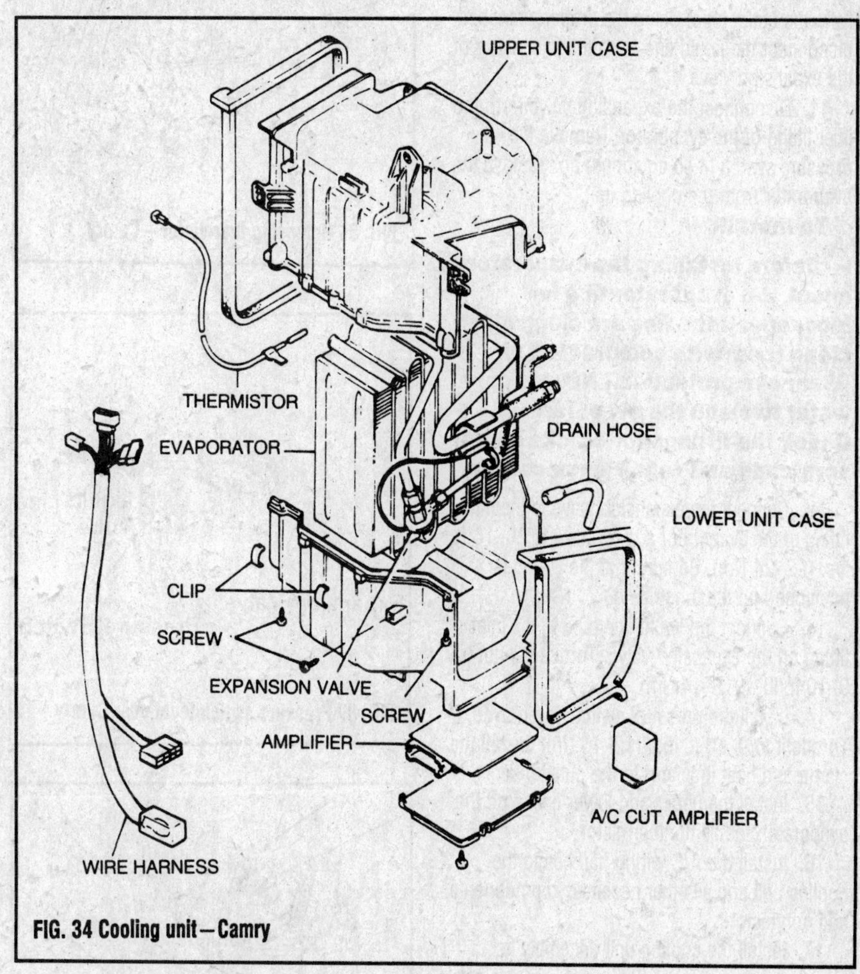

FIG. 34 Cooling unit—Camry

4. Remove the grommets from the inlet and outlet fittings.

5. Remove the glove box with the under cover, then disconnect all necessary connectors, such as the pressure switch connector, thermistor connector and the A/C harness.

6. Remove the 2 or 3 cooling unit attaching nuts and the 4 bolts. Remove the cooling unit from the vehicle.

7. Place the cooling unit on a suitable work bench and unscrew the thermistor, if so equipped.

8. Using suitable tools, carefully remove the cooling unit case clamps and retaining screws.

9. Remove the electrical components, if equipped, that prevent removing the upper cooling unit case half and remove the upper case from the evaporator.

10. Remove the heat insulator and the clamp from the outlet tube. Using the proper wrenches, disconnect the liquid line from the inlet fitting of the expansion valve.

11. Disconnect the expansion valve from the inlet fitting of the evaporator. Remove the pressure switch (if so equipped) and remove the evaporator from the cooling unit.

To install:

➡ Before installing the evaporator, check the evaporator fins for blockage. If the fins are clogged, clean them with compressed air (Wear eye protection.) Never use water to clean the evaporator. Check the fittings for cracks and or scratches and repair as necessary.

12. Connect the expansion valve to the inlet fitting of the evaporator and torque it to 16–18 ft. lbs. (22–24 Nm). Be sure that the O-ring is positioned on the tube fitting.

13. Connect the liquid line tube to the inlet fitting on the expansion valve. Torque the nut to 9–10 ft. lbs. (12–14 Nm).

14. Install the pressure switch, if removed. Torque it to 9–10 ft. lbs. (12–14 Nm). Install the clamp and heat insulator to the outlet tube.

15. Install the upper and lower cases on the evaporator. Install the thermistor.

16. Install the A/C wiring harness to the cooling unit and all other necessary components and connectors.

17. Install the cooling unit assembly its retaining nuts and bolts. Be careful not to pinch the wiring harness while installing the cooling unit.

18. Install the glove box and the grommets on the inlet and outlet fittings.

19. Connect the liquid line to the cooling unit inlet fittings and torque it to 9–11 ft. lbs. (12–15 Nm).

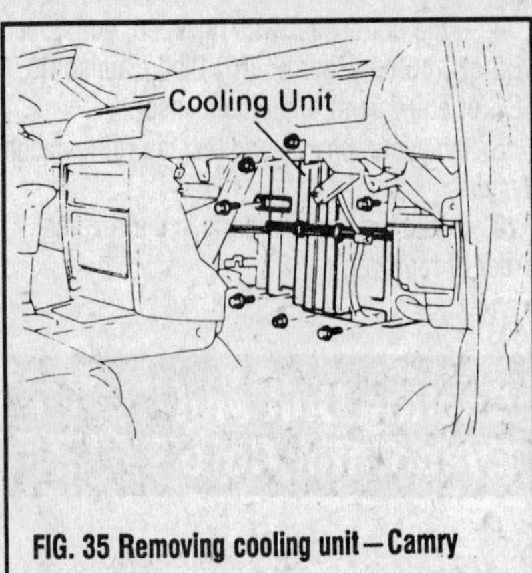

FIG. 35 Removing cooling unit—Camry

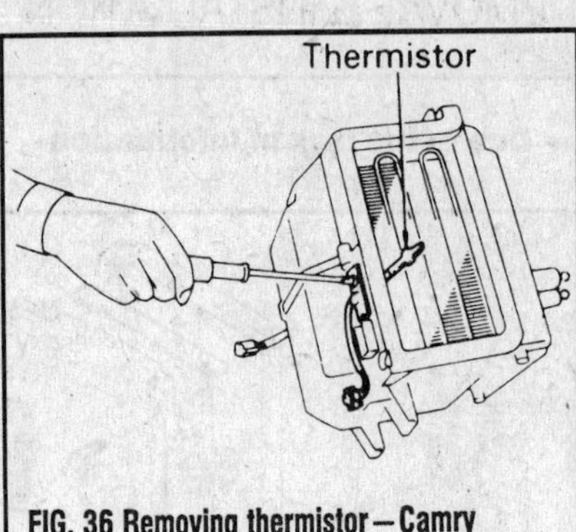

FIG. 36 Removing thermistor—Camry

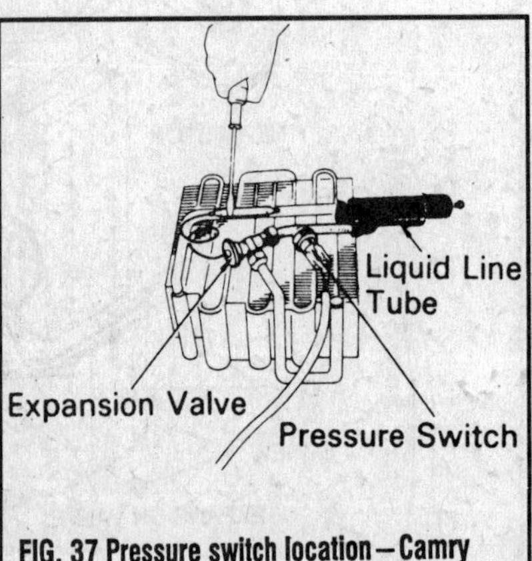

FIG. 37 Pressure switch location—Camry

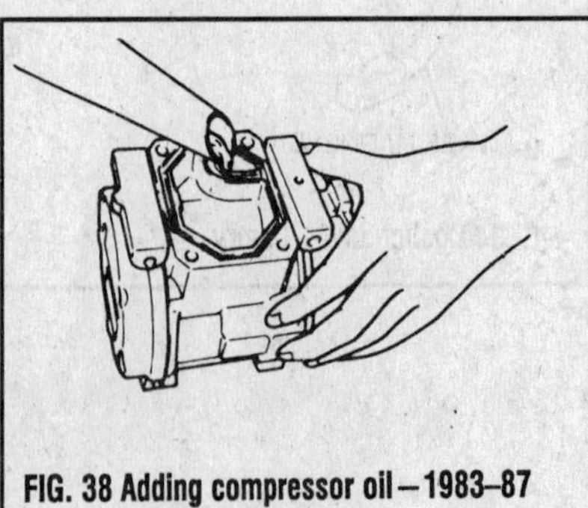

FIG. 38 Adding compressor oil—1983–87

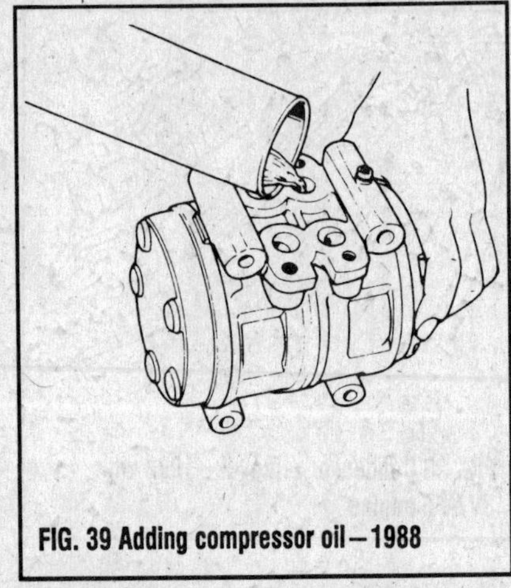

FIG. 39 Adding compressor oil—1988

20. Connect the suction tube to the cooling unit outlet fitting and torque to 22–25 ft. lbs. (30–34 Nm).

21. If the evaporator was replaced, add 1.4-1.7 ounces of compressor oil (ND OIL 6, SUNISO No. 5 GS or equivalent) to the compressor on 1983–89 models, or into the LOW side on 1990–91 models. Use new compressor seal ring(s) and lubricate with compressor oil when installing. Torque the sealing ring(s) cover bolts evenly to 19 ft. lbs. (25 Nm) on 1983–89 models.

22. Connect the negative battery cable.

23. Evacuate, charge and test the refrigeration system.

➡ Rotate the compressor several times by hand before starting the engine to insure that hydrolic lock-up will not occur, which would damage the compressor.

1992

➧ SEE FIGS. 40-42

1. Disconnect the negative battery cable.

2. Disconnect the negative battery cable, then discharge and recover the refrigerant from the air conditioning system, using the proper procedures.

3. Remove the blower unit.

4. Remove the 2 bolts for the liquid and suction tubes.

5. Remove the 8 evaporator cover screws and the cover.

6. Carefully pull and remove the evaporator.

7. Remove the 2 bolts using a hexagon key and separate the evaporator and the expansion valve.

To install:

8. Inspect the fins for blockage. If they are blocked, clean them with compressed air (Wear eye protection). Also, inspect the fittings for cracks or scratches.

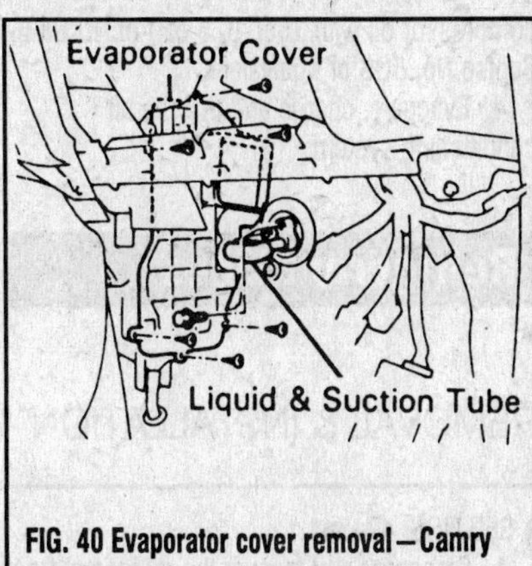

FIG. 40 Evaporator cover removal – Camry

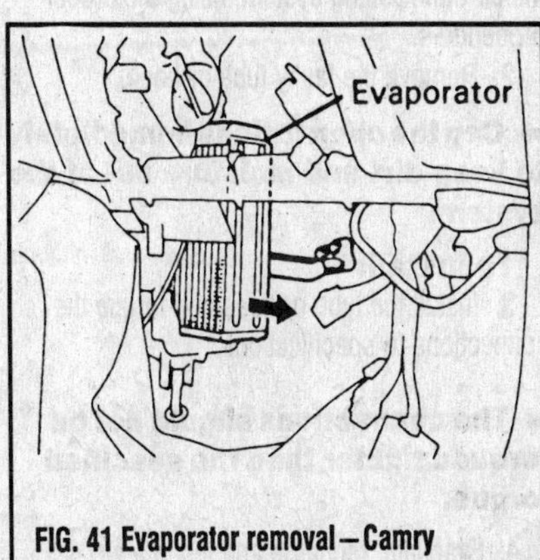

FIG. 41 Evaporator removal – Camry

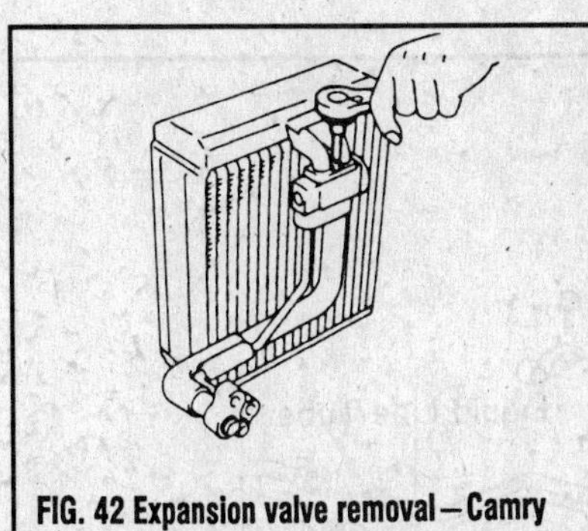
FIG. 42 Expansion valve removal – Camry

➡ **Do not use water to clean the evaporator.**

9. Install the expansion valve onto the evaporator and torque the bolts to 4 ft. lbs. (5.4 Nm).

10. Install the evaporator and cover and torque the bolts used to install the liquid and suction tubes to 7 ft. lbs. (9.8 Nm).

11. If the evaporator was replaced, replenish the compressor oil with 45cc (1.6 oz.) of ND OIL 6, SUNISO No. 5 GS or equivalent.

12. The remaining installation is the reverse of removal.

13. Evacuate, charge and test the air conditioning system.

➡ **Rotate the compressor several times by hand before starting the engine to insure that hydrolic lock-up will not occur, which would damage the compressor.**

Expansion Valve

REMOVAL & INSTALLATION

Follow the procedures for removal and installation of the evaporator core.

Receiver

REMOVAL & INSTALLATION

➧ SEE FIGS. 43–46

1983–88

1. Discharge and recover the refrigerant from the air conditioning system, using the proper procedures.

2. Disconnect the 2 liquid line tubes from the receiver.

➡ **Cap the open fittings immediately to keep moisture and dirt out of the system.**

3. Remove the receiver from the receiver holder after loosening the clamp bolt, if equipped.

1989–91

1. Discharge and recover the refrigerant from the air conditioning system, using the proper procedures.

2. Remove the battery, the reserve tank and the ignitor bracket.

3. Disconnect the 2 liquid line tubes from the receiver.

➡ **Cap the open fittings immediately to keep moisture and dirt out of the system.**

4. Remove the receiver from the receiver holder after loosening the clamp bolt, if equipped.

1992

1. Discharge and recover the refrigerant from the air conditioning system, using the proper procedures.

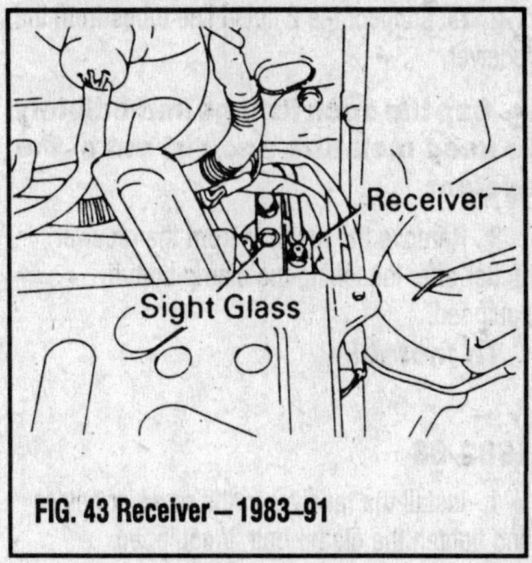

FIG. 43 Receiver – 1983–91

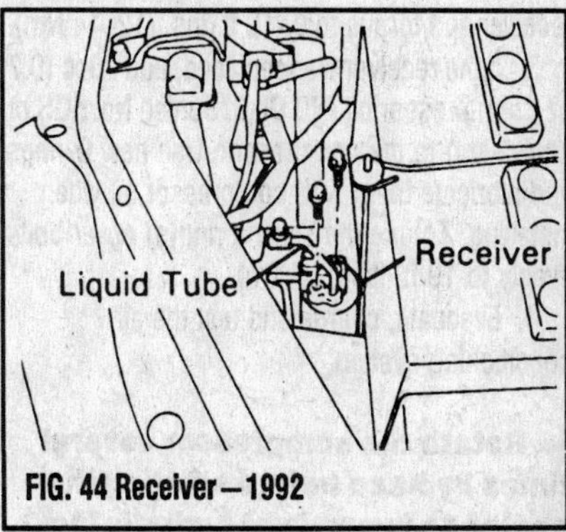

FIG. 44 Receiver – 1992

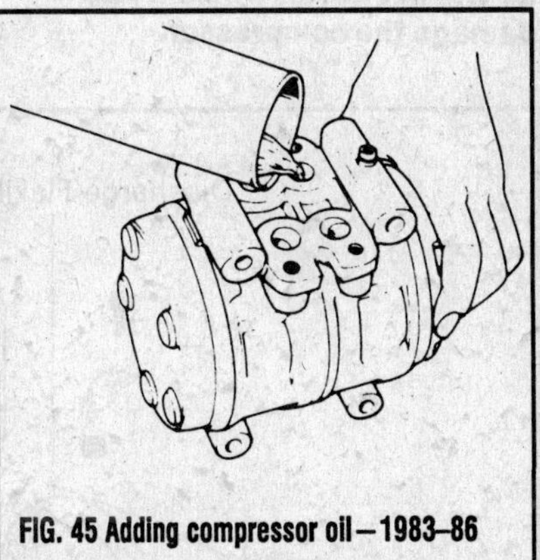
FIG. 45 Adding compressor oil – 1983–86

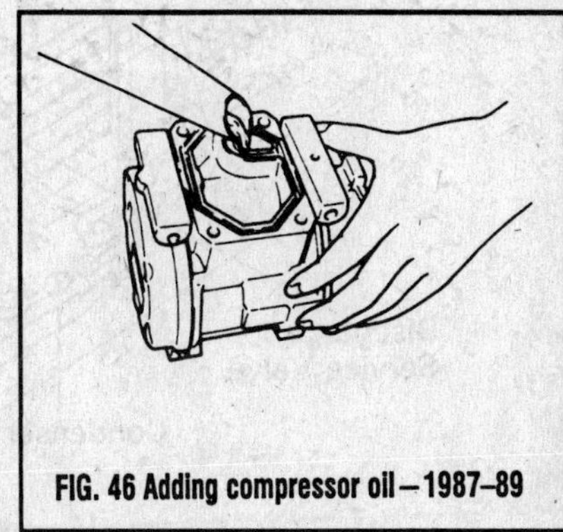
FIG. 46 Adding compressor oil – 1987–89

2. Disconnect the 2 liquid line tubes from the receiver.

➡ Cap the open fittings immediately to keep moisture and dirt out of the system.

3. Remove the receiver from the receiver holder after loosening the clamp bolt, if equipped.

To install:

1983–88

1. Install the receiver in the receiver holder and tighten the clamp bolt, if equipped.
2. Connect the 2 liquid line tubes to the receiver and torque to 9–10 ft. lbs. (12–14 Nm).
3. If the receiver was replaced, add 20cc (0.7 oz.) compressor oil (ND Oil 6, Suniso No. 5GS or equivalent) to the compressor. Use new O-rings and lubricate them with compressor oil when installing. Torque the sealing ring(s) cover bolts evenly to 19 ft. lbs. (25 Nm).
4. Evacuate, charge and test the air conditioning system.

➡ Rotate the compressor several times by hand before starting the engine to insure that hydrolic lock-up will not occur, which would damage the compressor.

1989–91

1. Install the receiver in the receiver holder and tighten the clamp bolt, if equipped.
2. Connect the 2 liquid line tubes to the receiver and torque to 4 ft. lbs. (5.4 Nm).
3. Install the battery (connecting the positive terminal first), the reserve tank and the ignitor bracket.
4. If the receiver was replaced, add 20cc (0.7 oz.) compressor oil (ND Oil 6, Suniso No. 5GS or equivalent) to the compressor on 1989 models or into the LOW side on 1990–91 models. Use a new seal ring and lubricate it with compressor oil when installing. Torque the sealing ring cover bolts evenly to 19 ft. lbs. (25 Nm) on 1989 models.
5. Evacuate, charge and test the air conditioning system.

➡ Rotate the compressor several times by hand before starting the engine to insure that hydrolic lock-up will not occur, which would damage the compressor.

1992

1. Install the receiver in the receiver holder and tighten the clamp bolt.
2. Connect the 2 liquid line tubes to the receiver and torque to 7 ft. lbs. (9.8 Nm).
3. If the receiver was replaced, replenish the compressor oil with 15cc (0.5 oz.) of ND Oil 6, Suniso No. 5GS or equivalent.
4. Evacuate, charge and test the air conditioning system.

Refrigerant Lines

REMOVAL & INSTALLATION

➧ SEE FIGS. 47–54

1. Discharge and recover the refrigerant from the air conditioning system, using the proper procedures.
2. Remove the faulty tube or hose.

➡ Cap the open fittings immediately to keep dirt and moisture out of the system.

To install:

3. Install the tube or hose and torque the connections to specifications.

➡ The connections should not be torqued tighter than the specified torque.

4. Evacuate, recharge and test the air conditioning system.

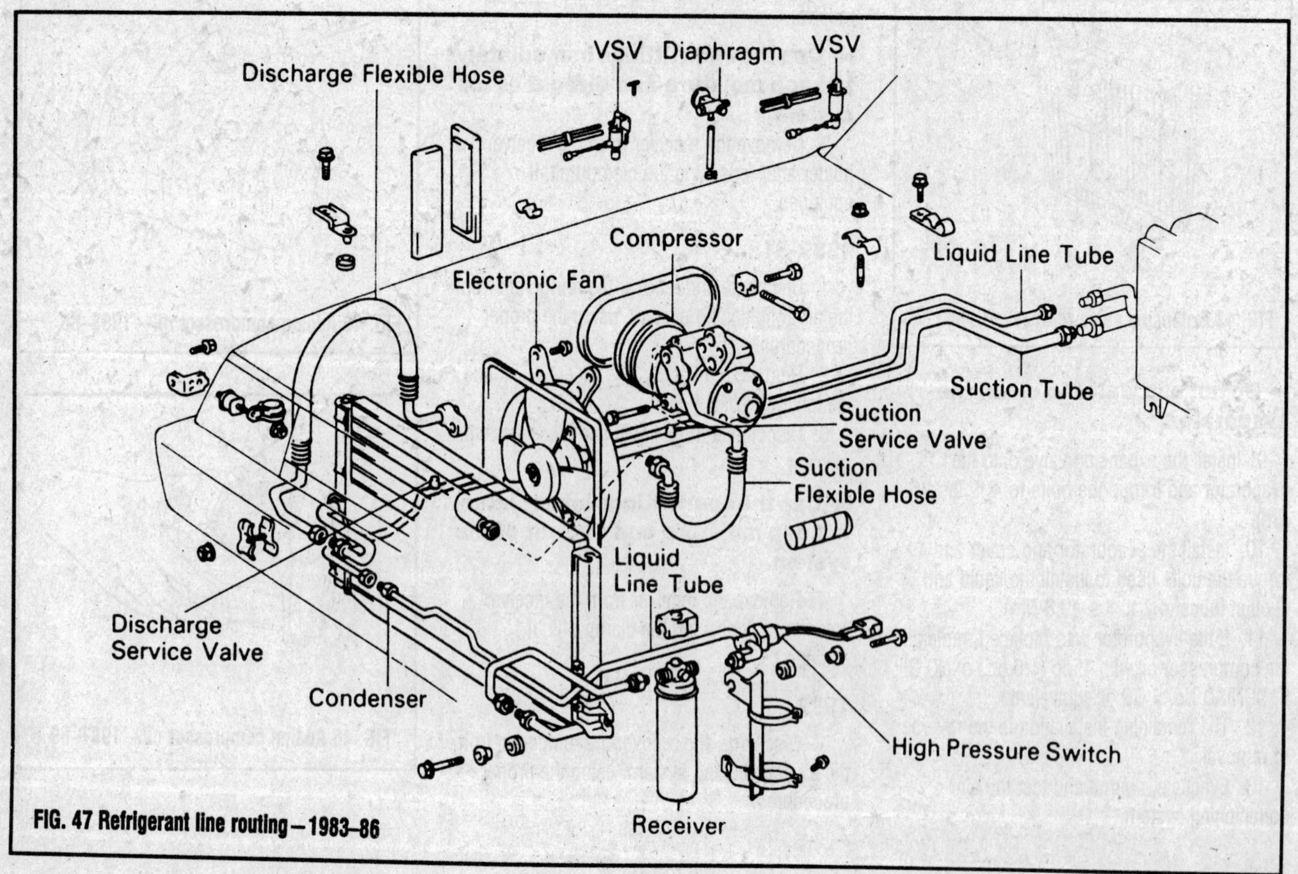

FIG. 47 Refrigerant line routing—1983–86

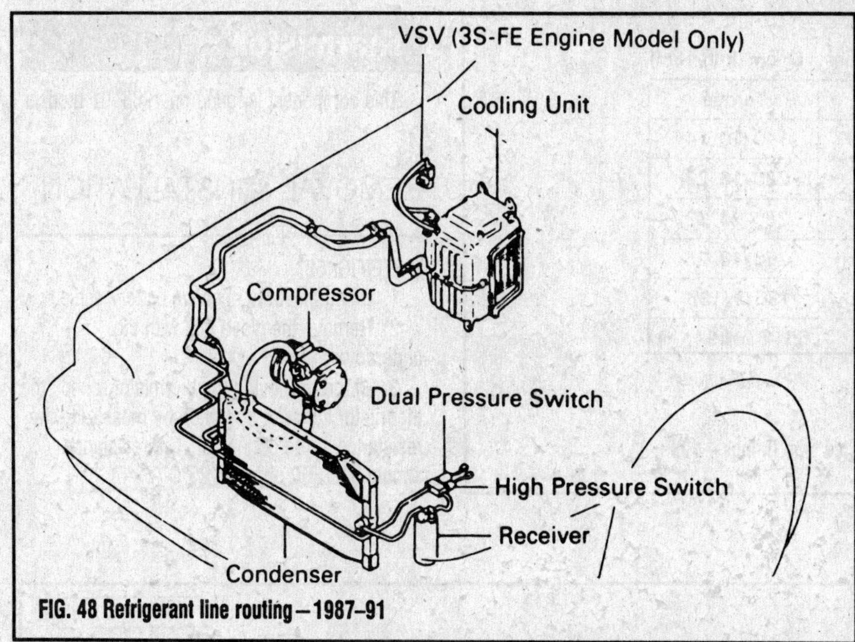

FIG. 48 Refrigerant line routing—1987-91

Fitting size
3/8 in. tube for liquid line 1/2 in. tube for discharge line 5/8 in. tube for suction line

Torque
120–150 kg-cm (9 – 10 ft-lb) 200–250 kg-cm (15 – 18 ft-lb) 300–350 kg-cm (22 – 25 ft-lb)

FIG. 50 Tightening torques for O-ring fittings—1983-86

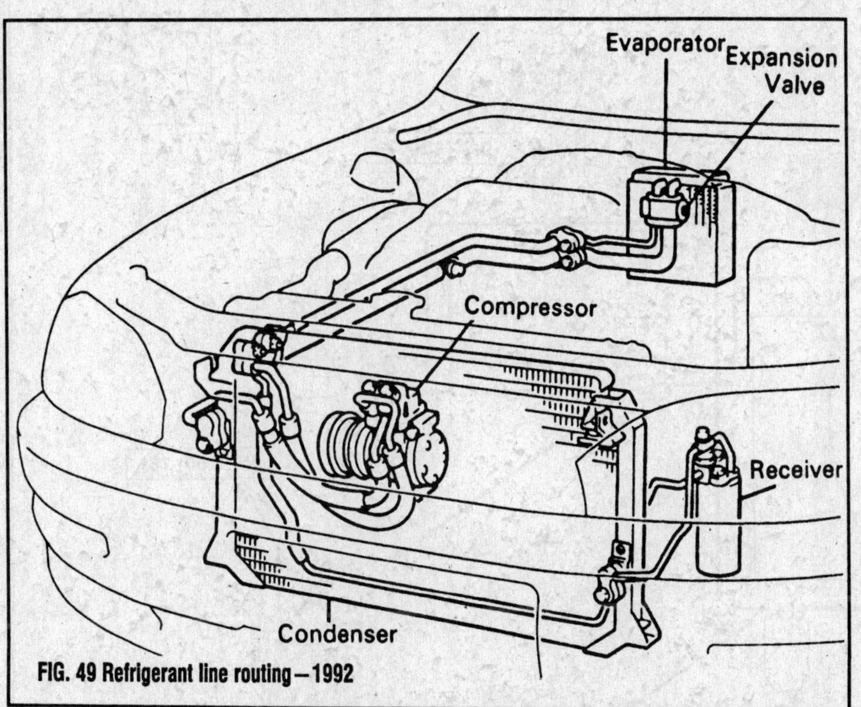

FIG. 49 Refrigerant line routing—1992

Fitting size
0.31 in. Tube
0.50 in. Tube
0.62 in. Tube
Bolted Type

Torque
135 kg-cm (10 ft-lb, 13 N·m)
225 kg-cm (16 ft-lb, 22 N·m)
325 kg-cm (24 ft-lb, 32 N·m)
250 kg-cm (18 ft-lb, 25 N·m)

FIG. 51 Tightening torques for O-ring fittings and bolted type fittings—1987

Fitting size		Torque
0.31 in. Tube		135 kg-cm (10 ft-lb, 13 N·m)
0.50 in. Tube		225 kg-cm (16 ft-lb, 22 N·m)
0.62 in. Tube		325 kg-cm (24 ft-lb, 32 N·m)
Bolted Type	(For Compressor)	280 kg-cm (20 ft-lb, 28 N·m)
	(For Condensor)	185 kg-cm (13 ft-lb, 18 N·m)
	(For Receiver)	110 kg-cm (8 ft-lb, 11 N·m)

FIG. 52 Tightening torques for O-ring fittings and bolted type fittings—1988

Specified Torque: kg-cm (ft-lb, N·m)

Fitting size		Torque
0.31 in. Tube		140 (10, 14)
0.50 in. Tube		230 (16, 22)
0.62 in. Tube		330 (24, 32)
Bolted Type	(For Compressor)	250 (18, 25)
	(For Condenser)	130 (9, 13)
	(For Receiver)	55 (48 in.-lb 5.4 N·m)

FIG. 53 Tightening torques for O-ring fittings and bolted type fittings—1989–91

Thermistor

This component is found on 1983–91 models.

REMOVAL & INSTALLATION

➧ SEE FIG. 55

1. Disconnect the negative battery cable.
2. Remove the glove box with the undercover.
3. Before removing the thermistor, check the thermistor installed operation by measuring the resistance at the connector. The resistance should be 1500 ohms at 25°C (77°F).

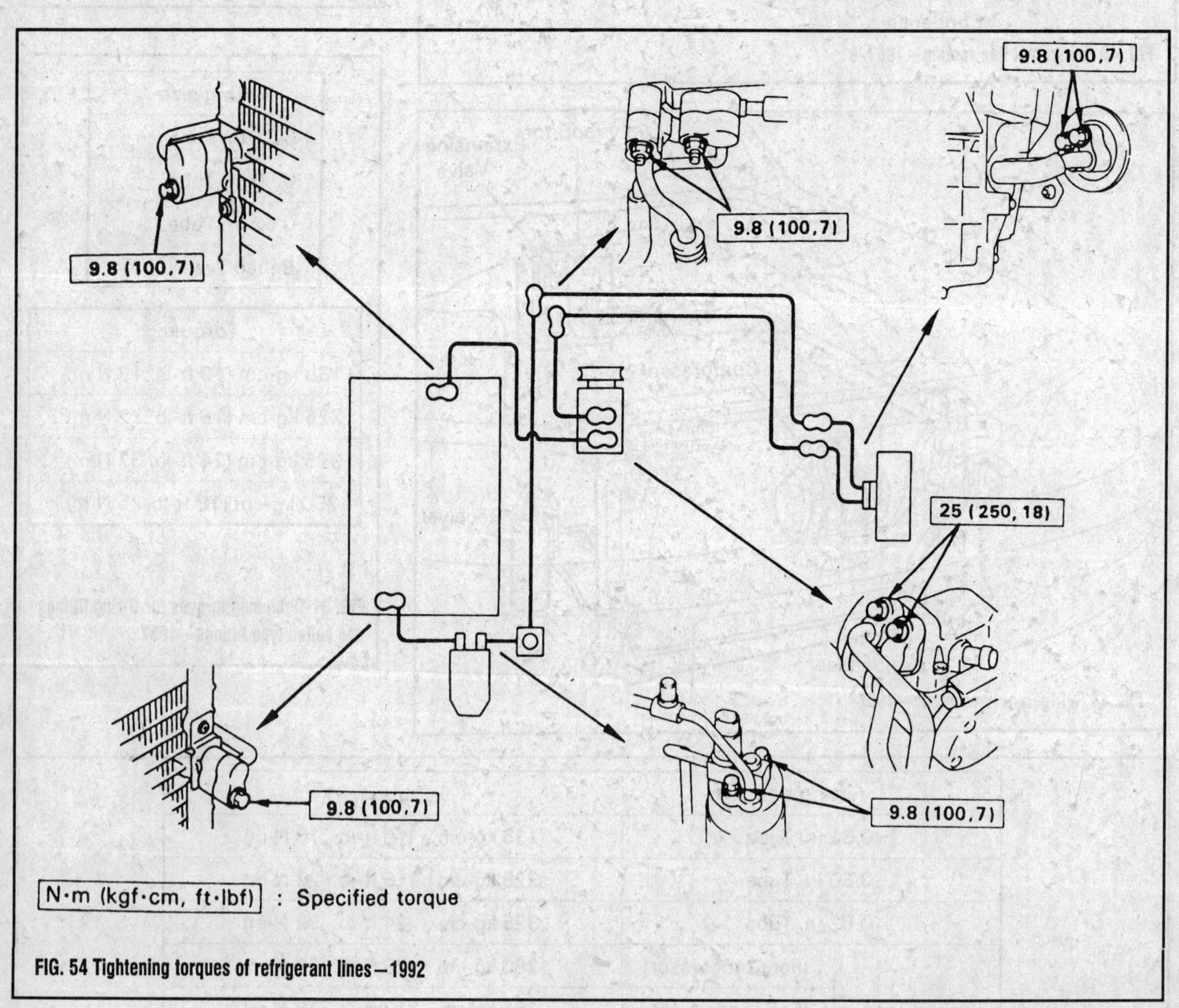

FIG. 54 Tightening torques of refrigerant lines—1992

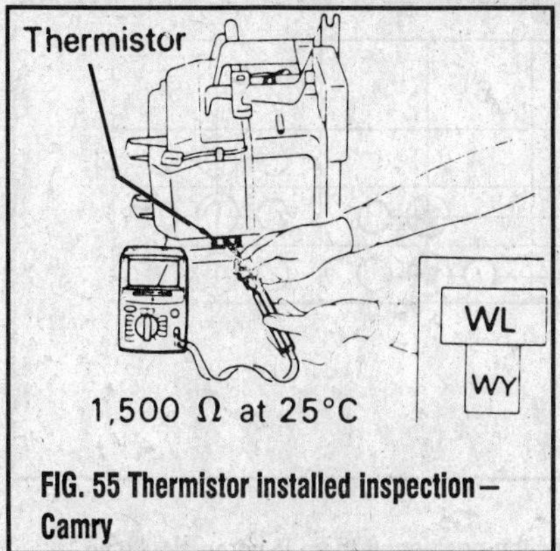

FIG. 55 Thermistor installed inspection—Camry

4. On 1983–86 models loosen or remove the cooling unit.

5. Remove the thermistor by disconnecting the connector and removing the screw securing the thermistor to the cooling unit.

To Install:

6. Installation is the reverse of removal.

TESTING

➧ SEE FIGS. 56 AND 57

1. Place the thermistor in cold water. While varying the temperature of the water, measure the resistance at the connector and, at the same time, measure the temperature of the water with a thermometer.

2. Compare the 2 readings on the chart. If the intersection is not between the 2 lines, replace the thermistor.

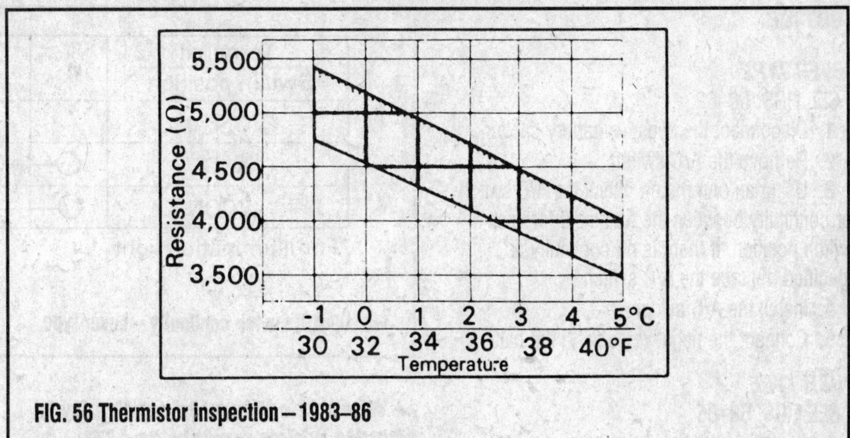

FIG. 56 Thermistor inspection—1983–86

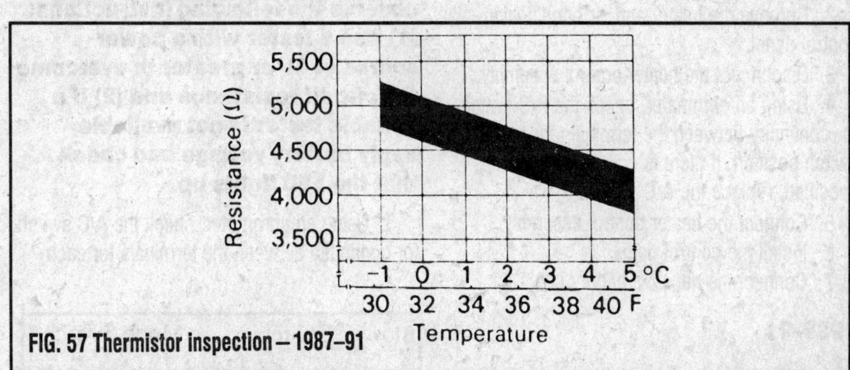

FIG. 57 Thermistor inspection—1987–91

Air Conditioning Switch

TESTING

1983–86

➧ SEE FIGS. 58 AND 59

1. Disconnect the negative battery cable.

2. Remove the heater and air conditioning control panel.

3. Disconnect the A/C switch connector.

4. Using an ohmmeter, check the continuity between the terminals for each switch position (ECONO and A/C). If there is no continuity as specified, replace the A/C switch.

5. Connect the A/C switch connector.

6. Install the control panel.

7. Connect the negative cable to the battery.

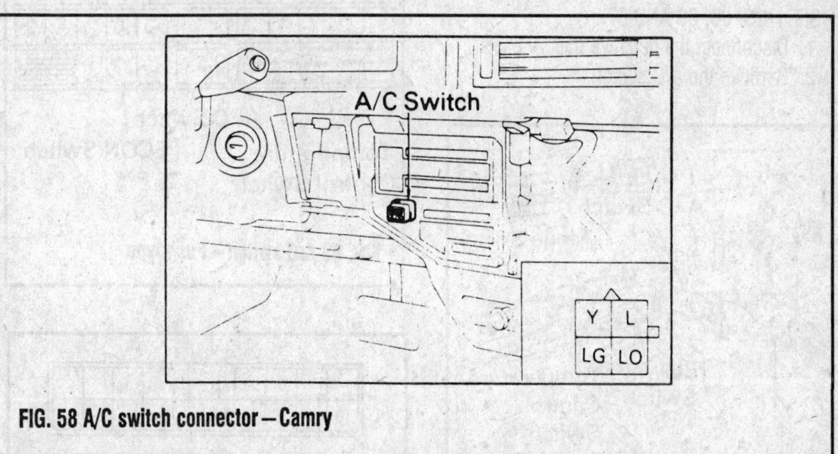

FIG. 58 A/C switch connector—Camry

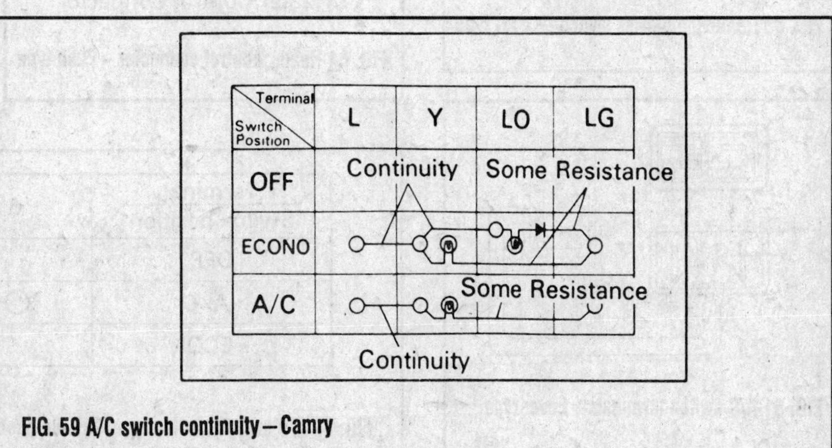

FIG. 59 A/C switch continuity—Camry

1987–88

LEVER TYPE

➧ SEE FIGS. 60–62

1. Disconnect the negative battery cable.
2. Remove the A/C switch.
3. Using an ohmmeter, check the A/C switch for continuity between the terminals for each switch position. If there is no continuity as specified, replace the A/C switch.
4. Install the A/C switch.
5. Connect the negative cable to the battery.

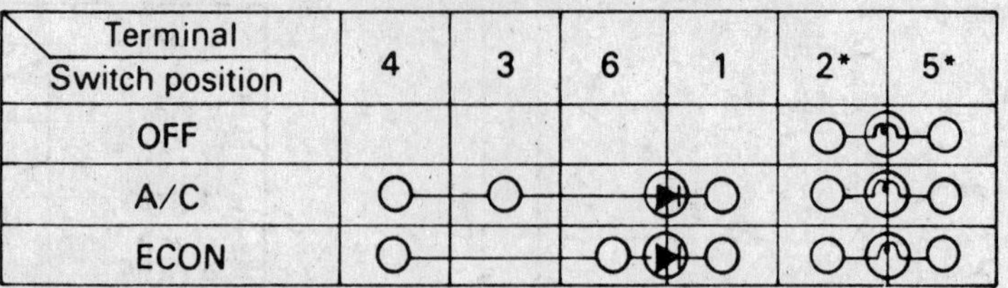

Terminal / Switch position	4	3	6	1	2*	5*
OFF					O	O
A/C	O	O		O	O	O
ECON	O		O	O	O	O

*For illumination light

FIG. 62 A/C switch continuity—Lever type

PUSH TYPE

➧ SEE FIGS. 63–65

1. Disconnect the negative battery cable.
2. Remove the heater and air conditioning control panel.
3. Disconnect the heater control assembly.
4. Using an ohmmeter, check the A/C switch for continuity between the terminals for each switch position. If there is no continuity as specified, replace the A/C switch.
5. Connect the heater control assembly.
6. Install the control panel.
7. Connect the negative battery cable.

1989–91

LEVER TYPE

➧ SEE FIGS. 60, 66 AND 67

1. Disconnect the negative battery cable.
2. Remove the A/C switch.

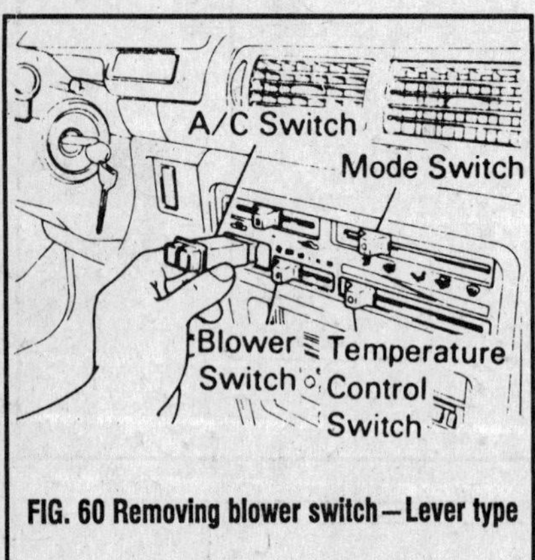

FIG. 60 Removing blower switch—Lever type

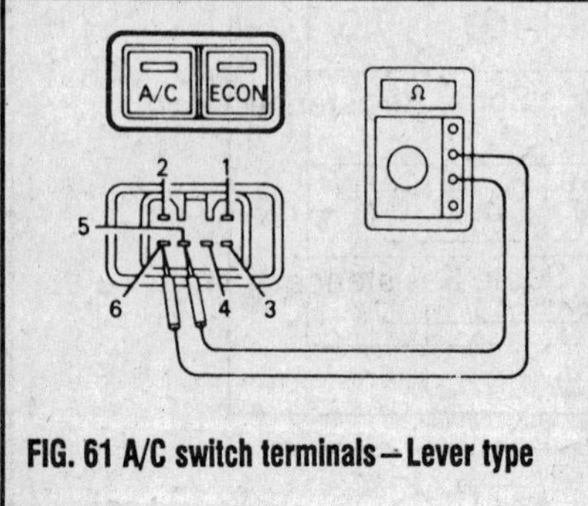

FIG. 61 A/C switch terminals—Lever type

➡ **When checking for continuity in circuits which contain an LED, observe the following instructions: (1) Use a tester with a power source of 3V or greater to overcome the circuit resistance and (2) if a suitable tester is not available, apply battery voltage and check that the LED lights up.**

3. Using an ohmmeter, check the A/C switch for continuity between the terminals for each switch position. If there is no continuity as specified, replace the A/C switch.
4. Install the A/C switch.
5. Connect the negative cable to the battery.

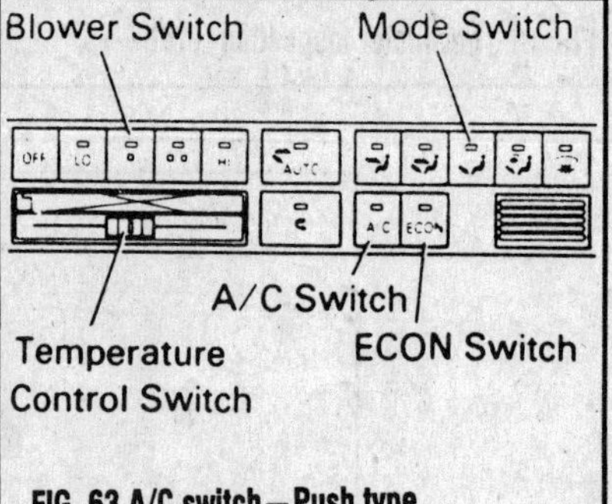

FIG. 63 A/C switch—Push type

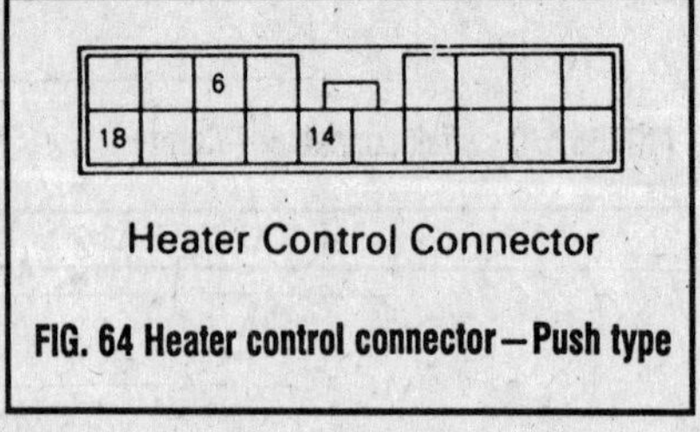

FIG. 64 Heater control connector—Push type

PUSH TYPE

➧ SEE FIGS. 63, 64 AND 68

1. Disconnect the negative battery cable.
2. Remove the heater and air conditioning control panel.
3. Disconnect the heater control assembly.
4. Using an ohmmeter, check the A/C switch for continuity between the terminals for each switch position. If there is no continuity as specified, replace the A/C switch.
5. Connect the heater control assembly.
6. Install the control panel.
7. Connect the negative battery cable.

1992

➧ SEE FIGS. 69–72

1. Disconnect the negative battery cable.
2. Remove the center cluster finish panel, using a suitable prying tool.

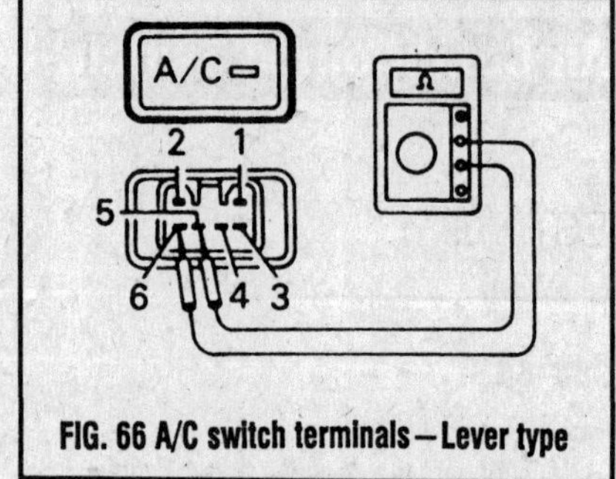

FIG. 66 A/C switch terminals—Lever type

Terminal / Switch position	6	14	18
OFF			
A/C	O	O	
ECON		O	O

FIG. 65 A/C switch continuity—1987–88 push type

Terminal / Switch position	2	3	5	6	Illumination 1	Illumination 4
OFF						
A/C	○	○	○	○	○	○

FIG. 67 A/C switch continuity—1989–91 lever type

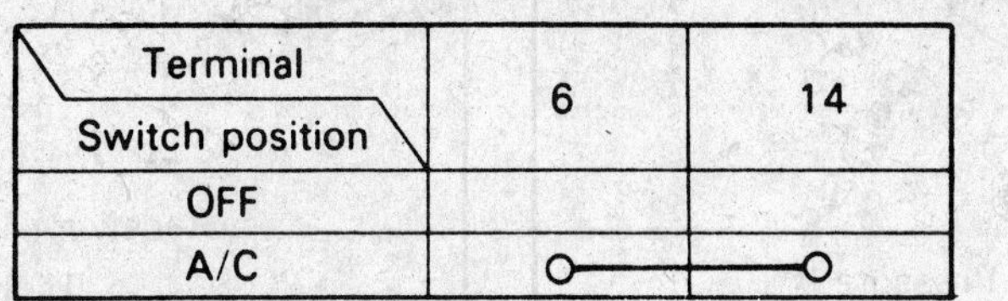

Terminal / Switch position	6	14
OFF		
A/C	○	○

FIG. 68 A/C switch continuity—1989–91 push type

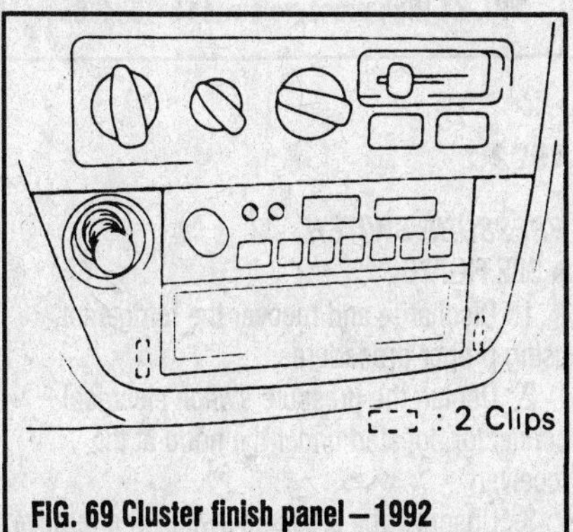

FIG. 69 Cluster finish panel—1992

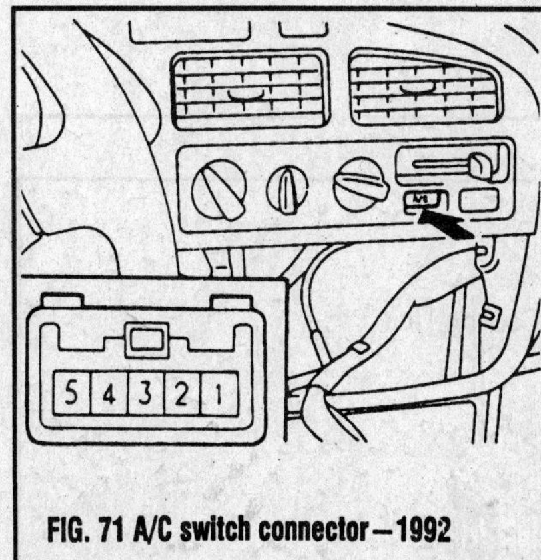

FIG. 71 A/C switch connector—1992

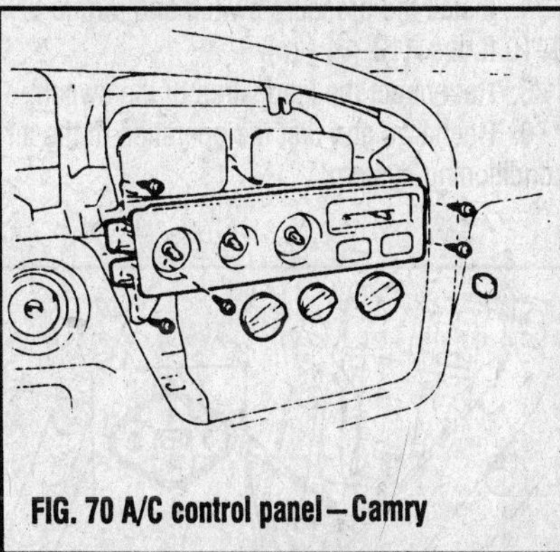

FIG. 70 A/C control panel—Camry

3. Remove the heater and air conditioning control panel.
4. Disconnect the A/C switch connector.
5. Using an ohmmeter, check the A/C switch for continuity between terminals 2 and 5 with the switch in the **ON** position. If there is no continuity as specified, replace the A/C switch.
6. Connect the A/C switch connector.
7. Install the control panel and the finish panel.
8. Connect the negative battery cable.

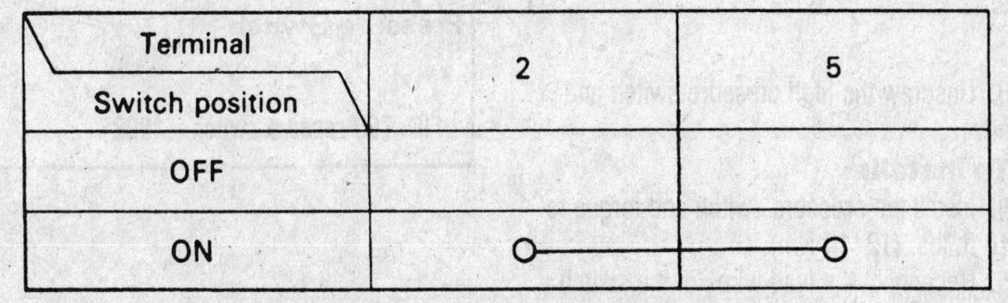

Terminal / Switch position	2	5
OFF		
ON	○	○

FIG. 72 A/C switch continuity—1992

Pressure Switch

REMOVAL & INSTALLATION

1983

➧ SEE FIG. 73

1. Discharge and recover the refrigerant, using proper procedures.
2. Remove the glove box with the undercover.
3. Disconnect the lead wires of the pressure switch.
4. Unscrew and remove the pressure switch.

To Install:

5. Install the pressure switch and torque to 9–10 ft. lbs. (12–14 Nm).
6. Reconnect the lead wires of the switch.
7. Install the glove box and undercover.
8. Recharge and test the operation of the air conditioning system.

1984–86

LOW PRESSURE SWITCH

➧ SEE FIG. 73

1. Discharge and recover the refrigerant, using proper procedures.
2. Remove the glove box with the undercover.
3. Disconnect the lead wires of the pressure switch.
4. Unscrew and remove the pressure switch.

To Install:

5. Install the pressure switch and torque to 9–10 ft. lbs. (12–14 Nm).
6. Reconnect the lead wires of the switch.
7. Install the glove box and undercover.
8. Recharge and test the operation of the air conditioning system.

HIGH PRESSURE SWITCH

➧ SEE FIG. 74

1. Discharge and recover the refrigerant, using proper procedures.
2. Unplug the high pressure switch electrical connector, located under the hood at the receiver.
3. Unscrew the high pressure switch and remove.

To Install:

4. Install the pressure switch and torque to 9–10 ft. lbs. (12–14 Nm).
5. Reconnect the lead wires of the switch.
6. Recharge and test the operation of the air conditioning system.

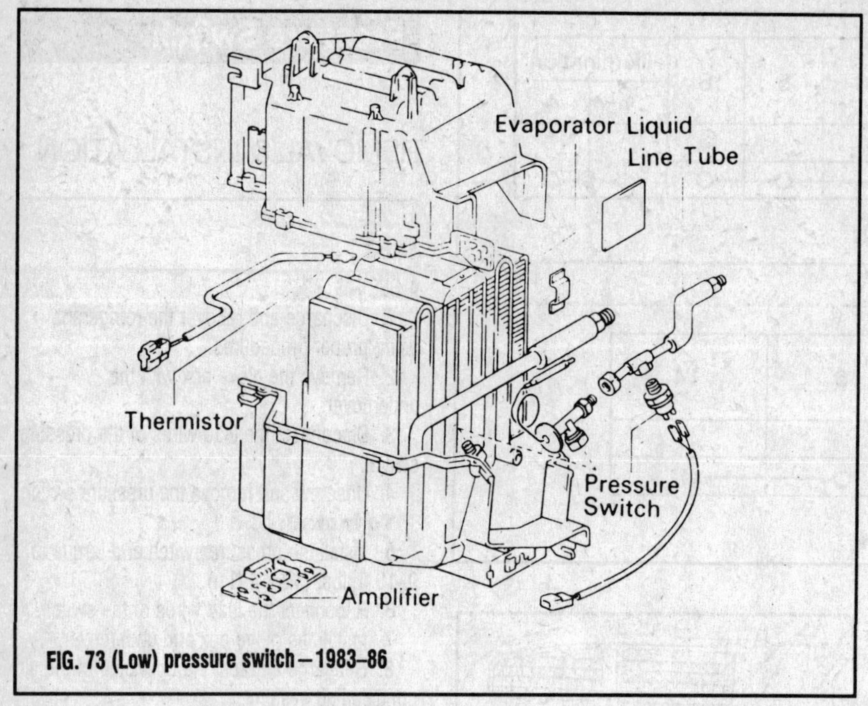

FIG. 73 (Low) pressure switch – 1983–86

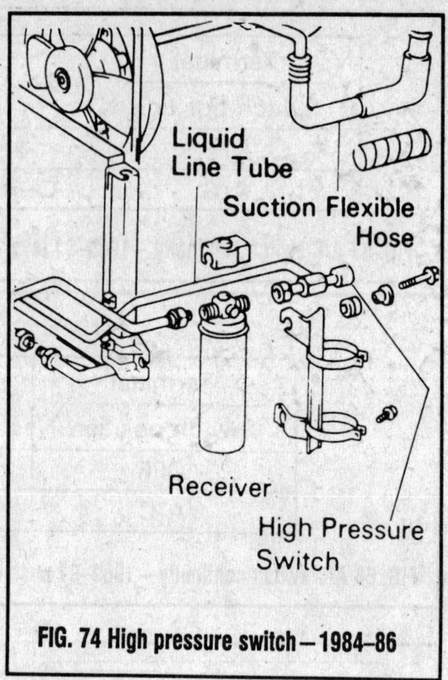

FIG. 74 High pressure switch – 1984–86

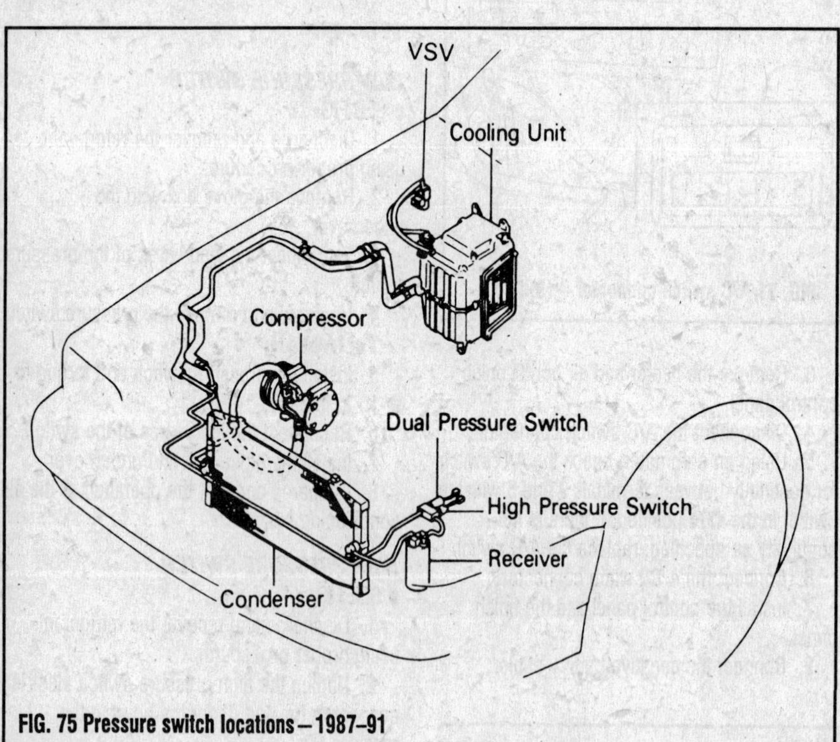

FIG. 75 Pressure switch locations – 1987–91

1987–91

DUAL AND HIGH PRESSURE SWITCHES

➧ SEE FIG. 75

1. Discharge and recover the refrigerant, using proper procedures.
2. Unplug the high pressure switch electrical connector, located under the hood at the receiver.
3. Unscrew the high pressure switch and remove.

To install:

4. Install the pressure switch and torque to 9–10 ft. lbs. (12–14 Nm).
5. Reconnect the lead wires of the switch.
6. Recharge and test the operation of the air conditioning system.

1992

PRESSURE SWITCH

➧ SEE FIG. 76

1. Discharge and recover the refrigerant, using proper procedures.
2. Unplug the pressure switch electrical connector, located under the hood at the receiver.
3. Unscrew the pressure switch and remove.

To install:

4. Install the pressure switch and torque to 9–10 ft. lbs. (12–14 Nm).
5. Reconnect the lead wires of the switch.
6. Recharge and test the operation of the air conditioning system.

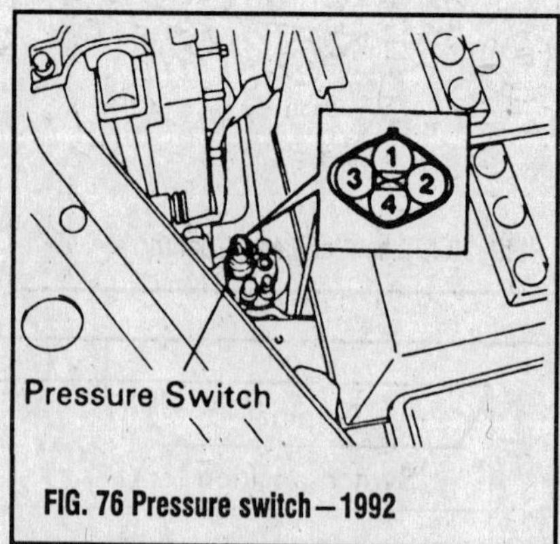

FIG. 76 Pressure switch – 1992

TESTING

1983-87

➧ SEE FIGS. 73-75, 77 AND 78

The Camry is equipped with a single (low pressure) switch in 1983, HIGH and LOW switches in 1984-86 and DUAL and HIGH switches in 1987. The testing procedures are the same.

1. Check the refrigerant pressure. The guage reading must be between 30-256 psi (206-1765 kpa) when the ambient temperature is higher than 0°C (32°F). If the pressure is too low, the system must be charged.
2. Remove the glove box and the undercover.
3. Disconnect the lead wires of the A/C harness.
4. Using an ohmmeter, check the continuity between the 2 terminals of the pressure switch.
5. If there is no continuity between the 2 terminals, replace the pressure switch.
6. Reinstall the removed parts in the reverse order of removal.

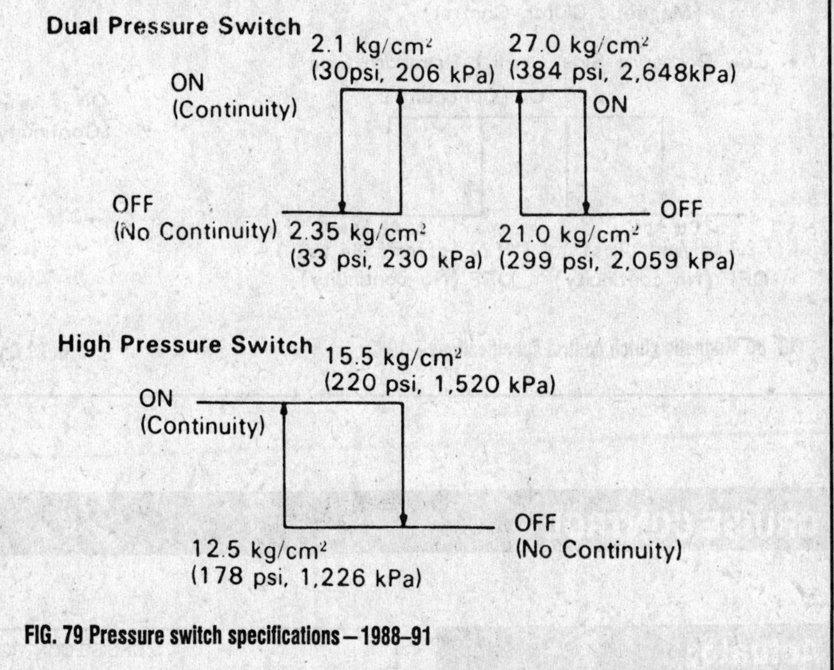

FIG. 79 Pressure switch specifications – 1988-91

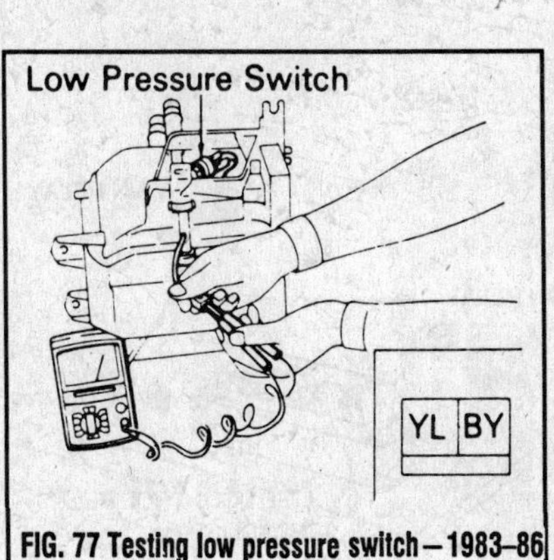

FIG. 77 Testing low pressure switch – 1983-86

1988-91

DUAL AND HIGH PRESSURE SWITCHES

➧ SEE FIGS. 78 AND 79

1. Disconnect the connector of the Dual or High pressure switch, located under the hood at the receiver.
2. Install a guage set and observe the continuity between the 2 terminals of the switch according to the pressure specifications.
3. If defective, replace the switch.
4. Connect the connector of the pressure switch.

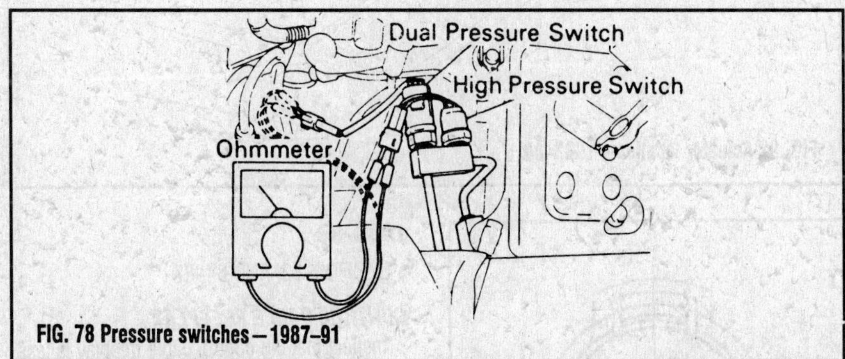

FIG. 78 Pressure switches – 1987-91

1992

PRESSURE SWITCH

➧ SEE FIGS. 76, 80 AND 81

1. Install a manifold guage set.
2. Disconnect the connector from the pressure switch.
3. Run the engine at approximately 2000 rpm.
4. Inspect the pressure switch operation (Magnetic Clutch Control):
   a. Connect the positive (+) lead from the ohmmeter to terminal 4 and negative (–) lead to terminal 1.
   b. Check the continuity between terminals when the refrigerant pressure is changed as shown. If the operation is not as specified, replace the pressure switch.
5. Inspect the pressure switch operation (Cooling Fan Control):
   a. Connect the positive (+) lead from the ohmmeter to terminal 2 and negative (–) lead to terminal 3.
   b. Check the continuity between terminals when the refrigerant pressure is changed as shown. If the operation is not as specified, replace the pressure switch.
6. Stop the engine and remove the manifold set.
7. Connect the connector to the pressure switch.

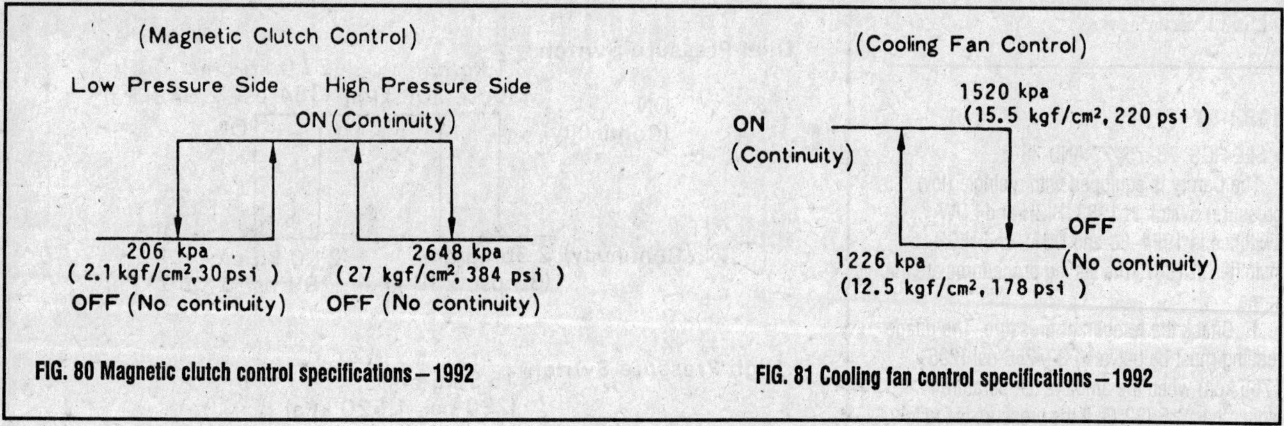

FIG. 80 Magnetic clutch control specifications – 1992

FIG. 81 Cooling fan control specifications – 1992

CRUISE CONTROL

Actuator

TESTING

1983–84

➧ SEE FIGS 82 AND 83

RESISTANCE

1. Disconnect the connector from the actuator lead wire.
2. Using an ohmmeter, measure the resistance between terminals S_1 and S_2. The resistance should be approximately 68 ohms. If the resistance is not as specified, replace the actuator.
3. Using an ohmmeter, measure the resistance between terminals S_1 and S_3. The resistance should be approximately 30 ohms. If the resistance is not as specified, replace the actuator.

OPERATION

4. Disconnect the accelerator cable from the throttle body.
5. Check the actuator operation:
   a. Check that the diaphragm makes a smooth reciprocation motion when either terminals S_2 and S_3 are connected to battery (+) terminal, and terminal S_1 is grounded to the body or, subsequently, terminal S_2 or S_3 is removed from the battery.
   b. Confirm that the cable does not return easily when pulled with a force of 2–3 kg (4.4–6.6 lbs.).
6. If the operation is not as specified, replace the actuator.

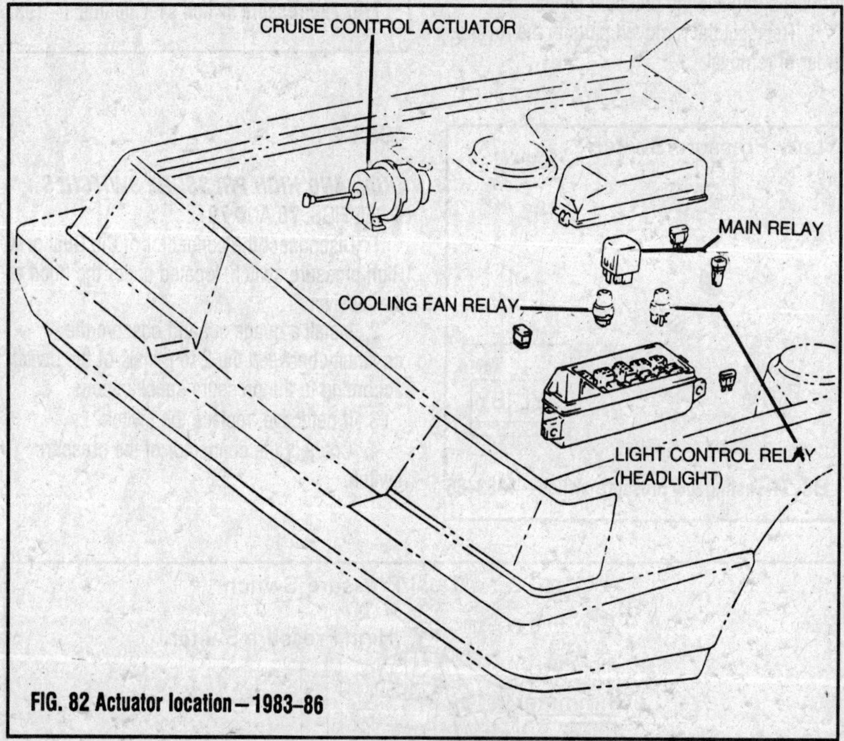

FIG. 82 Actuator location – 1983–86

FIG. 83 Actuator connector – 1983–84

1985–86

➧ SEE FIGS. 82, AND 84–87

CONTROL CABLE FREEPLAY

Inspect that the control cable freeplay is less than 10mm (0.39 in.). If necessary, adjust the freeplay.

RESISTANCE

1. Disconnect the connector from the actuator lead wire.
2. Using an ohmmeter, measure the resistance between terminals 1 and 2. The

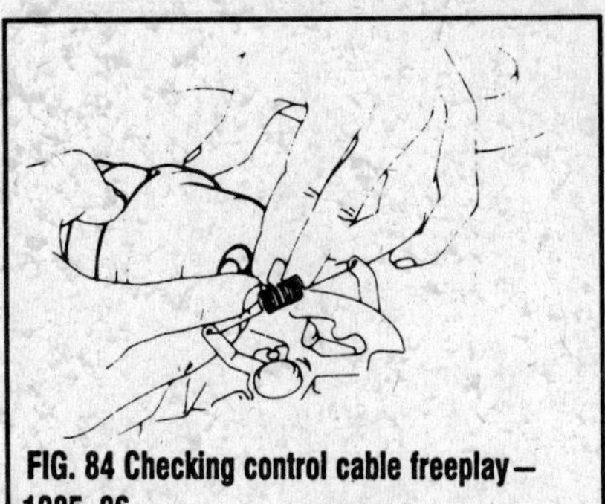
FIG. 84 Checking control cable freeplay–1985–86

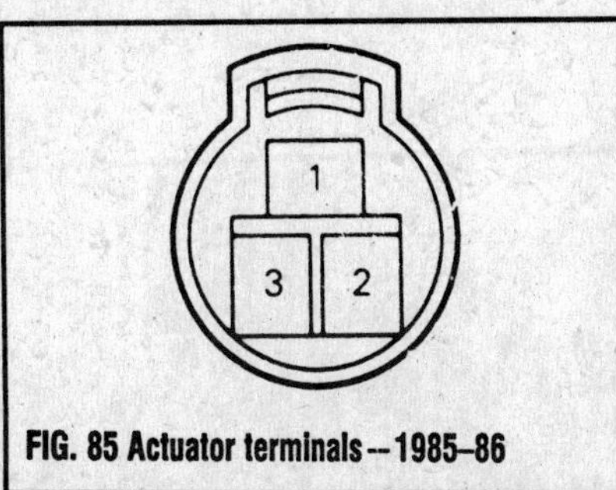

FIG. 85 Actuator terminals--1985–86

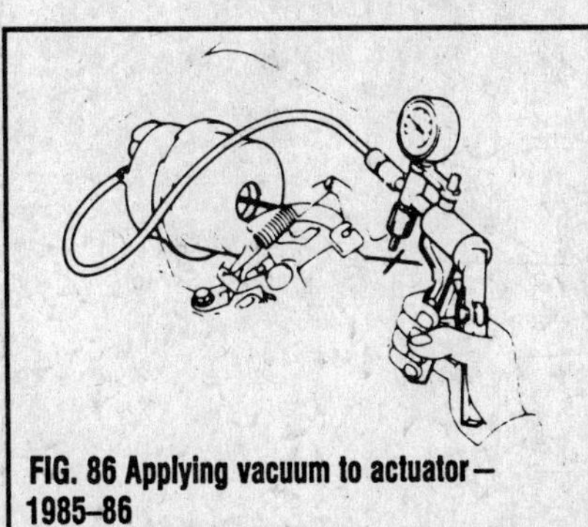
FIG. 86 Applying vacuum to actuator–1985–86

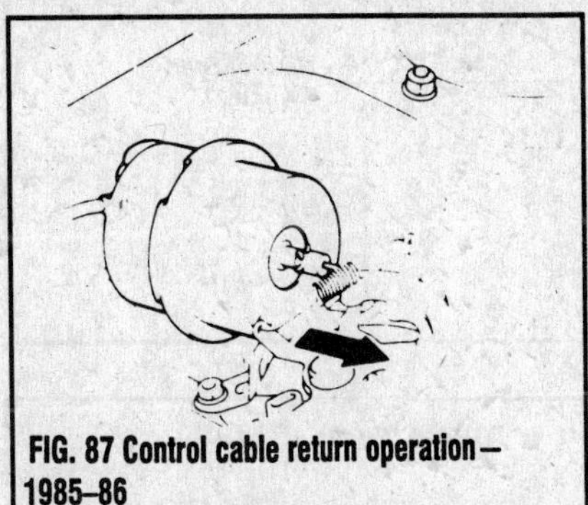
FIG. 87 Control cable return operation–1985–86

resistance should be approximately 68 ohms. If the resistance is not as specified, replace the actuator.

3. Using an ohmmeter, measure the resistance between terminals 1 and 3. The resistance should be approximately 30 ohms. If the resistance is not as specified, replace the actuator.

OPERATION

1. Connect the positive (+) lead from the battery to terminals 2 and 3. Connect the negative (–) lead to terminal 1.
   a. Slowly apply vacuum from 0–300mm Hg (0–40 kpa), and check that the control cable can be pulled smoothly.
   b. With the vacuum stabilized, check that the control cable does not return.
   c. Disconnect terminal 2 or 3 and check that the control cable returns to its original position and the vacuum returns to 0 mmHg (0 kpa).
2. If operation is not as described, replace the actuator.

1987–91

➧ SEE FIGS. 88–92

CONTROL CABLE FREEPLAY

1. Measure the cable stroke to where the throttle valve begins to open.
2. Inspect that the control cable freeplay is within 10mm (0.39 in.) with a slight amount of freeplay. If necessary, adjust the freeplay.

RESISTANCE

1. Disconnect the connector from the actuator lead wire.
2. Using an ohmmeter, measure the resistance between terminals 2 and 3. The resistance should be approximately 30 ohms. If the resistance is not as specified, replace the actuator.
3. Using an ohmmeter, measure the resistance between terminals 1 and 3. The resistance should be approximately 68 ohms. If the resistance is not as specified, replace the actuator.

OPERATION

1. Connect the positive (+) lead from the battery to terminals 1 and 2. Connect the negative (–) lead to terminal 3.
   a. Slowly apply vacuum from 0–300mm Hg (0–40 kpa), and check that the control cable can be pulled smoothly.
   b. Disconnect terminal 1 or 2 and check

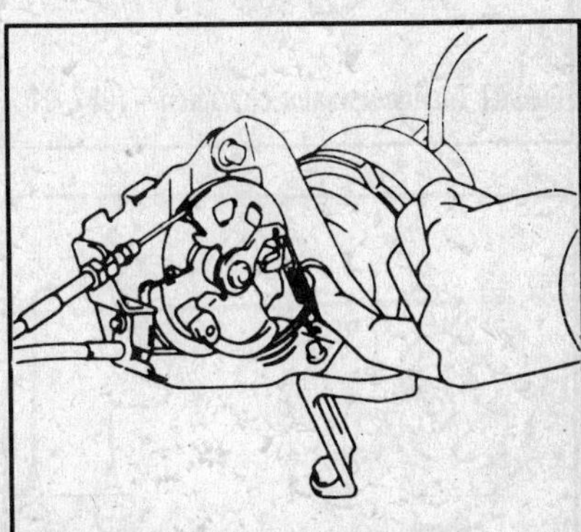
FIG. 89 Checking control cable freeplay–1987–91

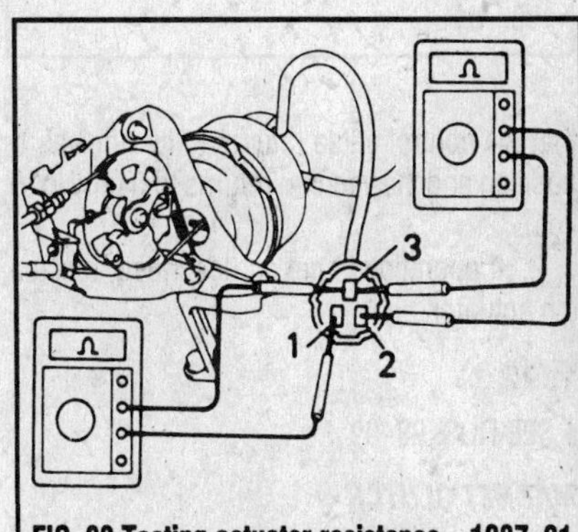

FIG. 90 Testing actuator resistance–1987–91

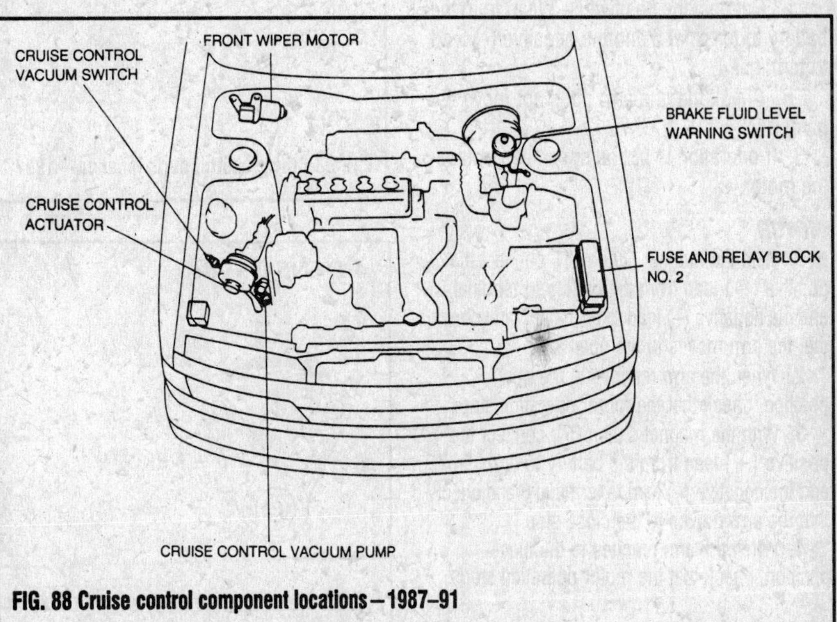

FIG. 88 Cruise control component locations–1987–91

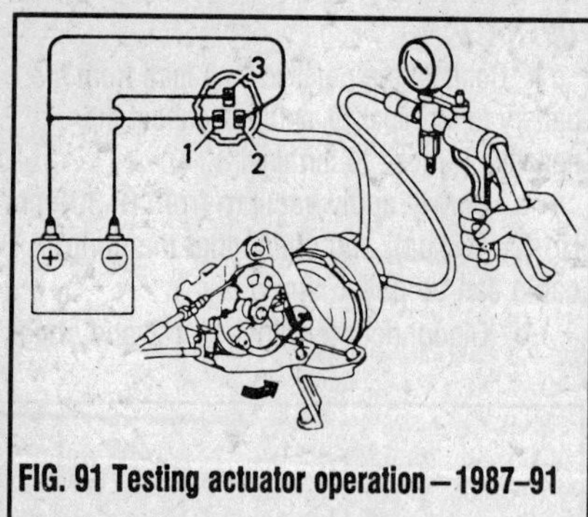

FIG. 91 Testing actuator operation—1987–91

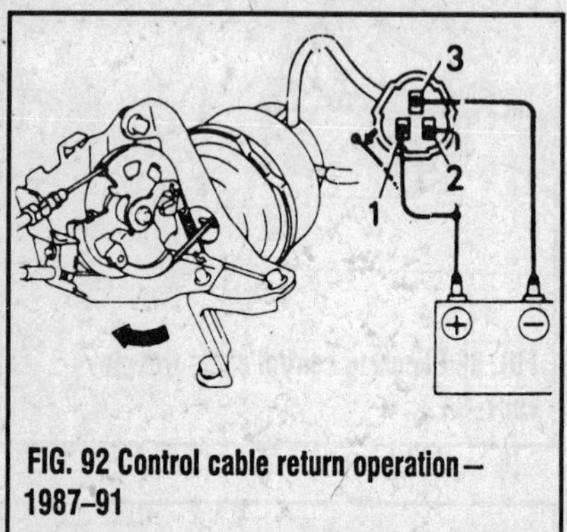

FIG. 92 Control cable return operation—1987–91

that the control cable returns to its original position and the vacuum returns to 0 mmHg (0 kpa).

2. If operation is not as described, replace the actuator.

1992

➧ SEE FIGS. 93–99

MAGNET CLUTCH

1. Check that the arm moves freely by hand.
2. Turn the magnet clutch **ON**:
   a. Connect the positive (+) lead from the battery to terminal 5 and the negative (–) lead to terminal 4.
   b. Check that the arm does not move by hand.
3. If operation is not as specified, replace the motor.

MOTOR

1. With the magnet clutch ON, connect the positive (+) lead from the battery to terminal 6 and the negative (–) lead to terminal 7 and check that the arm moves to the open side.
2. When the arm reaches to the open position, check that the motor operation stops.
3. With the magnet clutch ON, connect the positive (+) lead from the battery to terminal 7 and the negative (–) lead to terminal 6 and check that the arm moves to the close side.
4. When the arm reaches to the close position, check that the motor operation stops.

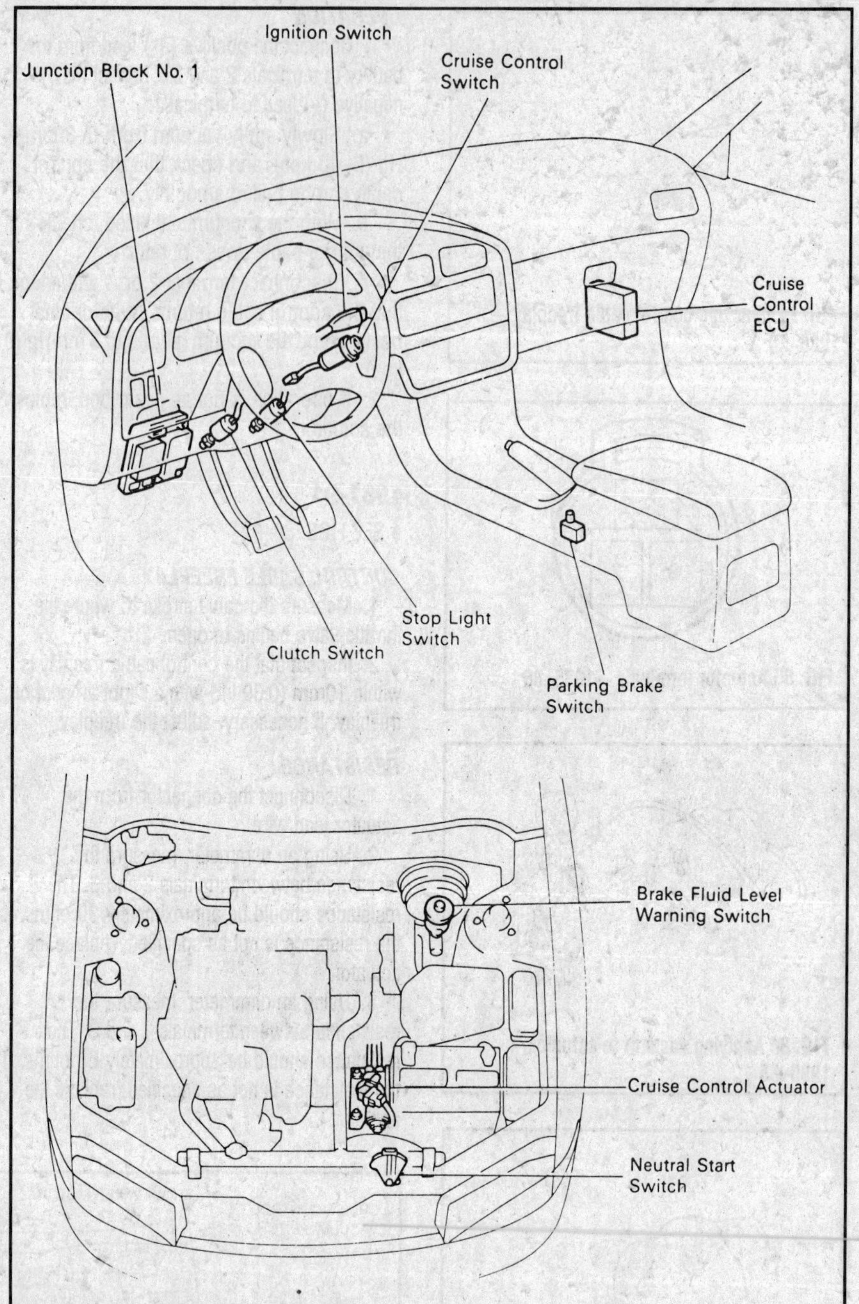

FIG. 93 Cruise control parts location—1992

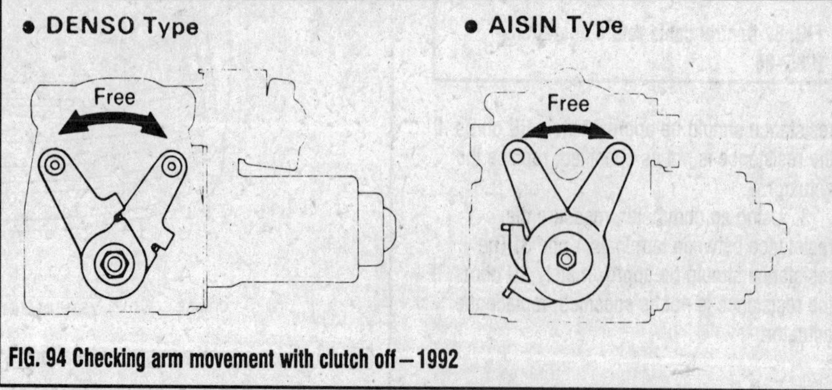

FIG. 94 Checking arm movement with clutch off—1992

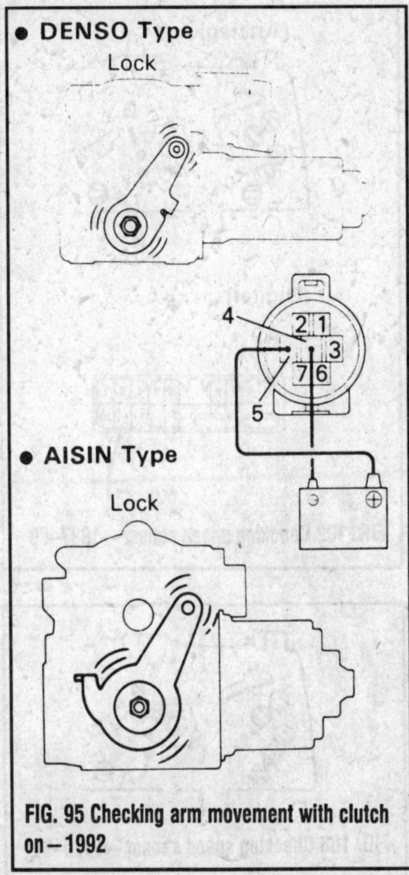

FIG. 95 Checking arm movement with clutch on—1992

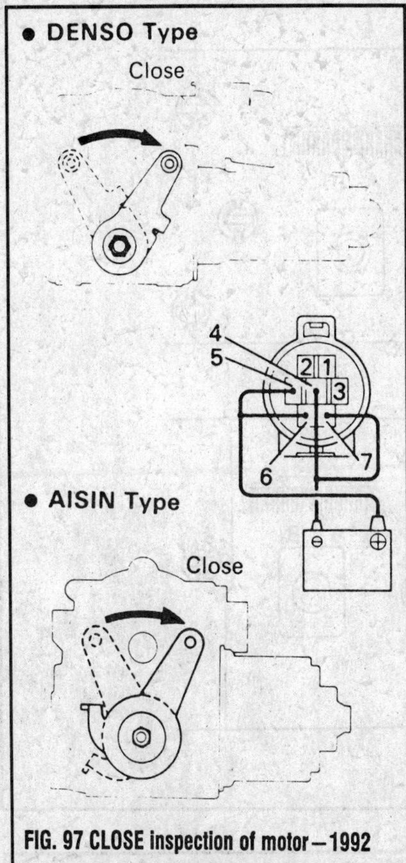

FIG. 97 CLOSE inspection of motor—1992

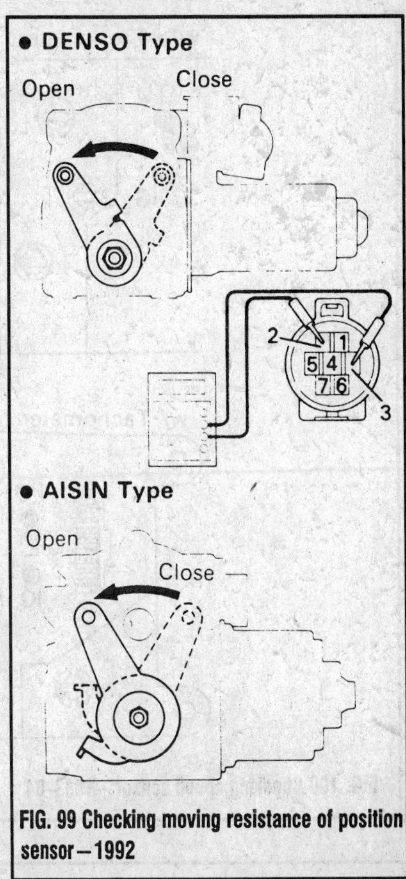

FIG. 99 Checking moving resistance of position sensor—1992

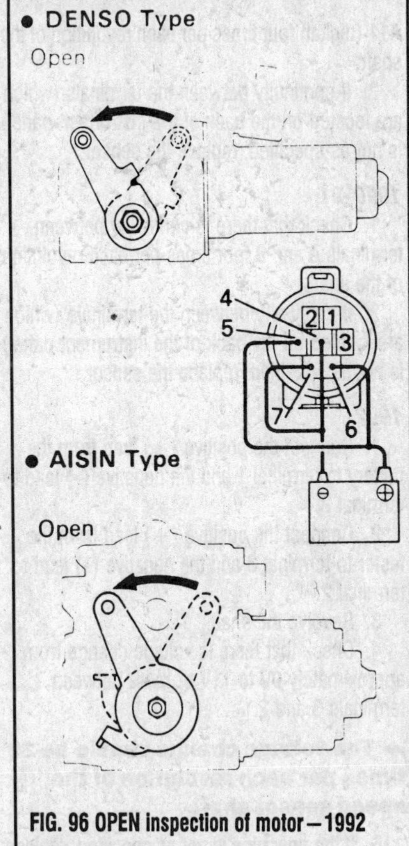

FIG. 96 OPEN inspection of motor—1992

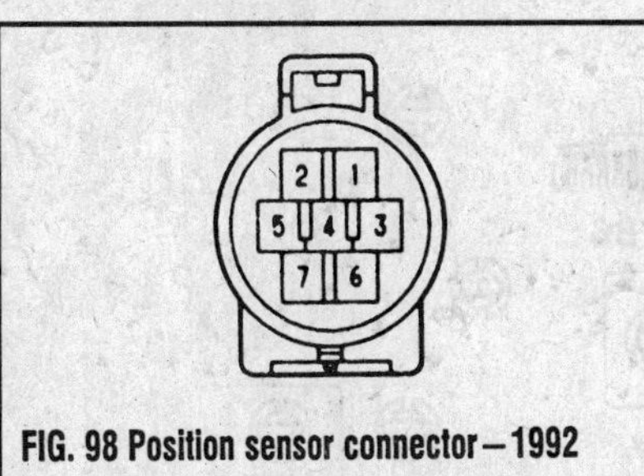

FIG. 98 Position sensor connector—1992

POSITION SENSOR

1. Measure the resistance between terminal 1 and 3. The resistance should be approximately 2000 ohms.
2. When the arm is moving from the closed to open position, check that resistance between terminals 2 and 3 increases from approximately 500 to 1800 ohms.
3. If operation is not as specified, replace the motor.

Speed Sensor

TESTING

➧ SEE FIGS. 100–104

1983–84

1. Using an ohmmeter, check to see that there is continuity between terminals A and B four times per each revolution of the meter shaft.
2. If the continuity between the terminals (which are located on the back of the instrument panel) is not as specified, replace the speedometer.

1985–86

This check applies to the analogue meter type sensor.

1. Using an ohmmeter, check to see that there is continuity between terminals B6 and B7 four times per each revolution of the meter shaft.
2. If the continuity between the terminals (which are located on the back of the instrument panel) is not as specified, replace the speedometer.

1987–89

1. Check that there is continuity between terminals A (analog), A9 (digital) and B (analog),

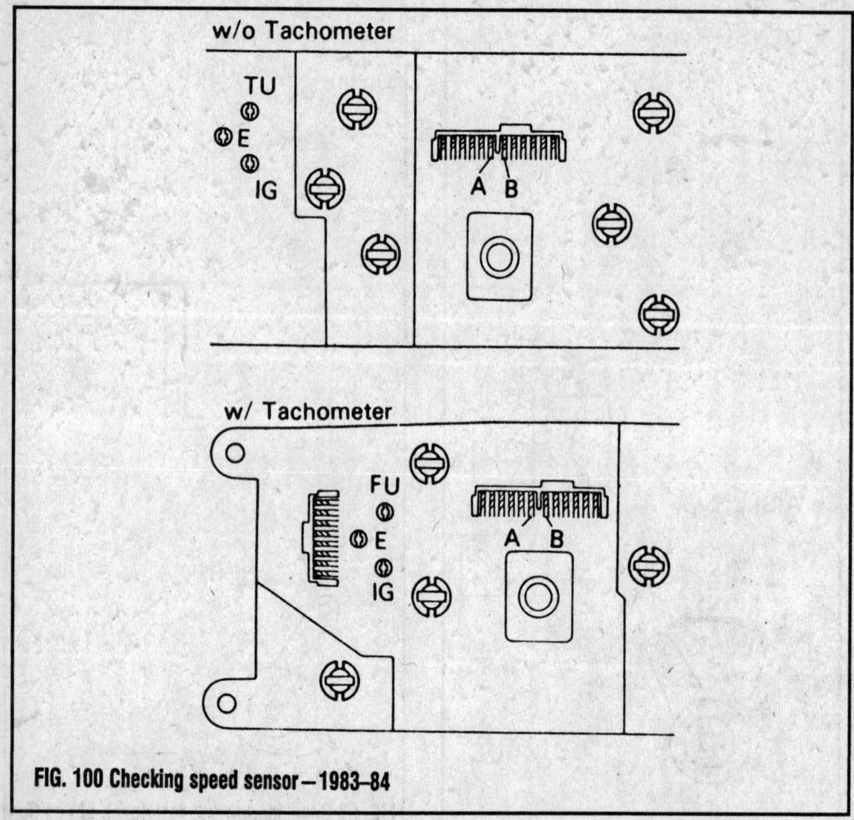

FIG. 100 Checking speed sensor—1983-84

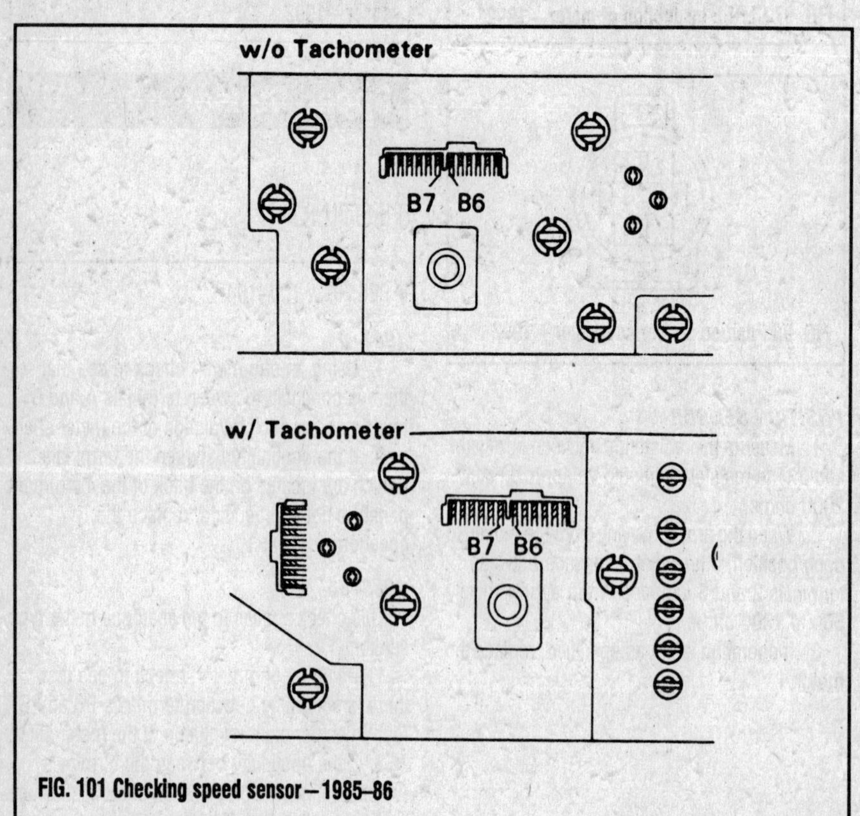

FIG. 101 Checking speed sensor—1985-86

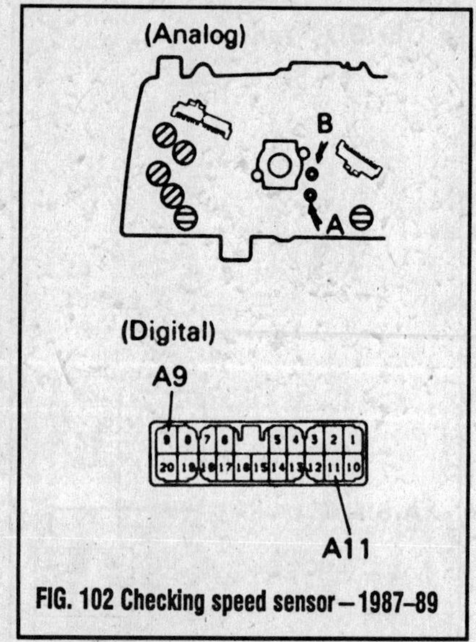

FIG. 102 Checking speed sensor—1987-89

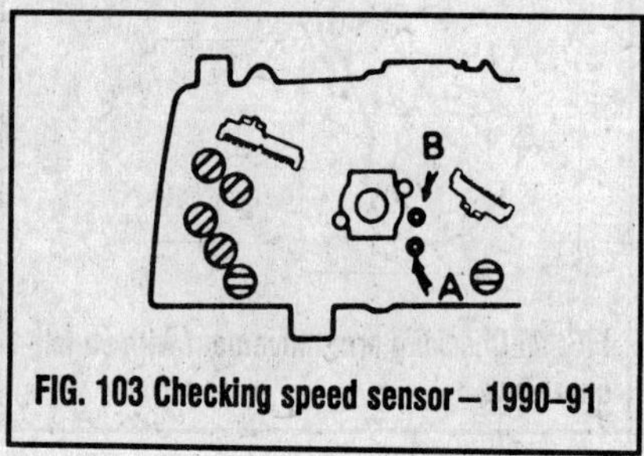

FIG. 103 Checking speed sensor—1990-91

A11 (digital) four times per each revolution of the shaft.

2. If continuity between the terminals (which are located on the back of the instrument panel) is not as specified, replace the sensor.

1990-91

1. Check that there is continuity between terminals A and B four times per each revolution of the shaft.

2. If continuity between the terminals (which are located on the back of the instrument panel) is not as specified, replace the sensor.

1992

1. Connect the positive (+) lead from the battery to terminal 1 and the negative (-) lead to terminal 2.

2. Connect the positive (+) lead from the tester to terminal 3 and the negative (-) lead to terminal 2.

3. Revolve the shaft.

4. Check that there is voltage change from approximately 0V to 11V or more between terminals 3 and 2.

➡ The voltage change should be 20 times per each revolution of the speed sensor shaft.

5. If the operation is not as specified, replace the sensor.

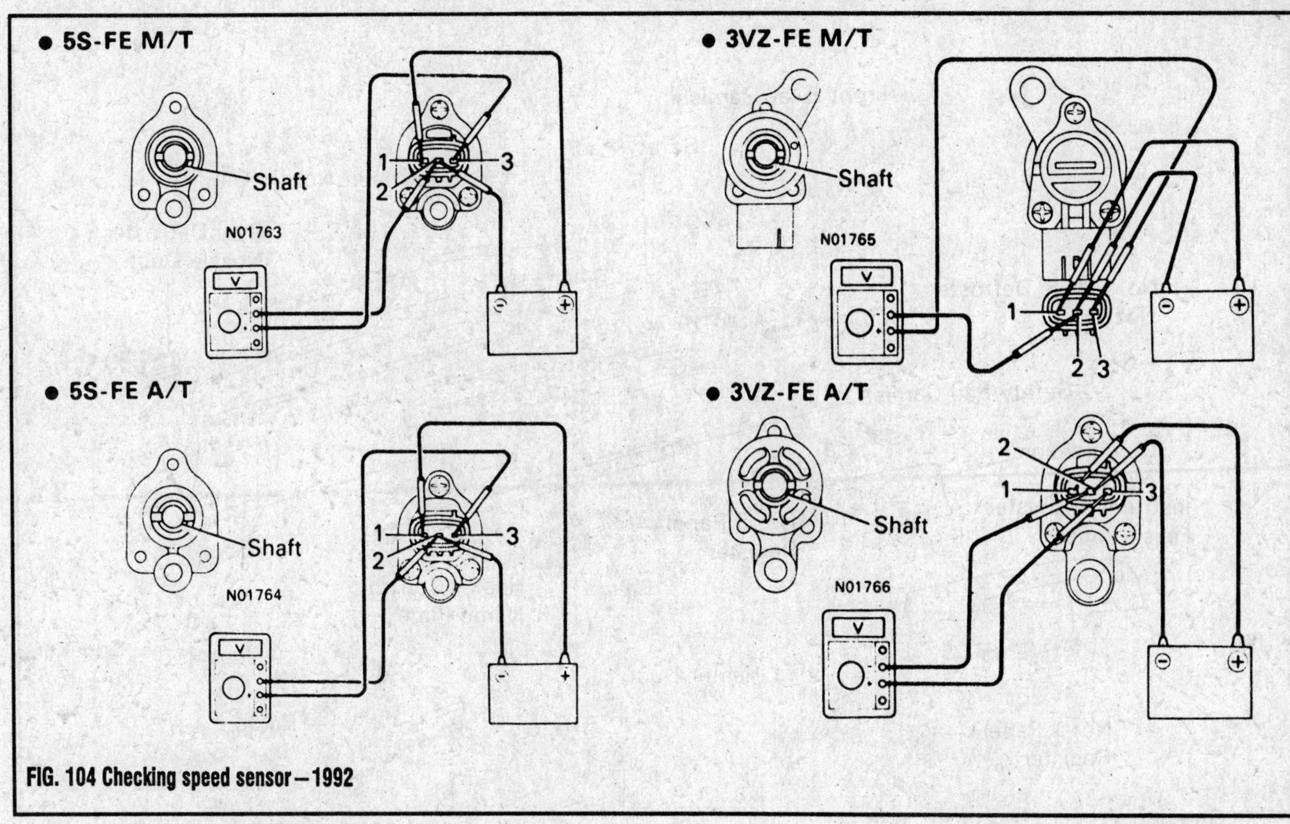

FIG. 104 Checking speed sensor—1992

ENTERTAINMENT SYSTEMS

Radio

REMOVAL & INSTALLATION

➡ **Due to the lack of information available at the time of this publication, a general radio removal and installation procedure is outlined for the Camry. The removal steps can be altered as required.**

➧ SEE FIGS. 105 AND 106

1. Disconnect the negative battery cable.
2. Remove the lower cluster finish panel.
3. Remove the screws that retain the radio.
4. Disconnect the antenna lead from the jack on the radio case and route the wiring off to the side.
5. Disconnect the wiring connectors and label them.
6. Label and detach the power and speaker leads.
7. Remove the radio.

To install:

8. Installation is the reverse of removal.

Speakers

REMOVAL & INSTALLATION

➡ **Due to the lack of information available at the time of this publication, a general speaker removal and installation procedure is outlined for the Camry. The removal steps can be altered as required.**

Dash Mounted

➧ SEE FIG. 107

1. Make sure that the radio is off.
2. Remove the speaker panel.
3. Remove the instrument panel box (some models).
4. Label and disconnect the speaker wires.
5. Remove the 2 screws and remove the speaker.

To install:

6. Installation is the reverse of removal.

Door mounted

➧ SEE FIGS.. 108 AND 109

1. Make sure that the radio is off.
2. Remove the 4 screws and the armrest.
3. Remove the clip and the screws securing the door pocket and remove the door pocket.
4. Remove the 2 screws and the speaker cover.
5. Remove the inner door panel.
6. Label and disconnect the speaker wires.
7. Remove the 4 screws and the speaker.

To install:

8. Installation is the reverse of removal.

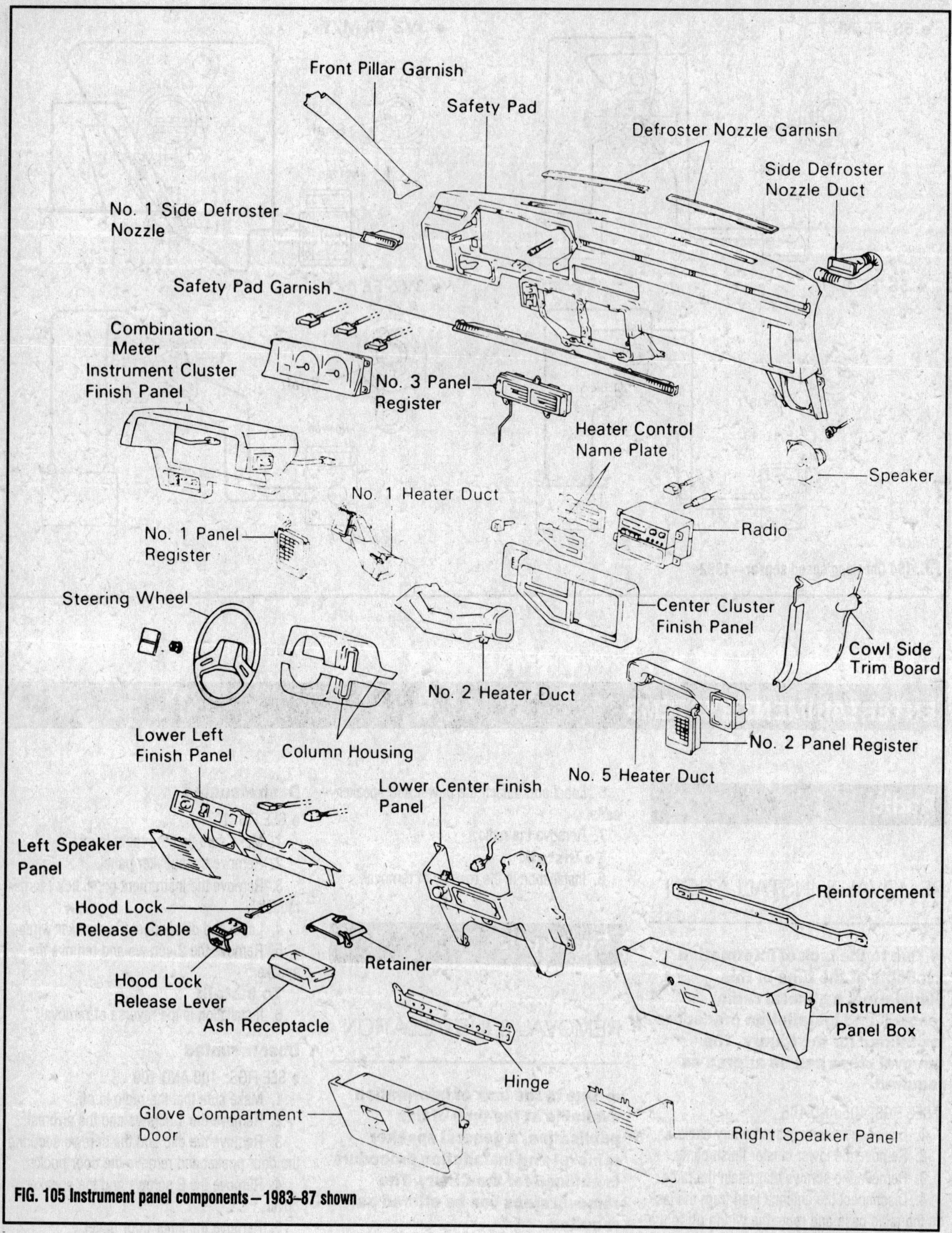

FIG. 105 Instrument panel components—1983–87 shown

Trunk Mounted

➧ SEE FIG. 110

1. Remove the package tray trim (some models).
2. Label and disconnect the speaker wires in the trunk (some models).
3. Remove the screws and the speaker.

To install:

4. Installation is the reverse of removal.

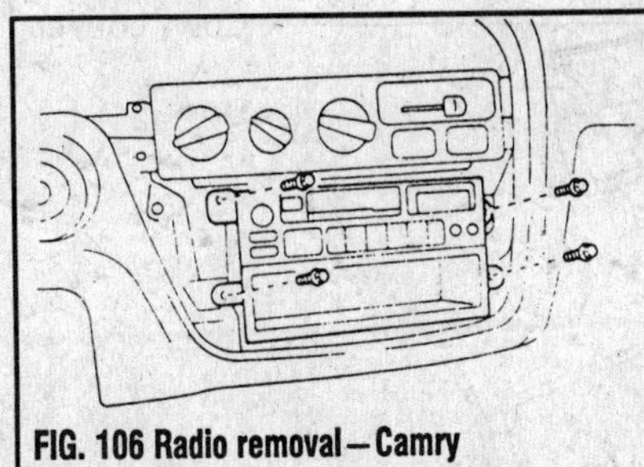

FIG. 106 Radio removal — Camry

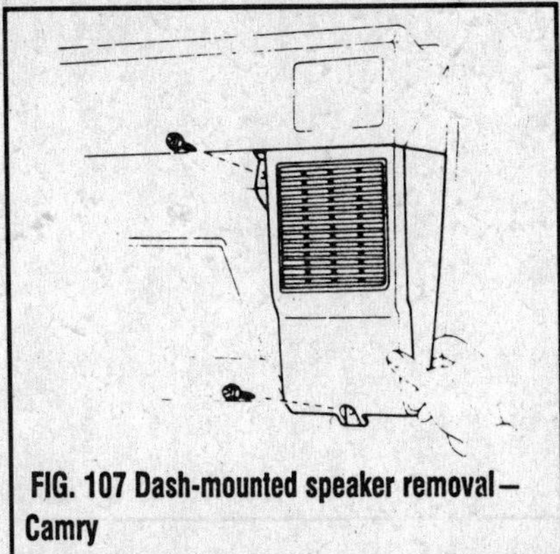

FIG. 107 Dash-mounted speaker removal — Camry

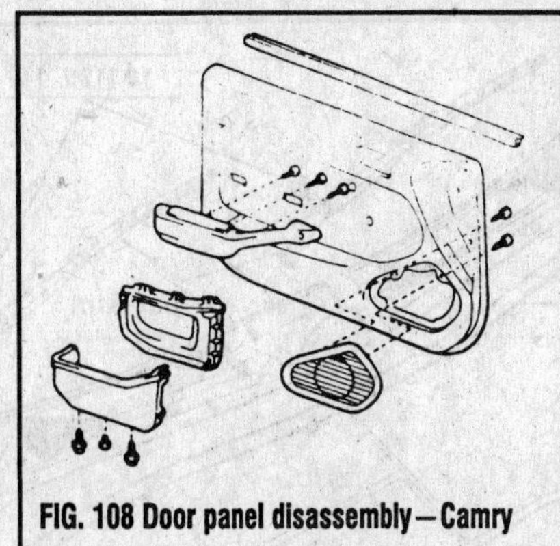

FIG. 108 Door panel disassembly — Camry

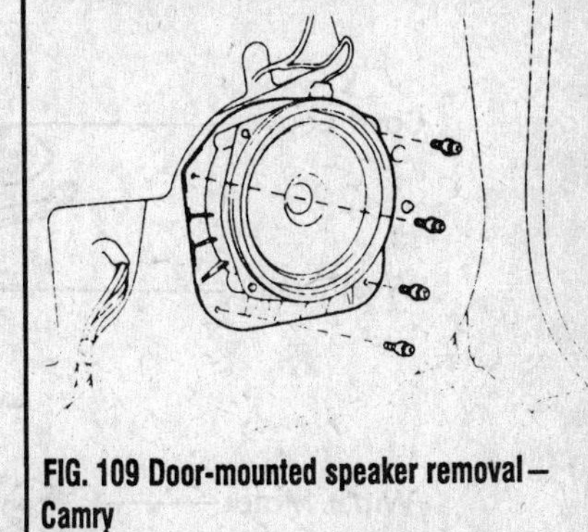

FIG. 109 Door-mounted speaker removal — Camry

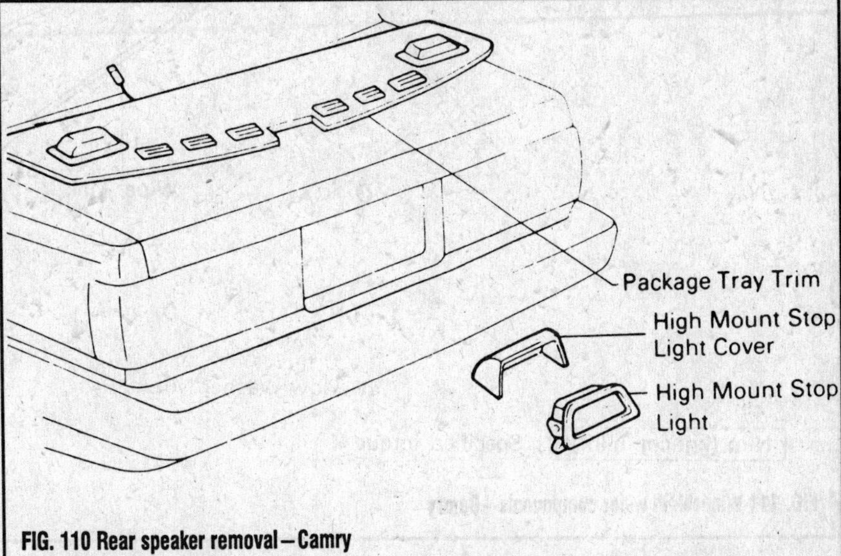

FIG. 110 Rear speaker removal — Camry

WINDSHIELD WIPERS AND WASHERS

Windshield Wiper Blade and Arm

REMOVAL & INSTALLATION

➧ SEE FIG. 111

1. Remove the wiper arm nut.

➡ **Hold the arm from moving when removing and installing the nuts so that the linkage will not be bent as a result of the torque.**

2. Mark the position of the wiper arm and remove.

To install:

3. Position the arm in the proper position.
4. Install the nuts and torque to 14 ft. lbs. (19 Nm).

Windshield Wiper Motor

REMOVAL & INSTALLATION

➧ SEE FIGS.. 112–114

1. Disconnect the negative battery cable.
2. Using a clip remover, remove the clips and the weatherstrip.
3. Remove the cowl louver.
4. Disconnect the wiper link.
5. Disconnect the wiper motor connector.
6. Remove the 4 bolts and remove the motor.

To install:

7. Installation is the reverse of removal.

➡ **Return the motor to the PARK position before installing by cycling the motor on and off once. Do this before connecting the linkage.**

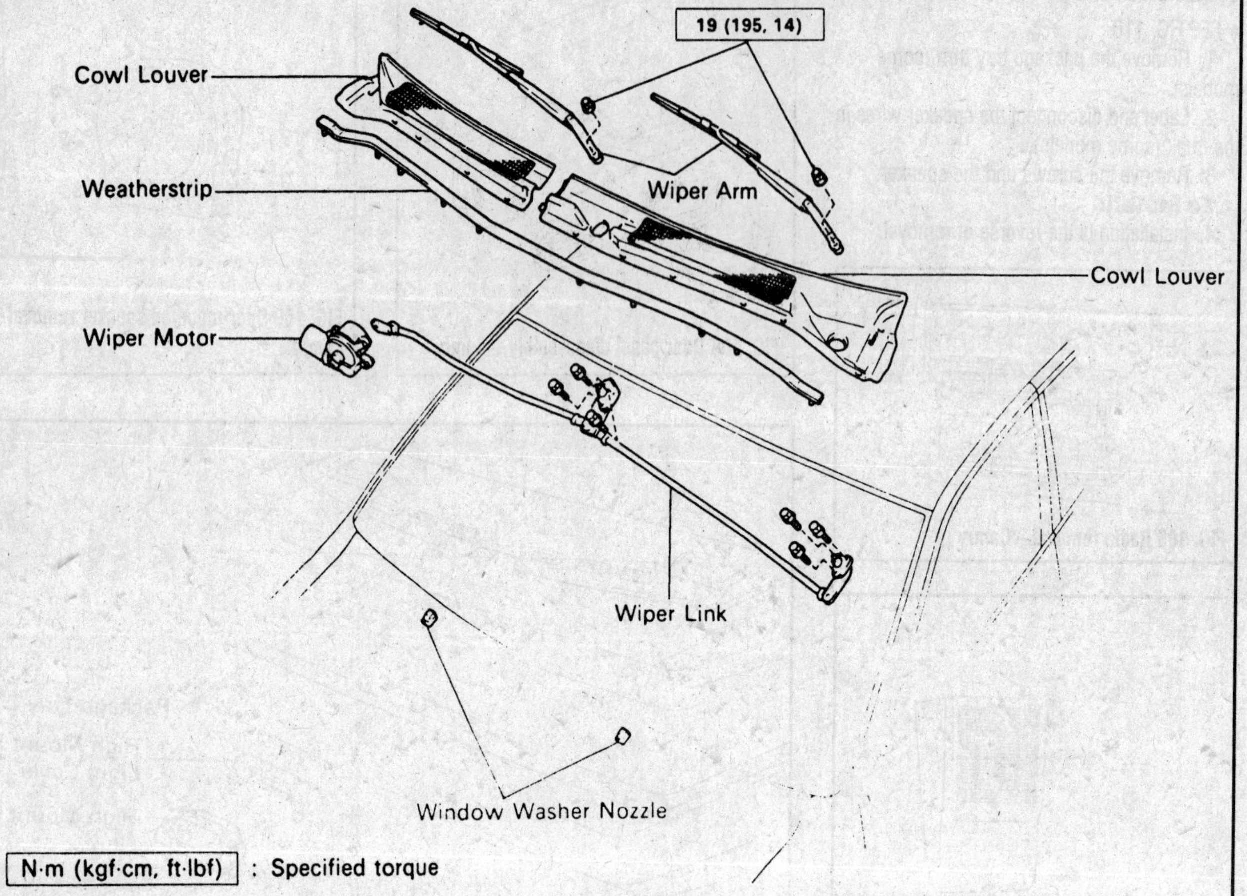

19 (195, 14)
Cowl Louver
Weatherstrip
Wiper Arm
Cowl Louver
Wiper Motor
Wiper Link
Window Washer Nozzle
N·m (kgf·cm, ft·lbf) : Specified torque

FIG. 111 Windshield wiper components—Camry

Wiper Motor
Washer Motor

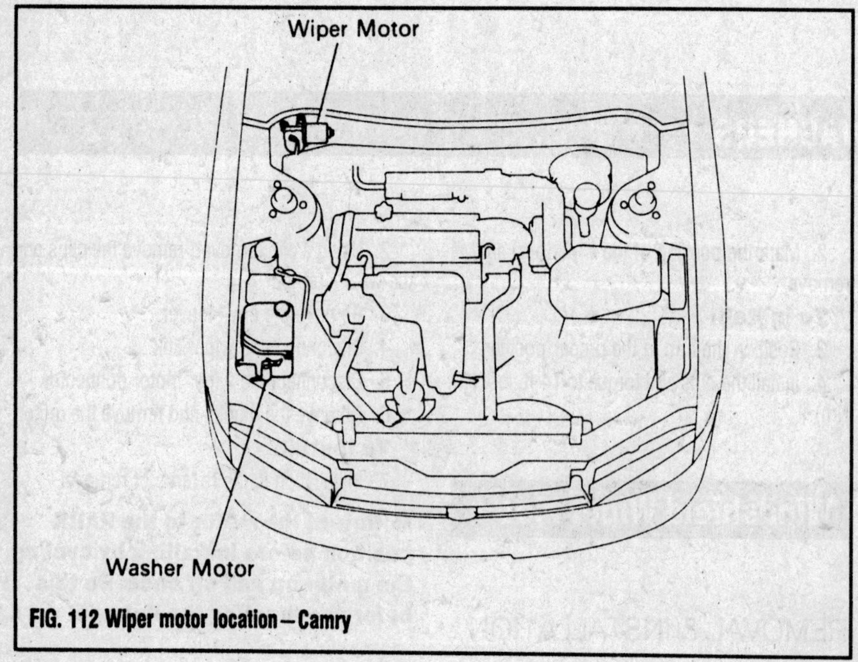

FIG. 112 Wiper motor location—Camry

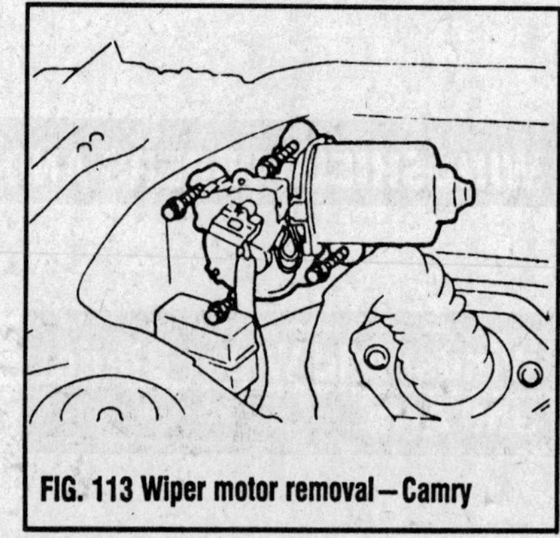

FIG. 113 Wiper motor removal—Camry

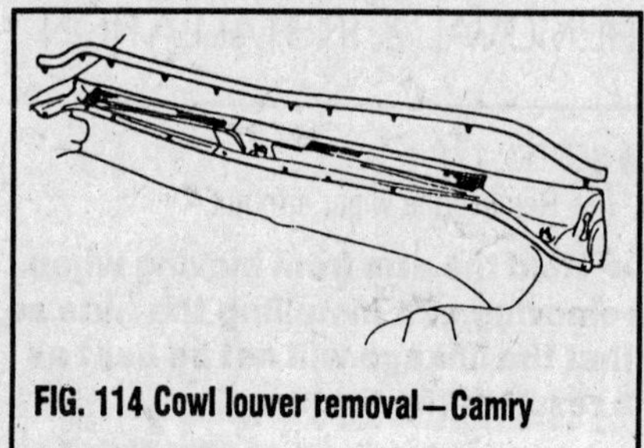

FIG. 114 Cowl louver removal—Camry

Rear Windshield Wiper Motor

REMOVAL & INSTALLATION

➡ **Due to the lack of information available at the time of this publication, a general rear wiper motor removal and installation procedure is outlined for the Camry. The removal steps can be altered as required.**

1. Disconnect the negative battery terminal.
2. Remove the wiper arm and rear door trim cover. Disconnect the wiper motor wire connector.
3. Remove the wiper motor bracket attaching bolts and the wiper motor along with the bracket.
4. Remove the mounting bracket from the old wiper motor and transfer it to the new motor.

To install:

5. Install the wiper motor and bracket with the attaching bolts.
6. Connect the wire connector and install the rear door trim cover and wiper arm.
7. Connect the negative battery cable and check the motor for proper operation.

Wiper Linkage

REMOVAL & INSTALLATION

➧ SEE FIG. 115

1. Using a clip remover, remove the clips and the weatherstrip.
2. Remove the cowl louver.
3. Disconnect the wiper link from the motor.
4. Remove the 6 bolts securing the wiper link pivots.
5. Remove the wiper link through the service hole.

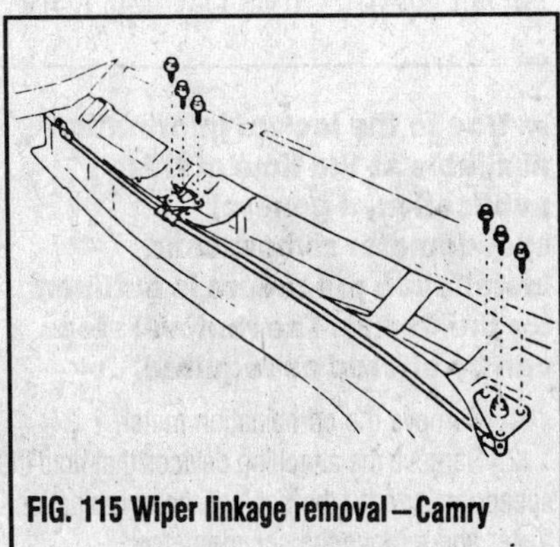

FIG. 115 Wiper linkage removal—Camry

To install:

6. Installation is the reverse of removal.

Window Washer Nozzle

REMOVAL & INSTALLATION

➧ SEE FIG. 116

1. Remove the cover.
2. Using a suitable tool, pry against the retaining tangs and remove the nozzle.

To install:

3. Installation is the reverse of removal.

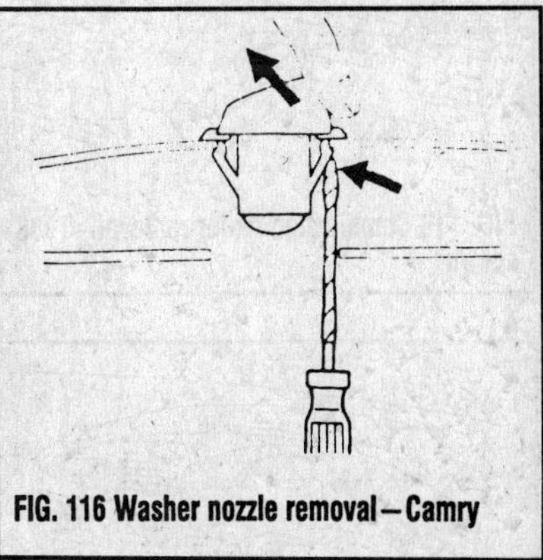

FIG. 116 Washer nozzle removal—Camry

INSTRUMENTS AND SWITCHES

➡ **For sending unit replacement refer to Sections 3 or 5 for the appropriate component.**

Instrument Cluster/ Combination Meter

➡ **When working around a digital or electronic cluster, make sure that the circuitry is not damaged due to static electricity discharge. To lessen the probability of this happening, touch both hands to ground frequently to discharge any static.**

REMOVAL & INSTALLATION

➡ **Due to the lack of information available at the time of this publication, a general instrument cluster/combination meter removal and installation procedure is outlined for the Camry. The removal steps can be altered as required.**

➧ SEE FIGS. 117–120

1. Disconnect the negative battery cable.
2. Remove the fuse box cover from under the left side of the instrument panel.
3. Remove the heater control knobs.
4. Using a screwdriver, carefully pry off the heater control panel.
5. Unscrew the cluster finish panel retaining screws and pull out the bottom of the panel.
6. Unplug all electrical connectors and unhook the speedometer cable.
7. Remove the combination meter.
8. To install, position the combination meter so that the connectors and speedometer cable can be easily connected. Connect the speedometer cable and connectors.
9. Install the cluster finish panel.
10. Install the heater control panel with the control knobs.
11. Install the fuse box cover and connect the negative battery cable.

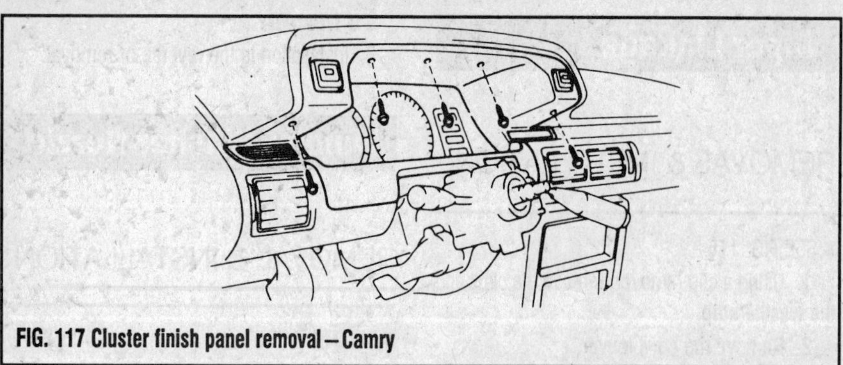
FIG. 117 Cluster finish panel removal — Camry

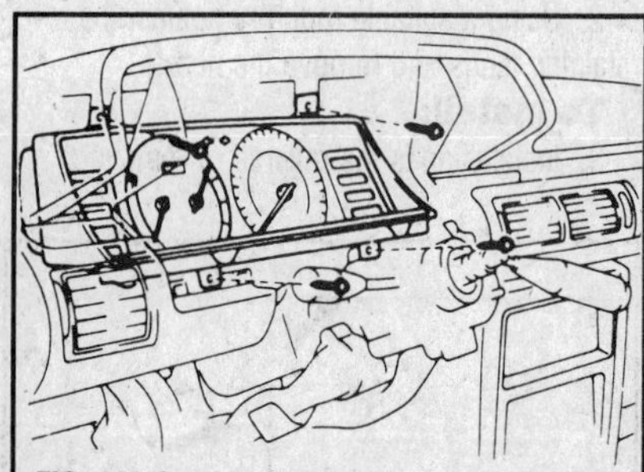
FIG. 118 Combination meter removal — 1988 shown

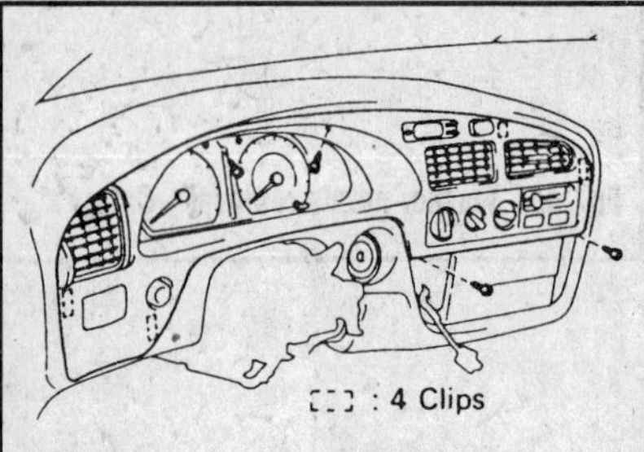

FIG. 119 Cluster finish panel removal — 1992 shown

FIG. 120 Combination meter removal — 1992 shown

Speedometer

REMOVAL & INSTALLATION

➡ **Due to the lack of information available at the time of this publication, a general speedometer removal and installation procedure is outlined for the Camry. The removal steps can be altered as required.**

1. Remove the combination meter.
2. Remove the attaching devices that hold the speedometer onto the back of the combination meter and remove the speedometer.
3. Installation is the reverse of removal.

➡ **Tire wear and over/under inflation will increase the indication error. Also, pointer vibration can be caused by a loose speedometer cable.**

Tachometer

REMOVAL & INSTALLATION

➡ **Due to the lack of information available at the time of this publication, a general tachometer removal and installation procedure is outlined for the Camry. The removal steps can be altered as required.**

1. Remove the combination meter.
2. Remove the attaching devices that hold the tachometer onto the back of the combination meter and remove the tachometer.
3. Installation is the reverse of removal.

➡ **When removing or installing the tachometer, be careful not to drop it or subject it to heavy shocks.**

Speedometer Cable

REMOVAL & INSTALLATION

➡ **Due to the lack of information available at the time of this publication, a general speedometer cable removal and installation procedure is outlined for the Camry. The removal steps can be altered as required.**

1. Disconnect the cable from the rear of the combination meter.
2. Unscrew the cable (at the transaxle end) from the speedometer driven gear housing on the transaxle.
3. Slip the cable through the grommet in the firewall or remove the grommet.
4. Installation is the reverse of removal.

➡ **When removing or installing the cable, be careful not to bend it to sharply or it will become kinked and require replacement.**

Oil Pressure, Fuel and Temperature Gauges

REMOVAL & INSTALLATION

➡ **Due to the lack of information available at the time of this publication, a general guage removal and installation procedure is outlined for the Camry. The removal steps can be altered as required.**

1. Remove the combination meter.
2. Remove the attaching devices that hold the guage onto the back of the combination meter and remove the guage.
3. Installation is the reverse of removal.

Voltmeter, Ammeter and Clock

REMOVAL & INSTALLATION

➡ Due to the lack of information available at the time of this publication, a general voltmeter, ammeter or clock removal and installation procedure is outlined for the Camry. The removal steps can be altered as required.

1. Remove the combination meter.
2. Remove the attaching devices that hold the instrument onto the back of the combination meter and remove the instrument.
3. Installation is the reverse of removal.

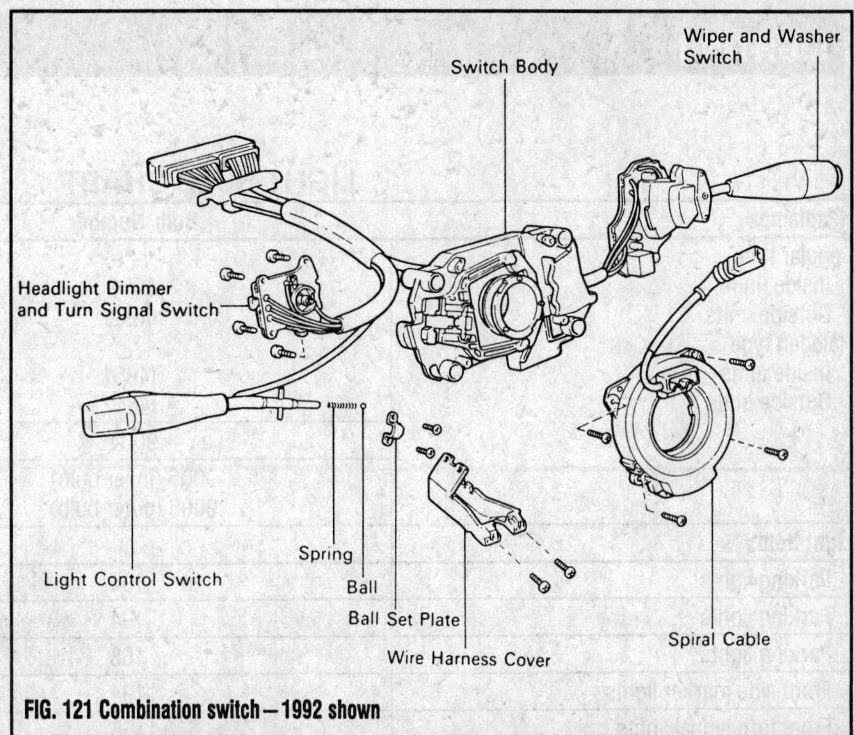

FIG. 121 Combination switch—1992 shown

Combination Switch

REMOVAL & INSTALLATION

➡ Due to the lack of information available at the time of this publication, a general combination switch removal and installation procedure is outlined for the Camry. The removal steps can be altered as required.

CAUTION

To prevent personal injury, work must be started after approximately 30 seconds or longer from the time the ignition switch is turned to the "LOCK" position and the negative (-) terminal cable is disconnected from the battery, so that the Air Bag will not deploy.

SEE FIGS. 121–123

1. Remove the steering wheel.
2. Remove the steering column cover screws and remove the cover.
3. Remove the combination switch screws and remove the switch.
4. Installation is the reverse of removal.

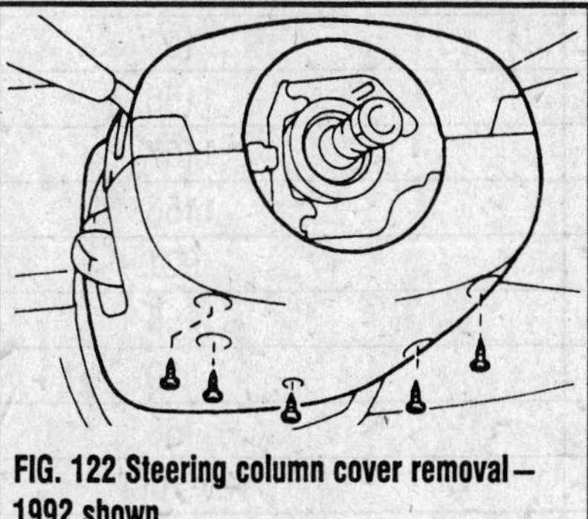
FIG. 122 Steering column cover removal—1992 shown

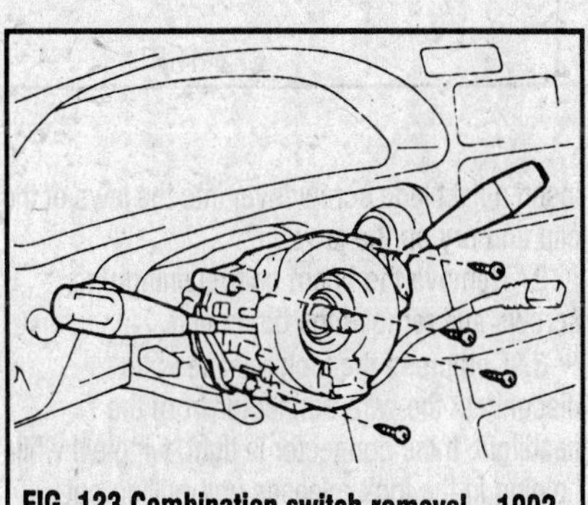
FIG. 123 Combination switch removal—1992 shown

Headlight Switch

See Combination Switch.

Windshield Wiper Switch

See Combination Switch.

Rear Windshield Wiper and Washer Switch

REMOVAL & INSTALLATION

➡ Due to the lack of information available at the time of this publication, a general Rear Wiper Switch removal and installation procedure is outlined for the Camry. The removal steps can be altered as required.

1. Disconnect the connector from the back of the switch behind the instrument panel.
2. Gently pry with a suitable tool and remove the switch from the front of the instrument panel.
3. Installation is the reverse of removal.

LIGHTING

LIGHT BULB CHART

Headlamps	Bulb Number	Year Applicable
Regular type Inside units Outside units Halogen type Inside units Outside units	4651 4652 H4651 H4652	1983-84
	9004	1985-91
	9005 (inner bulb) 9006 (outer bulb)	1992
Light Bulbs		
Parking lights	194	1983-84
Parking lights	194	1985-86
Parking lights	168	1987-92
Front side marker lights	194	
Front turn signal lights	1156	1983-90, 92
Front turn signal lights	1156 NA	1991
Rear side marker lights	194	
Rear turn signal lights	1156	
Stop and tail lights	1157	
High mounted stop-light	1156	1986-91
High mounted stop-light	921	1992
Back-up lights	1156	
License plate lights	89	1983-91
License plate lights	168	1992
Interior lights	12V-10CP	1983-86
Luggage compartment light	12V-3CP	1983-86
Trunk room light	168	1983-86

Headlights

REMOVAL & INSTALLATION

Sealed Beam

SEE FIGS. 124 AND 125

➡ **Before making a headlight replacement, make sure that the headlight switch is in the OFF position.**

1. Loosen the screws, release the clips and remove the headlight door. To release the clips, insert a flat blade screwdriver into the jaws of the clip and pry on the jaws.
2. Remove the beam unit retaining ring screws and remove the beam unit.
3. Compress the lock releases and disconnect the wire connector from the headlight. If the connector is tight, wiggle it while holding in the lock releases and pulling out.

➡ **Never try to loosen the aim adjusting screws. If the screws are loosened, the headlights will have to be re-aimed by a qualified technician.**

4. To install, use only a sealed beam unit with the same part number and wattage.

Bulb Element Type

SEE FIGS. 126–130

➡ **Before making a headlight replacement, make sure that the headlight switch is in the OFF position.**

1. Open the hood and unplug the connector while pressing down on the lock release on 1988–92 models.
2. On 1985–91 models, turn the bulb retaining ring clockwise and take the bulb out. On the 1992, just turn the bulb and remove it.
3. To install the new bulb, align the cut outs on the bulb socket with the protrusions on the headlight body. Use a bulb with the same part number and wattage rating.

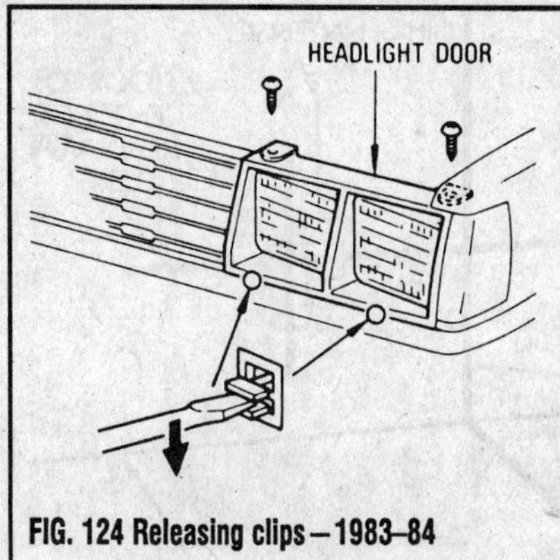

FIG. 124 Releasing clips—1983–84

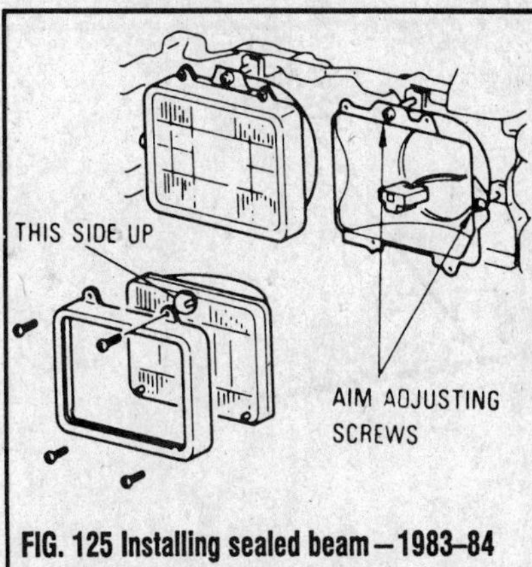

FIG. 125 Installing sealed beam—1983–84

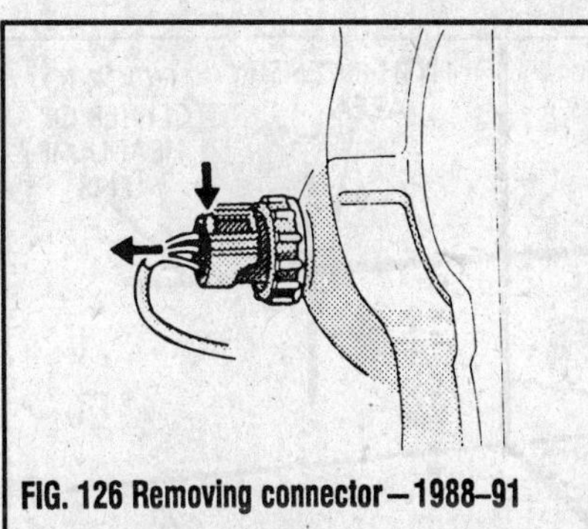

FIG. 126 Removing connector—1988–91

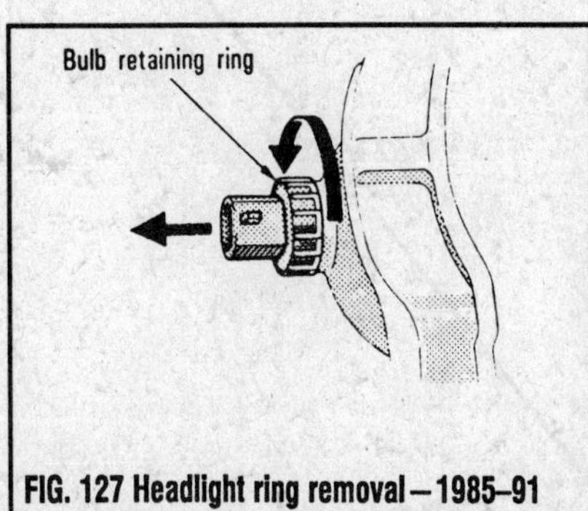

FIG. 127 Headlight ring removal—1985–91

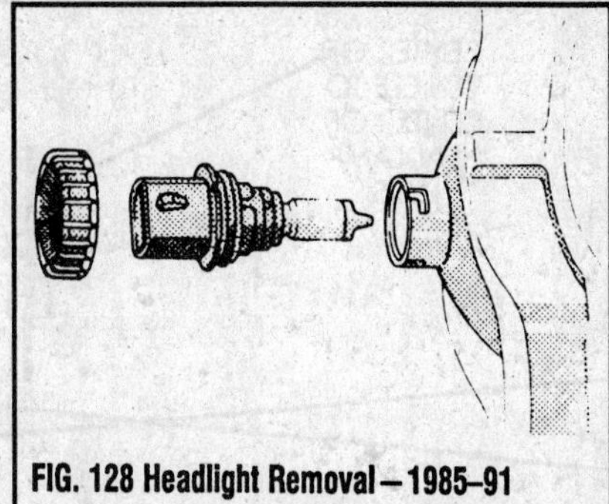

FIG. 128 Headlight Removal—1985–91

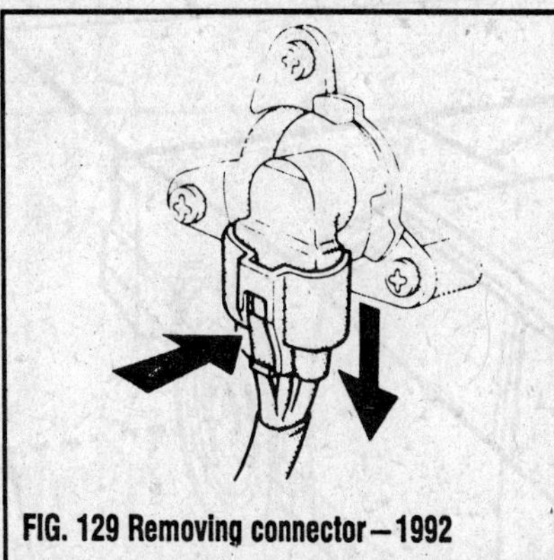

FIG. 129 Removing connector—1992

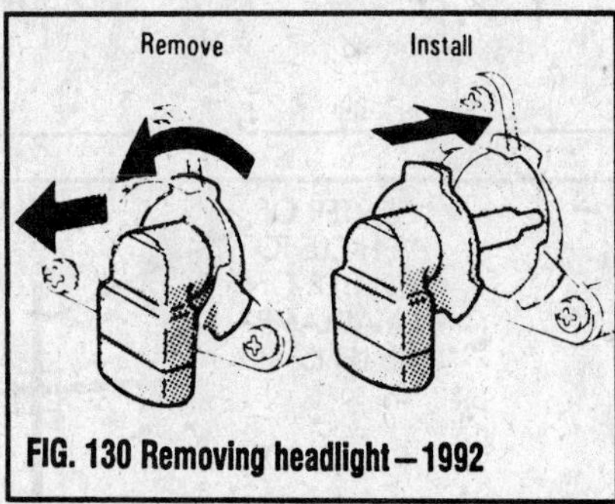

FIG. 130 Removing headlight—1992

➡ **Do not tough the glass portion of the new bulb with bare hands. If you do, clean the glass with alcohol and a clean, lint-free rag.**

4. Lock the locking ring, if equipped, and connect the connector.
5. Have the headlight aiming checked by a qualified technician.

AIMING

➧ SEE FIGS. 131 AND 132

Headlight Alignment Preparation

➡ **HEADLAMPS SHOULD BE ADJUSTED WITH A SPECIAL ALIGNMENT TOOL. STATE REGULATIONS MAY VARY ON THIS PROCEDURE. USE THIS PROCEDURE BELOW ONLY FOR TEMPORARY ADJUSTMENTS.**

Verify the headlamp dimmer and high beam indicator operation. Inspect and correct all components that could interfere with the proper headlamp alignment.

Verify proper tire inflation on all wheels. Clean headlamp lenses and make sure that there are no heavy loads in the trunk or hatch luggage area. The fuel tank should be FULL. Add 6.5 lbs. of weight over the fuel tank for each estimated gallon of missing fuel.

Alignment Screen Preparation

1. Position the vehicle on a LEVEL surface perpendicular to a flat wall 25 feet away.
2. From the floor UP, tape a line on the wall at the centerline of the vehicle. Sight along the centerline of the vehicle (from the rear of the vehicle forward) to verify accuracy of the the line placement.
3. Rock the vehicle side to side and up and down (on front bumper assembly) a few times to allow the suspension to stabilize.
4. Measure the distance from the center of the headlamp lens to the floor. Transfer measurements to the alignment screen with tape. Use this mark for UP/DOWN adjustment reference.
5. Measure distance from the centerline of the vehicle to the center of each headlamp being aligned. Transfer measurements to screen with tape to each side of the vehicle centerline. Use this mark for LEFT/RIGHT adjustment reference.

Headlight Adjustment

A properly aimed low beam headlamp will project the top edge of high intensity pattern on the the alignment screen from 2 inches (50mm) above to 2 inches (50mm) below the headlamp centerline. The side-to-side outboard edge of high intensity pattern should be from 2 inches (50mm) left to 2 inches (50mm) right of the headlamp centerline.

THE PREFERRED HEADLAMP ALIGNMENT IS "0" FOR THE UP/DOWN ADJUSTMENT AND "0" FOR THE LEFT/RIGHT.

The high beam pattern should be correct when the low beams are aligned properly. The high beam pattern on vehicles with multiple sealed beam headlamps should be aligned with the low beam lamp covered (do not cover illuminated headlamp for more than 15 seconds) or disconnected.

To adjust headlamps, adjust the alignment screws to achieve the specified high intensity pattern.

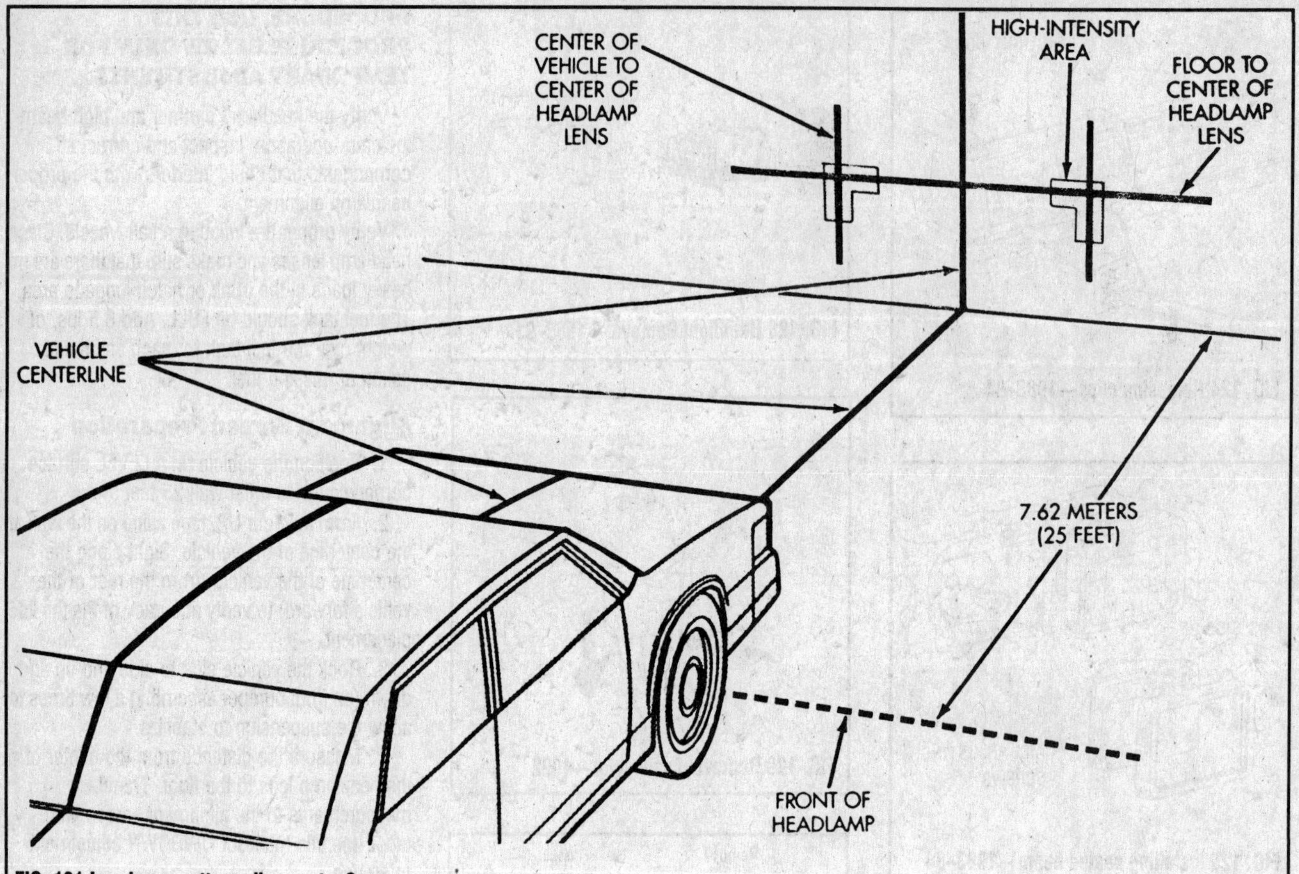

FIG. 131 Low beam pattern alignment—Camry

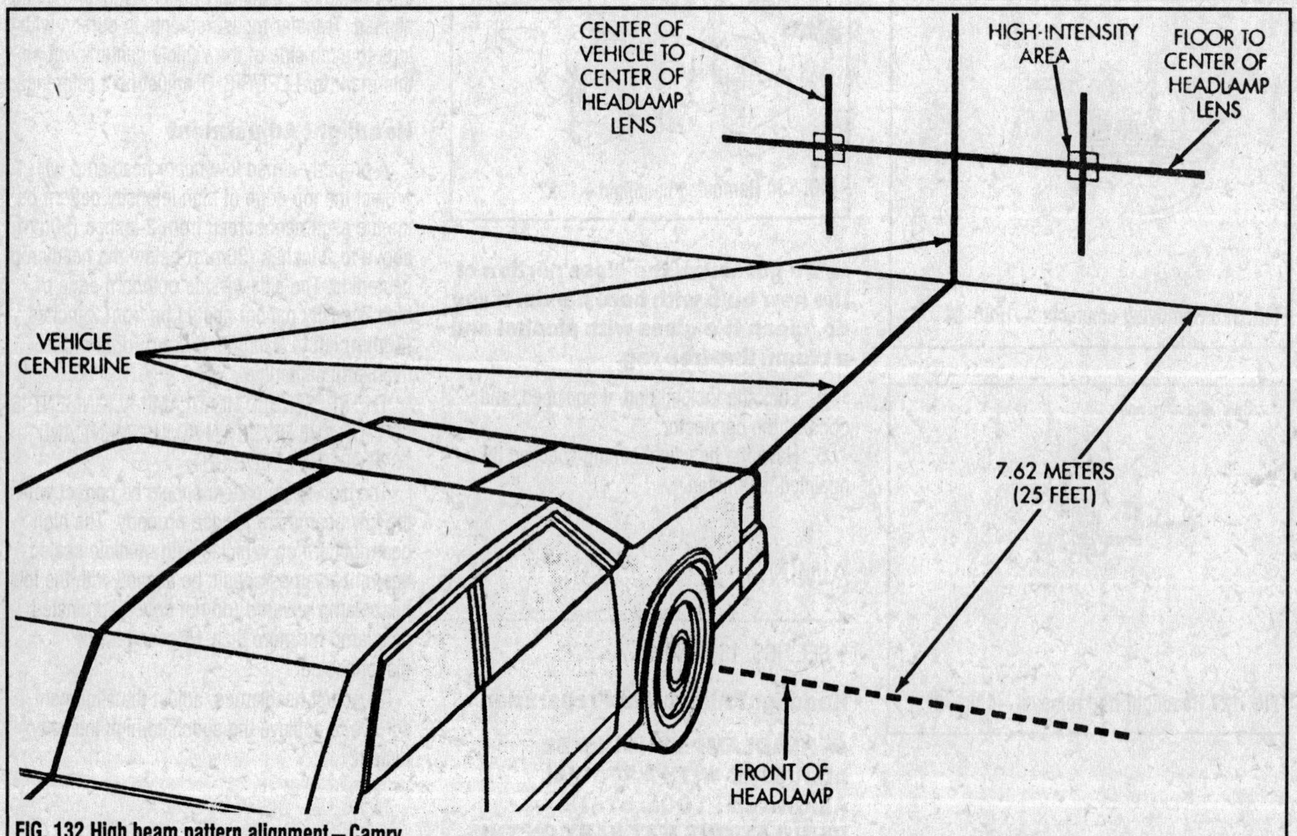

FIG. 132 High beam pattern alignment—Camry

Signal and Marker Lights

REMOVAL & INSTALLATION

Front Turn Signal and Parking Lights

➧ SEE FIGS. 133–137

1983–91

1. Remove the 2 or 3 screws retaining the lens and remove the lens.
2. Pull the bulb or bulbs straight out of the socket for parking lights, and push in and turn to remove the turn signal bulb.
3. Installation is the reverse of removal.

1992

1. Remove the parking light cover clips to gain access to the parking light lens screws, if replacing that bulb.
2. Remove the lens screws and the parking light lens or the turn signal lens.
3. Pull the bulb straight out of the socket for parking lights, and push in and turn to remove the turn signal bulb.
4. Installation is the reverse of removal.

Rear Side Marker Lights

➧ SEE FIGS. 138–140

1983–91 EXCEPT 1986 SEDAN AND HATCHBACK

1. Remove the 2 screws retaining the lens and remove the lens.
2. Pull the bulb straight out of the socket.
3. Installation is the reverse of removal.

1986 SEDAN AND HATCHBACK

1. Gain access to the bulb socket from the luggage compartment inside the vehicle.
2. Twist the socket and pull out from the inner lens housing.
3. Pull the bulb straight out of the socket.
4. Installation is the reverse of removal.

1992

See rear turn signal, brake and parking lights.

Rear Turn Signal, Brake and Parking Lights

➧ SEE FIGS. 141–147

1983–86

1. Remove the access covers in the luggage compartment.
2. Push in and rotate the bulb and remove.
3. Installation is the reverse of removal.

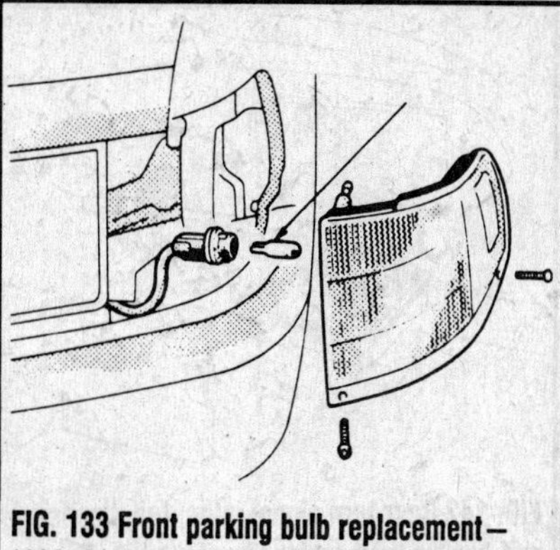

FIG. 133 Front parking bulb replacement–1983–91

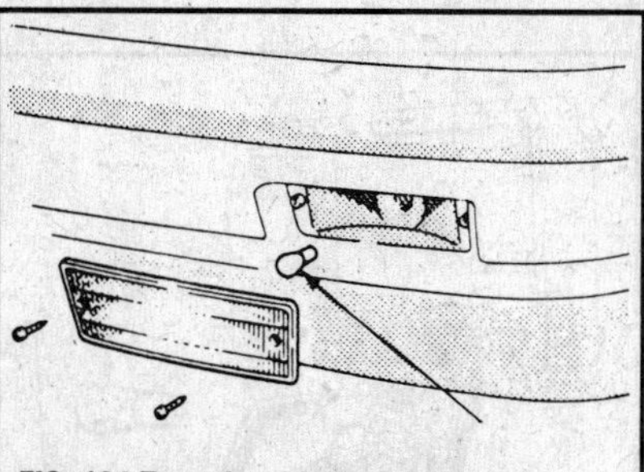

FIG. 134 Turn signal bulb replacement–1983–91

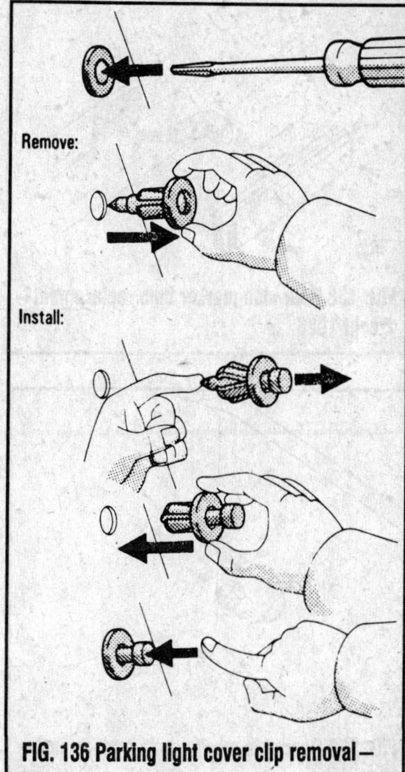

FIG. 136 Parking light cover clip removal–Camry

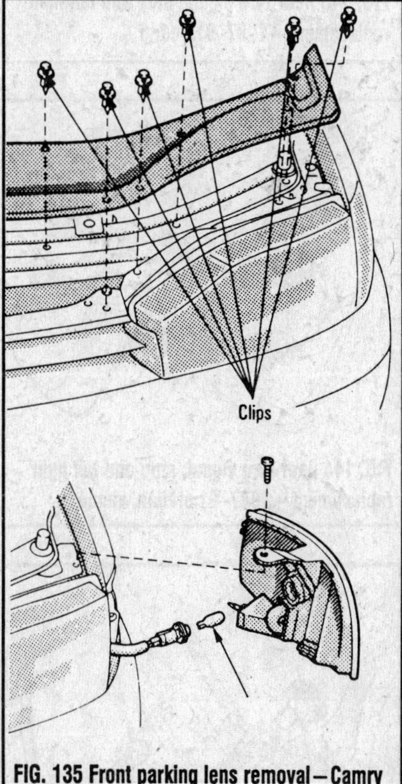

FIG. 135 Front parking lens removal–Camry

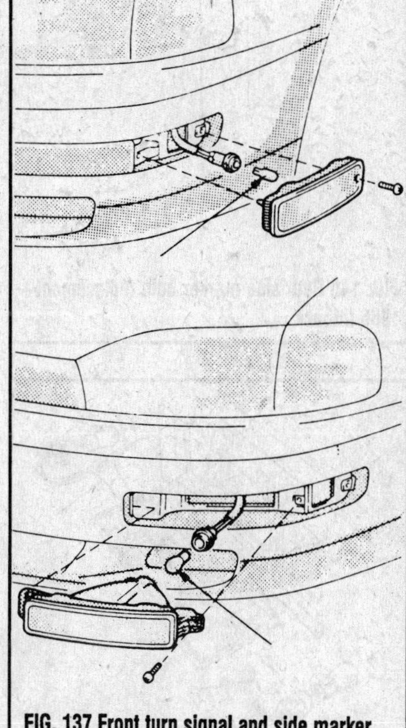

FIG. 137 Front turn signal and side marker bulb replacement–Camry

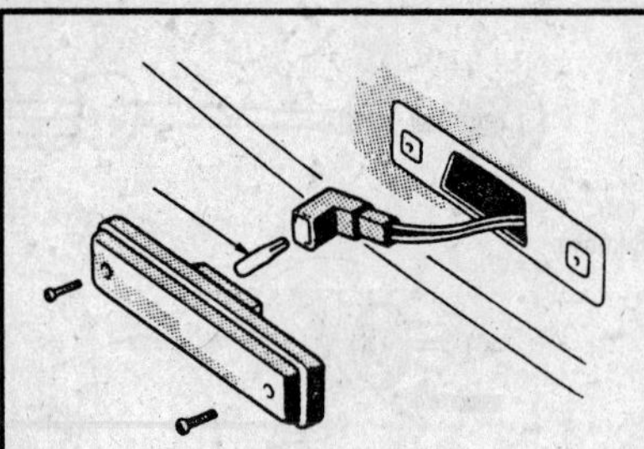
FIG. 138 Rear side marker bulb replacement—except 1986

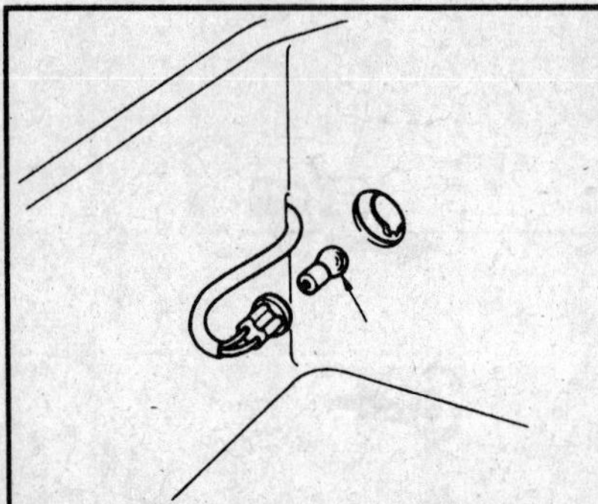
FIG. 139 Rear side marker bulb replacement—1986 sedan

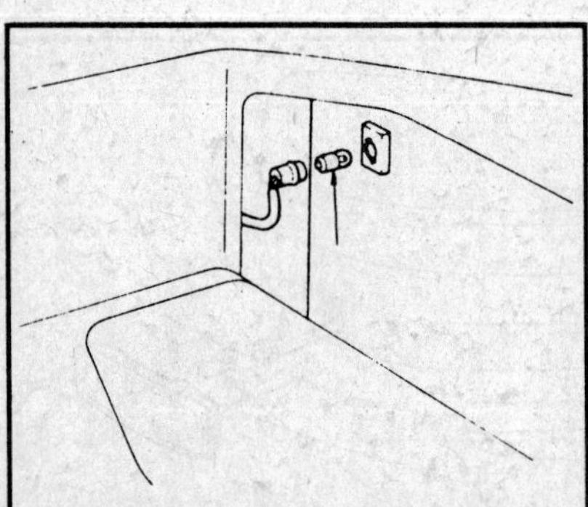
FIG. 140 Rear side marker bulb replacement—1986 liftback

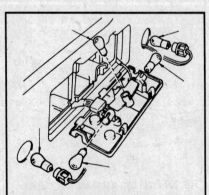

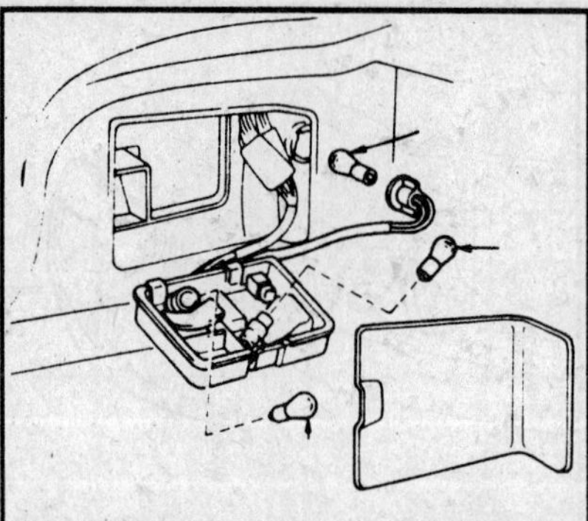
FIG. 142 Rear turn signal, stop, tail, license and backup light replacement—1983–86 liftback

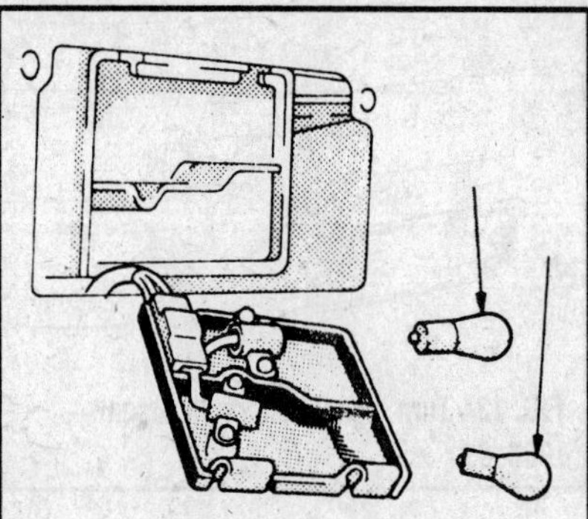
FIG. 143 Rear turn signal, stop and tail light replacement—1987–91 sedan

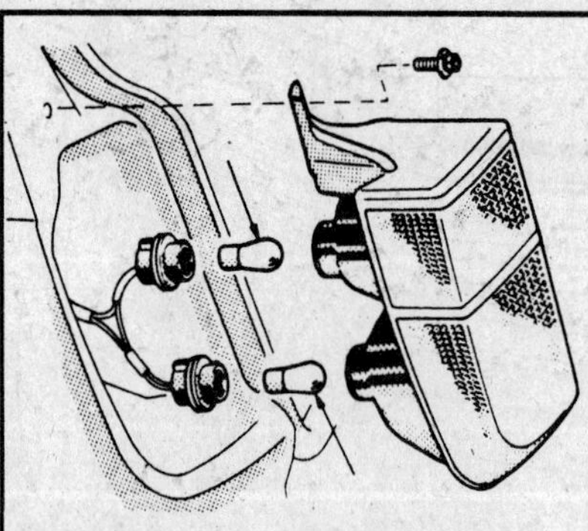
FIG. 144 Rear turn signal, stop and tail light replacement—1987–91 station wagon

FIG. 141 Rear turn signal, stop, tail, license and backup light replacement—1983–86 sedan

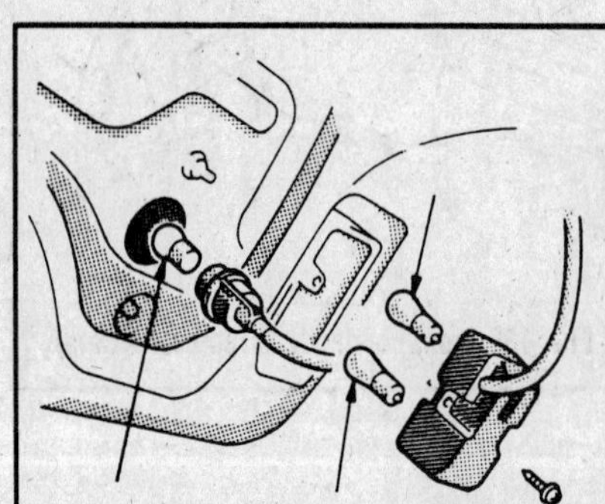
FIG. 145 Stop, tail, backup and licence plate light replacement—1987–91 sedan

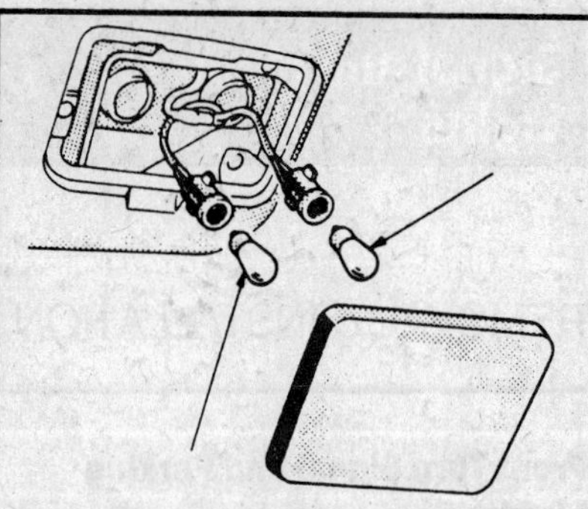
FIG. 146 Stop, tail, backup and licence plate light replacement—1987–91 station wagon

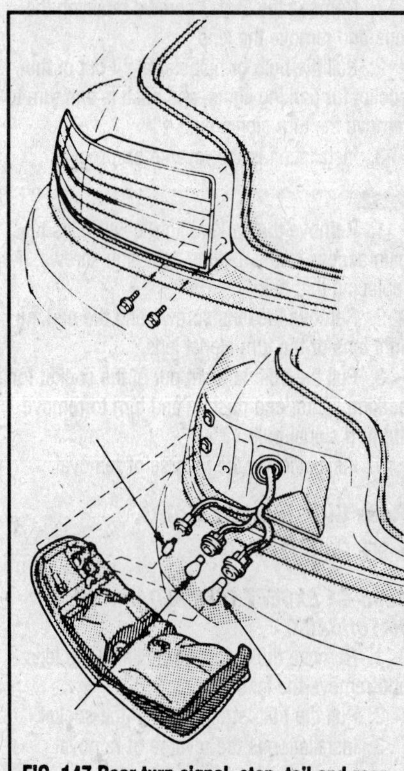
FIG. 147 Rear turn signal, stop, tail and rear side marker light replacement—1992

1987–92

1. Remove the access cover in the luggage compartment or remove the screws that secure the lens on the outside of the vehicle.
2. Push in and rotate the bulb and remove.
3. Installation is the reverse of removal.

High-mount Brake Light

➧ SEE FIGS. 148–152

1. Gently remove the lens with a suitable prying tool or remove the stop light cover screws and remove the cover.
2. Push in and rotate the bulb and remove on 1986–91 models or just pull the bulb straight out on 1992 models.
3. Installation is the reverse of removal.

Dome Light

➧ SEE FIG 153

1. Gently remove the lens with a suitable prying tool.
2. Gently remove the bulb with a suitable removal tool.
3. Installation is the reverse of removal.

✲✲ CAUTION

Make sure that the dome light switch is off and that the doors are shut. Also, wear eye protection to avoid eye injury in case of broken glass.

Cargo and Passenger Area Lamps

➧ SEE FIGS. 154–162

1. Twist, unscrew or gently remove the lens with a suitable prying tool.
2. Push in and turn, or pull the bulb strait out.
3. Installation is the reverse of removal.

License Plate Lights

➧ SEE FIGS. 141, 145 AND 159–162

1. Gain access to the bulbs by removing the inner cover or the lens.
2. Push in and turn, or pull the bulb strait out.
3. Installation is the reverse of removal.

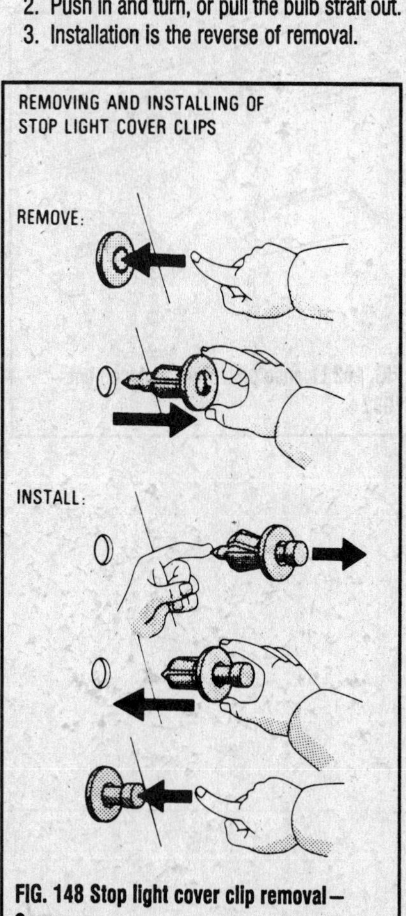

FIG. 148 Stop light cover clip removal—Camry

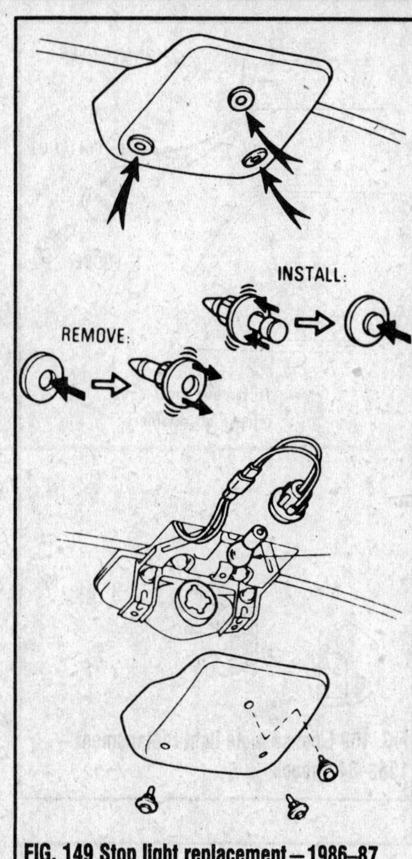

FIG. 149 Stop light replacement—1986–87 liftback

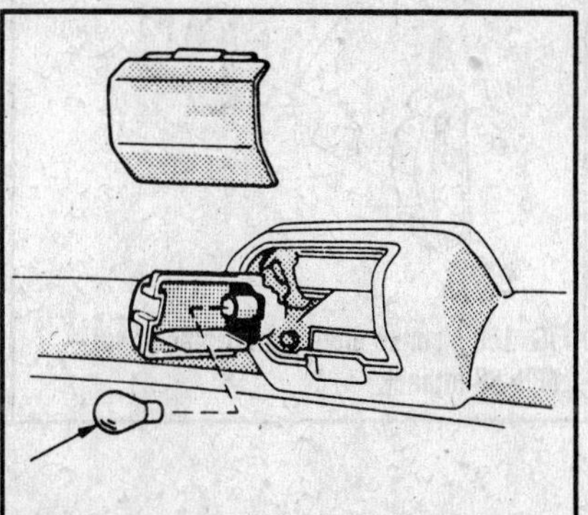

FIG. 150 High mount stop light replacement—station wagon

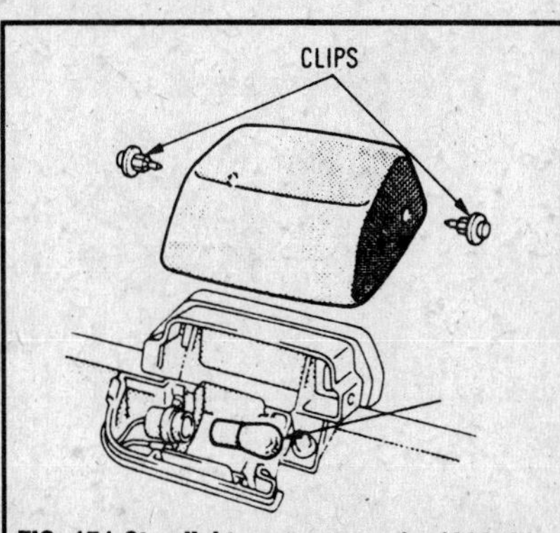

FIG. 151 Stop light cover removal—1986–91 sedan

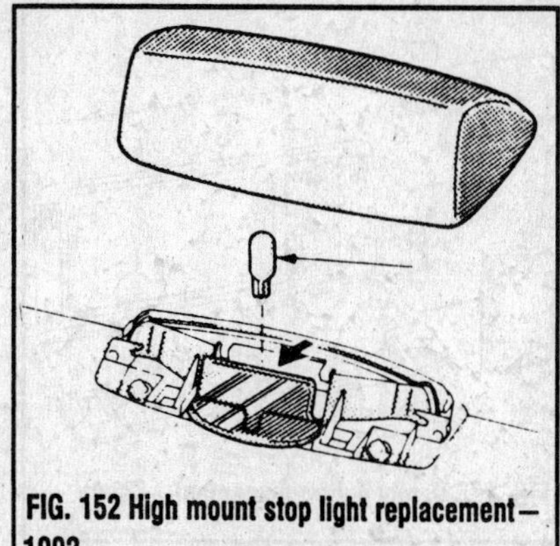

FIG. 152 High mount stop light replacement—1992

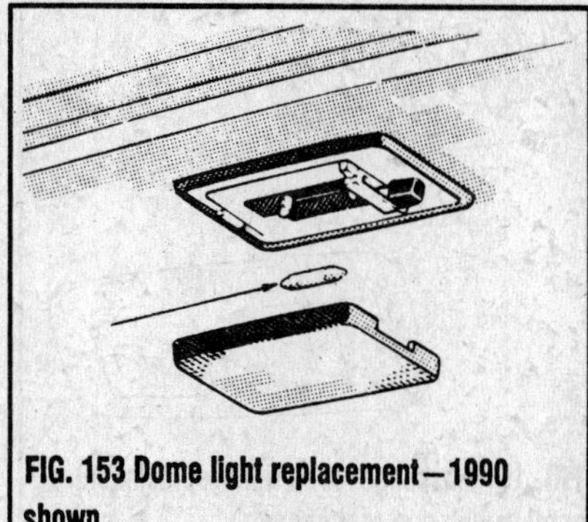

FIG. 153 Dome light replacement—1990 shown

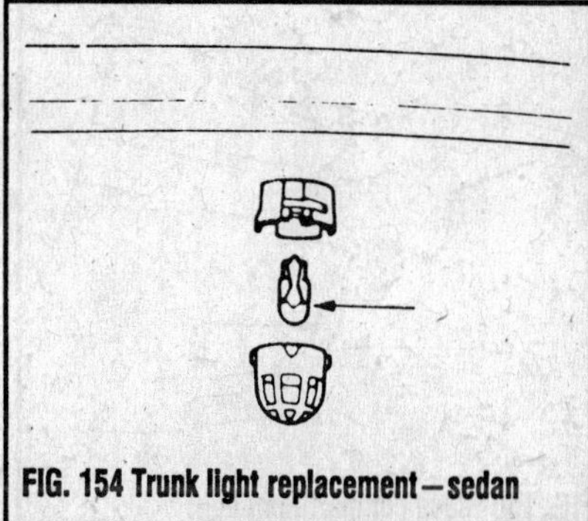

FIG. 154 Trunk light replacement—sedan

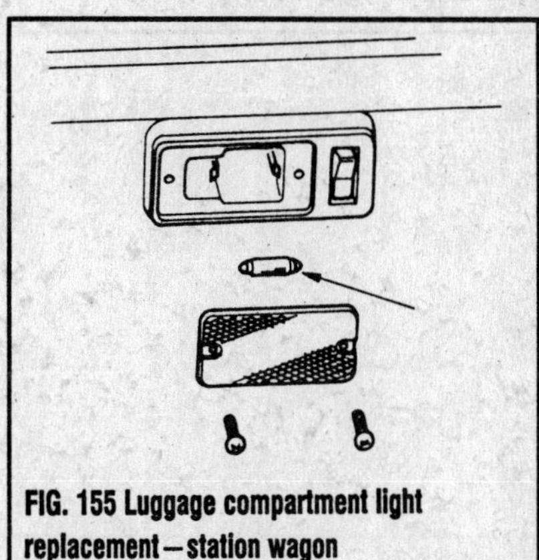

FIG. 155 Luggage compartment light replacement—station wagon

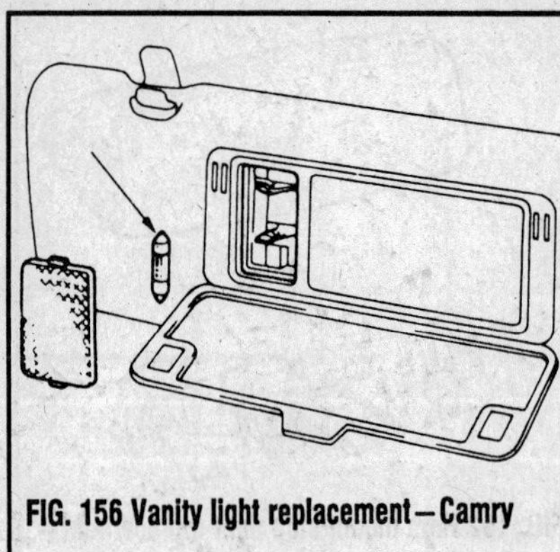
FIG. 156 Vanity light replacement—Camry

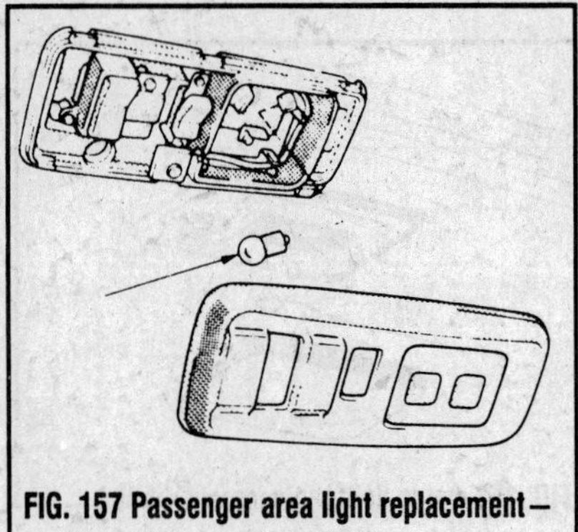
FIG. 157 Passenger area light replacement—models with sun roof shown

FIG. 158 Glove compartment light replacement—1992 shown

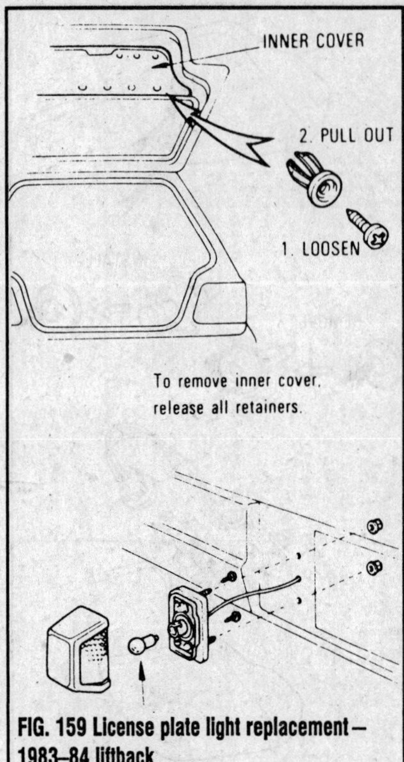

FIG. 159 License plate light replacement—1983–84 liftback

FIG. 160 License plate light replacement—1985–86 liftback

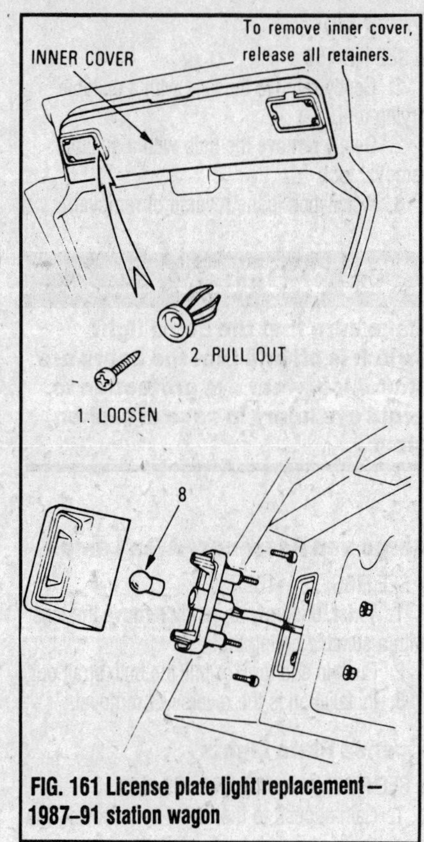

FIG. 161 License plate light replacement—1987–91 station wagon

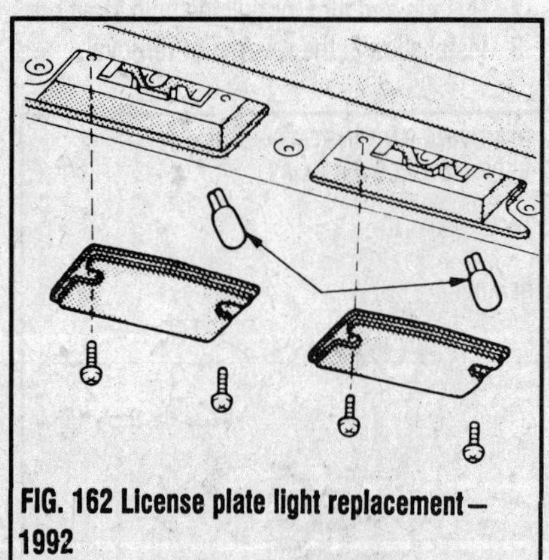
FIG. 162 License plate light replacement—1992

TRAILER WIRING

➧ SEE FIG. 163

Wiring the car for towing is fairly easy. There are a number of good wiring kits available and these should be used, rather than trying to design your own. All trailers will need brake lights and turn signals as well as tail lights and side marker lights. Most states require extra marker lights for overly wide trailers. Also, most states have recently required back-up lights for trailers, and most trailer manufacturers have been building trailers with back-up lights for several years.

Additionally, some Class I, most Class II and just about all Class III trailers will have electric brakes.

Add to this number an accessories wire, to operate trailer internal equipment or to charge the trailer's battery, and you can have as many as seven wires in the harness.

Determine the equipment on your trailer and buy the wiring kit necessary. The kit will contain all the wires needed, plus a plug adapter set which included the female plug, mounted on the bumper or hitch, and the male plug, wired into, or plugged into the trailer harness.

When installing the kit, follow the manufacturer's instructions. On the Camry, wire colors are coded alphabetically as follows:

- **B** = Black
- **BR** = Brown
- **G** = Green
- **GR** = Gray
- **L** = Blue
- **LG** = Light Green
- **O** = Orange
- **P** = Pink
- **R** = Red
- **V** = Voilet
- **W** = White
- **Y** = Yellow

One point to note, most foreign vehicles have separate turn signals. On most domestic vehicles, the brake lights and rear turn signals operate with the same bulb. For those vehicles with separate turn signals, you can purchase an isolation unit so that the brake lights won't blink whenever the turn signals are operated, or, you can go to your local electronics supply house and buy four diodes to wire in series with the brake and turn signal bulbs. Diodes will isolate the brake and turn signals. The choice is yours. The isolation units are simple and quick to install, but far more expensive than the diodes. The diodes, however, require more work to install properly, since they require the cutting of each bulb's wire and soldering in place of the diode.

One final point, the best kits are those with a spring loaded cover on the vehicle mounted socket. This cover prevents dirt and moisture from corroding the terminals. Never let the vehicle socket hang loosely. Always mount it securely to the bumper or hitch.

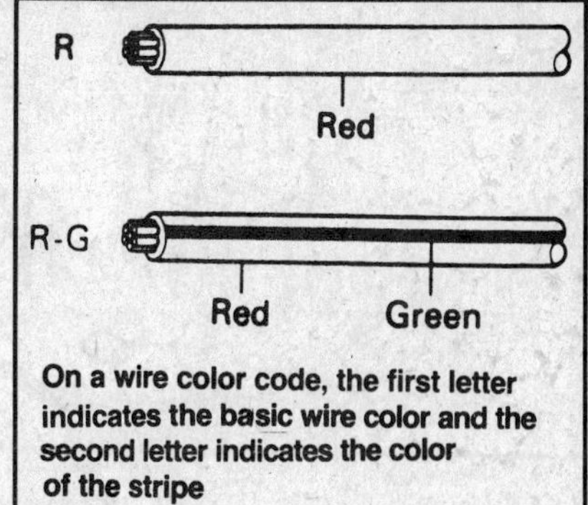

CIRCUIT PROTECTION

➧ SEE FIGS. 164A–179 AND FUSE APPLICATION CHART

Fuses

There are several fuse blocks. They are located in the engine compartment, behind the right side kick panel, under the instrument panel or behind the left side kick panel.

REPLACEMENT

If any light or electrical component in the vehicle does not work, its fuse may be blown. To determine the fuse that is the source of the problem, look on the lid of the fuse box as it will give the name and the circuit serviced by each fuse. To inspect a suspected blown fuse, pull the fuse straight out with the pull-out tool and look at the fuse carefully. If the thin wire that bridges the fuse terminals is broken, the fuse is bad and

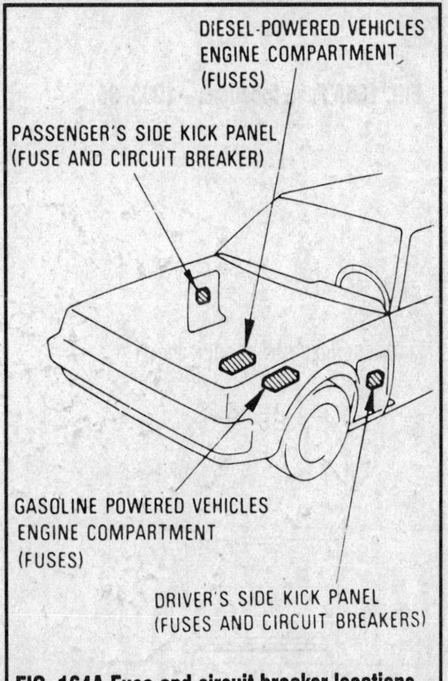

FIG. 164A Fuse and circuit breaker locations — 1983–90

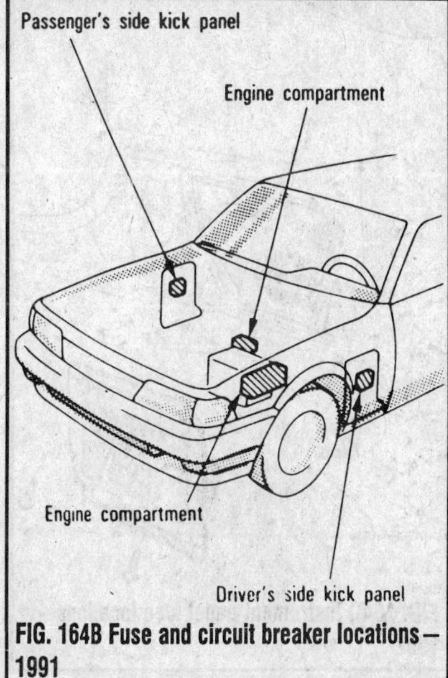

FIG. 164B Fuse and circuit breaker locations — 1991

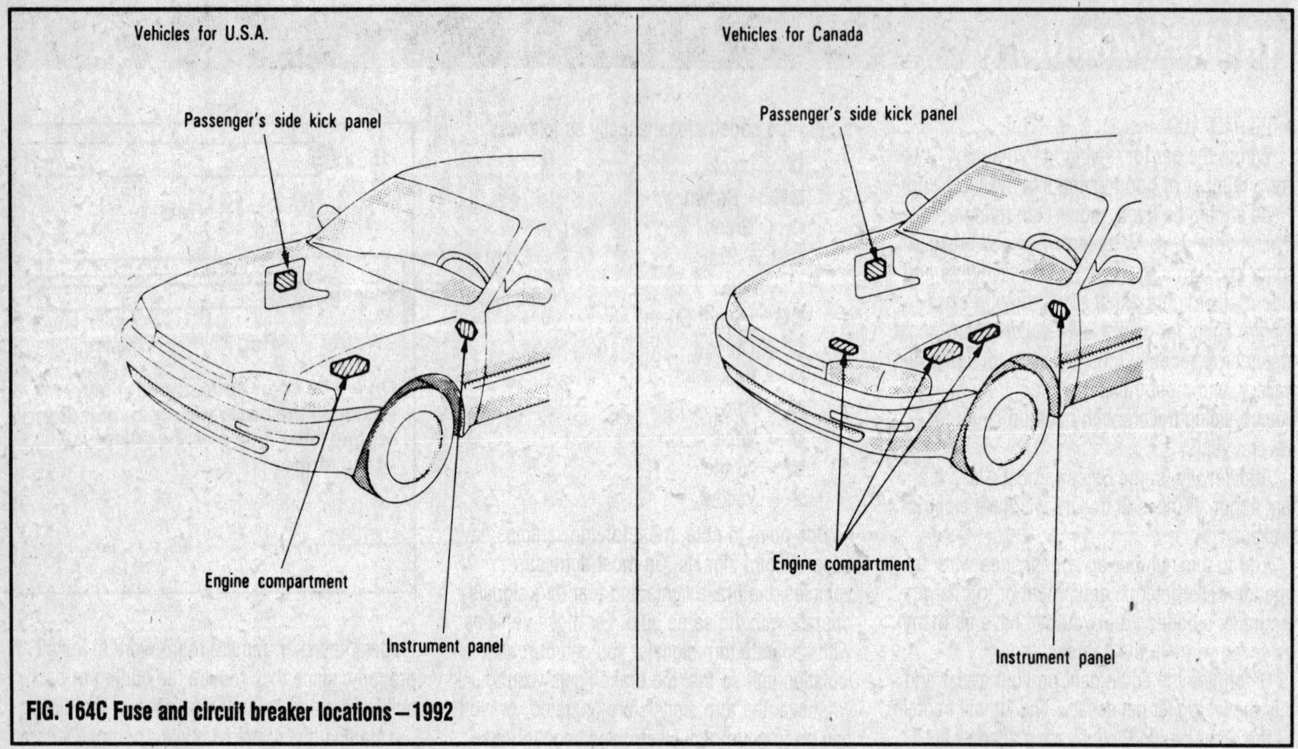

FIG. 164C Fuse and circuit breaker locations—1992

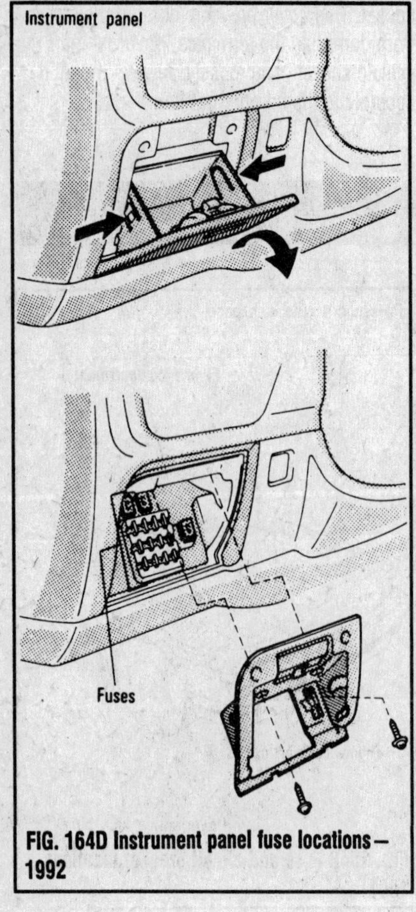

FIG. 164D Instrument panel fuse locations—1992

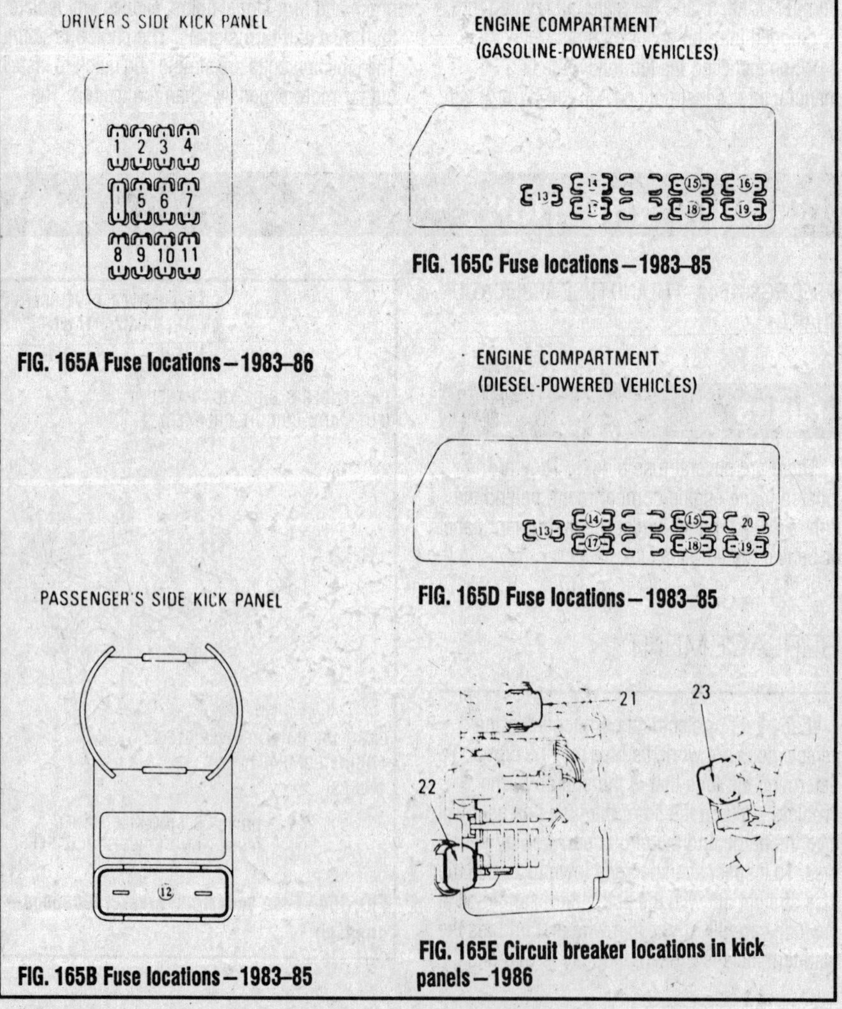

FIG. 165A Fuse locations—1983–86

FIG. 165B Fuse locations—1983–85

FIG. 165C Fuse locations—1983–85

FIG. 165D Fuse locations—1983–85

FIG. 165E Circuit breaker locations in kick panels—1986

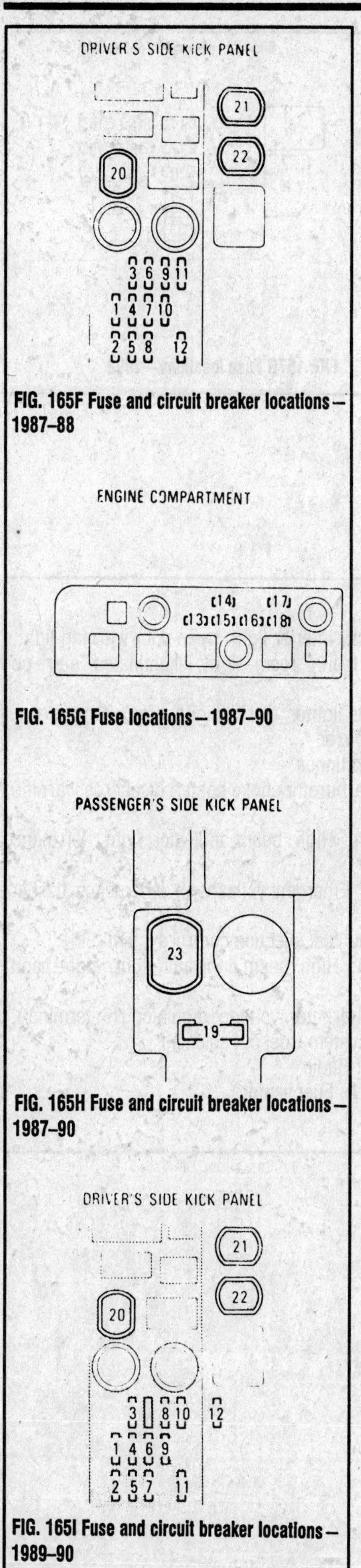

FIG. 165F Fuse and circuit breaker locations—1987–88

FIG. 165G Fuse locations—1987–90

FIG. 165H Fuse and circuit breaker locations—1987–90

FIG. 165I Fuse and circuit breaker locations—1989–90

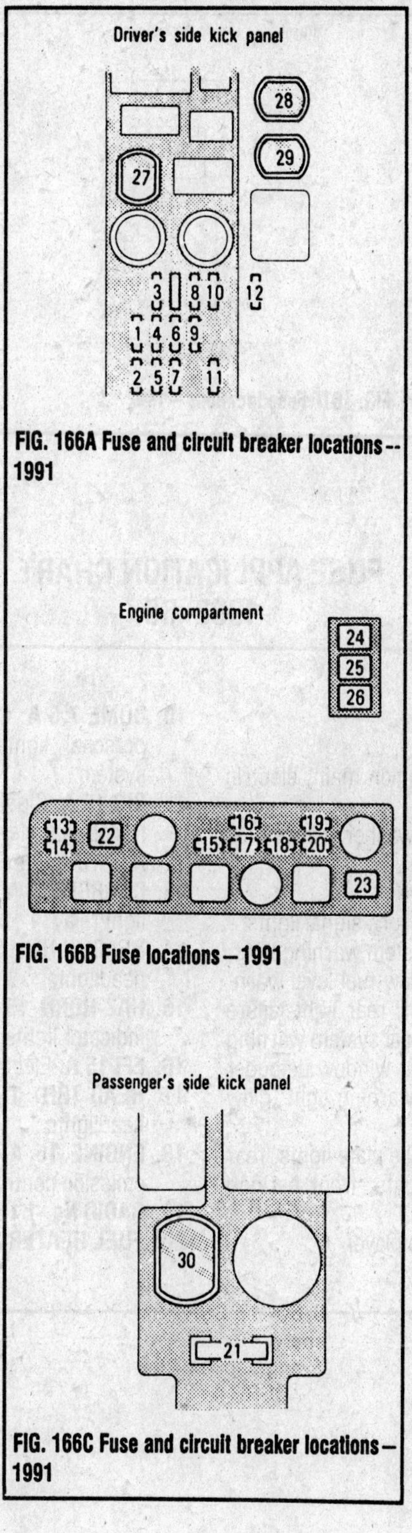

FIG. 166A Fuse and circuit breaker locations—1991

FIG. 166B Fuse locations—1991

FIG. 166C Fuse and circuit breaker locations—1991

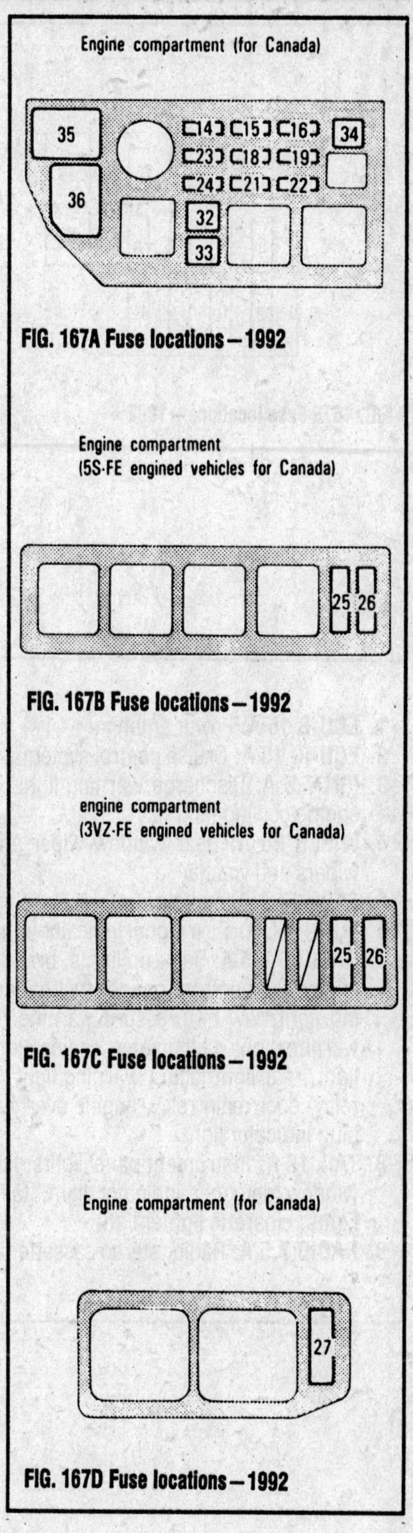

FIG. 167A Fuse locations—1992

FIG. 167B Fuse locations—1992

FIG. 167C Fuse locations—1992

FIG. 167D Fuse locations—1992

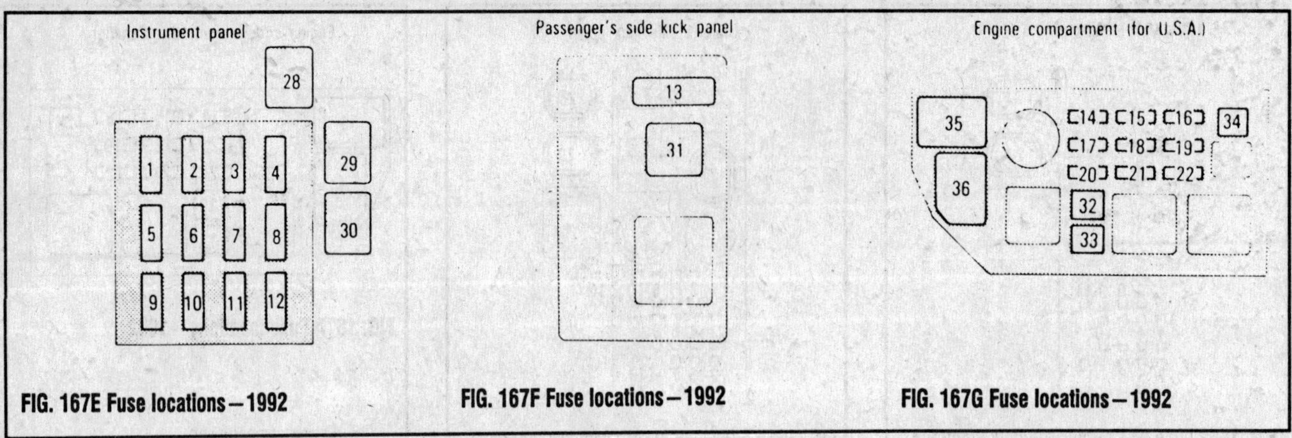

FIG. 167E Fuse locations—1992

FIG. 167F Fuse locations—1992

FIG. 167G Fuse locations—1992

FUSE APPLICATION CHART
1983-85

1. **ECU-B 15 A:** Power antenna
2. **ECU-IG 15 A:** Cruise control system
3. **IGN 7.5 A:** Discharge warning light, ignition main, electric engine cooling fan relay
4. **WIPER 20 A:** Rear window wiper and washer, windshield wipers and washer
5. **STOP 15 A:** Stop lights
6. **TURN 7.5 A:** Turn signal indicator lights, turn signal lights
7. **GAUGES 7.5 A:** Back-up lights, brake system warning light, engine temperature gauge, fuel gauge, low fuel level warning light, low oil pressure warning light, rear light failure warning light, tachometer, engine electrical system warning light, rear light failure warning light, rear window defogger relay, door main relay, engine overheat warning light, glow plug indicator light
8. **TAIL 15 A:** Instrument panel lights, license plate lights, rear window defogger indicator light, tail lights, front parking lights, cigarette lighter light
9. **RADIO 7.5 A:** Radio, stereo cassette tape player
10. **DOME 7.5 A:** Clock, interior light, open door warning light, personal lights, trunk room light, illuminated start-up system
11. **CIG 15 A:** Cigarette lighter, clock (digital type), remote controlled rear view mirror
12. **A/C 10 A:** Air conditioner
13. **CHARGE 7.5 A:** Carburetor choke heater, discharge warning light relay
14. **HEAD (LH) 15 A:** High beam indicator light, left-hand headlights
15. **HAZ-HORN 15 A:** Emergency flashers, emergency flasher indicator lights
16. **EFI 15 A:** Electronic fuel injection control system (EFI)
17. **HEAD (RH) 15 A:** High beam indicator light, right-hand headlights
18. **ENGINE 15 A:** Alternator voltage regulator (IG terminal), emission control system, fuel cut solenoid
19. **RADIO No. 1 15 A:** Radio
20. **FUEL HEATER 30 A:** Fuel heater

FUSE AND CIRCUIT BREAKER APPLICATION CHART 1986

Fuses

1. **ECU-B 15 A:** Power antenna, electronically controlled automatic transmission system
2. **ECU-IG 15 A:** Electronically controlled automatic transmission system
3. **IGN 7.5 A:** Charging system, discharge warning light, electric underhood cooling fans, electronic fuel injection system
4. **WIPER 20 A:** Windshield wipers and washer, rear window wiper and washer
5. **STOP 20 A:** Stop lights, cruise control system cancel device
6. **TURN 7.5 A:** Turn signal lights
7. **GAUGES 7.5 A:** Gauges and meters, warning lights (except discharge and open door warning lights), automatic transmission overdrive system, rear window defogger
8. **TAIL 15 A:** Tail lights, parking lights, side marker lights, license plate lights, instrument panel lights
9. **RADIO 7.5 A:** Radio, cassette tape player, graphic equalizer
10. **DOME 7.5 A:** Interior light, personal lights, luggage compartment light, trunk room light, ignition switch light, clock, open door warning light

Fuses

11. **CIG 15 A:** Cigarette lighter, digital clock display, power rear view mirrors
12. **A/C 10 A:** Environmental control system
13. **CHARGE 7.5 A:** Charging system, discharge warning light
14. **HEAD (LH) 15 A:** Left-hand headlight
15. **HAZ-HORN 15 A:** Emergency flashers, horns
16. **EFI 15 A:** Electronic fuel injection system
17. **HEAD (RH) 15 A:** Right-hand headlight
18. **ENGINE 15 A:** Charging system, emission control system
19. **RADIO 15 A:** Charging system, emission control system
20. **FUEL HEATER 30 A:** Fuel heater

SPARE: Spare fuse (7.5 A)
SPARE: Spare fuse (15 A)

Circuit breakers

21. **DEFOG C.B. 30 A:** Rear window defogger
22. **POWER C.B. 30 A:** Electric sun roof, power windows, power door lock system
23. **HEATER C.B. 30 A:** Environmental control system

FUSE AND CIRCUIT BREAKER APPLICATION CHART 1987-88

Fuses

1. **CIG 15 A:** Cigarette lighter, digital clock display
2. **ENGINE 10 A:** Charging system, emission control system
3. **GAUGE 7.5 A:** Gauges and meters, warning lights (except discharge and open door warning lights), back-up lights, automatic transmission overdrive system, rear window defogger, power windows, power door lock system, automatic shoulder belt
4. **RADIO No. 2 7.5 A:** Radio, cassette tape player, power rear view mirrors
5. **WIPER 20 A:** Windshield wipers and washer, rear window wiper and washer
6. **DOME 7.5 A:** Interior light, personal lights, door courtesy lights, luggage compartment light, trunk room light, ignition switch light, open door warning light
7. **TURN 7.5 A:** Turn signal lights
8. **ECU-IG 15 A:** Cruise control system, electronically controlled automatic transmission system
9. **STOP 20 A:** Stop lights
10. **DEF-I/UP 10 A:** Engine idle up system
11. **TAIL 15 A:** Tail lights, parking lights, side marker lights, license plate lights, instrument panel lights, glovebox light

Fuses

12. **IGN 7.5 A:** Charging system, discharge warning light, emission control system, electric underhood cooling fans, electronic fuel injection system
13. **CHARGE 7.5 A:** Charging system, discharge warning light
14. **RADIO No. 1 15 A:** Radio, cassette tape player, clock, electronically controlled automatic transmission system, power antenna
15. **EFI 15 A:** Electronic fuel injection system
16. **HAZ-HORN 15 A:** Emergency flashers, horns
17. **HEAD (RH) 15 A:** Right-hand headlight
18. **HEAD (LH) 15 A:** Left-hand headlight
19. **10 A:** Air Conditioning cooling system

Circuit breakers

20. **30 A:** Rear window defogger
21. **30 A:** Electric sun roof, power windows, power door lock system
22. **30 A:** Automatic shoulder belt
23. **30 A:** Air Conditioning control system

FUSE AND CIRCUIT BREAKER APPLICATION CHART 1989-90

Fuses

1. **CIG 15 A:** Cigarette lighter, digital clock display, shift lock system (automatic transmission)
2. **ENGINE 10 A:** Charging system, emission control system
3. **GAUGE 7.5 A:** Gauges and meters, warning lights (except discharge and open door warning lights), back-up lights, automatic transmission overdrive system, rear window defogger, power windows, power door lock system, automatic shoulder belt
4. **RADIO 7.5 A:** Radio, cassette tape player, power rear view mirrors
5. **WIPER 20 A:** Windshield wipers and washer, rear window wiper and washer
6. **TURN 7.5 A:** Turn signal lights
7. **ECU-IG 15 A:** Cruise control system, electronically controlled automatic transmission system, shift lock system (automatic transmission)
8. **STOP 20 A:** Stop lights
9. **DEF-I/UP 10 A:** Engine idle up system
10. **TAIL 15 A:** Tail lights, parking lights, side marker lights, license plate lights, instrument panel lights, glovebox light
11. **IGN 7.5 A:** Charging system, discharge warning light, emission control system, electric underhood cooling fans, electronic fuel injection system
12. **ECU-B 10 A:** Rear window defogger, anti-lock brake system
13. **CHARGE 7.5 A:** Charging system, discharge warning light

Fuses

14. **DOME 20 A:** Radio, cassette tape player, clock, electronically controlled automatic transmission system, power antenna, interior light, personal lights, door courtesy lights, trunk room light, ignition switch light, open door warning light
15. **EFI 15 A:** Electronic fuel injection system
16. **HAZ-HORN 15 A:** Emergency flashers, horns
17. **HEAD (RH) 15 A:** Right-hand headlight
18. **HEAD (LH) 15 A:** Left-hand headlight
19. **10 A:** Air Conditioning cooling system

Circuit breakers

20. **30 A:** Rear window defogger
21. **30 A:** Electric sun roof, power windows, power door lock system
22. **30 A:** Automatic shoulder belt
23. **40 A:** Air conditioning system

must be replaced. On a good fuse fuse, the wire will be intact.

Sometimes it is difficult to make an accurate determination. If this is the case, try replacing the fuse with one that you know is good. If the fuse blows repeatedly, then this suggests that a short circuit lies somewhere in the electrical system and you should have the system checked.

CAUTION

When making emergency replacements, only use fuses that have an equal or lower amperage rating than the one that is blown, to avoid damage and fire.

When installing a new fuse, use one with the same amperage rating as the one being replaced. To install the a new fuse, first turn off all the electrical components and the ignition switch. Always use the fuse pull-out tool and install the fuse straight. Twisting of the fuse could cause the terminals to separate too much which may result in a bad connection. It may be a good idea to purchase some extra fuses and put them in the box in case of an emergency.

Fusible Links

In case of an overload in the circuits from the battery, the fusible links are designed to melt before damage to the engine wiring harness occurs. Headlight and other electrical component failure usually requires checking the fusible links for melting. Fusible links are located in the engine compartment next to the battery.

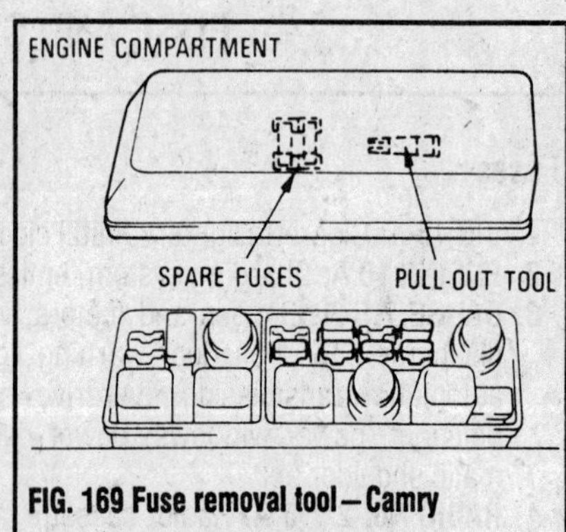

FIG. 169 Fuse removal tool—Camry

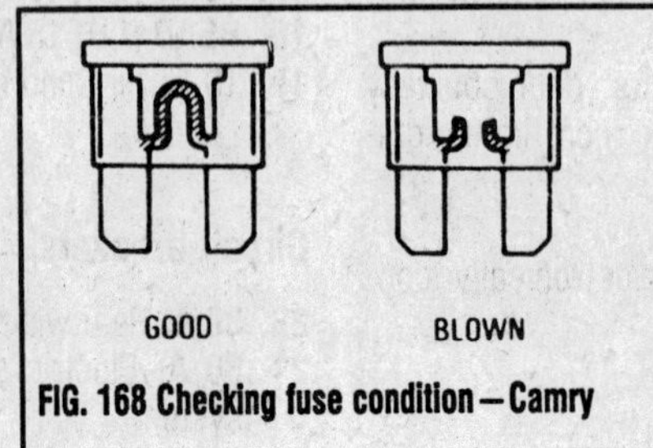

FIG. 168 Checking fuse condition—Camry

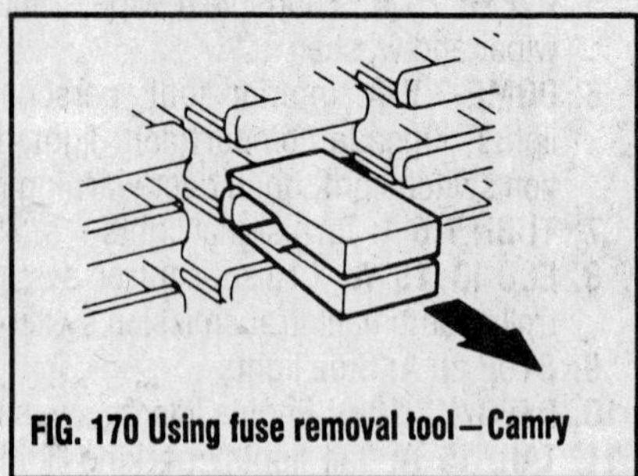

FIG. 170 Using fuse removal tool—Camry

FUSE AND CIRCUIT BREAKER APPLICATION CHART 1991

Fuses (type A)

1. **CIG 15 A:** Cigarette lighter, digital clock display, shift lock system (automatic transmission)
2. **ENGINE 10 A:** Charging system, emission control system
3. **GAUGE 7.5 A:** Gauges and meters, warning lights (except discharge and open door warning lights), back-up lights, automatic transmission overdrive system, rear window defogger, power windows, power door lock system, automatic shoulder belt
4. **RADIO 7.5 A:** Radio, cassette tape player, power rear view mirrors
5. **WIPER 20 A:** Windshield wipers and washer, rear window wiper and washer
6. **TURN 7.5 A:** Turn signal lights
7. **ECU-IG 15 A:** Cruise control system, electronically controlled automatic transmission system, shift lock system (automatic transmission)
8. **STOP 20 A:** Stop lights and high mounted stoplight
9. **DEF-I/UP 10 A:** Engine idle up system
10. **TAIL 15 A:** Tail lights, parking lights, side marker lights, license plate lights, instrument panel lights, glovebox light
11. **IGN 7.5 A:** Charging system, discharge warning light, emission control system, electric underhood cooling fans, electronic fuel injection system
12. **ECU-B 10 A:** Rear window defogger, anti-lock brake system
13. **HEAD-HI (RH) 15 A (vehicles sold in Canada):** Right-hand headlight (high beam)
14. **HEAD-HI (LH) 15 A (vehicles sold in Canada):** Left-hand headlight (high beam)
15. **CHARGE 7.5 A:** Charging system, discharge warning light
16. **DOME 20 A:** Radio, cassette tape player, clock, electronically controlled automatic transmission system, power antenna, interior light, personal lights, door courtsey lights, trunk room light, ignition switch light, open door warning light

Fuses (type A)

17. **EFI 15 A:** Electronic fuel injection system
18. **HAZ-HORN 15 A:** Emergency flashers, horns
19. **HEAD (RH) 15 A (vehicles sold in U.S.A.):** Right-hand headlight
    HEAD-LO (RH) 15 A (vehicles sold in Canada): Right-hand headlight (low beam)
20. **HEAD (LH) 15 A (vehicles sold in U.S.A.):** Left-hand headlight
    HEAD-LO (LH) 15 A (vehicles sold in Canada): Left-hand headlight (low beam)
21. **A/C 10 A:** Air conditioning cooling system

Fuses (type B)

22. **CDS 30 A:** Condenser fan motor
23. **FAN 30 A:** Radiator fan motor
24. **MAIN 40 A:** "DOME", "EFI", "HAZ-HORN", "HEAD-HI (RH)", "HEAD-HI (LH)", "HEAD (RH)", "HEAD-LO (RH)", "HEAD (LH), "HEAD-LO (LH)", and "A/C" fuses
25. **ALT 80 A:** "CIG", "ENGINE", "GAUGE", "RADIO", "WIPER", "TURN", "ECU-IG", "STOP", "DEF-I/UP", "TAIL", "ECU-B", "CDS", "FAN" fuses, and "DEFOG", "PWR", "AUTOMATIC SHOULDER BELT", "HEATER" circuit breakers
26. **AM 2 30 A:** "IGN" and "CHARGE" fuses

Circuit breakers

27. **DEFOG 30 A:** Rear window defogger
28. **PWR 30 A:** Electric moon roof, power windows, power door lock system
29. **AUTOMATIC SHOULDER BELT 30 A:** Automatic shoulder belt
30. **HEATER 40 A:** Air conditioning system

FUSE AND CIRCUIT BREAKER APPLICATION CHART 1992

Type A fuses

1. **ECU-IG 15 A:** Electronically controlled automatic transmission system, cruise control system, anti-lock brake system
2. **GAUGE 10 A:** Gauges and meters, back-up lights, air conditioning control system, rear window defogger, warning lights, daytime running light system, tilt steering
3. **STOP 25 A:** Stop lights, cruise control system, anti-lock brake system, shift lock system
4. **SEAT HTR 15 A:** No circuit
5. **WIPER 20 A:** Windshield wipers and washer, air bag system
6. **TURN 7.5 A:** Turn signal lights and emergency flashers
7. **IGN 7.5 A:** Electronic fuel injection system, charging system, radiator cooling fan, air bag system
8. **CIG/RADIO 15 A:** Audio system, daytime running light system, clock, cigarette lighter, air bag system, shift lock system
9. **MIR. HTR 10 A:** Outside rear view mirror heater
10. **TAIL 15 A:** Tail lights, parking lights, license plate lights, instrument panel lights, rear light failure warning system
11. **ECU-B 15 A:** Anti-lock brake system, daytime running light system, air bag system
12. **FOG 15 A:** No circuit
13. **A/C 10 A:** Air conditioning control system
14. **STARTER 10 A:** Starter system, electronic fuel injection system
15. **ALT-S 7.5 A:** Charging system
16. **EFI 15 A:** Electroind fuel injection system
17. **HEAD (RH) 15 A (U.S.A.):** Right-hand headlight
18. **DOME 20 A:** Audio system, interior light, clock, ignition switch light, personal light, trunk room light, vanity mirror light, electric moon roof
19. **HAZ-HORN 15 A:** turn signal lights, emergency flasher, horn

Type A fuses

20. **HEAD (LH) 15 A (U.S.A.):** Left-hand headlight
21. **TRAC 7.5:** Electronically controlled automatic transmission system
22. **AM2 30 A:** Headlights
23. **HEAD HI (RH) 15 A (Canada):** Right-hand headlight (high beam)
24. **HEAD HI (LH) 15 A (Canada):** Left-hand headlight (high beam)
25. **HEAD LO (RH) 15 A (Canada):** Right-hand headlight (low beam)
26. **HEAD LO (LH) 15 A (Canada):** Left-hand headlight (low beam)
27. **DRL 7.5 A (Canada):** Daytime running light system

Type B fuses

28. **AM1 40 A:** Starting system
29. **P/W 30 A:** Electric moon roof, power windows, tilt steering, power door lock controls
30. **DEFOG 40 A:** Rear window defogger
31. **HTR 40 A:** Air conditioning control system
32. **CDS 30 A:** Condenser cooling fan
33. **FAN 30 A:** Radiator cooling fan
34. **ST MAIN 30 A:** Starting system

Type C fuses

35. **ALT 100 A:** Charging system
36. **A.B.S. 60 A:** Anti-lock brake system

REPLACEMENT

The fusible link is replaced in a similar manner as the regular fuse, but a removal tool is not required.

CAUTION

Never install a wire in place of a fusible link. Extensive damage and fire may occur.

Circuit Breakers

In the event the rear window defogger, enviornmental control system, power windows, power door locks, power tail gate lock, sunroof

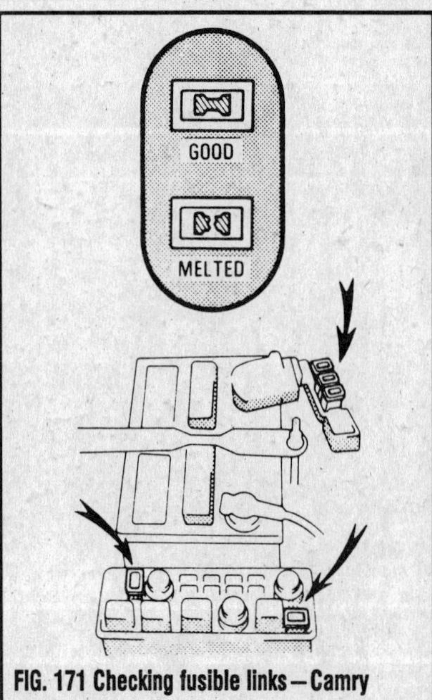

FIG. 171 Checking fusible links—Camry

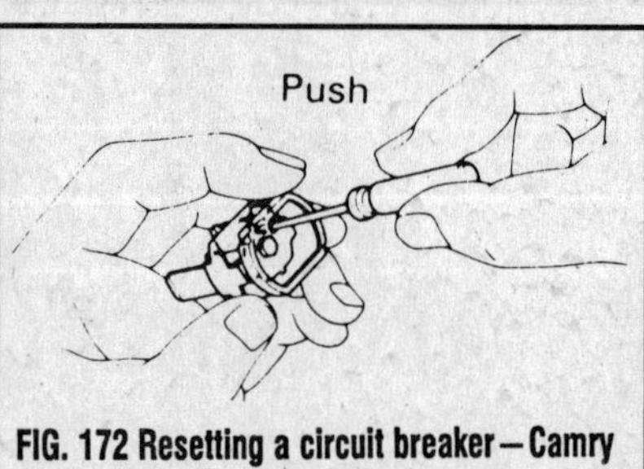

FIG. 172 Resetting a circuit breaker—Camry

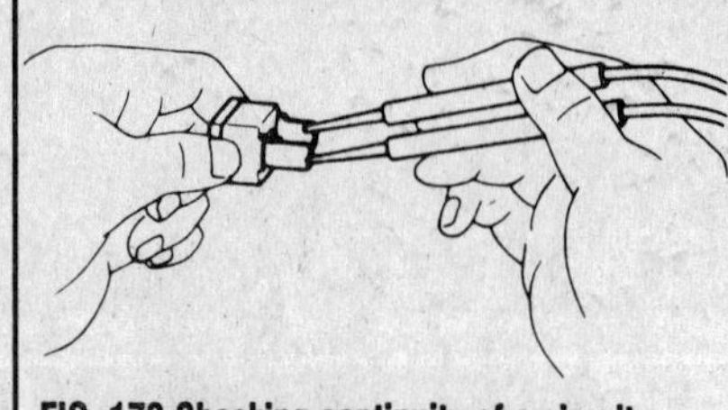
FIG. 173 Checking continuity of a circuit breaker—Camry

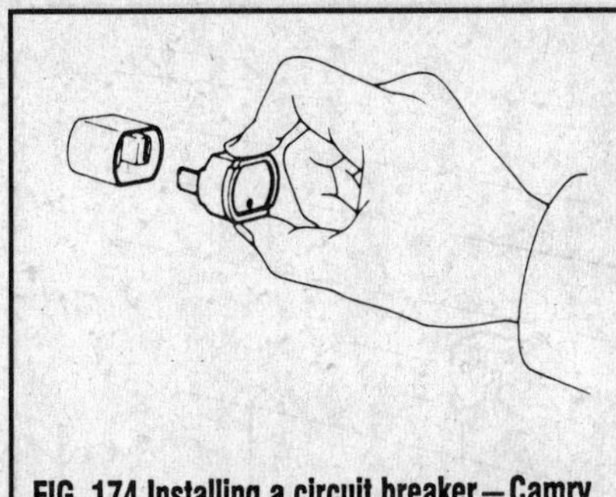

FIG. 174 Installing a circuit breaker — Camry

or automatic shoulder belt does not work, check its circuit breaker. Circuit breakers are located in the passenger's or driver's side kick panel with the fuses.

REMOVAL & INSTALLATION

1. Turn the ignition switch to the **OFF** position.
2. Disconnect the negative battery cable.
3. Remove the circuit breaker by unlocking its stopper and pulling it from its socket.

To Install:

4. Installation is the reverse of removal.

➡ Always use a new circuit breaker with the same amperage as the old one. If the circuit breaker immediately trips or the component does not operate, the electrical system must be checked.

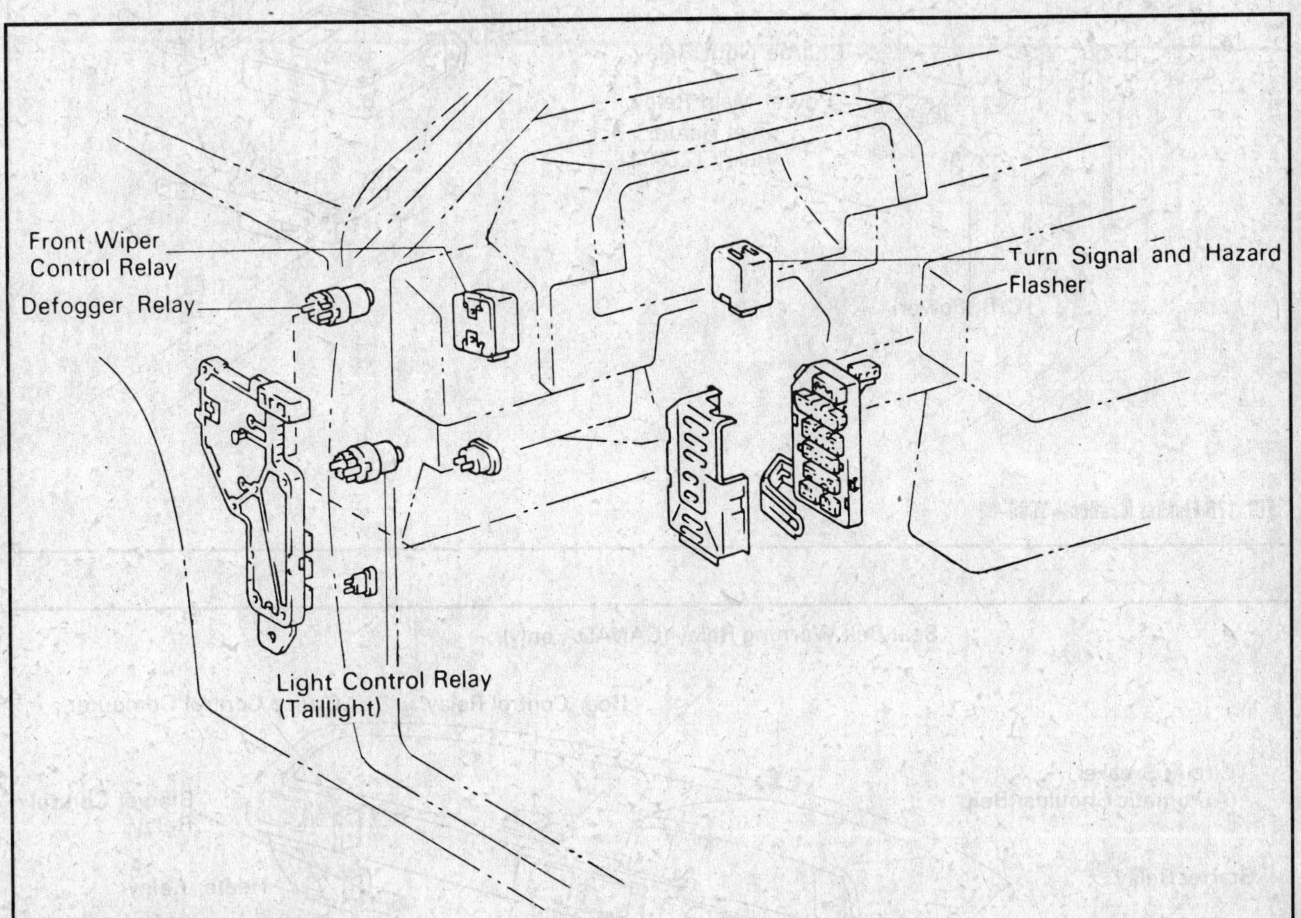

FIG. 175 Flasher location — 1983–84

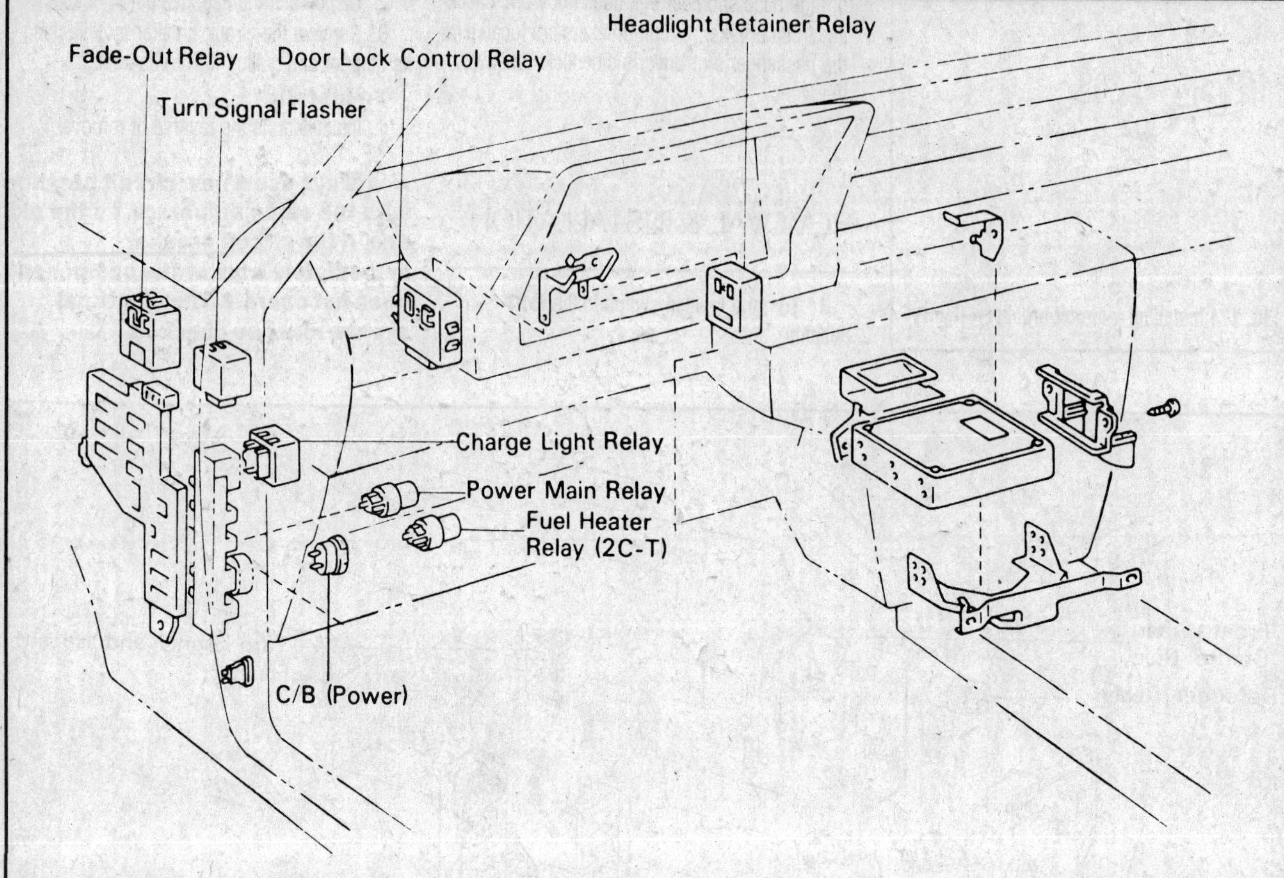

Headlight Retainer Relay
Fade-Out Relay
Door Lock Control Relay
Turn Signal Flasher
Charge Light Relay
Power Main Relay
Fuel Heater
Relay (2C-T)
C/B (Power)

FIG. 176 Flasher location—1985–86

Seat Belt Warning Relay (CANADA only)
Door Control Relay
Cruise Control Computer
Circuit Breaker
(Automatic Shoulder Belt)
Blower Control
Relay
Starter Relay
Heater Relay
Horn Relay
Turn Signal
Flasher
Circuit Breaker
(Heater)
Fuse (A/C)
Circuit
Braker
(Power)
Circuit Breaker (Defogger)
Defogger Relay
Automatic Shoulder
Belt Computer (USA
only)
Taillight Relay
Integration Relay
• Headlight Auto Cut System
• Interior Light Fade Out System
Fuse and Relay Block No.1

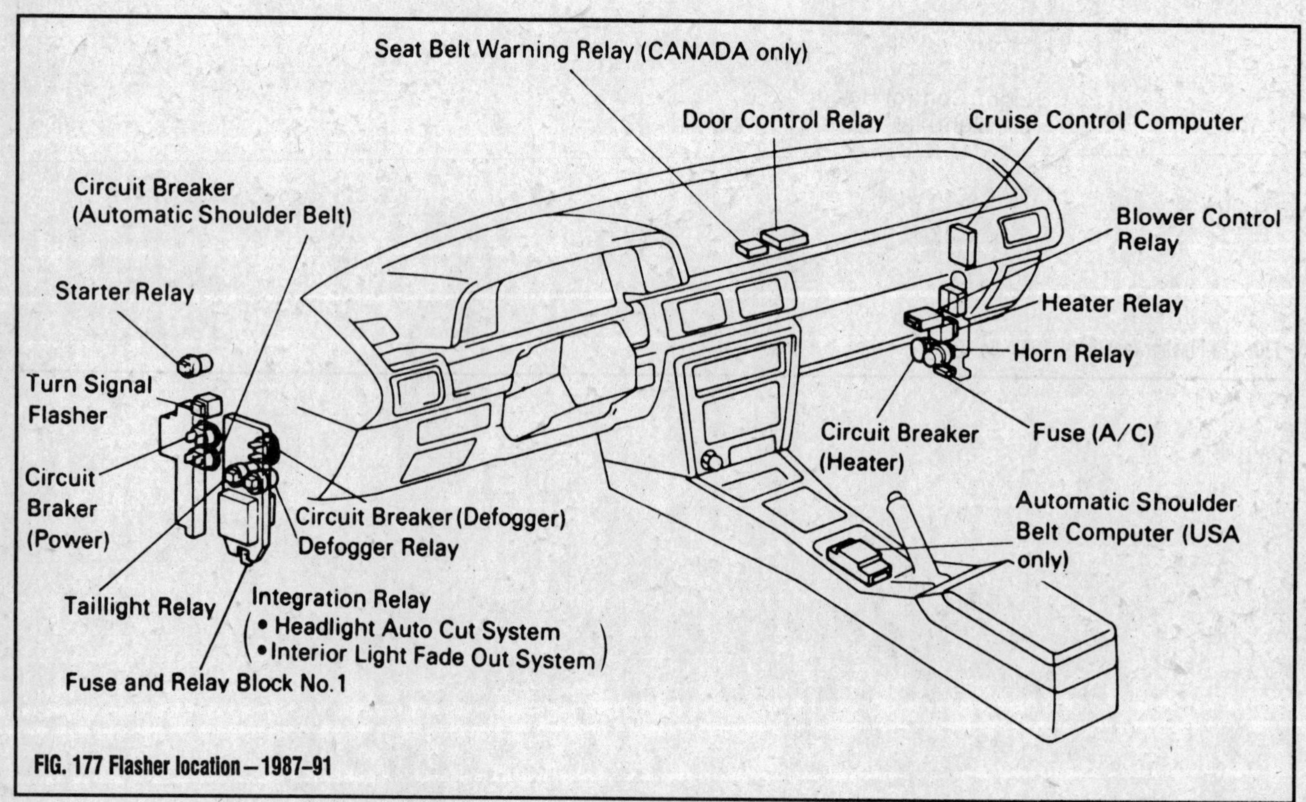

FIG. 177 Flasher location—1987–91

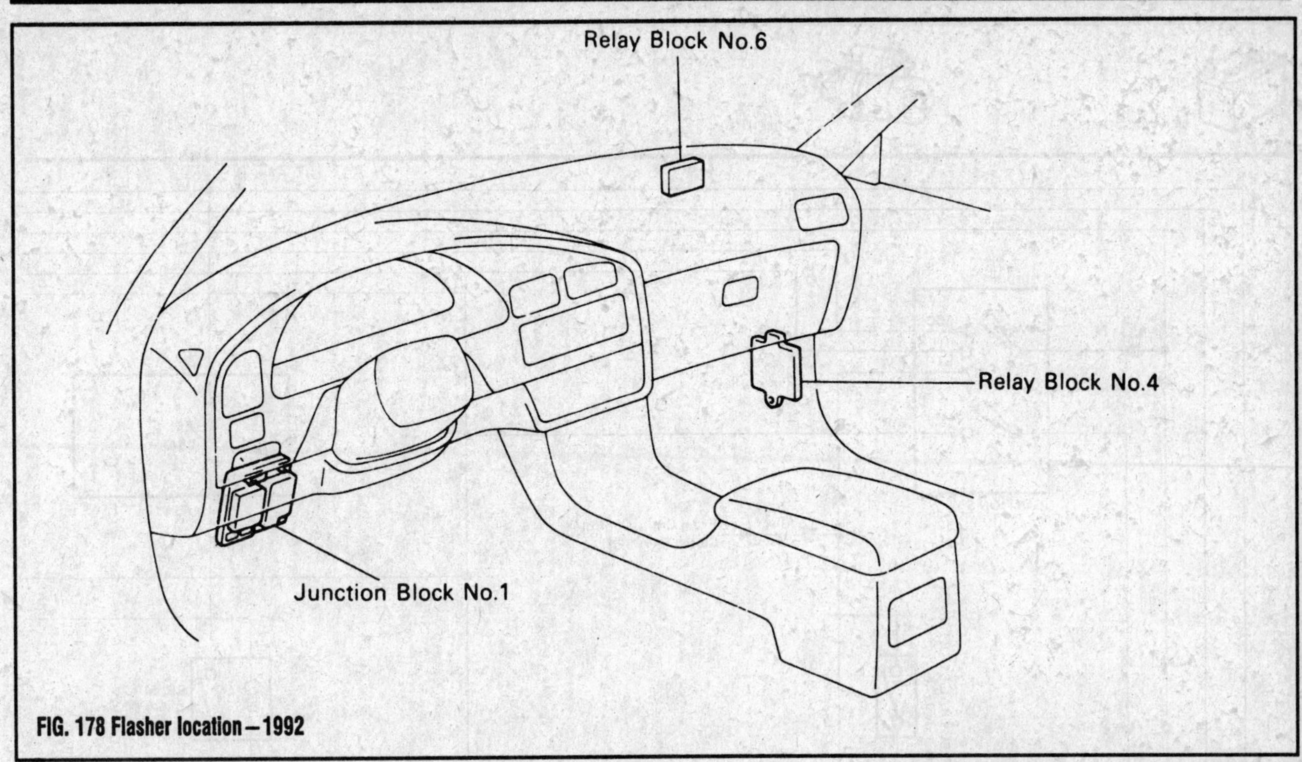

FIG. 178 Flasher location—1992

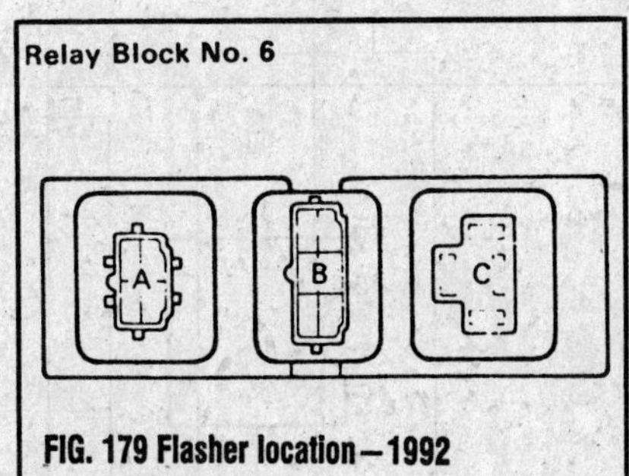

FIG. 179 Flasher location—1992

RESETTING

1. Insert a thin object into the reset hole and push until a click is heard.
2. Using an ohmmeter, check that there is continuity between both terminals of the circuit breaker. If continuity is not as specified, replace the circuit breaker.

Flashers

REMOVAL & INSTALLATION

Locate the flasher and pull it from its socket. Install a new one and check its operation. The location on 1992 models is position "C" in relay block 6.

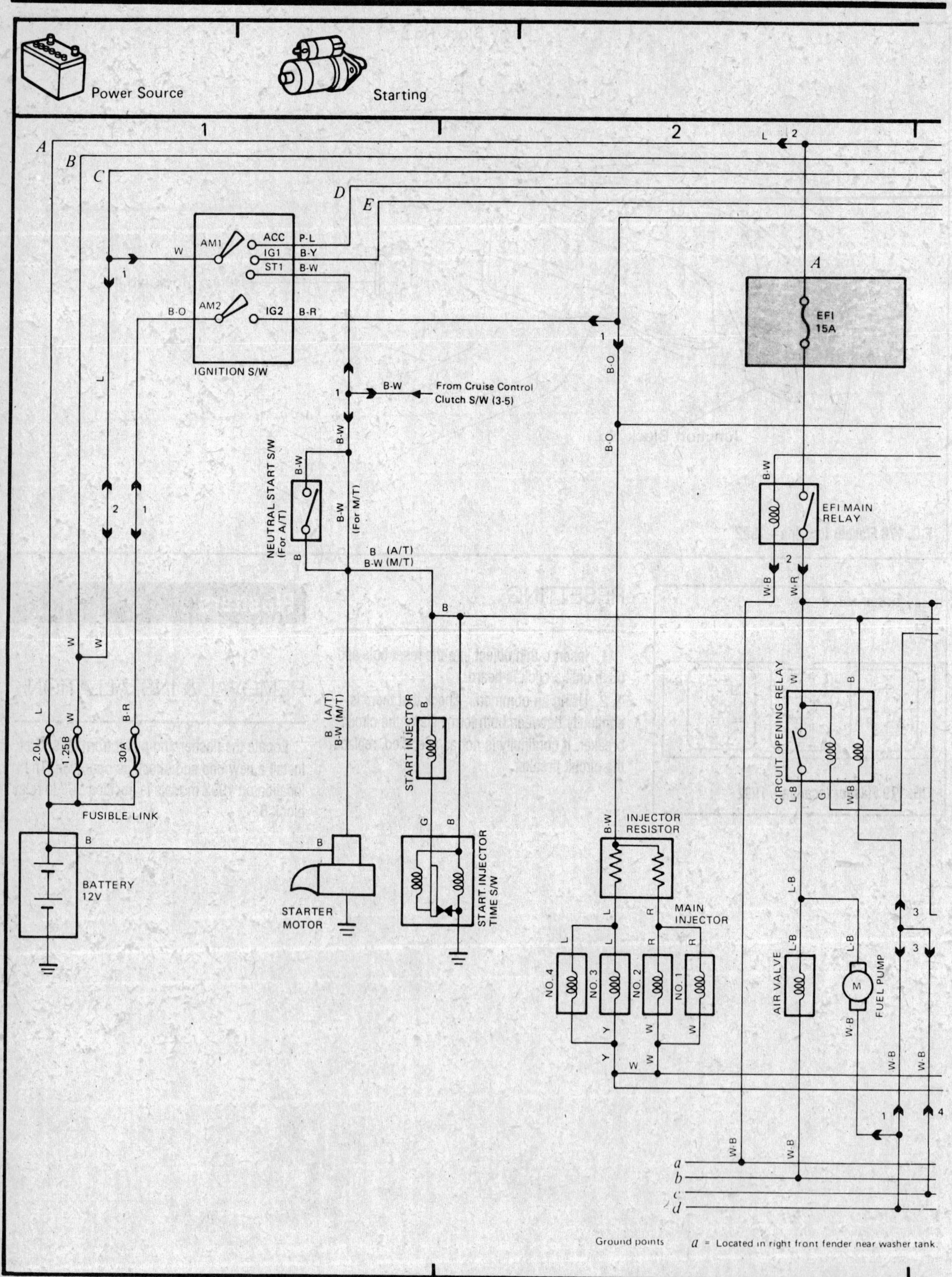

Wiring diagram—1983

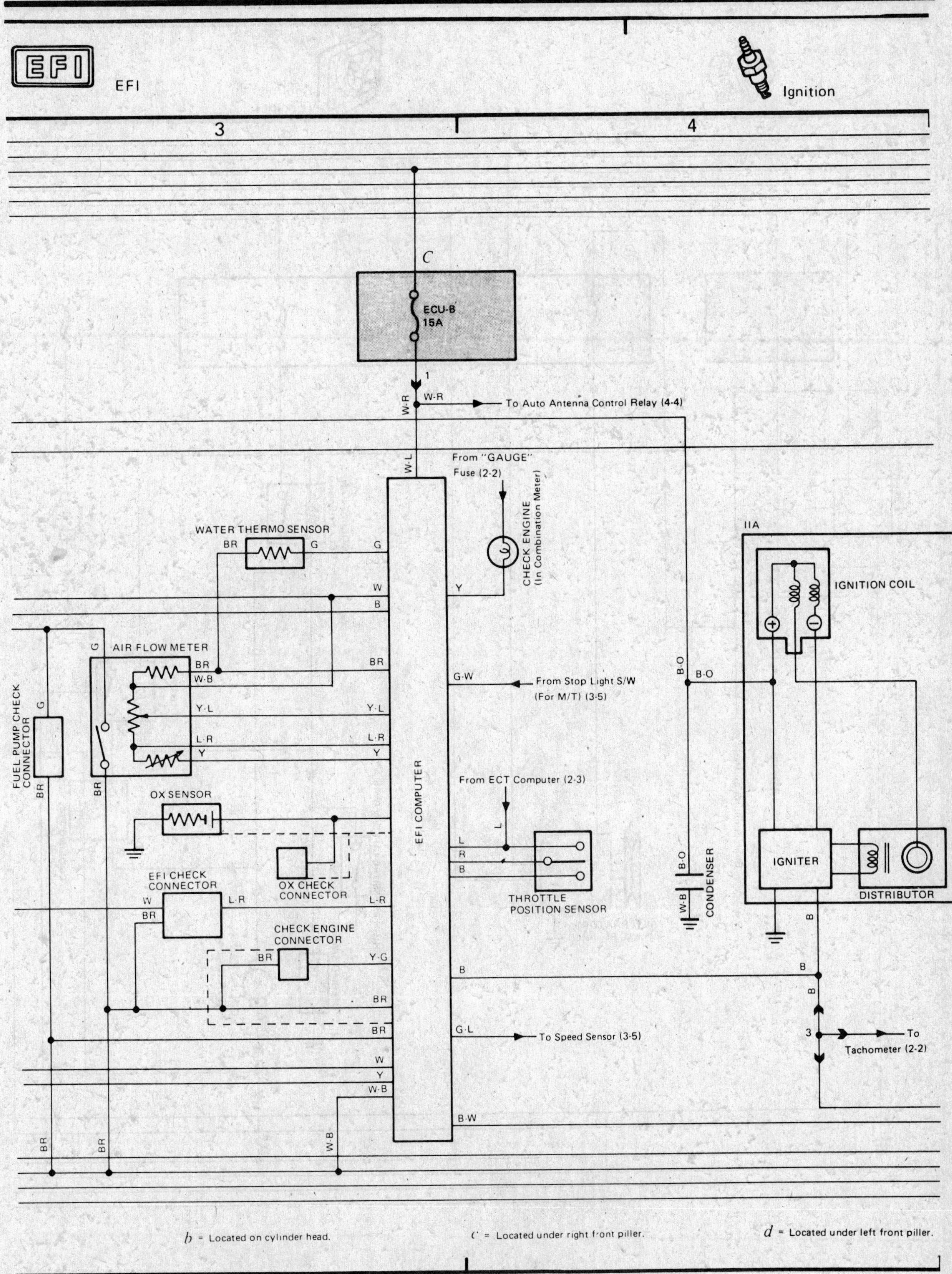

b = Located on cylinder head.
c = Located under right front piller.
d = Located under left front piller.

Wiring diagram—1983

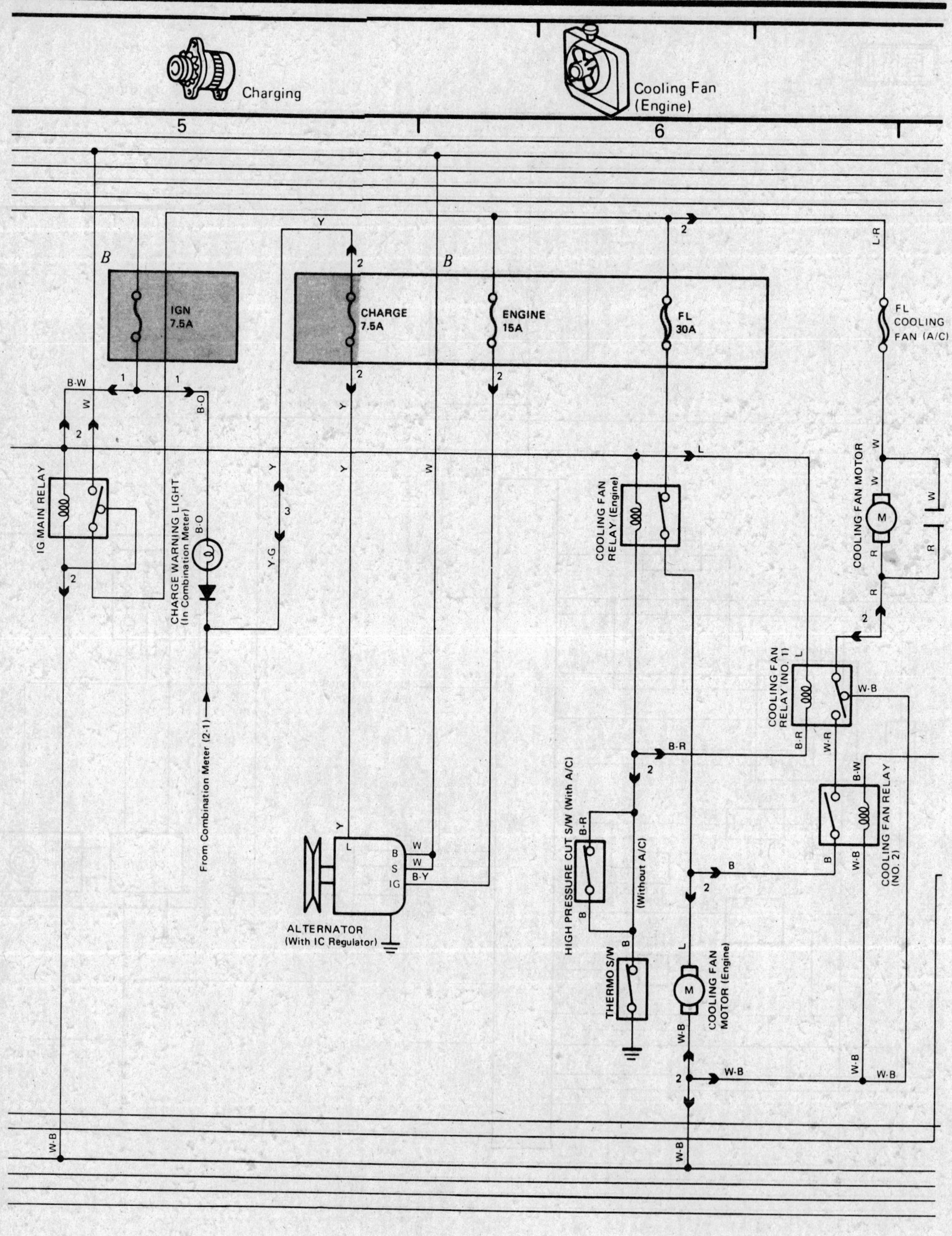

Wiring diagram—1983

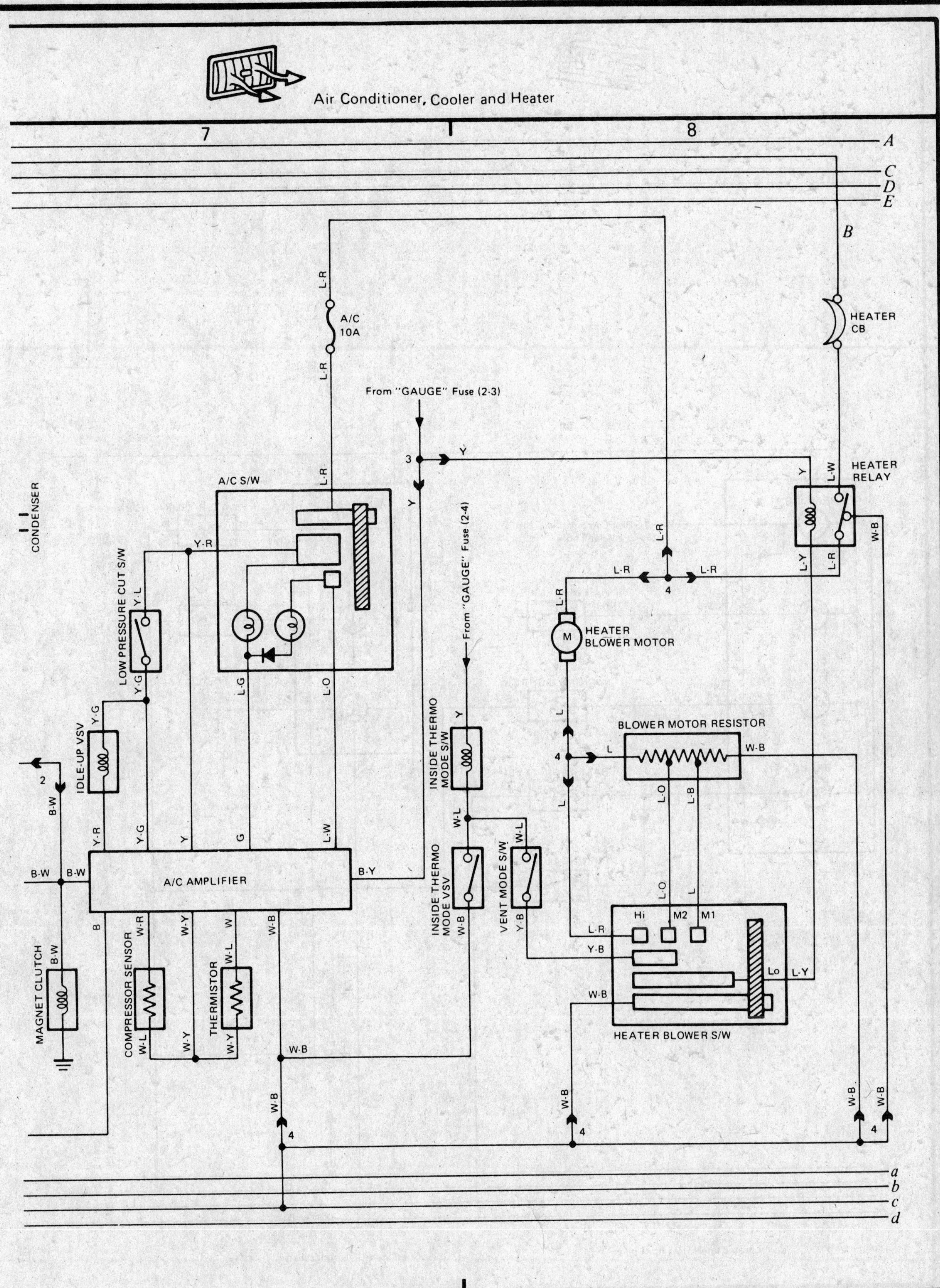

Wiring diagram—1983

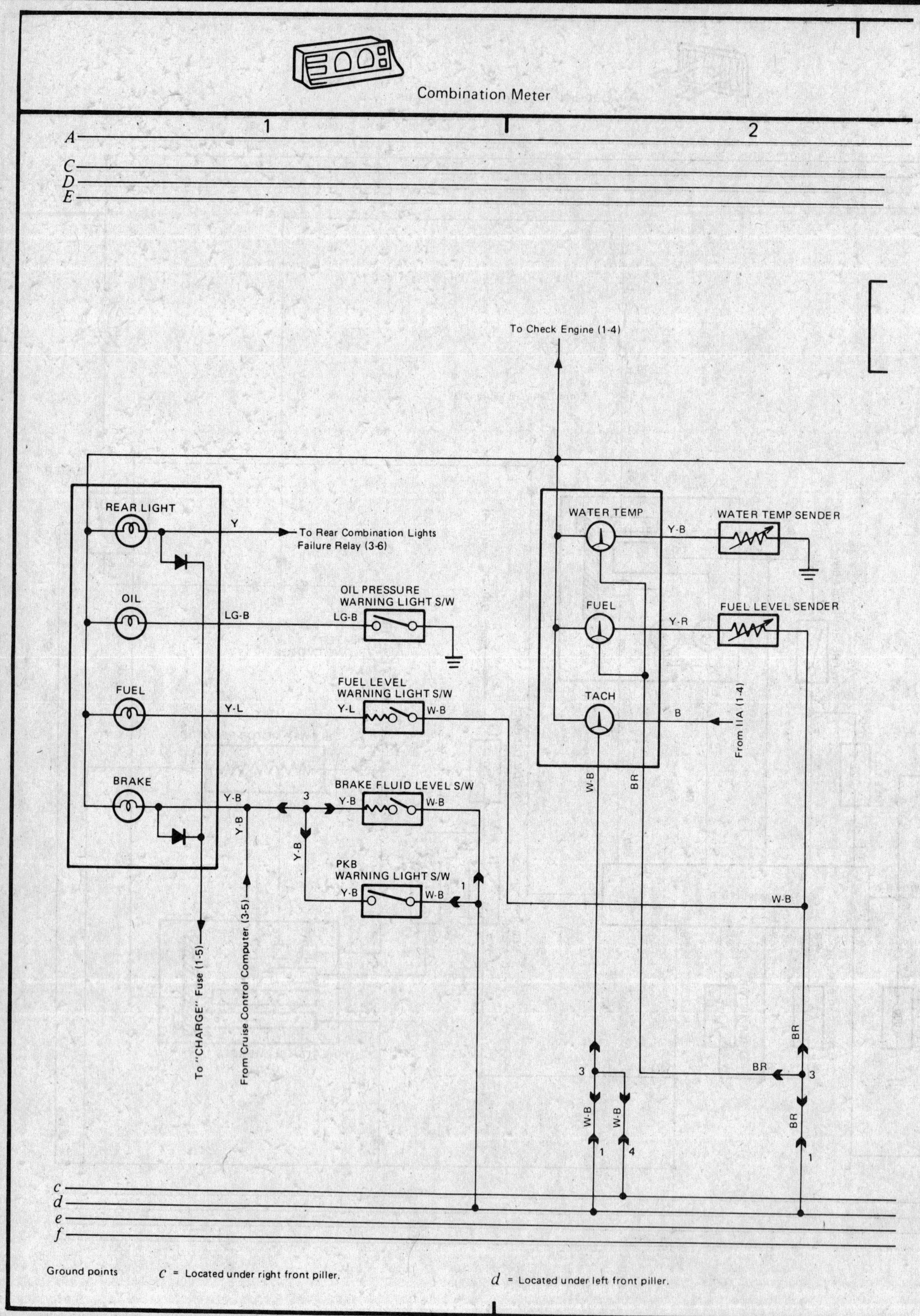

Wiring diagram—1983

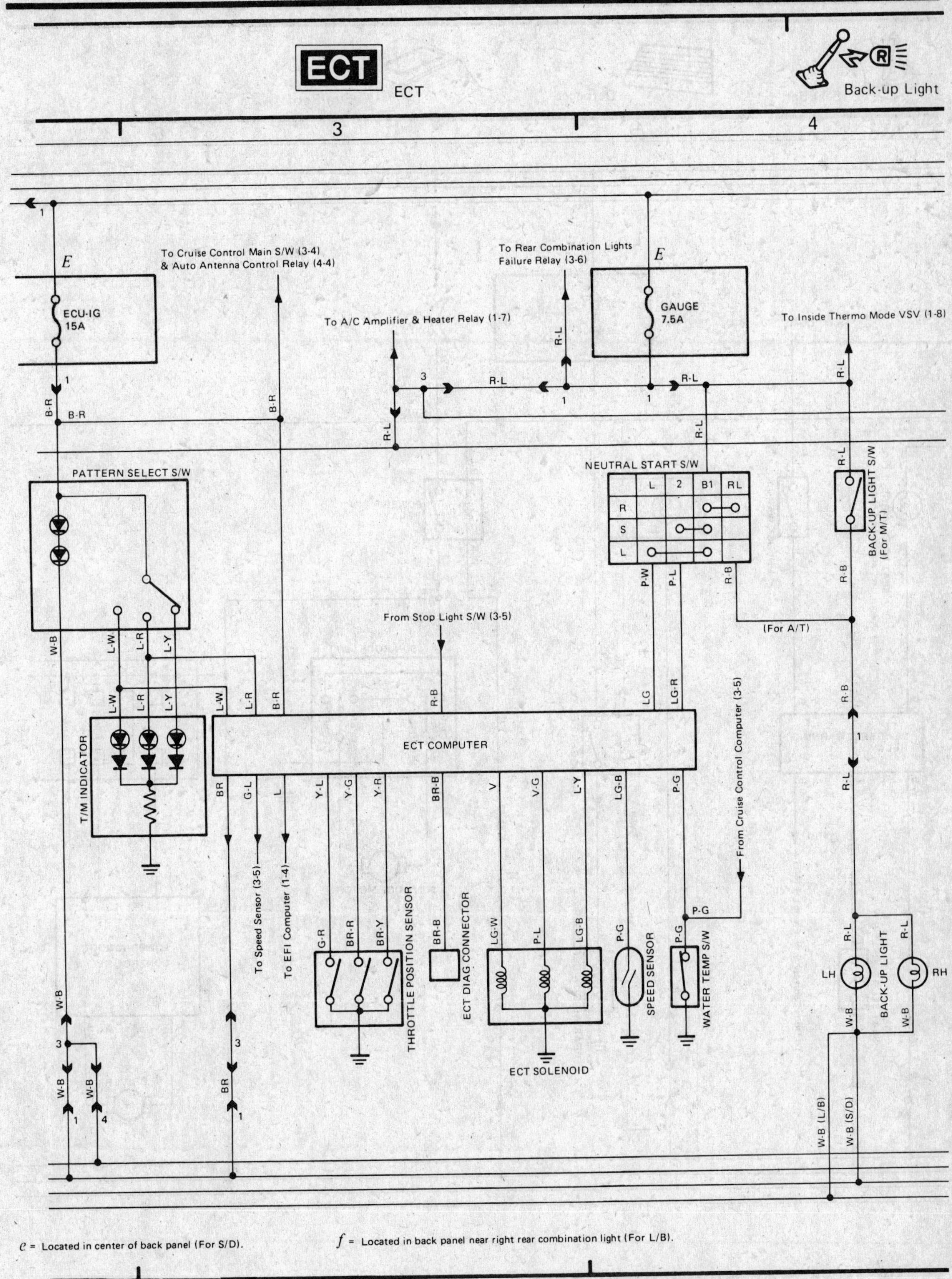

e = Located in center of back panel (For S/D).

f = Located in back panel near right rear combination light (For L/B).

Wiring diagram—1983

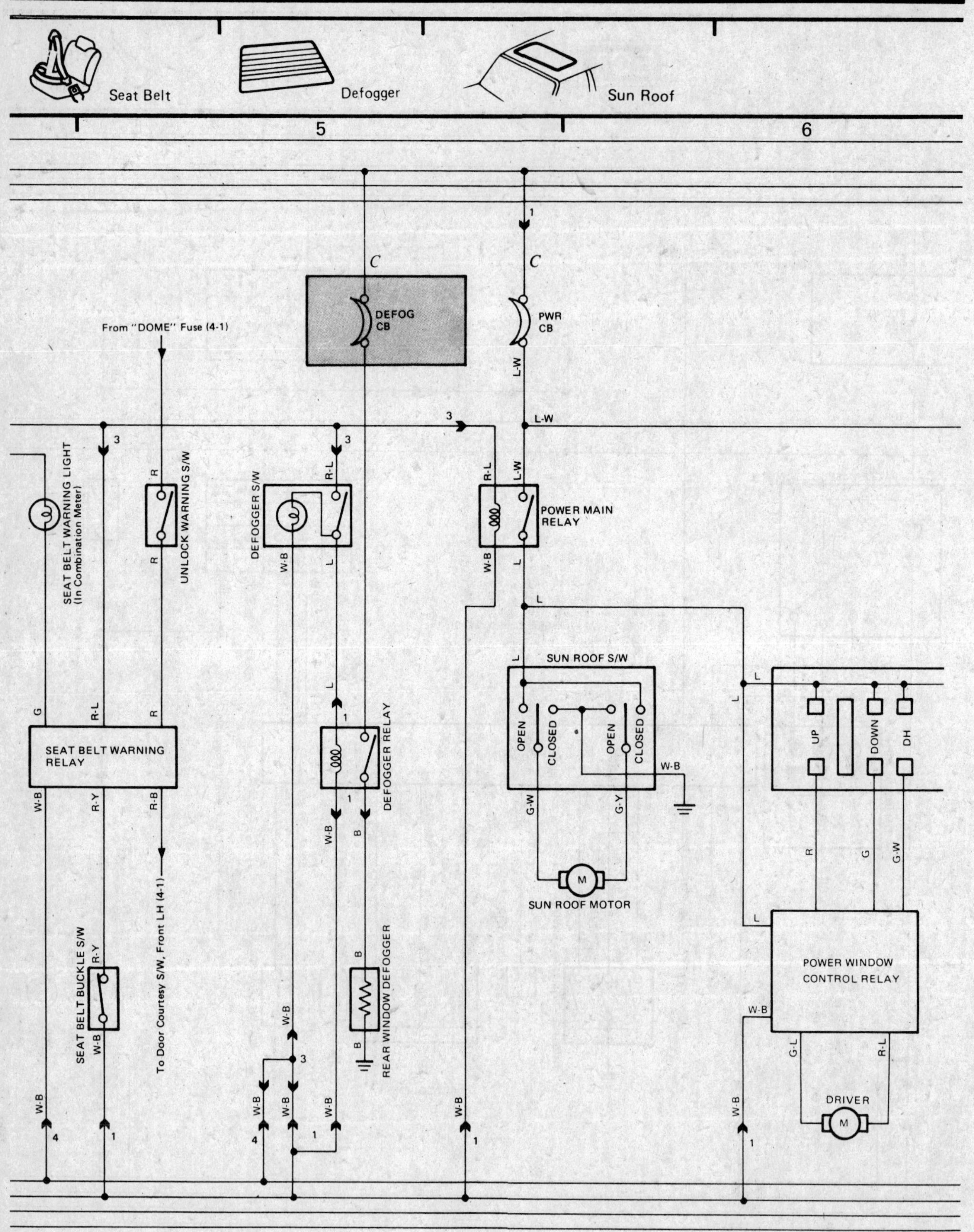

Wiring diagram—1983

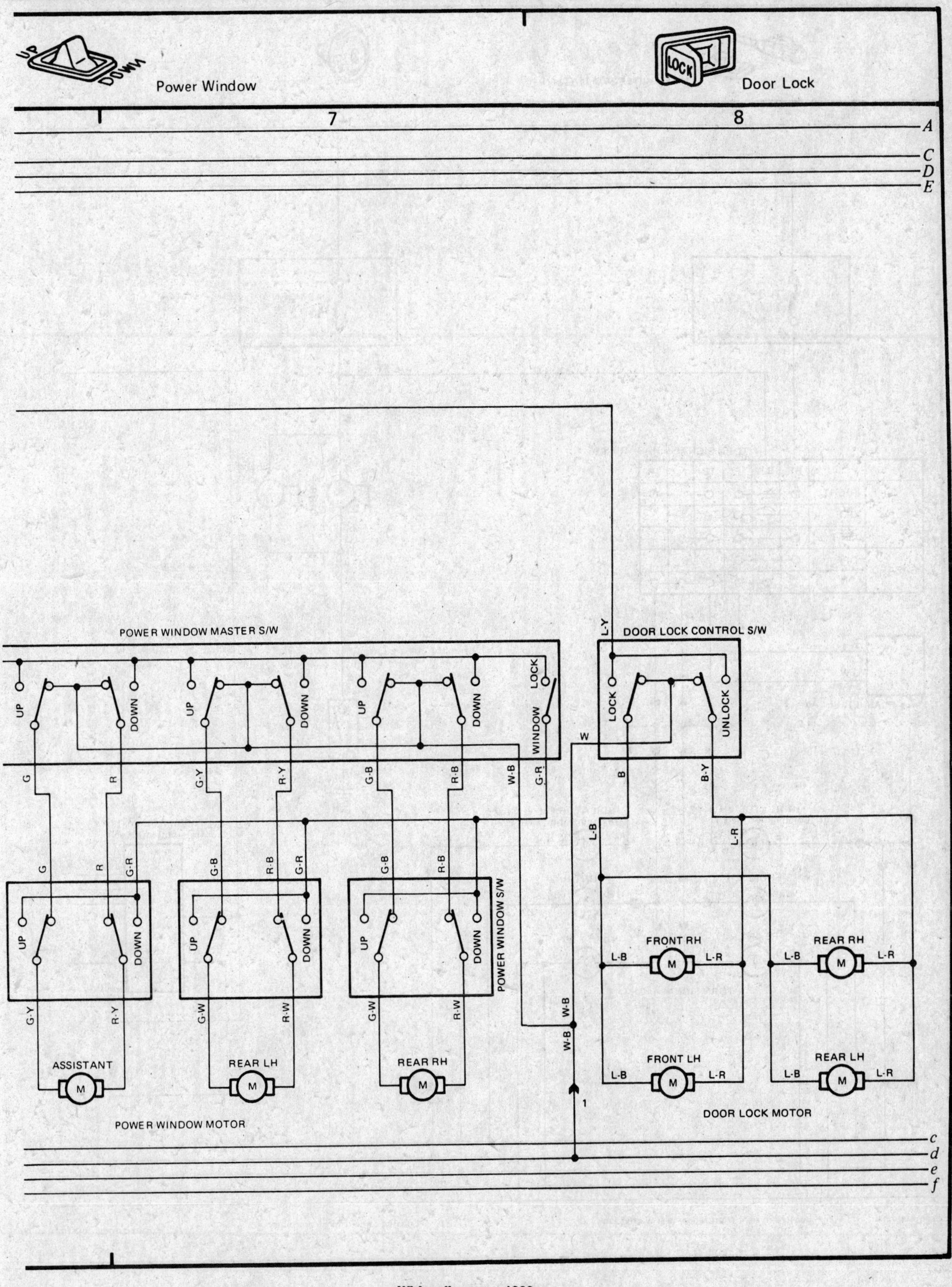

POWER WINDOW MASTER S/W
DOOR LOCK CONTROL S/W
UP DOWN UP DOWN UP DOWN LOCK WINDOW
LOCK UNLOCK
L-Y W B B-Y
G R G-Y R-Y G-B R-B W-B G-R
L-B L-R
G R G-R G-B R-B G-R G-B R-B
UP DOWN UP DOWN UP DOWN
POWER WINDOW S/W
G-Y R-Y G-W R-W G-W R-W W-B W-B
FRONT RH REAR RH
L-B L-R L-B L-R
ASSISTANT REAR LH REAR RH
FRONT LH REAR LH
L-B L-R L-B L-R
POWER WINDOW MOTOR
DOOR LOCK MOTOR
1
c d e f

Wiring diagram—1983

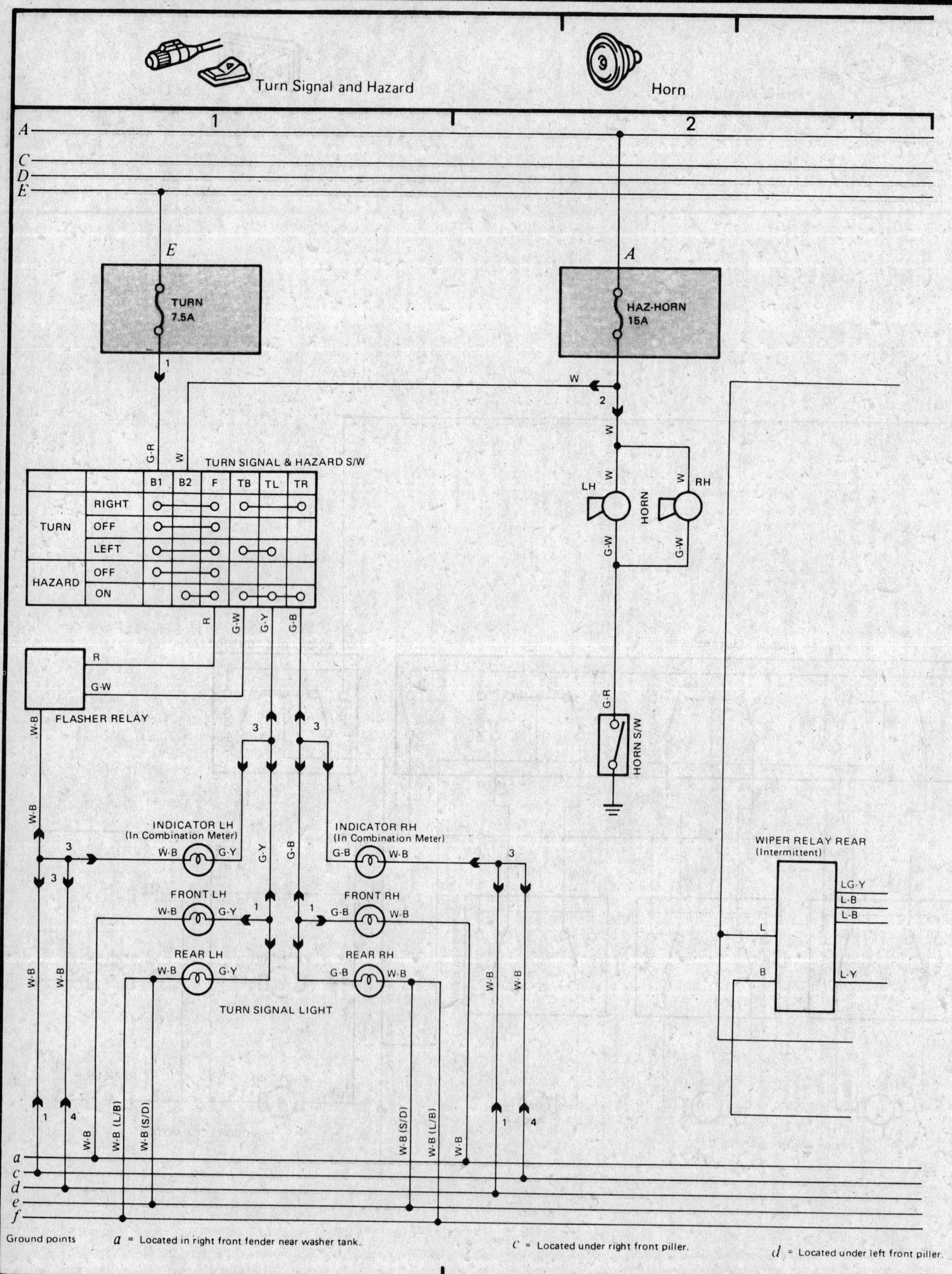

		B1	B2	F	TB	TL	TR
TURN	RIGHT	○	—	○	○	—	○
	OFF	○	—	○			
	LEFT	○	—	○	○	○	
HAZARD	OFF	○	—	○			
	ON		○	○	○	○	○

Wiring diagram—1983

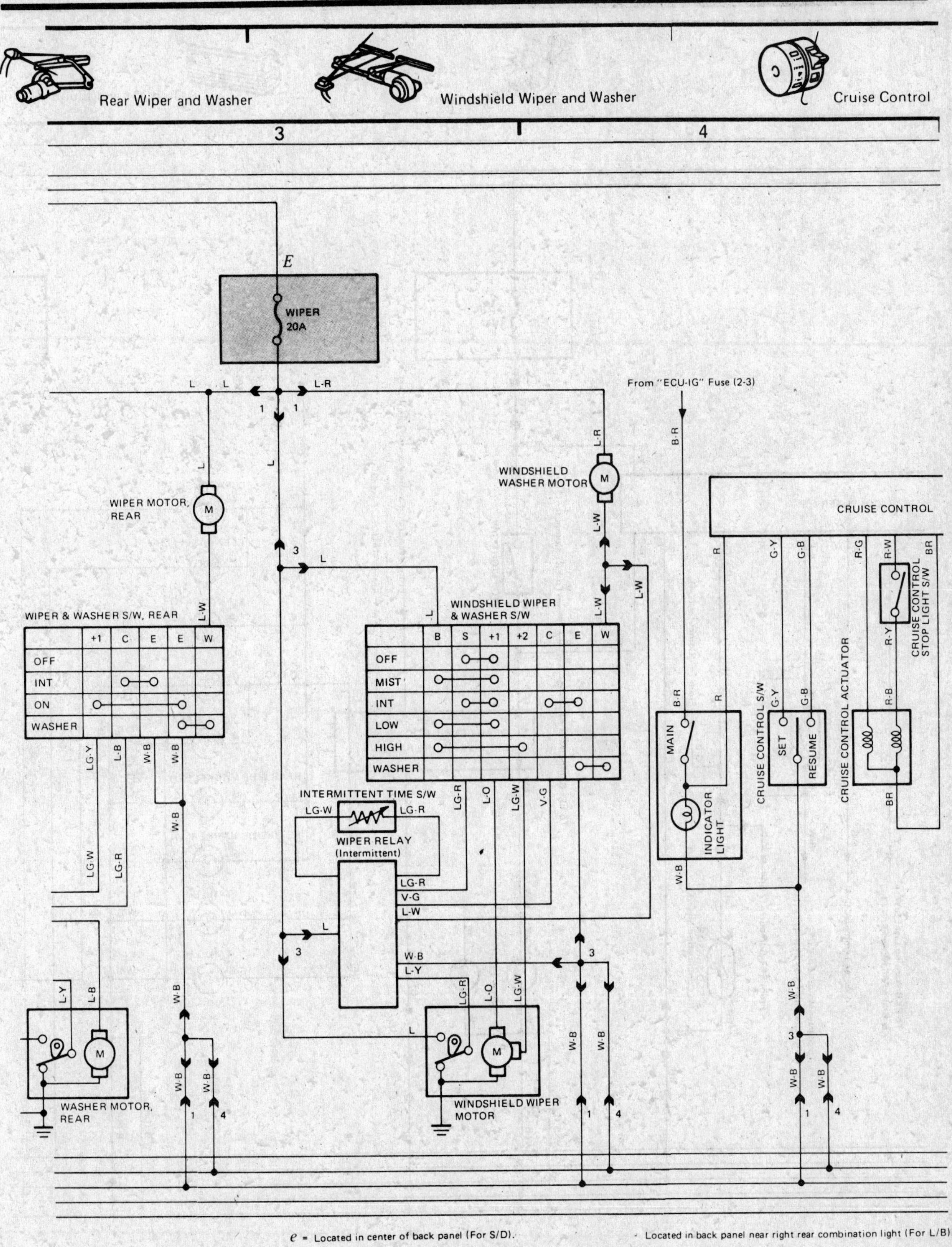

e = Located in center of back panel (For S/D).

· Located in back panel near right rear combination light (For L/B).

Wiring diagram—1983

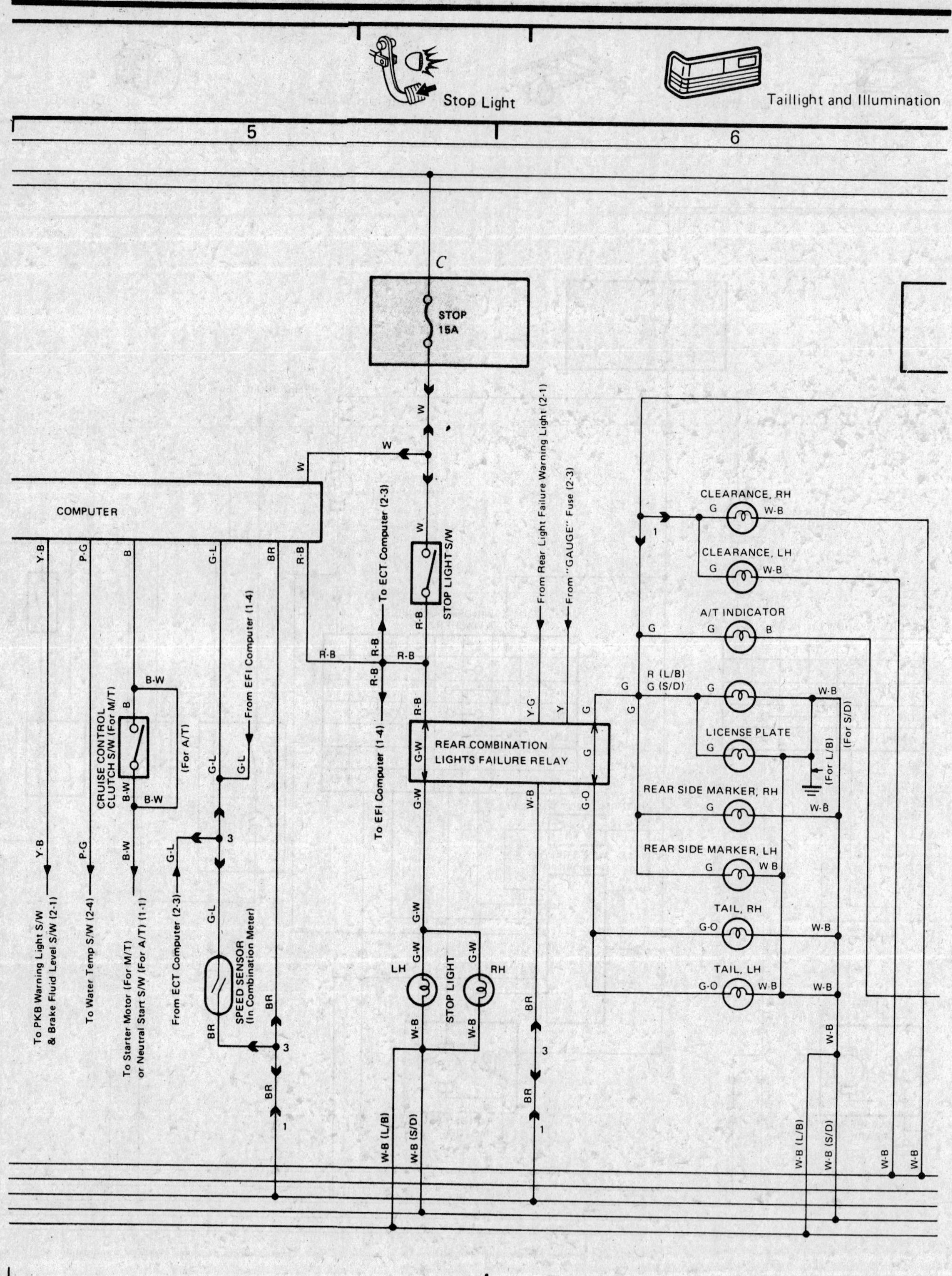

Wiring diagram—1983

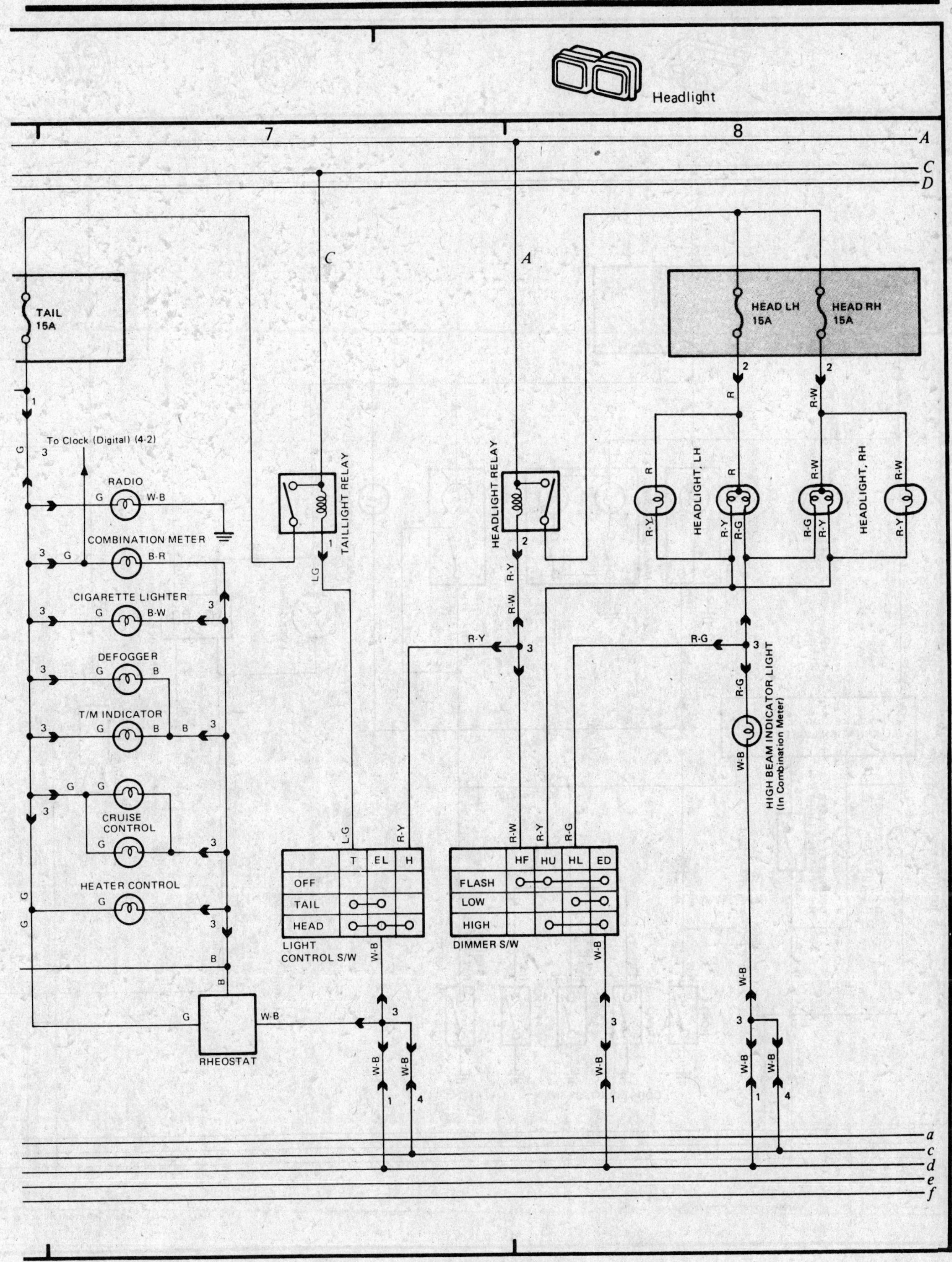

Wiring diagram—1983

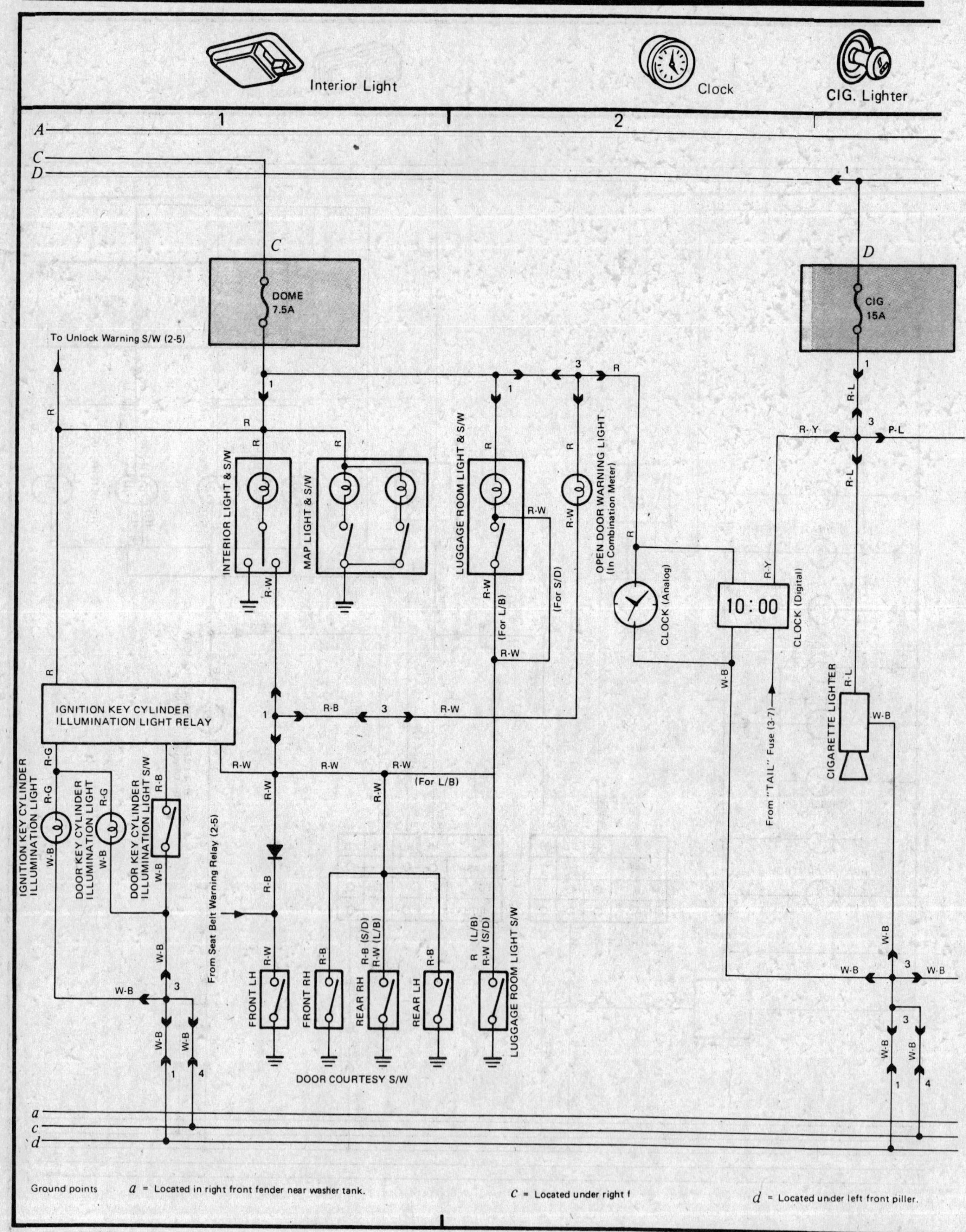

Wiring diagram—1983

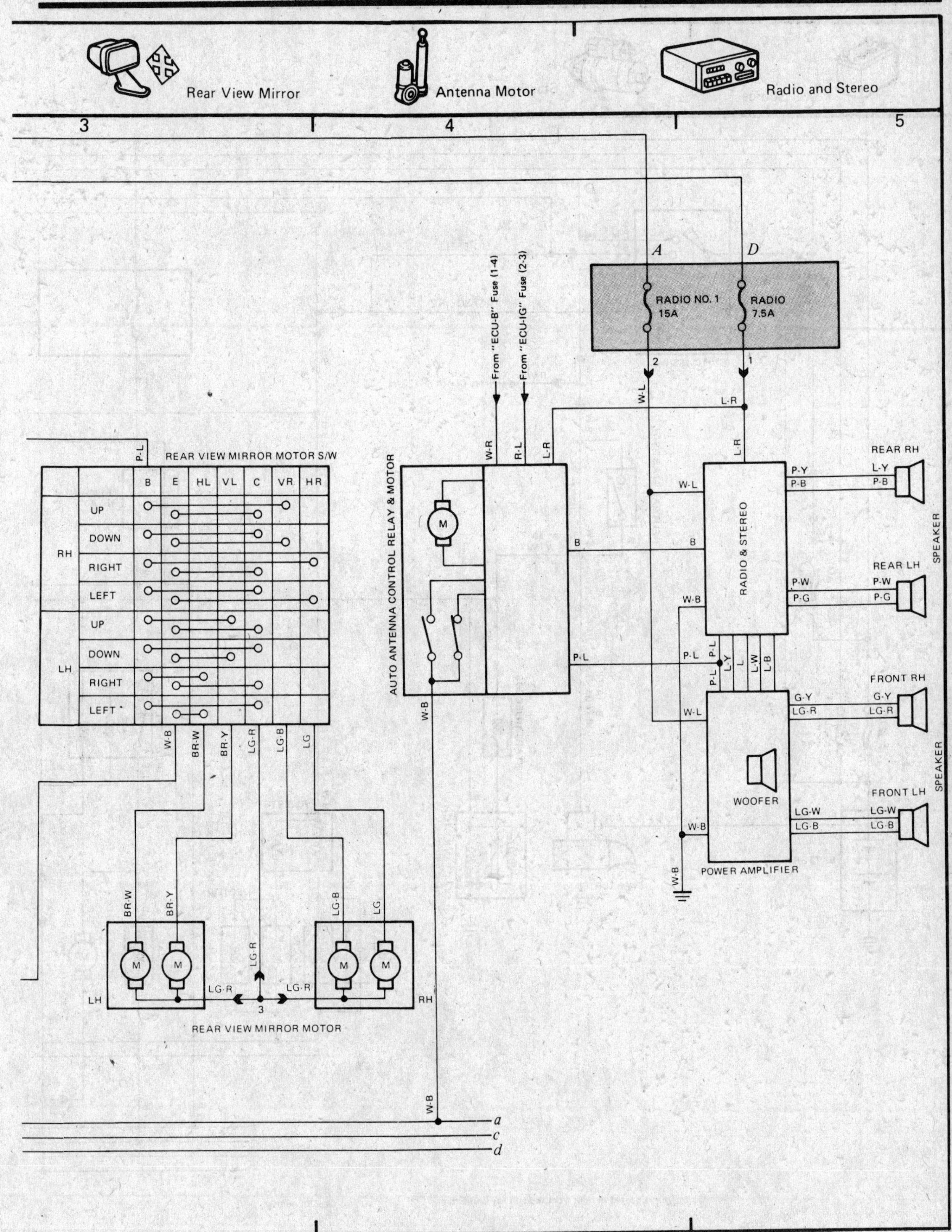

Wiring diagram—1983

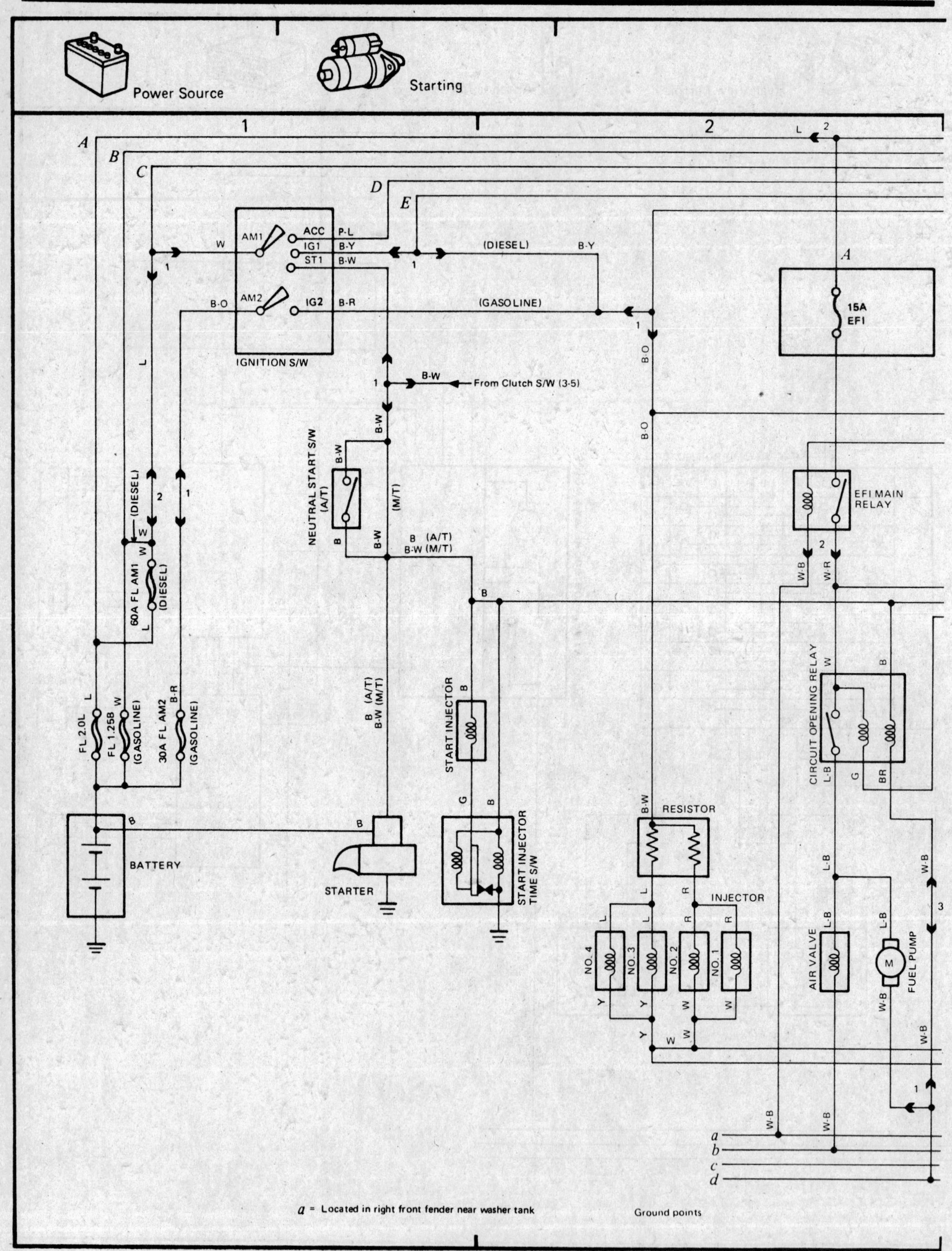

Wiring diagram—1984

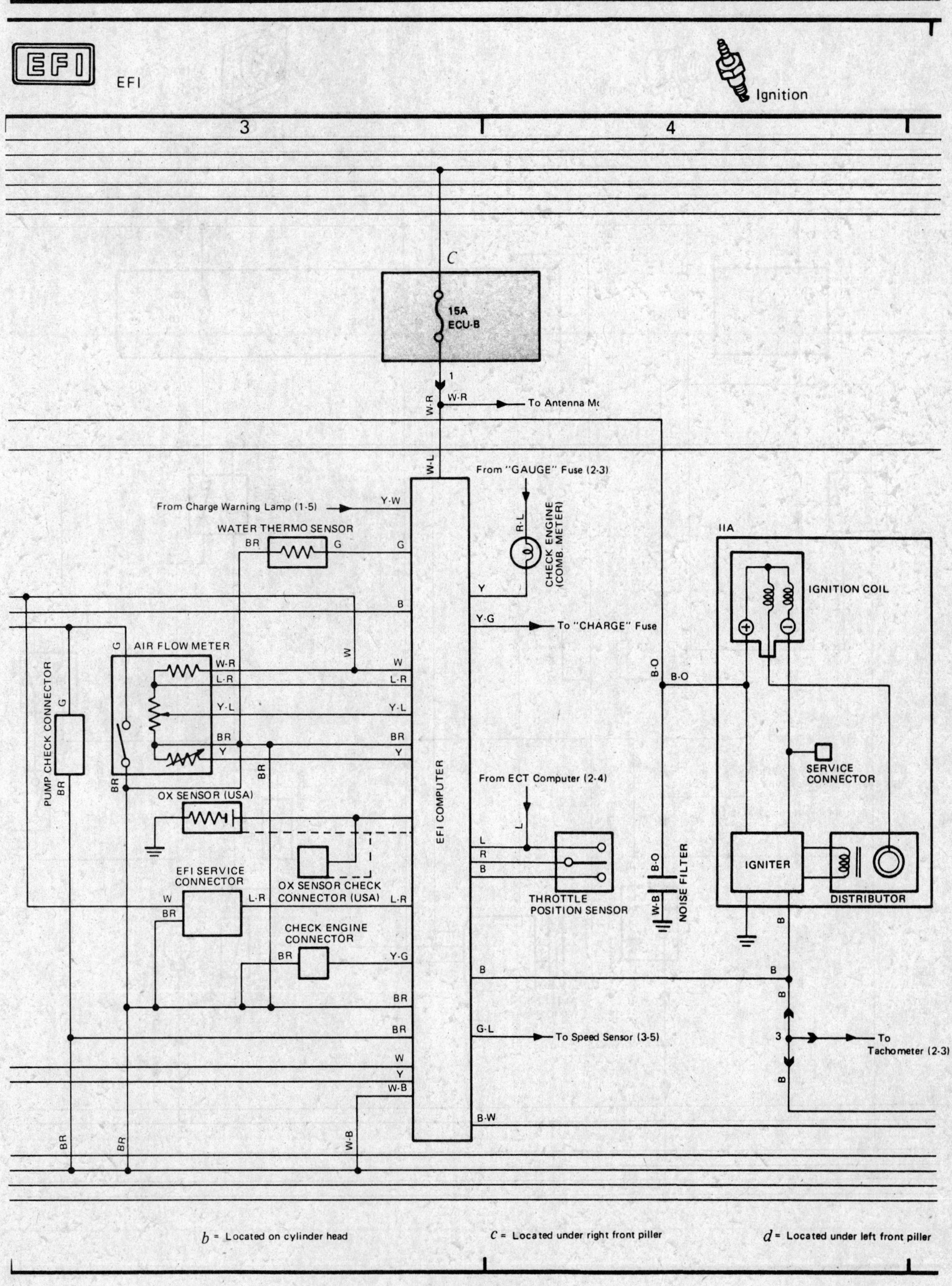
EFI
EFI
Ignition
3
4
C
15A
ECU-B
1
W-R
W-R
To Antenna Mc
W-L
From "GAUGE" Fuse (2-3)
R-L
CHECK ENGINE (COMB. METER)
From Charge Warning Lamp (1-5)
Y-W
WATER THERMO SENSOR
BR
G
G
Y
B
Y-G
To "CHARGE" Fuse
AIR FLOW METER
G
W
W-R
W
L-R
L-R
Y-L
Y-L
BR
BR
Y
Y
PUMP CHECK CONNECTOR
G
BR
BR
BR
OX SENSOR (USA)
EFI COMPUTER
From ECT Computer (2-4)
L
L
R
B
THROTTLE POSITION SENSOR
EFI SERVICE CONNECTOR
W
BR
L-R
OX SENSOR CHECK CONNECTOR (USA)
L-R
CHECK ENGINE CONNECTOR
BR
Y-G
B
B
BR
BR
G-L
To Speed Sensor (3-5)
W
Y
W-B
B-W
BR
BR
W-B
B-O
B-O
B-O
W-B
NOISE FILTER
IIA
IGNITION COIL
SERVICE CONNECTOR
IGNITER
DISTRIBUTOR
B
B
3
To Tachometer (2-3)
B
b = Located on cylinder head
C = Located under right front piller
d = Located under left front piller

Wiring diagram—1984

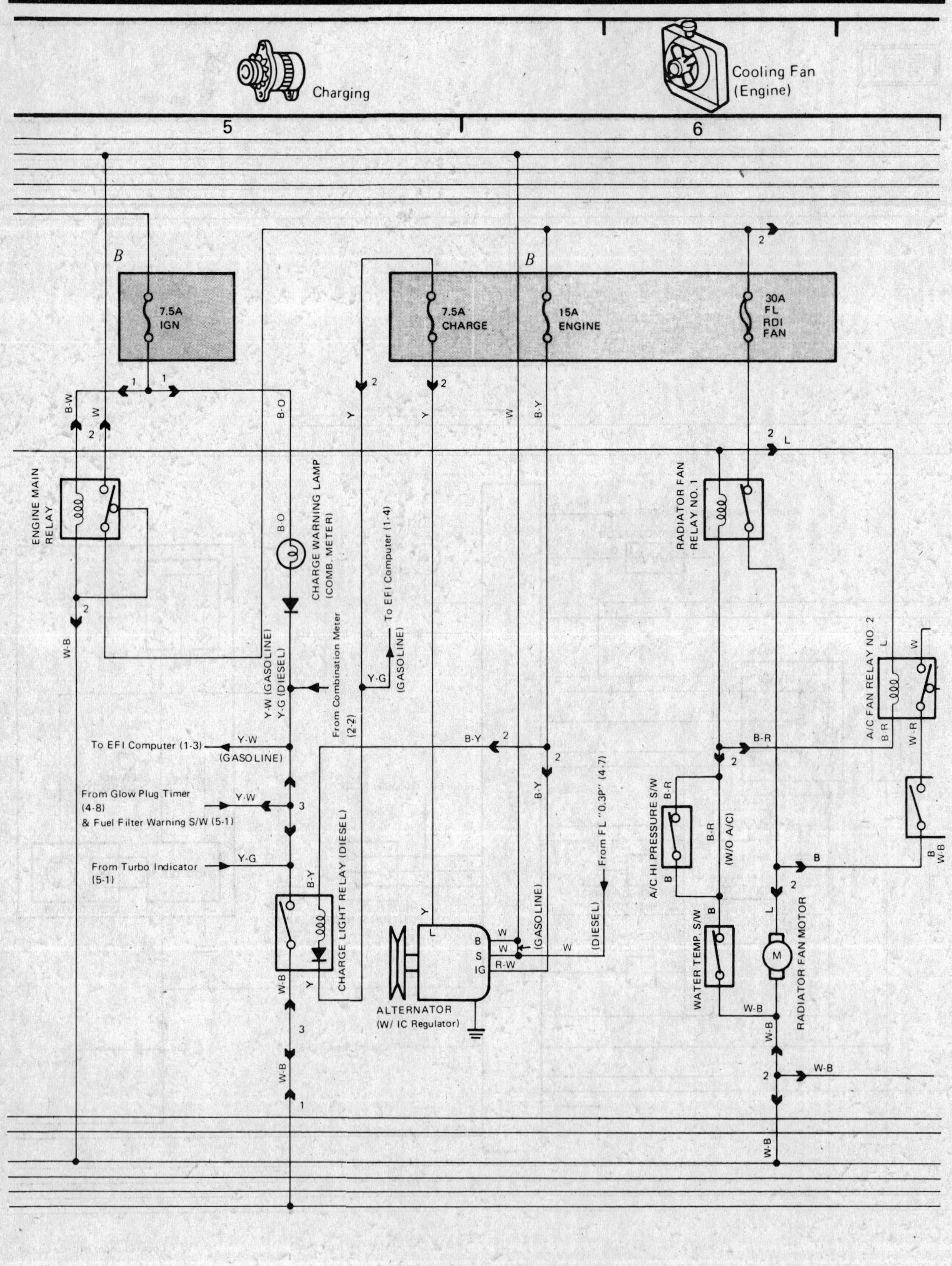

Charging
Cooling Fan (Engine)
5
6
B
7.5A IGN
7.5A CHARGE
15A ENGINE
30A FL RDI FAN
ENGINE MAIN RELAY
CHARGE WARNING LAMP (COMB. METER)
To EFI Computer (1-4)
From Combination Meter (2-2)
Y-W (GASOLINE)
Y-G (DIESEL)
To EFI Computer (1-3)
(GASOLINE)
From Glow Plug Timer (4-8)
& Fuel Filter Warning S/W (5-1)
From Turbo Indicator (5-1)
CHARGE LIGHT RELAY (DIESEL)
ALTERNATOR (W/ IC Regulator)
From FL "0.3P" (4-7)
(GASOLINE)
(DIESEL)
RADIATOR FAN RELAY NO. 1
A/C FAN RELAY NO. 2
A/C HI PRESSURE S/W
(W/O A/C)
WATER TEMP. S/W
RADIATOR FAN MOTOR

Wiring diagram—1984

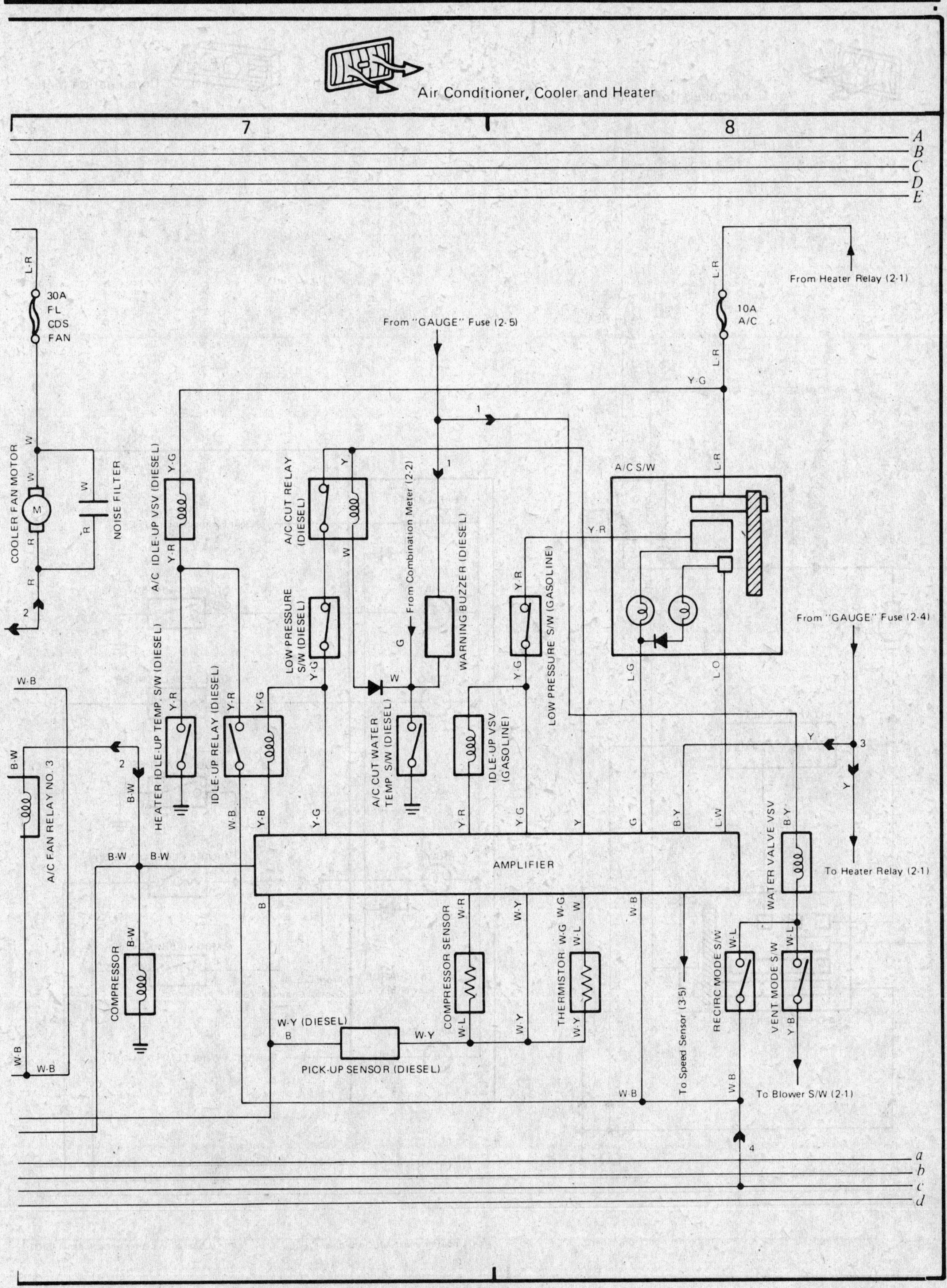

Wiring diagram—1984

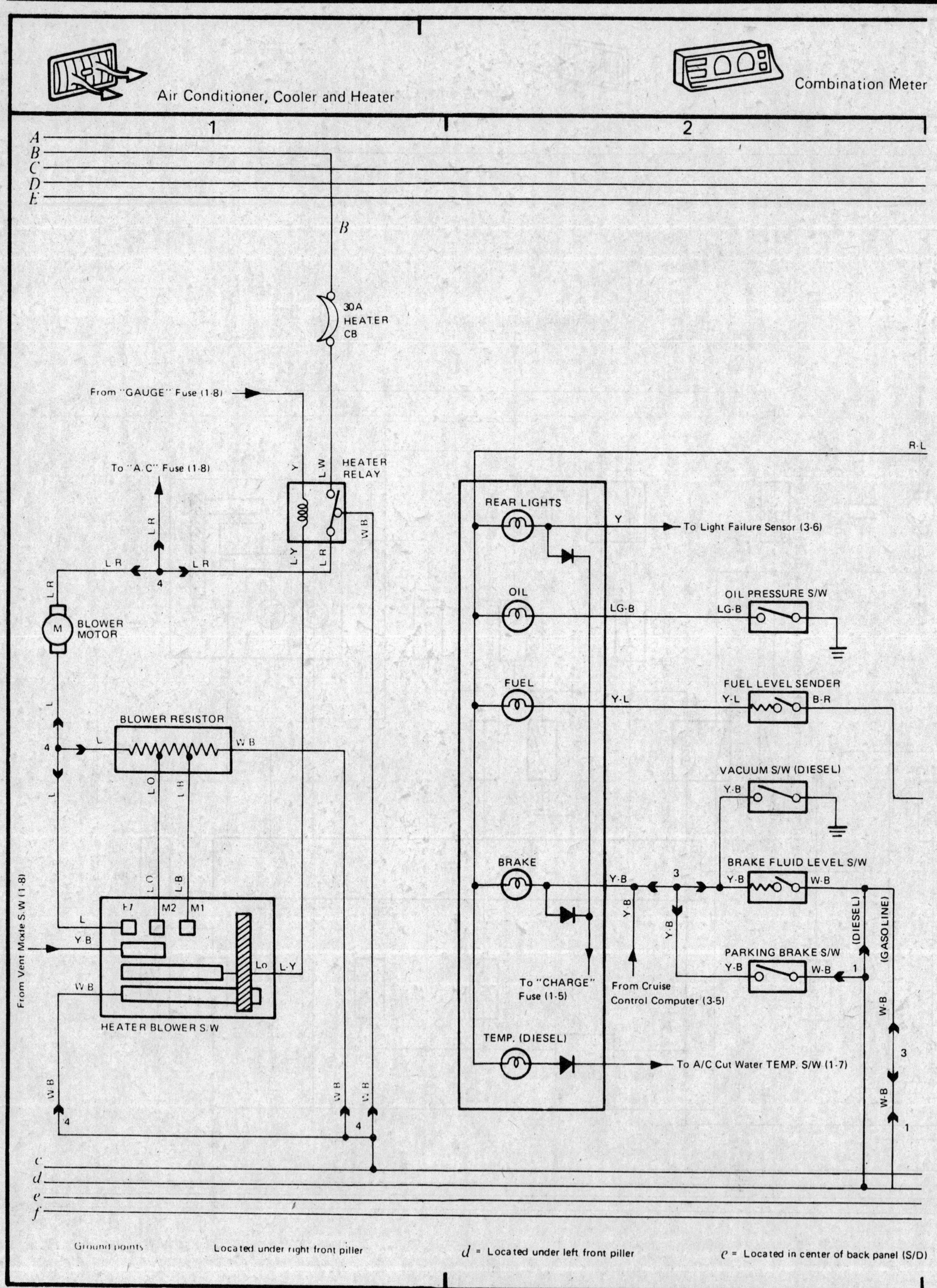

Wiring diagram—1984

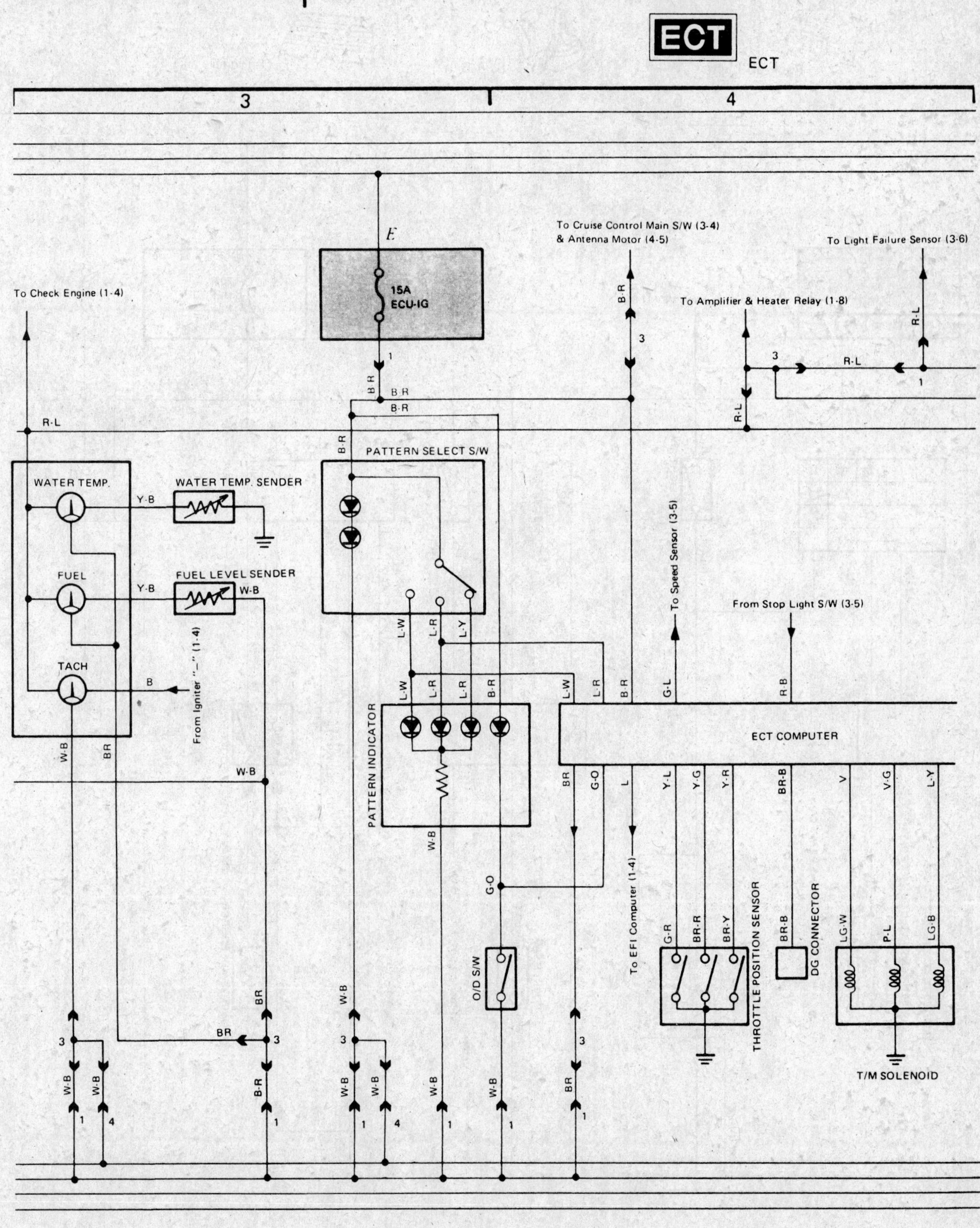

f = Located in back panel near right rear combination light (L/B)

Wiring diagram—1984

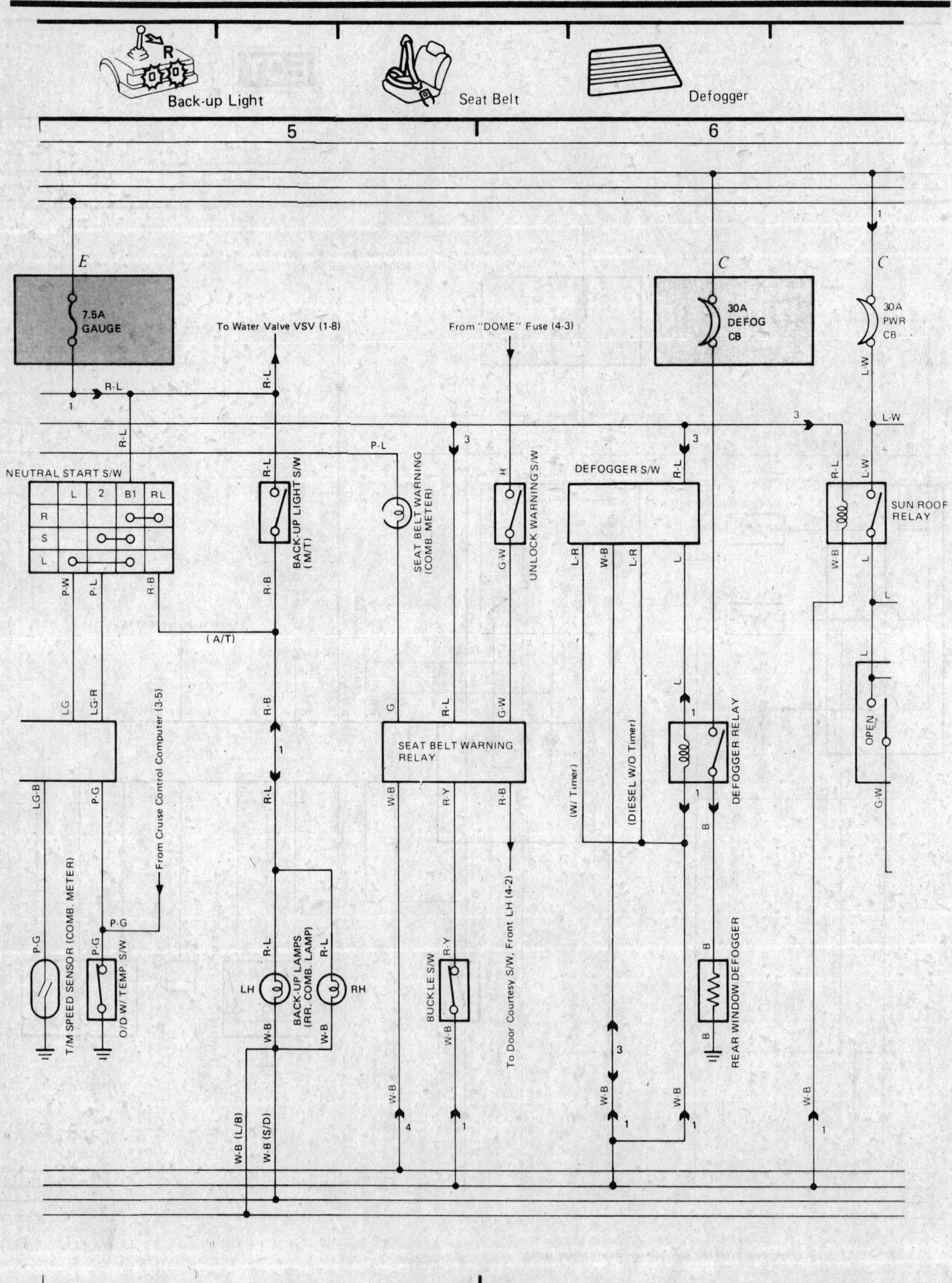

Wiring diagram—1984

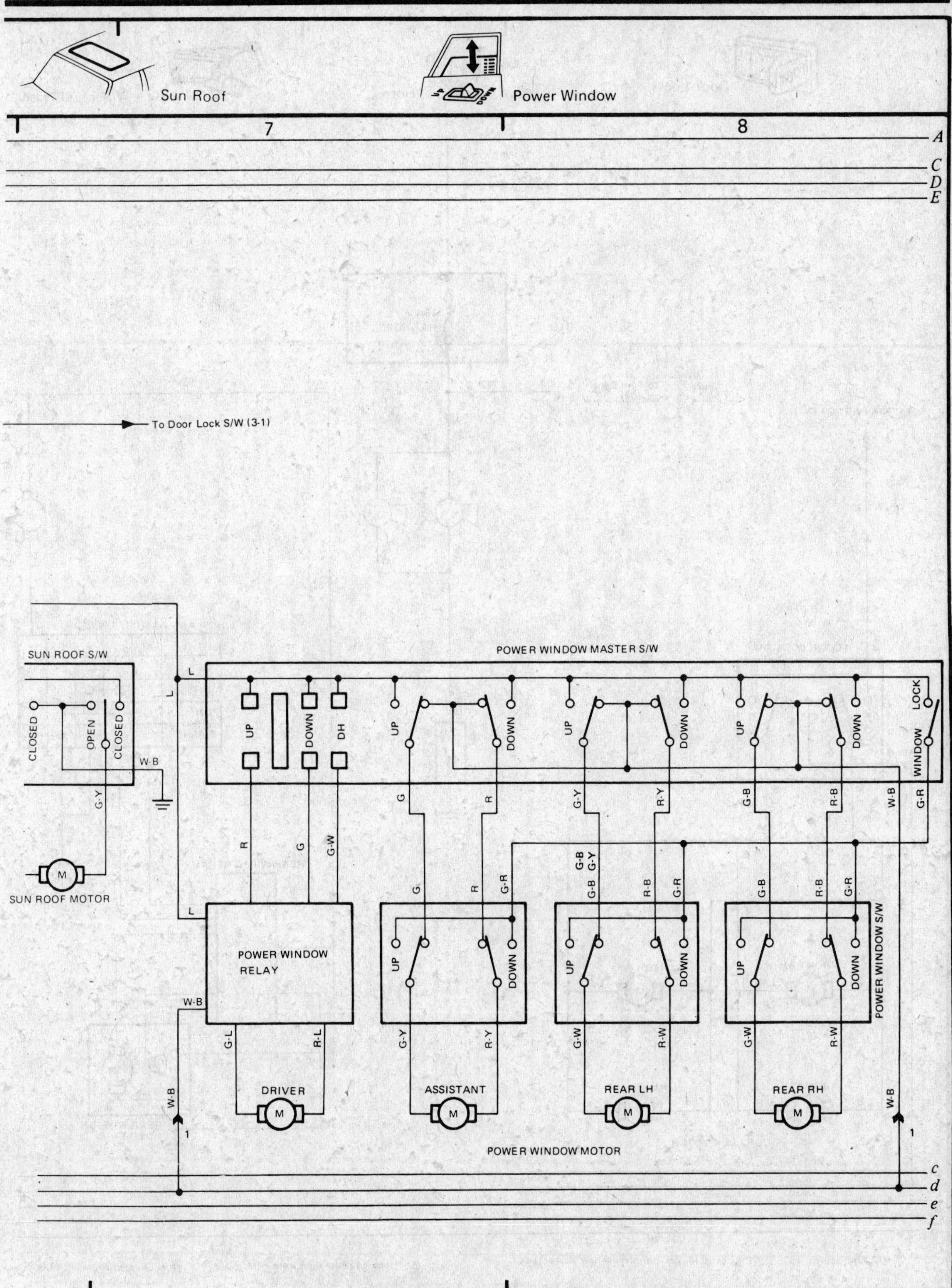

Wiring diagram—1984

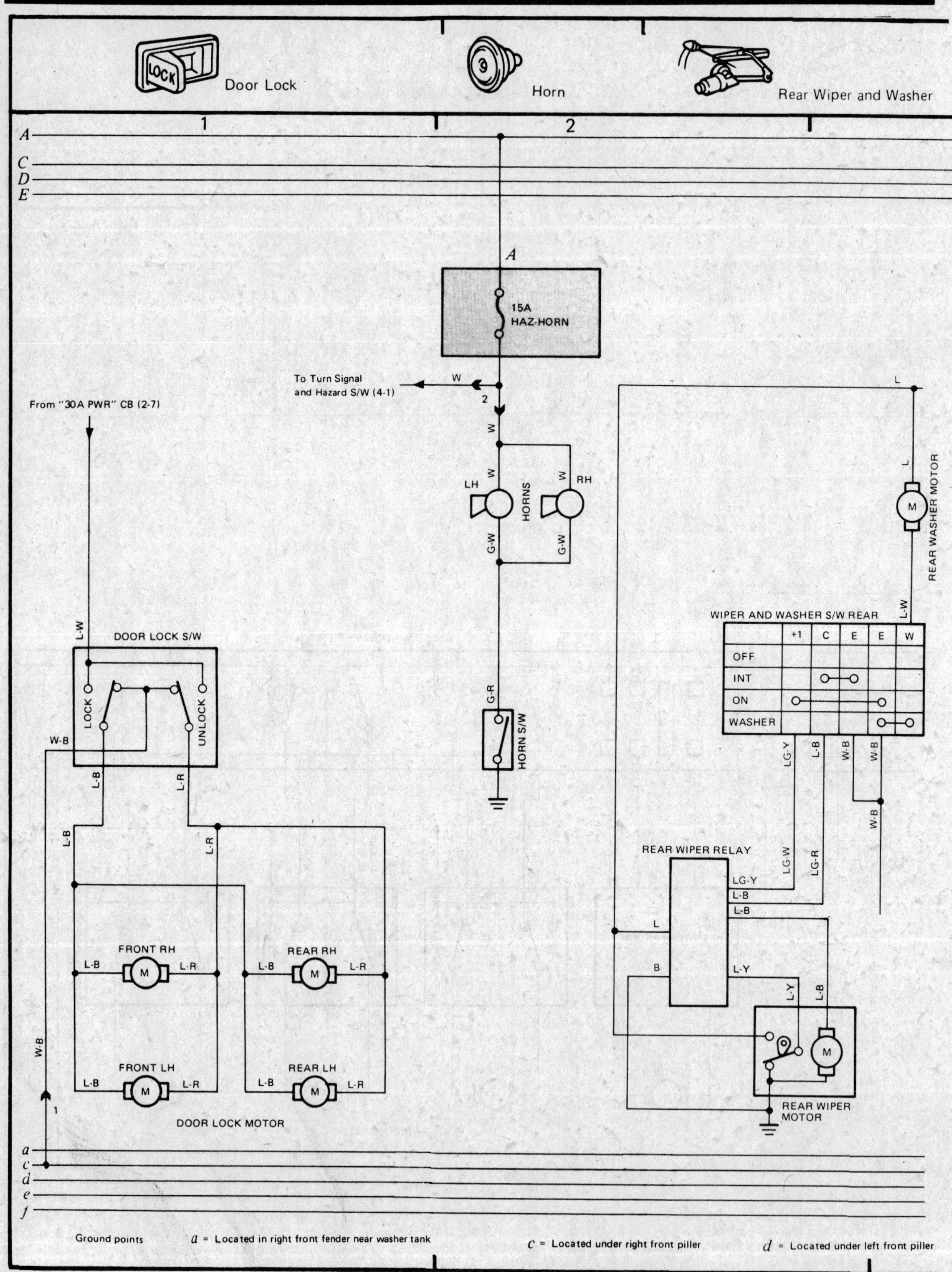

Ground points a = Located in right front fender near washer tank c = Located under right front piller d = Located under left front piller

Wiring diagram—1984

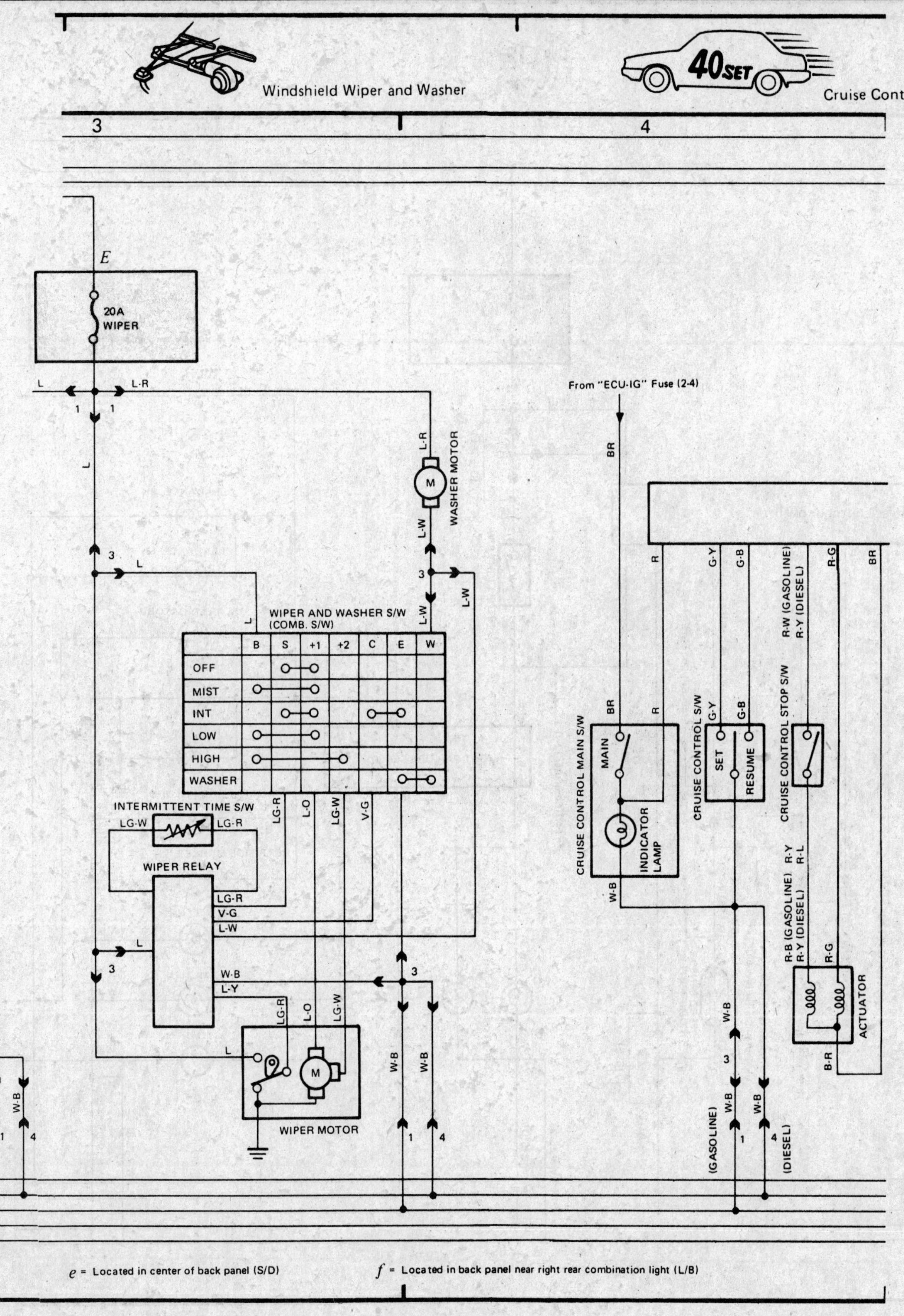

e = Located in center of back panel (S/D)

f = Located in back panel near right rear combination light (L/B)

Wiring diagram—1984

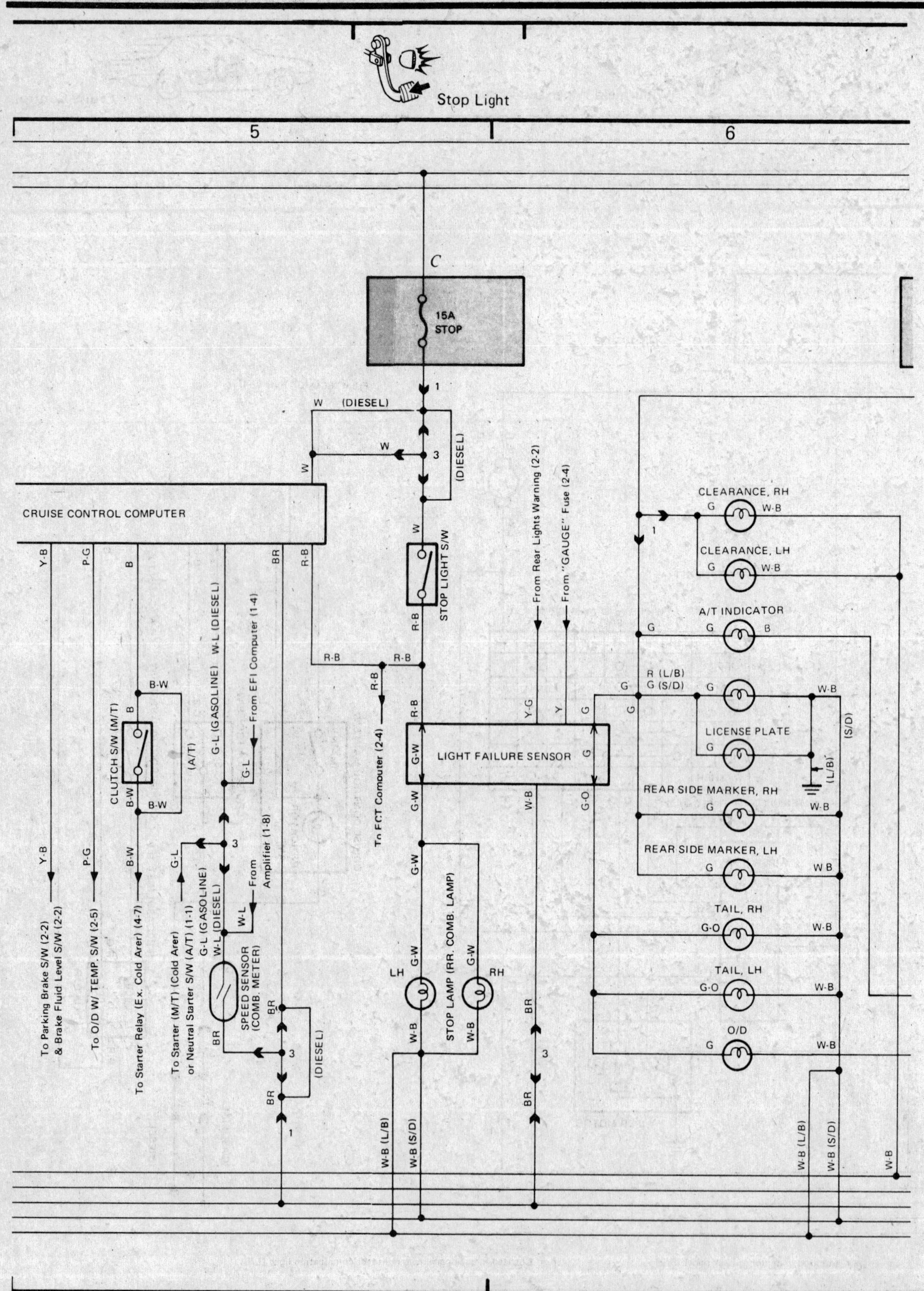

Wiring diagram—1984

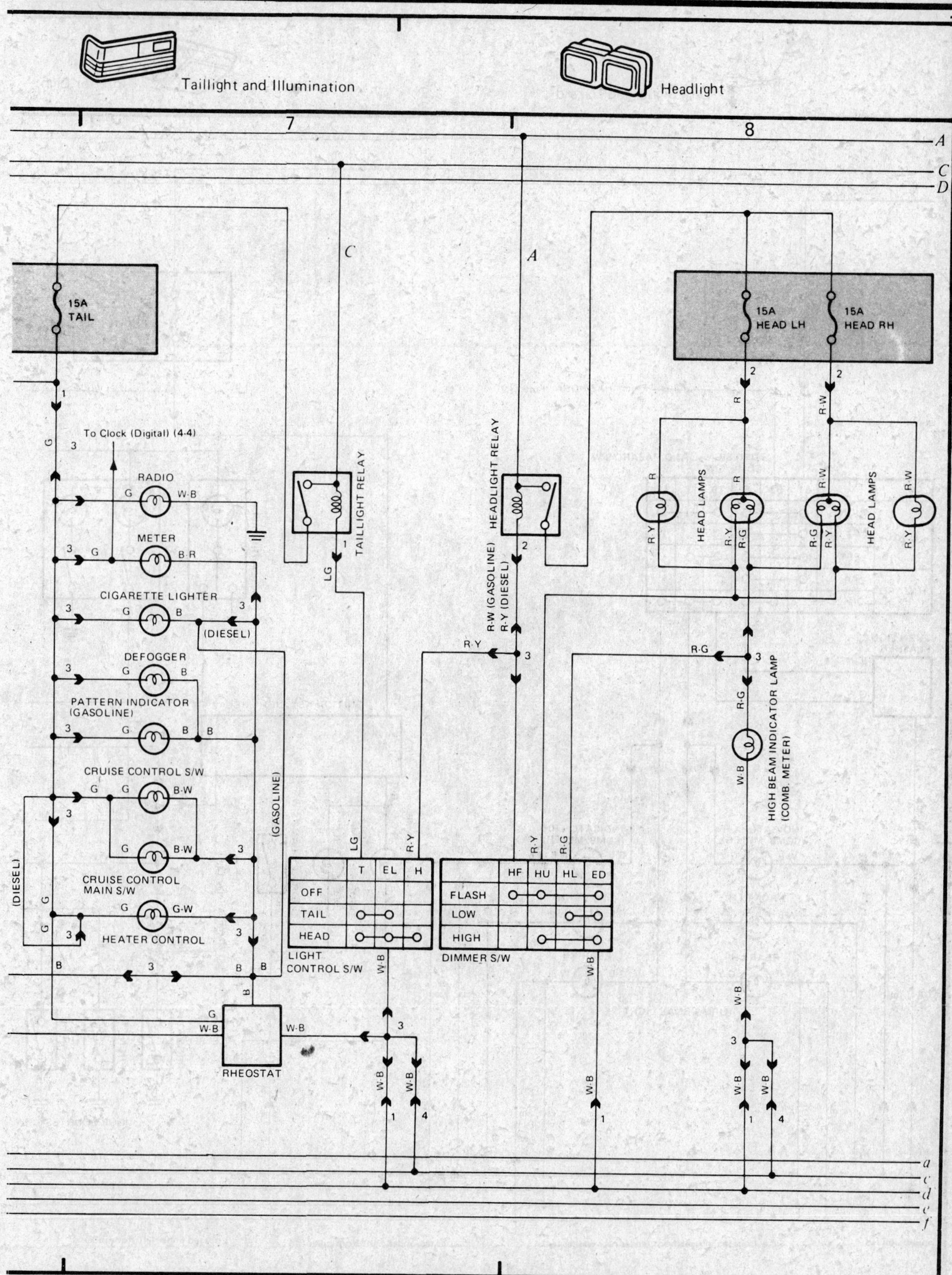

Wiring diagram—1984

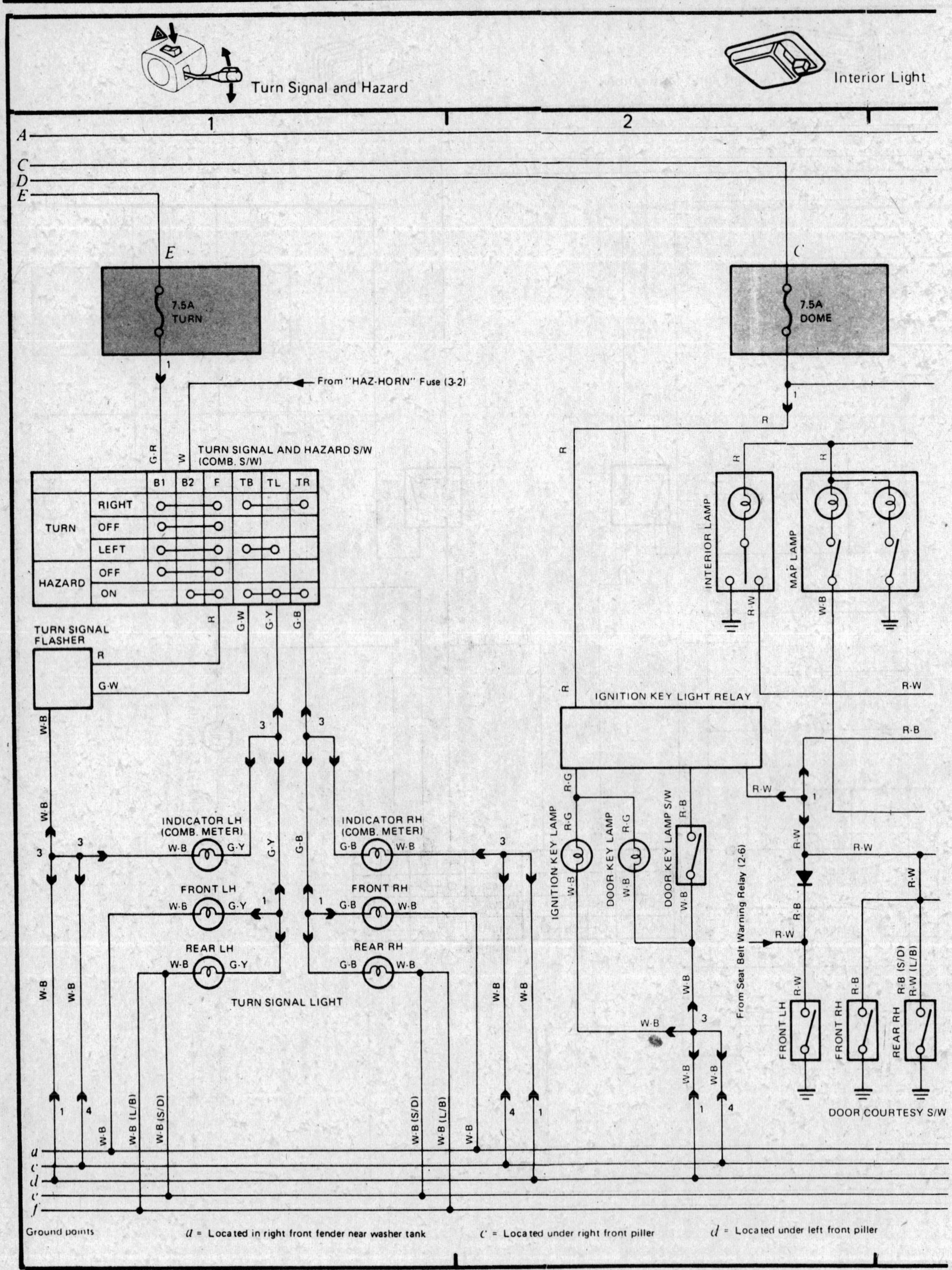

Wiring diagram—1984

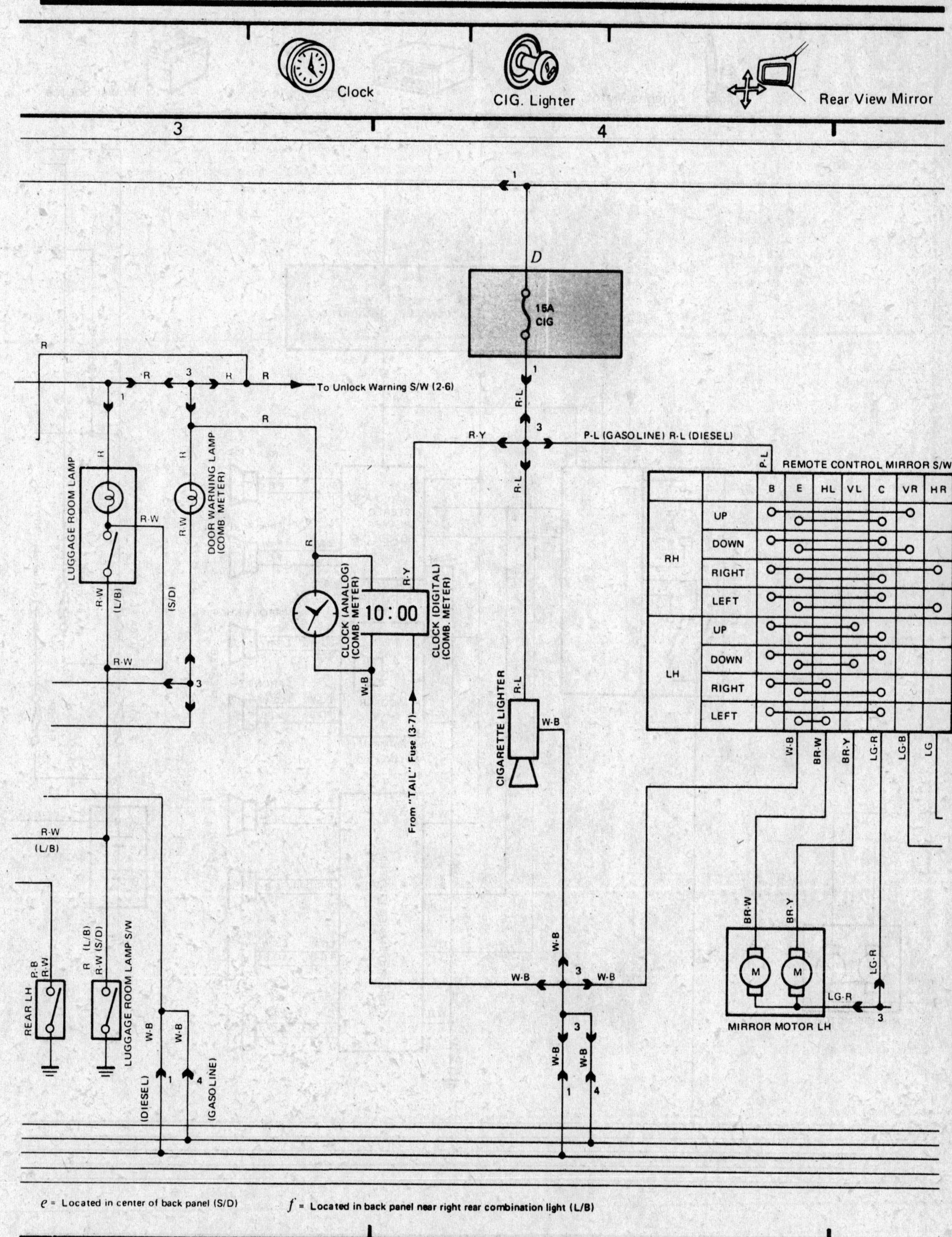

e = Located in center of back panel (S/D)

f = Located in back panel near right rear combination light (L/B)

Wiring diagram—1984

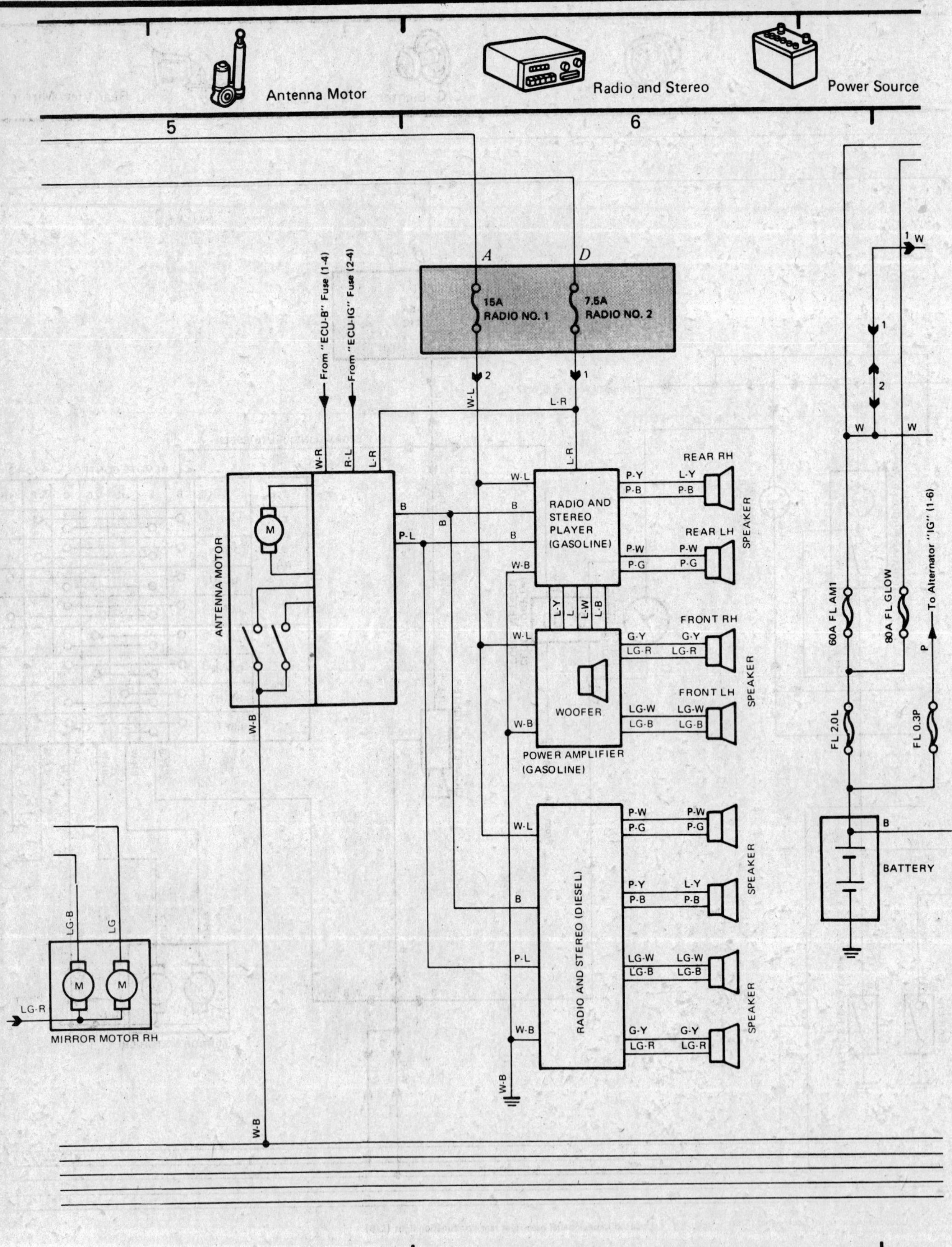

Wiring diagram—1984

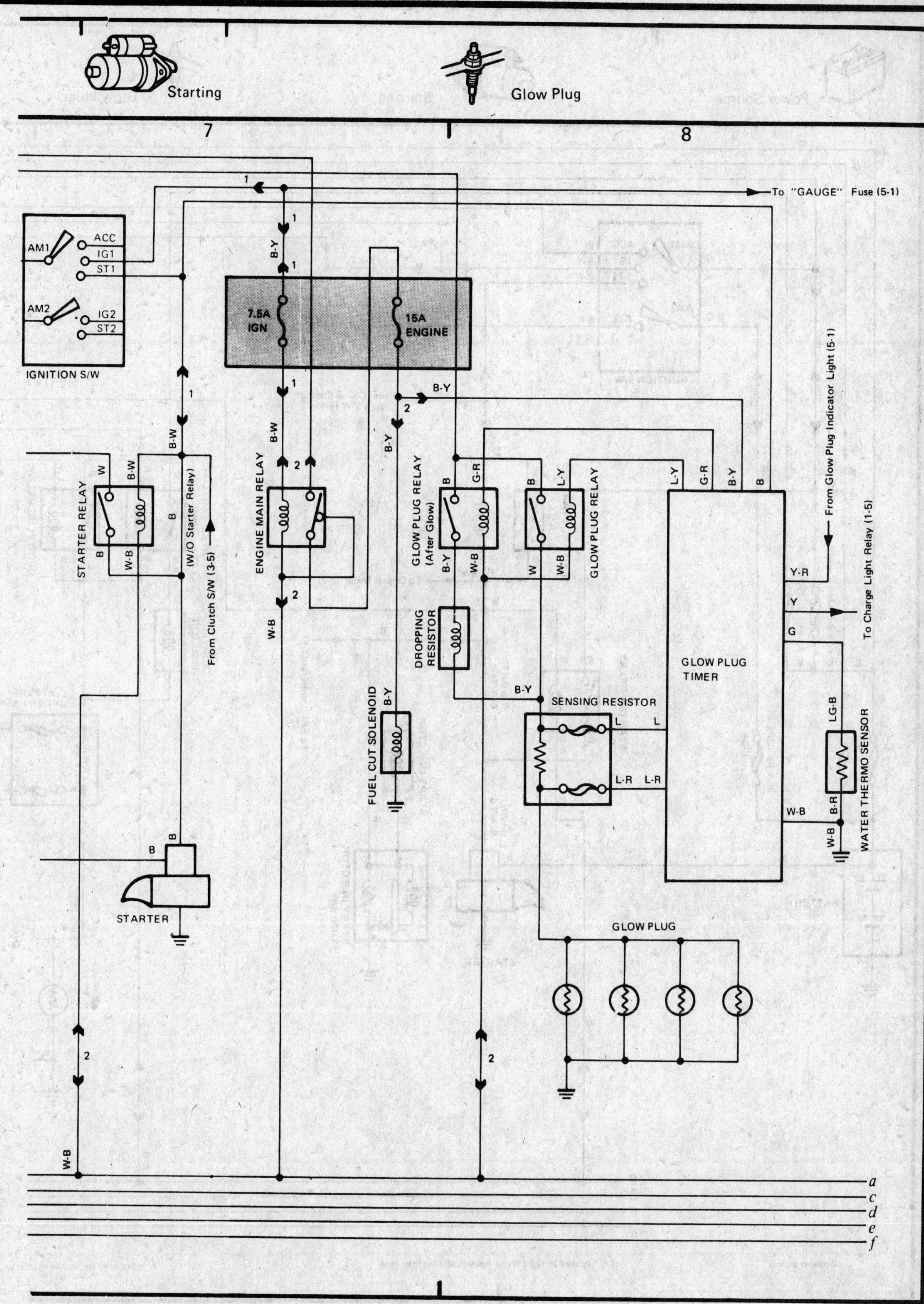

Wiring diagram—1984

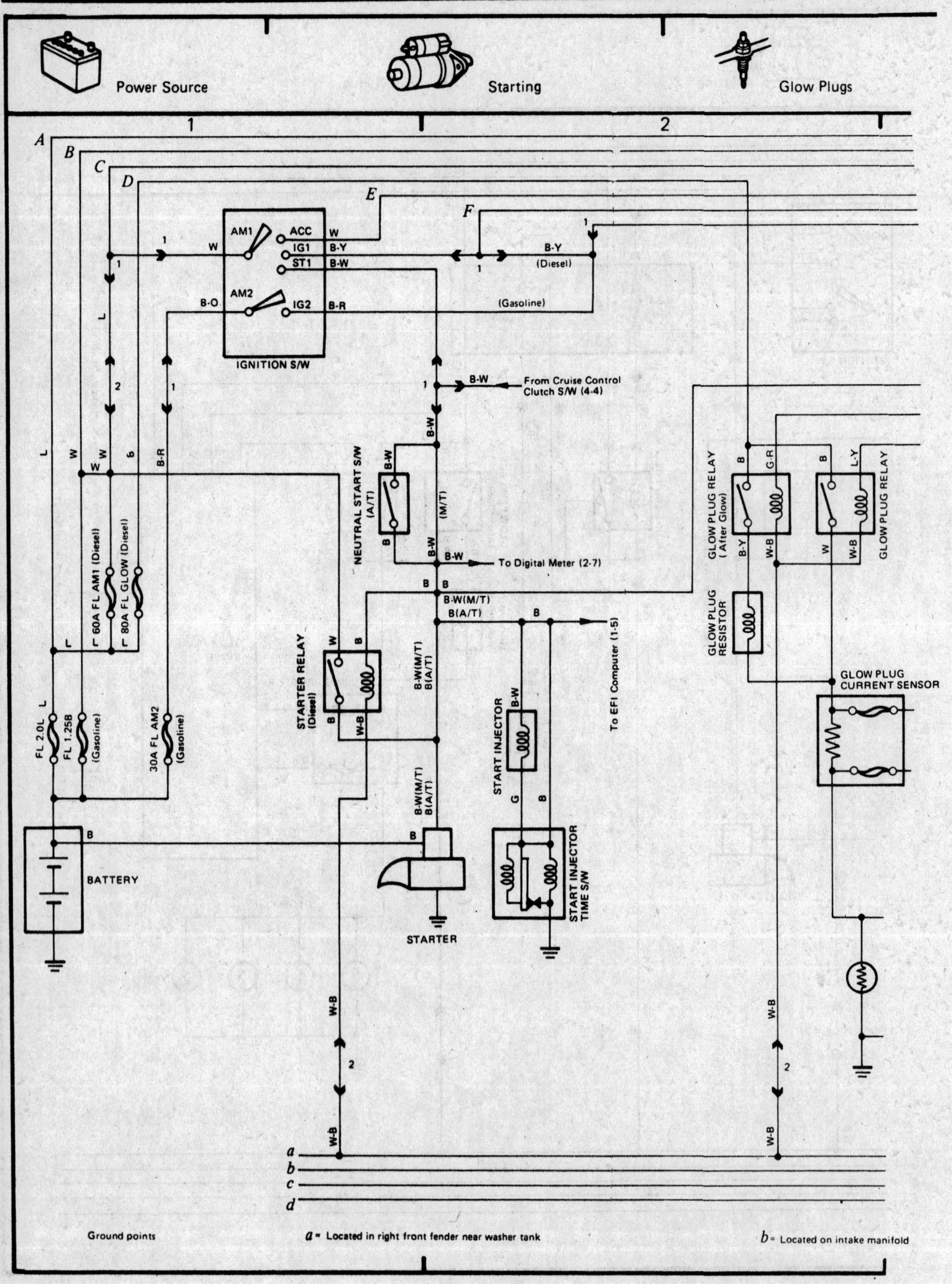

Wiring diagram—1985

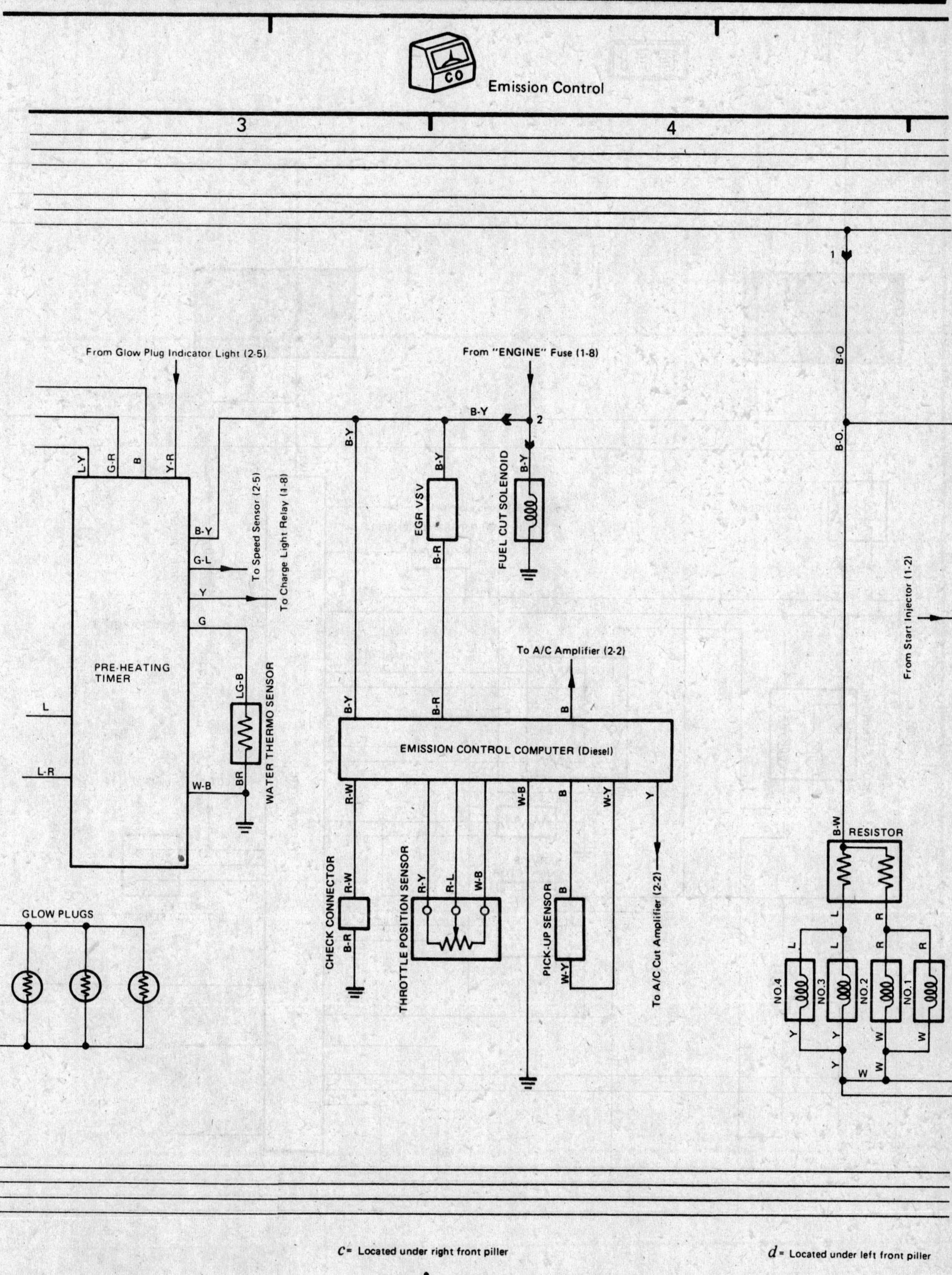

Emission Control
CO
3
4
From Glow Plug Indicator Light (2-5)
From "ENGINE" Fuse (1-8)
PRE-HEATING TIMER
To Speed Sensor (2-5)
To Charge Light Relay (1-8)
WATER THERMO SENSOR
EGR VSV
FUEL CUT SOLENOID
To A/C Amplifier (2-2)
EMISSION CONTROL COMPUTER (Diesel)
CHECK CONNECTOR
THROTTLE POSITION SENSOR
PICK-UP SENSOR
To A/C Cut Amplifier (2-2)
From Start Injector (1-2)
RESISTOR
GLOW PLUGS
NO.4
NO.3
NO.2
NO.1
c = Located under right front piller
d = Located under left front piller

Wiring diagram—1985

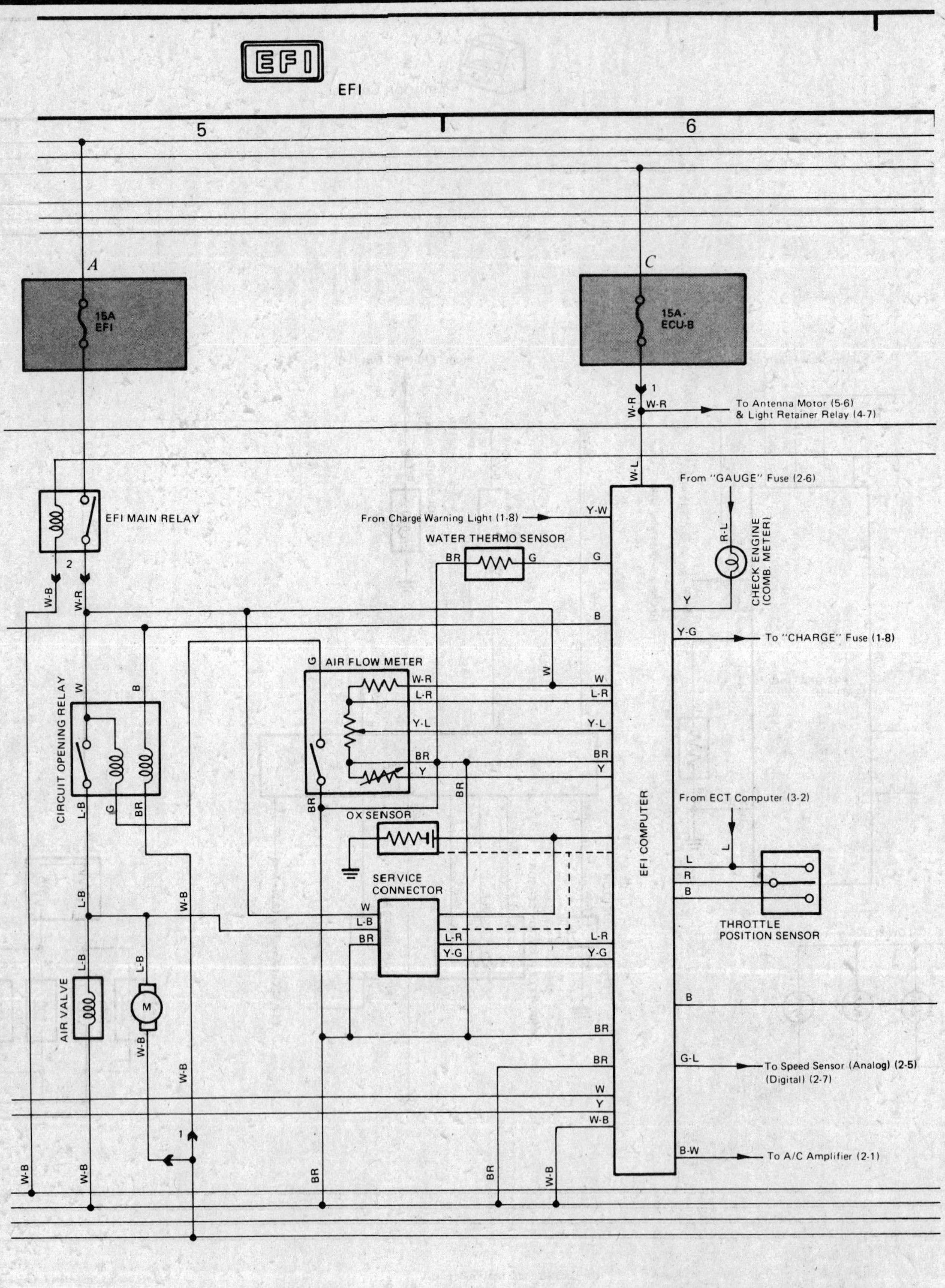

Wiring diagram—1985

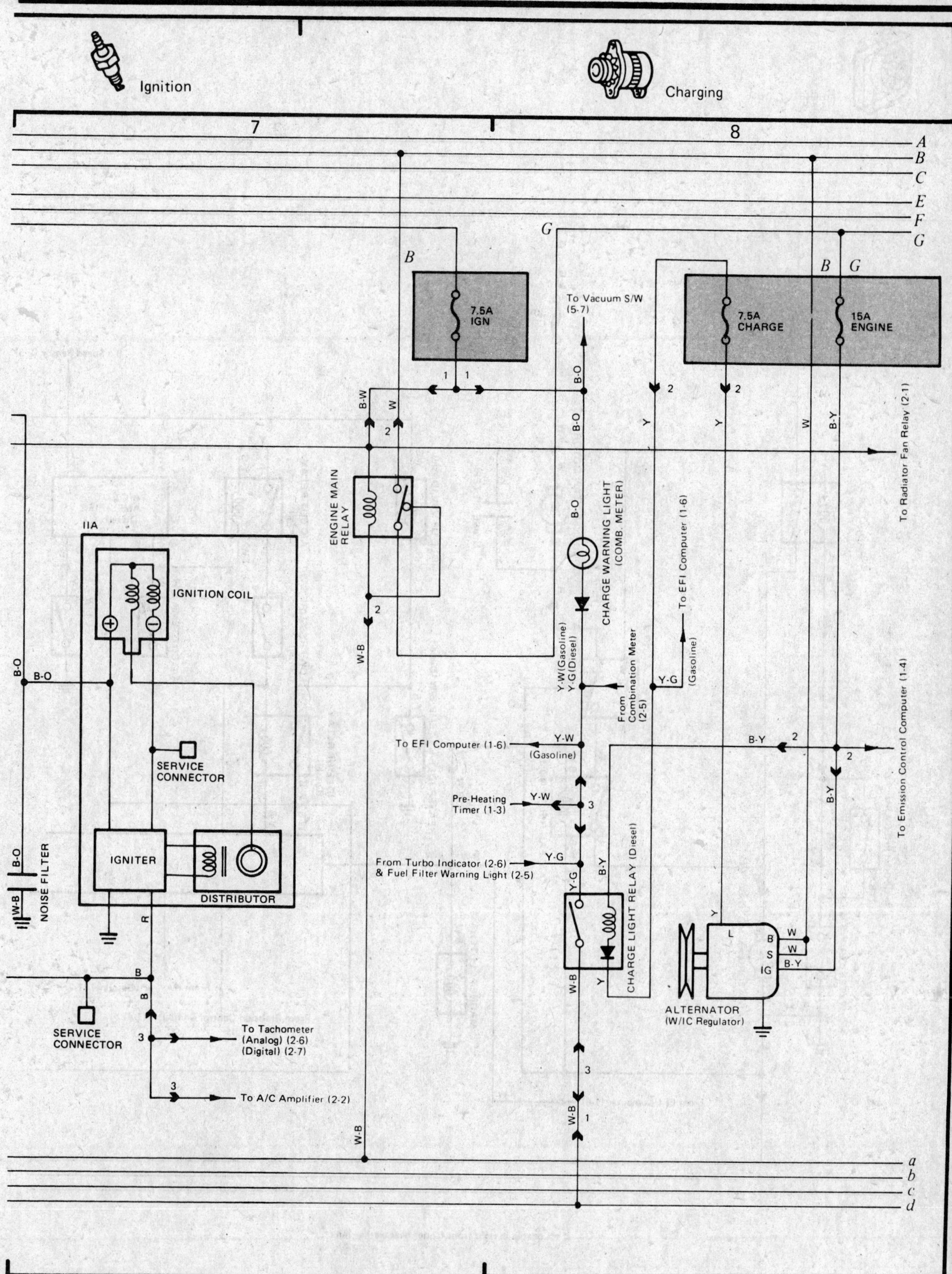

Wiring diagram—1985

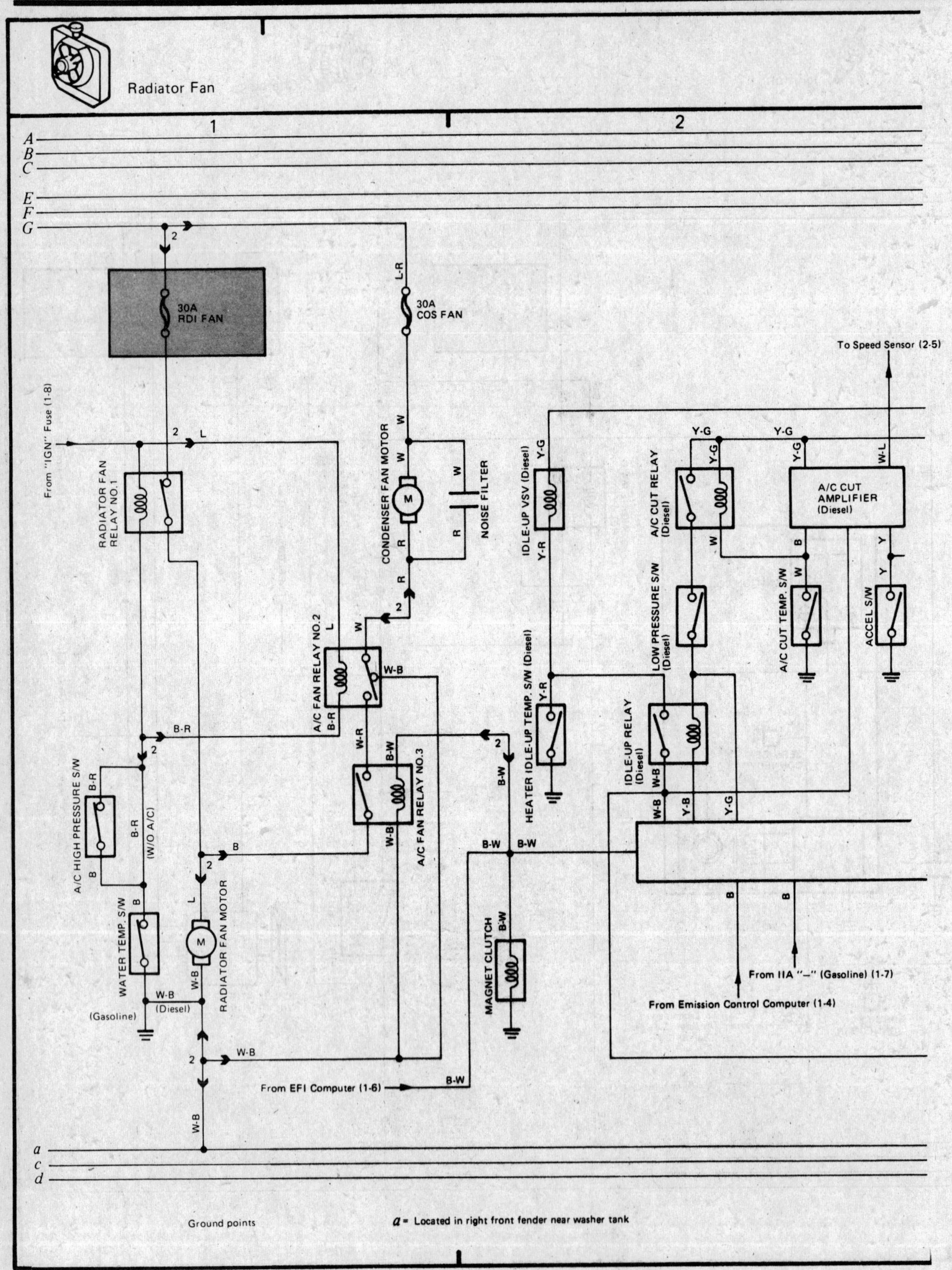

Wiring diagram—1985

Air Conditioner, Cooler and Heater

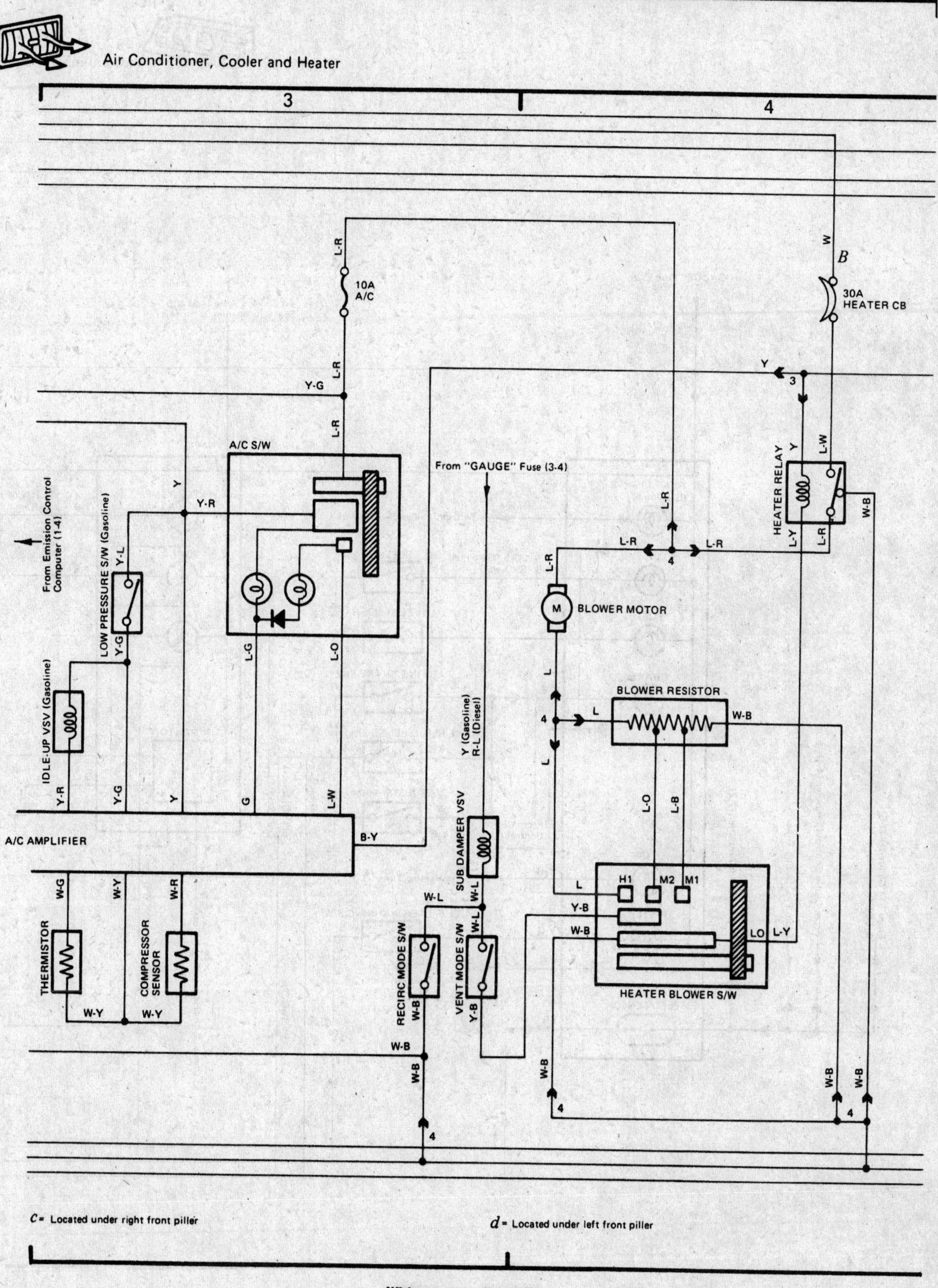

C = Located under right front piller

d = Located under left front piller

Wiring diagram—1985

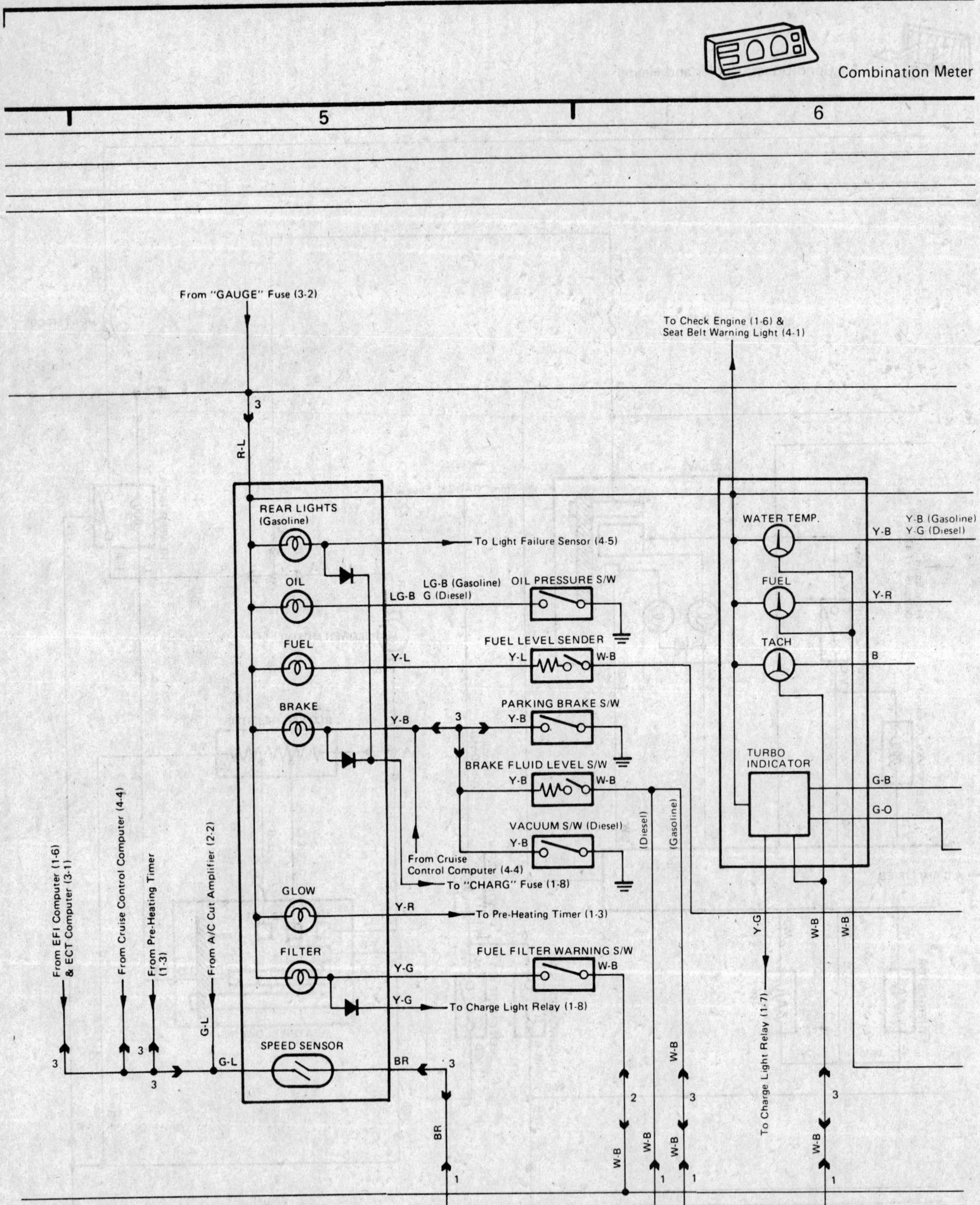

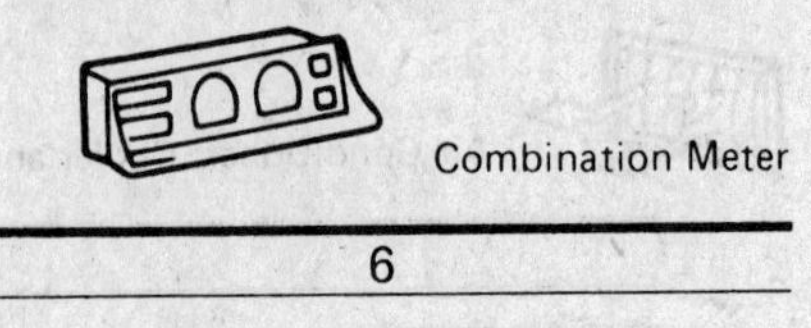

Combination Meter

5

6

From "GAUGE" Fuse (3-2)

To Check Engine (1-6) &
Seat Belt Warning Light (4-1)

3

R-L

REAR LIGHTS
(Gasoline)

To Light Failure Sensor (4-5)

OIL

LG-B

LG-B (Gasoline)
G (Diesel)

OIL PRESSURE S/W

FUEL

Y-L

FUEL LEVEL SENDER

Y-L

W-B

BRAKE

Y-B

3

PARKING BRAKE S/W

Y-B

BRAKE FLUID LEVEL S/W

Y-B

W-B

VACUUM S/W (Diesel)

Y-B

From Cruise
Control Computer (4-4)

To "CHARG" Fuse (1-8)

(Diesel)

(Gasoline)

GLOW

Y-R

To Pre-Heating Timer (1-3)

FILTER

Y-G

FUEL FILTER WARNING S/W

W-B

Y-G

To Charge Light Relay (1-8)

SPEED SENSOR

G-L

BR

3

BR

From EFI Computer (1-6)
& ECT Computer (3-1)

From Cruise Control Computer (4-4)

From Pre-Heating Timer
(1-3)

From A/C Cut Amplifier (2-2)

G-L

3

3

3

2

3

W-B

W-B

W-B

W-B

1

1

1

WATER TEMP.

Y-B

Y-B (Gasoline)
Y-G (Diesel)

FUEL

Y-R

TACH

B

TURBO
INDICATOR

G-B

G-O

Y-G

W-B

W-B

To Charge Light Relay (1-7)

3

W-B

1

Wiring diagram—1985

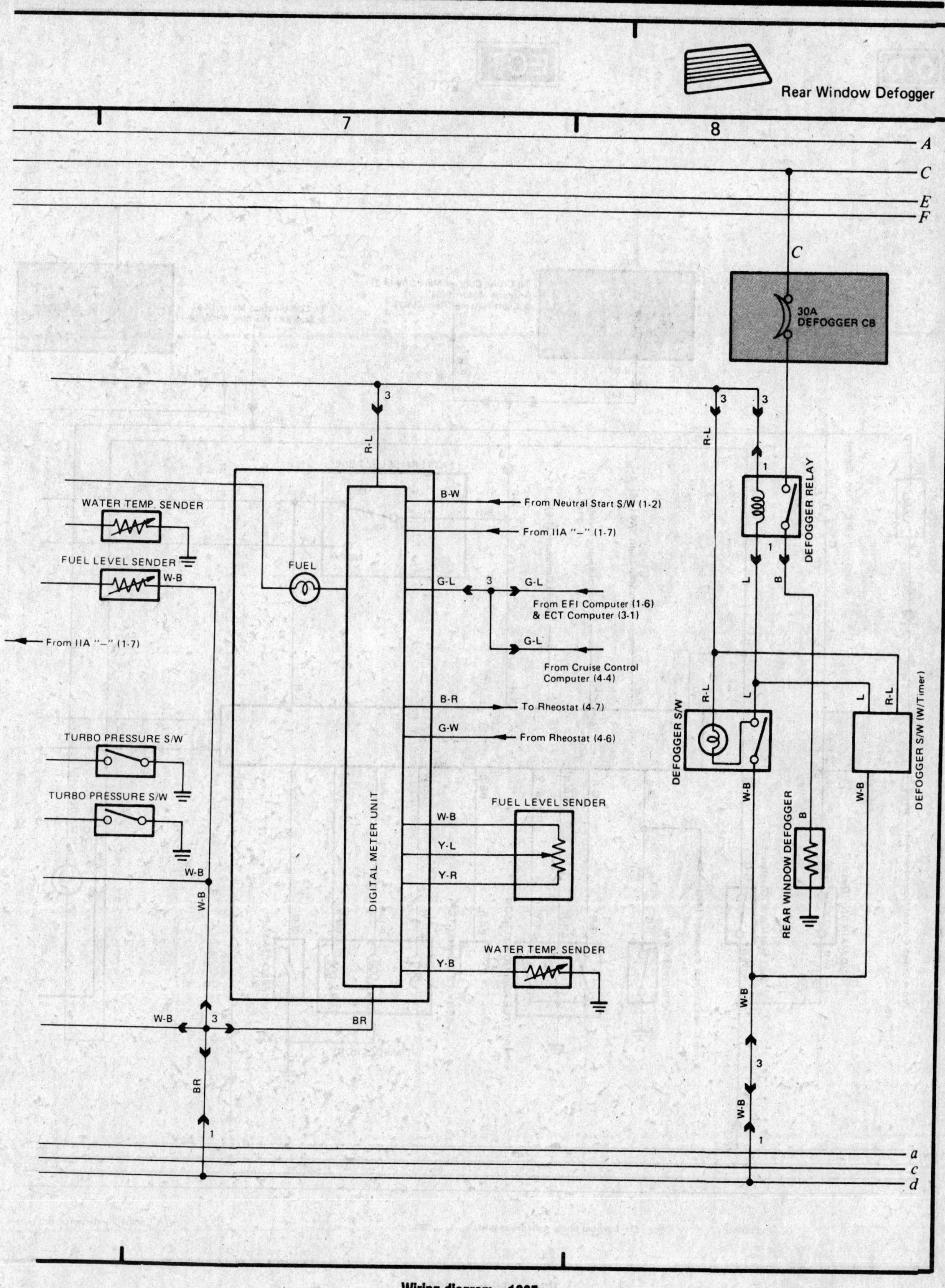

Rear Window Defogger
7
8
A
C
E
F
30A DEFOGGER CB
DEFOGGER RELAY
WATER TEMP. SENDER
FUEL LEVEL SENDER
FUEL
From Neutral Start S/W (1-2)
From IIA "–" (1-7)
From EFI Computer (1-6) & ECT Computer (3-1)
From Cruise Control Computer (4-4)
To Rheostat (4-7)
From Rheostat (4-6)
From IIA "–" (1-7)
TURBO PRESSURE S/W
TURBO PRESSURE S/W
DIGITAL METER UNIT
FUEL LEVEL SENDER
WATER TEMP. SENDER
DEFOGGER S/W
DEFOGGER S/W (W/Timer)
REAR WINDOW DEFOGGER
a
c
d

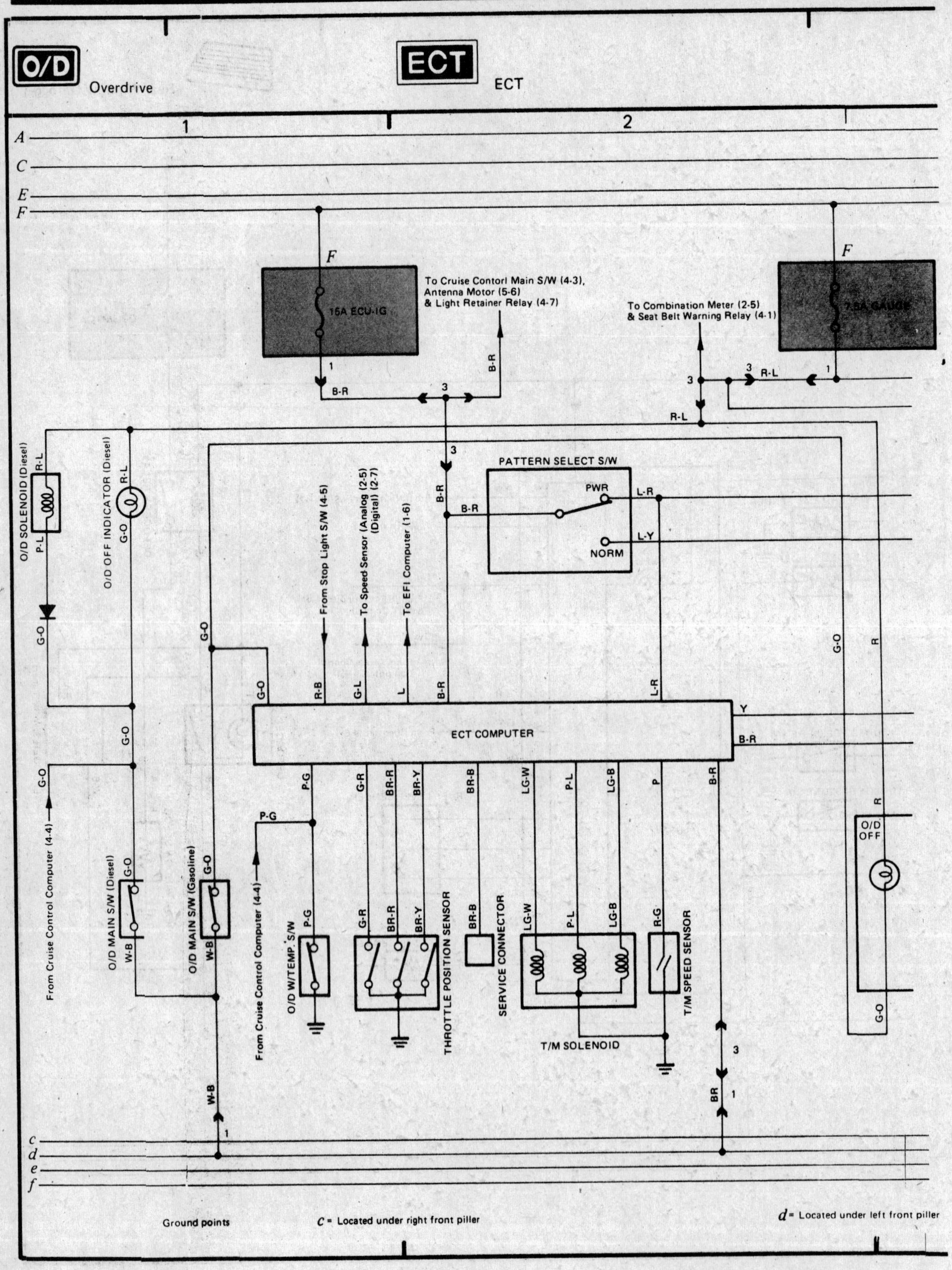

Wiring diagram—1985

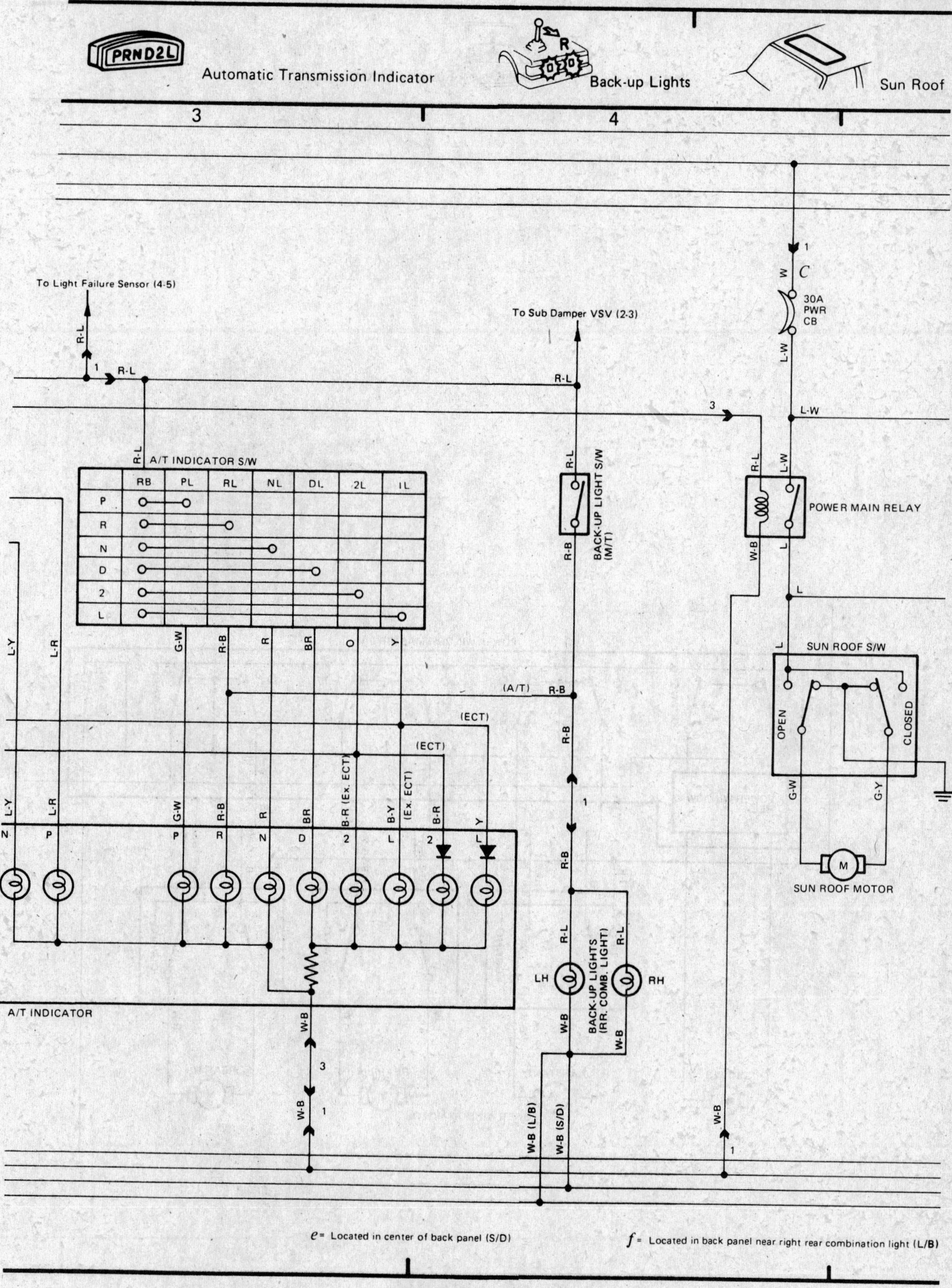

e = Located in center of back panel (S/D)

f = Located in back panel near right rear combination light (L/B)

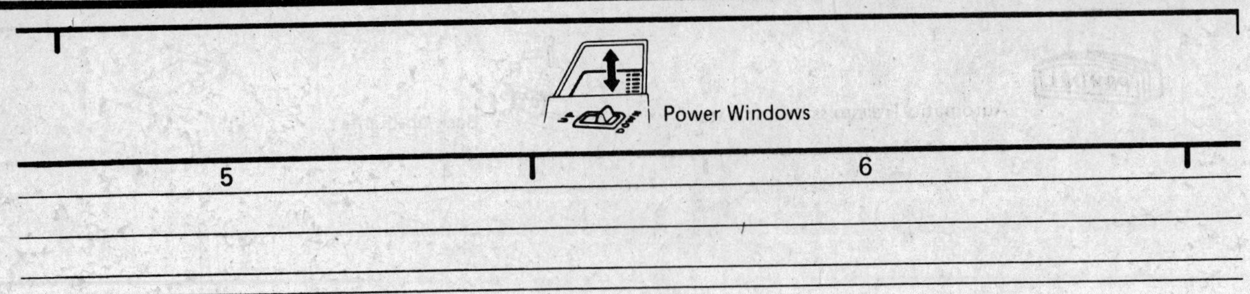

POWER WINDOW MASTER S/W
L
L
UP
DOWN
UP
DOWN
UP
DOWN
UP
DOWN
LOCK S/W
POWER WINDOW RELAY
G
R
G-Y
R-Y
G-B
R-B
G-L
R-L
G-R
G
R
G-Y
G-B
G-Y
R-B
G-R
G-B
G-Y
R-Y
R-B
UP
DOWN
UP
DOWN
UP
DOWN
G-L
R-L
G-Y
R-Y
G-W
R-W
G-W
R-W
DRIVER
ASSISTANT
REAR LH
REAR RH
M
M
M
M
POWER WINDOW MOTOR
1

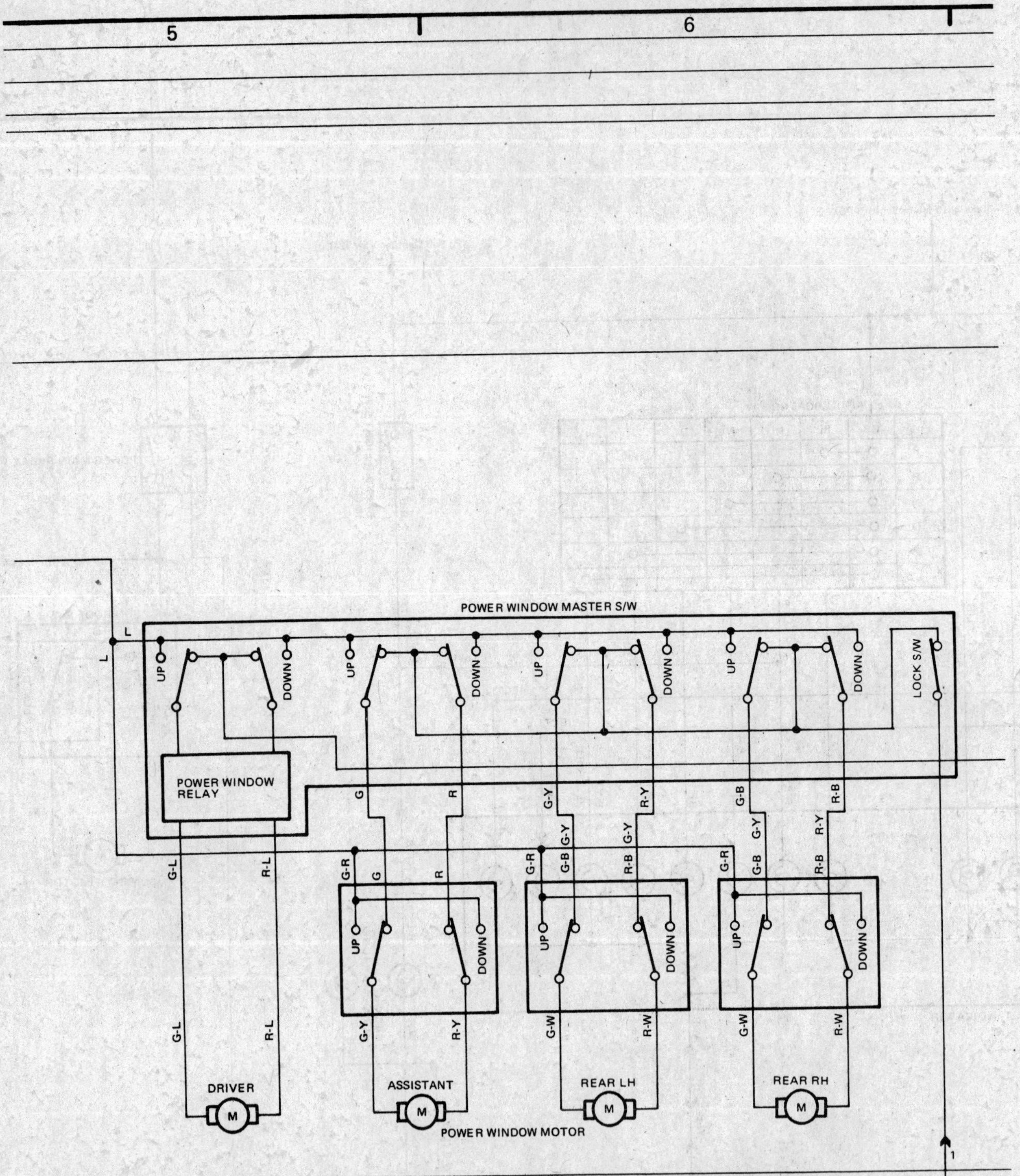

Wiring diagram—1985

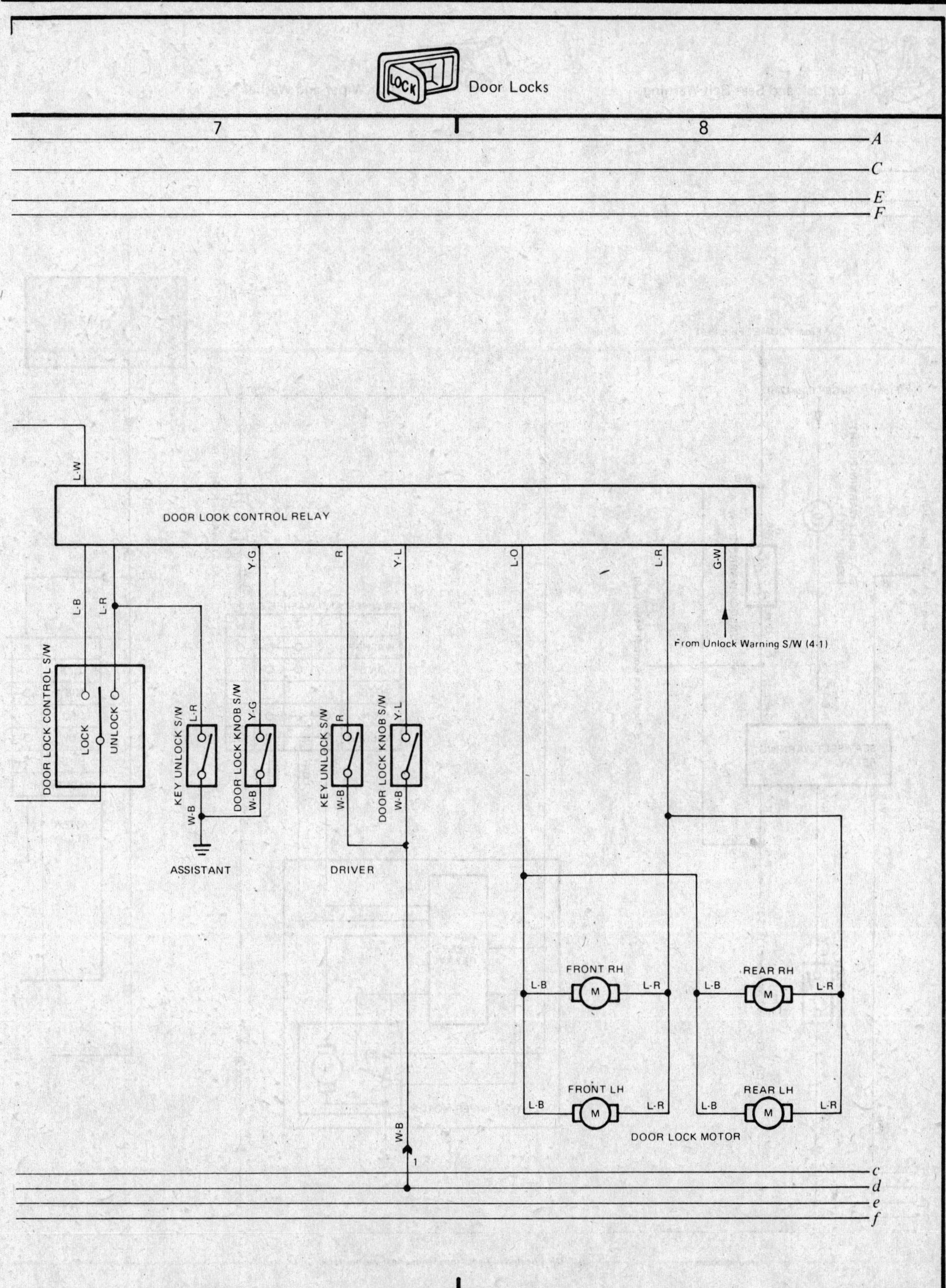

Wiring diagram—1985

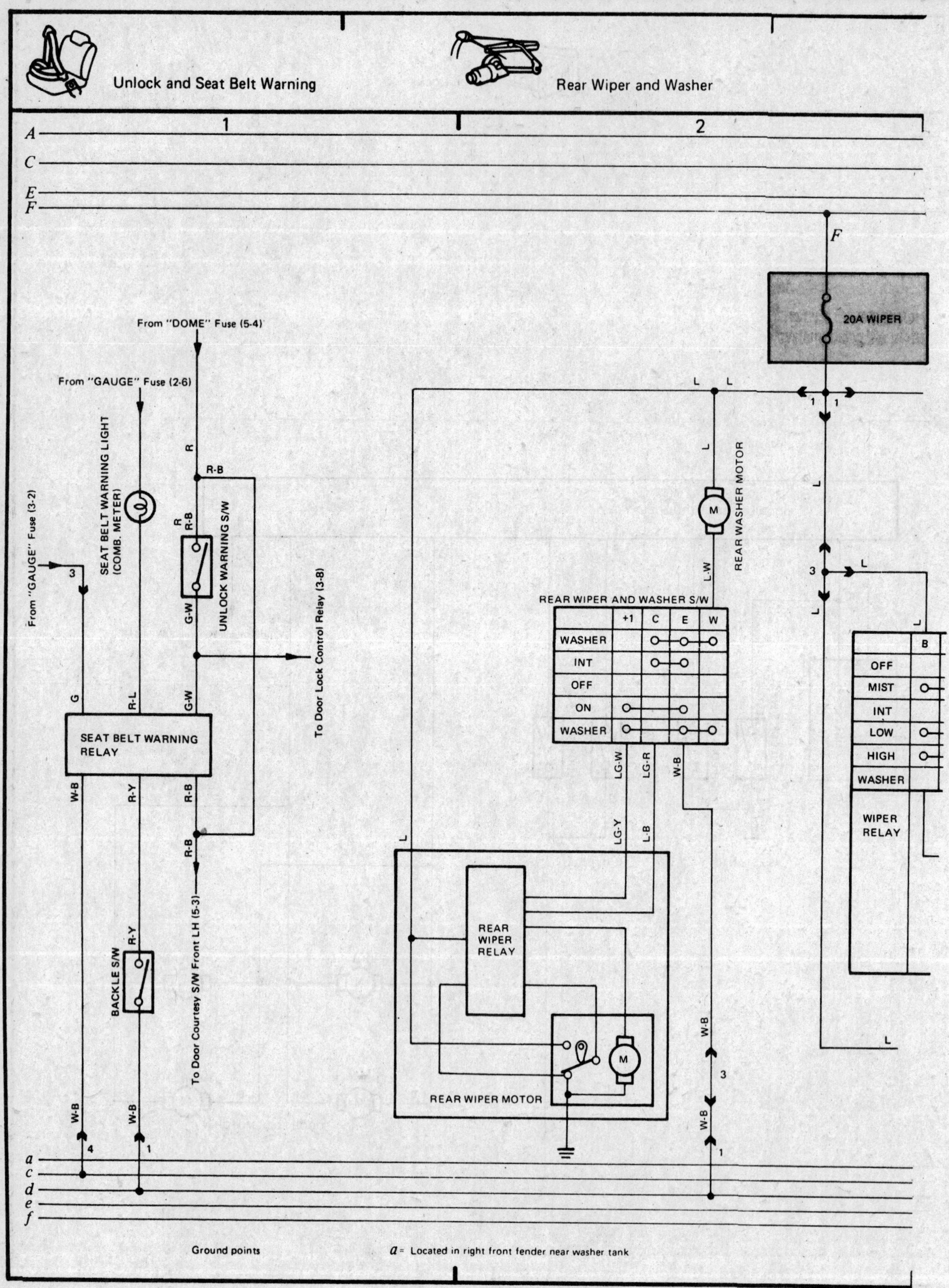

Wiring diagram—1985

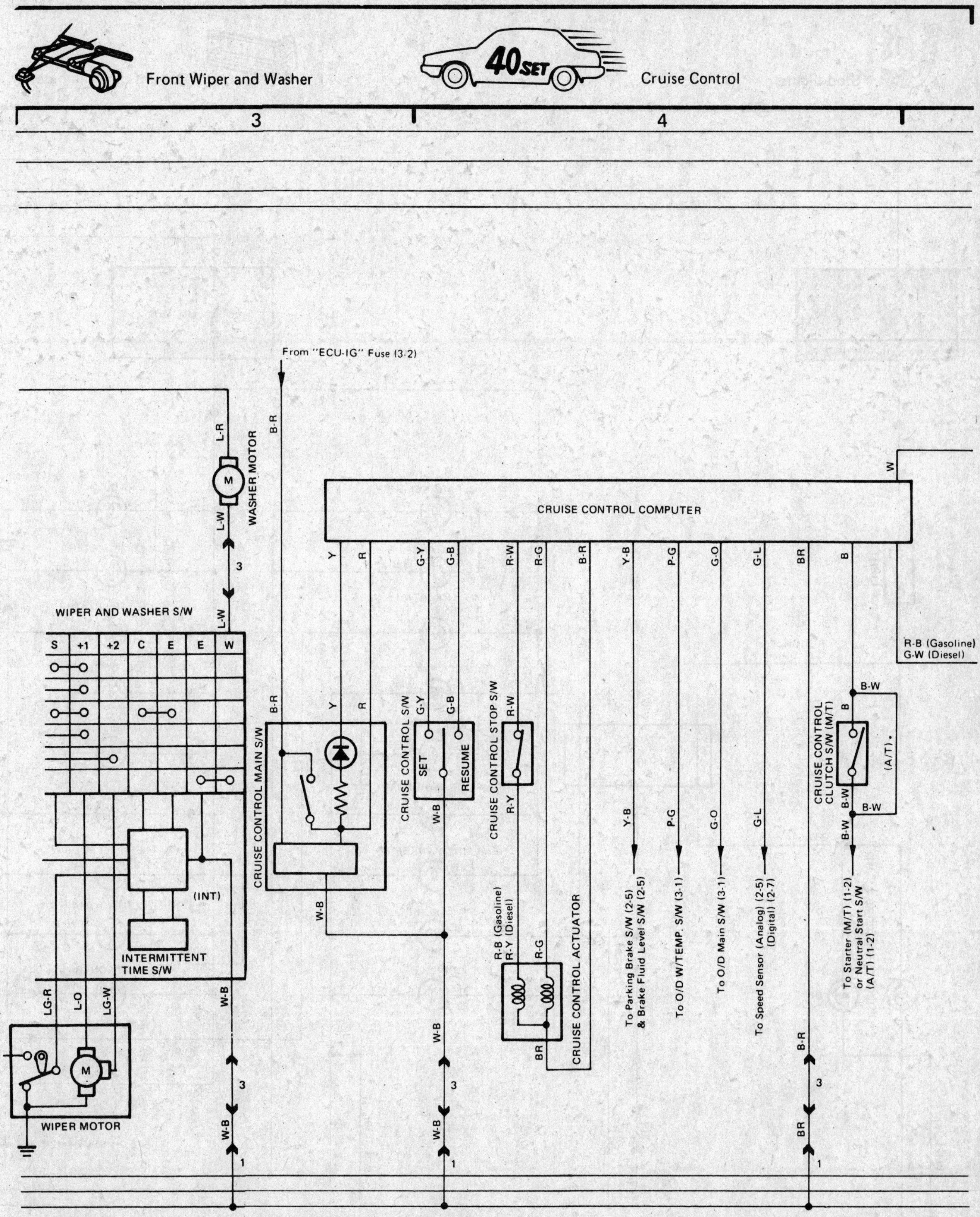

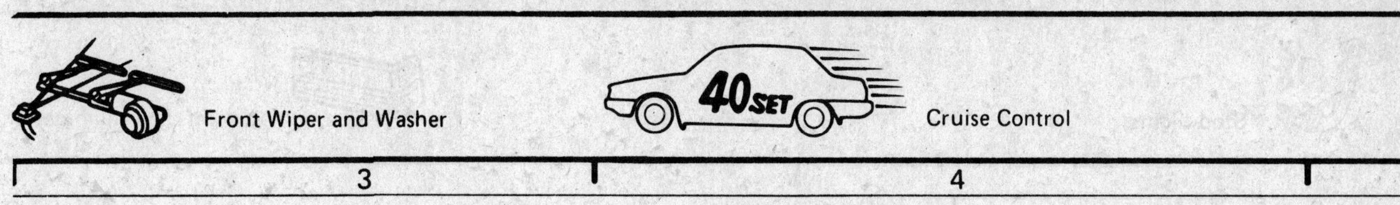

3

4

From "ECU-IG" Fuse (3-2)

B-R

L-R

WASHER MOTOR

L-W

3

WIPER AND WASHER S/W

S	+1	+2	C	E	E	W

(INT)

INTERMITTENT TIME S/W

LG-R LG-O LG-W

W-B

WIPER MOTOR

CRUISE CONTROL COMPUTER

W

Y R G-Y G-B R-W R-G B-R Y-B P-G G-O G-L BR B

R-B (Gasoline)
G-W (Diesel)

CRUISE CONTROL MAIN S/W

CRUISE CONTROL S/W

SET

RESUME

CRUISE CONTROL STOP S/W

R-Y

R-B (Gasoline)
R-Y (Diesel)

CRUISE CONTROL ACTUATOR

To Parking Brake S/W (2-5) & Brake Fluid Level S/W (2-5)

To O/D W/TEMP. S/W (3-1)

To O/D Main S/W (3-1)

To Speed Sensor (Analog) (2-5) (Digital) (2-7)

CRUISE CONTROL CLUTCH S/W (M/T)

B-W

(A/T)

To Starter (M/T) (1-2) or Neutral Start S/W (A/T) (1-2)

c = Located under right front piller

d = Located under left front piller

e = Located in center of back panel (S/D)

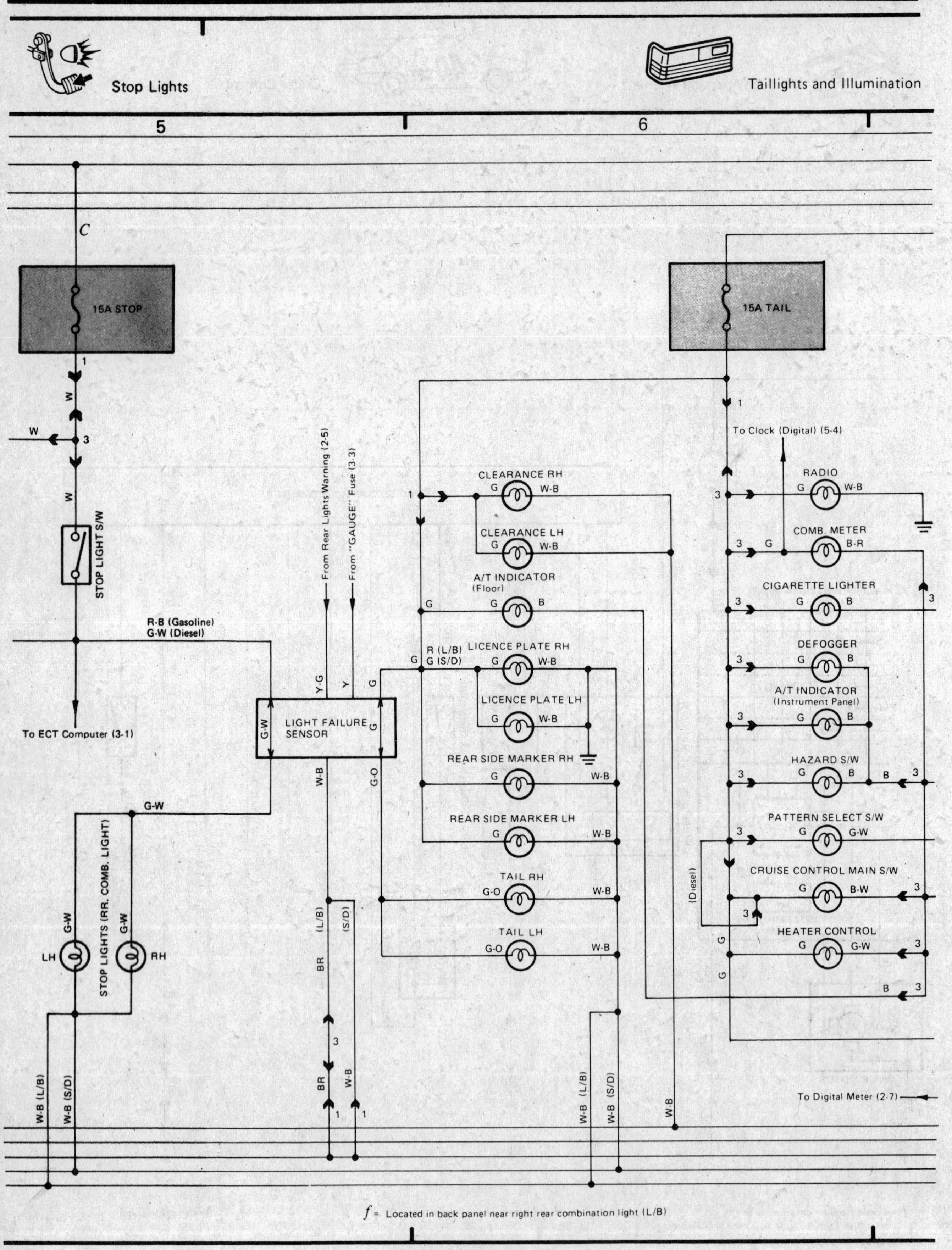

f = Located in back panel near right rear combination light (L/B)

Wiring diagram—1985

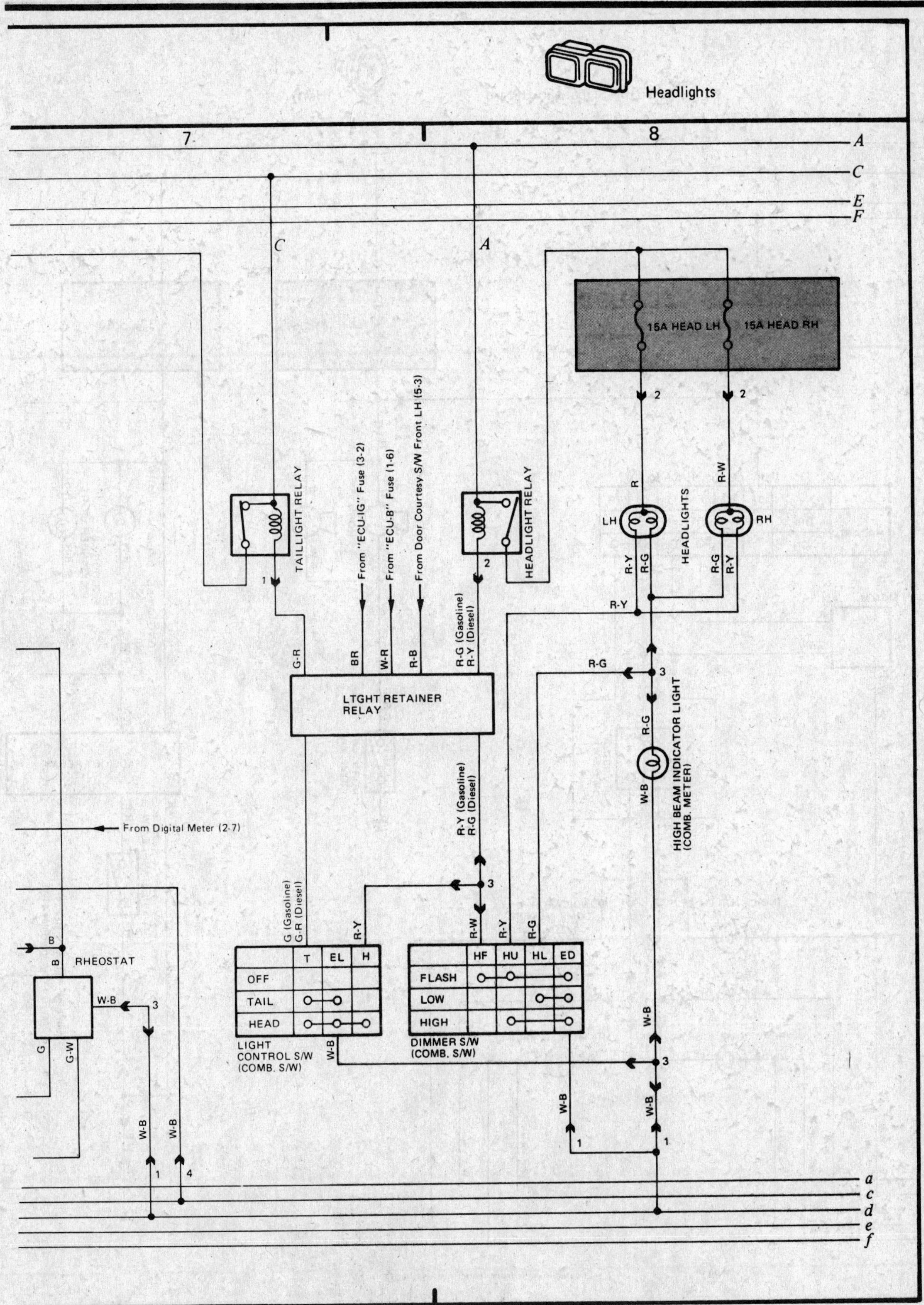

Wiring diagram—1985

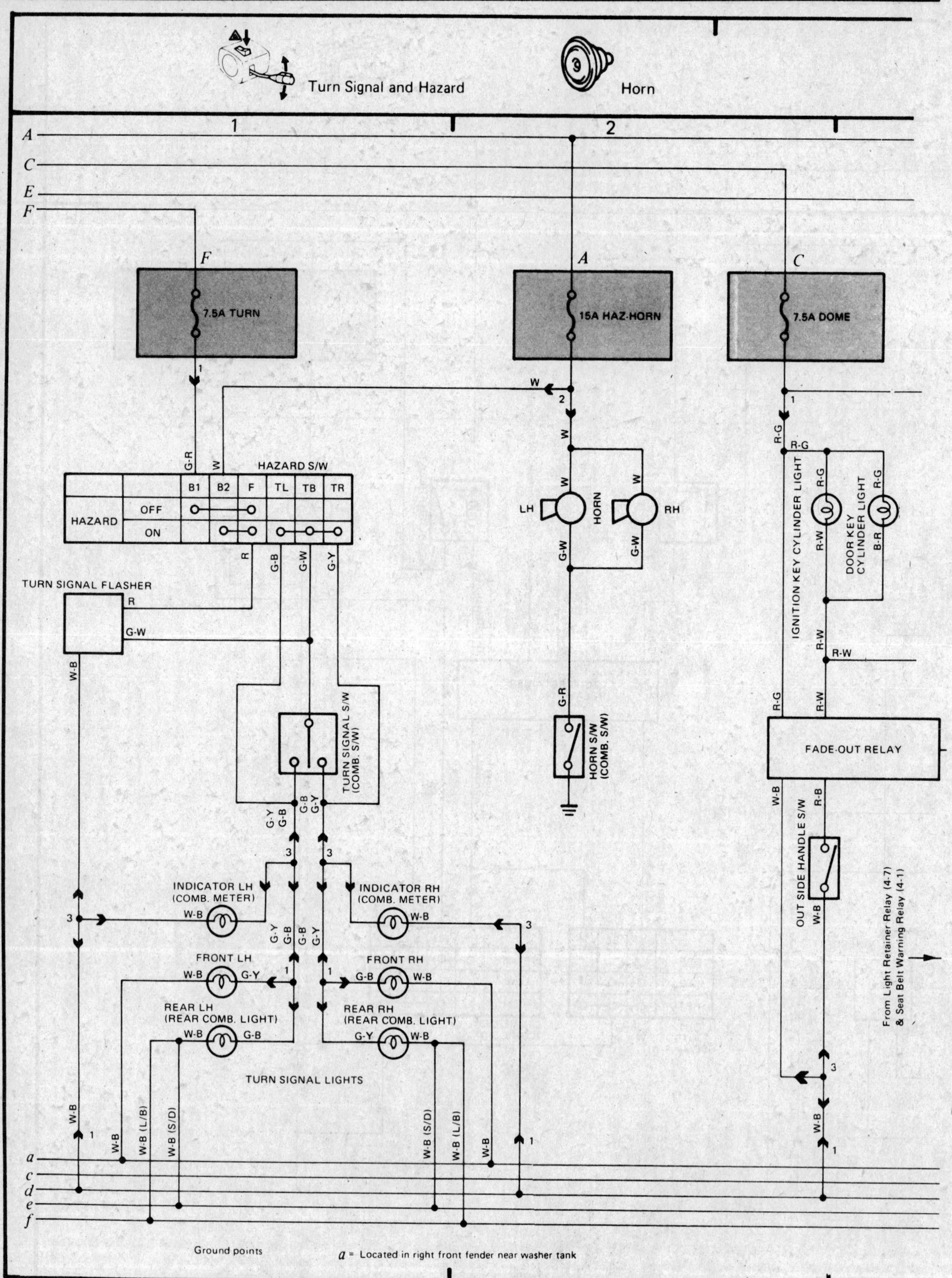

Wiring diagram—1985

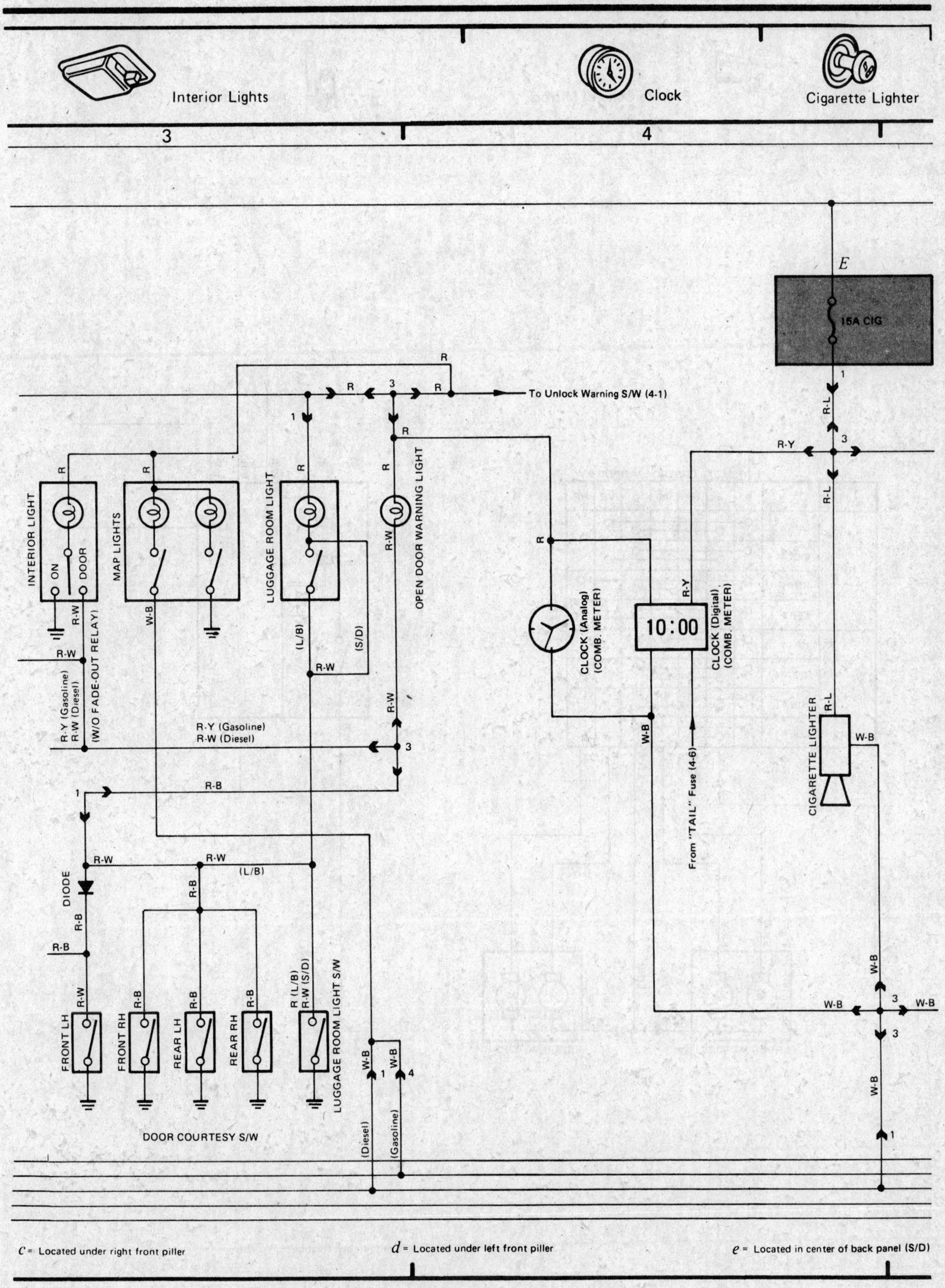

c = Located under right front piller

d = Located under left front piller

e = Located in center of back panel (S/D)

Wiring diagram—1985

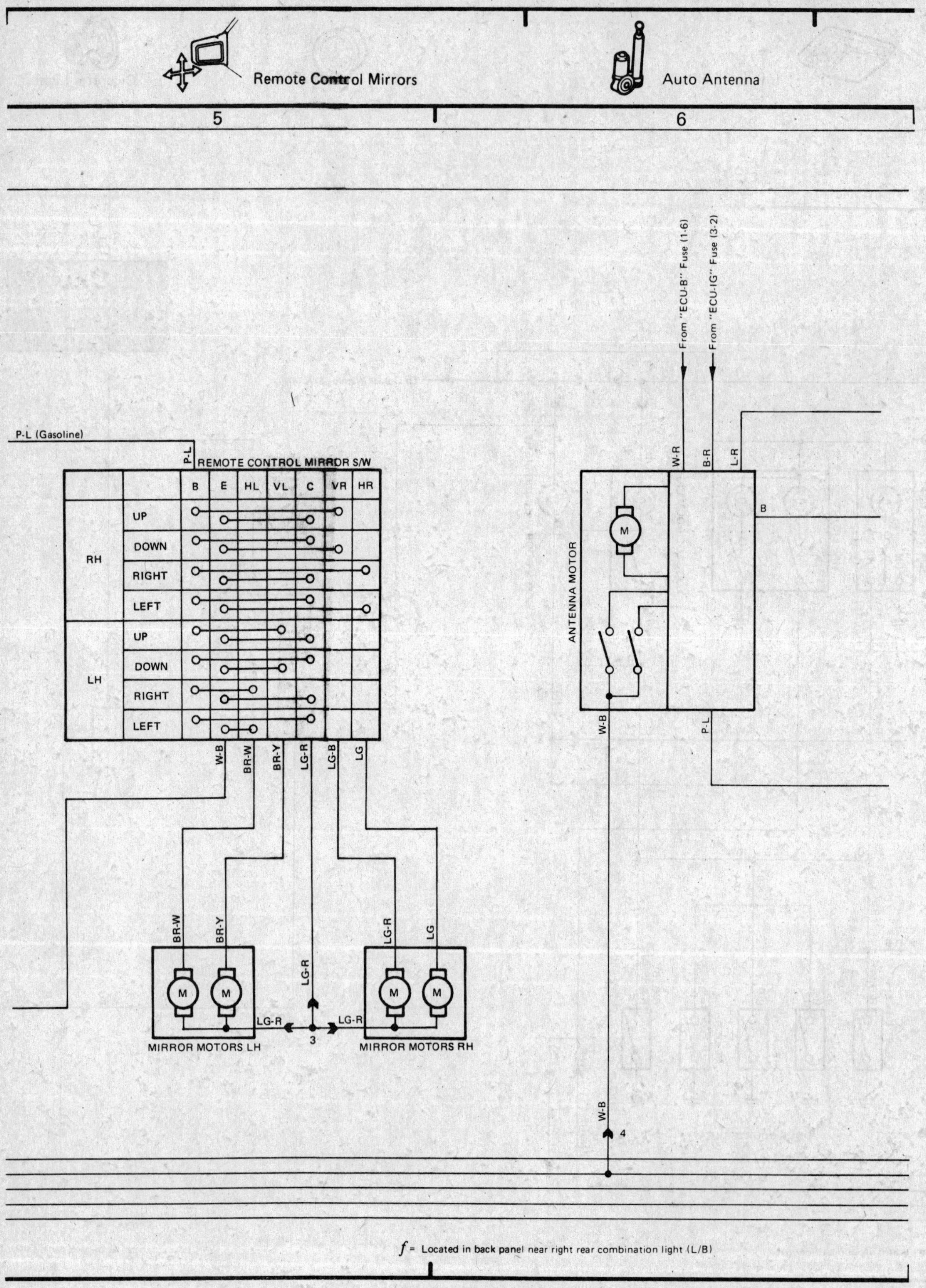

f = Located in back panel near right rear combination light (L/B)

Wiring diagram—1985

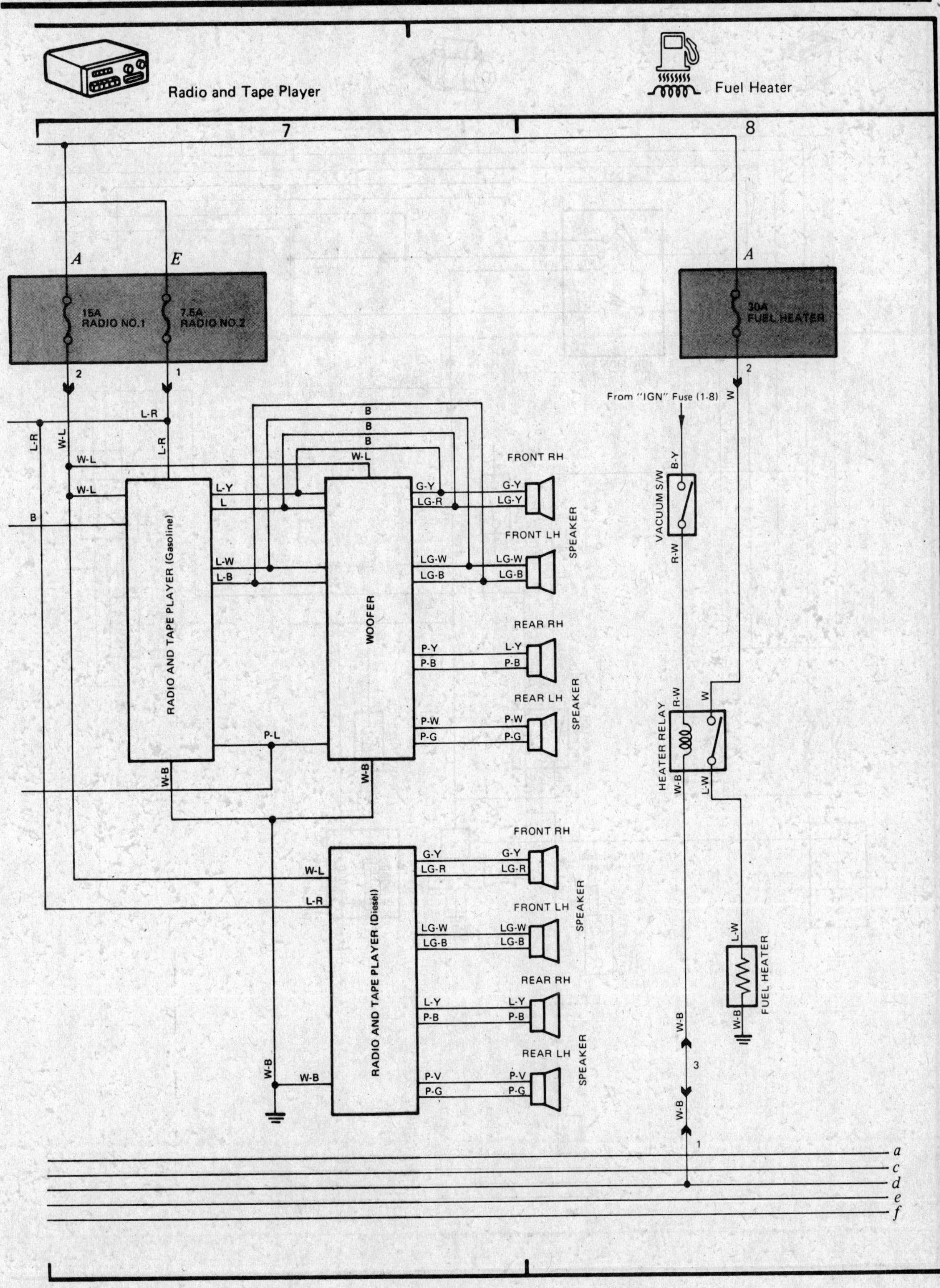

Wiring diagram—1985

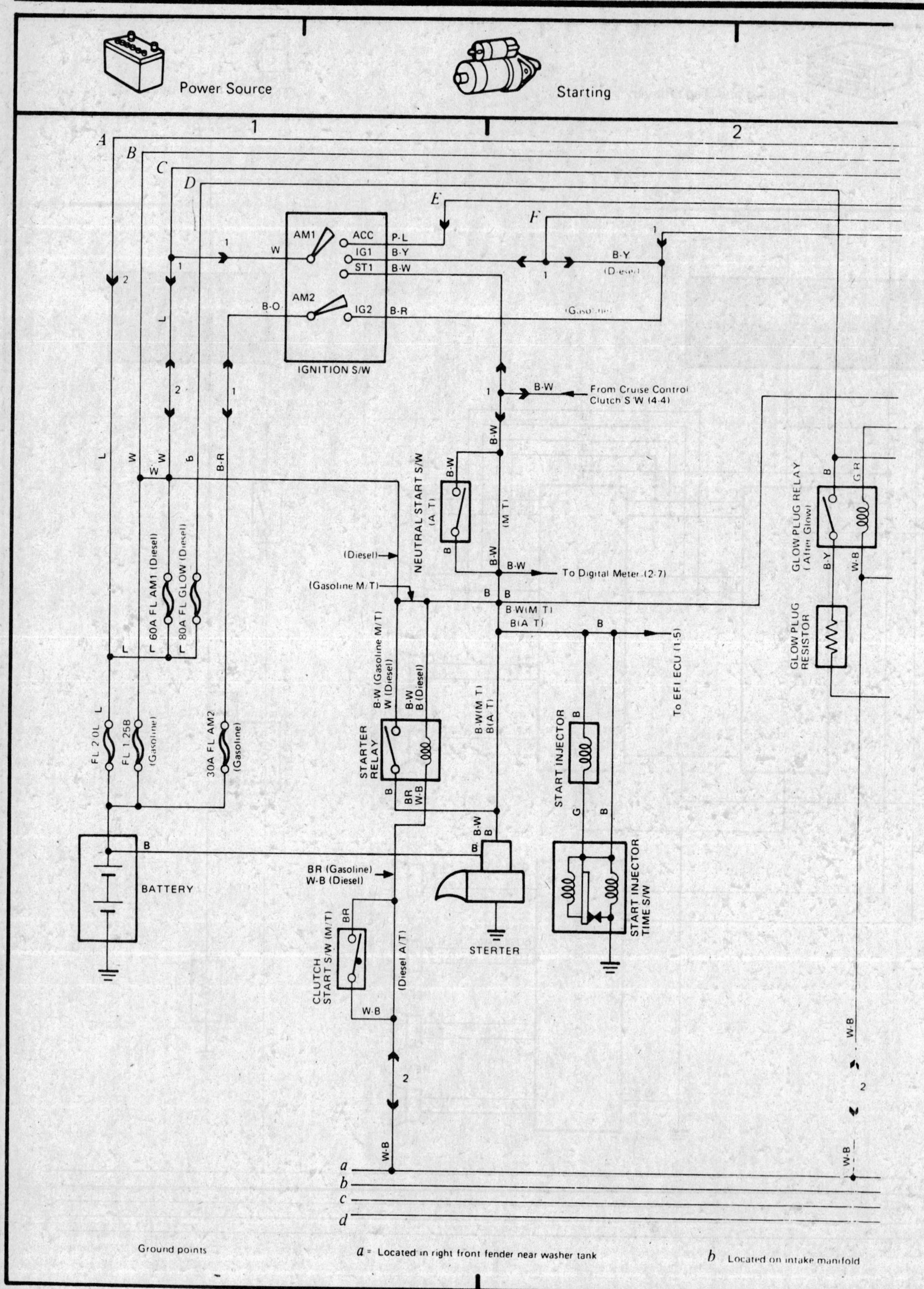

Wiring diagram—1986

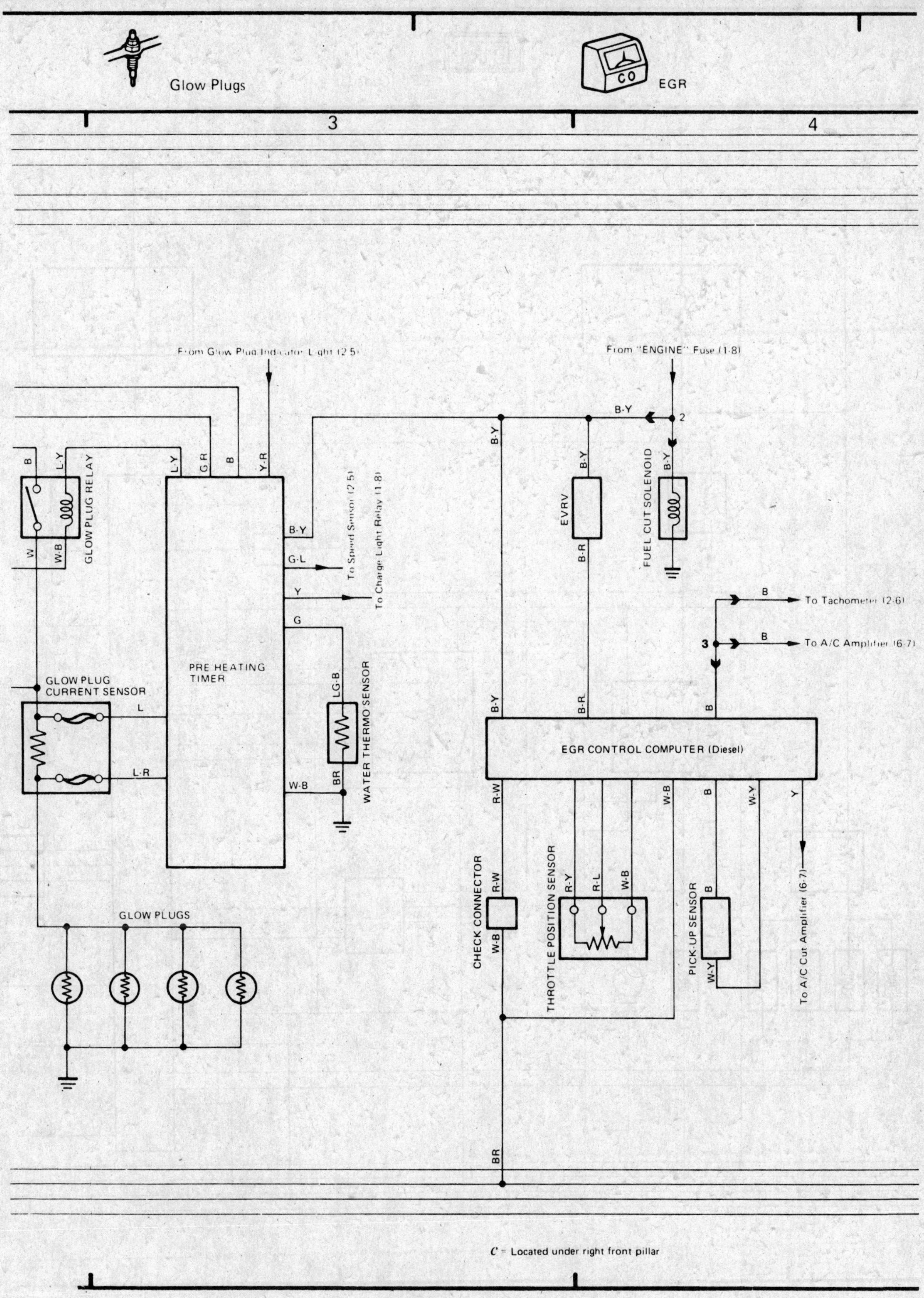

From Glow Plug Indicator Light (2·5)
From "ENGINE" Fuse (1·8)
B·Y
2
B
L·Y
GLOW PLUG RELAY
W
W·B
L·Y
G·R
B
Y·R
B·Y
G·L
To Speed Sensor (2·5)
Y
To Charge Light Relay (1·8)
G
PRE HEATING TIMER
LG·B
WATER THERMO SENSOR
BR
W·B
GLOW PLUG CURRENT SENSOR
L
L·R
GLOW PLUGS
B·Y
EVRV
B·R
FUEL CUT SOLENOID
B
To Tachometer (2·6)
3
To A/C Amplifier (6·7)
EGR CONTROL COMPUTER (Diesel)
R·W
W·B
W·Y
Y
CHECK CONNECTOR
THROTTLE POSITION SENSOR
R·Y
R·L
PICK-UP SENSOR
To A/C Cut Amplifier (6·7)
BR

C = Located under right front pillar

Wiring diagram—1986

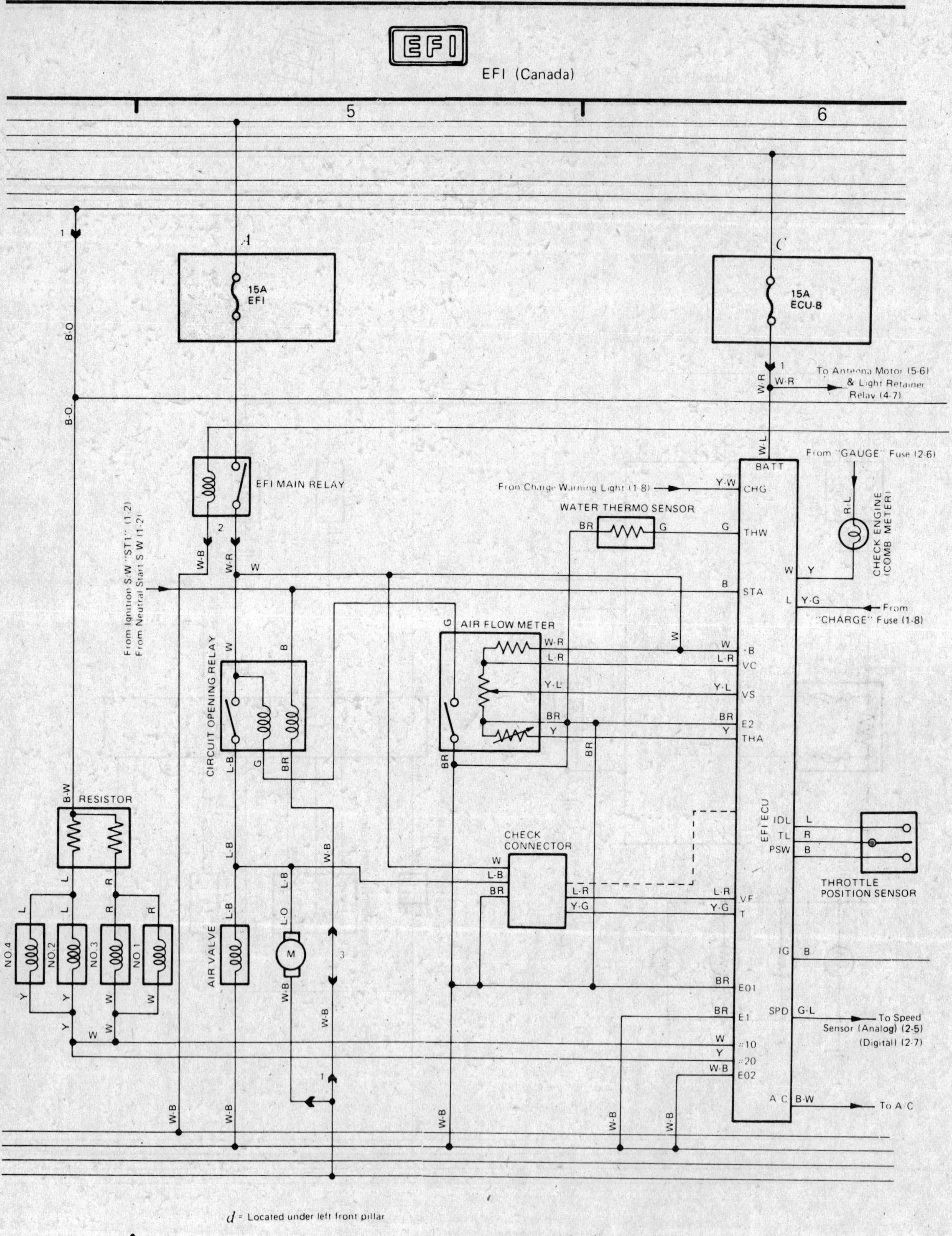

d = Located under left front pillar

Wiring diagram—1986

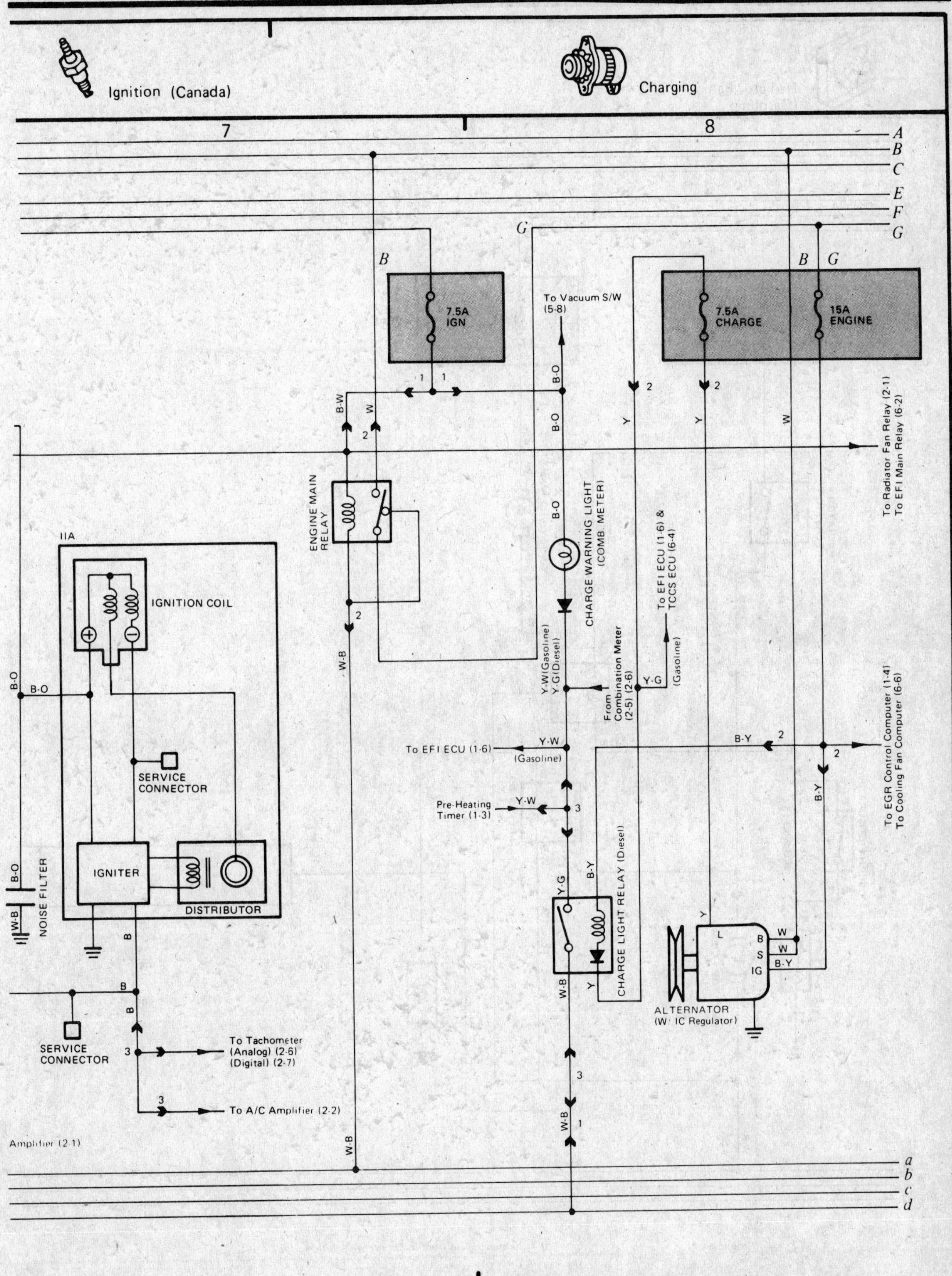

Wiring diagram—1986

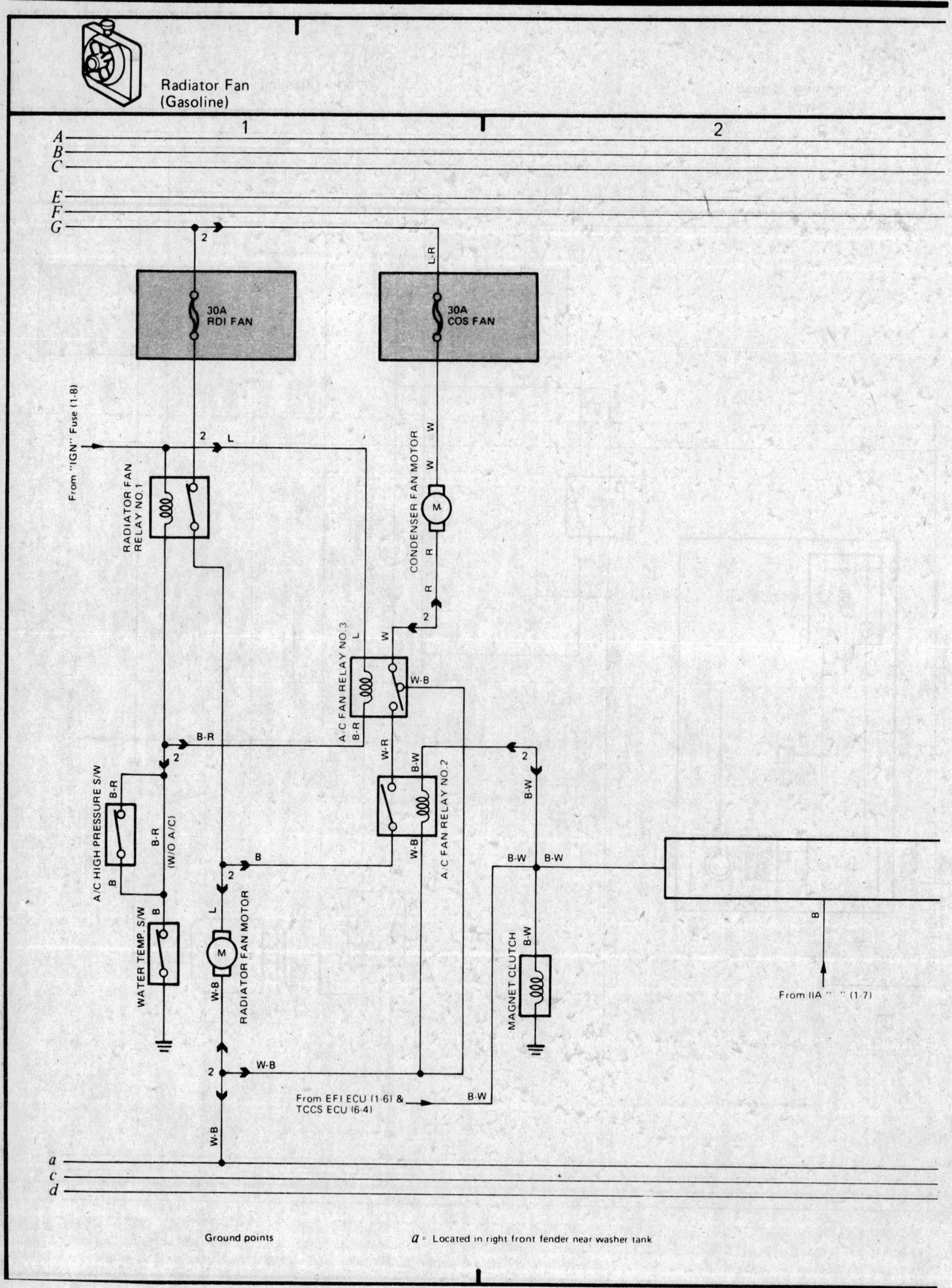

Wiring diagram—1986

Air Conditioner, Cooler and Heater (Gasoline)

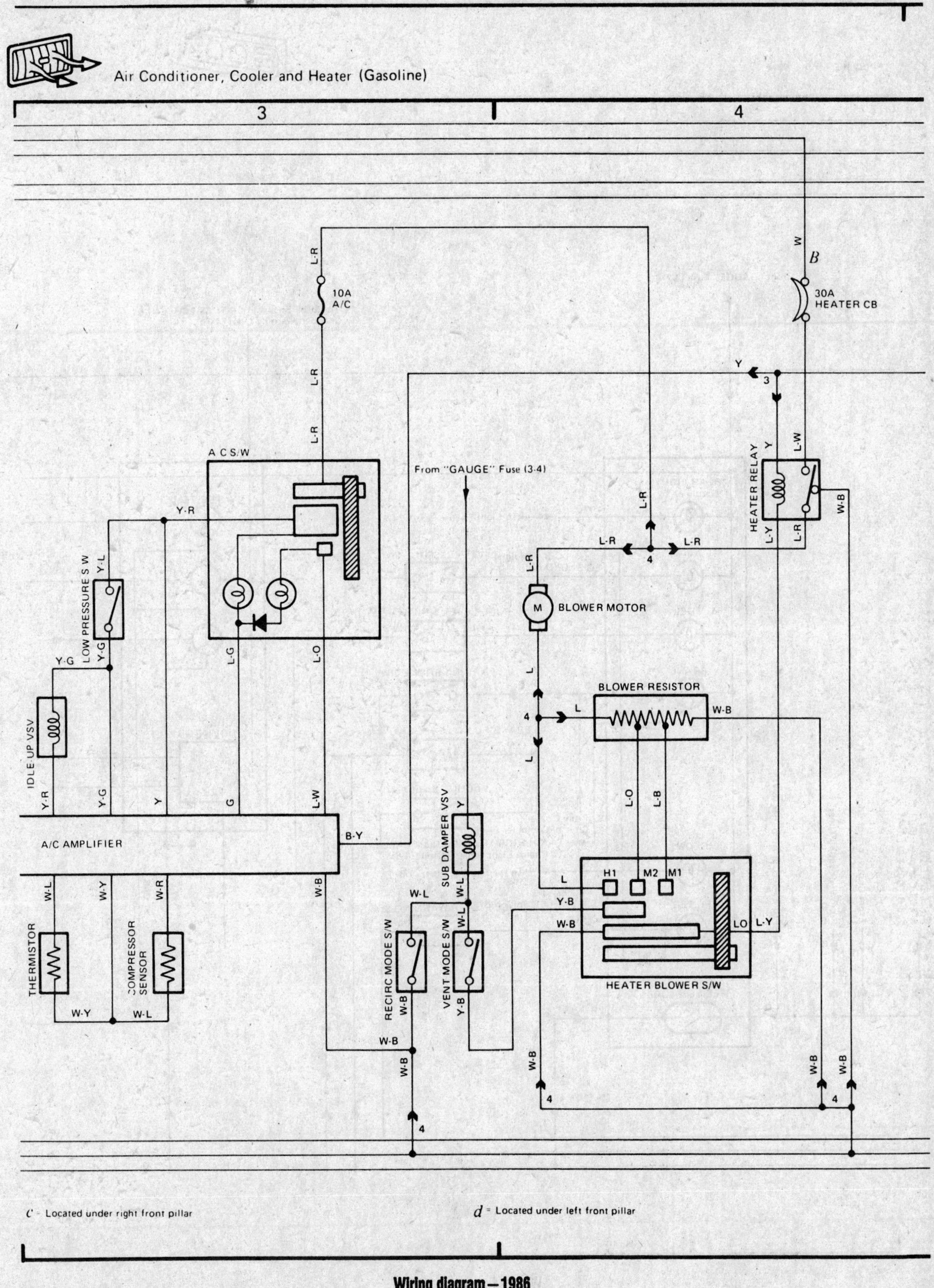

C - Located under right front pillar

d = Located under left front pillar

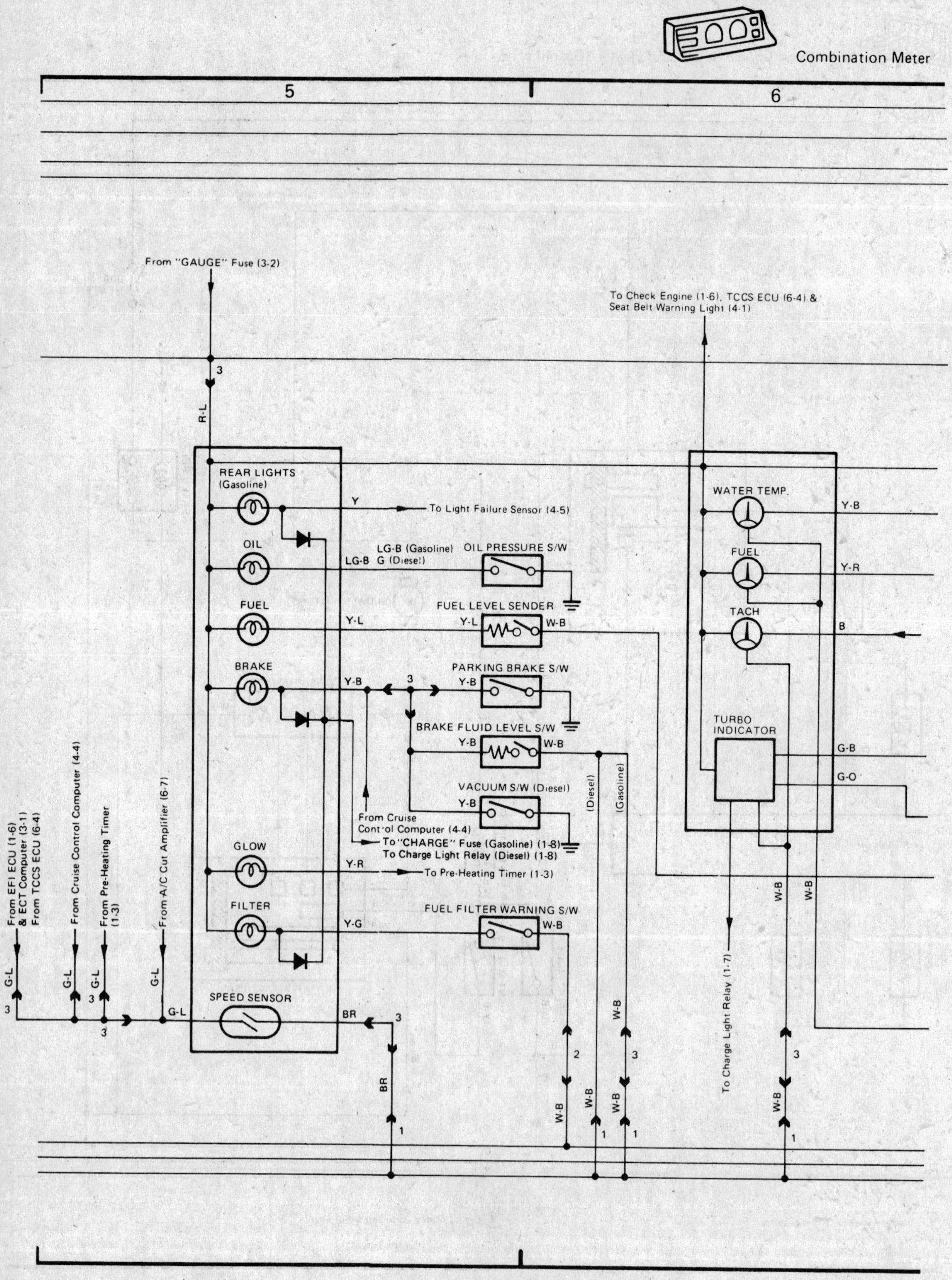

Combination Meter

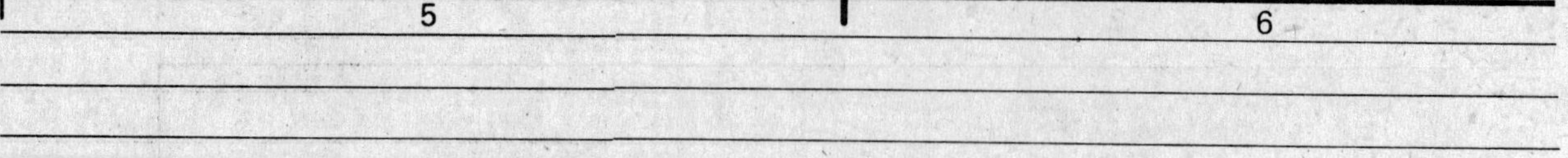
5
6
From "GAUGE" Fuse (3-2)
To Check Engine (1-6), TCCS ECU (6-4) &
Seat Belt Warning Light (4-1)
R-L
REAR LIGHTS
(Gasoline)
Y
To Light Failure Sensor (4-5)
OIL
LG-B
LG-B (Gasoline)
G (Diesel)
OIL PRESSURE S/W
FUEL
Y-L
FUEL LEVEL SENDER
W-B
BRAKE
Y-B
PARKING BRAKE S/W
BRAKE FLUID LEVEL S/W
VACUUM S/W (Diesel)
From Cruise
Control Computer (4-4)
To "CHARGE" Fuse (Gasoline) (1-8)
To Charge Light Relay (Diesel) (1-8)
GLOW
Y-R
To Pre-Heating Timer (1-3)
FILTER
Y-G
FUEL FILTER WARNING S/W
SPEED SENSOR
BR
G-L
From EFI ECU (1-6)
& ECT Computer (3-1)
From TCCS ECU (6-4)
From Cruise Control Computer (4-4)
From Pre-Heating Timer
(1-3)
From A/C Cut Amplifier (6-7)
(Diesel)
(Gasoline)
WATER TEMP.
Y-B
FUEL
Y-R
TACH
B
TURBO
INDICATOR
G-B
G-O
To Charge Light Relay (1-7)

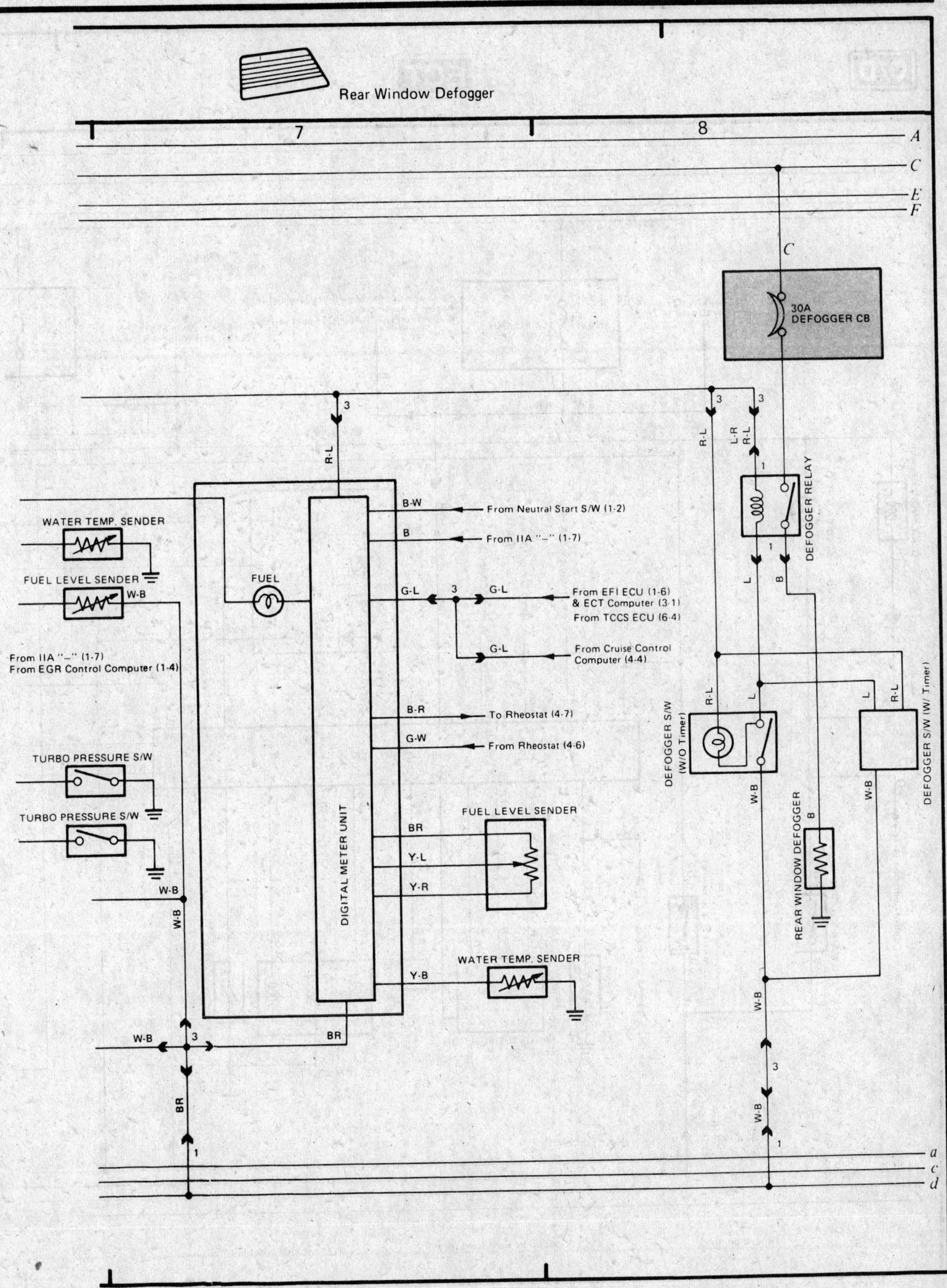

Wiring diagram—1986

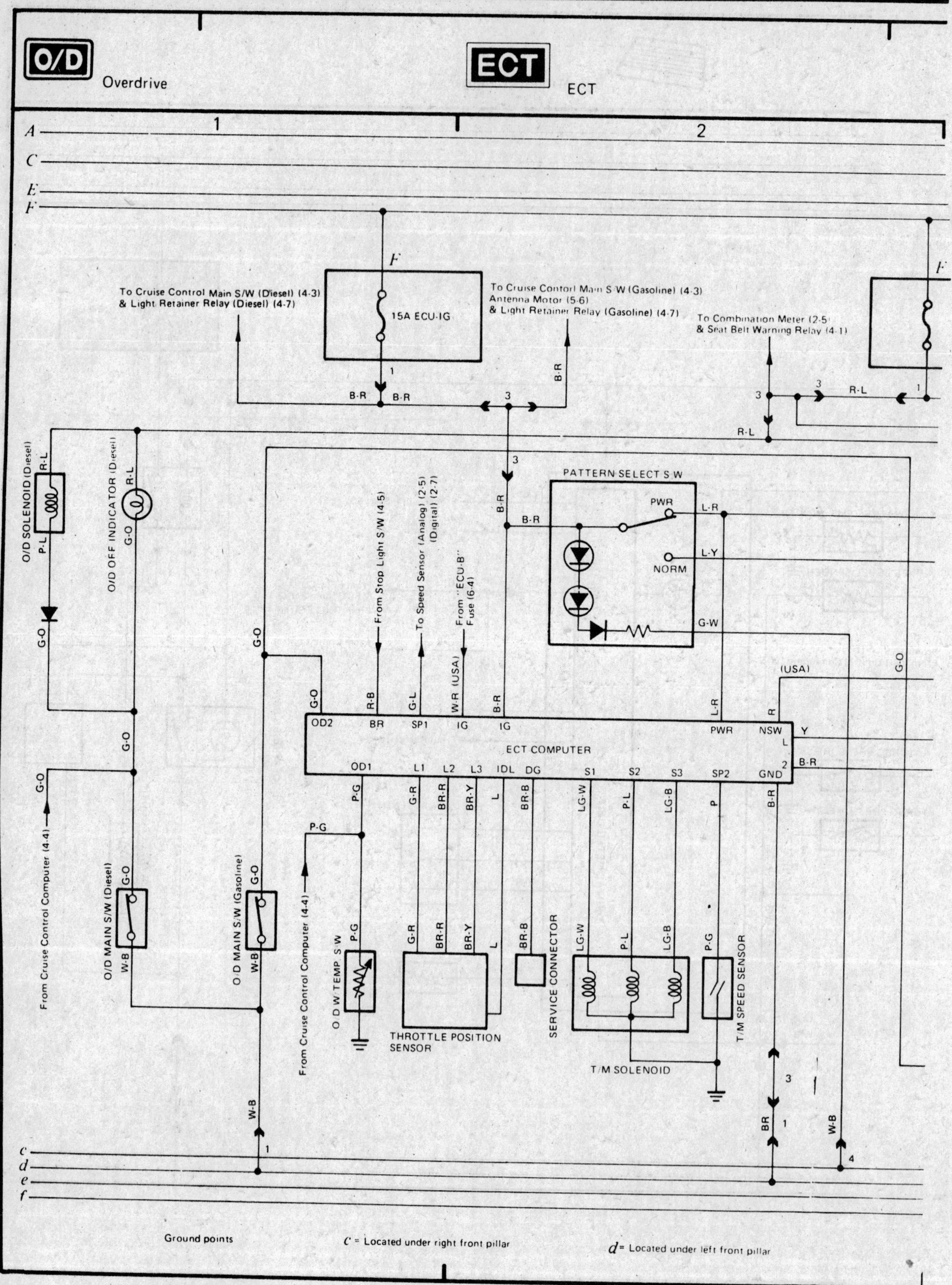

O/D
Overdrive
ECT
ECT
15A ECU-IG
To Cruise Control Main S/W (Diesel) (4-3) & Light Retainer Relay (Diesel) (4-7)
To Cruise Control Main S/W (Gasoline) (4-3) Antenna Motor (5-6) & Light Retainer Relay (Gasoline) (4-7)
To Combination Meter (2-5) & Seat Belt Warning Relay (4-1)
O/D SOLENOID (Diesel)
O/D OFF INDICATOR (Diesel)
PATTERN SELECT S/W
PWR
NORM
From Stop Light S/W (4-5)
To Speed Sensor (Analog) (2-5) (Digital) (2-7)
From "ECU-B" Fuse (6-4)
ECT COMPUTER
From Cruise Control Computer (4-4)
O/D MAIN S/W (Diesel)
O/D MAIN S/W (Gasoline)
O/D W/TEMP S/W
THROTTLE POSITION SENSOR
SERVICE CONNECTOR
T/M SOLENOID
T/M SPEED SENSOR
Ground points
c = Located under right front pillar
d = Located under left front pillar

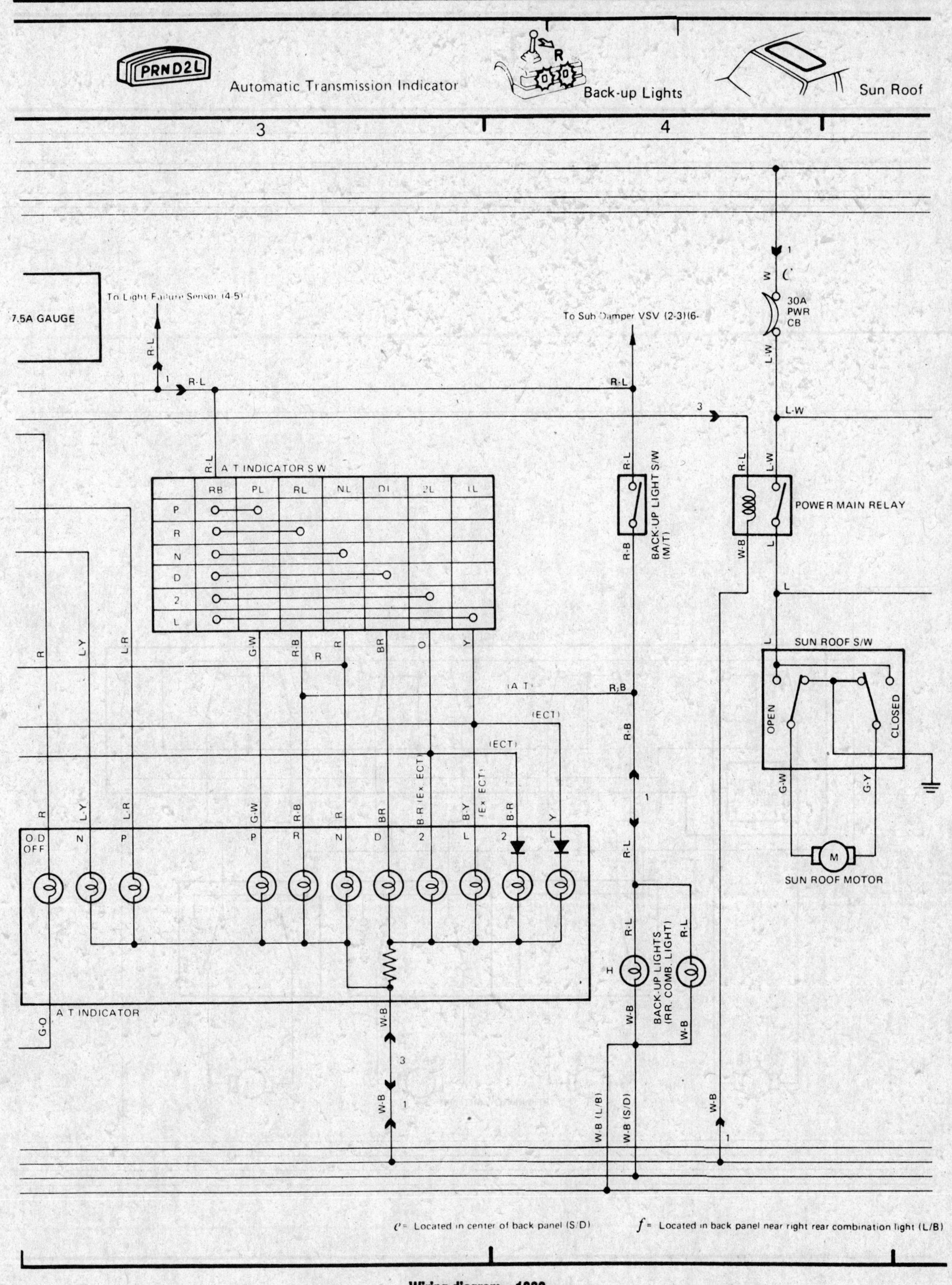

C = Located in center of back panel (S/D) *f* = Located in back panel near right rear combination light (L/B)

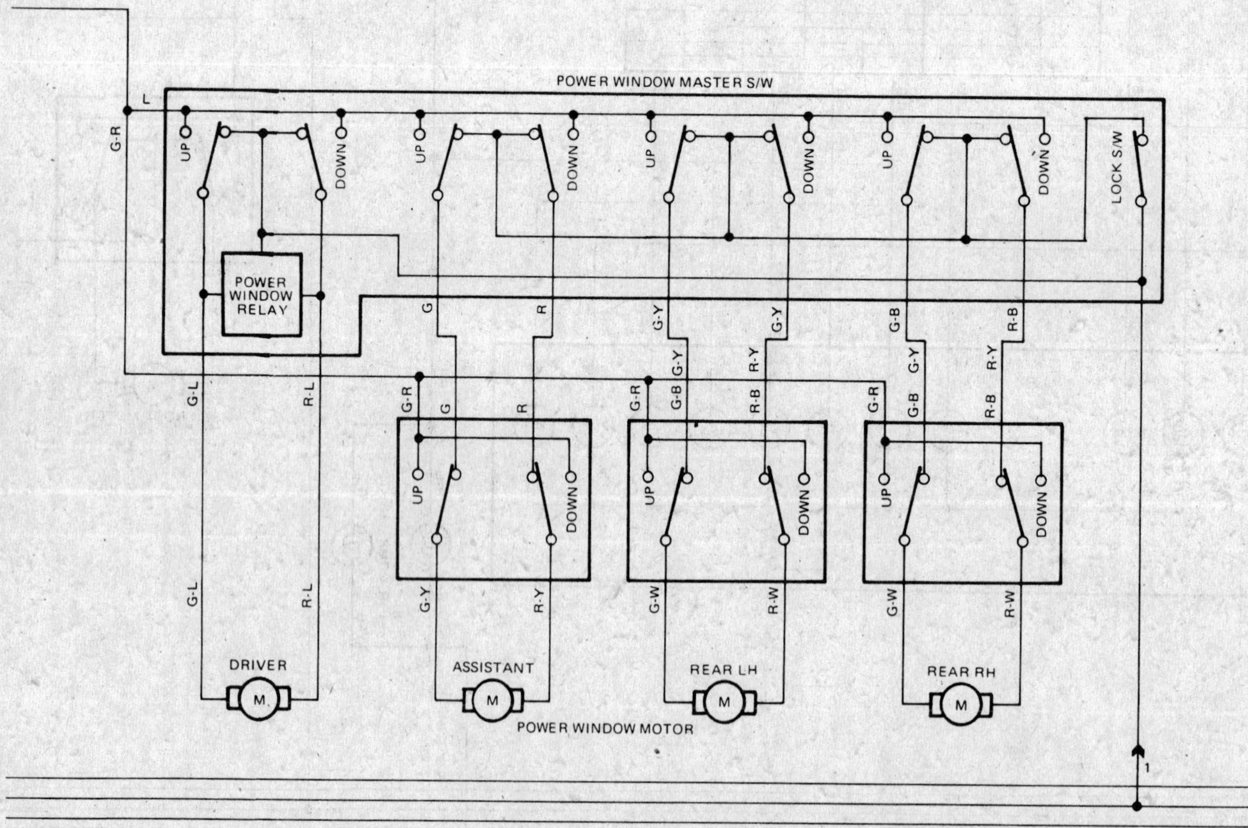

Wiring diagram—1986

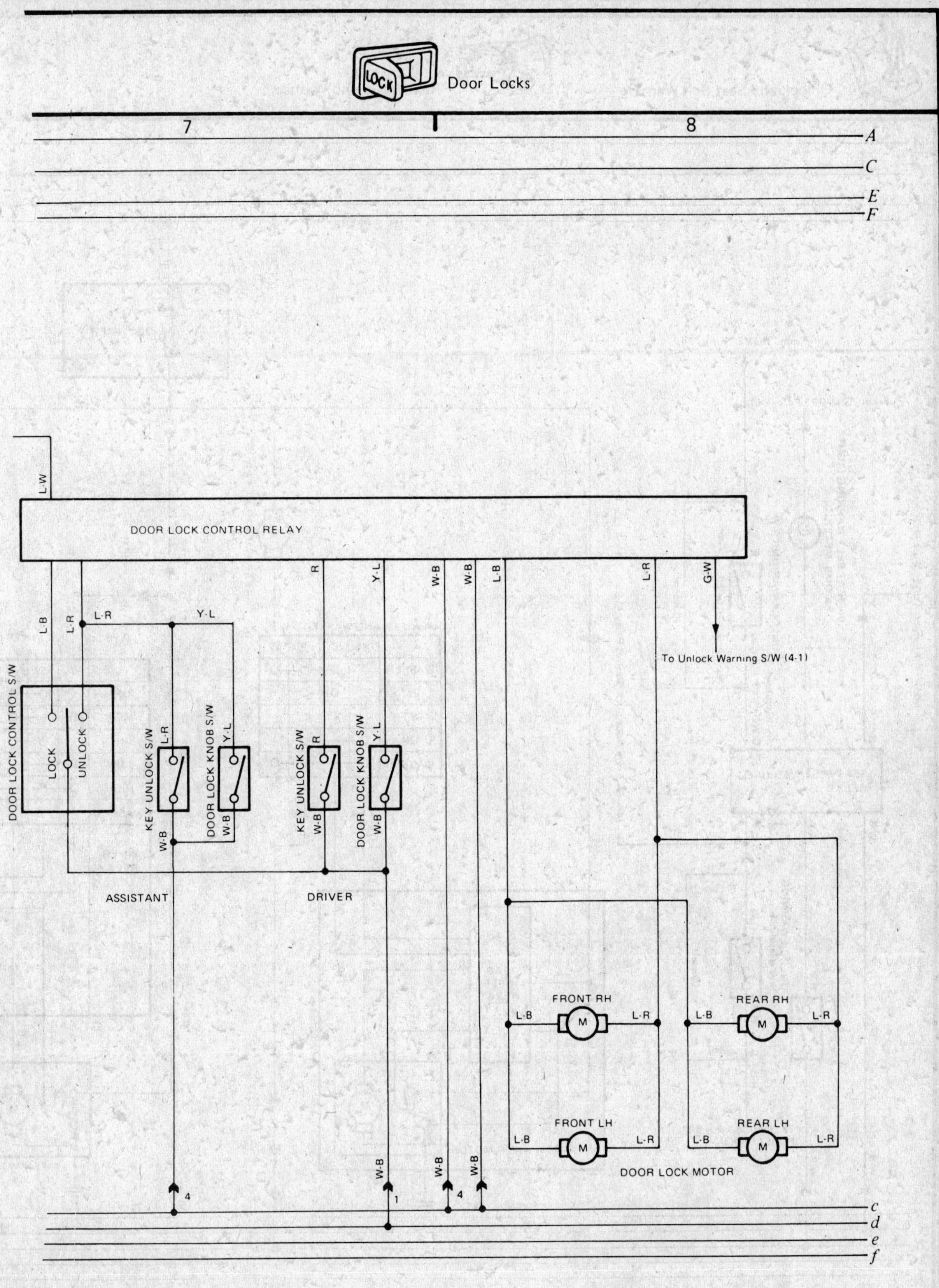

Wiring diagram—1986

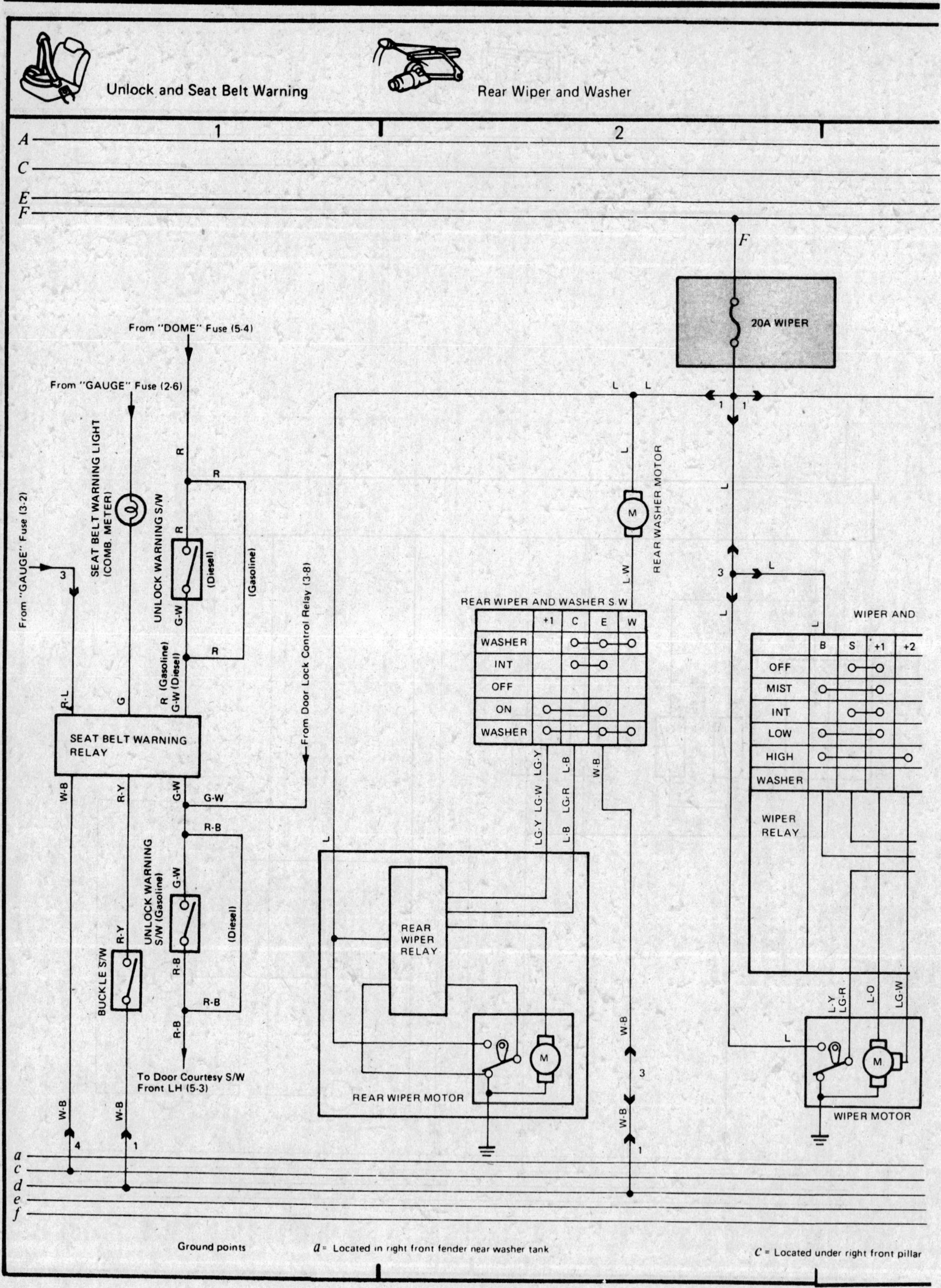

Wiring diagram—1986

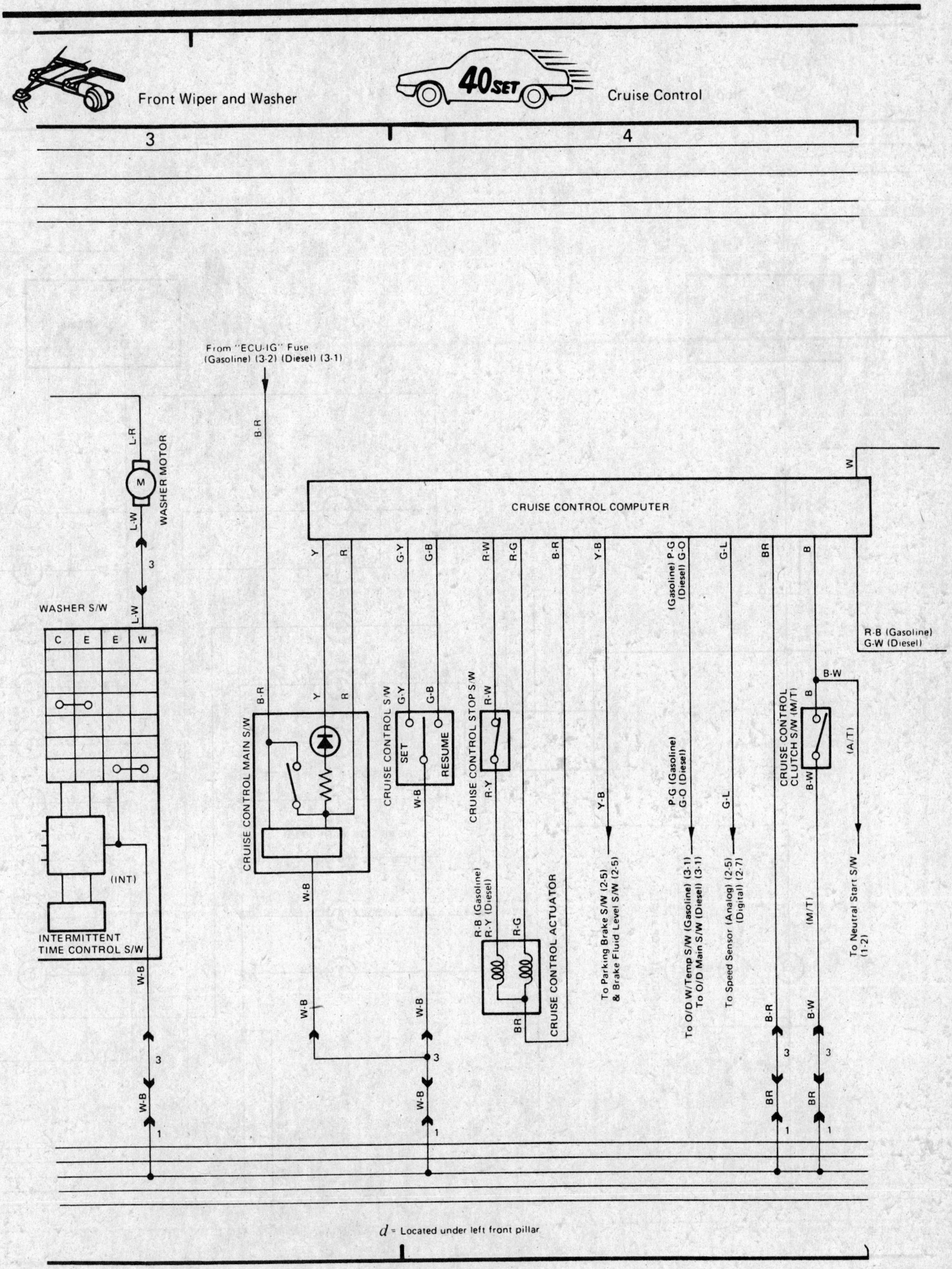

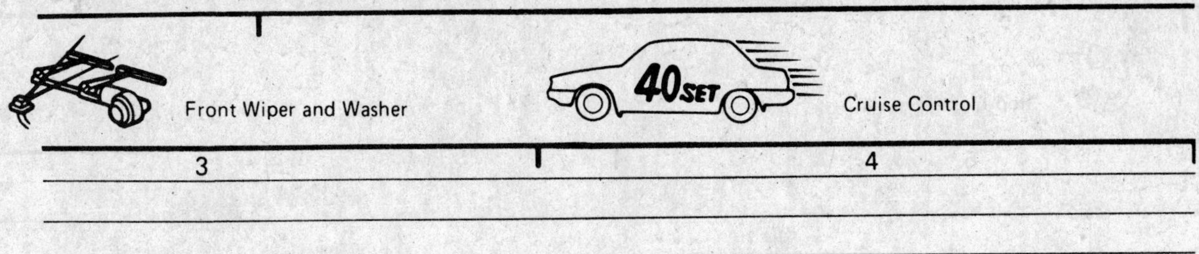

Front Wiper and Washer
Cruise Control
3
4
From "ECU-IG" Fuse
(Gasoline) (3-2) (Diesel) (3-1)
WASHER MOTOR
WASHER S/W
C E E W
(INT)
INTERMITTENT
TIME CONTROL S/W
CRUISE CONTROL COMPUTER
CRUISE CONTROL MAIN S/W
CRUISE CONTROL S/W
SET
RESUME
CRUISE CONTROL STOP S/W
R-B (Gasoline)
R-Y (Diesel)
CRUISE CONTROL ACTUATOR
To Parking Brake S/W (2-5)
& Brake Fluid Level S/W (2-5)
(Gasoline) P-G
(Diesel) G-O
To O/D W/Temp S/W (Gasoline) (3-1)
To O/D Main S/W (Diesel) (3-1)
To Speed Sensor (Analog) (2-5)
(Digital) (2-7)
CRUISE CONTROL
CLUTCH S/W (M/T)
(M/T)
(A/T)
R-B (Gasoline)
G-W (Diesel)
To Neutral Start S/W
(1-2)
d = Located under left front pillar

Wiring diagram—1986

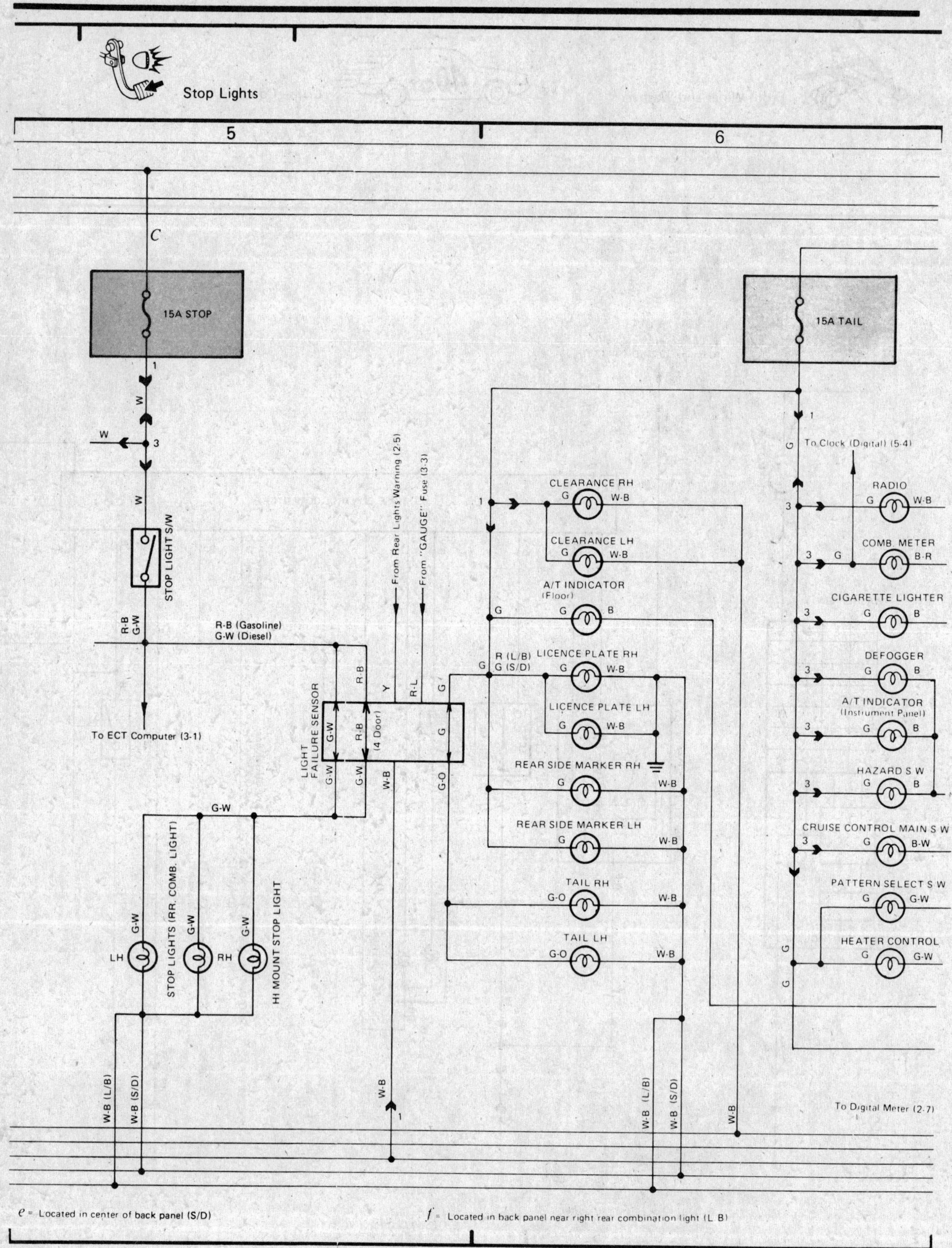

Wiring diagram—1986

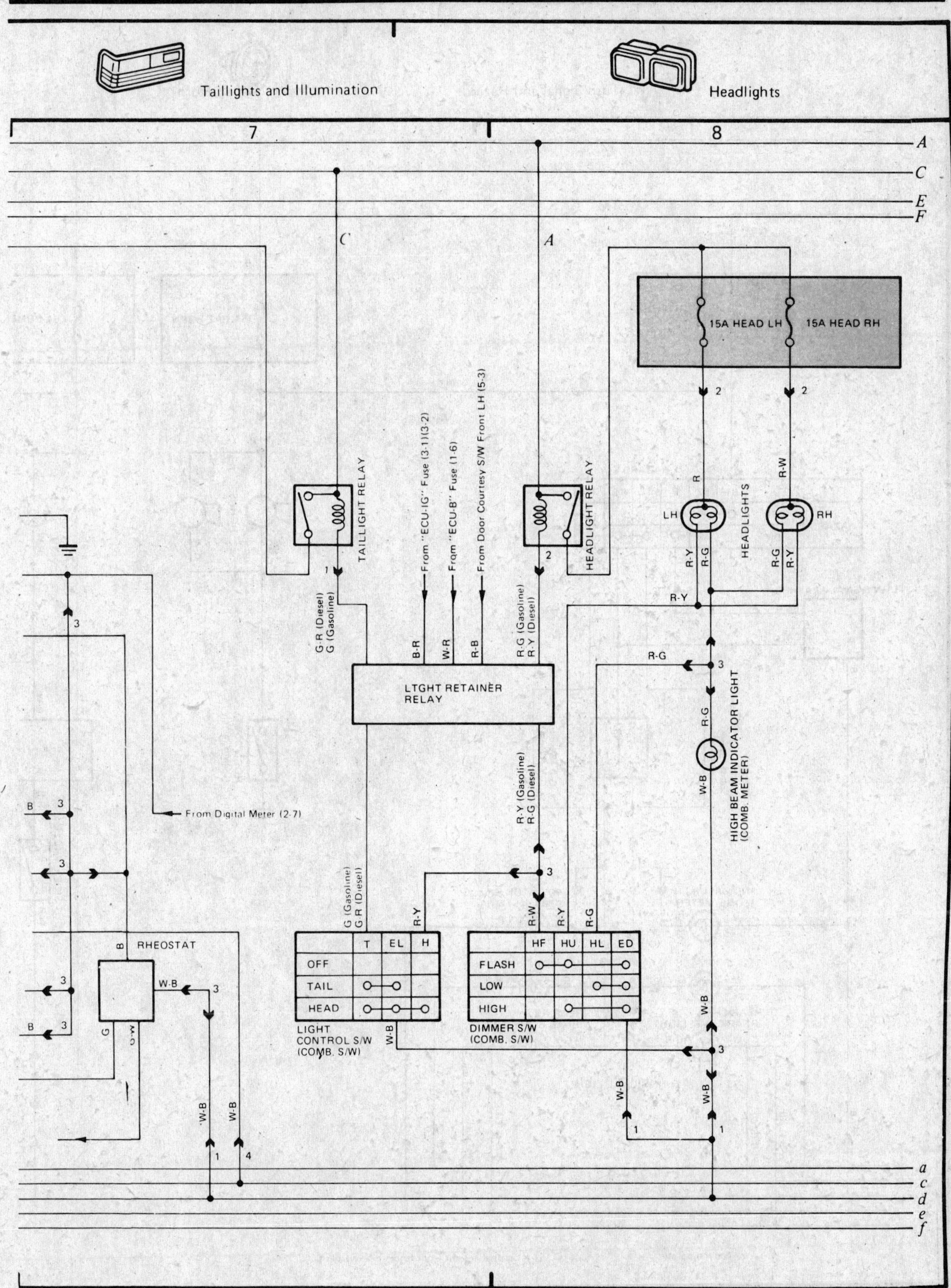

Wiring diagram—1986

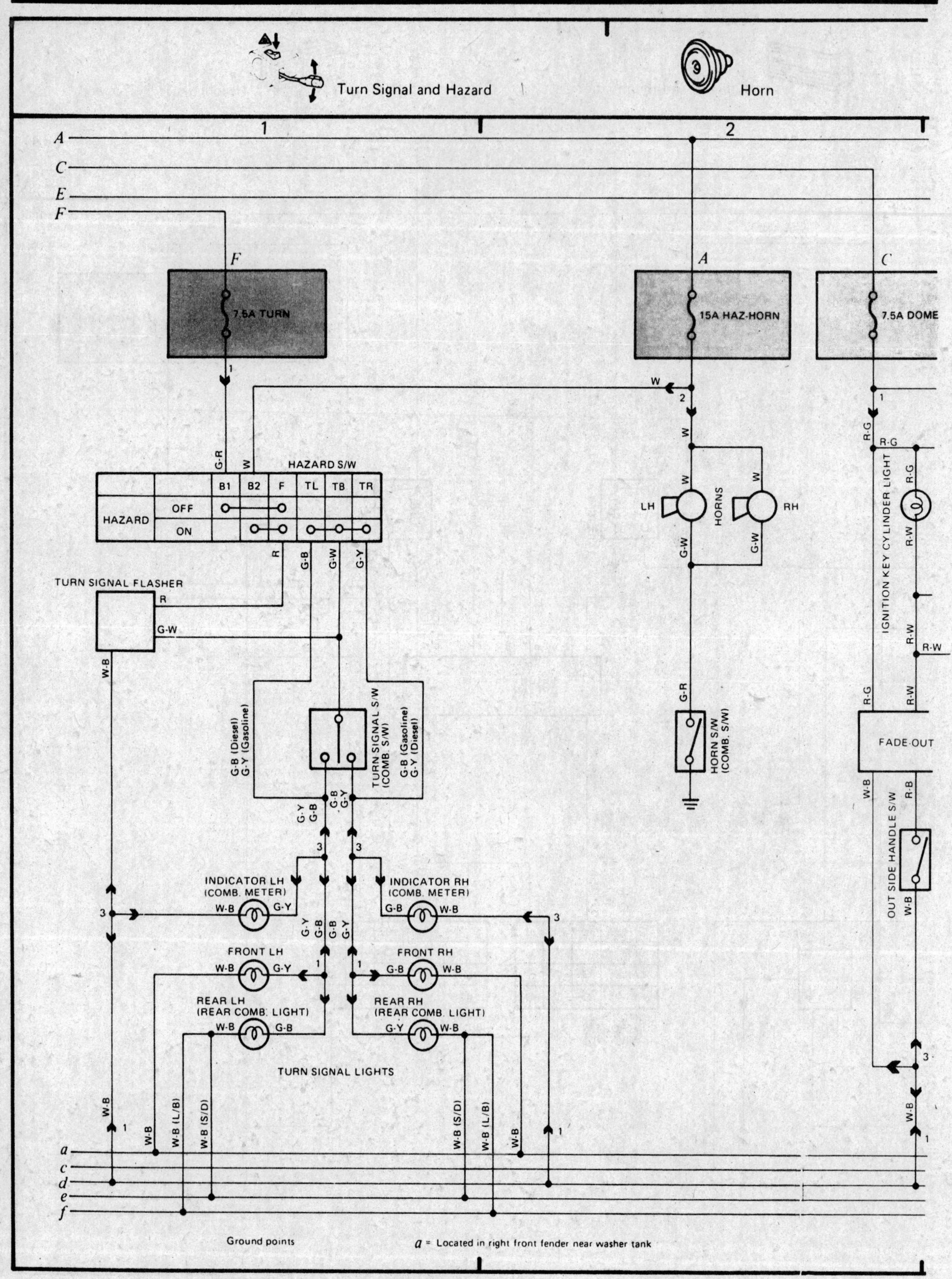

Wiring diagram—1986

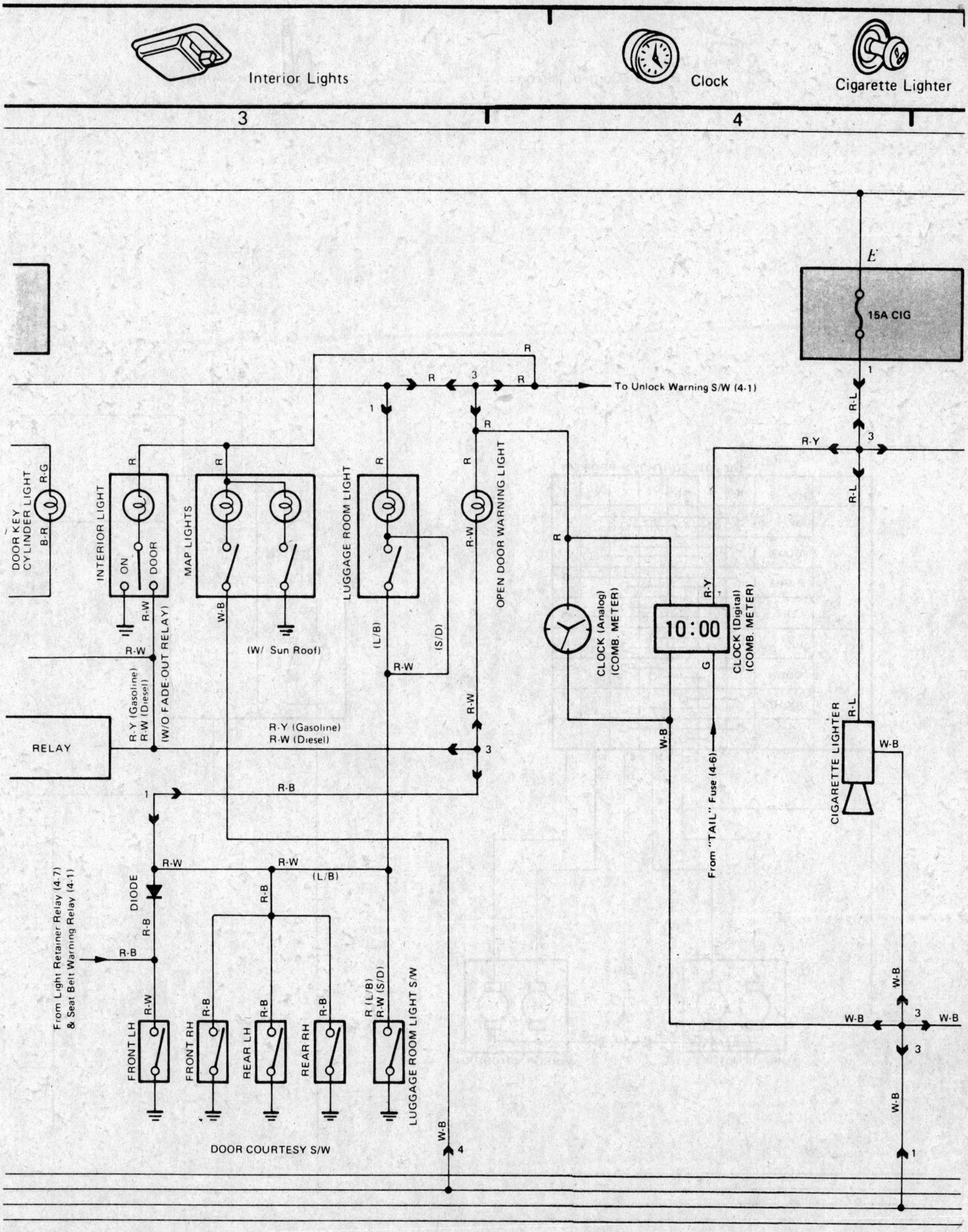

c - Located under right front pillar

d - Located under left front pillar

e = Located in center of back panel (S/D)

Wiring diagram—1986

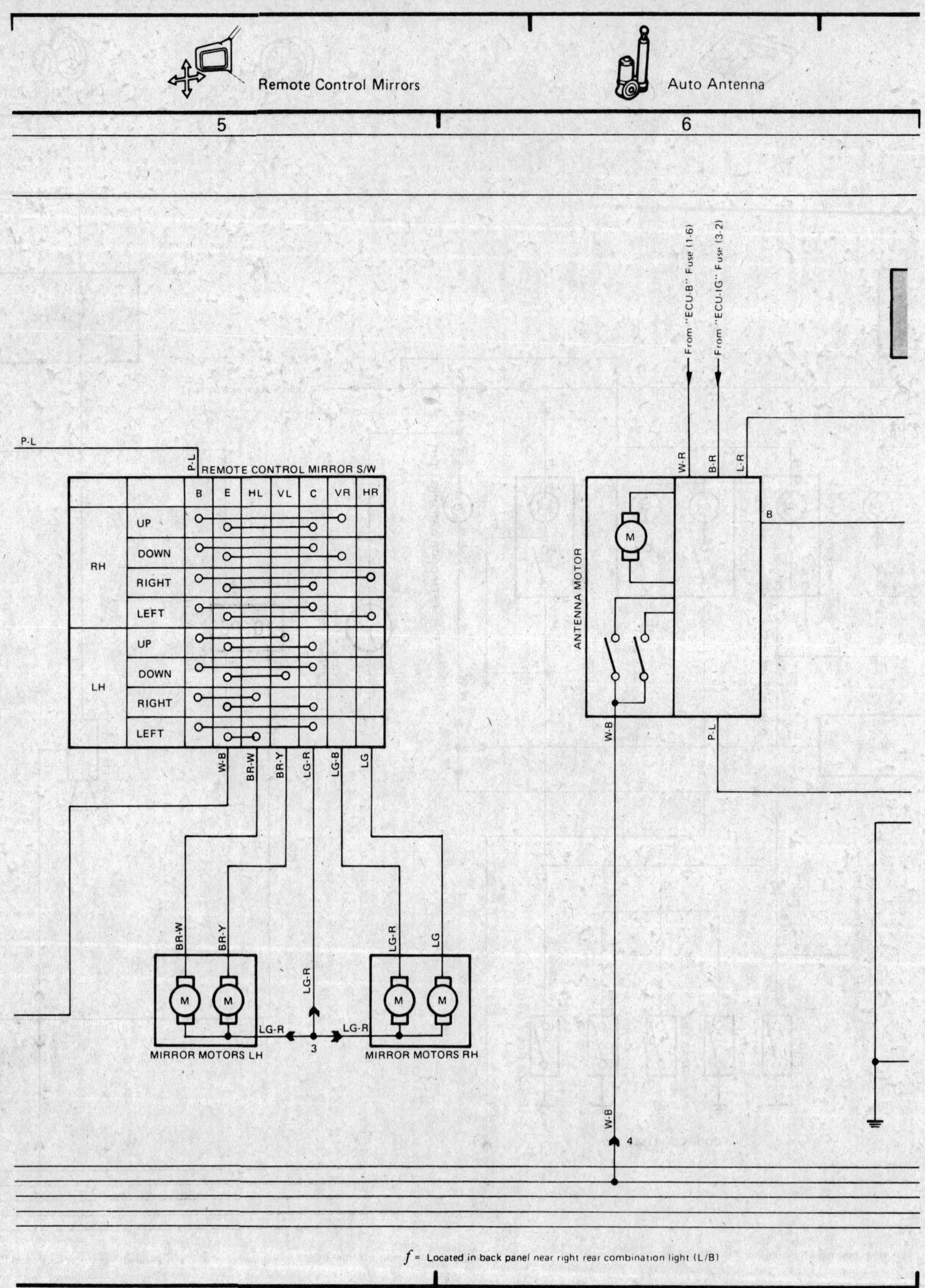

f = Located in back panel near right rear combination light (L/B)

Wiring diagram—1986

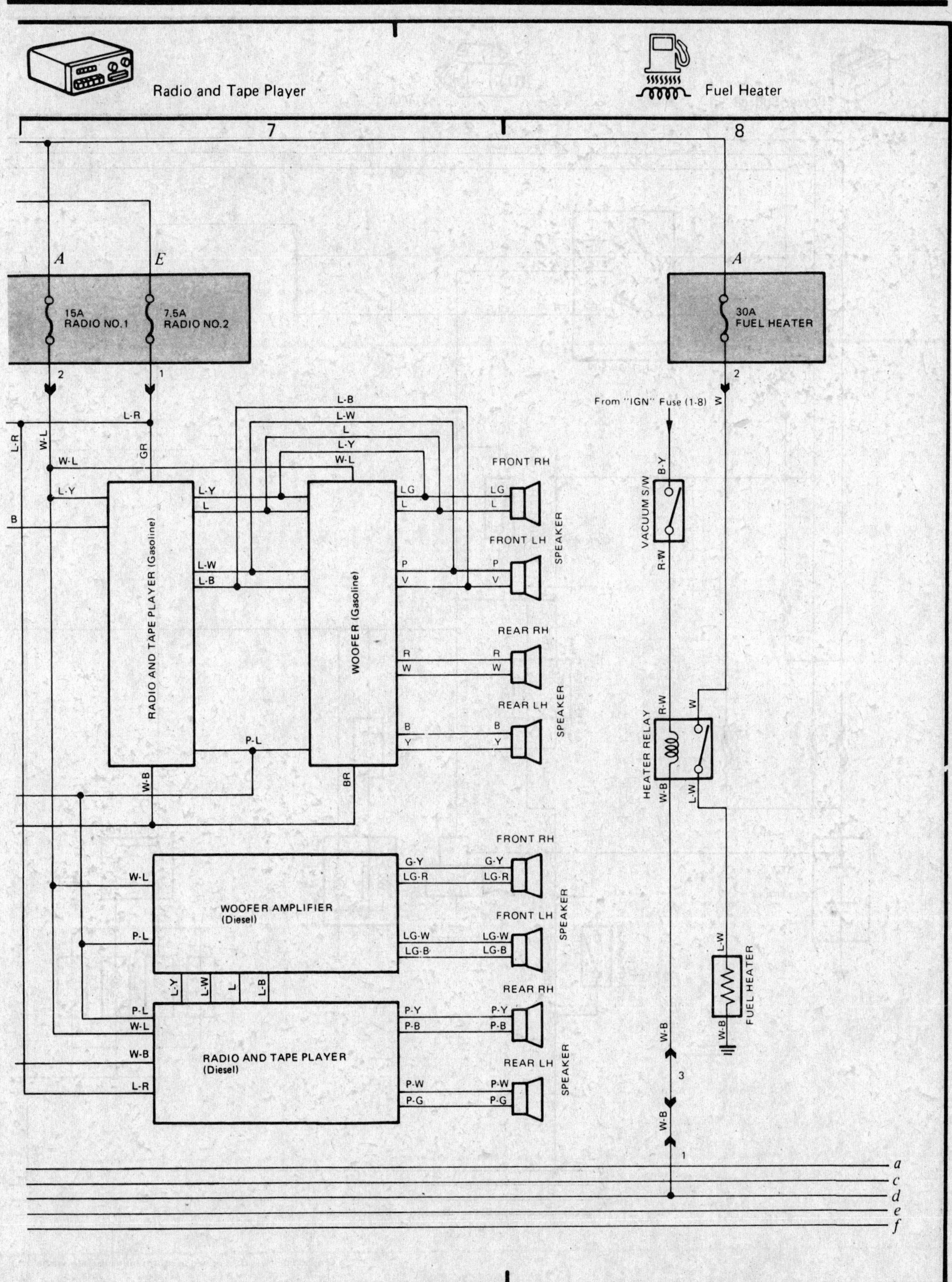

Wiring diagram—1986

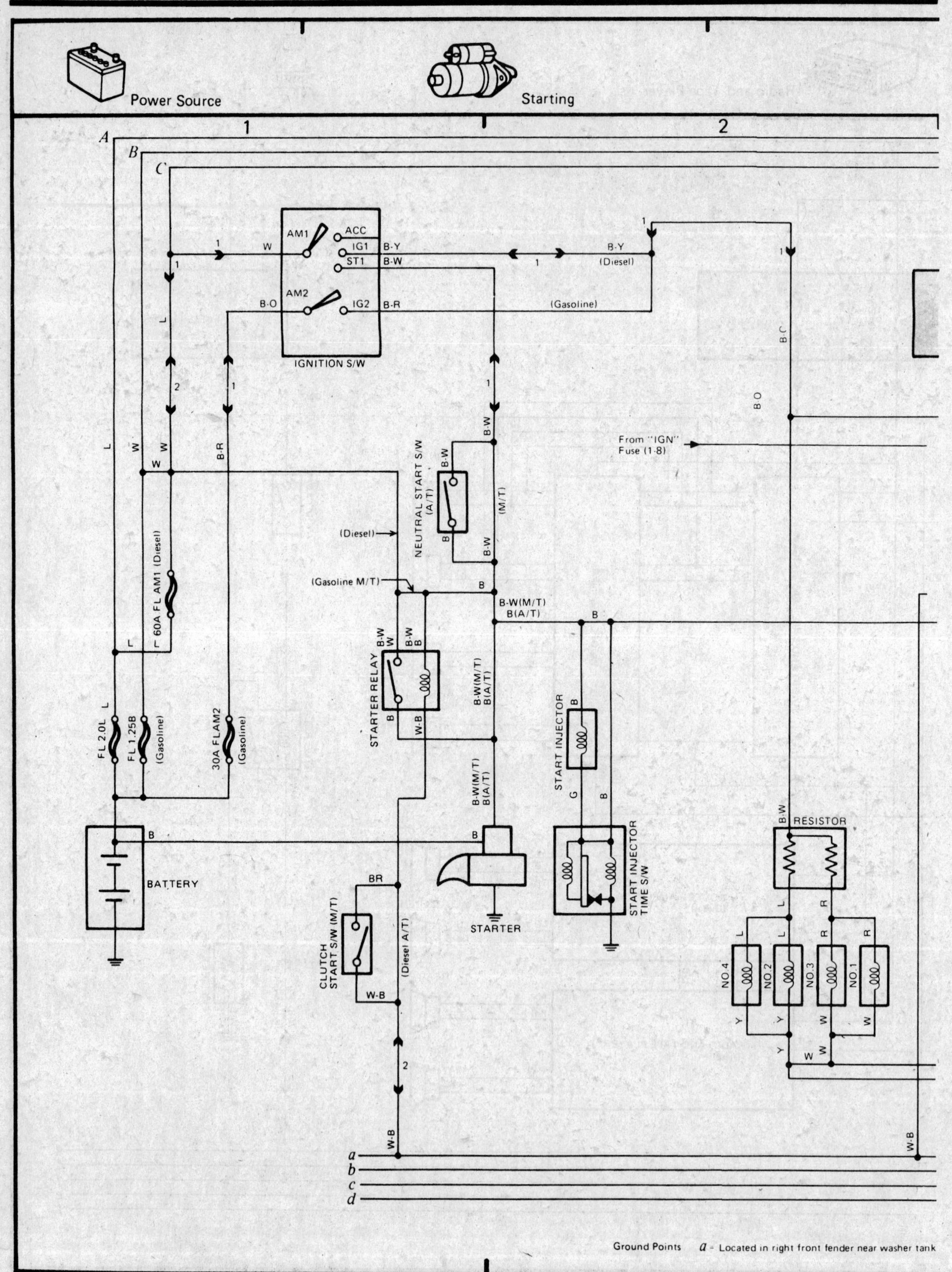

Wiring diagram—1986

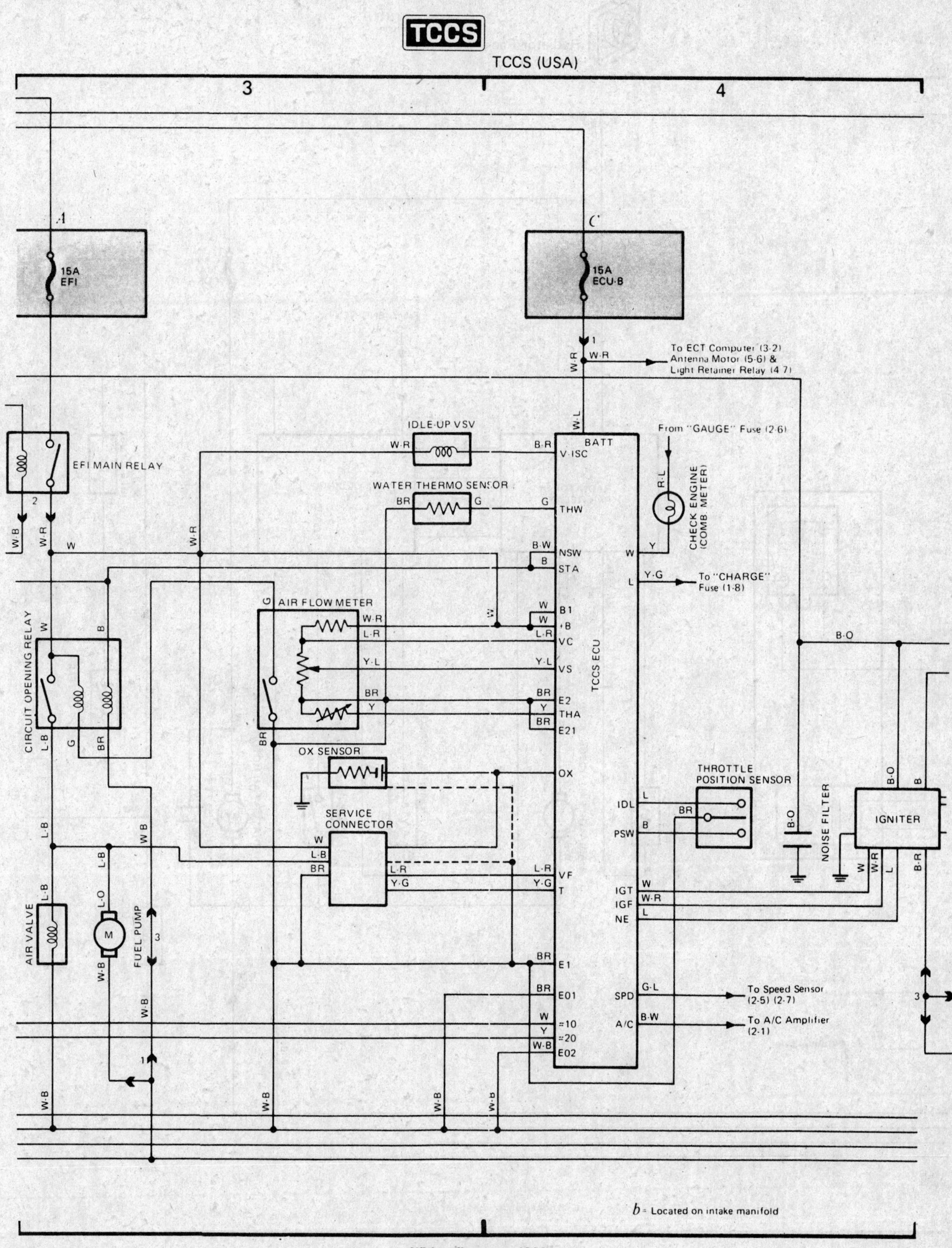

Wiring diagram—1986

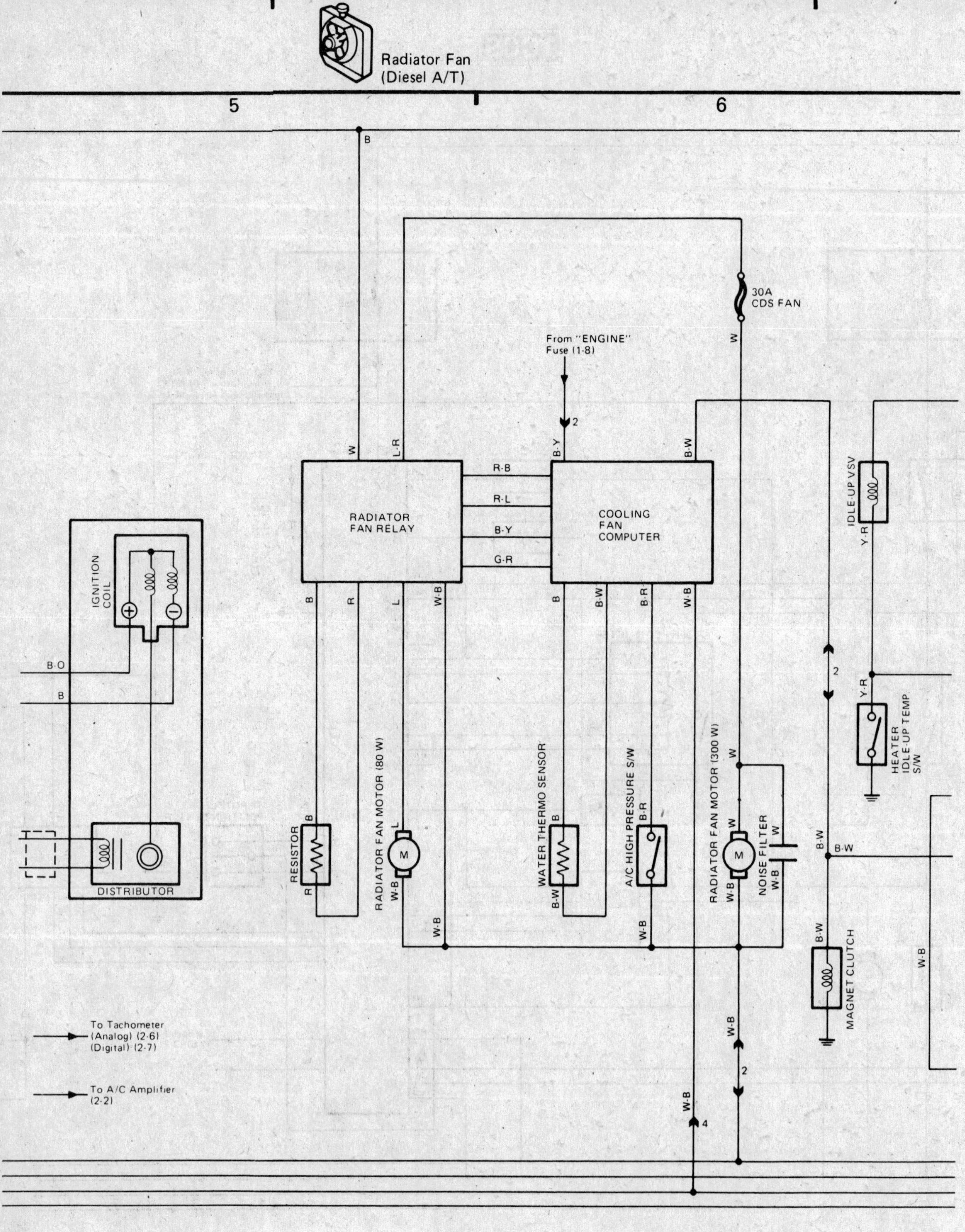

C = Located under right front pillar

Wiring diagram—1986

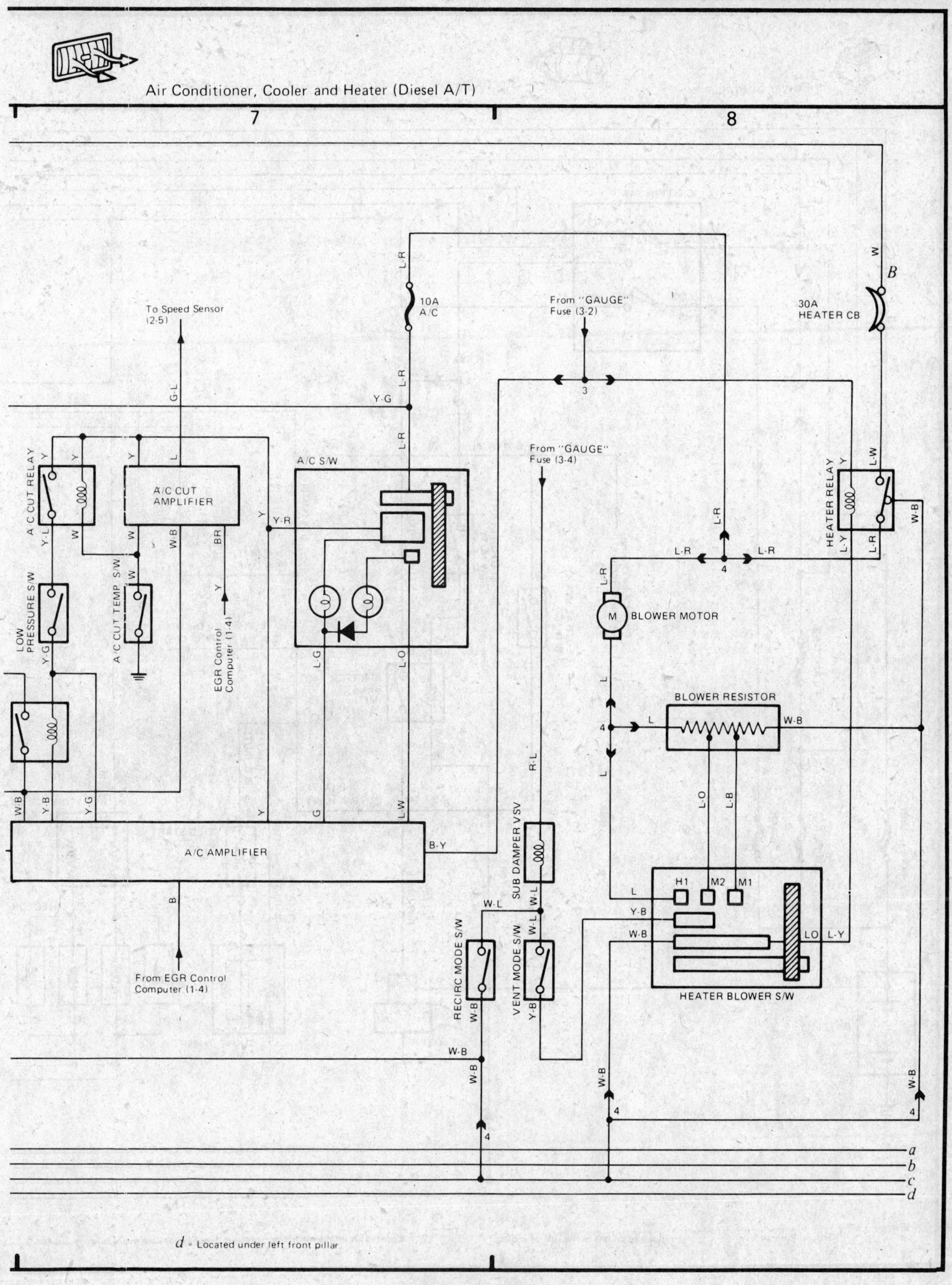

Wiring diagram—1986

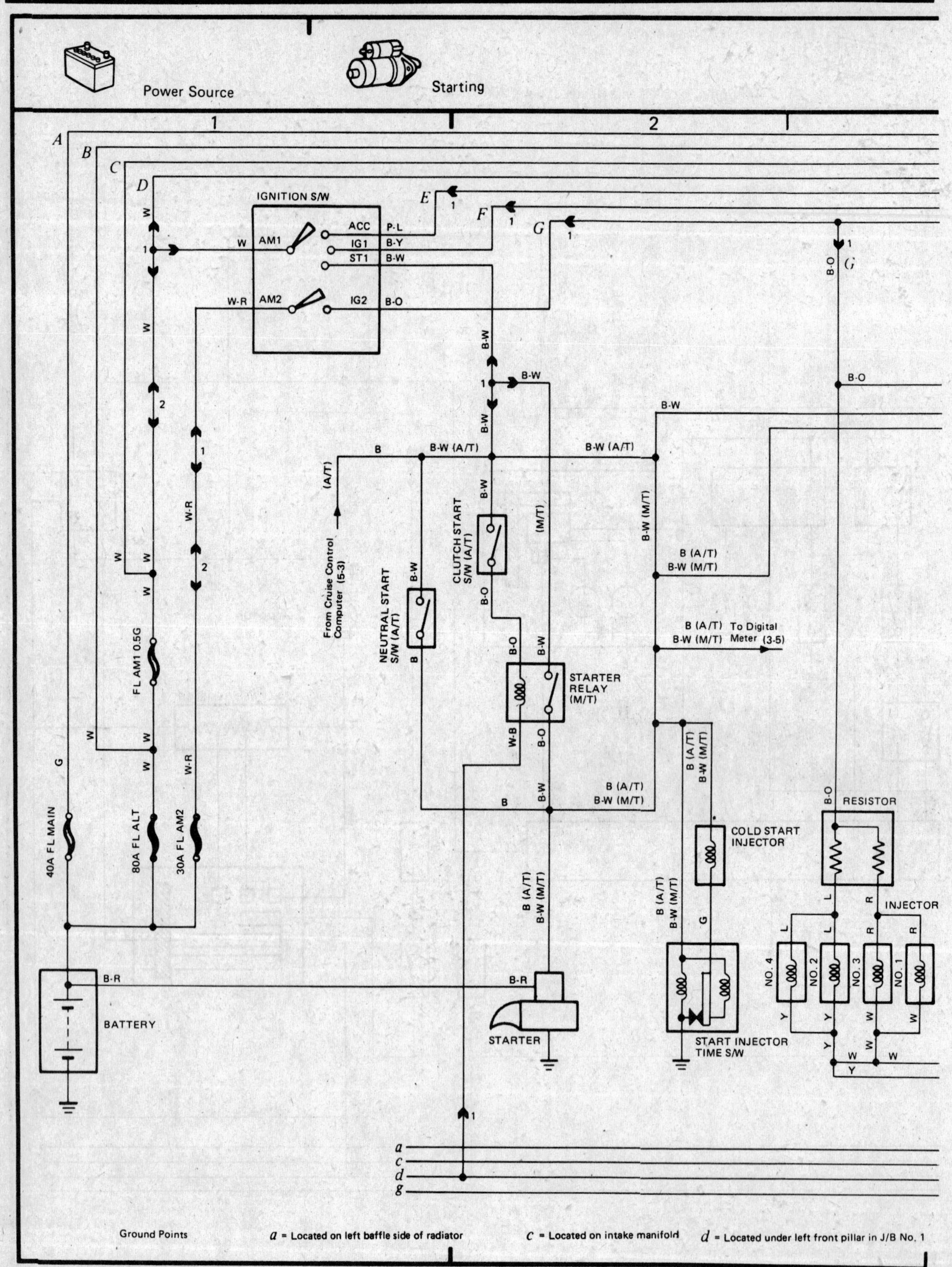

Wiring diagram—1987

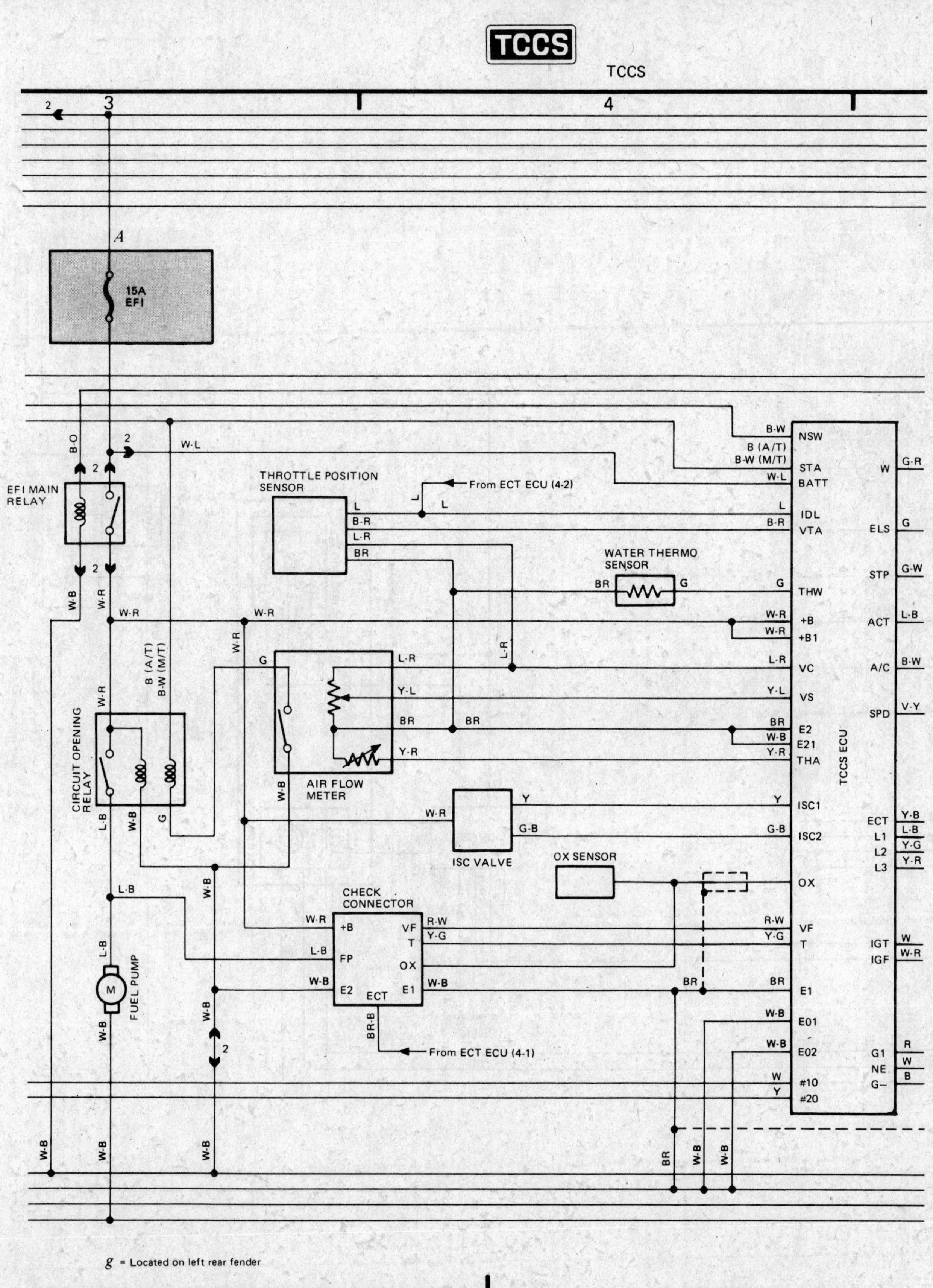

Wiring diagram—1987

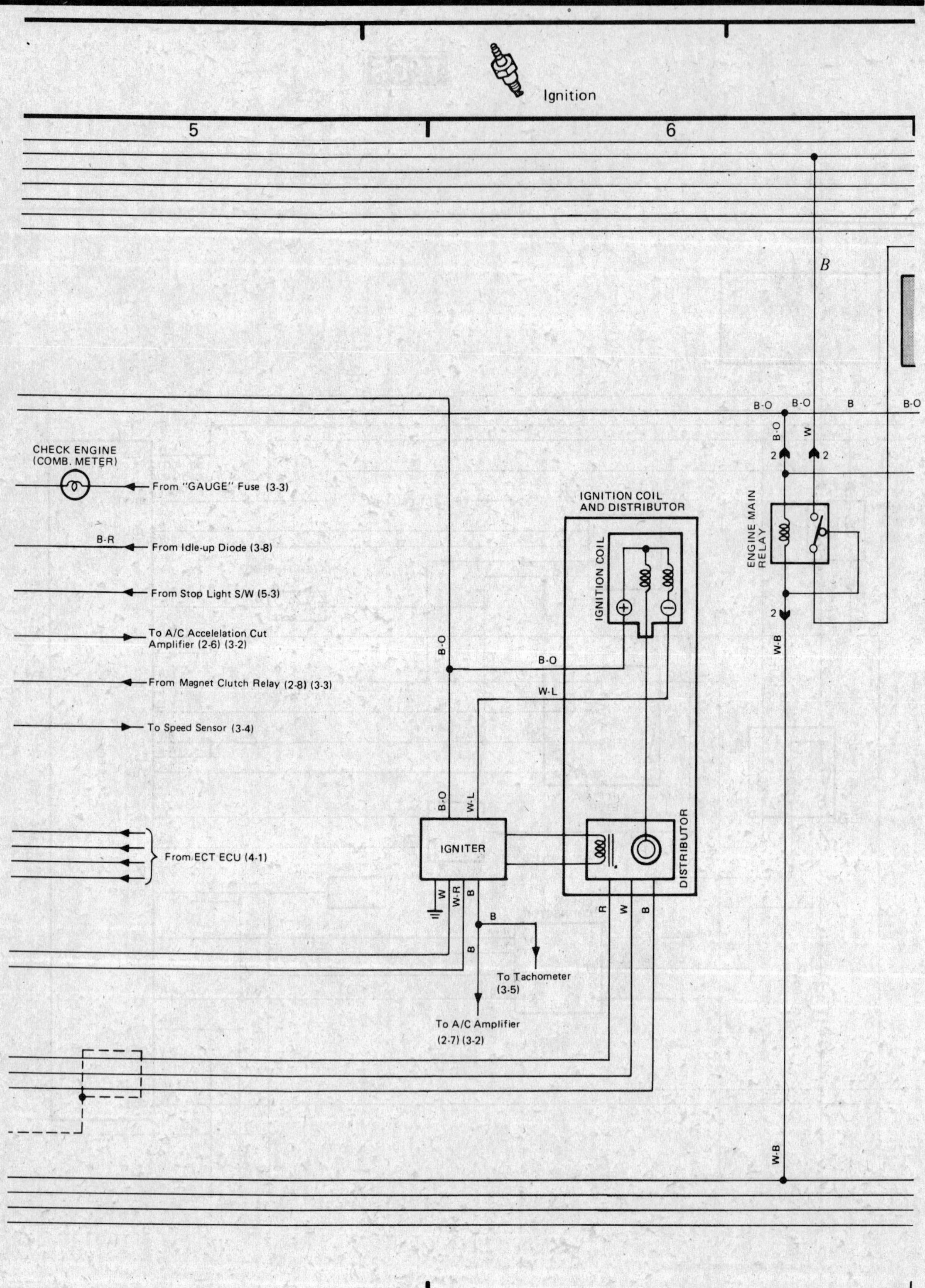
Ignition
5
6
B
B-O
B-O
B
B-O
B-O
W
2
2
CHECK ENGINE
(COMB. METER)
From "GAUGE" Fuse (3-3)
B-R
From Idle-up Diode (3-8)
From Stop Light S/W (5-3)
To A/C Accelelation Cut
Amplifier (2-6) (3-2)
From Magnet Clutch Relay (2-8) (3-3)
To Speed Sensor (3-4)
IGNITION COIL
AND DISTRIBUTOR
IGNITION COIL
ENGINE MAIN
RELAY
2
W-B
B-O
B-O
W-L
B-O
W-L
From ECT ECU (4-1)
IGNITER
DISTRIBUTOR
W
W-R
B
B
R
W
B
B
To Tachometer
(3-5)
To A/C Amplifier
(2-7) (3-2)
W-B

Wiring diagram—1987

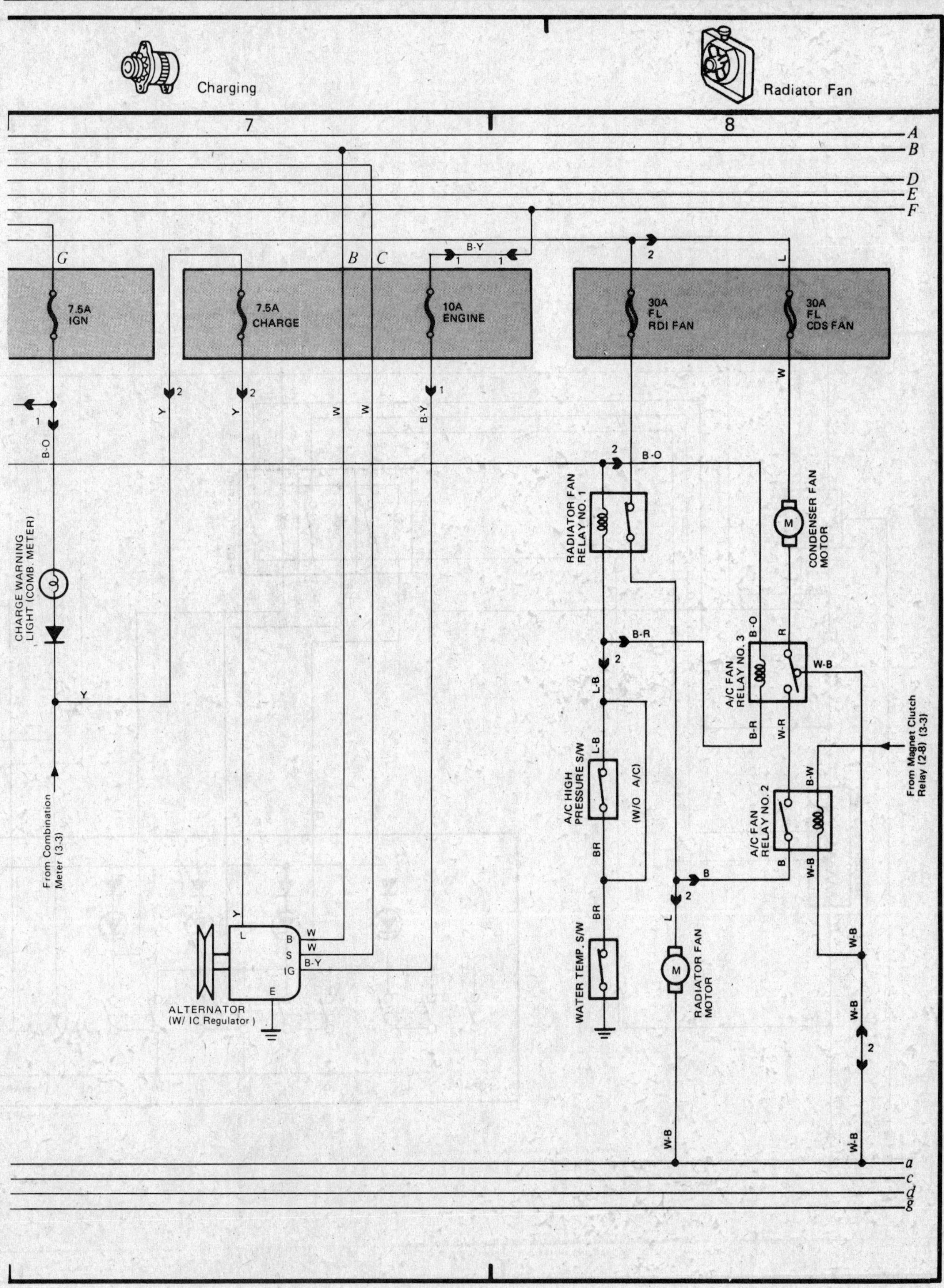

Wiring diagram—1987

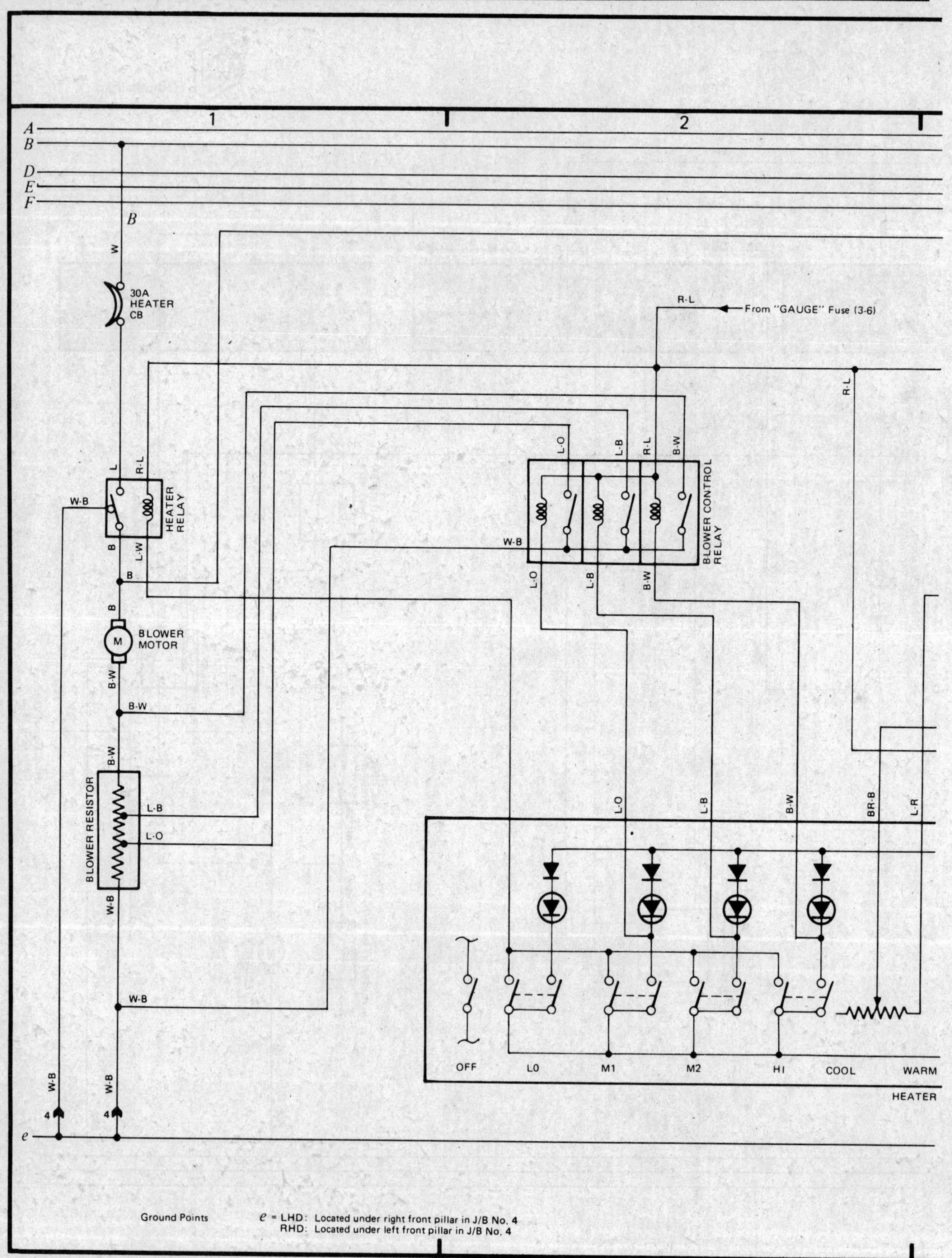

Ground Points   e = LHD: Located under right front pillar in J/B No. 4
RHD: Located under left front pillar in J/B No. 4

Wiring diagram—1987

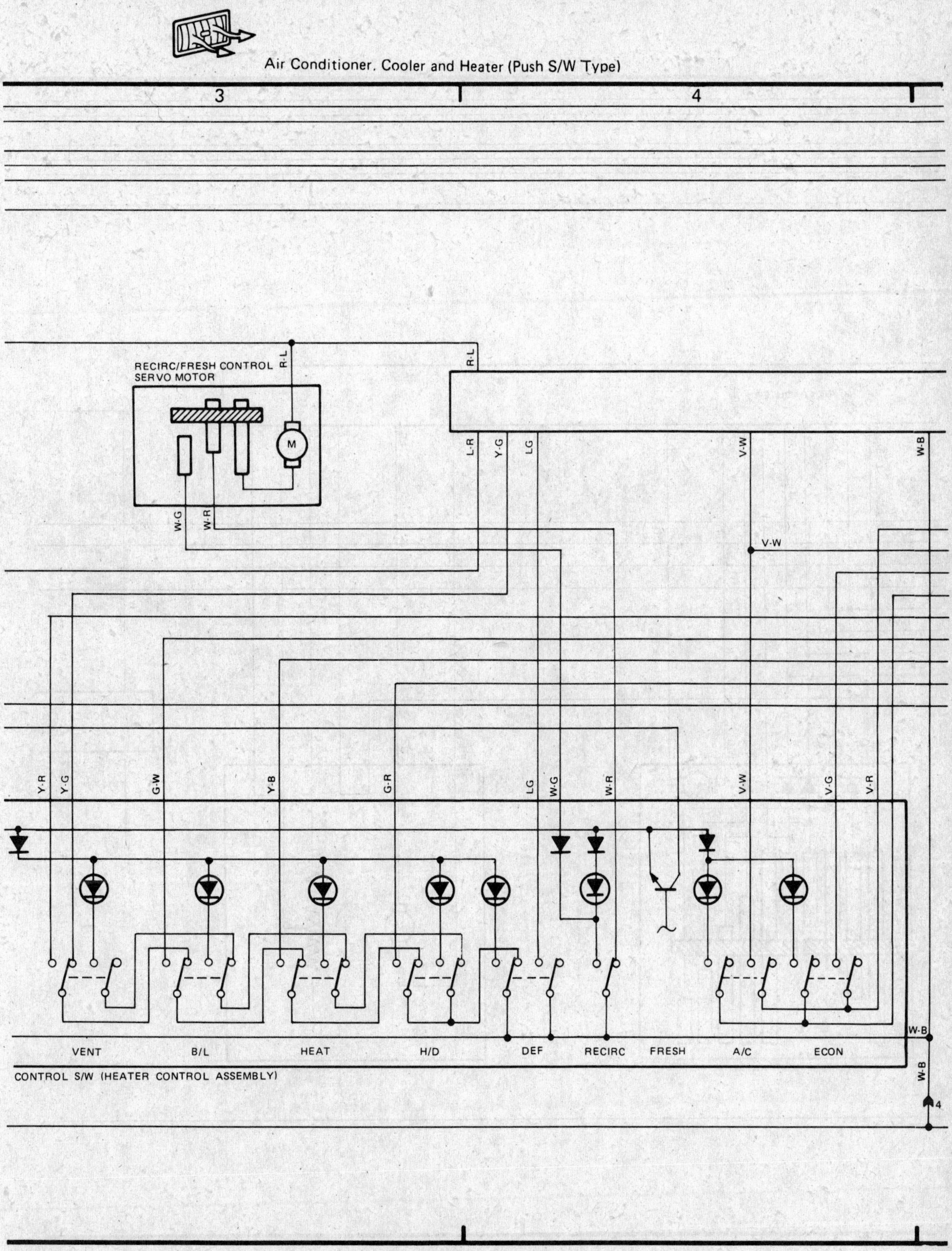

Air Conditioner, Cooler and Heater (Push S/W Type)

3

4

RECIRC/FRESH CONTROL SERVO MOTOR

R-L

R-L

M

L-R

Y-G

LG

V-W

W-B

W-G

W-R

V-W

Y-R

Y-G

G-W

Y-B

G-R

LG

W-G

W-R

V-W

V-G

V-R

VENT

B/L

HEAT

H/D

DEF

RECIRC

FRESH

A/C

ECON

W-B

CONTROL S/W (HEATER CONTROL ASSEMBLY)

W-B

4

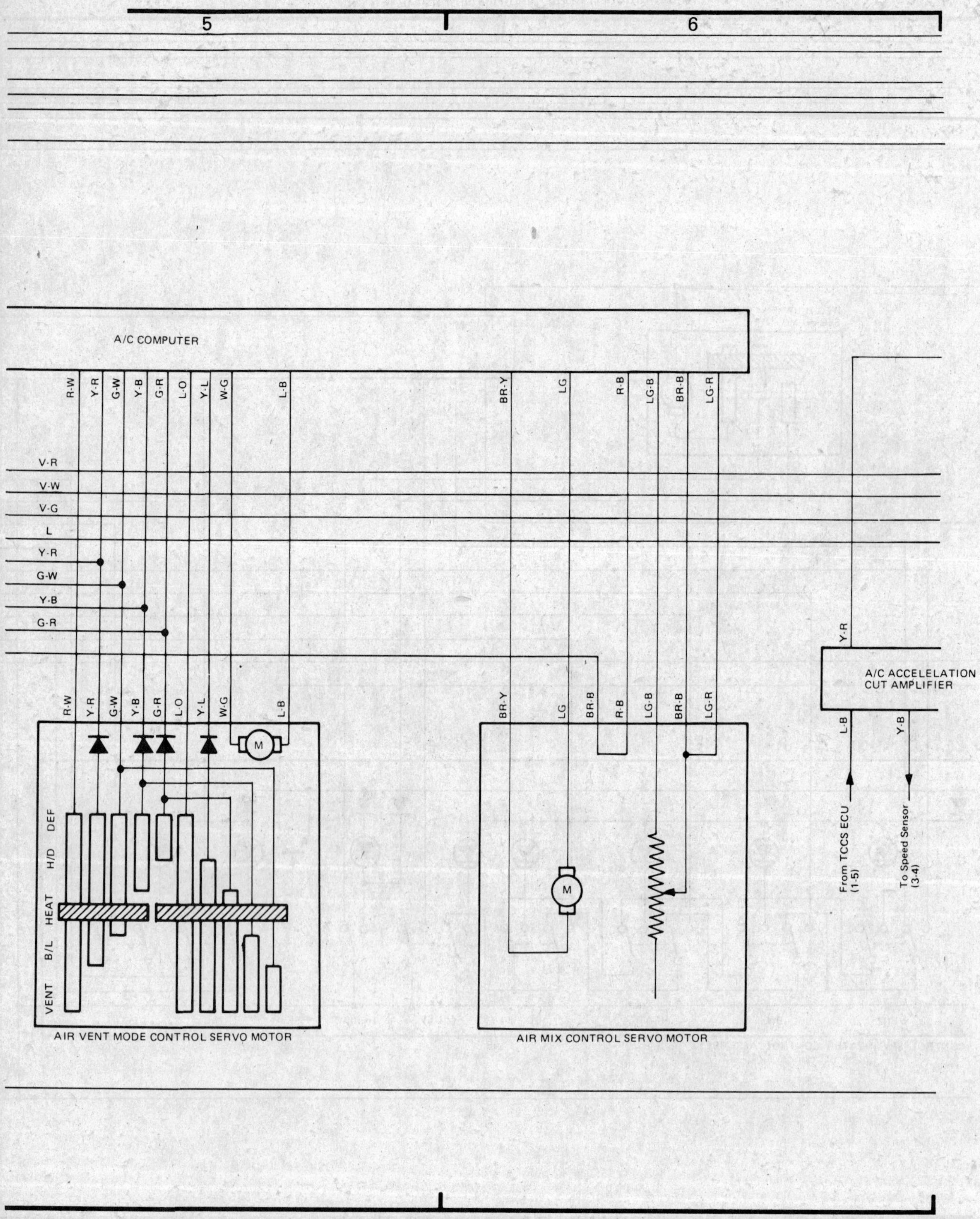

Wiring diagram—1987

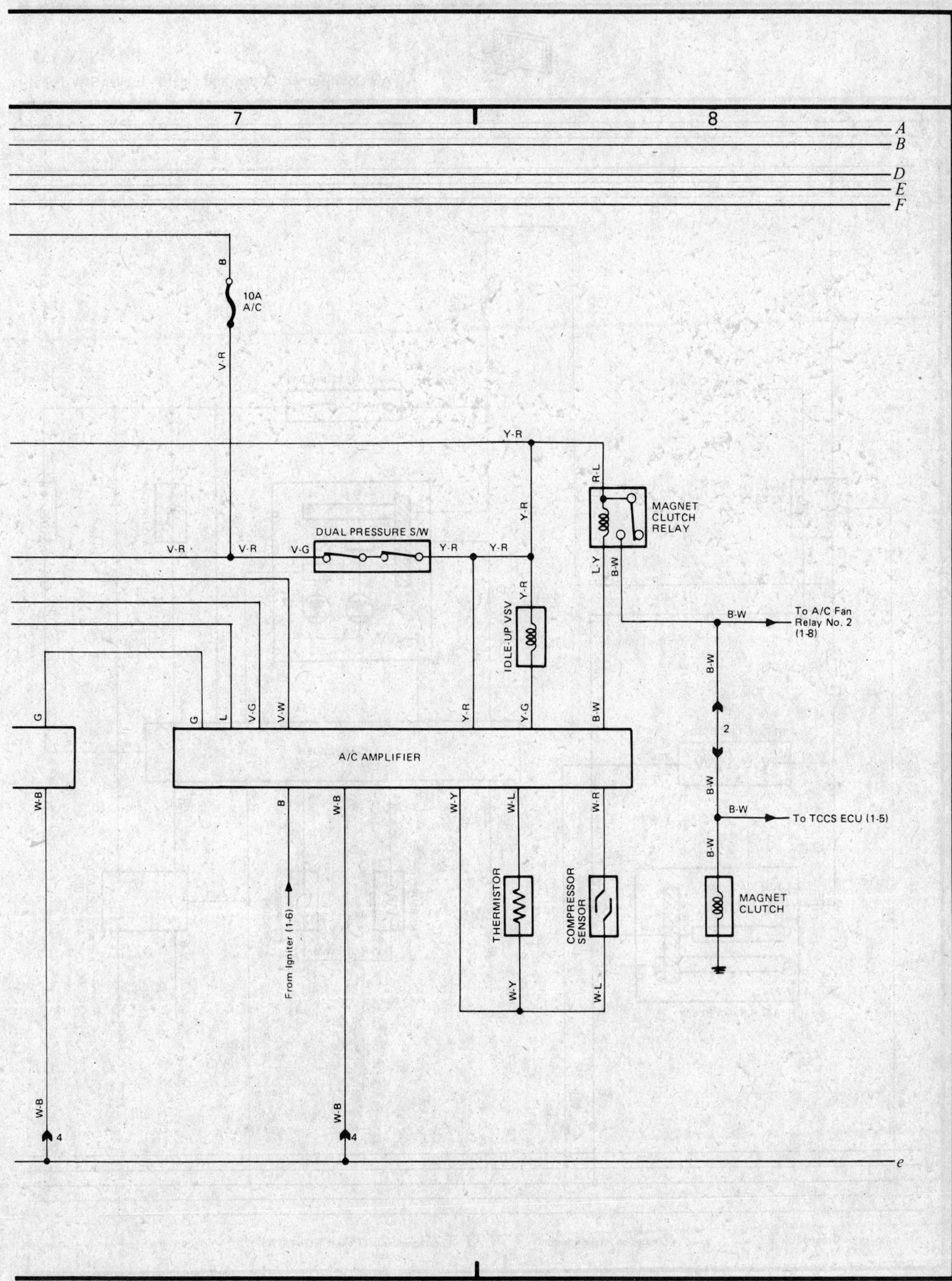

Wiring diagram—1987

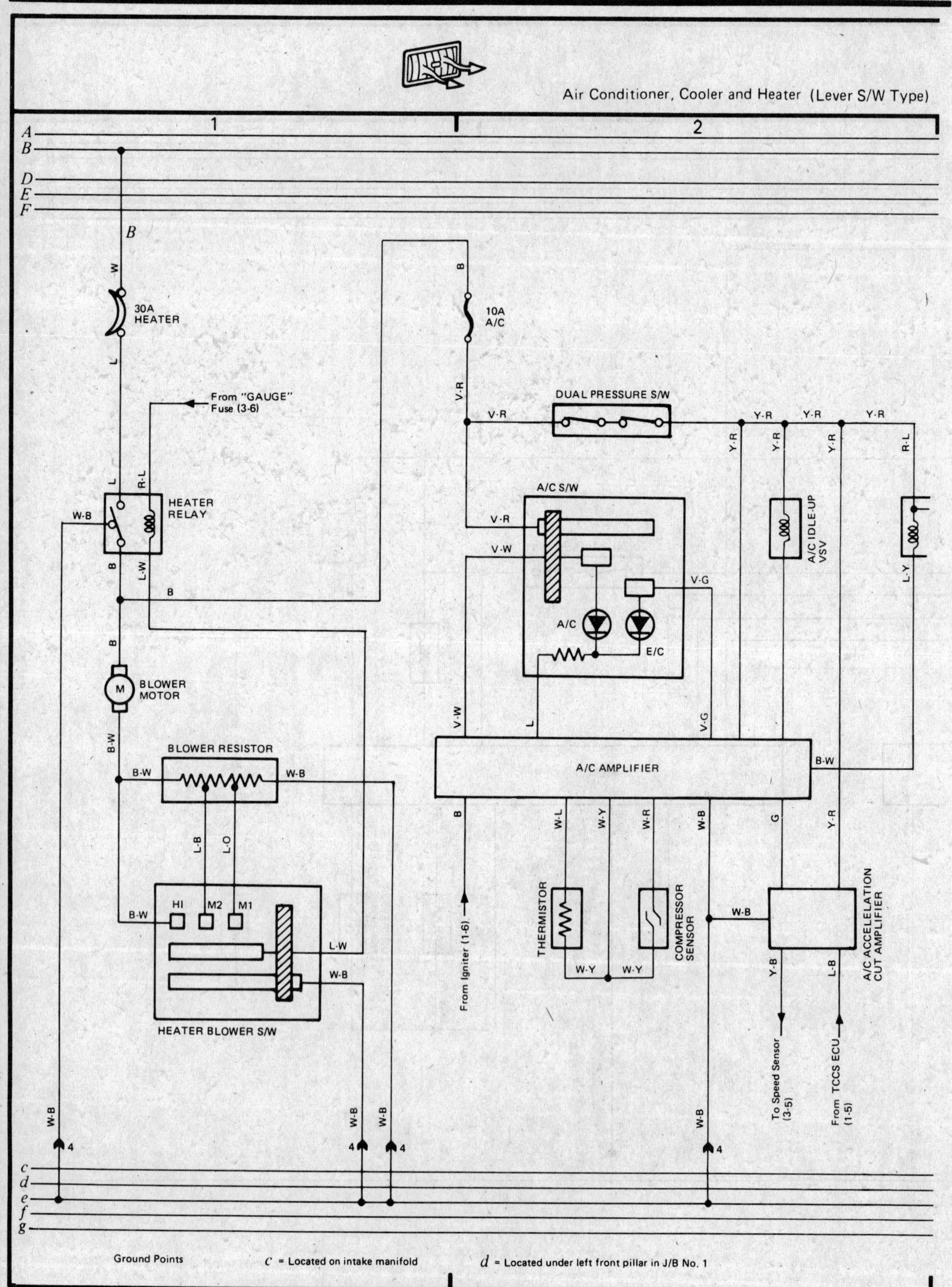

Wiring diagram—1987

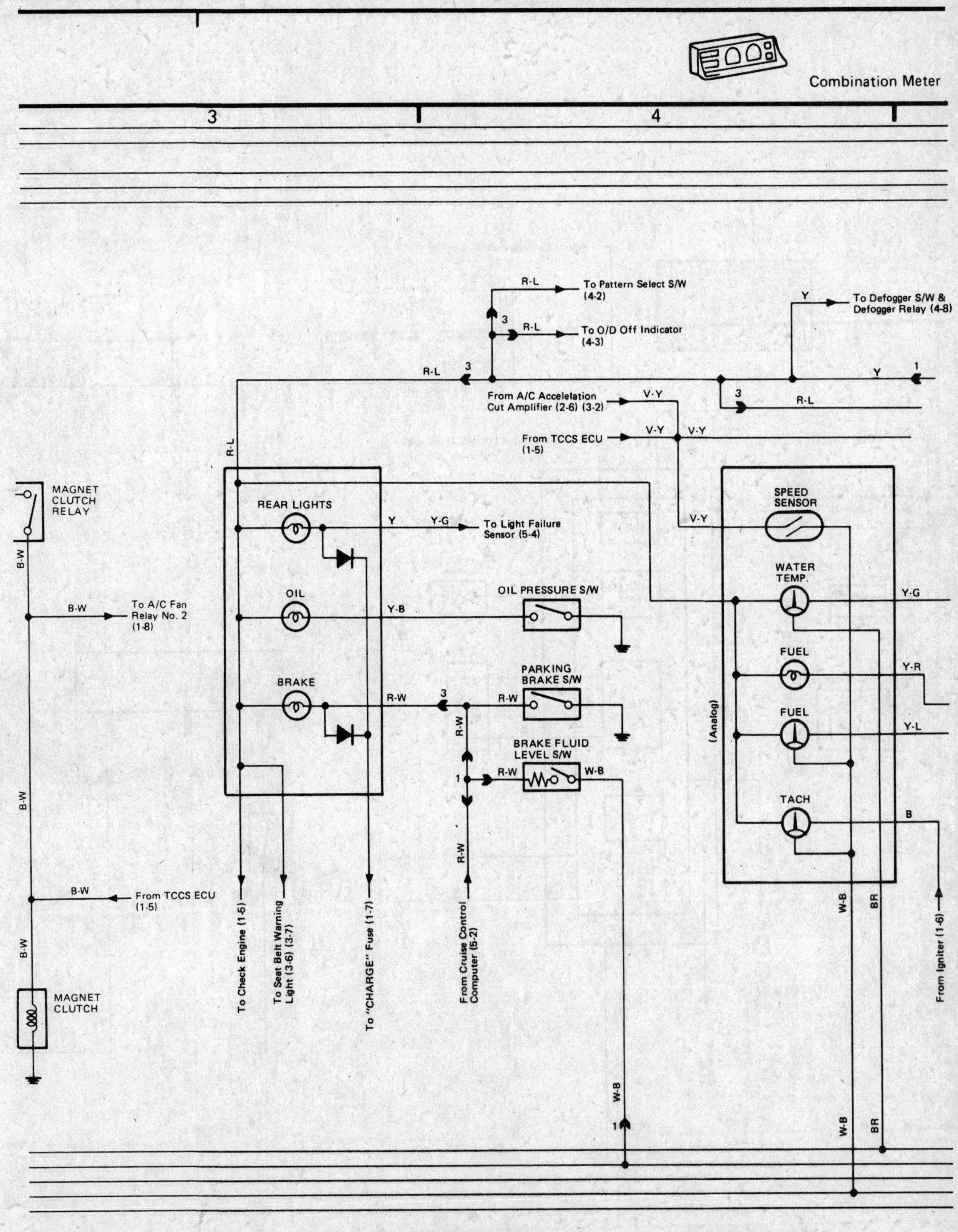

Combination Meter

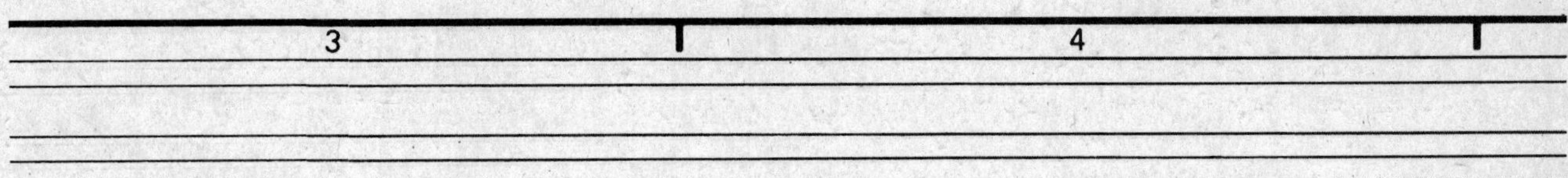

R-L
To Pattern Select S/W (4-2)
3
R-L
To O/D Off Indicator (4-3)
Y
To Defogger S/W & Defogger Relay (4-8)
R-L 3
Y 1
From A/C Accelelation Cut Amplifier (2-6) (3-2)
V-Y
3
R-L
From TCCS ECU (1-5)
V-Y
V-Y
R-L
MAGNET CLUTCH RELAY
REAR LIGHTS
Y
Y-G
To Light Failure Sensor (5-4)
V-Y
SPEED SENSOR
WATER TEMP.
Y-G
B-W
OIL
OIL PRESSURE S/W
B-W
To A/C Fan Relay No. 2 (1-8)
Y-B
FUEL
Y-R
PARKING BRAKE S/W
BRAKE
R-W
3
R-W
(Analog)
FUEL
Y-L
R-W
BRAKE FLUID LEVEL S/W
1
R-W
W-B
B-W
TACH
B
R-W
B-W
From TCCS ECU (1-5)
W-B
BR
B-W
To Check Engine (1-5)
To Seat Belt Warning Light (3-6) (3-7)
To "CHARGE" Fuse (1-7)
From Cruise Control Computer (5-2)
From Igniter (1-6)
MAGNET CLUTCH
W-B
1
W-B
BR

e = Located under right front pillar in R/B No. 4

f = Located under left front pillar

g = Located on left rear fender

Wiring diagram—1987

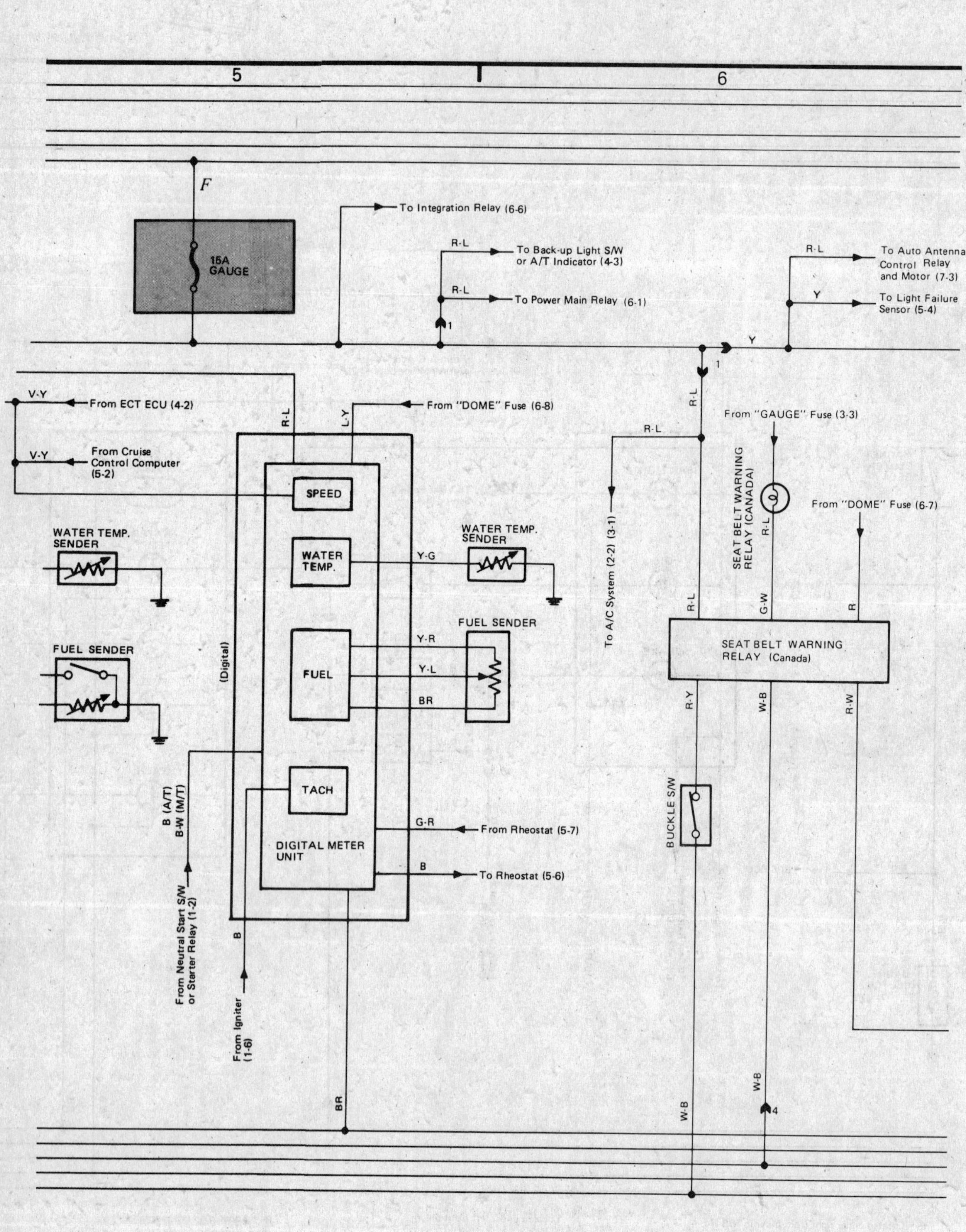

Wiring diagram—1987

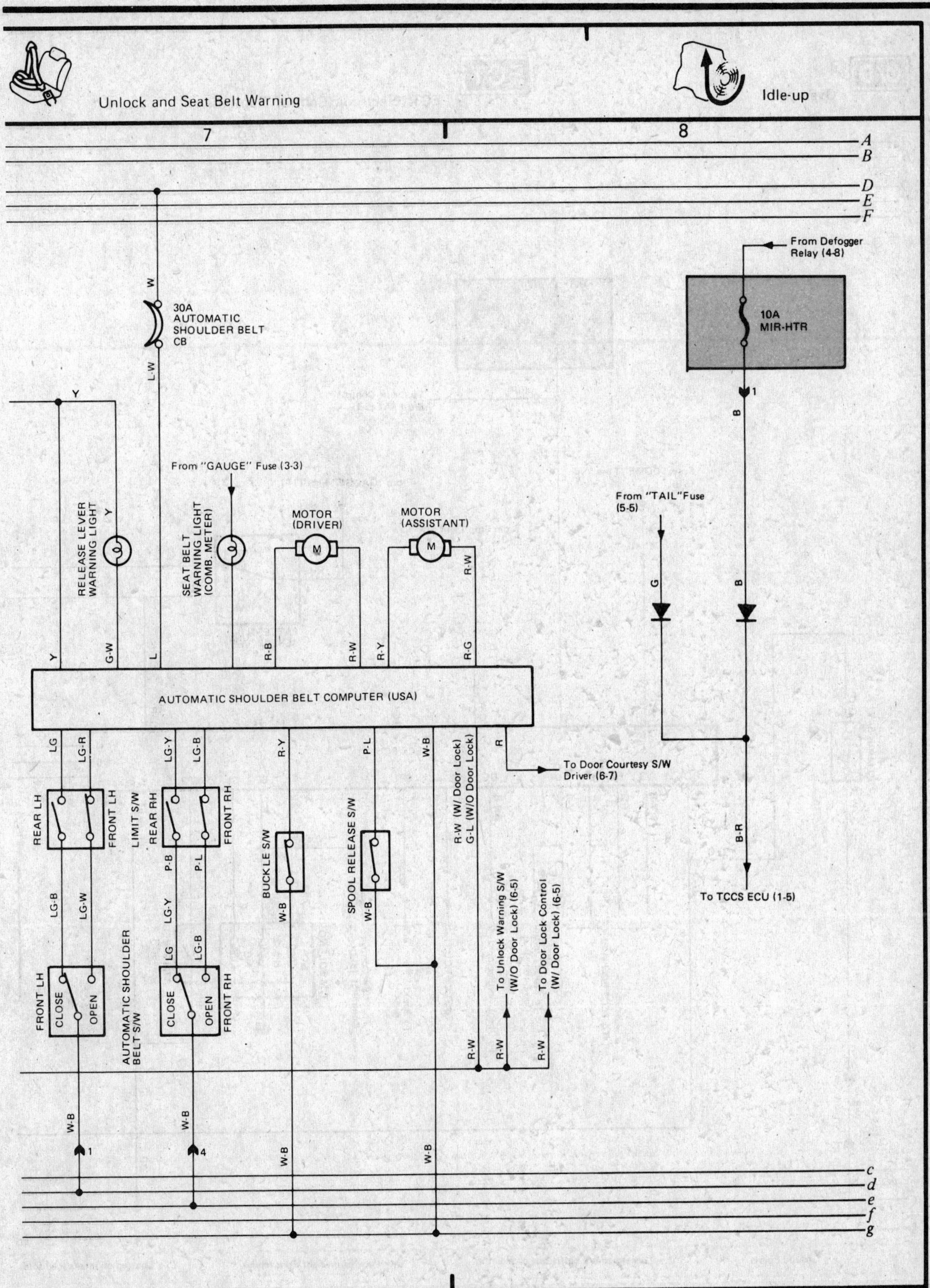

Wiring diagram—1987

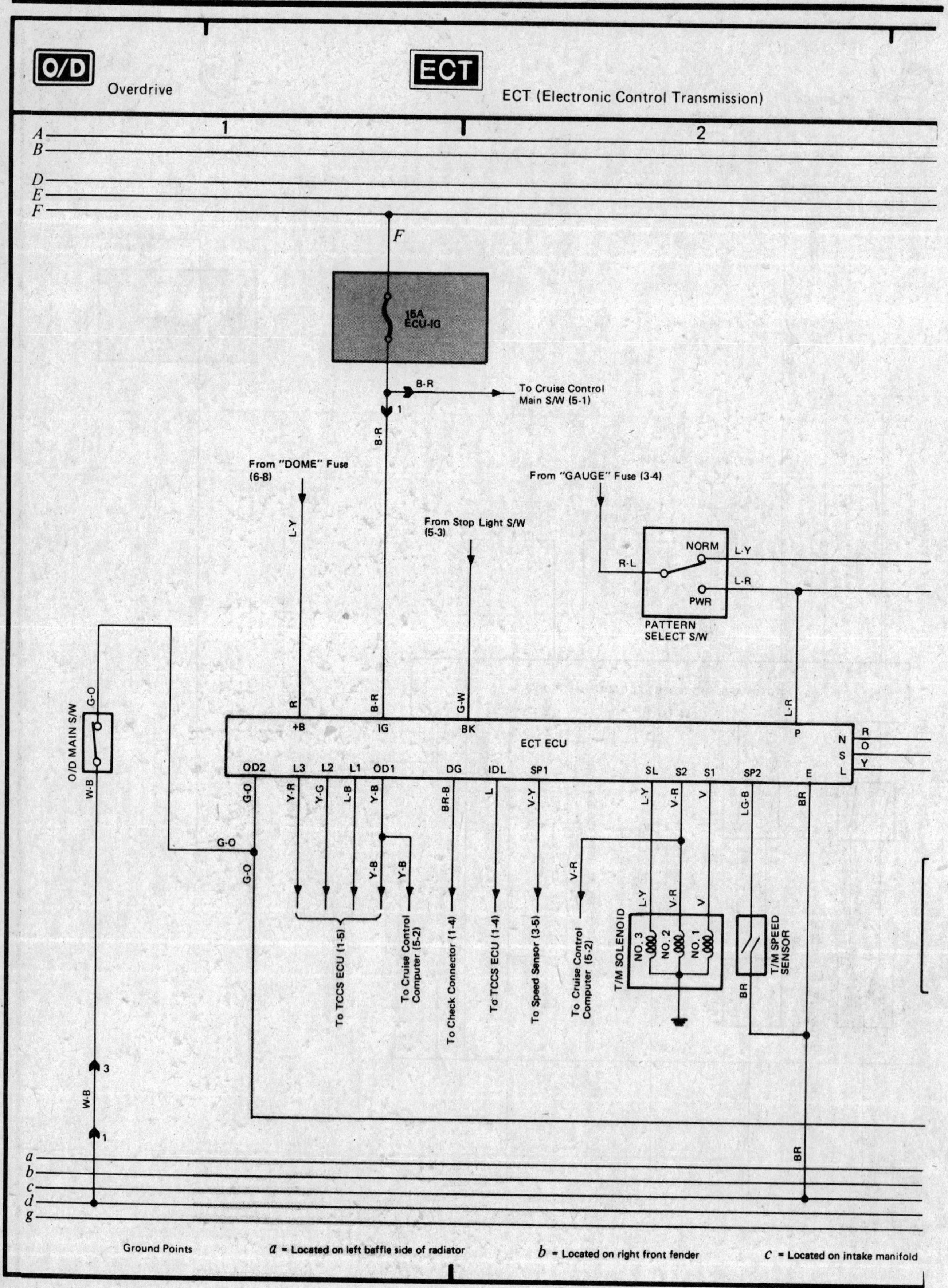

Wiring diagram—1987

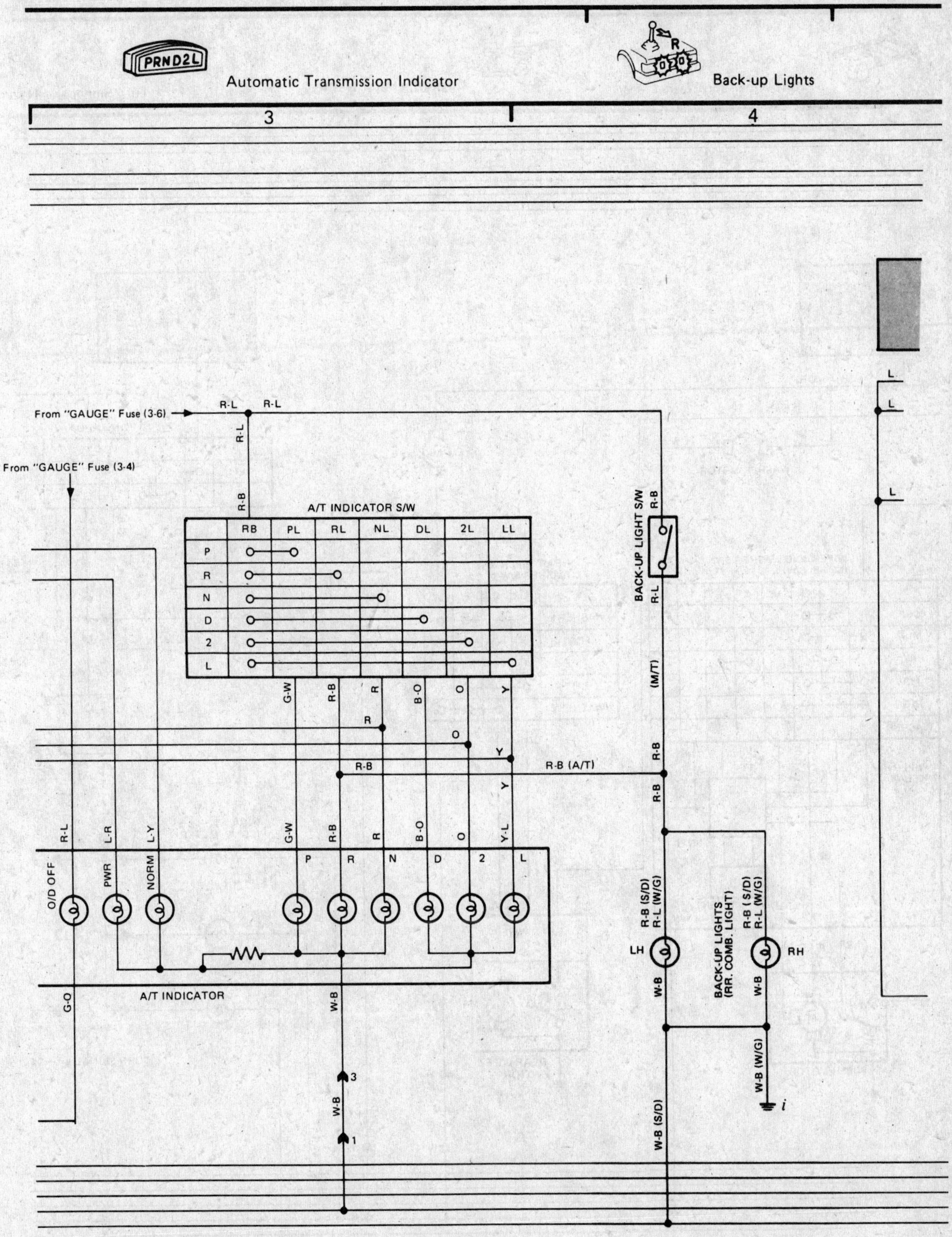

Automatic Transmission Indicator

Back-up Lights

3

4

From "GAUGE" Fuse (3-6)
R-L
R-L
From "GAUGE" Fuse (3-4)
R-B
A/T INDICATOR S/W

	RB	PL	RL	NL	DL	2L	LL
P	○	○					
R	○		○				
N	○			○			
D	○				○		
2	○					○	
L	○						○

G-W R-B R B-O O Y
R
O
Y
R-B
R-B (A/T)
R-L L-R L-Y G-W R-B R B-O O Y-L
O/D OFF PWR NORM P R N D 2 L
A/T INDICATOR
G-O
W-B
3
W-B
1

BACK-UP LIGHT S/W
R-B
R-L
(M/T)
R-B
R-B
R-B (S/D)
R-L (W/G)
LH
W-B
BACK-UP LIGHTS
(RR. COMB. LIGHT)
R-B (S/D)
R-L (W/G)
RH
W-B
W-B (W/G)
i
W-B (S/D)

L
L
L

d = Located under left front pillar in J/B No. 1

g = Located on left rear fender

h = Located on center of back panel (S/D)
Located on right of deck (W/G)

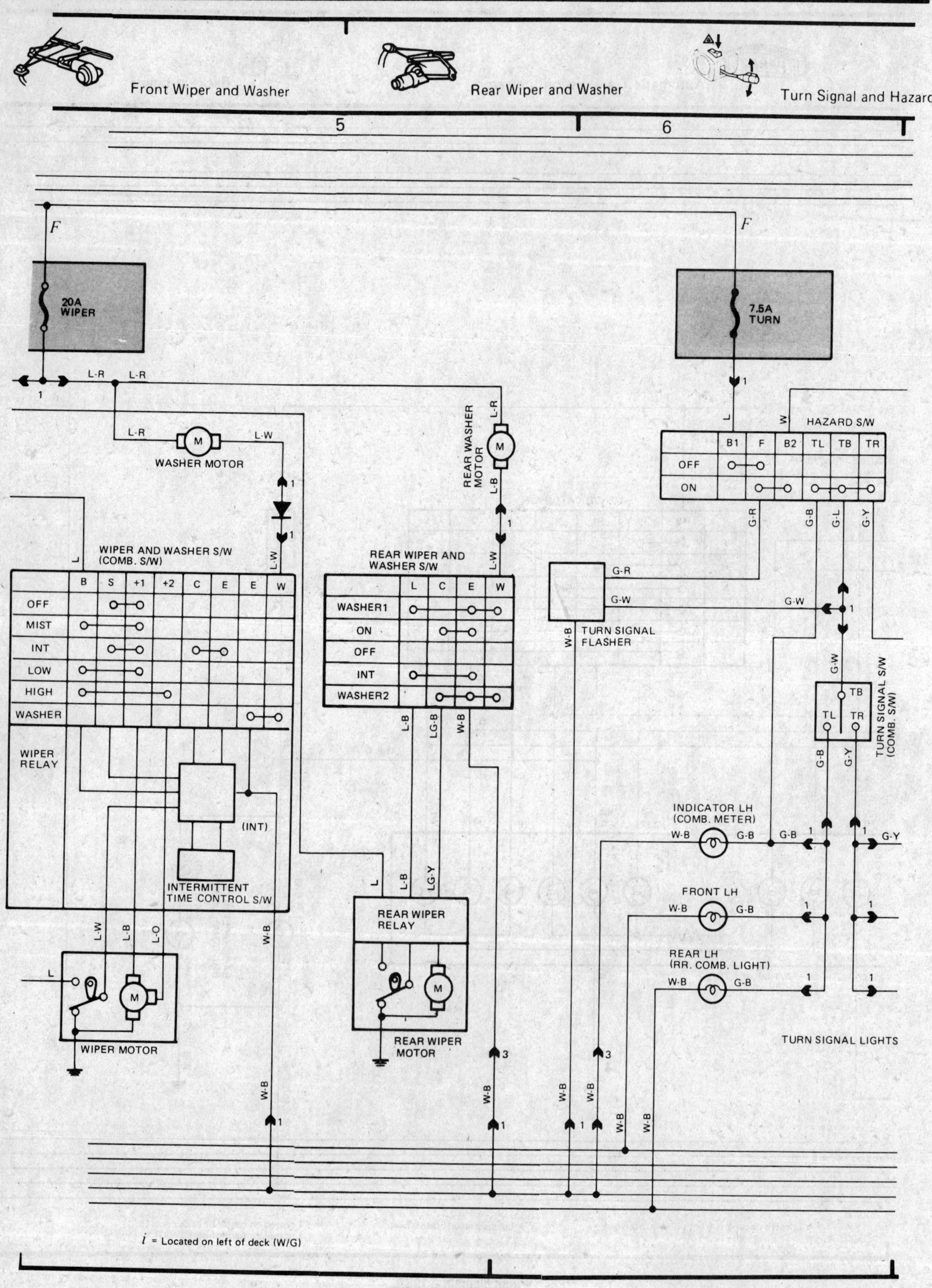

Wiring diagram—1987

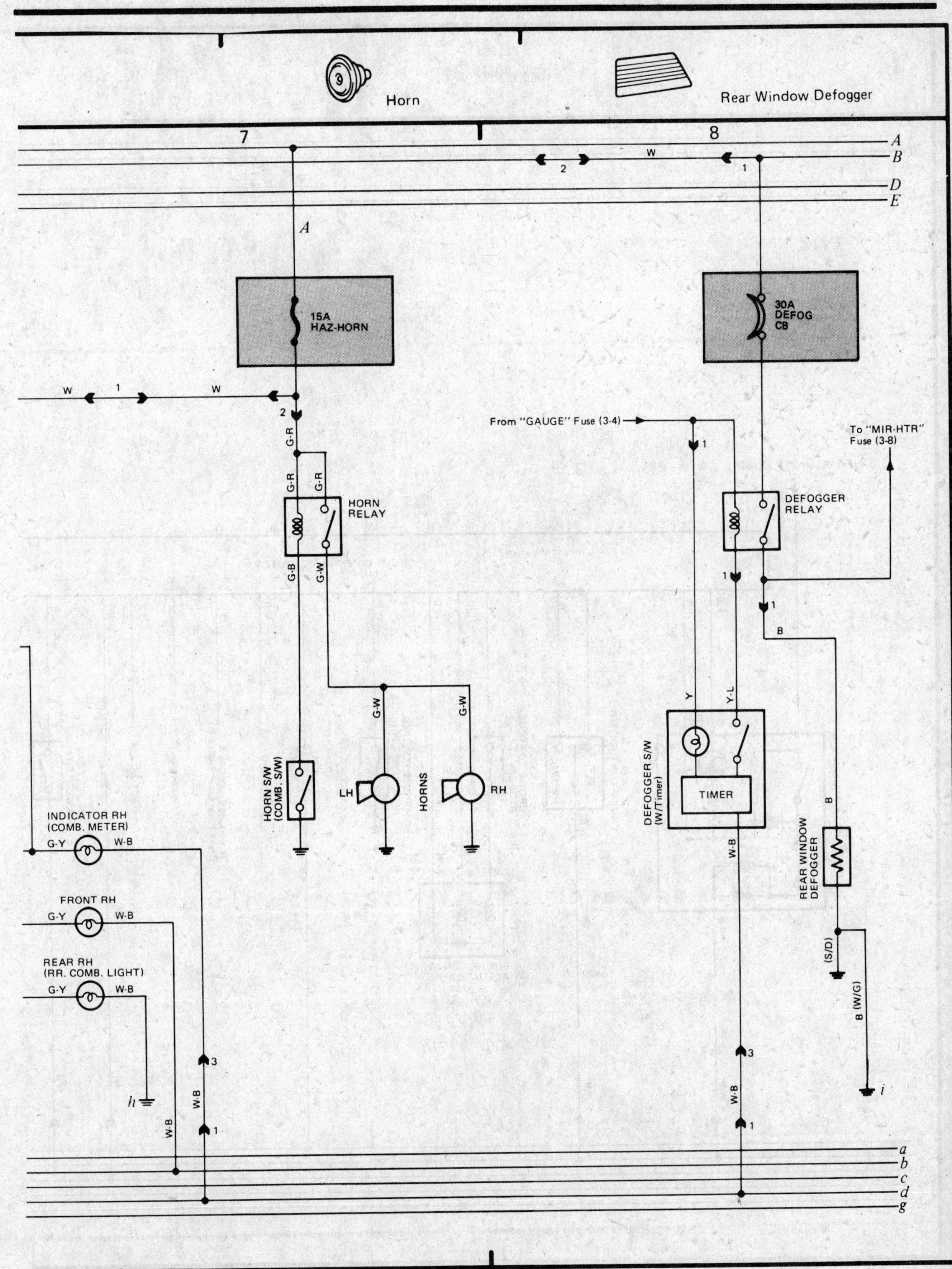

Wiring diagram—1987

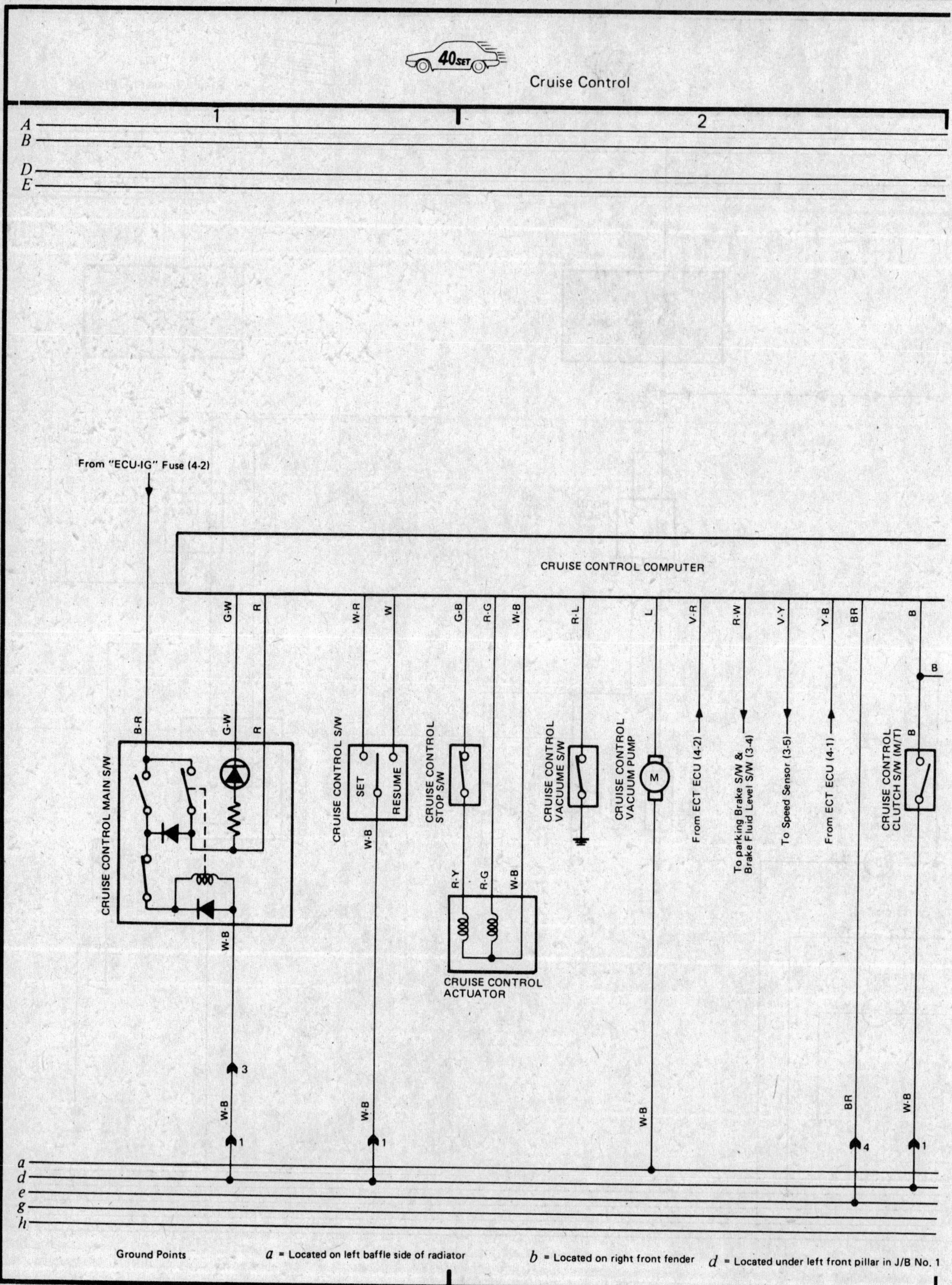

40SET
Cruise Control
1
2
A
B
D
E
From "ECU-IG" Fuse (4-2)
CRUISE CONTROL COMPUTER
G-W
R
W-R
W
G-B
R-G
W-B
R-L
L
V-R
R-W
V-Y
Y-B
BR
B
CRUISE CONTROL MAIN S/W
B-R
CRUISE CONTROL S/W
SET
RESUME
CRUISE CONTROL STOP S/W
R-Y
CRUISE CONTROL ACTUATOR
CRUISE CONTROL VACUUME S/W
CRUISE CONTROL VACUUM PUMP
M
From ECT ECU (4-2)
To parking Brake S/W &
Brake Fluid Level S/W (3-4)
To Speed Sensor (3-5)
From ECT ECU (4-1)
CRUISE CONTROL CLUTCH S/W (M/T)
3
1
4
a
d
e
g
h
Ground Points
a = Located on left baffle side of radiator
b = Located on right front fender
d = Located under left front pillar in J/B No. 1

Wiring diagram—1987

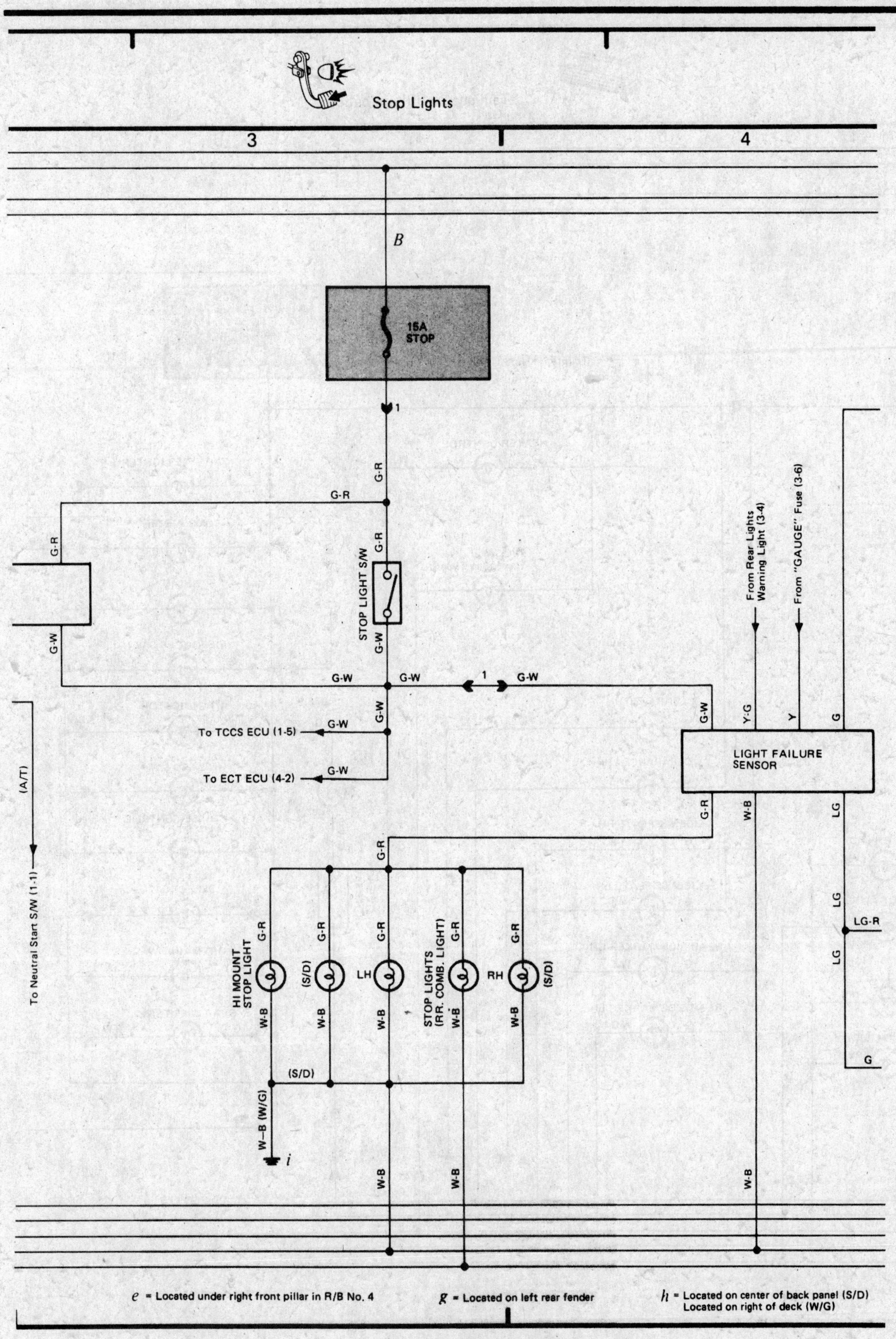

e = Located under right front pillar in R/B No. 4

g = Located on left rear fender

h = Located on center of back panel (S/D)
Located on right of deck (W/G)

Wiring diagram—1987

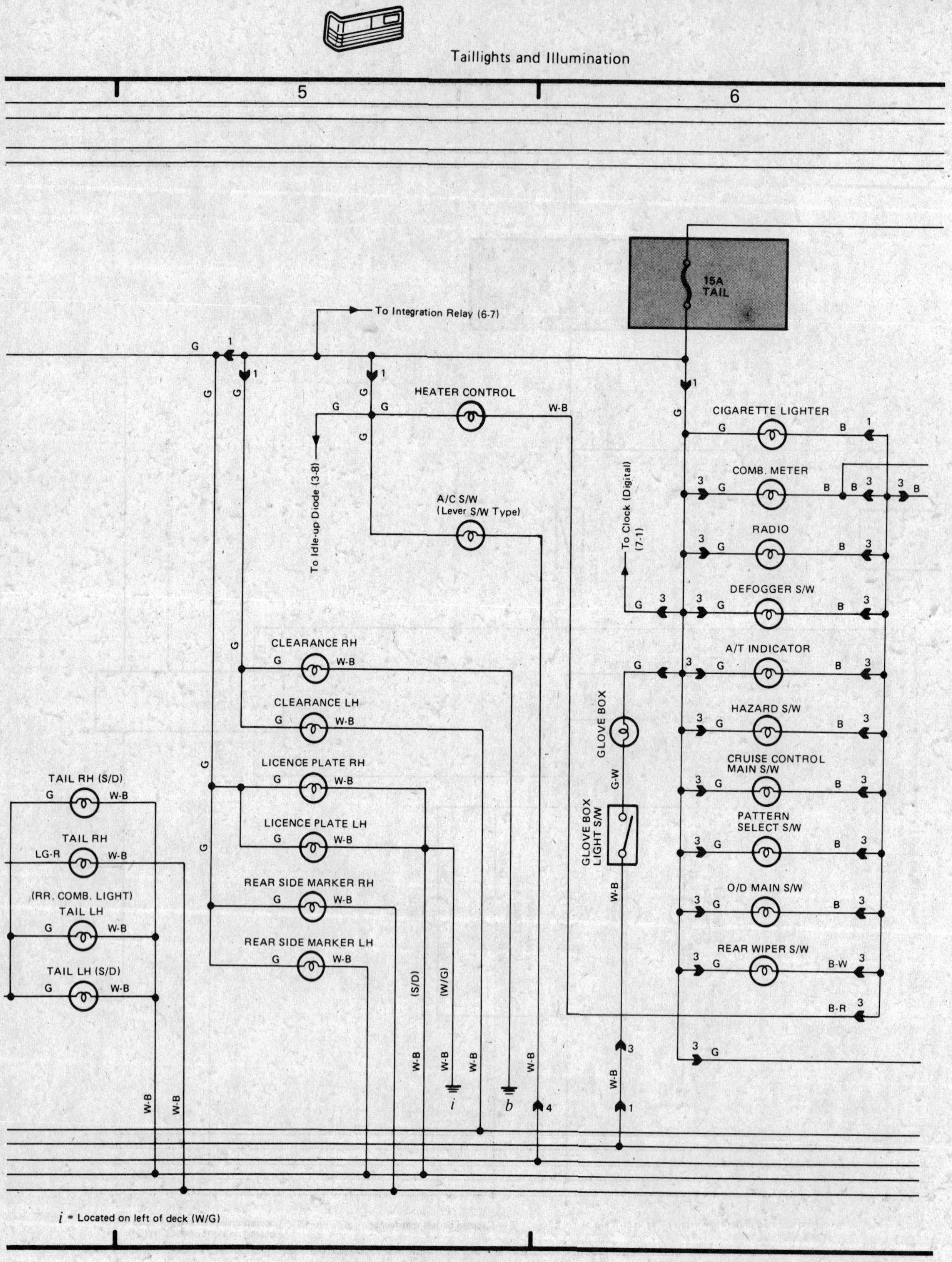

Taillights and Illumination

5

6

15A TAIL

To Integration Relay (6-7)

HEATER CONTROL

To Idle-up Diode (3-8)

A/C S/W
(Lever S/W Type)

To Clock (Digital)
(7-1)

CIGARETTE LIGHTER

COMB. METER

RADIO

DEFOGGER S/W

A/T INDICATOR

HAZARD S/W

CRUISE CONTROL
MAIN S/W

PATTERN
SELECT S/W

O/D MAIN S/W

REAR WIPER S/W

GLOVE BOX

GLOVE BOX
LIGHT S/W

CLEARANCE RH

CLEARANCE LH

LICENCE PLATE RH

LICENCE PLATE LH

REAR SIDE MARKER RH

REAR SIDE MARKER LH

TAIL RH (S/D)

TAIL RH

(RR. COMB. LIGHT)
TAIL LH

TAIL LH (S/D)

(S/D)

(W/G)

i = Located on left of deck (W/G)

Wiring diagram—1987

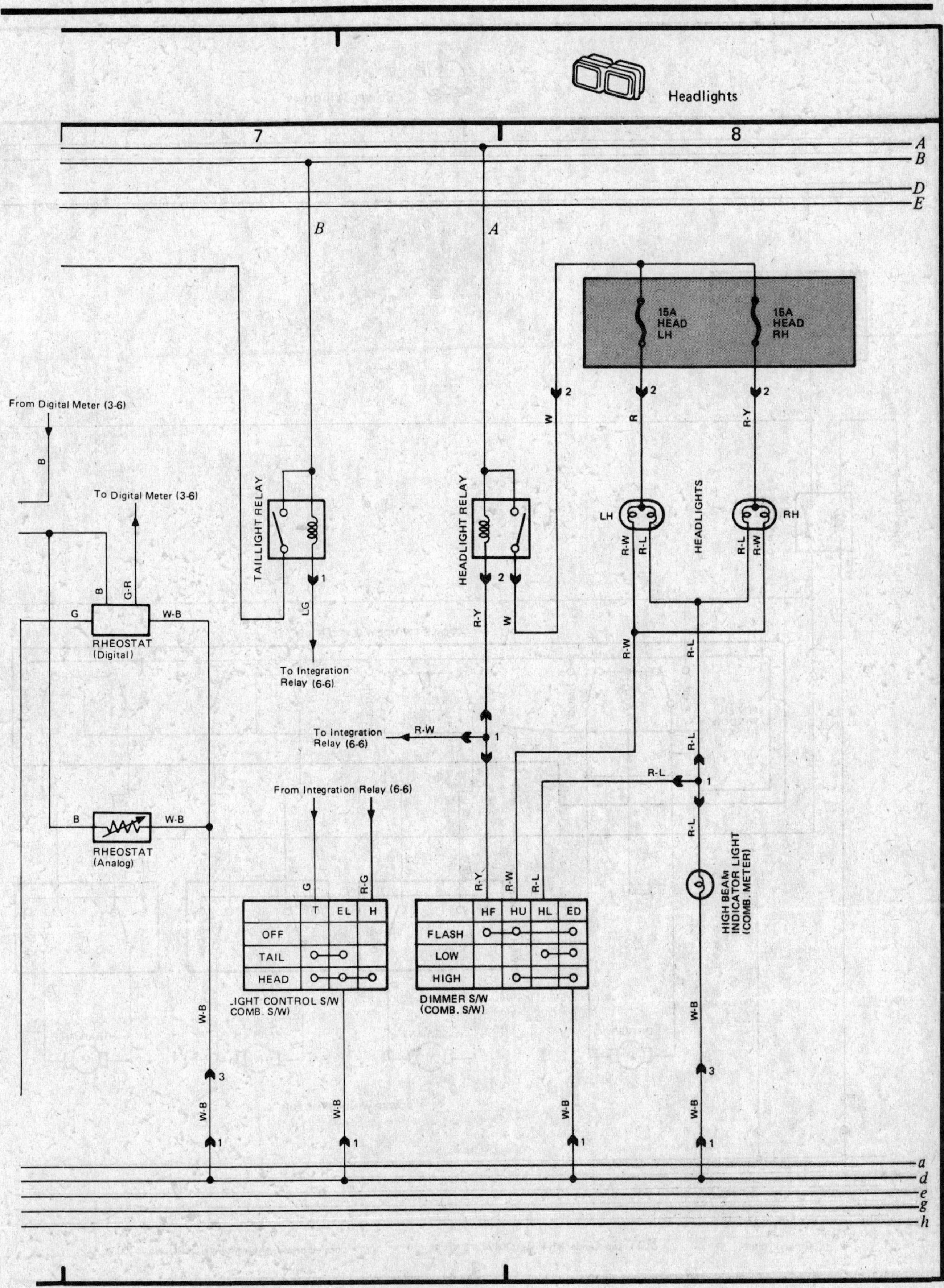

Wiring diagram—1987

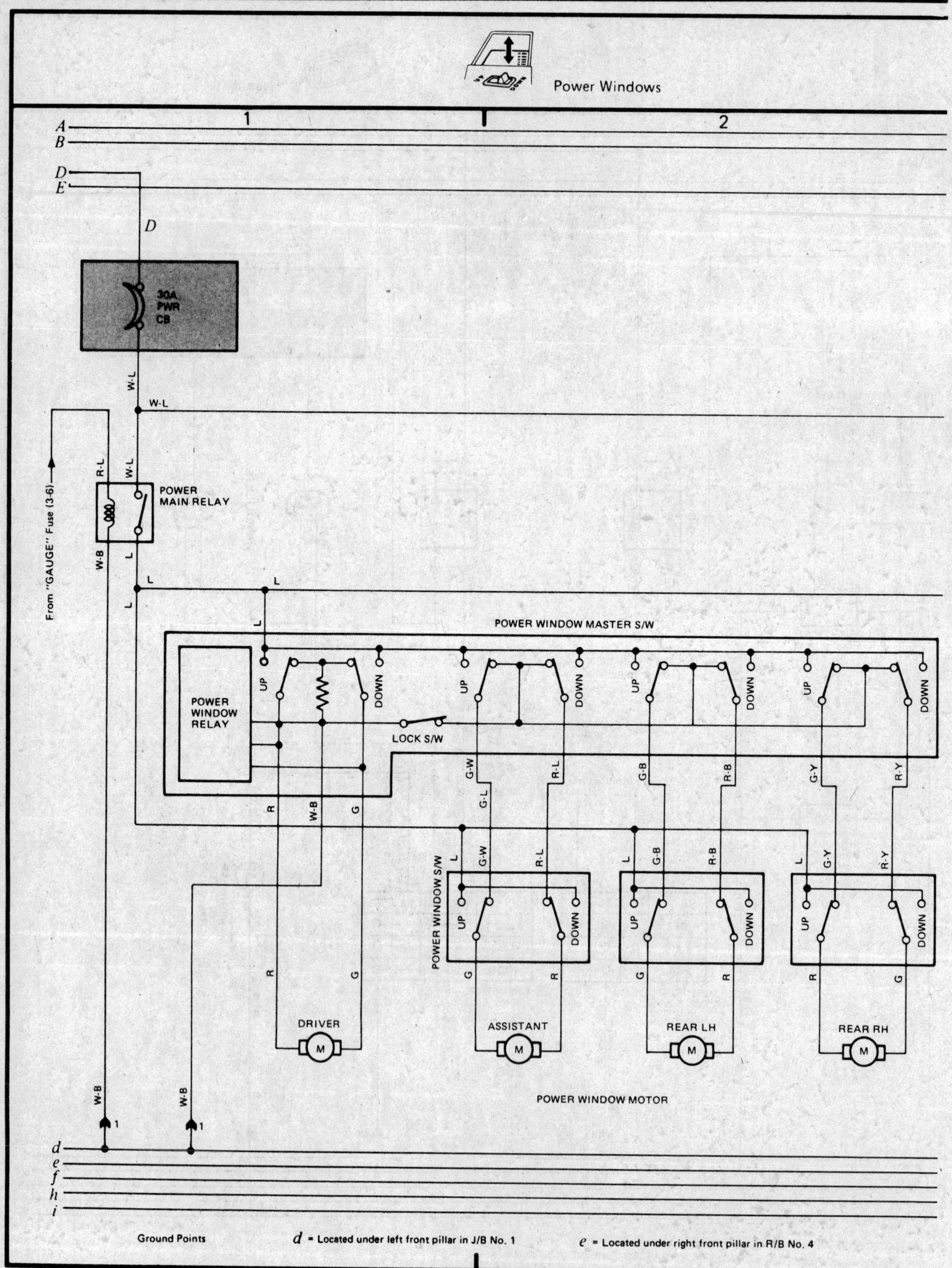

Wiring diagram—1987

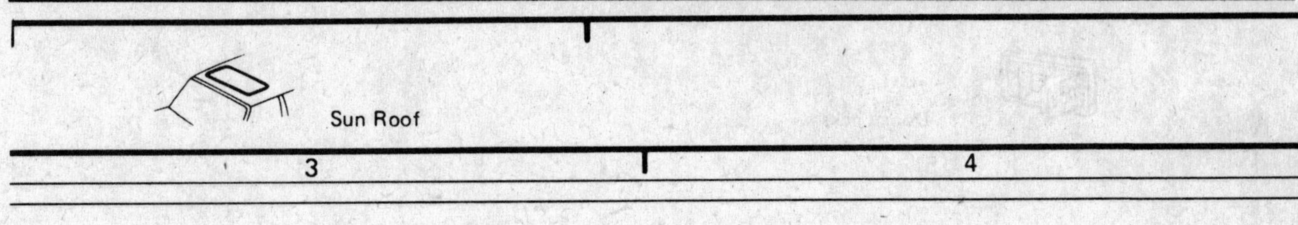

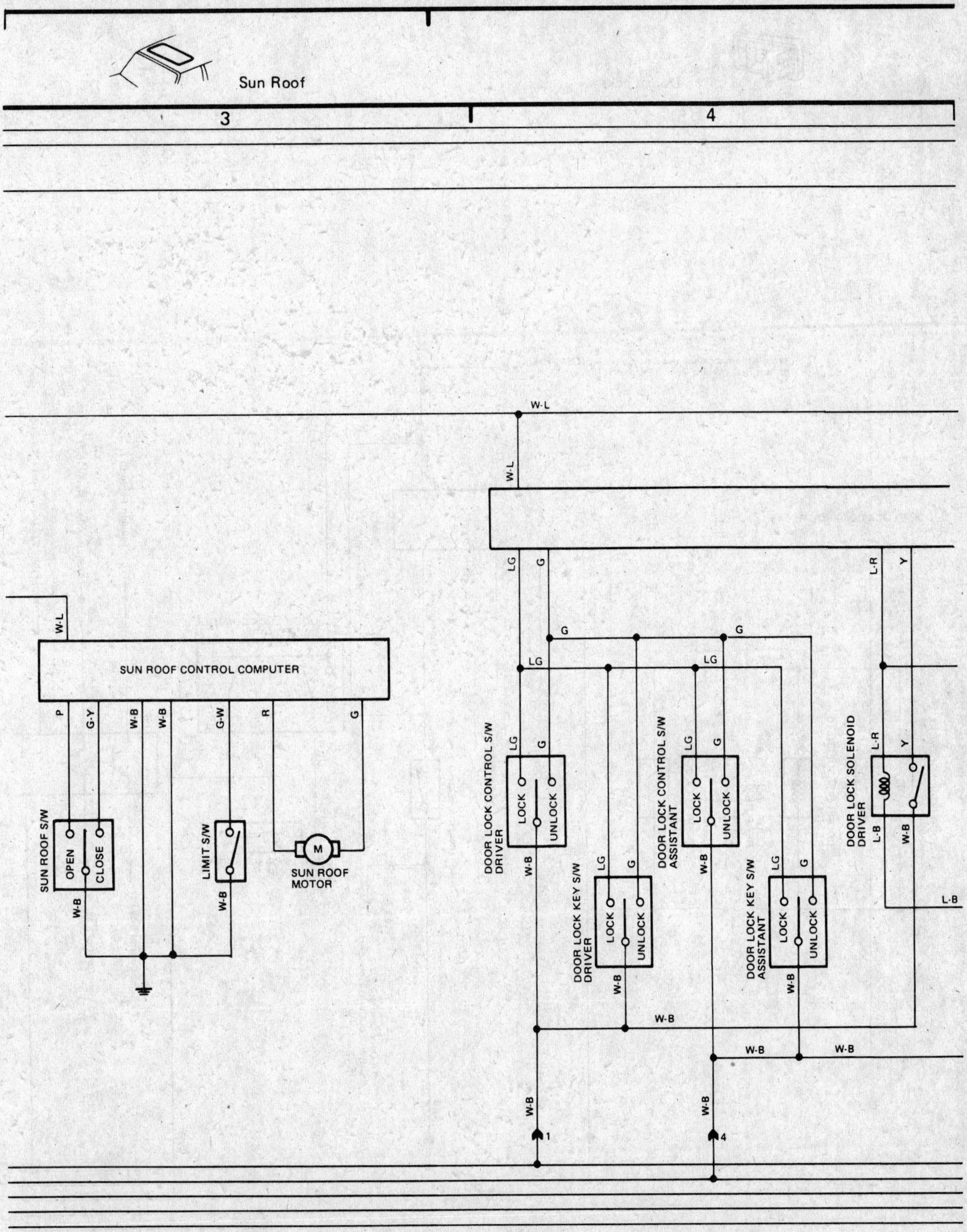

W-L
SUN ROOF CONTROL COMPUTER
P G-Y W-B W-B G-W R G
SUN ROOF S/W
OPEN
CLOSE
W-B
LIMIT S/W
W-B
M
SUN ROOF MOTOR

W-L
LG G
LG G
DOOR LOCK CONTROL S/W DRIVER
LOCK UNLOCK
W-B
DOOR LOCK KEY S/W DRIVER
LOCK UNLOCK
W-B
DOOR LOCK CONTROL S/W ASSISTANT
LOCK UNLOCK
W-B
DOOR LOCK KEY S/W ASSISTANT
LOCK UNLOCK
W-B
L-R Y
DOOR LOCK SOLENOID DRIVER
L-B W-B
L-B
W-B
W-B W-B
1
4

f = Located under left front pillar

h = Located on center of back panel (S/D)
Located on right of deck (W/G)

i = Located on left of deck (W/G)

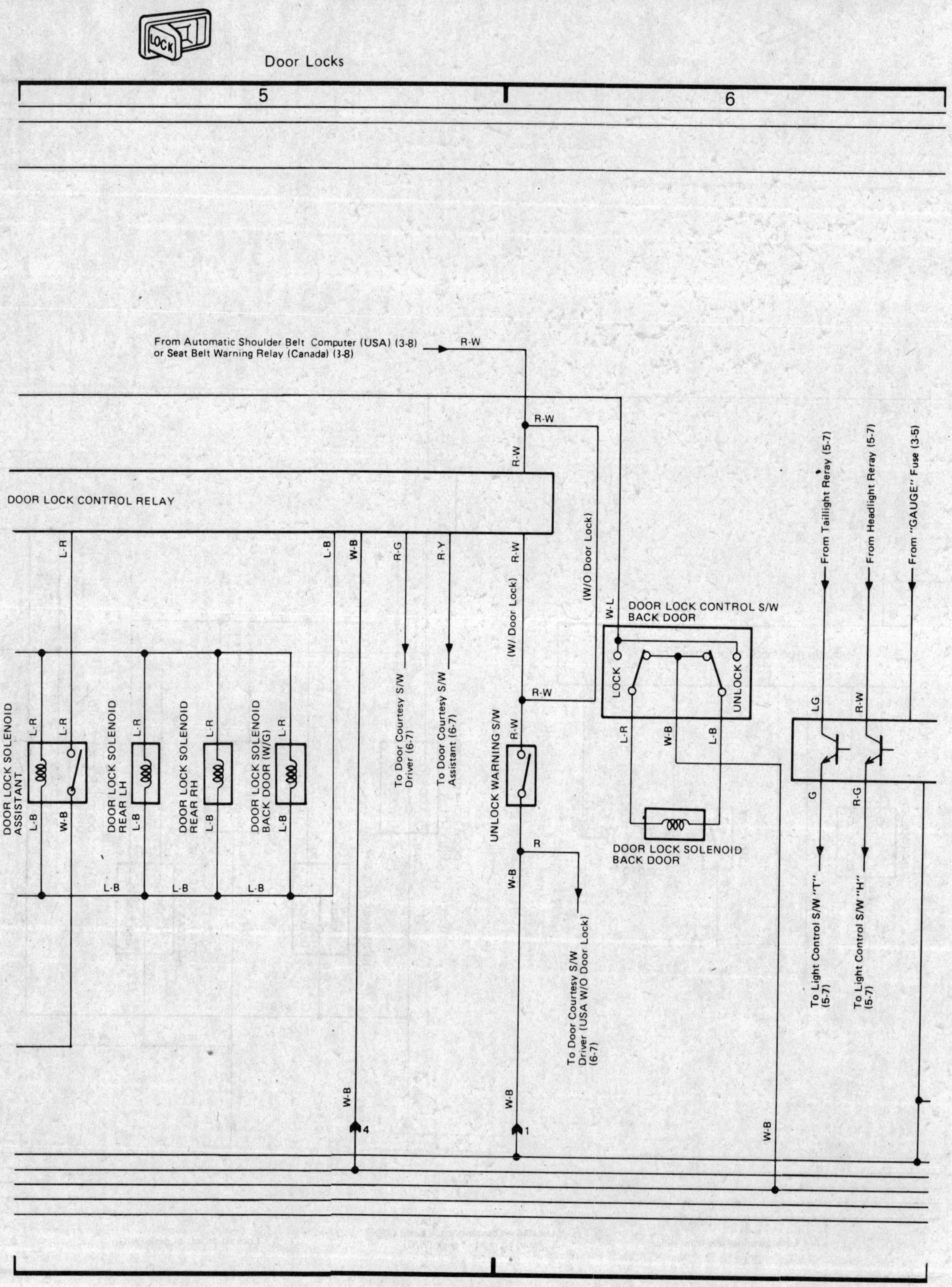

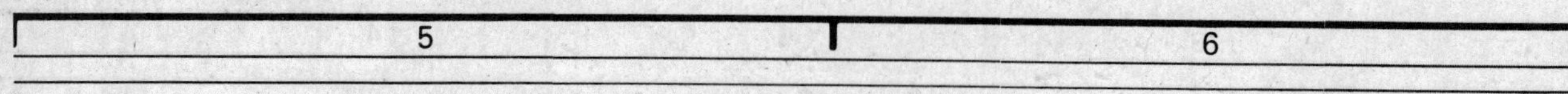

Door Locks

5

6

From Automatic Shoulder Belt Computer (USA) (3-8)
or Seat Belt Warning Relay (Canada) (3-8)
R-W
R-W
R-W
DOOR LOCK CONTROL RELAY
L-R
L-B
W-B
R-G
R-Y
R-W
(W/ Door Lock)
(W/O Door Lock)
W-L
DOOR LOCK CONTROL S/W
BACK DOOR
LOCK
UNLOCK
L-R
W-B
L-B
From Taillight Reray (5-7)
From Headlight Reray (5-7)
From "GAUGE" Fuse (3-5)
LG
R-W
G
R-G
DOOR LOCK SOLENOID
ASSISTANT
DOOR LOCK SOLENOID
REAR LH
DOOR LOCK SOLENOID
REAR RH
DOOR LOCK SOLENOID
BACK DOOR (W/G)
To Door Courtesy S/W
Driver (6-7)
To Door Courtesy S/W
Assistant (6-7)
UNLOCK WARNING S/W
R-W
R
W-B
DOOR LOCK SOLENOID
BACK DOOR
To Door Courtesy S/W
Driver (USA W/O Door Lock)
(6-7)
To Light Control S/W "T"
(5-7)
To Light Control S/W "H"
(5-7)
L-B
W-B
W-B
4
W-B
1
W-B

Wiring diagram—1987

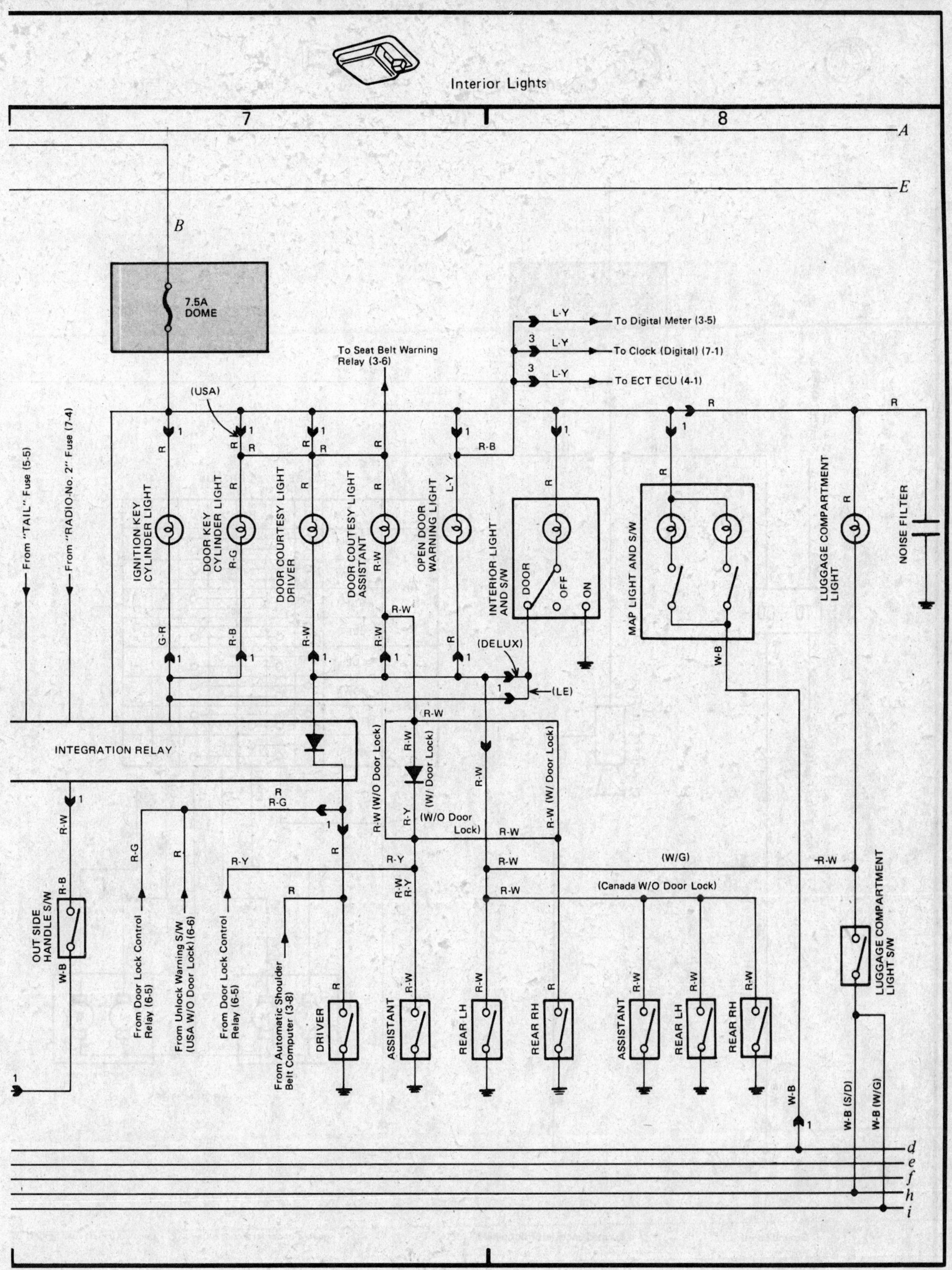

Wiring diagram—1987

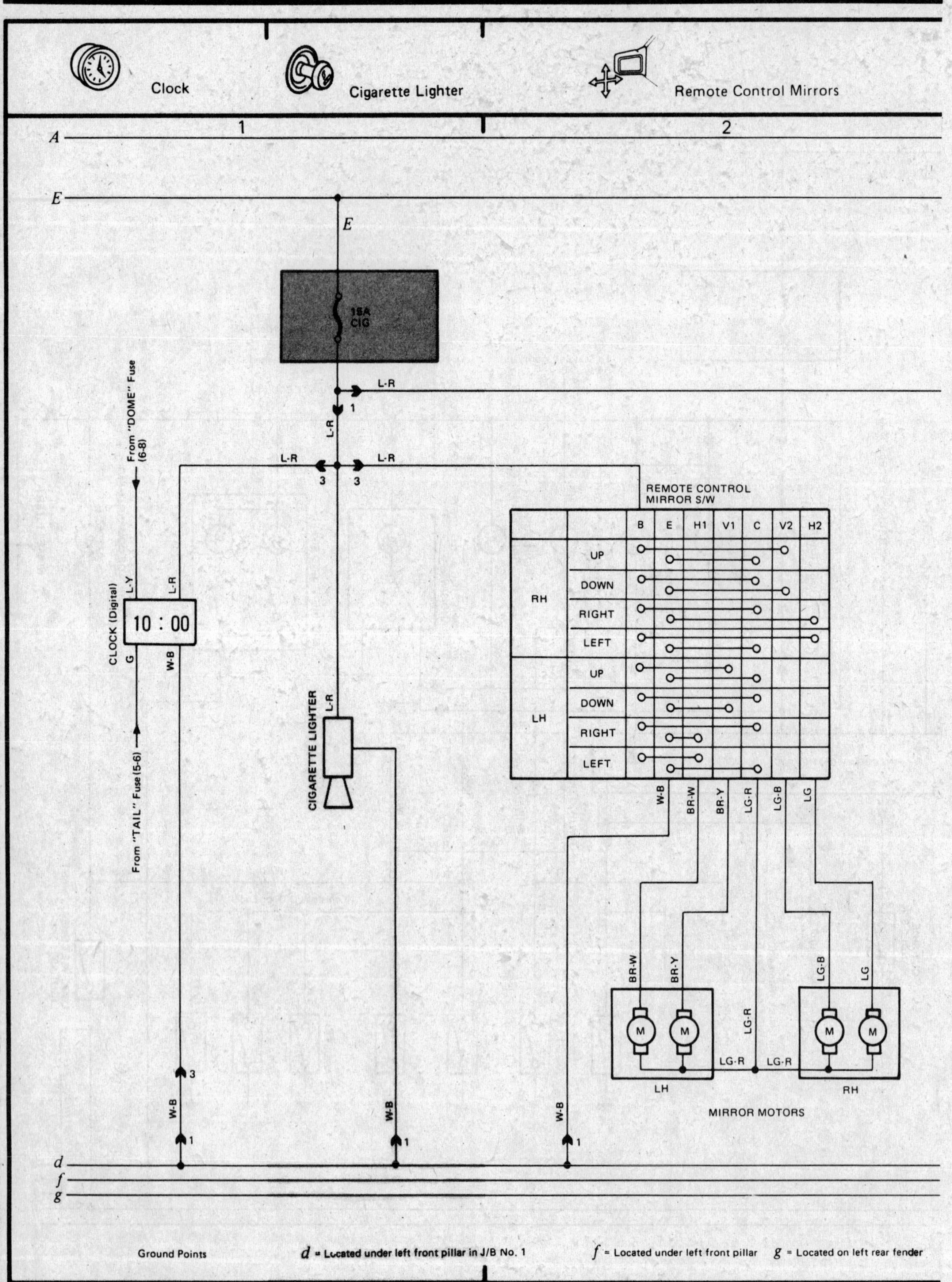

Ground Points *d* = Located under left front pillar in J/B No. 1 *f* = Located under left front pillar *g* = Located on left rear fender

Wiring diagram—1987

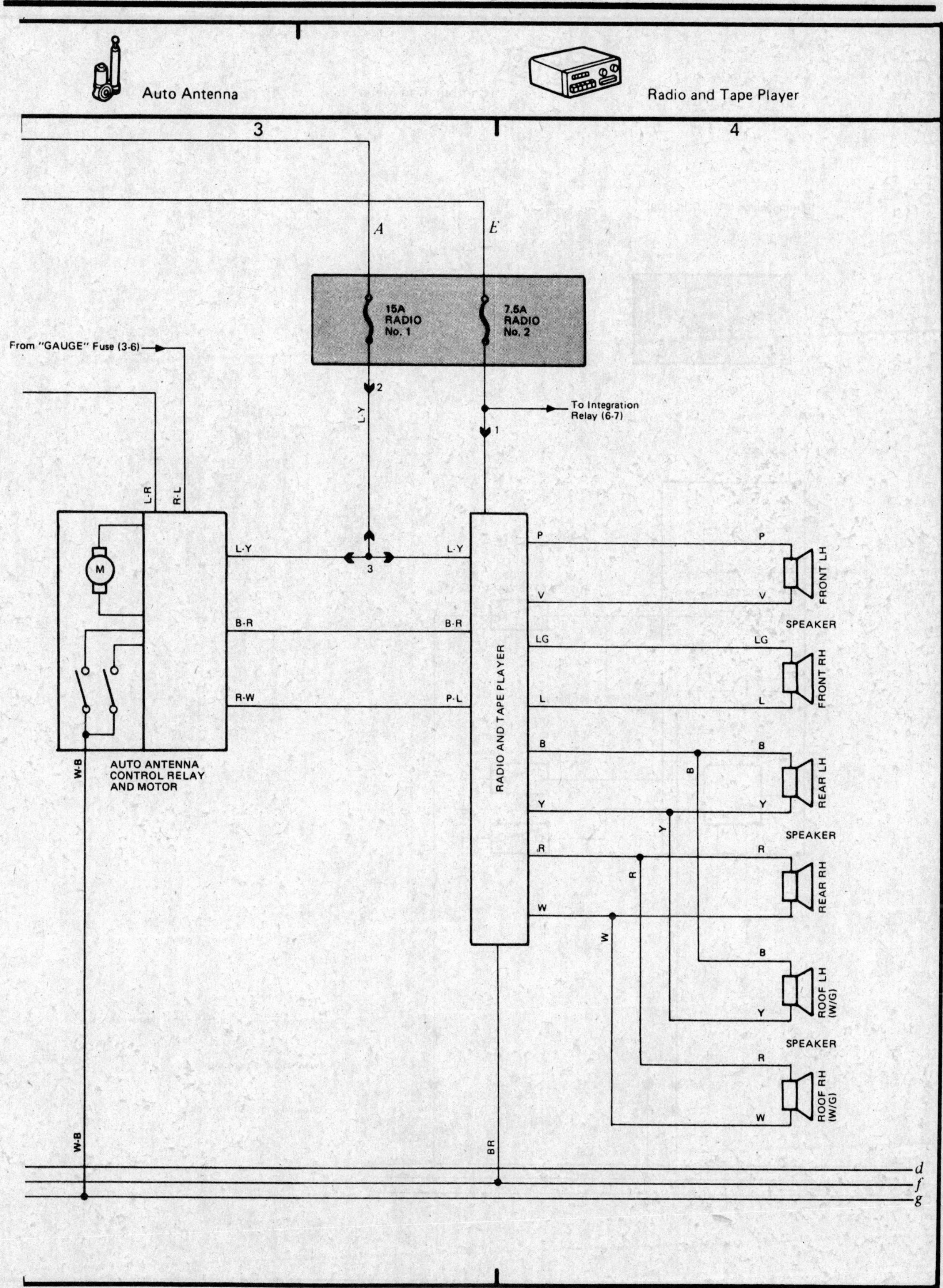

Wiring diagram—1987

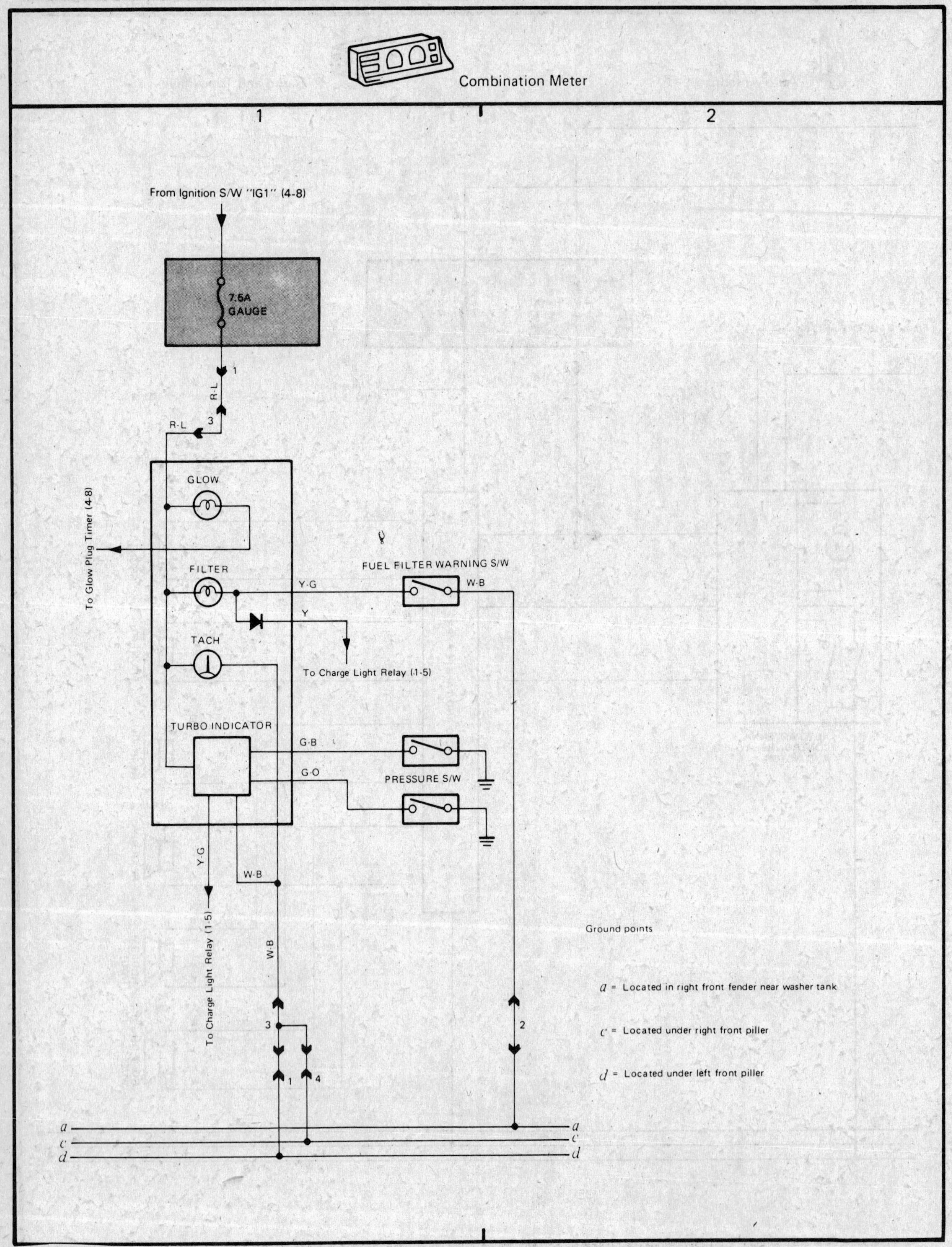
Combination Meter
1
2
From Ignition S/W "IG1" (4-8)
7.5A
GAUGE
R-L
R-L
GLOW
To Glow Plug Timer (4-8)
FILTER
Y-G
FUEL FILTER WARNING S/W
W-B
Y
TACH
To Charge Light Relay (1-5)
TURBO INDICATOR
G-B
G-O
PRESSURE S/W
Y-G
W-B
W-B
To Charge Light Relay (1-5)
Ground points
a = Located in right front fender near washer tank
c = Located under right front piller
d = Located under left front piller

Wiring diagram—1984

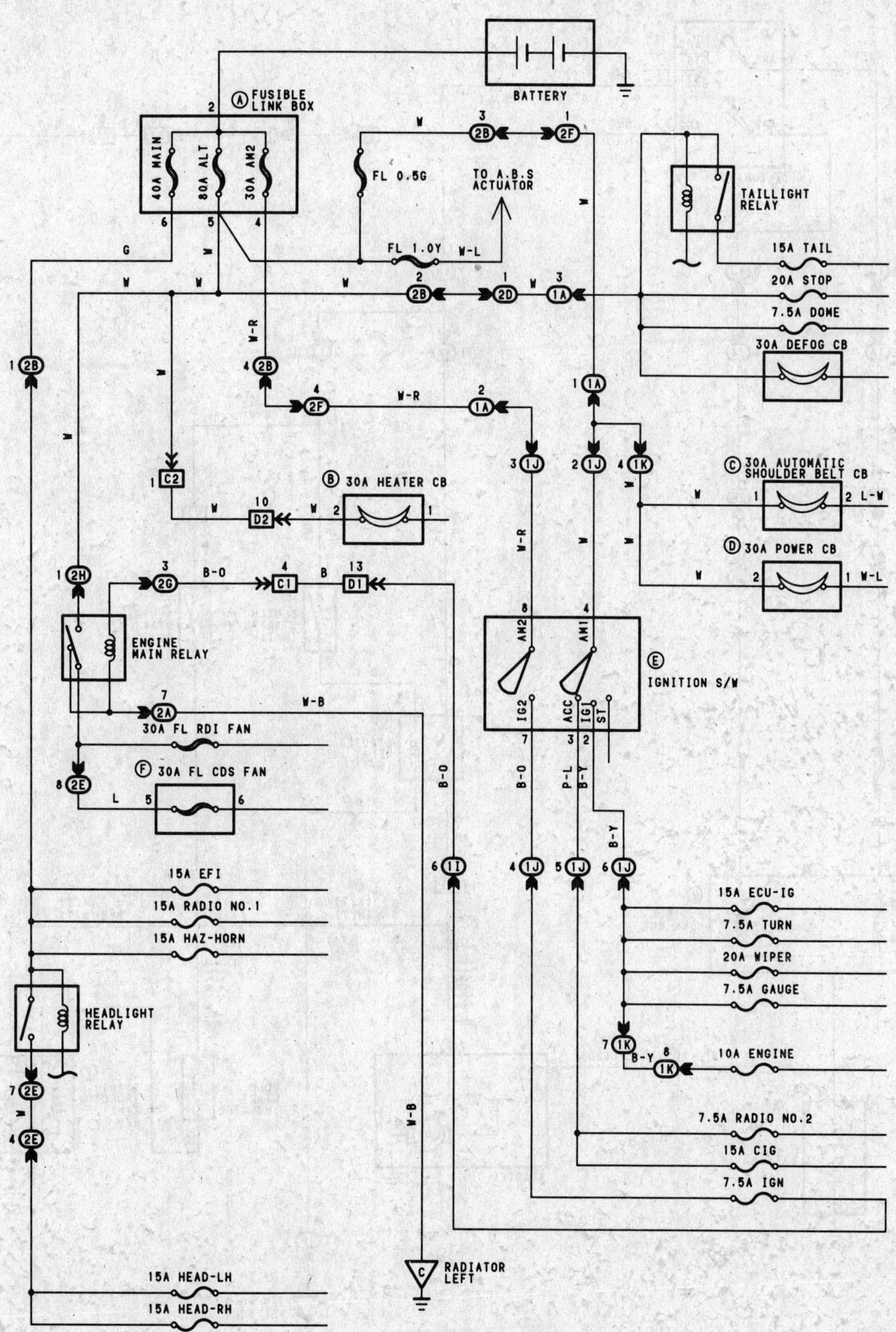

Power source—1988 wiring diagram

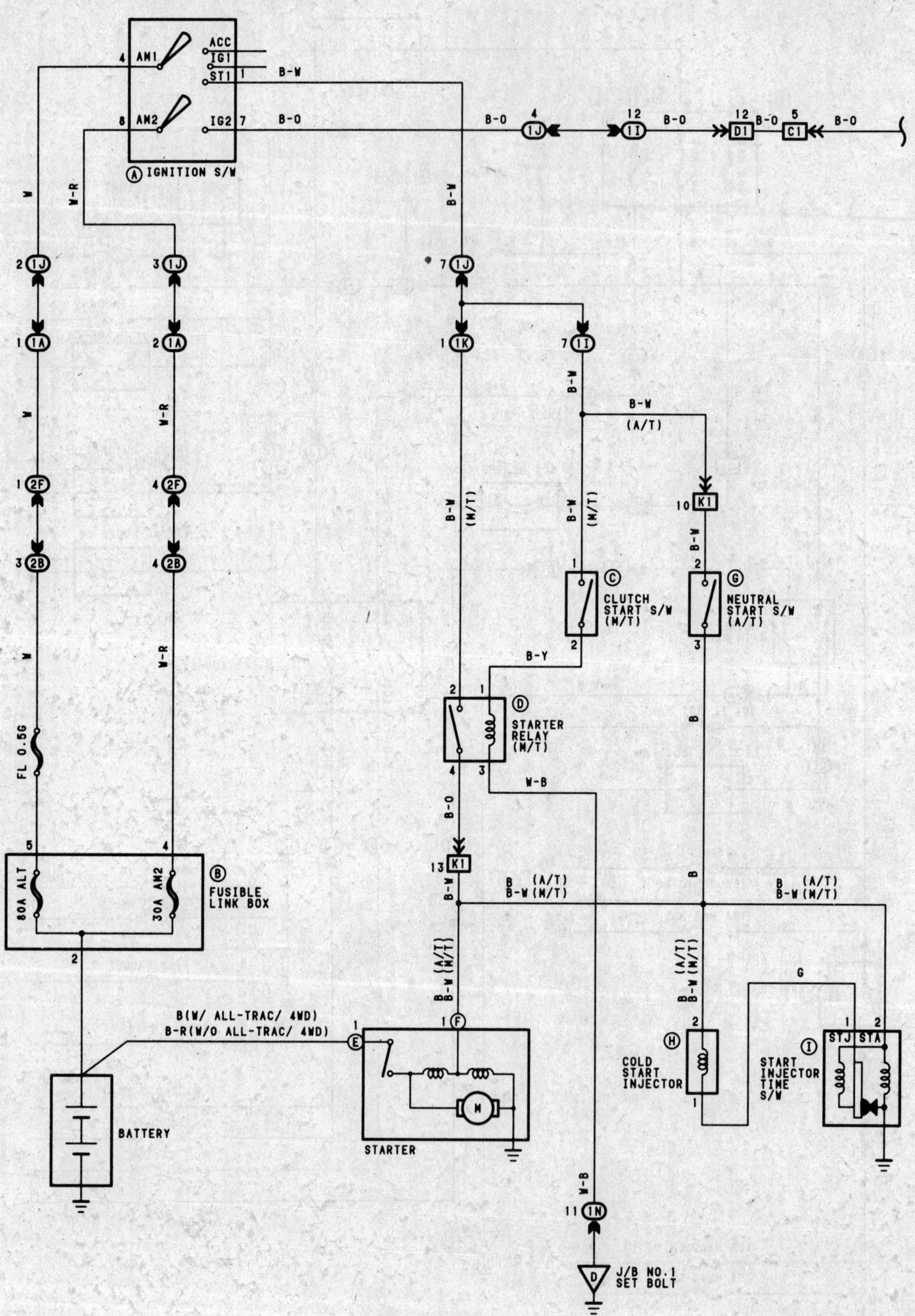

Starting and ignition systems—1988 wiring diagram

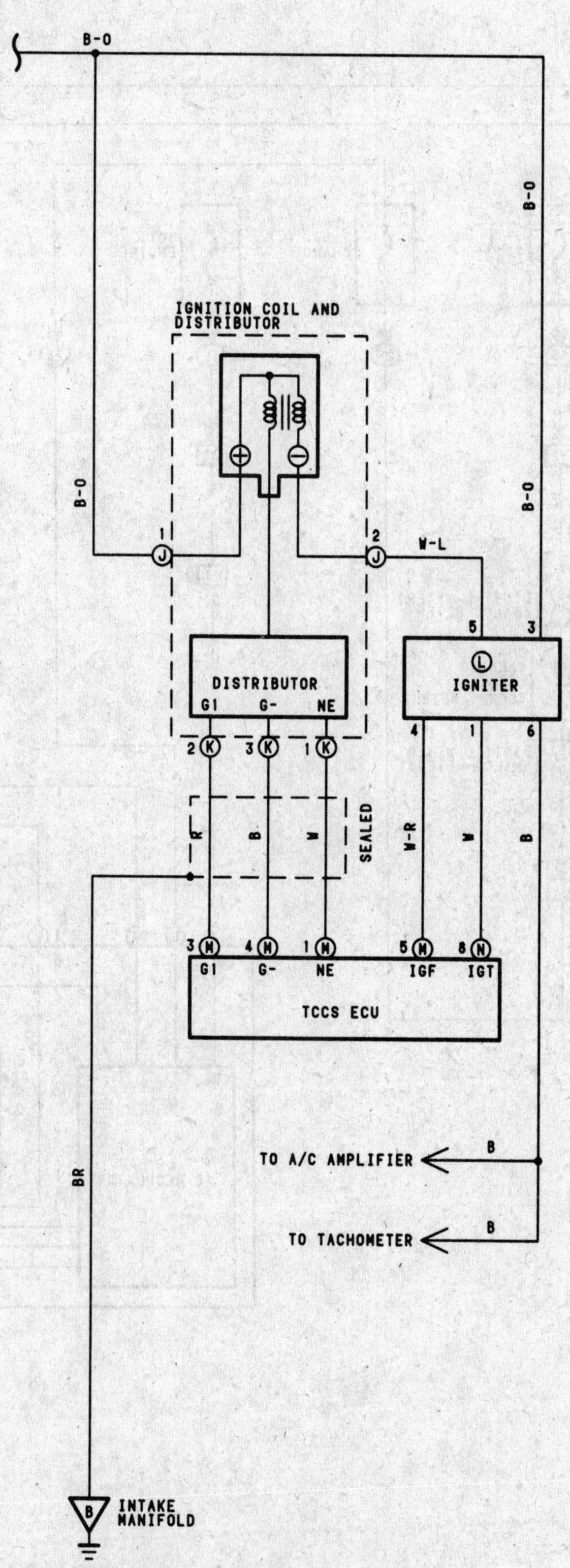

Starting and ignition systems—1988 wiring diagram

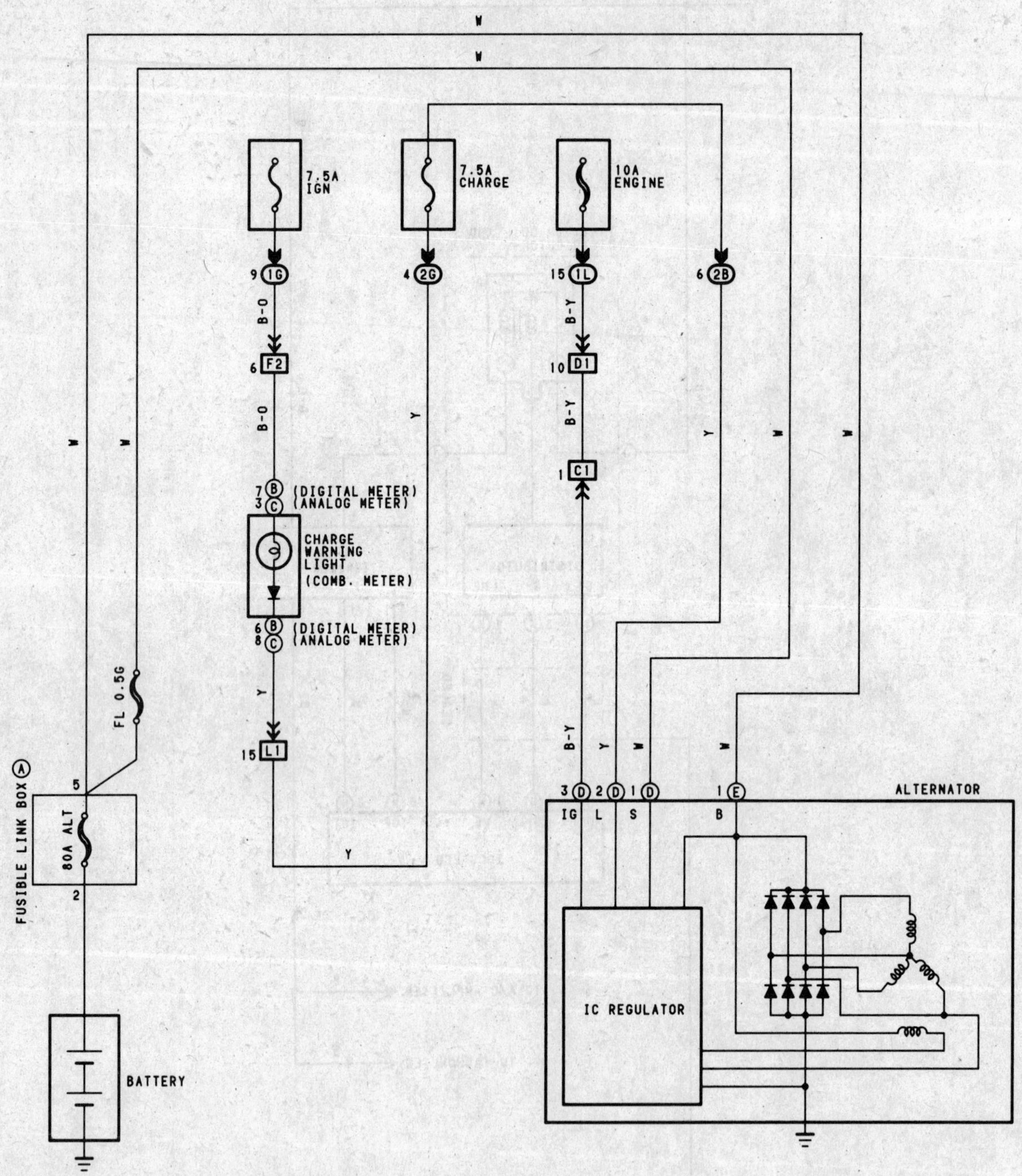

Charging system—1988 wiring diagram

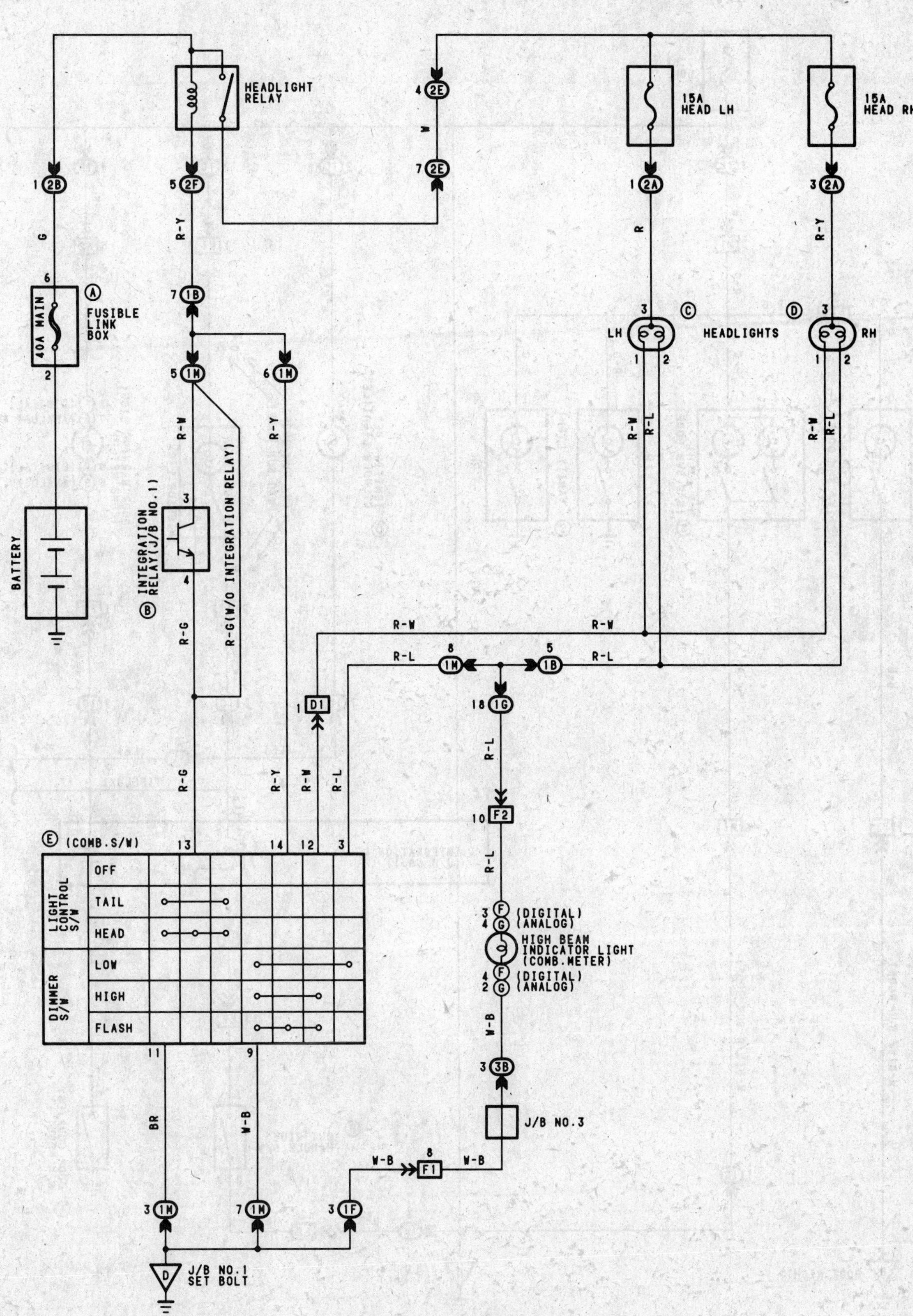

Headlights—1988 wiring diagram

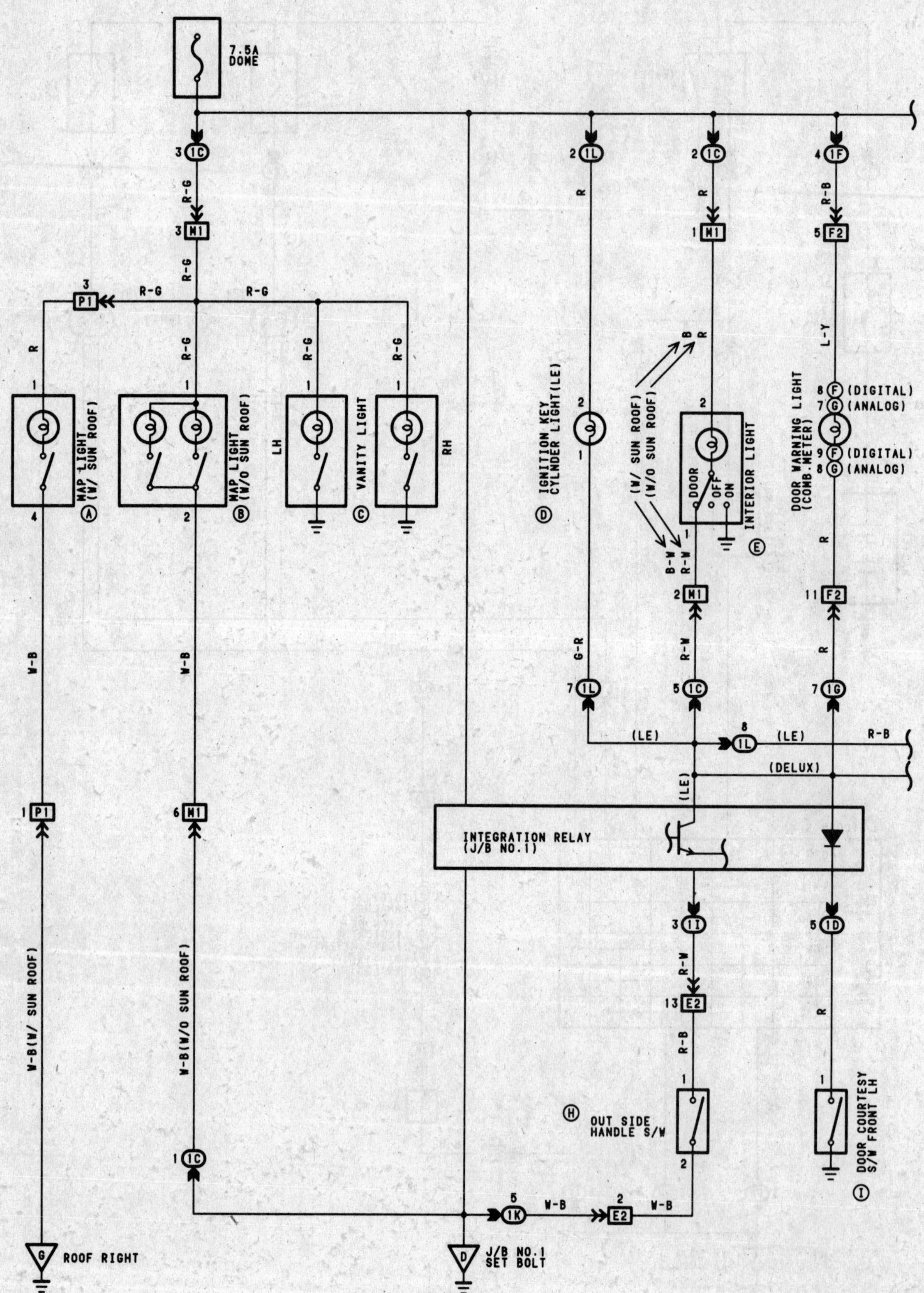

Interior lights with door locks—1988 wiring diagram

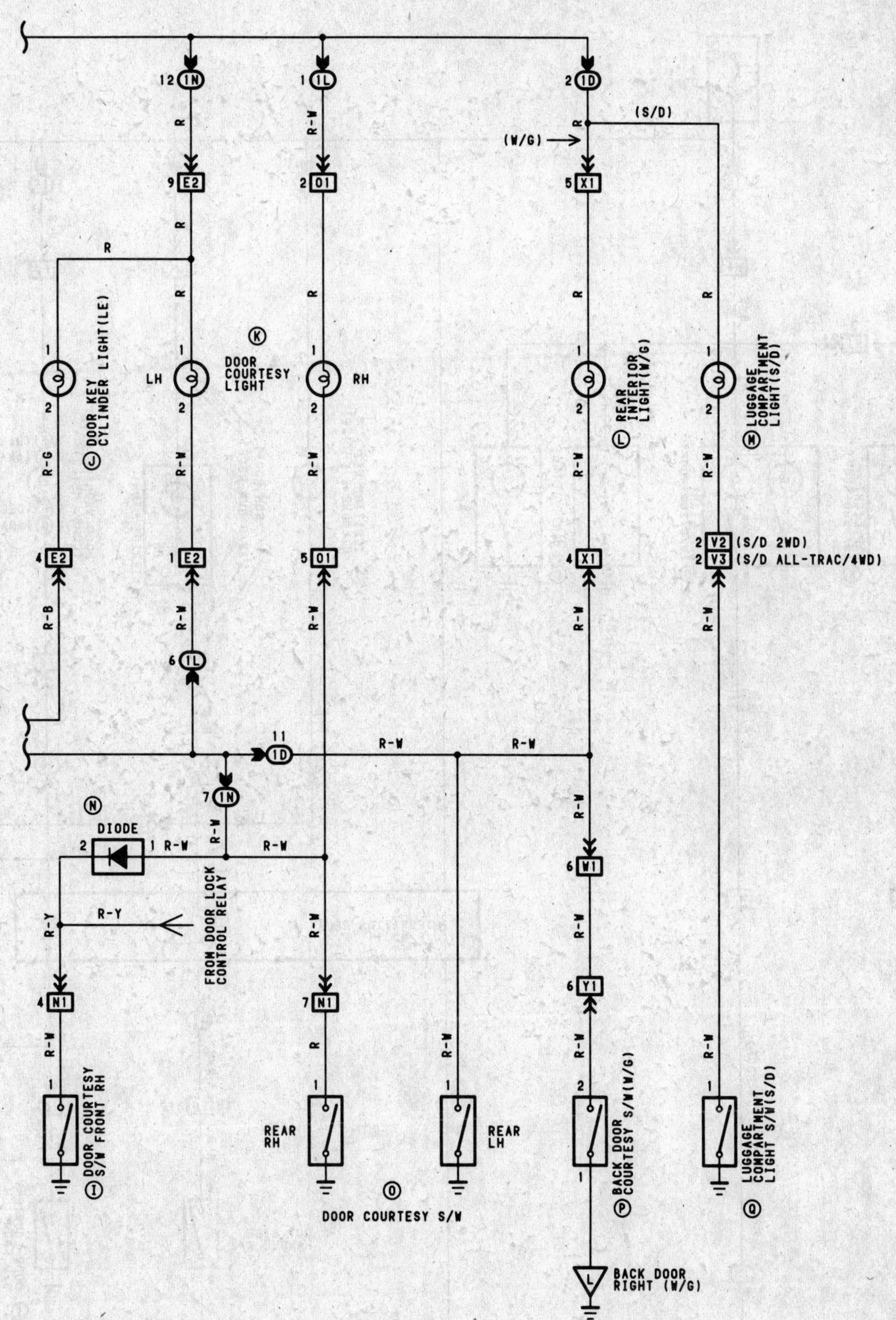

Interior lights with door locks—1988 wiring diagram

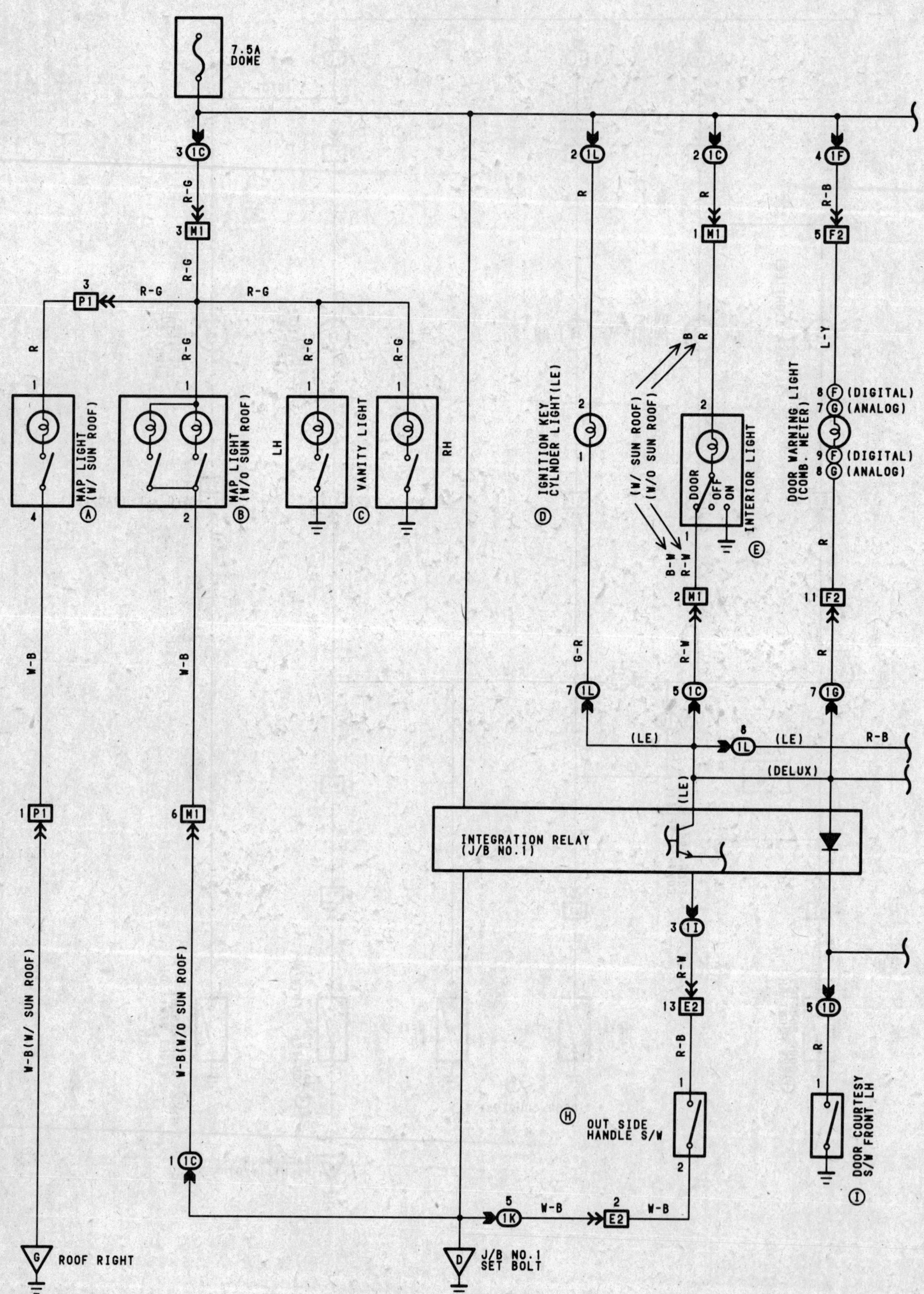

Interior lights without door locks—1988 wiring diagram

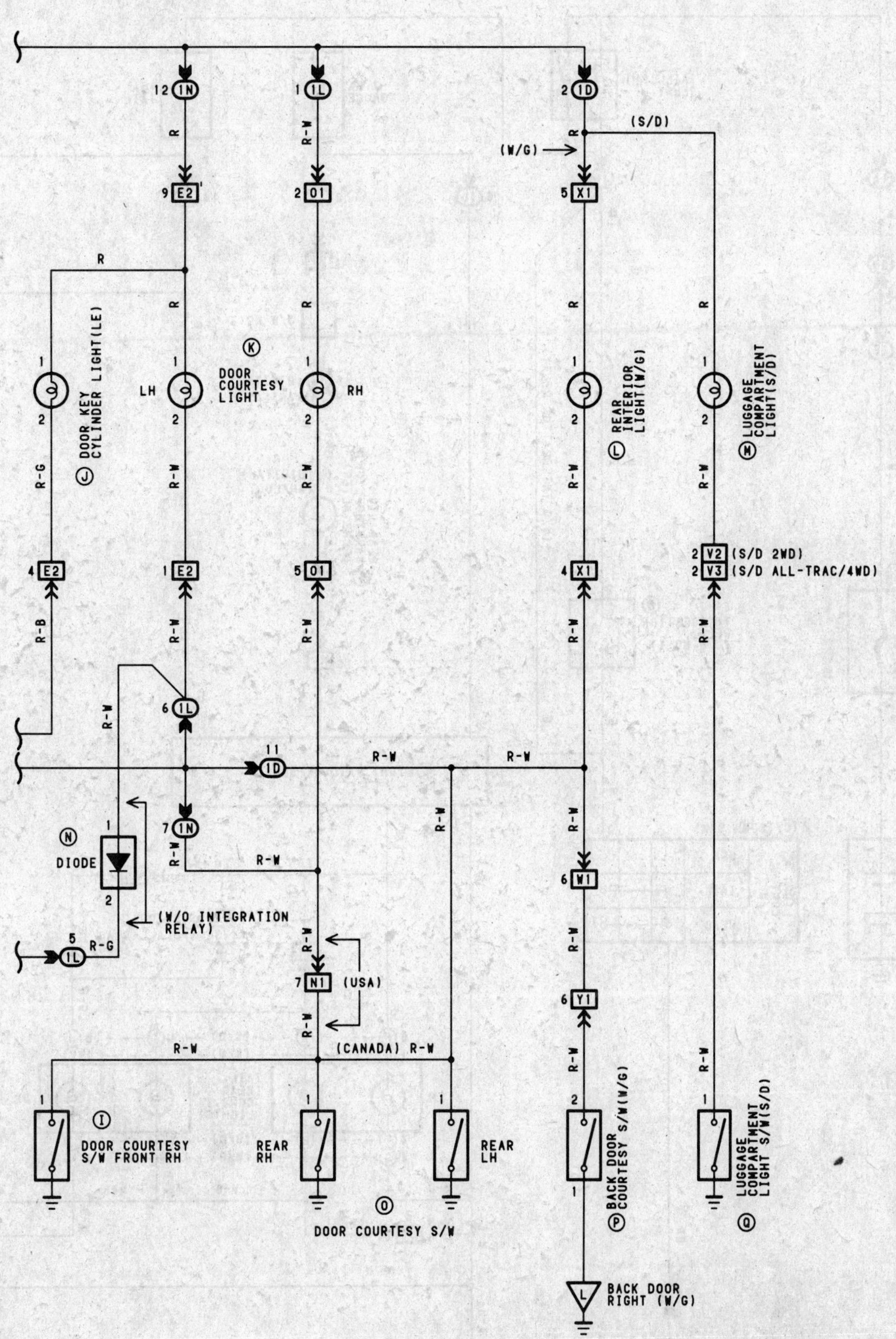

Interior lights without door locks—1988 wiring diagram

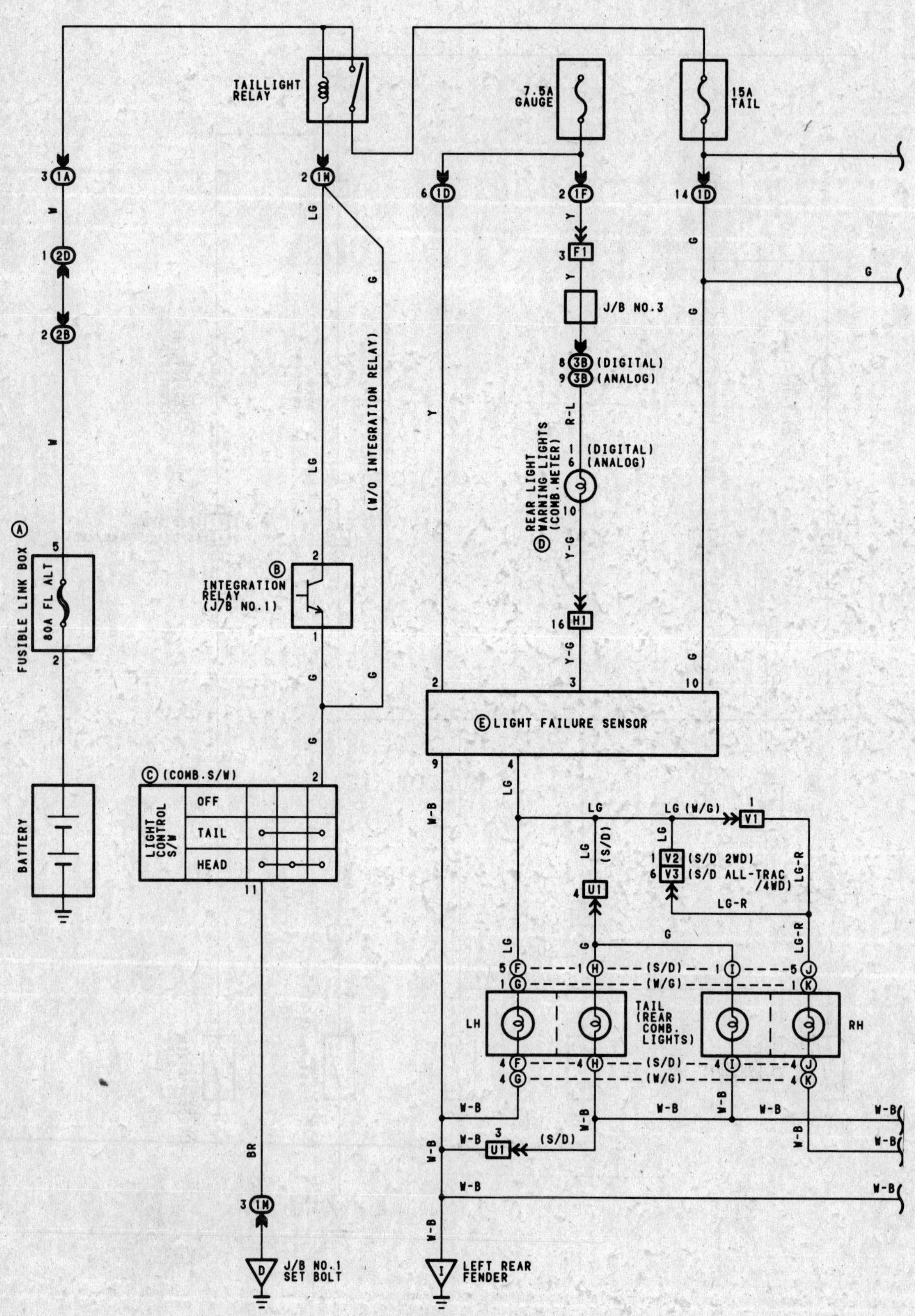

Taillights – 1988 wiring diagram

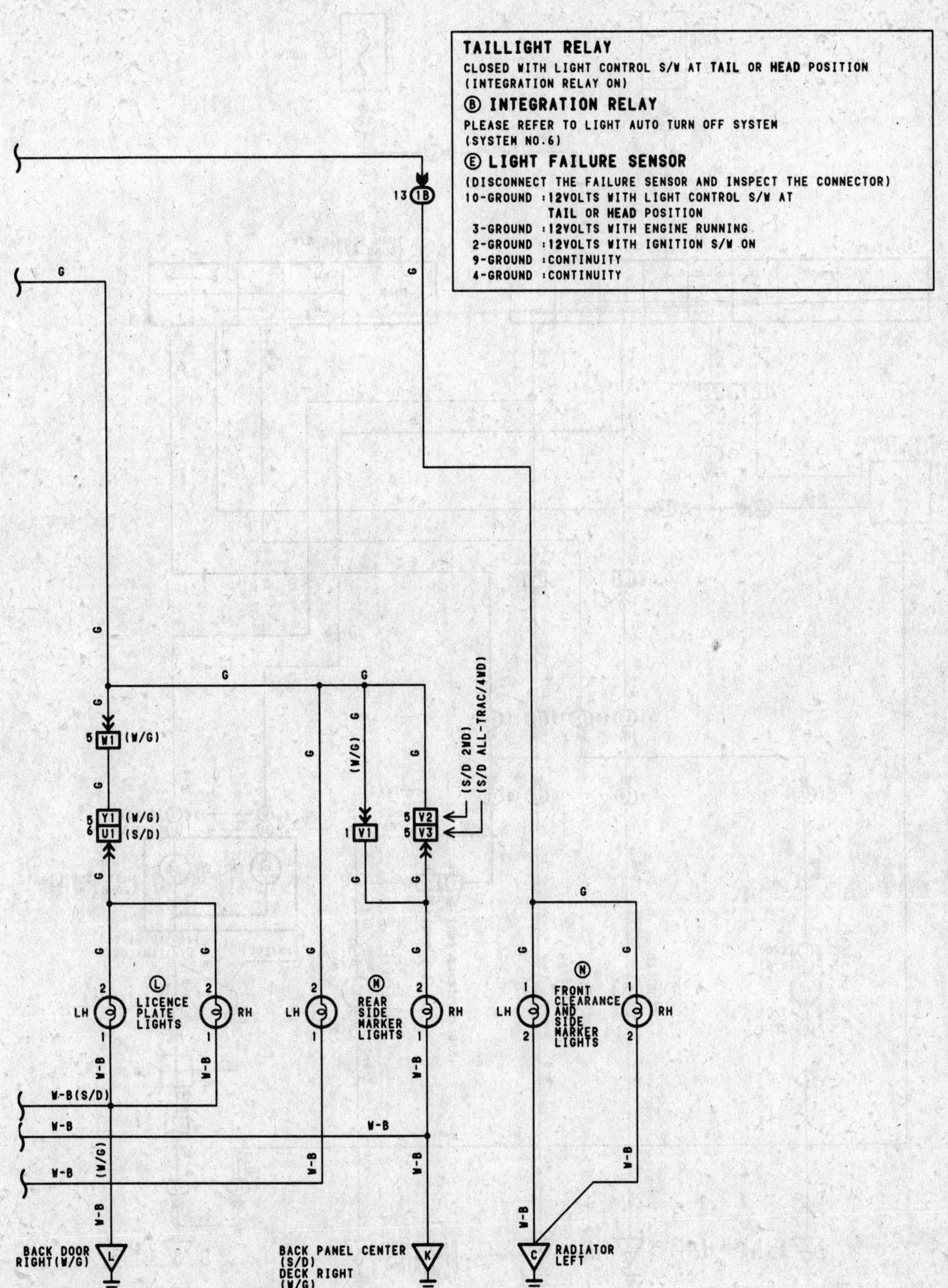
TAILLIGHT RELAY
CLOSED WITH LIGHT CONTROL S/W AT TAIL OR HEAD POSITION
(INTEGRATION RELAY ON)
Ⓑ INTEGRATION RELAY
PLEASE REFER TO LIGHT AUTO TURN OFF SYSTEM
(SYSTEM NO.6)
Ⓔ LIGHT FAILURE SENSOR
(DISCONNECT THE FAILURE SENSOR AND INSPECT THE CONNECTOR)
10-GROUND :12VOLTS WITH LIGHT CONTROL S/W AT TAIL OR HEAD POSITION
3-GROUND :12VOLTS WITH ENGINE RUNNING
2-GROUND :12VOLTS WITH IGNITION S/W ON
9-GROUND :CONTINUITY
4-GROUND :CONTINUITY
13 1B
G
W1 (W/G)
Y1 (W/G)
U1 (S/D)
V1
V2
V3
(S/D 2WD)
(S/D ALL-TRAC/4WD)
W-B
W-B(S/D)
(W/G)
LH
RH
Ⓛ LICENCE PLATE LIGHTS
Ⓜ REAR SIDE MARKER LIGHTS
Ⓝ FRONT CLEARANCE AND SIDE MARKER LIGHTS
BACK DOOR RIGHT(W/G)
BACK PANEL CENTER (S/D)
DECK RIGHT (W/G)
RADIATOR LEFT

Taillights—1988 wiring diagram

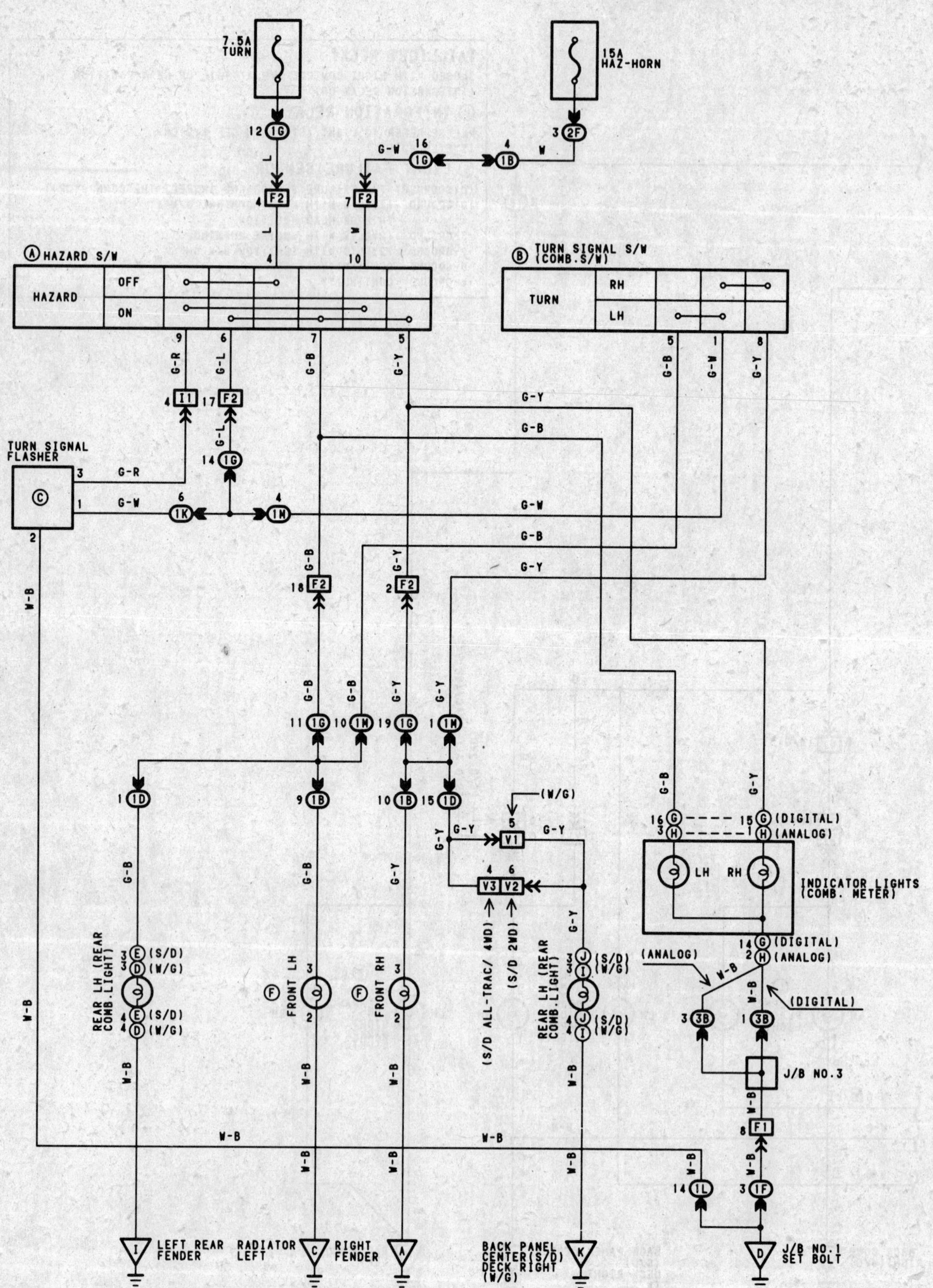

Turn signal and hazard warning lights—1988 wiring diagram

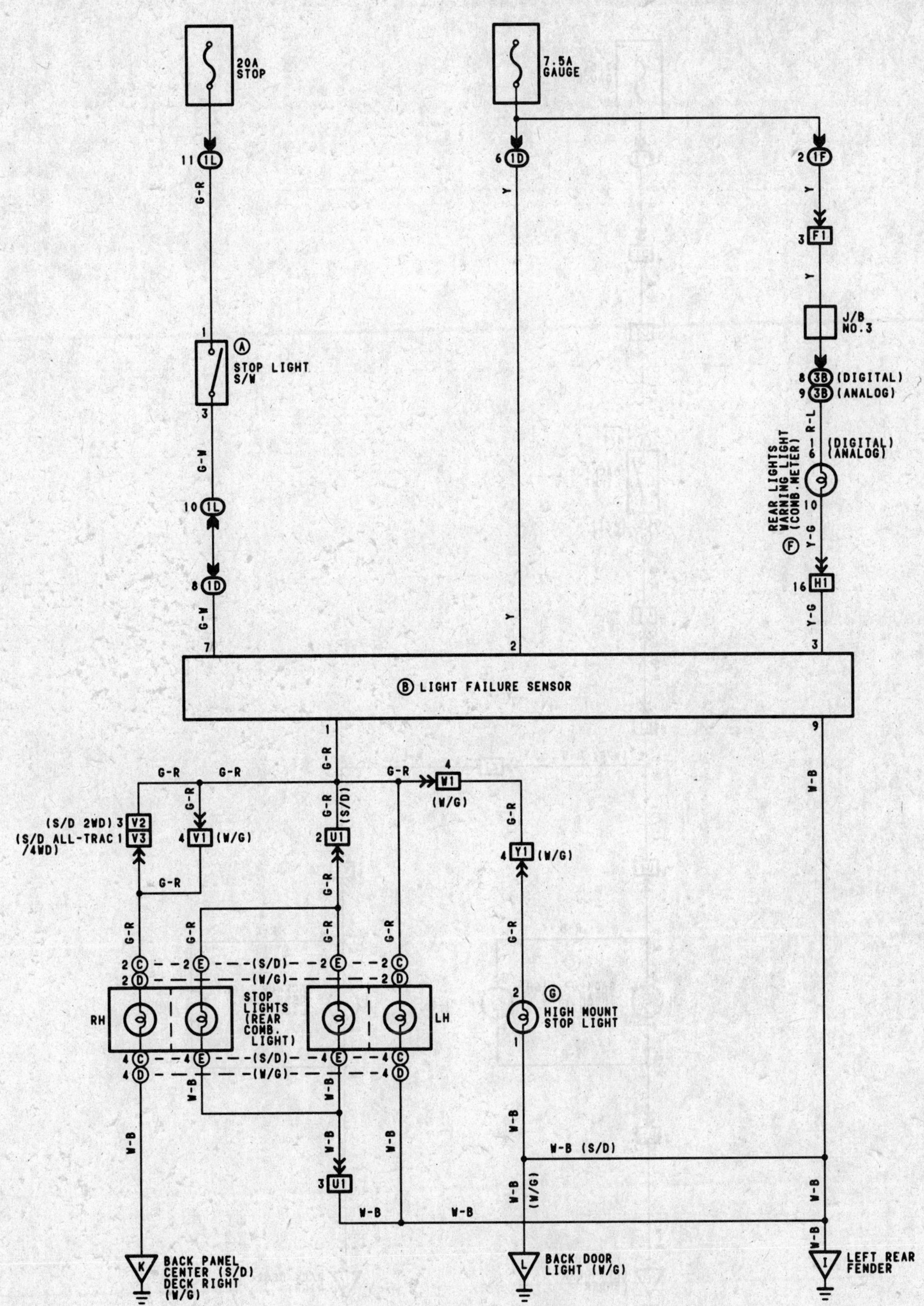

Stop lights—1988 wiring diagram

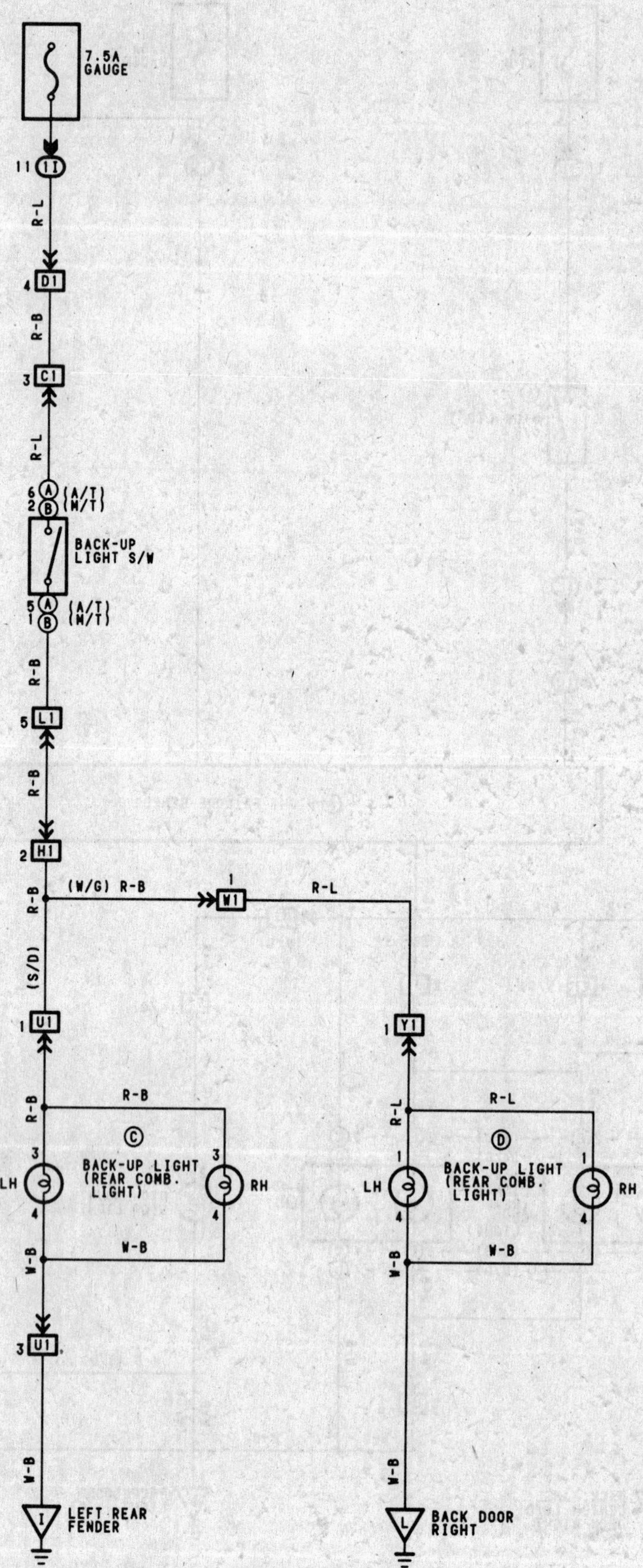

Back-up lights—1988 wiring wiring diagram

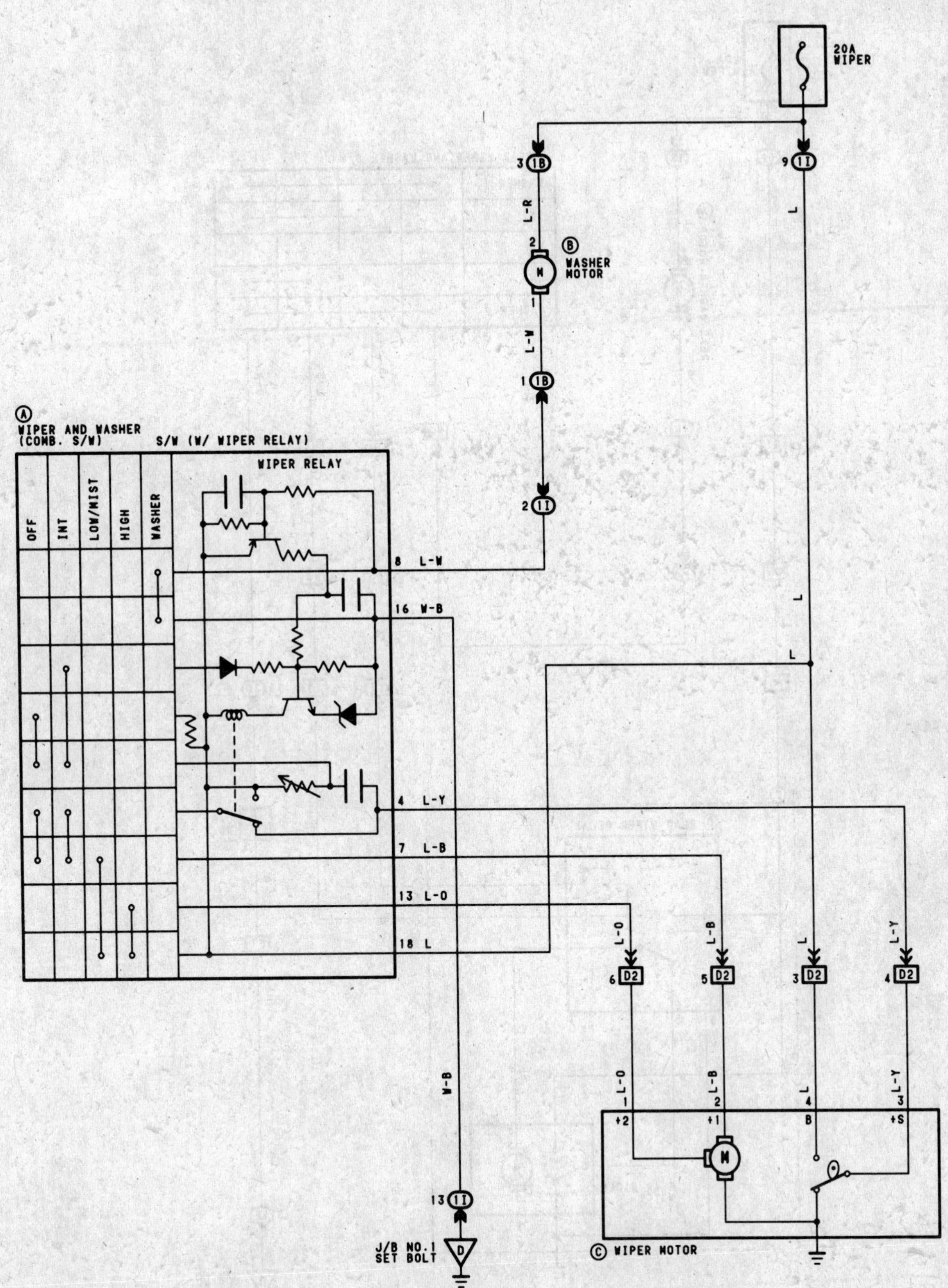

Front wiper and washer—1988 wiring diagram

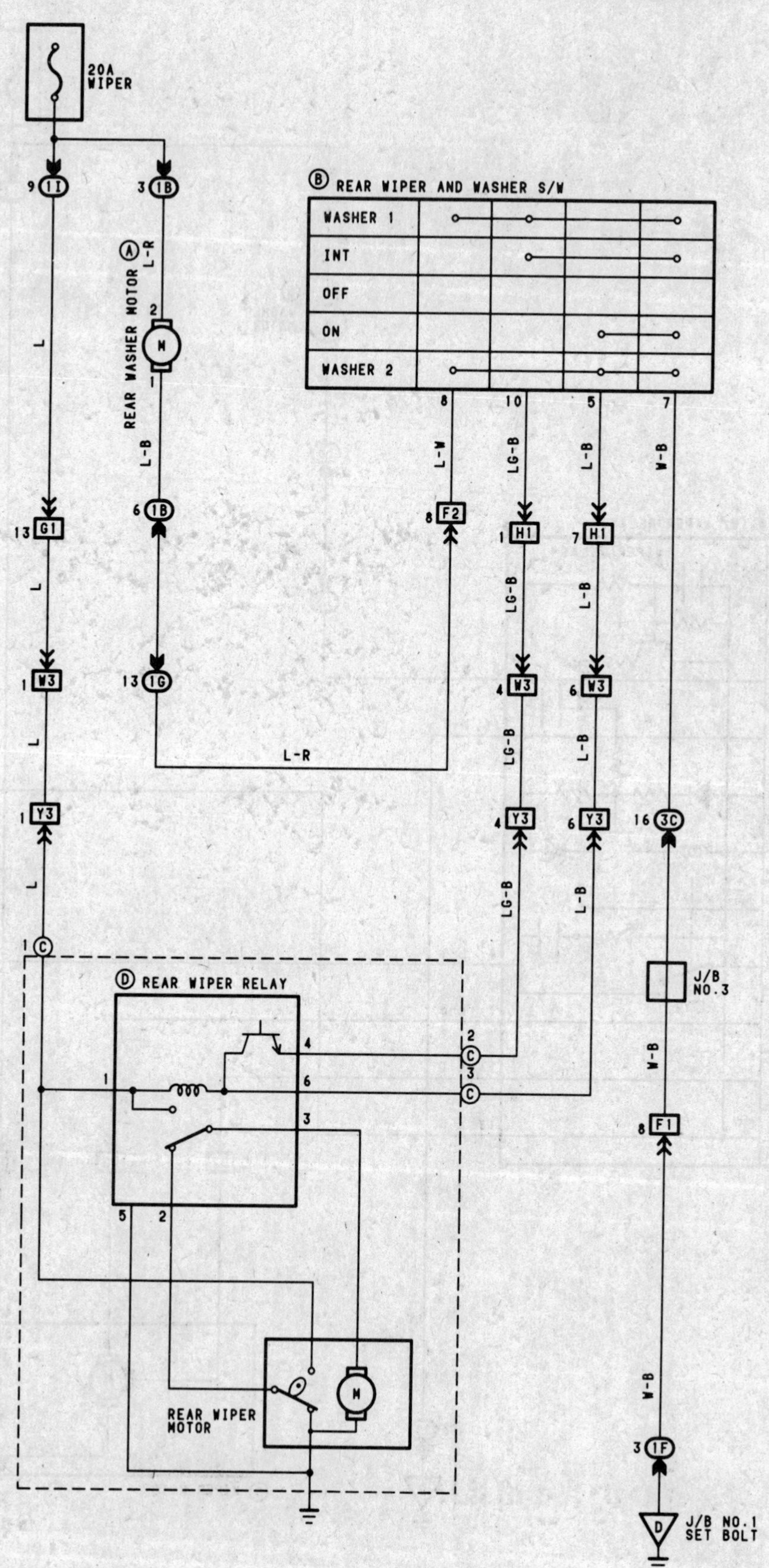

Rear wiper and washer—1988 wiring diagram

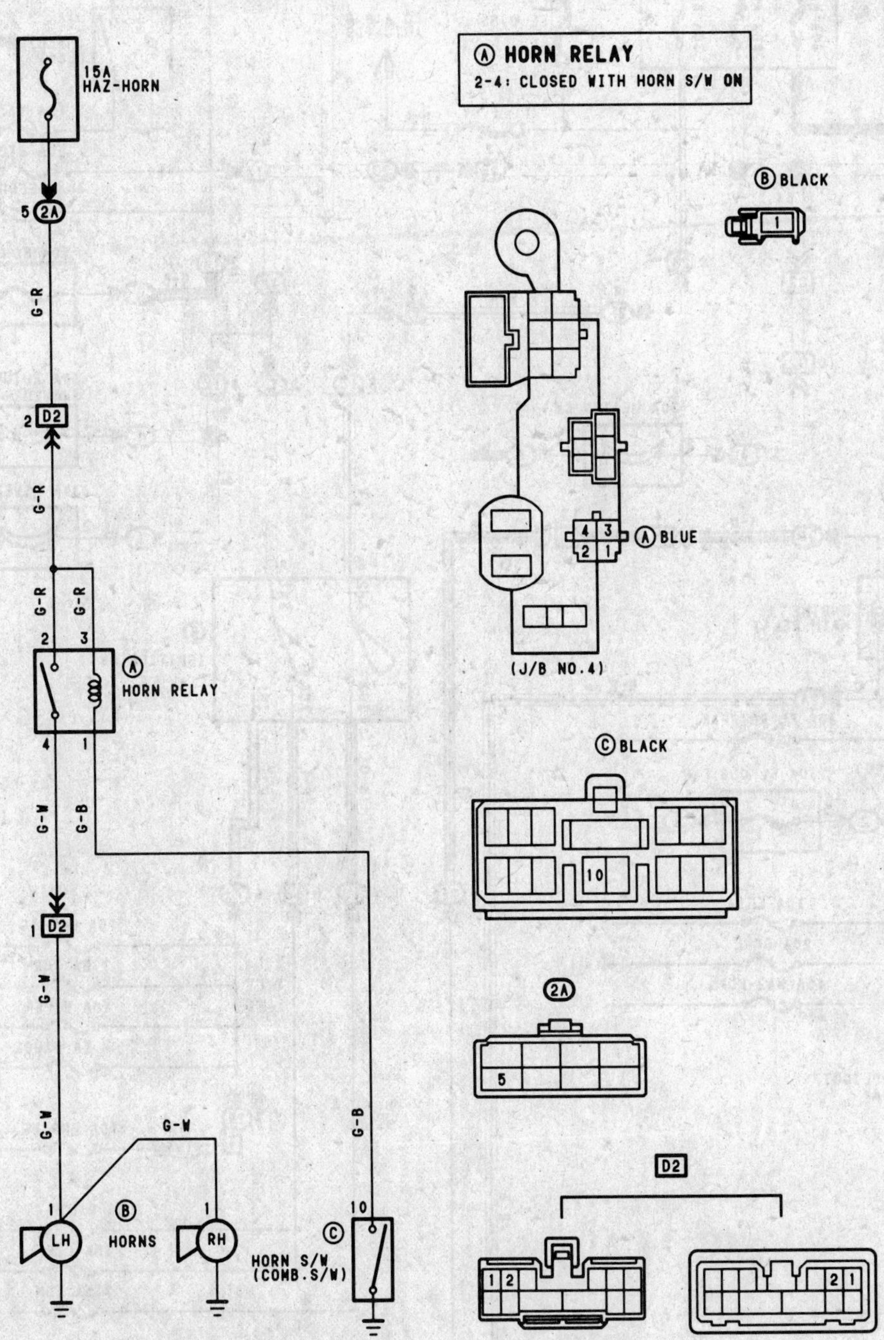

Horns—1988 wiring diagram

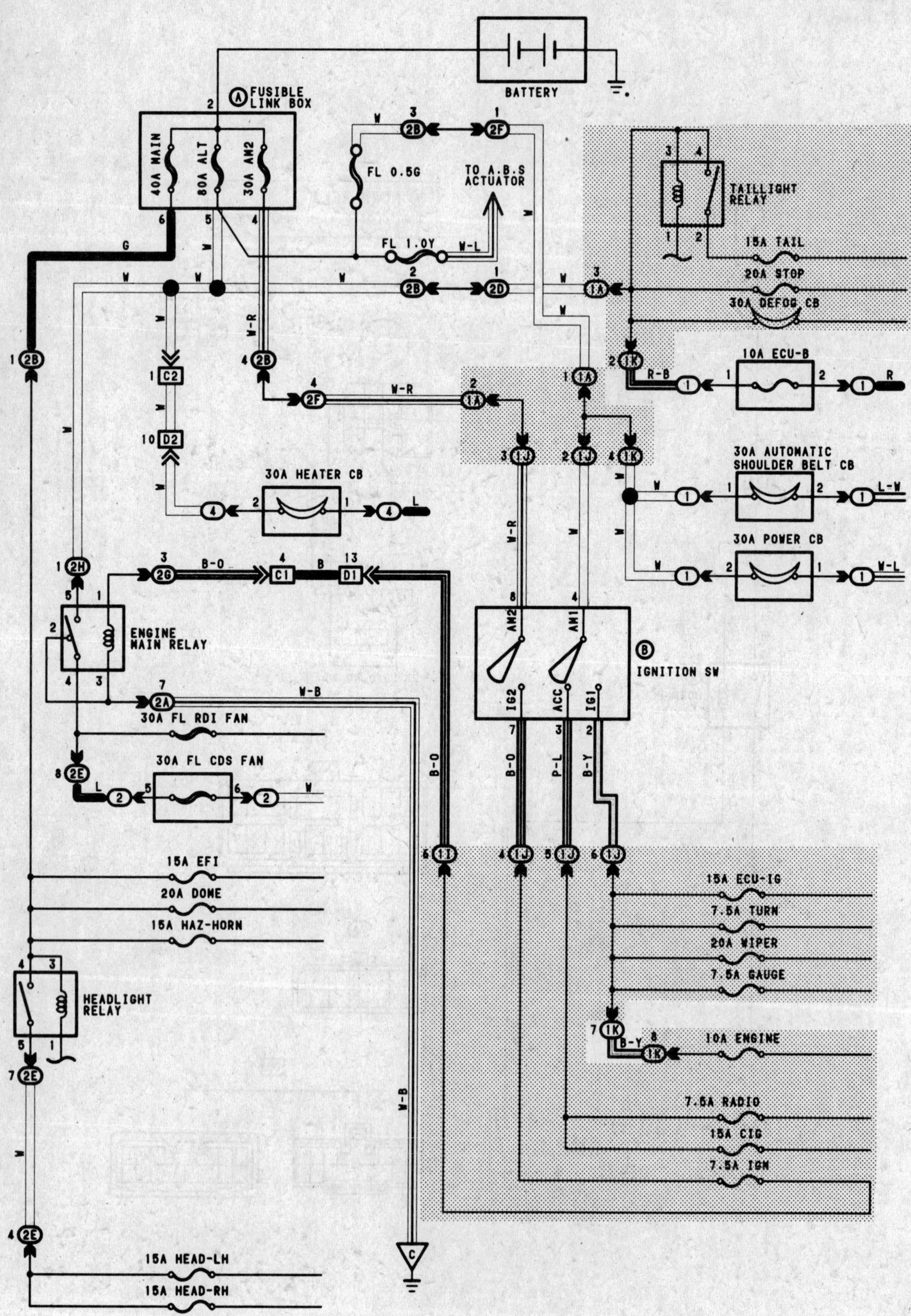

Power source—1989 wiring diagram

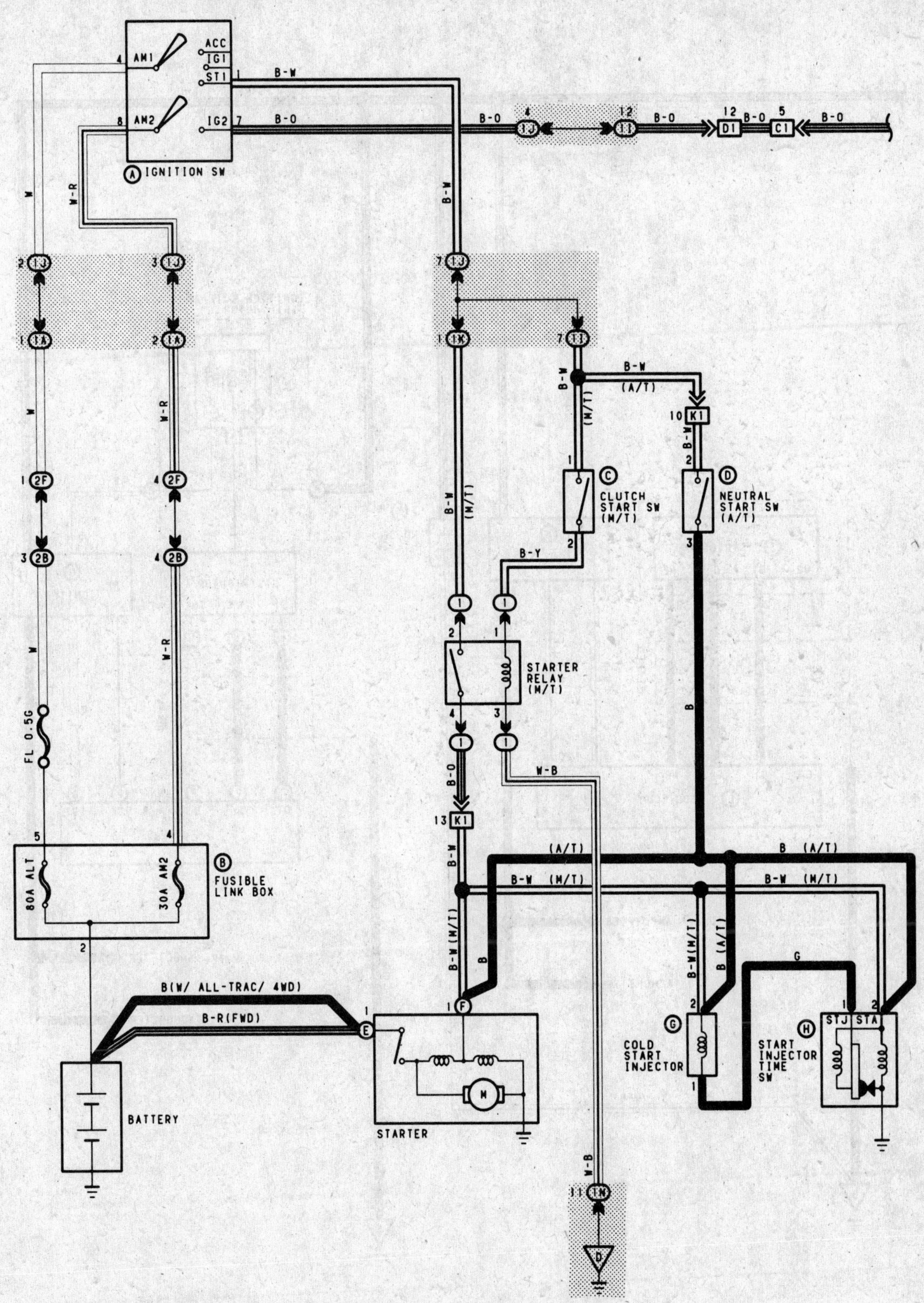

Starting and ignition—1989 wiring diagram

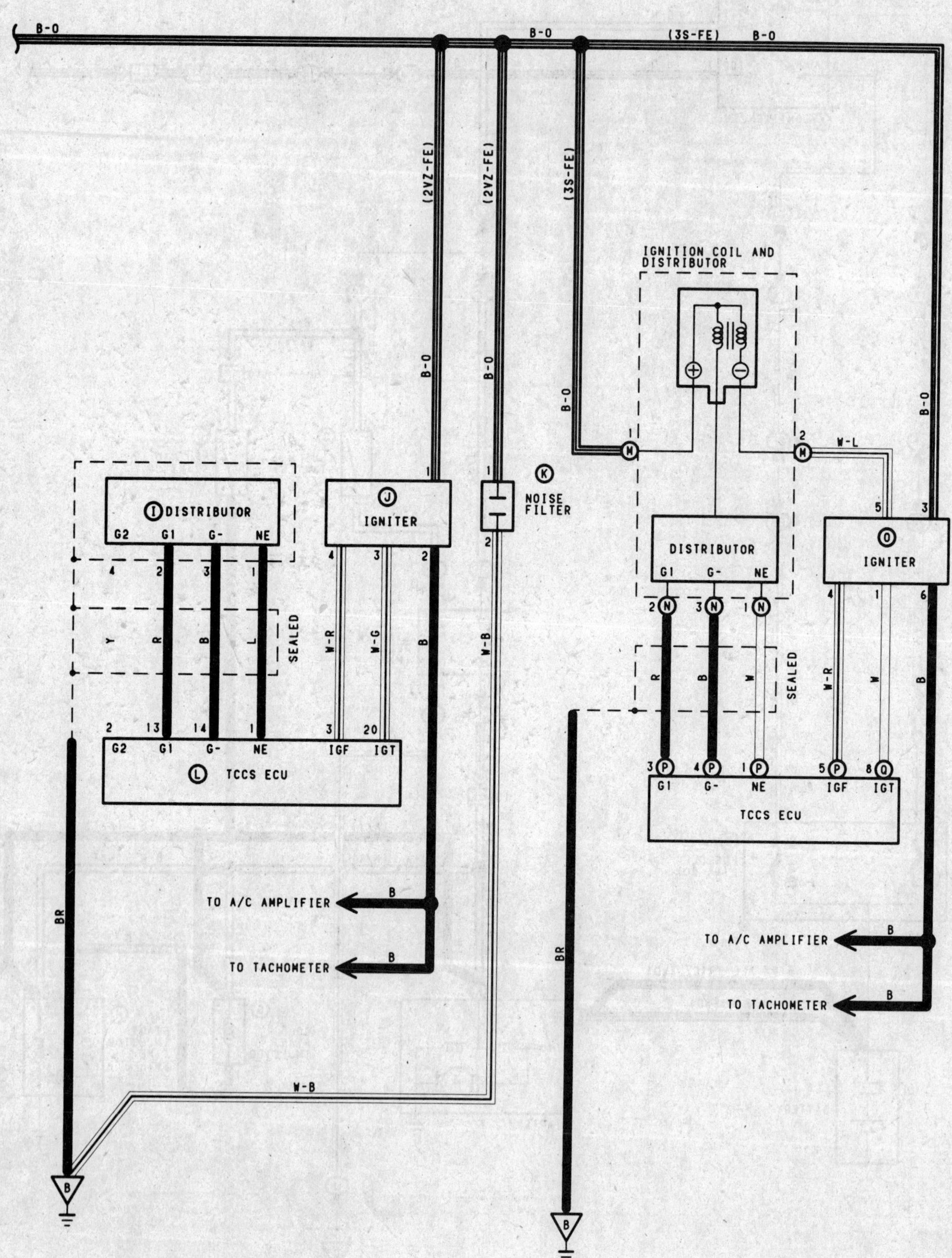

Starting and ignition—1989 wiring diagram

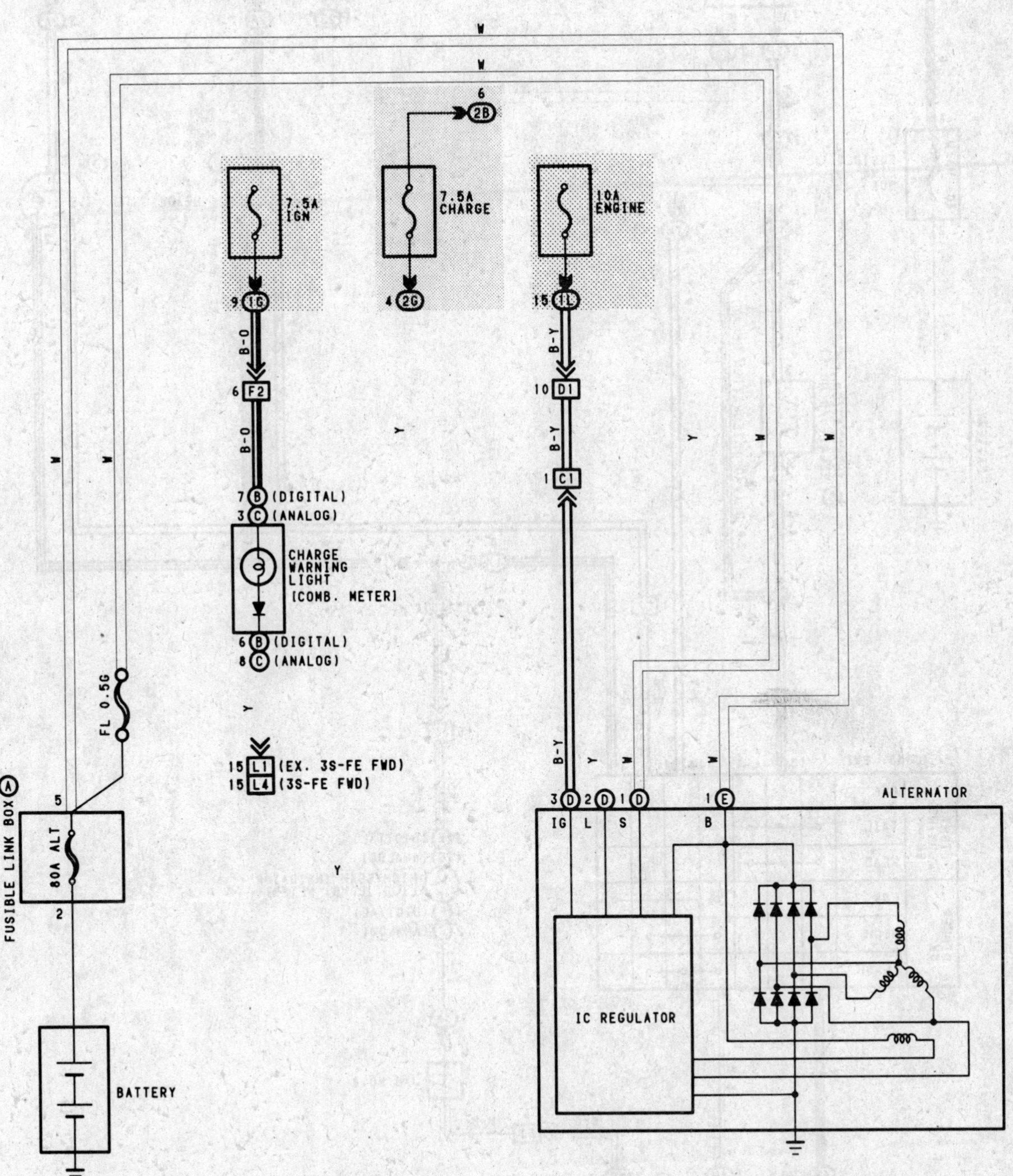

Charging system — 1989 wiring diagram

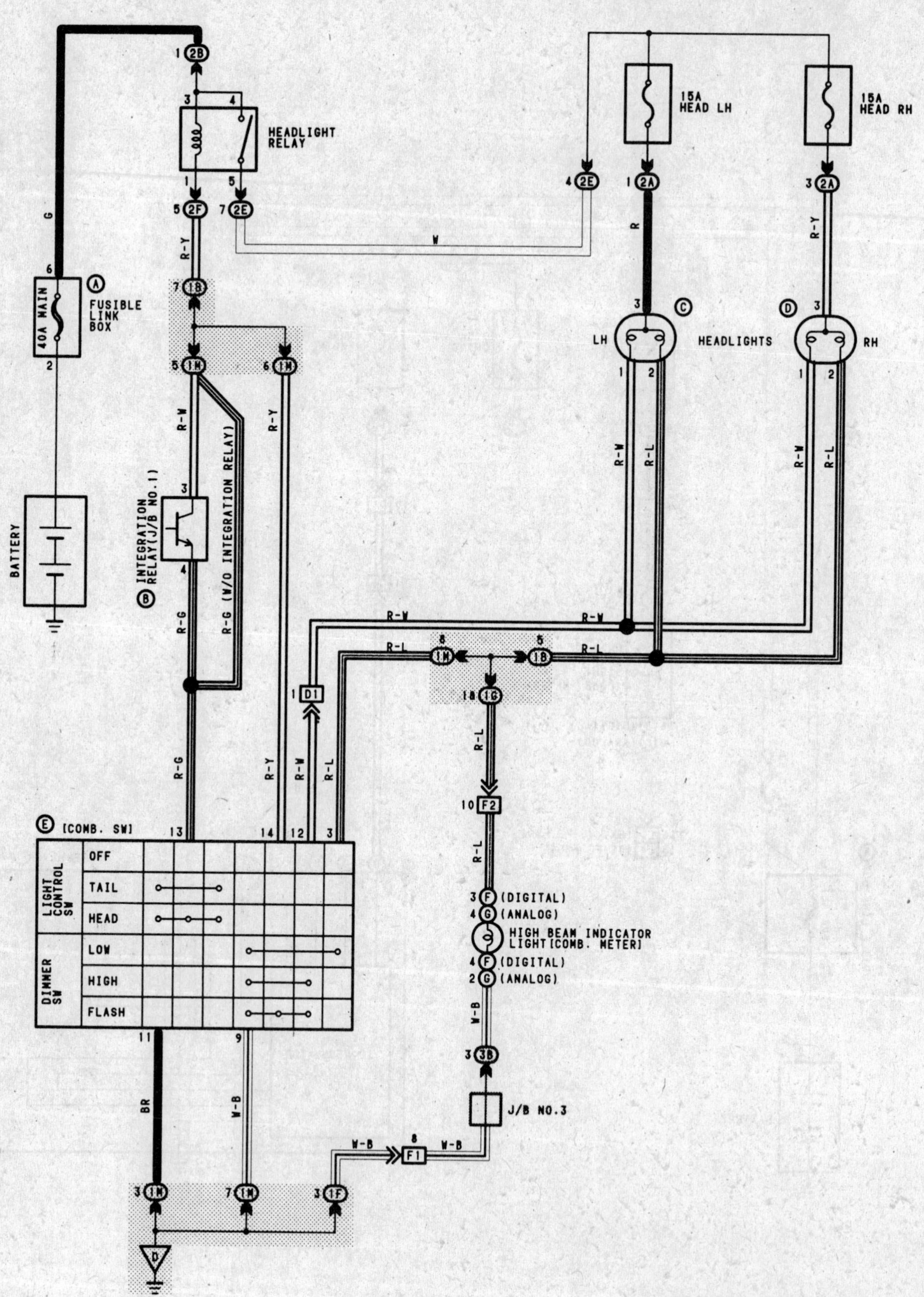

Headlights—1989 wiring diagram

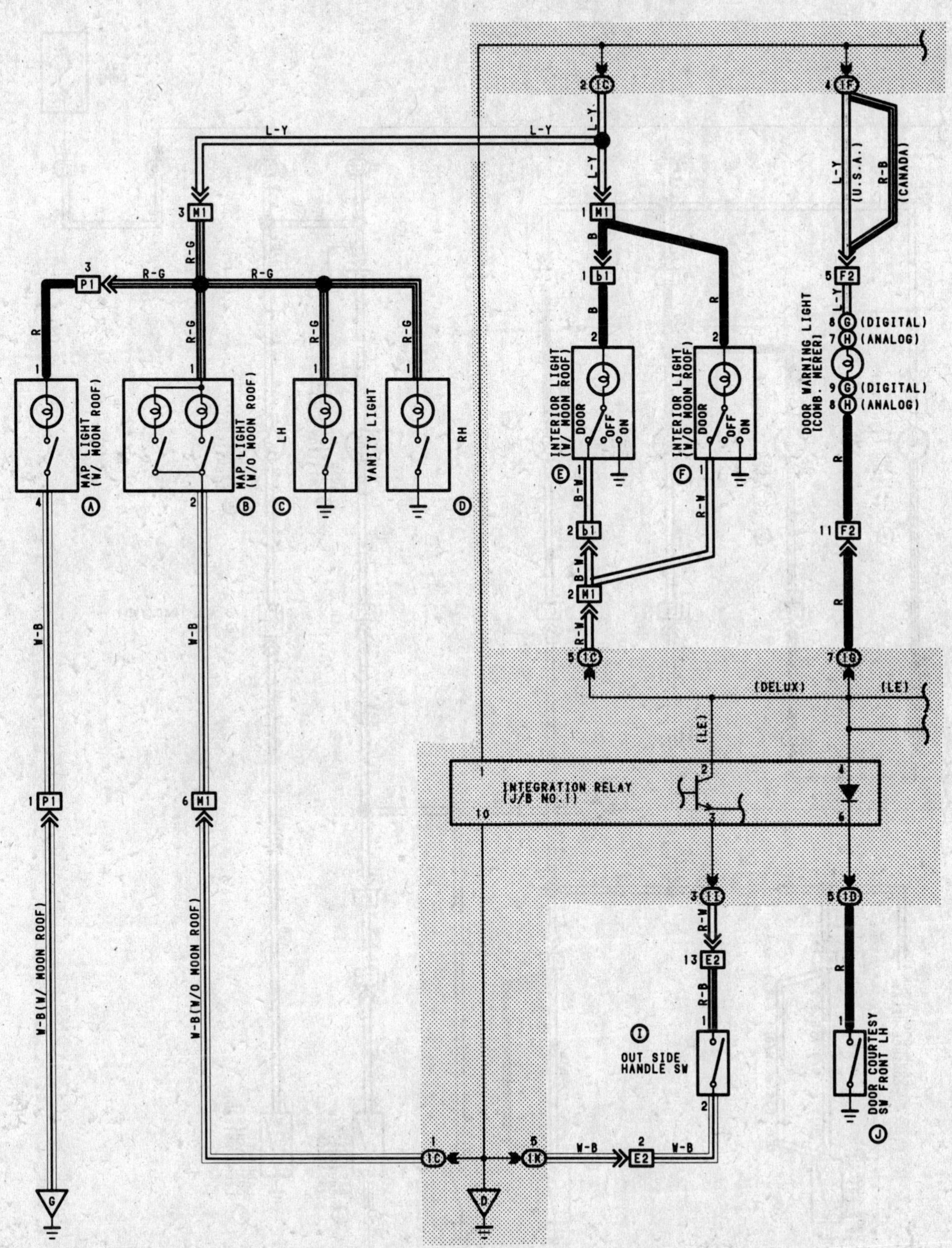

Interior lights with door locks—1989 wiring diagram

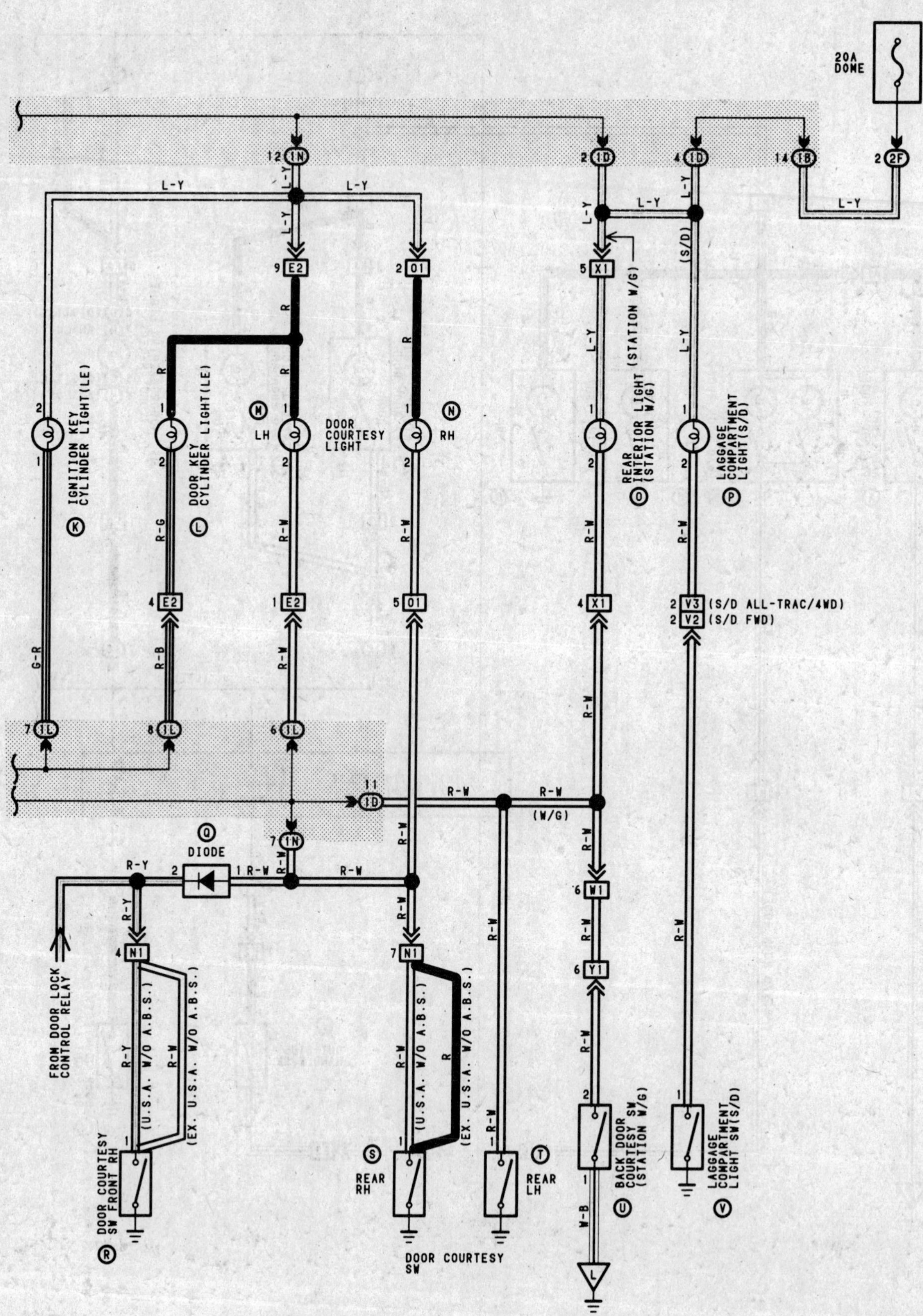

Interior lights with door locks — 1989 wiring diagram

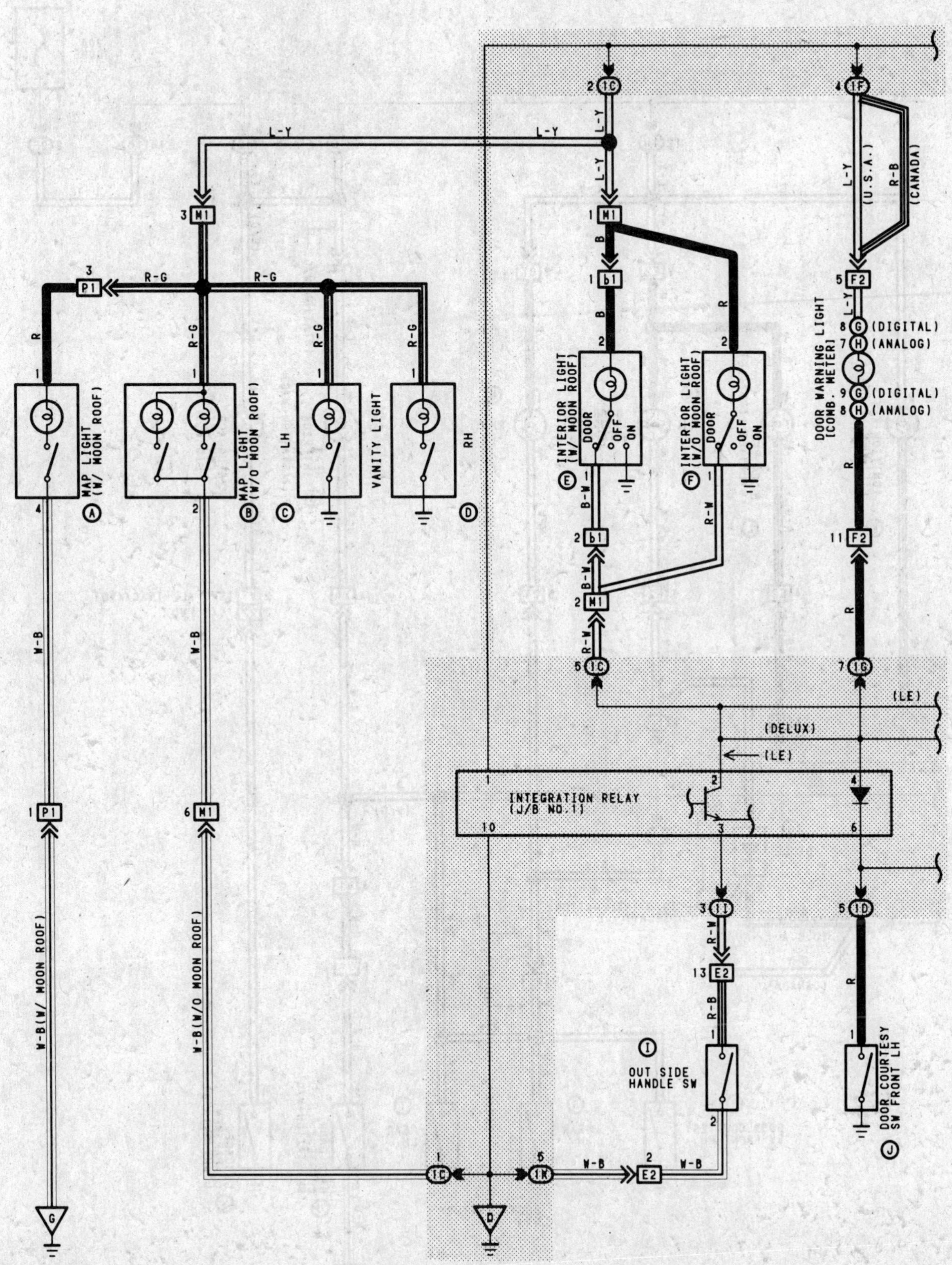

Interior lights without door locks—1989 wiring diagram

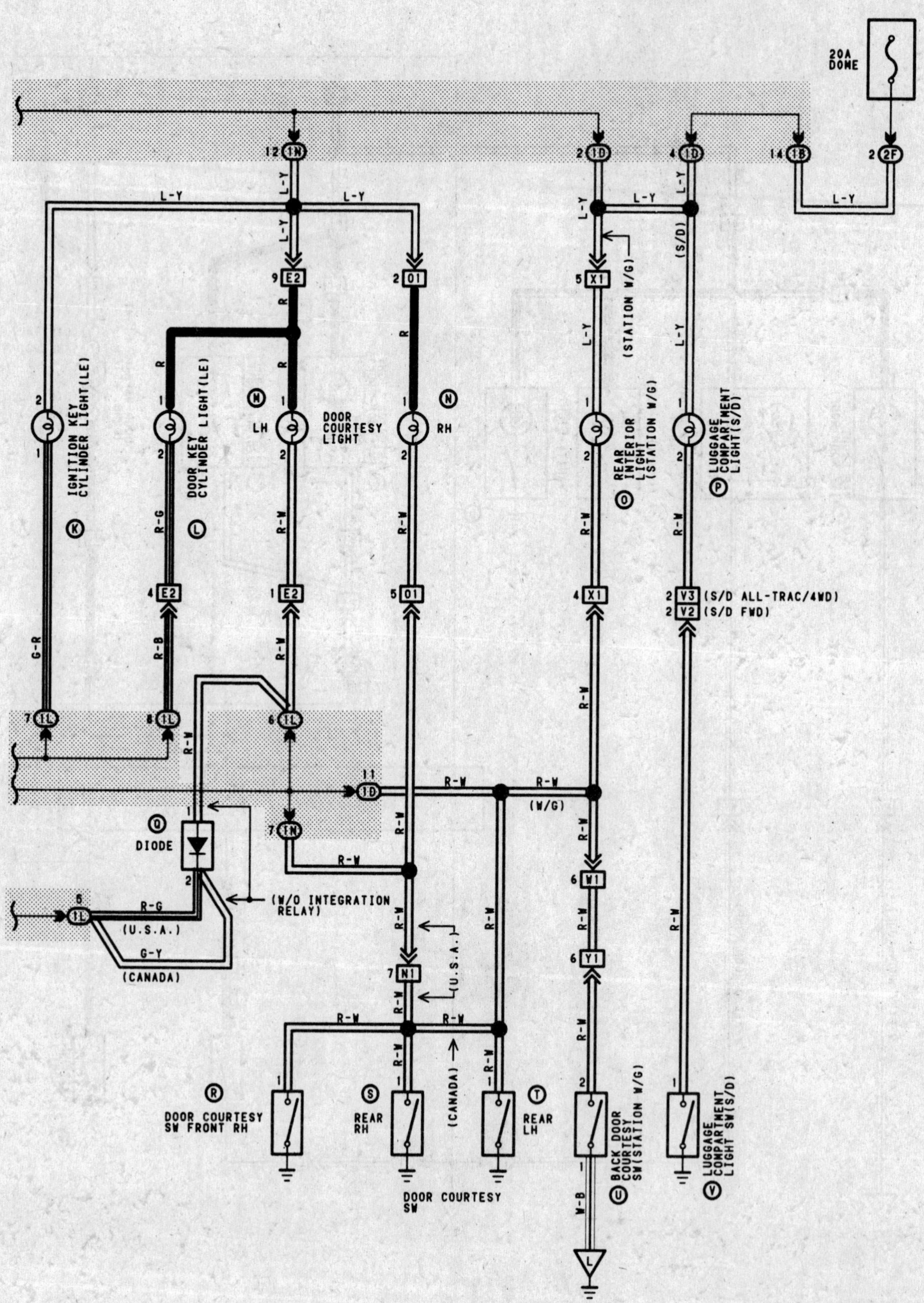

Interior lights without door locks—1989 wiring diagram

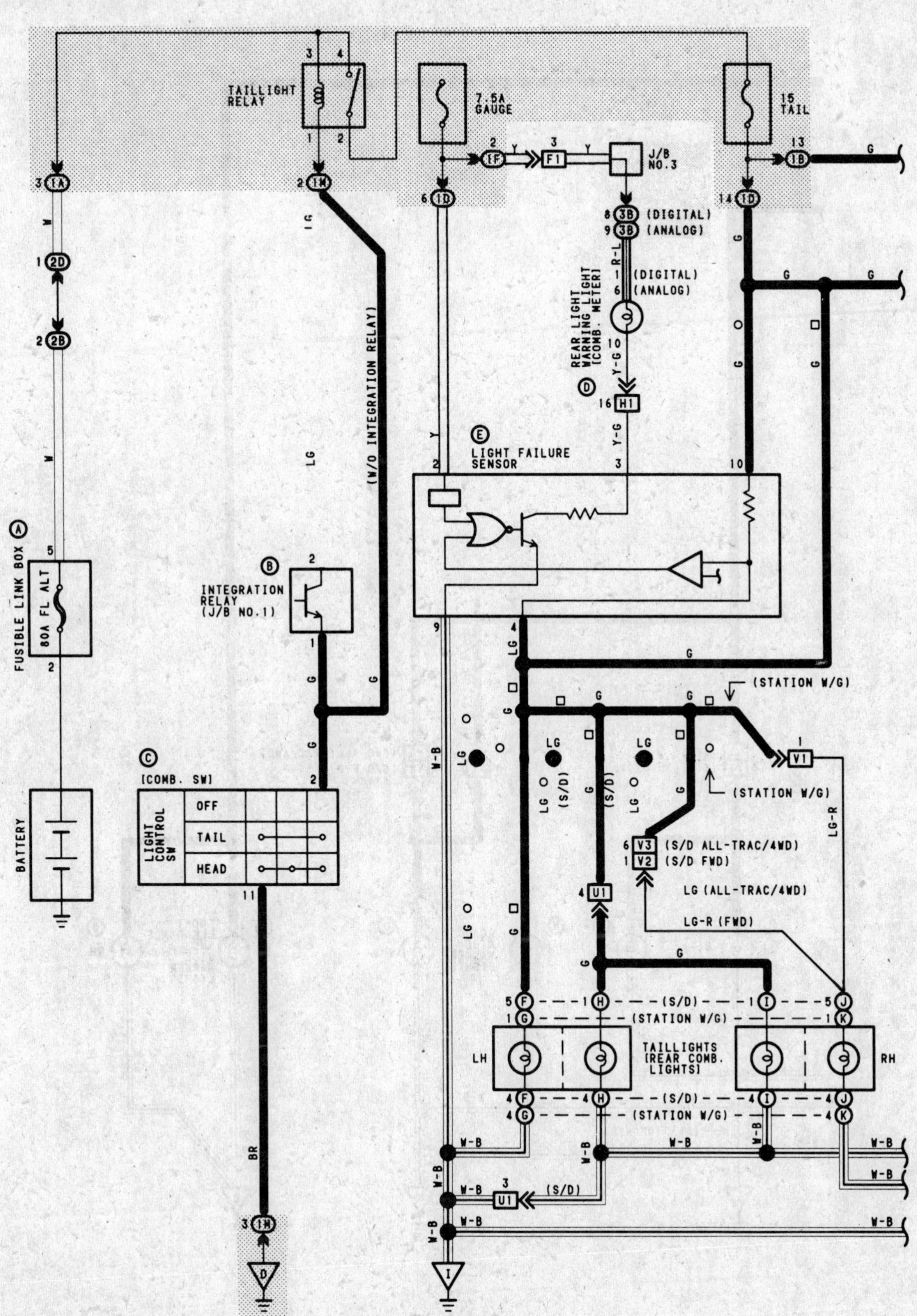

Taillights—1989 wiring diagram

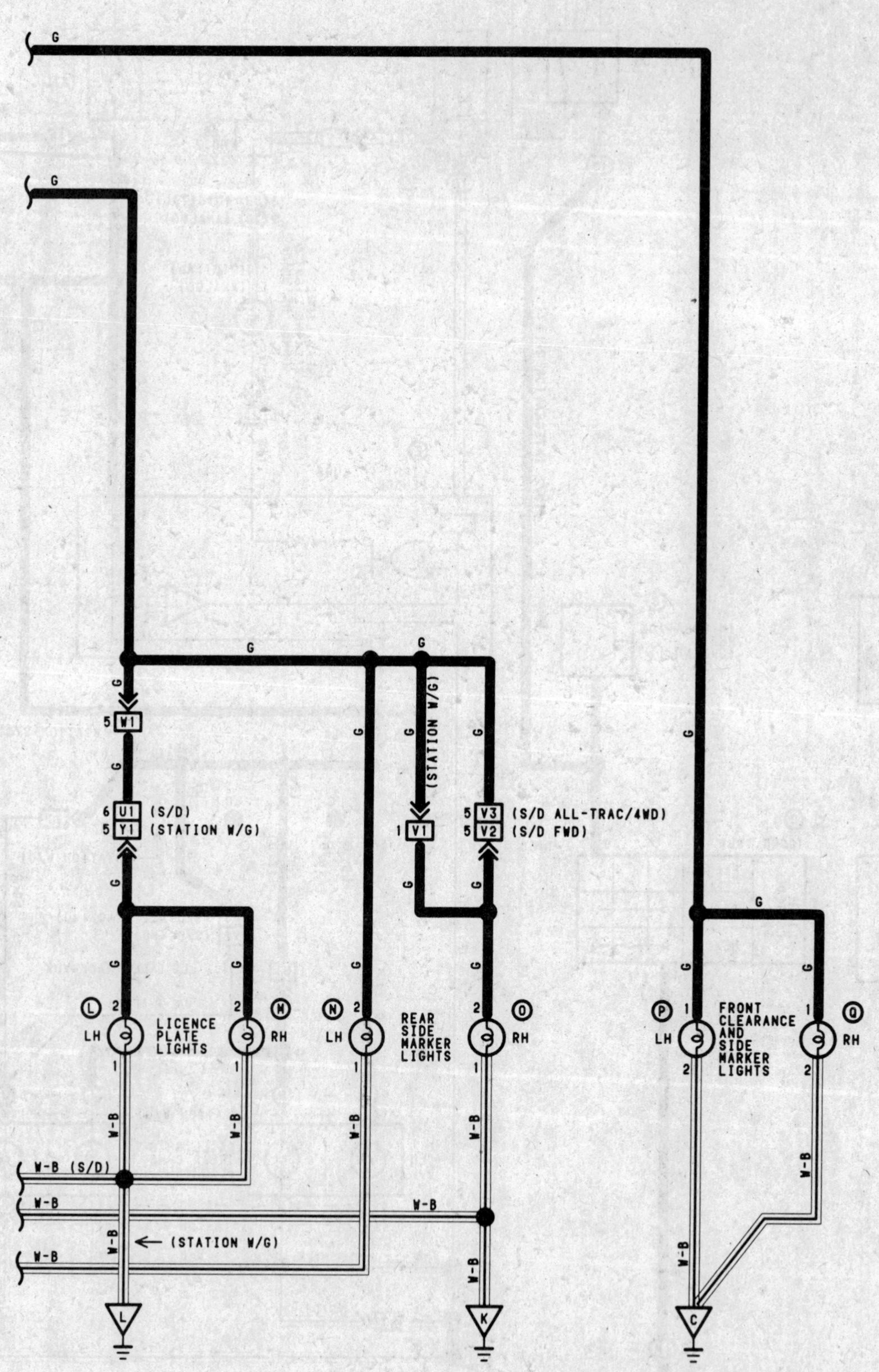

Taillights—1989 wiring diagram

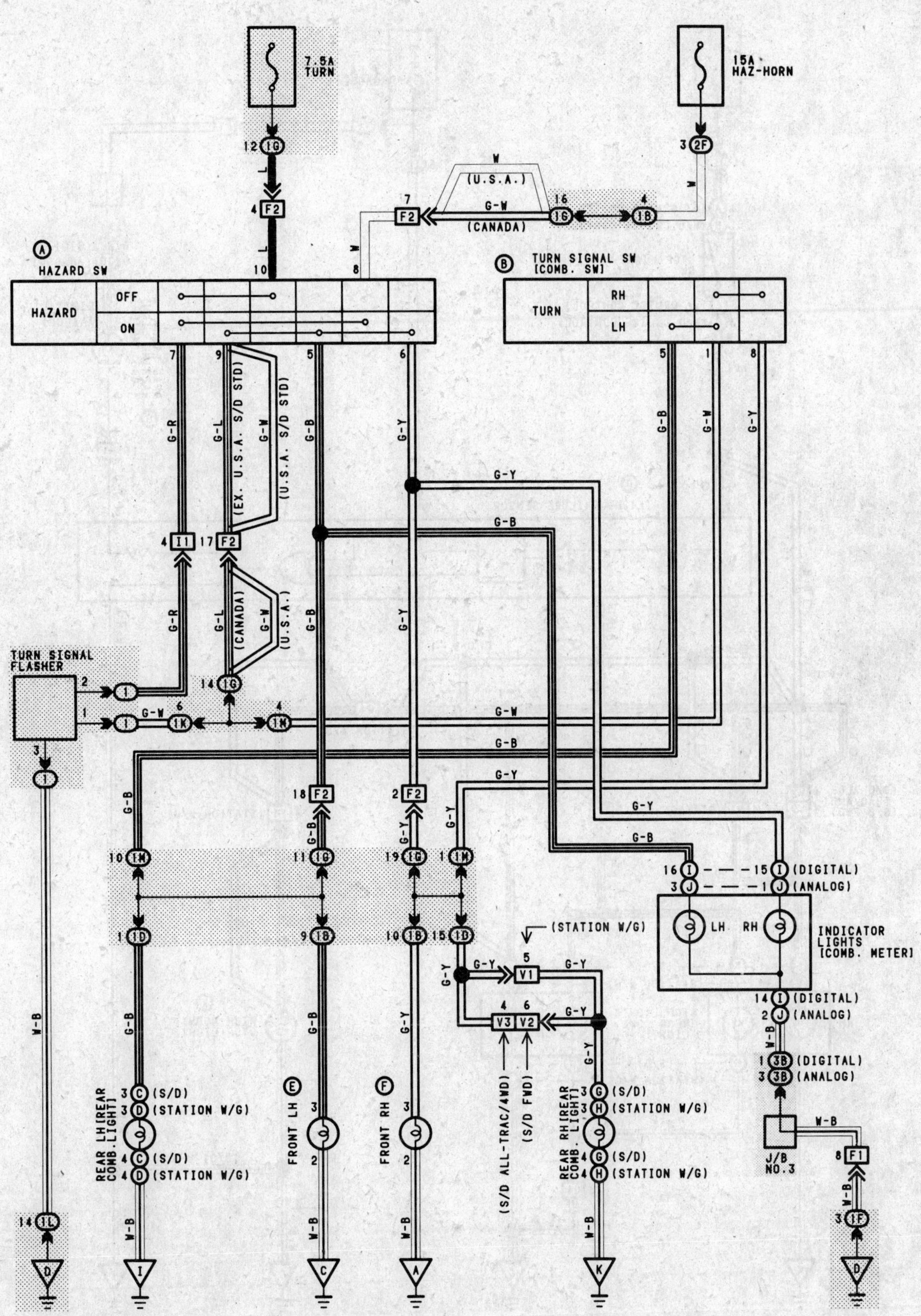

Turnsignal and hazard warning lights—1989 wiring diagram

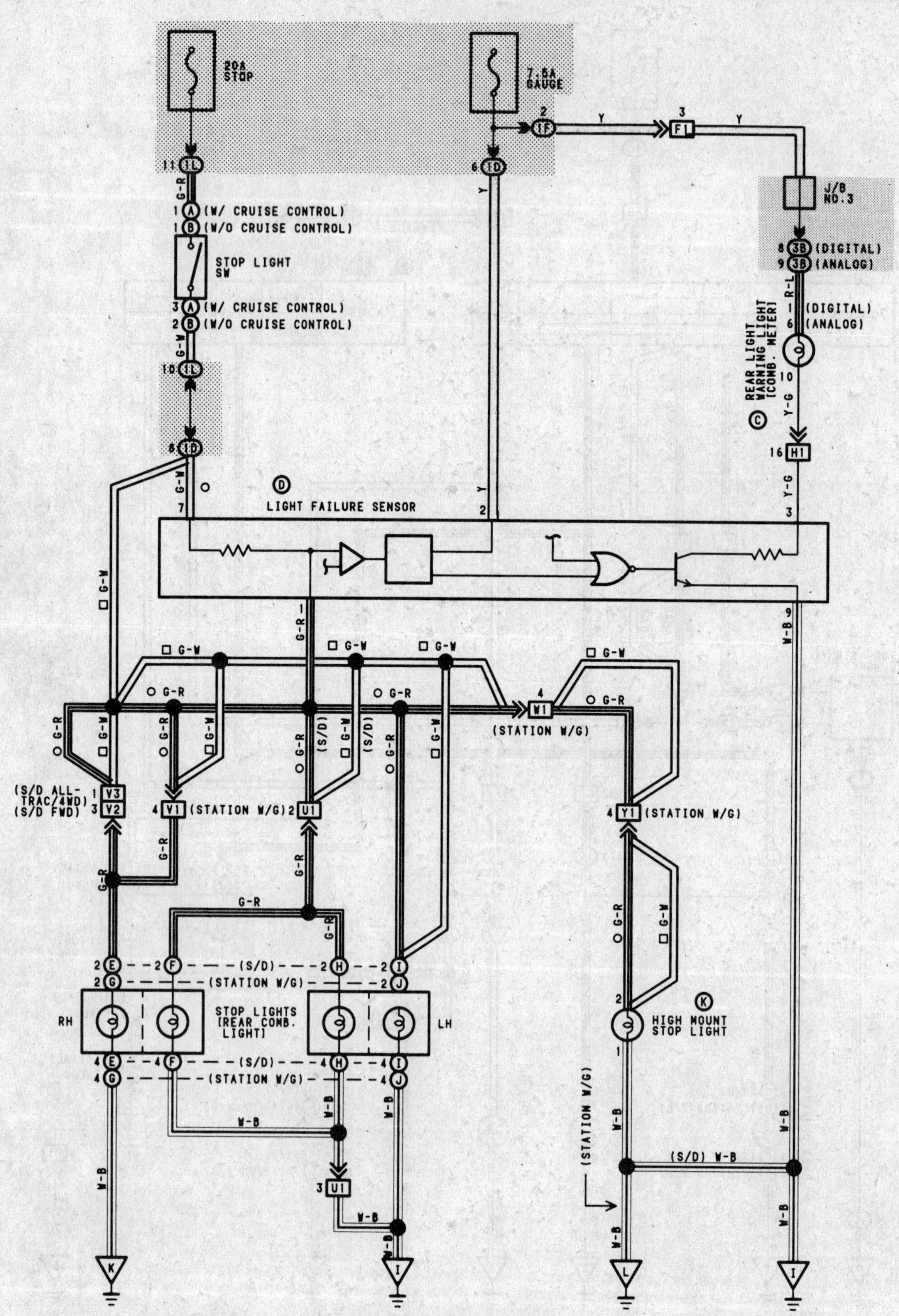

Stop lights—1989 wiring diagram

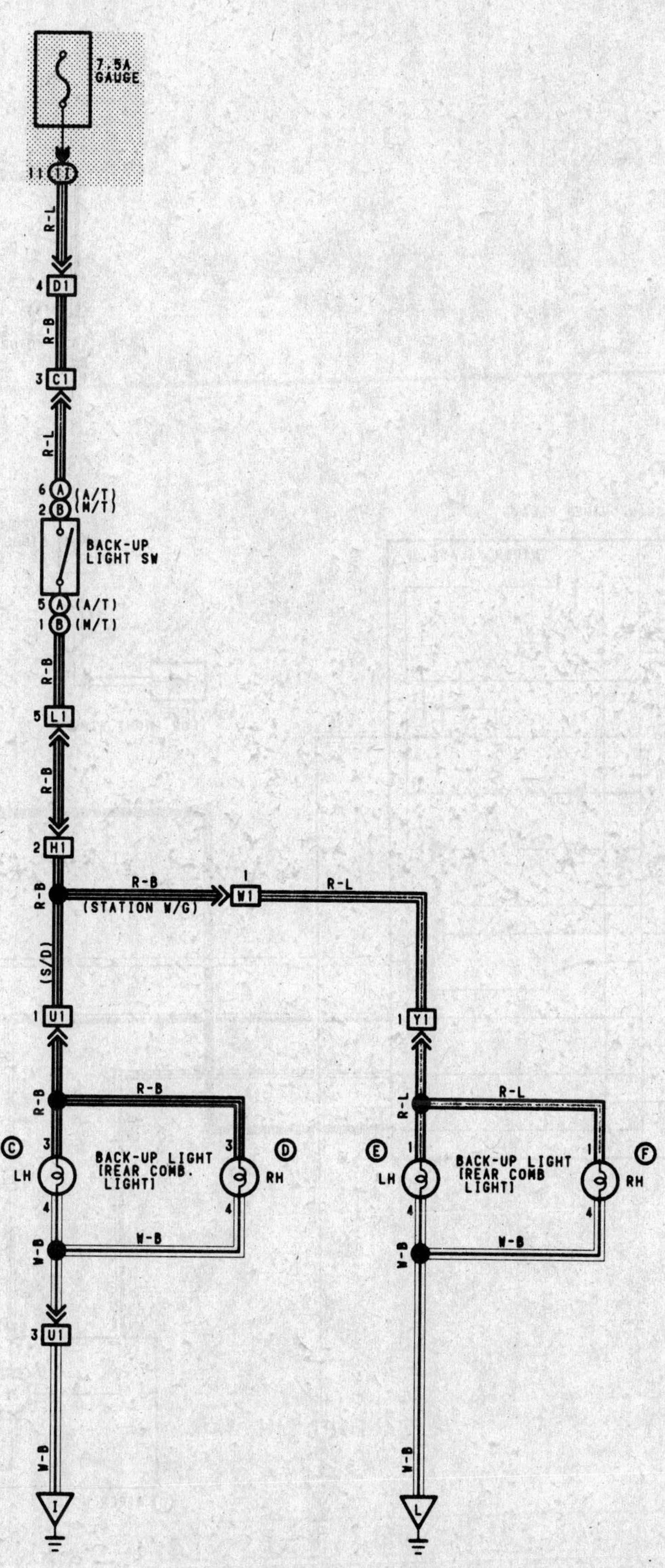

Back-up lights—1989 wiring diagram

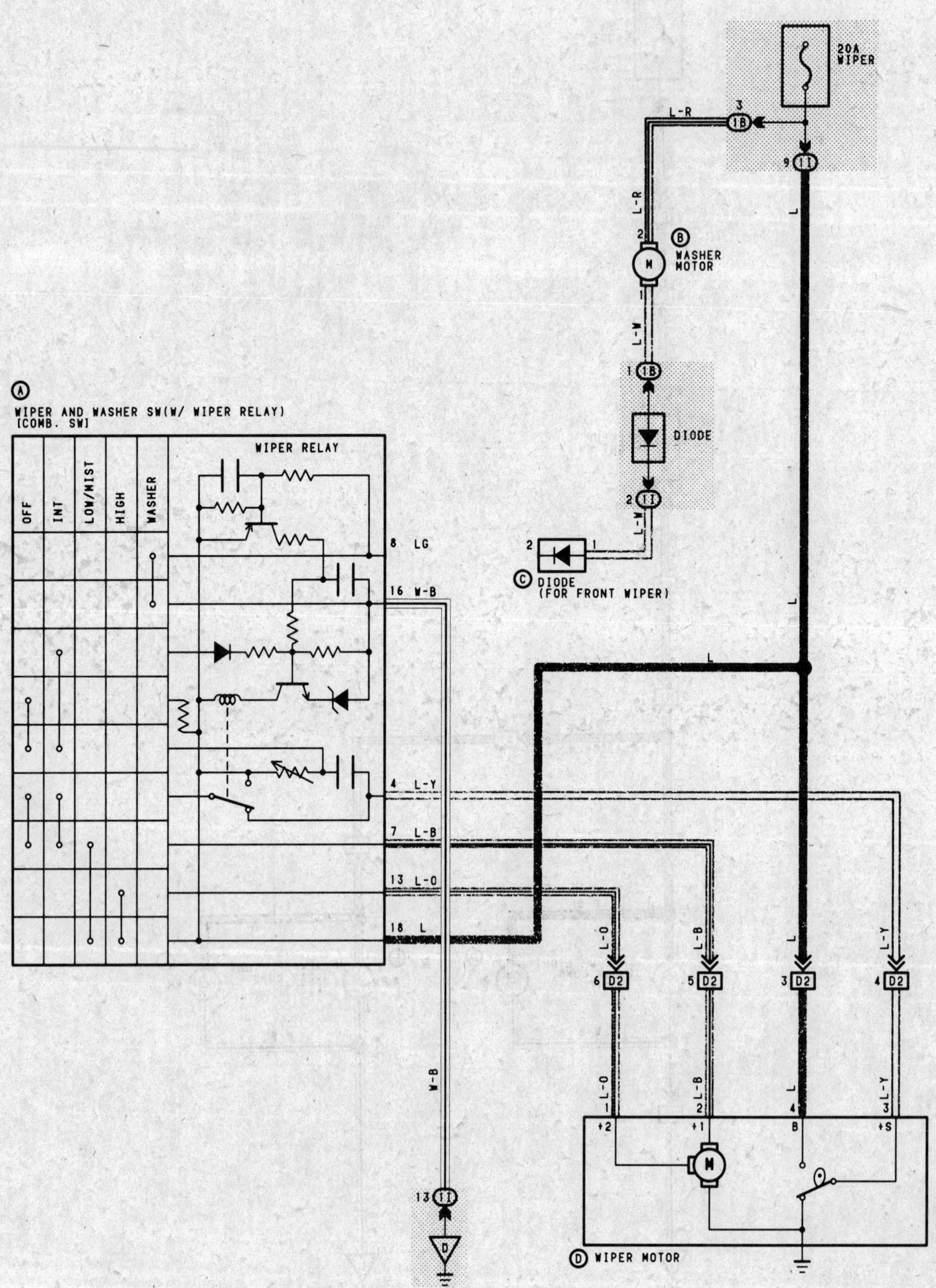

Front wiper and washer—1989 wiring diagram

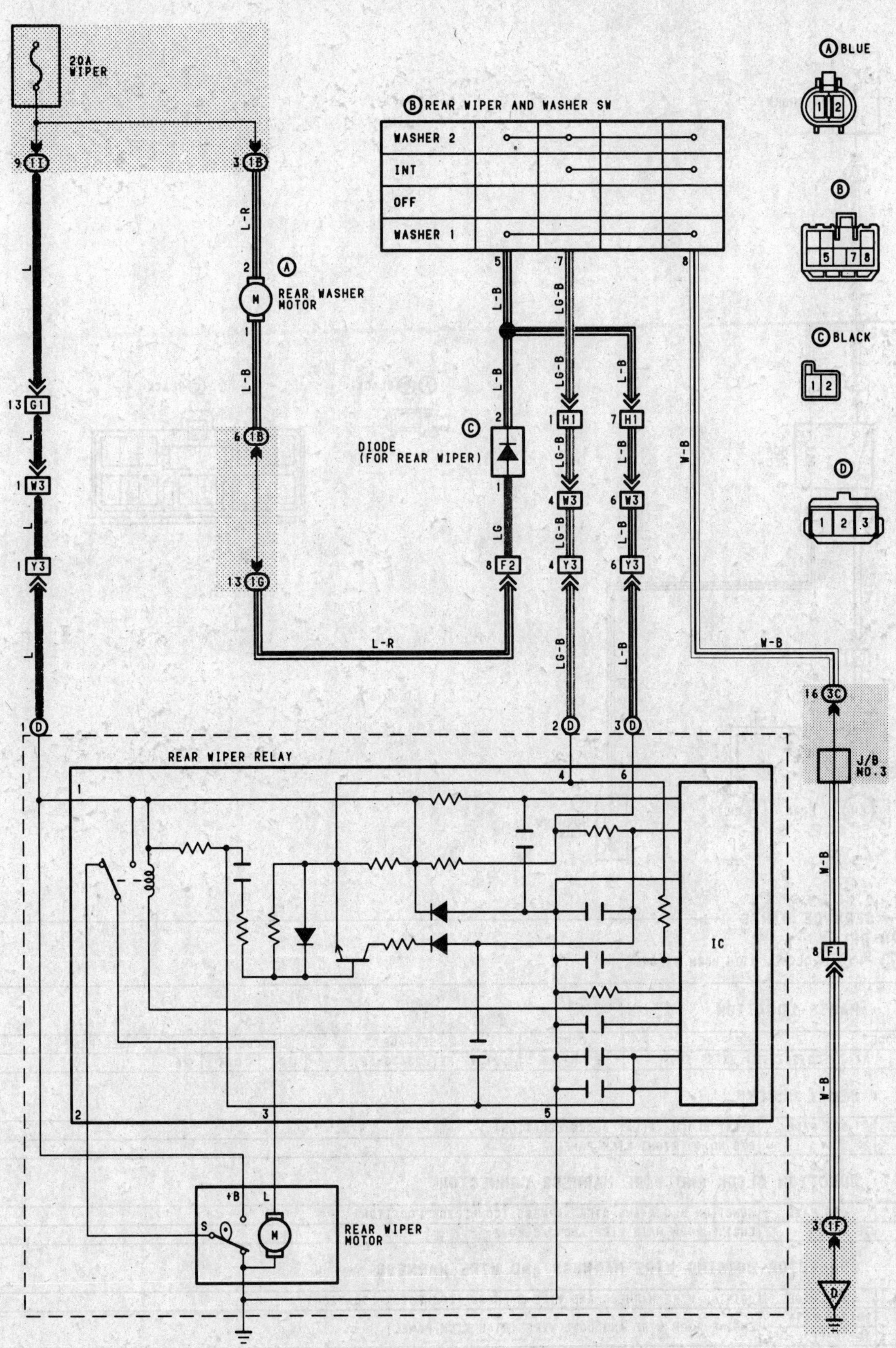

Rear wiper and washer—1989 wiring diagram

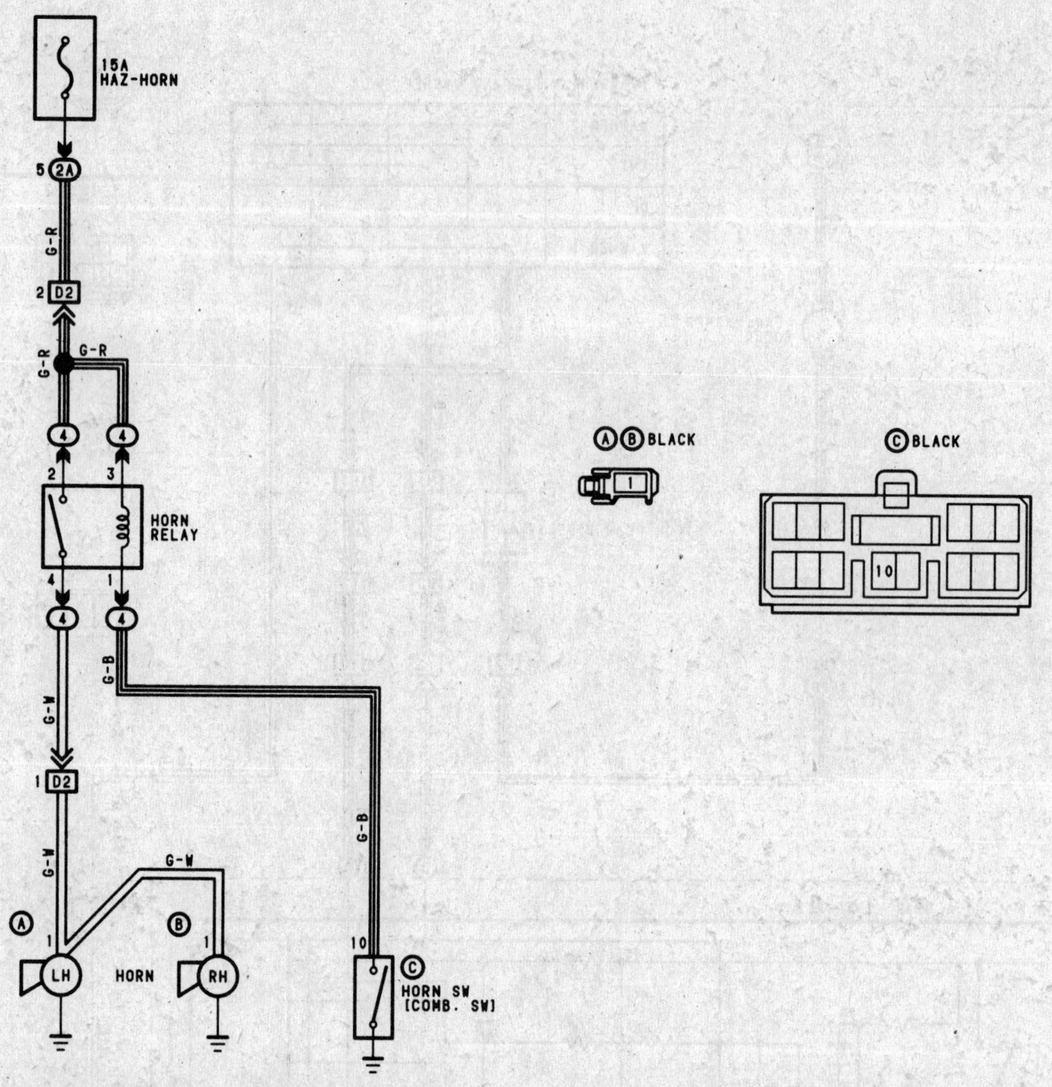

SERVICE HINTS

HORN RELAY

2 (4) -4 (4) :CLOSED WITH HORN SW ON

○ : PARTS LOCATION

CODE		SEE PAGE	CODE		SEE PAGE	CODE		SEE PAGE
A	H4	22(2VZ-FE),23(3S-FE)	B	H3	22(2VZ-FE),23(3S-FE)	C	C14	26

⬭ : RELAY BLOCKS

CODE	SEE PAGE	RELAY BLOCK (RELAY BLOCK LOCATION)
4	21	R/B NO.4 (RIGHT KICK PANEL)

⬭ : JUNCTION BLOCK AND WIRE HARNESS CONNECTOR

CODE	SEE PAGE	JUNCTION BLOCK AND WIRE HARNESS (CONNECTOR LOCATION)
2A	18	ENGINE ROOM MAIN WIRE AND J/B NO.2

□ : CONNECTOR JOINING WIRE HARNESS AND WIRE HARNESS

CODE	SEE PAGE	JOINING WIRE HARNESS AND WIRE HARNESS (CONNECTOR LOCATION)
D2	20(2VZ-FE) 30(3S-FE)	ENGINE ROOM WIRE AND COWL WIRE (RIGH KICK PANEL)

Horn—1989 wiring diagram

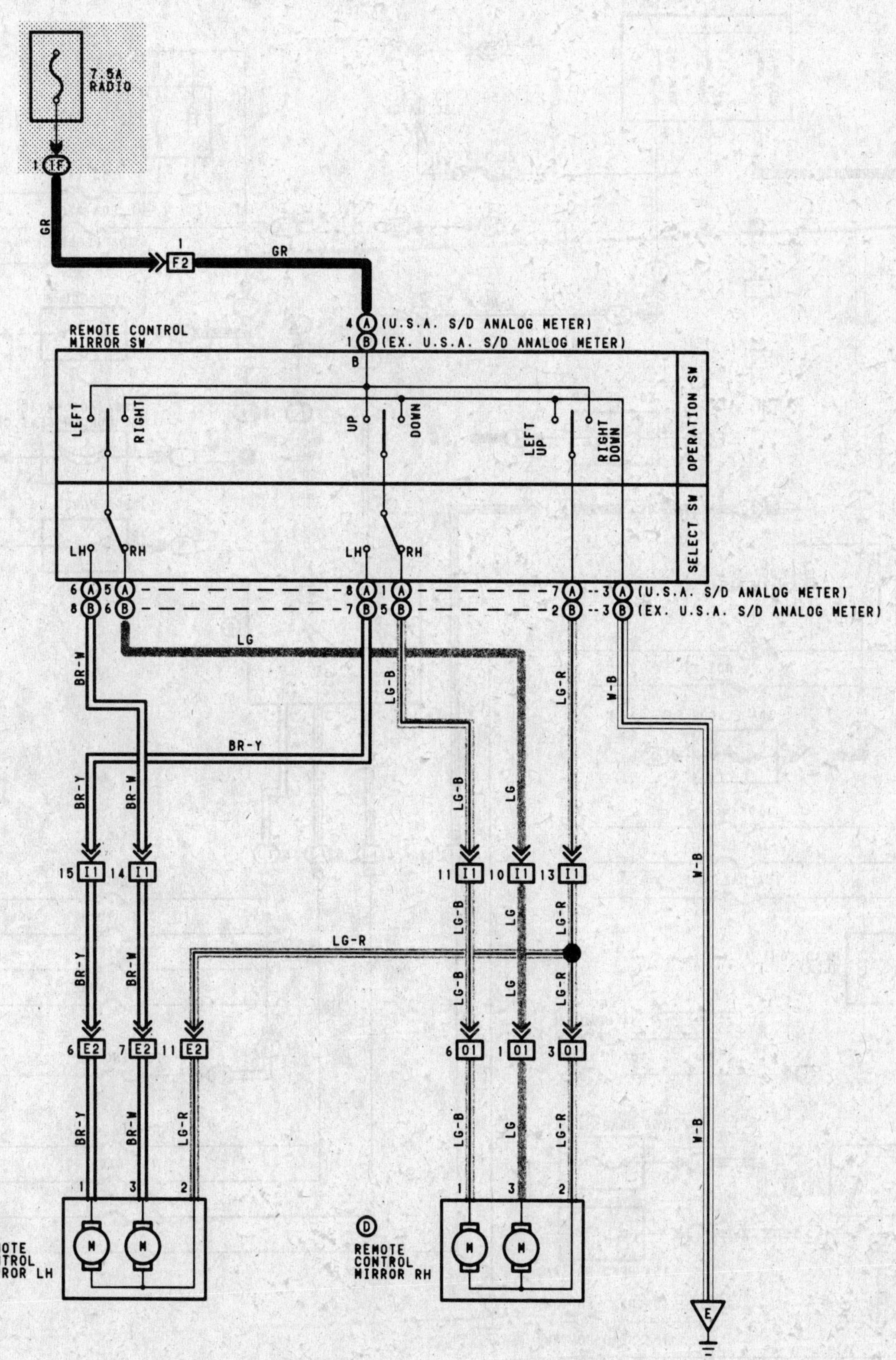

Remote control mirrors—1989 wiring diagram

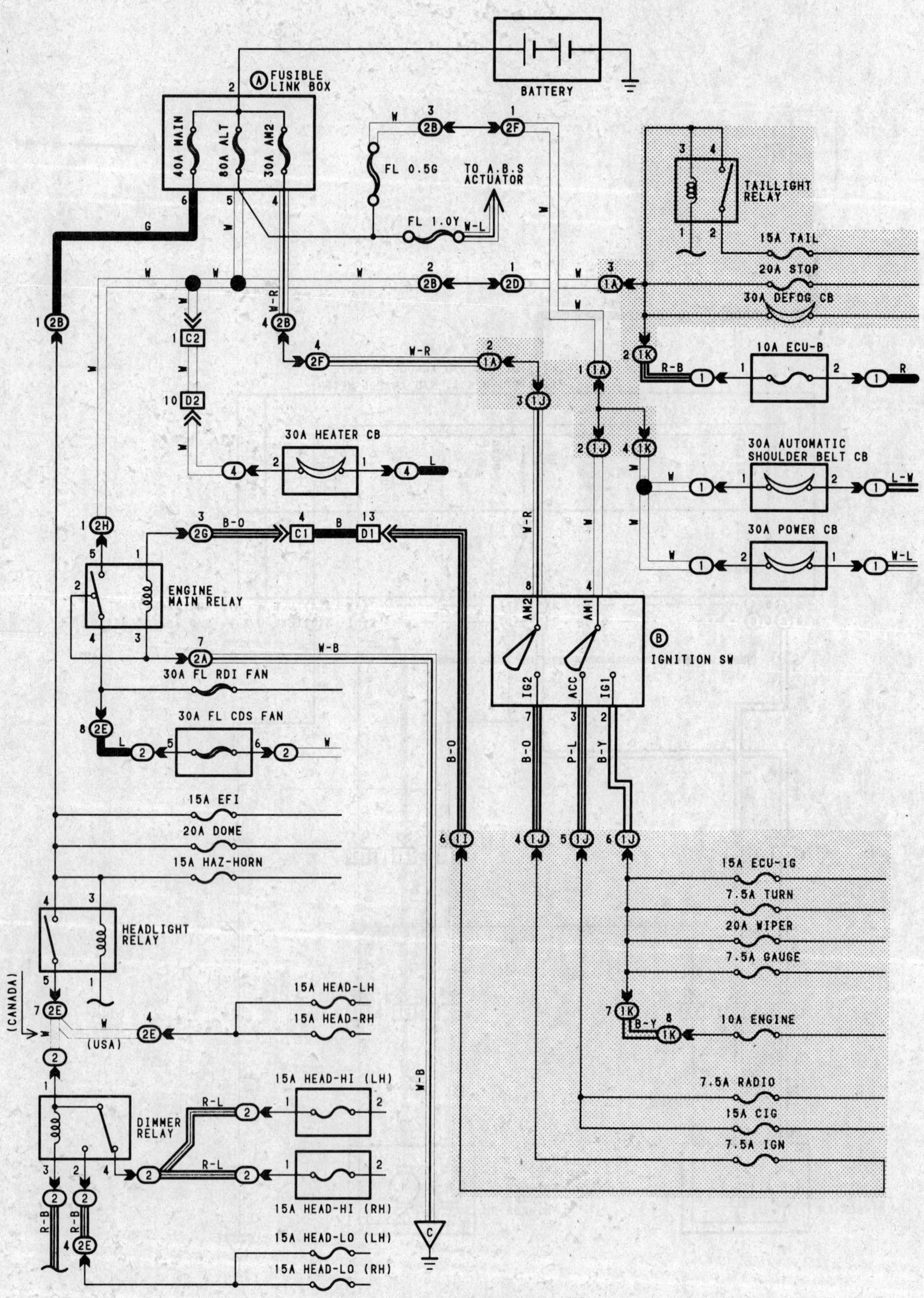

Power source—1990 wiring diagram

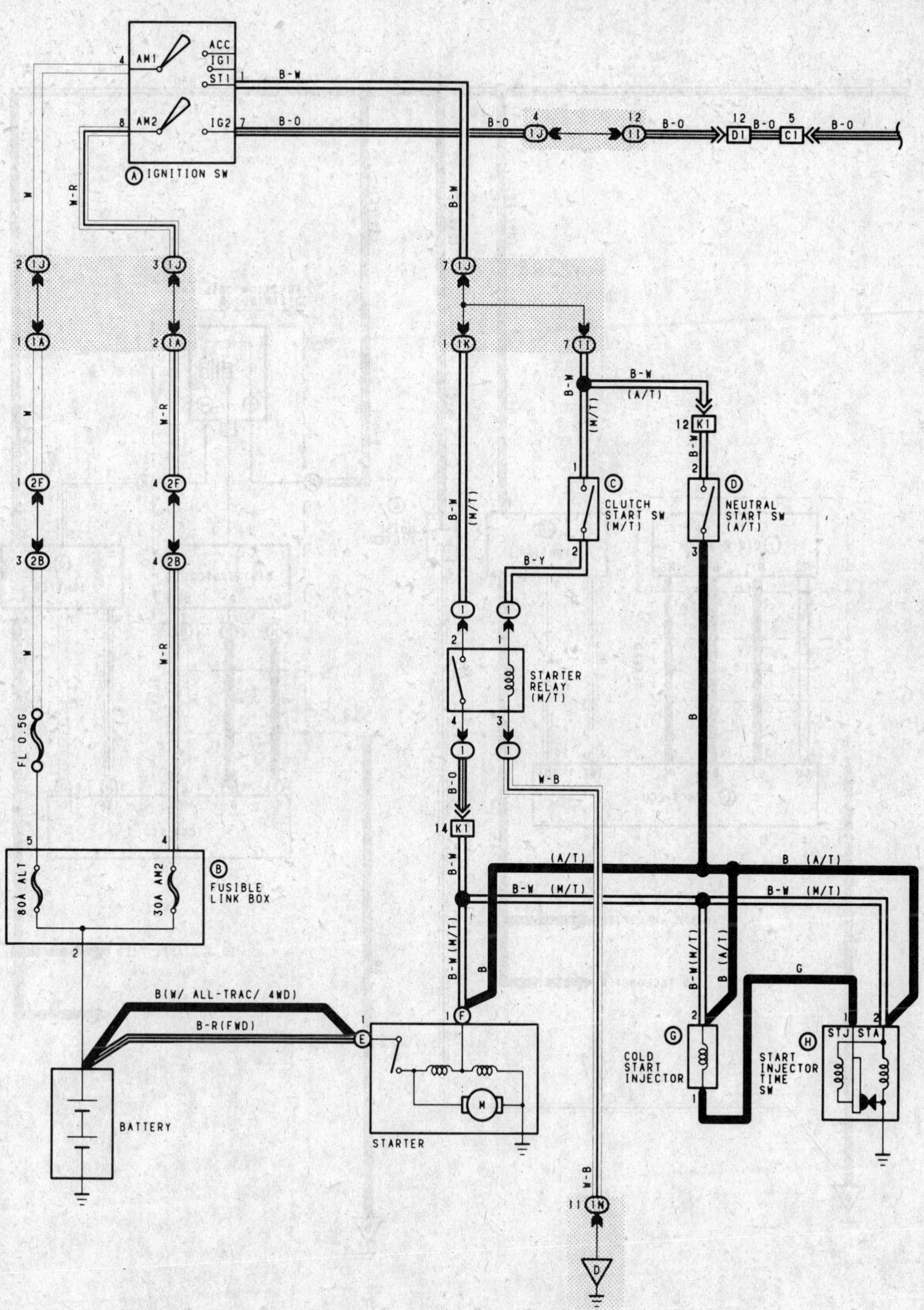

Starting and ignition—1990 wiring diagram

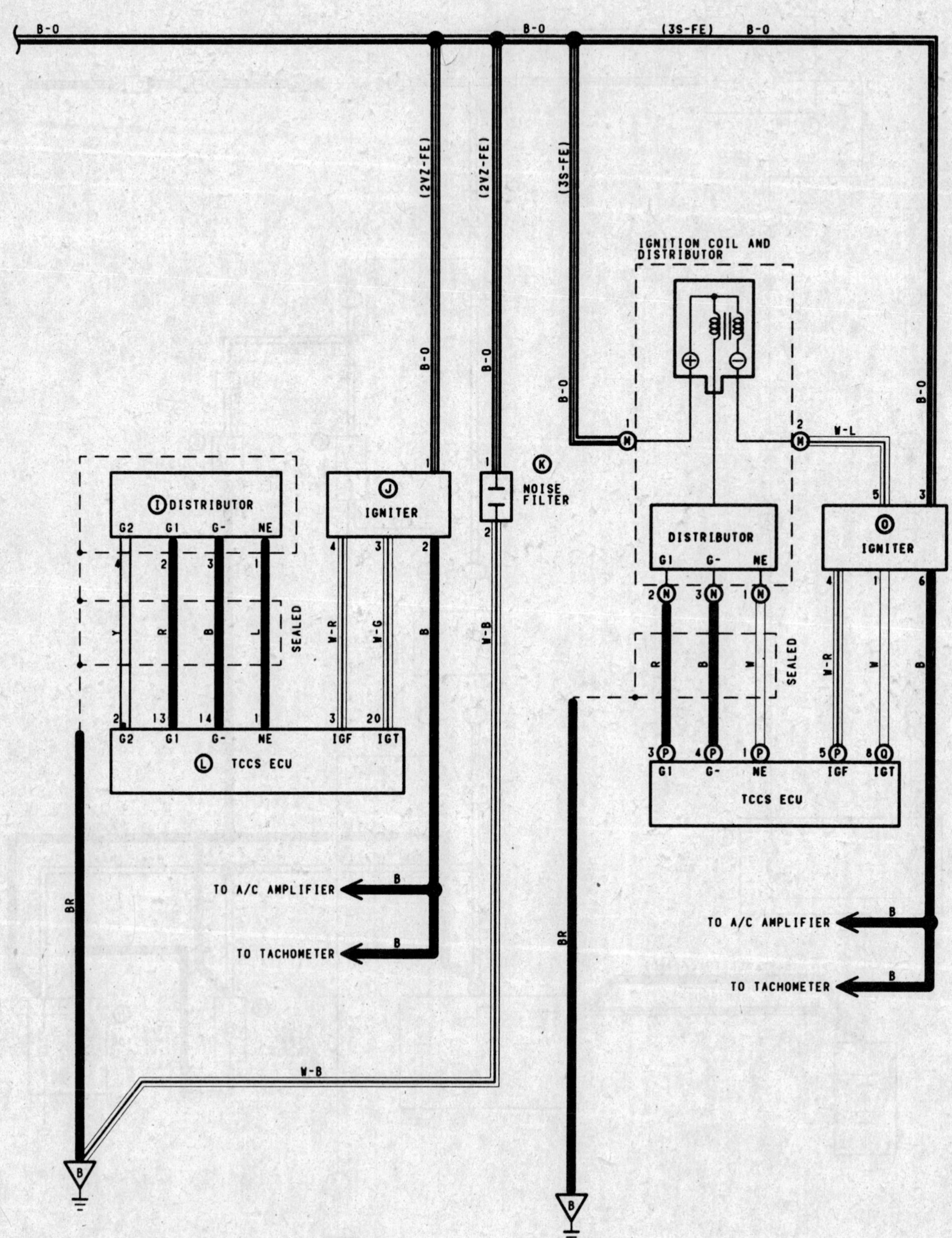

Starting and ignition—1990 wiring diagram

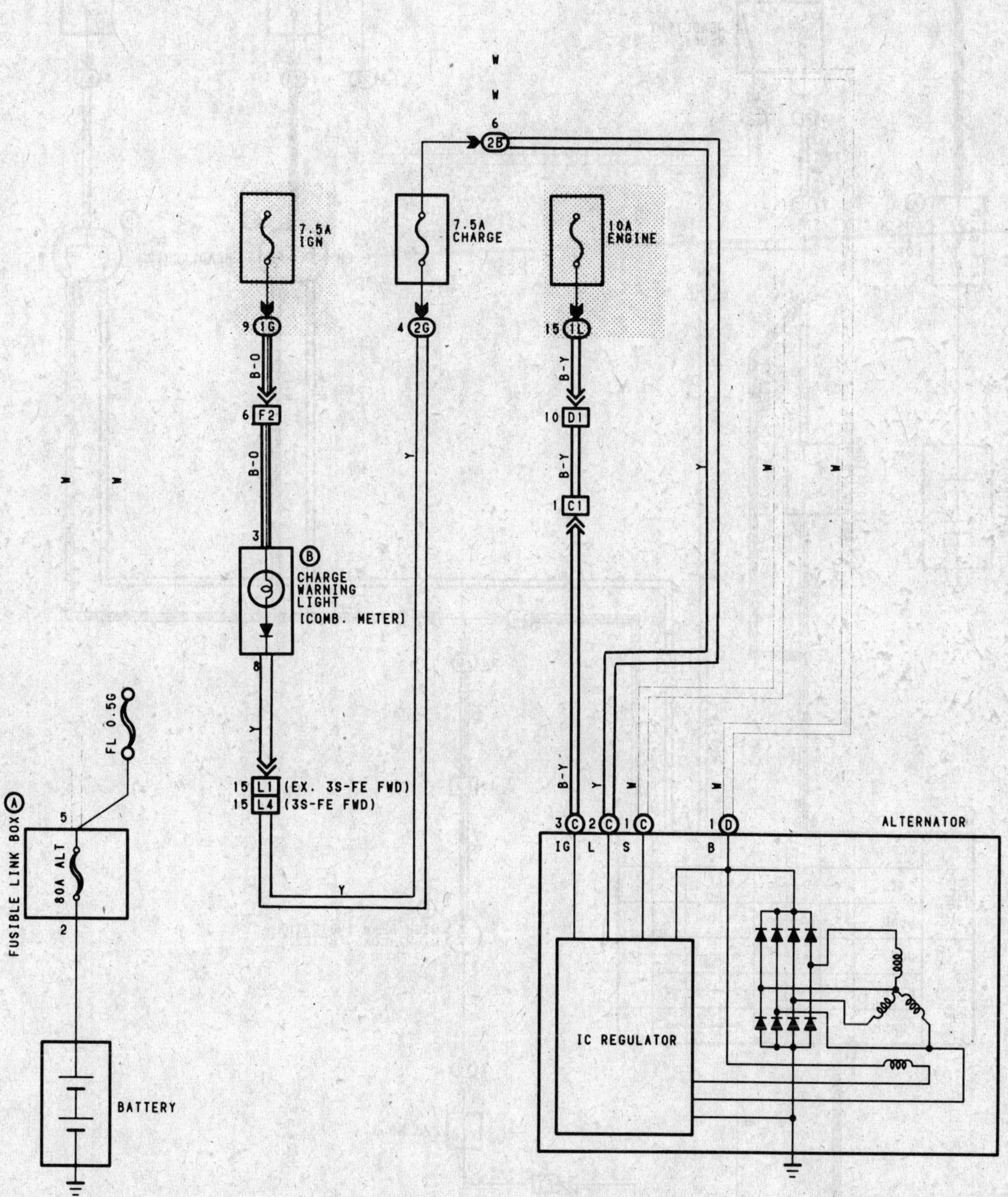

Charging system—1990 wiring diagram

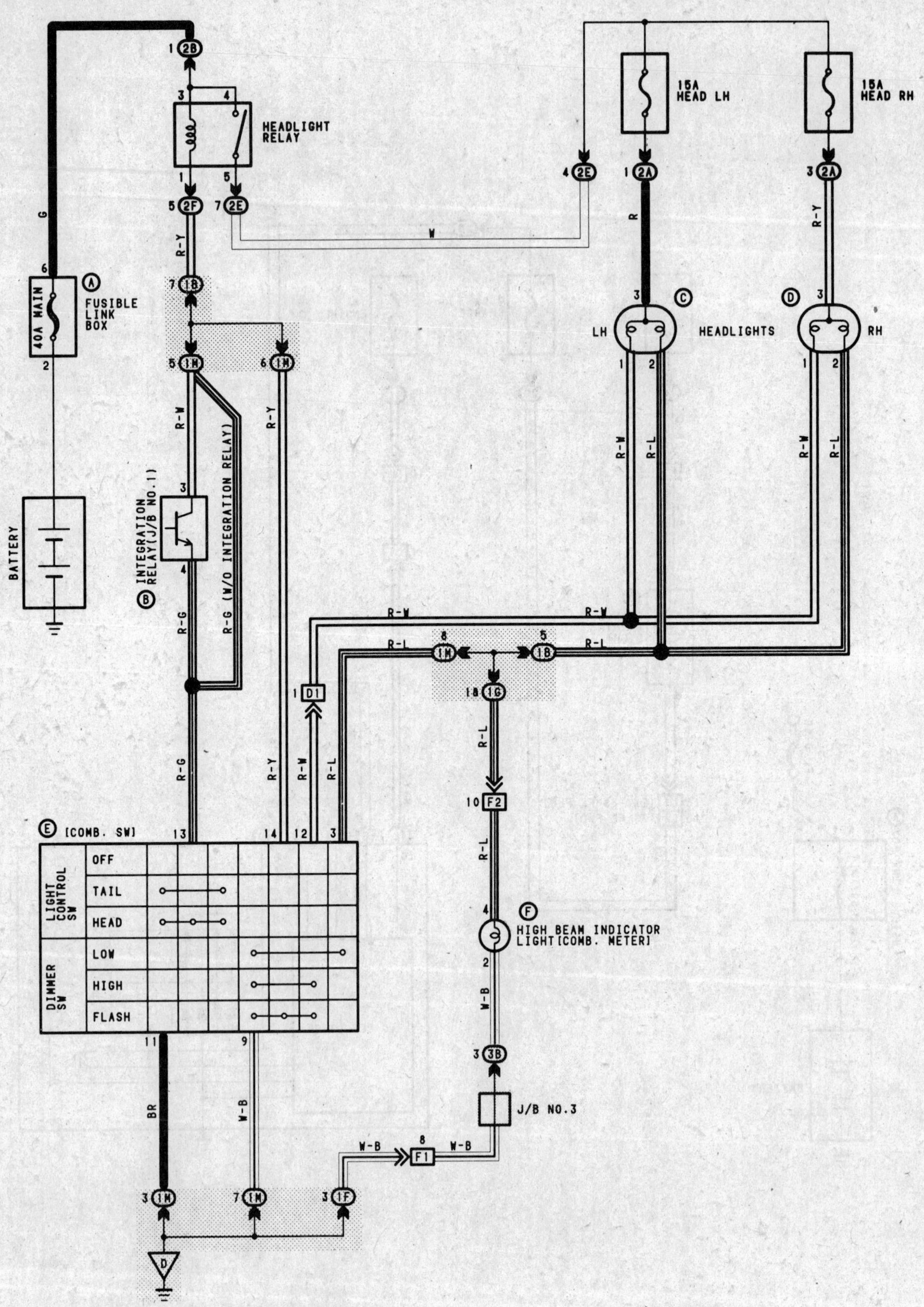

Headlights (USA) — 1990 wiring diagram

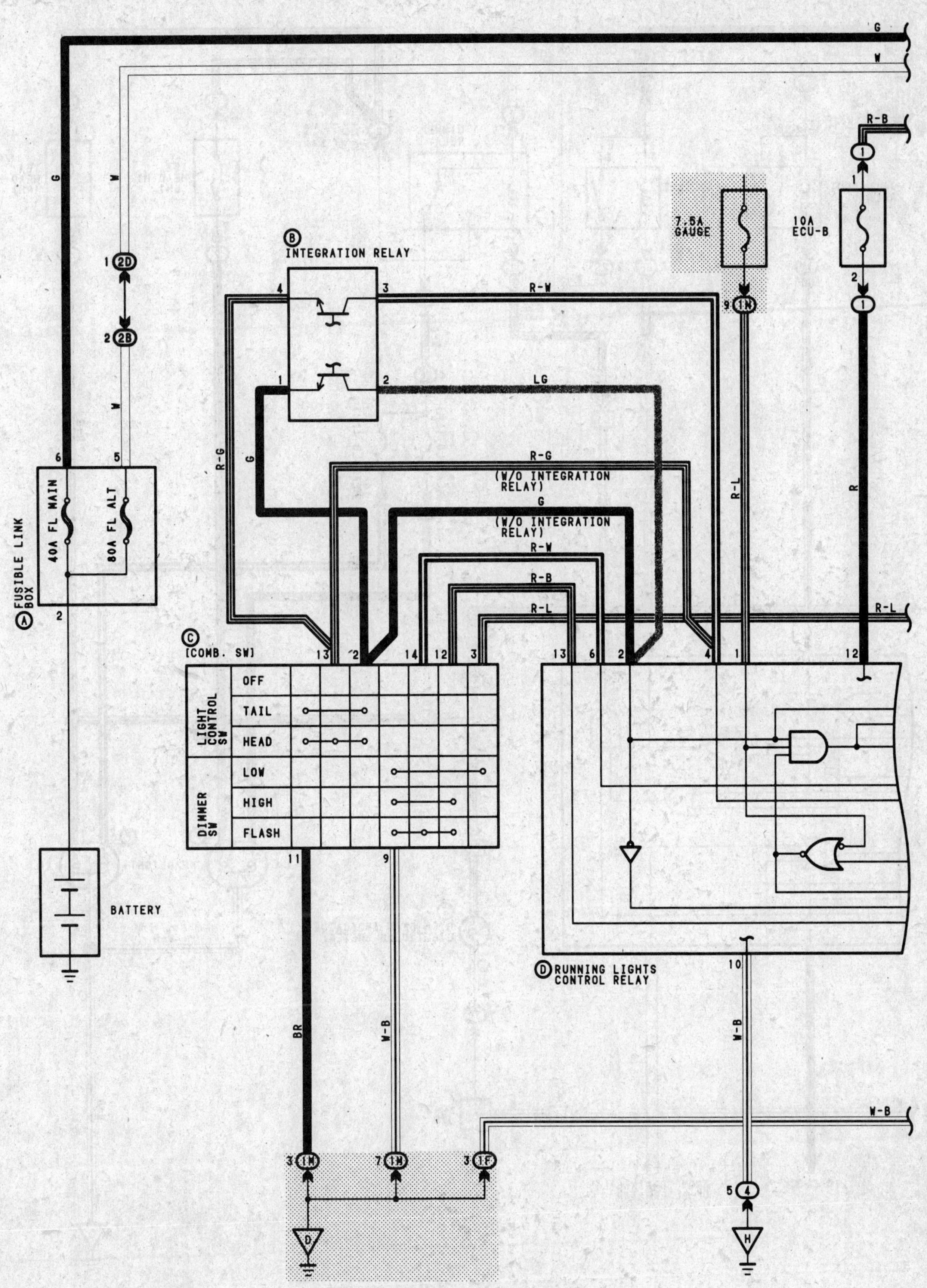

Headlights (Canada)—1990 wiring diagram

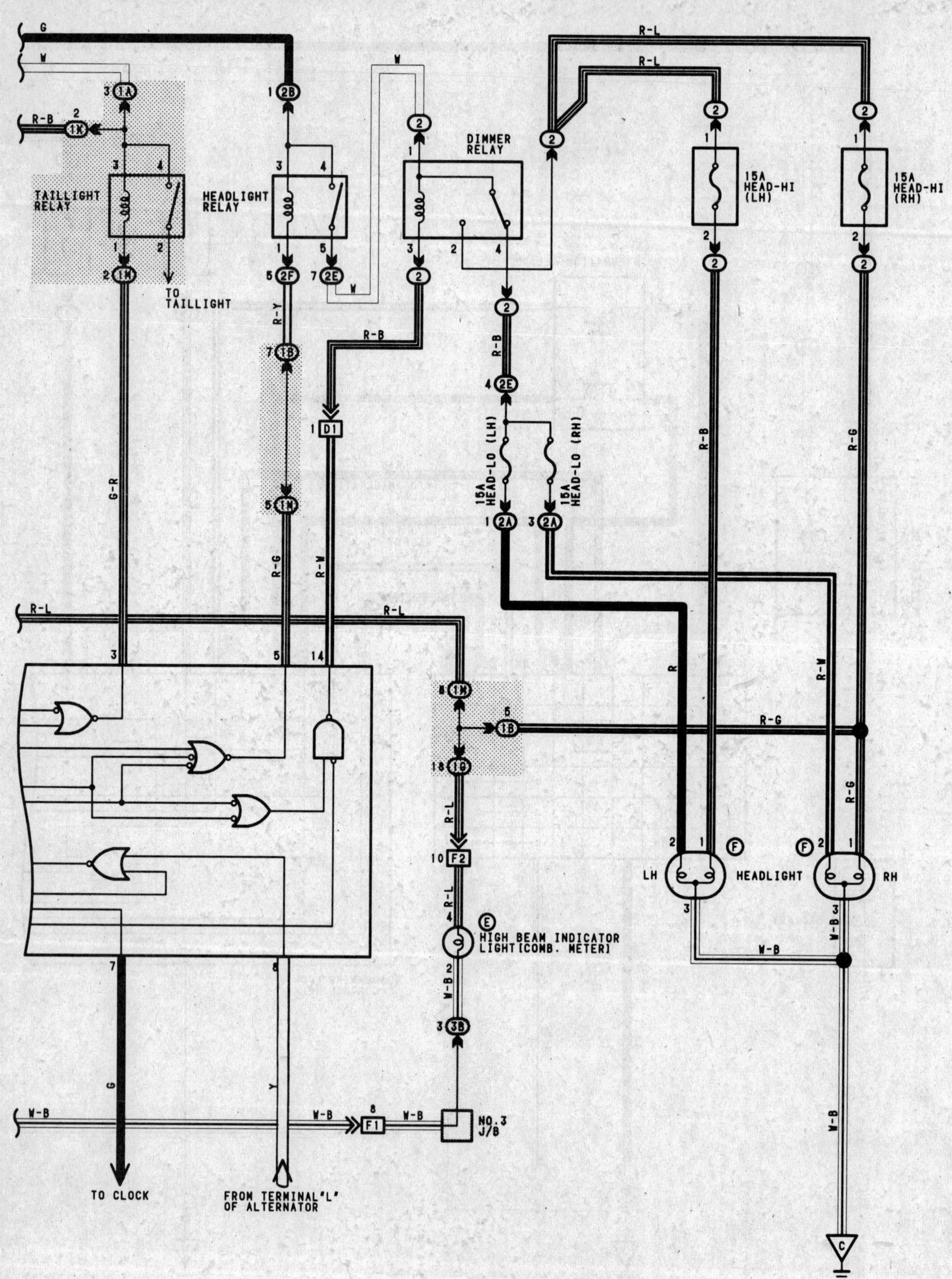

Headlights (Canada) — 1990 wiring diagram

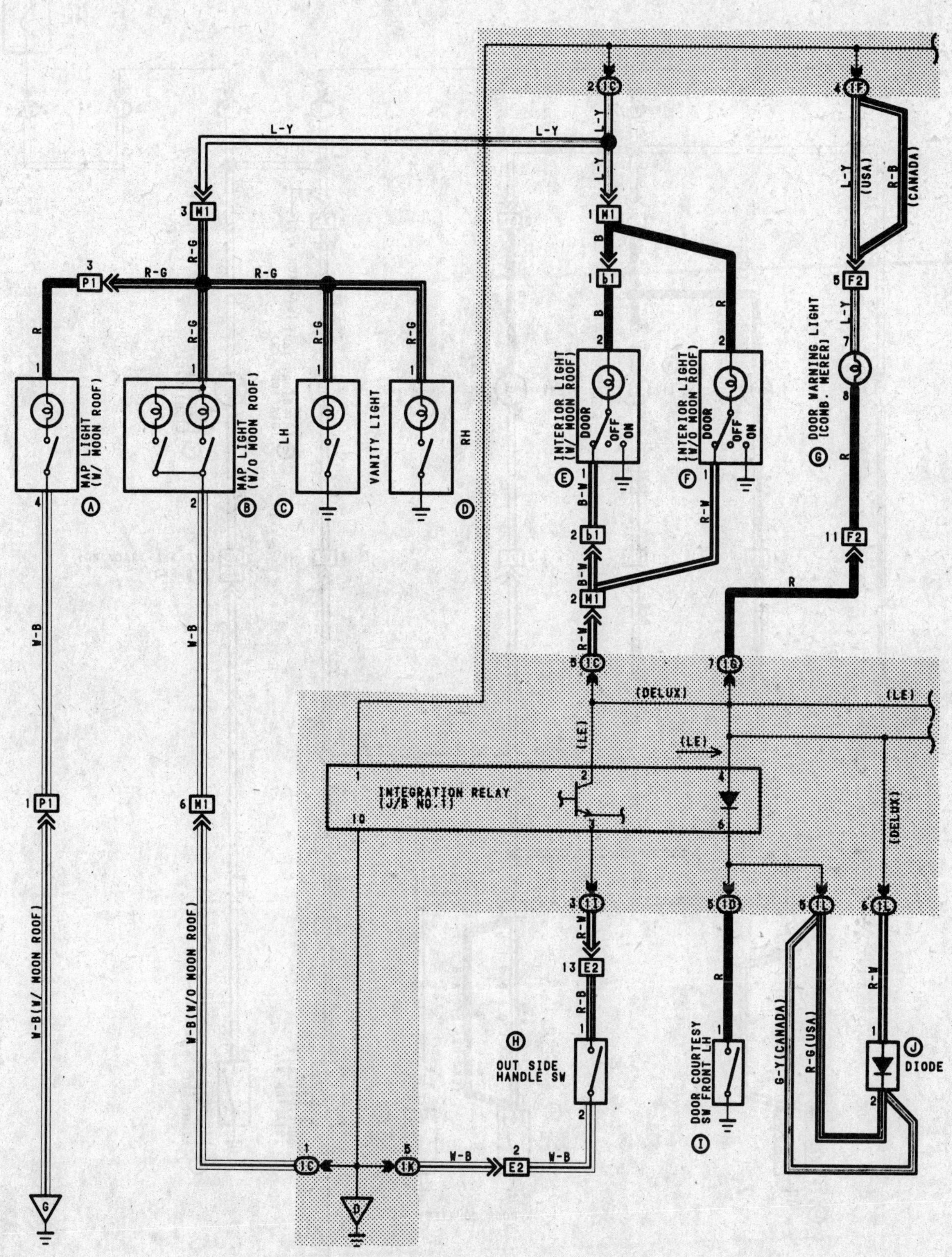

Interior lights with door locks—1990 wiring diagram

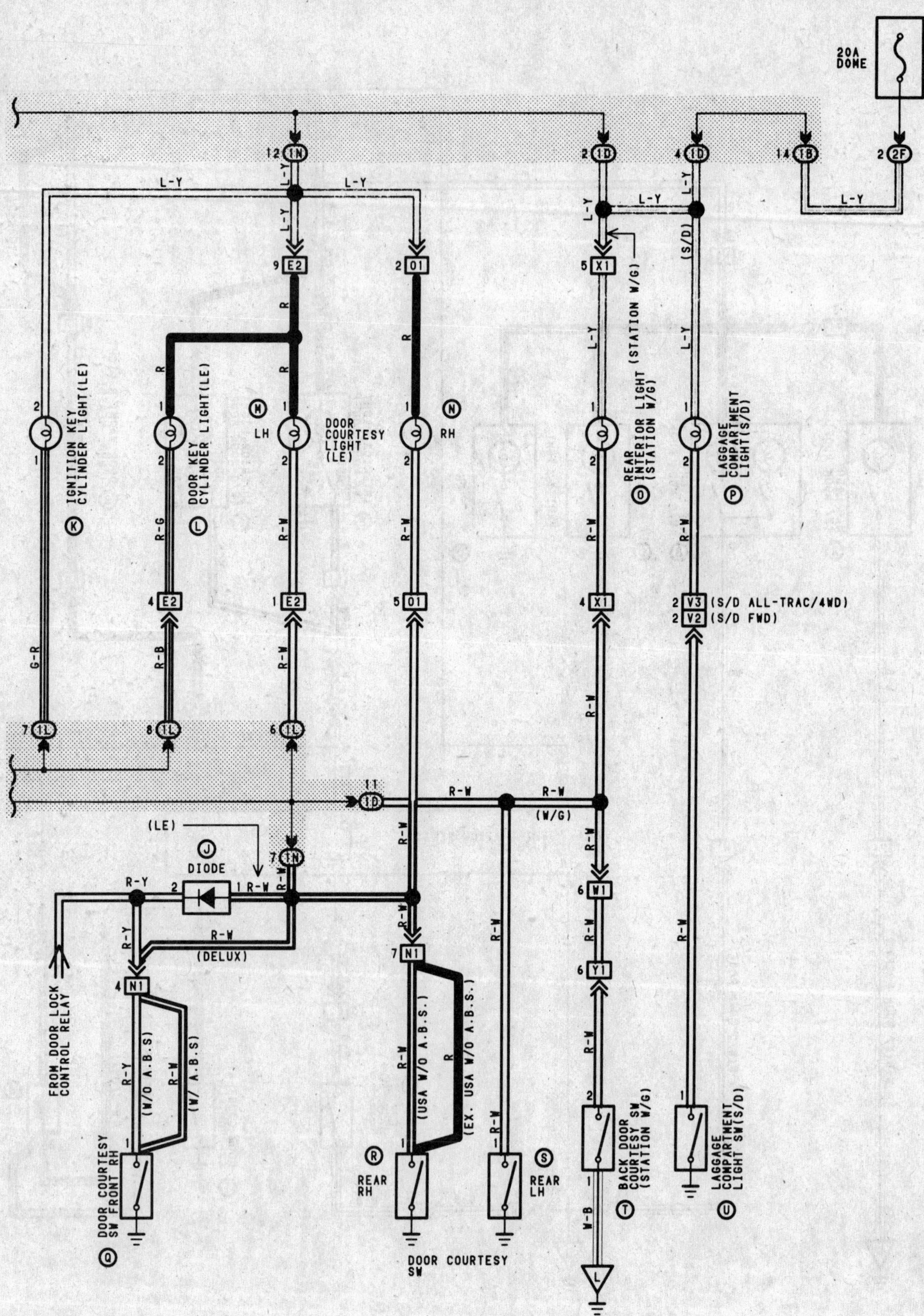

Interior lights with door locks—1990 wiring diagram

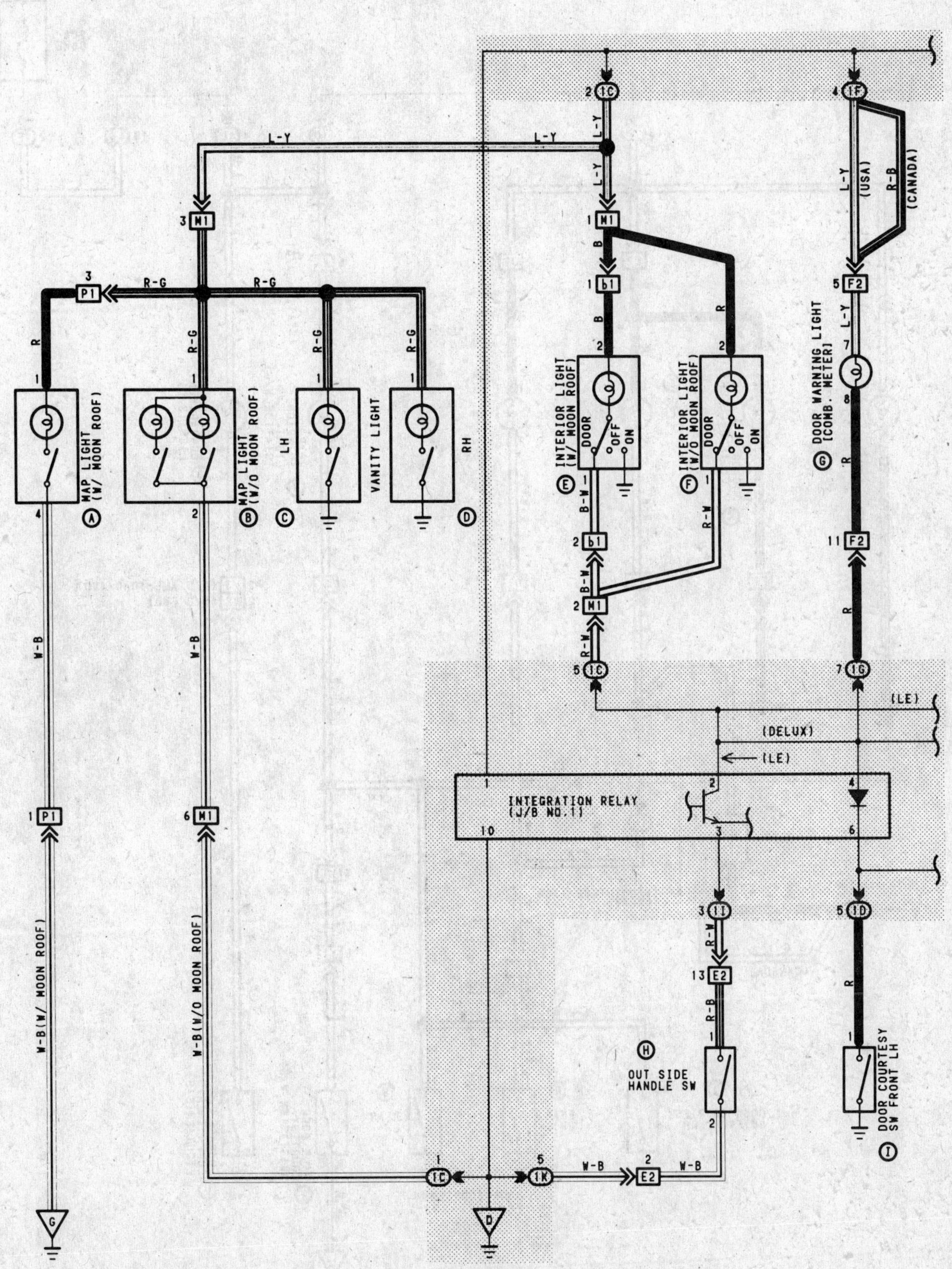

Interior lights without door locks—1990 wiring diagram

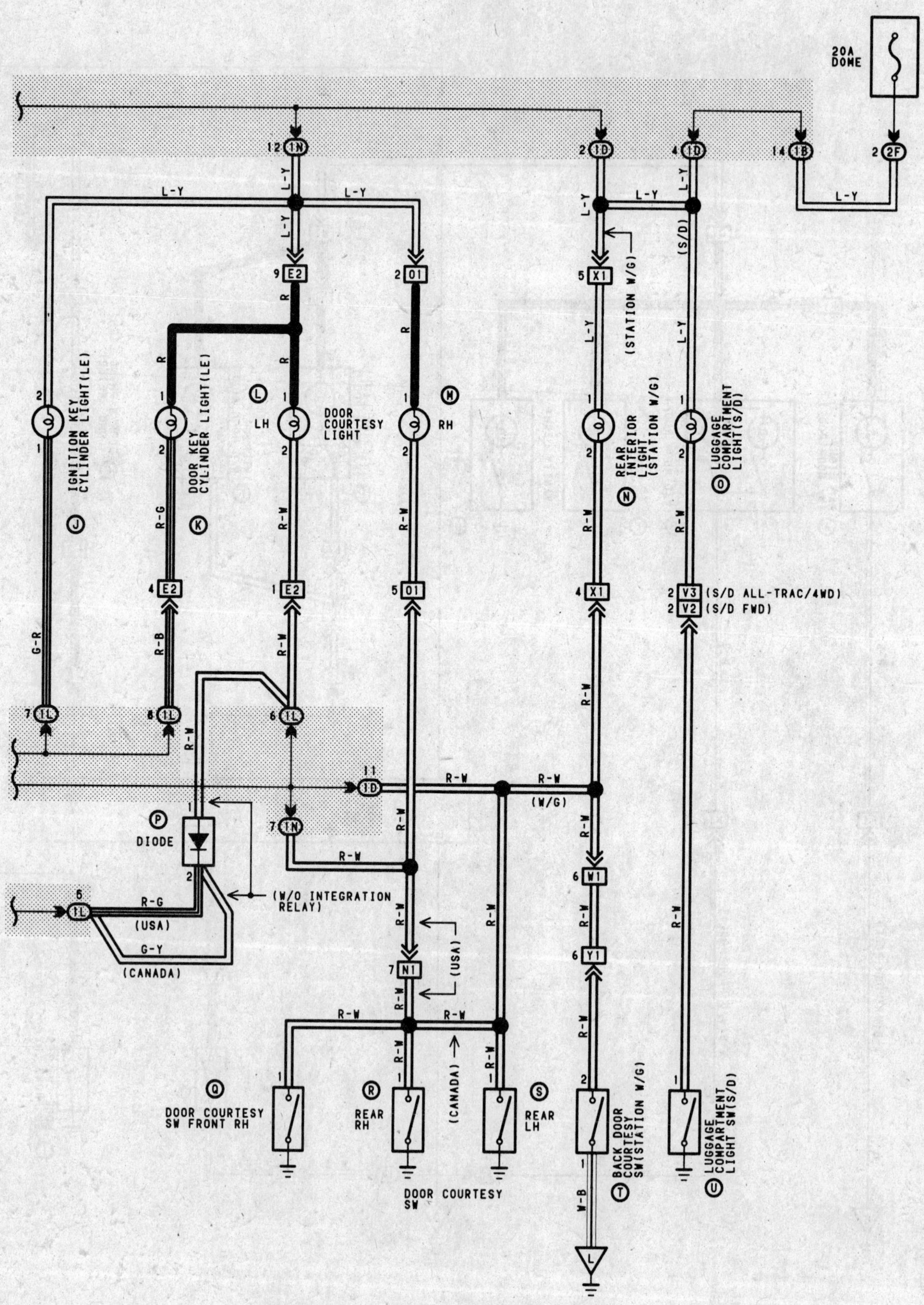

Interior lights without door locks—1990 wiring diagram

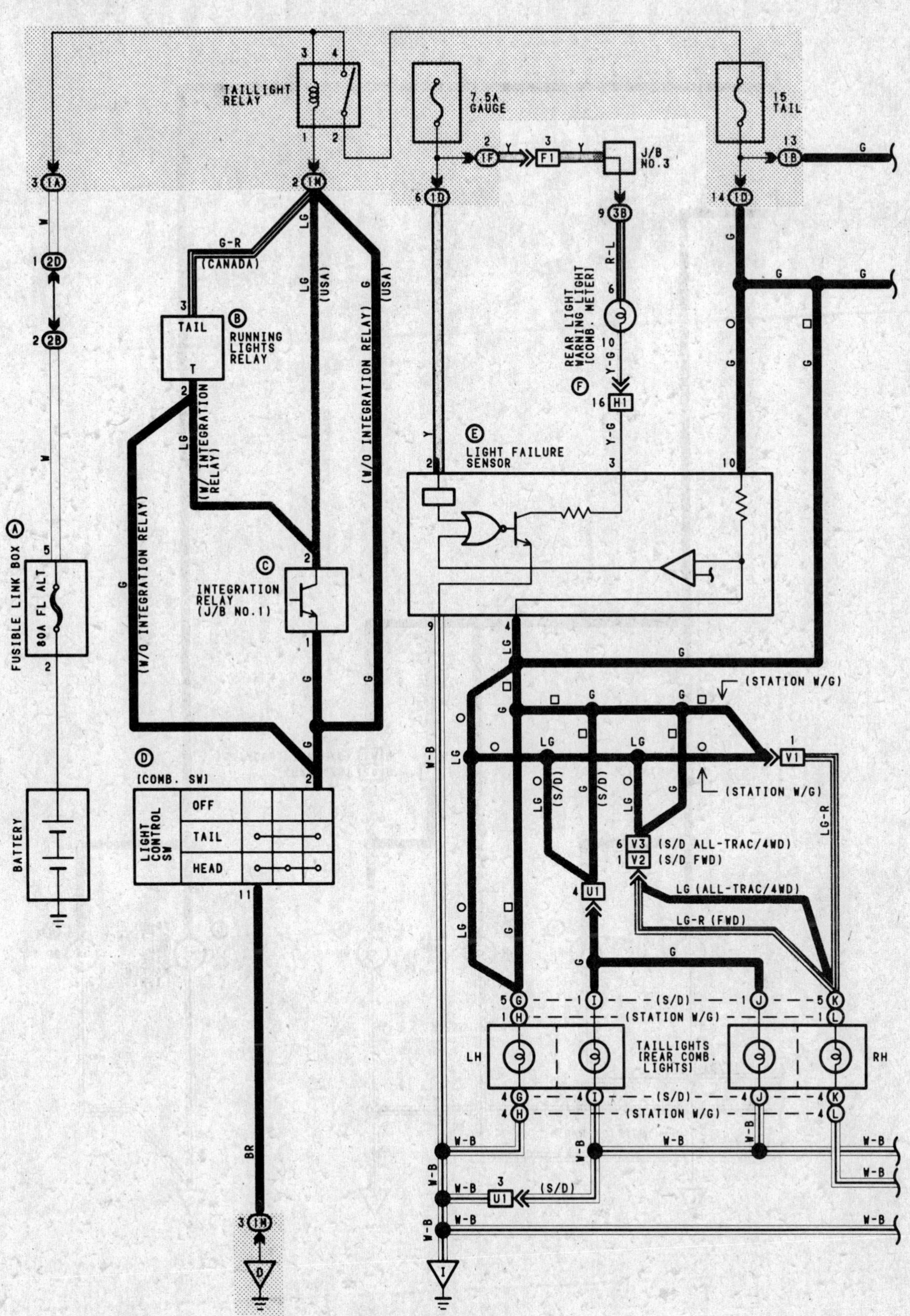

Taillights—1990 wiring diagram

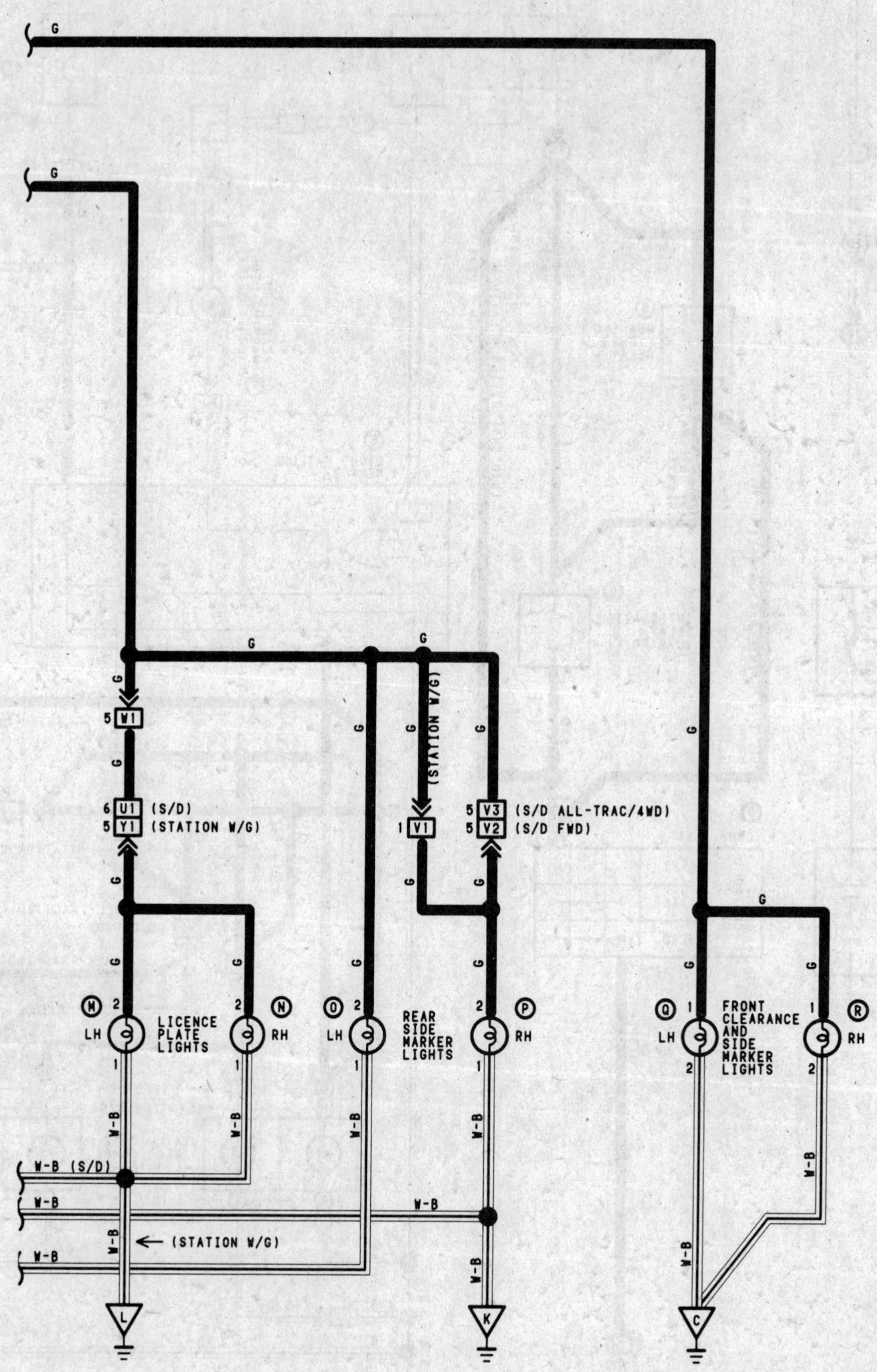

Taillights—1990 wiring diagram

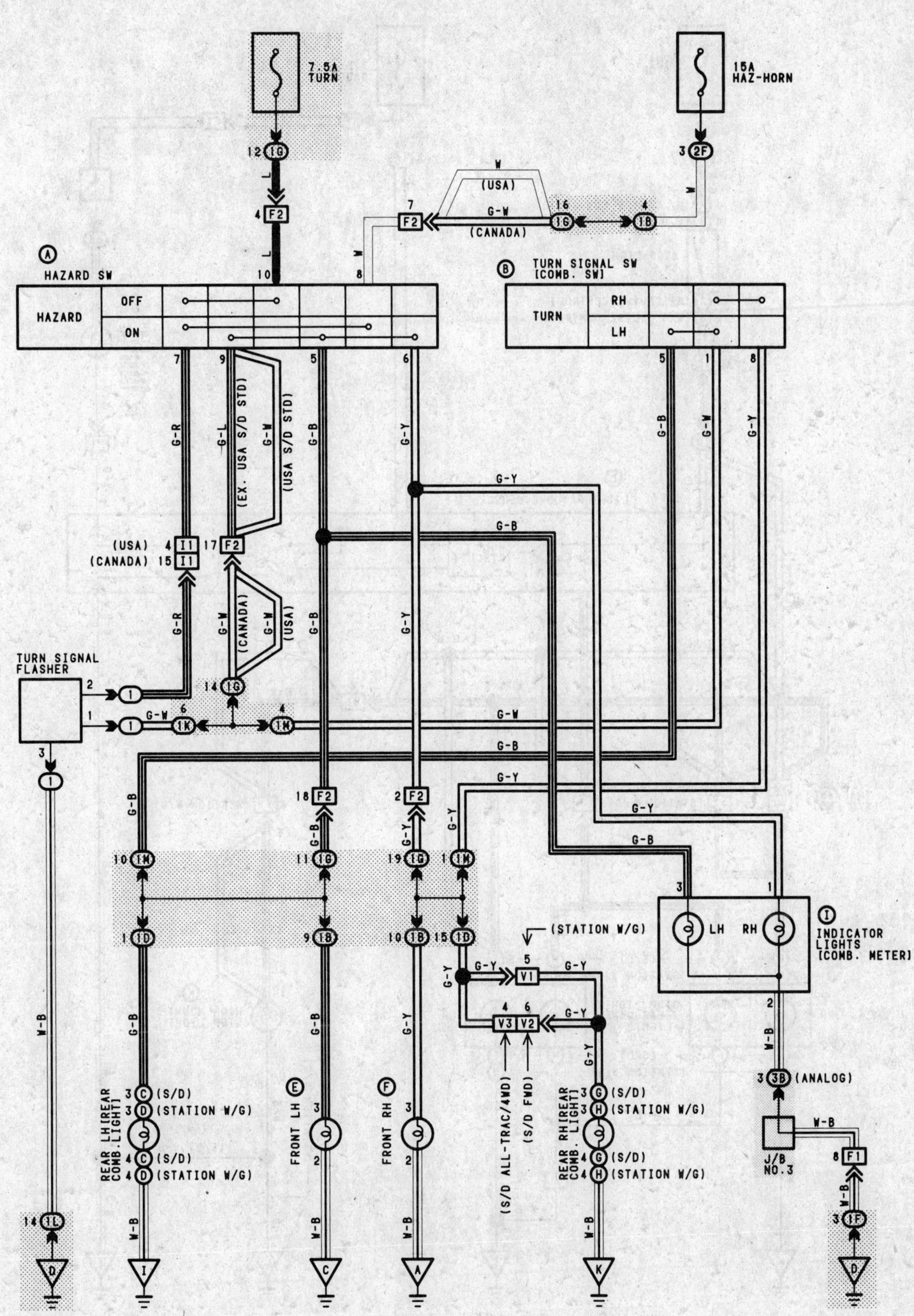

Turnsignal and hazard warning lights—1990 wiring diagram

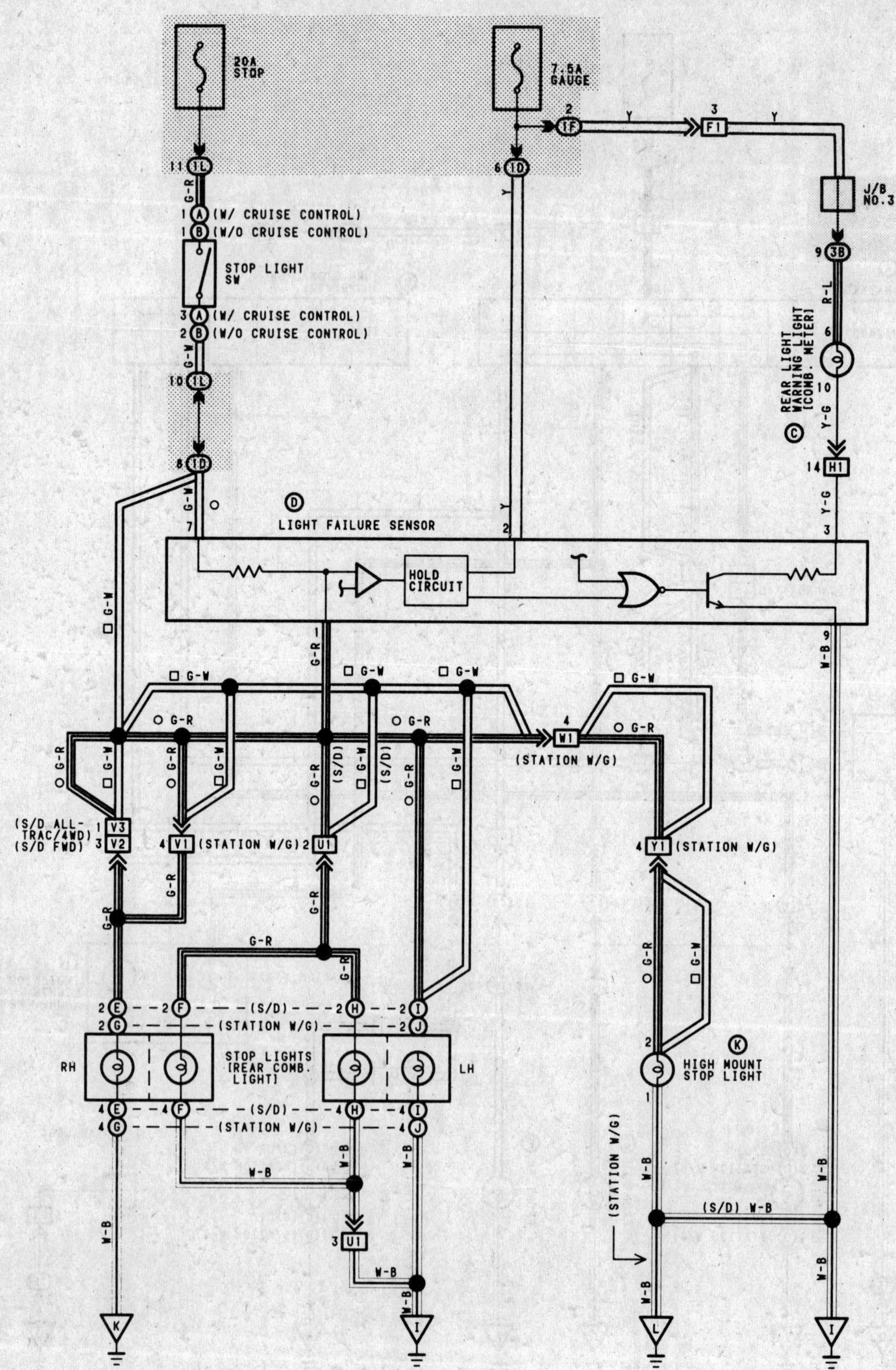

Stop lights—1990 wiring diagram

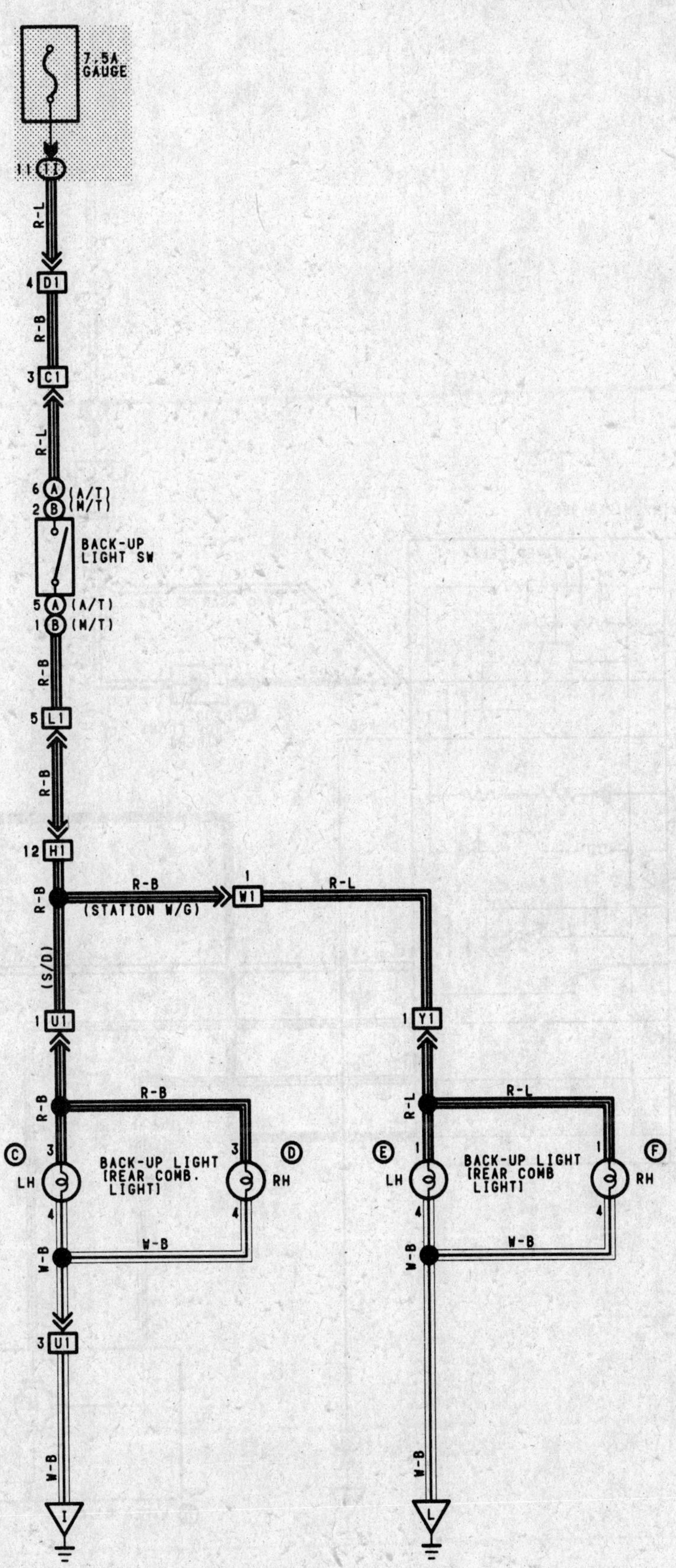

Back-up lights—1990 wiring diagram

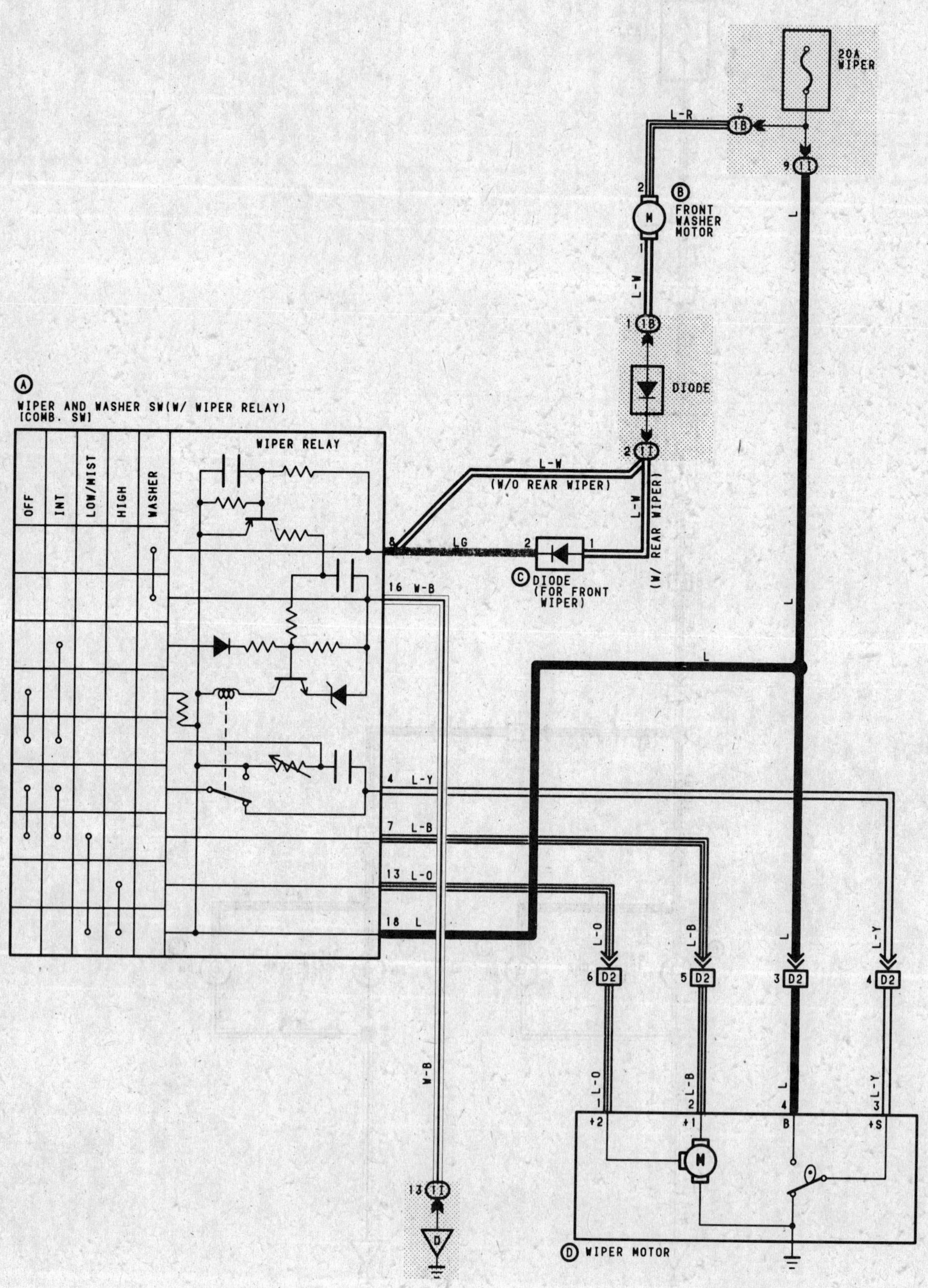

Front wiper and washer—1990 wiring diagram

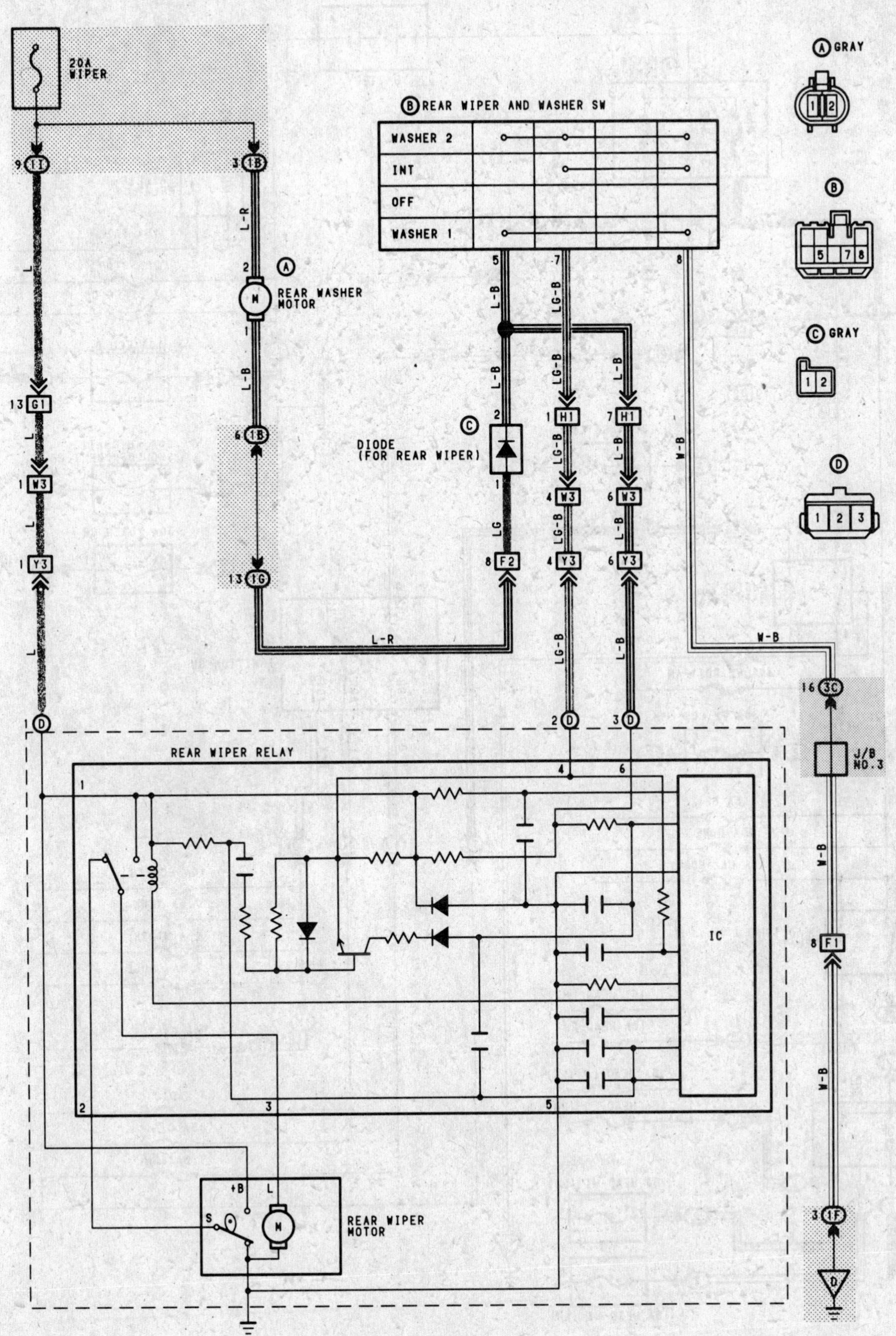

Rear wiper and washer—1990 wiring diagram

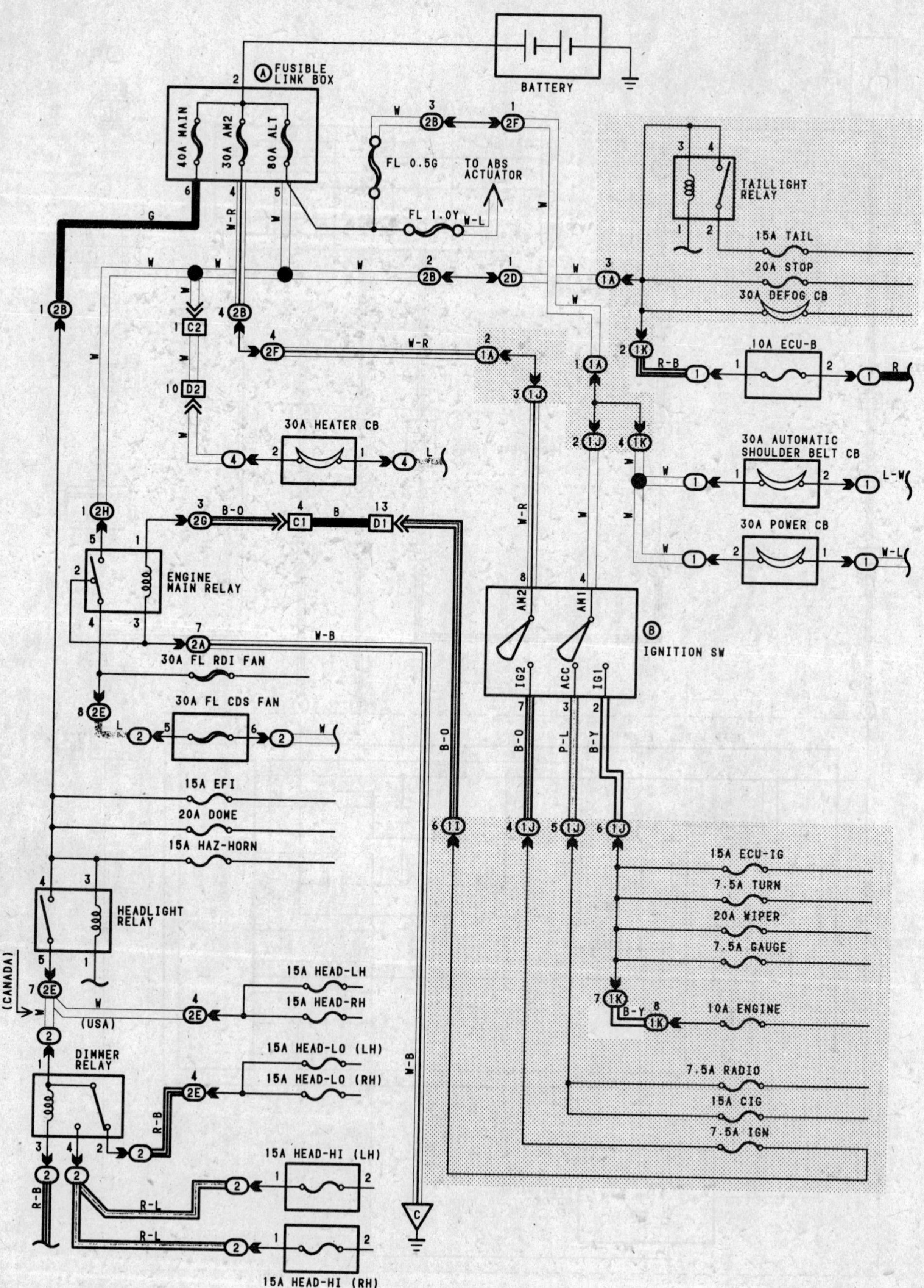

Power Source—1991 wiring diagram

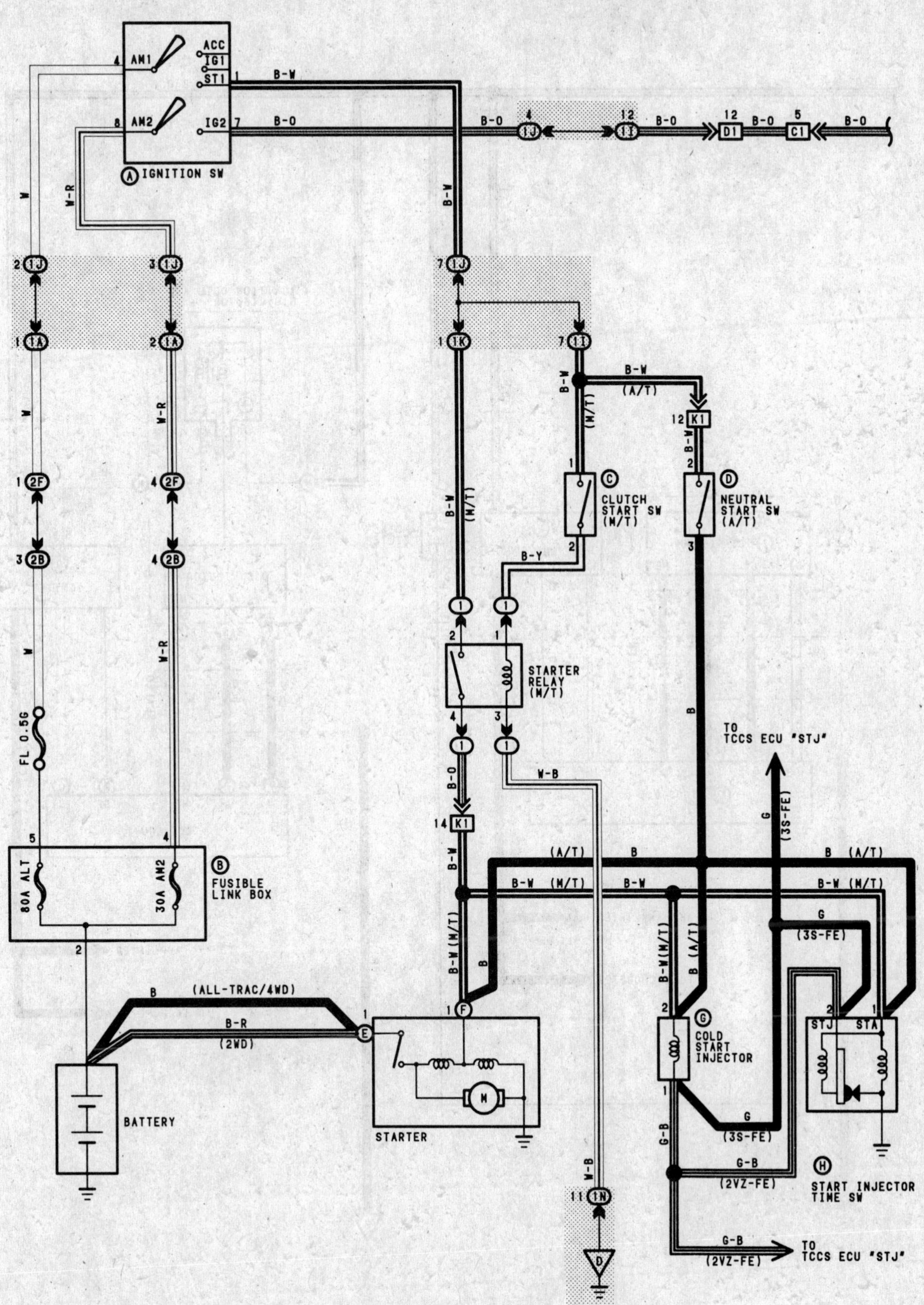

Starting and ignition—1991 wiring diagram

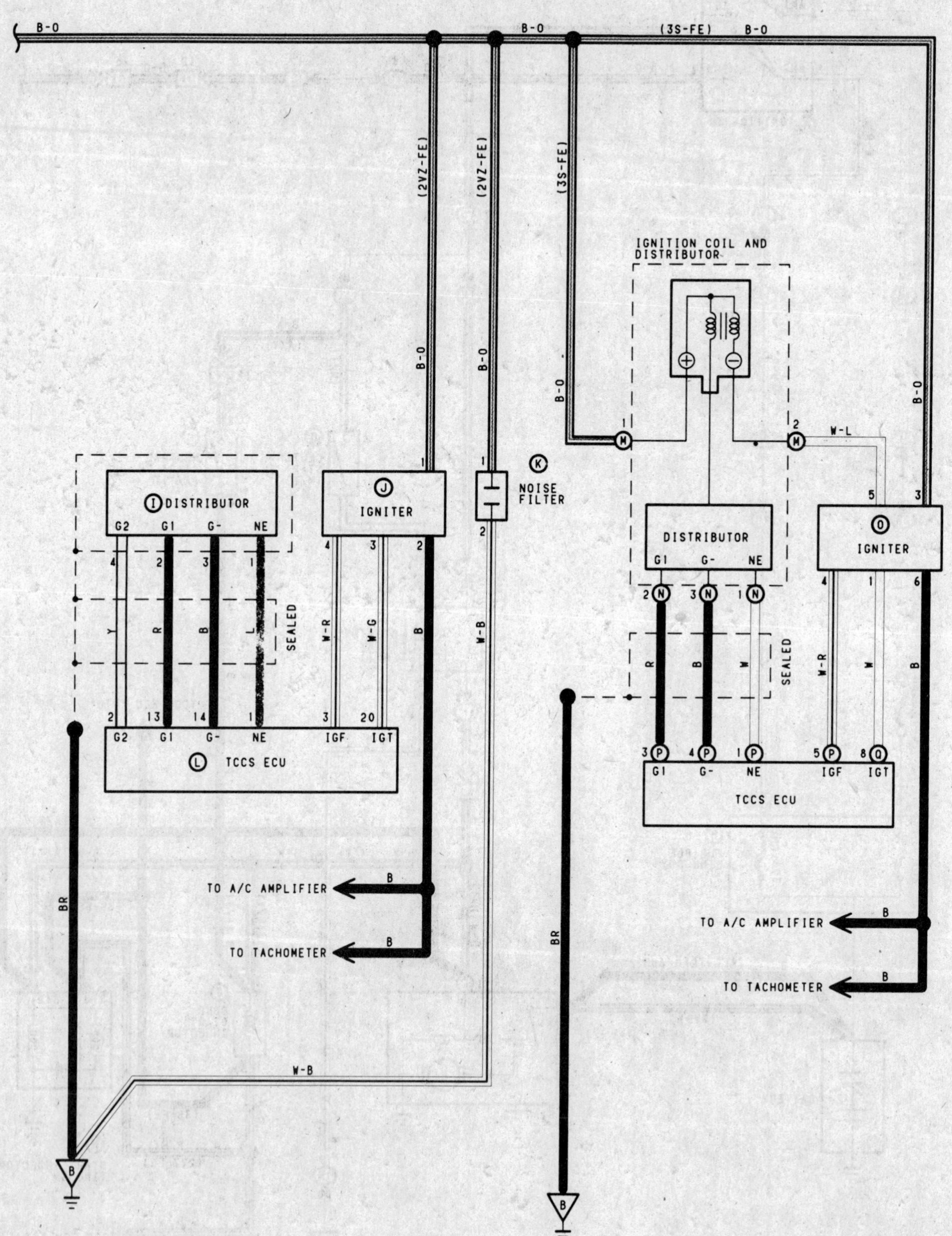

Starting and ignition—1991 wiring diagram

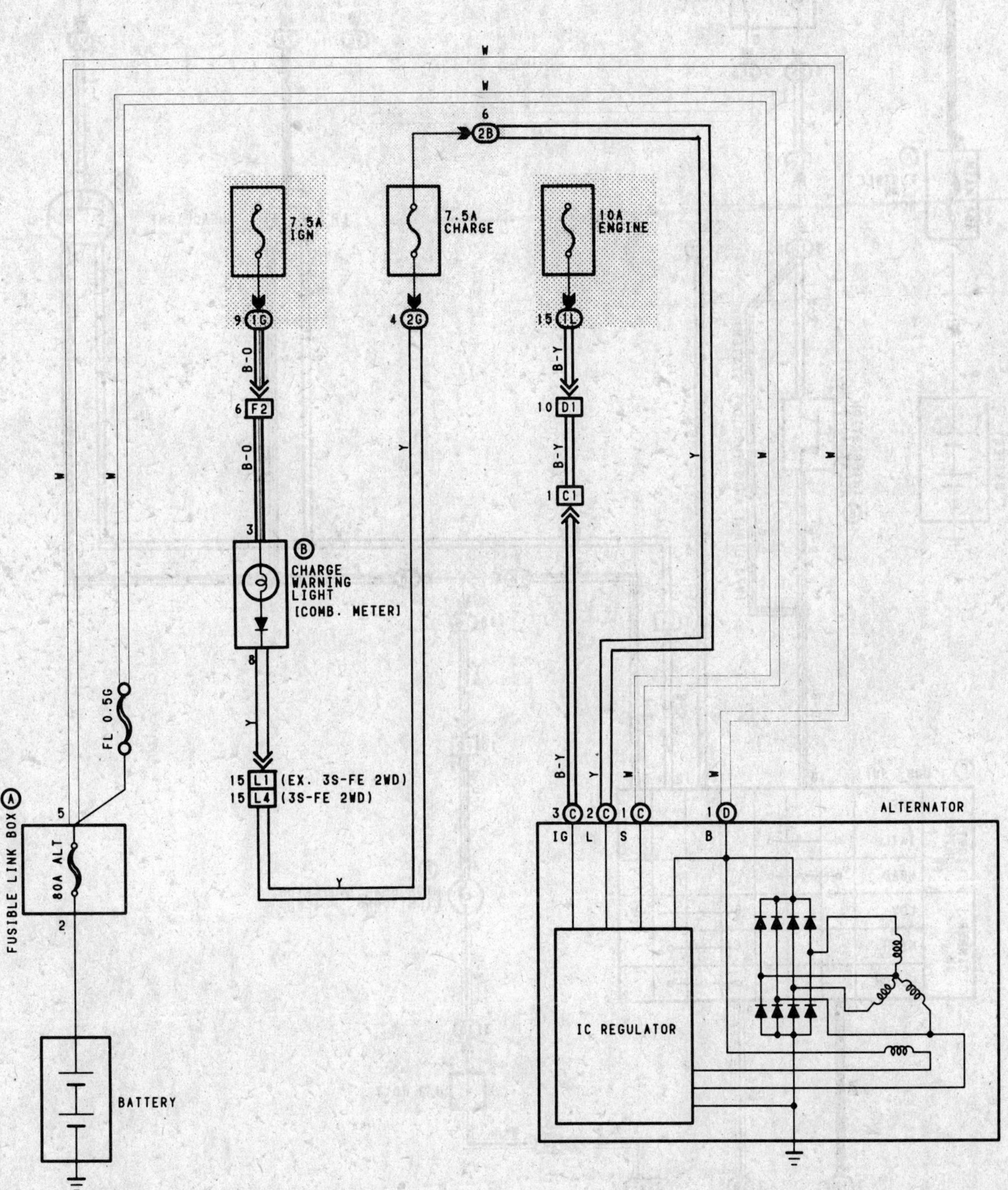

Charging—1991 wiring diagram

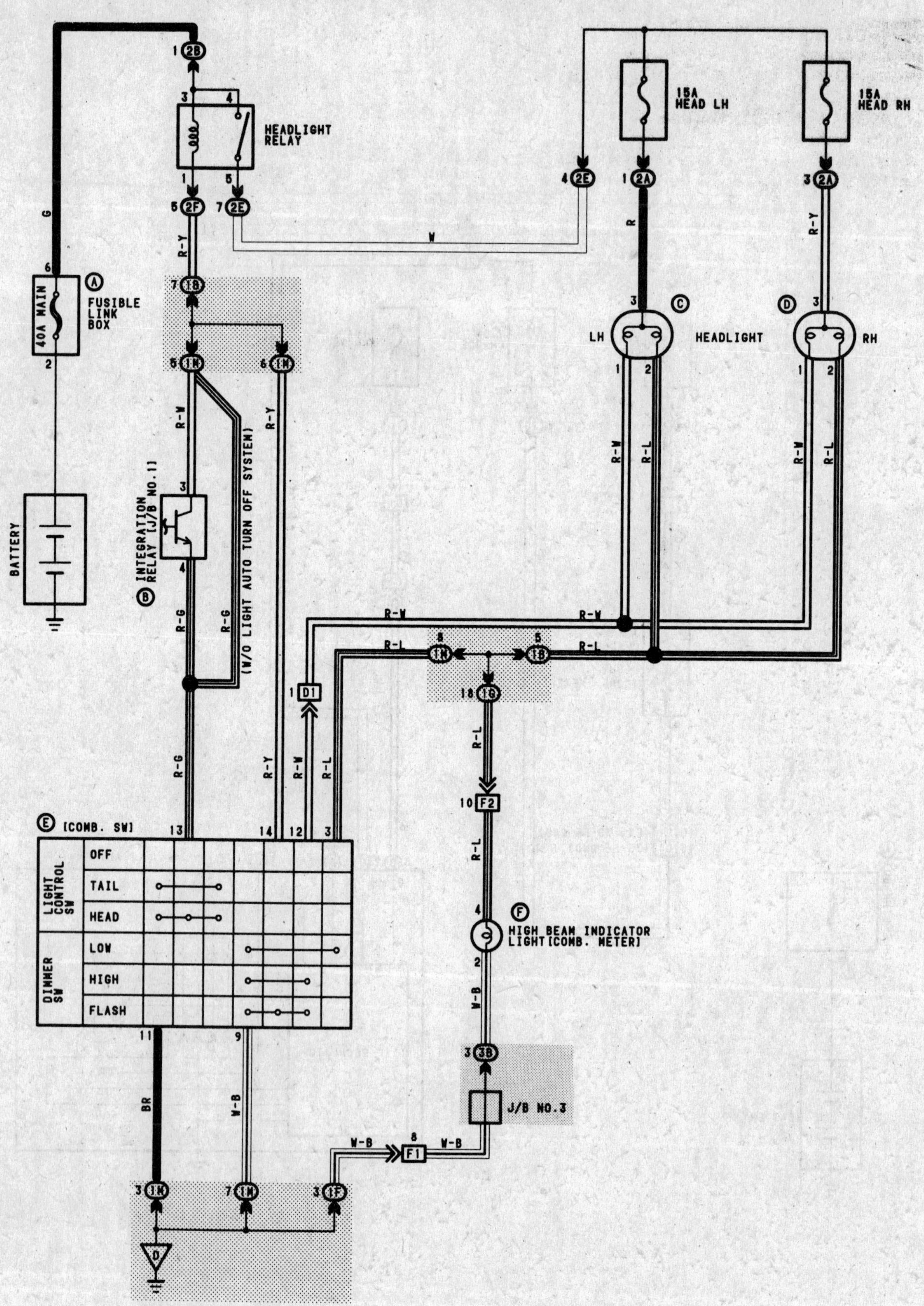

Headlight (USA)—1991 wiring diagram

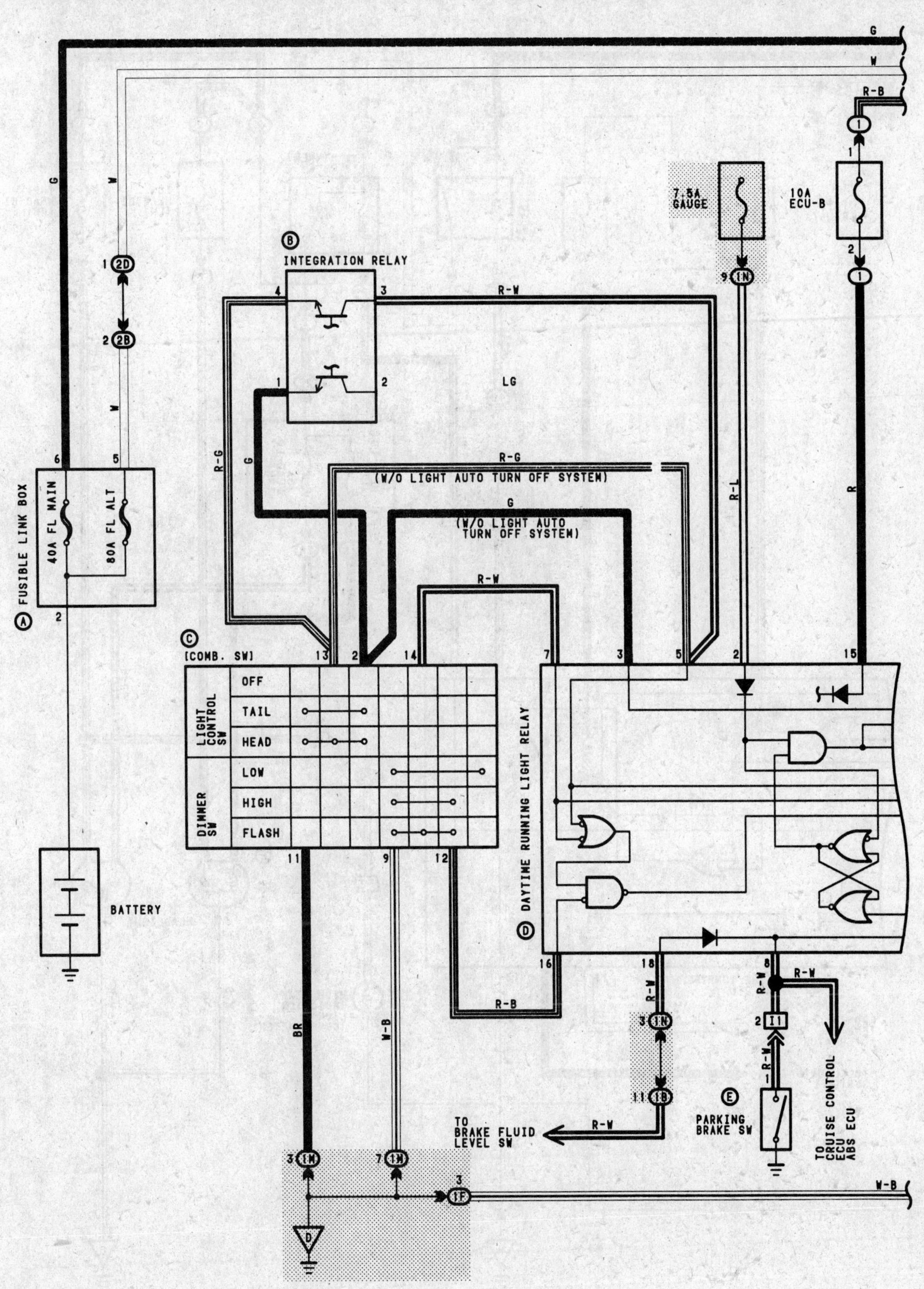

Headlight (Canada)—1991 wiring diagram

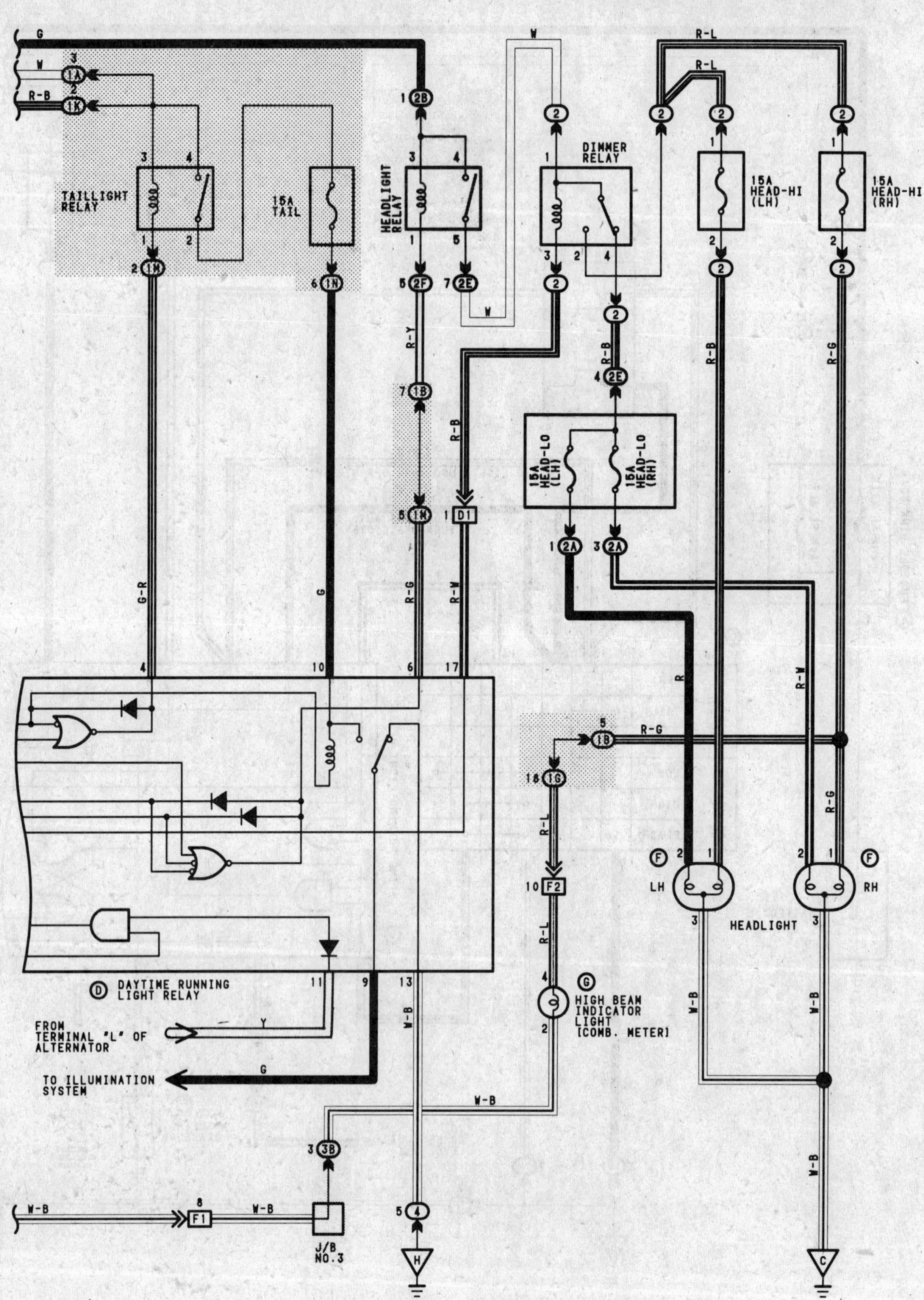

Headlight (Canada) – 1991 wiring diagram

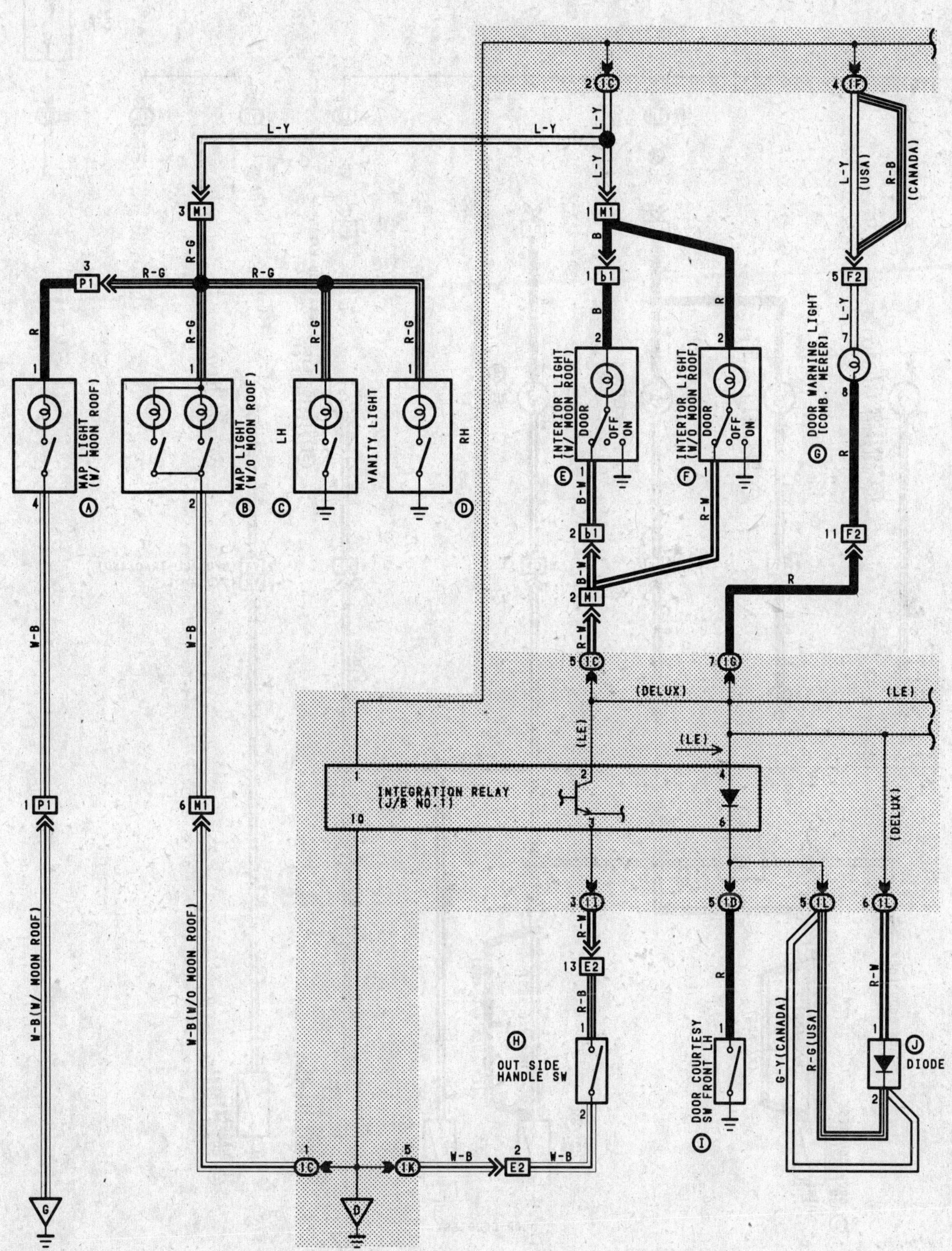

Interior light with door lock—1991 wiring diagram

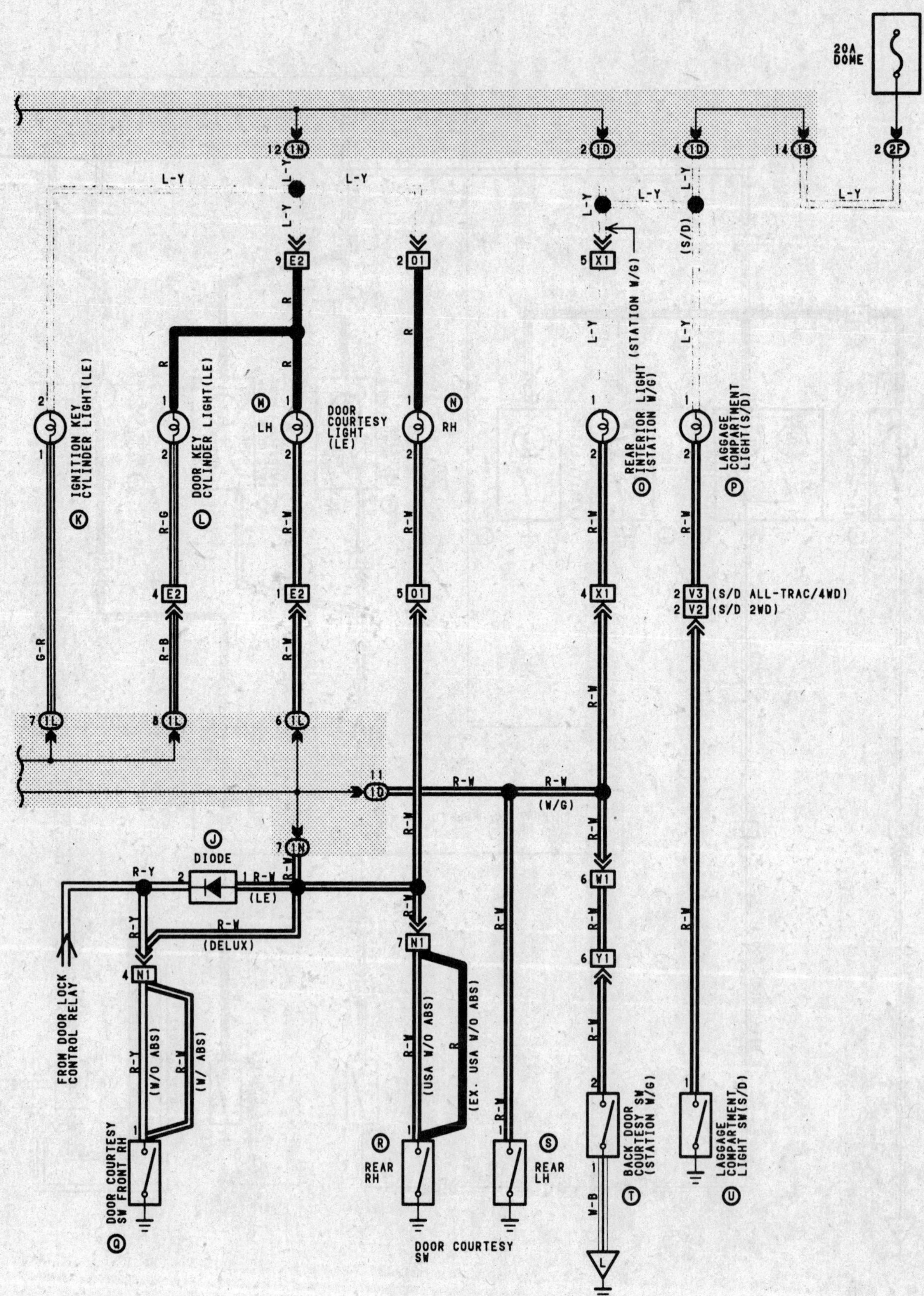

Interior light with door lock—1991 wiring diagram

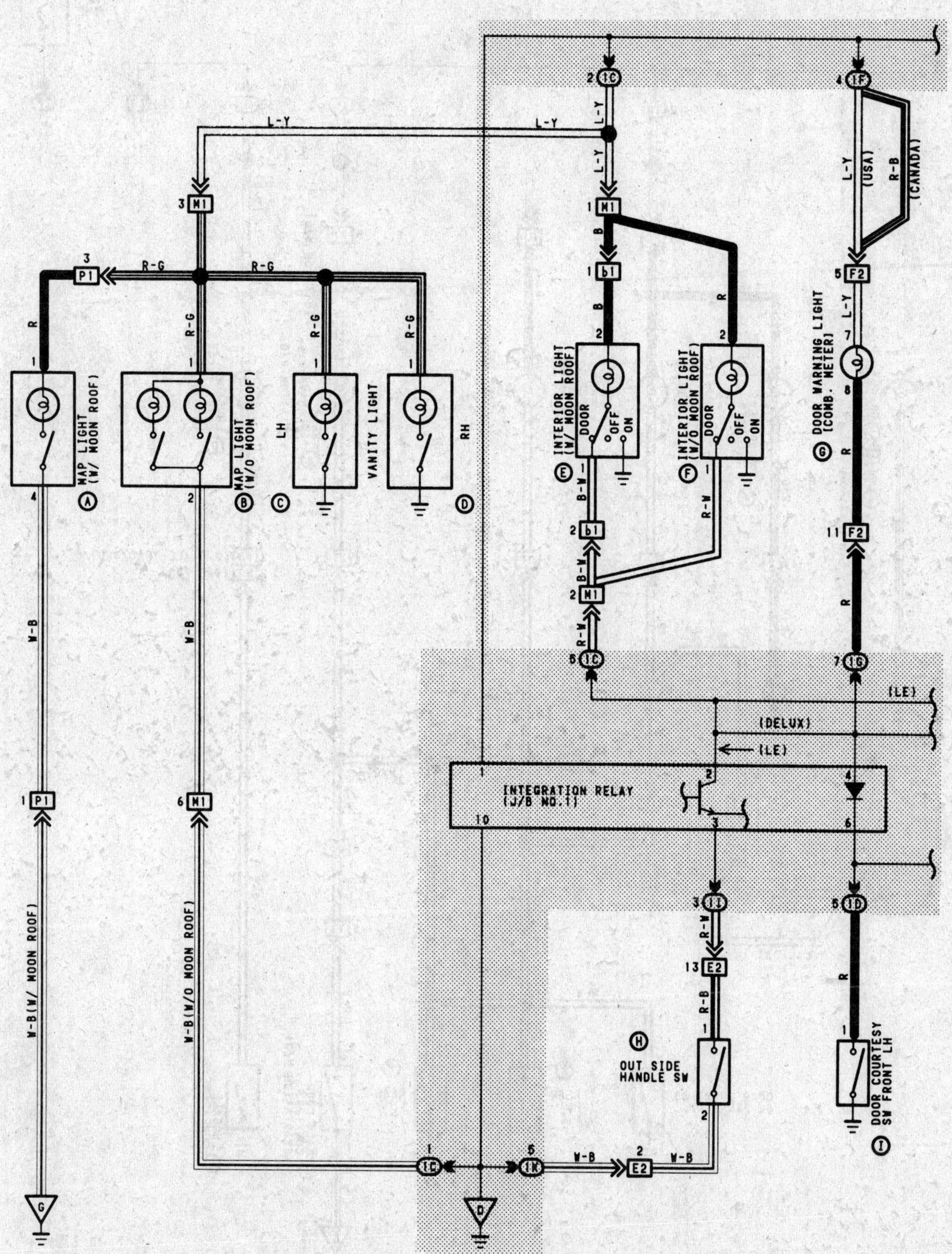

Interior light without door lock—1991 wiring diagram

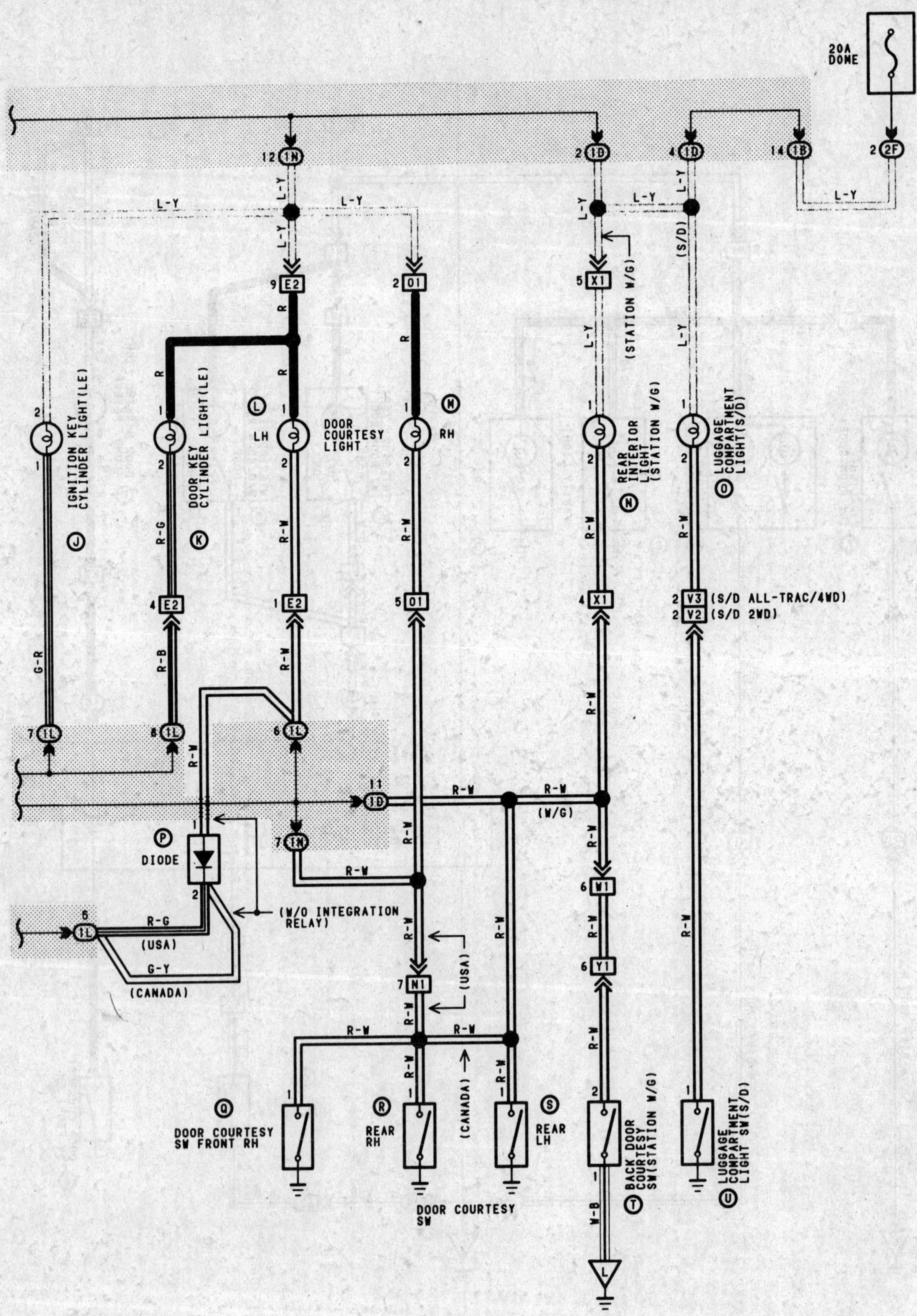

Interior light without door lock—1991 wiring diagram

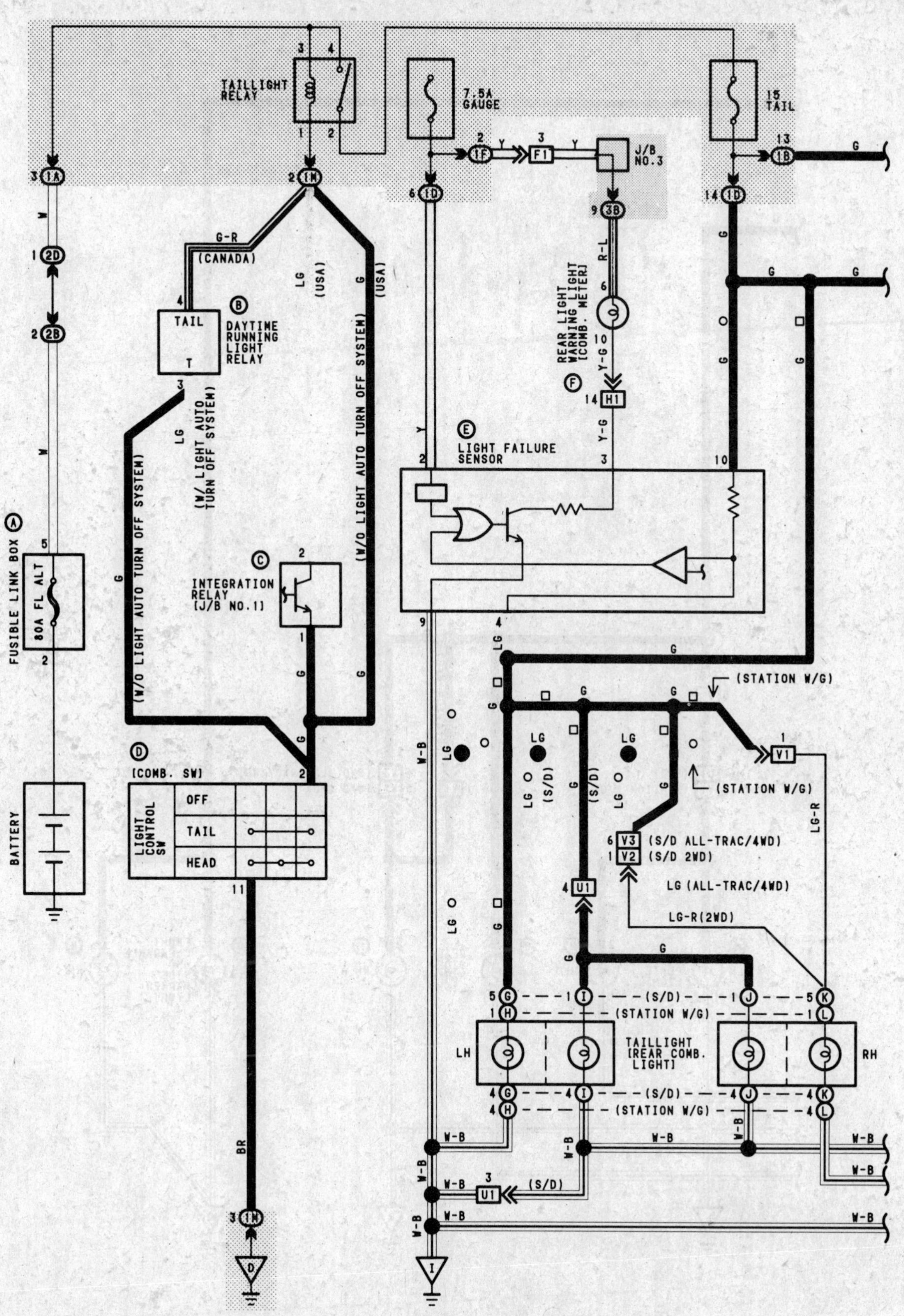

Taillight—1991 wiring diagram

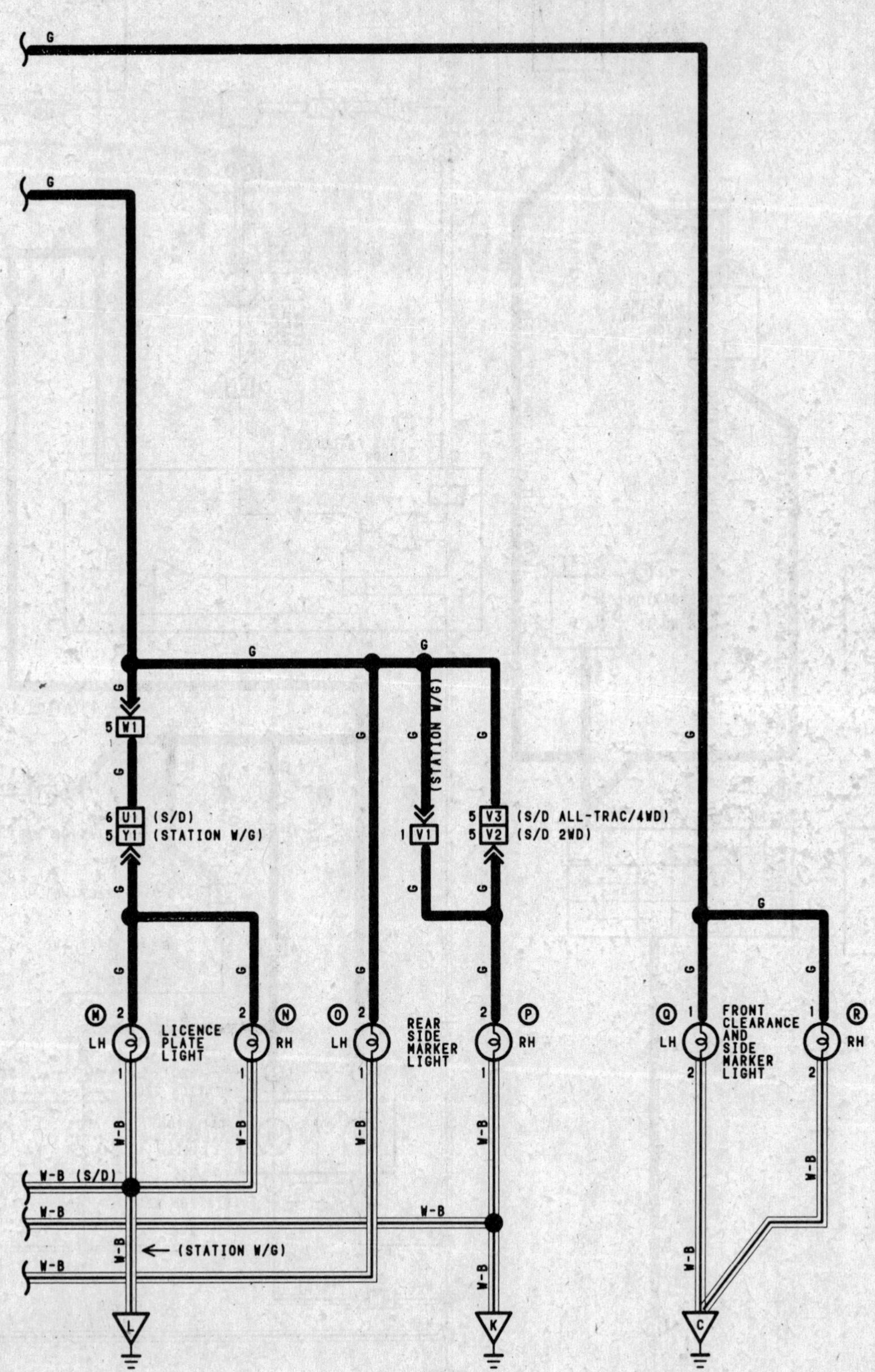

Taillight—1991 wiring diagram

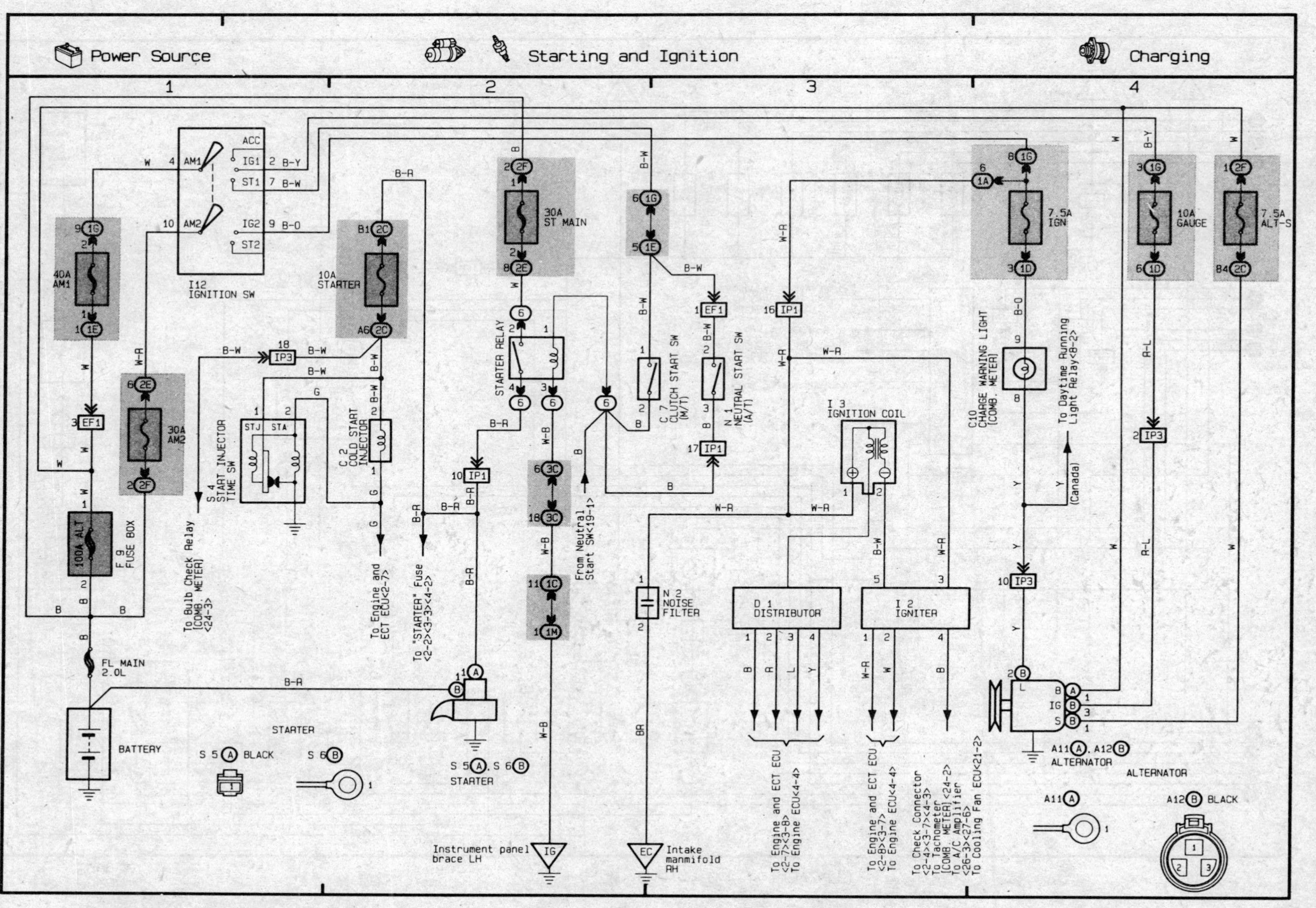
Power Source
Starting and Ignition
Charging
BATTERY
FL MAIN 2.0L
F 9 FUSE BOX
100A ALT
40A AM1
30A AM2
I12 IGNITION SW
10A STARTER
30A ST MAIN
7.5A IGN
10A GAUGE
7.5A ALT-S
STARTER RELAY
S 4 START INJECTOR TIME SW
C 2 COLD START INJECTOR
C 7 CLUTCH START SW (M/T)
N 1 NEUTRAL START SW (A/T)
N 2 NOISE FILTER
D 1 DISTRIBUTOR
I 3 IGNITION COIL
I 2 IGNITER
C10 CHARGE WARNING LIGHT [COMB. METER]
A11 A, A12 B ALTERNATOR
STARTER
S 5 A, S 6 B STARTER
Instrument panel brace LH
Intake manmifold RH
S 5 A BLACK
S 6 B
ALTERNATOR
A11 A
A12 B BLACK
To Bulb Check Relay [COMB. METER] <24-3>
To Engine and ECT ECU<2-7>
To "STARTER" Fuse <2-2><3-3><4-2>
From Neutral Start SW<19-1>
To Engine and ECT ECU <2-7><3-8>
To Engine ECU<4-4>
To Engine and ECT ECU <2-8><3-7>
To Engine ECU<4-4>
To Check Connector <2-4><3-7><4-3>
To Tachometer [COMB. METER]<24-2>
To A/C Amplifier <26-3><27-6>
To Cooling Fan ECU<21-2>
To Daytime Running Light Relay<8-2>
(Canada)

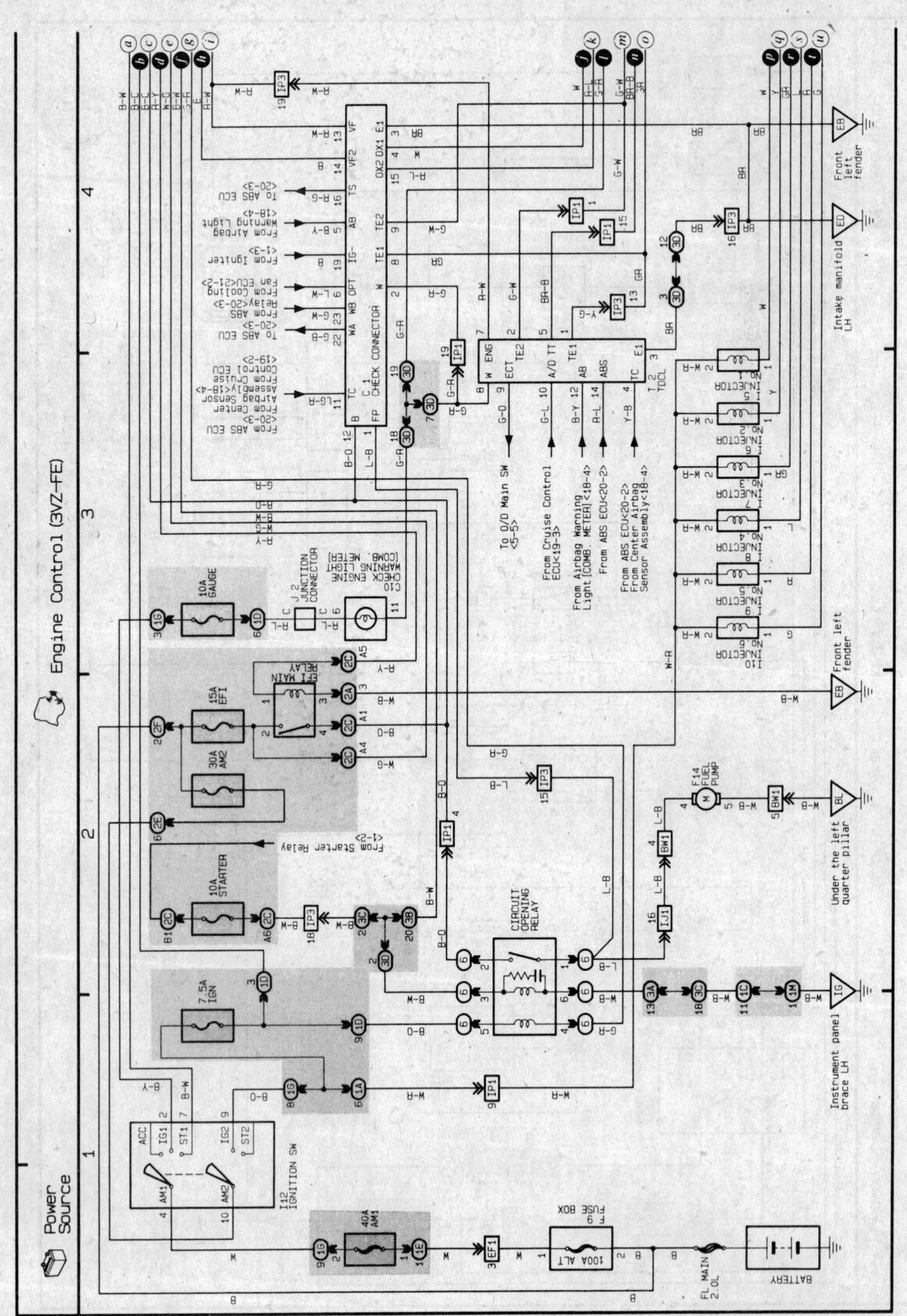
Power Source
Engine Control (3VZ-FE)
BATTERY
FL MAIN 2.0L
F 9 FUSE BOX
100A ALT
40A AM1
I12 IGNITION SW
7.5A IGN
10A STARTER
30A AM2
15A EFI
EFI MAIN RELAY
10A GAUGE
J 2 JUNCTION CONNECTOR
C10 CHECK ENGINE WARNING LIGHT [COMB. METER]
C 1 CHECK CONNECTOR
CIRCUIT OPENING RELAY
F14 FUEL PUMP
From Starter Relay <1-2>
To O/D Main SW <5-5>
From Cruise Control ECU<19-3>
From Airbag Warning Light [COMB. METER]<18-4>
From ABS ECU<20-2>
From ABS ECU<20-2>
From Center Airbag Sensor Assembly<18-4>
INJECTOR NO.1
INJECTOR NO.2
INJECTOR NO.3
INJECTOR NO.4
INJECTOR NO.5
INJECTOR NO.6
Front left fender
Intake manifold LH
Under the left quarter pillar
Instrument panel brace LH

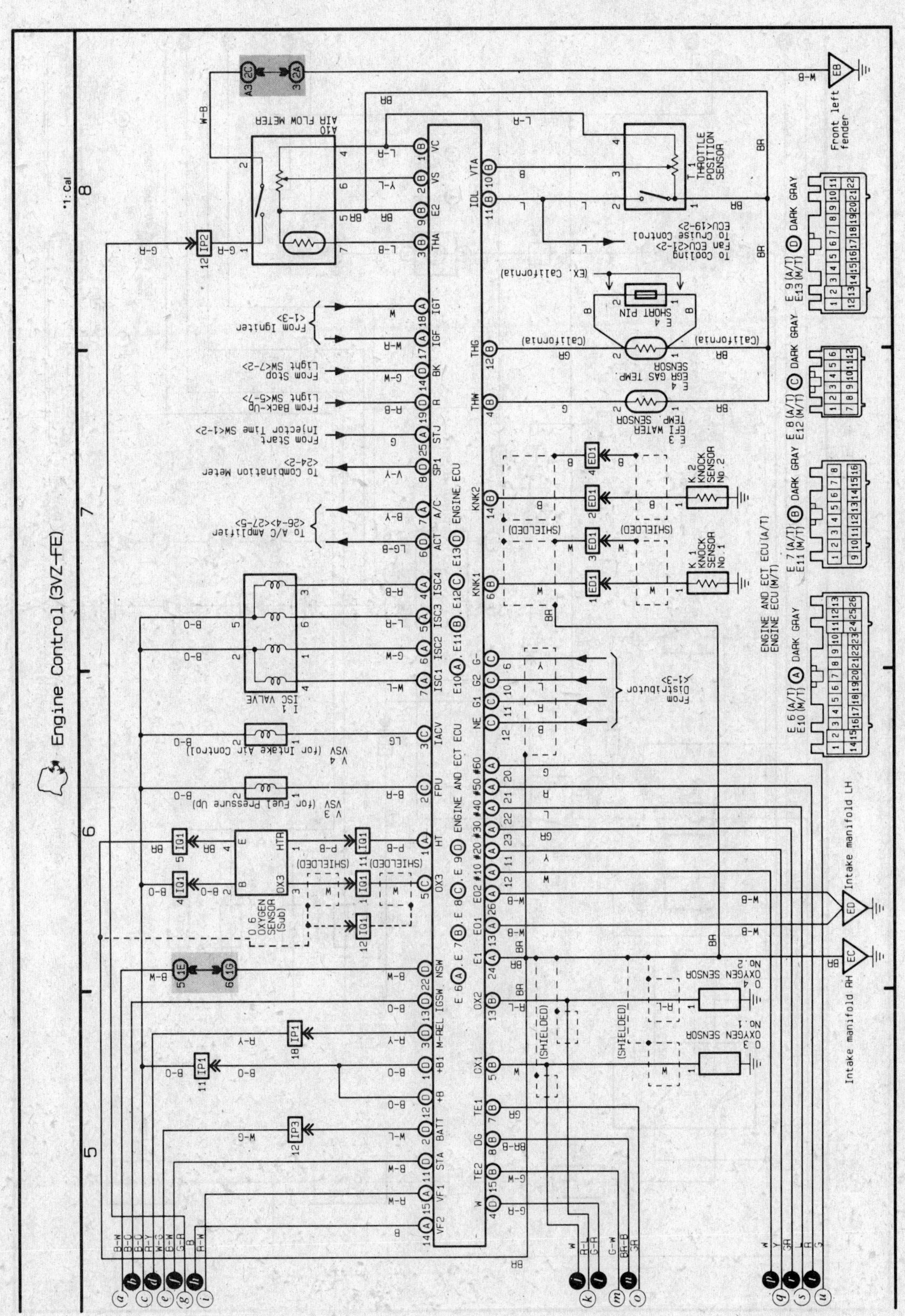

Wiring Diagram—1992

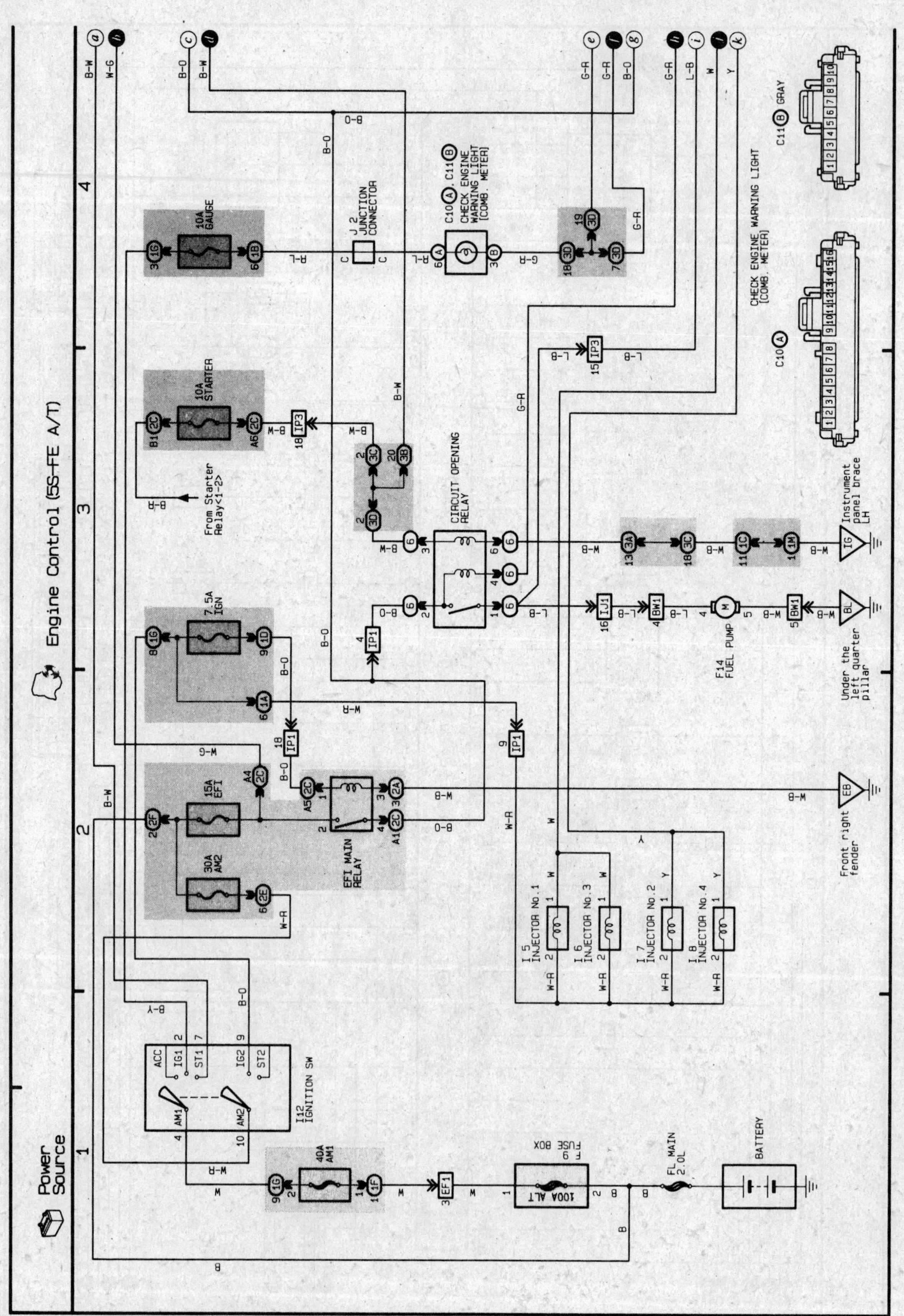
Power Source
Engine Control (5S-FE A/T)
10A GAUGE
10A STARTER
7.5A IGN
15A EFI
30A AM2
40A AM1
100A ALT
F 9
FUSE BOX
FL MAIN 2.0L
BATTERY
I12 IGNITION SW
ACC
IG1
ST1
IG2
ST2
AM1
AM2
EFI MAIN RELAY
CIRCUIT OPENING RELAY
J 2 JUNCTION CONNECTOR
C10 (A), C11 (B) CHECK ENGINE WARNING LIGHT [COMB. METER]
From Starter Relay<1-2>
F14 FUEL PUMP
I 5 INJECTOR No.1
I 6 INJECTOR No.3
I 7 INJECTOR No.2
I 8 INJECTOR No.4
Front right fender
Under the left quarter pillar
Instrument panel brace LH
CHECK ENGINE WARNING LIGHT [COMB. METER]
C10 (A)
C11 (B) GRAY

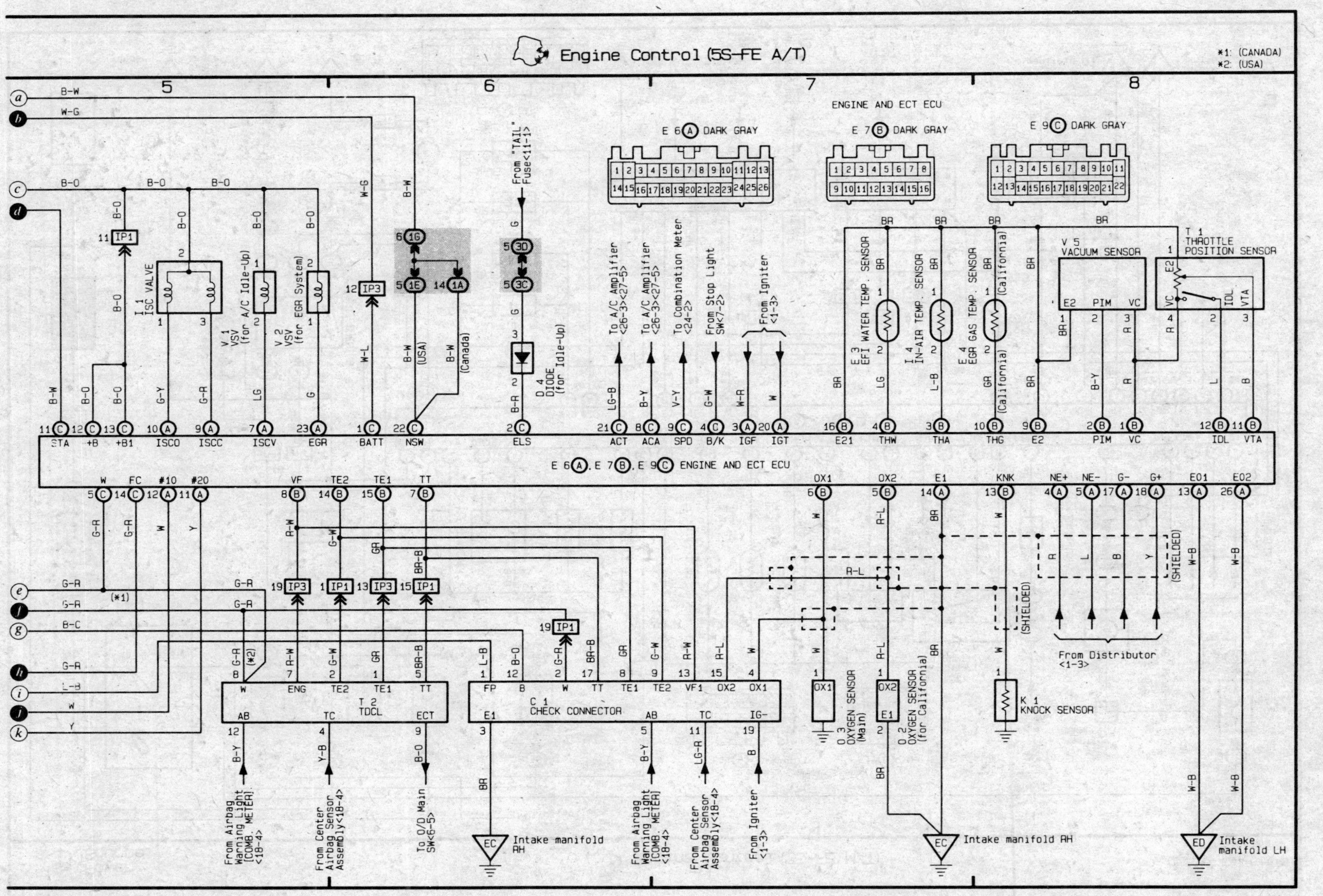
Engine Control (5S-FE A/T)
*1: (CANADA)
*2: (USA)
ENGINE AND ECT ECU
E 6 (A) DARK GRAY
E 7 (B) DARK GRAY
E 9 (C) DARK GRAY
E 6 (A), E 7 (B), E 9 (C) ENGINE AND ECT ECU
I 1 ISC VALVE
V 1 VSV (for A/C Idle-Up)
V 2 VSV (for EGR System)
From "TAIL" Fuse<11-1>
D 4 DIODE (for Idle-Up)
To A/C Amplifier <26-3><27-5>
To A/C Amplifier <26-3><27-5>
To Combination Meter <24-2>
From Stop Light SW<7-2>
From Igniter <1-3>
E 3 EFI WATER TEMP. SENSOR
I 4 IN-AIR TEMP. SENSOR
E 4 EGR GAS TEMP. SENSOR
(California)
V 5 VACUUM SENSOR
T 1 THROTTLE POSITION SENSOR
T 2 TDCL
C 1 CHECK CONNECTOR
O 3 OXYGEN SENSOR (Main)
O 2 OXYGEN SENSOR (for California)
K 1 KNOCK SENSOR
(SHIELDED)
From Distributor <1-3>
From Airbag Warning Light [COMB. METER] <18-4>
From Center Airbag Sensor Assembly<18-4>
To O/D Main SW<6-5>
From Igniter <1-3>
Intake manifold RH
Intake manifold LH

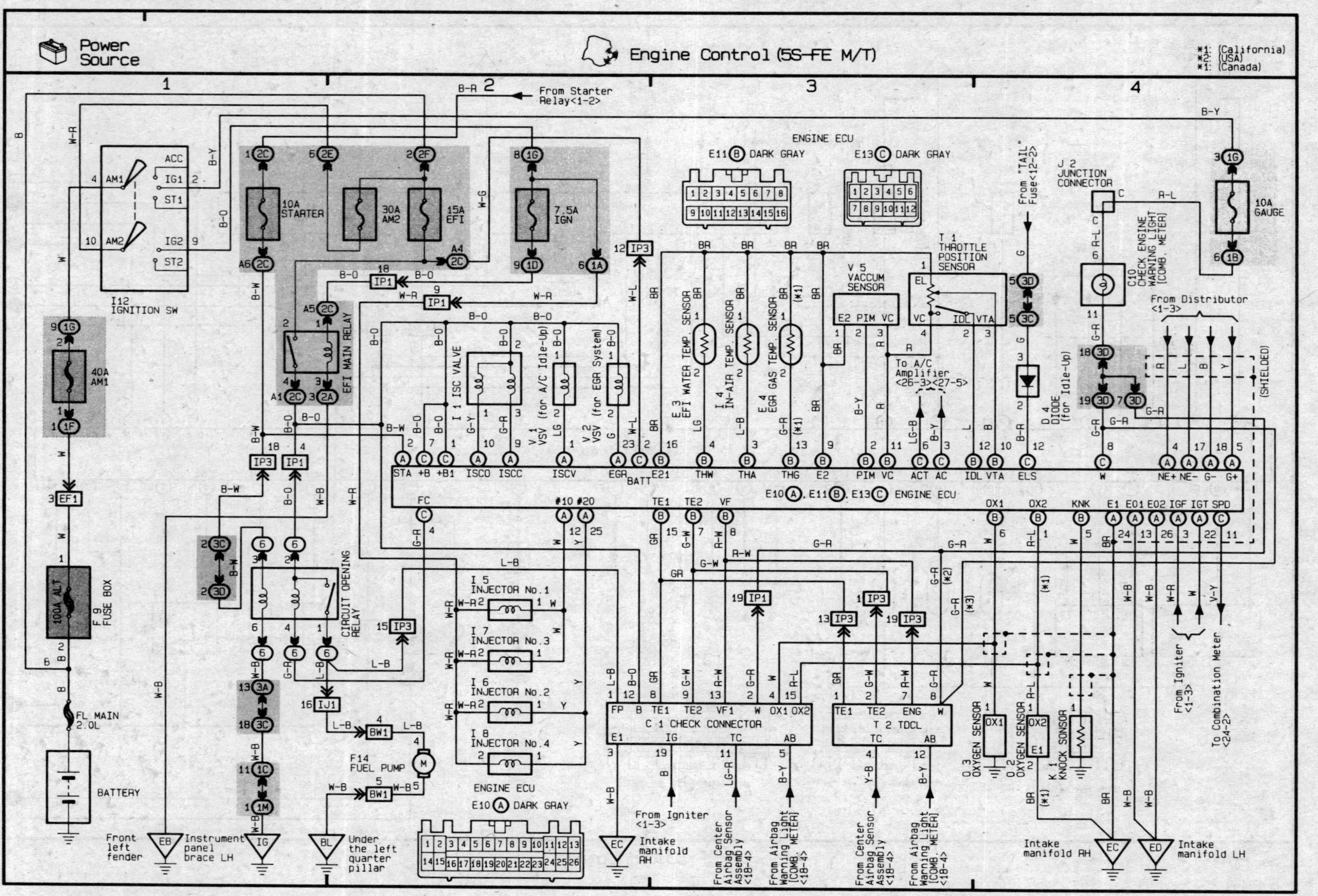
Power Source
Engine Control (5S-FE M/T)
*1: (California)
*2: (USA)
*1: (Canada)
ENGINE ECU
E11 B DARK GRAY
E13 C DARK GRAY
E10 A DARK GRAY
I12 IGNITION SW
BATTERY
F 9 FUSE BOX
FL MAIN 2.0L
40A AM1
100A ALT
10A STARTER
30A AM2
15A EFI
7.5A IGN
10A GAUGE
EFI MAIN RELAY
CIRCUIT OPENING RELAY
F14 FUEL PUMP
C 1 CHECK CONNECTOR
T 2 TDCL
I 1 ISC VALVE
V 1 VSV (for A/C Idle-Up)
V 2 VSV (for EGR System)
E 3 EFI WATER TEMP. SENSOR
I 4 IN-AIR TEMP. SENSOR
E 4 EGR GAS TEMP. SENSOR
V 5 VACCUM SENSOR
T 1 THROTTLE POSITION SENSOR
D 4 DIODE (for Idle-Up)
C10 CHECK ENGINE WARNING LIGHT [COMB. METER]
J 2 JUNCTION CONNECTOR
O 3 OXYGEN SENSOR
O 2 OXYGEN SENSOR
K 1 KNOCK SONSOR
I 5 INJECTOR No.1
I 7 INJECTOR No.3
I 6 INJECTOR No.2
I 8 INJECTOR No.4
From Starter Relay<1-2>
From "TAIL" Fuse<12-2>
To A/C Amplifier <26-3><27-5>
From Distributor <1-3>
(SHIELDED)
From Igniter <1-3>
To Combination Meter <24-2>
From Center Airbag Sensor Assembly <18-4>
From Airbag Warning Light [COMB. METER] <18-4>
Front left fender
Instrument panel brace LH
Under the left quarter pillar
Intake manifold RH
Intake manifold LH

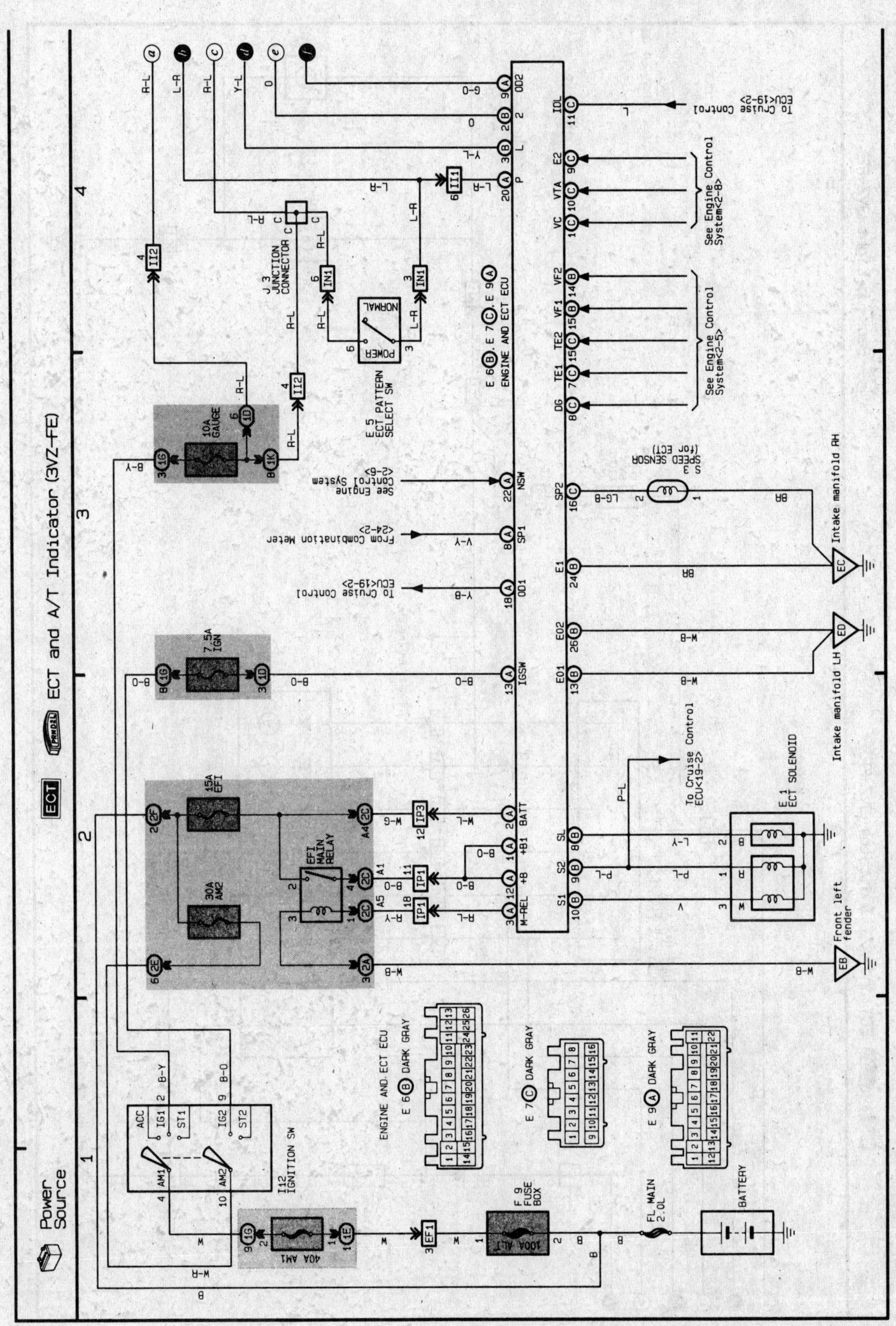

ECT and A/T Indicator (3VZ-FE)
Power Source
I 12 IGNITION SW
40A AM1
F 9 FUSE BOX
100A ALT
FL MAIN 2.0L
BATTERY
30A AM2
15A EFI
EFI MAIN RELAY
7.5A IGN
10A GAUGE
J 3 JUNCTION CONNECTOR
E 5 ECT PATTERN SELECT SW
POWER
NORMAL
E 6 B, E 7 C, E 9 A ENGINE AND ECT ECU
S 3 SPEED SENSOR (for ECT)
E 1 ECT SOLENOID
To Cruise Control ECU<19-2>
From Combination Meter <24-2>
See Engine Control System<2-6>
See Engine Control System<2-5>
See Engine Control System<2-8>
Front left fender
Intake manifold LH
Intake manifold RH
ENGINE AND ECT ECU E 6 B DARK GRAY
E 7 C DARK GRAY
E 9 A DARK GRAY

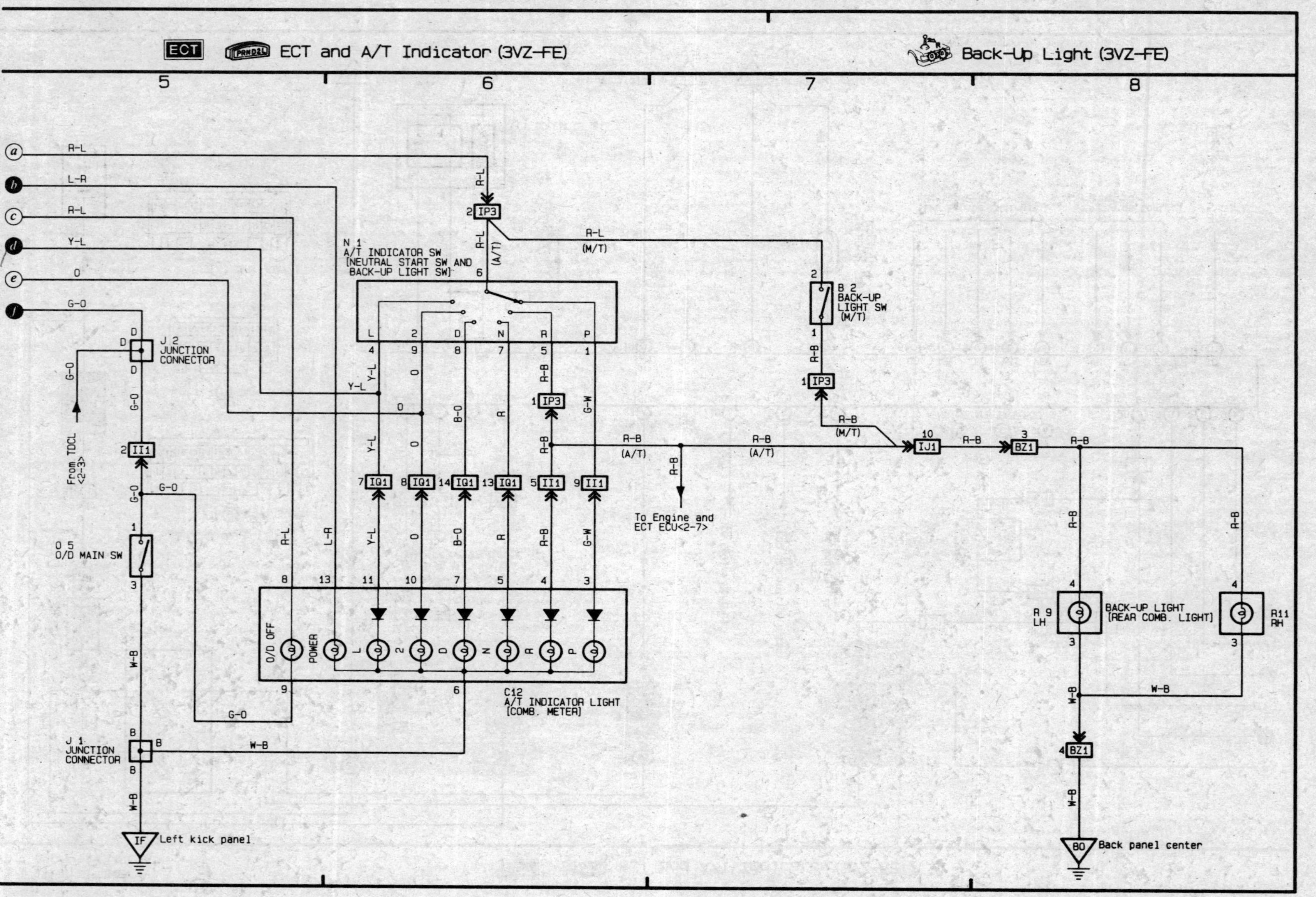
ECT
ECT and A/T Indicator (3VZ-FE)
Back-Up Light (3VZ-FE)
5
6
7
8
N 1 A/T INDICATOR SW [NEUTRAL START SW AND BACK-UP LIGHT SW]
B 2 BACK-UP LIGHT SW (M/T)
J 2 JUNCTION CONNECTOR
From TDCL <2-3>
O 5 O/D MAIN SW
To Engine and ECT ECU<2-7>
C12 A/T INDICATOR LIGHT [COMB. METER]
O/D OFF
POWER
J 1 JUNCTION CONNECTOR
Left kick panel
R 9 LH
BACK-UP LIGHT [REAR COMB. LIGHT]
R11 RH
Back panel center

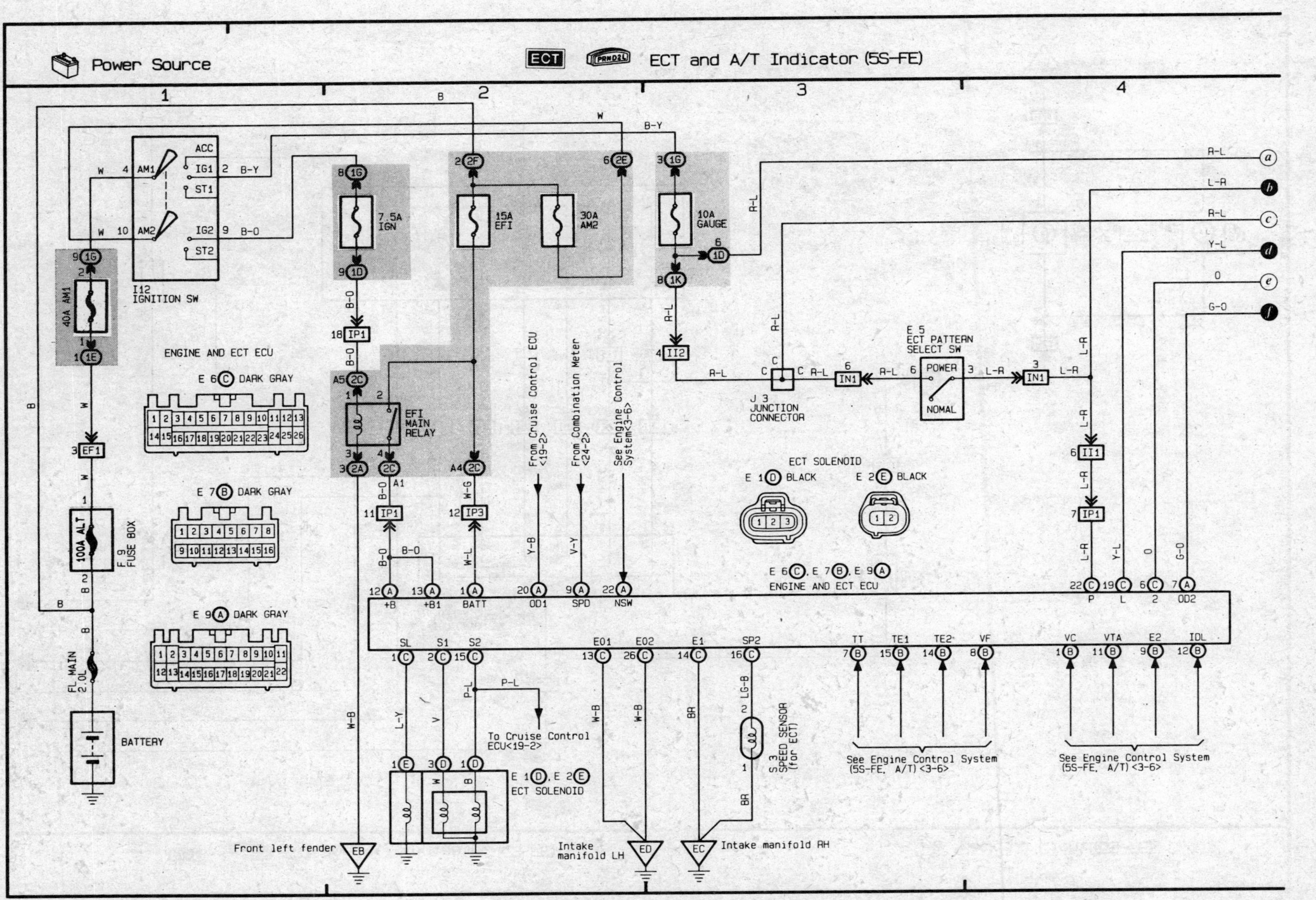
Power Source
ECT
ECT and A/T Indicator (5S-FE)
I12 IGNITION SW
7.5A IGN
15A EFI
30A AM2
10A GAUGE
40A AM1
EFI MAIN RELAY
E 5 ECT PATTERN SELECT SW
POWER
NOMAL
J 3 JUNCTION CONNECTOR
ENGINE AND ECT ECU
E 6 C DARK GRAY
E 7 B DARK GRAY
E 9 A DARK GRAY
ECT SOLENOID
E 1 D BLACK
E 2 E BLACK
E 6 C, E 7 B, E 9 A ENGINE AND ECT ECU
E 1 D, E 2 E ECT SOLENOID
From Cruise Control ECU <19-2>
From Combination Meter <24-2>
See Engine Control System<3-6>
To Cruise Control ECU<19-2>
S 3 SPEED SENSOR (for ECT)
See Engine Control System (5S-FE, A/T)<3-6>
See Engine Control System (5S-FE, A/T)<3-6>
100A ALT
F 9 FUSE BOX
FL MAIN 2.0L
BATTERY
Front left fender
Intake manifold LH
Intake manifold RH

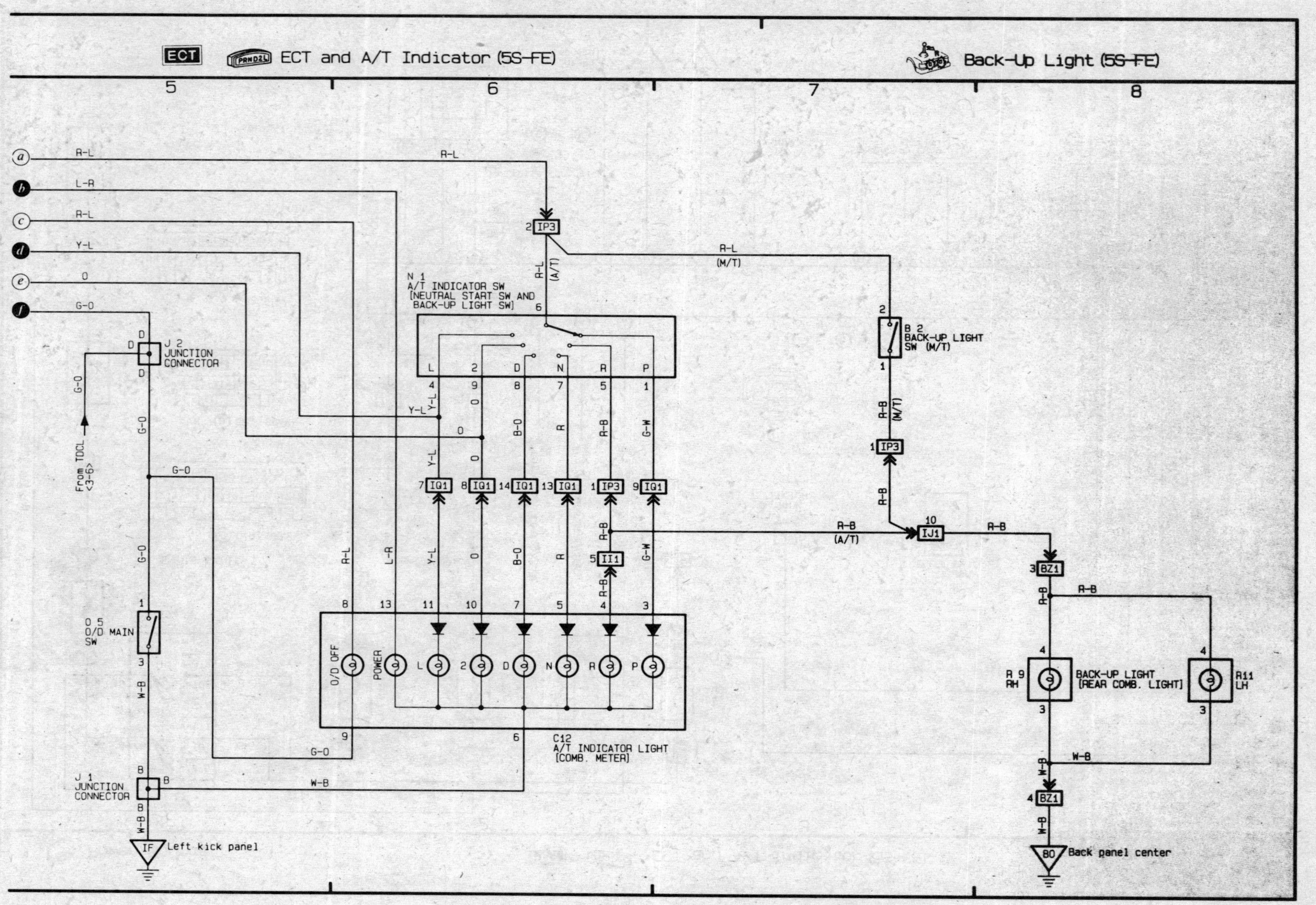

ECT
ECT and A/T Indicator (5S-FE)
Back-Up Light (5S-FE)
N 1
A/T INDICATOR SW
[NEUTRAL START SW AND
BACK-UP LIGHT SW]
B 2
BACK-UP LIGHT
SW (M/T)
C12
A/T INDICATOR LIGHT
[COMB. METER]
R 9
RH
R11
LH
BACK-UP LIGHT
[REAR COMB. LIGHT]
Back panel center
J 2
JUNCTION
CONNECTOR
J 1
JUNCTION
CONNECTOR
O 5
O/D MAIN
SW
Left kick panel
From TDCL
<3-6>
POWER
O/D OFF

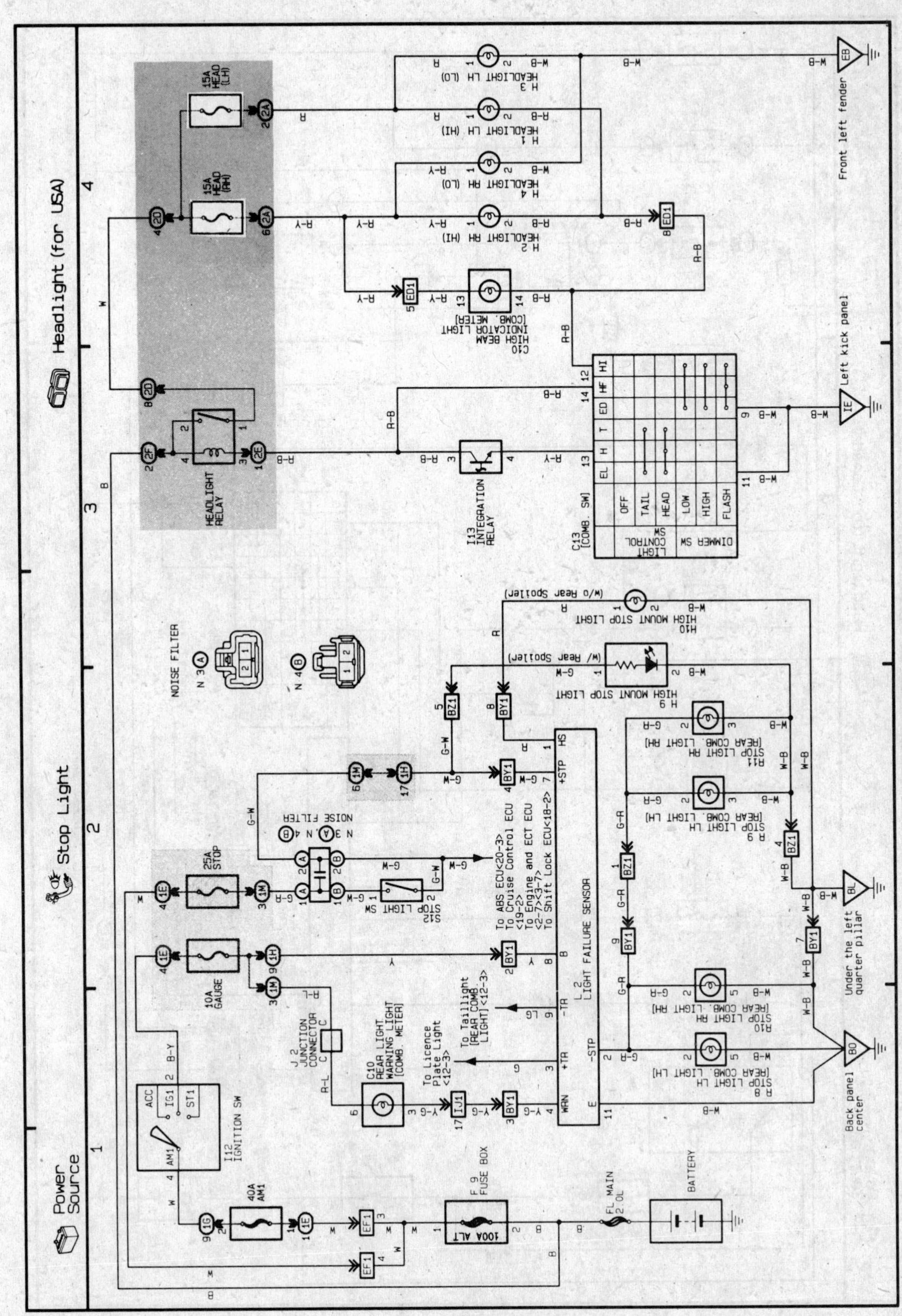

Power Source
Stop Light
Headlight (for USA)
I12 IGNITION SW
40A AM1
F 9 FUSE BOX
100A ALT
FL MAIN 2.0L
BATTERY
10A GAUGE
25A STOP
J 2 JUNCTION CONNECTOR
C10 REAR LIGHT WARNING LIGHT [COMB. METER]
S12 STOP LIGHT SW
NOISE FILTER
To ABS ECU<20-3>
To Cruise Control ECU <19-2>
To Engine and ECT ECU <2-7><3-7>
To Shift Lock ECU<18-2>
To Licence Plate Light <12-3>
To Taillight [REAR COMB. LIGHT] <12-3>
L 2 LIGHT FAILURE SENSOR
R 8 STOP LIGHT LH [REAR COMB. LIGHT LH]
R10 STOP LIGHT RH [REAR COMB. LIGHT RH]
R 9 STOP LIGHT LH [REAR COMB. LIGHT LH]
R11 STOP LIGHT RH [REAR COMB. LIGHT RH]
H 9 HIGH MOUNT STOP LIGHT (W/ Rear Spoiler)
H10 HIGH MOUNT STOP LIGHT (W/o Rear Spoiler)
Back panel center
Under the left quarter pillar
HEADLIGHT RELAY
I13 INTEGRATION RELAY
C13 [COMB. SW]
LIGHT CONTROL SW
DIMMER SW
OFF
TAIL
HEAD
LOW
HIGH
FLASH
C10 HIGH BEAM INDICATOR LIGHT [COMB. METER]
15A HEAD (RH)
15A HEAD (LH)
H 2 HEADLIGHT RH (HI)
H 4 HEADLIGHT RH (LO)
H 1 HEADLIGHT LH (HI)
H 3 HEADLIGHT LH (LO)
Left kick panel
Front left fender

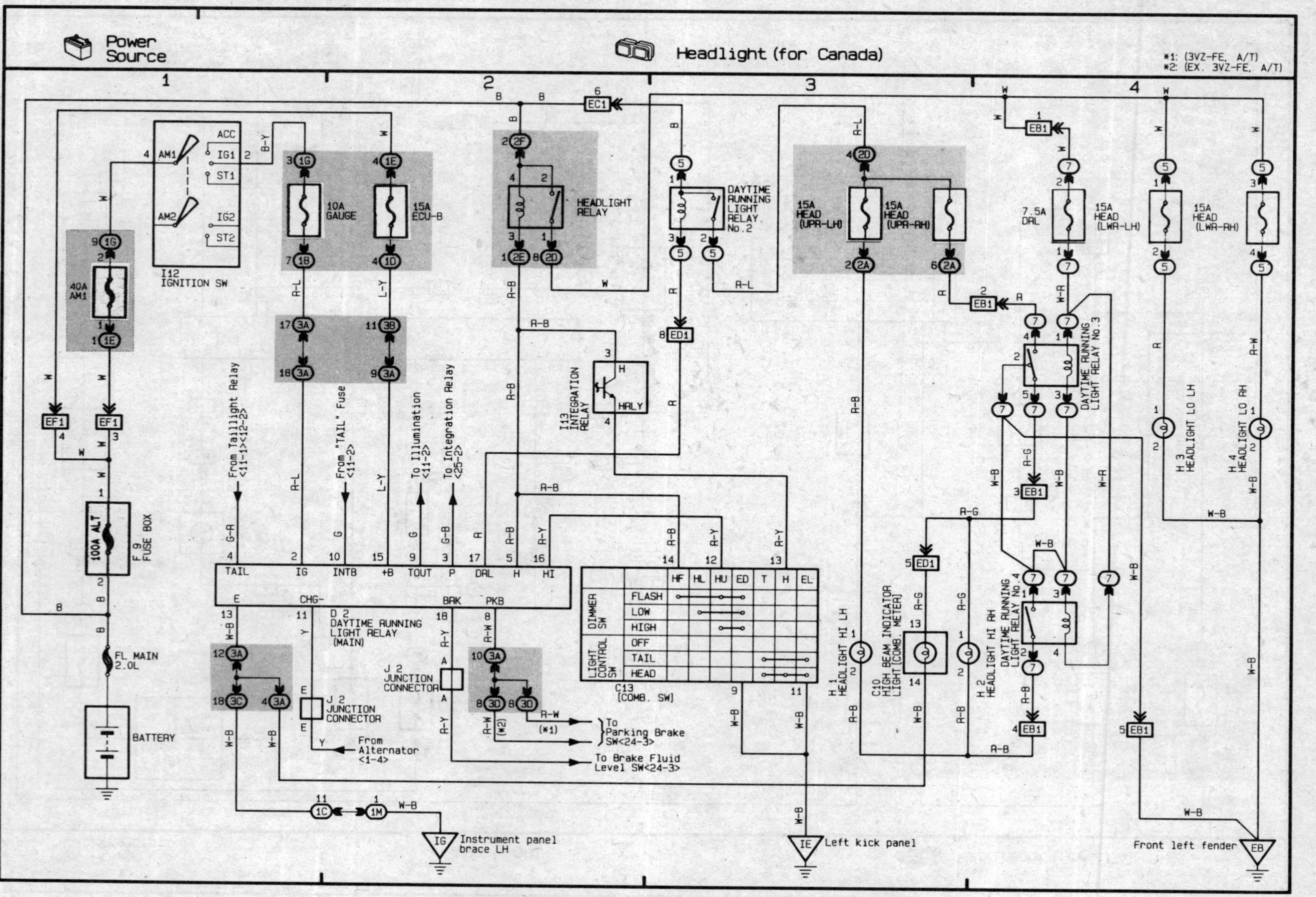
Power Source
Headlight (for Canada)
*1: (3VZ-FE, A/T)
*2: (EX. 3VZ-FE, A/T)
I12 IGNITION SW
BATTERY
FL MAIN 2.0L
F 9 FUSE BOX
100A ALT
40A AM1
10A GAUGE
15A ECU-B
HEADLIGHT RELAY
DAYTIME RUNNING LIGHT RELAY No.2
I13 INTEGRATION RELAY
15A HEAD (UPR-LH)
15A HEAD (UPR-RH)
7.5A DRL
15A HEAD (LWR-LH)
15A HEAD (LWR-RH)
DAYTIME RUNNING LIGHT RELAY No.3
DAYTIME RUNNING LIGHT RELAY No.4
H 3 HEADLIGHT LO LH
H 4 HEADLIGHT LO RH
H 1 HEADLIGHT HI LH
H 2 HEADLIGHT HI RH
C10 HIGH BEAM INDICATOR LIGHT [COMB. METER]
C13 [COMB. SW]
DIMMER SW
LIGHT CONTROL SW
D 2 DAYTIME RUNNING LIGHT RELAY (MAIN)
J 2 JUNCTION CONNECTOR
From Taillight Relay <11-1><12-2>
From "TAIL" Fuse <11-2>
To Illumination <11-2>
To Integration Relay <25-2>
From Alternator <1-4>
To Parking Brake SW<24-3>
To Brake Fluid Level SW<24-3>
Front left fender
Left kick panel
Instrument panel brace LH

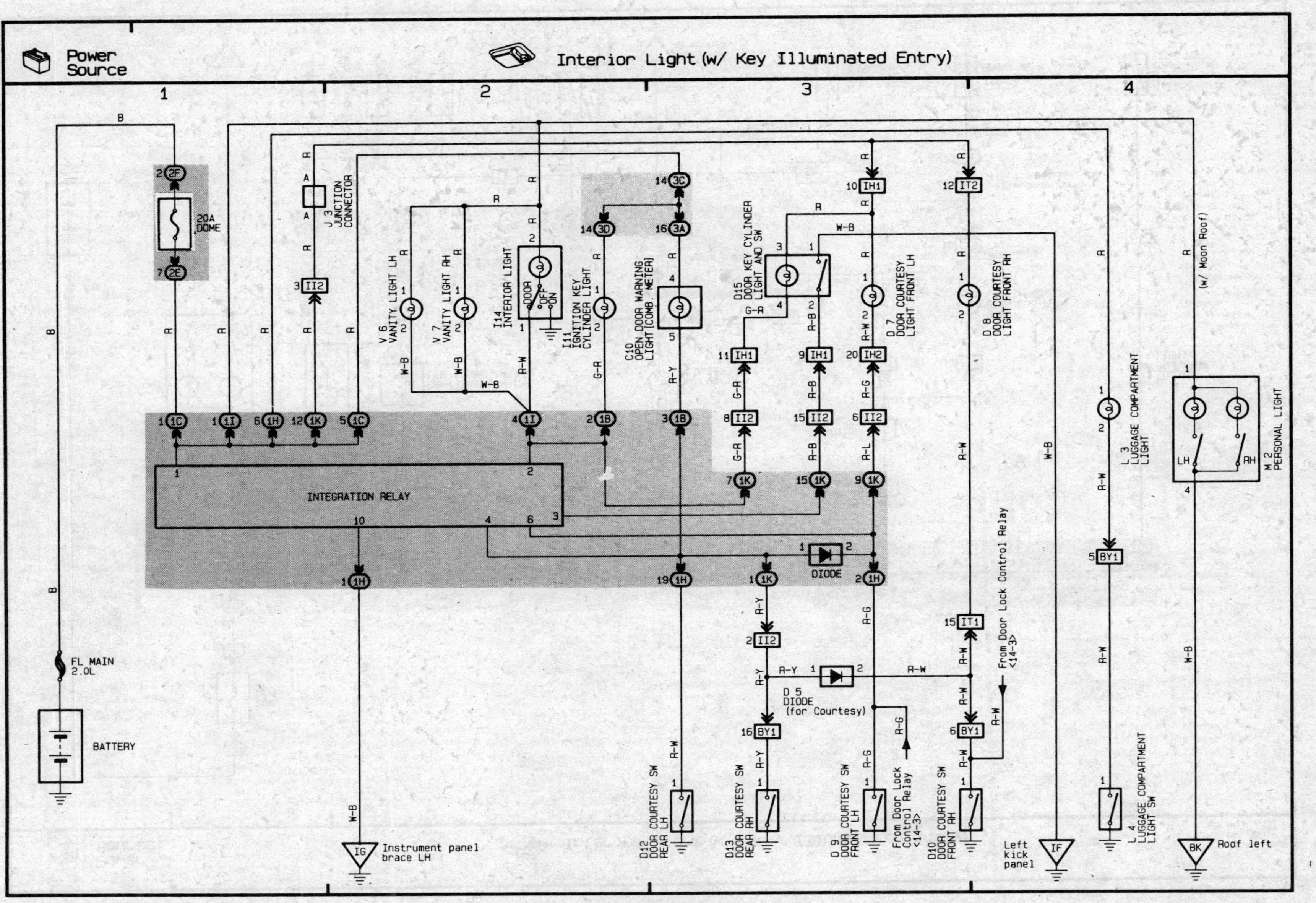
Power Source
Interior Light (w/ Key Illuminated Entry)
BATTERY
FL MAIN 2.0L
20A DOME
INTEGRATION RELAY
J 3 JUNCTION CONNECTOR
V 6 VANITY LIGHT LH
V 7 VANITY LIGHT RH
I14 INTERIOR LIGHT
I11 IGNITION KEY CYLINDER LIGHT
C10 OPEN DOOR WARNING LIGHT (COMB. METER)
D15 DOOR KEY CYLINDER LIGHT AND SW
D 7 DOOR COURTESY LIGHT FRONT LH
D 8 DOOR COURTESY LIGHT FRONT RH
L 3 LUGGAGE COMPARTMENT LIGHT
M 2 PERSONAL LIGHT
(w/ Moon Roof)
DIODE
D 5 DIODE (for Courtesy)
D12 DOOR COURTESY SW REAR LH
D13 DOOR COURTESY SW REAR RH
D 9 DOOR COURTESY SW FRONT LH
D10 DOOR COURTESY SW FRONT RH
L 4 LUGGAGE COMPARTMENT LIGHT SW
From Door Lock Control Relay <14-3>
Instrument panel brace LH
Left kick panel
Roof left

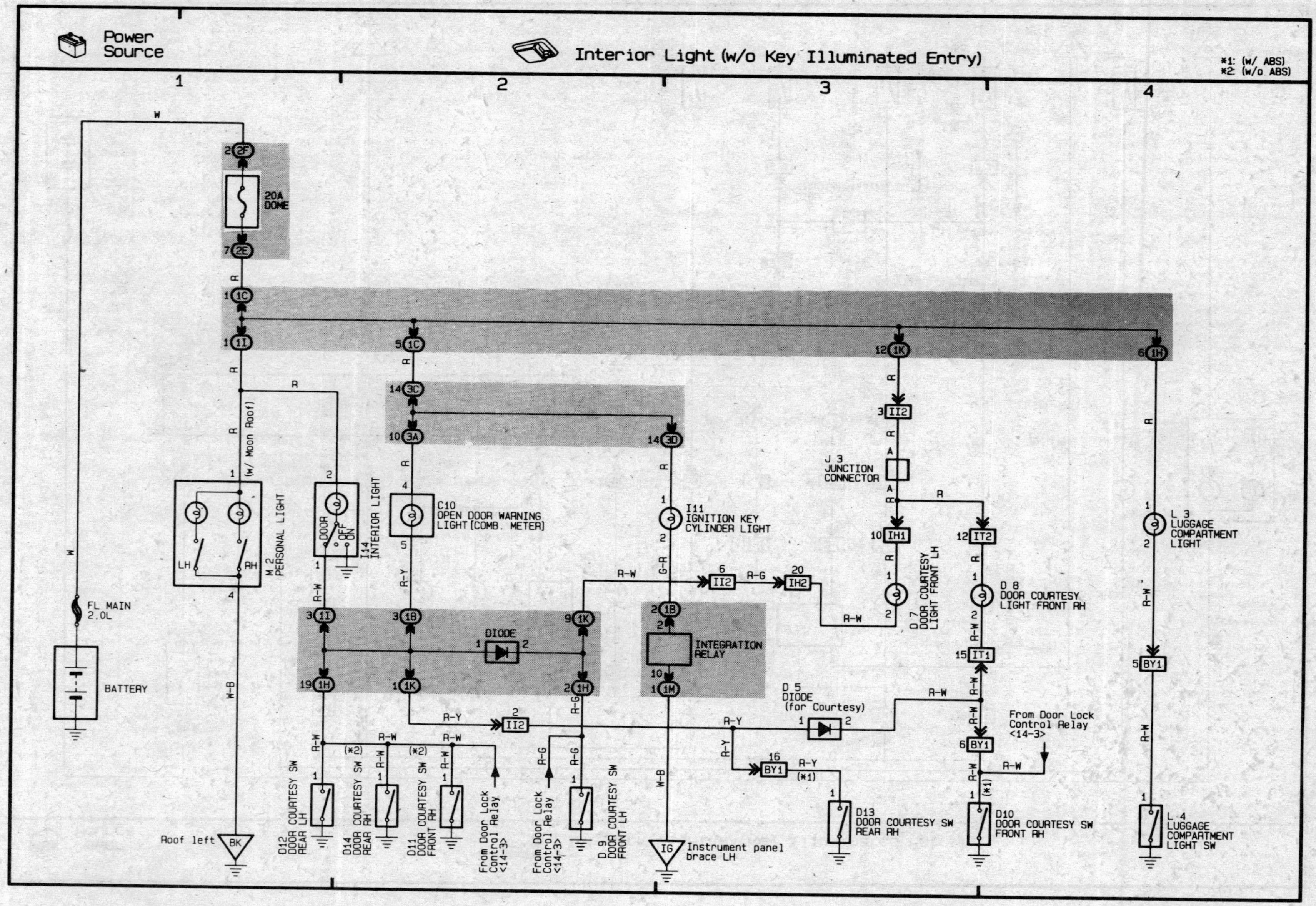
Power Source
Interior Light (w/o Key Illuminated Entry)
*1: (w/ ABS)
*2: (w/o ABS)
20A DOME
FL MAIN 2.0L
BATTERY
M 2 PERSONAL LIGHT
(w/ Moon Roof)
I14 INTERIOR LIGHT
DOOR OFF ON
C10 OPEN DOOR WARNING LIGHT [COMB. METER]
DIODE
I11 IGNITION KEY CYLINDER LIGHT
INTEGRATION RELAY
J 3 JUNCTION CONNECTOR
D 7 DOOR COURTESY LIGHT FRONT LH
D 8 DOOR COURTESY LIGHT FRONT RH
D 5 DIODE (for Courtesy)
L 3 LUGGAGE COMPARTMENT LIGHT
From Door Lock Control Relay <14-3>
Roof left
D12 DOOR COURTESY SW REAR LH
D14 DOOR COURTESY SW REAR RH
D11 DOOR COURTESY SW FRONT RH
D 9 DOOR COURTESY SW FRONT LH
Instrument panel brace LH
D13 DOOR COURTESY SW REAR RH
D10 DOOR COURTESY SW FRONT RH
L 4 LUGGAGE COMPARTMENT LIGHT SW

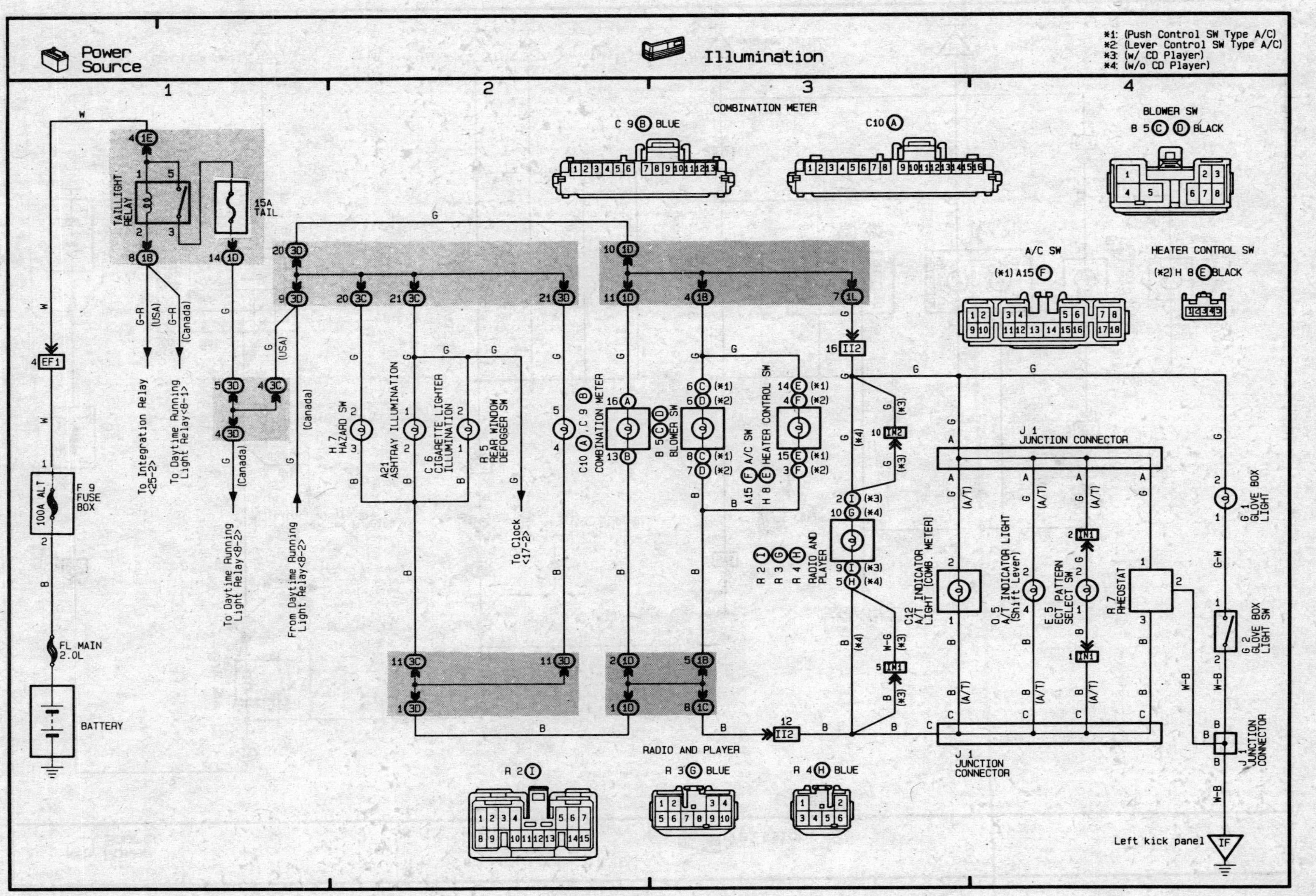
Power Source
Illumination
*1: (Push Control SW Type A/C)
*2: (Lever Control SW Type A/C)
*3: (w/ CD Player)
*4: (w/o CD Player)
TAILLIGHT RELAY
15A TAIL
F 9 FUSE BOX
100A ALT
FL MAIN 2.0L
BATTERY
To Integration Relay <25-2>
To Daytime Running Light Relay<8-1>
To Daytime Running Light Relay<8-2>
From Daytime Running Light Relay<8-2>
H 7 HAZARD SW
A21 ASHTRAY ILLUMINATION
C 6 CIGARETTE LIGHTER ILLUMINATION
R 5 REAR WINDOW DEFOGGER SW
To Clock <17-2>
C10 (A), C 9 (B) COMBINATION METER
B 5 (C) (D) BLOWER SW
A15 (F) A/C SW
H 8 (E) HEATER CONTROL SW
R 2 (I) R 3 (G) R 4 (H) RADIO AND PLAYER
C12 A/T INDICATOR LIGHT (COMB. METER)
O 5 A/T INDICATOR LIGHT (Shift Lever)
E 5 ECT PATTERN SELECT SW
R 7 RHEOSTAT
J 1 JUNCTION CONNECTOR
G 1 GLOVE BOX LIGHT
G 2 GLOVE BOX LIGHT SW
Left kick panel
COMBINATION METER
C 9 (B) BLUE
C10 (A)
BLOWER SW
B 5 (C) (D) BLACK
A/C SW
(*1) A15 (F)
HEATER CONTROL SW
(*2) H 8 (E) BLACK
RADIO AND PLAYER
R 2 (I)
R 3 (G) BLUE
R 4 (H) BLUE

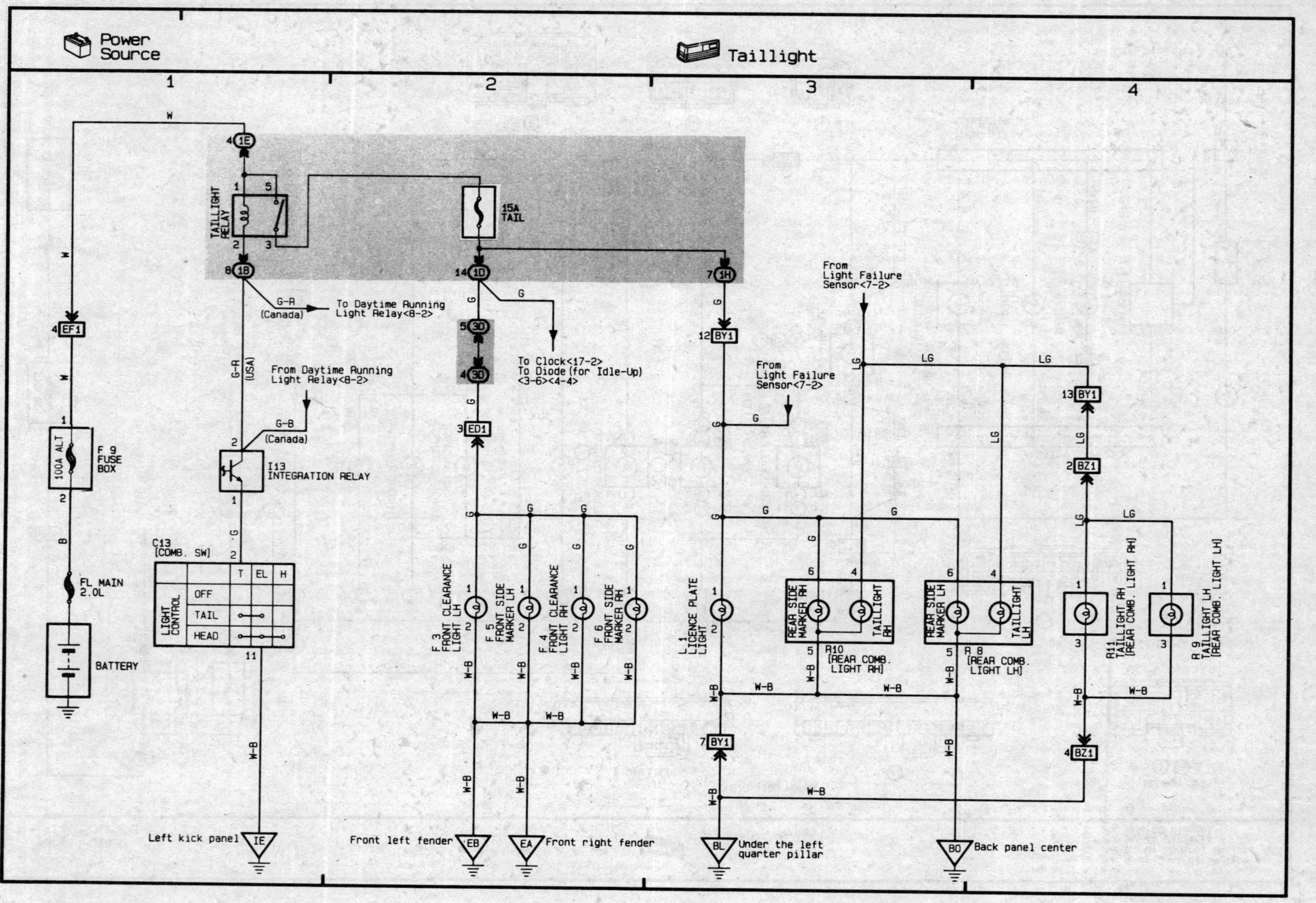

Power Source
Taillight
TAILLIGHT RELAY
15A TAIL
BATTERY
FL MAIN 2.0L
F 9 FUSE BOX
100A ALT
C13 [COMB. SW]
LIGHT CONTROL
OFF
TAIL
HEAD
I13 INTEGRATION RELAY
To Daytime Running Light Relay<8-2>
From Daytime Running Light Relay<8-2>
To Clock<17-2>
To Diode (for Idle-Up) <3-6><4-4>
From Light Failure Sensor<7-2>
F 3 FRONT CLEARANCE LIGHT LH
F 5 FRONT SIDE MARKER LH
F 4 FRONT CLEARANCE LIGHT RH
F 6 FRONT SIDE MARKER RH
L 1 LICENCE PLATE LIGHT
REAR SIDE MARKER RH
TAILLIGHT RH
R10 [REAR COMB. LIGHT RH]
REAR SIDE MARKER LH
TAILLIGHT LH
R 8 [REAR COMB. LIGHT LH]
R11 TAILLIGHT RH [REAR COMB. LIGHT RH]
R 9 TAILLIGHT LH [REAR COMB. LIGHT LH]
Left kick panel
Front left fender
Front right fender
Under the left quarter pillar
Back panel center

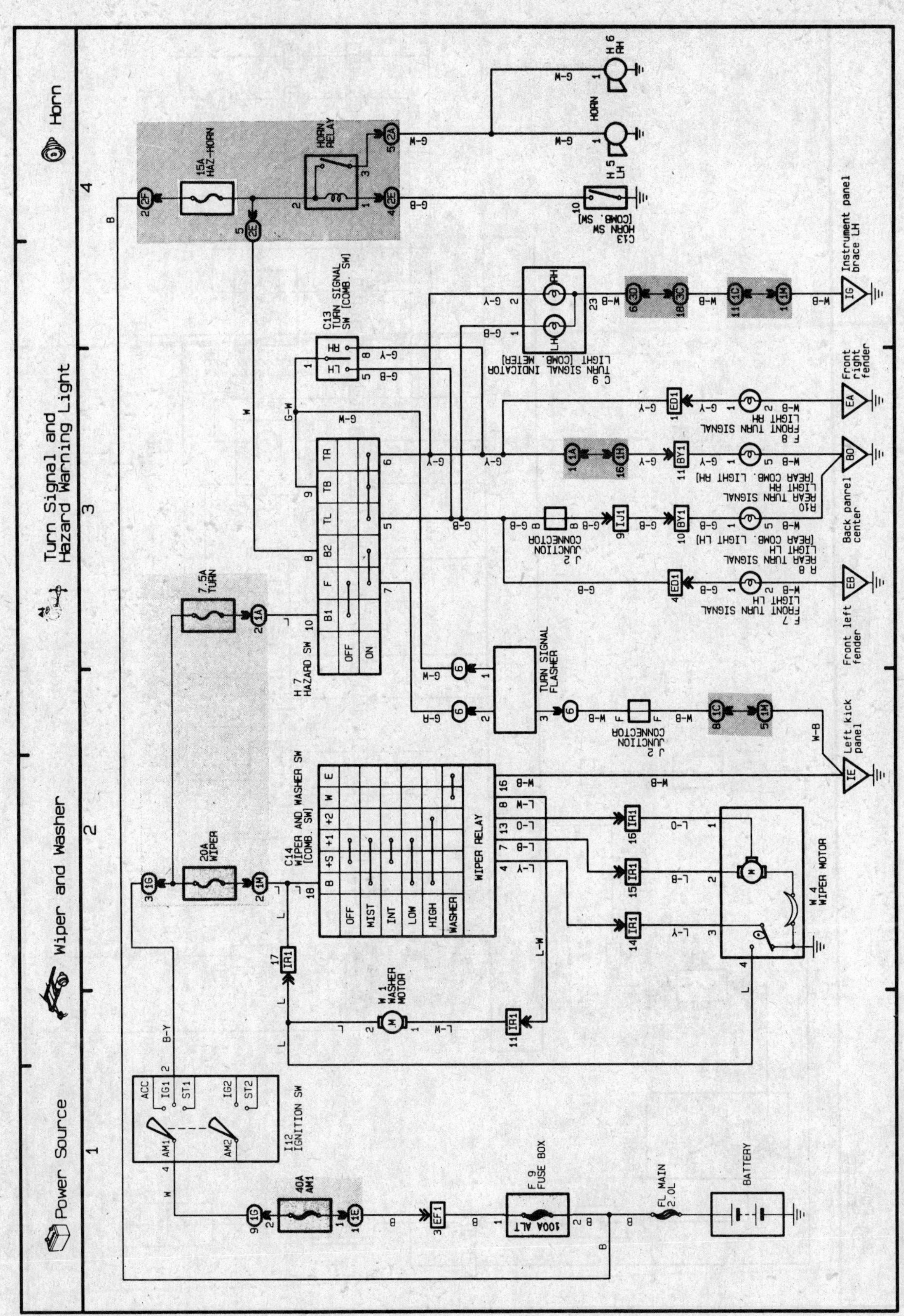

Wiring Diagram—1992

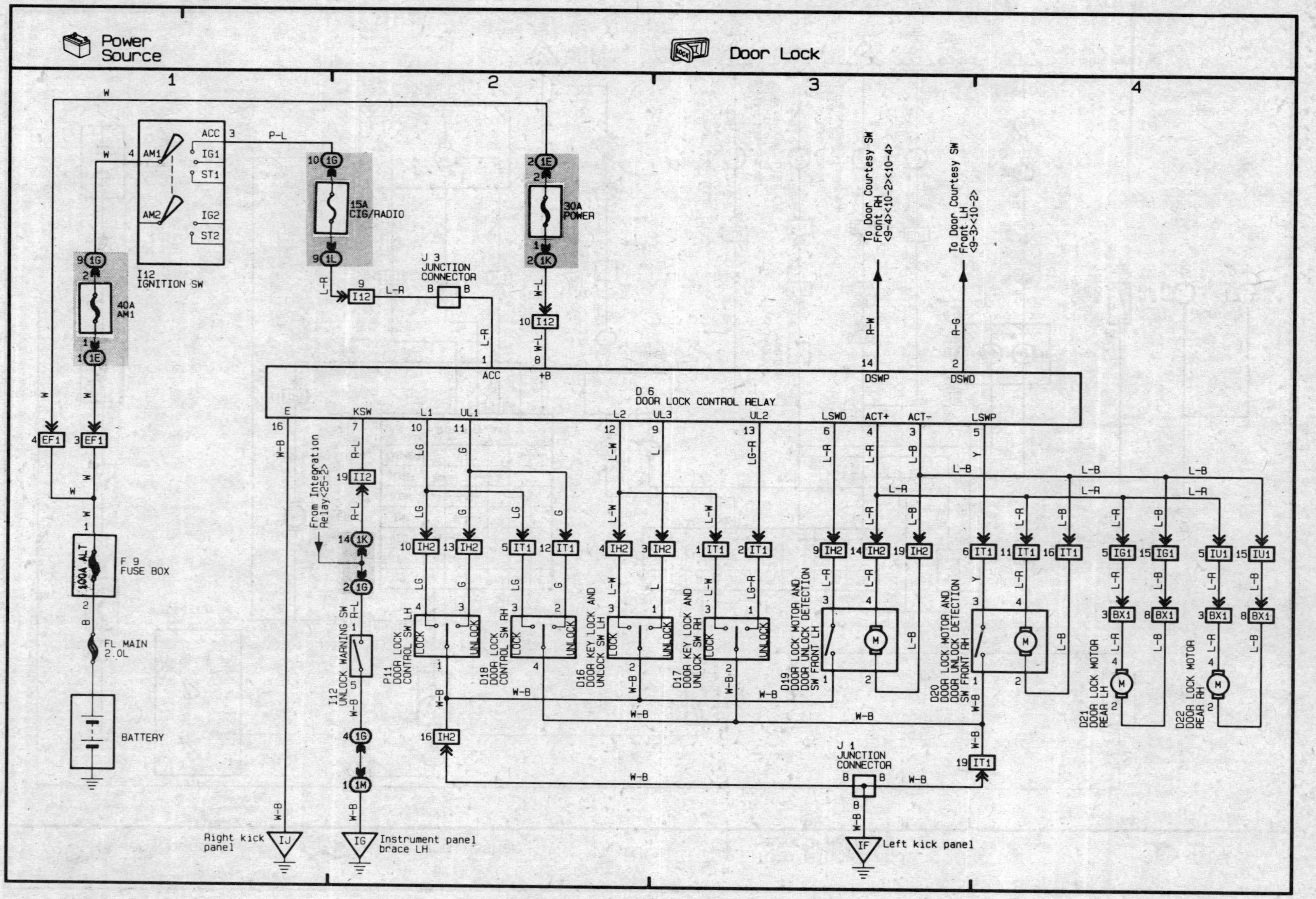

Wiring Diagram—1992

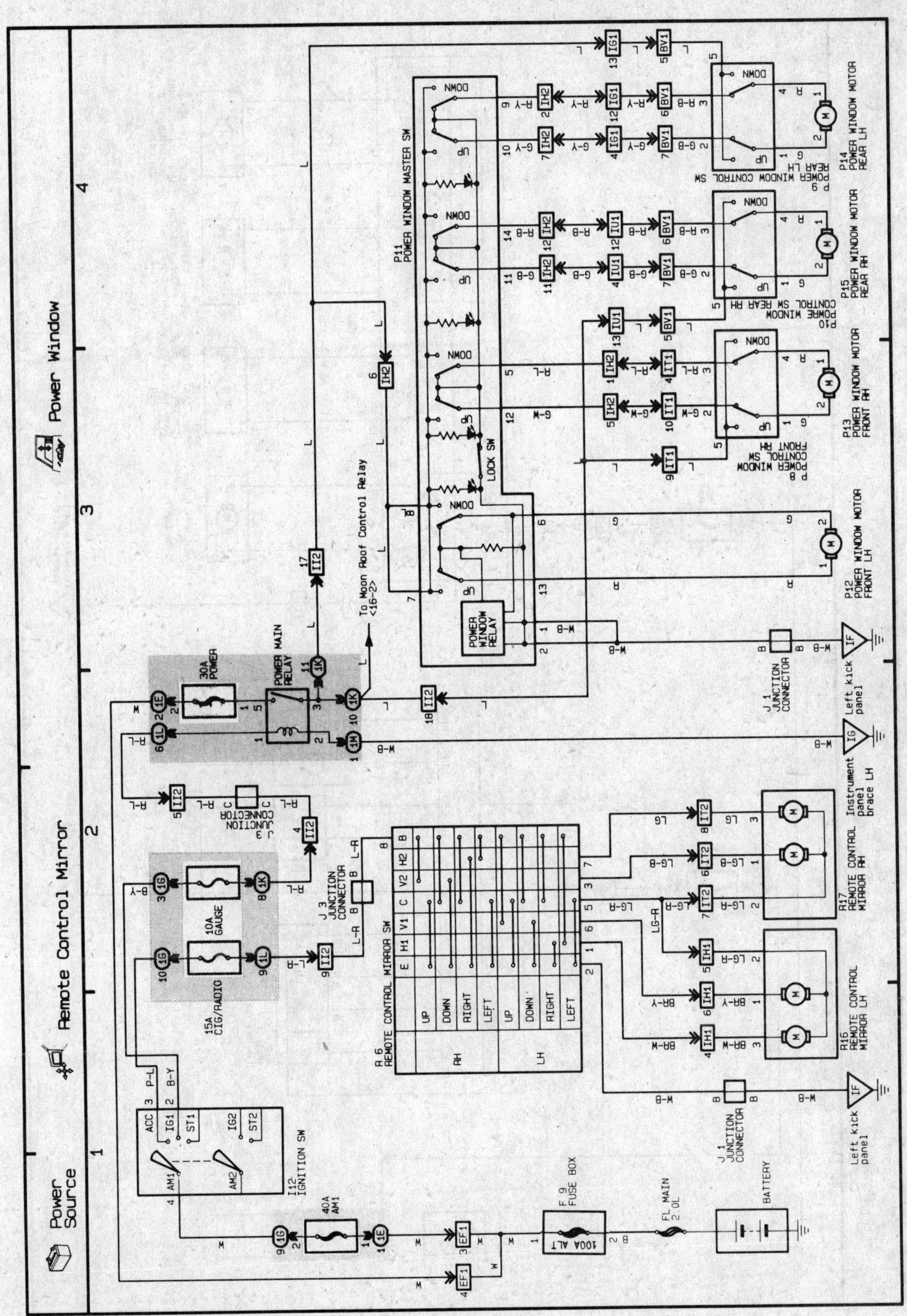

Wiring Diagram—1992

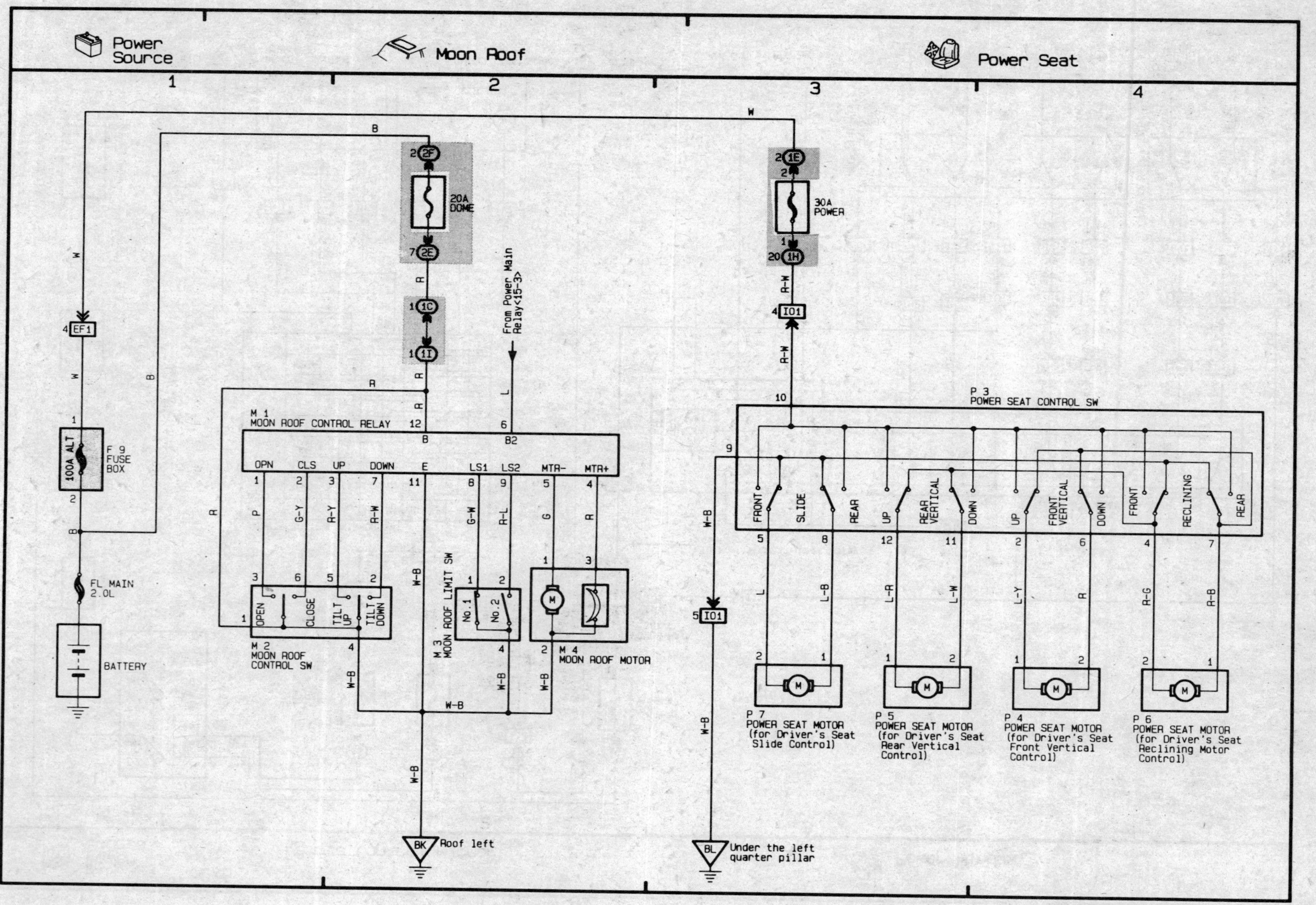
Power Source
Moon Roof
Power Seat
1
2
3
4
EF1
F 9
FUSE BOX
100A ALT
FL MAIN
2.0L
BATTERY
20A
DOME
From Power Main
Relay<15-3>
M 1
MOON ROOF CONTROL RELAY
OPN
CLS
UP
DOWN
E
B
B2
LS1
LS2
MTR-
MTR+
OPEN
CLOSE
TILT UP
TILT DOWN
M 2
MOON ROOF
CONTROL SW
No.1
No.2
M 3
MOON ROOF LIMIT SW
M 4
MOON ROOF MOTOR
Roof left
30A
POWER
P 3
POWER SEAT CONTROL SW
FRONT
SLIDE
REAR
UP
REAR VERTICAL
DOWN
UP
FRONT VERTICAL
DOWN
FRONT
RECLINING
REAR
P 7
POWER SEAT MOTOR
(for Driver's Seat
Slide Control)
P 5
POWER SEAT MOTOR
(for Driver's Seat
Rear Vertical
Control)
P 4
POWER SEAT MOTOR
(for Driver's Seat
Front Vertical
Control)
P 6
POWER SEAT MOTOR
(for Driver's Seat
Reclining Motor
Control)
Under the left
quarter pillar

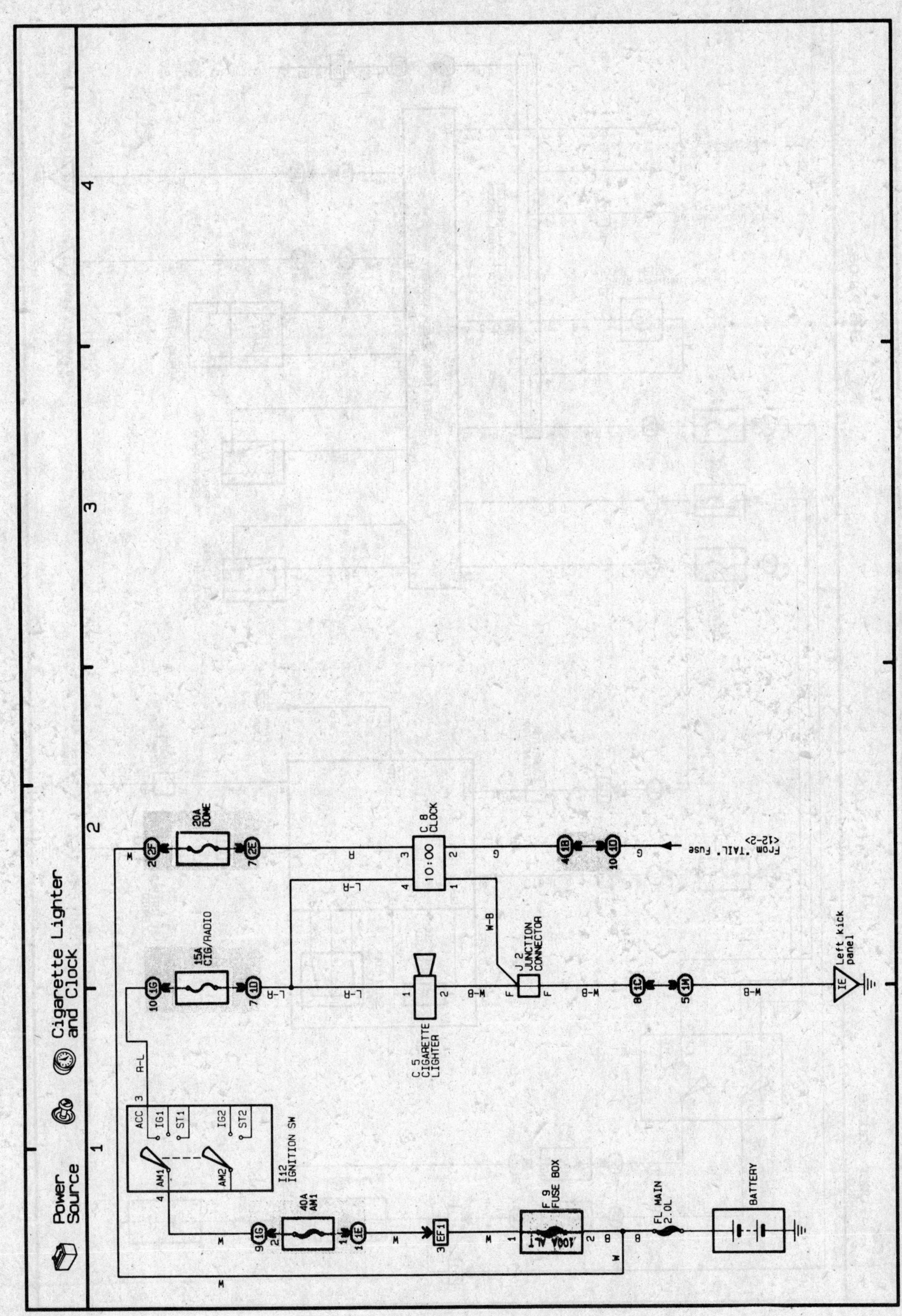
Power Source
Cigarette Lighter and Clock
1
2
3
4
I12
IGNITION SW
AM1
AM2
ACC
IG1
ST1
IG2
ST2
40A
AM1
F 9
FUSE BOX
100A ALT
FL MAIN
2.0L
BATTERY
EF1
15A
CIG/RADIO
20A
DOME
R-L
L-R
W-B
C 5
CIGARETTE
LIGHTER
J 2
JUNCTION
CONNECTOR
C 8
CLOCK
10:00
Left kick panel
IE
From 'TAIL' Fuse
<12-2>

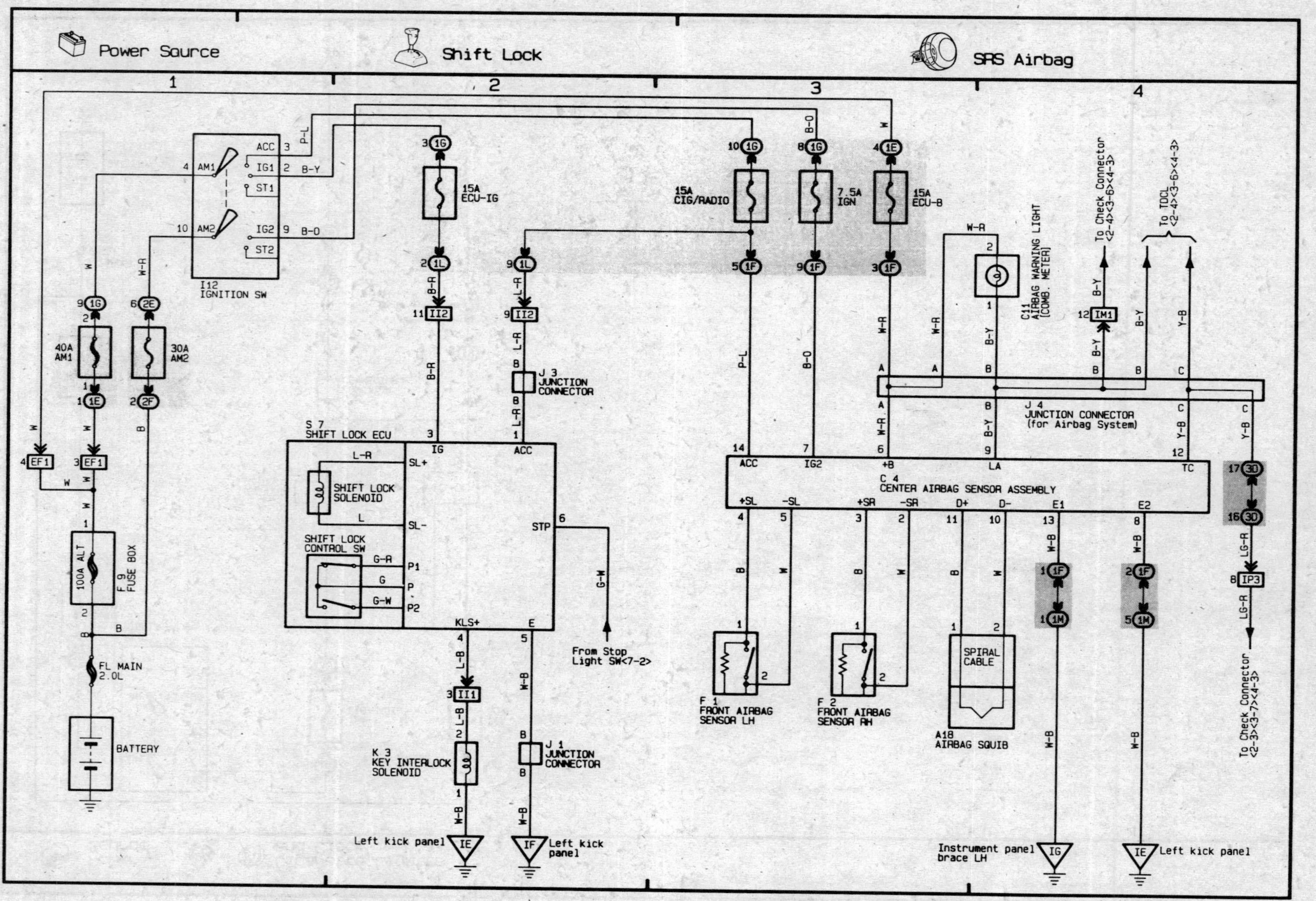

Wiring Diagram—1992

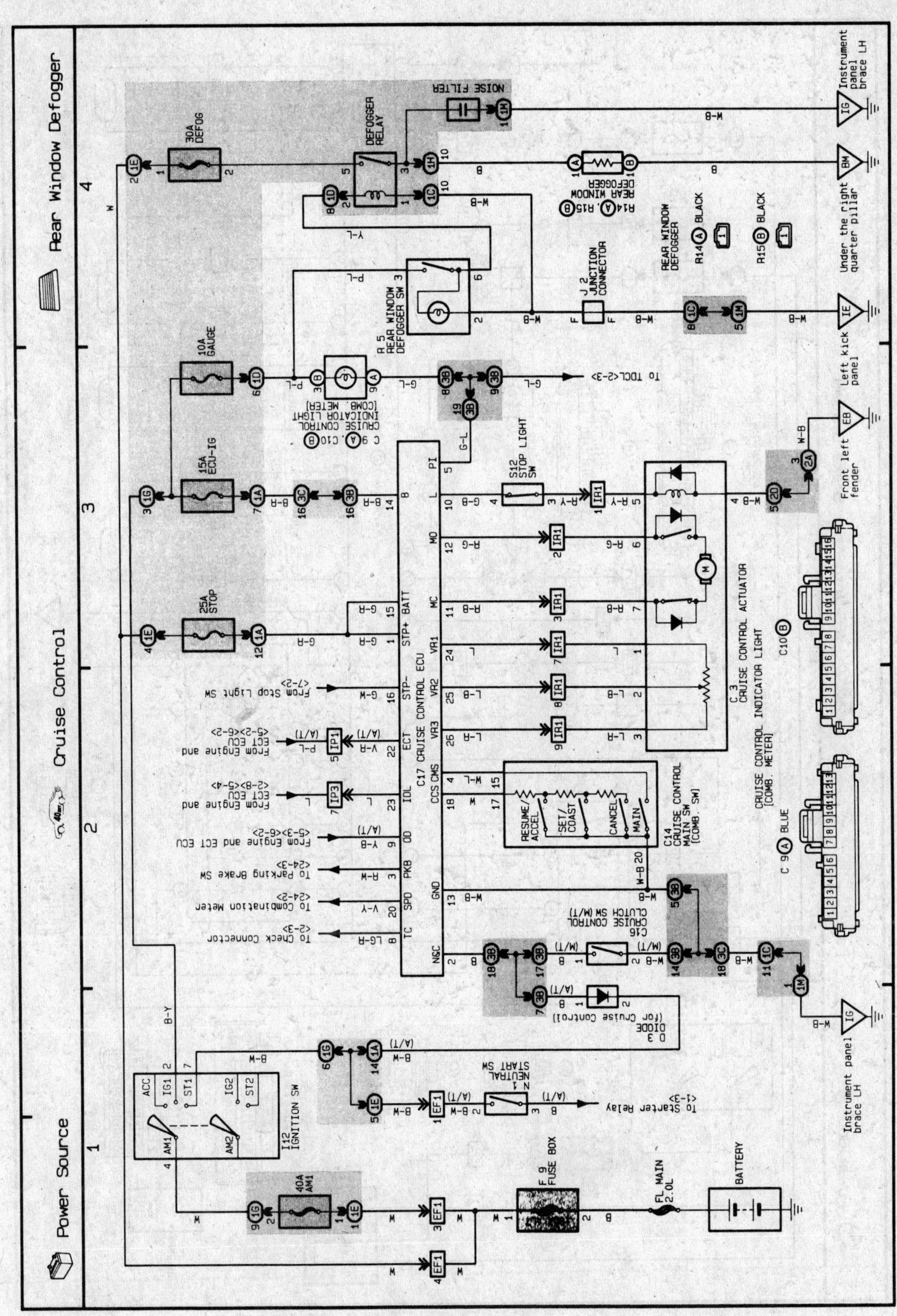
Power Source
Cruise Control
Rear Window Defogger
BATTERY
FL MAIN 2.0L
F 9 FUSE BOX
40A AM1
I12 IGNITION SW
N 1 NEUTRAL START SW
To Starter Relay <1-3>
D 3 DIODE (for Cruise Control)
C16 CRUISE CONTROL CLUTCH SW (M/T)
C14 CRUISE CONTROL MAIN SW [COMB. SW]
RESUME/ ACCEL
SET/ COAST
CANCEL
MAIN
C17 CRUISE CONTROL ECU
To Check Connector <2-3>
To Combination Meter <24-2>
To Parking Brake SW <24-3>
From Engine and ECT ECU <5-3><6-2>
From Engine and ECT ECU <2-8><5-4>
From Engine and ECT ECU <5-2><6-2>
From Stop Light SW <7-2>
25A STOP
15A ECU-IG
10A GAUGE
30A DEFOG
S12 STOP LIGHT SW
C 3 CRUISE CONTROL ACTUATOR
C 9 (A), C10 (B) CRUISE CONTROL INDICATOR LIGHT [COMB. METER]
To TDCL <2-3>
R 5 REAR WINDOW DEFOGGER SW 3
J 2 JUNCTION CONNECTOR
DEFOGGER RELAY
NOISE FILTER
R14 (A), R15 (B) REAR WINDOW DEFOGGER
REAR WINDOW DEFOGGER R14 (A) BLACK
R15 (B) BLACK
C 9 (A) BLUE
C10 (B)
CRUISE CONTROL INDICATOR LIGHT [COMB. METER]
Instrument panel brace LH
Front left fender
Left kick panel
Under the right quarter pillar
Instrument panel brace LH

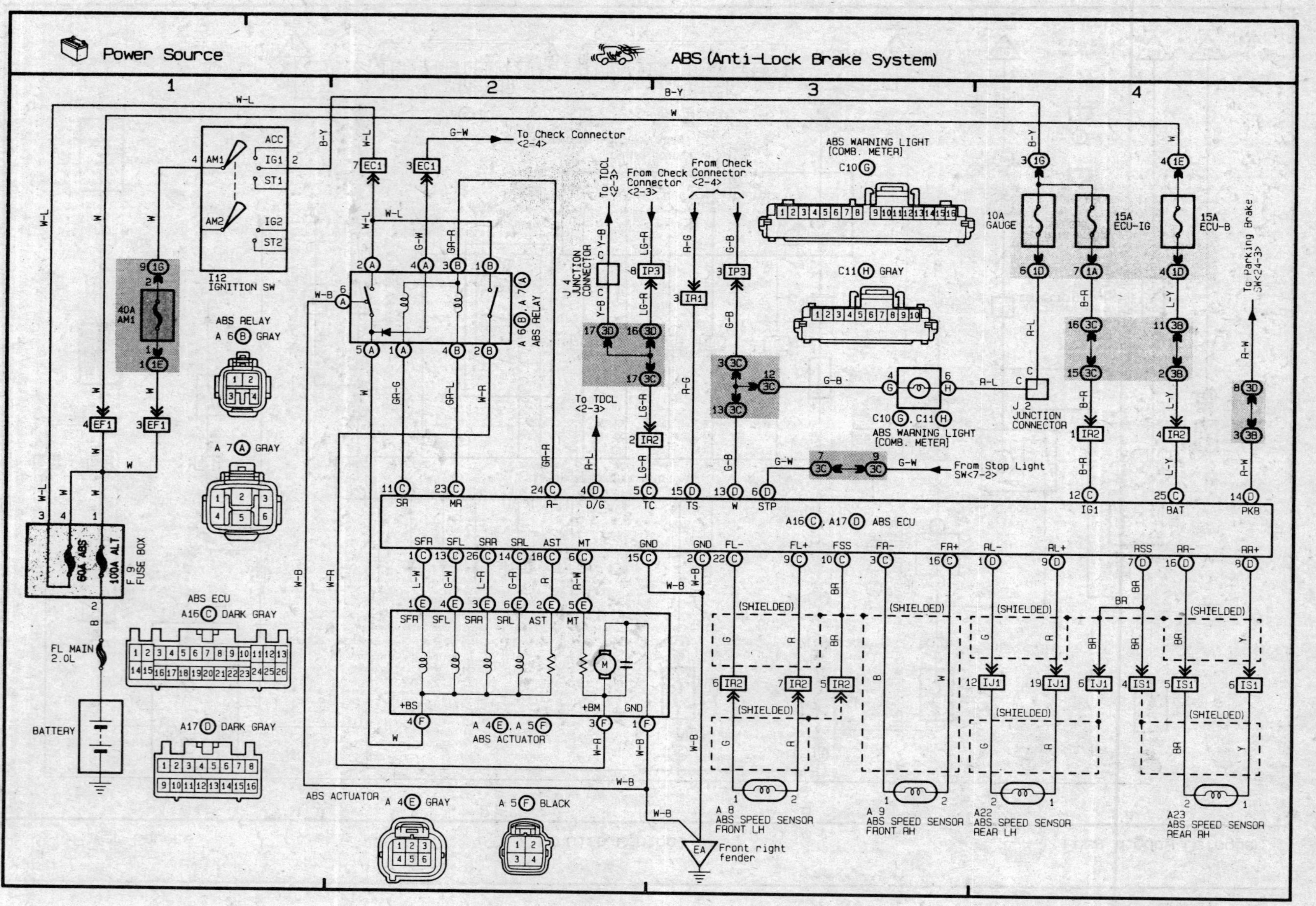
Power Source
ABS (Anti-Lock Brake System)
I12 IGNITION SW
ABS RELAY
A 6(B) GRAY
A 7(A) GRAY
ABS ECU
A16(C) DARK GRAY
A17(D) DARK GRAY
A16(C), A17(D) ABS ECU
A 4(E), A 5(F) ABS ACTUATOR
ABS ACTUATOR A 4(E) GRAY
A 5(F) BLACK
A 8 ABS SPEED SENSOR FRONT LH
A 9 ABS SPEED SENSOR FRONT RH
A22 ABS SPEED SENSOR REAR LH
A23 ABS SPEED SENSOR REAR RH
BATTERY
FL MAIN 2.0L
F 9 FUSE BOX
100A ALT
60A ABS
40A AM1
10A GAUGE
15A ECU-IG
15A ECU-B
ABS WARNING LIGHT [COMB. METER] C10(G)
C11(H) GRAY
C10(G), C11(H) ABS WARNING LIGHT [COMB. METER]
J 2 JUNCTION CONNECTOR
J 4 JUNCTION CONNECTOR
From Stop Light SW<7-2>
To Parking Brake SW<24-3>
To Check Connector <2-4>
From Check Connector <2-3>
From Check Connector <2-4>
To TDCL <2-3>
Front right fender

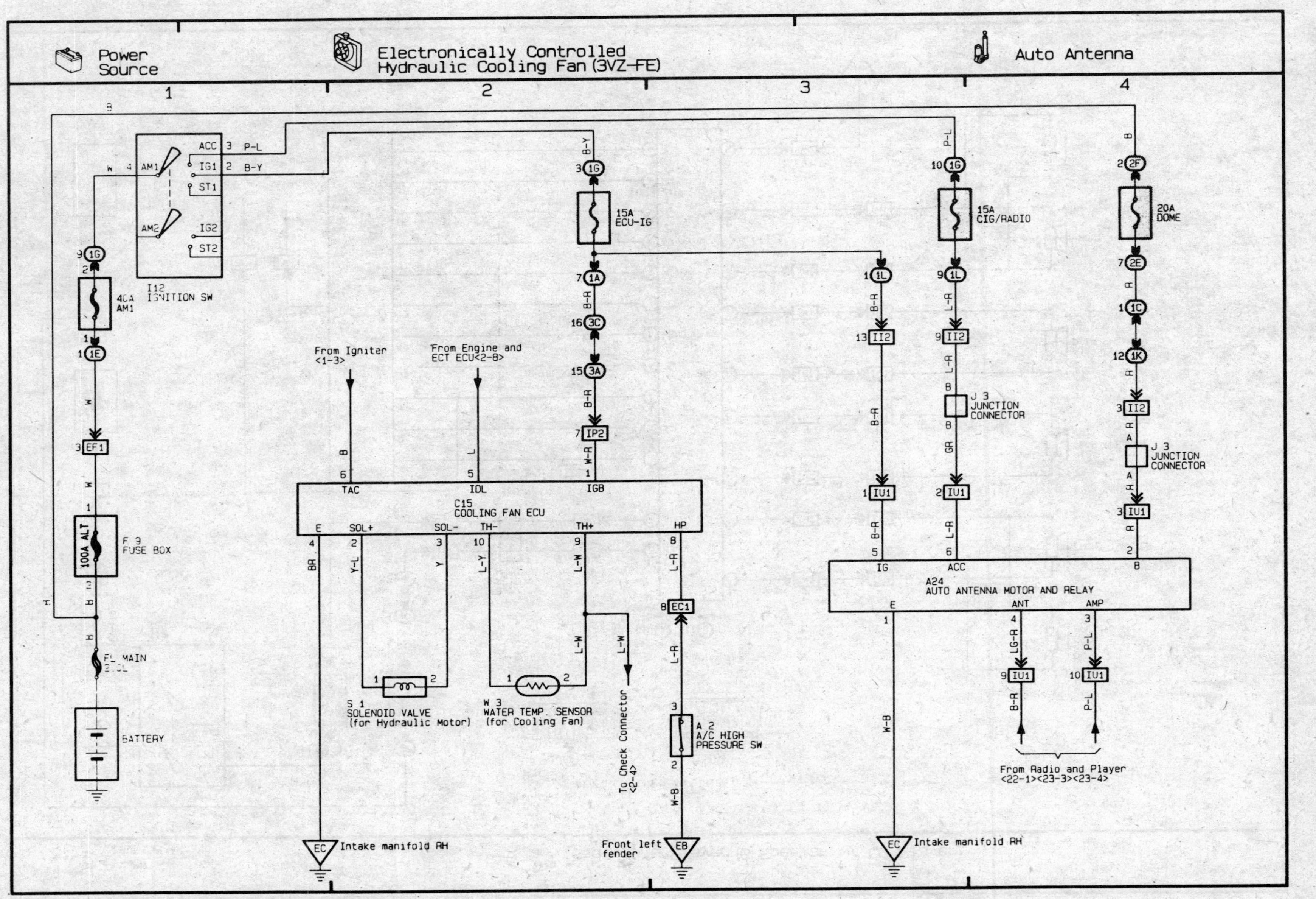
Power Source
Electronically Controlled Hydraulic Cooling Fan (3VZ-FE)
Auto Antenna
1
2
3
4
I12 IGNITION SW
ACC
IG1
ST1
IG2
ST2
AM1
AM2
40A AM1
F 3 FUSE BOX
100A ALT
FL MAIN
BATTERY
15A ECU-IG
15A CIG/RADIO
20A DOME
J 3 JUNCTION CONNECTOR
C15 COOLING FAN ECU
TAC
IDL
IGB
SOL+
SOL-
TH-
TH+
HP
E
From Igniter <1-3>
From Engine and ECT ECU<2-8>
S 1 SOLENOID VALVE (for Hydraulic Motor)
W 3 WATER TEMP. SENSOR (for Cooling Fan)
To Check Connector <2-4>
A 2 A/C HIGH PRESSURE SW
A24 AUTO ANTENNA MOTOR AND RELAY
IG
ACC
ANT
AMP
From Radio and Player <22-1><23-3><23-4>
Intake manifold RH
Front left fender
Intake manifold RH

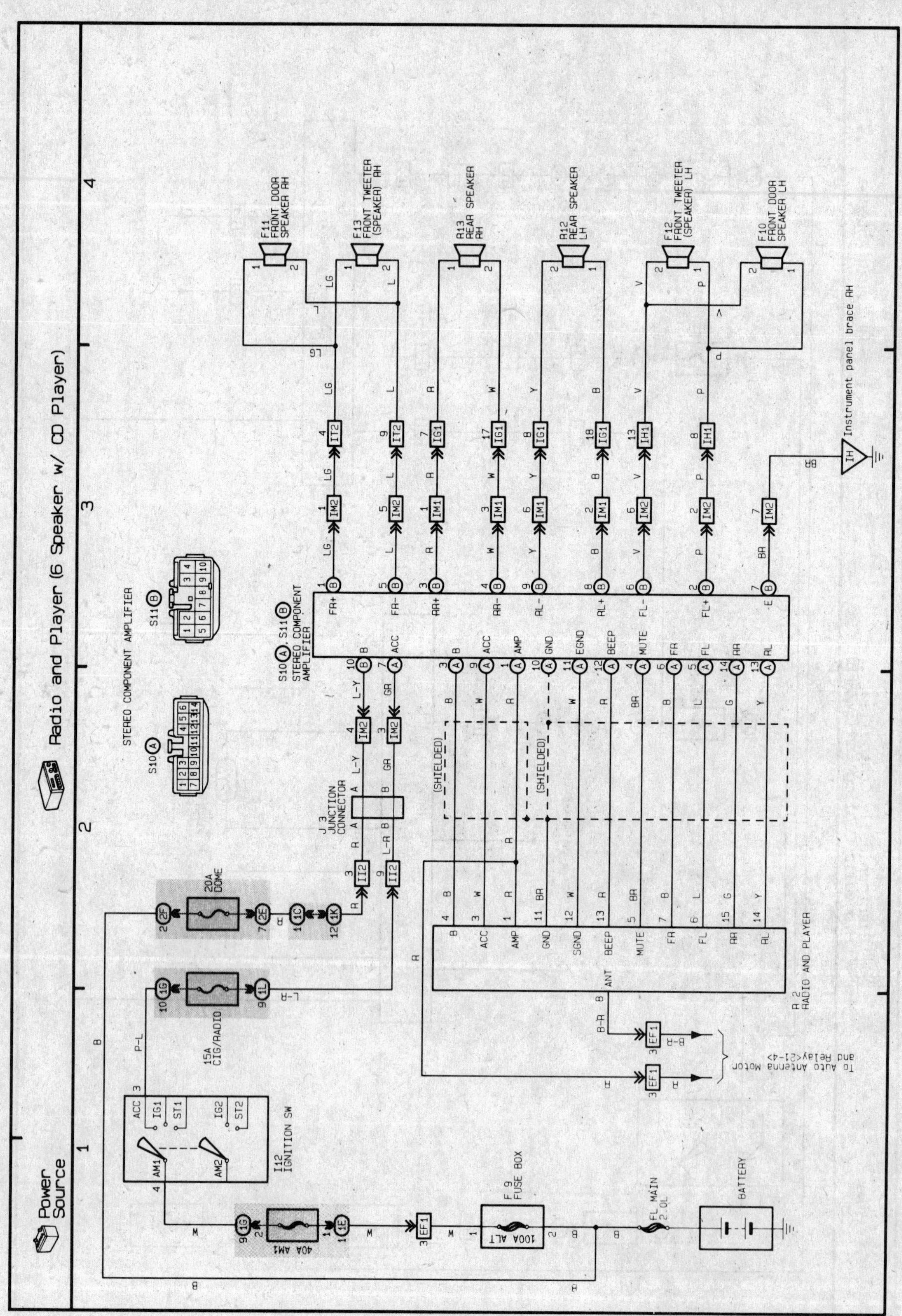

Radio and Player (6 Speaker w/ CD Player)
Power Source
STEREO COMPONENT AMPLIFIER
S10 A
S11 B
S10 A , S11 B STEREO COMPONENT AMPLIFIER
J 3 JUNCTION CONNECTOR
(SHIELDED)
20A DOME
15A CIG/RADIO
40A AM1
100A ALT
F 9 FUSE BOX
FL MAIN 2.0L
BATTERY
I12 IGNITION SW
R 2 RADIO AND PLAYER
To Auto Antenna Motor and Relay<21-4>
Instrument panel brace RH
F11 FRONT DOOR SPEAKER RH
F13 FRONT TWEETER (SPEAKER) RH
R13 REAR SPEAKER RH
R12 REAR SPEAKER LH
F12 FRONT TWEETER (SPEAKER) LH
F10 FRONT DOOR SPEAKER LH

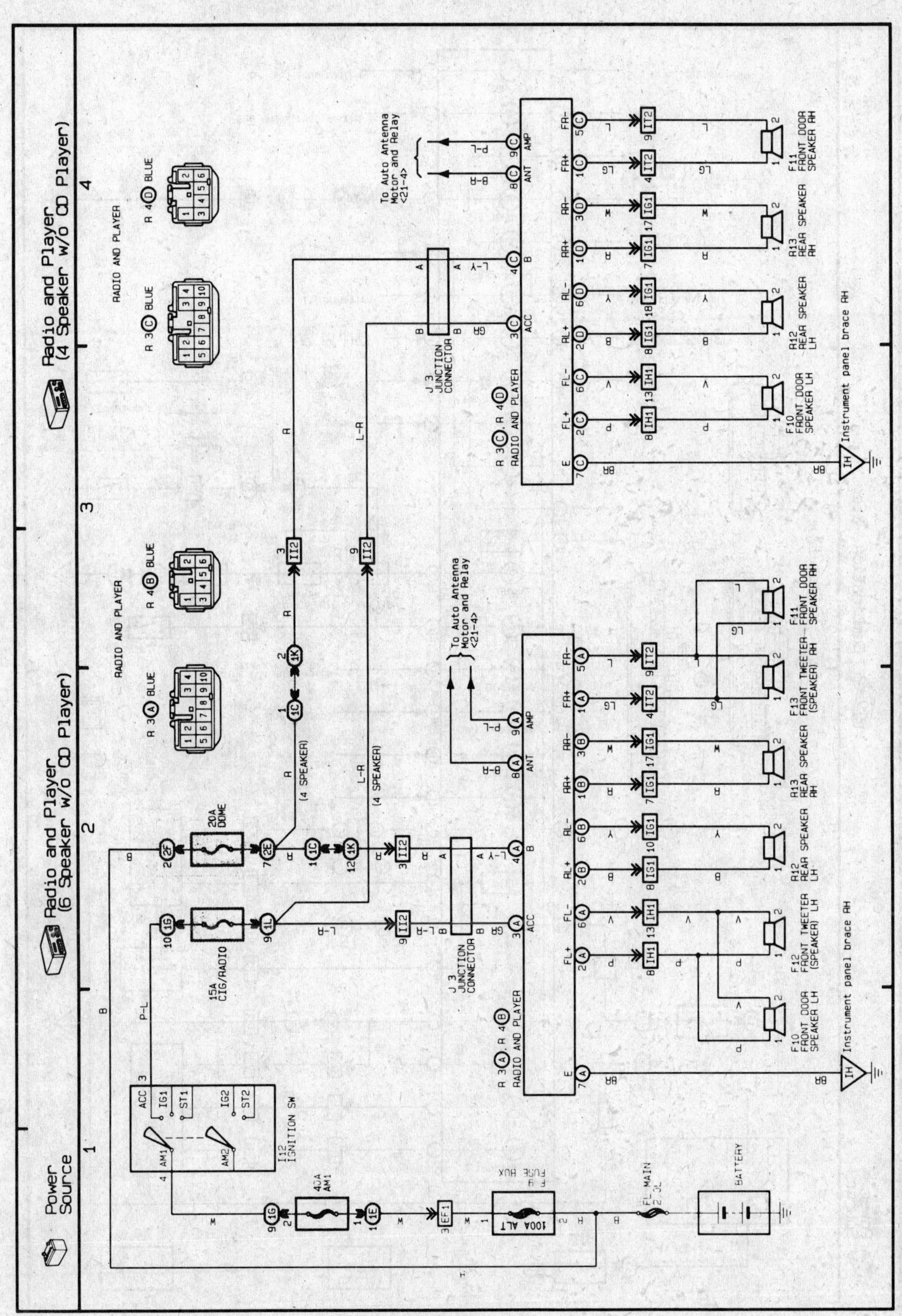

Wiring Diagram—1992

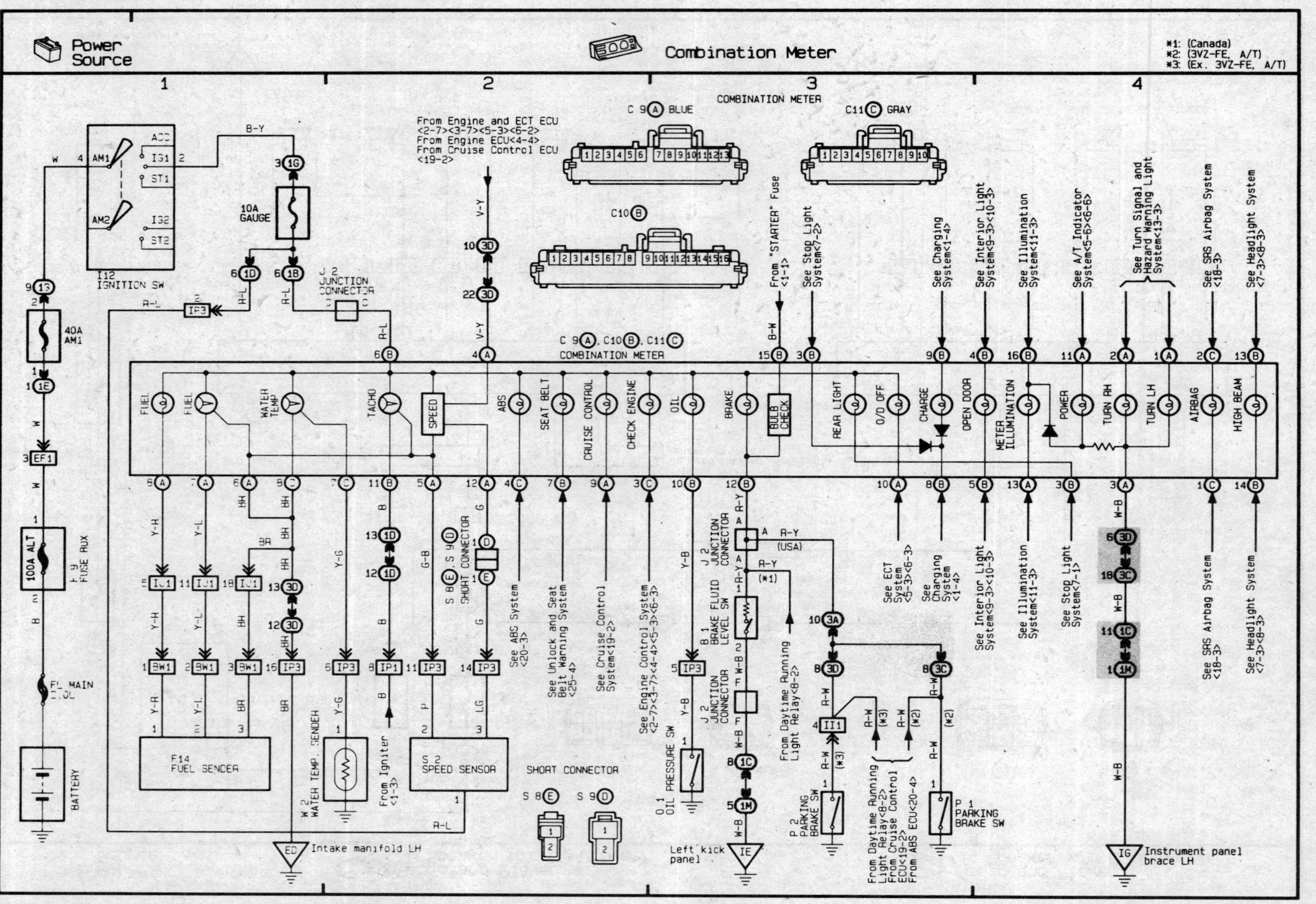
Power Source
Combination Meter
*1: (Canada)
*2: (3VZ-FE, A/T)
*3: (Ex. 3VZ-FE, A/T)
COMBINATION METER
C 9 (A) BLUE
C10 (B)
C11 (C) GRAY
C 9 (A), C10 (B), C11 (C) COMBINATION METER
From Engine and ECT ECU <2-7><3-7><5-3><6-2>
From Engine ECU<4-4>
From Cruise Control ECU <19-2>
From "STARTER" Fuse <1-1>
See Stop Light System<7-2>
See Charging System<1-4>
See Interior Light System<9-3><10-3>
See Illumination System<11-3>
See A/T Indicator System<5-6><6-6>
See Turn Signal and Hazard Warning Light System<13-3>
See SRS Airbag System <18-3>
See Headlight System <7-3><8-3>
FUEL
WATER TEMP
TACHO
SPEED
ABS
SEAT BELT
CRUISE CONTROL
CHECK ENGINE
OIL
BRAKE
BULB CHECK
REAR LIGHT
O/D OFF
CHARGE
OPEN DOOR
METER ILLUMINATION
POWER
TURN RH
TURN LH
AIRBAG
HIGH BEAM
I12 IGNITION SW
10A GAUGE
40A AM1
100A ALT
F 9 FUSE BOX
FL MAIN
BATTERY
J 2 JUNCTION CONNECTOR
F14 FUEL SENDER
W 2 WATER TEMP. SENDER
From Igniter <1-3>
S 2 SPEED SENSOR
S 8 (E), S 9 (D) SHORT CONNECTOR
SHORT CONNECTOR
See ABS System <20-3>
See Unlock and Seat Belt Warning System <25-4>
See Cruise Control System<19-2>
See Engine Control System <2-7><3-7><4-4><5-3><6-3>
O 1 OIL PRESSURE SW
B 1 BRAKE FLUID LEVEL SW
From Daytime Running Light Relay<8-2>
P 2 PARKING BRAKE SW
P 1 PARKING BRAKE SW
From Daytime Running Light Relay<8-2>
From Cruise Control ECU<19-2>
From ABS ECU<20-4>
See ECT System <5-3><6-3>
See Charging System <1-4>
See Interior Light System<9-3><10-3>
See Illumination System<11-3>
See Stop Light System<7-1>
See SRS Airbag System <18-3>
See Headlight System <7-3><8-3>
Intake manifold LH
Left kick panel
Instrument panel brace LH

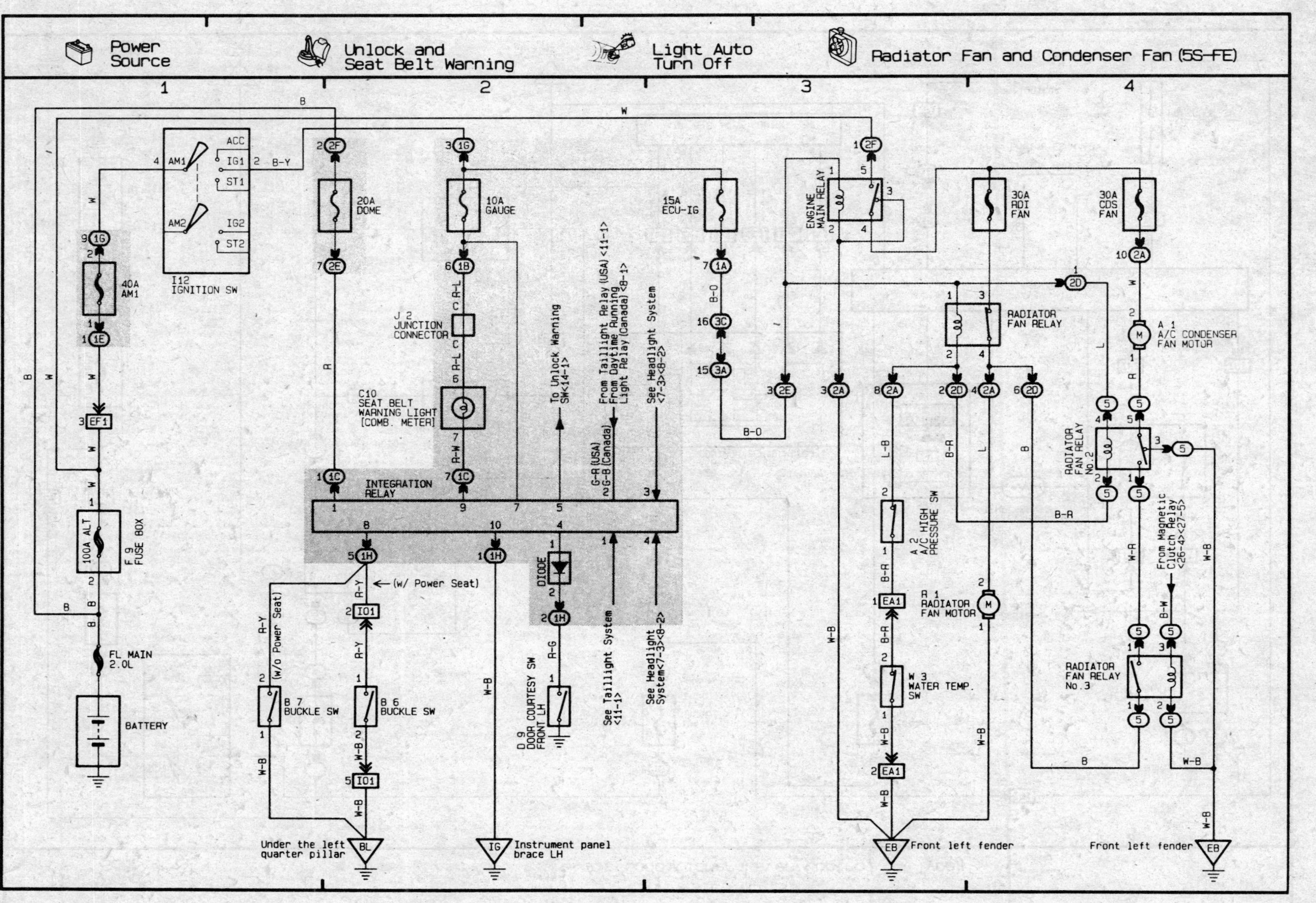
Power Source
Unlock and Seat Belt Warning
Light Auto Turn Off
Radiator Fan and Condenser Fan (5S-FE)
40A AM1
I12 IGNITION SW
ACC
IG1
ST1
IG2
ST2
AM1
AM2
F 9 FUSE BOX
100A ALT
FL MAIN 2.0L
BATTERY
20A DOME
10A GAUGE
15A ECU-IG
30A RDI FAN
30A CDS FAN
J 2 JUNCTION CONNECTOR
C10 SEAT BELT WARNING LIGHT [COMB. METER]
INTEGRATION RELAY
DIODE
D 9 DOOR COURTESY SW FRONT LH
B 6 BUCKLE SW
B 7 BUCKLE SW
(w/ Power Seat)
(w/o Power Seat)
To Unlock Warning SW<14-1>
From Taillight Relay (USA) <11-1>
From Daytime Running Light Relay (Canada) <8-1>
See Headlight System <7-3><8-2>
See Taillight System <11-1>
G-R (USA)
G-B (Canada)
ENGINE MAIN RELAY
RADIATOR FAN RELAY
RADIATOR FAN RELAY No.2
RADIATOR FAN RELAY No.3
A 2 A/C HIGH PRESSURE SW
R 1 RADIATOR FAN MOTOR
W 3 WATER TEMP. SW
A 1 A/C CONDENSER FAN MOTOR
From Magnetic Clutch Relay <26-4><27-5>
Under the left quarter pillar
Instrument panel brace LH
Front left fender
Front left fender

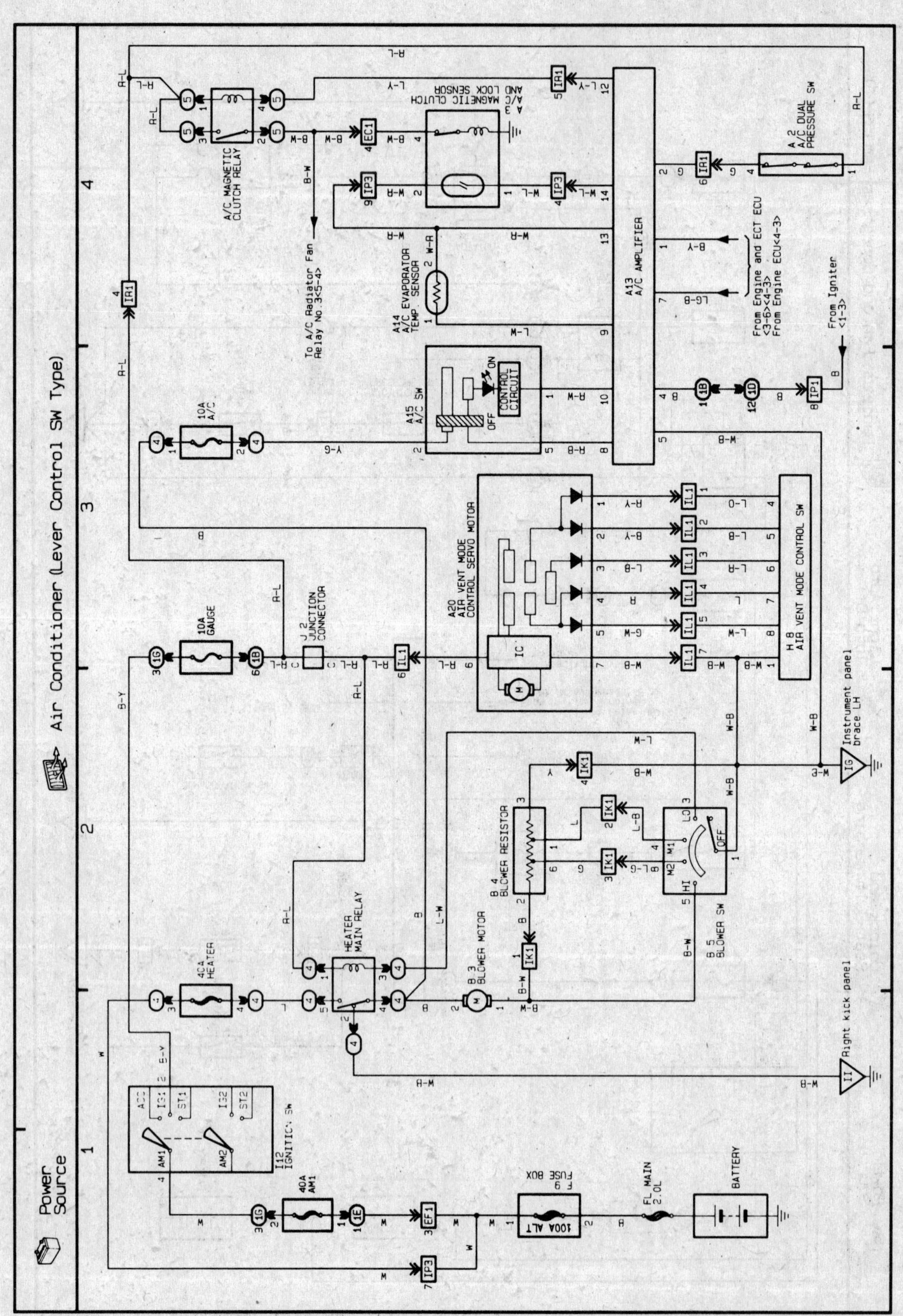
Air Conditioner (Lever Control SW Type)
Power Source
A/C MAGNETIC CLUTCH RELAY
A 3 A/C MAGNETIC CLUTCH AND LOCK SENSOR
A 2 A/C DUAL PRESSURE SW
A14 A/C EVAPORATOR TEMP. SENSOR
To A/C Radiator Fan Relay No.3<5-4>
A13 A/C AMPLIFIER
From Engine and ECT ECU <3-6><4-3> From Engine ECU<4-3>
From Igniter <1-3>
A15 A/C SW
CONTROL CIRCUIT
10A A/C
10A GAUGE
J 2 JUNCTION CONNECTOR
A20 AIR VENT MODE CONTROL SERVO MOTOR
H 8 AIR VENT MODE CONTROL SW
Instrument panel brace LH
40A HEATER
HEATER MAIN RELAY
B 3 BLOWER MOTOR
B 4 BLOWER RESISTOR
B 5 BLOWER SW
Right kick panel
I12 IGNITION SW
40A AM1
F 9 FUSE BOX
100A ALT
FL MAIN 2.0L
BATTERY

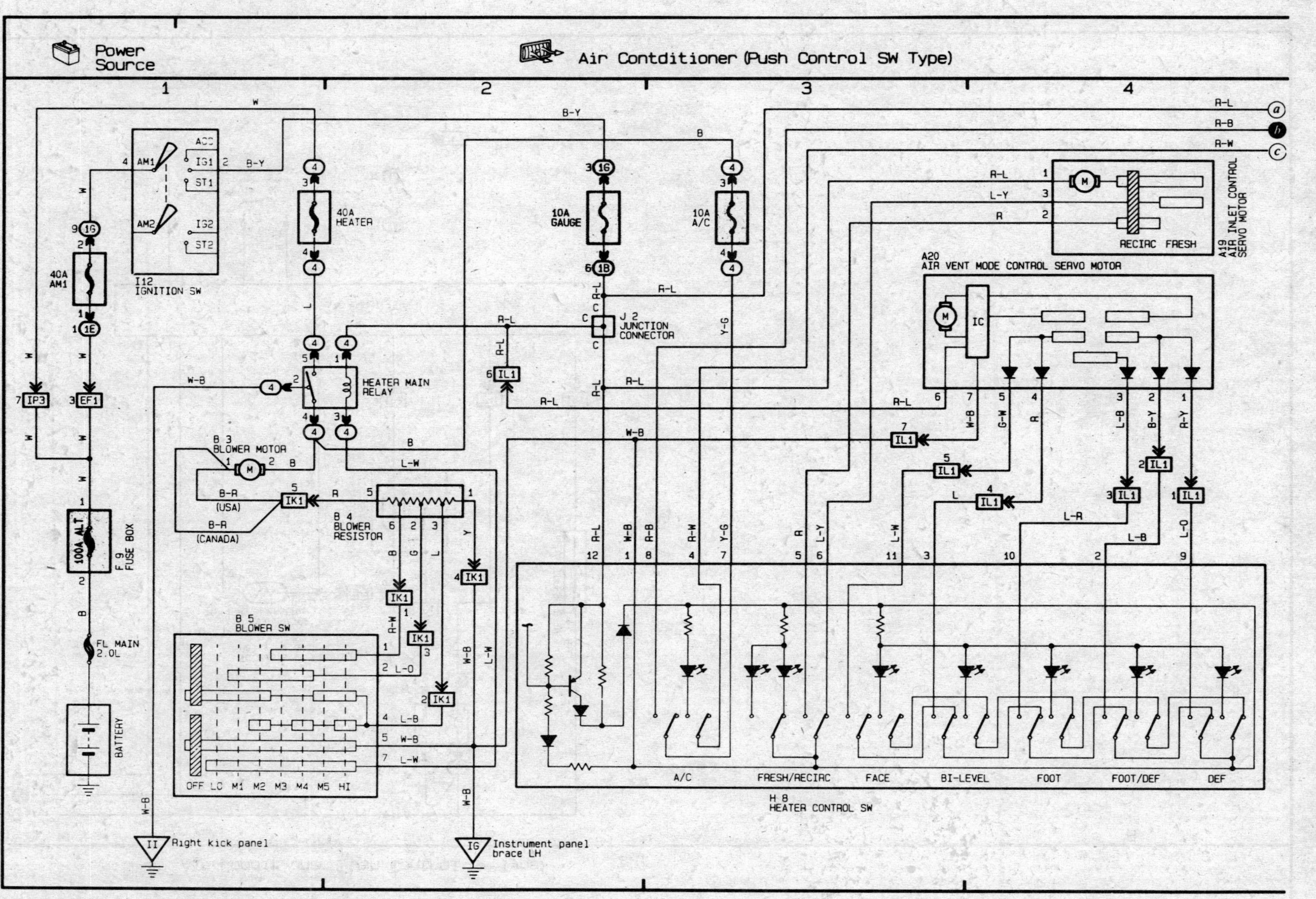
Power Source
Air Contditioner (Push Control SW Type)
1
2
3
4
40A AM1
I12 IGNITION SW
ACC
IG1
ST1
AM1
AM2
IG2
ST2
40A HEATER
10A GAUGE
10A A/C
J 2 JUNCTION CONNECTOR
HEATER MAIN RELAY
B 3 BLOWER MOTOR
(USA)
(CANADA)
B 4 BLOWER RESISTOR
B 5 BLOWER SW
OFF LO M1 M2 M3 M4 M5 HI
100A ALT
F 9 FUSE BOX
FL MAIN 2.0L
BATTERY
Right kick panel
Instrument panel brace LH
A19 AIR INLET CONTROL SERVO MOTOR
RECIRC FRESH
A20 AIR VENT MODE CONTROL SERVO MOTOR
IC
H 8 HEATER CONTROL SW
A/C
FRESH/RECIRC
FACE
BI-LEVEL
FOOT
FOOT/DEF
DEF

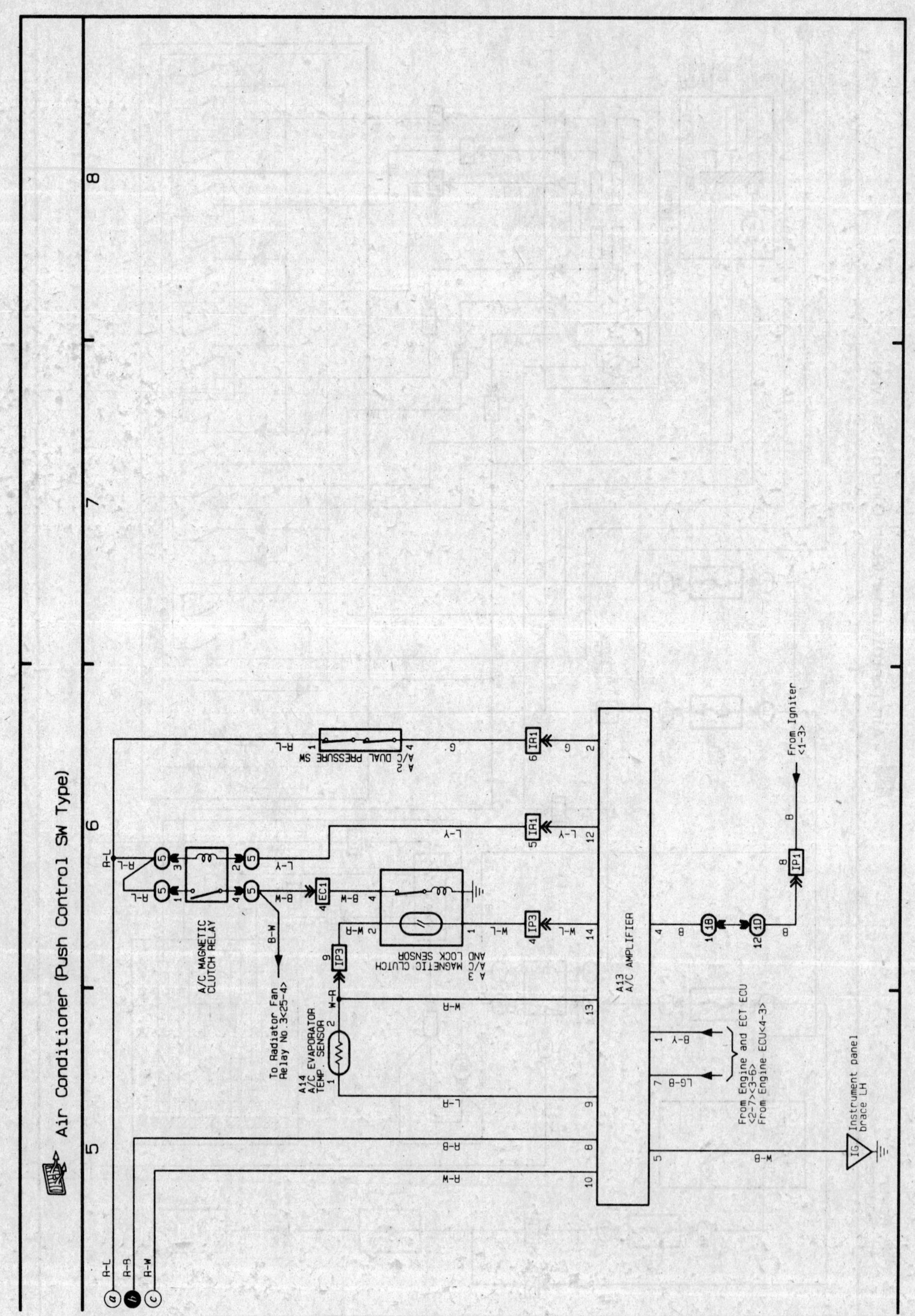

Air Conditioner (Push Control SW Type)
A/C MAGNETIC CLUTCH RELAY
A/C DUAL PRESSURE SW
A 2
A 3
A/C MAGNETIC CLUTCH AND LOCK SENSOR
A14
A/C EVAPORATOR TEMP. SENSOR
A13
A/C AMPLIFIER
To Radiator Fan Relay No.3<25-4>
From Igniter <1-3>
From Engine and ECT ECU <2-7><3-6>
From Engine ECU<4-3>
Instrument panel brace LH
R-L
R-B
R-W
L-Y
B-W
B-W
W-R
W-L
L-R
B-Y
LG-B
W-B

Troubleshooting Basic Turn Signal and Flasher Problems

Most problems in the turn signals or flasher system can be reduced to defective flashers or bulbs, which are easily replaced. Occasionally, problems in the turn signals are traced to the switch in the steering column, which will require professional service.

F = Front R = Rear ● = Lights off ○ = Lights on

Problem		Solution
Turn signals light, but do not flash	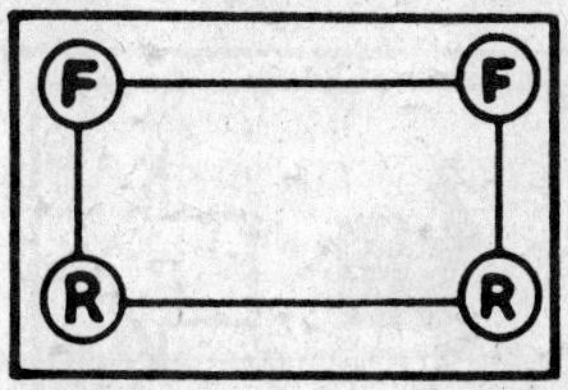 F F R R	• Replace the flasher
No turn signals light on either side	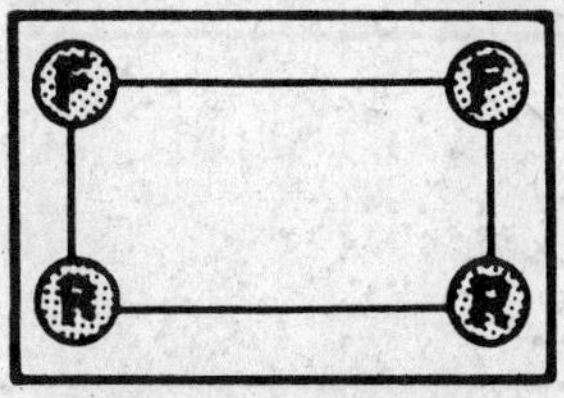 F F R R	• Check the fuse. Replace if defective. • Check the flasher by substitution • Check for open circuit, short circuit or poor ground
Both turn signals on one side don't work	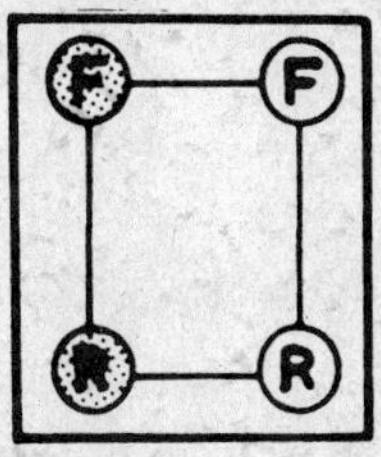 F F R R	• Check for bad bulbs • Check for bad ground in both housings
One turn signal light on one side doesn't work	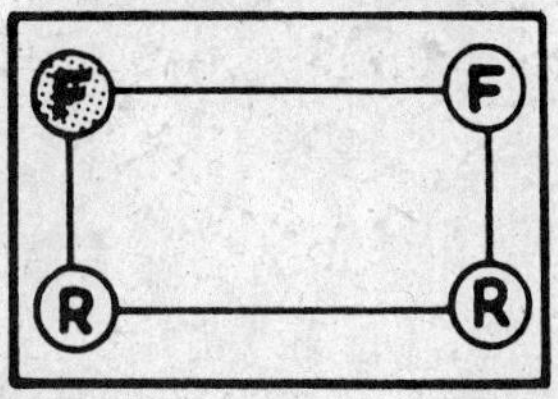 F F R R	• Check and/or replace bulb • Check for corrosion in socket. Clean contacts. • Check for poor ground at socket
Turn signal flashes too fast or too slow	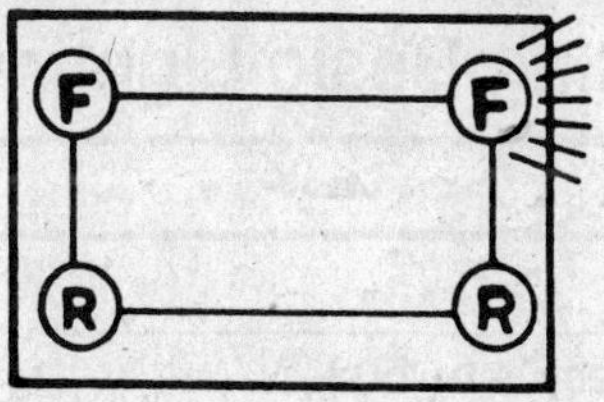 F F R R	• Check any bulb on the side flashing too fast. A heavy-duty bulb is probably installed in place of a regular bulb. • Check the bulb flashing too slow. A standard bulb was probably installed in place of a heavy-duty bulb. • Check for loose connections or corrosion at the bulb socket
Indicator lights don't work in either direction		• Check if the turn signals are working • Check the dash indicator lights • Check the flasher by substitution

Troubleshooting Basic Turn Signal and Flasher Problems

Most problems in the turn signals or flasher system can be reduced to defective flashers or bulbs, which are easily replaced. Occasionally, problems in the turn signals are traced to the switch in the steering column, which will require professional service.

F = Front R = Rear • = Lights off o = Lights on

Problem	Solution
One indicator light doesn't light	• On systems with 1 dash indicator: See if the lights work on the same side. Often the filaments have been reversed in systems combining stoplights with taillights and turn signals. Check the flasher by substitution • On systems with 2 indicators: Check the bulbs on the same side Check the indicator light bulb Check the flasher by substitution

Troubleshooting Basic Lighting Problems

Problem	Cause	Solution
Lights		
One or more lights don't work, but others do	• Defective bulb(s) • Blown fuse(s) • Dirty fuse clips or light sockets • Poor ground circuit	• Replace bulb(s) • Replace fuse(s) • Clean connections • Run ground wire from light socket housing to car frame
Lights burn out quickly	• Incorrect voltage regulator setting or defective regulator • Poor battery/alternator connections	• Replace voltage regulator • Check battery/alternator connections
Lights go dim	• Low/discharged battery • Alternator not charging • Corroded sockets or connections • Low voltage output	• Check battery • Check drive belt tension; repair or replace alternator • Clean bulb and socket contacts and connections • Replace voltage regulator

Troubleshooting Basic Lighting Problems

Problem	Cause	Solution
Lights		
Lights flicker	• Loose connection • Poor ground • Circuit breaker operating (short circuit)	• Tighten all connections • Run ground wire from light housing to car frame • Check connections and look for bare wires
Lights "flare"—Some flare is normal on acceleration—if excessive, see "Lights Burn Out Quickly"	• High voltage setting	• Replace voltage regulator
Lights glare—approaching drivers are blinded	• Lights adjusted too high • Rear springs or shocks sagging • Rear tires soft	• Have headlights aimed • Check rear springs/shocks • Check/correct rear tire pressure
Turn Signals		
Turn signals don't work in either direction	• Blown fuse • Defective flasher • Loose connection	• Replace fuse • Replace flasher • Check/tighten all connections
Right (or left) turn signal only won't work	• Bulb burned out • Right (or left) indicator bulb burned out • Short circuit	• Replace bulb • Check/replace indicator bulb • Check/repair wiring
Flasher rate too slow or too fast	• Incorrect wattage bulb • Incorrect flasher	• Flasher bulb • Replace flasher (use a variable load flasher if you pull a trailer)
Indicator lights do not flash (burn steadily)	• Burned out bulb • Defective flasher	• Replace bulb • Replace flasher
Indicator lights do not light at all	• Burned out indicator bulb • Defective flasher	• Replace indicator bulb • Replace flasher

Troubleshooting Basic Dash Gauge Problems

Problem	Cause	Solution
Coolant Temperature Gauge		
Gauge reads erratically or not at all	• Loose or dirty connections	• Clean/tighten connections
	• Defective sending unit	• Bi-metal gauge: remove the wire from the sending unit. Ground the wire for an instant. If the gauge registers, replace the sending unit.
	• Defective gauge	• Magnetic gauge: disconnect the wire at the sending unit. With ignition ON gauge should register COLD. Ground the wire; gauge should register HOT.
Ammeter Gauge—Turn Headlights ON (do not start engine). Note reaction		
Ammeter shows charge	• Connections reversed on gauge	• Reinstall connections
Ammeter shows discharge	• Ammeter is OK	• Nothing
Ammeter does not move	• Loose connections or faulty wiring	• Check/correct wiring
	• Defective gauge	• Replace gauge
Oil Pressure Gauge		
Gauge does not register or is inaccurate	• On mechanical gauge, Bourdon tube may be bent or kinked	• Check tube for kinks or bends preventing oil from reaching the gauge
	• Low oil pressure	• Remove sending unit. Idle the engine briefly. If no oil flows from sending unit hole, problem is in engine.
	• Defective gauge	• Remove the wire from the sending unit and ground it for an instant with the ignition ON. A good gauge will go to the top of the scale.
	• Defective wiring	• Check the wiring to the gauge. If it's OK and the gauge doesn't register when grounded, replace the gauge.
	• Defective sending unit	• If the wiring is OK and the gauge functions when grounded, replace the sending unit
All Gauges		
All gauges do not operate	• Blown fuse	• Replace fuse
	• Defective instrument regulator	• Replace instrument voltage regulator
All gauges read low or erratically	• Defective or dirty instrument voltage regulator	• Clean contacts or replace
All gauges pegged	• Loss of ground between instrument voltage regulator and car	• Check ground
	• Defective instrument regulator	• Replace regulator

Troubleshooting Basic Dash Gauge Problems

Problem	Cause	Solution
Warning Lights		
Light(s) do not come on when ignition is ON, but engine is not started	• Defective bulb • Defective wire • Defective sending unit	• Replace bulb • Check wire from light to sending unit • Disconnect the wire from the sending unit and ground it. Replace the sending unit if the light comes on with the ignition ON.
Light comes on with engine running	• Problem in individual system • Defective sending unit	• Check system • Check sending unit (see above)

Troubleshooting the Heater

Problem	Cause	Solution
Blower motor will not turn at any speed	• Blown fuse • Loose connection • Defective ground • Faulty switch • Faulty motor • Faulty resistor	• Replace fuse • Inspect and tighten • Clean and tighten • Replace switch • Replace motor • Replace resistor
Blower motor turns at one speed only	• Faulty switch • Faulty resistor	• Replace switch • Replace resistor
Blower motor turns but does not circulate air	• Intake blocked • Fan not secured to the motor shaft	• Clean intake • Tighten security
Heater will not heat	• Coolant does not reach proper temperature • Heater core blocked internally • Heater core air-bound • Blend-air door not in proper position	• Check and replace thermostat if necessary • Flush or replace core if necessary • Purge air from core • Adjust cable
Heater will not defrost	• Control cable adjustment incorrect • Defroster hose damaged	• Adjust control cable • Replace defroster hose

Troubleshooting Basic Windshield Wiper Problems

Problem	Cause	Solution
Electric Wipers		
Wipers do not operate— Wiper motor heats up or hums	• Internal motor defect • Bent or damaged linkage • Arms improperly installed on linking pivots	• Replace motor • Repair or replace linkage • Position linkage in park and reinstall wiper arms
Electric Wipers		
Wipers do not operate— No current to motor	• Fuse or circuit breaker blown • Loose, open or broken wiring • Defective switch • Defective or corroded terminals • No ground circuit for motor or switch	• Replace fuse or circuit breaker • Repair wiring and connections • Replace switch • Replace or clean terminals • Repair ground circuits
Wipers do not operate— Motor runs	• Linkage disconnected or broken	• Connect wiper linkage or replace broken linkage
Vacuum Wipers		
Wipers do not operate	• Control switch or cable inoperative • Loss of engine vacuum to wiper motor (broken hoses, low engine vacuum, defective vacuum/fuel pump) • Linkage broken or disconnected • Defective wiper motor	• Repair or replace switch or cable • Check vacuum lines, engine vacuum and fuel pump • Repair linkage • Replace wiper motor
Wipers stop on engine acceleration	• Leaking vacuum hoses • Dry windshield • Oversize wiper blades • Defective vacuum/fuel pump	• Repair or replace hoses • Wet windshield with washers • Replace with proper size wiper blades • Replace pump

AUTOMATIC TRANSMISSION
Adjustments 7-69
Back-up light switch 7-70
Fluid and filter change 7-69
Identification 7-68
Neutral safety switch 7-69
Removal and installation 7-70
Throttle cable adjustment 7-69
AXLE
Front 7-46
Rear 7-85
BACK-UP LIGHT SWITCH
Automatic transmission 7-69
Manual transmission 7-4
CLUTCH
Adjustment 7-63
Hydraulic system bleeding 7-68
Master cylinder 7-64
Pedal 7-63
Pilot bearing 7-65
Removal and installation 7-64
Slave cylinder 7-67
Switch 7-4
Troubleshooting 7-93
DIFFERENTIAL
Front 7-7
Rear 7-86
DRIVE AXLE (FRONT)
Axle shaft 7-46, 71
Differential 7-7
Removal and installation 7-46
DRIVE AXLE (REAR)
Axle housing 7-88
Axle shaft and bearing 7-85
Removal and installation 7-86
Driveshaft 7-82
GEARSHIFT LINKAGE
Automatic transmission 7-69
Manual transmission 7-2
HALFSHAFTS 7-46, 71
MANUAL TRANSMISSION
Adjustments 7-2
Back-up light switch 7-4
Identification 7-2
Linkage 7-2
Overhaul 7-7
5-speed 7-7
Removal and installation 7-5
Troubleshooting 7-91
MASTER CYLINDER 7-64
NEUTRAL SAFETY SWITCH 7-69
SLAVE CYLINDER 7-67
TRANSFER CASE
Removal and installation 7-78
Seals 7-78
TROUBLESHOOTING CHARTS
Automatic transmission 7-94
Clutch 7-93
Clutch switch 7-4
Manual transmission 7-91
Noise 7-91
Torque converter 7-94
U-JOINTS
Removal 7-84
Overhaul 7-84

Automatic Transmission 7-68
Clutch 7-63
Driveline 7-82
Front Drive Axle 7-46, 71
Manual Transmission 7-2
Rear Axle 7-85
Transfer Case 7-77

MANUAL TRANSAXLE

Identification

The transaxle model identification number is located on the bottom of the Vehicle Identification Number (VIN) plate. Since 1983 several types of manual transaxles have been used on the Camry: S51 (1983–88 2WD, 1989–92 2WD with 4-cyl.), E52 (1989–91 2WD with 6-cyl.), E53 (1992 2WD with 6-cyl.), E56F2 (1988 4WD) and E56F5 (1988–90 4WD).

The S51 has been the standard equipment transaxle and has remained basically unchanged since 1983. The major changes to the Camry powertrain came with the introduction of the 1988 All-Trac 4-Wheel Drive 5-speed transaxles with the model designations of E56F2 and E56F5. All-Trac was used from 1988–90.

Both the E56F5 and E56F2 transaxles have the same compact design in which the transmission, center differential, front differential and transfer are arranged on the same quadruple cased axle. The center differential on both models compensates for the difference between the front and rear wheel rotation through the use of a bevel gear that evenly distributes the power transmitted from the engine to the transmission to both the front and rear axles. The center differential on the E56F2 is equipped with a viscous coupling that is a type of fluid clutch. The coupling uses viscous resistance to control the operation of the differential. The E56F5 center differential is equipped with a lock mechanism that enables the vehicle to get out of a bad spot more easily when one of the four wheels spins on snowy, icy, muddy roads etc.

Adjustments

SHIFTER LEVER FREEPLAY

All Manual Transaxles

1983–92

➧ SEE FIGS 1-3

1. Adjust the shifter lever seat clearance by selecting a shim that will provide a 0.1-0.2 lb. preload at the top of the lever.
2. When the proper shim is selected, install the shim in the shifter lever seat.

CABLE STROKE

S51 Transaxle

➡ This procedure only applies to 1983 models.

1. Remove the console box.
2. Loosen the adjusting locknut.
3. Insert a 5mm diameter guide pin into the shift lever hole and turn the turn buckle to align the the shift lever hole with the shift lever support hole. The proper size Phillips head screwdriver can be used as the guide pin.
4. Tighten the adjusting locknut and remove the guide pin.
5. Install the console box.

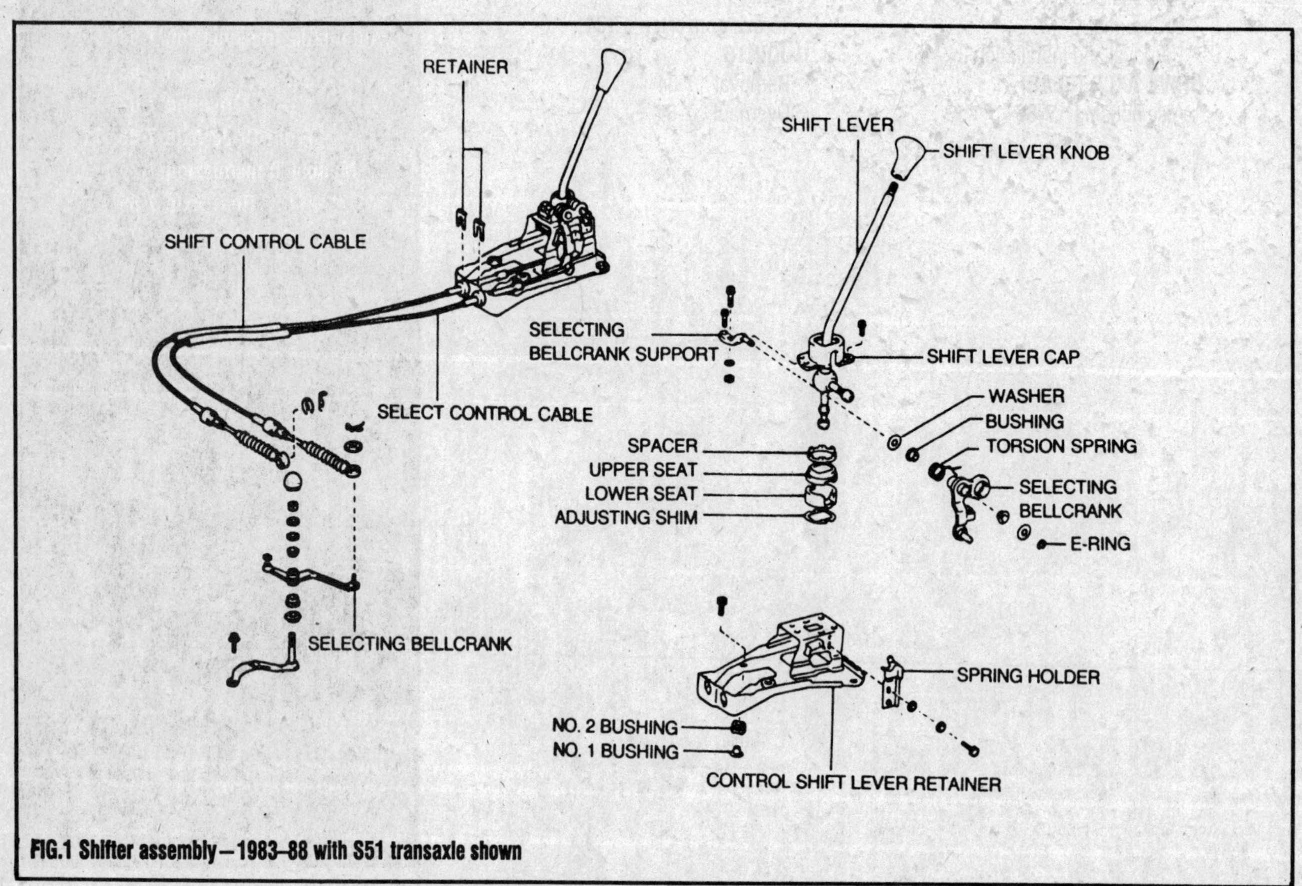

FIG.1 Shifter assembly—1983–88 with S51 transaxle shown

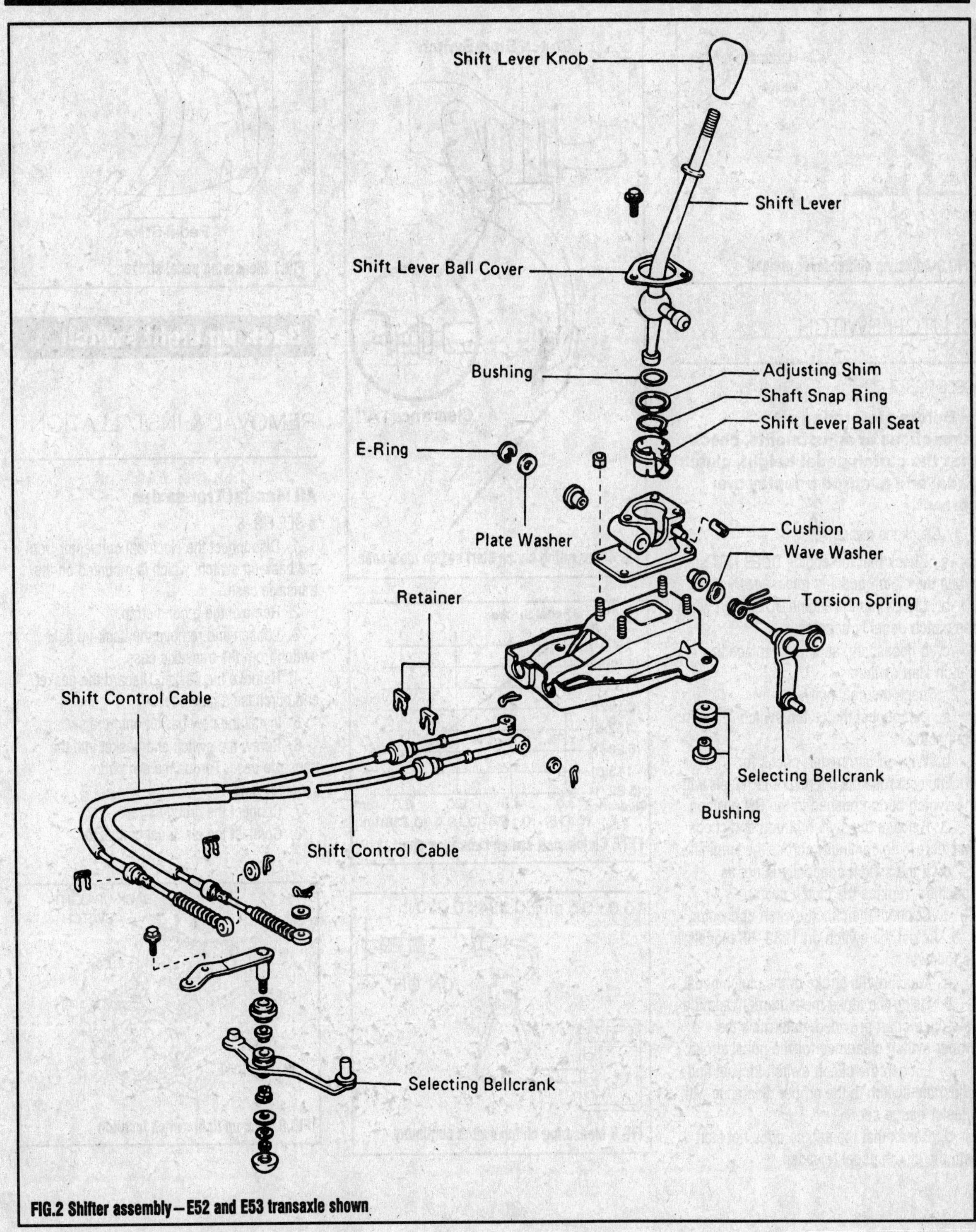

FIG.2 Shifter assembly—E52 and E53 transaxle shown

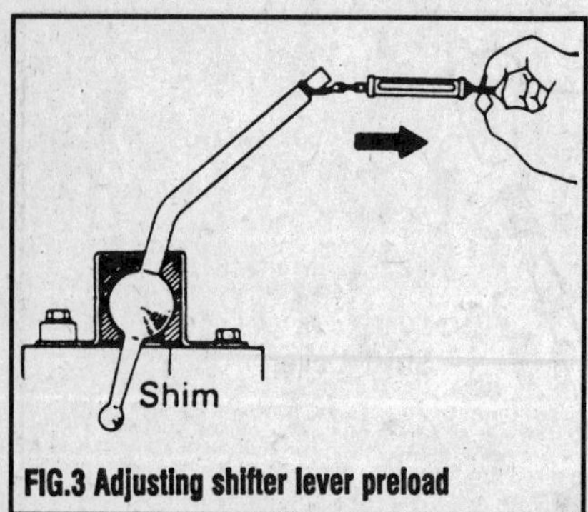

FIG.3 Adjusting shifter lever preload

CLUTCH SWITCH

➧ SEE FIGS. 4–7

➡ **Before preforming any inspections or adjustments, check that the clutch pedal height, clutch pedal and pushrod freeplay are correct.**

1. Check the clearance:

a. Check that the engine DOES NOT start when the clutch pedal is released.

b. Check that the engine DOES start when the clutch pedal is depressed.

c. If necessary, adjust or replace the clutch start switch.

2. Check the continuity:

a. Disconnect the clutch switch connector.

b. With an ohmmeter, check for continuity across the connector terminals with the switch button pushed in the ON position.

c. Release the switch button and check that there is no continuity across the terminals.

d. If the switch continuity is not as specified, replace the clutch switch.

e. Connect the clutch switch connector.

3. Adjust the switch on 1983–88 models as follows:

a. Measure the stroke of the clutch pedal.

b. Using the stoke measurement and the clearance chart provided, determine the proper switch clearance for the pedal stroke.

c. Loosen the clutch switch locknut and adjust the switch to the proper clearance with a feeler gauge set.

d. Check that the engine does not start with the clutch pedal released.

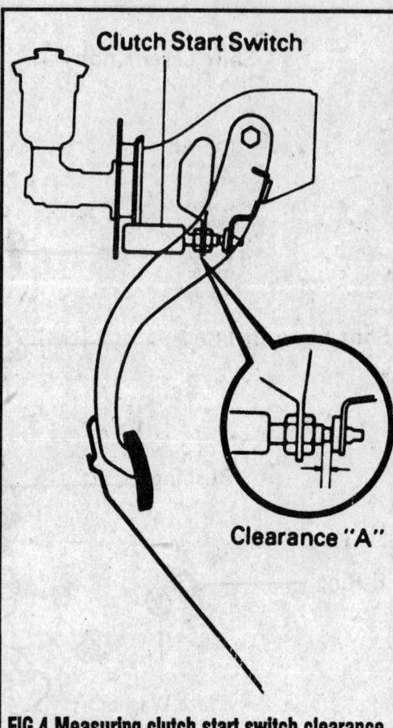

FIG.4 Measuring clutch start switch clearance

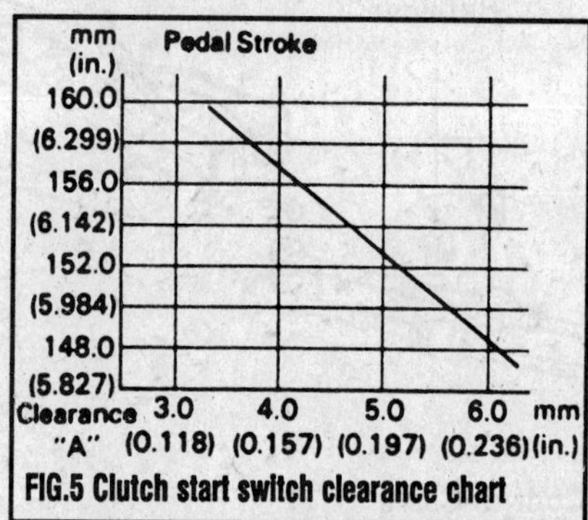

FIG.5 Clutch start switch clearance chart

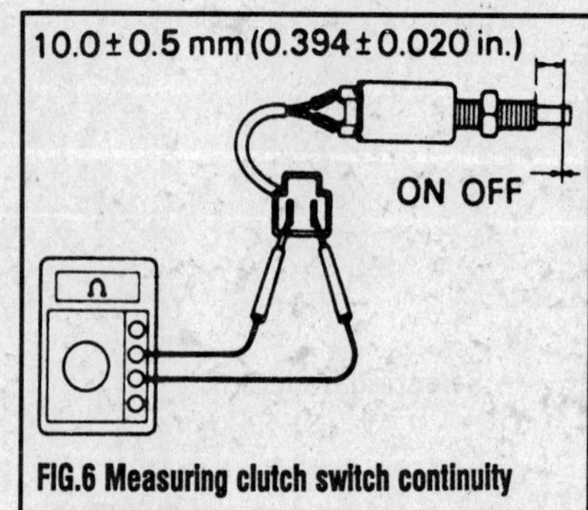

FIG.6 Measuring clutch switch continuity

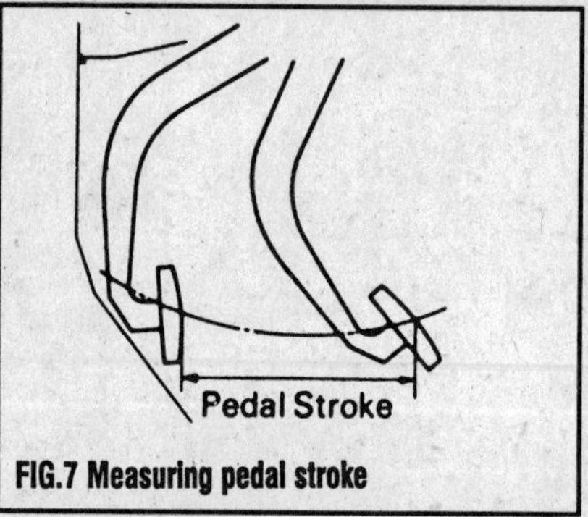

FIG.7 Measuring pedal stroke

Back-up Light switch

REMOVAL & INSTALLATION

All Manual Transaxles

➧ SEE FIG. 8

1. Disconnect the electrical connector from the back-up switch, which is mounted on the transaxle case.
2. Remove the ground strap.
3. Loosen and remove the back-up light switch from the transaxle case.
4. Remove the gasket. Discard the gasket and purchase a new one.
5. Install the new gasket onto the switch.
6. Screw the switch and gasket into the transaxle case. Torque the switch to specifications.
7. Connect the ground strap.
8. Connect the electrical connector.

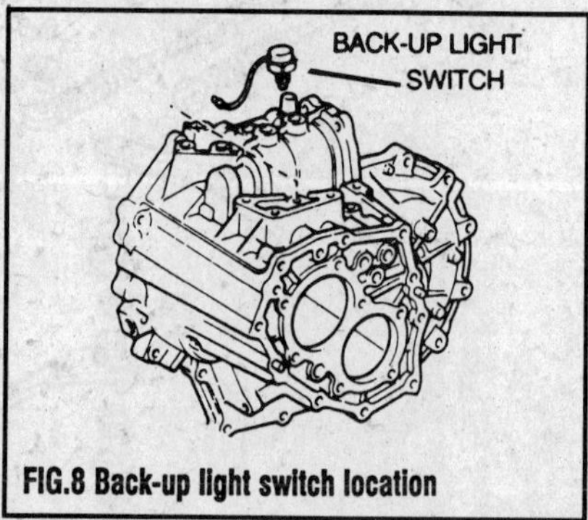

FIG.8 Back-up light switch location

Transaxle

REMOVAL & INSTALLATION

➡ The following procedures cover removal and installation of the transaxle without removing the engine. If the transaxle and engine are to removed as an assembly, refer to "Engine, Removal and Installation" as described in Section 3.

S51 Transaxle

1983-86

1. Disconnect the negative battery cable and drain the oil from the transaxle.
2. Remove the front and rear mounting.
3. Remove the left hand mounting bracket.
4. Remove the side gear shaft and front drive center shaft or universal joint (if equipped). On SV series vehicles, use SST Nos. 09520-32010 and 09520-32030 to drive out the universal joint. On CV series vehicles, drive out the side gear shaft using SST No. 09520-32011.
5. Remove the starter.

➡ Before removing the transaxle mounting bolts, support the engine either on wood blocks or with the use of an engine hoist.

6. Support the transaxle properly with a transaxle jack.
7. Remove the transaxle mounting bolts and locking plate.
8. Remove the transaxle from the engine.

To Install:

9. Install the front and rear mounting.
10. Install the side gear shaft, drive center shaft or universal joint.
11. Connect the transaxle to the engine temporarily by installing the locking plate and a mounting bolt. Support the transmission with the transaxle jack.
12. Install the remaining mounting bolts. Torque the 10mm bolts to 29 ft. lbs. and the 12mm bolts to 47 ft. lbs.
13. Install the starter motor.
14. Fill the transaxle with the proper grade oil to the proper level.

1987–92

1. Disconnect the negative battery cable and remove the air assembly for added working room.
2. Remove the clutch release cylinder and tube clamp and the cruise control actuator, if equipped.
3. Remove the retainer from the clutch tube bracket and unbolt and remove the bracket.
4. Remove the clips and washers that attach the transaxle control cables to the control levers. Remove the retaining clips and disconnect the transaxle control cables.
5. Remove the starter.
6. Disconnect the back-up light switch connector and ground strap.
7. Remove the upper transaxle mounting bolts.
8. Raise the vehicle and support it safely.
9. Remove the under covers.
10. Drain the fluid from the transaxle.
11. Disconnect the speedometer cable or sensor connector.
12. Remove the lower suspension crossmember.
13. Remove the front and rear engine mounting bolts and remove the engine mounting center member.
14. Have an assistant depress the brake pedal. Loosen the six mounting bolts and disconnect both driveshafts.
15. Remove the snapring from the center driveshaft bearing bracket. Remove the bearing bracket bolt and pull out the center driveshaft through the center bearing bracket. Discard the bolt and purchase a new one.
16. Disconnect the left steering knuckle from the lower arm. Pull the steering knuckle outward and remove the driveshaft.
17. Remove the stabilizer bar. On 1992 models, disconnect the steering gear housing from the front suspension member and disconnect the exhaust.
18. With a transaxle jack and block of wood, raise the transaxle and engine slightly and disconnect the left engine mounting.
19. Remove the transaxle mounting bolts from the engine.
20. Lower the left side of the engine and remove the transaxle. On 1992 models, remove the remaining components from the front suspension member and remove it. Then remove the engine as described.
21. Clean the mating surfaces of grease and dirt in preparation for reinstallation.

To Install:

22. Move the transaxle into position so that the input shaft spline is aligned with the clutch disc.
23. Install the transaxle into the engine and secure with the lower mounting bolts. Torque the 10mm mounting bolts to 47 ft. lbs. and 12mm bolts to 34 ft. lbs.
24. Connect the left engine mounting and torque the mounting bolts to specifications. On 1992 models, install the front suspension member and other components related to it and torque to specifications.
25. Insert the center driveshaft into the transaxle through the center bearing bracket. Secure the center driveshaft with the snapring. Install the new bolt into the bearing bracket and torque the bolt to specifications.
26. Connect both driveshafts and install the six retaining bolts. Have an assistant depress the brake pedal and torque the bolts to specifications.
27. Connect the left steering knuckle to the lower arm. Torque the bolts to specifications.
28. Install the engine mounting center member with the four bolts. Torque the bolts to specifications.
29. Install the front and rear engine mounting bolts and torque the bolts to specifications.
30. Install the suspension lower cross member. Torque the bolts to specifications.
31. Connect the speedometer cable.
32. Fill the transaxle to the proper level with a good grade of Dexron®II transmission fluid.
33. Install the under covers.
34. Install the upper transaxle mounting bolts and torque to specifications.
35. Connect the ground cable and electrical connector to the back-up switch.
36. Install the starter.
37. Connect the control levers.
38. Install the clutch tube bracket with the clutch release cylinder and tube clamp.
39. Connect the negative battery cable, the air cleaner and the cruise control actuator, if removed.
40. Check the front wheel alignment.
41. Perform a road test and check for any unusual noises or vibrations.

1988 E56F2 and E56F5 (All-Trac 4-Wheel Drive)

➧ SEE FIGS. 9 AND 10

➡ The transaxle on the All-Trac 4-Wheel Drive models is removed with the engine. For engine removal and installation procedures refer to Section 3.

The cylinder block rib on these model engines contacts the transfer case. When disconnecting the transaxle from the engine the following points must be observed.

- After the engine has been secured to a suitable engine holding fixture, pull the transaxle straight out until there is approximately 50-75mm clearance between the engine and the transaxle case.

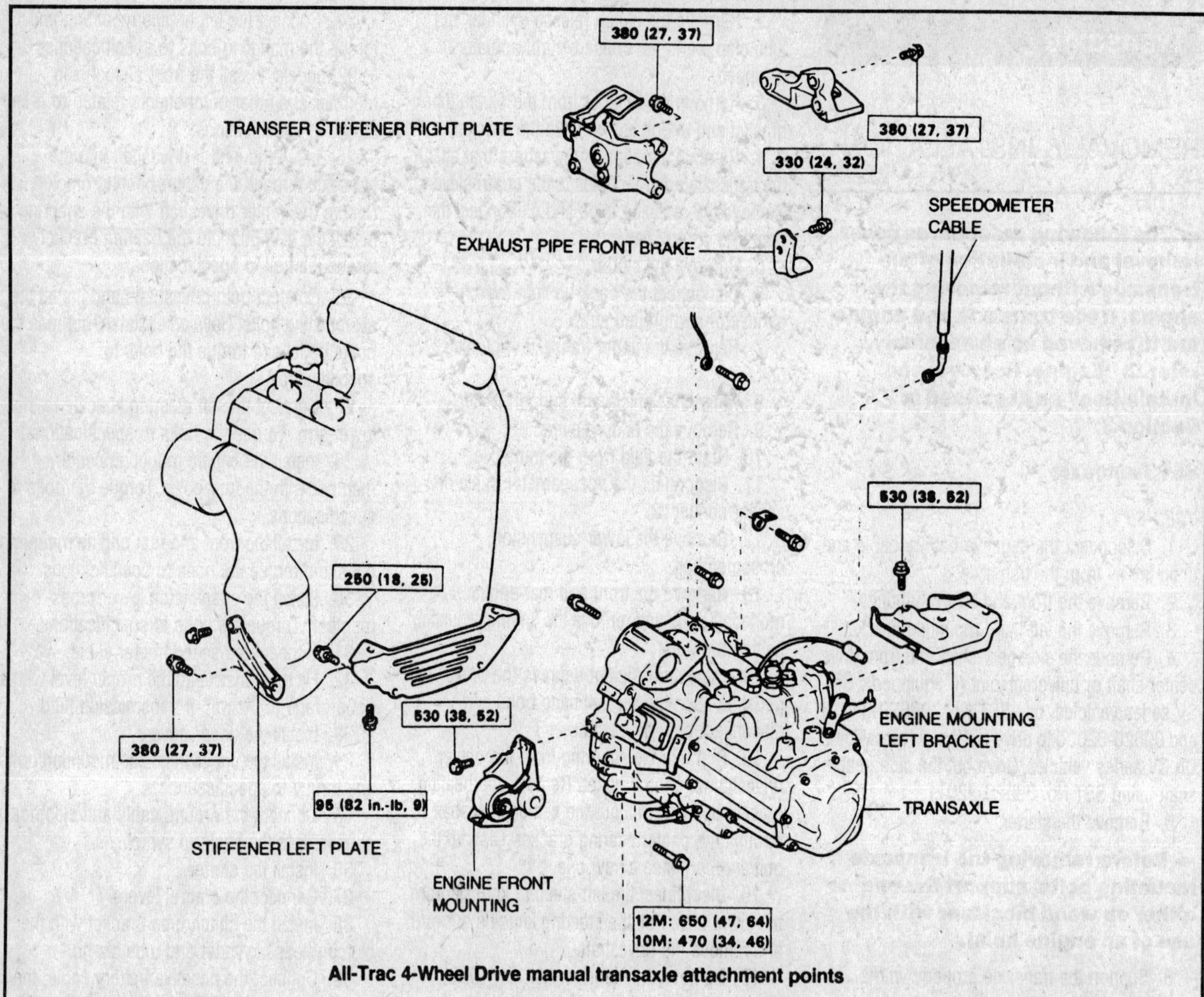

FIG.9 All-Trac 4-wheel drive manual transaxle attachment points

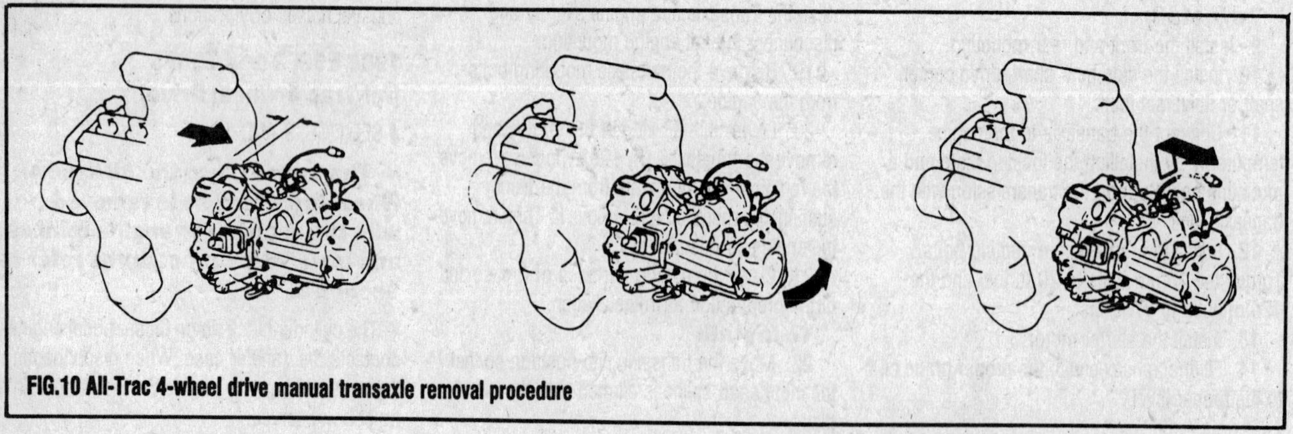

FIG.10 All-Trac 4-wheel drive manual transaxle removal procedure

• Move the transmission case cover in the proper direction (follow directional arrow on the illustration).

• Support the transfer output shaft and pull out the entire transaxle assembly.

1989-90 E56F5 (All-Trac 4-Wheel Drive)

➧ SEE FIGS. 9 AND 10

1. Remove the engine/transaxle assembly.
2. Remove the transfer case stiffener plate and the exhaust pipe front brake.
3. Remove the left stiffener plate and the front engine mount.
4. Remove the left engine mount bracket and then separate the transaxle from the engine.
5. Installation is in the reverse order of removal. Tighten the 12mm transaxle-to-engine mounting bolts to 47 ft. lbs. (64 Nm) and the 10mm bolts to 34 ft. lbs. (46 Nm).

E52 Transaxle

➧ SEE FIGS. 11 AND 12

1. Disconnect the negative battery cable. Remove the clutch release cylinder and tube clamp. Remove the clutch tube bracket.
2. Disconnect the control cables. Disconnect the back-up light switch electrical connector. Remove the ground strap.
3. Remove the starter assembly. Remove the transaxle upper mounting bolts.
4. Raise and support the vehicle safely. Remove the under covers. Drain the transaxle fluid. Disconnect the speedometer cable.
5. Remove the suspension lower crossmember. Remove the engine mounting centermember.
6. Disconnect both driveshafts. Remove the center driveshaft. Disconnect the left steering knuckle from the lower control arm. Remove the stabilizer bar.
7. Properly support the engine and remove the left engine mount.
8. Properly support the transaxle assembly. Remove the engine-to-transaxle bolts, lower the left side of the engine and carefully ease the transaxle out of the engine compartment.

To Install:

9. Install the transaxle and tighten the 12mm mounting bolts to 47 ft. lbs. (64 Nm) and the 10mm bolts to 34 ft. lbs. (46 Nm).
10. Tighten the left engine mount to 38 ft. lbs. (52 Nm). Tighten the 4 center engine mount bolts to 29 ft. lbs. (39 Nm). Tighten the front and rear engine mount bolts to 32 ft. lbs. (43 Nm).
11. Tighten the lower crossmember bolts to 153 ft. lbs. (207 Nm) – 4 outer bolts; and, 29 ft. lbs. (39 Nm) – 2 inner bolts.
12. Fill the transaxle with gear oil and perform road test.

E53 Transaxle

➧ SEE FIGS. 13 AND 14

1. Disconnect the negative battery cable. Remove the air cleaner assembly and the cruise control actuator.
2. Remove the clutch release cylinder and bracket. Remove the clutch accumulator and the tube clamp.
3. Remove the starter assembly. Disconnect the back-up light switch electrical connector. Remove the ground straps.
4. Disconnect the control cables.
5. Remove the upper 3 transaxle mounting bolts.
6. Disconnect the vehicle speed sensor connector.
7. Raise and support the vehicle safely. Remove the under covers. Drain the transaxle fluid.
8. Remove the exhaust front pipe and driveshaft.
9. Remove the steering gear housing from the front suspension member.
10. Remove the stiffener plate and the engine shock absorber.
11. Remove the engine front and rear mounting set bolts and nuts.
12. Remove the engine left mounting, the steering cooler set bolts, then remove the front suspension member.
13. Properly support the transaxle assembly. Remove the engine-to-transaxle bolts, lower the left side of the engine and carefully ease the transaxle out of the engine compartment.

To Install:

14. Installation is the reverse of removal. Tighten all fasteners to specifications.
15. Fill the transaxle with gear oil and perform road test.

OVERHAUL

1983-92 S51 Transaxle Disassembly

➧ SEE FIGS. 15–25

1. Remove the release fork, bearing, back-up light switch and speedometer driven gear.
2. Remove the front bearing retainer.
3. Remove the transmission case cover.
4. Remove No.3 shift fork lock bolt.
5. Using a dial indicator, measure the 5th gear thrust clearance. Standard clearance is 0.20-0.40mm with a maximum clearance of 0.45mm.
6. Loosen the locknut and remove the lock ball.
7. Remove the selecting bellcrank.
8. Remove the shift and select lever assembly.
9. Unstake the output shaft locknut using a small cold chisel.
10. Engage the gear double meshing.
11. Remove the lock nut.

➡ The locknut has left-hand threads.

12. Disengage the gear double meshing.
13. Using 2 prybars and a hammer, tap out the No. 3 hub sleeve snapring.
14. Remove the No.3 shift fork shifting key retainer.
15. Using 3 case cover set bolts, tighten the 3 bolts a little at a time and remove hub sleeve No. 3 and shift fork.
16. Remove 5th gear, synchronizer ring, needle roller bearing and spacer.
17. Remove 5th driven gear using SST No. 09950-20017 or equivalent puller.
18. Remove rear bearing retainer.
19. Remove 2 bearing snaprings by using snapring pliers.
20. Remove reverse idler gear shaft lock bolt.
21. Remove differential side bearing retainer and shim.
22. To remove transmission case, remove the seventeen bolts and tap off the case with a plastic hammer.
23. Shift the reverse fork shaft into reverse.
24. Remove the two bolts and pull off the reverse shift arm.
25. Remove reverse idler gear and shaft by pulling out the shaft.
26. Remove shift fork shaft No. 1, shift head No. 1, shift forks No. 1 and No. 2.
27. Drive out the slotted spring pin from fork shaft No. 1.
28. Drive out the slotted spring pin from shift head and fork shaft No. 1.
29. Pull out fork shaft No. 1 with the shift head and shift forks.
30. Remove reverse shift fork and interlock pin.
31. Remove the No.2 fork shaft straight screw plug.
32. Using a pin punch and hammer, drive out the No.2 fork shaft slotted spring pin.
33. Pull out the No.2 fork shaft.
34. Remove input and output shaft together from transaxle case.
35. Remove differential assembly.
36. Remove the magnet from the transaxle.
37. Using a feeler gauge, measure the 3rd and 4th gear thrust clearance.

Standard clearance:

• 3rd gear — 0.10-0.25mm
• 4th gear — 0.20-0.45mm

Maximum clearance:

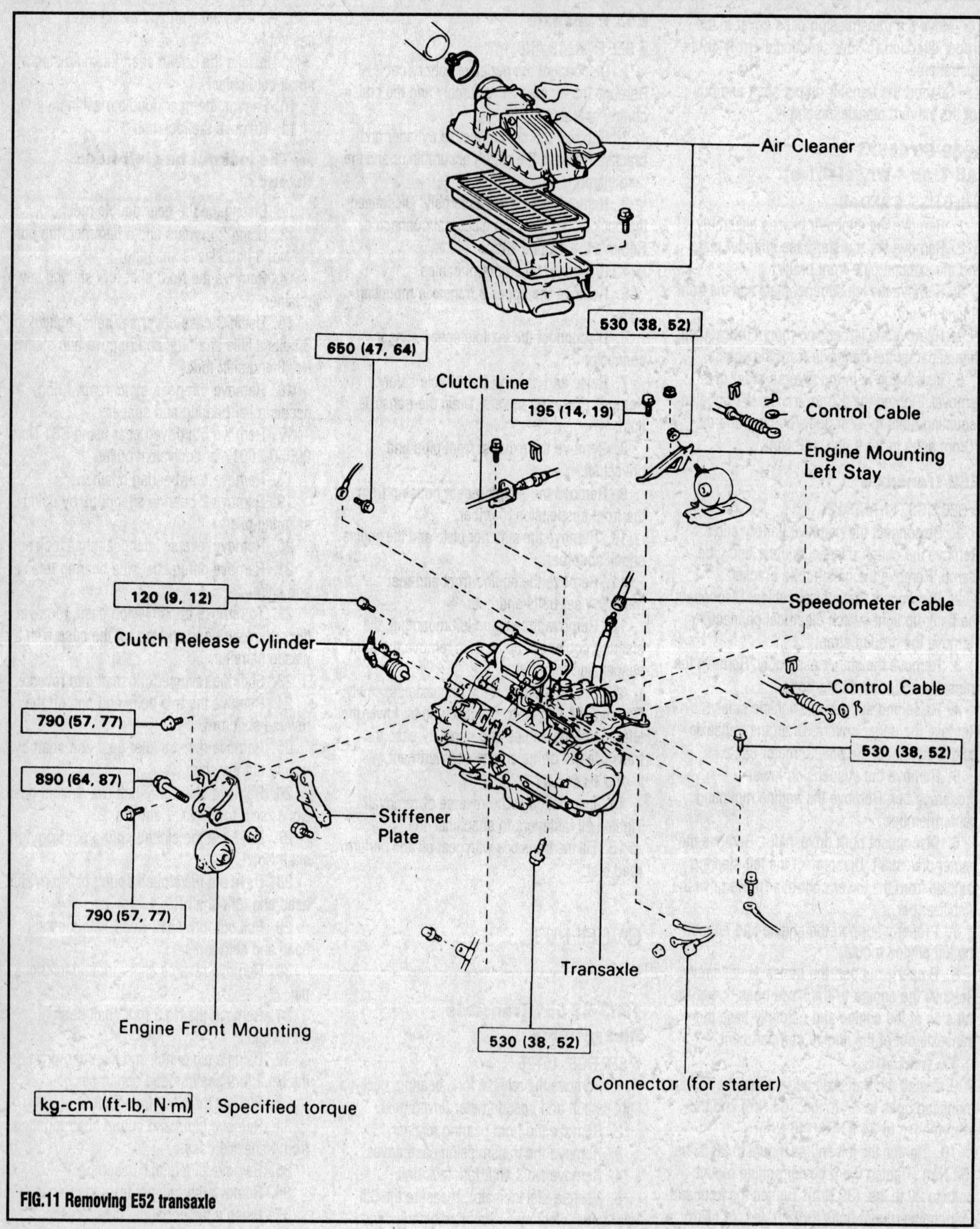
Air Cleaner
530 (38, 52)
650 (47, 64)
Clutch Line
195 (14, 19)
Control Cable
Engine Mounting
Left Stay
120 (9, 12)
Speedometer Cable
Clutch Release Cylinder
Control Cable
790 (57, 77)
530 (38, 52)
890 (64, 87)
Stiffener
Plate
790 (57, 77)
Transaxle
Engine Front Mounting
530 (38, 52)
Connector (for starter)
kg-cm (ft-lb, N·m) : Specified torque

FIG.11 Removing E52 transaxle

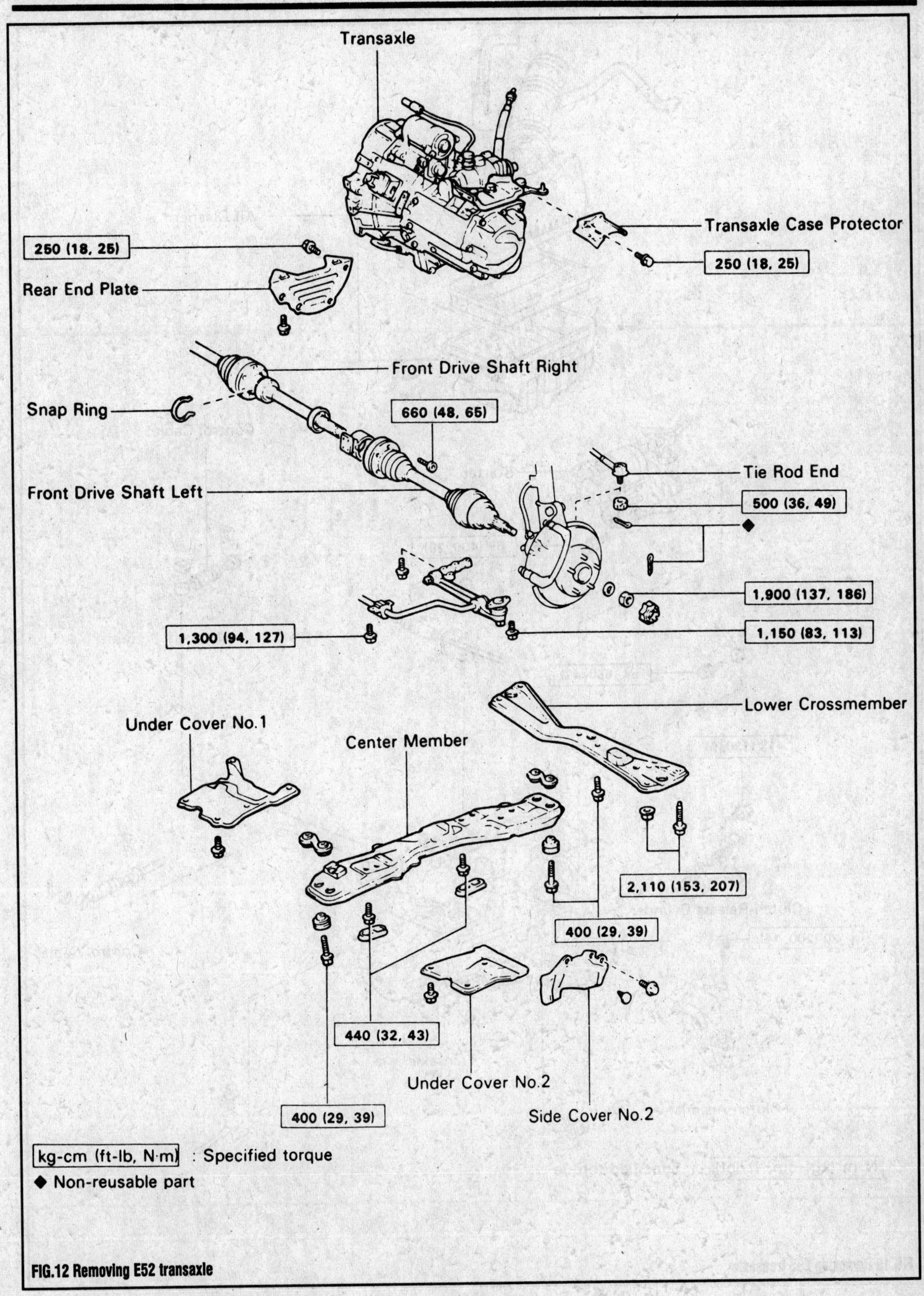
Transaxle
Transaxle Case Protector
250 (18, 25)
250 (18, 25)
Rear End Plate
Front Drive Shaft Right
Snap Ring
660 (48, 65)
Tie Rod End
Front Drive Shaft Left
500 (36, 49)
◆
1,900 (137, 186)
1,300 (94, 127)
1,150 (83, 113)
Lower Crossmember
Under Cover No.1
Center Member
2,110 (153, 207)
400 (29, 39)
440 (32, 43)
Under Cover No.2
400 (29, 39)
Side Cover No.2
kg-cm (ft-lb, N·m) : Specified torque
◆ Non-reusable part

FIG.12 Removing E52 transaxle

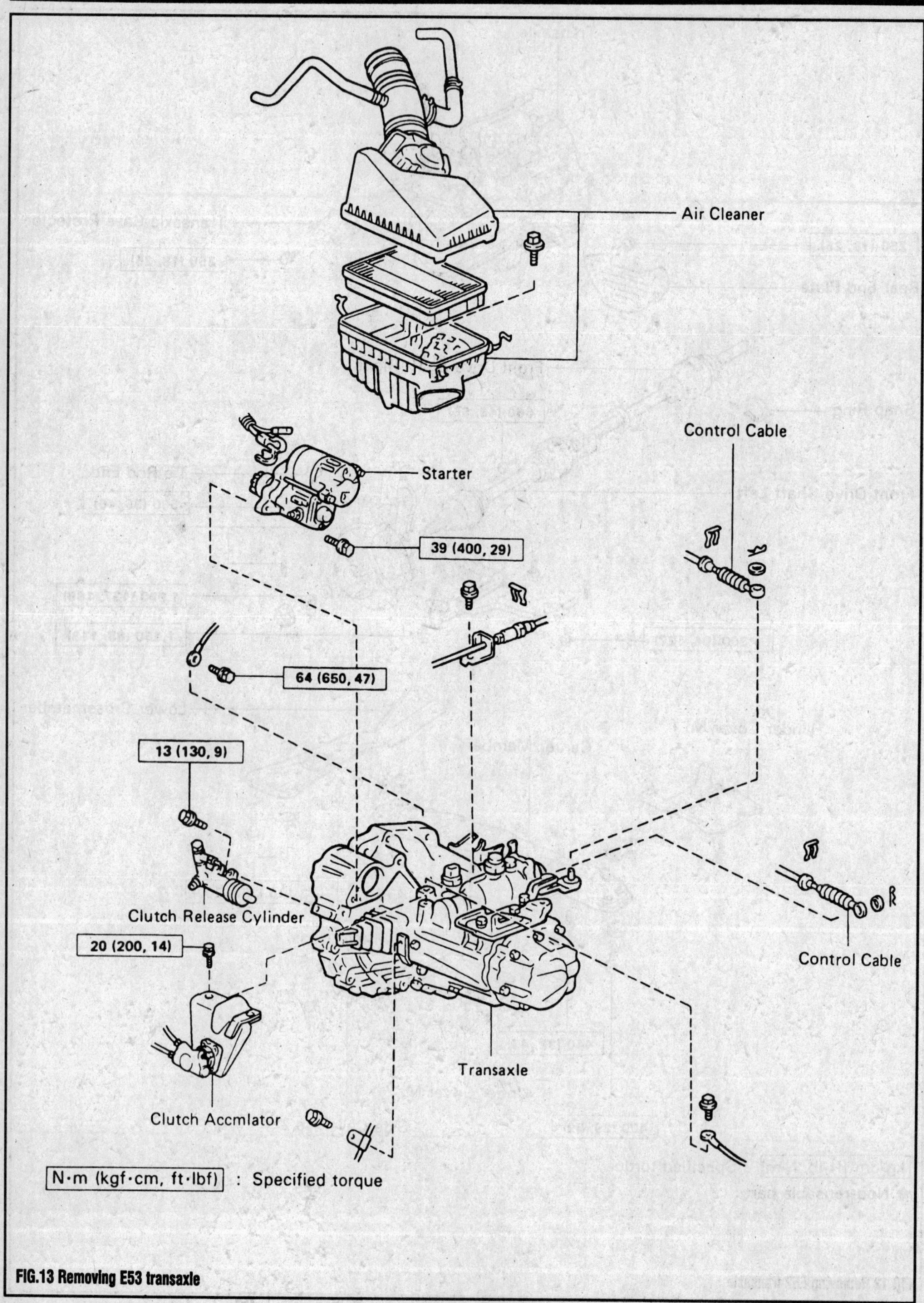

FIG.13 Removing E53 transaxle

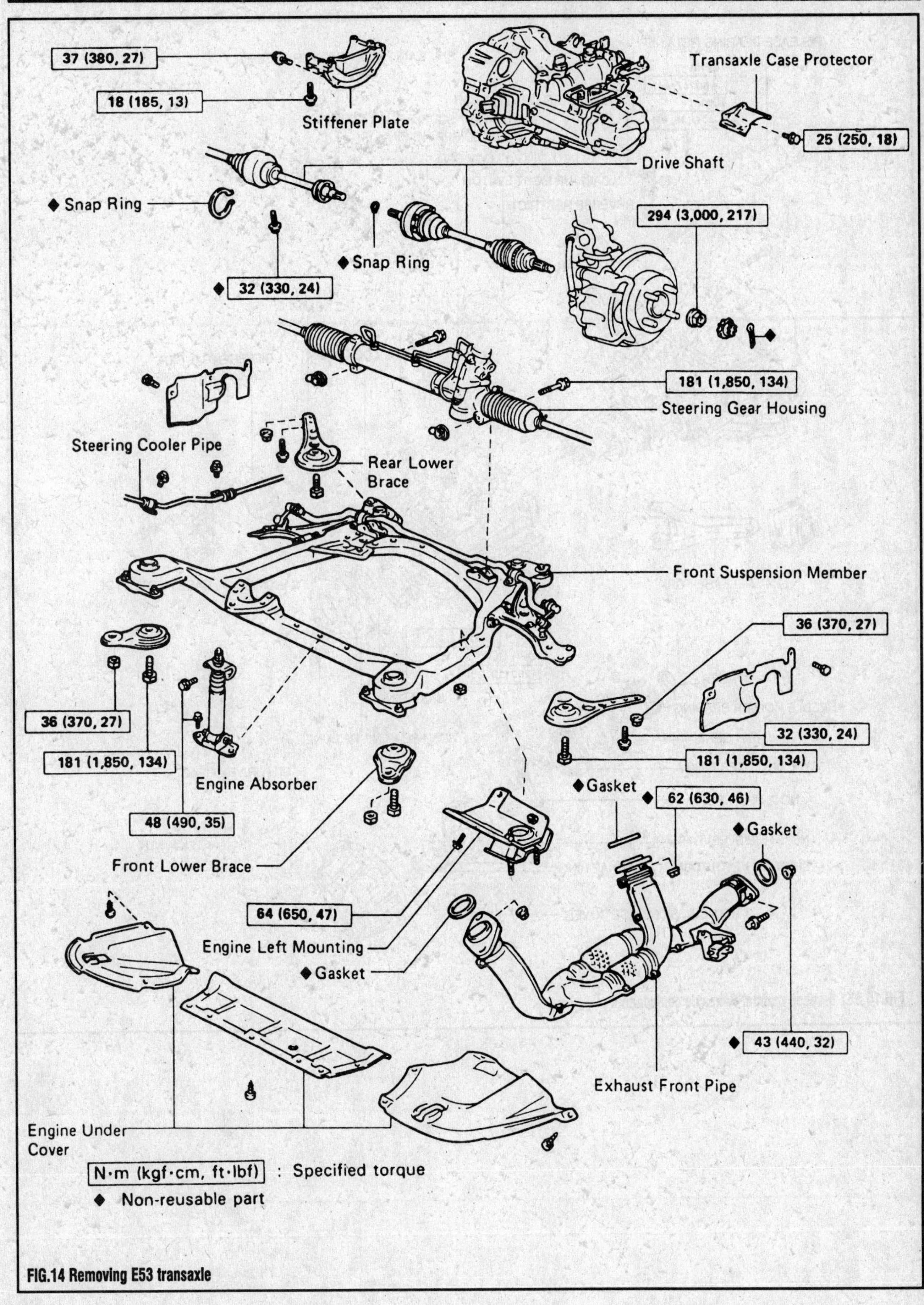
37 (380, 27)
18 (185, 13)
Stiffener Plate
Transaxle Case Protector
25 (250, 18)
Drive Shaft
◆ Snap Ring
◆ Snap Ring
294 (3,000, 217)
◆ 32 (330, 24)
181 (1,850, 134)
Steering Gear Housing
Steering Cooler Pipe
Rear Lower Brace
Front Suspension Member
36 (370, 27)
36 (370, 27)
32 (330, 24)
181 (1,850, 134)
181 (1,850, 134)
Engine Absorber
◆Gasket
◆ 62 (630, 46)
48 (490, 35)
◆Gasket
Front Lower Brace
64 (650, 47)
Engine Left Mounting
◆Gasket
◆ 43 (440, 32)
Exhaust Front Pipe
Engine Under Cover
N·m (kgf·cm, ft·lbf) : Specified torque
◆ Non-reusable part

FIG.14 Removing E53 transaxle

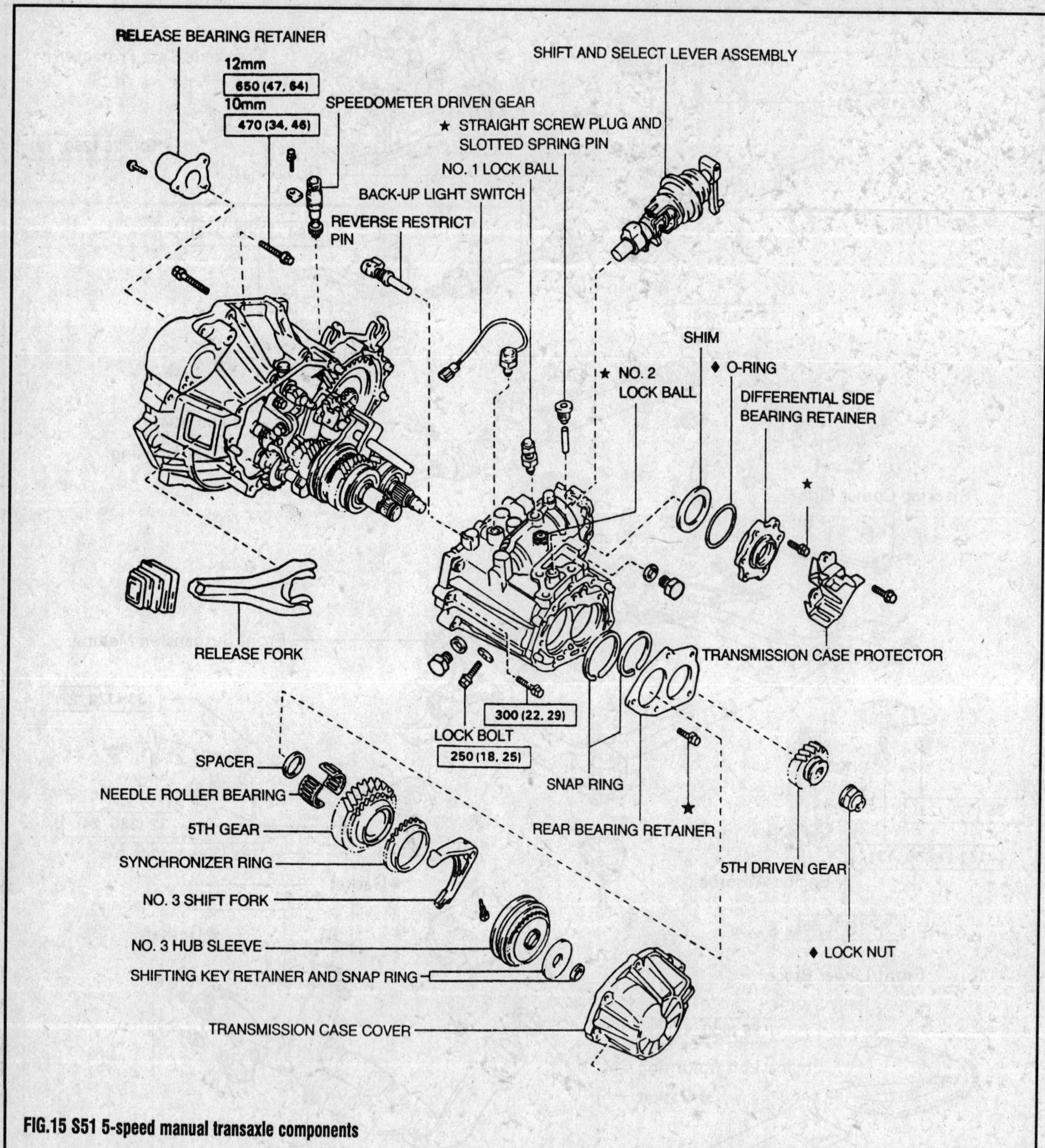
RELEASE BEARING RETAINER
12mm
650 (47, 64)
10mm
470 (34, 46)
SPEEDOMETER DRIVEN GEAR
SHIFT AND SELECT LEVER ASSEMBLY
★ STRAIGHT SCREW PLUG AND SLOTTED SPRING PIN
NO. 1 LOCK BALL
BACK-UP LIGHT SWITCH
REVERSE RESTRICT PIN
SHIM
♦ O-RING
★ NO. 2 LOCK BALL
DIFFERENTIAL SIDE BEARING RETAINER
★
RELEASE FORK
TRANSMISSION CASE PROTECTOR
300 (22, 29)
LOCK BOLT
250 (18, 25)
SPACER
NEEDLE ROLLER BEARING
SNAP RING
★
5TH GEAR
REAR BEARING RETAINER
SYNCHRONIZER RING
5TH DRIVEN GEAR
NO. 3 SHIFT FORK
NO. 3 HUB SLEEVE
♦ LOCK NUT
SHIFTING KEY RETAINER AND SNAP RING
TRANSMISSION CASE COVER

FIG.15 S51 5-speed manual transaxle components

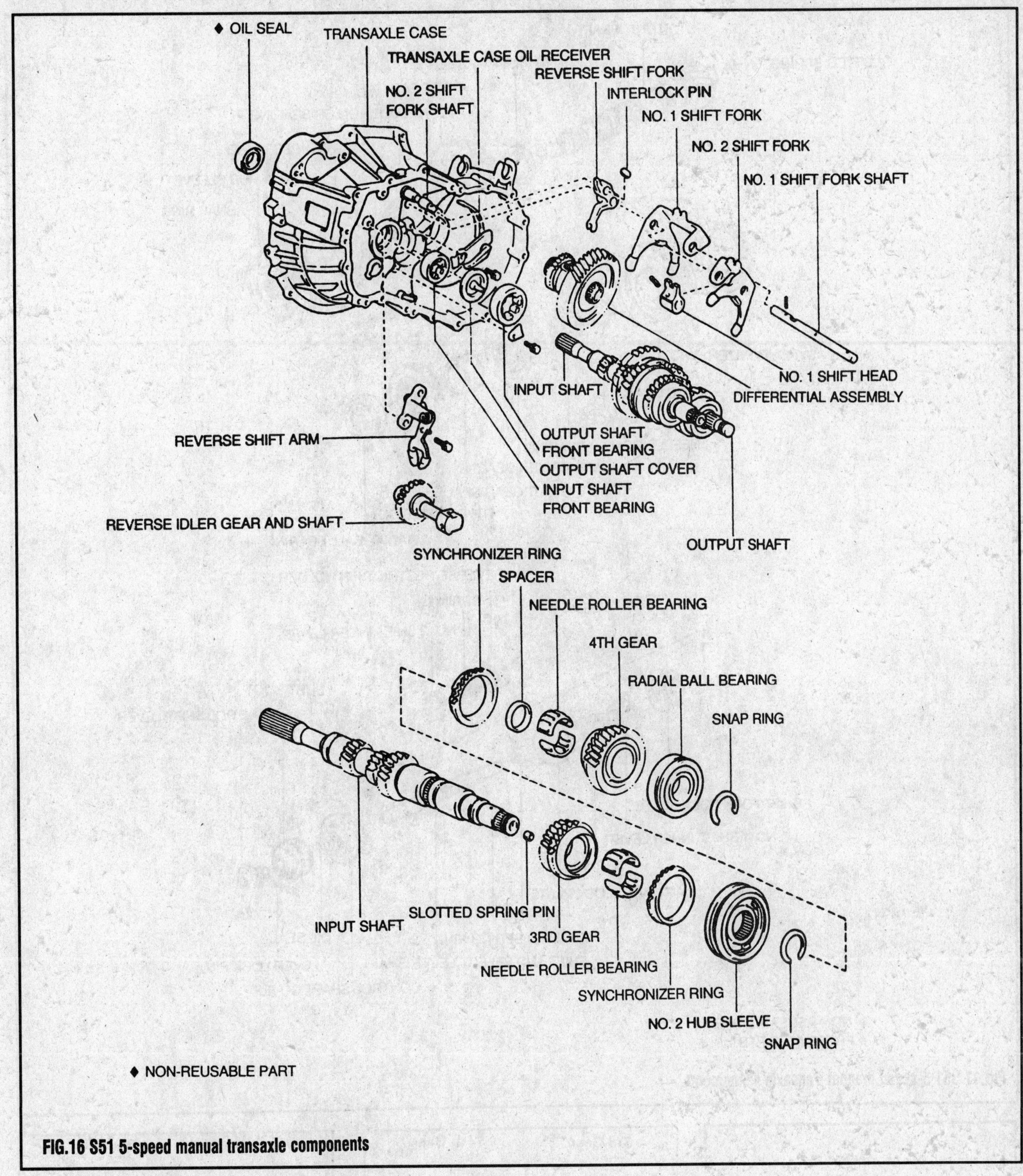
♦ OIL SEAL
TRANSAXLE CASE
TRANSAXLE CASE OIL RECEIVER
REVERSE SHIFT FORK
NO. 2 SHIFT FORK SHAFT
INTERLOCK PIN
NO. 1 SHIFT FORK
NO. 2 SHIFT FORK
NO. 1 SHIFT FORK SHAFT
NO. 1 SHIFT HEAD
DIFFERENTIAL ASSEMBLY
INPUT SHAFT
OUTPUT SHAFT FRONT BEARING
OUTPUT SHAFT COVER
INPUT SHAFT FRONT BEARING
REVERSE SHIFT ARM
REVERSE IDLER GEAR AND SHAFT
OUTPUT SHAFT
SYNCHRONIZER RING
SPACER
NEEDLE ROLLER BEARING
4TH GEAR
RADIAL BALL BEARING
SNAP RING
INPUT SHAFT
SLOTTED SPRING PIN
3RD GEAR
NEEDLE ROLLER BEARING
SYNCHRONIZER RING
NO. 2 HUB SLEEVE
SNAP RING
♦ NON-REUSABLE PART

FIG.16 S51 5-speed manual transaxle components

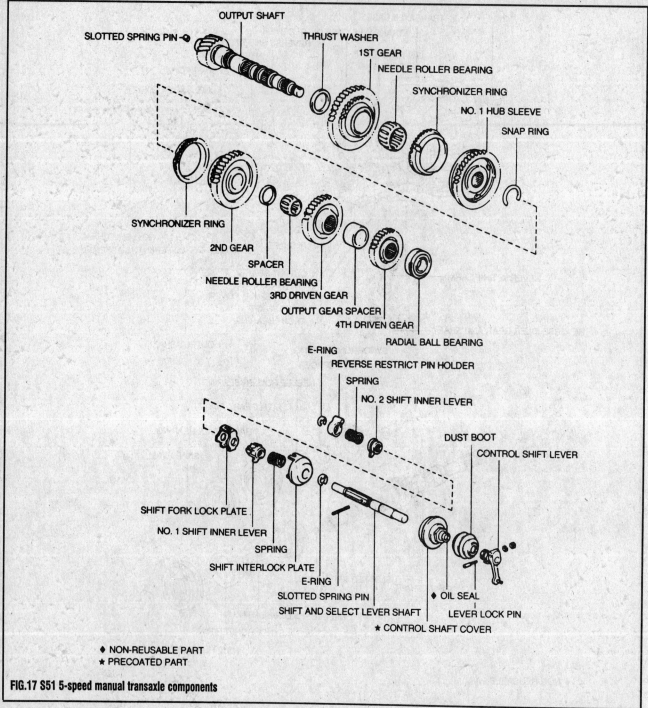

OUTPUT SHAFT
SLOTTED SPRING PIN
THRUST WASHER
1ST GEAR
NEEDLE ROLLER BEARING
SYNCHRONIZER RING
NO. 1 HUB SLEEVE
SNAP RING
SYNCHRONIZER RING
2ND GEAR
SPACER
NEEDLE ROLLER BEARING
3RD DRIVEN GEAR
OUTPUT GEAR SPACER
4TH DRIVEN GEAR
RADIAL BALL BEARING
E-RING
REVERSE RESTRICT PIN HOLDER
SPRING
NO. 2 SHIFT INNER LEVER
DUST BOOT
CONTROL SHIFT LEVER
SHIFT FORK LOCK PLATE
NO. 1 SHIFT INNER LEVER
SPRING
SHIFT INTERLOCK PLATE
E-RING
SLOTTED SPRING PIN
SHIFT AND SELECT LEVER SHAFT
♦ OIL SEAL
LEVER LOCK PIN
★ CONTROL SHAFT COVER

♦ NON-REUSABLE PART
★ PRECOATED PART

FIG.17 S51 5-speed manual transaxle components

FIG.18 Measuring 5th gear thrust clearance

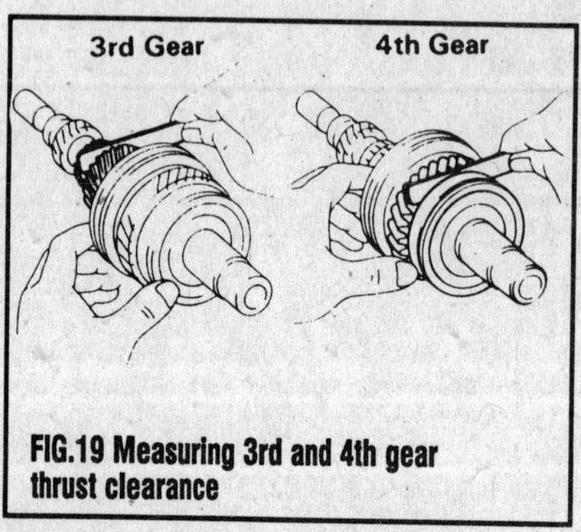

FIG.19 Measuring 3rd and 4th gear thrust clearance

FIG.20 Measuring 1st and 2nd gear thrust clearance

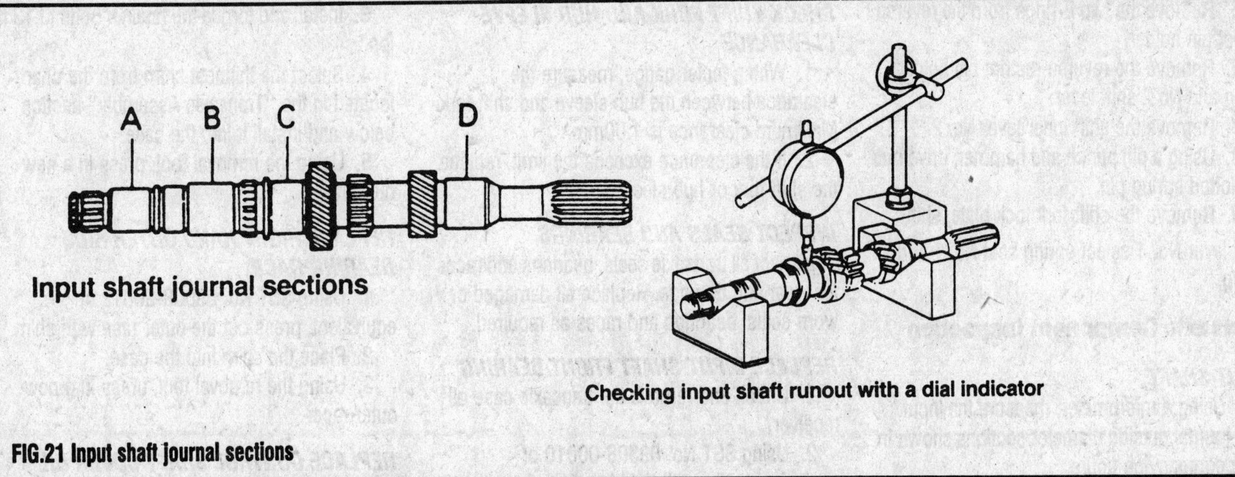

FIG.21 Input shaft journal sections

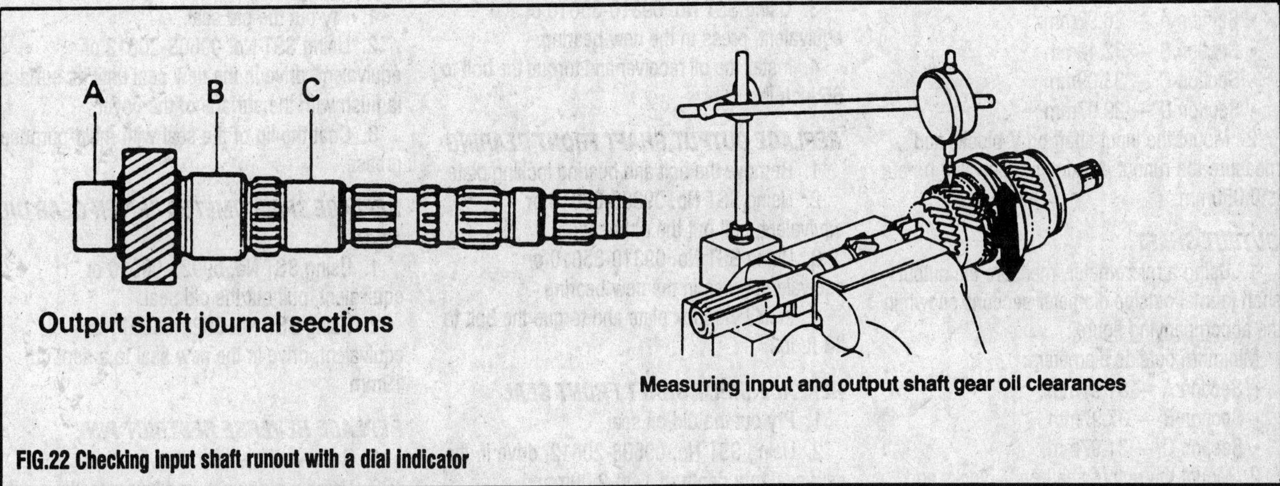

FIG.22 Checking input shaft runout with a dial indicator

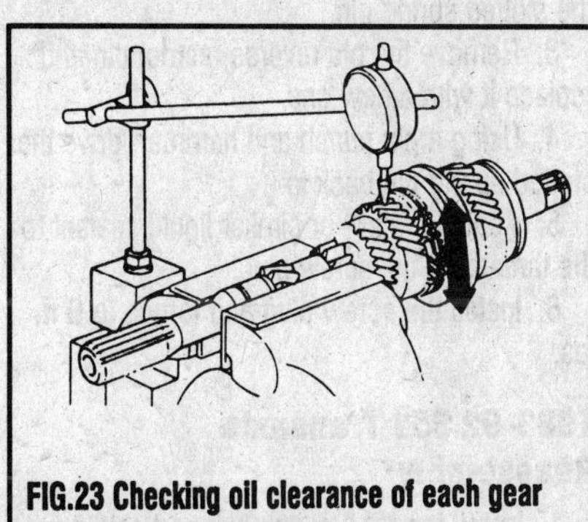
FIG.23 Checking oil clearance of each gear

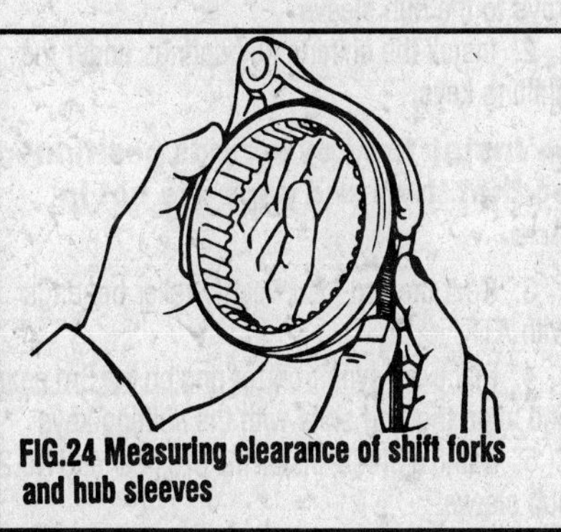
FIG.24 Measuring clearance of shift forks and hub sleeves

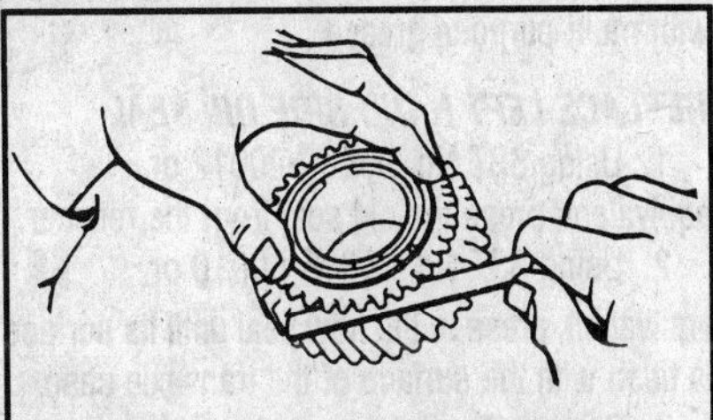
FIG.25 Measuring clearance between the synchronizer ring back and the gear spline end

- 3rd gear — 0.30mm
- 4th gear — 0.50mm

38. Remove snapring from input shaft.
39. Using a press, remove the radial ball bearing and 4th gear.
40. Remove the needle roller bearings, synchronizer ring and spacer.
41. Remove the snapring with snapring pliers.
42. Remove hub sleeve No. 2 assembly, 3rd gear, synchronizer ring and needle roller bearing.
43. Measure 1st/2nd gear thrust clearance by using a feeler gauge.

Standard Clearance
- 1st gear — 0.10-0.29mm
- 2nd gear — 0.20-0.44mm

Maximum clearance:
- 1st gear — 0.35mm
- 2nd gear — 0.50mm

44. Using a press, remove the radial ball bearing, 4th driven gear and spacer.
45. Shift hub sleeve No. 1 into 1st gear.
46. Using a press, remove the 3rd driven gear and 2nd gear.
47. Remove the needle roller bearing, spacer and synchronizer ring.
48. Remove the snapring.
49. Using a press, remove the No.1 hub sleeve, 1st gear and synchronizer ring.
50. Remove the needle roller bearing and spacer.
51. Remove the shift lever lock pin and nut.
52. Remove the control shift lever.
53. Remove the control shaft cover dust boot.
54. Remove the control shaft cover.

55. Remove the two E-rings from the reverse restrict pin holder.

56. Remove the reverse restrict pin holder, spring and No.2 shift lever.

57. Remove the shift inner lever No. 2.

58. Using a pin punch and hammer, drive out the slotted spring pin.

59. Remove the shift fork lock plate, shift inner lever No. 1 select spring seat No. 1 and spring.

Transaxle Component Inspection

INPUT SHAFT

1. Using a micrometer, measure the input shaft journal outside diameter sections shown in the accompanying figure.

Minimum outer diameters:

- Section A — 26.97mm
- Section B — 32.42mm
- Section C — 33.09mm
- Section D — 29.97mm

2. Mount the input shaft on V-blocks and measure the runout. Maximum allowable runout is 0.050mm.

OUTPUT SHAFT

1. Using a micrometer, measure the output shaft journal outside diameter sections shown in the accompanying figure.

Minimum outside diameters:

- Section A — 31.97mm
- Section B — 37.97mm
- Section C — 31.97mm

2. Mount the output shaft on V-blocks and measure the runout. Maximum allowable runout is 0.050mm.

CHECK GEAR OIL CLEARANCE

Using a dial indicator, measure the oil clearance between the gear and the input or output shaft with the needle roller bearing installed.

Standard clearance:

- 1st, 2nd, 3rd, 4th gears — 0.009-0.053mm
- 5th gear — 0.009-0.050mm

Maximum clearance:

- All gears — 0.07mm

If the clearance exceeds the maximum limit, replace the gear, bearing or shaft.

INSPECT SYNCHRONIZER RINGS

1. Turn the ring and push it in to check the braking action.

2. With a feeler gauge, measure the clearance between the back of the ring and gear spline end. Minimum clearance is 0.6mm.

3. If the clearance is less than the limit, replace the ring.

CHECK SHIFT FORK AND HUB SLEEVE CLEARANCE

1. With a feeler gauge, measure the clearance between the hub sleeve and shift fork. Maximum clearance is 1.00mm.

2. If the clearance exceeds the limit, replace the shift fork or hub sleeve.

INSPECT SEALS AND BEARINGS

Inspect all transaxle seals, bearings and races for wear and damage. Replace all damaged or worn seals, bearings and races as required.

REPLACE INPUT SHAFT FRONT BEARING

1. Unbolt and remove the transaxle case oil receiver.

2. Using SST No. 09308-00010 or equivalent, pull out the old bearing.

3. Using SST No. 09310-35010 or equivalent, press in the new bearing.

4. Install the oil receiver and torque the bolt to 65 inch lbs.

REPLACE OUTPUT SHAFT FRONT BEARING

1. Remove the bolt and bearing locking plate.

2. Using SST No. 09308-00010 or equivalent, pull out the old bearing.

3. Using SST No. 09310-35010 or equivalent, press in the new bearing.

4. Install the lock plate and torque the bolt to 13 ft. lbs.

REPLACE INPUT SHAFT FRONT SEAL

1. Pry out the old oil seal.

2. Using SST No. 09608-20012, drive in the new seal to a depth of 1.00-2.00mm.

3. Once installed, coat the lip of the new seal with multi-purpose grease.

REPLACE LEFT HAND SIDE OIL SEAL

1. Using SST No. 09608-20012 or equivalent, press the old seal from the retainer.

2. Using SST No. 09316-60010 or equivalent, press in the new seal until its surface is flush with the surface of the transaxle case.

3. Coat the lip of the new seal with multi-purpose grease.

REPLACE RIGHT HAND SIDE OIL SEAL

1. Drive the old seal from the retainer with a screwdriver or punch.

2. Using SST No. 09316-60010 or equivalent, press in the new seal until its surface is flush with the surface of the transaxle case.

3. Coat the lip of the new seal with multi-purpose grease.

REPLACE LEFT HAND OUTER SIDE BEARING RACE

1. Using SST No. 09608-20012 or equivalent, press out the outer race.

2. Install the bearing retainer without the O-ring.

3. Install and torque the retainer bolts to 13 ft. lbs.

4. Select the thinnest shim from the chart located in the "Transaxle Assembly" section below and install it into the case.

5. Using the removal tool, press in a new outer race.

REPLACE RIGHT HAND OUTER SIDE BEARING RACE

1. Using SST No. 09608-20012 or equivalent, press out the outer race with shim.

2. Place the shim into the case.

3. Using the removal tool, press in a new outer race.

REPLACE CONTROL SHAFT COVER OIL SEAL

1. Pry out the old seal.

2. Using SST No. 09608-20012 or equivalent, drive in the new seal until its surface is flush with the surface of the cover.

3. Coat the lip of the seal with multi-purpose grease.

REPLACE SPEEDOMETER DRIVEN GEAR OIL SEAL

1. Using SST No. 09921-00010 or equivalent, pull out the old seal.

2. Using SST No. 09201-60011 or equivalent, drive in the new seal to a depth of 19mm.

REPLACE REVERSE RESTRICT PIN

1. Remove the screw plug.

2. Using a pin punch and hammer, drive out the slotted spring pin.

3. Remove the old reverse restrict pin and replace it with a new one.

4. Using a pin punch and hammer, drive the slotted spring pin back in.

5. Apply Loctite® or similar liquid sealant to the threads of the screw plug.

6. Install the screw plug and torque to 9 ft. lbs.

1983–92 S51 Transaxle Reassembly

1. Install the No.2 clutch hub and shifting keys to the hub sleeve.

2. Install the shifting key springs under the shifting keys.

➡ Install the key springs positioned so that their end gaps are not in line.

3. Coat the 3rd gear needle roller bearings with ATF.

4. Place the synchronizer ring on the 3rd gear and align the ring slots with the shifting keys.

5. Using a press, install the 3rd gear and No.2 hub sleeve.

6. Select a snapring that will allow minimum axial play and install it on the shaft.

7. Using a feeler gauge, measure the 3rd gear thrust clearance.

- Standard clearance: 0.10-0.25mm
- Maximum clearance: 0.30mm

8. Install the synchronizer ring spacer.

9. Coat the needle roller bearing with ATF.

10. Place the synchronizer ring on the gear and align the ring slots with the shifting keys.

11. Press in the radial ball bearing.

12. Select a snapring that will allow minimum axial play and install it on the shaft.

13. Measure 4th gear thrust clearance by using a feeler gauge and measure the 4th gear thrust clearance.

- Standard clearance: 0.20-0.45mm
- Maximum clearance: 0.50mm

14. Install the No.1 clutch hub and shifting keys to the No.1 hub sleeve.

15. Install the shifting key springs under the shifting keys.

➡ Install the key springs positioned so that their end gaps are not in line.

16. Coat the 1st gear needle roller bearing with ATF.

17. Place the 1st gear synchronizer ring on the gear and align the ring slots with the shifting keys.

18. Using a press, install the 1st gear and hub sleeve No. 1.

19. Install snapring and select a snapring that will allow minimum axial play and install it on the shaft.

20. Measure 1st gear thrust clearance by using a feeler gauge and measure the 1st gear thrust clearance.

- Standard clearance: 0.10-0.30mm
- Maximum clearance: 0.35mm

21. Install the 2nd gear spacer.

22. Place the synchronizer ring on the 2nd gear and align the ring slots with the shifting keys.

23. Coat the the 2nd gear needle roller bearing with ATF.

24. Install the 2nd gear.

25. Using a press, install the 3rd driven gear.

26. Using a feeler gauge, measure the 2nd gear thrust clearance.

- Standard clearance: 0.20-0.44mm
- Maximum clearance: 0.50mm

27. Install the output gear spacer.

28. Press in the 4th driven gear and bearing.

29. Install the transaxle magnet.

30. Adjust differential side bearing preload by performing the following:

a. Install the differential to the transaxle case.

b. Install the transmission case with the used gasket.

c. Install and torque the case bolts. Torque the bolts to 22 ft. lbs.

d. Install the thinnest shim into the transmission case.

e. Install the bearing retainer without an O-ring.

f. Install and torque the retainer bolts. Torque the bolts to 13 ft. lbs..

g. Measure the preload. Preload (starting): 8.7-13.9 inch lbs.

h. If the preload is not within specification, remove the bearing retainer.

i. Reselect a adjusting shim.

➡ The preload will change about 2.6-3.5 inch lbs. with each shim thickness.

31. If the preload is adjusted within specification, remove the bearing retainer, shim and transmission case with gasket. Be careful not to lose the adjusted shim.

32. Install the input and output shaft together.

33. Insert the No.2 fork shaft into the transaxle case and align the slotted spring pin.

34. Using a pin punch and hammer drive in the slotted spring pin.

35. Install the straight screw plug and torque it to 9 ft. lbs.

36. Insert the interlock pin to the reverse shift fork hole.

37. Install the reverse shift fork onto fork shaft No. 2.

38. Put the reverse shift arm pivot into the reverse shift fork and install the reverse shift arm to the transaxle case.

39. Shift the reverse shift arm into reverse.

40. Install and torque the retaining bolts to 13 ft. lbs.

41. Install reverse idler gear and shaft by aligning the transaxle case slot and slotted spring pin.

42. Place shift forks No. 1 and No. 2 into the groove of hub sleeve No. 1 and No. 2.

43. Hold shift head No. 1 and insert fork shaft No. 1 into the transaxle case through shift fork No. 1, No. 2, shift head No. 1 and reverse shift fork.

44. Using a pin punch and hammer, drive the slotted spring pin into shift head No. 1 and fork shaft No. 1.

45. Shift the fork shaft into reverse.

46. Using a pin punch and hammer, drive the slotted spring pin into fork shaft No. 1.

47. Install the transmission case retaining bolts and torque them 22 ft. lbs.

48. Install the O-ring on the side bearing retainer.

49. Install the shim and side bearing retainer.

50. Install and torque the bearing retainer bolts to 13 ft. lbs.

51. Install and torque reverse idler gear shaft lock bolt to 18 ft. lbs.

52. Install the two bearing snaprings.

53. Install rear bearing retainer and torque the five bolts to 13 ft. lbs. Apply Loctite® or similar thread sealant to the bolt threads before installing them.

54. Using SST No. 09309, install the 5th driven gear.

55. Install the 5th gear spacer.

56. Coat the 5th gear needle roller bearings with ATF.

57. Install the 5th gear with the needle roller bearings and synchronizer ring.

58. Install the No.3 clutch hub and shifting keys to the No.3 hub sleeve.

59. Install the shifting key springs under the shifting keys.

➡ Install the key springs positioned so that their end gaps are not in line.

60. Support the tip of the input shaft with a spacer to raise the transaxle.

61. Drive in hub sleeve No. 3 with shift fork No. 3.

➡ Align the synchronizer ring slots with the shifting keys.

62. Using a dial indicator, measure 5th gear thrust clearance.

- Standard clearance: 0.20-0.40mm
- Maximum clearance: 0.45mm

63. Install the shifting key retainer.

64. Select a snapring that will allow minimum axial play and install it on the shaft.

65. Engage the gear double meshing and install the locknut. Torque the nut to 90 ft. lbs.

➡ The lock nut has left hand threads.

66. Disengage the gear double meshing and stake the lock nut with a small cold chisel.

67. Coat the shift lever shaft with ATF.

68. Install select spring seat No. 1, spring and E-ring.

69. Install shift inner lever No. 1 with the shift fork lock plate.

70. Align shift inner lever No. 2 with No. 1 and install it.

71. Install select spring seat No. 2 spring and E-ring.

72. Using a pin punch and hammer, drive in the slotted spring pin.

73. Install the control shaft cover and dust boot making sure that the air bleed is facing downward.

74. Install the control shift lever and insert the lever lock pin to the lever. Install the washer and lock nut.

75. Apply liquid sealer to the control shaft cover.

76. Install the shift and select lever and torque the control shaft cover to 27 ft. lbs.

77. Apply Loctite® sealant to the lock ball assembly threads. Install and torque the lock ball assembly to 17 ft. lbs.

78. Fully loosen the No.1 lock nut.

79. Screw in the lock ball fully.

80. Turn the lock ball to where the play at the shift outer lever tip is 0.10-0.50mm.

81. Hold the lock ball and torque the lock nut to 27 ft. lbs.

82. Check the shift outer level tip play. Acceptable tip play range is 0.10-0.50mm.

83. Install the selecting bellcrank.

84. Install the No.3 shift fork locking bolt and torque it to 13 ft. lbs.

85. Install the transmission case cover with the eight retaining bolts. Torque the bolts to 13 ft. lbs.

86. Install front bearing retainer and torque to 65 inch lbs.

87. Apply molybdenum disulphide lithium base grease to the following parts: release bearing hub inside groove, input shaft spline and release fork contact surface.

88. Install back-up light switch and torque to 33 ft. lbs.

89. Install speedometer driven gear.

1988–90 E56F5 and E56F2 Transaxle Disassembly

➧ SEE FIGS. 24–44

1. Remove the transmission from the vehicle and position it in a suitable holding fixture.

2. Remove the three bolts and five nuts attaching the transfer assembly to the transaxle. Using a rubber mallet, separate the transfer assembly from the transaxle.

3. Screw in a suitable bolt and washer into the side gear intermediate shaft and remove the shaft using SST No. 09910-00015 or equivalent.

4. Remove the release fork, bearing and boot.

5. Remove the back-up light switch and gasket from the transaxle case.

6. Remove the speedometer driven gear.

7. Remove the No. 2 selecting bellcrank and support.

8. Remove the shift and and select lever shaft lock bolt. Remove the gasket from the bolt.

9. Unbolt and remove the shift and select lever shaft assembly with the gasket.

10. Unbolt the transmission case cover (ten bolts). Using a rubber mallet, separate the cover from the transaxle.

11. Unstake and remove the output shaft lock nut with a small cold chisel. Disengage the double gear meshing.

12. Unbolt and remove the No. 3 hub sleeve and No. 3 shift fork.

13. Using SST. No. 09310-17010 or equivalent, remove the 5th driven gear.

14. Using a dial indicator, measure and record the 5th gear thrust clearance. Standard clearance is 0.10-0.57mm and maximum clearance is 0.65mm.

15. Using a dial indicator, measure and record the 5th gear oil clearance. Standard oil clearance is 0.010-0.057mm and maximum clearance is 0.07mm.

16. Tap out the snapring and using SST No. 09310-17010 or equivalent. Remove the No. 3 clutch hub with synchronizer ring and 5th gear.

17. Remove the needle roller bearing and spacer.

18. Remove the seven Torx® bolts and remove the rear bearing retainer and adjusting shim.

19. Remove the snapring from the input shaft rear bearing and remove the snaprings from the shift fork shafts.

20. Using SST No. 09313-30021 or equivalent, remove the plug, seat, spring and locking ball.

21. Remove the reverse idler gear shaft retaining bolt and bolt gasket.

22. Unbolt and remove the transmission case using a rubber mallet to coax the case loose.

➡ Fourteen bolts retain the transmission case side and three bolts retain the transaxle case side.

23. Remove the output shaft rear bearing outer race using a rubber mallet.

24. Remove the No. 2 oil pipe with gasket. Discard the gasket and purchase a new one.

25. Unbolt and remove the reverse shift arm bracket.

26. Remove the reverse idler gear, thrust washer and shaft.

27. Remove the plugs, seats, springs and balls.

28. Remove the three set bolts.

29. Pull up on the No. 3 shift fork shaft and remove the No. 1 shift fork shaft.

30. Remove the interlock roller from the reverse shift fork using a magnetic finger.

31. Remove the No.2 shift fork shaft, shift head and shift fork.

32. Remove the No. 3 shift fork shaft with reverse shift fork and No. 2 shift fork.

33. Remove the snapring and reverse shift fork from the No. 3 shift fork shaft.

34. Remove the input and output shaft assembly.

35. Remove the differential case assembly with the oil pump drive gear.

36. Remove the magnet from the transaxle case assembly.

37. Unbolt and remove the oil pump assembly with the oil pipe.

PRE-DISASSEMBLY TRANSAXLE COMPONENT INSPECTION

➡ The pre-disassmbly inspection of the transaxle components has been broken down to treat each component separately and for the sake of simplicity. Perform each operation in the order shown. No inspection procedure should be neglected or deleted, as they are all important to ensuring the proper operation of the transaxle. Inspection of the major transaxle components (i.e., input shaft) is included with "Transaxle Component Disassembly and Assembly".

INSPECT 5TH GEAR SYNCHRONIZER RING

1. Visually inspect the gear ring for wear or damage.

2. Rotate the ring and push it in to check that the braking action id functioning properly.

3. Measure the clearance between the synchronizer ring back and the gear spline end. Standard clearance is 0.75-1.65mm.

4. Inspect the clearance of the gears whole circumference. if the clearance is less than the specified limit, replace the ring.

CHECK SHIFT FORK AND HUB SLEEVE CLEARANCE

1. Using a feeler gauge, measure the clearance between the hub sleeve and shift fork. The maximum clearance is 1.00mm.

2. If the clearance exceeds the limit, replace the shift fork or the hub sleeve.

SEAL INSPECTION

Inspect all the oil seals, races and pins for wear and damage. Replace any worn or damaged seals as required.

REPLACEMENT OF INPUT SHAFT AND FRONT BEARING OIL SEAL

1. Remove the three bolts and the transaxle case receiver.

2. Using SST No. 09612-65014 or equivalent bearing puller, pull the bearing out from the transaxle case.

3. Remove the oil seal with a suitable prying tool. Discard the seal.

4. Using SST No. 09608-12010, drive in the new oil seal and coat the lip of the new seal with multi-purpose grease.

5. Using SST No. 09608-12010 or equivalent, drive in a new bearing.

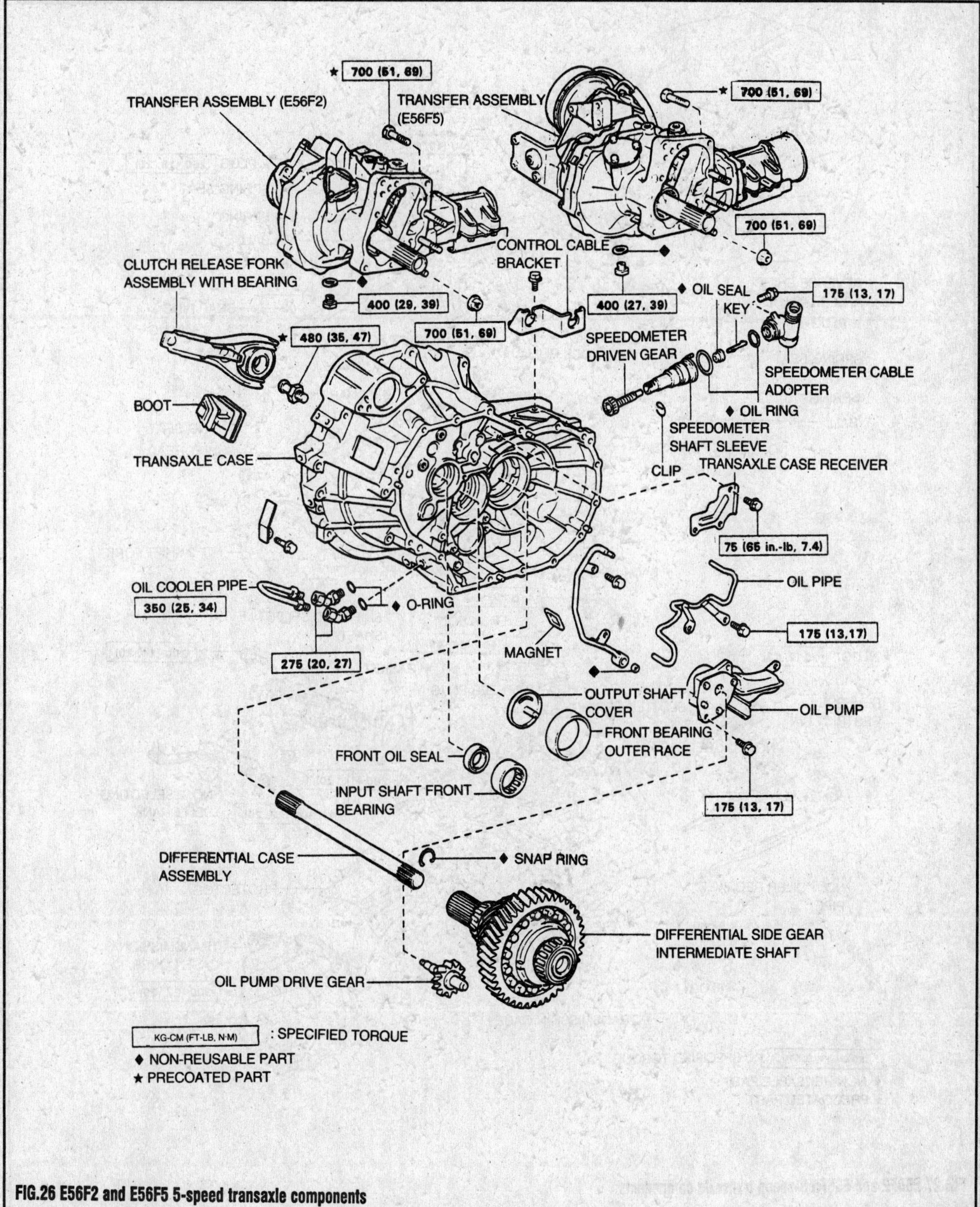
★ 700 (51, 69)
TRANSFER ASSEMBLY (E56F2)
TRANSFER ASSEMBLY (E56F5)
★ 700 (51, 69)
700 (51, 69)
CONTROL CABLE BRACKET
CLUTCH RELEASE FORK ASSEMBLY WITH BEARING
400 (29, 39)
400 (27, 39)
◆ OIL SEAL
175 (13, 17)
KEY
★ 480 (35, 47)
700 (51, 69)
SPEEDOMETER DRIVEN GEAR
SPEEDOMETER CABLE ADOPTER
◆ OIL RING
BOOT
SPEEDOMETER SHAFT SLEEVE
TRANSAXLE CASE
CLIP
TRANSAXLE CASE RECEIVER
75 (65 in.-lb, 7.4)
OIL COOLER PIPE
350 (25, 34)
◆ O-RING
OIL PIPE
175 (13,17)
MAGNET
275 (20, 27)
OUTPUT SHAFT COVER
OIL PUMP
FRONT BEARING OUTER RACE
FRONT OIL SEAL
INPUT SHAFT FRONT BEARING
175 (13, 17)
DIFFERENTIAL CASE ASSEMBLY
◆ SNAP RING
DIFFERENTIAL SIDE GEAR INTERMEDIATE SHAFT
OIL PUMP DRIVE GEAR
KG-CM (FT-LB, N·M) : SPECIFIED TORQUE
◆ NON-REUSABLE PART
★ PRECOATED PART

FIG.26 E56F2 and E56F5 5-speed transaxle components

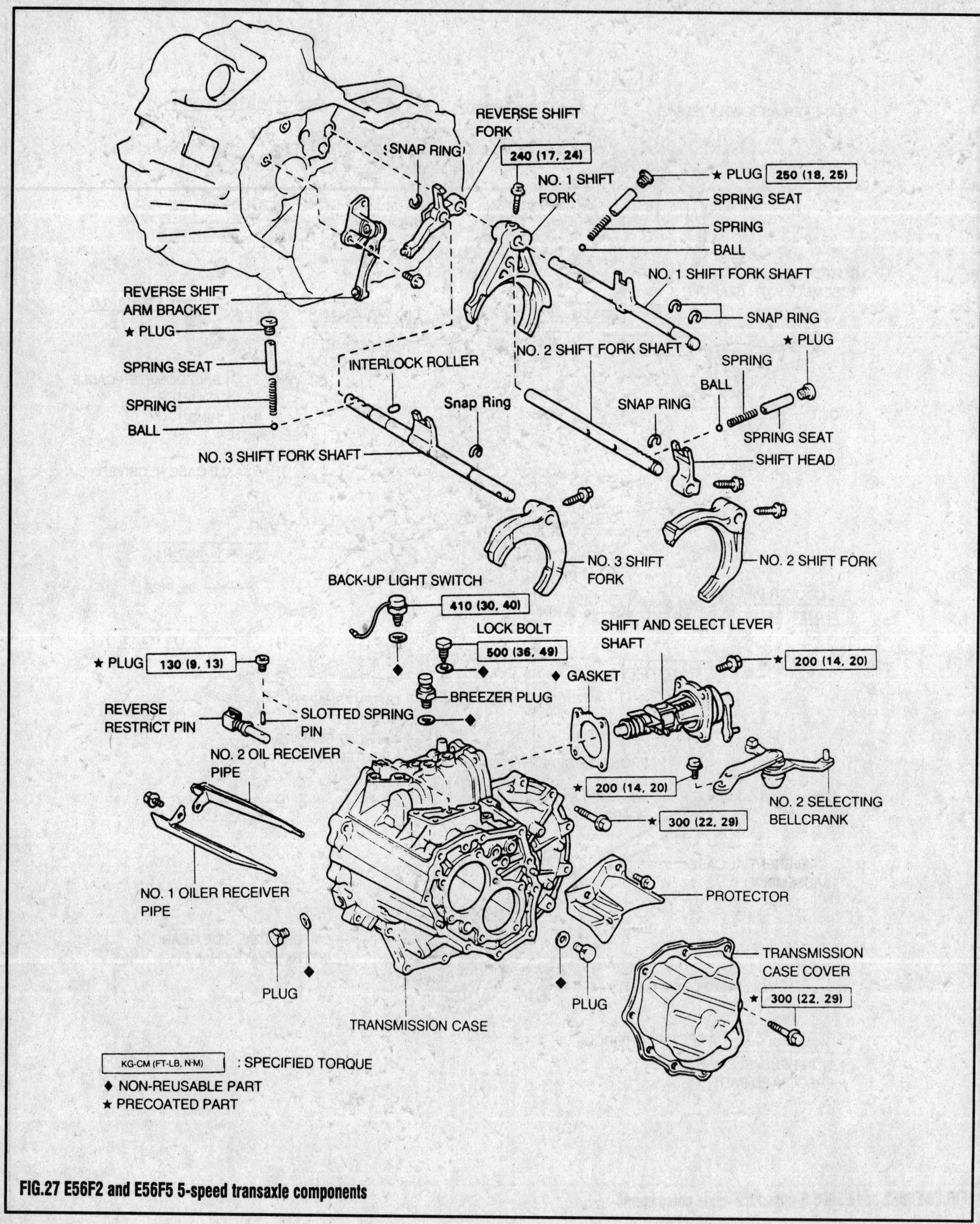
REVERSE SHIFT FORK
SNAP RING
240 (17, 24)
NO. 1 SHIFT FORK
★ PLUG 250 (18, 25)
SPRING SEAT
SPRING
BALL
NO. 1 SHIFT FORK SHAFT
SNAP RING
★ PLUG
REVERSE SHIFT ARM BRACKET
★ PLUG
SPRING SEAT
SPRING
BALL
INTERLOCK ROLLER
NO. 2 SHIFT FORK SHAFT
SPRING
BALL
Snap Ring
SNAP RING
SPRING SEAT
SHIFT HEAD
NO. 3 SHIFT FORK SHAFT
NO. 3 SHIFT FORK
NO. 2 SHIFT FORK
BACK-UP LIGHT SWITCH
410 (30, 40)
LOCK BOLT
500 (36, 49)
SHIFT AND SELECT LEVER SHAFT
★ 200 (14, 20)
★ PLUG 130 (9, 13)
◆ GASKET
BREEZER PLUG
REVERSE RESTRICT PIN
SLOTTED SPRING PIN
NO. 2 OIL RECEIVER PIPE
★ 200 (14, 20)
NO. 2 SELECTING BELLCRANK
★ 300 (22, 29)
NO. 1 OILER RECEIVER PIPE
PROTECTOR
TRANSMISSION CASE COVER
★ 300 (22, 29)
PLUG
PLUG
TRANSMISSION CASE
KG-CM (FT-LB, N·M) : SPECIFIED TORQUE
◆ NON-REUSABLE PART
★ PRECOATED PART

FIG.27 E56F2 and E56F5 5-speed transaxle components

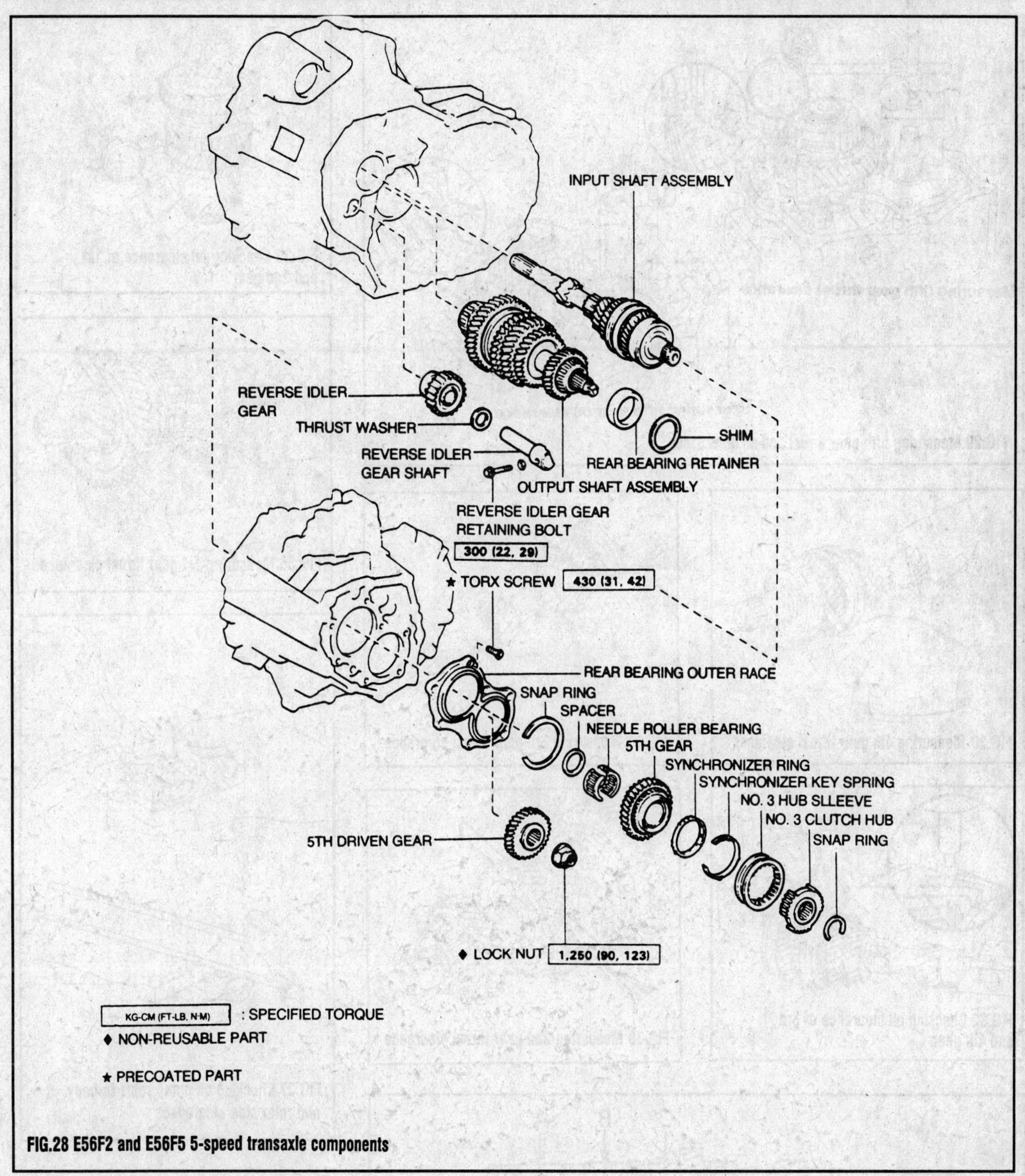

FIG.28 E56F2 and E56F5 5-speed transaxle components

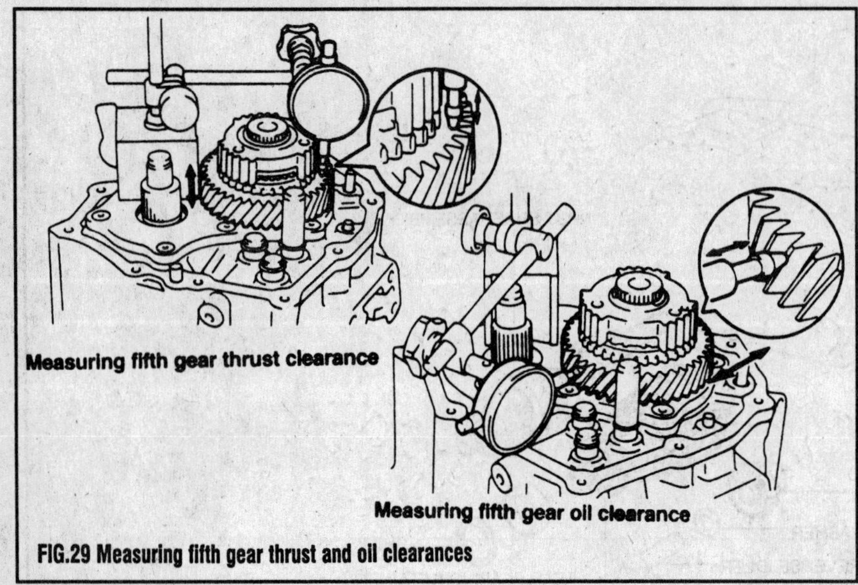

FIG.29 Measuring fifth gear thrust and oil clearances

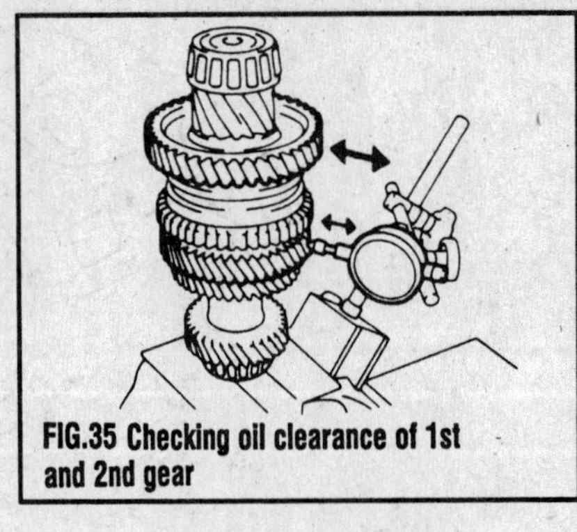
FIG.35 Checking oil clearance of 1st and 2nd gear

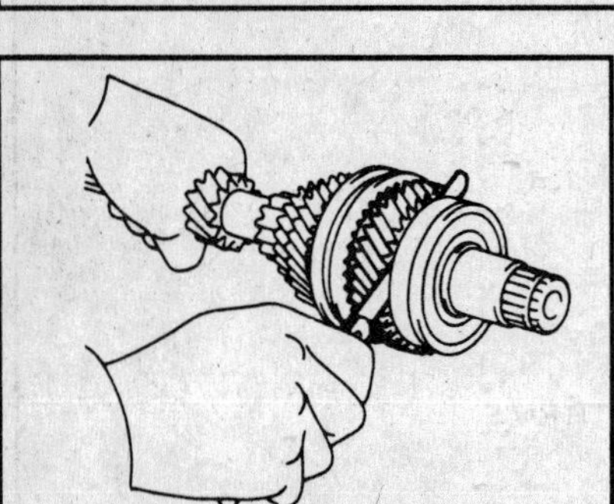
FIG.30 Measuring 4th gear thrust clearance

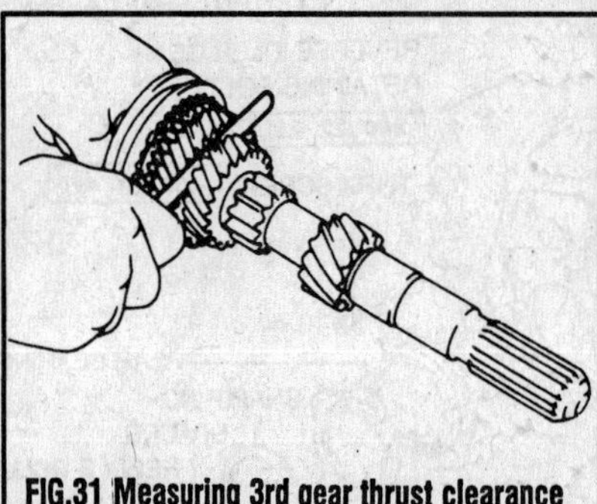
FIG.31 Measuring 3rd gear thrust clearance

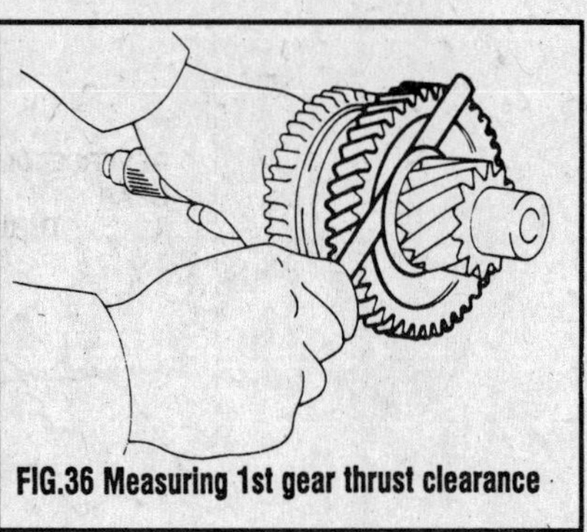
FIG.36 Measuring 1st gear thrust clearance

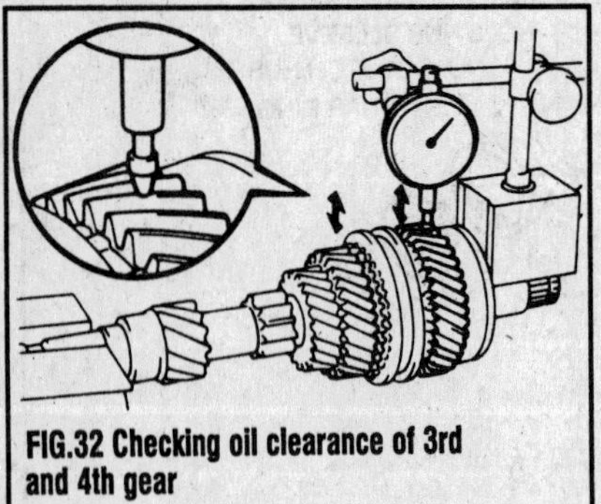
FIG.32 Checking oil clearance of 3rd and 4th gear

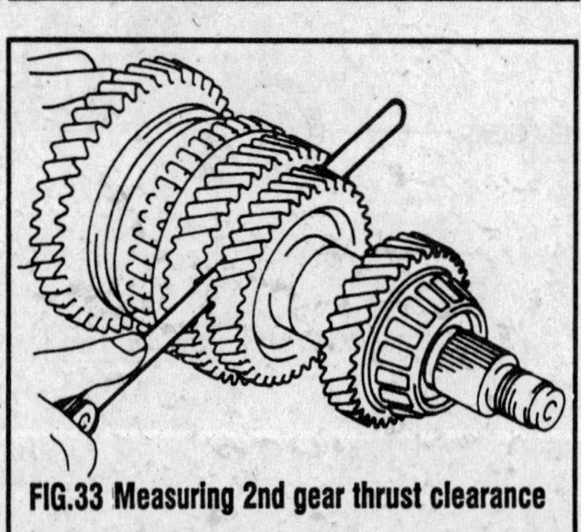
FIG.33 Measuring 2nd gear thrust clearance

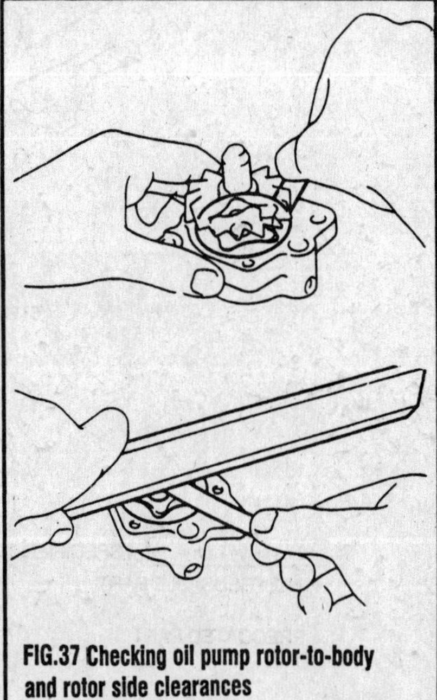
FIG.37 Checking oil pump rotor-to-body and rotor side clearances

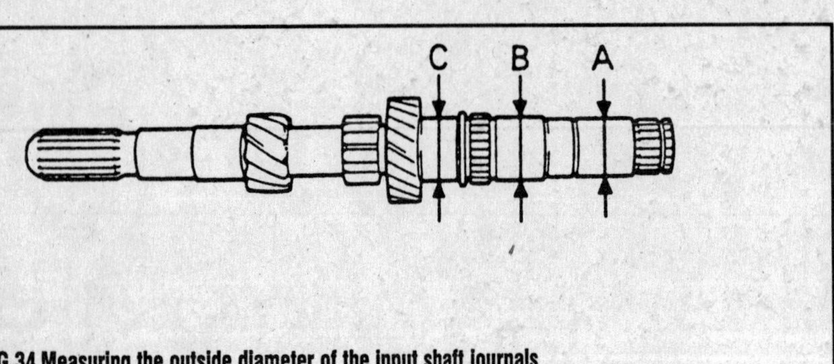

FIG.34 Measuring the outside diameter of the input shaft journals

NEEDLE ROLLER BEARING
3RD GEAR
SYNCHRONIZER RING
KEY
NO. 2 CLUTCH HUB
SPRING
SPACER
NO. 2 HUB SLEEVE
SNAP RING
NEEDLE ROLLER BEARING
SYNCHRONIZER RING
4TH GEAR
REAR BEARING
SNAP RING

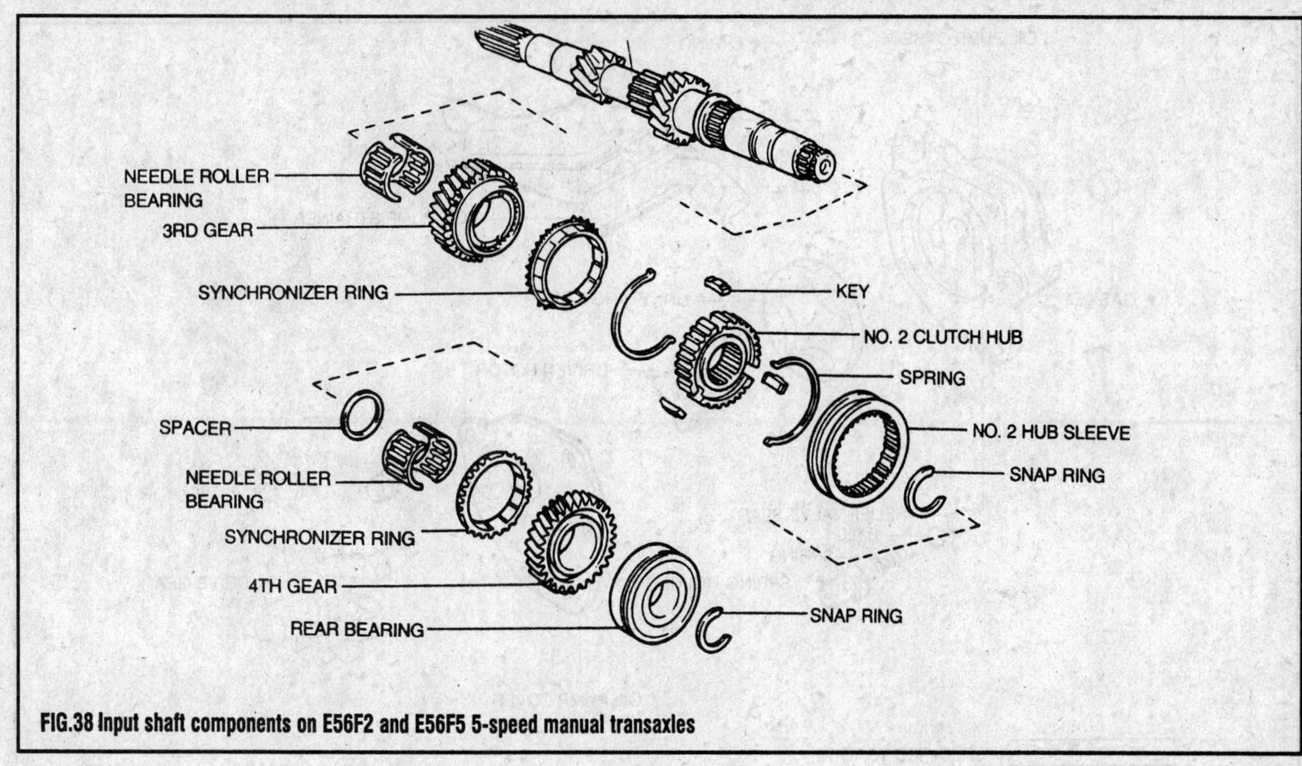

FIG.38 Input shaft components on E56F2 and E56F5 5-speed manual transaxles

♦ OUTPUT SHAFT FRONT BEARING
1ST GEAR
OUTPUT SHAFT
SYNCHRONIZER RING
NO. 1 HUB SLEEVE
NEEDLE ROLLER BEARING
BALL
SPRING
KEY
2ND GEAR
NO. 1 CLUTCH HUB
3RD DRIVEN GEAR
SECOND GEAR BUSHING
SPACER
NEEDLE ROLLER BEARING
4TH DRIVEN GEAR
SYNCHRONIZER RING
OUTPUT SHAFT REAR BEARING
♦ NON-REUSABLE PART

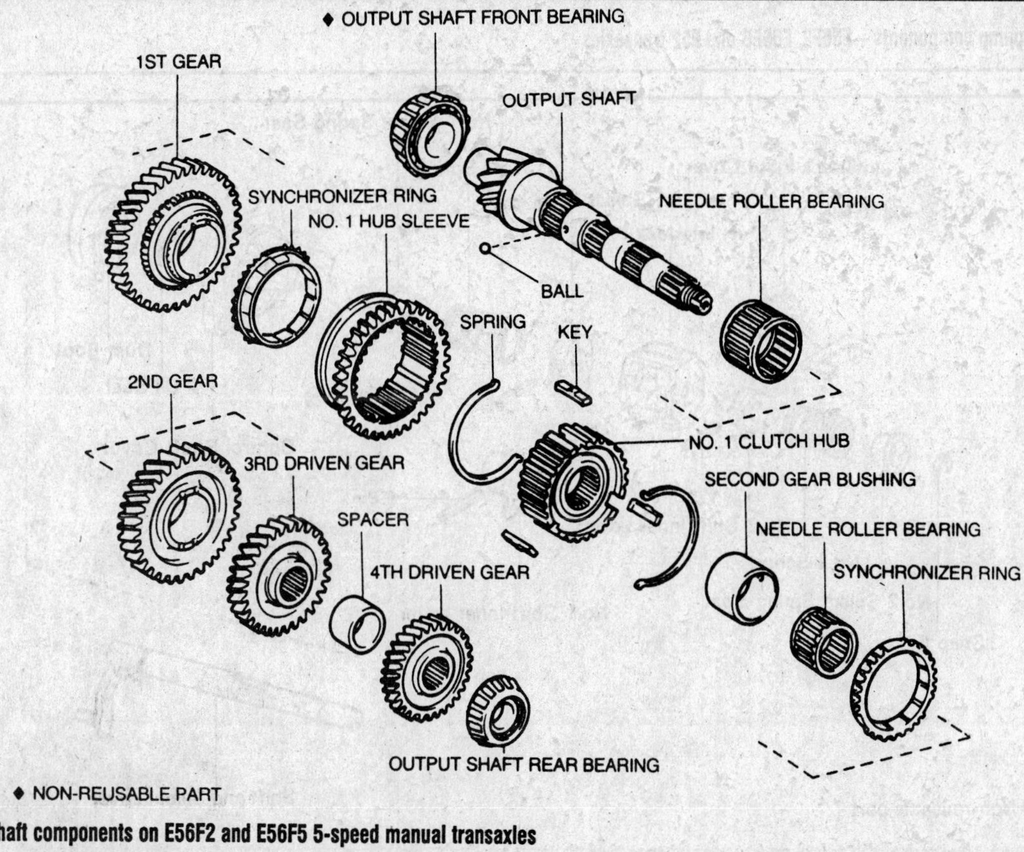

FIG.39 Output shaft components on E56F2 and E56F5 5-speed manual transaxles

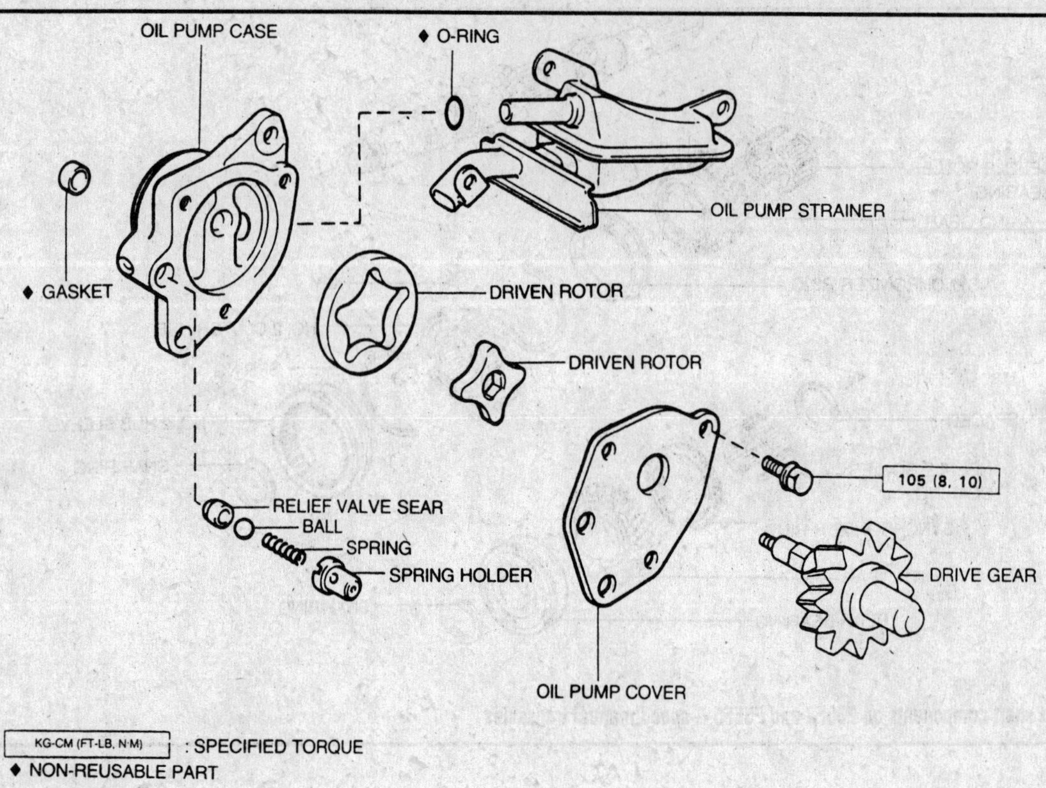

FIG.40 Oil pump components – E56F2, E56F5 and E52 transaxles

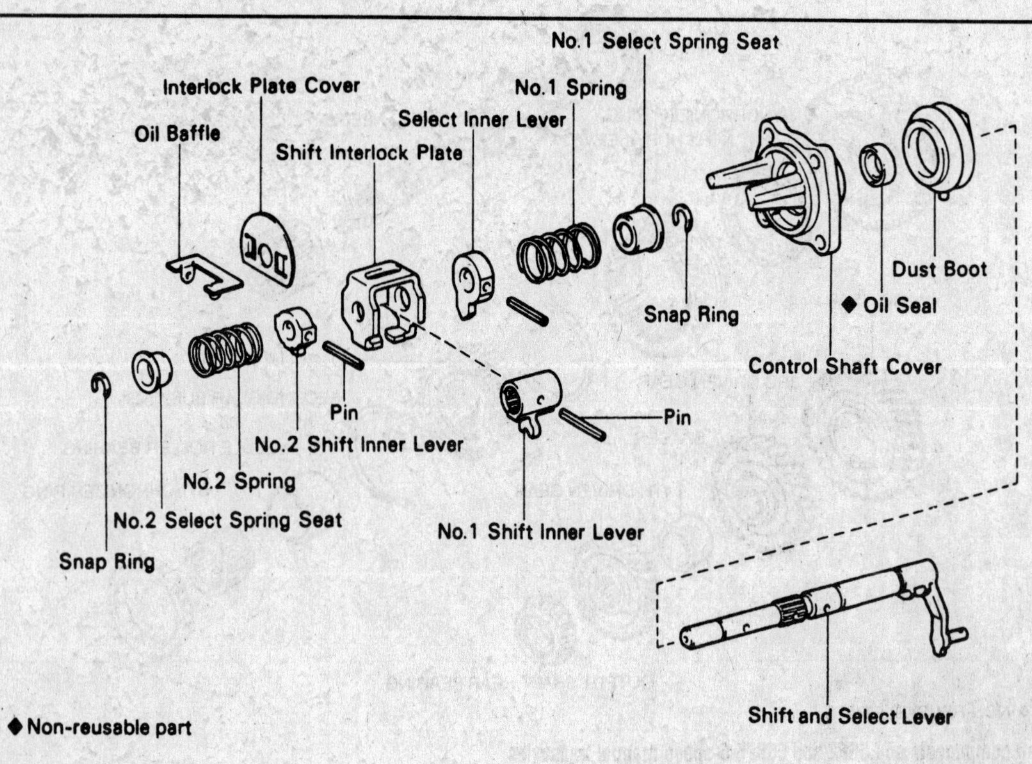

FIG.41 Shift and select lever shaft components on E56F2 and E56F5 5-speed manual transaxles

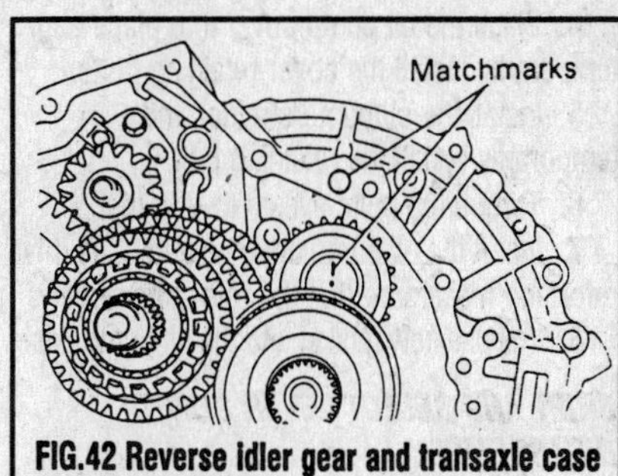

FIG.42 Reverse idler gear and transaxle case matchmark alignment

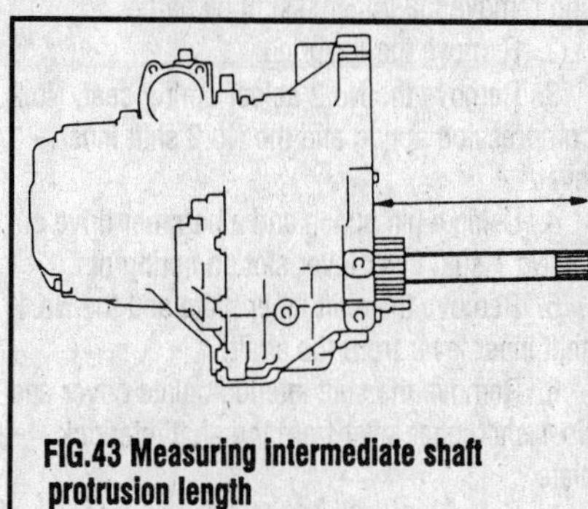
FIG.43 Measuring intermediate shaft protrusion length

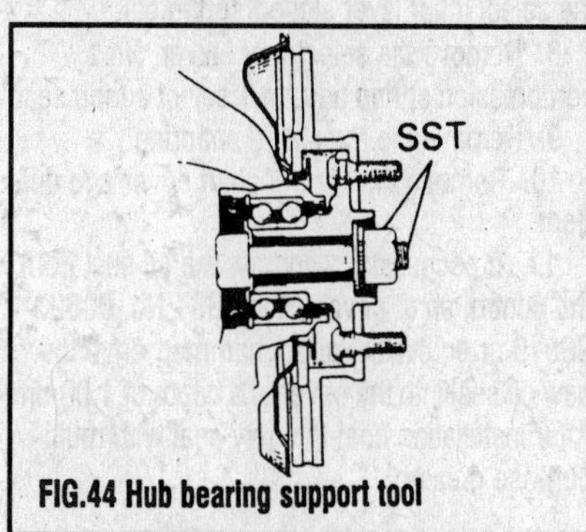

FIG.44 Hub bearing support tool

REPLACEMENT OF OUTPUT SHAFT FRONT BEARING OUTER RACE

1. Using SST No. 09308-00010 or equivalent, pull out the outer race.
2. Remove the output shaft cover.
3. Install the output shaft cover so that the projection is installed into the case side groove.
4. Using SST No. 09316-60010 or equivalent, press in a new outer race.
5. Install the transaxle case receiver and torque the bolts to 65 inch lbs.

REPLACEMENT OF SPEEDOMETER DRIVEN GEAR OIL SEAL

1. Using SST No. 09921-00010 or equivalent, pull out the speedometer driven gear oil seal.
2. Using SST. 09201-60011 or equivalent, drive in a new oil seal. Coat the lip of the seal with multi-purpose grease.

REPLACEMENT OF REVERSE RESTRICT PIN

1. Remove the screw plug using SST No. 09313-30021 or equivalent.
2. Drive out the slotted spring pin using a pin punch and hammer.
3. Replace the reverse restrict pin.
4. Drive in the slotted spring pin using a pin punch and a hammer.
5. Apply Loctite® or equivalent liquid sealant to the threads of the plug and install and tighten the plug.

INPUT SHAFT DISASSEMBLY

1. Using a feeler gauge, measure the 3rd and 4th gear thrust clearances. Standard clearance for the 3rd gear is 0.10-0.35mm and the maximum clearance is 0.40mm. Standard forth gear clearance is 0.10-0.55mm and the maximum clearance is 0.60mm.
2. Using a dial indicator, measure the clearance between the 3rd and forth gear shaft. 3rd gear standard clearance is 0.010-0.050mm with a maximum clearance of 0.078mm. 4th gear standard clearance is 0.010-0.050mm with a maximum clearance of 0.078mm. If the clearance exceeds the limit, replace the gear, needle roller bearing or shaft.
3. Remove the snapring.
4. Remove the input shaft rear bearing and the 4th gear using SST No. 09950-00020 or equivalent and a press.
5. Remove the needle roller bearings, spacer and synchronizer ring.
6. Remove the snapring.
7. Using a press, remove the No. 2 hub sleeve, 3rd gear, synchronizer ring and needle roller bearings.
8. Remove the needle roler bearing.
9. Remove the input shaft front bearing inner race using SST No. 09950-00020 and a press.

INPUT SHAFT INPECTION

1. Check the synchronizer rings for damage or wear.
2. Turn and push in on the synchronizer ring to check the bearing action.
3. Measure the clearance between the synchronizer ring back and gear spline end. Minimum clearance is 0.60mm. If the clearance is less than specified, replace the ring.
4. Using a feeler gauge, measure the clearance between the No. 2 shift fork and the hub sleeve. Maximum clearance is 1.00mm. If the clearance exceeds specification, replace the shift fork or the hub sleeve.
5. Check the input shaft for damage or wear.
6. With a micrometer, measure the outer diameter of the input shaft journal surface. The minimum outer diameter for Section **A** (as shown in the figure) is 33mm and Sections **B** and **C** is 36mm.
7. Place the input shaft on V-blocks and check the shaft runout. Maximum runout is 0.06mm.

INPUT SHAFT REASSEMBLY

➡ **Before assembling the input shaft, coat all the sliding and rotating surfaces with fresh gear oil.**

1. Install the clutch hub and shifting keys into the No. 2 clutch hub sleeve. Install the shifting key springs under the shifting keys so that the end gaps are staggered (not in line).
2. Coat the 3rd gear needle roller bearing with multi-purpose grease.
3. Install the 3rd gear.
4. Place the 3rd gear synchronizer ring on the gear and align the ring slots with the shifting keys.
5. Using SST No. 09506-3501 or equivalent and a press, install the 3rd gear and the No.2 hub sleeve.
6. Select a snapring (using the accompanying chart) that will allow minimum axial thrust and install it on the shaft.
7. Using a feeler gauge, measure the 3rd gear thrust clearance. Standard clearance is 0.10-0.35mm.
8. Install the 4th gear spacer.
9. Coat the 4th gear needle roller bearings with multi-purpose grease.
10. Place the 4th gear synchronizer ring on the gear and align the ring slots with the shifting keys.
11. Using SST No. 09506-3501 or equivalent and a press, install the radial ball bearing.
12. Select a snapring (using the accompanying chart) that will allow minimum axial thrust and install it on the shaft.
13. Using a feeler gauge, measure the 4th gear thrust clearance. Standard thrust clearance is 0.10-0.55mm.
14. Using SST No. 09316 and a suitable press, install the input shaft front bearing inner race.

OUTPUT SHAFT DISASSEMBLY

1. Using a feeler gauge, measure the 1st and 2nd gear thrust clearance. Fist gear standard clearance is 0.10-0.35mm with a maximum clearance of 0.40mm. 2nd gear standard clearance is 0.010-0.45mm with a maximum of 0.50mm.
2. Using a dial indicator, measure the clearance between the 1st and 2nd gear and the shaft. 1st gear standard clearance is 0.010-0.050mm. 2nd gear standard clearance is 0.010-0.050mm. Both gears have a maximum oil clearance of 0.078mm. If the oil clearance exceeds the maximum limit, replace the gear, needle roller bearing or the shaft.

3. Using a suitable press, remove the output shaft rear bearing and 4th driven gear. Remove the spacer.

4. Using SST No. 09950-00020 and a suitable press, remove the 3rd driven gear and 2nd gear.

5. Remove the needle roller bearing, 2nd gear bushing and ball.

6. Remove the synchronizer ring.

7. Using a suitable press, remove the No.1 hub sleeve and 1st gear.

8. Remove the synchronizer ring and needle roller bearing.

OUTPUT SHAFT INSPECTION

1. Visually inspect the synchronizer rings for wear and damage.

2. Turn and push in on the synchronizer ring to check the bearing action.

3. Measure the clearance between the synchronizer ring back and gear spline end. Minimum clearance is 0.60mm. If the clearance is less than specified, replace the ring.

4. Using a feeler gauge, measure the clearance between the hub sleeve and shift fork. Maximum clearance is 1.00mm. If the clearance exceeds specification, replace the shift fork or the hub sleeve.

5. Check the input shaft for damage or wear.

6. With a micrometer, measure the outer diameter of the output shaft journal surface and the 2nd gear bushing. The minimum outer diameter 39.5mm.

7. Place the input shaft on V-blocks and check the shaft runout. Maximum runout is 0.06mm.

8. If necessary, replace the output shaft front bearing. Press the old bearing out using SST Nos. 09307-12101 and 09950-00020 or their equivalents and press in the new bearing using SST No. 09316-00070.

OUTPUT SHAFT REASSEMBLY

➡ Before assembling the input shaft, coat all the sliding and roating surfaces with fresh gear oil.

1. Install the clutch hub and shifting keys into the No. 1 clutch hub sleeve. Install the shifting key springs under the shifting keys so that the end gaps are staggered (not in line).

2. Coat the 1st gear needle roller bearing with multi-purpose grease.

3. Install the 1st gear.

4. Place the 1st gear synchronizer ring on the gear and align the ring slots with the shifting keys.

5. Using SST No. 09316-60010 or equivalent and a press, install the 1st gear and the No.1 hub sleeve.

6. Using a feeler gauge, measure the 1st gear thrust clearance. Standard clearance is 0.10-0.35mm.

7. Install the 2nd gear ball and bushing.

8. Coat the 2nd gear needle roller bearing with mutli-purpose grease and install the bearing.

9. Place the 2nd gear synchronizer ring on the gear and align the ring slots with the shifting keys.

10. Install the 2nd gear.

11. Using a press, install the 2nd gear.

12. Using a feeler gauge, measure the 2nd gear thrust clearance. Standard clearance is 0.10-0.45mm.

13. Install the 4th gear spacer and press the 4th driven gear into place.

14. Using SST No. 09506-30012 and a press, install the output shaft rear taper roller bearing.

OIL PUMP DISASSEMBLY

1. Insert the oil pump drive gear into the drive rotor and check that the rotor turns smoothly.

2. Withdraw the gasket from the pump case. Discard the gasket and purchase a new one.

3. Remove the oil strainer retaining bolt. Hold the pump cover stationary, remove the two cover bolts and cover.

4. Withdraw the spring holder, spring, ball and relief valve seat from the oil pump case.

OIL PUMP INSPECTION

1. Mate the oil pump drive gear with the drive rotor.

2. Using a feeler gauge, measure the clearance between the drive rotor and the oil pump case. The standard clearance is 0.010-0.160mm and the maximum oil clearance is 0.30mm.

3. Using a feeler gauge, measure the clearance between the drive and driven rotors. The standard oil clearance is 0.078-0.100mm with a maximum clearance of 0.30mm.

4. Using a machinists straight edge and a feeler gauge, measure the side clearance of both rotors. Standard side clearance is 0.030-0.078mm with a maximum of 0.15mm.

5. Remove the oil pump drive and driven rotors.

6. Remove the O-ring from the oil pump case using a machinists scribe or screwdriver. Discard the O-ring and replace with new. Coat the new O-ring with clean gear oil and install the O-ring into the oil pump case.

OIL PUMP REASSEMBLY

1. Install the drive and driven rotors.

2. Wipe the relief valve bore out with a clean lint-free rag.

3. Install the relief valve seat, ball, spring and spring holder into the oil pump case.

4. Place the oil pump cover into place and temporarily install the cover retaining bolts.

5. Install the oil pump strainer and temporarily install the retaining bolt.

6. Torque the bolts evenly to 8 ft. lbs.

7. Insert the oil pump drive gear into the drive rotor and make sure that the rotor turns freely.

8. Install a new gasket into the oil pump case.

SHIFT AND SELECT LEVER SHAFT DISASSEMBLY

1. Using a pin punch and a hammer, drive the out the No.2 shift inner lever slotted spring pin and remove the transmission oil baffle.

2. Remove the snapring.

3. Remove the No.2 select spring seat, No.2 compression spring and the No.2 shift inner lever.

4. Using a pin punch and a hammer drive out the No.1 shift inner lever slotted spring pin.

5. Remove the shift inner plate and the No.1 shift inner lever from the shaft.

6. Remove the shift interlock plate cover and No.1 shift inner lever from the shift interlock plate.

7. Using a pin punch and a hammer drive out the select inner lever slotted spring pin.

8. Remove the select inner lever, No.1 compression spring and No.1 select spring seat.

9. Remove the remaining snapring.

10. Remove the control shaft cover and dust boot.

11. If necessary, withdraw the oil seal from the control shaft cover. Using SST No. 09620-30010 or equivalent and a hammer, drive the new oil seal into the cover to a depth of 1.00mm. After installation coat the new seal with multi-purpose grease.

SHIFT AND SELECT LEVER SHAFT REASSEMBLY

1. Lightly coat all sliding, mating and splined surfaces with multi-purpose grease.

2. Install the dust boot cover onto the control shaft cover.

3. Install the shift select lever onto the control shaft cover.

4. Using a piece of brass stock and a hammer, install the snapring and spring seat.

5. Install the No.1 spring seat, No.1 select spring and select inner lever in the proper order.

6. Using a pin punch and a hammer, drive in the select inner lever slotted spring pin.

7. Place the No.1 shift inner lever into the interlock plate and install the interlock cover.

8. Using a pin punch and a hammer, drive in the No.1 shift inner lever slotted spring pin.

9. Make sure that the shift interlock plate turns smoothly.

10. Install the No.2 shift inner lever, No.2 compression spring, transmission oil baffle and No.2 select spring seat in the proper order.

11. Install the snapring.
12. Using a pin punch and a hammer, drive in the No.2 shift inner lever slotted spring pin.

1988–90 E56F5 and E56F2 Transaxle Reassembly

➡ Prior to assembling the transaxle, coat all the moving and sliding parts with clean gear oil.

1. Install the output shaft assembly to the transaxle case.
2. Install the transmission case to the transaxle case. If necessary, use a rubber mallet to coax the transaxle into place.
3. Install the seventeen transaxle case retaining bolts and torque the bolts to 22 ft. lbs.
4. Install the output shaft rear bearing outer race.
5. Install the adjusting shim.

➡ If the output shaft rear bearing is being re-used, install a shim of the same thickness as the old shim. If a new bearing is being installed, select a shim of lesser thickness than the old shim.

6. Install the seven Torx® screws and torque them to 31 ft. lbs.
7. Install a new locknut onto the output shaft.
8. Rotate the output shaft counterclockwise and clockwise a few times.
9. Using a torque meter, measure the preload of the output shaft. Preload for a new bearing is 6.9-13.9 inch lbs. and 4.3-8.7 inch lbs. for a used bearing. If the preload is not within specification, select the proper thickness shim to adjust the preload.

➡ Pre-load changes 3.5-4.3 inch lbs. with each shim thickness.

10. Remove the locknut, seven Torx® screws and the adjusting shim.
11. Remove the seventeen retaining bolts and tap the case off with a rubber mallet.
12. Remove the output shaft rear bearing outer race.
13. Remove the output shaft assembly.
14. Install the oil pump assembly and temporarily install the two retaining bolts. Be careful not to drop the oil pump gasket.
15. Install the oil pipe with the two retaining bolts.
16. Torque the oil pipe and oil pump retaining bolts to 13 ft. lbs.
17. Install the transaxle case magnet.
18. Install the differential case assembly.
19. Install the oil pump drive gear.
20. Lift the differential case up slightly and install the output shaft assembly.
21. Lean the output shaft assembly towards the differential case side and install the input shaft assembly.

➡ When installing the input shaft assembly, be careful not to damage the oil seal.

22. Install the reverse shift fork onto the No.3 shift fork. Install and seat the snapring with a rubber mallet.
23. Place the No.2 shift fork into the groove of the No.2 hub sleeve.
24. Install the No.3 shift fork shaft with the reverse shift fork into the transaxle case.
25. Place the No.1 shift fork into the groove of the No.1 hub sleeve.
26. Place the shift head onto the No.1 shift fork.
27. Install the No.2 shift fork shaft into the transaxle case through the No.2 shift fork, the shift head and the No.1 shift fork.
28. Using a magnetic finger, install the interlock roller into the reverse shift fork by aligning the groove of the No.1 shift fork shaft with the interlock roller hole of the reverse shift fork.
29. Install the No.1 shift fork shaft into the transaxle case through the No.1 and reverse shift forks. If this is difficult to do, pull up on the No.3 shift fork shaft and then try to install the No.1 shift fork again.
30. Install the three set bolts and torque them to 17 ft. lbs.
31. Install the two locking balls, springs and spring seats.
32. Coat the threads of the two screw plugs with Loctite® sealant or equivalent liquid sealant. Install the two plugs and torque them to 18 ft. lbs.
33. Install the reverse idler gear shaft (with the gear and thrust washer) into the transaxle case.
34. Align the matchmarks on the gear with the matchmarks on the case as shown in the accompanying figure.
35. Place the reverse shift fork into the reverse shift arm. Connect the reverse shift arm bracket to the transaxle case and temporarily install the retaining bolt.
36. Install the No.2 oil pipe and torque the two retaining bolts and the reverse shift arm bracket bolt to 13 ft. lbs.
37. Install a new gasket onto the No.2 oil pipe.
38. Remove any old packing material from the transaxle case contact surfaces and apply a bead of new seal apcking No. 08826-00090, THREE BOND® 1281 or equivalent to the case.
39. As soon as the sealant is applied, install the transmission case with the seventeen retaining bolts. Torque the bolts to 22 ft. lbs.
40. Install the reverse idler gear retaining bolt and gasket. Torque the bolt to 22 ft. lbs.
41. Install the locking ball, spring and spring seat.
42. Coat the threads of the screw plug with Loctite® 242 or equivalent sealer, install and torque the plug to 18 ft. lbs.
43. Using a rubber mallet, install the two snaprings onto the shift fork shafts.
44. Install the output shaft rear bearing outer race.
45. Install the adjust shim.
46. Using snapring pliers, install the snapring onto the input shaft bearing.
47. Coat the threads of the seven Torx® screws with Loctite® 242 sealant or equivalnet. Install the screws and torque them to 31 ft. lbs.
48. Install the spacer, needle roller bearings and the 5th gear.
49. Install the synchronizer ring and the key spring onto the No.3 clutch hub.
50. Using SST No. 09310-17010 or equivalent, install the No.3 clutch hub with synchronizer ring and key spring.
51. Select a snapring that will allow minimum axial play and install onot the shaft using a brass bar and a hammer.
52. Using a dial indicator, measure the 5th gear thrust clearance. The standard thrust clearance is 0.10-0.55mm.
53. Using SST No.09310-17010 or equivalent, install the 5th driven gear.
54. Install the No.3 hub sleeve and the No.3 shift fork with the set bolt. Torque the set bolt to 17 ft. lbs.
55. Engage the gear double meshing and install the new locknut. Torque the locknut to 90 ft. lbs, stake the nut with a small cold chisel and disengage the double meshing.
56. Remove any old packing material from the transmission case cover contact surfaces and apply a bead of new seal packing No. 08826-00090, THREE BOND® 1281 or equivalent to the cover.
57. As soon as the sealant is applied, install the cover with the retaining bolts. Torque the retaining bolts to 22 ft. lbs.
58. Install the shift shaft select lever assembly with new gasket and coat the threads of the bolts with Loctite® 242 or equivalent. Install the bolts and torque them to 14 ft. lbs. Install the lock bolt with new gasket and torque it to 36 ft. lbs.
59. Install the No.2 selecting bellcrank with the support. Coat the threads of the two retaining bolts with Loctite® 242 or equivalent. Install and torque torque the bolts to 14 ft. lbs.
60. Install the back-up light switch and torque it to 30 ft. lbs.
61. Install the speedometer driven gear.

62. Coat the release bearing inside hub, input shaft spline and release fork contact surface with molybdenum disulfide lithium based grease.

63. Coat the front surface of the release bearing with multi-purpose grease.

64. Coat the intermediate shaft with multi-purpose grease.

65. With a rubber mallet, drive the intermediate shaft straight into the top of the shaft touches the differential pinion shaft.

66. Measure the protrusion length of the shaft. For E56F2 transaxles, the protrusion length should be 255mm. For E56F5 transaxles, the protrusion length is 255.5mm.

67. Remove any of the old packing material from the transfer assembly contact surfaces. Apply a bead of new seal packing No. 08826-00090, THREE BOND® 1281 or equivalent to the transfer assembly.

68. As soon as the sealant is applied, install the transfer assembly to the transaxle by shifting into 4th gear and installing the transfer assembly while turning the transaxle input shaft.

69. Coat the threads of the transfer case retaining bolts with Loctite® 242 or equivalent sealant. Install the three bolts and two nuts and torque them to 51 ft. lbs.

70. Move the select lever to the viscous mode position and lock it in place with the lock bolt.

1989–91 E52 Transaxle Disassembly

➧ SEE FIGS. 24–25, 29, 31–33, 36–37, 39–40, 42, and 45–51

1. Remove the release fork, bearing and back-up light switch.
2. Remove the speedometer driven gear.
3. Remove the transmission case cover.
4. Remove the selecting bellcrank.
5. Remove shift lever lock bolt.
6. Remove the 4 bolts securing the select lever assembly.
7. Remove the shift and select lever assembly.
8. Unstake the output shaft locknut using a small cold chisel.
9. Engage the gear double meshing.
10. Remove the lock nut and disengage the gear double meshing.
11. Remove the No. 3 shift fork set bolt, then the No. 3 hub sleeve and the shift fork.
12. Using a puller, remove the fifth driven gear.
13. Using a dial indicator, measure the 5th gear thrust clearance. Standard clearance is 0.10-0.57mm with a maximum clearance of 0.65mm.
14. Measure the oil clearance. Standard clearance is 0.009-0.050mm with a maximum clearance of 0.070mm.
15. Using 2 prybars and a hammer, tap out the No. 3 clutch hub snapring.
16. Using a puller, remove 5th gear, synchronizer ring and the No. 3 clutch hub.
17. Remove the needle roller bearing and spacer.
18. Remove the 7 screws, remove the rear bearing retainer and the adjust shim.
19. Remove the 3 small and 1 large snaprings by using suitable tools.
20. Remove the plug, seat, spring and locking ball, using a magnet.
21. Remove reverse idler gear shaft retaining bolt.
22. To remove transmission case, remove the 17 bolts and tap off the case with a plastic hammer.
23. Remove the output shaft rear tapered roller bearing outer race by driving out the outer race, then remove the oil pipe.
24. Remove the two bolts and pull off the reverse shift arm bracket.
25. Remove reverse idler gear and shaft by pulling out the shaft.
26. Remove the straight screw, locking balls and springs.
27. Remove the shift fork set bolt.
28. Pull up the No. 3 shift fork shaft and remove the No. 1 shift fork shaft.
29. Remove the interlock roller, using a magnet.
30. Remove the No.2 fork shaft.
31. Remove the shift head and the No. 1 shift fork.
32. Pull out the No. 3 shift fork shaft with the reverse shift fork.
33. Pull out the No.2 fork shaft.
34. Carefully remove input and output shaft together from transaxle case.
35. Remove the oil pump drive gear.
36. Remove differential assembly.
37. Remove the magnet from the transaxle case.
38. Remove the 2 oil pump assembly bolts and the oil pipe.

Transaxle Component Inspection

1. Inspect the synchronizer ring for fifth gear by turning the ring and pushing it in to check the braking action.

2. With a feeler gauge, measure the clearance between the back of the ring and gear spline end. Minimum clearance is 0.6mm.

3. If the clearance is less than the limit, replace the ring.

4. Check the shift fork and the hub clearance.

a. With a feeler gauge, measure the clearance between the hub sleeve and shift fork. Maximum clearance is 1.00mm.

b. If the clearance exceeds the limit, replace the shift fork or hub sleeve.

5. Inspect all transaxle seals, bearings and races for wear and damage. Replace all damaged or worn seals, bearings and races as required.

6. Replace the input shaft front bearing.

a. Unbolt and remove the transaxle case oil receiver.

b. Using SST No. 09612-65014 or equivalent, pull out the old bearing.

c. Replace the oil seal, coating the lip with grease.

d. Using SST No. 09608-12010 or equivalent, press in the new bearing.

7. Replace the output shaft front outer race and output shaft cover.

a. Using SST No. 09308-00010 or equivalent, pull out the old race.

b. Remove the output shaft cover.

c. Install the output shaft front cover, installing the shaft cover projection into the case side groove.

d. Using SST 09316–60010, press in a new outer race.

8. Install and torque the transaxle case receiver to 65 inch lbs. (7.4 Nm).

9. Replace the speedometer driven gear oil seal.

a. Using SST No. 09921-00010 or equivalent, pull out the old seal.

b. Using SST No. 09201-60011 or equivalent, drive in the new seal to a depth of 33mm and coat the lip with grease.

10. Replace the reverse restrict pin.

a. Remove the screw plug.

b. Using a pin punch and hammer, drive out the slotted spring pin.

c. Remove the reverse restrict pin.

d. Using a pin punch and hammer, drive the slotted spring pin back in.

e. Apply Loctite® or similar liquid sealant to the threads of the screw plug.

f. Install the screw plug.

INPUT SHAFT DISASSEMBLY

1. Using a feeler gauge, measure the 3rd and 4th gear thrust clearance.

Standard clearance:
- 3rd gear — 0.10-0.35mm
- 4th gear — 0.10-0.55mm

Maximum clearance:
- 3rd gear — 0.40mm
- 4th gear — 0.60mm

2. Check the oil clearance of the 3rd and 4th gear. Using a dial indicator, measure the oil clearance between the gear and the shaft.

Standard clearance:
- 3rd gear — 0.009-0.053mm
- 4th gear — 0.009-0.051mm

Maximum clearance:

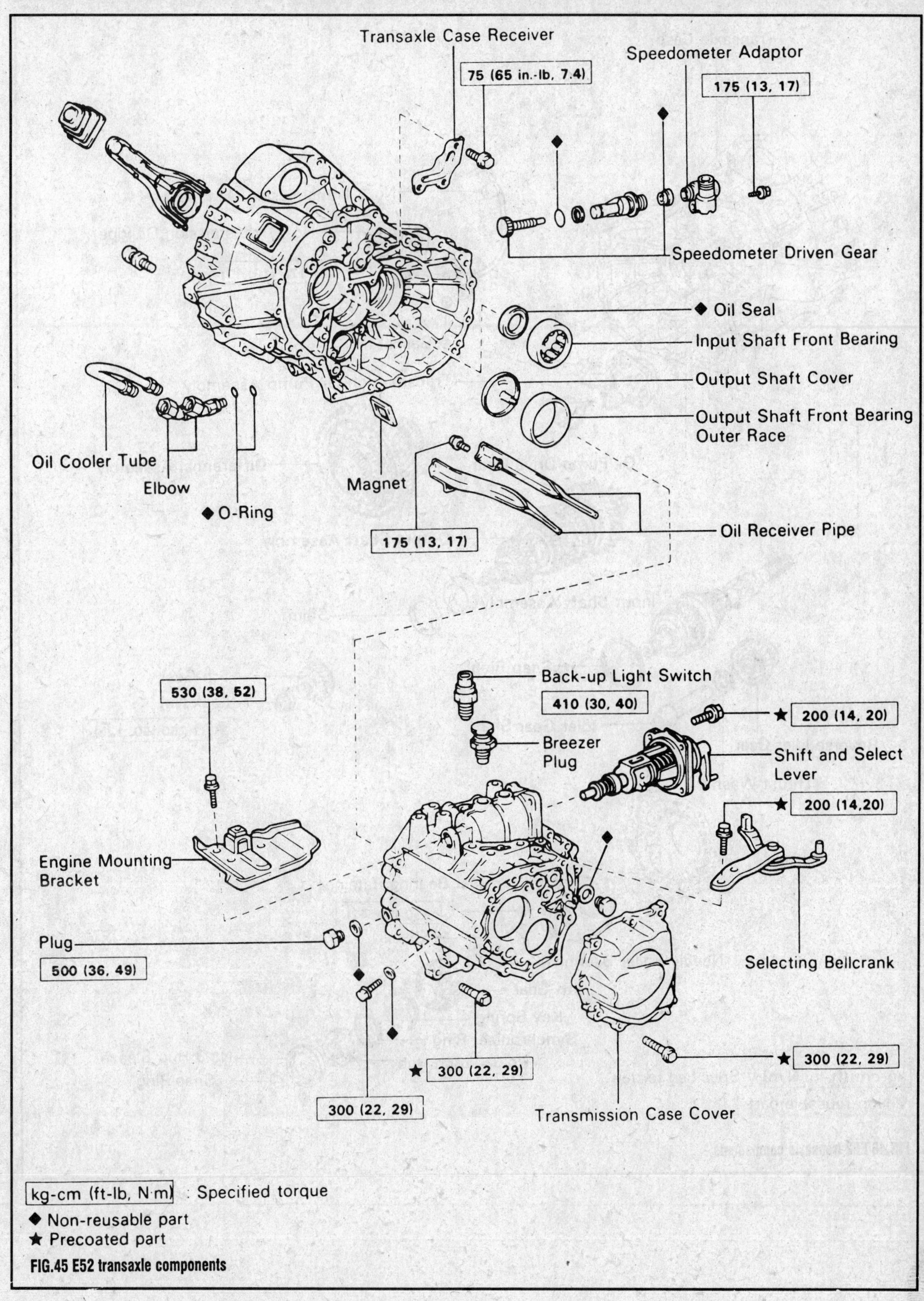
Transaxle Case Receiver
75 (65 in.-lb, 7.4)
Speedometer Adaptor
175 (13, 17)
Speedometer Driven Gear
Oil Seal
Input Shaft Front Bearing
Output Shaft Cover
Output Shaft Front Bearing Outer Race
Oil Cooler Tube
Elbow
O-Ring
Magnet
175 (13, 17)
Oil Receiver Pipe
530 (38, 52)
Back-up Light Switch
410 (30, 40)
200 (14, 20)
Breezer Plug
Shift and Select Lever
200 (14,20)
Engine Mounting Bracket
Plug
500 (36, 49)
Selecting Bellcrank
300 (22, 29)
300 (22, 29)
300 (22, 29)
Transmission Case Cover
kg-cm (ft-lb, N·m) : Specified torque
Non-reusable part
Precoated part

FIG.45 E52 transaxle components

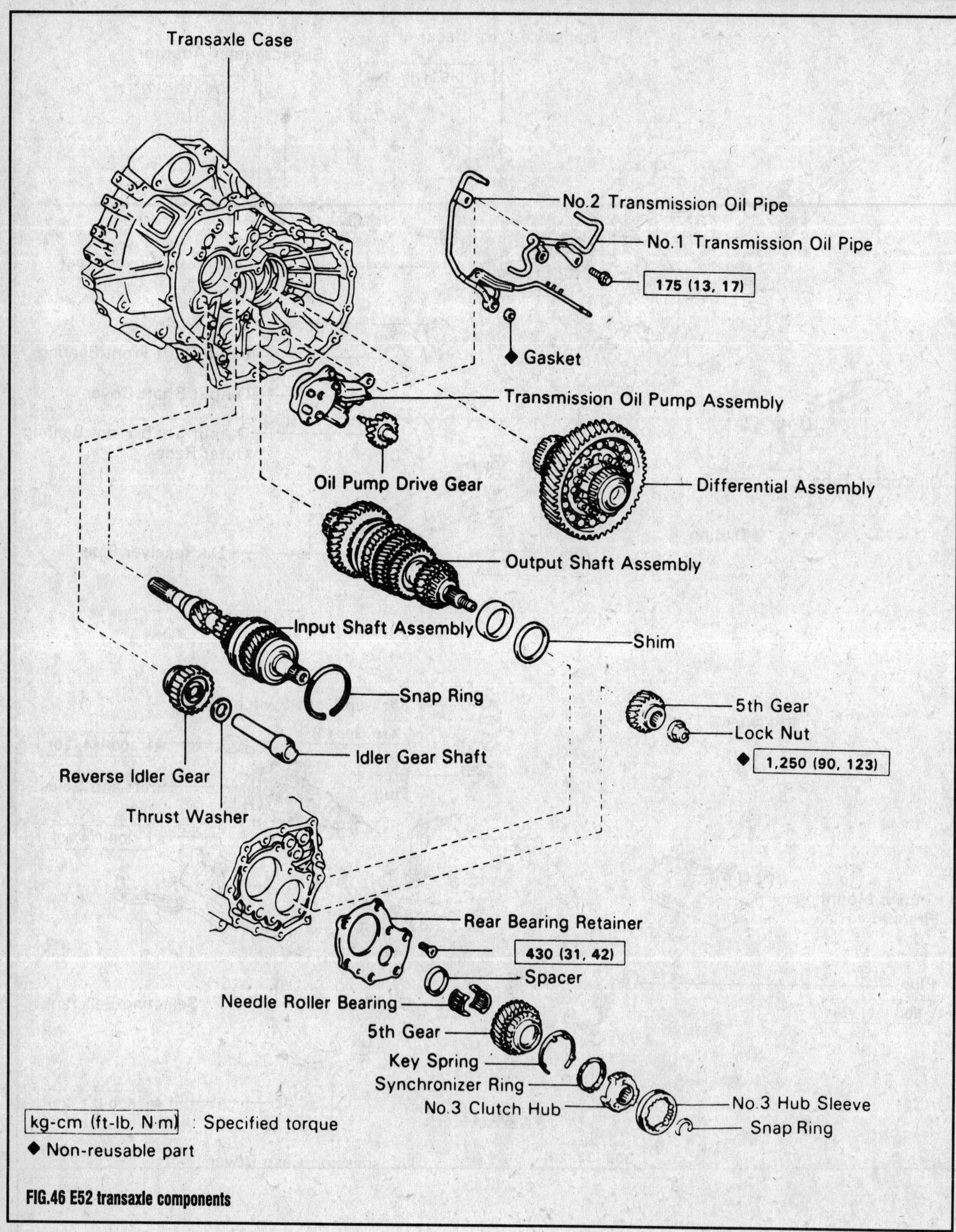
Transaxle Case
No.2 Transmission Oil Pipe
No.1 Transmission Oil Pipe
175 (13, 17)
◆ Gasket
Transmission Oil Pump Assembly
Oil Pump Drive Gear
Differential Assembly
Output Shaft Assembly
Input Shaft Assembly
Shim
Snap Ring
5th Gear
Lock Nut
◆ 1,250 (90, 123)
Idler Gear Shaft
Reverse Idler Gear
Thrust Washer
Rear Bearing Retainer
430 (31, 42)
Spacer
Needle Roller Bearing
5th Gear
Key Spring
Synchronizer Ring
No.3 Clutch Hub
No.3 Hub Sleeve
Snap Ring
kg-cm (ft-lb, N·m) : Specified torque
◆ Non-reusable part

FIG.46 E52 transaxle components

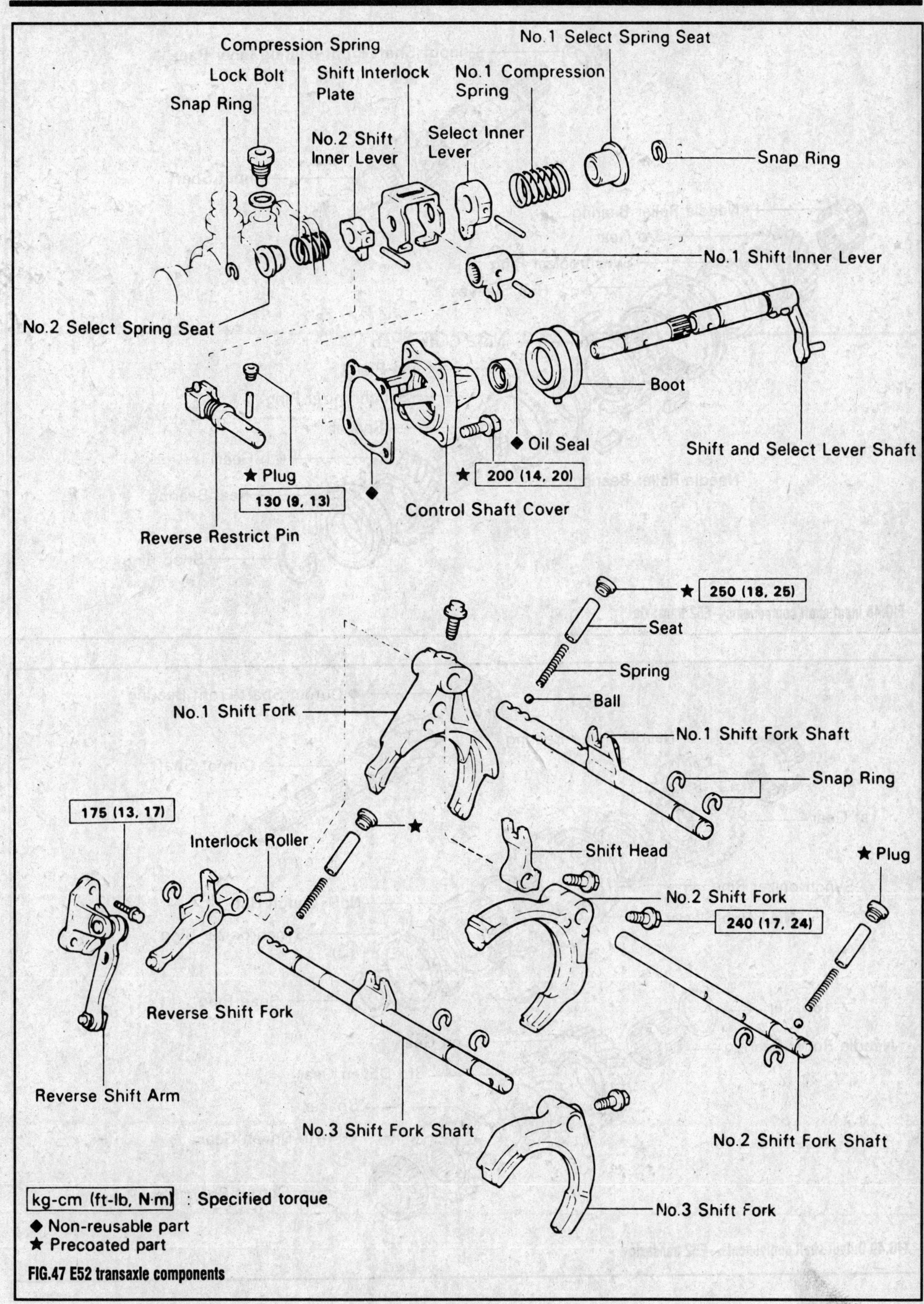
Compression Spring
Lock Bolt
Snap Ring
Shift Interlock Plate
No.1 Select Spring Seat
No.1 Compression Spring
No.2 Shift Inner Lever
Select Inner Lever
Snap Ring
No.1 Shift Inner Lever
No.2 Select Spring Seat
Boot
◆ Oil Seal
Shift and Select Lever Shaft
★ Plug
130 (9, 13)
★ 200 (14, 20)
Control Shaft Cover
Reverse Restrict Pin
★ 250 (18, 25)
Seat
Spring
Ball
No.1 Shift Fork
No.1 Shift Fork Shaft
Snap Ring
175 (13, 17)
Interlock Roller
Shift Head
★ Plug
No.2 Shift Fork
240 (17, 24)
Reverse Shift Fork
Reverse Shift Arm
No.3 Shift Fork Shaft
No.2 Shift Fork Shaft
No.3 Shift Fork
kg-cm (ft-lb, N·m) : Specified torque
◆ Non-reusable part
★ Precoated part

FIG.47 E52 transaxle components

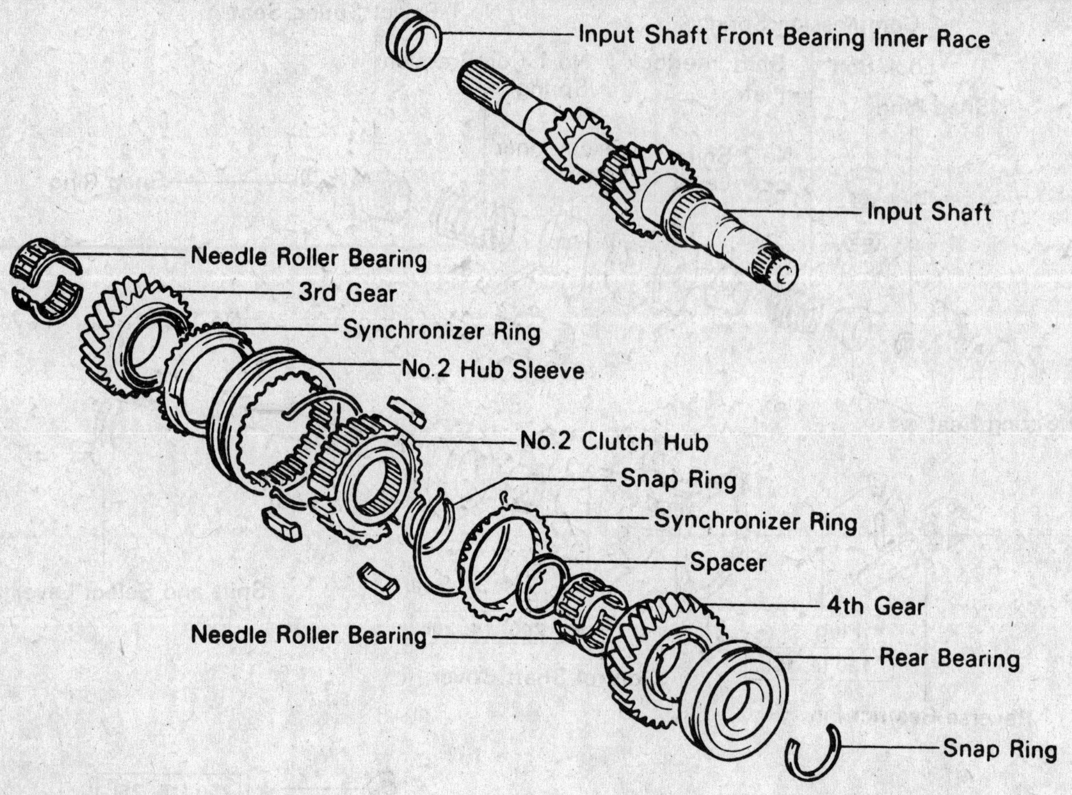

Input Shaft Front Bearing Inner Race
Input Shaft
Needle Roller Bearing
3rd Gear
Synchronizer Ring
No.2 Hub Sleeve
No.2 Clutch Hub
Snap Ring
Synchronizer Ring
Spacer
4th Gear
Needle Roller Bearing
Rear Bearing
Snap Ring

FIG.48 Input shaft components – E52 transaxle

◆ Output Shaft Front Bearing
Needle Roller Bearing
Output Shaft
1st Gear
Synchronizer Ring
No.1 Clutch Hub
No.1 Hub Sleeve
Synchronizer Ring
Snap Ring
Spacer
Needle Roller Bearing
2nd Gear
3rd Driven Gear
Spacer
4th Driven Gear
Output Shaft Rear Bearing

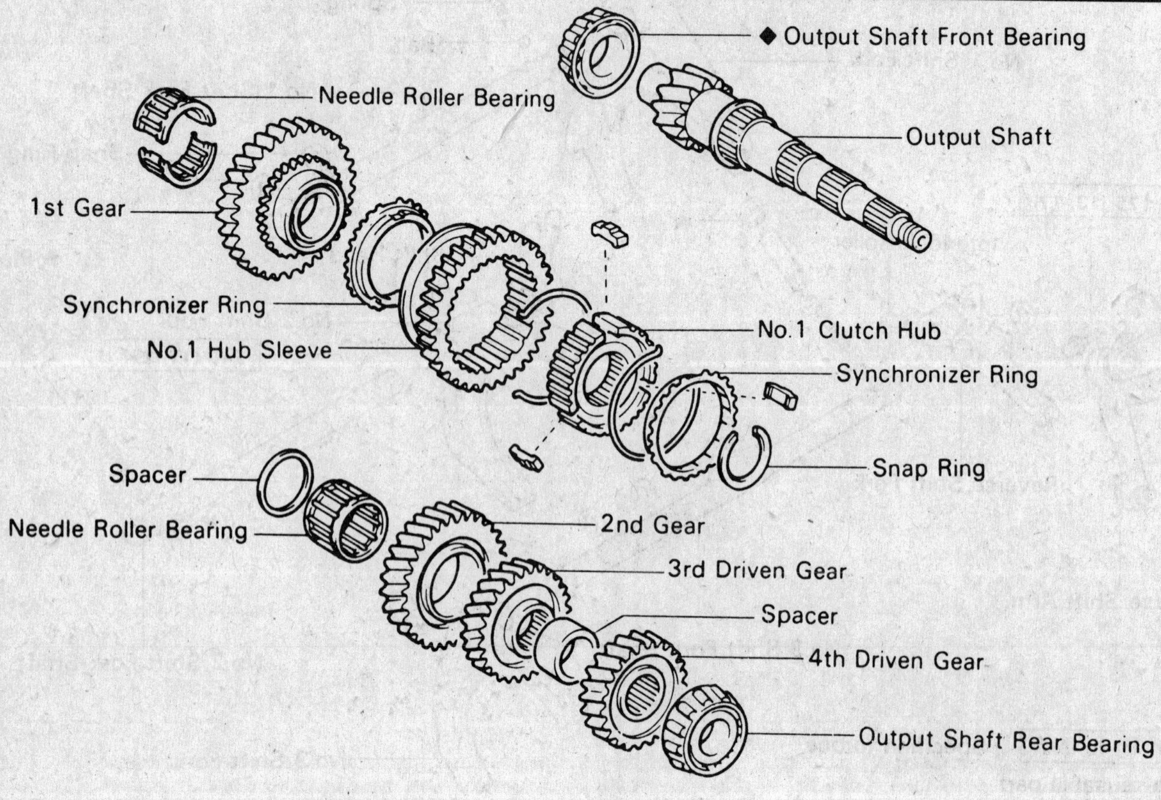

FIG.49 Output shaft components – E52 transaxle

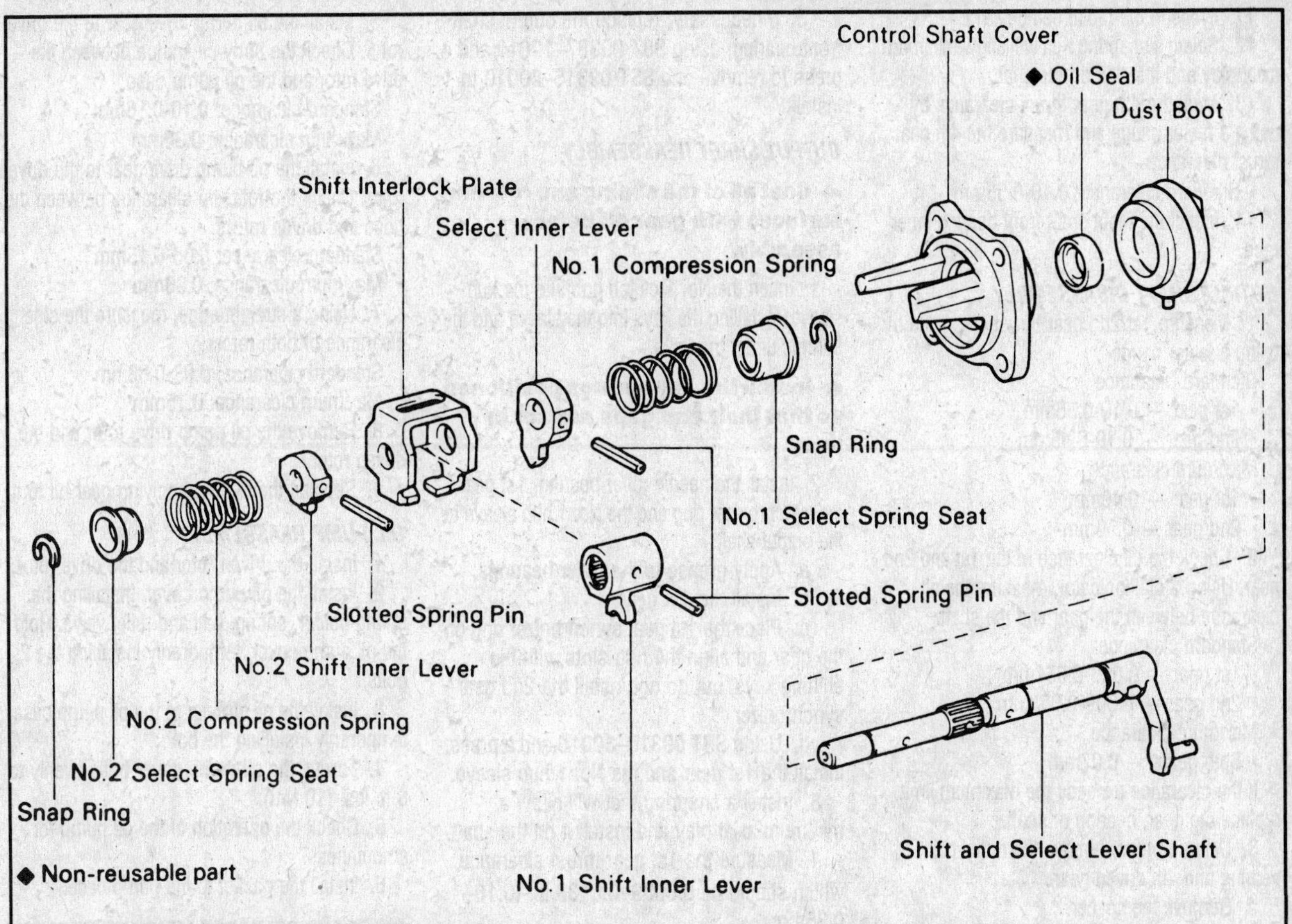

FIG.50 Shift and select lever components – E52 transaxle

FIG.51 Measuring 4th gear thrust clearance

- Both gears — 0.07mm

If the clearance exceeds the maximum limit, replace the gear, bearing or shaft.

3. Remove snapring from input shaft.
4. Using a press, remove the radial ball bearing and 4th gear.
5. Remove the needle roller bearings, synchronizer ring and spacer.
6. Remove the snapring with snapring pliers.
7. Remove No. 2 clutch hub assembly, 3rd gear, synchronizer ring and needle roller bearing.
8. Remove the input shaft front bearing inner race, using SST 09950–00020 and a press.
9. Inspect the synchronizer ring for fifth gear by turning the ring and pushing it in to check the braking action.
10. With a feeler gauge, measure the clearance between the back of the ring and gear spline end. Minimum clearance is 0.6mm.
11. If the clearance is less than the limit, replace the ring.
12. Check the shift fork and the hub clearance.
   a. With a feeler gauge, measure the clearance between the hub sleeve and shift fork. Maximum clearance is 1.00mm.
   b. If the clearance exceeds the limit, replace the shift fork or hub sleeve.
13. Using a micrometer, measure the input shaft journal outside diameter sections.
   Minimum outer diameters:
   - Section A — 32.93mm
   - Sections B and c — 35.95mm
14. Mount the input shaft on V-blocks and measure the runout. Maximum allowable runout is 0.050mm.

INPUT SHAFT REASSEMBLY

➡ **Coat all the sliding and rotating surfaces with gear oil before assembly.**

1. Install the No.2 clutch hub and shifting keys to the hub sleeve.
2. Install the shifting key springs under the shifting keys.

➡ **Install the key springs positioned so that their end gaps are not in line.**

3. Coat the 3rd gear needle roller bearings with grease.
4. Place the synchronizer ring on the 3rd gear and align the ring slots with the shifting keys.
5. Using a press, install the 3rd gear and No.2 hub sleeve.
6. Select a snapring that will allow minimum axial play and install it on the shaft.
7. Using a feeler gauge, measure the 3rd gear thrust clearance.
   - Standard clearance: 0.10-0.35mm
8. Install the synchronizer ring spacer.
9. Coat the needle roller bearing with grease.
10. Place the synchronizer ring on the gear and align the ring slots with the shifting keys and install the 4th gear.

11. Press in the radial ball bearing.

12. Select a snapring that will allow minimum axial play and install it on the shaft.

13. Measure 4th gear thrust clearance by using a feeler gauge and measure the 4th gear thrust clearance.

- Standard clearance: 0.10-0.55mm

14. Install the input shaft front bearing inner race.

OUTPUT SHAFT DISASSEMBLY

1. Measure 1st/2nd gear thrust clearance by using a feeler gauge.

Standard Clearance
- 1st gear — 0.10-0.35mm
- 2nd gear — 0.10-0.45mm

Maximum clearance:
- 1st gear — 0.40mm
- 2nd gear — 0.50mm

2. Check the oil clearance of the 1st and 2nd gear. Using a dial indicator, measure the oil clearance between the gear and the shaft.

Standard clearance:
- 1st gear — 0.009-0.051mm
- 2nd gear — 0.009-0.053mm

Maximum clearance:
- Both gears — 0.07mm

If the clearance exceeds the maximum limit, replace the gear, bearing or shaft.

3. Using a press, remove the radial ball bearing and 4th driven gear.

4. Remove the spacer.

5. Using a press, remove the 3rd driven gear and 2nd gear.

6. Remove the needle roller bearing, spacer and synchronizer ring.

7. Remove the snapring.

8. Using a press, remove the No.1 hub sleeve and 1st gear.

9. Remove the needle roller bearing and synchronizer ring.

10. Inspect the synchronizer rings by turning and pushing in to check the braking action.

11. With a feeler gauge, measure the clearance between the back of the ring and gear spline end. Minimum clearance is 0.6mm.

11. If the clearance is less than the limit, replace the ring.

12. Check the No. 1 shift fork and the hub clearance.

a. With a feeler gauge, measure the clearance between the hub sleeve and shift fork. Maximum clearance is 1.00mm.

b. If the clearance exceeds the limit, replace the shift fork or hub sleeve.

13. Using a micrometer, measure the output shaft journal outside diameter sections.

Minimum outer diameters:
- Both sections — 38.95mm

14. Mount the input shaft on V-blocks and measure the runout. Maximum allowable runout is 0.060mm.

15. If necessary, replace the output shaft front bearing, using SST 09307–12010 and a press to remove and SST 09316–60010 to install.

OUTPUT SHAFT REASSEMBLY

➡ Coat all of the sliding and rotating surfaces with gear oil before assembly.

1. Insert the No. 1 clutch hub into the hub sleeve, installing the keys into the sleeve and the springs under the keys.

➡ Install the key springs positioned so that their end gaps are not in line.

2. Install the needle roller bearing, 1st gear, the synchronizer ring and the No. 1 hub sleeve to the output shaft.

a. Apply grease to the roller bearings.

b. Install the 1st gear.

c. Place the 1st gear synchronizer ring on the gear and align the ring slots with the shifting keys, but do not install the 2nd gear synchronizer.

d. Using SST 09316–60010 and a press, install the 1st gear and the No. 1 hub sleeve.

3. Install a snapring that will allow a minimum axial play and install it on the shaft.

4. Measure the 1st gear thrust clearance, which should be 0.0039–0.0138 in. (0.10–0.35mm).

5. Install the spacer, needle roller bearing, synchronizer ring, 2nd gear and the 3rd driven gear.

a. Install the spacer.

b. Apply grease to the roller bearings.

c. Place the 2nd gear synchronizer ring on the gear and align the ring slots with the shifting keys, but do not install the 1st gear synchronizer.

d. Install the 2nd gear.

e. Using a press, install the 3rd driven gear.

6. Measure the 2nd gear thrust clearance, which should be 0.0039–0.0177 in. (0.10–0.45mm).

7. Install the spacer and the 4th driven gear, using a press.

8. Using SST 09506–30012 and a press, install the output shaft rear bearing.

OIL PUMP DISASSEMBLY

1. Install the oil pump drive gear to the drive rotor, then check that the drive rotor turns smoothly.

2. Remove the gasket to the oil pump case.

3. Remove the bolt and the oil strainer.

4. Hold the oil pump cover, remove the 2 bolts and the cover, then remove the spring holder, spring, ball and relief valve seat.

5. Install the oil pump drive gear to the drive rotor. Check the body clearance between the drive rotor and the oil pump case.

Standard clearance: 0.10-0.16mm
Maximum clearance: 0.30mm

6. Install the oil pump drive gear to the drive rotor. Check the rotor tip clearance between the drive and driven rotors.

Standard clearance: 0.08-0.15mm
Maximum clearance: 0.30mm

7. Using a straight edge, measure the side clearance of both rotors.

Standard clearance: 0.03-0.08mm
Maximum clearance: 0.15mm

8. Remove the oil pump drive rotor and the driven rotor.

9. Replace the O-ring, applying gear oil to it.

OIL PUMP REASSEMBLY

1. Install the driven rotor and the drive rotor.

2. Install the oil pump cover, installing the spring holder, spring, ball and relief valve. Hold the oil pump cover, temporarily installing the 2 bolts.

3. Install the oil strainer to the oil pump case, temporarily installing the bolt.

4. Torque the oil pump cover bolts evenly to 8 ft. lbs. (10 Nm).

5. Check the operation of the oil pump for smoothness.

6. Install the gasket to the pump case.

SHIFT AND SELECTOR LEVER COMPONENT DISASSEMBLY

1. Using a pin punch and a hammer, drive the out the slotted spring pin.

2. Remove the snapring.

3. Remove the No.2 select spring seat.

4. Remove the No.2 compression spring and the No.2 shift inner lever.

5. Using a pin punch and a hammer drive out the No.1 shift inner lever slotted spring pin.

6. Remove the shift interlock plate and the No.1 shift inner lever from the shaft.

7. Using a pin punch and a hammer drive out the select inner lever slotted spring pin.

8. Remove the select inner lever, No.1 compression spring and No.1 select spring seat.

9. Remove the remaining snapring.

10. Remove the control shaft cover and dust boot.

11. If necessary, withdraw the oil seal from the control shaft cover. Using SST No. 09620-30010 or equivalent and a hammer, drive the new oil seal into the cover to a depth of 0.5 mm ± 0.5mm. After installation coat the new seal lip with multi-purpose grease.

SHIFT AND SELECT LEVER SHAFT REASSEMBLY

1. Lightly coat all sliding, mating and splined surfaces with multi-purpose grease.

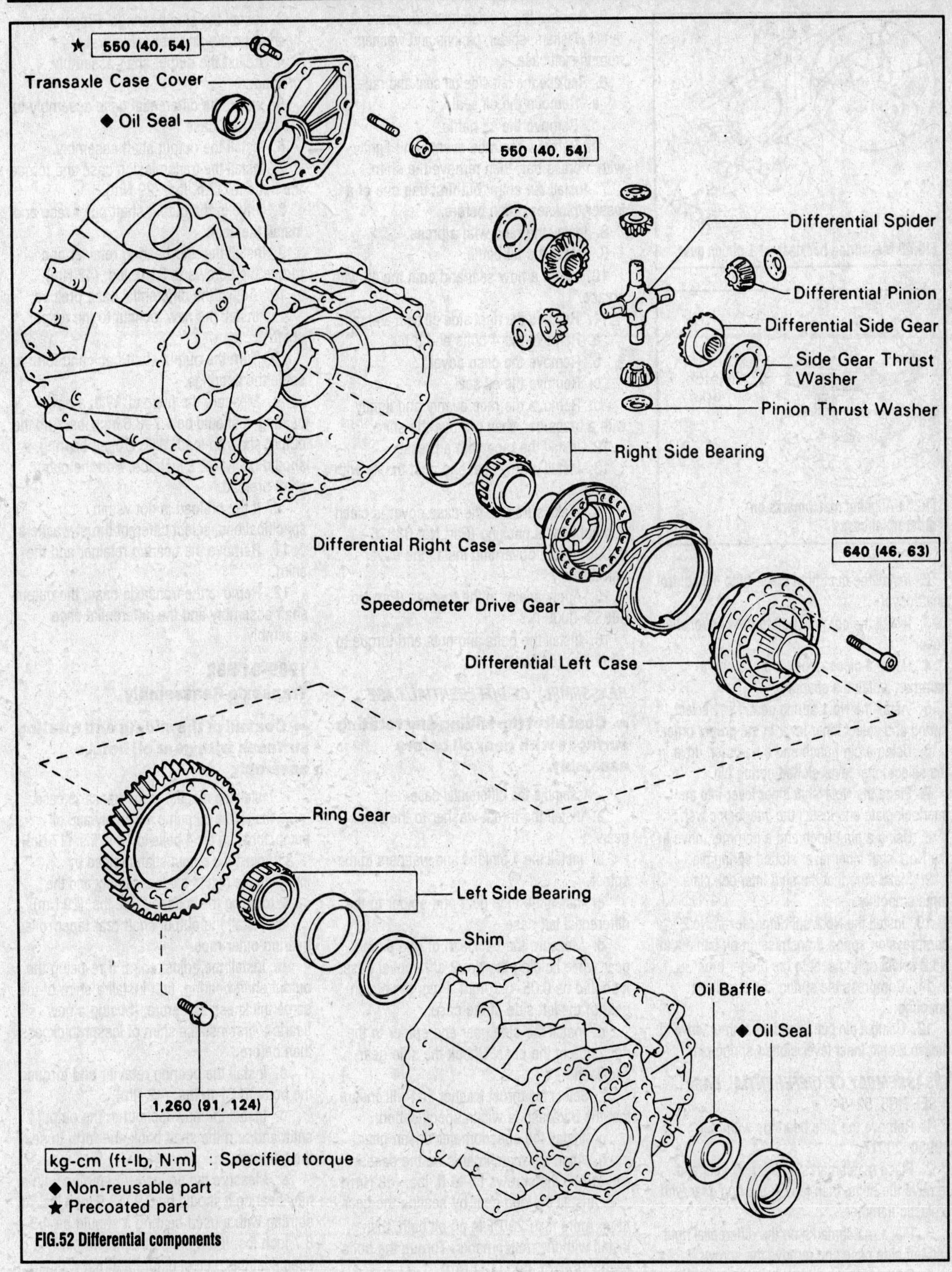
★ 550 (40, 54)
Transaxle Case Cover
◆ Oil Seal
550 (40, 54)
Differential Spider
Differential Pinion
Differential Side Gear
Side Gear Thrust Washer
Pinion Thrust Washer
Right Side Bearing
640 (46, 63)
Differential Right Case
Speedometer Drive Gear
Differential Left Case
Ring Gear
Left Side Bearing
Shim
Oil Baffle
◆ Oil Seal
1,260 (91, 124)
kg-cm (ft-lb, N·m) : Specified torque
◆ Non-reusable part
★ Precoated part

FIG.52 Differential components

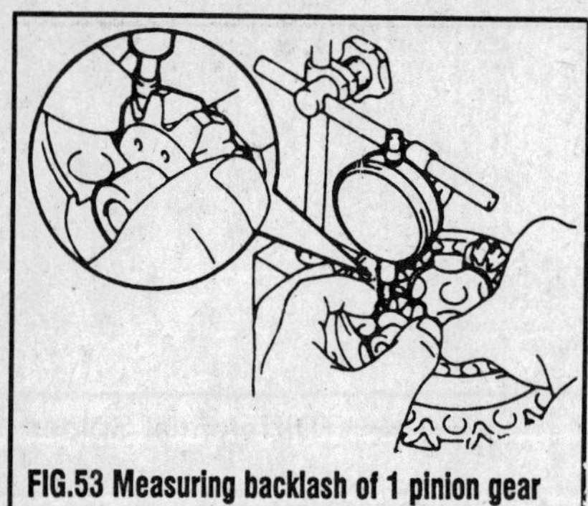
FIG.53 Measuring backlash of 1 pinion gear

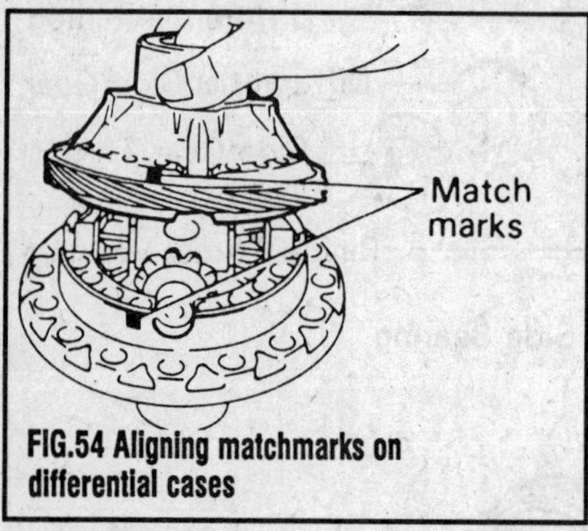

FIG.54 Aligning matchmarks on differential cases

2. Install the dust boot cover onto the control shaft cover.

3. Install the control shaft to the control shaft cover.

4. Using a piece of brass stock and a hammer, install the snapring.

5. Install the No.1 spring seat, No.1 select spring and select inner lever in the proper order.

6. Using a pin punch and a hammer, drive in the select inner lever slotted spring pin.

7. Place the No.1 shift inner lever into the interlock plate and install the interlock cover.

8. Using a pin punch and a hammer, drive in the No.1 shift inner lever slotted spring pin.

9. Make sure that the shift interlock plate turns smoothly.

10. Install the No.2 shift inner lever, No.2 compression spring, transmission oil baffle and No.2 select spring seat in the proper order.

11. Compress the spring and install the snapring.

12. Using a pin punch and a hammer, drive in the No.2 shift inner lever slotted spring pin.

DISASSEMBLY OF DIFFERENTIAL CASE

➧ SEE FIGS. 52–54

1. Remove the side bearings with SST 09950–20017.

2. Place matchmarks on the ring gear and remove the bolts, then tap off the ring gear with a plastic hammer.

3. Place matchmarks on the differential right and left side case and remove the screws.

4. Remove the speedometer drive gear from the differential right case.

5. Remove the 2 differential side gears, 2 thrust washers, spider, pinions and washers from the left case.

6. Replace the left side oil seal and race.
   a. Remove the oil seal.
   b. Remove the oil baffle.
   c. Remove the race evenly and lightly with a brass bar, then remove the shim.

7. Install the shim, but first use one of a lesser thickness than before.

8. Install the race with a press.

9. Install the oil baffle.

10. Install a new seal and coat the lip with grease.

11. Replace the right side oil seal and race.
   a. Remove the 4 bolts and 3 nut.
   b. Remove the case cover.
   c. Remove the oil seal.
   d. Remove the race evenly and lightly with a brass bar, then remove the shim.

12. Install the race with a press.

13. Install a new seal and coat the lip with grease.

14. Make sure that the case cover is clean and apply seal packing (Part No. 08826–00090) to the cover and install the cover immediately.

15. Apply sealer to the threads (Part No. 08833–00090).

16. Install the bolts and nuts and torque to 40 ft. lbs. (54 Nm).

REASSEMBLY OF DIFFERENTIAL CASE

➡ **Coat all of the sliding and rotating surfaces with gear oil before assembly.**

1. Assemble the differential case.
   a. Install the thrust washer to the side gear.
   b. Install the 4 pinions and washers to the spider.
   c. Install the side gear and spider to the differential left case.
   d. Measure the backlash of one pinion gear while holding the No. 2 differential case. It should be 0.05–0.20mm. Push the pinion gear of the left side of the case.
   e. Install the side gear and spider to the right side of the case. Check the side gear backlash.
   f. Select the thrust washer that will ensure that the backlash is within specification.
   g. Install the speedometer driven gear.
   h. Align the matchmarks on the cases and torque the screws to 46 ft. lbs. (63 Nm).

2. Install the ring gear by heating the gear to no more than 230°F in an oil bath, then install with the matchmarks. Torque the bolts evenly to 91 ft. lbs. (124 Nm).

3. Install the side bearings. Press the bearing on the ring gear side first.

4. Adjust the output shaft assembly preload.

5. Install the differential case assembly to the transaxle case.

6. Install the output shaft assembly.

7. Install the transmission case and torque the bolts to 22 ft. lbs. (29 Nm).

8. Drive in the output shaft outer race and install the shim.

9. Install the rear bearing retainer and torque the screws to 31 ft. lbs. (42 Nm).

10. Adjust the differential case preload.
   a. Install the new locknut to the output shaft.
   b. Turn the output shaft back and forth to settle the bearings.
   c. Measure the preload. With a new bearing, it should be 1.7–3.6 inch lbs. Add the output shaft preload. With a used bearing, it should be 1.1–2.2 inch lbs. Add the output shaft preload.
   d. If the preload is not within specifications, select different thrust washers.

11. Remove the bearing retainer and the shim.

12. Remove the transaxle case, the output shaft assembly and the differential case assembly.

1989–91 E52

Transaxle Reassembly

➡ **Coat all of the sliding and rotating surfaces with gear oil before assembly.**

1. Install the magnet to the transaxle case.

2. Install the oil pump assembly and oil pump, torquing the 4 bolts to 13 ft. lbs. (17 Nm).

3. Adjust the output shaft preload by installing the output shaft assembly and the case, torquing the bolts to 22 ft. lbs. (29 Nm).
   a. Install the output shaft rear taper roller bearing outer race.
   b. Install the adjust shim. If re-using the output shaft bearing, first install a shim of the same thickness as before. If using a new bearing, first install a shim of lesser thickness than before.
   c. Install the bearing retainer and torque the bolts to 31 ft. lbs. (42 Nm).
   d. Install the new locknut to the output shaft and turn the shaft back and forth to seat the bearings.
   e. Measure the preload. At starting with a new bearing it should be 6.9–13.9 inch lbs. At starting with a used bearing it should be 4.3–8.7 inch lbs. If the preload is not within specifications, select different thrust washers.

f. Remove the lock nut.

g. Remove the rear bearing retainer, shim, transmission case and output shaft assembly.

4. Install the differential case assembly.

5. Install the oil pump drive gear.

6. Install the output shaft assembly.

7. Install the snaprings to the 1, 2 and 3 shift fork shafts and install the reverse shift fork and snapring to the No. 3 shift fork shaft.

8. Install the No. 2 shift fork to the No. 2 hub sleeve and the reverse shift fork with fork shaft No. 3.

9. Install the No. 1 shift fork, shift head and the No. 2 shift fork shaft by installing the No. 1 fork to the No. 1 hub sleeve. Put the shift head onto the No. 1 shift fork. Then install the No. 2 shift fork shaft to the transaxle case, through the shift head and the No. 1 fork.

10. Install the interlock roller to the reverse shift fork.

11. Install the shift fork No. 1 to the case through shift fork No. 1 and reverse shift fork.

12. Install the 3 set bolts and torque to 17 ft. lbs. (24 Nm).

13. Install the locking balls, springs, seats and plugs. Apply sealing to the plugs and torque to 18 ft. lbs. (25 Nm).

14. Install reverse idler gear and shaft by aligning the reference points.

15. Install the reverse shift fork pivot into the reverse shift arm and install the reverse shift arm bracket to the transaxle case. Install the bolt, the No. 2 oil pipe and torque the bolts to 13 ft. lbs. (17 Nm). Use a new pipe gasket.

16. Install the transaxle case, applying sealer and assembling immediately. Torque the bolts to 22 ft. lbs. (29 Nm).

17. Install and torque the reverse idler gear shaft retaining bolt to 22 ft. lbs. (29 Nm).

18. Install the locking ball, spring and seat. Apply sealer to the plug and torque to 18 ft. lbs. (25 Nm).

19. Install the 3 snaprings.

20. Install the output shaft rear taper roller bearing outer race.

21. Install the shim.

22. Install the snapring to the input shaft rear bearing.

23. Install rear bearing retainer and torque the bolts to 31 ft. lbs.

24. Install the spacer, needle roller bearing and 5th gear.

25. Install the synchronizer ring with key spring to the No. 3 clutch hub.

26. Install the No.3 clutch hub with the synchronizer ring and key spring.

27. Install a snapring that will allow minimum axial play and install it on the shaft.

28. Using a dial indicator, measure 5th gear thrust clearance.

- Standard clearance: 0.10-0.57mm

29. Install the 5th driven gear.

30. Install the No. 3 hub sleeve with the No. 3 shift fork.

31. Install and torque the set bolt to 17 ft. lbs. (24 Nm).

32. Engage the gear double meshing and install the locknut. Torque the nut to 90 ft. lbs. Disengage the meshing and stake the lock nut.

33. Apply sealer to the transaxle case, then immediately install the transmission case cover with the retaining bolts. Torque the bolts to 22 ft. lbs.

34. Install the shift and selector lever shaft assembly.

a. Place a new gasket on the control shaft cover and install it.

b. Apply sealer to the bolt threads.

c. Torque the bolts to 14 ft. lbs. (20 Nm).

35. Install and torque the lock bolt to 36 ft. lbs. (49 Nm).

36. Install and torque the selecting bellcrank to 14 ft. lbs. (20 Nm).

37. Install back-up light switch and torque to 30 ft. lbs.

38. Install speedometer driven gear.

39. Apply molybdenum disulphide lithium base grease to the following parts: input shaft spline and release fork contact surface.

1992 E53 Transaxle

Disassembly

➧ SEE FIGS. 24, 25, 31–34, 37–40, 49, 55–64

1. Remove the release fork, bearing and back-up light switch.

2. Remove the speedometer driven gear.

3. Remove the speed sensor and the shift control bracket.

4. Remove the selecting bellcrank and the breather plug.

5. Remove shift lever lock bolt.

6. Remove the 4 bolts securing the shift and select lever assembly and remove.

7. Remove the transmission case cover.

8. Unstake the output shaft locknut using a small cold chisel.

9. Engage the gear double meshing.

10. Remove the lock nut and disengage the gear double meshing.

11. Remove the No. 3 shift fork set bolt, then the No. 3 hub sleeve and the shift fork.

12. Using SST kit 09310–17010, remove the fifth driven gear.

13. Using a dial indicator, measure the 5th gear thrust clearance. Standard clearance is 0.10-0.57mm with a maximum clearance of 0.65mm.

14. Measure the oil clearance. Standard clearance is 0.009-0.050mm with a maximum clearance of 0.070mm.

15. Using 2 prybars and a hammer, tap out the No. 3 clutch hub snapring.

16. Using a puller, remove 5th gear, synchronizer ring and the No. 3 clutch hub.

17. Remove the needle roller bearing.

18. Remove the 7 screws, remove the rear bearing retainer and the adjust shim.

19. Remove the 3 small and 1 large snaprings by using suitable tools.

20. Remove the plug, seat, spring and locking ball, using a magnet.

21. Remove reverse idler gear shaft retaining bolt.

22. To remove transmission case, remove the 17 bolts and tap off the case with a plastic hammer.

23. Remove the output shaft rear tapered roller bearing outer race by driving out the outer race, then remove the oil pipe.

24. Remove the two bolts and pull off the reverse shift arm bracket.

25. Remove reverse idler gear and thrust washer and shaft by pulling out the shaft.

26. Remove the 2 plugs, locking balls and springs.

27. Remove the No. 1 shift fork set bolt.

28. Pull up the No. 3 shift fork shaft and remove the No. 1 shift fork shaft.

29. Remove the interlock roller from the reverse shift fork, using a magnet.

30. Remove the No.2 fork shaft.

31. Remove the shift head and the No. 1 shift fork.

32. Pull out the No. 3 shift fork shaft with the reverse shift fork.

33. Pull out the No.2 fork shaft and remove all snaprings.

34. Carefully remove input and output shaft together from transaxle case.

35. Remove the oil pump drive gear.

36. Remove differential assembly.

37. Remove the magnet from the transaxle case.

38. Remove the 2 oil pump assembly bolts and the oil pipe.

39. Remove the No. 5 synchronizer ring with the key spring from the No. 3 clutch hub, removing the snapring.

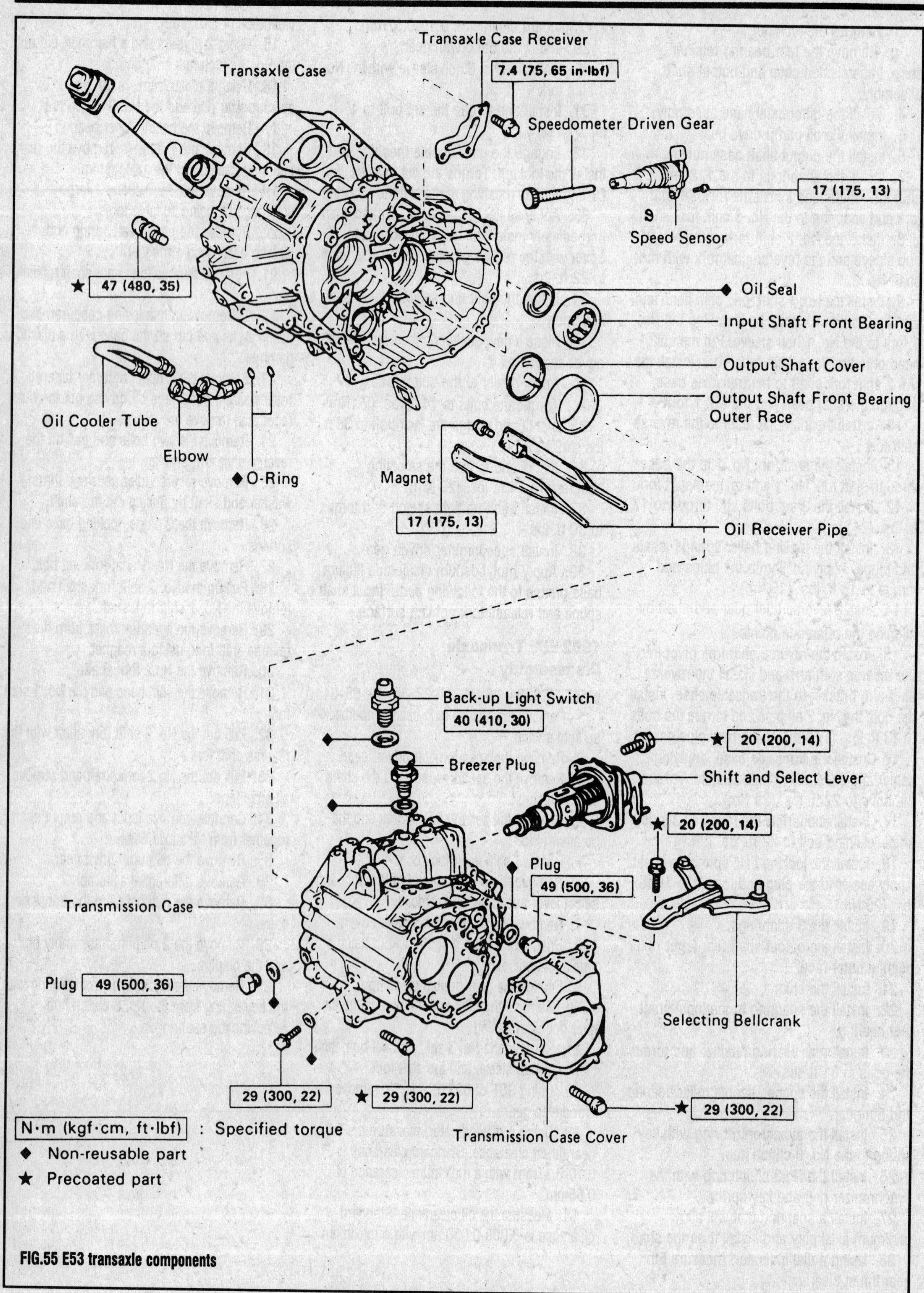

Transaxle Case Receiver
7.4 (75, 65 in·lbf)
Transaxle Case
Speedometer Driven Gear
17 (175, 13)
Speed Sensor
★ 47 (480, 35)
◆ Oil Seal
Input Shaft Front Bearing
Output Shaft Cover
Output Shaft Front Bearing Outer Race
Oil Cooler Tube
Elbow
◆ O-Ring
Magnet
17 (175, 13)
Oil Receiver Pipe
Back-up Light Switch
40 (410, 30)
★ 20 (200, 14)
Breezer Plug
Shift and Select Lever
★ 20 (200, 14)
Plug
49 (500, 36)
Transmission Case
Plug 49 (500, 36)
Selecting Bellcrank
29 (300, 22)
★ 29 (300, 22)
★ 29 (300, 22)
N·m (kgf·cm, ft·lbf) : Specified torque
◆ Non-reusable part
★ Precoated part
Transmission Case Cover

FIG.55 E53 transaxle components

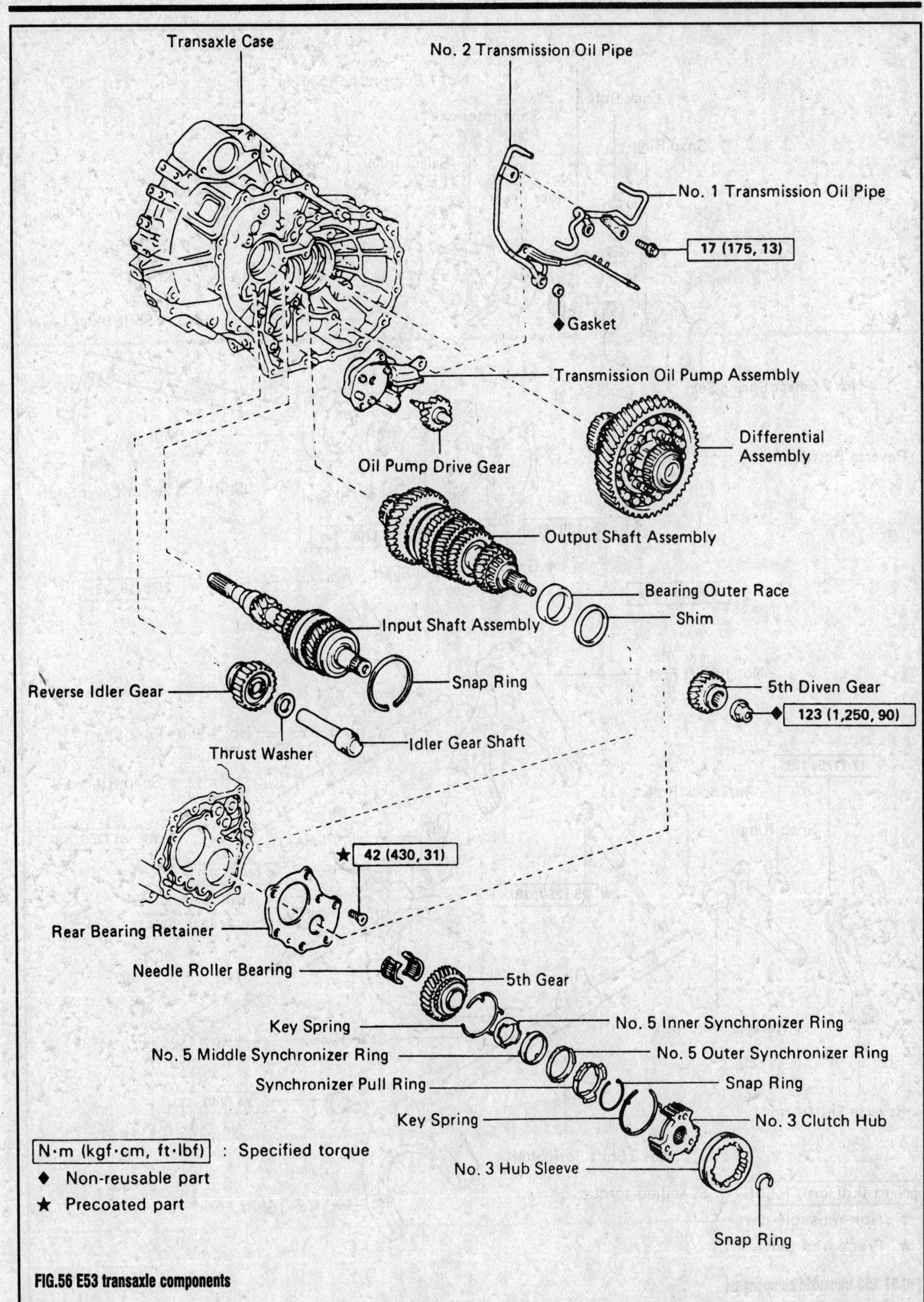
Transaxle Case
No. 2 Transmission Oil Pipe
No. 1 Transmission Oil Pipe
17 (175, 13)
◆ Gasket
Transmission Oil Pump Assembly
Differential Assembly
Oil Pump Drive Gear
Output Shaft Assembly
Bearing Outer Race
Shim
Input Shaft Assembly
Snap Ring
Reverse Idler Gear
5th Diven Gear
123 (1,250, 90)
Thrust Washer
Idler Gear Shaft
★ 42 (430, 31)
Rear Bearing Retainer
Needle Roller Bearing
5th Gear
Key Spring
No. 5 Inner Synchronizer Ring
No. 5 Middle Synchronizer Ring
No. 5 Outer Synchronizer Ring
Synchronizer Pull Ring
Snap Ring
Key Spring
No. 3 Clutch Hub
N·m (kgf·cm, ft·lbf) : Specified torque
◆ Non-reusable part
★ Precoated part
No. 3 Hub Sleeve
Snap Ring

FIG.56 E53 transaxle components

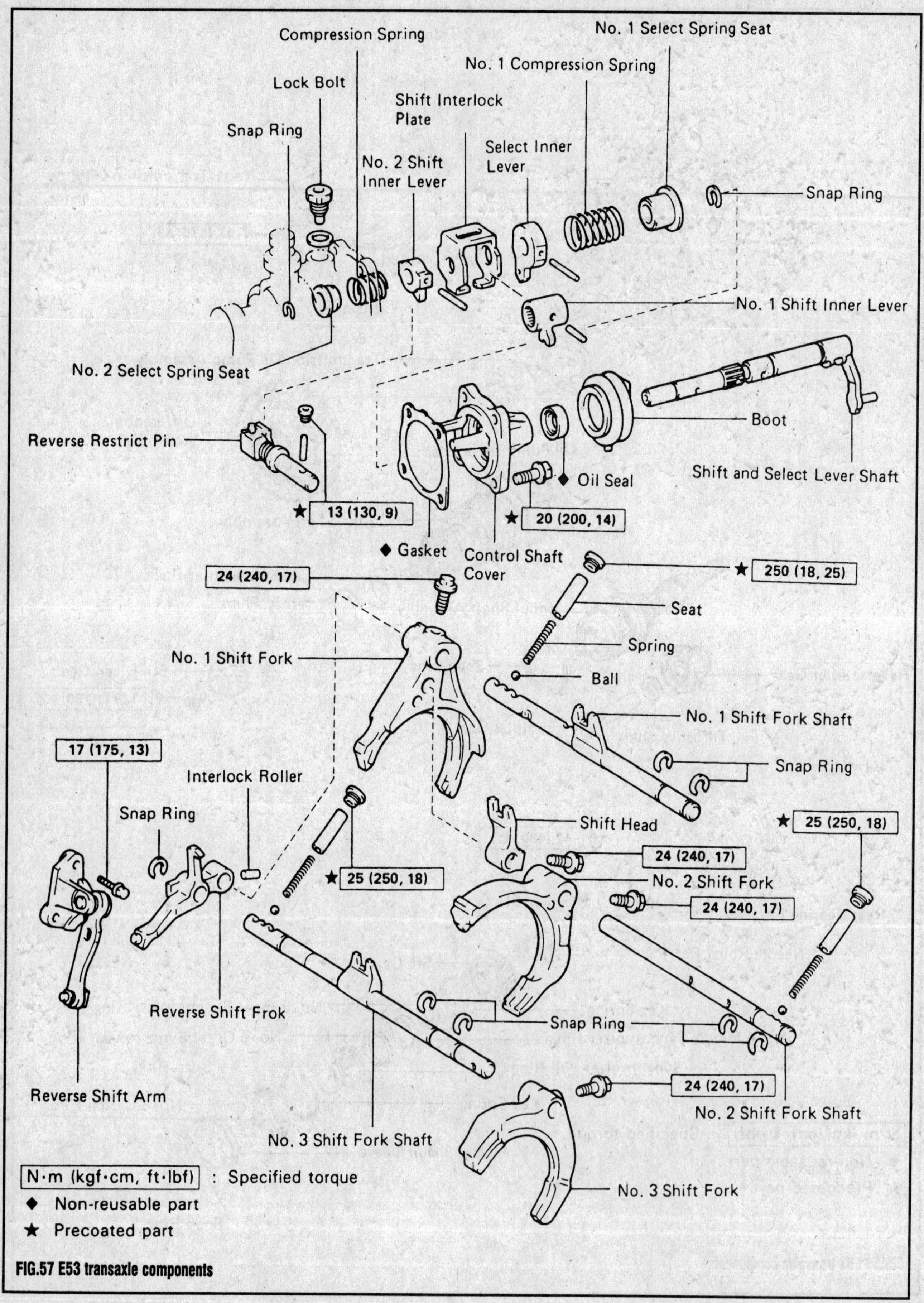
Compression Spring
No. 1 Select Spring Seat
No. 1 Compression Spring
Lock Bolt
Shift Interlock Plate
Snap Ring
Select Inner Lever
No. 2 Shift Inner Lever
Snap Ring
No. 1 Shift Inner Lever
No. 2 Select Spring Seat
Boot
Reverse Restrict Pin
Shift and Select Lever Shaft
Oil Seal
★ 13 (130, 9)
★ 20 (200, 14)
◆ Gasket
Control Shaft Cover
24 (240, 17)
★ 250 (18, 25)
Seat
Spring
No. 1 Shift Fork
Ball
No. 1 Shift Fork Shaft
17 (175, 13)
Snap Ring
Interlock Roller
Snap Ring
★ 25 (250, 18)
Shift Head
★ 25 (250, 18)
24 (240, 17)
No. 2 Shift Fork
24 (240, 17)
Reverse Shift Frok
Snap Ring
Reverse Shift Arm
24 (240, 17)
No. 2 Shift Fork Shaft
No. 3 Shift Fork Shaft
N·m (kgf·cm, ft·lbf) : Specified torque
◆ Non-reusable part
★ Precoated part
No. 3 Shift Fork

FIG.57 E53 transaxle components

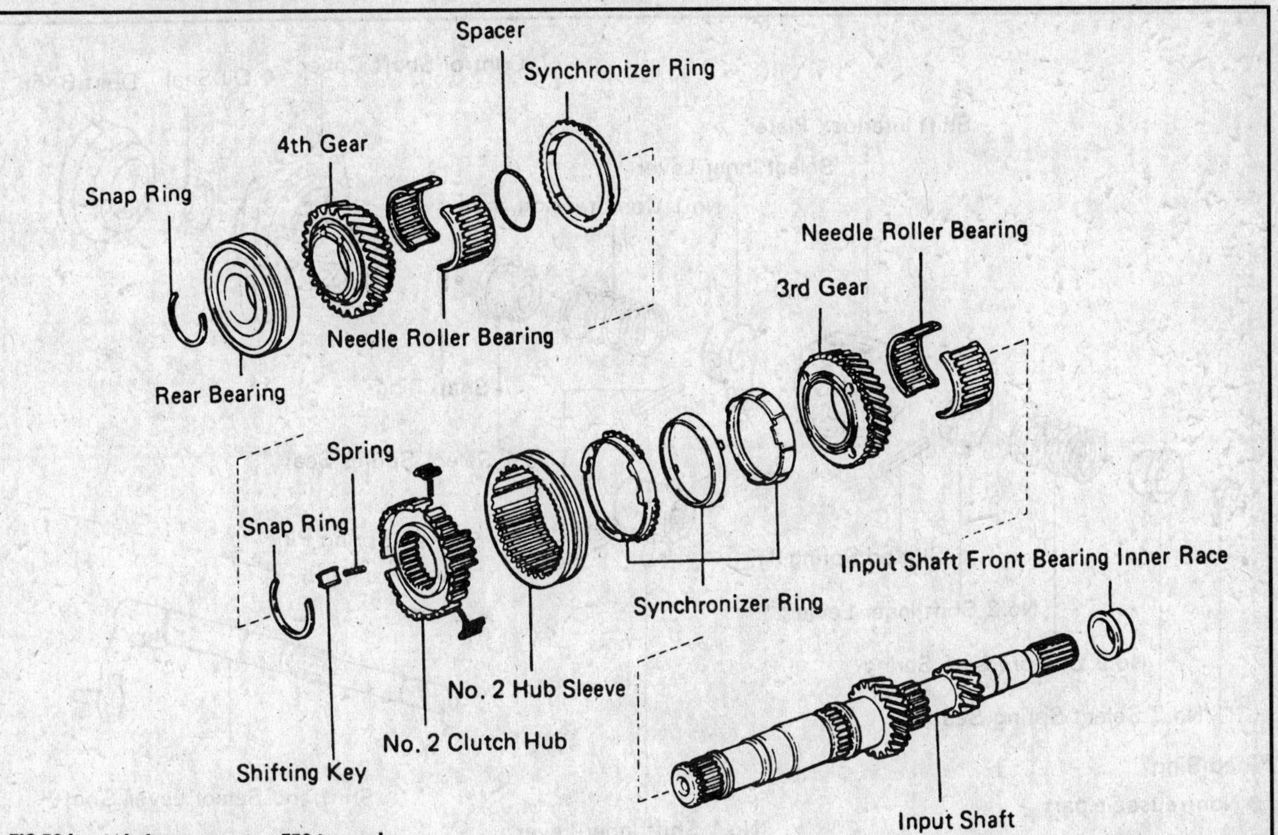

FIG.58 Input shaft components – E53 transaxle

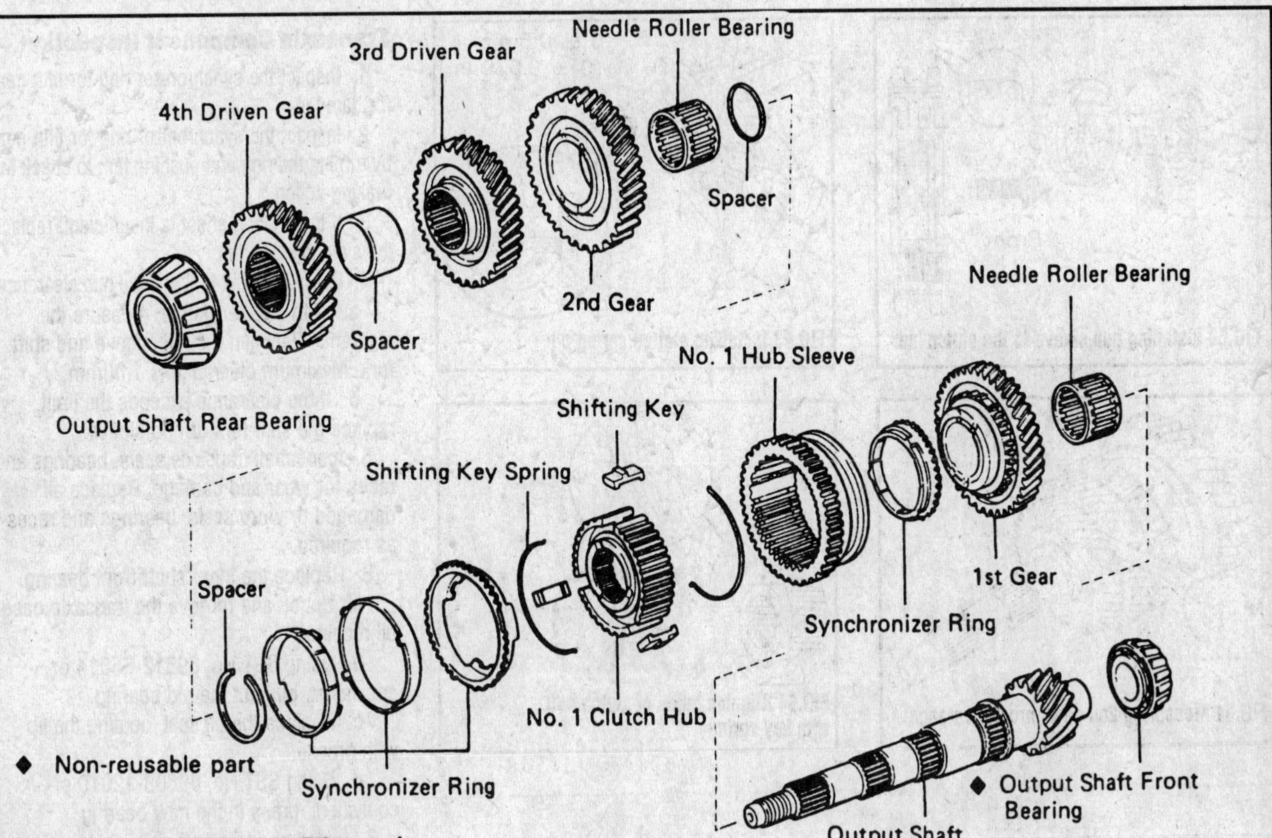

FIG.60 Output shaft components – E53 transaxle

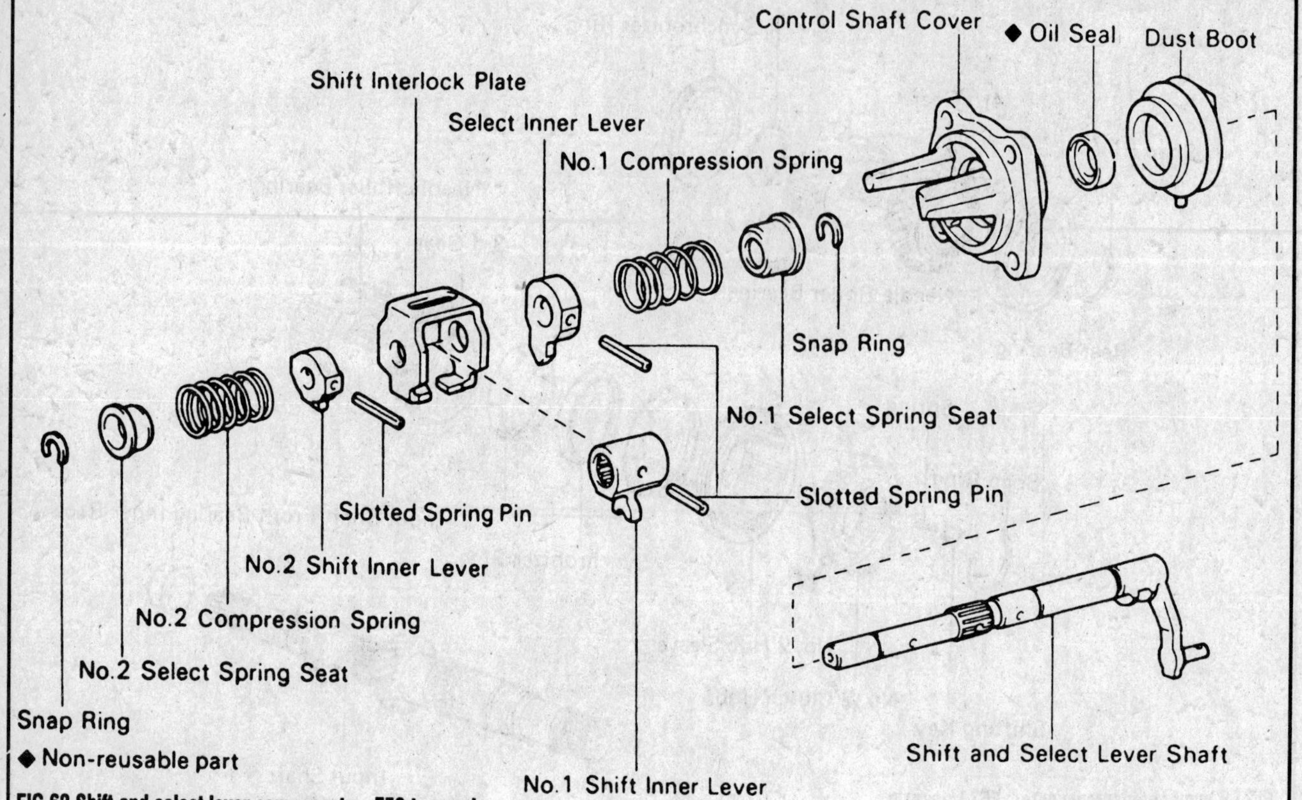

Control Shaft Cover
◆ Oil Seal
Dust Boot
Shift Interlock Plate
Select Inner Lever
No.1 Compression Spring
Snap Ring
No.1 Select Spring Seat
Slotted Spring Pin
Slotted Spring Pin
No.2 Shift Inner Lever
No.2 Compression Spring
No.2 Select Spring Seat
Snap Ring
Shift and Select Lever Shaft
No.1 Shift Inner Lever
◆ Non-reusable part

FIG.62 Shift and select lever components—E53 transaxle

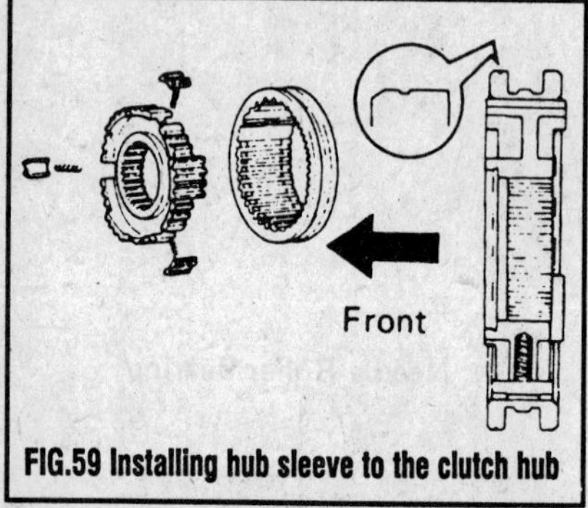

FIG.59 Installing hub sleeve to the clutch hub

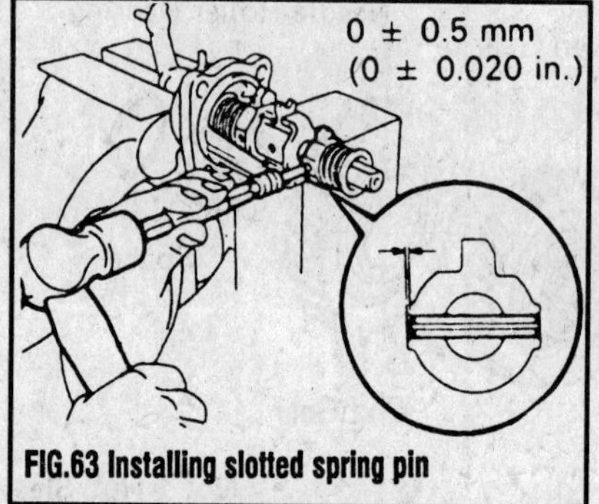

FIG.63 Installing slotted spring pin

FIG.61 Measuring 2nd gear thrust clearance

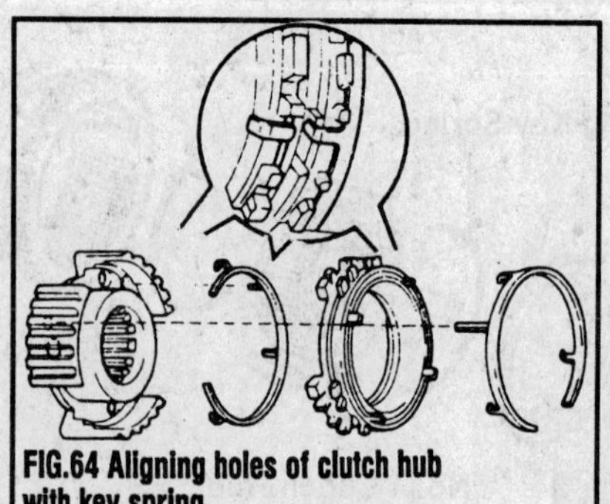

FIG.64 Aligning holes of clutch hub with key spring

Transaxle Component Inspection

1. Inspect the synchronizer ring for fifth gear for damage.
2. Inspect the synchronizer ring for fifth gear by turning the ring and pushing it in to check the braking action.
3. If the braking effect is insufficient, replace the synchronizer ring.
4. Check the shift fork and the hub clearance.
   a. With a feeler gauge, measure the clearance between the hub sleeve and shift fork. Maximum clearance is 1.00mm.
   b. If the clearance exceeds the limit, replace the shift fork or hub sleeve.
5. Inspect all transaxle seals, bearings and races for wear and damage. Replace all damaged or worn seals, bearings and races as required.
6. Replace the input shaft front bearing.
   a. Unbolt and remove the transaxle case oil receiver.
   b. Using SST No. 09612-65014 or equivalent, pull out the old bearing.
   c. Replace the oil seal, coating the lip with grease.
   d. Using SST No. 09608-12010 or equivalent, press in the new bearing.
7. Install and torque the transaxle case receiver to 65 inch lbs. (7.4 Nm).

8. Remove the inner race with SST 09950–00020, then install one with SST 09316–60010 and a press.

9. Replace the output shaft front bearing and output shaft front cover.

a. Using SST No. 09308-00010 or equivalent, pull out the output shaft front bearing outer race.

b. Remove the output shaft front cover.

c. Install the output shaft front cover, installing the shaft cover projection into the case side groove.

d. Using SST 09316–60010, press in a new outer race.

e. Using SST's 09950–00020 and 09950–00030, remove the output shaft front bearing.

f. Using SST 09316–60010, press in a new output shaft front bearing.

10. Replace the reverse restrict pin.

a. Remove the screw plug.

b. Using a pin punch and hammer, drive out the slotted spring pin.

c. Remove the reverse restrict pin.

d. Using a pin punch and hammer, drive the slotted spring pin back in.

e. Apply Loctite® or similar liquid sealant to the threads of the screw plug.

f. Install the screw plug.

INPUT SHAFT DISASSEMBLY AND INSPECTION

1. Using a feeler gauge, measure the 3rd and 4th gear thrust clearance.

Standard clearance:
- 3rd gear — 0.10-0.45mm
- 4th gear — 0.10-0.55mm

Maximum clearance:
- 3rd gear — 0.50mm
- 4th gear — 0.60mm

2. Check the oil clearance of the 3rd and 4th gear. Using a dial indicator, measure the oil clearance between the gear and the shaft.

Standard clearance:
- 3rd gear — 0.009-0.053mm
- 4th gear — 0.009-0.051mm

Maximum clearance:
- Both gears — 0.07mm

If the clearance exceeds the maximum limit, replace the gear, bearing or shaft.

3. Remove snapring from input shaft.

4. Using a press, remove the radial ball bearing and 4th gear.

5. Remove the needle roller bearings, synchronizer ring and spacer.

6. Remove the snapring with snapring pliers.

7. Remove No. 2 clutch hub assembly, 3rd gear and synchronizer ring.

8. Remove the needle roller bearing.

9. Inspect the synchronizer ring for 3rd gear by turning the ring and pushing it in to check the braking action. With a feeler gauge, measure the clearance between the back of the ring and gear spline end. Minimum clearance is 0.7mm.

10. Inspect the synchronizer ring for 4th gear by turning the ring and pushing it in to check the braking action. With a feeler gauge, measure the clearance between the back of the ring and gear spline end. Minimum clearance is 0.6mm.

11. If the clearance is less than the limit, replace the ring.

12. Check the No. 2 shift fork and the hub sleeve clearance.

a. With a feeler gauge, measure the clearance between the hub sleeve and shift fork. Maximum clearance is 1.00mm.

b. If the clearance exceeds the limit, replace the shift fork or hub sleeve.

13. Using a micrometer, measure the input shaft journal outside diameter sections.

Minimum outer diameters:
- Section A — 27.95mm
- Sections B and c — 35.95mm

14. Mount the input shaft on V-blocks and measure the runout. Maximum allowable runout is 0.050mm.

INPUT SHAFT REASSEMBLY

➡ Coat all the sliding and rotating surfaces with gear oil before assembly.

1. Install the 3 shifting key springs and the shifting keys to the No. 2 clutch hub.

2. Install the hub sleeve to the clutch hub.

➡ Direct the identification groove of the hub sleeve to the front of the transaxle.

3. Coat the 3rd gear needle roller bearings with grease.

4. Place the synchronizer ring on the 3rd gear and align the ring slots with the shifting keys.

5. Using a press, install the 3rd gear and No.2 hub sleeve.

6. Select a snapring that will allow minimum axial play and install it on the shaft and install it.

7. Using a feeler gauge, measure the 3rd gear thrust clearance.
- Standard clearance: 0.10-0.45mm

8. Install the synchronizer ring spacer.

9. Coat the needle roller bearing with grease.

10. Place the synchronizer ring on the gear and align the ring slots with the shifting keys and install the 4th gear.

11. Press in the radial ball bearing.

12. Select a snapring that will allow minimum axial play and install it on the shaft.

13. Measure 4th gear thrust clearance by using a feeler gauge and measure the 4th gear thrust clearance.
- Standard clearance: 0.10-0.55mm

OUTPUT SHAFT DISASSEMBLY AND INSPECTION

1. Measure 1st/2nd gear thrust clearance by using a feeler gauge.

Standard Clearance
- 1st gear — 0.10-0.35mm
- 2nd gear — 0.10-0.45mm

Maximum clearance:
- 1st gear — 0.40mm
- 2nd gear — 0.50mm

2. Check the oil clearance of the 1st and 2nd gear. Using a dial indicator, measure the oil clearance between the gear and the shaft.

Standard clearance:
- 1st gear — 0.009-0.051mm
- 2nd gear — 0.009-0.053mm

Maximum clearance:
- Both gears — 0.07mm

If the clearance exceeds the maximum limit, replace the gear, bearing or shaft.

3. Using a press, remove the radial ball bearing and 4th driven gear.

4. Remove the spacer.

5. Using a press, remove the 3rd driven gear and 2nd gear.

6. Remove the needle roller bearing, spacer and synchronizer ring.

7. Remove the snapring.

8. Using a press, remove the No.1 hub sleeve and 1st gear.

9. Remove the needle roller bearing and synchronizer ring, then remove the output shaft front bearing.

10. Inspect the synchronizer rings by turning and pushing in to check the braking action.

11. With a feeler gauge, measure the clearance between the back of the ring and gear spline end. Minimum clearance is 0.6mm for 1st gear and 0.7mm for 2nd gear.

12. If the clearance is less than the limit, replace the ring.

13. Check the No. 1 shift fork and the hub clearance.

a. With a feeler gauge, measure the clearance between the hub sleeve and shift fork. Maximum clearance is 1.00mm.

b. If the clearance exceeds the limit, replace the shift fork or hub sleeve.

14. Using a micrometer, measure the output shaft journal outside diameter sections.

Minimum outer diameters:
- Both sections — 38.95mm

15. Mount the input shaft on V-blocks and measure the runout. Maximum allowable runout is 0.060mm.

OUTPUT SHAFT REASSEMBLY

➡ Coat all of the sliding and rotating surfaces with gear oil before assembly.

1. Insert the No. 1 clutch hub into the hub sleeve, installing the keys into the sleeve and the springs under the keys.

➡ **Install the key springs positioned so that their end gaps are not in line.**

2. Install the needle roller bearing, 1st gear, the synchronizer ring and the No. 1 hub sleeve to the output shaft.
   a. Apply grease to the roller bearings.
   b. Install the 1st gear.
   c. Place the 1st gear synchronizer ring on the gear and align the ring slots with the shifting keys, but do not install the 2nd gear synchronizer.
   d. Using SST 09316-60010 and a press, install the 1st gear and the No. 1 hub sleeve.
3. Install a snapring that will allow a minimum axial play and install it on the shaft.
4. Measure the 1st gear thrust clearance, which should be 0.0039–0.0138 in. (0.10–0.35mm).
5. Install the spacer, needle roller bearing, synchronizer ring, 2nd gear and the 3rd driven gear.
   a. Install the spacer.
   b. Apply grease to the roller bearings.
   c. Place the 2nd gear synchronizer ring on the gear and align the ring slots with the shifting keys, but do not install the 1st gear synchronizer.
   d. Install the 2nd gear.
   e. Using a press, install the 3rd driven gear, aligning the clutch hub grooves with the projections on the synchronizer ring.
6. Measure the 2nd gear thrust clearance, which should be 0.0039–0.0177 in. (0.10–0.45mm).
7. Install the spacer and the 4th driven gear, using a press.
8. Using SST 09506-30012 and a press, install the output shaft rear bearing.
9. Using SST 09316-60010 and a press, install the output shaft front bearing.

OIL PUMP DISASSEMBLY

1. Install the oil pump drive gear to the drive rotor, then check that the drive rotor turns smoothly.
2. Remove the gasket to the oil pump case.
3. Remove the bolt and the oil strainer.
4. Hold the oil pump cover, remove the 2 bolts and the cover, then remove the spring holder, spring, ball and relief valve seat.
5. Install the oil pump drive gear to the drive rotor. Check the body clearance between the drive rotor and the oil pump case.
   Standard clearance: 0.10-0.16mm
   Maximum clearance: 0.30mm
6. Install the oil pump drive gear to the drive rotor. Check the rotor tip clearance between the drive and driven rotors.
   Standard clearance: 0.08-0.15mm
   Maximum clearance: 0.30mm
7. Using a straight edge, measure the side clearance of both rotors.
   Standard clearance: 0.03-0.08mm
   Maximum clearance: 0.15mm
8. Remove the oil pump drive rotor and the driven rotor.
9. Replace the O-ring, applying gear oil to it.

OIL PUMP REASSEMBLY

1. Install the driven rotor and the drive rotor.
2. Install the oil pump cover, installing the spring holder, spring, ball and relief valve. Hold the oil pump cover, temporarily installing the 2 bolts.
3. Install the oil strainer to the oil pump case, temporarily installing the bolt.
4. Torque the oil pump cover bolts evenly to 8 ft. lbs. (10 Nm).
5. Check the operation of the oil pump for smoothness.
6. Install the gasket to the pump case.

SHIFT AND SELECTOR LEVER COMPONENT DISASSEMBLY

1. Using a pin punch and a hammer, drive the out the slotted spring pin.
2. Remove the snapring.
3. Remove the No.2 select spring seat.
4. Remove the No.2 compression spring and the No.2 shift inner lever.
5. Using a pin punch and a hammer drive out the No.1 shift inner lever slotted spring pin.
6. Remove the shift interlock plate and the No.1 shift inner lever from the shaft.
7. Using a pin punch and a hammer drive out the select inner lever slotted spring pin.
8. Remove the select inner lever, No.1 compression spring and No.1 select spring seat.
9. Remove the remaining snapring.
10. Remove the control shaft cover and dust boot.
11. If necessary, withdraw the oil seal from the control shaft cover. Using SST No. 09620-30010 or equivalent and a hammer, drive the new oil seal into the cover to a depth of 0.5 ± 0.5mm. After installation coat the new seal lip with multi-purpose grease.

SHIFT AND SELECT LEVER SHAFT REASSEMBLY

1. Lightly coat all sliding, mating and splined surfaces with multi-purpose grease.
2. Install the dust boot cover onto the control shaft cover.
3. Install the control shaft to the control shaft cover.
4. Using a piece of brass stock and a hammer, install the snapring.
5. Install the No.1 spring seat, No.1 select spring and select inner lever in the proper order.
6. Using a pin punch and a hammer, drive in the select inner lever slotted spring pin.
7. Place the No.1 shift inner lever into the interlock plate and install the interlock cover.
8. Using a pin punch and a hammer, drive in the No.1 shift inner lever slotted spring pin.
9. Make sure that the shift interlock plate turns smoothly.
10. Install the No.2 shift inner lever, No.2 compression spring, transmission oil baffle and No.2 select spring seat in the proper order.
11. Compress the spring and install the snapring.
12. Using a pin punch and a hammer, drive in the No.2 shift inner lever slotted spring pin.

DISASSEMBLY OF DIFFERENTIAL CASE

➧ SEE FIGS. 52–54

1. Remove the side bearings with SST 09950-20017.
2. Place matchmarks on the ring gear and remove the bolts, then tap off the ring gear with a plastic hammer.
3. Place matchmarks on the differential right and left side case and remove the screws.
4. Remove the speedometer drive gear from the differential right case.
5. Remove the 2 differential side gears, 2 thrust washers, spider, pinions and washers from the left case.
6. Replace the left side oil seal and race.
   a. Remove the oil seal.
   b. Remove the oil baffle.
   c. Remove the race evenly and lightly with a brass bar, then remove the shim.
7. Install the shim, but first use one of a lesser thickness than before.
8. Install the race with a press.
9. Install the oil baffle, installing the projection into the case side cutout.
10. Install a new seal and coat the lip with grease.
11. Replace the right side oil seal and race.
   a. Remove the 4 bolts and 3 nut.
   b. Remove the case cover.
   c. Remove the oil seal.
   d. Remove the race evenly and lightly with a brass bar, then remove the shim.
12. Install the race with a press.
13. Install a new seal and coat the lip with grease.
14. Make sure that the case cover is clean and apply seal packing (Part No. 08826-00090) to the cover and install the cover immediately.
15. Apply sealer to the threads (Part No. 08833-00090).
16. Install the bolts and nuts and torque to 40 ft. lbs. (54 Nm).

REASSEMBLY OF DIFFERENTIAL CASE

➡ Coat all of the sliding and rotating surfaces with gear oil before assembly.

1. Assemble the differential case.

a. Install the thrust washer to the side gear.

b. Install the 4 pinions and washers to the spider.

c. Install the side gear and spider to the differential left case.

d. Measure the backlash of one pinion gear while holding the No. 2 differential case. It should be 0.05–0.20mm. Push the pinion gear of the left side of the case.

e. Install the side gear and spider to the right side of the case. Check the side gear backlash.

f. Select the thrust washer that will ensure that the backlash is within specification.

g. Install the speedometer driven gear.

h. Align the matchmarks on the cases and torque the screws to 46 ft. lbs. (63 Nm).

2. Install the ring gear by heating the gear to no more than 230°F in an oil bath, then install with the matchmarks. Torque the bolts evenly to 91 ft. lbs. (124 Nm).

3. Install the side bearings. Press the bearing on the ring gear side first.

4. Adjust the output shaft assembly preload.

5. Install the differential case assembly to the transaxle case.

6. Install the output shaft assembly.

7. Install the transmission case and torque the bolts to 22 ft. lbs. (29 Nm).

8. Drive in the output shaft outer race and install the shim.

9. Install the rear bearing retainer and torque the screws to 31 ft. lbs. (42 Nm).

10. Adjust the differential case side bearing preload.

a. Install the new locknut to the output shaft.

b. Turn the output shaft back and forth to settle the bearings.

c. Measure the preload. With a new bearing, it should be 1.7–3.6 inch lbs. Add the output shaft preload. With a used bearing, it should be 1.1–2.2 inch lbs. Add the output shaft preload.

d. If the preload is not within specifications, select different thrust washers.

11. Remove the bearing retainer and the shim.

12. Remove the transaxle case, the output shaft assembly and the differential case assembly.

1992 E53 Transaxle Reassembly

➡ Coat all of the sliding and rotating surfaces with gear oil before assembly.

1. Install the magnet to the transaxle case.

2. Install the oil pump assembly and oil pump, torquing the 4 bolts to 13 ft. lbs. (17 Nm).

3. Adjust the output shaft preload by installing the output shaft assembly and the case, torquing the bolts to 22 ft. lbs. (29 Nm).

a. Install the output shaft rear taper roller bearing outer race.

b. Install the adjust shim. If re-using the output shaft bearing, first install a shim of the same thickness as before. If using a new bearing, first install a shim of lesser thickness than before.

c. Install the bearing retainer and torque the bolts to 31 ft. lbs. (42 Nm).

d. Install the new locknut to the output shaft and turn the shaft back and forth to seat the bearings.

e. Measure the preload. At starting with a new bearing it should be 6.9–13.9 inch lbs. At starting with a used bearing it should be 4.3–8.7 inch lbs. If the preload is not within specifications, select different thrust washers.

f. Remove the lock nut.

g. Remove the rear bearing retainer, shim, transmission case and output shaft assembly.

4. Install the differential case assembly.

5. Install the oil pump drive gear.

6. Install the output shaft assembly.

7. Install the snaprings to the 1, 2 and 3 shift fork shafts and install the reverse shift fork and snapring to the No. 3 shift fork shaft.

8. Install the No. 2 shift fork to the No. 2 hub sleeve and the reverse shift fork with fork shaft No. 3.

9. Install the No. 1 shift fork, shift head and the No. 2 shift fork shaft by installing the No. 1 fork to the No. 1 hub sleeve. Put the shift head onto the No. 1 shift fork. Then install the No. 2 shift fork shaft to the transaxle case, through the shift head and the No. 1 fork.

10. Install the interlock roller to the reverse shift fork.

11. Install the shift fork No. 1 to the case through shift fork No. 1 and reverse shift fork.

12. Install the 3 set bolts and torque to 17 ft. lbs. (24 Nm).

13. Install the locking balls, springs, seats and plugs. Apply sealing to the plugs and torque to 18 ft. lbs. (25 Nm).

14. Install reverse idler gear and shaft by aligning the reference points.

15. Install the reverse shift fork pivot into the reverse shift arm and install the reverse shift arm bracket to the transaxle case. Install the bolt, the No. 2 oil pipe and torque the bolts to 13 ft. lbs. (17 Nm). Use a new pipe gasket.

16. Install the transaxle case, applying sealer and assembling immediately. Torque the bolts to 22 ft. lbs. (29 Nm).

17. Install and torque the reverse idler gear shaft retaining bolt to 22 ft. lbs. (29 Nm).

18. Install the locking ball, spring and seat. Apply sealer to the plug and torque to 18 ft. lbs. (25 Nm).

19. Install the 3 snaprings.

20. Install the output shaft rear taper roller bearing outer race.

21. Install the shim.

22. Install the snapring to the input shaft rear bearing.

23. Install rear bearing retainer and torque the bolts to 31 ft. lbs.

24. Install the spacer, needle roller bearing and 5th gear.

25. Install the synchronizer ring with key spring to the No. 3 clutch hub.

26. Install the No.3 clutch hub with the synchronizer ring and key spring.

27. Install a snapring that will allow minimum axial play and install it on the shaft.

28. Using a dial indicator, measure 5th gear thrust clearance.

- Standard clearance: 0.10-0.57mm

29. Install the 5th driven gear.

30. Install the No. 3 hub sleeve with the No. 3 shift fork.

31. Install and torque the set bolt to 17 ft. lbs. (24 Nm).

32. Engage the gear double meshing and install the locknut. Torque the nut to 90 ft. lbs. Disengage the meshing and stake the lock nut.

33. Apply sealer to the transaxle case, then immediately install the transmission case cover with the retaining bolts. Torque the bolts to 22 ft. lbs.

34. Install the shift and selector lever shaft assembly.

a. Place a new gasket on the control shaft cover and install it.

b. Apply sealer to the bolt threads.

c. Torque the bolts to 14 ft. lbs. (20 Nm).

35. Install and torque the lock bolt to 36 ft. lbs. (49 Nm).

36. Install and torque the selecting bellcrank to 14 ft. lbs. (20 Nm).

37. Install back-up light switch and torque to 30 ft. lbs.

38. Install speedometer driven gear and torque to 65 inch lbs.

39. Apply molybdenum disulphide lithium base grease to the following parts: input shaft spline and release fork contact surface.

40. Install the breather plug and torque to 36 ft. lbs. (49 Nm).

Halfshafts

REMOVAL & INSTALLATION

1983-84

1. Raise and support the front end on jackstands.
2. Remove the cotter pin, locknut cap and locknut from the hub.
3. Remove the six nuts attaching the halfshaft to the transaxle.
4. Remove the caliper and support it out of the way with a wire.
5. Remove the rotor.
6. Remove the left side case shield.
7. Remove the axle hub from the shaft with a puller.
8. Unbolt the right side intermediate shaft from the block bracket.
9. Remove the intermediate shaft from the U-joint.
10. With a slide hammer, pull the U-joint from the case.

To install the driveshafts:

11. Using the slide hammer, drive the U-joint in to the point where the joint and the differential pinion shaft touch.
12. Connect the intermediate shaft to the U-joint.
13. Install the bearing bracket onto the cylinder block. Torque the retaining bolts to 40 ft. lbs.
14. Install the outboard side of the driveshaft to the axle hub.

➡ Be careful not to damage the boots.

15. Install the six nuts that hold the driveshaft to the intermediate shaft or side differential side shaft and make them finger tight.
16. Install the left hand transmission case protector.
17. Install the disc rotor.
18. Connect the brake caliper to the steering knuckle.
19. Have an assistant depress the brake pedal and torque the bearing locknut to 137 ft. lbs.
20. Install the locknut cap and a new cotter pin. Separate the ends of the cotter pin with pliers.
21. Depress the brake pedal and torque the six driveshaft nuts to 25 ft. lbs.
22. Fill the transaxle to the proper level with the appropriate lubricant.

1985-86

➡ The hub bearing could be damaged if subjected to the full weight of the vehicle, such as if the vehicle is moved without the driveshafts. If it is absolutely necessary to place the full vehicle weight on the hub bearing, first support the bearing with SST No. 09608-16042.

1. Raise the front of the vehicle and support it safely.
2. Remove the front wheels.
3. Remove the cotter pin and locknut cap.
4. Have an assistant depress the brake pedal and loosen the bearing locknut.
5. On vehicles equipped with manual transaxle, remove the transaxle case protector.

➡ Cover the boot with cloth to prevent damage.

6. Have an assistant depress the brake pedal and loosen the six nuts holding the front driveshaft to the center driveshaft or differential side gear shaft.
7. Remove the brake caliper from the steering knuckle and support with wire.
8. Remove the disc rotor.
9. On CV series vehicles:
   a. Remove the two bolts that attach the ball joint to the steering knuckle.
   b. Lower the lower control arm and pull the shock absorber outward.
   c. Disconnect the driveshaft from the transaxle.
10. Using SST No. 09950-20015 or equivalent, push the front driveshaft from the axle hub.
11. On SV series vehicles right hand shaft:
    a. Drain the fluid from the center driveshaft.
    b. With pliers, remove the snapring and pull out the center driveshaft.

To install the driveshafts:

12. On SV series vehicles right hand shaft:
    a. Coat the transaxle the lip of the transxle oil seal with multi-purpose grease.
    b. Insert the center driveshaft into the transaxle through the bearing bracket and secure with the snapring.
13. Install the outboard side of the driveshaft to the axle hub.

➡ Be careful not to damage the boots.

14. Install the six nuts that hold the driveshaft to the intermediate shaft or side differential side shaft and make them finger tight.
15. On CV series vehicles:
    a. Connect the steering knuckle to the ball joint.
    b. Install the two bolts and torque them to 83 ft. lbs.
16. Install the disc rotor.
17. Install the brake caliper to the steering knuckle to the steering knuckle and torque the two bolts to 83 ft. lbs.
18. Have an assistant depress the brake pedal and torque the bearing locknut to 137 ft. lbs.
19. Install the locknut cap and a new cotter pin. Separate the ends of the cotter pin with pliers.
20. Depress the brake pedal and torque the six driveshaft nuts to 27 ft. lbs.
21. On manual transaxle equipped vehicles, install the case protector.
22. Fill the transaxle to the proper level with lubricant.

1987 With S51 Transaxle

➡ The hub bearing could be damaged if subjected to the full weight of the vehicle, such as if the vehicle is moved without the driveshafts. If it is absolutely necessary to place the full vehicle weight on the hub bearing, first support the bearing with SST No. 09608-16041.

1. Raise the front of the vehicle and support it safely.
2. Remove the front wheels.
3. Remove the cotter pin and locknut cap.
4. Have an assistant depress the brake pedal and loosen the bearing locknut.
5. Remove the engine under cover.
6. Remove the fender apron seal.
7. Loosen the six nuts holding the front driveshaft to the center driveshaft or differential side gear shaft.
8. Remove the two bolts and disconnect the steering knuckle from the lower ball joint.
9. Drain the transaxle fluid or differential oil.
10. Loosen the center driveshaft locknut.
11. Remove the bearing bracket snapring and pull out the center driveshaft.

To install the driveshafts:

12. Coat the transaxle the lip of the transxle oil seal with multi-purpose grease.
13. Insert the center driveshaft into the transaxle through the bearing bracket and secure with the snapring.
14. Install a new center bearing lock bolt and torque it 24 ft. lbs.
15. Install the outboard side of the driveshaft to the axle hub.

➡ Be careful not to damage the boots.

16. Install the six nuts that hold the driveshaft to the intermediate shaft or side differential side shaft and make them finger tight.
17. Connect the steering knuckle to the ball joint and torque the bolts to 94 ft. lbs.
18. Have an assistant depress the brake pedal and torque the bearing locknut to 137 ft. lbs.
19. Install the locknut cap and a new cotter pin. Separate the ends of the cotter pin with pliers.
20. Depress the brake pedal and torque the six driveshaft nuts to 27 ft. lbs.
21. Fill the transaxle to the proper level with gear oil or fluid.
22. Install the fender apron.
23. Install the engine under cover.
24. Check the front wheel alignment.

1988 With S51 Transaxle

1. Raise and support the vehicle safely.
2. Remove the wheels.
3. Remove the cotter pin, cap and locknut from the hub.
4. Remove the transaxle gravel shield, if with manual transaxle. Remove the engine under cover and front fender apron seal.
5. Loosen the 6 nuts attaching the inner end of the halfshaft to the transaxle or center shaft.

➡ Wrap the exposed end of the halfshaft in an old shop cloth to prevent damage to it.

6. Remove the brake caliper with the hydraulic line still attached, position it aside and suspend it with a wire. Remove the rotor.
7. Remove the 2 bolts attaching the ball joint to the steering knuckle. Pull the lower control arm down while pulling the strut outward; this will disconnect the inner end of the halfshaft from the transaxle.
8. Using a 2-armed puller, or the like, press the outer end of the halfshaft from the steering knuckle and then remove the halfshaft.
9. Drain the transaxle fluid, remove the snapring with pliers and pull the shaft out of the transaxle case.

To Install:

10. When installing the center halfshaft, coat the transaxle oil seal with grease, insert the halfshaft through the bearing bracket and secure it with a new snapring.
11. Press the outer end of the halfshaft into the steering knuckle, position the inner end and install the 6 nuts finger-tight.
12. Reconnect the ball joint to the steering knuckle, if disconnected, and tighten the bolts to 94 ft. lbs. (127 Nm).
13. Install the rotor and brake caliper. Tighten the caliper-to-knuckle bolts to 65 ft. lbs. (88 Nm).
14. Tighten the wheel bearing locknut to 137 ft. lbs. (186 Nm) while depressing the brake pedal. Install the locknut cap and use a new cotter pin.
15. Tighten the 6 inner end nuts to 27 ft. lbs. (36 Nm) while depressing the brake pedal.
16. Install the transaxle gravel shield, if equipped.
17. Fill the transaxle to the proper level.

1989–92 With S51 Transaxle

1. Raise and support the vehicle safely.
2. Remove the front wheels.
3. Remove the cotter pin, cap and locknut from the hub.
4. Remove the engine under covers.
5. Drain the transmission fluid or the differential fluid on the wagon.
6. Remove the transaxle gravel shield on the wagon.
7. Loosen the 6 nuts attaching the inner end of the halfshaft to transaxle, all except wagon.

➡ Wrap the exposed end of the halfshaft in an old shop cloth to prevent damage to it.

8. Remove the cotter pin from the tie end rod and then press the tie rod out of the steering knuckle. Remove the bolt and 2 nuts and disconnect the steering knuckle from the lower arm control.
9. On all except 4-cylinder wagon, use a 2-armed gear puller or equivalent, and press the halfshaft out of the steering knuckle.
10. On the 4-cylinder wagon, mark a spot somewhere on the left halfshaft and measure the distance between the spot and the transaxle case. Using the proper tool, pull the halfshaft out of the transaxle.
11. On the 4-cylinder wagon, use a 2-armed puller and press the outer end of the right halfshaft out of the steering knuckle. Remove the snapring at the inner end and pull the halfshaft out of the center driveshaft.
12. On all except the 4-cylinder wagon, remove the snapring on the center shaft and pull the center shaft out of the transaxle case.

To Install:

13. When installing the center driveshaft on sedan, coat the transaxle oil seal with grease, insert the halfshaft through the bearing bracket and secure it with a new snapring.
14. Repeat Step 13 when installing the inner end of the right halfshaft on the 4-cylinder wagon.
15. On the right halfshaft of the 4-cylinder wagon, use a new snapring, coat the transaxle oil seal with grease and then press the inner end of the shaft into the differential housing. Check that the measurement made in Step 10 is the same. Check that there is 0.08–0.12 in. (2–3mm) of axial play. Check also that the halfshaft will not come out by trying to pull it by hand.
16. Press the outer end of each halfshaft into the steering knuckle on the 4-cylinder wagon.
17. On all except the 4-cylinder wagon, press the outer end of the halfshafts into the steering knuckle and then finger-tighten the nuts on the inner end.
18. Connect the steering knuckle to the lower control arm and tighten the bolts to 83 ft. lbs. (113 Nm).
19. Connect the tie rod end to the steering knuckle and tighten the nut to 36 ft. lbs. (49 Nm). Install a new cotter pin.
20. Tighten the hub locknut to 137 ft. lbs. (186 Nm) while depressing the brake pedal. Install the cap and use a new cotter pin.
21. On all except the 4-cylinder wagon, tighten the 6 nuts on the inner halfshaft ends to 27 ft. lbs. (36 Nm) while depressing the brake pedal.
22. Install the transaxle gravel shield on the wagon.
23. Fill the transaxle with gear oil or fluid.
24. Install the engine under cover.

1988 With E56F2 Transaxle (AWD) – Front

➧ SEE FIG 65

➡ The hub bearing could be damaged if subjected to the full weight of the vehicle, such as if the vehicle is moved without the driveshafts. If it is absolutely necessary to place the full vehicle weight on the hub bearing, first support the bearing with SST No. 09608-16041.

1. Raise the front of the vehicle and support it safely.
2. Remove the front wheels.
3. Remove the cotter pin and locknut cap.
4. Have an assistant depress the brake pedal and loosen the bearing locknut.
5. Remove the right and left engine under covers.
6. Remove the cotter pin and nut from the tie rod end.
7. Disconnect the tie rod end from the steering knuckle using SST No. 09011-22012 or equivalent.
8. Matchmark the driveshaft and side gear with paint or chalk. Do not use a punch.
9. Depress the brake pedal and remove the 6 hex bolts and 3 washers holding the front driveshaft to the differential side gear shaft.

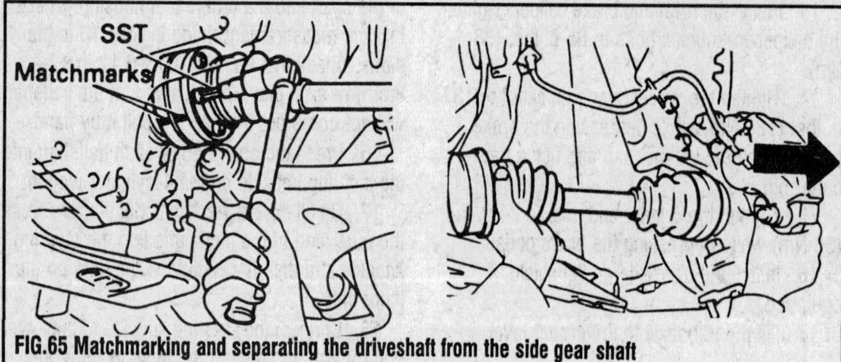

FIG.65 Matchmarking and separating the driveshaft from the side gear shaft

➡ **Use SST No. 09923-0020 or equivalent to remove the driveshaft hex bolts.**

10. Push the front axle carrier towards the outside of the vehicle and separate the driveshaft from the side gear shaft.

➡ **When moving the driveshaft, take care not to compress the inboard shaft.**

11. Remove the joint end cover gasket from the driveshaft.
12. Install the driveshaft bolts, nuts and washers to keep the inboard joint together and make the bolts hand tight.
13. Cover the inboard and side gear shafts with a plastic bag to keep out dust and sand.
14. Using a rubber or plastic mallet, tap the driveshaft from the axle hub.
15. Drain the gear oil.
16. Push the side gear shaft toward the differential. Measure and record the distance between the transaxle case and the side gear shaft.
17. Using SST No. 09520-32012, drive the side gear shaft out.

To install the driveshafts:

18. Install a new O-ring onto the right hand side gear shaft.
19. Properly install a new snapring into the groove of the side gear shaft.

➡ **Before installing the driveshaft, set the snapring opening side face downward.**

20. With a brass bar and hammer, gently tap in the driveshaft until it makes contact with the pinion shaft.

➡ **Wether or not the driveshaft is making contact with the pinion can be determined by sound or feel when driving it in.**

21. Check that the side gear shaft will not come out if it is pulled by hand.
22. Push the side gear shaft toward the differential. Measure and record the distance between the transaxle case and the side gear shaft.
23. Make sure that the distance is the same as the measurement that was recorded previously.
24. Pack about 40 grams of grease into the side gear shaft. Normally the grease is provided with the boot kit but grease that carries Part No. 90999-94029 may also be used.
25. Install the outboard joint side of the driveshaft into the axle hub being careful not to damage the boot, oil seal, and deflector.
26. Push the differential carrier outward and away from the vehicle and lift up the inboard joint.

➡ **When moving the driveshaft, take care not to compress the inboard shaft.**

27. Remove the plastic bag, 6 hex bolts and 3 washers from the inboard joint.
28. Place the new gasket onto the inboard joint.
29. Align the matchmarks on the side gear shaft and the inboard joint.
30. Connect the drive and side gear shafts with the hex bolts and washers and make them finger tight.
31. Connect the tie rod to the steering knuckle and torque the nut to 36 ft. lbs. Make sure hole in the nut aligns with the hole in the rod. Tighten the nut as required to obtain this alignment.
32. Connect the steering knuckle to the lower arm and torque the bolt to 94 ft. lbs.
33. Depress the brake pedal and torque the six hex bolts to 48 ft. lbs.
34. Measure the distance between the right and left gear shafts as shown in the figure. The distance should be less than 70.5cm.
35. Depress the brake pedal and torque the bearing locknut to 137 ft. lbs.
36. Install the locknut cap and a new cotter pin. Separate the ends of the cotter pin with pliers.
37. Fill the transaxle to the proper level with gear oil.
38. Install the left and right engine under covers.
39. Check the front wheel alignment.

1988 With E56F5 Transaxle (AWD) – Front

1. Raise and safely support the vehicle.
2. Remove the wheels.
3. Remove the cotter pin, cap and locknut from the hub.
4. Remove the transaxle gravel shield. Remove the engine under cover and front fender apron seal.
5. Remove the cotter pin and nut from the tie rod end and then disconnect it from the steering knuckle.
6. Remove the bolt and 2 nuts and disconnect the steering knuckle from the lower control arm.
7. Loosen the 6 nuts attaching the inner end of the halfshaft to the transaxle side gear shaft.
8. Grasp the halfshaft and push the axle carrier outward until the shaft can be removed from the side gear shaft.

➡ **Wrap the exposed end of the halfshaft in an old shop cloth to prevent damage to it.**

9. Use a rubber mallet and tap the outer end of the shaft from the axle hub.

To install:

10. Press the outer end of the halfshaft into the axle hub, position the inner end and install the 6 nuts finger-tight.
11. Connect the tie rod end to the steering knuckle and tighten the nut to 36 ft. lbs. (49 Nm). Install a new cotter pin. If the cotter pin holes do not align, tighten the nut until they align. Never loosen it.
12. Connect the steering knuckle to the lower control arm and tighten to 94 ft. lbs. (127 Nm).
13. Tighten the 6 inner shaft mounting nuts to 48 ft. lbs. (65 Nm). Measure the distance between the right and left side shafts; it must be less then 27.75 in. (704.7mm).
14. With the brake pedal depressed, install the bearing locknut and tighten it to 137 ft. lbs. (186 Nm). Install the cap and a new cotter pin.
15. Install the wheels and lower the vehicle.

1989–90 With E56F5 Transaxle (AWD) – Front

1. Raise and support the vehicle safely.
2. Remove the wheels.
3. Remove the cotter pin, cap and locknut from the hub.
4. Remove the engine undercovers.
5. Disconnect the tie rod end from the steering knuckle.

6. Disconnect the lower control arm at the steering knuckle and pull it down and aside.

7. Use a plastic hammer and carefully tap the outer end of the halfshaft until it frees itself from the axle hub.

8. Cover the outer boot with a rag and then remove the inner end of the halfshaft from the transaxle. Use the proper tools.

To install:

9. Coat the lip of the oil seal with grease and then carefully drive the inner end of the shaft into the transaxle until it makes contact with the pinion shaft.

➡ **Be careful not to damage the boots when installing the halfshafts; also, position the boot snapring so the opening is facing downward.**

10. Put the outer end of each shaft into the axle hub, being careful not to damage the boots.

11. Check that there is 0.08–0.12 in. (2–3mm) of axial play. Check also that the halfshaft will not come out by hand.

12. Connect the lower control arm to the steering arm and tighten the bolt to 83 ft. lbs. (113 Nm).

13. Connect the tie rod to the steering knuckle and tighten the nut to 36 ft. lbs. (49 Nm). Use a new cotter pin to secure it.

14. Install the axle bearing locknut and tighten it to 137 ft. lbs. (186 Nm) while stepping on the brake pedal. Install the locknut cap and then a new cotter pin.

15. Fill the transaxle with gear oil or fluid, install the undercovers and wheels. Lower the [illegible]hicle and check the front end alignment.

[illegible]91 With E52 Transaxle

[illegible] front of the vehicle and use jack stands to safely secure the vehicle.

2. Remove the front wheel and remove the axle nut cotter pin, the lock nut cap and the lock nut, while depressing the brake pedal.

3. Remove the engine under covers.

4. Remove the tie rod cotter pin and nut, then disconnect the tie rod end using tool 09628–62011, or equivalent.

5. Disconnect the steering knuckle from the lower arm by removing the 2 bolts.

6. Place matchmarks on the driveshaft and side gear shaft or center driveshaft, using paint and not a punch.

7. Loosen, but do not remove yet, the 6 bolts holding the driveshaft to the inner shaft.

8. Using a plastic hammer, disconnect the driveshaft from the axle hub and cover the boot with a protective cover.

➡ **Do not subject the hub bearing to the weight of the vehicle with a driveshaft removed.**

9. Remove the axle shaft.

10. To remove the LEFT shaft, remove the 6 bolts and remove the shaft, but do not compress the inboard boot allowing the inside balls to drop out.

11. To remove the RIGHT shaft, do the following:

a. Drain out the gear oil.

b. Remove the bearing lock bolt.

c. Using a suitable tool, remove the snap ring, and pull out the driveshaft with the center driveshaft, tapping out the driveshaft with a brass hammer, if necessary.

To install:

12. When installing the driveshafts, pack the side gear shaft or to the center driveshaft with grease (part no. 90999–94029. The grease capacity is 43–53g (0.09–0.12 lbs.).

13. Place a new gasket on the inboard joint, insert and finger tighten the 6 bolts with the 3 washers, making sure that the matchmarks are aligned.

14. Reverse the remaining removal steps to complete installation, tightening fasteners to specifications.

15. Fill the transaxle with gear oil, check front end alignment and test drive.

➡ **Do not compress the inboard boot when moving either driveshaft. If the cotter pin holes do not line up, always correct by TIGHTENING the nut until the next hole lines up. Then install a new cotter pin.**

1992 With E53 Transaxle

1. Raise the front of the vehicle and use jack stands to safely secure the vehicle.

2. Remove the front wheel and remove the axle nut cotter pin, the lock nut cap and the lock nut, while depressing the brake pedal.

3. Remove the front fender apron.

4. Remove the tie rod cotter pin and nut, then disconnect the tie rod end using tool 09628–62011, or equivalent.

5. Drain the gear oil.

6. Disconnect the stabilizer bar link from the lower arm.

7. Remove the bolt and the 2 nuts, then disconnect the steering knuckle from the lower ball joint.

8. Place matchmarks on the driveshaft and side gear shaft or center driveshaft, using paint and not a punch.

9. Loosen, but do not remove yet, the 6 bolts holding the driveshaft to the inner shaft.

10. Using a plastic hammer, disconnect the driveshaft from the axle hub and cover the boot with a protective cover.

➡ **Do not subject the hub bearing to the weight of the vehicle with a driveshaft removed.**

11. Using a suitable tool, pry out and remove the left axle shaft.

12. To remove the left driveshaft, remove the bearing lock bolt, remove the snapring and pull out the driveshaft.

To install:

13. To install the left driveshaft, do the following:

a. Install a new snapring on the end of the shaft.

b. Coat gear oil to the side gear shaft and differential case sliding surface.

c. Using a brass bar and hammer, tap in the driveshaft until it makes contact with the pinion shaft.

➡ **Before installing the driveshaft, set the snapring opening side facing downward. Whether or not the side gear shaft is making contact with the pinion shaft can be known by the sound or feeling when driving it inward.**

d. Check that there is 2–3mm (0.08–0.12 in.) of play in the axial direction and check that the driveshaft will not come out by trying to pull it completely out by hand.

14. To install the right driveshaft, do the following:

a. Coat gear oil to the side gear shaft and differential case sliding surface.

b. Install the driveshaft to the transaxle through the bearing bracket, without damaging the oil seal lip.

c. Using a suitable tool, install a new snapring.

d. Install a new bearing lock bolt and tighten it to 32 Nm (24 ft. lbs.).

15. Reverse the remaining removal procedures to complete installation, tightening fasteners to specifications.

16. Fill the transaxle with gear oil, install the fender apron, check front end alignment and test drive.

➡ **If the cotter pin holes do not line up, always correct by TIGHTENING the nut until the next hole lines up. Then install a new cotter pin**

CV-JOINT OVERHAUL

1983–91 With 4-cylinder Engine And AWD Front driveshaft Except E56F2 Manual Transaxle

♦ SEE FIGS. 66–82

DISASSEMBLY

1. Mount the front driveshaft in a vise and check that there is no play in the inboard and outboard joint.
2. Make sure that the inboard joint slides smoothly in the thrust direction.
3. Make sure that there is no excessive play in the radial direction of the inboard joint.
4. Inspect the boots for damage (rips, punctures and cracks).
5. Remove the inboard joint boot clips.
6. With chalk or paint, matchmark the inboard joint tulip and tripod. DO NOT use a punch.
7. Remove the inboard joint tulip from the driveshaft.
8. Remove the snapring.
9. Using a brass rod and hammer, evenly drive the tripod joint off the driveshaft without hitting the joint roller.
10. Remove the inboard joint boot.
11. Remove the clamp and driveshaft damper (1983-86 CV series right shaft only).
12. Remove the clamps and the outboard drive boot. DO NOT disassemble the outboard joint.
13. On 1987-91 vehicles, press out the transaxle and driveshaft side dust covers from the center driveshaft.
14. On 1987-91 vehicles, remove the center driveshaft snapring, press the bearing from the shaft and remove the remaining snapring.
15. Inspect the inside and the outside of the boots for damage.

REASSEMBLY

➡ Before installing the boot, wrap the spline end of the shaft with masking tape to prevent damage to the boot.

1. On 1987-91 vehicles, install the center driveshaft snapring, press in a new bearing and install a new snapring over the bearing.
2. On 1987-91 vehicles, press in the transaxle side and driveshaft bearing side dust covers.

➡ The clearance between the dust cover and the bearing should be 1.00mm.

3. Install the driveshaft damper with a new clamp (1983-86 CV series right shaft only).

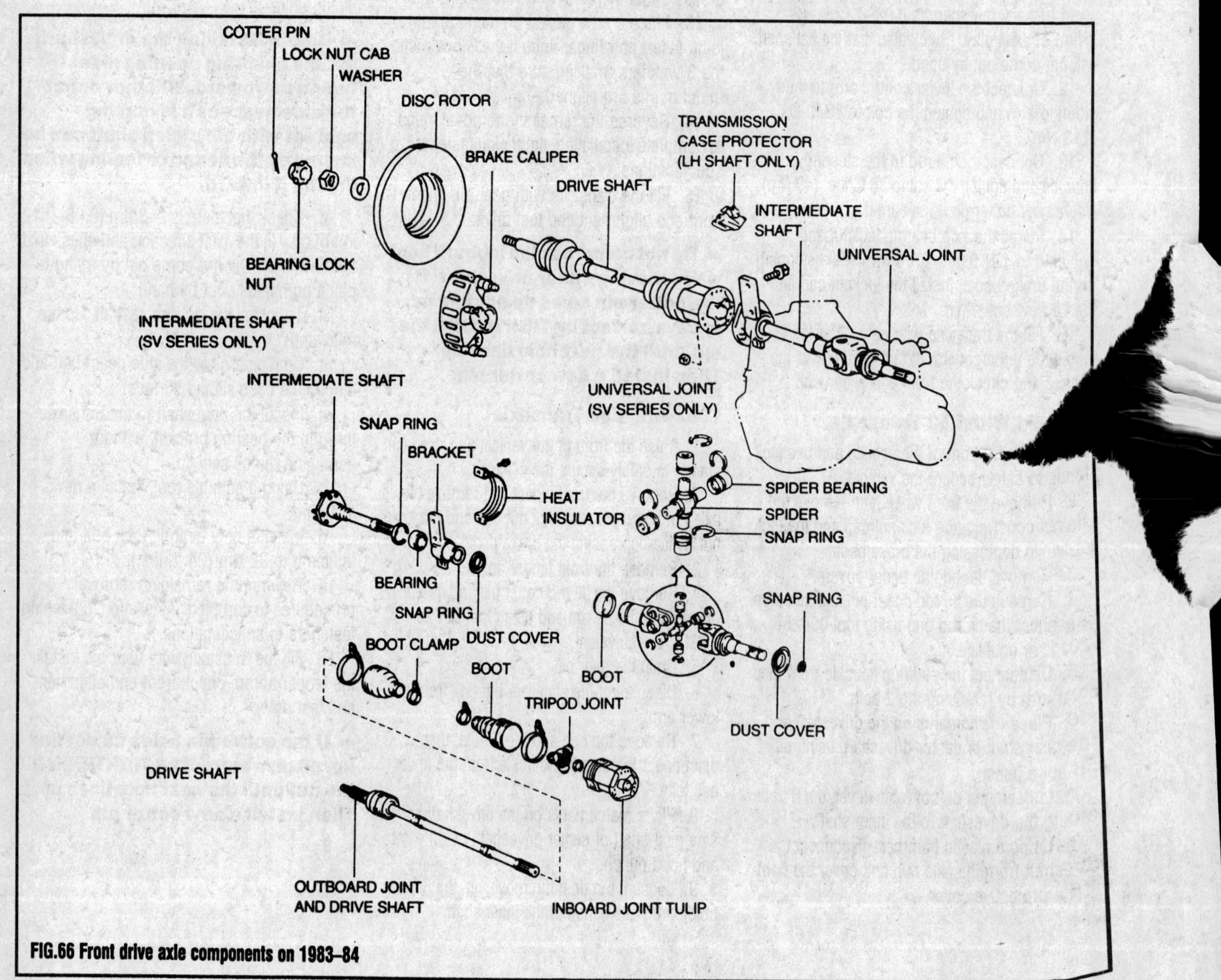

FIG.66 Front drive axle components on 1983–84

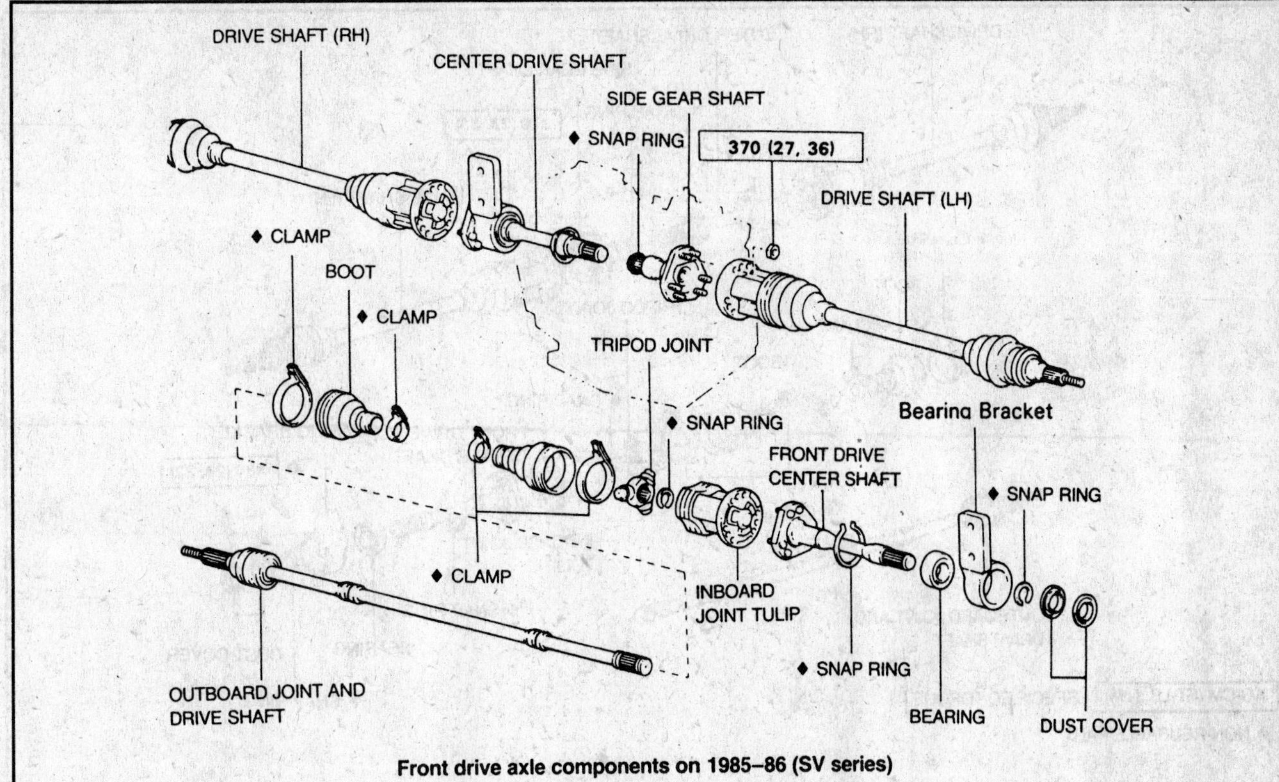

Front drive axle components on 1985–86 (SV series)

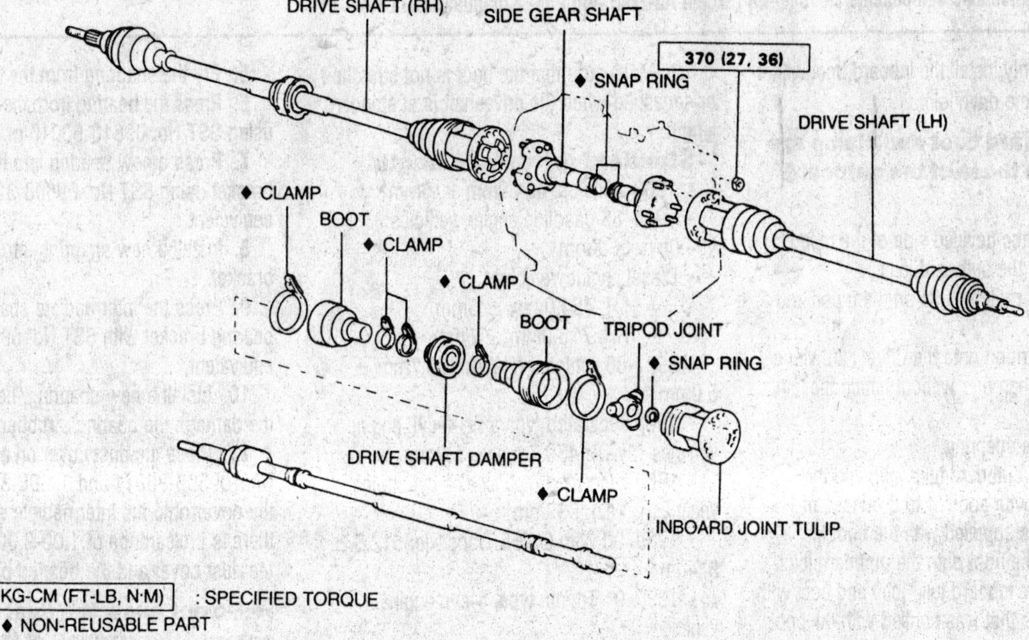

FIG.67 Front drive axle components on 1985–86 (CV series)

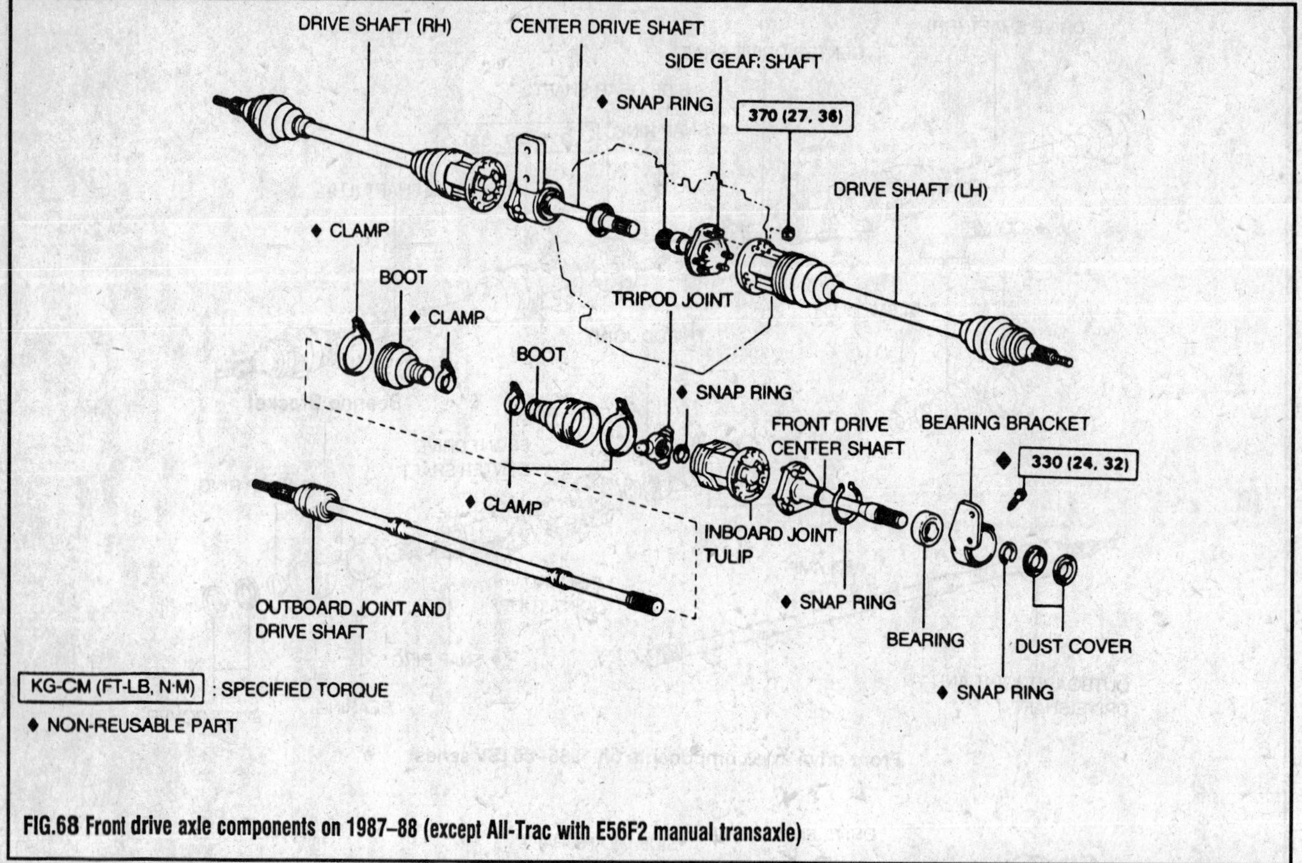

FIG.68 Front drive axle components on 1987–88 (except All-Trac with E56F2 manual transaxle)

4. Temporarily install the inboard boot with new clamp to the drive joint.

➡ **The inboard boot and clamp are larger than those of the outboard boot.**

5. Position the beveled side of the tripod spline towards the outboard joint.
6. Align the matchmarks on the tripod and driveshaft.
7. Tap the tripod onto the driveshaft with a brass rod and hammer without hitting the joint roller.
8. Install the snapring.
9. Pack the outboard tulip joint and the outboard boot with about 4 to 5 ounces of grease that was supplied with the boot kit.
10. Install the boot onto the outboard joint.
11. Pack the inboard tulip joint and boot with 1/2 lb. of grease that was suplied with the boot kit.
12. Align the matchmarks on the tulip joint and tripod.
13. Install the inboard tulip joint onto the driveshaft.
14. Install the boot onto the driveshaft.
15. Make sure that the boot is properly installed on the driveshaft.
16. Before checking the standard length, bend the band and lock it as shown in the illustration.
17. Make sure that the boot is not stretched or squashed when the driveshaft is at standard length.

Standard driveshaft length

- 1983 vehicles: 454.0mm ± 5mm
- 1984–86 gasoline engine vehicles: 454.0mm ± 5mm
- Diesel engine vehicles
  LH: 454.0mm ± 5mm
  RH: 716.0mm ± 5mm
- 1987-88 vehicles (2WD): 450.7mm ± 5.0mm
- 1989 separated type axle, 4-cyl. engine vehicles (2WD): 450.7mm ± 5.0mm
- 1989 integrated type axle, 4-cyl engine vehicles (2WD): 937mm
- 1989–90 With E56F5 Transaxle: 512.5 ± 5.0mm
- 1990–91 Toyota type, 4-cyl. engine vehicles
  LH: 558.7mm ± 5.0mm
  RH: 845.2mm ± 5.0mm
- 1990–91 GKN type, 4-cyl. engine vehicles
  LH: 652.0mm ± 6.0mm
  RH: 937.0mm ± 6.0mm

1983–84 INTERMEDIATE SHAFT OVERHAUL

1. Remove the heat insulator.
2. Remove the dust cover.
3. Remove the snapring.
4. Remove the intermediate shaft using SST No. 09950-20014 or equivalent.
5. Pry the snapring from the bearing bracket.
6. Press the bearing from the bearing bracket using SST No. 09618-60010 or equivalent.
7. Press a new bearing into the bearing bracket using SST No. 09608-32030 or equivalent.
8. Install a new snapring into the bearing bracket.
9. Press the intermediate shaft into the bearing bracket with SST No. 09608-32030 or equivalent.
10. Install a new snapring, being careful not the damage the bearing's rubber seal.
11. Place the dust cover on a press with SST No.s 09506-30011 and 09608-32030 and press the cover onto the intermediate shaft so that there is a clearance of 1.00-2.00mm between the dust cover and the bearing bracket.

➡ **Do not allow the dust cover to contact the surface of the bearing.**

12. Install the heat insulator.

1985–86 CENTER DRIVESHAFT OVERHAUL GASOLINE ENGINE

1. Press the transxle side dust cover from the shaft with a suitable press.
2. Using a press and SST No. 09950-00020 and a press, remove the driveshaft side dust cover.
3. Remove the snapring that retains the bearing.

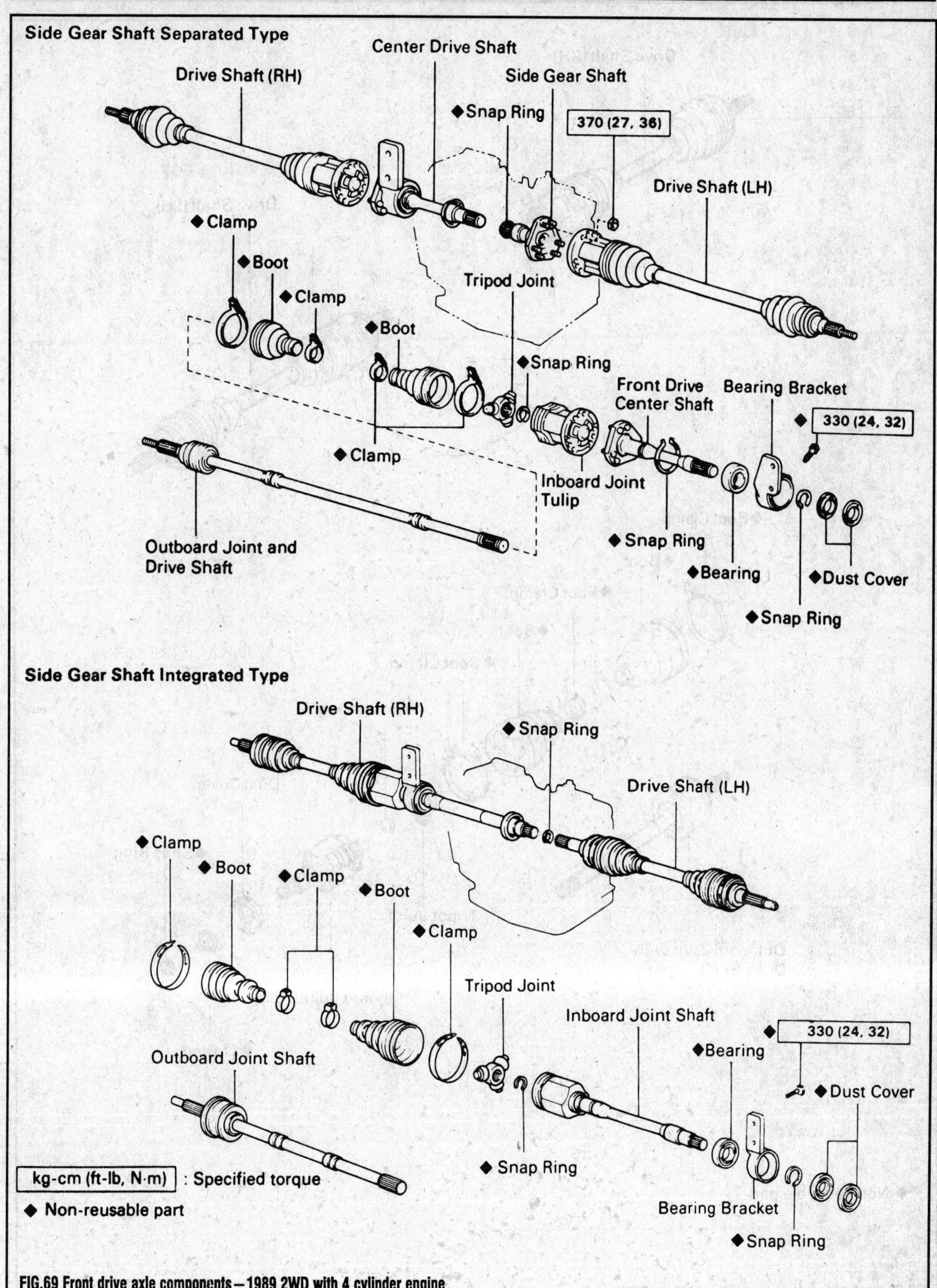

FIG.69 Front drive axle components—1989 2WD with 4 cylinder engine

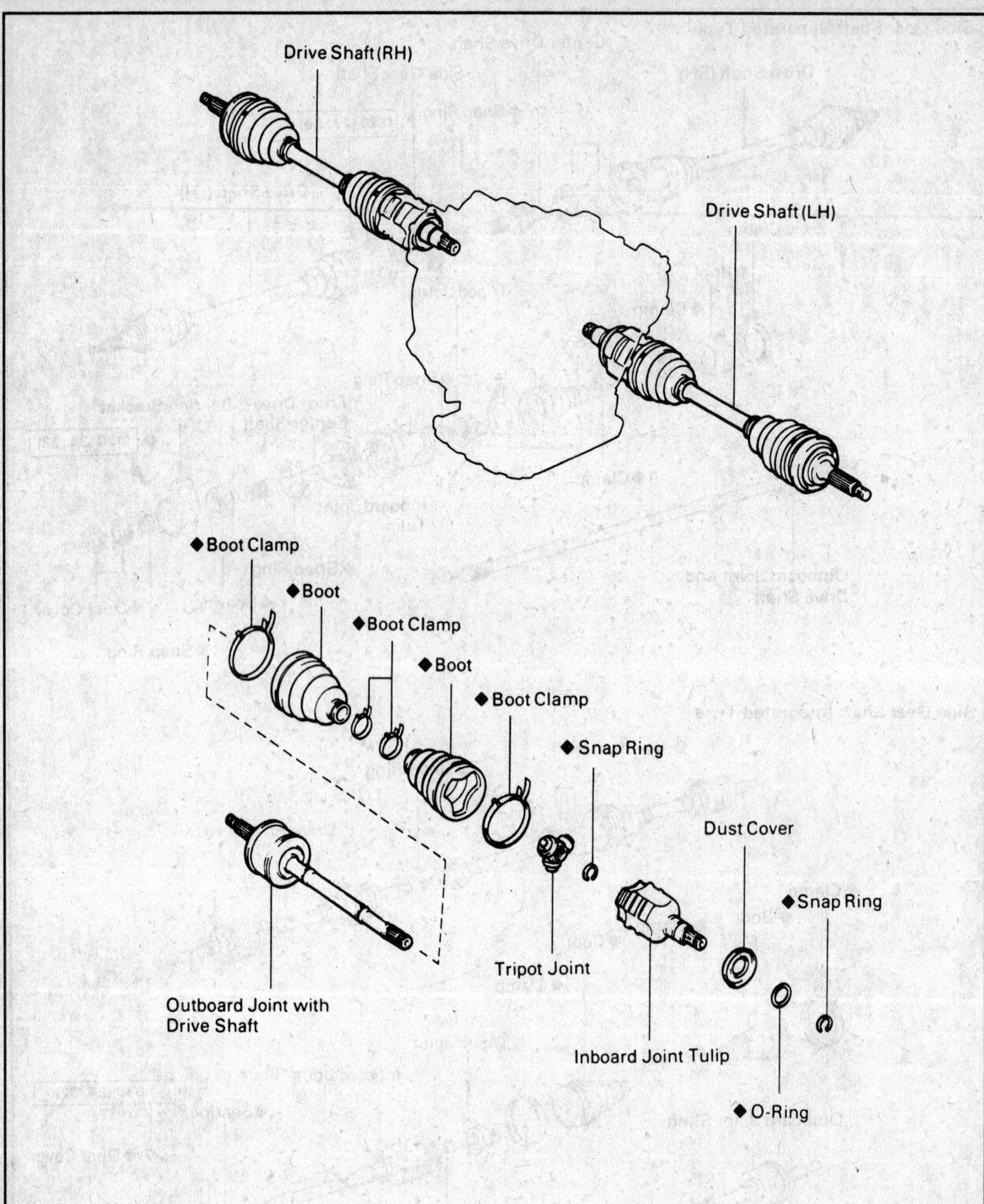

FIG.70 Front drive axle components—1989–91 AWD

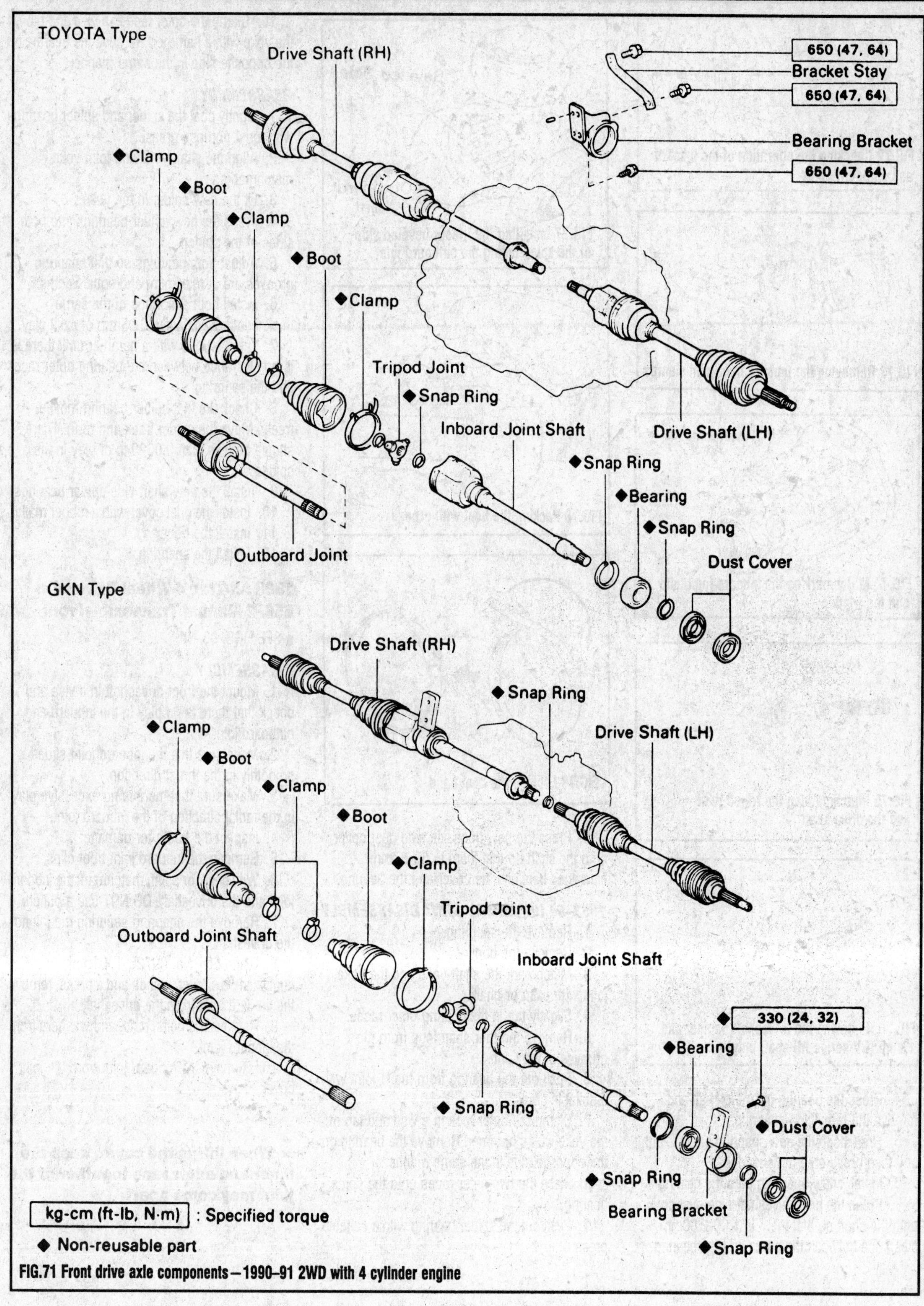

FIG.71 Front drive axle components—1990–91 2WD with 4 cylinder engine

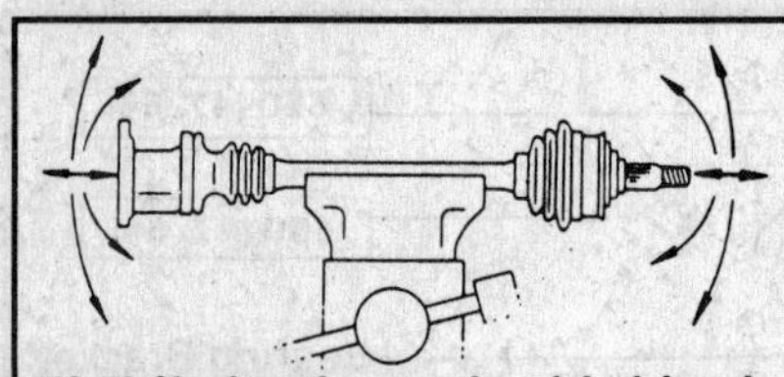
FIG.72 Checking the operation of the inboard and outboard joints

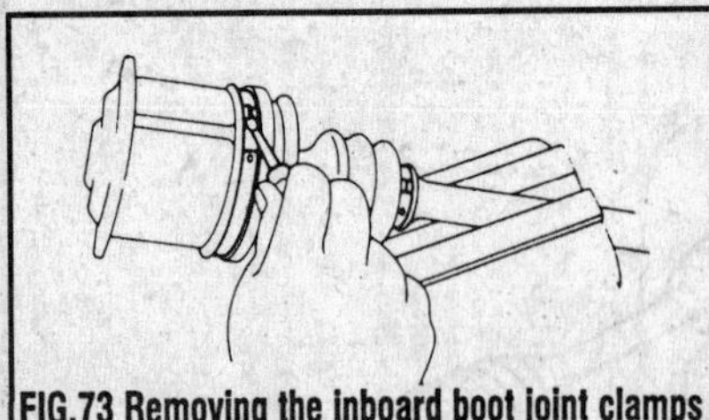
FIG.73 Removing the inboard boot joint clamps

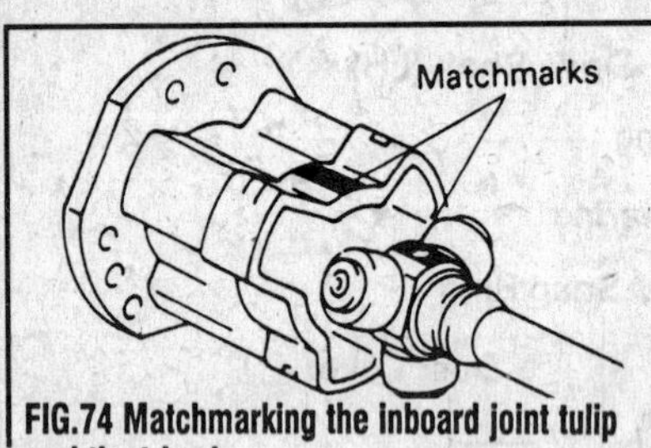

FIG.74 Matchmarking the inboard joint tulip and the tripod

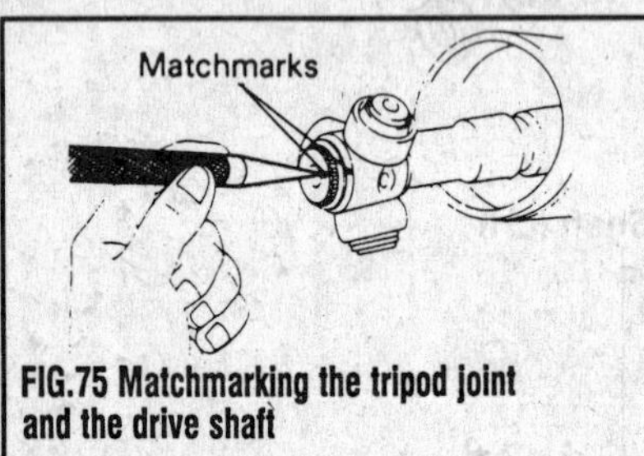

FIG.75 Matchmarking the tripod joint and the drive shaft

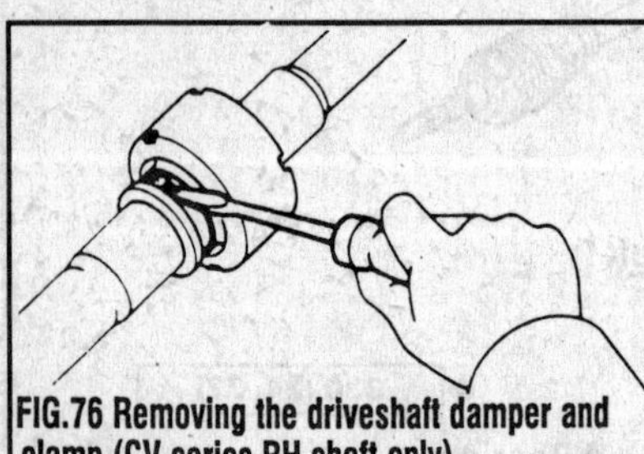
FIG.76 Removing the driveshaft damper and clamp (CV series RH shaft only)

4. Press the bearing from the shaft and remove the remaining snapring.
5. First, insert the new snapring onto the shaft and then press on a new bearing.
6. Install anew snapring onto the bearing.
7. Press the new driveshaft side dust cover onto the shaft so that there is 1.00-2.00mm clearance between the cover and the bearing.

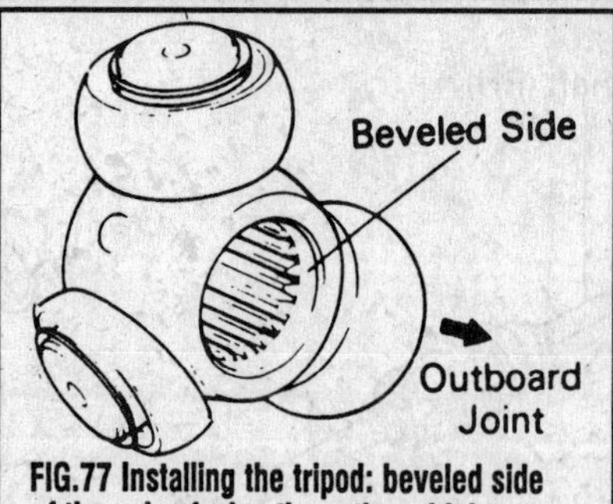

FIG.77 Installing the tripod: beveled side of the spine facing the outboard joint

FIG.78 Packing the boot with grease

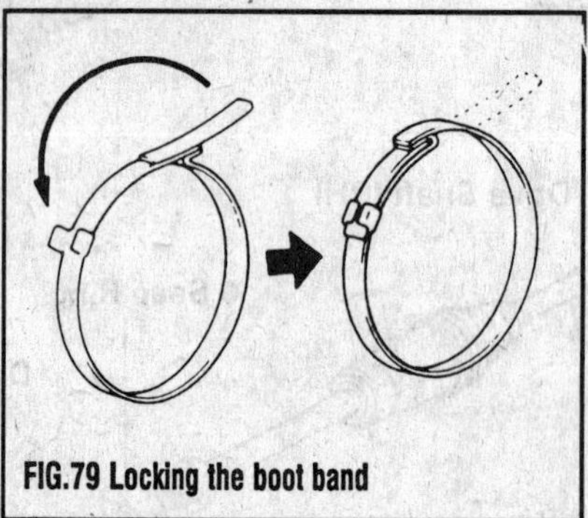
FIG.79 Locking the boot band

8. Press the new transaxle side dust cover onto the shaft so that there is 86-87mm clearance between the cover and the bearing.

1983–84 UNIVERSAL JOINT DISASSEMBLY

1. Remove the snapring.
2. Remove the boot.
3. Matchmark the shaft yoke and the yoke joint with paint or chalk.
4. Slightly tap in the bearing outer races.
5. Remove the four snaprings from the grooves of the joint.
6. Push out the bearing from the U-joint with a suitable press.
7. Clamp the outer race in a vise and tap off the yoke with a hammer. Remove the bearing on the opposite side in the same manner.
8. Place the two outer races onto the spider bearing.
9. Push out the spider bearing with a suitable press.
10. Clamp the outer race in a vise and tap off the yoke with a hammer. Remove the bearing on the opposite side in the same manner.

REASSEMBLY

1. Lightly coat the spider and spider bearings with multi-purpose grease.
2. Align the shaft yoke and joint yoke matchmarks.
3. Fit the new spider in the yoke.
4. Press the new spider bearings into both sides of the spider.
5. Adjust both bearings so that snapring grooves are at maximum and equal widths.
6. Install both snaprings of the same thickness that will allow 0.05mm of axial play.
7. Tap the yoke with a hammer until there is no clearance between the bearing outer race and the sanpring.
8. Check the that spider bearing moves freely. Move the spider back and forth. There should be less than 0.0020 in of play in the spider.
9. Install the new shaft side spider bearings.
10. Install the dust cover with a rubber mallet.
11. Install the boot.
12. Install the snapring.

1988 All-Trac 4-Wheel Drive with E56F2 Manual Transaxle – Front

➧ SEE FIGS. 83–84

DISASSEMBLY

1. Mount the front driveshaft in a vise and check that there is no play in the inboard and outboard joint.
2. Make sure that the inboard joint slides smoothly in the thrust direction.
3. Make sure that there is no excessive play in the radial direction of the inboard joint.
4. Inspect the boots for damage.
5. Remove the inboard joint boot clips.
6. With chalk or paint, matchmark the inboard joint and the driveshaft. DO NOT use a punch.
7. Remove the snapring securing the jointto the driveshaft.
8. Using SST No. 09726-10010 or equivalent, a socket wrench and a press, remove the inboard joint from the driveshaft.
9. Remove the bolts, nuts, and washers from the inboard joint.
10. Remove the inboard joint from the joint cover.

➡ When lifting the cover, keep the inner and outer race together or the joint may come apart.

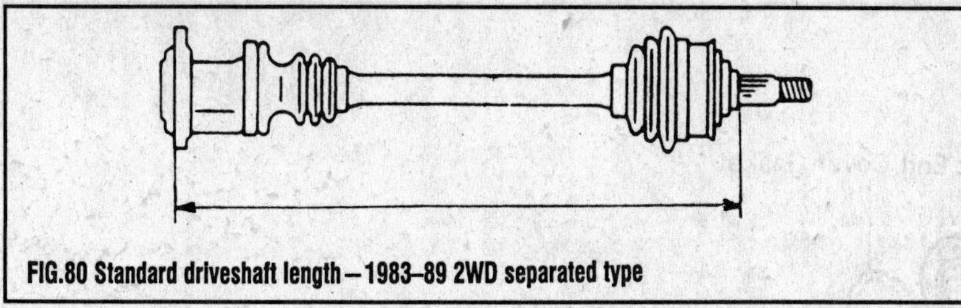
FIG.80 Standard driveshaft length—1983–89 2WD separated type

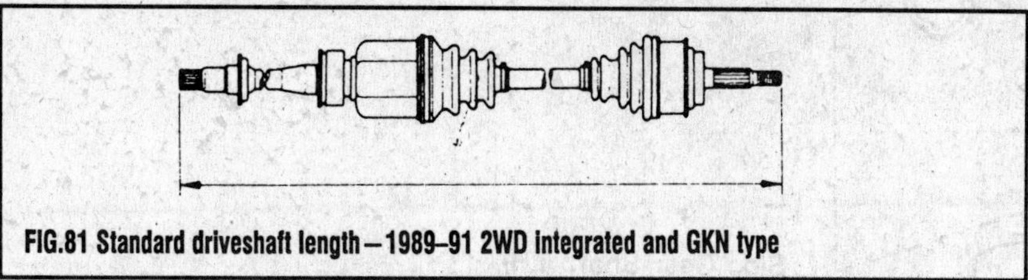
FIG.81 Standard driveshaft length—1989–91 2WD integrated and GKN type

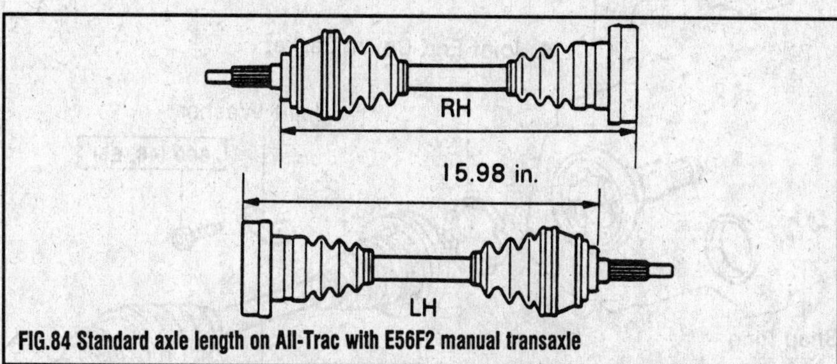

FIG.84 Standard axle length on All-Trac with E56F2 manual transaxle

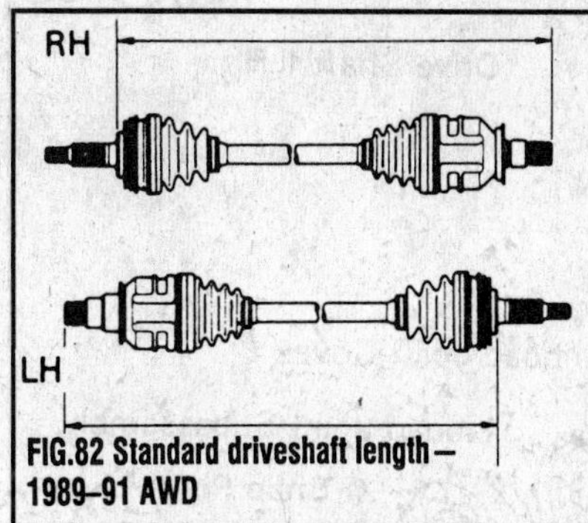

FIG.82 Standard driveshaft length—1989–91 AWD

11. Should the joint come apart, assemble it in the following manner:

a. Align the matchmarks.

b. Insert a spark plug wrench into the inner race.

c. Lift the outer race and cage and insert the six ball bearings.

d. Jiggle the outer race and cage to seat the balls in their respective grooves.

e. Lower the outer race and cage so that they fit tightly with the inner race.

12. Remove the inboard and outboard joint boots.

13. Check the inside and outside of the boots for damage.

REASSEMBLY

➡ **Before installing the boot, wrap the spline end of the shaft with masking tape to prevent damage to the boot.**

1. Temporarily install the inboard and outboard joint boots with the new clamps.

2. Apply a bead of seal packing No. 08826-00801 or equivalent to the inboard joint cover. A thin bead will do, avoid applying too much.

3. Align the bolt holes of the cover with the holes of the inboard joint and then insert the bolts.

4. Tap the rim of the inboard joint into place with a plastic or rubber mallet in a criss-cross pattern. Repeat the pattern several times until the cover is properly seated.

5. Hold the inboard joint together with the bolts, nuts and washers. Make the bolts finger tight as not to scratch the flange surface.

6. Align the matchmarks made in the driveshaft and joint.

7. Tap the inboard joint onto the driveshaft with a brass bar and a hammer.

➡ **Make sure to tap the inner race of the joint and not the cage.**

8. Install a new snapring.

9. Pack the outboard joint with about 3 to 4 ounces of the grease supplied in the boot kit.

10. Pack the inboard tulip joint with about 2 to 3 ounces of the grease supplied in the boot kit.

11. Install the inboard boot the the inboard joint.

12. Make sure that the boot is properly installed on the driveshaft.

13. Make sure that the boot is not stretched or squashed when the driveshaft is at standard length.

Standard driveshaft length: 406mm (15.98 in.).

14. To lock the boot bands, bend the band back and close the locking tabs.

15. Mount the driveshaft in vise and check that there is no play in the inboard or outboard joints. Check that the inboard joint slides smoothly in the thrust direction.

1992 With 4-cylinder Engine

➧ SEE FIGS. 85–86

DISASSEMBLY

1. Mount the front driveshaft in a vise and check that there is no play in the inboard and outboard joint.

2. Make sure that the inboard joint slides smoothly in the thrust direction.

3. Make sure that there is no excessive play in the radial direction of the inboard joint.

4. Inspect the boots for damage.

5. Disconnect the center driveshaft or the side gear shaft by removing the 6 bolts and the 3 washers.

➡ **Do not compress the inboard boot.**

6. Remove the joint end cover gasket and use the bolts and washers to keep the inboard joint together. Tighten the bolts only hand tight.

7. Remove the inboard and outboard joint boot clamps.

8. Place painted, not punched, matchmarks on the inboard joint and the driveshaft, then remove the snapring.

9. Using special service tool 09726–10010 (09726–00030), a socket wrench and a press, remove the inboard joint from the driveshaft.

10. Using suitable tools, remove the inboard joint from the inboard joint cover, holding onto races when lifting the inboard joint.

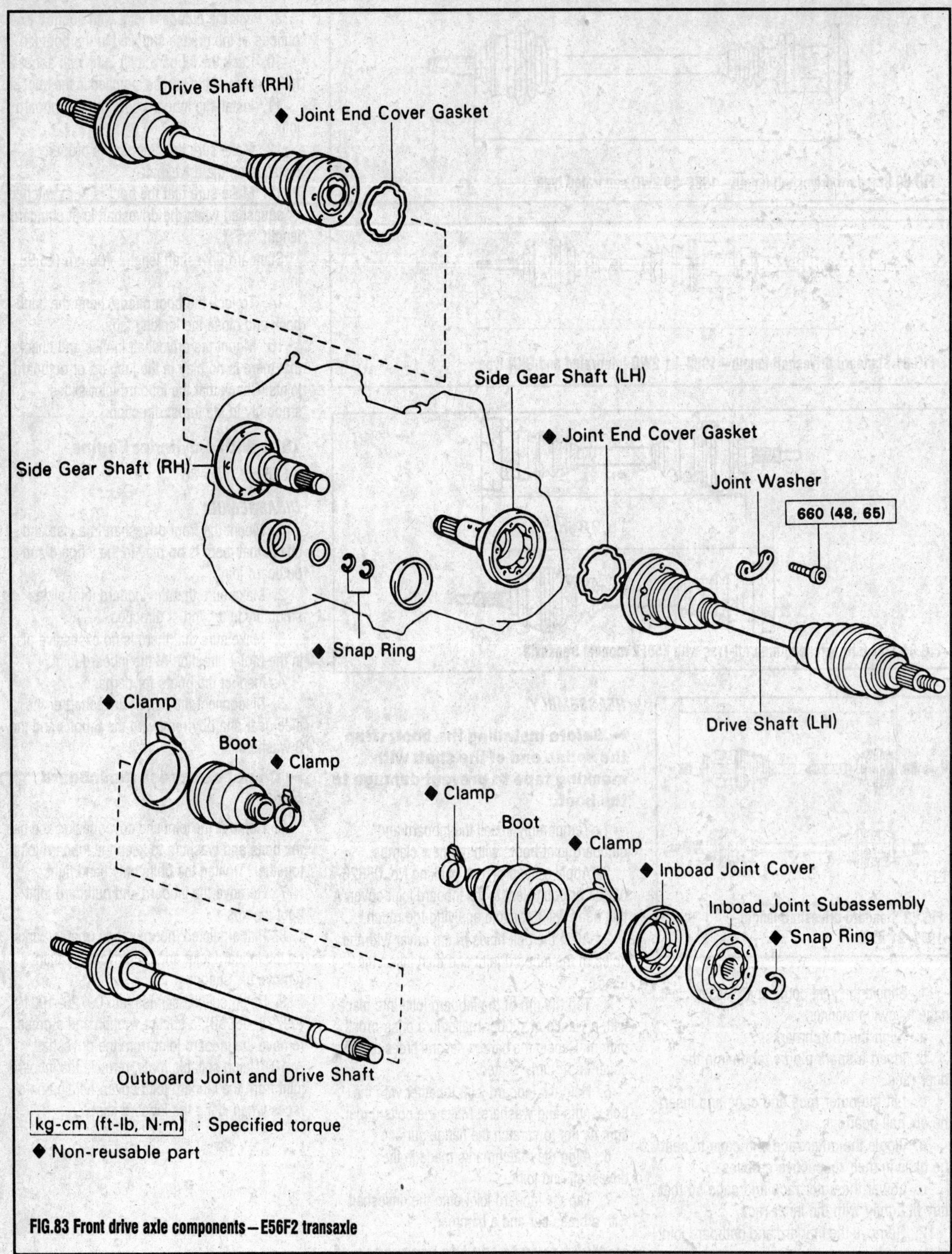

FIG.83 Front drive axle components—E56F2 transaxle

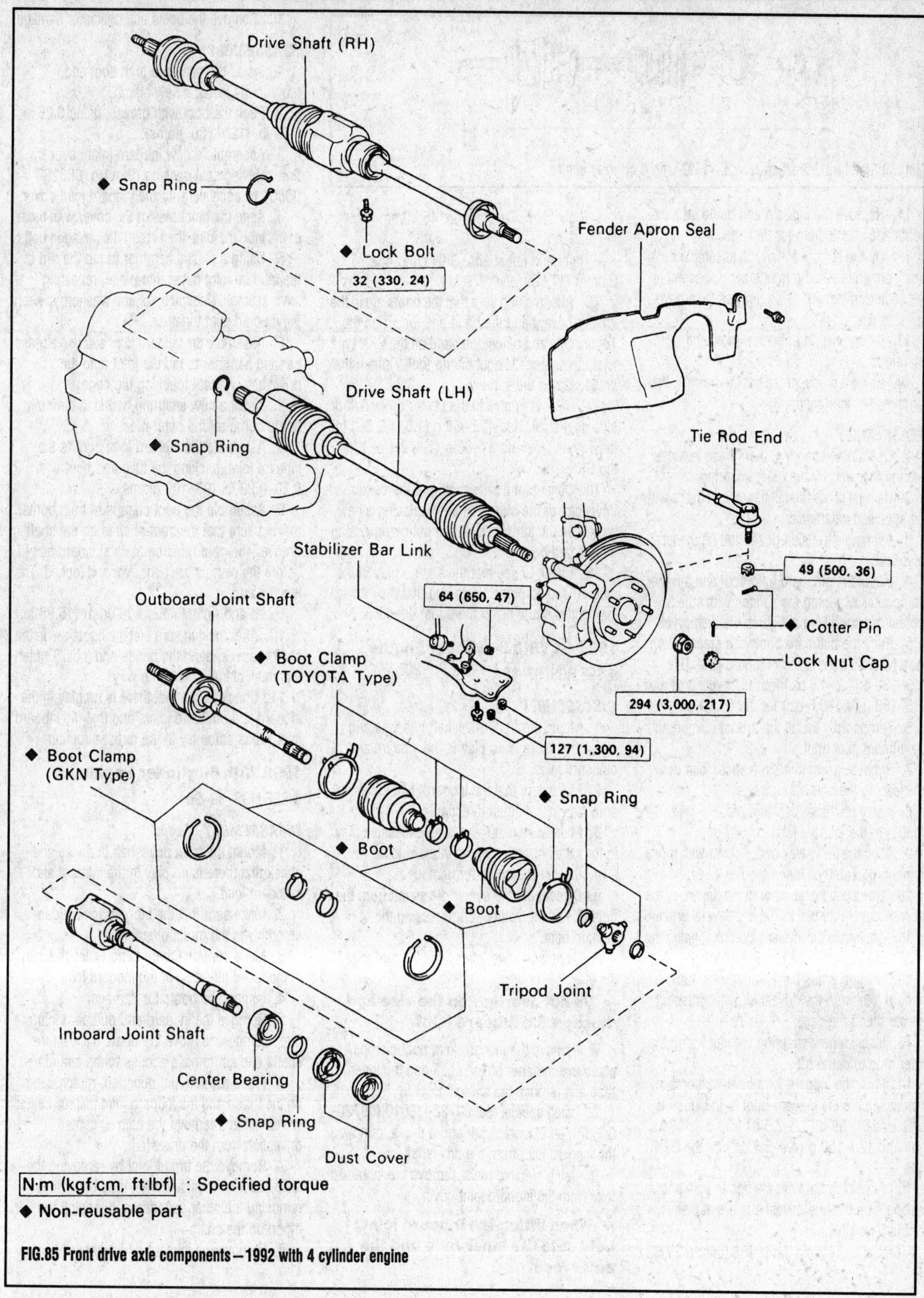

FIG.85 Front drive axle components—1992 with 4 cylinder engine

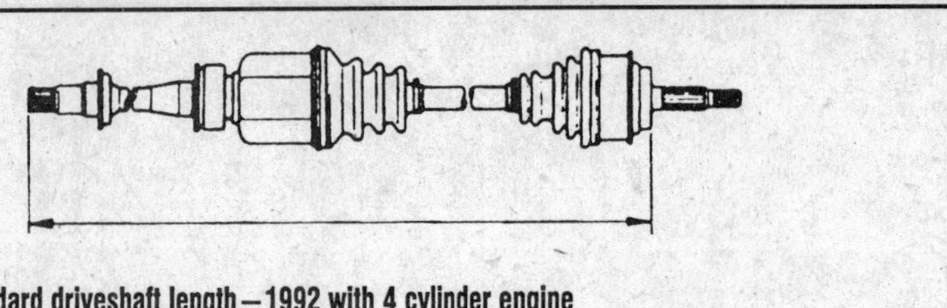

FIG.86 Standard driveshaft length—1992 with 4 cylinder engine

11. Remove the inboard and outboard joint boots and check them for damage.

12. On the left driveshaft, disassemble the side gear shaft. On the right side, disassemble the center driveshaft, using a press to remove the side dust cover.

13. Using snapring pliers, remove the snapring.

14. Using a press, press out the bearing, then remove the other snapring.

REASSEMBLY

1. Use a new snapring, then press in a new bearing followed by the other snapring.

2. Using a press, install new dust covers with the specified clearances.

3. Assemble the side gear shaft on the left driveshaft.

4. Install the outboard joint boot and a new clamp after wrapping the splines with tape to protect the boot. Do not tighten the clamp yet.

5. Pack the outboard boot with grease, then assemble the boot to the outboard joint. Use 119–130 g (4.2–4.6 oz.) for the Toyota type and 136–156 g (4.8–5.5 oz.) for the GKN type.

6. Temporarily install the 2 boot clamps and the inboard joint boot.

7. Begin to assemble the inboard joint cover by cleaning the contact surfaces.

8. Apply new seal packing, part No. 08826–00801, to the inboard joint cover.

9. Align the bolt holes of the cover with those of inboard joint, then insert the hex bolts.

10. Use a plastic hammer to tap the rim of the inboard cover into place. Repeat several times.

11. Assemble the inboard joint by aligning the match marks placed before disassembly.

12. Using a brass bar and hammer, tap the inboard joint onto the driveshaft without letting the bar touch the cage.

13. Install a new snapring without letting the outer race to come off.

14. Pack the inboard joint boot with grease, then assemble the inboard boot to the inboard joint. Use 91–99 g (3.2–3.5 oz.) for the Toyota type and 139–150 g (4.9–5.3 oz.) for the GKN type.

15. Assemble the boot clamps to both boots, making sure that the driveshafts are at their standard lengths:

- Left shaft, Toyota type: 456.0mm (17.953 in.)
- Right shaft, Toyota type: 456.0mm (17.953 in.)
- Right and left shafts, GKN type: 452.35 ± 2.0mm (17.809 ± 0.079 in.)

16. After making sure that the boots are in the shaft groove, bend the band and lock it on the Toyota type and pincer the band on the GKN type with the proper CV boot clamp tool. Tighten the small clamps the same way.

17. Pack in grease to the center driveshaft or side gear shaft. Use 42.5–54 g (1.5–1.9 oz.) for the Toyota type and 51–60 g (1.8–2.1 oz.) for the GKN type.

18. Connect the driveshaft and the center driveshaft or the side gear shaft, placing a new gasket on the inboard joint without compressing the inboard boot.

19. Check to see that there is no play in the inboard and outboard joints and that the inboard joint slides smoothly in the thrust direction.

1989–91 With 6-cylinder Engine

➧ SEE FIGS. 87–88

DISASSEMBLY

1. Mount the front driveshaft in a vise and check that there is no play in the inboard and outboard joint.

2. Make sure that the inboard joint slides smoothly in the thrust direction.

3. Make sure that there is no excessive play in the radial direction of the inboard joint.

4. Inspect the boots for damage.

5. Disconnect the center driveshaft from the right driveshaft, without compressing the inboard boot.

6. Using soft jaws, clamp the inboard joint in the vise.

➡ Do not overtighten the vise and damage the inboard joint.

7. Remove the inboard joint boot clamps, place matchmarks on the shaft and the inner race and remove the snapring.

8. Using special tool 09726–10010 (09726–00030), an extension bar and a press, remove the inboard joint from the driveshaft.

9. Using suitable tools, remove the inboard joint from the inboard joint cover.

➡ When lifting the inboard joint, hold onto the inner race and the outer race.

10. Remove the boots and check for damage.

REASSEMBLY

1. Install the outboard joint boot and temporarily install a new clamp.

2. Pack the boot with grease, using 0.26–0.29 lb. (120–130 grams).

3. Assemble a new inboard joint cover by first applying seal packing (Part No. 08826–00801 or equivalent) to the inboard joint cover.

4. Align the bolt holes of the cover with those of the inboard joint, then insert the hexagon bolts.

5. Using a plastic hammer to tap the rim of the inboard joint cover into place, repeating several times. Use the bolts and washers to keep the inboard joint together.

6. Assemble the inboard joint and use a brass bar and hammer to tap the joint onto the driveshaft, without touching the cage.

7. Install a new snapring, working carefully not to come off the outer race.

8. Assemble the inboard joint boot to the inboard joint, packing the tulip and boot with 0.20–0.22 lb. (90–100 grams).

9. Assemble the boot clamps to both boots, making sure that the boot shaft is on the shaft groove. The boot must be at its standard length before the clamps are bent over and locked. The lengths are:

- Left and right shafts: 406.0mm (15.98 in.)

10. After making sure that the boots are in the shaft grooves, bend the bands and lock. Tighten the small clamps the same way.

11. Check to see that there is no play in the inboard and outboard joints and that the inboard joint slides smoothly in the thrust direction.

1992 With 6-cylinder Engine

➧ SEE FIGS. 89–90

DISASSEMBLY

1. Mount the front driveshaft in a vise and check that there is no play in the inboard and outboard joint.

2. Make sure that the inboard joint slides smoothly in the thrust direction.

3. Make sure that there is no excessive play in the radial direction of the inboard joint.

4. Inspect the boots for damage.

5. Remove the inboard and outboard joint boot clamps and move the boots back on the shafts enough to have access to the snaprings.

6. Place painted, not punched, matchmarks on the tripod and the inboard joint tulip or center driveshaft and remove the tulip or center driveshaft from the driveshaft.

7. Remove the tripod joint by removing the visible snapring, sliding the tripod back, then removing the other snapring and tapping the tripod off the shaft.

8. Remove the inboard and outboard boots.

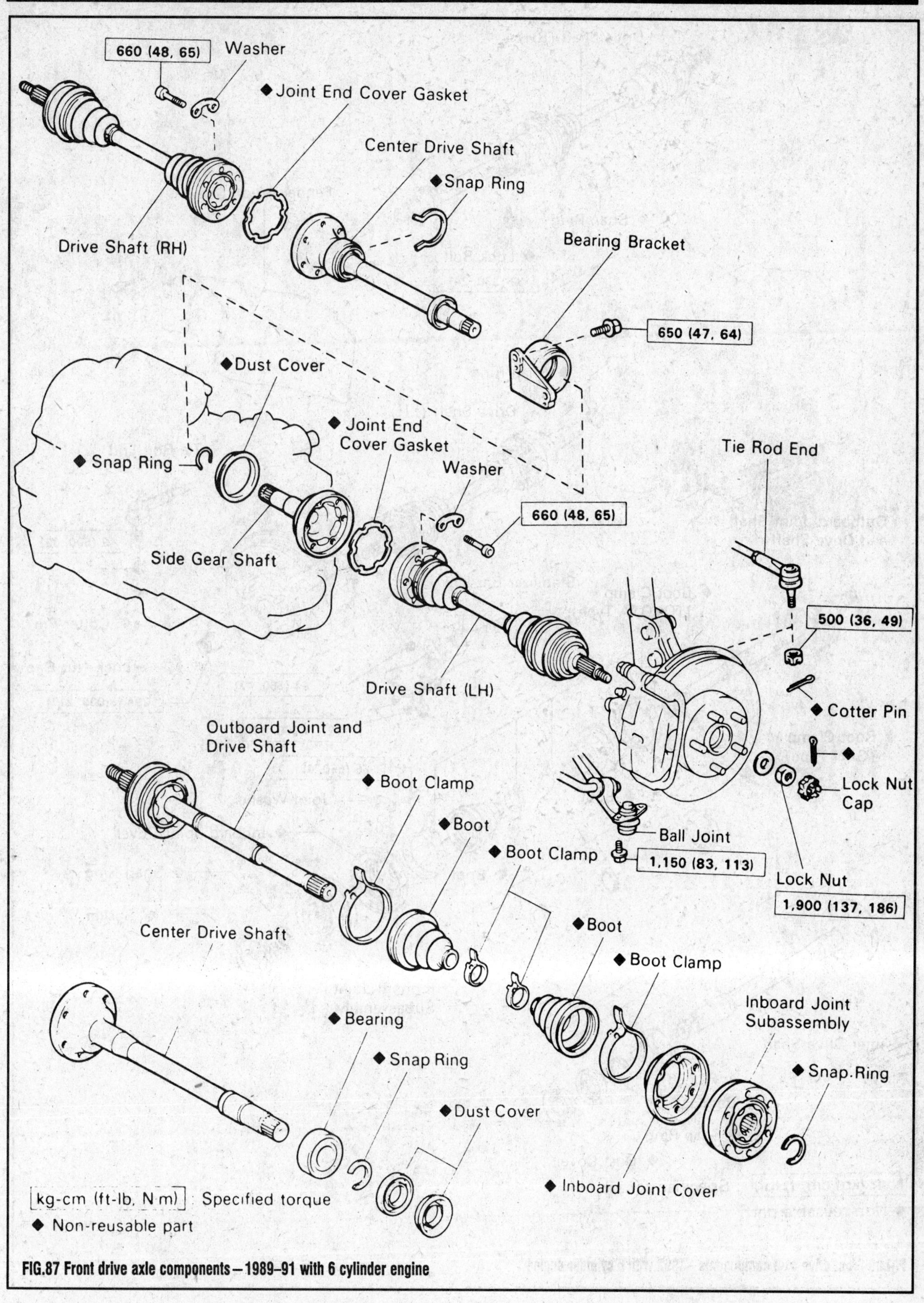

FIG.87 Front drive axle components—1989–91 with 6 cylinder engine

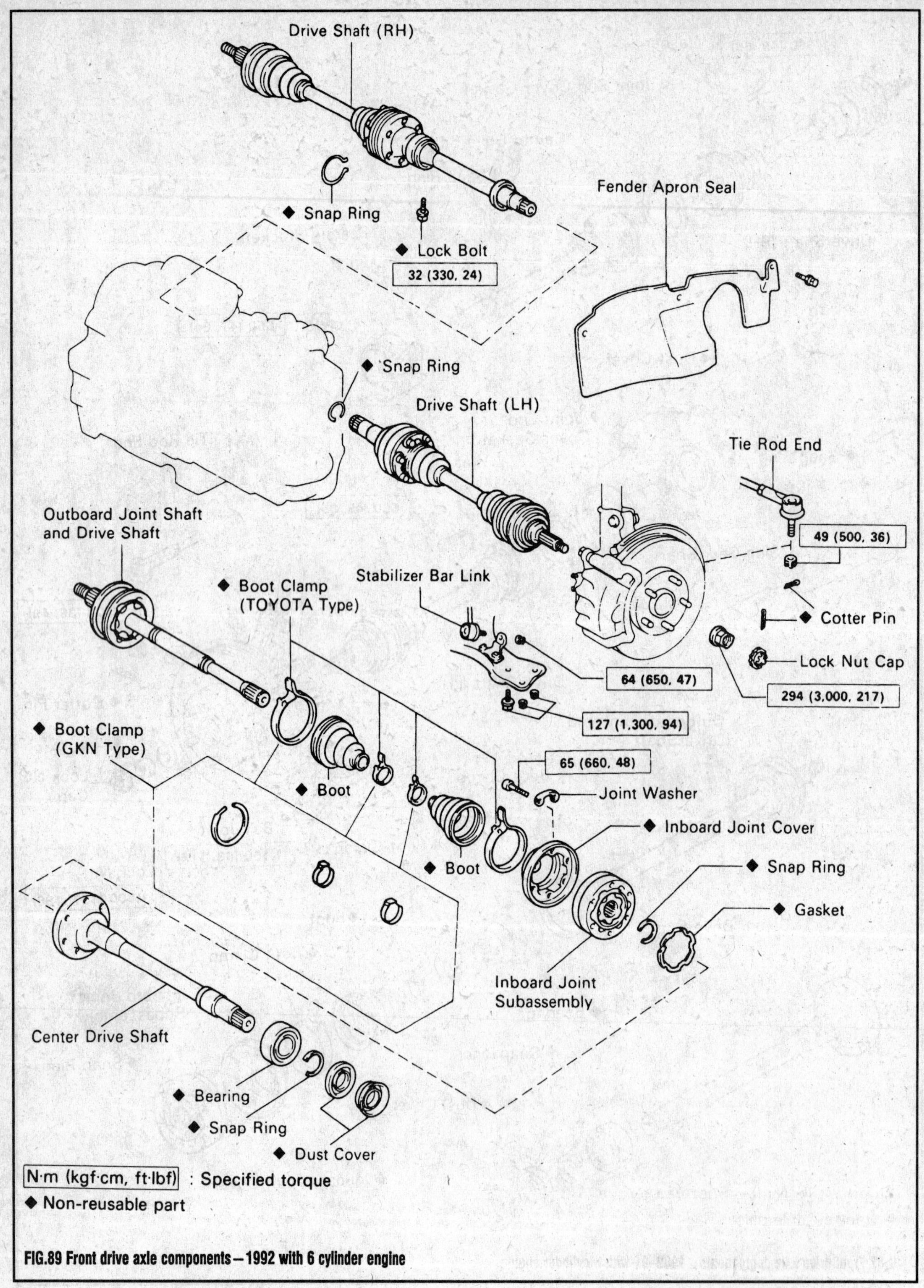

FIG.89 Front drive axle components—1992 with 6 cylinder engine

➡ **Do not disassemble the outboard joint.**

9. Remove the dust cover from the left inboard joint tulip and from the right center driveshaft with a press.
10. On the right side, disassemble the center driveshaft, using a press to remove the side dust cover.
11. Using snapring pliers, remove the snapring.
12. Using a press, press out the bearing, then remove the other snapring.

REASSEMBLY

1. Use a new snapring, then press in a new bearing followed by the other snapring on the center shaft.
2. Using a press, install new dust cover with the specified clearance.
3. Install a new dust cover on the left driveshaft tulip with the specified clearance.
4. Temporarily install both boots with clamps onto the shaft.
5. Reverse the removal procedure to install the tripod joint, aligning the matchmarks.
6. Fill grease into the outboard joint, using 119–130 g (4.2–4.6 oz.) for the Toyota type and 139–159 g (4.9–5.6 oz.) for the GKN type.
7. Fill grease into the inboard joint and boot, using 232–241 g (8.2–8.5 oz.) for the Toyota type and 184–215 g (6.5–7.6 oz.) for the GKN type and slide the tulip onto the driveshaft.
8. Assemble the boot clamps to both boots, making sure that the driveshafts are at their standard lengths:

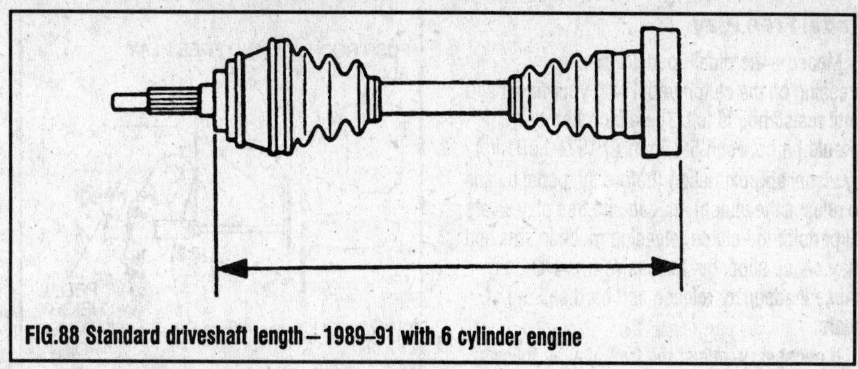

FIG.88 Standard driveshaft length—1989–91 with 6 cylinder engine

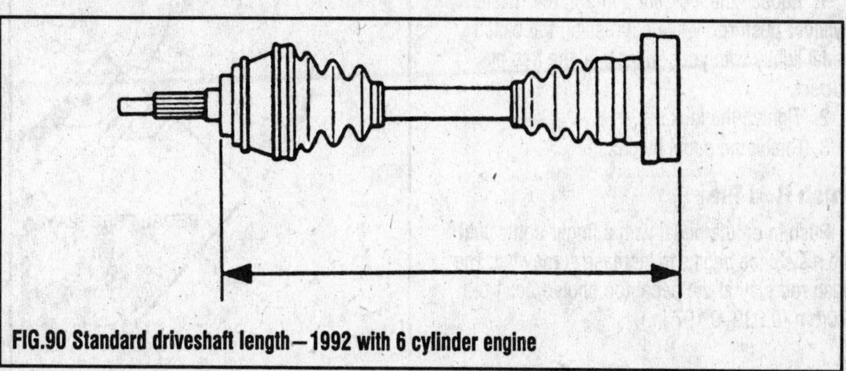

FIG.90 Standard driveshaft length—1992 with 6 cylinder engine

- Left shaft, Toyota type: 608.1 ± 5.0mm (23.94 ± 0.197 in.)
- Right shaft, Toyota type: 866.2 ± 5.0mm (34.1 ± 0.197 in.)
- Left shaft, GKN type: 609.2 ± 2.0mm (23.98 ± 0.079 in.)
- Right shaft, GKN type: 880.8 ± 2.0mm (34.67 ± 0.079 in.)

9. After making sure that the boots are in the shaft groove, bend the band and lock it on the Toyota type and pincer the band on the GKN type with the proper CV boot clamp tool. Tighten the small clamps the same way.
10. Check to see that there is no play in the inboard and outboard joints and that the inboard joint slides smoothly in the thrust direction.

CLUTCH

➧ SEE FIGS. 91–96

Adjustments

1983–88 WITH S51 TRANSAXLE

Linkage

No external adjustments are needed or possible.

Pedal height

Check that the height of the clutch pedal is correct by measuring from the top of the pedal to the asphalt sheet on the kick panel. The pedal height should be within these specifications:

- 1983–85: 7.54–7.94 in. (191.5–201.5mm)
- 1986: 8.0–8.4 in. (203–213mm)
- 1987–89: 7.5–7.9 in. (191–201mm)
- 1990–91: 7.1–7.5 in. (181–191mm)
- 1992 with 5S-FE engine: 6.3–6.7 in. (160.8–170.8mm)
- 1992 with 3VZ-FE engine: 6.5–6.9 in. (164.7–174.7mm)

TO ADJUST

1. Remove the lower instrument finish panel and disconnect the air duct, if necessary.
2. On vehicles except 1987–91 with cruise control, loosen the lock nut and turn the stopper bolt until the pedal height is correct and tighten the lock nut.
3. On 1987–91 vehicles with cruise control, loosen the lock nut on the clutch start switch, disconnect the connector and adjust the switch position to correct the pedal height. Tighten the lock nut and reconnect the connector.
4. Connect the air duct and reinstall the lower instrument finish panel, if removed.
5. After the pedal height is adjusted, check the free play.

Pedal Free Play

Measure the clutch pedal free play by pressing on the clutch pedal with your finger and until resistance is felt. The clutch free play should be between 5-15mm (0.197–0.591 in.) by visual approximation (before the pedal begins to release the clutch). Inadequate free play wears all parts of the clutch releasing mechanisms and may cause slippage. Excessive free play may cause inadequate release and hard shifting of gears.

If necessary, adjust the free play as follows:

1. Loosen the lock nut and turn the master cylinder push rod while depressing the clutch pedal lightly with your finger until the free play is correct.
2. Tighten the lock nut.
3. Check the pedal height.

Push Rod Play

Push in on the pedal with a finger softly until the resistance begins to increase somewhat. The push rod play at the pedal top should be: 1.0–5.0mm (0.039–0.197 in.).

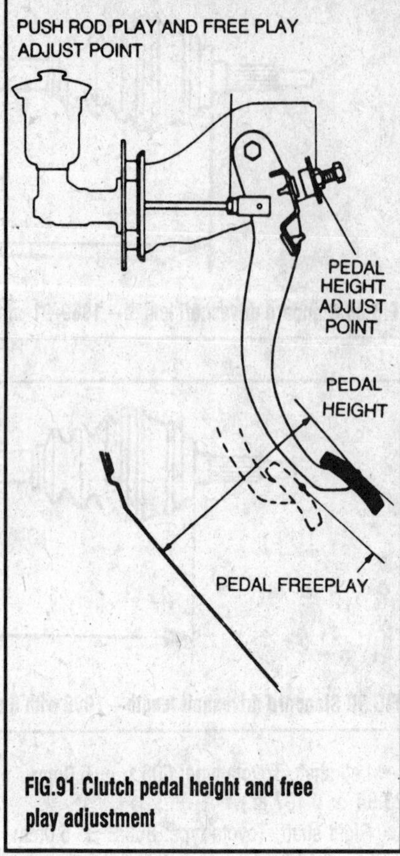

FIG.91 Clutch pedal height and free play adjustment

Driven Disc and Pressure Plate

The clutch is a single dry disc type, with a diaphragm spring pressure plate. Clutch release bearings are sealed ball bearing units which need no lubrication and should never be washed in any kind of solvent.

REMOVAL & INSTALLATION

CAUTION

The clutch driven disc contains asbestos, which has been determined to be a cancer causing agent. Never clean clutch surfaces with compressed air! Avoid inhaling any dust from any clutch surface! When cleaning clutch surfaces, use a commercially available brake cleaning fluid.

1983-88

1. Remove the transaxle from the vehicle.
2. Matchmark the flywheel and the clutch cover with paint or chalk.
3. Loosen each set bolt one at a time until the spring tension is relieved.
4. Remove the set bolts completely and pull off the clutch cover with the clutch disc.

➡ **Do not drop the clutch disc. Do not allow grease or oil to get on any of the disc, pressure plate, or flywheel surfaces.**

5. Unfasten the release fork bearing clips. Withdraw the release bearing assembly with the fork and then separate them.
6. Remove the release fork boot.
7. Using calipers, measure the rivet head depth. Minimum depth is 0.30mm. If not within the limit, replace the clutch disc.
8. Using a dial indicator and V-blocks, measure the clutch disc runout. Maximum allowable runout is 0.78mm. If the runout is excessive, replace the clutch disc.
9. Using a dial indicator, measure the flywheel runout. Maximum runout is 0.10mm. If the runout is excessive, machine or replace the flywheel.
10. Using calipers, measure the diaphragm spring for depth and width and wear. Maximum depth is 0.60mm and maximum width is 5mm. Replace the clutch cover as necessary.
11. Grasp the release bearing and turn it while applying force in the axial direction. Replace the bearing and hub as required.

To install the clutch:

12. Insert proper alignment tool into the clutch disc and set them and the clutch cover in position.
13. Install the clutch disc bolts and tighten them evenly and gradually in a criss-cross pattern in several passes around the cover until they are snug.
14. Once the bolts are snug, torque them in sequence to 14 ft. lbs.
15. Using a dial indicator with a roller attachment, measure the diaphragm spring tip alignment. Maximum non-alignment is 0.05mm. Adjust the alignment as necessary using SST No. 09333-00013.
16. Apply molybdenum disulphide lithium base grease (NLGI No.2) to the following parts:
    a. Release fork and hub contact point.
    b. Release fork and push rod contact point.
    c. Release fork pivot point.
    d. Clutch disc spline.
    e. Inside groove of the release bearing hub.
17. Install the bearing assembly on the fork and then install them to the transaxle.
18. Install the boot.
19. Install the transaxle to the engine.

Master Cylinder

REMOVAL & INSTALLATION

1983-88

1. Wipe off and remove the reservoir tank cap.
2. Draw the fluid from the master cylinder with a syringe.
3. Disconnect the clutch line tube fitting, using a line wrench.
4. On 1983-86 vehicles, remove the pedal return spring.
5. On 1886-91 vehicles, remove the lower instrument panel finish panel and disconnect the air duct from the panel.
6. Remove the clip and clevis pin with the spring washer. The spring washer is found on 1987-91 vehicles.

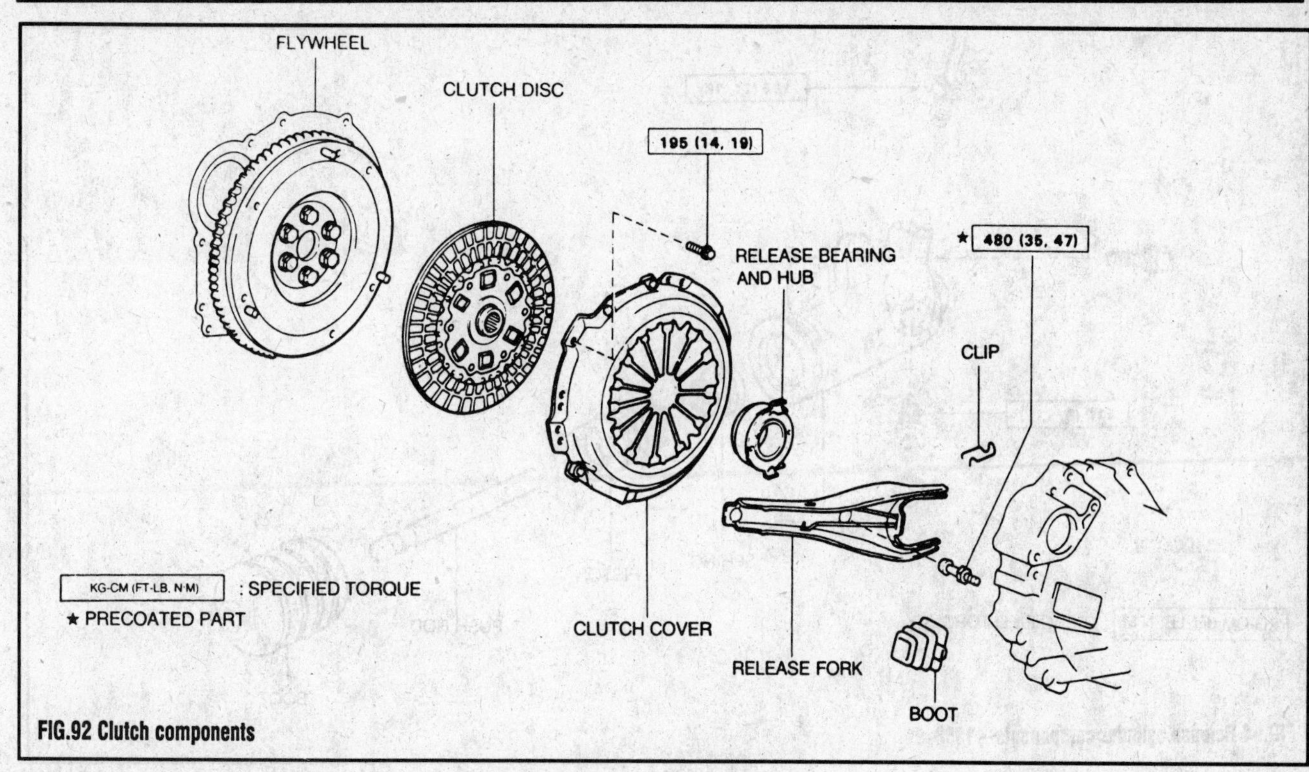

FIG.92 Clutch components

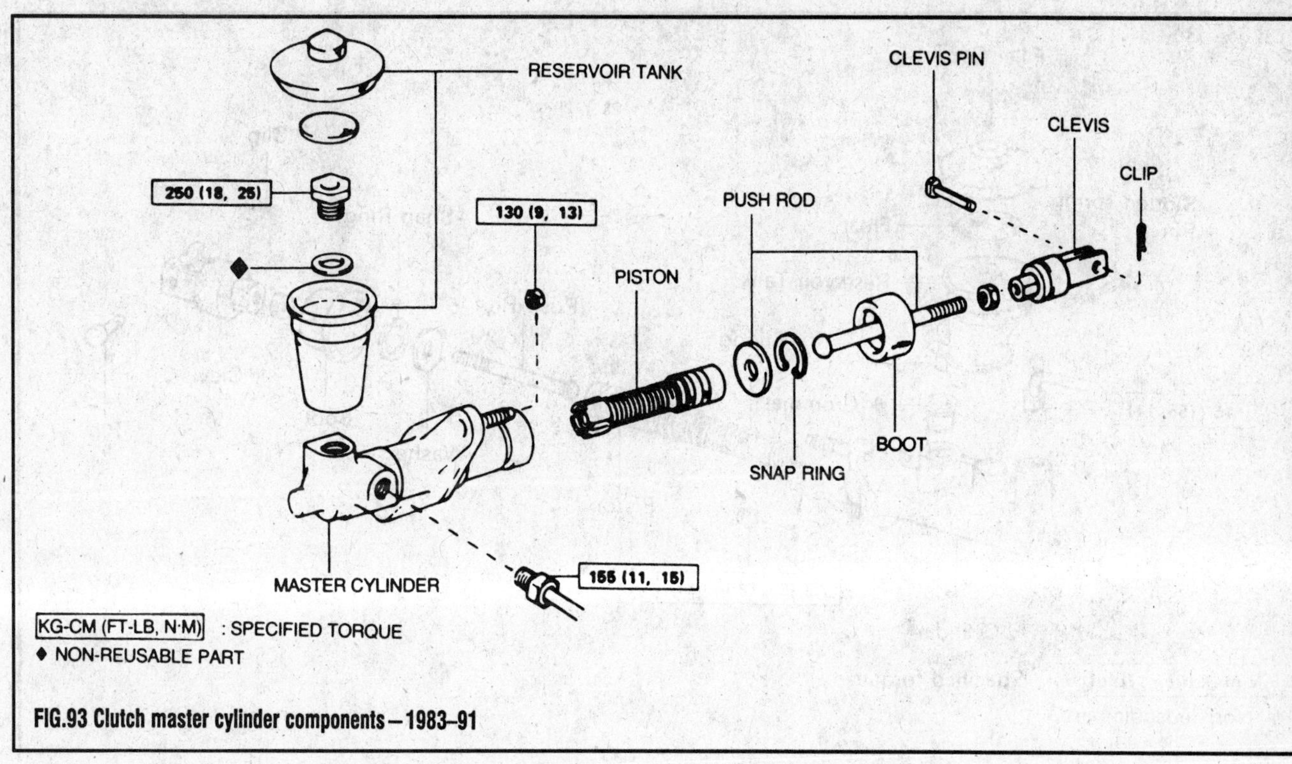

FIG.93 Clutch master cylinder components—1983–91

155 (11, 15)
110 (8, 11)
CYLINDER
SPRING
PISTON
PUSH ROD
BOOT
KG-CM (FT-LB, N·M) : SPECIFIED TORQUE

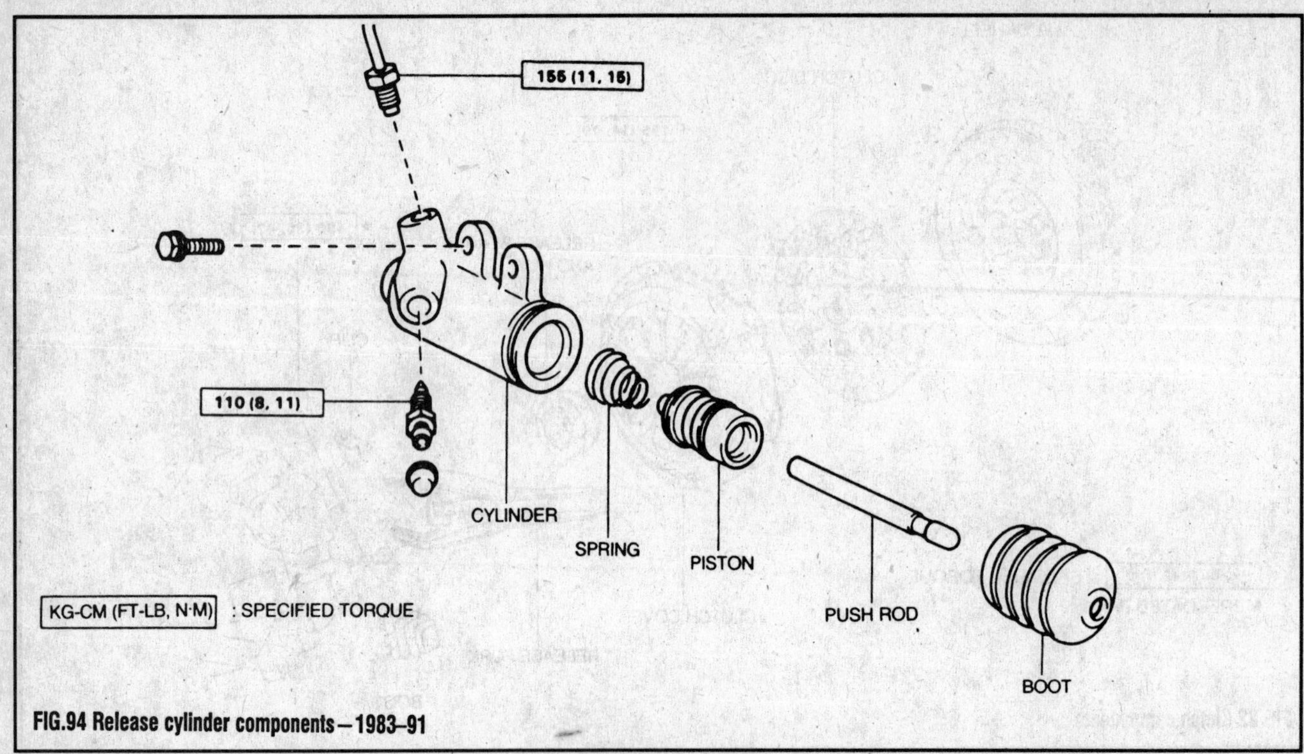

FIG.94 Release cylinder components—1983–91

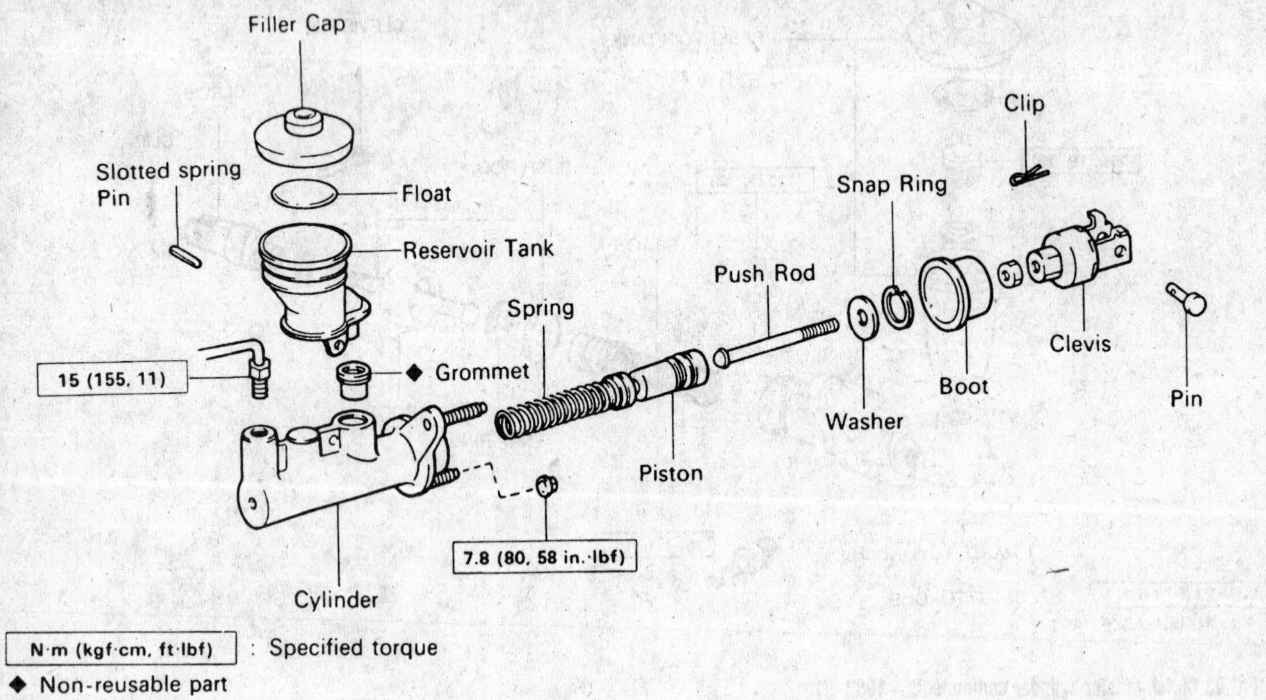

Filler Cap
Slotted spring Pin
Float
Reservoir Tank
Clip
Snap Ring
Push Rod
Spring
15 (155, 11)
◆ Grommet
Clevis
Boot
Pin
Washer
Piston
7.8 (80, 58 in.·lbf)
Cylinder
N·m (kgf·cm, ft·lbf) : Specified torque
◆ Non-reusable part

FIG.95 Clutch master cylinder components—1992

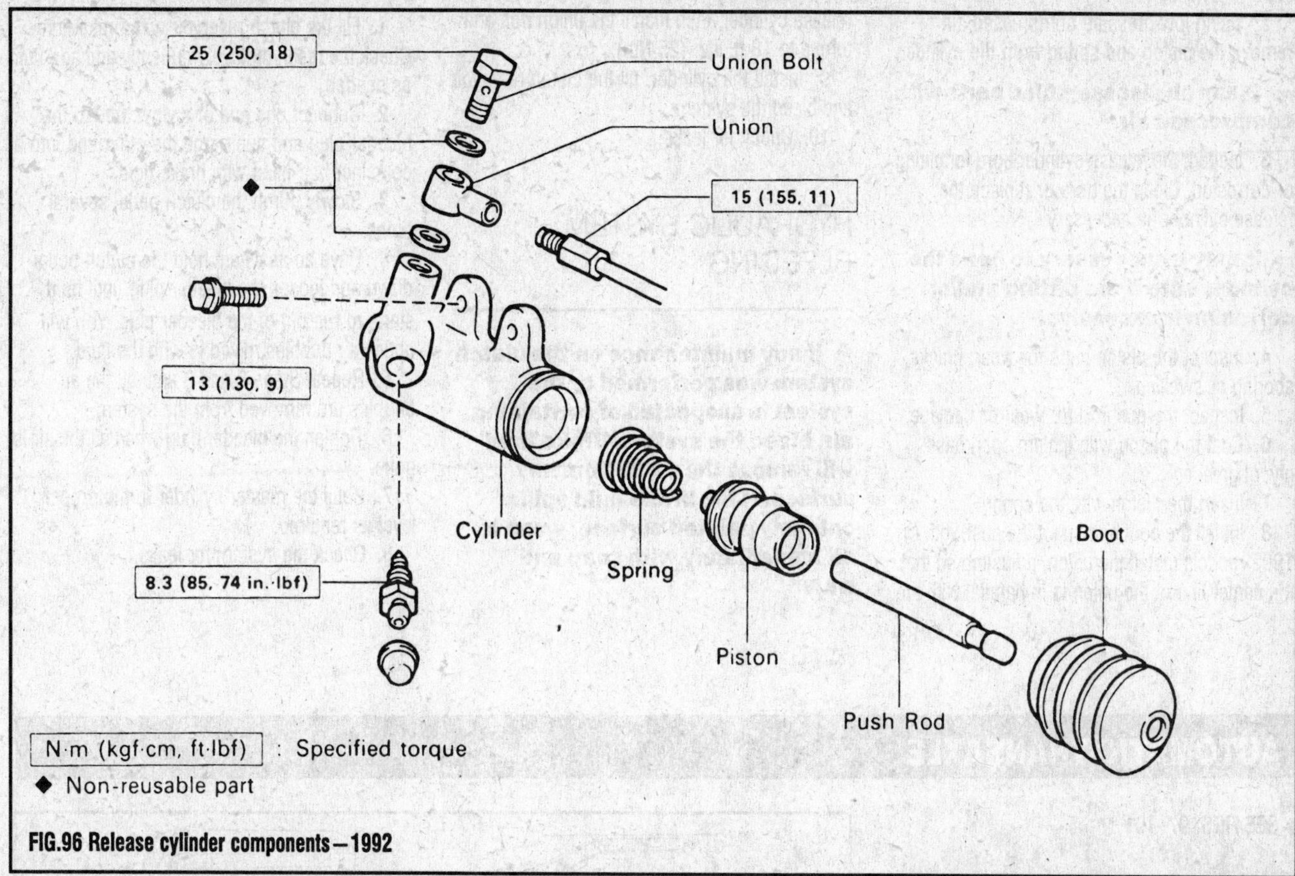

FIG.96 Release cylinder components—1992

7. Remove the mounting nuts and remove the master cylinder.

To install the master cylinder:

8. Install the master cylinder and tighten the mounting nuts to specifications.
9. Connect the clutch line tube and tighten the fitting to specifications.
10. Connect the clevis and secure the clevis pin with the clip.
11. On 1983-86 vehicles, install he pedal return spring.
12. Fill the reservoir with brake fluid and bleed the clutch system as described in this Section. Install the cap.
13. Check for leaks.
14. Check and adjust the clutch pedal.
15. On 1987-91 vehicles, connect the air duct to the lower instrument panel and install the panel.

OVERHAUL

1983-88

1. Remove the clutch master cylinder, clamp perpendicularly in a soft jaw vise (so that bore is not squeezed) and remove the reservoir by removing the bolt, or pin with a punch (1992).
2. Peel back the rubber boot and remove the snapring with snapring pliers.
3. Pull out the pushrod.
4. Apply low-pressure compressed air into the clutch line tube fitting and remove the piston.
5. Inspect the master cylinder bore for pitting or corrosion. Clean the bore or replace the master cylinder as necessary.

➡ It may be necessary to hone the cylinder bore if the pitting and/or corrosion is excessive.

6. Coat the piston with lithium soap base glycol grease.
7. Install the pushrod asembly with the snapring.
8. Install the reservoir tank and torque to 18 ft. lbs. (25 Nm), or on 1992 models, drive in the slotted spring pin with a pin punch and hammer.
9. Install the master cylinder.
10. Fill the reservoir with brake fluid and bleed the clutch sysem as described in this Section. Install the cap.
11. Check for leaks.
12. Check and adjust the clutch pedal.

Release Cylinder

REMOVAL & INSTALLATION

1. Place a small plastic container under the clutch line tube fitting and disconnect it, using a line wrench.
2. Remove the two retaining bolts.
3. Pull the release cylinder from its mounting.

To install:

4. Install the release cylinder onto it mounting.
5. Install and tighten the two bolts to specifications.
6. Connect and tighten the clutch line tube to specifications.
7. Fill the reservoir with brake fluid and bleed the clutch system as described in this Section.
8. Check for leaks.

OVERHAUL

1. Remove the release cylinder and loosely clamp in a soft jaw vise.

2. Using low pressure compressed air, remove the piston and spring from the cylinder.

➡ **Clean all disassembled parts with compressed air.**

3. Inspect the release cylinder bore for pitting or corrosion. Clean the bore or replace the release cylinder as necessary.

➡ **It may be necessary to hone the cylinder bore if the pitting and/or corrosion is excessive.**

4. Inspect the piston cups for wear, cracks, scoring or swelling.
5. Inspect the pushrod for wear or damage.
6. Coat the piston with lithium soap base glycol grease.
7. Insert the piston with the spring.
8. Install the boot and insert the push rod. On 1992 models install the union, adjusting so that the center line of the union is in parallel with the release cylinder, then install the union bolt and torque to 18 ft. lbs. (25 Nm).
9. Install the cylinder, fill the clutch reservoir and bleed the system.
10. Check for leaks.

HYDRAULIC SYSTEM BLEEDING

➡ **If any maintenance on the clutch system was performed or the system is suspected of containing air, bleed the system. Brake fluid will remove the paint from any surface. If the brake fluid spills onto any painted surface, wash it off immediately with soap and water.**

1. Fill the clutch reservoir with brake fluid. Check the reservoir level frequently and add fluid as needed.
2. Connect one end of a vinyl tube to the bleeder plug and submerge the other end into a container half-filled with brake fluid.
3. Slowly pump the clutch pedal several times.
4. Have an assistant hold the clutch pedal down and loosen the bleeder plug until fluid starts to run out of the bleeder plug. You will notice air bubbles mixed in with the fluid.
5. Repeat Steps 2 and 3 until all the air bubbles are removed from the system.
6. Tighten the bleeder plug when all the air is gone.
7. Refill the master cylinder to the proper level as required.
8. Check the system for leaks.

AUTOMATIC TRANSAXLE

➧ SEE FIGS. 97–101

Identification

The automatic transaxle identification code is stamped on the VIN plate under the hood.

The A140E transaxle, an electronically controlled transaxle, differs from the oil pressure control type transaxle (A140L) in that it is controlled by a microcomputer. The A540E transaxle, used beginning in 1989 on vehicles with V6 engines, is also a computer controlled transaxle. Vehicles produced from 1989–91 equipped with All-Trac/4WD have the A540H transaxle.

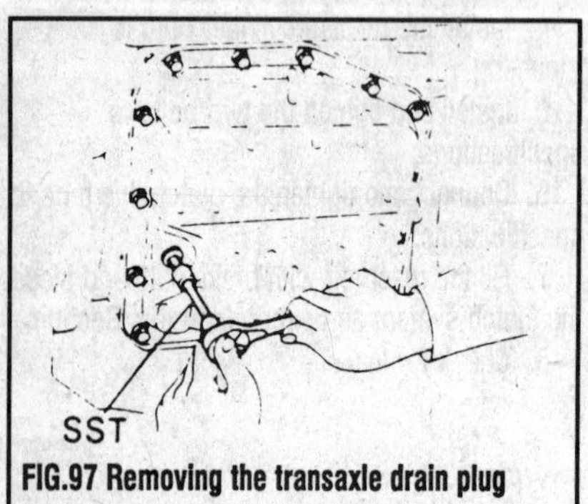

FIG.97 Removing the transaxle drain plug

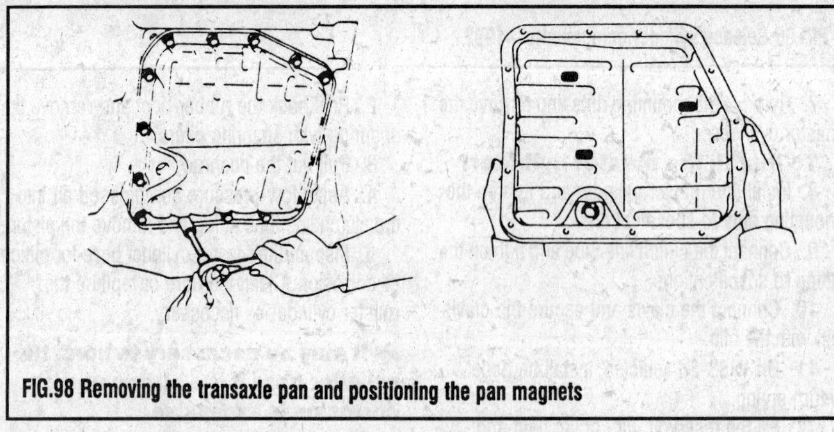

FIG.98 Removing the transaxle pan and positioning the pan magnets

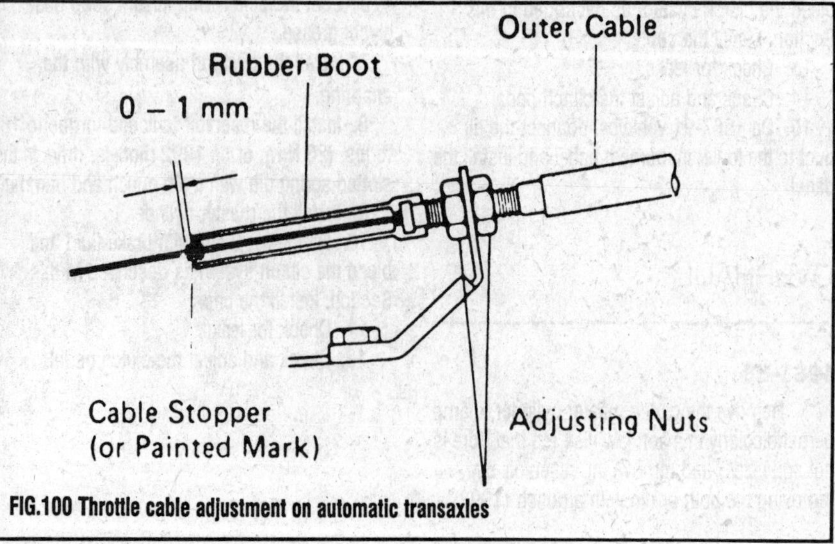

FIG.100 Throttle cable adjustment on automatic transaxles

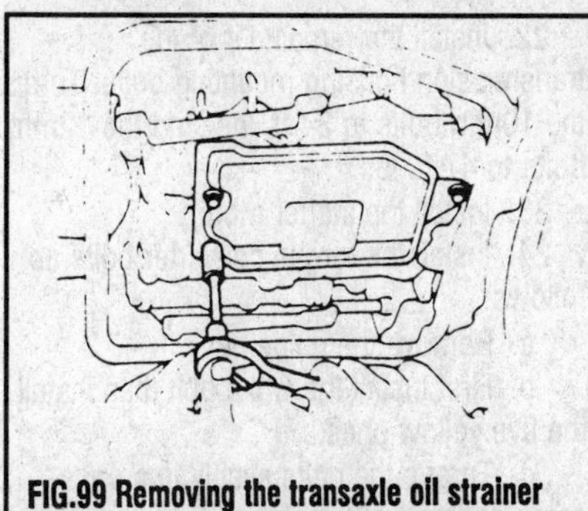
FIG.99 Removing the transaxle oil strainer

Fluid Pan

REMOVAL & INSTALLATION

FILTER SERVICE

➡ The removal of the transaxle oil pan drain plug requires the use of either Toyota special tool #SST 09043-38100 or its equivalent (a 10mm hex head wrench).

1. To avoid contamination of the transaxle, thoroughly clean the exterior of the oil pan and surrounding area to remove any deposits of dirt and grease.
2. Position a suitable drain pan under the oil pan and remove the drain plug. Allow the oil to drain from the pan. Set the drain plug aside.
3. Loosen and remove all but two of the oil pan retaining bolts.
4. Support the pan by hand and slowly remove the remaining two bolts.
5. Carefully lower the pan to the ground.

CAUTION

There will be some fluid still inside the pan and it may be hot. Allow the fluid to cool down before removing the pan and wear eye protection to avoid personal injury.

6. Remove the 3 oil strainer (filter) attaching bolts and carefully remove the strainer. The strainer will also contain some fluid.

➡ One of the 3 oil strainer bolts is slightly longer than the other 2. Make a note of where the longer bolt goes so that it may be reinstalled in the original position.

7. Discard the strainer. Remove the gasket from the pan and discard it.
8. Drain the remainder of the fluid from the oil pan and wipe the pan clean with a lint-free rag. With a gasket scraper, remove any old gasket material from the flanges of the pan and the transaxle. Remove the gasket from the drain plug and replace it with a new one.

➡ Depending on the year and maintenance schedule of the vehicle, there may be from one to three small magnets on the bottom of the pan. These magnets were installed by the manufacturer at the time the transaxle was assembled. The magnets function to collect metal chips and filings from clutch plates, bushings and bearings that accumulate during the normal break-in process that a new transaxle experiences. Clean the magnets and reinstall them. They can be useful tools for determining transaxle component wear.

To install the filter and pan:

9. Install the new oil strainer. Install and tighten the retaining bolts to 7–8 ft lbs. (10–11 Nm) in their proper locations.
10. Install the new gasket onto the oil pan making sure that the holes in the gasket are aligned evenly with those of the pan. Position the magnets so that they will not interfere with the oil tubes.
11. Raise the pan and gasket into position on the transaxle and install the retaining bolts. Torque the retaining bolts in a criss-cross pattern to 43 inch lbs. (4.9 Nm).
12. Install and tighten the drain plug to 36 ft. lbs. (49 Nm).
13. Fluid is added only through the dipstick tube. Use only the proper automatic transmission fluid.

➡ Do not overfill the transaxle. Do not race the engine when adding fluid.

14. Replace the dipstick after filling. Start the engine and allow it to idle.
15. After the engine has idled for a few minutes, shift the transmission slowly through the gears and then return it to **P**. With the engine still idling, check the fluid level on the dipstick. If necessary, add more fluid to raise the level to where it is supposed to be.

➡ Before discarding the used fluid, check the color of the fluid. It should always be a bright red color. It if is discolored (brown or black), or smells burnt, serious transmission troubles, possibly due to overheating, should be suspected. The transmission should be inspected by a qualified service technician to locate the cause of the burnt fluid.

Adjustments

THROTTLE CABLE

1983–88

To inspect the throttle cable operation, remove the air cleaner and depress the accelerator cable all the way. Check that the throttle valve opens fully. If the throttle valve does not open fully, adjust the accelerator link as follows:

1. Remove the air cleaner.
2. Fully depress the accelerator cable.
3. Loosen the adjustment nuts.
4. Adjust the cable housing so that the distance between the end of boot and the stopper is 0–.04 in. (0–1mm).
5. Tighten the adjusting nuts.
6. Recheck the adjustment.

SHIFT CABLE

1. Loosen the control cable lever swivel nut.
2. Push the control lever to the right as far as it will go.
3. Bring the lever back two notches to the Neutral position.
4. Place the shifter in Neutral.
5. Hold the lever, lightly, toward the **R** range side and tighten the swivel nut.

Neutral Safety Switch

The neutral safety switch is connected to the throttle cable and the manual shift lever on the transaxle. The switch, in addition to preventing vehicle start with the transaxle in gear, also actuates the back-up warning lights.

REMOVAL & INSTALLATION

1. Disconect the neutral start switch connector.

2. With a pair of needle nose pliers, remove the clip that connects the manual control cable to the manual shift lever.

3. Unstake the lock nut and remove the manual shift lever.

4. Remove the neutral start switch with the seal gasket.

5. Install the neutral start switch making sure that the lip of the seal gasket is facing inward.

6. Install the manual shift lever.

7. Install the locknut and torque to 61 inch lbs. (6.9 Nm). Stake the nut with the locking plate.

8. Connect the switch connector.

9. Adjust the neutral start switch.

10. Connect the transmission shift cable and install the clip.

11. Adjust the transmission shift cable.

12. Check the operation of the switch and adjust as necessary.

ADJUSTMENT

If the engine starts with the shift selector in any position except Park or Neutral, adjust the switch as follows:

1. Loosen the two neutral start switch retaining bolts and move the shift selector to the Neutral range.

2. On 1983-85 vehicles, disconnect the neutral start switch connector and connect an ohmmeter across the terminals. Adjust the switch to the point at which there is continuity across the terminals.

3. On 1986-92 vehicles, align the groove and the neutral basic line. Maintain the alignment and torque the bolts to 48 inch lbs. (5.4 Nm).

Back-Up light Switch

The neutral start switch functions as the back-up light switch. See removal, installation and adjustment procedures for the neutral safety switch as previously detailed in this Section.

Automatic Transaxle

REMOVAL & INSTALLATION

1983-86

1. Support the engine and remove the front and rear mounting

2. Remove the left hand dust cover.

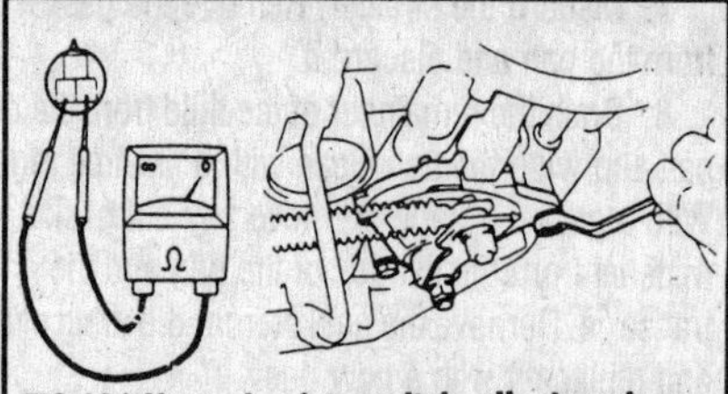

FIG.101 Neutral safety switch adjustment on 1983–85

3. Remove the left hand mounting bracket.

4. Remove the side gear shaft and center drive from the transaxle.

5. Unbolt and remove the control cable bracket.

6. Remove the stiffener plate (A140E transxles).

7. Remove the torque converter dust cover.

8. Remove the torque converter mounting bolts as follows:

a. Turn the crankshaft to gain access to each bolt.

b. Hold the crankshaft pulley nut stationary with a wrench.

c. Loosen and remove each bolt. There are five yellow bolts and one white one.

9. Remove the starter motor.

10. Remove the mounting bolts from the transaxle.

11. Fabricate a guide pin by cutting off the head of a bolt approximately the same size as one of the transaxle mounting bolts.

12. Install the guide pin in one of the vacant torque converter holes. The guide pin aids in keeping the transmission located to the converter during removal.

13. With a small prybar or equivalent, pry on the end of the guide pin to move the transmission and the converter away from the engine.

14. Remove the transaxle assembly away from the engine.

15. Remove the torque converter from the transmission.

To install the transaxle:

16. If the torque converter was drained and washed, refill with new Dexron®II. Install the torque converter into the transmission.

17. Using calipers and a straight edge, measure from the installed surface to the front of the transmission housing. The correct distance is 1.3mm.

18. Install the guide pin into the torque converter.

19. Align the guide pin with one of the drive plate holes.

20. Align the two knockpins on the block with the converter housing.

21. Temporarily install one of the mounting bolts.

22. Install the remainder of the transmission housing mounting bolts. Torque the 10mm bolts to 34 ft. lbs. and the 12mm bolts to 47 ft. lbs.

23. Install the starter motor.

24. Install the torque converter bolts as follows:

a. Remove the guide pin.

b. First install the white bolt then install the five yellow ones.

c. Torque the bolts evenly in a criss-cross pattern to 20 ft. lbs.

25. Install the torque converter dust cover. Lock the transaxle mounting bolt near the differential with the locking plate and one dust cover mounting bolt.

26. On A140E transaxles, install the stiffener plate and torque the bolts to 27 ft. lbs.

27. Install the control cable bracket.

28. Install the side gear shaft and center driveshaft.

29. Install the left hand dust cover.

30. Install the front and rear mounting.

1987-88

1. Disconnect the negative battery cable.

2. Remove the air flow meter and the air cleaner.

3. Disconnect the transmission wire and neutral start switch connectors.

4. Disconnect the ground strap.

5. Disconnect the throttle from the throttle cable linkage and bracket.

6. Remove the transmission case protector.

7. Disconnect the speedometer cable.

8. Remove the clip, retainer and disconnect the control cable.

9. Disconnect the oil cooler hoses.

10. Remove the starter motor set bolts.

11. Remove the two transmission housing set bolts.

12. Remove the rear mount insulator bracket set bolt.

13. Raise the vehicle and drain the transaxle.

14. Remove the left hand front apron seal.

15. Have an assistant depress the brake pedal and loosen the six driveshaft retaining nuts. Disconnect both driveshafts.

16. Remove the suspension lower crossmember.

17. Remove the snapring, bearing bracket bolt and pull out the center driveshaft.

18. Disconnect the control cable clamp.

19. Remove the ten bolts and the engine mounting center member.

20. Remove the stabilizer bar.

21. Disconnect the steering knuckle from the lower arm.

22. Pull the steering knuckle towards the outside and remove the driveshaft.

23. Remove the engine rear end plate.

24. Remove the six torque converter mounting bolts as follows:

a. Turn the crankshaft to gain access to each bolt.

b. Hold the crankshaft pulley nut stationary with a wrench.

c. Loosen and remove each bolt. There is one gray bolt and five black ones.

25. Hold the transaxle stationary with two jacks, or a chain, block and a jack.

26. Lower the rear end of the transaxle and remove the three transaxle housing mounting bolts.

27. Remove the transaxle from the engine.

28. Remove the torque converter from the transaxle.

To install the transaxle:

29. Install the torque converter into the transmission.

30. Using calipers and a straight edge, measure from the installed surface to the front of the transmission housing. The correct distance is 1.3mm.

31. Align the two knockpins on the block with the converter housing.

32. Temporarily install one of the mounting bolts.

33. Install the remainder of the transmission housing mounting bolts. Torque the 10mm bolts to 34 ft. lbs. and the 12mm bolts to 47 ft. lbs.

34. Install the rear transmission housing mounting bolts.

35. First install the grey bolt then install the five black ones.

36. Torque the bolts evenly in a criss-cross pattern to 20 ft. lbs.

37. Install the engine rear end plate.

38. Install the left hand driveshaft and connect the steering knuckle to the lower arm. Torque the bolt to 94 ft. lbs.

39. Install the stabilizer bar.

40. Install the engine mounting center member with the ten retaining bolts. Torque the four outside bolts to 29 ft. lbs. and the six inside bolts to 32 ft. lbs.

41. Connect the control cable clamp.

42. Coat the transaxle oil seal lip with multi-purpose grease.

43. Insert the center driveshaft into the transaxle through the bearing bracket.

44. Install the snapring.

45. Install a new bearing bracket bolt and torque it to 24 ft. lbs.

46. Install the lower suspension crossmember. Torque the four outside bolts to 153 ft. lbs. and the two inside bolts to 29 ft. lbs.

47. Connect both driveshafts and torque the retaining nuts to 27 ft. lbs.

48. Fill the differential with 1.7 qts. of Dexron®II.

49. Install the left hand front apron seal.

50. Install the rear mount insulator bracket set bolt.

51. Install the two transmission housing set bolts and torque to 47 ft. lbs.

52. Install the starter motor set bolts.

53. Connect the two oil cooler hoses.

54. Connect the control cable.

55. Connect the speedometer cable.

56. Install the transmission case protector.

57. Connect the ground strap.

58. Connect the throttle cable to the throttle linkage and bracket.

59. Adjust the throttle cable as described in this Section.

60. Connect the transmission and neutral start connectors.

61. Install the air cleaner and air flow meter.

62. Connect the negative battery cable.

63. Fill the transaxle with Dexron®II and check the fluid level.

1989-92

The A540E and A540H transaxles should be removed along with the engine assembly. Refer to Section 3.

1. Disconnect the negative battery cable. Remove the air flow meter and the air cleaner assembly.

2. Disconnect the transaxle wire connector. Disconnect the neutral safety switch electrical connector and the cruise control actuator connector and cover, if equipped.

3. Disconnect the transaxle ground strap. Disconnect the throttle cable from the throttle linkage and disconnect the speed sensor connectors, if equipped.

4. Remove the transaxle case protector. Disconnect the speedometer cable and control cable.

5. Disconnect the oil cooler hoses. Remove the upper starter retaining bolts, as required remove the starter assembly. Remove the upper transaxle housing bolts. Remove the engine rear mount insulator bracket set bolt.

6. Raise and support the vehicle safely. Drain the transaxle fluid.

7. Remove the left front fender apron seal. Disconnect both driveshafts and remove the exhaust pipe on 1992 vehicles .

8. Remove the suspension lower crossmember assembly. Remove the center driveshaft.

9. Remove the engine mounting center crossmember. Remove the stabilizer bar. Remove the left steering knuckle from the lower control arm.

10. Remove the torque converter cover. Remove the torque converter retaining bolts. On 1992 vehicles, remove the steering gear housing.

11. Properly support the engine and transaxle assembly. Remove the rear engine mounting bolts. Remove the remaining transaxle to engine retaining bolts.

12. Carefully remove the transaxle assembly from the vehicle.

To install:

13. Install the transaxle and tighten the 12mm transaxle housing bolts to 47 ft. lbs. (64 Nm); tighten the 10mm bolts to 34 ft. lbs. (46 Nm). Tighten the rear engine mount set bolts to 38 ft. lbs. (52 Nm). Tighten the torque converter mounting bolts to 20 ft. lbs. (27 Nm).

14. Install the transaxle cables, linkage and halfshafts.

15. Refill the transaxle with the approved fluid and check for leaks.

16. Lower the vehicle. Road test the vehicle and check operation.

Halfshafts

REMOVAL & INSTALLATION

➡ For illustrations and exploded views of the halfshafts and related components, refer to the the Manual Transaxle section in this Section.

1983-84

1. Raise and support the front end on jackstands.

2. Remove the cotter pin, locknut cap and locknut from the hub.

3. Remove the six nuts attaching the halfshaft to the transaxle.

4. Remove the caliper and support it out of the way with a wire.

5. Remove the rotor.

6. Remove the left side case shield.

7. Remove the axle hub from the shaft with a puller.

8. Unbolt the right side intermediate shaft from the block bracket.

9. Remove the intermediate shaft from the U-joint.

10. With a slide hammer, pull the U-joint from the case.

To install the driveshafts:

11. Using the slide hammer, drive the U-joint in to the point where the joint and the differential pinion shaft touch.

12. Connect the intermediate shaft to the U-joint.

13. Install the bearing bracket onto the cylinder block. Torque the retaining bolts to 40 ft. lbs.

14. Install the outboard side of the driveshaft to the axle hub.

➡ **Be careful not to damage the boots.**

15. Install the six nuts that hold the driveshaft to the intermediate shaft or side differential side shaft and make them finger tight.

16. Install the left hand transmission case protector.

17. Install the disc rotor.

18. Connect the brake caliper to the steering knuckle.

19. Have an assistant depress the brake pedal and torque the bearing locknut to 137 ft. lbs.

20. Install the locknut cap and a new cotter pin. Separate the ends of the cotter pin with pliers.

21. Depress the brake pedal and torque the six driveshaft nuts to 25 ft. lbs.

22. Fill the transaxle to the proper level with Dexron®II.

1985-86

➡ **The hub bearing could be damaged if subjected to the full weight of the vehicle, such as if the vehicle is moved without the driveshafts. If it is absolutely necessary to place the full vehicle weight on the hub bearing, first support the bearing with SST No. 09608-16042.**

1. Raise the front of the vehicle and support it safely.

2. Remove the front wheels.

3. Remove the cotter pin and locknut cap.

4. Have an assistant depress the brake pedal and loosen the bearing locknut.

5. On vehicles equipped with manual transaxle, remove the transaxle case protector.

➡ **Cover the boot with cloth to prevent damage.**

6. Have an assistant depress the brake pedal and loosen the six nuts holding the front driveshaft to the center driveshaft or differential side gear shaft.

7. Remove the brake caliper from the steering knuckle and support with wire.

8. Remove the disc rotor.

9. On CV series vehicles and left side of SV series vehicles with automatic transaxle:

a. Remove the two bolts that attach the ball joint to the steering knuckle.

b. Lower the lower control arm and pull the shock absorber outward.

c. Disconnect the driveshaft from the transaxle.

10. Using SST No. 09950-20015 or equivalent, push the front driveshaft from the axle hub.

11. On SV series vehicles right hand shaft:

a. Drain the fluid from the center driveshaft.

b. With pliers, remove the snapring and pull out the center driveshaft.

To install the driveshafts:

12. On SV series vehicles right hand shaft:

a. Coat the transaxle the lip of the transxle oil seal with multi-purpose grease.

b. Insert the center driveshaft into the transaxle through the bearing bracket and secure with the snapring.

13. Install the outboard side of the driveshaft to the axle hub.

➡ **Be careful not to damage the boots.**

14. Install the six nuts that hold the driveshaft to the intermediate shaft or side differential side shaft and make them finger tight.

15. On CV series vehicles and left side of SV series vehicles with auto trans:

a. Connect the steering knuckle to the ball joint.

b. Install the two bolts and torque them to 83 ft. lbs.

16. Install the disc rotor.

17. Install the brake caliper to the steering knuckle to the steering knuckle and torque the two bolts to 83 ft. lbs.

18. Have an assistant depress the brake pedal and torque the bearing locknut to 137 ft. lbs.

19. Install the locknut cap and a new cotter pin. Separate the ends of the cotter pin with pliers.

20. Depress the brake pedal and torque the six driveshaft nuts to 27 ft. lbs.

21. On manual transaxle equipped vehicles, install the case protector.

22. Fill the transaxle to the proper level with Dexron®II (SV series only).

1987

➡ **The hub bearing could be damaged if subjected to the full weight of the vehicle, such as if the vehicle is moved without the driveshafts. If it is absolutely necessary to place the full vehicle weight on the hub bearing, first support the bearing with SST No. 09608-16041.**

1. Raise the front of the vehicle and support it safely.

2. Remove the front wheels.

3. Remove the cotter pin and locknut cap.

4. Have an assistant depress the brake pedal and loosen the bearing locknut.

5. Remove the engine under cover.

6. Remove the fender apron seal.

7. Loosen the six nuts holding the front driveshaft to the center driveshaft or differential side gear shaft.

8. Remove the two bolts and disconnect the steering knuckle from the lower ball joint.

9. Drain the transaxle fluid or differential oil.

10. Loosen the center driveshaft locknut.

11. Remove the bearing bracket snapring and pull out the center driveshaft.

To install the driveshafts:

12. Coat the transaxle the lip of the transxle oil seal with multi-purpose grease.

13. Insert the center driveshaft into the transaxle through the bearing bracket and secure with the snapring.

14. Install a new center bearing lock bolt and torque it 24 ft. lbs.

15. Install the outboard side of the driveshaft to the axle hub.

➡ **Be careful not to damage the boots.**

16. Install the six nuts that hold the driveshaft to the intermediate shaft or side differential side shaft and make them finger tight.

17. Connect the steering knuckle to the ball joint and torque the bolts to 94 ft. lbs.

18. Have an assistant depress the brake pedal and torque the bearing locknut to 137 ft. lbs.

19. Install the locknut cap and a new cotter pin. Separate the ends of the cotter pin with pliers.

20. Depress the brake pedal and torque the six driveshaft nuts to 27 ft. lbs.

21. Fill the transaxle to the proper level with gear oil or fluid.

22. Install the fender apron.

23. Install the engine under cover.

24. Check the front wheel alignment.

1988

1. Raise and support the vehicle safely.

2. Remove the wheels.

3. Remove the cotter pin, cap and locknut from the hub.

4. Remove the engine under cover and front fender apron seal.

5. Loosen the 6 nuts attaching the inner end of the halfshaft to the transaxle or center shaft.

➡ **Wrap the exposed end of the halfshaft in an old shop cloth to prevent damage to it.**

6. Remove the brake caliper with the hydraulic line still attached, position it aside and suspend it with a wire. Remove the rotor.

7. Remove the 2 bolts attaching the ball joint to the steering knuckle. Pull the lower control arm down while pulling the strut outward; this will disconnect the inner end of the halfshaft from the transaxle.

8. Using a 2-armed puller, or the like, press the outer end of the halfshaft from the steering knuckle and then remove the halfshaft.

9. Drain the transaxle fluid, remove the snapring with pliers and pull the shaft out of the transaxle case.

To install:

10. When installing the center halfshaft, coat the transaxle oil seal with grease, insert the halfshaft through the bearing bracket and secure it with a new snapring.

11. Press the outer end of the halfshaft into the steering knuckle, position the inner end and install the 6 nuts finger-tight.

12. Reconnect the ball joint to the steering knuckle, if disconnected, and tighten the bolts to 94 ft. lbs. (127 Nm).

13. Install the rotor and brake caliper. Tighten the caliper-to-knuckle bolts to 65 ft. lbs. (88 Nm).

14. Tighten the wheel bearing locknut to 137 ft. lbs. (186 Nm) while depressing the brake pedal. Install the locknut cap and use a new cotter pin.

15. Tighten the 6 inner end nuts to 27 ft. lbs. (36 Nm) while depressing the brake pedal.

16. Fill the transaxle to the proper level.

17. Install the transaxle apron seal.

18. Test drive and check for unusual vibrations.

1989–92 With 4-cylinder Engine 2 Wheel Drive

1. Raise and support the vehicle safely.
2. Remove the front wheels.
3. Remove the cotter pin, cap and locknut from the hub.
4. Remove the engine under covers.
5. Drain the transmission fluid or the differential fluid on the wagon.
6. Remove the transaxle gravel shield on the wagon.
7. Loosen the 6 nuts attaching the inner end of the halfshaft to transaxle, all except wagon.

➡ Wrap the exposed end of the halfshaft in an old shop cloth to prevent damage to it.

8. Remove the cotter pin from the tie end rod and then press the tie rod out of the steering knuckle.

9. Remove the bolt and 2 nuts and disconnect the steering knuckle from the lower arm control.

10. On the 4-cylinder wagon, mark a spot somewhere on the left halfshaft and measure the distance between the spot and the transaxle case. Using the proper tool, pull the halfshaft out of the transaxle.

11. On the 4-cylinder wagon, use a 2-armed puller and press the outer end of the right halfshaft out of the steering knuckle.

12. Remove the snapring at the inner end and pull the halfshaft out of the center driveshaft.

To install:

13. When installing the center driveshaft on sedan, coat the transaxle oil seal with grease, insert the halfshaft through the bearing bracket and secure it with a new snapring.

14. Repeat Step 13 when installing the inner end of the right halfshaft on the 4-cylinder wagon.

15. On the right halfshaft of the 4-cylinder wagon, use a new snapring, coat the transaxle oil seal with grease and then press the inner end of the shaft into the differential housing. Check that the measurement made in Step 10 is the same. Check that there is 0.08–0.12 in. (2–3mm) of axial play. Check also that the halfshaft will not come out by trying to pull it by hand.

16. Press the outer end of each halfshaft into the steering knuckle on the 4-cylinder wagon.

17. On all except the 4-cylinder wagon, press the outer end of the halfshafts into the steering knuckle and then finger-tighten the nuts on the inner end.

18. Connect the steering knuckle to the lower control arm and tighten the bolts to 83 ft. lbs. (113 Nm).

19. Connect the tie rod end to the steering knuckle and tighten the nut to 36 ft. lbs. (49 Nm). Install a new cotter pin.

20. Tighten the hub locknut to 137 ft. lbs. (186 Nm) while depressing the brake pedal. Install the cap and use a new cotter pin.

21. On all except the 4-cylinder wagon, tighten the 6 nuts on the inner halfshaft ends to 27 ft. lbs. (36 Nm) while depressing the brake pedal.

22. Install the transaxle gravel shield on the wagon.

23. Fill the transaxle with gear oil or fluid.

24. Install the engine under cover.

1989–91 With All-Trac/4WD Front

1. Raise and support the vehicle safely.
2. Remove the wheels.
3. Remove the cotter pin, cap and locknut from the hub.
4. Remove the engine undercovers.
5. Disconnect the tie rod end from the steering knuckle.
6. Disconnect the lower control arm at the steering knuckle and pull it down and aside.
7. Use a plastic hammer and carefully tap the outer end of the halfshaft until it frees itself from the axle hub.
8. Cover the outer boot with a rag and then remove the inner end of the halfshaft from the transaxle. Use the proper tools.

To install:

9. Coat the lip of the oil seal with grease and then carefully drive the inner end of the shaft into the transaxle until it makes contact with the pinion shaft.

➡ Be careful not to damage the boots when installing the halfshafts; also, position the boot snapring so the opening is facing downward.

10. Put the outer end of each shaft into the axle hub, being careful not to damage the boots.

11. Check that there is 0.08–0.12 in. (2–3mm) of axial play. Check also that the halfshaft will not come out by hand.

12. Connect the lower control arm to the steering arm and tighten the bolt to 83 ft. lbs. (113 Nm).

13. Connect the tie rod to the steering knuckle and tighten the nut to 36 ft. lbs. (49 Nm). Use a new cotter pin to secure it.

14. Install the axle bearing locknut and tighten it to 137 ft. lbs. (186 Nm) while stepping on the brake pedal. Install the locknut cap and then a new cotter pin.

15. Fill the transaxle with gear oil or fluid, install the undercovers and wheels. Lower the vehicle and check the front end alignment.

1989–91 With 6-cylinder Engine – Front

1. Raise the front of the vehicle and use jack stands to safely secure the vehicle.
2. Remove the front wheel and remove the axle nut cotter pin, the lock nut cap and the lock nut, while depressing the brake pedal.
3. Remove the engine under covers.
4. Remove the tie rod cotter pin and nut, then disconnect the tie rod end using tool 09628–62011, or equivalent.
5. Disconnect the steering knuckle from the lower arm by removing the 2 bolts.
6. Place matchmarks on the driveshaft and side gear shaft or center driveshaft, using paint and not a punch.
7. Loosen, but do not remove yet, the 6 bolts holding the driveshaft to the inner shaft.
8. Using a plastic hammer, disconnect the

driveshaft from the axle hub and cover the boot with a protective cover.

➡ **Do not subject the hub bearing to the weight of the vehicle with a driveshaft removed.**

9. Remove the axle shaft.
10. To remove the LEFT shaft, remove the 6 bolts and remove the shaft, but do not compress the inboard boot allowing the inside balls to drop out.
11. To remove the RIGHT shaft, do the following:
  a. Drain out the gear oil.
  b. Remove the bearing lock bolt.
  c. Using a suitable tool, remove the snap ring, and pull out the driveshaft with the center driveshaft, tapping out the driveshaft with a brass hammer, if necessary.

To install:

12. When installing the driveshafts, pack the side gear shaft or to the center driveshaft with grease (part no. 90999–94029. The grease capacity is 43–53g (1.44–1.92 oz.).
13. Place a new gasket on the inboard joint, insert and finger tighten the 6 bolts with the 3 washers, making sure that the matchmarks are aligned.
14. Reverse the remaining removal steps to complete installation, tightening fasteners to specifications.
15. Fill the transaxle with gear oil, check front end alignment and test drive.

➡ **Do not compress the inboard boot when moving either driveshaft. If the cotter pin holes do not line up, always correct by TIGHTENING the nut until the next hole lines up. Then install a new cotter pin.**

1992 With 6-cylinder Engine

1. Raise the front of the vehicle and use jack stands to safely secure the vehicle.
2. Remove the front wheel and remove the axle nut cotter pin, the lock nut cap and the lock nut, while depressing the brake pedal.
3. Remove the front fender apron.
4. Remove the tie rod cotter pin and nut, then disconnect the tie rod end using tool 09628–62011, or equivalent.
5. Drain the gear oil.
6. Disconnect the stabilizer bar link from the lower arm.
7. Remove the bolt and the 2 nuts, then disconnect the steering knuckle from the lower ball joint.
8. Place matchmarks on the driveshaft and side gear shaft or center driveshaft, using paint and not a punch.
9. Loosen, but do not remove yet, the 6 bolts holding the driveshaft to the inner shaft.
10. Using a plastic hammer, disconnect the driveshaft from the axle hub and cover the boot with a protective cover.

➡ **Do not subject the hub bearing to the weight of the vehicle with a driveshaft removed.**

11. Using a suitable tool, pry out and remove the left axle shaft.
12. To remove the left driveshaft, remove the bearing lock bolt, remove the snapring and pull out the driveshaft.

To install:

13. To install the left driveshaft, do the following:
  a. Install a new snapring on the end of the shaft.
  b. Coat gear oil to the side gear shaft and differential case sliding surface.
  c. Using a brass bar and hammer, tap in the driveshaft until it makes contact with the pinion shaft.

➡ **Before installing the driveshaft, set the snapring opening side facing downward. Whether or not the side gear shaft is making contact with the pinion shaft can be known by the sound or feeling when driving it inward.**

  d. Check that there is 2–3mm (0.08–0.12 in.) of play in the axial direction and check that the driveshaft will not come out by trying to pull it completely out by hand.
14. To install the right driveshaft, do the following:
  a. Coat gear oil to the side gear shaft and differential case sliding surface.
  b. Install the driveshaft to the transaxle through the bearing bracket, without damaging the oil seal lip.
  c. Using a suitable tool, install a new snapring.
  d. Install a new bearing lock bolt and tighten it to 32 Nm (24 ft. lbs.).
15. Reverse the remaining removal procedures to complete installation, tightening fasteners to specifications.
16. Fill the transaxle with gear oil, install the fender apron, check front end alignment and test drive.

➡ **If the cotter pin holes do not line up, always correct by TIGHTENING the nut until the next hole lines up. Then install a new cotter pin**

CV-JOINT OVERHAUL

➧ SEE FIGS. 66–90

1983–91 With 4-cylinder Engine Or All-Trac/4WD 20Front Driveshaft

DISASSEMBLY

1. Mount the front driveshaft in a vise and check that there is no play in the inboard and outboard joint.
2. Make sure that the inboard joint slides smoothly in the thrust direction.
3. Make sure that there is no excessive play in the radial direction of the inboard joint.
4. Inspect the boots for damage (rips, punctures and cracks).
5. Remove the inboard joint boot clips.
6. With chalk or paint, matchmark the inboard joint tulip and tripod. DO NOT use a punch.
7. Remove the inboard joint tulip from the driveshaft.
8. Remove the snapring.
9. Using a brass rod and hammer, evenly drive the tripod joint off the driveshaft without hitting the joint roller.
10. Remove the inboard joint boot.
11. Remove the clamp and driveshaft damper (1983-86 with Diesel engine only).
12. Remove the clamps and the outboard drive boot.

➡ **Do not disassemble the outboard joint.**

13. On 1987-91 vehicles, press out the transaxle and driveshaft side dust covers from the center driveshaft.
14. On 1987-91 vehicles, remove the center driveshaft snapring, press the bearing from the shaft and remove the remaining snapring.
15. Inspect the inside and the outside of the boots for damage.

REASSEMBLY

➡ **Before installing the boot, wrap the spline end of the shaft with masking tape to prevent damage to the boot.**

1. On 1987-91 vehicles, install the center driveshaft snapring, press in a new bearing and install a new snapring over the bearing.
2. On 1987-91 vehicles, press in the transaxle side and driveshaft bearing side dust covers.

➡ **The clearance between the dust cover and the bearing should be 1.00mm.**

3. Install the driveshaft damper with a new clamp (1983-86 CV series right shaft only).

4. Temporarily install the inboard boot with new clamp to the drive joint.

➡ **The inboard boot and clamp are larger than those of the outboard boot.**

5. Position the beveled side of the tripod spline towards the outboard joint.

6. Align the matchmarks on the tripod and driveshaft.

7. Tap the tripod onto the driveshaft with a brass rod and hammer without hitting the joint roller.

8. Install the snapring.

9. Pack the outboard tulip joint and the outboard boot with about 4 to 5 ounces of grease that was supplied with the boot kit.

10. Install the boot onto the outboard joint.

11. Pack the inboard tulip joint and boot with 1/2 lb. of grease that was suplied with the boot kit.

12. Align the matchmarks on the tulip joint and tripod.

13. Install the inboard tulip joint onto the driveshaft.

14. Install the boot onto the driveshaft.

15. Make sure that the boot is properly installed on the driveshaft.

16. Before checking the standard length, bend the band and lock it as shown in the illustration.

17. Make sure that the boot is not stretched or squashed when the driveshaft is at standard length.

Standard driveshaft length

- 1983 vehicles: 454.0mm ± 5mm
- 1984–86 gasoline engine vehicle: 454.0mm ± 5mm
- diesel engine vehicle
  LH 454.0mm ± 5mm
  RH 716.0mm ± 5mm
- 1987-88: 450.7mm ± 5.0mm
- 1989 separated type, 4-cyl. engine: 450.7mm ± 5.0mm
- 1989 integrated type, 4-cyl engine: 937mm
- 1989–91 AWD, LH: 512.5 ± 5.0mm
- 1989–91 AWD, RH: 515.5 ± 5.0mm
- 1990–91 Toyota type, LH, 4-cyl. engine: 558.7mm ± 5.0mm
- 1990–91 Toyota type, RH, 4-cyl. engine: 845.2mm ± 5.0mm
- 1990–91 GKN type, LH, 4-cyl. engine: 652.0mm ± 6.0mm
- 1990–91 GKN type, RH, 4-cyl. engine: 937.0mm ± 6.0mm

1983–84 INTERMEDIATE DRIVESHAFT OVERHAUL

1. Remove the heat insulator.
2. Remove the dust cover.
3. Remove the snapring.
4. Remove the intermediate shaft using SST No. 09950-20014 or equivalent.
5. Pry the snapring from the bearing bracket.
6. Press the bearing from the bearing bracket using SST No. 09618-60010 or equivalent.
7. Press a new bearing into the bearing bracket using SST No. 09608-32030 or equivalent.
8. Install a new snapring into the bearing bracket.
9. Press the intermediate shaft into the bearing bracket with SST No. 09608-32030 or equivalent.
10. Install a new snapring, being careful not the damage the bearing's rubber seal.
11. Place the dust cover on a press with SST No.s 09506-30011 and 09608-32030 and press the cover onto the intermediate shaft so that there is a clearance of 1.00-2.00mm between the dust cover and the bearing bracket.

➡ **Do not allow the dust cover to contact the surface of the bearing.**

12. Install the heat insulator.

1985–86 CENTER DRIVESHAFT OVERHAUL GASOLINE ENGINE

1. Press the transxle side dust cover from the shaft with a suitable press.
2. Using a press and SST No. 09950-00020 and a press, remove the driveshaft side dust cover.
3. Remove the snapring that retains the bearing.
4. Press the bearing from the shaft and remove the remaining snapring.
5. First, insert the new snapring onto the shaft and then press on a new bearing.
6. Install anew snapring onto the bearing.
7. Press the new driveshaft side dust cover onto the shaft so that there is 1.00-2.00mm clearance between the cover and the bearing.
8. Press the new transaxle side dust cover onto the shaft so that there is 86-87mm clearance between the cover and the bearing.

1983–84 UNIVERSAL JOINT DISASSEMBLY

1. Remove the snapring.
2. Remove the boot.
3. Matchmark the shaft yoke and the yoke joint with paint or chalk.
4. Slightly tap in the bearing outer races.
5. Remove the four snaprings from the grooves of the joint.
6. Push out the bearing from the U-joint with a suitable press.
7. Clamp the outer race in a vise and tap off the yoke with a hammer. Remove the bearing on the opposite side in the same manner.
8. Place the two outer races onto the spider bearing.
9. Push out the spider bearing with a suitable press.
10. Clamp the outer race in a vise and tap off the yoke with a hammer. Remove the bearing on the opposite side in the same manner.

REASSEMBLY

1. Lightly coat the spider and spider bearings with multi-purpose grease.
2. Align the shaft yoke and joint yoke matchmarks.
3. Fit the new spider in the yoke.
4. Press the new spider bearings into both sides of the spider.
5. Adjust both bearings so that snapring grooves are at maximum and equal widths.
6. Install both snaprings of the same thickness that will allow 0.05mm of axial play.
7. Tap the yoke with a hammer until there is no clearance between the bearing outer race and the sanpring.
8. Check the that spider bearing moves freely. Move the spider back and forth. There should be less than 0.0020 in of play in the spider.
9. Install the new shaft side spider bearings.
10. Install the dust cover with a rubber mallet.
11. Install the boot.
12. Install the snapring.

1992 With 4-cylinder Engine

DISASSEMBLY

1. Mount the driveshaft in a vise and check that there is no play in the inboard and outboard joint.
2. Make sure that the inboard joint slides smoothly in the thrust direction.
3. Make sure that there is no excessive play in the radial direction of the inboard joint.
4. Inspect the boots for damage.
5. Disconnect the center driveshaft or the side gear shaft by removing the 6 bolts and the 3 washers.

➡ **Do not compress the inboard boot.**

6. Remove the joint end cover gasket and use the bolts and washers to keep the inboard joint together. Tighten the bolts only hand tight.
7. Remove the inboard and outboard joint boot clamps.
8. Place painted, not punched, matchmarks on the inboard joint and the driveshaft, then remove the snapring.

9. Using special service tool 09726–10010 (09726–00030), a socket wrench and a press, remove the inboard joint from the driveshaft.

10. Using suitable tools, remove the inboard joint from the inboard joint cover, holding onto races when lifting the inboard joint.

11. Remove the inboard and outboard joint boots and check them for damage.

12. On the left driveshaft, disassemble the side gear shaft. On the right side, disassemble the center driveshaft, using a press to remove the side dust cover.

13. Using snapring pliers, remove the snapring.

14. Using a press, press out the bearing, then remove the other snapring.

REASSEMBLY

1. Use a new snapring, then press in a new bearing followed by the other snapring.

2. Using a press, install new dust covers with the specified clearances.

3. Assemble the side gear shaft on the left driveshaft.

4. Install the outboard joint boot and a new clamp after wrapping the splines with tape to protect the boot. Do not tighten the clamp yet.

5. Pack the outboard boot with grease, then assemble the boot to the outboard joint. Use 119–130 g (4.2–4.6 oz.) for the Toyota type and 136–156 g (4.8–5.5 oz.) for the GKN type.

6. Temporarily install the 2 boot clamps and the inboard joint boot.

7. Begin to assemble the inboard joint cover by cleaning the contact surfaces.

8. Apply new seal packing, part No. 08826–00801, to the inboard joint cover.

9. Align the bolt holes of the cover with those of inboard joint, then insert the hex bolts.

10. Use a plastic hammer to tap the rim of the inboard cover into place. Repeat several times.

11. Assemble the inboard joint by aligning the match marks placed before disassembly.

12. Using a brass bar and hammer, tap the inboard joint onto the driveshaft without letting the bar touch the cage.

13. Install a new snapring without letting the outer race to come off.

14. Pack the inboard joint boot with grease, then assemble the inboard boot to the inboard joint. Use 91–99 g (3.2–3.5 oz.) for the Toyota type and 139–150 g (4.9–5.3 oz.) for the GKN type.

15. Assemble the boot clamps to both boots, making sure that the driveshafts are at their standard lengths:

- Left shaft, Toyota type: 456.0mm (17.953 in.)
- Right shaft, Toyota type: 456.0mm (17.953 in.)
- Right and left shafts, GKN type: 452.35 ± 2.0mm (17.809 ± 0.079 in.)

16. After making sure that the boots are in the shaft groove, bend the band and lock it on the Toyota type and pincer the band on the GKN type with the proper CV boot clamp tool. Tighten the small clamps the same way.

17. Pack in grease to the center driveshaft or side gear shaft. Use 42.5–54 g (1.5–1.9 oz.) for the Toyota type and 51–59 g (1.8–2.1 oz.) for the GKN type.

18. Connect the driveshaft and the center driveshaft or the side gear shaft, placing a new gasket on the inboard joint without compressing the inboard boot.

19. Check to see that there is no play in the inboard and outboard joints and that the inboard joint slides smoothly in the thrust direction.

1989–91 With 6-cylinder Engine Front

DISASSEMBLY

1. Mount the driveshaft in a vise and check that there is no play in the inboard and outboard joint.

2. Make sure that the inboard joint slides smoothly in the thrust direction.

3. Make sure that there is no excessive play in the radial direction of the inboard joint.

4. Inspect the boots for damage.

5. Disconnect the center driveshaft from the right driveshaft, without compressing the inboard boot.

6. Using soft jaws, clamp the inboard joint in the vise.

➡ Do not overtighten the vise and damage the inboard joint.

7. Remove the inboard joint boot clamps, place matchmarks on the shaft and the inner race and remove the snapring.

8. Using special tool 09726–10010 (09726–00030), an extension bar and a press, remove the inboard joint from the driveshaft.

9. Using suitable tools, remove the inboard joint from the inboard joint cover.

➡ When lifting the inboard joint, hold onto the inner race and the outer race.

10. Remove the boots and check for damage.

REASSEMBLY

1. Install the outboard joint boot and temporarily install a new clamp.

2. Pack the boot with grease, using 0.26–0.29 lb. (120–130 grams).

3. Assemble a new inboard joint cover by first applying seal packing (Part No. 08826–00801 or equivalent) to the inboard joint cover.

4. Align the bolt holes of the cover with those of the inboard joint, then insert the hexagon bolts.

5. Using a plastic hammer to tap the rim of the inboard joint cover into place, repeating several times. Use the bolts and washers to keep the inboard joint together.

6. Assemble the inboard joint and use a brass bar and hammer to tap the joint onto the driveshaft, without touching the cage.

7. Install a new snapring, working carefully not to come off the outer race.

8. Assemble the inboard joint boot to the inboard joint, packing the tulip and boot with 0.20–0.22 lb. (90–100 grams).

9. Assemble the boot clamps to both boots, making sure that the boot shaft is on the shaft groove. The boot must be at its standard length before the clamps are bent over and locked. The lengths are:

- Left and right shafts: 406.0mm (15.98 in.)

10. After making sure that the boots are in the shaft grooves, bend the bands and lock. Tighten the small clamps the same way.

11. Check to see that there is no play in the inboard and outboard joints and that the inboard joint slides smoothly in the thrust direction.

1992 With 6-cylinder Engine

DISASSEMBLY

1. Mount the driveshaft in a vise and check that there is no play in the inboard and outboard joint.

2. Make sure that the inboard joint slides smoothly in the thrust direction.

3. Make sure that there is no excessive play in the radial direction of the inboard joint.

4. Inspect the boots for damage.

5. Remove the inboard and outboard joint boot clamps and move the boots back on the shafts enough to have access to the snaprings.

6. Place painted, not punched, matchmarks on the tripod and the inboard joint tulip or center driveshaft and remove the tulip or center driveshaft from the driveshaft.

7. Remove the tripod joint by removing the visible snapring, sliding the tripod back, then removing the other snapring and tapping the tripod off the shaft.

8. Remove the inboard and outboard boots.

➡ Do not disassemble the outboard joint.

9. Remove the dust cover from the left inboard joint tulip and from the right center driveshaft with a press.

10. On the right side, disassemble the center driveshaft, using a press to remove the side dust cover.

11. Using snapring pliers, remove the snapring.

12. Using a press, press out the bearing, then remove the other snapring.

REASSEMBLY

1. Use a new snapring, then press in a new bearing followed by the other snapring on the center shaft.
2. Using a press, install new dust cover with the specified clearance.
3. Install a new dust cover on the left driveshaft tulip with the specified clearance.
4. Temporarily install both boots with clamps onto the shaft.
5. Reverse the removal procedure to install the tripod joint, aligning the matchmarks.
6. Fill grease into the outboard joint, using 119–130 g (4.2–4.6 oz.) for the Toyota type and 139–159 g (4.9–5.6 oz.) for the GKN type.
7. Fill grease into the inboard joint and boot, using 232–241 g (8.2–8.5 oz.) for the Toyota type and 184–215 g (6.5–7.6 oz.) for the GKN type and slide the tulip onto the driveshaft.
8. Assemble the boot clamps to both boots, making sure that the driveshafts are at their standard lengths:
   - Left shaft, Toyota type: 608.1 ± 5.0mm (23.94 ± 0.197 in.)
   - Right shaft, Toyota type: 866.2 ± 5.0mm (34.1 ± 0.197 in.)
   - Left shaft, GKN type: 609.2 ± 2.0mm (23.98 ± 0.079 in.)
   - Right shaft, GKN type: 880.8 ± 2.0mm (34.67 ± 0.079 in.)
9. After making sure that the boots are in the shaft groove, bend the band and lock it on the Toyota type and pincer the band on the GKN type with the proper CV boot clamp tool. Tighten the small clamps the same way.
10. Check to see that there is no play in the inboard and outboard joints and that the inboard joint slides smoothly in the thrust direction.

TRANSFER CASE

➧ SEE FIGS. 102–111

Identification

The E56F2 can be differentiated from the E56F5 by the indicator light type on the dash board.

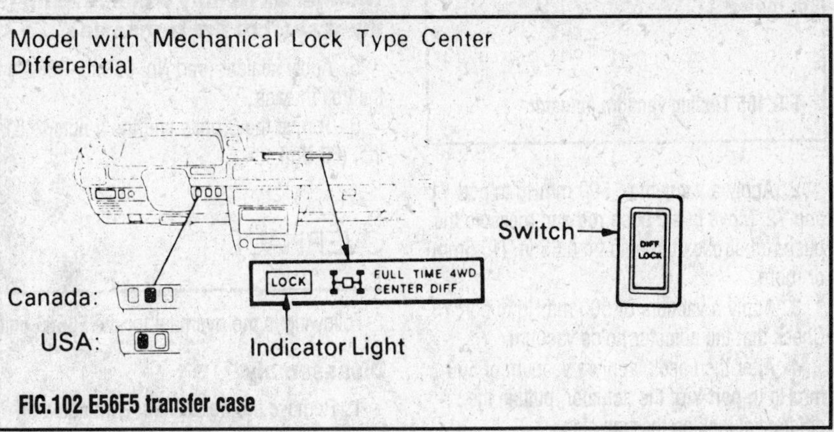

FIG.102 E56F5 transfer case

Transfer Vacuum Actuator

REMOVAL & INSTALLATION

1. Remove and tag the 4 vacuum hoses from the actuator.
2. Remove the stiffener center plate and the actuator bracket bolts and then remove the actuator.

To Install:

3. Install the transfer vacuum actuator, tightening the 3 bolts, then install the stiffener center plate and actuator bracket bolts and torque to 27 ft. lbs. (37 Nm).
4. Reinstall the vacuum hoses in their proper positions.

TESTING

1. Apply a vacuum of 500 mmHg to port Z. Move out the push rod.

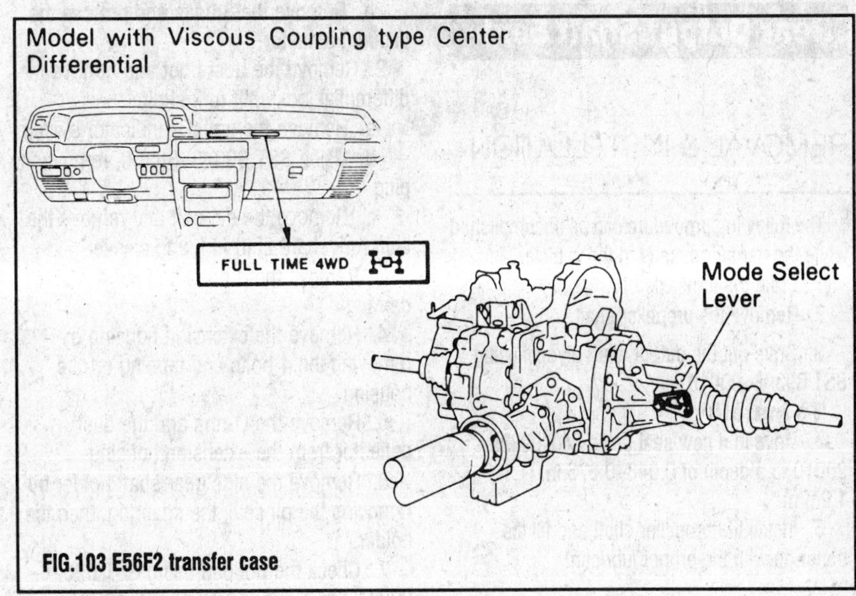

FIG.103 E56F2 transfer case

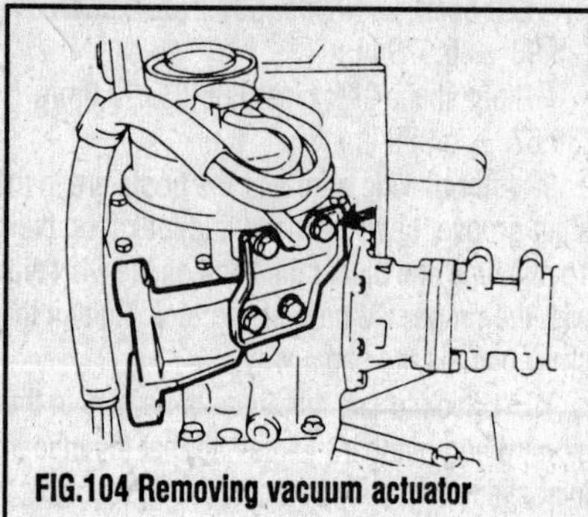

FIG.104 Removing vacuum actuator

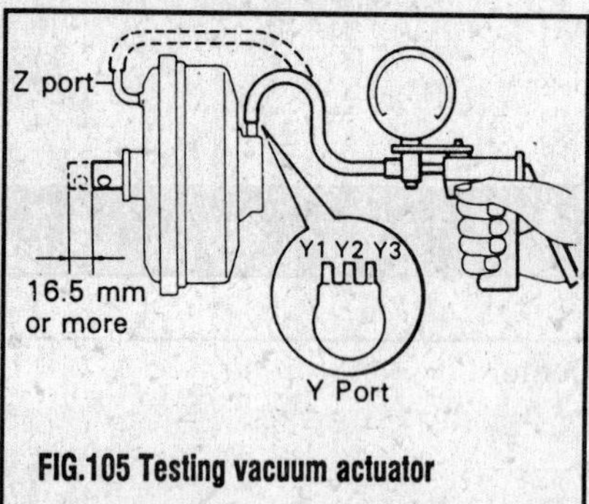

FIG.105 Testing vacuum actuator

2. Apply a vacuum of 500 mmHg to port Y1 and Y2. Move in the push rod and measure the push rod stroke. It should be 0.65 in. (16.5mm) or more.
3. Apply a vacuum of 500 mmHg to port Y3. Check that the actuator holds vacuum.
4. After the check, apply a vacuum of 500 mmHg to port Y of the actuator, putting the differential lock on the free side.

Rear Output Shaft Seal

REMOVAL & INSTALLATION

The following procedure can be accomplished while the transfer case is in the vehicle.

1. Drain the transaxle oil.
2. Remove the propeller shaft.
3. Drive out the output shaft oil seal using SST 09308–00010.

To Install:

4. Drive in a new seal using SST 09325–20010 to a depth of 0.043–0.075 in. (1.1–1.9mm).
5. Install the propeller shaft and fill the transaxle with the proper lubricant.

Transfer Case

REMOVAL & INSTALLATION

For ease of removal, the entire transaxle should be removed first.

1. Remove the 3 bolts and the 5 nuts.
2. Using a plastic hammer, remove the transfer assembly from the transaxle.

To Install:

3. Make sure that the contact surfaces are clean and oil-free.
4. Apply seal packing (part No. 08826–00090 or equivalent) to the transfer and install the transfer as soon as the packing is applied.

➡ Shift into 4th gear, and install the transfer assembly while turning the input shaft of the transaxle.

5. Apply sealant (part No. 08833–00080) to the bolt threads.
6. Torque the 3 bolts and the 5 nuts to 51 ft. lbs. (69 Nm).

OVERHAUL

Following is the overhaul for the E56F5 unit.

Disassembly

1. Remove the transfer vacuum actuator.
   a. Remove the 4 bolts and remove the actuator bracket and the stiffener center plate.
   b. Remove the 3 bolts and remove the vacuum actuator.
2. Remove the dust boot and remove the differential lock shift fork shaft.
   a. Remove the transfer indicator switch.
   b. Using SST 09043–38100, remove the plug.
   c. Remove the set bolt and remove the shift fork shaft, shift fork and sleeve.
3. Remove the 4 bolts and the dynamic damper.
4. Remove the extension housing by removing the 4 bolts and tapping off the housing.
5. Remove the O-ring and the dust deflector from the extension housing.
6. Remove the side gear shaft holder by removing the oil seal, the snapring, then the holder.
7. Check the preload using SST 09326–20011 and a spring tension guage. Measure the driven pinion preload of the backlash, between the driven pinion and the ring gear. At starting it should be 2–3 lbs. (9–14 Nm). Now measure the total preload. At starting it should be 1–2 lbs. (5–9 Nm). Add the driven preload.
8. Remove the 3 bolts and remove the transfer inspection hole cover.
9. Check the ring gear backlash, using a dial indicator. It should be 0.0051–0.0071 in. (0.13–0.18mm).
10. Check the tooth contact pattern.
11. Remove the driven pinion bearing cage assembly by removing the 6 bolts and tapping off with a plastic hammer. Remove the O-ring and the shim from the driven pinion bearing cage.
12. Remove the transfer right case by removing the 10 bolts and tapping off with a hammer.
13. Remove the ring gear mounting case assembly.
14. Using snapring pliers, remove the adjusting lock plate from the transfer right case
15. Replace the extension housing oil seal, driving it to a depth of 0.043–0.075 in. (1.1–1.9mm). Coat the lip of the seal with grease.
16. Replace the shift fork shaft oil seal, driving it to a height of 0.295–0.335 in. (7.5–8.5mm). Coat the lip of the seal with grease.
17. Replace the side gear shaft holder bearing, using snapring pliers, SST 09316–60010 and a press.
18. Replace the transfer oil tube, installing a new cushion and torquing the bolt to 9 ft. lbs. (13 Nm).
19. Replace the ring gear mounting case side bearing outer race. For the right side:
    a. Using SST 09318–20010, turn the bearing adjusting nut, remove the outer race and bearing adjusting nut.
    b. Install the bearing adjusting nut until it touches the lip of the case. If the nut is difficult to turn, use SST 09318–20010.
    c. Using SST kit 09608–35014 and a press, install the race until it is almost touching the bearing adjusting nut.
20. For the left side:
    a. Using a brass bar and a hammer, drive out the bearing outer race lightly and evenly.
    b. Remove and inspect the plate washer.
    c. Install the plate washer, one of the same thickness as before at first.
    d. Using SST kit 09316–60010 and a press, install the outer race.
21. Measure the clearance between the differential lock shift fork and sleeve. The maximum clearance should be 0.039 in. (1.0mm).

DISASSEMBLY OF DRIVEN PINION BEARING CAGE

1. Unstake the lock nut and remove with SST 09326–20011.

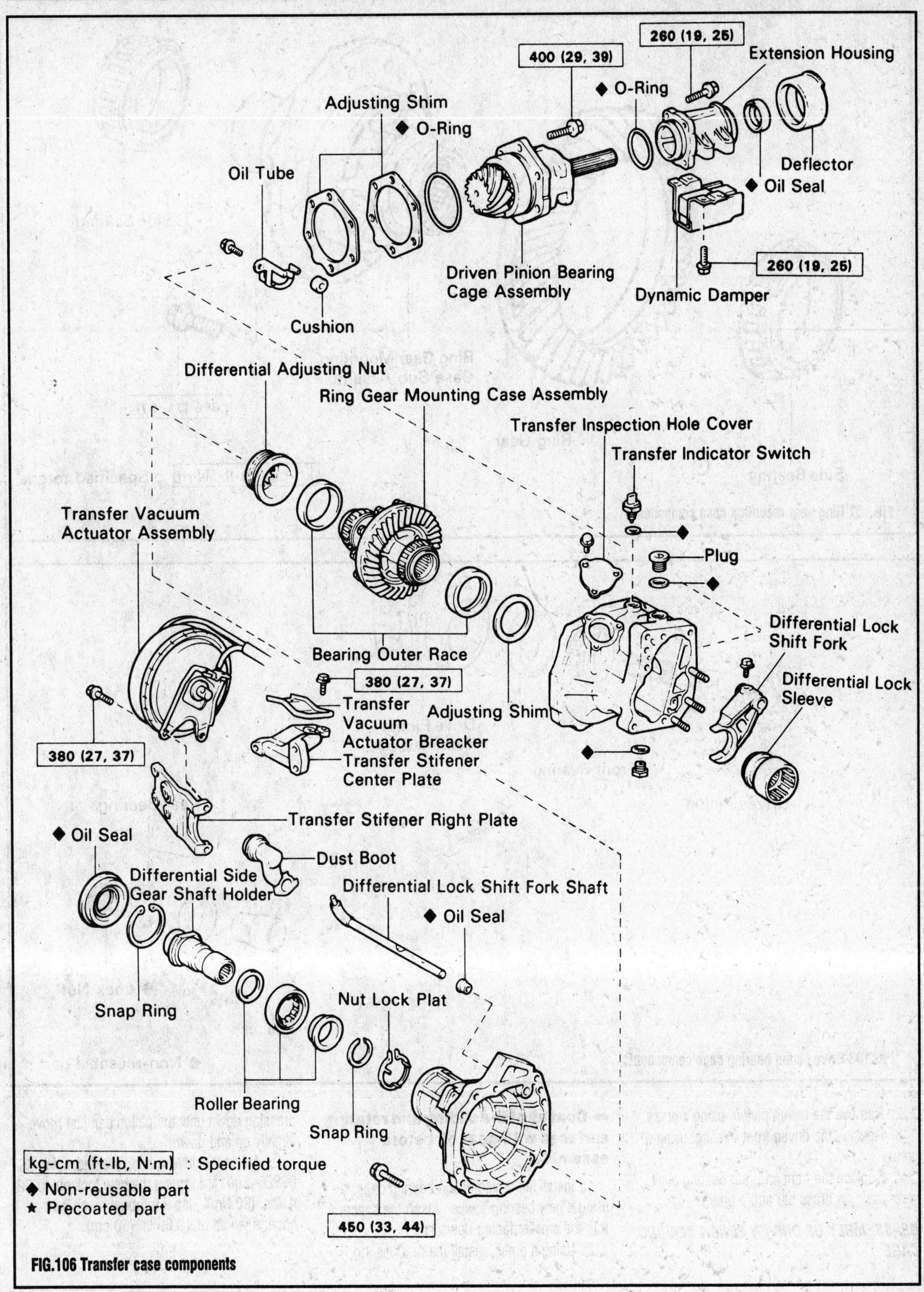

260 (19, 25)
Extension Housing
400 (29, 39)
◆ O-Ring
Adjusting Shim
◆ O-Ring
Deflector
Oil Tube
◆ Oil Seal
Driven Pinion Bearing
Cage Assembly
260 (19, 25)
Dynamic Damper
Cushion
Differential Adjusting Nut
Ring Gear Mounting Case Assembly
Transfer Inspection Hole Cover
Transfer Indicator Switch
Transfer Vacuum
Actuator Assembly
Plug
Differential Lock
Shift Fork
Bearing Outer Race
380 (27, 37)
Differential Lock
Sleeve
Transfer
Vacuum
Actuator Breacker
Adjusting Shim
380 (27, 37)
Transfer Stifener
Center Plate
Transfer Stifener Right Plate
◆ Oil Seal
Dust Boot
Differential Side
Gear Shaft Holder
Differential Lock Shift Fork Shaft
◆ Oil Seal
Snap Ring
Nut Lock Plat
Roller Bearing
Snap Ring
kg-cm (ft-lb, N·m) : Specified torque
◆ Non-reusable part
★ Precoated part
450 (33, 44)

FIG.106 Transfer case components

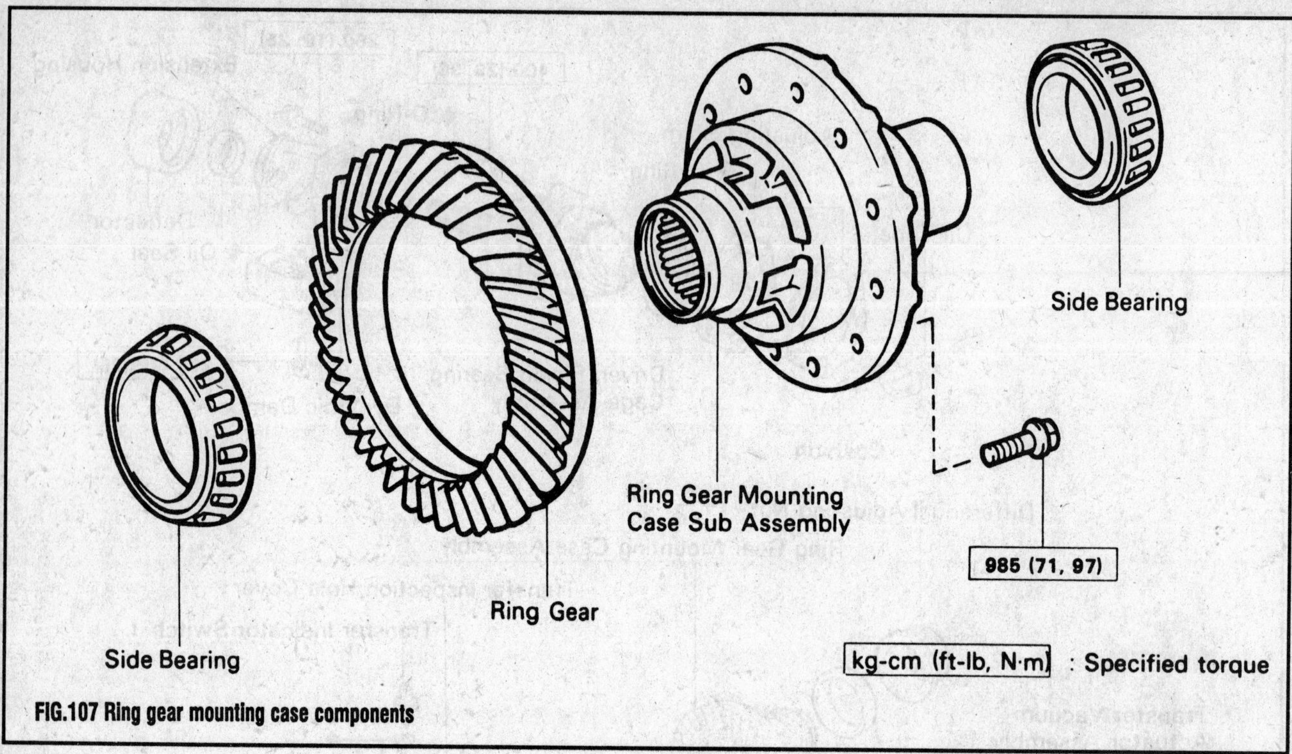

FIG.107 Ring gear mounting case components

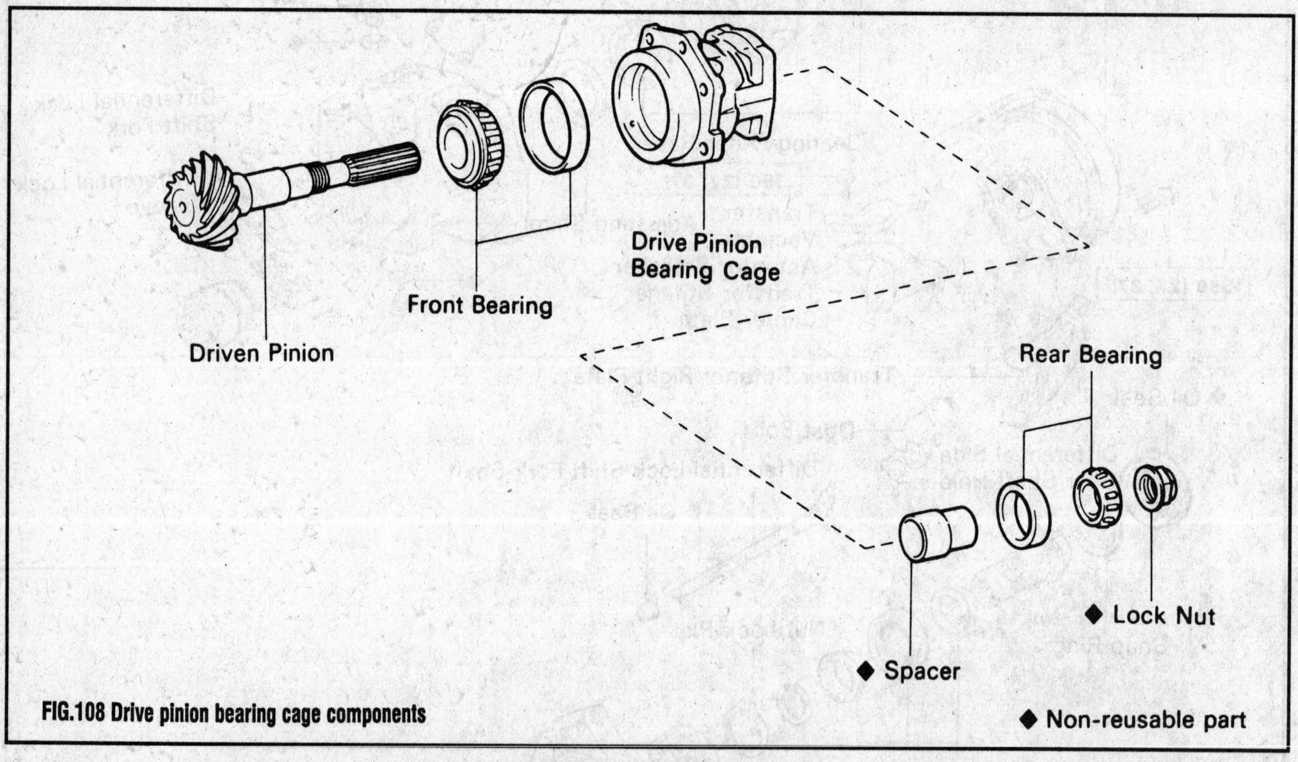

FIG.108 Drive pinion bearing cage components

2. Remove the driven pinion, using a press.

3. Replace the driven front bearing, using a press.

4. Replace the front and rear bearing outer races, using a brass bar and a press.

REASSEMBLY OF DRIVEN PINION BEARING CAGE

➡ Coat all of the sliding and rotating surfaces with gear oil before assembly.

1. Install the driven pinion bearing cage, using a new bearing spacer. Insert the spacer with the smaller facing upwards.

2. Using a press, install the rear bearing, pressing down until the pinion can just move slightly up and down.

3. Adjust the driven pinion preload, using SST 09326–20011, torquing the new lock nut to 72 ft. lbs. (90 Nm). Use a torque wrench with a fulcrum length of 19.69 in. (50 cm).

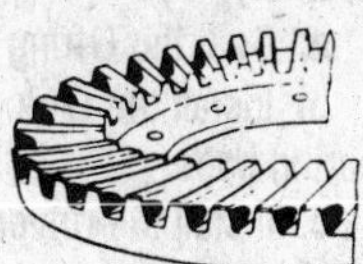
Heel Contact
Face Contact

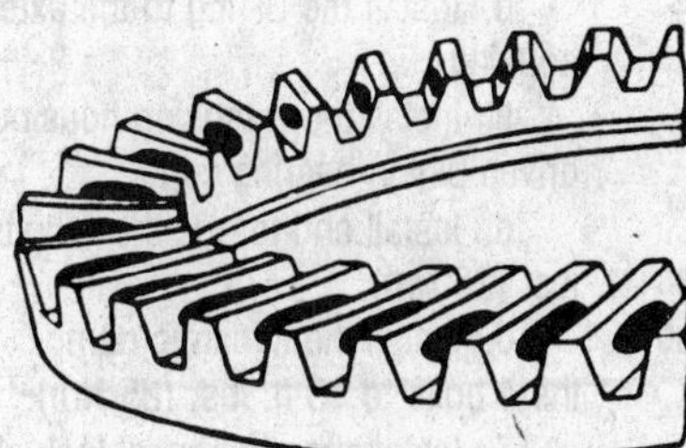
Proper Contact

Select an adjusting shim that will bring the driven pinion closer to the ring gear.

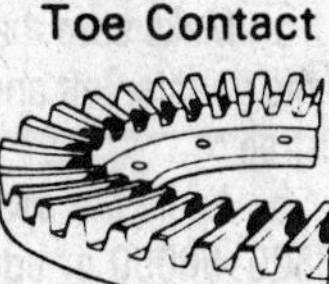
Toe Contact
Flank Contact

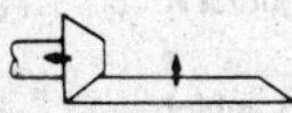
Select an adjusting shim that will shift the driven pinion away from the ring gear.

FIG.109 Checking ring gear tooth contact

4. Using the SST and a spring tension guage, measure the driven pinion preload.

➡ Turn the driven pinion right and left 2 or 3 times to allow the bearings to settle.

5. The preload at starting should be 4.0–6.4 lbs. with a new bearing and 2.0–3.1 lbs. with a used one. If the preload is greater than specification, replace the bearing spacer. If the preload is less, retighten the nut 5–10 degrees at a time until the proper specification is reached.

➡ If the maximum torque of 159 ft. lbs. (216 Nm) is exceeded while retightening the nut, replace the bearing spacer and repeat the preload procedure. Do not back off the pinion nut to reduce the preload.

6. Stake the lock nut.

DISASSEMBLY OF THE RING GEAR MOUNTING CASE

1. Remove the mounting case side bearing, using SST 09950–20017.
2. Check the ring gear runout. The maximum is 0.004 in. (0.1mm). If out of specification, check the runout of the mounting case for the limit.
3. Remove the ring gear after placing matchmarks on both the case and the gear.

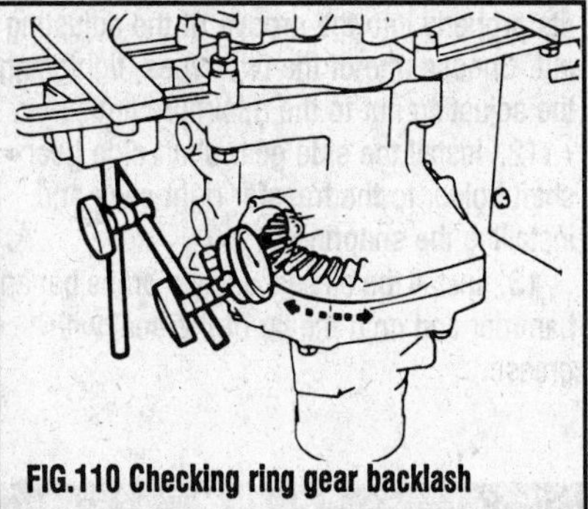

FIG.110 Checking ring gear backlash

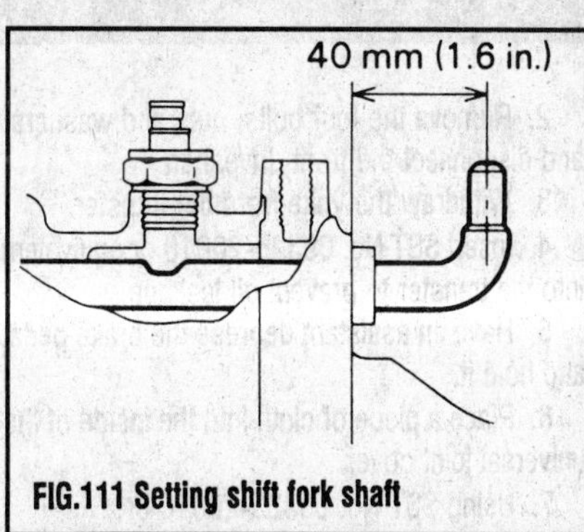
40 mm (1.6 in.)

FIG.111 Setting shift fork shaft

REASSEMBLY OF THE RING GEAR MOUNTING CASE

1. Install the ring gear, heating it to no more than 230°F (110°C) in an oil bath for installation.
2. Coat the set bolts with gear oil and torque them evenly a little at a time to 71 ft. lbs. (97 Nm). Recheck the runout.
3. Install the mounting case side bearings, using a press.

➡ The ring gear tooth side bearing inner diameter is 55mm, while the ring gear back side bearing inner diameter is 54mm.

Reassembly of Transfer Component Parts

➡ Coat all of the sliding and rotating surfaces with gear oil before assembly.

1. Adjust the ring gear backlash.
   a. Install the adjust shim to the driven pinion bearing cage assembly, first installing a shim of the same thickness as before.
   b. Install the driven pinion bearing cage assembly to the transfer left case.
   c. Install and torque the 6 bolts to 29 ft. lbs. (39 Nm), but do not install the O-ring.
   d. Install the ring gear mounting case assembly to the transfer left case.
   e. Measure the ring gear backlash, which should be 0.0051–0.0071 in. (0.13–0.18mm). If necessary, replace shims. The backlash will change about 0.0008 in.

(0.02mm) with each shim thickness.

2. Adjust the total preload.

a. Install the transfer right case.

b. Install and torque the 12 bolts to 33 ft. lbs. (44 Nm).

c. Adjust the total preload by tightening the bearing adjusting nut with SST 09318–20010. Measure the preload while tightening a little at a time.

d. Turn the output shaft back and forth several times, then check the total preload using SST 09326–20011 and a spring tension guage. At starting it should be 2.9–3.1 lbs. (12.7–13.7 Nm) with a new bearing. With a used bearing measure the total preload. At starting it should be 1.1–2 lbs. (4.9–8.8 Nm). Add the driven preload.

e. When the standard value for the total preload is exceeded, remove the transfer right case, push in the adjusting nut and outer race. Again adjust the total preload.

3. Check the ring gear backlash, which should be 0.0051–0.0071 in. (0.13–0.18mm). When the backlash is outside the standard value, select a different washer and adjust the backlash and the total preload.

4. Check the tooth contact by coating 3 of 4 teeth at 4 different positions on the ring gear with red lead and rotating it. If poor contact, select the proper shim and plate.

5. Remove the ring gear mounting case assembly by removing the 12 bolts and the transfer right case.

6. Remove the driven pinion bearing cage by removing the 6 bolts.

7. Install the driven pinion bearing cage assembly.

a. Coat the O-ring with gear oil.

b. Install the O-ring to the driven pinion bearing cage.

c. Install the driven pinion bearing cage with the adjust shim (previously selected) to the transfer left case.

d. Install and torque the 6 bolts to 29 ft. lbs. (39 Nm).

8. Install the ring gear mounting case assembly.

9. Install the transfer right case.

a. Make sure that the contacting surfaces of the transfer left and right case are clean and oil-free.

b. Apply the seal packing (part No. 08826–00090 or equivalent) to the transfer left case and install the transfer right case as soon as the packing is applied.

c. Apply sealant (part No. 08833–00080 or equivalent) to the bolt threads, then install and torque the 12 bolts to 33 ft. lbs. (44 Nm).

10. Check the total preload.

11. Using snapring pliers, install the lock plate so that the projection from the lock plate fits properly into the groove of the adjusting nut. Choose one of the two types, tightening the adjusting nut to the minimum limit.

12. Install the side gear shaft side gear shaft holder to the transfer right case and installing the snapring.

13. Install the oil seal using a brass bar and hammer and coat the lip of the seal with grease.

14. Install the transfer inspection hole cover, making sure that the surfaces are clean. Apply packing (part No. 08826–00090 or equivalent) and install the cover as soon as it is applied. Torque the bolts to 12 ft. lbs. (16 Nm).

15. Install the extension housing.

a. Coat the O-ring with gear oil.

b. Install the O-ring to the extension housing.

c. Install the extension housing to the driven pinion bearing cage.

d. Install and torque the 4 bolts to 19 ft. lbs. (25 Nm).

16. Install the dynamic damper and torque the 4 bolts to 19 ft. lbs. (25 Nm).

17. Install the differential lock shift fork shaft.

a. Install the differential lock sleeve with the shift fork.

b. Install and torque the set bolt to 12 ft. lbs. (16 Nm).

c. Using SST 09043–36100, install and torque the plug to 29 ft. lbs. (39 Nm).

d. Install and torque the indicator switch to 29 ft. lbs. (39 Nm).

e. Set the shift fork shaft to specifications.

18. Install the dust boot.

19. Install the transfer vacuum actuator, tightening the 3 bolts, then install the stiffener center plate and actuator bracket bolts and torque to 27 ft. lbs. (37 Nm).

DRIVELINE

➧ SEE FIGS. 112–117

Propeller Shaft

The three piece driveshaft is a four joint type shaft. No. 1, 2 and 4 joints are hooked joints and the No.3 joint is a cross groove type constant velocity joint that ensures good flexibility and reduces vibration and noise. The driveshaft also uses two center support bearings to control vibration and suppress noise.

REMOVAL & INSTALLATION

All-Trac 4-Wheel Drive Only

1. Matchmark the both front driveshaft flanges.

2. Remove the four bolts, nuts and washers and disconnect the front driveshaft.

3. Withdraw the yoke from the transfer.

4. Insert SST No. 09325-20010 or equivalent into the transfer to prevent oil leakage.

5. Have an assistant depress the brake pedal and hold it.

6. Place a piece of cloth into the inside of the universal joint cover.

7. Using SST No. 09325-20010 or equivalent, loosen the cross groove joint set bolts ½ turn.

8. Matchmark the intermediate and rear driveshafts.

9. Remove the four bolts, nuts and washers.

10. Remove the two bolts from the front center support bearing and remove the bearing and the washer.

11. Remove the rear front center support bearing and washers.

To install the driveshaft:

12. Install the center support bearing temporarily with the two bolts.

13. Align the matchmarks on the rear and intermediate flanges and connect the shafts with the four nuts, bolts and washers. Torque the bolts to 54 ft. lbs.

14. Remove the special tool from the transfer and insert the yoke.

15. Align the matchmarks on both flanges. Install the bolts, nuts and washers and torque to 54 ft. lbs.

16. Have an assistant depress the brake pedal and hold it.

17. Using the removal tool, torque the cross groove joint set bolts to 20 ft. lbs.

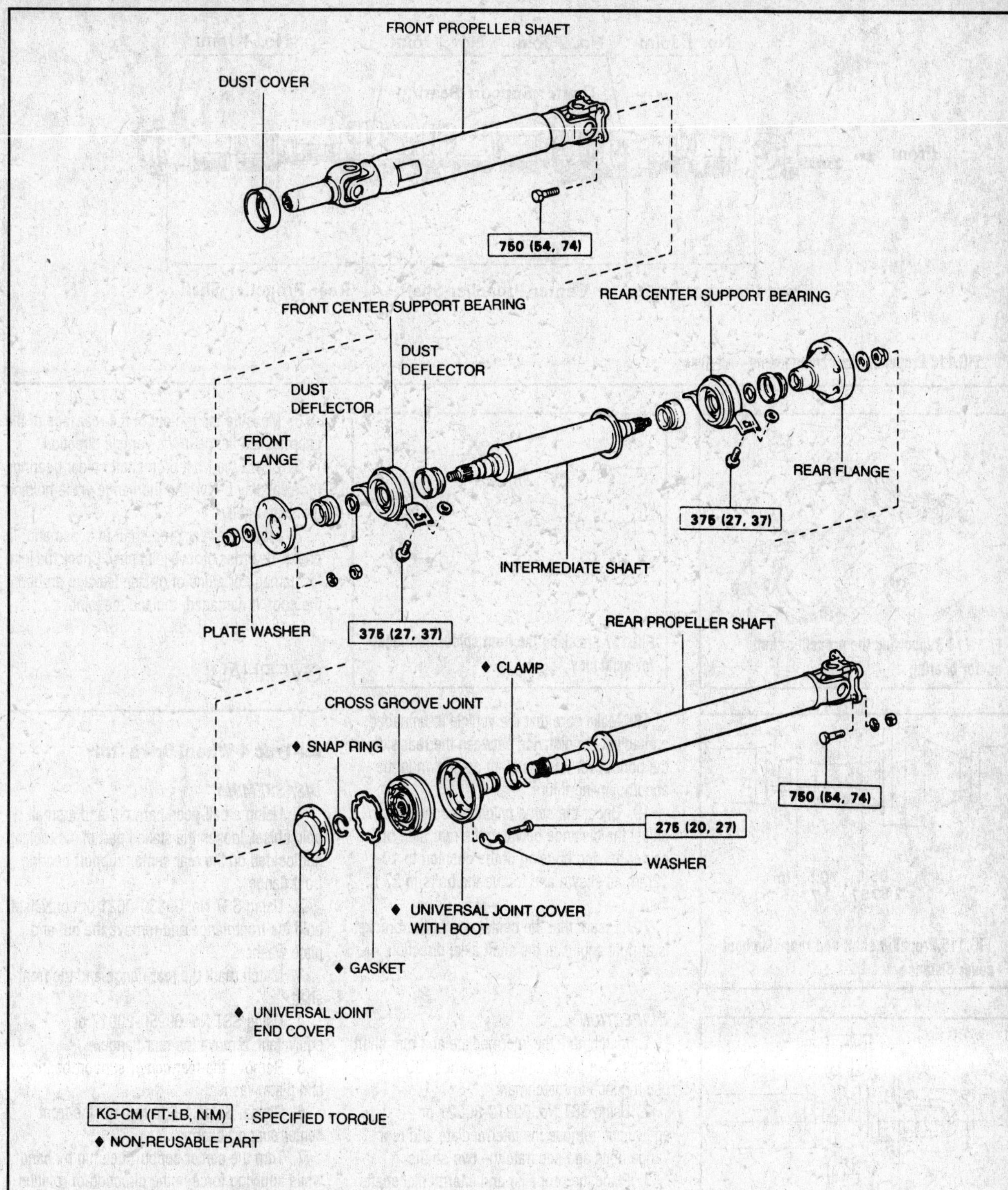
FRONT PROPELLER SHAFT
DUST COVER
750 (54, 74)
FRONT CENTER SUPPORT BEARING
REAR CENTER SUPPORT BEARING
DUST DEFLECTOR
DUST DEFLECTOR
FRONT FLANGE
REAR FLANGE
375 (27, 37)
INTERMEDIATE SHAFT
PLATE WASHER
375 (27, 37)
REAR PROPELLER SHAFT
◆ CLAMP
CROSS GROOVE JOINT
◆ SNAP RING
750 (54, 74)
275 (20, 27)
WASHER
◆ UNIVERSAL JOINT COVER WITH BOOT
◆ GASKET
◆ UNIVERSAL JOINT END COVER
KG-CM (FT-LB, N·M) : SPECIFIED TORQUE
◆ NON-REUSABLE PART

FIG.112 Propeller shaft components—All-Trac

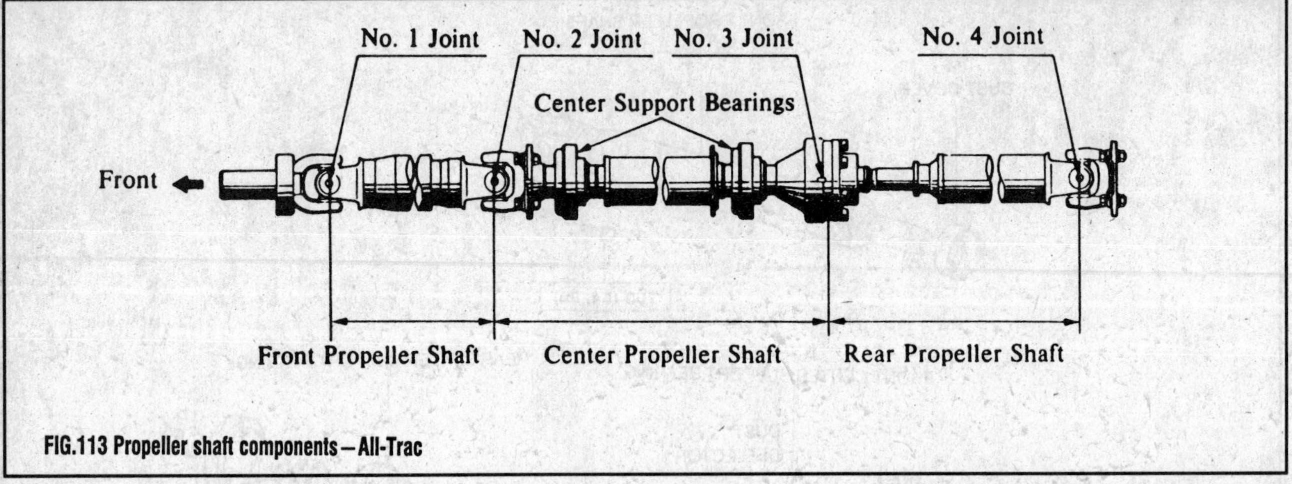

FIG.113 Propeller shaft components—All-Trac

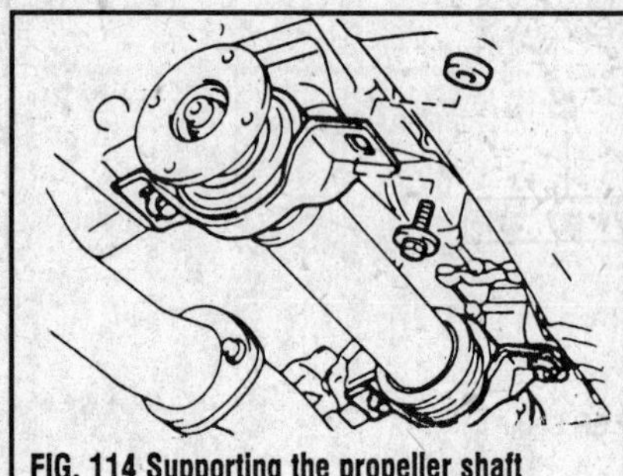

FIG. 114 Supporting the propeller shaft center bearing

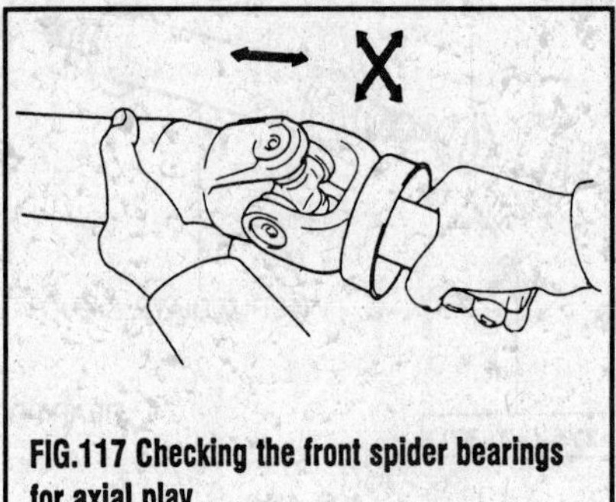

FIG.117 Checking the front spider bearings for axial play

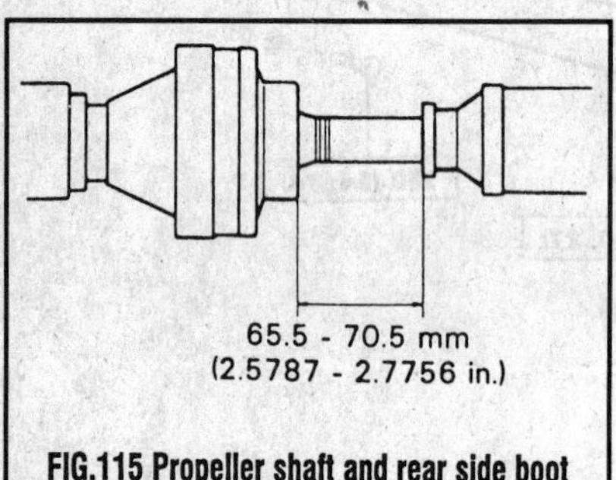

FIG.115 Propeller shaft and rear side boot cover distance

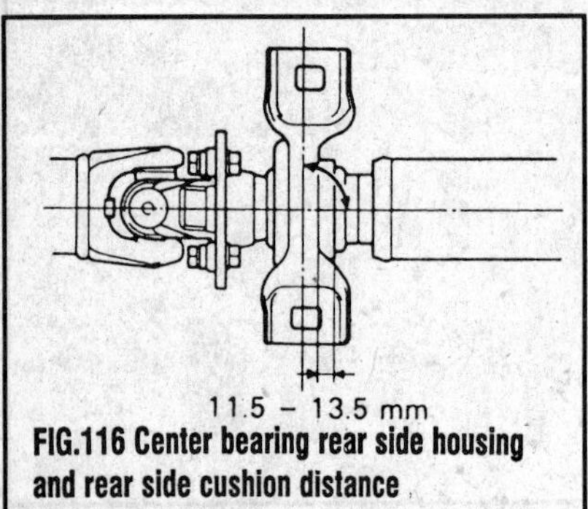

FIG.116 Center bearing rear side housing and rear side cushion distance

18. Make sure that the vehicle is unloaded, and adjust the distance between the rear side of the boot cover and the shaft as shown in the accompanying figure.

19. Under the same unloaded conditions, adjust the distance between the rear side of the center bearing housing of the cushion to 10-12mm as shown and torque the bolts to 27 ft. lbs.

20. Ensure that the center line of the bracket is at right angles at the shaft axial direction.

INSPECTION

1. Matchmark the intermediate and rear shaft flanges. Use paint, chalk or a scribe. DO NOT use a punch to matchmark.
2. Using SST No. 09313-30021 or equivalent, remove the intermediate and rear flange bolts and separate the two shafts.
3. Place the propeller and intermedial shafts on V-blocks and check the run out with a dial indicator. If the run out exceeds 0.075mm replace the shaft.
4. Measure the run out of the face of the intermediate shaft flange. If the runout exceeds 0.10mm, replace the shaft.
5. Measure the run out of the rear face of the intermediate flange in the verticle direction.
6. Check the front prop shaft spider bearings for axial play by turning the flange while holding the shaft tightly.
7. Mount the rear prop shaft in a vise and check the cross groove joint play. Check the joint for damage or signs of grease leakage around the boot. If damaged, replace the joint.

OVERHAUL

All-Trac 4-Wheel Drive Only

DISASSEMBLY

1. Using a ball-peen hammer and a small cold chisel, loosen the staked part of the locking nut located on the rear center support bearing front flange.
2. Using SST No. 09330-0021 or equivalent, hold the front flange and remove the nut and plate washer.
3. Match mark the rear flange and the front shaft.
4. Using SST No. 09950-20017 or equivalent, remove the rear flange.
5. Remove the rear center support bearing and plate washer.
6. Repeat Steps 1-5 to remove the front center support bearing.
7. Turn the center support bearing by hand while applying force in the direction of rotation. Check the bearing smooth play.
8. Inspect both support seals for cracks and damage.
9. Remove the cross groove joint end cover using a brass bar and ball-peen hammer.
10. With a small punch, matchmark the inner race and the cross groove joint shaft.
11. Remove the snapring that retains the joint to the shaft.

12. Using SST No. 09527-21011, extension bar and press, remove the cross groove joint.

13. Remove the joint end cover and gasket.

14. Loosen the clamp and remove the universal joint cover and boot.

15. Discard the locking nuts, washers, snapring, gaskets. boot cover and boot clamp and replace with new.

REASSEMBLY

1. Set the front center support bearing onto the intermediate shaft.

2. Install the plate washer.

3. Align the matchmark and install the bearing flange onto the shaft.

4. Using SST No. 09330-00021 or equivalent to hold the flange, press the bearing into place by tightening the new locking nut and washer to 134 ft. lbs.

5. Loosen the locking nut.

6. Torque the nut again to 51 ft. lbs. and stake the nut with a ball-peen hammer and small cold chisel.

7. Repeat Steps 1-6 to install the rear center support bearing.

8. Apply a 1/8 in. (3mm) bead of sealant to the new boot cover. Use sealant No. 08828-00801 or equivalent.

9. Wrap the end of the shaft with masking tape to prevent damage to the boot.

10. Install the universal joint cover and boot onto the shaft.

11. Align the matchmarks on the cross groove joint shaft and inner race.

12. Place the brass bar on the inner race and tap the cross groove joint onto the shaft.

13. Secure the joint onto the shaft with a new snapring.

14. Using a bolt for alignment, press the universal joint cover with boot into place using a steel plate and press.

15. Install a new boot clamp.

16. Pack the joint with about 4 ounces of grease.

17. Remove the backing paper and install the new joint end cover gasket.

18. Install the joint end cover.

19. Align the matchmarks and install the universal joint flange onto the cross groove joint cover.

20. Tighten the flange bolts evenly in an alternate pattern to press the joint end cover.

21. Mount the rear prop shaft in a vise and check the cross groove joint play.

22. Using SST No. 09313-30021 or equivalent, temporarily tighten the six bolts and three washers using a piece of cloth on the inside of the joint cover.

Center Support Bearings

Two center support bearings are used on All-Trac 4-Wheel Drive vehicles to control driveshaft noise and vibration and as a means of support for the intermediate driveshaft. The bearings use cushion rubber to bend the driveshaft to allow passage through the center of the bearing.

REMOVAL & INSTALLATION

See, "Propeller Shaft".

REAR AXLE

➧ SEE FIGS. 109, 118–124

Axle Shaft

REMOVAL & INSTALLATION

The following procedure applies to all 1988–91 rear axles.

1. Raise and support the vehicle safely. Remove the rear wheels.

2. Remove the cotter pin, locknut cap and bearing nut.

3. Scribe matchmarks on the inner joint tulip and the side gear shaft flange. Loosen and remove the 4 nuts.

4. Disconnect the inner end of the shaft by punching it upward and then pull the outer end from the axle carrier. Remove the halfshaft.

To install:

5. Position the halfshaft into the axle carrier and pull the inner end down until the matchmarks are aligned.

6. Connect the halfshaft to the side gear shaft and tighten the nuts to 51 ft. lbs. (69 Nm).

7. Install the bearing nut and tighten it to 137 ft. lbs. (186 Nm) with the brake pedal depressed. Install the cap and a new cotter pin.

8. Install the wheels and lower the vehicle.

OVERHAUL

Disassembly

1. Mount the driveshaft in a vise and check that there is no play in the inboard and outboard joint.

2. Make sure that the inboard joint slides smoothly in the thrust direction.

3. Make sure that there is no excessive play in the radial direction of the inboard joint.

4. Inspect the boots for damage.

5. Remove the inboard joint boot clamps, then remove the inboard joint boot from the inboard joint tulip.

6. Paint (Do not punch) matchmarks on the inboard joint tulip and the driveshaft and remove the tulip from the driveshaft.

7. Place matchmarks on the shaft and the tripod, remove the snapring and tap the tripod from the shaft.

8. Remove the outboard boot clamps, then both boots from the driveshaft.

➡ Do not disassemble the outboard joint.

Reassembly

1. Temporarily install the boots and clamps in the correct order onto the shaft.

2. Install the tripod joint in the reverse order of removal.

3. Install the inboard joint tulip to the driveshaft after packing 0.4 lb. (180 grams) of grease into the tulip.

4. Install the outboard joint boot after packing 0.26 lb. (120 grams) of grease into the boot.

5. Make sure that the boot is properly installed in the grooves on the driveshaft.

6. Make sure that the boot is not stretched or squashed when the driveshaft is at standard length.

Standard driveshaft length: 557.7mm (21.957 in.).

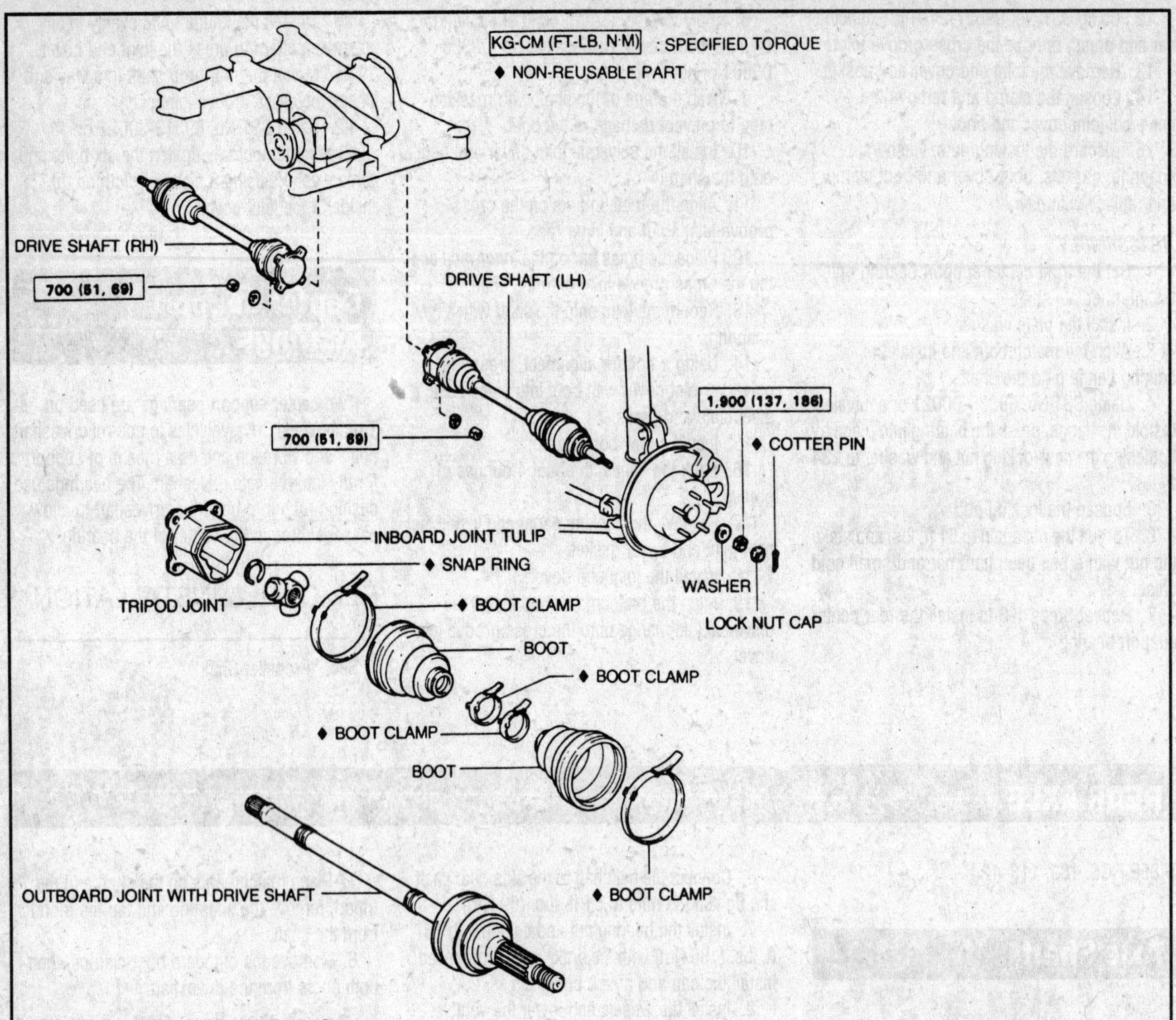

KG-CM (FT-LB, N·M) : SPECIFIED TORQUE
◆ NON-REUSABLE PART
DRIVE SHAFT (RH)
700 (51, 69)
DRIVE SHAFT (LH)
1,900 (137, 186)
700 (51, 69)
◆ COTTER PIN
INBOARD JOINT TULIP
◆ SNAP RING
WASHER
TRIPOD JOINT
◆ BOOT CLAMP
LOCK NUT CAP
BOOT
◆ BOOT CLAMP
◆ BOOT CLAMP
BOOT
OUTBOARD JOINT WITH DRIVE SHAFT
◆ BOOT CLAMP

FIG.119 Rear driveshaft on All-Trac—Camry

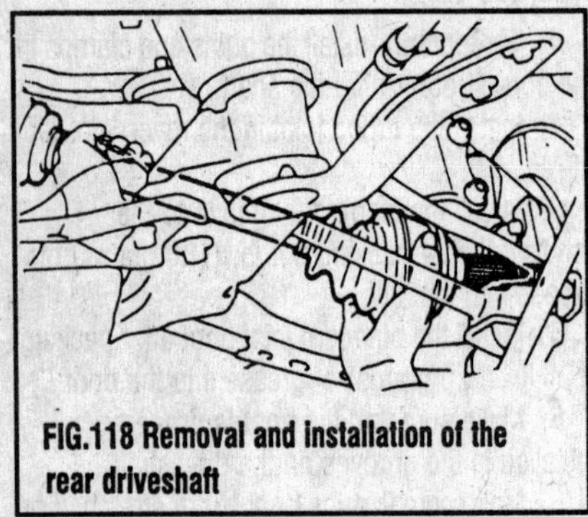

FIG.118 Removal and installation of the rear driveshaft

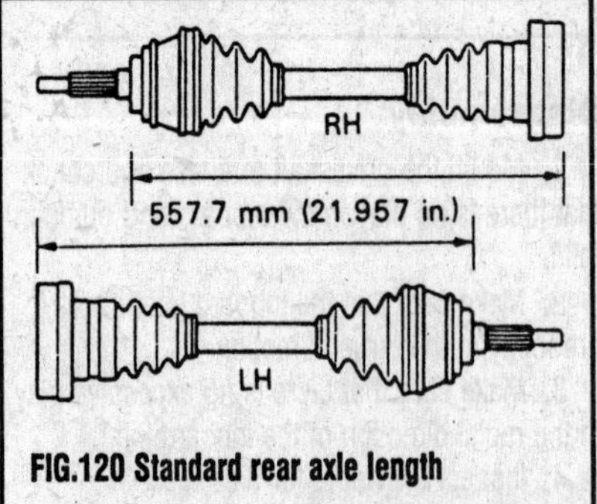

FIG.120 Standard rear axle length

7. To lock the boot bands, bend the band back and close the locking tabs.

8. Mount the driveshaft in vise and check that there is no play in the inboard or outboard joints. Check that the inboard joint slides smoothly in the thrust direction.

Differential Carrier

REMOVAL & INSTALLATION

All-Trac 4-Wheel Drive Only

1. Remove the drain plug and drain the oil from the differential into a drain pan.
2. Remove the rear driveshafts as described in this Section.
3. Unbolt and remove the rear crossmember.
4. Matchmark the differential and driveshaft flanges.
5. Remove the four flange bolts, nuts and washers.
6. Disconnect the driveshaft from the differential.
7. Raise the differential slighlty with a transaxle jack and a block of wood.
8. Remove the six bolts and four mounting nuts from the differential.
9. Remove the differential from the body.

To install the differential carrier:

10. Position the differential into place and install the mounting bolts and nuts. Torque the gruop of four nuts and bolts to 70 ft. lbs.

11. Torque the two bolts to 108 ft. lbs.

12. Align the driveshaft and differential flange matchmarks.

13. Install the flange bolts and torque to 54 ft. lbs.

14. Install the rear crossmember and torque the retaining bolts to 53 ft. lbs.

15. Install the rear driveshafts.

16. Install the drain plug with a new gasket and torque the plug to 36 ft. lbs.

17. Fill the differential to the proper level with new API GL-5 hyploid gear oil.

18. Install the filler plug with a new gasket and torque to 29 ft. lbs.

Differential Front Oil Seal and Bearing

REMOVAL & INSTALLATION

All-Trac 4-Wheel Drive Only

1. Unbolt and remove the rear crossmember.

2. Matchmark the differential and driveshaft flanges.

3. Remove the four flange bolts, nuts and washers.

4. Disconnect the driveshaft from the differential.

5. With a hammer and a cold chisel, loosen the staked part of the locking nut.

6. Using SST No. 09330-00021 or equivalent to hold the flange, remove the lockin nut.

7. Remove the plate washer.

8. Using SST No. 09557-22022 or equivalent, remove the companion flange.

9. Using SST No. 09308-10010 or equivalent seal puller, remove the front oil seal and then remove the oils slinger.

10. Using SST No. 09556-22010 or equivalent bearing puller, remove the front bearing.

11. Remove the front bearing spacer. Purchase a new spacer, bearing and oil seal as required.

To install the front seal and bearing

12. Install a new bearing spacer and bearing onto the shaft.

13. Install the oils slinger onto the shaft.

14. Using SST No. 09554-22010 or equivalent, drive in the new oil seal to a depth of 2mm.

15. Coat the lip of the new oil seal with multi-purpose grease.

16. Using the removal tool, install the companion flange.

17. Install the plate washer.

18. Coat the threads of the new nut with gear oil.

19. Using the removal tool to hold the flange, torque the companion flange to 80 ft. lbs.

20. Check and adjust the drive pinion preload as follows:

a. Using a inch lb. torque wrench, measure the preload of the backlash between the drive pinion and the ring gear. Preload for a new bearing is 8.7-13.9 inch lbs. and 4.3-6.9 inch lbs. for a used bearing.

b. If the preload is greater that the specified limit, replace the bearing spacer.

c. If the preload is less than specification, re-torque the nut in 9 ft. lb. increments until the specified preload is reached. Do not exceed a maximum torque of 174 ft. lbs.

d. If the maximum torque is exceeded, replace the bearing spacer and repeat the bearing prelopad procedure. Preload CANNOT be reduced by simply backing off on the pinion nut.

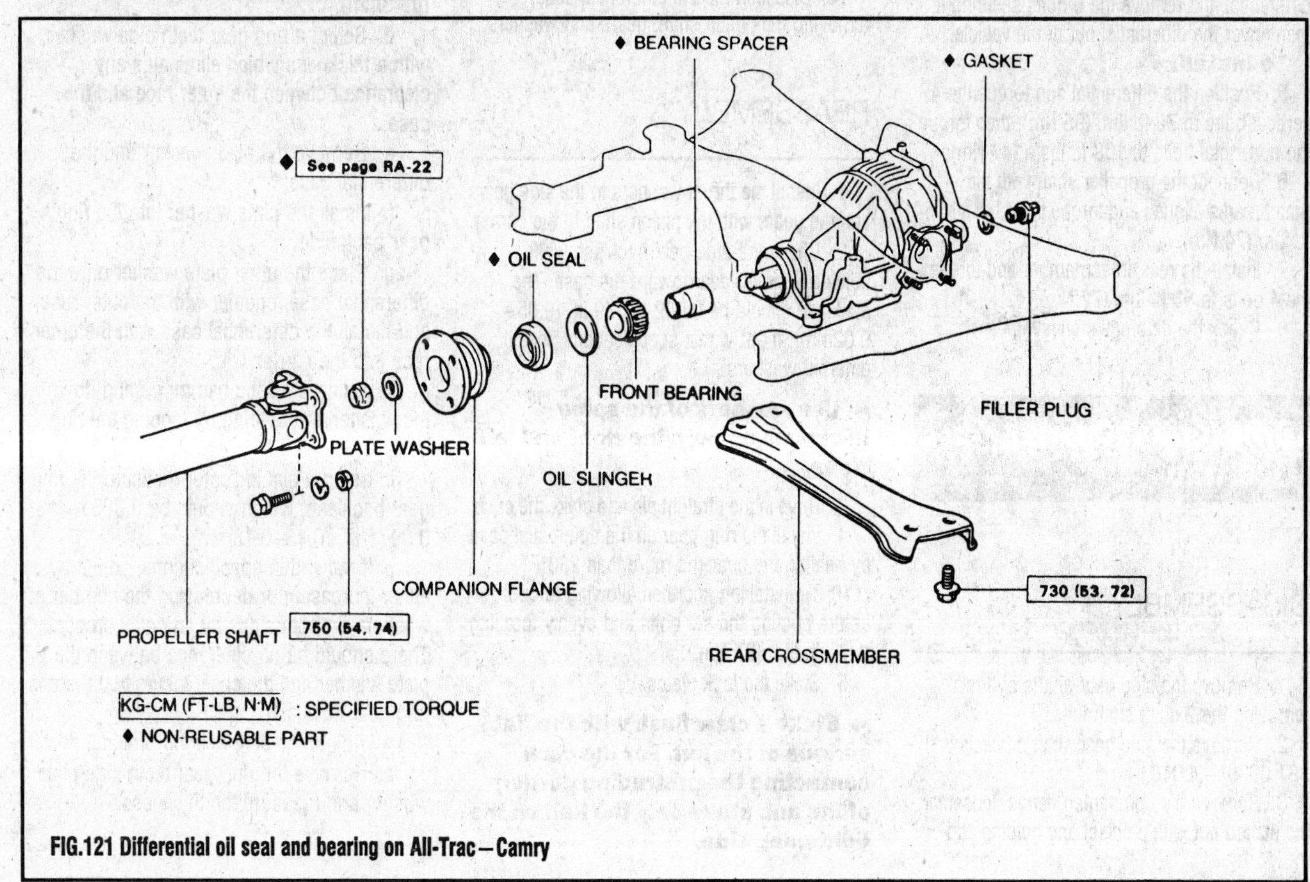

FIG.121 Differential oil seal and bearing on All-Trac—Camry

21. Stake the drive pinion nut.
22. Align the driveshaft and differential flange matchmarks.
23. Install the flange bolts and torque to 54 ft. lbs.
24. Install the rear crossmember and torque the retaining bolts to 53 ft. lbs.
25. Remove the differential FILL plug (the uppermost plug) and check the oil level. Fill the differential to the proper level with new API GL-5 hyploid gear oil.
26. Install and tighten the fill plug with a new gasket. Torque the plug to 29 ft. lbs.
27. Take the vehicle for a road test and inspect for leaks.

Axle Housing

REMOVAL & INSTALLATION

1. Matchmark and disconnect the driveshafts from the differential.
2. Remove the rear crossmember by removing the 4 bolts.
3. Matchmark and disconnect the propeller shaft.
4. Position a suitable jack under the differential and remove the 6 bolts securing it, then lower the differential out of the vehicle.

To install:

5. Position the differential and torque the 4 vertical bolts to 70 ft. lbs. (95 Nm), then torque the horizontal bolts to 108 ft. lbs. (147 Nm).
6. Connect the propeller shaft with the matchmarks aligned and torque the 4 bolts to 54 ft. lbs. (74 Nm).
7. Install the rear crossmember and torque the 4 bolts to 53 ft. lbs. (72 Nm).
8. Check the differential oil level.

Differential Carrier Overhaul

DISASSEMBLY

1. Remove the side gear shafts by first removing the 2 shaft snaprings.
2. Remove the side gear shaft oil seals with SST 09308–00010.
3. Remove the companion flange, loosening the staked nut with a chisel and holding and removing the flange with SST's 09330–00021 and 09557–22022, respectively.
4. Remove the front oil seal and oil slinger, using SST 09308–10010.
5. Remove the front bearing and the bearing spacer with SST 09556–22010.
6. Place matchmarks on the bearing cap and differential carrier and remove the caps.
7. Using SST 09504–22011, remove the 2 side bearing preload adjusting plate.

➡ Measure the adjusting plate washer and note the thickness.

8. Remove the differential case and bearing outer race from the carrier, tagging the bearing outer races for reassembly.
9. Remove the drive pinion from the differential carrier.
10. Remove the drive pinion bearing and the plate washer, using SST 09950–00020 and a press.

➡ If the pinion or the ring gear are damaged, replace them as a set.

11. Remove the front and rear bearing outer races, using a brass bar.
12. Place matchmarks on the ring gear and the differential case, unstake the lock plates and remove the bolts and the ring gear.
13. Remove the side bearings, using SST 09950–20017.
14. Disassemble the differential case, removing the pinion shaft, gears and washers.

REASSEMBLY

1. Install the thrust washers to the side gears and the gears with the pinion shaft to the carrier.
2. Check the side gear backlash while holding 1 pinion gear toward the case. The backlash should be 0.002–0.079 in. (0.05–0.02mm). If not within specifications, install different washers.

➡ Use washers of the same thickness on both the right and left sides.

3. Drive in the straight pin and stake the case.
4. Install the ring gear on the differential case by heating the gear (no more than 230°F (110°C), installing and then allowing to cool before coating the set bolts and evenly torquing to 71 ft. lbs. (97 Nm.).
5. Stake the lock plates.

➡ Stake 1 claw flush with the flat surface of the nut. For the claw contacting the protruding portion of the nut, stake only the half on the tightening side.

6. Install the side bearings into the case with SST 09710–22020.
7. With no play in the bearings, check the ring gear runout, which should be no more than 0.0028 in. (0.07mm).
8. Install the front and rear bearing outer races, using SST's and a press.
9. Install with a press the plate washer and the rear bearing to the drive pinion with the chamfered end of the plate washer facing the pinion gear.
10. Temporarily adjust the drive pinion preload by tightening the companion flange nut.

➡ Assemble the spacer, oil slinger and the oil seal after adjusting the gear contact pattern.

11. Using a torque wrench, measure the preload. At starting, with a new bearing, it should be 8.7–13.9 inch lbs. With a used bearing it should be 4.3–6.9 inch lbs.
12. Install the case into the carrier.
13. Adjust the ring gear backlash.
    a. Install only the plate washer on the ring gear backside, insuring that the ring gear has backlash.
    b. Snug down the washer and the bearing by tapping on the ring gear with a plastic hammer.
    c. Using a dial indicator measure the backlash, which should be 0.0051 in. (0.13mm).
    d. Select a ring gear teeth side washer with a thickness which eliminates any clearance between the outer race and the case.
    e. Remove the plate washer and the differential case.
    f. Install the plate washer into the ring gear back side.
    g. Place the other plate washer onto the differential case together with the outer race, and install the differential case with the outer race into the carrier.
    h. Using a plastic hammer, snug down the washer and bearing by tapping the ring gear.
    i. Using a dial indicator measure the ring gear backlash, which should be 0.0051–0.0071 in. (0.13–0.18mm).
    j. If not within specifications, adjust by either increasing or decreasing the number of washers on both sides by an equal amount. There should be no clearance between the plate washer and the case. Insure that there is ring gear backlash.
14. Adjust the side bearing preload.
    a. Remove the ring gear teeth side plate washer and measure the thickness.

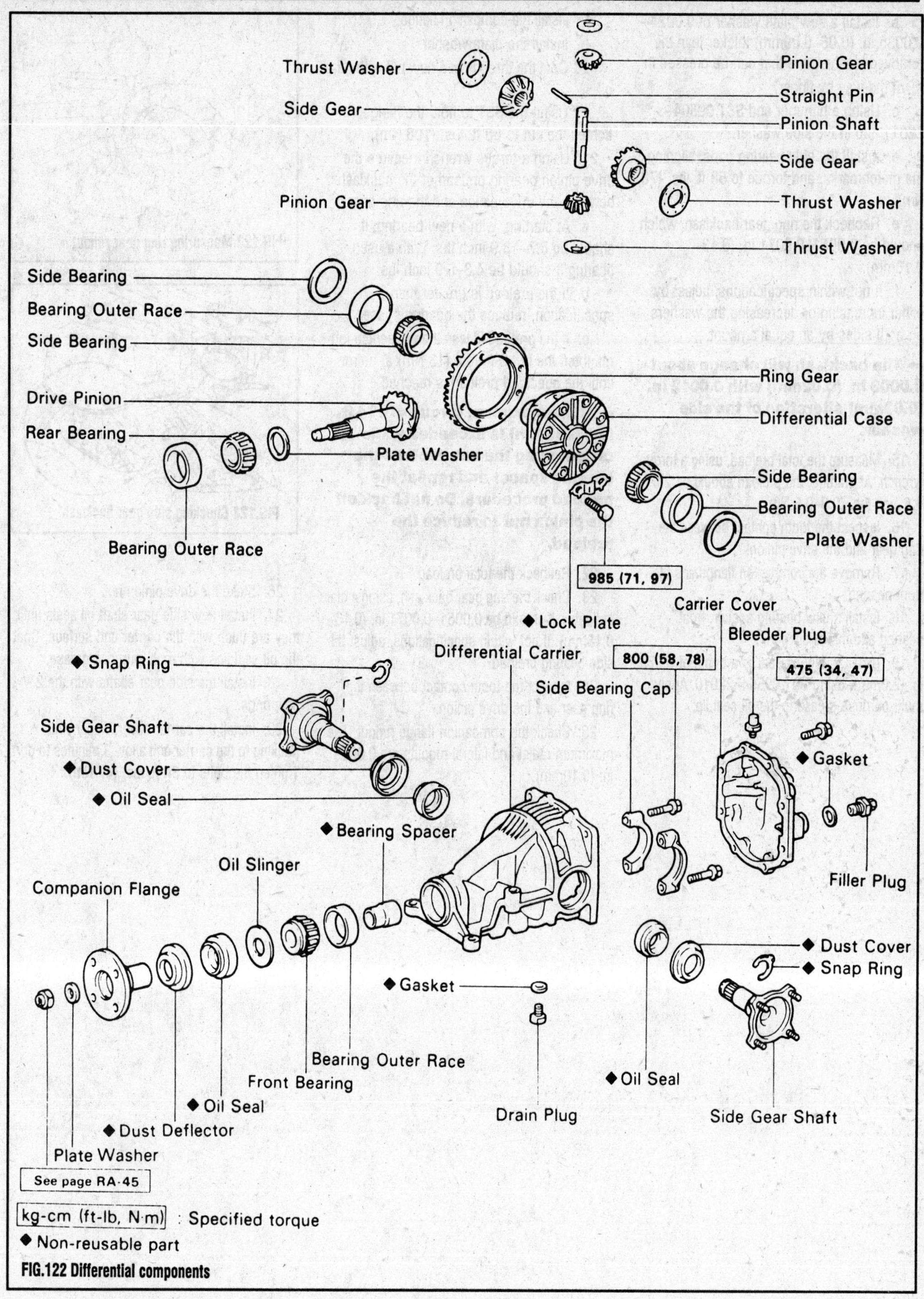
Thrust Washer
Pinion Gear
Side Gear
Straight Pin
Pinion Shaft
Side Gear
Pinion Gear
Thrust Washer
Thrust Washer
Side Bearing
Bearing Outer Race
Side Bearing
Ring Gear
Drive Pinion
Differential Case
Rear Bearing
Plate Washer
Side Bearing
Bearing Outer Race
Plate Washer
Bearing Outer Race
985 (71, 97)
Carrier Cover
◆ Lock Plate
Bleeder Plug
Differential Carrier
800 (58, 78)
475 (34, 47)
◆ Snap Ring
Side Bearing Cap
Side Gear Shaft
◆ Gasket
◆ Dust Cover
◆ Oil Seal
◆ Bearing Spacer
Oil Slinger
Filler Plug
Companion Flange
◆ Dust Cover
◆ Snap Ring
◆ Gasket
Bearing Outer Race
Front Bearing
◆ Oil Seal
◆ Oil Seal
Drain Plug
Side Gear Shaft
◆ Dust Deflector
Plate Washer
See page RA-45
kg-cm (ft-lb, N·m) : Specified torque
◆ Non-reusable part

FIG.122 Differential components

b. Install a new plate washer of 0.0024–0.0035 in. (0.06–0.09mm) thicker than the removed washer, one that can be pressed in 2/3 of the way by finger.

c. Using a hammer and SST 09504–22011, tap in the side washer.

d. Install the side bearing caps, aligning the matchmarks, and torque to 58 ft. lbs. (78 Nm).

e. Recheck the ring gear backlash, which should be 0.0051–0.0071 in. (0.13–0.18mm).

f. If not within specifications, adjust by either increasing or decreasing the washers on both sides by an equal amount.

➡ The backlash will change about 0.0008 in. (0.02mm) with 0.0012 in. (0.03mm) alteration of the side washer.

15. Measure the total preload, using a torque wrench. At starting, the preload should be 2.6–4.3 inch lbs. (0.3–0.5 Nm).

16. Inspect the tooth contact between the ring gear and the drive pinion.

17. Remove the companion flange and the front bearing.

18. Install a new bearing spacer, front bearing and the oil slinger.

19. Install a new oil seal to a depth of 0.079 in. (2.0mm), using SST 09554–22010. Apply multi-purpose grease to the oil seal lip.

20. Install the companion flange.

a. Install the plate washer.

b. Coat the threads of a new nut with gear oil.

c. Using the SST to hold the flange, tighten the nut to 80 ft. lbs. (108 Nm).

21. Using a torque wrench measure the drive pinion bearing preload of the backlash between the drive pinion and the ring gear.

a. At starting, with a new bearing, it should be 8.7–13.9 inch lbs. With a used bearing it should be 4.3–6.9 inch lbs.

b. If the preload is greater than specification, replace the bearing spacer.

c. If the preload is less than specification, retighten the nut 9 ft. lbs. (13 Nm) at a time until the specified preload is reached.

➡ If the maximum torque of 174 ft. lbs. (235 Nm) is exceeded while retightening the nut, replace the bearing spacer and repeat the preload procedure. Do not back off the pinion nut to reduce the preload.

22. Recheck the total preload.

23. Check the ring gear backlash, using a dial indicator. It should be 0.0051–0.0071 in. (0.13–0.18mm). If not within specifications, adjust the side bearing preload.

24. Inspect the tooth contact between the ring gear and the drive pinion.

25. Check the companion flange runout. The maximum radial and lateral runouts are 0.0039 in. (0.10mm).

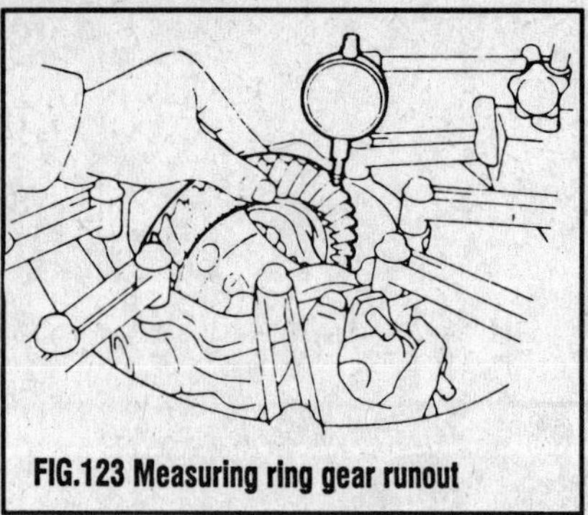

FIG.123 Measuring ring gear runout

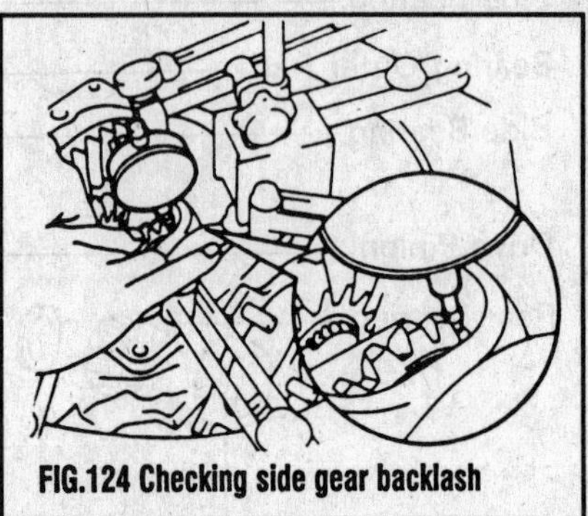

FIG.124 Checking side gear backlash

26. Stake the drive pinion nut.

27. Install new side gear shaft oil seals until they are flush with the carrier end surface. Coat the oil seal lips with multi-purpose grease.

28. Install the side gear shafts with the 2 snaprings.

29. Install the carrier cover. Apply seal packing to the carrier and allow 3 minutes to dry. Tighten the bolts to 34 ft. lbs. (47 Nm).

Troubleshooting the Manual Transmission

Problem	Cause	Solution
Transmission shifts hard	• Clutch adjustment incorrect	• Adjust clutch
	• Clutch linkage or cable binding	• Lubricate or repair as necessary
	• Shift rail binding	• Check for mispositioned selector arm roll pin, loose cover bolts, worn shift rail bores, worn shift rail, distorted oil seal, or extension housing not aligned with case. Repair as necessary.
	• Internal bind in transmission caused by shift forks, selector plates, or synchronizer assemblies	• Remove, dissemble and inspect transmission. Replace worn or damaged components as necessary.
	• Clutch housing misalignment	• Check runout at rear face of clutch housing
	• Incorrect lubricant	• Drain and refill transmission
	• Block rings and/or cone seats worn	• Blocking ring to gear clutch tooth face clearance must be 0.030 inch or greater. If clearance is correct it may still be necessary to inspect blocking rings and cone seats for excessive wear. Repair as necessary.
Gear clash when shifting from one gear to another	• Clutch adjustment incorrect	• Adjust clutch
	• Clutch linkage or cable binding	• Lubricate or repair as necessary
	• Clutch housing misalignment	• Check runout at rear of clutch housing
	• Lubricant level low or incorrect lubricant	• Drain and refill transmission and check for lubricant leaks if level was low. Repair as necessary.
	• Gearshift components, or synchronizer assemblies worn or damaged	• Remove, disassemble and inspect transmission. Replace worn or damaged components as necessary.
Transmission noisy	• Lubricant level low or incorrect lubricant	• Drain and refill transmission. If lubricant level was low, check for leaks and repair as necessary.
	• Clutch housing-to-engine, or transmission-to-clutch housing bolts loose	• Check and correct bolt torque as necessary
	• Dirt, chips, foreign material in transmission	• Drain, flush, and refill transmission
	• Gearshift mechanism, transmission gears, or bearing components worn or damaged	• Remove, disassemble and inspect transmission. Replace worn or damaged components as necessary.
	• Clutch housing misalignment	• Check runout at rear face of clutch housing

Troubleshooting the Manual Transmission

Problem	Cause	Solution
Jumps out of gear	• Clutch housing misalignment	• Check runout at rear face of clutch housing
	• Gearshift lever loose	• Check lever for worn fork. Tighten loose attaching bolts.
	• Offset lever nylon insert worn or lever attaching nut loose	• Remove gearshift lever and check for loose offset lever nut or worn insert. Repair or replace as necessary.
	• Gearshift mechanism, shift forks, selector plates, interlock plate, selector arm, shift rail, detent plugs, springs or shift cover worn or damaged	• Remove, disassemble and inspect transmission cover assembly. Replace worn or damaged components as necessary.
	• Clutch shaft or roller bearings worn or damaged	• Replace clutch shaft or roller bearings as necessary
Jumps out of gear (cont.)	• Gear teeth worn or tapered, synchronizer assemblies worn or damaged, excessive end play caused by worn thrust washers or output shaft gears	• Remove, disassemble, and inspect transmission. Replace worn or damaged components as necessary.
	• Pilot bushing worn	• Replace pilot bushing
Will not shift into one gear	• Gearshift selector plates, interlock plate, or selector arm, worn, damaged, or incorrectly assembled	• Remove, disassemble, and inspect transmission cover assembly. Repair or replace components as necessary.
	• Shift rail detent plunger worn, spring broken, or plug loose	• Tighten plug or replace worn or damaged components as necessary
	• Gearshift lever worn or damaged	• Replace gearshift lever
	• Synchronizer sleeves or hubs, damaged or worn	• Remove, disassemble and inspect transmission. Replace worn or damaged components.
Locked in one gear—cannot be shifted out	• Shift rail(s) worn or broken, shifter fork bent, setscrew loose, center detent plug missing or worn	• Inspect and replace worn or damaged parts
	• Broken gear teeth on countershaft gear, clutch shaft, or reverse idler gear	• Inspect and replace damaged part
	Gearshift lever broken or worn, shift mechanism in cover incorrectly assembled or broken, worn damaged gear train components	• Disassemble transmission. Replace damaged parts or assemble correctly.

Troubleshooting Basic Clutch Problems

Problem	Cause
Excessive clutch noise	Throwout bearing noises are more audible at the lower end of pedal travel. The usual causes are: • Riding the clutch • Too little pedal free-play • Lack of bearing lubrication A bad clutch shaft pilot bearing will make a high pitched squeal, when the clutch is disengaged and the transmission is in gear or within the first 2″ of pedal travel. The bearing must be replaced. Noise from the clutch linkage is a clicking or snapping that can be heard or felt as the pedal is moved completely up or down. This usually requires lubrication. Transmitted engine noises are amplified by the clutch housing and heard in the passenger compartment. They are usually the result of insufficient pedal free-play and can be changed by manipulating the clutch pedal.
Clutch slips (the car does not move as it should when the clutch is engaged)	This is usually most noticeable when pulling away from a standing start. A severe test is to start the engine, apply the brakes, shift into high gear and SLOWLY release the clutch pedal. A healthy clutch will stall the engine. If it slips it may be due to: • A worn pressure plate or clutch plate • Oil soaked clutch plate • Insufficient pedal free-play
Clutch drags or fails to release	The clutch disc and some transmission gears spin briefly after clutch disengagement. Under normal conditions in average temperatures, 3 seconds is maximum spin-time. Failure to release properly can be caused by: • Too light transmission lubricant or low lubricant level • Improperly adjusted clutch linkage
Low clutch life	Low clutch life is usually a result of poor driving habits or heavy duty use. Riding the clutch, pulling heavy loads, holding the car on a grade with the clutch instead of the brakes and rapid clutch engagement all contribute to low clutch life.

Troubleshooting Basic Automatic Transmission Problems

Problem	Cause	Solution
Fluid leakage	• Defective pan gasket	• Replace gasket or tighten pan bolts
	• Loose filler tube	• Tighten tube nut
	• Loose extension housing to transmission case	• Tighten bolts
	• Converter housing area leakage	• Have transmission checked professionally
Fluid flows out the oil filler tube	• High fluid level	• Check and correct fluid level
	• Breather vent clogged	• Open breather vent
	• Clogged oil filter or screen	• Replace filter or clean screen (change fluid also)
	• Internal fluid leakage	• Have transmission checked professionally
Transmission overheats (this is usually accompanied by a strong burned odor to the fluid)	• Low fluid level	• Check and correct fluid level
	• Fluid cooler lines clogged	• Drain and refill transmission. If this doesn't cure the problem, have cooler lines cleared or replaced.
	• Heavy pulling or hauling with insufficient cooling	• Install a transmission oil cooler
	• Faulty oil pump, internal slippage	• Have transmission checked professionally
Buzzing or whining noise	• Low fluid level	• Check and correct fluid level
	• Defective torque converter, scored gears	• Have transmission checked professionally
No forward or reverse gears or slippage in one or more gears	• Low fluid level	• Check and correct fluid level
	• Defective vacuum or linkage controls, internal clutch or band failure	• Have unit checked professionally
Delayed or erratic shift	• Low fluid level	• Check and correct fluid level
	• Broken vacuum lines	• Repair or replace lines
	• Internal malfunction	• Have transmission checked professionally

Lockup Torque Converter Service Diagnosis

Problem	Cause	Solution
Vibration when revved in neutral	• Torque converter out of balance	• Replace torque converter
Overheating: oil blows out of dip stick tube or pump seal	• Plugged cooler, cooler lines or fittings	• Flush or replace cooler and flush lines and fittings
	• Stuck switch valve	• Repair switch valve in valve body or replace valve body
Shudder after lockup engagement	• Faulty oil pump	• Replace oil pump
	• Plugged cooler, cooler lines or fittings	• Flush or replace cooler and flush lines and fittings
	• Valve body malfunction	• Repair or replace valve body or its internal components as necessary
	• Faulty torque converter	• Replace torque converter
	• Fail locking clutch	• Replace torque converter
	• Exhaust system strikes underbody	• Align exhaust system
	• Engine needs tune-up	• Tune engine
	• Throttle linkage misadjusted	• Adjust throttle linkage

Lockup Torque Converter Service Diagnosis

Problem	Cause	Solution
No lockup	• Faulty oil pump • Sticking governor valve • Valve body malfunction (a) Stuck switch valve (b) Stuck lockup valve (c) Stuck fail-safe valve • Failed locking clutch • Leaking turbine hub seal • Faulty input shaft or seal ring	• Replace oil pump • Repair or replace as necessary • Repair or replace valve body or its internal components as necessary • Replace torque converter • Replace torque converter • Repair or replace as necessary
Will not unlock	• Sticking governor valve • Valve body malfunction (a) Stuck switch valve (b) Stuck lockup valve (c) Stuck fail-safe valve	• Repair or replace as necessary • Repair or replace valve body or its internal components as necessary
Stays locked up at too low a speed in direct	• Sticking governor valve • Valve body malfunction (a) Stuck switch valve (b) Stuck lockup valve (c) Stuck fail-safe valve	• Repair or replace as necessary • Repair or replace valve body or its internal components as necessary
Locks up or drags in low or second	• Faulty oil pump • Valve body malfunction (a) Stuck switch valve (b) Stuck fail-safe valve	• Replace oil pump • Repair or replace valve body or its internal components as necessary
Sluggish or stalls in reverse	• Faulty oil pump • Plugged cooler, cooler lines or fittings • Valve body malfunction (a) Stuck switch valve (b) Faulty input shaft or seal ring	• Replace oil pump as necessary • Flush or replace cooler and flush lines and fittings • Repair or replace valve body or its internal components as necessary
Loud chatter during lockup engagement (cold)	• Faulty torque converter • Failed locking clutch • Leaking turbine hub seal	• Replace torque converter • Replace torque converter • Replace torque converter
Vibration or shudder during lockup engagement	• Faulty oil pump • Valve body malfunction • Faulty torque converter • Engine needs tune-up	• Repair or replace oil pump as necessary • Repair or replace valve body or its internal components as necessary • Replace torque converter • Tune engine
Vibration after lockup engagement	• Faulty torque converter • Exhaust system strikes underbody • Engine needs tune-up • Throttle linkage misadjusted	• Replace torque converter • Align exhaust system • Tune engine • Adjust throttle linkage

Transmission Fluid Indications

The appearance and odor of the transmission fluid can give valuable clues to the overall condition of the transmission. Always note the appearance of the fluid when you check the fluid level or change the fluid. Rub a small amount of fluid between your fingers to feel for grit and smell the fluid on the dipstick.

If the fluid appears:	It indicates:
Clear and red colored	• Normal operation
Discolored (extremely dark red or brownish) or smells burned	• Band or clutch pack failure, usually caused by an overheated transmission. Hauling very heavy loads with insufficient power or failure to change the fluid, often result in overheating. Do not confuse this appearance with newer fluids that have a darker red color and a strong odor (though not a burned odor).
Foamy or aerated (light in color and full of bubbles)	• The level is too high (gear train is churning oil) • An internal air leak (air is mixing with the fluid). Have the transmission checked professionally.
Solid residue in the fluid	• Defective bands, clutch pack or bearings. Bits of band material or metal abrasives are clinging to the dipstick. Have the transmission checked professionally.
Varnish coating on the dipstick	• The transmission fluid is overheating

TORQUE SPECIFICATIONS

Component	U.S.	Metric
Manual Transmission		
S51		
Back-up light switch:	33 ft. lbs.	45 Nm
Center drive shaft-to-cylinder block (1985–86):	40 ft. lbs.	54 Nm
Control shift cover:	27 ft. lbs.	37 Nm
Drain plug:	29 ft. lbs.	39 Nm
Drive shaft-to-side gear shaft (1989–91):	27 ft. lbs.	36 Nm
Drive shaft center bearing bracket (1989–91):	24 ft. lbs.	32 Nm
5th driven gear lock nut:	90 ft. lbs.	122 Nm
Filler plug:	29 ft. lbs.	39 Nm
Front wheel bearing lock nut (1983–91):	137 ft. lbs,	186 Nm
Front wheel bearing lock nut (1992):	217 ft. lbs.	294 Nm
Intermediate shaft bearing bracket-to-cylinder block:	40 ft. lbs.	54 Nm
Intermediate shaft-to-drive shaft:	25 ft. lbs.	34 Nm
Lock ball assembly (1983–86):	27 ft. lbs.	37 Nm
No. 1 lock ball assembly lock nut (1987–88, 1992):	27 ft. lbs.	37 Nm
No. 2 lock ball assembly (1987–88):	13 ft. lbs.	18 Nm
No. 2 lock ball assembly (1992):	17 ft. lbs.	23 Nm
Output shaft bearing lock plate:	13 ft. lbs.	18 Nm
Rear bearing retainer (1983–89):	13 ft. lbs.	18 Nm
Rear bearing retainer (1990–92):	31 ft. lbs.	42 Nm
Reverse idler shaft lock bolt (1983–88):	18 ft. lbs.	24 Nm
Reverse idler shaft lock bolt (1989–92):	22 ft. lbs.	29 Nm
Reverse restrict pin holder:	9 ft. lbs.	12 Nm
Reverse shift arm bracket:	13 ft. lbs.	18 Nm
Reverse shift arm pivot:	13 ft. lbs.	18 Nm
Ring gear-to-differential case:	71 ft. lbs.	96 Nm
Shift fork No. 3:	9 ft. lbs.	12 Nm
Shift fork No. 3-to-shift fork shaft (1987–88, 1992):	13 ft. lbs.	18 Nm
Side bearing retainer:	13 ft. lbs.	18 Nm
Stabilizer bar link-to-lower arm (1992):	47 ft. lbs.	64 Nm
Steering knuckle-to-lower arm (1992):	94 ft. lbs.	127 Nm
Straight screw plug (shift fork shaft No. 2):	9 ft. lbs.	12 Nm
Transaxle case-to-transaxle case:	22 ft. lbs.	30 Nm
Transaxle case-to-case cover (1983–84):	13 ft. lbs.	18 Nm
Transaxle case-to-case cover (1985–92):	22 ft. lbs.	30 Nm
Transaxle case protector:	13 ft. lbs.	18 Nm
Transaxle case-to-lock plate:	18 ft. lbs.	24 Nm
Wheel nut:	76 ft. lbs.	103 Nm
E56F2 AND E56F5		
Back-up light switch:	33 ft. lbs.	45 Nm
Bell crank-to-transaxle case:	14 ft. lbs.	20 Nm
Differential lock indicator switch (E56F5):	29 ft. lbs.	39 Nm
Differential lock sleeve-to-shift fork:	12 ft. lbs.	16 Nm
Driven pinion cage-to-extension housing:	19 ft. lbs.	25 Nm
Driven pinion cage-to-transaxle case:	29 ft. lbs.	39 Nm
Extension housing-to-dynamic damper:	19 ft. lbs.	25 Nm
Oil pipe-to-housing	13 ft. lbs.	17 Nm
Oil pump-to-cover:	8 ft. lbs.	10 Nm
Oil pump-to-transaxle case:	13 ft. lbs.	17 Nm
Rear bearing retainer-to-transaxle case:	31 ft. lbs.	42 Nm
Ring gear-to-differential case:	91 ft. lbs.	124 Nm
Ring gear-to-ring gear mounting cage:	71 ft. lbs.	97 Nm
Shift and select lever shaft assembly-to-transaxle case:	14 ft. lbs.	20 Nm
Shift fork-to-shaft	17 ft. lbs.	24 Nm
Transaxle assembly-to-transfer assembly:	51 ft. lbs.	69 Nm
Transaxle case-to-transaxle case:	22 ft. lbs.	29 Nm
Transaxle case-to-transaxle case cover:	22 ft. lbs.	29 Nm

TORQUE SPECIFICATIONS

Component	U.S.	Metric
Transfer case-to-actuator bracket (E56F5):	27 ft. lbs.	37 Nm
Transfer case-to-transaxle right case:	33 ft. lbs.	44 Nm
Transfer case-to-inspection hole cover:	12 ft. lbs.	16 Nm
Transfer right case-to-transfer case cover:	13 ft. lbs.	17 Nm
E52		
Back-up light switch:	30 ft. lbs.	40 Nm
Center driveshaft bearing lock nut:	24 ft. lbs.	32 Nm
Control shaft-to-lock bolt:	14 ft. lbs.	20 Nm
Differential case-to-differential case:	46 ft. lbs.	63 Nm
Drain plug:	29 ft. lbs.	39 Nm
Driveshaft bearing bracket-to-bracket stay:	48 ft. lbs.	65 Nm
Driveshaft-to-center drive shaft:	48 ft. lbs.	65 Nm
Driveshaft-to-side gear shaft:	48 ft. lbs.	65 Nm
Elbow-to-transaxle:	20 ft. lbs.	27 Nm
Elbow-to-oil cooler tube:	25 ft. lbs.	34 Nm
Engine left mounting-to-left stay:	38 ft. lbs.	52 Nm
Engine mounting bracket-to-body bracket:	38 ft. lbs.	52 Nm
5th driven gear lock nut:	90 ft. lbs.	122 Nm
Filler plug:	29 ft. lbs.	39 Nm
Front wheel bearing lock nut:	137 ft. lbs.	186 Nm
Insulator-to-engine front mounting:	58 ft. lbs.	78 Nm
Oil pump-to-cover:	8 ft. lbs.	10 Nm
Reverse idler shaft lock bolt:	22 ft. lbs.	29 Nm
Reverse restrict pin holder:	9 ft. lbs.	13 Nm
Reverse shift arm bracket:	13 ft. lbs.	18 Nm
Ring gear-to-differential case:	91 ft. lbs.	124 Nm
Selecting bell crank set bolt:	14 ft. lbs.	20 Nm
Shift and select lever lock bolt:	36 ft. lbs.	49 Nm
Shift fork-to-lock bolt:	17 ft. lbs.	24 Nm
Straight screw plug:	18 ft. lbs.	25 Nm
Transaxle case-to-transaxle case:	22 ft. lbs.	30 Nm
Transaxle case-to-case cover:	22 ft. lbs.	29 Nm
Transaxle case-to-oil pump:	13 ft. lbs.	17 Nm
Transaxle case-to-rear bearing retainer:	31 ft. lbs.	42 Nm
Transaxle-to-engine front mounting:	38 ft. lbs.	52 Nm
Transaxle-to-stiffener plate:	27 ft. lbs.	37 Nm
Transaxle-to-engine mounting left stay:	38 ft. lbs.	52 Nm
Transaxle-to-rear end plate:	18 ft. lbs.	25 Nm
Transaxle-to-case protector:	18 ft. lbs.	25 Nm
Wheel nut:	76 ft. lbs.	103 Nm
E53		
Back-up light switch:	30 ft. lbs.	40 Nm
Differential case-to-differential case:	46 ft. lbs.	63 Nm
Driveshaft-to-side gear shaft:	48 ft. lbs.	65 Nm
Engine-to-stiffener plate:	13 ft. lbs.	18 Nm
5th driven gear lock nut:	90 ft. lbs.	122 Nm
Front suspension member-to-body:	134 ft. lbs.	181 Nm
Front suspension member-to-engine front mounting:	58 ft. lbs.	78 Nm
Front wheel bearing lock nut:	217 ft. lbs.	294 Nm
Oil pump-to-cover:	8 ft. lbs.	10 Nm
Reverse idler gear lock bolt:	22 ft. lbs.	29 Nm
Ring gear-to-differential case:	91 ft. lbs.	124 Nm
Selecting bell crank set bolt:	14 ft. lbs.	20 Nm
Shift and select lever lock bolt:	14 ft. lbs.	20 Nm
Shift lever lock bolt:	36 ft. lbs.	49 Nm
Speed sensor lock bolt:	5 ft. lbs.	7 Nm

TORQUE SPECIFICATIONS

Component	U.S.	Metric
Stabilizer bar link-to-lower arm:	47 ft. lbs.	64 Nm
Steering knuckle-to-lower arm:	94 ft. lbs.	127 Nm
Transaxle case-to-transaxle case:	46 ft. lbs.	63 Nm
Transaxle case-to-case cover:	40 ft. lbs.	54 Nm
Transaxle case-to-oil pump:	13 ft. lbs.	17 Nm
Transaxle case-to-rear bearing retainer:	31 ft. lbs.	42 Nm
Transmission case-to-case cover:	22 ft. lbs.	29 Nm
Transaxle-to-stiffener plate:	27 ft. lbs.	37 Nm
Transaxle-to-starter:	29 ft. lbs.	39 Nm
Wheel nut:	76 ft. lbs.	103 Nm
Clutch		
Bleeder plug (1986–87):	8 ft. lbs.	11 Nm
Bleeder plug (1992):	6 ft. lbs.	8 Nm
Clutch cover-to-flywheel:	14 ft. lbs.	19 Nm
Clutch line union (1988):	11 ft. lbs.	15 Nm
Flywheel-to-crankshaft:	65 ft. lbs.	88 Nm
Master cylinder set bolt (1983–91):	9 ft. lbs.	12 Nm
Master cylinder set bolt (1992):	5 ft. lbs.	8 Nm
Release cylinder set bolt:	9 ft. lbs.	12 Nm
Release fork support (1989–91):	35 ft. lbs.	47 Nm
Release fork support (1992 with 4 cylinder engine):	29 ft. lbs.	39 Nm
Release fork support (1992 with 6 cylinder engine):	35 ft. lbs.	47 Nm
Reservoir tank-to-master cylinder (1986–87):	18 ft. lbs.	24 Nm
Starter-to-transaxle:	29 ft. lbs.	39 Nm
Transaxle-to-engine		
12mm bolts:	47 ft. lbs.	64 Nm
10mm bolts:	32 ft. lbs.	43 Nm
Automatic Transmission		
Cooler pipe union plug:	25 ft. lbs.	34 Nm
Drain plug (1983–85):	22 ft. lbs.	30 Nm
Drain plug (1986–92):	36 ft. lbs.	49 Nm
Drive plate-to-crankshaft:	61 ft. lbs.	83 Nm
Drive plate-to-crankshaft (1986 Diesel):	65 ft. lbs.	85 Nm
Neutral start switch bolt:	48 inch lbs.	6 Nm
Neutral start switch nut:	61 inch lbs.	7 Nm
Oil pan:	43 inch lbs.	5 Nm
Oil strainer:	7 ft. lbs.	10 Nm
Testing plug:	65 inch lbs.	7 Nm
Torque converter-to-drive plate:	20 ft. lbs.	27 Nm
Transaxle-to-engine		
12mm bolts:	47 ft. lbs.	64 Nm
10mm bolts:	32 ft. lbs.	43 Nm
Driveline		
Center support bearing-to-body:	27 ft. lbs.	37 Nm
Cross groove joint set bolt:	20 ft. lbs.	27 Nm
Intermediate shaft-to-center support bearing-to-joint flange:		
1st:	134 ft. lbs.	181 Nm
3rd:	51 ft. lbs.	69 Nm
Propeller shaft-to-differential:	54 ft. lbs.	74 Nm
Propeller shaft-to-intermediate shaft:	54 ft. lbs.	74 Nm

TORQUE SPECIFICATIONS

Component	U.S.	Metric
Rear Axle		
Axle shaft bearing lock nut:	137 ft. lbs.	186 Nm
Axle shaft-to-side gear shaft:	51 ft. lbs.	69 Nm
Carrier-to-side bearing cap:	58 ft. lbs.	78 Nm
Carrier-to-carrier cover:	34 ft. lbs.	47 Nm
Companion flange-to-propeller shaft:	54 ft. lbs.	74 Nm
Differential-to-support member (under side):	70 ft. lbs.	95 Nm
Differential-to-support member (rear side):	108 ft. lbs.	147 Nm
Drain plug:	36 ft. lbs.	49 Nm
Fill plug:	29 ft. lbs.	39 Nm
Ring gear-to-differential case:	71 ft. lbs.	97 Nm

ALIGNMENT (WHEEL)
Front 8-15
Rear 8-24
COMBINATION SWITCH 8-25
FRONT SUSPENSION
Ball joints
Lower 8-6
Axle hub and bearings 8-12
Strut rod 8-22
Lower control arm 8-9
MacPherson struts 8-27
Stabilizer bar 8-9
Steering knuckle 8-12
Wheel lug studs 8-2
Wheel alignment 8-15
FRONT WHEEL BEARINGS 8-12
IGNITION SWITCH AND LOCK CYLINDER 8-25
LOWER BALL JOINT 8-6
LOWER CONTROL ARM 8-9
MANUAL STEERING GEAR
Adjustments 8-28
Removal and installation 8-29
POWER STEERING GEAR
Adjustments 8-28
Removal and installation 8-29
POWER STEERING PUMP
Adjustments 8-35
Bleeding 8-35
Removal and installation 8-32
REAR SUSPENSION
Rear wheel bearings 8-22
Rear strut rod 8-22
Rear suspension arm 8-19
MacPherson struts 8-17
Stabilizer bar 8-22
SPECIFICATIONS CHARTS
Wheel alignment 8-16
STABILIZER BAR
Front 8-9
Rear 8-22
STEERING COLUMN
Removal and installation 8-26
STEERING GEAR
Manual 8-28
Power 8-28
STEERING LINKAGE
Tie rod ends 8-28
STEERING WHEEL 8-24
TIE ROD ENDS 8-28
TROUBLESHOOTING CHARTS
Ignition switch 8-25
Power steering pump 8-38, 39, 40
Turn signal switch 8-36, 37, 38
WHEEL ALIGNMENT
Front 8-15
Rear 8-24
Specifications 8-16

8

SUSPENSION AND STEERING

Front Suspension 8-2
Rear Suspension 8-17
Steering 8-24
Front Wheel Alignment Specifications 8-39

WHEELS

Wheels

REMOVAL & INSTALLATION

1. If using a lug wrench, loosen the lug nuts before raising the vehicle.
2. Raise the vehicle and support safely.
3. Remove the lug nuts and wheel from the vehicle.

To install:

4. Install the wheel and hand tighten the lug nuts until they are snug.
5. Lower the vehicle and torque the lug nuts to 76–90 ft. lbs. (103–122 Nm).

Wheel Lug Studs

REPLACEMENT

Front Wheel

1. Raise and support the vehicle safely. Remove the front wheels.
2. Remove the cotter pin from the bearing locknut cap and then remove the cap.
3. Depress the brake pedal and loosen the bearing locknut.
4. Remove the brake caliper mounting nuts, position the caliper aside with the hydraulic line still attached and suspend it with a wire.
5. Remove the brake disc.
6. Remove the cotter pin and nut from the tie rod end and then, using a tie rod end removal tool, remove the tie rod.
7. Place matchmarks on the shock absorber lower mounting bracket and the camber adjustment cam, remove the bolts and separate the steering knuckle from the strut.
8. Remove the 2 ball joint attaching nuts and disconnect the lower control arm from the steering knuckle.
9. Carefully grasp the axle hub and knuckle assembly and pull it out from the halfshaft using the proper tool.

➡ Cover the halfshaft boot with a shop rag to protect it from any damage.

10. Clamp the steering knuckle in a vise and remove the dust deflector. Remove the nut holding the steering knuckle to the ball joint. Press the ball joint out of the steering knuckle.
11. Remove the dust deflector from the hub.
12. Pry out the bearing inner oil seal and then remove the hole snap-ring.
13. Remove the 3 bolts attaching the steering knuckle to the disc brake dust cover.
14. Remove the axle hub from the steering knuckle using the proper tool.
15. If equipped with ABS, unbolt the ABS sensor control rotor using appropriate Torx® wrench and remove from axle hub.
16. Drive the lug from the hub using a hammer or press.

To install:

17. Install the new lug bolt and draw into place using the nut and a stack of washers.
18. Install the ABS sensor control rotor as required.
19. Install the disc brake dust cover onto the knuckle.
20. Apply grease between the oil seal lip, oil seal and the bearing and then press the axle hub into the steering knuckle.
21. Install a new hole snap-ring into the knuckle.
22. Press a new oil seal onto the knuckle and coat the contact surface of the seal and the halfshaft with grease. Press a new dust deflector into the knuckle.
23. Position the ball joint on the steering knuckle and tighten the nut to 14 ft. lbs. (20 Nm). Remove the nut, install a new one and torque the nut to 94 ft. lbs. (127 Nm).
24. Connect the knuckle assembly to the lower strut bracket. Insert the mounting bolts from the rear and make sure the matchmarks made earlier are in alignment. Tighten the nuts as follows:
   - 152 ft. lbs. (206 Nm) on 1983–87 vehicles.
   - 166 ft. lbs. (226 Nm) on 1988 vehicle.
   - 224 ft. lbs. (304 Nm) on 1989–91 vehicles.
   - 156 ft. lbs. (211 Nm) on 1992 vehicle.
25. Connect the tie rod end to the knuckle, tighten the nut to 36 ft. lbs. (49 Nm) and install a new cotter pin.
26. Connect the ball joint to the lower control arm and tighten the retainer as follows:
   - Lower ball joint to knuckle mounting nut on 1986 Camry—67 ft. lbs. (91 Nm).
   - Lower ball joint to knuckle mounting nut on 1989–92 Camry—90 ft. lbs. (123 Nm).
27. Install the brake disc and the caliper. Tighten the caliper mounting bolts to 86 ft. lbs. (117 Nm).
28. Install the bearing locknut while having someone depress the brake pedal. Tighten it to 137 ft. lbs. (186 Nm). Install the adjusting nut cap and insert a new cotter pin.
29. Check the front end alignment.

Rear

DRUM BRAKES

1. Raise the vehicle and support safely.
2. Remove the wheel.
3. Remove the brake drum from the vehicle.
4. Drive the lug bolt out of the axle flange.

To install:

5. Draw the lug bolt into the brake drum using the nut and a stack of washers.
6. Install the brake drum onto the vehicle.
7. Install the wheel, lower the vehicle and check operation.

REAR DISC BRAKES

1. Raise the vehicle and support safely.
2. Remove the rear wheel.
3. Remove the caliper and brake rotor as outlined in section 9.
4. Remove the wheel lug bolt by tapping bolt through hub with a hammer. Be careful not to damage the ABS rotor which is located oh the back side of the hub.

To install:

5. Draw the new lug bolt into the hub using the nut and a stack of washers.
6. Install the caliper and brake rotor as outlined in section 9.
7. Install the rear wheel and lower the vehicle.

FRONT SUSPENSION

MacPherson Struts

REMOVAL & INSTALLATION

1983-86

➧ SEE FIGS. 1 AND 2

1. Raise and support the front end on jackstands placed under the frame pads.
2. Remove the front wheels.
3. Using a line nut wrench, disconnect the brake tube and flexible hose from the clamp. Drain the brake fluid into a plastic container.
4. Using needle nose pliers, remove the two clips and E-rings from the brake tube support bracket.
5. Remove the two retaining bolts and separate the brake pad from the brake caliper.

➡ Do not disconnect the brake hose from the caliper.

6. Matchmark the shock absorber lower mounting bracket with the camber adjusting cam.
7. Remove the nuts and bolts and disconnect the steering knuckle and the shock absorber.
8. Remove the three bolts from the top of the suspension support.
9. Remove the shock absorber from the body.

➡ Cover the driveshaft boot with a cloth to prevent damage.

To install:

10. Position the shock absorber onto the body and install the three nuts. Torque the nuts to 27 ft. lbs. (36 Nm).
11. Coat the threads of the steering knuckle retaining nuts with clean engine oil.
12. Connect the steering knuckle to the shock absorber lower bracket.
13. Insert the mounting bolts from the rear side and align the matchmarks made on the camber adjusting cam. Torque the nuts to 157 ft. lbs.
14. There is a bearing located under the suspension support dust cover. Remove the dust cover and pack the bearing with multi-purpose grease. Once packed, reinstall the dust cover.
15. Install the brake caliper and torque the retaining bolts to 65 ft. lbs.
16. Install the two clips and E-rings.
17. Connect the brake tube to the flexible hose.
18. Bleed the brake lines as described in Section 9.
19. Have the front wheel alignment checked.

1987-88

➧ SEE FIG. 3

1. Raise and support the front end on jackstands placed under the frame pads.
2. Remove the front wheels.
3. Disconnect the brake from the caliper by removing the union bolt from the banjo fitting. Drain the brake fluid into a plastic container.

➡ The union bolt uses gaskets to seal the bolt to the caliper. Discard the bolt gaskets and purchase new ones.

4. Using needle nose pliers, remove the clip from the brake tube support bracket.
5. Pull the brake hose from the support bracket.
6. Matchmark the shock absorber lower mounting bracket with the camber adjusting cam.
7. Remove the nuts and bolts and disconnect the steering knuckle and the shock absorber.
8. Remove the three bolts from the top of the suspension support.
9. Remove the shock absorber from the body.

➡ Cover the driveshaft boot with a cloth to prevent damage.

To install:

10. Position the shock absorber onto the body and install the three nuts. Torque the nuts to 47 ft. lbs. (64 Nm).
11. Coat the threads of the steering knuckle retaining nuts with clean engine oil.
12. Connect the steering knuckle to the shock absorber lower bracket.
13. Insert the mounting bolts from the rear side and align the matchmarks made on the camber adjusting cam. Torque the nuts to 166 ft. lbs.
14. There is a bearing located under the suspension support dust cover. Remove the dust cover and pack the bearing with multi-purpose grease. Once packed, reinstall the dust cover.
15. Route the brake hose through the bracket and secure with the clip.
16. Connect the brake hose with the union bolt and new gaskets to the brake caliper. Torque the union bolt to 22 ft. lbs. (29 Nm).

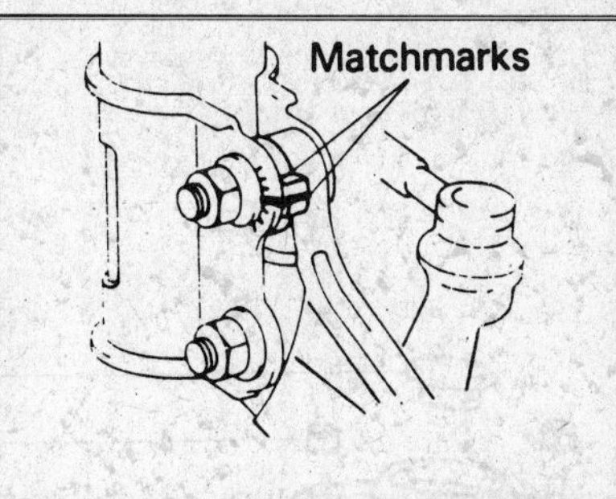

FIG. 1 Camber adjusting cam alignment marks

➡ When connecting the brake hose banjo fitting to the caliper, make sure that the peg on the brake hose fitting aligns with the locating hole on the caliper.

17. Install the hose clip.
18. Bleed the brake lines as described in Section 9.
19. Align the front suspension.

1989-92

➧ SEE FIG. 4

1. Remove the hubcap and loosen the lug nuts.
2. Raise and support the vehicle safely.

➡ Do not support the weight of the vehicle on the suspension arm; the arm will deform under its weight.

3. Unfasten the lug nuts and remove the wheel.
4. Remove the brake hose and the ABS speed sensor wire from the shock absorber.
5. Matchmark on the strut lower bracket and camber adjust cam, if equipped. Remove the 2 bolts and nuts which attach the strut lower end to the steering knuckle lower arm.
6. Remove the 3 nuts which secure the upper strut mounting plate to the top of the wheel arch and remove the shock absorber with coil spring.

To install:

7. Align the hole in the upper suspension support with the shock absorber piston or end, so they fit properly.
8. Always use a new nut and nylon washer on the shock absorber piston rod end when securing it to the upper suspension support. Torque the nut to 29–40 ft. lbs. (39–54 Nm).

➡ Do not use an impact wrench to tighten the nut.

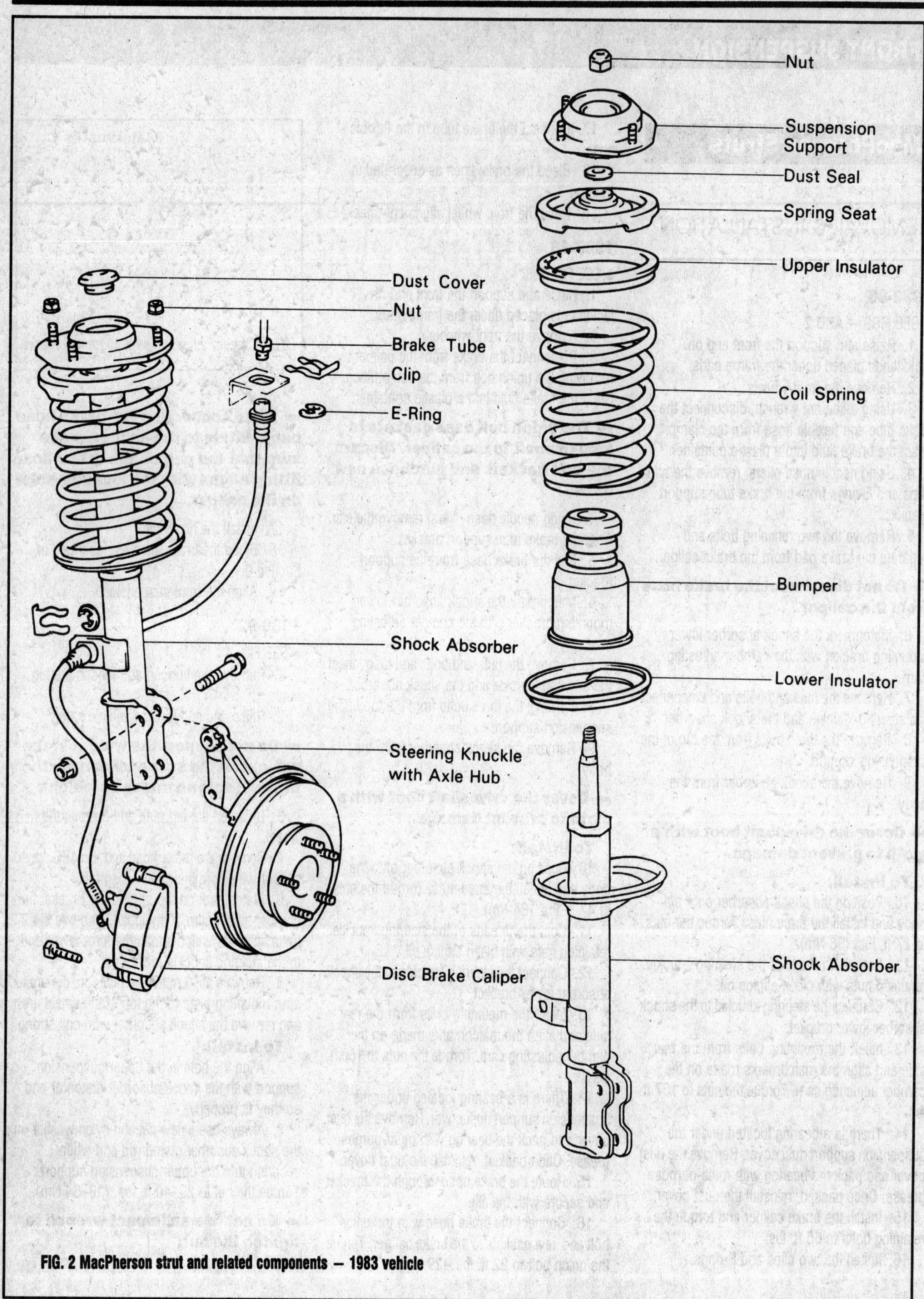

FIG. 2 MacPherson strut and related components — 1983 vehicle

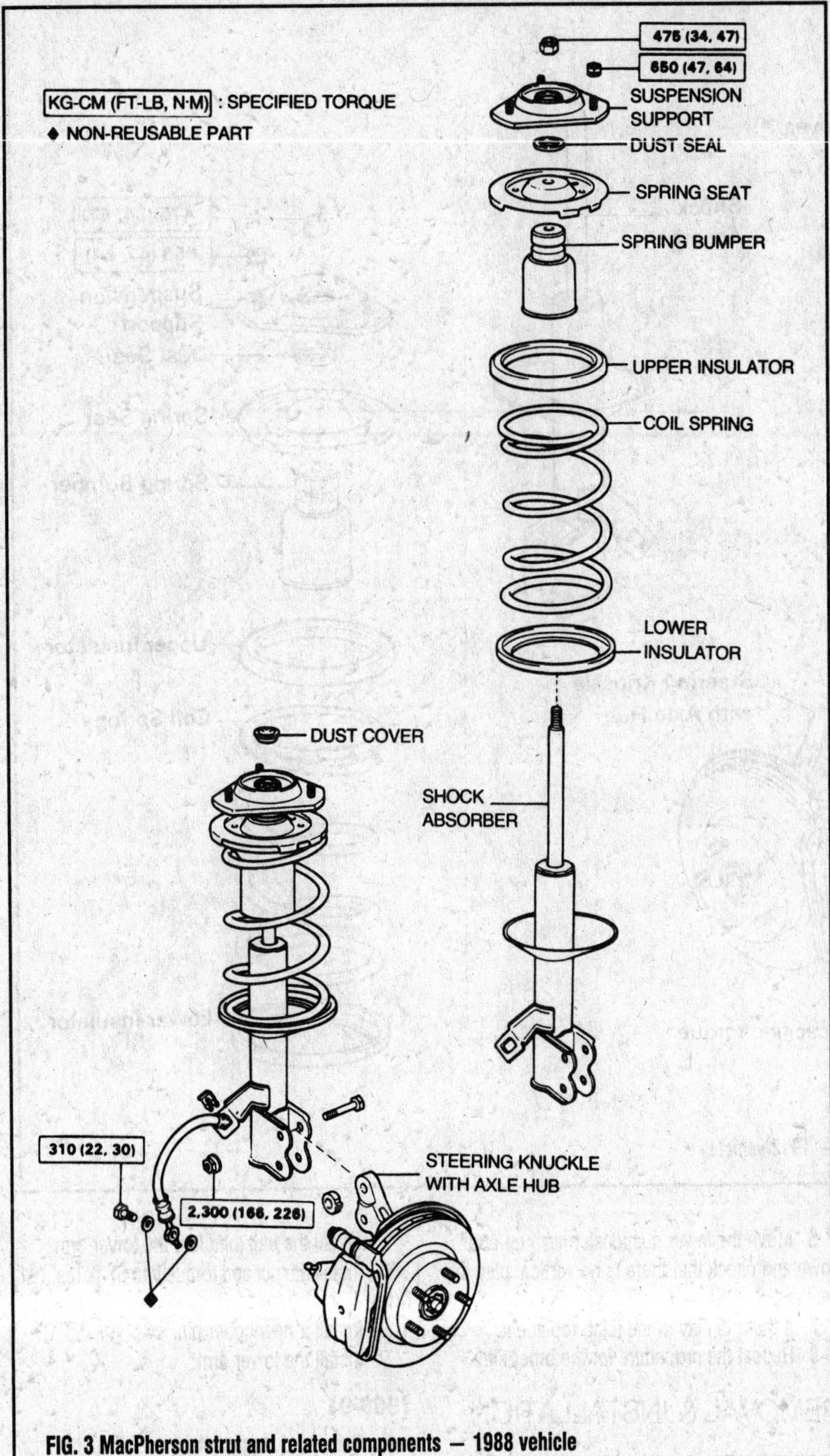

FIG. 3 MacPherson strut and related components — 1988 vehicle

9. Coat the suspension support bearing with multipurpose grease prior to installation. Pack the space in the upper support with multipurpose grease, also, after installation.
10. Tighten 3 suspension support-to-wheel arch nuts to 47 ft. lbs. (64 Nm). On 1992 models torque to 59 ft. lbs. (80 Nm).
11. Tighten the shock absorber-to-steering knuckle arm bolts to 224 ft. lbs. (304 Nm) on 1989–91 models and 156 ft. lbs. (211 Nm) on 1992 models.
12. Install the ABS speed sensor and the brake hose to the shock absorber, if equipped.
13. Install the front tire and wheel assembly. Have the front wheel alignment checked.

DISASSEMBLY

All Models

1. Remove the strut from the vehicle.
2. Position a bolt (about the size of a 14mm socket) and two nuts between the bracket at the lower portion of the shock absorber shell and clamp shock absorber in a vise. The bolt acts as a spacer to allow for clamping without crushing the bracket.
3. Using SST No. 09727-22032 or a suitable spring compressor, compress the coil spring.

CAUTION

Failure to fully compress the spring and hold it securely is extremely hazardous.

4. Using SST No. 09727-22032 or suitable clamping device, hold the spring seat so that it will not turn and remove the center nut. Discard the nut.
5. Slowly release the coil spring tension.
6. Remove the suspension support, spring seat, spring insulators and bumper.
7. While pushing on the piston rod, make sure that the pull stroke is even and that there is no unusual noise or resistance.
8. Push the piston rod in and then release it. Make sure that the return rate is constant.
9. If the shock absorber does not operate as described, replace it.

Before discarding the shock absorber, first loosen the ring nut, if equipped, about two or three turns to allow the gas inside to be released.

ASSEMBLY

1. Install the bumper onto the piston rod.
2. Compress the coil spring with the spring compressor.
3. Install the lower insulator.
4. Align the coil spring end with the lower seat hollow and install.
5. Install the upper insulator.
6. Face the **OUT** mark of the spring seat toward the outside of the vehicle.
7. Install the dust seal onto the spring seat.
8. Install the suspension support.
9. Install a new suspension support nut and torque.
10. Release the spring compressor and install the strut into the vehicle.

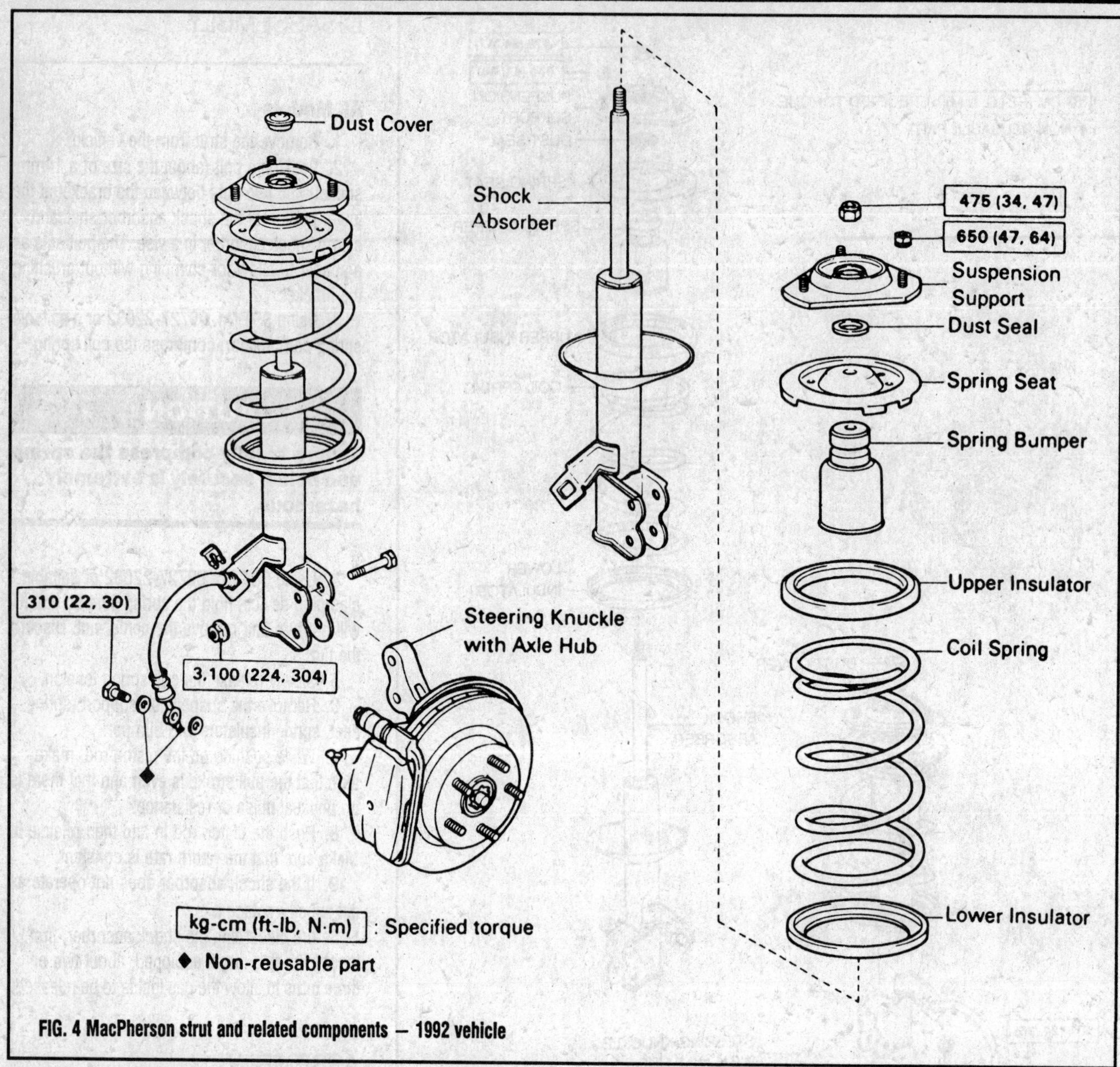

FIG. 4 MacPherson strut and related components — 1992 vehicle

Lower Ball Joint

➧ SEE FIGS. 5–8

INSPECTION

1. Make the front wheels straight and jack up the front of the vehicle.
2. Place an 8 in. (203mm) wooden block under one front tire.
3. Slowly lower the jack until there is about half a load on the front coil spring.
4. Support the front of the vehicle with jackstands for safety.
5. Make sure that the front wheels are still straight and block them.
6. Move the lower suspension arm up and down and check that there is no vertical play in the joint.
7. If there is play in the joint, replace it.
8. Repeat the procedure for the other side.

REMOVAL & INSTALLATION

1983-87

1. Remove the lower suspension arm as described in this Section.
2. Clamp the lower arm in a vise.
3. Remove the cotter pin and the nut.
4. On 1983-86 vehicles, temporarily install the nut to prevent the ball joint from falling out.
5. Using the proper tool or puller, remove the ball joint from the lower arm.
6. Install the ball joint into the lower arm.
7. Install the nut and torque it to 67 ft. lbs. (91 Nm).
8. Install a new cotter pin.
9. Install the lower arm.

1988-91

1. Raise and support the vehicle safely. Remove the wheels.
2. Remove the bolts attaching the ball joint to the steering knuckle.
3. Remove the stabilizer bar nut, retainer and cushion.
4. Remove the nut attaching the lower arm shaft to the lower arm.
5. Remove the lower suspension crossmember (2 bolts and 4 nuts).
6. Remove the lower control arm and lower arm shaft as an assembly.

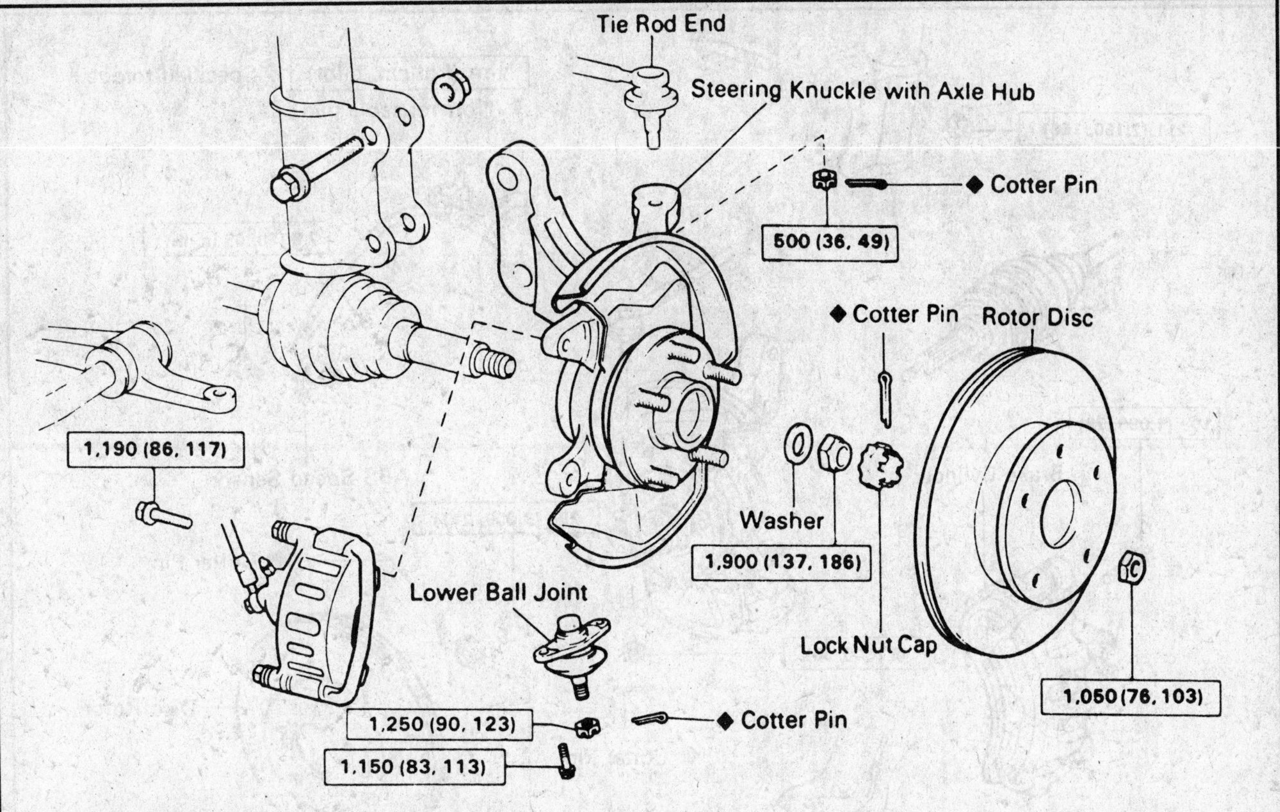

FIG. 5 Ball joint and related components — 1990 vehicle

7. Grip the lower arm assembly in a vise and remove the ball joint cotter pin and retaining nut. With a ball joint removal tool, pull the ball joint out of the control arm.

To install:

8. Position the ball joint in the lower arm and tighten the nut to 67 ft. lbs. (91 Nm) for 1988 or 90 ft. lbs. (123 Nm) for 1989–92. Install a new cotter pin.

9. Install the lower arm to the stabilizer bar and then install the lower arm shaft to the body. Install the lower arm nut and retainer. Screw on a new stabilizer bar end nut and retainer.

10. Connect the ball joint to the steering knuckle and tighten the bolts to 94 ft. lbs. (127 Nm) for 1988 or 83 ft. lbs. (113 Nm) for 1989–92.

11. Install the suspension lower crossmember. Tighten the inner bolts to 32 ft. lbs. (43 Nm) and the outer ones to 153 ft. lbs. (207 Nm).

12. Install the wheels and lower the vehicle. Bounce it several times to set the suspension.

13. Tighten the stabilizer bar end nut and the lower arm shaft-to-lower arm bolt to 156 ft. lbs. (212 Nm).

1992

1. Raise the front of the vehicle and support it safely. Remove the front wheels.

2. Remove side fender apron seal.

3. Remove the steering knuckle with the axle hub, from the vehicle. See appropriate section of this Section for aid in removing the knuckle.

4. Pry the dust deflector from the knuckle using a screw driver.

5. Remove the cotter pin and the nut from the ball joint stud.

6. Using puller, remove the lower ball joint from the steering knuckle.

To install:

7. Install the lower ball joint onto the steering knuckle and tighten nut to 90 ft. lbs. (123 Nm). Install new cotter pin.

8. Using the appropriate driver, install new dust deflector.

9. Install the steering knuckle onto the vehicle.

10. Install the fender apron seal and the front wheels.

FIG. 6 Inspecting the ball joint for vertical play

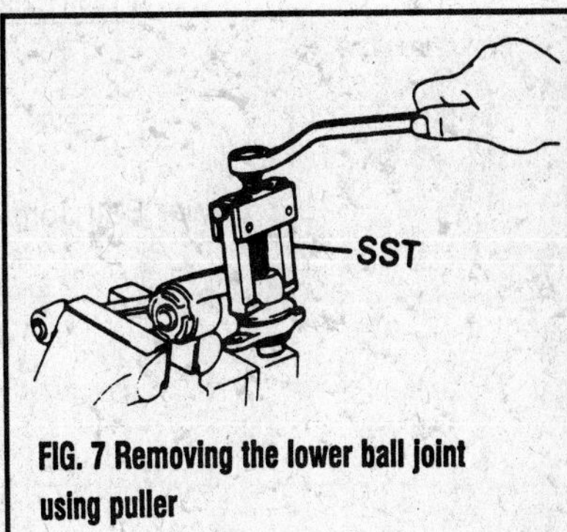

FIG. 7 Removing the lower ball joint using puller

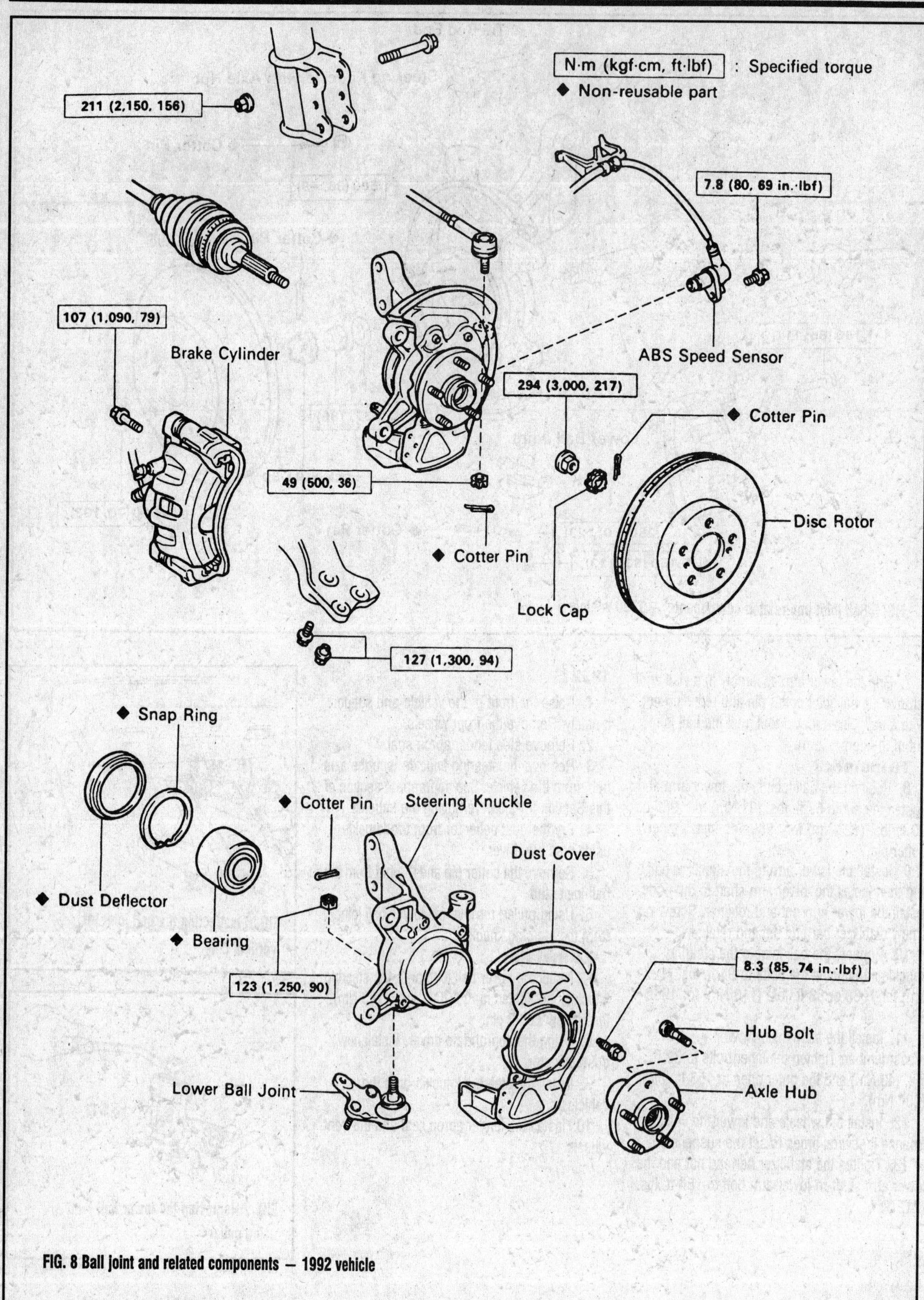

FIG. 8 Ball joint and related components — 1992 vehicle

Stabilizer Bar

REMOVAL & INSTALLATION

1983-86

1. Remove the engine under covers.
2. On 1985-86 vehicles, remove the center support member as follows:
   a. Remove the two access hole covers from the center engine mounting member.
   b. Remove the bolts from the front and rear mountings.
   c. Unbolt the center mounting member.
3. Remove both stabilizer bar brackets from the body.
4. On one side, disconnect the lower stabilizer end from the lower arm.
5. Remove the lower arm on the other side.
6. Remove the stabilizer bar, retainer and spacer.

To install:

7. Install the spacer first and then the retainer.
8. Make the nut finger tight.
9. Pry the bar forward and install the brackets.
10. Torque the bracket retaining bolts to 83 ft. lbs.
11. Install the lower arm on one side and torque the stabilizer bar nut to 86 ft. lbs.
12. On 1985-86 vehicles, install the center support member as follows:
    a. Position the members and install the mounting bolts. Torque the mounting bolts to 29 ft. lbs. (39 Nm).
    b. Install the front and rear mountings and torque the bolts to 29 ft. lbs. (39 Nm).
    c. Install the access covers.
13. Install the engine under covers.
14. Have the front wheel alignment checked.

1987-91

1. Raise the front of the vehicle and support it safely. Remove the front wheels.
2. Unbolt and remove the suspension lower crossmember from the bottom of the vehicle.
3. Remove the nuts attaching the stabilizer bar to the lower arm.
4. Remove the stabilizer bar bracket.
5. Remove the control cable clamp from the engine center mounting member.
6. Unbolt and remove the center mounting member.
7. Withdraw the stabilizer bar from the lower suspension arms.
8. Note their position and remove the spacers and retainers from the bar.

To install:

9. Install the spacers and retainers onto the stabilizer bar in their original order.
10. Connect the stabilizer bar to the lower arms.
11. Install the retainers and temporarily install two new nuts onto the stabilizer bar. They will be tightened later.
12. Install the stabilizer bar brackets with cushions. Torque the retaining bolts to 94 ft. lbs. (127 Nm).
13. Install the engine center mounting member and torque the outside bolts to 153 ft. lbs. (206 Nm) and the inside bolts to 32 ft. lbs. (43 Nm).
14. Install the suspension lower cross member. Torque the outside bolts to 153 ft. lbs. (207 Nm) and the inside bolts to 32 ft. lbs. (43 Nm).
15. Install the wheels and lower the vehicle.
16. Bounce the vehicle up and down a few times to stabilize the suspension.
17. Torque the stabilizer bar nuts to 156 ft. lbs. (212 Nm).
18. Have the front wheel alignment checked.

1992

1. Raise the front of the vehicle and support it safely. Remove the front wheels.
2. Remove both right and left side fender apron seals.
3. Remove the cotter pin and the nut from both side tie rod end studs. Using puller, disconnect right and left tie rod ends from the steering knuckle
4. Remove stabilizer bar links (bolts) from each control arm.
5. Remove the right and left bushing retainers and the bar bushings.
6. Remove the front exhaust pipe.
7. Remove the steering gear box mounting bolts and nuts.
8. Lift the steering gear box and remove the stabilizer bar from the vehicle.

To install:

9. Lift the steering gear box and install bar into position.
10. Install the steering gear box mounting bolts and nuts and torque to 134 ft. lbs. (181 Nm).
11. Install the front exhaust pipe.
12. Install the left and the right stabilizer bar bushings, bushing retainers, and secure with the retaining bolts. Torque the retainer bolts to 14 ft. lbs. (19 Nm).
13. Install both side stabilizer bar links and torque to 47 ft. lbs. (64 Nm).
14. Connect both side tie rod ends to the steering knuckles and tighten the nut to 36 ft. lbs. (49 Nm).
15. Install the left and the right fender apron seals and the front wheels.

Lower Control Arm

SEE FIGS. 9 AND 10

REMOVAL & INSTALLATION

1983-86

1. Raise the front of the vehicle and support it with jackstands. Remove the front wheels.
2. Loosen and remove the two bolts attaching the ball joint to the steering knuckle.
3. Remove the nut that holds the stabilizer bar to the lower control arm.
4. Loosen the lower control arm bolt.
5. Wiggle the stabilizer bar back and forth and pull out the bolt.
6. Remove the lower control arm.

CAUTION

Do not pull on the driveshaft!

7. Remove the retainer and the spacer from the stabilizer bar.
8. Remove and install the ball joint, if necessary.
9. Install the spacer first and then the retainer.
10. Pass the lower arm through the stabilizer.
11. While pushing on the bar and having an assistant pry on the arm with a cresent wrench, temporarily install the bolt.
12. Install the retainer and finger tighten the stabilizer bar nut.
13. Connect the lower arm to the steering knuckle and torque the bolts to 83 ft. lbs. (112 Nm).
14. Install the front wheels and lower the vehicle.
15. Bounce the vehicle up and down several times to settle the suspension.
16. Torque the stabilizer bar nut to 86 ft. lbs. (116 Nm).
17. Torque the lower arm bolt to 83 ft. lbs. (112 Nm).
18. Have the front wheel alignment checked.

1987

1. Raise the front of the vehicle and support it safely.
2. Remove the front wheels.
3. Disconnect the lower ball joint from the steering knuckle.
4. Remove the nut holding the stabilizer bar to the lower arm.
5. Remove the nut holding the lower arm shaft to the lower arm.
6. Unbolt and remove the lower suspension crossmember.

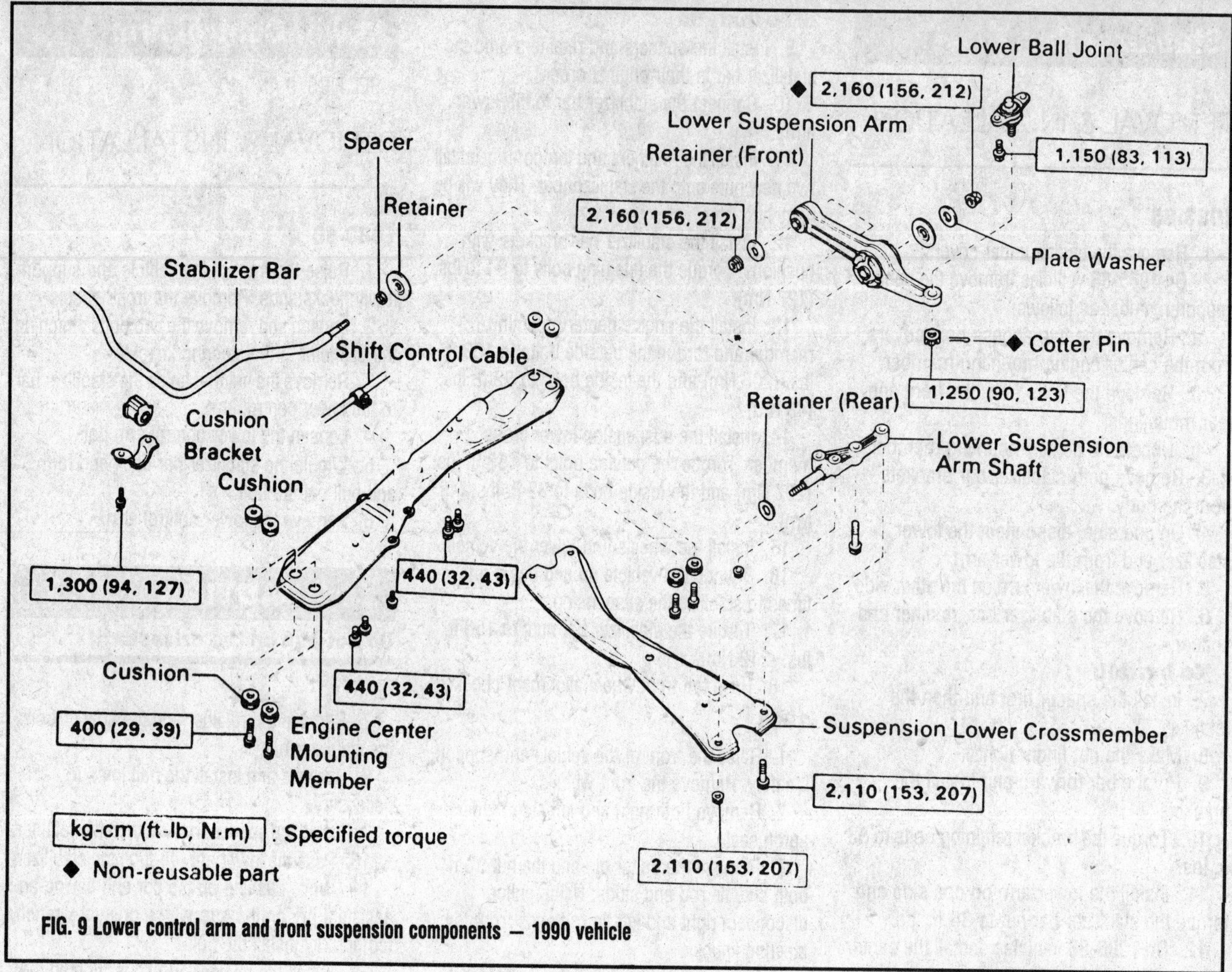

FIG. 9 Lower control arm and front suspension components — 1990 vehicle

7. Remove the lower arm shaft mounting nut and bolt.
8. Remove the lower arm with the lower arm shaft.
9. Remove and install the ball joint as necessary.
10. First insert the lower arm into the stabilizer bar, and then install the lower arm shaft into the body.
11. Temporarily install the lower arm nut and retainer.
12. Temporarily install the new stabilizer nut with the retainer to hold the stabilizer bar to the lower arm.
13. Connect the steering knuckle to the lower ball joint and torque the two bolts to 94 ft. lbs. (127 Nm).
14. Temporarily install the lower arm shaft to the body.
15. Install the suspension lower cross member. Torque the outside bolts to 153 ft. lbs. (207 Nm) and the inside bolts to 32 ft. lbs. (43 Nm).
16. Install the front wheels and lower the vehicle.
17. Bounce the vehicle up and down several times to settle the suspension.
18. Torque the lower suspension arm nuts to 156 ft. lbs. (212 Nm).
19. Have the front wheel alignment checked.

1988–91

1. Raise the vehicle and support safely. Remove the front wheels and the fender apron seal.
2. Disconnect the lower arm from the steering knuckle, at the ball joint.
3. Disconnect the stabilizer bar from the lower arm.
4. Remove the crossmember and lower arm as an assembly. Remove the lower suspension with the lower suspension arm shaft.

To install:

5. Install the crossmember and lower arm assemblies. Loosely install the lower arm bushing bolts. Torque the crossmember bolts to 112 ft. lbs. (152 Nm).
6. Install the ball joint bolts and torque to 90 ft. lbs. (123 Nm).
7. Install the stabilizer nut loosely.
8. Install the front wheels and lower the vehicle. Bounce up and down to stabilize the suspension. With the vehicle weight on the suspension, torque the lower control arm bushing and stabilizer nuts to 156 ft. lbs. (212 Nm).
9. Align the front end.

1992

1. Raise the vehicle and support safely. Remove the front wheels and the fender apron seal.
2. While applying the front brakes, remove the drive shaft lock nut.
3. Disconnect and separate the tie rod end from the steering knuckle.
4. Remove the left and right stabilizer end brackets from the lower arms.
5. Remove the 2 nuts and disconnect the lower arm from the ball joint.
6. Remove the drive shaft from the axle hub. Secure the shaft out of the way using wire. Be careful not to damage the shaft boot or ABS sensor rotor.

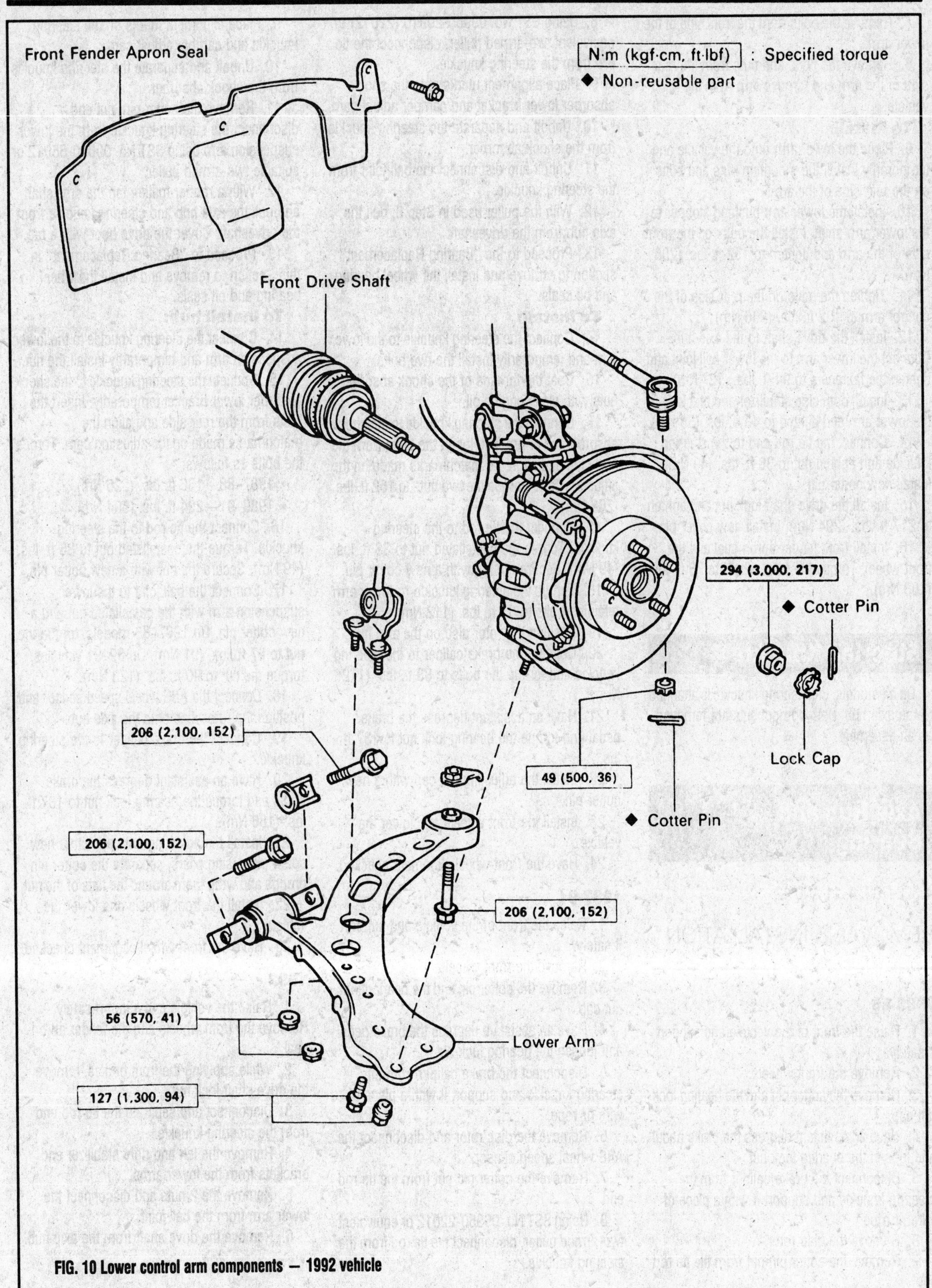

FIG. 10 Lower control arm components — 1992 vehicle

7. Remove the bolts from the front side of the lower arm.

8. Remove the bolts and nuts from the rear side of the arm and remove arm from the vehicle.

To Install:

9. Place the lower arm onto the vehicle and temporarily install the mounting nuts and bolts on the rear side of the arm.

10. Install the lower arm bushing stopper to the lower arm shaft. Install the bolts on the front side of the arm and tighten to 152 ft. lbs. (206 Nm).

11. Tighten the bolts on the rear side of the control arm to 152 ft. lbs. (206 Nm).

12. Install the drive shaft to the axle hub. Connect the lower arm to the lower ball joint and tighten the fasteners to 94 ft. lbs. (127 Nm).

13. Install both side stabilizer end brackets to the lower arm and tighten to 43 ft. lbs. (58 Nm).

14. Connect the tie rod end to the steering knuckle and tighten nut to 36 ft. lbs. (49 Nm). Install new cotter pin.

15. Install the drive shaft lock nut and tighten to 217 ft. lbs. (294 Nm). Install new cotter pin.

16. Install front fender apron seal and the front wheel. Torque the front wheel to 76 ft. lbs. (103 Nm).

Steering Knuckle

On all models, the steering knuckle is attached to the axle hub. Both components are removed as an assembly.

Axle Hub and Bearing

➧ SEE FIGS. 4, 11 AND 12

REMOVAL & INSTALLATION

1983-86

1. Raise the front of the vehicle and support it safely.

2. Remove the front wheels.

3. Remove the cotter pin and the bearing lock nut cap.

4. Have an assistant depress the brake pedal and loosen the bearing lock nut.

5. Disconnect the brake caliper from the steering knuckle and support it with a piece of wire or rope.

6. Remove the disc rotor.

7. Remove the cotter pin nut from the tie rod end.

8. Using SST No. 09950-20016 (22012) or equivalent two-armed puller, disconnect the tie rod from the steering knuckle.

9. Place alignment marks onto the shock absorber lower bracket and camber adjust cam.

10. Unbolt and separate the steering knuckle from the shock absorber.

11. Unbolt and disconnect the ball joint from the steering knuckle.

12. With the puller used in Step 8, pull the axle hub from the driveshaft.

13. Proceed to the "Bearing Replacement" section to remove and install the wheel bearing and oil seals.

To Install:

14. Connect the steering knuckle to the lower arm and temporarily install the two bolts.

15. Coat the threads of the shock absorber nuts with clean engine oil.

16. Connect the steering knuckle to the shock absorber lower bracket. Insert the bolts from the rear side and align the matchmarks made on the adjusting cam. Torque the two nuts to 152 ft. lbs. (206 Nm).

17. Connect the tie rod to the steering knuckle. Torque the castellated nut to 36 ft. lbs. (49 Nm). Secure the nut with a new cotter pin.

18. Torque the steering knuckle-to-lower arm retaining bolts to 83 ft. lbs. (112 Nm).

19. Position the rotor disc on the axle hub.

20. Connect the brake caliper to the steering knuckle and torque the bolts to 83 ft. lbs. (112 Nm).

21. Have an assistant depress the brake pedal and torque the bearing lock nut to 137 ft. lbs.

22. Install the adjusting nut cap with a new cotter pin.

23. Install the front wheels and lower the vehicle.

24. Have the front wheel alignment checked.

1987-91

1. Raise the front of the vehicle and support it safely.

2. Remove the front wheels.

3. Remove the cotter pin and the bearing lock nut cap.

4. Have an assistant depress the brake pedal and loosen the bearing lock nut.

5. Disconnect the brake caliper from the steering knuckle and support it with a piece of wire or rope.

6. Remove the disc rotor and disconnect the ABS wheel speed sensor.

7. Remove the cotter pin nut from the tie rod end.

8. Using SST No. 09950-22012 or equivalent two-armed puller, disconnect the tie rod from the steering knuckle.

9. Place alignment marks on the steering knuckle and camber adjust cam.

10. Unbolt and separate the steering knuckle from the shock absorber.

11. Remove the cotter pin, nut and disconnect the steering knuckle from the lower suspension arm using SST No. 09610-55012 or suitable two-armed puller.

12. With a rubber mallet, tap the driveshaft and pull the axle hub and steering knuckle from the driveshaft. Cover the drive boot with a rag.

13. Proceed to "Bearing Replacement" in this Section to remove and install the wheel bearing and oil seals.

To install hub:

14. Connect the steering knuckle to the lower suspension arm and temporarily install the nut.

15. Connect the steering knuckle to the shock absorber lower bracket temporarily. Insert the bolts from the rear side and align the matchmarks made on the adjusting cam. Torque the bolts as follows:

- 1987–88 – 166 ft. lbs. (226 Nm).
- 1989–91 – 224 ft. lbs. (304 Nm).

16. Connect the tie rod to the steering knuckle. Torque the castellated nut to 36 ft. lbs. (49 Nm). Secure the nut with a new cotter pin.

17. Connect the ball joint to the lower suspension arm with the castellated nut and a new cotter pin. On 1987–88 models, torque the nut to 67 ft. lbs. (91 Nm). On 89–91 vehicles, torque the nut to 90 ft. lbs. (123 Nm).

18. Connect the ABS wheel speed sensor and position the rotor disc onto the axle hub.

19. Connect the brake caliper to the steering knuckle.

20. Have an assistant depress the brake pedal and torque the bearing lock nut to 137 ft. lbs. (186 Nm).

21. Install the adjusting nut cap with a new cotter pin. Using pliers, separate the cotter pin prongs and wrap them around the flats of the nut.

22. Install the front wheels and lower the vehicle.

23. Have the front wheel alignment checked.

1992

1. Raise the vehicle and support safely. Remove the front wheels and the fender apron seal.

2. While applying the front brakes, remove the drive shaft lock nut.

3. Disconnect and separate the tie rod end from the steering knuckle.

4. Remove the left and right stabilizer end brackets from the lower arms.

5. Remove the 2 nuts and disconnect the lower arm from the ball joint.

6. Remove the drive shaft from the axle hub.

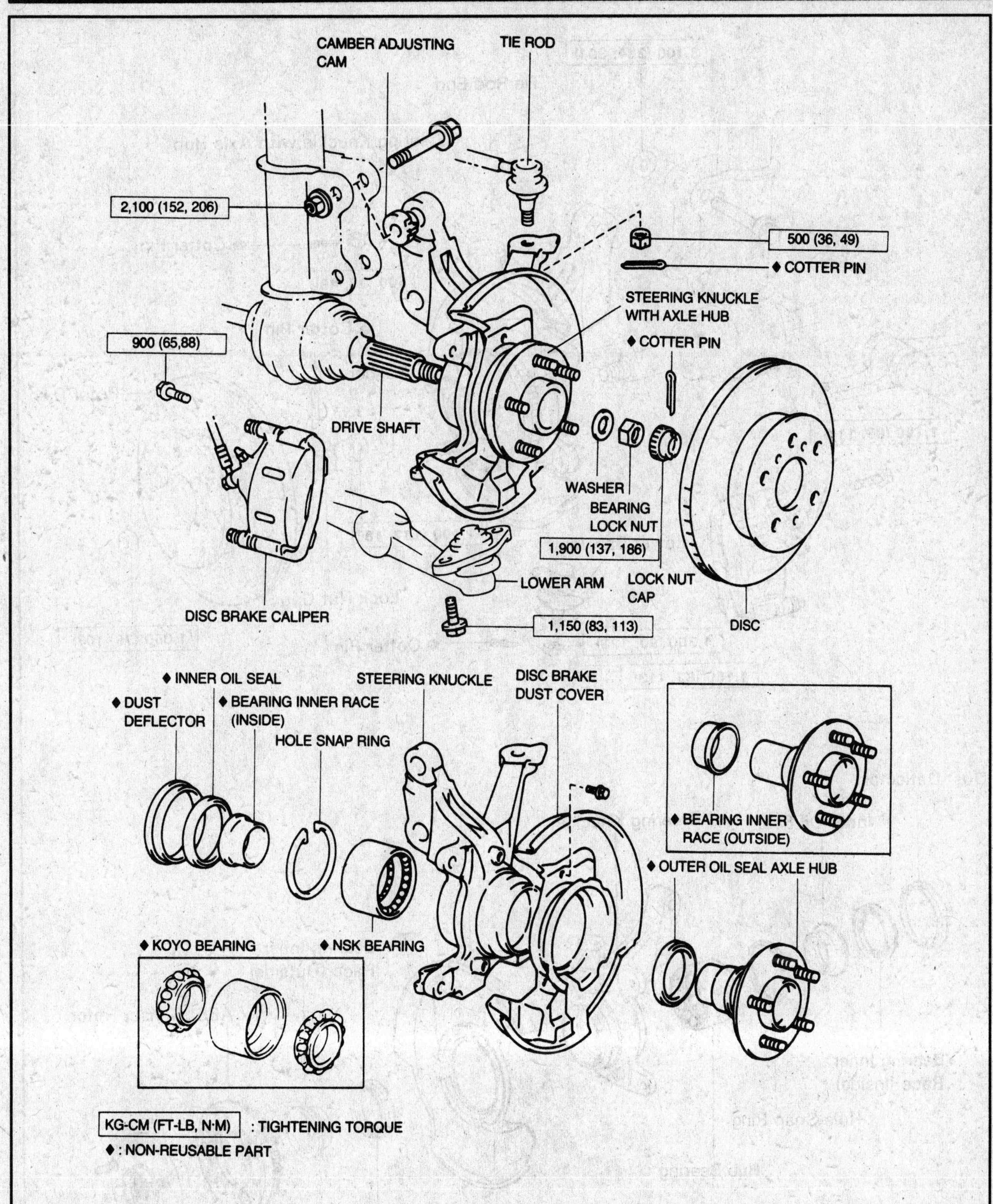

FIG. 11 Axle hub and bearing components — 1988 vehicle

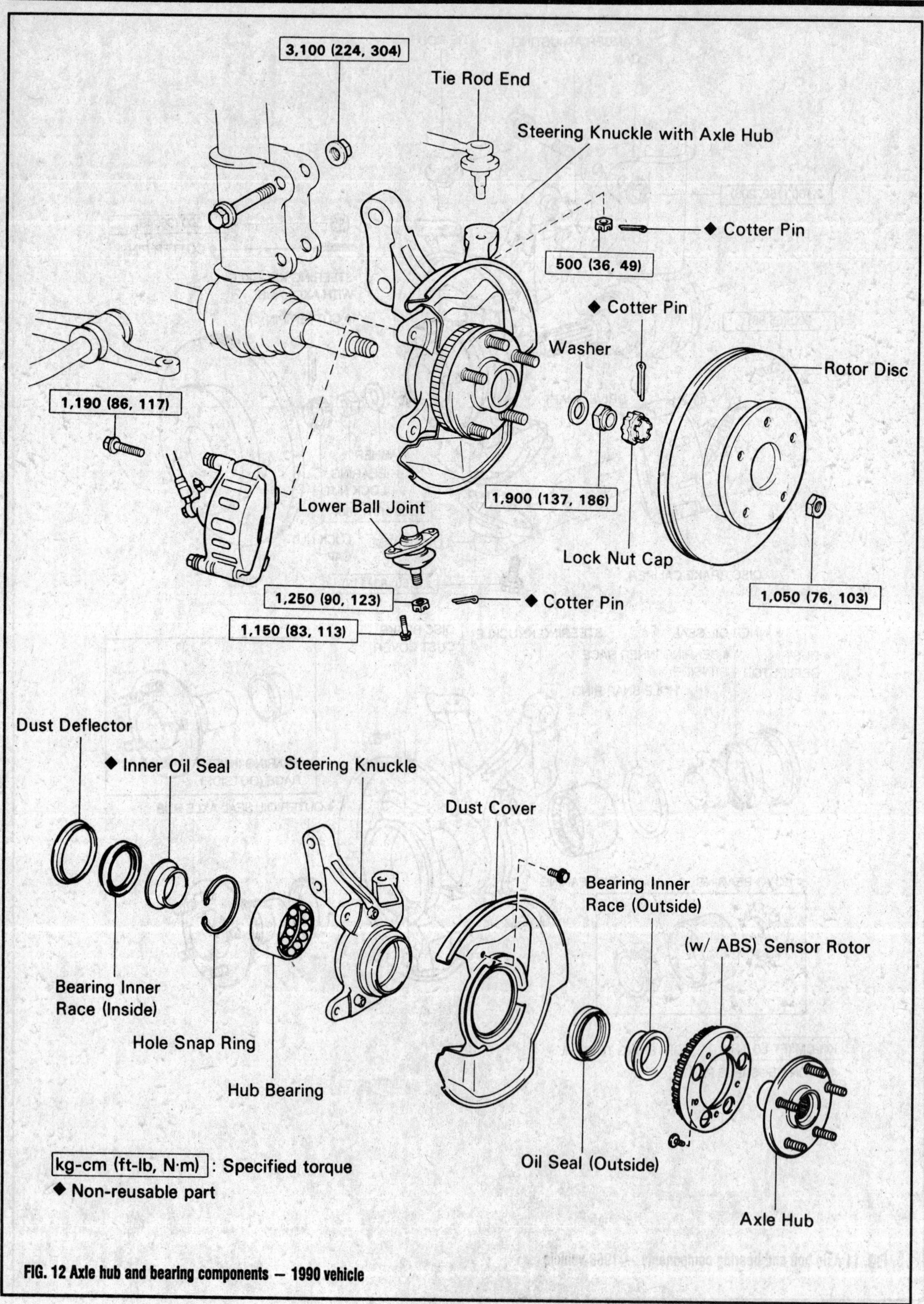

FIG. 12 Axle hub and bearing components — 1990 vehicle

Secure the shaft out of the way using wire. Be careful not to damage the shaft boot or ABS sensor rotor.

7. Remove the 2 brake cylinder mounting bolts and remove the cylinder. Support cylinder from the vehicle using wire. Remove the disc rotor.

8. If equipped with ABS, remove the sensor from the steering knuckle.

9. Remove the 2 nuts on the lower end of the shock and remove the steering knuckle.

To install:

10. Install the steering knuckle onto the vehicle and temporarily install the lower shock bolts.

11. Connect the lower ball joint to the lower arm and tighten the bolt and nuts to 94 ft. lbs. (127 Nm).

12. Connect the tie rod to the knuckle and tighten the nut to 36 ft. lbs. (49 Nm). Install new cotter pin.

13. Torque the nuts on the lower end of the shock to 156 ft. lbs. (211 Nm).

14. Install both side stabilizer end brackets to the lower arm and tighten to 43 ft. lbs. (58 Nm).

15. Install the front ABS sensor and torque to 69 inch lbs. (7.8 Nm).

16. Install the front brake rotor and cylinder. Tighten the cylinder mounting bolts to 79 ft. lbs. (107 Nm).

17. Install the drive shaft locknut, and while applying the brakes, torque to 217 ft. lbs. (294 Nm). Install lock cap and new cotter pin.

18. Install front fender apron seal and the front wheel. Torque the front wheel to 76 ft. lbs. (103 Nm).

BEARING REPLACEMENT

1. Clamp the steering knuckle in a vise with soft jaws to protect the knuckle.

2. Using screw driver, carefully pry the dust deflector from the hub.

3. Drive out the bearing inner oil seal from the knuckle. On 1983-86 vehicles the seal is extracted with a puller. On 1887-92 vehicles, the seal is pried from the knuckle bore.

4. After the seal is removed, use snapring pliers to remove the hole snapring from the knuckle bore.

5. Unbolt and separate the dust deflector from the steering knuckle.

6. Using a two-armed mechanical puller, pull the axle hub from the dust deflector.

7. Using the puller, remove the inner (inside) bearing race from the bearing.

8. Using Torx® wrench, remove the sensor control rotor from the axle hub.

9. Using the puller, remove the outer bearing race. Set the outer race aside.

10. Remove the outer bearing seal in the same manner as the inner seal.

11. Take the inner (outside) race and install it inside the bearing.

12. With a piece of brass stock, tap the bearing from the steering knuckle.

To install bearing:

13. Clean all the oil seal and bearing seating surfaces with a clean, dry rag.

14. Install SST No. 09608-32010 into the bore of the steering knuckle and press the bearing into the bore. Leave the tool in place.

15. Turn and insert the side lip of the new outer oil seal into the factory tool and drive the seal into the steering knuckle.

16. Connect the brake disc cover to the steering knuckle with the bolts.

17. Apply multi-purpose grease between the oil seal lip, oil seal and bearing and press the hub into the knuckle.

18. Install a new snapring in the knuckle.

19. Press a new oil seal into the knuckle and coat the seal with multi-purpose grease.

20. Press the dust deflector into the knuckle.

21. Connect the ball joint to the steering knuckle and torque the bolts to 94 ft. lbs. (127 Nm).

22. Install the steering knuckle onto the vehicle as described earlier in this Section.

Front End Alignment

Front end alignment measurements require the use of special equipment. We recommend that you leave front end alignment adjustments to professional alignment technicians.

CASTER

Caster is the tilt of the front steering axis either forward or backward away from the front of the vehicle. Rearward tilt is referred to as a positive caster, while forward tilt is referred to as negative caster.

CAMBER

Camber is the slope of the front wheels from the vertical when viewed from the front of the vehicle. When the wheels tilt outward at the top, the camber is positive (+). When the wheels tilt inward at the top, the camber is negative (−). The amount of positive and negative camber is measured in degrees from the vertical and the measurement is called camber angle. Camber is preset at the factory, therefore, it is not adjustable.

TOE-IN

Toe-in is the amount, measured in a fraction of an inch, that the front wheels are closer together at one end than the other. Toe-in means that the front wheels are closer together at the front of the tire than at the rear; toe-out means that the rear of the tires are closer together than the front.

The wheels must be dead straight ahead. The car must have a full tank of gas, all fluids must be at their proper levels, all other suspension and steering adjustments must be correct and the tires must be properly inflated to their cold specifications.

FRONT WHEEL ALIGNMENT

Year	Model	Caster Range (deg.)	Caster Preferred Setting (deg.)	Camber Range (deg.)	Camber Preferred Setting (deg.)	Toe-in (in.)	Steering Axis Inclination (deg.)
1983	Camry	①	②	0–1P	1/2P	③	12 1/2
1984	Camry	①	②	0–1P	1/2P	③	12 1/2
1985	Camry	①	②	0–1P	1/2P	③	12 1/2
1986	Camry	7/16P–1 3/4P	1P	3/16N–1 1/4P	9/16P	0–0.16	12 1/2
1987	Camry						
	Sedan	15/16P–2 7/16P	1 11/16P	3/16N–1 5/16P	9/16P	0.04 out–0.12 in	12 3/4
	Wagon	1/4P–1 3/4P	1P	1/4N–1 1/4P	1/2P	0.04 out–0.12 in	13
1988	Camry						
	Sedan	15/16P–2 7/16P	1 11/16P	3/16N–1 5/16P	9/16P	0.04 out–0.12 in	12 3/4
	Wagon	1/4P–1 3/4P	1P	1/4N–1 1/4P	1/2P	0.04 out–0.12 in	13
1989	Camry						
	Sedan	15/16P–2 7/16P	1 11/16P	3/16N–1 5/16P	9/16P	0.04 out–0.12 in	12 3/4
	Wagon	1/4P–1 3/4P	1P	1/4N–1 1/4P	1/2P	0.04 out–0.12 in	13
1990	Camry						
	Sedan	1 3/16P–2 3/16P	1 11/16P	1/16P–1 1/16P	9/16P	0.04 out–0.04 in	12 3/4
	Wagon	1/2P–1 1/2P	1P	0–1P	1/2P	0.04 out–0.04 in	12 13/16
1991	Camry						
	Sedan	1 3/16P–2 3/16P	1 11/16P	1/16P–1 1/16P	9/16P	0.04 out–0.04 in	12 3/4
	Wagon	1/2P–1 1/2P	1P	0–1P	1/2P	0.04 out–0.04 in	12 13/16
1992	Camry	1 3/16P–2 3/16P	1 11/16P	1/16P–1 1/16P	9/16P	0.04 out–0.04 in	12 3/4

① Manual steering: 1/2P–1 1/2P
Power steering: 2P–3P

② Manual steering: 1P
Power steering: 2 1/2P

③ Manual steering: 0
Power steering: 0.08

REAR WHEEL ALIGNMENT

Year	Model	Caster Range (deg.)	Caster Preferred Setting (deg.)	Camber Range (deg.)	Camber Preferred Setting (deg.)	Toe-in (in.)	Steering Axis Inclination (deg.)
1983	Camry	—	—	0–1P	1/2P	0	—
1984	Camry	—	—	0–1P	1/2P	0	—
1985	Camry	—	—	0–1P	1/2P	0	—
1986	Camry	—	—	1/4N–1 1/4P	1/2P	0.08 in–0.24 in	—
1987	Camry	—	—	1/16N–1 1/16P	9/16N	0.08 in–0.24 in	—
1988	Camry	—	—	1/16N–1 1/16P	9/16N	0.08 in–0.24 in	—
1989	Sedan 2WD	—	—	1/16N–1 1/16P	9/16N	0.08 in–0.24 in	—
	Wagon 2WD	—	—	0.04–0.12N	0.08N	0.4 in–0.20 in	—
	4WD	—	—	0–1N	1/2N	0.08 in–0.20 in	—
1990	Sedan 2WD	—	—	3/16N–1 5/16P	9/16N	0.12 in–0.2 in	—
	Wagon 2WD	—	—	0.04–0.12N	0.08N	0.12 in–0.2 in	—
	4WD	—	—	0–1N	1/2N	0.08 in–0.24 in	—
1991	Sedan 2WD	—	—	3/16P–1 5/16N	9/16N	0.12 in–0.2 in	—
	Wagon 2WD	—	—	0.04–0.12N	0.08N	0.12 in–0.2 in	—
	4WD	—	—	0.25P–1.25N	1/2N	0.08 in–0.24 in	—
1992		—	—	0.25P–1.25N	1/2N	0.08 in–0.24 in	—

REAR SUSPENSION

MacPherson Struts

➧ SEE FIG. 13

REMOVAL & INSTALLATION

1983-86

1. On 4-door sedan, remove the package tray and vent duct.
2. On hatchback, remove the speaker grilles.
3. Disconnect the brake line from the wheel cylinder.
4. Remove the brake line from the brake hose.
5. Disconnect the brake hose from its bracket on the strut.
6. Loosen, but do not remove, the nut holding the suspension support to the strut.
7. Unbolt the strut from the rear arm.
8. Unbolt the strut from the body.

To install the strut:

9. Connect the shock absorber to the body and torque the nuts to 17 ft. lbs. (25 Nm).
10. Engage the shock absorber bracket with the carrier and install the hardware. Torque the nuts to 119 ft. lbs. (162 Nm).
11. Torque the center suspension support nut to 36 ft. lbs. There is a bearing located under the suspension support dust cover. Remove the dust cover and pack the bearing with multi-purpose grease. Once packed, reinstall the dust cover.
12. Connect the flexible hose to the shock absorber bracket.
13. Install the brake tube.
14. Fill the brake reservoir with brake fluid and bleed the brakes as described in Section 8.
15. Have the rear wheel alignment checked.
16. On Sedans, install the quarter bent duct and package tray.
17. On Liftbacks, install the speaker grille.

1987-88

1. On Wagon models, remove the tonneau cover holder.
2. Loosen the rear wheel lug nuts, raise the rear of the vehicle and support it safely. Block the front wheels.
3. Remove the rear wheels.
4. Using the proper size flare nut wrench, disconnect the backing plate hardware.
5. With a flare nut and a back-up wrench, disconnect the brake tube from the brake hose and use a small plastic container to collect the brake fluid.
6. Undo the clip and disconnect the brake hose from the shock absorber.

➡ Before the axle bolts are removed, the axle carrier must be supported with a jack.

7. Support the axle carrier with a floor jack and remove the mounting bolts and nut. Disconnect the axle carrier from the shock absorber.
8. Support the shock absorber firmly by hand and remove the three mounting nuts. Remove the shock absorber from the body.

To install:

9. Position the shock absorber onto the body and support it firmly by hand. Install the three nuts and torque them to 23 ft. lbs. (31 Nm).
10. Attach the axle carrier to the shock absorber with the nuts and bolts. Torque the **nuts** to 166 ft. lbs. (226 Nm).
11. Connect the brake tube to the backing plate and brake tube and make the union nuts hand tight.
12. Install the brake hose clip.
13. Torque the brake tube union nuts to 11 ft. lbs. (16 Nm).
14. Install the tonneau cover on Wagon models.
15. Remove the floor jack, install the wheels and lower the vehicle.
16. Bleed the brake lines as described in Section 9.
17. Have the rear wheel alignment checked.

1989-92

2WD

1. On the 4-door sedan, remove the package tray and vent duct. On 1992 models, it will be necessary to remove the rear seat back.
2. On the hatchback, remove the speaker grilles.
3. Disconnect the brake hose and the ABS speed sensor from the shock absorber.
4. If equipped with ABS, disconnect the LSPV spring from the lower arm.
5. Disconnect the stabilizer bar link from the strut.
6. Support the rear axle and remove the 2 bolts from the lower end of the strut.
7. Unbolt the strut from the body and remove from the vehicle.

To install:

8. Install the strut assembly onto the vehicle.
9. Connect the brake hose and the ABS speed sensor to the strut.
10. Connect the stabilizer bar link to the strut.
11. Install the wheel and tire assembly.
12. During installation, please observe the following torque specifications:
    a. Tighten the strut-to-body bolts to 23 ft. lbs. (31 Nm) on 1988 vehicles and 29 ft. lbs. (39 Nm) on 1989–92 vehicles.
    b. Tighten the strut-to-axle carrier bolts 166 ft. lbs. (226 Nm) on 1988–91 vehicles and 188 ft. lbs. (155 Nm) on 1992 vehicles.
    c. Tighten the suspension support-to-strut nut to 36 ft. lbs. (49 Nm) on 1988–91 vehicles. On 1992 models, tighten the stabilizer bar link to strut retainers to 47 ft. lbs. (64 Nm).
13. Install the rear seat back, vent duct and the package tray as required.

DISASSEMBLY

1. Remove the strut from the vehicle.
2. Position a bolt (about the size of a 14mm socket) and two nuts between the bracket at the lower portion of the shock absorber shell and clamp shock absorber in a vise. The bolt acts as a spacer to allow for clamping without crushing the bracket. Remove the suspension support cover.
3. Using SST No. 09727-22032 or a suitable spring compressor, compress the coil spring.

⁂ CAUTION

Failure to fully compress the spring and hold it securely is extremely hazardous.

4. Using SST No. 09727-22032 or suitable clamping device, hold the spring seat so that it will not turn and remove the center nut. Discard the nut.
5. Slowly release the coil spring tension.
6. Scribe alignment marks on the suspension support and the shock absorber. Remove the suspension support, spring seat, spring insulators and bumper.

INSPECTION

1. While pushing on the piston rod, make sure that the pull stroke is even and that there is no unusual noise or resistance.
2. Push the piston rod in and then release it. Make sure that the return rate is constant.
3. If the shock absorber does not operate as described, replace it.

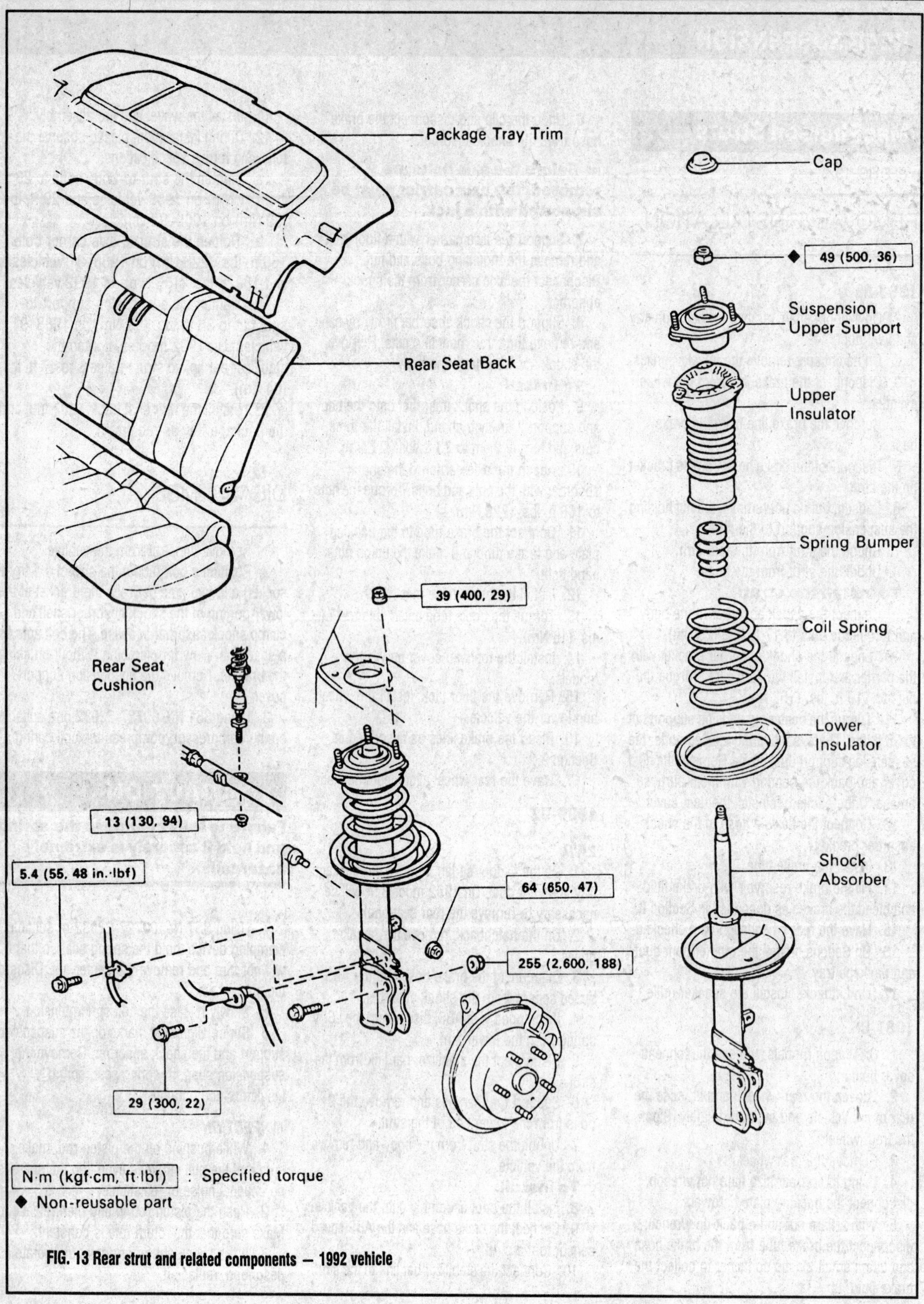

FIG. 13 Rear strut and related components — 1992 vehicle

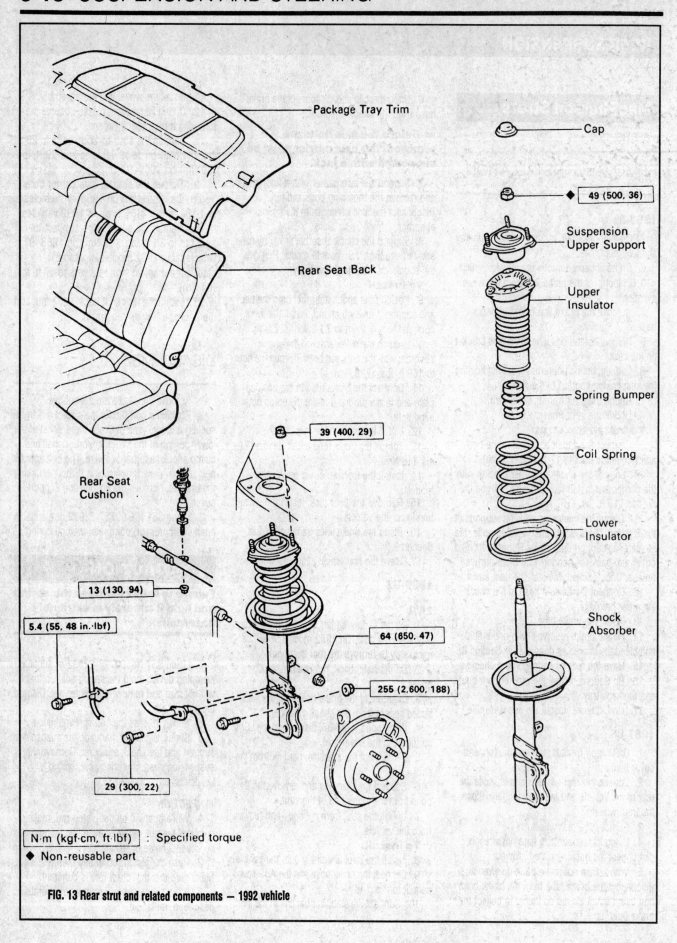

ASSEMBLY

1. Install the bumper onto the piston rod.
2. Slowly compress the coil spring with the spring compressor.
3. Install the lower insulator onto the shock absorber.
4. Align the coil spring end with the lower seat hollow and install it.
5. Install the spring bumper onto the shock absorber piston rod.
6. Install the upper insulator. Match the bolt of the upper support with the cut-off part of the insulator.
7. Install into the upper suspension support and align with the shock absorber scribe marks.
8. Install a new suspension support nut and torque it to 36 ft. lbs. (49 Nm).
9. Install the strut onto the body.

Suspension Arm

REMOVAL & INSTALLATION

1983-86

1. Loosen the rear wheel lug nuts. Raise the rear of the vehicle with a floor jack and support the body with safety stands. Remove the rear wheels.
2. Remove the nut and bolt that connects the No. 2 suspension arm to the axle carrier.
3. Note and record the position of the cam plate mark, then remove the nut and bolt that connects the No. 2 suspension arm to the body. Remove the No. 2 suspension arm.
5. On 1984-86 vehicles, remove the nut, retainer and cushion that connects the No. 1 suspension arm to the stabilizer bar link. Discard the nut and purchase a new one.
6. Disconnect the No. 1 suspension arm from the axle carrier by removing the nut and bolt. Remove the nut and bolt that connects the No. 2 suspension arm to the body.
7. Press the old side body bushing from the No. 1 suspension arm and press in a new bushing. The new bushing need not be lubricated to install it.
8. To install, engage the No. 1 suspension arm with the body and install the nut and bolt so that it is finger tight. The lip of the nut should be resting on the flange of the bracket and not over it.
9. On 1984-86 vehicles, connect the stabilizer link to the No. 1 suspension arm with the cushions, retainers and the new nut. Torque the nut to 11 ft. lbs. (16 Nm).
10. Engage the No. 1 suspension arm with the axle carrier and install the nut and bolt so that they are finger tight. When doing this, insert the lip of the nut into the hole in the arm.
11. Position the No. 2 suspension arm onto the body and temporarily install the cam and bolt.
12. Align the cam plate mark with its original position. Temporarily install the nut and bolt that connects the suspension arm to the body.
13. Install the rear wheels and remove the safety stands.
14. Lower the vehicle and bounce the rear end a few to times to allow the rear suspension to stabilize.
15. Now that the vehicle weight is on the suspension, torque all the previously finger tightened bolts to 64 ft. lbs. (87 Nm).
16. Have the rear alignment checked.

1987-88

1. Loosen the rear wheel lug nuts. Raise the rear of the vehicle with a floor jack and support the body with safety stands. Remove the rear wheels.
2. Disconnect the strut rod from the axle carrier by removing the nut and bolt.
3. Remove the bolt and nut that runs through the No. 1 and No. 2 suspension arms.
4. Remove the fuel tank protector by unlocking the two clips and removing the two retaining bolts.
5. Scribe alignment marks on the No. 2 suspension arm adjusting cam and body. Remove the cam, cam bolt and No. 2 suspension arm.
6. Remove the No. 1 suspension arm by removing the nut and retainer.
7. To install, position the No. 1 suspension arm so that the bushing with the slit side is facing towards the rear and connect the arm to the body temporarily with the bolt, plate and nut. The right and left suspension arms have been stamped at the factory **R** and **L** respectively for positive identification.
8. Position the No. 2 suspension arm in the same manner as the No. 1 arm. Install the No. 2 arm so that the small paint mark is facing toward the outside of the vehicle. When the arm is in position, temporarily install the cam bolt and cam.
9. Connect the No. 1 and No. 2 arms to the axle carrier with the through bolt and two retainers. Install the nut finger tight.
10. Connect the strut rod to the axle carrier and install the nut and bolt finger tight.
11. Install the rear wheels and remove the safety stands.
12. Lower the vehicle and bounce the rear end a few to times to allow the rear suspension to stabilize.
13. Now that the vehicle weight is on the suspension, align the matchmarks on the cam with the body and torque the No. 1 and No. 2 suspension arm bolts to 83 ft. lbs. (113 Nm).
14. Torque the through bolt to 134 ft. lbs. (181 Nm).
15. Torque the strut rod bolt to 83 ft. lbs. (113 Nm).
16. Install the fuel tank protector with the two bolts and two clips.
17. Have the rear alignment checked.

1989-92

➧ SEE FIGS. 14–17

1. Raise the vehicle and support safely. Remove the rear wheels.
2. Remove the nut from the axle carrier. Remove the mounting bolts from the strut rod and disconnect from the carrier.
3. Disconnect LSPV spring from the lower arm if equipped.
4. Disconnect No. 1 and No. 2 suspension arms from the axle carrier.
5. Remove the fasteners and pull the fuel tank protector down from the vehicle.
6. Place matchmarks on the toe adjust cam and suspension member.
7. Remove the service hole cover(s). Loosen the bolt and remove the toe adjust plate No. 2.
8. Remove the bolt with toe adjust cam, disconnect the No. 2 suspension arm and remove from the vehicle.
9. Remove the nut retainer from the body and remove the No. 1 suspension arm.

To Install:

10. Install the stamped suspension arm No. 1 with the identification mark **L** for left and **R** for right on the proper side. Temporarily install the suspension arms with the bolt, washer and nut. Do not tighten at this time. Install with the bushing slit side towards the rear.
11. Face the paint mark on the No. 2 suspension arms toward the rear of the vehicle. Install the bushing with the slit side towards the rear of the vehicle.
12. Loosely install the bolt into the axle carrier. Connect the LSPV spring to the lower arm.
13. Connect the strut bar to the axle carrier and temporarily install the bolt and nut.
14. Install the fuel tank protector, rear wheels and lower the vehicle. Bounce the suspension up and down a few times.
15. Torque the strut rod bolts to 83 ft. lbs. (113 Nm) and the suspension arm nuts (inside and outside) to 134 ft. lbs. (181 Nm).
16. Have the rear wheel alignment checked.

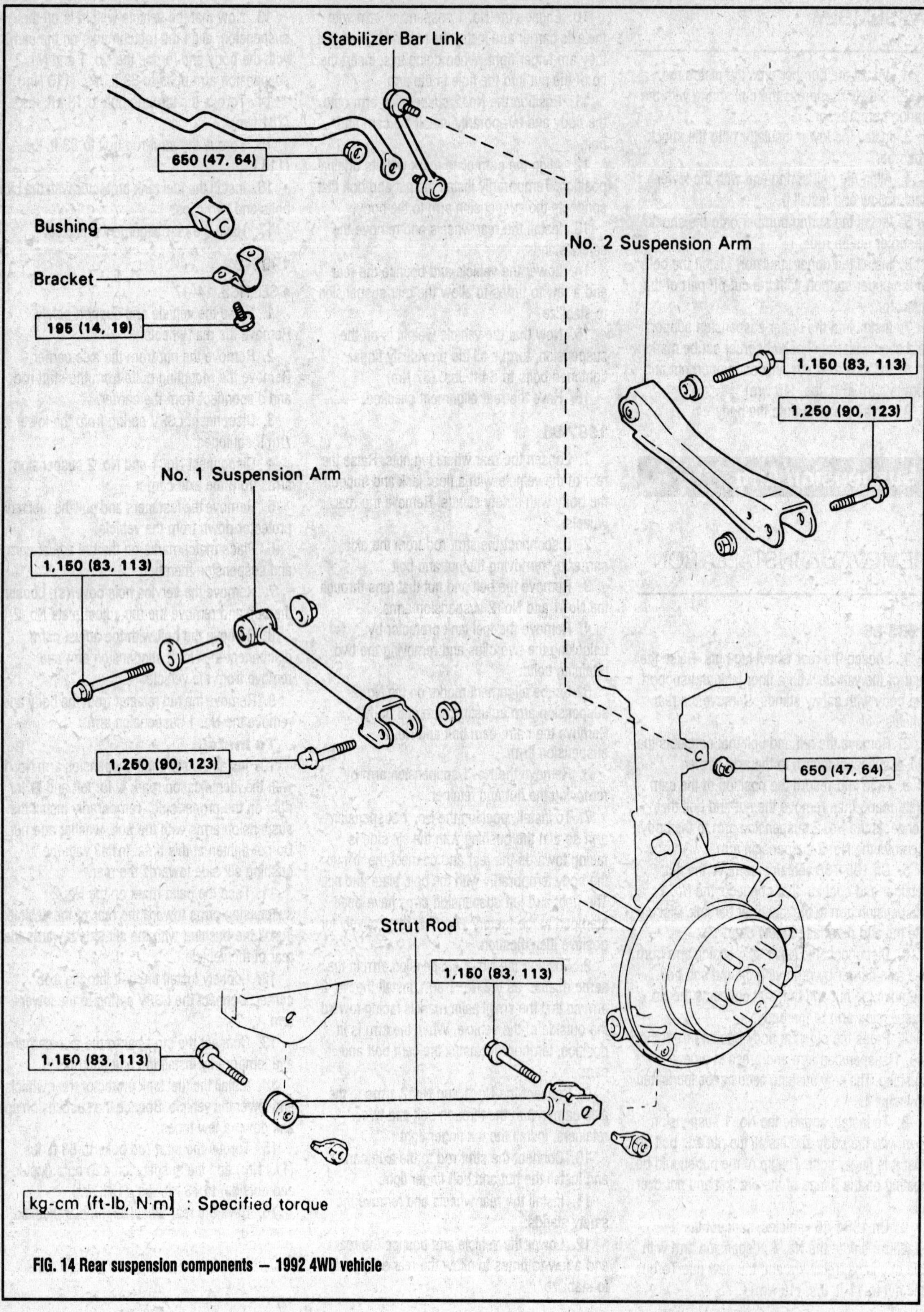

FIG. 14 Rear suspension components — 1992 4WD vehicle

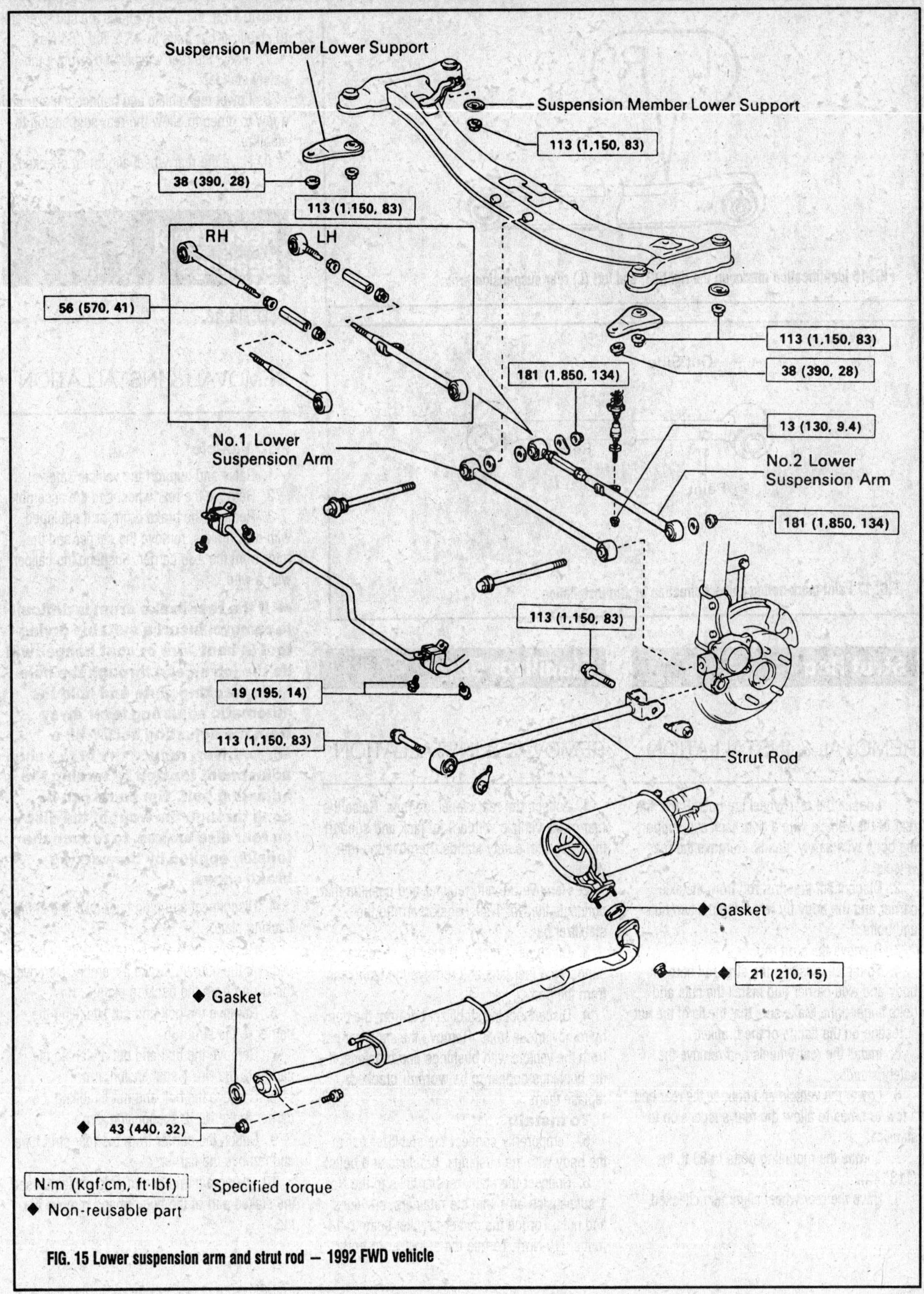

FIG. 15 Lower suspension arm and strut rod — 1992 FWD vehicle

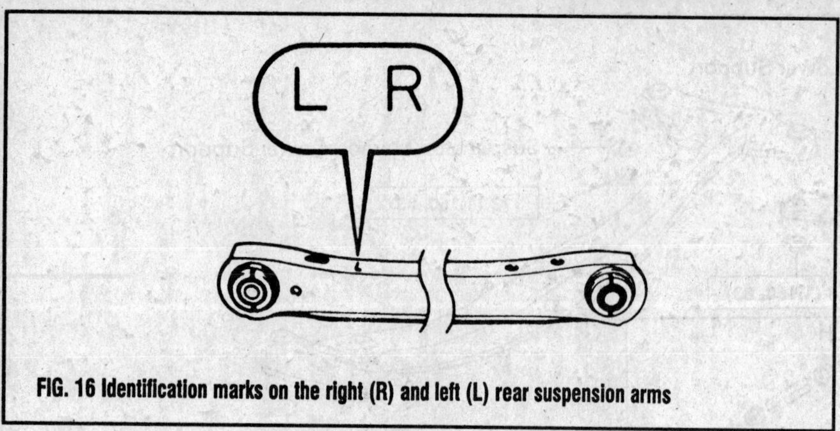

FIG. 16 Identification marks on the right (R) and left (L) rear suspension arms

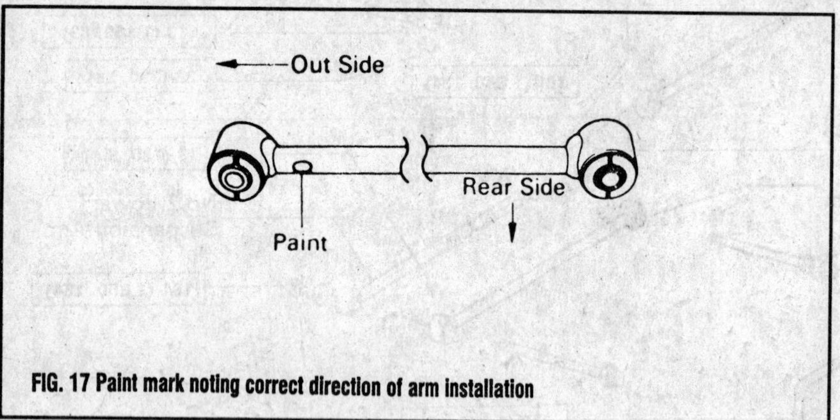

FIG. 17 Paint mark noting correct direction of arm installation

Strut Rod

REMOVAL & INSTALLATION

1. Loosen the rear wheel lug nuts. Raise the rear of the vehicle with a floor jack and support the body with safety stands. Remove the rear wheels.
2. Disconnect the strut rod from the axle carrier and the body by removing the two nuts and bolts.
3. Remove the strut rod.
4. To install, position the strut rod onto the body and axle carrier and install the nuts and bolts finger tight. Make sure that the lip of the nut is resting on the flange of the bracket.
5. Install the rear wheels and remove the safety stands.
6. Lower the vehicle and bounce the rear end a few to times to allow the rear suspension to stabilize.
7. Torque the mounting bolts to 83 ft. lbs. (113 Nm).
8. Have the rear wheel alignment checked.

Stabilizer Bar

REMOVAL & INSTALLATION

1. Loosen the rear wheel lug nuts. Raise the rear of the vehicle with a floor jack and support the body with safety stands. Remove the rear wheels.
2. Remove the nut, retainer and cushion that connects the No. 1 suspension arm to the stabilizer bar.
3. On some vehicles, it may be necessary to support the fuel tank and remove the tank band from the body.
4. Disconnect the stabilizer bar from the body by removing the bolts. Remove the stabilizer bar from the vehicle with bushings and brackets. If the bushings appear to be worn or cracked, replace them.

To Install:

5. Temporarily connect the stabilizer bar to the body with the bushings, brackets and bolts.
6. Connect the stabilizer bar links to the No. 1 suspension arm with the retainers, cushions and nuts. Torque the center bracket bolts to 14 ft. lbs. (19 Nm). Torque the stabilizer-to-body bolts to 14 ft. lbs. (19 Nm) and the stabilizer link to stabilizer bar bolts to 47 ft. lbs. (64 Nm).
7. Install the rear wheels and remove the safety stands.
8. Lower the vehicle and bounce the rear end a few to times to allow the rear suspension to stabilize.
9. Have the rear wheel alignment checked.

Rear Wheel Bearings

➧ SEE FIG. 18

REMOVAL & INSTALLATION

FWD Vehicle

1. Raise and support the vehicle safely.
2. Remove the rear wheel and tire assembly.
3. Remove the brake drum or if equipped with disc brakes, remove the caliper and the rotor from the axle carrier. Suspend the caliper with a wire.

➡ If the rear brake drum is difficult to remove, insert a suitable prying tool (a bent wire or coat hanger will do the job nicely) through the hole in the backing plate and hold the automatic adjusting lever away from the adjusting bolt. With a screwdriver, reduce the brake shoe adjustment tension by turning the adjusting bolt. The same can be done through the front of the disc on rear disc brakes, to reduce the tension applied by the parking brake shoes.

4. Disconnect and plug the brake line at the backing plate.
5. Remove the 4 axle hub-to-carrier bolts and slide off the hub and brake assembly. Remove the O-ring from the backing plate.
6. Remove the bolt and nut attaching the carrier to the strut rod.
7. Remove the bolt and nut attaching the carrier to the No. 1 suspension arm.
8. Remove the bolt and nut attaching the carrier to the No. 2 suspension arm.
9. Unbolt the carrier from the rear strut tube and remove the carrier.
10. Using a hammer and cold chisel, loosen the staked part of the hub nut and remove the nut.

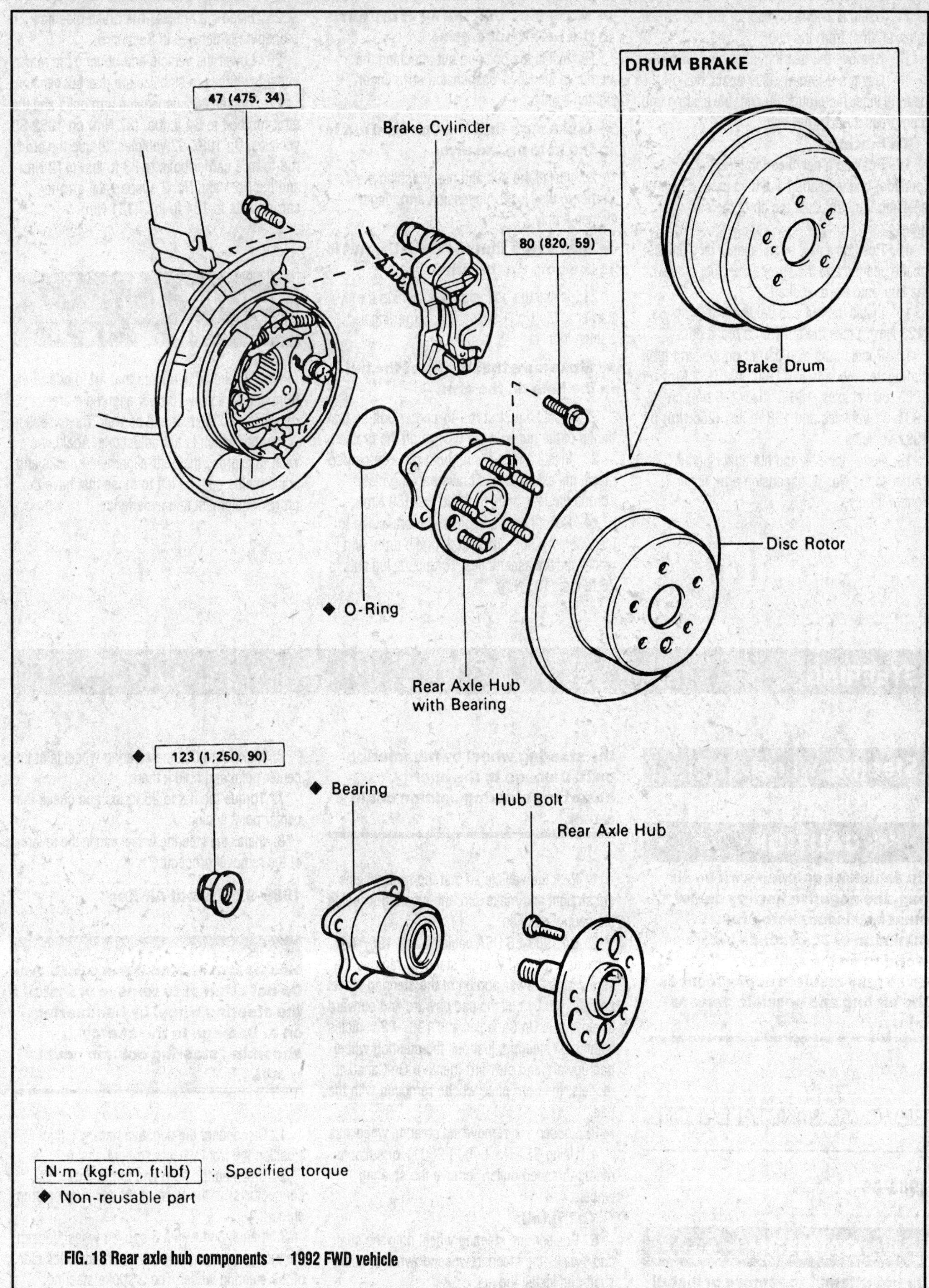

FIG. 18 Rear axle hub components — 1992 FWD vehicle

11. Using a 2-armed puller or the like, press the axle shaft from the hub.
12. Remove the bearing inner race (inside).
13. Using a 2-armed puller again, pull off the bearing inner race (outside) over the bearing and then press it out of the hub.

To install:

14. Position a new bearing inner race (outside) on the bearing and then press a new oil seal into the hub. Coat the lip of the seal with grease.
15. Position a new bearing inner race (inside) on the bearing and then press the inner race with the hub onto the axle shaft.
16. Install the nut and tighten it to 90 ft. lbs. (123 Nm). Stake the nut with a brass drift.
17. Position the axle carrier on the strut tube and tighten the nuts to 119 ft. lbs. (162 Nm) on 1983–86 vehicles, 166 ft. lbs. (226 Nm) on 1987–91 vehicles and 188 ft. lbs. (255 Nm) on 1992 vehicles.
18. Install the bolt and nut attaching the carrier to the No. 2 suspension arm; finger tighten it only.

➡ Make sure that the lip of the nut is in the hole on the arm.

19. Install the bolt and nut attaching the carrier to the No. 1 suspension arm; finger tighten it only.

➡ Make sure that the lip of the nut is in the hole on the arm.

20. Install the bolt and nut attaching the carrier to the No. 2 suspension arm; finger tighten it only.

➡ Make sure that the lip of the nut is in the hole on the arm.

21. Install the bolt and nut attaching the carrier to the No. 1 suspension arm; finger tighten it only.

➡ Make sure that the lip of the nut is in the hole on the arm.

22. Install the strut rod-to-carrier bolt so that the lip of the nut is in the groove on the bracket.
23. Install a new O-ring onto the axle carrier. Install the axle hub and brake backing plate. Torque the four bolts to 59 ft. lbs. (80 Nm).
24. Reconnect and tighten the brake line to the wheel cylinder. Install the brake drum and wheel and tire assemblies. Torque the lug nuts to 76 ft. lbs. (103 Nm).
25. Bleed the brakes. The brake bleeding procedure is detailed in Section 9.
26. Lower the vehicle and bounce the rear end a few times to stabilize the rear suspension.
27. Tighten the suspension arm bolts and the strut rod bolt to 64 ft. lbs. (87 Nm) on 1983-86 vehicles. On 1987-92 vehicles, torque the strut rod-to-axle carrier bolts to 83 ft. lbs. (112 Nm) and the No.1 and No. 2 suspension arm-to-carrier bolts to 134 ft. lbs. (181 Nm).

Rear End Alignment

Most of the adjustments that are made to the front end to achieve proper alignment are performed on the rear end as well. The exception is camber which is not adjustable. Again, we wish to express that rear alignment checks and adjustments best be left to those that have the proper equipment and experience.

STEERING

Steering Wheel

⁂ CAUTION

On vehicles equipped with an air bag, the negative battery cable must be disconnected for a minimum of 30 seconds before working on the system. Failure to do so may result in deployment of the air bag and possible personal injury.

REMOVAL & INSTALLATION

1983–88

⁂ CAUTION

Do not attempt to remove or install the steering wheel by hammering on it. Damage to the energy absorbing steering column could result.

1. Park the vehicle so that the front wheels are straight and make sure the steering wheel in the neutral position.
2. On 1983-86 USA vehicles and 1987-88 vehicles equipped with tilt steering, remove the screw at the lower portion of the steering wheel pad and **gently** pull the pad upward and outward to remove it. On Canadian and 1987-88 vehicles without tilt steering, just pull the steering wheel pad upward and outward (gently). On Canadian models, the horn plate will be removed with the pad.
3. Loosen and remove the steering wheel nut.
4. Using SST No. 09609-20011 or suitable metric threaded puller, remove the steering wheel.

To install:

5. Position the steering wheel onto the shaft and "walk" the steering wheel down the main shaft and install the nut.
6. Make sure that the steering wheel is at the center point and hold it there.
7. Torque the nut to 25 ft. lbs and check the center point again.
8. Install the steering wheel pad in the reverse of the removal procedure.

1989–92 Without Air Bag

⁂ CAUTION

Do not attempt to remove or install the steering wheel by hammering on it. Damage to the energy-absorbing steering column could result.

1. Disconnect the negative battery cable. Position the front wheels straight ahead.
2. Unfasten the horn and turn signal multi-connector(s) at the base of the steering column shroud.
3. If equipped with a 3 spoked wheel, loosen the trim pad retaining screws from the back side of the steering wheel. The 2 spoke steering

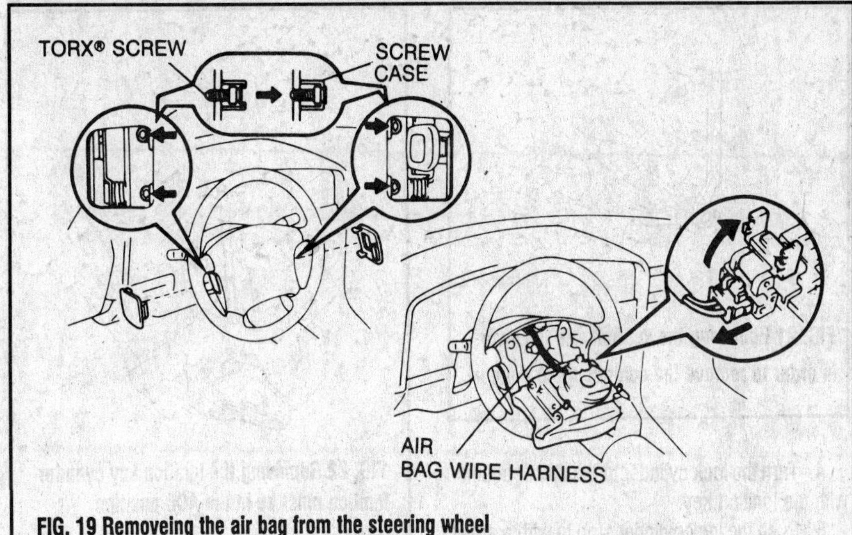

FIG. 19 Removeing the air bag from the steering wheel

wheel is removed in the same manner as the three spoke, except that the trim pad should be pried off with a small prybar. Remove the pad by lifting it toward the top of the wheel.

4. Lift the trim pad and horn button assembly from the wheel.
5. Remove the steering wheel hub retaining nut.
6. Scribe matchmarks on the hub and shaft to aid in correct installation.
7. Use a suitable puller to remove the steering wheel.
8. Installation is the reverse of removal. Tighten the wheel retaining nut to 26 ft. lbs. (35 Nm).

With Air Bag

➧ SEE FIG. 19

CAUTION

Air bag equipped vehicles: Work must be started after 30 seconds or longer from the time the ignition switch is turned to the LOCK position and the negative battery terminal is disconnected. If the air bag system is disconnected with the ignition switch at the ON or ACC, diagnostic codes will be recorded.

1. Disconnect the negative battery cable.
2. Place the front wheels facing straight ahead.
3. Remove the steering wheel screw covers.
4. Using a Torx® wrench T30, loosen the screws until the groove trailing the screw circumference catches on the screw case.
5. Pull the wheel pad out from the steering wheel and disconnect the air bag connector.
6. Remove the steering wheel nut. Place matchmarks on the wheel and steering shaft.
7. Using a steering wheel puller SST 09213-31021 or equivalent, remove the steering wheel.

To install:

8. Turn the spiral cable on the combination switch counterclockwise by hand until it becomes harder to turn. Then rotate the cable clockwise about 3 turns to align the alignment mark.
9. Install the steering wheel, align the matchmarks and torque the nut to 26 ft. lbs. (35 Nm).
10. Connect the air bag connector and install the steering pad.
11. Torque the Torx® screws to 78 inch lbs. (8.8 Nm).
12. Install the screw covers.
13. Connect the battery cable, check operation and the steering wheel center point.

Turn Signal Switch (Combination Switch)

REMOVAL & INSTALLATION

1. Disconnect the negative battery cable. On vehicles equipped with an air bag, wait at least 30 seconds before working on the vehicle.
2. Remove the steering wheel, as outlined in this Section.
3. Remove the instrument lower finish panel (as required), air duct and upper and lower column covers.
4. Disconnect the combination switch connector.
5. On air bag equipped vehicles, disconnect the cable connectors, remove the spiral cable housing attaching screws and slide the cable assembly from the front of the combination switch.
6. Remove the screws that attach the combination switch to its mounting brackets and remove the combination switch from the vehicle.

To install:

7. Position the combination switch onto the mounting bracket and install the retaining screws.
8. Connect the electrical connector.
9. Install the upper/lower column covers, air duct and instrument lower finish panel.
10. Turn the spiral cable on the combination switch counterclockwise by hand until it becomes harder to turn. Then rotate the cable clockwise about 3 turns to align the alignment mark.
11. Install the steering wheel onto the shaft and torque nut to 26 ft. lbs. (35 Nm).
12. Connect the air bag connector and install the steering pad.
13. Connect the battery cable, check operation and the steering wheel center point.
14. Connect the negative battery cable. Check all combination switch functions for proper operation. Check the steering wheel center point.

Ignition Lock/Switch

REMOVAL & INSTALLATION

1983–87

➧ SEE FIGS. 20–22

1. Disconnect the negative battery cable. Remove the steering column from the vehicle as outlined in this Section.
2. Mount the steering column in vise padded with rags to prevent damage to the column.
3. Using needle nose pliers, pull the torsion springs upward and remove the grommets. Loosen the anchor bolt and remove the spring.
4. Unbolt and remove the tilt lever. This bolt will have left hand threads.
5. Remove the adjusting nut, washer and pull the lock bolt out.
6. Remove the 2 screws and remove the column upper support.
7. On the tilt steering support, remove the two nuts and pawl set bolts. Remove the bushings, O-rings and the tilt steering support.

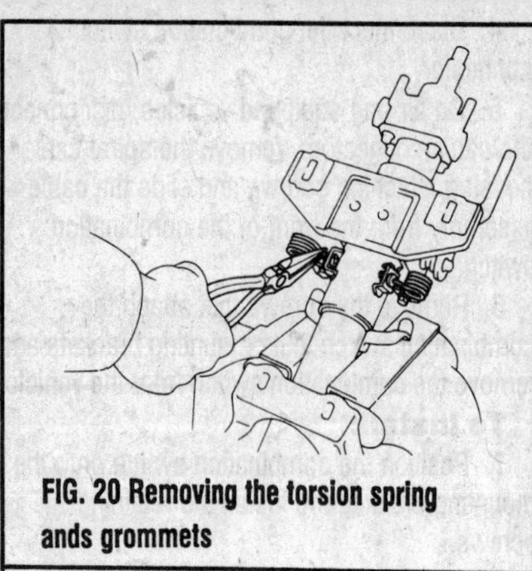

FIG. 20 Removing the torsion spring ands grommets

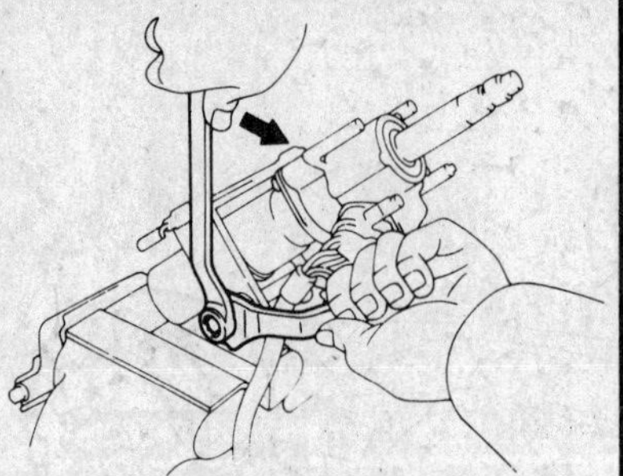

FIG. 21 Removing the set bolt and tilt lever in order to remove the column upper support.

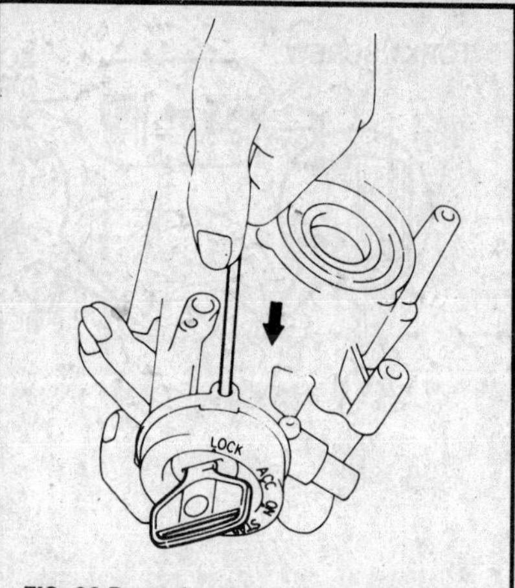

FIG. 22 Removing the ignition key cylinder Ignition must be in the ACC position.

8. Turn the ignition lock cylinder to the **ACC** position.

9. Push the lock cylinder stop in with a small, round object (cotter pin, punch, etc).

10. Withdraw the lock cylinder from the lock housing while depressing the stop tab.

To install:

11. Align the locking cam with the hole in the ignition switch and insert the switch in the lock housing.

12. Make sure that both the lock cylinder and the column lock are in the **ACC** position. Slide the cylinder into the lock housing until the stop tab engages the hole in the lock.

13. Lubricate the bushings O-rings and install the 2 bushings to the steering column tube. Install the tilt steering support and pawl set bolts with bushings and O-ring. Torque the nut to 9 ft. lbs. (12 Nm).

14. Install the column upper support and the lock bolt. Provisionally install the washer and the adjusting nut, which has left hand threads. Adjust the bracket so the lock bolt is in the center of the oval hole of the bracket and the upper surface of the bracket is parallel with the column tube. Tighten the adjusting nut to 8 ft. lbs. (10 Nm). (If there is any play in the support, tighten the adjusting nut to eliminate the play)

15. Place the tilt lever in position and torque the set bolt, which also has left hand threads, to 25 ft. lbs. (33 Nm).

16. Install the torsion springs and grommets. Install the steering column into the vehicle as described in this Section.

1988–1992

1. Disconnect the negative battery cable. If equipped with an air bag, wait at least 20 seconds before working on the vehicle.

2. Remove the lower steering column cover. Unfasten the ignition switch connector under the instrument panel.

3. Remove the screws which secure the upper and lower halves of the steering column cover.

4. Turn the lock cylinder to the **ACC** position with the ignition key.

5. Push the lock cylinder stop in with a small, round object (cotter pin, punch, etc.).

➡ **On some vehicles, it may be necessary to remove the steering wheel and combination switch first.**

6. Withdraw the lock cylinder from the lock housing while depressing the stop tab.

7. To remove the ignition switch, unfasten its securing screws and withdraw the switch from the lock housing.

To install:

8. Align the locking cam with the hole in the ignition switch and insert the switch into the lock housing.

9. Secure the switch with its screw(s).

10. Make sure both the lock cylinder and column lock are in the **ACC** position. Slide the cylinder into the lock housing until the stop tab engages the hole in the lock.

11. Install the steering column covers.

12. Connect the ignition switch connector.

13. Connect the negative battery cable.

Steering Column

➧ SEE FIGS. 23 AND 24

REMOVAL & INSTALLATION

CAUTION

Air bag equipped vehicles: Work must be started after 20 seconds or longer from the time the ignition switch is turned to the LOCK and the negative battery terminal is disconnected. If the air bag system is disconnected with the ignition switch at the ON or ACC, diagnostic codes will be recorded.

1. Disconnect the negative battery cable.

2. Remove the two set bolts from the universal joint.

3. First disengage the universal joint from the gear housing, then pull it straight out from the main shaft.

4. Remove the steering wheel as outlined in this Section.

5. Remove the instrument lower finish panel (as required), air duct and upper and lower column covers.

6. Disconnect all electrical connections for ignition switch and combination switch. Remove the combination switch as outlined in this Section.

7. Loosen the clamp bolt from the hole cover.

8. Remove the four mounting nuts and support bolt. Pull the mainshaft out and remove the steering column from the vehicle. The support bolt is found only on 1987-88 vehicles with tilt steering columns.

To install:

9. Position the steering column inside the vehicle so that the main shaft can be inserted in the hole cover. Then, position the main shaft so that the ends of the tilt steering support holes touch the mounting bolts.

10. Support the column while installing the mounting nuts finger tight. Tighten the right upper nut through the bond cable. Torque the nuts evenly to 19 ft. lbs. and the support bolt (1987-88) to 9 ft. lbs.

11. Tighten the hole cover clamp bolt.

12. Connect the switch connectors and install the combination switch, if removed.

13. Install the column covers, air duct and lower instrument panel finish panel.

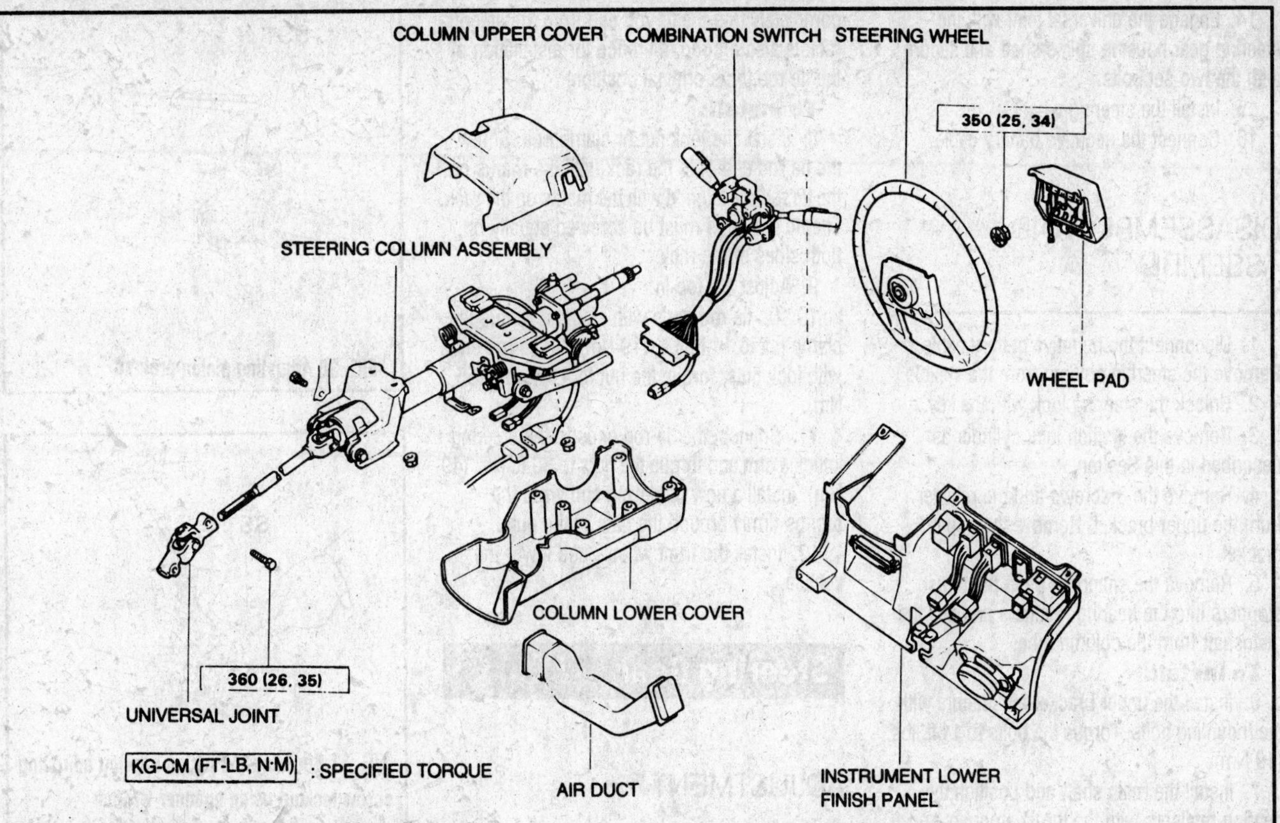

COLUMN UPPER COVER
COMBINATION SWITCH
STEERING WHEEL
350 (25, 34)
STEERING COLUMN ASSEMBLY
WHEEL PAD
COLUMN LOWER COVER
360 (26, 35)
UNIVERSAL JOINT
KG-CM (FT-LB, N·M) : SPECIFIED TORQUE
AIR DUCT
INSTRUMENT LOWER FINISH PANEL

FIG. 23 Steering column components without tilt steering

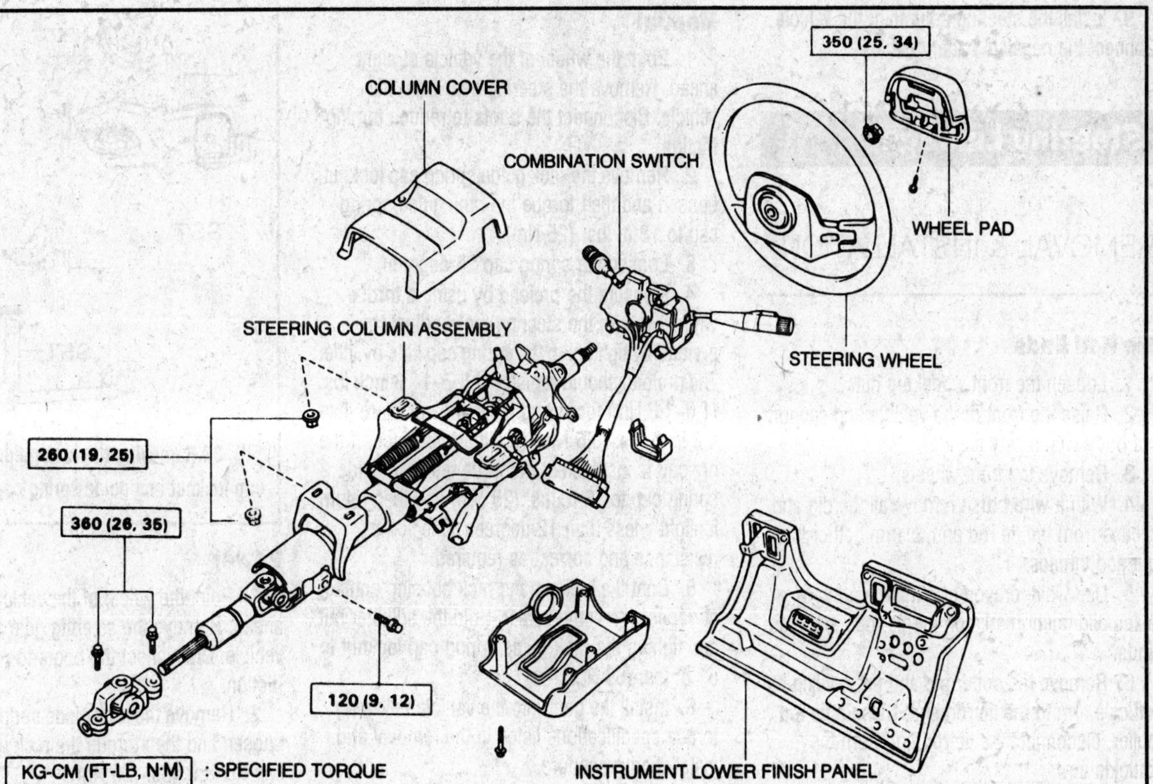

350 (25, 34)
COLUMN COVER
COMBINATION SWITCH
WHEEL PAD
STEERING COLUMN ASSEMBLY
STEERING WHEEL
260 (19, 25)
360 (26, 35)
120 (9, 12)
KG-CM (FT-LB, N·M) : SPECIFIED TORQUE
INSTRUMENT LOWER FINISH PANEL

FIG. 24 Steering column components with tilt steering

14. Engage the universal joint with the steering gear housing spline shaft and secure with the two set bolts.
15. Install the steering wheel.
16. Connect the negative battery cable.

DISASSEMBLY AND ASSEMBLY

1. Disconnect the negative battery cable. Remove the steering column from the vehicle.
2. Unlock the steering lock with the key.
3. Remove the ignition lock cylinder as described in this Section.
4. Remove the 3 screws and the retainer from the upper bracket. Remove the upper bracket.
5. Remove the snapring, push the thrust stoppers into the bearing retainers and pull the mainshaft from the column tube.

To Install:

6. Install the upper bracket and secure with the mounting bolts. Torque the bolts to 14 ft. lbs. (19 Nm).
7. Install the main shaft and position the bearing retainers with the thrust stoppers and install the snapring.
8. Install the ignition lock cylinder into the column as described in this Section.
9. Install the steering column in the vehicle. Connect the negative battery cable.

Steering Linkage

REMOVAL & INSTALLATION

Tie Rod Ends

1. Loosen the front wheel lug nuts.
2. Raise the front of the vehicle and support the body with safety stands.
3. Remove the front wheels.
4. With a wire brush remove all the dirt and grease from the tie rod end, clamp bolt or lock nut and threads.
5. Use white crayon or similar marker to place alignment marks on the tie rods and rack ends.
6. Remove the cotter pin and nut holding the knuckle arm to the tie rod end. Using a tie rod puller, disconnect the tie rod end from the knuckle arm.
7. Loosen the lock nut or the clamp bolt and unscrew the tie rod end from the steering rack. Counting the number of turns it takes to completely free the tie rod end from the steering rack is also a good reference for installation of the tie rod to its original position.

To Install:

8. Install the lock nut or clamp bolt. Screw the tie rod end onto the rack until the marks on the tie rod are aligned with the marks on the rack. The tie rod ends must be screwed equally on both sides of the rack.
9. Adjust the toe-in.
10. On tie rod ends with clamps, torque the clamp nut to 14 ft. lbs. (19 Nm). On tie rod ends with lock nuts, torque the nut to 41 ft. lbs. (55 Nm).
11. Connect the tie rod ends to the steering knuckle arm and torque the nuts to 36 ft. lbs. (49 Nm). Install a new cotter pin and wrap the prongs firmly around the flats of the nuts.
12. Install the front wheels and lower the vehicle.

Steering Gear

ADJUSTMENT

(Total Preload)

➧ SEE FIGS. 30–32

Manual

1. Point the wheel of the vehicle straight ahead. Remove the steering gear from the vehicle. Disconnect the boots to reduce turning friction.
2. Remove the rack guide spring cap locknut. Loosen and then torque the rack guide spring cap to 18 ft. lbs. (25 Nm).
3. Loosen the spring cap 25 degrees.
4. Measure the preload by using a torque wrench to turn the steering rack. Adjust the preload by tightening the spring cap little by little. The preload should register at 8.7–11.3 inch lbs. (1.0–1.3 Nm) for strong resistance or more than 4.3 inch lbs. (0.5 Nm) for little resistance. If the preload is insufficient, retorque the rack guide spring cap to 18 ft. lbs. (25 Nm) and then return it slightly less than 12 degrees. Check the resistance and correct as required.
5. Coat the locknut and rack housing contact surfaces with liquid sealer. Hold the adjuster nut and tighten the rack guide spring cap locknut to 51 ft. lbs. (69 Nm).
6. Install the gear into the vehicle following torque specifications listed in the removal and installation procedure.

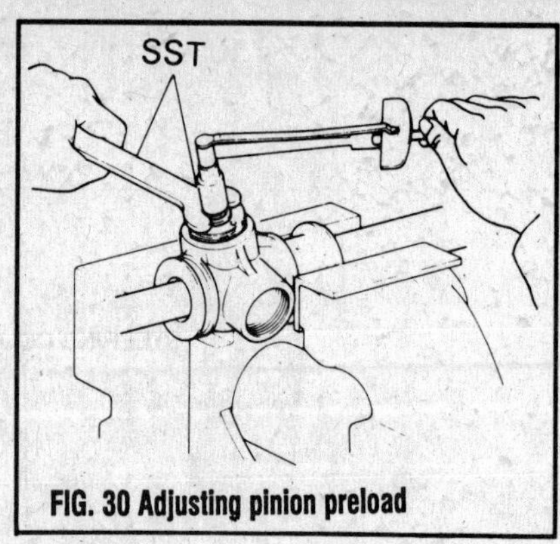

FIG. 30 Adjusting pinion preload

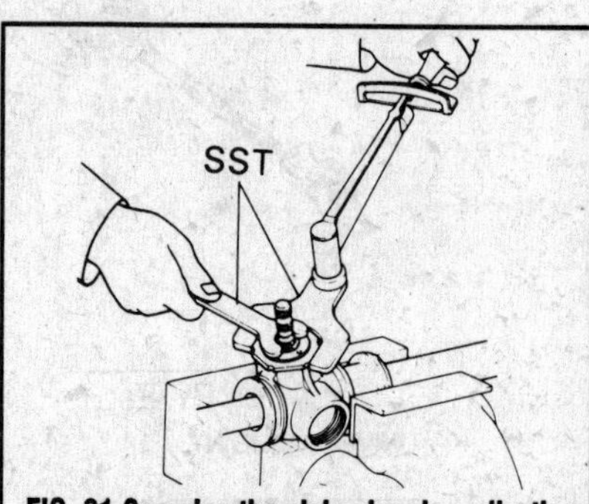

FIG. 31 Securing the pinion bearing adjusting screw locknut using spanner wrench (special tool)

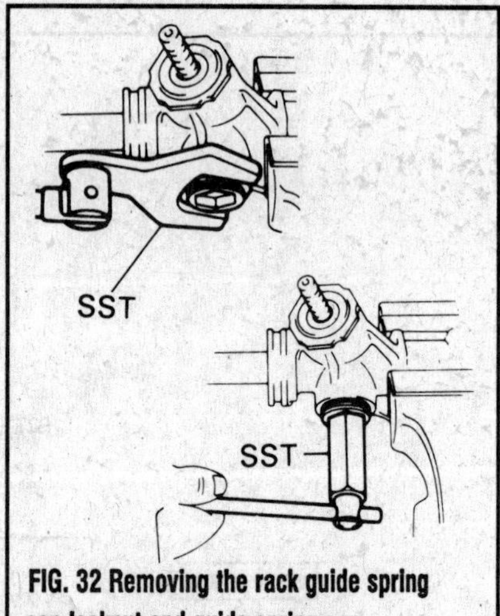

FIG. 32 Removing the rack guide spring cap locknut and guide spring cap

Power

1. Point the wheel of the vehicle straight ahead. Remove the steering gear from the vehicle. Disconnect the boots to reduce turning friction.
2. Remove the rack guide spring cap locknut. Loosen and then torque the rack guide spring cap to 18 ft. lbs. (25 Nm).
3. Loosen the spring cap 12 degrees.
4. Turn the control valve shaft and operate the steering rack 2 full strokes to snug it down.

5. Return the spring cap until there is no more tension on the spring. Measure the preload by using a torque wrench to turn the steering rack. Adjust the preload by tightening the spring cap slowly. The preload should register at 10.4 inch lbs. (1.2 Nm). Recheck the preload and adjust as required.

6. Coat the locknut and rack housing contact surfaces with liquid sealer. Hold the adjuster nut and tighten the rack guide spring cap locknut to 51 ft. lbs. (69 Nm).

7. Install the gear into the vehicle following torque specifications listed in the removal and installation procedure.

REMOVAL & INSTALLATION

FWD

➧ SEE FIG. 25

1. Raise and support the vehicle safely. Remove the front wheels. Open the hood. Remove the 2 set bolts, and remove the sliding yoke from between the steering rack housing and the steering column shaft.

2. Remove the cotter pin and nut holding the knuckle arm to the tie rod end. Using a tie rod puller, disconnect the tie rod end from the knuckle arm.

3. If equipped with power steering, remove the lower crossmember, remove the engine under cover, center engine mount member and the rear engine mount.

4. On 1983-86 vehicles equipped with manual transaxle, remove the four retaining clips and disconnect the two control cables from the trasaxle.

5. Using SST No. 09631-22020 or equivalent, disconnect the return line and the pressure line from the control valve housing. Use a small plastic container to catch the fluid.

6. Remove the rear engine mounting and bracket as required.

7. Remove the steering gear housing brackets. Slide the gear housing to the right side and then to the left side to remove the housing.

To install:

8. Install the grommets to the gear housing.

9. Install the steering gear onto the body and support by hand.

10. On 1983-86 vehicles, install the left mounting bracket so that the flat surface is facing upward (paint mark on left side of the bracket down). On 1987-92 vehicles, install the brackets in the same way they were removed. Install the nuts and bolts and torque them to 43 ft. lbs. (58 Nm).

11. Install the rear engine mounting bracket and torque the retaining bolts to 38 ft. lbs. (52 Nm).

12. On 1983-86 vehicles, connect the mounting to the bracket and torque the bolts to 58 ft. lbs. (78 Nm).

13. Install the center member with the mounting bolts. Torque the body mount bolts to 29 ft. lbs. and the engine mount bolts to 32 ft. lbs.

14. On 1987-88 vehicles, install the lower cross member and torque the outer bolts to 129 ft. lbs., inner bolts to 29 ft. lbs. (39 Nm) and install the engine under covers. On 1992 vehicles, install the lower cross member and torque the outer bolts to 153 ft. lbs. (207 Nm).

15. Connect the pressure and return lines and torque the connector nuts to 33 ft. lbs. (44 Nm).

16. Install the universal joint and torque the retaining bolts to 26–33 ft. lbs. (35–44 Nm).

18. Connect the tie rods to the steering knuckle with the castellated nut. Torque the nut to 36 ft. lbs. and install a new cotter pin. The prongs of the cotter pin should be firmly wrapped around the flats of the nut.

19. On 1983-86 vehicles, connect the transaxle control cables.

20. Install the front wheels and lower the vehicle.

21. Fill the power steering reservoir tank to the proper level with Dexron®II ATF.

22. Bleed the system as described in this Section.

23. Check for leaks, adjust the toe-in and check the steering wheel center point.

AWD

➧ SEE FIG. 26

1. Loosen the front wheel lug nuts. Raise the front of the vehicle and support the body with safety stands. Remove the front wheels.

2. Matchmark the universal joint with the control valve shaft. Loosen the upper U-joint set bolt and remove the lower bolt. Pull the U-joint upward from the control valve shaft.

3. Remove the cotter pin and nut holding the knuckle arm to the tie rod end. Using a tie rod puller, disconnect the tie rod end from the knuckle arm.

4. Disconnect the speedometer cable. Removal of the front exhaust pipe is required on some models.

5. Using SST No. 09631-22020 or equivalent flare nut wrench, disconnect the return line and the pressure line from the control valve housing. Use a small plastic container to catch the fluid.

6. Matchmark the driveshaft to the intermediate shaft flange. Remove the flange bolts, separate the flanges and pull the prop shaft out. Install SST No. 09325-20010 into the intermediate shaft.

7. If more clearance is required to remove the gear, jack up the front of the engine carefully. DO NOT over-tilt the engine.

8. Disconnect the steering gear support brackets. Slide the gear housing to the right to position the left tie rod end in the body panel. Then, pull the steering gear assembly through the opening in the left lower side of the vehicle body.

⁂ CAUTION

Be careful not to damage the pressure tubes and transaxle control cables.

9. Remove the gear housing grommets.

To install:

10. Install the grommets to the gear housing.

11. Install the steering gear onto the body and torque the mounting bracket bolts and nuts to 43 ft. lbs. (59 Nm).

12. Install the drive shaft making sure to align the matchmarks. Torque the bolts to 54 ft. lbs. (74 Nm).

13. Connect the return line and the pressure line to the control valve housing and torque the line union nuts to 33 ft. lbs. (45 Nm).

14. Connect the tie rod end to the knuckle arm and torque to 36 ft. lbs. (49 Nm) Install new cotter pin.

15. Align the matchmark on the universal joint and the control valve shaft.

Push the U-joint downward onto the control valve shaft. Tighten the bolt to 26 ft. lbs. (35 Nm).

16. Install the front wheels onto the vehicle.

OVERHAUL

To correctly overhaul the steering gear, a number of special tools are required. Unfortunately, some of the tools are specific to steering gear repairs and substitutes are not available. Incorrect installation of components with a tool that looks comparable to a specific tool will prevent successful overhaul of the unit and possibly pose a threat to the safe operation of the vehicle. It is recommended that the overhaul of a steering gear be performed by qualified steering gear rebuilders. The cost for specific components, the time invested in the repair, and an unsuccessful result may not be as cost effective as purchasing a rebuilt unit.

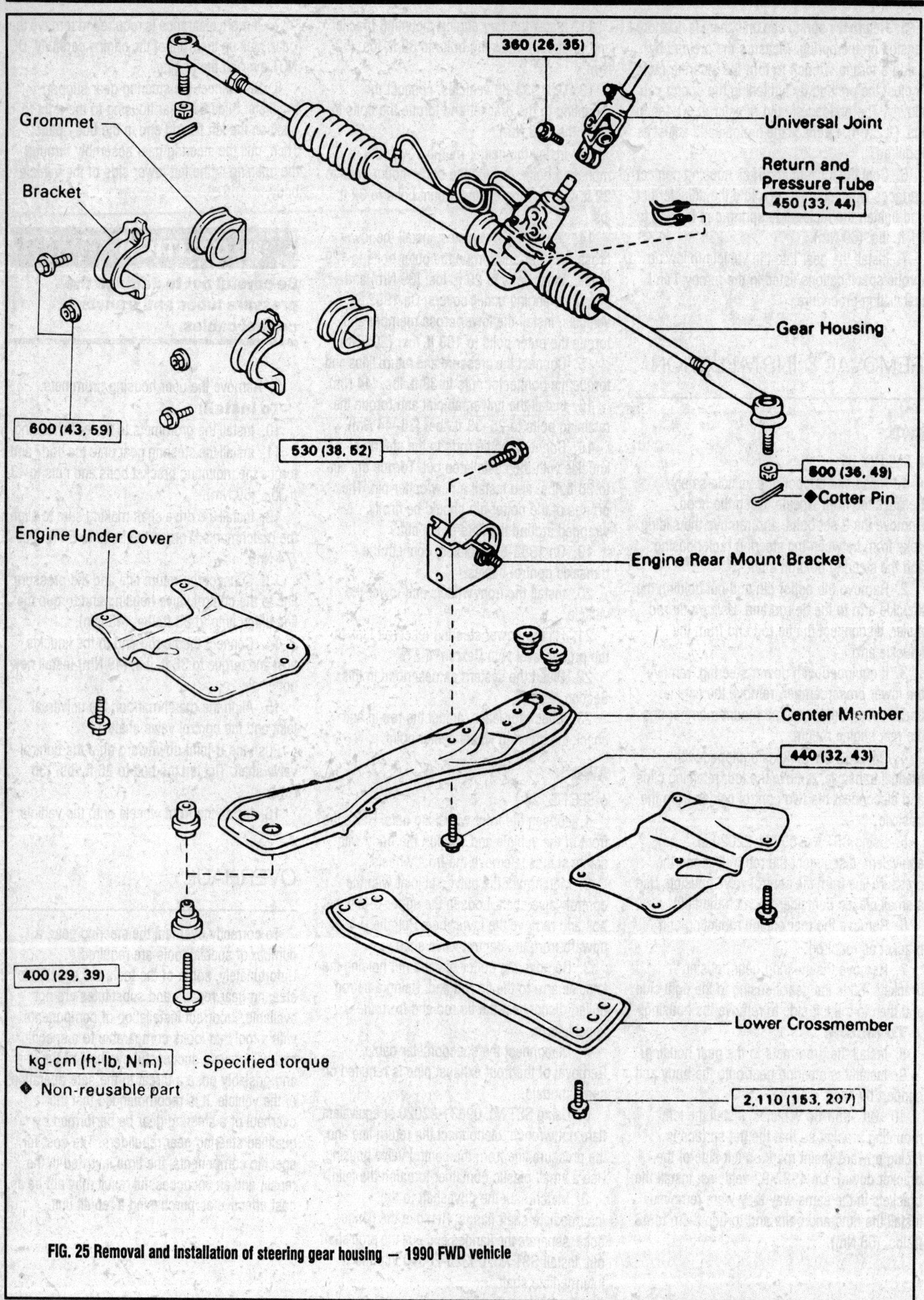

FIG. 25 Removal and installation of steering gear housing — 1990 FWD vehicle

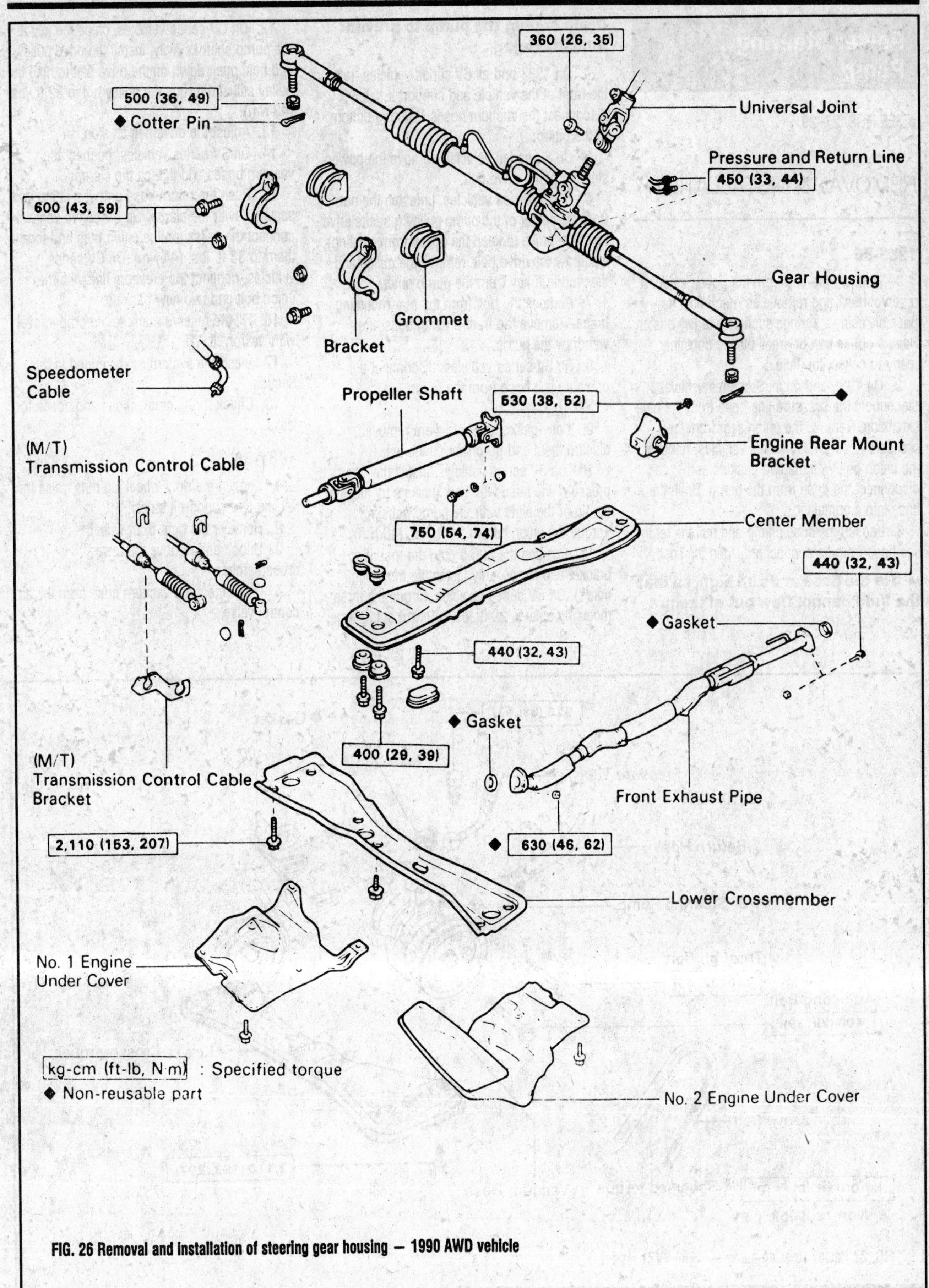

FIG. 26 Removal and installation of steering gear housing — 1990 AWD vehicle

Power Steering Pump

➧ SEE FIGS. 27–29

REMOVAL & INSTALLATION

1983-86

1. Remove the cap from the power steering reservoir tank and remove as much fluid as possible using a syringe such as a turkey baster. Have a coffee can or small plastic container ready to collect the fluid.
2. On 1983 and on all SV series vehicles, disconnect the pressure line hose from the pipe extension. Remove the union seat from the pressure hose. On CV series vehicles, remove the union bolt with the two gaskets and disconnect the hose from the pump. Drain the hose into a container.
3. Loosen the hose clamp and pull the return line hose from its connection. Drain the hose.

➡ **Tie the hose ends up high, so that the fluid cannot flow out of them. Drain or plug the pump to prevent fluid leakage.**

4. On 1983 and all SV series vehicles, raise the front of the vehicle and support it safely; disconnect the vacuum hoses from the bottom of the pump.
5. On SV series vehicles, remove the power steering pump drive belt.
6. Ov CV series vehicles, unfasten the nut from the center of the pump pulley (use the drive belt as a brake to keep the pulley from rotating), withdraw the drive belt, remove the pulley and the woodruff key from the pump shaft.
7. Remove the bolt from the rear mounting brace. Remove the front bracket bolts and withdraw the pump.
8. On SV series vehicles, disconnect the pressure line hose from the pump.

To install:

9. If any gasket or seals were removed, discard them and purchase new ones.
10. On SV series vehicles, install the pressure line hose with new gaskets by aligning the tip of the plate with the pump housing. Torque the union bolt to 34 ft. lbs. (46 Nm).
11. Position the pump onto the mounting bracket and temporarily install the mounting bolt(s). On CV series vehicles, torque the three mounting bolts to 29 ft. lbs. (39 Nm) at this time.
12. On CV series vehicles, place the key in the pump shaft keyway, install the drive pulley and belt, push down on the drive belt to hold the pulley still and torque the pulley nut to 32 ft. lbs. (43 Nm).
13. Adjust the drive belt tension.
14. On SV series vehicles, connect the vacuum hoses and tighten the clamps.
15. Push the return hose onto it's fitting and secure it with the clamp. On SV series vehicles, connect the pressure line union nuts and torque them to 33 ft. lbs. (44 Nm). On CV series vehicles, connect the pressure line with the union bolt and two new gaskets.
16. Fill the reservoir tank to the proper level with Dexron®II ATF.
17. Bleed the system as described in this Section.
18. Check for all connections and hoses for leaks.

1987-88

1. Loosen the right wheel lug nuts, raise the vehicle and support it safely.
2. Remove the right front wheel.
3. Unbolt and remove the lower crossmember.
4. Disconnect the vacuum hose from the air control valve.

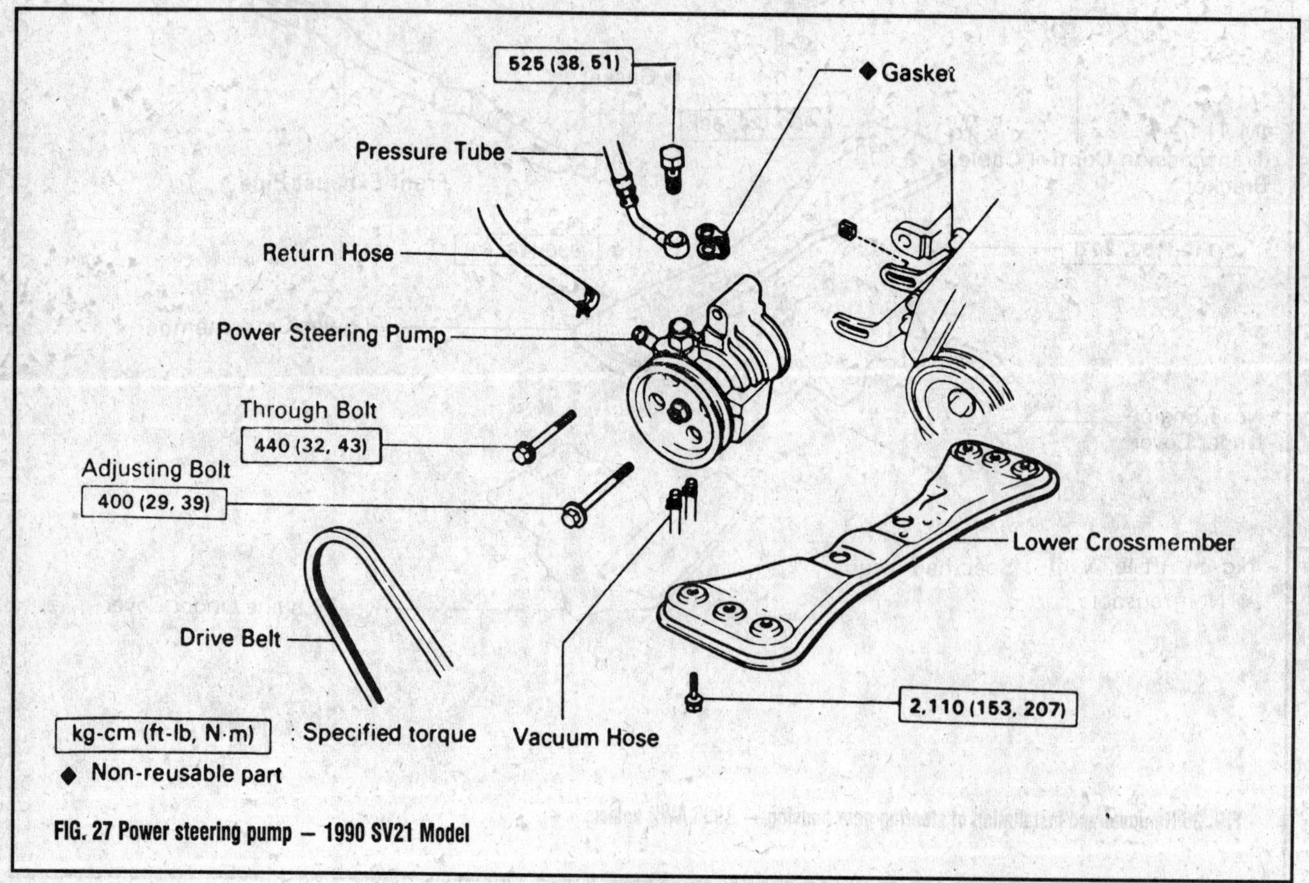

FIG. 27 Power steering pump — 1990 SV21 Model

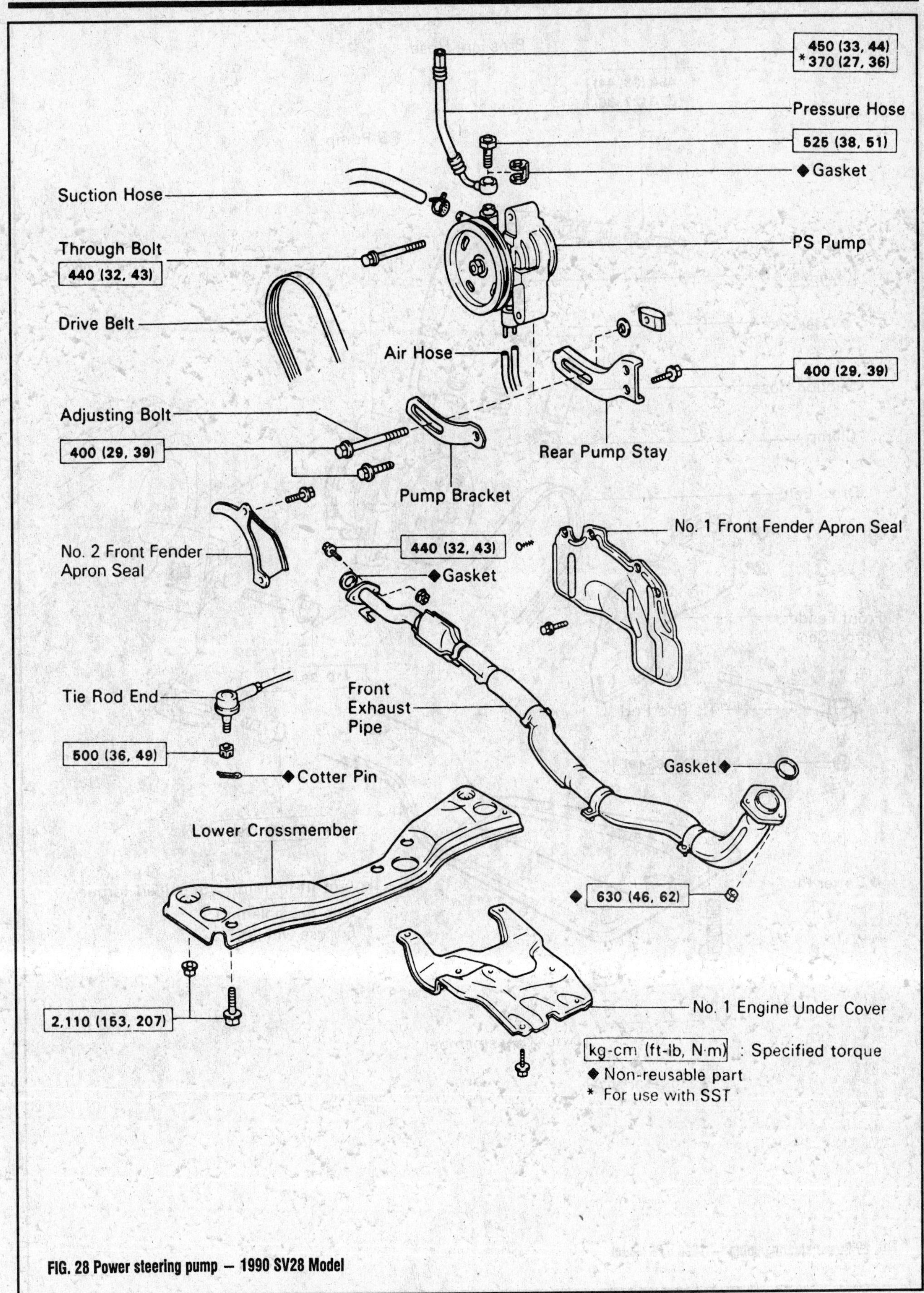
450 (33, 44)
*370 (27, 36)
Pressure Hose
525 (38, 51)
◆Gasket
Suction Hose
PS Pump
Through Bolt
440 (32, 43)
Drive Belt
Air Hose
400 (29, 39)
Adjusting Bolt
400 (29, 39)
Rear Pump Stay
Pump Bracket
No. 1 Front Fender Apron Seal
No. 2 Front Fender Apron Seal
440 (32, 43)
◆Gasket
Tie Rod End
Front Exhaust Pipe
500 (36, 49)
◆Cotter Pin
Gasket◆
Lower Crossmember
◆ 630 (46, 62)
2,110 (153, 207)
No. 1 Engine Under Cover
kg-cm (ft-lb, N·m) : Specified torque
◆ Non-reusable part
* For use with SST

FIG. 28 Power steering pump — 1990 SV28 Model

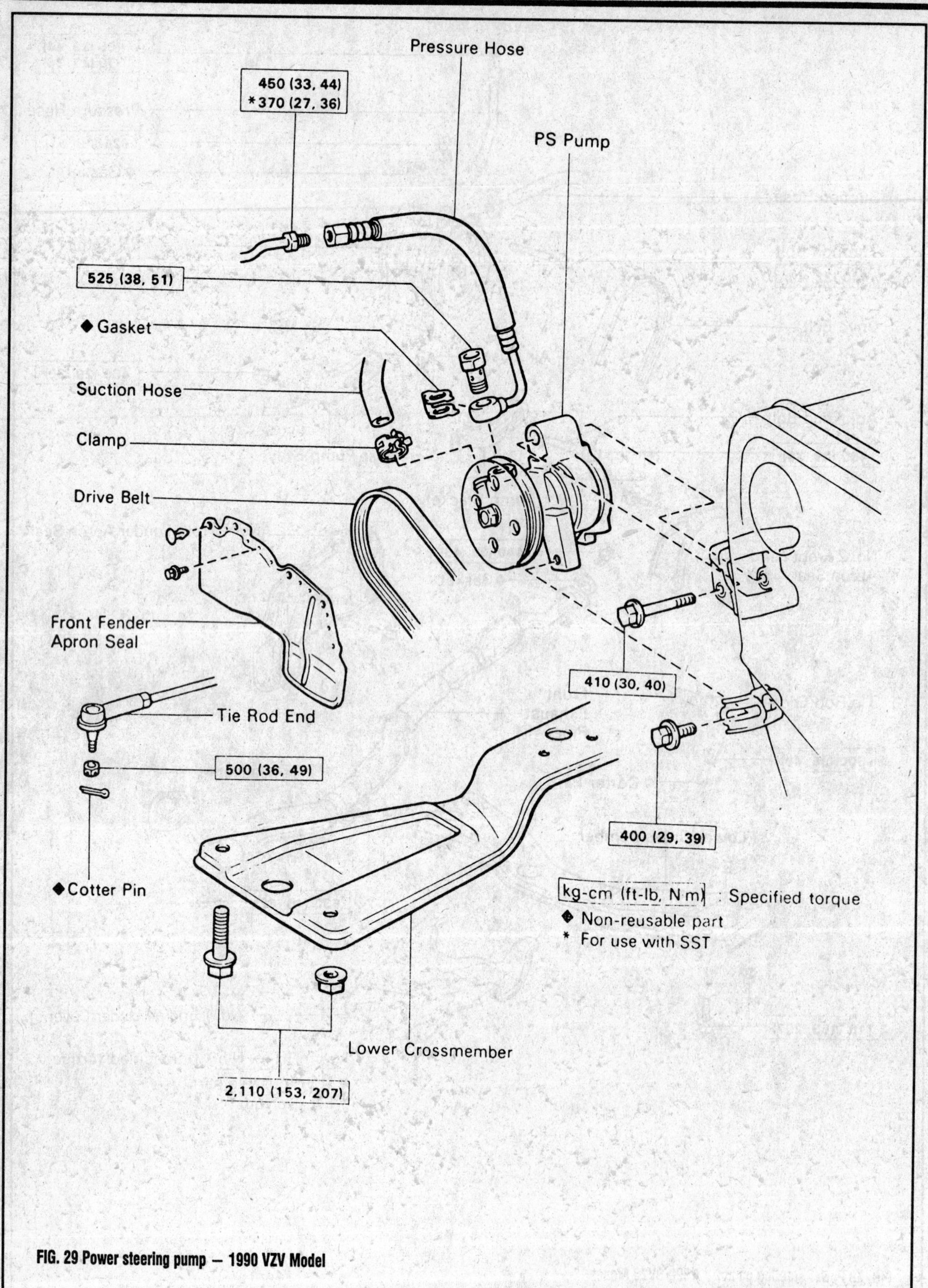

FIG. 29 Power steering pump — 1990 VZV Model

5. Loosen the clamp on the return hose and pull the hose from it's connection.

6. Remove the union bolt with the two gaskets and disconnect the return hose from the pump.

7. Loosen the two mounting bolts and push the pump downward until you can remove the drive belt from the pulley. Remove the bolts completely and remove the pump.

To Install:

8. Connect the pump to the mounting bracket temporarily with the two bolts and slip the drive belt over the pulley. Adjust the drive belt tension and tighten the bolts to 29 ft. lbs. (39 Nm).

9. Connect the pressure tube to the pump with two new gaskets. Torque the union bolt to 38 ft. lbs. (52 Nm).

10. Connect the return hose to the pump and tighten the clamp.

11. Connect the vacuum hose to the air control valve.

12. Install the cross member. Torque the center bolts to 29 ft. lbs. (39 Nm) and the outer bolts to 153 ft. lbs. (207 Nm).

13. Install the right front wheel and lower the vehicle.

14. Fill the reservoir tank to the proper level with Dexron®II ATF.

15. Bleed the system as described in this Section.

16. Check for all connections and hoses for leaks.

1989–92

1. Raise and support the vehicle safely. Remove the fan shroud.

2. Remove the right front wheel and the engine under cover. Remove the lower suspension crossmember.

3. Unfasten the nut from the center of the pump pulley. Disconnect the vacuum hose from the air control valve, if equipped.

➡ **Use the drive belt as a brake to keep the pulley from rotating.**

4. Withdraw the drive belt. On vehicles with SV pump, it will be necessary to disconnect the right tie rod from the steering knuckle.

5. If equipped with an idler pulley, push on the drive belt to hold the pulley in place and remove the pulley set nut. Loosen the idler pulley set nut and adjusting bolt. Remove the drive belt and loosen the drive pulley to remove the Woodruff key.

6. Remove the pulley and the Woodruff key from the pump shaft.

7. Detach and plug the intake and outlet hoses from the pump reservoir.

➡ **Tie the hose ends up high so the fluid cannot flow out of them. Drain or plug the pump to prevent fluid leakage.**

8. Remove the bolt from the rear mounting brace.

9. Remove the front bracket bolts and withdraw the pump from the lower side of the vehicle.

To Install:

10. Tighten the pump pulley mounting bolt to 25–39 ft. lbs. (34–53 Nm).

11. Tighten the 5 outer mounting bolts on the lower crossmember to 154 ft. lbs. (209 Nm).

12. Adjust the pump drive belt tension. The belt should deflect 0.13–0.93 in. (3.3–23.6mm) under thumb pressure applied midway between the air pump and the power steering pump.

13. Fill the reservoir with Dexron®II automatic transmission fluid. Bleed the air from the system.

BELT ADJUSTMENT

1. Inspect the power steering drive belt to see that it is not cracked or worn. Be sure its surfaces are free of grease or oil.

2. Push down on the belt halfway between the fan and the alternator pulleys (or crankshaft pulley) with thumb pressure. Belt deflection should be $^3/_8$–$^1/_2$ in. (10–13mm).

3. If the belt tension requires adjustment, loosen the adjusting link bolt and move the power steering pump until the proper belt tension is obtained.

4. Do not over-tighten the belt, as damage to the power steering pump bearings could result. Tighten the adjusting link bolt.

5. Drive the vehicle and re-check the belt tension. Adjust as necessary.

BLEEDING

1. Raise and support the vehicle safely.

2. Fill the pump reservoir with the proper fluid.

3. Rotate the steering wheel from lock-to-lock several times. Add fluid if necessary.

4. With the steering wheel turned fully to one lock, crank the starter while watching the fluid level in the reservoir.

➡ **Do not start the engine. Operate the starter with a remote starter switch or have an assistant do it from inside the vehicle. Do not run the starter for prolonged periods.**

5. Repeat Step 4 with the steering wheel turned to the opposite lock.

6. Start the engine. With the engine idling, turn the steering wheel from lock-to-lock several times.

7. Lower the front of the vehicle and repeat Step 6.

8. Center the wheel at the midpoint of its travel. Stop the engine.

9. The fluid level should not have risen more than 0.2 in. (5mm). If it does, repeat Step 7.

10. Check for fluid leakage.

Troubleshooting the Turn Signal Switch

Problem	Cause	Solution
Turn signal will not cancel	• Loose switch mounting screws • Switch or anchor bosses broken • Broken, missing or out of position detent, or cancelling spring	• Tighten screws • Replace switch • Reposition springs or replace switch as required
Turn signal difficult to operate	• Turn signal lever loose • Switch yoke broken or distorted • Loose or misplaced springs • Foreign parts and/or materials in switch • Switch mounted loosely	• Tighten mounting screws • Replace switch • Reposition springs or replace switch • Remove foreign parts and/or material • Tighten mounting screws
Turn signal will not indicate lane change	• Broken lane change pressure pad or spring hanger • Broken, missing or misplaced lane change spring • Jammed wires	• Replace switch • Replace or reposition as required • Loosen mounting screws, reposition wires and retighten screws
Turn signal will not stay in turn position	• Foreign material or loose parts impeding movement of switch yoke • Defective switch	• Remove material and/or parts • Replace switch
Hazard switch cannot be pulled out	• Foreign material between hazard support cancelling leg and yoke	• Remove foreign material. No foreign material impeding function of hazard switch—replace turn signal switch.
No turn signal lights	• Inoperative turn signal flasher • Defective or blown fuse • Loose chassis to column harness connector • Disconnect column to chassis connector. Connect new switch to chassis and operate switch by hand. If vehicle lights now operate normally, signal switch is inoperative • If vehicle lights do not operate, check chassis wiring for opens, grounds, etc.	• Replace turn signal flasher • Replace fuse • Connect securely • Replace signal switch • Repair chassis wiring as required

Troubleshooting the Turn Signal Switch (cont.)

Problem	Cause	Solution
Instrument panel turn indicator lights on but not flashing	• Burned out or damaged front or rear turn signal bulb	• Replace bulb
	• If vehicle lights do not operate, check light sockets for high resistance connections, the chassis wiring for opens, grounds, etc.	• Repair chassis wiring as required
	• Inoperative flasher	• Replace flasher
	• Loose chassis to column harness connection	• Connect securely
	• Inoperative turn signal switch	• Replace turn signal switch
	• To determine if turn signal switch is defective, substitute new switch into circuit and operate switch by hand. If the vehicle's lights operate normally, signal switch is inoperative.	• Replace turn signal switch
Stop light not on when turn indicated	• Loose column to chassis connection	• Connect securely
	• Disconnect column to chassis connector. Connect new switch into system without removing old.	• Replace signal switch
Stop light not on when turn indicated (cont.)	Operate switch by hand. If brake lights work with switch in the turn position, signal switch is defective.	
	• If brake lights do not work, check connector to stop light sockets for grounds, opens, etc.	• Repair connector to stop light circuits using service manual as guide
Turn indicator panel lights not flashing	• Burned out bulbs	• Replace bulbs
	• High resistance to ground at bulb socket	• Replace socket
	• Opens, ground in wiring harness from front turn signal bulb socket to indicator lights	• Locate and repair as required
Turn signal lights flash very slowly	• High resistance ground at light sockets	• Repair high resistance grounds at light sockets
	• Incorrect capacity turn signal flasher or bulb	• Replace turn signal flasher or bulb
	• If flashing rate is still extremely slow, check chassis wiring harness from the connector to light sockets for high resistance	• Locate and repair as required
	• Loose chassis to column harness connection	• Connect securely
	• Disconnect column to chassis connector. Connect new switch into system without removing old. Operate switch by hand. If flashing occurs at normal rate, the signal switch is defective.	• Replace turn signal switch

Troubleshooting the Turn Signal Switch (cont.)

Problem	Cause	Solution
Hazard signal lights will not flash—turn signal functions normally	• Blow fuse • Inoperative hazard warning flasher • Loose chassis-to-column harness connection • Disconnect column to chassis connector. Connect new switch into system without removing old. Depress the hazard warning lights. If they now work normally, turn signal switch is defective. • If lights do not flash, check wiring harness "K" lead for open between hazard flasher and connector. If open, fuse block is defective	• Replace fuse • Replace hazard warning flasher in fuse panel • Conect securely • Replace turn signal switch • Repair or replace brown wire or connector as required

Troubleshooting the Power Steering Pump

Problem	Cause	Solution
Chirp noise in steering pump	• Loose belt	• Adjust belt tension to specification
Belt squeal (particularly noticeable at full wheel travel and stand still parking)	• Loose belt	• Adjust belt tension to specification
Growl noise in steering pump	• Excessive back pressure in hoses or steering gear caused by restriction	• Locate restriction and correct. Replace part if necessary.
Growl noise in steering pump (particularly noticeable at stand still parking)	• Scored pressure plates, thrust plate or rotor • Extreme wear of cam ring	• Replace parts and flush system • Replace parts
Groan noise in steering pump	• Low oil level • Air in the oil. Poor pressure hose connection.	• Fill reservoir to proper level • Tighten connector to specified torque. Bleed system by operating steering from right to left—full turn.
Rattle noise in steering pump	• Vanes not installed properly • Vanes sticking in rotor slots	• Install properly • Free up by removing burrs, varnish, or dirt
Swish noise in steering pump	• Defective flow control valve	• Replace part
Whine noise in steering pump	• Pump shaft bearing scored	• Replace housing and shaft. Flush system.

Troubleshooting the Power Steering Pump (cont.)

Problem	Cause	Solution
Hard steering or lack of assist	• Loose pump belt • Low oil level in reservoir **NOTE:** Low oil level will also result in excessive pump noise • Steering gear to column misalignment • Lower coupling flange rubbing against steering gear adjuster plug • Tires not properly inflated	• Adjust belt tension to specification • Fill to proper level. If excessively low, check all lines and joints for evidence of external leakage. Tighten loose connectors. • Align steering column • Loosen pinch bolt and assemble properly • Inflate to recommended pressure
Foaming milky power steering fluid, low fluid level and possible low pressure	• Air in the fluid, and loss of fluid due to internal pump leakage causing overflow	• Check for leaks and correct. Bleed system. Extremely cold temperatures will cause system aeriation should the oil level be low. If oil level is correct and pump still foams, remove pump from vehicle and separate reservoir from body. Check welsh plug and body for cracks. If plug is loose or body is cracked, replace body.
Low pump pressure	• Flow control valve stuck or inoperative • Pressure plate not flat against cam ring	• Remove burrs or dirt or replace. Flush system. • Correct
Momentary increase in effort when turning wheel fast to right or left	• Low oil level in pump • Pump belt slipping • High internal leakage	• Add power steering fluid as required • Tighten or replace belt • Check pump pressure. (See pressure test)
Steering wheel surges or jerks when turning with engine running especially during parking	• Low oil level • Loose pump belt • Steering linkage hitting engine oil pan at full turn • Insufficient pump pressure	• Fill as required • Adjust tension to specification • Correct clearance • Check pump pressure. (See pressure test). Replace flow control valve if defective.

Troubleshooting the Power Steering Pump (cont.)

Problem	Cause	Solution
Steering wheel surges or jerks when turning with engine running especially during parking (cont.)	· Sticking flow control valve	· Inspect for varnish or damage, replace if necessary
Excessive wheel kickback or loose steering	· Air in system	· Add oil to pump reservoir and bleed by operating steering. Check hose connectors for proper torque and adjust as required.
Low pump pressure	· Extreme wear of cam ring	· Replace parts. Flush system.
	· Scored pressure plate, thrust plate, or rotor	· Replace parts. Flush system.
	· Vanes not installed properly	· Install properly
	· Vanes sticking in rotor slots	· Freeup by removing burrs, varnish, or dirt
	· Cracked or broken thrust or pressure plate	· Replace part

TORQUE SPECIFICATIONS

Component	U.S.	Metric
Brake hose union bolt	22 ft. lbs.	29 Nm
Brake tube union nuts	11 ft. lbs.	16 Nm
Caliper mounting bolts	86 ft. lbs.	117 Nm
Center bracket bolts	14 ft. lbs.	19 Nm
Front shock absorber to body nuts		
1983-86	27 ft. lbs.	36 Nm
1987-91	47 ft. lbs.	64 Nm
1992	59 ft. lbs.	80 Nm
Knuckle assembly to lower strut bracket		
1983–87:	152 ft. lbs.	206 Nm
1988:	166 ft. lbs.	226 Nm
1989–91:	224 ft. lbs.	304 Nm
1992:	156 ft. lbs.	211 Nm
Lower ball joint to knuckle mounting nut		
1986	67 ft. lbs.	91 Nm
1988–91		
Lower arm shaft-to-lower arm bolt	156 ft. lbs.	212 Nm
Stabilizer bar end nut	156 ft. lbs.	212 Nm
1989–92	90 ft. lbs.	123 Nm
Lower ball joint to steering knuckle nut	94 ft. lbs.	127 Nm
Lug nuts		
steel wheels	100 ft. lbs.	136 Nm
aluminum wheels	90 ft. lbs.	122 Nm
Rear shock to body nuts		
1983–86	17 ft. lbs.	25 Nm
1987–88	23 ft. lbs.	31 Nm
1989–92	29 ft. lbs.	39 Nm
Rear shock absorber bracket o axle carrier nuts		
1983–86	119 ft. lbs.	162 Nm
1987–91	166 ft. lbs.	226 Nm
1992	188 ft. lbs.	155 Nm
Suspension support-to-strut nut		
1988–91	36 ft. lbs.	49 Nm
Stabilizer bar link to strut retainers		
1992	47 ft. lbs.	64 Nm
Tie rod end to knuckle nut	36 ft. lbs.	49 Nm

ANTI-LOCK BRAKE SYSTEM
Actuator 9-38
Bleeding 9-39
Control relays 9-36
Decelerator sensor 9-37
Front wheel speed sensor 9-36
Operation 9-27
Rear wheel speed sensor 9-37
BRAKES
Adjustments
Brake pedal 9-25
Bleeding 9-8
Brake light switch 9-3
Master cylinder 9-3
DISC BRAKES (FRONT)
Caliper 9-12
Pads 9-9
Rotor (Disc) 9-13
DISC BRAKES (REAR)
Caliper 9-23
Pads 9-23
Rotor 9-25
DRUM BRAKES
Adjustment 9-2
Drum 9-14
Shoes 9-16
Wheel cylinder 9-22
HOSES AND LINES 9-9
MASTER CYLINDER 9-3
PARKING BRAKE
Adjustment 9-25
Cables 9-25
Removal and installation 9-25
POWER BOOSTER
Removal and installation 9-4
PROPORTIONING VALVE 9-7
SPECIFICATIONS 9-39
TROUBLESHOOTING 9-40

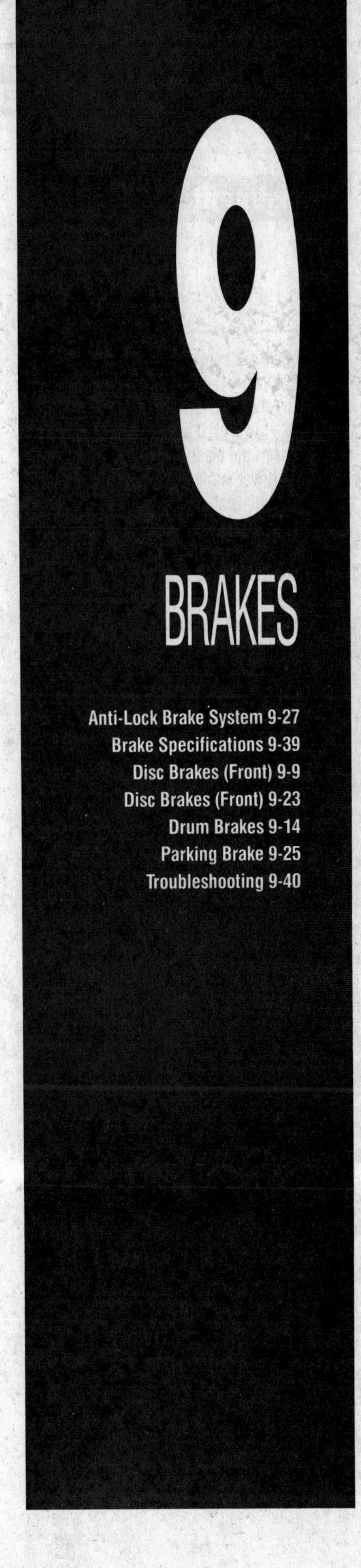

9 BRAKES

Anti-Lock Brake System 9-27
Brake Specifications 9-39
Disc Brakes (Front) 9-9
Disc Brakes (Front) 9-23
Drum Brakes 9-14
Parking Brake 9-25
Troubleshooting 9-40

BRAKE OPERATING SYSTEM

Adjustment

REAR DRUM BRAKES

All models are equipped with self-adjusting rear drum brakes. Under normal conditions, adjustment of the rear brake shoes should not be necessary. However, if an initial adjustment is required insert the blade of a brake adjuster tool or a screw driver into the hole in the brake drum and turn the adjuster slowly. The tension is set correctly if the tire and wheel assembly will rotate approximately 3 times when spun with moderate force. Do not over adjust the brake shoes. Before adjusting the rear drum brake shoes, make sure emergency brake is in the OFF position, and all cables are free.

BRAKE PEDAL

➧ SEE FIGS. 1 AND 2

Before adjusting the pedal height, measure the distance from the top of the pedal rubber to the carpet. On 1983–85 vehicles this distance should be approximately 7.4–7.8 in. (188–198mm) and 6.9–7.4 in. (178–188mm) for 1986–91 vehicles. For 1992 vehicles, this distance should be approximately 5.8–6.2 in. (147–158 Nm). If the actual measurement does not agree with the range given, the pedal height **and** the pedal freeplay must be adjusted.

To adjust the pedal height perform the following:

1. If necessary, remove the instrument lower finish panel, air duct and floor mats to gain access to the pedal and pedal linkages.
2. Loosen the stop light switch locknut and loosen the stop light switch until it can be moved freely by hand.
3. Loosen the push rod locknut and adjust the height of the pedal by rotating the push rod as needed. Torque the push rod locknut to 19 ft. lbs. (25 Nm).
4. Return the stop light switch until it lightly contacts the pedal stop and tighten the two locknuts.
5. Start the engine.
6. Depress the pedal and have an assistant verify the stop lights illuminate.

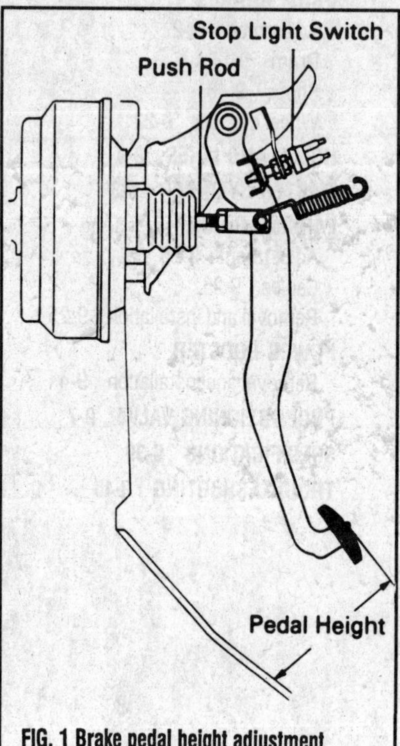

FIG. 1 Brake pedal height adjustment

7. Now, stop the engine adjust the pedal freeplay

To check and adjust pedal freeplay, perform the following:

8. With the engine off depress the brake pedal several times until all the vacuum is removed from the booster.
9. Push the pedal by hand until resistance can just be felt and measure the distance from the top of the pedal rubber to the bottom of the carpet. The distance should be 3–6mm for all models.
10. If the freeplay is not correct, loosen the push rod locknut until the freeplay is within the given range.
11. Start the engine and verify that there is freeplay in the pedal. Check the pedal height again to make sure that is has not been disturbed. To check the pedal height after a freeplay adjustment, depress the pedal by foot and measure the pedal reserve distance with the engine running. The pedal reserve distance should be more than 2.76 in. (70mm) with a moderate force applied to the pedal.
12. If the pedal reserve distance is not correct, troubleshoot the brake system.
13. If all adjustments are satisfactory, install the air duct and lower instrument finish panel.

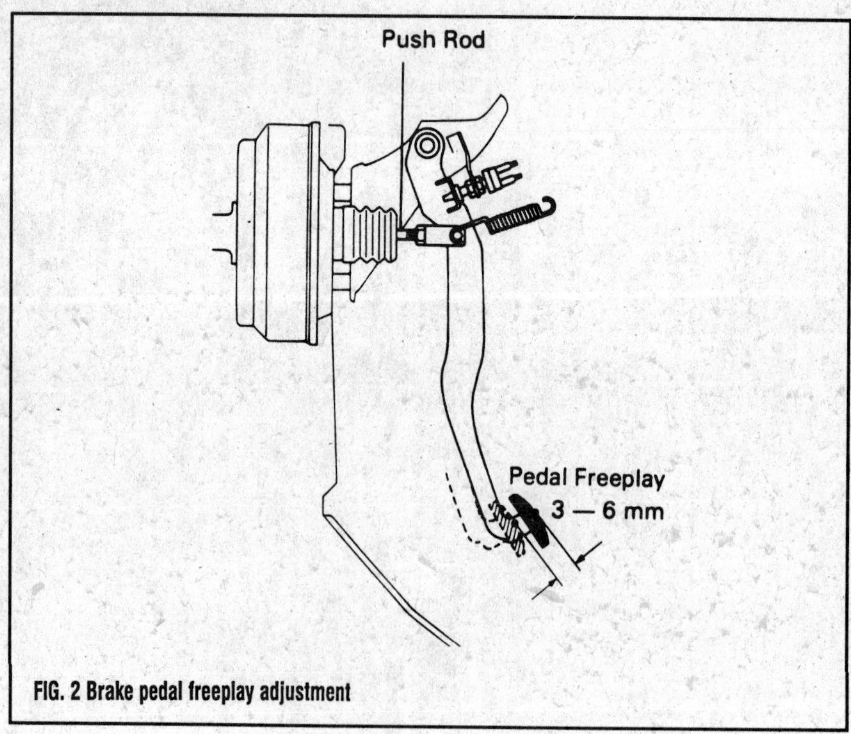

FIG. 2 Brake pedal freeplay adjustment

Brake Light Switch

REMOVAL & INSTALLATION

1. Disconnect the negative battery cable.
2. Remove the instrument lower finish panel and the air duct if required to gain access to the stoplight switch.
3. Disconnect the stoplight switch connector.
4. Remove the switch mounting nut, then slide the switch from the mounting bracket on the pedal.

To install:

5. Install the switch into the mounting bracket and adjust.
6. Connect the switch connector and reconnect the negative battery cable.
7. Depress the brake pedal and verify that the brake lights illuminate.
8. Install the air duct and the lower finish panel, if removed.

Brake Pedal

REMOVAL & INSTALLATION

1. Disconnect the negative battery cable.
2. Remove the instrument lower finish panel and the lower air duct, as required.
3. Remove the brake pedal return spring. Disconnect and remove the brake light switch.
4. Remove clip and clevis pin.
5. Unbolt and remove the brake pedal assembly from the vehicle.
6. The installation is the reverse of the removal procedure. Check and adjust the brake pedal as required. Assure that the brake lights are fully functional.

Master Cylinder

REMOVAL & INSTALLATION

SEE FIGS. 3 AND 4

Before the master cylinder is reinstalled, the brake booster pushrod must be adjusted. This adjustment requires the use of factory special tool SST No. 09397-00010 or its equivalent.

1. Open the hood and disconnect the level warning switch connector. Disconnect the negative battery cable.
2. Remove the cap from the master cylinder and drain the fluid out with the use a turkey baster or similar syringe. Deposit the fluid into a container.
3. Disconnect the brake tubes from the

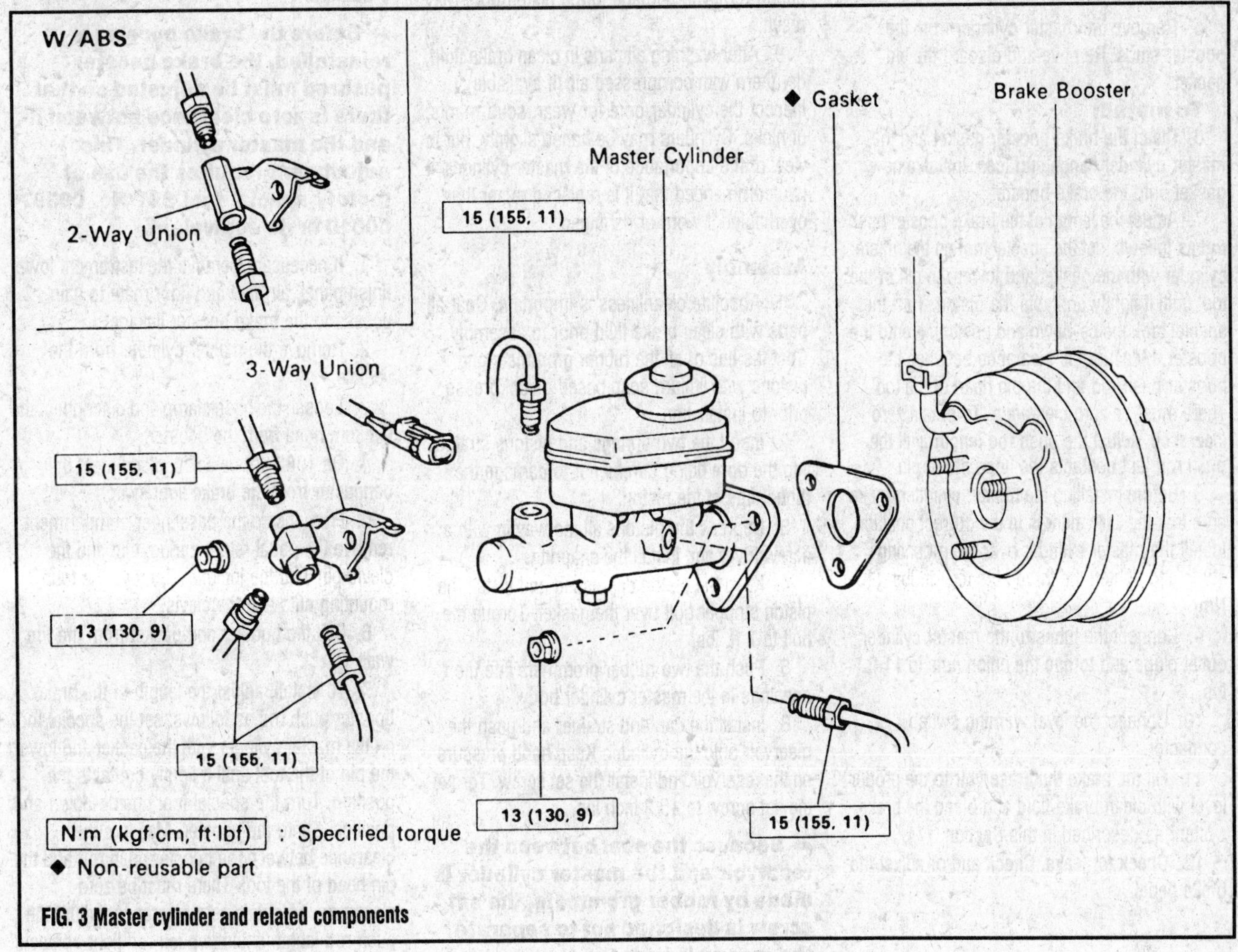

FIG. 3 Master cylinder and related components

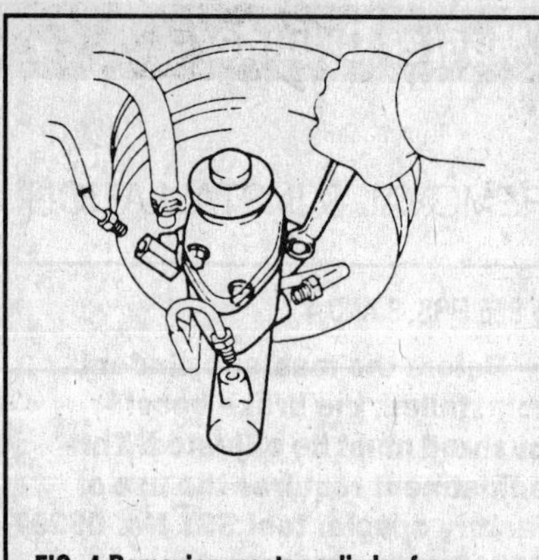

FIG. 4 Removing master cylinder from brake booster

master cylinder. Drain the fluid from the lines into the container. Plug the lines to prevent fluid from leaking onto and damaging painted surfaces or the entry of moisture into the brake system.

4. Remove the three nuts that attach the master cylinder and 3-way union to the brake booster.

5. Remove the master cylinder from the booster studs. Remove and discard the old gasket.

To install:

6. Clean the brake booster gasket and the master cylinder flange surfaces. Install a new gasket onto the brake booster.

7. Adjust the length of the brake booster push rod as follows: set the special tool on the master cylinder with the gasket and lower the pin of the tool until it lightly contacts the piston. Turn the special tool upside-down and position it onto the booster. Measure the clearance between the booster push rod and the pin head of the tool. There must be zero clearance. To obtain zero clearance, adjust the push rod length until the push rod just contacts the head of the pin.

8. Before installing the master cylinder, make sure that the **UP** mark is in the correct position. Install the master cylinder over the mounting studs and tighten the three nuts to 9 ft. lbs. (13 Nm).

9. Connect the tubes to the master cylinder outlet plugs and torque the union nuts to 11 ft. lbs.

10. Connect the level warning switch connector.

11. Fill the brake fluid reservoir to the proper level with clean brake fluid and bleed the brake system as described in this Section.

12. Check for leaks. Check and/or adjust the brake pedal.

OVERHAUL

Disassembly

➧ SEE FIG. 5

1. Remove the master cylinder from the vehicle.

2. Remove the setscrew at the bottom of the reservoir tank and pull the reservoir from the body. Remove the cap and strainer.

3. Remove the two rubber grommets from the housing.

4. Clamp the master cylinder body in a vise.

5. Push the pistons all the way in with a screwdriver and remove the piston stopper bolt and gasket.

6. Keep the piston depressed and remove the snapring using snapring pliers.

7. Place a rag on two blocks of wood and **lightly** tap the flange of the body against the blocks until the tip of the piston is visible.

8. Pull the pistons with springs by hand straight out of the bore. If the piston(s) is cocked during removal, damage to the piston bore may result.

9. After washing all parts in clean brake fluid, dry them with compressed air (if available). Inspect the cylinder bore for wear, scuff marks, or nicks. Cylinders may be honed slightly, but in view of the importance of the master cylinder, it is recommended that it is replaced rather than overhauled if worn or damaged.

Assembly

1. Absolute cleanliness is important. Coat all parts with clean brake fluid prior to assembly. Coat the lips of all the rubber grommets and pistons with lithium soap based glycol grease prior to installation.

2. Insert the two springs and pistons straight into the bore being careful not to damage the rubber lips of the piston.

3. Depress the pistons all the way in with a screwdriver and install the snapring.

4. Keep the piston depressed and install the piston stopper bolt over the gasket. Torque the bolt to 7 ft. lbs.

5. Push the two rubber grommets into the openings in the master cylinder body.

6. Install the cap and strainer and push the reservoir onto the cylinder. Keep hand pressure on the reservoir and install the set screw. Torque the set screw to 15.2 inch lbs.

➡ Because the seal between the reservoir and the master cylinder is made by rubber grommets, the set screw is designed not to separate the reservoir from the cylinder and will not tighten down the reservoir. Due to the nature of this type of seal, there will be a clearance between the head of the screw and the body. This clearance is normal and no attempt should be made to shim it up with washers or a spacer.

7. Install the master cylinder onto the vehicle.

8. Fill the brake fluid reservoir to the proper level with clean brake fluid and bleed the master cylinder as described in this Section.

9. Check for leaks. Check and/or adjust the brake pedal as required.

Power Brake Booster

REMOVAL & INSTALLATION

➧ SEE FIG. 6

➡ Before the brake booster is reinstalled, the brake booster pushrod must be adjusted so that there is zero clearance between it and the master cylinder. This adjustment requires the use of factory special tool SST No. 09397-00010 or its equivalent.

1. If necessary, remove the instrument lower finish panel, air duct and floor mats to gain access to the brake booster linkage.

2. Remove the master cylinder from the vehicle.

3. Loosen the hose clamp and disconnect the vacuum hose from the booster.

4. On 1983–86 vehicles, disconnect the connector from the brake light switch.

5. From inside the passenger compartment, remove the pedal return spring, clip and the clevis pin with the locknut. Remove the four mounting nuts and the clevis.

6. Pull the booster and gasket from the fire wall.

7. To install, adjust the length of the brake booster push rod as follows: set the special tool on the master cylinder with the gasket and lower the pin of the tool until it lightly contacts the position. Turn the special tool upside-down and position it onto the booster. Measure the clearance between the booster push rod and the pin head of the tool. There must be zero clearance. To obtain zero clearance, adjust the push rod length until the push rod light contacts the head of the pin.

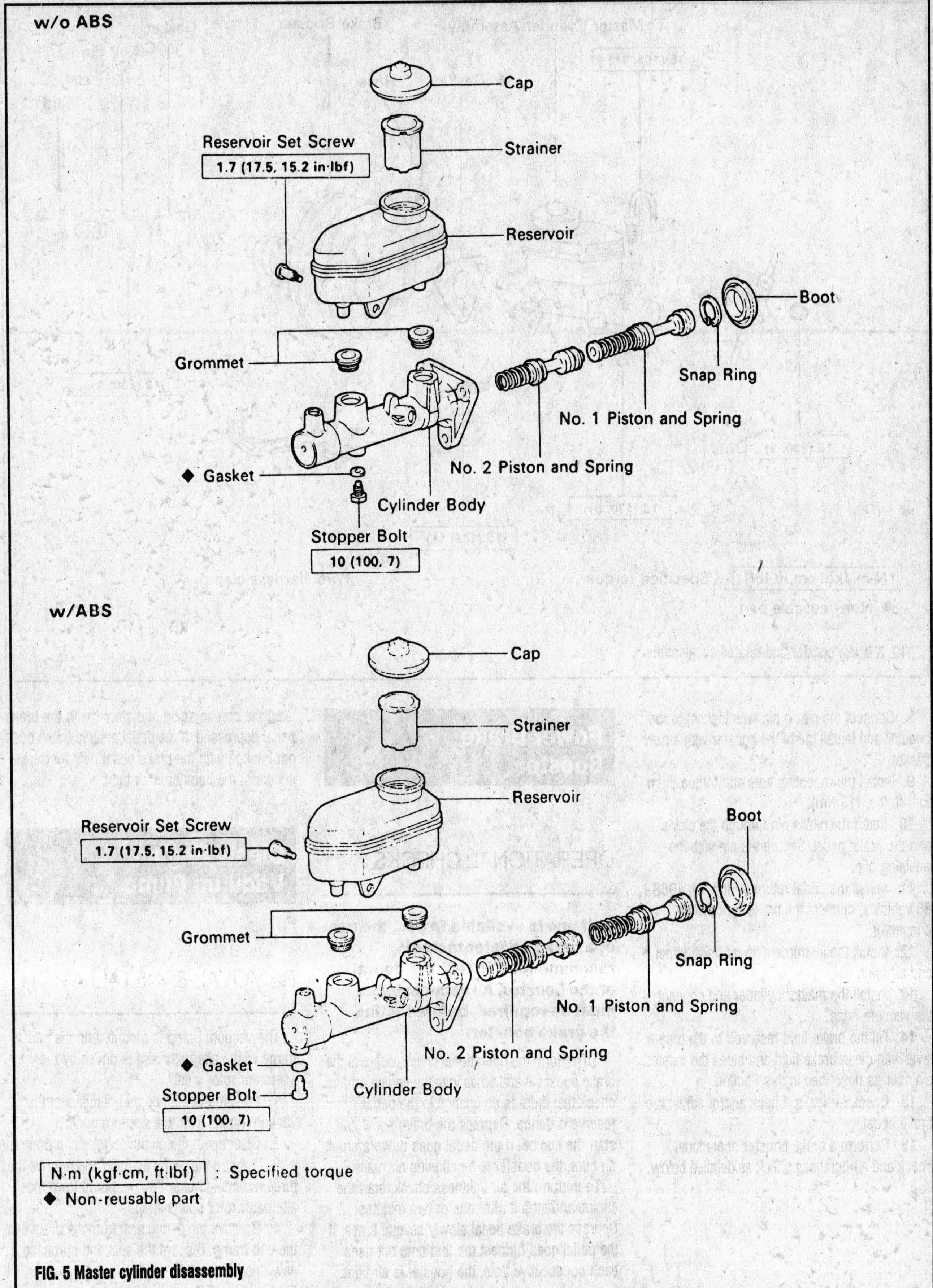

FIG. 5 Master cylinder disassembly

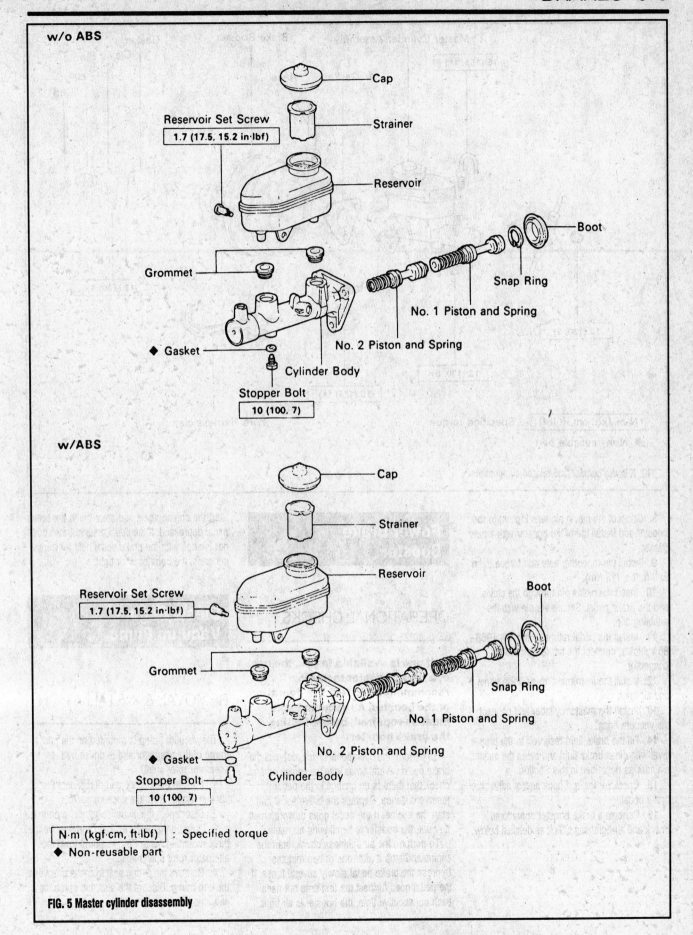

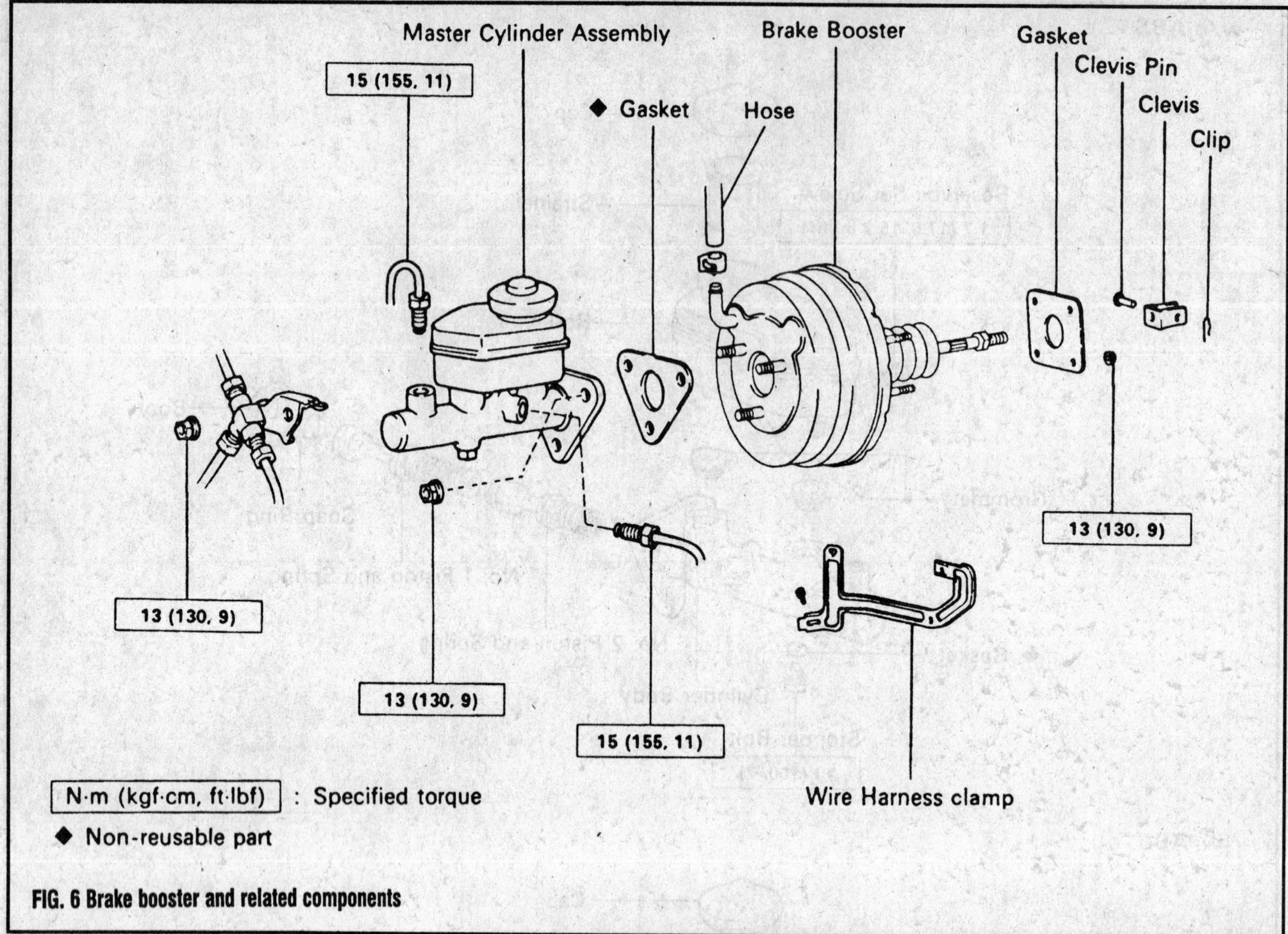

FIG. 6 Brake booster and related components

8. Connect the clevis pin with locknut to the booster and install the brake booster with a new gasket.

9. Install the mounting nuts and torque them to 9 ft. lbs. (13 Nm).

10. Insert the clevis pin through the clevis and the brake pedal. Secure the pin with the retaining clip.

11. Install the pedal return spring. On 1983–86 vehicles, connect the brake light switch connector.

12. Install the instrument lower finish panel and air duct.

13. Install the master cylinder and connect the vacuum hose.

14. Fill the brake fluid reservoir to the proper level with clean brake fluid and bleed the master cylinder as described in this Section.

15. Check for leaks. Check and/or adjust the brake pedal.

16. Perform a brake booster operational check and air tightness check as detailed below.

Power Brake Booster

OPERATIONAL CHECKS

➡ If one is available to you, the use of a brake booster tester is recommended to test the operation of the booster. All vacuum leaks must be repaired, before testing the brake booster.

To perform the operational check, depress the brake pedal several times with the engine off and check that there is no change in the pedal reserve distance. Depress the brake pedal and start the engine. If the pedal goes down a small amount, the booster is functioning normally.

To perform the air tightness check, start the engine and stop it after one or two minutes. Depress the brake pedal slowly several times. If the pedal goes furthest the first time but rises each consecutive time, the booster is air tight. Start the engine again and stop it with the brake pedal depressed. If the pedal reserve travel does not change with the brake pedal held for thirty seconds, the booster is air tight.

Diesel Engine Vacuum Pump

REMOVAL & INSTALLATION

The vacuum pump is mounted on the end frame of the alternator and is driven by the alternator rotor shaft.

1. Loosen the clamps and disconnect the vacuum hoses from the vacuum pump.

2. Disconnect the oil outlet hose and drain it.

3. Support the pump by hand and remove the three mounting bolts. Pull the pump from the alternator rotor spline shaft.

4. Remove the O-ring seal from the groove in the end frame. Discard the seal and purchase a new one.

To Install:

5. Install a new O-ring into the end frame groove.

6. Coat the rotor spline shaft with multi-purpose grease.

7. Engage the pump with the spline shaft and secure with the mounting bolts. Torque the mounting bolts to 69 inch lbs.

8. Connect all the hoses and check the vacuum pump operation.

Proportioning Valve

A proportioning valve is used to reduce the hydraulic pressure to the rear brakes because of weight transfer during high speed stops. This helps to keep the rear brakes from locking up by improving front to rear brake balance.

REMOVAL & INSTALLATION

1. Disconnect the brake lines from the valve unions.

2. Remove the valve mounting bolt, if used, and remove the valve.

➡ If the proportioning valve is defective, it must be replaced as an assembly; it cannot be rebuilt.

3. Installation is the reverse of removal. Bleed the brake system after it is completed.

Load Sensing Proportioning Valve (LSPV)

REMOVAL & INSTALLATION

➧ SEE FIGS. 7

1. Disconnect the brake lines from the valve body.

2. Remove the locknut and disconnect the adjusting bolt from the rear suspension arm.

3. Remove the 2 mounting bolts and remove the LSPV from the vehicle.

To Install:

4. Install the valve and secure with the 2 mounting bolts. Tighten the bolts to 9 ft. lbs. (13 Nm).

5. Install the adjusting bolt and then install the adjusting bolt lock bolt to the rear suspension arm with the adjusting bolt locknut.

6. Set the shaft length (end opposite the adjusting nut) to the initial set length of 1.08 inch (27.5mm) and temporarily tighten the bolt lock nut.

7. Connect the brake lines to the valve body. Torque the tubes to 11 ft. lbs. (15 Nm).

8. Fill the master cylinder with clean brake fluid and bleed the brake system.

9. Check the system for leaks and repair as required. Check and adjust the fluid pressure and bleed the brake system. Refill the master cylinder with clean fluid and check for leaks.

FLUID PRESSURE INSPECTION

1. Begin the procedure by setting the rear axle load. To do this, set the vehicle to its curb weight of approximately 68 lbs.

2. Install LSPV gauge tool 09709-29017 or equivalent, and bleed the brake system.

3. Raise the front brake pressure to 1,565 psi (10,791 kpa) and check the rear pressure, which should be 1,013–1,154 psi (6.985–7957 kpa).

4. If necessary, adjust the pressures as follows:

a. To raise the pressure, adjust the LSPV locknut to increase the length of the upper portion of the shaft (end opposite the adjusting nut).

b. To decrease the pressure, adjust the

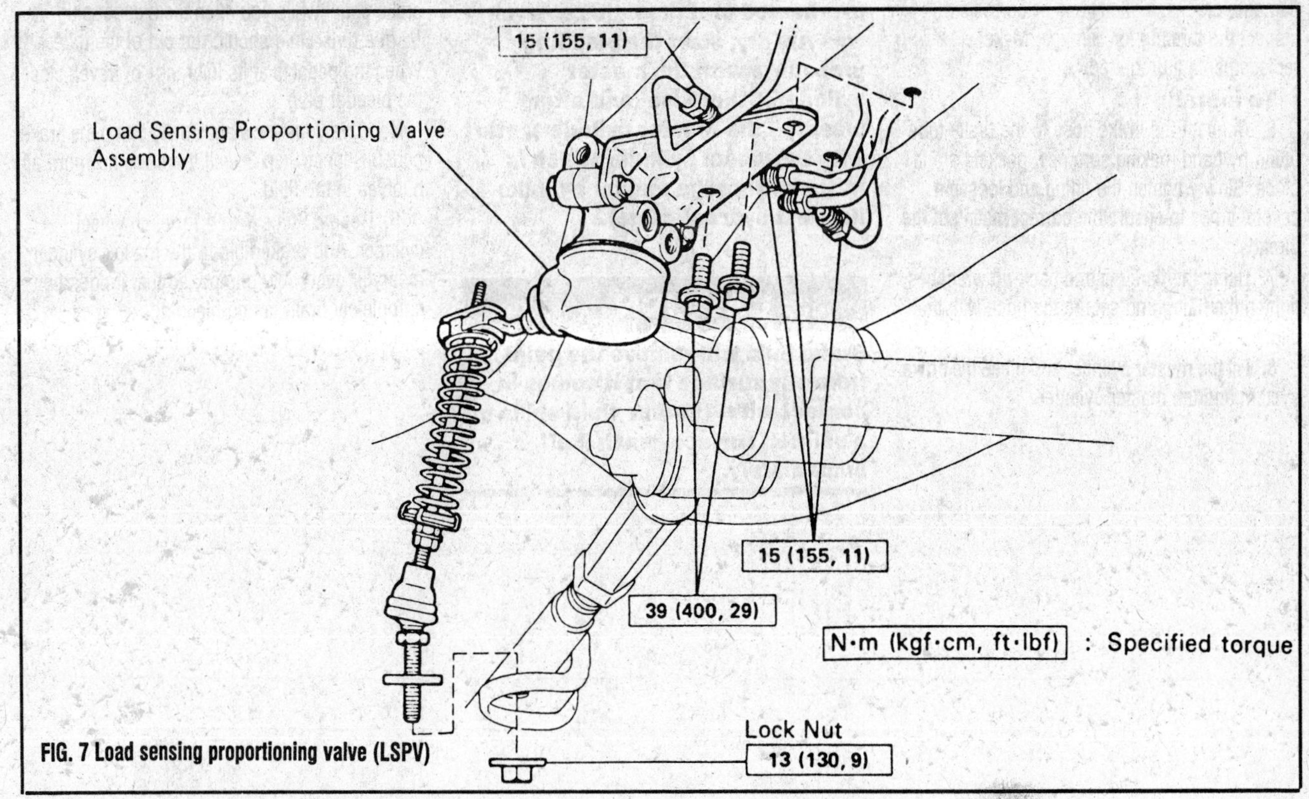

FIG. 7 Load sensing proportioning valve (LSPV)

LSPV locknut to decrease the length of the upper portion of the shaft (end opposite the adjusting nut).

c. As a guide, the fluid pressure is adjusted 45.5 psi (313.7 kpa) for each revolution of the adjusting nut.

5. Torque the locknut to 9 ft. lbs. (13 Nm).
6. If it can not be adjusted, replace the valve.

Brake Hoses

REMOVAL & INSTALLATION

1. Remove the brake line clip.
2. Using a back-up wrench to hold the hose, loosen the connector nut with the proper size flare nut wrench and disconnect the hose from the fitting.
3. Drain the hose into a plastic container. If equipped with gaskets on either side of the hose connections, discard old gaskets and replace with new.
4. Visually inspect the brake hose for signs of cracking, damage and swelling. Inspect the fitting threads for damage. Minor thread damage may be repaired with a jeweler's file. Make replacements as required. If a repair is questionable, replace the part.
5. Visually inspect the brake tubes for damage, cracks, indentations or corrosion. Inspect the threads for damage. Make replacements as required.

To install:

6. Connect the brake hose to the brake tube fitting by hand making sure new gaskets are in place. Slowly tighten the fitting and loosen it several times to ensure the correct mating of the threads.
7. Using the flare nut and back-up wrenches, tighten the fitting and secure the hose with the clip.
8. Fill the master cylinder and bleed the brake system and the master cylinder.

BRAKE PIPE FLARING

Flaring steel lines is a skill that needs to be practiced before it should be done on a line to be used on a vehicle. It is essential that the flare be done uniformly to prevent any leaks when the brake system is under pressure. It is also recommended that the flare be a "double flare" (rolled twice). With the supply of parts available today, a preflared steel brake line should be available to fit your needs. Due to the high pressures in the brake system and the serious injuries that could occur if the brake system (flare in a brake line) should fail, it is strongly advised that preflared lines are installed when repairing the braking system. If a line were to leak brake fluid due to an defective flare, and the leak was to go undetected, brake failure would result

Bleeding the Brake System

On vehicles equipped with anti-lock brakes (ABS), please refer to the appropriate procedure in a later section of this Section.

➡ **If any maintenance or repairs were performed on the brake system, or if air is suspected in the system, the system must be bled. If the master cylinder has been overhauled or if the fluid reservoir was run dry, start the bleeding procedure with the master cylinder. Otherwise (and after bleeding the master cylinder), start with the wheel cylinder which is farthest from the master cylinder (longest hydraulic line).**

CAUTION

Brake fluid will remove the paint from any surface that it comes in contact with. If brake fluid spills on a painted surface, wash it off immediately.

MASTER CYLINDER

1. Check the fluid level in the master cylinder reservoir and add fluid as required to bring to the proper level.
2. Loosen the two brake tubes from the master cylinder.
3. Have an assistant depress the brake pedal and hold it in the down position.
4. While the pedal is depressed, tighten the fluid lines and then release the brake pedal.
5. Repeat the procedure three or four times.
6. Bleed the brake system, if needed.

BRAKE SYSTEM

➡ **Start the brake system bleeding procedure on the wheel cylinder that is the furthest away from the master cylinder. To bleed the brakes you will need a supply of brake fluid, a long piece of clear vinyl tubing and a small container that is half full of brake fluid.**

1. Clean all the dirt and grease from the wheel cylinder bleeder plug and remove the protective cap. Connect one end of a clear vinyl tube to the fitting.
2. Insert the other end of the tube into a jar which is half filled with brake fluid.
3. Have an assistant slowly depress the brake pedal while you open the bleeder plug $1/3$–$1/2$ of a turn. Fluid should run out of the tube. When the pedal is at its full range of travel, close the bleeder plug.
4. Have your assistant slowly pump the brake pedal. Repeat Step 3 until there are no more air bubbles in the fluid.
5. Repeat Steps 1 to 4 for each wheel cylinder. Add brake fluid to the master cylinder reservoir every few pumps, so that it does not completely drain during bleeding.

FRONT DISC BRAKES

⁂ CAUTION

Brake shoes contain asbestos, which has been determined to be a cancer causing agent. Never clean the brake surfaces with compressed air! Avoid inhaling any dust from any brake surfaces. When cleaning brake surfaces, use a commercially available brake cleaning fluid.

Brake Pads

REMOVAL & INSTALLATION

➧ SEE FIGS. 9–12

1983–88

1. Loosen the front wheel lugs slightly, then raise and safely support the front of the car. Remove the front wheel(s) and temporarily attach the rotor disc with two of the wheel nuts.
2. Remove the two bolts from the torque plate.
3. Remove the brake cylinder and suspend it with a piece of wire from the strut spring so that the brake hose in not under stress. DO NOT disconnect the brake hose.
4. Remove the two anti-squeal springs, two brake pads, two anti-squeal shims, two wear indicator plates and four pad support plates. Note the various positions of the parts removed to make installation easier.
5. Check the rotor thickness and disc runout as described in this Section.

To Install:

6. Install the four pad support plates and a new pad wear indicator plate on the inside brake pad.

➡ Make sure that the arrow on the pad wear indicator is pointing in the rotating direction of the disc.

7. Install the new brake pads onto the support plates, then install the two anti-squeal springs. Do not allow oil and grease to come in contact with the surface of the pads.
8. Remove the master cylinder cap and take a small amount of brake fluid from the reservoir. Force the piston back into the caliper bore using a large C-type clamp to accommodate the greater thickness of the new brake pads. Always do one wheel at a time, because at this point there is the possibility of the opposite piston extending out of the caliper bore. If the piston is difficult to push into the caliper, loosen the bleeder plug and allow fluid to exit the caliper while depressing the piston into the caliper bore.
9. Remove the supporting wire and position the brake cylinder carefully to avoid wedging the dust boot. Install the cylinder installation bolts. On 1983–86 vehicles, torque the bolts to 18 ft. lbs. (24 Nm) and 29 ft. lbs. (39 Nm) on 1987–88 vehicles.
10. Install the front wheels and lower the vehicle.
11. Check the master cylinder level to ensure that it is on the **MAX** line. Before moving the vehicle, make sure to pump the brake pedal to seat the pads against the rotors.

1989–92

1. Raise and support the vehicle safely.
2. Remove the wheels.
3. Siphon a sufficient quantity of brake fluid from the master cylinder reservoir to prevent any brake fluid from overflowing the master cylinder when removing or installing new pads. This is necessary as the piston must be forced into the caliper bore to provide sufficient clearance when installing the pads.
4. Grasp the caliper from behind and carefully pull it to seat the piston in its bore.
5. Loosen and remove the 2 caliper mounting pins (bolts) and then remove the caliper assembly. Position it aside. Do not disconnect the brake line.
6. Slide out the old brake pads along with any anti-squeal shims, springs, pad wear indicators and pad support plates. Make sure to note the position of all assorted pad hardware.

To Install:

7. Check the brake disc (rotor) for thickness and run-out. Inspect the caliper and piston assembly for breaks, cracks, fluid seepage or other damage. Overhaul or replace as necessary.
8. Install the pad support plates into the torque plate.
9. Install the pad wear indicators onto the pads. Be sure the arrow on the indicator plate is pointing in the direction of rotation.
10. Install the anti-squeal shims on the outside of each pad and then install the pad assemblies into the torque plate.
11. Position the caliper back down over the pads. If it won't fit, use a C-clamp or hammer handle and carefully force the piston into its bore.
12. Install and tighten the caliper mounting bolts to 29 ft. lbs. (39 Nm) on 1989–91 vehicles, and 25 ft. lbs (34 Nm) on 1992 vehicles.
13. Install the wheels and lower the vehicle. Check the brake fluid level. Before moving the vehicle, make sure to pump the brake pedal to seat the pads against the rotors.

INSPECTION

If you hear a squealing noise coming from the front brakes while driving, check the brake lining thickness and pad wear indicator by looking into the inspection hole on the brake cylinder with the front wheels removed and the vehicle properly supported. The wear indicator is designed to emit the squealing noise when the brake pad wears down to 2.5mm at which time the pad wear plate and the rotor disc rub against each other. If there are traces of the pad wear indicator contacting the rotor disc, the brake pads should be replaced.

To inspect the brake lining thickness, look through the inspection hole and measure the lining thickness using a machinists rule. Also looks for signs of uneven wear. Standard thickness is 10mm. The **minimum** allowable thickness is 0.039 in. (1mm) at which time the brake pads must be replaced.

➡ Always replace the pads on both front wheels. When inspecting or replacing the brake pads, check the surface of the disc rotors for scoring, wear and runout. The rotors should be resurfaced if badly scored or replaced if badly worn.

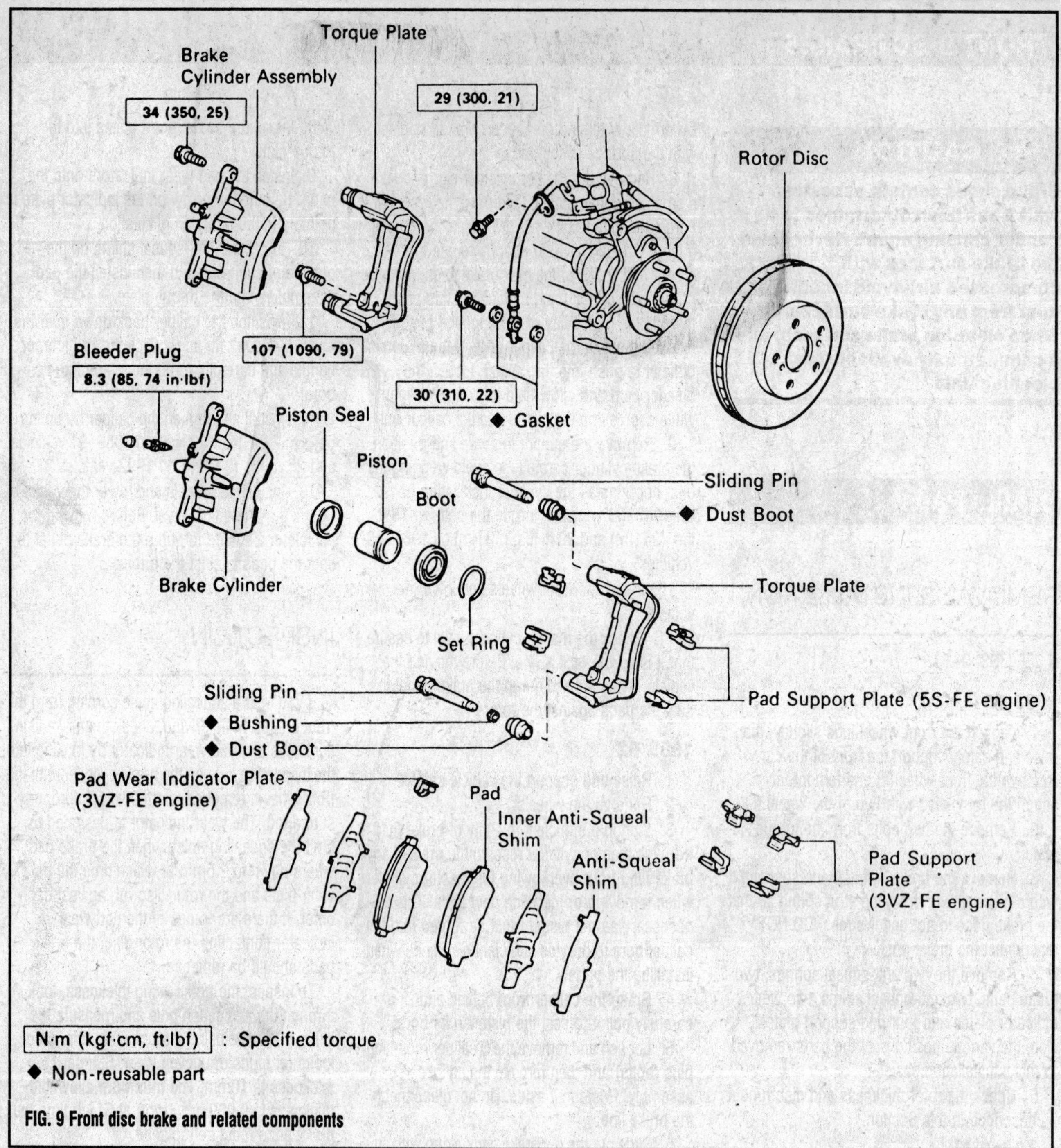

FIG. 9 Front disc brake and related components

FIG. 10 Brake pads and anti-squeal springs

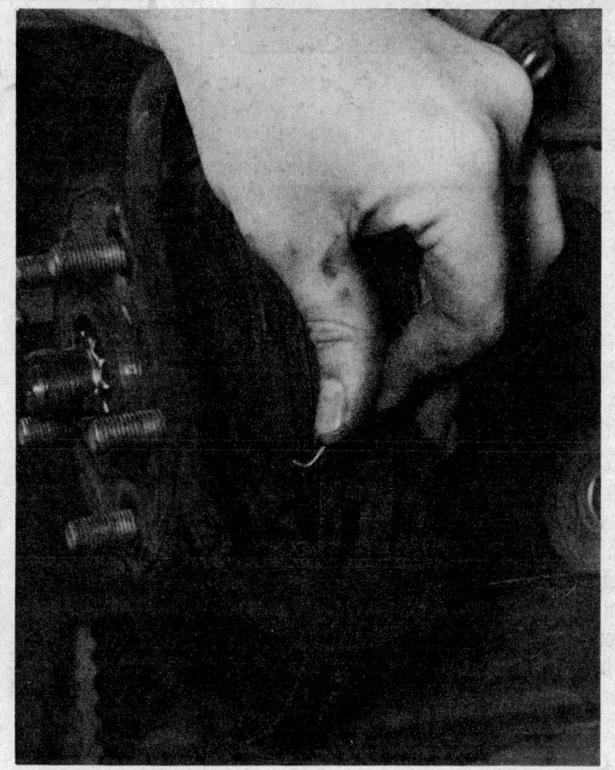

FIG. 11 Removing anti-squeal springs

FIG. 12 Disc brake pads, anti-squeal springs and wear indicator plates

FIG. 13 Front disc brake caliper

Brake Caliper

REMOVAL & INSTALLATION

➧ SEE FIGS. 13–16

1. Raise and support the vehicle safely.
2. Remove the front or rear wheels.
3. Disconnect the brake hose from the caliper. Plug the end of the hose to prevent loss of fluid.
4. Remove the bolts that attach the caliper to the torque plate.
5. Lift up and remove the caliper assembly.
6. Installation is the reverse of the removal procedure. Grease the caliper slides and bolts with Lithium grease or equivalent. Torque the caliper bolt(s) to 20–27 ft. lbs. (27–41 Nm) on front disc brakes. Fill and bleed the system. Before moving the vehicle, make sure to pump the brake pedal to seat the pads against the rotors.

OVERHAUL

1. Remove the caliper from the vehicle.
2. Withdraw the two slide bushings from their respective bores.
3. Remove the dust boots and sliding pins from the torque plate.
4. Gently pry the cylinder boot set ring from the boot and remove the boot.
5. Place a folded towel between the piston and housing. Apply compressed air to the brake line union fitting to force the piston out of its bore. Be careful, the piston may come out forcefully.

***** CAUTION**

Do not attempt to catch the piston with your fingers. Let the towel do this for you.

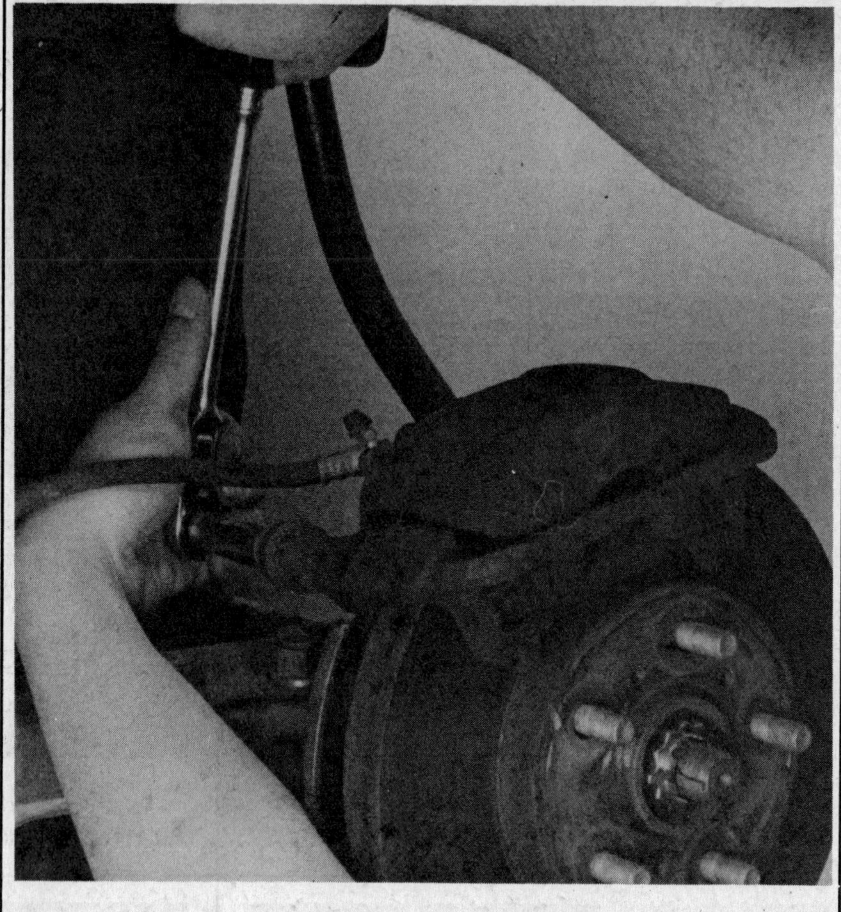

FIG. 14 Loosening caliper attaching bolts

6. Pry the piston seal from the bore with a machinists scribe.
7. Check the piston and cylinder bore for wear and/or corrosion. Replace components if excess wear or corrosion is present.
8. To assemble, coat all the bore, dust boot, collar, slide bushing, piston and piston seal surfaces with lithium soap base glycol grease.
9. Install the piston seal into the bore and install the piston using a hammer handle or equivalent.
10. Install the boot and set ring.
11. Install the collar, dust boots and boot bushings in the torque plate. Make sure that the boots are secured firmly to each brake cylinder and bushing groove.
12. Install the brake pads into the cylinder and install the cylinder onto the torque plate. Torque the caliper bolt(s) to 20–27 ft. lbs. (27–41 Nm) on front disc brakes.
13. Fill the master cylinder reservoir and bleed the brake system.
14. Pump the brake pedal and check the brake system for leaks.

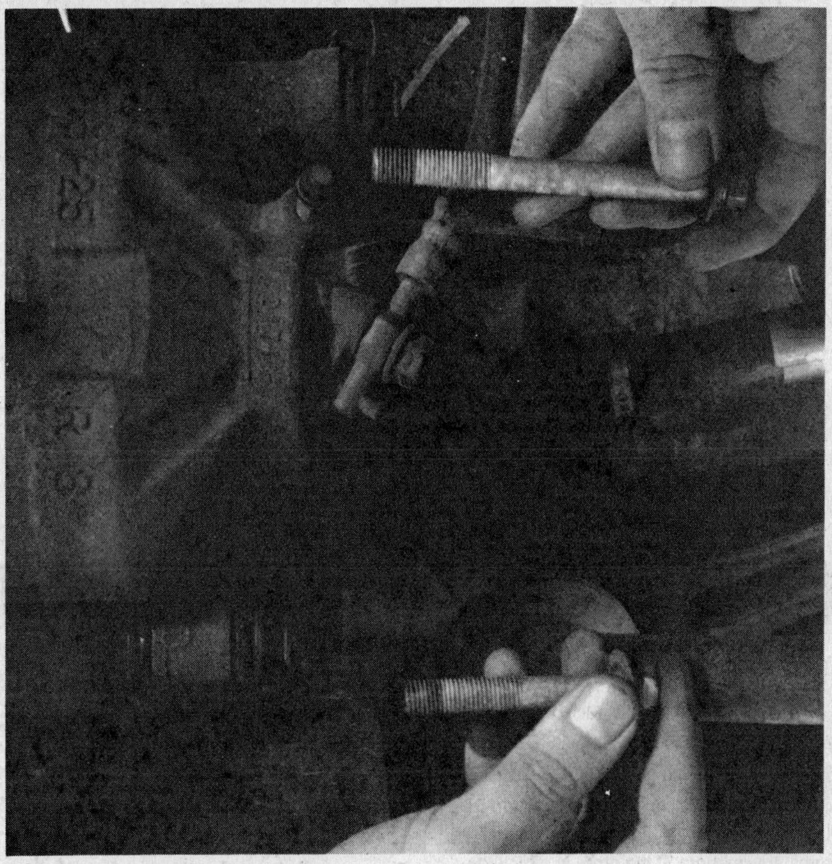

FIG. 15 Removing caliper attaching bolts

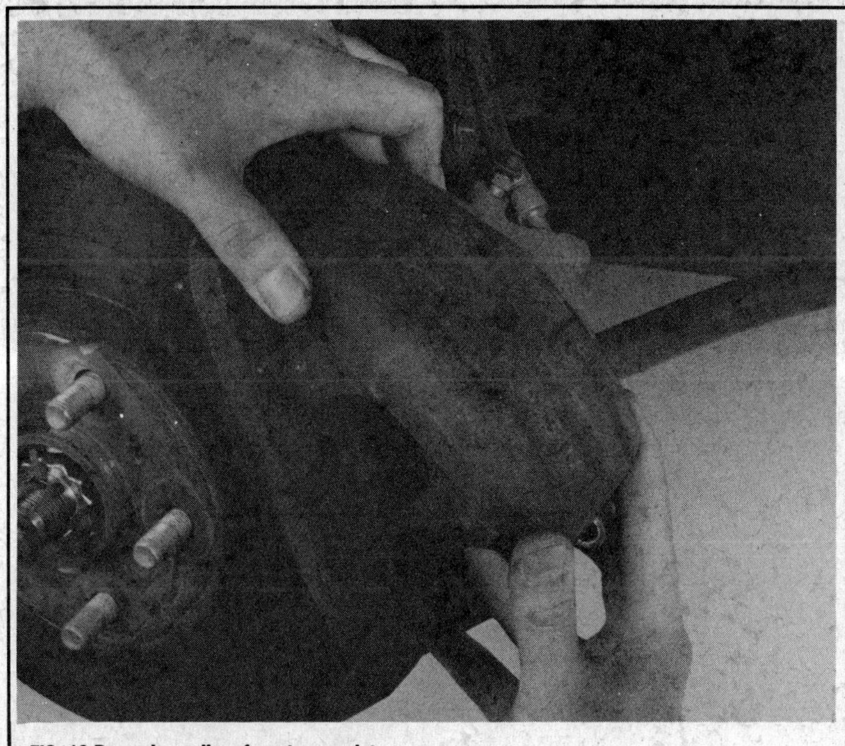

FIG. 16 Removing caliper from torque plate

Brake Disc (Rotor)

REMOVAL & INSTALLATION

1. Loosen the front wheel lugs slightly, then raise and safely support the front of the car. Remove the front wheel(s) and temporarily attach the rotor disc with two of the wheel nuts.
2. Unbolt and remove the torque plate from the steering knuckle.
3. Remove the two wheel nuts and pull the disc from the axle hub.

To install:

4. Position the new rotor disc onto the axle hub and reinstall the two wheel nuts temporarily.
5. Install the torque plate onto the steering knuckle. On 1983–84 vehicles, torque the plate bolts to 70 ft. lbs. (95 Nm); 1985–86, 65 ft. lbs (88 Nm); 1987–92, 79 ft. lbs. (107 Nm).
6. Remove the wheel nuts and install the front wheels. Secure the wheel lugs. Before moving the vehicle, make sure to pump the brake pedal to seat the brake pads against the rotors.

INSPECTION

➧ SEE FIGS. 17 AND 18

Examine the disc. If it is worn, warped or scored, it must be replaced. Check the thickness of the disc against the specifications given in the Disc and Pad Specifications chart. If it is below specifications, replace it. Use a micrometer to measure the thickness.

The disc run-out should be measured before the disc is removed and again, after the disc is installed. Use a dial indicator mounted on a magnet type stand (attached to the shock absorber shaft) to determine runout. Position the dial so the stylus is 10mm from the outer edge of the rotor disc. The maximum allowable runout on 1983–86 and 1989 vehicles is 0.15mm. The maximum allowable runout for 1987–88 vehicles is 0.08mm. The maximum allowable runout on 1990–91 vehicles is 0.07mm. The maximum allowable runout on 1992 vehicles is 0.05mm. If runout exceeds the specification, replace the disc.

➡ **Be sure that the wheel bearing nut is properly tightened. If it is not, an inaccurate run-out reading may be obtained. If different run-out readings are obtained with the same disc, between removal and installation, this is probably the cause.**

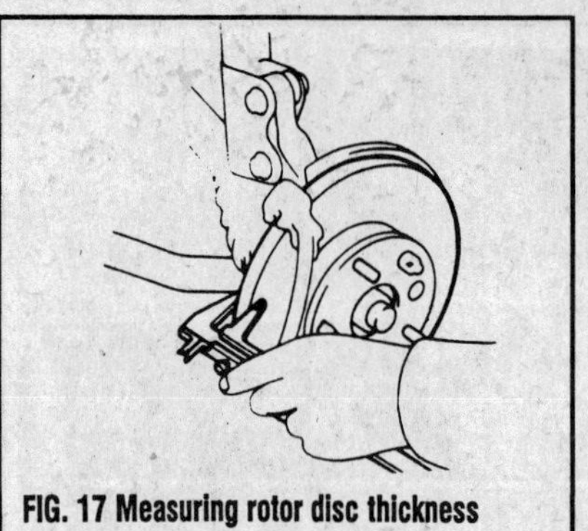

FIG. 17 Measuring rotor disc thickness

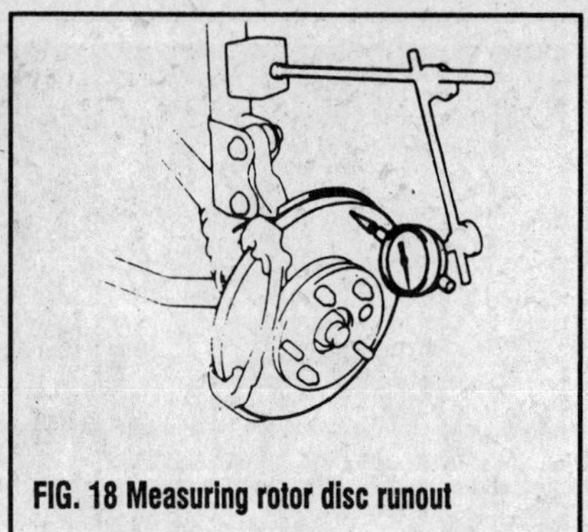

FIG. 18 Measuring rotor disc runout

REAR DRUM BRAKES

⁂ CAUTION

Brake shoes contain asbestos, which has been determined to be a cancer causing agent. Never clean the brake surfaces with compressed air! Avoid inhaling any dust from any brake surface. When cleaning brake surfaces, use a commercially available brake cleaning fluid.

Brake Drums

REMOVAL & INSTALLATION

➧ SEE FIGS. 19–23

1. Loosen the rear wheel lug nuts slightly. Release the parking brake.
2. Block the front wheels, raise the rear of the car, and safely support it with jackstands.
3. Remove the lug nuts and the wheel.
4. Tap the drum lightly with a mallet to free the drum if resistance is felt. Sometimes brake drums are stubborn. If the drum is difficult to remove, perform the following: Insert the end of a bent wire (a coat hanger will do nicely) through the hole in the brake drum and hold the automatic adjusting lever away from the adjuster. Reduce the brake shoe adjustment by turning the adjuster bolt with a screwdriver. The drum should now be loose enough to remove without much effort.
5. Clean the drum and inspect it as detailed in this Section.
6. Hold the brake drum so that the hole on the drum is aligned with the large hole on the axle carrier and install the drum.
7. If the adjuster was loosened to remove the drum, turn the adjuster bolt to adjust the length to the shortest possible amount.
8. Install the rear wheels, tighten the lug nuts and lower the vehicle.
9. Retighten the lug nuts and pump the brake pedal before moving the vehicle.

INSPECTION

1. Remove the inspection hole plug from the backing plate, and with the aide of a flashlight, check the lining thickness. The minimum lining thickness is 0.039 in. (1.0mm). If the lining does not meet the minimum specification, replace the shoes.
2. Remove the brake drum and clean it thoroughly.
3. Inspect the drum for scoring, cracks, grooves and out-of-roundness. Replace or turn the drum, as required. Light scoring may be removed by dressing the drum with fine grit emery cloth. Heavy scoring will require the use of a brake drum lathe to turn the drum.
4. Using inside calipers, measure the inside diameter of the drum. The maximum allowable diameter for 1983–86 vehicles is 201mm. The maximum allowable diameter for 1987–92 vehicles is 230.6mm. If the drum exceeds the maximum diameter, replace it.

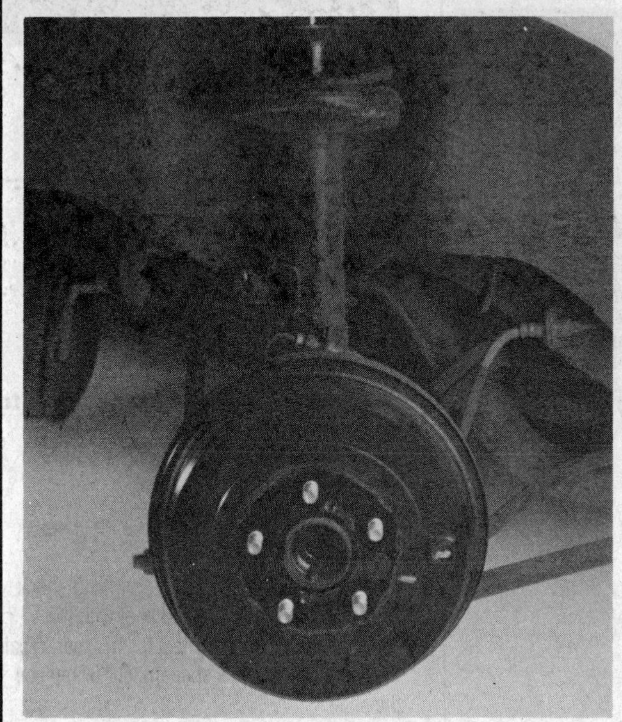

FIG. 19 Rear brake drum

FIG. 20 Removing adjuster access hole plug from the drum

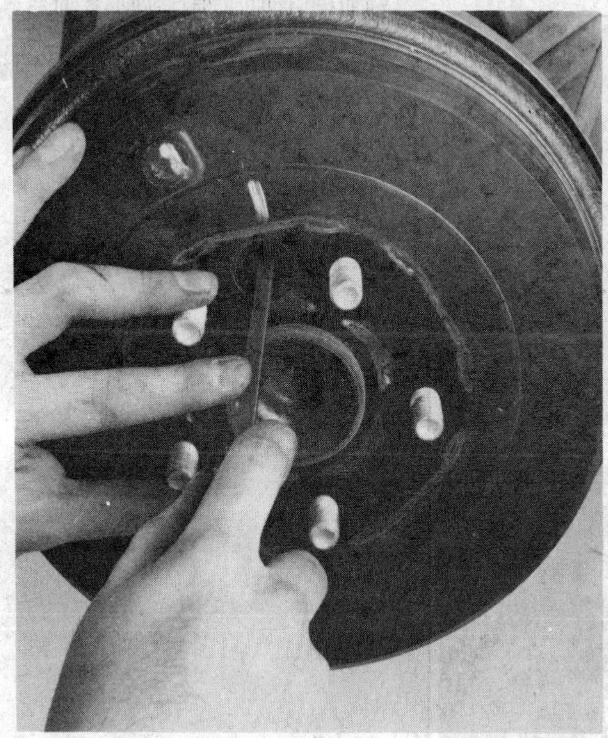

FIG. 21 Loosening the brake shoe adjuster

FIG. 22 Removing the drum retaining bolt

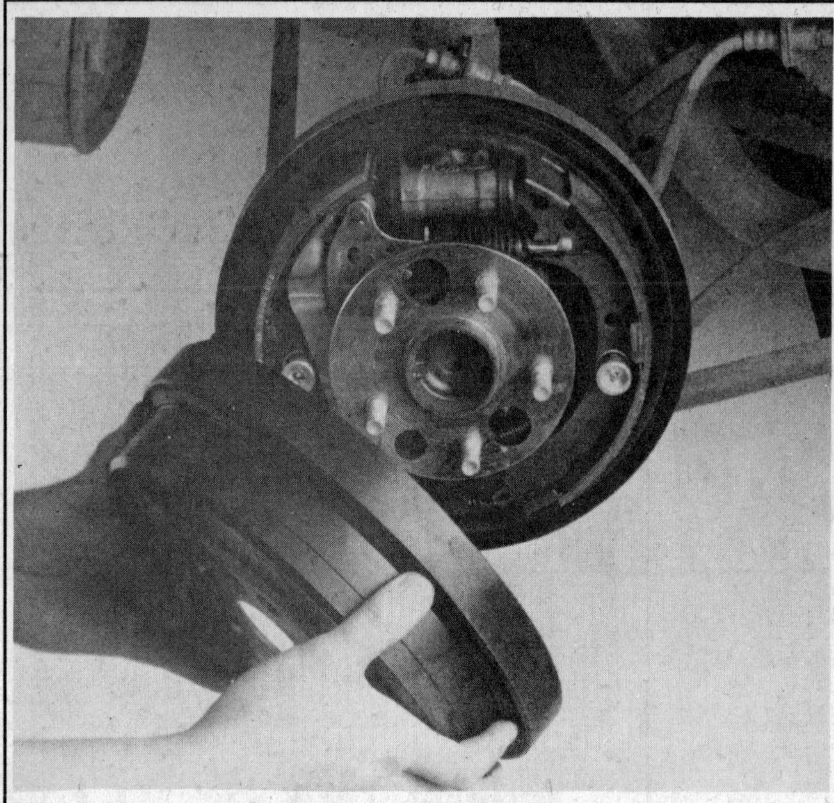

FIG. 23 Removing the rear brake drum

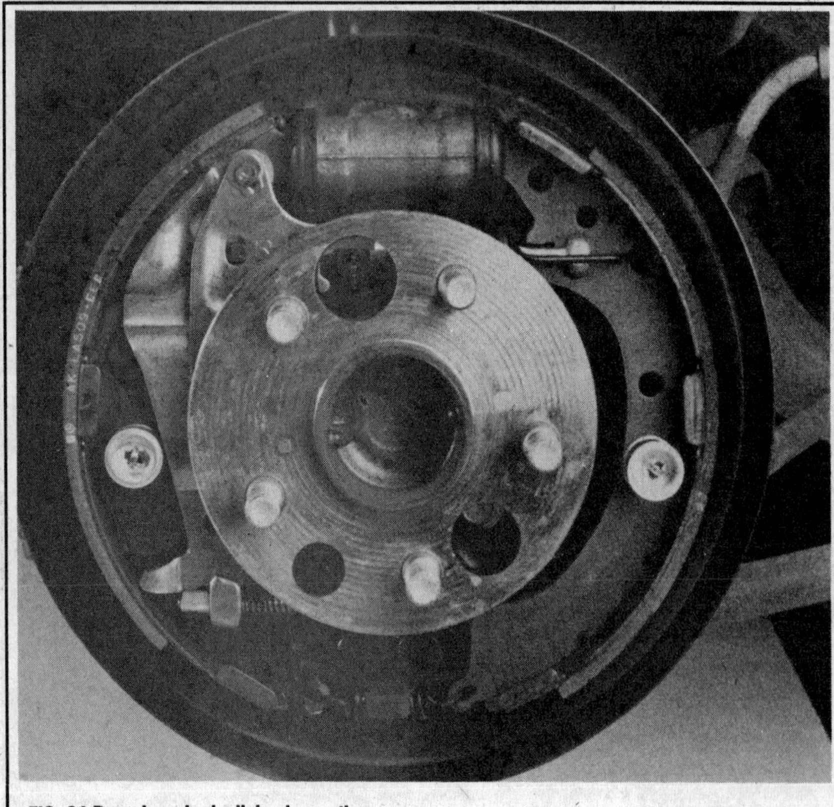

FIG. 24 Rear drum brake lining inspection

Brake Shoes

INSPECTION

SEE FIG. 24

1. Inspect all parts for rust and damage.
2. Measure the lining thickness. The minimum allowable thickness is 0.039 in. (1.0mm). If the lining does not meet the minimum specification, replace it.

If one of the brake shoes needs to be replaced, replace all the rear shoes in order to maintain even braking.

3. Measure inside diameter of the drum as detailed in this Section.
4. Place the shoe into the drum and check that the lining is in proper contact with the drum's surface. If the contact is improper, repair the lining with a brake shoe grinder or replace the shoe.
5. To measure the clearance between brake shoe and parking brake lever, temporarily install the parking brake and automatic adjusting levers onto the rear shoe, using a new C-washer. With a feeler gauge, measure the clearance between the shoe and the lever. The clearance should be within 0-0.35mm. If the clearance is not as specified, use a shim to adjust it. When the clearance is correct, stake the C-washer with pliers.

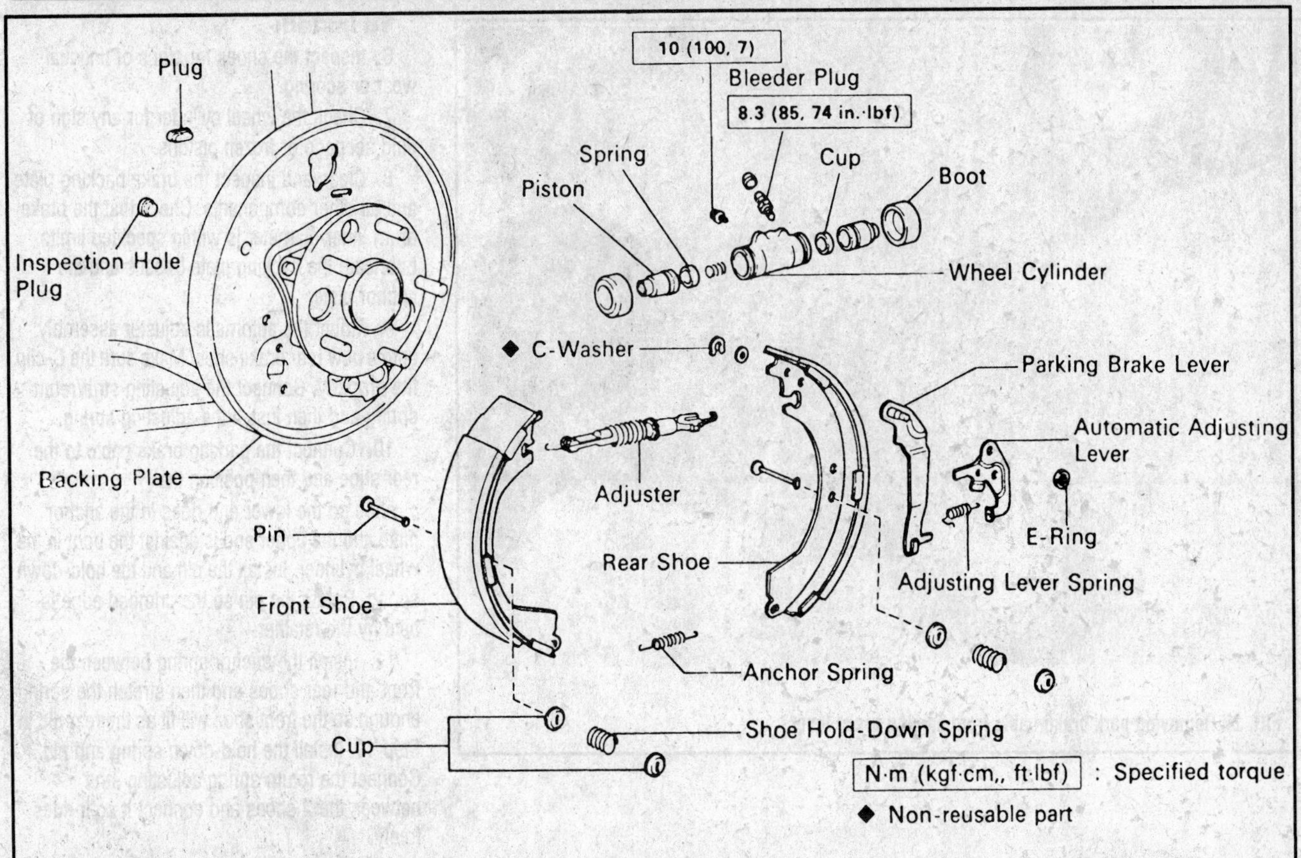

10 (100, 7)
Bleeder Plug
8.3 (85, 74 in.·lbf)
Plug
Spring
Cup
Boot
Piston
Inspection Hole Plug
Wheel Cylinder
◆ C-Washer
Parking Brake Lever
Automatic Adjusting Lever
Adjuster
Backing Plate
Pin
E-Ring
Rear Shoe
Adjusting Lever Spring
Front Shoe
Anchor Spring
Shoe Hold-Down Spring
Cup
N·m (kgf·cm,, ft·lbf) : Specified torque
◆ Non-reusable part

FIG. 25 Rear drum brake components

FIG. 26 Brake shoes installed

REMOVAL AND INSTALLATION

➧ SEE FIGS. 25–41

1. Raise and support the vehicle safely. Remove the wheels.
2. Perform the brake drum removal procedure as previously detailed. Do one set of shoes at a time. Note the position and direction of each component part so that they may be reinstalled in the correct order.

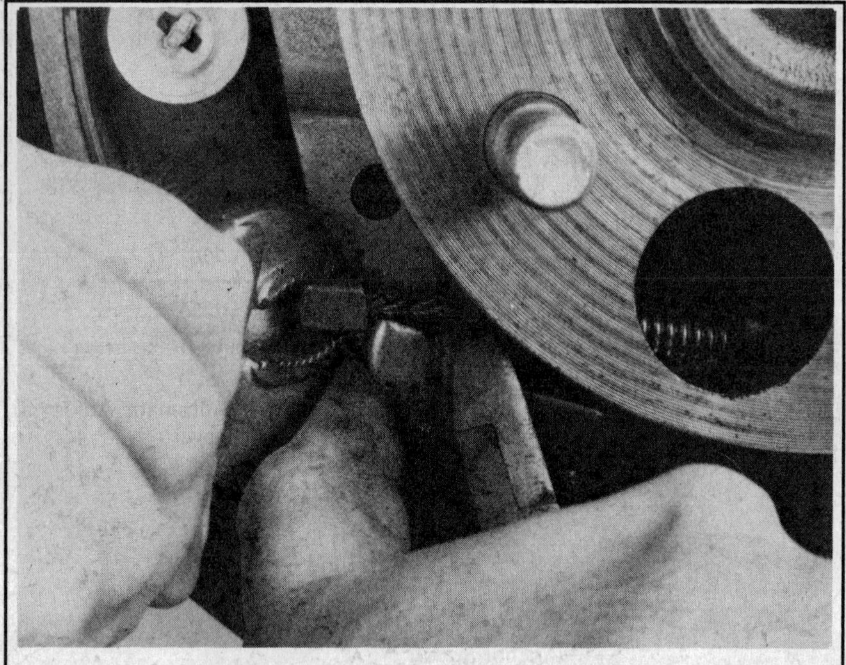

FIG. 27 Removing park brake cable from parking brake lever

➡ **Do not depress the brake pedal once the brake drum has been removed.**

3. Carefully unhook the return spring from the leading (front) brake shoe. Grasp the hold-down spring pin with pliers and turn it until its in line with the slot in the hold-down spring. Remove the hold-down spring and the pin. Pull out the brake shoe and unhook the anchor spring from the lower edge.

4. Remove the hold-down spring from the trailing (rear) shoe. Pull the shoe out with the adjuster strut, automatic adjuster assembly and springs attached and disconnect the parking brake cable. Unhook the return spring and then remove the adjusting strut. Remove the anchor spring.

5. Remove the adjusting strut. Unhook the adjusting lever spring from the rear shoe and then remove the automatic adjuster assembly by popping out the C-clip.

To install:

6. Inspect the shoes for signs of unusual wear or scoring.

7. Check the wheel cylinder for any sign of fluid seepage or frozen pistons.

8. Clean and inspect the brake backing plate and all other components. Check that the brake drum inner diameter is within specified limits. Lubricate the backing plate bosses and the anchor plate.

9. Mount the automatic adjuster assembly onto a new rear brake shoe. Make sure the C-clip fits properly. Connect the adjusting strut/return spring and then install the adjusting spring.

10. Connect the parking brake cable to the rear shoe and then position the shoe so the lower end rides in the anchor plate and the upper end is against the boot in the wheel cylinder. Install the pin and the hold-down spring. Rotate the pin so the crimped edge is held by the retainer.

11. Install the anchor spring between the front and rear shoes and then stretch the spring enough so the front shoe will fit as the rear did in Step 10. Install the hold-down spring and pin. Connect the return spring/adjusting strut between the 2 shoes and connect it so it rides freely.

12. Check that the automatic adjuster is operating properly; the adjusting bolt should turn when the parking brake lever (in the brake assembly, not in the vehicle!) is moved. Adjust the strut as short as possible and then install the

FIG. 28 Removing return spring

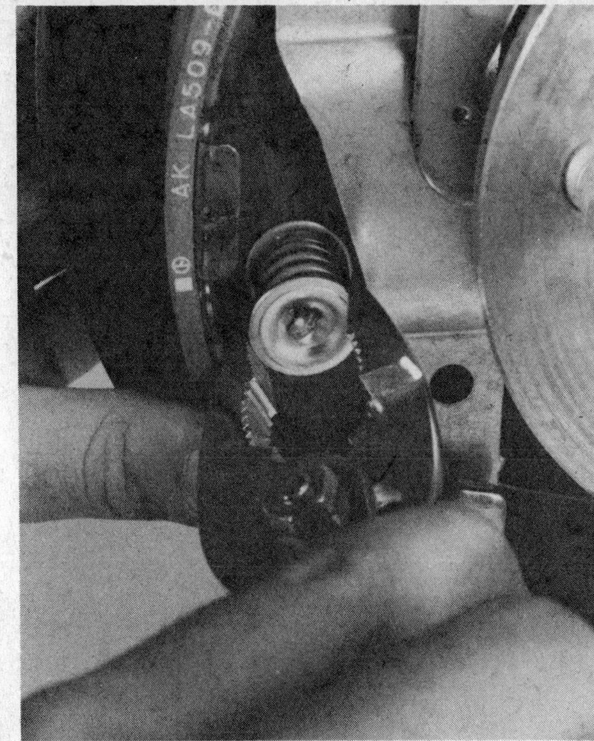

FIG. 29 Removing shoe hold down spring

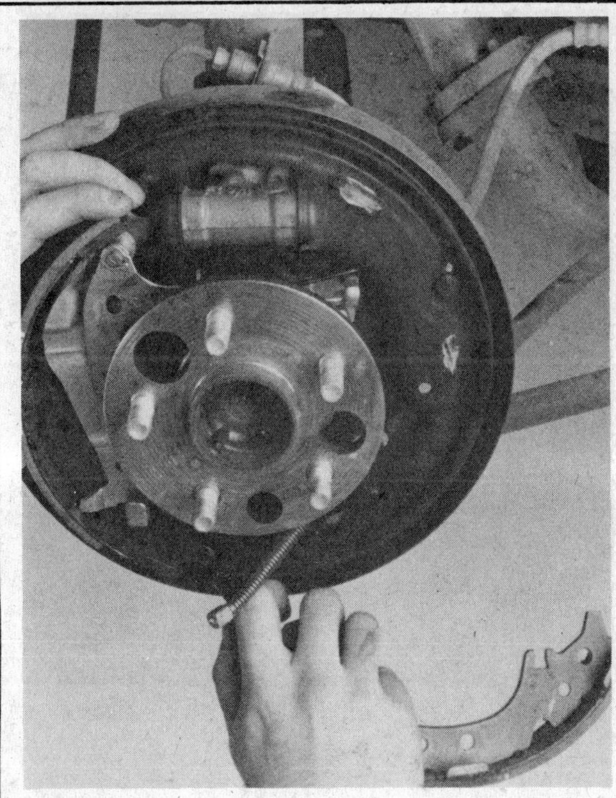

FIG. 30 Removing front shoe from backing plate

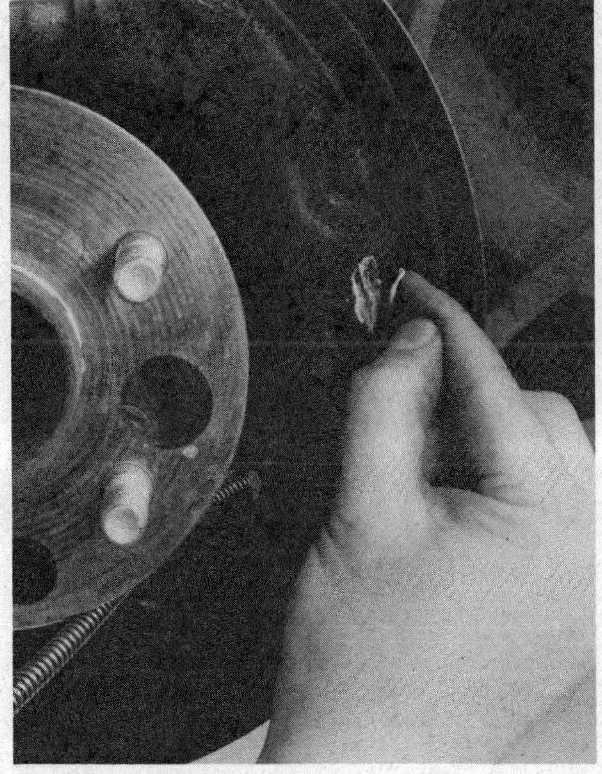

FIG. 31 Lubricating backing plate boss

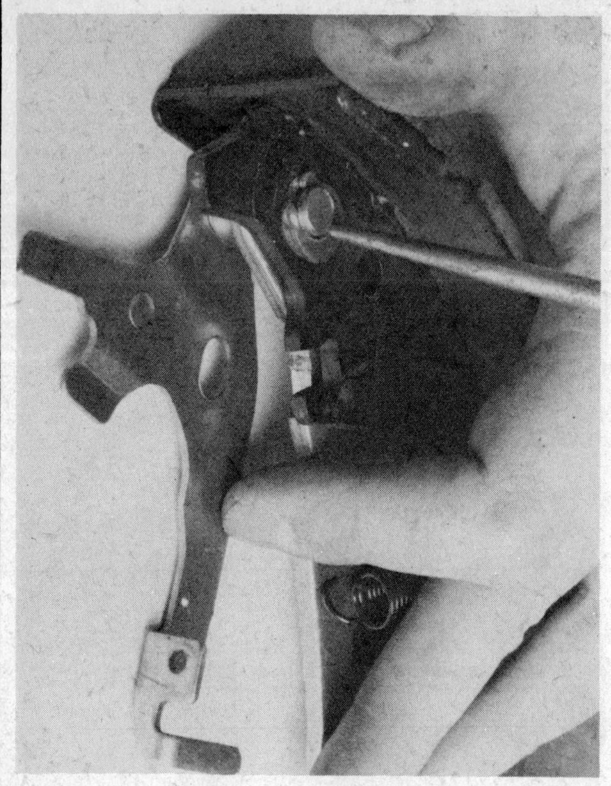

FIG. 32 Removing C-washer to remove the parking brake lever from the brake shoe

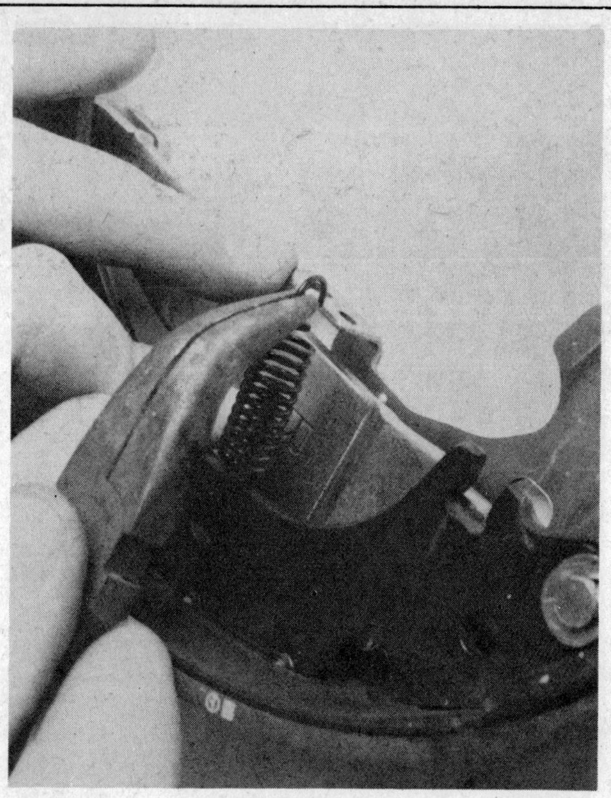

FIG. 33 Installing adjusting lever spring

FIG. 34 Installing adjuster onto rear shoe

FIG. 35 Connecting return spring

FIG. 36 Installing shoe hold-down spring

FIG. 37 Installing shoe hold-down spring retainer cup

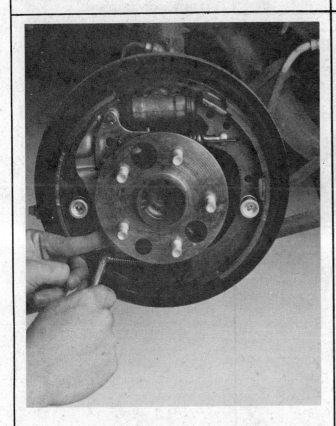

FIG. 38 Connecting parking brake cable to parking brake lever on rear shoe

FIG. 39 Adjusting the rear brake shoes

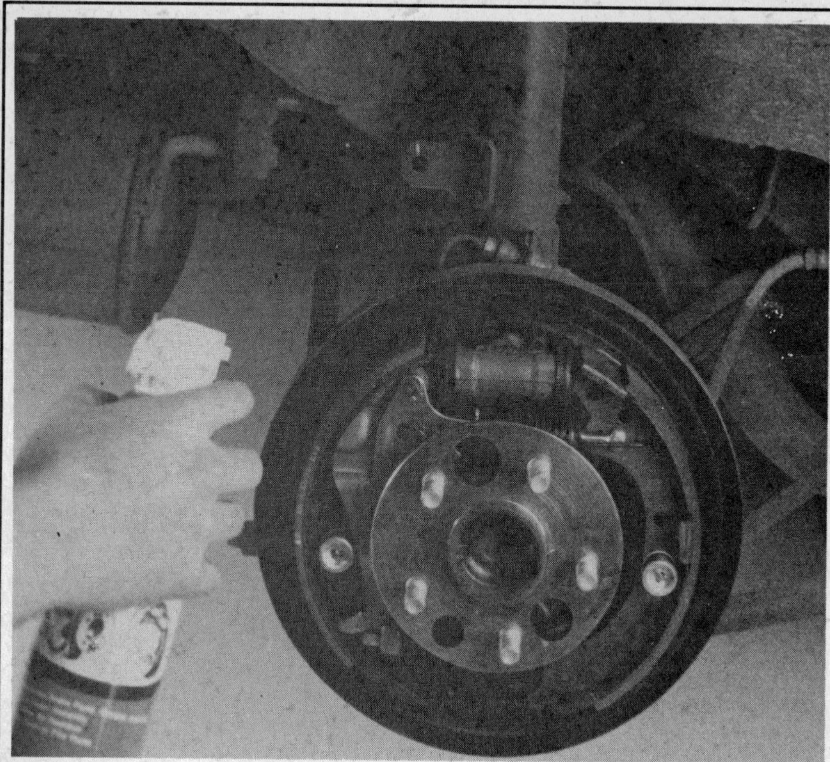

FIG. 40 Cleaning the brake shoes with commercial brake cleaning solution

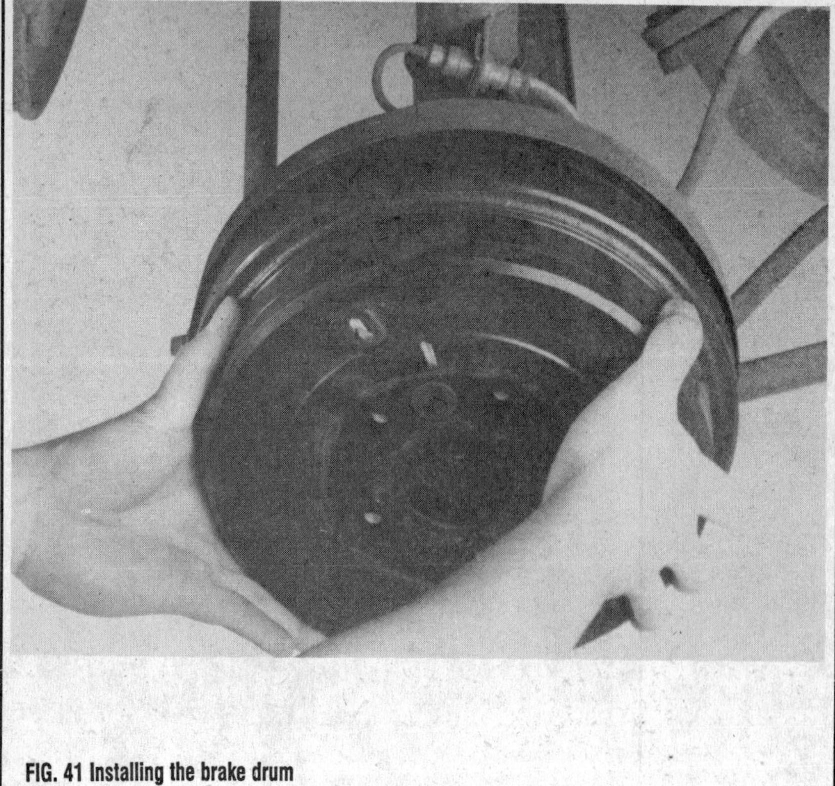

FIG. 41 Installing the brake drum

brake drum. Set and release the parking brake several times.

13. Install the wheel and lower the vehicle. Check the level of brake fluid in the master cylinder.

Wheel Cylinder

REMOVAL & INSTALLATION

1. Plug the master cylinder inlet to prevent hydraulic fluid from leaking. Raise and safely support the vehicle.
2. Remove the brake drums and shoes.
3. Working from behind the backing plate, disconnect the hydraulic line from the wheel cylinder.
4. Unfasten the screws retaining the wheel cylinder and withdraw the cylinder.

To install:

5. Attach the wheel cylinder to the backing plate. Torque the bolts to 7 ft. lbs.
6. Connect the hydraulic line to the wheel cylinder and tighten it.
7. Install the brake shoes and drums. Make all the necessary adjustments.
8. Fill the master cylinder to the proper level with clean brake fluid bleed the brake system. Check the brake system for leaks.

REAR DISC BRAKES

⁂ CAUTION

Brake shoes contain asbestos, which has been determined to be a cancer causing agent. Never clean the brake surfaces with compressed air! Avoid inhaling any dust from any brake surface. When cleaning brake surfaces, use a commercially available brake cleaning fluid.

Brake Pads

REMOVAL & INSTALLATION

➧ SEE FIG. 42

1. Raise and safely support the vehicle.
2. Remove the wheels. Remove the flexible hose bracket.
3. Siphon a sufficient quantity of brake fluid from the master cylinder reservoir to prevent any brake fluid from overflowing the master cylinder when removing or installing new pads. This is necessary as the piston must be forced into the caliper bore to provide sufficient clearance when installing the pads.
4. Grasp the caliper from behind and carefully pull it to seat the piston in its bore.
5. Loosen and remove the caliper mounting pin(s) or bolt(s), and then remove the caliper assembly. Position it aside. Do not disconnect the brake line.
6. Slide out the old brake pads along with any anti-squeal shims, springs, pad wear indicators and pad support plates. Make sure to note the position of all assorted pad hardware.

To install:

7. Check the brake disc (rotor) for thickness and run-out. Inspect the caliper and piston assembly for breaks, cracks, fluid seepage or other damage. Overhaul or replace as necessary.
8. Install the pad support plates into the torque plate.
9. Install the pad wear indicators onto the pads. Be sure the arrow on the indicator plate is pointing in the direction of rotation.
10. Install the anti-squeal shims on the outside of each pad and then install the pad assemblies into the torque plate.
11. Position the caliper back down over the pads. If it won't fit, use a C-clamp or hammer handle and carefully force the piston into its bore.
12. Install and tighten the caliper installation bolt(s) to 14 ft. lbs. (20 Nm).
13. Install the wheels and lower the vehicle. Check the brake fluid level. Make sure to pump the brake pedal before moving the vehicle. This will seat the brake pads against the rotors.

INSPECTION

If you hear a squealing noise coming from the front brakes while driving, check the brake lining thickness and pad wear indicator by looking into the inspection hole on the brake cylinder with the front wheels removed and the vehicle properly supported. The wear indicator is designed to emit the squealing noise when the brake pad wears down to 2.5mm at which time the pad wear plate and the rotor disc rub against each other. If there are traces of the pad wear indicator contacting the rotor disc, the brake pads should be replaced.

To inspect the brake lining thickness, look through the inspection hole and measure the lining thickness using a machinists rule. Also looks for signs of uneven wear. Standard thickness is 10mm. The **minimum** allowable thickness is 0.039 in. (1.0mm), at which time the brake pads must be replaced.

Brake Caliper

REMOVAL & INSTALLATION

1. Raise and support the vehicle safely.
2. Remove the rear wheels.
3. Disconnect the brake hose from the caliper. Plug the end of the hose to prevent loss of fluid. Discard the union bolt gaskets and replace with new ones.
4. Remove the bolts that attach the caliper to the torque plate.
5. Lift up and remove the caliper assembly.
6. Installation is the reverse of the removal procedure. Grease the caliper slides and bolts with Lithium grease or equivalent. Torque the caliper bolts to 14 ft. lbs. (20 Nm) for rear disc brakes. Fill and bleed the system.

OVERHAUL

1. Remove the caliper from the vehicle.
2. Withdraw the two slide bushings from their respective bores.
3. Remove the dust boots and sliding pins from the torque plate.
4. Gently pry the cylinder boot set ring from the boot and remove the boot.
5. Place a folded towel between the piston and housing. Apply compressed air to the brake line union fitting to force the piston out of its bore. Be careful, the piston may come out forcefully.

⁂ CAUTION

Do not attempt to catch the piston with your fingers. Let the towel do this for you.

6. Pry the piston seal from the bore with a machinists scribe.
7. Check the piston and cylinder bore for wear and/or corrosion. Replace components if excess wear or corrosion is present.
8. To assemble, coat all the bore, dust boot, collar, slide bushing, piston and piston seal surfaces with lithium soap base glycol grease.
9. Install the piston seal into the bore and install the piston using a hammer handle or equivalent.
10. Install the boot and set ring.
11. Install the collar, dust boots and boot bushings in the torque plate. Make sure that the boots are secured firmly to each brake cylinder and bushing groove.
12. Install the brake pads into the cylinder and install the cylinder onto the torque plate. Torque the caliper bolt(s) to 14 ft. lbs. (20 Nm).
13. Fill the master cylinder reservoir and bleed the brake system.
14. Pump the brake pedal and check the brake system for leaks.

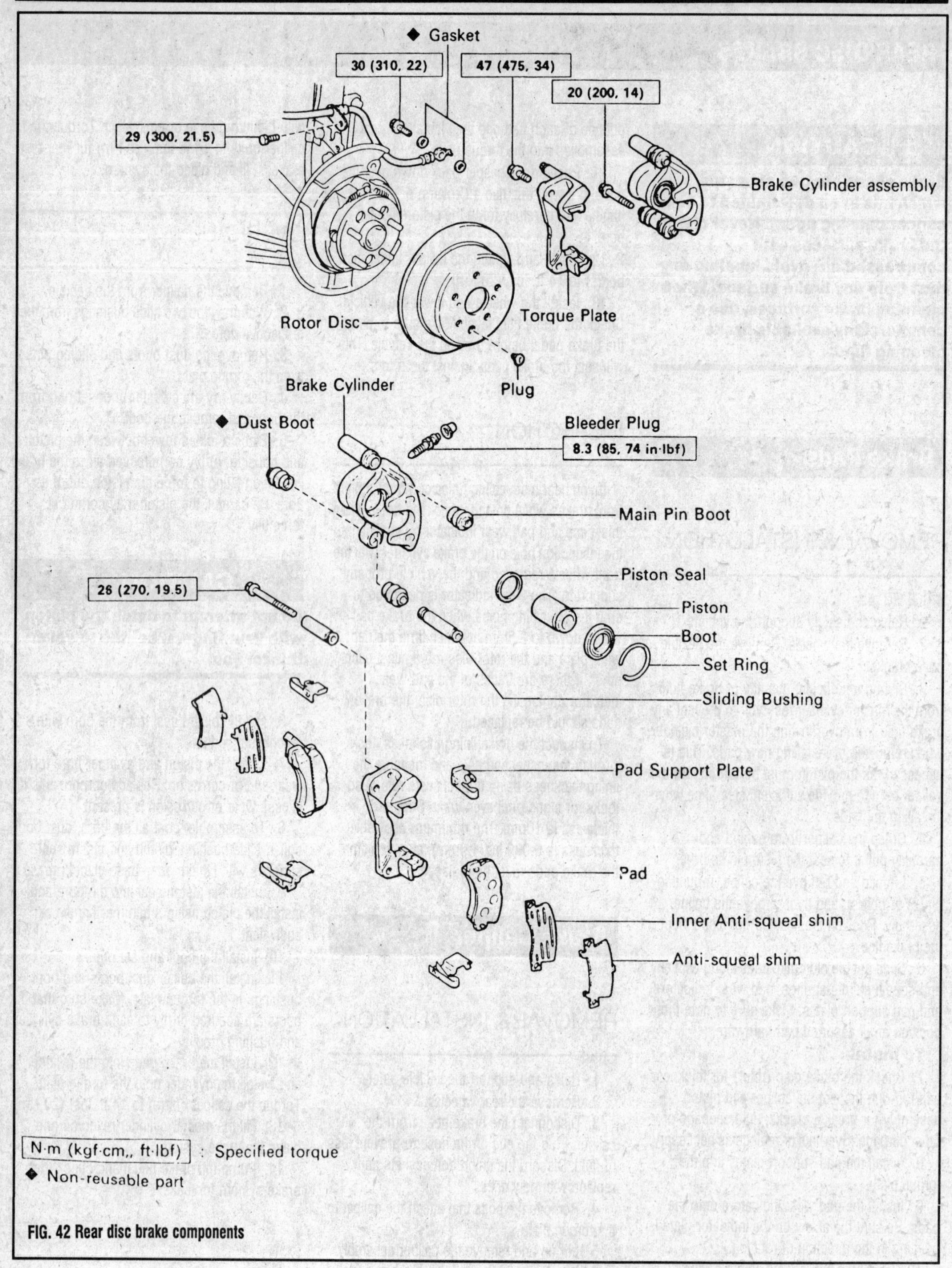
◆ Gasket
30 (310, 22)
47 (475, 34)
20 (200, 14)
29 (300, 21.5)
Brake Cylinder assembly
Rotor Disc
Torque Plate
Plug
Brake Cylinder
◆ Dust Boot
Bleeder Plug
8.3 (85, 74 in·lbf)
Main Pin Boot
Piston Seal
26 (270, 19.5)
Piston
Boot
Set Ring
Sliding Bushing
Pad Support Plate
Pad
Inner Anti-squeal shim
Anti-squeal shim
N·m (kgf·cm,, ft·lbf) : Specified torque
◆ Non-reusable part

FIG. 42 Rear disc brake components

Brake Disc (Rotor)

REMOVAL & INSTALLATION

➧ SEE FIG. 42

1. Loosen the rear wheel lugs slightly, then raise and safely support the rear of the vehicle. Remove the rear wheel(s) and temporarily attach the rotor disc with two of the wheel nuts.
2. Unbolt and remove the torque plate from the steering knuckle.
3. Remove the two wheel nuts and pull the disc from the axle hub. If the disc is difficult to remove, return the shoe adjuster until the disc spins freely, and remove the disc.
4. Before installing the disc, lightly polish the disc and shoe surfaces with a fine grit emery cloth.

To install:

5. Position the new rotor disc onto the axle hub so that the hole on the rear axle shaft is aligned with the service hole on the disc. Reinstall the two wheel nuts temporarily.
6. Install the torque plate onto the steering knuckle. Torque the plate bolts to 34 ft. lbs. (47 Nm).
7. Reinstall the rear wheels and lower the vehicle.

INSPECTION

Examine the disc. If it is worn, warped or scored, it must be replaced. Check the thickness of the disc against the specifications given in the Disc and Pad Specifications chart. If it is below specifications, replace it. Use a micrometer to measure the thickness.

The disc run-out should be measured before the disc is removed and again, after the disc is installed. Use a dial indicator mounted on a magnet type stand (attached to the shock absorber shaft) to determine runout. Position the dial so the stylus is 10mm from the outer edge of the rotor disc. The maximum allowable runout 0.0059 in. (0.15mm). If the runout exceeds the specification, replace the disc.

PARKING BRAKE

Cables

REMOVAL & INSTALLATION

Pedal Operated Front Cable

1. Disconnect the negative battery cable.
2. Remove the left inner kick panel to access the parking brake pedal assembly.
3. Remove the retainer clip from the pin on the pedal assembly and withdraw
   the pin from the bracket and the eye of the cable.
4. Remove the spring clip holding the cable to the brake pedal assembly and remove the cable.
5. Disconnect the rear portion of the front parking brake wire and remove from the vehicle.
6. Installation is the reverse of the removal procedure.

Lever Operated Intermediate Wire

1. Raise and safely support the vehicle.
2. Remove the parking brake lever console box.
3. Remove the retainer nut located on the top of the lever shaft.
4. From under the vehicle disconnect the cable from the equalizer and extract the intermediate cable from the lever assembly. Remove the cable from the vehicle.
5. Installation is the reverse the removal procedure. Torque the cable retainer nut to 9 ft. lbs. (13 Nm).

Rear Cable

1. Raise and safely support the vehicle.
2. Remove the tire and wheel assembly from the vehicle.
3. Working from underneath of the car, loosen the locknut on the parking brake cable equalizer.
4. Remove the brake drum or rotor from the vehicle.
5. Removal of the rear brake shoe and disconnect the parking brake cable from the shoe.
6. Remove the rear cable from the equalizer assembly and remove the cable from the vehicle.
7. Installation is the reverse of the removal procedure.

ADJUSTMENT

➡ **Before any adjustment is attempted, make sure that the rear brake shoe clearance is correct and that the automatic self adjuster is properly adjusted.**

1. If the brake system requires adjustment, loosen the cable adjusting nut cap which is located at the rear of the parking brake lever. On some vehicles, the adjustment and lock nuts are located under the vehicle, beneath the lever assembly. Raise and safely support the vehicle as required.
2. Take up the slack in the parking brake cable by rotating the adjusting nut with another open end wrench.
   a. To loosen the brake cable, turn the nut counterclockwise.
   b. To increase the tension on the brake cable, turn the nut clockwise.
5. Tighten the adjusting cap, using care not to disturb the setting of the adjusting nut.
6. Check the rotation of the rear wheels to be sure the brakes are not dragging.

Brake Pedal

REMOVAL & INSTALLATION

1. Disconnect the negative battery cable.
2. Remove the left inner kick panel to access the parking brake pedal assembly.
3. Remove the retainer clip from the pin on the pedal assembly and withdraw
   the pin from the bracket and the eye of the cable.
4. Remove the spring clip holding the cable to the brake pedal assembly and remove the cable.
5. Disconnect the electrical connector from the parking brake switch.
6. Remove the release cable retainer bolts and the park brake assembly mounting bolts. Remove the assembly from the vehicle.

To install:

7. Position the parking brake assembly in the vehicle and install the retainer bolts. Torque to 45 ft. lbs. (61 Nm).

8. Connect the electrical connector to the parking brake switch.

9. Install the park brake cable into the brake assembly. Install the lower C-clip, cable retainer pin and clip.

10. Install the release cable retainer bolts and tighten to 4 ft. lbs. (5 Nm).

11. Install the left inner kick panel and reconnect the negative battery cable. Adjust the parking brake cable as required.

Brake Lever

REMOVAL & INSTALLATION

1. Remove the parking brake lever console box.

2. Remove the retainer nut located on the top of the lever shaft. Disconnect the electrical connector.

3. Remove the 4 retaining bolts in the lower bracket and remove the mechanism from the vehicle. Raise and safely support the vehicle as required.

4. Installation is the reverse of the removal procedure. Adjust the parking brake cable after installation.

Brake Shoes

REMOVAL & INSTALLATION

➧ SEE FIG. 43

➡ Some of the parking brake assembly springs are color coded green, blue, white. The remainder of the springs have no color. Make sure that all springs are installed in their proper locations.

1. Loosen the rear wheel lugs slightly and raise the rear of the vehicle and support it safely. Remove the rear wheels.

2. Remove the two mounting bolts and disconnect the rear disc brake assembly. Suspend the disc with wire from the strut spring or a convenient location on the body.

3. Pull the rotor disc from the axle hub. If the rotor disc is stubborn, return the shoe adjuster until the wheel spins freely, and remove the disc.

4. Using a suitable spring removal tool, remove the return springs.

5. Remove the shoe strut with the adjuster spring.

6. Slide the front shoe out and remove the adjuster. Unhook the tension spring and remove the front shoe.

7. Slide the rear shoe out and remove the tension spring. Disconnect the parking brake cable from the lever. Remove the shoe hold down spring cups, springs and pins.

To install:

8. Lubricate all shoe sliding surfaces of the backing plate and the threads and head of the adjuster with a high temperature Lithium grease or equivalent.

9. Connect the parking brake cable to the to the rear shoe lever. Install the shoe hold down springs, cups and pins.

10. Slide the rear shoe in between the hold down spring cup and the backing plate.

CAUTION

Do not allow the brake shoe rubbing surface to come in contact with the grease on the backing plate.

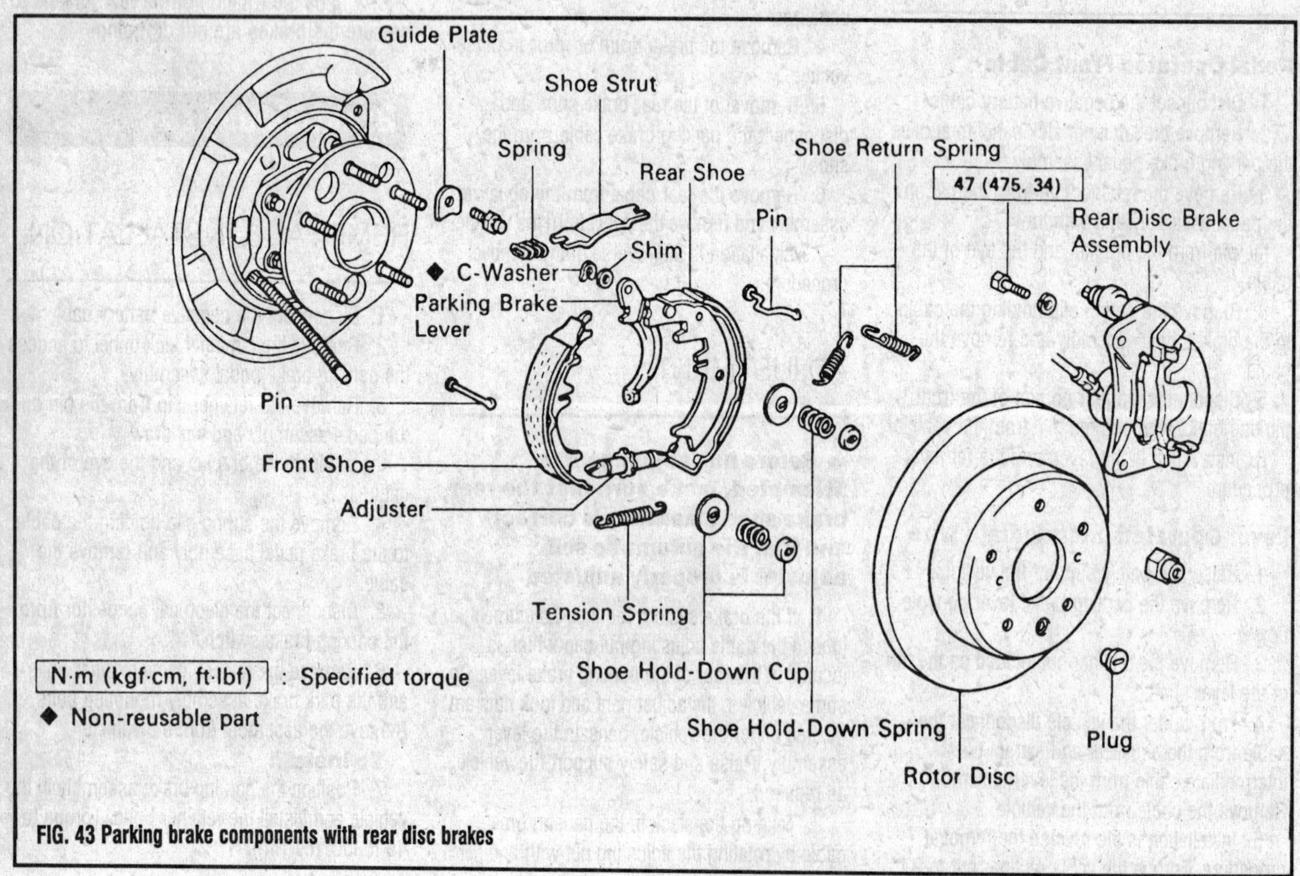

FIG. 43 Parking brake components with rear disc brakes

11. Hook the one end of the tension spring to the rear shoe and connect the front shoe to the other end of the spring. Install the adjuster between the front and rear shoes. Slide the front shoe in between the hold down spring cup and the backing plate.

12. Install the strut so that the spring end is forward.

13. Install the front and then the rear return springs using the removal tool.

14. Before installing the disc, lightly polish the disc and shoe surfaces with a fine grit emery cloth. Position the rotor disc onto the axle hub so that the hole on the rear axle shaft is aligned with the service hole on the disc.

15. Adjust the parking brake shoe clearance: Temporarily install two of the wheel nuts and remove the hole plug from the face of the disc. Turn the adjuster clockwise to expand the brake shoes until the disc locks. Return the adjuster eight notches and install the hole plug.

16. Attach the disc brake assembly to the backing plate and torque the bolt to 34 ft. lbs. (47 Nm).

17. Install the rear wheels and lower the vehicle.

ANTI-LOCK BRAKE SYSTEM (A.B.S)

➧ SEE FIGS. 44 AND 45

Description and Operation

Anti-lock braking systems are designed to prevent locked-wheel skidding during hard braking or during braking on slippery surfaces. The front wheels of a vehicle cannot apply steering force if they are locked and sliding; the vehicle will continue in its previous direction of travel. The four wheel anti-lock brake systems found on Toyota vehicles hold the individual wheels just below the point of locking. By preventing wheel lock-up, maximum braking effort is maintained while preventing loss of directional control. Additionally, some steering capability is maintained during the stop. The ABS system will operate regardless of road surface conditions.

There are conditions for which the ABS system provides no benefit. Hydroplaning occurs when the tires ride on a film of water, losing contact with the paved surface. This renders the vehicle uncontrollable until road contact is regained. Extreme steering maneuvers at high speed or cornering beyond the limits of tire adhesion can result in skidding which is independent of vehicle braking. For this reason, the system is named anti–lock rather than anti–skid.

Under normal braking conditions, the ABS system functions in the same manner as a standard brake system. The system is a combination of electrical and hydraulic components, working together to control the flow of brake fluid to the wheels when necessary.

The Anti-lock Brake System Computer (ABS ECU) is the electronic brain of the system, receiving and interpreting speed signals from the speed sensors. The ABS ECU will enter anti-lock mode when it senses impending wheel lock at any wheel and immediately controls the brake line pressure(s) to the affected wheel(s). The actuator assembly is separate from the master cylinder and booster. It contains the wheel circuit valves used to control the brake fluid pressure to each wheel circuit.

During anti-lock braking, line pressures are controlled or modulated by the rapid cycling of electronic valves within the actuator. These valves can allow pressures within the system to increase, remain constant or decrease depending on the needs of the moment as registered by the ABS ECU. The front wheels are controlled individually. Depending on the model, the rear wheel circuits may receive the same electrical signal or be under individual control.

The operator may hear a popping or clicking sound as the pump and/or control valves cycle on and off during normal operation. The sounds are due to normal operation and are not indicative of a system problem. Under most conditions, the sounds are only faintly audible. If ABS is engaged, the operator may notice some pulsation in the body of the vehicle during a hard stop; this is generally due to suspension shudder as the brake pressures are altered rapidly and the forces transfer to the vehicle.

Although the ABS system prevents wheel lock–up under hard braking, as brake pressure increases, wheel slip is allowed to increase as well. This slip will result in some tire chirp during ABS operation. The sound should not be interpreted as lock–up but rather than as indication of the system holding the wheel(s) just outside the point of lock–up. Additionally, the final few feet of an ABS–engaged stop may be completed with the wheels locked; the electronic controls do not operate below 4 mph (6.4 kph).

The speed of each wheel (or the front wheels and driveshaft in 3 sensor systems) is monitored by the speed sensor. A toothed wheel rotates in front of the sensor, generating a small AC voltage which is transmitted to the ABS controller. The ABS computer compares the signals and reacts to rapid loss of wheel speed at a particular wheel by engaging the ABS system. Each speed sensor is individually removable. In most cases, the toothed wheels may be replaced if damaged, but disassembly of other components such as hub and knuckle, constant velocity joints or axles may be required.

A computer interprets inputs from the speed sensors, the brake lights, the brake warning lamp circuit, and, on some vehicles, the fuel injection system and/or a deceleration sensor. After processing the inputs, the computer controls output electrical signals to the hydraulic control solenoids, causing them to increase, decrease or hold brake line pressures. Additionally, the computer oversees operation of the pump motor and the ABS warning lamp.

Additionally, the computer constantly monitors system signals, performs a system actuation test immediately after engine start-up and can assign and store diagnostic fault codes if any errors are noted.

The ABS actuator, also called the hydraulic unit, contains the control solenoids for each brake circuit. The pump which maintains the system pressure during ABS braking is also within this unit. The solenoid relay and pump motor relays are mounted externally on the actuator. The ABS actuator can only be changed as a unit; with the exception of the relays, individual components cannot be replaced.

The deceleration sensor, used only on 4WD vehicles, advises the computer of vehicle deceleration. The computer uses this information in addition to the wheel speed sensor signals to decide if ABS control is necessary.

The ABS or ANTILOCK dashboard warning lamp is controlled by the ABS controller. The lamp will illuminate briefly when the ignition switch is turned **ON** as a bulb check. The lamp should then extinguish and remain out during vehicle operation. If only the ABS warning lamp illuminates while driving, the controller has noted a fault within the ABS system. ABS function is halted, but normal braking is maintained.

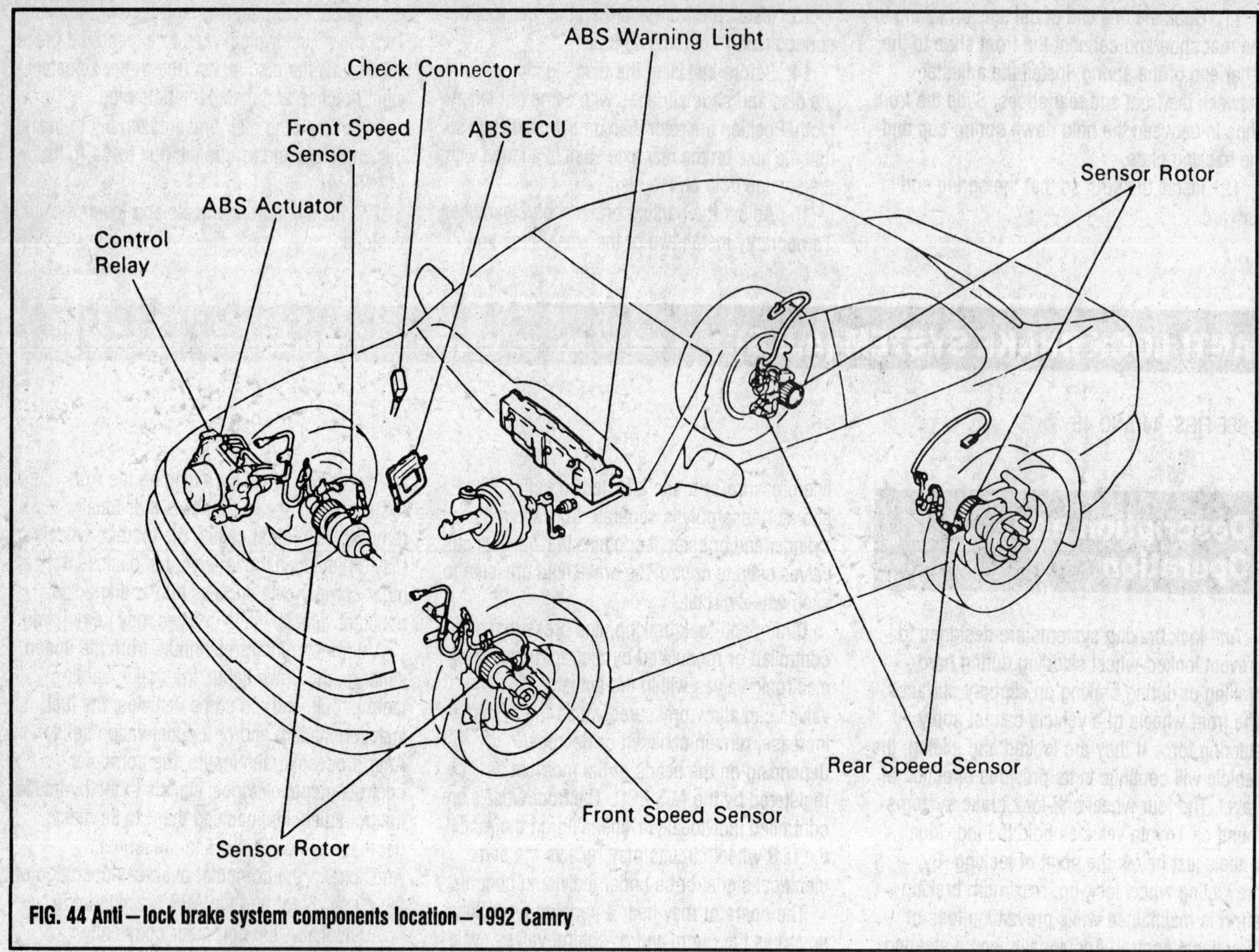

FIG. 44 Anti–lock brake system components location–1992 Camry

System Precautions

- Certain components within the ABS system are not intended to be serviced or repaired individually. Only those components with removal and installation procedures should be serviced.
- Do not use rubber hoses or other parts not specifically specified for the ABS system. When using repair kits, replace all parts included in the kit. Partial or incorrect repair may lead to functional problems and require the replacement of components.
- Lubricate rubber parts with clean, fresh brake fluid to ease assembly. Do not use lubricated shop air to clean parts; damage to rubber components may result.
- Use only DOT 3 brake fluid from an unopened container.
- If any hydraulic component or line is removed or replaced, it may be necessary to bleed the entire system.
- A clean repair area is essential. Always clean the reservoir and cap thoroughly before removing the cap. The slightest amount of dirt in the fluid may plug an orifice and impair the system function. Perform repairs after components have been thoroughly cleaned; use only denatured alcohol to clean components. Do not allow ABS components to come into contact with any substance containing mineral oil; this includes shop rags.
- The anti-lock brake controller is a microprocessor similar to other computer units in the vehicle. Insure that the ignition switch is **OFF** before removing or installing controller harnesses. Avoid static electricity discharge at or near the controller.
- If any arc welding is to be done on the

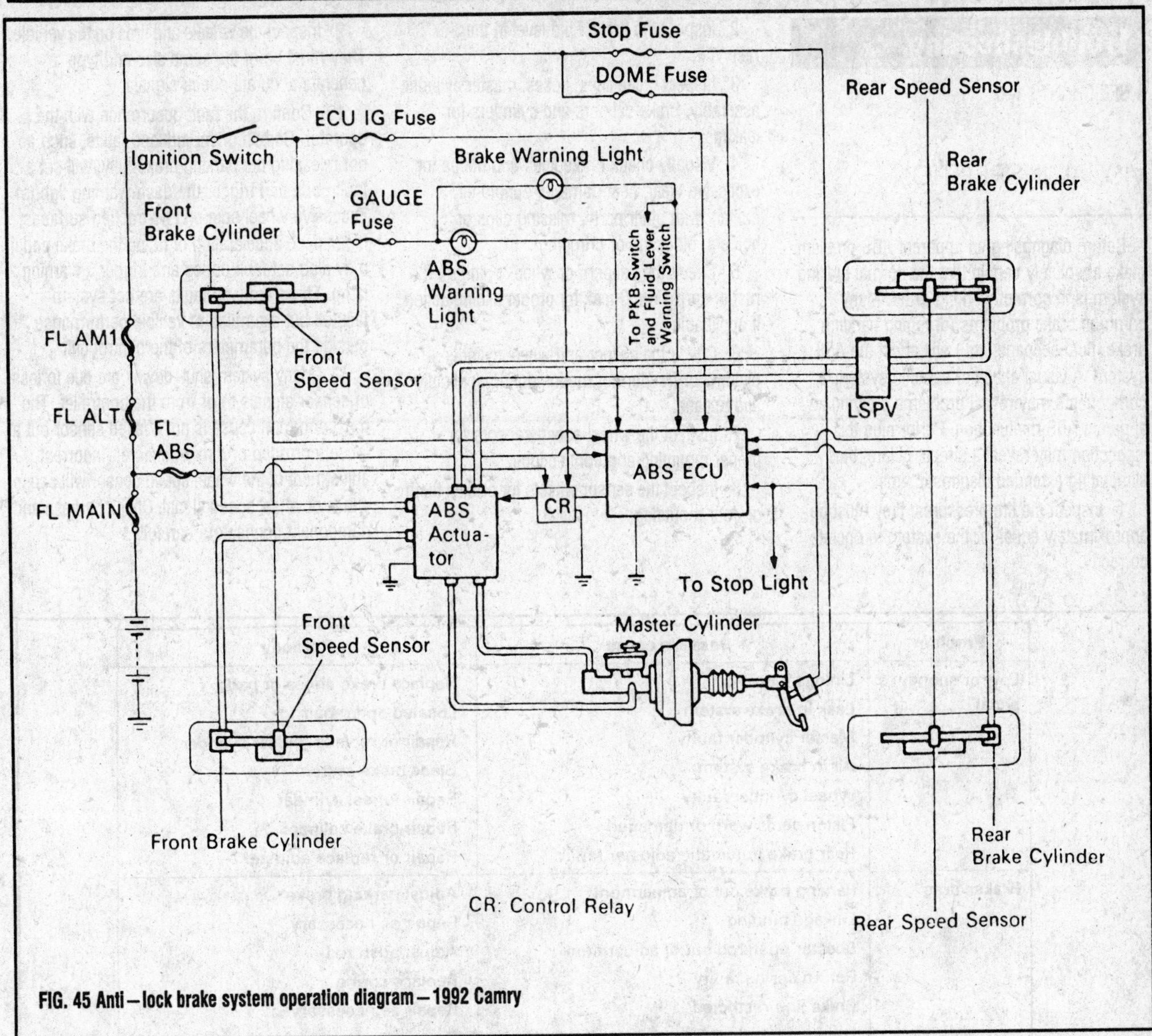

FIG. 45 Anti-lock brake system operation diagram—1992 Camry

vehicle, the ABS controller should be disconnected before welding operations begin.

- If the vehicle is to be baked after paint repairs, disconnect and remove the ABSC from the vehicle.

Diagnostic Codes

If a malfunction occurs, the system will identify the problem and the computer will assign and store a fault code for the fault(s). The dashboard warning lamp will be illuminated to inform the driver that a fault has been found.

During diagnostics, the system will transmit the stored code(s) by flashing the dashboard warning lamp. If two or more codes are stored, they will be displayed from lowest number to highest, regardless of the order of occurrence. The system does not display the diagnostic codes while the vehicle is running.

Troubleshooting

➧ SEE CHARTS 1–6

VISUAL INSPECTION

Before diagnosing an apparent ABS problem, make absolutely certain that the normal braking system is in correct working order. Many common brake problems (dragging parking brake, fluid seepage, etc.) will affect the ABS system. A visual check of specific system components may reveal problems creating an apparent ABS malfunction. Performing this inspection may reveal a simple failure, thus eliminating extended diagnostic time.

1. Inspect the tire pressures; they must be approximately equal for the system to operate correctly.
2. Inspect the brake fluid level in the reservoir.
3. Inspect brake lines, hoses, master cylinder assembly, brake calipers and cylinders for leakage.
4. Visually check brake lines and hoses for excessive wear, heat damage, punctures, contact with other parts, missing clips or holders, blockage or crimping.
5. Check the calipers or wheel cylinders for rust or corrosion. Check for proper sliding action if applicable.
6. Check the caliper and wheel cylinder pistons for freedom of motion during application and release.
7. Inspect the wheel speed sensors for proper mounting and connections.
8. Inspect the sensor wheels for broken teeth or poor mounting.
9. Inspect the wheels and tires on the vehicle. They must be of the same size and type to generate accurate speed signals.
10. Confirm the fault occurrence with the operator. Certain driver induced faults, such as not releasing the parking brake fully, will set a fault code and trigger the dash warning light(s). Excessive wheel spin on low-traction surfaces, high speed acceleration or riding the brake pedal may also set fault codes and trigger a warning lamp. These induced faults are not system failures but examples of vehicle performance outside the parameters of the control unit
11. Many system shut–downs are due to loss of sensor signals to or from the controller. The most common cause is not a failed sensor but a loose, corroded or dirty connector. Incorrect adjustment of the wheel speed sensor will cause a loss of wheel speed signal. Check harness and component connectors carefully.

Problem	Possible cause	Remedy
Low or spongy pedal	Linings worn	Replace brake shoes or pads
	Leak in brake system	Located and repair
	Master cylinder faulty	Repair or replace master cylinder
	Air in brake system	Bleed brake system
	Wheel cylinder faulty	Repair wheel cylinder
	Piston seals worn or damaged	Repair brake calipers
	Rear brake automatic adjuster faulty	Repair or replace adjuster
Brakes drag	Parking brake out of adjustment	Adjust parking brake
	Linkage binding	Repair as necessary
	Booster push rod out of adjustment	Adjust push rod
	Return spring faulty	Replace spring
	Brake line restricted	Repair as necessary
	Lining cracked or distorted	Replace brake shoes and pads
	Wheel cylinder or caliper piston sticking	Repair as necessary
	Automatic adjuster broken	Replace adjuster
	Master cylinder faulty	Repair or replace master cylinder
Brakes pull	Tires improperly inflated	Inflate tires to proper pressure
	Oil or grease on linings	Check for cause/Replace shoes or pads
	Brake shoes distorted, linings worn or glazed	Replace brake shoes
	Drum or disc out of round	Replace drum or disc
	Return spring faulty	Replace spring
	Wheel cylinder faulty	Repair wheel cylinder
	Piston frozen in caliper	Repair caliper
	Disc brake pad sticking	Replace pads
Brakes grab/chatter	Oil or grease on linings	Check for cause/Replace shoes or pads
	Drum or disc scored or out of round	Replace drum or disc
	Brake shoes distorted, linings worn or glazed	Replace brake shoes
	Wheel cylinder faulty	Repair wheel cylinder
	Disc brake pad sticking	Replace pads
	Brake booster faulty	Repair booster

Problem	Possible cause	Remedy
Hard pedal but brakes inefficient	Oil or grease on linings	Check for cause/Replace shoes or pads
	Brake shoes distorted, linings worn or glazed, drums worn	Replace brake shoes
	Disc brake pads worn	Replace pads
	Piston frozen in caliper	Repair caliper
	Brake booster faulty	Repair booster
	Brake line restricted	Repair as necessary
	Vacuum system leaking	Repair or replace
Snapping or clicking noise when brakes are applied	Drum brakes-brake shoes binding at backing plate ledges	Lubricate
	Drum brakes-backing plate ledges worn	Replace and lubricate ledges
	Drum brakes-loose or missing hold down spring	Replace
	Drum brakes-loose set bolt at backing plate	Tighten
	Disc brakes-rust on front edge of inboard shoes	Inspect, lubricate/Replace if necessary
	Disc brakes-loose or missing pad support plate	Replace or insert
	Disc brakes-loose installation bolt	Tighten
	Disc brakes-wear on slide bushing	Replace
	Pad wear and pad wear indicator making contact with the rotor	Replace
Scraping or grinding noise when brakes are applied	Worn brake linings	Replace/Refinish drums or rotors if heavily scored
	Caliper to wheel or rotor interference	Replace as required
	Dust cover to rotor or drum interference	Correct or replace
	Other brake system components: Warped or bent brake backing plate, cracked drums or rotors	Inspect and repair or replace
	Tires rubbing against chassis and body	Inspect and repair or replace
	Pad wear and pad wear indicator making contact with the rotor	Replace

Problem	Possible cause	Remedy
Squealing, groaning or chattering noise when brakes are applied Note: Brake friction materials inherently generate noise and heat in order to dissipate energy. As a result, occasional squeal is normal and is aggravated by severe environmental coditions such as cold, heat, wetness, snow, salt, mud, etc. This occasional squeal is not a functional problem and does not indicate any loss of brake effectiveness	Brake drums and linings, rotors and pads worn or scored	Inspect, service or replace
	Disc brakes-missing or damaged brake pad anti-squeal shim	Replace
	Disc brakes-burred or rusted calipers	Clean or deburr
	Dirty, greased, contaminated or glazed linings	Clean or replace
	Improper lining parts	Check for correct parts/Replace
	Maladjustment of brake pedal or booster push rod	Inspect and adjust
	Drum brakes-weak damaged or incorrect shoe hold down springs, loose or damaged shoe hold down pins and springs and grooved backing plate ledges	Inspect, repair or replace
Squealing noise when brakes are not applied	Bent or warped backing plate causing interference with drum	Repair or replace
	Improper machining of drum causing interference with backing plate or shoe	Replace drum
	Maladjustment of brake pedal or booster push rod	Inspect and adjust
	Poor return of brake booster or master cylinder or wheel cylinder	Inspect, repair or replace
	Disc brakes-rusted, stuck	Inspect/Lubricate if necessary
	Other brake system components: Loose or extra parts in brakes Rear drum adjustment too tight causing lining to glaze Worn, damaged or insufficiently lubricated wheel bearings	Inspect, repair or replace as required
	Drum brakes-weak, damaged or incorrect shoe retracting springs	Inspect, repair or replace
	Drum brakes-grooved backig plate ledges	
	Improper positioning of pads in caliper	Inspect and repair
	Outside diameter of rotor rubbing caliper housing	Inspect, correct or replace
	Housing installation of disc brake pad support plate	Correct

Problem	Possible cause	Remedy
Groaning, clicking or rattling noise when brakes are not applied	Stones or foreign material trapped inside wheel covers	Remove foreign material
	Loose wheel hub nuts	Tighten to correct torque. Replace if stud holes are elongated
	Disc brakes-failure of shim	Inspect. Replace if necessary
	Disc brakes-wear on sliding bushing	Inspect. Replace if necessary
	Disc brakes-loose installation bolt	Inspect. Tighten if necessary
	Maladjustment of brake pedal or booster push rod	Inspect and adjust
	Disc brakes-poor return of piston	Inspect, repair or replace
	Drum brakes-loose or extra parts	Inspect, repair or replace
	Worn, damaged or dry wheel bearings	Inspect, lubricate or replace

Code No.	Light Pattern	Diagnosis	Trouble Part
11	ON OFF	Open circuit in solenoid relay circuit	● Actuator inside wire harness ● Control relay ● Wire harness and connector of solenoid relay circuit
12		Short circuit in solenoid relay circuit	
13		Open circuit in pump motor relay circuit	● Actuator inside wire harness ● Control relay ● Wire harness and connector of pump motor relay circuit
14		Short circuit in pump motor relay circuit	
21		Open or short circuit in 3 position solenoid of front right wheel	● Actuator solenoid ● Wire harness and connector of actuator solenoid circuit
22		Open or short circuit in 3 position solenoid of front left wheel	
23		Open or short circuit in 3 position solenoid of rear right wheel	
24		Open or short circuit 3 position solenoid of rear left wheel	
31		Front right wheel speed sensor signal malfunction	● Speed sensor ● Sensor rotor ● Wire harness and connector of speed sensor
32		Front left wheel speed sensor signal malfunction	
33		Rear right wheel speed sensor signal malfunction	
34		Rear left wheel speed sensor signal malfunction	
35		Open circuit in front left or rear right wheel speed sensor	
36		Open circuit in front right or rear left wheel speed sensor	
37		Wrong both rear axle hubs	● Rear sensor rotors
41		Abnormal battery voltage (less than 9.5 V/more than 16.2 V)	● Battery ● Voltage regulator
51		Pump motor of actuator locked or open circuit in pump motor circuit in actuator	● Pump motor, relay and battery ● Wire harness, connector and ground bolt or actuator pump motor circuit
Always on		Malfunction in ECU	● ECU

Code No.	Light Pattern	Diagnosis	Malfunctioning Part
	ON / OFF (continuous flashing)	All speed sensors and sensor rotors are normal	
71		Low voltage of front right speed sensor signal	• Front right speed sensor • Sensor installation
72		Low voltage of front left speed sensor signal	• Front left speed sensor • Sensor installation
73		Low voltage of rear right speed sensor signal	• Rear right speed sensor • Sensor installation
74		Low voltage of rear left speed sensor signal	• Rear left speed sensor • Sensor installation
75		Abnormal change of front right speed sensor signal	• Front right sensor rotor
76		Abnormal change of front left speed sensor signal	• Front left sensor rotor
77		Abnormal change of rear right speed sensor signal	• Rear right sensor rotor
78		Abnormal change of rear left speed sensor signal	• Rear left sensor rotor

Actuator and Diagnostic System

TESTING

➧ SEE FIGS. 46–48

1. Start the engine and drive at a speed over 4 mph (6.4 kph). Listen carefully for actuator operation as the vehicle passes 4 mph (6.4 kph). If the brake is not applied, the controller cycles each solenoid and operates the pump motor briefly as an initial system check.

2. Return the vehicle to the workplace and turn the ignition switch **OFF**. Check battery condition; approximately 12 volts is required to operate the system.

3. Turn the ignition switch **ON** and check that the dashboard warning lamp (ABS or ANTILOCK) comes on for 3–4 seconds. If the lamp does not come on, repair the fuse, bulb or wiring.

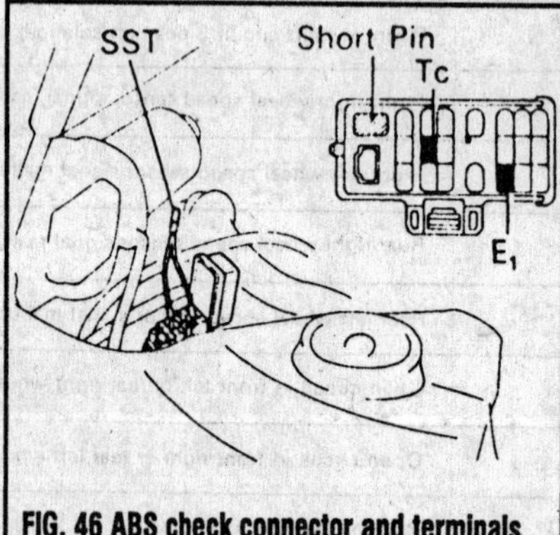

FIG. 46 ABS check connector and terminals Tc and E1 locations

4. On 1989–91 vehicles, read the stored diagnostic code(s), if any, as follows:

a. With the ignition **ON**, disconnect the service connector at the actuator.

b. If a fault code has been set, the dashboard warning lamp will begin to blink 4 seconds later. The number of flashes corresponds to the first digit of a 2–digit code; after a 1.5 second pause, the second digit is transmitted. If a second code is stored, it will be displayed after a 2.5 second pause. Once all codes have been displayed, the entire series will repeat after a 4 second pause.

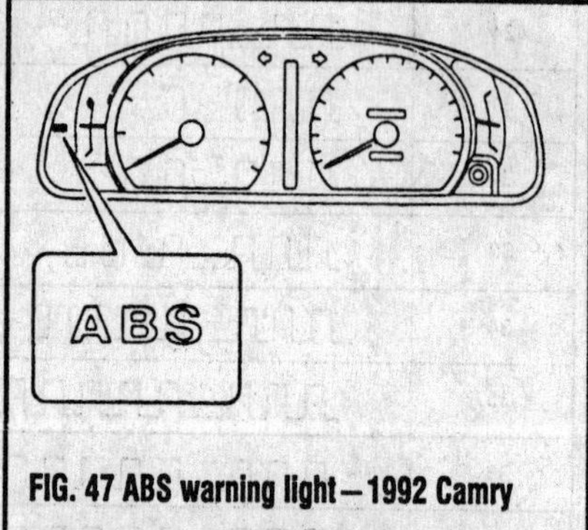

FIG. 47 ABS warning light—1992 Camry

c. If no codes have been stored, the warning lamp will flash continuously every 1/2 second with no variation.

5. On 1992 vehicles, read the stored diagnostic code(s), if any as follows:

a. With the ignition **ON**, disconnect the service connector at the actuator.

b. Using special tool SST 09843–18020 or equivalent, connect terminals **Tc** and **E1** of the check connector. Remove the short pin

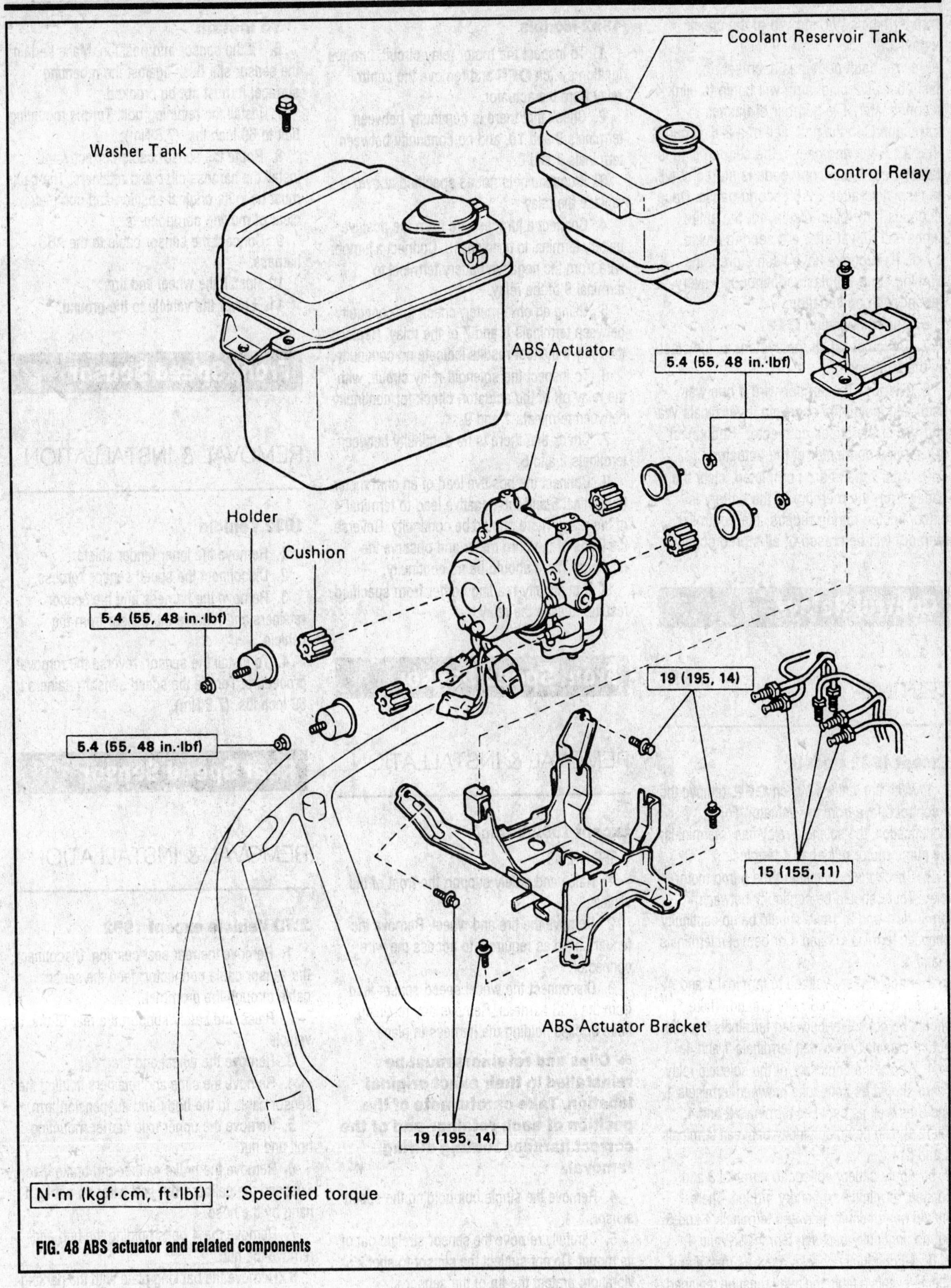

FIG. 48 ABS actuator and related components

from terminals Wa and Wb of the check connector.

c. If a fault code has been set, the dashboard warning lamp will begin to blink 4 seconds later. The number of flashes corresponds to the first digit of a 2-digit code; after a 1.5 second pause, the second digit is transmitted. If a second code is stored, it will be displayed after a 2.5 second pause. Once all codes have been displayed, the entire series will repeat after a 4 second pause.

d. If no codes have been stored, the warning lamp will flash continuously every 1/2 second with no variation.

6. Turn the ignition **OFF**.

7. Check or repair the system as indicated by the fault code.

8. Remove the jumper wire if one was used and install the short pin in terminals Wa and Wb of the check connector. Reconnect the service connector at the actuator.

9. After repairs are completed, clear the codes from the memory. If the battery is disconnected during repairs, the controller memory will be erased of all stored codes.

Control Relays

TESTING

Except 1992 Models

1. With the ignition switch **OFF**, remove the 2 control relays from the actuator. For identification, the solenoid relay has 5 terminals; the pump motor relay has 4 terminals.

2. Check the continuity of the pump motor relay. There should be continuity between terminals 1 and 2. There should be no continuity between terminals 3 and 4 or between terminals 1 and 4.

3. Apply battery voltage to terminal 1 and connect terminal 2 to battery ground. There should be continuity between terminals 3 and 4 but no continuity between terminals 1 and 4.

4. Check the continuity of the solenoid relay. There should be continuity between terminals 1 and 3 as well as between terminals 2 and 4. There should be no continuity between terminals 4 and 5.

5. Apply battery voltage to terminal 3 and connect terminal 1 to battery ground. There should be continuity between terminals 4 and 5 but no continuity between terminals 2 and 4.

6. All continuity checks must be met; if any check reveals a fault, the relay must be replaced.

1992 Models

1. To inspect the motor relay circuit, turn the ignition switch **OFF** and remove the control relay from the actuator.

2. Check that there is continuity between terminals 9 and 10, and no continuity between terminals 7 and 8.

3. If continuity is not as specified above, replace the relay.

4. Connect a jumper wire from the positive battery terminal to terminal 10. Connect a jumper wire from the negative battery terminal to terminal 9 of the relay.

5. Using an ohm meter, check for continuity between terminals 8 and 7 of the relay. Replace the relay if the test results indicate no continuity.

6. To inspect the solenoid relay circuit, with the relay off of the actuator, check for continuity between terminals 1 and 9.

7. Check that there is no continuity between terminals 2 and 5.

8. Connect the positive lead of an ohm meter to terminal 5 and the negative lead to terminal 4 of the relay. There should be continuity. Reverse the leads of the ohm meter and observe the readings. There should be no continuity.

9. If continuity readings differ from specified results, replace the relay.

Front Speed Sensor

REMOVAL & INSTALLATION

Except 1992 Vehicle

➧ SEE FIG. 49

1. Raise and safely support the front of the vehicle.

2. Remove the tire and wheel. Remove the fender shield as required, to access the wire connector.

3. Disconnect the wheel speed sensor lead from the ABS harness. Remove any retaining bolts or clips holding the harness in place.

➡ Clips and retainers must be reinstalled in their exact original location. Take careful note of the position of each retainer and of the correct harness routing during removal.

4. Remove the single bolt holding the speed sensor.

5. Carefully remove the sensor straight out of its mount. Do not subject the sensor to shock or vibration; protect the tip of the sensor at all times.

To Install:

6. Fit the sensor into position. Make certain the sensor sits flush against the mounting surface; it must not be crooked.

7. Install the retaining bolt. Torque mounting bolt to 69 inch lbs. (7.8 Nm).

8. Route the sensor cable correctly and install the harness clips and retainers. The cable must be in its original position and completely clear of moving components.

9. Connect the sensor cable to the ABS harness.

10. Install the wheel and tire.

11. Lower the vehicle to the ground.

Front Speed Sensor

REMOVAL & INSTALLATION

1992 Vehicle

1. Remove the inner fender shield.

2. Disconnect the speed sensor harness.

3. Remove the harness and the sensor retainers and remove the sensor from the vehicle.

4. To install the sensor, reverse the removal procedure. Torque the speed sensor retainers to 69 inch lbs. (7.8 Nm).

Rear Speed Sensor

REMOVAL & INSTALLATION

2WD Vehicle except 1992

1. Remove the rear seat cushion. Disconnect the sensor cable connector; feed the sensor cable through the grommet.

2. Raise and safely support the rear of the vehicle.

3. Remove the wheel and tire.

4. Remove the clips and retainers holding the sensor cable to the body and suspension arm.

5. Remove the upper axle carrier mounting bolt and nut.

6. Remove the brake caliper and brake disc. Suspend the caliper from stiff wire; do not let it hang by the hose.

7. Remove the 4 bolts holding the hub and remove the hub.

8. Remove the backing plate with the parking brake assembly and O-ring.

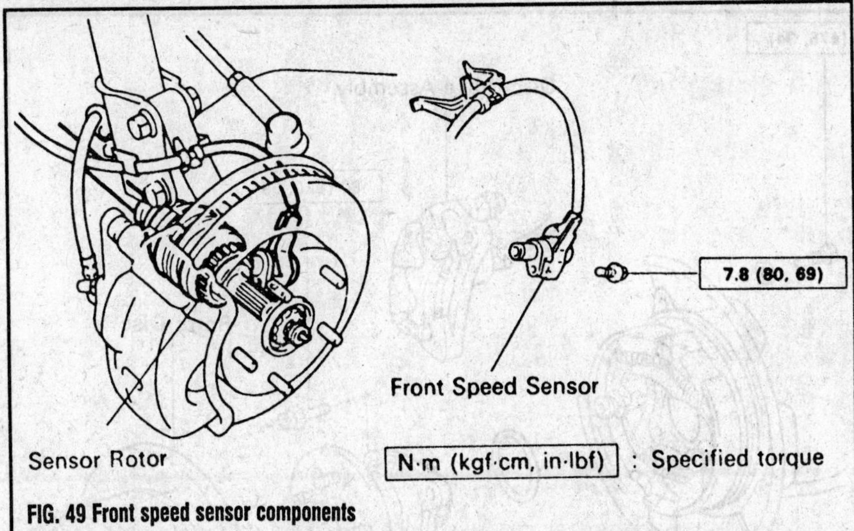

FIG. 49 Front speed sensor components

9. Remove the speed sensor retaining bolt and remove the sensor from the backing plate.

To install:

10. Position the sensor on the backing plate and install the retaining bolt. Tighten the bolt to 69 inch lbs. (7.8 Nm).
11. Install the backing plate with the parking brake assembly in place.
12. Install a new O-ring on the axle carrier. Install the hub and tighten the 4 mounting bolts to 59 ft. lbs. (80 Nm).
13. Align the hole on the axle hub and the service hole on the brake disc. Install the disc.
14. Install the brake caliper; tighten the mounting bolts to 34 ft. lbs. (47 Nm).
15. Install the upper axle carrier bolt and nut. Tighten to 152 ft. lbs. (206 Nm)
16. Install the sensor cable into the clips and retainers. Make certain the cable is clear of all moving components.
17. Insert the sensor cable through the grommet into the vehicle.
18. Install the wheel and tire. Lower the vehicle to the ground.
19. Connect the sensor cable to the ABS harness.
20. Install the rear seat cushion.

Rear Speed Sensor

REMOVAL & INSTALLATION

1992 Vehicle

➧ SEE FIG. 50

1. Remove the rear seat cushion. Disconnect the sensor cable connector; feed the sensor cable through the grommet.
2. Raise and safely support the rear of the vehicle.
3. Remove the wheel and tire.
4. Remove the clips and retainers holding the sensor cable to the body and suspension arm. Remove the sensor from the vehicle.
5. Installation is the reverse of the removal procedure. Torque the mounting bolt to 69 inch lbs. (7.8 Nm).

Rear Speed Sensor

REMOVAL & INSTALLATION

4WD Vehicle

1. Raise and safely support the rear of the vehicle.
2. Remove the tire and wheel.
3. Disconnect the wheel speed sensor lead from the ABS harness. Remove any retaining bolts or clips holding the harness in place.

➡ Clips and retainers must be reinstalled in their exact original location. Take careful note of the position of each retainer and of the correct harness routing during removal.

4. Remove the single bolt holding the speed sensor.
5. Carefully remove the sensor straight out of its mount. Do not subject the sensor to shock or vibration; protect the tip of the sensor at all times.

To install:

6. Before installation, make certain all traces of paint are removed from the hub carrier surface. A clean metal-to-metal contact is required. Fit the sensor into position. Make certain the sensor sits flush against the mounting surface; it must not be crooked.
7. Install the retaining bolt. Tighten the bolt to 69 inch lbs. (7.8 Nm).
8. Route the sensor cable correctly and install the harness clips and retainers. The cable must be in its original position and completely clear of moving components.
9. Connect the sensor cable to the ABS harness.
10. Install the wheel and tire.
11. Lower the vehicle to the ground.

Deceleration Sensor

TESTING

➡ The following procedures require driving the vehicle while it is in the diagnostic mode. The anti-lock system will be disabled; only normal braking function will be available.

1. Check the battery voltage with the engine off; voltage should be approximately 12 volts.
2. With the ignition switch **ON**, make certain the ABS warning lamp comes on for about 3 seconds and then goes out. Turn the ignition switch **OFF**.
3. Remove the rubber cap from the Ts connector located in front of the actuator. Use a jumper wire to connect the 2 terminals.
4. Apply the parking brake fully, depress the brake pedal and start the engine.
5. After a short delay, the ABS dashboard warning lamp should flash about once every second. This is slower than the usual system flashing when transmitting a code.
6. Release the parking brake and drive the vehicle straight ahead at 12.4 mph (20 kph) or greater speed. Lightly depress the brake pedal; there should be no change in the flashing dashboard lamp.
7. Continue to drive at the same speed and apply the brakes moderately. The warning lamp should stop flashing and remain on during braking only. Once the brake is released, flashing continues at the previous rate.
8. Continue driving at the same speed; apply the brakes strongly. The dash warning lamp should remain on during the braking period and

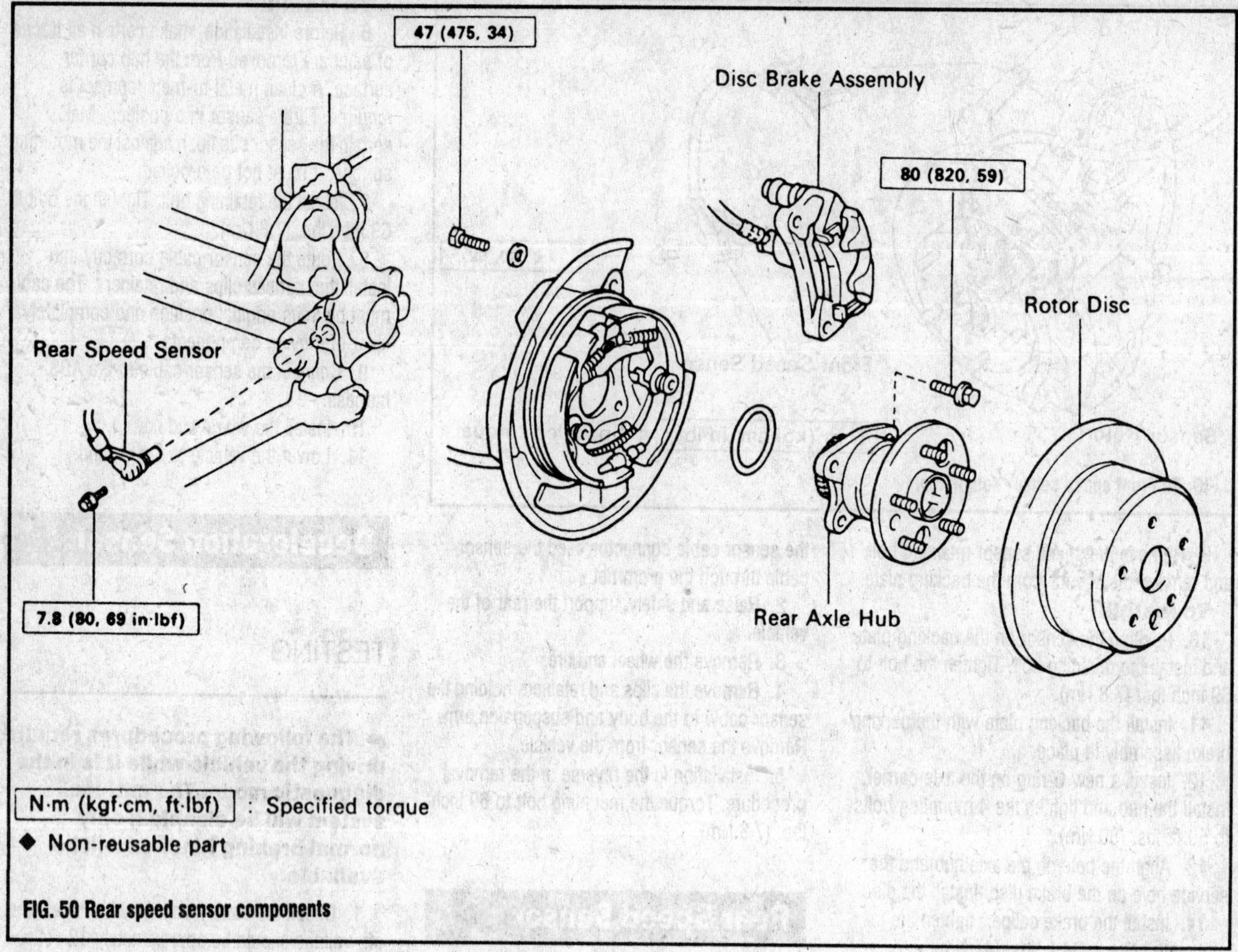

FIG. 50 Rear speed sensor components

change to a rapid flash when the brakes are released.

9. If the warning lamp display does not meet specifications, check the installation of the deceleration sensor. It must be correctly and securely installed. If installation is proper, replace the sensor and retest the system.

10. Stop the vehicle and turn the ignition switch **OFF**. Remove the jumper wire from the check connector.

Deceleration Sensor

REMOVAL & INSTALLATION

1. Remove the ABS ECU cover and the ECU from the mounting bracket.
2. Disconnect the electrical connector from the ECU and remove the computer from the vehicle.
3. Remove the 2 mounting screws from the deceleration sensor and remove the sensor from the vehicle.
4. Installation is the reverse of the removal procedure.

ABS Actuator

REMOVAL & INSTALLATION

➧ SEE FIG. 48

1. Disconnect the negative battery cable. Label and disconnect the electrical connectors.
2. Remove the fluid in the brake actuator with a suitable syringe.
3. Remove the engine coolant reserve tank and the windshield washer tank as required.
4. Disconnect the hydraulic lines from the brake actuator. Plug the ends of the lines to prevent loss of fluid.
5. Detach the hydraulic fluid pressure differential switch wiring connectors.
6. Loosen the brake actuator reservoir mounting nuts.
7. Unfasten the nuts and remove the ABS actuator assembly.

To Install:

8. Before tightening the mounting nuts or bolts, screw the hydraulic line into the cylinder body a few turns.
9. Install the actuator. Torque the hydraulic lines to 11 ft. lbs. (15 Nm).
10. Install the engine coolant reserve tank and the windshield washer tank as required.
11. After installation is completed, fill the reservoir and bleed the brake system.

Sensor Ring (Rotor)

➧ SEE FIG. 49 AND 50

The wheel mounted sensor rings are integral parts of either the wheel hub or the axle shaft; if the ring is damaged, the hub or shaft must be replaced. For axle shaft and wheel hub removal and installation procedures, please refer to the appropriate section of this repair manual.

Filling and Bleeding System

The brake fluid reservoir is located on top of the master cylinder. While no special procedures are needed to fill the fluid, the reservoir cap and surrounding area must be wiped clean of all dirt and debris before removing the cap. The slightest dirt in the fluid can cause a system malfunction. Use only DOT 3 fluid from an unopened container. Use of old, polluted or non-approved fluid can seriously impair the function of the system.

Bleeding is performed in the usual manner, using either a pressure bleeder or the 2-person manual method. If a pressure bleeder is used, it must be of the diaphragm type with an internal diaphragm separating the air chamber from the fluid. Tighten each bleeder plug to 74 inch lbs. (8.3 Nm).

Always begin the bleeding with the longest brake line, then the next longest, and so on. If the master cylinder has been repaired or if the reservoir has been emptied, the master cylinder will need to be bled before the individual lines and calipers. During any bleeding procedure, make certain to maintain the fluid level above the MIN line on the reservoir. When the bleeding procedure is complete, fill the reservoir to the MAX line before reinstalling the cap.

BRAKE SPECIFICATIONS

All measurements in inches unless noted.

			Brake Disc			Brake Drum Diameter			Minimum Lining Thickness	
Year	Model	Master Cylinder Bore	Original Thickness	Minimum Thickness	Maximum Runout	Original Inside Diameter	Max. Wear Limit	Maximum Machine Diameter	Front	Rear
1983	Camry	①	0.866	0.827	0.0059	7.874	7.913	①	0.039	0.039
1984	Camry	①	0.866	0.827	0.0059	7.874	7.913	①	0.039	0.039
1985	Camry	①	0.866	0.827	0.0059	7.874	7.913	①	0.039	0.039
1986	Camry	①	0.866	0.827	0.0059	7.874	7.913	①	0.039	0.039
1987	Camry	①	0.866	0.827	0.0051	9.000	9.079	①	0.039	0.039
1988	Camry	①	0.984	0.945	0.0031	9.000	9.079	①	0.039	0.039
1989	Camry	①	0.984②	0.945②	0.0028②	9.000	9.079	①	0.039	0.039
1990	Camry	①	0.984②	0.945②	0.0028②	9.000	9.079	①	0.039	0.039
1991	Camry	①	0.984②	0.945②	0.0028②	9.000	9.079	①	0.039	0.039
1992	Camry	①	1.102②	1.024②	0.0020②	9.000	9.079	①	0.039	0.039

① Not specified by manufacturer
② Rear disc original thickness—0.394
Rear disc minimum thickness—0.354

Troubleshooting the Brake System

Problem	Cause	Solution
Low brake pedal (excessive pedal travel required for braking action.)	• Excessive clearance between rear linings and drums caused by inoperative automatic adjusters	• Make 10 to 15 alternate forward and reverse brake stops to adjust brakes. If brake pedal does not come up, repair or replace adjuster parts as necessary.
	• Worn rear brakelining	• Inspect and replace lining if worn beyond minimum thickness specification
	• Bent, distorted brakeshoes, front or rear	• Replace brakeshoes in axle sets
	• Air in hydraulic system	• Remove air from system. Refer to Brake Bleeding.
Low brake pedal (pedal may go to floor with steady pressure applied.)	• Fluid leak in hydraulic system	• Fill master cylinder to fill line; have helper apply brakes and check calipers, wheel cylinders, differential valve tubes, hoses and fittings for leaks. Repair or replace as necessary.
	• Air in hydraulic system	• Remove air from system. Refer to Brake Bleeding.
	• Incorrect or non-recommended brake fluid (fluid evaporates at below normal temp).	• Flush hydraulic system with clean brake fluid. Refill with correct-type fluid.
	• Master cylinder piston seals worn, or master cylinder bore is scored, worn or corroded	• Repair or replace master cylinder
Low brake pedal (pedal goes to floor on first application—o.k. on subsequent applications.)	• Disc brake pads sticking on abutment surfaces of anchor plate. Caused by a build-up of dirt, rust, or corrosion on abutment surfaces	• Clean abutment surfaces
Fading brake pedal (pedal height decreases with steady pressure applied.)	• Fluid leak in hydraulic system	• Fill master cylinder reservoirs to fill mark, have helper apply brakes, check calipers, wheel cylinders, differential valve, tubes, hoses, and fittings for fluid leaks. Repair or replace parts as necessary.
	• Master cylinder piston seals worn, or master cylinder bore is scored, worn or corroded	• Repair or replace master cylinder
Spongy brake pedal (pedal has abnormally soft, springy, spongy feel when depressed.)	• Air in hydraulic system	• Remove air from system. Refer to Brake Bleeding.
	• Brakeshoes bent or distorted	• Replace brakeshoes
	• Brakelining not yet seated with drums and rotors	• Burnish brakes
	• Rear drum brakes not properly adjusted	• Adjust brakes

Troubleshooting the Brake System (cont.)

Problem	Cause	Solution
Decreasing brake pedal travel (pedal travel required for braking action decreases and may be accompanied by a hard pedal.)	• Caliper or wheel cylinder pistons sticking or seized • Master cylinder compensator ports blocked (preventing fluid return to reservoirs) or pistons sticking or seized in master cylinder bore • Power brake unit binding internally	• Repair or replace the calipers, or wheel cylinders • Repair or replace the master cylinder • Test unit according to the following procedure: (a) Shift transmission into neutral and start engine (b) Increase engine speed to 1500 rpm, close throttle and fully depress brake pedal (c) Slow release brake pedal and stop engine (d) Have helper remove vacuum check valve and hose from power unit. Observe for backward movement of brake pedal. (e) If the pedal moves backward, the power unit has an internal bind—replace power unit
Grabbing brakes (severe reaction to brake pedal pressure.)	• Brakelining(s) contaminated by grease or brake fluid • Parking brake cables incorrectly adjusted or seized • Incorrect brakelining or lining loose on brakeshoes • Caliper anchor plate bolts loose • Rear brakeshoes binding on support plate ledges • Incorrect or missing power brake reaction disc • Rear brake support plates loose	• Determine and correct cause of contamination and replace brakeshoes in axle sets • Adjust cables. Replace seized cables. • Replace brakeshoes in axle sets • Tighten bolts • Clean and lubricate ledges. Replace support plate(s) if ledges are deeply grooved. Do not attempt to smooth ledges by grinding. • Install correct disc • Tighten mounting bolts
Chatter or shudder when brakes are applied (pedal pulsation and roughness may also occur.)	• Brakeshoes distorted, bent, contaminated, or worn • Caliper anchor plate or support plate loose • Excessive thickness variation of rotor(s)	• Replace brakeshoes in axle sets • Tighten mounting bolts • Refinish or replace rotors in axle sets
Noisy brakes (squealing, clicking, scraping sound when brakes are applied.)	• Bent, broken, distorted brakeshoes • Excessive rust on outer edge of rotor braking surface	• Replace brakeshoes in axle sets • Remove rust

Troubleshooting the Brake System (cont.)

Problem	Cause	Solution
Hard brake pedal (excessive pedal pressure required to stop vehicle. May be accompanied by brake fade.)	• Loose or leaking power brake unit vacuum hose	• Tighten connections or replace leaking hose
	• Incorrect or poor quality brake-lining	• Replace with lining in axle sets
	• Bent, broken, distorted brakeshoes	• Replace brakeshoes
	• Calipers binding or dragging on mounting pins. Rear brakeshoes dragging on support plate.	• Replace mounting pins and bushings. Clean rust or burrs from rear brake support plate ledges and lubricate ledges with molydisulfide grease. **NOTE:** If ledges are deeply grooved or scored, do not attempt to sand or grind them smooth—replace support plate.
	• Caliper, wheel cylinder, or master cylinder pistons sticking or seized	• Repair or replace parts as necessary
	• Power brake unit vacuum check valve malfunction	• Test valve according to the following procedure: (a) Start engine, increase engine speed to 1500 rpm, close throttle and immediately stop engine (b) Wait at least 90 seconds then depress brake pedal (c) If brakes are not vacuum assisted for 2 or more applications, check valve is faulty
	• Power brake unit has internal bind	• Test unit according to the following procedure: (a) With engine stopped, apply brakes several times to exhaust all vacuum in system (b) Shift transmission into neutral, depress brake pedal and start engine (c) If pedal height decreases with foot pressure and less pressure is required to hold pedal in applied position, power unit vacuum system is operating normally. Test power unit. If power unit exhibits a bind condition, replace the power unit.

Troubleshooting the Brake System (cont.)

Problem	Cause	Solution
Hard brake pedal (excessive pedal pressure required to stop vehicle. May be accompanied by brake fade.)	• Master cylinder compensator ports (at bottom of reservoirs) blocked by dirt, scale, rust, or have small burrs (blocked ports prevent fluid return to reservoirs).	• Repair or replace master cylinder **CAUTION:** Do not attempt to clean blocked ports with wire, pencils, or similar implements. Use compressed air only.
	• Brake hoses, tubes, fittings clogged or restricted	• Use compressed air to check or unclog parts. Replace any damaged parts.
	• Brake fluid contaminated with improper fluids (motor oil, transmission fluid, causing rubber components to swell and stick in bores	• Replace all rubber components, combination valve and hoses. Flush entire brake system with DOT 3 brake fluid or equivalent.
	• Low engine vacuum	• Adjust or repair engine
Dragging brakes (slow or incomplete release of brakes)	• Brake pedal binding at pivot	• Loosen and lubricate
	• Power brake unit has internal bind	• Inspect for internal bind. Replace unit if internal bind exists.
	• Parking brake cables incorrrectly adjusted or seized	• Adjust cables. Replace seized cables.
	• Rear brakeshoe return springs weak or broken	• Replace return springs. Replace brakeshoe if necessary in axle sets.
	• Automatic adjusters malfunctioning	• Repair or replace adjuster parts as required
	• Caliper, wheel cylinder or master cylinder pistons sticking or seized	• Repair or replace parts as necessary
	• Master cylinder compensating ports blocked (fluid does not return to reservoirs).	• Use compressed air to clear ports. Do not use wire, pencils, or similar objects to open blocked ports.
Vehicle moves to one side when brakes are applied	• Incorrect front tire pressure	• Inflate to recommended cold (reduced load) inflation pressure
	• Worn or damaged wheel bearings	• Replace worn or damaged bearings
	• Brakelining on one side contaminated	• Determine and correct cause of contamination and replace brakelining in axle sets
	• Brakeshoes on one side bent, distorted, or lining loose on shoe	• Replace brakeshoes in axle sets
	• Support plate bent or loose on one side	• Tighten or replace support plate
	• Brakelining not yet seated with drums or rotors	• Burnish brakelining
	• Caliper anchor plate loose on one side	• Tighten anchor plate bolts
	• Caliper piston sticking or seized	• Repair or replace caliper
	• Brakelinings water soaked	• Drive vehicle with brakes lightly applied to dry linings
	• Loose suspension component attaching or mounting bolts	• Tighten suspension bolts. Replace worn suspension components.
	• Brake combination valve failure	• Replace combination valve

Troubleshooting the Brake System (cont.)

Problem	Cause	Solution
Noisy brakes (squealing, clicking, scraping sound when brakes are applied.) (cont.)	• Brakelining worn out—shoes contacting drum of rotor	• Replace brakeshoes and lining in axle sets. Refinish or replace drums or rotors.
	• Broken or loose holdown or return springs	• Replace parts as necessary
	• Rough or dry drum brake support plate ledges	• Lubricate support plate ledges
	• Cracked, grooved, or scored rotor(s) or drum(s)	• Replace rotor(s) or drum(s). Replace brakeshoes and lining in axle sets if necessary.
	• Incorrect brakelining and/or shoes (front or rear).	• Install specified shoe and lining assemblies
Pulsating brake pedal	• Out of round drums or excessive lateral runout in disc brake rotor(s)	• Refinish or replace drums, re-index rotors or replace

TORQUE SPECIFICATIONS

Component	U.S.	Metric
ABS actuator bracket bolts	14 ft. lbs.	19 Nm
Bleeder plug	74 inch lbs.	8.3 Nm
Brake booster mounting nuts	9 ft. lbs.	13 Nm
Brake pedal push rod locknut	19 ft. lbs.	25 Nm
Brake tube union nut	11 ft. lbs.	15 Nm
Cylinder installation bolts		
1983–86 vehicles	18 ft. lbs.	24 Nm
1987–88 vehicles	29 ft. lbs.	39 Nm
1989–91 vehicles	29 ft. lbs.	39 Nm
1992 vehicles	25 ft. lbs 34 Nm	
Front disc brake torque plate-to-steering knuckle	79 ft. lbs.	107 Nm
Front speed sensor bolts	69 inch lbs.	7.8 Nm
LSPV mounting bolts	9 ft. lbs.	13 Nm
Master cylinder mounting nuts	9 ft. lbs.	13 Nm
Master cylinder piston stopper bolt	7 ft. lbs.	10 Nm
Rear axle hub installation bolts	59 ft. lbs.	80 Nm
Rear disc brake installation bolts	14 ft. lbs.	20 Nm
Rear disc brake torque plate mounting bolts	34 ft. lbs.	47 Nm
Rear speed sensor bolts	69 inch lbs.	7.8 Nm
Wheel cylinder mounting bolts	7 ft. lbs.	10 Nm

EXTERIOR
- Antenna 10-10
- Bumpers 10-7
- Doors 10-2
- Fenders 10-11
- Grille 10-8
- Hood 10-4
- Outside Mirrors 10-10
- Sunroof/Moonroof 10-11
- Tailgate, Hatch, Trunk Lid 10-5

INTERIOR
- Console 10-13
- Door glass & regulator 10-17
- Door locks 10-17
- Door panels 10-14
- Electric window motor 10-18
- Headliner 10-15
- Heater & a/c ducts 10-17
- Inside mirror 10-21
- Instrument Panel & Pad 10-12
- Interior trim panels 10-15
- Seat belt systems 10-22
- Seats 10-21
- Stationary glass 10-20
- Vent windows 10-
- Windshield glass 10-18

STAIN REMOVAL 10-28

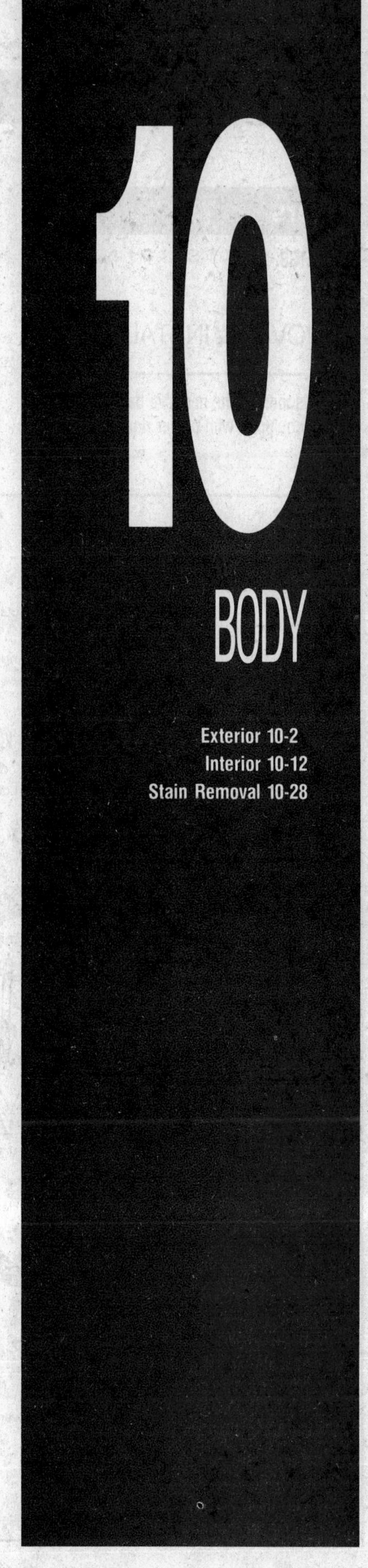

10

BODY

Exterior 10-2
Interior 10-12
Stain Removal 10-28

EXTERIOR

Doors

SEE FIGS. 1–2

REMOVAL & INSTALLATION

1. Disconnect the negative battery terminal.
2. If equipped with power door locks, windows or any other power option located on the door, remove the inner door panel and disconnect the electrical components.
3. Remove the wire harness retainers and extract the harness from the door.
4. Disconnect the door check rod. To prevent the rod from falling inside the door, install the retainer into the hole in the end of the check rod.
5. Matchmark the position of both the upper and lower door hinge to aid in installation. While supporting the door, remove the door-to-hinge bolts and lift the door from the vehicle.

To Install:

6. Position the door on the vehicle and loosely install the hinge bolts.
7. Align each hinge to the matchmarks and secure the bolts.
8. Install and connect the electrical wire harness and secure to the door (if removed).
9. Connect the door check rod and reinstall the interior door trim panel(if removed).
10. Close the door slowly and check for proper alignment. Adjust the door as required and reconnect the negative battery cable.

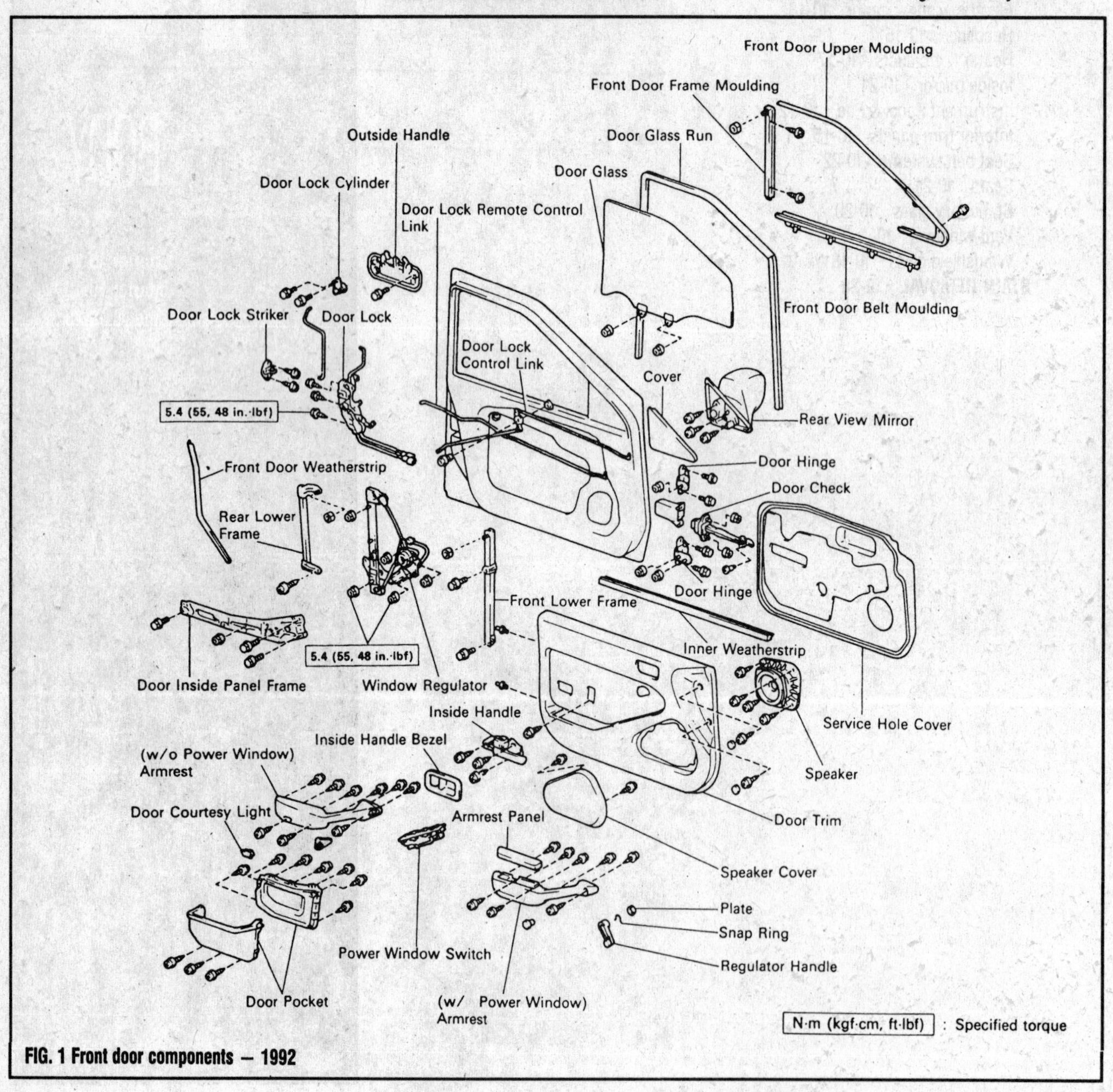

FIG. 1 Front door components — 1992

ADJUSTMENT

➧ SEE FIGS. 3–7

To adjust the door in forward, rearward and vertical directions, perform the following adjustment:

1. Loosen the body side hinge bolts located on the front fender.
2. Adjust the door to the desired position.
3. Secure the body side hinge bolts and check the door for proper alignment.

To adjust the door in left, right and vertical directions, perform the following adjustments:

1. Loosen the door side hinge bolts slightly.
2. Adjust the door to the desired position.
3. Secure the door side hinge bolts and check the door for proper alignment.

To adjust the door lock striker, perform the following procedure:

1. Check that the door fit and the door lock linkages are adjusted properly.
2. Slightly loosen the striker mounting screws and tap striker with a hammer until the desired position is obtained.
3. Tighten the striker mounting screws.

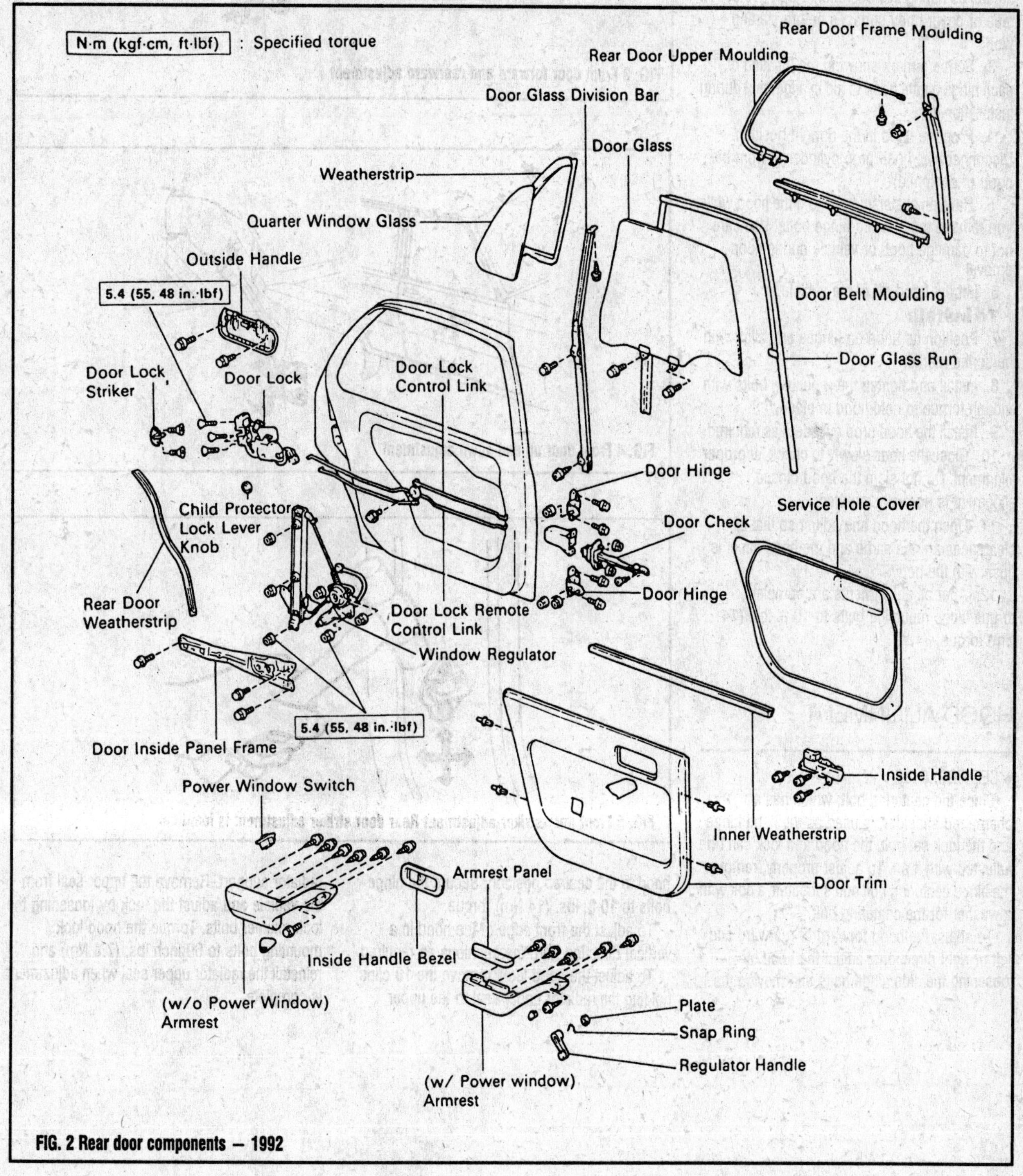

FIG. 2 Rear door components — 1992

Hood

REMOVAL & INSTALLATION

1. Open the hood completely.
2. Protect the cowl panel and hood from scratches during this operation. Apply protection tape or cover body surfaces before starting work.
3. Scribe a mark showing the location of each hinge on the hood to aid in alignment during installation.
4. Prop the hood in the upright position. Disconnect the hood prop cylinder(s) from the hood (if equipped).
5. Have an assistant help hold the hood while you remove the hood-to-hinge bolts. Use care not to damage hood or vehicle during hood removal.
6. Lift the hood off of the vehicle.

To install:

7. Position he hood on hinges and align with the scribe marks.
8. Install and tighten the mounting bolts with enough torque to hold hood in place.
9. Install the hood prop cylinders as required.
10. Close the hood slowly to check for proper alignment. Do not slam the hood closed, alignment is normally required.
11. Open the hood and adjust so that all clearances are the same and the hood panel is flush with the body.
12. After all adjustments are complete, torque hinge mounting bolts to 10 ft. lbs. (14 Nm) torque.

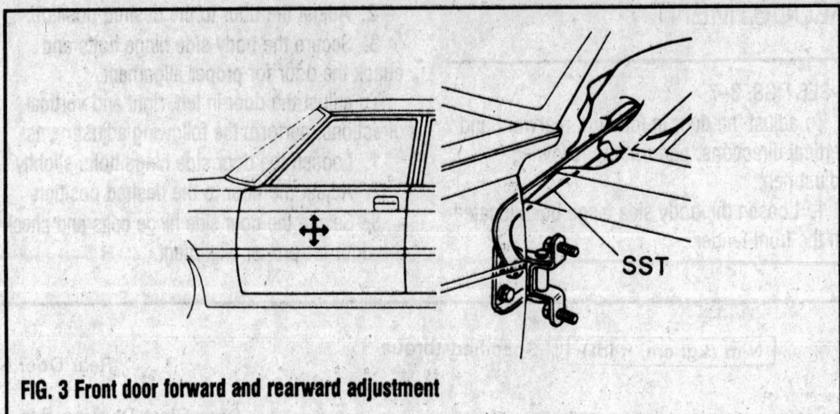

FIG. 3 Front door forward and rearward adjustment

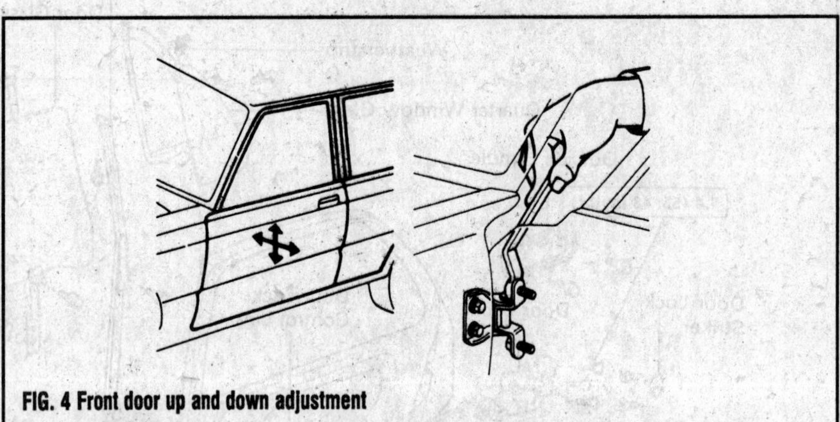
FIG. 4 Front door up and down adjustment

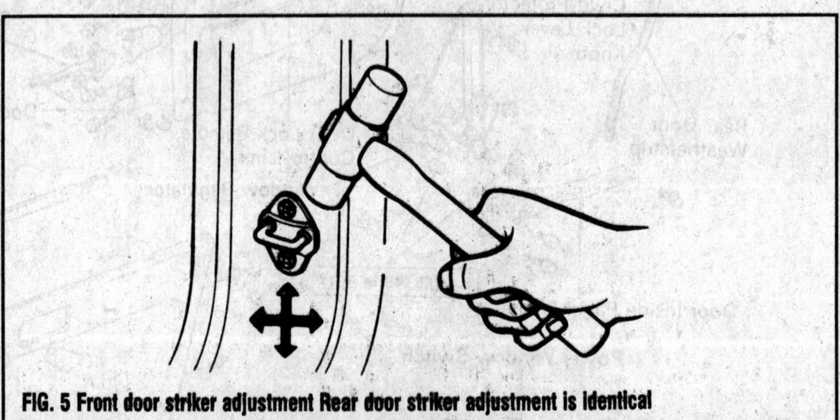
FIG. 5 Front door striker adjustment Rear door striker adjustment is identical

HOOD ALIGNMENT

➧ SEE FIGS. 8–12

Since the centering bolt, which has a chamfered shoulder, is used as the hood hinge and the lock set bolt, the hood and lock can't be adjusted with it on. To adjust properly, remove the hinge centering bolt and substitute a bolt with a washer for the centering bolt.

To adjust the hood forward or rearward and left or right directions, adjust the hood by loosening the side hinge bolts and moving the hood to the desired position. Secure the hinge bolts to 10 ft. lbs. (14 Nm) torque.

To adjust the front edge of the hood in a vertical direction, turn the cushions as required.

To adjust the hood lock, remove the 10 clips holding the radiator upper seal to the upper radiator support. Remove the upper seal from the vehicle and adjust the lock by loosening the lock retainer bolts. Torque the hood lock mounting bolts to 69 inch lbs. (7.8 Nm) and reinstall the radiator upper seal when adjustment is complete.

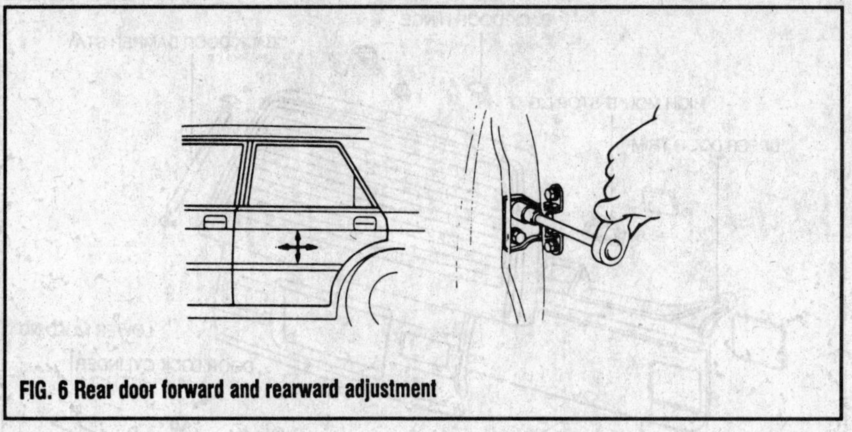
FIG. 6 Rear door forward and rearward adjustment

FIG. 7 Rear door up and down adjustment

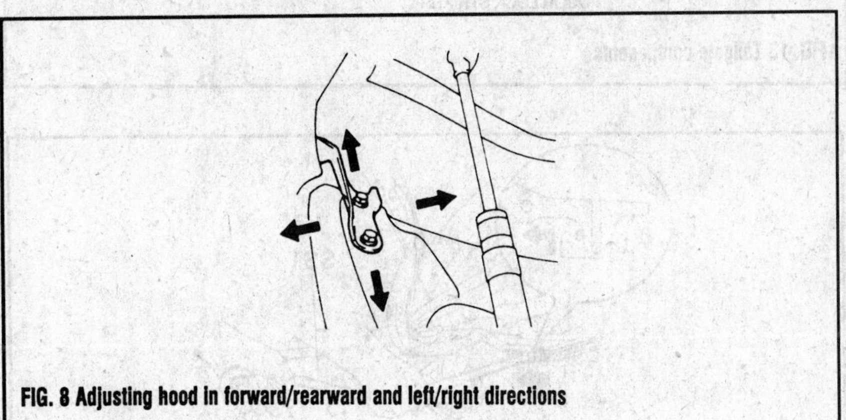
FIG. 8 Adjusting hood in forward/rearward and left/right directions

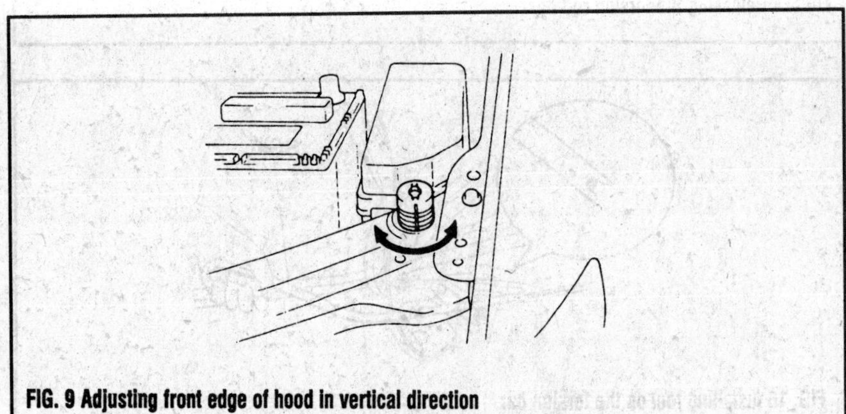
FIG. 9 Adjusting front edge of hood in vertical direction

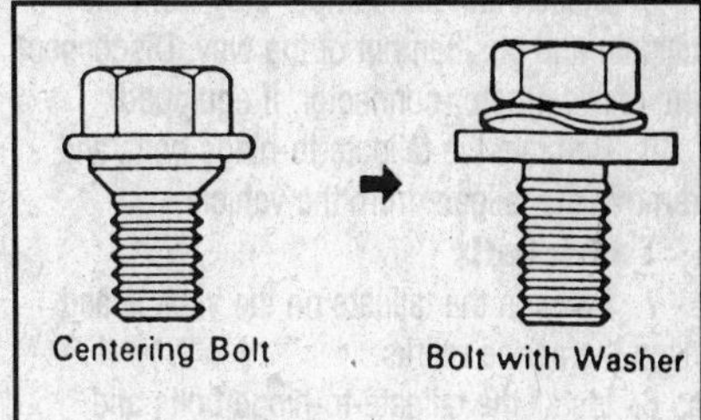

FIG. 10 Shouldered centering bolt which is to be removed during hood adjustment

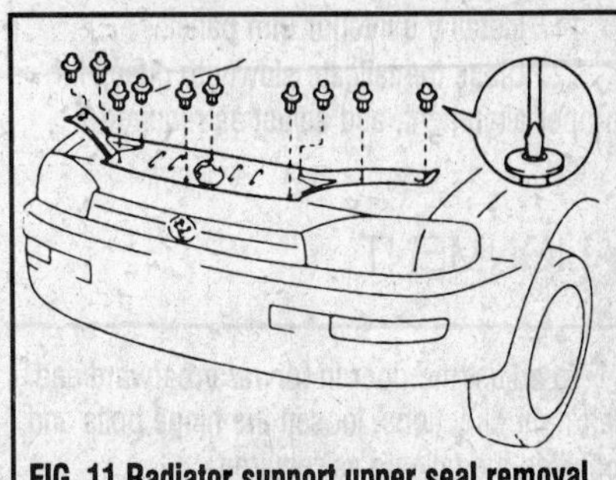
FIG. 11 Radiator support upper seal removal and installation

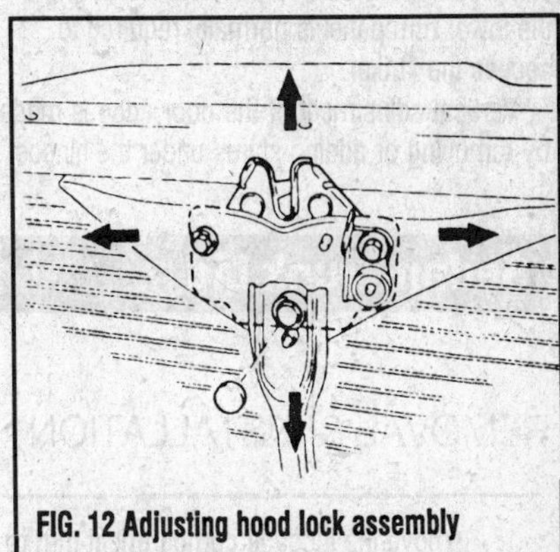
FIG. 12 Adjusting hood lock assembly

Tailgate

SEE FIG. 13

REMOVAL & INSTALLATION

1. Open the tailgate completely.
2. Remove the inner trim panel.
3. Disconnect the electrical connector from the combination light and the electric solenoid as required. Remove the harness and position out of the way.
4. Scribe the hinge location on the tailgate to aid in installation.

5. Disconnect the damper stay from the tailgate and position out of the way. Disconnect the rear defroster connector, if equipped.
6. Remove the tailgate-to-hinge bolts and remove the tailgate from the vehicle.

To Install:

7. Position the tailgate on the vehicle and align the scribe marks.
8. Install the tailgate-to-hinge bolts and secure tightly.
9. Install the damper stay to the tailgate attaching the upper end to the tailgate first.
10. Reconnect the electrical harness as required.
11. Install the interior trim panel.
12. Close the tailgate slowly to check for proper alignment, and adjust as required.

ALIGNMENT

To adjust the door in forward/rearward and left/right directions, loosen the hinge bolts and position the tailgate as required.

To adjust the tailgate lock striker, loosen the mounting bolts and using a plastic hammer, tap the striker to the desired position. Removing of the lower trim panel is normally required to access the striker.

Vertical adjustment of the door edge is made by removing or adding shims under the hinges.

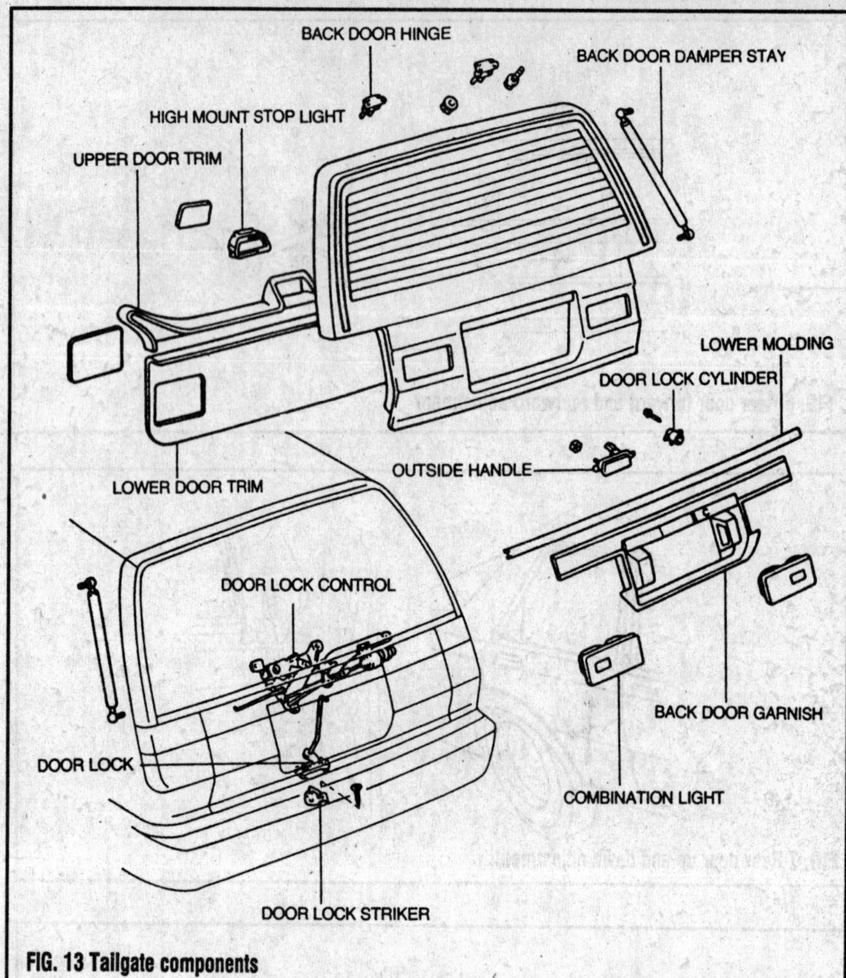

FIG. 13 Tailgate components

Sedan Trunk Lid

REMOVAL & INSTALLATION

1. Remove the luggage compartment trim to access the hinge bolts.
2. Using tool SST 09804–24010 or its equivalent, push down on the torsion bar at one end and pull the luggage compartment lid hinge from the torsion bar.
3. Slowly lift the tool and remove the torsion bar from the bracket.
4. Repeat steps 2 and 3 on the other side of the trunk lid to remove that torsion bar.
5. Prop the hood in the upright position and scribe the hinge locations in the trunk lid.
6. Remove the hinge-to-trunk lid mounting bolts and remove the trunk lid from the vehicle.

To Install:

7. Position the trunk lid on the vehicle and loosely install the retainer bolts.
8. Align the scribe marks on the tailgate and secure the fasteners.
9. Install the torsion bar to the side and center

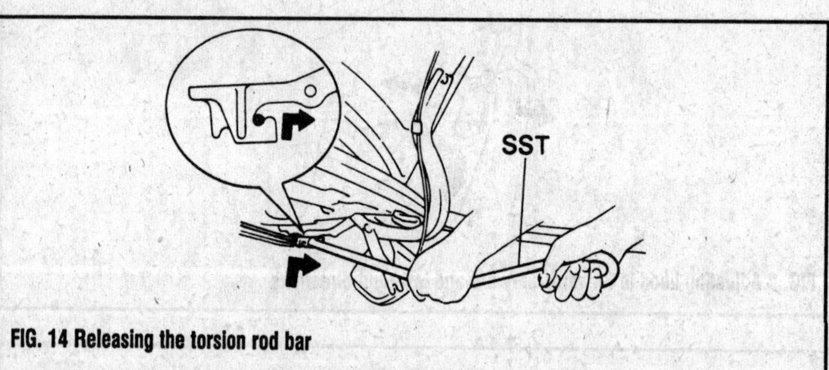

FIG. 14 Releasing the torsion rod bar

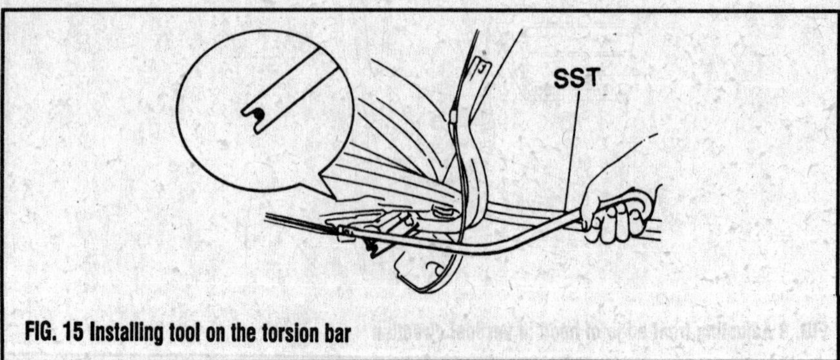

FIG. 15 Installing tool on the torsion bar

brackets, and using tool SST 09804–24010 or its equivalent, install the torsion bar to the hinges.

10. Install the luggage compartment trim that was removed to access the hinge bolts.

ALIGNMENT

To adjust the door in forward/rearward and left/right directions, loosen the hinge bolts and position the tailgate as required. Tighten the hinge bolts to 69 inch lbs. (7.8 Nm).

To adjust the tailgate lock striker, loosen the mounting bolts and using a plastic hammer and a brass bar, tap the striker to the desired position.

Vertical adjustment of the door edge is made by removing or adding washes to shim the hinge bolts.

Bumpers

REMOVAL & INSTALLATION

Front

➧ SEE FIGS. 16–20

1. Remove the radiator support upper seal, if equipped.

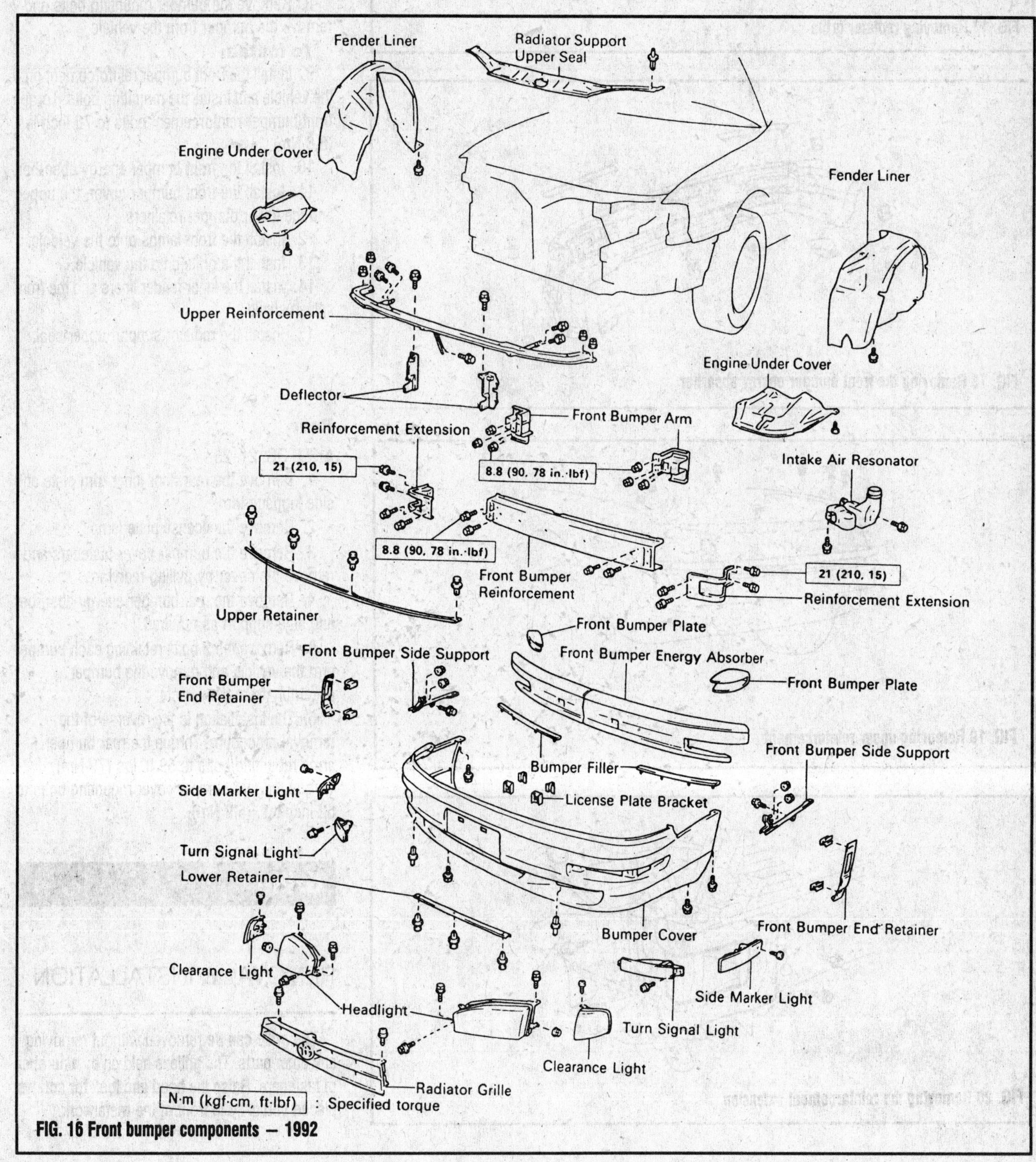

FIG. 16 Front bumper components — 1992

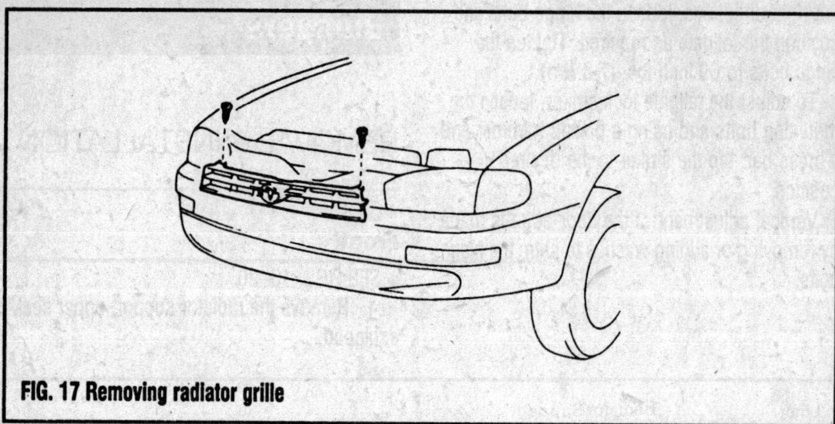
FIG. 17 Removing radiator grille

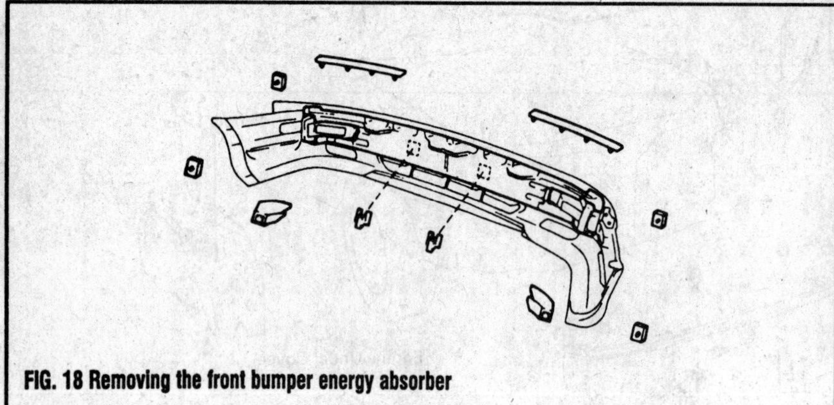
FIG. 18 Removing the front bumper energy absorber

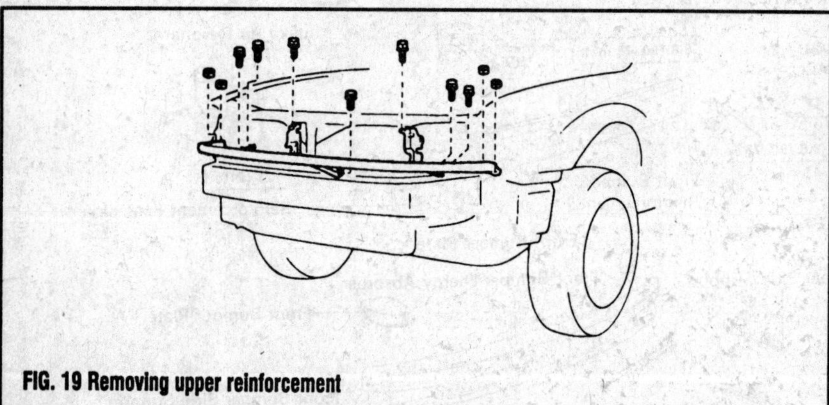
FIG. 19 Removing upper reinforcement

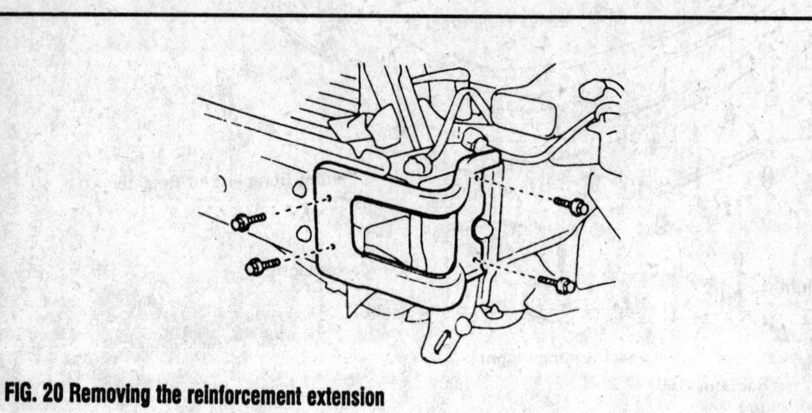
FIG. 20 Removing the reinforcement extension

2. Remove the front inner fender liners.
3. Remove the front lamp assemblies and disconnect the wiring to each.
4. Remove the retaining screws and the grille from the vehicle.
5. If equipped with an air resonator, located under the vehicle near the front left tire, remove it from the vehicle.
6. Remove the front bumper energy absorber.
7. Remove the upper and the lower bumper reinforcements.
8. Remove the bumper mounting bolts and remove the bumper from the vehicle.

To install:

9. Install the front bumper reinforcement onto the vehicle and install the mounting bolts. Torque front bumper reinforcement bolts to 78 inch lbs. (8.8 Nm).
10. Install the front bumper energy absorber.
11. Install the front bumper cover, the upper and the lower bumper retainers.
12. Install the front lamps onto the vehicle.
13. Install the grille onto the vehicle.
14. Install the inner fender liners and the front splash shield.
15. Install the radiator support upper seal.

Rear

➧ SEE FIG. 21–25

1. Remove the rear floor inner trim plate and side luggage trim.
2. Remove the license plate lamp.
3. Remove the bumper cover fasteners and remove the cover by pulling rearward.
4. Remove the rear bumper energy absorber and side support as required.
5. Remove the 2 bolts retaining each bumper arm the vehicle and remove the bumper assembly from the vehicle.
6. The installation is the reverse of the removal procedure. Torque the rear bumper arms mounting bolts to 59 ft. lbs (79 Nm). Torque the rear bumper cover mounting bolts to 52 inch lbs. (5.9 Nm).

Grille

REMOVAL & INSTALLATION

The grille can be removed without removing any other parts. The grille is held on by a number of fasteners. Raise the hood and look for screws placed vertically in front of the metalwork.

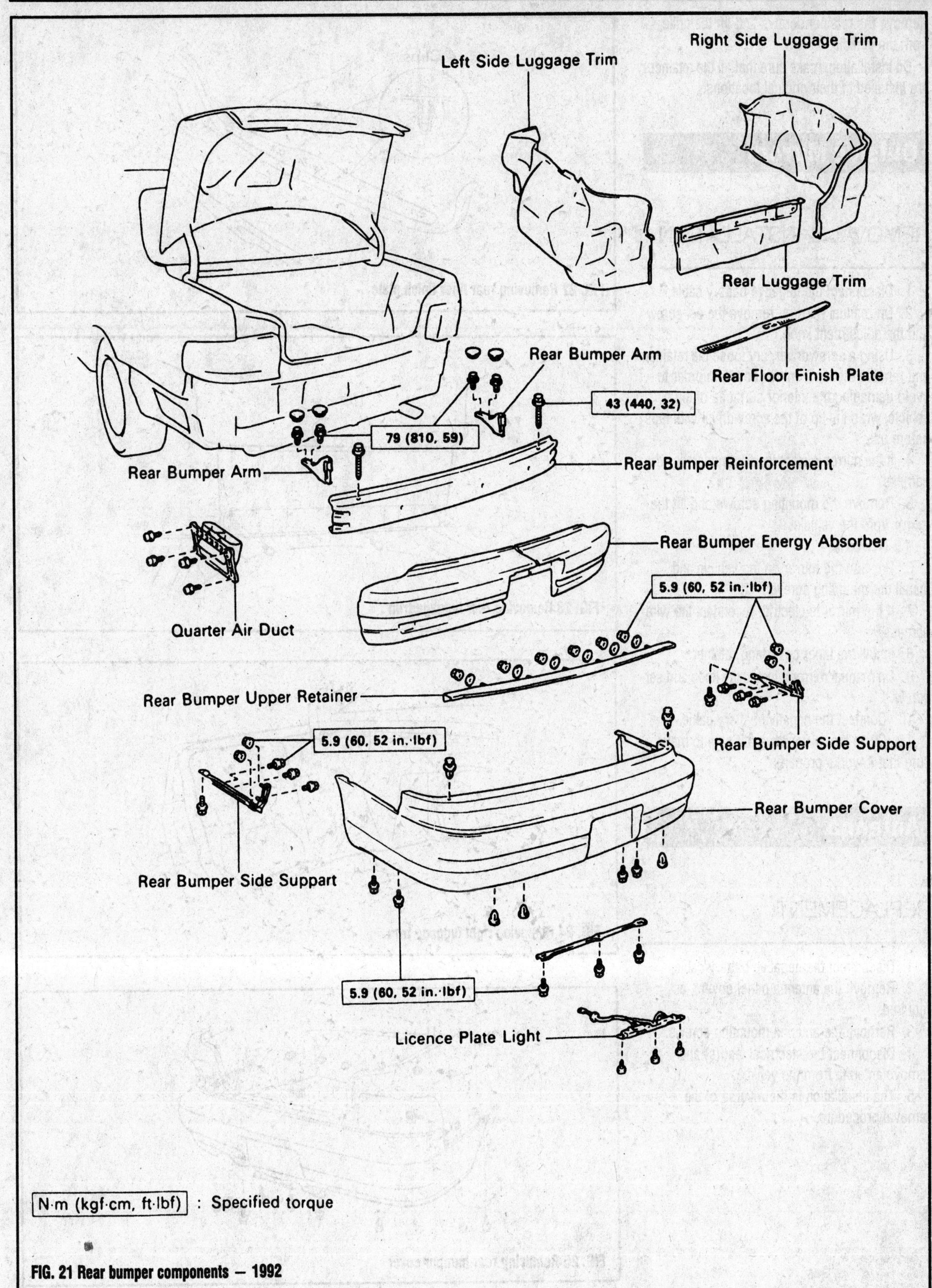
Right Side Luggage Trim
Left Side Luggage Trim
Rear Luggage Trim
Rear Floor Finish Plate
Rear Bumper Arm
43 (440, 32)
79 (810, 59)
Rear Bumper Arm
Rear Bumper Reinforcement
Rear Bumper Energy Absorber
Quarter Air Duct
5.9 (60, 52 in.·lbf)
Rear Bumper Upper Retainer
Rear Bumper Side Support
5.9 (60, 52 in.·lbf)
Rear Bumper Cover
Rear Bumper Side Suppart
5.9 (60, 52 in.·lbf)
Licence Plate Light
N·m (kgf·cm, ft·lbf) : Specified torque

FIG. 21 Rear bumper components — 1992

Remove the retainer screws and lift the grille from the vehicle.

On installation, make sure that all the retainers are installed in their original locations.

Outside Mirrors

REMOVAL & INSTALLATION

1. Disconnect the negative battery cable.
2. On manual mirrors, remove the set screw and the adjustment knob.
3. Using a screwdriver, pry loose the retainer and remove the inner mirror cover. In order to avoid damaging the interior surfaces of the vehicle, wrap the tip of the screwdriver with tape before use.
4. If the mirror is electric, disconnect the wire harness.
5. Remove the mounting screws and lift the mirror from the vehicle.

To install:

6. Position the mirror on the vehicle and install the mounting screws.
7. If the mirror is electric, reconnect the wire harness.
8. Install the inner cover and retainer.
9. On manual mirrors, install the knob and set screw.
10. Connect the negative battery cable.
11. Cycle the mirror several times to make sure that it works properly.

Antenna

REPLACEMENT

1. Disconnect the negative battery cable.
2. Remove the antenna panel covers, as required.
3. Remove the antenna mounting screws.
4. Disconnect the electrical lead(s) and remove antenna from the vehicle.
5. The installation is the reverse of the removal procedure.

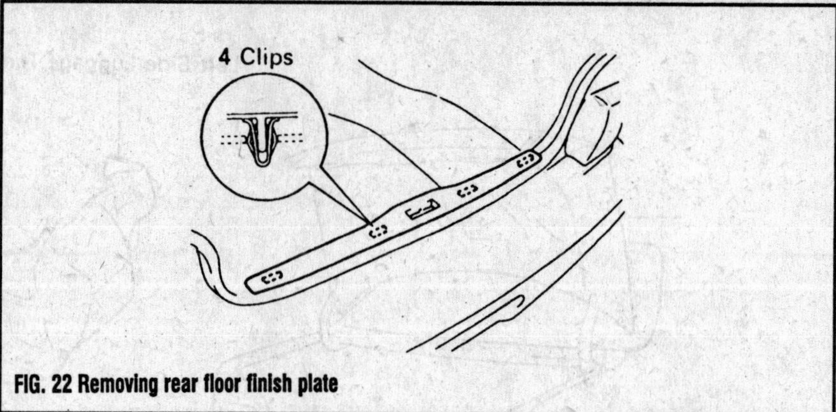

FIG. 22 Removing rear floor finish plate

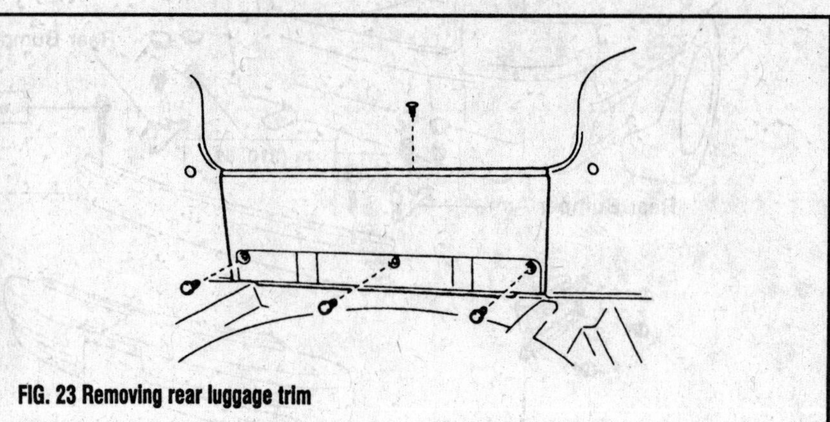
FIG. 23 Removing rear luggage trim

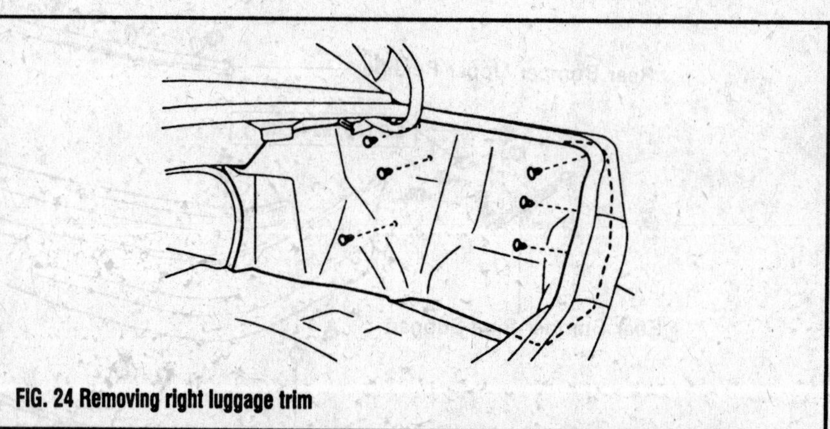
FIG. 24 Removing right luggage trim

FIG. 25 Removing rear bumper cover

Fenders

REMOVAL & INSTALLATION

1. Remove of disconnect all electrical items attached to the fender to be removed.
2. Remove the inner fender liner and the front bumper assembly.
3. Remove all bolts attaching the fender and the brace to the firewall and the radiator/grille panel.
4. Remove the rear attaching bolts through the pillar opening and remove the fender from he vehicle.
5. To install, reverse the removal procedure.

Power Sunroof

➧ SEE FIG. 26

REMOVAL & INSTALLATION

1. Disconnect the negative battery cable. Wait at least 30 seconds from the time the negative battery was disconnected to start work.
2. Using a screwdriver, remove the cover and the power roof switch.
3. Remove the inner rear view mirror, sun visors, and the front assist grip, if equipped.
4. Remove the front pillar garnishes and remove the front side of the headliner. On models prior to 1992, it may be necessary to remove the upper and the lower side garnishes to allow enough clearance for the headliner.
5. On models prior to 1992, remove 4 screws from the wind deflector and remove from the vehicle.

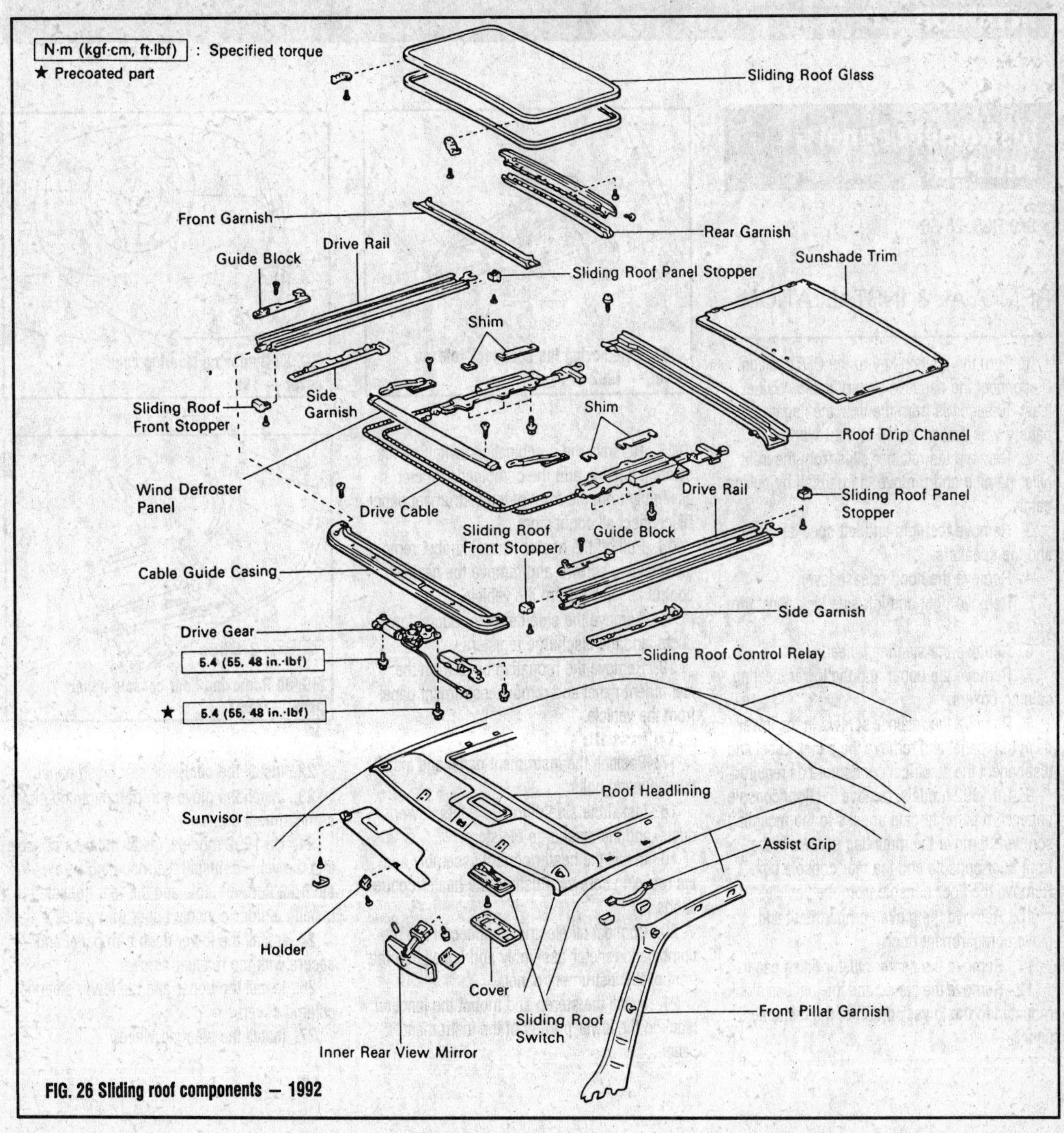

FIG. 26 Sliding roof components — 1992

6. On 1992 models, disconnect and remove the sliding roof control relay.

7. Disconnect the electrical connector, remove the fasteners and remove the drive motor.

8. Remove the side guide rail trim covers.

9. Apply tape to the vehicle to protect the finish and remove the screws holding the glass into the roof.

10. Remove the roof from the vehicle lifting outward and slightly forward. Take notice of shim positioning and install in original location on installation.

To Install:

11. Install the roof onto the vehicle from above. Take notice of shim positioning and install in original location.

12. Install the screws holding the glass into the roof.

13. Install the side guide rail trim covers.

14. Connect the electrical connector, install the drive motor and install the fasteners.

15. On 1992 models, connect and install the sliding roof control relay.

16. On models prior to 1992, install the wind deflector and secure on the vehicle with the retaining screws.

17. Install the front side of the headliner and install the front pillar garnishes. Install the upper and the lower side garnishes, if removed.

18. Install the inner rear view mirror, sun visors, and the front assist grip, if equipped.

19. Install the roof switch and cover.

20. Connect the negative battery cable.

INTERIOR

Instrument Panel and Pad

➧ SEE FIGS. 28-36

REMOVAL & INSTALLATION

1. Turn the ignition key to the OFF position. Disconnect the negative battery cable. Wait at least 30 seconds from the time the negative battery was disconnected to start work.

2. Remove the retainer clips from the front pillar garnish and remove the garnish by pulling gently.

3. Remove the right and left speaker covers and the speakers.

4. Remove the hood release lever.

5. Remove right and left side kick panel trim covers.

6. Remove the steering wheel.

7. Remove the upper and the lower steering column covers.

8. Remove the retainer screws in the lower dash trim panel and remove the panel. Label and disconnect the electrical connectors as required.

9. On 1992 models, remove the floor console upper trim panel to gain access to the mounting screws. Remove the mounting screws in the front floor console and the rear console box. Remove the floor console from the vehicle.

10. Remove the glove compartment and glove compartment door.

11. Remove the center cluster finish panel.

12. Remove the stereo and the junction block mounted to the lower portion of the instrument panel.

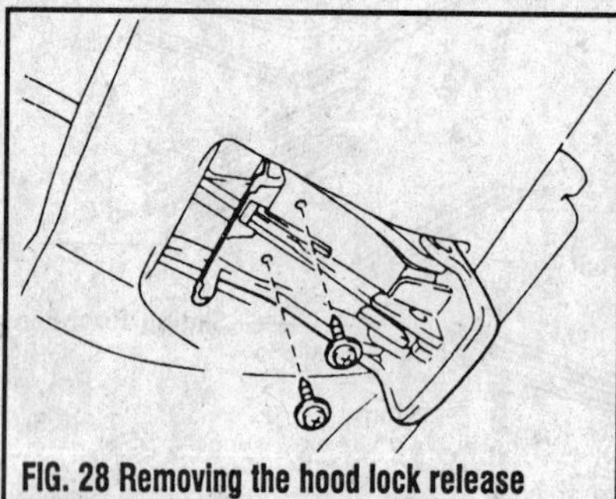

FIG. 28 Removing the hood lock release lever — 1992

13. Remove the combination switch on the steering column and the combination meter assembly from the front of the instrument panel. Disconnect all connectors.

14. Pull off the heater control knobs, remove the retaining screws and remove the heater control assembly from the vehicle.

15. Remove the side defroster ducts, lower ducts, and the discharge registers.

16. Remove the mounting bolts from the instrument panel and remove instrument panel from the vehicle.

To Install:

17. Position the instrument panel and install the mounting bolts.

18. Install the side defroster ducts, lower ducts, and the discharge registers.

19. Install the heater control assembly and the retaining screws. Push on the heater control knobs.

20. Connect all electrical connectors to the combination meter assembly and install into the front of the instrument panel.

21. Install the stereo and mount the junction block to the lower portion of the instrument panel.

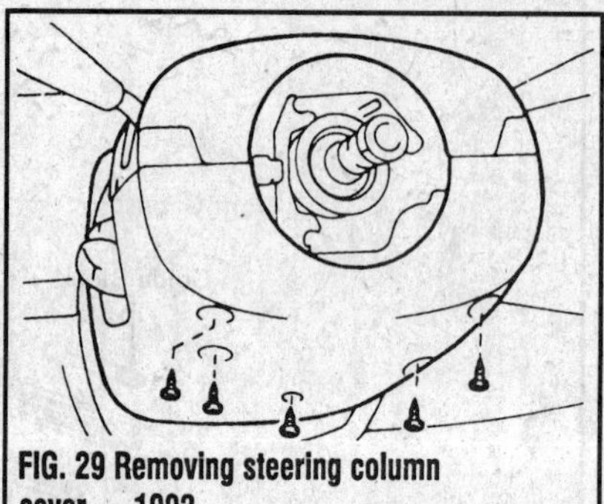

FIG. 29 Removing steering column cover — 1992

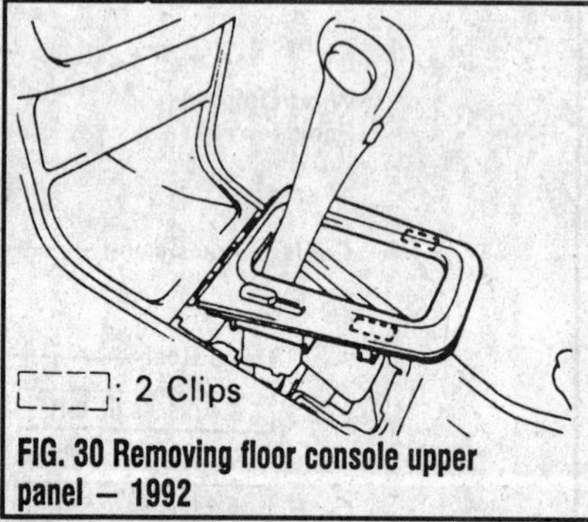

FIG. 30 Removing floor console upper panel — 1992

22. Install the center cluster finish panel.

23. Install the glove compartment and glove compartment door.

24. On 1992 models, install the floor console into the vehicle. Install the mounting screws in the front floor console and the rear console box. Install the floor console upper trim panel.

25. Install the lower dash trim panel and secure with the retainer screws.

26. Install the upper and the lower steering column covers.

27. Install the steering wheel.

28. Install right and left side kick panel trim covers.
29. Install the hood release lever.
30. Install the right and left speakers and the speaker covers.
31. Install the front pillar garnish by pushing gently into position. Install the retainers.
32. Connect the negative battery cable.

Center Console

REMOVAL & INSTALLATION

1. Disconnect the negative battery cable.

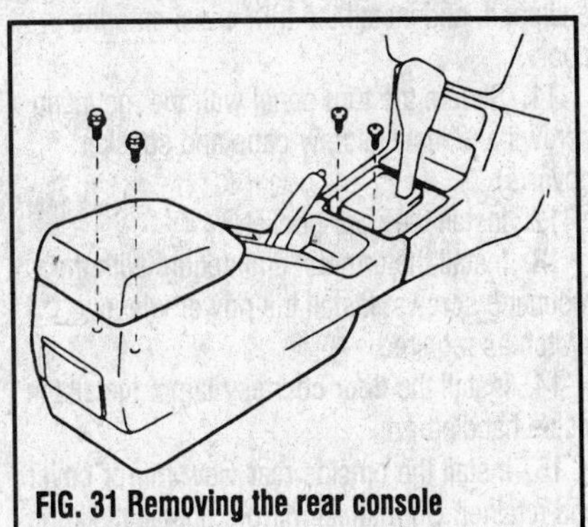

FIG. 31 Removing the rear console box — 1992

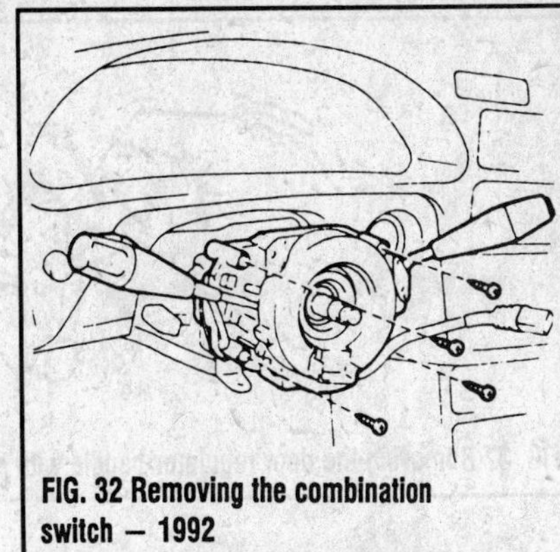

FIG. 32 Removing the combination switch — 1992

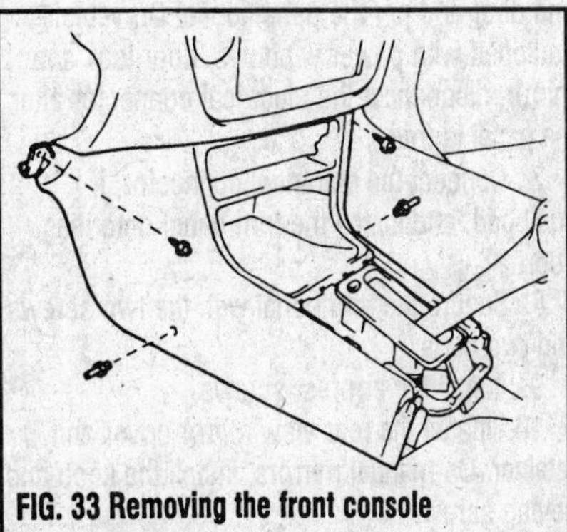

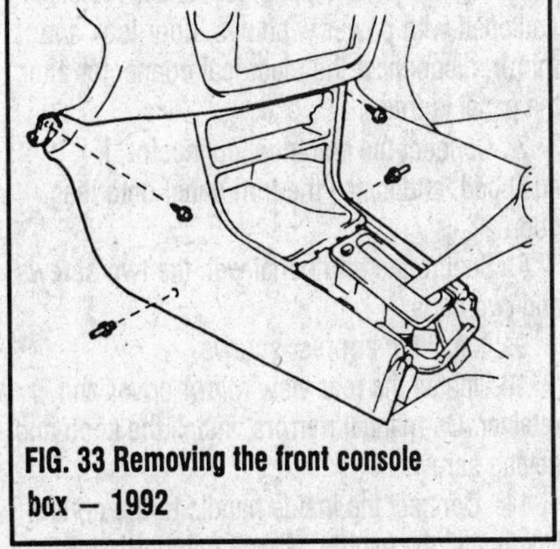

FIG. 33 Removing the front console box — 1992

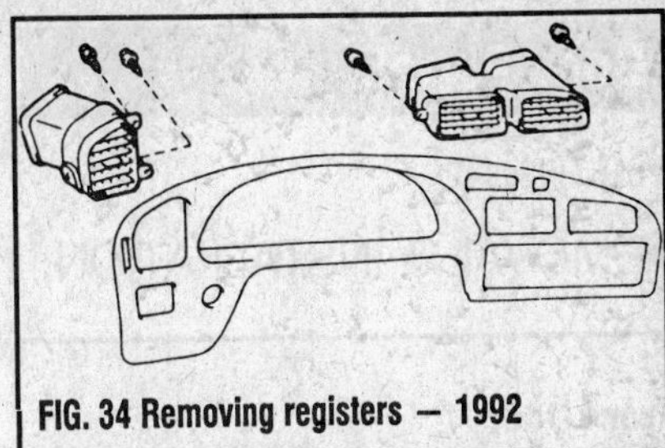

FIG. 34 Removing registers — 1992

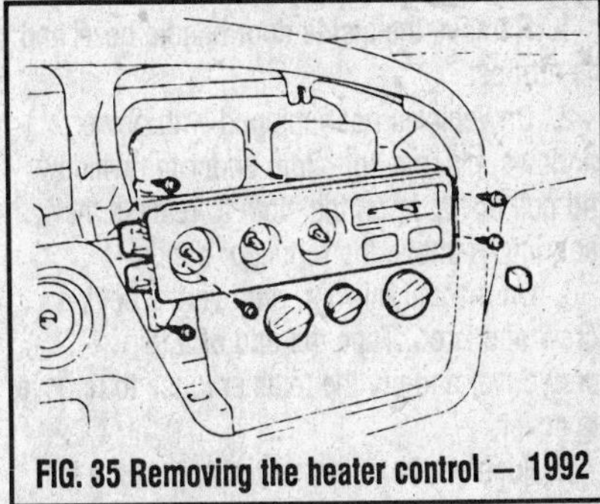

FIG. 35 Removing the heater control — 1992

Wait at least 30 seconds from the time the negative battery was disconnected to start work.

2. Remove the floor console upper trim panel to gain access to the mounting screws.
3. Remove the mounting screws in the front floor console and in the rear console box.
4. Remove the floor console from the vehicle.
5. Reverse the removal procedure to install.

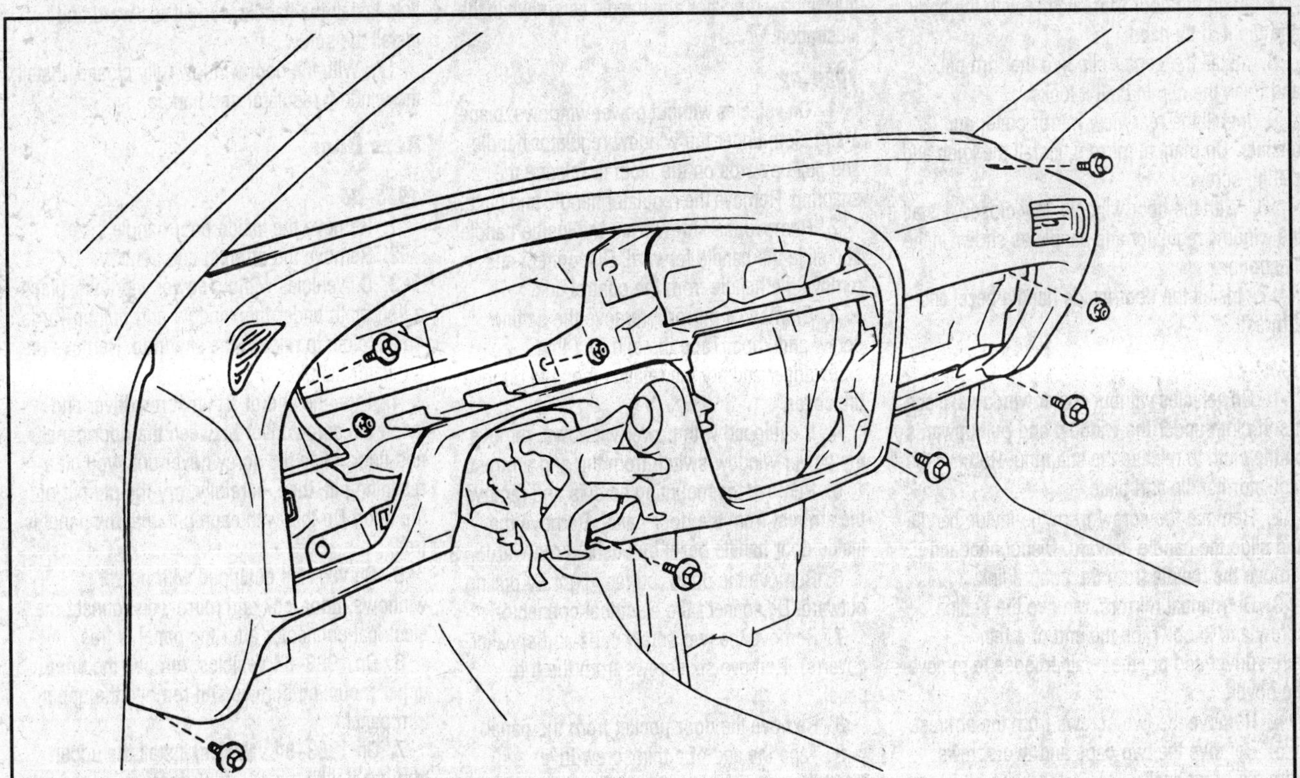

FIG. 36 Instrument panel pad mounting bolts — 1992

Door Panels

➧ SEE FIGS. 1–2

REMOVAL & INSTALLATION

Front Door

1983–86

1. Remove the inside door handle bezel and the armrest.
2. On vehicles not equipped with power windows, place a soft cloth under the window and pull upwards on the cloth to release the snapring. Remove the regulator handle.
3. On manual mirrors, remove the setting screw and knob. Tape the end of a thin screwdriver and pry the retainer loose to remove the cover.
4. Push on the center of the clip with a thin object to remove it.
5. Tape the end of a thin screwdriver and insert the screwdriver between the door panel and door. Slide the screwdriver until you hit a retaining pin, then, carefully, pry the pin out of the door. Do this with each pin until the panel is free. On vehicles equipped with power windows, disconnect the electrical connector after the panel is free.
6. On vehicles equipped with electric windows, connect the electrical connector.
7. Align the door trim retainer with the body and tap it in by hand.
8. Install the center clip into the trim panel and push the clip in until it locks.
9. Install the rear view mirror cover and retainer. On manual mirrors, install the knob and setting screw.
10. With the door window fully closed, install the window regulator and handle as shown in the illustration.
11. Install the door inside handle bezel and armrest.

1987–88

1. On vehicles without power windows, place a soft cloth under the window and pull upwards on the cloth to release the snapring. Remove the regulator handle and plate.
2. Remove the screw from the inside handle and slide the handle forward. Disconnect and remove the handle from the control link.
3. On manual mirrors, remove the setting screw and knob. Tape the end of a thin screwdriver and pry the retainer loose to remove the cover.
4. Remove the two screws from the armrest.
5. Remove the two caps and two screws from the trim panel.

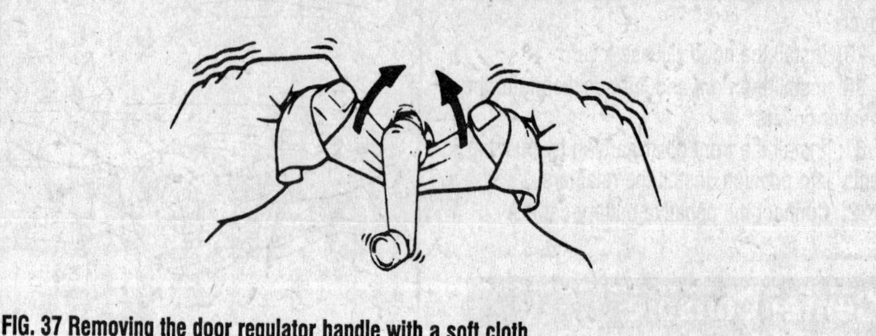

FIG. 37 Removing the door regulator handle with a soft cloth

6. Tape the end of a thin screwdriver and insert the screwdriver between the door panel and door and pry the panel loose. On vehicles equipped with power windows, door lock and mirror, disconnect the electrical connector after the panel is free.
7. Connect the electrical connector, if equipped, and install the trim panel onto the door.
8. Secure the trim panel with the two screws and two caps.
9. Install the armrest screws.
10. Install the rear view mirror cover and retainer. On manual mirrors, install the knob and setting screw.
11. Connect the inside handle to the control link. Install the handle, slide it rearward and install the screw.
12. With the door window fully closed, install the window regulator and handle as shown in the illustration.

1989–92

1. On vehicles without power windows, place a soft cloth under the window regulator handle and pull upwards on the cloth to release the snapring. Remove the regulator handle and plate.
2. Remove the screw from the inside handle and slide the handle forward. Disconnect and remove the handle from the control link.
3. On manual mirrors, remove the setting screw and knob. Tape the end of a thin screwdriver and pry the retainer loose to remove the cover.
4. If equipped with power windows, remove the power window switch from the and armrest.
5. Remove the mounting screws and remove the armrest from the door panel. Remove the inside door handle bezel by pushing rearward.
6. Remove the door courtesy light by pulling outward. Disconnect the electrical connector.
7. Remove the two screw caps and speaker cover(s). Remove six screws from the trim panel.
8. Remove the door pocket from the panel.
9. Tape the end of a thin screwdriver and insert the screwdriver between the door panel and door and pry the panel outward. Disconnect the electrical connector after the panel is free and remove the panel from the vehicle.

To install:

10. Connect the electrical connectors, if equipped, and install the trim panel onto the door.
11. Secure the trim panel with the mounting screws and install screw caps and speaker cover(s).
12. Install the door pocket.
13. Install the armrest and secure with the mounting screws. Install the power window switch as required.
14. Install the door courtesy lamp. Install the inside handle bezel.
15. Install the outside rear view mirror cover and retainer. On manual mirrors, install the knob and setting screw.
16. Connect the inside handle to the control link. Install the handle, slide it rearward and install the screw.
17. With the door window fully closed, install the window regulator and handle.

Rear Door

1983–86

1. Remove the inside door handle bezel.
2. Remove the armrest and ashtray.
3. On vehicles without power windows, place a soft cloth under the window and pull upwards on the cloth to release the snapring. Remove the regulator handle.
4. Tape the end of a thin screwdriver and insert the screwdriver between the door panel and door. Slide the screwdriver until you hit a retaining pin, then, carefully, pry the pin out of the door. Do this with each pin until the panel is free.
5. On vehicles equipped with power windows, door lock and mirror, disconnect the electrical connector after the panel is free.
6. On 1983–84 vehicles, remove the three upper mounting screws and remove the upper trim panel.
7. On 1983–84 vehicles, install the upper trim panel with the attaching screws.
8. Connect the electrical connector, if

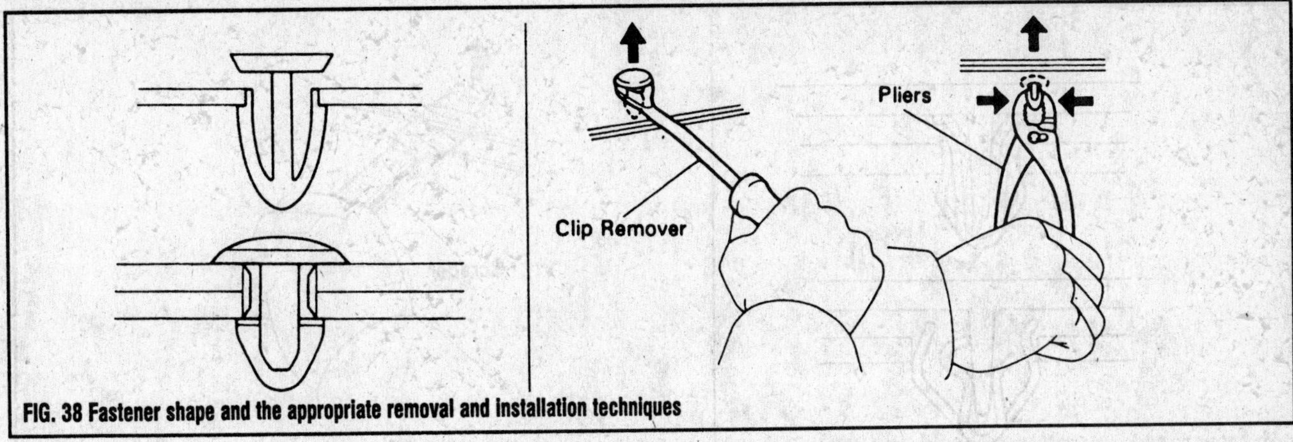

FIG. 38 Fastener shape and the appropriate removal and installation techniques

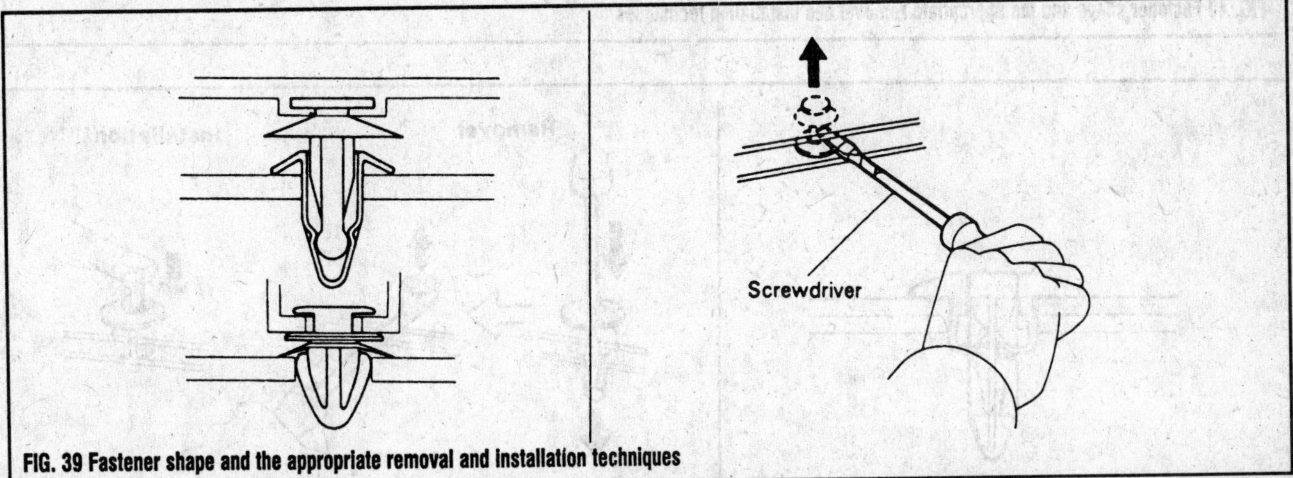

FIG. 39 Fastener shape and the appropriate removal and installation techniques

equipped, and install the trim panel onto the door.

9. With the door window fully closed, install the window regulator and handle as shown in the illustration.

1987–88

1. On vehicles without power windows, place a soft cloth under the window and pull upwards on the cloth to release the snapring. Remove the regulator handle and plate.
2. Remove the screw from the inside handle and slide the handle forward. Disconnect and remove the handle from the control link.
3. Remove the two screws from the armrest.
4. Tape the end of a screwdriver and insert it between the trim retainers and the door panel to pry it loose.
5. Once released, remove the door trim with the inner weatherstrip.
6. Install the door trim with the weatherstrip.
7. Connect the inside handle to the control link. Install the handle, slide it rearward and install the screw.
8. With the door window fully closed, install the window regulator and handle as shown in the illustration.

1989–92

1. On vehicles without power windows, place a soft cloth under the window and pull upwards on the cloth to release the snapring. Remove the regulator handle and plate.
2. If equipped with power windows, tape the end of a screwdriver and insert it between the window switch and the armrest. Pry the switch from the armrest and disconnect the connector.
4. Tape the end of a screwdriver and pry the inside door handle bezel rearward and remove.
5. Remove the screw caps and remove the retaining screws.
6. Tape the end of a screwdriver and insert it between the trim retainers and the door panel to pry it loose.
7. Pull the trim panel upwards and remove from the door.

To install:

8. Install the door trim panel onto the door from above. Tap the top of the door panel to insure it is fully seated on door panel.
9. Install all trim retainers and secure.
10. Install the power window switch onto the armrest and secure.
11. With the door window fully closed, install the window regulator and handle.

Interior Trim Panel

➧ SEE FIGS. 38-42

REMOVAL & INSTALLATION

The interior trim panels are generally retained by screws, push type or spring loaded fasteners. To remove the spring type fasteners, apply light hand pressure to separate the trim. To remove the push type fasteners, insert a clip remover tool or the blade of a screwdriver that has been taped between the trim panel and the fastener to be removed, and pry the retainer upward.

Headliner

REMOVAL & INSTALLATION

1. Turn the ignition key to the OFF position. Disconnect the negative battery cable. Wait at

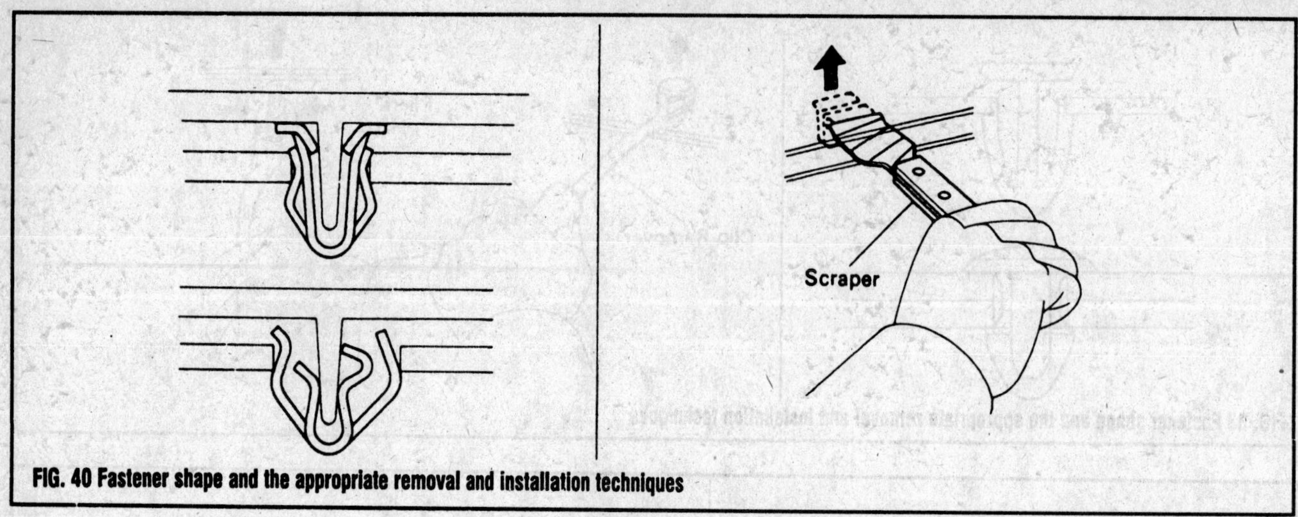

FIG. 40 Fastener shape and the appropriate removal and installation techniques

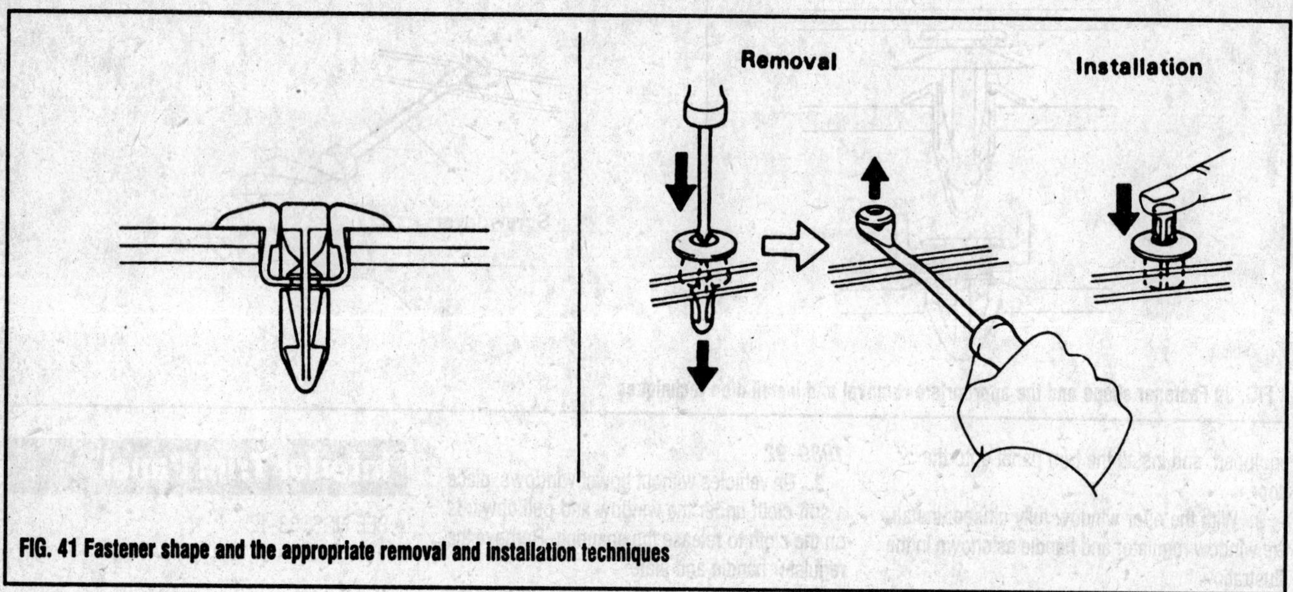

FIG. 41 Fastener shape and the appropriate removal and installation techniques

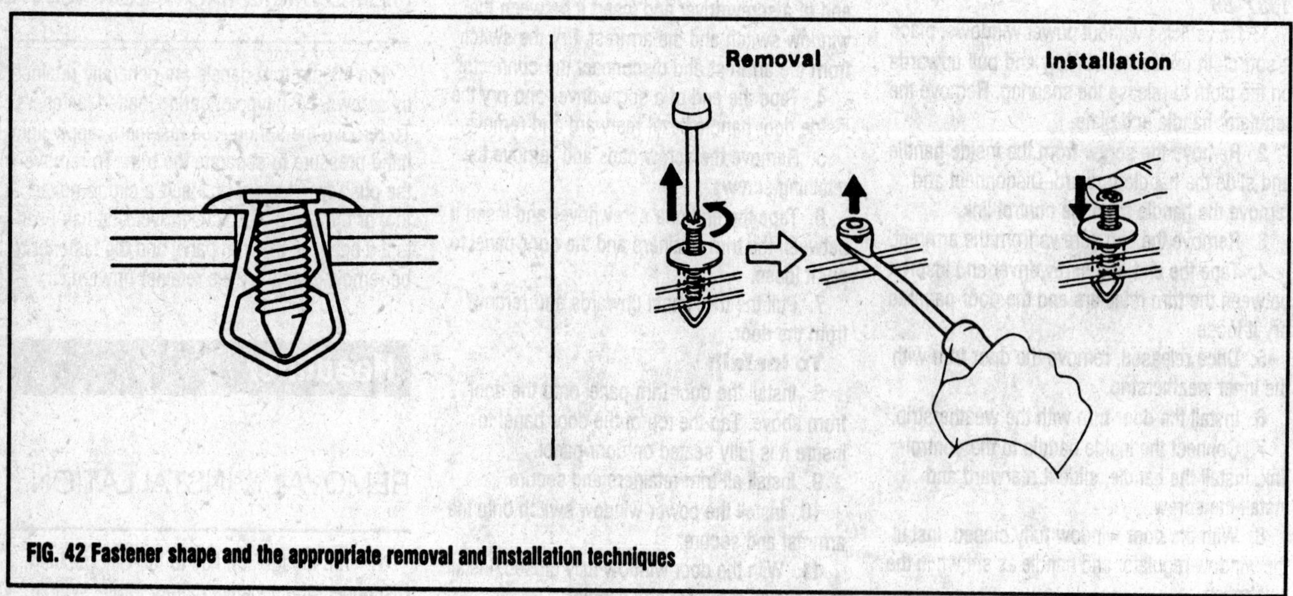

FIG. 42 Fastener shape and the appropriate removal and installation techniques

least 30 seconds from the time the negative battery was disconnected to start work.

2. Remove the front sunvisors and the inner rear view mirror.
3. Remove both front pillar garnish moldings by pulling the retainer clips out by hand and pulling garnish rearward.
4. Remove the side and rear trim in the same manner.
5. If equipped with sliding roof, remove the roof control switch and the opening trim.
6. Remove the side assist grips, if equipped.
7. Remove the headliner from the vehicle taking care not to bend or distort the liner.

To Install:

8. Install the headliner into the vehicle taking care not to bend or distort the liner.
9. Install the side assist grips, if equipped.
10. If equipped with sliding roof, install the roof control switch and the opening trim.
11. Install both front pillar garnish moldings and the retainer clips.
12. Install the side and rear trim.
13. Install the front sunvisors and the inner rear view mirror.
14. Connect the negative battery cable.

Heater/AC Registers

REMOVAL & INSTALLATION

1. Turn the ignition key to the OFF position. Disconnect the negative battery cable. Wait at least 30 seconds from the time the negative battery was disconnected to start work.
2. Remove the cluster finish panel.
3. From the rear of the cluster finish panel, extract the 2 mounting screws and remove the register.
4. The installation is the reverse of the removal procedure.

Defroster Nozzle

REMOVAL & INSTALLATION

To remove the nozzle, tape the end of a screwdriver and insert it between the defroster nozzle and the panel. Gently pry the nozzle out. To install, push into place by hand.

Heater Ducts

REMOVAL & INSTALLATION

To remove the ducts, remove the retainer clips, if equipped, and separate the ductwork. To install, position pieces of duct together assuring tight connection between pieces and install the retainers as required.

Door Locks

REMOVAL & INSTALLATION

Front or Rear Doors

1. Turn the ignition key to the OFF position. Disconnect the negative battery cable. If equipped with an air bag, wait at least 30 seconds from the time the negative battery was disconnected to start work.
2. Remove the door panel and watershield. Remove the service hole cover.
3. Disconnect the door outside opening linkage. Remove the two mounting bolts and remove the door handle if in need of replacement.
4. Disconnect the lock cylinder control linkage.
5. Remove the lock knob and the child protector lock lever knob.
6. Remove the three lock assembly retaining screws and remove the door lock. If equipped with power locks, disconnect the electrical connector.
7. To remove the lock cylinder, remove the lock cylinder retaining clip and pull the cylinder from the door.

To Install:

8. Coat all the door lock sliding surfaces with multi-purpose grease.
9. Install the outside handle with the two retaining bolts, if removed.
10. Install the door lock solenoid linkage to the door lock.
11. Connect the link to the outside handle.
12. Install the lock knob and the child protector lock lever knob.
13. Install the door opening control link.
14. Install the door lock cylinder control linkage.
15. Install the door panel and watershield.
16. Reconnect the negative battery cable.

Tailgate Lock

REMOVAL & INSTALLATION

1. Turn the ignition key to the OFF position. Disconnect the negative battery cable.
2. Remove the back door inside garnish.
3. Remove the link protector.
4. Disconnect the links from the door control and door lock cylinder.
5. Remove the bolts and the door lock control with the solenoid.
6. To remove the door lock cylinder, remove the retaining screws and then remove the cylinder.

To Install:

7. Install the door lock cylinder and secure with the retaining screws.
8. Install the bolts and the door lock control with the solenoid.
9. Connect the links to the door control and door lock cylinder.
10. Install the link protector.
11. Install the back door inner garnish.
12. Connect the negative battery cable.

Sedan Trunk Lock

REMOVAL & INSTALLATION

1. Disconnect the negative battery cable.
2. Remove the inside trunk garnish.
3. Remove the bolts and the door lock control with the solenoid, if equipped.
4. The installation is the reverse of the removal procedure.

Door Glass and Regulator

REMOVAL & INSTALLATION

Front Door

1. Disconnect the negative battery cable.
2. Remove the front door panel to gain access to the regulator assembly.

3. Remove the service hole cover.

4. Lower the regulator until the door glass is in the fully open position.

5. Remove the two glass channel mount bolts.

6. Pull the glass up and out of the door.

7. If equipped, unbolt and remove the inside door panel frame.

8. If equipped with power windows, disconnect the electrical connector.

9. Remove the equalizer arm bracket mounting bolts.

10. Remove the window regulator mounting bolts and remove the regulator (with the power window motor attached) through the service hole.

To Install:

11. Coat all the window regulator sliding surfaces with multi-purpose grease.

12. Place the regulator (with the power window motor) through the service hole and install the mounting bolts. Connect the power window connector if equipped.

13. Place the door glass into the door cavity.

14. Connect the glass to the regulator with the channel mount bolts.

15. With the equalizer arm, raise the glass to the almost closed position and make sure that the leading and trailing edges of the glass are equidistant from the top of the glass channel. If not, adjust the equalizer arm to achieve an even fit.

16. Install the service hole cover.

17. Install the door panel and reconnect the negative battery cable.

Rear Door

1. Disconnect the negative battery cable.

2. Remove the front door panel to gain access to the regulator assembly.

3. Remove the service hole cover.

4. Remove the clips from the outer edge of the belt molding and remove the rear door belt molding from the vehicle.

5. Remove the door glass run.

6. Remove the division bar by removing the two screws under the weatherstripping, the screw from the panel and pulling the glass run from the division bar. Pull the bar from the door.

7. Remove the glass mounting screws and remove the door glass.

8. To remove the quarter window, remove the glass along with the weatherstrip by pulling assembly forward.

9. To remove the regulator, unbolt from door panel and remove from vehicle. If equipped with power windows, disconnect the electrical connector and remove the regulator with the power window motor attached.

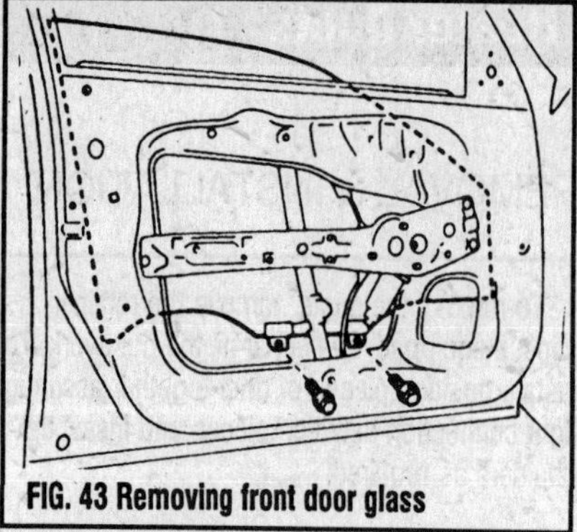

FIG. 43 Removing front door glass

To Install:

10. Install the glass down into the door cavity.

11. Install the quarter window and weatherstrip into the door frame.

12. Place the regulator (with the power window motor) through the service hole and install the mounting bolts.

13. Place the door glass in the door cavity.

14. Connect the glass to the regulator with the channel mount bolts.

15. Install the rear door belt molding and the door glass run.

16. With the equalizer arm, raise the glass to the almost closed position and make sure that the leading and trailing edges of the glass are equidistant from the top of the glass channel. If not, adjust the equalizer arm to achieve an even fit.

17. With the door glass fully closed, adjust the door glass stopper so it lightly makes contact with the glass plate.

18. Install the division bar in the door and secure with the two screws and the bolt.

19. Install the service hole cover.

20. Install the door panel and connect the negative battery cable.

21. Reconnect the negative battery cable.

Electric Window Motor

The power window motor, if equipped, is attached to the window regulator. If service is required, remove the window regulator from the inside of the door panel and detach the motor from the regulator. Removal and installation of the regulator is described in this Section.

Windshield Glass

Extreme care must be taken when removing, installing or resealing a windshield. The windshield will crack if a stress in the wrong

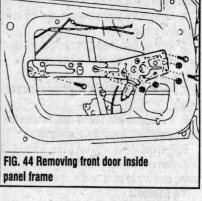

FIG. 44 Removing front door inside panel frame

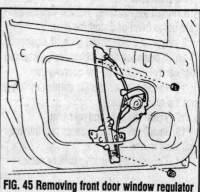

FIG. 45 Removing front door window regulator

direction is exerted, even if the pressure is very slight. Undesirable stress on the windshield could take place during a number of operations. Damage could occur days after the repair has been completed, caused by the body of the vehicle flexing during normal vehicle operation, or during the removal of the outer moldings before any repair work has been done. This should be realized before the job of removing a windshield is undertaken.

REMOVAL & INSTALLATION

1. Disconnect the negative battery cable.

2. Remove the sunvisors, holders and the front assist grips.

3. Remove the inner rear view mirror.

4. Remove the front pillar garnishes.

5. Remove the hood, wiper arms and the cowl panel (louver).

6. Remove the hood weatherstrip by pulling upward. Take care not to tear the weatherstrip during removal.

7. Remove the retainer screws and the outside windshield molding.

8. Tape the end of a scraper and insert between the body and the upper windshield molding. Pry the molding upward and remove from the clips. Remove the molding from the vehicle.

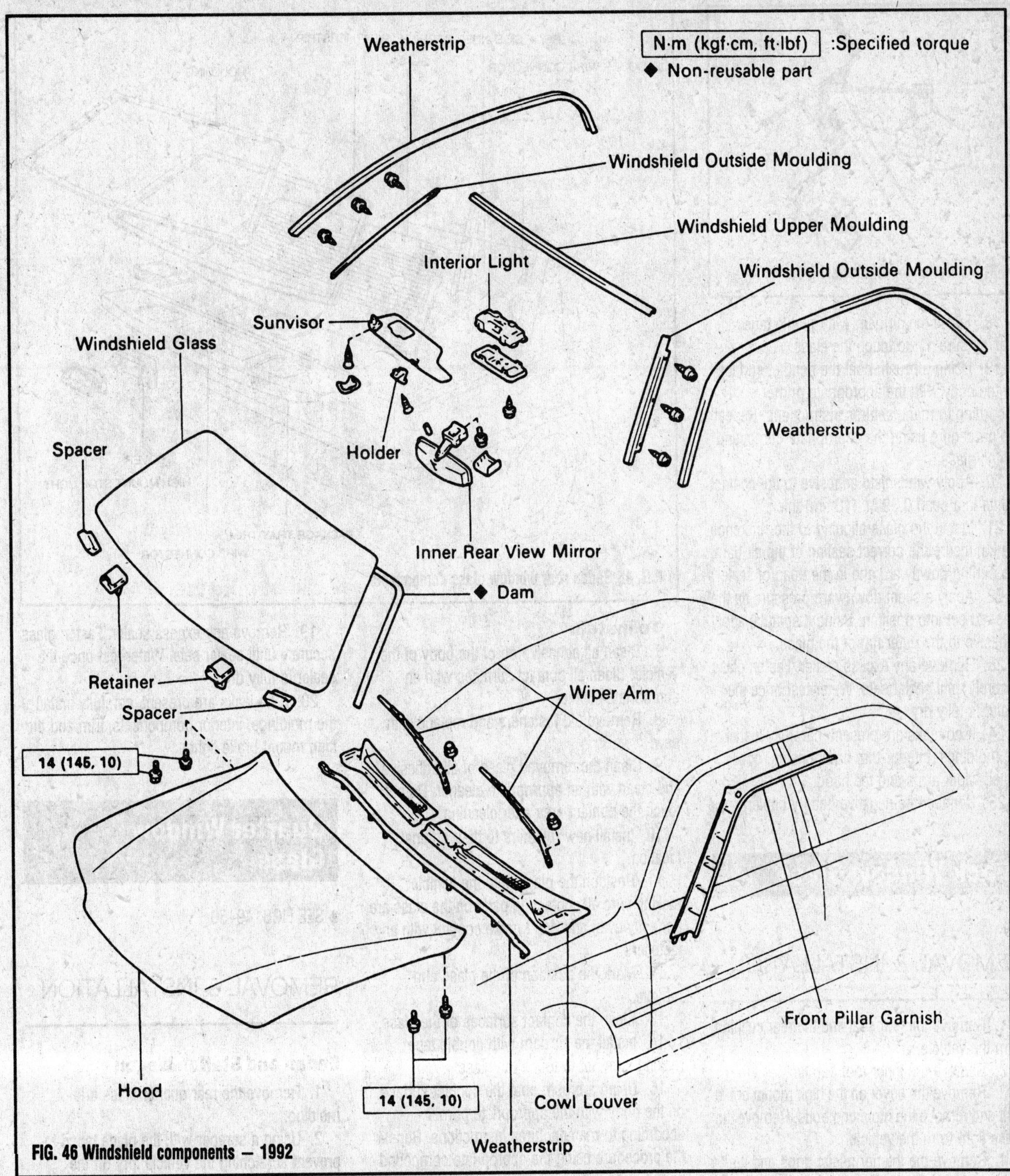

FIG. 46 Windshield components — 1992

9. Push piano wire from the interior of the vehicle outward and tie object to act as a handle to each end of the wire. Apply tape to the outer body surfaces to avoid scratching the finish. Cut the adhesive by pulling the piano wire, with the aid of a helper, around the windshield.

10. Carefully remove the glass from the vehicle.

To Install:

11. Clean all adhesive off of the body of the vehicle. Clean all contact surfaces with an appropriate cleaner.

12. Remove old fasteners and replace with new.

13. Clean the removed glass of all adhesive and clean with an appropriate cleaner. Do not touch the contact area after cleaning.

14. Install new retainers to their original location. Install the spacer.

15. Position the glass onto the vehicle making sure all contacting parts of the glass are perfectly even and don't make contact with any fasteners.

16. Mark the position of the glass and remove.

17. Clean the contact surfaces of the glass.

FIG. 47 Removing windshield glass

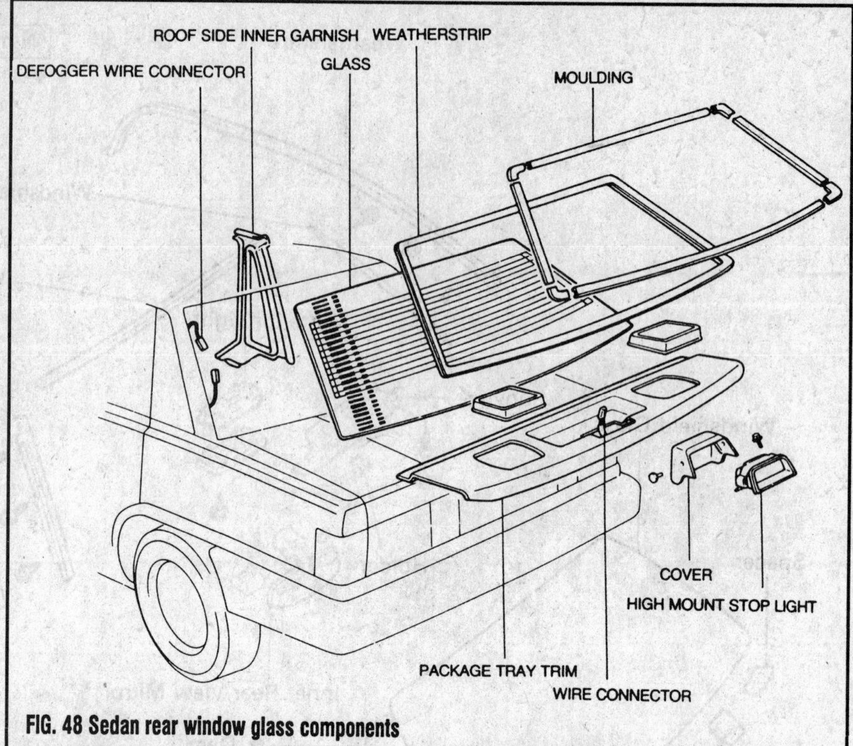

FIG. 48 Sedan rear window glass components

18. Install the air dam with double tape making sure not to touch the glass.
19. Using a brush, coat the contact surface on the body with the appropriate primer according to manufactures instructions. Repeat the procedure using the appropriate compound on the glass.
20. Apply windshield adhesive to the contact points in a bead 0.39 in. (10mm) thick.
21. Install the glass aligning to the reference marks. Insure the correct sealing of the air dam. (lip curling downward and in the bead of sealer)
22. Apply a slight downward pressure on the glass to set into position. Using a spatula, apply adhesive to the outer rim of the glass.
23. Remove any excess sealer. Fasten glass securely until sealer sets. Water test once the sealer is fully dry.
24. If no leaks are present, carefully install the moldings, interior trim components, cowl panel, wiper arms and the hood.
25. Connect the negative battery cable.

Back Window Glass

REMOVAL & INSTALLATION

1. Remove the rear seat and the rear cushion from the vehicle.
2. Remove the inner roof garnish.
3. Remove the cover on the high mount brake light and remove the mounting bolts. Remove the brake light from the vehicle.
4. Remove the interior assist grips and the rear portion of the headlining.
5. Using a knife, remove the back window molding by cutting off lip portion of the molding which is over the glass.
6. Remove the back glass in the same manner as the front windshield (using the piano wire) and remove the glass retainers.

To install:

7. Clean all adhesive off of the body of the vehicle. Clean all contact surfaces with an appropriate cleaner.
8. Remove old fasteners and replace with new.
9. Clean the removed glass of all adhesive and clean with an appropriate cleaner. Do not touch the contact area after cleaning.
10. Install new retainers to their original location.
11. Position the glass onto the vehicle making sure all contacting parts on the glass are perfectly even and don't make contact with any fasteners.
12. Mark the position of the glass and remove.
13. Clean the contact surfaces of the glass.
14. Install the air dam with double tape making sure not to touch the glass.
15. Using a brush, coat the contact surface on the body with the appropriate primer according to manufactures instructions. Repeat the procedure using the appropriate compound on the glass.
16. Apply the glass adhesive to the contact points on the body in a bead 0.39 in. (10mm) thick.
17. Install the glass aligning to the reference marks. Insure the correct sealing of the air dam. (lip curling downward and in the bead of sealer)
18. Apply a slight downward pressure on the glass to set into position. Using a spatula, apply adhesive to the outer rim of the glass.
19. Remove any excess sealer. Fasten glass securely until sealer sets. Water test once the sealer is fully dry.
20. If no leaks are present, carefully install the moldings, interior components, trim and the high mount brake light.

Quarter Window Glass

➧ SEE FIGS. 49–50

REMOVAL & INSTALLATION

Sedan and Station Wagon

1. Remove the rear quarter glass drip molding.
2. Using a scraper with the blade taped to prevent scratching the vehicle, pry off the window upper molding.
3. Pull off, by hand, the belt molding.
4. Remove the rear seat back from the vehicle. Disconnect the rear defroster, if equipped.
5. Remove the rear inside upper trim and the rear pillar upper garnish.
6. Remove the mounting nuts and pull the rear molding from the quarter window.

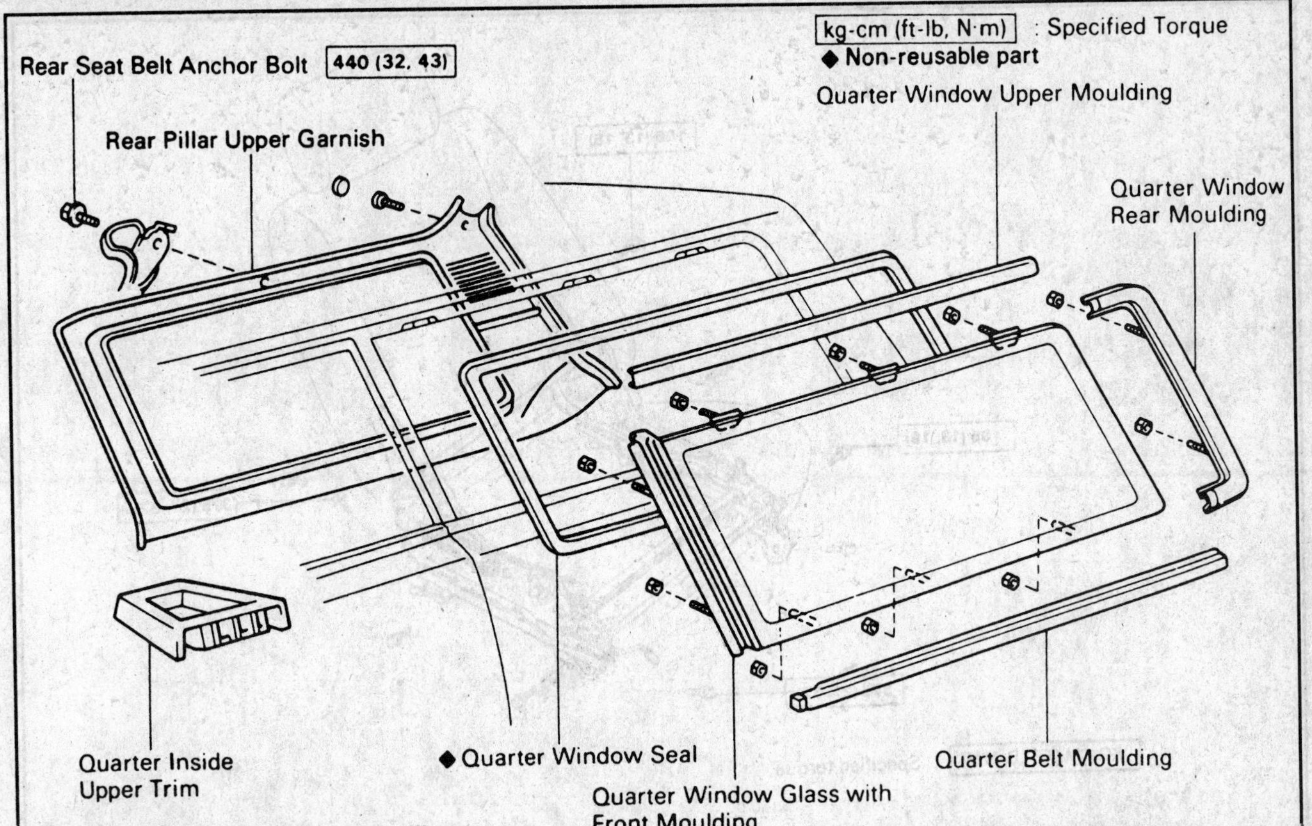

FIG. 49 Quarter window glass — Station Wagon

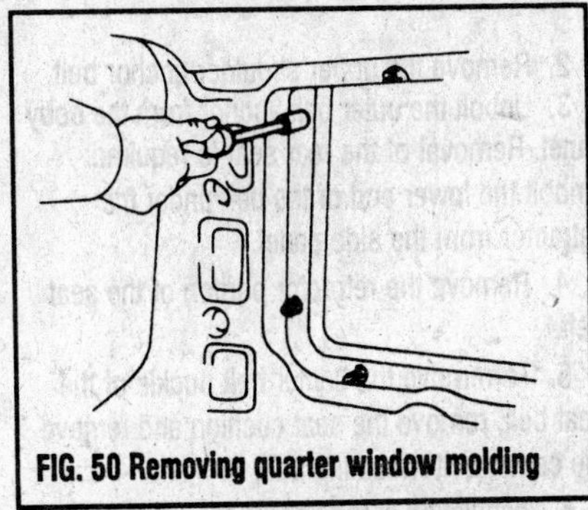

FIG. 50 Removing quarter window molding

7. Remove the window glass set nuts and remove the glass with the molding. Cut the sealer loose as required to remove the glass.

To Install:

8. Clean all adhesive off of the body of the vehicle. Clean all contact surfaces with an appropriate cleaner.

9. Clean the removed glass of all adhesive and clean with an appropriate cleaner. Do not touch the contact area after cleaning.

10. Using a brush, coat the contact surface on the body with the appropriate primer according to manufactures instructions. Repeat the procedure using the appropriate compound on the glass.

11. Apply the glass adhesive to the contact points on the body in a bead 0.39 in. (10mm) thick and overlapping the bead approximately 2.0 in. (50mm).

12. Install the glass with the molding attached. Install the window glass set nuts and the moldings.

13. Push on the outer rear molding and install the mounting nuts.

14. Install the rear inside upper trim and the rear pillar upper garnish and the belt molding.

15. Install the rear seat back from the vehicle. Connect the rear defroster electrical connector, as required.

16. Install the window upper molding.

17. Leak test the window when the sealer is completely dry.

Inside Rear View Mirror

REMOVAL & INSTALLATION

Remove the inner rear view mirror by loosening the set screw on the mirror stem and lifting mirror off of the base, which is glued onto the windshield. The installation is the reverse of the removal procedure.

Seats

➧ SEE FIGS. 51-53

REMOVAL & INSTALLATION

Front seats are held to the floor with four bolts each.

The sedan rear seat is retained by two clips at the front and two bolts at the rear.

The hatchback rear seat cushion is retained by four bolts, while the seat back is bolted to its hinges.

When installing the seats, torque the front seat bolts to 27 ft. lbs; the sedan rear seat bolts to 9 ft. lbs.; the hatchback seat cushion front bolts to 27 ft. lbs.; the hatchback seat cushion rear bolts to 14 ft. lbs.; the seat back-to-center hinge bolts to 69 inch lbs.; the seat back-to-side hinge bolts to 13 ft. lbs.

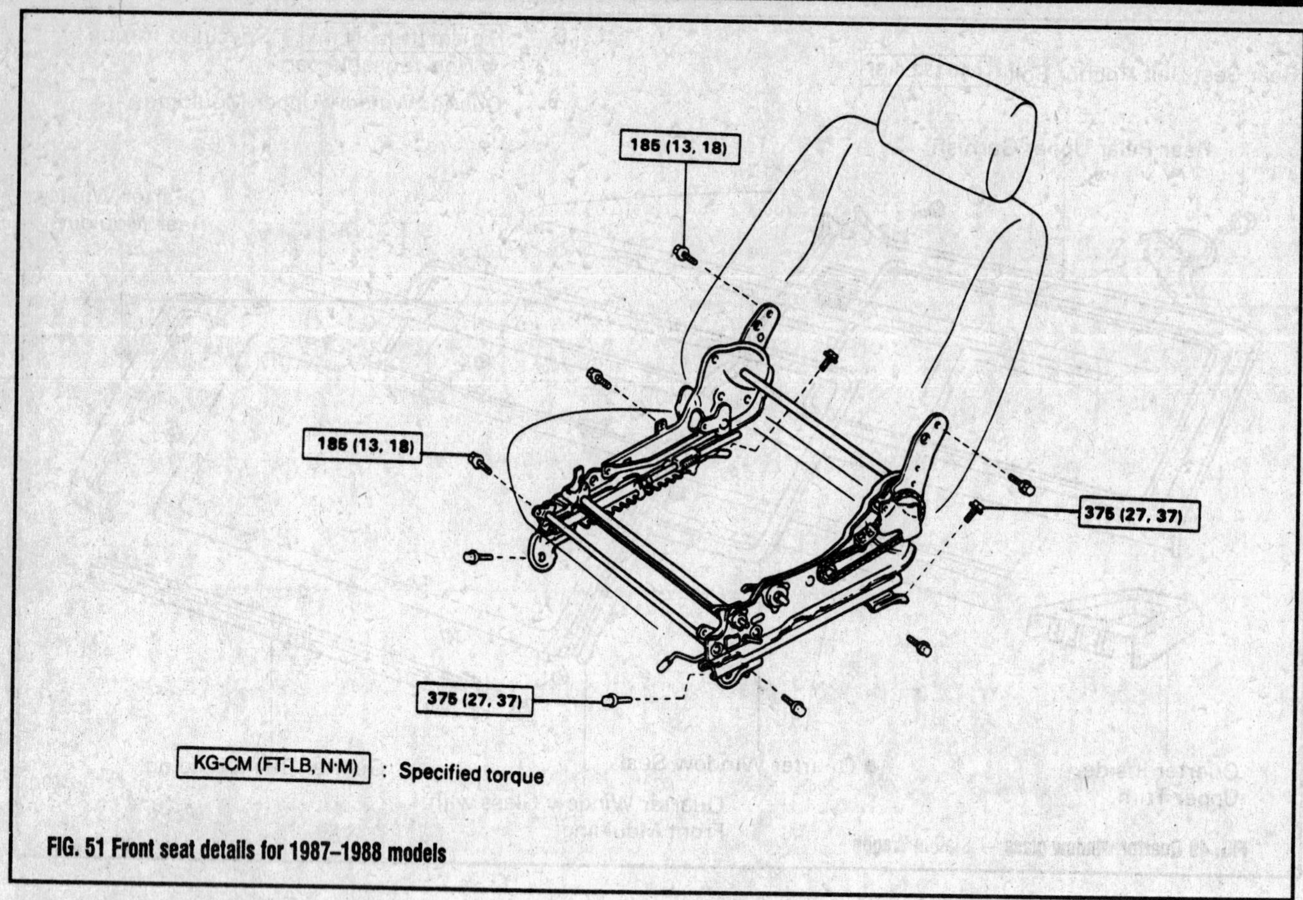

FIG. 51 Front seat details for 1987–1988 models

Seat Belt System

REMOVAL & INSTALLATION

Front Seat

1. Remove the trim cover at the upper shoulder anchor bolt.
2. Remove the anchor bolt.
3. Remove the lower cover on the outer retractor. Unbolt the retractor from the inner floor panel.
4. Remove the retractor portion of the seat belt.
5. To remove the buckle end of the seat belt, remove the cover on the base of the belt and remove the mounting bolt.
6. Installation of the belts is the reverse of the removal procedure. Torque the upper shoulder mounting bolt to 32 ft. lbs. (43 Nm), the lower retractor mounting bolt to 69 inch lbs. (8.0 Nm), and the buckle retainer bolt to 32 ft. lbs. (43 Nm).

Do not remove safety belts from any vehicle. Inspection of the seat belts for proper operation is recommended for the safety of the vehicle's occupants and is required in most states by law.

Rear Seat

1. Remove the trim cover at the upper shoulder anchor bolt.
2. Remove the upper shoulder anchor bolt.
3. Unbolt the outer belt anchor from the body panel. Removal of the rear seat is required. Unbolt the lower end of the belt under the retractor from the side panel.
4. Remove the retractor portion of the seat belt.
5. To remove the center belt buckle of the seat belt, remove the seat cushion and remove the center belt mounting bolt.
6. Installation of the belts is the reverse of the removal procedure. Torque all mounting bolts on the belt to 32 ft. lbs. (43 Nm).

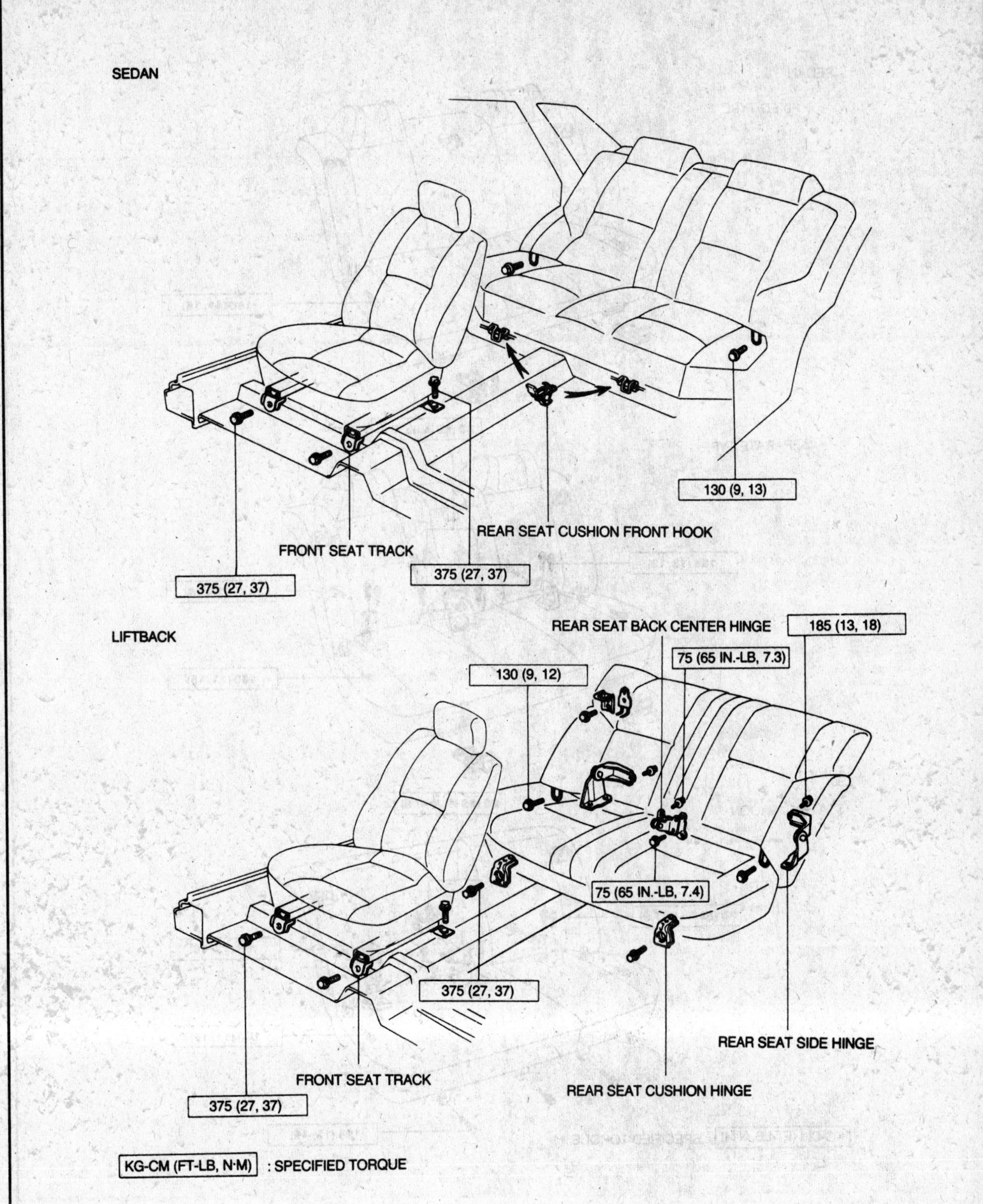

FIG. 52 Front and rear seat details 1987–88 models

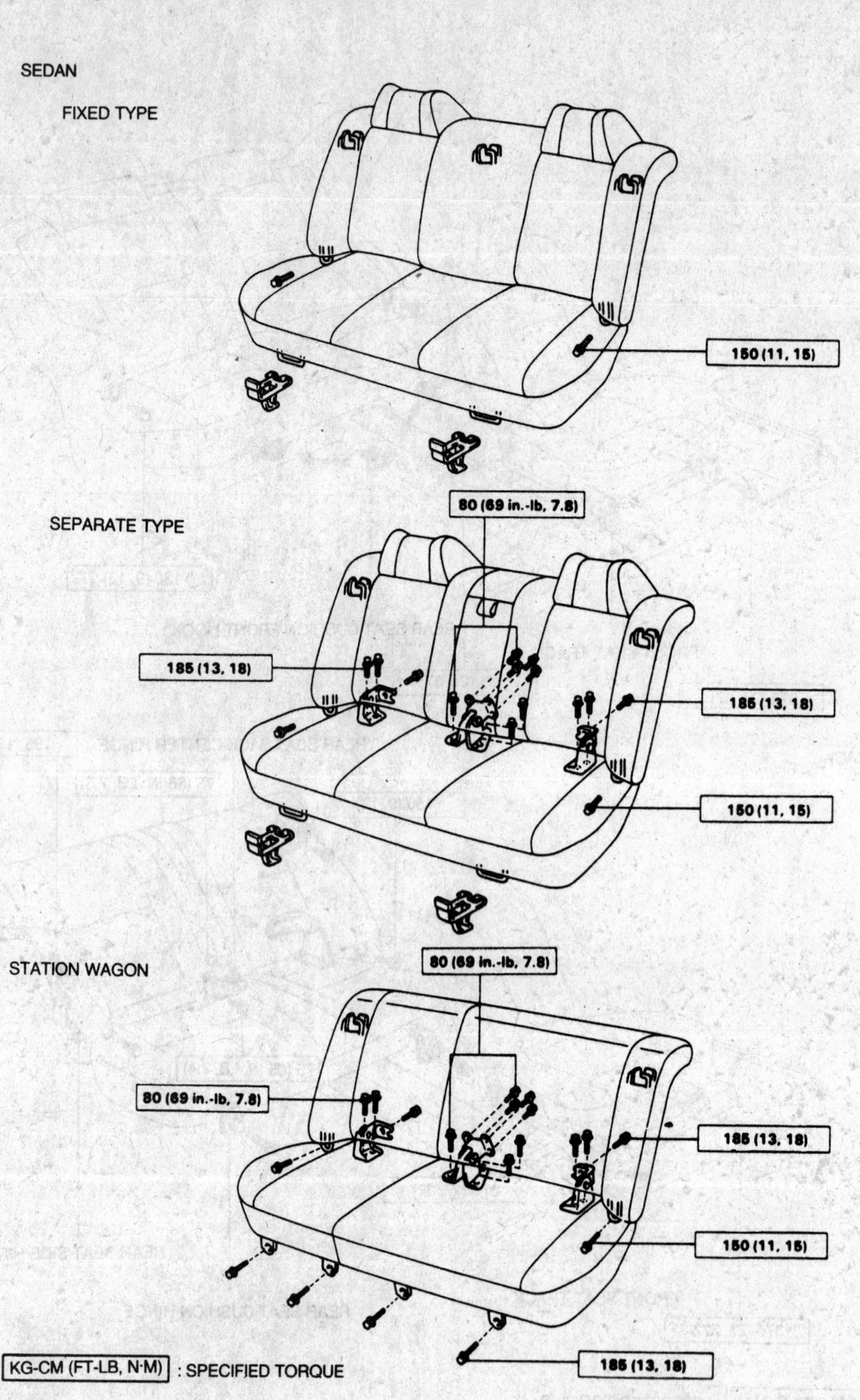

FIG. 53 Rear seat details 1987–1988 models

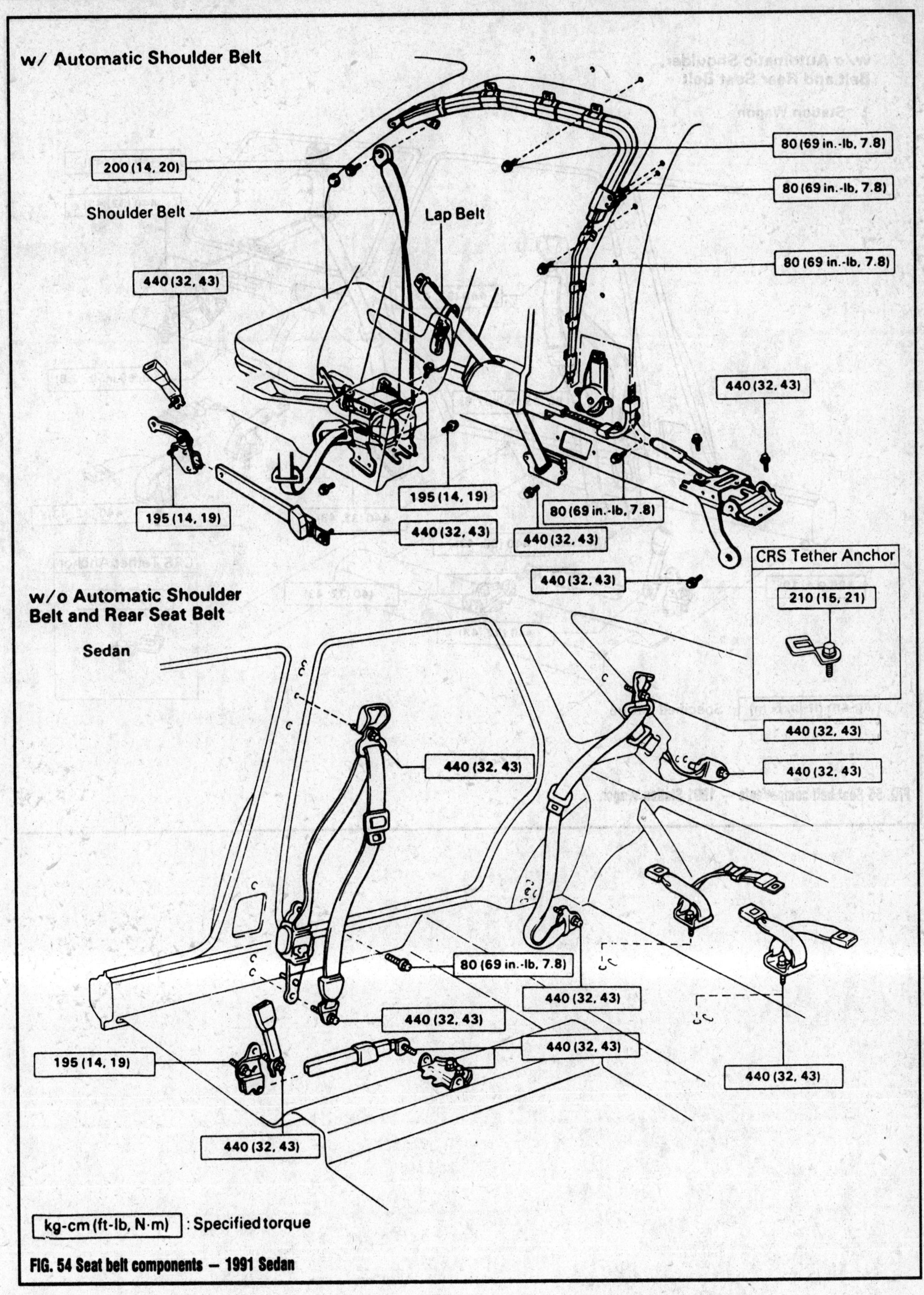

FIG. 54 Seat belt components — 1991 Sedan

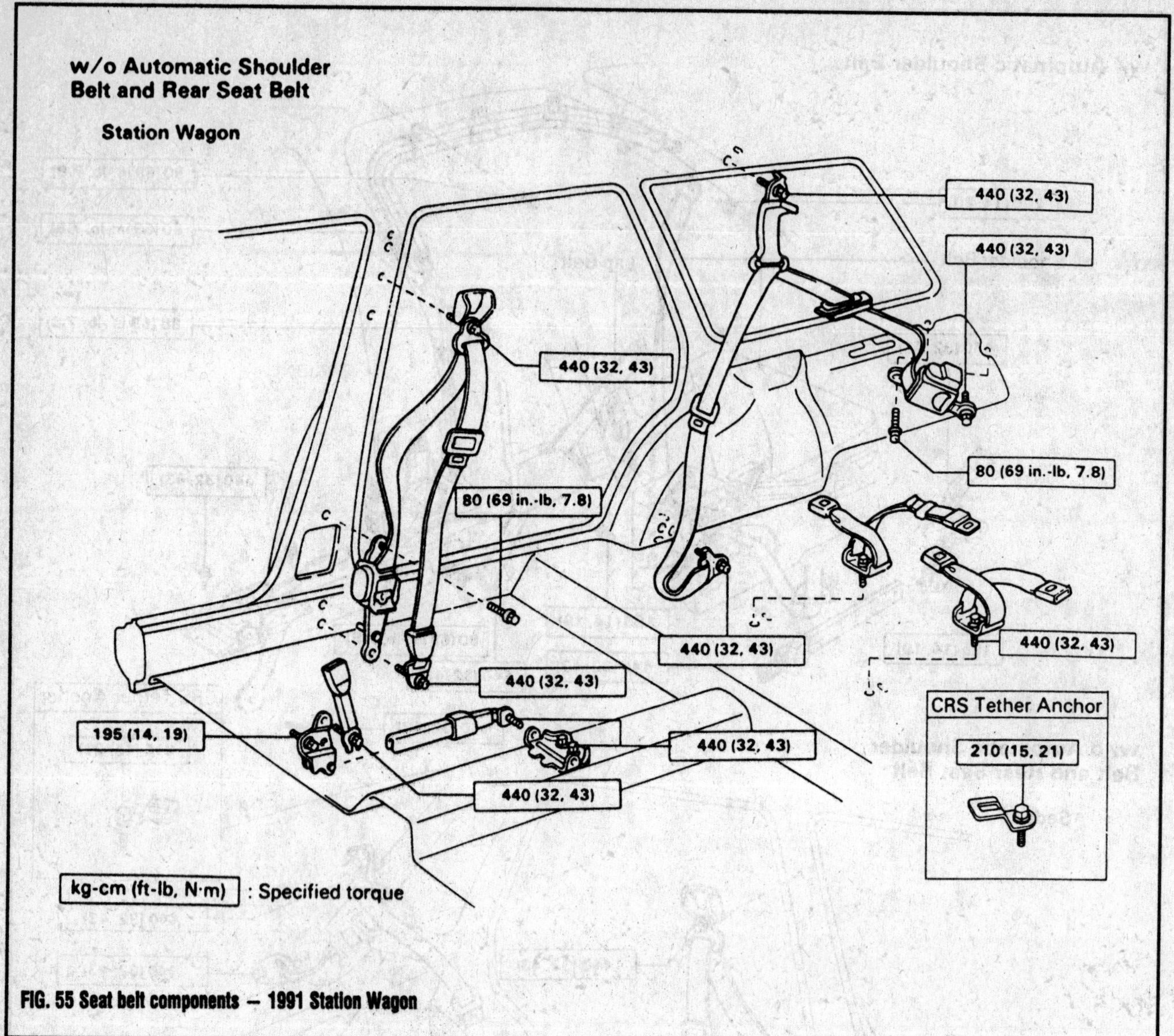

FIG. 55 Seat belt components — 1991 Station Wagon

Hood, Trunk Lid, Hatch Lid, Glass and Doors

Problem	Possible Cause	Correction
HOOD/TRUNK/HATCH LID		
Improper closure.	• Striker and latch not properly aligned.	• Adjust the alignment.
Difficulty locking and unlocking.	• Striker and latch not properly aligned.	• Adjust the alignment.
Uneven clearance with body panels.	• Incorrectly installed hood or trunk lid.	• Adjust the alignment.
WINDOW/WINDSHIELD GLASS		
Water leak through windshield	• Defective seal. • Defective body flange.	• Fill sealant • Correct.
Water leak through door window glass.	• Incorrect window glass installation. • Gap at upper window frame.	• Adjust position. • Adjust position.
Water leak through quarter window.	• Defective seal. • Defective body flange.	• Replace seal. • Correct.
Water leak through rear window.	• Defective seal. • Defective body flange.	• Replace seal. • Correct.
FRONT/REAR DOORS		
Door window malfunction.	• Incorrect window glass installation. • Damaged or faulty regulator.	• Adjust position. • Correct or replace.
Water leak through door edge.	• Cracked or faulty weatherstrip.	• Replace.
Water leak from door center.	• Drain hole clogged. • Inadequate waterproof skeet contact or damage.	• Remove foreign objects. • Correct or replace.
Door hard to open.	• Incorrect latch or striker adjustment.	• Adjust.
Door does not open or close completely.	• Incorrect door installation. • Defective door check strap. • Door check strap and hinge require grease.	• Adjust position. • Correct or replace. • Apply grease.
Uneven gap between door and body.	• Incorrect door installation.	• Adjust position.
Wind noise around door.	• Improperly installed weatherstrip. • Improper clearance between door glass and door weatherstrip. • Deformed door.	• Repair or replace. • Adjust. • Repair or replace.

How to Remove Stains from Fabric Interior

For best results, spots and stains should be removed as soon as possible. Never use gasoline, lacquer thinner, acetone, nail polish remover or bleach. Use a 3′ x 3″ piece of cheesecloth. Squeeze most of the liquid from the fabric and wipe the stained fabric from the outside of the stain toward the center with a lifting motion. Turn the cheesecloth as soon as one side becomes soiled. When using water to remove a stain, be sure to wash the entire section after the spot has been removed to avoid water stains. Encrusted spots can be broken up with a dull knife and vacuumed before removing the stain.

Type of Stain	How to Remove It
Surface spots	Brush the spots out with a small hand brush or use a commercial preparation such as K2R to lift the stain.
Mildew	Clean around the mildew with warm suds. Rinse in cold water and soak the mildew area in a solution of 1 part table salt and 2 parts water. Wash with upholstery cleaner.
Water stains	Water stains in fabric materials can be removed with a solution made from 1 cup of table salt dissolved in 1 quart of water. Vigorously scrub the solution into the stain and rinse with clear water. Water stains in nylon or other synthetic fabrics should be removed with a commercial type spot remover.
Chewing gum, tar, crayons, shoe polish (greasy stains)	Do not use a cleaner that will soften gum or tar. Harden the deposit with an ice cube and scrape away as much as possible with a dull knife. Moisten the remainder with cleaning fluid and scrub clean.
Ice cream, candy	Most candy has a sugar base and can be removed with a cloth wrung out in warm water. Oily candy, after cleaning with warm water, should be cleaned with upholstery cleaner. Rinse with warm water and clean the remainder with cleaning fluid.
Wine, alcohol, egg, milk, soft drink (non-greasy stains)	Do not use soap. Scrub the stain with a cloth wrung out in warm water. Remove the remainder with cleaning fluid.
Grease, oil, lipstick, butter and related stains	Use a spot remover to avoid leaving a ring. Work from the outisde of the stain to the center and dry with a clean cloth when the spot is gone.
Headliners (cloth)	Mix a solution of warm water and foam upholstery cleaner to give thick suds. Use only foam—liquid may streak or spot. Clean the entire headliner in one operation using a circular motion with a natural sponge.
Headliner (vinyl)	Use a vinyl cleaner with a sponge and wipe clean with a dry cloth.
Seats and door panels	Mix 1 pint upholstery cleaner in 1 gallon of water. Do not soak the fabric around the buttons.
Leather or vinyl fabric	Use a multi-purpose cleaner full strength and a stiff brush. Let stand 2 minutes and scrub thoroughly. Wipe with a clean, soft rag.
Nylon or synthetic fabrics	For normal stains, use the same procedures you would for washing cloth upholstery. If the fabric is extremely dirty, use a multi-purpose cleaner full strength with a stiff scrub brush. Scrub thoroughly in all directions and wipe with a cotton towel or soft rag.

GLOSSARY

AIR/FUEL RATIO: The ratio of air to gasoline by weight in the fuel mixture drawn into the engine.

AIR INJECTION: One method of reducing harmful exhaust emissions by injecting air into each of the exhaust ports of an engine. The fresh air entering the hot exhaust manifold causes any remaining fuel to be burned before it can exit the tailpipe.

ALTERNATOR: A device used for converting mechanical energy into electrical energy.

AMMETER: An instrument, calibrated in amperes, used to measure the flow of an electrical current in a circuit. Ammeters are always connected in series with the circuit being tested.

AMPERE: The rate of flow of electrical current present when one volt of electrical pressure is applied against one ohm of electrical resistance.

ANALOG COMPUTER: Any microprocessor that uses similar (analogous) electrical signals to make its calculations.

ARMATURE: A laminated, soft iron core wrapped by a wire that converts electrical energy to mechanical energy as in a motor or relay. When rotated in a magnetic field, it changes mechanical energy into electrical energy as in a generator.

ATMOSPHERIC PRESSURE: The pressure on the Earth's surface caused by the weight of the air in the atmosphere. At sea level, this pressure is 14.7 psi at 32°F (101 kPa at 0°C).

ATOMIZATION: The breaking down of a liquid into a fine mist that can be suspended in air.

AXIAL PLAY: Movement parallel to a shaft or bearing bore.

BACKFIRE: The sudden combustion of gases in the intake or exhaust system that results in a loud explosion.

BACKLASH: The clearance or play between two parts, such as meshed gears.

BACKPRESSURE: Restrictions in the exhaust system that slow the exit of exhaust gases from the combustion chamber.

BAKELITE: A heat resistant, plastic insulator material commonly used in printed circuit boards and transistorized components.

BALL BEARING: A bearing made up of hardened inner and outer races between which hardened steel balls roll.

BALLAST RESISTOR: A resistor in the primary ignition circuit that lowers voltage after the engine is started to reduce wear on ignition components.

BEARING: A friction reducing, supportive device usually located between a stationary part and a moving part.

BIMETAL TEMPERATURE SENSOR: Any sensor or switch made of two dissimilar types of metal that bend when heated or cooled due to the different expansion rates of the alloys. These types of sensors usually function as an on/off switch.

BLOWBY: Combustion gases, composed of water vapor and unburned fuel, that leak past the piston rings into the crankcase during normal engine operation. These gases are removed by the PCV system to prevent the buildup of harmful acids in the crankcase.

BRAKE PAD: A brake shoe and lining assembly used with disc brakes.

BRAKE SHOE: The backing for the brake lining. The term is, however, usually applied to the assembly of the brake backing and lining.

BUSHING: A liner, usually removable, for a bearing; an anti-friction liner used in place of a bearing.

BYPASS: System used to bypass ballast resistor during engine cranking to increase voltage supplied to the coil.

CALIPER: A hydraulically activated device in a disc brake system, which is mounted straddling the brake rotor (disc). The caliper contains at least one piston and two brake pads. Hydraulic pressure on the piston(s) forces the pads against the rotor.

CAMSHAFT: A shaft in the engine on which are the lobes (cams) which operate the valves. The camshaft is driven by the crankshaft, via a belt, chain or gears, at one half the crankshaft speed.

CAPACITOR: A device which stores an electrical charge.

CARBON MONOXIDE (CO): A colorless, odorless gas given off as a normal byproduct of combustion. It is poisonous and extremely dangerous in confined areas, building up slowly to toxic levels without warning if adequate ventilation is not available.

CARBURETOR: A device, usually mounted on the intake manifold of an engine, which mixes the air and fuel in the proper proportion to allow even combustion.

CATALYTIC CONVERTER: A device installed in the exhaust system, like a muffler, that converts harmful byproducts of combustion into carbon dioxide and water vapor by means of a heat-producing chemical reaction.

CENTRIFUGAL ADVANCE: A mechanical method of advancing the spark timing by using fly weights in the distributor that react to centrifugal force generated by the distributor shaft rotation.

CHECK VALVE: Any one-way valve installed to permit the flow of air, fuel or vacuum in one direction only.

CHOKE: A device, usually a movable valve, placed in the intake path of a carburetor to restrict the flow of air.

CIRCUIT: Any unbroken path through which an electrical current can flow. Also used to describe fuel flow in some instances.

CIRCUIT BREAKER: A switch which protects an electrical circuit from overload by opening the circuit when the current flow exceeds a predetermined level. Some circuit breakers must be reset manually, while most reset automatically

COIL (IGNITION): A transformer in the ignition circuit which steps up the voltage provided to the spark plugs.

COMBINATION MANIFOLD: An assembly which includes both the intake and exhaust manifolds in one casting.

COMBINATION VALVE: A device used in some fuel systems that routes fuel vapors to a charcoal storage canister instead of venting them into the atmosphere. The valve relieves fuel tank pressure and allows fresh air into the tank as the fuel level drops to prevent a vapor lock situation.

COMPRESSION RATIO: The comparison of the total volume of the cylinder and combustion chamber with the piston at BDC and the piston at TDC.

CONDENSER: 1. An electrical device which acts to store an electrical charge, preventing voltage surges.
2. A radiator-like device in the air conditioning system in which refrigerant gas condenses into a liquid, giving off heat.

CONDUCTOR: Any material through which an electrical current can be transmitted easily.

CONTINUITY: Continuous or complete circuit. Can be checked with an ohmmeter.

COUNTERSHAFT: An intermediate shaft which is rotated by a mainshaft and transmits, in turn, that rotation to a working part.

CRANKCASE: The lower part of an engine in which the crankshaft and related parts operate.

CRANKSHAFT: The main driving shaft of an engine which receives reciprocating motion from the pistons and converts it to rotary motion.

CYLINDER: In an engine, the round hole in the engine block in which the piston(s) ride.

CYLINDER BLOCK: The main structural member of an engine in which is found the cylinders, crankshaft and other principal parts.

CYLINDER HEAD: The detachable portion of the engine, fastened, usually, to the top of the cylinder block, containing all or most of the combustion chambers. On overhead valve engines, it contains the valves and their operating parts. On overhead cam engines, it contains the camshaft as well.

DEAD CENTER: The extreme top or bottom of the piston stroke.

DETONATION: An unwanted explosion of the air/fuel mixture in the combustion chamber caused by excess heat and compression, advanced timing, or an overly lean mixture. Also referred to as "ping".

DIAPHRAGM: A thin, flexible wall separating two cavities, such as in a vacuum advance unit.

DIESELING: A condition in which hot spots in the combustion chamber cause the engine to run on after the key is turned off.

DIFFERENTIAL: A geared assembly which allows the transmission of motion between drive axles, giving one axle the ability to turn faster than the other.

DIODE: An electrical device that will allow current to flow in one direction only.

DISC BRAKE: A hydraulic braking assembly consisting of a brake disc, or rotor, mounted on an axle, and a caliper assembly containing, usually two brake pads which are activated by hydraulic pressure. The pads are forced against the sides of the disc, creating friction which slows the vehicle.

DISTRIBUTOR: A mechanically driven device on an engine which is responsible for electrically firing the spark plug at a predetermined point of the piston stroke.

DOWEL PIN: A pin, inserted in mating holes in two different parts allowing those parts to maintain a fixed relationship.

DRUM BRAKE: A braking system which consists of two brake shoes and one or two wheel cylinders, mounted on a fixed backing plate, and a brake drum, mounted on an axle, which revolves around the assembly. Hydraulic action applied to the wheel cylinders forces the shoes outward against the drum, creating friction, slowing the vehicle.

DWELL: The rate, measured in degrees of shaft rotation, at which an electrical circuit cycles on and off.

ELECTRONIC CONTROL UNIT (ECU): Ignition module, amplifier or igniter. See Module for definition.

ELECTRONIC IGNITION: A system in which the timing and firing of the spark plugs is controlled by an electronic control unit, usually called a module. These systems have no points or condenser.

ENDPLAY: The measured amount of axial movement in a shaft.

ENGINE: A device that converts heat into mechanical energy.

EXHAUST MANIFOLD: A set of cast passages or pipes which conduct exhaust gases from the engine.

FEELER GAUGE: A blade, usually metal, of precisely predetermined thickness, used to measure the clearance between two parts. These blades usually are available in sets of assorted thicknesses.

F-HEAD: An engine configuration in which the intake valves are in the cylinder head, while the camshaft and exhaust valves are located in the cylinder block. The camshaft operates the intake valves via lifters and pushrods, while it operates the exhaust valves directly.

FIRING ORDER: The order in which combustion occurs in the cylinders of an engine. Also the order in which spark is distributed to the plugs by the distributor.

FLATHEAD: An engine configuration in which the camshaft and all the valves are located in the cylinder block.

FLOODING: The presence of too much fuel in the intake manifold and combustion chamber which prevents the air/fuel mixture from firing, thereby causing a no-start situation.

FLYWHEEL: A disc shaped part bolted to the rear end of the crankshaft. Around the outer perimeter is affixed the ring gear. The starter drive engages the ring gear, turning the flywheel, which rotates the crankshaft, imparting the initial starting motion to the engine.

FOOT POUND (ft.lb. or sometimes, ft. lbs.): The amount of energy or work needed to raise an item weighing one pound, a distance of one foot.

FUSE: A protective device in a circuit which prevents circuit overload by breaking the circuit when a specific amperage is present. The device is constructed around a strip or wire of a lower amperage rating than the circuit it is designed to protect. When an amperage higher than that stamped on the fuse is present in the circuit, the strip or wire melts, opening the circuit.

GEAR RATIO: The ratio between the number of teeth on meshing gears.

GENERATOR: A device which converts mechanical energy into electrical energy.

HEAT RANGE: The measure of a spark plug's ability to dissipate heat from its firing end. The higher the heat range, the hotter the plug fires.

HUB: The center part of a wheel or gear.

HYDROCARBON (HC): Any chemical compound made up of hydrogen and carbon. A major pollutant formed by the engine as a byproduct of combustion.

HYDROMETER: An instrument used to measure the specific gravity of a solution.

INCH POUND (in.lb. or sometimes, in. lbs.): One twelfth of a foot pound.

INDUCTION: A means of transferring electrical energy in the form of a magnetic field. Principle used in the ignition coil to increase voltage.

INJECTION PUMP: A device, usually mechanically operated, which meters and delivers fuel under pressure to the fuel injector.

INJECTOR: A device which receives metered fuel under relatively low pressure and is activated to inject the fuel into the engine under relatively high pressure at a predetermined time.

INPUT SHAFT: The shaft to which torque is applied, usually carrying the driving gear or gears.

INTAKE MANIFOLD: A casting of passages or pipes used to conduct air or a fuel/air mixture to the cylinders.

JOURNAL: The bearing surface within which a shaft operates.

KEY: A small block usually fitted in a notch between a shaft and a hub to prevent slippage of the two parts.

MANIFOLD: A casting of passages or set of pipes which connect the cylinders to an inlet or outlet source.

MANIFOLD VACUUM: Low pressure in an engine intake manifold formed just below the throttle plates. Manifold vacuum is highest at idle and drops under acceleration.

MASTER CYLINDER: The primary fluid pressurizing device in a hydraulic system. In automotive use, it is found in brake and hydraulic clutch systems and is pedal activated, either directly or, in a power brake system, through the power booster.

MODULE: Electronic control unit, amplifier or igniter of solid state or integrated design which controls the current flow in the ignition primary circuit based on input from the pick- up coil. When the module opens the primary circuit, the high secondary voltage is induced in the coil.

NEEDLE BEARING: A bearing which consists of a number (usually a large number) of long, thin rollers.

OHM:(Ω) The unit used to measure the resistance of conductor to electrical flow. One ohm is the amount of resistance that limits current flow to one ampere in a circuit with one volt of pressure.

OHMMETER: An instrument used for measuring the resistance, in ohms, in an electrical circuit.

OUTPUT SHAFT: The shaft which transmits torque from a device, such as a transmission.

OVERDRIVE: A gear assembly which produces more shaft revolutions than that transmitted to it.

OVERHEAD CAMSHAFT (OHC): An engine configuration in which the camshaft is mounted on top of the cylinder head and operates the valves either directly or by means of rocker arms.

OVERHEAD VALVE (OHV): An engine configuration in which all of the valves are located in the cylinder head and the camshaft is located in the cylinder block. The camshaft operates the valves via lifters and pushrods.

OXIDES OF NITROGEN (NOx): Chemical compounds of nitrogen produced as a byproduct of combustion. They combine with hydrocarbons to produce smog.

OXYGEN SENSOR: Used with the feedback system to sense the presence of oxygen in the exhaust gas and signal the computer which can reference the voltage signal to an air/fuel ratio.

PINION: The smaller of two meshing gears.

PISTON RING: An open ended ring which fits into a groove on the outer diameter of the piston. Its chief function is to form a seal between the piston and cylinder wall. Most automotive pistons have three rings: two for compression sealing; one for oil sealing.

PRELOAD: A predetermined load placed on a bearing during assembly or by adjustment.

PRIMARY CIRCUIT: Is the low voltage side of the ignition system which consists of the ignition switch, ballast resistor or resistance wire, bypass, coil, electronic control unit and pick-up coil as well as the connecting wires and harnesses.

PRESS FIT: The mating of two parts under pressure, due to the inner diameter of one being smaller than the outer diameter of the other, or vice versa; an interference fit.

RACE: The surface on the inner or outer ring of a bearing on which the balls, needles or rollers move.

REGULATOR: A device which maintains the amperage and/or voltage levels of a circuit at predetermined values.

RELAY: A switch which automatically opens and/or closes a circuit.

RESISTANCE: The opposition to the flow of current through a circuit or electrical device, and is measured in ohms. Resistance is equal to the voltage divided by the amperage.

RESISTOR: A device, usually made of wire, which offers a preset amount of resistance in an electrical circuit.

RING GEAR: The name given to a ring-shaped gear attached to a differential case,or affixed to a flywheel or as part a planetary gear set.

ROLLER BEARING: A bearing made up of hardened inner and outer races between which hardened steel rollers move.

ROTOR: 1. The disc-shaped part of a disc brake assembly, upon which the brake pads bear; also called, brake disc.
2. The device mounted atop the distributor shaft, which passes current to the distributor cap tower contacts.

SECONDARY CIRCUIT: The high voltage side of the ignition system, usually above 20,000 volts. The secondary includes the ignition coil, coil wire, distributor cap and rotor, spark plug wires and spark plugs.

SENDING UNIT: A mechanical, electrical, hydraulic or electromagnetic device which transmits information to a gauge.

SENSOR: Any device designed to measure engine operating conditions or ambient pressures and temperatures. Usually electronic in nature and designed to send a voltage signal to an on-board computer, some sensors may operate as a simple on/off switch or they may provide a variable voltage signal (like a potentiometer) as conditions or measured parameters change.

SHIM: Spacers of precise, predetermined thickness used between parts to establish a proper working relationship.

SLAVE CYLINDER: In automotive use, a device in the hydraulic clutch system which is activated by hydraulic force, disengaging the clutch.

SOLENOID: A coil used to produce a magnetic field, the effect of which is to produce work.

SPARK PLUG: A device screwed into the combustion chamber of a spark ignition engine. The basic construction is a conductive core inside of a ceramic insulator, mounted in an outer conductive base. An electrical charge from the spark plug wire travels along the conductive core and jumps a preset air gap to a grounding point or points at the end of the conductive base. The resultant spark ignites the fuel/air mixture in the combustion chamber.

SPLINES: Ridges machined or cast onto the outer diameter of a shaft or inner diameter of a bore to enable parts to mate without rotation.

TACHOMETER: A device used to measure the rotary speed of an engine, shaft, gear, etc., usually in rotations per minute.

THERMOSTAT: A valve, located in the cooling system of an engine, which is closed when cold and opens gradually in response to engine heating, controlling the temperature of the coolant and rate of coolant flow.

TOP DEAD CENTER (TDC): The point at which the piston reaches the top of its travel on the compression stroke.

TORQUE: The twisting force applied to an object.

TORQUE CONVERTER: A turbine used to transmit power from a driving member to a driven member via hydraulic action, providing changes in drive ratio and torque. In automotive use, it links the driveplate at the rear of the engine to the automatic transmission.

TRANSDUCER: A device used to change a force into an electrical signal.

TRANSISTOR: A semi-conductor component which can be actuated by a small voltage to perform an electrical switching function.

TUNE-UP: A regular maintenance function, usually associated with the replacement and adjustment of parts and components in the electrical and fuel systems of a vehicle for the purpose of attaining optimum performance.

TURBOCHARGER: An exhaust driven pump which compresses intake air and forces it into the combustion chambers at higher than atmospheric pressures. The increased air pressure allows more fuel to be burned and results in increased horsepower being produced.

VACUUM ADVANCE: A device which advances the ignition timing in response to increased engine vacuum.

VACUUM GAUGE: An instrument used to measure the presence of vacuum in a chamber.

VALVE: A device which control the pressure, direction of flow or rate of flow of a liquid or gas.

VALVE CLEARANCE: The measured gap between the end of the valve stem and the rocker arm, cam lobe or follower that activates the valve.

VISCOSITY: The rating of a liquid's internal resistance to flow.

VOLTMETER: An instrument used for measuring electrical force in units called volts. Voltmeters are always connected parallel with the circuit being tested.

WHEEL CYLINDER: Found in the automotive drum brake assembly, it is a device, actuated by hydraulic pressure, which, through internal pistons, pushes the brake shoes outward against the drums.

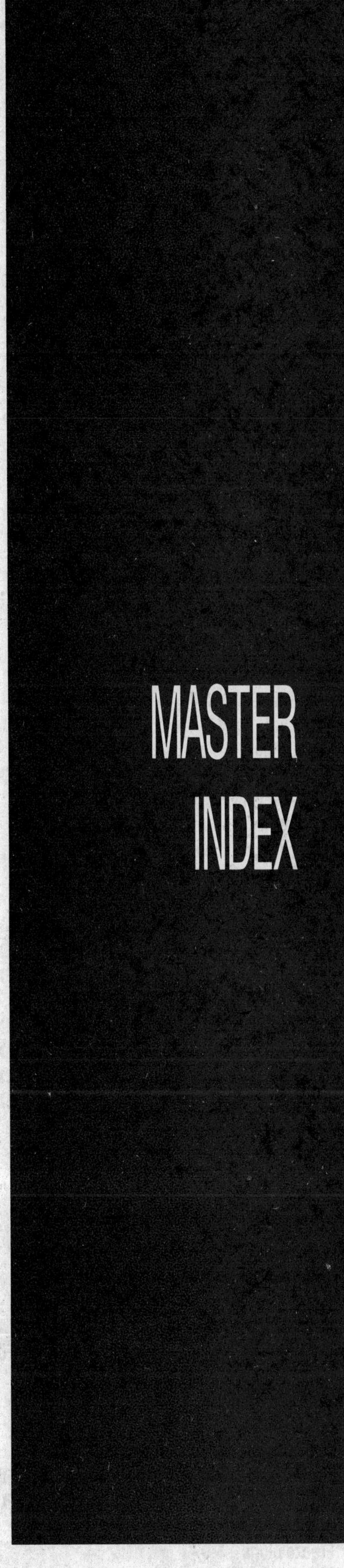

AIR CLEANER 1-14
AIR CONDITIONING
A/C switch 6-23
Blower 6-9
Charging 1-17
Compressor 6-14
Condenser 6-16
Control panel 6-13
Discharging 1-37
Evacuating 1-37
Evaporator 6-17
Gauge sets 1-36
General service 1-33
Inspection 1-35
Pressure switch 6-25
Receiver 6-19
Refrigerant lines 6-20
Safety precautions 1-14
Troubleshooting 1-87
Water control valve 6-11
AIR FLOW METER 4-19
ALIGNMENT (WHEEL)
Front 8-15
Rear 8-24
ALTERNATOR
Alternator precautions 3-12
Brush replacement 3-15
Removal and installation 3-13
Specifications 3-17
ANTI-LOCK BRAKE SYSTEM
Actuator 9-38
Bleeding 9-39
Control relays 9-36
Decelerator sensor 9-37
Front wheel speed sensor 9-36
Operation 9-27
Rear wheel speed sensor 9-37
ANTIFREEZE 1-59
AUTOMATIC TRANSMISSION
Adjustments 7-69
Application chart 1-9
Back-up light switch 7-70
Fluid and filter change 7-69
Fluid change 1-52
Identification 7-68
Neutral safety switch 7-69
Removal and installation 7-70
Throttle cable adjustment 7-69
AXLE
Front 7-46
Rear 7-85
BACK-UP LIGHT SWITCH
Automatic transmission 7-69
Manual transmission 7-4
BATTERY
Cables 1-24
Fluid level and maintenance 1-23
General maintenance 1-23
Jump starting 1-26
Replacement 1-25
Testing 1-24
BATTERY 3-16
BELTS 1-27
BLOWER MOTOR 6-9
BRAKES
Adjustments 9-2
Bleeding 9-8
Brake light switch 9-3
Disc brakes
Front 9-9
Rear 9-23
Drum brakes 9-14
Hoses and lines 9-9
Master cylinder 9-3
Parking brake 9-25
Power booster 9-4
Proportioning valve 9-7
Specifications 9-39
CAMSHAFT 3-82
CAPACITIES CHART 1-74
CATALYTIC CONVERTER 3-103
CHARGING SYSTEM 3-12
CHASSIS ELECTRICAL SYSTEM
Circuit breakers 6-47
Control panel 6-34
Cruise control 6-28
Flashers 6-57
Fuses 6-47
Fusible links 6-52
Headlight switch 6-39
Headlights 6-40
Heater and air conditioning 6-9
Instrument cluster 6-37
Lighting 6-44
Windshield wipers 6-35
CHASSIS LUBRICATION 1-65
CHECK ENGINE LIGHT 4-13
CLUTCH
Adjustment 7-63
Hydraulic system bleeding 7-68
Master cylinder 7-64
Pedal 7-63
Pilot bearing 7-65
Removal and installation 7-64
Slave cylinder 7-67
Switch 7-4
Troubleshooting 7-93
COIL (IGNITION) 3-5
COMBINATION SWITCH 8-25
COMPRESSION TESTING 3-25
CONNECTING RODS AND BEARINGS
Service 3-88
Specifications 3-28
COOLING SYSTEM 1-59
CRANKCASE VENTILATION VALVE 1-19, 4-6

CRANKSHAFT
Service 3-98
Specifications 3-28
CYLINDER HEAD
Removal and installation 3-53
Resurfacing 3-62
DIESEL FUEL SYSTEM
Glow plugs 5-21
Injection lines 5-18
Injection pump 5-20
Injection timing 5-21
Injectors 5-19
DIFFERENTIAL
Front 7-7
Rear 7-86
DISC BRAKES (FRONT)
Caliper 9-12
Pads 9-9
Rotor (Disc) 9-13
DISC BRAKES (REAR)
Caliper 9-23
Pads 9-23
DISTRIBUTOR 3-8
DRIVE AXLE (FRONT)
Axle shaft 7-46
Differential 7-7
Removal and installation 7-46
DRIVE AXLE (REAR)
Axle housing 7-88
Axle shaft and bearing 7-85
Driveshaft 7-82
Removal and installation 7-86
DRUM BRAKES
Adjustment 9-2
Drum 9-14
Shoes 9-16
Wheel cylinder 9-22
EGR VALVE 4-8
ELECTRONIC ENGINE CONTROLS 4-13
ELECTRONIC FUEL INJECTION
Fuel pressure relief 5-3
Fuel pump 5-3
Idle speed control valve 5-9
Injectors 5-9
Throttle body 5-5
Throttle position sensor 5-17
ELECTRONIC IGNITION 2-8
ENGINE
Camshaft 3-82
Compression testing 3-25
Connecting rods and bearings 3-88
Crankshaft 3-98
Cylinder head 3-53
Cylinders 3-96
Exhaust manifold 3-41
Fan 3-45
Flywheel 3-102
Freeze plugs 3-97
Front (timing) cover 3-72
Front seal 3-72
Intake manifold 3-39
Main bearings 3-101
Oil pan 3-67
Oil pump 3-69
Overhaul techniques 3-23
Piston pin 3-95
Pistons 3-88
Rear main seal 3-98
Removal and installation 3-30
Ring gear 3-102
Rings 3-95
Rocker arms 3-38
Specifications 3-26
Thermostat 3-38
Timing belt 3-78
Timing covers 3-72
Timing gears 3-81
Turbocharger 3-44
Valve (rocker) cover 3-36
Valve guides 3-66
Valve seats 3-65
Valve springs 3-65
Valves 3-62
Water pump 3-49
ENGINE EMISSION CONTROLS
Evaporative canister 4-6
Exhaust gas recirculation (EGR) system 4-8
Oxygen (O_2) sensor 4-15
PCV valve 4-6
EVAPORATIVE CANISTER 1-17, 4-6
EXHAUST EMISSION CONTROLS 4-3
EXHAUST GAS RECIRCULATION (EGR) SYSTEM 4-8
EXHAUST MANIFOLD 3-41
EXHAUST PIPE 3-103
EXHAUST SYSTEM 3-103
EXTERIOR
Antenna 10-10
Bumpers 10-7
Doors 10-2
Fenders 10-11
Grille 10-8
Hood 10-4
Outside Mirrors 10-10
Sunroof/Moonroof 10-11
FAN 3-45
FILTERS
Air 1-14
Crankcase 1-19
Fuel 1-17
Oil 1-48
FIRING ORDERS 2-7
FLUIDS AND LUBRICANTS
Automatic transmission 1-52
Battery 1-23
Chassis greasing 1-65
Coolant 1-60
Engine oil 1-45
Fuel recommendations 1-46
Manual transmission 1-51
Master cylinder 1-62
Power steering pump 1-63
Transfer case 1-55
FLYWHEEL AND RING GEAR 3-102
FREEZE PLUGS 3-97
FRONT SUSPENSION
Axle hub and bearings 8-12
Lower control arm 8-9
MacPherson struts 8-27
Stabilizer bar 8-9
Steering knuckle 8-12
Strut rod 8-22
Wheel alignment 8-15
Wheel lug studs 8-2
FRONT WHEEL BEARINGS 8-12
FUEL FILTER 1-17
FUEL PUMP 5-3
FUEL SYSTEM
Diesel 5-18
Fuel injection 5-2
FUEL TANK 5-18
GEARSHIFT LINKAGE
Automatic transmission 7-69
Manual transmission 7-2
HALFSHAFTS 7-46, 71
HEATER
Blower 6-9
Blower switch 6-13
Control cable 6-12
Control panel 6-13
Core 6-10
HISTORY 1-6
HOSES 1-32
HOW TO USE THIS BOOK 1-2
IC REGULATOR 3-15
IDENTIFICATION
Drive axle 1-8
Engine 1-8
Model 1-6
Serial number 1-6
Vehicle 1-6
IDLE SPEED AND MIXTURE ADJUSTMENT 2-23
IDLE SPEED CONTROL VALVE 4-22
IGNITER 3-7
IGNITION COIL 3-5
IGNITION SWITCH AND LOCK CYLINDER 8-25
IGNITION TIMING 2-10
INSTRUMENTS AND SWITCHES
Cluster 6-37
Gauges 6-38
Panel 6-34

Radio 6-33
Speakers 6-33
Speedometer 6-38
INTAKE MANIFOLD 3-39
INTERIOR
Console 10-13
Door glass & regulator 10-17
Door locks 10-17
Door panels 10-14
Electric window motor 10-18
Headliner 10-15
Heater & A/C ducts 10-17
Inside mirror 10-21
Instrument Panel & Pad 10-12
Interior trim panels 10-15
Seat belt systems 10-22
Seats 10-21
Stationary glass 10-20
Windshield glass 10-18
JACKING POINTS 1-5, 69
JUMP STARTING 1-26
LIGHTING
Headlights 6-40
License plate light 6-45
Light bulb application chart 6-40
Marker lights 6-43
Signal and marker lights 6-43
LOWER BALL JOINT 8-6
LOWER CONTROL ARM 8-9
MAIN BEARINGS 3-101
MAIN RELAYS 4-24
MAINTENANCE INTERVALS CHART 1-75
MANIFOLD PRESSURE SENSOR 4-20
MANIFOLDS
Exhaust 3-41
Intake 3-39
MANUAL STEERING GEAR
Adjustments 8-28
Removal and installation 8-29
MANUAL TRANSMISSION
Adjustments 7-2
Back-up light switch 7-4
Identification 7-2
Linkage 7-2
Overhaul 7-7
Removal and installation 7-5
Troubleshooting 7-91
MASTER CYLINDER 1-62, 7-64, 9-3
MODEL IDENTIFICATION 1-6
MUFFLER 3-104
NEUTRAL SAFETY SWITCH 7-69
OIL AND FILTER CHANGE (ENGINE) 1-48
OIL AND FUEL RECOMMENDATIONS 1-45
OIL COOLER 3-70
OIL LEVEL CHECK
Differential 1-57
Engine 1-47
Tranqmission 1-51
Transfer case 1-55
OIL PAN 3-67
OIL PUMP 3-69
OXYGEN (O_2) SENSOR 4-15
PARKING BRAKE
Adjustment 9-25
Cables 9-25
Removal and installation 9-25
PCV VALVE 1-19, 4-6
PICKUP COIL 3-5
PISTON PIN 3-95
PISTONS 3-88
POWER BOOSTER 9-4
POWER STEERING GEAR
Adjustments 8-28
Removal and installation 8-29
POWER STEERING PUMP
Adjustments 8-35
Bleeding 8-35
Removal and installation 8-32
POWER STEERING PUMP 1-63
PROPORTIONING VALVE 9-7
PUSHING 1-67
RADIATOR 1-62, 3-47
RADIO 6-33
REAR MAIN OIL SEAL 3-98
REAR SUSPENSION
MacPherson struts 8-17
Rear strut rod 8-22
Rear suspension arm 8-19
Rear wheel bearings 8-22
Stabilizer bar 8-22
RING GEAR 3-102
RINGS 3-95
ROCKER ARMS 3-38
ROUTINE MAINTENANCE 1-10
SAFETY MEASURES 1-5
SENDING UNITS & SENSORS 3-22
SERIAL NUMBER LOCATION 1-6
SLAVE CYLINDER 7-67
SPARK PLUG WIRES 2-5
SPARK PLUGS 2-3
SPECIAL TOOLS 1-3
SPECIFICATIONS CHARTS
Alternator and regulator 3-17
Brakes 9-39
Camshaft 3-27
Capacities 1-74
Crankshaft and connecting rod 3-28
General engine 3-26
Piston and ring 3-29
Preventive Maintenance 1-75
Starter 3-17
Torque 3-30
Tune-up 2-2
Valves 3-26
Wheel alignment 8-16
SPEEDOMETER CABLE 6-38
STABILIZER BAR
Front 8-9
Rear 8-22
STAIN REMOVAL 10-28
STARTER
Overhaul 3-21
Removal and installation 3-19
Solenoid or relay replacement 3-21
Specifications 3-17
STEERING COLUMN 8-26
STEERING GEAR
Manual 8-28
Power 8-28
STEERING LINKAGE 8-28
STEERING WHEEL 8-24
STRIPPED THREADS 3-24
SWITCHES
Headlight 6-39
Windshield wiper 6-39
TAILPIPE 3-104
THERMOSTAT 3-38
THROTTLE POSITION SENSOR 4-17
TIE ROD ENDS 8-28
TIMING 2-10
TIMING BELT 3-78
TIMING GEARS 3-81
TIRES
Inflation 1-44
Rotation 1-43
Storage 1-44
Tread depth 1-43
Troubleshooting 1-89
Usage 1-43
Wear problems 1-43
TOOLS AND EQUIPMENT 1-3
TORQUE SPECIFICATIONS 3-30, 114
TOWING 1-67
TRAILER TOWING 1-65
TRAILER WIRING 6-47
TRANSFER CASE
Fluid level 1-55
Removal and installation 7-78
Seals 7-78
TRANSMISSION
Application charts 1-9
Routine maintenance 1-51
TROUBLESHOOTING
Air conditioning 1-87
Air conditioning switch 6-23
Automatic transmission 7-94
Brakes 9-40
Clutch 7-93
Clutch switch 7-4
Cruise control 6-28

Gauges 6-260
Heater 6-261
Ignition switch 8-25
Lights 6-258
Manual transmission 7-91
Noise 7-91
Pressure switch 6-27
Power steering pump 8-38
Speed sensor & ratio controller 6-31
Thermistor 6-22
Tires 1-89
Torque converter 7-94
Turn signal switch 8-36
Turn signals and flashers 6-257
Wheels 1-89
Windshield wipers 6-262

TUNE-UP
Idle speed and mixture 2-23
Ignition timing 2-10
Procedures 2-2
Spark plug wires 2-5
Spark plugs 2-3
Specifications 2-2
Troubleshooting 2-29
Valve lash adjustment 2-13
U-JOINTS 7-84
VACUUM DIAGRAMS 4-26
VACUUM SOLENOID VALVES 4-22
VALVE GUIDES 3-66
VALVE SEATS 3-65
VALVE SERVICE 3-62
VALVE SPECIFICATIONS 3-26

VALVE SPRINGS 3-65
VEHICLE IDENTIFICATION 1-6
WATER PUMP 3-49
WHEEL ALIGNMENT
Front 8-15
Rear 8-24
Specifications 8-16
WHEEL BEARINGS 1-65
WHEELS 1-43
WINDSHIELD WIPERS
Arm and blade 6-35
Linkage and motor 6-35
Switch 6-39
WINDSHIELD WIPERS 1-39
WIRING DIAGRAMS 6-58